Collins
Discovery
Encyclopedia

HarperCollins Publishers
Westerhill Road
Bishopbriggs
Glasgow
G64 2QT

First Edition 2005

© HarperCollins Publishers 2005

UK Edition ISBN 0–00–7203225

Collins® is a registered trademark
of HarperCollins Publishers Limited

www.collins.co.uk

A catalogue record for this book is
available from the British Library.

Designed by Mark Thomson

Typeset by Market House Books Ltd,
Aylesbury, England

Printed and bound in Great Britain
by Clays Ltd, St Ives plc

Acknowledgments

We would like to thank those authors and
publishers who kindly gave permission for
copyright material to be used in the Collins
Word Web. We would also like to thank Times
Newspapers Ltd for providing valuable data.

About the type

This dictionary is typeset in CollinsFedra, a
special version of the Fedra family of types
designed by Peter Bil'ak. CollinsFedra has
been customized especially for Collins
dictionaries; it includes both sans serif (for
headwords) and serif (entries) versions, in
several different weights. Its large x-height,
its open 'eye', and its basis in the tradition of
humanist letterforms make CollinsFedra
both familiar and easy to read at small sizes.
It has been designed to use the minimum
space without sacrificing legibility, as well as
including a number of characters and signs
that are specific to dictionary typography. Its
companion phonetic type is the first of its
kind to be drawn according to the same
principles as the regular typeface, rather
than assembled from rotated and reflected
characters from other types.

Peter Bil'ak (born 1973, Slovakia) is a graphic
and type designer living in the Netherlands.
He is the author of two books, *Illegibility* and
Transparency. As well as the Fedra family, he
has designed several other typefaces
including Eureka. His typotheque.com
website has become a focal point for
research and debate around contemporary
type design.

EDITORIAL STAFF

EDITORS
Justin Crozier
Andrew Holmes
Cormac McKeown
Elspeth Summers

CONTRIBUTORS
John Daintith
Alan Isaacs
Jonathan Law
Elizabeth Martin
Dave Mumford
Roger Pountain
Anne Stibbs

FOR THE PUBLISHERS
Morven Dooner
Elaine Higgleton
Lorna Knight

Contents

William Collins' dream of knowledge for all began with the publication of his first book in 1819. A self-educated mill worker, he not only enriched millions of lives, but also founded a flourishing publishing house. Today, staying true to this spirit, Collins books are packed with inspiration, innovation, and practical expertise. They place you at the centre of a world of possibility and give you exactly what you need to explore it.

Language is the key to this exploration, and at the heart of Collins Dictionaries is language as it is really used. New words, phrases, and meanings spring up every day, and all of them are captured and analysed by the Collins Word Web. Constantly updated, and with over 2.5 billion entries, this living language resource is unique to our dictionaries.

Words are tools for life. And a Collins Dictionary makes them work for you.

Collins. Do more.

Foreword

In today's Information Age, facts are at a premium. With huge amounts of information of varying quality available to us on the internet, and in print and broadcast media, a reliable resource for fact-finding and checking is vital. This is precisely what this first edition of **Collins Discovery Encylopedia** does, allowing you to find the basic facts that you need on a broad range of topics, as well as useful weblinks so that you can pursue a given subject to whatever degree of detail you require.

Drawing on Collins' vast information resources, the **Discovery Encylopedia** provides a wealth of reference material, and is the perfect fact-finder for the home, office, or classroom. Thousands of entries cover a comprehensive array of subjects: geography, history, flora and fauna, biographical information, and science and technology. You will find everything from the population of **Aalborg** to the fundamentals of **Zoroastrianism**. Population estimates for towns, cities, regions, and countries are recent and reliable, while biographical entries include birth and death dates where these are known.

Many entries are supplemented by internet links, providing easy access to handpicked websites where you will find in-depth information on the topic in which you are interested. The following section provides useful hints and tips on using the internet safely and efficiently, enabling you to conduct your online research with precision and speed.

Whether you require facts to complete a report, finish an essay, pursue an interest, or win an argument, the **Collins Discovery Encylopedia** is the perfect reference tool, taking you to information you need swiftly, clearly and in depth.

Abbreviations

AD	anno Domini
Anat	anatomy
Architect	architecture
Astrol	astrology
Austral	Australia(n)
BC	before Christ
Biol	biology
Brit	British
Chem	chemistry
C of E	Church of England
E	East
eg	for example
esp	especially
etc	et cetera
Geom	geometry
Hist	history
Lit	literary
Med	medicine
Meteorol	meteorology
Mil	military
N	North
Naut	nautical
NZ	New Zealand
Pathol	pathology
Photog	photography
Physiol	physiology
Psychol	psychology
S	South
S African	South Africa(n)
Scot	Scottish
US	United States
W	West
zool	zoology

Using the internet safely

This section offers advice chiefly to parents concerned with the online safety of their children. Hints and tips for safe surfing are provided as is a list of websites dealing with this subject in more detail.

The Internet contains an inconceivably large amount of information, much of it free, on a vast range of topics. It does not belong to and is not controlled by any single organization, government, or nation. Although the absence of centralized control is occasionally lamented as anarchic, the lack of a top-down structure provides many benefits.

The Internet offers the chance for anyone with a computer and a modem to communicate with and learn from any person, group, or organization similarly equipped. Libraries, museums, art galleries, governments, universities, research institutes, and many other bodies provide open access to their data and links to the online resources of other organizations.

This availability of information and the unparalleled potential for communication and the spread of ideas provides Internet users with incalculable benefits, but there are downsides. As the Internet is unregulated and decentralized there is no quality-control mechanism; the only barrier preventing someone from setting up a website is technical ability. There is much of little merit on the Internet.

More worrying is the potential for criminal misuse. The Internet's accessibility and inclusiveness is exploited by those who wish to disseminate hate or obscenity or to take advantage of the vulnerable or gullible. As 70 per cent of UK households with school-age children are online it is important that parents and carers are aware of the potential dangers as well as the benefits.

Tips for safe use of the Internet and chatrooms

▷ Find out as much as possible about the Internet, chatrooms, instant messaging, and email. A number of websites dealing with the concerns of parents are listed at the bottom of this section.

▷ Make Internet surfing a family event as often as possible.

▷ Limit the amount of time your children spend online. Encourage them to maintain their other interests and hobbies.

▷ Keep the computer in a family room so that you can check how long your children have been using the Internet.

▷ Make sure your child doesn't give out personal details, phone numbers, addresses, or any other information that could be used to identify him or her, such as information about your family or the school he or she goes to.

▷ Make sure that any chatroom used by your child is monitored to prevent publication of offensive material or personal contact details.

▷ Online contacts should not be taken at face value. They may not be what they seem.

▷ Warn children never to arrange to meet someone only ever previously met on the Internet without first telling you. Accompany your child to any meetings and make sure they are held in a public place.

▷ Children should not accept files from people they don't know and trust offline, since the files could contain viruses or self-extracting software which could reveal personal information to the sender.

▷ Video-conferencing and webcams allow the transmission of voice and live images. Children should be discouraged from using this technology unsupervised and with people they don't know and trust offline.

▷ Talk with your children if they are made uncomfortable or feel threatened by anything they see online.

▷ Warn your children never to respond directly to anything they find disturbing. Encourage them to log off and report what they found to an adult.

▷ Discuss with your children news stories concerning the dangers of chatrooms and the Internet. The website www.chatdanger.com has a number of such reports.

▷ Consider using Internet filtering software and child-friendly search engines. Use your browser's controls, as some offer varying degrees of security for each family member.

▷ Investigate your Internet Service Provider's (ISP) child-protection services. Do they filter out spam (unwanted email), for instance?

▷ Investigate Internet safety in greater detail at the following websites:

> ▷ www.chatdanger.com
> ▷ http://safety.ngfl.gov.uk
> ▷ www.childnet-int.org/links/index.html
> ▷ www.internetcrimeforum.org.uk/chatwise_streetwise.html
> ▷ www.nspcc.org.uk/html/home/needadvice/
> ▷ helpyourchildsurfinsafety.htm

Aa

a *or* **A** the first in a series, esp the highest grade or mark, as in an examination

A1, A-1, *or* **A-one** (of a vessel) with hull and equipment in first-class condition

Aalborg *or* **Ålborg** a city and port in Denmark, in N Jutland. Pop: 121 549 (2004 est)

Aalto Alvar 1898–1976, Finnish architect and furniture designer, noted particularly for his public and industrial buildings, in which wood is much used. He invented bent plywood furniture (1932)

Aarau a town in N Switzerland, capital of Aargau canton: capital of the Helvetic Republic from 1798 to 1803. Pop: 15 470 (2000)

aardvark a nocturnal mammal, *Orycteropus afer*, the sole member of its family (*Orycteropodidae*) and order (*Tubulidentata*). It inhabits the grasslands of Africa, has long ears and snout, and feeds on termites

Aargau a canton in N Switzerland. Capital: Aarau. Pop: 556 200 (2002 est). Area: 1404 sq km (542 sq miles)

Aarhus *or* **Århus** a city and port in Denmark, in E Jutland. Pop: 228 547 (2004 est)

Aaron *Old Testament* the first high priest of the Israelites, brother of Moses (Exodus 4:14)

abacus 1 a counting device that consists of a frame holding rods on which a specific number of beads are free to move. Each rod designates a given denomination, such as units, tens, hundreds, etc, in the decimal system, and each bead represents a digit or a specific number of digits 2 *Architect* the flat upper part of the capital of a column

Abaddon 1 the Devil (Revelation 9:11) 2 (in rabbinical literature) a part of Gehenna; Hell

Abakan a city in S central Russia, capital of the Khakass Republic, at the confluence of the Yenisei and Abakan Rivers. Pop: 167 000 (2005 est)

abalone any of various edible marine gastropod molluscs of the genus *Haliotis*, having an ear-shaped shell that is perforated with a row of respiratory holes. The shells are used for ornament or decoration

Abba¹ Swedish pop group (1972–82): comprised Benny Andersson (born 1946), Agnetha Faltskog (born 1950), Anni-Frid Lyngstad (born 1945), and Bjorn Ulvaeus (born 1945); numerous hit singles included "Waterloo" (1974), "Dancing Queen" (1977), and "The Winner Takes It All" (1980)

Abba² 1 *New Testament* father (used of God) 2 a title given to bishops and patriarchs in the Syrian, Coptic, and Ethiopian Churches

abbacy the office, term of office, or jurisdiction of an abbot or abbess

Abbado Claudio born 1933, Italian conductor; principal conductor of the London Symphony Orchestra (1979–88); director of the Vienna State Opera (1986–91), and the Berlin Philharmonic (1989–2001)

abbé 1 a French abbot 2 a title used in addressing any other French cleric, such as a priest

Abbe Ernst 1840–1905, German physicist, noted for his work in optics and the microscope condenser known as the **Abbe condenser**

abbess the female superior of a convent

abbey 1 a building inhabited by a community of monks or nuns governed by an abbot or abbess 2 a church built in conjunction with such a building 3 such a community of monks or nuns

abbot the superior of an abbey of monks

abdomen 1 the region of the body of a vertebrate that contains the viscera other than the heart and lungs. In mammals it is separated from the thorax by the diaphragm 2 (in arthropods) the posterior part of the body behind the thorax, consisting of up to ten similar segments

abdominoplasty the surgical removal of excess skin and fat from the abdomen

Abdul-Hamid II 1842–1918, sultan of Turkey (1876–1909), deposed by the Young Turks, noted for his brutal suppression of the Armenian revolt (1894–96)

Abednego *Old Testament* one of Daniel's three companions who, together with Shadrach and Meshach, was miraculously saved from destruction in Nebuchadnezzar's fiery furnace (Daniel 3:12–30)

Abel *Old Testament* the second son of Adam and Eve, a shepherd, murdered by his brother Cain (Genesis 4:1–8)

Abelard Peter French name *Pierre Abélard*. 1079–1142, French scholastic philosopher and theologian whose works include *Historia Calamitatum* and *Sic et Non* (1121). His love for Hëloïse is recorded in their correspondence

Abeokuta a town in W Nigeria, capital of Ogun state. Pop: 487 000 (2005 est)

Aberdare a town in South Wales, in Rhondda, Cynon, Taff county borough. Pop: 31 705 (2001)

Aberdeen¹ George Hamilton-Gordon, 4th Earl of. 1784–1860, British statesman. He was foreign secretary under Wellington (1828) and Peel (1841–46); became prime minister of a coalition ministry in 1852 but was compelled to resign after mismanagement of the Crimean War (1855)

Aberdeen² 1 a city in NE Scotland, on the North Sea: centre for processing North Sea oil and gas; university (1494). Pop: 184 788 (2001) 2 **City of** a council area in NE Scotland, established in 1996. Pop: 206 600 (2003 est). Area: 186 sq km (72 sq miles)

Aberdeen Angus a black hornless breed of beef cattle originating in Scotland

Aberdeenshire a council area and historical county of N Scotland, on the North Sea: became part of Grampian Region in 1975 but reinstated as an independent unitary authority (with adjusted borders) in 1996: rises to the Grampian and Cairngorm Mountains in the SW: chiefly agricultural (esp sheep and stock raising). Administrative centre: Aberdeen. Pop: 229 330 (2003 est). Area 6319 sq km (2439 sq miles)

Aberfan a former coal-mining village in S Wales, in Merthyr Tydfil county borough: scene of a disaster in 1966 when a slag heap collapsed onto part of the village killing 144 people (including 116 children)

aberration 1 *Optics* a defect in a lens or mirror that causes the formation of either a distorted image or one with coloured fringes (see **chromatic aberration**) 2 *Astronomy* the apparent displacement of a celestial body due to the finite speed of light and the motion of the observer with the earth

Aberystwyth a resort and university town in Wales, in Ceredigion on Cardigan Bay. Pop: 15 935 (2001)

abeyance *Law* an indeterminate state of ownership, as when the person entitled to an estate has not been ascertained

Abia a state of SE Nigeria. Capital: Umuahia. Pop: 2 569 362 (1995 est). Area (including Imo state): 11 850 sq km (4575 sq miles)

Abidjan a port in Côte d'Ivoire, on the Gulf of Guinea: the legislative capital (Yamoussoukro became the administrative capital in 1983). Pop: 3 516 000 (2005 est)

Abigail *Old Testament* the woman who brought provisions to David and his followers and subsequently became his wife (I Samuel 25:1–42)

Abingdon a market town in S England, in Oxfordshire. Pop: 36 010 (2001)

Abkhazia an administrative division of NW Georgia, between the Black Sea and the Caucasus Mountains: a subtropical region, with mountains rising over 3900 m (13 000 ft); Abkhazian separatists seized control of the region in 1993. Capital: Sukhumi. Pop: 516 600 (1993 est). Area: 8600 sq km (3320 sq miles)

ablation 1 *Medicine* the surgical removal of an organ, structure, or part 2 *Astronautics* the melting or wearing away of an expendable part, such as the heat shield of a space re-entry vehicle on passing through the earth's atmosphere 3 *Geology* the wearing away of a rock or glacier

able *Law* qualified, competent, or authorized to do some specific act

able-bodied seaman an ordinary seaman, esp one in the merchant navy, who has been trained in certain skills

able rating (esp in the Royal Navy) a rating who is qualified to perform certain duties of seamanship

abolition *History* 1 (in British territories) the ending of the slave trade (1807) or the ending of slavery (1833): accomplished after a long campaign led by William Wilberforce 2 (in the US) the emancipation of the slaves, accomplished by the Emancipation Proclamation issued in 1863 and ratified in 1865

abominable snowman a large legendary manlike or apelike creature, alleged to inhabit the Himalayan Mountains

Aboriginal 1 of, relating to, or characteristic of the native peoples of Australia 2 another word for an Australian **Aborigine**

aborigine an original inhabitant of a country or region who has been there from the earliest known times

Aborigine 1 a member of a dark-skinned hunting and gathering people who were living in Australia when European settlers arrived 2 any of the languages of this people

abortion pill a drug, such as mifepristone, used to terminate a pregnancy in its earliest stage

Aboukir Bay *or* **Abukir Bay** a bay on the N coast of Egypt, where the Nile enters the Mediterranean: site of the Battle of the Nile (1798), in which Nelson defeated the French fleet

Abraham 1 *Old Testament* the first of the patriarchs, the father of Isaac and the founder of the Hebrew people (Genesis 11–25) 2 **Abraham's bosom** the place where the just repose after death (Luke 16:22)

abrasion *Geography* the effect of mechanical erosion of rock, esp a river bed, by rock fragments scratching and scraping it; wearing down

abrupt 1 *Botany* shaped as though a part has been cut off; truncate 2 *Geology* (of strata) cropping out suddenly

Abruzzi *or* **Abruzzo** a region of S central Italy, between the Apennines and the Adriatic: separated from the former administrative region **Abruzzi e Molise** in 1965. Capital: Aquila. Pop: 1 273 284 (2003 est). Area: 10 794 sq km (4210 sq miles)

Absalom *Old Testament* the third son of David, who rebelled against his father and was eventually killed by Joab (II Samuel 15–18)

abscess a localized collection of pus formed as the product of inflammation and usually caused by bacteria

abscissa the horizontal or x-coordinate of a point in a two-dimensional system of Cartesian coordinates. It is the distance from the y-axis measured parallel to the x-axis

absinthe *or* **absinth** 1 another name for **wormwood** (the plant) 2 a potent green alcoholic drink, technically a gin, originally having high wormwood content

absolute 1 *Physics* **a** (of a pressure measurement) not relative to atmospheric pressure **b** denoting absolute or thermodynamic temperature 2 *Maths* **a** (of a constant) never changing in value **b** (of an inequality) unconditional **c** (of a term) not containing a variable 3 *Law* (of a court order or decree) coming into effect immediately and not liable to be modified; final 4 *Law* (of a title to property, etc) not subject to any encumbrance or condition

absolute majority a number of votes totalling over 50

per cent, such as the total number of votes or seats obtained by a party that beats the combined opposition

absolute pitch 1 the ability to identify exactly the pitch of a note without comparing it to another 2 the exact pitch of a note determined by its number of vibrations per second

absolute zero the lowest temperature theoretically attainable, at which the particles constituting matter would be in the lowest energy states available; the zero of thermodynamic temperature; zero on the International Practical Scale of Temperature: equivalent to –273.15°C or –459.67°F

absolution *Christianity* a a formal remission of sin pronounced by a priest in the sacrament of penance b the prescribed form of words granting such a remission

absolutism 1 *Philosophy* a any theory which holds that truth or moral or aesthetic value is absolute and universal and not relative to individual or social differences b the doctrine that reality is unitary and unchanging and that change and diversity are mere illusion 2 *Christianity* an uncompromising form of the doctrine of predestination

absorption 1 *Physiol* a normal assimilation by the tissues of the products of digestion b the passage of a gas, fluid, drug, etc, through the mucous membranes or skin 2 *Physics* a reduction of the intensity of any form of radiated energy as a result of energy conversion in a medium, such as the conversion of sound energy into heat 3 *Immunol* the process of removing superfluous antibodies or antigens from a mixture using a reagent

abstention *Politics* the act of withholding one's vote

abstinence *Chiefly RC Church* the practice of refraining from specific kinds of food or drink, esp from meat, as an act of penance

abstract 1 denoting art characterized by geometric, formalized, or otherwise nonrepresentational qualities 2 *Philosophy* (of an idea) functioning for some empiricists as the meaning of a general term 3 an abstract painting, sculpture, etc.

abstraction 1 *Logic* an operator that forms a class name or predicate from any given expression 2 an abstract painting, sculpture, etc.

absurd *Philosophy* the conception of the world, esp in Existentialist thought, as neither designed nor predictable but irrational and meaningless

Abu Dhabi a sheikhdom (emirate) of SE Arabia, on the S coast of the Persian Gulf: the chief sheikhdom and capital of the United Arab Emirates, consisting principally of the port of Abu Dhabi and a desert hinterland; contains major oilfields. Pop: 476 000 (2005 est). Area: 67 350 sq km (25 998 sq miles)

Abuja the federal capital of Nigeria, in the centre of the country. Pop: 467 000 (2005 est)

abundance 1 *Chem* the extent to which an element or ion occurs in the earth's crust or some other specified environment: often expressed in parts per million or as a percentage 2 *Physics* the ratio of the number of atoms of a specific isotope in a mixture of isotopes of an element to the total number of atoms present: often expressed as a percentage 3 a call in solo whist undertaking to make nine tricks

Abu Simbel a former village in S Egypt: site of two tem-

ples of Rameses II, which were moved to higher ground (1966–67) before the area behind the Aswan High Dam was flooded

abutment *or* **abuttal** *Architect, Civil engineering* a construction that takes the thrust of an arch or vault or supports the end of a bridge

Abydos 1 an ancient town in central Egypt: site of many temples and tombs 2 an ancient Greek colony on the Asiatic side of the Dardanelles (Hellespont): scene of the legend of Hero and Leander

abyss 1 a very deep or unfathomable gorge or chasm 2 hell or the infernal regions conceived of as a bottomless pit

acacia 1 any shrub or tree of the tropical and subtropical leguminous genus *Acacia*, having compound or reduced leaves and small yellow or white flowers in dense inflorescences 2 **false acacia** another name for **locust** 3 **gum acacia** another name for **gum arabic**

academic 1 belonging or relating to a place of learning, esp a college, university, or academy 2 relating to studies such as languages, philosophy, and pure science, rather than applied, technical, or professional studies 3 a member of a college or university

academy 1 an institution or society for the advancement of literature, art, or science 2 a secondary school: now used only as part of a name, and often denoting a private school

Acadia 1 a the Atlantic Provinces of Canada b the French-speaking areas of these provinces 2 (formerly) a French colony in the present-day Atlantic Provinces: ceded to Britain in 1713

Acadian 1 denoting or relating to Acadia or its inhabitants 2 any of the early French settlers in Nova Scotia, many of whom were deported to Louisiana in the 18th century

acanthus 1 any shrub or herbaceous plant of the genus *Acanthus*, native to the Mediterranean region but widely cultivated as ornamental plants, having large spiny leaves and spikes of white or purplish flowers: family *Acanthaceae* 2 a carved ornament based on the leaves of the acanthus plant, esp as used on the capital of a Corinthian column

Acapulco a port and resort in SW Mexico, in Guerrero state. Pop: 761 000 (2005 est)

ACAS *or* **Acas** in Britain Advisory Conciliation and Arbitration Service
▷www.acas.org.uk

accelerando *Music* 1 (to be performed) with increasing speed 2 an increase in speed

acceleration the rate of increase of speed or the rate of change of velocity.

accelerator 1 a device for increasing speed, esp a pedal for controlling the fuel intake in a motor vehicle; throttle 2 *Physics* a machine for increasing the kinetic energy of subatomic particles or atomic nuclei and focusing them on a target 3 *Chem* a substance that increases the speed of a chemical reaction, esp one that increases the rate of vulcanization of rubber, the rate of development in photography, the rate of setting of synthetic resins, or the rate of setting of concrete; catalyst 4 *Economics* (in an economy) the relationship between the rate of change in output or sales and the consequent change in the level of investment **5** *Anatomy* a muscle or nerve that increases the rate of a function

accent 1 *Music* **a** stress placed on certain notes in a piece of music, indicated by a symbol printed over the note concerned **b** the rhythmic pulse of a piece or passage, usually represented as the stress on the first beat of each bar **2** *Maths* either of two superscript symbols indicating a specific unit, such as feet ('), inches ("), minutes of arc ('), or seconds of arc (")

acceptance 1 *Commerce* **a** a formal agreement by a debtor to pay a draft, bill, etc. **b** the document so accepted **2** *Austral and NZ* a list of horses accepted as starters in a race **3** *Contract law* words or conduct by which a person signifies his assent to the terms and conditions of an offer or agreement

accessible *Logic* (of a possible world) surveyable from some other world so that the truth value of statements about it can be known. A statement *possibly p* is true in a world W if and only if *p* is true in some worlds accessible to W

accession 1 *Property law* **a** an addition to land or property by natural increase or improvement **b** the owner's right to the increased value of such land **2** *International law* the formal acceptance of a convention or treaty

accessory 1 *Law* a person who incites someone to commit a crime or assists the perpetrator of a crime, either before or during its commission **2** assisting in or having knowledge of an act, esp a crime

access road a road providing a means of entry into a region or of approach to another road, esp a motorway

access time *Computing* the time required to retrieve a piece of stored information

accident 1 *Logic, Philosophy* a nonessential attribute or characteristic of something (as opposed to substance) **2** *Metaphysics* a property as contrasted with the substance in which it inheres **3** *Geology* a surface irregularity in a natural formation, esp in a rock formation or a river system

accidental 1 *Music* denoting sharps, flats, or naturals that are not in the key signature of a piece **2** *Logic* (of a property) not essential; contingent **3** *Music* a symbol denoting a sharp, flat, or natural that is not a part of the key signature

acclamation by acclamation a by an overwhelming majority without a ballot **b** *Canadian* (of an election or electoral victory) without opposition

accolade 1 the ceremonial gesture used to confer knighthood, originally an embrace, now a touch on the shoulder with a sword **2** *Architect* a curved ornamental moulding, esp one having the shape of an ogee arch

accommodation *Physiol* the automatic or voluntary adjustment of the shape of the lens of the eye for far or near vision

accommodation address an address on letters, etc, to a person or business that does not wish or is not able to receive post at a permanent or actual address

accompaniment *Music* a subordinate part for an instrument, voices, or an orchestra

accordion 1 a portable box-shaped instrument of the reed organ family, consisting of metallic reeds that are made to vibrate by air from a set of bellows controlled by the player's hands. Notes are produced by means of studlike keys **2** short for **piano accordion**

account 1 a a regular client or customer, esp a firm that purchases commodities on credit **b** an area of business assigned to another **2 on account a** on credit **b** as partial payment **3 settle** *or* **square accounts with** to pay or receive a balance due

Accra the capital of Ghana, a port on the Gulf of Guinea: built on the site of three 17th-century trading fortresses founded by the English, Dutch, and Danish. Pop: 1 970 000 (2005 est)

accretion 1 *Botany* the growing together of normally separate plant or animal parts **2** *Pathol* **a** abnormal union or growing together of parts; adhesion **b** a mass of foreign matter collected in a cavity **3** *Law* an increase in the share of a beneficiary in an estate, as when a co-beneficiary fails to take his share **4** *Astronomy* the process in which matter under the influence of gravity is attracted to and increases the mass of a celestial body. The matter usually forms an **accretion disc** around the accreting object **5** *Geology* the process in which a continent is enlarged by the tectonic movement and deformation of the earth's crust

accumulation the taking of a first and an advanced university degree simultaneously

accumulator 1 a rechargeable device for storing electrical energy in the form of chemical energy, consisting of one or more separate secondary cells **2** *Horse racing, Brit* a collective bet, esp on four or more races, in which the stake and winnings on each successive race are carried forward to become the stake on the next, so that both stakes and winnings accumulate progressively so long as the bet continues to be a winning one **3 a** a register in a computer or calculator used for holding the results of a computation or data transfer **b** a location in a computer store in which arithmetical results are produced

accuracy *Physics, Chem* the degree of agreement between a measured or computed value of a physical quantity and the standard or accepted value for that quantity

accurate *Maths* **a** (to n significant digits) representing the first n digits of the given number starting with the first nonzero digit, but approximating to the nearest digit in the final position **b** (to n decimal places) giving the first n digits after the decimal point without further approximation

accusation *Law* a formal charge brought against a person stating the crime that he is alleged to have committed

accused *Law* the defendant or defendants appearing on a criminal charge

ace 1 *Tennis* a winning serve that the opponent fails to reach **2** *Golf, chiefly US* a hole in one

Aceh an autonomous region of N Indonesia, in N Sumatra; mountainous with rain forests; scene of separatist conflict since the later 1990s; coastal areas suffered badly in the Indian Ocean tsunami of December 2004. Capital: Banda Aceh. Pop: 3 930 905 (2000). Area: 55 392 sq km (21 381 sq miles)

acetaldehyde a colourless volatile pungent liquid, miscible with water, used in the manufacture of organic compounds and as a solvent and reducing agent. Formula: CH_3CHO

acetate 1 any salt or ester of acetic acid, containing the monovalent ion CH_3COO^- or the group CH_3COO- **2** consisting of, containing, or concerned with the group CH_3COO- **3** short for **cellulose acetate 4** a sound recording disc composed of an acetate lacquer coating on an aluminium or plastic base: used for demonstration or other short-term purposes

acetic of, containing, producing, or derived from acetic acid or vinegar

acetic acid a colourless pungent liquid, miscible with water, widely used in the manufacture of acetic anhydride, vinyl acetate, plastics, pharmaceuticals, dyes, etc. Formula: CH_3COOH

acetone a colourless volatile flammable pungent liquid, miscible with water, used in the manufacture of chemicals and as a solvent and thinner for paints, varnishes, and lacquers. Formula: CH_3COCH_3

acetylene a colourless flammable gas used in the manufacture of organic chemicals and in cutting and welding metals. Formula: C_2H_2

Achaea *or* **Achaia 1** a department of Greece, in the N Peloponnese. Capital: Patras. Pop: 318 928 (2001). Area: 3209 sq km (1239 sq miles) **2** a province of ancient Greece, in the N Peloponnese on the Gulf of Corinth: enlarged as a Roman province in 27 BC

Achebe Chinua born 1930, Nigerian novelist. His works include *Things Fall Apart* (1958), *A Man of the People* (1966), and *Anthills of the Savannah* (1987)

Acheson Dean (**Gooderham**). 1893–1971, US lawyer and statesman: secretary of state (1949–53) under President Truman

Achilles tendon the fibrous cord that connects the muscles of the calf to the heelbone

Achill Island an island in the Republic of Ireland, off the W coast of Co. Mayo. Area: 148 sq km (57 sq miles). Pop: 2620 (2002)

achromatic 1 capable of reflecting or refracting light without chromatic aberration **2** *Cytology* a not staining with standard dyes **b** of or relating to achromatin **3** *Music* **a** involving no sharps or flats **b** another word for **diatonic 4** denoting a person who is an achromat

acid 1 any substance that dissociates in water to yield a sour corrosive solution containing hydrogen ions, having a pH of less than 7, and turning litmus red **2** a slang name for **LSD 3** *Chem* **a** of, derived from, or containing acid **b** being or having the properties of an acid **4** (of rain, snow, etc) containing pollutant acids in solution **5** (of igneous rocks) having a silica content of more than 60 of the total and containing at least one tenth quartz **6** *Metallurgy* of or made by a process in which the furnace or converter is lined with an acid material

Acid House *or* **Acid** a type of funk-based electronically edited disco music of the late 1980s, which has hypnotic sound effects and is associated with hippy culture and the use of the drug ecstasy

acidity 1 the amount of acid present in a solution, often expressed in terms of pH

acid rain rain that contains a high concentration of pollutants, chiefly sulphur dioxide and nitrogen oxide, released into the atmosphere by the burning of fossil fuels such as coal or oil

acne a chronic skin disease common in adolescence, involving inflammation of the sebaceous glands and characterized by pustules on the face, neck, and upper trunk

acolyte *Christianity* an officer who attends or assists a priest

Aconcagua a mountain in W Argentina: the highest peak in the Andes and in the W Hemisphere. Height: 6960 m (22 835 ft)

aconite *or* **aconitum 1** any of various N temperate plants of the ranunculaceous genus *Aconitum*, such as monkshood and wolfsbane, many of which are poisonous **2** the dried poisonous root of many of these plants, sometimes used as an antipyretic

acorn the fruit of an oak tree, consisting of a smooth thick-walled nut in a woody scaly cuplike base

acoustic *or* **acoustical 1** of or related to sound, the sense of hearing, or acoustics **2** designed to respond to, absorb, or control sound **3** (of a musical instrument or recording) without electronic amplification

acoustics 1 the scientific study of sound and sound waves **2** the characteristics of a room, auditorium, etc, that determine the fidelity with which sound can be heard within it

acquaintance *Philosophy* the relation between a knower and the object of his knowledge, as contrasted with knowledge by description (esp in the phrase **knowledge by acquaintance**)

acre a unit of area used in certain English-speaking countries, equal to 4840 square yards or 4046.86 square metres

Acre 1 a state of W Brazil: mostly unexplored tropical forests; acquired from Bolivia in 1903. Capital: Rio Branco. Pop: 586 942 (2002). Area: 152 589 sq km (58 899 sq miles) **2** a city and port in N Israel, strategically situated on the **Bay of Acre** in the E Mediterranean: taken and retaken during the Crusades (1104, 1187, 1191, 1291), taken by the Turks (1517), by Egypt (1832), and by the Turks again (1839). Pop: 45 600 (2001)

acrobat an entertainer who performs acts that require skill, agility, and coordination, such as tumbling, swinging from a trapeze, or walking a tightrope

acrophobia abnormal fear or dread of being at a great height

acropolis the citadel of an ancient Greek city

acrostic a a number of lines of writing, such as a poem, certain letters of which form a word, proverb, etc. A **single acrostic** is formed by the initial letters of the lines, a **double acrostic** by the initial and final letters, and a **triple acrostic** by the initial, middle, and final letters **b** the word, proverb, etc, so formed **c** (*as modifier*): *an acrostic sonnet*

acrylic acid a colourless corrosive pungent liquid, miscible with water, used in the manufacture of acrylic resins. Formula: $CH_2:CHCOOH$

acrylic resin any of a group of polymers or copolymers of acrylic acid, its esters, or amides, used as synthetic rubbers, textiles, paints, adhesives, and as plastics such as Perspex

act 1 the formally codified result of deliberation by a legislative body; a law, edict, decree, statute, etc. **2** a formal written record of transactions, proceedings, etc, as of a society, committee, or legislative body **3** a major division of a dramatic work **4 a** a short performance of

5

skill, a comic sketch, dance, etc, esp one that is part of a programme of light entertainment **b** those giving such a performance **5** *Philosophy* an occurrence effected by the volition of a human agent, usually opposed at least as regards its explanation to one which is causally determined

ACT (in New Zealand) Association of Consumers and Taxpayers: a small political party of the right

acting **1** intended for stage performance; provided with directions for actors **2** the art or profession of an actor

▷www.linksnorth.com/acting

▷www.myactingagent.com

▷www.caryn.com/acting

actinide series a series of 15 radioactive elements with increasing atomic numbers from actinium to lawrencium

actinium a radioactive element of the actinide series, occurring as a decay product of uranium. It is used as an alpha-particle source and in neutron production. Symbol: Ac; atomic no.: 89; half-life of most stable isotope,[227]Ac: 21.6 years; relative density: 10.07; melting pt.: 1051°C; boiling pt.: 3200 ± 300°C

action **1** *Law* **a** a legal proceeding brought by one party against another, seeking redress of a wrong or recovery of what is due; lawsuit **b** the right to bring such a proceeding **2** the operating mechanism, esp in a piano, gun, watch, etc. **3** (of a guitar) the distance between the strings and the fingerboard **4** (of keyboard instruments) the sensitivity of the keys to touch **5** the force applied to a body **6** *Physics* **a** a property of a system expressed as twice the mean kinetic energy of the system over a given time interval multiplied by the time interval **b** the product of work or energy and time, usually expressed in joule seconds **7** *Philosophy* behaviour which is voluntary and explicable in terms of the agent's reasons, as contrasted with that which is coerced or determined causally

actionable *Law* affording grounds for legal action

action painting a development of abstract expressionism evolved in the 1940s, characterized by broad vigorous brush strokes and accidental effects of thrown, smeared, dripped, or spattered paint

Actium a town of ancient Greece that overlooked the naval battle in 31 BC at which Octavian's fleet under Agrippa defeated that of Mark Antony and Cleopatra

active **1** (of a volcano) erupting periodically; not extinct **2** *Astronomy* (of the sun) exhibiting a large number of sunspots, solar flares, etc, and a marked variation in intensity and frequency of radio emission **3** *Commerce* **a** producing or being used to produce profit, esp in the form of interest **b** of or denoting stocks or shares that have been actively bought and sold as recorded in the Official List of the London Stock Exchange **4** *Electronics* **a** containing a source of power **b** capable of amplifying a signal or controlling some function

activity **1** the number of disintegrations of a radioactive substance in a given unit of time, usually expressed in curies or disintegrations per second **2 a** the capacity of a substance to undergo chemical change **b** the effective concentration of a substance in a chemical system. The **absolute activity** of a substance B, λ_B, is defined as $\exp(\mu_B RT)$ where μ_B is the chemical potential

act of God *Law* a sudden and inevitable occurrence caused by natural forces and not by the agency of man, such as a flood, earthquake, or a similar catastrophe

acupuncture the insertion of the tips of needles into the skin at specific points for the purpose of treating various disorders by stimulating nerve impulses. Originally Chinese, this method of treatment is practised in many parts of the world

acute **1** *Maths* **a** (of an angle) less than 90° **b** (of a triangle) having all its interior angles less than 90° **2** of a disease **a** arising suddenly and manifesting intense severity **b** of relatively short duration **3** (of a hospital, hospital bed, or ward) intended to accommodate short-term patients with acute illnesses

Ada a high-level computer programming language designed for dealing with real-time processing problems: used for military and other systems

adagio *Music* **1** (to be performed) slowly **2** a movement or piece to be performed slowly **3** *Ballet* a slow section of a pas de deux

Adam[1] **1** Adolphe 1803–56, French composer, best known for his romantic ballet *Giselle* (1841) **2** Robert 1728–92, Scottish architect and furniture designer. Assisted by his brother, **James**, 1730–94, he emulated the harmony of classical and Italian Renaissance architecture **3** in the neoclassical style made popular by Robert Adam

Adam[2] *Old Testament* the first man, created by God: the progenitor of the human race (Genesis 2–3)

Adam in the neoclassical style made popular by Robert Adam (1728–92), Scottish architect and furniture designer

adamant a legendary stone said to be impenetrable, often identified with the diamond or loadstone

Adams[1] **1** Gerry, full name *Gerrard Adams*. born 1948, Northern Ireland politician; president of Sinn Féin from 1983: negotiated the Irish Republican Army ceasefires in 1994–96 and 1997 **2** Henry (Brooks). 1838–1918, US historian and writer. His works include *Mont Saint Michel et Chartres* (1913) and his autobiography *The Education of Henry Adams* (1918) **3** John 1735–1826, second president of the US (1797–1801); US ambassador to Great Britain (1785–88); helped draft the Declaration of Independence (1776) **4** John Coolidge born 1947, US composer; works include the operas *Nixon in China* (1987) and *The Death of Klinghoffer* (1991) **5** John Couch 1819–92, British astronomer who deduced the existence and position of the planet Neptune **6** John Quincey son of John Adams. 1767–1848, sixth president of the US (1825–29); secretary of state (1817–25) **7** Richard born 1920, British author; his novels include *Watership Down* (1972), *The Plague Dogs* (1977), and *Traveller* (1988) **8** Samuel 1722–1803, US revolutionary leader; one of the organizers of the Boston Tea Party; a signatory of the Declaration of Independence

Adams[2] a mountain in SW Washington, in the Cascade Range. Height: 3751 m (12 307 ft)

Adam's apple the visible projection of the thyroid cartilage of the larynx at the front of the neck

Adana a city in S Turkey, capital of Adana province. Pop: 1 248 000 (2005 est)

adaptation **1** *Biology* an inherited or acquired modification in organisms that makes them better suited to survive and reproduce in a particular environment **2** *Physiol* the decreased response of a sense organ to a repeated or sustained stimulus **3** *Psychol* (in learning theory) the weakening of a response to a stimulus with repeated presentation of the stimulus without reinforcement; applied mainly to innate responses **4** *Social welfare* alteration to a dwelling to make it suitable for a disabled person, as by replacing steps with ramps

adaptor *or* **adapter 1** any device for connecting two parts, esp ones that are of different sizes or have different mating fitments **2 a** a plug used to connect an electrical device to a mains supply when they have different types of terminals **b** a device used to connect several electrical appliances to a single mains socket

Addams Jane 1860–1935, US social reformer, feminist, and pacifist, who founded Hull House, a social settlement in Chicago: Nobel peace prize 1931

addendum 1 the radial distance between the major and pitch cylinders of an external screw thread **2** the radial distance between the pitch circle and tip of a gear tooth

adder¹ 1 a common viper, *Vipera berus*, that is widely distributed in Europe, including Britain, and Asia and is typically dark greyish in colour with a black zigzag pattern along the back **2** any of various similar venomous or nonvenomous snakes

adder² a person or thing that adds, esp a single element of an electronic computer, the function of which is to add a single digit of each of two inputs

addict a person who is addicted, esp to narcotic drugs
▷www.addictionsearch.com
▷www.adpana.com
▷www.alcoholicsanonymous.org

Addington Henry, 1st Viscount Sidmouth. 1757–1844, British statesman; prime minister (1801–04) and Home Secretary (1812–21)

Addis Ababa the capital of Ethiopia, on a central plateau 2400 m (8000 ft) above sea level: founded in 1887; became capital in 1896. Pop: 2 899 000 (2005 est)

Addison Joseph 1672–1719, English essayist and poet who, with Richard Steele, founded *The Spectator* (1711–14) and contributed most of its essays, including the *de Coverley Papers*

addition a mathematical operation in which the sum of two numbers or quantities is calculated. Usually indicated by the symbol +

add-on a feature that can be added to a standard model or package to give increased benefits

address 1 *Computing* a number giving the location of a piece of stored information **2** *Brit, Government* a statement of the opinions or wishes of either or both Houses of Parliament that is sent to the sovereign **3** the alignment or position of a part, component, etc, that permits correct assembly or fitting

Adelaide the capital of South Australia: Port Adelaide, 11 km (7 miles) away on St. Vincent Gulf, handles the bulk of exports. Pop: 1 002 127 (2001)

Aden 1 the main port and commercial capital of Yemen, on the N coast of the **Gulf of Aden**, an arm of the Indian Ocean at the entrance to the Red Sea: capital of South Yemen until 1990: formerly an important port of call on shipping routes to the East. Pop: 584 000 (2005 est) **2** a former British colony and protectorate on the S coast of

the Arabian Peninsula: became part of South Yemen in 1967, now part of Yemen. Area: 195 sq km (75 sq miles)

Adenauer Konrad 1876–1967, German statesman; chancellor of West Germany (1949–63)

adhesion 1 an attraction or repulsion between the molecules of unlike substances in contact: distinguished from *cohesion* **2** *Pathol* abnormal union of structures or parts

adipose 1 of, resembling, or containing fat; fatty **2** animal fat

adjacent 1 *Maths* **a** (of a pair of vertices in a graph) joined by a common edge **b** (of a pair of edges in a graph) meeting at a common vertex **2** *Geometry* the side lying between a specified angle and a right angle in a right-angled triangle

adjective (of law) relating to court practice and procedure, as opposed to the principles of law dealt with by the courts

Adler 1 Alfred 1870–1937, Austrian psychiatrist, noted for his descriptions of overcompensation and inferiority feelings **2** Larry, full name *Lawrence Cecil Adler*. 1914–2001, US harmonica player

administration 1 the conduct of the affairs of government **2** the executive branch of government along with the public service; the government as a whole **3** *Chiefly US* the political executive, esp of the US; the government **4** *Chiefly US* a government board, agency, authority, etc. **5** *Property law* **a** the conduct or disposal of the estate of a deceased person **b** the management by a trustee of an estate subject to a trust

administrator 1 *Property law* a person authorized to manage an estate, esp when the owner has died intestate or without having appointed executors **2** a person who manages a computer system

admiral any of various nymphalid butterflies, esp the red admiral or white admiral

Admiralty Range a mountain range in Antarctica, on the coast of Victoria Land, northwest of the Ross Sea

admissible *Law* (esp of evidence) capable of being or bound to be admitted in a court of law

admittance 1 **2** *Electrical engineering* the reciprocal of impedance, usually measured in siemens. It can be expressed as a complex quantity, the real part of which is the conductance and the imaginary part the susceptance

Adonai *Judaism* a name for God

Adonis *Greek myth* a handsome youth loved by Aphrodite. Killed by a wild boar, he was believed to spend part of the year in the underworld and part on earth, symbolizing the vegetative cycle

ADP *Biochem* adenosine diphosphate; a nucleotide derived from ATP with the liberation of energy that is then used in the performance of muscular work

adrenal 1 on or near the kidneys **2** of or relating to the adrenal glands or their secretions **3** an adrenal gland

Adrian IV original name *Nicholas Breakspear*. ?1100–59, the only English pope (1154–59)

Adriatic 1 of or relating to the Adriatic Sea, or to the inhabitants of its coast or islands **2 the** short for the **Adriatic Sea**

Adriatic Sea an arm of the Mediterranean between Italy and the Balkan Peninsula

adrift floating without steering or mooring; drifting

adult 1 a mature fully grown animal or plant **2** *Law* a person who has attained the age of legal majority (18 years for most purposes)

adultery voluntary sexual intercourse between a married man or woman and a partner other than the legal spouse

Aduwa *or* **Adowa** a town in N Ethiopia: Emperor Menelik II defeated the Italians here in 1896. Pop: 17 476 (1989 est)

advance 1 *Commerce* **a** the supplying of commodities or funds before receipt of an agreed consideration **b** the commodities or funds supplied in this manner **c** (*as modifier*): *an advance supply* **2** a money payment made before it is legally due

advancement *Property law* the use during a testator's lifetime of money or property for the benefit of a child or other person who is a prospective beneficiary in the testator's will

advantage *Tennis* **a** the point scored after deuce **b** the resulting state of the score

advection the transference of heat energy in a horizontal stream of gas, esp of air

Advent *Christianity* the season including the four Sundays preceding Christmas or (in Eastern Orthodox churches) the forty days preceding Christmas

Adventist a member of any of the Christian groups, such as the **Seventh-Day Adventists** that hold that the Second Coming of Christ is imminent

adventitious (of a plant or animal part) developing in an abnormal position, as a root that grows from a stem

adverse (of leaves, flowers, etc) facing the main stem

advocaat a liqueur having a raw egg base

advocate 1 a person who pleads his client's cause in a court of law **2** *Scots Law* the usual word for **barrister**

Adygei Republic *or* **Adygea** a constituent republic of SW Russia, bordering on the Caucasus Mountains: chiefly agricultural but with some mineral resources. Capital: Maikop. Pop: 447 000 (2002). Area: 7600 sq km (2934 sq miles)

adze *or US* **adz** a heavy hand tool with a steel cutting blade attached at right angles to a wooden handle, used for dressing timber

Adzhar Autonomous Republic *or* **Adzharia** an administrative division of SW Georgia, on the Black Sea: part of Turkey from the 17th century until 1878; mostly mountainous, reaching 2805 m (9350 ft), with a subtropical coastal strip. Capital: Batumi. Pop: 386 700 (1993 est). Area: 3000 sq km (1160 sq miles)

Aegean 1 of or relating to the Aegean Sea or Islands **2** of or relating to the Bronze Age civilization of Greece, Asia Minor, and the Aegean Islands

Aegean Sea an arm of the Mediterranean between Greece and Turkey

Aegina 1 an island in the Aegean Sea, in the Saronic Gulf. Area: 85 sq km (33 sq miles) **2** a town on the coast of this island: a city-state of ancient Greece **3 Gulf of** another name for the **Saronic Gulf**

aegis *or sometimes US* **egis** *Greek myth* the shield of Zeus, often represented in art as a goatskin

Aegospotami a river of ancient Thrace that flowed into the Hellespont. At its mouth the Spartan fleet under Lysander defeated the Athenians in 405 BC, ending the Peloponnesian War

aeolian harp a stringed instrument that produces a musical sound when a current of air or wind passes over the strings

Aeolis *or* **Aeolia** the ancient name for the coastal region of NW Asia Minor, including the island of Lesbos, settled by the Aeolian Greeks (about 1000 BC)

aeon *or esp US* **eon 1** a period of one thousand million years **2** *Gnosticism* one of the powers emanating from the supreme being and culminating in the demiurge

aerial 1 of or relating to aircraft **2** the part of a radio or television system having any of various shapes, such as a dipole, Yagi, long-wire, or vertical aerial, by means of which radio waves are transmitted or received

aerobic 1 (of an organism or process) depending on oxygen **2** of or relating to aerobes

aerodrome *or US* **airdrome** a landing area, esp for private aircraft, that is usually smaller than an airport

aerodynamics the study of the dynamics of gases, esp of the forces acting on a body passing through air

aero engine an engine for powering an aircraft

aerofoil *or US and Canadian* **airfoil** a cross section of an aileron, wing, tailplane, or rotor blade

aeronautics the study or practice of all aspects of flight through the air

   ▷www.sae.org/technology/aerospace.htm
   ▷www.aeronautics.ru/links.htm

aeroplane *or US and Canadian* **airplane** a heavier-than-air powered flying vehicle with fixed wings

aerosol a colloidal dispersion of solid or liquid particles in a gas; smoke or fog

aerospace 1 the atmosphere and space beyond **2** of or relating to rockets, missiles, space vehicles, etc, that fly or operate in aerospace

   ▷www.airspacemag.com
   ▷www.janes.com/aerospace/civil/

Aeschylus ?525–?456 BC, Greek dramatist, regarded as the father of Greek tragedy. Seven of his plays are extant, including *Seven Against Thebes*, *The Persians*, *Prometheus Bound*, and the trilogy of the *Oresteia*

Aesop ?620–564 BC, Greek author of fables in which animals are given human characters and used to satirize human failings

aesthetic *or sometimes US* **esthetic 1** connected with aesthetics or its principles **2** a principle of taste or style adopted by a particular person, group, or culture

aesthetics *or sometimes US* **esthetics 1** the branch of philosophy concerned with the study of such concepts as beauty, taste, etc. **2** the study of the rules and principles of art

aetiology *or* **etiology 1** the study of the causes of diseases **2** the cause of a disease

Aetolia a mountainous region forming (with the region of Acarnania) a department of W central Greece, north of the Gulf of Patras: a powerful federal state in the 3rd century BC. Chief city: Missolonghi. Pop. (with Acarnania): 219 092 (2001). Area: 5461 sq km (2108 sq miles)

Afars and the Issas **Territory of the a** former name (1967–77) of Djibouti

affect *Psychol* the emotion associated with an idea or set of ideas

affection 1 *Pathol* any disease or pathological condition 2 *Psychol* any form of mental functioning that involves emotion

affidavit *Law* a declaration in writing made upon oath before a person authorized to administer oaths, esp for use as evidence in court

affinity 1 similarity in structure, form, etc, between different animals, plants, or languages 2 *Chem* **a** the tendency for two substances to combine; chemical attraction **b** a measure of the tendency of a chemical reaction to take place expressed in terms of the free energy change. 3 *Biology* a measure of the degree of interaction between two molecules, such as an antigen and antibody or a hormone and its receptor

affirmative 1 *Logic* **a** (of a categorial proposition) affirming the satisfaction by the subject of the predicate, as in *all birds have feathers; some men are married* **b** not containing negation 2 *Logic* an affirmative proposition

affray *Law* a fight, noisy quarrel, or disturbance between two or more persons in a public place

Afghan *or* **Afghani** a native, citizen, or inhabitant of Afghanistan

Afghan hound a tall graceful breed of hound with a long silky coat

Afghanistan a republic in central Asia: became independent in 1919; occupied by Soviet troops, 1979–89; controlled by mujaheddin forces from 1992 until 1996 when Taliban forces seized power; in the US-led 'war against terrorism' (2001) the Taliban were overthrown and replaced by an interim administration; generally arid and mountainous, with the Hindu Kush range rising over 7500 m (25 000 ft) and fertile valleys of the Amu Darya, Helmand, and Kabul Rivers. Official languages: Pashto and Dari (Persian), Tajik also widely spoken. Religion: Muslim. Currency: afghani. Capital: Kabul. Pop: 24 926 000 (2004 est). Area: 657 500 sq km (250 000 sq miles)

aficionado a devotee of bullfighting

Africa the second largest of the continents, on the Mediterranean in the north, the Atlantic in the west, and the Red Sea, Gulf of Aden, and Indian Ocean in the east. The Sahara desert divides the continent unequally into North Africa (an early centre of civilization, in close contact with Europe and W Asia, now inhabited chiefly by Arabs) and Africa south of the Sahara (relatively isolated from the rest of the world until the 19th century and inhabited chiefly by Negroid peoples). It was colonized mainly in the 18th and 19th centuries by Europeans and now comprises independent nations. The largest lake is Lake Victoria and the chief rivers are the Nile, Niger, Congo, and Zambezi. Pop: 887 964 000 (2005 est). Area: about 30 300 000 sq km (11 700 000 sq miles)

African 1 denoting or relating to Africa or any of its peoples, languages, nations, etc. 2 a native, inhabitant, or citizen of any of the countries of Africa 3 a member or descendant of any of the peoples of Africa, esp a Black person

African violet any of several tropical African plants of the genus *Saintpaulia*, esp *S. ionantha*, cultivated as house plants, with violet, white, or pink flowers and hairy leaves: family *Gesneriaceae*

Afrikaans one of the official languages of the Republic of South Africa, closely related to Dutch

Afrikaner a White native of the Republic of South Africa whose mother tongue is Afrikaans

aft *Chiefly nautical* towards or at the stern or rear

after 07 *Nautical* further aft

afterbirth the placenta and fetal membranes expelled from the uterus after the birth of the offspring

aftercare 1 support services by a welfare agency for a person discharged from an institution, such as hospital, hostel, or prison 2 *Med* the care before and after discharge from hospital of a patient recovering from an illness or operation 3 any system of maintenance or upkeep of an appliance or product

afterdamp a poisonous mixture of gases containing carbon dioxide, carbon monoxide, and nitrogen formed after the explosion of firedamp in coal mines

aftereffect 1 *Med* any delayed response to a stimulus or agent 2 *Psychol* any illusory sensation caused by a stimulus that has ceased

afterglow 1 the glow left after a light has disappeared, such as that sometimes seen after sunset 2 the glow of an incandescent metal after the source of heat has been removed 3 *Physics* luminescence persisting on the screen of a cathode-ray tube or in a gas-discharge tube after the power supply has been disconnected

aftershock one of a series of minor tremors occurring after the main shock of an earthquake

Agadir a port in SW Morocco, which became the centre of an international crisis (1911), when a gunboat arrived to protect German interests. Britain issued a strong warning to Germany but the French negotiated and war was averted. In 1960 the town was virtually destroyed by an earthquake, about 10 000 people being killed. Pop: 385 000 (2003)

Aga Khan IV Prince Karim born 1936, spiritual leader of the Ismaili sect of Muslims from 1957

agar a complex gelatinous carbohydrate obtained from seaweeds, esp those of the genus *Gelidium*, used as a culture medium for bacteria, a laxative, in food such as ice cream as a thickening agent (E406), etc.

agaric 1 any saprotrophic basidiomycetous fungus of the family *Agaricaceae*, having gills on the underside of the cap. The group includes the edible mushrooms and poisonous forms such as the fly agaric 2 the dried spore-producing bodies of certain fungi, esp *Polyphorus officinalis* (or *Boletus laricis*), formerly used in medicine

Agartala a city in NE India, capital of the state of Tripura. Pop: 189 327 (2001)

Agassi Andre born 1970, US tennis player: won the Wimbledon men's singles in 1992 and the US Open in 1994 and 1999

agate 1 an impure microcrystalline form of quartz consisting of a variegated, usually banded chalcedony, used as a gemstone and in making pestles and mortars, burnishers, and polishers. Formula: SiO_2 2 a playing marble of this quartz or resembling it

agave any plant of the genus *Agave*, native to tropical America, with tall flower stalks rising from a massive, often armed, rosette of thick fleshy leaves: family *Agavaceae*. Some species are the source of fibres such as sisal or of alcoholic beverages such as pulque and tequila

age 1 a a period of history marked by some feature or characteristic; era b (*capital when part of a name*): *the Middle Ages; the Space Age* 2 *Geology, palaeontol* a a period of the earth's history distinguished by special characteristics b the period during which a stage of rock strata is formed; a subdivision of an epoch 3 *Myth* any of the successive periods in the legendary history of man, which were, according to Hesiod, the golden, silver, bronze, heroic, and iron ages 4 *Psychol* the level in years that a person has reached in any area of development, such as mental or emotional, compared with the normal level for his chronological age 5 **of age** adult and legally responsible for one's actions (usually at 18 or, formerly, 21 years)

aged *Geography* having reached an advanced stage of erosion

Agee James 1909–55, US novelist, poet, and film critic. His works include the autobiographical novel *A Death in the Family* (1957)

ageing or **aging** the change of properties that occurs in some metals after heat treatment or cold working

agency 1 a business or other organization providing a specific service 2 the place where an agent conducts business 3 the business, duties, or functions of an agent 4 one of the administrative organizations of a government

agent a person representing a business concern, esp a travelling salesman

agglomerate a rock consisting of angular fragments of volcanic lava

aggravated *Law* (of a criminal offence) made more serious by its circumstances

aggregate 1 (of fruits and flowers) composed of a dense cluster of carpels or florets 2 *Geology* a rock, such as granite, consisting of a mixture of minerals 3 a group of closely related biotypes produced by apomixis, such as brambles, which are the *Rubus fruticosus* aggregate

aggression 1 an attack or harmful action, esp an unprovoked attack by one country against another 2 *Psychol* a hostile or destructive mental attitude or behaviour

agitprop 1 (formerly) a bureau of the Central Committee of the Communist Party of the Soviet Union, in charge of agitation and propaganda on behalf of Communism 2 a any promotion, as in the arts, of political propaganda, esp of a Communist nature b (*as modifier*): *agitprop theatre*

Agnes Saint ?292–?304 AD, Christian child martyr under Diocletian. Feast day: Jan 21

Agnesi Maria Gaetana 1718–99, Italian mathematician and philosopher, noted for her work on differential calculus

agnostic a person who holds that knowledge of a Supreme Being, ultimate cause, etc, is impossible

agoraphobia a pathological fear of being in public places, often resulting in the sufferer becoming housebound

Agra a city in N India, in W Uttar Pradesh on the Jumna River: a capital of the Mogul empire until 1658; famous for its Mogul architecture, esp the Taj Mahal. Pop: 1 259 979 (2001)

agrarian a person who favours the redistribution of landed property

Agricola Gnaeus Julius 40–93 AD, Roman general; governor of Britain who advanced Roman rule north to the Firth of Forth

Agrigento a town in Italy, in SW Sicily: site of six Greek temples. Pop: 54 619 (2001)

agrimony 1 any of various N temperate rosaceous plants of the genus *Agrimonia*, which have compound leaves, long spikes of small yellow flowers, and bristly burlike fruits 2 any of several other plants, such as hemp agrimony

Agrippa Marcus Vipsanius 63–12 BC, Roman general: chief adviser and later son-in-law of Augustus

Agrippina 1 called *the Elder. c* 14 BC–33 AD, Roman matron: granddaughter of Augustus, wife of Germanicus, mother of Caligula and Agrippina the Younger 2 called *the Younger.* 15–59 AD, mother of Nero, who put her to death after he became emperor

Aguascalientes 1 a state in central Mexico. Pop: 943 506 (2000). Area: 5471 sq km (2112 sq miles) 2 a city in central Mexico, capital of Aguascalientes state, about 1900 m (6200 ft) above sea level, with hot springs. Pop: 830 000 (2005 est)

ague a fever with successive stages of fever and chills esp when caused by malaria

Ahab *Old Testament* the king of Israel from approximately 869 to 850 BC and husband of Jezebel: rebuked by Elijah (I Kings 16:29–22:40)

Ahasuerus *Old Testament* a king of ancient Persia and husband of Esther, generally identified with Xerxes

Ahern Bertie born 1951, Irish politician; leader of the Fianna Fáil party from 1994; prime minister of the Republic of Ireland from 1997

Ahithophel or **Achitophel** *Old Testament* a member of David's council, who became one of Absalom's advisers in his rebellion and hanged himself when his advice was overruled (II Samuel 15:12–17:23)

Ahmedabad or **Ahmadabad** a city in W India, in Gujarat: famous for its mosque. Pop: 3 515 361 (2001)

Ahmednagar or **Ahmadnagar** a city in W India, in Maharashtra: formerly one of the kingdoms of Deccan. Pop: 307 455 (2001)

Ahwaz or **Ahvaz** a town in SW Iran, on the Karun River. Pop: 967 000 (2005 est)

aid 1 *Mountaineering* any of various devices such as piton or nut when used as a direct help in the ascent 2 (in medieval Europe; in England after 1066) a feudal payment made to the king or any lord by his vassals, usually on certain occasions such as the marriage of a daughter or the knighting of an eldest son

Aidan Saint died 651 AD, Irish missionary in Northumbria, who founded the monastery at Lindisfarne (635). Feast day: Aug 31

aide *Social welfare* an unqualified assistant to a professional welfare worker

AIDS or **Aids** acquired immune (or immuno-) deficiency syndrome: a condition, caused by a virus, in which certain white blood cells (lymphocytes) are destroyed, resulting in loss of the body's ability to protect itself against disease. AIDS is transmitted by sexual intercourse, through infected blood and blood products, and

through the placenta
▷www.aids.org
▷www.amfar.org

aileron a flap hinged to the trailing edge of an aircraft wing to provide lateral control, as in a bank or roll

Ain 1 a department in E central France, in Rhône-Alpes region. Capital: Bourg. Pop: 539 006 (2003 est). Area: 5785 sq km (2256 sq miles) **2** a river in E France, rising in the Jura Mountains and flowing south to the Rhône. Length: 190 km (118 miles)

Aintree a suburb of Liverpool, in Merseyside: site of the racecourse over which the Grand National steeplechase has been run since 1839

air 1 the mixture of gases that forms the earth's atmosphere. At sea level dry air has a density of 1.226 kilograms per cubic metre and consists of 78.08 per cent nitrogen, 20.95 per cent oxygen, 0.93 per cent argon, 0.03 per cent carbon dioxide, with smaller quantities of ozone and inert gases; water vapour varies between 0 and 4 per cent and in industrial areas sulphur gases may be present as pollutants **2** *Music* **a** a simple tune for either vocal or instrumental performance **b** another word for **aria 3** *Austral, informal* the height gained when getting airborne in surfing, snowboarding, etc **4** *Astrology* of or relating to a group of three signs of the zodiac, Gemini, Libra, and Aquarius

airborne (of aircraft) flying; in the air

air brake 1 a brake operated by compressed air, esp in heavy vehicles and trains **2** an articulated flap or small parachute for reducing the speed of an aircraft **3** a rotary fan or propeller connected to a shaft to reduce its speed

airbrush an atomizer for spraying paint or varnish by means of compressed air

air conditioning a system or process for controlling the temperature and sometimes the humidity and purity of the air in a house, etc.

aircraft any machine capable of flying by means of buoyancy or aerodynamic forces, such as a glider, helicopter, or aeroplane
▷www.aerospaceweb.org/aircraft/index.shtml

air cushion 1 the pocket of air that supports a hovercraft **2** a form of pneumatic suspension consisting of a constricted volume of air

Airdrie a town in W central Scotland, in North Lanarkshire, E of Glasgow: manufacturing and pharmaceutical industries. Pop: 36 326 (2001)

Aire a river in N England rising in the Pennines and flowing southeast to the Ouse. Length: 112 km (70 miles)

Airedale a large rough-haired tan-coloured breed of terrier characterized by a black saddle-shaped patch covering most of the back

airfield a landing and taking-off area for aircraft, usually with permanent buildings

air hostess a stewardess on an airliner

airlift the transportation by air of passengers, troops, cargo, etc, esp when other routes are blocked

airline 1 a a system or organization that provides scheduled flights for passengers or cargo **b** (*as modifier*): *an airline pilot* **2** a hose or tube carrying air under pressure
▷http://routesinternational.com/air.htm

▷http://airlines.afriqonline.com

airliner a large passenger aircraft
▷www.airliners.net/info

airlock 1 a bubble in a pipe causing an obstruction or stoppage to the flow **2** an airtight chamber with regulated air pressure used to gain access to a space that has air under pressure

airplane *US and Canadian* a heavier-than-air powered flying vehicle with fixed wings

air pocket a localized region of low air density or a descending air current, causing an aircraft to suffer an abrupt decrease in height

airport a landing and taking-off area for civil aircraft, usually with surfaced runways and aircraft maintenance and passenger facilities
▷http://routesinternational.com/airports.htm
▷www.internationalairportguide.com

air pump a device for pumping air in or out of something

airship a lighter-than-air self-propelled craft
▷http://spot.colorado.edu/~dziadeck/ airship.html

airsick sick or nauseated from travelling in an aircraft

airside the part of an airport nearest the aircraft, the boundary of which is the security check, customs, passport control, etc.

airspeed the speed of an aircraft relative to the air in which it moves

airstrip a cleared area for the landing and taking off of aircraft; runway

air terminal 1 *Brit* a building in a city from which air passengers are taken by road or rail to an airport or the terminal building of an airport **2** a building at an airport from which air passengers depart or at which they arrive

airway 1 an air route, esp one that is fully equipped with emergency landing fields, navigational aids, etc. **2** a passage down which air travels from the nose or mouth to the lungs **3** *Med* a tubelike device inserted via the throat to keep open the airway of an unconscious patient

airworthy (of an aircraft) safe to fly

Aisha *or* **Ayesha** ?613–678 AD, the favourite wife of Mohammed; daughter of Abu Bekr

aisle a lateral division in a church flanking the nave or chancel

Aisne 1 a department of NE France, in Picardy region. Capital: Laon. Pop: 535 326 (2003 est). Area: 7428 sq km (2897 sq miles) **2** a river in N France, rising in the Argonne Forest and flowing northwest and west to the River Oise: scene of a major Allied offensive in 1918 which turned the tide finally against Germany in World War I. Length: 282 km (175 miles)

aitchbone the rump bone or floor of the pelvis in cattle

Aitken Robert Grant 1864–1951, US astronomer who discovered over three thousand double stars

Aix-en-Provence a city and spa in SE France: the medieval capital of Provence. Pop: 134 222 (1999)

Aix-les-Bains a town in E France: a resort with sulphurous springs. Pop: 25 732 (1999)

Ajaccio the capital of Corsica, a port on the W coast. Pop: 52 880 (1999)

Ajmer a city in NW India, in Rajasthan: textile centre. Pop: 485 197 (2001)

Akbar called *Akbar the Great*. 1542–1605, Mogul emperor of India (1556–1605), who extended the Mogul empire to include N India

Akhenaten or **Akhenaton** original name *Amenhotep IV*. died ?1358 BC, king of Egypt, of the 18th dynasty; he moved his capital from Thebes to Tell El Amarna and introduced the cult of Aten

Akhmatova Anna pseudonym of *Anna Gorenko*. 1889–1966, Russian poet: noted for her concise and intensely personal lyrics

Akihito born 1933, Emperor of Japan from 1989

Akkad or **Accad** 1 a city on the Euphrates in N Babylonia, the centre of a major empire and civilization (2360–2180 BC) 2 an ancient region lying north of Babylon, from which the Akkadian language and culture is named

Akure a city in SW Nigeria, capital of Ondo state: agricultural trade centre. Pop: 434 000 (2005 est)

Alabama 1 a state of the southeastern US, on the Gulf of Mexico: consists of coastal and W lowlands crossed by the Tombigbee, Black Warrior, and Alabama Rivers, with parts of the Tennessee Valley and Cumberland Plateau in the north; noted for producing cotton and white marble. Capital: Montgomery. Pop: 4 500 752 (2003 est). Area: 131 333 sq km (50 708 sq miles) 2 a river in Alabama, flowing southwest to the Mobile and Tensaw Rivers. Length: 507 km (315 miles)

alabaster 1 a fine-grained usually white, opaque, or translucent variety of gypsum used for statues, vases, etc. 2 a variety of hard semitranslucent calcite, often banded like marble

Ala Dağ or **Ala Dagh** 1 the E part of the Taurus Mountains, in SE Turkey, rising over 3600 m (12 000 ft) 2 a mountain range in E Turkey, rising over 3300 m (11 000 ft) 3 a mountain range in NE Turkey, rising over 3000 m (10 000 ft)

Alagna Roberto born 1963, Italian opera singer, born in France; a lyric tenor, he is married to the soprano Angela Gheorghiu

Alagoas a state in NE Brazil, on the Atlantic coast. Capital: Maceió. Pop: 2 887 535 (2002). Area: 30 776 sq km (11 031 sq miles)

Alai a mountain range in central Asia, in SW Kyrgyzstan, running from the Tian Shan range in China into Tajikistan. Average height: 4800 m (16 000 ft), rising over 5850 m (19 500 ft)

Alain-Fournier real name *Henri-Alban Fournier*. 1886–1914, French novelist; author of *Le Grand Meaulnes* (1913; translated as *The Lost Domain*, 1959)

Alamo the a mission in San Antonio, Texas, the site of a siege and massacre in 1836 by Mexican forces under Santa Anna of a handful of American rebels fighting for Texan independence from Mexico

Alanbrooke Alan Francis Brooke, 1st Viscount. 1883–1963, British field marshal; chief of Imperial General Staff (1941–46)

Alaric ?370–410 AD, king of the Visigoths, who served under the Roman emperor Theodosius I but later invaded Greece and Italy, capturing Rome in 410

alarm *Fencing* a warning or challenge made by stamping the front foot

Alaska 1 the largest state of the US, in the extreme northwest of North America: the aboriginal inhabitants are Inuit and Yupik; the earliest White settlements were made by the Russians; it was purchased by the US from Russia in 1867. It is mostly mountainous and volcanic, rising over 6000 m (20 000 ft), with the Yukon basin in the central region; large areas are covered by tundra; it has important mineral resources (chiefly coal, oil, and natural gas). Capital: Juneau. Pop: 648 818 (2003 est). Area: 1 530 694 sq km (591 004 sq miles) 2 **Gulf of** the N part of the Pacific, between the Alaska Peninsula and the Alexander Archipelago

Alaska Highway a road extending from Dawson Creek, British Columbia, to Fairbanks, Alaska: built by the US Army (1942). Length: 2452 km (1523 miles)

Alaska Peninsula an extension of the mainland of SW Alaska between the Pacific and the Bering Sea, ending in the Aleutian Islands. Length: about 644 km (400 miles)

Alaska Range a mountain range in S central Alaska. Highest peak: Mount McKinley, 6194 m (20 320 ft)

alb *Christianity* a long white linen vestment with sleeves worn by priests and others

albacore a tunny, *Thunnus alalunga*, occurring mainly in warm regions of the Atlantic and Pacific. It has very long pectoral fins and is a valued food fish

Alba Longa a city of ancient Latium, southeast of modern Rome: the legendary birthplace of Romulus and Remus

Alban Saint 3rd century AD, the first English martyr. He was beheaded by the Romans on the site on which St Alban's Abbey now stands, for admitting his conversion to Christianity. Feast day: June 17

Albania a republic in SE Europe, on the Balkan Peninsula: became independent in 1912 after more than four centuries of Turkish rule; established as a republic (1946) under Communist rule; multiparty constitution adopted in 1991. It is generally mountainous, rising over 2700 m (9000 ft), with extensive forests. Language: Albanian. Religion: Muslim majority. Currency: lek. Capital: Tirana. Pop: 3 193 000 (2004 est). Area: 28 749 sq km (11 100 sq miles)

Albanian 1 the official language of Albania: of uncertain relationship within the Indo-European family, but thought to be related to ancient Illyrian 2 a a native, citizen, or inhabitant of Albania b a native speaker of Albanian

Albany 1 a city in E New York State, on the Hudson River: the state capital. Pop: 93 919 (2003 est) 2 a river in central Canada, flowing east and northeast to James Bay. Length: 982 km (610 miles) 3 a port in southwest Western Australia: founded as a penal colony. Pop: 22 415 (2001)

albatross 1 any large oceanic bird of the genera *Diomedea* and *Phoebetria*, family *Diomedeidae*, of cool southern oceans: order *Procellariiformes* (petrels). They have long narrow wings and are noted for a powerful gliding flight 2 *Golf* a score of three strokes under par for a hole

Albee Edward born 1928, US dramatist. His plays include *Who's Afraid of Virginia Woolf?* (1962), *Seascape* (1975), *Marriage Play* (1986), *Three Tall Women* (1990), and *Goat* (2004)

Albemarle Sound an inlet of the Atlantic in NE North Carolina. Length: about 96 km (60 miles)

Albers Josef 1888–1976, US painter, designer, and poet, born in Germany. His works include a series of abstract paintings entitled *Homage to the Square*

Albert¹ Prince full name *Albert Francis Charles Augustus Emmanuel of Saxe-Coburg-Gotha*. 1819–61, Prince Consort of Queen Victoria of Great Britain and Ireland

Albert² Lake a lake in E Africa, between the Democratic Republic of Congo (formerly Zaïre) and Uganda in the great Rift Valley, 660 m (2200 ft) above sea level: a source of the Nile, fed by the Victoria Nile, which leaves as the Albert Nile. Area: 5345 sq.km (2064 sq miles)

Alberta a province of W Canada: mostly prairie, with the Rocky Mountains in the southwest. Capital: Edmonton. Pop: 3 201 895 (2004 est). Area: 661 188 sq km (255 285 sq miles)

Albertan 1 of or relating to Alberta or its inhabitants 2 a native or inhabitant of Alberta

Albert Edward a mountain in SE New Guinea, in the Owen Stanley Range. Height: 3993 m (13 100 ft)

Albert I 1 *c* 1255–1308, king of Germany (1298–1308) 2 1875–1934, king of the Belgians (1909–34) 3 called *Albert the Bear.c* 1100–70. German military leader: first margrave of Brandenburg

Alberti Leon Battista 1404–72, Italian Renaissance architect, painter, writer, and musician; among his architectural designs are the façades of Sta. Maria Novella at Florence and S. Francesco at Rimini

Albertus Magnus Saint original name *Albert, Count von Böllstadt*. ?1193–1280, German scholastic philosopher; teacher of Thomas Aquinas and commentator on Aristotle. Feast day: Nov 15

Albi a town in S France: connected with the Albigensian heresy and the crusade against it. Pop: 46 274 (1999)

albino 1 a person with congenital absence of pigmentation in the skin, eyes, and hair 2 any animal or plant that is deficient in pigment

Albinoni Tomaso 1671–1750, Italian composer and violinist. He wrote concertos and over 50 operas

Albion *Archaic or poetic* Britain or England

album 1 a booklike holder containing sleeves for gramophone records 2 *Chiefly Brit* an anthology, usually large and illustrated

albumin *or* **albumen** any of a group of simple watersoluble proteins that are coagulated by heat and are found in blood plasma, egg white, etc.

Albuquerque¹ Afonso de 1453–1515, Portuguese navigator who established Portuguese colonies in the East by conquering Goa, Ceylon, Malacca, and Ormuz

Albuquerque² a city in central New Mexico, on the Rio Grande. Pop: 471 856 (2003 est)

Albury-Wodonga a town in SE Australia, in S central New South Wales, on the Murray River: commercial centre of an agricultural region. Pop: 69 880 (2001)

Alcaeus 7th century BC, Greek lyric poet who wrote hymns, love songs, and political odes

Alcatraz an island in W California, in San Francisco Bay: a federal prison until 1963

Alcazar de San Juan a town in S central Spain: associated with Cervantes and Don Quixote. Pop: 27 229 (2003 est)

alchemy the pseudoscientific predecessor of chemistry that sought a method of transmuting base metals into gold, an elixir to prolong life indefinitely, a panacea or universal remedy, and an alkahest or universal solvent

Alchevsk a city in E Ukraine. Pop: 117 000 (2005 est)

Alcibiades 450–404 BC, Athenian statesman and general in the Peloponnesian War: brilliant, courageous, and unstable, he defected to the Spartans in 415, but returned and led the Athenian victories at Abydos (411) and Cyzicus (410)

Alcock Sir John William 1892–1919, English aviator who with A.W. Brown made the first nonstop flight across the Atlantic (1919)

alcohol 1 a colourless flammable liquid, the active principle of intoxicating drinks, produced by the fermentation of sugars, esp glucose, and used as a solvent and in the manufacture of organic chemicals. Formula: C_2H_5OH 2 a drink or drinks containing this substance 3 *Chem* any one of a class of organic compounds that contain one or more hydroxyl groups bound to carbon atoms. The simplest alcohols have the formula ROH, where R is an alkyl group

alcoholic a person affected by alcoholism
▷www.ias.org.uk
▷www.alcoholconcern.org.uk

alcoholism a condition in which dependence on alcohol harms a person's health, social functioning, or family life

Alcott Louisa May 1832–88, US novelist, noted for her children's books, esp *Little Women* (1869)

alcove any recessed usually vaulted area, as in a garden wall

Alcuin *or* **Albinus** 735–804 AD, English scholar and theologian; friend and adviser of Charlemagne

Aldabra an island group in the Indian Ocean: part of the British Indian Ocean Territory (1965–76); now administratively part of the Seychelles

Aldan a river in E Russia in the SE Sakha Republic, rising in the Aldan Mountains and flowing north and west to the Lena River. Length: about 2700 km (1700 miles)

Aldeburgh a small resort in SE England, in Suffolk: site of an annual music festival established in 1948 by Benjamin Britten. Pop: 2654 (2001)

aldehyde 1 any organic compound containing the group -CHO. Aldehydes are oxidized to carboxylic acids and take part in many addition reactions 2 consisting of, containing, or concerned with the group -CHO

alder 1 any N temperate betulaceous shrub or tree of the genus *Alnus*, having toothed leaves and conelike fruits. The bark is used in dyeing and tanning and the wood for bridges, etc because it resists underwater rot 2 any of several similar trees or shrubs

Aldermaston a village in S England, in West Berkshire unitary authority, Berkshire, SW of Reading: site of the Atomic Weapons Research Establishment and starting point of the Aldermaston marches (1958–63), organized by the Campaign for Nuclear Disarmament. Pop: 2157 (1987 est)

Alderney 1 one of the Channel Islands, in the English Channel: separated from the French coast by a dangerous tidal channel (the **Race of Alderney**). Pop: 2294

13

(2001). Area: 8 sq km (3 sq miles) **2** an early, but now extinct, breed of dairy cattle originating from the island of Alderney

Aldershot a town in S England, in Hampshire: site of a large military camp. Pop: 58 170 (2001)

Aldington Richard 1892–1962, English poet, novelist, and biographer. His novels include *Death of a Hero* (1929) and *The Colonel's Daughter* (1931), which reflect postwar disillusion following World War I

Aldiss Brian W(ilson). born 1925, British novelist, best known for his science fiction. His works include *Non-Stop* (1958), *Enemies of the System* (1978), *The Helliconia Trilogy* (1983–86), *Forgotten Life* (1988), and *The Detached Retina* (1995)

Aldridge-Brownhills a town in central England, in Walsall unitary authority, West Midlands: formed by the amalgamation of neighbouring towns in 1966. Pop: 35 525 (2001)

Aldrin Edwin Eugene Jr, known as *Buzz*. born 1930, US astronaut; the second man to set foot on the moon on July 20, 1969, during the Apollo 11 flight

Aldus Manutius 1450–1515, Italian printer, noted for his fine editions of the classics. He introduced italic type

ale 1 a beer fermented in an open vessel using yeasts that rise to the top of the brew **2** (formerly) an alcoholic drink made by fermenting a cereal, esp barley, but differing from beer by being unflavoured by hops **3** *Chiefly Brit* another word for **beer**

Aleichem Sholom, real name *Solomon Rabinowitz*. 1859–1916, US Jewish writer, born in Russia. His works include *Tevye the Milkman*, which was adapted for the stage musical *Fiddler on the Roof*

Aleixandre Vicente 1898–1984, Spanish poet, whose collections include *La destrucción o el amor* (1935; Destruction or Love): Nobel prize for literature 1977

alembic an obsolete type of retort used for distillation

Aleppo an ancient city in NW Syria: industrial and commercial centre. Pop: 2 505 000 (2005 est)

Alessandria a town in NW Italy, in Piedmont. Pop: 85 438 (2001)

A level in Britain **1 a** a public examination in a subject taken for the General Certificate of Education (**GCE**), usually at the age of 17–18 **b** the course leading to this examination **c** (*as modifier*): *A-level maths* **2** a pass in a particular subject at A level

Alexander Harold (Rupert Leofric George), Earl Alexander of Tunis. 1891–1969, British field marshal in World War II, who organized the retreat from Dunkirk and commanded in North Africa (1943) and Sicily and Italy (1944–45); governor general of Canada (1946–52); British minister of defence (1952–54)

Alexander Archipelago a group of over 1000 islands along the coast of SE Alaska

Alexander I 1 *c*1080–1124, king of Scotland (1107–24), son of Malcolm III **2** 1777–1825, tsar of Russia (1801–25), who helped defeat Napoleon and formed the Holy Alliance (1815)

Alexander II 1 1198–1249, king of Scotland (1214–49), son of William (the Lion) **2** 1818–81, tsar of Russia (1855–81), son of Nicholas I, who emancipated the serfs (1861). He was assassinated by the Nihilists

Alexander III 1 1241–86, king of Scotland (1249–86), son

of Alexander II **2** original name *Orlando Bandinelli*. died 1181, pope (1159–81), who excommunicated Barbarossa **3** 1845–94, tsar of Russia (1881–94), son of Alexander II

Alexander I Island an island of Antarctica, west of Palmer Land, in the Bellingshausen Sea. Length: about 378 km (235 miles)

Alexander technique a technique for developing awareness of one's posture and movement in order to improve it

Alexander VI original name *Rodrigo Borgia*. 1431–1503, pope (1492–1503): noted for his extravagance and immorality as well as for his patronage of the arts; father of Cesare and Lucrezia Borgia, with whom he is said to have committed incest

Alexander Nevski Saint ?1220–63, Russian prince and military leader, who defeated the Swedes at the River Neva (1240) and the Teutonic knights at Lake Peipus (1242)

Alexander the Great 356–323 BC, king of Macedon, who conquered Greece (336), Egypt (331), and the Persian Empire (328), and founded Alexandria

Alexandra 1 1844–1925, queen consort of Edward VII of Great Britain and Ireland **2** 1872–1918, the wife of Nicholas II of Russia; her misrule while Nicholas was supreme commander of the Russian forces during World War I precipitated the Russian Revolution

Alexandria the chief port of Egypt, on the Nile Delta: cultural centre of ancient times, founded by Alexander the Great (332 BC). Pop: 3 760 000 (2005 est)

Alexis Mikhailovich 1629–76, tsar of Russia (1645–76); father of Peter the Great

alfalfa a leguminous plant, *Medicago sativa*, of Europe and Asia, having compound leaves with three leaflets and clusters of small purplish flowers. It is widely cultivated for forage and as a nitrogen fixer and used as a commercial source of chlorophyll

al Fayed Mohamed born 1933, Egyptian-born businessman; owner of the Harrods department store from 1985 and of the Ritz Hotel, Paris, from 1979: his son Dodi Fayed (1956–97) died in the same Paris car crash as Diana, Princess of Wales

Alfonso VI died 1109, king of Léon (1065–1109) and of Castile (1072–1109). He appointed his vassal, the Spanish hero El Cid, ruler of Valencia

Alfonso XIII 1886–1941, king of Spain (1886–1931), who was forced to abdicate on the establishment of the republic in 1931

Alfred the Great 849–99, king of Wessex (871–99) and overlord of England, who defeated the Danes and encouraged learning and writing in English

Algarve the an area in the south of Portugal, on the Atlantic; it approximately corresponds to the administrative district of Faro: fishing and tourism important

algebra a branch of mathematics in which arithmetical operations and relationships are generalized by using alphabetic symbols to represent unknown numbers or members of specified sets of numbers

Algeciras a port and resort in SW Spain, on the Strait of Gibraltar: scene of a conference of the Great Powers in 1906. Pop: 108 779 (2003 est)

Algeria a republic in NW Africa, on the Mediterranean: became independent in 1962, after more than a century of French rule; one-party constitution adopted in 1976; religious extremists led a campaign of violence from 1988 until 2000; consists chiefly of the N Sahara, with the Atlas Mountains in the north, and contains rich deposits of oil and natural gas. Official languages: Arabic and Berber; French also widely spoken. Religion: Muslim. Currency: dinar. Capital: Algiers. Pop: 32 339 000 (2004 est). Area: about 2 382 800 sq km (920 000 sq miles)

Algerian 1 of or relating to Algeria or its inhabitants **2** a native or inhabitant of Algeria

Algiers the capital of Algeria, an ancient port on the Mediterranean; until 1830 a centre of piracy. Pop: 3 260 000 (2005 est)

Algonquin *or* **Algonkin 1** a member of a North American Indian people formerly living along the St Lawrence and Ottawa Rivers in Canada **2** the language of this people, a dialect of Ojibwa

algorism 1 the Arabic or decimal system of counting **2** the skill of computation using any system of numerals **3** another name for **algorithm**

algorithm 1 a logical arithmetical or computational procedure that if correctly applied ensures the solution of a problem **2** *Logic, Maths* a recursive procedure whereby an infinite sequence of terms can be generated

Algren Nelson 1909–81, US novelist. His novels, mostly set in Chicago, include *Never Come Morning* (1942) and *The Man with the Golden Arm* (1949)

Alhambra a citadel and palace in Granada, Spain, built for the Moorish kings during the 13th and 14th centuries: noted for its rich ornamentation

Al Hufuf *or* **Al Hofuf** a town in E Saudi Arabia: a trading centre with nearby oilfields and oases. Pop: 331 000 (2005 est)

Ali 1 7600–661 AD, fourth caliph of Islam (656–61 AD), considered the first caliph by the Shiites: cousin and son-in-law of Mohammed **2** Mehemet See **Mehemet Ali 3** Muhammad See **Muhammad Ali**

alibi *Law* **a** a defence by an accused person that he was elsewhere at the time the crime in question was committed **b** the evidence given to prove this

Alicante a port in SE Spain: commercial centre. Pop: 305 911 (2003 est)

Alice Springs a town in central Australia, in the Northern Territory, in the Macdonnell Ranges. Pop: 23 640 (2001)

alien 1 a person owing allegiance to a country other than that in which he lives; foreigner **2** (in science fiction) a being from another world, sometimes specifically an extraterrestrial

alienable *Law* (of property) transferable to another owner

Aligarh a city in N India, in W Uttar Pradesh, with a famous Muslim university (1920). Pop: 667 732 (2001)

alimentary *Scots Law* free from the claims of creditors

alimentary canal *or* **tract** the tubular passage extending from the mouth to the anus, through which food is passed and digested

alimony *Law* (formerly) an allowance paid under a court order by one spouse to another when they are separated but not divorced

Ali Pasha known as *the Lion of Janina*. 1741–1822, Turkish pasha and ruler of Albania (1787–1820), who was deposed and assassinated after intriguing against Turkey

aliphatic (of an organic compound) not aromatic, esp having an open chain structure, such as alkanes, alkenes, and alkynes

aliquant *Maths* of, signifying, or relating to a quantity or number that is not an exact divisor of a given quantity or number

aliquot 1 *Maths* of, signifying, or relating to an exact divisor of a quantity or number **2** consisting of equal quantities **3** an aliquot part

alkali 1 *Chem* a soluble base or a solution of a base **2** a soluble mineral salt that occurs in arid soils and some natural waters

alkaline having the properties of or containing an alkali

alkaloid any of a group of nitrogenous basic compounds found in plants, typically insoluble in water and physiologically active. Common examples are morphine, strychnine, quinine, nicotine, and caffeine

alkane a any saturated aliphatic hydrocarbon with the general formula C_nH_{2n+2} **b** (*as modifier*): *alkane series*

alkene a any unsaturated aliphatic hydrocarbon with the general formula C_nH_{2n} **b** (*as modifier*): *alkene series*

Alkmaar a city in the W Netherlands, in North Holland. Pop: 93 000 (2003 est)

Allah *Islam* the Muslim name for God; the one Supreme Being

Allahabad a city in N India, in SE Uttar Pradesh at the confluence of the Ganges and Jumna Rivers: Hindu pilgrimage centre. Pop: 990 298 (2001)

allegiance (in feudal society) the obligations of a vassal to his liege lord

allegory 1 a poem, play, picture, etc, in which the apparent meaning of the characters and events is used to symbolize a deeper moral or spiritual meaning **2** the technique or genre that this represents **3** use of such symbolism to illustrate truth or a moral

allegretto *Music* **1** (to be performed) fairly quickly or briskly **2** a piece or passage to be performed in this manner

Allegri Gregorio 1582–1652, Italian composer and singer. His compositions include a *Miserere* for nine voices

allegro *Music* **1** (to be performed) quickly, in a brisk lively manner **2** a piece or passage to be performed in this manner

allele any of two or more variants of a gene that have the same relative position on homologous chromosomes and are responsible for alternative characteristics, such as smooth or wrinkled seeds in peas

alleluia a song of praise to God

Allen¹ 1 Ethan 1738–89, American soldier during the War of Independence who led the Green Mountain Boys of Vermont **2** Sir **Thomas** born 1944, British operatic baritone **3 Woody** real name *Allen Stewart Konigsberg*. born 1935, US film comedian, screenwriter, and director. His films as an actor and director include *Annie Hall* (1977), *Manhattan* (1979), *Hannah and Her Sisters* (1986), *Bullets over Broadway* (1994), and *Anything Else* (2003)

Allen² 1 Bog of a region of peat bogs in central Ireland, west of Dublin. Area: over 10 sq km (3.75 sq miles) **2**

Lough a lake in Ireland, in county Leitrim

Allenby Edmund Henry Hynman, 1st Viscount. 1861–1936, British field marshal who captured Palestine and Syria from the Turks in 1918; high commissioner in Egypt (1919–25)

Allende 1 Isabel born 1942, Chilean writer, born in Peru; her works include *Eva Luna* (1989), *Paula* (1995), and *Daughter of Fortune* (1999) 2 Salvador 1908–73, Chilean Marxist politician; president of Chile from 1970 until 1973, when the army seized power and he was killed

allergen any substance capable of inducing an allergy

allergy a hypersensitivity to a substance that causes the body to react to any contact with that substance. Hay fever is an allergic reaction to pollen
▷www.aafa.org

alley¹ *Tennis, chiefly US* the space between the singles and doubles sidelines

alley² a large playing marble

alliance *Botany* a taxonomic category consisting of a group of related families; subclass

Allier 1 a department of central France, in Auvergne region. Capital: Moulins. Pop: 342 307 (2003 est). Area: 7382 sq km (2879 sq miles) 2 a river in S central France, rising in the Cévennes and flowing north to the Loire. Length: over 403 km (250 miles)

alligator 1 a large crocodilian, *Alligator mississipiensis*, of the southern US, having powerful jaws and sharp teeth and differing from the crocodiles in having a shorter and broader snout: family *Alligatoridae* (alligators and caymans) 2 a similar but smaller species, *A. sinensis*, occurring in China near the Yangtse River 3 any crocodilian belonging to the family *Alligatoridae* 4 any of various tools or machines having adjustable toothed jaws, used for gripping, crushing, or compacting

Allingham Margery 1904–66, British author of detective stories, featuring Albert Campion. Her works include *Tiger in the Smoke* (1952) and *The Mind Readers* (1965)

alliteration the use of the same consonant (**consonantal alliteration**) or of a vowel, not necessarily the same vowel (**vocalic alliteration**), at the beginning of each word or each stressed syllable in a line of verse, as in *around the rock the ragged rascal ran*

Alloa a town in E central Scotland, the administrative centre of Clackmannanshire. Pop: 18 989 (2001)

allopathy the orthodox medical method of treating disease, by inducing a condition different from or opposed to the cause of the disease

allotrope any of two or more physical forms in which an element can exist

allotropy *or* **allotropism** the existence of an element in two or more physical forms. The most common elements having this property are carbon, sulphur, and phosphorus

allowance *Brit, Education* a salary supplement given to a teacher who is appointed to undertake extra duties and responsibilities

Alloway a village in Scotland, in South Ayrshire, S of Ayr: birthplace of Robert Burns

alloy a metallic material, such as steel, brass, or bronze, consisting of a mixture of two or more metals or of metallic elements with nonmetallic elements. Alloys often have physical properties markedly different from

those of the pure metals

All Saints' Day a Christian festival celebrated on Nov 1 to honour all the saints

All Souls' Day *RC Church* a day of prayer (Nov 2) for the dead in purgatory

allspice a tropical American myrtaceous tree, *Pimenta officinalis*, having small white flowers and aromatic berries

alluvial 1 of or relating to alluvium 2 another name for **alluvium** 3 *Austral and NZ* alluvium containing any heavy mineral, esp gold

alluvium a fine-grained fertile soil consisting of mud, silt, and sand deposited by flowing water on flood plains, in river beds, and in estuaries

ally a plant, animal, substance, etc, closely related to another in characteristics or form

Almada a town in S central Portugal, on the S bank of the Tagus estuary opposite Lisbon: statue of Christ 110 m (360 ft) high, erected 1959. Pop: 160 826 (2001)

Al Marj an ancient town in N Libya: founded in about 550 BC. Pop: 25 166 (latest est)

Alma-Tadema Sir Lawrence 1836–1912, Dutch-English painter of studies of Greek and Roman life

Almaty a city in SE Kazakhstan; capital of Kazakhstan (1991–97): an important trading centre. Pop: 1 103 000 (2005 est)

almond 1 a small widely cultivated rosaceous tree, *Prunus amygdalus*, that is native to W Asia and has pink flowers and a green fruit containing an edible nutlike seed 2 a a pale yellowish-brown colour b (*as adjective*): *an almond shirt* 3 a yellowish-green colour b (*as adjective*)

almoner (formerly) a person who distributes alms or charity on behalf of a household or institution

almshouse *Brit, History* a privately supported house offering accommodation to the aged or needy

aloe any plant of the liliaceous genus *Aloe*, chiefly native to southern Africa, with fleshy spiny-toothed leaves and red or yellow flowers

aloe vera a juice obtained from the leaves of a liliaceous plant, *Aloe vera*, used as an emollient in skin and hair preparations

alopecia loss of hair, esp on the head; baldness

Aloysius Saint full name *Aloysius Luigi Gonzaga*. 1568–91, Italian Jesuit who died nursing plague victims; the patron saint of youth. Feast day: June 21

alp 1 (in the European Alps) an area of pasture above the valley bottom but below the mountain peaks 2 a high mountain

alpaca¹ 1 a domesticated cud-chewing artiodactyl mammal, *Lama pacos*, closely related to the llama and native to South America: family *Camelidae*. Its dark shaggy hair is a source of wool 2 the cloth made from the wool of this animal 3 a glossy fabric simulating this, used for linings, etc.

alpaca² *or sometimes* **alpacca** a type of nickel silver used in jewellery

alpenstock an early form of ice axe, consisting of a stout stick with an iron tip and sometimes having a pick and adze at the head, formerly used by mountain climbers

Alpes-de-Haute-Provence a department of SE France in Provence-Alpes-Côte-d'Azur region. Capital: Digne.

Pop: 144 508 (2003 est). Area: 6988 sq km (2725 sq miles)

alpha 1 the first letter in the Greek alphabet (A, α), a vowel transliterated as *a* 2 *Brit* the highest grade or mark, as in an examination 3 **a** involving or relating to helium-4 nuclei **b** relating to one of two or more allotropes or crystal structures of a solid **c** relating to one of two or more isomeric forms of a chemical compound, esp one in which a group is attached to the carbon atom to which the principal group is attached

alphanumeric *or* **alphameric** (of a character set, code, or file of data) consisting of alphabetical and numerical symbols

alpha particle a helium-4 nucleus, containing two neutrons and two protons, emitted during some radioactive transformations

alpha ray ionizing radiation consisting of a stream of alpha particles

alpine 1 (of plants) growing on mountains, esp above the limit for tree growth 2 connected with or used in mountaineering in medium-sized glaciated mountain areas such as the Alps 3 *Skiing* of or relating to racing events on steep prepared slopes, such as the slalom and downhill 4 a plant that is native or suited to alpine conditions

alpinist a mountaineer who climbs in medium-sized glaciated mountain areas such as the Alps

Alsace a region and former province of NE France, between the Vosges mountains and the Rhine: famous for its wines. Area: 8280 sq km (3196 sq miles)

Alsace-Lorraine an area of NE France, comprising the modern regions of Alsace and Lorraine: under German rule 1871–1919 and 1940–44. Area: 14 522 sq km (5607 sq miles)

Alsatia 1 the ancient name for **Alsace** 2 an area around Whitefriars, London, in the 17th century, which was a sanctuary for criminals and debtors

Alsatian 1 a large wolflike breed of dog often used as a guard or guide dog and by the police 2 a native or inhabitant of Alsace 3 (in the 17th century) a criminal or debtor who took refuge in the Whitefriars area of London 4 of or relating to Alsace or its inhabitants

Altamira a cave in N Spain, SW of Santander, noted for Old Stone Age wall drawings

altar 1 a raised place or structure where sacrifices are offered and religious rites performed 2 (in Christian churches) the communion table 3 a step in the wall of a dry dock upon which structures supporting a vessel can stand

altarpiece a work of art set above and behind an altar; a reredos

Altdorf a town in central Switzerland, capital of Uri canton: setting of the William Tell legend. Pop: 8541 (2000)

alternate *Botany* **a** (of leaves, flowers, etc) arranged singly at different heights on either side of the stem **b** (of parts of a flower) arranged opposite the spaces between other parts

alternating current a continuous electric current that periodically reverses direction, usually sinusoidally

alternative energy a form of energy derived from a natural source, such as the sun, wind, tides, or waves

alternator an electrical machine that generates an alternating current

altimeter an instrument that indicates height above sea level, esp one based on an aneroid barometer and fitted to an aircraft

Altiplano a plateau of the Andes, covering two thirds of Bolivia and extending into S Peru: contains Lake Titicaca. Height: 3000 m (10 000 ft) to 3900 m (13 000 ft)

altitude 1 *Geometry* the perpendicular distance from the vertex to the base of a geometrical figure or solid 2 *Astronomy, navigation* the angular distance of a celestial body from the horizon measured along the vertical circle passing through the body

alto 1 the highest adult male voice; countertenor 2 (in choral singing) a shortened form of **contralto** 3 a singer with such a voice 4 another name for **viola** 5 a flute, saxophone, etc, that is the third or fourth highest instrument in its group 6 denoting a flute, saxophone, etc, that is the third or fourth highest instrument in its group

Altrincham a residential town in NW England, in Trafford unitary authority, Greater Manchester. Pop: 40 695 (2001)

altruism the philosophical doctrine that right action is that which produces the greatest benefit to others

alum 1 a colourless soluble hydrated double sulphate of aluminium and potassium used in the manufacture of mordants and pigments, in dressing leather and sizing paper, and in medicine as a styptic and astringent. Formula: $K_2SO_4.Al_2(SO_4)_3.24H_2O$ 2 any of a group of isomorphic double sulphates of a monovalent metal or group and a trivalent metal. Formula: $X_2SO_4.Y_2(SO_4)_3.24H_2O$, where X is monovalent and Y is trivalent

aluminium *or US and Canadian* **aluminum** a light malleable ductile silvery-white metallic element that resists corrosion; the third most abundant element in the earth's crust (8.1 per cent), occurring only as a compound, principally in bauxite. It is used, esp in the form of its alloys, in aircraft parts, kitchen utensils, etc. Symbol: Al; atomic no.: 13; atomic wt.: 26.9815; valency: 3; relative density: 2.699; melting pt.: 660.45°C; boiling pt.: 2520°C

alumnus *Chiefly US and Canadian* a graduate of a school, college, etc.

Alva *or* **Alba** Duke of, title of *Fernando Alvarez de Toledo*. 1508–82, Spanish general and statesman who suppressed the Protestant revolt in the Netherlands (1567–72) and conquered Portugal (1580)

Alvarez Luis Walter 1911–88, US physicist. He made (with Felix Bloch) the first measurement of the neutron's magnetic moment (1939). Nobel prize for physics 1968

alveolus 1 any small pit, cavity, or saclike dilation, such as a honeycomb cell 2 any of the sockets in which the roots of the teeth are embedded 3 any of the tiny air sacs in the lungs at the end of the bronchioles, through which oxygen is taken into the blood

Alwyn William 1905–85, British composer. His works include the oratorio *The Marriage of Heaven and Hell* (1936) and the *Suite of Scottish dances* (1946)

alyssum any widely cultivated herbaceous garden plant

of the genus *Alyssum*, having clusters of small yellow or white flowers: family *Brassicaceae* (crucifers)

Alzheimer's disease a disorder of the brain resulting in a progressive decline in intellectual and physical abilities and eventual dementia
▷www.zarcrom.com/users/yeartorem
▷www.alz.org

Amalfi a town in Italy: a major Mediterranean port from the 10th to the 18th century, now a resort

amalgam 1 an alloy of mercury with another metal, esp with silver 2 a rare white metallic mineral that consists of silver and mercury and occurs in deposits of silver and cinnabar

amandla *South African* a political slogan calling for power to the Black population

Amanullah Khan 1892–1960, emir (1919–26) and king (1926–29) of Afghanistan; he obtained Afghan independence from Britain (1919)

amaranth any of numerous tropical and temperate plants of the genus *Amaranthus*, having tassel-like heads of small green, red, or purple flowers: family *Amaranthaceae*

amaryllis 1 an amaryllidaceous plant, *Amaryllis belladonna*, native to southern Africa and having large lily-like reddish or white flowers 2 any of several related plants, esp hippeastrum

Amati 1 a family of Italian violin makers, active in Cremona in the 16th and 17th centuries, esp **Nicolò**, 1596–1684, who taught Guarneri and Stradivari 2 a violin or other stringed instrument made by any member of this family

Amazon¹ 1 *Greek myth* one of a race of women warriors of Scythia near the Black Sea 2 one of a legendary tribe of female warriors of South America

Amazon² a river in South America, rising in the Peruvian Andes and flowing east through N Brazil to the Atlantic: in volume, the largest river in the world; navigable for 3700 km (2300 miles). Length: over 6440 km (4000 miles). Area of basin: over 5 827 500 sq km (2 250 000 sq miles)

Amazonas a state of W Brazil, consisting of the central Amazon basin: vast areas of unexplored tropical rainforest. Capital: Manaus. Pop: 2 961 801 (2002). Area: 1 542 277 sq km (595 474 sq miles)

Amazonia the land around the Amazon river

Ambala a city in N India, in Haryana: site of archaeological remains of a prehistoric Indian civilization: grain, cotton, food processing. Pop: 139 222 (2001)

ambassador 1 short for **ambassador extraordinary and plenipotentiary**; a diplomatic minister of the highest rank, accredited as permanent representative to another country or sovereign 2 **ambassador extraordinary** a diplomatic minister of the highest rank sent on a special mission 3 **ambassador plenipotentiary** a diplomatic minister of the first rank with treaty-signing powers 4 **ambassador-at-large** *US* an ambassador with special duties who may be sent to more than one government

amber 1 a yellow or yellowish-brown hard translucent fossil resin derived from extinct coniferous trees that occurs in Tertiary deposits and often contains trapped insects. It is used for jewellery, ornaments, etc. 2 a medium to dark brownish-yellow colour, often some-

what orange, similar to that of the resin

ambergris a waxy substance consisting mainly of cholesterol secreted by the intestinal tract of the sperm whale and often found floating in the sea: used in the manufacture of perfumes

Ambler Eric 1909–1998, English novelist. His thrillers include *The Mask of Dimitrios* (1939), *Journey into Fear* (1940), *A Kind of Anger* (1964), and *Doctor Frigo* (1974)

Ambleside a town in NW England, in Cumbria: a tourist centre for the Lake District. Pop: 3064 (2001)

Amboina 1 an island in Indonesia, in the Moluccas. Capital: Amboina. Area: 1000 sq km (386 sq miles) 2 a port in the Moluccas, the capital of Amboina island

Amboise a town in NW central France, on the River Loire: famous castle, a former royal residence. Pop: 11 457 (1999)

Ambrose Saint ?340–397 AD, bishop of Milan; built up the secular power of the early Christian Church; also wrote music and Latin hymns. Feast day: Dec 7 or April 4 1 **Curtly** born 1963, Antiguan cricketer; played for the West Indies 1987–2000

ambrosia 1 *Classical myth* the food of the gods, said to bestow immortality 2 any of various herbaceous plants constituting the genus *Ambrosia*, mostly native to America but widely naturalized: family *Asteraceae* (composites). The genus includes the ragweeds

ambulatory 1 able to walk 2 *Law* (esp of a will) capable of being altered or revoked 3 *Architect* a an aisle running around the east end of a church, esp one that passes behind the sanctuary b a place for walking, such as an aisle or a cloister

amen the use of the word *amen*, as at the end of a prayer

Amenhotep III or **Amenhotpe III** Greek name *Amenophis*. ?1411–?1375 BC, Egyptian pharaoh who expanded Egypt's influence by peaceful diplomacy and erected many famous buildings

Amen-Ra *Egyptian myth* the sun-god; the principal deity during the period of Theban hegemony

America 1 short for the **United States of America** 2 the American continent, including North, South, and Central America

American football 1 a team game similar to rugby, with 11 players on each side. Forward passing is allowed and planned strategies and formations for play are decided during the course of the game 2 the oval-shaped inflated ball used in this game
▷www.nfl.com

American Indian 1 a member of any of the indigenous peoples of North, Central, or South America, having Mongoloid affinities, notably straight black hair and a yellow to brown skin 2 of or relating to any of these peoples, their languages, or their cultures

American Samoa the part of Samoa administered by the US Capital: Pago Pago. Pop: 67 000 (2003 est). Area: 197 sq km (76 sq miles)

americium a white metallic transuranic element artificially produced from plutonium. It is used as an alpha-particle source. Symbol: Am; atomic no.: 95; half-life of most stable isotope, ^{243}Am: 7.4×10^3 years; valency: 2,3,4,5, or 6; relative density: 13.67; melting pt.: 1176°C; boiling pt.: 2607°C (est)

amethyst 1 a purple or violet transparent variety of

quartz used as a gemstone. Formula: SiO_2 **2** a purple variety of sapphire; oriental amethyst **3** the purple colour of amethyst

Amhara 1 a region of NW Ethiopia: formerly a kingdom **2** an inhabitant of the former kingdom of Amhara

Amharic the official language of Ethiopia, belonging to the SE Semitic subfamily of the Afro-Asiatic family

Amherst Jeffrey, 1st Baron Amherst. 1717–97, British general who defeated the French in Canada (1758–60): governor general of British North America (1761–63)

amide 1 any organic compound containing the functional group -$CONH_2$ **2** consisting of, containing, or concerned with the group -$CONH_2$ **3** an inorganic compound having the general formula $M(NH_2)_x$, where M is a metal atom

amidships *Nautical* at, near, or towards the centre of a vessel

Amiens a city in N France: its Gothic cathedral is the largest church in France. Pop: 135 501 (1999)

Amin[1] Idi 1925–2003, Ugandan soldier; dictator and head of state (1971–79). Notorious for his brutality, he was overthrown and exiled

Amin[2] Lake a former official name for (Lake) **Edward**

amine an organic base formed by replacing one or more of the hydrogen atoms of ammonia by organic groups

amino acid any of a group of organic compounds containing one or more amino groups, -NH_2, and one or more carboxyl groups, -COOH. The alpha-amino acids $RCH(NH_2)COOH$ (where R is either hydrogen or an organic group) are the component molecules of proteins; some can be synthesized in the body (**nonessential amino acids**) and others cannot and are thus essential components of the diet (**essential amino acids**)

Amis 1 Sir Kingsley 1922–95, British novelist and poet, noted for his novels *Lucky Jim* (1954), *Jake's Thing* (1978), *Stanley and the Women* (1984), *The Old Devils* (1986), and *The Folks that Live on the Hill* (1990) **2** his son, **Martin** born 1949, British novelist. His works include *The Rachel Papers* (1974), *Money* (1984), *London Fields* (1989), *The Information* (1994), and *Yellow Dog* (2003)

Amman the capital of Jordan, northeast of the Dead Sea: ancient capital of the Ammonites, rebuilt by Ptolemy in the 3rd century BC. Pop: 1 292 000 (2005 est)

ammeter an instrument for measuring an electric current in amperes

Ammon *Old Testament* the ancestor of the Ammonites

ammonia 1 a colourless pungent highly soluble gas mainly used in the manufacture of fertilizers, nitric acid, and other nitrogenous compounds, and as a refrigerant and solvent. Formula: NH_3 **2** a solution of ammonia in water, containing the compound ammonium hydroxide

ammonite[1] 1 any extinct marine cephalopod mollusc of the order *Ammonoidea*, which were common in Mesozoic times and generally had a coiled partitioned shell. Their closest modern relative is the pearly nautilus **2** the shell of any of these animals, commonly occurring as a fossil

ammonite[2] 1 an explosive consisting mainly of ammonium nitrate with smaller amounts of other substances, such as TNT **2** a nitrogenous fertilizer made from animal wastes

ammonium of, consisting of, or containing the monovalent group NH_4– or the ion NH_4^+

amnesia a defect in memory, esp one resulting from pathological cause, such as brain damage or hysteria

amnesty *Law* a pardon granted by the Crown or Executive and effected by statute

amnion the innermost of two membranes enclosing an embryonic reptile, bird, or mammal

amoeba *or US* **ameba** any protozoan of the phylum *Rhizopoda*, esp any of the genus *Amoeba*, able to change shape because of the movements of cell processes (pseudopodia). They live in fresh water or soil or as parasites in man and animals

amorphous (of chemicals, rocks, etc) not having a crystalline structure

Amos *Old Testament* **1** a Hebrew prophet of the 8th century BC **2** the book containing his oracles

Amoy 1 a port in SE China, in Fujian province on **Amoy Island**, at the mouth of the Jiulong River opposite Taiwan: one of the first treaty ports opened to European trade (1842). Pop: 746 000 (2005 est) **2** the dialect of Chinese spoken in Amoy, Taiwan, and elsewhere: a Min dialect

amp 1 an ampere **2** *Informal* an amplifier

amperage the magnitude of an electric current measured in amperes, esp the rated current of an electrical component or device

ampere 1 the basic SI unit of electric current; the constant current that, when maintained in two parallel conductors of infinite length and negligible cross section placed 1 metre apart in free space, produces a force of 2×10^{-7} newton per metre between them. 1 ampere is equivalent to 1 coulomb per second **2** a former unit of electric current (**international ampere**); the current that, when passed through a solution of silver nitrate, deposits silver at the rate of 0.001118 gram per second. 1 international ampere equals 0.999835 ampere

amphetamine a synthetic colourless volatile liquid used medicinally as the white crystalline sulphate, mainly for its stimulant action on the central nervous system, although it also stimulates the sympathetic nervous system. It can have unpleasant or dangerous side effects and drug dependence can occur; 1-phenyl-2-aminopropane. Formula: $C_6H_5CH_2CH(NH_2)CH_3$

amphibian 1 any cold-blooded vertebrate of the class *Amphibia*, typically living on land but breeding in water. Their aquatic larvae (tadpoles) undergo metamorphosis into the adult form. The class includes the newts and salamanders, frogs and toads, and caecilians **2** a type of aircraft able to land and take off from both water and land **3** any vehicle able to travel on both water and land **4** another word for **amphibious**

amphibious able to live both on land and in the water, as frogs, toads, etc.

amphitheatre *or US* **amphitheater 1** a building, usually circular or oval, in which tiers of seats rise from a central open arena, as in those of ancient Rome **2** any level circular area of ground surrounded by higher ground **3 a** the first tier of seats in the gallery of a theatre **b** any similarly designated seating area in a theatre

amphora an ancient Greek or Roman two-handled narrow-necked jar for oil, wine, etc.

amplifier 1 an electronic device used to increase the strength of the signal fed into it 2 such a device used for the amplification of audio frequency signals in a radio, etc. 3 *Photog* an additional lens for altering the focal length of a camera lens

amplitude 1 *Astronomy* the angular distance along the horizon measured from true east or west to the point of intersection of the vertical circle passing through a celestial body 2 *Maths* (of a complex number) the angle that the vector representing the complex number makes with the positive real axis. If the point (x, y) has polar coordinates (r, θ), the amplitude of $x + iy$ is θ, that is, arctan y/x 3 *Physics* the maximum variation from the zero or mean value of a periodically varying quantity

ampoule *or esp US* **ampule** *Med* a small glass vessel in which liquids for injection are hermetically sealed

ampulla 1 *Anatomy* the dilated end part of certain ducts or canals, such as the end of a uterine tube 2 *Christianity* a a vessel for containing the wine and water used at the Eucharist b a small flask for containing consecrated oil 3 a Roman two-handled bottle for oil, wine, or perfume

amputee a person who has had a limb amputated

Amritsar a city in India, in NW Punjab: centre of the Sikh religion; site of a massacre in 1919 of unarmed supporters of Indian self-government by British troops; in 1984 the Golden Temple, fortified by Sikhs, was attacked by Indian troops with the loss of many Sikh lives. Pop: 975 695 (2001)

Amsterdam the commercial capital of the Netherlands, a major industrial centre and port on the IJsselmeer, connected with the North Sea by canal: built on about 100 islands within a network of canals. Pop: 737 000 (2003 est)

Amu Darya a river in central Asia, rising in the Pamirs and flowing northwest through the Hindu Kush and across Turkmenistan and Uzbekistan to its delta in the Aral Sea: forms much of the N border of Afghanistan and is important for irrigation. Length: 2400 km (1500 miles)

Amundsen Roald 1872–1928, Norwegian explorer and navigator, who was the first man to reach the South Pole (1911)

Amundsen Sea a part of the South Pacific Ocean, in Antarctica off Byrd Land

Amur a river in NE Asia, rising in N Mongolia as the Argun and flowing southeast, then northeast to the Sea of Okhotsk: forms the boundary between Manchuria and Russia. Length: about 4350 km (2700 miles)

amylase any of several enzymes that hydrolyse starch and glycogen to simple sugars, such as glucose. They are present in saliva

Anabaptist 1 a member of any of various 16th-century Protestant movements that rejected infant baptism, insisted that adults be rebaptized, and sought to establish Christian communism 2 a member of a later Protestant sect holding the same doctrines, esp with regard to baptism

anabolic steroid any of a group of synthetic steroid hormones (androgens) used to stimulate muscle and bone growth for therapeutic or athletic purposes

anabolism a metabolic process in which complex molecules are synthesized from simpler ones with the storage of energy; constructive metabolism

anaconda a very large nonvenomous arboreal and semiaquatic snake, *Eunectes murinus*, of tropical South America, which kills its prey by constriction: family *Boidae* (boas)

Anacreon ?572–?488 BC, Greek lyric poet, noted for his short songs celebrating love and wine

Anadyr 1 a town in Russia, in NE Siberia at the mouth of the Anadyr River. Pop: 6586 (1993 est) 2 a mountain range in Russia, in NE Siberia, rising over 1500 m (5000 ft) 3 a river in Russia, rising in mountains on the Arctic Circle, south of the Anadyr Range, and flowing east to the Gulf of Anadyr. Length: 725 km (450 miles) 4 **Gulf of** an inlet of the Bering Sea, off the coast of NE Russia

anaemia *or US* **anemia** a deficiency in the number of red blood cells or in their haemoglobin content, resulting in pallor, shortness of breath, and lack of energy

anaerobe *or* **anaerobium** an organism that does not require oxygen for respiration

anaesthesia *or US* **anesthesia** 1 local or general loss of bodily sensation, esp of touch, as the result of nerve damage or other abnormality 2 loss of sensation, esp of pain, induced by drugs: called **general anaesthesia** when consciousness is lost and **local anaesthesia** when only a specific area of the body is involved

anaesthetic *or US* **anesthetic** a substance that causes anaesthesia

anaesthetist 1 *Brit* a qualified doctor specializing in the administration of anaesthetics 2 *US* a person qualified to administer anaesthesia, often a nurse or someone other than a physician

anal *Psychoanal* a relating to a stage of psychosexual development during which the child's interest is concentrated on the anal region and excremental functions b designating personality traits in the adult, such as orderliness, meanness, stubbornness, etc, due to fixation at the anal stage of development

analgesia *or* **analgia** 1 inability to feel pain 2 the relief of pain

analgesic 1 of or causing analgesia 2 a substance that produces analgesia

analogous *Biology* (of organs and parts) having the same function but different evolutionary origin

analogue *or sometimes US* **analog** 1 a a physical object or quantity, such as a pointer on a dial or a voltage, used to measure or represent another quantity b *(as modifier)*: *analogue watch* 2 *Biology* an analogous part or organ 3 *Chem* a an organic chemical compound related to another by substitution of hydrogen atoms with alkyl groups b an organic compound that is similar in structure to another organic compound

analogy 1 *Biology* the relationship between analogous organs or parts 2 *Logic, maths* a form of reasoning in which a similarity between two or more things is inferred from a known similarity between them in other respects

analysis 1 short for **psychoanalysis** 2 *Chem* a the decomposition of a substance into its elements, radicals, or other constituents in order to determine the kinds of constituents present (**qualitative analysis**) or the amount of each constituent (**quantitative analysis**) **b** the result obtained by such a determination **3** *Maths* the branch of mathematics principally concerned with the properties of functions, largely arising out of calculus **4** *Philosophy* (in the writings of Kant) the separation of a concept from another that contains it

Anambra a state of S Nigeria, formed in 1976 from part of East-Central State. Capital: Enugu. Pop: 3 094 783 (1995 est). Area: 4844 sq km (1870 sq miles)

Ananda 5th century BC, the first cousin, favourite disciple, and personal attendant of the Buddha

Ananias *New Testament* a Jewish Christian of Jerusalem who was struck dead for lying (Acts 5)

anaphylactic shock a severe, sometimes fatal, reaction to a substance to which a person has an extreme sensitivity, often involving respiratory difficulty and circulation failure

anarchism *Political theory* a doctrine advocating the abolition of government

anarchist a person who advocates the abolition of government and a social system based on voluntary cooperation

anarchy 1 *Political theory* general lawlessness and disorder, esp when thought to result from an absence or failure of government **2** the absence or lack of government **3** the theory or practice of political anarchism

Anastasia Grand Duchess 1901–?18, daughter of Tsar Nicholas II, believed to have been executed by the Bolsheviks in 1918, although several women subsequently claimed to be her

anastigmat a lens or system of lenses designed to be free of astigmatism

anathema a formal ecclesiastical curse of excommunication or a formal denunciation of a doctrine

Anatolia the Asian part of Turkey, occupying the peninsula between the Black Sea, the Mediterranean, and the Aegean: consists of a plateau, largely mountainous, with salt lakes in the interior

anatomist an expert in anatomy

anatomy 1 the science concerned with the physical structure of animals and plants **2** the physical structure of an animal or plant or any of its parts **3** a book or treatise on this subject **4** dissection of an animal or plant
▷http://omni.ac.uk/subject-listing/QS4.html
▷www.bartleby.com/107

Anaxagoras ?500–428 BC, Greek philosopher who maintained that all things were composed of minute particles arranged by an eternal intelligence

Anaximander 611–547 BC, Greek philosopher, astronomer, and mathematician who believed the first principle of the world to be the Infinite

ancestor an early type of animal or plant from which a later, usually dissimilar, type has evolved

ancestral *Logic* a relation that holds between *x* and *y* if there is a chain of instances of a given relation leading from *x* to *y*. Thus the ancestral of *parent of* is *ancestor of*, since *x* is the ancestor of *y* if and only if *x* is a parent of... a parent of...a parent of *y*

anchor 1 any of several devices, usually of steel, attached to a vessel by a cable and dropped overboard so as to grip the bottom and restrict the vessel's move-

ment **2 a** the rear person in a tug-of-war team **b** short for **anchorman 3 at anchor** (of a vessel) anchored **4 cast, come to,** *or* **drop anchor** to anchor a vessel **5 drag anchor** See **drag 6 ride at anchor** to be anchored **7 weigh anchor** to raise a vessel's anchor or (of a vessel) to have its anchor raised in preparation for departure

Anchorage the largest city in Alaska, a port in the south, at the head of Cook Inlet. Pop: 270 951 (2003 est)

anchor ice *Canadian* ice that forms at the bottom of a lake or river

anchorite a person who lives in seclusion, esp a religious recluse; hermit

anchorman (in broadcasting) a person in a central studio who links up and maintains contact with various outside camera units, reporters, etc.

anchovy any of various small marine food fishes of the genus *Engraulis* and related genera, esp *E. encrasicolus* of S Europe: family *Clupeidae* (herrings). They have a salty taste and are often tinned or made into a paste or essence

ancient 1 of the far past, esp before the collapse of the Western Roman Empire (476 AD) **2** *Law* having existed since before the time of legal memory **3** a member of a civilized nation in the ancient world, esp a Greek, Roman, or Hebrew **4** one of the classical authors of Greek or Roman antiquity

Ancient of Days a name for God, originating in the Authorized Version of the Old Testament (Daniel 7:9)

Ancohuma one of the two peaks of Mount **Sorata**

Ancona a port in central Italy, on the Adriatic, capital of the Marches: founded by Greeks from Syracuse in about 390 BC. Pop: 100 507 (2001)

Andalusia a region of S Spain, on the Mediterranean and the Atlantic, with the Sierra Morena in the north, the Sierra Nevada in the southeast, and the Guadalquivir River flowing over fertile lands between them; a centre of Moorish civilization; an autonomous region in 1981. Area: about 87 280 sq km (33 700 sq miles)

Andaman Sea part of the Bay of Bengal, between the Andaman and Nicobar Islands and the Malay Peninsula

andante *Music* **1** (to be performed) at a moderately slow tempo **2** a passage or piece to be performed in this manner

andantino *Music* **1** (to be performed) slightly faster, or slightly more slowly, than andante **2** a passage or piece to be performed in this manner

Andersen Hans Christian 1805–75, Danish author of fairy tales, including *The Ugly Duckling, The Tin Soldier*, and *The Snow Queen*

Anderson[1] 1 Carl David 1905–91, US physicist, who discovered the positron in cosmic rays (1932): Nobel prize for physics 1936 **2** Elizabeth Garrett 1836–1917, English physician and feminist: a campaigner for the admission of women to the professions **3** John 1893–1962, Australian philosopher, born in Scotland, whose theories are expounded in *Studies in Empirical Philosophy* (1962) **4** Dame **Judith**, real name *Frances Margaret Anderson*. 1898–1992, Australian stage and film actress **5** Lindsay (Gordon) 1923–94, British film and theatre director: his films include *This Sporting Life* (1963), *If* (1968), *O Lucky*

Man! (1973), and *The Whales of August* (1987) **6 Marian** 1902–93, US contralto, the first Black permanent member of the Metropolitan Opera Company, New York **7 Philip Warren** born 1923, US physicist, noted for his work on solid-state physics. Nobel prize for physics 1977 **8 Sherwood** 1874–1941, US novelist and short-story writer, best known for *Winesburg Ohio* (1919), a collection of short stories illustrating small-town life

Anderson² a river in N Canada, in the Northwest Territories, rising in lakes north of Great Bear Lake and flowing west and north to the Beaufort Sea. Length: about 580 km (360 miles)

Andhra Pradesh a state of SE India, on the Bay of Bengal: formed in 1953 from parts of Madras and Hyderabad states. Capital: Hyderabad. Pop: 75 727 541 (2001). Area: about 275 068 sq km (106 204 sq miles)

Andong a port in E China, in Liaoning province at the mouth of the Yalu River. Pop: 730 000 (2005 est)

Andorra a mountainous principality in SW Europe, between France and Spain: according to tradition, given independence by Charlemagne in the 9th century for helping to fight the Moors; placed under the joint sovereignty of the Comte de Foix and the Spanish bishop of Urgel in 1278; under the joint overlordship of the French head of state and the bishop of Urgel from the 16th century; adopted a constitution reducing the powers of the overlords in 1993. Languages: Catalan (official), French, and Spanish. Religion: Roman Catholic. Currency: euro. Capital: Andorra la Vella. Pop: 71 000 (2003 est). Area: 464 sq km (179 sq miles)

Andorra la Vella the capital of Andorra, situated in the west of the principality. Pop: 22 035 (2003 est)

Andrew *New Testament* **Saint** one of the twelve apostles of Jesus; the brother of Peter; patron saint of Scotland. Feast day: Nov 30

Andrewes Lancelot 1555–1626, English bishop and theologian

Andrews Thomas 1813–85, Irish physical chemist, noted for his work on the liquefaction of gases

Andrić Ivo 1892–1975, Serbian novelist; author of *The Bridge on the Drina* (1945): Nobel prize for literature 1961

androgynous 1 *Botany* having male and female flowers in the same inflorescence, as cuckoo pint **2** having male and female characteristics; hermaphrodite

android (in science fiction) a robot resembling a human being

andrology the branch of medicine concerned with diseases in men, esp of the reproductive organs

Andropov Yuri Vladimirovich 1914–84, Soviet statesman; president of the Soviet Union (1983–84)

Andros 1 an island in the Aegean Sea, the northernmost of the Cyclades: long famous for wine. Capital: Andros. Pop: 10 009 (2001). Area: about 311 sq km (120 sq miles) **2** an island in the N Caribbean, the largest of the Bahamas. Pop: 7686 (2000). Area: 4144 sq km (1600 sq miles)

Aneirin 6th century AD, Welsh poet. His *Y Gododdin*, preserved in *The Book of Aneirin* (?1250), is one of the earliest surviving Welsh poems

anemometer an instrument for recording the speed and often the direction of winds

anemone any ranunculaceous woodland plant of the genus *Anemone* of N temperate regions, such as the white-flowered *A. nemorosa* (**wood anemone** or **windflower**). Some cultivated anemones have lilac, pale blue, pink, purple, or red flowers. See also **pasqueflower**. Compare **sea anemone** (an animal).

aneroid barometer a device for measuring atmospheric pressure without the use of fluids. It consists of a partially evacuated metal chamber, the thin corrugated lid of which is displaced by variations in the external air pressure. This displacement is magnified by levers and made to operate a pointer

Aneto Pico de a mountain in N Spain, near the French border: the highest in the Pyrenees. Height: 3404 m (11 168 ft)

aneurysm *or* **aneurism** a sac formed by abnormal dilation of the weakened wall of a blood vessel

Anfinsen Christian Boehmer 1916–95, US biochemist, noted for his research on the structure of enzymes. Nobel prize for chemistry 1972

Angara a river in S Russia, in Siberia, flowing from Lake Baikal north and west to the Yenisei River: important for hydroelectric power. Length: 1840 km (1150 miles)

angel 1 *Theol* one of a class of spiritual beings attendant upon God. In medieval angelology they are divided by rank into nine orders: seraphim, cherubim, thrones, dominations (or dominions), virtues, powers, principalities (or princedoms), archangels, and angels **2** a divine messenger from God **3** a former English gold coin with a representation of the archangel Michael on it, first minted in Edward IV's reign

Angel Falls a waterfall in SE Venezuela, on the Caroní River. Height (probably the highest in the world): 979 m (3211 ft)

angelfish 1 any of various small tropical marine percoid fishes of the genus *Pomacanthus* and related genera, which have a deep flattened brightly coloured body and brushlike teeth: family *Chaetodontidae* **2** a South American cichlid, *Pterophyllum scalare*, of the Amazon region, having a compressed body and large dorsal and anal fins: a popular aquarium fish

angelic of or relating to angels

angelica any tall umbelliferous plant of the genus *Angelica*, having compound leaves and clusters of small white or greenish flowers, esp *A. archangelica*, the aromatic seeds, leaves, and stems of which are used in medicine and cookery

Angelico Fra , original name *Guido di Pietro;* monastic name *Fra Giovanni da Fiesole.* ?1400–55, Italian fresco painter and Dominican friar

Angell Sir Norman, real name *Ralph Norman Angell Lane.* 1874–1967, English writer, pacifist, and economist, noted for his work on the economic futility of war, *The Great Illusion* (1910): Nobel peace prize 1933

Angelou Maya, real name *Marguerite Johnson.* born 1928, US Black novelist, poet, and dramatist. Her works include the autobiographical novel *I Know Why the Caged Bird Sings* (1970) and its sequels

Angelus *RC Church* **1** a series of prayers recited in the morning, at midday, and in the evening, commemorating the Annunciation and Incarnation **2** the bell (**Angelus bell**) signalling these prayers

Angers a city in W France, on the River Maine. Pop:

151 279 (1999)

Angevin 1 a native or inhabitant of Anjou 2 *History* a member of the Plantagenet royal line descended from Geoffrey, Count of Anjou, esp one of the kings of England from Henry II to John (1154–1216) 3 of or relating to Anjou or its inhabitants 4 of or relating to the Plantagenet kings of England between 1154 and 1216

angina 1 any disease marked by painful attacks of spasmodic choking, such as Vincent's angina and quinsy 2 a sudden intense pain in the chest, often accompanied by feelings of suffocation, caused by momentary lack of adequate blood supply to the heart muscle

Angkor a large area of ruins in NW Cambodia, containing **Angkor Thom**, the capital of the former Khmer Empire, and **Angkor Wat**, a three-storey temple, which were overgrown with dense jungle from the 14th to 19th centuries

angle 1 the space between two straight lines that diverge from a common point or between two planes that extend from a common line 2 the shape formed by two such lines or planes 3 the extent to which one such line or plane diverges from another, measured in degrees or radians

angler 1 a person who fishes with a rod and line 2 any spiny-finned fish of the order *Pediculati* (or *Lophiiformes*). They live at the bottom of the sea and typically have a long spiny movable dorsal fin with which they lure their prey

Anglesey an island and county of N Wales, formerly part of Gwynedd (1974–96), separated from the mainland by the Menai Strait. Administrative centre: Llangefni. Pop: 59 500 (2003 est). Area: 720 sq km (278 sq miles)

Anglican 1 denoting or relating to the Anglican communion 2 a member of the Church of England or one of the Churches in full communion with it
▷www.anglicancommunion.org

angling a the art or sport of catching fish with a rod and line and a baited hook or other lure, such as a fly; fishing b (*as modifier*): *an angling contest*
▷www.cips-fips.org

Anglo-French the Norman-French language of medieval England

Anglo-Norman *History* 1 relating to the Norman conquerors of England, their society, or their language 2 a Norman inhabitant of England after 1066 3 the Anglo-French language

Anglo-Saxon 1 a member of any of the West Germanic tribes (Angles, Saxons, and Jutes) that settled in Britain from the 5th century AD and were dominant until the Norman conquest 2 the language of these tribes

Angola a republic in SW Africa, on the Atlantic: includes the enclave of Cabinda, north of the River Congo; a Portuguese possession from 1575 until its independence in 1975; multiparty constitution adopted in 1991; factional violence. It consists of a narrow coastal plain with a large fertile plateau in the east. Currency: kwanza. Religion: Christian majority. Capital: Luanda. Pop: 14 078 000 (2004 est). Area: 1 246 693 sq km (481 351 sq miles)

angora a the long soft hair of the outer coat of the Angora goat or the fur of the Angora rabbit b yarn,

cloth, or clothing made from this hair c a material made to resemble this yarn or cloth d (*as modifier*): *an angora sweater*

angst (in Existentialist philosophy) the dread caused by man's awareness that his future is not determined but must be freely chosen

angstrom a unit of length equal to 10^{-10} metre, used principally to express the wavelengths of electromagnetic radiations. It is equivalent to 0.1 nanometre.

Anguilla an island in the Caribbean, in the Leeward Islands: part of the British associated state of St Kitts-Nevis-Anguilla from 1967 until 1980, when it reverted to the status of a British dependency and is now a UK Overseas Territory. Pop: 12 000 (2003 est). Area: 90 sq km (35 sq miles)

angular 1 having an angle or angles 2 measured by an angle or by the rate at which an angle changes

Angus a council area of E Scotland on the North Sea: the historical county of Angus became part of Tayside region in 1975; reinstated as a unitary authority (excluding City of Dundee) in 1996. Administrative centre: Forfar. Pop: 107 520 (2003 est). Area: 2181 sq km (842 sq miles)

Anhalt a former duchy and state of central E Germany, now part of the state of Saxony-Anhalt: part of East Germany until 1990

Anhui *or* **Anhwei** a province of E China, crossed by the Yangtze River. Capital: Hefei. Pop: 64 100 000 (2003 est). Area: 139 860 sq km (54 000 sq miles)

anhydride 1 a compound that has been formed from another compound by dehydration 2 a compound that forms an acid or base when added to water 3 any organic compound containing the group -CO.O.CO- formed by removal of one water molecule from two carboxyl groups

anhydrous containing no water, esp no water of crystallization

Aniakchak an active volcanic crater in SW Alaska, on the Alaska Peninsula: the largest explosion crater in the world. Height: 1347 m (4420 ft). Diameter: 9 km (6 miles)

anil a leguminous West Indian shrub, *Indigofera suffruticosa*: a source of indigo

aniline a colourless oily pungent poisonous liquid used in the manufacture of dyes, plastics, pharmaceuticals, and explosives. Formula: $C_6H_5NH_2$

animal *Zoology* any living organism characterized by voluntary movement, the possession of cells with non-cellulose cell walls and specialized sense organs enabling rapid response to stimuli, and the ingestion of complex organic substances such as plants and other animals
▷www.biosis.org.uk/free_resources/classifn/classifn.html
▷http://animaldiversity.ummz.umich.edu/index.html
▷www.a25.com/animals.html
▷www.itis.usda.gov

animalcule *or* **animalculum** a microscopic animal such as an amoeba or rotifer

animalism the doctrine or belief that man lacks a spiritual nature

animated cartoon a film produced by photographing a series of gradually changing drawings, etc, which give the illusion of movement when the series is projected rapidly
▷www.cliphoto.com/disney.htm
▷www.artie.com
▷www.aaascreensavers.com/cartoonscreensavers.phtml

animation a the techniques used in the production of animated cartoons b a variant of **animated cartoon**

animator or **animater** an artist who produces animated cartoons

animism 1 the belief that natural objects, phenomena, and the universe itself have desires and intentions 2 (in the philosophies of the Greek philosophers Plato (?427–?347 BC) and Pythagoras (?580–?500 BC)) the hypothesis that there is an immaterial force that animates the universe
▷www.wikipedia.org/wiki/Animism

animus (in Jungian psychology) the masculine principle present in the female unconscious

anion a negatively charged ion; an ion that is attracted to the anode during electrolysis

anise a Mediterranean umbelliferous plant, *Pimpinella anisum*, having clusters of small yellowish-white flowers and liquorice-flavoured seeds (see **aniseed**)

aniseed the liquorice-flavoured aromatic seeds of the anise plant, used medicinally for expelling intestinal gas and in cookery as a flavouring, esp in cakes and confections

Anjou a former province of W France, in the Loire valley: a medieval countship from the 10th century, belonging to the English crown from 1154 until 1204; annexed by France in 1480

Ankara the capital of Turkey: an ancient city in the Anatolian highlands: first a capital in the 3rd century BC, in the Celtic kingdom of Galatia. Pop: 3 593 000 (2005 est)

ankylosis or **anchylosis** abnormal adhesion or immobility of the bones in a joint, as by a direct joining of the bones, a fibrous growth of tissues within the joint, or surgery

anna a former Indian copper coin, worth one sixteenth of a rupee

Annaba a port in NE Algeria: site of the Roman city of Hippo Regius. Pop: 382 000 (2005 est)

Annan Kofi born 1938, Ghanaian international civil servant; secretary-general of the United Nations from 1997: Nobel peace prize 2001 with the UN

Annapolis the capital of Maryland, near the mouth of the Severn River on Chesapeake Bay: site of the US Naval Academy. Pop: 36 178 (2003 est)

Annapolis Royal a town in SE Canada in W Nova Scotia on an arm of the Bay of Fundy: the first settlement in Canada (1605). Pop: 550 (2001)

Annapurna or **Anapurna** a massif of the Himalayas, in Nepal. Highest peak: 8078 m (26 502 ft)

Ann Arbor a city in SE Michigan: seat of the University of Michigan. Pop: 114 498 (2003 est)

Anne 1 Princess, the Princess Royal. born 1950, daughter of Elizabeth II of Great Britain and Northern Ireland; a noted horsewoman and president of the Save the Children Fund 2 Queen 1665–1714, queen of Great Britain and Ireland (1702–14), daughter of James II, and the last of the Stuart monarchs 3 Saint (in Christian tradition) the mother of the Virgin Mary. Feast day: July 26 or 25

Annecy 1 a city and resort in E France, on Lake Annecy. Pop: 50 348 (1999) 2 Lake a lake in E France, in the Alps

annelid 1 any worms of the phylum *Annelida*, in which the body is divided into segments both externally and internally. The group includes the earthworms, lugworm, ragworm, and leeches 2 of, relating to, or belonging to the *Annelida*

Anne of Austria 1601–66, wife of Louis XIII of France and daughter of Philip III of Spain: regent of France (1643–61) for her son Louis XIV

Anne of Cleves 1515–57, the fourth wife of Henry VIII of England: their marriage (1540) was annulled after six months

Annigoni Pietro 1910–88, Italian painter; noted esp for his portraits of President Kennedy (1961) and Queen Elizabeth II (1955 and 1970)

annual a plant that completes its life cycle in less than one year

annular eclipse an eclipse of the sun in which the moon does not cover the entire disc of the sun, so that a ring of sunlight surrounds the shadow of the moon

annulment a formal invalidation, as of a marriage, judicial proceeding, etc.

Annunciation 1 the *New Testament* the announcement of the Incarnation by the angel Gabriel to the Virgin Mary (Luke 1:26–38) 2 the festival commemorating this, held on March 25 (Lady Day)

anode 1 the positive electrode in an electrolytic cell 2 the positively charged electrode in an electronic valve 3 the negative terminal of a primary cell

anodyne a drug that relieves pain; analgesic

anointing of the sick RC Church a sacrament in which a person who is seriously ill or dying is anointed by a priest with consecrated oil

anomaly 1 *Astronomy* a the angle between a planet, the sun, and the previous perihelion of the planet b the angle between the periapsis of a particular point on a circle round the orbit as seen from the centre of the orbit. This point is obtained by producing a perpendicular to the major axis of the ellipse through the orbiting body until it reaches the circumference of the circle c the angle between the periapsis of an orbit and the position of an imaginary body orbiting at a constant angular speed and in the same period as the real orbiting body 2 *Geology* a a deviation from the normal value of gravity at the earth's surface, caused by density differences at depth, for example those caused by a buried mineral body b a magnetic field, for example one produced by a buried mineral body, that deviates from an expected or standard value, usually that of the earth's magnetic field

anorexia 1 loss of appetite 2 a disorder characterized by fear of becoming fat and refusal of food, leading to debility and even death

Anouilh Jean 1910–87, French dramatist, noted for his reinterpretations of Greek myths: his works include *Eurydice* (1942), *Antigone* (1944), and *Becket* (1959)

Anqing or **Anking** a city in E China, in SW Anhui province on the Yangtze River: famous seven-storeyed pagoda. Pop: 686 000 (2005 est)

Anselm Saint 1033–1109, Italian Benedictine monk; archbishop of Canterbury (1093–1109): one of the founders of scholasticism; author of *Cur Deus Homo? (Why did God become Man?)*. Feast day: Aug 21

Ansermet Ernest 1883–1969, Swiss orchestral conductor; principal conductor of Diaghilev's Ballet Russe

answer 1 *Law* **a** a party's written reply to his opponent's interrogatories **b** (in divorce law) the respondent's written reply to the petition 2 a musical phrase that follows the subject of a fugue, reproducing it a fifth higher or a fourth lower

ant 1 any small social insect of the widely distributed hymenopterous family *Formicidae*, typically living in highly organized colonies of winged males, wingless sterile females (workers), and fertile females (queens), which are winged until after mating 2 **white ant** another name for a **termite**

antacid 1 a substance used to neutralize acidity, esp in the stomach 2 having the properties of this substance

antagonism 1 *Physiol* the normal opposition between certain muscles 2 *Biology* the inhibition or interference of growth of one kind of organism by another

antagonist 1 any muscle that opposes the action of another 2 a drug that counteracts the effects of another drug

antalkali a substance that neutralizes alkalis, esp one used to treat alkalosis

Antananarivo the capital of Madagascar, on the central plateau: founded in the 17th century by a Hova chief; university (1961). Pop: 1 808 000 (2005 est)

Antarctic 1 the Also called: **Antarctic Zone** Antarctica and the surrounding waters 2 of or relating to the south polar regions

Antarctica a continent around the South Pole: consists of an ice-covered plateau, 1800–3000 m (6000 ft to 10 000 ft) above sea level, and mountain ranges rising to 4500 m (15 000 ft) with some volcanic peaks; average temperatures all below freezing and human settlement is confined to research stations. All political claims to the mainland are suspended under the Antarctic Treaty of 1959

Antarctic Circle the imaginary circle around the earth, parallel to the equator, at latitude 66° 32′ S; it marks the southernmost point at which the sun appears above the level of the horizon at the winter solstice

Antarctic Ocean the sea surrounding Antarctica, consisting of the most southerly parts of the Pacific, Atlantic, and Indian Oceans

Antarctic Peninsula the largest peninsula of Antarctica, between the Weddell Sea and the Pacific: consists of Graham Land in the north and the Palmer Peninsula in the south

ante the gaming stake put up before the deal in poker by the players

anteater 1 any toothless edentate mammal of the family *Myrmecophagidae* of Central and South America, esp *Myrmecophaga tridactyla* (or *jubata*) (**giant anteater**), having a long tubular snout used for eating termites 2 **scaly anteater** another name for **pangolin** 3 **spiny**

anteater another name for **echidna** 4 **banded anteater** another name for **numbat**

antecedent 1 *Logic* the hypothetical clause, usually introduced by "if", in a conditional statement: that which implies the other 2 *Maths* an obsolescent name for **numerator** 3 **denying the antecedent** *Logic* the fallacy of inferring the falsehood of the consequent of a conditional statement, given the truth of the conditional and the falsehood of its antecedent, as *if there are five of them, there are more than four: there are not five, so there are not more than four*

antediluvian belonging to the ages before the biblical Flood (Genesis 7, 8)

antelope 1 any bovid mammal of the subfamily *Antilopinae*, of Africa and Asia. They are typically graceful, having long legs and horns, and include the gazelles, springbok, impala, gerenuk, blackbuck, and dik-diks 2 any of various similar bovids of Africa and Asia

antenna 1 one of a pair of mobile appendages on the heads of insects, crustaceans, etc, that are often whip-like and respond to touch and taste but may be specialized for swimming or attachment 2 another name for **aerial**

ante-post *Brit* (of a bet) placed before the runners in a race are confirmed

anterior 1 *Zoology* of or near the head end 2 *Botany* (of part of a flower or leaf) situated farthest away from the main stem

anteroom a room giving entrance to a larger room, often used as a waiting room

anthem 1 a song of loyalty or devotion, as to a nation or college 2 a musical composition for a choir, usually set to words from the Bible, sung as part of a church service 3 a religious chant sung antiphonally

anther the terminal part of a stamen consisting usually of two lobes each containing two sacs in which the pollen matures

ant hill 1 a mound of soil, leaves, etc, near the entrance of an ants' nest, carried and deposited there by the ants while constructing the nest 2 a mound of earth, usually about 2 metres high, built up by termites in forming a nest

anthology a collection of literary passages or works, esp poems, by various authors

Anthony Saint ?251–?356 AD, Egyptian hermit, commonly regarded as the founder of Christian monasticism. Feast day: Jan 17

Anthony of Padua Saint 1195–1231, Franciscan friar, who preached in France and Italy. Feast day: June 13

anthracite a hard jet-black coal that burns slowly with a nonluminous flame giving out intense heat. Fixed carbon content: 86–98 per cent; calorific value: 3.14×10^7–3.63×10^7 J/kg

anthrax 1 a highly infectious and often fatal disease of herbivores, esp cattle and sheep, characterized by fever, enlarged spleen, and swelling of the throat. Carnivores are relatively resistant. It is caused by the spore-forming bacterium *Bacillus anthracis* and can be transmitted to man 2 a pustule or other lesion caused by this disease

anthropoid any primate of the suborder *Anthropoidea*,

including monkeys, apes, and man

anthropology the study of humans, their origins, physical characteristics, institutions, religious beliefs, social relationships, etc.
▷http://vlib.anthrotech.com
▷www.sosig.ac.uk/ ethnology_ethnography_anthropology
▷www.rai.anthropology.org.uk

Antibes a port and resort in SE France, on the Mediterranean: an important Roman town. Pop: 72 412 (1999)

antibiotic any of various chemical substances, such as penicillin, streptomycin, chloramphenicol, and tetracycline, produced by various microorganisms, esp fungi, or made synthetically and capable of destroying or inhibiting the growth of microorganisms, esp bacteria

antibody any of various proteins produced in the blood in response to the presence of an antigen. By becoming attached to antigens on infectious organisms antibodies can render them harmless or cause them to be destroyed

Antichrist 1 *New Testament* the antagonist of Christ, expected by early Christians to appear and reign over the world until overthrown at Christ's Second Coming 2 an enemy of Christ or Christianity

anticipation *Music* an unstressed, usually short note introduced before a downbeat and harmonically related to the chord immediately following it

anticline a formation of stratified rock raised up, by folding, into a broad arch so that the strata slope down on both sides from a common crest

anticoagulant 1 acting to prevent or impair coagulation, esp of blood 2 an agent, such as warfarin, that prevents or impairs coagulation

Anticosti an island of E Canada, in the Gulf of St Lawrence; part of Quebec. Area: 7881 sq km (3043 sq miles)

anticyclone *Meteorol* a body of moving air of higher pressure than the surrounding air, in which the pressure decreases away from the centre. Winds circulate around the centre in a clockwise direction in the N hemisphere and anticlockwise in the S hemisphere

antidepressant any of a class of drugs used to alleviate depression

antidote *Med* a drug or agent that counteracts or neutralizes the effects of a poison

antifreeze a liquid, usually ethylene glycol (ethanediol), added to cooling water to lower its freezing point, esp for use in an internal-combustion engine

antigen a substance that stimulates the production of antibodies

Antigua an island in the Caribbean, one of the Leeward Islands: a British colony, with its dependency Barbuda, until 1967, when it became a British associated state; it became independent in 1981 as part of the state of Antigua and Barbuda. Area: 279 sq km (108 sq miles)

Antigua and Barbuda a state in the Caribbean, comprising the islands of Antigua, Barbuda, and Redonda: gained independence in 1981: a member of the Commonwealth. Official language: English. Religion: Christian majority. Currency: East Caribbean dollar.

Capital: St John's. Pop: 73 000 (2003 est). Area: 442 sq km (171 sq miles)

antihero a central character in a novel, play, etc, who lacks the traditional heroic virtues

antihistamine any drug that neutralizes the effects of histamine, used esp in the treatment of allergies

antiknock a compound, such as lead tetraethyl, added to petrol to reduce knocking in the engine

Anti-Lebanon a mountain range running north and south between Syria and Lebanon, east of the Lebanon Mountains. Highest peak: Mount Hermon, 2814 m (9232 ft)

antilogarithm a number whose logarithm to a given base is a given number

antimatter a form of matter composed of antiparticles, such as antihydrogen, consisting of antiprotons and positrons

antimony a toxic metallic element that exists in two allotropic forms and occurs principally in stibnite. The stable form is a brittle silvery-white crystalline metal that is added to alloys to increase their strength and hardness and is used in semiconductors. Symbol: Sb; atomic no.: 51; atomic wt.: 121.757; valency: 0, −3, +3, or +5; relative density: 6.691; melting pt.: 630.76°C; boiling pt.: 1587°C

antinomy *Philosophy* contradiction existing between two apparently indubitable propositions; paradox

antinovel a type of prose fiction in which conventional or traditional novelistic elements are rejected

Antioch a city in S Turkey, on the Orontes River: ancient commercial centre and capital of Syria (300–64 BC); early centre of Christianity. Pop: 155 000 (2005 est)

Antiochus III known as *Antiochus the Great*. 242–187 BC, king of Syria (223–187), who greatly extended the Seleucid empire but was forced (190) to surrender most of Asia Minor to the Romans

Antiochus IV ?215–164 BC, Seleucid king of Syria (175–164), who attacked the Jews and provoked the revolt of the Maccabees

antioxidant 1 any substance that retards deterioration by oxidation, esp of fats, oils, foods, petroleum products, or rubber 2 *Biology* a substance, such as vitamin C, vitamin E, or beta carotene, that counteracts the damaging effects of oxidation in a living organism

antiparticle any of a group of elementary particles that have the same mass and spin as their corresponding particle but have opposite values for all other nonzero quantum numbers. When a particle collides with its antiparticle, mutual annihilation occurs

antiperspirant an astringent substance applied to the skin to reduce or prevent perspiration

antiphon 1 a short passage, usually from the Bible, recited or sung as a response after certain parts of a liturgical service 2 a psalm, hymn, etc, chanted or sung in alternate parts

antipope a rival pope elected in opposition to one who has been canonically chosen

antipyretic a remedy or drug that prevents or alleviates fever

antiquary a person who collects, deals in, or studies antiques, ancient works of art, or ancient times

antique 1 a a decorative object, piece of furniture, or

other work of art created in an earlier period, that is collected and valued for its beauty, workmanship, and age **b** (*as modifier*): *an antique shop* **2** any object made in an earlier period **3 the** the style of ancient art, esp Greek or Roman art, or an example of it **4** made in or in the style of an earlier period
▷www.antiqueweb.com
▷http://antiquerestorers.com
▷www.pbs.org/wgbh/pages/roadshow/speak/ index.htm

antirrhinum any scrophulariaceous plant of the genus *Antirrhinum*, esp the snapdragon, which have two-lipped flowers of various colours

Antisana a volcano in N central Ecuador, in the Andes. Height: 5756 m (18 885 ft)

antiscorbutic a remedy or agent that prevents or cures scurvy

antiseptic an agent or substance that prevents infection by killing germs

antiserum blood serum containing antibodies against a specific antigen, used to treat or provide immunity to a disease

antistatic (of a substance, textile, etc) retaining sufficient moisture to provide a conducting path, thus avoiding the effects of static electricity

antithesis *Philosophy* the second stage in the **Hegelian dialectic** contradicting the **thesis** before resolution by the **synthesis**

antitoxin **1** an antibody that neutralizes a toxin **2** blood serum that contains a specific antibody

antitrust *Chiefly US* regulating or opposing trusts, monopolies, cartels, or similar organizations, esp in order to prevent unfair competition

antitype a person or thing that is foreshadowed or represented by a type or symbol, esp a character or event in the New Testament prefigured in the Old Testament

antivirus a piece of software designed to prevent viruses entering a computer system or network

antler one of a pair of bony outgrowths on the heads of male deer and some related species of either sex. The antlers are shed each year and those of some species grow more branches as the animal ages

Antonello da Messina ?1430–?79, Italian painter, born in Sicily. His paintings include *St Jerome in His Study* and *Portrait of a Man*

Antonescu Ion 1882–1946, Romanian general and statesman; appointed prime minister (1940) by King Carol II. He was executed for war crimes

Antoninus Pius 86–161 AD, emperor of Rome (138–161); adopted son and successor of Hadrian

Antonioni Michelangelo born 1912, Italian film director; his films include *L'Avventura* (1959), *La Notte* (1961), *Blow-Up* (1966), *Zabriskie Point* (1970), *Beyond the Clouds* (1995), and *Just To Be Together* (2002)

Antony Mark Latin name *Marcus Antonius*. ?83–30 BC, Roman general who served under Julius Caesar in the Gallic wars and became a member of the second triumvirate (43). He defeated Brutus and Cassius at Philippi (42) but having repudiated his wife for Cleopatra, queen of Egypt, he was defeated by his brother-in-law Octavian (Augustus) at Actium (31)

Antrim **1** a historical county of NE Northern Ireland,

famous for the Giant's Causeway on the N coast: in 1973 it was replaced for administrative purposes by the districts of Antrim, Ballymena, Ballymoney, Carrickfergus, Larne, Moyle, Newtownabbey, and parts of Belfast and Lisburn. Area: 3100 sq km (1200 sq miles) **2** a district of Northern Ireland, in Co. Antrim. Pop: 49 260 (2003 est). Area: 415 sq km (160 sq miles)

antrum *Anatomy* a natural cavity, hollow, or sinus, esp in a bone

Antwerp **1** a province of N Belgium. Pop: 1 668 812 (2004 est). Area: 2859 sq km (1104 sq miles) **2** a port in N Belgium, capital of Antwerp province, on the River Scheldt: a major European port. Pop: 455 148 (2004 est)

Anubis *Egyptian myth* a deity, a son of Osiris, who conducted the dead to judgment. He is represented as having a jackal's head and was identified by the Greeks with Hermes

Anuradhapura a town in Sri Lanka: ancient capital of Ceylon; site of the sacred bo tree and place of pilgrimage for Buddhists. Pop: 42 600 (1995 est)

anus the excretory opening at the end of the alimentary canal

anvil **1** a heavy iron or steel block on which metals are hammered during forging **2** the fixed jaw of a measurement device against which the piece to be measured is held

anxiety *Psychol* a state of intense apprehension or worry often accompanied by physical symptoms such as shaking, intense feelings in the gut, etc, common in mental illness or after a very distressing experience

Anyang a town in E China, in Henan province: archaeological site and capital of the Shang dynasty. Pop: 808 000 (2005 est)

Anzac **1** (in World War I) a soldier serving with the Australian and New Zealand Army Corps **2** (now) any Australian or New Zealand soldier **3** the Anzac landing at Gallipoli in 1915
▷www.anzacs.net
▷www.awm.gov.au

Anzio a port and resort on the W coast of Italy: site of Allied landings in World War II. Pop: 36 952 (2001)

aorta the main vessel in the arterial network, which conveys oxygen-rich blood from the heart to all parts of the body except the lungs

Aosta a town in NW Italy, capital of Valle d'Aosta region: Roman remains. Pop: 34 062 (2001)

Apache **1** a member of a North American Indian people, formerly nomadic and warlike, inhabiting the southwestern US N Mexico **2** the language of this people, belonging to the Athapascan group of the Na-Dene phylum

apartheid (in South Africa) the official government policy of racial segregation; officially renounced in 1992
▷www.apartheidmuseum.org
▷http://racerelations.about.com/cs/apartheid

ape **1** any of various primates, esp those of the family *Pongidae*, in which the tail is very short or absent **2** any monkey

Apeldoorn a town in the Netherlands, in central Gelderland province: nearby is the summer residence of the Dutch royal family. Pop: 156 000 (2003 est)

Apelles 4th century BC, Greek painter of mythological

subjects, none of whose work survives, his fame resting on the testimony of Pliny and other writers

apeman any of various extinct apelike primates thought to have been the forerunners, or closely related to the forerunners, of modern man

aperient *Med* a mild laxative

aperture *Physics* **a** a usually circular and often variable opening in an optical instrument or device that controls the quantity of radiation entering or leaving it **b** the diameter of such an opening

apex 1 the highest point; vertex 2 *Astronomy* the point on the celestial sphere, lying in the constellation Hercules, towards which the sun appears to move at a velocity of 20 kilometres per second relative to the nearest stars

aphasia a disorder of the central nervous system characterized by partial or total loss of the ability to communicate, esp in speech or writing

aphelion the point in its orbit when a planet or comet is at its greatest distance from the sun

aphid any of the small homopterous insects of the family *Aphididae*, which feed by sucking the juices from plants

aphrodisiac a drug, food, etc, that excites sexual desire

Aphrodite *Greek myth* the goddess of love and beauty, daughter of Zeus

Apo the highest mountain in the Philippines, on SE Mindanao: active volcano with three peaks. Height: 2954 m (9690 ft)

Apocalypse *Bible* (in the Vulgate and Douay versions of the Bible) the Book of Revelation

Apocrypha the the 14 books included as an appendix to the Old Testament in the Septuagint and the Vulgate but not included in the Hebrew canon. They are not printed in Protestant versions of the Bible
  ▷www.sacred-texts.com/chr/apo

apocryphal of or like the Apocrypha

apogee the point in its orbit around the earth when the moon or an artificial satellite is at its greatest distance from the earth

Apollinaire Guillaume , real name *Wilhelm Apollinaris de Kostrowitzki*. 1880–1918, French poet, novelist, and dramatist, regarded as a precursor of surrealism; author of *Alcoöls* (1913) and *Calligrammes* (1918)

Apollo *Classical myth* the god of light, poetry, music, healing, and prophecy: son of Zeus and Leto

Apollyon *New Testament* the destroyer, a name given to the Devil (Revelation 9:11)

apologetics the branch of theology concerned with the defence and rational justification of Christianity

apoplexy sudden loss of consciousness, often followed by paralysis, caused by rupture or occlusion of a blood vessel in the brain

a posteriori *Logic* 1 relating to or involving inductive reasoning from particular facts or effects to a general principle 2 derived from or requiring evidence for its validation or support; empirical; open to revision

apostle 1 one of the 12 disciples chosen by Christ to preach his gospel 2 any prominent Christian missionary, esp one who first converts a nation or people 3 *Mormon Church* a member of a council of twelve officials appointed to administer and preside over the Church

Apostolic See 1 *RC Church* the see of the pope regarded as the successor to Saint Peter 2 a see established by one of the Apostles

apothecary 1 an archaic word for **pharmacist** 2 *Law* a chemist licensed by the Society of Apothecaries of London to prescribe, prepare, and sell drugs

apotheosis the elevation of a person to the rank of a god; deification

Appalachia a highland region of the eastern US, containing the Appalachian Mountains, extending from Pennsylvania to Alabama

apparatus 1 a collection of instruments, machines, tools, parts, or other equipment used for a particular purpose 2 a machine having a specific function 3 *Anatomy* any group of organs having a specific function

apparel *Nautical* a vessel's gear and equipment

apparent *Physics* as observed but ignoring such factors as the motion of the observer, changes in the environment, etc.

appeal 1 *Law* **a** the judicial review by a superior court of the decision of a lower tribunal **b** a request for such review **c** the right to such review 2 *Cricket* a verbal request to the umpire from one or more members of the fielding side to declare a batsman out 3 *English law* (formerly) a formal charge or accusation

appearance 1 *Law* **a** the formal attendance in court of a party in an action **b** formal notice that a party or his legal representative intends to maintain or contest the issue 2 *Philosophy* **a** the outward or phenomenal manifestation of things **b** the world as revealed by the senses, as opposed to its real nature

Appel Karel born 1921, Dutch abstract expressionist painter

appellant 1 *Law* the party who appeals to a higher court from the decision of a lower tribunal 2 *Law* another word for **appellate**

appellate *Law* 1 of or relating to appeals 2 (of a tribunal) having jurisdiction to review cases on appeal and to reverse decisions of inferior courts

appendage 1 *Zoology* any organ that projects from the trunk of animals such as arthropods 2 *Botany* any subsidiary part of a plant, such as a branch or leaf

appendicectomy *or esp US and Canadian* **appendectomy** surgical removal of any appendage, esp the vermiform appendix

appendicitis inflammation of the vermiform appendix

appendix 1 a body of separate additional material at the end of a book, magazine, etc, esp one that is documentary or explanatory 2 *Anatomy* See **vermiform appendix**

Appenzell 1 a canton of NE Switzerland, divided in 1597 into the Protestant demicanton of **Appenzell Outer Rhodes** and the Catholic demicanton of **Appenzell Inner Rhodes**. Capitals: Herisau and Appenzell. Pop: 53 200 and Pop: 15 000 (2002 est) respectively. Areas: 243 sq km (94 sq miles) and 171 sq km (66 sq miles) respectively 2 a town in NE Switzerland, capital of Appenzell Inner Rhodes demicanton. Pop: 5447 (2000)

appetence *or* **appetency** an attraction or affinity

Appian Way a Roman road in Italy, extending from Rome to Brindisi: begun in 312 BC by Appius Claudius Caecus. Length: about 560 km (350 miles)

apple 1 a rosaceous tree, *Malus sieversii*, native to Central

Asia but widely cultivated in temperate regions in many varieties, having pink or white fragrant flowers and firm rounded edible fruits **2** the fruit of this tree, having red, yellow, or green skin and crisp whitish flesh **3** any of several unrelated trees that have fruits similar to the apple, such as the custard apple, sugar apple, and May apple

Apple Isle the *Austral, informal* Tasmania

applet *Computing* a computer program that runs within a page on the World Wide Web

Appleton Sir **Edward** (**Victor**). 1892–1965, English physicist, noted particularly for his research on the ionosphere: Nobel prize for physics 1947

appliance 1 any piece of equipment having a specific function **2** a device fitted to a machine or tool to adapt it for a specific purpose **3** another name for a **fire engine**

application 1 something, such as a healing agent or lotion, that is applied, esp to the skin **2** *Logic, maths* the process of determining the value of a function for a given argument

applicator a device, such as a spatula or rod, for applying a medicine, glue, etc.

appointment *Property law* nomination to an interest in property under a deed or will

apposition *Biology* growth in the thickness of a cell wall by the deposition of successive layers of material

apprehension the act of capturing or arresting

après-ski a social activity following a day's skiing **b** (*as modifier*): *an après-ski outfit*

apricot 1 a rosaceous tree, *Prunus armeniaca*, native to Africa and W Asia, but widely cultivated for its edible fruit **2** the downy yellow juicy edible fruit of this tree, which resembles a small peach

a priori 1 *Logic* relating to or involving deductive reasoning from a general principle to the expected facts or effects **2** *Logic* known to be true independently of or in advance of experience of the subject matter; requiring no evidence for its validation or support

apron 1 the part of a stage extending in front of the curtain line; forestage **2** a hard-surfaced area in front of or around an aircraft hangar, terminal building, etc, upon which aircraft can stand **3** a continuous conveyor belt composed usually of slats linked together **4** a protective plate screening the operator of a machine, artillery piece, etc. **5** a ground covering of concrete or other material used to protect the underlying earth from water erosion **6** *Geology* a sheet of sand, gravel, etc, deposited at the front of a moraine **7** *Golf* the part of the fairway leading onto the green **8** *Machinery* the housing for the lead screw gears of a lathe

apse 1 a domed or vaulted semicircular or polygonal recess, esp at the east end of a church **2** *Astronomy* another name for **apsis**

apsis 1 either of two points lying at the extremities of an eccentric orbit of a planet, satellite, etc, such as the aphelion and perihelion of a planet or the apogee and perigee of the moon. The **line of apsides** connects two such points and is the principal axis of the orbit **2** another name for **apse**

apteryx another name for **kiwi**

Apuleius Lucius 2nd century AD, Roman writer, noted for his romance *The Golden Ass*

Apulia a region of SE Italy, on the Adriatic. Capital: Bari. Pop: 4 023 957 (2003 est). Area: 19 223 sq km (7422 sq miles)

Aqaba *or* **Akaba** the only port in Jordan, in the southwest, on the **Gulf of Aqaba**. Pop: 46 090 (1990 est)

aqua 1 water: used in compound names of certain liquid substances (as in **aqua regia**) or solutions of substances in water (as in **aqua ammoniae**), esp in the names of pharmacological solutions **2** short for **aquamarine**

aqualung breathing apparatus used by divers, etc, consisting of a mouthpiece attached to air cylinders strapped to the back

aquamarine 1 a pale greenish-blue transparent variety of beryl used as a gemstone **2 a** a pale blue to greenish-blue colour **b** (*as adjective*): *an aquamarine dress*

aquaplane a single board on which a person stands and is towed by a motorboat at high speed, as in water skiing

aqua regia a yellow fuming corrosive mixture of one part nitric acid and three to four parts hydrochloric acid, used in metallurgy for dissolving metals, including gold

aquarium 1 a tank, bowl, or pool in which aquatic animals and plants are kept for pleasure, study, or exhibition **2** a building housing a collection of aquatic life, as for exhibition

Aquarius 1 *Astronomy* a zodiacal constellation in the S hemisphere lying between Pisces and Capricorn on the ecliptic **2** *Astrology* **a** the eleventh sign of the zodiac, symbol ≈, having a fixed air classification and ruled by the planets Saturn and Uranus. The sun is in this sign between about Jan 20 and Feb 18 **b** a person born during a period when the sun is in this sign **3** *Astrology* born under or characteristic of Aquarius

aquatic a marine or freshwater animal or plant

aquatint 1 a technique of etching copper with acid to produce an effect resembling the flat tones of wash or watercolour. The tone or tint is obtained by acid (aqua) biting through the pores of a ground that only partially protects the copper **2** an etching made in this way

aqueduct 1 a conduit used to convey water over a long distance, either by a tunnel or more usually by a bridge **2** a structure, usually a bridge, that carries such a conduit or a canal across a valley or river **3** a channel in an organ or part of the body, esp one that conveys a natural body fluid

aqueous 1 of, like, or containing water **2** dissolved in water **3** (of rocks, deposits, etc) formed from material laid down in water

aqueous humour *Physiol* the watery fluid within the eyeball between the cornea and the lens

aquifer a porous deposit of rock, such as a sandstone, containing water that can be used to supply wells

Aquinas Saint **Thomas** 1225–74, Italian theologian, scholastic philosopher, and Dominican friar, whose works include *Summa contra Gentiles* (1259–64) and *Summa Theologiae* (1267–73), the first attempt at a comprehensive theological system. Feast day: Jan 28

Aquino Corazón, born 1933, Philippine stateswoman: president (1986–92)

Aquitaine a region of SW France, on the Bay of Biscay: a former Roman province and medieval duchy. It is generally flat in the west, rising to the slopes of the Massif Central in the northeast and the Pyrenees in the south; mainly agricultural

Arab 1 a member of a Semitic people originally inhabiting Arabia, who spread throughout the Middle East, N Africa, and Spain during the seventh and eighth centuries AD 2 a lively intelligent breed of horse, mainly used for riding

arabesque 1 *Ballet* a classical position in which the dancer has one leg raised behind and both arms stretched out in one of several conventional poses 2 *Music* a piece or movement with a highly ornamented or decorated melody 3 *Arts* **a** a type of curvilinear decoration in painting, metalwork, etc, with intricate intertwining leaf, flower, animal, or geometrical designs **b** a design of flowing lines 4 designating, of, or decorated in this style

Arabia a great peninsula of SW Asia, between the Red Sea and the Persian Gulf: consists chiefly of a desert plateau, with mountains rising over 3000 m (10 000 ft) in the west and scattered oases; includes the present-day countries of Saudi Arabia, Yemen, Oman, Bahrain, Qatar, Kuwait, and the United Arab Emirates. Area: about 2 600 000 sq km (1 000 000 sq miles)

Arabian Desert 1 a desert in E Egypt, between the Nile, the Gulf of Suez, and the Red Sea: mountainous parts rise over 1800 m (6000 ft). Area: about 220 000 sq km (85 000 sq miles) 2 a desert, mainly in Saudi Arabia, forming the desert area of the Arabian Peninsula, esp in the north. Area: about 2 330 000 sq km (900 000 sq miles)

Arabian Sea the NW part of the Indian Ocean, between Arabia and India

Arabic the language of the Arabs, spoken in a variety of dialects; the official language of Algeria, Egypt, Iraq, Jordan, the Lebanon, Libya, Morocco, Saudi Arabia, the Sudan, Syria, Tunisia, and Yemen. It is estimated to be the native language of some 75 million people throughout the world. It belongs to the Semitic subfamily of the Afro-Asiatic family of languages and has its own alphabet, which has been borrowed by certain other languages such as Urdu

arachnid any terrestrial chelicerate arthropod of the class *Arachnida*, characterized by simple eyes and four pairs of legs. The group includes the spiders, scorpions, ticks, mites, and harvestmen

Arafat¹ Yasser born 1929, Palestinian leader; cofounder of Al Fatah (1956), leader from 1968 of the Palestine Liberation Organization, president of the Palestinian National Authority from 1996: signed a peace agreement with Israel (1993); Nobel peace prize 1994 with Shimon Peres and Yitzhak Rabin

Arafat² a hill in W Saudi Arabia, near Mecca: a sacred site of Islam, visited by pilgrims performing the hajj

Arafura Sea a part of the W Pacific Ocean, between N Australia and SW New Guinea

Aragats Mount a volcanic mountain in NW Armenia. Height: 4090 m (13 419 ft)

Aragon¹ Louis 1897–1982, French poet, essayist, and novelist; an early surrealist, later a committed Communist. His works include the verse collections *Le Crève-Coeur* (1941) and *Les Yeux d'Elsa* (1942) and the series of novels *Le Monde réel* (1933–51)

Aragon² an autonomous region of NE Spain: independent kingdom from the 11th century until 1479, when it was united with Castile to form modern Spain. Pop: 1 059 600 (2003 est). Area: 47 609 sq km (18 382 sq miles)

Araguaia or **Araguaya** a river in central Brazil, rising in S central Mato Grosso state and flowing north to the Tocantins River. Length: over 1771 km (1100 miles)

Arakan Yoma a mountain range in Myanmar, between the Irrawaddy River and the W coast: forms a barrier between Myanmar and India; teak forests

Aral Sea a lake in Kazakhstan and Uzbekistan, east of the Caspian Sea, formerly the fourth largest lake in the world: shallow and saline, now badly polluted; use of its source waters for irrigation led to a loss of over 50 of its area between 1967 and 1997, after which the reduction began to be slowed. Area originally (to 1960) about 68 000 sq km (26 400 sq miles); water area reduced by 2003 to 26 687 sq km (11 076 sq miles) and the lake divided into two sections

Aram the biblical name for ancient Syria

Aramaic an ancient language of the Middle East, still spoken in parts of Syria and the Lebanon, belonging to the NW Semitic subfamily of the Afro-Asiatic family. Originally the speech of Aram, in the 5th century BC it spread to become the lingua franca of the Persian empire

Aran made of thick undyed wool with its natural oils retained

Ararat an extinct volcanic mountain massif in E Turkey: two main peaks; **Great Ararat** 5155 m (16 916 ft), said to be the resting place of Noah's Ark after the Flood (Genesis 8:4), and **Little Ararat** 3914 m (12 843 ft)

Aras a river rising in mountains in E Turkey and flowing east to the Caspian Sea: forms part of the E border of Turkey and the N border of Iran. Length: about 1100 km (660 miles)

Araucania a region of central Chile, inhabited by Araucanian Indians

Arbela an ancient city in Assyria, near which the **Battle of Arbela** took place (331 BC), in which Alexander the Great defeated the Persians

Arber Werner born 1929, Swiss microbiologist, noted for his work on restriction enzymes. Nobel prize for physiology or medicine 1978

arbiter a person empowered to judge in a dispute; referee; arbitrator

arbitrary 1 *Maths* not representing any specific value 2 *Law* (esp of a penalty or punishment) not laid down by statute; within the court's discretion

arbitration 1 *Law* the hearing and determination of a dispute, esp an industrial dispute, by an impartial referee selected or agreed upon by the parties concerned 2 *International law* the procedure laid down for the settlement of international disputes

arbor 1 a rotating shaft in a machine or power tool on which a milling cutter or grinding wheel is fitted 2 a rotating shaft or mandrel on which a workpiece is fitted for machining 3 *Metallurgy* a part, piece, or structure used to reinforce the core of a mould

arboreal 1 of, relating to, or resembling a tree 2 living in or among trees

arboretum a place where trees or shrubs are cultivated for their scientific or educational interest

arboriculture the cultivation of trees or shrubs, esp for the production of timber

arbor vitae any of several Asian and North American evergreen coniferous trees of the genera *Thuja* and *Thujopsis*, esp *Thuja occidentalis*, having tiny scalelike leaves and egglike cones

arbour 1 a leafy glade or bower shaded by trees, vines, shrubs, etc, esp when trained about a trellis 2 *Obsolete* an orchard, garden, or lawn

Arbroath a port and resort in E Scotland, in Angus: scene of the barons of Scotland's declaration of independence to Pope John XXII in 1320. Pop: 22 785 (2001)

Arbus Diane, original name *Diane Nemerov*. 1923–71, US photographer, noted esp for her portraits of vagrants, dwarfs, transvestites, etc.

Arbuthnot John 1667–1735, Scottish physician and satirist: author of *The History of John Bull* (1712) and, with others, of the *Memoirs of Martinus Scriblerus* (1741)

arbutus any of several temperate ericaceous shrubs of the genus *Arbutus*, esp the strawberry tree of S Europe. They have clusters of white or pinkish flowers, broad evergreen leaves, and strawberry-like berries

arc 1 a luminous discharge that occurs when an electric current flows between two electrodes or any other two surfaces separated by a small gap and a high potential difference 2 *Astronomy* a circular section of the apparent path of a celestial body 3 *Maths* a section of a curve, graph, or geometric figure

ARC AIDS-related complex: an early condition in which a person infected with the AIDS virus may suffer from such mild symptoms as loss of weight, fever, etc.

arcade 1 a set of arches and their supporting columns 2 a covered and sometimes arched passageway, usually with shops on one or both sides 3 a building, or part of a building, with an arched roof

Arcadia 1 a department of Greece, in the central Peloponnese. Capital: Tripolis. Pop: 91 326 (2001). Area: 4367 sq km (1686 sq miles) 2 the traditional idealized rural setting of Greek and Roman bucolic poetry and later in the literature of the Renaissance

arch 1 a curved structure, normally in the vertical plane, that spans an opening 2 a structure in the form of an arch that serves as a gateway 3 a any of various parts or structures of the body having a curved or archlike outline, such as the transverse portion of the aorta (**arch of the aorta**) or the raised bony vault formed by the tarsal and metatarsal bones (**arch of the foot**) b one of the basic patterns of the human fingerprint, formed by several curved ridges one above the other

archaeobotany or **archeobotany** the analysis and interpretation of plant remains found at archaeological sites

archaeology or **archeology** the study of man's past by scientific analysis of the material remains of his cultures
▷www.britac.ac.uk/portal/
 bysection.asp?section=H7
▷http://ads.ahds.ac.uk/catalogue
▷http://archnet.asu.edu/
▷www.serve.com/archaeology

archaeopteryx any of several extinct primitive birds constituting the genus *Archaeopteryx*, esp *A. lithographica*, which occurred in Jurassic times and had teeth, a long tail, well-developed wings, and a body covering of feathers

archaism an archaic word, expression, style, etc.

archangel 1 a principal angel, a member of the order ranking immediately above the angels in medieval angelology 2 another name for **angelica** 3 **yellow archangel** a Eurasian herbaceous plant (*Lamiastrum luteum*) that has yellow helmet-shaped flowers: family *Lamiaceae* (labiates) 4 a bronze-coloured breed of domestic pigeon with black markings

Archangel a port in NW Russia, on the Dvina River: major centre for the timber trade and White Sea fisheries. Pop: 345 000 (2005 est)

archbishop a bishop of the highest rank

archbishopric 1 the rank, office, or jurisdiction of an archbishop 2 the area governed by an archbishop

archdeacon 1 an Anglican clergyman ranking just below a bishop and having supervisory duties under the bishop 2 a clergyman of similar rank in other Churches

archdiocese the diocese of an archbishop

archduchess 1 the wife or widow of an archduke 2 (since 1453) a princess of the Austrian imperial family, esp a daughter of the Austrian emperor

archduke a chief duke, esp (since 1453) a prince of the Austrian imperial dynasty

Archer 1 Frederick Scott 1813–57, British inventor and sculptor. He developed (1851) the wet collodion photographic process, enabling multiple copies of pictures to be made 2 **Jeffrey** (**Howard**), Baron Archer of Weston-Super-Mare. born 1940, British novelist and Conservative politician. He was an MP from 1969 until 1974. His novels include *Kane and Abel* (1979), *Honour Among Thieves* (1993), and *The Fourth Estate* (1996): in 2000 he was imprisoned for perjury and attempting to pervert the course of justice 3 **William** 1856–1924, Scottish critic and dramatist: made the first English translations of Ibsen

archery 1 the art or sport of shooting with bows and arrows 2 archers or their weapons collectively
▷www.archery.org

archetype 1 *Psychoanal* one of the inherited mental images postulated by Jung as the content of the collective unconscious 2 a constantly recurring symbol or motif in literature, painting, etc.

Archimedes ?287–212 BC, Greek mathematician and physicist of Syracuse, noted for his work in geometry, hydrostatics, and mechanics

Archimedes' principle a law of physics stating that the apparent upward force (buoyancy) of a body immersed in a fluid is equal to the weight of the displaced fluid

archipelago 1 a group of islands 2 a sea studded with islands

architect 1 a person qualified to design buildings and to superintend their erection 2 a person similarly qualified in another form of construction

architecture 1 the art and science of designing and superintending the erection of buildings and similar structures **2** a style of building or structure **3** buildings or structures collectively **4** the internal organization of a computer's components with particular reference to the way in which data is transmitted **5** the arrangement of the various devices in a complete computer system or network

▷www.architecture.com
▷www.architectureweek.com
▷http://architecture.about.com
▷www.bluffton.edu/sullivanm/index

architrave *Architect* **1** the lowest part of an entablature that bears on the columns **2** a moulding around a doorway, window opening, etc.

archive *Computing* data transferred to a tape or disk for long-term storage rather than frequent use

arctic of or relating to the Arctic

Arctic 1 the Also called: **Arctic Zone** the regions north of the Arctic Circle **2** of or relating to the regions north of the Arctic Circle

Arctic Circle the imaginary circle round the earth, parallel to the equator, at latitude 66° 32′ N; it marks the northernmost point at which the sun appears above the level of the horizon on the winter solstice

arctic hare a large hare, *Lepus arcticus*, of the Canadian Arctic whose fur is white in winter

Arctic Ocean the ocean surrounding the North Pole, north of the Arctic Circle. Area: about 14 100 000 sq km (5 440 000 sq miles)

arctic willow a low-growing shrub, *Salix arctica*, of the tundra

arc welding a technique in which metal is welded by heat generated by an electric arc struck between two electrodes or between one electrode and the metal workpiece

Arden¹ John born 1930, British dramatist and novelist. His plays include *Serjeant Musgrave's Dance* (1959) and *The Workhouse Donkey* (1963); novels include *Silence Among the Weapons* (1982): he often works in collaboration with his wife Margaretta D'Arcy

Arden² Forest of a region of N Warwickshire, part of a former forest: scene of Shakespeare's *As You Like It*

Ardennes 1 a department of NE France, in Champagne-Ardenne region. Capital: Mézières. Pop: 288 806 (2003 est). Area: 5253 sq km (2049 sq miles) **2** the a wooded plateau in SE Belgium, Luxembourg, and NE France: scene of heavy fighting in both World Wars

Ards a district of Northern Ireland, in Co. Down. Pop: 74 369 (2003 est). Area: 368 sq km (142 sq miles)

are a unit of area equal to 100 sq metres or 119.599 sq yards; one hundredth of a hectare.

area 1 a the extent of a two-dimensional surface enclosed within a specified boundary or geometric figure **b** the two-dimensional extent of the surface of a solid, or of some part thereof, esp one bounded by a closed curve **2** *Anatomy* any of the various regions of the cerebral cortex **3** *Computing* any part of a computer memory assigned to store data of a specified type

arena *Ancient history* the central area of an ancient Roman amphitheatre, in which gladiatorial contests and other spectacles were held

Arendt Hannah 1906–75, US political philosopher, born in Germany. Her publications include *The Origins of*

Totalitarianism (1951) and *Eichmann in Jerusalem* (1961)

areola *Anatomy* any small circular area, such as the pigmented ring around the human nipple or the inflamed area surrounding a pimple

Areopagus 1 a the hill to the northwest of the Acropolis in Athens **b** (in ancient Athens) the judicial council whose members (Areopagites) met on this hill **2** *Literary* any high court

Arequipa a city in S Peru, at an altitude of 2250 m (7500 ft): founded in 1540 on the site of an Inca city. Pop: 791 000 (2005 est)

Ares *Greek myth* the god of war, born of Zeus and Hera

arête a sharp ridge separating two cirques or glacial valleys in mountainous regions

Arezzo a city in central Italy, in E Tuscany. Pop: 91 589 (2001)

Argenteuil a suburb of Paris, France, with a convent (656) that became famous when Héloïse was abbess (12th century). Pop: 93 961 (1999)

Argentina a republic in southern South America: colonized by the Spanish from 1516 onwards; gained independence in 1816 and became a republic in 1852; ruled by military dictatorships for much of the 20th century; civilian rule restored in 1983; consists chiefly of subtropical plains and forests (the Chaco) in the north, temperate plains (the pampas) in the central parts, the Andes in the west, and an infertile plain extending to Tierra del Fuego in the south (Patagonia); an important meat producer. Language: Spanish. Religion: Roman Catholic. Currency: peso. Capital: Buenos Aires. Pop: 38 871 000 (2004 est). Area: 2 776 653 sq km (1 072 067 sq miles)

Argentine 1 the another name for **Argentina 2** a native or inhabitant of Argentina

Argerich Martha born 1941, Argentinian concert pianist

Argive 1 (in Homer, Virgil, etc) of or relating to the Greeks besieging Troy, esp those from Argos **2** of or relating to Argos or Argolis **3** a literary word for **Greek 4** an ancient Greek, esp one from Argos or Argolis

Argolis 1 a department and ancient region of Greece, in the NE Peloponnese. Capital: Nauplion. Pop: 102 392 (2001). Area: 2261 sq km (873 sq miles) **2** Gulf of an inlet of the Aegean Sea, in the E Peloponnese

argon an extremely unreactive colourless odourless element of the rare gas series that forms almost 1 per cent (by volume) of the atmosphere. It is used in electric lights. Symbol: Ar; atomic no.: 18; atomic wt.: 39.948; density: 1.7837 kg/m³; freezing pt.: –189.3°C; boiling pt.: –185.9°C

Argonne the a wooded region of NE France: scene of major battles in both World Wars

Argos an ancient city in SE Greece, in the NE Peloponnese: one of the oldest Greek cities, it dominated the Peloponnese in the 7th century BC. Pop: 22 000 (1995 est)

argosy *Archaic or poetic* a large abundantly laden merchant ship, or a fleet of such ships

argument 1 *Logic* **a** a process of deductive or inductive reasoning that purports to show its conclusion to be true **b** formally, a sequence of statements one of which is the conclusion and the remainder the premises **2** *Logic* an obsolete name for the middle term of a syllogism **3** *Maths* **a** an element to which an operation, function, predicate, etc, applies, esp the independent variable of a function **b** another name for **amplitude** (sense 2) of a complex number

argumentation *Logic* the process of reasoning methodically

Argyll and Bute a council area in W Scotland on the Atlantic Ocean: in 1975 the historical counties of Argyllshire and Bute became part of Strathclyde region; in 1996 they were reinstated as a single unitary authority. Argyll and Bute is mountainous and includes the islands of Bute, Mull, Islay, and Jura. Administrative centre: Lochgilphead. Pop: 91 300 (2003 est). Area: 6930 sq km (2676 sq miles)

Argyllshire (until 1975) a county of W Scotland, part of Strathclyde region (1975–96), now part of Argyll and Bute

aria an elaborate accompanied song for solo voice from a cantata, opera, or oratorio

Arica a port in extreme N Chile: awarded to Chile in 1929 after the lengthy Tacna-Arica dispute with Peru; outlet for Bolivian and Peruvian trade. Pop: 180 000 (2005 est)

Aries 1 *Astronomy* a small zodiacal constellation in the N hemisphere lying between Taurus and Pisces on the ecliptic and having a second-magnitude star **2** *Astrology* **a** the first sign of the zodiac, symbol ♈, having a cardinal fire classification, ruled by the planet Mars. The sun is in this sign between about March 21 and April 19 **b** a person born during the period when the sun is in this sign **3** *Astrology* born under or characteristic of Aries

Arimathea *or* **Arimathaea** a town in ancient Palestine: location unknown

Ariosto Ludovico 1474–1533, Italian poet, famous for his romantic epic *Orlando Furioso* (1516)

aristocracy 1 a privileged class of people usually of high birth; the nobility **2** such a class as the ruling body of a state **3** government by such a class **4** a state governed by such a class

aristocrat 1 a member of the aristocracy; a noble **2** a person who advocates aristocracy as a form of government

aristocratic relating to or characteristic of aristocracy or an aristocrat

Aristophanes ?448–?380 BC, Greek comic dramatist, who satirized leading contemporary figures such as Socrates and Euripides. Eleven of his plays are extant, including *The Clouds*, *The Frogs*, *The Birds*, and *Lysistrata*

Aristotelian 1 of or relating to Aristotle (384–322 BC), the Greek philosopher or his philosophy **2** (of a philosophical position) derived from that of Aristotle, or incorporating such of his major doctrines as the distinctions between matter and form, and substance and accident, or the primacy of individuals over universals

Aristotle 384–322 BC, Greek philosopher; pupil of Plato, tutor of Alexander the Great, and founder of the Peripatetic school at Athens; author of works on logic, ethics, politics, poetics, rhetoric, biology, zoology, and metaphysics. His works influenced Muslim philosophy and science and medieval scholastic philosophy

arithmetic 1 the branch of mathematics concerned with numerical calculations, such as addition, subtraction, multiplication, and division **2** one or more calculations involving numerical operations

arithmetic mean an average value of a set of integers, terms, or quantities, expressed as their sum divided by their number

arithmetic progression a sequence of numbers or quantities, each term of which differs from the succeeding term by a constant amount, such as 3,6,9,12

Arius ?250–336 AD, Greek Christian theologian, originator of the doctrine of Arianism

Arizona a state of the southwestern US: consists of the Colorado plateau in the northeast, including the Grand Canyon, divided from desert in the southwest by mountains rising over 3750 m (12 500 ft). Capital: Phoenix. Pop: 5 580 811 (2003 est). Area: 293 750 sq km (113 417 sq miles)

ark the vessel that Noah built and in which he saved himself, his family, and a number of animals and birds during the Flood (Genesis 6–9)

Ark *Judaism* **1** the cupboard at the front of a synagogue, usually in the eastern wall, in which the Torah scrolls are kept **2** the most sacred symbol of God's presence among the Hebrew people, carried in their journey from Sinai to the Promised Land (Canaan) and eventually enshrined in the holy of holies of the Temple in Jerusalem

Arkansas 1 a state of the southern US: mountainous in the north and west, with the alluvial plain of the Mississippi in the east; has the only diamond mine in the US; the chief US producer of bauxite. Capital: Little Rock. Pop: 2 725 714 (2003 est). Area: 134 537 sq km (51 945 sq miles) **2** a river in the S central US, rising in central Colorado and flowing east and southeast to join the Mississippi in Arkansas. Length: 2335 km (1450 miles)

Arkwright Sir Richard 1732–92, English cotton manufacturer: inventor of the spinning frame (1769) which produced cotton thread strong enough to be used as a warp

Arles 1 a city in SE France, on the Rhône: Roman amphitheatre. Pop: 50 513 (1999) **2 Kingdom of** a kingdom in SE France which had dissolved by 1378: known as the Kingdom of Burgundy until about 1200

Arlington a county of N Virginia: site of **Arlington National Cemetery**

Arlon a town in SE Belgium, capital of Luxembourg province. Pop: 25 766 (2004 est)

armadillo any edentate mammal of the family *Dasypodidae* of Central and South America and S North America, such as *Priodontes giganteus* (**giant armadillo**). They are burrowing animals, with peglike rootless teeth and a covering of strong horny plates over most of the body

Armageddon *New Testament* the final battle at the end of the world between the forces of good and evil, God against the kings of the earth (Revelation 16:16)

Armagh 1 a historical county of S Northern Ireland: in 1973 it was replaced for administrative purposes by the districts of Armagh and Craigavon. Area: 1326 sq km (512 sq miles) **2** a district in Northern Ireland, in Co. Armagh. Pop: 55 449 (2003 est). Area: 667 sq km (258 sq miles) **3** a town in S Northern Ireland, in Armagh district, Co. Armagh: seat of Roman Catholic and Protestant archbishops. Pop: 14 590 (2001)

Armani Giorgio born 1936, Italian fashion designer,

noted for his restrained classical style

armature 1 a revolving structure in an electric motor or generator, wound with the coils that carry the current **2** any part of an electric machine or device that moves under the influence of a magnetic field or within which an electromotive force is induced **3** a soft iron or steel bar placed across the poles of a permanent magnet to close the magnetic circuit **4** such a bar placed across the poles of an electromagnet to transmit mechanical force **5** *Sculpture* a framework to support the clay or other material used in modelling **6** the protective outer covering of an animal or plant

Armenia 1 a republic in NW Asia: originally part of the historic Armenian kingdom; acquired by Russia in 1828; became the Armenian Soviet Socialist Republic in 1936; gained independence in 1991. It is mountainous, rising over 4000 m (13 000 ft). Language: Armenian. Religion: Christian (Armenian Apostolic) majority. Currency: dram. Capital: Yerevan. Pop: Pop: 3 052 000 (2004 est). Area: 29 800 sq km (11 490 sq miles) **2** a former kingdom in W Asia, between the Black Sea and the Caspian Sea, south of Georgia **3** a town in central Colombia: centre of a coffee-growing district. Pop: 349 000 (2005 est)

Armenian 1 the language of the Armenians: an Indo-European language probably belonging to the Thraco-Phrygian branch, but containing many non-Indo-European elements **2** an adherent of the Armenian Church or its doctrines

Armidale a town in Australia, in NE New South Wales: a centre for tourism. Pop: 20 271 (2001)

Armitage Simon (**Robert**). born 1963, British poet and writer, whose collections include *Zoom!* (1989), *Killing Time* (1999), and *Universal Home Doctor* (2002)

armour *or US* **armor 1** *Nautical* the watertight suit of a diver **2** *Engineering* permanent protection for an underwater structure

Armstrong 1 Edwin Howard 1890–1954, US electrical engineer; invented the superheterodyne radio receiver and the FM radio **2** (Daniel) **Louis**, known as *Satchmo*. 1900–71, US jazz trumpeter, bandleader, and singer **3** **Gillian** born 1950, Australian film director; her films include *My Brilliant Career* (1978), *Little Women* (1994), and *Charlotte Gray* (2001) **4** **Neil** (**Alden**). born 1930, US astronaut; commanded Apollo 11 on the first manned lunar landing during which he became the first man to set foot on the moon on July 20, 1969 **5** **Lance** born 1971, US cyclist, winner of 6 Tour de France titles, 1999–2004

Arnaud Yvonne 1892–1958, French actress, who was well-known on the London stage and in British films. A theatre in Guildford is named after her

Arne Thomas (**Augustine**). 1710–78, English composer, noted for his setting of Shakespearean songs and for his song *Rule Britannia*

Arnhem a city in the E Netherlands, capital of Gelderland province, on the Rhine: site of a World War II battle. Pop: 142 000 (2003 est)

Arnhem Land a region of N Australia in the N Northern Territory, large areas of which are reserved for native Australians

Arnim Achim von 1781–1831, German romantic poet. He published, with Clemens Brentano, the collection of folk songs, *Des Knaben Wunderhorn* (1805–08)

Arno a river in central Italy, rising in the Apennines and flowing through Florence to the Ligurian Sea. Length: about 240 km (150 miles)

Arnold[1] 1 Sir Malcolm born 1921, English composer, esp of orchestral works in a traditional idiom **2** Matthew 1822–88, English poet, essayist, and literary critic, noted particularly for his poems *Sohrab and Rustum* (1853) and *Dover Beach* (1867), and for his *Essays in Criticism* (1865) and *Culture and Anarchy* (1869) **3** his father, Thomas 1795–1842, English historian and educationalist, headmaster of Rugby School, noted for his reforms in public-school education

Arnold[2] a town in N central England, in S Nottinghamshire. Pop: 37 402 (2001)

aromatherapy the use of fragrant essential oils extracted from plants as a treatment in complementary medicine to relieve tension and cure certain minor ailments

aromatic *Chemistry* (of an organic compound) having an unsaturated ring containing alternating double and single bonds, esp containing a benzene ring; exhibiting aromaticity

Arp Jean *or* Hans 1887–1966, Alsatian sculptor, painter, and poet, cofounder of the Dada movement in Zürich, noted particularly for his abstract organic sculptures based on natural forms

arpeggio 1 a chord whose notes are played in rapid succession rather than simultaneously **2** an ascending and descending figuration used in practising the piano, voice, etc.

Arran an island off the SW coast of Scotland, in the Firth of Clyde. Pop: 5045 (2001). Area: 427 sq km (165 sq miles)

arrangement 1 an adaptation of a piece of music for performance in a different way, esp on different instruments from those for which it was originally composed **2** an adaptation (of a play, etc) for broadcasting

Arras a town in N France: formerly famous for tapestry; severely damaged in both World Wars. Pop: 40 590 (1999)

Arrau Claudio 1903–91, Chilean pianist

array 1 *Maths* a sequence of numbers or symbols in a specified order **2** *Maths* a set of numbers or symbols arranged in rows and columns, as in a determinant or matrix **3** *Electronics* an arrangement of aerials spaced to give desired directional characteristics, used esp in radar **4** *Law* a panel of jurors **5** *Computing* a regular data structure in which individual elements may be located by reference to one or more integer index variables, the number of such indices being the number of dimensions in the array

arrest 1 the act of taking a person into custody, esp under lawful authority **2** the act of seizing and holding a ship under lawful authority **3** the state of being held, esp under lawful authority

arrow a long slender pointed weapon, usually having feathers fastened at the end as a balance, that is shot from a bow

arrowhead any aquatic herbaceous plant of the genus *Sagittaria*, esp *S. sagittifolia*, having arrow-shaped aerial leaves and linear submerged leaves: family *Alismataceae*

arrowroot 1 a white-flowered West Indian plant,

Maranta arundinacea, whose rhizomes yield an easily digestible starch: family *Marantaceae* **2** any of several other plants whose rhizomes or roots yield starch **3** the starch obtained from this plant

Arroyo Gloria Macapagal born 1948, Filipino stateswoman; president of the Philippines from 2001; vice-president (1998–2001)

arsenic a toxic metalloid element, existing in several allotropic forms, that occurs principally in realgar and orpiment and as the free element. It is used in transistors, lead-based alloys, and high-temperature brasses. Symbol: As; atomic no.: 33; atomic wt.: 74.92159; valency: –3, 0, +3, or +5; relative density: 5.73 (grey); melting pt.: 817°C at a pressure of 3MN/m^2 (grey); sublimes at 613°C (grey)

arson *Criminal law* the act of intentionally or recklessly setting fire to another's property or to one's own property for some improper reason

Artaud Antonin 1896–1948, French stage director and dramatist, whose concept of the theatre of cruelty is expounded in *Manifeste du théâtre de la cruauté* (1932) and *Le Théâtre et son double* (1938)

Artaxerxes II died ?358 BC, king of Persia (?404–?358). He defeated his brother Cyrus the Younger at Cunaxa (401)

Art Deco a a style of interior decoration, jewellery, architecture, etc, at its height in the 1930s and characterized by geometrical shapes, stylized natural forms, and symmetrical utilitarian designs adapted to mass production **b** (*as modifier*): *an Art-Deco carpet*
▷www.art-deco.com
▷www.artcyclopedia.com/history/art-deco.htm
▷www.adsw.org/resource/websites.htm

artefact *or* **artifact** *Cytology* a structure seen in tissue after death, fixation, staining, etc, that is not normally present in the living tissue

Artemis *Greek myth* the virgin goddess of the hunt and the moon: the twin sister of Apollo

arterial 1 of, relating to, or affecting an artery or arteries **2** denoting or relating to the usually bright red reoxygenated blood returning from the lungs or gills that circulates in the arteries

arteriosclerosis a pathological condition of the circulatory system characterized by thickening and loss of elasticity of the arterial walls

artery any of the tubular thick-walled muscular vessels that convey oxygenated blood from the heart to various parts of the body

artesian well a well sunk through impermeable strata into strata receiving water from an area at a higher altitude than that of the well, so that there is sufficient pressure to force water to flow upwards

arthritis inflammation of a joint or joints characterized by pain and stiffness of the affected parts, caused by gout, rheumatic fever, etc.

arthropod any invertebrate of the phylum *Arthropoda*, having jointed limbs, a segmented body, and an exoskeleton made of chitin. The group includes the crustaceans, insects, arachnids, and centipedes

Arthur a legendary king of the Britons in the sixth century AD, who led Celtic resistance against the Saxons: possibly based on a historical figure; represented as leader of the Knights of the Round Table at

Camelot **2 Chester Alan** 1830–86, 21st president of the US (1881–85)

artichoke 1 a thistle-like Eurasian plant, *Cynara scolymus*, cultivated for its large edible flower head containing many fleshy scalelike bracts: family *Asteraceae* (composites) **2** the unopened flower head of this plant, which can be cooked and eaten **3** See **Jerusalem artichoke**

article 1 a clause or section in a written document such as a treaty, contract, statute, etc. **2** in **articles** formerly, undergoing training, according to the terms of a written contract, in the legal profession

articled bound by a written contract, such as one that governs a period of training

articular of or relating to joints or to the structural components in a joint

articulate *Zoology* (of arthropods and higher vertebrates) possessing joints or jointed segments

articulation 1 *Zoology* **a** a joint such as that between bones or arthropod segments **b** the way in which jointed parts are connected **2** *Botany* the part of a plant at which natural separation occurs, such as the joint between leaf and stem

artificial *Biology* relating to superficial characteristics not based on the interrelationships of organisms

artificial insemination introduction of spermatozoa into the vagina or uterus by means other than sexual union

artificial intelligence the study of the modelling of human mental functions by computer programs

artificial respiration 1 any of various methods of restarting breathing after it has stopped, by manual rhythmic pressure on the chest, mouth-to-mouth breathing, etc. **2** any method of maintaining respiration artificially, as by use of an iron lung

artistry 1 artistic workmanship, ability, or quality **2** artistic pursuits

Art Nouveau a a style of art and architecture of the 1890s, characterized by swelling sinuous outlines and stylized natural forms, such as flowers and leaves **b** (*as modifier*): *an Art-Nouveau mirror*
▷http://kubos.org/AN/en
▷www.artchive.com/artchive/art_nouveau.htm

Aruba an island in the Caribbean, off the NW coast of Venezuela, a dependency of the Netherlands with special status; part of the Netherlands Antilles until 1986. Chief town: Oranjestad. Pop: 100 000 (2003 est). Area: about 181 sq km (70 sq miles)

Arunachal Pradesh a state in NE India, formed in 1986 from the former Union Territory. Capital: Itanagar. Pop: 1 091 117 (2001). Area: 83 743 sq km (32 648 sq miles)

Arundel a town in S England, in West Sussex: 11th-century castle. Pop: 3297 (2001)

Aryan *or* **Arian 1** (in Nazi ideology) a Caucasian of non-Jewish descent, esp of the Nordic type **2** a member of any of the peoples supposedly descended from the Indo-Europeans, esp a speaker of an Iranian or Indic language in ancient times **3** of, relating to, or characteristic of an Aryan or Aryans **4** *Archaic* Indo-European

as *History* **1** an ancient Roman unit of weight approximately equal to 1 pound troy (373 grams) **2** the standard monetary unit and copper coin of ancient Rome

asafoetida *or* **asafetida** a bitter resin with an unpleasant onion-like smell, obtained from the roots of some umbelliferous plants of the genus *Ferula:* formerly used as a carminative, antispasmodic, and expectorant

asbestos **a** any of the fibrous amphibole and serpentine minerals, esp chrysotile and tremolite, that are incombustible and resistant to chemicals. It was formerly widely used in the form of fabric or board as a heat-resistant structural material **b** (*as modifier*): *asbestos matting*

asbestosis inflammation of the lungs resulting from chronic inhalation of asbestos particles

ASBO *Brit* anti-social behaviour order: a civil order made against a persistently anti-social individual which restricts his or her activities or movements, a breach of which results in criminal charges

ascendant *or* **ascendent** *Astrology* **a** a point on the ecliptic that rises on the eastern horizon at a particular moment and changes as the earth rotates on its axis **b** the sign of the zodiac containing this point

ascension *Astronomy* the rising of a star above the horizon

Ascension¹ *New Testament* the passing of Jesus Christ from earth into heaven (Acts 1:9)

Ascension² an island in the S Atlantic, northwest of St Helena: uninhabited until claimed by Britain in 1815. Pop: 1122 (2003 est). Area: 88 sq km (34 sq miles)

Ascension Day *Christianity* the 40th day after Easter, when the Ascension of Christ into heaven is celebrated

ascetic **1** a person who practises great self-denial and austerities and abstains from worldly comforts and pleasures, esp for religious reasons **2** (in the early Christian Church) a monk

Asch **Sholem** 1880–1957, US writer, born in Poland, who wrote in Yiddish. His works include biblical novels

Aschaffenburg a city in Germany, on the River Main in Bavaria: seat of the Imperial Diet (1447); ceded to Bavaria in 1814. Pop: 68 607 (2003 est)

Ascham **Roger** ?1515–68, English humanist writer and classical scholar: tutor to Queen Elizabeth I

ASCII American standard code for information interchange: a computer code for representing alphanumeric characters

ascorbic acid a white crystalline vitamin present in plants, esp citrus fruits, tomatoes, and green vegetables. A deficiency in the diet of man leads to scurvy. Formula: $C_6H_8O_6$

Ascot a town in S England, in Bracknell Forest unitary authority, Berkshire: noted for its horse-race meetings, esp **Royal Ascot**, a four-day meeting held in June. Pop: 8755 (2001)

aseptic **1** free from living pathogenic organisms; sterile **2** aiming to achieve a germ-free condition

asexual **1** having no apparent sex or sex organs **2** (of reproduction) not involving the fusion of male and female gametes, as in vegetative reproduction, fission, or budding

ash¹ **1** the nonvolatile products and residue formed when matter is burnt **2** any of certain compounds formed by burning **3** fine particles of lava thrown out by an erupting volcano **4** a light silvery grey colour, often with a brownish tinge

ash² **1** any oleaceous tree of the genus *Fraxinus*, esp *F. excelsior* of Europe and Asia, having compound leaves, clusters of small greenish flowers, and winged seeds **2** the close-grained durable wood of any of these trees, used for tool handles, etc. **3** any of several trees resembling the ash, such as the mountain ash **4** *Austral* any of several Australian trees resembling the ash, esp of the eucalyptus genus

Ashanti an administrative region of central Ghana: former native kingdom, suppressed by the British in 1900 after four wars. Capital: Kumasi. Pop: 3 187 607 (2000). Area: 24 390 sq km (9417 sq miles)

Ashcroft Dame **Peggy** 1907–91, English stage and film actress

Ashdod a town in central Israel, on the Mediterranean coast: an important city in the Philistine Empire, with its artificial harbour (1961) it is now a major port. Pop: 192 000 (2003 est)

Ashe **Arthur** (**Robert**). 1943–93, US tennis player: US champion 1968; Wimbledon champion 1975

ashen¹ of a pale greyish colour

ashen² of, relating to, or made from the ash tree or its timber

Asher the son of Jacob and ancestor of one of the 12 tribes of Israel

Ashford a market town in SE England, in central Kent. Pop: 58 936 (2001)

Ashkenazy **Vladimir** born 1937, Soviet-born Icelandic pianist and conductor

Ashkhabad *or* **Ashgabat** the capital of Turkmenistan. Pop: 598 000 (2005 est)

Ashley **1 Jack**, Baron. born 1922, British Labour politician and campaigner for deaf and disabled people **2 Laura** 1925–85, British designer, who built up a successful chain of retail stores selling dresses and fabrics based on traditional English patterns

ashram a religious retreat or community where a Hindu holy man lives

Ashton Sir **Frederick** 1906–88, British ballet dancer and choreographer. His ballets include *Façade* (1931), to music by Walton, *La Fille mal gardée* (1960), *The Dream* (1964), and *A Month in the Country* (1976)

Ashton-under-Lyne a town in NW England, in Tameside unitary authority, Greater Manchester. Pop: 43 236 (2001)

Ash Wednesday the first day of Lent, named from the practice of Christians of placing ashes on their heads as a sign of penitence

Asia the largest of the continents, bordering on the Arctic Ocean, the Pacific Ocean, the Indian Ocean, and the Mediterranean and Red Seas in the west. It includes the large peninsulas of Asia Minor, India, Arabia, and Indochina and the island groups of Japan, Indonesia, the Philippines, and Ceylon (Sri Lanka); contains the mountain ranges of the Hindu Kush, Himalayas, Pamirs, Tian Shan, Urals, and Caucasus, the great plateaus of India, Iran, and Tibet, vast plains and deserts, and the valleys of many large rivers including the Mekong, Irrawaddy, Indus, Ganges, Tigris, and Euphrates. Pop: 3 917 508 000 (2005 est). Area: 44 391 162 sq km (17 139 445 sq miles)

Asian pear **1** a tropical pear tree, esp any of several varieties of Japanese pear *Pyrus serotina* **2** the fruit of the Japanese pear, which resembles a large yellow apple, has crisp juicy flesh, and is cultivated in Japan, Korea, the US, and New Zealand

aside *Theatre* something spoken by an actor, intended to be heard by the audience, but not by the others on stage

Asimov Isaac 1920–92, US writer and biochemist, born in Russia. His science-fiction works include *Foundation Trilogy* (1951–53; sequel 1982) and the collection of stories *I, Robot* (1950)

Asir a region of SW Saudi Arabia, in the Southern Province on the Red Sea: under Turkish rule until 1933. Area: 81 000 sq km (31 000 sq miles)

Askey Arthur 1900–82, British comedian

asking price *Commerce* the price suggested by a seller but usually considered to be subject to bargaining

Askja a volcano in E central Iceland: active in 1961; largest crater in Iceland. Height: 1510 m (4954 ft). Area of crater: 88 sq km (34 sq miles)

Asmara the capital of Eritrea; cathedral (1922); Grand Mosque (1937); university (1958). Pop: 615 000 (2005 est)

Aso a group of five volcanic cones in Japan on central Kyushu, one of which, Naka-dake, has the largest crater in the world, between 16 km (10 miles) and 24 km (15 miles) in diameter. Highest cone: 1592 m (5223 ft)

asp **1** the venomous snake, probably *Naja haje* (Egyptian cobra), that caused the death of Cleopatra and was formerly used by the Pharaohs as a symbol of their power over life and death **2** a viper, *Vipera aspis*, that occurs in S Europe and is very similar to but smaller than the adder

asparagus **1** any Eurasian liliaceous plant of the genus *Asparagus*, esp the widely cultivated *A. officinalis*, having small scaly or needle-like leaves **2** the succulent young shoots of *A. officinalis*, which may be cooked and eaten **3 asparagus fern** a fernlike species of asparagus, *A. plumosus*, native to southern Africa

aspartame an artificial sweetener produced from aspartic acid. Formula: $C_{14}H_{18}N_2O_5$

aspect **1** *Astrology* any of several specific angular distances between two planets or a planet and the Ascendant or Midheaven measured, from the earth, in degrees along the ecliptic **2** *Botany* **a** the compass direction to which a plant habitat is exposed, or the degree of exposure **b** the effect of the seasons on the appearance of plants

aspen any of several trees of the salicaceous genus *Populus*, such as *P. tremula* of Europe, in which the leaves are attached to the stem by long flattened stalks so that they quiver in the wind

asperity *Physics* the elastically compressed region of contact between two surfaces caused by the normal force

aspersion *Rare* the act of sprinkling, esp of water in baptism

asphalt **1** any of several black semisolid substances composed of bitumen and inert mineral matter. They occur naturally in parts of America and as a residue from petroleum distillation: used as a waterproofing material and in paints, dielectrics, and fungicides **2** a mixture of this substance with gravel, used in road-surfacing and roofing materials

asphodel **1** any of various S European liliaceous plants of the genera *Asphodelus* and *Asphodeline*, having clusters of white or yellow flowers **2** any of various other plants, such as the daffodil **3** an unidentified flower of Greek legend, probably a narcissus, said to cover the Elysian fields

asphyxia lack of oxygen in the blood due to restricted respiration; suffocation. If severe enough and prolonged, it causes death

aspic either of two species of lavender, *Lavandula spica* or *L. latifolia*, that yield an oil used in perfumery: family *Lamiaceae* (labiates)

aspidistra any Asian plant of the liliaceous genus *Aspidistra*, esp *A. lurida*, a popular house plant with long tough evergreen leaves and purplish flowers borne on the ground

aspiration **1 a** the act of breathing **b** a breath **2** removal of air or fluid from a body cavity by suction **3** *Med* **a** the sucking of fluid or foreign matter into the air passages of the body **b** the removal of air or fluid from the body by suction

aspirator a device employing suction, such as a jet pump or one for removing fluids from a body cavity

aspirin **1** a white crystalline compound widely used in the form of tablets to relieve pain and fever, to reduce inflammation, and to prevent strokes. Formula: $CH_3COOC_6H_4COOH$ **2** a tablet of aspirin

Asquith Herbert Henry, 1st Earl of Oxford and Asquith. 1852–1928, British statesman; prime minister (1908–16); leader of the Liberal Party (1908–26)

ass **1** either of two perissodactyl mammals of the horse family (*Equidae*), *Equus asinus* (**African wild ass**) or *E. hemionus* (**Asiatic wild ass**). They are hardy and sure-footed, having longer ears than the horse **2** the domesticated variety of the African wild ass; donkey

Assad **1** Hafiz al born 1928, Syrian statesman and general; president of Syria (1971–2000) **2** his son, **Bashar al** born 1965, Syrian statesman; president of Syria from 2000

Assam a state of NE India, situated in the central Brahmaputra valley: tropical forest, with the heaviest rainfall in the world; produces large quantities of tea. Capital: Dispur. Pop: 26 638 407 (2001 est). Area: 78 438 sq km (30 673 sq miles)

assault *Law* an intentional or reckless act that causes another person to expect to be subjected to immediate and unlawful violence

assault and battery *Criminal law* a threat of attack to another person followed by actual attack, which need amount only to touching with hostile intent

assay **1 a** an analysis, esp a determination of the amount of metal in an ore or the amounts of impurities in a precious metal **b** (*as modifier*): *an assay office* **2** a substance undergoing an analysis **3** a written report on the results of an analysis

assegai *or* **assagai** a southern African cornaceous tree, *Curtisia faginea*, the wood of which is used for making spears

assemblage *Art* a three-dimensional work of art that combines various objects into an integrated whole

assembler a type of computer program that converts a program written in assembly language into machine code

assembly *Machinery* a group of mating components before or after fitting together

assembly line a sequence of machines, tools, operations, workers, etc, in a factory, arranged so that at each stage a further process is carried out

assemblyman *Politics* a member of an assembly, esp a legislature

Assen a city in the N Netherlands, capital of Drenthe province. Pop: 62 000 (2003 est)

assessor 1 a person who evaluates the merits, importance, etc, of something, esp (in Britain) work prepared as part of a course of study 2 a person with technical expertise called in to advise a court on specialist matters

asset-stripping *Commerce* the practice of taking over a failing company at a low price and then selling the assets piecemeal

assign *Law* a person to whom property is assigned; assignee

assignment 1 *Law* a the transfer to another of a right, interest, or title to property, esp personal property b the document effecting such a transfer c the right, interest, or property transferred 2 *Law* (formerly) the transfer, esp by an insolvent debtor, of property in trust for the benefit of his creditors 3 *Logic* a function that associates specific values with each variable in a formal expression

Assiniboine a river in W Canada, rising in E Saskatchewan and flowing southeast and east to the Red River at Winnipeg. Length: over 860 km (500 miles)

Assisi a town in central Italy, in Umbria: birthplace of St Francis, who founded the Franciscan religious order here in 1208. Pop: 25 304 (2001)

assist *Baseball* the act of a player who throws or deflects a batted ball in such a way that a team is enabled to put out an opponent

association 1 *Psychol* the mental process of linking ideas so that the recurrence of one idea automatically recalls the other 2 *Chem* the formation of groups of molecules and ions, esp in liquids, held together by weak chemical bonds 3 *Ecology* a group of similar plants that grow in a uniform environment and contain one or more dominant species

associative *Maths, logic* being independent of the grouping of numbers, symbols, or terms within a given set, as in conjunction or in an expression such as $(2 \times 3) \times 4 = 2 \times (3 \times 4)$

assonance the use of the same vowel sound with different consonants or the same consonant with different vowels in successive words or stressed syllables, as in a line of verse. Examples are *time* and *light* or *mystery* and *mastery*

assumption *Logic* a statement that is used as the premise of a particular argument but may not be otherwise accepted

Assumption *Christianity* 1 the taking up of the Virgin Mary (body and soul) into heaven when her earthly life was ended 2 the feast commemorating this, celebrated by Roman Catholics on Aug 15

Assur, Asur, Asshur *or* **Ashur** 1 the supreme national god of the ancient Assyrians, chiefly a war god, whose symbol was an archer within a winged disc 2 one of the chief cities of ancient Assyria, on the River Tigris about 100 km (60 miles) downstream from the present-day city of Mosul

Assyria an ancient kingdom of N Mesopotamia: it established an empire that stretched from Egypt to the Persian Gulf, reaching its greatest extent between 721 and 633 BC. Its chief cities were Assur and Nineveh

Assyrian 1 an inhabitant of ancient Assyria 2 a modern-day descendant of the ancient Assyrians 3 a the language of the ancient Assyrians, belonging to the E Semitic subfamily of the Afro-Asiatic family and regarded as a dialect of Akkadian b a dialect of Aramaic, spoken by modern Assyrians

Astaire Fred, real name *Frederick Austerlitz*. 1899–1987, US dancer, singer, and actor, whose films include *Top Hat* (1935), *Swing Time* (1936), and *The Band Wagon* (1953)

Astana the capital of Kazakhstan, in the N of the country; replaced Almaty as capital in 1997; an important railway junction. Pop: 335 000 (2005 est)

astatine a radioactive element of the halogen series: a decay product of uranium and thorium that occurs naturally in minute amounts and is artificially produced by bombarding bismuth with alpha particles. Symbol: At; atomic no.: 85; half-life of most stable isotope, ^{210}At: 8.1 hours; probable valency: 1,3,5, or 7; melting pt.: 302°C; boiling pt.: 337°C (est)

Astbury John 1688–1743, English potter; earliest of the great Staffordshire potters

aster 1 any plant of the genus *Aster*, having white, blue, purple, or pink daisy-like flowers: family *Asteraceae* (composites) 2 **China aster** a related Chinese plant, *Callistephus chinensis*, widely cultivated for its showy brightly coloured flowers 3 *Cytology* a group of radiating microtubules that surrounds the centrosome before and during mitosis

asteroid 1 any of numerous small celestial bodies that move around the sun mainly between the orbits of Mars and Jupiter. Their diameters range from 930 kilometres (Ceres) to less than one kilometre 2 any echinoderm of the class *Asteroidea*; a starfish

asthma a respiratory disorder, often of allergic origin, characterized by difficulty in breathing, wheezing, and a sense of constriction in the chest

Asti a town in NW Italy: famous for its sparkling wine (Asti spumante). Pop: 71 276 (2001)

astigmatism *or* **astigmia** 1 a defect of a lens resulting in the formation of distorted images; caused by the curvature of the lens being different in different planes 2 faulty vision resulting from defective curvature of the cornea or lens of the eye

Aston Francis William 1877–1945, English physicist and chemist, who developed the first mass spectrograph, using it to investigate the isotopic structures of elements: Nobel prize for chemistry 1922

Astor 1 John Jacob, 1st Baron Astor of Hever. 1886–1971, British proprietor of *The Times* (1922–66) 2 Nancy (Witcher), Viscountess, original name *Nancy Langhorne*. 1879–1964, British Conservative politician, born in the US; the first woman to sit in the British House of Commons

astrakhan 1 a fur, usually black or grey, made of the closely curled wool of lambs from Astrakhan 2 a cloth with curled pile resembling this

Astrakhan a city in SE Russia, on the delta of the Volga River, 21 m (70 ft) below sea level. Pop: 507 000 (2005 est)

astral 1 relating to, proceeding from, consisting of, or resembling the stars 2 *Biology* of or relating to the aster occurring in dividing cells 3 *Theosophy* denoting or relating to a supposed supersensible substance believed to form the material of a second body for each person, taking the form of an aura discernible to certain gifted individuals

astringent a drug or medicine causing contraction of body tissues, checking blood flow, or restricting secretions of fluids

astrolabe an instrument used by early astronomers to measure the altitude of stars and planets and also as a navigational aid. It consists of a graduated circular disc with a movable sighting device

astrology 1 the study of the motions and relative positions of the planets, sun, and moon, interpreted in terms of human characteristics and activities 2 the primitive study of celestial bodies, which formed the basis of astronomy

   ▷www.astrology-numerology.com

astronomical unit a unit of distance used in astronomy equal to the mean distance between the earth and the sun. 1 astronomical unit is equivalent to 1.495×10^{11} metres or about 9.3×10^7 miles

astronomy the scientific study of the individual celestial bodies (excluding the earth) and of the universe as a whole. Its various branches include astrometry, astrodynamics, cosmology, and astrophysics

   ▷www.astronomy.net
   ▷www.astronomytoday.com
   ▷www.astronomynow.com
   ▷www.popastro.com/home.htm
   ▷www.bbc.co.uk/science/space
   ▷www.rog.nmm.ac.uk

astrophysics the branch of physics concerned with the physical and chemical properties, origin, and evolution of the celestial bodies

Asturias¹ Miguel Ángel 1899–1974, Guatemalan novelist and poet. His novels include *El Señor Presidente* (1946). Nobel prize for literature 1967

Asturias² a region and former kingdom of NW Spain, consisting of a coastal plain and the Cantabrian Mountains: a Christian stronghold against the Moors (8th to 13th centuries); rich mineral resources

Aswan, Assuan, or **Assouan** an ancient town in SE Egypt, on the Nile, just below the First Cataract. Pop: 249 000 (2005 est)

Aswan High Dam a dam on the Nile forming a reservoir (Lake Nasser) extending 480 km (300 miles) from the First to the Third Cataracts: opened in 1971, it was built 6 km (4 miles) upstream from the old Aswan Dam (built in 1902 and twice raised). Height of dam: 109 m (365 ft)

asylum 1 *International law* refuge afforded to a person whose extradition is sought by a foreign government 2 *Obsolescent* an institution for the shelter, treatment, or confinement of individuals, esp a mental hospital (formerly termed **lunatic asylum**)

asymmetry lack or absence of symmetry in spatial arrangements or in mathematical or logical relations

asymptote a straight line that is closely approached by a plane curve so that the perpendicular distance between them decreases to zero as the distance from the origin increases to infinity

at a Laotian monetary unit worth one hundredth of a kip.

Atacama Desert a desert region along the W coast of South America, mainly in N Chile: a major source of nitrates. Area: about 80 000 sq km (31 000 sq miles)

Atahualpa or **Atabalipa** ?1500–33, the last Inca emperor of Peru (1525–33), who was put to death by the Spanish under Pizarro

atavism the recurrence in a plant or animal of certain primitive characteristics that were present in an ancestor but have not occurred in intermediate generations

ataxia or **ataxy** *Pathol* lack of muscular coordination

Atbara 1 a town in NE Sudan. Pop: 110 000 (2005 est) 2 a river in NE Africa, rising in N Ethiopia and flowing through E Sudan to the Nile at Atbara. Length: over 800 km (500 miles)

Atget (Jean) Eugène Auguste 1856–1927, French photographer, noted for his pictures of Parisian life

Athabaska or **Athabasca** 1 Lake a lake in W Canada, in NW Saskatchewan and NE Alberta. Area: about 7770 sq km (3000 sq miles) 2 a river in W Canada, rising in the Rocky Mountains and flowing northeast to Lake Athabaska. Length: 1230 km (765 miles)

Athanasius Saint ?296–373 AD, patriarch of Alexandria who championed Christian orthodoxy against Arianism. Feast day: May 2

atheism rejection of belief in God or gods

Athelstan ?895–939 AD, king of Wessex and Mercia (924–939 AD), who extended his kingdom to include most of England

Athena or **Athene** *Greek myth* a virgin goddess of wisdom, practical skills, and prudent warfare. She was born, fully armed, from the head of Zeus

Athenian a native or inhabitant of Athens

Athens the capital of Greece, in the southeast near the Saronic Gulf: became capital after independence in 1834; ancient city-state, most powerful in the 5th century BC; contains the hill citadel of the Acropolis. Pop: 3 238 000 (2005 est)

atherosclerosis a degenerative disease of the arteries characterized by patchy thickening of the inner lining of the arterial walls, caused by deposits of fatty material; a form of arteriosclerosis

athlete 1 a person trained to compete in sports or exercises involving physical strength, speed, or endurance 2 *Chiefly Brit* a competitor in track and field events

athlete's foot a fungal infection of the skin of the foot, esp between the toes and on the soles

athletics 1 a track and field events b (*as modifier*): *an athletics meeting* 2 sports or exercises engaged in by athletes 3 the theory or practice of athletic activities and training

   ▷www.iaaf.org

Athos Mount a mountain in NE Greece, in Macedonia Central region: site of the Monastic Republic of Mount Athos, autonomous since 1927 and inhabited by Greek

Orthodox Basilian monks in 20 monasteries founded in the 10th century. Pop: 1942 (2001)

Atkins Robert C 1930–2003, US physician, cardiologist, and nutritionist. An advocate of complementary medicine, he devised a widely-used diet (the Atkins diet) based on controlled intake of carbohydrates for weight management and disease prevention

Atkinson Sir Harry Albert 1831–92, New Zealand statesman, born in England: prime minister of New Zealand (1876–77; 1883–84; 1887–91)

Atlanta a city in N Georgia: the state capital. Pop: 423 019 (2003 est)

Atlantic 1 the short for the **Atlantic Ocean** 2 of or relating to or bordering the Atlantic Ocean 3 of or relating to Atlas or the Atlas Mountains

Atlantic City a resort in SE New Jersey on Absecon Beach, an island on the Atlantic coast. Pop: 40 385 (2003 est)

Atlantic Intracoastal Waterway a system of inland and coastal waterways along the Atlantic coast of the US from Cape Cod to Florida Bay. Length: 2495 km (1550 miles)

Atlanticism advocacy of close cooperation in military, political, and economic matters between Western Europe, esp the UK and the US

Atlantic Ocean the world's second largest ocean, bounded in the north by the Arctic, in the south by the Antarctic, in the west by North and South America, and in the east by Europe and Africa. Greatest depth: 9220 m (30 246 ft). Area: about 81 585 000 sq km (31 500 000 sq miles)

Atlantis (in ancient legend) a continent said to have sunk beneath the Atlantic Ocean west of the Straits of Gibraltar

atlas *Anatomy* the first cervical vertebra, attached to and supporting the skull in man

atmosphere 1 the gaseous envelope surrounding the earth or any other celestial body 2 the prevailing tone or mood of a novel, symphony, painting, or other work of art 3 any local gaseous environment or medium 4 a unit of pressure; the pressure that will support a column of mercury 760 mm high at 0°C at sea level. 1 atmosphere is equivalent to 101 325 newtons per square metre or 14.72 pounds per square inch

atoll a circular coral reef or string of coral islands surrounding a lagoon

atom 1 a the smallest quantity of an element that can take part in a chemical reaction b this entity as a source of nuclear energy 2 the hypothetical indivisible particle of matter postulated by certain ancient philosophers as the fundamental constituent of matter

atomic 1 of, using, or characterized by atomic bombs or atomic energy 2 of, related to, or comprising atoms 3 *Logic* (of a sentence, formula, etc) having no internal structure at the appropriate level of analysis. In predicate calculus, *Fa* is an **atomic sentence** and *Fx* an **atomic predicate**

atomic bomb *or* **atom bomb** a type of bomb in which the energy is provided by nuclear fission. Uranium-235 and plutonium-239 are the isotopes most commonly used in atomic bombs

atomic mass unit a unit of mass used to express atomic and molecular weights that is equal to one twelfth of the mass of an atom of carbon-12. It is equivalent to 1.66×10^{-27} kg

atomic number the number of protons in the nucleus of an atom of an element.

atomic theory 1 any theory in which matter is regarded as consisting of atoms, esp that proposed by John Dalton postulating that elements are composed of atoms that can combine in definite proportions to form compounds 2 the current concept of the atom as an entity with a definite structure

atomizer *or* **atomiser** a device for reducing a liquid to a fine spray, such as the nozzle used to feed oil into a furnace or an enclosed bottle with a fine outlet used to spray perfumes or medicines

atonal *Music* having no established key

atonement 1 *Christian theol* a the reconciliation of man with God through the life, sufferings, and sacrificial death of Christ b the sufferings and death of Christ 2 *Christian Science* the state in which the attributes of God are exemplified in man

atrium 1 the open main court of a Roman house 2 a central often glass-roofed hall that extends through several storeys in a building, such as a shopping centre or hotel 3 a court in front of an early Christian or medieval church, esp one flanked by colonnades 4 *Anatomy* a cavity or chamber in the body, esp the upper chamber of each half of the heart

atrophy a wasting away of an organ or part, or a failure to grow to normal size as the result of disease, faulty nutrition, etc.

atropine *or* **atropin** a poisonous alkaloid obtained from deadly nightshade, having an inhibitory action on the autonomic nervous system. It is used medicinally in pre-anaesthetic medication, to speed a slow heart rate, and as an emergency first-aid counter to exposure to chemical warfare nerve agents. Formula: $C_{17}H_{23}NO_3$

attaché 1 a specialist attached to a diplomatic mission 2 *Brit* a junior member of the staff of an embassy or legation

attachment 1 a the arrest of a person for disobedience to a court order b the lawful seizure of property and placing of it under control of a court c a writ authorizing such arrest or seizure 2 *Law* the binding of a debt in the hands of a garnishee until its disposition has been decided by the court

attack 1 *Music* decisiveness in beginning a passage, movement, or piece 2 *Music* the speed with which a note reaches its maximum volume

attar, otto, *or* **ottar** an essential oil from flowers, esp the damask rose, used pure or as a base for perfume

Attenborough 1 Sir David born 1926, British naturalist and broadcaster; noted esp for his TV series *Life on Earth* (1978), *The Living Planet* (1983), and *The Life of Birds* (1998) 2 his brother, **Richard,** Baron Attenborough. born 1923, British film actor, director, and producer; his films include *Gandhi* (1982), *Cry Freedom* (1987), and *Shadowlands* (1993)

attention *Psychol* the act of concentrating on any one of a set of objects or thoughts

attic *Architect* a storey or low wall above the cornice of a classical façade

Attic the dialect of Ancient Greek spoken and written in Athens: the chief literary dialect of classical Greek

Attica a region and department of E central Greece: in ancient times the territory of Athens. Capital: Athens. Pop: 3 336 700 (2001). Area: 14 157 sq km (5466 sq miles)

Attila ?406–453 AD, king of the Huns, who devastated much of the Roman Empire, invaded Gaul in 451 AD, but was defeated by the Romans and Visigoths at Châlons-sur-Marne

attire *Zoology* the antlers of a mature male deer

attitude 1 *Aeronautics* the orientation of an aircraft's axes in relation to some plane, esp the horizontal 2 *Ballet* a classical position in which the body is upright and one leg raised and bent behind

Attlee Clement Richard, 1st Earl Attlee. 1883–1967, British statesman; prime minister (1945–51); leader of the Labour party (1935–55). His government instituted the welfare state, with extensive nationalization

attorney 1 a person legally appointed or empowered to act for another 2 *US* a lawyer qualified to represent clients in legal proceedings 3 *South African* a solicitor

attorney general 1 a country's chief law officer and senior legal adviser to its government 2 (in the US) the chief law officer and legal adviser of a state government 3 (in some states of the US) a public prosecutor

attraction a force by which one object attracts another, such as the gravitational or electrostatic force

attribute *Logic* the property, quality, or feature that is affirmed or denied concerning the subject of a proposition

attributive *Philosophy* relative to an understood domain, as *small* in *that elephant is small*

attrition 1 *Geography* the grinding down of rock particles by friction during transportation by water, wind, or ice 2 *Theol* sorrow for sin arising from fear of damnation, esp as contrasted with contrition, which arises purely from love of God

Attu the westernmost of the Aleutian Islands, off the coast of SW Alaska: largest of the Near Islands

ATV all-terrain vehicle: a vehicle with treads or wheels designed to travel on rough uneven ground

Atwood Margaret (Eleanor) born 1939, Canadian poet and novelist. Her novels include *Lady Oracle* (1976), *The Handmaid's Tale* (1986), *Alias Grace* (1996), the Booker Prize-winning *The Blind Assassin* (2000), and *Oryx and Crake* (2003)

Aube 1 a department of N central France, in Champagne-Ardenne region. Capital: Troyes. Pop: 293 925 (2003 est). Area: 6026 sq km (2350 sq miles) 2 a river in N central France, flowing northwest to the Seine. Length: about 225 km (140 miles)

aubergine 1 a tropical Old World solanaceous plant, *Solanum melongena*, widely cultivated for its egg-shaped typically dark purple fruit 2 the fruit of this plant, which is cooked and eaten as a vegetable 3 a dark purple colour

Aubrey John 1626–97, English antiquary and author, noted for his vivid biographies of his contemporaries, *Brief Lives* (edited 1898)

aubrietia, aubrieta, or **aubretia** any trailing purple-flowered plant of the genus *Aubrieta*, native to European mountains but widely planted in rock gardens: family

Brassicaceae (crucifers)

auburn a moderate reddish-brown colour

Aubusson 1 a town in central France, in the Creuse department: a centre for flat-woven carpets and for tapestries since the 16th century. Pop: 4662 (1999) 2 denoting or relating to these carpets or tapestries

Auckland the chief port of New Zealand, in the northern part of North Island: former capital of New Zealand (1840–65). Pop: 420 700 (2004 est)

auction the competitive calls made in bridge and other games before play begins, undertaking to win a given number of tricks if a certain suit is trumps

auctioneer a person who conducts an auction by announcing the lots and controlling the bidding

Aude a department of S France on the Gulf of Lions, in Languedoc-Roussillon region. Capital: Carcassonne. Pop: 321 734 (2003 est). Area: 6342 sq km (2473 sq miles)

Auden W(ystan) H(ugh). 1907–73, US poet, dramatist, critic, and librettist, born in Britain; noted for his lyric and satirical poems and for plays written in collaboration with Christopher Isherwood

audible *American football* a change of playing tactics called by the quarterback when the offense is lined up at the line of scrimmage

audio 1 of or relating to sound or hearing 2 relating to or employed in the transmission, reception, or reproduction of sound 3 of, concerned with, or operating at audio frequencies

audio frequency a frequency in the range 20 hertz to 20 000 hertz. A sound wave of this frequency would be audible to the human ear

audiometer an instrument for testing the intensity and frequency range of sound that is capable of detection by the human ear

audition *Physiology* the act, sense, or power of hearing

auditor *Austral, US and Canadian* a registered student who attends a class that is not an official part of his course of study, without actively participating in it

auditorium the area of a concert hall, theatre, school, etc, in which the audience sits

auditory *Physiology* of or relating to hearing, the sense of hearing, or the organs of hearing

Audubon John James 1785–1851, US naturalist and artist, noted particularly for his paintings of birds in *Birds of America* (1827–38)

Auerbach Frank (Helmuth). born 1931, British painter, born in Germany, noted esp for his use of impasto

auger a hand tool with a bit shaped like a corkscrew, for boring holes in wood 2 a larger tool of the same kind for boring holes in the ground

Augsburg a city in S Germany, in Bavaria: founded by the Romans in 14 BC; site of the diet that produced the **Peace of Augsburg** (1555), which ended the struggles between Lutherans and Catholics in the Holy Roman Empire and established the principle that each ruler should determine the form of worship in his lands. Pop: 259 217 (2003 est)

augur (in ancient Rome) a religious official who observed and interpreted omens and signs to help guide the making of public decisions

Augusta 1 a town in the US, in Georgia. Pop: 193 316 (2003 est) (including Richmond) 2 a port in S Italy, in E

Sicily. Pop: 33 820 (2001) **3** a city in the US, in Maine: the state capital; founded (1628) as a trading post; timber industry. Pop: 18 618 (2003 est)

Augustan 1 characteristic of, denoting, or relating to the Roman emperor Augustus Caesar (63 BC–14 AD), his period, or the poets, notably Virgil, Horace, and Ovid, writing during his reign **2** of, relating to, or characteristic of any literary period noted for refinement and classicism, esp the late 17th century in France (the period of the dramatists Corneille, Racine, and Molière) or the 18th century in England (the period of Swift, Pope, and Johnson, much influenced by Dryden) **3** an author in an Augustan Age **4** a student of or specialist in Augustan literature

Augustine 1 Saint 354–430 AD, one of the Fathers of the Christian Church; bishop of Hippo in North Africa (396–430), who profoundly influenced both Catholic and Protestant theology. His most famous works are *Confessions*, a spiritual autobiography, and *De Civitate Dei*, a vindication of the Christian Church. Feast day: Aug 28 **2 Saint** died 604 AD, Roman monk, sent to Britain (597 AD) to convert the Anglo-Saxons to Christianity and to establish the authority of the Roman See over the native Celtic Church; became the first archbishop of Canterbury (601–604). Feast day: May 26 or 27 **3** a member of an Augustinian order

Augustus original name *Gaius Octavianus*; after his adoption by Julius Caesar (44 BC) known as *Gaius Julius Caesar Octavianus*. 63 BC–14 AD, Roman statesman, a member of the second triumvirate (43 BC). After defeating Mark Antony at Actium (31 BC), he became first emperor of Rome, adopting the title Augustus (27 BC)

auk 1 any of various diving birds of the family *Alcidae* of northern oceans having a heavy body, short tail, narrow wings, and a black-and-white plumage: order *Charadriiformes* **2 little auk** a small short-billed auk, *Plautus alle*, abundant in Arctic regions

Aulis an ancient town in E central Greece, in Boeotia: traditionally the harbour from which the Greeks sailed at the beginning of the Trojan war

Aung San Suu Kyi born 1945, Burmese politician; cofounder (1988) and general secretary (1988–91; 1995–) of the National League for Democracy: Nobel peace prize 1991

aura 1 *Pathol* strange sensations, such as noises in the ears or flashes of light, that immediately precede an attack, esp of epilepsy **2** (in parapsychology) an invisible emanation produced by and surrounding a person or object: alleged to be discernible by individuals of supernormal sensibility

aural *Physiology* of or relating to the sense or organs of hearing; auricular

aureate (of a style of writing or speaking) excessively elaborate or ornate; florid

Aurelian Latin name *Lucius Domitius Aurelianus*. ?212–275 AD, Roman emperor (270–275), who conquered Palmyra (273) and restored political unity to the Roman Empire

aureole *or* **aureola 1** (esp in paintings of Christian saints and the deity) a border of light or radiance enveloping the head or sometimes the whole of a figure represented as holy **2** another name for **corona**

auric of or containing gold in the trivalent state

Auric Georges 1899–1983, French composer; one of *les Six*. His works include ballet and film music

auricle 1 a the upper chamber of the heart; atrium **b** a small sac in the atrium of the heart **2** *Anatomy* the external part of the ear **3** *Biology* an ear-shaped part or appendage, such as that occurring at the join of the leaf blade and the leaf sheath in some grasses

auricula a widely cultivated alpine primrose, *Primula auricula*, with leaves shaped like a bear's ear

auriferous (of rock) containing gold; gold-bearing

Auriol Vincent 1884–1966, French statesman; president of the Fourth Republic (1947–54)

aurochs a recently extinct member of the cattle tribe, *Bos primigenius*, that inhabited forests in N Africa, Europe, and SW Asia. It had long horns and is thought to be one of the ancestors of modern cattle

aurora an atmospheric phenomenon consisting of bands, curtains, or streamers of light, usually green, red, or yellow, that move across the sky in polar regions. It is caused by collisions between air molecules and charged particles from the sun that are trapped in the earth's magnetic field

aurora australis the aurora seen around the South Pole

aurora borealis the aurora seen around the North Pole

Auschwitz an industrial town in S Poland; site of a Nazi concentration camp during World War II. Pop: 45 400 (latest est)

auscultation the diagnostic technique in medicine of listening to the various internal sounds made by the body, usually with the aid of a stethoscope

Austen Jane 1775–1817, English novelist, noted particularly for the insight and delicate irony of her portrayal of middle-class families. Her completed novels are *Sense and Sensibility* (1811), *Pride and Prejudice* (1813), *Mansfield Park* (1814), *Emma* (1816), *Northanger Abbey* (1818), and *Persuasion* (1818)

austerity *Economics* **a** reduced availability of luxuries and consumer goods, esp when brought about by government policy **b** (*as modifier*): *an austerity budget*

Austerlitz a town in the Czech Republic, in Moravia: site of Napoleon's victory over the Russian and Austrian armies in 1805. Pop: 4747 (latest est)

Austin[1] 1 Herbert, 1st Baron. 1866–1941, British automobile engineer, who founded the Austin Motor Company **2** John 1790–1859, British jurist, whose book *The Province of Jurisprudence Determined* (1832) greatly influenced legal theory and the English legal system **3** J(ohn) L(angshaw). 1911–60, English philosopher, whose lectures *Sense and Sensibilia* and *How to do Things with Words* were published posthumously in 1962

Austin[2] a city in central Texas, on the Colorado River: state capital since 1845. Pop: 672 011 (2003 est)

austral[1] of or coming from the south

austral[2] a former monetary unit of Argentina equal to 100 centavos, replaced by the peso

Australasia 1 Australia, New Zealand, and neighbouring islands in the S Pacific Ocean **2** (loosely) the whole of Oceania

Australia a country and the smallest continent, situated between the Indian Ocean and the Pacific: a former British colony, now an independent member of the Commonwealth, constitutional links with Britain formally abolished in 1986; consists chiefly of a low plateau, mostly arid in the west, with the basin of the Murray River and the Great Dividing Range in the east and the Great Barrier Reef off the NE coast. Official language: English. Religion: Christian majority. Currency: dollar. Capital: Canberra. Pop: 19 913 000 (2004 est). Area: 7 682 300 sq km (2 966 150 sq miles)

Australia Day a public holiday in Australia, commemorating the landing of the British in 1788: observed on the first Monday after January 26

Australian Antarctic Territory the area of Antarctica, other than Adélie Land, that is administered by Australia (claims are suspended under the Antarctic Treaty), lying south of latitude 60°S and between longitudes 45°E and 160°E

Australian Capital Territory a territory of SE Australia, within New South Wales: consists of two exclaves, one containing Canberra, the capital of Australia, and one at Jervis Bay (the latter sometimes regarded as a separate entity). Pop: 322 579 (2003 est)

Austrasia the eastern region of the kingdom of the Merovingian Franks that had its capital at Metz and lasted from 511 AD until 814 AD. It covered the area now comprising NE France, Belgium, and western Germany

Austria a republic in central Europe: ruled by the Hapsburgs from 1282 to 1918; formed a dual monarchy with Hungary in 1867 and became a republic in 1919; a member of the European Union; contains part of the Alps, the Danube basin in the east, and extensive forests. Official language: German. Religion: Roman Catholic majority. Currency: euro. Capital: Vienna. Pop: 8 120 000 (2004 est). Area: 83 849 sq km (32 374 sq miles)

Austronesia the islands of the central and S Pacific, including Indonesia, Melanesia, Micronesia, and Polynesia

autarchy 1 unlimited rule; autocracy 2 self-government; self-rule

autarky 1 (esp of a political unit) a system or policy of economic self-sufficiency aimed at removing the need for imports 2 an economically self-sufficient country

authentic 1 (of a deed or other document) duly executed, any necessary legal formalities having been complied with 2 *Music* **a** using period instruments and historically researched scores and playing techniques in an attempt to perform a piece as it would have been played at the time it was written **b** (*in combination*) 3 *Music* **a** (of a mode as used in Gregorian chant) commencing on the final and ending an octave higher **b** (of a cadence) progressing from a dominant to a tonic chord

authority 1 a public board or corporation exercising governmental authority in administering some enterprise 2 *Law* **a** a judicial decision, statute, or rule of law that establishes a principle; precedent **b** legal permission granted to a person to perform a specified act

Authorized Version the English translation of the Bible published in 1611 under James I

autism *Psychiatry* abnormal self-absorption, usually affecting children, characterized by lack of response to people and actions and limited ability to communicate

autobahn a motorway in German-speaking countries

autobiography an account of a person's life written or otherwise recorded by that person

autoclave 1 a strong sealed vessel used for chemical reactions at high pressure 2 an apparatus for sterilizing objects (esp surgical instruments) or for cooking by means of steam under pressure 3 *Civil engineering* a vessel in which freshly cast concrete or sand-lime bricks are cured very rapidly in high-pressure steam

autocracy 1 government by an individual with unrestricted authority 2 the unrestricted authority of such an individual 3 a country, society, etc, ruled by an autocrat

autocrat a ruler who possesses absolute and unrestricted authority

autocross a form of motor sport in which cars race over a half-mile circuit of rough grass

auto-da-fé 1 *History* a ceremony of the Spanish Inquisition including the pronouncement and execution of sentences passed on sinners or heretics 2 the burning to death of people condemned as heretics by the Inquisition

autogiro or **autogyro** a self-propelled aircraft supported in flight mainly by unpowered rotating horizontal blades

autograph **a** a book, document, etc, handwritten by its author; original manuscript; holograph **b** (*as modifier*): *an autograph letter*

automat a machine that automatically dispenses goods, such as cigarettes, when money is inserted

automatic 1 **a** (of a device, mechanism, etc) able to activate, move, or regulate itself **b** (of an act or process) performed by such automatic equipment 2 (of the action of a muscle, gland, etc) involuntary or reflex 3 a motor vehicle having automatic transmission 4 a machine that operates automatically

automatic pilot a device that automatically maintains an aircraft on a preset course

automatic transmission a transmission system in a motor vehicle, usually incorporating a fluid clutch, in which the gears change automatically

automation 1 the use of methods for controlling industrial processes automatically, esp by electronically controlled systems, often reducing manpower 2 the extent to which a process is so controlled

automaton a mechanical device operating under its own hidden power; robot

autonomy 1 the right or state of self-government, esp when limited 2 a state, community, or individual possessing autonomy 3 *Philosophy* **a** the doctrine that the individual human will is or ought to be governed only by its own principles and laws **b** the state in which one's actions are autonomous

autopsy dissection and examination of a dead body to determine the cause of death

autoroute a French motorway

autostrada an Italian motorway

autosuggestion a process of suggestion in which the person unconsciously supplies or consciously attempts to supply the means of influencing his own behaviour or beliefs

Auvergne a region of S central France: largely mountainous, rising over 1800 m (6000 ft)

Auxerre a town in central France, capital of Yonne

department; Gothic cathedral. Pop: 37 790 (1999)

auxiliary 1 *Nautical* (of a sailing vessel) having an engine 2 *Nautical* a a sailing vessel with an engine b the engine of such a vessel 3 *Navy* a vessel such as a tug, hospital ship, etc, not used for combat

avalanche 1 a a fall of large masses of snow and ice down a mountain b a fall of rocks, sand, etc. 2 *Physics* a group of ions or electrons produced by a single ion or electron as a result of a collision with some other form of matter

avatar 1 *Hinduism* the manifestation of a deity, notably Vishnu, in human, superhuman, or animal form 2 a movable image that represents a person in a virtual reality environment or in cyberspace

Ave *RC Church* 1 short for **Ave Maria**: see **Hail Mary** 2 the time for the Angelus to be recited, so called because of the threefold repetition of the Ave Maria in this devotion 3 the beads of the rosary used to count the number of Ave Marias said

Avebury a village in Wiltshire, site of an extensive Neolithic stone circle

Aveiro a port in N central Portugal, on the **Aveiro lagoon**: ancient Roman town; linked by canal with the Atlantic Ocean. Pop: 73 335 (2001)

Aventine one of the seven hills on which Rome was built

average 1 the result obtained by adding the numbers or quantities in a set and dividing the total by the number of members in the set 2 (of a continuously variable ratio, such as speed) the quotient of the differences between the initial and final values of the two quantities that make up the ratio 3 *Maritime law* a a loss incurred or damage suffered by a ship or its cargo at sea b the equitable apportionment of such loss among the interested parties

Averno a crater lake in Italy, near Naples: in ancient times regarded as an entrance to hell

averse *Botany* (of leaves, flowers, etc) turned away from the main stem

Avesta a collection of sacred writings of Zoroastrianism, including the Songs of Zoroaster

Aveyron a department of S France in Midi-Pyrénées region. Capital: Rodez. Pop: 266 940 (2003 est). Area: 8771 sq km (3421 sq miles)

aviation a the art or science of flying aircraft b the design, production, and maintenance of aircraft
▷www.icao.int

aviator *Old-fashioned* the pilot of an aeroplane or airship; flyer

Avicenna Arabic name *ibn-Sina*. 980–1037, Arab philosopher and physician whose philosophical writings, which combined Aristotelianism with neo-Platonist ideas, greatly influenced scholasticism, and whose medical work *Qanun* was the greatest single influence on medieval medicine

Aviemore a winter sports resort in Scotland, in Moray between the Monadhliath and Cairngorm Mountains. Pop: 2397 (2001)

Avignon a city in SE France, on the Rhône: seat of the papacy (1309–77); famous 12th-century bridge, now partly destroyed. Pop: 85 935 (1999)

avocado 1 a pear-shaped fruit having a leathery green or blackish skin, a large stony seed, and a greenish-yellow edible pulp 2 the tropical American lauraceous tree, *Persea americana*, that bears this fruit 3 a dull greenish colour resembling that of the fruit

avocet any of several long-legged shore birds of the genus *Recurvirostra*, such as the European *R. avosetta*, having black-and-white plumage and a long upward-curving bill: family *Recurvirostridae*, order *Charadriiformes*

Avogadro Amedeo , *Conte di Quaregna*. 1776–1856, Italian physicist, noted for his work on gases

avoirdupois *or* **avoirdupois weight** a system of weights used in many English-speaking countries. It is based on the pound, which contains 16 ounces or 7000 grains. 100 pounds (US) or 112 pounds (Brit) is equal to 1 hundredweight and 20 hundredweights equals 1 ton

Avon[1] **Earl of** title of (Anthony) **Eden**

Avon[2] 1 a former county of SW England, created in 1974 from areas of N Somerset and S Gloucestershire: replaced in 1996 by the unitary authorities of Bath and North East Somerset (Somerset), North Somerset (Somerset), South Gloucestershire (Gloucestershire), and Bristol 2 a river in central England, rising in Northamptonshire and flowing southwest through Stratford-on-Avon to the River Severn at Tewkesbury. Length: 154 km (96 miles) 3 a river in SW England, rising in Gloucestershire and flowing south and west through Bristol to the Severn estuary at Avonmouth. Length: 120 km (75 miles) 4 a river in S England, rising in Wiltshire and flowing south to the English Channel. Length: about 96 km (60 miles)

award *Law* a the decision of an arbitrator b a grant made by a court of law, esp of damages in a civil action

awash *Nautical* 1 at a level even with the surface of the sea 2 washed over by the waves

away 1 *Golf* (of a ball or player) farthest from the hole 2 *Baseball* (of a player) having been put out 3 *Horse racing* relating to the outward portion or first half of a race

aweigh *Nautical* (of an anchor) no longer hooked into the bottom; hanging by its rode

awl a pointed hand tool with a fluted blade used for piercing wood, leather, etc.

awn any of the bristles growing from the spikelets of certain grasses, including cereals

awning a roof of canvas or other material supported by a frame to provide protection from the weather, esp one placed over a doorway or part of a deck of a ship

axe *or US* **ax** 1 a hand tool with one side of its head forged and sharpened to a cutting edge, used for felling trees, splitting timber, etc. 2 **the axe** *Informal* a dismissal, esp from employment; the sack (esp in the phrase **get the axe**) b *Brit* severe cutting down of expenditure, esp the removal of unprofitable sections of a public service 3 *US, slang* any musical instrument, esp a guitar or horn

axil the angle between the upper surface of a branch or leafstalk and the stem from which it grows

axiom 1 a generally accepted proposition or principle, sanctioned by experience; maxim 2 a self-evident statement 3 *Logic, maths* a statement or formula that is stipulated to be true for the purpose of a chain of reasoning: the foundation of a formal deductive system

axiomatic or **axiomatical** (of a logical system) consisting of a set of axioms from which theorems are derived by **transformation rules**

axis[1] **1** a real or imaginary line about which a body, such as an aircraft, can rotate or about which an object, form, composition, or geometrical construction is symmetrical **2** one of two or three reference lines used in coordinate geometry to locate a point in a plane or in space **3** *Anatomy* the second cervical vertebra **4** *Botany* the main central part of a plant, typically consisting of the stem and root, from which secondary branches and other parts develop **5** an alliance between a number of states to coordinate their foreign policy **6** *Optics* the line of symmetry of an optical system, such as the line passing through the centre of a lens **7** *Geology* an imaginary line along the crest of an anticline or the trough of a syncline **8** *Crystallog* one of three lines passing through the centre of a crystal and used to characterize its symmetry

axis[2] any of several S Asian deer of the genus *Axis*, esp *A. axis*. They typically have a reddish-brown white-spotted coat and slender antlers

axle a bar or shaft on which a wheel, pair of wheels, or other rotating member revolves

axolotl 1 any of several aquatic salamanders of the North American genus *Ambystoma*, esp *A. mexicanum* (**Mexican axolotl**), in which the larval form (including external gills) is retained throughout life under natural conditions (see **neoteny**): family *Ambystomidae* **2** any of various other North American salamanders in which neoteny occurs or is induced

Ayacucho a city in SE Peru: nearby is the site of the battle (1824) that won independence for Peru. Pop: 150 000 (2005 est)

ayatollah one of a class of Iranian Shiite religious leaders

Ayckbourn Sir Alan born 1939, English dramatist. His plays include *Absurd Person Singular* (1973), the trilogy *The Norman Conquests* (1974), *A Chorus of Disapproval* (1985), and *House and Garden* (2000)

Aycliffe a town in Co. Durham: founded as a new town in 1947. Pop. (including Newton Aycliffe): 25 655 (2001)

Aydin or **Aidin** a town in SW Turkey: an ancient city of Lydia. Pop: 160 000 (2000)

Ayer Sir Alfred Jules 1910–89, English positivist philosopher, noted particularly for his antimetaphysical work *Language, Truth, and Logic* (1936)

Ayia Napa a coastal resort in SE Cyprus. Pop: 9500 (2004 est)

Aykroyd Dan born 1952, Canadian film actor and screenwriter, best known for the television show *Saturday Night Live* (1975–80) and the films *The Blues Brothers* (1980), *Ghostbusters* (1984), and *Driving Miss Daisy* (1989)

Aylesbury a town in SE central England, administrative centre of Buckinghamshire. Pop: 69 021 (2001)

Aylward Gladys 1903–70, English missionary in China

Ayr a port in SW Scotland, in South Ayrshire. Pop: 46 431 (2001)

Ayrshire 1 a historical county of SW Scotland, formerly part of Strathclyde region (1975–96), now divided into the council areas of North Ayrshire, South Ayrshire, and East Ayrshire **2** any one of a hardy breed of brown-and-white dairy cattle

Ayub Khan Mohammed 1907–74, Pakistani field marshal; president of Pakistan (1958–69)

Ayutthaya a city in S Thailand, on the Chao Phraya River: capital of the country until 1767; noted for its canals and ruins. Pop: 61 185 (1990)

azalea any ericaceous plant of the group *Azalea*, formerly a separate genus but now included in the genus *Rhododendron*: cultivated for their showy pink or purple flowers

Azerbaijan 1 a republic in NW Asia: the region was acquired by Russia from Persia in the early 19th century; became the Azerbaijan Soviet Socialist Republic in 1936 and gained independence in 1991; consists of dry subtropical steppes around the Aras and Kura rivers, surrounded by the Caucasus; contains the extensive Baku oilfields. Language: Azerbaijani (or Azeri). Religion: Shiite Muslim. Currency: manat. Capital: Baku. Pop: Pop: 8 447 000 (2004 est). Area: 86 600 sq km (33 430 sq miles) **2** a mountainous region of NW Iran, separated from the republic of Azerbaijan by the Aras River: divided administratively into **Eastern Azerbaijan** and **Western Azerbaijan**. Capitals: Tabriz and Orumiyeh. Pop: 2 119 524 (2002 est)

Azikiwe Nnamdi 1904–96, Nigerian statesman; first president of Nigeria (1963–66)

azimuth *Astronomy, navigation* the angular distance usually measured clockwise from the north point of the horizon to the intersection with the horizon of the vertical circle passing through a celestial body

Azov Sea of a shallow arm of the Black Sea, to which it is connected by the Kerch Strait: almost entirely landlocked; fed chiefly by the River Don. Area: about 37 500 sq km (14 500 sq miles)

Aztec 1 a member of a Mexican Indian people who established a great empire, centred on the valley of Mexico, that was overthrown by Cortés and his followers in the mid 16th century **2** the language of the Aztecs
  ▷www.aztecempire.com
  ▷www.indians.org/welker/aztec.html

azure 1 a deep blue, occasionally somewhat purple, similar to the colour of a clear blue sky **2** of the colour azure; serene

Bb

Ba *Egyptian myth* the soul, represented as a bird with a human head

Baalbek a town in E Lebanon: an important city in Phoenician and Roman times; extensive ruins. Pop: 150 000 (1998 est)

Baal Shem Tov *or* **Baal Shem Tob** original name *Israel ben Eliezer* ?1700–60, Jewish religious leader, teacher, and healer in Poland: founder of modern Hasidism

baaskap *or* **baasskap** (in South Africa) control by Whites of non-Whites

Bab the title of *Mirza Ali Mohammed* 1819–50, Persian religious leader: founded Babism; executed as a heretic of Islam

babaco 1 a subtropical parthenocarpic tree, *Carica pentagona*, originating in South America, cultivated for its fruit: family *Caricaceae* 2 the greenish-yellow egg-shaped fruit of this tree, having a delicate fragrance and no pips

Babbage *Charles* 1792–1871, English mathematician and inventor, who built a calculating machine that anticipated the modern electronic computer

Babel¹ *Issak Emmanuilovich* 1894–1941, Russian short-story writer, whose works include *Stories from Odessa* (1924) and *Red Cavalry* (1926)

Babel² *Old Testament* a a tower presumptuously intended to reach from earth to heaven, the building of which was frustrated when Jehovah confused the language of the builders (Genesis 11:1–10) b the city, probably Babylon, in which this tower was supposedly built

Bab el Mandeb a strait between SW Arabia and E Africa, connecting the Red Sea with the Gulf of Aden

Baber, Babar, *or* **Babur** original name *Zahir ud-Din Mohammed* 1483–1530, founder of the Mogul Empire: conquered India in 1526

Babeuf *François Noël* 1760–97, French political agitator: plotted unsuccessfully to destroy the Directory and establish a communistic system

Babington *Anthony* 1561–86, English conspirator, executed for organizing an unsuccessful plot (1586) to assassinate Elizabeth I and place Mary, Queen of Scots, on the English throne

baboon any of several medium-sized omnivorous Old World monkeys of the genus *Papio* (or *Chaeropithecus*) and related genera, inhabiting open rocky ground or wooded regions of Africa. They have an elongated muzzle, large teeth, and a fairly long tail

baby a a newborn or recently born animal b (*as modifier*): *baby rabbits*

baby bonus *Canadian, informal* family allowance

Babylon 1 the chief city of ancient Mesopotamia: first settled around 3000 BC 2 *Derogatory* (in Protestant polemic) the Roman Catholic Church, regarded as the seat of luxury and corruption

Babylonia the southern kingdom of ancient Mesopotamia: a great empire from about 2200–538 BC, when it was conquered by the Persians

Bacău a city in E Romania on the River Bistrila: oil refining, textiles, paper. Pop: 128 000 (2005 est)

baccalaureate 1 the university degree of Bachelor or Arts, Bachelor of Science, etc. 2 an internationally recognized programme of study, comprising different subjects, offered as an alternative to a course of A levels in Britain 3 *US* a farewell sermon delivered at the commencement ceremonies in many colleges and universities

baccarat a card game in which two or more punters gamble against the banker

Bacchus (in ancient Greece and Rome) a god of wine and giver of ecstasy, identified with Dionysus

Bach 1 *Johann Christian*, 11th son of J. S. Bach. 1735–82, German composer, called *the English Bach*, resident in London from 1762 2 *Johann Christoph* 1642–1703, German composer: wrote oratorios, cantatas, and motets, some of which were falsely attributed to J S Bach, of whom he was a distant relative 3 *Johann Sebastian* 1685–1750, German composer: church organist at Arnstadt (1703–07) and Mühlhausen (1707–08); court organist at Weimar (1708–17); musical director for Prince Leopold of Köthen (1717–28); musical director for the city of Leipzig (1728–50). His output was enormous and displays great vigour and invention within the northern European polyphonic tradition. His works include nearly 200 cantatas and oratorios, settings of the *Passion according to St John* (1723) and *St Matthew* (1729), the six *Brandenburg Concertos* (1720–21), the 48 preludes and fugues of the *Well-tempered Clavier* (completed 1744), and the *Mass in B Minor* (1733–38) 4 *Karl* (*or* **Carl**) *Philipp Emanuel*, 3rd son of J S Bach. 1714–88, German composer, chiefly of symphonies, keyboard sonatas, and church music 5 *Wilhelm Friedemann*, eldest son of J S Bach. 1710–84, German composer: wrote nine symphonies and much keyboard and religious music

bachelor 1 **a** a person who holds the degree of Bachelor of Arts, Bachelor of Education, Bachelor of Science, etc **b** the degree itself 2 (in the Middle Ages) a young knight serving a great noble 3 **bachelor seal** a young male seal, esp a fur seal, that has not yet mated

Bachelor of Arts a degree conferred on a person who has successfully completed his undergraduate studies, usually in a branch of the liberal arts or humanities

back¹ 1 *Ball games* **a** a mainly defensive player behind a forward **b** the position of such a player 2 the upper surface of a joist, rafter, slate, tile, etc, when in position

back² a large tub or vat, esp one used by brewers

backbencher *Brit, Austral, NZ* a Member of Parliament who does not hold office in the government or opposition

back boiler a tank or series of pipes at the back of a fireplace for heating water

backbone 1 a nontechnical name for **spinal column** 2 the main or central mountain range of a country or region 3 *Nautical* the main longitudinal members of a vessel, giving structural strength 4 *Computing* (in computer networks) a large-capacity, high-speed central section by which other network segments are connected

backcloth a large painted curtain hanging at the back of a stage set

backfire 1 in an internal-combustion engine **a** an explosion of unburnt gases in the exhaust system **b** a premature explosion in a cylinder or inlet manifold 2 a controlled fire started to create a barren area that will halt an advancing forest or prairie fire

backgammon 1 a game for two people played on a board with pieces moved according to throws of the dice 2 the most complete form of win in this game
▷www.worldbackgammonfederation.com

background 1 *Art* **a** the plane or ground in a picture upon which all other planes or forms appear superimposed **b** the parts of a picture that appear most distant 2 *Physics* low-intensity radiation as, for example, from small amounts of radioisotopes in soil, air, building materials, etc. 3 *Electronics* unwanted effects, such as noise, occurring in a measuring instrument, electronic device, etc. **b** (*as modifier*): *background interference*

backhand 1 *Sport* **a** a stroke made across the body with the back of the hand facing the direction of the stroke **b** (*as modifier*): *a backhand return* 2 the side on which backhand strokes are made

backing 1 *Theatre* a scenic cloth or flat placed behind a window, door, etc, in a set to mask the offstage space 2 the support in gold or precious metals for a country's issue of money in notes 3 *Meteorol* an anticlockwise change in wind direction

backing dog *NZ and Australia* a dog that moves a flock of sheep by jumping on their backs

backlash 1 a reaction or recoil between interacting worn or badly fitting parts in a mechanism 2 the play between parts

back office **a** the administrative and support staff of a financial institution or other business **b** (*as modifier*): *back-office operations*

backpack a pack carried on the back of an astronaut, containing oxygen cylinders, essential supplies, etc

back passage the rectum

Back River a river in N Canada, flowing northeast through Nunavut to the Arctic Ocean. Length: about 966 km (600 miles)

backside *Informal* the buttocks

backstage situated backstage

backstroke 1 *Swimming* **a** a stroke performed on the back, using backward circular strokes of each arm and flipper movements of the feet **b** (*as modifier*): *the backstroke champion* 2 *Chiefly US* a backhanded stroke 3 *Bellringing* the upward movement of the bell rope as the bell swings back and forth

back up *Computing* a file or set of files copied for security purposes

backward *Chess* (of a pawn) behind neighbouring pawns and unable to be supported by them

backwash 1 a sucking movement of water, such as that of retreating waves 2 water washed backwards by the motion of oars or other propelling devices 3 the backward flow of air set up by an aircraft's engines

backwater a body of stagnant water connected to a river

Bacolod a town in the Philippines, on the NW coast of Negros Island. Pop: 468 000 (2005 est)

Bacon 1 Francis, Baron Verulam, Viscount St. Albans. 1561–1626, English philosopher, statesman, and essayist; described the inductive method of reasoning: his works include *Essays* (1625), *The Advancement of Learning* (1605), and *Novum Organum* (1620) 2 Francis 1909–92, British painter, born in Dublin, noted for his distorted, richly coloured human figures, dogs, and carcasses 3 Roger ?1214–92, English Franciscan monk, scholar, and scientist: stressed the importance of experiment, demonstrated that air is required for combustion, and first used lenses to correct vision. His *Opus Majus* (1266) is a compendium of all the sciences of his age

Bactria an ancient country of SW Asia, between the Hindu Kush mountains and the Oxus River: forms the present Balkh region in N Afghanistan

Bactrian camel a two-humped camel, *Camelus bactrianus*, used as a beast of burden in the cold deserts of central Asia

Badajoz a city in SW Spain: strategically positioned near the frontier with Portugal. Pop: 138 415 (2003 est)

Badalona a port in NE Spain: an industrial suburb of Barcelona. Pop: 214 440 (2003 est)

Baden a former state of West Germany, now part of Baden-Württemberg

Baden-Baden a spa in SW Germany, in Baden-Württemberg. Pop: 53 938 (2003 est)

Baden-Powell Robert Stephenson Smyth , 1st Baron Baden-Powell. 1857–1941, British general, noted for his defence of Mafeking (1899–1900) in the Boer War; founder of the Boy Scouts (1908) and (with his sister Agnes) the Girl Guides (1910)

Bader Sir Douglas 1910–82, British fighter pilot. Despite losing both legs after a flying accident (1931), he became a national hero as a pilot in World War II

badger any of various stocky omnivorous musteline mammals of the subfamily *Melinae*, such as *Meles meles* (**Eurasian badger**), occurring in Europe, Asia, and North America: order *Carnivora* (carnivores). They are typically large burrowing animals, with strong claws and a thick coat striped black and white on the head

badminton a game played with rackets and a shuttlecock, which is hit back and forth across a high net
▷www.intbadfed.org

Badminton a village in SW England, in South Gloucestershire unitary authority, Gloucestershire: site of Badminton House, seat of the Duke of Beaufort; annual horse trials

Baez Joan born 1941, US rock and folk singer and songwriter, noted for the pure quality of her voice and for her committed pacifist and protest songs

Baffin Bay part of the Northwest Passage, situated between Baffin Island and Greenland

Baffin Island the largest island of the Canadian Arctic, between Greenland and Hudson Bay. Area: 476 560 sq km (184 000 sq miles)

baffle a plate or mechanical device designed to restrain or regulate the flow of a fluid, the emission of light or sound, or the distribution of sound, esp in a loudspeaker or microphone

bag 1 any of various measures of quantity, such as a bag containing 1 hundredweight of coal 2 any pouch or sac forming part of the body of an animal, esp the udder of a cow 3 *Hunting* the quantity of quarry taken in a single hunting trip or by a single hunter

bagatelle 1 a board game in which balls are struck into holes, with pins as obstacles; pinball 2 a short light piece of music, esp for piano

Bagehot Walter 1826–77, English economist and journalist: editor of *The Economist*; author of *The English Constitution* (1867) *Physics and Politics* (1872), and *Lombard Street* (1873)

Baghdad or **Bagdad** the capital of Iraq, on the River Tigris: capital of the Abbasid Caliphate (762–1258). Pop: 5 910 000 (2005 est)

Bagnold Enid (**Algerine**). 1889–1981, British novelist and playwright; her works include the novel *National Velvet* (1935) and the play *The Chalk Garden* (1955)

Bagram an air base in NE Afghanistan, near Kabul; now under the control of US forces

Baguio a city in the N Philippines, on N Luzon: summer capital of the Republic. Pop: 287 000 (2005 est)

Bahawalpur an industrial city in Pakistan: cotton, soap. Pop: 563 000 (2005 est)

Bahia 1 a state of E Brazil, on the Atlantic coast. Capital: Salvador. Pop: 13 323 212 (2002). Area: about 562 000 sq km (217 000 sq miles) 2 the former name of **San Salvador**

Bahrain or **Bahrein** an independent sheikhdom on the Persian Gulf, consisting of several islands: under British protection until the declaration of independence in 1971. It has large oil reserves. Language: Arabic. Religion: Muslim. Currency: dinar. Capital: Manama. Pop: 739 000 (2004 est). Area: 678 sq km (262 sq miles)

Baikal Lake a lake in Russia, in SE Siberia: the largest freshwater lake in Eurasia and the deepest in the world. Greatest depth: over 1500 m (5000 ft). Area: about 33 670 sq km (13 000 sq miles)

Baikonur a launching site for spacecraft in central Kazakhstan; formerly the centre for the Soviet space

programme, now leased from Kazakhstan by Russia

bail¹ *Law* 1 a sum of money by which a person is bound to take responsibility for the appearance in court of another person or himself, forfeited if the person fails to appear 2 the person or persons so binding themselves; surety 3 the system permitting release of a person from custody where such security has been taken 4 **jump bail** or (*formal*) **forfeit bail** to fail to appear in court to answer to a charge 5 **stand** or **go bail** to act as surety (for someone)

bail² *Cricket* either of two small wooden bars placed across the tops of the stumps to form the wicket

bail or **bale** 1 a semicircular support for a canopy 2 a movable bar on a typewriter that holds the paper against the platen

Bailey 1 David born 1938, English photographer 2 Nathan or Nathaniel died 1742, English lexicographer: compiler of *An Universal Etymological English Dictionary* (1721–27)

Bailey bridge a temporary bridge made of prefabricated steel panels that can be rapidly assembled

bailiff *Chiefly Brit* (formerly) a high official having judicial powers

bailiwick *Law* the area over which a bailiff has jurisdiction

Bainbridge Beryl born 1934, British novelist and playwright. Novels include *The Dressmaker* (1973), *Injury Time* (1977), *Master Georgie* (1998), and *According to Queeney* (2001)

Baird John Logie 1888–1946, Scottish engineer: inventor of a 240-line mechanically scanned system of television, replaced in 1935 by a 405-line electrically scanned system

baize a woollen fabric resembling felt, usually green, used mainly for the tops of billiard tables

Baja California Norte a state of NW Mexico, in the N part of the Lower California peninsula. Capital: Mexicali. Pop: 2 487 700 (2000). Area: about 71 500 sq km (27 600 sq miles)

Baja California Sur a state of NW Mexico, in the S part of the Lower California peninsula. Capital: La Paz. Pop: 423 516 (2000). Area: 73 475 sq km (28 363 sq miles)

bakeapple *Canadian* the fruit of the cloudberry

Bakelite *Trademark* any one of a class of thermosetting resins used as electric insulators and for making plastic ware, telephone receivers, etc

Baker 1 Sir Benjamin 1840–1907, British engineer who, with Sir John Fowler, designed and constructed much of the London underground railway, the Forth Railway Bridge, and the first Aswan Dam 2 Chet, full name Chesney H. Baker. 1929–88, US jazz trumpeter and singer 3 Dame Janet born 1933, British mezzo-soprano 4 Sir Samuel White 1821–93, British explorer: discovered Lake Albert (1864)

Bakewell Robert 1725–95, English agriculturist: radically improved livestock breeding, esp of cattle and sheep

Bakhtaran a city in W Iran, in the valley of the Qareh Su: oil refinery. Pop: 832 000 (2005 est)

bakkie *South African* a small truck with an open body and low sides

Bakst Leon Nikolayevich 1866–1924, Russian painter and stage designer, noted particularly for his richly coloured sets for Diaghilev's *Ballet Russe* (1909–21)

Baku or **Baki** the capital of Azerbaijan, a port on the Caspian Sea: important for its extensive oilfields. Pop: 1 830 000 (2005 est)

Bakunin Mikhail 1814–76, Russian anarchist and writer: a prominent member of the First International, expelled from it after conflicts with Marx

Bala Lake a narrow lake in Gwynedd: the largest natural lake in Wales. Length: 6 km (4 miles)

Balaam Old Testament a Mesopotamian diviner who, when summoned to curse the Israelites, prophesied future glories for them instead, after being reproached by his ass (Numbers 22–23)

Balakirev Mily Alexeyevich 1837–1910, Russian composer, whose works include two symphonic poems, two symphonies, and many arrangements of Russian folk songs

Balaklava or **Balaclava** a small port in Ukraine, in S Crimea: scene of an inconclusive battle (1854), which included the charge of the Light Brigade, during the Crimean War

balalaika a plucked musical instrument, usually having a triangular body and three strings: used chiefly for Russian folk music

balance 1 a weighing device, generally consisting of a horizontal beam pivoted at its centre, from the ends of which two pans are suspended. The substance to be weighed is placed in one pan and known weights are placed in the other until the beam returns to the horizontal 2 Chem the state of a chemical equation in which the number, kind, electrical charges, etc, of the atoms on opposite sides are equal 3 short for **spring balance**

balance of payments Economics the difference over a given time between total payments to foreign nations, arising from imports of goods and services and transfers abroad of capital, interest, grants, etc, and total receipts from foreign nations, arising from exports of goods and services and transfers from abroad of capital, interest, grants, etc.

balance of power the distribution of power among countries so that no one nation can seriously threaten the fundamental interests of another

balance of trade Economics the difference in value between total exports and total imports of goods

Balanchine George 1904–83, US choreographer, born in Russia

Balaton Lake a large shallow lake in W Hungary. Area: 689 sq km (266 sq miles)

Balboa¹ Vasco Núñez de ?1475–1519, Spanish explorer, who discovered the Pacific Ocean in 1513

Balboa² a port in Panama at the Pacific end of the Panama Canal: the administrative centre of the former Canal Zone. Pop: 2750 (1990)

Balcon Sir Michael 1896–1977, British film producer; his films made at Ealing Studios include the comedies Kind Hearts and Coronets (1949) and The Lavender Hill Mob (1951)

balcony 1 a platform projecting from the wall of a building with a balustrade or railing along its outer edge, often with access from a door or window 2 a gallery in a theatre or auditorium, above the dress circle 3 US and Canadian any circle or gallery in a theatre or auditorium including the dress circle

bald 1 having no hair or fur, esp (of a man) having no hair on all or most of the scalp 2 (of certain birds and other animals) having white markings on the head and face 3 (of a tyre) having a worn tread

Baldwin 1 James Arthur 1924–87, US Black writer, whose works include the novel Go Tell it on the Mountain (1954) 2 Stanley, 1st Earl Baldwin of Bewdley. 1867–1947, British Conservative statesman: prime minister (1923–24, 1924–29, 1935–37)

Baldwin I 1058–1118, crusader and first king of Jerusalem (1100–18), who captured Acre (1104), Beirut (1109), and Sidon (1110)

bale 1 US 500 pounds of cotton 2 a group of turtles

baleen whalebone

Balenciaga Cristobal 1895–1972, Spanish couturier

Balfour Arthur James, 1st Earl of Balfour. 1848–1930, British Conservative statesman: prime minister (1902–05); foreign secretary (1916–19)

Bali an island in Indonesia, east of Java: mountainous, rising over 3000 m (10 000 ft). Capital: Denpasar. Pop: 2 902 200 (1995 est). Area: 5558 sq km (2146 sq miles)

Balikpapan a city in Indonesia, on the SE coast of Borneo. Pop: 409 023 (2000)

Baliol or **Balliol** 1 Edward ?1283–1364, king of Scotland (1332, 1333–56) 2 his father, John 1249–1315, king of Scotland (1292–96): defeated and imprisoned by Edward I of England (1296)

balk or **baulk** 1 a roughly squared heavy timber beam 2 a timber tie beam of a roof 3 Baseball an illegal motion by a pitcher towards the plate or towards the base when there are runners on base, esp without delivering the ball

Balkan of, denoting, or relating to the Balkan States or their inhabitants, the Balkan Peninsula, or the Balkan Mountains

Balkan Peninsula a large peninsula in SE Europe, between the Adriatic and Aegean Seas

Balkh a region of N Afghanistan, corresponding to ancient Bactria. Chief town: Mazar-i-Sharif

Balkhash Lake a salt lake in SE Kazakhstan: fed by the Ili River. Area: about 18 000 sq km (7000 sq miles)

ball 1 a round or roundish body, either solid or hollow, of a size and composition suitable for any of various games, such as football, golf, billiards, etc 2 Cricket a single delivery of the ball by the bowler to the batsman 3 Baseball a single delivery of the ball by a pitcher outside certain limits and not swung at by the batter 4 Horticulture the hard mass of roots and earth removed with the rest of the plant during transplanting

Ball John died 1381, English priest: executed as one of the leaders of the Peasants' Revolt (1381)

ballad 1 a narrative song with a recurrent refrain 2 a narrative poem in short stanzas of popular origin, originally sung to a repeated tune

ballade 1 Prosody a verse form consisting of three stanzas and an envoy, all ending with the same line. The first three stanzas commonly have eight or ten lines each and the same rhyme scheme 2 Music an instrumental composition, esp for piano, based on or intended to evoke a narrative

Ballance John 1839–93, New Zealand statesman, born in Northern Ireland: prime minister of New Zealand

(1891–93)

ball-and-socket joint *or* **ball joint** 1 a coupling between two rods, tubes, etc, that consists of a spherical part fitting into a spherical socket, allowing free movement within a specific conical volume 2 *Anatomy* a bony joint, such as the hip joint, in which a rounded head fits into a rounded cavity, allowing a wide range of movement

Ballarat a town in SE Australia, in S central Victoria: originally the centre of a gold-mining region. Pop: 72 999 (2001)

Ballard J(ames) G(raham). born 1930, British novelist, born in China; his books include *Crash* (1973), *The Unlimited Dream Company* (1979), *Empire of the Sun* (1984), *Cocaine Nights* (1996), and *Super-Cannes* (2000)

ballast 1 any dense heavy material, such as lead or iron pigs, used to stabilize a vessel, esp one that is not carrying cargo 2 crushed rock, broken stone, etc, used for the foundation of a road or railway track 3 *Electronics* a device for maintaining the current in a circuit

ball bearing 1 a bearing consisting of a number of hard steel balls rolling between a metal sleeve fitted over the rotating shaft and an outer sleeve held in the bearing housing, so reducing friction between moving parts while providing support for the shaft 2 a metal ball, esp one used in such a bearing

ball boy (esp in tennis) a person who retrieves balls that go out of play

ball cock a device for regulating the flow of a liquid into a tank, cistern, etc, consisting of a floating ball mounted at one end of an arm and a valve on the other end that opens and closes as the ball falls and rises

ballerina 1 a female ballet dancer 2 US the principal female dancer of a ballet company

ballet 1 a a classical style of expressive dancing based on precise conventional steps with gestures and movements of grace and fluidity b (*as modifier*): *ballet dancer* 2 a theatrical representation of a story or theme performed to music by ballet dancers 3 a troupe of ballet dancers 4 a piece of music written for a ballet
▷www.ballet.co.uk
▷www.culturekiosque.com/dance

ball game *US and Canadian* a game of baseball

ballistics the study of the flight dynamics of projectiles, either through the interaction of the forces of propulsion, the aerodynamics of the projectile, atmospheric resistance, and gravity (**exterior ballistics**), or through these forces along with the means of propulsion, and the design of the propelling weapon and projectile (**interior ballistics**)

balloon 1 a large impermeable bag inflated with a lighter-than-air gas, designed to rise and float in the atmosphere. It may have a basket or gondola for carrying passengers, etc 2 *Chem* a round-bottomed flask 3 *Surgery* a an inflatable plastic tube used for dilating obstructed blood vessels or parts of the alimentary canal b (*as modifier*): *balloon angioplasty*
▷www.fai.org/ballooning

ballot 1 the democratic practice of selecting a representative, a course of action, or deciding some other choice by submitting the options to a vote of all qualified persons 2 an instance of voting, usually in secret using ballot papers or a voting machine 3 a list of candidates standing for office 4 the number of votes cast in an election 5 a random selection of successful applicants for something in which the demand exceeds the supply, esp for shares in an oversubscribed new issue

ballot box a box into which ballot papers are dropped after voting

ballot paper a paper used for voting in a ballot, esp (in a parliamentary or local government election) one having the names of the candidates printed on it

ballpark *US and Canadian* a stadium used for baseball games

ballroom dancing social dancing, popular since the beginning of the 20th century, to dances in conventional rhythms (**ballroom dances**) such as the foxtrot and the quickstep
▷www.ballroomdancers.com
▷www.dancesport.uk.com

Ballymena a district in central Northern Ireland, in Co. Antrim. Pop: 59 516 (2003 est). Area: 634 sq km (247 sq miles)

Ballymoney a district in N Northern Ireland, in Co. Antrim. Pop: 27 809 (2003 est). Area: 417 sq km (161 sq miles)

balm 1 any of various oily aromatic resinous substances obtained from certain tropical trees and used for healing and soothing 2 any plant yielding such a substance, esp the balm of Gilead 3 an aromatic Eurasian herbaceous plant, *Melissa officinalis*, having clusters of small fragrant white two-lipped flowers: family *Lamiaceae* (labiates) 4 any aromatic or oily substance used for healing or soothing

Balmain Pierre Alexandre 1914–82, French couturier

Balmoral a castle in NE Scotland, in SW Aberdeenshire: a private residence of the British sovereign

balsa 1 a bombacaceous tree, *Ochroma lagopus*, of tropical America 2 the very light wood of this tree, used for making rafts, etc 3 a light raft

balsam 1 any of various fragrant oleoresins, such as balm or tolu, obtained from any of several trees and shrubs and used as a base for medicines and perfumes 2 any of various similar substances used as medicinal or ceremonial ointments 3 any of certain aromatic resinous turpentines 4 any plant yielding balsam 5 any of several balsaminaceous plants of the genus *Impatiens*, esp *I. balsamina*, cultivated for its brightly coloured flowers

Balthazar one of the Magi, the others being Caspar and Melchior

Balthus real name *Balthasar Klossowski de Rola*. 1908–2001, French painter of Polish descent, noted esp for his paintings of adolescent girls

Baltic 1 a branch of the Indo-European family of languages consisting of Lithuanian, Latvian, and Old Prussian 2 a freight-chartering market in the City of London, which formerly also dealt in some commodities

Baltic Sea a sea in N Europe, connected with the North Sea by the Skagerrak, Kattegat, and Öresund; shallow, with low salinity and small tides

Baltimore[1] 1 David born 1938, US molecular biologist: shared the Nobel prize for physiology or medicine (1975)

for his discovery of reverse transcriptase **2 Lord.** See (Sir George) **Calvert**

Baltimore² a port in N Maryland, on Chesapeake Bay. Pop: Pop: 628 670 (2003 est)

Baluchistan *or* **Balochistan 1** a mountainous region of SW Asia, in SW Pakistan and SE Iran **2** a province of SW Pakistan: a former territory of British India (until 1947). Capital: Quetta. Pop: Pop: 7 450 000 (2003 est)

baluster 1 any of a set of posts supporting a rail or coping **2** (of a shape) swelling at the base and rising in a concave curve to a narrow stem or neck

balustrade an ornamental rail or coping with its supporting set of balusters

Balzac Honoré de 1799–1850, French novelist: author of a collection of novels under the general title *La Comédie humaine*, including *Eugénie Grandet* (1833), *Le Père Goriot* (1834), and *La Cousine Bette* (1846)

Bamako the capital of Mali, in the south, on the River Niger. Pop: 1 379 000 (2005 est)

Bamberg a town in S Germany, in N Bavaria: seat of independent prince-bishops of the Holy Roman Empire (1007–1802). Pop: 69 899 (2003 est)

bamboo 1 any tall treelike tropical or semitropical fast-growing grass of the genus *Bambusa*, having hollow woody-walled stems with ringed joints and edible young shoots (**bamboo shoots**) **2** the stem of any of these plants, used for building, poles, and furniture **3** any of various bamboo-like grasses of the genera *Arundinaria, Phyllostachys* or *Dendrocalamus*

ban¹ *Law* an official proclamation or public notice, esp of prohibition

ban² (in feudal England) the summoning of vassals to perform their military obligations

ban³ a monetary unit of Romania and Moldova worth one hundredth of a leu

Banaba an island in the SW Pacific, in the Republic of Kiribati. Phosphates were mined by Britain (1900–79). Area: about 5 sq km (2 sq miles). Pop: 284 (1990)

banana 1 any of several tropical and subtropical herbaceous treelike plants of the musaceous genus *Musa*, esp *M. sapientum*, a widely cultivated species propagated from suckers and having hanging clusters of edible fruit **2** the crescent-shaped fruit of any of these plants

banana republic *Informal and derogatory* a small country, esp in Central America, that is politically unstable and has an economy dominated by foreign interest, usually dependent on one export, such as bananas

Banat a fertile plain extending through Hungary, Romania, and Serbia

Banbridge a district in S Northern Ireland, in Co. Down. Pop: 43 083 (2003 est). Area: 442 sq km (170 sq miles)

Banbury a town in central England, in N Oxfordshire: telecommunications, financial services. Pop: 43 867 (2001)

band¹ 1 a group of musicians playing either brass and percussion instruments only (**brass band**) or brass, woodwind, and percussion instruments (**concert band** or **military band**) **2** a group of instrumentalists generally; orchestra **3** *Canadian* a formally recognized group of Indians on a reserve **4** *Anthropol* a division of a tribe; a family group or camp group

band² 1 a driving belt in machinery **2** a range of values

that are close or related in number, degree, or quality **3** *Computing* one or more tracks on a magnetic disk or drum **4** *Anatomy* any structure resembling a ribbon or cord that connects, encircles, or binds different parts **5** *Architect* a strip of flat panelling, such as a fascia or plinth, usually attached to a wall

Banda Hastings Kamuzu 1906–97, Malawi statesman. As first prime minister of Nyasaland (from 1963), he led his country to independence (1964) as Malawi: president (1966–94)

Banda Aceh a city in N Indonesia, in N Sumatra; the capital of Aceh region; suffered badly in the Indian Ocean tsunami of December 2004. Pop: 154 767 (2000)

Bandaranaike 1 Sirimavo 1916–2000, prime minister of Sri Lanka, formerly Ceylon (1960–65; 1970–77; 1994–2000); the world's first woman prime minister **2** her husband, **Solomon** 1899–1959, prime minister of Ceylon (1956–59); assassinated

Bandar Seri Begawan the capital of Brunei. Pop: 64 000 (2005 est)

Banda Sea a part of the Pacific in Indonesia, between Sulawesi and New Guinea

banderole, banderol, *or* **bannerol 1** a long narrow flag, usually with forked ends, esp one attached to the masthead of a ship; pennant **2** a ribbon-like scroll or sculptured band bearing an inscription, found esp in Renaissance architecture

bandicoot 1 any agile terrestrial marsupial of the family *Peramelidae* of Australia and New Guinea. They have a long pointed muzzle and a long tail and feed mainly on small invertebrates **2 bandicoot rat** any of three burrowing rats of the genera *Bandicota* and *Nesokia*, of S and SE Asia: family *Muridae*

band saw a power-operated saw consisting of an endless toothed metal band running over and driven by two wheels

Bandung a city in Indonesia, in SW Java. Pop: 2 136 260 (2000)

bandy 1 an early form of hockey, often played on ice **2** a stick, curved at one end, used in the game of bandy **3** an old form of tennis

Banff 1 a town in NE Scotland, in Aberdeenshire. Pop: 3991 (2001) **2** a town in Canada, in SW Alberta, in the Rocky Mountains: surrounded by **Banff National Park.** Pop: 7135 (2001)

Banffshire (until 1975) a county of NE Scotland: formerly (1975–96) part of Grampian region, now part of Aberdeenshire

Bangalore a city in S India, capital of Karnataka state: printing, textiles, pharmaceuticals. Pop: 4 292 223 (2001)

Bangka *or* **Banka** an island in Indonesia, separated from Sumatra by the **Bangka Strait.** Chief town: Pangkalpinang. Area: about 11 914 sq km (4600 sq miles)

Bangkok the capital and chief port of Thailand, on the Chao Phraya River: became a royal city and the capital in 1782. Pop: 6 604 000 (2005 est)

Bangladesh a republic in S Asia: formerly the Eastern Province of Pakistan; became independent in 1971 after civil war and the defeat of Pakistan by India; consists of the plains and vast deltas of the Ganges and

Brahmaputra Rivers; prone to flooding: economy based on jute and jute products (over 70 per cent of world production); a member of the Commonwealth. Language: Bengali. Religion: Muslim. Currency: taka. Capital: Dhaka. Pop: 149 665 000 (2004 est). Area: 142 797 sq km (55 126 sq miles)

Bangor 1 a university town in NW Wales, in Gwynedd, on the Menai Strait. Pop: 15 280 (2001) **2** a town in SE Northern Ireland, in North Down district, Co. Down, on Belfast Lough. Pop: 58 388 (2001)

Bangui the capital of the Central African Republic, in the south part, on the Ubangi River. Pop: 732 000 (2005 est)

Bangweulu Lake a shallow lake in NE Zambia, discovered by David Livingstone, who died there in 1873. Area: about 9850 sq km (3800 sq miles), including swamps

Banja Luka a city in NW Bosnia-Herzegovina, on the Vrbas River: scene of battles between the Austrians and Turks in 1527, 1688, and 1737; besieged by Serb forces (1992–95). Pop: 182 000 (2005 est)

Banjarmasin, Banjermasin, Bandjarmasin or **Bandjermasin** a port in Indonesia, in SW Borneo. Pop: 527 415 (2000)

banjo a stringed musical instrument with a long neck (usually fretted) and a circular drumlike body overlaid with parchment, plucked with the fingers or a plectrum

Banjul the capital of The Gambia, a port at the mouth of the Gambia River. Pop: 392 000 (2005 est)

bank¹ 1 the funds held by a gaming house or a banker or dealer in some gambling games **2** in various games **a** the stock, as of money, pieces, tokens, etc, on which players may draw **b** the player holding this stock

bank² 1 a slope, as of a hill **2** the sloping side of any hollow in the ground, esp when bordering a river **3 a** an elevated section, rising to near the surface, of the bed of a sea, lake, or river **b** (in combination): sandbank **4** the lateral inclination of an aircraft about its longitudinal axis during a turn **5** a bend on a road or on a railway, athletics, cycling, or other track having the outside built higher than the inside in order to reduce the effects of centrifugal force on vehicles, runners, etc, rounding it at speed and in some cases to facilitate drainage **6** the cushion of a billiard table

bank³ a a tier of oars in a galley **b** a bench for the rowers in a galley

banker¹ 1 an official or player in charge of the bank in any of various games, esp gambling games **2** a result that has been forecast identically in a series of entries on a football pool coupon

banker² 1 a fishing vessel of Newfoundland **2** a fisherman in such a vessel **3** Brit a locomotive that is used to help a heavy train up a steep gradient

banker³ a craftsman's workbench

Bankhead Tallulah (Brockman). 1902–68, US stage and film actress; her successes included the plays The Little Foxes (1939) and The Skin of Our Teeth (1942)

bankrupt a person adjudged insolvent by a court, his property being transferred to a trustee and administered for the benefit of his creditors

Banks 1 Iain (Menzies). born 1954, Scottish novelist and science fiction writer. His novels include The Wasp

Factory (1984), The Crow Road (1992), and Dead Air (2002); science-fiction (under the name Iain M Banks) includes Look to Windward (2000) **2** Sir **Joseph** 1743–1820, British botanist and explorer: circumnavigated the world with James Cook (1768–71)

banksia any shrub or tree of the Australian genus Banksia, having long leathery evergreen leaves and dense cylindrical heads of flowers that are often red or yellowish: family Proteaceae

Banks Island 1 an island of N Canada, in the Northwest Territories: the westernmost island of the Arctic Archipelago. Area: about 67 340 sq km (26 000 sq miles) **2** an island of W Canada, off British Columbia. Length: about 72 km (45 miles)

banner Computing an advertisement, often animated, that extends across the width of a web page

Bannister Sir Roger (Gilbert). born 1929, British athlete and doctor: first man to run a mile in under four minutes (1954)

Bannockburn a village in central Scotland, south of Stirling; nearby is the site of a victory (1314) of the Scots, led by Robert the Bruce, over the English. Pop: 7396 (2001)

banshee (in Irish folklore) a female spirit whose wailing warns of impending death

Banstead a town in S England, in NE Surrey. Pop: 19 332 (2001)

bantam 1 any of various very small breeds of domestic fowl **2** Boxing short for **bantamweight 3** Canadian an age level of between 13 and 15 in amateur sport, esp ice hockey **b** (as modifier): bantam hockey

bantamweight 1 a a professional boxer weighing 112–118 pounds (51–53.5 kg) **b** an amateur boxer weighing 51–54 kg (112–119 pounds) **c** (as modifier): the bantamweight champion **2** a wrestler in a similar weight category (usually 115–126 pounds (52–57 kg))

Banting Sir Frederick Grant 1891–1941, Canadian physiologist: discovered the insulin treatment for diabetes with Best and Macleod (1922) and shared the Nobel prize for physiology or medicine with Macleod (1923)

Bantock Sir Granville 1868–1946, British composer. His works include the Hebridean Symphony (1915), five ballets, and three operas

Bantu 1 a group of languages of Africa, including most of the principal languages spoken from the equator to the Cape of Good Hope, but excluding the Khoisan family: now generally regarded as part of the Benue-Congo branch of the Niger-Congo family **2** South African, derogatory a Black speaker of a Bantu language

Bantustan (formerly, in South Africa) an area reserved for occupation by a Black African people, with limited self-government; abolished in 1993

banyan or **banian 1** a moraceous tree, Ficus benghalensis, of tropical India and the East Indies, having aerial roots that grow down into the soil forming additional trunks **2** a member of the Hindu merchant caste of N and W India

baobab a bombacaceous tree, Adansonia digitata, native to Africa, that has a very thick trunk, large white flowers, and a gourdlike fruit with an edible pulp called monkey bread

Baoding, Paoting, or **Pao-ting** a city in NE China, in

N Hebei province. Pop: 810 000 (2005 est).

Baotou *or* **Paotow** an industrial city in N China, in the central Inner Mongolia AR on the Yellow River. Pop: 1 367 000 (2005 est)

baptism a Christian religious rite consisting of immersion in or sprinkling with water as a sign that the subject is cleansed from sin and constituted as a member of the Church

baptism of fire *Christianity* the penetration of the Holy Ghost into the human spirit to purify, consecrate, and strengthen it, as was believed to have occurred initially at Pentecost

Baptist 1 a member of any of various Christian sects that affirm the necessity of baptism (usually of adults and by immersion) following a personal profession of the Christian faith 2 **the Baptist**. See **John the Baptist**
▷http://www.baptist.org/
▷http://www.baptist.org.uk/
▷http://baptist.org.au/
▷http://www.baptist.org.nz/
▷http://www.baptist.org.nz/

bar a cgs unit of pressure equal to 10^6 dynes per square centimetre. 1 bar is equivalent to 10^5 newtons per square metre

Bar the 1 (in England and elsewhere) barristers collectively 2 *US* the legal profession collectively 3 **be called to** *or* **go to the Bar** *Brit* to become a barrister 4 **be called within the Bar** *Brit* to be appointed as a Queen's Counsel

Barabbas *New Testament* a condemned robber who was released at the Passover instead of Jesus (Matthew 27:16)

barachois (in the Atlantic Provinces of Canada) a shallow lagoon formed by a sand bar

Barak Ehud born 1942, Israeli Labour politician, prime minister (1999–2001)

Baranof Island an island off SE Alaska, in the western part of the Alexander Archipelago. Area: 4162 sq km (1607 sq miles)

barb¹ 1 any of the numerous hairlike filaments that form the vane of a feather 2 a beardlike growth in certain animals 3 a hooked hair or projection on certain fruits 4 any small cyprinid fish of the genus *Barbus* (or *Puntius*) and related genera, such as *B. conchonius* (**rosy barb**) 5 any of the small fleshy protuberances beneath the tongue in horses and cattle

barb² *Austral* a breed of horse of North African origin, similar to the Arab but less spirited

barb³ *Austral* a black kelpie (see **kelpie¹**)

Barbadian 1 of or relating to Barbados or its inhabitants 2 a native or inhabitant of Barbados

Barbados an island in the Caribbean, in the E Lesser Antilles: a British colony from 1628 to 1966, now an independent state within the Commonwealth. Language: English. Currency: Barbados dollar. Capital: Bridgetown. Pop: 271 000 (2004 est). Area: 430 sq km (166 sq miles)

barbarian a member of a primitive or uncivilized people

Barbarossa 1 the nickname of the Holy Roman Emperor **Frederick I** 2 real name *Khair ed-Din. c* 1465–1546, Turkish pirate and admiral: conquered Tunis for the Ottomans (1534)

Barbary a historic name for a region of N Africa extending from W Egypt to the Atlantic and including the former **Barbary States** of Tripolitania, Tunisia, Algeria, and Morocco

Barbary Coast the the Mediterranean coast of North Africa: a centre of piracy against European shipping from the 16th to the 19th centuries

barbel 1 any of several slender tactile spines or bristles that hang from the jaws of certain fishes, such as the catfish and carp 2 any of several European cyprinid fishes of the genus *Barbus*, esp *B. barbus*, that resemble the carp but have a longer body and pointed snout

barbell a metal rod to which heavy discs are attached at each end for weightlifting exercises

Barber Samuel 1910–81, US composer: his works include an *Adagio for Strings*, adapted from the second movement of his string quartet No 1 (1936) and the opera *Vanessa* (1958)

barberry 1 any spiny berberidaceous shrub of the widely distributed genus *Berberis*, esp *B. vulgaris*, having clusters of yellow flowers and orange or red berries: widely cultivated as hedge plants 2 the fruit of any of these plants

Barbican the a building complex in the City of London: includes residential developments and the Barbican Arts Centre (completed 1982) housing concert and exhibition halls, theatres, cinemas, etc

Barbirolli Sir John 1899–1970, English conductor of the Hallé Orchestra (1943–68)

barbiturate a derivative of barbituric acid, such as phenobarbital, used in medicine as a sedative, hypnotic, or auticonvulsant

barbituric acid a white crystalline solid used in the preparation of barbiturate drugs. Formula: $C_4H_4N_2O_3$

Barbuda a coral island in the E Caribbean, in the Leeward Islands: part of the independent state of Antigua and Barbuda. Area: 160 sq km (62 sq miles)

Barbusse Henri 1873–1935, French novelist and poet. His novels include *L'Enfer* (1908) and *Le Feu* (1916), reflecting the horror of World War I

barcarole *or* **barcarolle** 1 a Venetian boat song in a time of six or twelve quaver beats to the bar 2 an instrumental composition resembling this

Barcelona the chief port of Spain, on the NE Mediterranean coast: seat of the Republican government during the Civil War (1936–39); the commercial capital of Spain. Pop: 1 582 738 (2003 est)

Barclay de Tolly Prince **Mikhail** 1761–1818, Russian field marshal: commander in chief against Napoleon in 1812

bar code *Commerce* a machine-readable arrangement of numbers and parallel lines of different widths printed on a package, which can be electronically scanned at a checkout to register the price of the goods and to activate computer stock-checking and reordering

Barcoo River a river in E central Australia, in SW Queensland: joins with the Thomson River to form Cooper Creek

bard 1 a (formerly) one of an ancient Celtic order of poets who recited verses about the exploits, often legendary, of their tribes b (in modern times) a poet who wins a verse competition at a Welsh eisteddfod 2 *Archaic or literary* any poet, esp one who writes lyric or heroic verse or is of national importance

Bardeen John 1908–91, US physicist and electrical engineer, noted for his research on electrical conduction in solids; shared Nobel prize for physics 1956 for research on semiconductors leading to the invention of the transistor; shared Nobel prize for physics 1972 for contributions to the theory of superconductivity

Bardot Brigitte born 1934, French film actress

Bareilly a city in N India, in N central Uttar Pradesh. Pop: 699 839 (2001)

Barenboim Daniel born 1942, Israeli concert pianist and conductor, born in Argentina

Barents Sea a part of the Arctic Ocean, bounded by Norway, Russia, and the islands of Novaya Zemlya, Spitsbergen, and Franz Josef Land

barge 1 a vessel, usually flat-bottomed and with or without its own power, used for transporting freight, esp on canals **2** a vessel, often decorated, used in pageants, for state occasions, etc. **3** Austral, informal a heavy or cumbersome surfboard

Bari a port in SE Italy, capital of Apulia, on the Adriatic coast. Pop: 316 532 (2001)

Baring Evelyn, 1st Earl of Cromer. 1841–1917, English administrator. As consul general in Egypt with plenipotentiary powers, he controlled the Egyptian government from 1883 to 1907

baritone 1 the second lowest adult male voice, having a range approximately from G an eleventh below middle C to F a fourth above it **2** a singer with such a voice **3** the second lowest instrument in the families of the saxophone, horn, oboe, etc.

barium a soft silvery-white metallic element of the alkaline earth group. It is used in bearing alloys and compounds are used as pigments. Symbol: Ba; atomic no.: 56; atomic wt.: 137.327; valency: 2; relative density: 3.5; melting pt.: 729°C; boiling pt.: 1805°C

barium meal a preparation of barium sulphate, which is opaque to X-rays, swallowed by a patient before X-ray examination of the upper part of the alimentary canal

bark 1 a protective layer of dead corky cells on the outside of the stems of woody plants **2** an informal name for cinchona

Barker 1 George (Granville). 1913–91, British poet: author of Calamiterror (1937) and The True Confession of George Barker (1950) **2** Howard born 1946, British playwright: his plays include Claw (1975), The Castle (1985), A Hard Heart (1992), and 13 Objects (2003) **3** Ronnie, full name Ronald William George Barker. born 1929, British comedian: known esp for his partnership with Ronnie Corbett (born 1930) in the TV series The Two Ronnies (1971–85)

Barking and Dagenham a borough of E Greater London. Pop: 165 900 (2003 est). Area: 34 sq km (13 sq miles)

Bar Kochba, Bar Kokhba, or **Bar Kosba** Simeon died 135 AD. Jewish leader who led an unsuccessful revolt against the Romans in Palestine

Barletta a port in SE Italy, in Apulia. Pop: 92 094 (2001)

barley 1 any of various erect annual temperate grasses of the genus Hordeum, esp H. vulgare, that have short leaves and dense bristly flower spikes and are widely cultivated for grain and forage **2** the grain of any of these grasses, used in making beer and whisky and for soups, puddings, etc.

barleycorn 1 a grain of barley, or barley itself **2** an obsolete unit of length equal to one third of an inch

barm 1 the yeasty froth on fermenting malt liquors **2** an archaic or dialect word for yeast

barn[1] US and Canadian a large shed for sheltering railroad cars, trucks, etc.

barn[2] a unit of nuclear cross section equal to 10^{-28} square metre.

Barnabas, Saint New Testament original name Joseph. a Cypriot Levite who supported Saint Paul in his apostolic work (Acts 4:36, 37). Feast day: June 11

barnacle any of various marine crustaceans of the subclass Cirripedia that, as adults, live attached to rocks, ship bottoms, etc. They have feathery food-catching cirri protruding from a hard shell

barnacle goose a N European goose, Branta leucopsis, that has a black-and-white head and body and grey wings

Barnard 1 Christiaan (Neethling). 1923–2001, South African surgeon, who performed the first human heart transplant (1967) **2** Edward Emerson 1857–1923, US astronomer: noted for his discovery of the fifth satellite of Jupiter and his discovery of comets, nebulae, and a red dwarf (1916)

Barnardo Dr Thomas John 1845–1905, British philanthropist, who founded homes for destitute children

Barnaul a city in S Russia, on the River Ob. Pop: 605 000 (2005 est)

barn dance 1 Brit a progressive round country dance **2** US and Canadian a party with hoedown music and square-dancing **3** a party featuring country dancing

Barnet a borough of N Greater London: scene of a Yorkist victory (1471) in the Wars of the Roses. Pop: 324 400 (2003 est). Area: 89 sq km (34 sq miles)

barn owl any owl of the genus Tyto, esp T. alba, having a pale brown and white plumage, long slender legs, and a heart-shaped face: family Tytonidae

Barnsley 1 an industrial town in N England, in Barnsley unitary authority, South Yorkshire. Pop: 71 599 (2001) **2** a unitary authority in N England, in South Yorkshire. Pop: 220 200 (2003 est). Area: 329 sq km (127 sq miles)

Barnstaple a town in SW England, in Devon, on the estuary of the River Taw: tourism, agriculture. Pop: 30 765 (2001)

Barnum P(hineas) T(aylor). 1810–91, US showman, who created The Greatest Show on Earth (1871) and, with J. A. Bailey, founded the Barnum and Bailey Circus (1881)

Baroda 1 a former state of W India, part of Gujarat since 1960 **2** the former name (until 1976) of **Vadodara**

barograph Meteorol a self-recording aneroid barometer

Baroja Pío 1872–1956, Spanish Basque novelist, who wrote nearly 100 novels, including a series of twenty-two under the general title Memorias de un Hombre de Acción (1944–49)

barometer an instrument for measuring atmospheric pressure, usually to determine altitude or weather changes

baron 1 (in Europe from the Middle Ages) originally any tenant-in-chief of a king or other overlord, who held land from his superior by honourable service; a landholding nobleman **2** a powerful businessman or financier **3** *English law* (formerly) the title held by judges of the Court of Exchequer

Baron-Cohen Sacha born 1970, British television comedian, best known for his creation of the character Ali G

baroque 1 a style of architecture and decorative art that flourished throughout Europe from the late 16th to the early 18th century, characterized by extensive ornamentation **2** a 17th-century style of music characterized by extensive use of the thorough bass and of ornamentation **3** any ornate or heavily ornamented style
▷witcombe.sbc.edu/ARTHbaroque.html
▷www.artlex.com/ArtLex/b/baroque.html
▷www.baroquemusic.org
▷classicalmus.hispeed.com/baroque.html
▷www.baroque-music.co.uk

barque *or esp US* **bark** a sailing ship of three or more masts having the foremasts rigged square and the aftermast rigged fore-and-aft

Barquisimeto a city in NW Venezuela. Pop: 1 009 000 (2005 est)

Barra an island in NW Scotland, in the Outer Hebrides: fishing, crofting, tourism. Pop: 1078 (2001)

barracuda any predatory marine teleost fish of the mostly tropical family *Sphyraenidae*, esp *Sphyraena barracuda*. They have an elongated body, strong teeth, and a protruding lower jaw

barrage 1 a usually gated construction, similar to a low dam, across a watercourse, esp one to increase the depth of water to assist navigation or irrigation **2** *Fencing* a heat or series of bouts in a competition

barramundi any of several large edible Australian fishes esp the percoid species *Lates calcarifer* (family Centropomidae) of NE coastal waters or the freshwater species *Scleropages leichardti* (family Osteoglossidae) of Queensland

Barranquilla a port in N Colombia, on the Magdalena River. Pop: 1 918 000 (2005 est)

Barrault Jean-Louis 1910–94, French actor and director, noted particularly as a mime

barrel 1 a unit of capacity used in brewing, equal to 36 Imperial gallons **2** a unit of capacity used in the oil and other industries, normally equal to 42 US gallons or 35 Imperial gallons **3** the trunk of a four-legged animal **4** the quill of a feather

barrel organ 1 an instrument consisting of a cylinder turned by a handle and having pins on it that interrupt the air flow to certain pipes, thereby playing any of a number of tunes **2** a similar instrument in which the projections on a rotating barrel pluck a set of strings

barren 1 incapable of producing offspring, seed, or fruit; sterile **2** (of rock strata) having no fossils

Barrie Sir James Matthew 1860–1937, Scottish dramatist and novelist, noted particularly for his popular children's play *Peter Pan* (1904)

barrier 1 a an exposed offshore sand bar separated from the shore by a lagoon **b** (*as modifier*): *a barrier beach* **2** that part of the Antarctic icecap extending over the sea

barrier reef a long narrow coral reef near and lying parallel to the shore, separated from it by deep water

barrister 1 (in England) a lawyer who has been called to the bar and is qualified to plead in the higher courts **2** (in Canada) a lawyer who pleads in court **3** *US* a less

common word for **lawyer**

barrow a heap of earth placed over one or more prehistoric tombs, often surrounded by ditches. **Long barrows** are elongated Neolithic mounds usually covering stone burial chambers; **round barrows** are Bronze Age, covering burials or cremations

Barrow 1 a river in SE Ireland, rising in the Slieve Bloom Mountains and flowing south to Waterford Harbour. Length: about 193 km (120 miles) **2** See **Barrow-in-Furness** and **Barrow Point**

Barrow-in-Furness an industrial town in NW England, in S Cumbria. Pop: 47 194 (2001)

Barrow Point the northernmost tip of Alaska, on the Arctic Ocean

Barry[1] **1** Sir Charles 1795–1860, English architect: designer of the Houses of Parliament in London **2** Comtesse du. See **du Barry 3** John, real name *John Barry Prendergast*. born 1933, British composer of film scores, including several for films in the James Bond series

Barry[2] a port in SE Wales, in Vale of Glamorgan county borough on the Bristol Channel. Pop: 50 661 (2001)

Barrymore a US family of actors, esp **Ethel** (1879–1959), **John** (1882–1942), and **Lionel** (1878–1954)

Bart Lionel 1930–99, British composer and playwright. His musicals include *Oliver* (1960)

barter trade by the exchange of goods

Barth 1 Heinrich 1821–65, German explorer: author of *Travels and Discoveries in North and Central Africa* (1857–58) **2** John (Simmons). born 1930, US novelist; his novels include *The Sot-Weed Factor* (1960), *Giles Goat-Boy* (1966), and *Once Upon a Time* (1994) **3** Karl 1886–1968, Swiss Protestant theologian. He stressed man's dependence on divine grace in such works as *Commentary on Romans* (1919)

Barthes Roland 1915–80, French writer and critic, who applied structuralist theory to literature and popular culture: his books include *Mythologies* (1957) and *Elements of Semiology* (1964)

Bartholdi Frédéric August 1834–1904, French sculptor and architect, who designed (1884) the Statue of Liberty

Bartholomew *New Testament* **Saint** one of the twelve apostles (Matthew 10:3). Feast day: Aug 24 or June 11

Bartoli Cecilia born 1966, Italian mezzo-soprano, noted for her performances in Mozart and Rossini operas

Bartolommeo Fra original name *Baccio della Porta*. 1472–1517, Italian painter of the Florentine school, noted for his austere religious works

Barton 1 Sir Derek (Harold Richard). 1918–98, British organic chemist: shared the Nobel prize for chemistry (1969) for his work on conformational analysis **2** Sir Edmund 1849–1920, Australian statesman; first prime minister of Australia (1901–03) **3** Elizabeth, known as the *Maid of Kent*. ?1506–34, English nun, who claimed the gift of prophecy. Her criticism of Henry VIII's attempt to annul his first marriage led to her execution **4** John (Bernard Adie). born 1928, British theatre director, noted esp for his productions of Shakespeare

Baruch *Bible* **a** a disciple of Jeremiah (Jeremiah 32–36) **b** the book of the Apocrypha said to have been written by him

baryon any of a class of elementary particles that have a mass greater than or equal to that of the proton, participate in strong interactions, and have a spin of ½. Baryons are either nucleons or hyperons. The **baryon number** is the number of baryons in a system minus the number of antibaryons

barytes a colourless or white mineral consisting of barium sulphate in orthorhombic crystalline form, occurring in sedimentary rocks and with sulphide ores: a source of barium. Formula: BaSO₄

basalt 1 a fine-grained dark basic igneous rock consisting of plagioclase feldspar, a pyroxene, and olivine: the most common volcanic rock and usually extrusive **2** a form of black unglazed pottery resembling basalt

bascule 1 a bridge with a movable section hinged about a horizontal axis and counterbalanced by a weight **2** a movable roadway forming part of such a bridge

base¹ 1 a chemical compound that combines with an acid to form a salt and water. A solution of a base in water turns litmus paper blue, produces hydroxyl ions, and has a pH greater than 7. Bases are metal oxides or hydroxides or amines **2** *Biochem.* any of the nitrogen-containing constituents of nucleic acids: adenine, thymine (in DNA), uracil (in RNA), guanine, or cytosine **3** the inorganic material on which the dye is absorbed in lake pigments; carrier **4** *Biology* **a** the part of an organ nearest to its point of attachment **b** the point of attachment of an organ or part **5** *Architect* **a** the lowest division of a building or structure **b** the lower part of a column or pier **6** the lower side or face of a geometric construction **7** *Maths* **a** the number of distinct single-digit numbers in a counting system, and so the number represented as 10 in a place-value system **b** (of a logarithm or exponential) the number whose powers are expressed **c** (of a mathematical structure) a substructure from which the given system can be generated **d** the initial instance from which a generalization is proven by mathematical induction **8** *Logic, Maths* the initial element of a recursive definition, that defines the first element of the infinite sequence generated thereby **9** *Electronics* the region in a transistor between the emitter and collector **10** *Photog* the glass, paper, or cellulose-ester film that supports the sensitized emulsion with which it is coated **11** a starting or finishing point in any of various games **12** *Baseball* any of the four corners of the diamond, which runners have to reach in order to score

base² 1 *English history* **a** (of land tenure) held by villein or other ignoble service **b** holding land by villein or other ignoble service **2** *Music* an obsolete spelling of **bass**

baseball 1 a team game with nine players on each side, played on a field with four bases connected to form a diamond. The object is to score runs by batting the ball and running round the bases **2** the hard rawhide-covered ball used in this game

▷ www.majorleaguebaseball.com
▷ www.baseball-links.com

baseline a line at each end of a tennis court that marks the limit of play

basement 1 a a partly or wholly underground storey of a building, esp the one immediately below the main floor **b** (*as modifier*): *a basement flat* **2** the foundation or substructure of a wall or building **3** *Geology* a part of the earth's crust formed of hard igneous or metamorphic

rock that lies beneath the cover of soft sedimentary rock, sediment, and soil

base metal any of certain common metals such as copper, lead, zinc, and tin, as distinct from the precious metals, gold, silver, and platinum

Bashkir Republic a constituent republic of E central Russia, in the S Urals: established as the first Soviet autonomous republic in 1919; rich mineral resources. Capital: Ufa. Pop: 4 012 900 (2002). Area: 143 600 sq km (55 430 sq miles)

Basho full name **Matsuo Basho**, originally *Matsuo Munefusa*. 1644–94, Japanese poet and travel writer, noted esp for his haiku

basic 1 *Chem* **a** of, denoting, or containing a base; alkaline **b** (of a salt) containing hydroxyl or oxide groups not all of which have been replaced by an acid radical **2** *Metallurgy* of, concerned with, or made by a process in which the furnace or converter is made of a basic material, such as magnesium oxide **3** (of such igneous rocks as basalt) containing between 52 and 45 per cent silica

BASIC or **Basic** a computer programming language that uses common English terms

basic slag a furnace slag produced in steel-making, containing large amounts of calcium phosphate: used as a fertilizer

Basie William, known as *Count Basie*. 1904–84, US jazz pianist, bandleader, and composer: associated particularly with the polished phrasing and style of big-band jazz

basil 1 a Eurasian plant, *Ocimum basilicum*, having spikes of small white flowers and aromatic leaves used as herbs for seasoning: family *Lamiaceae* (labiates) **2** a European plant, *Satureja vulgaris* (or *Clinopodium vulgare*), with dense clusters of small pink or whitish flowers: family *Lamiaceae* **3** **basil-thyme** a European plant, *Acinos arvensis*, having clusters of small violet-and-white flowers: family *Lamiaceae*

Basil Saint, called *the Great*, ?329–379 AD, Greek patriarch: an opponent of Arianism and one of the founders of monasticism. Feast day: Jan 2, June 14, or Jan 1

Basilan 1 a group of islands in the Philippines, SW of Mindanao **2** the main island of this group, separated from Mindanao by the **Basilan Strait**. Area: 1282 sq km (495 sq miles) **3** a city on Basilan Island. Pop: 381 000 (2005 est)

Basildon a town in SE England, in S Essex: designated a new town in 1955. Pop: 99 876 (2001)

basilica 1 a Roman building, used for public administration, having a large rectangular central nave with an aisle on each side and an apse at the end **2** a rectangular early Christian or medieval church, usually having a nave with clerestories, two or four aisles, one or more vaulted apses, and a timber roof **3** a Roman Catholic church having special ceremonial rights

Basilicata a region of S Italy, between the Tyrrhenian Sea and the Gulf of Taranto. Capital: Potenza. Pop: 596 821 (2003 est). Area: 9985 sq km (3855 sq miles)

basilisk 1 (in classical legend) a serpent that could kill by its breath or glance **2** any small arboreal semiaquatic lizard of the genus *Basiliscus* of tropical America: family *Iguanidae* (iguanas). The males have an inflatable head crest, used in display

basin 1 any partially enclosed or sheltered area where vessels may be moored or docked 2 the catchment area of a particular river and its tributaries or of a lake or sea 3 a depression in the earth's surface 4 *Geology* a part of the earth's surface consisting of rock strata that slope down to a common centre

Basingstoke a town in S England, in N Hampshire. Pop: 90 171 (2001)

basis *Maths* (of a vector space) a maximal set of linearly independent vectors, in terms of which all the elements of the space are uniquely expressible, and the number of which is the dimension of the space

basket *Basketball* a an open horizontal metal hoop fixed to the backboard, through which a player must throw the ball to score points b a point or points scored in this way

basketball 1 a game played by two opposing teams of five men (or six women) each, usually on an indoor court. Points are scored by throwing the ball through an elevated horizontal metal hoop 2 the inflated ball used in this game
▷www.basketball.com
▷www.nba.com

basket weave a weave of two or more yarns together, resembling that of a basket, esp in wool or linen fabric

basking shark a very large plankton-eating shark, *Cetorhinus maximus*, often floating at the sea surface: family *Cetorhinidae*

Basle *or* **Basel** 1 a canton of NW Switzerland, divided into the demicantons of **Basle-Landschaft** and **Basle-Stadt**. Pops.: 263 200 and 186 900 (2002 est). Areas: 427 sq km (165 sq miles) and 36 sq km (14 sq miles) respectively 2 a city in NW Switzerland, capital of Basle canton, on the Rhine: oldest university in Switzerland. Pop: 165 000 (2002 est)

Basque 1 a member of a people of unknown origin living around the W Pyrenees in France and Spain 2 the language of this people, of no known relationship with any other language

Basque Provinces an autonomous region of N Spain, comprising the provinces of Álava, Guipúzcoa, and Vizcaya: inhabited mainly by Basques, who retained virtual autonomy from the 9th to the 19th century. Pop: 1 840 700 (2003 est). Area: about 7250 sq km (2800 sq miles)

Basra, Basrah, Busra *or* **Busrah** a port in SE Iraq, on the Shatt-al-Arab. Pop: 1 187 000 (2005 est)

bas-relief sculpture in low relief, in which the forms project slightly from the background but no part is completely detached from it

Bas-Rhin a department of NE France in Alsace region. Capital: Strasbourg. Pop: 1 052 698 (2003 est). Area: 4793 sq km (1869 sq miles)

bass[1] 1 the lowest adult male voice usually having a range from E a 13th below middle C to D a tone above it 2 a singer with such a voice 3 **the bass** the lowest part in a piece of harmony 4 the low-frequency component of an electrical audio signal, esp in a record player or tape recorder

bass[2] 1 any of various sea perches, esp *Morone labrax*, a popular game fish with one large spiny dorsal fin separate from a second smaller one 2 another name for the

European perch (see **perch**[2] (sense 1)) 3 any of various predatory North American freshwater percoid fishes, such as *Micropterus salmoides*, (**largemouth bass**): family *Centrarchidae* (sunfishes, etc)

bass[3] a bast fibre bag for holding an angler's catch

bass clef the clef that establishes F a fifth below middle C on the fourth line of the staff.

bass drum a large shallow drum of low and indefinite pitch

Bassein a city in Myanmar, on the Irrawaddy delta: a port on the **Bassein River** (the westernmost distributary of the Irrawaddy). Pop: 231 000 (2005 est)

Basse-Normandie a region of NW France, on the English Channel: consists of the Cherbourg peninsula in the west rising to the Normandy hills in the east; mainly agricultural.

Bassenthwaite a lake in NW England, in Cumbria near Keswick. Length: 6 km (4 miles)

Basseterre a port in the Caribbean, on St Kitts in the Leeward Islands: the capital of St Kitts-Nevis. Pop: 13 220 (2001)

Basse-Terre 1 a mountainous island in the Caribbean, in the Leeward Islands, comprising part of Guadeloupe. Area: 848 sq km (327 sq miles) 2 a port in W Guadeloupe, on Basse-Terre Island: the capital of the French Overseas Department of Guadeloupe. Pop: 12 410 (1999)

bass guitar a guitar that has the same pitch and tuning as a double bass, usually electrically amplified

basso (esp in operatic or solo singing) a singer with a bass voice

bassoon a woodwind instrument, the tenor of the oboe family. Range: about three and a half octaves upwards from the B flat below the bass staff

Bass Strait a channel between mainland Australia and Tasmania, linking the Indian Ocean and the Tasman Sea

bastard a hybrid, esp an accidental or inferior one

Bastia a port in NE Corsica: the main commercial and industrial town of the island: capital of Haute-Corse department. Pop: 37 884 (1999)

Bastille a fortress in Paris, built in the 14th century: a prison until its destruction in 1789, at the beginning of the French Revolution

Bastogne a town in SE Belgium: of strategic importance to Allied defences during the Battle of the Bulge; besieged by the Germans during the winter of 1944–45. Pop: 14 070 (2004 est)

bat[1] 1 any of various types of club with a handle, used to hit the ball in certain sports, such as cricket, baseball, or table tennis 2 a flat round club with a short handle, resembling a table-tennis bat, used by a man on the ground to guide the pilot of an aircraft when taxiing 3 *Cricket* short for **batsman** 4 *Austral* a small board used for tossing the coins in the game of two-up

bat[2] any placental mammal of the order *Chiroptera*, being a nocturnal mouselike animal flying with a pair of membranous wings (patagia). The group is divided into the *Megachiroptera* (**fruit bats**) and *Microchiroptera* (**insectivorous bats**)

Bataan a peninsula in the Philippines, in W Luzon: scene of the surrender of US and Philippine forces to the Japanese during World War II, later retaken by

American forces

Batangas a port in the Philippines, in SW Luzon. Pop: 293 000 (2005 est)

Batavia 1 an ancient district of the Netherlands, on an island at the mouth of the Rhine 2 an archaic or literary name for **Holland** 3 a former name for **Jakarta**

batch processing a system by which the computer programs of a number of individual users are submitted to the computer as a single batch

Bates 1 Sir **Alan (Arthur)**. 1934–2003, British film and stage actor. His films include *A Kind of Loving* (1962), *Women in Love* (1969), *The Go-Between* (1971), and *The Cherry Orchard* (1999) 2 H(erbert) E(rnest). 1905–74, English writer of short stories and novels, which include *The Darling Buds of May* (1958), *A Moment in Time* (1964), and *The Triple Echo* (1970)

bath[1] a vessel in which something is immersed to maintain it at a constant temperature, to process it photographically, electrolytically, etc, or to lubricate it

bath[2] an ancient Hebrew unit of liquid measure equal to about 8.3 Imperial gallons or 10 US gallons

Bath a city in SW England, in Bath and North East Somerset unitary authority, Somerset, on the River Avon: famous for its hot springs; a fashionable spa in the 18th century; Roman remains, notably the baths; university (1966). Pop: 90 144 (2001)

Bath and North East Somerset a unitary authority in SW England, in Somerset; formerly (1974–96) part of the county of Avon. Pop: 170 900 (2003 est). Area: 351 sq km (136 sq miles)

bathos *Lit* a sudden ludicrous descent from exalted to ordinary matters or style in speech or writing

Bathsheba *Old Testament* the wife of Uriah, who committed adultery with David and later married him and became the mother of his son Solomon (II Samuel 11–12)

Bathurst 1 a city in SE Australia, in E New South Wales: scene of a gold rush in 1851. Pop: 27 036 (2001) 2 a port in E Canada, in NE New Brunswick: rich mineral resources discovered in 1953. Pop: 16 427 (2001) 3 the former name (until 1973) of **Banjul**

bathyscaph, bathyscaphe, or **bathyscape** a submersible vessel having a flotation compartment with an observation capsule underneath, capable of reaching ocean depths of over 10 000 metres (about 5000 fathoms)

bathysphere a strong steel deep-sea diving sphere, lowered by cable

Batista Fulgencio , full name *Batista y Zaldívar*. 1901–73, Cuban military leader and dictator: president of Cuba (1940–44, 1952–59); overthrown by Fidel Castro

Batley a town in N England, in Kirklees unitary authority, West Yorkshire. Pop: 49 448 (2001)

baton 1 a thin stick used by the conductor of an orchestra, choir, etc, to indicate rhythm or expression 2 *Athletics* a short bar carried by a competitor in a relay race and transferred to the next runner at the end of each stage 3 a long stick with a knob on one end, carried, twirled, and thrown up and down by a drum major or drum majorette, esp at the head of a parade

Baton Rouge the capital of Louisiana, in the SE part on the Mississippi River. Pop: 225 090 (2003 est)

batsman *Cricket* a person who bats or whose turn it is

to bat **b** a player who specializes in batting

batten 1 a narrow flat length of wood or plastic inserted in pockets of a sail to give it proper shape 2 a lath used for holding a tarpaulin along the side of a raised hatch on a ship 3 *Theatre* **a** a row of lights **b** the strip or bar supporting them 4 NZ an upright part of a fence made of wood or other material, designed to keep wires at equal distances apart

Batten Jean 1909–82, New Zealand aviator: the first woman to fly single-handed from Australia to Britain (1935)

Battersea a district in London, in Wandsworth: noted for its dogs' home, power station (now a leisure centre), and park

battery 1 **a** two or more primary cells connected together, usually in series, to provide a source of electric current **b** short for **dry battery** 2 another name for **accumulator** 3 *Criminal law* unlawful beating or wounding of a person or mere touching in a hostile or offensive manner 4 *Chiefly Brit* **a** a large group of cages for intensive rearing of poultry **b** *(as modifier): battery hens* 5 *Psychol* a series of tests 6 *Chess* two men of the same colour placed so that one can unmask an attack by the other by moving 7 the percussion section in an orchestra 8 *Baseball* the pitcher and the catcher considered together

Battle[1] Kathleen born 1948, US opera singer: a coloratura soprano, she made her professional debut in 1972 and sang with New York City's Metropolitan Opera (1977–94)

Battle[2] a town in SE England, in East Sussex: site of the Battle of Hastings (1066); medieval abbey. Pop: 5190 (2001)

battledore 1 an ancient racket game 2 a light racket, smaller than a tennis racket, used for striking the shuttlecock in this game 3 (formerly) a wooden utensil used for beating clothes, in baking, etc.

Batum or **Batumi** a city in Georgia: capital of the Adzhar Autonomous Republic; a major Black Sea port. Pop: 118 000 (2005 est)

bauble (formerly) a mock staff of office carried by a court jester

Bauchi 1 a state of N Nigeria: formed in 1976 from part of North-Eastern State; tin mining. Capital: Bauchi. Pop: 446 000 (2005 est). Area: 64 605 sq km (24 944 sq miles) 2 a town in N central Nigeria, capital of Bauchi state. Pop: 76 070 (1991 est)

baud a unit used to measure the speed of electronic code transmissions, equal to one unit interval per second

Baudelaire Charles Pierre 1821–67, French poet, noted for his macabre imagery; author of *Les fleurs du mal* (1857)

Baudouin I 1930–93, king of Belgium (1951–93)

Baudrillard Jean born 1929, French sociologist and theorist of postmodernism; his books include *Seduction* (1979), *America* (1986), and *The Spirit of Terrorism* (2002)

bauera any small evergreen Australian shrub of the genus *Bauera*, having pink or purple flowers

Bauhaus a a German school of architecture and applied arts founded in 1919 by Walter Gropius on experimental principles of functionalism and truth to materials. After being closed by the Nazis in 1933, its ideas were widely disseminated by its students and staff, includ-

ing Kandinsky, Klee, Feininger, Moholy-Nagy, and Mies van der Rohe **b** (*as modifier*): *Bauhaus wallpaper*
▷www.cs.umb.edu
▷http://alilley/bauhaus.html

Bautzen a city in E Germany, in Saxony: site of an indecisive battle in 1813 between Napoleon's army and an allied army of Russians and Prussians. Pop: 42 160 (2003 est)

bauxite a white, red, yellow, or brown amorphous claylike substance comprising aluminium oxides and hydroxides, often with such impurities as iron oxides. It is the chief ore of aluminium. General formula: $Al_2O_3.nH_2O$

Bavaria a state of S Germany: a former duchy and kingdom; mainly wooded highland, with the Alps in the south. Capital: Munich. Pop: 12 155 000 (2000 est). Area: 70 531 sq km (27 232 sq miles)

Bax Sir Arnold (**Edward Trevor**). 1883–1953, English composer of romantic works, often based on Celtic legends, including the tone poem *Tintagel* (1917)

Baxter 1 James (**Keir**). 1926–72, New Zealand lyric poet. His works include *The Fallen House* (1953) and *In Fires of No Return* (1958) **2** Richard 1615–91, English Puritan divine and devotional writer: prominent in church affairs during the Restoration

bay¹ 1 a wide semicircular indentation of a shoreline, esp between two headlands or peninsulas **2** an extension of lowland into hills that partly surround it **3** *US* an extension of prairie into woodland

bay² 1 an alcove or recess in a wall **2** See **bay window 3** a compartment in an aircraft, esp one used for a specified purpose **4** *Nautical* a compartment in the forward part of a ship between decks, often used as the ship's hospital **5** *Brit* a tracked recess in the platform of a railway station, esp one forming the terminus of a branch line

bay³ 1 a small evergreen Mediterranean laurel, *Laurus nobilis*, with glossy aromatic leaves, used for flavouring in cooking, and small blackish berries **2** any of various other trees with strongly aromatic leaves used in cooking, esp a member of the genera *Myrica* or *Pimenta* **3** any of several magnolias **4** any of certain other trees or shrubs, esp bayberry

bay⁴ a a moderate reddish-brown colour **b** (*as adjective*): *a bay horse*

bayberry *or* **bay 1** any of several North American aromatic shrubs or small trees of the genus *Myrica*, that bear grey waxy berries: family *Myricaceae* **2** a tropical American myrtaceous tree, *Pimenta racemosa*, that yields an oil used in making bay rum **3** the fruit of any of these plants

Bayeux a town in NW France, on the River Aure: its museum houses the Bayeux tapestry and there is a 13th-century cathedral: dairy foods, plastic. Pop: 14 961 (1999)

Baylis 1 Lillian Mary 1874–1937, British theatre manager: founded the Old Vic (1912) and the Sadler's Wells company for opera and ballet (1931) **2** Trevor (**Graham**). born 1937, British inventor of the clockwork radio (1992)

Bay of Pigs a bay on the SW coast of Cuba: scene of an unsuccessful invasion of Cuba by US-backed troops (April 17, 1961)

bayonet 1 a blade that can be attached to the muzzle of

a rifle for stabbing in close combat. **2** a type of fastening in which a cylindrical member is inserted into a socket against spring pressure and turned so that pins on its side engage in slots in the socket

Bayonne a port in SW France: a commercial centre for the Basque region. Pop: 40 078 (1999)

Bayreuth a city in E Germany, in NE Bavaria: home and burial place of Richard Wagner; annual festivals of his music. Pop: 74 818 (2003 est)

bay rum 1 an aromatic liquid, used in medicines and cosmetics, originally obtained by distilling the leaves of the bayberry tree (*Pimenta racemosa*) with rum: now also synthesized from alcohol, water, and various oils **2** **bay rum tree** another name for **bayberry**

bay window a window projecting from the wall of a building and forming an alcove of a room

bazaar *or* **bazar 1** (esp in the Orient) a market area, esp a street of small stalls **2** a sale in aid of charity, esp of miscellaneous secondhand or handmade articles **3** a shop where a large variety of goods is sold

beach an extensive area of sand or shingle sloping down to a sea or lake, esp the area between the high- and low-water marks on a seacoast

beachcomber a long high wave rolling onto a beach

Beachy Head a headland in East Sussex, on the English Channel, consisting of chalk cliffs 171 m (570 ft) high

beacon 1 a hill on which such fires were lit **2** a lighthouse, signalling buoy, etc, used to warn or guide ships in dangerous waters **3** a radio or other signal marking a flight course in air navigation **4** short for **Belisha beacon 5** a stone set by a surveyor to mark a corner or line of a site boundary, etc.

Beaconsfield¹ 1st Earl of title of (Benjamin) **Disraeli**

Beaconsfield² a town in SE England, in Buckinghamshire. Pop: 12 292 (2001)

bead 1 *Architect, Furniture* a small convex moulding having a semicircular cross section **2** *Chem* a small solid globule made by fusing a powdered sample with borax or a similar flux on a platinum wire. The colour of the globule serves as a test for the presence of certain metals (**bead test**) **3** *Metallurgy* a deposit of welding metal on the surface of a metal workpiece, often used to examine the structure of the weld zone **4** *RC Church* one of the beads of a rosary

beading 1 another name for **bead 2** a narrow strip of some material used for edging or ornamentation

beadle 1 (formerly, in the Church of England) a minor parish official who acted as an usher and kept order **2** (in Scotland) a church official attending on the minister **3** *Judaism* a synagogue attendant **4** an official in certain British universities and other institutions

beagle a small sturdy breed of hound, having a smooth dense coat usually of white, tan, and black; often used (esp formerly) for hunting hares

Beaglehole John 1901–71, New Zealand historian and author. His works include *Exploration of the Pacific* (1934) and *The Journals of James Cook* (1955)

beak 1 the projecting jaws of a bird, covered with a horny sheath; bill **2** any beaklike mouthpart in other animals, such as turtles **3** *Architect* the upper surface of a cornice, which slopes out to throw off water **4** *Chem* the part of a still or retort through which vapour passes to the condenser **5** *Nautical* another word for **ram**

beaker a cylindrical flat-bottomed container used in laboratories, usually made of glass and having a pouring lip

Beale **Dorothea** 1831–1906, British schoolmistress, a champion of women's education and suffrage. As principal of Cheltenham Ladies' College (1858–1906) she introduced important reforms

beam **1** any rigid member or structure that is loaded transversely **2** the breadth of a ship or boat taken at its widest part, usually amidships **3** one of the two cylindrical rollers on a loom, one of which holds the warp threads before weaving, the other the finished work **4** the main stem of a deer's antler from which the smaller branches grow **5** a narrow unidirectional flow of electromagnetic radiation or particles **6** the horizontal centrally pivoted bar in a balance **7 off (the) beam** not following a radio beam to maintain a course **8 on the beam a** following a radio beam to maintain a course **b** *Nautical* opposite the beam of a vessel; abeam

bean **1** any of various leguminous plants of the widely cultivated genus *Phaseolus* producing edible seeds in pods **2** any of several other leguminous plants that bear edible pods or seeds, such as the broad bean and soya bean **3** any of various other plants whose seeds are produced in pods or podlike fruits **4** the seed or pod of any of these plants **5** any of various beanlike seeds, such as coffee

bear **1** any plantigrade mammal of the family *Ursidae*: order *Carnivora* (carnivores). Bears are typically massive omnivorous animals with a large head, a long shaggy coat, and strong claws **2** any of various bearlike animals, such as the koala and the ant bear

bear-baiting (formerly) an entertainment in which dogs attacked and enraged a chained bear

beard **1** the hair growing on the lower parts of a man's face **2** any similar growth in animals **3** a tuft of long hairs in plants such as barley and wheat; awn **4** the gills of an oyster

Beardsley **Aubrey (Vincent).** 1872–98, English illustrator: noted for his stylized black-and-white illustrations, esp those for Oscar Wilde's *Salome* and Pope's *Rape of the Lock*

bear hug **1** a wrestling hold in which the arms are locked tightly round an opponent's chest and arms **2** *Commerce* an approach to the board of one company by another to indicate that an offer is to be made for their shares

bearing **1** a support, guide, or locating piece for a rotating or reciprocating mechanical part **2** the angular direction of a line, point, or course measured from true north or south (**true bearing**), magnetic north or south (**magnetic bearing**), or one's own position **3** the position or direction, as of a ship, fixed with reference to two or more known points

bearskin **1** the pelt of a bear, esp when used as a rug **2** a rough shaggy woollen cloth, used for overcoats

beat **1** *Physics* the low regular frequency produced by combining two sounds or electrical signals that have similar frequencies **2** *Prosody* the accent, stress, or ictus in a metrical foot **3** *Nautical* a course that steers a sailing vessel as close as possible to the direction from

which the wind is blowing **4 a** the act of scouring for game by beating **b** the organized scouring of a particular woodland so as to rouse the game in it **c** the woodland where game is so roused **5** *Fencing* a sharp tap with one's blade on an opponent's blade to deflect it

beatific of, conferring, or relating to a state of celestial happiness

beatitude an honorific title of the Eastern Christian Church, applied to those of patriarchal rank

Beatitude *New Testament* any of eight distinctive sayings of Jesus in the Sermon on the Mount (Matthew 5:3–11) in which he declares that the poor, the meek, those that mourn, the merciful, the peacemakers, the pure of heart, those that thirst for justice, and those that are persecuted will, in various ways, receive the blessings of heaven

Beaton **Sir Cecil (Walter Hardy).** 1904–80, British photographer, noted esp for his society portraits

Beatrix full name *Beatrix Wilhelmina Armgard*. born 1938, queen of the Netherlands from 1980

Beatty **1 David,** 1st Earl Beatty. 1871–1936, British admiral of the fleet in World War I **2 Warren,** full name *Henry Warren Beatty.* Born 1937, US film actor and director: his films include *Bonnie and Clyde* (1967), *Heaven Can Wait* (1978), *Reds* (1981, also directed), *Bugsy* (1991), and *Bulworth* (1998, also wrote and directed)

Beaufort **1 Henry** ?1374–1447, English cardinal, half-brother of Henry IV; chancellor (1403–04, 1413–17, 1424–26) **2 Lady Margaret,** Countess of Richmond and Derby. ?1443–1509, mother of Henry VII. She helped to found two Cambridge colleges and was a patron of Caxton

Beaufort scale *Meteorol* an international scale of wind velocities ranging for practical purposes from o (calm) to 12 (hurricane force). In the US an extension of the scale, from 13 to 17 for winds over 64 knots, is used

Beaufort Sea part of the Arctic Ocean off the N coast of North America

Beauharnais **1 Alexandre** , Vicomte de. 1760–94, French general, who served in the War of American Independence and the French Revolutionary wars; first husband of Empress Joséphine: guillotined **2** his son, **Eugène de** 1781–1824, viceroy of Italy (1805–14) for his stepfather Napoleon I **3 Hortense de** 1783–1837, queen of Holland (1806–10) as wife of Louis Bonaparte; daughter of Alexandre Beauharnais and sister of Eugène: mother of Napoleon III **4 Joséphine de** . See (Empress) **Josephine**

Beaulieu a village in S England, in Hampshire: site of Palace House, seat of Lord Montagu and once the gatehouse of the ruined 13th-century abbey; the National Motor Museum is in its grounds. Pop: 1200 (latest est)

Beaumarchais **Pierre Augustin Caron de** 1732–99, French dramatist, noted for his comedies *The Barber of Seville* (1775) and *The Marriage of Figaro* (1784)

Beaumaris a resort in N Wales, on the island of Anglesey: 13th-century castle. Pop: 1513 (2001)

Beaumont[1] **Francis** l584–1616, English dramatist, who collaborated with John Fletcher on plays including *The Knight of the Burning Pestle* (l607) and *The Maid's Tragedy* (1611)

Beaumont[2] a city in SE Texas. Pop: 112 434 (2003 est)

Beaune 1 a city in E France, near Dijon: an important trading centre for Burgundy wines. Pop: 21 923 (1999) 2 a wine produced in this district

beauty spot a mole or other similar natural mark on the skin

Beauvais a market town in N France, 64 km (40 miles) northwest of Paris. Pop: 55 392 (1999)

Beauvoir Simone de 1908–86, French existentialist novelist and feminist, whose works include *Le sang des autres* (1944), *Le deuxième sexe* (1949), and *Les mandarins* (1954)

beaver 1 a large amphibious rodent, *Castor fiber*, of Europe, Asia, and North America: family *Castoridae*. It has soft brown fur, a broad flat hairless tail, and webbed hind feet, and constructs complex dams and houses (lodges) in rivers 2 the fur of this animal 3 **mountain beaver** a burrowing rodent, *Aplodontia rufa*, of W North America: family *Aplodontidae* 4 a woollen napped cloth resembling beaver fur, formerly much used for overcoats, etc 5 a greyish- or yellowish-brown

Beaverbrook 1st Baron, title of *William Maxwell Aitken*. 1879–1964, British newspaper proprietor and Conservative politician, born in Canada, whose newspapers included the *Daily Express*; minister of information (1918); minister of aircraft production (1940–41)

Bebington a town in NW England, in Wirral unitary authority, Merseyside: docks and chemical works. Pop: 57 066 (2001)

becalmed (of a sailing boat or ship) motionless through lack of wind

Bechet Sidney (Joseph). 1897–1959, US jazz soprano saxophonist and clarinettist

Bechstein Karl 1826–1900, German piano maker; founder (1853) of the Bechstein company of piano manufacturers in Berlin

beck (in N England) a stream, esp a swiftly flowing one

Beckenbauer Franz born 1945, German footballer: team captain when West Germany won the World Cup (1974): manager of West Germany (1984–90), coaching the team to success in the 1990 World Cup

Becker Boris born 1967, German tennis player: Wimbledon champion 1985, 1986, and 1989: the youngest man ever to win Wimbledon

Becket Saint Thomas à 1118–70, English prelate; chancellor (1155–62) to Henry II; archbishop of Canterbury (1162–70): murdered following his opposition to Henry's attempts to control the clergy. Feast day: Dec 29 or July 7

Beckett 1 Margaret Mary born 1943, British Labour politician: leader of the House of Commons (1998–2001); secretary of state for environment, food, and rural affairs (2001–) 2 Samuel (Barclay). 1906–89, Irish dramatist and novelist writing in French and English, whose works portray the human condition as insignificant or absurd in a bleak universe. They include the plays *En attendant Godot* (*Waiting for Godot*, 1952), *Fin de partie* (*Endgame*, 1957), and *Not I* (1973) and the novel *Malone meurt* (*Malone Dies*, 1951): Nobel prize for literature 1969

Beckford William 1759–1844, English writer and dilettante; author of the oriental romance *Vathek* (1787)

Beckham David born 1975, British footballer; captain of England from 2000: married to the pop singer Victoria Beckham ("Posh Spice" of the Spice Girls)

Beckmann 1 Ernst Otto 1853–1923, German chemist: devised the Beckmann thermometer, used for measuring small temperature changes in liquids 2 Max 1884–1950, German expressionist painter

becoming (in the philosophy of Aristotle) any change from the lower level of potentiality to the higher level of actuality

becquerel the derived SI unit of radioactivity equal to one disintegration per second.

Becquerel Antoine Henri 1852–1908, French physicist, who discovered the photographic action of the rays emitted by uranium salts and so instigated the study of radioactivity: Nobel prize for physics 1903

bed 1 *Med* a unit of potential occupancy in a hospital or residential institution 2 a plot of ground in which plants are grown, esp when considered together with the plants in it 3 the bottom of a river, lake, or sea 4 a layer of crushed rock, gravel, etc, used as a foundation for a road, railway, etc 5 a layer of rock, esp sedimentary rock 6 a layer of solid particles of an absorbent, catalyst, or reagent through which a fluid is passed during the course of a chemical reaction or other process 7 a machine base on which a moving part carrying a tool or workpiece slides 8 **go to bed** *Journalism, Printing* (of a newspaper, magazine, etc) to go to press; start printing 9 **put to bed** a *Journalism* to finalize work on (a newspaper, magazine, etc) so that it is ready to go to press b *Printing* to lock up the type forme of (a publication) in the press before printing

bedbug any of several bloodsucking insects of the heteropterous genus *Cimex*, esp *C. lectularius* of temperate regions, having an oval flattened wingless body and infesting dirty houses: family *Cimicidae*

bedding 1 something acting as a foundation, such as mortar under a brick 2 the arrangement of a mass of rocks into distinct layers; stratification

Beddoes Thomas Lovell 1803–49, British poet, noted for his macabre imagery, esp in *Death's Jest-Book* (1850)

Bede Saint, known as *the Venerable Bede*. ?673–735 AD, English monk, scholar, historian, and theologian, noted for his Latin *Ecclesiastical History of the English People* (731). Feast day: May 27 or 25

Bedford¹ 1 David born 1937, British composer, influenced by rock music 2 Duke of, title of *John of Lancaster*. 1389–1435, son of Henry IV of England: protector of England and regent of France (1422–35)

Bedford² 1 a town in SE central England, administrative centre of Bedfordshire, on the River Ouse. Pop: 82 488 (2001) 2 short for **Bedfordshire**

Bedfordshire a county of S central England: mainly low-lying, with the Chiltern Hills in the south: the geographical county includes Luton, which became a separate unitary authority in 1997. Administrative centre: Bedford. Pop. (excluding Luton): 388 600 (2003 est). Area (excluding Luton): 1192 sq km (460 sq miles)

bedlam *Archaic* a lunatic asylum; madhouse

Bedouin *or* **Beduin** a member of any of the nomadic tribes of Arabs inhabiting the deserts of Arabia, Jordan, and Syria, as well as parts of the Sahara

bedrock the solid unweathered rock that lies beneath the loose surface deposits of soil, alluvium, etc

bedstraw any of numerous rubiaceous plants of the genus *Galium*, which have small white or yellow flowers and prickly or hairy fruits: some species formerly used as straw for beds as they are aromatic when dry

Bedworth a town in central England, in N Warwickshire. Pop: 30 001 (2001)

bee¹ any hymenopterous insect of the superfamily *Apoidea*, which includes social forms such as the honeybee and solitary forms such as the carpenter bee

bee² *Nautical* a small sheave with one cheek removed and the pulley and other cheek fastened flat to a boom or another spar, used for reeving outhauls or stays

beech 1 any N temperate tree of the genus *Fagus*, esp *F. sylvatica* of Europe, having smooth greyish bark: family *Fagaceae* 2 any tree of the related genus *Nothofagus*, of temperate Australasia and South America 3 the hard wood of any of these trees, used in making furniture, etc 4 See copper beech

Beecham Sir Thomas 1879–1961, English conductor who did much to promote the works of Delius, Sibelius, and Richard Strauss

beechnut the small brown triangular edible nut of the beech tree. Collectively, the nuts are often termed beech mast, esp when lying on the ground

beef 1 the flesh of a cow, bull, or ox. 2 an adult ox, bull, cow, etc, reared for its meat

Beelzebub *Old Testament* a god of the Philistines (2 Kings 1:2)

beer 1 an alcoholic drink brewed from malt, sugar, hops, and water and fermented with yeast 2 a slightly fermented drink made from the roots or leaves of certain plants

▷www.realbeer.com
▷www.howstuffworks.com/beer.htm
▷www.beerinfo.com/vlib
▷www.camra.org.uk
▷www.history-of-beer.com

Beerbohm Sir (Henry) Max(imilian). 1872–1956, English critic, wit, and caricaturist, whose works include *Zuleika Dobson* (1911), a satire on Oxford undergraduates

Beersheba a town in S Israel: commercial centre of the Negev. In biblical times it marked the southern limit of Palestine. Pop: 183 000 (2003 est)

beeswax a a yellowish or dark brown wax secreted by honeybees for constructing honeycombs b this wax after refining, purifying, etc, used in polishes, ointments, and for modelling

beet 1 any chenopodiaceous plant of the genus *Beta*, esp the Eurasian species *B. vulgaris*, widely cultivated in such varieties as the sugar beet, mangelwurzel, beetroot, and spinach beet 2 the leaves of any of several varieties of this plant, which are cooked and eaten as a vegetable 3 red beet the US name for beetroot

Beethoven Ludwig van 1770–1827, German composer, who greatly extended the form and scope of symphonic and chamber music, bridging the classical and romantic traditions. His works include nine symphonies, 32 piano sonatas, 16 string quartets, five piano concertos, a violin concerto, two masses, the opera *Fidelio* (1805), and choral music

beetle¹ 1 any insect of the order *Coleoptera*, having biting mouthparts and forewings modified to form shell-like protective elytra 2 a game played with dice in which the players draw or assemble a beetle-shaped form

beetle² 1 a heavy hand tool, usually made of wood, used for ramming, pounding, or beating 2 a machine used to finish cloth by stamping it with wooden hammers

Beeton Isabella Mary, known as *Mrs Beeton*. 1836–65, British cookery writer, author of *The Book of Household Management* (1861)

beetroot 1 a variety of the beet plant, *Beta vulgaris*, that has a bulbous dark red root that may be eaten as a vegetable, in salads, or pickled 2 the root of this plant

beet sugar the sucrose obtained from sugar beet, identical in composition to cane sugar

Begin Menachem 1913–92, Israeli statesman, born in Poland. In Palestine after 1942, he became a leader of the militant Zionists; prime minister of Israel (1977–83); Nobel peace prize jointly with Sadat 1978. In 1979 he concluded the Camp David treaty with Anwar Sadat of Egypt

begonia any plant of the genus *Begonia*, of warm and tropical regions, widely cultivated for their ornamental leaves and waxy flowers: family *Begoniaceae*

beguine 1 a dance of South American origin in bolero rhythm 2 a piece of music in the rhythm of this dance

Behan Brendan 1923–64, Irish writer, noted esp for his plays *The Quare Fellow* (1954) and *The Hostage* (1958) and for an account of his detention as a member of the Irish Republican Army, *Borstal Boy* (1958)

behaviour *or US* **behavior** *Psychol* a the aggregate of all the responses made by an organism in any situation b a specific response of a certain organism to a specific stimulus or group of stimuli

behavioural science the application of scientific methods to the study of the behaviour of organisms

behaviourism *or US* **behaviorism** 1 a school of psychology that regards the objective observation of the behaviour of organisms (usually by means of automatic recording devices) as the only proper subject for study and that often refuses to postulate any intervening mechanisms between the stimulus and the response 2 *Philosophy* the doctrine that the mind has no separate existence but that statements about the mind and mental states can be analysed into statements about actual and potential behaviour

behemoth *Old Testament* a gigantic beast, probably a hippopotamus, described in Job 40:15

behind *Australian Rules football* a score of one point made by kicking the ball over the behind line between a goalpost and one of the smaller outer posts (behind posts)

Behistun, Bisitun, *or* **Bisutun** a village in W Iran by the ancient road from Ecbatana to Babylon. On a nearby cliff is an inscription by Darius in Old Persian, Elamite, and Babylonian describing his enthronement

Behn Aphra 1640–89, English dramatist and novelist, best known for her play *The Rover* (1678) and her novel *Oroonoko* (1688)

Behrens Peter 1868–1940, German architect

Behring 1 Emil (Adolf) von 1854–1917, German bacteriologist, who discovered diphtheria and tetanus antitoxins: Nobel prize for physiology or medicine 1901 2

Beiderbecke Leon Bismarcke, known as *Bix*. 1903–31, US jazz cornettist, composer, and pianist

beige 1 a a very light brown, sometimes with a yellow-ish tinge, similar to the colour of undyed wool **b** (as adjective): *beige gloves* **2** a fabric made of undyed or unbleached wool

Beijing the capital of the People's Republic of China, in the northeast in central Hebei province: dates back to the 12th century BC; consists of two central walled cities, the Outer City (containing the commercial quarter) and the Inner City, which contains the Imperial City, within which is the Purple or Forbidden City; three universities. Pop: 10 849 000 (2005 est)

being (in the philosophy of Aristotle) actuality

Beira a port in E Mozambique: terminus of a transcontinental railway from Lobito, Angola, through the Democratic Republic of Congo (formerly Zaïre), Zambia, and Zimbabwe. Pop: 566 000 (2005 est)

Beirut *or* **Beyrouth** the capital of Lebanon, a port on the Mediterranean: part of the Ottoman Empire from the 16th century until 1918; four universities (Lebanese, American, French, and Arab). Pop: 1 875 000 (2005 est)

Bekaa *or* **Beqaa** a broad valley in central Lebanon, between the Lebanon and Anti-Lebanon Mountains

bel a unit for comparing two power levels, equal to the logarithm to the base ten of the ratio of the two powers.

Belarus, Byelorussia, *or* **Belorussia** a republic in E Europe; part of the medieval Lithuanian and Polish empires before occupied by Russia; a Soviet republic (1919–91); in 1997 formed a close political and economic union with Russia: mainly low-lying and forested. Languages: Belarussian; Russian. Religion: believers are mostly Christian. Currency: rouble. Capital: Minsk. Pop: 9 851 000 (2004 est). Area: 207 600 sq km (80 134 sq miles)

Belarussian, Belarusian, Byelorussian *or* **Belorussian 1** of, relating to, or characteristic of Belarus, its people, or their language **2** the official language of Belarus: an East Slavonic language closely related to Russian **3** a native or inhabitant of Belarus

belay *Mountaineering* the attachment (of a climber) to a mountain by tying the rope off round a rock spike, piton, nut, etc, to safeguard the party in the event of a fall

Belfast 1 the capital of Northern Ireland, a port on Belfast Lough in Belfast district, Co. Antrim and Co. Down: became the centre of Irish Protestantism and of the linen industry in the 17th century; seat of the Northern Ireland assembly and executive. Pop: 276 459 (2001) **2** a district of W Northern Ireland, in Co. Antrim and Co. Down. Pop: 271 596 (2003 est). Area: 115 sq km (44 sq miles)

Belfort 1 Territoire de a department of E France, now in Franche-Comté region: the only part of Alsace remaining to France after 1871. Capital: Belfort. Pop: Pop: 139 383 (2003 est). Area: 608 sq km (237 sq miles) **2** a fortress town in E France: strategically situated in the **Belfort Gap** between the Vosges and the Jura mountains. Pop: 50 417 (1999)

belfry 1 the part of a tower or steeple in which bells are hung **2** a tower or steeple **3** the timber framework inside a tower or steeple on which bells are hung

Belgaum a city in India, in Karnataka: cotton, furniture, leather. Pop: 399 600 (2001)

Belgian Congo a former name (1908–60) of (Democratic Republic of) **Congo** (sense 1)

Belgium a federal kingdom in NW Europe: at various times under the rulers of Burgundy, Spain, Austria, France, and the Netherlands before becoming an independent kingdom in 1830. It formed the Benelux customs union with the Netherlands and Luxembourg in 1948 and and was a founder member of the Common Market, now the European Union. It consists chiefly of a low-lying region of sand, woods, and heath (the Campine) in the north and west, and a fertile undulating central plain rising to the Ardennes Mountains in the southeast. Languages: French, Flemish (Dutch), German. Religion: Roman Catholic majority. Currency: euro. Capital: Brussels. Pop: 10 339 000 (2004 est). Area: 30 513 sq km (11 778 sq miles)

Belgorod-Dnestrovski *or* **Byelgorod-Dnestrovski** a port in SW Ukraine, on the Dniester estuary: belonged to Romania from 1918 until 1940; under Soviet rule (1944–91). Pop: 56 800 (1991 est)

Belgrade the capital of the Union of Serbia and Montenegro and of Serbia, in the E part at the confluence of the Danube and Sava Rivers: became the capital of Serbia in 1878 and of Yugoslavia in 1929. Pop: 1 280 639 (2002)

Belgravia a fashionable residential district of W central London, around Belgrave Square

Belial 1 a demon mentioned frequently in apocalyptic literature: identified in the Christian tradition with the devil or Satan **2** (in the Old Testament and rabbinical literature) worthlessness or wickedness

Belisarius ?505–565 AD, Byzantine general under Justinian I. He recovered North Africa from the Vandals and Italy from the Ostrogoths and led forces against the Persians

Belisha beacon a flashing light in an orange globe mounted on a post, indicating a pedestrian crossing on a road

Belize a state in Central America, on the Caribbean Sea: site of a Mayan civilization until the 9th century AD; colonized by the British from 1638; granted internal self-government in 1964; became an independent state within the Commonwealth in 1981. Official language: English; Carib and Spanish are also spoken. Currency: Belize dollar. Capital: Belmopan. Pop: 261 000 (2004 est). Area: 22 965 sq km (8867 sq miles)

Belize City a port and the largest city in Belize, on the Caribbean coast: capital until 1973, when that function was transferred inland to Belmopan owing to hurricane risk. Pop: 53 000 (2005 est)

bell¹ 1 a hollow, usually metal, cup-shaped instrument that emits a musical ringing sound when struck, often by a clapper hanging inside it **2** an electrical device that rings or buzzes as a signal **3** the bowl-shaped termination of the tube of certain musical wind instruments, such as the trumpet or oboe **4** any musical percussion instrument emitting a ringing tone, such as a glockenspiel, one of a set of hand bells, etc **5** *Nautical* a signal rung on a ship's bell to count the number of half-hour intervals during each of six four-hour watches reckoned from midnight. Thus, one bell may signify 12.30, 4.30, or 8.30 am or pm **6** See **diving bell 7** *Biology* a structure resembling a bell in shape, such as the corolla of certain flowers or the body of a jellyfish **8 bell, book, and candle** instruments used formerly in excommunications and other ecclesiastical acts

bell² a bellowing or baying cry, esp that of a hound or a male deer in rut

Bell 1 Acton, Currer, and **Ellis** pen names of the sisters Anne, Charlotte, and Emily **Brontë 2 Alexander Graham** 1847–1922, US scientist, born in Scotland, who invented the telephone (1876) **3** Sir **Francis Henry Dillon** 1851–1936, New Zealand statesman; prime minister of New Zealand (1925) **4 Gertrude (Margaret Lowthian)**. 1868–1926, British traveller, writer, and diplomat; secretary to the British High Commissioner in Baghdad (1917–26) **5 Joshua** born 1967, US violinist **6 (Susan) Jocelyn**, married name *Jocelyn Burnell*, born 1943, British radio astronomer, who discovered the first pulsar **7 Vanessa**, original name *Vanessa Stephen*. 1879–1961, British painter; a member of the Bloomsbury group, sister of Virginia Woolf and wife of the art critic Clive Bell (1881–1964)

belladonna 1 either of two alkaloid drugs, atropine or hyoscyamine, obtained from the leaves and roots of the deadly nightshade **2** another name for **deadly nightshade**

Bellarmine Saint Robert 1542–1621, Italian Jesuit theologian and cardinal; an important influence during the Counter-Reformation

Bellay Joachim du 1522–60, French poet, a member of the Pléiade

Belleau Wood a forest in N France: site of a battle (1918) in which the US Marines halted a German advance on Paris

Belle Isle an island in the Atlantic, at the N entrance to the **Strait of Belle Isle**, between Labrador and Newfoundland. Area: about 39 sq km (15 sq miles)

belles-lettres literary works, esp essays and poetry, valued for their aesthetic rather than their informative or moral content

Bellingshausen Sea an area of the S Pacific Ocean off the coast of Antarctica

Bellini 1 Giovanni ?1430–1516, Italian painter of the Venetian school, noted for his altarpieces, landscapes, and Madonnas. His father **Jacopo** (?1400–70) and his brother **Gentile** (?1429–1507) were also painters **2 Vincenzo** 1801–35, Italian composer of operas, esp *La Sonnambula* (1831) and *Norma* (1831)

Bellinzona a town in SE central Switzerland, capital of Ticino canton. Pop: 16 463 (2000)

Belloc Hilaire 1870–1953, British poet, essayist, and historian, born in France, noted particularly for his verse for children in *The Bad Child's Book of Beasts* (1896) and *Cautionary Tales* (1907)

bellow the characteristic noise of a bull

Bellow Saul 1915–2005, US novelist, born in Canada. His works include *Dangling Man* (1944), *The Adventures of Angie March* (1954), *Herzog* (1964), *Humboldt's Gift* (1975), *The Dean's December* (1981), and *Ravelstein* (2000): Nobel prize for literature 1976

bellows 1 an instrument consisting of an air chamber with flexible sides or end, a means of compressing it, an inlet valve, and a constricted outlet that is used to create a stream of air, as for producing a draught for a fire or for sounding organ pipes **2** *Photog* a telescopic light-tight sleeve, connecting the lens system of some cameras to the body of the instrument **3** a flexible corrugated element used as an expansion joint, pump, or means of transmitting axial motion

belly 1 the lower or front part of the body of a vertebrate, containing the intestines and other abdominal organs; abdomen **2** the surface of a stringed musical instrument over which the strings are stretched **3** the thick central part of certain muscles **4** *Austral and NZ* the wool from a sheep's belly **5** *Archery* the surface of the bow next to the bowstring

belly dance a sensuous and provocative dance of Middle Eastern origin, performed by women, with undulating movements of the hips and abdomen

Belmopan (since 1973) the capital of Belize, about 50 miles inland: founded in 1970. Pop: 10 000 (2005 est)

Belo Horizonte a city in SE Brazil, the capital of Minas Gerais state. Pop: 5 304 000 (2005 est)

Belsen a village in NE Germany: with Bergen, the site of a Nazi concentration camp (1943–45)

Belshazzar 6th century BC, the son of Nabonidus, coregent of Babylon with his father for eight years: referred to as king and son of Nebuchadnezzar in the Old Testament (Daniel 5:1, 17; 8:1); described as having received a divine message of doom written on a wall at a banquet (**Belshazzar's Feast**)

belt 1 See **seat belt 2** a band of flexible material between rotating shafts or pulleys to transfer motion or transmit goods **3** short for **beltcourse** (see **cordon**(sense 4)) **4 below the belt** *Boxing* below the waist, esp in the groin

beluga 1 a large white sturgeon, *Acipenser* (or *Huso*) *huso*, of the Black and Caspian Seas: a source of caviar and isinglass **2** a small white-toothed whale, *Delphinapterus leucas*, of northern waters: family *Monodontidae*

belvedere a building, such as a summerhouse or roofed gallery, sited to command a fine view

Bembo Pietro 1470–1547, Italian scholar, poet, and cardinal (1539). His treatise *Prose della volgar lingua* (1525) helped to establish a standard form of literary Italian

ben¹ *Scot* an inner room in a house or cottage

ben² **1** any of several Asiatic trees of the genus *Moringa*, esp *M. oleifera* of Arabia and India, whose seeds yield **oil of ben**, used in manufacturing perfumes and cosmetics, lubricating delicate machinery, etc.: family *Moringaceae* **2** the seed of such a tree

ben³ *Scot, Irish* a mountain peak (esp in place names)

Ben Bella Mohammed Ahmed born 1916, Algerian statesman: first prime minister (1962–65) and president (1963–65) of independent Algeria: overthrown and imprisoned (1965–80)

Benbow John 1653–1702, English admiral, noted esp for his heroic death during the War of the Spanish Succession

bench 1 the bench a a judge or magistrate sitting in court in a judicial capacity **b** judges or magistrates collectively **2** *Geology* a flat narrow platform of land, esp one marking a former shoreline

bench press a weight-training exercise in which a person lies on a bench and pushes a barbell upwards with both hands from chest level until the arms are straight, then lowers it again

bend *Nautical* a knot or eye in a line for joining it to another or to an object

Bendigo a city in SE Australia, in central Victoria: founded in 1851 after the discovery of gold. Pop: 68 715 (2001)

Benedict Saint ?480–?547 AD, Italian monk: founded the Benedictine order at Monte Cassino in Italy in about 540 AD. His *Regula Monachorum* became the basis of the rule of all Western Christian monastic orders. Feast day: July 11 or March 14

Benedictine 1 a monk or nun who is a member of a Christian religious community founded by or following the rule of Saint Benedict (?480–?547 AD), the Italian monk 2 a greenish-yellow liqueur made from a secret formula developed at the Benedictine monastery at Fécamp in France in about 1510

benediction 1 an invocation of divine blessing, esp at the end of a Christian religious ceremony 2 a Roman Catholic service in which the congregation is blessed with the sacrament

Benedict XV original name *Giacomo della Chiesa*. 1854–1922, pope (1914–22); noted for his repeated attempts to end World War I and for his organization of war relief

benefice 1 *Christianity* an endowed Church office yielding an income to its holder; a Church living 2 the property or revenue attached to such an office 3 (in feudal society) a tenement (piece of land) held by a vassal from a landowner on easy terms or free, esp in return for military support

Benedict XVI original name *Joseph Ratzinger*. born 1927, pope from 2005

beneficial *Law* entitling a person to receive the profits or proceeds of property

beneficiary 1 *Law* a person entitled to receive funds or other property under a trust, will, or insurance policy 2 the holder of an ecclesiastical or other benefice 3 NZ a person who receives government assistance

benefit an allowance paid by the government for sickness, unemployment, etc, to which a person is entitled under social security or the national insurance scheme

Benelux 1 the customs union formed by Belgium, the Netherlands, and Luxembourg in 1948; became an economic union in 1960 2 these countries collectively

Beneš Eduard 1884–1948, Czech statesman; president of Czechoslovakia (1935–38; 1946–48) and of its government in exile (1939–45)

Benevento a city in S Italy, in N Campania: at various times under Samnite, Roman, Lombard, Saracen, Norman, and papal rule. Pop: 61 791 (2001)

benevolence (in the Middle Ages) a forced loan or contribution exacted by English kings from their nobility and subjects

Benfleet a town in SE England, in S Essex on an inlet of the Thames estuary. Pop: 48 539 (2001)

Bengal 1 a former province of NE India, in the great deltas of the Ganges and Brahmaputra Rivers: in 1947 divided into West Bengal (belonging to India) and East Bengal (Bangladesh) 2 **Bay of** a wide arm of the Indian

Ocean, between India and Myanmar 3 a breed of medium-large cat with a spotted or marbled coat

Bengali 1 a member of a people living chiefly in Bangladesh and in West Bengal. The West Bengalis are mainly Hindus; the East Bengalis of Bangladesh are mainly Muslims 2 the language of this people: the official language of Bangladesh and the chief language of West Bengal; it belongs to the Indic branch of the Indo-European family

Bengbu, Pengpu, or **Pang-fou** a city in E China, in Anhui province. Pop: 779 000 (2005 est)

Benghazi or **Bengasi** a port in N Libya, on the Gulf of Sidra: centre of Italian colonization (1911–42); scene of much fighting in World War II. Pop: 1 080 500 (2002 est)

Benguela a port in W Angola: founded in 1617; a terminus (with Lobito) of the railway that runs from Beira in Mozambique through the Copper Belt of Zambia and Zimbabwe. Pop: 41 000 (latest est)

Ben-Gurion David, original name *David Gruen*. 1886–1973, Israeli socialist statesman, born in Poland; first prime minister of Israel (1948–53; 1955–63)

Beni a river in N Bolivia, rising in the E Cordillera of the Andes and flowing north to the Marmoré River. Length: over 1600 km (1000 miles)

benign *Pathol* (of a tumour, etc) not threatening to life or health; not malignant

Beni Hasan a village in central Egypt, on the Nile, with cliff-cut tombs dating from 2000 BC

Benin 1 a republic in W Africa, on the **Bight of Benin**, a section of the Gulf of Guinea: in the early 19th century a powerful kingdom, famed for its women warriors; became a French colony in 1893, gaining independence in 1960. It consists chiefly of coastal lagoons and swamps in the south, a fertile plain and marshes in the centre, and the Atakora Mountains in the northwest. Official language: French. Religion: animist majority. Currency: franc. Capital: Porto Novo (the government is based in Cotonou). Pop: 6 918 000 (2004 est). Area: 112 622 sq km (43 474 sq miles) 2 a former kingdom of W Africa, powerful from the 14th to the 17th centuries: now a province of S Nigeria: noted for its bronzes

Benin City a city in S Nigeria, capital of Edo state: former capital of the kingdom of Benin. Pop: 1 022 000 (2005 est)

Benjamin¹ 1 Arthur 1893–1960, Australian composer. In addition to *Jamaican Rumba* (1938), he wrote five operas and a harmonica concerto (1953) 2 **Walter** 1892–1940, German critic and cultural theorist

Benjamin² *Old Testament* a the youngest and best-loved son of Jacob and Rachel (Genesis 35:16–18; 42:4) b the tribe descended from this patriarch c the territory of this tribe, northwest of the Dead Sea

Ben Lomond 1 a mountain in W central Scotland, on the E side of Loch Lomond. Height: 973 m (3192 ft) 2 a mountain in NE Tasmania. Height: 1527 m (5010 ft) 3 a mountain in SE Australia, in NE New South Wales. Height: 1520 m (4986 ft)

Bennett 1 Alan born 1934, British actor and playwright. His plays include *Forty Years On* (1968), *The Old Country* (1977), *The Madness of George III* (1991), *The History Boys* (2004), and the monologues for television *Talking Heads*

(1987, 1998) **2 (Enoch) Arnold** 1867–1931, British novelist, noted for *The Old Wives' Tale* (1908), *Clayhanger* (1910), and other works set in the Staffordshire Potteries **3 James Gordon** 1837–1931, US newspaper editor, born in Scotland. He founded (1835) the *New York Herald* and introduced techniques of modern news reporting **4 Jill** 1931–90, British actress **5 Richard Bedford**, 1st Viscount. 1870–1947, Canadian Conservative statesman; prime minister (1930–35) **6 Sir Richard Rodney** born 1936, British composer, noted for film music and his operas *The Mines of Sulphur* (1965) and *Victory* (1970)

Ben Nevis a mountain in W Scotland, in the Grampian mountains: highest peak in Great Britain. Height: 1344 m (4408 ft)

Bennington a town in SW Vermont: the site of a British defeat (1777) in the War of American Independence. Pop: 15 637 (2003 est)

Benny Jack, real name *Benjamin Kubelsky*. 1894–1974, US comedian

Benoni a city in NE South Africa: gold mines. Pop: 94 341 (2001)

bent *Civil engineering* a framework placed across a structure to stiffen it

Bentham Jeremy 1748–1832, British philosopher and jurist: a founder of utilitarianism. His works include *A Fragment on Government* (1776) and *Introduction to the Principles of Morals and Legislation* (1789)

Benthamism the philosophy of utilitarianism as first expounded by the British philosopher and jurist Jeremy Bentham (1748–1832) in terms of an action being good that has a greater tendency to augment the happiness of the community than to diminish it

Bentinck Lord **William Cavendish** 1774–1839, British statesman, governor general of Bengal (1828–35)

Bentley Edmund Clerihew 1875–1956, English journalist, noted for his invention of the clerihew

Benue 1 a state of SE Nigeria, formed in 1976 from part of Benue-Plateau state. Capital: Makurdi. Pop: 3 108 754 (1995 est). Area: 34 059 sq km (13 150 sq miles) **2** a river in W Africa, rising in N Cameroon and flowing west across Nigeria: chief tributary of the River Niger. Length: 1400 km (870 miles)

Benxi, Penchi, *or* **Penki** an industrial city in SE China, in S Liaoning province. Pop: 967 000 (2005 est)

Benz Karl (**Friedrich**). 1844–1929, German engineer; designed and built the first car to be driven by an internal-combustion engine (1885)

benzene a colourless flammable toxic aromatic liquid used in the manufacture of styrene, phenol, etc, as a solvent for fats, resins, etc, and as an insecticide. Formula: C_6H_6

benzine *or* **benzin** a volatile mixture of the lighter aliphatic hydrocarbon constituents of petroleum

bequest *Law* a gift of property by will, esp personal property

Berar a region of W central India: part of Maharashtra state since 1956; important for cotton growing

Berber 1 a member of a Caucasoid Muslim people of N Africa **2** the language of this people, forming a subfamily of the Afro-Asiatic family of languages. There are extensive differences between dialects

Berbera a port in N Somalia, on the Gulf of Aden. Pop:

70 000 (1990 est)

berberis any shrub of the berberidaceous genus *Berberis*

berceuse 1 a cradlesong or lullaby **2** an instrumental piece suggestive of this, in six-eight time

Berchtesgaden a town in Germany, in SE Bavaria: site of the fortified mountain retreat of Adolf Hitler. Pop: 7667 (2003 est)

Berezina a river in Belarus, rising in the north and flowing south to the River Dnieper: linked with the River Dvina and the Baltic Sea by the **Berezina Canal**. Length: 563 km (350 miles)

Berezniki a city in E Russia: chemical industries. Pop: 169 000 (2005 est)

Berg 1 Alban (**Maria Johannes**). 1885–1935, Austrian composer: a pupil of Schoenberg. His works include the operas *Wozzeck* (1921) and *Lulu* (1935), a violin concerto (1935), chamber works, and songs **2 Paul** born 1926, US molecular biologist, the first to identify transfer RNA (1956). Nobel prize for chemistry 1980

Bergamo a walled city in N Italy, in Lombardy. Pop: 113 143 (2001)

bergamot 1 a small Asian spiny rutaceous tree, *Citrus bergamia*, having sour pear-shaped fruit **2** essence of bergamot a fragrant essential oil from the fruit rind of this plant, used in perfumery and some teas (including Earl Grey) **3** a Mediterranean mint, *Mentha citrata*, that yields an oil similar to essence of bergamot **4 a wild bergamot** a North American plant, *Monarda fistulosa*, with clusters of purple flowers: family *Lamiaceae* (labiates) **b** a garden plant of the same genus, usually *M. didyma* (bee balm), grown for its scarlet or pink flowers **5** a variety of pear

Bergen 1 a port in SW Norway: chief city in medieval times. Pop: 237 430 (2004 est) **2** the Flemish name for **Mons**

Bergius Friedrich (**Karl Rudolph**). 1884–1949, German chemist, who invented a process for producing oil by high-pressure hydrogenation of coal: Nobel prize for chemistry 1931

Bergman 1 (**Ernst**) **Ingmar** born 1918, Swedish film and stage director, whose films include *The Seventh Seal* (1956), *Wild Strawberries* (1957), *Persona* (1966), *Scenes from a Marriage* (1974), *Autumn Sonata* (1978), and *Fanny and Alexander* (1982) **2 Ingrid** 1915–82, Swedish film and stage actress, working in Hollywood 1938–48; noted for her leading roles in many films, including *Casablanca* (1942), *For Whom the Bell Tolls* (1943), *Anastasia* (1956), and *The Inn of the Sixth Happiness* (1958)

Bergson Henri Louis 1859–1941, French philosopher, who sought to bridge the gap between metaphysics and science. His main works are *Memory and Matter* (1896, trans. 1911) and *Creative Evolution* (1907, trans. 1911): Nobel prize for literature 1927

Beria Lavrenti Pavlovich 1899–1953, Soviet chief of secret police; killed by his associates shortly after Stalin's death

Bering *or* **Behring** Vitus 1681–1741, Danish navigator, who explored the N Pacific for the Russians and discovered Bering Island and the Bering Strait

Bering Sea a part of the N Pacific Ocean, between NE Siberia and Alaska. Area: about 2 275 000 sq km (878 000 sq miles)

Bering Strait a strait between Alaska and Russia, connecting the Bering Sea and the Arctic Ocean

Berkeley¹ **1** Busby real name *William Berkeley Enos*. 1895–1976, US dance director, noted esp for his elaborate choreography in film musicals **2** George 1685–1753, Irish philosopher and Anglican bishop, whose system of subjective idealism was expounded in his works *A Treatise concerning the Principles of Human Knowledge* (1710) and *Three Dialogues between Hylas and Philonous* (1713). He also wrote *Essay towards a New Theory of Vision* (1709) **3** Sir Lennox (**Randal Francis**). 1903–89, British composer; his works include four symphonies, four operas, and the *Serenade for Strings* (1939)

Berkeley² a city in W California, on San Francisco Bay: seat of the University of California. Pop: 102 049 (2003 est)

berkelium a metallic transuranic element produced by bombardment of americium. Symbol: Bk; atomic no.: 97; half-life of most stable isotope, ²⁴⁷Bk: 1400 years; valency: 3 or 4; relative density: 14 (est)

Berkshire **1** a historic county of S England: since reorganization in 1974 the River Thames has marked the N boundary while the **Berkshire Downs** occupy central parts; the county council was replaced by six unitary authorities in 1998. Area: 1259 sq km (486 sq miles) **2** a rare breed of pork and bacon pig having a black body and white points

Berlin¹ **1** Irving original name *Israel Baline*, 1888–1989, US composer and writer of lyrics, born in Russia. His musical comedies include *Annie Get Your Gun* (1946); his most popular song is *White Christmas* **2** Sir **Isaiah** 1909–97, British philosopher, born in Latvia, historian, and diplomat. His books include *Historical Inevitability* (1954) and *The Magus of the North* (1993)

Berlin² the capital of Germany (1871–1945 and from 1990), formerly divided (1945–90) into the eastern sector, capital of East Germany, and the western sectors, which formed an exclave in East German territory closely affiliated with West Germany: a wall dividing the sectors was built in 1961 by the East German authorities to stop the flow of refugees from east to west; demolition of the wall began in 1989 and the city was formally reunited in 1990: formerly (1618–1871) the capital of Brandenburg and Prussia. Pop: 3 388 477 (2003 est)

Berlioz Hector (**Louis**). 1803–69, French composer, regarded as a pioneer of modern orchestration. His works include the cantata *La Damnation de Faust* (1846), the operas *Les Troyens* (1856–59) and *Béatrice et Bénédict* (1860–62), the *Symphonie fantastique* (1830), and the oratorio *L'Enfance du Christ* (1854)

Berlusconi Silvio born 1936, Italian politician and media tycoon: prime minister of Italy (1994, from 2001)

Bermejo a river in Argentina, rising in the northwest and flowing southeast to the Paraguay River. Length: about 1600 km (1000 miles)

Bermuda a UK Overseas Territory consisting of a group of over 150 coral islands (**the Bermudas**) in the NW Atlantic: discovered in about 1503, colonized by the British by 1612, although not acquired by the British crown until 1684. Capital: Hamilton. Pop: 82 000 (2003 est). Area: 53 sq km (20 sq miles)

Bermuda Triangle an area in the Atlantic Ocean bounded by Bermuda, Puerto Rico, and Florida where ships and aeroplanes are alleged to have disappeared mysteriously

Bern **1** the capital of Switzerland, in the W part, on the Aar River: entered the Swiss confederation in 1353 and became the capital in 1848. Pop: 122 700 (2002 est) **2** a canton of Switzerland, between the French frontier and the Bernese Alps. Capital: Bern. Pop: 950 200 (2002 est). Area: 6884 sq km (2658 sq miles)

Bernadette of Lourdes Saint original name *Marie Bernarde Soubirous*. 1844–79, French peasant girl born in Lourdes, whose visions of the Virgin Mary led to the establishment of Lourdes as a centre of pilgrimage, esp for the sick or crippled. Feast day: Feb 18

Bernadotte **1** Folke , Count. 1895–1948, Swedish diplomat, noted for his work with the Red Cross during World War II and as United Nations mediator in Palestine (1948). He was assassinated by Jewish terrorists **2** Jean Baptiste Jules 1764–1844, French marshal under Napoleon; king of Norway and Sweden (1818–44) as Charles XIV

Bernard **1** Claude 1813–78, French physiologist, noted for his research on the action of secretions of the alimentary canal and the glycogenic function of the liver **2** Saint, known as *Bernard of Menthon* and the *Apostle of the Alps*. 923–1008, French monk who founded hospices in the Alpine passes. Feast day: Aug 20

Bernard of Clairvaux Saint ?1090–1153, French abbot and theologian, who founded the stricter branch of the Cistercians in 1115

Bernese Alps *or* **Oberland** a mountain range in SW Switzerland, the N central part of the Alps. Highest peak: Finsteraarhorn, 4274 m (14 022 ft)

Bernhardt Sarah original name *Rosine Bernard*. 1844–1923, French actress, regarded as one of the greatest tragic actresses of all time

Bernina Piz a mountain in SE Switzerland, the highest peak of the **Bernina Alps** in the S Rhaetian Alps. Height: 4049 m (13 284 ft)

Bernina Pass a pass in the Alps between SE Switzerland and N Italy, east of Piz Bernina. Height: 2323 m (7622 ft)

Bernini Gian Lorenzo 1598–1680, Italian painter, architect, and sculptor: the greatest exponent of the Italian baroque

Bernoulli *or* **Bernouilli** **1** Daniel , son of Jean Bernoulli. 1700–82, Swiss mathematician and physicist, who developed an early form of the kinetic theory of gases and stated the principle of conservation of energy in fluid dynamics **2** Jacques *or* Jakob 1654–1705, Swiss mathematician, noted for his work on calculus and the theory of probability **3** his brother, Jean *or* Johann 1667–1748, Swiss mathematician who developed the calculus of variations

Bernstein Leonard 1918–90, US conductor and composer, whose works include *The Age of Anxiety* (1949), the score of the musical *West Side Story* (1957), and *Mass* (1971)

berry **1** any of various small edible fruits such as the blackberry and strawberry **2** *Botany* an indehiscent fruit with two or more seeds and a fleshy pericarp, such as the grape or gooseberry **3** any of various seeds or dried kernels, such as a coffee bean **4** the egg of a lobster, crayfish, or similar animal

Berry 1 Chuck, full name *Charles Edward Berry*. born 1926, US rock-and-roll guitarist, singer, and songwriter. His frequently covered songs include "Maybellene" (1955), "Roll over Beethoven" (1956), "Johnny B. Goode" (1958), "Memphis, Tennessee" (1959), and "Promised Land" (1964) **2 Jean de France**, Duc de. 1340–1416, French prince, son of King John II; coregent (1380–88) for Charles VI and a famous patron of the arts

berserk a member of a class of ancient Norse warriors who worked themselves into a frenzy before battle and fought with insane fury and courage

berth *Nautical* **1** a place assigned to a ship at a mooring **2** sufficient distance from the shore or from other ships or objects for a ship to manoeuvre **3** accommodation on a ship

Bertolucci Bernardo born 1940, Italian film director: his films include *The Spider's Stratagem* (1970), *The Conformist* (1970), *1900* (1976), *The Last Emperor* (1987), *The Sheltering Sky* (1990), and *The Dreamers* (2003)

Berwick James Fitzjames, Duke of Berwick. 1670–1734, marshal of France and illegitimate son of James II of England. He led French forces during the War of the Spanish Succession (1701–14)

Berwickshire (until 1975) a county of SE Scotland: part of the Borders region from 1975 to 1996, now part of Scottish Borders council area

Berwick-upon-Tweed a town in N England, in N Northumberland at the mouth of the Tweed: much involved in border disputes between England and Scotland between the 12th and 16th centuries; neutral territory 1551–1885. Pop: 12 870 (2001)

beryl a white, blue, yellow, green, or pink mineral, found in coarse granites and igneous rocks. It is a source of beryllium and used as a gemstone; the green variety is emerald, the blue is aquamarine. Composition: beryllium aluminium silicate. Formula: $Be_3Al_2Si_6O_{18}$. Crystal structure: hexagonal

beryllium a corrosion-resistant toxic silvery-white metallic element that occurs chiefly in beryl and is used mainly in X-ray windows and in the manufacture of alloys. Symbol: Be; atomic no.: 4; atomic wt.: 9.012; valency: 2; relative density: 1.848; melting pt.: 1289°C; boiling pt.: 2472°C

Berzelius Baron Jöns Jakob 1779–1848, Swedish chemist, who invented the present system of chemical symbols and formulas, discovered several elements, and determined the atomic and molecular weight of many substances

Besant Annie, *née* Wood 1847–1933, British theosophist, writer, and political reformer in England and India

besom *Curling* a broom or brush used to sweep the ice in front of the stone to make it slide farther

Bessarabia a region in E Europe, mostly in Moldova and Ukraine: long disputed by the Turks and Russians; a province of Romania from 1918 until 1940. Area: about 44 300 sq km (17 100 sq miles)

Bessel Friedrich Wilhelm 1784–1846, German astronomer and mathematician. He made the first authenticated measurement of a star's distance (1841) and systematized a series of mathematical functions used in physics

Best 1 Charles Herbert 1899–1978, Canadian physiologist: associated with Banting and Macleod in their discovery of insulin in 1922 **2 George** born 1946, Northern Ireland footballer

bestiality sexual activity between a person and an animal

bestiary a moralizing medieval collection of descriptions of real and mythical animals

beta 1 the second letter in the Greek alphabet (B or β), a consonant, transliterated as *b* **2 a** involving or relating to electrons **b** relating to one of two or more allotropes or crystal structures of a solid **c** relating to one of two or more isomeric forms of a chemical compound

beta-blocker *Medicine* any of a class of drugs, such as propranolol, that inhibit the activity of the nerves that are stimulated by adrenaline; they therefore decrease the contraction and speed of the heart: used in the treatment of high blood pressure and angina pectoris

beta particle *Physics* a high-speed electron or positron emitted by a nucleus during radioactive decay or nuclear fission

betatron *Physics* a type of particle accelerator for producing high-energy beams of electrons, having an alternating magnetic field to keep the electrons in a circular orbit of fixed radius and accelerate them by magnetic induction. It produces energies of up to about 300 MeV

betel an Asian piperaceous climbing plant, *Piper betle*, the leaves of which are chewed, with the betel nut, by the peoples of SE Asia

Bethany a village in the West Bank, near Jerusalem at the foot of the Mount of Olives: in the New Testament, the home of Lazarus and the lodging place of Jesus during Holy Week

Bethe Hans Albrecht born 1906, US physicist, born in Germany; noted for his research on astrophysics and nuclear physics: Nobel prize for physics 1967

Bethel 1 an ancient town in the West Bank, near Jerusalem: in the Old Testament, the place where the dream of Jacob occurred (Genesis 28:19) **2** a chapel of any of certain Nonconformist Christian sects

Bethesda 1 *New Testament* a pool in Jerusalem reputed to have healing powers, where a paralytic was healed by Jesus (John 5:2) **2** a chapel of any of certain Nonconformist Christian sects

Bethlehem a town in the West Bank, near Jerusalem: birthplace of Jesus and early home of King David

Bethmann Hollweg Theobald von 1856–1921, chancellor of Germany (1909–17)

Bethsaida a ruined town in N Israel, near the N shore of the Sea of Galilee

Betjeman Sir John 1906–84, English poet, noted for his nostalgic and humorous verse and essays and for his concern for the preservation of historic buildings, esp of the Victorian era. Poet laureate (1972–84)

betterment *Property law* an improvement effected on real property that enhances the value of the property

Betws-y-Coed a village in N Wales, in Conwy county borough, on the River Conwy: noted for its scenery. Pop: 2860 (1991)

Beulah *Old Testament* the land of Israel (Isaiah 62:4)

Bevan Aneurin , known as *Nye*. 1897–1960, British Labour statesman, born in Wales: noted for his oratory. As minister of health (1945–51) he introduced the National Health Service (1948)

bevel gear a gear having teeth cut into a conical surface known as the pitch zone. Two such gears mesh together to transmit power between two shafts at an angle to each other

Beveridge William Henry, 1st Baron Beveridge. 1879–1963, British economist, whose *Report on Social Insurance and Allied Services* (1942) formed the basis of social-security legislation in Britain

Beverley a market town in NE England, the administrative centre of the East Riding of Yorkshire. Pop: 29 110 (2001)

Beverly Hills a city in SW California, near Los Angeles: famous as the home of film stars. Pop: 34 941 (2003 est)

Bevin Ernest 1881–1951, British Labour statesman and trade unionist, who was largely responsible for the creation of the Transport and General Workers' Union (1922): minister of labour (1940–45); foreign secretary (1945–51)

bevy 1 a flock of quails 2 a group of roedeer

Bewick Thomas 1753–1828, English wood engraver; his best-known works are *Chillingham Bull* (1789), a large woodcut, *Aesop's Fables* (1818), and his *History of British Birds* (1797–1804)

Bexley a borough of SE Greater London. Pop: 219 100 (2003 est). Area: 61 sq km (23 sq miles)

bey (in the Ottoman Empire) a title given to senior officers, provincial governors, certain other officials or nobles, and (sometimes) Europeans

Beyoğlu a district of Istanbul, north of the Golden Horn: the European quarter

Beza or **de Bèze** Théodore1519–1605, French Calvinist theologian and scholar, who lived in Switzerland. He succeeded Calvin as leader of the Swiss Protestants

bezel 1 the sloping face adjacent to the working edge of a cutting tool 2 a retaining outer rim used in vehicle instruments, eg in tachometers and speedometers 3 a small indicator light used in vehicle instrument panels

bezique 1 a card game for two or more players with tricks similar to whist but with additional points scored for honours and sequences: played with two packs with nothing below a seven 2 (in this game) the queen of spades and jack of diamonds declared together

Bhagalpur a city in India, in Bihar: agriculture, textiles, university (1960). Pop: 340 349 (2001)

bhang or **bang** a preparation of the leaves and flower tops of Indian hemp, which has psychoactive properties: much used in India

Bhaskar Sanjeev born 1964, British actor and writer of Asian origin, known for the TV comedy series *Goodness Gracious Me* (1998) and *The Kumars at No. 42* (2001–02)

Bhatpara a city in NE India, in West Bengal on the Hooghly River: jute and cotton mills. Pop: 441 956 (2001)

Bhavnagar a port in W India, in S Gujarat. Pop: 510 958 (2001)

Bhopal a city in central India, the capital of Madhya Pradesh state and of the former state of Bhopal: site of a poisonous gas leak from a US-owned factory, which killed over 7000 people in 1984 and was implicated in a

further 15 000 deaths afterwards. Pop: 1 433 875 (2001)

Bhubaneswar an ancient city in E India, the capital of Orissa state: many temples built between the 7th and 16th centuries. Pop: 647 302 (2001)

Bhutan a kingdom in central Asia: disputed by Tibet, China, India, and Britain since the 18th century, the conflict now being chiefly between China and India (which is responsible for Bhutan's external affairs); contains inaccessible stretches of the E Himalayas in the north. Official language: Dzongka; Nepali is also spoken. Official religion: Mahayana Buddhist. Currencies: ngultrum and Indian rupee. Capital: Thimbu. Pop: 2 325 000 (2004 est). Area: about 46 600 sq km (18 000 sq miles)

Biafra 1 a region of E Nigeria, formerly a local government region: seceded as an independent republic (1967–70) during the Civil War, but defeated by Nigerian government forces 2 **Bight of** former name (until 1975) of (the Bight of) **Bonny**

Biak an island in Indonesia, north of West Irian: the largest of the Schouten Islands. Area: 2455 sq km (948 sq miles)

Białystok a city in E Poland: belonged to Prussia (1795–1807) and to Russia (1807–1919). Pop: 315 000 (2005 est)

Biarritz a town in SW France, on the Bay of Biscay: famous resort, patronized by Napoleon III and by Queen Victoria and Edward VII of Great Britain and Ireland. Pop: 30 055 (1999)

bias 1 *Electronics* the voltage applied to an electronic device or system to establish suitable working conditions 2 *Bowls* a a bulge or weight inside one side of a bowl b the curved course of such a bowl on the green 3 an inaudible high-frequency signal used to improve the quality of a tape recording

bib a light-brown European marine gadoid food fish, *Gadus* (or *Trisopterus*) *luscus*, with a barbel on its lower jaw

Bible a the the sacred writings of the Christian religion, comprising the Old and New Testaments and, in the Roman Catholic Church, the Apocrypha b (*as modifier*): a *Bible reading*

▷http://unbound.biola.edu/
▷www.yallop.org/synopsis/
▷www.bible-history.com/

Biblicist or **Biblist** 1 a biblical scholar 2 a person who takes the Bible literally

bibliomancy prediction of the future by interpreting a passage chosen at random from a book, esp the Bible

bicameral *Politics* (of a legislature) consisting of two chambers

bicarbonate 1 a salt of carbonic acid containing the ion HCO_3^-; an acid carbonate 2 consisting of, containing, or concerned with the ion HCO_3^-

bicarbonate of soda sodium bicarbonate, esp when used as a medicine or as a raising agent in baking

biceps *Anatomy* any muscle having two heads or origins, esp the muscle that flexes the forearm

bicuspid or **bicuspidate** 1 having or terminating in two cusps or points 2 a bicuspid tooth; premolar

bicycle a vehicle with a tubular metal frame mounted on two spoked wheels, one behind the other. The rider sits on a saddle, propels the vehicle by means of pedals

that drive the rear wheel through a chain, and steers with handlebars on the front wheel
▷www.ibike.org

bid 1 *Commerce* a a statement by a buyer, in response to an offer by a seller, of the more favourable terms that would be acceptable b the price or other terms so stated 2 *Bridge* a the number of tricks a player undertakes to make b a player's turn to make a bid

bidding *Bridge* a group of bids considered collectively, esp those made on a particular deal

Biel 1 a town in NW Switzerland, on Lake Biel. Pop: 48 655 (2000) 2 *Lake* a lake in NW Switzerland: remains of lake dwellings were discovered here in the 19th century. Area: 39 sq km (15 sq miles)

Bielefeld a city in Germany, in NE North Rhine-Westphalia: food, textiles. Pop: 328 452 (2003 est)

Bielsko-Biała a town in S Poland: created in 1951 by the union of Bielsko and Biala Krakowska; a leading textile centre since the 16th century. Pop: 356 000 (2005 est)

Bien Hoa a town in S Vietnam: a former capital of Cambodia. Pop: 520 000 (2005 est)

biennial a plant, such as the carrot, that completes its life cycle within two years, developing vegetative storage parts during the first year and flowering and fruiting in its second year

Bierce Ambrose (Gwinett). 1842–?1914, US journalist and author of humorous sketches, horror stories, and tales of the supernatural: he disappeared during a mission in Mexico (1913)

bifocal 1 *Optics* having two different focuses 2 relating to a compound lens permitting near and distant vision

bigamy the crime of marrying a person while one is still legally married to someone else

big-bang theory a cosmological theory postulating that approximately 12 billion years ago all the matter of the universe, packed into a small superdense mass, was hurled in all directions by a cataclysmic explosion. As the fragments slowed down, the galaxies and stars evolved but the universe is still expanding

big end *Brit Engineering* 1 the larger end of a connecting rod in an internal-combustion engine 2 the bearing surface between the larger end of a connecting rod and the crankpin of the crankshaft

bight a wide indentation of a shoreline, or the body of water bounded by such a curve

Bight the *Austral, informal* the major indentation of the S coast of Australia, from Cape Pasley in W Australia to the Eyre Peninsula in S Australia

Bihar a state of NE India: consists of part of the Ganges plain; important for rice: lost the S to the new state of Jharkhand in 2000. Capital: Patna. Pop: 82 878 796 (2001). Area: 99 225 sq km (38 301 sq miles)

Bijapur an ancient city in W India, in N Mysore: capital of a former kingdom, which fell at the end of the 17th century: cotton. Pop: 245 946 (2001)

Bikaner a walled city in NW India, in Rajasthan: capital of the former state of Bikaner, on the edge of the Thar Desert. Pop: 529 007 (2001)

Bikini an atoll in the N Pacific; one of the Marshall Islands: site of a US atomic-bomb test in 1946

Biko Steven Bantu, known as *Steve*. 1946–77, Black South African civil rights leader: founder of the South African

Students Organization. His death in police custody caused worldwide concern

Bilbao a port in N Spain, on the Bay of Biscay: the largest city in the Basque Provinces: famous since medieval times for the production of iron and steel goods: modern buildings include the Guggenheim Art Museum (1997). Pop: 353 567 (2003 est)

bilberry 1 any of several ericaceous shrubs of the genus *Vaccinium*, having edible blue or blackish berries 2 a the fruit of any of these plants b (*as modifier*): bilberry pie

bile 1 a bitter greenish to golden brown alkaline fluid secreted by the liver and stored in the gall bladder. It is discharged during digestion into the duodenum, where it aids the emulsification and absorption of fats 2 *Archaic* either of two bodily humours, one of which (**black bile**) was thought to cause melancholy and the other (**yellow bile**) anger

bilge 1 *Nautical* the parts of a vessel's hull where the vertical sides curve inwards to form the bottom 2 the parts of a vessel between the lowermost floorboards and the bottom 3 the dirty water that collects in a vessel's bilge 4 the widest part of the belly of a barrel or cask

biliary of or relating to bile, to the ducts that convey bile, or to the gall bladder

bilious affected with or denoting any disorder related to excess secretion of bile

bill¹ a statute in draft, before it becomes law

bill² 1 the mouthpart of a bird, consisting of projecting jaws covered with a horny sheath; beak. It varies in shape and size according to the type of food eaten and may also be used as a weapon 2 any beaklike mouthpart in other animals 3 a narrow promontory 4 *Nautical* the pointed tip of the fluke of an anchor

billabong *Austral* 1 a backwater channel that forms a lagoon or pool 2 a branch of a river running to a dead end

billboard a fitting at the bow of a vessel for securing an anchor

billet¹ a space or berth allocated, esp for slinging a hammock, in a ship

billet² 1 *Metallurgy* a a metal bar of square or circular cross section b an ingot cast into the shape of a prism 2 *Architect* a carved ornament in a moulding, with short cylinders or blocks evenly spaced

billhook a cutting tool with a wooden handle and a curved blade terminating in a hook at its tip, used for pruning, chopping, etc

billiards 1 any of various games in which long cues are used to drive balls now made of composition or plastic. It is played on a rectangular table covered with a smooth tight-fitting cloth and having raised cushioned edges 2 a version of this, played on a rectangular table having six pockets let into the corners and the two longer sides. Points are scored by striking one of three balls with the cue to contact the other two or one of the two
▷http://moveto/wbfsuperstars

Billingsgate the largest fish market in London, on the N bank of the River Thames; moved to new site on the Isle of Dogs in 1982

billion 1 one thousand million: it is written as 1 000 000 000 or 10^9 2 (formerly, in Britain) one million million: it is written as 1 000 000 000 000 or 10^{12}

Billiton an island of Indonesia, in the Java Sea between Borneo and Sumatra. Chief town: Tanjungpandan. Area: 4833 sq km (1866 sq miles)

bill of health a certificate, issued by a port officer, that attests to the health of a ship's company

bill of lading (in foreign trade) a document containing full particulars of goods shipped or for shipment

billow 1 a large sea wave 2 a large atmospheric wave, usually in the lee of a hill

Billy the Kid nickname of *William H Bonney*. 1859–81, US outlaw

bimetallic consisting of two metals

bin *Brit* **a** a storage place for bottled wine **b** one particular bottling of wine

binary 1 *Maths, Computing* of, relating to, or expressed in binary notation or binary code 2 (of a compound or molecule) containing atoms of two different elements 3 *Metallurgy* (of an alloy) consisting of two components or phases 4 (of an educational system) consisting of two parallel forms of education such as the grammar school and the secondary modern in Britain 5 *Maths, Logic* (of a relation, expression, or operation) applying to two elements of its domain; having two argument places; dyadic 6 *Astronomy* See **binary star**

binary star a double star system comprising two stars orbiting around their common centre of mass. A **visual binary** can be seen through a telescope. A **spectroscopic binary** can only be observed by the spectroscopic Doppler shift as each star moves towards or away from the earth

Binchy Maeve born 1940, Irish novelist and journalist; her bestselling novels include *Circle of Friends* (1990) and *Quentins* (2002)

bind 1 *Music* another word for **tie** 2 *Fencing* a pushing movement with the blade made to force one's opponent's sword from one line into another 3 *Chess* a position in which one player's pawns have a hold on the centre that makes it difficult for the opponent to advance there

binder 1 a tie, beam, or girder, used to support floor joists 2 the nonvolatile component of the organic media in which pigments are dispersed in paint

bindweed 1 any convolvulaceous plant of the genera *Convolvulus* and *Calystegia* that twines around a support 2 any of various other trailing or twining plants, such as black bindweed

Bingen a town in W Germany on the Rhine: wine trade and tourist centre. Pop: 24 716 (2003 est)

bingo a gambling game, usually played with several people, in which numbers selected at random are called out and the players cover the numbers on their individual cards. The first to cover a given arrangement of numbers is the winner

bin Laden Osama born 1957, Saudi-born leader of the al-Qaida terrorist network: presumed architect of the terrorist attacks on New York and Washington of September 11 2001

binnacle a housing for a ship's compass

binomial 1 a mathematical expression consisting of two terms, such as $3x + 2y$ 2 a two-part taxonomic name for an animal or plant 3 referring to two names or terms

binomial theorem a mathematical theorem that gives the expansion of any binomial raised to a positive integral power, n. It contains $n+1$ terms: $(x+a)^n = x^n + nx^{n-1}a + [n(n-1)/2]x^{n-2}a^2 + ... + \binom{n}{k}x^{n-k}a^k + ... + a^n$, where $\binom{n}{k} = n!/(n-k)!k!$, the number of combinations of k items selected from n

Binyon (Robert) Laurence 1869–1943, British poet and art historian, best known for his elegiac war poems "For the Fallen" (1914) and "The Burning of the Leaves" (1944)

biochemistry the study of the chemical compounds, reactions, etc, occurring in living organisms
 ▷http://restools.sdsc.edu/
 ▷www.geocities.com/peterroberts.geo/biology.htm#bioch

biocide a chemical, such as a pesticide, capable of killing living organisms

biocoenosis *or* **biocenosis** a diverse community inhabiting a single biotope

biodegradable (of sewage constituents, packaging material, etc) capable of being decomposed by bacteria or other biological means

biodiversity the existence of a wide variety of plant and animal species in their natural environments, which is the aim of conservationists concerned about the indiscriminate destruction of rainforests and other habitats
 ▷www.biosis.org.uk/zrdocs/zoolinfo/biodiv.htm
 ▷www.eti.uva.nl
 ▷www.biodiv.org

bioengineering 1 the design and manufacture of aids, such as artificial limbs, to rectify defective body functions 2 the design, manufacture, and maintenance of engineering equipment used in biosynthetic processes, such as fermentation

biogenesis the principle that a living organism must originate from a parent organism similar to itself

Bioko an island in the Gulf of Guinea, off the coast of Cameroon: part of Equatorial Guinea. Capital: Malabo. Area: 2017 sq km (786 sq miles)

biological *or archaic* **biologic** 1 of or relating to biology 2 (of a detergent) containing enzymes said to be capable of removing stains of organic origin from items to be washed 3 a drug, such as a vaccine, that is derived from a living organism

biological clock 1 an inherent periodicity in the physiological processes of living organisms that is not dependent on the periodicity of external factors 2 the hypothetical mechanism responsible for this periodicity

biological control the control of destructive organisms by the use of other organisms, such as the natural predators of the pests

biology 1 the study of living organisms, including their structure, functioning, evolution, distribution, and interrelationships 2 the structure, functioning, etc, of a particular organism or group of organisms 3 the animal and plant life of a particular region
 ▷http://mcb.harvard.edu/BioLinks
 ▷http://biology-online.org/
 ▷http://cellbiol.com/
 ▷www.webref.org/biology/biology.htm

biomass 1 the total number of living organisms in a given area, expressed in terms of living or dry weight per unit area 2 vegetable matter used as a source of energy

biomechanics the study of the mechanics of the movement of living organisms

biomedicine 1 the medical study of the effects of unusual environmental stress on human beings, esp in connection with space travel 2 the study of herbal remedies

biometric 1 a relating to the analysis of biological data using mathematical and statistical methods b relating to digital scanning of the physiological or behavioural characteristics of individuals as a means of identification 2 relating to the statistical calculation of the probable duration of human life

biometry *or* **biometrics** 1 a the analysis of biological data using mathematical and statistical methods b the practice of digitally scanning the physiological or behavioural characteristics of individuals as a means of identification 2 the statistical calculation of the probable duration of human life

bionic 1 of or relating to bionics 2 (in science fiction) having certain physiological functions augmented or replaced by electronic equipment

bionics 1 the study of certain biological functions, esp those relating to the brain, that are applicable to the development of electronic equipment, such as computer hardware, designed to operate in a similar manner 2 the technique of replacing a limb or body part by an artificial limb or part that is electronically or mechanically powered

biophysics the physics of biological processes and the application of methods used in physics to biology

biopic a film based on the life of a famous person, esp one giving a popular treatment

biopsy 1 examination, esp under a microscope, of tissue from a living body to determine the cause or extent of a disease 2 the sample taken for such an examination

biorhythm a cyclically recurring pattern of physiological states in an organism or organ, such as alpha rhythm or circadian rhythm; believed by some to affect physical and mental states and behaviour

bioscope 1 a kind of early film projector 2 a South African word for **cinema**

biosphere the part of the earth's surface and atmosphere inhabited by living things

biosynthesis the formation of complex compounds from simple substances by living organisms

biotech a short for **biotechnology** b (*as modifier*): *a biotech company*

biotechnology 1 (in industry) the technique of using microorganisms, such as bacteria, to perform chemical processing, such as waste recycling, or to produce other materials, such as beer and wine, cheese, antibiotics, and (using genetic engineering) hormones, vaccines, etc 2 another name for **ergonomics**
  ▷www.cato.com/biotech
  ▷www.academicinfo.net/biotechmeta.html
  ▷www.bio.com

biotin a vitamin of the B complex, abundant in egg yolk and liver, deficiency of which causes dermatitis and loss of hair. Formula: $C_{10}H_{16}N_2O_3S$

bipartisan consisting of or supported by two political parties

bipartite 1 affecting or made by two parties; bilateral 2 *Botany* (esp of some leaves) divided into two parts almost to the base

biped 1 any animal with two feet 2 having two feet

biplane a type of aeroplane having two sets of wings, one above the other

bipolar 1 having two poles 2 relating to or found at the North and South Poles 3 (of a transistor) utilizing both majority and minority charge carriers 4 *Psychiatry* suffering from bipolar manic-depressive disorder

birch 1 any betulaceous tree or shrub of the genus *Betula*, having thin peeling bark 2 the hard close-grained wood of any of these trees 3 of, relating to, or belonging to the birch 4 consisting or made of birch

bird any warm-blooded egg-laying vertebrate of the class *Aves*, characterized by a body covering of feathers and forelimbs modified as wings. Birds vary in size between the ostrich and the humming bird

birdie *Golf* a score of one stroke under par for a hole

birdlime a sticky substance, prepared from holly, mistletoe, or other plants, smeared on twigs to catch small birds

bird of paradise 1 any songbird of the family *Paradisaeidae* of New Guinea and neighbouring regions, the males of which have brilliantly coloured ornate plumage 2 **bird-of-paradise flower** any of various banana-like plants of the genus *Strelitzia*, esp *S. reginae*, that are native to tropical southern Africa and South America and have purple bracts and large orange or yellow flowers resembling birds' heads: family *Strelitziaceae*

bird of prey a bird, such as a hawk, eagle, or owl, that hunts and kills other animals, esp vertebrates, for food. It has strong talons and a sharp hooked bill

biretta *or* **berretta** *RC Church* a stiff clerical cap having either three or four upright pieces projecting outwards from the centre to the edge: coloured black for priests, purple for bishops, red for cardinals, and white for certain members of religious orders

Birgitta Saint. See (Saint) **Bridget** (sense 2)

Birkbeck George 1776–1841, British educationalist, who helped to establish vocational training for working men: founder and first president of the London Mechanics Institute (1824), which later became Birkbeck College

Birkenhead[1] Frederick Edwin Smith, 1st Earl of, known as *F. E. Smith*. 1872–1930, British Conservative statesman, lawyer, and orator

Birkenhead[2] a port in NW England, in Wirral unitary authority, Merseyside: former shipbuilding centre. Pop: 83 729 (2001)

Birmingham 1 an industrial city in central England, in Birmingham unitary authority, in the West Midlands: the second largest city in Great Britain; two cathedrals; three universities (1900, 1966, 1992). Pop: 970 892 (2001) 2 a unitary authority in central England, in the West Midlands. Pop: 992 100 (2003 est). Area: 283 sq km (109 sq miles) 3 an industrial city in N central Alabama: rich local deposits of coal, iron ore, and other minerals. Pop: 236 620 (2003 est)

Birobidzhan *or* **Birobijan** 1 a city in SE Russia: capital of the Jewish Autonomous Region. Pop: 82 000 (1994) 2 another name for the **Jewish Autonomous Region**

Birtwistle Sir **Harrison** born 1934, English composer, whose works include the operas *Punch and Judy* (1967), *The Mask of Orpheus* (1984), *Gawain* (1991), and *Exody* (1998)

Biscay Bay of a large bay of the Atlantic Ocean between W France and N Spain: notorious for storms

bisexual 1 (of some plants and animals) having both male and female reproductive organs 2 a bisexual organism; a hermaphrodite

Bishkek the capital of Kyrgyzstan. Pop: 828 000 (2005 est)

bishop 1 (in the Roman Catholic, Anglican, and Greek Orthodox Churches) a clergyman having spiritual and administrative powers over a diocese or province of the Church 2 (in some Protestant Churches) a spiritual overseer of a local church or a number of churches 3 a chesspiece, capable of moving diagonally over any number of unoccupied squares of the same colour 4 mulled wine, usually port, spiced with oranges, cloves, etc

Bishop Auckland a town in N England, in central Durham: seat of the bishops of Durham since the 12th century: light industries. Pop: 24 764 (2001)

bishopric the see, diocese, or office of a bishop

Biskra a town and oasis in NE Algeria, in the Sahara. Pop: 204 000 (2005 est)

Bisley a village in SE England, in Surrey: annual meetings of the National Rifle Association

Bismarck¹ Prince **Otto** (**Eduard Leopold**) **von** , called *the Iron Chancellor*. 1815–98, German statesman; prime minister of Prussia (1862–90). Under his leadership Prussia defeated Austria and France, and Germany was united. In 1871 he became the first chancellor of the German Reich

Bismarck² a city in North Dakota, on the Missouri River: the state capital. Pop: 56 344 (2003 est)

Bismarck Archipelago a group of over 200 islands in the SW Pacific, northeast of New Guinea: part of Papua New Guinea. Main islands: New Britain, New Ireland, Lavongai, and the Admiralty Islands. Chief town: Rabaul, on New Britain. Pop: 424 000 (1995 est). Area: 49 658 sq km (19 173 sq miles)

bismuth a brittle pinkish-white crystalline metallic element having low thermal and electrical conductivity, which expands on cooling. It is widely used in alloys, esp low-melting alloys in fire safety devices; its compounds are used in medicines. Symbol: Bi; atomic no.: 83; atomic wt.: 208.98037; valency: 3 or 5; relative density: 9.747; melting pt.: 271.4°C; boiling pt.: 1564±5°C

bison 1 a member of the cattle tribe, *Bison bison*, formerly widely distributed over the prairies of W North America but now confined to reserves and parks, with a massive head, shaggy forequarters, and a humped back 2 a closely related and similar animal, *Bison bonasus*, formerly widespread in Europe

bisque¹ 1 a a pink to yellowish tan colour b (*as adjective*): *a bisque tablecloth* 2 *Ceramics* another name for **biscuit**

bisque² *Tennis, Golf, croquet* an extra point, stroke, or turn allowed to an inferior player, usually taken when desired

Bissau *or* **Bissão** a port on the Atlantic, the capital of Guinea-Bissau (until 1974 Portuguese Guinea). Pop: 369 000 (2005 est)

bistable 1 having two stable states 2 *Computing* another name for **flip-flop**

bit¹ 1 a metal mouthpiece, for controlling a horse on a bridle 2 a cutting or drilling tool, part, or head in a brace, drill, etc 3 the blade of a woodworking plane 4 the part of a pair of pincers designed to grasp an object 5 the copper end of a soldering iron 6 the part of a key that engages the levers of a lock

bit² *Maths, Computing* 1 a single digit of binary notation, represented either by 0 or by 1 2 the smallest unit of information, indicating the presence or absence of a single feature 3 a unit of capacity of a computer, consisting of an element of its physical structure capable of being in either of two states, such as a switch with *on* and *off* positions, or a microscopic magnet capable of alignment in two directions

bite 1 *Angling* an attempt by a fish to take the bait or lure 2 the depth of cut of a machine tool 3 the grip or hold applied by a tool or chuck to a workpiece 4 *Dentistry* the angle or manner of contact between the upper and lower teeth when the mouth is closed naturally 5 the surface of a file or rasp with cutting teeth 6 the corrosive action of acid, as on a metal etching plate

Bithynia an ancient country on the Black Sea in NW Asia Minor

bitmap *Computing* a picture created on a visual display unit where each pixel corresponds to one or more bits in memory, the number of bits per pixel determining the number of available colours

Bitolj *or* **Bitola** a city in SW Macedonia: under Turkish rule from 1382 until 1913 when it was taken by the Serbs. Pop: 77 000 (2005 est)

bitstream *Computing* a sequence of digital data transmitted electronically

bitter *Brit* beer with a high hop content, with a slightly bitter taste

bittern¹ any wading bird of the genera *Ixobrychus* and *Botaurus*, related and similar to the herons but with shorter legs and neck, a stouter body, and a booming call: family *Ardeidae*, order *Ciconiiformes*

bittern² the bitter liquid remaining after common salt has been crystallized out of sea water: a source of magnesium, bromine, and iodine compounds

bittersweet any of several North American woody climbing plants of the genus *Celastrus*, esp *C. scandens*, having orange capsules that open to expose scarlet-coated seeds: family *Celastraceae*

bitumen 1 any of various viscous or solid impure mixtures of hydrocarbons that occur naturally in asphalt, tar, mineral waxes, etc.: used as a road surfacing and roofing material 2 the constituents of coal that can be extracted by an organic solvent 3 any liquid suitable for coating aggregates 4 **the bitumen** a *Austral and NZ, informal* any road with a bitumen surface b *Austral, informal* the road in the Northern Territory between Darwin and Alice Springs 5 a transparent brown pigment or glaze made from asphalt

bituminous coal a soft black coal, rich in volatile hydrocarbons, that burns with a smoky yellow flame.

Fixed carbon content: 46–86 per cent; calorific value: $1.93 \times 10^7 - 3.63 \times 10^7$ J/kg

bivalve 1 any marine or freshwater mollusc of the class *Pelecypoda* (formerly *Bivalvia* or *Lamellibranchia*), having a laterally compressed body, a shell consisting of two hinged valves, and gills for respiration. The group includes clams, cockles, oysters, and mussels 2 of, relating to, or belonging to the *Pelecypoda* 3 *Biology* having or consisting of two valves or similar parts

Biysk, Biisk, *or* **Bisk** a city in SW Russia, at the foot of the Altai Mountains. Pop: 216 000 (2005 est)

Bizerte *or* **Bizerta** a port in N Tunisia, on the Mediterranean at the canalized outlet of **Lake Bizerte**. Pop: 118 000 (2005 est)

Bizet Georges 1838–75, French composer, whose works include the opera *Carmen* (1875) and incidental music to Daudet's *L'Arlésienne* (1872)

black 1 of the colour of jet or carbon black, having no hue due to the absorption of all or nearly all incident light 2 *Chess, Draughts* **a** a black or dark-coloured piece or square **b** the player playing with such pieces 3 a black ball in snooker, etc 4 (in roulette and other gambling games) one of two colours on which players may place even bets, the other being red 5 *Archery* a black ring on a target, between the outer and the blue, scoring three points

Black¹ 1 Sir James **(Whyte)**. born 1924, British biochemist. He discovered beta-blockers and drugs for peptic ulcers: Nobel prize for physiology or medicine 1988 2 Joseph 1728–99, Scottish physician and chemist, noted for his pioneering work on carbon dioxide and heat

Black² *Sometimes derogatory* a member of a dark-skinned race, esp someone of Negroid or Australoid origin

black-and-white 1 **a** a photograph, picture, sketch, etc, in black, white, and shades of grey rather than in colour **b** (*as modifier*): *black-and-white film* 2 the neutral tones of black, white, and intermediate shades of grey

black-backed gull 1 either of two common black-and-white European coastal gulls, *Larus fuscus* (**lesser black-backed gull**) and *L. marinus* (**great black-backed gull**) 2 a southern gull, *larus dominicanus*, with black feathers on its back

black bear 1 American black bear a bear, *Euarctos* (or *Ursus*) *americanus*, inhabiting forests of North America. It is smaller and less ferocious than the brown bear 2 **Asiatic black bear** a bear, *Selenarctos thibetanus*, of central and E Asia, whose coat is black with a pale V-shaped mark on the chest

black belt 1 *Martial Arts* **a** a black belt worn by an instructor or expert competitor in the dan grades, usually from first to fifth dan **b** a person entitled to wear this 2 **the a** a region of the southern US extending from Georgia across central Alabama and Mississippi, in which the population contains a large number of Blacks: also noted for its fertile black soil

blackberry 1 any of several woody plants of the rosaceous genus *Rubus*, esp *R. fruticosus*, that have thorny stems and black or purple glossy edible berry-like fruits (drupelets) 2 **a** the fruit of any of these plants **b** (*as modifier*): *blackberry jam* 3 **blackberry lily** an ornamental Chinese iridaceous plant, *Belamcanda chinensis*, that has red-spotted orange flowers and clusters of black seeds that resemble blackberries

blackbird 1 a common European thrush, *Turdus merula*, in which the male has a black plumage and yellow bill and the female is brown 2 any of various American orioles having a dark plumage, esp any of the genus *Agelaius* 3 *History* a person, esp a South Sea Islander, who was kidnapped and sold as a slave, esp in Australia

blackboard a hard or rigid surface made of a smooth usually dark substance, used for writing or drawing on with chalk, esp in teaching

black box 1 a self-contained unit in an electronic or computer system whose circuitry need not be known to understand its function 2 an informal name for **flight recorder**

Blackburn 1 a city in NW England, in Blackburn with Darwen unitary authority, Lancashire: formerly important for textiles, now has mixed industries. Pop: 105 085 (2001) 2 **Mount** a mountain in SE Alaska, the highest peak in the Wrangell Mountains. Height: 5037 m (16 523 ft)

Blackburn with Darwen a unitary authority in NW England, in Lancashire. Pop: 139 800 (2003 est). Area: 137 sq km (53 sq miles)

blackcap 1 a brownish-grey Old World warbler, *Sylvia atricapilla*, the male of which has a black crown 2 any of various similar birds, such as the black-capped chickadee (*Parus atricapillus*) 3 *Brit* (formerly) the cap worn by a judge when passing a death sentence

blackcock the male of the black grouse

Black Country the the formerly heavily industrialized region of central England, northwest of Birmingham

blackcurrant 1 a N temperate shrub, *Ribes nigrum*, having red or white flowers and small edible black berries: family *Grossulariaceae* 2 **a** the fruit of this shrub **b** (*as modifier*): *blackcurrant jelly*

Black Death the a form of bubonic plague pandemic in Europe and Asia during the 14th century, when it killed over 50 million people

black economy that portion of the income of a nation that remains illegally undeclared either as a result of payment in kind or as a means of tax avoidance

Blackett Patrick Maynard Stuart, Baron. 1897–1974, English physicist, noted for his work on cosmic radiation and his discovery of the positron. Nobel prize for physics 1948

Black Forest the the hilly wooded region of SW Germany, in Baden-Württemberg: a popular resort area

Black Friar a Dominican friar

blackhead 1 a black-tipped plug of fatty matter clogging a pore of the skin, esp the duct of a sebaceous gland 2 an infectious and often fatal disease of turkeys and some other fowl caused by the parasitic protozoa *Histomonas meleagridis* 3 any of various birds, esp gulls or ducks, with black plumage on the head

Blackheath a residential district in SE London, mainly in the boroughs of Lewisham and Greenwich: a large heath formerly notorious for highwaymen

black hole *Astronomy* an object in space so dense that its escape velocity exceeds the speed of light

black ice a thin transparent layer of new ice on a road or similar surface

Black Isle the a peninsula in NE Scotland, in Highland

council area, between the Cromarty and Moray Firths

blackjack¹ *Cards* **1** pontoon or any of various similar card games **2** the ace of spades

blackjack² a dark iron-rich variety of the mineral sphalerite

blackjack³ a small oak tree, *Quercus marilandica*, of the southeastern US, with blackish bark and fan-shaped leaves

blackleg an acute infectious disease of cattle, sheep, and pigs, characterized by gas-filled swellings, esp on the legs, caused by *Clostridium* bacteria

Black Maria a police van for transporting prisoners

black market 1 a any system in which goods or currencies are sold and bought illegally, esp in violation of controls or rationing **b** (*as modifier*): *black market lamb* **2** the place where such a system operates

Blackmore R(ichard) D(oddridge). 1825–1900, English novelist; author of *Lorna Doone* (1869)

Black Mountain the a mountain range in S Wales, in E Carmarthenshire and W Powys. Highest peak: Carmarthen Van, 802 m (2632 ft)

blackout 1 a momentary loss of consciousness, vision, or memory **2** a temporary electrical power failure or cut *Electronics* **3** a temporary loss of sensitivity in a valve following a short strong pulse **4** a temporary loss of radio communications between a spacecraft and earth, esp on re-entry into the earth's atmosphere

Blackpool 1 a town and resort in NW England, in Blackpool unitary authority, Lancashire on the Irish Sea: famous for its tower, 158 m (518 ft) high, and its illuminations. Pop: 142 283 (2001) **2** a unitary authority in NW England, in Lancashire. Pop: 142 400 (2003 est). Area: 35 sq km (13 sq miles)

Black Power a social, economic, and political movement of Black people, esp in the US, to obtain equality with Whites

Black Prince the. See Edward¹ (sense 1)

Black Rod 1 (in Britain) an officer of the House of Lords and of the Order of the Garter, whose main duty is summoning the Commons at the opening and proroguing of Parliament **2** a similar officer in any of certain other legislatures

Black Sea an inland sea between SE Europe and Asia: connected to the Aegean Sea by the Bosporus, the Sea of Marmara, and the Dardanelles, and to the Sea of Azov by the Kerch Strait. Area: about 415 000 sq km (160 000 sq miles)

Blackshirt *History* (in Europe) a member of a fascist organization, esp a member of the Italian Fascist party before and during World War II

blackthorn a thorny Eurasian rosaceous shrub, *Prunus spinosa*, with black twigs, white flowers, and small sour plumlike fruits

Black Volta a river in W Africa, rising in SW Burkina-Faso and flowing northeast, then south into Lake Volta: forms part of the border of Ghana with Burkina-Faso and with the Ivory Coast. Length: about 800 km (500 miles)

black widow an American spider, *Latrodectus mactans*, the female of which is black with red markings, highly venomous, and commonly eats its mate

Blackwood Algernon (Henry). 1869–1951, British novel-

ist and short- story writer; noted for his supernatural tales

bladder 1 *Anatomy* a distensible membranous sac, usually containing liquid or gas, esp the urinary bladder **2** a blister, cyst, vesicle, etc, usually filled with fluid **3** a hollow vesicular or saclike part or organ in certain plants, such as the bladderwort or bladderwrack

blade 1 the flattened expanded part of a leaf, sepal, or petal **2** the long narrow leaf of a grass or related plant **3** *Archaeol* a long thin flake of flint, possibly used as a tool

Blaenau Gwent a county borough of SE Wales, created in 1996 from NW Gwent. Administrative centre: Ebbw Vale. Pop: 68 900 (2003 est). Area: 109 sq km (42 sq miles)

Blagoveshchensk a city and port in E Russia, in Siberia on the Amur River. Pop: 222 000 (2005 est)

blain a blister, blotch, or sore on the skin

Blair Tony, full name *Anthony Charles Lynton Blair*. born 1953, British politician; leader of the Labour Party from 1994; prime minister from 1997

Blake 1 Sir Peter born 1932, British painter, a leading exponent of pop art in the 1960s: co-founder of the Brotherhood of Ruralists (1969) **2 Quentin** (Saxby). born 1932, British artist, illustrator, and children's writer; noted esp for his illustrations to books by Roald Dahl **3 Robert** 1599–1657, English admiral, who commanded Cromwell's fleet against the Royalists, the Dutch, and the Spanish **4 William** 1757–1827, English poet, painter, engraver, and mystic. His literary works include *Songs of Innocence* (1789) and *Songs of Experience* (1794), *The Marriage of Heaven and Hell* (1793), and *Jerusalem* (1820). His chief works in the visual arts include engravings of a visionary nature, such as the illustrations for *The Book of Job* (1826), for Dante's poems, and for his own *Prophetic Books* (1783–1804)

Blanc¹ (Jean Joseph Charles) Louis 1811–82, French socialist and historian: author of *L'Organisation du travail* (1840), in which he advocated the establishment of cooperative workshops subsidized by the state

Blanc² 1 Mont. See Mont Blanc **2 Cape** a headland in N Tunisia: the northernmost point of Africa **3 Cape.** Also called: **Cape Blanco** a peninsula in Mauritania, on the Atlantic coast

Blanchett Cate , full name *Catherine Elise Blanchett*. born 1969, Australian actress; her films include *Elizabeth* (1998) and the *Lord of the Rings* trilogy (2001–03)

Blanco Serge born 1958, French Rugby Union footballer

blank 1 a plate or plug used to seal an aperture **2** a piece of material prepared for stamping, punching, forging, etc **3** *Archery* the white spot in the centre of a target

blanket *Physics* a layer of a fertile substance placed round the core of a nuclear reactor as a reflector and absorber and often to breed new fissionable fuel

blank verse *Prosody* unrhymed verse, esp in iambic pentameters

Blantyre-Limbe a city in S Malawi: largest city in the country; formed in 1956 from the adjoining towns of Blantyre and Limbe. Pop: 647 000 (2005 est)

blasphemy *Law* the crime committed if a person insults, offends, or vilifies the deity, Christ, or the Christian religion

blast 1 a the rapid movement of air away from the centre of an explosion, combustion of rocket fuel, etc **b** a wave of overpressure caused by an explosion; shock wave 2 any of several diseases of plants and animals, esp one producing withering in plants

blast furnace a vertical cylindrical furnace for smelting iron, copper, lead, and tin ores. The ore, scrap, solid fuel, and slag-forming materials are fed through the top and a blast of preheated air is forced through the charge from the bottom. Metal and slag are run off from the base

Blavatsky Elena Petrovna , called *Madame Blavatsky*. 1831–91, Russian theosophist; author of *Isis Unveiled* (1877)

Blaydon an industrial town in NE England, in Gateshead unitary authority, Tyne and Wear. Pop: 14 648 (2001)

blaze a light-coloured marking on the face of a domestic animal, esp a horse

bleaching powder a white powder with the odour of chlorine, consisting of chlorinated calcium hydroxide with an approximate formula $CaCl(OCl).4H_2O$. It is used in solution as a bleaching agent and disinfectant

bleak any slender silvery European cyprinid fish of the genus *Alburnus*, esp *A. lucidus*, occurring in slow-flowing rivers

Bleasdale Alan born 1946, British playwright, best known for his television series *The Boys From the Blackstuff* (1983) and *GBH* (1991)

blende any of several sulphide ores, such as antimony sulphide

Blenheim a village in SW Germany, site of a victory of Anglo-Austrian forces under the Duke of Marlborough and Prince Eugène of Savoy that saved Vienna from the French and Bavarians (1704) during the War of the Spanish Succession

blenny 1 any blennioid fish of the family *Blenniidae* of coastal waters, esp of the genus *Blennius*, having a tapering scaleless body, a long dorsal fin, and long raylike pelvic fins 2 any of various related fishes

blessed 1 *RC Church* (of a person) beatified by the pope 2 the blessed *Christianity* the dead who are already enjoying heavenly bliss

blessing *Judaism* a a short prayer prescribed for a specific occasion and beginning "Blessed art thou, O Lord..." b a section of the liturgy including a similar formula

Blida a city in N Algeria, on the edge of the Mitidja Plain. Pop: 269 000 (2005 est)

Bligh William 1754–1817, British admiral; Governor of New South Wales (1806–9), deposed by the New South Wales Corps: as a captain, commander of *HMS Bounty* when the crew mutinied in 1789

blimp 1 a small nonrigid airship, esp one used for observation or as a barrage balloon 2 *Films* a soundproof cover fixed over a camera during shooting

blind 1 done without being able to see, relying on instruments for information 2 (of cultivated plants) having failed to produce flowers or fruits 3 *Poker* a stake put up by a player before he examines his cards 4 *Hunting, chiefly US and Canadian* a screen of brush or undergrowth, in which hunters hide to shoot their quarry
▷www.eyecarefoundation.org

blindfold *Chess* not seeing the board and pieces

blind spot *Anatomy* a small oval-shaped area of the reti-

na in which vision is not experienced. It marks the nonphotosensitive site of entrance into the eyeball of the optic nerve

blinker a flashing light for sending messages, as a warning device, etc, such as a direction indicator on a road vehicle

Bliss Sir Arthur 1891–1975, British composer; Master of the Queen's Musick (1953–75). His works include the *Colour Symphony* (1922), film and ballet music, and a cello concerto (1970)

blister 1 a small bubble-like elevation of the skin filled with serum, produced as a reaction to a burn, mechanical irritation, etc 2 a transparent dome or any bulge on the fuselage of an aircraft, such as one used for observation

blitz *American football* a defensive charge on the quarterback

Blitz the the systematic night-time bombing of the British in 1940–41 by the German Luftwaffe

Blixen Karen. See (Isak) **Dinesen**

blizzard a strong bitterly cold wind accompanied by a widespread heavy snowfall

bloat *Vet science* an abnormal distention of the abdomen in cattle, sheep, etc, caused by accumulation of gas in the stomach

bloc a group of people or countries combined by a common interest or aim

Bloch 1 Ernest 1880–1959, US composer, born in Switzerland, who found inspiration in Jewish liturgical and folk music: his works include the symphonies *Israel* (1916) and *America* (1926) 2 Felix 1905–83, US physicist, born in Switzerland: Nobel prize for physics (1952) for his work on the magnetic moments of atomic particles 3 Konrad Emil 1912–2000, US biochemist, born in Germany: shared the Nobel prize for physiology or medicine in 1964 for his work on fatty-acid metabolism 4 Marc 1886–1944, French historian and Resistance fighter; author of *Feudal Society* (1935) and *Strange Defeat* (1940), an essay on the fall of France: killed by the Nazis outside Lyons, France

block 1 a casing housing one or more freely rotating pulleys 2 *Pathol* interference in the normal physiological functioning of an organ or part 3 *Psychol* a short interruption of perceptual or thought processes 4 *Computing* a group of words treated as a unit of data on a tape, disk, etc 5 *Cricket* a mark made near the popping crease by a batsman to indicate his position in relation to the wicket

blockade *Med* the inhibition of the effect of a hormone or a drug, a transport system, or the action of a nerve by a drug

block and tackle a hoisting device in which a rope or chain is passed around a pair of blocks containing one or more pulleys. The upper block is secured overhead and the lower block supports the load, the effort being applied to the free end of the rope or chain

Bloemfontein a city in central South Africa: capital of Free State province and judicial capital of the country. Pop: 111 698 (2001)

blog a journal written on-line and accessible to users of the internet

Blois a city in N central France, on the Loire: 13th-century castle. Pop: 49 171 (1999)

blonde a French pillow lace, originally of unbleached cream-coloured Chinese silk, later of bleached or black-dyed silk

Blondin Charles, real name *Jean-François Gravelet*. 1824–97, French acrobat and tightrope walker; best known for walking a tightrope across Niagara Falls (1859)

blood 1 a reddish fluid in vertebrates that is pumped by the heart through the arteries and veins, supplies tissues with nutrients, oxygen, etc, and removes waste products. It consists of a fluid containing cells (erythrocytes, leucocytes, and platelets) 2 a similar fluid in such invertebrates as annelids and arthropods 3 *Obsolete* one of the four bodily humours

blood bank a place where whole blood, blood plasma, or other blood products are stored until required in transfusion

blood count the number of red and white blood corpuscles and platelets in a specific sample of blood

blood group any one of the various groups into which human blood is classified on the basis of its agglutinogens

blood heat the normal temperature of the human body, 98.4°F or 37°C

bloodhound a large breed of hound having a smooth glossy coat of red, tan, or black and loose wrinkled skin on its head: formerly much used in tracking and police work

blood-letting the therapeutic removal of blood, as in relieving congestive heart failure

blood orange a variety of orange all or part of the pulp of which is dark red when ripe

blood pressure the pressure exerted by the blood on the inner walls of the arteries, being relative to the elasticity and diameter of the vessels and the force of the heartbeat

blood relation *or* **relative** a person related to another by birth, as distinct from one related by marriage

bloodshot (of an eye) inflamed

blood sport any sport involving the killing of an animal, esp hunting

bloodstock thoroughbred horses, esp those bred for racing

bloodstream the flow of blood through the vessels of a living body

bloodsucker an animal that sucks blood, esp a leech or mosquito

blood vessel an artery, capillary, or vein

bloom¹ 1 a fine whitish coating on the surface of fruits, leaves, etc, consisting of minute grains of a waxy substance 2 *Ecology* a visible increase in the algal constituent of plankton, which may be seasonal or due to excessive organic pollution

bloom² a rectangular mass of metal obtained by rolling or forging a cast ingot

Bloomfield Leonard 1887–1949, US linguist, influential for his strictly scientific and descriptive approach to comparative linguistics; author of *Language* (1933)

Bloomington a city in central Indiana: seat of the University of Indiana (1820). Pop: 70 642 (2003 est)

Bloomsbury a district of central London in the borough of Camden: contains the British Museum, part of the

University of London, and many publishers' offices

blossom the flower or flowers of a plant, esp conspicuous flowers producing edible fruit

blot *Backgammon* a man exposed by being placed alone on a point and therefore able to be taken by the other player

blow *Archaic Metallurgy* a a stage in the Bessemer process in which air is blasted upwards through molten pig iron b the quantity of metal treated in a Bessemer converter

blower 1 a low-pressure rotary compressor, esp in a furnace or internal-combustion engine 2 an informal name for a **whale**

blowfly any of various dipterous flies of the genus *Calliphora* and related genera that lay their eggs in rotting meat, dung, carrion, and open wounds: family *Calliphoridae*

blowhole 1 the nostril, paired or single, of whales, situated far back on the skull 2 a hole in ice through which whales, seals, etc, breathe 3 a bubble-like defect in an ingot resulting from gas being trapped during solidification 4 *Geology* a hole in a cliff top leading to a sea cave through which air is forced by the action of the sea

blow out 1 the sudden melting of an electrical fuse 2 a sudden burst in a tyre 3 the failure of a jet engine, esp when in flight

blowpipe 1 a tube for blowing air or oxygen into a flame to intensify its heat and direct it onto a small area 2 a long narrow iron pipe used to gather molten glass and blow it into shape

blowtorch a small burner that produces a very hot flame, used to remove old paint, melt soft metal, etc

blubber 1 a thick insulating layer of fatty tissue below the skin of aquatic mammals such as the whale: used by man as a source of oil 2 *Austral* an informal name for **jellyfish**

blue 1 any of a group of colours, such as that of a clear unclouded sky, that have wavelengths in the range 490–445 nanometres. Blue is the complementary colour of yellow and with red and green forms a set of primary colours 2 a a sportsman who represents or has represented Oxford or Cambridge University and has the right to wear the university colour (dark blue for Oxford, light blue for Cambridge) b the honour of so representing one's university 3 *Brit* an informal name for **Tory** 4 any of numerous small blue-winged butterflies of the genera *Lampides*, *Polyommatus*, etc.: family *Lycaenidae* 5 *Archery* a blue ring on a target, between the red and the black, scoring five points 6 a blue ball in snooker, etc

blue baby a baby born with a bluish tinge to the skin because of lack of oxygen in the blood, esp caused by a congenital defect of the heart

bluebell 1 a European liliaceous woodland plant, *Hyacinthoides* (or *Endymion*) *non-scripta*, having a one-sided cluster of blue bell-shaped flowers 2 a similar and related plant, *hispanica*, widely grown in gardens and becoming naturalized 3 a Scot name for **harebell** 4 any of various other plants with blue bell-shaped flowers

blueberry 1 any of several North American ericaceous shrubs of the genus *Vaccinium*, such as *V. pennsylvanicum*, that have blue-black edible berries with tiny seeds 2 a the fruit of any of these plants **b** (*as modifier*): blueberry pie

bluebird 1 any North American songbird of the genus *Sialia*, having a blue or partly blue plumage: subfamily *Turdinae* (thrushes) **2 fairy bluebird** any songbird of the genus *Irena*, of S and SE Asia, having a blue-and-black plumage: family *Irenidae* **3** any of various other birds having a blue plumage

bluebottle any of various blue-flowered plants, esp the cornflower

blue chip a gambling chip with the highest value

blue heeler *Austral and NZ* a cattle dog that controls cattle by biting their heels

Blue Nile a river in E Africa, rising in central Ethiopia as the Abbai and flowing southeast, then northwest to join the White Nile. Length: about 1530 km (950 miles)

blue peter *Nautical* a signal flag of blue with a white square at the centre, displayed by a vessel about to leave port

blueprint a photographic print of plans, technical drawings, etc, consisting of white lines on a blue background

blue ribbon (in Britain) a badge of blue silk worn by members of the Order of the Garter

bluetit a common European tit, *Parus caeruleus*, having a blue crown, wings, and tail, yellow underparts, and a black and grey head

blue whale the largest mammal: a widely distributed bluish-grey whalebone whale, *Sibbaldus* (or *Balaenoptera*) *musculus*, closely related and similar to the rorquals: family *Balaenopteridae*

bluff 1 a steep promontory, bank, or cliff, esp one formed by river erosion on the outside bend of a meander **2** (of a bank, cliff, etc) presenting a steep broad face

Blum Léon 1872–1950, French socialist statesman; premier of France (1936–37; 1938; 1946–47)

Blunden Edmund (**Charles**). 1896–1974, British poet and scholar, noted esp for *Undertones of War* (1928), a memoir of World War I in verse and prose

Blunkett David born 1947, British Labour politician; secretary of state for education and employment (1997–2001); home secretary (2001–2004)

Blunt 1 Anthony 1907–83, British art historian and Soviet spy **2** Wilfred Scawen 1840–1922, British poet, traveller, and anti-imperialist

blush 1 a reddish or pinkish tinge **2** a cloudy area on the surface of freshly applied gloss paint

Blyth¹ Sir Chay born 1940, British yachtsman. He sailed round the world alone (1970–71) and won many races

Blyth² a port in N England, in SE Northumberland, on the North Sea. Pop: 35 691 (2001)

Blyton Enid (**Mary**). 1897–1968, British writer of children's books; creator of Noddy and the *Famous Five* series of adventure stories

B-movie a film originally made (esp in Hollywood in the 1940s and 50s) as a supporting film, now often considered as a genre in its own right

boa any large nonvenomous snake of the family *Boidae*, most of which occur in Central and South America and the Caribbean. They have vestigial hind limbs and kill their prey by constriction

boa constrictor a very large snake, *Constrictor constrictor*, of tropical America and the Caribbean, that kills its prey by constriction: family *Boidae* (boas)

boar an uncastrated male pig

board 1 the boards the acting profession; the stage **2** short for **blackboard, chessboard, springboard, surfboard 3** *Nautical* **a** the side of a ship **b** the leg that a sailing vessel makes on a beat to windward **4 a** any of various portable surfaces specially designed for indoor games such as chess, backgammon, etc **b** (*as modifier*): *board games* **5 a** a set of hands in duplicate bridge **b** a wooden or metal board containing four slots, or often nowadays, a plastic wallet, in which the four hands are placed so that the deal may be replayed with identical hands **6** the hull of a sailboard, usually made of plastic, to which the mast is jointed and on which a windsurfer stands **7 sweep the board** (in gambling) to win all the cards or money

boarder 1 *Brit* a pupil who lives at school during term time **2** *US* a child who lives away from its parents and is cared for by a person or organization receiving payment **3** a person who boards a ship, esp one who forces his way aboard in an attack **4** *Informal* a person who takes part in sailboarding or snowboarding
▷boardgames.about.com

boarding house *Austral* a house for boarders at a school

boarding school a school providing living accommodation for some or all of its pupils

boardroom a a room where the board of directors of a company meets **b** (*as modifier*): *a boardroom power struggle*

boast *Squash* a stroke in which the ball is hit on to one of the side walls before hitting the front wall

boat 1 a small vessel propelled by oars, paddle, sails, or motor for travelling, transporting goods, etc, esp one that can be carried aboard a larger vessel **2** (not in technical use) another word for **ship 3** a small boat-shaped container for incense, used in some Christian churches

boatswain, bosun, or **bo's'n** a petty officer on a merchant ship or a warrant officer on a warship who is responsible for the maintenance of the ship and its equipment

Boa Vista a town in N Brazil, capital of the state of Roraima, on the Rio Branco. Pop: 275 000 (2005 est)

Boaz *Old Testament* a kinsman of Naomi, who married her daughter-in-law Ruth (Ruth 2–4); one of David's ancestors

bob¹ 1 *Bell-ringing* a particular set of changes **2** *Angling* the topmost fly on a cast of three, often fished bobbing at the surface

bob² 1 a dangling or hanging object, such as the weight on a pendulum or on a plumb line **2** a polishing disc on a rotating spindle. It is usually made of felt, leather, etc, impregnated with an abrasive material **3** *Angling* a small knot of worms, maggots, etc, used as bait **4** *Prosody* a very short line of verse at the end of a stanza or preceding a rhyming quatrain (the wheel) at the end of a stanza **5** a refrain or burden with such a short line or lines **6** a docked tail, esp of a horse

bobbejaan *South African* **1** a baboon **2** a large black spider **3** a monkey wrench

bobbin 1 a spool or reel on which thread or yarn is wound, being unwound as required; spool; reel **2** narrow braid or cord used as binding or for trimming **3 a** a spool on which insulated wire is wound to form the coil of a small electromagnetic device, such as a bell or buzzer **b** the coil of such a spool

Bobo-Dioulasso a city in W Burkina-Faso. Pop: 396 000 (2005 est)

Bobruisk or **Bobruysk** a port in Belarus, on the River Berezina: engineering, timber, tyre manufacturing. Pop: 219 000 (2005 est)

bobtail 1 a docked or diminutive tail **2** an animal with such a tail **3** having the tail cut short

Boccaccio Giovanni 1313–75, Italian poet and writer, noted particularly for his *Decameron*(1353), a collection of 100 short stories. His other works include *Filostrato*(?1338) and *Teseida* (1341)

Boccherini Luigi 1743–1805, Italian composer and cellist

Bochum an industrial city in NW Germany, in W North Rhine-Westphalia: university (1965). Pop: 387 283 (2003 est)

bodega a shop selling wine and sometimes groceries, esp in a Spanish-speaking country

Bodhidharma 6th century AD, Indian Buddhist monk, who taught in China (from 520): considered to be the founder of Zen Buddhism

Bodmin a market town in SW England, in Cornwall, near **Bodmin Moor**, a granite upland rising to 420 m (1375 ft). Pop: 12 778 (2001)

body 1 the entire physical structure of an animal or human being **2** the trunk or torso, not including the limbs, head, or tail **3** *Maths* a three-dimensional region with an interior **4** *Physics* an object or substance that has three dimensions, a mass, and is distinguishable from surrounding objects **5** the sound box of a guitar, violin, or similar stringed instrument **6** (in water-colour painting) a white filler mixed with pigments to make them opaque

body building the practice of performing regular exercises designed to make the muscles of the body conspicuous

bodycheck *Wrestling* the act of blocking a charging opponent with the body

body language the nonverbal imparting of information by means of conscious or subconscious bodily gestures, posture, etc.

body politic the the people of a nation or the nation itself considered as a political entity; the state

body search a form of search by police, customs officials, etc, that involves examination of a prisoner's or suspect's bodily orifices

body shop a place where the bodywork of motor vehicles is built or repaired

bodywork 1 the external shell of a motor vehicle **2** any form of therapy in which parts of the body are manipulated, such as massage

Boeotia a region of ancient Greece, northwest of Athens. It consisted of ten city-states, which formed the Boeotian League, led by Thebes: at its height in the 4th century BC

Boeotian 1 a native or inhabitant of Boeotia, a region of ancient Greece **2** of or relating to Boeotia or its inhabitants

Boer a descendant of any of the Dutch or Huguenot colonists who settled in South Africa, mainly in Cape Colony, the Orange Free State, and the Transvaal **b** (as modifier): *a Boer farm*
▷www.wikipedia.org/wiki/Boer_War
▷www.nationmaster.com/encyclopedia/Boer-War

Boethius Anicius Manlius Severinus ?480–?524 AD, Roman philosopher and statesman, noted particularly for his work *De Consolatione Philosophiae*. He was accused of treason and executed by Theodoric

bog wet spongy ground consisting of decomposing vegetation, which ultimately forms peat

Bogarde Sir Dirk, real name *Derek Jules Gaspard Ulric Niven van den Bogaerde*. 1920–99, British film actor and writer: his films include *The Servant* (1963) and *Death in Venice* (1970). His writings include the autobiographical *A Postillion Struck by Lightning* (1977) and the novel *A Period of Adjustment* (1994)

Bogart Humphrey (**DeForest**). nicknamed *Bogie*. 1899–1957, US film actor: his films include *High Sierra* (1941), *Casablanca* (1942), *The Big Sleep* (1946), *The African Queen* (1951), and *The Caine Mutiny* (1954)

bogey or **bogy** *Golf* **a** a score of one stroke over par on a hole **b** *Obsolete* a standard score for a hole or course, regarded as one that a good player should make

bogie or **bogy 1** an assembly of four or six wheels forming a pivoted support at either end of a railway coach. It provides flexibility on curves **2** *Chiefly Brit* a small railway truck of short wheelbase, used for conveying coal, ores, etc.

bogle a rhythmic dance, originating in the early 1990s, performed to ragga music

Bognor Regis a resort in S England, in West Sussex on the English Channel: electronics industries. *Regis* was added to the name after King George V's convalescence there in 1929. Pop: 62 141 (2001)

Bogor a city in Indonesia, in W Java: botanical gardens and research institutions. Pop: 750 819 (2000)

Bohai or **Pohai** a large inlet of the Yellow Sea on the coast of NE China. Also called: (Gulf of) **Chihli**

Bohemia 1 a former kingdom of central Europe, surrounded by mountains: independent from the 9th to the 13th century; belonged to the Hapsburgs from 1526 until 1918 **2** an area of the W Czech Republic, formerly a province of Czechoslovakia (1918–1949). From 1939 until 1945 it formed part of the German protectorate of **Bohemia-Moravia**

Bohemian Forest a mountain range between the SW Czech Republic and SE Germany. Highest peak: Arber, 1457 m (4780 ft)

Bohol an island of the central Philippines. Chief town: Tagbilaran. Pop: 1 139 130 (2000). Area: about 3900 sq km (1500 sq miles)

Bohr 1 Aage Niels born 1922, Danish physicist, noted for his work on nuclear structure. He shared the Nobel prize for physics 1975 **2** his father, **Niels** (**Henrik David**). 1885–1962, Danish physicist, who applied the quantum theory to Rutherford's model of the atom to explain spectral lines: Nobel prize for physics 1922

bohrium a transuranic element artificially produced in minute quantities by bombarding ^{204}Bi atoms with ^{54}Cr nuclei. Symbol: Bh; atomic no.: 107

boil a red painful swelling with a hard pus-filled core

caused by bacterial infection of the skin and subcutaneous tissues, esp at a hair follicle

Boileau Nicolas full name *Nicolas Boileau-Despréaux*. 1636–1711, French poet and critic; author of satires, episties, and *L'Art poétique* (1674), in which he laid down the basic principles of French classical literature

boiler a closed vessel or arrangement of enclosed tubes in which water is heated to supply steam to drive an engine or turbine or provide heat

boiling point the temperature at which a liquid boils at a given pressure, usually atmospheric pressure at sea level; the temperature at which the vapour pressure of a liquid equals the external pressure

Bois de Boulogne a large park in W Paris, formerly a forest: includes the racecourses of Auteuil and Longchamp

Boise *or* **Boise City** a city in SW Idaho: the state capital. Pop: 190 117 (2003 est)

Boito Arrigo 1842–1918, Italian operatic composer and librettist, whose works include the opera *Mefistofele* (1868) and the librettos for Verdi's *Otello* and *Falstaff*

Bokassa I original name *Jean Bedel Bokassa*. 1921–96, president of the Central African Republic (1972–76); emperor of the renamed Central African Empire from 1976 until overthrown in 1979

Boland an area of high altitude in S South Africa

Bolan Pass a mountain pass in W central Pakistan through the Brahui Range, between Sibi and Quetta, rising to 1800 m (5900 ft)

Boldrewood Rolf, real name *Thomas Alexander Browne*. 1826–1915, Australian writer, born in the UK, noted for his novels of the Australian outback, esp *Robbery Under Arms* (1882–3)

bole[1] the trunk of a tree

bole[2] *or* **bolus** a moderate reddish-brown colour

bolero 1 a Spanish dance, often accompanied by the guitar and castanets, usually in triple time 2 a piece of music composed for or in the rhythm of this dance

Boleyn Anne 1507–36, second wife of Henry VIII of England; mother of Elizabeth I. She was executed on a charge of adultery

Bolingbroke 1 the surname of **Henry IV** of England 2 **Henry St John**, 1st Viscount Bolingbroke. 1678–1751, English politician; fled to France in 1714 and acted as secretary of state to the Old Pretender; returned to England in 1723. His writings include *A Dissertation on Parties* (1733–34) and *Idea of a Patriot King* (1738)

Bolivar Simon 1783–1830, South American soldier and liberator. He drove the Spaniards from Venezuela, Colombia, Ecuador, and Peru and hoped to set up a republican confederation, but was prevented by separatist movements in Venezuela and Colombia (1829–30). Upper Peru became a separate state and was called Bolivia in his honour

Bolivia an inland republic in central S America: original Aymará Indian population conquered by the Incas in the 13th century; colonized by Spain from 1538; became a republic in 1825; consists of low plains in the east, with ranges of the Andes rising to over 6400 m (21 000 ft) and the Altiplano, a plateau averaging 3900 m (13 000 ft) in the west; contains some of the world's highest inhabited regions; important producer of tin

and other minerals. Official languages: Spanish, Quechua, and Aymara. Religion: Roman Catholic. Currency: boliviano. Capital: La Paz (administrative); Sucre (judicial). Pop: 8 973 000 (2004 est). Area: 1 098 580 sq km (424 260 sq miles)

boll the fruit of such plants as flax and cotton, consisting of a rounded capsule containing the seeds

bollard 1 a strong wooden or metal post mounted on a wharf, quay, etc, used for securing mooring lines 2 *Brit* a small post or marker placed on a kerb or traffic island to make it conspicuous to motorists 3 *Mountaineering* an outcrop of rock or pillar of ice that may be used to belay a rope

Bologna[1] Giovanni da. See **Giambologna**

Bologna[2] a city in N Italy, at the foot of the Apennines: became a free city in the Middle Ages; university (1088). Pop: 371 217 (2001)

Bolshevik (formerly) a Russian Communist
▷www.imternationalist.org/
stalinism&bolshevism.html
▷www.1upinfo.com/encyclopedia/B/
Bolshevism.html

bolster a cold chisel having a broad blade splayed towards the cutting edge, used for cutting stone slabs, etc

bolt an arrow, esp for a crossbow

Bolt Robert (Oxton). 1924–95, British playwright. His plays include *A Man for All Seasons* (1960) and he also wrote a number of screenplays

Bolton 1 a town in NW England, in Bolton unitary authority, Greater Manchester: centre of the woollen trade since the 14th century; later important for cotton. Pop: 139 403 (2001) 2 a unitary authority in NW England, in Greater Manchester. Pop: 263 800 (2003 est). Area: 140 sq km (54 sq miles)

Boltzmann Ludwig 1844–1906, Austrian physicist. He established the principle of the equipartition of energy and developed the kinetic theory of gases with J. C. Maxwell

Bolzano a city in NE Italy, in Trentino-Alto Adige: belonged to Austria until 1919. Pop: 94 989 (2001)

Boma a port in the Democratic Republic of Congo (formerly Zaïre), on the Congo River, capital of the Belgian Congo until 1926: forest products. Pop: 607 000 (2005 est)

bomb 1 **the bomb** a a hydrogen or atomic bomb considered as the ultimate destructive weapon b *Slang* something excellent 2 a round or pear-shaped mass of volcanic rock, solidified from molten lava that has been thrown into the air 3 *Med* a container for radioactive material, applied therapeutically to any part of the body 4 *American football* a very long high pass
▷www.fas.org/man/dod-101/sys/dumb

bombardier any of various small carabid beetles of the genus *Brachinus*, esp *B. crepitans* of Europe, which defend themselves by ejecting a jet of volatile fluid

Bombardier *Trademark, Canadian* a snow tractor, typically having caterpillar tracks at the rear and skis at the front

Bombay 1 a port in W India, capital of Maharashtra state, on the Arabian Sea: ceded by Portugal to England in 1661 and of major importance in British India; com-

mercial and industrial centre, esp for cotton. Pop:
11 914 398 (2001) **2** a breed of black short-haired medium-sized cat

Bombay duck a teleost fish, *Harpodon nehereus*, that resembles and is related to the lizard fishes: family *Harpodontidae*. It is eaten dried with curry dishes as a savoury

bombazine *or* **bombasine** a twilled fabric, esp one with a silk warp and worsted weft, formerly worn dyed black for mourning

Bomu *or* **Mbomu** a river in central Africa, rising in the SE Central African Republic and flowing west into the Uele River, forming the Ubangi River. Length: about 800 km (500 miles)

Bon Cape a peninsula of NE Tunisia

Bona Mount a mountain in S Alaska, in the Wrangell Mountains. Height: 5005 m (16 420 ft)

Bonaire an island in the S Caribbean, in the E Netherlands Antilles: one of the Leeward Islands. Chief town: Kralendijk. Pop: 10 185 (2004 est). Area: about 288 sq km (111 sq miles)

Bonaparte **1** Jérôme , brother of Napoleon I. 1784–1860, king of Westphalia (1807–13) **2** Joseph , brother of Napoleon I. 1768–1844, king of Naples (1806–08) and of Spain (1808–13) **3** Louis , brother of Napoleon I. 1778–1846, king of Holland (1806–10) **4** Lucien , brother of Napoleon I. 1775–1840, prince of Canino

Bonaventura *or* **Bonaventure** Saint, called *the Seraphic Doctor*. 1221–74, Italian Franciscan monk, mystic, theologian, and philosopher; author of a *Life of St Francis* and *Journey of the Soul to God* Feast day: July 14

bond **1** *Law* a written acknowledgment of an obligation to pay a sum or to perform a contract **2 in bond** *Commerce* deposited in a bonded warehouse

Bond Edward born 1934, British dramatist: his plays, including *Saved* (1965), *Lear* (1971), *Restoration* (1981), and *In the Company of Men* (1990), are noted for their violent imagery and socialist commitment

bondage (in medieval Europe) the condition and status of unfree peasants who provided labour and other services for their lord in return for holdings of land

bonded *Commerce* deposited in a bonded warehouse; placed or stored in bond

Bondi Sir Hermann born 1919, British mathematician and cosmologist, born in Austria; joint originator (with Sir Fred Hoyle and Thomas Gold) of the steady-state theory of the universe

Bondi Beach a beach in Sydney, Australia, popular with surfers

bone **1** any of the various structures that make up the skeleton in most vertebrates **2** the porous rigid tissue of which these parts are made, consisting of a matrix of collagen and inorganic salts, such as calcium phosphate, interspersed with canals and small holes

bone china porcelain containing bone ash

bongo¹ a rare spiral-horned antelope, *Boocercus* (or *Taurotragus*) *eurycerus*, inhabiting forests of central Africa. The coat is bright red-brown with narrow cream stripes

bongo² a small bucket-shaped drum, usually one of a pair, played by beating with the fingers

Bonhoeffer Dietrich 1906–45, German Lutheran theologian: executed by the Nazis

Boniface Saint original name *Wynfrith*. ?680–?755 AD. Anglo-Saxon missionary: archbishop of Mainz (746–755). Feast day: June 5

Boniface VIII original name *Benedict Caetano*. ?1234–1303, pope (1294–1303)

Bonington **1** Sir Chris(tian John Storey). born 1934, British mountaineer and writer; led 1970 Annapurna I and 1975 Everest expeditions; reached Everest summit in 1985 **2** Richard Parkes 1801–28, British painter of landscapes and historical scenes

bonito **1** any of various small tunny-like marine food fishes of the genus *Sarda*, of warm Atlantic and Pacific waters: family *Scombridae* (tunnies and mackerels) **2** any of various similar or related fishes, such as *Katsuwonus pelamis* (**oceanic bonito**), the flesh of which is dried and flaked and used in Japanese cookery

Bonn a city in W Germany, in North Rhine-Westphalia on the Rhine: the former capital (1949–90) of West Germany; university (1786). Pop: 311 052 (2003 est)

Bonnard Pierre 1867–1947, French painter and lithographer, noted for the effects of light and colour in his landscapes and sunlit interiors

bonnet **1** the hinged metal part of a motor vehicle body that provides access to the engine, or to the luggage space in a rear-engined vehicle **2** a cowl on a chimney **3** *Nautical* a piece of sail laced to the foot of a foresail to give it greater area in light winds

Bonnie Prince Charlie See (Charles Edward) **Stuart**

Bonny Bight of a wide bay at the E end of the Gulf of Guinea off the coasts of Nigeria and Cameroon

bonsai the art of growing dwarfed ornamental varieties of trees or shrubs in small shallow pots or trays by selective pruning, etc
> www.bonsai4me.com
> www.bonsaiweb.com
> http://geocities.com/bonsai_enthusiasts/index.html
> www.saba.org.za

Bonynge Richard born 1930, Australian conductor, esp of opera; married to the soprano Joan Sutherland

booby any of several tropical marine birds of the genus *Sula*: family *Sulidae*, order *Pelecaniformes* (pelicans, cormorants, etc). They have a straight stout bill and the plumage is white with darker markings

boogie-woogie a style of piano jazz using a dotted bass pattern, usually with eight notes in a bar and the harmonies of the 12-bar blues
> www.jazzinamerica.org

book **1** the script of a play or the libretto of an opera, musical, etc **2** a major division of a written composition, as of a long novel or of the Bible **3** *Bookmaking* a record of the bets made on a horse race or other event **4** (in card games) the number of tricks that must be taken by a side or player before any trick has a scoring value **5 the book** the Bible

booking *Theatre* an engagement for the services of an actor or acting company

bookmaker a person who as an occupation accepts bets, esp on horseraces, and pays out to winning betters

bookmark *Computing* **a** an address for a website stored on a computer so that the user can easily return to the site **b** an identifier placed in a document so that part of the document can be accessed easily

bookworm any of various small insects that feed on the binding paste of books, esp the book louse

Boole George 1815–64, English mathematician. In *Mathematical Analysis of Logic* (1847) and *An Investigation of the Laws of Thought* (1854), he applied mathematical formulae to logic, creating Boolean algebra

Boolean algebra a system of symbolic logic devised by George Boole to codify logical operations. It is used in computers

boom¹ **1** the cry of certain animals, esp the bittern **2** *Economics* a period of high economic growth characterized by rising wages, profits, and prices, full employment, and high levels of investment, trade, and other economic activity

boom² **1** *Nautical* a spar to which a sail is fastened to control its position relative to the wind **2** a beam or spar pivoting at the foot of the mast of a derrick, controlling the distance from the mast at which a load is lifted or lowered **3** a pole, usually extensible, carrying an overhead microphone and projected over a film or television set **4** a barrier across a waterway, usually consisting of a chain of connected floating logs, to confine free-floating logs, protect a harbour from attack, etc

boomer *Austral* a large male kangaroo

boomslang a large greenish venomous arboreal colubrid snake, *Dispholidus typus*, of southern Africa

boost the amount by which the induction pressure of a supercharged internal-combustion engine exceeds that of the ambient pressure

booster **1** *Radio, Television* **a** a radio-frequency amplifier connected between an aerial and a receiver to amplify weak incoming signals **b** a radio-frequency amplifier that amplifies incoming signals, retransmitting them at higher power **2** another name for **supercharger**

boot **1** an enclosed compartment of a car for holding luggage, etc, usually at the rear **2** a protective covering over a mechanical device, such as a rubber sheath protecting a coupling joining two shafts **3** *US and Canadian* a rubber patch used to repair a puncture in a tyre **4** a protective covering for the lower leg of a horse

Booth **1** Edwin Thomas, son of Junius Brutus Booth. 1833–93, US actor **2** John Wilkes, son of Junius Brutus Booth. 1838–65, US actor; assassin of Abraham Lincoln **3** Junius Brutus 1796–1852, US actor, born in England **4** William 1829–1912, British religious leader; founder and first general of the Salvation Army (1878)

Boothia Peninsula a peninsula of N Canada: the northernmost part of the mainland of North America, lying west of the Gulf of Boothia, an arm of the Arctic Ocean

Bootle a port in NW England, in Sefton unitary authority, Merseyside; on the River Mersey adjoining Liverpool. Pop: 59 123 (2001)

booty *Slang* the buttocks

Bophuthatswana (formerly) a Bantu homeland in N South Africa: consisted of six separate areas; granted independence by South Africa in 1977 although this was not internationally recognized; abolished in 1993. Capital: Mmabatho

bora¹ a violent cold north wind blowing from the moun-

tains to the E coast of the Adriatic, usually in winter

bora² an initiation ceremony of native Australians, introducing youths to manhood

Bora Bora an island in the S Pacific, in French Polynesia, in the Society Islands: one of the Leeward Islands. Area: 39 sq km (15 sq miles)

borage **1** a European boraginaceous plant, *Borago officinalis*, with star-shaped blue flowers. The young leaves have a cucumber-like flavour and are sometimes used in salads or as seasoning **2** any of several related plants

borax **1** a soluble readily fusible white mineral consisting of impure hydrated disodium tetraborate in monoclinic crystalline form, occurring in alkaline soils and salt deposits. Formula: $Na_2B_4O_7.10H_2O$ **2** pure disodium tetraborate

Bordeaux **1** a port in SW France, on the River Garonne: a major centre of the wine trade. Pop: 215 363 (1999) **2** any of several red, white, or rosé wines produced around Bordeaux

border **1** the dividing line or frontier between political or geographic regions **2 a** a region straddling such a boundary **b** (*as modifier*): *border country* **3 a** a design or ornamental strip around the edge or rim of something, such as a printed page or dinner plate **b** (*as modifier*): *a border illustration* **4** a long narrow strip of ground planted with flowers, shrubs, trees, etc, that skirts a path or wall or surrounds a lawn or other area

Border¹ Allan (Robert). born 1955, Australian cricketer; captain of Australia (1985–94)

Border² the **1** the area straddling the border between England and Scotland **2** the area straddling the border between Northern Ireland and the Republic of Ireland **3** the region in S South Africa around East London

Borders Region a former local government region in S Scotland, formed in 1975 from Berwick, Peebles, Roxburgh, Selkirk, and part of Midlothian; replaced in 1996 by Scottish Borders council area

bore¹ **a** a circular hole in a material produced by drilling, turning, or drawing **b** the diameter of such a hole

bore² a high steep-fronted wave moving up a narrow estuary, caused by the tide

Borg Björn born 1956, Swedish tennis player: Wimbledon champion 1976–80

Borgerhout a city in N Belgium, near Antwerp. Pop: 40 142 (2002 est)

Borges Jorge Luis 1899–1986, Argentinian poet, short-story writer, and literary scholar. The short stories collected in *Ficciones* (1944) he described as "games with infinity"

Borgia **1** Cesare , son of Rodrigo Borgia (Pope Alexander VI). 1475–1507, Italian cardinal, politician, and military leader; model for Machiavelli's *The Prince* **2** his sister, Lucrezia , daughter of Rodrigo Borgia. 1480–1519, Italian noblewoman. After her third marriage (1501), to the Duke of Ferrara, she became a patron of the arts and science **3** Rodrigo . See Alexander VI

boric of or containing boron

boric acid **1** a white soluble weakly acid crystalline solid used in the manufacture of heat-resistant glass and porcelain enamels, as a fireproofing material, and as a mild antiseptic. Formula: H_3BO_3 **2** any other acid containing boron

Bormann Martin 1900–45, German Nazi politician; Hitler's adviser and private secretary (1942–45): committed suicide

Born Max 1882–1970, British nuclear physicist, born in Germany, noted for his fundamental contribution to quantum mechanics: Nobel prize for physics 1954

born-again having experienced conversion, esp to evangelical Christianity

Borneo an island in the W Pacific, between the Sulu and Java Seas, part of the Malay Archipelago: divided into Kalimantan (**Indonesian Borneo**), the Malaysian states of Sarawak and Sabah, and the sultanate of Brunei; mountainous and densely forested. Area: about 750 000 sq km (290 000 sq miles)

Bornholm an island in the Baltic Sea, south of Sweden: administratively part of Denmark. Chief town: Rønne. Pop: 43 956 (2003 est). Area: 588 sq km (227 sq miles)

Borno a state of NE Nigeria, on Lake Chad: the second largest state, formed in 1976 from part of North-Eastern State. Capital: Maiduguri. Pop: 2 903 238 (1995 est). Area: 70 898 sq km (27 374 sq miles)

Borodin Aleksandr Porfirevich 1834–87, Russian composer, whose works include the unfinished opera *Prince Igor*, symphonies, songs, and chamber music

Borodino a village in E central Russia, about 110 km (70 miles) west of Moscow: scene of a battle (1812) in which Napoleon defeated the Russians but irreparably weakened his army

boron a very hard almost colourless crystalline metalloid element that in impure form exists as a brown amorphous powder. It occurs principally in borax and is used in hardening steel. The naturally occurring isotope **boron-10** is used in nuclear control rods and neutron detection instruments. Symbol: B; atomic no.: 5; atomic wt.: 10.81; valency: 3; relative density: 2.34 (crystalline), 2.37 (amorphous); melting pt.: 2092°C; boiling pt.: 4002°C

boronia any aromatic rutaceous shrub of the Australian genus *Boronia*

borough 1 a town, esp (in Britain) one that forms the constituency of an MP or that was originally incorporated by royal charter 2 any of the 32 constituent divisions that together with the City of London make up Greater London 3 any of the five constituent divisions of New York City 4 (in the US) a self-governing incorporated municipality 5 (in medieval England) a fortified town or village or a fort 6 (in New Zealand) a small municipality with a governing body

Borromini Francesco, original name *Francesco Castelli*. 1599–1667, Italian baroque architect, working in Rome: his buildings include the churches of San Carlo (1641) and Sant' Ivo (1660)

borrow 1 *Golf* a deviation of a ball from a straight path because of the slope of the ground 2 material dug from a borrow pit to provide fill at another

Borrow George (Henry). 1803–81, English traveller and writer. His best-known works are the semiautobiographical novels of Gypsy life and language, *Lavengro* (1851) and its sequel *The Romany Rye* (1857)

borzoi a tall graceful fast-moving breed of dog with a long silky coat, originally used in Russia for hunting

wolves

Bosch 1 Carl 1874–1940, German chemist, who adapted the Haber process to produce ammonia for industrial use. He shared the Nobel prize for chemistry 1931 2 Hieronymus , original name probably *Jerome van Aken* (or *Aeken*). ?1450–1516, Dutch painter, noted for his macabre allegorical representations of biblical subjects in brilliant transparent colours, esp the triptych *The Garden of Earthly Delights*

Bose 1 Sir Jagadis Chandra 1858–1937, Indian physicist and plant physiologist 2 Satyendra Nath 1894–1974, Indian physicist, who collaborated with Einstein in devising Bose-Einstein statistics 3 Subhas Chandra , known as *Netaji*. 1897–1945, Indian nationalist leader; president of the Indian National Congress (1938–39); organized the Indian National Army, with Japanese support, in Singapore to free India from British Rule

bosh 1 the lower tapering portion of a blast furnace, situated immediately above the air-inlet tuyères 2 the deposit of siliceous material that occurs on the surfaces of vessels in which copper is refined 3 a water tank for cooling glass-making tools, etc

Bosnia a region of central Bosnia-Herzegovina: belonged to Turkey (1463–1878), to Austria-Hungary (1879–1918), then to Yugoslavia (1918–91)

Bosnia-Herzegovina *or esp US* **Bosnia and Herzegovina** a country in SW Europe; a constituent republic of Yugoslavia until 1991; in a state of civil war (1992–95); Serbian and Croatian forces were also involved: mostly barren and mountainous, with forests in the east. Language: Serbo-Croatian (sometimes now divided into Serbian, Croatian and Bosnian). Religion: Muslim, Serbian Orthodox, and Roman Catholic. Currency: marka (pegged to the euro). Capital: Sarajevo. Pop: 4 186 000 (2004 est). Area: 51 129 sq km (19 737 sq miles)

Bosporus *or* **Bosphorus** the a strait between European and Asian Turkey, linking the Black Sea and the Sea of Marmara

boss¹ *Informal Chiefly US* a professional politician who controls a party machine or political organization, often using devious or illegal methods

boss² 1 *Biology* any of various protuberances or swellings in plants and animals 2 a an area of increased thickness, usually cylindrical, that strengthens or provides room for a locating device on a shaft, hub of a wheel, etc b a similar projection around a hole in a casting or fabricated component 3 an exposed rounded mass of igneous or metamorphic rock, esp the uppermost part of an underlying batholith

bossa nova a dance similar to the samba, originating in Brazil

Boston 1 a port in E Massachusetts, the state capital. Pop: 581 616 (2003 est) 2 a port in E England, in SE Lincolnshire. Pop: 35 124 (2001)

Boswell James 1740–95, Scottish author and lawyer, noted particularly for his *Life of Samuel Johnson* (1791)

Bosworth Field *English history* the site, two miles south of Market Bosworth in Leicestershire, of the battle that ended the Wars of the Roses (August 1485). Richard III was killed and Henry Tudor was crowned king as Henry VII

botany 1 the study of plants, including their classification, structure, physiology, ecology, and economic importance 2 the plant life of a particular region or time 3 the biological characteristics of a particular group of plants
▷www.ou.edu/cas/botany-micro/www-vl
▷www.botany.net/IDB
▷www.academicinfo.net/bot.html

Botany Bay 1 an inlet of the Tasman Sea, on the SE coast of Australia: surrounded by the suburbs of Sydney 2 (in the 19th century) a British penal settlement that was in fact at Port Jackson, New South Wales

Botha 1 Louis 1862–1919, South African statesman and general; first prime minister of the Union of South Africa (1910–19) 2 P(ieter) W(illem). born 1916, South African politician; defence minister (1965–78); prime minister (1978–84); state president (1984–89)

Botham Ian (Terence). born 1955, English cricketer: played for Somerset (1973–86), Worcestershire (1987–91), and Durham (1991–93); captained England (1980–81)

Bothnia Gulf of an arm of the Baltic Sea, extending north between Sweden and Finland

Bothwell Earl of, title of *James Hepburn*. 1535–78, Scottish nobleman; third husband of Mary Queen of Scots. He is generally considered to have instigated the murder of Darnley (1567)

Botox *Trademark* a preparation of botulinum toxin used to treat muscle spasm and to remove wrinkles

Botswana a republic in southern Africa: established as the British protectorate of Bechuanaland in 1885 as a defence against the Boers; became an independent state within the Commonwealth in 1966; consists mostly of a plateau averaging 1000 m (3300 ft), with the extensive Okavango swamps in the northwest and the Kalahari Desert in the southwest. Languages: English and Tswana. Religion: animist majority. Currency: pula. Capital: Gaborone. Pop: 1 795 000 (2004 est). Area: about 570 000 sq km (220 000 sq miles)

Botticelli Sandro , original name *Alessandro di Mariano Filipepi*. 1444–1510, Italian (Florentine) painter, illustrator, and engraver, noted for the graceful outlines and delicate details of his mythological and religious paintings

bottleneck a narrow stretch of road or a junction at which traffic is or may be held up

bottlenose dolphin any dolphin of the genus *Tursiops*, esp *T. truncatus*, some of which have been kept in captivity and trained to perform tricks

bottle tree 1 any of several Australian sterculiaceous trees of the genus *Sterculia* (or *Brachychiton*) that have a bottle-shaped swollen trunk 2 another name for baobab

bottom 1 *Nautical* touch bottom to run aground 2 *Nautical* the parts of a vessel's hull that are under water 3 (in literary and commercial contexts) a boat or ship 4 *Billiards, Snooker* a strike in the centre of the cue ball 5 a dry valley or hollow 6 *US and Canadian* the low land bordering a river

bottom line the last line of a financial statement that shows the net profit or loss of a company or organization

Bottrop an industrial city in W Germany, in North

Rhine-Westphalia in the Ruhr. Pop: 120 324 (2003 est)

botulism severe poisoning from ingestion of botulin, which affects the central nervous system producing difficulty in swallowing, visual disturbances, and respiratory paralysis: often fatal

Boucher François 1703–70, French rococo artist, noted for his delicate ornamental paintings of pastoral scenes and mythological subjects

Boudicca died 62 AD, a queen of the Iceni, who led a revolt against Roman rule in Britain; after being defeated she poisoned herself

Boudin Eugène 1824–98, French painter: one of the first French landscape painters to paint in the open air; a forerunner of impressionism

Bougainville[1] Louis Antoine de 1729–1811, French navigator

Bougainville[2] an island in the W Pacific, in Papua New Guinea: the largest of the Solomon Islands: unilaterally declared independence in 1990; occupied by government troops in 1992, and granted autonomy in 2001. Chief town: Kieta. Area: 10 049 sq km (3880 sq miles)

bougainvillea *or* **bougainvillaea** any tropical woody nyctaginaceous widely cultivated climbing plant of the genus *Bougainvillea*, having inconspicuous flowers surrounded by showy red or purple bracts

Boulanger 1 Georges 1837–91, French general and minister of war (1886–87). Accused of attempting a coup d'état, he fled to Belgium, where he committed suicide 2 Nadia (Juliette). 1887–1979, French teacher of musical composition: her pupils included Elliott Carter, Aaron Copland, Darius Milhaud, and Virgil Thomson. She is noted also for her work in reviving the works of Monteverdi

boulder 1 a smooth rounded mass of rock that has a diameter greater than 25cm and that has been shaped by erosion and transported by ice or water from its original position 2 *Geology* a rock fragment with a diameter greater than 256 mm and thus bigger than a cobble

boulder clay an unstratified glacial deposit consisting of fine clay, boulders, and pebbles

boulevard *Chiefly Canadian* a a grass strip between the pavement and road b the strip of ground between the edge of a private property and the road c the centre strip of a road dividing traffic travelling in different directions

Boulez Pierre born 1925, French composer and conductor, whose works employ total serialism

Boulogne a port in N France, on the English Channel. Pop: 44 859 (1999)

Boulogne-Billancourt an industrial suburb of SW Paris. Pop: 106 367 (1999)

Boult Sir Adrian (Cedric). 1889–1983, English conductor

Boulton Matthew 1728–1809, British engineer and manufacturer, who financed Watt's steam engine and applied it to various industrial purposes

bounce the bounce *Australian Rules football* the start of play at the beginning of each quarter or after a goal

bound[1] *Logic* (of a variable) occurring within the scope of a quantifier that indicates the degree of generality of the open sentence in which the variable occurs: in (x) (Fx → bxy), x is bound and y is free

bound[2] *Maths* a a number which is greater than all the members of a set of numbers (an **upper bound**), or less than all its members (a **lower bound**) **b** more generally, an element of an ordered set that has the same ordering relation to all the members of a given subset **c** whence, an estimate of the extent of some set

boundary *Cricket* **a** the marked limit of the playing area **b** a stroke that hits the ball beyond this limit **c** the four runs scored with such a stroke, or the six runs if the ball crosses the boundary without touching the ground

bourbon a whiskey distilled, chiefly in the US, from maize, esp one containing at least 51 per cent maize (the rest being malt and rye) and aged in charred white-oak barrels

Bourbon **a** a member of the European royal line that ruled in France from 1589 to 1793 (when Louis XVI was executed by the revolutionaries) and was restored in 1815, continuing to rule in its Orleans branch from 1830 until 1848. Bourbon dynasties also ruled in Spain (1700–1808; 1813–1931) and Naples and Sicily (1734–1806; 1815–1860) **b** (*as modifier*): *the Bourbon kings*

bourgeoisie the (in Marxist thought) the ruling class of the two basic classes of capitalist society, consisting of capitalists, manufacturers, bankers, and other employers. The bourgeoisie owns the most important of the means of production, through which it exploits the working class

Bourges a city in central France. Pop: 72 480 (1999)

Bourguiba Habib ben Ali 1903–2000, Tunisian statesman: president of Tunisia (1957–87); a moderate and an advocate of gradual social change. He was deposed in a coup and kept under house arrest for the rest of his life

bourn *. Chiefly southern Brit* a stream, esp an intermittent one in chalk areas

Bournemouth **1** a resort in S England, in Bournemouth unitary authority, Dorset, on the English Channel. Pop: 167 527 (2001) **2** a unitary authority in SE Dorset. Pop: 163 700 (2003 est). Area: 46 sq km (17 sq miles)

bouzouki a Greek long-necked stringed musical instrument related to the mandolin

bovine **1** of, relating to, or belonging to the *Bovini* (cattle), a bovid tribe including domestic cattle **2** any animal belonging to the *Bovini*

bow¹ **1** a weapon for shooting arrows, consisting of an arch of flexible wood, plastic, metal, etc bent by a string (**bowstring**) fastened at each end **2** a long slightly curved stick across which are stretched strands of horsehair, used for playing the strings of a violin, viola, cello, or related instrument **3** *US* **a** a frame of a pair of spectacles **b** a sidepiece of the frame of a pair of spectacles that curls round behind the ear **4** a metal ring forming the handle of a pair of scissors or of a large old-fashioned key **5** *Architect* part of a building curved in the form of a bow

bow² **1** *Chiefly nautical* **a** the forward end or part of a vessel **b** (*as modifier*): *the bow mooring line* **2** **on the port** (or **starboard**) **bow** *Nautical* within 45 degrees to the port (or starboard) of straight ahead

bowel **1** an intestine, esp the large intestine in man **2** innards; entrails

Bowen Elizabeth (**Dorothea Cole**). 1899–1973, British novelist and short-story writer, born in Ireland. Her novels include *The Death of the Heart* (1938) and *The Heat of*

the Day (1949)

bower¹ *Nautical* a vessel's bow anchor

bower² a jack in euchre and similar card games

bowerbird any of various songbirds of the family *Ptilonorhynchidae*, of Australia and New Guinea. The males build bower-like display grounds in the breeding season to attract the females

Bowery the a street in New York City noted for its cheap hotels and bars, frequented by vagrants and drunks

Bowie **1** David, real name *David Jones*. born 1947, British rock singer, songwriter, and film actor. His recordings include "Space Oddity" (1969), *The Rise and Fall of Ziggy Stardust and the Spiders from Mars* (1972), *Heroes* (1977), *Let's Dance* (1983), and *Heathen* (2002) **2** James, known as *Jim Bowie*. 1796–1836, US frontiersman. A hero of the Texas Revolution against Mexico (1835–36), he died at the Battle of the Alamo

bowie knife a stout hunting knife with a short hilt and a guard for the hand

bowl¹ **1** *Chiefly US* a bowl-shaped building or other structure, such as a football stadium or amphitheatre **2** a bowl-shaped depression of the land surface

bowl² **1** a wooden ball used in the game of bowls, having flattened sides, one side usually being flatter than the other in order to make it run on a curved course **2** a large heavy ball with holes for gripping with the fingers and thumb, used in tenpin bowling

Bowles Paul 1910–99, US novelist, short-story writer, and composer, living in Tangiers. His novels include *The Sheltering Sky* (1949) and *The Spider's House* (1955)

bowline *Nautical* a line for controlling the weather leech of a square sail when a vessel is close-hauled

bowling **1** any of various games in which a heavy ball is rolled down a special alley, usually made of wood, at a group of wooden pins, esp the games of tenpin bowling (tenpins) and skittles (ninepins) **2** the game of bowls **3** *Cricket* the act of delivering the ball to the batsman

bowls **1** **a** a game played on a bowling green in which a small bowl (the jack) is pitched from a mark and two opponents or opposing teams take turns to roll biased wooden bowls towards it, the object being to finish as near the jack as possible **b** (*as modifier*): *a bowls tournament* **2** skittles or tenpin bowling
▷www.wbc.org.uk
▷www.lawnbowls.com

bowsprit *Nautical* a spar projecting from the bow of a vessel, esp a sailing vessel, used to carry the headstay as far forward as possible

bowstring the string of an archer's bow, usually consisting of three strands of hemp

bow window a bay window in the shape of a curve

box¹ **1** a separate compartment in a public place for a small group of people, as in a theatre or certain restaurants **2** an enclosure within a courtroom **3** a compartment for a horse in a stable or a vehicle **4** *Brit* a small country house occupied by sportsmen when following a field sport, esp shooting **5** a protective housing for machinery or mechanical parts **b** the contents of such a box **6** the central part of a computer or the casing enclosing it **7** short for **penalty box 8** *Baseball* either of the designated areas for the batter or the pitcher **9** the raised seat on which the driver sits in a horse-drawn coach

box² 1 a dense slow-growing evergreen tree or shrub of the genus *Buxus*, esp *B. sempervirens*, which has small shiny leaves and is used for hedges, borders, and garden mazes: family *Buxaceae* 2 the wood of this tree 3 any of several trees the timber or foliage of which resembles this tree, esp various species of *Eucalyptus* with rough bark

boxer a medium-sized smooth-haired breed of dog with a short nose and a docked tail

boxing a the act, art, or profession of fighting with the fists, esp the modern sport practised under Queensberry rules b *(as modifier): a boxing enthusiast*
    ▷www.ibf-usba-boxing.com
    ▷www.wbaonline.com
    ▷www.wbcboxing.com
    ▷www.ibuboxing.com
    ▷www.aiba.net
    ▷www.wibf.org

boxwood 1 the hard close-grained yellow wood of the box tree, used to make tool handles, small turned or carved articles, etc 2 the box tree

Boyce William ?1710–79, English composer, noted esp for his church music and symphonies

Boycott Geoff(rey). born 1940, English cricketer: captained Yorkshire (1970–78); played for England (1964–74, 1977–82)

Boyd 1 **Arthur** 1920–99, Australian painter and sculptor, noted for his large ceramic sculptures and his series of engravings 2 **Martin (A'Beckett).** 1893–1972, Australian novelist, author of *Lucinda Brayford* (1946) and of the Langton tetralogy *The Cardboard Crown* (1952), *A Difficult Young Man* (1955), *Outbreak of Love* (1957), and *When Blackbirds Sing* (1962) 3 **Michael** born 1955, British theatre director; artistic director of the Royal Shakespeare Company from 2003

Boyer Charles, known as *the Great Lover*. 1899–1978, French film actor

Boyle Robert 1627–91, Irish scientist who helped to dissociate chemistry from alchemy. He established that air has weight and studied the behaviour of gases; author of *The Sceptical Chymist* (1661)

Boyne a river in the E Republic of Ireland, rising in the Bog of Allen and flowing northeast to the Irish Sea: William III of England defeated the deposed James II in a battle (**Battle of the Boyne**) on its banks in 1690, completing the overthrow of the Stuart cause in Ireland. Length: about 112 km (70 miles)

Brabant 1 a former duchy of W Europe: divided when Belgium became independent (1830), the south forming the Belgian provinces of Antwerp and Brabant and the north forming the province of North Brabant in the Netherlands 2 a former province of central Belgium; replaced in 1995 by the provinces of **Flemish Brabant** and **Walloon Brabant**

Brabham Sir John Arthur, known as *Jack*. born 1926, Australian motor-racing driver: world champion 1959, 1960, and 1966

brace 1 a hand tool for drilling holes, with a socket to hold the drill at one end and a cranked handle by which the tool can be turned 2 a sliding loop, usually of leather, attached to the cords of a drum: used to change its tension 3 a line or bracket connecting two or more staves of music 4 an appliance of metal bands and wires that can be tightened to maintain steady pressure on the teeth for correcting uneven alignment 5 *Med* any of various appliances for supporting the trunk, a limb, or teeth 6 (in square-rigged sailing ships) a rope that controls the movement of a yard and thus the position of a sail

brace and bit a hand tool for boring holes, consisting of a cranked handle into which a drilling bit is inserted

brachiopod any marine invertebrate animal of the phylum *Brachiopoda*, having a ciliated feeding organ (lophophore) and a shell consisting of dorsal and ventral valves

brachium 1 *Anatomy* the arm, esp the upper part 2 a corresponding part, such as a wing, in an animal 3 *Biology* a branching or armlike part

bracken 1 any of various large coarse ferns, esp *Pteridium aquilinum*, having large fronds with spore cases along the undersides and extensive underground stems 2 a clump of any of these ferns

bracket 1 *Architect* a support projecting from the side of a wall or other structure 2 a general name for **square bracket** 3 the distance between two preliminary shots of artillery fire in range-finding 4 a skating figure consisting of two arcs meeting at a point, tracing the shape ⋎

Bracknell a town in SE England, in Bracknell Forest unitary authority, Berkshire, designated a new town in 1949. Pop: 70 795 (2001)

Bracknell Forest a unitary authority in SE England, in E Berkshire. Pop: 110 100 (2003 est). Area: 109 sq km (42 sq miles)

bract a specialized leaf, usually smaller than the foliage leaves, with a single flower or inflorescence growing in its axil

brad a small tapered nail having a small head that is either symmetrical or formed on one side only

Bradbury 1 Sir **Malcolm (Stanley).** 1932–2000, British novelist and critic. His novels include *The History Man* (1975), *Rates of Exchange* (1983), *Cuts* (1988), and *Doctor Criminale* (1992) 2 **Ray** born 1920, US science-fiction writer. His novels include *Fahrenheit 451* (1953), *Death is a Lonely Business* (1986), and *A Graveyard for Lunatics* (1990)

Bradford 1 an industrial city in N England, in Bradford unitary authority, West Yorkshire: a centre of the woollen industry from the 14th century and of the worsted trade from the 18th century; university (1966). Pop: 293 717 (2001) 2 a unitary authority in West Yorkshire. Pop: 477 800 (2003 est). Area: 370 sq km (143 sq miles)

Bradley 1 **A(ndrew) C(ecil).** 1851–1935, English critic; author of *Shakespearian Tragedy* (1904) 2 **F(rancis) H(erbert).** 1846–1924, English idealist philosopher and metaphysical thinker; author of *Ethical Studies* (1876), *Principles of Logic* (1883), and *Appearance and Reality* (1893) 3 **Henry** 1845–1923, English lexicographer; one of the editors of the *Oxford English Dictionary* 4 **James** 1693–1762, English astronomer, who discovered the aberration of light and the nutation of the earth's axis

Bradman Sir Don(ald George). 1908–2001, Australian cricketer: an outstanding batsman

Braemar a village in NE Scotland, in Aberdeenshire; Balmoral Castle is nearby: site of the Royal Braemar Gathering, an annual Highland Games meeting

brag a card game: an old form of poker

Braga a city in N Portugal: capital of the Roman province of Lusitania; 12th-century cathedral, seat of the Primate of Portugal. Pop: 164 193 (2001)

Bragg 1 **Billy** born 1957, British rock singer and songwriter, noted for his political protest songs; recordings include *Between the Wars* (1985), *Workers' Playtime* (1988), *Mermaid Avenue* (1998), and *England, Half English* (2002) 2 **Melvyn**, Baron. born 1939, British novelist, broadcaster, and television executive; presenter of *The South Bank Show* since 1978 3 Sir **William Henry**, 1862–1942, British physicist, who shared a Nobel prize for physics (1915) with his son, for their study of crystal structures by means of X-rays 4 his son, Sir (**William**) **Lawrence**, 1890–1971, British physicist

Brahe **Tycho** 1546–1601, Danish astronomer, who designed and constructed instruments that he used to plot accurately the positions of the planets, sun, moon, and stars

Brahma[1] 1 a Hindu god: in later Hindu tradition, the Creator who, with Vishnu, the Preserver, and Shiva, the Destroyer, constitutes the triad known as the Trimurti 2 another name for **Brahman**

Brahma[2] a heavy breed of domestic fowl with profusely feathered legs and feet

Brahman 1 a member of the highest or priestly caste in the Hindu caste system 2 *Hinduism* the ultimate and impersonal divine reality of the universe, from which all being originates and to which it returns 3 another name for **Brahma**

Brahmaputra a river in S Asia, rising in SW Tibet as the Tsangpo and flowing through the Himalayas and NE India to join the Ganges at its delta in Bangladesh. Length: about 2900 km (1800 miles)

Brahms **Johannes** 1833–97, German composer, whose music, though classical in form, exhibits a strong lyrical romanticism. His works include four symphonies, four concertos, chamber music, and *A German Requiem* (1868)

Bräila a port in E Romania: belonged to Turkey (1544–1828). Pop: 192 000 (2005 est)

Braille **Louis** 1809–52, French inventor, musician, and teacher of the blind, who himself was blind from the age of three and who devised the Braille system of raised writing

brain 1 the soft convoluted mass of nervous tissue within the skull of vertebrates that is the controlling and coordinating centre of the nervous system and the seat of thought, memory, and emotion. It includes the cerebrum, brainstem, and cerebellum 2 the main neural bundle or ganglion of certain invertebrates

brain death irreversible cessation of respiration due to irreparable brain damage, even though the heart may continue beating with the aid of a mechanical ventilator: widely considered as the criterion of death

Braine **John** (**Gerard**). 1922–86, English novelist, whose works include *Room at the Top* (1957) and *Life at the Top* (1962)

brain wave any of the fluctuations of electrical potential in the brain as represented on an electroencephalogram. They vary in frequency from 1 to 30 hertz

brak *South African* a mongrel dog

brake[1] 1 a a device for slowing or stopping a vehicle, wheel, shaft, etc, or for keeping it stationary, esp by means of friction b (*as modifier*): *the brake pedal* 2 a machine or tool for crushing or breaking flax or hemp to separate the fibres 3 an open four-wheeled horse-drawn carriage

brake[2] an area of dense undergrowth, shrubs, brushwood, etc.; thicket

brake horsepower the rate at which an engine does work, expressed in horsepower. It is measured by the resistance of an applied brake

brake light a red light attached to the rear of a motor vehicle that lights up when the brakes are applied, serving as a warning to following drivers

brake shoe 1 the curved metal casting to which the brake lining is riveted in a drum brake 2 the curved metal casting together with the attached brake lining

Brakpan a city in E South Africa: gold-mining centre. Pop: 62 116 (2001)

Bramante **Donato** ?1444–1514, Italian architect and artist of the High Renaissance. He modelled his designs for domed centrally planned churches on classical Roman architecture

bramble 1 any of various prickly herbaceous plants or shrubs of the rosaceous genus *Rubus*, esp the blackberry 2 *Scot* a a blackberry b (*as modifier*): *bramble jelly* 3 any of several similar and related shrubs

bran husks of cereal grain separated from the flour by sifting

branch 1 a secondary woody stem arising from the trunk or bough of a tree or the main stem of a shrub 2 a subdivision of the stem or root of any other plant 3 *US* any small stream 4 *Maths* a section of a curve separated from the rest of the curve by discontinuities or special points 5 *Computing* a departure from the normal sequence of programmed instructions into a separate program area 6 *Physics* an alternative route in an atomic or nuclear decay series

Brancusi **Constantin** 1876–1957, Romanian sculptor, noted for his streamlined abstractions of animal forms

Brandenburg 1 a state in NE Germany, part of East Germany until 1990. A former electorate, it expanded under the Hohenzollerns to become the kingdom of Prussia (1701). The district east of the Oder River became Polish in 1945. Capital: Potsdam. Pop: 2 575 000 (2003 est). Area: 29 481 sq km (11 219 sq miles) 2 a city in NE Germany: former capital of the Prussian province of Brandenburg. Pop: 75 485 (2003 est)

Brando **Marlon** 1924–2004, US actor; his films include *On the Waterfront* (1954) and *The Godfather* (1972), for both of which he won Oscars, *Last Tango in Paris* (1972), *Apocalypse Now* (1979), *A Dry White Season* (1989), and *Don Juan de Marco* (1995)

Brandt 1 **Bill**, full name *William Brandt*. 1905–83, British photographer. His photographic books include *The English at Home* (1936) and *Perspectives of Nudes* (1961) 2 **Georg** 1694–1768, Swedish chemist, who isolated cobalt (1742) and exposed fraudulent alchemists 3 **Willy** 1913–92, German statesman; socialist chancellor of

West Germany (1969–74); chairman of the Social Democratic party (1964–87). His policy of détente and reconciliation with E Europe brought him international acclaim. Nobel peace prize 1971

brandy 1 an alcoholic drink consisting of spirit distilled from grape wine 2 a distillation of wines made from other fruits

Branson Sir **Richard** born 1950, British entrepreneur. In 1969 he founded the Virgin record company, adding other interests later, including Virgin Atlantic Airways (1984), Virgin Radio (1993), and the Virgin Rail Group (1996): made the fastest crossing of the Atlantic by boat (1986) and the first of the Pacific by hot-air balloon (1991)

Brantford a city in central Canada, in SW Ontario. Pop: 86 417 (2001)

Braque Georges 1882–1963, French painter who developed cubism (1908–14) with Picasso

Braşov an industrial city in central Romania: formerly a centre for expatriate Germans; ceded by Hungary to Romania in 1920. Pop: 249 000 (2005 est)

brass 1 an alloy of copper and zinc containing more than 50 per cent of copper. **Alpha brass** (containing less than 35 per cent of zinc) is used for most engineering materials requiring forging, pressing, etc. **Alpha-beta brass** (35–45 per cent zinc) is used for hot working and extrusion. **Beta brass** (45–50 per cent zinc) is used for castings. Small amounts of other metals, such as lead or tin, may be added 2 a the large family of wind instruments including the trumpet, trombone, French horn, etc, each consisting of a brass tube blown directly by means of a cup- or funnel-shaped mouthpiece b instruments of this family forming a section in an orchestra 3 a renewable sleeve or bored semicylindrical shell made of brass or bronze, used as a liner for a bearing 4 Brit an engraved brass memorial tablet or plaque, set in the wall or floor of a church

brassica any plant of the genus *Brassica*, such as cabbage, rape, turnip, and mustard: family *Brassicaceae* (crucifers)

brass rubbing the taking of an impression of an engraved brass tablet or plaque by placing a piece of paper over it and rubbing the paper with graphite, heelball, or chalk

Bratislava the capital of Slovakia since 1918, a port on the River Danube; capital of Hungary (1541–1784) and seat of the Hungarian parliament until 1848. Pop: 428 672 (2001)

Brattain Walter Houser 1902–87, US physicist, who shared the Nobel prize for physics (1956) with W. B. Shockley and John Bardeen for their invention of the transistor

Braun 1 **Eva** 1910–45, Adolf Hitler's mistress, whom he married shortly before their suicides in 1945 2 **Karl Ferdinand** 1850–1918, German physicist, who invented crystal diodes (leading to the development of crystal radio) and the oscilloscope. He shared the Nobel prize for physics (1909) with Marconi

bravura *Music* a brilliance of execution b *(as modifier)*: a *bravura passage*

brawl a dance: the English version of the branle

braze the high-melting solder or alloy used in brazing

brazil or **brasil** 1 the red wood obtained from various tropical leguminous trees of the genus *Caesalpinia*, such as *C. echinata* of America: used for cabinetwork 2 short for **brazil nut**

Brazil a republic in South America, comprising about half the area and half the population of South America: colonized by the Portuguese from 1500 onwards; became independent in 1822 and a republic in 1889; consists chiefly of the tropical Amazon basin in the north, semiarid scrub in the northeast, and a vast central tableland; an important producer of coffee and minerals, esp iron ore. Official language: Portuguese. Religion: Roman Catholic majority. Currency: real. Capital: Brasília. Pop: 180 655 000 (2004 est). Area: 8 511 957 sq km (3 286 470 sq miles)

brazil nut 1 a tropical South American tree, *Bertholletia excelsa*, producing large globular capsules, each containing several closely packed triangular nuts: family *Lecythidaceae* 2 the nut of this tree, having an edible oily kernel and a woody shell

Brazzaville the capital of Congo-Brazzaville, in the south on the River Congo. Pop: 1 153 000 (2005 est)

breach 1 the act of a whale in breaking clear of the water 2 the breaking of sea waves on a shore or rock 3 an obsolete word for **wound**

breach of promise *Law* (formerly) failure to carry out one's promise to marry

breach of the peace *Law* an offence against public order causing an unnecessary disturbance of the peace

bread *Christianity* a small loaf, piece of bread, or wafer of unleavened bread used in the Eucharist
▷www.howstuffworks.com/bread.htm
▷www.breadrecipe.com
▷www.breadnet.net

breadboard an experimental arrangement of electronic circuits giving access to components so that modifications can be carried out easily

breadfruit 1 a moraceous tree, *Artocarpus communis* (or *A. altilis*), of the Pacific Islands, having large round edible starchy usually seedless, fruit 2 the fruit of this tree, which is eaten baked or roasted and has a texture like bread

breakage *Commerce* compensation or allowance for goods damaged while in use, transit, etc

breakaway *Sport* a a sudden attack, esp from a defensive position, in football, hockey, etc b an attempt to get away from the rest of the field in a race

break dance an acrobatic dance style originating in the 1980s

break down 1 short for **nervous breakdown** 2 the sudden electrical discharge through an insulator or between two electrodes in a vacuum or gas discharge tube 3 *Electrical engineering* the sudden transition, dependent on the bias magnitude, from a high to a low dynamic resistance in a semiconductor device 4 a lively American country dance

breaker[1] 1 a large wave with a white crest on the open sea or one that breaks into foam on the shore 2 *Electronics* short for **circuit breaker** 3 *Textiles* a machine for extracting fibre preparatory to carding

breaker[2] a small water cask for use in a boat

break in *Law* a the illegal entering of a building, esp by thieves **b** (*as modifier*): *the break-in plans*

breakwater 1 a massive wall built out into the sea to protect a shore or harbour from the force of waves **2** another name for **groyne**

bream *or Austral* **brim 1** any of several Eurasian freshwater cyprinid fishes of the genus *Abramis*, esp *A. brama*, having a deep compressed body covered with silvery scales **2** **white** *or* **silver bream** a similar cyprinid, *Blicca bjoerkna*

Bream Julian (Alexander). born 1933, English guitarist and lutenist

breast 1 the front part of the body from the neck to the abdomen; chest **2** either of the two soft fleshy milk-secreting glands on the chest in sexually mature human females **3** a similar organ in certain other mammals **4** a projection from the side of a wall, esp that formed by a chimney

breastplate 1 the strap of a harness covering a horse's breast **2** *Judaism* an ornamental silver plate hung on the scrolls of the Torah **3** *Old Testament* a square vestment ornamented with 12 precious stones, representing the 12 tribes of Israel, worn by the high priest when praying before the holy of holies

breaststroke a swimming stroke in which the arms are extended in front of the head and swept back on either side while the legs are drawn up beneath the body and thrust back together

breath 1 the intake and expulsion of air during respiration **2** the air inhaled or exhaled during respiration **3** a single respiration or inhalation of air, etc

breathable (of a material) allowing air to pass through so that perspiration can evaporate

Breathalyser *or* **Breathalyzer** *Trademark* a device for estimating the amount of alcohol in the breath: used in testing people suspected of driving under the influence of alcohol

breather a vent in a container to equalize internal and external pressure, such as the pipe in the crankcase of an internal-combustion engine

breath test *Brit* a chemical test of a driver's breath to determine the amount of alcohol he has consumed

Brecht Bertolt 1898–1956, German dramatist, theatrical producer, and poet, who developed a new style of "epic" theatre and a new theory of theatrical alienation, notable also for his wit and compassion. His early works include *The Threepenny Opera* (1928) and *Rise and Fall of the City of Mahagonny* (1930) (both with music by Kurt Weill). His later plays are concerned with moral and political dilemmas and include *Mother Courage and her Children* (1941), *The Good Woman of Setzuan* (1943), and *The Caucasian Chalk Circle* (1955)

Brecon *or* **Brecknock 1** a town in SE Wales, in Powys: textile and leather industries. Pop: 7901 (2001) **2** short for **Breconshire**

Breconshire *or* **Brecknockshire** (until 1974) a county of SE Wales, now mainly in Powys: over half its area forms the **Brecon Beacons National Park**

Breda a city in the S Netherlands, in North Brabant province: residence of Charles II of England during his exile. Pop: 164 000 (2003 est)

breech 1 the lower dorsal part of the human trunk; buttocks; rump **2** the lower portion of a pulley block, esp

the part to which the rope or chain is secured

breeches buoy a ring-shaped life buoy with a support in the form of a pair of short breeches, in which a person is suspended for safe transfer from a ship

breed 1 a group of organisms within a species, esp a group of domestic animals, originated and maintained by man and having a clearly defined set of characteristics **2** a lineage or race
▷www.ansi.okstate.edu/library
▷www.fanciers.com
▷www.the-kennel-club.org.uk

breeder reactor a type of nuclear reactor that produces more fissionable material than it consumes

breeding *Physics* a process occurring in a nuclear reactor as a result of which more fissionable material is produced than is used up

breeze *Meteorol* a wind of force two to six inclusive on the Beaufort scale

Bregenz a resort in W Austria, the capital of Vorarlberg province. Pop: 26 752 (2001)

Bremen 1 a state of NW Germany, centred on the city of Bremen and its outport Bremerhaven; formerly in West Germany. Pop: 663 000 (2003 est). Area: 404 sq km (156 sq miles) **2** an industrial city and port in NW Germany, on the Weser estuary. Pop: 544 853 (2003 est)

Bremerhaven a port in NW Germany: an outport for Bremen. Pop: 118 276 (2003 est)

Brendel Alfred born 1931, Austrian pianist and poet

Brennan Christopher John 1870–1932, Australian poet and classical scholar, disciple of Mallarmé and exponent of French symbolism in Australian verse

Brenner Pass a pass over the E Alps, between Austria and Italy. Highest point: 1372 m (4501 ft)

Brent a borough of NW Greater London. Pop: 267 800 (2003 est). Area: 44 sq km (17 sq miles)

Brenton Howard born 1942, British dramatist, author of such controversial plays as *The Churchill Play* (1974), *The Romans in Britain* (1980), (with David Hare) *Pravda* (1985), and several topical satires with Tariq Ali

Brentwood a residential town in SE England, in SW Essex near London. Pop: 47 593 (2001)

Brescia a city in N Italy, in Lombardy: at its height in the 16th century. Pop: 187 567 (2001)

Brest 1 a port in NW France, in Brittany: chief naval station of the country, planned by Richelieu in 1631 and fortified by Vauban. Pop: 149 634 (1999) **2** a city in SW Belarus: Polish until 1795 and from 1921 to 1945. Pop: 299 000 (2005 est)

Breton[1] André 1896–1966, French poet and art critic: founder and chief theorist of surrealism, publishing the first surrealist manifesto in 1924

Breton[2] **1** a native or inhabitant of Brittany, esp one who speaks the Breton language **2** the indigenous language of Brittany, belonging to the Brythonic subgroup of the Celtic family of languages

Breuer 1 Josef 1842–1925, Austrian physician: treated the mentally ill by hypnosis **2** Marcel Lajos 1902–81, US architect and furniture designer, born in Hungary. He developed bent plywood and tubular metal furniture and designed the UNESCO building in Paris (1953–58)

breve 1 *Music* a note, now rarely used, equivalent in time value to two semibreves **2** *RC Church* a less common word for **brief** (papal letter)

breviary 1 *RC Church* a book of psalms, hymns, prayers, etc, to be recited daily by clerics in major orders and certain members of religious orders as part of the divine office 2 a similar book in the Orthodox Church

Brezhnev Leonid Ilyich 1906–82, Soviet statesman; president of the Soviet Union (1977–82); general secretary of the Soviet Communist Party (1964–82)

Brian Havergal 1876–1972, English composer, who wrote 32 symphonies, including the large-scale *Gothic Symphony* (1919–27)

Brian Boru ?941–1014, king of Ireland (1002–14): killed during the defeat of the Danes at the battle of Clontarf

Briand Aristide 1862–1932, French socialist statesman: prime minister of France 11 times. He was responsible for the separation of Church and State (1905) and he advocated a United States of Europe. Nobel peace prize 1926

briar *or* **brier** 1 an ericaceous shrub, *Erica arborea*, of S Europe, having a hard woody root (briarroot) 2 a tobacco pipe made from the root of this plant

bribe a length of flawed or damaged cloth removed from the main piece

bridge¹ 1 a structure that spans and provides a passage over a road, railway, river, or some other obstacle 2 a the hard ridge at the upper part of the nose, formed by the underlying nasal bones b any anatomical ridge or connecting structure 3 a dental plate containing one or more artificial teeth that is secured to the surrounding natural teeth 4 a platform athwartships and above the rail, from which a ship is piloted and navigated 5 a piece of wood, usually fixed, supporting the strings of a violin, guitar, etc, and transmitting their vibrations to the sounding board 6 a passage in a musical, literary, or dramatic work linking two or more important sections 7 *Electronics* any of several networks, such as a Wheatstone bridge, consisting of two branches across which a measuring device is connected. The resistance, capacitance, etc, of one component can be determined from the known values of the others when the voltage in each branch is balanced 8 *Computing* a device that connects networks and sends packets between them 9 *Billiards, Snooker* a a support for a cue made by placing the fingers on the table and raising the thumb b a cue rest with a notched end for shots beyond normal reach 10 *Theatre* a a platform of adjustable height above or beside the stage for the use of stagehands, light operators, etc b *Chiefly Brit* a part of the stage floor that can be raised or lowered 11 a partition in a furnace or boiler to keep the fuel in place
▷www.worldbridge.org

bridge² a card game for four players, based on whist, in which one hand (the dummy) is exposed and the trump suit decided by bidding between the players
▷www.worldbridge.org

Bridge Frank 1879–1941, English composer, esp of chamber music. He taught Benjamin Britten

Bridgend a county borough in S Wales, created in 1996 from S Mid Glamorgan. Administrative centre: Bridgend. Pop: 129 900 (2003 est). Area: 264 sq km (102 sq miles)

Bridge of Sighs a covered 16th-century bridge in Venice, between the Doges' Palace and the prisons, through which prisoners were formerly led to trial or execution

Bridgeport a port in SW Connecticut, on Long Island Sound. Pop: 139 664 (2003 est)

Bridges Robert (Seymour). 1844–1930, English poet: poet laureate (1913–30)

Bridget, Saint 1 453–523 AD, Irish abbess; a patron saint of Ireland. Feast day: Feb 1 2 ?1303-73, Swedish nun and visionary; patron saint of Sweden. Feast day: July 23

Bridgetown the capital of Barbados, a port on the SW coast. Pop: 144 000 (2005 est)

bridgework a a partial denture attached to the surrounding teeth

Bridgwater a town in SW England, in central Somerset. Pop: 36 563 (2001)

Bridie James, real name *Osborne Henry Mavor*. 1888–1951, Scottish physician and dramatist, who founded the Glasgow Citizens' Theatre. His plays include *The Anatomist* (1930)

bridle 1 a headgear for a horse, etc, consisting of a series of buckled straps and a metal mouthpiece (bit) by which the animal is controlled through the reins 2 a Y-shaped cable, rope, or chain, used for holding, towing, etc 3 *Machinery* a device by which the motion of a component is limited, often in the form of a linkage or flange

Brie a mainly agricultural area in N France, between the Rivers Marne and Seine: noted esp for its cheese

brief 1 *Law* a document containing all the facts and points of law of a case by which a solicitor instructs a barrister to represent a client 2 *RC Church* a letter issuing from the Roman court written in modern characters, as contrasted with a papal bull; papal brief

brier *or* **briar** any of various thorny shrubs or other plants, such as the sweetbriar and greenbrier

brig *Nautical* a two-masted square-rigger

brigalow *Austral* a any of various acacia trees b *(as modifier)*: brigalow country

brigantine a two-masted sailing ship, rigged square on the foremast and fore-and-aft with square topsails on the mainmast

Briggs Henry 1561–1631, English mathematician: introduced common logarithms

Brighouse¹ Harold 1882–1958, British novelist and dramatist, best known for his play *Hobson's Choice* (1915)

Brighouse² a town in N England, in Calderdale unitary authority, West Yorkshire: machine tools, textiles, engineering. Pop: 32 360 (2001)

bright a thin flat paintbrush with a straight sharp edge used for highlighting in oil painting

Bright John 1811–89, British liberal statesman, economist, and advocate of free trade: with Richard Cobden he led the Anti-Corn-Law League (1838–46)

Brighton a coastal resort in S England, in Brighton and Hove unitary authority, East Sussex: patronized by the Prince Regent, who had the Royal Pavilion built (1782); seat of the University of Sussex (1966) and the University of Brighton (1992). Pop: 134 293 (2001)

Brighton and Hove a city and unitary authority in S England, in East Sussex. Pop: 251 500 (2003 est). Area: 72 sq km (28 sq miles)

brill a European food fish, *Scophthalmus rhombus*, a flatfish similar to the turbot but lacking tubercles on the body: family *Bothidae*

brilliant 1 (of a colour) having a high saturation and reflecting a considerable amount of light; vivid 2 *Music* (of the tone of an instrument) having a large proportion of high harmonics above the fundamental

brilliantine *Chiefly US* a glossy fabric made of mohair and cotton

brimstone 1 an obsolete name for **sulphur** 2 a common yellow butterfly, *Gonepteryx rhamni*, of N temperate regions of the Old World: family *Pieridae*

Brindisi a port in SE Italy, in SE Apulia: important naval base in Roman times and a centre of the Crusades in the Middle Ages. Pop: 89 081 (2001)

brindled brown or grey streaked or patched with a darker colour

Brindley James 1716–72, British canal builder, who constructed (1759–61) the Bridgewater Canal, the first in England

brine 1 the sea or its water 2 *Chem* a a concentrated solution of sodium chloride in water b any solution of a salt in water

brinkmanship the art or practice of pressing a dangerous situation, esp in international affairs, to the limit of safety and peace in order to win an advantage from a threatening or tenacious foe

Brisbane a port in E Australia, the capital of Queensland: founded in 1824 as a penal settlement; vast agricultural hinterland. Pop: 1 508 161 (2001)

brisket the breast of a four-legged animal

bristle any short stiff hair of an animal or plant

Bristol 1 City of a port and industrial city in SW England, mainly in Bristol unitary authority, on the River Avon seven miles from its mouth on the Bristol Channel: a major port, trading with America, in the 17th and 18th centuries; the modern port consists chiefly of docks at Avonmouth and Portishead; noted for the **Clifton Suspension Bridge** (designed by I K Brunel, 1834) over the Avon gorge; Bristol university (1909) and University of the West of England (1992). Pop: 420 556 (2001) 2 City of a unitary authority in SW England, created in 1996 from part of Avon county. Pop: 391 500 (2003 est). Area: 110 sq km (42 sq miles)

Bristol Channel an inlet of the Atlantic, between S Wales and SW England, merging into the Severn estuary. Length: about 137 km (85 miles)

Britain another name for **Great Britain** or the **United Kingdom**

Britannia 1 a female warrior carrying a trident and wearing a helmet, personifying Great Britain or the British Empire 2 (in the ancient Roman Empire) the S part of Great Britain

Britannia metal an alloy of low melting point consisting of tin with 5–10 per cent antimony, 1–3 per cent copper, and sometimes small quantities of zinc, lead, or bismuth: used for decorative purposes and for bearings

British 1 relating to or denoting the English language as spoken and written in Britain, esp the S dialect generally regarded as standard 2 relating to or denoting the ancient Britons 3 the natives or inhabitants of Britain 4 the extinct Celtic language of the ancient Britons

British Antarctic Territory a UK Overseas Territory in the S Atlantic (claims are suspended under the Antarctic Treaty): created in 1962 and consisting of the South Shetland Islands, the South Orkney Islands, and Graham Land; formerly part of the Falkland Islands Dependencies

British Columbia a province of W Canada, on the Pacific coast: largely mountainous with extensive forests, rich mineral resources, and important fisheries. Capital: Victoria. Pop: 4 196 383 (2004 est). Area: 930 532 sq km (359 279 sq miles)

British East Africa the former British possessions of Uganda, Kenya, Tanganyika, and Zanzibar, before their independence in the 1960s

British India the 17 provinces of India formerly governed by the British under the British sovereign: ceased to exist in 1947 when the independent states of India and Pakistan were created

British Indian Ocean Territory a UK Overseas Territory in the Indian Ocean: consists of the Chagos Archipelago (formerly a dependency of Mauritius) and formerly included (until 1976) Aldabra, Farquhar, and Des Roches, now administratively part of the Seychelles. Diego Garcia is an important US naval base

British North America (formerly) Canada or its constituent regions or provinces that formed part of the British Empire

British Somaliland a former British protectorate (1884–1960) in E Africa, on the Gulf of Aden: united with Italian Somaliland in 1960 to form the Somali Republic

British West Africa the former British possessions of Nigeria, The Gambia, Sierra Leone, and the Gold Coast, and the former trust territories of Togoland and Cameroons

Briton 1 a native or inhabitant of Britain 2 a citizen of the United Kingdom 3 *History* any of the early Celtic inhabitants of S Britain who were largely dispossessed by the Anglo-Saxon invaders after the 5th century AD

Brittany a region of NW France, the peninsula between the English Channel and the Bay of Biscay: settled by Celtic refugees from Wales and Cornwall during the Anglo-Saxon invasions; disputed between England and France until 1364

Britten (Edward) Benjamin, Baron Britten. 1913–76, English composer, pianist, and conductor. His works include the operas *Peter Grimes* (1945) and *Billy Budd* (1951), the choral works *Hymn to St Cecilia* (1942) and *A War Requiem* (1962), and numerous orchestral pieces

Brno a city in the Czech Republic; formerly the capital of Moravia: the country's second largest city. Pop: 375 000 (2005 est)

broach 1 a long tapered toothed cutting tool for enlarging holes 2 a roof covering the corner triangle on the top of a square tower having an octagonal spire 3 a pin, forming part of some types of lock, that registers in the hollow bore of a key 4 a tool used for tapping casks

broad *Woodwork* a wood-turning tool used for shaping the insides and bottoms of cylinders

broad bean 1 an erect annual Eurasian bean plant, *Vicia faba*, cultivated for its large edible flattened seeds, used as a vegetable 2 the seed of this plant

broad gauge a railway track with a greater distance

between the lines than the standard gauge of 56½ inches (about 1.44 metres) used now by most mainline railway systems

broad-leaved denoting trees other than conifers, most of which have broad rather than needle-shaped leaves

broadloom of or designating carpets or carpeting woven on a wide loom to obviate the need for seams

broadside 1 *Nautical* the entire side of a vessel, from stem to stern and from waterline to rail **2** a ballad or popular song printed on one side of a sheet of paper and sold by hawkers, esp in 16th-century England

Broadway a thoroughfare in New York City, famous for its theatres: the centre of the commercial theatre in the US

brocade a a rich fabric woven with a raised design, often using gold or silver threads **b** (*as modifier*): *brocade curtains*

broccoli 1 a cultivated variety of cabbage, *Brassica oleracea italica*, having branched greenish flower heads **2** the flower head of this plant, eaten as a vegetable before the buds have opened **3** a variety of this plant that does not form a head, whose stalks are eaten as a vegetable

Brocken a mountain in central Germany, formerly in East Germany: the highest peak of the Harz Mountains; important in German folklore. Height: 1142 m (3747 ft). The **Brocken Bow** or **Brocken Spectre** is an atmospheric phenomenon in which an observer, when the sun is low, may see his enlarged shadow against the clouds, often surrounded by coloured lights

Broglie 1 Prince **Louis Victor de** 1892–1987, French physicist, noted for his research in quantum mechanics and his development of wave mechanics: Nobel prize for physics 1929 **2** his brother, **Maurice** , Duc de Broglie. 1875–1960, French physicist, noted for his research into X-ray spectra

broken 1 varying in direction or intensity, as of pitch **2** (of colour) having a multicoloured decorative effect, as by stippling paint onto a surface

broken chord *Music* a chord played as an arpeggio

Broken Hill a city in SE Australia, in W New South Wales: mining centre for lead, silver, and zinc. Pop: 19 834 (2001)

brolga a large grey Australian crane, *Grus rubicunda*, having a red-and-green head and a trumpeting call

bromide 1 any salt of hydrobromic acid, containing the monovalent ion Br⁻ (**bromide ion**) **2** any compound containing a bromine atom, such as methyl bromide **3** a dose of sodium or potassium bromide given as a sedative

bromide paper a type of photographic paper coated with an emulsion of silver bromide usually containing a small quantity of silver iodide

bromine a pungent dark red volatile liquid element of the halogen series that occurs in natural brine and is used in the production of chemicals, esp ethylene dibromide. Symbol: Br; atomic no.: 35; atomic wt.: 79.904; valency: 1, 3, 5, or 7; relative density 3.12; density (gas): 7.59 kg/m³; melting pt.: –7.2°C; boiling pt.: 58.78°C

Bromley a borough of SE Greater London. Pop: 298 300 (2003 est). Area: 153 sq km (59 sq miles)

Bromsgrove a town in W central England, in N Worcestershire. Pop: 29 237 (2001)

bronchiole any of the smallest bronchial tubes, usually ending in alveoli

bronchitis inflammation of the bronchial tubes, characterized by coughing, difficulty in breathing, etc, caused by infection or irritation of the respiratory tract

bronchus either of the two main branches of the trachea, which contain cartilage within their walls

bronco *or* **broncho** (in the US and Canada) a wild or partially tamed pony or mustang of the western plains

Brontë 1 **Anne**, pen name *Acton Bell*. 1820—49, English novelist; author of *The Tenant of Wildfell Hall* (1847) **2** her sister, **Charlotte**, pen name *Currer Bell*. 1816—55, English novelist, author of *Jane Eyre* (1847), *Villette* (1853), and *The Professor* (1857) **3** her sister, **Emily (Jane)**, pen name *Ellis Bell*. 1818—48, English novelist and poet; author of *Wuthering Heights* (1847)

brontosaurus *or* **brontosaur** any very large herbivorous quadrupedal dinosaur of the genus *Apatosaurus*, common in North America during Jurassic times, having a long neck and long tail: suborder *Sauropoda* (sauropods)

Bronx the a borough of New York City, on the mainland, separated from Manhattan by the Harlem River. Pop: 1 363 198 (2003 est)

bronze 1 a any hard water-resistant alloy consisting of copper and smaller proportions of tin and sometimes zinc and lead **b** any similar copper alloy containing other elements in place of tin, such as aluminium bronze, beryllium bronze, etc **2** a yellowish-brown colour or pigment

Bronze Age *Archaeol* **a** a technological stage between the Stone and Iron Ages, beginning in the Middle East about 4500 BC and lasting in Britain from about 2000 to 500 BC, during which weapons and tools were made of bronze and there was intensive trading **b** (*as modifier*): *a Bronze-Age tool*

Bronzino **II**, real name *Agnolo di Cosimo*. 1503–72, Florentine mannerist painter

Brooke 1 **Alan Francis**. See (1st Viscount) **Alanbrooke 2** Sir **James** 1803–68, British soldier; first rajah of Sarawak (1841–63) **3** **Rupert** (**Chawner**). 1887–1915, British lyric poet, noted for his idealistic war poetry, which made him a national hero

Brooklyn a borough of New York City, on the SW end of Long Island. Pop: 2 465 326 (2000)

Brooks 1 **Mel**, real name *Melvyn Kaminsky*. born 1926, US comedy writer, actor, and film director. His films include *The Producers* (1968), *Blazing Saddles* (1974), *High Anxiety* (1977), and *Dracula: Dead and Loving It* (1996) **2** (**Troyal**) **Garth** born 1962, US country singer and songwriter; his bestselling records include *Ropin' the Wind* (1991) and *Scarecrow* (2001)

Brooks Range a mountain range in N Alaska. Highest peak: Mount Isto, 2761 m (9058 ft)

broom 1 any of various yellow-flowered Eurasian leguminous shrubs of the genera *Cytisus*, *Genista*, and *Spartium*, esp *C. scoparius* **2** any of various similar Eurasian plants of the related genera *Genista* and *Spartium*

brother *Christianity* **a** a member of a male religious order who undertakes work for the order without actually being in holy orders **b** a lay member of a male religious order

brougham 1 a four-wheeled horse-drawn closed carriage having a raised open driver's seat in front **2** *Obsolete* a large car with an open compartment at the front for the driver **3** *Obsolete* an early electric car

brown 1 any of various colours, such as those of wood or earth, produced by low intensity light in the wavelength range 620–585 nanometres **2** brown cloth or clothing **3** any of numerous mostly reddish-brown butterflies of the genera *Maniola, Lasiommata*, etc, such as *M. jurtina* (**meadow brown**): family *Satyridae* **4** of the colour brown

Brown 1 Sir **Arthur Whitten** 1886–1948, British aviator who with J W Alcock made the first flight across the Atlantic (1919) **2 Ford Madox** 1821–93, British painter, associated with the Pre-Raphaelite Brotherhood. His paintings include *The Last of England* (1865) and *Work* (1865) **3 George** (**Alfred**), Lord George-Brown. 1914–85, British Labour politician; vice-chairman and deputy leader of the Labour party (1960–70); foreign secretary 1966–68 **4 George Mackay** 1921–96, Scottish poet, novelist, and short-story writer. His works, which include the novels *Greenvoe* (1972) and *Magnus* (1973), reflect the history and culture of Orkney **5** (**James**) **Gordon** born 1951, British Labour politician; Chancellor of the Exchequer from 1997 **6 Herbert Charles** born 1912, US chemist, who worked on the compounds of boron. Nobel prize for chemistry 1979 **7 James** born 1933, US soul singer and songwriter, noted for his dynamic stage performances and for his commitment to Black rights **8 John** 1800–59, US abolitionist leader, hanged after leading an unsuccessful rebellion of slaves at Harper's Ferry, Virginia **9 Lancelot**, called *Capability Brown*. 1716–83, British landscape gardener **10 Michael** (**Stuart**). born 1941, US physician: shared the Nobel prize for physiology or medicine (1985) for work on cholesterol **11 Robert** 1773–1858, Scottish botanist who was the first to observe the Brownian movement in fluids

brown bear a large ferocious brownish bear, *Ursus arctos*, inhabiting temperate forests of North America, Europe, and Asia

brown coal a low-quality coal intermediate in grade between peat and lignite

Browne 1 Coral (**Edith**). 1913–91, Australian actress: married to Vincent Price **2 Hablot Knight**. See **Phiz 3** Sir **Thomas** 1605–82, English physician and author, noted for his magniloquent prose style. His works include *Religio Medici* (1642) and *Hydriotaphia or Urn Burial* (1658)

brownie (in folklore) an elf said to do helpful work at night, esp household chores

Browning 1 Elizabeth Barrett 1806–61, English poet and critic; author of the *Sonnets from the Portuguese* (1850) **2** her husband, **Robert** 1812–89, English poet, noted for his dramatic monologues and *The Ring and the Book* (1868–69)

brown rice unpolished rice, in which the grains retain the outer yellowish-brown layer (bran)

Brown Shirt (in Nazi Germany) a storm trooper

brown trout a common brownish variety of the trout *Salmo trutta* that occurs in the rivers of N Europe and has been successfully introduced in North America

browse the young twigs, shoots, leaves, etc, on which

certain animals feed

browser *Computing* a software package that enables a user to find and read hypertext files, esp on the World Wide Web

Broz Josip original name of (Marshal) **Tito**

Brubeck Dave born 1920, US modern jazz pianist and composer; formed his own quartet in 1951

Bruce 1 James 1730–94, British explorer, who discovered the source of the Blue Nile (1770) **2 Lenny** 1925–66, US comedian, whose satirical sketches, esp of the sexual attitudes of his contemporaries, brought him prosecutions for obscenity, but are now regarded as full of insight as well as wit **3 Robert the**. See **Robert I 4 Stanley Melbourne**, 1st Viscount Bruce of Melbourne. 1883–1967, Australian statesman; prime minister, in coalition with Sir Earle Page's Country Party, of Australia (1923–29)

brucellosis an infectious disease of cattle, goats, dogs, and pigs, caused by bacteria of the genus *Brucella* and transmittable to man (eg by drinking contaminated milk): symptoms include fever, chills, and severe headache

Bruch Max 1838–1920, German composer, noted chiefly for his three violin concertos

Bruckner Anton 1824–96, Austrian composer and organist in the Romantic tradition. His works include nine symphonies, four masses, and a Te Deum

Brudenell James Thomas. See (7th Earl of) **Cardigan**

Brueghel, Bruegel, *or* **Breughel 1 Jan** 1568–1625, Flemish painter, noted for his detailed still lifes and landscapes **2** his father, **Pieter**, called *the Elder*. ?1525–69, Flemish painter, noted for his landscapes, his satirical paintings of peasant life, and his allegorical biblical scenes **3** his son, **Pieter**, called *the Younger*. ?1564–1637, Flemish painter, noted for his gruesome pictures of hell

Bruges a city in NW Belgium, capital of West Flanders province: centre of the medieval European wool and cloth trade. Pop: 117 025 (2004 est)

brumby *Austral* a wild horse, esp one descended from runaway stock

Brummell George Bryan, called *Beau Brummell*. 1778–1840, English dandy: leader of fashion in the Regency period

Brunei 1 a sultanate in NW Borneo, consisting of two separate areas on the South China Sea, otherwise bounded by Sarawak: controlled all of Borneo and parts of the Philippines and the Sulu Islands in the 16th century; under British protection since 1888; internally self-governing since 1971; became fully independent in 1984 as a member of the Commonwealth. The economy depends chiefly on oil and natural gas. Official language: Malay; English is also widely spoken. Religion: Muslim. Currency: Brunei dollar. Capital: Bandar Seri Begawan. Pop: 366 000 (2004 est). Area: 5765 sq km (2226 sq miles) **2** the former name of **Bandar Seri Begawan**

Brunel 1 Isambard Kingdom 1806–59, English engineer: designer of the Clifton Suspension Bridge (1828), many railway lines, tunnels, bridges, etc, and the steamships *Great Western* (1838), *Great Britain* (1845), and *Great Eastern* (1858) **2** his father, Sir **Marc Isambard** 1769–1849, French engineer in England

Brunelleschi Filippo 1377–1446, Italian architect, whose works in Florence include the dome of the cathedral, the Pazzi chapel of Santa Croce, and the church of San Lorenzo

Brunswick 1 a former duchy (1635–1918) and state (1918–46) of central Germany, now part of the state of Lower Saxony; formerly (1949–90) part of West Germany **2** a city in central Germany: formerly capital of the duchy and state of Brunswick. Pop: 245 076 (2003 est)

brush¹ 1 a device made of bristles, hairs, wires, etc, set into a firm back or handle: used to apply paint, clean or polish surfaces, groom the hair, etc **2** the bushy tail of a fox, often kept as a trophy after a hunt, or of certain breeds of dog **3** an electric conductor, esp one made of carbon, that conveys current between stationary and rotating parts of a generator, motor, etc **4** a dark brush-shaped region observed when a biaxial crystal is viewed through a microscope, caused by interference between beams of polarized light

brush² 1 a thick growth of shrubs and small trees; scrub **2** land covered with scrub **3** broken or cut branches or twigs; brushwood **4** wooded sparsely populated country; backwoods

brushed *Textiles* treated with a brushing process to raise the nap and give a softer, warmer finish

brush turkey any of several gallinaceous birds, esp *Alectura lathami*, of New Guinea and Australia, having a black plumage: family *Megapodidae* (megapodes)

brushwood 1 cut or broken-off tree branches, twigs, etc **2** another word for **brush**

Brussels the capital of Belgium, in the central part: became capital of Belgium in 1830; seat of the European Commission. Pop: 999 899 (2004 est)

Brussels sprout 1 a variety of cabbage, *Brassica oleracea gemmifera*, having a stout stem studded with budlike heads of tightly folded leaves, resembling tiny cabbages **2** the head of this plant, eaten as a vegetable

brutalism an austere style of architecture characterized by emphasis on such structural materials as undressed concrete and unconcealed service pipes
▷http://students.open.ac.uk/open2net/
   modernity/4_15.htm
▷www.skyscrapers.com/re/en/ab/ds/pd/bu/
   ca/sy/mo/br

Bruton John Gerard born 1947, Irish politician: leader of the Fine Gael party from 1990; prime minister of the Republic of Ireland (1994–97)

Brutus 1 Lucius Junius late 6th century BC, Roman statesman who ousted the tyrant Tarquin (509) and helped found the Roman republic **2 Marcus Junius** ?85–42 BC, Roman statesman who, with Cassius, led the conspiracy to assassinate Caesar (44): committed suicide after being defeated by Antony and Octavian (Augustus) at Philippi (42)

Bryansk a city in W Russia. Pop: 428 000 (2005 est)

bryony *or* **briony** any of several herbaceous climbing plants of the cucurbitaceous genus *Bryonia*, of Europe and N Africa

Brythonic the S group of Celtic languages, consisting of Welsh, Cornish, and Breton

BSE bovine spongiform encephalopathy: a fatal slow-developing disease of cattle, affecting the nervous system. It is caused by a prion protein and is thought to be transmissable to humans, causing a variant form of Creutzfeldt-Jakob disease

bubble car (in Britain, formerly) a small car, often having three wheels, with a transparent bubble-shaped top

Buber Martin 1878–1965, Jewish theologian, existentialist philosopher, and scholar of Hasidism, born in Austria, whose works include *I and Thou* (1923), *Between Man and Man* (1946), and *Eclipse of God* (1952)

bubo *Pathol* inflammation and swelling of a lymph node, often with the formation of pus, esp in the region of the armpit or groin

bubonic plague an acute infectious febrile disease characterized by chills, prostration, delirium, and formation of buboes: caused by the bite of a rat flea infected with the bacterium *Yersinia pestis*

Bucaramanga a city in N central Colombia, in the Cordillera Oriental: centre of a district growing coffee, tobacco, and cotton. Pop: 1 069 000 (2005 est)

buccaneer a pirate, esp one who preyed on the Spanish colonies and shipping in America and the Caribbean in the 17th and 18th centuries

Buchan John, 1st Baron Tweedsmuir. 1875–1940, Scottish statesman, historian, and writer of adventure stories, esp *The Thirty-Nine Steps* (1915) and *Greenmantle* (1916); governor general of Canada (1935–40)

Buchanan 1 George 1506–82, Scottish historian, who was tutor to Mary, Queen of Scots and James VI; author of *History of Scotland* (1582) **2 James** 1791–1868, 15th president of the US (1857–61)

Bucharest the capital of Romania, in the southeast. Pop: 2 001 000 (2005 est)

Buchenwald a village in E central Germany, near Weimar; site of a Nazi concentration camp (1937–45)

buck¹ 1 a the male of various animals including the goat, hare, kangaroo, rabbit, and reindeer **b** (*as modifier*): *a buck antelope* **2** *South African* an antelope or deer of either sex

buck² 1 *US, Canadian, and Austral, informal* a dollar **2** *South African, informal* a rand

buck³ 1 *Gymnastics* a type of vaulting horse **2** *US and Canadian* a stand for timber during sawing

buck⁴ *Poker* a marker in the jackpot to remind the winner of some obligation when his turn comes to deal

Buck Pearl S(ydenstricker). 1892–1973, US novelist, noted particularly for her novel of Chinese life *The Good Earth* (1931): Nobel prize for literature 1938

bucket 1 any of various bucket-like parts of a machine, such as the scoop on a mechanical shovel **2** a cupped blade or bucket-like compartment on the outer circumference of a water wheel, paddle wheel, etc **3** *Computing* a unit of storage on a direct-access device from which data can be retrieved **4** *Chiefly US* a turbine rotor blade

bucket shop *Chiefly Brit* any small business that cannot be relied upon, esp one selling cheap airline tickets

Buckingham¹ 1 George Villiers, 1st Duke of 1592–1628, English courtier and statesman; favourite of James I and Charles I: his arrogance, military incompetence, and greed increased the tensions between the King and Parliament that eventually led to the Civil War **2** his son, **George Villiers, 2nd Duke of** 1628–87, English courtier and writer; chief minister of Charles II and member of the Cabal (1667–73)

Buckingham² a town in S central England, in Buckinghamshire; university (1975). Pop: 12 512 (2001)

Buckingham Palace the London residence of the British sovereign: built in 1703, rebuilt by John Nash in 1821–36 and partially redesigned in the early 20th century

Buckinghamshire a county in SE central England, containing the Vale of Aylesbury and parts of the Chiltern Hills: the geographic and ceremonial county includes Milton Keynes, which became an independent unitary authority in 1997. Administrative centre: Aylesbury. Pop. (excluding Milton Keynes): 478 000 (2003 est). Area (excluding Milton Keynes): 1568 sq km (605 sq miles)

Buckland William 1784–1856, English geologist; he became a proponent of the idea of catastrophic ice ages

buckskin 1 the skin of a male deer 2 a stiffly starched cotton cloth 3 a strong satin-woven woollen fabric 4 greyish-yellow

buckthorn any of several thorny small-flowered shrubs of the genus *Rhamnus*, esp the Eurasian species *R. cathartica*, whose berries were formerly used as a purgative: family *Rhamnaceae*

buckwheat 1 any of several polygonaceous plants of the genus *Fagopyrum*, esp *F. esculentum*, which has fragrant white flowers and is cultivated, esp in the US, for its seeds 2 the edible seeds of this plant, ground into flour or used as animal fodder 3 the flour obtained from these seeds

bucolic a pastoral poem, often in the form of a dialogue

bud 1 a swelling on a plant stem consisting of overlapping immature leaves or petals 2 any small budlike outgrowth 3 an asexually produced outgrowth in simple organisms, such as yeasts, and the hydra that develops into a new individual 4 in bud at the stage of producing buds

Budapest the capital of Hungary, on the River Danube: formed in 1873 from the towns of Buda and Pest. Traditionally Buda, the old Magyar capital, was the administrative and Pest the trade centre: suffered severely in the Russian siege of 1945 and in the unsuccessful revolt against the Communist regime (1956). Pop: 1 719 342 (2003 est)

Buddh Gaya, Buddha Gaya, *or* **Bodh Gaya** a town in NE India, in Bihar: site of the sacred bo tree under which Gautama Siddhartha attained enlightenment and became the Buddha; pilgrimage centre. Pop: 30 883 (2001)

Buddhism a religious teaching propagated by the Buddha and his followers, which declares that by destroying greed, hatred, and delusion, which are the causes of all suffering, man can attain perfect enlightenment

▷www.buddhanet.net/

buddleia any ornamental shrub of the genus *Buddleia*, esp *B. davidii*, which has long spikes of mauve flowers and is frequently visited by butterflies: family *Buddleiaceae*

buddy 1 a volunteer who visits and gives help and support to a person suffering from AIDS 2 a volunteer who gives help and support to a person who has become disabled but is returning to work

budge a lambskin dressed for the fur to be worn on the outer side

budgerigar a small green Australian parrot, *Melopsittacus undulatus*: a popular cagebird that is bred in many different coloured varieties

Budget the an estimate of British government expenditures and revenues and the financial plans for the ensuing fiscal year presented annually to the House of Commons by the Chancellor of the Exchequer

budget deficit *Economics* the amount by which government expenditure exceeds income from taxation, customs duties, etc, in any one fiscal year

Buenaventura a major port in W Colombia, on the Pacific coast. Pop: 250 000 (2005 est)

Buena Vista a village in NE Mexico, near Saltillo: site of the defeat of the Mexicans by US forces (1847)

Buenos Aires the capital of Argentina, a major port and industrial city on the Río de la Plata estuary: became capital in 1880; university (1821). Pop: 13 349 000 (2005 est)

buff a a cloth or pad of material used for polishing an object b a flexible disc or wheel impregnated with a fine abrasive for polishing metals, etc, with a power tool

buffalo 1 a member of the cattle tribe, *Syncerus caffer*, mostly found in game reserves in southern and eastern Africa and having upward-curving horns 2 short for **water buffalo** 3 *US and Canadian* a member of the cattle tribe, *Bison bison*, formerly widely distributed over the prairies of W North America but now confined to reserves and parks, with a massive head, shaggy forequarters, and a humped back

Buffalo a port in W New York State, at the E end of Lake Erie. Pop: 285 018 (2003 est)

Buffalo Bill nickname of *William Frederick Cody*. 1846–1917, US showman who toured Europe and the US with his famous *Wild West Show*

buffer¹ 1 one of a pair of spring-loaded steel pads attached at both ends of railway vehicles and at the end of a railway track to reduce shock due to contact 2 *Chem* a an ionic compound, usually a salt of a weak acid or base, added to a solution to resist changes in its acidity or alkalinity and thus stabilize its pH b a solution containing such a compound 3 *Computing* a memory device for temporarily storing data 4 *Electronics* an isolating circuit used to minimize the reaction between a driving and a driven circuit

buffer² 1 any device used to shine, polish, etc.; buff 2 a person who uses such a device

buffer state *Politics* a small neutral state between two rival powers

buffet aerodynamic excitation of an aircraft structure by separated flows

Buffet Bernard 1928–99, French painter and engraver. His works are characterized by sombre tones and thin angular forms

bug¹ 1 any insect of the order *Hemiptera*, esp any of the suborder *Heteroptera*, having piercing and sucking mouthparts specialized as a beak (rostrum) 2 *Chiefly US and Canadian* any insect, such as the June bug or the Croton bug 3 *Informal* an error or fault, as in a machine or system, esp in a computer or computer program 4 *US* (in poker) a joker used as an ace or wild card to complete a straight or flush

bug² *Obsolete* an evil spirit or spectre; hobgoblin

Bug 1 a river in E Europe, rising in W Ukraine and flowing southeast to the Dnieper estuary and the Black Sea. Length: 853 km (530 miles) 2 a river in E Europe, rising in SW Ukraine and flowing northwest to the River Vistula in Poland, forming part of the border between Poland and Ukraine. Length: 724 km (450 miles)

Buganda a region of Uganda: a powerful Bantu kingdom from the 17th century

Bugatti Ettore (Arco Isidoro). 1881–1947, Italian car manufacturer; founder of the Bugatti car factory at Molsheim (1909)

bugbear (in English folklore) a goblin said to eat naughty children and thought to be in the form of a bear

buggy 1 a light horse-drawn carriage having either four wheels (esp in the US and Canada) or two wheels (esp in Britain and India) 2 a small motorized vehicle designed for a particular purpose

bugle¹ *Music* a brass instrument similar to the cornet but usually without valves: used for military fanfares, signal calls, etc.

bugle 2 any of several Eurasian plants of the genus *Ajuga*, esp *A. reptans*, having small blue or white flowers: family *Lamiaceae* (labiates)

bugle³ a tubular glass or plastic bead sewn onto clothes for decoration

builder a substance added to a soap or detergent as a filler or abrasive

built-up 1 having many buildings (esp in the phrase built-up area) 2 denoting a beam, girder, or stanchion constructed of sections welded, riveted, or bolted together, etc.

Bujumbura the capital of Burundi, a port at the NE end of Lake Tanganyika. Pop: 419 000 (2005 est)

Bukavu a port in E Democratic Republic of Congo (formerly Zaïre), on Lake Kivu: commercial and industrial centre. Pop: 294 000 (2005 est)

Bukhara *or* **Bokhara** 1 a city in S Uzbekistan. Pop: 299 000 (2005 est) 2 a former emirate of central Asia: a powerful kingdom and centre of Islam; became a territory of the Soviet Union (1920) and was divided between the former Uzbek, Tajik, and Turkmen Soviet Socialist Republics

Bukovina *or* **Bucovina** a region of E central Europe, part of the NE Carpathians: the north was seized by the Soviet Union (1940) and later became part of Ukraine; the south remained Romanian

Bulawayo a city in SW Zimbabwe founded (1893) on the site of the kraal of Lobengula, the last Matabele king; the country's main industrial centre. Pop: 693 000 (2005 est)

bulb 1 a rounded organ of vegetative reproduction in plants such as the tulip and onion: a flattened stem bearing a central shoot surrounded by fleshy nutritive inner leaves and thin brown outer leaves 2 a plant, such as a hyacinth or daffodil, that grows from a bulb 3 See light bulb 4 a rounded part of an instrument such as a syringe or thermometer 5 *Anatomy* a rounded expansion of a cylindrical organ or part, such as the

medulla oblongata 6 *Nautical* a bulbous protuberance at the forefoot of a ship to reduce turbulence

Bulgakov Mikhail Afanaseyev 1891–1940, Soviet novelist, dramatist, and short-story writer; his novels include *The Master and Margarita* (1966–67)

Bulganin Nikolai Aleksandrovich 1895–1975, Soviet statesman and military leader; chairman of the council of ministers (1955–58)

Bulgaria a republic in SE Europe, on the Balkan Peninsula on the Black Sea: under Turkish rule from 1395 until 1878; became an independent kingdom in 1908 and a republic in 1946; consists chiefly of the Danube valley in the north and the Balkan Mountains in the central part, separated from the Rhodope Mountains of the south by the valley of the Maritsa River. Language: Bulgarian. Religion: Christian (Bulgarian Orthodox) majority. Currency: lev. Capital: Sofia. Pop: 7 829 000 (2004 est). Area: 110 911 sq km (42 823 sq miles)

Bulgarian the official language of Bulgaria, belonging to the S Slavonic branch of the Indo-European family

bulimia 1 pathologically insatiable hunger, esp when caused by a brain lesion 2 a disorder characterized by compulsive overeating followed by vomiting: sometimes associated with anxiety about gaining weight

bulk 1 unpackaged cargo or goods 2 a ship's cargo or hold 3 in bulk a (of a cargo, etc) unpackaged

bulk buying 1 *Commerce* the purchase at one time, and often at a reduced price, of a large quantity of a particular commodity 2 the purchase of the whole or greater part of the output of a commodity of a country or state by a single buyer, usually another country or state; state trading

bulkhead 1 any upright wall-like partition in a ship, aircraft, vehicle, etc. 2 a wall or partition built to hold back earth, fire, water, etc.

bull¹ 1 any male bovine animal, esp one that is sexually mature 2 the uncastrated adult male of any breed of domestic cattle 3 the male of various other animals including the elephant and whale 4 *Chiefly Brit* short for bull's-eye 5 short for bulldog *or* bull terrier 6 male; masculine

bull² a formal document issued by the pope, written in antiquated characters and often sealed with a leaden bulla

Bull John 1563–1628, English composer and organist

bulldog 1 a sturdy thickset breed of dog with an undershot jaw, short nose, broad head, and a muscular body 2 (at Oxford University) an official who accompanies the proctors on ceremonial occasions

bulldog clip *Trademark* a clip for holding papers together, consisting of two T-shaped metal clamps held in place by a cylindrical spring

bulldozer a powerful tractor fitted with caterpillar tracks and a blade at the front, used for moving earth, rocks, etc.

bulletin board *Computing* a facility on a computer network allowing any user to leave messages that can be read by any other user, and to download software and information to the user's own computer

bullfight a traditional Spanish, Portuguese, and Latin American spectacle in which a matador, assisted by banderilleros and mounted picadors, baits and usually kills a bull in an arena

bullfinch 1 a common European finch, *Pyrrhula pyrrhula*: the male has a bright red throat and breast, black crown, wings, and tail, and a grey-and-white back **2** any of various similar finches

bullfrog any of various large frogs, such as *Rana catesbeiana* (**American bullfrog**), having a loud deep croak

bullion 1 gold or silver in mass **2** gold or silver in the form of bars and ingots, suitable for further processing **3** a thick gold or silver wire or fringed cord used as a trimming, as on military uniforms

bullock 1 a gelded bull; steer **2** *Archaic* a bull calf

bull terrier a breed of terrier having a muscular body and thick neck, with a short smooth often white coat: developed by crossing the bulldog with various terriers

bully any of various small freshwater fishes of the genera *Gobiomorphus* and *Philynodon* of New Zealand

bully-off *Hockey* a method by which a game is restarted after a stoppage. Two opposing players stand with the ball between them and alternately strike their sticks together and against the ground three times before trying to hit the ball

bulrush 1 a grasslike cyperaceous marsh plant, *Scirpus lacustris*, used for making mats, chair seats, etc. **2** a biblical word for **papyrus** (the plant)

bulwark 1 *Nautical* a solid vertical fencelike structure along the outward sides of a deck **2** a breakwater or mole

bumblebee *or* **humblebee** any large hairy social bee of the genus *Bombus* and related genera, of temperate regions: family *Apidae*

bump 1 *Anatomy* any of the natural protuberances of the human skull, said by phrenologists to indicate underlying faculties and character **2** a rising current of air that gives an aircraft a severe upward jolt **3** *Rowing* the act of bumping **4** *Cricket* **bump ball** a ball that bounces into the air after being hit directly into the ground by the batsman

bumper 1 a horizontal metal bar attached to the front or rear end of a car, lorry, etc, to protect against damage from impact **2** *Cricket* a ball bowled so that it bounces high on pitching; bouncer

Bundaberg a city in E Australia, near the E coast of Queensland: centre of a sugar-growing area, with a nearby deep-water port. Pop: 44 556 (2001)

Bundelkhand a region of central India: formerly native states, now mainly part of Madhya Pradesh

bundle 1 *Biology* a collection of strands of specialized tissue such as nerve fibres **2** *Textiles* a measure of yarn or cloth; 60 000 yards of linen yarn; 5 or 10 pounds of cotton hanks

bung a stopper, esp of cork or rubber, for a cask, piece of laboratory glassware, etc.

bungalow 1 a one-storey house, sometimes with an attic **2** (in India) a one-storey house, usually surrounded by a veranda

bungee jumping *or* **bungy jumping** a sport in which a participant jumps from a high bridge, building, etc, secured only by a rubber cord attached to the ankles

bunion swelling of the first joint of the big toe, which is displaced to one side. An inflamed bursa forms over the joint

bunker an obstacle on a golf course, usually a sand-filled hollow bordered by a ridge

Bunsen Robert Wilhelm 1811–99, German chemist who with Kirchhoff developed spectrum analysis and discovered the elements caesium and rubidium. He invented the Bunsen burner and the ice calorimeter

Bunsen burner a gas burner, widely used in scientific laboratories, consisting of a metal tube with an adjustable air valve at the base

bunting any of numerous seed-eating songbirds of the families *Fringillidae* (finches, etc) or *Emberizidae*, esp those of the genera *Emberiza* of the Old World and *Passerina* of North America. They all have short stout bills

bunya a tall dome-shaped Australian coniferous tree, *Araucaria bidwillii*, having edible cones (**bunya nuts**) and thickish flattened needles

Bunyan John 1628–88, English preacher and writer, noted particularly for his allegory *The Pilgrim's Progress* (1678)

bunyip *Austral* a legendary monster said to inhabit swamps and lagoons of the Australian interior

buoy a distinctively shaped and coloured float, anchored to the bottom, for designating moorings, navigable channels, or obstructions in a body of water

buoyant (of a liquid or gas) able to keep a body afloat or cause it to rise

Buraydah *or* **Buraida** a town and oasis in central Saudi Arabia. Pop: 462 000 (2005 est)

Burbage 1 James ?1530–97, English actor and theatre manager, who built (1576) the first theatre in England **2** his son, **Richard** ?1567–1619, English actor, associated with Shakespeare

burble turbulence in the airflow around a body

burbot a freshwater gadoid food fish, *Lota lota*, that has barbels around its mouth and occurs in Europe, Asia, and North America

Burckhardt Jacob Christoph 1818–97, Swiss art and cultural historian; author of *The Civilisation of the Renaissance in Italy* (1860)

burden[1] *Nautical* **a** the cargo capacity of a ship **b** the weight of a ship's cargo

burden[2] a line of words recurring at the end of each verse of a ballad or similar song; chorus or refrain

burdock a coarse weedy Eurasian plant of the genus *Arctium*, having large heart-shaped leaves, tiny purple flowers surrounded by hooked bristles, and burlike fruits: family *Asteraceae* (composites)

burette *or US* **buret** a graduated glass tube with a stopcock on one end for dispensing and transferring known volumes of fluids, esp liquids

Burgas a port in SE Bulgaria on an inlet of the Black Sea. Pop: 177 000 (2005 est)

Burgenland a state of E Austria. Capital: Eisenstadt. Pop: 276 419 (2003 est). Area: 3965 sq km (1531 sq miles)

burgeon *or* **bourgeon** a bud of a plant

Burgess 1 Anthony, real name *John Burgess Wilson*. 1917–93, English novelist and critic: his novels include *A Clockwork Orange* (1962), *Tremor of Intent* (1966), *Earthly Powers* (1980), and *Any Old Iron* (1989) **2 Guy** 1911–63, British spy, who fled to the Soviet Union (with Donald Maclean) in 1951

Burgess Shale a bed of Cambrian sedimentary rock in the Rocky Mountains in British Columbia containing many unique invertebrate fossils

burgh 1 (in Scotland) a town, esp one incorporated by charter, that enjoyed a degree of self-government until the local-government reorganization of 1975 2 an archaic form of **borough**

burgher 1 a member of the trading or mercantile class of a medieval city 2 *Archaic* a citizen or inhabitant of a corporate town, esp on the Continent 3 *South African, History* a a citizen of the Cape Colony or of one of the Transvaal and Free State republics b *(as modifier)*: burgher troops

Burghley *or* **Burleigh** William Cecil, 1st Baron Burghley. 1520–98, English statesman: chief adviser to Elizabeth I; secretary of state (1558–72) and Lord High Treasurer (1572–98)

burglary *English criminal law* the crime of either entering a building as a trespasser with the intention of committing theft, rape, grievous bodily harm, or damage, or, having entered as a trespasser, of committing one or more of these offences

burgomaster the chief magistrate of a town in Austria, Belgium, Germany, or the Netherlands; mayor

Burgos a city in N Spain, in Old Castile: cathedral. Pop: 169 317 (2003 est)

Burgoyne John 1722–92, British general in the War of American Independence who was forced to surrender at Saratoga (1777)

Burgundy 1 a region of E France famous for its wines, lying west of the Saône: formerly a semi-independent duchy; annexed to France in 1482 2 a monarchy (1384–1477) of medieval Europe, at its height including the Low Countries, the duchy of Burgundy, and Franche-Comté 3 **Kingdom of** a kingdom in E France, established in the early 6th century AD, eventually including the later duchy of Burgundy, Franche-Comté, and the Kingdom of Provence: known as the Kingdom of Arles from the 13th century 4 a any red or white wine produced in the region of Burgundy, around Dijon b any heavy red table wine 5 a blackish-purple to purplish-red colour

burin 1 a chisel of tempered steel with a sharp lozenge-shaped point, used for engraving furrows in metal, wood, or marble 2 an engraver's individual style 3 *Archaeol* a prehistoric flint tool with a very small transverse edge

Burke 1 Edmund 1729–97, British Whig statesman, conservative political theorist, and orator, born in Ireland: defended parliamentary government and campaigned for a more liberal treatment of the American colonies; denounced the French Revolution 2 **Robert O'Hara** 1820–61, Irish explorer, who led the first expedition (1860–61) across Australia from south to north. He was accompanied by W. J. Wills, George Grey, and John King; King alone survived the return journey 3 **William** 1792–1829, Irish murderer and body snatcher; associate of William Hare

Burkina-Faso an inland republic in W Africa: dominated by Mossi kingdoms (10th–19th centuries); French protectorate established in 1896; became an independent republic in 1960; consists mainly of a flat savanna plateau. Official language: French; Mossi and other African languages also widely spoken. Religion: mostly animist, with a large Muslim minority. Currency: franc. Capital: Ouagadougou. Pop: 13 393 000 (2004 est). Area: 273 200 sq km (105 900 sq miles)

burl 1 a small knot or lump in wool 2 a roundish warty outgrowth from the trunk, roots, or branches of certain trees

burlesque 1 an artistic work, esp literary or dramatic, satirizing a subject by caricaturing it 2 a play of the 17th–19th centuries that parodied some contemporary dramatic fashion or event 3 *US and Canadian, Theatre* a bawdy comedy show of the late 19th and early 20th centuries: the striptease eventually became one of its chief elements

Burlington 1 a city in S Canada on Lake Ontario, northeast of Hamilton. Pop: 150 836 (2001) 2 a city in NW Vermont on Lake Champlain: largest city in the state; University of Vermont (1791). Pop: 39 148 (2003 est)

Burmese the official language of Burma (Myanmar), belonging to the Sino-Tibetan family

burn 1 an injury caused by exposure to heat, electrical, chemical, or radioactive agents. Burns are classified according to the depth of tissue affected: **first-degree burn**: skin surface painful and red; **second-degree burn**: blisters appear on the skin; **third-degree burn**: destruction of both epidermis and dermis 2 a hot painful sensation in a muscle, experienced during vigorous exercise 3 *Austral and NZ* a controlled fire to clear an area of scrub

Burne-Jones Sir Edward 1833–98, English Pre-Raphaelite painter and designer of stained-glass windows and tapestries

Burnet 1 Gilbert 1643–1715, Scottish bishop and historian, who played a prominent role in the Glorious Revolution (1688–89); author of *The History of My Own Times* (2 vols: 1724 and 1734) 2 Sir (**Frank**) **Macfarlane** 1899–1985, Australian physician and virologist, who shared a Nobel prize for physiology or medicine in 1960 with P B Medawar for their work in immunology 3 **Thomas** 1635–1715, English theologian who tried to reconcile science and religion in his *Sacred theory of the Earth* (1680–89)

Burnett Frances Hodgson 1849–1924, US novelist, born in England; author of *Little Lord Fauntleroy* (1886) and *The Secret Garden* (1911)

Burney 1 Charles 1726–1814, English composer and music historian, whose books include *A General History of Music* (1776–89) 2 his daughter, **Frances** known as *Fanny*; married name *Madame D'Arblay*. 1752–1840, English novelist and diarist: author of *Evelina* (1778). Her *Diaries and Letters* (1768–1840) are of historical interest

burning 1 a form of heat treatment used to harden and finish ceramic materials or to prepare certain ores for further treatment by calcination 2 overheating of an alloy during heat treatment in which local fusion or excessive oxide formation and penetration occur, weakening the alloy

burning bush *Old Testament* the bush that burned without being consumed, from which God spoke to Moses (Exodus 3:2–4)

burning glass a convex lens for concentrating the sun's

rays into a small area to produce heat or fire

Burnley an industrial town in NW England, in E Lancashire. Pop: 73 021 (2001)

burn out 1 *Engineering* the failure of a mechanical device from excessive heating **2** *Psychology* a total loss of energy and interest and an inability to function effectively, experienced as a result of excessive demands upon one's resources or chronic overwork

Burns Robert 1759–96, Scottish lyric poet. His verse, written mostly in dialect, includes love songs, nature poetry, and satires. *Auld Lang Syne* and *Tam o' Shanter* are among his best known poems

burr¹ *or* **bur 1** a washer fitting around the end of a rivet **2** a blank punched out of sheet metal

burr², buhr, *or* **bur** a mass of hard siliceous rock surrounded by softer rock

burrawang any of several Australian cycads of the genus *Macrozamia*, having an edible nut

Burren the a limestone area on the North Clare coast in the Irish Republic, famous for its wild flowers, caves, and dolmens

Burroughs 1 Edgar Rice 1875–1950, US novelist, author of the *Tarzan* stories **2 William S(eward)**. 1914–97, US novelist, noted for his experimental works exploring themes of drug addiction, violence, and homosexuality. His novels include *Junkie* (1953), *The Naked Lunch* (1959), and *Interzone* (1989)

Bursa a city in NW Turkey: founded in the 2nd century BC; seat of Bithynian kings. Pop: 1 413 000 (2005 est)

bursar 1 an official in charge of the financial management of a school, college, or university **2** *Chiefly Scot and NZ* a student holding a bursary

bursary 1 a scholarship or grant awarded esp in Scottish and New Zealand schools, universities etc. **2** *Brit* **a** the treasury of a college, etc. **b** the bursar's room in a college

burton *Nautical* a kind of light hoisting tackle

Burton 1 Sir Richard Francis 1821–90, English explorer, Orientalist, and writer who discovered Lake Tanganyika with John Speke (1858); produced the first unabridged translation of *The Thousand Nights and a Night* (1885–88) **2 Richard**, real name *Richard Jenkins*. 1925–84, Welsh stage and film actor: films include *Becket* (1964), *Who's Afraid of Virginia Woolf?* (1966), and *Equus* (1977) **3 Robert**, pen name *Democritus Junior*. 1577–1640, English clergyman, scholar, and writer, noted for his *Anatomy of Melancholy* (1621) **4 Tim** born 1958, US film director whose work includes *Beetlejuice* (1988), *Batman* (1989), *Ed Wood* (1994), and *Big Fish* (2003)

Burton-upon-Trent a town in W central England, in E Staffordshire: famous for brewing. Pop: 43 784 (2001)

Burundi a republic in E central Africa: inhabited chiefly by the Hutu, Tutsi, and Twa (Pygmy); made part of German East Africa in 1899; part of the Belgian territory of Ruanda-Urundi from 1923 until it became independent in 1962; ethnic violence has erupted at times; consists mainly of high plateaus along the main Nile-Congo dividing range, dropping rapidly to the Great Rift Valley in the west. Official languages: Kirundi and French. Religion: Christian majority. Currency: Burundi franc. Capital: Bujumbura. Pop: 7 068 000 (2004 est). Area: 27 731 sq km (10 707 sq miles)

Bury 1 a town in NW England, in Bury unitary authority, Greater Manchester: an early textile centre. Pop: 60 178 (2001) **2** a unitary authority in NW England, in Greater Manchester. Pop: 181 900 (2003 est). Area: 99 sq km (38 sq miles)

Buryat Republic *or* **Buryatia** a constituent republic of SE central Russia, on Lake Baikal: mountainous, with forests covering over half the total area. Capital: Ulan-Ude. Pop: 981 000 (2002). Area: 351 300 sq km (135 608 sq miles)

Bury St Edmunds a market town in E England, in Suffolk. Pop: 36 218 (2001)

bus a large motor vehicle designed to carry passengers between stopping places along a regular route
▷http://routesinternational.com/buslines.htm
▷www.busesintl.com

Busby Sir Matthew, known as *Matt*. 1909–94, British footballer. He managed Manchester United (1946–69)

bush¹ 1 a dense woody plant, smaller than a tree, with many branches arising from the lower part of the stem; shrub **2** a dense cluster of such shrubs; thicket **3 a** an uncultivated or sparsely settled area, esp in Africa, Australia, New Zealand, or Canada: usually covered with trees or shrubs, varying from open shrubby country to dense rainforest **b** (*as modifier*): *bush flies* **4** a forested area; woodland **5** a fox's tail; brush

bush² a thin metal sleeve or tubular lining serving as a bearing or guide

Bush 1 George born 1924, US Republican politician; vice president of the US (1981–89): 41st president of the US (1989–93) **2** his son, **George W(alker)** born 1946, US Republican statesman: 43rd president of the US (from 2001)

bushbaby any agile nocturnal arboreal prosimian primate of the genera *Galago* and *Euoticus*, occurring in Africa south of the Sahara: family *Lorisidae* (lorises). They have large eyes and ears and a long tail

bushel 1 a Brit unit of dry or liquid measure equal to 8 Imperial gallons. 1 Imperial bushel is equivalent to 0.036 37 cubic metres **2** a US unit of dry measure equal to 64 US pints. 1 US bushel is equivalent to 0.035 24 cubic metres

Bushire a port in SW Iran, on the Persian Gulf. Pop: 166 000 (2005 est)

Bushman 1 a member of a hunting and gathering people of southern Africa, esp the Kalahari region, typically having leathery yellowish skin, short stature, and prominent buttocks **2** any language of this people, belonging to the Khoisan family

bushveld the an area of low altitude in N South Africa, having scrub vegetation

business 1 an industrial, commercial, or professional operation; purchase and sale of goods and services **2** a commercial or industrial establishment, such as a firm or factory **3** commercial activity; dealings (esp in the phrase **do business**) **4** volume or quantity of commercial activity **5** commercial policy or procedure **6** *Theatre* an incidental action, such as lighting a pipe, performed by an actor for dramatic effect **7** a group of ferrets

business park an area specially designated and landscaped to accommodate business offices, warehouses, light industry, etc.

Buss Frances Mary 1827–94, British educationalist; a pioneer of secondary education for girls, who campaigned for women's admission to university

Bussell Darcey **(Andrea)**. born 1969, British ballet dancer, principal ballerina with the Royal Ballet from 1989

bust 1 the chest of a human being, esp a woman's bosom 2 *Art* a sculpture of the head, shoulders, and upper chest of a person

bustard any terrestrial bird of the family *Otididae*, inhabiting open regions of the Old World: order *Gruiformes* (cranes, rails, etc). They have long strong legs, a heavy body, a long neck, and speckled plumage

butane a colourless flammable gaseous alkane that exists in two isomeric forms, both of which occur in natural gas. The stable isomer, *n*-butane, is used mainly in the manufacture of rubber and fuels (such as Calor Gas). Formula: C_4H_{10}

butcherbird 1 a shrike, esp one of the genus *Lanius* 2 any of several Australian magpies of the genus *Cracticus* that impale their prey on thorns

Bute[1] John Stuart, 3rd Earl of Bute. 1713–92, British Tory statesman; prime minister (1762–63)

Bute[2] an island off the coast of SW Scotland, in Argyll and Bute council area: situated in the Firth of Clyde, separated from the Cowal peninsula by the **Kyles of Bute**. Chief town: Rothesay. Pop: 7228 (2001). Area: 121 sq km (47 sq miles)

Butenandt Adolf Frederick Johann 1903–95, German organic chemist. He shared the Nobel prize for chemistry (1939) for his pioneering work on sex hormones

Buteshire (until 1975) a county of SW Scotland, consisting of islands in the Firth of Clyde and Kilbrannan Sound: formerly part of Strathclyde region (1975–96), now part of Argyll and Bute council area

Buthelezi Mangosouthu Gatsha , known as *Chief Buthelezi*. born 1928, Zulu leader, chief minister of the KwaZulu territory of South Africa from 1970 until its abolition in 1994; founder of the Inkatha movement and advocate of Zulu autonomy; minister of home affairs from 1994

Butler 1 Joseph 1692–1752, English bishop and theologian, author of *Analogy of Religion* (1736) 2 Josephine **(Elizabeth)**. 1828–1906, British social reformer, noted esp for her campaigns against state regulation of prostitution 3 **Reg**, full name *Reginald Cotterell Butler*. 1913–81, British metal sculptor; his works include *The Unknown Political Prisoner* (1953) 4 R(ichard) A(usten), Baron Butler of Saffron Walden, known as *Rab Butler*. 1902–82, British Conservative politician: Chancellor of the Exchequer (1951–55); Home Secretary (1957–62); Foreign Secretary (1963–64) 5 **Samuel** 1612–80, English poet and satirist; author of *Hudibras* (1663–78) 6 **Samuel** 1835–1902, British novelist, noted for his satirical work *Erewhon* (1872) and his autobiographical novel *The Way of All Flesh* (1903)

butt[1] 1 *Shooting, Archery* a a mound of earth behind the target on a target range that stops bullets or wide shots b the target itself c the target range 2 a low barrier, usually of sods or peat, behind which sportsmen shoot game birds, esp grouse

butt[2] 1 a large cask, esp one with a capacity of two hogsheads, for storing wine or beer 2 a US unit of liquid measure equal to 126 US gallons

butter bean a variety of lima bean that has large pale flat edible seeds and is grown in the southern US

buttercup any of various yellow-flowered ranunculaceous plants of the genus *Ranunculus*, such as *R. acris* (meadow buttercup), which is native to Europe but common throughout North America

Butterfield William 1814–1900, British architect of the Gothic Revival; his buildings include Keble College, Oxford (1870) and All Saints, Margaret Street, London (1849–59)

butterfly 1 any diurnal insect of the order *Lepidoptera* that has a slender body with clubbed antennae and typically rests with the wings (which are often brightly coloured) closed over the back 2 a swimming stroke in which the arms are plunged forward together in large circular movements

Buttermere a lake in NW England, in Cumbria, in the Lake District, southwest of Keswick. Length: 2 km (1.25 miles)

Butterworth 1 George 1885–1916, British composer, noted for his interest in folk song and his settings of Housman's poems 2 **Nick** born 1946, English writer and illustrator of children's books, many of which feature Percy, the animal-loving park keeper

buttery 1 a room for storing foods or wines 2 *Brit* (in some universities) a room in which food is supplied or sold to students

buttock 1 either of the two large fleshy masses of thick muscular tissue that form the human rump 2 the analogous part in some mammals

button 1 a small disc that completes an electric circuit when pushed, as one that operates a doorbell or machine 2 *Computing* a symbolic representation of a button on the screen of a computer that is notionally depressed by manipulating the mouse to initiate an action 3 *Biology* any rounded knoblike part or organ, such as an unripe mushroom 4 *Fencing* the protective knob fixed to the point of a foil 5 a small amount of metal, usually lead, with which gold or silver is fused, thus concentrating it during assaying 6 the piece of a weld that pulls out during the destructive testing of spot welds 7 *Rowing* a projection around the loom of an oar that prevents it slipping through the rowlock

buttress 1 a construction, usually of brick or stone, built to support a wall 2 either of the two pointed rear parts of a horse's hoof

Butung an island of Indonesia, southeast of Sulawesi: hilly and forested. Chief town: Baubau. Pop: 317 124 (latest est). Area: 4555 sq km (1759 sq miles)

butyl of, consisting of, or containing any of four isomeric forms of the group C_4H_9-

Buxtehude Dietrich 1637–1707, Danish composer and organist, resident in Germany from 1668, who influenced Bach and Handel

Buxton a town in N England, in NW Derbyshire in the Peak District: thermal springs. Pop: 20 836 (2001)

buy in *Business* the purchase of a company by a manager or group who does not work for that company

buzzard any diurnal bird of prey of the genus *Buteo*, typically having broad wings and tail and a soaring flight: family *Accipitridae* (hawks, etc)

Byatt Dame A(ntonia) S(usan). born 1936, British novelist; her books include *The Virgin in the Garden* (1978), *Possession* (1990), and *A Whistling Woman* (2002)

Bydgoszcz an industrial city and port in N Poland: under Prussian rule from 1772 to 1919. Pop: 579 000 (2005 est)

bye 1 *Sport* the situation in which a player or team in an eliminatory contest wins a preliminary round by virtue of having no opponent 2 *Golf* one or more holes of a stipulated course that are left unplayed after the match has been decided 3 *Cricket* a run scored off a ball not struck by the batsman: allotted to the team as an extra and not to the individual batsman

by-election *or* **bye-election** 1 (in the United Kingdom and other countries of the Commonwealth) an election held during the life of a parliament to fill a vacant seat in the lower chamber 2 (in the US) a special election to fill a vacant elective position with an unexpired term

Byelovo *or* **Belovo** a city in W central Russia. Pop: 65 000 (2005 est)

bylaw *or* **bye-law** 1 a rule made by a local authority for the regulation of its affairs or management of the area it governs 2 a regulation of a company, society, etc. 3 a subsidiary law

Byng 1 **George**, Viscount Torrington. 1663–1733, British admiral: defeated fleet of James Edward Stuart, the Old Pretender, off Scotland (1708); defeated Spanish fleet off Messina (1717) 2 his son **John** 1704–57, English admiral: executed after failing to relieve Minorca 3 **Julian Hedworth George**, 1st Viscount Byng of Vimy. 1862–1935, British general in World War I; governor general of Canada (1921–26)

bypass 1 a main road built to avoid a city or other congested area 2 any system of pipes or conduits for redirecting the flow of a liquid 3 a means of redirecting the flow of a substance around an appliance through which it would otherwise pass 4 *Surgery* a the redirection of blood flow, either to avoid a diseased blood vessel or in order to perform heart surgery b (*as modifier*): *bypass surgery* 5 *Electronics* a an electrical circuit, esp one containing a capacitor, connected in parallel around one or more components, providing an alternative path for certain frequencies b (*as modifier*): *a bypass capacitor*

by-play *Theatre* secondary action or talking carried on apart while the main action proceeds, esp in a play

Byrd 1 **Richard Evelyn** 1888–1957, US rear admiral, aviator, and polar explorer 2 **William** 1543–1623, English composer and organist, noted for his madrigals, masses, and music for virginals

Byrd Land a part of Antarctica, east of the Ross Ice Shelf and the Ross Sea: claimed for the US by Admiral Richard E. Byrd in 1929, though all claims are suspended under the Antarctic Treaty of 1959

Byron **George Gordon**, 6th Baron. 1788–1824, British Romantic poet, noted also for his passionate and disastrous love affairs. His major works include *Childe Harold's Pilgrimage* (1812–18), and *Don Juan* (1819–24). He spent much of his life abroad and died while fighting for Greek independence

Bytom an industrial city in SW Poland, in Upper Silesia: under Prussian and German rule from 1742 to 1945. Pop: 205 560 (1999 est)

Byzantine 1 of, characteristic of, or relating to Byzantium or the Byzantine Empire 2 of, relating to, or characterizing the Orthodox Church or its rites and liturgy 3 of or relating to the highly coloured stylized form of religious art developed in the Byzantine Empire 4 of or relating to the style of architecture developed in the Byzantine Empire, characterized by massive domes with square bases, rounded arches, spires and minarets, and the extensive use of mosaics 5 denoting the Medieval Greek spoken in the Byzantine Empire

  ▷www.archaeolink.com/
    byzantine_civilization.htm
  ▷www.metmuseum.org/explore/Byzantium/
    art.html
  ▷http://historymedren.about.com/cs/
    byzantinestudies

Byzantine Church another name for the **Orthodox Church**

Byzantine Empire the continuation of the Roman Empire in the East, esp after the deposition of the last emperor in Rome (476 AD). It was finally extinguished by the fall of Constantinople, its capital, in 1453

Byzantium an ancient Greek city on the Bosporus: founded about 660 BC; rebuilt by Constantine I in 330 AD and called Constantinople; present-day Istanbul

Cc

C a computer programming language combining the advantages of a high-level language with the ability to address the computer at a level comparable with that of an assembly language

cab¹ 1 a taxi **2** the enclosed compartment of a lorry, locomotive, crane, etc, from which it is driven or operated **3** (formerly) a light horse-drawn vehicle used for public hire

cab² or kab an ancient Hebrew measure equal to about 2.3 litres (4 pints)

cabal 1 a small group of intriguers, esp one formed for political purposes **2** a secret plot, esp a political one; conspiracy; intrigue

cabbage 1 any of various cultivated varieties of the plant *Brassica oleracea capitata*, typically having a short thick stalk and a large head of green or reddish edible leaves: family *Brassicaceae* (crucifers) **2 wild cabbage** a European plant, *Brassica oleracea*, with broad leaves and a long spike of yellow flowers: the plant from which the cabbages, cauliflower, broccoli, and Brussels sprout have been bred **3 a** the head of a cabbage **b** the edible leaf bud of the cabbage palm

cabbage tree 1 a tree, *Cordyline australis*, of New Zealand having a tall branchless trunk and a palmlike top **2** any of several other similar trees of the genus *Cordyline*

cabbage white any large white butterfly of the genus *Pieris*, esp the Eurasian species *P. brassicae*, the larvae of which feed on the leaves of cabbages and related vegetables: family *Pieridae*

caber *Scot* a heavy section of trimmed tree trunk thrown in competition at Highland games

Cabernet Sauvignon 1 a black grape originally grown in the Bordeaux area of France, and now throughout the wine-producing world **2** any of various red wines made from this grape

cabin 1 a room used as an office or living quarters in a ship **2** a covered compartment used for shelter or living quarters in a small boat **3** (in a warship) the compartment or room reserved for the commanding officer **4** *Brit* another name for **signal box 5 a** the enclosed part of a light aircraft in which the pilot and passengers sit **b** the part of an airliner in which the passengers are carried **c** the section of an aircraft used for cargo

cabin cruiser a power boat fitted with a cabin and comforts for pleasure cruising or racing

Cabinda an exclave of Angola, separated from the rest of the country by part of the Democratic Republic of Congo (formerly Zaïre). Pop: 174 000 (1993 est). Area: 7270 sq km (2807 sq miles)

cabinet a the executive and policy-making body of a country, consisting of all government ministers or just the senior ministers **b** an advisory council to a president, sovereign, governor, etc. **c** (*as modifier*): *a cabinet reshuffle*

cable 1 *Nautical* an anchor chain or rope **2 a** a unit of distance in navigation, equal to one tenth of a sea mile (about 600 feet) **b** a unit of length in nautical use that has various values, including 100 fathoms (600 feet). **3** a wire or bundle of wires that conducts electricity

cable car 1 a cabin suspended from and moved by an overhead cable in a mountain area **2** a cableway **3** a passenger car on a cable railway

caboose 1 *Railways, US and Canadian* a guard's van, esp one with sleeping and eating facilities for the train crew **2** *Nautical* **a** a deckhouse for a galley aboard ship or formerly in Canada, on a lumber raft **b** *Chiefly Brit* the galley itself

Cabot 1 John Italian name *Giovanni Caboto*. 1450–98, Italian explorer, who landed in North America in 1497, under patent from Henry VII of England, and explored the coast from Nova Scotia to Newfoundland **2** his son, Sebastian ?1476–1557, Italian navigator and cartographer, who served the English and Spanish crowns: explored the La Plata region of Brazil (1526–30)

Cabral Pedro Álvarez ?1460–?1526, Portuguese navigator: discovered and took possession of Brazil for Portugal in 1500.

cacao a small tropical American evergreen tree, *Theobroma cacao*, having yellowish flowers and reddish-brown seed pods from which cocoa and chocolate are prepared: family *Sterculiaceae*

cache *Computing* a small high-speed memory that improves computer performance

cachet 1 an official seal on a document, letter, etc. **2** *Philately* **a** a mark stamped by hand on mail for commemorative purposes **b** a small mark made by dealers and experts on the back of postage stamps **3** a hollow wafer, formerly used for enclosing an unpleasant-tasting medicine

cactus 1 any spiny succulent plant of the family *Cactaceae* of the arid regions of America. Cactuses have swollen tough stems, leaves reduced to spines or scales, and often large brightly coloured flowers **2 cactus dahlia** a double-flowered variety of dahlia

cadaver *Med* a corpse

Cadbury George 1839–1922, British Quaker industrialist and philanthropist. He established, with his brother **Richard Cadbury** (1835–99), the chocolate-making company Cadbury Brothers and the garden village Bournville, near Birmingham, for their workers.

caddie *or* **caddy** *Golf* an attendant who carries clubs, etc, for a player

caddis fly any small mothlike insect of the order *Trichoptera*, having two pairs of hairy wings and aquatic larvae (caddis worms)

Cade Jack died 1450, English leader of the Kentish rebellion against the misgovernment of Henry VI (1450)

cadence *or* **cadency 1** a rhythm or rhythmic construction in verse or prose; measure **2** the close of a musical phrase or section

cadenza a virtuoso solo passage occurring near the end of a piece of music, formerly improvised by the soloist but now usually specially composed

cadet *History* (in England and in France before 1789) a gentleman, usually a younger son, who entered the army to prepare for a commission

cadi *or* **kadi** a judge in a Muslim community

cadmium a malleable ductile toxic bluish-white metallic element that occurs in association with zinc ores. It is used in electroplating, alloys, and as a neutron absorber in the control of nuclear fission. Symbol: Cd; atomic no.: 48; atomic wt.: 112.411; valency: 2; relative density: 8.65; melting pt.: 321.1°C; boiling pt.: 767°C

Cadwalader 7th century AD, legendary king of the Britons, probably a confusion of several historical figures

caecum *or* US **cecum** *Anatomy* any structure or part that ends in a blind sac or pouch, esp the pouch that marks the beginning of the large intestine

Caelian the southeasternmost of the Seven Hills of Rome

Caen an industrial city in NW France. Pop: 113 987 (1999)

Caernarfon, Caernarvon, *or* **Carnarvon** a port and resort in NW Wales, in Gwynedd on the Menai Strait: 13th-century castle. Pop: 9726 (2001)

Caernarvonshire (until 1974) a county of NW Wales, now part of Gwynedd

Caerphilly 1 a market town in SE Wales, in Caerphilly county borough: site of the largest castle in Wales (13th–14th centuries). Pop: 31 060 (2001) **2** a county borough in SE Wales, created in 1996 from parts of Mid Glamorgan and Gwent. Pop: 170 200 (2003 est). Area: 275 sq km (106 sq miles)

Caesar[1] **1** Gaius Julius 100–44 BC, Roman general, statesman, and historian. He formed the first triumvirate with Pompey and Crassus (60), conquered Gaul (58–50), invaded Britain (55–54), mastered Italy (49), and defeated Pompey (46). As dictator of the Roman Empire (49–44) he destroyed the power of the corrupt Roman nobility. He also introduced the Julian calendar and planned further reforms, but fear of his sovereign power led to his assassination (44) by conspirators led by Marcus Brutus and Cassius Longinus **2** any Roman emperor **3** a title of the Roman emperors from

Augustus to Hadrian **4** in the Roman Empire **a** a title borne by the imperial heir from the reign of Hadrian **b** the heir, deputy, and subordinate ruler to either of the two emperors under Diocletian's system of government

Caesar[2] **1** any Roman emperor **2** a title of the Roman emperors from Augustus to Hadrian **3** in the Roman Empire **a** a title borne by the imperial heir from the reign of Hadrian **b** the heir, deputy, and subordinate ruler to either of the two emperors under Diocletian's system of government

Caesarea an ancient port in NW Israel, capital of Roman Palestine: founded by Herod the Great

Caesarean, Caesarian, US **Cesarean** *or* **Cesarian 1** of or relating to any of the Caesars, esp Julius Caesar (100–44 BC), Roman general, statesman, and historian **2** *Surgery* **a** short for **Caesarean section b** (*as modifier*): *Caesarean birth*

Caesarean section surgical incision through the abdominal and uterine walls in order to deliver a baby

caesium *or* US **cesium** a ductile silvery-white element of the alkali metal group that is the most electropositive metal. It occurs in pollucite and lepidolite and is used in photocells. The radioisotope **caesium-137**, with a half-life of 30.2 years, is used in radiotherapy. Symbol: Cs; atomic no.: 55; atomic wt.: 132.90543; valency: 1; relative density: 1.873; melting pt.: 28.39±0.01°C; boiling pt.: 671°C

caesura 1 (in modern prosody) a pause, esp for sense, usually near the middle of a verse line. **2** (in classical prosody) a break between words within a metrical foot, usually in the third or fourth foot of the line

Caetano Marcello 1906–80, prime minister of Portugal from 1968 until he was replaced by an army coup in 1974.

caffeine *or* **caffein** a white crystalline bitter alkaloid responsible for the stimulant action of tea, coffee, and cocoa: a constituent of many tonics and analgesics. Formula: $C_8H_{10}N_4O_2$

cage 1 *Engineering* a skeleton ring device that ensures that the correct amount of space is maintained between the individual rollers or balls in a rolling bearing **2** *Informal* the basket used in basketball **3** *Informal* the goal in ice hockey

Cage John 1912–92, US composer of experimental music for a variety of conventional, modified, or invented instruments. He evolved a type of music apparently undetermined by the composer, such as in *Imaginary Landscape* (1951) for 12 radio sets. Other works include *Reunion* (1968), *Apartment Building 1776* (1976), and *Europeras 3 and 4* (1990)

Cagliari[1] Paolo , original name of (Paolo) **Veronese**

Cagliari[2] a port in Italy, the capital of Sardinia, on the S coast. Pop: 164 249 (2001)

Cagney James 1899–1986, US film actor, esp in gangster roles; his films include *The Public Enemy* (1931), *Angels with Dirty Faces* (1938), *The Roaring Twenties* (1939), and *Yankee Doodle Dandy* (1942) for which he won an Oscar.

Caiaphas *New Testament* the high priest at the beginning of John the Baptist's preaching and during the trial of Jesus (Luke 3:2; Matthew 26)

Caine Sir Michael real name *Maurice Micklewhite*. born 1933, British film actor. His films include *The Ipcress File*

(1965), *Get Carter* (1971), *Educating Rita* (1983), *Hannah and Her Sisters* (1986), and *The Cider House Rules* (1999).

Caird Coast a region of Antarctica: a part of Coats Land on the SE coast of the Weddell Sea; now included in the British Antarctic Territory (claim suspended under the Antarctic Treaty of 1959)

cairn a small rough-haired breed of terrier originally from Scotland

cairngorm a smoky yellow, grey, or brown variety of quartz, used as a gemstone

Cairns a port in NE Australia, in Queensland. Pop: 98 981 (2001)

Cairo the capital of Egypt, on the Nile: the largest city in Africa and in the Middle East; industrial centre; site of the university and mosque of Al Azhar (founded in 972). Pop: 11 146 000 (2005 est)

caisson 1 a watertight chamber open at the bottom and containing air under pressure, used to carry out construction work under water 2 a similar unpressurized chamber 3 a watertight float filled with air, used to raise sunken ships 4 a watertight structure placed across the entrance of a basin, dry dock, etc, to exclude water from it 5 another name for **coffer**

Caithness (until 1975) a county of NE Scotland, now part of Highland

Calabar a port in SE Nigeria, capital of Cross River state. Pop: 418 000 (2005 est)

calabash 1 a tropical American evergreen tree, *Crescentia cujete*, that produces large round gourds: family *Bignoniaceae* 2 the gourd of either of these plants 3 the dried hollow shell of a gourd used as the bowl of a tobacco pipe, a bottle, rattle, etc. 4 **calabash nutmeg** a tropical African shrub, *Monodora myristica*, whose oily aromatic seeds can be used as nutmegs: family *Annonaceae*

calabrese a variety of green sprouting broccoli

Calabria 1 a region of SW Italy: mostly mountainous and subject to earthquakes. Chief town: Reggio di Calabria. Pop: 2 007 392 (2003 est). Area: 15 080 sq km (5822 sq miles) 2 an ancient region of extreme SE Italy (3rd century BC to about 668 AD); now part of Apulia

Calais a port in N France, on the Strait of Dover: the nearest French port to England; belonged to England 1347–1558. Pop: 77 333 (1999)

calamine a pink powder consisting of zinc oxide and ferric oxide, (iron(III) oxide), used medicinally in the form of soothing lotions or ointments

Calamity Jane real name **Martha Canary** ?1852–1903, US frontierswoman, noted for her skill at shooting and riding

calciferol a fat-soluble steroid, found esp in fish-liver oils, produced by the action of ultraviolet radiation on ergosterol. It increases the absorption of calcium from the intestine and is used in the treatment of rickets. Formula: $C_{28}H_{43}OH$

calcite a colourless or white mineral (occasionally tinged with impurities), found in sedimentary and metamorphic rocks, in veins, in limestone, and in stalagmites and stalactites. It is used in the manufacture of cement, plaster, paint, glass, and fertilizer. Composition: calcium carbonate. Formula: $CaCO_3$. Crystal structure: hexagonal (rhombohedral)

calcium a malleable silvery-white metallic element of the alkaline earth group; the fifth most abundant element in the earth's crust (3.6 per cent), occurring esp as forms of calcium carbonate. It is an essential constituent of bones and teeth and is used as a deoxidizer in steel. Symbol: Ca; atomic no.: 20; atomic wt.: 40.078; valency: 2; relative density: 1.55; melting pt.: 842±2°C; boiling pt.: 1494°C

calcium carbonate a white crystalline salt occurring in limestone, chalk, marble, calcite, coral, and pearl: used in the production of lime and cement. Formula: $CaCO_3$

calcium hydroxide a white crystalline slightly soluble alkali with many uses, esp in cement, water softening, and the neutralization of acid soils. Formula: $Ca(OH)_2$

calcium oxide a white crystalline base used in the production of calcium hydroxide and bleaching powder and in the manufacture of glass, paper, and steel. Formula: CaO

calculator 1 a device for performing mathematical calculations, esp an electronic device that can be held in the hand 2 a set of tables used as an aid to calculations

calculus 1 a branch of mathematics, developed independently by Newton and Leibniz. Both **differential calculus** and **integral calculus** are concerned with the effect on a function of an infinitesimal change in the independent variable as it tends to zero. 2 any mathematical system of calculation involving the use of symbols 3 *Logic* an uninterpreted formal system 4 *Pathol* a stonelike concretion of minerals and salts found in ducts or hollow organs of the body

Calcutta a port in E India, capital of West Bengal state, on the Hooghly River: former capital of the country (1833–1912); major commercial and industrial centre; three universities. Pop: 4 580 544 (2001)

Calder Alexander 1898–1976, US sculptor, who originated mobiles and stabiles (moving or static abstract sculptures, generally suspended from wire).

Calderdale a unitary authority in N England, in West Yorkshire. Pop: 193 200 (2003 est). Area: 364 sq km (140 sq miles)

Caldwell Erskine 1903–87, US novelist whose works include *Tobacco Road* (1933)

Caledonia the Roman name for **Scotland**: used poetically in later times

Caledonian of or denoting a period of mountain building in NW Europe in the Palaeozoic era

Caledonian Canal a canal in N Scotland, linking the Atlantic with the North Sea through the Great Glen: built 1803–47; now used mostly for leisure boating

calender[1] a machine in which paper or cloth is glazed or smoothed by passing between rollers

calender[2] a member of a mendicant order of dervishes in Turkey, Iran, and India

calendula 1 any Eurasian plant of the genus *Calendula*, esp the pot marigold, having orange-and-yellow rayed flowers: family *Asteraceae* (composites) 2 the dried flowers of the pot marigold, formerly used medicinally and for seasoning

calf[1] 1 the young of cattle, esp domestic cattle 2 the young of certain other mammals, such as the buffalo, elephant, giraffe, and whale 3 a large piece of floating ice detached from an iceberg, etc.

calf² the thick fleshy part of the back of the leg between the ankle and the knee

Calgary a city in Canada, in S Alberta: centre of a large agricultural region; oilfields. Pop: 879 277 (2001)

calico 1 a white or unbleached cotton fabric with no printed design 2 *Chiefly US* a coarse printed cotton fabric 3 made of calico

California 1 a state on the W coast of the US: the third largest state in area and the largest in population; consists of a narrow, warm coastal plain rising to the Coast Range, deserts in the south, the fertile central valleys of the Sacramento and San Joaquin Rivers, and the mountains of the Sierra Nevada in the east; major industries include the growing of citrus fruits and grapes, fishing, oil production, electronics, information technology, and films. Capital: Sacramento. Pop: 35 484 453 (2003 est). Area: 411 015 sq km (158 693 sq miles) 2 Gulf of an arm of the Pacific Ocean, between Sonora and Lower California

californium a metallic transuranic element artificially produced from curium. Symbol: Cf; atomic no.: 98; half-life of most stable isotope, ^{251}Cf: 800 years (approx.)

Caligula original name *Gaius Caesar*, son of Germanicus. 12–41 AD, Roman emperor (37–41), noted for his cruelty and tyranny; assassinated

caliph, calif, kalif *or* **khalif** *Islam* the title of the successors of Mohammed as rulers of the Islamic world, later assumed by the Sultans of Turkey

caliphate, califate, *or* **kalifate** the office, jurisdiction, or reign of a caliph

call 1 *Hunting* any of several notes or patterns of notes, blown on a hunting horn as a signal 2 *Hunting* a an imitation of the characteristic cry of a wild animal or bird to lure it to the hunter b an instrument for producing such an imitation 3 *Brit* the summons to the bar of a student member of an Inn of Court 4 *Theatre* a notice to actors informing them of times of rehearsals 5 (in square dancing) an instruction to execute new figures 6 *Commerce* a a demand for repayment of a loan b (*as modifier*): *call money* 7 *Billiards* a demand to an opponent to say what kind of shot he will play 8 *Poker* a demand for a hand or hands to be exposed 9 *Bridge* a bid, or a player's turn to bid 10 *Sport* a decision of an umpire or referee regarding a shot, pitch, etc. 11 *Business* **on call** a (of a loan, etc) repayable on demand b available to be called for work outside normal working hours

Callaghan (**Leonard**) **James,** Baron Callaghan of Cardiff. 1912–2005, British Labour statesman; prime minister (1976–79)

Callas Maria, real name *Maria Anna Cecilia Kalageropoulos.* 1923–77, Greek operatic soprano, born in the US

Callicrates 5th century BC, Greek architect: with Ictinus, designed the Parthenon

calligraphy handwriting, esp beautiful handwriting considered as an art

   ▷www.chinapage.com/callig1.htm
   ▷www.sakkal.com/ArtArabicCalligraphy.htm
   ▷www.islamicart.com/main/calligraphy

Callimachus 1 late 5th century BC, Greek sculptor, reputed to have invented the Corinthian capital 2 ?305–?240 BC, Greek poet of the Alexandrian School; author of

hymns and epigrams

Calliope *Greek myth* the Muse of epic poetry

calliper *or US* **caliper** 1 an instrument for measuring internal or external dimensions, consisting of two steel legs hinged together 2 *Med* a splint consisting of two metal rods with straps attached, for supporting or exerting tension on the leg

callisthenics *or* **calisthenics** light exercises designed to promote general fitness, develop muscle tone, etc.

callow *Rare* (of a young bird) unfledged and usually lacking feathers

callus 1 an area of skin that is hard or thick, esp on the palm of the hand or sole of the foot, as from continual friction or pressure 2 an area of bony tissue formed during the healing of a fractured bone 3 *Botany* a a mass of hard protective tissue produced in woody plants at the site of an injury b an accumulation of callose in the sieve tubes 4 *Biotechnology* a mass of undifferentiated cells produced as the first stage in tissue culture

calm *Meteorol* of force 0 on the Beaufort scale; without wind

Calor Gas *Trademark* butane gas liquefied under pressure in portable containers for domestic use

caloric *Obsolete* a hypothetical elastic fluid formerly postulated as the embodiment of heat

calorie *or* **calory** a unit of heat, equal to 4.1868 joules (**International Table calorie**): formerly defined as the quantity of heat required to raise the temperature of 1 gram of water by 1°C under standard conditions. It has now largely been replaced by the joule for scientific purposes

Calorie 1 a unit of heat, equal to one thousand calories, often used to express the heat output of an organism or the energy value of food 2 the amount of a specific food capable of producing one thousand calories of energy

Calvados 1 a department of N France in the Basse-Normandie region. Capital: Caen. Pop: 659 893 (2003 est). Area: 5693 sq km (2198 sq miles) 2 an apple brandy distilled from cider in this region

Calvary the place just outside the walls of Jerusalem where Jesus was crucified

Calvert 1 Sir **George,** 1st Baron Baltimore. ?1580–1632, English statesman; founder of the colony of Maryland 2 his son, **Leonard** 1606–47, English statesman; first colonial governor of Maryland (1634–47)

Calvin 1 **John,** original name *Jean Cauvin, Caulvin,* or *Chauvin.* 1509–64, French theologian: a leader of the Protestant Reformation in France and Switzerland, establishing the first presbyterian government in Geneva. His theological system is described in his *Institutes of the Christian Religion* (1536) 2 **Melvin** 1911–97, US chemist, noted particularly for his research on photosynthesis: Nobel prize for chemistry 1961

Calvinism the theological system of John Calvin (original name *Jean Cauvin, Caulvin,* or *Chauvin.;* 1509–64), the French theologian and leader of the Protestant Reformation, and his followers, characterized by emphasis on the doctrines of predestination, the irresistibility of grace, and justification by faith

Calvino Italo 1923–85, Italian novelist and short-story writer. His works include *Our Ancestors* (1960) and *Invisible*

Cities (1972)

calypso¹ 1 a popular type of satirical, usually topical, West Indian ballad, esp from Trinidad, usually extemporized to a percussive syncopated accompaniment 2 a dance done to the rhythm of this song

calypso² a rare N temperate orchid, *Calypso* (or *Cytherea*) *bulbosa*, whose flower is pink or white with purple and yellow markings

calyx 1 the sepals of a flower collectively, forming the outer floral envelope that protects the developing flower bud 2 any cup-shaped cavity or structure, esp any of the divisions of the human kidney (**renal calyx**) that form the renal pelvis

cam a slider or roller attached to a rotating shaft to give a particular type of reciprocating motion to a part in contact with its profile

Cam a river in E England, in Cambridgeshire, flowing through Cambridge to the River Ouse. Length: about 64 km (40 miles)

Camargue la a delta region in S France, between the channels of the Grand and Petit Rhône: cattle, esp bulls for the Spanish bullrings, and horses are reared

Cambay Gulf of an inlet of the Arabian Sea on the W coast of India, southeast of the Kathiawar Peninsula.

camber 1 another name for **bank** 2 *Engineering* an outward inclination of the front wheels of a road vehicle so that they are slightly closer together at the bottom than at the top 3 *Aeronautics* aerofoil curvature expressed by the ratio of the maximum height of the aerofoil mean line to its chord

Cambodia a country in SE Asia: became part of French Indochina in 1887; achieved self-government in 1949 and independence in 1953; civil war (1970–74) ended in victory for the Khmer Rouge, who renamed the country Kampuchea (1975) and carried out extreme-radical political and economic policies resulting in a considerable reduction of the population; Vietnamese forces ousted the Khmer Rouge in 1979 and set up a pro-Vietnamese government who reverted (1981) to the name Cambodia; after Vietnamese withdrawal in 1989 a peace settlement with exiled factions was followed in 1993 by the adoption of a democratic monarchist constitution restoring Prince Sihanouk to the throne. The country contains the central plains of the Mekong River and the Cardamom Mountains in the SW. Official language: Khmer; French is also widely spoken. Currency: riel. Capital: Phnom Penh. Pop: 14 482 000 (2004 est). Area: 181 000 sq km (69 895 sq miles)

Cambrai a town in NE France: textile industry: scene of a battle in which massed tanks were first used and broke through the German line (November, 1917). Pop: 33 738 (1999)

Cambrian of, denoting, or formed in the first 65 million years of the Palaeozoic era, during which marine invertebrates, esp trilobites, flourished

cambric a fine white linen or cotton fabric

Cambridge 1 a city in E England, administrative centre of Cambridgeshire, on the River Cam: centred around the university, founded in the 12th century: electronics, biotechnology. Pop: 117 717 (2001) 2 short for **Cambridgeshire** 3 a city in the US, in E Massachusetts: educational centre, with Harvard University (1636) and the Massachusetts Institute of Technology. Pop: 101 587 (2003 est)

Cambridgeshire a county of E England, in East Anglia: includes the former counties of the Isle of Ely and Huntingdon and lies largely in the Fens: Peterborough became an independent unitary authority in 1998. Administrative centre: Cambridge. Pop. (excluding Peterborough): 571 000 (2003 est). Area (excluding Peterborough): 3068 sq km (184 sq miles)

Cambyses died ?522 BC, king of Persia (529–522 BC), who conquered Egypt (525); son of Cyrus the Great

Camden¹ William 1551–1623, English antiquary and historian; author of *Britannia* (1586)

Camden² a borough of N Greater London. Pop: 210 700 (2003 est). Area: 21 sq km (8 sq miles)

came a grooved strip of lead used to join pieces of glass in a stained-glass window or a leaded light

camel 1 either of two cud-chewing artiodactyl mammals of the genus *Camelus* (see **Bactrian camel**): family *Camelidae*. They are adapted for surviving long periods without food or water in desert regions, esp by using humps on the back for storing fat 2 a float attached to a vessel to increase its buoyancy 3 a raft or float used as a fender between a vessel and a wharf 4 a a fawn colour b *(as adjective)*: *a camel coat*

camellia any ornamental shrub of the Asian genus *Camellia*, esp *C. japonica*, having glossy evergreen leaves and showy roselike flowers, usually white, pink or red in colour: family *Theaceae*

cameo 1 a a medallion, as on a brooch or ring, with a profile head carved in relief b *(as modifier)*: *a cameo necklace* 2 a a single and often brief dramatic scene played by a well-known actor or actress in a film or television play b *(as modifier)*: *a cameo role* 3 a a short literary work or dramatic sketch b *(as modifier)*: *a cameo sketch*

camera 1 an optical device consisting of a lens system set in a light-proof construction inside which a light-sensitive film or plate can be positioned 2 *Television* the equipment used to convert the optical image of a scene into the corresponding electrical signals 3 See **camera obscura** 4 a judge's private room 5 **in camera** a *Law* relating to a hearing from which members of the public are excluded b in private 6 **off camera** not within an area being filmed 7 **on camera** (esp of an actor) being filmed

camera obscura a darkened chamber or small building in which images of outside objects are projected onto a flat surface by a convex lens in an aperture

Cameron 1 (Mark) James (Walter). 1911–85, British journalist, author, and broadcaster. His books include *Witness in Vietnam* (1966) and *Point of Departure* (1967). 2 James born 1954, Canadian film director and screenwriter; his films include *The Terminator* (1984), *Aliens* (1986) and *Titanic* (1997) 3 Julia Margaret 1815–79, British photographer, born in India, renowned for her portrait photographs.

Cameroon 1 a republic in West Africa, on the Gulf of Guinea: became a German colony in 1884; divided in 1919 into the **Cameroons** (administered by Britain) and **Cameroun** (administered by France); Cameroun and the S part of the Cameroons formed a republic in 1961 (the N part joined Nigeria); became a member of the

Commonwealth in 1995. Official languages: French and English. Religions: Christian, Muslim, and animist. Currency: franc. Capital: Yaoundé. Pop: 16 296 000 (2004 est). Area: 475 500 sq km (183 591 sq miles) **2** an active volcano in W Cameroon: the highest peak on the West African coast. Height: 4070 m (13 352 ft)

camomile *or* **chamomile 1** any aromatic plant of the Eurasian genus *Anthemis*, esp *A. nobilis*, whose finely dissected leaves and daisy-like flowers are used medicinally: family *Asteraceae* (composites) **2** any plant of the related genus *Matricaria*, esp *M. chamomilla* (**German** or **wild camomile**) **3 camomile tea** a medicinal beverage made from the fragrant leaves and flowers of any of these plants

camouflage the means by which animals escape the notice of predators, usually because of a resemblance to their surroundings: includes cryptic and apatetic coloration

camp *Informal* consciously artificial, exaggerated, vulgar, or mannered; self-parodying, esp when in dubious taste

Campagna a low-lying plain surrounding Rome, Italy: once fertile, it deteriorated to malarial marshes; recently reclaimed. Area: about 2000 sq km (800 sq miles)

campaign *Politics, Business* a series of coordinated activities, such as public speaking and demonstrating, designed to achieve a social, political, or commercial goal

Campanella Tommaso 1568–1639, Italian philosopher and Dominican friar. During his imprisonment by the Spaniards (1599–1626) he wrote his celebrated utopian fantasy, *La città del sole*.

Campania a region of SW Italy: includes the islands of Capri and Ischia. Chief town: Naples. Pop: 5 725 098 (2003 est). Area: 13 595 sq km (5248 sq miles)

campanile (esp in Italy) a bell tower, not usually attached to another building

campanology the art or skill of ringing bells musically

campanula any N temperate plant of the campanulaceous genus *Campanula*, typically having blue or white bell-shaped flowers

Campbell 1 Sir **Colin**, Baron Clyde. 1792–1863, British field marshal who relieved Lucknow for the second time (1857) and commanded in Oudh, suppressing the Indian Mutiny **2 Donald** 1921–67, English water speed record-holder **3** Sir **Malcolm**, father of Donald Campbell. 1885–1948, English racing driver and land speed record-holder **4** Mrs **Patrick**, original name *Beatrice Stella Tanner*. 1865–1940, English actress **5 Roy** 1901–57, South African poet. His poetry is often satirical and includes *The Flaming Terrapin* (1924) **6 Thomas** 1777–1844, Scottish poet and critic, noted particularly for his war poems *Hohenlinden* and *Ye Mariners of England*

Campbell-Bannerman Sir **Henry** 1836–1908, British statesman and leader of the Liberal Party (1899–1908); prime minister (1905–08), who granted self-government to the Transvaal and the Orange River Colony

Camp David the US president's retreat in the Appalachian Mountains, Maryland: scene of the **Camp David Agreement** (Sept, 1978) between Anwar Sadat of Egypt and Menachem Begin of Israel, mediated by Jimmy Carter, which outlined a framework for establishing peace in the Middle East. This agreement was the basis of the peace treaty between Israel and Egypt signed in Washington (March, 1979).

Campeche 1 a state of SE Mexico, on the SW of the Yucatán peninsula: forestry and fishing. Capital: Campeche. Pop: 205 000 (2005 est). Area: 56 114 sq km (21 666 sq miles) **2** a port in SE Mexico, capital of Campeche state. Pop: 195 000 (2000 est) **3 Bay of** Also called: **Gulf of Campeche** the SW part of the Gulf of Mexico.

Campese David born 1962, Australian rugby union player

camphor a whitish crystalline aromatic terpene ketone obtained from the wood of the camphor tree or made from pinene: used in the manufacture of celluloid and in medicine as a liniment and treatment for colds. Formula: $C_{10}H_{16}O$

Campin Robert 1379–1444, Flemish painter, noted esp for his altarpieces: usually identified with the so-called Master of Flémalle.

campion any of various caryophyllaceous plants of the genera *Silene* and *Lychnis*, having red, pink, or white flowers

Campion 1 Saint Edmund 1540–81, English Jesuit martyr. He joined the Jesuits in 1573 and returned to England (1580) as a missionary. He was charged with treason and hanged **2 Jane** born 1954, New Zealand film director and screenwriter: her films include *An Angel at My Table* (1990), *The Piano* (1993), *Holy Smoke* (1999), and *In the Cut* (2003) **3 Thomas** 1567–1620, English poet and musician, noted particularly for his songs for the lute

Campobello an island in the Bay of Fundy, off the coast of SE Canada: part of New Brunswick province. Area: about 52 sq km (20 sq miles). Pop: 1195 (2001)

Campo Formio a village in NE Italy, in Friuli-Venezia Giulia: scene of the signing of a treaty in 1797 that ended the war between revolutionary France and Austria

Campo Grande a city in SW Brazil, capital of Mato Grosso do Sul state on the São Paulo–Corumbá railway: market centre. Pop: 746 000 (2005 est)

campus 1 the grounds and buildings of a university **2** *Chiefly US* the outside area of a college, university, etc.

Cam Ranh a port in SE Vietnam: large natural harbour, in recent years used as a naval base by French, Japanese, US, and Russian forces successively. Pop: 114 041 (1992 est)

camshaft *Engineering* a shaft having one or more cams attached to it, esp one used to operate the valves of an internal-combustion engine

Camus Albert 1913–60, French novelist, dramatist, and essayist, noted for his pessimistic portrayal of man's condition of isolation in an absurd world: author of the novels *L'Étranger* (1942) and *La Peste* (1947), the plays *Le Malentendu* (1945) and *Caligula* (1946), and the essays *Le Mythe de Sisyphe* (1942) and *L'Homme révolté* (1951): Nobel prize for literature 1957.

can 1 a shallow cylindrical metal container of varying size used for storing and handling film **2 in the can** (of a film, piece of music, etc) having been recorded, processed, edited, etc.

Cana *New Testament* the town in Galilee, north of Nazareth, where Jesus performed his first miracle by changing water into wine (John 2:1, 11)

Canaan an ancient region between the River Jordan and the Mediterranean, corresponding roughly to Israel: the Promised Land of the Israelites

Canaanite 1 a member of an ancient Semitic people who occupied the land of Canaan before the Israelite conquest 2 the extinct language of this people, belonging to the Canaanitic branch of the Semitic subfamily of the Afro-Asiatic family 3 (in later books of the Old Testament) a merchant or trader (Job 40:30; Proverbs 31:24)

Canada a country in North America: the second largest country in the world; first permanent settlements by Europeans were made by the French from 1605; ceded to Britain in 1763 after a series of colonial wars; established as the Dominion of Canada in 1867; a member of the Commonwealth. It consists generally of sparsely inhabited tundra regions, rich in natural resources, in the north, the Rocky Mountains in the west, the Canadian Shield in the east, and vast central prairies; the bulk of the population is concentrated along the US border and the Great Lakes in the south. Languages: English and French. Religion: Christian majority. Currency: Canadian dollar. Capital: Ottawa. Pop: 31 743 000 (2004 est). Area: 9 976 185 sq km (3 851 809 sq miles)

Canada goose a large common greyish-brown North American goose, *Branta canadensis*, with a black neck and head and a white throat patch

Canada jay a large common jay of North America, *Perisoreus canadensis*, with a grey body, and a white-and-black crestless head

Canadian football a game resembling American football, played on a grass pitch between two teams of 12 players
▷www.cfl.ca

Canadian River a river in the southern US, rising in NE New Mexico and flowing east to the Arkansas River in E Oklahoma. Length: 1458 km (906 miles)

Canadian Shield (in Canada) the wide area of Precambrian rock extending west from the Labrador coast to the basin of the Mackenzie and north from the Great Lakes to Hudson Bay and the Arctic: rich in minerals

canal 1 an artificial waterway constructed for navigation, irrigation, water power, etc. 2 any of various tubular passages or ducts 3 any of various elongated intercellular spaces in plants 4 *Astronomy* any of the indistinct surface features of Mars originally thought to be a network of channels but not seen on close-range photographs. They are caused by an optical illusion in which faint geological features appear to have a geometric structure

Canaletto original name *Giovanni Antonio Canale*. 1697–1768, Italian painter and etcher, noted particularly for his highly detailed paintings of cities, esp Venice, which are marked by strong contrasts of light and shade

Canal Zone a former administrative region of the US, on the Isthmus of Panama around the Panama Canal: bordered on each side by the Republic of Panama, into which it was incorporated in 1979

canard an aircraft in which the tailplane is mounted in front of the wing

canary a small finch, *Serinus canaria*, of the Canary Islands and Azores: a popular cagebird noted for its singing. Wild canaries are streaked yellow and brown, but most domestic breeds are pure yellow

canasta 1 a card game for two to six players who seek to amass points by declaring sets of cards 2 a declared set in this game, containing seven or more like cards, worth 500 points if the canasta is pure or 300 if wild (containing up to three jokers)

Canaveral Cape a cape on the E coast of Florida: site of the US Air Force Missile Test Centre, from which the majority of US space missions have been launched. Former name (1963–73): Cape **Kennedy**

Canberra the capital of Australia, in Australian Capital Territory: founded in 1913 as a planned capital. Pop: 309 799 (2001)

cancan a high-kicking dance performed by a female chorus, originating in the music halls of 19th-century Paris

cancer any type of malignant growth or tumour, caused by abnormal and uncontrolled cell division: it may spread through the lymphatic system or blood stream to other parts of the body
▷www.jasperweb.com/texascanceronline
▷www.cancercare.org

Cancer 1 *Astronomy* a small faint zodiacal constellation in the N hemisphere, lying between Gemini and Leo on the ecliptic and containing the star cluster Praesepe 2 *Astrology* **a** the fourth sign of the zodiac, symbol ♋, having a cardinal water classification and ruled by the moon. The sun is in this sign between about June 21 and July 22 **b** a person born during a period when the sun is in this sign 3 tropic of Cancer See **tropic** 4 *Astrology* born under or characteristic of Cancer

candela the basic SI unit of luminous intensity; the luminous intensity in a given direction of a source that emits monochromatic radiation of frequency 540×10^{12} hertz and that has a radiant intensity in that direction of (1/683) watt per steradian.

Candela Felix born 1910, Mexican architect, noted for his naturalistic modern style and thin prestressed concrete roofs

Candiot *or* **Candiote** 1 of or relating to Candia (Iráklion) or Crete; Cretan 2 a native or inhabitant of Crete; a Cretan

Candlemas *Christianity* Feb 2, the Feast of the Purification of the Virgin Mary and the presentation of Christ in the Temple: the day on which the church candles are blessed. In Scotland it is one of the four quarter days

candlepower the luminous intensity of a source of light in a given direction: now expressed in candelas but formerly in terms of the international candle

candlewick unbleached cotton or muslin into which loops of yarn are hooked and then cut to give a tufted pattern. It is used for bedspreads, dressing gowns, etc.

Candolle Augustin Pyrame de 1778–1841, Swiss botanist; his *Théorie élémentaire de la botanique* (1813) introduced a new system of plant classification

candy-striped (esp of clothing fabric) having narrow coloured stripes on a white background

candytuft either of two species of *Iberis* grown as annual garden plants for their umbels ("tufts") of white, red, or purplish flowers

cane¹ 1 a the long jointed pithy or hollow flexible stem of the bamboo, rattan, or any similar plant **b** any plant having such a stem **2** the woody stem of a reed, young grapevine, blackberry, raspberry, or loganberry **3** any of several grasses with long stiff stems, esp *Arundinaria gigantea* of the southeastern US **4** See **sugar cane**

cane² *Dialect* a female weasel

Canea or **Chania** the chief port of Crete, on the NW coast. Pop: 50 000 (latest est)

cane sugar the sucrose obtained from sugar cane, which is identical to that obtained from sugar beet

Canetti Elias 1905–94, British novelist and writer, born in Bulgaria, who usually wrote in German. His works include the novel *Auto da Fé* (1935). Nobel prize for literature 1981

canine 1 of, relating to, or belonging to the *Canidae*, a family of mammals, including dogs, jackals, wolves, and foxes, typically having a bushy tail, erect ears, and a long muzzle: order *Carnivora* (carnivores) **2** of or relating to any of the four teeth, two in each jaw, situated between the incisors and the premolars **3** a canine tooth

canker 1 an ulceration, esp of the lips or lining of the oral cavity **2** *Vet science* **a** a disease of horses in which the horn of the hoofs becomes soft and spongy **b** an inflammation of the lining of the external ear, esp in dogs and cats, resulting in a discharge and sometimes ulceration **c** ulceration or abscess of the mouth, eyelids, ears, or cloaca of birds

cannabis 1 another name for **hemp** (the plant), esp Indian hemp (*Cannabis indica*) **2** the drug obtained from the dried leaves and flowers of the hemp plant, which is smoked or chewed for its psychoactive properties. It produces euphoria and relaxation; repeated use may lead to psychological dependence

Cannae an ancient city in SE Italy: scene of a victory by Hannibal over the Romans (216 BC)

Cannes a port and resort in SE France: developed in the 19th century from a fishing village; annual film festival. Pop: 67 304 (1999)

cannibal a a person who eats the flesh of other human beings **b** (*as modifier*): *cannibal tribes*

Canning 1 Charles John, 1st Earl Canning. 1812–62, British statesman; governor general of India (1856–58) and first viceroy (1858–62) **2** his father, **George** 1770–1827, British Tory statesman; foreign secretary (1822–27) and prime minister (1827)

Cannock a town in W central England, in S Staffordshire: **Cannock Chase** (a public area of heathland, once a royal preserve) is just to the east. Pop: 65 022 (2001)

cannon 1 a heavy tube or drum, esp one that can rotate freely on the shaft by which it is supported **2** the metal loop at the top of a bell, from which it is suspended **3** *Billiards* a shot in which the cue ball is caused to contact one object ball after another

cannonball 1 *Tennis* **a** a very fast low serve **b** (*as modifier*): *a cannonball serve* **2** a jump into water by a person who has his arms tucked into the body to form a ball

canoe a light narrow open boat, propelled by one or more paddles

canon¹ 1 *Christianity* a Church decree enacted to regulate morals or religious practices **2** *RC Church* the complete list of the canonized saints **3** the prayer in the Mass in which the Host is consecrated **4** a list of writings, esp sacred writings, officially recognized as genuine **5** a piece of music in which an extended melody in one part is imitated successively in one or more other parts **6** a list of the works of an author that are accepted as authentic

canon² 1 one of several priests on the permanent staff of a cathedral, who are responsible for organizing services, maintaining the fabric, etc. **2** *RC Church* a member of either of two religious orders, the Augustinian or Premonstratensian Canons, living communally as monks but performing clerical duties

canonical hour 1 *RC Church* **a** one of the seven prayer times appointed for each day by canon law **b** the services prescribed for these times, namely matins, prime, terce, sext, nones, vespers, and compline **2** *Church of England* any time between 8:00 am and 6:00 pm at which marriages may lawfully be celebrated

canon law the law governing the affairs of a Christian Church, esp the law created or recognized by papal authority in the Roman Catholic Church

Canopus a port in ancient Egypt east of Alexandria where granite monuments have been found inscribed with the name of Rameses II and written in languages similar to those of the Rosetta stone

canopy 1 a rooflike covering over an altar, niche, etc. **2** a roofed structure serving as a sheltered passageway or area **3** the nylon or silk hemisphere that forms the supporting surface of a parachute **4** the transparent cover of an aircraft cockpit **5** the highest level of branches and foliage in a forest, formed by the crowns of the trees

cantabile *Music* **1** (to be performed) in a singing style, i.e. flowingly and melodiously **2** a piece or passage performed in this way

Cantal a department of S central France, in the Auvergne region. Capital: Aurillac. Pop: 148 359 (2003 est). Area: 5779 sq km (2254 sq miles)

cantaloupe or **cantaloup 1** a cultivated variety of muskmelon, *Cucumis melo cantalupensis*, with ribbed warty rind and orange flesh **2** any of several other muskmelons

cantata a musical setting of a text, esp a religious text, consisting of arias, duets, and choruses interspersed with recitatives

Canteloube (Marie) Joseph 1879–1957, French composer, best known for his *Chants d'Auvergne* (1923–30)

canter an easy three-beat gait of horses, etc, between a trot and a gallop in speed

Canterbury 1 a city in SE England, in E Kent: starting point for St Augustine's mission to England (597 AD); cathedral where St Thomas à Becket was martyred (1170); seat of the archbishop and primate of England; seat of the University of Kent (1965). Pop: 43 552 (2001) **2**

a regional council area of New Zealand, on E central South Island on **Canterbury Bight**: mountainous with coastal lowlands; agricultural. Chief town: Christchurch. Pop: 520 500 (2004 est). Area: 43 371 sq km (16 742 sq miles)

canticle 1 a nonmetrical hymn, derived from the Bible and used in the liturgy of certain Christian churches 2 a song, poem, or hymn, esp one that is religious in character

cantilever 1 a a beam, girder, or structural framework that is fixed at one end and is free at the other b (as modifier): a cantilever wing 2 a wing or tailplane of an aircraft that has no external bracing or support 3 a part of a beam or a structure projecting outwards beyond its support

cantilever bridge a bridge having spans that are constructed as cantilevers and often a suspended span or spans, each end of which rests on one end of a cantilever span

canto a main division of a long poem

canton 1 any of the 23 political divisions of Switzerland 2 a subdivision of a French arrondissement

Canton 1 a port in SE China, capital of Guangdong province, on the Zhu Jiang (Pearl River): the first Chinese port open to European trade. Pop: 3 881 000 (2005 est) 2 a city in the US, in NE Ohio. Pop: 80 806 (2000)

Cantonese the Chinese language spoken in the city of Canton, Guangdong and Guanxi provinces, Hong Kong, and elsewhere outside China

cantonment Military esp formerly History a permanent military camp in British India

cantor 1 Judaism a man employed to lead synagogue services, esp to traditional modes and melodies 2 Christianity the leader of the singing in a church choir

Canuck US and Canadian, informal a a Canadian b (formerly) esp a French Canadian

Canute, Cnut, or **Knut** died 1035, Danish king of England (1016–35), Denmark (1018–35), and Norway (1028–35). He defeated Edmund II of England (1016), but divided the kingdom with him until Edmund's death. An able ruler, he invaded Scotland (1027) and drove Olaf II from Norway (1028)

canvas 1 a a heavy durable cloth made of cotton, hemp, or jute, used for sails, tents, etc. b (as modifier): a canvas bag 2 a a piece of canvas or a similar material on which a painting is done, usually in oils b a painting on this material, esp in oils 3 Nautical any cloth of which sails are made 4 Nautical the sails of a vessel collectively 5 the floor of a boxing or wrestling ring 6 Rowing the tapering covered part at either end of a racing boat, sometimes referred to as a unit of length 7 under canvas Nautical with sails unfurled

canvass a solicitation of opinions, votes, sales orders, etc.

canyon or **cañon** a gorge or ravine, esp in North America, usually formed by the down-cutting of a river in a dry area where there is insufficient rainfall to erode the sides of the valley

cap 1 Sport, chiefly Brit a an emblematic hat or beret given to someone chosen for a representative team b a player chosen for such a team 2 the upper part of a pedestal in

a classical order 3 Botany the pileus of a mushroom or toadstool 4 Hunting a money contributed to the funds of a hunt by a follower who is neither a subscriber nor a farmer, in return for a day's hunting b a collection taken at a meet of hounds, esp for a charity 5 Anatomy a the natural enamel covering a tooth b an artificial protective covering for a tooth 6 an upper financial limit 7 a mortarboard when worn with a gown at an academic ceremony (esp in the phrase **cap and gown**) 8 Meteorol a the cloud covering the peak of a mountain b the transient top of detached clouds above an increasing cumulus

CAP Common Agricultural Policy: (in the EU) the system for supporting farm incomes by maintaining agricultural prices at agreed levels

Capa Robert, real name André Friedmann. 1913–54, Hungarian photographer, who established his reputation as a photojournalist during the Spanish Civil War.

Capablanca José Raúl , called Capa or the Chess Machine 1888–1942, Cuban chess player; world champion 1921–27.

capacitance 1 Electronics the property of a system that enables it to store electric charge 2 a measure of this, equal to the charge that must be added to such a system to raise its electrical potential by one unit.

capacitor a device for accumulating electric charge, usually consisting of two conducting surfaces separated by a dielectric

capacity 1 a measure of the electrical output of a piece of apparatus such as a motor, generator, or accumulator 2 Electronics a former name for **capacitance** 3 Computing a the number of words or characters that can be stored in a particular storage device b the range of numbers that can be processed in a register 4 the bit rate that a communication channel or other system can carry 5 legal competence

cape a headland or promontory

Cape the 1 the SW region of South Africa, in Western Cape province 2 See **Cape of Good Hope**

Cape Breton Island an island off SE Canada, in NE Nova Scotia, separated from the mainland by the Strait of Canso: its easternmost point is **Cape Breton**. Pop: 120 098 (1991). Area: 10 280 sq km (3970 sq miles)

Cape Cod 1 a long sandy peninsula in SE Massachusetts, between **Cape Cod Bay** and the Atlantic 2 a one-storey cottage of timber construction with a simple gable roof and a large central chimney: originated on Cape Cod in the 18th century

Cape Colony the name from 1652 until 1910 of the former **Cape Province** of South Africa

Cape Horn a rocky headland on an island at the extreme S tip of South America, belonging to Chile. It is notorious for gales and heavy seas; until the building of the Panama Canal it lay on the only sea route between the Atlantic and the Pacific

Čapek Karel 1890–1938, Czech dramatist and novelist; author of R.U.R. (1921), which introduced the word "robot", and (with his brother **Josef**) The Insect Play (1921).

Cape of Good Hope a cape in SW South Africa south of Cape Town

Cape Peninsula (in South Africa) the peninsula and the part of the mainland on which Cape Town and most of its suburbs are located

Cape Province a former province of S South Africa; replaced in 1994 by the new provinces of Northern Cape, Western Cape, Eastern Cape and part of North-West. Capital: Cape Town

caper 1 a spiny trailing Mediterranean capparidaceous shrub, *Capparis spinosa*, with edible flower buds 2 any of various similar plants or their edible parts

capercaillie *or* **capercailzie** a large European woodland grouse, *Tetrao urogallus*, having a black plumage and fan-shaped tail in the male

Capernaum a ruined town in N Israel, on the NW shore of the Sea of Galilee: closely associated with Jesus Christ during his ministry

Capet Hugh or Hugues ?938–996 AD, king of France (987–96); founder of the Capetian dynasty.

Cape Town the legislative capital of South Africa and capital of Western Cape province, situated in the southwest on Table Bay: founded in 1652, the first White settlement in southern Africa; important port. Pop: 827 219 (2001)

Cape Verde a republic in the Atlantic off the coast of West Africa, consisting of a group of ten islands and five islets: an overseas territory of Portugal until 1975, when the islands became independent. Official language: Portuguese. Religion: Christian (Roman Catholic) majority; animist minority. Currency: Cape Verdean escudo. Capital: Praia. Pop: 472 000 (2004 est). Area: 4033 sq km (1557 sq miles)

Cape York the northernmost point of the Australian mainland, in N Queensland on the Torres Strait at the tip of **Cape York Peninsula** (a peninsula between the Coral Sea and the Gulf of Carpentaria).

Cap-Haitien a port in N Haiti: capital during the French colonial period. Pop: 134 000 (2005 est)

capillarity *Physics* a phenomenon caused by surface tension and resulting in the distortion, elevation, or depression of the surface of a liquid in contact with a solid

capillary 1 (of tubes) having a fine bore 2 *Anatomy* of or relating to any of the delicate thin-walled blood vessels that form an interconnecting network between the arterioles and the venules 3 *Physics* of or relating to capillarity 4 *Anatomy* any of the capillary blood vessels 5 a fine hole or narrow passage in any substance

capital¹ 1 a the seat of government of a country or other political unit b (*as modifier*): *a capital city* 2 material wealth owned by an individual or business enterprise 3 wealth available for or capable of use in the production of further wealth, as by industrial investment 4 the capitalist class or their interests 5 *Law* involving or punishable by death

capital² the upper part of a column or pier that supports the entablature

capitalism an economic system based on the private ownership of the means of production, distribution, and exchange, characterized by the freedom of capitalists to operate or manage their property for profit in competitive conditions

capital punishment the punishment of death for a crime; death penalty

capital stock the total physical capital existing in an economy at any moment of time

capitation a tax levied on the basis of a fixed amount per head

Capitol 1 a another name for the **Capitoline** b the temple on the Capitoline 2 **the** the main building of the US Congress 3 (in the US) the building housing any state legislature

Capitoline **the** the most important of the Seven Hills of Rome. The temple of Jupiter was on the southern summit and the ancient citadel on the northern summit

capo¹ a device fitted across all the strings of a guitar, lute, etc, so as to raise the pitch of each string simultaneously

capo² the presumed title of a leader in the Mafia

capoeira a movement discipline combining martial art and dance, which originated among African slaves in 19th-century Brazil

Capone Alphonse, called *Al*. 1899–1947, US gangster in Chicago during Prohibition

Capote Truman 1924–84, US writer; his novels include *Other Voices, Other Rooms* (1948) and *In Cold Blood* (1964), based on an actual multiple murder

Capp Al, full name *Alfred Caplin*. 1909–79, US cartoonist, famous for his comic strip *Li'l Abner*

Cappadocia an ancient region of E Asia Minor famous for its horses

Capra Frank 1896–1992, US film director born in Italy. His films include *It Happened One Night* (1934), *It's a Wonderful Life* (1946), and several propaganda films during World War II.

Capri an island off W Italy, in the Bay of Naples: resort since Roman times. Pop: 8000 (latest est). Area: about 13 sq km (5 sq miles)

Capricorn 1 *Astrology* a the tenth sign of the zodiac, symbol ♑, having a cardinal earth classification and ruled by the planet Saturn. The sun is in this sign between about Dec 22 and Jan 19 b a person born during the period when the sun is in this sign 2 **tropic of Capricorn** See **tropic** 3 *Astrology* born under or characteristic of Capricorn

Capricornia the regions of Australia in the tropic of Capricorn

capriole 1 *Dressage* a high upward but not forward leap made by a horse with all four feet off the ground 2 *Dancing* a leap from bent knees

capsicum 1 any tropical American plant of the solanaceous genus *Capsicum*, such as *C. frutescens*, having mild or pungent seeds enclosed in a pod-shaped or bell-shaped fruit 2 the fruit of any of these plants, used as a vegetable or ground to produce a condiment

capstan 1 a machine with a drum that rotates round a vertical spindle and is turned by a motor or lever, used for hauling in heavy ropes, etc. 2 any similar device, such as the rotating shaft in a tape recorder that pulls the tape past the head

capstone *or* **copestone** *Mountaineering* a chockstone occurring at the top of a gully or chimney

capsule 1 a soluble case of gelatine enclosing a dose of medicine 2 a thin metal cap, seal, or cover, such as the foil covering the cork of a wine bottle 3 *Botany* a a dry fruit that liberates its seeds by splitting, as in the violet, or through pores, as in the poppy b the spore-producing organ of mosses and liverworts **4** *Anatomy* **a** a cartilaginous, fibrous, or membranous envelope surrounding any of certain organs or parts **b** a broad band of white fibres (**internal capsule**) near the thalamus in each cerebral hemisphere **5** an aeroplane cockpit that can be ejected in a flight emergency, complete with crew, instruments, etc.

captain **1** the person in charge of and responsible for a vessel **2** the officer in command of a civil aircraft, usually the senior pilot **3** the leader of a team in games **4** US a policeman in charge of a precinct

caption **1** graphic material, usually containing lettering, used in television presentation **2** another name for **subtitle** **3** the formal heading of a legal document stating when, where, and on what authority it was taken or made

capture **1** *Physics* a process by which an atom, molecule, ion, or nucleus acquires an additional particle **2** *Geography* the process by which the headwaters of one river are diverted into another through erosion caused by the second river's tributaries **3** *Computing* the act or process of inserting or transferring data into a computer

Capua a town in S Italy, in NW Campania: strategically important in ancient times, situated on the Appian Way. Pop: 19 041 (2001)

Capuana Luigi 1839–1915, Italian realist novelist, dramatist, and critic. His works include the novel *Giacinta* (1879) and the play *Malìa* (1895)

capuchin **1** any agile intelligent New World monkey of the genus *Cebus*, inhabiting forests in South America, typically having a cowl of thick hair on the top of the head **2** a rare variety of domestic fancy pigeon

Capuchin **a** a friar belonging to a strict and autonomous branch of the Franciscan order founded in 1525 **b** (*as modifier*): *a Capuchin friar*

capybara the largest rodent: a pig-sized amphibious hystricomorph, *Hydrochoerus hydrochaeris*, resembling a guinea pig and inhabiting river banks in Central and South America: family *Hydrochoeridae*

car **1** **a** a self-propelled road vehicle designed to carry passengers, esp one with four wheels that is powered by an internal-combustion engine **b** (*as modifier*): *car coat* **2** *Brit* a railway vehicle for passengers only, such as a sleeping car or buffet car **3** *Chiefly US and Canadian* a railway carriage or van

▷www.planet-cars.net
▷www.britishcarlinks.com

caracal **1** a lynxlike feline mammal, *Lynx caracal*, inhabiting deserts of N Africa and S Asia, having long legs, a smooth coat of reddish fur, and black-tufted ears. **2** the fur of this animal

Caracalla real name *Marcus Aurelius Antoninus*, original name *Bassianus*. 188–217 AD, Roman emperor (211–17): ruled with cruelty and extravagance; assassinated

Caracas the capital of Venezuela, in the north: founded in 1567; major industrial and commercial centre, notably for oil companies. Pop: 3 276 000 (2005 est)

carafe a an open-topped glass container for serving water or wine at table **b** (*as modifier*): *a carafe wine*

carambola **1** a tree, *Averrhoa carambola*, probably native to Brazil but cultivated in the tropics, esp SE Asia, for its

edible fruit **2** the smooth-skinned yellow fruit of this tree, which is star-shaped on cross section

carapace the thick hard shield, made of chitin or bone, that covers part of the body of crabs, lobsters, tortoises, etc.

carat **1** a measure of the weight of precious stones, esp diamonds. It was formerly defined as 3.17 grains, but the international carat is now standardized as 0.20 grams **2** a measure of the proportion of gold in an alloy, expressed as the number of parts of gold in 24 parts of the alloy

Caratacus, Caractacus, *or* **Caradoc** died ?54 AD, British chieftain: led an unsuccessful resistance against the Romans (43–50)

Caravaggio Michelangelo Merisi da 1571–1610, Italian painter, noted for his realistic depiction of religious subjects and for his dramatic use of chiaroscuro.

caraway **1** an umbelliferous Eurasian plant, *Carum carvi*, having finely divided leaves and clusters of small whitish flowers. **2 caraway seed** the pungent aromatic one-seeded fruit of this plant, used in cooking and in medicine

carbide a binary compound of carbon with a more electropositive element

carbohydrate any of a large group of organic compounds, including sugars, such as sucrose, and polysaccharides, such as cellulose, glycogen, and starch, that contain carbon, hydrogen, and oxygen, with the general formula $C_m(H_2O)_n$: an important source of food and energy for animals

carbon **1 a** a nonmetallic element existing in the three crystalline forms: graphite, diamond, and buckminsterfullerene: occurring in carbon dioxide, coal, oil, and all organic compounds. The isotope **carbon-12** has been adopted as the standard for atomic wt.; **carbon-14**, a radioisotope with a half-life of 5700 years, is used in radiocarbon dating and as a tracer. Symbol: C; atomic no.: 6; atomic wt.: 12.011; valency: 2, 3, or 4; relative density: 1.8–2.1 (amorphous), 1.9–2.3 (graphite), 3.15–3.53 (diamond); sublimes at 3367±25°C; boiling pt.: 4827°C. **b** (*as modifier*): *a carbon compound* **2** a carbon electrode used in a carbon-arc light or in carbon-arc welding **3** a rod or plate, made of carbon, used in some types of battery

carbonate a salt or ester of carbonic acid. Carbonate salts contain the divalent ion CO_3^{2-}

carbon black a black finely divided form of amorphous carbon produced by incomplete combustion of natural gas or petroleum: used to reinforce rubber and in the manufacture of pigments and ink

carbon dioxide a colourless odourless incombustible gas present in the atmosphere and formed during respiration, the decomposition and combustion of organic compounds, and in the reaction of acids with carbonates: used in carbonated drinks, fire extinguishers, and as dry ice for refrigeration. Formula: CO_2

carbonic acid a weak acid formed when carbon dioxide combines with water: obtained only in aqueous solutions, never in the pure state. Formula: H_2CO_3

Carboniferous of, denoting, or formed in the fifth period of the Palaeozoic era, between the Devonian and Permian periods, lasting for nearly 64 million years during which coal measures were formed

carbon monoxide a colourless odourless poisonous flammable gas formed when carbon compounds burn in insufficient air and produced by the action of steam on hot carbon: used as a reducing agent in metallurgy and as a fuel. Formula: CO

carbon tax a tax on the emissions caused by the burning of coal, gas, and oil, aimed at reducing the production of greenhouse gases

carbon tetrachloride a colourless volatile nonflammable sparingly soluble liquid made from chlorine and carbon disulphide; tetrachloromethane. It is used as a solvent, cleaning fluid, and insecticide. Formula: CCl$_4$

Carborundum *Trademark* **a** any of various abrasive materials, esp one consisting of silicon carbide **b** (*as modifier*): *a Carborundum wheel*

carboxyl group *or* **radical** the monovalent group –COOH, consisting of a carbonyl group bound to a hydroxyl group: the functional group in organic acids

carbuncle 1 an extensive skin eruption, similar to but larger than a boil, with several openings: caused by staphylococcal infection **2** a dark reddish-greyish-brown colour

carburettor, carburetter, *or US* **carburetor** a device used in petrol engines for atomizing the petrol, controlling its mixture with air, and regulating the intake of the air-petrol mixture into the engine

Carcassonne a city in SW France: extensive remains of medieval fortifications. Pop: 43 950 (1999)

carcinogen *Pathol* any substance that produces cancer

carcinoma *Pathol* **1** any malignant tumour derived from epithelial tissue **2** another name for **cancer**

card (formerly) a machine or comblike tool for carding fabrics or for raising the nap on cloth

cardamom, cardamum, *or* **cardamon 1** a tropical Asian zingiberaceous plant, *Elettaria cardamomum*, that has large hairy leaves **2** a related East Indian plant, *Amomum cardamomum*, whose seeds are used as a substitute for cardamom seeds.

card-carrying being an official member of a specified organization

Cardenal Ernesto born 1925, Nicaraguan poet, revolutionary, and Roman Catholic priest; an influential figure in the Sandinista movement.

cardiac 1 of or relating to the heart **2** of or relating to the portion of the stomach connected to the oesophagus **3** a person with a heart disorder **4** *Obsolete* a drug that stimulates the heart muscle

Cardiff 1 the capital of Wales, situated in the southeast, in Cardiff county borough: formerly an important port; seat of the Welsh assembly (1999); university (1883). Pop: 292 150 (2001) **2** a county borough in SE Wales, created in 1996 from part of South Glamorgan. Pop: 315 100 (2003 est). Area: 139 sq km (54 sq miles)

Cardigan 7th Earl of, title of *James Thomas Brudenell*. 1797–1868, British cavalry officer. He led the charge of the Light Brigade at Balaklava (1854) during the Crimean War.

Cardigan Bay an inlet of St George's Channel, on the W coast of Wales

Cardiganshire a former county of W Wales: became part of Dyfed in 1974; reinstated as **Ceredigion** in 1996

cardinal 1 *RC Church* any of the members of the Sacred College, ranking next after the pope, who elect the pope and act as his chief counsellors **2** a deep vivid red colour **3** See **cardinal number 4** a crested North American bunting, *Richmondena* (or *Pyrrhuloxia*) *cardinalis*, the male of which has a bright red plumage and the female a brown one **5** a fritillary butterfly, *Pandoriana pandora*, found in meadows of southern Europe **6** of a deep vivid red colour **7** *Astrology* of or relating to the signs Aries, Cancer, Libra, and Capricorn

cardinal number *or* **numeral 1** a number denoting quantity but not order in a set **2** *Maths, Logic* **a** a measure of the size of a set that does not take account of the order of its members **b** a particular number having this function

cardiograph 1 an instrument for recording the mechanical force and form of heart movements **2** short for **electrocardiograph**

cardiology the branch of medical science concerned with the heart and its diseases

cardiovascular of or relating to the heart and the blood vessels

Cardoso Fernando Henrique born 1931, Brazilian statesman; president (1995–2002)

cards a any game or games played with cards, esp playing cards **b** the playing of such a game
▷http://thehouseofhttp://thehouseofcards.com

cardsharp *or* **cardsharper** a professional card player who cheats

Cardus Sir Neville 1889–1975, British music critic and cricket writer

card vote *Brit* a vote by delegates, esp at a trade-union conference, in which each delegate's vote counts as a vote by all his constituents

care in (*or into*) **care** *Social welfare* made the legal responsibility of a local authority by order of a court

caretaker *Social welfare* a person who takes care of a vulnerable person, often a close relative

Carew Thomas ?1595–?1639, English Cavalier poet

Carey 1 George (Leonard). born 1935, Archbishop of Canterbury (1991–2002) **2** Peter born 1943, Australian novelist and writer; his novels include *Illywhacker* (1985), *Oscar and Lucinda* (1988), and *The True History of the Kelly Gang* (2001) **3** William 1761–1834, British orientalist and pioneer Baptist missionary in India

Carey Street (formerly) the street in which the London bankruptcy court was situated

Carib 1 a member of a group of American Indian peoples of NE South America and the Lesser Antilles **2** the family of languages spoken by these peoples

Caribbean 1 the the states and islands of the Caribbean Sea, including the West Indies, when considered as a geopolitical region **2** short for the **Caribbean Sea 3** a member of any of the peoples inhabiting the islands of the Caribbean Sea, such as a West Indian or a Carib

Caribbean Sea an almost landlocked sea, part of the Atlantic Ocean, bounded by the Caribbean islands, Central America, and the N coast of South America. Area: 2 718 200 sq km (1 049 500 sq miles)

Cariboo the *Canadian* a region in the W foothills of the Cariboo Mountains, scene of a gold rush beginning in 1860

caribou a large deer, *Rangifer tarandus*, of Arctic regions of

North America, having large branched antlers in the male and female: also occurs in Europe and Asia, where it is called a reindeer.

caries progressive decay of a bone or a tooth

carillon *Music* **1** a set of bells usually hung in a tower and played either by keys and pedals or mechanically **2** a tune played on such bells **3** an organ stop giving the effect of a bell **4** a form of celesta or keyboard glockenspiel

caring the practice or profession of providing social or medical care

Carinthia a state of S Austria: an independent duchy from 976 to 1276; mainly mountainous, with many lakes and resorts. Capital: Klagenfurt. Pop: 559 440 (2003 est). Area: 9533 sq km (3681 sq miles)

Carlisle a city in NW England, administrative centre of Cumbria: railway and industrial centre. Pop: 71 773 (2001)

Carlow **1** a county of SE Republic of Ireland, in Leinster: mostly flat, with barren mountains in the southeast. County town: Carlow. Pop: 46 014 (2002). Area: 896 sq km (346 sq miles) **2** a town in SE Republic of Ireland, county town of Co. Carlow. Pop: 18 487 (2002)

Carling Will(iam). born 1965, Scottish Rugby Union footballer; captain of England (1988–96)

Carlos Don full name *Carlos María Isidro de Borbón*. 1788–1855, second son of Charles IV: pretender to the Spanish throne and leader of the Carlists.

Carlota original name *Marie Charlotte Amélie Augustine Victoire Clémentine Léopoldine*. 1840–1927, wife of Maximilian; empress of Mexico (1864–67)

Carlyle **1** Robert born 1961, Scottish actor; his work includes the television series *Cracker* and *Hamish Macbeth* and the films *Trainspotting* (1996), *The Full Monty* (1997), and *The Beach* (2000) **2** Thomas 1795–1881, Scottish essayist and historian. His works include *Sartor Resartus* (1833–34), *The French Revolution* (1837), lectures *On Heroes, Hero-Worship, and the Heroic in History* (1841), and the *History of Frederick the Great* (1858–65)

Carmarthen a market town in S Wales, the administrative centre of Carmarthenshire: Norman castle. Pop: 14 648 (2001)

Carmarthenshire a county of S Wales, formerly part of Dyfed (1974–96): on Carmarthen Bay, with the Cambrian Mountains in the N: generally agricultural (esp dairying). Administrative centre: Carmarthen. Pop: 176 000 (2003 est). Area: 2398 sq km (926 sq miles)

Carmel Mount a mountain ridge in NW Israel, extending from the Samarian Hills to the Mediterranean. Highest point: about 540 m (1800 ft)

Carmelite *RC Church* **1** a member of an order of mendicant friars founded about 1154; a White Friar **2** a member of a corresponding order of nuns founded in 1452, noted for its austere rule

Carmichael Hoaglund Howard , known as *Hoagy*. 1899--1981, US pianist, singer, and composer of such standards as "Star Dust" (1929).

carminative a drug used to relieve flatulence

carmine a vivid red colour, sometimes with a purplish tinge

Carnac a village in NW France: noted for its many megalithic monuments, including alignments of stone menhirs

Carnap Rudolf 1891–1970, US logical positivist philosopher, born in Germany: attempted to construct a formal language for the empirical sciences that would eliminate ambiguity

carnation **1** a Eurasian caryophyllaceous plant, *Dianthus caryophyllus*, cultivated in many varieties for its white, pink, or red flowers, which have a fragrant scent of cloves. **2** the flower of this plant **3 a** a pink or reddish-pink colour **b** (*as adjective*): *a carnation dress* **4** a flesh tint in painting

Carnegie Andrew 1835–1919, US steel manufacturer and philanthropist, born in Scotland: endowed public libraries, education, and research trusts

Carnegie Hall a famous concert hall in New York (opened 1891); endowed by Andrew Carnegie (1835–1919), Scots-born US steel manufacturer and philanthropist

carnelian a red or reddish-yellow translucent variety of chalcedony, used as a gemstone

carnet **a** a customs licence authorizing the temporary importation of a motor vehicle **b** an official document permitting motorists to cross certain frontiers

Carniola a region of N Slovenia: a former duchy and crownland of Austria (1335–1919); divided between Yugoslavia and Italy in 1919; part of Yugoslavia (1947–92)

carnivore **1** any placental mammal of the order *Carnivora*, typically having large pointed canine teeth and sharp molars and premolars, specialized for eating flesh. The order includes cats, dogs, bears, raccoons, hyenas, civets, and weasels **2** any other animal or any plant that feeds on animals

Carnot **1** Lazare (Nicolas Marguerite) , known as *the Organizer of Victory*. 1753–1823, French military engineer and administrator: organized the French Revolutionary army (1793–95) **2** Nicolas Léonard Sadi 1796–1832, French physicist, whose work formed the basis for the second law of thermodynamics, enunciated in 1850; author of *Réflexions sur la puissance motrice du feu* (1824).

Caro **1** Sir Antony born 1924, British sculptor, best known for his abstract steel sculptures **2** Joseph (ben Ephraim) 1488–1575, Jewish legal scholar and mystic, born in Spain; compiler of the *Shulhan Arukh* (1564–65), the most authoritative Jewish legal code.

carob an evergreen leguminous Mediterranean tree, *Ceratonia siliqua*, with compound leaves and edible pods

carol **1** a joyful hymn or religious song, esp one (a **Christmas carol**) celebrating the birth of Christ **2** *Archaic* an old English circular dance

Carol II 1893–1953, king of Romania (1930–40), who was deposed by the Iron Guard

Carolina a former English colony on the E coast of North America, first established in 1663: divided in 1729 into North and South Carolina, which are often referred to as **the Carolinas**

carotene *or* **carotin** any of four orange-red isomers of an unsaturated hydrocarbon present in many plants (β-carotene is the orange pigment of carrots) and converted to vitamin A in the liver. Formula: $C_{40}H_{56}$

carotid either one of the two principal arteries that supply blood to the head and neck

carousel 1 a circular magazine in which slides for a projector are held: it moves round as each slide is shown 2 *History* a tournament in which horsemen took part in races and various manoeuvres in formation

carp 1 a freshwater teleost food fish, *Cyprinus carpio*, having a body covered with cycloid scales, a naked head, one long dorsal fin, and two barbels on each side of the mouth: family *Cyprinidae* 2 any other fish of the family *Cyprinidae*; a cyprinid

Carpaccio Vittore ?1460–?1525, Italian painter of the Venetian school

carpal a any bone of the wrist b *(as modifier)*: *carpal bones*

carpel the female reproductive organ of flowering plants, consisting of an ovary, style (sometimes absent), and stigma. The carpels are separate or fused to form a single pistil

Carpentaria Gulf of a shallow inlet of the Arafura Sea, in N Australia between Arnhem Land and Cape York Peninsula

carpenter a person skilled in woodwork, esp in buildings, ships, etc.

Carpenter John Alden 1876–1951, US composer, who used jazz rhythms in orchestral music: his works include the ballet *Skyscrapers* (1926) and the orchestral suite *Adventures in a Perambulator* (1915)

Carpentier Georges , known as *Gorgeous Georges*. 1894–1975, French boxer: world light-heavyweight champion (1920–22)

carpentry 1 the art or technique of working wood 2 the work produced by a carpenter; woodwork

carpetbagger 1 a politician who seeks public office in a locality where he has no real connections 2 *US* a Northern White who went to the South after the Civil War to profit from Reconstruction

carpet snake *or* **python** a large nonvenomous Australian snake, *Morelia variegata*, having a carpetlike pattern on its back

carpus 1 the technical name for **wrist** 2 the eight small bones of the human wrist that form the joint between the arm and the hand 3 the corresponding joint in other tetrapod vertebrates

Carracci a family of Italian painters, born in Bologna: **Agostino** (1557–1602); his brother, **Annibale** (1560–1609), noted for his frescoes, esp in the Palazzo Farnese, Rome; and their cousin, **Ludovico** (1555–1619). They were influential in reviving the classical tradition of the Renaissance and founded a teaching academy (1582) in Bologna

carrageen, carragheen, *or* **carageen** an edible red seaweed, *Chondrus crispus*, of North America and N Europe

Carrara a town in NW Italy, in NW Tuscany: famous for its marble. Pop: 65 034 (2001)

Carrel Alexis 1873–1944, French surgeon and biologist, active in the US (1905–39): developed a method of suturing blood vessels, making the transplantation of arteries and organs possible: Nobel prize for physiology or medicine 1912

Carreras José born 1947, Spanish tenor

Carrey Jim born 1962, Canadian-born Hollywood actor noted for his comedy roles; films include *Ace Ventura, Pet Detective* (1994), *Liar Liar* (1997), *The Truman Show* (1998), and *The Majestic* (2001)

carriage 1 *Brit* a railway coach for passengers 2 the moving part of a machine that bears another part

carriageway *Brit* the part of a road along which traffic passes in a single line moving in one direction only

Carrickfergus 1 a town in E Northern Ireland, in Carrickfergus district, Co. Antrim; historic settlement of Scottish Protestants on Belfast Lough; Norman castle. Pop: 27 201 (2001) 2 a district of E Northern Ireland, in Co. Antrim. Pop: 37 659 (2001). Area: 83 sq km (32 sq miles)

carrier 1 a mechanism by which something is carried or moved, such as a device for transmitting rotation from the faceplate of a lathe to the workpiece 2 *Pathol* another name for **vector** 3 *Pathol* a person or animal that, without having any symptoms of a disease, is capable of transmitting it to others 4 *Physics* an electron, ion, or hole that carries the charge in a conductor or semiconductor 5 *Chem* a the inert solid on which a dyestuff is adsorbed in forming a lake b a substance, such as kieselguhr or asbestos, used to support a catalyst c an inactive substance containing a radioisotope used in radioactive tracing d an inert gas used to transport the sample through a gas-chromatography column e a catalyst that effects the transfer of an atom or group from one molecule to another 6 a breed of domestic fancy pigeon having a large walnut-shaped wattle over the beak; a distinct variety of pigeon from the homing or carrier pigeon 7 a US name for **roof rack**

carrier pigeon any homing pigeon, esp one used for carrying messages

Carrington 1 Dora, known as *Carrington*. 1893–1932, British painter, engraver, and letter writer; a member of the Bloomsbury Group 2 Peter (**Alexander Rupert**), 6th Baron. born 1919, British Conservative politician: secretary of state for defence (1970–74); foreign secretary (1979–82); secretary general of NATO (1984–88)

carrion dead and rotting flesh

carrion crow a common predatory and scavenging European crow, *Corvus corone*, similar to the rook but having a pure black bill

Carroll Lewis real name *the Reverend Charles Lutwidge Dodgson*. 1832–98, English writer; an Oxford mathematics don who wrote *Alice's Adventures in Wonderland* (1865) and *Through the Looking-Glass* (1872) and the nonsense poem *The Hunting of the Snark* (1876)

carrot 1 an umbelliferous plant, *Daucus carota sativa*, with finely divided leaves and flat clusters of small white flowers 2 the long tapering orange root of this plant, eaten as a vegetable

carroty of a reddish or yellowish-orange colour

carry the distance travelled by a ball, etc, esp (in golf) the distance from where the ball is struck to where it first touches the ground

Carson 1 Christopher, known as *Kit Carson*. 1809–68, US frontiersman, trapper, scout, and Indian agent 2 Edward Henry, Baron. 1854–1935, Anglo-Irish politician and lawyer; led northern Irish resistance to the British government's plan for home rule for Ireland 3 Rachel (Louise). 1907–64, US marine biologist and science writer; author of *Silent Spring* (1962) 4 Willie, full name *William Hunter Fisher Carson*. born 1942, Scottish jockey;

retired in 1997

Carson City a city in W Nevada, capital of the state. Pop: 55 311 (2003 est)

Carstensz Mount a former name of (Mount) **Jaya**

Cartagena 1 a port in NW Colombia, on the Caribbean: centre for the Inquisition and the slave trade in the 16th century; chief oil port of Colombia. Pop: 1 002 000 (2005 est) **2** a port in SE Spain, on the Mediterranean: important since Carthaginian and Roman times for its minerals. Pop: 194 203 (2003 est)

carte blanche *Cards* a piquet hand containing no court cards: scoring ten points

cartel 1 *Economics* a collusive international association of independent enterprises formed to monopolize production and distribution of a product or service, control prices, etc. **2** *Politics* an alliance of parties or interests to further common aims

Carter 1 Angela 1940–92, British novelist and writer; her novels include *The Magic Toyshop* (1967) and *Nights at the Circus* (1984) **2 Elliot** (**Cook**). born 1908, US composer. His works include the *Piano Sonata* (1945–46), four string quartets, and other orchestral pieces: Pulitzer Prize 1960, 1973 **3 Howard** 1873–1939, English Egyptologist: excavated the tomb of the Pharaoh Tutankhamen **4 James Earl**, known as *Jimmy*. born 1924, US Democratic statesman; 39th president of the US (1977–81)

Carteret John, 1st Earl Granville. 1690–1763, British statesman, diplomat, and orator who led the opposition to Walpole (1730–42), after whose fall he became a leading minister as secretary of state (1742–44)

Cartesian 1 of or relating to the works of René Descartes (1596–1650), the French philosopher and mathematician **2** of, relating to, or used in Descartes' mathematical system **3** of, relating to, or derived from Descartes' philosophy, esp his contentions that personal identity consists in the continued existence of a unique mind and that the mind and body are connected causally

Carthage an ancient city state, on the N African coast near present-day Tunis. Founded about 800 BC by Phoenician traders, it grew into an empire dominating N Africa and the Mediterranean. Destroyed and then rebuilt by Rome, it was finally razed by the Arabs in 697 AD

Carthaginian 1 of or relating to Carthage (an ancient N African city state) or its inhabitants **2** a native or inhabitant of Carthage

carthorse a large heavily built horse kept for pulling carts or carriages

Carthusian *RC Church* **a** a member of an austere monastic order founded by Saint Bruno in 1084 near Grenoble, France **b** (*as modifier*): *a Carthusian monastery*

Cartier Jacques 1491–1557, French navigator and explorer in Canada, who discovered the St Lawrence River (1535)

Cartier-Bresson Henri 1908–2004, French photographer

cartilage a tough elastic tissue composing most of the embryonic skeleton of vertebrates. In the adults of higher vertebrates it is mostly converted into bone, remaining only on the articulating ends of bones, in the thorax, trachea, nose, and ears

Cartland Dame Barbara (**Hamilton**). 1901–2000, British novelist, noted for her prolific output of popular romantic fiction

cartography *or* **chartography** the art, technique, or practice of compiling or drawing maps or charts

carton 1 *Shooting* **a** a white disc at the centre of a target **b** a shot that hits this disc

cartoon 1 See **animated cartoon 2** a full-size preparatory sketch for a fresco, tapestry, mosaic, etc, from which the final work is traced or copied

cartouche *or* **cartouch 1** a carved or cast ornamental tablet or panel in the form of a scroll, sometimes having an inscription **2** an oblong figure enclosing characters expressing royal or divine names in Egyptian hieroglyphics **3** the paper case holding combustible materials in certain fireworks

cartridge 1 an electromechanical transducer in the pick-up of a record player, usually either containing a piezoelectric crystal (**crystal cartridge**) or an electromagnet (**magnetic cartridge**) **2** a container for magnetic tape that is inserted into a tape deck in audio or video systems. It is about four times the size of a cassette **3** *Photog* a light-tight film container that enables a camera to be loaded and unloaded in normal light **4** *Computing* a removable unit in a computer, such as an integrated circuit, containing software

cartridge paper a heavy paper used in making cartridges or as drawing or printing paper

cartwheel an acrobatic movement in which the body makes a sideways revolution supported on the hands with arms and legs outstretched

Cartwright 1 Edmund 1743–1823, British clergyman, who invented the power loom **2 Dame Silvia** (née *Poulter*). born 1943, New Zealand lawyer. She became a High Court judge in 1993 and governor general of New Zealand in 2001.

Caruso Enrico 1873–1921, an outstanding Italian operatic tenor; one of the first to make gramophone records

carving a figure or design produced by carving stone, wood, etc.

Cary (**Arthur**) **Joyce** (*Lunel*). 1888–1957, British novelist; author of *Mister Johnson* (1939), *A House of Children* (1941), and *The Horse's Mouth* (1944)

caryatid a column, used to support an entablature, in the form of a draped female figure

Casablanca a port in NW Morocco, on the Atlantic: largest city in the country; industrial centre. Pop: 3 523 000 (2003)

Casals Pablo 1876–1973, Spanish cellist and composer, noted for his interpretation of J S Bach's cello suites

Casanova Giovanni Jacopo 1725–98, Italian adventurer noted for his *Mémoires*, a vivid account of his sexual adventures and of contemporary society

cascade 1 a waterfall or series of waterfalls over rocks **2 a** a consecutive sequence of chemical or physical processes **b** (*as modifier*): *cascade liquefaction* **3** a series of stages in the processing chain of an electrical signal where each operates the next in turn **b** (*as modifier*): *a cascade amplifier* **4** the cumulative process responsible for the formation of an electrical discharge, cosmic-ray shower, or Geiger counter avalanche in a gas **5** the sequence of spontaneous decays by an excited atom or ion

Cascade Range a chain of mountains in the US and Canada: a continuation of the Sierra Nevada range from N California through Oregon and Washington to British Columbia. Highest peak: Mount Rainier, 4392 m (14 408 ft)

cascading style sheet *Computing* a file recording style details, such as fonts, colours, etc, that is read by browsers so that style is consistent over multiple web pages

cascara a shrub or small tree, *Rhamnus purshiana* of NW North America, whose bark is a source of cascara sagrada: family *Rhamnaceae*

case¹ a an action or suit at law or something that forms sufficient grounds for bringing an action b the evidence offered in court to support a claim

case² 1 *Architect* another word for **casing** 2 *Metallurgy* the surface of a piece of steel that has been case-hardened

case history a record of a person's background, medical history, etc, esp one used for determining medical treatment

casein a phosphoprotein, precipitated from milk by the action of rennin, forming the basis of cheese: used in the manufacture of plastics and adhesives

case law law established by following judicial decisions given in earlier cases

caseload the number of cases constituting the work of a doctor, solicitor, social worker, etc over a specified period

casement 1 a window frame that is hinged on one side 2 a window containing frames hinged at the side or at the top or bottom

Casement Sir Roger (David). 1864–1916, British diplomat and Irish nationalist: hanged by the British for treason in attempting to gain German support for Irish independence

Caserta a town in S Italy, in Campania: centre of Garibaldi's campaigns for the unification of Italy (1860); Allied headquarters in World War II. Pop: 75 208 (2001)

casework social work based on close study of the personal histories and circumstances of individuals and families

Cash Johnny 1932–2003, US country-and-western singer, guitarist, and songwriter. His recordings include the hits "I Walk the Line" (1956), "Ring of Fire" (1963), "A Boy named Sue" (1969), and the *American Recordings* series of albums (1994–2003)

cash-and-carry 1 sold or operated on a basis of cash payment for merchandise that is not delivered but removed by the purchaser 2 a wholesale store, esp for groceries, that operates on this basis

cashback a a discount offered in return for immediate payment b *(as modifier): cashback price £519.99 — save £30!*

cash desk a counter or till in a shop where purchases are paid for

cash discount *Commerce* a discount granted to a purchaser who pays before a stipulated date

cashew 1 a tropical American anacardiaceous evergreen tree, *Anacardium occidentale*, bearing kidney-shaped nuts that protrude from a fleshy receptacle 2 the edible nut of this tree

cashmere *or* **kashmir** 1 a fine soft wool from goats of the Kashmir area 2 a cloth or knitted material made from this or similar wool b *(as modifier): a cashmere sweater*

cash on delivery *Commerce* a service entailing cash payment to the carrier on delivery of merchandise

cash register a till with a keyboard that operates a mechanism for displaying and adding the amounts of cash received in individual sales

casing 1 a frame containing a door, window, or staircase 2 the outer cover of a pneumatic tyre 3 a pipe or tube used to line a hole or shaft 4 the outer shell of a steam or gas turbine

cask 1 a strong wooden barrel used mainly to hold alcoholic drink 2 *Austral* a lightweight cardboard container with plastic lining and a small tap, used to hold and serve wine 3 *Engineering* another name for **flask**

Caspar *or* **Gaspar** (in Christian tradition) one of the Magi, the other two being Melchior and Balthazar

Caspian Sea a salt lake between SE Europe and Asia: the largest inland sea in the world; fed mainly by the River Volga. Area: 394 299 sq km (152 239 sq miles)

Cassatt Mary 1845–1926, US impressionist painter, who lived in France

cassava any tropical euphorbiaceous plant of the genus *Manihot*, esp the widely cultivated American species *M. esculenta* (or *utilissima*) (**bitter cassava**) and *M. dulcis* (**sweet cassava**)

cassette 1 a a plastic container for magnetic tape, as one inserted into a tape deck b *(as modifier): a cassette recorder* 2 *Photog* another term for **cartridge** 3 *Films* a container for film used to facilitate the loading of a camera or projector, esp when the film is used in the form of a loop 4 *Biology* the injection of genes from one species into the fertilized egg of another species

cassia 1 any plant of the mainly tropical leguminous genus *Cassia*, esp *C. fistula*, whose pods yield **cassia pulp**, a mild laxative 2 a lauraceous tree, *Cinnamomum cassia*, of tropical Asia

Cassini Giovanni Domenico 1625–1712, French astronomer, born in Italy. He discovered (1675) **Cassini's division**, the gap that divides Saturn's rings into two parts, and four of Saturn's moons

Cassiodorus Flavius Magnus Aurelius ?490–?585 AD, Roman statesman, writer, and monk; author of *Variae*, a collection of official documents written for the Ostrogoths

Cassirer Ernst 1874–1945, German neo-Kantian philosopher. *The Philosophy of Symbolic Forms* (1923–29) analyses the symbols that underlie all manifestations, including myths and language, of human culture

Cassius Longinus Gaius died 42 BC, Roman general: led the conspiracy against Julius Caesar (44); defeated at Philippi by Antony (42)

Cassivelaunus 1st century BC, British chieftain, king of the Catuvellauni tribe, who organized resistance to Caesar's invasion of Britain (54 BC)

cassock *Christianity* an ankle-length garment, usually black, worn by priests and choristers

Casson Sir Hugh (Maxwell). 1910–99, British architect; president of the Royal Academy of Arts (1976–84)

cassowary any large flightless bird of the genus *Casuarius*, inhabiting forests in NE Australia, New Guinea, and adjacent islands, having a horny head crest, black plumage, and brightly coloured neck and wattles: order *Casuariiformes*

cast 1 a a throw at dice b the resulting number shown 2 *Angling* a a trace with a fly or flies attached b the act or an instance of casting 3 a the actors in a play collectively b (*as modifier*): *a cast list* 4 a an object made of metal, glass, etc, that has been shaped in a molten state by being poured or pressed into a mould b the mould used to shape such an object 5 a fixed twist or defect, esp in the eye 6 *Surgery* a rigid encircling casing, often made of plaster of Paris, for immobilizing broken bones while they heal 7 *Pathol* a mass of fatty, waxy, cellular, or other material formed in a diseased body cavity, passage, etc. 8 the act of casting a pack of hounds 9 *Falconry* a pair of falcons working in combination to pursue the same quarry 10 *Archery* the speed imparted to an arrow by a particular bow 11 a computation or calculation 12 *Palaeontol* a replica of an organic object made of nonorganic material, esp a lump of sediment that indicates the internal or external surface of a shell or skeleton 13 *Palaeontol* a sedimentary structure representing the infilling of a mark or depression in a soft layer of sediment (or bed)

Castalia a spring on Mount Parnassus: in ancient Greece sacred to Apollo and the Muses and believed to be a source of inspiration

caste 1 a any of the four major hereditary classes, namely the Brahman, Kshatriya, Vaisya, and Sudra into which Hindu society is divided b the system or basis of such classes c the social position or rank conferred by this system 2 *Entomol* any of various types of specialized individual, such as the worker, in social insects (hive bees, ants, etc)

Castellammare di Stabia a port and resort in SW Italy, in Campania on the Bay of Naples: site of the Roman resort of Stabiae, which was destroyed by the eruption of Vesuvius in 79 AD. Pop: 66 929 (2001)

castellated *Architecture* 1 having turrets and battlements, like a castle 2 having indentations similar to battlements

Castiglione Count **Baldassare** 1478–1529, Italian diplomat and writer, noted particularly for his dialogue on ideal courtly life, *Il Libro del Cortegiano* (The Courtier) (1528)

Castile *or* **Castilla** a former kingdom comprising most of modern Spain: originally part of León, it became an independent kingdom in the 10th century and united with Aragon (1469), the first step in the formation of the Spanish state

Castilian the Spanish dialect of Castile; the standard form of European Spanish

casting 1 an object or figure that has been cast, esp in metal from a mould 2 the process of transferring molten steel to a mould 3 the choosing of actors for a production 4 *Hunting* the act of directing a pack of hounds over ground where their quarry may recently have passed so that they can quest for, discover, or recapture its scent 5 *Zoology* another word for **cast** *or* **pellet**

cast iron iron containing so much carbon (1.7 to 4.5 per cent) that it cannot be wrought and must be cast into shape

Castlebar the county town of Co. Mayo, Republic of Ireland; site of the battle (1798) between the French and British known as Castlebar Races. Pop: 11 371 (2002)

Castlereagh[1] **Viscount** title of *Robert Stewart*, Marquis of Londonderry. 1769–1822, British statesman: as foreign secretary (1812–22) led the Grand Alliance against Napoleon and attended the Congress of Vienna (1815)

Castlereagh[2] a district of E Northern Ireland, in Co. Down. Pop: 66 076 (2003 est). Area.: 85 sq km (33 sq miles)

Castner HamiltonYoung 1858–98, US chemist, who devised the **Castner process** for extracting sodium from sodium hydroxide

castor 1 the brownish aromatic secretion of the anal glands of a beaver, used in perfumery and medicine 2 the fur of the beaver 3 a less common name for **beaver**

castor oil a colourless or yellow glutinous oil obtained from the seeds of the castor-oil plant and used as a fine lubricant and as a cathartic

castrato (in 17th- and 18th-century opera) a male singer whose testicles were removed before puberty, allowing the retention of a soprano or alto voice

Castries the capital and chief port of St Lucia. Pop: 14 000 (2005 est)

Castro Fidel full name *Fidel Castro Ruz.* born 1927, Cuban statesman: prime minister from 1959, when he led the Communist overthrow of Batista and president from 1976

casualty a hospital department in which victims of accidents, violence, etc, are treated

casuarina any tree of the genus *Casuarina*, of Australia and the East Indies, having jointed leafless branchlets: family *Casuarinaceae*

casuistry *Philosophy* the resolution of particular moral dilemmas, esp those arising from conflicting general moral rules, by careful distinction of the cases to which these rules apply

cat[1] 1 a small domesticated feline mammal, *Felis catus* (or *domesticus*), having thick soft fur and occurring in many breeds in which the colour of the fur varies greatly: kept as a pet or to catch rats and mice 2 any of the larger felines, such as a lion or tiger 3 any wild feline mammal of the genus *Felis*, such as the lynx or serval, resembling the domestic cat 4 *Nautical* a heavy tackle for hoisting an anchor to the cathead 5 a short sharpended piece of wood used in the game of tipcat

cat[2] short for **catalytic converter**

catabolism *or* **katabolism** a metabolic process in which complex molecules are broken down into simple ones with the release of energy; destructive metabolism

cataclysm 1 a disastrous flood; deluge 2 *Geology* another name for **catastrophe**

Catalan a language of Catalonia, quite closely related to Spanish and Provençal, belonging to the Romance group of the Indo-European family

catalepsy a state of prolonged rigid posture, occurring for example in schizophrenia or in hypnotic trances

catalogue *or US* **catalog** 1 a book, usually illustrated, containing details of items for sale, esp as used by mail-order companies 2 *US and Canadian* a publication issued by a university, college, etc, listing courses offered, reg-.

ulations, services, etc.

Catalonia a region of NE Spain, with a strong separatist tradition: became an autonomous region with its own parliament in 1979; an important agricultural and industrial region, with many resorts. Pop: 7 012 600 (2003 est). Area: 31 929 sq km (12 328 sq miles)

catalpa any bignoniaceous tree of the genus *Catalpa* of North America and Asia, having large leaves, bell-shaped whitish flowers, and long slender pods

catalysis acceleration of a chemical reaction by the action of a catalyst

catalyst a substance that increases the rate of a chemical reaction without itself suffering any permanent chemical change

catalytic converter a device using three-way catalysts to reduce the obnoxious and poisonous components of the products of combustion (mainly oxides of nitrogen, carbon monoxide, and unburnt hydrocarbons) from the exhausts of motor vehicles

catalytic cracker a unit in an oil refinery in which mineral oils with high boiling points are converted to fuels with lower boiling points by a catalytic process

catamaran 1 a sailing, or sometimes motored, vessel with twin hulls held parallel by a rigid framework 2 a primitive raft made of logs lashed together

Catania a port in E Sicily, near Mount Etna. Pop: 313 110 (2001)

cataract 1 a large waterfall or rapids 2 *Pathol* a partial or total opacity of the crystalline lens of the eye b the opaque area

catarrh 1 inflammation of a mucous membrane with increased production of mucus, esp affecting the nose and throat in the common cold 2 the mucus so formed

catastrophe 1 *Theatre* the denouement of a play, esp a classical tragedy 2 any sudden and violent change in the earth's surface caused by flooding, earthquake, or some other rapid process

catatonia a state of muscular rigidity and stupor, sometimes found in schizophrenia

catch 1 a game in which a ball is thrown from one player to another 2 *Cricket* the catching of a ball struck by a batsman before it touches the ground, resulting in him being out 3 *Music* a type of round popular in the 17th, 18th, and 19th centuries, having a humorous text that is often indecent or bawdy and hard to articulate

catchment a structure in which water is collected

catchment area the area of land bounded by watersheds draining into a river, basin, or reservoir

catchword *Theatre* an actor's cue to speak or enter

catechism instruction by a series of questions and answers, esp a book containing such instruction on the religious doctrine of a Christian Church

category 1 *Metaphysics* any one of the most basic classes into which objects and concepts can be analysed 2 a (in the philosophy of Aristotle) any one of ten most fundamental modes of being, such as quantity, quality, and substance b (in the philosophy of Kant) one of twelve concepts required by human beings to interpret the empirical world c any set of objects, concepts, or expressions distinguished from others within some logical or linguistic theory by the intelligibility of a specific set of statements concerning them

catena a connected series, esp of patristic comments on the Bible

caterpillar the wormlike larva of butterflies and moths, having numerous pairs of legs and powerful biting jaws. It may be brightly coloured, hairy, or spiny

Catesby Robert 1573–1605, English conspirator, leader of the Gunpowder Plot (1605): killed while resisting arrest

catfish any of numerous mainly freshwater teleost fishes having whisker-like barbels around the mouth, esp the silurids of Europe and Asia and the horned pouts of North America

catharsis 1 (in Aristotelian literary criticism) the purging or purification of the emotions through the evocation of pity and fear, as in tragedy 2 *Psychoanal* the bringing of repressed ideas or experiences into consciousness, thus relieving tensions 3 purgation, esp of the bowels

cathartic a purgative drug or agent

cathedral a the principal church of a diocese, containing the bishop's official throne b (*as modifier*): *a cathedral city*

Cather Willa (Sibert). 1873–1947, US novelist, whose works include *O Pioneers!* (1913) and *My Ántonia* (1918)

Catherine Saint died 307 AD, legendary Christian martyr of Alexandria, who was tortured on a spiked wheel and beheaded

Catherine I ?1684–1727, second wife of Peter the Great, whom she succeeded as empress of Russia (1725–27)

Catherine II known as *Catherine the Great*. 1729–96, empress of Russia (1762–96), during whose reign Russia extended her boundaries at the expense of Turkey, Sweden, and Poland: she was a patron of literature and the arts

Catherine of Aragon 1485–1536, first wife of Henry VIII of England and mother of Mary I. The annulment of Henry's marriage to her (1533) against papal authority marked an initial stage in the English Reformation

Catherine of Braganza 1638–1705, wife of Charles II of England, daughter of John IV of Portugal

Catherine of Siena Saint 1347–80, Italian mystic and ascetic; patron saint of the Dominican order. Feast day: April 29

Catherine wheel a circular window having ribs radiating from the centre

catheter *Med* a long slender flexible tube for inserting into a natural bodily cavity or passage for introducing or withdrawing fluid, such as urine or blood

cathode 1 the negative electrode in an electrolytic cell; the electrode by which electrons enter a device from an external circuit 2 the negatively charged electron source in an electronic valve 3 the positive terminal of a primary cell

cathode-ray tube a valve in which a beam of high-energy electrons is focused onto a fluorescent screen to give a visible spot of light. The device, with appropriate deflection equipment, is used in television receivers, visual display units, oscilloscopes, etc.

Catholic *Christianity* 1 denoting or relating to the entire body of Christians, esp to the Church before separation into the Greek or Eastern and Latin or Western Churches 2 denoting or relating to the Latin or

Western Church after this separation **3** denoting or relating to the Roman Catholic Church **4** denoting or relating to any church, belief, etc, that claims continuity with or originates in the ancient undivided Church

Catiline Latin name *Lucius Sergius Catilina*. ?108–62 BC, Roman politician: organized an unsuccessful conspiracy against Cicero (63–62)

cation a positively charged ion; an ion that is attracted to the cathode during electrolysis

catkin an inflorescence consisting of a spike, usually hanging, of much reduced flowers of either sex: occurs in birch, hazel, etc.

catmint a Eurasian plant, *Nepeta cataria*, having spikes of purple-spotted white flowers and scented leaves of which cats are fond: family *Lamiaeae* (labiates)

Cato 1 Marcus Porcius , known as *Cato the Elder* or *the Censor*. 234–149 BC, Roman statesman and writer, noted for his relentless opposition to Carthage **2** his great-grandson, **Marcus Porcius,** known as *Cato the Younger* or *Uticensis*. 95–46 BC, Roman statesman, general, and Stoic philosopher; opponent of Catiline and Caesar

cattle 1 bovid mammals of the tribe *Bovini* (bovines), esp those of the genus *Bos* **2** any domesticated bovine mammals, esp those of the species *Bos taurus* (domestic ox)

catty *or* **cattie** a unit of weight, used esp in China, equal to about one and a half pounds or about 0.67 kilogram

Catullus Gaius Valerius ?84–?54 BC, Roman lyric poet, noted particularly for his love poems

catwalk a narrow ramp extending from the stage into the audience in a theatre, nightclub, etc, esp as used by models in a fashion show

Cauca a river in W Colombia, rising in the northwest and flowing north to the Magdalena River. Length: about 1350 km (840 miles)

Caucasia a region in SW Russia, Georgia, Armenia, and Azerbaijan, between the Caspian Sea and the Black Sea: contains the Caucasus Mountains, dividing it into Ciscaucasia in the north and Transcaucasia in the south; one of the most complex ethnic areas in the world, with over 50 different peoples

Caucasian *or* **Caucasic 1** a member of the Caucasoid race; a white man **2** a native or inhabitant of Caucasia **3** any of three possibly related families of languages spoken in the Caucasus: **North-West Caucasian,** including Circassian and Abkhaz, **North-East Caucasian,** including Avar, and **South Caucasian** including Georgian

Caucasus the 1 a mountain range in SW Russia, running along the N borders of Georgia and Azerbaijan, between the Black Sea and the Caspian Sea: mostly over 2700 m (9000 ft). Highest peak: Mount Elbrus, 5642 m (18 510 ft) **2** another name for **Caucasia**

Cauchy Augustin Louis , Baron Cauchy. 1789–1857, French mathematician, noted for his work on the theory of functions and the wave theory of light

caucus 1 *Chiefly US and Canadian* **a** a closed meeting of the members of one party in a legislative chamber, etc, to coordinate policy, choose candidates, etc. **b** such a bloc of politicians **2** *Chiefly US* **a** a group of leading politicians of one party **b** a meeting of such a group **3** *Chiefly*

US a local meeting of party members **4** *Brit* a group or faction within a larger group, esp a political party, who discuss tactics, choose candidates, etc. **5** *Austral* a meeting of the members of the Federal parliamentary Labor Party **6** *NZ* a formal meeting of all Members of Parliament belonging to one political party

caudal 1 *Anatomy* of or towards the posterior part of the body **2** *Zoology* relating to, resembling, or in the position of the tail

caul *Anatomy* **1** a portion of the amniotic sac sometimes covering a child's head at birth **2** a large fold of peritoneum hanging from the stomach across the intestines; the large omentum

Caulfield Patrick (Joseph). born 1936, British painter and printmaker

cauliflower 1 a variety of cabbage, *Brassica oleracea botrytis*, having a large edible head of crowded white flowers on a very short thick stem **2** the flower head of this plant, used as a vegetable

cauliflower ear permanent swelling and distortion of the external ear as the result of ruptures of the blood vessels: usually caused by blows received in boxing

causal *Philosophy* (of a theory) explaining a phenomenon or analysing a concept in terms of some causal relation

cause 1 a a ground for legal action; matter giving rise to a lawsuit **b** the lawsuit itself **2** (in the philosophy of Aristotle) any of four requirements for a thing's coming to be, namely material (material cause), its nature (formal cause), an agent (efficient cause), and a purpose (final cause)

causeway 1 a raised path or road crossing water, marshland, sand, etc. **2** a paved footpath **3** a road surfaced with setts

caustic 1 capable of burning or corroding by chemical action **2** of, relating to, or denoting light that is reflected or refracted by a curved surface **3** a surface that envelopes the light rays reflected or refracted by a curved surface **4** a curve formed by the intersection of a caustic surface with a plane **5** *Chem* a caustic substance, esp an alkali

caution 1 *Law, chiefly Brit* a formal warning given to a person suspected or accused of an offence that his words will be taken down and may be used in evidence **2** a notice entered on the register of title to land that prevents a proprietor from disposing of his land without a notice to the person who entered the caution

Cavafy Constantine Greek name *Kavafis*.1863–1933, Greek poet of Alexandria in Egypt

Cavalcanti Guido ?1255–1300, Italian poet, noted for his love poems

cavalier 1 a gallant or courtly gentleman, esp one acting as a lady's escort **2** *Archaic* a horseman, esp one who is armed

Cavalier a supporter of Charles I during the English Civil War

Cavallini Pietro ?1250–?1330, Italian fresco painter and mosaicist. His works include the mosaics of the *Life of the Virgin* in Santa Maria, Trastevere, Rome

Cavan 1 a county of N Republic of Ireland: hilly, with many small lakes and bogs. County town: Cavan. Pop: 56 546 (2002). Area: 1890 sq km (730 sq miles) **2** a market town in N Republic of Ireland, county town of Co. Cavan. Pop: 6098 (2002)

cave 1 an underground hollow with access from the ground surface or from the sea, often found in limestone areas and on rocky coastlines 2 *Brit, History* a secession or a group seceding from a political party on some issue

caveat *Law* a formal notice requesting the court or officer to refrain from taking some specified action without giving prior notice to the person lodging the caveat

Cavell Edith Louisa 1865–1915, English nurse: executed by the Germans in World War I for helping Allied prisoners to escape

caveman a man of the Palaeolithic age

Cavendish Henry 1731–1810, British physicist and chemist: recognized hydrogen, determined the composition of water, and calculated the density of the earth by an experiment named after him

cavern a cave, esp when large and formed by underground water, or a large chamber in a cave

caving the sport of climbing in and exploring caves

cavity 1 *Dentistry* a soft decayed area on a tooth 2 any empty or hollow space within the body

Cavour Conte Camillo Benso di 1810–61, Italian statesman and premier of Piedmont-Sardinia (1852–59; 1860–61): a leader of the movement for the unification of Italy

Cawley Evonne (née *Goolagong*). born 1951, Australian tennis player: Wimbledon champion 1971 and 1980; Australian champion 1974–76

Caxton William ?1422–91, English printer and translator: published, in Bruges, the first book printed in English (1475) and established the first printing press in England (1477)

cay a small low island or bank composed of sand and coral fragments, esp in the Caribbean area

Cayenne the capital of French Guiana, on an island at the mouth of the Cayenne River: French penal settlement from 1854 to 1938. Pop: 50 594 (1999)

Cayley 1 Arthur 1821–93, British mathematician, who invented matrices 2 Sir George 1773–1857, British engineer and pioneer of aerial navigation. He constructed the first man-carrying glider (1853) and invented the caterpillar tractor

cayman *or* **caiman** any tropical American crocodilian of the genus *Caiman* and related genera, similar to alligators but with a more heavily armoured belly: family *Alligatoridae* (alligators, etc)

CD player a device for playing compact discs

CD-ROM compact disc read-only memory; a compact disc used with a computer system as a read-only optical disk

CD-video a compact-disc player that, when connected to a television and hi-fi, produces high-quality stereo sound and synchronized pictures from a disc resembling a large compact audio disc

Ceauşescu Nicolae 1918–89, Romanian statesman; chairman of the state council (1967–89) and president of Romania (1974–89): deposed and executed

Cecil Lord David 1902–86, English literary critic and biographer

Cecilia Saint died ?230 AD, Roman martyr; patron saint of music. Feast day: Nov 22

cedar 1 any Old World coniferous tree of the genus *Cedrus*, having spreading branches, needle-like evergreen leaves, and erect barrel-shaped cones: family *Pinaceae* See also **deodar** 2 any of various other conifers, such as the red cedars and white cedars 3 the wood of any of these trees 4 any of certain other plants, such as the Spanish cedar

ceiling 1 the inner upper surface of a room 2 a an upper limit, such as one set by regulation on prices or wages b (*as modifier*): *ceiling prices* 3 the upper altitude to which an aircraft can climb measured under specified conditions 4 *Meteorol* the highest level in the atmosphere from which the earth's surface is visible at a particular time, usually the base of a cloud layer 5 a wooden or metal surface fixed to the interior frames of a vessel for rigidity

Cela Camilo José 1916–2002, Spanish novelist and essayist. His works include *The Family of Pascual Duarte* (1942), *La Colmena* (1951), and *La Cruz de San Andres* (1994). Nobel prize for literature 1989

Celan Paul, real name *Paul Antschel*. 1920–70, Romanian Jewish poet, writing in German, whose work reflects the experience of Nazi persecution

celandine either of two unrelated plants, *Chelidonium majus* or *Ranunculus ficaria*

Celebes Sea the part of the Pacific Ocean between Sulawesi, Borneo, and Mindanao

celebrant *Christianity* an officiating priest, esp at the Eucharist

celeriac a variety of celery, *Apium graveolens rapaceum*, with a large turnip-like root, used as a vegetable

celery 1 an umbelliferous Eurasian plant, *Apium graveolens dulce*, whose blanched leafstalks are used in salads or cooked as a vegetable 2 **wild celery** a related and similar plant, *Apium graveolens*

celesta *or* **celeste** *Music* a keyboard percussion instrument consisting of a set of steel plates of graduated length that are struck with key-operated hammers. The tone is an ethereal tinkling sound. Range: four octaves upwards from middle C

celestial equator the great circle lying on the celestial sphere the plane of which is perpendicular to the line joining the north and south celestial poles

celestial sphere an imaginary sphere of infinitely large radius enclosing the universe so that all celestial bodies appear to be projected onto its surface

cell 1 *Biology* the basic structural and functional unit of living organisms. It consists of a nucleus, containing the genetic material, surrounded by the cytoplasm in which are mitochondria, lysosomes, ribosomes, and other organelles. All cells are bounded by a cell membrane; plant cells have an outer cell wall in addition 2 *Biology* any small cavity or area, such as the cavity containing pollen in an anther 3 a device for converting chemical energy into electrical energy, usually consisting of a container with two electrodes immersed in an electrolyte 4 a small religious house dependent upon a larger one 5 a small group of persons operating as a nucleus of a larger political, religious, or other organization 6 *Maths* a small unit of volume in a mathematical coordinate system 7 *Zoology* one of the areas on an insect wing bounded by veins

cellar 1 an underground room, rooms, or storey of a building, usually used for storage 2 a place where wine is stored 3 a stock of bottled wines

Cellini Benvenuto 1500–71, Italian sculptor, goldsmith, and engraver, noted also for his autobiography

cello *Music* a bowed stringed instrument of the violin family. Range: more than four octaves upwards from C below the bass staff. It has four strings, is held between the knees, and has an extendible metal spike at the lower end, which acts as a support

cellular 1 of, relating to, resembling, or composed of a cell or cells 2 having cells or small cavities; porous 3 *Textiles* woven with an open texture

cellulite a name sometimes given to subcutaneous fat alleged to resist dieting

celluloid 1 a flammable thermoplastic material consisting of cellulose nitrate mixed with a plasticizer, usually camphor: used in sheets, rods, and tubes for making a wide range of articles 2 a a cellulose derivative used for coating film b one of the transparent sheets on which the constituent drawings of an animated film are prepared c a transparent sheet used as an overlay in artwork d cinema film

cellulose a polysaccharide consisting of long unbranched chains of linked glucose units: the main constituent of plant cell walls and used in making paper, rayon, and film

cellulose acetate nonflammable material made by acetylating cellulose: used in the manufacture of film, dopes, lacquers, and artificial fibres

cellulose nitrate a compound made by treating cellulose with nitric and sulphuric acids, used in plastics, lacquers, and explosives: a nitrogen-containing ester of cellulose

Celsius scale a scale of temperature in which 0° represents the melting point of ice and 100° represents the boiling point of water

Celt *or* **Kelt** 1 a person who speaks a Celtic language 2 a member of an Indo-European people who in pre-Roman times inhabited Britain, Gaul, Spain, and other parts of W and central Europe
▷www.ibiblio.org/gaelic/celts.html
▷http://celt.net/Celtic/celtopedia/indices/encyintro.html

Celtic *or* **Keltic** a branch of the Indo-European family of languages that includes Gaelic, Welsh, and Breton, still spoken in parts of Scotland, Ireland, Wales, and Brittany. Modern Celtic is divided into the Brythonic (southern) and Goidelic (northern) groups

Celtic Sea the relatively shallow part of the Atlantic Ocean lying between S Ireland, SW Wales, Cornwall, and W Brittany

cement 1 *Dentistry* any of various materials used in filling teeth 2 mineral matter, such as silica and calcite, that binds together particles of rock, bones, etc, to form a solid mass of sedimentary rock

Cenis Mont a pass over the Graian Alps in SE France, between Lanslebourg (France) and Susa (Italy): nearby tunnel, opened in 1871. Highest point: 2082 m (6831 ft)

cenotaph a monument honouring a dead person or persons buried elsewhere

Cenozoic, Caenozoic, *or* **Cainozoic** of, denoting, or relating to the most recent geological era, which began 65 000 000 years ago: characterized by the development and increase of the mammals

censer a container for burning incense, esp one swung at religious ceremonies

censor 1 (in republican Rome) either of two senior magistrates elected to keep the list of citizens up to date, control aspects of public finance, and supervise public morals 2 *Psychoanal* the postulated factor responsible for regulating the translation of ideas and desires from the unconscious to the conscious mind

censorship *Psychoanal* the activity of the mind in regulating impulses, etc, from the unconscious so that they are modified before reaching the conscious mind

census 1 an official periodic count of a population including such information as sex, age, occupation, etc. 2 (in ancient Rome) a registration of the population and a property evaluation for purposes of taxation
▷www.census.gov/ipc/www/idbnew.html

cent 1 a monetary unit of American Samoa, Andorra, Antigua and Barbuda, Aruba, Australia, Austria, the Bahamas, Barbados, Belgium, Belize, Bermuda, Bosnia and Hercegovina, Brunei, Canada, the Cayman Islands, Cyprus, Dominica, East Timor, Ecuador, El Salvador, Ethiopia, Fiji, Finland, France, French Guiana, Germany, Greece, Grenada, Guadeloupe, Guam, Guyana, Hong Kong, Ireland, Jamaica, Kenya, Kiribati, Kosovo, Liberia, Luxembourg, Malaysia, Malta, the Marshall Islands, Martinique, Mauritius, Mayotte, Micronesia, Monaco, Montenegro, Namibia, Nauru, the Netherlands, the Netherlands Antilles, New Zealand, the Northern Mariana Islands, Palau, Portugal, Puerto Rico, Réunion, Saint Kitts and Nevis, Saint Lucia, Saint Vincent and the Grenadines, San Marino, the Seychelles, Sierra Leone, Singapore, the Solomon Islands, Somalia, South Africa, Spain, Sri Lanka, Surinam, Swaziland, Taiwan, Tanzania, Trinidad and Tobago, Tuvalu, Uganda, the United States, the Vatican City, the Virgin Islands, and Zimbabwe. It is worth one hundredth of their respective standard units 2 an interval of pitch between two frequencies f_2 and f_1 equal to 3986.31 log (f_2/f_1); one twelve-hundredth of the interval between two frequencies having the ratio 1:2 (an octave)

centaur *Greek myth* one of a race of creatures with the head, arms, and torso of a man, and the lower body and legs of a horse

centavo 1 a monetary unit of Argentina, Bolivia, Brazil, Cape Verde, Chile, Colombia, Cuba, the Dominican Republic, Guatemala, Guinea-Bissau, Honduras, Mexico, Mozambique, Nicaragua, and the Philippines. It is worth one hundredth of their respective standard units 2 a former monetary unit of Ecuador, El Salvador, and Portugal, worth one hundredth of their former standard units.

centesimal 1 hundredth 2 relating to division into hundredths

centigrade a unit of angle equal to one hundredth of a grade

centigram *or* **centigramme** one hundredth of a gram

centilitre *or* US **centiliter** one hundredth of a litre

centime 1 a monetary unit of Algeria, Benin, Burkina-Faso, Burundi, Cameroon, the Central African Republic, Chad, Comoros, Democratic Republic of Congo, Congo-Brazzaville, Côte d'Ivoire, Djibouti, Equatorial Guinea, French Polynesia, Gabon, Guinea, Guinea-Bissau, Haiti, Liechtenstein, Madagascar, Mali, Mayotte, Morocco, New Caledonia, Niger, Rwanda, Senegal, Switzerland, and Togo. It is worth one hundredth of their respective standard units 2 a former monetary unit of Andorra, Belgium, France, French Guiana, Guadeloupe, Luxembourg, Martinique, Monaco, and Réunion, worth one hundredth of a franc

centimetre *or US* **centimeter** one hundredth of a metre

centipede any carnivorous arthropod of the genera *Lithobius, Scutigera*, etc, having a body of between 15 and 190 segments, each bearing one pair of legs: class *Chilopoda*

central 1 a of or relating to the central nervous system b of or relating to the centrum of a vertebra 2 (of a force) directed from or towards a point

Central African Republic a landlocked country of central Africa: joined with Chad as a territory of French Equatorial Africa in 1910; became an independent republic in 1960; a parliamentary monarchy (1976–79); consists of a huge plateau, mostly savanna, with dense forests in the south; drained chiefly by the Shari and Ubangi Rivers. Official language: French; Sango is the national language. Religion: Christian and animist. Currency: franc. Capital: Bangui. Pop: 3 912 000 (2004 est). Area: 622 577 sq km (240 376 sq miles)

Central America an isthmus joining the continents of North and South America, extending from the S border of Mexico to the NW border of Colombia and consisting of Belize, Guatemala, Honduras, El Salvador, Nicaragua, Costa Rica, and Panama. Area: about 518 000 sq km (200 000 sq miles)

central heating a system for heating the rooms of a building by means of radiators or air vents connected by pipes or ducts to a central source of heat

centralism the principle or act of bringing something under central control; centralization

Central Karoo an arid plateau of S central South Africa, in Cape Province, separated from the Little Karoo to the southwest by the Swartberg range. Average height: 750 m (2500 ft)

central locking a system by which all the doors of a motor vehicle can be locked simultaneously when the driver's door is locked

central nervous system the mass of nerve tissue that controls and coordinates the activities of an animal. In vertebrates it consists of the brain and spinal cord

central processing unit the part of a computer that performs logical and arithmetical operations on the data as specified in the instructions

Central Region a former local government region in central Scotland, formed in 1975 from Clackmannanshire, most of Stirlingshire, and parts of Perthshire, West Lothian, Fife, and Kinross-shire; in 1996 it was replaced by the council areas of Stirling, Clackmannanshire, and Falkirk

centre *or US* **center** 1 *Geometry* a the midpoint of any line or figure, esp the point within a circle or sphere that is equidistant from any point on the circumference or surface b the point within a body through which a specified force may be considered to act, such as the centre of gravity 2 the point, axis, or pivot about which a body rotates 3 *Politics* a a political party or group favouring moderation, esp the moderate members of a legislative assembly b *(as modifier): a Centre-Left alliance* 4 *Physiol* any part of the central nervous system that regulates a specific function 5 a bar with a conical point upon which a workpiece or part may be turned or ground 6 a punch mark or small conical hole in a part to be drilled, which enables the point of the drill to be located accurately 7 *Basketball* a the position of a player who jumps for the ball at the start of play b the player in this position 8 *Archery* a the ring around the bull's eye b a shot that hits this ring

Centre 1 the the sparsely inhabited central region of Australia 2 a region of central France: generally low-lying; drained chiefly by the Rivers Loire, Loir, and Cher

centreboard *Nautical* a supplementary keel for a sailing vessel, which may be adjusted by raising and lowering

centre half *or* **centre back** *Soccer* a defender who plays in the middle of the defence

centre of gravity the point through which the resultant of the gravitational forces on a body always acts

centre pass *Hockey* a push or hit made in any direction to start the game or to restart the game after a goal has been scored

centrifugal 1 acting, moving, or tending to move away from a centre 2 of, concerned with, or operated by centrifugal force 3 *Botany* (esp of certain inflorescences) developing outwards from a centre 4 any device that uses centrifugal force for its action 5 the rotating perforated drum in a centrifuge

centrifugal force a fictitious force that can be thought of as acting outwards on any body that rotates or moves along a curved path

centrifuge 1 any of various rotating machines that separate liquids from solids or dispersions of one liquid in another, by the action of centrifugal force 2 any of various rotating devices for subjecting human beings or animals to varying accelerations for experimental purposes

centripetal 1 acting, moving, or tending to move towards a centre 2 of, concerned with, or operated by centripetal force 3 *Botany* (esp of certain inflorescences) developing from the outside towards the centre

centripetal force a force that acts inwards on any body that rotates or moves along a curved path and is directed towards the centre of curvature of the path or the axis of rotation

centrist a person holding moderate political views

centurion the officer commanding a Roman century

century 1 (in ancient Rome) a unit of foot soldiers, originally 100 strong, later consisting of 60 to 80 men 2 (in ancient Rome) a division of the people for purposes of voting

Cephalonia a mountainous island in the Ionian Sea, the largest of the Ionian Islands, off the W coast of Greece. Pop: 36 404 (2001). Area: 935 sq km (365 sq miles)

cephalopod any marine mollusc of the class

Cephalopoda., characterized by well-developed head and eyes and a ring of sucker-bearing tentacles. The group also includes the octopuses, squids, cuttlefish, and pearly nautilus

ceramic 1 a hard brittle material made by firing clay and similar substances 2 an object made from such a material 3 of, relating to, or made from a ceramic 4 of or relating to ceramics

ceramics the art and technique of producing articles of clay, porcelain, etc.
▷www.acers.org
▷www.ceramicsmonthly.org
▷www.ceramicstoday.com

Cerberus *Greek myth* a dog, usually represented as having three heads, that guarded the entrance to Hades

cereal 1 any grass that produces an edible grain, such as oat, rye, wheat, rice, maize, sorghum, and millet 2 the grain produced by such a plant 3 of or relating to any of these plants or their products

cerebellum one of the major divisions of the vertebrate brain, situated in man above the medulla oblongata and beneath the cerebrum, whose function is coordination of voluntary movements and maintenance of bodily equilibrium

cerebral palsy a nonprogressive impairment of muscular function and weakness of the limbs, caused by lack of oxygen to the brain immediately after birth, brain injury during birth, or viral infection

cerebrospinal of or relating to the brain and spinal cord

cerebrovascular of or relating to the blood vessels and the blood supply of the brain

cerebrum 1 the anterior portion of the brain of vertebrates, consisting of two lateral hemispheres joined by a thick band of fibres: the dominant part of the brain in man, associated with intellectual function, emotion, and personality 2 the brain considered as a whole 3 the main neural bundle or ganglion of certain invertebrates

Ceredigion a county of W Wales, on Cardigan Bay: created in 1996 from part of Dyfed; corresponds to the former Cardiganshire (abolished 1974): mainly agricultural, with the Cambrian Mountains in the E and N. Administrative centre: Aberaeron. Pop: 77 200 (2003 est). Area: 1793 sq km (692 sq miles)

ceremonial *Christianity* a the prescribed order of rites and ceremonies b a book containing this

Ceres[1] the Roman goddess of agriculture

Ceres[2] the largest asteroid and the first to be discovered. It has a diameter of 930 kilometres

cerise a a moderate to dark red colour b *(as adjective): a cerise scarf*

cerium a malleable ductile steel-grey element of the lanthanide series of metals, used in lighter flints and as a reducing agent in metallurgy. Symbol: Ce; atomic no.: 58; atomic wt.: 140.115; valency: 3 or 4; relative density: 6.770; melting pt.: 798°C; boiling pt.: 3443°C

CERN Conseil Européen pour la Recherche Nucléaire; an organization of European states with a centre in Geneva for research in high-energy particle physics, now called the European Laboratory for Particle Physics
▷http://public.web.cern.ch/public

Cernuda Luis 1902–63, Spanish poet. His major work is the autobiographical *Reality and Desire* (1936–64)

Cerro de Pasco a town in central Peru, in the Andes: one of the highest towns in the world, 4400 m (14 436 ft) above sea level; mining centre. Pop: 62 749 (1993)

certified *Law, Psychiatry* (of a person) declared legally insane

Cervantes Miguel de , full surname *Cervantes Saavedra.* 1547–1616, Spanish dramatist, poet, and prose writer, most famous for *Don Quixote* (1605), which satirizes the chivalric romances and greatly influenced the development of the novel

Cervin Mont the French name for the **Matterhorn**

cervix 1 the technical name for **neck** 2 any necklike part of an organ, esp the lower part of the uterus that extends into the vagina

cetacean 1 of, relating to, or belonging to the *Cetacea*, an order of aquatic placental mammals having no hind limbs and a blowhole for breathing: includes toothed whales (dolphins, porpoises, etc) and whalebone whales (rorquals, right whales, etc) 2 a whale

cetane a colourless insoluble liquid alkane hydrocarbon used in the determination of the cetane number of diesel fuel. Formula: $C_{16}H_{34}$

cetane number a measure of the quality of a diesel fuel expressed as the percentage of cetane in a mixture of cetane and 1-methylnapthalene of the same quality as the given fuel

Cetinje a city in Serbia and Montenegro, in SW Montenegro: former capital of Montenegro (until 1945); palace and fortified monastery, residences of Montenegrin prince-bishops. Pop: 15 924 (1991)

Cetshwayo *or* **Cetewayo** ?1826–84, king of the Zulus (1873–79): defeated the British at Isandhlwana (1879) but was overwhelmed by them at Ulundi (1879); captured, he stated his case in London, and was reinstated as ruler of part of Zululand (1883)

Ceuta an enclave in Morocco on the Strait of Gibraltar, consisting of a port and military station: held by Spain since 1580. Pop: 74 931 (2003 est)

Ceylon 1 the former name (until 1972) of **Sri Lanka** 2 an island in the Indian Ocean, off the SE coast of India: consists politically of the republic of Sri Lanka. Area: 64 644 sq km (24 959 sq miles)

Chablis a dry white burgundy wine made around Chablis, in central France

Chabrier (Alexis) Emmanuel 1841–94, French composer; noted esp for the orchestral rhapsody *España* (1883)

Chabrol Claude born 1930, French film director, whose films, such as *Le Beau Serge* (1958), *Les Biches* (1968), *Le Boucher* (1969), *Au coeur du mensonge* (1999), and *La Fleur du mal* (2003) explore themes of jealousy, guilt, and murder

chaconne 1 a musical form consisting of a set of continuous variations upon a ground bass 2 *Archaic* a dance in slow triple time probably originating in Spain

Chad 1 a republic in N central Africa: made a territory of French Equatorial Africa in 1910; became independent in 1960; contains much desert and the Tibesti Mountains, with Lake Chad in the west; produces chiefly cotton and livestock; suffered intermittent civil war from 1963 and prolonged drought. Official languages: Arabic; French. Religion: Muslim majority, also Christian and animist. Currency: franc. Capital:

Ndjamena. Pop: 8 854 000 (2004 est). Area: 1 284 000 sq km (495 750 sq miles) **2 Lake** a lake in N central Africa: fed chiefly by the Shari River, it has no apparent outlet. Area: at fullest extent 10 000 to 26 000 sq km (4000 to 10 000 sq miles), varying seasonally; it has shrunk considerably in recent years

Chadwick 1 Sir **Edwin** 1800–90, British social reformer, known for his *Report on the Sanitary Condition of the Labouring Population of Great Britain* (1842) **2** Sir **James** 1891–1974, British physicist: discovered the neutron (1932): Nobel prize for physics 1935 **3 Lynn (Russell).** born 1914, British sculptor in metal

chafer any of various scarabaeid beetles, such as the cockchafer and rose chafer

chaff the dry membranous bracts enclosing the flowers of certain composite plants

chaffinch a common European finch, *Fringilla coelebs*, with black and white wings and, in the male, a reddish body and blue-grey head

Chagall Marc 1887–1985, French painter and illustrator, born in Russia, noted for his richly coloured pictures of men, animals, and objects in fantastic combinations and often suspended in space: his work includes 12 stained glass windows for a synagogue in Jerusalem (1961) and the decorations for the ceiling of the Paris Opera House (1964)

chain 1 a set of metal links that fit over the tyre of a motor vehicle to increase traction and reduce skidding on an icy surface **2 a** a number of establishments such as hotels, shops, etc, having the same owner or management **b** (*as modifier*): *a chain store* **3** a series of deals in which each depends on a purchaser selling before being able to buy **4** *Logic* (of reasoning) a sequence of arguments each of which takes the conclusion of the preceding as a premise **5** a unit of length equal to 22 yards **6** a unit of length equal to 100 feet **7** *Chem* two or more atoms or groups bonded together so that the configuration of the resulting molecule, ion, or radical resembles a chain **8** *Geography* a series of natural features, esp approximately parallel mountain ranges

Chain Sir **Ernst Boris** 1906–79, British biochemist, born in Germany: purified and adapted penicillin for clinical use; with Fleming and Florey shared the Nobel prize for physiology or medicine 1945

chain gang *US* a group of convicted prisoners chained together, usually while doing hard labour

chain reaction 1 a process in which a neutron colliding with an atomic nucleus causes fission and the ejection of one or more other neutrons, which induce other nuclei to split **2** a chemical reaction in which the product of one step is a reactant in the following step

chain saw a motor-driven saw, usually portable, in which the cutting teeth form links in a continuous chain

chair 1 a professorship **2** *Railways* an iron or steel cradle bolted to a sleeper in which the rail sits and is locked in position **3** short for **sedan chair**

chaise a gold coin first issued in France in the 14th century, depicting the king seated on a throne

chalcedony a microcrystalline often greyish form of quartz with crystals arranged in parallel fibres: a gemstone. Formula: SiO_2

Chalcidice a peninsula of N central Greece, in Macedonia Central, ending in the three promontories of Kassandra, Sithonia, and Akti. Area: 2945 sq km (1149 sq miles)

Chalcis a city in SE Greece, at the narrowest point of the Euripus strait: important since the 7th century BC, founding many colonies in ancient times. Pop: 47 600 (1995 est)

Chaldea *or* **Chaldaea 1** an ancient region of Babylonia; the land lying between the Euphrates delta, the Persian Gulf, and the Arabian desert **2** another name for **Babylonia**

chalet a type of wooden house of Swiss origin, typically low, with wide projecting eaves **2** a similar house used esp as a ski lodge, garden house, etc.

Chaliapin Fyodor Ivanovich 1873–1938, Russian operatic bass singer

chalice 1 *Christianity* a gold or silver cup containing the wine at Mass **2** the calyx of a flower, esp a cup-shaped calyx

chalk 1 a soft fine-grained white sedimentary rock consisting of nearly pure calcium carbonate, containing minute fossil fragments of marine organisms, usually without a cementing material **2** *Billiards, Snooker* a small cube of prepared chalk or similar substance for rubbing the tip of a cue

challenge 1 *US* an assertion that a person is not entitled to vote or that a vote is invalid **2** *Law* a formal objection to a person selected to serve on a jury (**challenge to the polls**) or to the whole body of jurors (**challenge to the array**)

chalybeate 1 containing or impregnated with iron salts **2** any drug containing or tasting of iron

chamber 1 a reception room or audience room in an official residence, palace, etc. **2 a** a legislative, deliberative, judicial, or administrative assembly **b** any of the houses of a legislature **3** the space between two gates of the locks of a canal, dry dock, etc. **4** *Obsolete* a place where the money of a government, corporation, etc, was stored; treasury

chamberlain 1 an officer who manages the household of a king **2** the steward of a nobleman or landowner **3** the treasurer of a municipal corporation

Chamberlain 1 Sir **(Joseph)** Austen 1863–1937, British Conservative statesman; foreign secretary (1924–29); awarded a Nobel peace prize for his negotiation of the Locarno Pact (1925) **2** his father, **Joseph** 1836–1914, British statesman; originally a Liberal, he resigned in 1886 over Home Rule for Ireland and became leader of the Liberal Unionists; a leading advocate of preferential trading agreements with members of the British Empire **3** his son, **(Arthur) Neville** 1869–1940, British Conservative statesman; prime minister (1937–40): pursued a policy of appeasement towards Germany; following the German invasion of Poland, he declared war on Germany on Sept 3, 1939 **4 Owen** born 1920, US physicist, who discovered the antiproton. Nobel prize for physics jointly with Emilio Segré 1959

chamber music music for performance by a small group of instrumentalists

chameleon any lizard of the family *Chamaeleontidae* of Africa and Madagascar, having long slender legs, a prehensile tail and tongue, and the ability to change colour

chamois 1 a sure-footed goat antelope, *Rupicapra rupicapra*, inhabiting mountains of Europe and SW Asia, having vertical horns with backward-pointing tips 2 a soft suede leather formerly made from the hide of this animal, now obtained from the skins of sheep and goats 3 a yellow to greyish-yellow colour

Chamonix a town in SE France, in the Alps at the foot of Mont Blanc: skiing and tourist centre. Pop: 9830 (1999)

champagne 1 a white sparkling wine produced around Reims and Epernay, France 2 (loosely) any effervescent white wine 3 a a colour varying from a pale orange-yellow to a greyish-yellow b (*as adjective*): *a champagne carpet*

▷www.champagne.com

Champagne-Ardenne a region of NE France: a countship and commercial centre in medieval times; it consists of a great plain, with sheep and dairy farms and many vineyards

Champaigne Philippe de 1602–74, French painter, born in Brussels: noted particularly for his portraits and historical and religious scenes

Champigny-sur-Marne a suburb of Paris, on the River Marne. Pop: 74 237 (1999)

champion (formerly) a warrior or knight who did battle for another, esp a king or queen, to defend their rights or honour

Champlain¹ Samuel de ?1567–1635, French explorer; founder of Quebec (1608) and governor of New France (1633–35)

Champlain² Lake a lake in the northeastern US, between the Green Mountains and the Adirondack Mountains: linked by the **Champlain Canal** to the Hudson River and by the Richelieu River to the St Lawrence; a major communications route in colonial times

Champollion Jean François 1790–1832, French Egyptologist, who deciphered the hieroglyphics on the Rosetta stone

chancel the part of a church containing the altar, sanctuary, and choir, usually separated from the nave and transepts by a screen

chancellery or **chancellory** 1 the building or room occupied by a chancellor's office 2 the position, rank, or office of a chancellor 3 US a the residence or office of an embassy or legation b the office of a consulate

chancellor 1 the head of the government in several European countries 2 US the president of a university or, in some colleges, the chief administrative officer 3 *Brit and Canadian* the honorary head of a university 4 US (in some states) the presiding judge of a court of chancery or equity 5 *Brit* the chief secretary of an embassy 6 *Christianity* a clergyman acting as the law officer of a bishop 7 *Archaic* the chief secretary of a prince, nobleman, etc.

Chancellor of the Exchequer *Brit* the cabinet minister responsible for finance

chancre *Pathol* a small hard nodular growth, which is the first diagnostic sign of acquired syphilis

Chandernagore a port in E India, in S West Bengal on the Hooghly River: a former French settlement

(1686–1950). Pop: 162 166 (2001)

Chandigarh a city and Union Territory of N India, joint capital of the Punjab and Haryana: modern city planned in the 1950s by Le Corbusier. Pop: Pop: 808 796 (2001), of city; 900 414 (2001), of union territory. Area (of union territory): 114 sq km (44 sq miles).

chandler 1 a dealer in a specified trade or merchandise 2 a person who makes or sells candles 3 *Brit, obsolete* a retailer of grocery provisions; shopkeeper

Chandler Raymond (Thornton). 1888–1959, US thriller writer: created Philip Marlowe, one of the first detective heroes in fiction

Chandragupta Greek name *Sandracottos*. died ?297 BC, ruler of N India, who founded the Maurya dynasty (325) and defeated Seleucus (?305)

Chandrasekhar Subrahmanyan 1910–95, US astronomer born in Lahore, India (now Pakistan). His work on stellar evolution led to an understanding of white dwarfs: shared the Nobel prize for physics 1983

Chanel Gabrielle , known as *Coco Chanel*. 1883–1971, French couturière and perfumer, who created "the little black dress" and the perfume Chanel No. 5

Changchun or **Ch'ang Ch'un** a city in NE China, capital of Jilin province: as Hsinking, capital of the Japanese state of Manchukuo (1932–45). Pop: 3 092 000 (2005 est)

Changde, Changteh, or **Ch'ang-te** a port in SE central China, in N Hunan province, near the mouth of the Yuan River: severely damaged by the Japanese in World War II. Pop: 1 483 000 (2005 est)

change 1 money given or received in return for its equivalent in a larger denomination or in a different currency 2 the balance of money given or received when the amount tendered is larger than the amount due 3 *Archaic* a place where merchants meet to transact business; an exchange 4 *Astronomy* the transition from one phase of the moon to the next 5 the order in which a peal of bells may be rung 6 *Sport* short for **changeover**

changeling a child believed to have been exchanged by fairies for the parents' true child

changeover 1 *Sport* a the act of transferring to or being relieved by a team-mate in a relay race, as by handing over a baton, etc. b the point in a relay race at which the transfer is made 2 *Sport, chiefly Brit* the exchange of ends by two teams, esp at half time

change up *Baseball* an unexpectedly slow ball thrown in order to surprise the batter

Changsha or **Ch'ang-sha** a port in SE China, capital of Hunan province, on the Xiang River. Pop: 2 051 000 (2005 est)

Chania or **Hania** the chief port of Crete, on the NW coast. Pop: 82 000 (2005 est)

channel¹ 1 a broad strait connecting two areas of sea 2 the bed or course of a river, stream, or canal 3 a navigable course through a body of water 4 *Electronics* a a band of radio frequencies assigned for a particular purpose, esp the broadcasting of a television signal b a path for an electromagnetic signal c a thin semiconductor layer between the source and drain of a field-effect transistor, the conductance of which is controlled by the gate voltage 5 a groove or flute, as in the shaft of a column 6 *Computing* a a path along which data can be transmitted between a central processing unit and one or more peripheral devices **b** one of the lines along the length of a paper tape on which information can be stored in the form of punched holes

channel² *Nautical* a flat timber or metal ledge projecting from the hull of a vessel above the chainplates to increase the angle of the shrouds

Channel the short for **English Channel**

Channel Country the an area of E central Australia, in SW Queensland: crossed by intermittent rivers and subject to both flooding and long periods of drought

chant **1** a simple song or melody **2** a short simple melody in which several words or syllables are assigned to one note, as in the recitation of psalms **3** a psalm or canticle performed by using such a melody

chanter the pipe on a set of bagpipes that is provided with finger holes and on which the melody is played

chanticleer *or* **chantecler** a name for a cock, used esp in fables

Chantilly **1** a town in N France, near the **Forest of Chantilly** formerly famous for lace and porcelain. Pop: 10 902 (1999) **2** a breed of medium-sized cat with silky semi-long hair

chaos the disordered formless matter supposed to have existed before the ordered universe

chaos theory a theory, applied in various branches of science, that apparently random phenomena have underlying order

chap a cracked or sore patch on the skin caused by chapping

chapel **1** a place of Christian worship in a larger building, esp a place set apart, with a separate altar, in a church or cathedral **2** a similar place of worship in or attached to a large house or institution, such as a college, hospital or prison **3** a church subordinate to a parish church **4** in Britain **a** a Nonconformist place of worship **b** Nonconformist religious practices or doctrine **c** (*as adjective*): *he is chapel, but his wife is church* **5** (in Scotland) a Roman Catholic church

chaplain a Christian clergyman attached to a private chapel of a prominent person or institution or ministering to a military body, professional group, etc

chaplet **1** *RC Church* **a** a string of prayer beads constituting one third of the rosary **b** the prayers counted on this string **2** a narrow convex moulding in the form of a string of beads; astragal **3** a metal support for the core in a casting mould, esp for the core of a cylindrical pipe

Chaplin Sir **Charles Spencer**, known as *Charlie Chaplin*. 1889–1977, English comedian, film actor, and director. He is renowned for his portrayal of a downtrodden little man with baggy trousers, bowler hat, and cane. His films, most of which were made in Hollywood, include *The Gold Rush* (1924), *Modern Times* (1936), and *The Great Dictator* (1940)

chapman *Archaic* a trader, esp an itinerant pedlar

Chapman George 1559–1634, English dramatist and poet, noted for his translation of Homer

Chappell Greg(ory Stephen). born 1948, Australian cricketer: first Australian to score over 7000 test runs

chapter **1** a numbered reference to that part of a Parliamentary session which relates to a specified Act of Parliament **2** the collective body or a meeting of the canons of a cathedral or collegiate church or of the

members of a monastic or knightly order **3** a general assembly of some organization

char *or* **charr** any of various troutlike fishes of the genus *Salvelinus*, esp *S. alpinus*, occurring in cold lakes and northern seas: family *Salmonidae* (salmon)

character **1** a person represented in a play, film, story, etc.; role **2** *Computing* any letter, numeral, etc, which is a unit of information and can be represented uniquely by a binary pattern **3** *Genetics* any structure, function, attribute, etc, in an organism, which may or may not be determined by a gene or group of genes **4** a short prose sketch of a distinctive type of person, usually representing a vice or virtue

characteristic *Maths* **a** the integral part of a common logarithm, indicating the order of magnitude of the associated number **b** another name for **exponent** (esp in number representation in computing)

charade an episode or act in the game of charades

charades a parlour game in which one team acts out each syllable of a word, the other team having to guess the word

charcoal **1** a black amorphous form of carbon made by heating wood or other organic matter in the absence of air: used as a fuel, in smelting metal ores, in explosives, and as an absorbent **2** a stick or pencil of this for drawing **3** a drawing done in charcoal

Charcot Jean Martin 1825–93, French neurologist, noted for his attempt using hypnotism to find an organic cause for hysteria, which influenced Freud

Chardin Jean-Baptiste Siméon 1699–1779, French still-life and genre painter, noted for his subtle use of scumbled colour

Chardonnay **1** a white grape originally grown in the Burgundy region of France, and now throughout the wine-producing world **2** any of various white wines made from this grape

Chardonnet (Louis Marie) **Hilaire Bernigaud**, Comte de. 1839–1924, French chemist and industrialist who produced rayon, the first artificial fibre

Charente **1** a department of W central France, in Poitou-Charentes region. Capital: Angoulême. Pop: 341 275 (2003 est). Area: 5972 sq km (2329 sq miles) **2** a river in W France, flowing west to the Bay of Biscay. Length: 362 km (225 miles)

Charente-Maritime a department of W France, in Poitou-Charentes region. Capital: La Rochelle. Pop: 576 855 (2003 est). Area: 7232 sq km (2820 sq miles)

charge **1** a price charged for some article or service; cost **2** an accusation or allegation, such as a formal accusation of a crime in law **3** *Physics* **a** the attribute of matter by which it responds to electromagnetic forces responsible for all electrical phenomena, existing in two forms to which the signs negative and positive are arbitrarily assigned **b** a similar property of a body or system determined by the extent to which it contains an excess or deficiency of electrons **c** a quantity of electricity determined by the product of an electric current and the time for which it flows, measured in coulombs **d** the total amount of electricity stored in a capacitor **e** the total amount of electricity held in an accumulator, usually measured in ampere-hours. **4** *Law* the address made by a judge to the jury at the conclusion of the evidence

charger¹ a device for charging or recharging an accumulator or rechargeable battery

charger² *Antiques* a large dish for serving at table or for display

Chari *or* **Shari** a river in N central Africa, rising in the N Central African Republic and flowing north to Lake Chad. Length: about 2250 km (1400 miles)

Charing Cross a district of London, in the city of Westminster: the modern cross (1863) in front of Charing Cross railway station replaces the one erected by Edward I (1290), the last of twelve marking the route of the funeral procession of his queen, Eleanor

chariot a two-wheeled horse-drawn vehicle used in ancient Egypt, Greece, Rome, etc, in war, races, and processions

charisma *or* **charism** *Christianity* a divinely bestowed power or talent

charismatic movement *Christianity* any of various groups, within existing denominations, that emphasize communal prayer and the charismatic gifts of speaking in tongues, healing, etc.

charity 1 a the giving of help, money, food, etc, to those in need **b** (*as modifier*): *a charity show* **2 a** an institution or organization set up to provide help, money, etc, to those in need **b** (*as modifier*): *charity funds* **3** the help, money, etc, given to the needy; alms

Charlemagne ?742–814 AD, king of the Franks (768–814) and, as Charles I, Holy Roman Emperor (800–814). He conquered the Lombards (774), the Saxons (772–804), and the Avars (791–799). He instituted many judicial and ecclesiastical reforms, and promoted commerce and agriculture throughout his empire, which extended from the Ebro to the Elbe. Under Alcuin his court at Aachen became the centre of a revival of learning

Charles 1 *Prince of Wales.* born 1948, son of Elizabeth II; heir apparent to the throne of Great Britain and Northern Ireland. He married (1981) Lady Diana Spencer; they separated in 1992 and were divorced in 1996; their son, Prince William of Wales, was born in 1982 and their second son, Prince Henry, in 1984. He (2005) married Camilla Parker Bowles **2 Ray** real name *Ray Charles Robinson.* 1930–2004, US singer, pianist, and songwriter, whose work spans jazz, blues, gospel, pop, and country music

Charles I 1 title as Holy Roman Emperor of Charlemagne **2** title as king of France of **Charles II** (Holy Roman Emperor) **3** title as king of Spain of **Charles V** (Holy Roman Emperor) **4** title of **Charles Stuart** 1600–49, king of England, Scotland, and Ireland (1625–49); son of James I. He ruled for 11 years (1629–40) without parliament, advised by his minister Strafford, until rebellion broke out in Scotland. Conflict with the Long Parliament led to the Civil War and after his defeat at Naseby (1645) he sought refuge with the Scots (1646). He was handed over to the English army under Cromwell (1647) and executed **5** 1887–1922, emperor of Austria, and, as Charles IV, king of Hungary (1916–18). The last ruler of the Austro-Hungarian monarchy, he was forced to abdicate at the end of World War I

Charles II 1 known as *Charles the Bald.* 823–877 AD, Holy Roman Emperor (875–877) and, as Charles I, king of

France (843–877) **2** the title as king of France of **Charles III** (Holy Roman Emperor) **3** 1630–85, king of England, Scotland, and Ireland (1660–85) following the Restoration (1660); son of Charles I. He did much to promote commerce, science, and the Navy, but his Roman Catholic sympathies caused widespread distrust **4** 1661–1700, the last Hapsburg king of Spain: his reign saw the end of Spanish power in Europe

Charles III 1 known as *Charles the Fat.* 839–888 AD, Holy Roman Emperor (881–887) and, as Charles II, king of France (884–887). He briefly reunited the empire of Charlemagne **2** 1716–88, king of Spain (1759–88), who curbed the power of the Church and tried to modernize his country

Charles IV 1 known as *Charles the Fair.* 1294–1328, king of France (1322–28): brother of Isabella of France, with whom he intrigued against her husband, Edward II of England **2** 1316–78, king of Bohemia (1346–78) and Holy Roman Emperor (1355–78) **3** 1748–1819, king of Spain (1788–1808), whose reign saw the domination of Spain by Napoleonic France: abdicated **4** title as king of Hungary of **Charles I** (sense 5)

charleston a fast rhythmic dance of the 1920s, characterized by kicking and by twisting of the legs from the knee down

Charleston 1 a city in central West Virginia: the state capital. Pop: 51 394 (2003 est) **2** a port in SE South Carolina, on the Atlantic: scene of the first action in the Civil War. Pop: 101 024 (2003 est)

Charles V 1 known as *Charles the Wise.* 1337–80, king of France (1364–80) during the Hundred Years' War **2** 1500–58, Holy Roman Emperor (1519–56), king of Burgundy and the Netherlands (1506–55), and, as Charles I, king of Spain (1516–56): his reign saw the empire threatened by Francis I of France, the Turks, and the spread of Protestantism; abdicated

Charles VI 1 known as *Charles the Mad* or *Charles the Well-Beloved.* 1368- -1422, king of France (1380–1422): defeated by Henry V of England at Agincourt (1415), he was forced by the Treaty of Troyes (1420) to recognize Henry as his successor **2** 1685–1740, Holy Roman Emperor (1711–40). His claim to the Spanish throne (1700) led to the War of the Spanish Succession

Charles VII 1 1403–61, king of France (1422–61), son of Charles VI. He was excluded from the French throne by the Treaty of Troyes, but following Joan of Arc's victory over the English at Orléans (1429), was crowned **2** 1697–1745, Holy Roman Emperor (1742–45) during the War of the Austrian Succession

Charles IX 1550–74, king of France (1560–74), son of Catherine de' Medici and Henry II: his reign was marked by war between Huguenots and Catholics

Charles X 1 title of *Charles Gustavus.* 1622–60, king of Sweden, who warred with Poland and Denmark in an attempt to create a unified Baltic state **2** 1757–1836, king of France (1824–30): his attempt to restore absolutism led to his enforced exile

Charles XIV the title as king of Sweden and Norway of (Jean Baptiste Jules) Bernadotte

Charles Martel grandfather of Charlemagne. ?688–741 AD, Frankish ruler of Austrasia (715–41), who checked the Muslim invasion of Europe by defeating the Moors at Poitiers (732)

charlock 1 a weedy Eurasian plant, *Sinapis arvensis* (or *Brassica kaber*), with hairy stems and foliage and yellow flowers: family: *Brassicaceae* (crucifers) 2 **white charlock** a related plant, *Raphanus raphanistrum*, with yellow, mauve, or white flowers and podlike fruits

Charlotte a city in S North Carolina: the largest city in the state. Pop: 584 658 (2003 est)

Charlotte Amalie the capital of the Virgin Islands of the United States, a port on St Thomas Island. Pop: 18 914 (2000)

Charlottenburg a district of Berlin (of West Berlin until 1990), formerly an independent city. Pop: 145 564 (latest est)

Charlottetown a port in SE Canada, capital of the province of Prince Edward Island. Pop: 38 114 (2001)

Charlton 1 **Bobby**, full name *Sir Robert Charlton*. born 1937, English footballer; played for England over 100 times 2 his brother, **Jack**, full name *John Charlton*. born 1935, English footballer; played for Leeds United (1952–73) and England; manager of the Republic of Ireland soccer team (1986–95)

charm *Physics* an internal quantum number of certain elementary particles, used to explain some scattering experiments

Charnley Sir **John** 1911–82, British surgeon noted for his invention of an artificial hip joint and his development of hip-replacement surgery

Charpentier 1 **Gustave** 1860–1956, French composer, whose best-known work is the opera *Louise* (1900) 2 **Marc-Antoine** ?1645–1704, French composer, best known for his sacred music, particularly the *Te Deum*

chart 1 a map designed to aid navigation by sea or air 2 an outline map, esp one on which weather information is plotted 3 a sheet giving graphical, tabular, or diagrammatical information 4 another name for **graph** 5 *Astrology* another word for **horoscope**

charter 1 a formal document from the sovereign or state incorporating a city, bank, college, etc, and specifying its purposes and rights 2 a formal document granting or demanding from the sovereign power of a state certain rights or liberties 3 the fundamental principles of an organization; constitution 4 **a** the hire or lease of transportation **b** the agreement or contract regulating this **c** (*as modifier*): *a charter flight* 5 a law, policy, or decision containing a loophole which allows a specified group to engage more easily in an activity considered undesirable

Charteris **Leslie**, original name *Leslie Charles Bowyer Yin*. 1907–93, British novelist, born in Singapore: created the character Simon Templar, known as The Saint, the central character in many adventure novels

Chartism *English history* the principles of the reform movement in England from 1838 to 1848, which included manhood suffrage, payment of Members of Parliament, equal electoral districts, annual parliaments, voting by ballot, and the abolition of property qualifications for MPs

Chartres a city in NW France: Gothic cathedral; market town. Pop: 40 361 (1999)

chartreuse 1 either of two liqueurs, green or yellow, made from herbs and flowers 2 **a** a colour varying from a clear yellowish-green to a strong greenish-yellow **b** (*as adjective*): *a chartreuse dress*

Charybdis a ship-devouring monster in classical mythology, identified with a whirlpool off the north coast of Sicily, lying opposite Scylla on the Italian coast

chase 1 *Brit* an unenclosed area of land where wild animals are preserved to be hunted 2 *Brit* the right to hunt a particular quarry over the land of others 3 **the chase** the act or sport of hunting 4 short for **steeplechase** 5 *Real Tennis* a ball that bounces twice, requiring the point to be played again

chaser¹ a drink drunk after another of a different kind, as beer after spirits

chaser² a lathe cutting tool for accurately finishing a screw thread, having a cutting edge consisting of several repetitions of the thread form

chasm a deep cleft in the ground; abyss

chassis 1 the steel frame, wheels, engine, and mechanical parts of a motor vehicle, to which the body is attached 2 *Electronics* a mounting for the circuit components of an electrical or electronic device, such as a radio or television 3 the landing gear of an aircraft

chasuble *Christianity* a long sleeveless outer vestment worn by a priest when celebrating Mass

chat¹ 1 any Old World songbird of the subfamily *Turdinae* (thrushes, etc) having a harsh chattering cry 2 any of various North American warblers, such as *Icteria virens* (**yellow-breasted chat**) 3 any of various Australian wrens (family *Muscicapidae*) of the genus *Ephthianura* and other genera

chat² *Archaic or dialect* a catkin, esp a willow catkin

chateau *or* **château** 1 a country house, castle, or manor house, esp in France 2 (in Quebec) the residence of a seigneur or (formerly) a governor 3 (in the name of a wine) estate or vineyard

Chateaubriand **François René**, Vicomte de Chateaubriand. 1768–1848, French writer and statesman: a precursor of the romantic movement in France; his works include *Le Génie du Christianisme* (1802) and *Mémoires d'outre-tombe* (1849–50)

Chatham¹ **1st Earl of** title of the elder (William) **Pitt**

Chatham² 1 a town in SE England, in N Kent on the River Medway: formerly royal naval dockyard. Pop: 73 468 (2001) 2 a city in SE Canada, in SE Ontario on the Thames River. Pop: 44 156 (2001)

Chattanooga a city in SE Tennessee, on the Tennessee River: scene of two battles during the Civil War, in which the North defeated the Confederates, cleared Tennessee, and opened the way to Georgia (1863). Pop: 154 887 (2003 est)

chatter the undulating pattern of marks in a machined surface from the vibration of the tool or workpiece

Chatterton **Thomas** 1752–70, British poet; author of spurious medieval verse and prose: he committed suicide at the age of 17

Chaucer **Geoffrey** ?1340–1400, English poet, noted for his narrative skill, humour, and insight, particularly in his most famous work, *The Canterbury Tales*. He was influenced by the continental tradition of rhyming verse. His other works include *Troilus and Criseyde*, *The Legende of Good Women*, and *The Parlement of Foules*

cheat *Law* the obtaining of another's property by fraudulent means

Cheb a town in the W Czech Republic, in W Bohemia on the Ohře River: 12th-century castle where Wallenstein was murdered (1634); a centre of the Sudeten-German movement after World War I. Pop: 31 847 (1991)

Cheboksary a port in W central Russia on the River Volga: capital of the Chuvash Republic. Pop: 446 000 (2005 est)

check 1 a fabric with a pattern of squares or crossed lines **b** (*as modifier*): *a check suit* **2** *Chess* the state or position of a king under direct attack, from which it must be moved or protected by another piece **3** part of the action of a piano that arrests the backward motion of a hammer after it has struck a string and holds it until the key is released **4** a chip or counter used in some card and gambling games **5** *Hunting* a pause by the hounds in the pursuit of their quarry owing to loss of its scent **6** *Angling* a ratchet fitted to a fishing reel to check the free running of the line **7** *Ice hockey* the act of impeding an opponent with one's body or stick

checkers *US and Canadian* a game for two players using a checkerboard and 12 checkers each. The object is to jump over and capture the opponent's pieces

checkmate *Chess* **a** the winning position in which an opponent's king is under attack and unable to escape **b** the move by which this position is achieved

checkup *Med* a medical examination, esp one taken at regular intervals to verify a normal state of health or discover a disease in its early stages

Cheddar a village in SW England, in N Somerset: situated near **Cheddar Gorge**, a pass through the Mendip Hills renowned for its stalactitic caverns and rare limestone flora. Pop: 4796 (2001)

cheek 1 a either side of the face, esp that part below the eye **b** either side of the oral cavity; side of the mouth **2** a side of a door jamb **3** *Nautical* one of the two fore-and-aft supports for the trestletrees on a mast of a sailing vessel, forming part of the hounds **4** one of the jaws of a vice

cheesecloth a loosely woven cotton cloth formerly used only for wrapping cheese

cheetah or **chetah** a large feline mammal, *Acinonyx jubatus*, of Africa and SW Asia: the swiftest mammal, having very long legs, nonretractile claws, and a black-spotted light-brown coat

Cheever John 1912–82, US novelist and short-story writer. His novels include *The Wapshot Chronicle* (1957) and *Bullet Park* (1969)

Cheju a volcanic island in the N East China Sea, southwest of Korea: constitutes a province (Cheju-do) of South Korea. Capital: Cheju. Pop: 302 000 (2005 est). Area: 1792 sq km (692 sq miles)

Chekhov or **Chekov** Anton Pavlovich 1860–1904, Russian dramatist and short-story writer. His plays include *The Seagull* (1896), *Uncle Vanya* (1900), *The Three Sisters* (1901), and *The Cherry Orchard* (1904)

Chelmsford a city in SE England, administrative centre of Essex: electronics, retail; university (1992). Pop: 99 962 (2001)

Chelsea a residential district of SW London, in the Royal Borough of Kensington and Chelsea: site of the Chelsea Royal Hospital for old and invalid soldiers (Chelsea Pensioners)

Cheltenham a town in W England, in central Gloucestershire: famous for its schools, racecourse, and saline springs (discovered in 1716). Pop: 98 875 (2001)

Chelyabinsk an industrial city in SW Russia. Pop: 1 067 000 (2005 est)

Chelyuskin Cape a cape in N central Russia, in N Siberia at the end of the Taimyr Peninsula: the northernmost point of Asia

chemical any substance used in or resulting from a reaction involving changes to atoms or molecules, especially one derived artificially for practical use

chemical engineering the branch of engineering concerned with the design, operation, maintenance, and manufacture of the plant and machinery used in industrial chemical processes
▷www.che.ufl.edu/www-che

chemin de fer a gambling game, a variation of baccarat

chemist 1 *Brit* a shop selling medicines, cosmetics, etc. **2** *Brit* a qualified dispenser of prescribed medicines **3** a person studying, trained in, or engaged in chemistry

chemistry 1 the branch of physical science concerned with the composition, properties, and reactions of substances **2** the composition, properties, and reactions of a particular substance
▷www.chemweb.com
▷www.psigate.ac.uk/newsite
▷http://people.ouc.bc.ca/woodcock/
  nomenclature/index-2.htm
▷www.psigate.ac.uk/newsite/reference/
  periodic-table.html

Chemnitz a city in E Germany, in Saxony, at the foot of the Erzgebirge: textiles, engineering. Pop: 249 922 (2003 est)

chemotherapy treatment of disease, esp cancer, by means of chemical agents

Chenab a river rising in the Himalayas and flowing southwest to the Sutlej River in Pakistan. Length: 1087 km (675 miles)

Cheney Richard B(ruce), known as *Dick*. born 1941, US Republican politician; vice-president from 2001

Chengde, Chengteh, or **Ch'eng-te** a city in NE China, in Hebei on the Luan River: summer residence of the Manchu emperors. Pop: 470 000 (2005 est)

Chengdu, Chengtu, or **Ch'eng-tu** a city in S central China, capital of Sichuan province. Pop: 3 478 000 (2005 est)

chenille 1 a thick soft tufty silk or worsted velvet cord or yarn used in embroidery and for trimmings, etc. **2** a fabric of such yarn

Cheops original name *Khufu*. Egyptian king of the fourth dynasty (?2613–?2494 BC), who built the largest pyramid at El Gîza

Chepstow a town in S Wales, in Monmouthshire on the River Wye: tourism, light industry. Pop: 10 821 (2001)

chequer or US **checker** any of the marbles, pegs, or other pieces used in the game of Chinese chequers

Cher 1 a department of central France, in E Centre region. Capital: Bourges. Pop: 312 277 (2003 est). Area: 7304 sq km (2849 sq miles) **2** a river in central France, rising in the Massif Central and flowing northwest to the Loire. Length: 354 km (220 miles)

Cherbourg a port in NW France, on the English Channel. Pop: 25 370 (1999)

Cherenkov or **Cerenkov** Pavel Alekseyevich 1904–90, Soviet physicist: noted for work on the effects produced by high-energy particles: shared Nobel prize for physics 1958

Chernenko Konstantin (**Ustinovich**). 1911–85, Soviet statesman; general secretary of the Soviet Communist Party (1984–85)

Chernobyl a town in N Ukraine; site of a nuclear power station accident in 1986

Chernovtsy a city in Ukraine on the Prut River: formerly under Polish, Austro-Hungarian, and Romanian rule; part of the Soviet Union (1947–91). Pop: 237 000 (2005 est)

Cherokee 1 a member of a North American Indian people formerly living in and around the Appalachian Mountains, now chiefly in Oklahoma; one of the Iroquois peoples 2 the language of this people, belonging to the Iroquoian family

cherry 1 any of several trees of the rosaceous genus *Prunus*, such as *P. avium* (**sweet cherry**), having a small fleshy rounded fruit containing a hard stone 2 the fruit or wood of any of these trees 3 any of various unrelated plants, such as the ground cherry and Jerusalem cherry 4 of or relating to the cherry fruit or wood 5 a a bright red colour; cerise b (*as adjective*): *a cherry coat*

Chertsey a town in S England, in N Surrey on the River Thames. Pop: 10 323 (2001)

cherub *Theol* a member of the second order of angels, whose distinctive gift is knowledge, often represented as a winged child or winged head of a child

Cherubini (**Maria**) **Luigi** (**Carlo Zenobio Salvatore**). 1760–1842, Italian composer, noted particularly for his church music and his operas.

chervil 1 an aromatic umbelliferous Eurasian plant, *Anthriscus cerefolium*, with small white flowers and aniseed-flavoured leaves used as herbs in soups and salads 2 **bur chervil** a similar and related plant, *Anthriscus caucalis* 3 a related plant, *Chaerophyllum temulentum*, having a hairy purple-spotted stem

Cherwell 1st Viscount title of *Frederick Alexander Lindemann*. 1886–1957, British physicist, born in Germany, noted for his research on heat capacity, aeronautics, and atomic physics. He was scientific adviser to Winston Churchill during World War II

Chesapeake Bay the largest inlet of the Atlantic in the coast of the US: bordered by Maryland and Virginia

Cheshire[1] Group Captain (**Geoffrey**) **Leonard** 1917–92, British philanthropist: awarded the Victoria Cross in World War II; founded the Leonard Cheshire Foundation Homes for the Disabled: married Sue, Baroness Ryder

Cheshire[2] a county of NW England: low-lying and undulating, bordering on the Pennines in the east; mainly agricultural: the geographic and ceremonial county includes Warrington and Halton, which became independent unitary authorities in 1998. Administrative centre: Chester. Pop. (excluding unitary authorities): 678 700 (2003 est). Area (excluding unitary authorites): 2077 sq km (802 sq miles)

chess[1] a game of skill for two players using a chessboard on which chessmen are moved. Initially each player has one king, one queen, two rooks, two bishops, two knights, and eight pawns, which have different types of moves according to kind. The object is to checkmate the opponent's king
▷www.fide.com

chess[2] a floorboard of the deck of a pontoon bridge
▷www.fide.com

chessboard a square board divided into 64 squares of two alternating colours, used for playing chess or draughts

chessman any of the eight pieces and eight pawns used by each player in a game of chess

chest 1 a the front part of the trunk from the neck to the belly b (*as modifier*): *a chest cold* 2 a sealed container or reservoir for a gas

Chester a city in NW England, administrative centre of Cheshire, on the River Dee: intact surrounding walls; 16th- and 17th-century double-tier shops. Pop: 80 121 (2001)

Chesterfield[1] Philip Dormer Stanhope, 4th Earl of Chesterfield. 1694–1773, English statesman and writer, noted for his elegance, suavity, and wit; author of *Letters to His Son* (1774)

Chesterfield[2] an industrial town in N central England, in Derbyshire: famous 14th-century church with twisted spire. Pop: 70 260 (2001)

Chesterton G(ilbert) K(eith). 1874–1936, English essayist, novelist, poet, and critic

chestnut 1 any N temperate fagaceous tree of the genus *Castanea*, such as *C. sativa* (**sweet** or **Spanish chestnut**), which produce flowers in long catkins and nuts in a prickly bur 2 the hard wood of any of these trees, used in making furniture, etc. 3 a a reddish-brown to brown colour b (*as adjective*): *chestnut hair* 4 a horse of a yellow-brown or golden-brown colour 5 a small horny callus on the inner surface of a horse's leg

chevalier 1 a member of certain orders of merit, such as the French Legion of Honour 2 *French history* a a mounted soldier or knight, esp a military cadet b the lowest title of rank in the old French nobility

Chevalier 1 Albert 1861–1923, British music hall entertainer, remembered for his cockney songs 2 **Maurice** 1888–1972, French singer and film actor

Cheviot 1 a large British breed of sheep reared for its wool 2 a rough twill-weave woollen suiting fabric

chevron an ornamental moulding having a zigzag pattern

Cheyenne a city in SE Wyoming, capital of the state. Pop: 54 374 (2003 est)

Chiang Ching-kuo or **Jiang Jing Guo** 1910–88, Chinese statesman; the son of Chiang Kai-shek. He was prime minister of Taiwan (1971–78); president (1978–88)

Chiang Kai-shek or **Jiang Jie Shi** original name *Chiang Chung-cheng*, 1887–1975, Chinese general: president of China (1928–31; 1943–49) and of the Republic of China (Taiwan) (1950–75). As chairman of the Kuomintang, he allied with the Communists against the Japanese (1937–45), but in the Civil War that followed was forced to withdraw to Taiwan after his defeat by the Communists (1949)

chianti a dry red wine produced in the Chianti region of Italy

Chiapas a state of S Mexico: mountainous and forested; Maya ruins in the northeast; rich mineral resources. Capital: Tuxtla Gutiérrez. Pop: 3 920 515 (2000). Area: 73 887 sq km (28 816 sq miles)

chiaroscuro *Art* **1** the artistic distribution of light and dark masses in a picture **2** monochrome painting using light and dark only, as in grisaille

Chiba an industrial city in central Japan, in SE Honshu on Tokyo Bay. Pop: 880 164 (2002 est)

Chicago a port in NE Illinois, on Lake Michigan: the third largest city in the US; it is a major railway and air traffic centre. Pop: 2 869 121 (2003 est)

chicane 1 a bridge or whist hand without trumps **2** *Motor racing* a short section of sharp narrow bends formed by barriers placed on a motor-racing circuit to provide an additional test of driving skill

Chichagof Island an island of Alaska, in the Alexander Archipelago. Area: 5439 sq km (2100 sq miles)

Chichester¹ Sir Francis 1901–72, British yachtsman, who sailed alone round the world in *Gipsy Moth IV* (1966–67)

Chichester² a city in S England, administrative centre of West Sussex: Roman ruins; 11th-century cathedral; Festival Theatre. Pop: 27 477 (2001)

chick the young of a bird, esp of a domestic fowl

chicken 1 a domestic fowl bred for its flesh or eggs, esp a young one **2** any of various similar birds, such as a prairie chicken **3** *Informal* any of various, often danger-ous, games or challenges in which the object is to make one's opponent lose his nerve

chickenpox a highly communicable viral disease most commonly affecting children, characterized by slight fever and the eruption of a rash

chickpea a bushy leguminous plant, *Cicer arietinum*, cul-tivated for its edible pealike seeds in the Mediterranean region, central Asia, and Africa

chickweed 1 any of various caryophyllaceous plants of the genus *Stellaria*, esp *S. media*, a common garden weed with small white flowers **2** **mouse-ear chickweed** any of various similar and related plants of the genus *Cerastium*

Chiclayo a city in NW Peru. Pop: 434 000 (2005 est)

chicory a blue-flowered plant, *Cichorium intybus*, cultivat-ed for its leaves, which are used in salads, and for its roots: family *Asteraceae* (composites)

chieftain the head or leader of a tribe or clan

chiffchaff a common European warbler, *Phylloscopus collybita*, with a yellowish-brown plumage

chiffon 1 a fine transparent or almost transparent plain-weave fabric of silk, nylon, etc. **2** made of chiffon

Chifley Joseph Benedict 1885–1951, Australian states-man; prime minister of Australia (1945–49)

chigoe a tropical flea, *Tunga penetrans*, the female of which lives on or burrows into the skin of its host, which includes man

Chigwell a town in S England, in W Essex. Pop: 10 128 (2001)

Chihli *Gulf of* another name for the **Bohai**

Chihuahua 1 a state of N Mexico: mostly high plateau;

important mineral resources, with many silver mines. Capital: Chihuahua. Pop: 728 000 (2005 est). Area: 247 087 sq km (153 194 sq miles). **2** a city in N Mexico, capital of Chihuahua state. Pop: 650 000 (2000 est) **3** a breed of tiny dog originally from Mexico, having short smooth hair, large erect ears, and protruding eyes

chilblain *Pathol* an inflammation of the fingers, toes, or ears, caused by prolonged exposure to moisture and cold

child benefit (in Britain and New Zealand) a regular government payment to the parents of children up to a certain age

Childers (Robert) Erskine 1870–1922, Irish politician, executed by the Irish Free State for his IRA activities: author of the spy story *The Riddle of the Sands* (1903)

Chile a republic in South America, on the Pacific, with a total length of about 4090 km (2650 miles) and an aver-age width of only 177 km (110 miles): gained indepen-dence from Spain in 1818; the government of President Allende (elected 1970) attempted the implementation of Marxist policies within a democratic system until overthrown by a military coup (1973); democracy restored 1988. Chile consists chiefly of the Andes in the east, the Atacama Desert in the north, a central fertile region, and a huge S region of almost uninhabitable mountains, glaciers, fjords, and islands; an important producer of copper, iron ore, nitrates, etc. Language: Spanish. Religion: Roman Catholic majority. Currency: peso. Capital: Santiago. Pop: 15 997 000 (2004 est). Area: 756 945 sq km (292 256 sq miles).

chill 1 a feverish cold **2** a metal plate placed in a sand mould to accelerate cooling and control local grain growth

Chilpancingo a town in S Mexico, capital of Guerrero state, in the Sierra Madre del Sur. Pop: 166 000 (2005 est)

Chilung *or* **Chi-lung** a port in N Taiwan: fishing and industrial centre. Pop: 406 000 (2005 est)

Chimborazo an extinct volcano in central Ecuador, in the Andes: the highest peak in Ecuador. Height: 6267 m (20 561 ft)

Chimbote a port in N central Peru: contains Peru's first steelworks (1958), using hydroelectric power from the Santa River. Pop: 328 000 (2005 est)

chime¹ 1 an individual bell or the sound it makes when struck **2** the machinery employed to sound a bell in this way **3** a percussion instrument consisting of a set of vertical metal tubes of graduated length, suspended in a frame and struck with a hammer

chime², **chimb**, *or* **chine** the projecting edge or rim of a cask or barrel

chimera *or* **chimaera 1** *Greek myth* a fire-breathing monster with the head of a lion, body of a goat, and tail of a serpent **2** a fabulous beast made up of parts taken from various animals **3** *Biology* an organism, esp a cul-tivated plant, consisting of at least two genetically dif-ferent kinds of tissue as a result of mutation, grafting, etc.

Chimkent a city in S Kazakhstan; a major railway junc-tion. Pop: 469 000 (2005 est)

chimney 1 *Geology* **a** a cylindrical body of an ore, which is usually oriented vertically **b** the vent of a volcano **2**

Mountaineering a vertical fissure large enough for a person's body to enter

chimpanzee a gregarious and intelligent anthropoid ape, *Pan troglodytes*, inhabiting forests in central W Africa

chin 1 the protruding part of the lower jaw **2** the front part of the face below the lips

china 1 ceramic ware of a type originally from China **2** any porcelain or similar ware **3** cups, saucers, etc, collectively **4** made of china
▷http://entertainment.howstuffworks.com/lenox.htm
▷www.pbs.org/wgbh/pages/roadshow/speak/china.html
▷www.netcentral.co.uk/steveb/types/bonechina.htm

China 1 People's Republic of Also called: **Communist China, Red China** a republic in E Asia: the third largest and the most populous country in the world; the oldest continuing civilization (beginning over 2000 years BC); republic established in 1911 after the overthrow of the Manchu dynasty by Sun Yat-sen; People's Republic formed in 1949; the 1980s and 1990s saw economic liberalization but a rejection of political reform; contains vast deserts, steppes, great mountain ranges (Himalayas, Kunlun, Tian Shan, and Nan Shan), a central rugged plateau, and intensively cultivated E plains. Language: Chinese in various dialects, the chief of which is Mandarin. Religion: nonreligious majority; Buddhist and Taoist minorities. Currency: yuan. Capital: Beijing. Pop: 1 300 000 000 (2005 est). Area: 9 560 990 sq km (3 691 502 sq miles) **2** Republic of Also called: **Nationalist China, Taiwan** a republic (recognized as independent by only 26 nations) in E Asia occupying the island of Taiwan, 13 nearby islands, and 64 islands of the Penghu (Pescadores) group: established in 1949 by the Nationalist government of China under Chiang Kai-shek after its expulsion by the Communists from the mainland; its territory claimed by the People's Republic of China since the political separation from the mainland; under US protection 1954–79; lost its seat at the UN to the People's Republic of China in 1971; state of war with the People's Republic of China formally ended in 1991, though tensions continue owing to the unresolved territorial claim. Language: Mandarin Chinese. Religion: nonreligious majority, Buddhist and Taoist minorities. Currency: New Taiwan dollar. Capital: Taipei. Pop: 22 610 000 (2003 est). Area: 35 981 sq km (13 892 sq miles)

Chinaman 1 *Archaic or derogatory* a native or inhabitant of China **2** *Cricket* a ball bowled by a left-handed bowler to a right-handed batsman that spins from off to leg

China Sea part of the Pacific Ocean off the coast of China: divided by Taiwan into the East China Sea in the north and the South China Sea in the south

Chinatown a quarter of any city or town outside China with a predominantly Chinese population

chinchilla 1 a small gregarious hystricomorph rodent, *Chinchilla laniger*, inhabiting mountainous regions of South America: family *Chinchillidae*. It has a stocky body and is bred in captivity for its soft silvery grey fur **2** the highly valued fur of this animal **3** mountain chinchilla

any of several long-tailed rodents of the genus *Lagidium*, having coarse poor quality fur **4** a breed of rabbit with soft silver-grey fur **5** a thick napped woollen cloth used for coats

Chindwin a river in N Myanmar, rising in the Kumôn Range and flowing northwest then south to the Irrawaddy, of which it is the main tributary. Length: about 966 km (600 miles)

chine 1 the backbone **2** a ridge or crest of land **3** (in some boats) a corner-like intersection where the bottom meets the side

Chinese any of the languages of China belonging to the Sino-Tibetan family, sometimes regarded as dialects of one language. They share a single writing system that is not phonetic but ideographic. A phonetic system using the Roman alphabet was officially adopted by the Chinese government in 1966

Chinese chequers a board game played with marbles or pegs

Chinese lantern an Asian solanaceous plant, *Physalis franchetii*, cultivated for its attractive orange-red inflated calyx

Chinese puzzle an intricate puzzle, esp one consisting of boxes within boxes

Chinese Turkestan the E part of the central Asian region of Turkestan: corresponds generally to the present-day Xinjiang Uygur Autonomous Region of China

chinoiserie 1 a style of decorative or fine art based on imitations of Chinese motifs **2** an object or objects in this style

Chinook 1 a North American Indian people of the Pacific coast near the Columbia River **2** the language of this people, probably forming a separate branch of the Penutian phylum

Chinook salmon a Pacific salmon, *Oncorhynchus tschawytscha*, valued as a food fish

chintz 1 a printed, patterned cotton fabric, with glazed finish **2** a painted or stained Indian calico

Chios 1 an island in the Aegean Sea, off the coast of Turkey: belongs to Greece. Capital: Chios. Pop: 51 936 (2001). Area: 904 sq km (353 sq miles) **2** a port on the island of Chios: in ancient times, one of the 12 Ionian city-states. Pop: 54 000 (1995 est)

chip 1 (in some games) a counter used to represent money **2** *Electronics* a tiny wafer of semiconductor material, such as silicon, processed to form a type of integrated circuit or component such as a transistor **3** a thin strip of wood or straw used for making woven hats, baskets, etc.

chipmunk any burrowing sciurine rodent of the genera *Tamias* of E North America and *Eutamias* of W North America and Asia, typically having black-striped yellowish fur and cheek pouches for storing food

Chippendale Thomas ?1718–79, English cabinet-maker and furniture designer
▷www.britainexpress.com/History/bio

chipset 1 a highly integrated circuit on the motherboard of a computer that controls many of its data transfer functions **2** *Computing* the main processing circuitry on many video cards

Chirac Jacques (René). born 1932, French Gaullist politician: president of France from 1995; prime minister

(1974–76 and 1986–88); mayor of Paris (1977–95)

Chirico Giorgio de 1888–1978, Italian artist born in Greece: profoundly influenced the surrealist movement

chiropractic a system of treating bodily disorders by manipulation of the spine and other parts, based on the belief that the cause is the abnormal functioning of a nerve

chisel a a hand tool for working wood, consisting of a flat steel blade with a cutting edge attached to a handle of wood, plastic, etc. It is either struck with a mallet or used by hand **b** a similar tool without a handle for working stone or metal

Chisimaio a port in S Somalia, on the Indian Ocean. Pop: 200 000 (latest est)

chit a voucher for a sum of money owed, esp for food or drink

Chita an industrial city in SE Russia, on the Trans-Siberian railway. Pop: 309 000 (2005 est)

chitin a polysaccharide that is the principal component of the exoskeletons of arthropods and of the bodies of fungi

Chittagong a port in E Bangladesh, on the Bay of Bengal: industrial centre. Pop: 4 171 000 (2005 est)

chivalry 1 the combination of qualities expected of an ideal knight, esp courage, honour, justice, and a readiness to help the weak **2** the medieval system and principles of knighthood

chloral hydrate a colourless crystalline soluble solid produced by the reaction of chloral with water and used as a sedative and hypnotic; 2,2,2-trichloro-1,1-ethanediol. Formula: $CCl_3CH(OH)_2$

chlorate any salt of chloric acid, containing the monovalent ion ClO_3^-

chloride 1 any salt of hydrochloric acid, containing the chloride ion Cl^- **2** any compound containing a chlorine atom, such as methyl chloride (chloromethane), CH_3Cl

chlorine *or* **chlorin** a toxic pungent greenish-yellow gas of the halogen group; the 15th most abundant element in the earth's crust, occurring only in the combined state, mainly in common salt: used in the manufacture of many organic chemicals, in water purification, and as a disinfectant and bleaching agent. Symbol: Cl; atomic no.: 17; atomic wt.: 35.4527; valency: 1, 3, 5, or 7; density: 3.214 kg/m³; relative density: 1.56; melting pt.: –101.03°C; boiling pt.: –33.9°C

chlorofluorocarbon *Chem* any of various gaseous compounds of carbon, hydrogen, chlorine, and fluorine, used as refrigerants, aerosol propellants, solvents, and in foam: some cause a breakdown of ozone in the earth's atmosphere

chloroform a heavy volatile liquid with a sweet taste and odour, used as a solvent and cleansing agent and in refrigerants; formerly used as an inhalation anaesthetic. Formula: $CHCl_3$

chlorophyll *or US* **chlorophyl** the green pigment of plants and photosynthetic algae and bacteria that traps the energy of sunlight for photosynthesis and exists in several forms, the most abundant being chlorophyll a ($C_{55}H_{72}O_5N_4Mg$): used as a colouring agent in medicines or food (**E140**)

chloroplast a plastid containing chlorophyll and other pigments, occurring in plants and algae that carry out photosynthesis

chock 1 *Nautical* **a** a fairlead consisting of a ringlike device with an opening at the top through which a rope is placed **b** a cradle-like support for a boat, barrel, etc. **2** *Mountaineering* See **nut**

chock-a-block *Nautical* with the blocks brought close together, as when a tackle is pulled as tight as possible

chocolate a a moderate to deep brown colour **b** (*as adjective*): *a chocolate carpet*

choir 1 an organized group of singers, esp for singing in church services **2 a** the part of a cathedral, abbey, or church in front of the altar, lined on both sides with benches, and used by the choir and clergy **b** (*as modifier*): *choir stalls* **3** a number of instruments of the same family playing together **4** one of the manuals on an organ controlling a set of soft sweet-toned pipes **5** any of the nine orders of angels in medieval angelology

choirboy one of a number of young boys who sing the treble part in a church choir

Choiseul[1] **Étienne François** , Duc de. 1719–85, French statesman; foreign minister (1758–70)

Choiseul[2] an island in the SW Pacific Ocean, in the Solomon Islands: hilly and densely forested. Area: 3885 sq km (1500 sq miles)

choke 1 a device in the carburettor of a petrol engine that enriches the petrol-air mixture by reducing the air supply **2** any constriction or mechanism for reducing the flow of a fluid in a pipe, tube, etc. **3** *Electronics* an inductor having a relatively high impedance, used to prevent the passage of high frequencies or to smooth the output of a rectifier

choko the cucumber-like fruit of a tropical American cucurbitaceous vine, *Sechium edule*: eaten as a vegetable in the Caribbean, Australia, and New Zealand

choler 1 *Archaic* one of the four bodily humours; yellow bile **2** *Obsolete* biliousness

cholera an acute intestinal infection characterized by severe diarrhoea, cramp, etc.: caused by ingestion of water or food contaminated with the bacterium *Vibrio comma*

cholesterol a sterol found in all animal tissues, blood, bile, and animal fats: a precursor of other body steroids. A high level of cholesterol in the blood is implicated in some cases of atherosclerosis, leading to heart disease. Formula: $C_{27}H_{45}OH$

Cholula a town in S Mexico, in Puebla state: ancient ruins, notably a pyramid, 53 m (177 ft) high. Pop: 37 791 (1990)

Chomsky (**Avram**) **Noam** born 1928, US linguist and political critic. His theory of language structure, transformational generative grammar, superseded the behaviourist view of Bloomfield

Chongqing, Chungking, *or* **Ch'ung-ch'ing** a river port in SW China, in Sichuan province at the confluence of the Yangtze and Jialing rivers: site of a city since the 3rd millennium BC; wartime capital of China (1938–45); major trade centre for W China. Pop: 4 975 000 (2005 est)

chop a design stamped on goods as a trademark, esp in the Far East

Chopin Frédéric (**François**). 1810–49, Polish composer and pianist active in France, who wrote chiefly for the piano: noted for his harmonic imagination and his lyrical and melancholy qualities

chopper 1 *Chiefly Brit* a small hand axe 2 a butcher's cleaver 3 an informal name for a **helicopter** 4 *Physics* a device for periodically interrupting an electric current or beam of radiation to produce a pulsed current or beam 5 a type of bicycle or motorcycle with very high handlebars and an elongated saddle 6 *NZ* a child's bicycle

chorale *or* **choral** 1 a slow stately hymn tune, esp of the Lutheran Church 2 *Chiefly US* a choir or chorus

chord the simultaneous sounding of a group of musical notes, usually three or more in number

chordate any animal of the phylum *Chordata*, including the vertebrates and protochordates, characterized by a notochord, dorsal tubular nerve cord, and pharyngeal gill slits

chorea a disorder of the central nervous system characterized by uncontrollable irregular brief jerky movements

choreography *or* **choregraphy** 1 the composition of dance steps and sequences for ballet and stage dancing 2 the steps and sequences of a ballet or dance 3 the notation representing such steps 4 the art of dancing
▷www.instchordance.com
▷www.culturekiosque.com/dance

chorister a singer in a choir, esp a choirboy

Chorley a town in NW England, in S Lancashire: cotton textiles. Pop: 33 424 (2001)

chorus 1 a large choir of singers or a piece of music composed for such a choir 2 a body of singers or dancers who perform together, in contrast to principals or soloists 3 a section of a song in which a soloist is joined by a group of singers, esp in a recurring refrain 4 *Jazz* any of a series of variations on a theme 5 in ancient Greece a a lyric poem sung by a group of dancers, originally as a religious rite b an ode or series of odes sung by a group of actors 6 a (in classical Greek drama) the actors who sang the chorus and commented on the action of the play b actors playing a similar role in any drama 7 a (esp in Elizabethan drama) the actor who spoke the prologue, etc. b the part of the play spoken by this actor

chorus girl a girl who dances or sings in the chorus of a musical comedy, revue, etc.

chose *Law* an article of personal property

Chosen the official name for **Korea** as a Japanese province (1910–45)

Chota Nagpur a plateau in E India, mainly in Jharkhand state since 2000: forested, with rich mineral resources and much heavy industry; produces chiefly lac (world's leading supplier), coal (half India's total output), and mica

Chou En-lai *or* **Zhou En Lai** 1898–1976, Chinese Communist statesman; foreign minister of the People's Republic of China (1949–58) and premier (1949–76)

chough 1 a large black passerine bird, *Pyrrhocorax pyrrhocorax*, of parts of Europe, Asia, and Africa, with a long downward-curving red bill: family *Corvidae* (crows) 2 **alpine chough** a smaller related bird, *Pyrrhocorax graculus*, with a shorter yellow bill

chrism *or* **chrisom** a mixture of olive oil and balsam used for sacramental anointing in the Greek Orthodox and Roman Catholic Churches

Christ 1 Jesus of Nazareth (Jesus Christ), regarded by Christians as fulfilling Old Testament prophecies of the Messiah 2 the Messiah or anointed one of God as the subject of Old Testament prophecies 3 an image or picture of Christ

Christchurch 1 a city in New Zealand, on E South Island: manufacturing centre of a rich agricultural region. Pop: 344 100 (2004 est) 2 a town and resort in S England, in SE Dorset. Pop: 40 208 (2001)

Christendom the collective body of Christians throughout the world or throughout history

Christian[1] **Charlie** 1919–42, US jazz guitarist

Christian[2] 1 a a person who believes in and follows Jesus Christ b a member of a Christian Church or denomination

Christian Era the period beginning with the year of Christ's birth. Dates in this era are labelled AD, those previous to it BC

Christianity 1 the Christian religion 2 Christian beliefs, practices or attitudes

Christian IV 1577–1648, king of Denmark and Norway (1588–1648): defeated in the Thirty Years' War (1629) and by Sweden (1645)

Christian Science the religious system and teaching of the Church of Christ, Scientist. It was founded by Mary Baker Eddy (1866) and emphasizes spiritual healing and the unreality of matter
▷www.tfccs.com

Christian X 1890–1947, king of Denmark (1912–47) and Iceland (1918–44)

Christie 1 Dame **Agatha** (**Mary Clarissa**). 1890–1976, British author of detective stories, many featuring Hercule Poirot, and several plays, including *The Mousetrap* (1952) 2 **John** (**Reginald Halliday**). 1898–1953, British murderer. His trial influenced legislation regarding the death penalty after he was found guilty of a murder for which Timothy Evans had been hanged 3 **Linford** born 1960, British athlete: Commonwealth (1990), Olympic (1992), World (1993), and European (1994) 100 metres gold medallist 4 **William** (**Lincoln**). born 1944, French harpsichord player, organist, and conductor, born in the US; founder (1979) and director of the early-music group Les Arts Florissants

Christina 1626–89, queen of Sweden (1632–54), daughter of Gustavus Adolphus, noted particularly for her patronage of literature

Christine de Pisan ?1364–?1430, French poet and prose writer, born in Venice. Her works include ballads, rondeaux, lays, and a biography of Charles V of France

Christmas 1 a the annual commemoration by Christians of the birth of Jesus Christ on Dec 25 b Dec 25, observed as a day of secular celebrations when gifts and greetings are exchanged c (*as modifier*): *Christmas celebrations* 2 the season of Christmas extending from Dec 24 (Christmas Eve) to Jan 6 (the festival of the Epiphany or Twelfth Night)

Christmas Island 1 the former name (until 1981) of **Kiritimati** 2 an island in the Indian Ocean, south of

Java: administered by Singapore (1900–58), now by Australia; phosphate mining. Pop: 1500 (2004 est). Area: 135 sq km (52 sq miles)

Christmas rose an evergreen ranunculaceous plant, *Helleborus niger*, of S Europe and W Asia, with white or pinkish winter-blooming flowers

Christmas tree 1 an evergreen tree or an imitation of one, decorated as part of Christmas celebrations **2** *Austral* any of various trees or shrubs flowering at Christmas and used for decoration

Christo full name **Christo Jaracheff** born 1935, US artist, born in Bulgaria; best known for works in which he wraps buildings, monuments, or natural features in canvas or plastic

Christoff **Boris** 1919–93, Bulgarian bass-baritone, noted esp for his performance in the title role of Mussorgsky's *Boris Godunov*

Christopher Saint 3rd century AD, Christian martyr; patron saint of travellers

chromate any salt or ester of chromic acid. Simple chromate salts contain the divalent ion, CrO_4^{2-}, and are orange

chromatic *Music* **a** involving the sharpening or flattening of notes or the use of such notes in chords and harmonic progressions **b** of or relating to the chromatic scale or an instrument capable of producing it

chromatics *or* **chromatology** the science of colour

chromatic scale *Music* a twelve-note scale including all the semitones of the octave

chromatin *Cytology* the part of the nucleus that consists of DNA and proteins, forms the chromosomes, and stains with basic dyes

chromatography *Chemistry* the technique of separating and analysing the components of a mixture of liquids or gases by selective adsorption in, for example, a column of powder (**column chromatography**) or on a strip of paper (**paper chromatography**)

chrome 1 a another word for **chromium** (esp when present in a pigment or dye) **b** (*as modifier*): *a chrome dye* **2** anything plated with chromium, such as fittings on a car body

chromite 1 a brownish-black mineral consisting of a ferrous chromic oxide in cubic crystalline form, occurring principally in basic igneous rocks: the only commercial source of chromium and its compounds. Formula: $FeCr_2O_4$ **2** a salt of chromous acid

chromium a hard grey metallic element that takes a high polish, occurring principally in chromite: used in steel alloys and electroplating to increase hardness and corrosion-resistance. Symbol: Cr; atomic no.: 24; atomic wt.: 51.9961; valency: 2, 3, or 6; relative density: 7.18–7.20; melting pt.: 1863±20°C; boiling pt.: 2672°C

chromosome any of the microscopic rod-shaped structures that appear in a cell nucleus during cell division, consisting of nucleoprotein arranged into units (genes) that are responsible for the transmission of hereditary characteristics

chromosphere *Astronomy* a gaseous layer of the sun's atmosphere extending from the photosphere to the corona and visible during a total eclipse of the sun

chronic *Medicine* (of a disease) developing slowly, or of long duration

chrysalis the object pupa of a moth or butterfly

chrysanthemum 1 any widely cultivated plant of the genus *Chrysanthemum*, esp *C. morifolium* of China, having brightly coloured showy flower heads: family *Asteraceae* (composites) **2** any other plant of the genus *Chrysanthemum*, such as oxeye daisy

Chrysostom Saint **John** ?345–407 AD, Greek patriarch; archbishop of Constantinople (398–404). Feast day: Sept 13 or Nov 13

chub 1 a common European freshwater cyprinid game fish, *Leuciscus* (or *Squalius*) *cephalus*, having a cylindrical dark greenish body **2** any of various North American fishes, esp certain whitefishes and minnows

chuck a a device that holds a workpiece in a lathe or tool in a drill, having a number of adjustable jaws geared to move in unison to centralize the workpiece or tool **b** a similar device having independently adjustable jaws for holding an unsymmetrical workpiece

chukka *or US* **chukker** *Polo* a period of continuous play, generally lasting 7½ minutes

chum¹ *Angling, chiefly US and Canadian* chopped fish, meal, etc, used as groundbait

chum² a Pacific salmon, *Oncorhynchus keta*

Chur a city in E Switzerland, capital of Graubünden canton. Pop: 32 989 (2000)

church 1 a building designed for public forms of worship, esp Christian worship **2** an occasion of public worship **3** the clergy as distinguished from the laity **4** institutionalized forms of religion as a political or social force **5** the collective body of all Christians **6** a particular Christian denomination or group of Christian believers **7** the Christian religion **8** (in Britain) the practices or doctrines of the Church of England and similar denominations

Church **Charlotte** born 1986, Welsh soprano, who made her name with the album *Voice of an Angel* (1998) when she was 12

churchgoer 1 a person who attends church regularly **2** an adherent of an established Church in contrast to a Nonconformist

Churchill¹ 1 Caryl born 1938, British playwright; her plays include *Cloud Nine* (1978), *Top Girls* (1982), *Serious Money* (1987), and *Far Away* (2000) **2 Charles** 1731–64, British poet, noted for his polemical satires. His works include *The Rosciad* (1761) and *The Prophecy of Famine* (1763) **3 Lord Randolph** 1849–95, British Conservative politician: secretary of state for India (1885–86) and chancellor of the Exchequer and leader of the House of Commons (1886) **4** his son, **Sir Winston (Leonard Spencer)**. 1874–1965, British Conservative statesman, orator, and writer, noted for his leadership during World War II. He held various posts under both Conservative and Liberal governments, including 1st Lord of the Admiralty (1911–15), before becoming prime minister (1940–45; 1951–55). His writings include *The World Crisis* (1923–29), *Marlborough* (1933–38), *The Second World War* (1948–54), and *History of the English-Speaking Peoples* (1956–58): Nobel prize for literature 1953

Churchill² 1 a river in E Canada, rising in SE Labrador and flowing north and southeast over Churchill Falls, then east to the Atlantic. Length: about 1000 km (600 miles) **2** a river in central Canada, rising in NW

Saskatchewan and flowing east through several lakes to Hudson Bay. Length: about 1600 km (1000 miles)

churchman 1 a clergyman 2 a male practising member of a church

Church of England the reformed established state Church in England, Catholic in order and basic doctrine, with the Sovereign as its temporal head

churchwarden 1 *Church of England, Episcopal Church* one of two assistants of a parish priest who administer the secular affairs of the church 2 a long-stemmed tobacco pipe made of clay

chute 1 a steep slope, used as a slide as for toboggans 2 a slide into a swimming pool 3 a rapid or waterfall

Chu Teh *or* **Zhu De** 1886–1976, Chinese military leader and politician; he became commander in chief of the Red Army (1931) and was chairman of the Standing Committee of the National People's Congress of the People's Republic of China (1959–76)

chutney a type of music popular in the Caribbean Asian community, much influenced by calypso

Chuvash Republic a constituent republic of W central Russia, in the middle Volga valley: generally low-lying with undulating plains and large areas of forest. Capital: Cheboksary. Pop: 1 313 900 (2002). Area: 18 300 sq km (7064 sq miles)

chyle a milky fluid composed of lymph and emulsified fat globules, formed in the small intestine during digestion

chyme the thick fluid mass of partially digested food that leaves the stomach

Ciano Galeazzo, full name *Conte Galeazzo Ciano di Cortellazzo*. 1903–44, Italian fascist politician; minister of foreign affairs (1936–43) and son-in-law of Mussolini, whose supporters shot him

Cibber Colley 1671–1757, English actor and dramatist; poet laureate (1730–57)

cicada *or* **cicala** any large broad insect of the homopterous family *Cicadidae*, most common in warm regions. Cicadas have membranous wings and the males produce a high-pitched drone by vibration of a pair of drumlike abdominal organs

cicatrix 1 the tissue that forms in a wound during healing; scar 2 a scar on a plant indicating the former point of attachment of a part, esp a leaf

Cicero Marcus Tullius 106–43 BC, Roman consul, orator, and writer. He foiled Catiline's conspiracy (63) and was killed by Mark Antony's agents after he denounced Antony in the *Philippics*. His writings are regarded as a model of Latin prose

Cid El *or* the original name *Rodrigo Diaz de Vivar*. ?1043–99, Spanish soldier and hero of the wars against the Moors

cider *or* **cyder** 1 an alcoholic drink made from the fermented juice of apples 2 *US and Canadian* an unfermented drink made from apple juice

cigar a cylindrical roll of cured tobacco leaves, for smoking

cigarette *or sometimes US* **cigaret** a short tightly rolled cylinder of tobacco, wrapped in thin paper and often having a filter tip, for smoking

cilium 1 any of the short thread-like projections on the surface of a cell, organism, etc, whose rhythmic beating causes movement of the organism or of the surrounding fluid 2 the technical name for **eyelash**

Cimarosa Domenico 1749–1801, Italian composer, chiefly remembered for his opera buffa *The Secret Marriage* (1792)

cinch[1] *US and Canadian* a band around a horse's belly to keep the saddle in position

cinch[2] a card game in which the five of trumps ranks highest

cinchona 1 any tree or shrub of the South American rubiaceous genus *Cinchona*, esp *C. calisaya*, having medicinal bark 2 the dried bark of any of these trees, which yields quinine and other medicinal alkaloids 3 any of the drugs derived from cinchona bark

Cincinnati a city in SW Ohio, on the Ohio River. Pop: 317 361 (2003 est)

Cincinnatus Lucius Quinctius ?519–438 BC, Roman general and statesman, regarded as a model of simple virtue; dictator of Rome during two crises (458; 439), retiring to his farm after each one

cinder 1 any solid waste from smelting or refining 2 fragments of volcanic lava; scoriae

cinema 1 *Chiefly Brit* a a place designed for the exhibition of films b (*as modifier*): *a cinema seat* 2 the cinema a the art or business of making films b films collectively
  ▷www.cinema.com
  ▷www.sensesofcinema.com
  ▷www.learner.org/exhibits/cinema
  ▷www.scoot.co.uk/cinemafinder/default.asp

cinematograph *Chiefly Brit* a combined camera, printer, and projector

cinematography the art or science of film (motion-picture) photography
  ▷www.cinematographersday.com
  ▷www.zerocut.com/tech/film_terms.html
  ▷www.cinematographer.com

cineraria a plant, *Senecio cruentus*, of the Canary Islands, widely cultivated for its blue, purple, red, or variegated daisy-like flowers: family *Asteraceae* (composites)

cinnabar 1 a bright red or brownish-red mineral form of mercuric sulphide (mercury(II) sulphide), found close to areas of volcanic activity and hot springs. It is the main commercial source of mercury. Formula: HgS. Crystal structure: hexagonal 2 the red form of mercuric sulphide (mercury(II) sulphide), esp when used as a pigment 3 a bright red to reddish-orange; vermilion 4 a large red-and-black European moth, *Callimorpha jacobaeae*: family *Arctiidae* (tiger moths, etc)

cinnamon 1 a tropical Asian lauraceous tree, *Cinnamomum zeylanicum*, having aromatic yellowish-brown bark 2 **Saigon cinnamon** an E Asian lauraceous tree, *Cinnamomum loureirii*, the bark of which is used as a cordial and to relieve flatulence 3 any of several similar or related trees or their bark 4 a light yellowish brown

cinquefoil 1 any plant of the N temperate rosaceous genus *Potentilla*, typically having five-lobed compound leaves 2 an ornamental carving in the form of five arcs arranged in a circle and separated by cusps

cipher *or* **cypher** 1 an obsolete name for **zero** 2 any of the Arabic numerals (0, 1, 2, 3, etc, to 9) or the Arabic system of numbering as a whole 3 *Music* a defect in an organ resulting in the continuous sounding of a pipe, the key of which has not been depressed

circadian of or relating to biological processes that occur regularly at about 24-hour intervals, even in the absence of periodicity in the environment

Circassia a region of S Russia, on the Black Sea north of the Caucasus Mountains

Circassian a language or languages spoken in Circassia, belonging to the North-West Caucasian family

circle 1 *Maths* a closed plane curve every point of which is equidistant from a given fixed point, the centre. Equation: $(x-h)^2 + (y-k)^2 = r^2$ where *r* is the radius and (*h*, *k*) are the coordinates of the centre; area πr^2; circumference: $2\pi r$ 2 the figure enclosed by such a curve 3 *Theatre* the section of seats above the main level of the auditorium, usually comprising the dress circle and the upper circle 4 a parallel of latitude 5 *History* one of a number of Neolithic or Bronze Age rings of standing stones, such as Stonehenge, found in Europe and thought to be associated with some form of ritual or astronomical measurement

circuit 1 a a complete path through which an electric current can flow b (*as modifier*): *a circuit diagram* 2 an administrative division of the Methodist Church comprising a number of neighbouring churches 3 *English law* one of six areas into which England is divided for the administration of justice 4 a number of theatres, cinemas, etc, under one management or in which the same film is shown or in which a company of performers plays in turn 5 *Chiefly Brit* a motor racing track, usually of irregular shape

circuit breaker a device that under abnormal conditions, such as a short circuit, interrupts the flow of current in an electrical circuit

circuitry 1 the design of an electrical circuit 2 the system of circuits used in an electronic device

circular *Logic* (of arguments) futile because the truth of the premises cannot be established independently of the conclusion

circular saw a power-driven saw in which a circular disc with a toothed edge is rotated at high speed

circulation 1 the transport of oxygenated blood through the arteries to the capillaries, where it nourishes the tissues, and the return of oxygen-depleted blood through the veins to the heart, where the cycle is renewed 2 the flow of sap through a plant 3 in **circulation** (of currency) serving as a medium of exchange

circumference 1 the boundary of a specific area or geometric figure, esp of a circle 2 the length of a closed geometric curve, esp of a circle. The circumference of a circle is equal to the diameter multiplied by π

circumflex *Anatomy* (of certain nerves, arteries, or veins) bending or curving around

circus 1 in ancient Rome a an open-air stadium, usually oval or oblong, for chariot races or public games b the games themselves 2 *Brit* a an open place, usually circular, in a town, where several streets converge b (*capital when part of a name*): *Picadilly Circus*
▷www.circusweb.com

Cirencester a market town in S England, in Gloucestershire: Roman amphitheatre. Pop: 15 861 (2001)

cirque 1 *Geography* a semicircular or crescent-shaped basin with steep sides and a gently sloping floor

formed in mountainous regions by the erosive action of a glacier 2 *Archaeol* an obsolete term for **circle**

cirrhosis any of various progressive diseases of the liver, characterized by death of liver cells, irreversible fibrosis, etc.: caused by inadequate diet, excessive alcohol, chronic infection, etc.

cirrocumulus *Meteorol* a high cloud of ice crystals grouped into small separate globular masses, usually occurring above 6000 metres (20 000 feet)

cirrostratus *Meteorol* a uniform layer of cloud above about 6000 metres (20 000 feet)

cirrus 1 *Meteorol* a thin wispy fibrous cloud at high altitudes, composed of ice particles 2 a plant tendril or similar part 3 *Zoology* a a slender tentacle or filament in barnacles and other marine invertebrates b a hairlike structure in other animals, such as a filament on the appendage of an insect or a barbel of a fish

cisalpine 1 on this (the southern) side of the Alps, as viewed from Rome 2 relating to a movement in the Roman Catholic Church to minimize the authority of the pope and to emphasize the independence of branches of the Church

Ciscaucasia the part of Caucasia north of the Caucasus Mountains

cisco any of various whitefish, esp *Coregonus artedi* (also called **lake herring**), of cold deep lakes of North America

Ciskei (formerly) a Bantustan in SE South Africa; granted independence in 1981 but this was not recognized outside South Africa; abolished in 1993. Capital: Bisho

Cistercian a a member of a Christian order of monks and nuns founded in 1098, which follows an especially strict form of the Benedictine rule b (*as modifier*): *a Cistercian monk*

citadel the headquarters of the Salvation Army

citation 1 *Law* a an official summons to appear in court b the document containing such a summons 2 *Law* the quoting of decided cases to serve as guidance to a court

citizen a native registered or naturalized member of a state, nation, or other political community

citrate any salt or ester of citric acid. Salts of citric acid are used in beverages and pharmaceuticals

citric of or derived from citrus fruits or citric acid

citric acid a water-soluble weak tribasic acid found in many fruits, esp citrus fruits, and used in pharmaceuticals and as a flavouring (**E330**). It is extracted from citrus fruits or made by fermenting molasses and is an intermediate in carbohydrate metabolism. Formula: $CH_2(COOH)C(OH)(COOH)CH_2COOH$

citron 1 a small Asian rutaceous tree, *Citrus medica*, having lemon-like fruit with a thick aromatic rind 2 the fruit of this tree 3 a variety of watermelon, *Citrullus vulgaris citroides*, that has an inedible fruit with a hard rind 4 a greenish-yellow colour

citronella 1 a tropical Asian grass, *Cymbopogon* (or *Andropogon*) *nardus*, with bluish-green lemon-scented leaves 2 the yellow aromatic oil obtained from this grass, used in insect repellents, soaps, perfumes, etc.

city 1 any large town or populous place 2 (in Britain) a large town that has received this title from the Crown: usually the seat of a bishop 3 (in the US) an incorporated urban centre with its own government and administration established by state charter 4 an ancient Greek city-state; polis

City the short for **City of London**: the original settlement of London on the N bank of the Thames; a municipality governed by the Lord Mayor and Corporation. Resident pop.: 7186 (2001)

city-state a state consisting of a sovereign city and its dependencies. Among the most famous are the great independent cities of the ancient world, such as Athens, Sparta, Carthage, and Rome

Ciudad Guayana an industrial conurbation in E Venezuela, on the River Orinoco: iron and steel processing, gold mining. Pop: 807 000 (2005 est)

Ciudad Victoria a city in E central Mexico, capital of Tamaulipas state. Pop: 285 000 (2005 est)

civet 1 any catlike viverrine mammal of the genus *Viverra* and related genera, of Africa and S Asia, typically having blotched or spotted fur and secreting a powerfully smelling fluid from anal glands 2 the yellowish fatty secretion of such an animal, used as a fixative in the manufacture of perfumes 3 the fur of such an animal

civic centre *Brit* the public buildings of a town, including recreational facilities and offices of local administration

civics 1 the study of the rights and responsibilities of citizenship 2 *US and Canadian* the study of government and its workings

civil 1 of the ordinary life of citizens as distinguished from military, legal, or ecclesiastical affairs 2 of or relating to the citizen as an individual 3 of or occurring within the state or between citizens 4 of or in accordance with Roman law 5 relating to the private rights of citizens

civil disobedience *Politics* a refusal to obey laws, pay taxes, etc.: a nonviolent means of protesting or of attempting to achieve political goals

civil law 1 the law of a state relating to private and civilian affairs 2 the body of law in force in ancient Rome, esp the law applicable to private citizens 3 any system of law based on the Roman system as distinguished from the common law and canon law 4 the law of a state as distinguished from international law

civil list (in Britain) the annuities voted by Parliament for the support of the royal household and the royal family

civil marriage *Law* a marriage performed by some official other than a clergyman

civil servant a member of the civil service

civil service the service responsible for the public administration of the government of a country. It excludes the legislative, judicial, and military branches. Members of the civil service have no official political allegiance and are not generally affected by changes of governments

clack *Engineering* a simple nonreturn valve using either a hinged flap or a ball

Clackmannanshire a council area and historical county of central Scotland; became part of the Central region in 1975 but reinstated as an independent unitary authority in 1996; mainly agricultural. Administrative centre: Alloa. Pop: 47 680 (2003 est). Area: 142 sq km (55 sq miles)

Clacton *or* **Clacton-on-Sea** a town and resort in SE England, in E Essex. Pop: 51 284 (2001)

cladding 1 the process of protecting one metal by bonding a second metal to its surface 2 the protective coating so bonded to metal

cladistics *Biology* a method of grouping animals that makes use of lines of descent rather than structural similarities

claim *Law* a document under seal, issued in the name of the Crown or a court, commanding the person to whom it is addressed to do or refrain from doing some specified act.

Clair René, real name *René Chomette*. 1898–1981, French film director; noted for his comedies including *An Italian Straw Hat* (1928) and pioneering sound films such as *Sous les toits de Paris* (1930); later films include *Les Belles de nuit* (1952)

clairvoyance the alleged power of perceiving things beyond the natural range of the senses

clam any of various burrowing bivalve molluscs of the genera *Mya*, *Venus*, etc. Many species, such as the quahog and soft-shell clam, are edible and *Tridacna gigas* is the largest known bivalve, nearly 1.5 metres long

clamp 1 a mechanical device with movable jaws with which an object can be secured to a bench or with which two objects may be secured together 2 *Nautical* a horizontal beam fastened to the ribs for supporting the deck beams in a wooden vessel

clan 1 a group of people interrelated by ancestry or marriage 2 a group of families with a common surname and a common ancestor, acknowledging the same leader, esp among the Scots and the Irish

Clancy Tom born 1947, US novelist; his thrillers, many of which have been filmed, include *The Hunt for Red October* (1984), *Clear and Present Danger* (1989), *Debt of Honour* (1994) and *Red Rabbit* (2002)

clapper 1 a contrivance for producing a sound of clapping, as for scaring birds 2 a slang word for **tongue**

clapperboard a pair of boards clapped together during film shooting in order to aid sound synchronization

Clapton Eric born 1945, British rock guitarist, noted for his virtuoso style, his work with the Yardbirds (1963–65), Cream (1966–68), and, with Derek and the Dominos, the album *Layla* (1970); later solo work includes *Unplugged* (1992)

claque *Theatre* a group of people hired to applaud

Clare[1] 1 Anthony (**Ward**). born 1942, Irish psychiatrist and broadcaster; presenter of the radio series *In the Psychiatrist's Chair* from 1982 2 John 1793–1864, English poet, noted for his descriptions of country life, particularly in *The Shepherd's Calendar* (1827) and *The Rural Muse* (1835). He was confined in a lunatic asylum from 1837

Clare[2] a county of W Republic of Ireland, in Munster between Galway Bay and the Shannon estuary. County town: Ennis. Pop: 103 277 (2002). Area: 3188 sq km (1231 sq miles)

Clarendon[1] 1st Earl of, title of *Edward Hyde*. 1609–74, English statesman and historian; chief adviser to Charles II (1660–67); author of *History of the Rebellion and Civil Wars in England* (1704–07)

Clarendon[2] a village near Salisbury in S England: site of a council held by Henry II in 1164 that produced a code of laws (the **Constitutions of Clarendon**) defining relations between church and state

Clare of Assisi Saint 1194–1253, Italian nun; founder of the Franciscan Order of Poor Clares. Feast day: Aug 11

claret 1 *Chiefly Brit* a red wine, esp one from the Bordeaux district of France 2 a a purplish-red colour b (*as adjective*): *a claret carpet*

clarinet *Music* a keyed woodwind instrument with a cylindrical bore and a single reed. It is a transposing instrument, most commonly pitched in A or B flat

clarion 1 a four-foot reed stop of trumpet quality on an organ 2 an obsolete, high-pitched, small-bore trumpet

Clark 1 **Helen** born 1950, New Zealand politician; Labour prime minister from 1999 2 **James,** known as *Jim.* 1936–68, Scottish racing driver; World Champion (1963, 1965) 3 **Kenneth,** Baron Clark of Saltwood. 1903–83, English art historian: his books include *Civilization* (1969), which he first presented as a television series 4 **William** 1770–1838, US explorer and frontiersman: best known for his expedition to the Pacific Northwest (1804–06) with Meriwether Lewis

Clarke 1 Sir **Arthur C(harles).** born 1917, British science-fiction writer, who helped to develop the first communications satellites. He scripted the film *2001, A Space Odyssey* (1968) 2 **Austin** 1896–1974, Irish poet and verse dramatist. His volumes include *The Vengeance of Fionn* (1917), *Night and Morning* (1938), and *Ancient Lights* (1955) 3 **Jeremiah** ?1673–1707, English composer and organist, best known for his *Trumpet Voluntary,* formerly attributed to Purcell 4 **Kenneth Harry** born 1940, British Conservative politician: secretary of state for health (1988–1990); secretary of state for education (1990–1992); home secretary (1992–93); chancellor of the exchequer (1993–97) 5 **Marcus (Andrew Hislop).** 1846–81, Australian novelist born in England, noted for his novel *For the Term of His Natural Life,* published in serial form (1870–72); other works include *Twixt Shadow and Shine* (1875)

Clarkson Thomas 1760–1846, British campaigner for the abolition of slavery

clasp knife a large knife with one or more blades or other devices folding into the handle

class 1 (in Marxist theory) a group of persons sharing the same relationship to the means of production 2 a a group of pupils or students who are taught and study together b a meeting of a group of students for tuition 3 *Chiefly US* a group of students who graduated in a specified year 4 *Brit* a grade of attainment in a university honours degree 5 a outstanding speed and stamina in a racehorse b (*as modifier*): *the class horse in the race* 6 *Biology* any of the taxonomic groups into which a phylum is divided and which contains one or more orders. *Amphibia, Reptilia,* and *Mammalia* are three classes of phylum *Chordata* 7 *Maths, Logic* a another name for **set** b **proper class** a class which cannot itself be a member of other classes

classic *Horse racing* a any of the five principal races for three-year-old horses in Britain, namely the One Thousand Guineas, Two Thousand Guineas, Derby, Oaks, and Saint Leger b a race equivalent to any of these in other countries

classical 1 of, relating to, or characteristic of the ancient Greeks and Romans or their civilization, esp in the period of their ascendancy 2 designating, following, or influenced by the art or culture of ancient Greece or Rome 3 *Music* a of, relating to, or denoting any music or its period of composition marked by stability of form, intellectualism, and restraint b denoting serious art music in general 4 *Music* of or relating to a style of music composed, esp at Vienna, during the late 18th and early 19th centuries. This period is marked by the establishment, esp by Haydn and Mozart, of sonata form 5 (of an education) based on the humanities and the study of Latin and Greek 6 *Physics* a not involving the quantum theory or the theory of relativity b obeying the laws of Newtonian mechanics or 19th-century physics 7 (of a logical or mathematical system) according with the law of excluded middle, so that every statement is known to be either true or false even if it is not known which

▷www.wilhelm-aerospace.org/Architecture/classical

▷www.le.ac.uk/ur/urarch5.html

▷www.classicalmus.hispeed.com/classical.html

classic car *Chiefly Brit* a car that is more than twenty-five years old

classicism *or* **classicalism** a style based on the study of Greek and Roman models, characterized by emotional restraint and regularity of form, associated esp with the 18th century in Europe

classification 1 *Biology* the placing of animals and plants in a series of increasingly specialized groups because of similarities in structure, origin, molecular composition, etc, that indicate a common relationship. The major groups are domain or superkingdom, kingdom, phylum (in animals) or division (in plants), class, order, family, genus, and species 2 *Government* the designation of an item of information as being secret and not available to people outside a restricted group

classified 1 *Government* (of information) not available to people outside a restricted group, esp for reasons of national security 2 (of British roads) having a number in the national road system. If the number is preceded by an M the road is a motorway, if by an A it is a first-class road, and if by a B it is a secondary road

Claude Lorrain real name *Claude Gelée.* 1600–82, French painter, esp of idealized landscapes, noted for his subtle depiction of light

Claudius full name *Tiberius Claudius Drusus Nero Germanicus.* 10 BC–54 AD, Roman emperor (41–54); invaded Britain (43); poisoned by his fourth wife, Agrippina

Claudius II full name *Marcus Aurelius Claudius,* called *Gothicus.* 214–270 AD, Roman emperor (268–270)

clause *Law* a section of a legal document such as a contract, will, or draft statute

Clausewitz Karl von 1780–1831, Prussian general, noted for his works on military strategy, esp *Vom Kriege* (1833)

Clausius Rudolf Julius 1822–88, German physicist and mathematician. He enunciated the second law of thermodynamics (1850) and developed the kinetic theory of gases

claustrophobia an abnormal fear of being closed in or of being in a confined space

clavichord a keyboard instrument consisting of a number of thin wire strings struck from below by brass tangents. The instrument is noted for its delicate tones, since the tangents do not rebound from the string until the key is released

clavicle *Anatomy* **1** either of the two bones connecting the shoulder blades with the upper part of the breast-bone **2** the corresponding structure in other verte-brates

claw 1 a curved pointed horny process on the end of each digit in birds, some reptiles, and certain mammals **2** a corresponding structure in some invertebrates, such as the pincer of a crab **3** *Botany* the narrow basal part of certain petals and sepals

claw back the recovery of a sum of money, esp by taxa-tion or a penalty

clay 1 a very fine-grained material that consists of hydrated aluminium silicate, quartz, and organic frag-ments and occurs as sedimentary rocks, soils, and other deposits. It becomes plastic when moist but hardens on heating and is used in the manufacture of bricks, cement, ceramics, etc. **2** *Poetic* the material of the human body

Clay Henry 1777–1852, US statesman and orator; secretary of state (1825–29)

clean 1 a (of a nuclear weapon) producing little or no radioactive fallout or contamination **b** uncontaminat-ed **2** (of a wound, etc) having no pus or other sign of infection **3** *Aeronautics* causing little turbulence; streamlined **4** (of an aircraft) having no projections, such as rockets, flaps, etc, into the airstream **5** *Nautical* of a vessel **a** having its bottom clean **b** having a satis-factory bill of health **6** *Old Testament* **a** (of persons) free from ceremonial defilement **b** (of animals, birds, and fish) lawful to eat **7** *New Testament* morally and spiritu-ally pure

clear 1 emptied of freight or cargo **2** (of timber) having a smooth, unblemished surface **3** *Showjumping* (of a round) ridden without any fences being knocked down or any points being lost

clearance 1 a the disposal of merchandise at reduced prices **b** (*as modifier*): *a clearance sale* **2** the act of clearing an area of land of its inhabitants by mass eviction **3** *Dentistry* the extraction of all of a person's teeth **4** a less common word for **clearing**

clearing an area with few or no trees or shrubs in wood-ed or overgrown land

clearway 1 *Brit* a stretch of road on which motorists may stop only in an emergency **2** an area at the end of a runway over which an aircraft taking off makes its ini-tial climb: it is under the control of the airport

cleat 1 a wedge-shaped block, usually of wood, attached to a structure to act as a support **2** *Nautical* a device con-sisting of two hornlike prongs projecting horizontally in opposite directions from a central base, used for securing lines on vessels, wharves, etc. **3** a small trian-gular-shaped nail used in glazing

cleavage 1 (of crystals) the act of splitting or the ten-dency to split along definite planes so as to yield smooth surfaces **2** *Embryol* (in animals) the repeated division of a fertilized ovum into a solid ball of cells (a morula), which later becomes hollow (a blastula) **3** the breaking of a chemical bond in a molecule to give smaller molecules or radicals **4** *Geology* the natural

splitting of certain rocks, or minerals such as slates, or micas along the planes of weakness

cleavers a Eurasian rubiaceous plant, *Galium aparine*, having small white flowers and prickly stems and fruits

Cleethorpes a resort in E England, in North East Lincolnshire unitary authority, Lincolnshire. Pop: 31 853 (2001)

clef *Music* one of several symbols placed on the left-hand side beginning of each stave indicating the pitch of the music written after it

cleft 1 a fissure or crevice **2** (of leaves) having one or more incisions reaching nearly to the midrib

cleft palate a congenital crack or fissure in the midline of the hard palate, often associated with a harelip

Cleland John 1709–89, British writer, best known for his bawdy novel *Fanny Hill* (1748–49)

clematis any N temperate ranunculaceous climbing plant or erect shrub of the genus *Clematis*, having plumelike fruits. Many species are cultivated for their large colourful flowers

Clemenceau Georges Eugène Benjamin 1841–1929, French statesman; prime minister of France (1906–09; 1917–20); negotiated the Treaty of Versailles (1919)

Clemens Samuel Langhorne

Clement I Saint, called *Clement of Rome*. pope (?88–?97 AD). Feast day: Nov 23

Clement V original name *Bertrand de Got*. ?1264–1314, pope (1305–14): removed the papal seat from Rome to Avignon in France (1309)

Clement VII original name *Giulio de' Medici*. 1478–1534, pope (1523–34): refused to authorize the annulment of the marriage of Henry VIII of England to Catherine of Aragon (1533)

clementine a citrus fruit thought to be either a variety of tangerine or a hybrid between a tangerine and sweet orange

Clement of Alexandria Saint original name *Titus Flavius Clemens*. ?150–?215 AD, Greek Christian theologian: head of the catechetical school at Alexandria; teacher of Origen. Feast day: Dec 5

clench a device that grasps or grips, such as a clamp

Cleon died 422 BC, Athenian demagogue and military leader

Cleopatra ?69–30 BC, queen of Egypt (51–30), renowned for her beauty: the mistress of Julius Caesar and later of Mark Antony. She killed herself with an asp to avoid capture by Octavian (Augustus)

clerestory *or* **clearstory 1** a row of windows in the upper part of the wall of a church that divides the nave from the aisle, set above the aisle roof **2** the part of the wall in which these windows are set

clergy the collective body of men and women ordained as religious ministers, esp of the Christian Church

clerihew a form of comic or satiric verse, consisting of two couplets of metrically irregular lines, containing the name of a well-known person

clerk 1 clerk to the justices (in England) a legally quali-fied person who sits in court with lay justices to advise them on points of law **2** an employee of a court, legisla-ture, board, corporation, etc, who keeps records and accounts, etc. **3** *Brit* a senior official of the House of

Commons **4** *Archaic* a cleric **5** a scholar

Clermont-Ferrand a city in S central France: capital of Puy-de-Dôme department; industrial centre. Pop: 137 140 (1999)

Cleveland¹ Stephen Grover 1837–1908, US Democratic politician; the 22nd and 24th president of the US (1885–89; 1893–97)

Cleveland² **1** a former county of NE England formed in 1974 from parts of E Durham and N Yorkshire; replaced in 1996 by the unitary authorities of Hartlepool (Durham), Stockton-on-Tees (Durham), Middlesbrough (North Yorkshire) and Redcar and Cleveland (North Yorkshire) **2** a port in NE Ohio, on Lake Erie: major heavy industries. Pop: 461 324 (2003 est) **3** a hilly region of NE England, extending from the **Cleveland Hills** to the River Tees

clianthus any Australian or New Zealand plant of the leguminous genus *Clianthus*, with ornamental clusters of slender scarlet flowers

click **1 a** the locking member of a ratchet mechanism, such as a pawl or detent **b** the movement of such a mechanism between successive locking positions **2** *US and Canadian, slang* a kilometre **3** *Computing* an act of pressing and releasing a button on a mouse

client **1** a customer **2** a person who is registered with or receiving services or financial aid from a welfare agency **3** *Computing* a program or work station that requests data or information from a server

cliff a steep high rock face, esp one that runs along the seashore and has the strata exposed

cliffhanger a situation of imminent disaster usually occurring at the end of each episode of a serialized film

climacteric **1** another name for **menopause 2** the period in the life of a man corresponding to the menopause, chiefly characterized by diminished sexual activity **3** *Botany* the period during which certain fruits, such as apples, ripen, marked by a rise in the rate of respiration

climate the long-term prevalent weather conditions of an area, determined by latitude, position relative to oceans or continents, altitude, etc.

climax **1** a decisive moment in a dramatic or other work **2** *Ecology* the stage in the development of a community during which it remains stable under the prevailing environmental conditions **3** (esp in referring to women) another word for **orgasm**

clime *Poetic* a region or its climate

clinch **1** *Boxing, Wrestling* an act or an instance in which one or both competitors hold on to the other to avoid punches, regain wind, etc. **2** *Nautical* a loop or eye formed in a line by seizing the end to the standing part

Cline Patsy, original name *Virginia Patterson Hensley*. 1932–63, US country singer; her bestselling records include "Walking After Midnight", "I Fall to Pieces", and "Leavin' On Your Mind".

clinic **1** a place in which outpatients are given medical treatment or advice, often connected to a hospital **2** a similar place staffed by physicians or surgeons specializing in one or more specific areas **3** *Brit* a private hospital or nursing home **4** *Obsolete* the teaching of medicine to students at the bedside **5** *US* a place in which medical lectures are given **6** *US* a clinical lecture

clinical thermometer a finely calibrated thermometer for determining the temperature of the body, usually placed under the tongue, in the armpit, or in the rectum

clink *Brit* a pointed steel tool used for breaking up the surface of a road before it is repaired

clinker the ash and partially fused residues from a coal-fired furnace or fire

clinker-built *or* **clincher-built** (of a boat or ship) having a hull constructed with each plank overlapping that below

Clinton **1** Bill, full name *William Jefferson*. born 1946, US Democrat politician; 42nd president of the US (1993–2001) **2** his wife, Hillary Rodham born 1947, US politician and lawyer: first lady (1993–2001); senator from 2001

Clio *Greek myth* the Muse of history

clip the pointed flange on a horseshoe that secures it to the front part of the hoof

clipboard *Computing* a temporary storage area in desktop publishing where text or graphics are held after the cut command or the copy command

clipper any fast sailing ship

clipping *Electronics* the distortion of an audio or visual signal in which the tops of peaks with a high amplitude are cut off, caused by, for example, overloading of amplifier circuits

clitoris a part of the female genitalia consisting of a small elongated highly sensitive erectile organ at the front of the vulva: homologous with the penis

Clive Robert, Baron Clive of Plassey. 1725–74, British general and statesman, whose victory at Plassey (1757) strengthened British control in India

cloaca a cavity in the pelvic region of most vertebrates, except higher mammals, and certain invertebrates, into which the alimentary canal and the genital and urinary ducts open

cloche a bell-shaped cover used to protect young plants

clock **1** a timepiece, usually free-standing, hanging, or built into a tower, having mechanically or electrically driven pointers that move constantly over a dial showing the numbers of the hours **2** any clocklike device for recording or measuring, such as a taximeter or pressure gauge **3** *Botany* the downy head of a dandelion that has gone to seed **4** an electrical circuit that generates pulses at a predetermined rate **5** *Computing* an electronic pulse generator that transmits streams of regular pulses to which various parts of the computer and its operations are synchronized **6** an informal word for **speedometer** *or* **mileometer 7 against the clock** (in certain sports, such as show jumping) timed by a stop clock

cloister **1** a covered walk, usually around a quadrangle in a religious institution, having an open arcade or colonnade on the inside and a wall on the outside **2** a place of religious seclusion, such as a monastery

clone **1** *Biology* a group of organisms or cells of the same genetic constitution that are descended from a common ancestor by asexual reproduction, as by cuttings, grafting, etc, in plants **2** a segment of DNA that has been isolated and replicated by laboratory manipulation: used to analyse genes and manufacture their products (proteins)

Clonmel the county town of Co. Tipperary, Republic of Ireland; birthplace of Laurence Sterne; meat processing and enamelware. Pop: 16 910 (2002)

Clooney George born 1961, US film actor; he starred in the television series ER (1994–99) and the films *The Perfect Storm* (2000), and *Ocean's Eleven* (2001), and *Confessions of a Dangerous Mind*, (2002, also directed)

close¹ restricted or prohibited as to the type of game or fish able to be taken

close² 1 *Law* private property, usually enclosed by a fence, hedge, or wall 2 *Brit* a courtyard or quadrangle enclosed by buildings or an entry leading to such a courtyard 3 *Brit* a small quiet residential road 4 the precincts of a cathedral or similar building 5 *Scot* the entry from the street to a tenement building 6 *Music* another word for **cadence**. A perfect cadence is called a **full close** an imperfect one a **half close**

closed 1 (of a hunting season, etc) close 2 *Maths* a (of a curve or surface) completely enclosing an area or volume b (of a set) having members that can be produced by a specific operation on other members of the same set

closed circuit a complete electrical circuit through which current can flow when a voltage is applied

closed-circuit television a television system in which signals are transmitted from a television camera to the receivers by cables or telephone links forming a closed circuit, as used in security systems, etc.

close harmony *Music* a type of singing in which all the parts except the bass lie close together and are confined to the compass of a tenth

close season *or* **closed season** the period of the year when it is prohibited to kill certain game or fish

close-up a photograph or film or television shot taken at close range

closure 1 *Politics* (in a deliberative body) a procedure by which debate may be halted and an immediate vote taken 2 *Geology* the vertical distance between the crest of an anticline and the lowest contour that surrounds it 3 *Logic* the closed sentence formed from a given open sentence by prefixing universal or existential quantifiers to bind all its free variables 4 *Maths* the smallest closed set containing a given set 5 *Psychol* the tendency, first noted by Gestalt psychologists, to see an incomplete figure like a circle with a gap in it as more complete than it is

cloth 1 a a fabric formed by weaving, felting or knitting wool, cotton, etc. b (*as modifier*): *a cloth bag* 2 a piece of such fabric used for a particular purpose, as for a dishcloth 3 a the clothes worn by a clergyman b the clergy 4 *Nautical* any of the panels of a sail 5 *Chiefly Brit* a piece of coloured fabric, used on the stage as scenery

cloud 1 a mass of water or ice particles visible in the sky, usually white or grey, from which rain or snow falls when the particles coagulate 2 a large number of insects or other small animals in flight

cloud chamber *Physics* an apparatus for detecting high-energy particles by observing their tracks through a chamber containing a supersaturated vapour. Each particle ionizes molecules along its path and small droplets condense on them to produce a visible track

Clough 1 Arthur Hugh 1819–61, British poet, author of *Amours de Voyage* (1858) and *Dipsychus* (1865) 2 Brian 1935–2004, English footballer and manager

clout *Archery* a the target used in long-distance shooting b the centre of this target c a shot that hits the centre

clove 1 a tropical evergreen myrtaceous tree, *Syzygium aromaticum*, native to the East Indies but cultivated elsewhere, esp Zanzibar 2 *Botany* any of the segments of a compound bulb that arise from the axils of the scales of a large bulb

Clovelly a village in SW England, in Devon on the Bristol Channel: famous for its steep cobbled streets: tourism, fishing. Pop: 500 (latest est)

cloven hoof *or* **foot** the divided hoof of a pig, goat, cow, deer, or related animal, which consists of the two middle digits of the foot

clover 1 any plant of the leguminous genus *Trifolium*, having trifoliate leaves and dense flower heads. Many species, such as red clover, white clover, and alsike, are grown as forage plants 2 any of various similar or related plants

Clovis I German name Chlodwig. ?466–511 AD, king of the Franks (481–511), who extended the Merovingian kingdom to include most of Gaul and SW Germany

clown a comic entertainer, usually grotesquely costumed and made up, appearing in the circus

club 1 a stick or bat used to strike the ball in various sports, esp golf 2 short for **Indian club** 3 a commercial establishment in which people can drink and dance; disco 4 a the black trefoil symbol on a playing card b a card with one or more of these symbols or (*when pl.*) the suit of cards so marked 5 *Nautical* a spar used for extending the clew of a gaff topsail beyond the peak of the gaff

club class 1 a class of air travel which is less luxurious than first class but more luxurious than economy class 2 of or relating to this class of travel

club foot 1 a congenital deformity of the foot, esp one in which the foot is twisted so that most of the weight rests on the heel 2 *Nautical* a boom attached to the foot of a jib

Cluj an industrial city in NW Romania, on the Someşul-Mic River: former capital of Transylvania. Pop: 297 000 (2005 est)

Cluniac of or relating to a reformed Benedictine order founded at the French town of Cluny in 910

Cluny a town in E central France: reformed Benedictine order founded here in 910; important religious and cultural centre in the Middle Ages. Pop: 4376 (1999)

cluster 1 *Astronomy* an aggregation of stars or galaxies moving together through space 2 *Chem* a a chemical compound or molecule containing groups of metal atoms joined by metal-to-metal bonds b the group of linked metal atoms present

clutch¹ a device that enables two revolving shafts to be joined or disconnected as required, esp one that transmits the drive from the engine to the gearbox in a vehicle

clutch² a hatch of eggs laid by a particular bird or laid in a single nest

Clutha a river in New Zealand, the longest river in

South Island; rising in the Southern Alps it flows southeast to the Pacific. Length: 338 km (210 miles)

clutter *Electronics* unwanted echoes that confuse the observation of signals on a radar screen

Clwyd a former county in NE Wales, formed in 1974 from Flintshire, most of Denbighshire, and part of Merionethshire; replaced in 1996 by Flintshire, Denbighshire, Wrexham county borough, and part of Conwy county borough

Clyde 1 Firth of, an inlet of the Atlantic in SW Scotland. Length: 103 km (64 miles) 2 a river in S Scotland, rising in South Lanarkshire and flowing northwest to the Firth of Clyde: formerly extensive shipyards. Length: 170 km (106 miles)

Clydebank a town in W Scotland, in West Dunbartonshire on the north bank of the River Clyde. Pop: 29 858 (2001)

Clydesdale a heavy powerful breed of carthorse, originally from Scotland

coach 1 a vehicle for several passengers, used for transport over long distances, sightseeing, etc. 2 a railway carriage carrying passengers 3 a trainer or instructor 4 a tutor who prepares students for examinations

coachman a fishing fly with white wings and a brown hackle

coachwork 1 the design and manufacture of car bodies 2 the body of a car

coagulate the solid or semisolid substance produced by coagulation

Coahuila a state of N Mexico: mainly plateau, crossed by several mountain ranges that contain rich mineral resources. Capital: Saltillo. Pop: 2 295 808 (2000). Area: 151 571 sq km (59 112 sq miles)

coal 1 a a combustible compact black or dark-brown carbonaceous rock formed from compaction of layers of partially decomposed vegetation: a fuel and a source of coke, coal gas, and coal tar b (*as modifier*): *coal cellar* 2 short for **charcoal**

coal gas a mixture of gases produced by the distillation of bituminous coal and used for heating and lighting: consists mainly of hydrogen, methane, and carbon monoxide

coal tar a black tar, produced by the distillation of bituminous coal, that can be further distilled to yield benzene, toluene, xylene, anthracene, phenol, etc.

coal tit a small European songbird, *Parus ater*, having a black head with a white patch on the nape: family *Paridae* (tits)

coaming *Nautical* a raised frame around the cockpit or hatchway of a vessel for keeping out water

coarse 1 (of a metal) not refined 2 (of a screw) having widely spaced threads

coarse fish a freshwater fish that is not a member of the salmon family

coast 1 a the line or zone where the land meets the sea or some other large expanse of water b (*in combination*): *coastland* 2 US a a slope down which a sledge may slide b the act or an instance of sliding down a slope

coaster 1 *Brit* a vessel or trader engaged in coastal commerce 2 *West African* a European resident on the coast

coastguard 1 a maritime force which aids shipping, saves lives at sea, prevents smuggling, etc. 2 a member

of such a force

coastline the outline of a coast, esp when seen from the sea, or the land adjacent to it

coat the hair, wool, or fur of an animal

Coates Joseph Gordon 1878–1943, New Zealand statesman; prime minister of New Zealand (1925–28)

coating a heavy fabric suitable for coats

coaxial *or* **coaxal** 1 having or being mounted on a common axis 2 *Geometry* (of a set of circles) having all the centres on a straight line 3 *Electronics* formed from, using, or connected to a coaxial cable

cob¹ 1 a male swan 2 a thickset short-legged type of riding and draught horse

cob² *or* **cobb** an archaic or dialect name for a **gull** esp the greater black-backed gull (*Larus marinus*)

cobalt a brittle hard silvery-white element that is a ferromagnetic metal: occurs principally in cobaltite and smaltite and is widely used in alloys. The radioisotope **cobalt-60**, with a half-life of 5.3 years, is used in radiotherapy and as a tracer. Symbol: Co; atomic no.: 27; atomic wt.: 58.93320; valency: 2 or 3; relative density: 8.9; melting pt.: 1495°C; boiling pt.: 2928°C

Cobbett William 1763–1835, English journalist and social reformer; founded *The Political Register* (1802); author of *Rural Rides* (1830)

cobble 1 short for **cobblestone** 2 *Geology* a rock fragment, often rounded, with a diameter of 64–256 mm and thus smaller than a boulder but larger than a pebble

cobbler a person who makes or mends shoes

cobblestone a rounded stone used for paving

Cobden Richard 1804–65, British economist and statesman: with John Bright a leader of the successful campaign to abolish the Corn Laws (1846)

Cobham Lord, title of (Sir John) **Oldcastle**

COBOL *or* **Cobol** a high-level computer programming language designed for general commercial use

cobra 1 any highly venomous elapid snake of the genus *Naja*, such as *N. naja* (**Indian cobra**), of tropical Africa and Asia. When alarmed they spread the skin of the neck region into a hood 2 any related snake, such as the king cobra

Coburg a city in E Germany, in N Bavaria. Pop: 42 257 (2003 est)

cobweb 1 a web spun by certain spiders, esp those of the family *Theridiidae*, often found in the corners of disused rooms 2 a single thread of such a web

coca 1 either of two shrubs, *Erythroxylon coca* or *E. truxiuense*, native to the Andes: family *Erythroxylaceae* 2 the dried leaves of these shrubs and related plants, which contain cocaine and are chewed by the peoples of the Andes for their stimulating effects

Coca-Cola *Trademark* a carbonated soft drink flavoured with coca leaves, cola nuts, caramel, etc.

cocaine *or* **cocain** an addictive narcotic drug derived from coca leaves or synthesized, used medicinally as a topical anaesthetic. Formula: $C_{17}H_{21}NO_4$

coccyx a small triangular bone at the end of the spinal column in man and some apes, representing a vestigial tail

Cochin 1 a region and former state of SW India: part of Kerala state since 1956 2 a port in SW India, on the

Malabar Coast: the first European settlement in India, founded by Vasco da Gama in 1502: shipbuilding, engineering. Pop: 596 473 (2001) **3** a large breed of domestic fowl, with dense plumage and feathered legs, that originated in Cochin China

Cochin China a former French colony of Indochina (1862–1948): now the part of Vietnam that lies south of Phan Thiet

cochineal 1 a Mexican homopterous insect, *Dactylopius coccus*, that feeds on cacti **2** a crimson substance obtained from the crushed bodies of these insects, used for colouring food and for dyeing

cochlea the spiral tube, shaped like a snail's shell, that forms part of the internal ear, converting sound vibrations into nerve impulses

cock 1 the male of the domestic fowl **2 a** any other male bird **b** the male of certain other animals, such as the lobster **c** (*as modifier*): *a cock sparrow*

cockabully any of several small freshwater fish of New Zealand

cockatoo any of various parrots of the genus *Kakatoe* and related genera, such as *K. galerita* (**sulphur-crested cockatoo**), of Australia and New Guinea. They have an erectile crest and most of them are light-coloured

cockatrice 1 a legendary monster, part snake and part cock, that could kill with a glance **2** another name for **basilisk**

cockchafer any of various Old World scarabaeid beetles, esp *Melolontha melolontha* of Europe, whose larvae feed on crops and grasses

Cockcroft Sir John Douglas 1897–1967, English nuclear physicist. With E. T. S. Walton, he produced the first artificial transmutation of an atomic nucleus (1932) and shared the Nobel prize for physics 1951

Cocker Edward 1631–75, English arithmetician

Cockerell Sir Christopher Sydney 1910–99, British engineer, who invented the hovercraft

cocker spaniel a small compact breed of spaniel having sleek silky fur, a domed head, and long fringed ears

cockfight a fight between two gamecocks fitted with sharp metal spurs

cockle¹ 1 any sand-burrowing bivalve mollusc of the family *Cardiidae*, esp *Cardium edule* (**edible cockle**) of Europe, typically having a rounded shell with radiating ribs **2** any of certain similar or related molluscs **3** short for **cockleshell 4** a small furnace or stove

cockle² any of several plants, esp the corn cockle, that grow as weeds in cornfields

cockleshell 1 the shell of the cockle **2** any of the valves of the shells of certain other bivalve molluscs, such as the scallop **3** any small light boat **4** a badge worn by pilgrims

cockney 1 a native of London, esp of the working class born in the East End, speaking a characteristic dialect of English. Traditionally defined as someone born within the sound of the bells of St. Mary-le-Bow church **2** *Austral* a young snapper fish

cockpit 1 the compartment in a small aircraft in which the pilot, crew, and sometimes the passengers sit **2** the driver's compartment in a racing car **3** *Nautical* **a** an enclosed or recessed area towards the stern of a small vessel from which it is steered **b** (formerly) an apartment in a warship used as quarters for junior officers and as a first-aid station during combat **4** an enclosure used for cockfights

cockroach any insect of the suborder *Blattodea* (or *Blattaria*), such as *Blatta orientalis* (**oriental cockroach** or **black beetle**): order *Dictyoptera*. They have an oval flattened body with long antennae and biting mouthparts and are common household pests

cockscomb *or* **coxcomb 1** an amaranthaceous garden or pot plant, *Celosia cristata*, with yellow, crimson, or purple feathery plumelike flowers in a broad spike resembling the comb of a cock **2** any similar species of *Celosia* **3** the comb of a domestic cock

cocktail¹ a any mixed drink with a spirit base, usually drunk before meals **b** (*as modifier*): *the cocktail hour*
▷www.cocktail.com
▷www.cocktail.uk.com

cocktail² 1 a horse with a docked tail **2** an animal of unknown or mixed breeding

cocoa *or* **cacao 1** a powder made from cocoa beans after they have been roasted, ground, and freed from most of their fatty oil **2** a hot or cold drink made from cocoa and milk or water

coconut *or* **cocoanut** the fruit of the coconut palm, consisting of a thick fibrous oval husk inside which is a thin hard shell enclosing edible white meat. The hollow centre is filled with a milky fluid (**coconut milk**)

cocoon 1 a a silky protective envelope secreted by silkworms and certain other insect larvae, in which the pupae develop **b** a similar covering for the eggs of the spider, earthworm, etc. **2** a protective spray covering used as a seal on machinery

Cocteau Jean 1889–1963, French dramatist, novelist, poet, critic, designer, and film director. His works include the novel *Les Enfants terribles* (1929) and the play *La Machine infernale* (1934)

cod 1 any of the gadoid food fishes of the genus *Gadus*, esp *G. morhua* (or *G. callarias*), which occurs in the North Atlantic and has a long body with three rounded dorsal fins: family *Gadidae*. They are also a source of cod-liver oil **2** any other fish of the family *Gadidae* **3** *Austral* any of various unrelated Australian fish, such as the Murray cod

coda 1 *Music* the final, sometimes inessential, part of a musical structure **2** a concluding part of a literary work, esp a summary at the end of a novel of further developments in the lives of the characters

codeine a white crystalline alkaloid prepared mainly from morphine and having a similar but milder action. It is used as an analgesic, an antidiarrhoeal, and to relieve coughing. Formula: $C_{18}H_{21}NO_3$

codex *Obsolete* a legal code

codfish a cod, esp *Gadus morhua*

codicil *Law* a supplement modifying a will or revoking some provision of it

codling¹ *or* **codlin** any unripe apple

codling² a codfish, esp a young one

cod-liver oil an oil extracted from the livers of cod and related fish, rich in vitamins A and D and used to treat deficiency of these vitamins

Coe Sebastian, Baron. born 1956, English middle-distance runner and Conservative politician: winner of the 1500 metres in the 1980 and 1984 Olympic Games; holds 1000 m record; held records at 800 m, 1500 m, and a mile: member of parliament (1992–97)

coeducation instruction in schools, colleges, etc, attended by both sexes

coefficient 1 *Maths* **a** a numerical or constant factor in an algebraic term **b** the product of all the factors of a term excluding one or more specified variables **2** *Physics* a value that relates one physical quantity to another

coelacanth a primitive marine bony fish of the genus *Latimeria* (subclass *Crossopterygii*), having fleshy limblike pectoral fins and occurring off the coast of E Africa: thought to be extinct until a living specimen was discovered in 1938

coelenterate 1 any invertebrate of the phylum *Cnidaria* (formerly *Coelenterata*), having a saclike body with a single opening (mouth), which occurs in polyp and medusa forms. Coelenterates include the hydra, jellyfishes, sea anemones, and corals **2** (loosely) any invertebrate of the phyla *Cnidaria* or *Ctenophora*

coeliac disease a chronic intestinal disorder of young children caused by sensitivity to the protein gliadin contained in the gluten of cereals, characterized by distention of the abdomen and frothy and pale foul-smelling stools

coenobite *or* **cenobite** a member of a religious order following a communal rule of life

Coetzee J(ohn) M(ichael). born 1940, South African novelist: his works include *Life and Times of Michael K* (1983), *Age of Iron* (1990), *Disgrace* (1999), and *Elizabeth Costello* (2003)

Coeur Jacques ?1395–1456, French merchant; councillor and court banker to Charles VII of France

coffee 1 a drink consisting of an infusion of the roasted and ground or crushed seeds of the coffee tree **2** the beanlike seeds of the coffee tree, used to make this beverage

▷www.coffeeresearch.org
▷www.ico.org
▷www.nationalgeographic.com/coffee
▷www.coffeescience.org/css.html
▷www.ineedcoffee.com
▷www.ncausa.org

coffee house a place where coffee is served, esp one that was a fashionable meeting place in 18th-century London

coffer 1 an ornamental sunken panel in a ceiling, dome, etc. **2** a watertight box or chamber **3** a short for **cofferdam b** a recessed panel in a concrete, metal, or timber soffit

cofferdam 1 a watertight structure, usually of sheet piling, that encloses an area under water, pumped dry to enable construction work to be carried out. Below a certain depth a caisson is required **2** (on a ship) a compartment separating two bulkheads or floors, as for insulation or to serve as a barrier against the escape of gas or oil

coffin the part of a horse's foot that contains the coffin bone

cog 1 any of the teeth or projections on the rim of a gearwheel or sprocket **2** a gearwheel, esp a small one

Cognac 1 a town in SW France: centre of the district famed for its brandy. Pop: 19 534 (1999) **2** a high-quality grape brandy

cognate related by blood or descended from a common maternal ancestor

cognition the mental act or process by which knowledge is acquired, including perception, intuition, and reasoning

cognizance *or* **cognisance** *Law* **a** the right of a court to hear and determine a cause or matter **b** knowledge of certain facts upon which the court must act without requiring proof **c** *Chiefly US* confession

cognomen (originally) an ancient Roman's third name or nickname, which later became his family name

Cohen 1 Leonard born 1934, Canadian singer, songwriter, and poet; recordings include *Songs of Leonard Cohen* (1968), *Songs of Love and Hate* (1971), *I'm Your Man* (1988), and *Ten New Songs* (2001) **2** Stanley born 1922, US biochemist: shared the Nobel prize for physiology or medicine 1986

coherent 1 *Physics* (of two or more waves) having the same phase or a fixed phase difference **2** (of a system of units) consisting only of units the quotient or product of any two of which yield the unit of the resultant quantity

cohesion 1 *Physics* the force that holds together the atoms or molecules in a solid or liquid, as distinguished from adhesion **2** *Botany* the fusion in some plants of flower parts, such as petals, that are usually separate

cohort *Biology* a taxonomic group that is a subdivision of a subclass (usually of mammals) or subfamily (of plants)

coif (formerly in England) the white cap worn by a serjeant at law

coil 1 an electrical conductor wound into the form of a spiral, sometimes with a soft iron core, to provide inductance or a magnetic field **2** the transformer in a petrol engine that supplies the high voltage to the sparking plugs

Coimbra a city in central Portugal: capital of Portugal from 1190 to 1260; seat of the country's oldest university. Pop: 148 474 (2001)

coinage 1 coins collectively **2** the act of striking coins **3** the currency of a country

coincidence *Electronics* of or relating to a circuit that produces an output pulse only when both its input terminals receive pulses within a specified interval

coir the fibre prepared from the husk of the coconut, used in making rope and matting

coke 1 a solid-fuel product containing about 80 per cent of carbon produced by distillation of coal to drive off its volatile constituents: used as a fuel and in metallurgy as a reducing agent for converting metal oxides into metals **2** any similar material, such as the layer formed in the cylinders of a car engine by incomplete combustion of the fuel

Coke 1 Sir Edward 1552–1634, English jurist, noted for his defence of the common law against encroachment from the Crown: the Petition of Right (1628) was largely his work **2** Thomas William, 1st Earl of Leicester, known as *Coke of Holkham*. 1752–1842, English agriculturist: pioneered agricultural improvement and considerably improved productivity at his Holkham estate in

Norfolk

col 1 *Geography* the lowest point of a ridge connecting two mountain peaks, often constituting a pass 2 *Meteorol* a pressure region between two anticyclones and two depressions, associated with variable weather

cola *or* **kola** 1 either of two tropical sterculiaceous trees, *Cola nitida* or *C. acuminata*, widely cultivated in tropical regions for their seeds 2 a sweet carbonated drink flavoured with cola nuts

Colbert 1 Claudette, real name *Claudette Lily Chauchoin*. 1905–96, French-born Hollywood actress, noted for her sophisticated comedy roles; her films include *It Happened One Night* (1934) and *The Palm Beach Story* (1942) 2 Jean Baptiste 1619–83, French statesman; chief minister to Louis XIV: reformed the taille and pursued a mercantilist policy, creating a powerful navy and merchant fleet and building roads and canals

Colchester a town in E England, in NE Essex; university (1964). Pop: 104 390 (2001)

Colchis an ancient country on the Black Sea south of the Caucasus; the land of Medea and the Golden Fleece in Greek mythology

cold 1 (of a colour) having violet, blue, or green predominating; giving no sensation of warmth 2 *Metallurgy* denoting or relating to a process in which work-hardening occurs as a result of the plastic deformation of a metal at too low a temperature for annealing to take place 3 (of a process) not involving heat, in contrast with traditional methods 4 an acute viral infection of the upper respiratory passages characterized by discharge of watery mucus from the nose, sneezing, etc.

cold-blooded (of all animals except birds and mammals) having a body temperature that varies with that of the surroundings

cold chisel a toughened steel chisel

cold frame *Horticulture* an unheated wooden frame with a glass top, used to protect young plants from the cold

cold front *Meteorol* 1 the boundary line between a warm air mass and the cold air pushing it from beneath and behind as it moves 2 the line on the earth's surface where the cold front meets it

Colditz a town in E Germany, on the River Mulde: during World War II its castle was used as a top-security camp for Allied prisoners of war; many daring escape attempts, some successful, were made

cold sore a cluster of blisters at the margin of the lips that sometimes accompanies the common cold, caused by a viral infection

Coldstream a town in SE Scotland, in Scottish Borders on the English border: the Coldstream Guards were formed here (1660). Pop: 1813 (2001)

cold sweat *Informal* a bodily reaction to fear or nervousness, characterized by chill and moist skin

cold turkey 1 *Slang* a method of curing drug addiction by abrupt withdrawal of all doses 2 the withdrawal symptoms, esp nausea and shivering, brought on by this method

cold war a state of political hostility and military tension between two countries or power blocs, involving propaganda, subversion, threats, economic sanctions, and other measures short of open warfare, esp that between the American and Soviet blocs after World War

II (the **Cold War**)
 ▷www.coldwar.org
 ▷www.fas.harvard.edu/~hpcws

cole any of various plants of the genus *Brassica*, such as the cabbage and rape

Cole Nat 'King', real name *Nathaniel Adams Cole*. 1917–65, US popular singer and jazz pianist

Coleman Ornette born 1930, US avant-garde jazz alto saxophonist and multi-instrumentalist

Coleraine 1 a town in N Northern Ireland, in Coleraine district, Co. Antrim, on the River Bann; light industries; university (1965). Pop: 24 089 (2001) 2 a district in N Northern Ireland, in Co. Antrim and Co. Londonderry. Pop: 56 024 (2003 est). Area: 485 sq km (187 sq miles)

Coleridge Samuel Taylor 1772–1834, English Romantic poet and critic, noted for poems such as *The Rime of the Ancient Mariner* (1798), *Kubla Khan* (1816), and *Christabel* (1816), and for his critical work *Biographia Literaria* (1817)

Coleridge-Taylor Samuel 1875–1912, British composer, best known for his trilogy of oratorios *Song of Hiawatha* (1898–1900)

Colet John ?1467–1519, English humanist and theologian; founder of St. Paul's School, London (1509)

Colette full name *Sidonie Gabrielle Claudine Colette*. 1873–1954, French novelist; her works include *Chéri* (1920), *Gigi* (1944), and the series of *Claudine* books

colic a condition characterized by acute spasmodic abdominal pain, esp that caused by inflammation, distention, etc, of the gastrointestinal tract

Coligny *or* **Coligni** Gaspard de , Seigneur de Châtillon. 1519–72, French Huguenot leader

Colima 1 a state of SW Mexico, on the Pacific coast: mainly a coastal plain, rising to the foothills of the Sierra Madre, with important mineral resources. Capital: Colima. Pop: 238 000 (2005 est). Area: 5455 sq km (2106 sq miles) 2 a city in SW Mexico, capital of Colima state, on the Colima River. Pop: 106 967 (1990) 3 Nevado de a volcano in SW Mexico, in Jalisco state. Height: 4339 m (14 235 ft)

colitis *or* **colonitis** inflammation of the colon

collage 1 an art form in which compositions are made out of pieces of paper, cloth, photographs, and other miscellaneous objects, juxtaposed and pasted on a dry ground 2 any work, such as a piece of music, created by combining unrelated styles

collagen a fibrous scleroprotein of connective tissue and bones that is rich in glycine and proline and yields gelatine on boiling

collar 1 *Biology* a marking or structure resembling a collar, such as that found around the necks of some birds or at the junction of a stem and a root 2 a section of a shaft or rod having a locally increased diameter to provide a bearing seat or a locating ring

collateral 1 a person, animal, or plant descended from the same ancestor as another but through a different line 2 descended from a common ancestor but through different lines

collation 1 *RC Church* a light meal permitted on fast days 2 the appointment of a clergyman to a benefice

collect¹ *Austral, informal* a winning bet

collect² *Christianity* a short Church prayer generally preceding the lesson or epistle in Communion and other services

collected (of a horse or a horse's pace) controlled so that movement is in short restricted steps

collection (at Oxford University) a college examination or an oral report by a tutor

collective a a cooperative enterprise or unit, such as a collective farm b the members of such a cooperative

collectivism the principle of ownership of the means of production, by the state or the people

collector 1 a person employed to collect debts, rents, etc. 2 the head of a district administration in India 3 a person who collects or amasses objects as a hobby 4 *Electronics* the region in a transistor into which charge carriers flow from the base

college 1 an institution of higher education; part of a university 2 a school or an institution providing specialized courses or teaching 3 the building or buildings in which a college is housed 4 the staff and students of a college 5 an organized body of persons with specific rights and duties 6 a body of clerics living in community and supported by endowment

collegian a current member of a college; student

collegiate 1 of or relating to a college or college students 2 (of a university) composed of various colleges of equal standing

collie any of several silky-coated breeds of dog developed for herding sheep and cattle

collier *Chiefly Brit* a a ship designed to transport coal b a member of its crew

Collins 1 Michael 1890–1922, Irish republican revolutionary: a leader of Sinn Féin; member of the Irish delegation that negotiated the treaty with Great Britain (1921) that established the Irish Free State 2 (William) Wilkie 1824–89, British author, noted particularly for his suspense novel *The Moonstone* (1868) 3 William 1721–59, British poet, noted for his odes; regarded as a precursor of romanticism

collision *Physics* an event in which two or more bodies or particles come together with a resulting change of direction and, normally, energy

colloid 1 a mixture having particles of one component, with diameters between 10^{-7} and 10^{-9} metres, suspended in a continuous phase of another component. The mixture has properties between those of a solution and a fine suspension 2 *Physiol* a gelatinous substance of the thyroid follicles that holds the hormonal secretions of the thyroid gland 3 *Pathol* of or relating to the gluelike translucent material found in certain degenerating tissues

colloquium an academic seminar

colloquy 1 a literary work in dialogue form 2 an informal conference on religious or theological matters

collusion a secret agreement between opponents at law in order to obtain a judicial decision for some wrongful or improper purpose

Colmar a city in NE France: annexed to Germany 1871–1919 and 1940–45; textile industry. Pop: 65 136 (1999)

Cologne an industrial city and river port in W Germany, in North Rhine-Westphalia on the Rhine: important commercially since ancient times; university (1388). Pop: 965 954 (2003 est)

Colombes an industrial and residential suburb of NW Paris. Pop: 76 757 (1999)

Colombia a republic in NW South America: inhabited by Chibchas and other Indians before Spanish colonization in the 16th century; independence won by Bolívar in 1819; became the Republic of Colombia in 1886; violence and unrest have been endemic since the 1970s. It consists chiefly of a hot swampy coastal plain, separated by ranges of the Andes from the pampas and the equatorial forests of the Amazon basin in the east. Language: Spanish. Religion: Roman Catholic majority. Currency: peso. Capital: Bogotá. Pop: 44 914 000 (2004 est). Area: 1 138 908 sq km (439 735 sq miles)

Colombo the capital and chief port of Sri Lanka, on the W coast, with one of the largest artificial harbours in the world. Pop: 653 000 (2005 est)

colon¹ (in classical prosody) a part of a rhythmic period with two to six feet and one principal accent or ictus

colon² the part of the large intestine between the caecum and the rectum

colonial 1 characteristic of or relating to the 13 British colonies that became the United States of America (1776) 2 of or relating to the colonies of the British Empire 3 denoting, relating to, or having the style of Neoclassical architecture used in the British colonies in America in the 17th and 18th centuries 4 of or relating to the period of Australian history before Federation (1901) 5 (of organisms such as corals and bryozoans) existing as a colony of polyps 6 (of animals and plants) having become established in a community in a new environment

colonialism the policy and practice of a power in extending control over weaker peoples or areas

colonnade 1 a set of evenly-spaced columns 2 a row of regularly spaced trees

Colonsay an island in W Scotland, in the Inner Hebrides. Area: about 41 sq km (16 sq miles)

colony 1 a body of people who settle in a country distant from their homeland but maintain ties with it 2 the community formed by such settlers 3 a subject territory occupied by a settlement from the ruling state 4 *Zoology* a a group of the same type of animal or plant living or growing together, esp in large numbers b an interconnected group of polyps of a colonial organism

Colorado 1 a state of the central US: consists of the Great Plains in the east and the Rockies in the west; drained chiefly by the Colorado, Arkansas, South Platte, and Rio Grande Rivers. Capital: Denver. Pop: 4 550 688 (2003 est). Area: 269 998 sq km (104 247 sq miles) 2 a river in SW North America, rising in the Rocky Mountains and flowing southwest to the Gulf of California: famous for the 1600 km (1000 miles) of canyons along its course. Length: about 2320 km (1440 miles) 3 a river in central Texas, flowing southeast to the Gulf of Mexico. Length: about 1450 km (900 miles) 4 a river in central Argentina, flowing southeast to the Atlantic. Length: about 850 km (530 miles)

Colorado beetle a black-and-yellow beetle, *Leptinotarsa decemlineata*, that is a serious pest of potatoes, feeding on the leaves: family *Chrysomelidae*

Colorado Desert an arid region of SE California and NW Mexico, west of the Colorado River. Area: over 5000

sq km (2000 sq miles)

Colorado Springs a city and resort in central Colorado. Pop: 370 448 (2003 est)

coloration *or* **colouration** 1 the colouring or markings of insects, birds, etc. 2 unwanted extraneous variations in the frequency response of a loudspeaker or listening environment

coloratura *or* **colorature** *Music* 1 a (in 18th- and 19th-century arias) a florid virtuoso passage b (*as modifier*): *a coloratura aria* 2 a lyric soprano who specializes in such music

colossal 1 (in figure sculpture) approximately twice life-size 2 *Architect* of or relating to the order of columns and pilasters that extend more than one storey in a façade

colostomy the surgical formation of an opening from the colon onto the surface of the body, which functions as an anus

colour *or* US **color** 1 a an attribute of things that results from the light they reflect, transmit, or emit in so far as this light causes a visual sensation that depends on its wavelengths b the aspect of visual perception by which an observer recognizes this attribute c the quality of the light producing this aspect of visual perception d (*as modifier*): *colour vision* 2 a a colour, such as red or green, that possesses hue, as opposed to achromatic colours such as white or black b (*as modifier*): *a colour television* 3 a the skin complexion of a person, esp as determined by his race b (*as modifier*): *colour prejudice* 4 the use of all the hues in painting as distinct from composition, form, and light and shade 5 the distinctive tone of a musical sound; timbre 6 *Physics* one of three characteristics of quarks, designated red, blue, or green, but having no relationship with the physical sensation

colour bar discrimination against people of a different race, esp as practised by Whites against Blacks

colour-blind 1 of or relating to any defect in the normal ability to distinguish certain colours 2 not discriminating on grounds of skin colour or ethnic origin

Coloured 1 an individual who is not a White person, esp a Black person 2 (in South Africa) a person of racially mixed parentage or descent 3 designating or relating to a Coloured person or Coloured people

colt a male horse or pony under the age of four

Coltrane John (William). 1926–67, US jazz tenor and soprano saxophonist and composer

coltsfoot a European plant, *Tussilago farfara*, with yellow daisy-like flowers and heart-shaped leaves: a common weed: family *Asteraceae* (composites)

Colum Padraic 1881–1972, Irish lyric poet, resident in the US (1914–72)

Columba Saint ?521–597 AD, Irish missionary: founded the monastery at Iona (563) from which the Picts were converted to Christianity. Feast day: June 9

Columbia 1 a river in NW North America, rising in the Rocky Mountains and flowing through British Columbia, then west to the Pacific. Length: about 1930 km (1200 miles) 2 a city in central South Carolina, on the Congaree River: the state capital. Pop: 117 357 (2003 est)

Columbian 1 of or relating to the United States 2 relating to Christopher Columbus (Spanish name *Cristóbal Colón*, Italian name *Cristoforo Colombo*.; 1451–1506), Italian navigator and explorer in the service of Spain, who discovered the New World (1492)

columbine any plant of the ranunculaceous genus *Aquilegia*, having purple, blue, yellow, or red flowers with five spurred petals

Columbus¹ Christopher Spanish name *Cristóbal Colón*, Italian name *Cristoforo Colombo*. 1451–1506, Italian navigator and explorer in the service of Spain, who discovered the New World (1492)

Columbus² 1 a city in central Ohio: the state capital. Pop: 728 432 (2003 est) 2 a city in W Georgia, on the Chattahoochee River. Pop: 185 702 (2003 est)

column 1 an upright post or pillar usually having a cylindrical shaft, a base, and a capital 2 a vertical array of numbers or mathematical terms 3 *Botany* a long structure in a flower, such as that of an orchid, consisting of the united stamens and style 4 *Anatomy, Zoology* any elongated structure, such as a tract of grey matter in the spinal cord or the stalk of a crinoid

Colwyn Bay a town and resort in N Wales, in Conwy county borough. Pop: 30 269 (2001)

coma¹ a state of unconsciousness from which a person cannot be aroused, caused by injury to the head, rupture of cerebral blood vessels, narcotics, poisons, etc.

coma² 1 *Astronomy* the luminous cloud surrounding the frozen solid nucleus in the head of a comet, formed by vaporization of part of the nucleus when the comet is close to the sun 2 *Botany* a a tuft of hairs attached to the seed coat of some seeds b the terminal crown of leaves of palms and moss stems 3 *Optics* a type of lens defect characterized by the formation of a diffuse pear-shaped image from a point object

comb 1 a tool or machine that separates, cleans, and straightens wool, cotton, etc. 2 the fleshy deeply serrated outgrowth on the top of the heads of certain birds, esp the domestic fowl 3 a currycomb 4 a honeycomb 5 the row of fused cilia in a ctenophore

comber 1 a person, tool, or machine that combs wool, flax, etc. 2 a long curling wave; roller

combination 1 a the set of numbers that opens a combination lock b the mechanism of this type of lock 2 *Brit* a motorcycle with a sidecar attached 3 *Maths* a an arrangement of the numbers, terms, etc, of a set into specified groups without regard to order in the group b a group formed in this way. The number of combinations of n objects taken r at a time is $n!/[(n-r)!r!]$. Symbol: $_nC_r$ 4 the chemical reaction of two or more compounds, usually to form one other compound 5 *Chess* a tactical manoeuvre involving a sequence of moves and more than one piece

combination lock a type of lock that can only be opened when a set of dials releasing the tumblers of the lock are turned to show a specific sequence of numbers

combine *Business* an association of enterprises, esp in order to gain a monopoly of a market

combo a small group of musicians, esp of jazz musicians

combustion 1 any process in which a substance reacts with oxygen to produce a significant rise in temperature and the emission of light 2 a chemical process in which two compounds, such as sodium and chlorine, react together to produce heat and light **3** a process in which a compound reacts slowly with oxygen to produce little heat and no light

Comecon (formerly) an association of Soviet-oriented Communist nations, founded in 1949 to coordinate economic development, etc.; it was disbanded in 1991 when free-market policies were adopted by its members

comedian 1 an entertainer who specializes in jokes, comic skits, etc. **2** an actor in comedy

comedy 1 a dramatic or other work of light and amusing character **2** the genre of drama represented by works of this type **3** (in classical literature) a play in which the main characters and motive triumph over adversity

▷www.comedy-zone.net

▷www.comedy.com

▷www.bbc.co.uk/comedy

comet a celestial body that travels around the sun, usually in a highly elliptical orbit: thought to consist of a solid frozen nucleus part of which vaporizes on approaching the sun to form a gaseous luminous coma and a long luminous tail

comfrey any hairy Eurasian boraginaceous plant of the genus *Symphytum*, having blue, purplish-pink, or white flowers

comic opera a play largely set to music, employing comic effects or situations

coming the return of Christ in glory

comity the policy whereby one religious denomination refrains from proselytizing the members of another

comma *Music* a minute interval

command *Computing* a word or phrase that can be selected from a menu or typed after a prompt in order to carry out an action

commander 1 an officer responsible for a district of the Metropolitan Police in London **2** *History* the administrator of a house, priory, or landed estate of a medieval religious order

commandment a divine command, esp one of the Ten Commandments of the Old Testament

commando 1 a an amphibious military unit trained for raiding **b** a member of such a unit **2** the basic unit of the Royal Marine Corps **3** (originally) an armed force raised by Boers during the Boer War

commencement a *US and Canadian* a ceremony for the presentation of awards at secondary schools **b** *US* a ceremony for the conferment of academic degrees

commensurable *Maths* **a** having a common factor **b** having units of the same dimensions and being related by whole numbers

commerce the activity embracing all forms of the purchase and sale of goods and services

commercial (of goods, chemicals, etc) of unrefined quality or presentation and produced in bulk for use in industry

commissar in the former Soviet Union **1** an official of the Communist Party responsible for political education, esp in a military unit **2** (before 1946) the head of a government department

commissariat 1 (in the former Soviet Union) a government department before 1946 **2 a** a military department in charge of food supplies, equipment, etc. **b** the offices of such a department **3** food supplies

commissary 1 *US* a shop supplying food or equipment, as in a military camp **2** *US* a snack bar or restaurant in a film studio **3** a representative or deputy, esp an official representative of a bishop

commission 1 a government agency or board empowered to exercise administrative, judicial, or legislative authority **2 a** the authority given to a person or organization to act as an agent to a principal in commercial transactions **b** the fee allotted to an agent for services rendered **3** *US* the head of a department of municipal government

commissioner *Government* **a** any of several types of civil servant **b** an ombudsman

commitment 1 the referral of a bill to a committee or legislature **2** *Law* a written order of a court directing that a person be imprisoned

commodity 1 an article of commerce **2** *Economics* an exchangeable unit of economic wealth, esp a primary product or raw material **3** *Obsolete* **a** a quantity of goods **b** convenience or expediency

commodore 1 the senior captain of a shipping line **2** the officer in command of a convoy of merchant ships **3** the senior flag officer of a yacht or boat club

Commodus Lucius Aelius Aurelius , son of Marcus Aurelius. 161–192 AD, Roman emperor (180–192), noted for his tyrannical reign

common 1 *Maths* **a** having a specified relationship with a group of numbers or quantities **b** (of a tangent) tangential to two or more circles **2** *Anatomy* **a** having branches **b** serving more than one function **3** *Christianity* of or relating to the common of the Mass or divine office **4** a tract of open public land, esp one now used as a recreation area **5** *Law* the right to go onto someone else's property and remove natural products, as by pasturing cattle or fishing (esp in the phrase **right of common**) **6** *Christianity* **a** a form of the proper of the Mass used on festivals that have no special proper of their own **b** the ordinary of the Mass

commonalty 1 the ordinary people as distinct from those with authority, rank, or title, esp when considered as a political and social unit or estate of the realm **2** *Business* the members of an incorporated society

common cold a mild viral infection of the upper respiratory tract, characterized by sneezing, coughing, watery eyes, nasal congestion, etc.

commoner 1 a person who does not belong to the nobility **2** a person who has a right in or over common land jointly with another or others **3** *Brit* a student at a university or other institution who is not on a scholarship

common law 1 the body of law based on judicial decisions and custom, as distinct from statute law **2** the law of a state that is of general application, as distinct from regional customs **3** denoting a marriage deemed to exist after a couple have cohabited for several years

Common Market the an informal name for the European Economic Community (now the **European Community**, part of the wider **European Union**) and its politics of greater economic cooperation between member states

commonplace a passage in a book marked for inclusion

in a commonplace book, etc.

common room *Chiefly Brit* a sitting room in schools, colleges, etc, for the relaxation of students or staff

commons 1 people not of noble birth viewed as forming a political order 2 the lower classes as contrasted to the ruling classes of society; the commonalty 3 *Brit* a building or hall for dining, recreation, etc, usually attached to a college 4 *Brit* food or rations (esp in the phrase **short commons**)

common time *Music* a time signature indicating four crotchet beats to the bar; four-four time.

commonwealth 1 the people of a state or nation viewed politically; body politic 2 a state or nation in which the people possess sovereignty; republic 3 the body politic organized for the general good

Commonwealth the 1 an association of sovereign states, almost all of which were at some time dependencies of the UK. All member states recognize the reigning British sovereign as **Head of the Commonwealth** 2 a the republic that existed in Britain from 1649 to 1660 b the part of this period up to 1653, when Cromwell became Protector 3 the official designation of Australia, four states of the US (Kentucky, Massachusetts, Pennsylvania, and Virginia), and Puerto Rico

▷www.thecommonwealth.org

commune 1 the smallest administrative unit in Belgium, France, Italy, and Switzerland, governed by a mayor and council 2 the government or inhabitants of a commune 3 a medieval town enjoying a large degree of autonomy

communicable (of a disease or its causative agent) capable of being passed on readily

communicant *Christianity* a person who receives Communion

communication cord *Brit* a cord or chain in a train which may be pulled by a passenger to stop the train in an emergency

communion 1 a religious group or denomination having a common body of beliefs, doctrines, and practices 2 the spiritual union held by Christians to exist between individual Christians and Christ, their Church, or their fellow Christians

Communion *Christianity* 1 the act of participating in the Eucharist 2 the celebration of the Eucharist, esp the part of the service during which the consecrated elements are received 3 a the consecrated elements of the Eucharist b (*as modifier*): *Communion cup*

communism 1 advocacy of a classless society in which private ownership has been abolished and the means of production and subsistence belong to the community 2 any social, economic, or political movement or doctrine aimed at achieving such a society 3 a political movement based upon the writings of Karl Marx, the German political philosopher (1818–83), that considers history in terms of class conflict and revolutionary struggle, resulting eventually in the victory of the proletariat and the establishment of a socialist order based on public ownership of the means of production 4 a social order or system of government established by a ruling Communist Party, esp in the former Soviet Union 5 *Chiefly US* any leftist political activity or

thought, esp when considered to be subversive 6 communal living; communalism

community 1 a the people living in one locality b the locality in which they live c (*as modifier*): *community spirit* 2 a group of nations having certain interests in common 3 (in Wales since 1974 and Scotland since 1975) the smallest unit of local government; a subdivision of a district 4 *Ecology* a group of interdependent plants and animals inhabiting the same region and interacting with each other through food and other relationships

community centre a building used by members of a community for social gatherings, educational activities, etc.

community charge (formerly in Britain) a flat-rate charge paid by each adult in a community to their local authority in place of rates

community service voluntary work, intended to be for the common good, usually done as part of an organized scheme

commutative *Maths, Logic* a (of an operator) giving the same result irrespective of the order of the arguments; thus disjunction and addition are commutative but implication and subtraction are not b relating to this property

commutator 1 a device used to reverse the direction of flow of an electric current 2 the segmented metal cylinder or disc mounted on the armature shaft of an electric motor, generator, etc, used to make electrical contact with the rotating coils and ensure unidirectional current flow

Como a city in N Italy, in Lombardy at the SW end of Lake Como: tourist centre. Pop: 78 680 (2001)

compact[1] 1 *Logic* (of a relation) having the property that for any pair of elements such that a is related to b, there is some element c such that a is related to c and c to b, as *less than* on the rational numbers. 2 *US and Canadian* (of a car) small and economical 3 *US and Canadian* a comparatively small and economical car 4 *Metallurgy* a mass of metal prepared for sintering by cold-pressing a metal powder

compact[2] *Law* an official contract or agreement

compact disc a small digital audio disc on which sound is recorded as a series of metallic pits enclosed in PVC; the disc is spun by the compact disc player and read by an optical laser system

companion[1] *Astronomy* the fainter of the two components of a double star

companion[2] *Nautical* a a raised frame on an upper deck with windows to give light to the deck below b (*as modifier*): *a companion ladder*

companionway *Nautical* a stairway or ladder leading from one deck to another in a boat or ship

company 1 a business enterprise 2 the members of an enterprise not specifically mentioned in the enterprise's title 3 a group of actors, usually including business and technical personnel 4 the officers and crew of a ship 5 a unit of Girl Guides 6 *English history* a medieval guild

compass 1 an instrument used for drawing circles, measuring distances, etc, that consists of two arms, joined at one end, one arm of which serves as a pivot or stationary reference point, while the other is extended or describes a circle **2** *Music* the interval between the lowest and highest note attainable by a voice or musical instrument

compatible 1 of plants **a** capable of forming successful grafts **b** capable of successful self-fertilization **2** (of pieces of machinery, computer equipment, etc) capable of being used together without special modification or adaptation

compendium 1 *Brit* a book containing a collection of useful hints **2** a concise but comprehensive summary of a larger work

compensation 1 the automatic movements made by the body to maintain balance **2** *Biology* abnormal growth and increase in size in one organ in response to the removal or inactivation of another

compere *Brit* a master of ceremonies who introduces cabaret, television acts, etc.

competence 1 *Law* the state of being legally competent or qualified **2** *Embryol* the ability of embryonic tissues to react to external conditions in a way that influences subsequent development

competent *Law* (of a witness) having legal capacity; qualified to testify, etc.

competition *Ecology* the struggle between individuals of the same or different species for food, space, light, etc, when these are inadequate to supply the needs of all

competitive *Business* sufficiently low in price or high in quality to be successful against commercial rivals

compiler a computer program by which a high-level programming language, such as COBOL or FORTRAN, is converted into machine language that can be acted upon by a computer

complainant *Law* a person who makes a complaint, usually before justices; plaintiff

complaint *English law* a statement by which a civil proceeding in a magistrates' court is commenced

complement 1 the officers and crew needed to man a ship **2** *Maths* the angle that when added to a specified angle produces a right angle **3** *Logic, Maths* the class of all things, or of all members of a given universe of discourse, that are not members of a given set **4** *Music* the inverted form of an interval that, when added to the interval, completes the octave

complementary or **complemental 1** forming a mathematical complement **2** *Maths, Logic* (of a pair of sets, etc) mutually exclusive and exhaustive, each being the complement of the other **3** (of genes) producing an effect in association with other genes

complementary medicine the treatment, alleviation, or prevention of disease by such techniques as osteopathy, homeopathy, aromatherapy, and acupuncture, allied with attention to such factors as diet and emotional stability, which can affect a person's wellbeing

complete 1 (of a logical system) constituted such that a contradiction arises on the addition of any proposition that cannot be deduced from the axioms of the system **2** (of flowers) having sepals, petals, stamens, and carpels

complex 1 *Maths* of or involving one or more complex numbers **2** *Psychoanal* a group of emotional ideas or impulses that have been banished from the conscious

mind but that continue to influence a person's behaviour **3** *Informal* an obsession or excessive fear **4** a chemical compound in which molecules, groups, or ions are attached to a central metal atom, esp a transition metal atom, by coordinate bonds **5** any chemical compound in which one molecule is linked to another by a coordinate bond

complex fraction *Maths* a fraction in which the numerator or denominator or both contain fractions

complex number any number of the form $a + ib$, where a and b are real numbers and $i = \sqrt{-1}$

compliance or **compliancy** a measure of the ability of a mechanical system to respond to an applied vibrating force, expressed as the reciprocal of the system's stiffness.

complicate *Biology* folded on itself

complication *Medicine* a disease or disorder arising as a consequence of another disease

component 1 any electrical device, such as a resistor, that has distinct electrical characteristics and that may be connected to other electrical devices to form a circuit **2** *Maths* **a** one of a set of two or more vectors whose resultant is a given vector **b** the projection of this given vector onto a specified line **3** *Chemistry* one of the minimum number of chemically distinct constituents necessary to describe fully the composition of each phase in a system

composite 1 *Maths* capable of being factorized or decomposed **2** of, relating to, or belonging to the plant family *Asteraceae* **3** denoting or relating to one of the five classical orders of architecture: characterized by a combination of the Ionic and Corinthian styles **4** any plant of the family *Asteraceae* (formerly *Compositae*), typically having flower heads composed of ray flowers (e.g. dandelion), disc flowers (e.g. thistle), or both (e.g. daisy)

composite school *Eastern Canadian* a secondary school offering both academic and nonacademic courses

composition 1 a work of music, art, or literature **2** the harmonious arrangement of the parts of a work of art in relation to each other and to the whole **3** a piece of writing undertaken as an academic exercise in grammatically acceptable writing; an essay **4** *Logic* the fallacy of inferring that the properties of the part are also true of the whole, as *every member of the team has won a prize, so the team will win a prize* **5** **a** a settlement by mutual consent, esp a legal agreement whereby the creditors agree to accept partial payment of a debt in full settlement **b** the sum so agreed **6** *Chem* the nature and proportions of the elements comprising a chemical compound

compost a mixture, normally of plant remains, peat, charcoal, etc, in which plants are grown, esp in pots

compound¹ 1 a substance that contains atoms of two or more chemical elements held together by chemical bonds **2** *Music* **a** denoting a time in which the number of beats per bar is a multiple of three **b** (of an interval) greater than an octave **3** *Zoology* another word for **colonial 4** (of a steam engine, turbine, etc) having multiple stages in which the steam or working fluid from one stage is used in a subsequent stage **5** (of a piston engine) having a turbocharger powered by a turbine in the exhaust stream

compound² (formerly in India, China, etc) the enclosure in which a European's house or factory stood

compound fracture a fracture in which the broken bone either pierces the skin or communicates with an open wound

comprehension 1 *Education* an exercise consisting of a previously unseen passage of text with related questions, designed to test a student's understanding esp of a foreign language 2 *Logic, obsolete* the attributes implied by a given concept or term; connotation

comprehensive school 1 *Chiefly Brit* a secondary school for children of all abilities from the same district 2 *Eastern Canadian* another name for **composite school**

compress 1 a wet or dry cloth or gauze pad with or without medication, applied firmly to some part of the body to relieve discomfort, reduce fever, drain a wound, etc. 2 a machine for packing material, esp cotton, under pressure

compression *Engineering* an increase in pressure of the charge in an engine or compressor obtained by reducing its volume

compressor 1 any reciprocating or rotating device that compresses a gas 2 the part of a gas turbine that compresses the air before it enters the combustion chambers 3 any muscle that causes compression of any part or structure 4 a medical instrument for holding down a part of the body 5 an electronic device for reducing the variation in signal amplitude in a transmission system

Compton 1 Arthur Holly 1892–1962, US physicist, noted for his research on X-rays, gamma rays, and nuclear energy: Nobel prize for physics 1927 2 **Denis** 1918–97, English cricketer, who played for Middlesex and England (1937–57); broke two records in 1947 scoring 3816 runs and 18 centuries in one season

Compton-Burnett Dame Ivy 1884–1969, English novelist. Her novels include *Men and Wives* (1931) and *Mother and Son* (1955)

compulsion *Psychiatry* an inner drive that causes a person to perform actions, often of a trivial and repetitive nature, against his or her will

compulsory purchase purchase of a house or other property by a local authority or government department for public use or to make way for development, regardless of whether or not the owner wishes to sell

computer a a device, usually electronic, that processes data according to a set of instructions

computer game any of various games, recorded on cassette or disc for use in a home computer, that are played by manipulating a mouse, joystick, or the keys on the keyboard of a computer in response to the graphics on the screen

comrade a fellow member of a political party, esp a fellow Communist or socialist

Comte (Isidore) Auguste (Marie François). 1798–1857, French mathematician and philosopher; the founder of positivism

con *or esp US* **conn** *Nautical* the place where a person who cons a vessel is stationed

Conakry *or* **Konakri** the capital of Guinea, a port on the island of Tombo. Pop: 1 465 000 (2005 est)

Conan Doyle Sir Arthur 1859–1930, British author of detective stories and historical romances and the creator of *Sherlock Holmes*

concave 1 *Physics* having one or two surfaces curved or ground in the shape of a section of the interior of a sphere, paraboloid, etc. 2 *Maths* (of a polygon) containing an interior angle greater than 180°

conceit *Literary* an elaborate image or far-fetched comparison, esp as used by the English Metaphysical poets

concentration 1 *Chemistry* the strength of a solution, esp the amount of dissolved substance in a given volume of solvent, usually expressed in moles per cubic metre or cubic decimetre (litre). 2 *Economics* the degree to which the output or employment in an industry is accounted for by only a few firms

concentration camp a guarded prison camp in which nonmilitary prisoners are held, esp one of those in Nazi Germany in which millions were exterminated

concept 1 *Philosophy* a general idea or notion that corresponds to some class of entities and that consists of the characteristic or essential features of the class 2 *Philosophy* a the conjunction of all the characteristic features of something b a theoretical construct within some theory c a directly intuited object of thought d the meaning of a predicate 3 *Engineering* (of a product, esp a car) created as an exercise to demonstrate the technical skills and imagination of the designers, and not intended for mass production or sale

conception *Biology* the fertilization of an ovum by a sperm in the Fallopian tube followed by implantation in the womb

concern a commercial company or enterprise

concert 1 a a performance of music by players or singers that does not involve theatrical staging b (*as modifier*): *a concert version of an opera* 2 **in concert** a (of musicians, esp rock musicians) performing live

concerted *Music* arranged in parts for a group of singers or players

concertina a small hexagonal musical instrument of the reed organ family in which metallic reeds are vibrated by air from a set of bellows operated by the player's hands. Notes are produced by pressing buttons

concerto a composition for an orchestra and one or more soloists. The classical concerto usually consisted of several movements, and often a cadenza

concert pitch *Music* the frequency of 440 hertz assigned to the A above middle C

concession 1 *Brit* a reduction in the usual price of a ticket granted to a special group of customers 2 any grant of rights, land, or property by a government, local authority, corporation, or individual 3 *US and Canadian* a the right to maintain a subsidiary business on a lessor's premises b the premises so granted or the business so maintained c a free rental period for such premises

concession road *Canadian* (esp in Ontario) one of a series of roads separating concessions in a township

conch 1 any of various tropical marine gastropod molluscs of the genus *Strombus* and related genera, esp *S. gigas* (giant conch), characterized by a large brightly coloured spiral shell 2 the shell of such a mollusc, used as a trumpet

concierge (esp in France) a caretaker of a block of flats, hotel, etc, esp one who lives on the premises

conciliation a method of helping the parties in a dispute to reach agreement, esp divorcing or separating couples to part amicably

conclave *RC Church* **a** the closed apartments where the college of cardinals elects a new pope **b** a meeting of the college of cardinals for this purpose

conclusion 1 the last main division of a speech, lecture, essay, etc. 2 *Logic* **a** a statement that purports to follow from another or others (the **premises**) by means of an argument **b** a statement that does validly follow from given premises 3 *Law* **a** an admission or statement binding on the party making it; estoppel **b** the close of a pleading or of a conveyance

concord *Music* a combination of musical notes, esp one containing a series of consonant intervals

Concord 1 a town in NE Massachusetts: scene of one of the opening military actions (1775) of the War of American Independence. Pop: 16 937 (2003 est) 2 a city in New Hampshire, the state capital: printing, publishing. Pop: 41 823 (2003 est)

concordat a pact or treaty, esp one between the Vatican and another state concerning the interests of religion in that state

concrete 1 a construction material made of a mixture of cement, sand, stone, and water that hardens to a stonelike mass 2 *Physics* a rigid mass formed by the coalescence of separate particles 3 relating to a particular instance or object; specific as opposed to general 4 formed by the coalescence of particles; condensed; solid

concretion 1 any of various rounded or irregular mineral masses formed by chemical precipitation around a nucleus, such as a bone or shell, that is different in composition from the sedimentary rock that surrounds it 2 *Pathol* another word for **calculus**

concubine (in polygamous societies) a secondary wife, usually of lower social rank

concurrence *Geometry* a point at which three or more lines intersect

concussion a jarring of the brain, caused by a blow or a fall, usually resulting in loss of consciousness

condensation 1 anything that has condensed from a vapour, esp on a window 2 *Chem* a type of reaction in which two organic molecules combine to form a larger molecule as well as a simple molecule such as water, methanol, etc. 3 *Psychoanal* **a** the fusion of two or more ideas, etc, into one symbol, occurring esp in dreams **b** the reduction of many experiences into one word or action, as in a phobia

condenser 1 **a** an apparatus for reducing gases to their liquid or solid form by the abstraction of heat **b** a device for abstracting heat, as in a refrigeration unit 2 a lens that concentrates light into a small area 3 another name for **capacitor**

condition 1 an ailment or physical disability 2 *Law* **a** a declaration or provision in a will, contract, etc, that makes some right or liability contingent upon the happening of some event **b** the event itself 3 *Logic* a statement whose truth is either required for the truth of a given statement (a **necessary condition**) or sufficient to guarantee the truth of the given statement (a **sufficient condition**) 4 *Maths, Logic* a presupposition, esp a

restriction on the domain of quantification, indispensable to the proof of a theorem and stated as part of it

conditional 1 **a** (of an equation or inequality) true for only certain values of the variable: $x^2 - 1 = x + 1$ is a conditional equation, only true for $x = 2$ or -1 **b** (of an infinite series) divergent when the absolute values of the terms are considered 2 *Logic* (of a proposition) consisting of two component propositions associated by the words *if...then* so that the proposition is false only when the antecedent is true and the consequent false. Usually written: $p \rightarrow q$ or $p \supset q$, where p is the antecedent, q the consequent, and $\rightarrow$ or $\supset$ symbolizes *implies* 3 *Logic* a conditional proposition

condominium *Politics* 1 joint rule or sovereignty 2 a country ruled by two or more foreign powers

condor either of two very large rare New World vultures, *Vultur gryphus* (**Andean condor**), which has black plumage with white around the neck, and *Gymnogyps californianus* (**California condor**), which is similar but nearly extinct

conductance the ability of a system to conduct electricity, measured by the ratio of the current flowing through the system to the potential difference across it; the reciprocal of resistance. It is measured in reciprocal ohms, mhos, or siemens.

conduction 1 the transfer of energy by a medium without bulk movement of the medium itself 2 the transmission of an electrical or chemical impulse along a nerve fibre 3 *Physics* another name for **conductivity**

conductivity 1 the property of transmitting heat, electricity, or sound 2 **a** a measure of the ability of a substance to conduct electricity; the reciprocal of resistivity **b** in the case of a solution, the electrolytic conductivity is the current density divided by the electric field strength, measured in siemens per metre

conductor 1 a person who conducts an orchestra, choir, etc. 2 *US and Canadian* a railway official in charge of a train 3 a substance, body, or system that conducts electricity, heat, etc. 4 See **lightning conductor**

conduit *Botany* a water-transporting element in a plant; a xylem vessel or a tracheid

cone 1 *Maths* **a** a geometric solid consisting of a plane base bounded by a closed curve, often a circle or an ellipse, every point of which is joined to a fixed point, the vertex, lying outside the plane of the base. A **right circular cone** has a vertex perpendicularly above or below the centre of a circular base. Volume of a cone: $\frac{1}{3}\pi r^2 h$, where r is the radius of the base and h is the height of the cone **b** a geometric surface formed by a line rotating about the vertex and connecting the peripheries of two closed plane bases, usually circular or elliptical, above and below the vertex 2 *Botany* **a** the reproductive body of conifers and related plants, made up of overlapping scales, esp the mature **female cone**, whose scales each bear a seed **b** a similar structure in horsetails, club mosses, etc. 3 a small cone-shaped bollard used as a temporary traffic marker on roads 4 *Anatomy* any one of the cone-shaped cells in the retina of the eye, sensitive to colour and bright light

Coney Island an island off the S shore of Long Island, New York: site of a large amusement park

confection a medicinal drug sweetened with sugar,

honey, etc.

confectioner a person who makes or sells sweets or confections

confederacy 1 *Politics* a union or combination of peoples, states, etc.; alliance; league 2 *Law* a combination of groups or individuals for unlawful purposes

Confederacy the another name for the **Confederate States of America**

Confederate States of America *US, History* the 11 Southern states (Alabama, Arkansas, Florida, Georgia, North Carolina, South Carolina, Texas, Virginia, Tennessee, Louisiana, and Mississippi) that seceded from the Union in 1861, precipitating a civil war with the North. The Confederacy was defeated in 1865 and the South reincorporated into the US

confederation 1 a loose alliance of political units. The union of the Swiss cantons is the oldest surviving confederation 2 (esp in Canada) another name for a **federation**

conference 1 a formal meeting of two or more states, political groups, etc, esp to discuss differences or formulate common policy 2 an assembly of the clergy or of clergy and laity of any of certain Protestant Christian Churches acting as representatives of their denomination

confession 1 *Christianity, Chiefly RC Church* the act of a penitent accusing himself of his sins 2 **confession of faith** a formal public avowal of religious beliefs 3 a religious denomination or sect united by a common system of beliefs

confessional 1 *Christianity, Chiefly RC Church* a small stall, usually enclosed and divided by a screen or curtain, where a priest hears confessions 2 a book of penitential prayers

confessor 1 *Christianity, Chiefly RC Church* a priest who hears confessions and sometimes acts as a spiritual counsellor 2 *History* a person who bears witness to his Christian religious faith by the holiness of his life, esp in resisting threats or danger, but does not suffer martyrdom

configuration 1 *Physics, Chem* a the shape of a molecule as determined by the arrangement of its atoms b the structure of an atom or molecule as determined by the arrangement of its electrons and nucleons 2 *Psychol* the unit or pattern in perception studied by Gestalt psychologists 3 *Computing* the particular choice of hardware items and their interconnection that make up a particular computer system

confirmation 1 a rite in several Christian churches that confirms a baptized person in his faith and admits him to full participation in the church 2 (in the philosophy of science) the relationship between an observation and the theory which it supposedly renders more probable

confirmed 1 having received the rite of confirmation 2 (of a disease) another word for **chronic**

confiscate 1 seized or confiscated; forfeit 2 having lost or been deprived of property through confiscation

conflict *Psychol* opposition between two simultaneous but incompatible wishes or drives, sometimes leading to a state of emotional tension and thought to be responsible for neuroses

conformation *Chem* a another name for **configuration** b one of the configurations of a molecule that can easily change its shape and can consequently exist in equilibrium with molecules of different configuration

conformity *or* **conformance** compliance with the practices of an established church

Confucianism the ethical system of Confucius, the Chinese philosopher and teacher of ethics (551–479 BC), emphasizing moral order, the humanity and virtue of China's ancient rulers, and gentlemanly education ▷http://www.wam.umd.edu/~tkang/

Confucius Chinese name *Kong Zi* or *K'ung Fu-tse.* 551–479 BC, Chinese philosopher and teacher of ethics (see **Confucianism**). His doctrines were compiled after his death under the title *The Analects of Confucius*

conga 1 a Latin American dance of three steps and a kick to each bar, usually performed by a number of people in single file 2 a large tubular bass drum, used chiefly in Latin American and funk music and played with the hands

congenital denoting or relating to any nonhereditary condition, esp an abnormal condition, existing at birth

conger any large marine eel of the family *Congridae*, esp *Conger conger*, occurring in temperate and tropical coastal waters

conglomerate 1 any coarse-grained sedimentary rock consisting of rounded fragments of rock embedded in a finer matrix 2 a large corporation consisting of a group of companies dealing in widely diversified goods, services, etc. 3 (of sedimentary rocks) consisting of rounded fragments within a finer matrix

Congo 1 **Democratic Republic of** a republic in S central Africa, with a narrow strip of land along the Congo estuary leading to the Atlantic in the west: Congo Free State established in 1885, with Leopold II of Belgium as absolute monarch; became the Belgian Congo colony in 1908; gained independence in 1960, followed by civil war and the secession of Katanga (until 1963); President Mobutu Sese Seko seized power in 1965; declared a one-party state in 1978, and was overthrown by rebels in 1997. The country consists chiefly of the Congo basin, with large areas of dense tropical forest and marshes, and the Mitumba highlands reaching over 5000 m (16 000 ft) in the east. Official language: French. Religion: Christian majority, animist minority. Currency: Congolese franc. Capital: Kinshasa. Pop: 54 417 000 (2004 est). Area: 2 344 116 sq km (905 063 sq miles) 2 **Republic of** the short name of Congo-Brazzaville 3 the second longest river in Africa, rising as the Lualaba on the Katanga plateau in the Democratic Republic of Congo and flowing in a wide northerly curve to the Atlantic: forms the border between Congo-Brazzaville and the Democratic Republic of Congo Length: about 4800 km (3000 miles). Area of basin: about 3 000 000 sq km (1 425 000 sq miles)

Congo-Brazzaville, Congo, *or* **Republic of Congo** a republic in W Central Africa: formerly the French colony of Middle Congo, part of French Equatorial Africa, it became independent in 1960; consists mostly of equatorial forest, with savanna and extensive swamps; drained chiefly by the Rivers Congo and

Ubangi. Official language: French. Religion: Christian majority. Currency: franc. Capital: Brazzaville. Pop: 3 818 000 (2004 est). Area: 342 000 sq km (132 018 sq miles)

congregation 1 a group of persons gathered for worship, prayer, etc, esp in a church or chapel 2 the group of persons habitually attending a given church, chapel, etc. 3 *RC Church* a a society of persons who follow a common rule of life but who are bound only by simple vows b an administrative subdivision of the papal curia c an administrative committee of bishops for arranging the business of a general council 4 *Chiefly Brit* an assembly of senior members of a university

Congregationalism a system of Christian doctrines and ecclesiastical government in which each congregation is self-governing and maintains bonds of faith with other similar local congregations
▷http://wikipedia.org/wiki/Congregationalism

congress 1 a meeting or conference, esp of representatives of a number of sovereign states 2 a national legislative assembly

Congress 1 the bicameral federal legislature of the US, consisting of the House of Representatives and the Senate 2 this body during any two-year term 3 (in India) a major political party, which controlled the Union government from 1947 to 1977

Congreve William 1670–1729, English dramatist, a major exponent of Restoration comedy; author of *Love for Love* (1695) and *The Way of the World* (1700)

congruent 1 *Maths* having identical shapes so that all parts correspond 2 of or concerning two integers related by a congruence

conic section one of a group of curves formed by the intersection of a plane and a right circular cone. It is either a circle, ellipse, parabola, or hyperbola, depending on the eccentricity, e, which is constant for a particular curve $e = 0$ for a circle; $e<1$ for an ellipse; $e = 1$ for a parabola; $e>1$ for a hyperbola.

conifer any gymnosperm tree or shrub of the phylum *Coniferophyta*, typically bearing cones and evergreen leaves. The group includes the pines, spruces, firs, larches, yews, junipers, cedars, cypresses, and sequoias

Coniston Water a lake in NW England, in Cumbria: scene of the establishment of world water speed records by Sir Malcolm Campbell (1939) and his son Donald Campbell (1959). Length: 8 km (5 miles)

conjugate 1 *Maths* a (of two angles) having a sum of 360° b (of two complex numbers) differing only in the sign of the imaginary part as $4 + 3i$ and $4 - 3i$ c (of two algebraic numbers) being roots of the same irreducible algebraic equation with rational coefficients d (of two elements of a square matrix) interchanged when the rows and columns are interchanged e (of two arcs) forming a complete circle or other closed curved figure 2 *Chem* of, denoting, or concerning the state of equilibrium in which two liquids can exist as two separate phases that are both solutions. The liquid that is the solute in one phase is the solvent in the other 3 *Chem* (of acids and bases) related by loss or gain of a proton 4 *Physics* a joined by a reciprocal relationship, such as in the case of two quantities, points, etc, that are interchangeable with respect to the properties of each of

them b (of points connected with a lens) having the property that an object placed at one point will produce an image at the other point 5 (of a compound leaf) having one pair of leaflets

conjugation 1 a type of sexual reproduction in ciliate protozoans involving the temporary union of two individuals and the subsequent migration and fusion of the gametic nuclei 2 (in bacteria) the direct transfer of DNA between two cells that are temporarily joined 3 the union of gametes, esp isogametes, as in some algae and fungi 4 the pairing of chromosomes in the early phase of a meiotic division 5 *Chem* the existence of alternating double or triple bonds in a chemical compound, with consequent electron delocalization over part of the molecule

conjunction 1 2 *Astronomy* a the position of any two bodies that appear to meet, such as two celestial bodies on the celestial sphere b the position of a planet or the moon when it is in line with the sun as seen from the earth. The inner planets are in **inferior conjunction** when the planet is between the earth and the sun and in **superior conjunction** when the sun lies between the earth and the planet 3 *Astrology* an exact aspect of 0° between two planets, etc, an orb of 8° being allowed 4 *Logic* a the operator that forms a compound sentence from two given sentences, and corresponds to the English *and* b a sentence so formed. Usually written $p \vartheta Q$, $p \wedge q$, or $p.q$, where p,q are the component sentences, it is true only when both these are true 5 the relation between such sentences

conjunctiva the delicate mucous membrane that covers the eyeball and the under surface of the eyelid

conjunctive *Logic* relating to, characterized by, or containing a conjunction

conjunctivitis inflammation of the conjunctiva

conjuror *or* **conjurer** a person who practises magic; sorcerer

conkers *Brit* a game in which a player swings a horse chestnut (conker), threaded onto a string, against that of another player to try to break it

Conn 2nd century AD, king of Leinster and high king of Ireland

Connacht *or* **Connaught** a province and ancient kingdom of NW Republic of Ireland: consists of the counties of Galway, Leitrim, Mayo, Roscommon, and Sligo. Pop: 464 296 (2002). Area: 17 122 sq km (6611 sq miles)

Connecticut 1 a state of the northeastern US, in New England. Capital: Hartford. Pop: 3 483 372 (2003 est). Area: 12 973 sq km (5009 sq miles). 2 a river in the northeastern US, rising in N New Hampshire and flowing south to Long Island Sound. Length: 651 km (407 miles)

connection *or* **connexion** 1 the persons owning or controlling a racehorse 2 a link, usually a wire or metallic strip, between two components in an electric circuit or system 3 *Slang* a supplier of illegal drugs, such as heroin 4 *Rare* a small sect or religious group united by a body of distinct beliefs or practices

connective tissue an animal tissue developed from the embryonic mesoderm that consists of collagen or elastic fibres, fibroblasts, fatty cells, etc, within a jelly-like matrix. It supports organs, fills the spaces between them, and forms tendons and ligaments

Connell Desmond born 1926, Irish cardinal; Archbishop of Dublin and primate of Ireland from 1988

Connemara a barren coastal region of W Republic of Ireland, in Co. Galway: consists of quartzite mountains, peat bogs, and many lakes; noted for its breed of pony originating from the hilly regions

Connery Sir Sean, real name *Thomas Connery*. born 1929, Scottish film actor, who played James Bond in such films as *Goldfinger* (1964). His later films include *The Name of the Rose* (1986), *Indiana Jones and the Last Crusade* (1989), and *Finding Forrester* (2000)

conning tower 1 a superstructure of a submarine, used as the bridge when the vessel is on the surface 2 the armoured pilot house of a warship

connivance *Law* the tacit encouragement of or assent to another's wrongdoing, esp (formerly) of the petitioner in a divorce suit to the respondent's adultery

connoisseur a person with special knowledge or appreciation of a field, esp in the arts

Connolly 1 **Billy** born 1942, Scottish comedian 2 **Cyril (Vernon)**. 1903–74, British critic and writer, founder and editor of *Horizon* (1939–50): his books include *Enemies of Promise* (1938) 3 **James** 1868–1916, Irish labour leader: executed by the British for his part in the Easter Rising (1916)

conquistador *History* an adventurer or conqueror, esp one of the Spanish conquerors of the New World in the 16th century

> ▷www.bbc.co.uk/history/discovery/
>   exploration/conquistadors
> ▷www.incaconquest.com

Conrad Joseph real name *Teodor Josef Konrad Korzeniowski*. 1857–1924, British novelist born in Poland, noted for sea stories such as *The Nigger of the Narcissus* (1897) and *Lord Jim* (1900) and novels of politics and revolution such as *Nostromo* (1904) and *Under Western Eyes* (1911)

conscience a the sense of right and wrong that governs a person's thoughts and actions b regulation of one's actions in conformity to this sense c a supposed universal faculty of moral insight

conscious denoting or relating to a part of the human mind that is aware of a person's self, environment, and mental activity and that to a certain extent determines his choices of action

consecutive *Music* another word for **parallel**

consent age of consent the lowest age at which the law recognizes the right of a person to consent to sexual intercourse

consequence *Logic* a a conclusion reached by reasoning b the conclusion of an argument c the relations between the conclusion and the premises of a valid argument

consequent 1 (of a river) flowing in the direction of the original slope of the land or dip of the strata 2 the resultant clause in a conditional sentence 3 **affirming the consequent** *Logic* the fallacy of inferring the antecedent of a conditional sentence, given the truth of the conditional and its consequent, as *if John is six feet tall, he's more than five feet: he's more than five feet so he's six feet* 4 an obsolete term for **denominator**

conservancy (in Britain) a court or commission with jurisdiction over a river, port, area of countryside, etc.

conservative 1 *Med* (of treatment) designed to alleviate symptoms 2 *Physics* a field of force, system, etc, in which the work done moving a body from one point to another is independent of the path taken between them

Conservative in Britain, Canada, and elsewhere 1 of, supporting, or relating to a Conservative Party 2 of, relating to, or characterizing Conservative Judaism

conservatoire an institution or school for instruction in music

conservatory 1 a greenhouse, esp one attached to a house 2 another word for **conservatoire**

consideration *Law* the promise, object, etc, given by one party to persuade another to enter into a contract

consignment 1 a shipment of goods consigned 2 **on consignment** for payment by the consignee after sale

consistency *or* **consistence** degree of viscosity or firmness

consistent 1 *Maths* (of two or more equations) satisfied by at least one common set of values of the variables 2 *Logic* a (of a set of statements) capable of all being true at the same time or under the same interpretation b (of a formal system) not permitting the deduction of a contradiction from the axioms

console 1 an ornamental bracket, esp one used to support a wall fixture, bust, etc. 2 the part of an organ comprising the manuals, pedals, stops, etc. 3 a unit on which the controls of an electronic system are mounted

consonance *or* **consonancy** 1 *Prosody* similarity between consonants, but not between vowels, as between the *s* and *t* sounds in *sweet silent thought* 2 *Music* a an aesthetically pleasing sensation or perception associated with the interval of the octave, the perfect fourth and fifth, the major and minor third and sixth, and chords based on these intervals b an interval or chord producing this sensation

consonant 1 a speech sound or letter of the alphabet other than a vowel; a stop, fricative, or continuant 2 *Music* characterized by the presence of a consonance

consort 1 esp formerly a a small group of instruments, either of the same type, such as viols, (a **whole consort**) or of different types (a **broken consort**) b (*as modifier*): *consort music* 2 the husband or wife of a reigning monarch 3 a ship that escorts another

consortium 1 an association of financiers, companies, etc, esp one formed for a particular purpose 2 *Law* the right of husband or wife to the company, assistance, and affection of the other

Constable John 1776–1837, English landscape painter, noted particularly for his skill in rendering atmospheric effects of changing light

constabulary *Chiefly Brit* the police force of a town or district

Constance 1 a city in S Germany, in Baden-Württemberg on Lake Constance: tourist centre. Pop: 80 716 (2003 est) 2 **Lake** a lake in W Europe, bounded by S Germany, W Austria, and N Switzerland, through which the Rhine flows. Area: 536 sq km. (207 sq miles)

constant 1 a specific quantity that is always invariable 2 a *Maths* a symbol representing an unspecified number that remains invariable throughout a particular series of operations **b** *Physics* a theoretical or experimental quantity or property that is considered invariable throughout a particular series of calculations or experiments

▷http://physics.nist.gov/cuu/Constants/index.html

Constanța a port and resort in SE Romania, on the Black Sea: founded by the Greeks in the 6th century BC and rebuilt by Constantine the Great (4th century); exports petroleum. Pop: 265 000 (2005 est)

Constantia *South African* **1** a region of the Cape Peninsula **2** any of several red or white wines produced around Constantia

Constantine a walled city in NE Algeria: built on an isolated rock; military and trading centre. Pop: 482 000 (2005 est)

Constantine I 1 known as *Constantine the Great*. Latin name *Flavius Valerius Aurelius Constantinus*. ?280–337 AD, first Christian Roman emperor (306–337): moved his capital to Byzantium, which he renamed Constantinople (330) **2** 1868–1923, king of Greece (1913–17; 1920–22): deposed (1917), recalled by a plebiscite (1920), but forced to abdicate again (1922) after defeat by the Turks

Constantine VII known as *Porphyrogenitus*. 905–59 AD, Byzantine emperor (913–59) and scholar: his writings are an important source for Byzantine history

Constantine XI 1404–53, last Byzantine emperor (1448–53): killed when Constantinople was captured by the Turks

constellation 1 any of the 88 groups of stars as seen from the earth and the solar system, many of which were named by the ancient Greeks after animals, objects, or mythological persons **2** *Psychoanal* a group of ideas felt to be related

constipation infrequent or difficult evacuation of the bowels, with hard faeces, caused by functional or organic disorders or improper diet

constituency 1 the whole body of voters who elect one representative to a legislature or all the residents represented by one deputy **2 a** a district that sends one representative to a legislature **b** (*as modifier*): *constituency organization*

constituent 1 having the power to frame a constitution or to constitute a government (esp in the phrases **constituent assembly, constituent power**) **2** *Becoming rare* electing or having the power to elect **3** a resident of a constituency, esp one entitled to vote **4** *Chiefly law* a person who appoints another to act for him, as by power of attorney

constitution 1 the fundamental political principles on which a state is governed, esp when considered as embodying the rights of the subjects of that state **2** (in certain countries, esp Australia and the US) a statute embodying such principles

▷www.psa.ac.uk/www/constitutions.htm

constitutive 1 having power to enact, appoint, or establish **2** *Chem* (of a physical property) determined by the arrangement of atoms in a molecule rather than by their nature **3** *Biochem* (of an enzyme) formed continuously, irrespective of the cell's needs

constriction *Genetics* a localized narrow region of a chromosome, esp at the centromere

constrictor 1 any of various nonvenomous snakes, such as the pythons, boas, and anaconda, that coil around and squeeze their prey to kill it **2** *Anatomy* any muscle that constricts or narrows a canal or passage; sphincter

construct *Psychol* a model devised on the basis of observation, designed to relate what is observed to some theoretical framework

construction 1 *Geometry* a drawing of a line, angle, or figure satisfying certain conditions, used in solving a problem or proving a theorem **2** an abstract work of art in three dimensions or relief

constructive 1 *Law* deduced by inference or construction; not expressed but inferred **2** *Law* having a deemed legal effect

consul 1 an official appointed by a sovereign state to protect its commercial interests and aid its citizens in a foreign city **2** (in ancient Rome) either of two annually elected magistrates who jointly exercised the highest authority in the republic **3** (in France from 1799 to 1804) any of the three chief magistrates of the First Republic

consulate 1 the business premises or residence of a consul **2** government by consuls **3** the office or period of office of a consul or consuls **4 a** the government of France by the three consuls from 1799 to 1804 **b** this period of French history **5 a** the consular government of the Roman republic **b** the office or rank of a Roman consul

consultant a a senior physician, esp a specialist, who is asked to confirm a diagnosis or treatment or to provide an opinion **b** a physician or surgeon holding the highest appointment in a particular branch of medicine or surgery in a hospital

consumer 1 a person who acquires goods and services for his or her own personal needs **2** *Ecology* an organism, esp an animal, within a community that feeds upon plants or other animals

consumerism 1 protection of the interests of consumers **2** advocacy of a high rate of consumption and spending as a basis for a sound economy

consumption 1 *Economics* expenditure on goods and services for final personal use **2** *Pathol* a condition characterized by a wasting away of the tissues of the body, esp as seen in tuberculosis of the lungs

consumptive 1 *Pathol* relating to or affected with consumption, esp tuberculosis of the lungs **2** *Pathol* a person who suffers from consumption

contact 1 a a junction of two or more electrical conductors **b** the part of the conductors that makes the junction **c** the part of an electrical device to which such connections are made **2** any person who has been exposed to a contagious disease **3** an informal name for **contact lens 4** of or relating to irritation or inflammation of the skin caused by touching the causative agent

contact lens a thin convex lens, usually of plastic, which floats on the layer of tears in front of the cornea to correct defects of vision

contagion 1 the transmission of disease from one person to another by direct or indirect contact **2** a contagious disease

contagious 1 (of a disease) capable of being passed on

by direct contact with a diseased individual or by handling clothing, etc, contaminated with the causative agent **2** (of an organism) harbouring or spreading the causative agent of a transmissible disease

container a a large cargo-carrying standard-sized container that can be loaded from one mode of transport to another **b** (as modifier): a container port

containment 1 the act or condition of containing, esp of restraining the ideological or political power of a hostile country or the operations of a hostile military force **2** (from 1947 to the mid-1970s) a principle of US foreign policy that sought to prevent the expansion of Communist power **3** Physics the process of preventing the plasma in a controlled thermonuclear reactor from reaching the walls of the reaction vessel, usually by confining it within a configuration of magnetic fields

contempt wilful disregard of or disrespect for the authority of a court of law or legislative body

content the meaning or significance of a poem, painting, or other work of art, as distinguished from its style or form

contentious Law relating to a cause or legal business that is contested, esp a probate matter

continent¹ 1 one of the earth's large land masses (Asia, Australia, Africa, Europe, North and South America, and Antarctica) **2** that part of the earth's crust that rises above the oceans and is composed of sialic rocks. Including the continental shelves, the continents occupy 30 per cent of the earth's surface **3** Obsolete **a** mainland as opposed to islands **b** a continuous extent of land

continent² able to control urination and defecation

Continent the the mainland of Europe as distinguished from the British Isles

continental climate a climate characterized by hot summers, cold winters, and little rainfall, typical of the interior of a continent

continental drift Geology the theory that the earth's continents move gradually over the surface of the planet on a substratum of magma. The present-day configuration of the continents is thought to be the result of the fragmentation of a single landmass, Pangaea, that existed 200 million years ago

continental quilt Brit a quilt, stuffed with down or a synthetic material and containing pockets of air, used as a bed cover in place of the top sheet and blankets

continental shelf the sea bed surrounding a continent at depths of up to about 200 metres (100 fathoms), at the edge of which the **continental slope** drops steeply to the ocean floor.

contingent 1 Logic (of a proposition) true under certain conditions, false under others; not necessary **2** Metaphysics (of some being) existing only as a matter of fact; not necessarily existing

continuance US the postponement or adjournment of a legal proceeding

continuity Film, TV **1** the comprehensive script or scenario of detail and movement in a film or broadcast **2** the continuous projection of a film, using automatic rewind

continuo 1 Music **a** a shortened form of **basso continuo b** (as modifier): a continuo accompaniment **2** the thorough-

bass part as played on a keyboard instrument, often supported by a cello, bassoon, etc.

continuous Maths (of a function or curve) changing gradually in value as the variable changes in value. A function f is continuous if at every value a of the independent variable the difference between $f(x)$ and $f(a)$ approaches zero as x approaches a

contortionist a performer who contorts his body for the entertainment of others

contour line a line on a map or chart joining points of equal height or depth

contraband 1 a goods that are prohibited by law from being exported or imported **b** illegally imported or exported goods **2** illegal traffic in such goods; smuggling **3** (during the American Civil War) a Black slave captured by the Union forces or one who escaped to the Union lines **4** of goods **a** forbidden by law from being imported or exported **b** illegally imported or exported

contract 1 a formal agreement between two or more parties **2** a document that states the terms of such an agreement **3** the branch of law treating of contracts **4** marriage considered as a formal agreement **5** See **contract bridge 6** Bridge **a** (in the bidding sequence before play) the highest bid, which determines trumps and the number of tricks one side must try to make **b** the number and suit of these tricks

contract bridge the most common variety of bridge, in which the declarer receives points counting towards game and rubber only for tricks he bids as well as makes, any overtricks receiving bonus points

contraction 1 Physiol any normal shortening or tensing of an organ or part, esp of a muscle, e.g. during childbirth **2** Pathol any abnormal tightening or shrinking of an organ or part

contractor 1 something that contracts, esp a muscle **2** Law a person who is a party to a contract **3** the declarer in bridge

contradictory 1 Logic (of a pair of statements) unable both to be true or both to be false under the same circumstances **2** Logic a statement that cannot be true when a given statement is true or false when it is false

contraflow Brit two-way traffic on one carriageway of a motorway, esp to allow maintenance work to be carried out or an accident to be cleared

contralto 1 Music the lowest female voice, usually having a range of approximately from F a fifth below middle C to D a ninth above it

contrapuntal Music characterized by counterpoint

contrary 1 (esp of wind) adverse; unfavourable **2** (of plant parts) situated at right angles to each other **3** Logic (of a pair of propositions) related so that they cannot both be true at once, although they may both be false together **4** Logic a statement that cannot be true when a given statement is true

contrast 1 (in painting) the effect of the juxtaposition of different colours, tones, etc. **2 a** (of a photographic emulsion) the degree of density measured against exposure used **b** the extent to which adjacent areas of an optical image, esp on a television screen or in a photographic negative or print, differ in brightness **3** Psychol the phenomenon that when two different but related stimuli are presented close together in space and/or time they are perceived as being more different than they really are

contretemps *Fencing* a feint made with the purpose of producing a counterthrust from one's opponent

contrite *Theol* remorseful for past sin and resolved to avoid future sin

control 1 a device or mechanism for operating a car, aircraft, etc. 2 a a device that regulates the operation of a machine. A **dynamic control** is one that incorporates a governor so that it responds to the output of the machine it regulates b *(as modifier): control panel* 3 *Spiritualism* an agency believed to assist the medium in a séance 4 a letter, or letter and number, printed on a sheet of postage stamps, indicating authenticity, date, and series of issue 5 one of a number of checkpoints on a car rally, orienteering course, etc, where competitors check in and their time, performance, etc, is recorded

controller the equipment concerned with controlling the operation of an electrical device

control tower a tower at an airport from which air traffic is controlled

contumacy *Law* the wilful refusal of a person to appear before a court or to comply with a court order

contusion an injury in which the skin is not broken; bruise

conurbation a large densely populated urban sprawl formed by the growth and coalescence of individual towns or cities

convalescence gradual return to health after illness, injury, or an operation, esp through rest

convection 1 a process of heat transfer through a gas or liquid by bulk motion of hotter material into a cooler region 2 *Meteorol* the process by which masses of relatively warm air are raised into the atmosphere, often cooling and forming clouds, with compensatory downward movements of cooler air 3 *Geology* the slow circulation of subcrustal material, thought to be the mechanism by which tectonic plates are moved

convector a space-heating device from which heat is transferred to the surrounding air by convection

convener *or* **convenor** *Politics* the chairman and civic head of certain Scottish councils

convent 1 a building inhabited by a religious community, usually of nuns 2 the religious community inhabiting such a building 3 a school in which the teachers are nuns

conventicle 1 a secret or unauthorized assembly for worship 2 a small meeting house or chapel for a religious assembly, esp of Nonconformists or Dissenters

convention 1 *US, Politics* an assembly of delegates of one party to select candidates for office 2 *Diplomacy* an international agreement second only to a treaty in formality 3 *Bridge* a bid or play not to be taken at its face value, which one's partner can interpret according to a prearranged bidding system

conventional 1 *Law* based upon the agreement or consent of parties 2 *Arts* represented in a simplified or generalized way; conventionalized 3 *Bridge* another word for **convention**

conversation piece 1 (esp in 18th-century Britain) a group portrait in a landscape or domestic setting 2 a play emphasizing dialogue

converse 1 *Logic* a a categorical proposition obtained from another by the transposition of subject and predicate, as *no bad man is bald* from *no bald man is bad* b a proposition so derived, possibly by weakening a universal proposition to the corresponding particular, as *some socialists are rich* from *all rich men are socialists* 2 *Logic, Maths* a relation that holds between two relata only when a given relation holds between them in reverse order: thus *father of* is the converse of *son of*

conversion 1 a change to another attitude or belief, as in a change of religion 2 *Maths* a change in the units or form of a number or expression 3 *Logic* a form of inference by which one proposition is obtained as the converse of another proposition 4 *Law* a unauthorized dealing with or the assumption of rights of ownership to another's personal property b the changing of real property into personalty or personalty into realty 5 *Rugby* a score made after a try by kicking the ball over the crossbar from a place kick 6 *Physics* a change of fertile material to fissile material in a reactor 7 a an alteration to a car engine to improve its performance b *(as modifier): a conversion kit* 8 *NZ* the unauthorized appropriation of a motor vehicle

convertible a car with a folding or removable roof

convex 1 *Physics* having one or two surfaces curved or ground in the shape of a section of the exterior of a sphere, paraboloid, ellipsoid, etc. 2 *Maths* (of a polygon) containing no interior angle greater than 180°

conveyance *Law* a a transfer of the legal title to property b the document effecting such a transfer

conveyor belt a flexible endless strip of fabric or linked plates driven by rollers and used to transport objects, esp in a factory

convict 1 a person found guilty of an offence against the law, esp one who is sentenced to imprisonment 2 a person serving a prison sentence

convocation 1 *Church of England* either of the synods of the provinces of Canterbury or York 2 *Episcopal Church* a an assembly of the clergy and part of the laity of a diocese b a district represented at such an assembly 3 (in some British universities) a legislative assembly composed mainly of graduates 4 (in India) a degree-awarding ceremony 5 (in Australia and New Zealand) the graduate membership of a university

convolution *Anatomy* any of the numerous convex folds or ridges of the surface of the brain

convolvulus any typically twining herbaceous convolvulaceous plant of the genus *Convolvulus*, having funnel-shaped flowers and triangular leaves

convoy a group of merchant ships with an escort of warships

convulsion a violent involuntary contraction of a muscle or muscles

Conwy 1 a market town and resort in N Wales, in Conwy county borough on the estuary of the River Conwy: medieval town walls, 13th-century castle. Pop: 3847 (2001) 2 a county borough in N Wales, created in 1996 from parts of Gwynedd and Clwyd. Pop: 110 900 (2003 est). Area: 1130 sq km (436 sq miles)

cony *or* **coney** 1 a rabbit or fur made from the skin of a rabbit 2 (in the Bible) another name for the **hyrax** (esp the Syrian rock hyrax)

Conybeare William Daniel 1787–1857, British geologist. He summarized all that was known about rocks at the time in *Outlines of the Geology of England and Wales* (1822)

Cooch Behar *or* **Kuch Bihar** 1 a former state of NE India: part of West Bengal since 1950 2 a city in India, in NE West Bengal: capital of the former state of Cooch Behar. Pop: 76 812 (2001)

Cook¹ 1 Captain **James** 1728–79, British navigator and explorer: claimed the E coast of Australia for Britain, circumnavigated New Zealand, and discovered several Pacific and Atlantic islands (1768–79) 2 Sir **Joseph** 1860–1947, Australian statesman, born in England: prime minister of Australia (1913–14) 3 **Peter** (**Edward**). 1937–95, British comedy actor and writer, noted esp for his partnership (1960–73) with Dudley Moore 4 **Robin,** full name *Robert Finlayson Cook*. born 1946, British Labour politician; foreign secretary (1997–2001), Leader of the House (2001-2003) 5 **Thomas** 1808–92, British travel agent; innovator of conducted excursions and founder of the travel agents Thomas Cook and Son

Cook², **Mount** 1 a mountain in New Zealand, in the South Island, in the Southern Alps: the highest peak in New Zealand. Height: reduced in 1991 by a rockfall from 3764 m (12 349 ft) to 3754 m (12 316 ft) 2 a mountain in SE Alaska, in the St. Elias Mountains. Height: 4194 m (13 760 ft)

Cooke Norman, real name *Quentin Cooke*, also known as *Fatboy Slim*. born 1963, British disc jockey, pop musician, and record producer; hit records include *You've Come a Long Way, Baby* (1998) and "Praise You" (2001)

Cookson Dame **Catherine** 1906-98, British novelist, known for her popular novels set in northeast England

Cookstown a district of central Northern Ireland, in Co. Tyrone. Pop: 33 387 (2003 est). Area: 622 sq km (240 sq miles)

Cook Strait the strait between North and South Islands, New Zealand. Width: 26 km (16 miles)

cool 1 (of a colour) having violet, blue, or green predominating; cold 2 (of jazz) characteristic of the late 1940s and early 1950s, economical and rhythmically relaxed

coolant 1 a fluid used to cool a system or to transfer heat from one part of it to another 2 a liquid, such as an emulsion of oil, water, and soft soap, used to lubricate and cool the workpiece and cutting tool during machining

cooler 1 a container, vessel, or apparatus for cooling, such as a heat exchanger 2 a drink consisting of wine, fruit juice, and carbonated water

Coolidge (**John**) **Calvin** 1872–1933, 30th president of the US (1923–29)

coolie *or* **cooly** 1 a cheaply hired unskilled Oriental labourer 2 *Derogatory* an Indian living in South Africa

cooling tower a tall hollow structure in which steam is condensed or water that is used as a coolant in some industrial process is allowed to cool for reuse by trickling down a surface

Coomaraswamy Ananda (**Kentish**). 1877–1947, Ceylonese art historian and interpreter of Indian culture to the West

coomb, combe, coombe *or* **comb** 1 *Chiefly Southern English* a short valley or deep hollow, esp in chalk areas 2 *Chiefly Northern English* another name for a **cirque**

coon 1 *Informal* short for **raccoon** 2 *Offensive slang* a Black or a native Australian 3 *South African, offensive* a person of mixed race

coop¹ a wicker basket for catching fish

coop² *or* **co-op** a cooperative, cooperative society, or shop run by a cooperative society

cooper a person skilled in making and repairing barrels, casks, etc.

Cooper 1 **Cary** (**Lynn**). born 1940, British psychologist, noted for his studies of behaviour at work and the causes and treatment of stress 2 **Gary,** real name *Frank James Cooper*. 1901–61, US film actor; his many films include *Sergeant York* (1941) and *High Noon* (1952), for both of which he won Oscars 3 Sir **Henry** born 1934, British boxer; European heavyweight champion (1964; 1968–71) 4 **James Fenimore** 1789–1851, US novelist, noted for his stories of American Indians, esp *The Last of the Mohicans* (1826) 5 **Leon Neil** born 1930, US physicist, noted for his work on the theory of superconductivity. He shared the Nobel prize for physics 1972 6 **Samuel** 1609–72, English miniaturist

cooperative *or* **co-operative** 1 a (of an enterprise, farm, etc) owned collectively and managed for joint economic benefit b (of an economy or economic activity) based on collective ownership and cooperative use of the means of production and distribution 2 a cooperative organization 3 *US* a block of flats belonging to a corporation in which shares are owned in proportion to the relative value of the flat occupied

cooperative society a commercial enterprise owned and managed by and for the benefit of customers or workers

Cooper Creek an intermittent river in E central Australia, in the Channel Country: rises in central Queensland and flows generally southwest, reaching Lake Eyre only during wet-year floods; scene of the death of the explorers Burke and Wills in 1861; the surrounding basin provides cattle pastures after the floods subside. Total length: 1420 km (880 miles)

coordinate *or* **co-ordinate** *Maths* any of a set of numbers that defines the location of a point in space

coot any aquatic bird of the genus *Fulica*, esp *F. atra* of Europe and Asia, having lobed toes, dark plumage, and a white bill with a frontal shield: family *Rallidae* (rails, crakes, etc)

cop a conical roll of thread wound on a spindle

copal a hard aromatic resin, yellow, orange, or red in colour, obtained from various tropical trees and used in making varnishes and lacquers

copartner a partner or associate, esp an equal partner in business

cope a large ceremonial cloak worn at solemn liturgical functions by priests of certain Christian sects

Copenhagen the capital of Denmark, a port on Zealand and Amager Islands on a site inhabited for some 6000 years: exports chiefly agricultural products; iron and steel works; university (1479). Pop: 501 664 (2004 est)

Copernicus Nicolaus . Polish name *Mikolaj Kopernik*. 1473–1543, Polish astronomer, whose theory of the solar system (the **Copernican system**) was published in 1543

copilot a second or relief pilot of an aircraft

coping saw a handsaw with a U-shaped frame used for

cutting curves in a material too thick for a fret saw

Copland Aaron 1900–90, US composer of orchestral and chamber music, ballets, and film music

copper 1 a a malleable ductile reddish metallic element occurring as the free metal, copper glance, and copper pyrites: used as an electrical and thermal conductor and in such alloys as brass and bronze. Symbol: Cu; atomic no.: 29; atomic wt.: 63.546; valency: 1 or 2; relative density: 8.96; melting pt.: 1084.87±+0.2°C; boiling pt.: 2563°C **b** (*as modifier*): *a copper coin* **2 a** the reddish-brown colour of copper **b** (*as adjective*): *copper hair* **3** *Informal* any copper or bronze coin **4** any of various small widely distributed butterflies of the genera *Lycaena*, *Heodes*, etc, typically having reddish-brown wings: family *Lycaenidae*

copper beech a cultivated variety of European beech that has dark purple leaves

Copper Belt a region of Central Africa, along the border between Zambia and the Democratic Republic of Congo: rich deposits of copper

copperhead 1 a venomous reddish-brown snake, *Agkistrodon contortrix*, of the eastern US: family *Crotalidae* (pit vipers) **2** a venomous reddish-brown Australian elapid snake, *Denisonia superba* **3** *US, History* a Yankee supporter of the South during the Civil War

copper sulphate a copper salt found naturally as chalcanthite and made by the action of sulphuric acid on copper oxide. It usually exists as blue crystals of the pentahydrate that form a white anhydrous powder when heated: used as a mordant, in electroplating, and in plant sprays. Formula: $CuSO_4$

coppice a thicket or dense growth of small trees or bushes, esp one regularly trimmed back to stumps so that a continual supply of small poles and firewood is obtained

Coppola Francis Ford born 1939, US film director. His films include *The Godfather* (1972), *Apocalypse Now* (1979), *Tucker* (1988), and *The Rainmaker* (1999)

copra the dried, oil-yielding kernel of the coconut

Copt 1 a member of the Coptic Church **2** an Egyptian descended from the ancient Egyptians

Coptic 1 an Afro-Asiatic language, written in the Greek alphabet but descended from ancient Egyptian. It was extinct as a spoken language by about 1600 AD but survives in the Coptic Church **2** of or relating to this language

copula *Logic* the often unexpressed link between the subject and predicate terms of a categorial proposition, as *are* in *all men are mortal*

copyright 1 the exclusive right to produce copies and to control an original literary, musical, or artistic work, granted by law for a specified number of years (in Britain, usually 70 years from the death of the author, composer, etc, or from the date of publication if later). **2** (of a work, etc) subject to or controlled by copyright

coquette any hummingbird of the genus *Lophornis*, esp the crested Brazilian species *L. magnifica*

coracle a small roundish boat made of waterproofed hides stretched over a wicker frame

coral 1 any marine mostly colonial coelenterate of the class *Anthozoa* having a calcareous, horny, or soft skeleton **2 a** the calcareous or horny material forming the skeleton of certain of these animals **b** (*as modifier*): *a coral reef* **3 a** a rocklike aggregation of certain of these animals or their skeletons, forming an island or reef **b** (*as modifier*): *a coral island* **4 a** a deep-pink to yellowish-pink colour **b** (*as adjective*): *a coral blouse*

Coral Sea the SW arm of the Pacific, between Australia, New Guinea, and Vanuatu

cor anglais *Music* a woodwind instrument, the alto of the oboe family. It is a transposing instrument in F. Range: two and a half octaves upwards from E on the third space of the bass staff

corbel *Architect* a bracket, usually of stone or brick

Corcovado 1 a volcano in S Chile, in the Andes. Height: 2300 m (7546 ft) **2** a mountain in SE Brazil, in SW Rio de Janeiro city, famous for a massive statue of Christ the Redeemer. Height: 704 m (2310 ft)

cord 1 string or thin rope made of several twisted strands **2** a length of woven or twisted strands of silk, etc, sewn on clothing or used as a belt **3** a ribbed fabric, esp corduroy **4** *US and Canadian* a flexible insulated electric cable, used esp to connect appliances to mains **5** *Anatomy* any part resembling a string or rope **6** a unit of volume for measuring cut wood, equal to 128 cubic feet

cordate heart-shaped

Corday Charlotte , full name *Marie Anne Charlotte Corday d'Armont*. 1768–93, French Girondist revolutionary, who assassinated Marat

corded 1 (of a fabric) ribbed **2** (of muscles) standing out like cords

cordial 1 a drink with a fruit base, usually sold in concentrated form and diluted with water before being drunk **2** another word for **liqueur**

cordless (of an electrical device) operated by an internal battery so that no connection to mains supply or other apparatus is needed

cordon 1 a cord or ribbon worn as an ornament or fastening **2** *Architect* an ornamental projecting band or continuous moulding along a wall **3** *Horticulture* a form of fruit tree consisting of a single stem bearing fruiting spurs, produced by cutting back all lateral branches

cordon bleu *French history* **a** the sky-blue ribbon worn by members of the highest order of knighthood under the Bourbon monarchy **b** a knight entitled to wear the cordon bleu

Cordovan 1 a native or inhabitant of Córdoba, Spain **2** of or relating to Córdoba, Spain

corduroy a heavy cotton pile fabric with lengthways ribs **b** (*as modifier*): *a corduroy coat*

core 1 the central part of certain fleshy fruits, such as the apple or pear, consisting of the seeds and supporting parts **2** a piece of magnetic material, such as soft iron, placed inside the windings of an electromagnet or transformer to intensify and direct the magnetic field **3** *Geology* the central part of the earth, beneath the mantle, consisting mainly of iron and nickel, which has an inner solid part surrounded by an outer liquid part **4** a cylindrical sample of rock, soil, etc, obtained by the use of a hollow drill **5** shaped body of material (in metal casting usually of sand) supported inside a mould to form a cavity of predetermined shape in the finished casting **6** *Physics* the region of a nuclear reactor in which the reaction takes place **7** *Computing* a ferrite ring formerly used in a computer memory to store one bit of information **8** *Archaeol* a lump of stone or flint from which flakes or blades have been removed **9** *Physics* the nucleus together with all complete electron shells of an atom

Corelli 1 Arcangelo 1653–1713, Italian violinist and composer of sonatas and concerti grossi **2 Marie** , real name *Mary Mackay*. 1854–1924, British novelist. Her melodramatic works include *The Sorrows of Satan* (1895) and *The Murder of Delicia* (1896)

co-respondent *Law* a person cited in divorce proceedings, who is alleged to have committed adultery with the respondent

Corfu 1 an island in the Ionian Sea, in the Ionian Islands: forms, with neighbouring islands, a department of Greece. Pop: 107 879 (2001). Area: 641 sq km (247 sq miles) **2** a port on E Corfu island. Pop: 107 879 (1995 est)

corgi either of two long-bodied short-legged sturdy breeds of dog, the Cardigan and the Pembroke

coriander a European umbelliferous plant, *Coriandrum sativum*, widely cultivated for its aromatic seeds and leaves, used in flavouring food, etc.

Corinth 1 a port in S Greece, in the NE Peloponnese: the modern town is near the site of the ancient city, the largest and richest of the city-states after Athens. Pop: 29 600 (1995 est) **2** a region of ancient Greece, occupying most of the Isthmus of Corinth and part of the NE Peloponnese **3 Gulf of** Also called: Gulf of **Lepanto** an inlet of the Ionian Sea between the Peloponnese and central Greece **4 Isthmus of** a narrow strip of land between the Gulf of Corinth and the Saronic Gulf: crossed by the **Corinth Canal** making navigation possible between the gulfs

Corinthian of, denoting, or relating to one of the five classical orders of architecture: characterized by a bell-shaped capital having carved ornaments based on acanthus leaves

▷www.ancientgreece.com/art/art.htm

Coriolanus Gaius Marcius 5th century BC, a legendary Roman general, who allegedly led an army against Rome but was dissuaded from conquering it by his mother and wife

cork 1 the thick light porous outer bark of the cork oak, used widely as an insulator and for stoppers for bottles, casks, etc. **2** an angling float **3** *Botany* a protective layer of dead impermeable cells on the outside of the stems and roots of woody plants, produced by the outer layer of the cork cambium

Cork 1 a county of SW Republic of Ireland, in Munster province: crossed by ridges of low mountains; scenic coastline. County town: Cork. Pop: 447 829 (2002). Area: 7459 sq km (2880 sq miles) **2** a city and port in S Republic of Ireland, county town of Co. Cork, at the mouth of the River Lee: seat of the University College of Cork (1849). Pop: 186 239 (2002)

corkage a charge made at a restaurant for serving wine, etc, bought off the premises

corked (of a wine) tainted through having a cork containing excess tannin

corkscrew 1 a device for drawing corks from bottles, typically consisting of a pointed metal spiral attached

to a handle or screw mechanism **2** *Boxing, slang* a blow that ends with a twist of the fist, esp one intended to cut the opponent

corm *Botany* an organ of vegetative reproduction in plants such as the crocus, consisting of a globular stem base swollen with food and surrounded by papery scale leaves

cormorant any aquatic bird of the family *Phalacrocoracidae*, of coastal and inland waters, having a dark plumage, a long neck and body, and a slender hooked beak: order *Pelecaniformes* (pelicans, etc)

corn¹ a a tall annual grass, *Zea mays*, cultivated for its yellow edible grains, which develop on a spike **b** the grain of this plant, used for food, fodder, and as a source of oil

corn² a hardening or thickening of the skin around a central point in the foot, caused by pressure or friction

corncrake a common Eurasian rail, *Crex crex*, of fields and meadows, with a buff speckled plumage and reddish wings

cornea the convex transparent membrane that forms the anterior covering of the eyeball and is continuous with the sclera

Corneille Pierre 1606–84, French tragic dramatist often regarded as the founder of French classical drama. His plays include *Médée* (1635), *Le Cid* (1636), *Horace* (1640), and *Polyeucte* (1642)

corner 1 a projecting angle of a solid object or figure **2** *Commerce* a monopoly over the supply of a commodity so that its market price can be controlled **3** *Soccer, Hockey* a free kick or shot from the corner of the field, taken against a defending team when the ball goes out of play over their goal line after last touching one of their players **4** either of two opposite angles of a boxing ring in which the opponents take their rests **5** *Mountaineering* a junction between two rock faces forming an angle of between 60° and 120° **6** *Logic* either of a pair of symbols used in the same way as ordinary quotation marks to indicate quasi quotation

Corner the *Informal* an area in central Australia, at the junction of the borders of Queensland and South Australia

cornflower a Eurasian herbaceous plant, *Centaurea cyanus*, with blue, purple, pink, or white flowers, formerly a common weed in cornfields: family *Asteraceae* (composites)

Cornforth Sir John Warcup born 1917, Australian chemist, who shared the 1975 Nobel prize for chemistry with Vladimir Prelog for their work on stereochemistry

cornice 1 *Architect* **a** the top projecting mouldings of an entablature **b** a continuous horizontal projecting course or moulding at the top of a wall, building, etc. **2** an overhanging ledge of snow formed by the wind on the edge of a mountain ridge, cliff, or corrie

Cornish a former language of Cornwall, belonging to the S Celtic branch of the Indo-European family and closely related to Breton: extinct by 1800; has experienced a revival since the early 20th century

Corno Monte a mountain in central Italy: the highest peak in the Apennines. Height: 2912 m (9554 ft)

cornucopia 1 *Greek myth* the horn of Amalthea, the goat that suckled Zeus **2** a representation of such a horn in painting, sculpture, etc, overflowing with fruit, vegetables, etc.; horn of plenty

Cornwall a county of SW England: hilly, with a deeply indented coastline. Administrative centre: Truro. Pop: 513 500 (2003 est). Area: 3564 sq km (1376 sq miles)

Cornwallis Charles, 1st Marquis Cornwallis. 1738–1805, British general in the War of American Independence: commanded forces defeated at Yorktown (1781): defeated Tipu Sahib (1791): governor general of Bengal (1786–93, 1805): negotiated the Treaty of Amiens (1801)

Cornwell Patricia D (aniels). born 1956, US crime novelist; her novels, many of which feature the pathologist Dr Kay Scarpetta, include *Postmortem* (1990), *The Last Precinct* (2000), and *Isle of Dogs* (2002)

corolla the petals of a flower collectively, forming an inner floral envelope

corollary *Logic* a proposition that follows directly from the proof of another proposition

Coromandel Coast the SE coast of India, along the Bay of Bengal, extending from Point Calimere to the mouth of the Krishna River

corona 1 a circle of light around a luminous body, usually the moon **2** the outermost region of the sun's atmosphere, visible as a faint halo during a solar eclipse **3** *Architect* the flat vertical face of a cornice just above the soffit **4** a circular chandelier suspended from the roof of a church **5** *Botany* **a** the trumpet-shaped part of the corolla of daffodils and similar plants; the crown **b** a crown of leafy outgrowths from inside the petals of some flowers **6** *Anatomy* a crownlike structure, such as the top of the head **7** *Zoology* the head or upper surface of an animal, such as the body of an echinoid or the disc and arms of a crinoid **8** a long cigar with blunt ends

coronary 1 *Anatomy* designating blood vessels, nerves, ligaments, etc, that encircle a part or structure **2** short for **coronary thrombosis**

coronary thrombosis a condition of interrupted blood flow to the heart due to a blood clot in a coronary artery, usually as a consequence of atherosclerosis: characterized by intense pain

coronation the act or ceremony of crowning a monarch

coronavirus a type of airborne virus accounting for 10-30 of all colds

coroner a public official responsible for the investigation of violent, sudden, or suspicious deaths and inquiries into treasure trove. The investigation (**coroner's inquest**) is held in the presence of a jury (**coroner's jury**)

coronet 1 the margin between the skin of a horse's pastern and the horn of the hoof **2** the knob at the base of a deer's antler

Corot Jean Baptiste Camille 1796–1875, French landscape and portrait painter

corporal¹ 1 a noncommissioned officer junior to a sergeant in the army, air force, or marines **2** (in the Royal Navy) a petty officer who assists the master-at-arms

corporal² *or* **corporale** a white linen cloth on which the bread and wine are placed during the Eucharist

corporation 1 a group of people authorized by law to act as a single personality and having its own powers, duties, and liabilities **2** the municipal authorities of a city or town

corporeal of the nature of the physical body; not spiritual

corps de ballet the members of a ballet company who dance together in a group

corpus 1 a collection or body of writings, esp by a single author or on a specific topic **2** *Anatomy* **a** any distinct mass or body **b** the main part of an organ or structure **3** *Botany* the inner layer or layers of cells of the meristem at a shoot tip, which produces the vascular tissue and pith

Corpus Christi a port in S Texas, on **Corpus Christi Bay**, an inlet of the Gulf of Mexico. Pop: 279 208 (2003 est)

corpuscle 1 any cell or similar minute body that is suspended in a fluid, esp any of the **red blood corpuscles** (see **erythrocyte**) or **white blood corpuscles** (see **leucocyte**). **2** *Anatomy* the encapsulated ending of a sensory nerve **3** *Physics* a discrete particle such as an electron, photon, ion, or atom

corral *Chiefly US* (formerly) a defensive enclosure formed by a ring of covered wagons

corrasion erosion of a rock surface by rock fragments transported over it by water, wind, or ice

correction *Science* a number or quantity added to or subtracted from a scientific or mathematical calculation or observation to increase its accuracy

Correggio Antonio Allegri da 1494–1534, Italian painter, noted for his striking use of perspective and foreshortening

Corregidor an island at the entrance to Manila Bay, in the Philippines: site of the defeat of American forces by the Japanese (1942) in World War II

correspondent *Commerce* a person or firm that has regular business relations with another, esp one in a different part of the country or abroad

corridor 1 a hallway or passage connecting parts of a building **2** a strip of land or airspace along the route of a road or river **3** a strip of land or airspace that affords access, either from a landlocked country to the sea (such as the **Polish corridor**, 1919-39, which divided Germany) or from a state to an exclave (such as the **Berlin corridor**, 1945-90, which passed through the former East Germany) **4** a passageway connecting the compartments of a railway coach **5 corridors of power** the higher echelons of government, the Civil Service, etc, considered as the location of power and influence **6** a flight path that affords safe access for intruding aircraft

corroboree *Austral* a native assembly of sacred, festive, or warlike character

corrosion a process in which a solid, esp a metal, is eaten away and changed by a chemical action, as in the oxidation of iron in the presence of water by an electrolytic process

corrupt 1 (of a text or manuscript) made meaningless or different in meaning from the original by scribal errors or alterations **2** (of computer programs or data) containing errors

corsair 1 a pirate **2** a privateer, esp of the Barbary Coast

Corsica an island in the Mediterranean, west of N Italy: forms, with 43 islets, a region of France; mountainous; settled by Greeks in about 560 BC; sold by Genoa to

France in 1768. Capital: Ajaccio. Pop: 265 999 (2003 est). Area: 8682 sq km (3367 sq miles)

cortex 1 *Anatomy* the outer layer of any organ or part, such as the grey matter in the brain that covers the cerebrum (**cerebral cortex**) or the outer part of the kidney (**renal cortex**) 2 *Botany* **a** the unspecialized tissue in plant stems and roots between the vascular bundles and the epidermis **b** the outer layer of a part such as the bark of a stem

cortisone a glucocorticoid hormone, the synthetic form of which has been used in treating rheumatoid arthritis, allergic and skin diseases, leukaemia, etc.; 17-hydroxy-11-dehydrocorticosterone. Formula: $C_{21}H_{28}O_5$

Cortona a town in central Italy, in Tuscany: Roman and Etruscan remains, 15th-century cathedral. Pop: 22 048 (2001)

Cortot Alfred 1877–1962, French pianist, born in Switzerland

corundum a white, grey, blue, green, red, yellow, or brown mineral, found in metamorphosed shales and limestones, in veins, and in some igneous rocks. It is used as an abrasive and as gemstone; the red variety is ruby, the blue is sapphire. Composition: aluminium oxide. Formula: Al_2O_3. Crystal structure: hexagonal (rhombohedral)

corymb *Botany* an inflorescence in the form of a flat-topped flower cluster with the oldest flowers at the periphery. This type of raceme occurs in the candytuft

cos *or* **cos lettuce** a variety of lettuce with a long slender head and crisp leaves

cosecant (of an angle) a trigonometric function that in a right-angled triangle is the ratio of the length of the hypotenuse to that of the opposite side; the reciprocal of sine

Cosgrave 1 Liam born 1920, Irish statesman; prime minister of the Republic of Ireland (1973–77) 2 his father, **W** (**illiam**) **T** (**homas**). 1880–1965, Irish statesman; first prime minister (president of the executive council) of the Irish Free State (1922–32)

cosh hyperbolic cosine; a hyperbolic function, cosh $z = \frac{1}{2}(e^z + e^{-z})$, related to cosine by the expression cosh iz = cos z, where i = $\sqrt{-1}$

cosignatory 1 a person, country, etc, that signs a document jointly with others 2 signing jointly with another or others

cosine of an angle a trigonometric function that in a right-angled triangle is the ratio of the length of the adjacent side to that of the hypotenuse; the sine of the complement

cosmic 1 of or relating to the whole universe 2 occurring or originating in outer space, esp as opposed to the vicinity of the earth, the solar system, or the local galaxy

cosmogony the study of the origin and development of the universe or of a particular system in the universe, such as the solar system

cosmology 1 the philosophical study of the origin and nature of the universe 2 the branch of astronomy concerned with the evolution and structure of the universe
▷www.damtp.cam.ac.uk/user/gr/public/cos_home.html
▷http://map.gsfc.nasa.gov/m_uni.html

cosmopolitan (of plants or animals) widely distributed

cosmos 1 the world or universe considered as an ordered system 2 any tropical American plant of the genus *Cosmos*, cultivated as garden plants for their brightly coloured flowers: family *Asteraceae* (composites)

Cossack (formerly) any of the free warrior-peasants of chiefly East Slavonic descent who lived in communes, esp in Ukraine, and served as cavalry under the tsars

cost 1 **a** the amount paid for a commodity by its seller **b** (*as modifier*): *the cost price* 2 *Law* the expenses of judicial proceedings

Costa Brava a coastal region of NE Spain along the Mediterranean, extending from Barcelona to the French border: many resorts

Costa Rica a republic in Central America: gained independence from Spain in 1821; mostly mountainous and volcanic, with extensive forests. Official language: Spanish. Official religion: Roman Catholic. Currency: colón. Capital: San José. Pop: 4 250 000 (2004 est). Area: 50 900 sq km (19 652 sq miles)

costive having constipation; constipated

cost of living 1 **a** the basic cost of the food, clothing, shelter, and fuel necessary to maintain life, esp at a standard regarded as basic or minimal **b** (*as modifier*): *the cost-of-living index* 2 the average expenditure of a person or family in a given period

cot¹ *Nautical* a hammock-like bed with a stiff frame

cot² 1 *Literary or archaic* a small cottage 2 another name for **fingerstall**

cotangent (of an angle) a trigonometric function that in a right-angled triangle is the ratio of the length of the adjacent side to that of the opposite side; the reciprocal of tangent

cot death the unexplained sudden death of an infant during sleep

cote *or* **cot** *Dialect, chiefly Brit* a small cottage

cotoneaster any Old World shrub of the rosaceous genus *Cotoneaster*: cultivated for their small ornamental white or pinkish flowers and red or black berries

Cotonou the chief port and official capital of Benin, on the Bight of Benin. Pop: 891 000 (2005 est)

Cotopaxi a volcano in central Ecuador, in the Andes: the world's highest active volcano. Height: 5896 m (19 344 ft)

cottage 1 a small simple house, esp in a rural area 2 *US and Canadian* a small house in the country or at a resort, used for holiday purposes

cottage industry an industry in which employees work in their own homes, often using their own equipment

cotter¹ *Machinery* 1 any part, such as a pin, wedge, key, etc, that is used to secure two other parts so that relative motion between them is prevented 2 short for **cotter pin**

cotter² 1 *English history* a villein in late Anglo-Saxon and early Norman times occupying a cottage and land in return for labour 2 a peasant occupying a cottage and land in the Scottish Highlands under the same tenure as an Irish cottier

cotter pin *Machinery* 1 a split pin secured, after passing through holes in the parts to be attached, by spreading the ends **2** a tapered pin threaded at the smaller end and secured by a nut after insertion

cotton 1 any of various herbaceous plants and shrubs of the malvaceous genus *Gossypium* cultivated in warm climates for the fibre surrounding the seeds and the oil within the seeds **2** the soft white downy fibre of these plants: used to manufacture textiles **3 a** a cloth or thread made from cotton fibres **b** (*as modifier*): *a cotton dress* **4** any substance, such as kapok (**silk cotton**), resembling cotton but obtained from other plants

Cotton Henry 1907–87, British golfer: three times winner of the British Open

cotton wool 1 *Chiefly Brit* bleached and sterilized cotton from which the gross impurities, such as the seeds and waxy matter, have been removed: used for surgical dressings, tampons, etc. **2** cotton in the natural state

cotyledon 1 *Botany* a simple embryonic leaf in seed-bearing plants, which, in some species, forms the first green leaf after germination **2** *Anatomy* a tuft of villi on the mammalian placenta

couch 1 a frame upon which barley is malted **2** a priming layer of paint or varnish, esp in a painting **3** *Papermaking* **a** a board on which sheets of handmade paper are dried by pressing **b** a felt blanket onto which sheets of partly dried paper are transferred for further drying **c** a roll on a papermaking machine from which the wet web of paper on the wire is transferred to the next section **4** *Archaic* the lair of a wild animal

couchette a bed in a railway carriage, esp one converted from seats

couch grass a grass, *Agropyron repens*, with a yellowish-white creeping underground stem by which it spreads quickly: a troublesome weed

coulomb the derived SI unit of electric charge; the quantity of electricity transported in one second by a current of 1 ampere.

Coulomb Charles Augustin de 1736–1806, French physicist: made many discoveries in the field of electricity and magnetism

council 1 a body of people elected or appointed to serve in an administrative, legislative, or advisory capacity **2** *Brit* the local governing authority of a town, county, etc. **3** *Brit* provided by a local council, esp (of housing) at a subsidized rent **4** *Austral* an administrative or legislative assembly, esp the upper house of a state parliament in Australia **5** *Christianity* an assembly of bishops, theologians, and other representatives of several churches or dioceses, convened for regulating matters of doctrine or discipline

councillor *or US* **councilor** a member of a council

council tax (in Britain) a tax, based on the relative value of property, levied to fund local council services

counsel 1 a barrister or group of barristers engaged in conducting cases in court and advising on legal matters **2** *Christianity* any of the **counsels of perfection** or **evangelical counsels**, namely poverty, chastity, and obedience

counsellor *or US* **counselor 1** a person, such as a social worker, who is involved in counselling **2** *US* a lawyer, esp one who conducts cases in court; attorney **3** a senior British diplomatic officer **4** a US diplomatic officer ranking just below an ambassador or minister **5** a

person who advises students or others on personal problems or academic and occupational choice

count¹ 1 the act of counting or reckoning **2** the number reached by counting; sum **3** *Law* a paragraph in an indictment containing a distinct and separate charge **4** *Physics* the total number of photons or ionized particles detected by a counter **5** *Boxing, Wrestling* the act of telling off a number of seconds by the referee, as when a boxer has been knocked down or a wrestler pinned by his opponent **6 out for the count** *Boxing* knocked out and unable to continue after a count of ten by the referee **7 take the count** *Boxing* to be unable to continue after a count of ten

count² 1 a nobleman in any of various European countries having a rank corresponding to that of a British earl **2** any of various officials in the late Roman Empire and under various Germanic kings in the early Middle Ages **3** a man who has received an honour (**papal knighthood**) from the Pope in recognition of good deeds, achievements, etc.

counter¹ 1 a a small flat disc of wood, metal, or plastic, used in various board games **b** a similar disc or token used as an imitation coin **2** a skating figure consisting of three circles

counter² 1 an apparatus that records the number of occurrences of events **2** any instrument for detecting or counting ionizing particles or photons

counter 1 a return attack, such as a blow in boxing **2** *Fencing* a parry in which the foils move in a circular fashion **3** the portion of the stern of a boat or ship that overhangs the water aft of the rudder **4** the part of a horse's breast under the neck and between the shoulders

counterbalance a weight or force that balances or offsets another

counterespionage activities designed to detect and counteract enemy espionage

counterpart a duplicate, esp of a legal document; copy

counterpoint 1 the technique involving the simultaneous sounding of two or more parts or melodies **2** a melody or part combined with another melody or part **3** the musical texture resulting from the simultaneous sounding of two or more melodies or parts **4 strict counterpoint** the application of the rules of counterpoint as an academic exercise **5** *Prosody* the use of a stress or stresses at variance with the regular metrical stress

countertenor an adult male voice with an alto range

countess 1 the wife or widow of a count or earl **2** a woman of the rank of count or earl

count noun *Linguistics, Logic* a noun that can be qualified by the indefinite article, and may be used in the plural, as *telephone* and *thing* but not *airs and graces* or *bravery*

country 1 a territory distinguished by its people, culture, language, geography, etc. **2** an area of land distinguished by its political autonomy; state **3** the people of a territory or state **4 a** the part of the land that is away from cities or industrial areas; rural districts **b** (*as modifier*): *country cottage* **5** one's native land or nation of citizenship **6 go** *or* **appeal to the country** *Chiefly Brit* to dissolve Parliament and hold an election

country dance a type of folk dance in which couples

are arranged in sets and perform a series of movements, esp facing one another in a line
▷www.cdss.org
▷www.cam.ac.uk/societies/round/dances/elements.htm

county 1 a any of the administrative or geographic subdivisions of certain states, esp any of the major units into which England and Wales are or have been divided for purposes of local government b (*as modifier*): *county cricket* 2 *NZ* an electoral division in a rural area 3 *Obsolete* the lands under the jurisdiction of a count or earl

Couperin François 1668–1733, French composer, noted for his harpsichord suites and organ music

Coupland Douglas born 1961, Canadian novelist and journalist; novels include *Generation X* (1991), *Girlfriend in a Coma* (1998), and *City of Glass* (2000)

couple 1 *Chiefly hunting or coursing* a a pair of collars joined by a leash, used to attach hounds to one another b two hounds joined in this way c the unit of reckoning for hounds in a pack 2 *Mechanics* a pair of equal and opposite parallel forces that have a tendency to produce rotation with a torque or turning moment equal to the product of either force and the perpendicular distance between them 3 *Physics* a two dissimilar metals, alloys, or semiconductors in electrical contact, across which a voltage develops b two dissimilar metals or alloys in electrical contact that when immersed in an electrolyte act as the electrodes of an electrolytic cell

couplet two successive lines of verse, usually rhymed and of the same metre

coupling 1 a mechanical device that connects two things 2 a device for connecting railway cars or trucks together 3 the part of the body of a horse, dog, or other quadruped that lies between the forequarters and the hindquarters 4 *Electronics* the act or process of linking two or more circuits so that power can be transferred between them usually by mutual induction, as in a transformer, or by means of a capacitor or inductor common to both circuits 5 *Physics* an interaction between different properties of a system, such as a group of atoms or nuclei, or between two or more systems 6 *Genetics* the occurrence of two specified nonallelic genes from the same parent on the same chromosome

coupon 1 *Commerce* a a detachable part of a ticket or advertisement entitling the holder to a discount, free gift, etc. b a detachable slip usable as a commercial order form c a voucher given away with certain goods, a certain number of which are exchangeable for goods offered by the manufacturers 2 *History* a ticket issued to facilitate rationing

Courantyne a river in N South America, rising in S Guyana and flowing north to the Atlantic, forming the boundary between Guyana and Surinam. Length: 765 km (475 miles)

Courbet Gustave 1819–77, French painter, a leader of the realist movement; noted for his depiction of contemporary life

courgette *chiefly Brit* a small variety of vegetable marrow, cooked and eaten as a vegetable

courier a special messenger, esp one carrying diplomatic correspondence

Cournand André (Frederic). 1895–1988, US physician, born in France: shared the 1956 Nobel prize for physiology or medicine for his work on heart catheterization

course 1 the path or channel along which something moves 2 a a prescribed number of lessons, lectures, etc, in an educational curriculum b the material covered in such a curriculum 3 a prescribed regimen to be followed for a specific period of time 4 *Nautical* any of the sails on the lowest yards of a square-rigged ship 5 (in medieval Europe) a charge by knights in a tournament 6 a a hunt by hounds relying on sight rather than scent b a match in which two greyhounds compete in chasing a hare 7 the part or function assigned to an individual bell in a set of changes 8 *Archaic* a running race

courser[1] 1 a person who courses hounds or dogs, esp greyhounds 2 a hound or dog trained for coursing

courser[2] *Literary* a swift horse; steed

courser a terrestrial plover-like shore bird, such as *Cursorius cursor* (cream-coloured courser), of the subfamily *Cursoriinae* of desert and semidesert regions of the Old World: family *Glareolidae*, order *Charadriiformes*

coursework written or oral work completed by a student within a given period, which is assessed as an integral part of an educational course

coursing 1 hunting with hounds or dogs that follow their quarry by sight 2 a sport in which hounds are matched against one another in pairs for the hunting of hares by sight

court 1 an area of ground wholly or partly surrounded by walls or buildings 2 *Brit* a a block of flats b a mansion or country house c a short street, sometimes closed at one end 3 a space inside a building, sometimes surrounded with galleries 4 a the residence, retinues, or household of a sovereign or nobleman b (*as modifier*): *a court ball* 5 a sovereign or prince and his retinue, advisers, etc. 6 any formal assembly, reception, etc, held by a sovereign or nobleman with his courtiers 7 *Law* a an authority having power to adjudicate in civil, criminal, military, or ecclesiastical matters b the regular sitting of such a judicial authority c the room or building in which such a tribunal sits 8 a a marked outdoor or enclosed area used for any of various ball games, such as tennis, squash, etc. b a marked section of such an area 9 a the board of directors or council of a corporation, company, etc. b *Chiefly Brit* the supreme council of some universities 10 **go to court** to take legal action 11 **out of court** a without a trial or legal case b too unimportant for consideration

Court Margaret (née *Smith*). born 1942, Australian tennis player: Australian champion 1960–66, 1969–71, and 1973; US champion 1962, 1965, 1969–70, and 1973; Wimbledon champion 1963, 1965, and 1970

court card (in a pack of playing cards) a king, queen, or jack of any suit

courtesan *or* **courtezan** (esp formerly) a prostitute, or the mistress of a man of rank

courthouse a public building in which courts of law are held

courtyard an open area of ground surrounded by walls or buildings; court

cousin *Etiquette* a title used by a sovereign when addressing another sovereign or a nobleman

Cousin **Victor** 1792–1867, French philosopher and educational reformer

Cousteau **Jacques Yves** 1910–97, French underwater explorer

covalency *or US* **covalence** *Chemistry* 1 the formation and nature of covalent bonds 2 the number of covalent bonds that a particular atom can make with other atoms in forming a molecule

cove¹ 1 a small bay or inlet, usually between rocky headlands 2 a narrow cavern formed in the sides of cliffs, mountains, etc, usually by erosion 3 *Architect* a concave curved surface between the wall and ceiling of a room

cove² *Austral, History* an overseer of convict labourers

covenant 1 *Law* a an agreement in writing under seal, as to pay a stated annual sum to a charity b a particular clause in such an agreement, esp in a lease 2 (in early English law) an action in which damages were sought for breach of a sealed agreement 3 *Bible* God's promise to the Israelites and their commitment to worship him alone

Covenanter a person upholding the National Covenant of 1638 or the Solemn League and Covenant of 1643 between Scotland and England to establish and defend Presbyterianism

▷www.tartans.com/articles/covmain.html
▷www.sorbie.net/covenanters.htm

Covent Garden 1 a district of central London: famous for its former fruit, vegetable, and flower market, now a shopping precinct 2 the Royal Opera House (built 1858) in Covent Garden

Coventry 1 a city in central England, in Coventry unitary authority, West Midlands: devastated in World War II; modern cathedral (1954–62); industrial centre, esp for motor vehicles; two universities (1965, 1992). Pop: 303 475 (2001) 2 a unitary authority in central England, in West Midlands. Pop: 305 000 (2003 est). Area: 97 sq km (37 sq miles)

cover 1 woods or bushes providing shelter or a habitat for wild creatures 2 a blanket used on a bed for warmth 3 *Philately* a an entire envelope that has been postmarked b **on cover** (of a postage stamp) kept in this form by collectors 4 *Pop music* a version by a different artist of a previously recorded musical item 5 *Cricket* a the area more or less at right angles to the pitch on the off side and usually about halfway to the boundary b (*as modifier*): *a cover drive by a batsman* c a fielder in such a position 6 *Ecology* the percentage of the ground surface covered by a given species of plant 7 **break cover** (esp of game animals) to come out from a shelter or hiding place

Coverdale **Miles** 1488–1568, the first translator of the complete Bible into English (1535)

covert 1 a thicket or woodland providing shelter for game 2 *Ornithol* any of the small feathers on the wings and tail of a bird that surround the bases of the larger feathers 3 a flock of coots

covey a small flock of grouse or partridge

cow 1 the mature female of any species of cattle, esp domesticated cattle 2 the mature female of various other mammals, such as the elephant, whale, and seal

3 any domestic species of cattle

Coward **Sir Noël (Pierce)**. 1899–1973, English dramatist, actor, and composer, noted for his sophisticated comedies, which include *Private Lives* (1930) and *Blithe Spirit* (1941)

cowbell a metal percussion instrument usually mounted on the bass drum or hand-held and struck with a drumstick

cowboy a conventional character of Wild West folklore, films, etc, esp one involved in fighting Indians

cowcatcher *US and Canadian* a metal frame on the front of a locomotive to clear the track of animals or other obstructions

Cowdrey **(Michael) Colin, Baron**. 1932–2000, English cricketer. He played for Kent and in 114 Test matches (captaining England 27 times)

Cowell **Simon** born 1959, British manager of pop groups and TV personality, best known as an outspoken judge on the TV talent contest *Pop Idol*

Cowes a town in S England, on the Isle of Wight: famous for its annual regatta. Pop: 19 110 (2001)

cowl 1 the part of a car body that supports the windscreen and the bonnet 2 *Aeronautics* another word for **cowling**

cowling a streamlined metal covering, esp one fitted around an aircraft engine

cow parsley a common Eurasian umbelliferous hedgerow plant, *Anthriscus sylvestris*, having umbrella-shaped clusters of white flowers

Cowper **William** 1731–1800, English poet, noted for his nature poetry, such as in *The Task* (1785), and his hymns

cowpox a contagious viral disease of cows characterized by vesicles on the skin, esp on the teats and udder. Inoculation of humans with this virus provides temporary immunity to smallpox. It can be transmitted to other species, esp cats

cowrie *or* **cowry** 1 any marine gastropod mollusc of the mostly tropical family *Cypraeidae*, having a glossy brightly marked shell with an elongated opening 2 the shell of any of these molluscs, esp the shell of *Cypraea moneta* (**money cowry**), used as money in parts of Africa and S Asia

cowslip a primrose, *Primula veris*, native to temperate regions of the Old World, having fragrant yellow flowers

cox a coxswain, esp of a racing eight or four

coxswain the helmsman of a lifeboat, racing shell, etc.

coyote 1 a predatory canine mammal, *Canis latrans*, related to but smaller than the wolf, roaming the deserts and prairies of North America 2 (in American Indian legends of the West) a trickster and culture hero represented as a man or as an animal

coypu an aquatic South American hystricomorph rodent, *Myocastor coypus*, introduced into Europe: family *Capromyidae*. It resembles a small beaver with a ratlike tail and is bred in captivity for its soft grey underfur

crab 1 any chiefly marine decapod crustacean of the genus *Cancer* and related genera (section *Brachyura*), having a broad flattened carapace covering the cephalothorax, beneath which is folded the abdomen. The first pair of limbs are modified as pincers 2 any of various similar or related arthropods, such as the hermit crab and horseshoe crab **3** short for **crab louse 4** *Aeronautics* a manoeuvre in which an aircraft flies slightly into the crosswind to compensate for drift **5** a mechanical lifting device, esp the travelling hoist of a gantry crane **6** **catch a crab** *Rowing* to make a stroke in which the oar either misses the water or digs too deeply, causing the rower to fall backwards

crab apple 1 any of several rosaceous trees of the genus *Malus* that have white, pink, or red flowers and small sour apple-like fruits **2** the fruit of any of these trees, used to make jam

Crabbe George 1754–1832, English narrative poet, noted for his depiction of impoverished rural life in *The Village* (1783) and *The Borough* (1810)

crab louse a parasitic louse, *Pthirus* (or *Phthirus*) *pubis*, that infests the pubic region in man

crack 1 a break or fracture without complete separation of the two parts **2** a physical or mental defect; flaw **3** a broken or cracked tone of voice, as a boy's during puberty **4** *Slang* a processed form of cocaine hydrochloride used as a stimulant. It is highly addictive **5** *Obsolete slang* a burglar or burglary

cracker 1 a decorated cardboard tube that emits a bang when pulled apart, releasing a toy, a joke, or a paper hat **2** *US* another word for **poor White**

cracking *Chemistry* the process in which molecules are cracked, esp the oil-refining process in which heavy oils are broken down into hydrocarbons of lower molecular weight by heat or catalysis

crackle 1 intentional crazing in the glaze of a piece of porcelain or pottery **2** porcelain or pottery so decorated

Cracow an industrial city in S Poland, on the River Vistula: former capital of the country (1320–1609); university (1364). Pop: 822 000 (2005 est)

-cracy indicating a type of government or rule

cradle 1 a frame, rest, or trolley made to support or transport a piece of equipment, aircraft, ship, etc. **2** a platform, cage, or trolley, in which workmen are suspended on the side of a building or ship **3** a holder connected to a computer allowing data to be transferred from a PDA, digital camera, etc. **4** another name for **creeper 5** a framework used to prevent the bedclothes from touching a sensitive part of an injured person

craft 1 an occupation or trade requiring special skill, esp manual dexterity **2 a** the members of such a trade, regarded collectively **b** (*as modifier*): *a craft guild* **3** a single vessel, aircraft, or spacecraft
▷www.craftsitedirectory.com
▷www.artpromote.com/craft.shtml

craftsman 1 a member of a skilled trade; someone who practises a craft; artisan **2** an artist skilled in the techniques of an art or craft

crag a steep rugged rock or peak

Craig Edward Gordon 1872–1966, English theatrical designer, actor, and director. His nonrealistic scenic design greatly influenced theatre in Europe and the US

Craigavon a district in central Northern Ireland, in Co. Armagh. Pop: 57 685 (2001). Area: 279 sq km (108 sq miles)

Craigie Sir William A(lexander). 1867–1957, Scottish lexicographer; joint editor of the *Oxford English Dictionary* (1901–33), and of *A Dictionary of American English on Historical Principles* (1938–44)

crake *Zoology* any of several rails that occur in the Old World, such as the corncrake and the spotted crake

crammer a person or school that prepares pupils for an examination, esp pupils who have already failed that examination

cramp¹ 1 a painful involuntary contraction of a muscle, typically caused by overexertion, heat, or chill **2** temporary partial paralysis of a muscle group **3** severe abdominal pain

cramp² 1 a strip of metal with its ends bent at right angles, used to bind masonry **2** a device for holding pieces of wood while they are glued; clamp

crampon 1 one of a pair of pivoted steel levers used to lift heavy objects; grappling iron **2** one of a pair of frames each with 10 or 12 metal spikes, strapped to boots for climbing or walking on ice or snow

Cranach Lucas , known as *the Elder*, real name *Lucas Müller*. 1472–1553, German painter, etcher, and designer of woodcuts

cranberry any of several trailing ericaceous shrubs of the genus *Vaccinium*, such as the European *V. oxycoccus*, that bear sour edible red berries

crane 1 any large long-necked long-legged wading bird of the family *Gruidae*, inhabiting marshes and plains in most parts of the world except South America, New Zealand, and Indonesia: order *Gruiformes* **2** any similar bird, such as a heron **3** a device for lifting and moving heavy objects, typically consisting of a moving boom, beam, or gantry from which lifting gear is suspended **4** *Films* a large trolley carrying a boom, on the end of which is mounted a camera

Crane 1 (**Harold**) Hart 1899–1932, US poet; author of *The Bridge* (1930) **2** Stephen 1871–1900, US novelist and short-story writer, noted particularly for his novel *The Red Badge of Courage* (1895) **3** Walter 1845–1915, British painter, illustrator of children's books, and designer of textiles and wallpaper

crane fly any dipterous fly of the family *Tipulidae*, having long legs, slender wings, and a narrow body

cranesbill any of various plants of the genus *Geranium*, having pink or purple flowers and long slender beaked fruits: family *Geraniaceae*

cranial of or relating to the skull

craniology the branch of science concerned with the shape and size of the human skull, esp with reference to variations between different races

cranium 1 the skull of a vertebrate **2** the part of the skull that encloses the brain

crank¹ 1 a device for communicating motion or for converting reciprocating motion into rotary motion or vice versa. It consists of an arm projecting from a shaft, often with a second member attached to it parallel to the shaft **2** a handle incorporating a crank, used to start an engine or motor

crank² or **cranky** (of a sailing vessel) easily keeled over by the wind; tender

crankcase the metal housing that encloses the crankshaft, connecting rods, etc, in an internal-combustion engine, reciprocating pump, etc.

Cranko John 1927–73, British choreographer, born in South Africa: director of the Stuttgart Ballet (1961–73)

crankpin a short cylindrical bearing surface fitted between two arms of a crank and set parallel to the main shaft of the crankshaft

crankshaft a shaft having one or more cranks, esp the main shaft of an internal-combustion engine to which the connecting rods are attached

Cranmer Thomas 1489–1556, the first Protestant archbishop of Canterbury (1533–56) and principal author of the Book of Common Prayer. He was burnt as a heretic by Mary I

Cranwell a village in E England, in Lincolnshire: Royal Air Force College (1920)

crap 1 a losing throw in the game of craps 2 another name for **craps**

craps 1 a gambling game using two dice, in which a player wins the bet if 7 or 11 is thrown first, and loses if 2, 3, or 12 is thrown 2 **shoot craps** to play this game

crash¹ 1 a sudden descent of an aircraft as a result of which it hits land or water 2 the sudden collapse of a business, stock exchange, etc, esp one causing further financial failure

crash² a coarse cotton or linen cloth used for towelling, curtains, etc.

Crashaw Richard 1613–49, English religious poet, noted esp for the *Steps to the Temple* (1646)

crash barrier a barrier erected along the centre of a motorway, around a racetrack, etc, for safety purposes

crash dive a sudden steep dive from the surface by a submarine

crash team a medical team with special equipment able to be mobilized quickly to treat cardiac arrest

Crassus Marcus Licinius ?115–53 BC, Roman general; member of the first triumvirate with Caesar and Pompey

-crat indicating a person who takes part in or is a member of a form of government or class

crater 1 the bowl-shaped opening at the top or side of a volcano or top of a geyser through which lava and gases are emitted 2 a similarly shaped depression formed by the impact of a meteorite or exploding bomb 3 any of the circular or polygonal walled formations covering the surface of the moon and some other planets, formed probably either by volcanic action or by the impact of meteorites. They can have a diameter of up to 240 kilometres (150 miles) and a depth of 8900 metres (29 000 feet) 4 a large open bowl with two handles, used for mixing wines, esp in ancient Greece

craw 1 a less common word for **crop** 2 the stomach of an animal

crawfish a variant (esp US) of **crayfish** (esp sense 2)

Crawford 1 Joan, real name *Lucille le Sueur*. 1908–77, US film actress, who portrayed ambitious women in such films as *Mildred Pierce* (1945) 2 Michael, real name *Michael Dumbell Smith*. born 1942, British actor

crawl *Swimming* a stroke in which the feet are kicked like paddles while the arms reach forward and pull back through the water

Crawley a town in S England, in NE West Sussex: designated a new town in 1956. Pop: 100 547 (2001)

crayfish *or esp US* **crawfish** 1 any freshwater decapod crustacean of the genera *Astacus* and *Cambarus*, resembling a small lobster 2 any of various similar crustaceans, esp the spiny lobster

crayon 1 a small stick or pencil of charcoal, wax, clay, or chalk mixed with coloured pigment 2 a drawing made with crayons

Crazy Horse Indian name *Ta-Sunko-Witko*. ?1849–77, Sioux Indian chief, remembered for his attempts to resist White settlement in Sioux territory

cream 1 **cream sherry** a full-bodied sweet sherry 2 a a yellowish-white colour b (*as adjective*): *cream wallpaper*

creamery a place where dairy products are sold

crease 1 *Cricket* any three lines near each wicket marking positions for the bowler or batsman 2 *Ice hockey* the small rectangular area in front of each goal cage 3 *Lacrosse* the circular area surrounding the goal

Creation *Theol* 1 God's act of bringing the universe into being 2 the universe as thus brought into being by God

Creator an epithet of God

credit 1 a sum of money or equivalent purchasing power, as at a shop, available for a person's use 2 a the practice of permitting a buyer to receive goods or services before payment b the time permitted for paying for such goods or services 3 reputation for solvency and commercial or financial probity, inducing confidence among creditors 4 *Education* a a distinction awarded to an examination candidate obtaining good marks b a section of an examination syllabus satisfactorily completed, as in higher and professional education 5 **on credit** with payment to be made at a future date

creditor a person or commercial enterprise to whom money is owed

creditworthy (of an individual or business enterprise) adjudged as meriting credit on the basis of such factors as earning power, previous record of debt repayment, etc.

creed 1 a concise, formal statement of the essential articles of Christian belief, such as the Apostles' Creed or the Nicene Creed 2 any statement or system of beliefs or principles

creek 1 *Chiefly Brit* a narrow inlet or bay, esp of the sea 2 *US, Canadian, Austral, and NZ* a small stream or tributary

creel 1 a wickerwork basket, esp one used to hold fish 2 a wickerwork trap for catching lobsters, etc.

creep 1 *Geology* the gradual downwards movement of loose rock material, soil, etc, on a slope 2 a slow relative movement of two adjacent parts, structural components, etc. 3 slow plastic deformation of metals

creeper 1 a plant, such as the ivy or periwinkle, that grows by creeping 2 *US and Canadian* any small songbird of the family *Certhiidae* of the N hemisphere, having a brown-and-white plumage and slender downward-curving bill. They creep up trees to feed on insects 3 a hooked instrument for dragging deep water 4 a flat board or framework mounted on casters, used to lie on when working under cars 5 *Cricket* a bowled ball that keeps low or travels along the ground

Cremona a city in N Italy, in Lombardy on the River Po: noted for the manufacture of fine violins in the 16th–18th centuries. Pop: 70 887 (2001)

crenellated *or US* **crenelated** (of a moulding, etc) having square indentations

creole a language that has its origin in extended contact between two language communities, one of which is generally European. It incorporates features from each and constitutes the mother tongue of a community

Creole 1 in the Caribbean and Latin America **a** a native-born person of European, esp Spanish, ancestry **b** a native-born person of mixed European and African ancestry who speaks a French or Spanish creole **c** a native-born Black person as distinguished from one brought from Africa **2** (in Louisiana and other Gulf States of the US) a native-born person of French ancestry **3** the creolized French spoken in Louisiana, esp in New Orleans ·

creosote 1 a colourless or pale yellow liquid mixture with a burning taste and penetrating odour distilled from wood tar, esp from beechwood, contains creosol and other phenols, and is used as an antiseptic **2** a thick dark liquid mixture prepared from coal tar, containing phenols: used as a preservative for wood

crepe or **crape a** a light cotton, silk, or other fabric with a fine ridged or crinkled surface **b** (as modifier): a crepe dress

crepuscular (of certain insects, birds, and other animals) active at twilight or just before dawn

crescendo Music **a** a gradual increase in loudness or the musical direction or symbol indicating this **b** (as modifier): a crescendo passage

crescent 1 the biconcave shape of the moon in its first or last quarters **2** Chiefly Brit a crescent-shaped street, often lined with houses of the same style **3 a** the emblem of Islam or Turkey **b** Islamic or Turkish power

cress any of various plants of the genera Lepidium, Cardamine, Arabis, etc, having pungent-tasting leaves often used in salads and as a garnish: family Brassicaceae (crucifers)

crest 1 a tuft or growth of feathers, fur, or skin along the top of the heads of some birds, reptiles, and other animals **2** a ridge on the neck of a horse, dog, lion, etc. **3** the mane or hair growing from this ridge **4** a ridge along the surface of a bone **5** Archery identifying rings painted around an arrow shaft

Cretaceous of, denoting, or formed in the last period of the Mesozoic era, between the Jurassic and Tertiary periods, lasting 80 million years during which chalk deposits were formed and flowering plants first appeared

Crete a mountainous island in the E Mediterranean, the largest island of Greece: of archaeological importance for the ruins of Minoan civilization. Pop: 601 131 (2001). Area: 8331 sq km (3216 sq miles)

cretinism a condition arising from a deficiency of thyroid hormone, present from birth, characterized by dwarfism and mental retardation

cretonne a a heavy cotton or linen fabric with a printed design, used for furnishing **b** (as modifier): cretonne chair covers

crevasse 1 a deep crack or fissure, esp in the ice of a glacier **2** US a break in a river embankment

crevice a narrow fissure or crack; split; cleft

crew Nautical a group of people assigned to a particular job or type of work

Crewe a town in NW England, in Cheshire: major railway junction. Pop: 67 683 (2001)

crewel a loosely twisted worsted yarn, used in fancy work and embroidery

crib 1 a representation of the manger in which the infant Jesus was laid at birth **2** Informal, chiefly Brit a translation of a foreign text or a list of answers used by students, often illicitly, as an aid in lessons, examinations, etc. **3** short for **cribbage 4** Cribbage the discard pile **5** a storage area for floating logs contained by booms

cribbage a game of cards for two to four, in which players try to win a set number of points before their opponents

Crichton James 1560–82, Scottish scholar and writer, called the Admirable Crichton because of his talents (John) Michael born 1942, US novelist, screenwriter, and film director; his thrillers, many of which have been filmed, include The Andromeda Strain (1969), Jurassic Park (1990), and Disclosure (1994)

Crick Francis Harry Compton 1916–2004, English molecular biologist: helped to discover the helical structure of DNA; Nobel prize for physiology or medicine shared with James Watson and Maurice Wilkins 1962

cricket¹ 1 any insect of the orthopterous family Gryllidae, having long antennae and, in the males, the ability to produce a chirping sound (stridulation) by rubbing together the leathery forewings **2** any of various related insects, such as the mole cricket

cricket² a a game played by two teams of eleven players on a field with a wicket at either end of a 22-yard pitch, the object being for one side to score runs by hitting a hard leather-covered ball with a bat while the other side tries to dismiss them by bowling, catching, running them out, etc. **b** (as modifier): a cricket bat

crime 1 an act or omission prohibited and punished by law **2 a** unlawful acts in general **b** (as modifier): crime wave

▷www.unodc.org/unodc/
crime_cicp_sitemap.html

Crimea a peninsula and autonomous region in Ukraine between the Black Sea and the Sea of Azov: a former autonomous republic of the Soviet Union (1921–45), part of the Ukrainian SSR from 1945 until 1991

criminal 1 a person charged with and convicted of crime **2** of, involving, or guilty of crime

criminology the scientific study of crime, criminal behaviour, law enforcement, etc.

crimp the natural wave of wool fibres

Crimplene Trademark a synthetic material similar to Terylene, characterized by its crease-resistance

crimson a a deep or vivid red colour **b** (as adjective): a crimson rose

crinoline a stiff fabric, originally of horsehair and linen used in lining garments

Crippen Hawley Harvey, known as Doctor Crippen. 1862–1910, US doctor living in England: executed for poisoning his wife; the first criminal to be apprehended by the use of radiotelegraphy

cripple US, dialect a dense thicket, usually in marshy land

Cripple Creek a village in central Colorado: gold-mining centre since 1891, once the richest in the world

Cripps Sir (Richard) Stafford 1889–1952, British Labour

statesman; Chancellor of the Exchequer (1947–50)

crisis *Pathol* a sudden change, for better or worse, in the course of a disease

Crispin Saint, 3rd century AD, legendary Roman Christian martyr, with his brother **Crispinian**: they are the patron saints of shoemakers. Feast day: Oct 25

criterion *Philosophy* a defining characteristic of something

critic a professional judge of art, music, literature, etc.

critical 1 *Informal* so seriously injured or ill as to be in danger of dying **2** *Physics* of, denoting, or concerned with a state in which the properties of a system undergo an abrupt change **3** **go critical** (of a nuclear power station or reactor) to reach a state in which a nuclear-fission chain reaction becomes self-sustaining

criticism 1 the analysis or evaluation of a work of art, literature, etc. **2** a work that sets out to evaluate or analyse **3** the investigation of a particular text, with related material, in order to establish an authentic text

critique a critical essay or commentary, esp on artistic work

Croatia a republic in SE Europe: settled by Croats in the 7th century; belonged successively to Hungary, Turkey, and Austria; formed part of Yugoslavia (1918–91); became independent in 1991 but was invaded by Serbia and fighting continued until 1995; involved in the civil war in Bosnia-Herzegovina (1991–95). Language: Croatian. Religion: Roman Catholic majority. Currency: kuna. Capital: Zagreb. Pop: 4 416 000 (2004 est). Area: 55 322 sq km (21 359 sq miles)

Croatian the language that is spoken in Croatia, a dialect of Serbo-Croat (Croato-Serb)

Croce Benedetto 1866–1952, Italian philosopher, critic, and statesman: an opponent of Fascism, he helped re-establish liberalism in postwar Italy

crochet *Zoology* a hooklike structure of insect larvae that aids locomotion

crock¹ 1 an earthen pot, jar, etc. **2** a piece of broken earthenware

crock² an old broken-down horse or ewe

Crockett David, known as *Davy Crockett*. 1786–1836, US frontiersman, politician, and soldier

crocodile 1 any large tropical reptile, such as C. *niloticus* (**African crocodile**), of the family *Crocodylidae*: order *Crocodilia* (crocodilians). They have a broad head, tapering snout, massive jaws, and a thick outer covering of bony plates **2** any other reptile of the order *Crocodilia*; a crocodilian

Crocodile River 1 a river in N South Africa, rising north of Johannesburg and flowing north-westerly into the Marico River on the Botswanan border; a tributary of the Limpopo **2** a river that rises in NE South Africa, in the Kruger National Park, and flows south-easterly into Mozambique

crocus 1 any plant of the iridaceous genus *Crocus*, widely cultivated in gardens, having white, yellow, or purple flowers **2** of a saffron yellow colour

Croesus died ?546 BC, the last king of Lydia (560–546), noted for his great wealth

Cromer a resort in E England, on the Norfolk coast: fishing. Pop: 8836 (2001)

cromlech 1 a circle of prehistoric standing stones **2** (no longer in technical usage) a megalithic chamber tomb or dolmen

Crompton 1 Richmal, full name *Richmal Crompton Lamburn*. 1890–1969, British children's author, best known for her *Just William* stories **2** **Samuel** 1753–1827, British inventor of the spinning mule (1779)

Cromwell 1 Oliver 1599–1658, English general and statesman. A convinced Puritan, he was an effective leader of the parliamentary army in the Civil War. After the execution of Charles I he quelled the Royalists in Scotland and Ireland, and became Lord Protector of the Commonwealth (1653–58) **2** his son, **Richard** 1626–1712, Lord Protector of the Commonwealth (1658–59) **3** **Thomas**,Earl of Essex. ?1485–1540, English statesman. He was secretary to Cardinal Wolsey (1514), after whose fall he became chief adviser to Henry VIII. He drafted most of the Reformation legislation, securing its passage through parliament, the power of which he thereby greatly enhanced. He was executed after losing Henry's favour

Cronin 1 A(rchibald) J(oseph). 1896–1981, British novelist and physician. His works include *Hatter's Castle* (1931), *The Judas Tree* (1961), and *Dr Finlay's Casebook*, a TV series based on his medical experiences **2** **James Watson** born 1931, US physicist; shared the Nobel prize for physics (1980) for his work on parity conservation in weak interactions

crook *Music* a piece of tubing added to a brass instrument in order to obtain a lower harmonic series

Crookes Sir William 1832–1919, English chemist and physicist: he investigated the properties of cathode rays and invented a type of radiometer and the lens named after him

crop 1 short for **riding crop 2 a** a pouchlike expanded part of the oesophagus of birds, in which food is stored or partially digested before passing on to the gizzard **b** a similar structure in insects, earthworms, and other invertebrates

cropper 1 a a cutting machine for removing the heads from castings and ingots **b** a guillotine for cutting lengths of bar or strip **2** a machine for shearing the nap from cloth **3** a variety of domestic pigeon with a puffed-out crop

croquet a game for two to four players who hit a wooden ball through iron hoops with mallets in order to hit a peg

▷www.croquet.org.uk
▷www.croquetamerica.com

Crosby¹ Bing, real name *Harry Lillis Crosby*. 1904–77, US singer and film actor; famous for his style of crooning: best known for the song "White Christmas" from the film *Holiday Inn* (1942)

Crosby² a town in NW England, in Sefton unitary authority, Merseyside. Pop: 51 789 (2001)

crosier *or* **crozier 1** a staff surmounted by a crook or cross, carried by bishops as a symbol of pastoral office **2** the tip of a young plant, esp a fern frond, that is coiled into a hook

cross 1 a representation of the Cross used as an emblem of Christianity or as a reminder of Christ's death **2** a sign representing the Cross made either by tracing a figure in the air or by touching the forehead, breast, and either shoulder in turn **3** any conventional variation of the Christian symbol, used emblematically, decoratively, or heraldically, such as a Maltese, tau, or Greek cross **4** Christianity or Christendom, esp as contrasted with non-Christian religions **5** the place in a town or village where a cross has been set up **6** *Biology* **a** the process of crossing; hybridization **b** an individual produced as a result of this process **7** *Boxing* a straight punch delivered from the side, esp with the right hand **8** *Football* the act or an instance of kicking or passing the ball from a wing to the middle of the field

Cross¹ Richard Assheton, 1st Viscount. 1823–1914, British Conservative statesman, home secretary (1874–80); noted for reforms affecting housing, public health, and the employment of women and children in factories

Cross² the **1** the cross on which Jesus Christ was crucified **2** the Crucifixion of Jesus

crossbar 1 a horizontal beam across a pair of goalposts **2** a horizontal bar mounted on vertical posts used in athletics or show-jumping **3** the horizontal bar on a man's bicycle that joins the handlebar and saddle supports

cross-bench *Brit* a seat in Parliament occupied by a neutral or independent member

crossbill any of various widely distributed finches of the genus *Loxia*, such as *L. curvirostra*, that occur in coniferous woods and have a bill with crossed mandible tips for feeding on conifer seeds

crossbreed the offspring produced by such a breeding

cross-country a long race held over open ground

crossing 1 a place, often shown by markings, lights, or poles, where a street, railway, etc, may be crossed **2** the intersection of the nave and transept in a church **3** the act or process of crossbreeding

Crossman Richard (Howard Stafford). 1907–74, British Labour politician. His diaries, published posthumously as the *Crossman Papers* (1975), revealed details of cabinet discussions

cross-ply (of a motor tyre) having the fabric cords in the outer casing running diagonally to stiffen the sidewalls

crossroad *US and Canadian* **1** a road that crosses another road **2** a road that crosses from one main road to another

crossroads an area or the point at which two or more roads cross each other

cross section 1 *Maths* a plane surface formed by cutting across a solid, esp perpendicular to its longest axis **2** a section cut off in this way **3** *Physics* a measure of the probability that a collision process will result in a particular reaction. It is expressed by the effective area that one participant presents as a target for the other

crossword puzzle a puzzle in which the solver deduces words suggested by numbered clues and writes them into corresponding boxes in a grid to form a vertical and horizontal pattern

▷www.crossword-puzzles.co.uk

crotch a the angle formed by the inner sides of the legs where they join the human trunk **b** the human external genitals or the genital area

c the corresponding part of a pair of trousers, pants, etc.

crotchet 1 *Music* a note having the time value of a quar-

ter of a semibreve **2** *Zoology* a small notched or hooked process, as in an insect

croup¹ a throat condition, occurring usually in children, characterized by a hoarse cough and laboured breathing, resulting from inflammation and partial obstruction of the larynx

croup² *or* **croupe** the hindquarters of a quadruped, esp a horse

croupier a person who deals cards, collects bets, etc, at a gaming table

crow 1 any large gregarious songbird of the genus *Corvus*, esp *C. corone* (**carrion crow**) of Europe and Asia: family *Corvidae*. Other species are the raven, rook, and jackdaw and all have a heavy bill, glossy black plumage, and rounded wings **2** any of various other corvine birds, such as the jay, magpie, and nutcracker **3** any of various similar birds of other families

crowbar a heavy iron lever with one pointed end, and one forged into a wedge shape

crowd *Music* an ancient bowed stringed instrument; crwth

Crowe Russell born 1964, Australian film actor, born in New Zealand. His films include *LA Confidential* (1997), *Gladiator* (2000), for which he won an Oscar, *A Beautiful Mind* (2001), and *Master and Commander* (2003)

crown 1 monarchy or kingship **2 a** *History* a coin worth 25 pence (five shillings) **b** any of several continental coins, such as the krona or krone, with a name meaning *crown* **3** the centre part of a road, esp when it is cambered **4** *Botany* **a** the leaves and upper branches of a tree **b** the junction of root and stem, usually at the level of the ground **c** another name for **corona 5** *Zoology* **a** the cup and arms of a crinoid, as distinct from the stem **b** the crest of a bird **6** *Dentistry* **a** the enamel-covered part of a tooth above the gum **b** **artificial crown** a substitute crown, usually of gold, porcelain, or acrylic resin, fitted over a decayed or broken tooth **7** *Nautical* the part of an anchor where the arms are joined to the shank **8** *Architecture* the highest part of an arch or vault

Crown 1 the sovereignty or realm of a monarch **2 a** the government of a constitutional monarchy **b** (*as modifier*): *Crown property*

crown colony a British colony whose administration and legislature is controlled by the Crown

crown court *English law* a court of criminal jurisdiction holding sessions in towns throughout England and Wales at which circuit judges hear and determine cases

Crown Derby a type of porcelain manufactured at Derby from 1784–1848

crown-of-thorns a thorny euphorbiaceous Madagascan shrub, *Euphorbia milii* var. *splendens*, cultivated as a hedging shrub or pot plant, having flowers with scarlet bracts

crown prince the male heir to a sovereign throne

Croydon a borough in S Greater London (since 1965): formerly important for its airport (1915–59). Pop: 336 700 (2003 est). Area: 87 sq km (33 sq miles)

crucible 1 a vessel in which substances are heated to high temperatures **2** the hearth at the bottom of a metallurgical furnace in which the metal collects

crucifix a cross or image of a cross with a figure of Christ upon it

Crucifixion 1 the crucifying of Christ at Calvary, regarded by Christians as the culminating redemptive act of his ministry **2** a picture or representation of this

cruciform a geometric curve, shaped like a cross, that has four similar branches asymptotic to two mutually perpendicular pairs of lines. Equation:$x^2y^2 - a^2x^2 - a^2y^2 = 0$, where $x = y = \pm a$ are the four lines.

crud *Slang* an undesirable residue from a process, esp one inside a nuclear reactor

Cruden Alexander 1701–70, Scottish bookseller and compiler of a well- known biblical concordance (1737)

crude oil petroleum before it has been refined

cruet *Christianity* either of a pair of small containers for the wine and water used in the Eucharist

Cruft Charles 1852–1938, British dog breeder, who organized the first (1886) of the annual dog shows known as Cruft's

Cruikshank George 1792–1878, English illustrator and caricaturist

cruiser 1 a high-speed, long-range warship of medium displacement, armed with medium calibre weapons or missiles **2** a pleasure boat, esp one that is power-driven and has a cabin **3** *Boxing* short for **cruiserweight** (see **light heavyweight**)

crummy *Canadian* a lorry that carries loggers to work from their camp

crupper 1 a strap from the back of a saddle that passes under the horse's tail to prevent the saddle from slipping forwards **2** the part of the horse's rump behind the saddle

crusade 1 any of the military expeditions undertaken in the 11th, 12th, and 13th centuries by the Christian powers of Europe to recapture the Holy Land from the Muslims **2** (formerly) any holy war undertaken on behalf of a religious cause
▷www.medievalcrusades.com
▷www.fordham.edu/halsall/sbook.1k.html

cruse a small earthenware container used, esp formerly, for liquids

crush *Vet science* a construction designed to confine and limit the movement of an animal, esp a large or dangerous animal, for examination or to perform a procedure on it

crust 1 *Geology* the solid outer shell of the earth, with an average thickness of 30–35 km in continental regions and 5 km beneath the oceans, forming the upper part of the lithosphere and lying immediately above the mantle, from which it is separated by the Mohorovičić discontinuity **2** the dry covering of a skin sore or lesion; scab **3** *Oenology* a layer of acid potassium tartrate deposited by some wine, esp port, on the inside of the bottle **4** *Biology* the hard outer layer of such organisms as lichens and crustaceans

crustacean any arthropod of the mainly aquatic class *Crustacea*, typically having a carapace hardened with lime and including the lobsters, crabs, shrimps, woodlice, barnacles, copepods, and water fleas

crutch 1 *Brit* another word for **crotch 2** *Nautical* **a** a forked support for a boom or oar, etc. **b** a brace for reinforcing the frames at the stern of a wooden vessel

crux *Mountaineering* the most difficult and often decisive part of a climb or pitch

cry 1 *Hunting* the baying of a pack of hounds hunting their quarry by scent **2** a pack of hounds

cryogenics the branch of physics concerned with the production of very low temperatures and the phenomena occurring at these temperatures

crypt 1 a cellar, vault, or underground chamber, esp beneath a church, where it is often used as a chapel, burial place, etc. **2** *Anatomy* any pitlike recess or depression

cryptic *or* **cryptical** *Zoology* (of the coloration of animals) tending to conceal by disguising or camouflaging the shape

cryptogam (in former plant classification schemes) any organism that does not produce seeds, including algae, fungi, mosses, and ferns

crystal 1 a piece of solid substance, such as quartz, with a regular shape in which plane faces intersect at definite angles, due to the regular internal structure of its atoms, ions, or molecules **2** a single grain of a crystalline substance **3 a** a highly transparent and brilliant type of glass, often used in cut-glass tableware, ornaments, etc. **b** (*as modifier*): *a crystal chandelier* **4** crystal glass articles collectively **5** *Electronics* **a** a crystalline element used in certain electronic devices as a detector, oscillator, transducer, etc. **b** (*as modifier*): *crystal pick-up*

crystal ball the glass globe used in crystal gazing

crystal gazing the act of staring into a crystal globe (**crystal ball**) supposedly in order to arouse visual perceptions of the future, etc.

crystalline 1 having the characteristics or structure of crystals **2** consisting of or containing crystals

crystallography the science concerned with the formation, properties, and structure of crystals

crystalloid 1 resembling or having the appearance or properties of a crystal or crystalloid **2** a substance that in solution can pass through a semipermeable membrane **3** *Botany* any of numerous crystals of protein occurring in certain seeds and other storage organs

CS gas a gas causing tears, salivation, and painful breathing, used in civil disturbances; *ortho*-chlorobenzal malononitrile. Formula: $C_6H_4ClCH{:}C(CN)_2$

CT scanner computerized tomography scanner: an X-ray machine that can produce stereographic images

cub the young of certain animals, such as the lion, bear, etc.

Cuba a republic and the largest island in the Caribbean, at the entrance to the Gulf of Mexico: became a Spanish colony after its discovery by Columbus in 1492; gained independence after the Spanish-American War of 1898 but remained subject to US influence until declared a people's republic under Castro in 1960; subject of an international crisis in 1962, when the US blockaded the island in order to compel the Soviet Union to dismantle its nuclear missile base. Sugar comprises about 80 per cent of total exports; the economy was badly affected by loss of trade following the collapse of the Soviet Union and by the continuing US trade embargo. Language: Spanish. Religion: nonreligious majority. Currency: peso. Capital: Havana. Pop: 11 328 000 (2004 est). Area: 110 922 sq km (42 827 sq miles)

cube¹ 1 a solid having six plane square faces in which the angle between two adjacent sides is a right angle **2**

the product of three equal factors: the cube of 2 is $2 \times 2 \times 2$ (usually written 2^3)

cube² any of various tropical American plants, esp any of the leguminous genus *Lonchocarpus*, the roots of which yield rotenone

cube root the number or quantity whose cube is a given number or quantity: 2 is the cube root of 8 (usually written $\sqrt[3]{8}$ or $8^{1/3}$)

cubic 1 having the shape of a cube 2 a having three dimensions **b** denoting or relating to a linear measure that is raised to the third power 3 *Maths* of, relating to, or containing a variable to the third power or a term in which the sum of the exponents of the variables is three 4 *Crystallog* relating to or belonging to the crystal system characterized by three equal perpendicular axes. The unit cell of cubic crystals is a cube with a lattice point at each corner (**simple cubic**) and one in the cube's centre (**body-centred cubic**), or a lattice point at each corner and one at the centre of each face (**face-centred cubic**). 5 *Maths* a a cubic equation, such as $x^3 + x + 2 = 0$ **b** a cubic term or expression

cubicle *Agriculture* an indoor construction designed to house individual cattle while allowing them free access to silage

cubic measure a system of units for the measurement of volumes, based on the cubic inch, the cubic centimetre, etc.

cubism a French school of painting, collage, relief, and sculpture initiated in 1907 by Pablo Picasso, the Spanish painter and sculptor (1881–1973) and Georges Braque, the French painter (1882–1963), which amalgamated viewpoints of natural forms into a multifaceted surface of geometrical planes
  ▷www.artlex.com/ArtLex/c/cubism.html
  ▷http://wwar.com/categories/Artists/Masters/
    Cubism
  ▷http://abstractart.20m.com/cubism.htm

cubit an ancient measure of length based on the length of the forearm

cuboid 1 the cubelike bone of the foot; the outer distal bone of the tarsus 2 *Maths* a geometric solid whose six faces are rectangles; rectangular parallelepiped

Cub Scout *or* **Cub** a member of a junior branch (for those aged 8–11 years) of the Scout Association
  ▷www.scoutbase.org.uk

cuckoo any bird of the family *Cuculidae*, having pointed wings, a long tail, and zygodactyl feet: order *Cuculiformes*. Many species, including the **European cuckoo** (*Cuculus canorus*), lay their eggs in the nests of other birds and have a two-note call

cuckoopint a European aroid plant, *Arum maculatum*, with arrow-shaped leaves, a spathe marked with purple, a pale purple spadix, and scarlet berries

cuckoo spit a white frothy mass on the stems and leaves of many plants, produced by froghopper larvae (**cuckoo spit insects**) which feed on the plant juices

cucumber 1 a creeping cucurbitaceous plant, *Cucumis sativus*, cultivated in many forms for its edible fruit 2 the cylindrical fruit of this plant, which has hard thin green rind and white crisp flesh 3 any of various similar or related plants or their fruits

cud partially digested food regurgitated from the first

stomach of cattle and other ruminants to the mouth for a second chewing

Cudlipp Hugh, Baron. 1913–98, British newspaper editor, a pioneer of tabloid journalism: editorial director of the *Daily Mirror* (1952–63)

cue 1 (in the theatre, films, music, etc) anything spoken or done that serves as a signal to an actor, musician, etc, to follow with specific lines or action 2 *Psychol* the part of any sensory pattern that is identified as the signal for a response

Cuernavaca a city in S central Mexico, capital of Morelos state: resort with nearby Cacahuamilpa Caverns. Pop: 723 000 (2005 est)

Culbertson Ely 1891–1955, US authority on contract bridge

cul-de-sac 1 a road with one end blocked off; dead end 2 *Anatomy* any tube-shaped bodily cavity or pouch closed at one end, such as the caecum

Culham a village in S central England, in Oxfordshire: site of the UK centre for thermonuclear reactor research and of the Joint European Torus (JET) programme

Cullen William Douglas, Baron. born 1935, Scottish judge who conducted public inquiries into the Piper Alpha disaster (1990), the Dunblane school shootings (1996), and the Ladbroke Grove rail disaster (1999)

Culloden a moor near Inverness in N Scotland: site of a battle in 1746 in which government troops under the Duke of Cumberland defeated the Jacobites under Prince Charles Edward Stuart

Culpeper Nicholas 1616–54, English herbalist and astrologer; his unauthorized translation (1649) of the College of Physicians' *Pharmacopoeia* and his *Herbal* (1653) popularized herbalism

culprit *Law* a person awaiting trial, esp one who has pleaded not guilty

cult 1 a specific system of religious worship, esp with reference to its rites and deity 2 a sect devoted to such a system

culture 1 the total range of activities and ideas of a group of people with shared traditions, which are transmitted and reinforced by members of the group 2 a particular civilization at a particular period 3 the artistic and social pursuits, expression, and tastes valued by a society or class, as in the arts, manners, dress, etc. 4 *Stockbreeding* the rearing and breeding of animals, esp with a view to improving the strain

culvert 1 a drain or covered channel that crosses under a road, railway, etc. 2 a channel for an electric cable 3 a tunnel through which water is pumped into or out of a dry dock

Cumberland¹ 1 Richard 1631–1718, English theologian and moral philosopher; bishop of Peterborough (1691–1718) 2 William Augustus, Duke of Cumberland, known as *Butcher Cumberland*. 1721–65, English soldier, younger son of George II, noted for his defeat of Charles Edward Stuart at Culloden (1746) and his subsequent ruthless destruction of Jacobite rebels

Cumberland² (until 1974) a county of NW England, now part of Cumbria

Cumbria (since 1974) a county of NW England comprising the former counties of Westmorland and

Cumberland together with N Lancashire: includes the Lake District mountain area and surrounding coastal lowlands with the Pennine uplands in the extreme east. Administrative centre: Carlisle. Pop: 489 800 (2003 est). Area: 6810 sq km (2629 sq miles)

cumin *or* **cummin** an umbelliferous Mediterranean plant, *Cuminum cyminum*, with finely divided leaves and small white or pink flowers

Cummings Edward Estlin , (preferred typographical representation of name **e e. cummings**). 1894–1962, US poet

cumulus 1 *Meteorol* a bulbous or billowing white or dark grey cloud associated with rising air currents 2 *Histology* the mass of cells surrounding a recently ovulated egg cell in a Graafian follicle

Cunaxa the site near the lower Euphrates where Artaxerxes II defeated Cyrus the Younger in 401 BC

cuneiform 1 of, relating to, or denoting the wedge-shaped characters employed in the writing of several ancient languages of Mesopotamia and Persia, esp Sumerian, Babylonian, etc. 2 of or relating to a tablet in which this script is employed 3 any one of the three tarsal bones

cunjevoi *Austral* 1 an aroid plant, *Alocasia macrorrhiza*, of tropical Asia and Australia, cultivated for its edible rhizome 2 a sea squirt

Cunningham Merce born 1919, US dancer and choreographer. His experimental ballets include *Suit for Five* (1956) and *Travelogue* (1977)

Cunninghame Graham R(obert) B(ontine). 1852–1936, Scottish traveller, writer, and politician, noted for his essays and short stories: first president (1928) of the Scottish Nationalist Party

Cunobelinus also called *Cymbeline*. died ?42 AD, British ruler of the Catuvellauni tribe (?10–?42); founder of Colchester (?10)

cup 1 a unit of capacity used in cooking equal to approximately half a pint, 8 fluid ounces, or about one quarter of a litre 2 a mixed drink with one ingredient as a base, usually served from a bowl 3 *Golf* the hole or metal container in the hole on a green 4 *Christian religion* the chalice or the consecrated wine used in the Eucharist

Cup Final 1 the annual final of the FA Cup soccer competition, played at Wembley, or the Scottish Cup, played at Hampden Park 2 the final of any cup competition

Cupid 1 the Roman god of love, represented as a winged boy with a bow and arrow 2 any similar figure, esp as represented in Baroque art

cupola 1 a roof or ceiling in the form of a dome 2 a small structure, usually domed, on the top of a roof or dome 3 a vertical air-blown coke-fired cylindrical furnace in which iron is remelted for casting

cupreous 1 of, consisting of, containing, or resembling copper; coppery 2 of the reddish-brown colour of copper

cupric of or containing copper in the divalent state

cupronickel any ductile corrosion-resistant copper alloy containing up to 40 per cent nickel: used in coins, condenser tubes, turbine blades, etc.

cup tie *Sport* an eliminating match or round between two teams in a cup competition

curacy the office or position of curate

curare *or* **curari** 1 black resin obtained from certain tropical South American trees, esp *Chondrodendron tomentosum*, acting on the motor nerves to cause muscular paralysis: used medicinally as a muscle relaxant and by South American Indians as an arrow poison 2 any of various trees of the genera *Chondrodendron* (family *Menispermaceae*) and *Strychnos* (family *Loganiaceae*) from which this resin is obtained

curate 1 a clergyman appointed to assist a parish priest 2 a clergyman who has the charge of a parish (**curate-in-charge**)

curator *Law, chiefly Scots* a guardian of a minor, mentally ill person, etc.

curb¹ 1 a a horse's bit with an attached chain or strap, which checks the horse b the chain or strap itself 2 a hard swelling on the hock of a horse

curb² *Vet science* a swelling on the leg of a horse, below the point of the hock, usually caused by a sprain

cure 1 a return to health, esp after specific treatment 2 any course of medical therapy, esp one proved effective in combating a disease 3 the spiritual and pastoral charge of a parish

curette *or* **curet** a surgical instrument for removing dead tissue, growths, etc, from the walls of certain body cavities

curfew 1 an official regulation setting restrictions on movement, esp after a specific time at night 2 in medieval Europe a the ringing of a bell to prompt people to extinguish fires and lights b the time at which the curfew bell was rung c the bell itself

curie a unit of radioactivity that is equal to 3.7×10^{10} disintegrations per second.

Curie 1 Marie 1867–1934, French physicist and chemist, born in Poland: discovered with her husband Pierre the radioactivity of thorium, and discovered and isolated radium and polonium. She shared a Nobel prize for physics (1903) with her husband and Henri Becquerel, and was awarded a Nobel prize for chemistry (1911) 2 her husband, **Pierre** 1859–1906, French physicist and chemist

curio a small article valued as a collector's item, esp something fascinating or unusual

Curitiba a city in SE Brazil, capital of Paraná state: seat of the University of Paraná (1946). Pop: 2 871 000 (2005 est)

curium a silvery-white metallic transuranic element artificially produced from plutonium. Symbol: Cm; atomic no.: 96; half-life of most stable isotope, ^{247}Cm: 1.6×10^7 years; valency: 3 and 4; relative density: 13.51 (calculated); melting pt.: 1345±400°C.

curl *Maths* a vector quantity associated with a vector field that is the vector product of the operator ∇ and a vector function A, where $\nabla = i\partial/\partial x + j\partial/\partial y + k\partial/\partial z$, i, j, and k being unit vectors. Usually written curl A, rot A

curlew any large shore bird of the genus *Numenius*, such as *N. arquata* of Europe and Asia: family *Scolopacidae* (sandpipers, etc), order *Charadriiformes*. They have a long downward-curving bill and occur in northern and arctic regions.

curling a game played on ice, esp in Scotland and Canada, in which heavy stones with handles (**curling stones**) are slid towards a target (**tee**)

▷http://icing.org

Curnow (Thomas) **Allen** (Monro). 1911–2001, New Zealand poet and anthologist

currant 1 any of several mainly N temperate shrubs of the genus *Ribes*, esp *R. rubrum* (redcurrant) and *R. nigrum* (blackcurrant): family *Grossulariaceae* **2** the small acid fruit of any of these plants

currawong any Australian crowlike songbird of the genus *Strepera*, having black, grey, and white plumage: family *Cracticidae*

currency 1 a metal or paper medium of exchange that is in current use in a particular country **2** *Austral* (formerly) the local medium of exchange, esp in the colonies, as distinct from sterling

current 1 a mass of air, body of water, etc, that has a steady flow in a particular direction **2** the rate of flow of such a mass **3** *Physics* **a** a flow of electric charge through a conductor **b** the rate of flow of this charge. It is measured in amperes

current account *Economics* that part of the balance of payments composed of the balance of trade and the invisible balance

curriculum 1 a course of study in one subject at a school or college **2** a list of all the courses of study offered by a school or college

currycomb a square comb consisting of rows of small teeth, used for grooming horses

curse an ecclesiastical censure of excommunication

cursor 1 the sliding part of a measuring instrument, esp a transparent sliding square on a slide rule **2** *Computing* any of various means, typically a flashing bar or underline, of identifying a particular position on a computer screen, such as the insertion point for text

curtain 1 a hanging cloth or similar barrier for concealing all or part of a theatre stage from the audience **2** the end of a scene of a play, opera, etc, marked by the fall or closing of the curtain **3** the rise or opening of the curtain at the start of a performance

curtain call the appearance of performers at the end of a theatrical performance to acknowledge applause

curtain-raiser *Theatre* a short dramatic piece presented before the main play

Curtin John Joseph 1885–1945, Australian statesman; prime minister of Australia (1941–45)

curvature 1 any normal or abnormal curving of a bodily part **2** *Geometry* the change in inclination of a tangent to a curve over unit length of arc. For a circle or sphere it is the reciprocal of the radius

curve 1 *Maths* **a** a system of points whose coordinates satisfy a given equation; a locus of points **b** the graph of a function with one independent variable **2** a line representing data, esp statistical data, on a graph

curvet *Dressage* a low leap with all four feet off the ground

curvilinear *or* **curvilineal 1** consisting of, bounded by, or characterized by a curved line **2** along a curved line **3** *Maths* (of a set of coordinates) determined by or determining a system of three orthogonal surfaces

Curzon 1 Sir **Clifford** 1907–82, English pianist **2** George **Nathaniel**, 1st Marquis Curzon of Kedleston. 1859–1925, British Conservative statesman; viceroy of India (1898–1905)

Cusack Cyril (James). 1910–93, Irish actor

cuscus any of several large nocturnal phalangers of the genus *Phalanger*, of N Australia, New Guinea, and adjacent islands, having dense fur, prehensile tails, large eyes, and a yellow nose

Cush *or* **Kush** *Old Testament* **1** the son of Ham and brother of Canaan (Genesis 10:6) **2** the country of the supposed descendants of Cush (ancient Ethiopia), comprising approximately Nubia and the modern Sudan, and the territory of southern (or Upper) Egypt

Cushing Harvey Williams 1869–1939, US neurosurgeon: identified a pituitary tumour as a cause of the disease named after him

cushion 1 the resilient felt-covered rim of a billiard table **2** short for **air cushion 3** a capital, used in Byzantine, Romanesque, and Norman architecture, in the form of a bowl with a square top

cusp 1 *Dentistry* any of the small elevations on the grinding or chewing surface of a tooth **2** *Anatomy* any of the triangular flaps of a heart valve **3** *Geometry* a point at which two arcs of a curve intersect and at which the two tangents are coincident **4** *Architect* a carving at the meeting place of two arcs **5** *Astronomy* either of the points of a crescent moon or of a satellite or inferior planet in a similar phase **6** *Astrology* any division between houses or signs of the zodiac

Custer George Armstrong 1839–76, US cavalry general: Civil War hero, killed fighting the Sioux Indians at Little Bighorn, Montana

custodian 1 a person who has custody, as of a prisoner, ward, etc. **2** a guardian or keeper, as of an art collection, etc.

custody 1 the act of keeping safe or guarding, esp the right of guardianship of a minor **2** the state of being held by the police; arrest (esp in the phrases **in custody, take into custody**)

custom 1 a a practice which by long-established usage has come to have the force of law **b** such practices collectively (esp in the phrase **custom and practice**) **2** habitual patronage, esp of a shop or business **3** the customers of a shop or business collectively **4** (in feudal Europe) a tribute paid by a vassal to his lord

customary 1 *Law* **a** founded upon long continued practices and usage rather than law **b** (of land, esp a feudal estate) held by custom **2 a** a statement in writing of customary laws and practices **b** a body of such laws and customs

custom house *or* **customs house** a government office, esp at a port, where customs are collected and ships cleared for entry

customs 1 duty on imports or exports **2** the government department responsible for the collection of these duties **3** the part of a port, airport, frontier station, etc, where baggage and freight are examined for dutiable goods and contraband **4** the procedure for examining baggage and freight, paying duty, etc. **5** (*as modifier*): *customs officer*

cut 1 *Botany* incised or divided **2** *Veterinary science* gelded or castrated **3** *Economics* a decrease in government finance in a particular department or area, usually leading to a reduction of services, staff numbers, etc. **4** short for **power cut 5** *Chiefly US and Canadian* a quantity of timber cut during a specific time or operation **6** *Sport* the spin of a cut ball **7** *Cricket* a stroke made with the bat in a roughly horizontal position **8** *Films* an immediate transition from one shot to the next, brought about by splicing the two shots together **9** *Chem* a fraction obtained in distillation, as in oil refining **10** the metal removed in a single pass of a machine tool **11 a** the shape of the teeth of a file **b** their coarseness or fineness **12** *Brit* a stretch of water, esp a canal **13 make the cut** *Golf* to better or equal the required score after two rounds in a strokeplay tournament, thus avoiding elimination from the final two rounds **14 miss the cut** *Golf* to achieve a greater score after the first two rounds of a strokeplay tournament than that required to play in the remaining two rounds

cutaneous of, relating to, or affecting the skin

cutaway **1 a** a drawing or model of a machine, engine, etc, in which part of the casing is omitted to reveal the workings **b** (*as modifier*): *a cutaway model* **2** *Films, Television* a shot separate from the main action of a scene, to emphasize something or to show simultaneous events

cut glass **a** glass, esp bowls, vases, etc, decorated by facet-cutting or grinding **b** (*as modifier*): *a cut-glass vase*

Cuthbert Saint ?635–87AD, English monk; bishop of Lindisfarne. Feast day: March 20

cuticle **1** dead skin, esp that round the base of a fingernail or toenail **2** another name for **epidermis** **3** any covering layer or membrane **4** the protective layer, containing cutin, that covers the epidermis of higher plants **5** the hard protective layer covering the epidermis of many invertebrates

cut in *Films* a separate shot or scene inserted at a relevant point

cutler a person who makes or sells cutlery

cutlery **1** implements used for eating, such as knives, forks, and spoons **2** instruments used for cutting **3** the art or business of a cutler

cut off **1** a device to terminate the flow of a fluid in a pipe or duct **2** the remnant of metal, plastic, etc, left after parts have been machined or trimmed **3** *Electronics* **a** the value of voltage, frequency, etc, below or above which an electronic device cannot function efficiently **b** (*as modifier*): *cutoff voltage* **4** *Geography* a channel cutting across the neck of a meander, which leaves an oxbow lake

cut out **1** a device that switches off or interrupts an electric circuit, esp a switch acting as a safety device **2** an impressed stamp cut out from an envelope for collecting purposes

cut-price *or esp US* **cut-rate** **1** available at prices or rates below the standard price or rate **2** offering goods or services at prices below the standard price

cutter **1** a sailing boat with its mast stepped further aft so as to have a larger foretriangle than that of a sloop **2** a ship's boat, powered by oars or sail, for carrying passengers or light cargo **3** a small lightly armed boat, as used in the enforcement of customs regulations

cut-throat (of some games) played by three people

cutting **1** *Horticulture* **a** a method of vegetative propagation in which a part of a plant, such as a stem or leaf, is induced to form its own roots **b** a part separated for this purpose **2** *Films* the editing process by which a film

is cut and made **3** *Civil Engineering* an excavation in a piece of high land for a road, railway, etc, enabling it to remain at approximately the same level

cuttlefish any cephalopod mollusc of the genus *Sepia* and related genera, which occur near the bottom of inshore waters and have a broad flattened body: order *Decapoda* (decapods)

Cuxhaven a port in NW Germany, at the mouth of the River Elbe. Pop: 52 876 (2003 est)

Cuyp *or* **Kuyp** Aelbert 1620–91, Dutch painter of landscapes and animals

Cuzco *or* **Cusco** a city in S central Peru: former capital of the Inca Empire, with extensive Inca remains; university (1692). Pop: 307 000 (2005 est)

cwm **1** (in Wales) a valley **2** *Geology* another name for cirque

cyanic acid a colourless poisonous volatile liquid acid that hydrolyses readily to ammonia and carbon dioxide. Formula: HOCN

cyanide *or* **cyanid** any salt of hydrocyanic acid. Cyanides contain the ion CN^- and are extremely poisonous

cyanogen an extremely poisonous colourless flammable gas with an almond-like odour: has been used in chemical warfare. Formula: $(CN)_2$

cyanosis *Pathol* a bluish-purple discoloration of skin and mucous membranes usually resulting from a deficiency of oxygen in the blood

cybernetics the branch of science concerned with control systems in electronic and mechanical devices and the extent to which useful comparisons can be made between man-made and biological systems

cyberspace all of the data stored in a large computer or network represented as a three-dimensional model through which a virtual-reality user can move

cyclamen **1** any Old World plant of the primulaceous genus *Cyclamen*, having nodding white, pink, or red flowers, with reflexed petals **2** of a dark reddish-purple colour

cycle **1** *Lit* a group of poems or prose narratives forming a continuous story about a central figure or event **2** a series of miracle plays **3** *Music* a group or sequence of songs **4** *Astronomy* the orbit of a celestial body **5** *Biology* a recurrent series of events or processes in plants and animals **6** *Physics* a continuous change or a sequence of changes in the state of a system that leads to the restoration of the system to its original state after a finite period of time **7** *Physics* one of a series of repeated changes in the magnitude of a periodically varying quantity, such as current or voltage **8** *Computing* **a** a set of operations that can be both treated and repeated as a unit **b** the time required to complete a set of operations **c** one oscillation of the regular voltage waveform used to synchronize processes in a digital computer
▷www.uci.ch
▷www.usacycling.org

cyclometer a device that records the number of revolutions made by a wheel and hence the distance travelled

cyclone **1** another name for **depression** **2** a violent tropical storm; hurricane

Cyclops *Classical myth* one of a race of giants having a single eye in the middle of the forehead, encountered by Odysseus in the *Odyssey*

cyclotron a type of particle accelerator in which the particles spiral inside two D-shaped hollow metal electrodes placed facing each other under the effect of a strong vertical magnetic field, gaining energy by a high-frequency voltage applied between these electrodes

cygnet a young swan

cylinder 1 *Maths* a solid consisting of two parallel planes bounded by identical closed curves, usually circles, that are interconnected at every point by a set of parallel lines, usually perpendicular to the planes. Volume *base area* × length. 2 a surface formed by a line moving round a closed plane curve at a fixed angle to it 3 *Engineering* the chamber in a reciprocating internal-combustion engine, pump, or compressor within which the piston moves 4 *Archaeology* a cylindrical seal of stone, clay, or precious stone decorated with linear designs, found in the Middle East and Balkans: dating from about 6000 BC

cymbal a percussion instrument of indefinite pitch consisting of a thin circular piece of brass, which vibrates when clashed together with another cymbal or struck with a stick

cyme an inflorescence in which the first flower is the terminal bud of the main stem and subsequent flowers develop as terminal buds of lateral stems

Cymric *or* **Kymric** 1 the Welsh language 2 the Brythonic group of Celtic languages 3 a breed of medium-sized cat with soft semi-long hair

Cynewulf, Kynewulf, *or* **Cynwulf** ?8th century AD, Anglo-Saxon poet; author of *Juliana, The Ascension, Elene,* and *The Fates of the Apostles*

cynic *Astronomy* of or relating to Sirius, the Dog Star

Cynic a member of a sect founded by Antisthenes that scorned worldly things and held that self-control was the key to the only good

cypress 1 any coniferous tree of the N temperate genus *Cupressus*, having dark green scalelike leaves and rounded cones: family *Cupressaceae* 2 any of several similar and related trees, such as the widely cultivated *Chamaecyparis lawsoniana* (**Lawson's cypress**), of the western US 3 any of various other coniferous trees, esp the swamp cypress 4 the wood of any of these trees

Cyprian¹ Saint ?200–258 AD, bishop of Carthage and martyr. Feast day: Sept 26 or 16

Cyprian² 1 of or relating to Cyprus 2 of or resembling the ancient orgiastic worship of Aphrodite on Cyprus

Cypriot *or* **Cypriote** 1 a native, citizen, or inhabitant of Cyprus 2 the dialect of Ancient or Modern Greek spoken in Cyprus

Cyprus an island in the E Mediterranean: ceded to Britain by Turkey in 1878 and made a colony in 1925; became an independent republic in 1960 as a member of the Commonwealth; invaded by Turkey in 1974 following a Greek-supported military coup, leading to the partition of the island. In 1983 the Turkish-controlled northern sector declared itself to be an independent state as the Turkish Republic of Northern Cyprus but failed to receive international recognition. Attempts by the U.N. to broker a reunification agreement have failed. Cyprus joined the EU in 2004. The UK maintains two enclaves as military bases (Akrotiri and Dhekelia Sovereign Base Areas), which are not included in Cyprus politically. Languages: Greek and Turkish. Religions: Greek Orthodox and Muslim. Currency: pound and Turkish lira. Capital: Nicosia. Pop. (Greek): 675 000 (2001 est); (Turkish): 198 000 (2001 est). Area: 9251 sq km (3571 sq miles)

Cyrano de Bergerac Savinien 1619–55, French writer and soldier, famous as a duellist and for his large nose. He became widely known through the verse drama *Cyrano de Bergerac* (1897) by Edmond Rostand

Cyrene an ancient Greek city of N Africa, near the coast of Cyrenaica: famous for its medical school

Cyril Saint ?827–869 AD, Greek Christian theologian, missionary to the Moravians and inventor of the Cyrillic alphabet; he and his brother Saint Methodius were called *the Apostles of the Slavs*. Feast day: Feb 14 or May 11

Cyrillic denoting or relating to the alphabet derived from that of the Greeks, supposedly by Saint Cyril, for the writing of Slavonic languages: now used primarily for Russian, Bulgarian, and the Serbian dialect of Serbo-Croat

Cyril of Alexandria Saint ?375–444 AD, Christian theologian and patriarch of Alexandria. Feast day: June 27 or June 9

Cyrus 1 known as *Cyrus the Great* or *Cyrus the Elder*. died ?529 BC, king of Persia and founder of the Persian empire 2 called *the Younger*. died 401 BC, Persian satrap of Lydia: revolted against his brother Artaxerxes II, but was killed at the battle of Cunaxa

cyst 1 *Pathol* any abnormal membranous sac or blister-like pouch containing fluid or semisolid material 2 *Anatomy* any normal sac or vesicle in the body 3 a thick-walled protective membrane enclosing a cell, larva, or organism

cystic fibrosis an inheritable disease of the exocrine glands, controlled by a recessive gene: affected children inherit defective alleles from both parents. It is characterized by chronic infection of the respiratory tract and by pancreatic insufficiency

cystitis inflammation of the urinary bladder

-cyte indicating a cell

Cythera 1 a Greek island off the SE coast of the Peloponnese: in ancient times a centre of the worship of Aphrodite. Pop: 3354 (2001). Area: about 285 sq km (110 sq miles) 2 the chief town of this island, on the S coast. Pop: 300 (latest est)

Cyzicus an ancient Greek colony in NW Asia Minor on the S shore of the Sea of Marmara: site of Alcibiades' naval victory over the Peloponnesians (410 BC)

Czech 1 a of, relating to, or characteristic of the Czech Republic, its people, or its language b of, relating to, or characteristic of Bohemia and Moravia, their people, or their language c (loosely) of, relating to, or characteristic of the former Czechoslovakia or its people 2 the official language of the Czech Republic, belonging to the West Slavonic branch of the Indo-European family; also spoken in Slovakia. Czech and Slovak are closely related and mutually intelligible 3 a a native or inhabitant of the Czech Republic b a native or inhabitant of Bohemia or Moravia c (loosely) a native, inhabitant, or citizen of the former Czechoslovakia

Czechoslovak (loosely) either of the two mutually intelligible languages of the former Czechoslovakia; Czech or Slovak

Czechoslovakia a former republic in central Europe: formed after the defeat of Austria-Hungary (1918) as a nation of Czechs in Bohemia and Moravia and Slovaks in Slovakia; occupied by Germany from 1939 until its liberation by the Soviet Union in 1945; became a people's republic under the Communists in 1948; invaded by Warsaw Pact troops in 1968, ending Dubček's attempt to liberalize communism; in 1989 popular unrest led to the resignation of the politburo and the formation of a non-Communist government. It consisted of two federal republics, the **Czech Republic** and **Slovakia**, which became independent in 1993.

Czech Republic a country in central Europe; formed part of Czechoslovakia until 1993; mostly wooded, with lowlands surrounding the River Morava, rising to the Bohemian plateau in the W and to highlands in the N; joined the EU in 2004. Language: Czech. Religion: Christian majority. Currency: koruna. Capital Prague. Pop: 10 226 000 (2004 est). Area: 78 864 sq km (30 450 sq miles).

Czerny Karl 1791–1857, Austrian pianist, composer, and teacher, noted for his studies

Dd

D *or* **D.** Deutsch: indicating the serial number in the catalogue (1951) of the musical compositions of Schubert made by Otto Deutsch (1883–1967)

dab 1 a small common European brown flatfish, *Limanda limanda*, covered with rough toothed scales: family *Pleuronectidae*: a food fish 2 any of various other small flatfish, esp flounders 3 a sand flounder, *Rhombosolea plebia*, common around New Zealand's South Island

dace 1 a European freshwater cyprinid fish, *Leuciscus leuciscus*, with a slender bluish-green body 2 any of various similar fishes

Dachau a town in S Germany, in Bavaria: site of a Nazi concentration camp. Pop: 39 474 (2003 est)

dachshund a long-bodied short-legged breed of dog

Dacia an ancient region bounded by the Carpathians, the Tisza, and the Danube, roughly corresponding to modern Romania. United under kings from about 60 BC, it later contained the Roman province of the same name (about 105 to 270 AD)

dactyl 1 *Prosody* a metrical foot of three syllables, one long followed by two short (–◡◡) 2 *Zoology* any digit of a vertebrate

Dada *or* **Dadaism** a nihilistic artistic movement of the early 20th century in W Europe and the US, founded on principles of irrationality, incongruity, and irreverence towards accepted aesthetic criteria
▷www.peak.org/~dadaist/English/Graphics

dado 1 the lower part of an interior wall that is decorated differently from the upper part 2 *Architect* the part of a pedestal between the base and the cornice

Dadra and Nagar Haveli a union territory of W India, on the Gulf of Cambay: until 1961 administratively part of Portuguese Damão. Capital: Silvassa. Pop: 220 451 (2001). Area: 489 sq km (191 sq miles)

daffodil 1 a widely cultivated Eurasian amaryllidaceous plant, *Narcissus pseudonarcissus*, having spring-blooming yellow flowers 2 any other plant of the genus *Narcissus*

Dafydd ap Gruffudd died 1283, Welsh leader. Claiming the title Prince of Wales (1282), he led an unsuccessful revolt against Edward I: executed

Dafydd ap Gwilym ?1320–?1380, Welsh poet

Dagenham part of the Greater London borough of Barking and Dagenham: engineering and chemicals

Dagestan Republic a constituent republic of S Russia, on the Caspian Sea: annexed from Persia in 1813; rich mineral resources. Capital: Makhachkala. Pop: 2 584 200 (2002). Area: 50 278 sq km (19 416 sq miles)

Dagon *Bible* a god worshipped by the Philistines, represented as half man and half fish

Daguerre Louis Jacques Mandé 1789–1851, French inventor, who devised one of the first practical photographic processes (1838)

daguerreotype one of the earliest photographic processes, in which the image was produced on iodine-sensitized silver and developed in mercury vapour

Dahl Roald 1916–90, British writer with Norwegian parents, noted for his short stories and such children's books as *Charlie and the Chocolate Factory* (1964)

dahlia 1 any herbaceous perennial plant of the Mexican genus *Dahlia*, having showy flowers and tuberous roots, esp any horticultural variety derived from *D. pinnata*: family *Asteraceae* (composites) 2 the flower or root of any of these plants

Daimler Gottlieb (Wilhelm) 1834–1900, German engineer and car manufacturer, who collaborated with Nikolaus Otto in inventing the first internal-combustion engine (1876)

dairy 1 a company that supplies milk and milk products 2 a a shop that sells provisions, esp milk and milk products b NZ a shop that remains open outside normal trading hours 3 a room or building where milk and cream are stored or made into butter and cheese

daisy 1 a small low-growing European plant, *Bellis perennis*, having a rosette of leaves and flower heads of yellow central disc flowers and pinkish-white outer ray flowers: family *Asteraceae* (composites) 2 a Eurasian composite plant, *Leucanthemum vulgare* having flower heads with a yellow centre and white outer rays 3 any of various other composite plants having conspicuous ray flowers, such as the Michaelmas daisy and Shasta daisy

daisywheel *Computing* a component of a computer printer in the shape of a wheel with many spokes that prints characters using a disk with characters around the circumference as the print element

Dakar the capital and chief port of Senegal, on the SE side of Cape Verde peninsula. Pop: 2 313 000 (2005 est)

Dakota a former territory of the US: divided into the states of North Dakota and South Dakota in 1889

Daladier Édouard 1884–1970, French radical socialist statesman; premier of France (1933; 1934; 1938–40) and signatory of the Munich Pact (1938)

Dalai Lama 1 (until 1959) the chief lama and ruler of

Tibet **2** born 1935, the 14th holder of this office (1940), who fled to India (1959): Nobel peace prize 1989

dale an open valley, usually in an area of low hills

Dale Sir **Henry Hallet** 1875–1968, English physiologist: shared a Nobel prize for physiology or medicine in 1936 with Otto Loewi for their work on the chemical transmission of nerve impulses

Dalglish Kenny, born 1951, Scottish footballer: a striker, he played for Celtic (1968–77) and for Liverpool (1977–89): manager of Liverpool (1985–91), of Blackburn Rovers (1991–95), and of Newcastle United (1997–98): Scotland's most-capped footballer

Dalhousie 1 9th Earl of, title of *George Ramsay*. 1770–1838, British general; governor of the British colonies in Canada (1819–28) **2** his son, 1st Marquis and 10th Earl of, title of *James Andrew Broun Ramsay*. 1812–60, British statesman: governor general of India (1848–56)

Dali Salvador 1904–89, Spanish surrealist painter

Dalian *or* **Talien** a city in NE China, at the end of the Liaodong Peninsula: with the adjoining city of Lüshun comprises the port complex of Lüda. Pop: 2 709 000 (2005 est)

Dallapiccola Luigi 1904–75, Italian composer of twelve-tone music. His works include the opera *Il Prigioniero* (1944–48) and the ballet *Marsia* (1948)

Dallas a city in NE Texas, on the Trinity River: scene of the assassination of President John F. Kennedy (1963). Pop: 1 208 318 (2003 est)

Dalmatia a region of W Croatia along the Adriatic: mountainous, with many offshore islands

Dalmatian a large breed of dog having a short smooth white coat with black or (in liver-spotted dalmatians) brown spots

Dalton John 1766–1844, English chemist and physicist, who formulated the modern form of the atomic theory and the law of partial pressures for gases. He also gave the first accurate description of colour blindness, from which he suffered

dam¹ 1 a barrier of concrete, earth, etc, built across a river to create a body of water for a hydroelectric power station, domestic water supply, etc. **2** a reservoir of water created by such a barrier

dam² the female parent of an animal, esp of domestic livestock

Daman a coastal town in W India, the chief town of Daman and Diu. Pop: 35 743 (2001)

Daman and Diu a union territory in W India: formerly a district of Portuguese India (1559–1961) then part of the union territory of Goa, Daman, and Diu (1961–87). Area: 112 sq km (43 sq miles). Pop: 158 059 (2001)

Damascene a variety of domestic fancy pigeon with silvery plumage

Damascus the capital of Syria, in the southwest: reputedly the oldest city in the world, having been inhabited continuously since before 2000 BC Pop: 2 317 000 (2005 est)

damask a reversible fabric, usually silk or linen, with a pattern woven into it. It is used for table linen, curtains, etc. **b** table linen made from this **c** (*as modifier*): *a damask tablecloth*

dame 1 a nun who has taken the vows of her order, esp a Benedictine **2** *Brit* the role of a comic old woman in a pantomime, usually played by a man

Damien Joseph , known as *Father Damien*. 1840–89, Belgian Roman Catholic missionary to the leper colony at Molokai, Hawaii

Damodar a river in NE India, rising in Jharkhand and flowing east through West Bengal to the Hooghly River: the Damodar Valley is an important centre of heavy industry.

damper 1 a movable plate to regulate the draught in a stove or furnace flue **2** a device to reduce electronic, mechanical, acoustic, or aerodynamic oscillations in a system **3** *Music* the pad in a piano or harpsichord that deadens the vibration of each string as its key is released

damson 1 a small rosaceous tree, *Prunus domestica instititia* (or *P. instititia*), cultivated for its blue-black edible plum-like fruit and probably derived from the bullace **2** the fruit of this tree

dan¹ a small buoy used as a marker at sea

dan² *Martial Arts* **1** any one of the 10 black-belt grades of proficiency **2** a competitor entitled to dan grading

Dan *Old Testament* **1 a** the fourth son of Jacob (Genesis 30:1–6) **b** the tribe descended from him **2** a city in the northern territory of Canaan

Dana James Dwight 1813–95, American geologist; noted for his work *The System of Mineralogy* (1837)

Da Nang a port in central Vietnam, on the South China Sea. Pop: 448 000 (2005 est)

dance 1 a series of rhythmic steps and movements, usually in time to music **2** an act of dancing **3 a** a social meeting arranged for dancing; ball **b** (*as modifier*): *a dance hall* **4** a piece of music in the rhythm of a particular dance form, such as a waltz **5** dancelike movements made by some insects and birds, esp as part of a behaviour pattern

▷www.culturekiosque.com/dance
▷www.streetswing.com/histmain/z3modrn.htm
▷www.sapphireswan.com/dance/links/modern.htm
▷www.artindia.net/modern.html
▷www.britisharts.co.uk/moddance.htm

dandelion 1 a plant, *Taraxacum officinale*, native to Europe and Asia and naturalized as a weed in North America, having yellow rayed flowers and deeply notched basal leaves, which are used for salad or wine: family *Asteraceae* (composites) **2** any of several similar related plants

dander small particles or scales of hair or feathers

dandruff loose scales of dry dead skin shed from the scalp

dandy *Nautical* a yawl or ketch

dandy-brush a stiff brush used for grooming a horse

Dane 1 a native, citizen, or inhabitant of Denmark **2** any of the Vikings who invaded England from the late 8th to the 11th century AD

Danelaw *or* **Danelagh** the northern, central and eastern parts of Anglo-Saxon England in which Danish law and custom were observed

Daniel¹ 1 Paul (Wilson). born 1958, British conductor; musical director of the English National Opera 1997–2003 **2** Samuel ?1562–1619, English poet and writer: author of the sonnet sequence *Delia* (1592)

Daniel[2] *Old Testament* **a** a youth who was taken into the household of Nebuchadnezzar, received guidance and apocalyptic visions from God, and was given divine protection when thrown into the lions' den **b** the book that recounts these experiences and visions (in full **The Book of the Prophet Daniel**)

Danish the official language of Denmark, belonging to the North Germanic branch of the Indo-European family

Dante full name **Dante Alighieri** 1265–1321, Italian poet famous for *La Divina Commedia* (?1309–?1320), an allegorical account of his journey through Hell, Purgatory, and Paradise, guided by Virgil and his idealized love Beatrice. His other works include *La Vita Nuova* (?1292), in which he celebrates his love for Beatrice

Danton Georges Jacques 1759–94, French revolutionary leader: a founder member of the Committee of Public Safety (1793) and minister of justice (1792–94). He was overthrown by Robespierre and guillotined

Danube a river in central and SE Europe, rising in the Black Forest in Germany and flowing to the Black Sea. Length: 2859 km (1776 miles)

Danzig 1 the German name for **Gdańsk** 2 a rare variety of domestic fancy pigeon originating in this area

Da Ponte Lorenzo , real name *Emmanuele Conegliano*. 1749–1838, Italian writer; Mozart's librettist for *The Marriage of Figaro* (1786), *Don Giovanni* (1787), and *Così fan tutte* (1790)

dapple-grey a horse with a grey coat having spots of darker colour

Darcy (James) **Les(lie)**. 1895–1917, Australian boxer and folk hero, who lost only five professional fights and was never knocked out, considered a martyr after his death from septicaemia during a tour of the United States

Dardanelles the strait between the Aegean and the Sea of Marmara, separating European from Asian Turkey

Dar es Salaam the chief port of Tanzania, on the Indian Ocean: capital of German East Africa (1891–1916); capital of Tanzania until 1983 when it was replaced by Dodoma; university (1963). Pop: 2 683 000 (2005 est)

Darfur a region of the W Sudan; an independent kingdom until conquered by Egypt in 1874

Darien 1 the E part of the Isthmus of Panama, between the **Gulf of Darien** on the Caribbean coast and the Gulf of San Miguel on the Pacific coast; chiefly within the republic of Panama but extending also into Colombia: site of a disastrous attempt to establish a Scottish colony in 1698 2 **Isthmus of** the former name of the Isthmus of **Panama**

Dario Rubén , real name *Félix Rubén Garcia Sarmiento*. 1867–1916, Nicaraguan poet whose poetry includes *Prosas Profanas* (1896)

Darius I known as *Darius the Great*, surname *Hystaspis*. ?550–486 BC, king of Persia (521–486), who extended the Persian empire and crushed the revolt of the Ionian city states (500). He led two expeditions against Greece but was defeated at Marathon (490)

Darjeeling a town in NE India, in West Bengal in the Himalayas, at an altitude of about 2250 m (7500 ft). Pop: 107 530 (2001)

Dark Continent the a term for Africa when it was relatively unexplored

dark horse 1 a competitor in a race or contest about whom little is known; an unknown 2 *US, Politics* a candidate who is unexpectedly nominated or elected

darkroom a room in which photographs are processed in darkness or safe light

Darlan Jean Louis Xavier François 1881–1942, French admiral and member of the Vichy government. He cooperated with the Allies after their invasion of North Africa; assassinated

Darling Grace 1815–42, English national heroine, famous for her rescue (1838) of some shipwrecked sailors with her father, a lighthouse keeper

Darling Range a ridge in SW Western Australia, parallel to the coast. Highest point: about 582 m (1669 ft)

Darling River a river in SE Australia, rising in the Eastern Highlands and flowing southwest to the Murray River. Length: 2740 km (1702 miles)

Darlington 1 an industrial town in NE England in Darlington unitary authority, S Durham: developed mainly with the opening of the Stockton-Darlington railway (1825). Pop: 86 082 (2001) 2 a unitary authority in NE England, in Durham. Pop: 98 200 (2003 est). Area: 198 sq km (77 sq miles)

Darmstadt an industrial city in central Germany, in Hesse: former capital of the grand duchy of Hesse-Darmstadt (1567–1945). Pop: 139 698 (2003 est)

darnel any of several grasses of the genus *Lolium*, esp *L. temulentum*, that grow as weeds in grain fields in Europe and Asia

Darnley Lord title of *Henry Stuart* (or *Stewart*). 1545–67, Scottish nobleman; second husband of Mary, Queen of Scots and father of James I of England. After murdering his wife's secretary, Rizzio (1566), he was himself assassinated (1567)

dart[1] 1 a small narrow pointed missile that is thrown or shot, as in the game of darts 2 *Zoology* a slender pointed structure, as in snails for aiding copulation or in nematodes for penetrating the host's tissues

dart[2] any of various tropical and semitropical marine fish

dartboard a circular piece of wood, cork, etc, used as the target in the game of darts. It is divided into numbered sectors with central inner and outer bull's-eyes

Dartford a town in SE England, in NW Kent. Pop: 56 818 (2001)

Dartmoor 1 a moorland plateau in SW England, in SW Devon: a national park since 1951. Area: 945 sq km (365 sq miles) 2 a prison in SW England, on Dartmoor: England's main prison for long-term convicts 3 a small strong breed of pony, originally from Dartmoor 4 a hardy coarse-woolled breed of sheep originally from Dartmoor

Dartmouth 1 a port in SW England, in S Devon: Royal Naval College (1905). Pop: 5512 (2001) 2 a city in SE Canada, in S Nova Scotia, on Halifax Harbour: oil refineries and shipyards. Pop: 65 741 (2001)

darts any of various competitive games in which darts are thrown at a dartboard
▷www.dartswdf.com

Darwin[1] 1 Charles (**Robert**). 1809–82, English naturalist who formulated the theory of evolution by natural selection, expounded in *On the Origin of Species* (1859) and applied to man in *The Descent of Man* (1871) **2** his grandfather, **Erasmus** 1731–1802, English physician and poet; author of *Zoonomia, or the Laws of Organic Life* (1794–96), anticipating Lamarck's views on evolution **3** Sir **George Howard**, son of Charles Darwin. 1845–1912, English astronomer and mathematician noted for his work on tidal friction

Darwin² a port in N Australia, capital of the Northern Territory: destroyed by a cyclone in 1974 but rebuilt on the same site. Pop: 71 347 (2001)

Darwinism *or* **Darwinian theory** the theory of the origin of animal and plant species by evolution through a process of natural selection

dashboard 1 the instrument panel in a car, boat, or aircraft **2** *Obsolete* a board at the side of a carriage or boat to protect against splashing

dasher the plunger in a churn, often with paddles attached

Dasht-i-Kavir *or* **Dasht-e-Kavir** a salt waste on the central plateau of Iran: a treacherous marsh beneath a salt crust

Dasht-i-Lut *or* **Dasht-e-Lut** a desert plateau in central and E central Iran

dasyure any small carnivorous marsupial, such as *Dasyurus quoll* (**eastern dasyure**), of the subfamily *Dasyurinae*, of Australia, New Guinea, and adjacent islands

database *Computing* a systematized collection of data that can be accessed immediately and manipulated by a data-processing system for a specific purpose

data capture any process for converting information into a form that can be handled by a computer

data processing a a sequence of operations performed on data, esp by a computer, in order to extract information, reorder files, etc. **b** (*as modifier*): *a data-processing centre*

date palm a feather palm, *Phoenix dactylifera*, probably native to N Africa and SW Asia and widely grown in other arid warm temperate and subtropical regions for its edible fruit (dates)

date rape 1 the act or an instance of a man raping a woman while they are on a date together **2** an act of sexual intercourse regarded as tantamount to rape, esp if the woman was encouraged to drink excessively or was subjected to undue pressure

datum a proposition taken for granted, often in order to construct some theoretical framework upon it; a given

daub an unskilful or crude painting

Daubigny Charles François 1817–78, French landscape painter associated with the Barbizon School

Daudet Alphonse 1840–97, French novelist, short-story writer, and dramatist: noted particularly for his humorous sketches of Provençal life, as in *Lettres de mon moulin* (1866)

Daugavpils a city in SE Latvia on the Western Dvina River: founded in 1274 by Teutonic Knights; ruled by Poland (1559–1772) and Russia (1772–1915); retaken by the Russians in 1940. Pop: 112 609 (2002 est)

Daumier Honoré 1808–79, French painter and lithographer, noted particularly for his political and social caricatures

dauphin (1349–1830) the title of the direct heir to the French throne; the eldest son of the king of France

Daventry a town in central England, in Northamptonshire: light industries, site of an important international radio transmitter. Pop: 21 731 (2001)

David 1 the second king of the Hebrews (about 1000–962 BC), who united Israel as a kingdom with Jerusalem as its capital **2 Elizabeth** 1914–92, British cookery writer. Her books include *Mediterranean Food* (1950) and *An Omelette and a Glass of Wine* (1984) **3 Jacques Louis** 1748–1825, French neoclassical painter of such works as the *Oath of the Horatii* (1784), *Death of Socrates* (1787), and *The Intervention of the Sabine Women* (1799). He actively supported the French Revolution and became court painter to Napoleon Bonaparte in 1804; banished at the Bourbon restoration **4 Saint** 6th century AD, Welsh bishop; patron saint of Wales. Feast day: March 1

David I 1084–1153, king of Scotland (1124–53) who supported his niece Matilda's claim to the English throne and unsuccessfully invaded England on her behalf

David II 1324–71, king of Scotland (1329–71): he was forced into exile in France (1334–41) by Edward de Baliol; captured following the battle of Neville's Cross (1346), and imprisoned by the English (1346–57)

Davies 1 Sir **John** 1569–1626, English poet, author of *Orchestra or a Poem of Dancing* (1596) and the philosophical poem *Nosce Teipsum* (1599) **2** Sir **Peter Maxwell** born 1934, British composer whose works include the operas *Taverner* (1967), *The Martyrdom of St Magnus* (1977), and *Resurrection* (1988), six symphonies, and the ten Strathclyde Concertos; appointed Master of the Queen's Music in 2004 (1987–95) **3** (**William**) **Robertson** 1913–95, Canadian novelist and dramatist. His novels include *Leaven of Malice* (1954), *The Rebel Angels* (1981), *What's Bred in the Bone* (1985), and *Murther and Walking Spirits* (1991) **4** W(illiam) H(enry). 1871–1940, Welsh poet, noted also for his *Autobiography of a Super-tramp* (1908)

Davis 1 Sir **Andrew** (**Frank**). born 1944, British conductor; chief conductor of the BBC Symphony Orchestra (1989–2000) and of the Chicago Lyric Opera from 2000 **2 Bette**, real name *Ruth Elizabeth Davis*. 1908–89, US film actress, whose films include *Of Human Bondage* (1934), *Jezebel* (1938) for which she won an Oscar, *All About Eve* (1950), *Whatever Happened to Baby Jane?* (1962), *The Nanny* (1965), and *The Whales of August* (1987) **3** Sir **Colin** (**Rex**). born 1927, English conductor, noted for his interpretation of the music of Berlioz **4 Jefferson** 1808–89, president of the Confederate States of America during the Civil War (1861–65) **5 Joe** 1901–78, English billiards and snooker player: world champion from 1927 to 1946 **6 John**. Also called: **John Davys** ?1550–1605, English navigator: discovered the Falkland Islands (1592); searched for a Northwest Passage **7 Miles** (**Dewey**). 1926–91, US jazz trumpeter and composer **8 Steve** born 1957, English snooker player: world champion 1981, 1983–84, 1987–89

Davisson Clinton Joseph 1881–1958, US physicist, noted for his discovery of electron diffraction; shared the Nobel prize for physics in 1937

Davis Strait a strait between Baffin Island, in Canada, and Greenland

davit a cranelike device, usually one of a pair, fitted

with a tackle for suspending or lowering equipment, esp a lifeboat

Davos a mountain resort in Switzerland: winter sports, site of the Parsenn ski run. Pop: 11 417 (2000). Height: about 1560 m (5118 ft)

Davy Sir **Humphry** 1778–1829, English chemist who isolated sodium, magnesium, chlorine, and other elements and suggested the electrical nature of chemical combination. He invented the **Davy lamp**

Dawes **Charles Gates** 1865–1951, US financier, diplomat, and statesman, who devised the Dawes Plan for German reparations payments after World War I; vice president of the US (1925–29); Nobel peace prize 1925

Dawkins **Richard** born 1941, British zoologist, noted for such works as *The Selfish Gene* (1976), *The Blind Watchmaker* (1986), and *River Out of Eden* (1995)

dawn chorus the singing of large numbers of birds at dawn

Dawson Creek a town in W Canada, in NE British Columbia: SE terminus of the Alaska Highway. Pop: 10 754 (2001)

day 1 the period of time, the **sidereal day** during which the earth makes one complete revolution on its axis relative to a particular star. The **mean sidereal day** lasts 23 hours 56 minutes 4.1 seconds of the mean solar day **2** the period of time, the **solar day** during which the earth makes one complete revolution on its axis relative to the sun. The **mean solar day** is the average length of the apparent solar day and is some four minutes (3 minutes 56.5 seconds of sidereal time) longer than the sidereal day **3** the period of time taken by a specified planet to make one complete rotation on its axis **4 day of rest** the Sabbath; Sunday

Dayan **Moshe** 1915–81, Israeli soldier and statesman; minister of defence (1967; 1969–74) and foreign minister (1977–79)

Day-Glo *Trademark* **a** a brand of fluorescent colouring materials, as of paint **b** (*as modifier*): *Day-Glo colours*

Day-Lewis *or* **Day Lewis** **C(ecil)**. 1904–72, British poet, critic, and (under the pen name *Nicholas Blake*) author of detective stories; poet laureate (1968–72)

day release *Brit* a system whereby workers are released for part-time education without loss of pay

day return a reduced fare for a journey (by train, etc) travelling both ways in one day

D-day the day, June 6, 1944, on which the Allied invasion of Europe began
▷www.dday.co.uk
▷www.ddaymuseum.org

DDT dichlorodiphenyltrichloroethane; a colourless odourless substance used as an insecticide. It is toxic to animals and is known to accumulate in the tissues. It is now banned in the UK

deacon *Christianity* **1** (in the Roman Catholic and other episcopal churches) an ordained minister ranking immediately below a priest **2** (in Protestant churches) a lay official appointed or elected to assist the minister, esp in secular affairs

deadbeat *Physics* **a** (of a system) returning to an equilibrium position with little or no oscillation **b** (of an instrument or indicator) indicating a true reading without oscillation

Dead Heart *Austral* the remote interior of Australia

dead heat a a race or contest in which two or more participants tie for first place **b** a tie between two or more contestants in any position

dead letter a law or ordinance that is no longer enforced but has not been formally repealed

deadly nightshade a poisonous Eurasian solanaceous plant, *Atropa belladonna*, having dull purple bell-shaped flowers and small very poisonous black berries

dead march a piece of solemn funeral music played to accompany a procession, esp at military funerals

dead-nettle any Eurasian plant of the genus *Lamium*, such as *L. alba* (white dead-nettle), having leaves resembling nettles but lacking stinging hairs: family *Lamiaceae* (labiates)

dead reckoning a method of establishing one's position using the distance and direction travelled rather than astronomical observations

Dead Sea a lake between Israel, Jordan, and the West Bank, 417 m (1373 ft) below sea level; originally 390 m (1285 ft): the lowest lake in the world, with no outlet and very high salinity; outline, esp at the southern end, reduced considerably in recent years. Area: originally about 950 sq km (365 sq miles); by 2003 about 625 sq km (240 sq miles)

dead set 1 the motionless position of a dog when pointing with its muzzle towards game **2** (of a hunting dog) in this position

dead weight 1 the difference between the loaded and the unloaded weights of a ship **2** (in shipping) freight chargeable by weight rather than by bulk

deaf partially or totally unable to hear
▷www.drf.org

deaf-and-dumb *Offensive* a deaf-mute person

deafblind unable to hear or see

deaf-mute 1 a person who is unable to hear or speak **2** unable to hear or speak

Deakin **Alfred** 1856–1919, Australian statesman. He was a leader of the movement for Australian federation; prime minister of Australia (1903–04; 1905- -08; 1909–10)

deal¹ *Cards* **a** the process of distributing the cards **b** a player's turn to do this **c** a single round in a card game

deal² **1** a plank of softwood timber, such as fir or pine, or such planks collectively **2** the sawn wood of various coniferous trees, such as that from the Scots pine (**red deal**) or from the Norway Spruce (**white deal**)

Deal a town in SE England, in Kent, on the English Channel: two 16th-century castles: tourism, light industries. Pop: 96 670 (2003 est)

dealer 1 a person or firm engaged in commercial purchase and sale; trader **2** *Cards* the person who distributes the cards **3** *Slang* a person who sells illegal drugs

dean 1 the chief administrative official of a college or university faculty **2** (at Oxford and Cambridge universities) a college fellow with responsibility for undergraduate discipline **3** *Chiefly Church of England* the head of a chapter of canons and administrator of a cathedral or collegiate church **4** *RC Church* the cardinal bishop senior by consecration and head of the college of cardinals

Dean¹ James (**Byron**). 1931–55, US film actor, who became a cult figure; his films include *East of Eden* and *Rebel Without a Cause* (both 1955). He died in a car crash

Dean² Forest of a forest in W England, in Gloucestershire, between the Rivers Severn and Wye: formerly a royal hunting ground

Deane Sir William Patrick born 1931, Australian lawyer. He became a High Court judge in 1982 and governor-general of Australia (1995–2001)

deanery 1 the office or residence of dean 2 the group of parishes presided over by a rural dean

death certificate a legal document issued by a qualified medical practitioner certifying the death of a person and stating the cause if known

death knell or **bell** a bell rung to announce a death

death mask a cast of a person's face taken shortly after death

Death Valley a desert valley in E California and W Nevada: the lowest, hottest, and driest area of the US. Lowest point: 86 m (282 ft) below sea level. Area: about 3885 sq km (1500 sq miles)

death warrant *Law* the official authorization for carrying out a sentence of death

Deauville a town and resort in NW France: casino. Pop: 4364 (1999)

debacle *Geography* 1 the breaking up of ice in a river during spring or summer, often causing flooding 2 a violent rush of water carrying along debris

debate *Politics* 1 a formal discussion, as in a legislative body, in which opposing arguments are put forward 2 the formal presentation and opposition of a specific motion, followed by a vote

debenture *Commerce* a customs certificate providing for a refund of excise or import duty

Deborah *Old Testament* 1 a prophetess and judge of Israel who fought the Canaanites (Judges 4, 5) 2 Rebecca's nurse (Genesis 35:8)

debris or **débris** a collection of loose material derived from rocks, or an accumulation of animal or vegetable matter

debug *Informal* something, esp a computer program, that locates and removes defects in (a device, system, etc)

Debussy (**Achille**) **Claude** 1862–1918, French composer and critic, the creator of impressionism in music and a profound influence on contemporary composition. His works include *Prélude à l'après- midi d'un faune* (1894) and *La Mer* (1905) for orchestra, the opera *Pelléas et Mélisande* (1902), and many piano pieces and song settings

debut the first public appearance of an actor, musician, etc, or the first public presentation of a show

Debye Peter Joseph Wilhelm 1884–1966, Dutch chemist and physicist, working in the US: Nobel prize for chemistry (1936) for his work on dipole moments

decade 1 a period of ten consecutive years 2 a group or series of ten

decagon a polygon having ten sides

decahedron a solid figure having ten plane faces

decalitre or US **decaliter** ten litres. One decalitre is equal to about 2.2 imperial gallons

decametre or US **decameter** ten metres

decanter a stoppered bottle, usually of glass, into which a drink, such as wine, is poured for serving

decapod 1 any crustacean of the mostly marine order *Decapoda*, having five pairs of walking limbs: includes the crabs, lobsters, shrimps, prawns, and crayfish 2 any cephalopod mollusc of the order *Decapoda*, having a ring of eight short tentacles and two longer ones: includes the squids and cuttlefish 3 (of any other animal) having ten limbs

decathlon an athletic contest for men in which each athlete competes in ten different events

decay 1 decomposition, as of vegetable matter 2 rotten or decayed matter 3 *Physics* a a spontaneous transformation of an elementary particle into two or more different particles b of an excited atom or molecule, losing energy by the spontaneous emission of photons 4 *Physics* a gradual decrease of a stored charge, magnetic flux, current, etc, when the source of energy has been removed 5 *Music* the fading away of a note

Deccan the 1 a plateau in S India, between the Eastern Ghats, the Western Ghats, and the Narmada River 2 the whole Indian peninsula south of the Narmada River

decennial 1 lasting for ten years 2 occurring every ten years

decibel 1 a unit for comparing two currents, voltages, or power levels, equal to one tenth of a bel 2 a similar unit for measuring the intensity of a sound. It is equal to ten times the logarithm to the base ten of the ratio of the intensity of the sound to be measured to the intensity of some reference sound, usually the lowest audible note of the same frequency

deciduous 1 *Botany* (of trees and shrubs) shedding all leaves annually at the end of the growing season and then having a dormant period without leaves 2 *Zoology* (of antlers, wings, teeth, etc) being shed at the end of a period of growth

decilitre or US **deciliter** one tenth of a litre

decimal 1 a fraction that has a denominator of a power of ten, the power depending on or deciding the decimal place. It is indicated by a decimal point to the left of the numerator, the denominator being omitted. Zeros are inserted between the point and the numerator, if necessary, to obtain the correct decimal place 2 any number used in the decimal system 3 a relating to or using powers of ten b of the base ten 4 expressed as a decimal

decimal currency a system of currency in which the monetary units are parts or powers of ten

decimal point a full stop or a raised full stop placed between the integral and fractional parts of a number in the decimal system

decimal system 1 the number system in general use, having a base of ten, in which numbers are expressed by combinations of the ten digits 0 to 9 2 a system of measurement, such as the metric system, in which the multiple and submultiple units are related to a basic unit by powers of ten

decimetre or US **decimeter** one tenth of a metre

deck 1 *Nautical* any of various platforms built into a vessel 2 a the horizontal platform that supports the turntable and pick-up of a record player b See tape deck 3 *Chiefly US* a pack of playing cards 4 *Computing*, *obsolete* a collection of punched cards relevant to a particular program **5** a raised wooden platform built in a garden to provide a seating area

decking a wooden deck or platform, esp one in a garden for deckchairs, etc.

declaration 1 the ruling of a judge or court on a question of law, esp in the chancery division of the High Court **2** *Law* an unsworn statement of a witness admissible in evidence under certain conditions **3** *Cricket* the voluntary closure of an innings before all ten wickets have fallen **4** *Contract bridge* the final contract **5** *Cards* an announcement of points made after taking a trick, as in bezique

declination *Astronomy* the angular distance, esp in degrees, of a star, planet, etc, from the celestial equator measured north (positive) or south (negative) along the great circle passing through the celestial poles and the body

decompression sickness *or* **illness** a disorder characterized by severe pain in muscles and joints, cramp, and difficulty in breathing, caused by a sudden and sustained decrease in air pressure, resulting in the deposition of nitrogen bubbles in the tissues

decongestant 1 relieving congestion, esp nasal congestion **2** a decongestant drug

Decorated style *or* **architecture** a 14th-century style of English architecture characterized by the ogee arch, geometrical tracery, and floral decoration
▷www.britainexpress.com/architecture/decorated.htm

decoy *Hunting* **1** a bird or animal, or an image of one, used to lure game into a trap or within shooting range **2** an enclosed space or large trap, often with a wide funnelled entrance, into which game can be lured for capture

decree 1 an edict, law, etc, made by someone in authority **2** an order or judgment of a court made after hearing a suit, esp in matrimonial proceedings

decree absolute *Law* the final decree in divorce proceedings, which leaves the parties free to remarry

decree nisi *Law* a provisional decree, esp in divorce proceedings, which will later be made absolute unless cause is shown why it should not

decretal *RC Church* a papal edict on doctrine or church law

Dedekind (Julius Wilhelm) Richard 1831–1916, German mathematician, who devised a way (the **Dedekind cut**) of according irrational and rational numbers the same status

dedicated *Computing* designed to fulfil one function

dedication a ceremony in which something, such as a church, is dedicated

deduction 1 the act or process of deducting or subtracting **2 a** the process of reasoning typical of mathematics and logic, whose conclusions follow necessarily from their premises **b** an argument of this type **c** the conclusion of such an argument **3** *Logic* a systematic method of deriving conclusions that cannot be false when the premises are true, esp one amenable to formalization and study by the science of logic

Dee[1] John 1527–1608, English mathematician, astrologer, and magician: best known for his preface

(1570) to the first edition of Euclid in English

Dee[2] 1 a river in N Wales and NW England, rising in S Gwynedd and flowing east and north to the Irish Sea. Length: about 112 km (70 miles) **2** a river in NE Scotland, rising in the Cairngorms and flowing east to the North Sea. Length: about 140 km (87 miles) **3** a river in S Scotland, flowing south to the Solway Firth. Length: about 80 km (50 miles)

deed *Law* a formal legal document signed, witnessed, and delivered to effect a conveyance or transfer of property or to create a legal obligation or contract

deed poll *Law* a deed made by one party only, esp one by which a person changes his name

deep 1 *Cricket* relatively far from the pitch **2** (of a colour) having an intense or dark hue **3** any deep place on land or under water, esp below 6000 metres (3000 fathoms) **4 the deep** *Cricket* the area of the field relatively far from the pitch **5** *Nautical* one of the intervals on a sounding lead, one fathom apart

Deep South the SE part of the US, esp South Carolina, Georgia, Alabama, Mississippi, and Louisiana

deep-vein thrombosis a blood clot in one of the major veins, usually in the legs or pelvis; can be caused by prolonged sitting in the same position, as on long-haul air flights.

deer 1 any ruminant artiodactyl mammal of the family *Cervidae*, including reindeer, elk, muntjacs, and roe deer, typically having antlers in the male **2** (in N Canada) another name for **caribou**

deerstalker a person who stalks deer, esp in order to shoot them

default 1 a failure to act, esp a failure to meet a financial obligation or to appear in a court of law at a time specified **2 judgment by default** *Law* a judgment in the plaintiff's favour when the defendant fails to plead or to appear **3** *Computing* **a** the preset selection of an option offered by a system, which will always be followed except when explicitly altered **b** (*as modifier*): *default setting*

defeat *Law* an annulment

defect *Crystallog* a local deviation from regularity in the crystal lattice of a solid

defence *or US* **defense 1** *Law* a defendant's denial of the truth of the allegations or charge against him **2** *Law* the defendant and his legal advisers collectively **3** *American football* **a** the team that does not have possession of the ball **b** the members of a team that play in such circumstances

defendant a person against whom an action or claim is brought in a court of law

deficiency *Biology* the absence of a gene or a region of a chromosome normally present

deficiency disease 1 *Med* any condition, such as pellagra, beriberi, or scurvy, produced by a lack of vitamins or other essential substances **2** *Botany* any disease caused by lack of essential minerals

defile *Geography* a narrow pass or gorge, esp one between two mountains

definite *Botany* **a** denoting a type of growth in which the main stem ends in a flower, as in a cymose inflorescence; determinate **b** (esp of flower parts) limited or fixed in number in a given species

definition *Optics* a measure of the clarity of an optical, photographic, or television image as characterized by its sharpness and contrast

definitive 1 *Zoology* fully developed; complete 2 (of postage stamps) permanently on sale

deflation 1 *Economics* a reduction in the level of total spending and economic activity resulting in lower levels of output, employment, investment, trade, profits, and prices 2 *Geology* the removal of loose rock material, sand, and dust by the wind

Defoe Daniel ?1660–1731, English novelist, journalist, spymaster, and pamphleteer, noted particularly for his novel *Robinson Crusoe* (1719). His other novels include *Moll Flanders* (1722) and *A Journal of the Plague Year* (1722)

defoliate (of a plant) having shed its leaves

De Forest Lee 1873–1961, US inventor of telegraphic, telephonic, and radio equipment: patented the first triode valve (1907)

deformity *Pathol* an acquired or congenital distortion of an organ or part

Degas Hilaire Germain Edgar 1834–1917, French impressionist painter and sculptor, noted for his brilliant draughtsmanship and ability to convey movement, esp in his studies of horse racing and ballet dancers

De Gasperi Alcide 1881–1954, Italian statesman; prime minister (1945–53). An antifascist, he led the Christian Democratic party during World War II from the Vatican City

de Gaulle Charles (André Joseph Marie). 1890–1970, French general and statesman. During World War II, he refused to accept Pétain's armistice with Germany and founded the Free French movement in England (1940). He was head of the provisional governments (1944–46) and, as first president of the Fifth Republic (1959–69), he restored political and economic stability to France

degenerate 1 *Physics* a (of the constituents of a system) having the same energy but different wave functions b (of a semiconductor) containing a similar number of electrons in the conduction band to the number of electrons in the conduction band of metals c (of a resonant device) having two or more modes of equal frequency 2 *Biology* (of a plant or animal) having undergone degeneration

degeneration 1 *Biology* the loss of specialization, function, or structure by organisms and their parts, as in the development of vestigial organs 2 *Biology* a impairment or loss of the function and structure of cells or tissues, as by disease or injury, often leading to death (necrosis) of the involved part b the resulting condition 3 *Electronics* negative feedback of a signal

degree 1 a stage in a scale of relative amount or intensity 2 an academic award conferred by a university or college on successful completion of a course or as an honorary distinction (**honorary degree**) 3 *Med* any of three categories of seriousness of a burn 4 (in the US) any of the categories into which a crime is divided according to its seriousness 5 *Music* any note of a diatonic scale relative to the other notes in that scale 6 a unit of temperature on a specified scale 7 *Geometry* a measure of angle equal to one three-hundred-and-sixtieth of the angle traced by one complete revolution of a line about one of its ends. 8 *Geography* a a unit of latitude or longitude, divided into 60 minutes, used to define points on the earth's surface or on the celestial sphere b a point or line defined by units of latitude and/or longitude. 9 a unit on any of several scales of measurement, as for alcohol content or specific gravity. 10 *Maths* a the highest power or the sum of the powers of any term in a polynomial or by itself b the greatest power of the highest order derivative in a differential equation 11 **degrees of frost** See **frost**

de Havilland Sir Geoffrey 1882–1965, British aircraft designer. He produced many military aircraft and the first jet airliners

Deighton Len born 1929, British thriller writer. His books include *The Ipcress File* (1962), *Bomber* (1970), and the trilogy *Berlin Game*, *Mexico Set*, and *London Match* (1983–85)

deism belief in the existence of God based solely on natural reason, without reference to revelation

deity 1 the state of being divine; godhead 2 the rank, status, or position of a god 3 the nature or character of God

Deity the the Supreme Being; God

deke *US and Canadian Sport* (esp in ice hockey) the act or an instance of feinting

Dekker *or* **Decker** Thomas ?1572–?1632, English dramatist and pamphleteer, noted particularly for his comedy *The Shoemaker's Holiday* (1600) and his satirical pamphlet *The Gull's Hornbook* (1609)

de Klerk F(rederik) W(illem). born 1936, South African statesman; president (1989–94), second executive deputy president (1994–97). In 1990 he legalized the ANC and released Nelson Mandela from prison, and initiated the abolition of apartheid: Nobel peace prize 1993 jointly with Mandela

Delacroix (Ferdinand Victor) Eugène 1798–1863, French romantic painter whose use of colour and free composition influenced impressionism. His paintings of historical and contemporary scenes include *The Massacre at Chios* (1824)

Delagoa Bay an inlet of the Indian Ocean, in S Mozambique

de la Mare Walter (John). 1873–1956, English poet and novelist, noted esp for his evocative verse for children. His works include the volumes of poetry *The Listeners and Other Poems* (1912) and *Peacock Pie* (1913) and the novel *Memoirs of a Midget* (1921)

Delaroche (Hippolyte) Paul 1797–1859, French painter of portraits and sentimental historical scenes, such as *The Children of Edward IV in the Tower* (1830)

Delaunay Robert 1885–1941, French painter, whose abstract use of colour characterized Orphism, an attempt to introduce more colour into austere forms of Cubism

Delaware 1 a state of the northeastern US, on the Delmarva Peninsula: mostly flat and low-lying, with hills in the extreme north and cypress swamps in the extreme south. Capital: Dover. Pop: 817 491 (2003 est). Area: 5004 sq km (1932 sq miles) 2 a river in the northeastern US, rising in the Catskill Mountains and flowing south into **Delaware Bay**, an inlet of the Atlantic. Length 660 km (410 miles)

De La Warr Baron, title of *Thomas West*, known as *Lord Delaware*. 1577–1618, English administrator in America;

first governor of Virginia (1610)

delegate *US, Government* a representative of a territory in the US House of Representatives

delegation *US, Politics* all the members of Congress from one state

Delft 1 a town in the SW Netherlands, in South Holland province. Pop: 97 000 (2003 est) 2 tin-glazed earthenware made in Delft since the 17th century, typically having blue decoration on a white ground 3 a similar earthenware made in England

Delhi 1 the capital of India, in the N central part, on the Jumna river: consists of **Old Delhi** (a walled city reconstructed in 1639 on the site of former cities of Delhi, which date from the 15th century BC) and **New Delhi** to the south, chosen as the capital in 1912, replacing Calcutta; university (1922). Pop: 9 817 439 (2001) 2 an administrative division (National Capital Territory) of N India, formerly a Union Territory. Capital: Delhi. Area: 1483 sq km (572 sq miles). Pop: 13 782 976 (2001)

Delibes (**Clément Philibert**) **Léo** 1836–91, French composer, noted particularly for his ballets *Coppélia* (1870) and *Sylvia* (1876), and the opera *Lakmé* (1883)

delicatessen a shop selling various foods, esp unusual or imported foods, already cooked or prepared

Delilah Samson's Philistine mistress, who deprived him of his strength by cutting off his hair (Judges 16:4–22)

delinquent 1 *Archaic* a person who fails in an obligation or duty 2 guilty of an offence or misdeed, esp one of a minor nature 3 failing in or neglectful of duty or obligation

delirium a state of excitement and mental confusion, often accompanied by hallucinations, caused by high fever, poisoning, brain injury, etc.

delirium tremens a severe psychotic condition occurring in some persons with chronic alcoholism, characterized by delirium, tremor, anxiety, and vivid hallucinations

Delius Frederick 1862–1934, English composer, who drew inspiration from folk tunes and the sounds of nature. His works include the opera *A Village Romeo and Juliet* (1901), *A Mass of Life* (1905), and the orchestral variations *Brigg Fair* (1907)

delivery 1 *Sport* a the act or manner of bowling or throwing a ball b the ball so delivered 2 *Law* an actual or symbolic handing over of property, a deed, etc. 3 *Engineering* the discharge rate of a compressor or pump 4 (in South Africa) the supply of basic services to communities deprived under apartheid

dell a small, esp wooded hollow

Deller Alfred (George). 1912–79, British countertenor

Del Mar Norman 1919–94, British conductor, associated esp with 20th- century British music

Delmarva Peninsula a peninsula of the northeast US, between Chesapeake Bay and the Atlantic

Delors Jacques (Lucien Jean). born 1925, French politician and economist, President of the European Commission (1985–94): originator of the **Delors plan** for closer European union

Delos a Greek island in the SW Aegean Sea, in the Cyclades: a commercial centre in ancient times; the legendary birthplace of Apollo and Artemis. Area: about

5 sq km (2 sq miles)

de los Angeles Victoria born 1923, Spanish soprano

Delphi an ancient Greek city on the S slopes of Mount Parnassus: site of the most famous oracle of Apollo

delphinium any ranunculaceous plant of the genus *Delphinium*: many varieties are cultivated as garden plants for their spikes of blue, pink, or white spurred flowers

delta 1 the fourth letter in the Greek alphabet (Δ or δ), a consonant transliterated as *d* 2 the flat alluvial area at the mouth of some rivers where the mainstream splits up into several distributaries 3 *Maths* a finite increment in a variable

delusion *Psychiatry* a belief held in the face of evidence to the contrary, that is resistant to all reason

demagogue *or sometimes US* **demagog** 1 a political agitator who appeals with crude oratory to the prejudice and passions of the mob 2 (esp in the ancient world) any popular political leader or orator

demand 1 *Economics* a willingness and ability to purchase goods and services b the amount of a commodity that consumers are willing and able to purchase at a specified price 2 *Law* a formal legal claim, esp to real property

demarcation *or* **demarkation** separation or distinction (often in the phrase **line of demarcation**)

dementia a state of serious emotional and mental deterioration, of organic or functional origin

Demerara the a river in Guyana, rising in the central forest area and flowing north to the Atlantic at Georgetown. Length: 346 km (215 miles)

demerit *US and Canadian* a mark given against a person for failure or misconduct, esp in schools or the armed forces

demesne 1 land, esp surrounding a house or manor, retained by the owner for his own use 2 *Property law* the possession and use of one's own property or land 3 the territory ruled by a state or a sovereign; realm; domain 4 a region or district; domain

Demeter *Greek myth* the goddess of agricultural fertility and protector of marriage and women

demigod a a mythological being who is part mortal, part god b a lesser deity

demijohn a large bottle with a short narrow neck, often with small handles at the neck and encased in wickerwork

De Mille Cecil B(lount). 1881–1959, US film producer and director

demise 1 *Property law* a a transfer of an estate by lease b the passing or transfer of an estate on the death of the owner 2 the immediate transfer of sovereignty to a successor upon the death, abdication, etc, of a ruler (esp in the phrase **demise of the crown**)

demi-sec (of wine, esp champagne) medium-sweet

demisemiquaver *Music* a note having the time value of one thirty-second of a semibreve

demo *Informal* 1 short for **demonstration** 2 a a demonstration record or tape, used for audition purposes b a demonstration of a prototype system

democracy 1 government by the people or their elected representatives 2 a political or social unit governed ultimately by all its members 3 the common people, esp as a political force

democrat 1 an advocate of democracy; adherent of democratic principles 2 a member or supporter of a democratic party or movement

Democrat (in the US) a member or supporter of the Democratic Party

democratic 1 of, characterized by, derived from, or relating to the principles of democracy 2 upholding or favouring democracy or the interests of the common people 3 popular with or for the benefit of all

Democritus ?460–?370 BC, Greek philosopher who developed the atomist theory of matter of his teacher, Leucippus

demodulation *Electronics* the act or process by which an output wave or signal is obtained having the characteristics of the original modulating wave or signal; the reverse of modulation

demography the scientific study of human populations, esp with reference to their size, structure, and distribution
▷www.un.org/popin/data.html
▷http://unstats.un.org/unsd/demographic/social/default.htm

demoniac a person possessed by an evil spirit or demon

demonolatry the worship of demons

demonology the study of demons or demonic beliefs

demonstration 1 proof or evidence leading to proof 2 a manifestation of grievances, support, or protest by public rallies, parades, etc. 3 *Maths* a logical presentation of the assumptions and equations used in solving a problem or proving a theorem

demonstrator 1 a person who takes part in a public demonstration 2 *Commerce* a piece of merchandise, such as a car that one test-drives, used to display merits or performance to prospective buyers

Demosthenes 384–322 BC, Athenian statesman, orator, and lifelong opponent of the power of Macedonia over Greece

demotic 1 of or relating to a simplified form of hieroglyphics used in ancient Egypt by the ordinary literate class outside the priesthood 2 the demotic script of ancient Egypt

Dempsey Jack real name *William Harrison Dempsey*. 1895–1983, US boxer; world heavyweight champion (1919–26)

den 1 the habitat or retreat of a lion or similar wild animal; lair 2 *Scot* a small wooded valley; dingle 3 *Scot and northern English, dialect* a place of sanctuary in certain catching games; home or base

denarius 1 a silver coin of ancient Rome, often called a penny in translation 2 a gold coin worth 25 silver denarii

denary 1 calculated by tens; based on ten; decimal 2 containing ten parts; tenfold

Denbighshire a county of N Wales: split between Clwyd and Gwynedd in 1974; reinstated with different boundaries in 1996: borders the Irish Sea, with the Cambrian Mountains in the south: chiefly agricultural. Administrative centre: Ruthin. Pop: 94 900 (2003 est). Area: 844 sq km (327 sq miles)

Dench Dame Judi (Olivia). born 1934, British actress and theatre director

dendrology the branch of botany that is concerned with the natural history of trees and shrubs

dene¹ *or* **dean** *Brit* a valley, esp one that is narrow and wooded

dene² *or* **dean** *Dialect, chiefly southern English* a sandy stretch of land or dune near the sea

Deneuve Catherine, original name *Catherine Dorléac*. born 1943, French film actress: her films include *Les Parapluies de Cherbourg* (1964), *Belle de Jour* (1967), *Indochine* (1992), and *Dancing in the Dark* (2000)

dengue *or* **dandy** an acute viral disease transmitted by mosquitoes, characterized by headache, fever, pains in the joints, and skin rash

Deng Xiaoping *or* **Teng Hsiao-ping** 1904–97, Chinese Communist statesman; deputy prime minister (1973–76; 1977–80) and the dominant figure in the Chinese government from 1977 until his death. He was twice removed from office (1967–73, 1976–77) and rehabilitated. He introduced economic liberalization, but suppressed demands for political reform, most notably in 1989 when over 2500 demonstrators were killed by the military in Tiananmen Square in Beijing

denial *Psychol* a psychological process by which painful truths are not admitted into an individual's consciousness

denier 1 a unit of weight used to measure the fineness of silk and man-made fibres, esp when woven into women's tights, etc. It is equal to 1 gram per 9000 metres 2 any of several former European coins of various denominations

denim *Textiles* 1 a a hard-wearing twill-weave cotton fabric used for trousers, work clothes, etc. b *(as modifier)*: *a denim jacket* 2 a a similar lighter fabric used in upholstery b *(as modifier)*: *denim cushion covers*

De Niro Robert born 1943, US film actor. His films include *Taxi Driver* (1976), *Raging Bull* (1980), *GoodFellas* (1990), *Casino* (1995), and *Analyze This* (1999)

Denis 1 Maurice 1870–1943, French painter and writer on art. One of the leading Nabis, he defined a picture as "essentially a flat surface covered with colours assembled in a certain order" 2 Saint 3rd century AD, first bishop of Paris; patron saint of France. Feast day: Oct 9

denizen 1 *Brit* an individual permanently resident in a foreign country where he enjoys certain rights of citizenship 2 *Biology* a plant or animal established in a place to which it is not native

Denmark a kingdom in N Europe, between the Baltic and the North Sea: consists of the mainland of Jutland and about 100 inhabited islands (chiefly Zealand, Lolland, Funen, Falster, Langeland, and Bornholm); extended its territory throughout the Middle Ages, ruling Sweden until 1523 and Norway until 1814, and incorporating Greenland as a province from 1953 to 1979; joined the Common Market (now the EU) in 1973; an important exporter of dairy produce. Language: Danish. Religion: Christian, Lutheran majority. Currency: krone. Capital: Copenhagen. Pop: 5 375 000 (2004 est). Area: 43 031 sq km (16 614 sq miles)

Denmark Strait a channel between SE Greenland and Iceland, linking the Arctic Ocean with the Atlantic

Dennis C(larence) J(ames). 1876–1938, the poet of the Australian larrikin, esp in *The Songs of a Sentimental Bloke*

(1915) and *The Moods of Ginger Mick* (1916)

denominate *Maths* (of a number) representing a multiple of a unit of measurement

denomination 1 a group having a distinctive interpretation of a religious faith and usually its own organization 2 a grade or unit in a series of designations of value, weight, measure, etc.

denominator the divisor of a fraction, as 8 in ⅞

denouement *or* **dénouement** *Theatre* a the final clarification or resolution of a plot in a play or other work b the point at which this occurs

dense 1 *Physics* having a high density 2 (of a photographic negative) having many dark or exposed areas 3 (of an optical glass, colour, etc) transmitting little or no light

density 1 a measure of the compactness of a substance, expressed as its mass per unit volume. It is measured in kilograms per cubic metre or pounds per cubic foot. 2 a measure of a physical quantity per unit of length, area, or volume

dent 1 a toothlike protuberance, esp the tooth of a sprocket or gearwheel 2 *Textiles* the space between two wires in a loom through which a warp thread is drawn

dental floss a soft usually flattened often waxed thread for cleaning the teeth and the spaces between them

dentate 1 having teeth or toothlike processes 2 (of leaves) having a toothed margin

dentifrice any substance, esp paste or powder, for use in cleaning the teeth

dentine *or* **dentin** the calcified tissue surrounding the pulp cavity of a tooth and comprising the bulk of the tooth

dentist a person qualified to practise dentistry

dentistry the branch of medical science concerned with the diagnosis and treatment of diseases and disorders of the teeth and gums

▷www.dental-health.com

▷http://dir.yahoo.com/Health/Medicine/
Dentistry

dentition 1 the arrangement, type, and number of the teeth in a particular species. Man has a **primary dentition** of deciduous teeth and a **secondary dentition** of permanent teeth 2 teething or the time or process of teething

Denton a town in NW England, in Tameside unitary authority, Greater Manchester. Pop: 26 866 (2001)

denture 1 a partial or full set of artificial teeth 2 *Rare* a set of natural teeth

denumerable *Maths* capable of being put into a one-to-one correspondence with the positive integers; countable

denunciation 1 *Law, obsolete* a charge or accusation of crime made by an individual before a public prosecutor or tribunal 2 a formal announcement of the termination of a treaty

Denver a city in central Colorado: the state capital. Pop: 557 478 (2003 est)

deodar a Himalayan cedar, *Cedrus deodara*, with drooping branches

Depardieu Gérard born 1948, French film actor. His films include *Jean de Florette* (1986), *Cyrano de Bergerac* (1990), *Green Card* (1991), *The Man in the Iron Mask* (1997),

and *Tais-toi* (2003)

department *Politics* 1 a major subdivision or branch of the administration of a government 2 a branch or subdivision of learning 3 a territorial and administrative division in several countries, such as France

department store a large shop divided into departments selling a great many kinds of goods

departure *Nautical* a the net distance travelled due east or west by a vessel b the latitude and longitude of the point from which a vessel calculates dead reckoning

dependency *or sometimes US* **dependancy** 1 *Politics* a territory subject to a state on which it does not border 2 *Psychol* overreliance by a person on another person or on a drug, etc.

depilatory a chemical that is used to remove hair from the body

deponent *Law* a a person who makes an affidavit b a person, esp a witness, who makes a deposition

deportation *Law* 1 the act of expelling an alien from a country; expulsion 2 the act of transporting someone from his country; banishment

deposit 1 money given in part payment or as security, as when goods are bought on hire-purchase 2 a consideration, esp money, given temporarily as security against loss of or damage to something borrowed or hired 3 *Geography* an accumulation of sediments, mineral ores, coal, etc. 4 *Chemistry* a coating produced on a surface, esp a layer of metal formed by electrolysis 5 a depository or storehouse 6 **on deposit** payable as the first instalment, as when buying on hire-purchase

deposition 1 *Law* a the giving of testimony on oath b the testimony so given c the sworn statement of a witness used in court in his absence 2 the act or instance of deposing

depot 1 a storehouse or warehouse 2 *Chiefly Brit* a building used for the storage and servicing of buses or railway engines 3 *US and Canadian* a a bus or railway station b *(as modifier)*: *a depot manager* 4 (of a drug or drug dose) designed for gradual release from the site of an injection so as to act over a long period

depreciation *Economics* a decrease in the exchange value of currency against gold or other currencies brought about by excess supply of that currency under conditions of fluctuating exchange rates

depressant 1 *Med* able to diminish or reduce nervous or functional activity 2 a depressant drug

depression 1 a mental disorder characterized by extreme gloom, feelings of inadequacy, and inability to concentrate 2 *Pathol* an abnormal lowering of the rate of any physiological activity or function, such as respiration 3 an economic condition characterized by substantial and protracted unemployment, low output and investment, etc.; slump 4 *Meteorol* a large body of rotating and rising air below normal atmospheric pressure, which often brings rain 5 (esp in surveying and astronomy) the angular distance of an object, celestial body, etc, below the horizontal plane through the point of observation

Depression *History* the worldwide economic depression of the early 1930s, when there was mass unemployment

depressive *Psychol* tending to be subject to periods of depression

depth *Nautical* the distance from the top of a ship's keel to the top of a particular deck

deputy *Politics* a member of the legislative assembly or of the lower chamber of the legislature in various countries, such as France

De Quincey Thomas 1785–1859, English critic and essayist, noted particularly for his *Confessions of an English Opium Eater* (1821)

derail *Chiefly US* a device designed to make rolling stock or locomotives leave the rails to avoid a collision or accident

Derain André 1880–1954, French painter, noted for his Fauvist pictures (1905–08)

Derby¹ Earl of title of *Edward George Geoffrey Smith Stanley*. 1799–1869, British statesman; Conservative prime minister (1852; 1858–59; 1866–68)

Derby² 1 **the** an annual horse race run at Epsom Downs, Surrey, since 1780: one of the English flat-racing classics 2 any of various other horse races 3 **local Derby** a football match between two teams from the same area

Derby 1 a city in central England, in Derby unitary authority, Derbyshire: engineering industries (esp aircraft engines and railway rolling stock); university (1991). Pop: 229 407 (2001) 2 a unitary authority in central England, in Derbyshire. Pop: 233 200 (2003 est). Area: 78 sq km (30 sq miles)

Derbyshire a county of N central England: contains the Peak District and several resorts with mineral springs: the geographical and ceremonial county includes the city of Derby, which became an independent unitary authority in 1997. Administrative centre: Matlock. Pop. (excluding Derby city): 743 000 (2003 est). Area (excluding Derby city): 2551 sq km (985 sq miles)

derelict 1 falling into ruins; neglected; dilapidated 2 a person abandoned or neglected by society; a social outcast or vagrant 3 property deserted or abandoned by an owner, occupant, etc. 4 *Nautical* a vessel abandoned at sea

dereliction *Law* a accretion of dry land gained by the gradual receding of the sea or by a river changing its course b the land thus left

derivation a the process of deducing a mathematical theorem, formula, etc, as a necessary consequence of a set of accepted statements b this sequence of statements c the operation of finding a derivative

derivative 1 *Chem* a compound that is formed from, or can be regarded as formed from, a structurally related compound 2 *Maths* a the change of a function, $f(x)$, with respect to an infinitesimally small change in the independent variable, x; the limit of $[f(a + \Delta x) - f(a)]/\Delta x$, at $x = a$, as the increment, Δx, tends to 0. Symbols: $df(x)/dx$, $f'(x)$, $Df(x)$ b the rate of change of one quantity with respect to another 3 *Psychoanal* an activity that represents the expression of hidden impulses and desires by channelling them into socially acceptable forms

dermatitis inflammation of the skin

dermatology the branch of medicine concerned with the skin and its diseases
  ▷www.aad.org

derrick a simple crane having lifting tackle slung from

a boom

Derrida Jacques 1930–2004, French philosopher and literary critic, regarded as the founder of deconstruction: author of *L'Écriture et la différence* (1967)

Derry 1 a district in NW Northern Ireland, in Co. Londonderry. Pop: 106 456 (2003 est). Area: 387 sq km (149 sq miles) 2 another name for **Londonderry**

derv a Brit name for **diesel oil** when used for road transport

dervish a member of any of various Muslim orders of ascetics, some of which (**whirling dervishes**) are noted for a frenzied, ecstatic, whirling dance

Derwent 1 a river in S Australia, in S Tasmania, flowing southeast to the Tasman Sea. Length: 172 km (107 miles) 2 a river in N central England, in N Derbyshire, flowing southeast to the River Trent. Length: 96 km (60 miles) 3 a river in N England, in Yorkshire, rising on the North York Moors and flowing south to the River Ouse. Length: 92 km (57 miles) 4 a river in NW England, in Cumbria, rising on the Borrowdale Fells and flowing north and west to the Irish Sea. Length: 54 km (34 miles)

Derwentwater a lake in NW England, in Cumbria in the Lake District. Area: about 8 sq km (3 sq miles)

Desai Morarji (Ranchhodji). 1896–1995, Indian statesman, noted for his asceticism. He founded the Janata party in opposition to Indira Gandhi, whom he defeated in the 1977 election; prime minister of India (1977–79)

desalination, desalinization, *or* **desalinisation** the process of removing salt, esp from sea water so that it can be used for drinking or irrigation

descant *Music* 1 a decorative counterpoint added above a basic melody 2 of or pertaining to the highest member in common use of a family of musical instruments

Descartes René 1596–1650, French philosopher and mathematician. He provided a mechanistic basis for the philosophical theory of dualism and is regarded as the founder of modern philosophy. He also founded analytical geometry and contributed greatly to the science of optics. His works include *Discours de la méthode* (1637), *Meditationes de Prima Philosophia* (1641), and *Principia Philosophiae* (1644)

descent 1 derivation from an ancestor or ancestral group; lineage 2 (in genealogy) a generation in a particular lineage 3 *Property law* (formerly) the transmission of real property to the heir on an intestacy

description *Geometry* the act of drawing a line or figure, such as an arc

desert 1 a region that is devoid or almost devoid of vegetation, esp because of low rainfall 2 an uncultivated uninhabited region

desertification a process by which fertile land turns into barren land or desert

desert island a small remote tropical island

de Sica Vittorio 1902–74, Italian film actor and director. His films, in the neorealist tradition, include *Shoeshine* (1946) and *Bicycle Thieves* (1948)

design 1 a plan, sketch, or preliminary drawing 2 the arrangement or pattern of elements or features of an artistic or decorative work 3 a finished artistic or decorative creation 4 the art of designing

designer (of cells, chemicals, etc) designed (or produced) to perform a specific function or combat a specific problem

▷www.fashion.net/sites/fashiondesigners

desktop denoting a computer system, esp for word processing, that is small enough to use at a desk

Des Moines 1 a city in S central Iowa: state capital. Pop: 196 093 (2003 est) 2 a river in the N central US, rising in SW Minnesota and flowing southeast to join the Mississippi. Length: 861 km (535 miles)

Desmoulins (Lucie Simplice) Camille (Benoît). 1760–94, French revolutionary leader, pamphleteer, and orator

De Soto Hernando ?1500–42, Spanish explorer, who discovered the Mississippi River (1541)

Despenser Hugh le, Earl of Winchester. 1262–1326, English statesman, a favourite of Edward II. Together with his son **Hugh**, *the Younger* (?1290–1326), he was executed by the king's enemies

despot 1 *Politics* an absolute or tyrannical ruler; autocrat or tyrant 2 *History* a title borne by numerous persons of rank in the later Roman, Byzantine, and Ottoman Empires

despotism the rule of a despot; arbitrary, absolute, or tyrannical government

Dessau an industrial city in E Germany, in Saxony-Anhalt: capital of Anhalt state from 1340 to 1918. Pop: 78 380 (2003 est)

dessertspoon a spoon intermediate in size between a tablespoon and a teaspoon

destitute lacking the means of subsistence; totally impoverished

detached *Ophthalmol* (of the retina) separated from the choroid layer of the eyeball to which it is normally attached, resulting in loss of vision in the affected part

detachment *Logic* the rule whereby the consequent of a true conditional statement, given the truth of its antecedent, may be asserted on its own

detail *Art* a small or accessory section or element in a painting, building, statue, etc, esp when considered in isolation

detection *Physics* the act or process of extracting information, esp at audio or video frequencies, from an electromagnetic wave

detention 1 *Law* a custody or confinement, esp of a suspect awaiting trial b (*as modifier*): *a detention order* 2 a form of punishment in which a pupil is detained after school

detention centre a place where persons (typically asylum seekers, illegal immigrants, or people awaiting trial) may be detained for short periods by order of a court

detergent a cleansing agent, esp a surface-active chemical such as an alkyl sulphonate, widely used in industry, laundering, shampoos, etc.

determinant *Maths* a square array of elements that represents the sum of certain products of these elements, used to solve simultaneous equations, in vector studies, etc.

determinate 1 a able to be predicted or deduced b (of an effect) obeying the law of causality 2 *Botany* (of an inflorescence) having the main and branch stems ending in flowers and unable to grow further; cymose

determination 1 *Law* the termination of an estate or

interest 2 *Law* the decision reached by a court of justice on a disputed matter 3 *Logic* a the process of qualifying or limiting a proposition or concept b the qualifications or limitations used in this process 4 *Biology* the condition of embryonic tissues of being able to develop into only one particular tissue or organ in the adult

determinism 1 the philosophical doctrine that all events including human actions and choices are fully determined by preceding events and states of affairs, and so that freedom of choice is illusory 2 the scientific doctrine that all occurrences in nature take place in accordance with natural laws 3 the principle in classical mechanics that the values of dynamic variables of a system and of the forces acting on the system at a given time, completely determine the values of the variables at any later time

detour a deviation from a direct, usually shorter route or course of action

detritus 1 a loose mass of stones, silt, etc, worn away from rocks 2 the organic debris formed from the decay of organisms

Detroit 1 a city in SE Michigan, on the Detroit River: a major Great Lakes port; largest car-manufacturing centre in the world. Pop: 911 402 (2003 est) 2 a river in central North America, flowing along the US-Canadian border from Lake St Clair to Lake Erie

detumescence the subsidence of a swelling, esp the return of a swollen organ, such as the penis, to the flaccid state

deuce 1 a a playing card or dice with two pips or spots; two b a throw of two in dice 2 *Tennis* a tied score (in tennis 40-all) that requires one player to gain two successive points to win the game

deuterium a stable isotope of hydrogen, occurring in natural hydrogen (156 parts per million) and in heavy water: used as a tracer in chemistry and biology. Symbol: D or ^{2}H; atomic no.: 1; atomic wt.: 2.014; boiling pt.:–249.7°C.

Deutsch Otto Erich 1883–1967, Austrian music historian and art critic, noted for his catalogue of Schubert's works (1951)

Deutschmark *or* **Deutsche Mark** the former standard monetary unit of Germany, divided into 100 pfennigs; replaced by the euro in 2002: until 1990 the standard monetary unit of West Germany

deutzia any saxifragaceous shrub of the genus *Deutzia*: cultivated for their clusters of white or pink spring-blooming flowers

de Valera Eamon 1882–1975, Irish statesman; president of Sinn Féin (1917–26) and of the Dáil (1918–22); formed the Fianna Fáil party (1927); prime minister (1937–48; 1951–54; 1957–59) and president (1959–73) of the Irish Republic

developer *Photog* a solution of a chemical reducing agent that converts the latent image recorded in the emulsion of a film or paper into a visible image

developing country a nonindustrialized poor country that is seeking to develop its resources by industrialization

development 1 an area or tract of land that has been developed 2 *Music* the section of a movement, usually in sonata form, in which the basic musical themes are developed **3** *Chess* **a** the process of developing pieces **b** the manner in which they are developed **c** the position of the pieces in the early part of a game with reference to their attacking potential or defensive efficiency

development area (in Britain) an area suffering from high unemployment and economic depression, because of the decline of its main industries, that is given government help to establish new industries

device 1 a machine or tool used for a specific task; contrivance **2** any ornamental pattern or picture, as in embroidery **3** computer hardware that is designed for a specific function **4** a particular pattern of words, figures of speech, etc, used in literature to produce an effect on the reader

devil 1 *Theol* the chief spirit of evil and enemy of God, often represented as the ruler of hell and often depicted as a human figure with horns, cloven hoofs, and tail **2** *Theol* one of the subordinate evil spirits of traditional Jewish and Christian belief **3** *Christian Science* the opposite of truth; an error, lie, or false belief in sin, sickness, and death **4** *Engineering* a portable furnace or brazier, esp one used in road-making or one used by plumbers **5** *Engineering* any of various mechanical devices, usually with teeth, such as a machine for making wooden screws or a rag-tearing machine **6** *Law* (in England) a junior barrister who does work for another in order to gain experience, usually for a half fee **7** *Meteorol* a small whirlwind in arid areas that raises dust or sand in a column

Devine George (Alexander Cassady). 1910–65, British stage director and actor: founded (1956) the English Stage Company in London's Royal Court Theatre

devise *Law* **1 a** a disposition of property by will **b** the property so transmitted **2** a will or clause in a will disposing of real property

Devizes a market town in S England, in Wiltshire: agricultural and dairy products. Pop: 14 379 (2001)

devolution *Politics* a transfer or allocation of authority, esp from a central government to regional governments or particular interests

Devon 1 a county of SW England, between the Bristol Channel and the English Channel, including the island of Lundy: the geographic and ceremonial county includes Plymouth and Torbay, which became independent unitary authorities in 1998; hilly, rising to the uplands of Exmoor and Dartmoor, with wooded river valleys and a rugged coastline. Administrative centre: Exeter. Pop. (excluding unitary authorities): 714 900 (2003 est). Area (excluding unitary authorities): 6569 sq km (2536 sq miles) **2** a breed of large red beef cattle originally from Devon

Devonian *Geology* of, denoting, or formed in the fourth period of the Palaeozoic era, between the Silurian and Carboniferous periods, lasting 60–70 million years during which amphibians first appeared

Devonshire 8th Duke of, title of *Spencer Compton Cavendish*. 1833–1908, British politician, also known (1858–91) as Lord Hartington. He led the Liberal Party (1874–80) and left it to found the Liberal Unionist Party (1886)

devotion 1 religious zeal; piety **2** religious observance or prayers

De Vries Hugo 1848–1935, Dutch botanist, who rediscovered Mendel's laws and developed the mutation theory of evolution

dew drops of water condensed on a cool surface, esp at night, from vapour in the air

Dewar 1 Donald 1937–2000, Scottish Labour politician; secretary of state for Scotland (1997–99); first minister of Scotland (1999–2000) **2** Sir James 1842–1923, Scottish chemist and physicist. He worked on the liquefaction of gases and the properties of matter at low temperature, invented the vacuum flask, and (with Sir Frederick Abel) was the first to prepare cordite

dewberry any trailing bramble, such as *Rubus hispidus* of North America and *R. caesius* of Europe and NW Asia, having blue-black fruits

dewclaw *Zoology* **1** a nonfunctional claw in dogs; the rudimentary first digit **2** an analogous rudimentary hoof in deer, goats, etc.

de Wet Christian Rudolf 1854–1922, Afrikaner military commander and politician, who led the Orange Free State army in the second Boer War (1899– 1902). He was imprisoned for treason (1914) after organizing an Afrikaner nationalist rebellion

Dewey John 1859–1952, US pragmatist philosopher and educator: an exponent of progressivism in education, he formulated an instrumentalist theory of learning through experience. His works include *The School and Society* (1899), *Democracy and Education* (1916), and *Logic: the Theory of Inquiry* (1938)

dewlap 1 a loose fold of skin hanging from beneath the throat in cattle, dogs, etc. **2** loose skin on an elderly person's throat

dexter a small breed of red or black beef cattle, originally from Ireland

dexterity *Rare* the characteristic of being right-handed

dextrin *or* **dextrine** any of a group of sticky substances that are intermediate products in the conversion of starch to maltose: used as thickening agents in foods and as gums

dextrose a white soluble sweet-tasting crystalline solid that is the dextrorotatory isomer of glucose, occurring widely in fruit, honey, and in the blood and tissue of animals. Formula: $C_6H_{12}O_6$

Dezhnev Cape a cape in NE Russia at the E end of Chukchi Peninsula: the northeasternmost point of Asia

Dhahran a town in E Saudi Arabia: site of the original discovery of oil in the country (1938)

Dhaka *or* **Dacca** the capital of Bangladesh, in the E central part: capital of Bengal (1608–39; 1660–1704) and of East Pakistan (1949–71); jute and cotton mills; university (1921). Pop: 12 560 000 (2005 est)

dhal, dal, *or* **dholl** a tropical African and Asian leguminous shrub, *Cajanus cajan*, cultivated in tropical regions for its nutritious pealike seeds

dharma 1 *Hinduism* social custom regarded as a religious and moral duty **2** *Hinduism* **a** the essential principle of the cosmos; natural law **b** conduct that conforms with this **3** *Buddhism* ideal truth as set forth in the teaching of Buddha

diabetes any of various disorders, esp diabetes mellitus, characterized by excretion of an abnormally large

amount of urine
▷www.insulinchoice.org
▷www.diabetes.org.uk

diabolism a activities designed to enlist the aid of devils, esp in witchcraft or sorcery b worship of devils or beliefs and teachings concerning them

diaconate the office, sacramental status, or period of office of a deacon

diaeresis *or* **dieresis** a pause in a line of verse occurring when the end of a foot coincides with the end of a word

Diaghilev Sergei Pavlovich 1872–1929, Russian ballet impresario. He founded (1909) and directed (1909–29) the *Ballet Russe* in Paris, introducing Russian ballet to the West

diagnosis 1 *Med* a the identification of diseases by the examination of symptoms and signs and by other investigations b an opinion or conclusion so reached 2 *Biology* a detailed description of an organism, esp a plant, for the purpose of classification

diagonal 1 *Maths* connecting any two vertices that in a polygon are not adjacent and in a polyhedron are not in the same face 2 *Maths* a diagonal line or plane 3 *Chess* any oblique row of squares of the same colour 4 cloth marked or woven with slanting lines or patterns 5 one front leg and the hind leg on the opposite side of a horse, which are on the ground together when the horse is trotting

diagram *Maths* a pictorial representation of a quantity or of a relationship

dial 1 the circular graduated disc of various measuring instruments 2 a the control on a radio or television set used to change the station or channel b the panel on a radio on which the frequency, wavelength, or station is indicated by means of a pointer

dialectic 1 disputation or debate, esp intended to resolve differences between two views rather than to establish one of them as true 2 *Philosophy* a the conversational Socratic method of argument b (in Plato) the highest study, that of the Forms 3 *Philosophy* (in the writings of Kant) the exposure of the contradictions implicit in applying empirical concepts beyond the limits of experience 4 *Philosophy* the process of reconciliation of contradiction either of beliefs or in historical processes

dialogue¹ *or often US* **dialog** 1 the lines spoken by characters in drama or fiction 2 a particular passage of conversation in a literary or dramatic work 3 a literary composition in the form of a dialogue 4 a political discussion between representatives of two nations or groups

dialogue² *or* **dialog box** *Computing* a window that may appear on a VDU display to prompt the user to enter further information or select an option

dialysis the separation of small molecules from large molecules and colloids in a solution by the selective diffusion of the small molecules through a semipermeable membrane

diamagnetism the phenomenon exhibited by substances that have a relative permeability less than unity and a negative susceptibility. It is caused by the orbital motion of electrons in the atoms of the material and is unaffected by temperature

diameter a a straight line connecting the centre of a

geometric figure, esp a circle or sphere, with two points on the perimeter or surface b the length of such a line

diamond 1 a a colourless exceptionally hard mineral (but often tinted yellow, orange, brown, or black by impurities), found in certain igneous rocks (esp the kimberlites of South Africa). It is used as a gemstone, as an abrasive, and on the working edges of cutting tools. Composition: carbon. Formula: C. Crystal structure: cubic b (*as modifier*): *a diamond ring* 2 *Geometry* a a figure having four sides of equal length forming two acute angles and two obtuse angles; rhombus b rhombic 3 a a red lozenge-shaped symbol on a playing card b a card with one or more of these symbols or (*when plural*) the suit of cards so marked 4 *Baseball* a the whole playing field b the square formed by the four bases 5 **black diamond** a figurative name for **coal** 6 **rough diamond** an unpolished diamond
▷www.adiamondisforever.com
▷www.amnh.org/exhibitions/diamonds

Diana¹ title *Diana, Princess of Wales*, original name *Lady Diana Frances Spencer*. 1961–97, she married Charles, Prince of Wales, in 1981; they were divorced in 1996: died in a car crash in Paris

Diana² the virginal Roman goddess of the hunt and the moon

diapason *Music* 1 either of two stops (**open** and **stopped diapason**) usually found throughout the compass of a pipe organ that give it its characteristic tone colour 2 the compass of an instrument or voice 3 chiefly in French usage a a standard pitch used for tuning, esp the now largely obsolete one of A above middle C = 435 hertz, known as **diapason normal** b a tuning fork or pitch pipe 4 (in classical Greece) an octave

diaper a a woven pattern on fabric consisting of a small repeating design, esp diamonds b fabric having such a pattern c such a pattern, used as decoration

diaphanous (usually of fabrics such as silk) fine and translucent

diaphoretic 1 relating to or causing sweat 2 a diaphoretic drug or agent

diaphragm 1 *Anatomy* any separating membrane, esp the dome-shaped muscular partition that separates the abdominal and thoracic cavities in mammals 2 *Optics* a disc with a fixed or adjustable aperture to control the amount of light or other radiation entering an optical instrument, such as a camera 3 *Chem* a a porous plate or cylinder dividing an electrolytic cell, used to permit the passage of ions and prevent the mixing of products formed at the electrodes b a semipermeable membrane used to separate two solutions in osmosis 4 *Botany* a transverse plate of cells that occurs in the stems of certain aquatic plants

diapositive a positive transparency; slide

diarist a person who keeps or writes a diary, esp one that is subsequently published

diarrhoea *or esp US* **diarrhea** frequent and copious discharge of abnormally liquid faeces

Dias *or* **Diaz** Bartholomeu ?1450–1500, Portuguese navigator who discovered the sea route from Europe to the East via the Cape of Good Hope (1488)

Diaspora 1 a the dispersion of the Jews after the Babylonian and Roman conquests of Palestine b the

Jewish communities outside Israel **c** the Jews living outside Israel **d** the extent of Jewish settlement outside Israel **2** (in the New Testament) the body of Christians living outside Palestine **3** a dispersion or spreading, as of people originally belonging to one nation or having a common culture

diastase any of a group of enzymes that hydrolyse starch to maltose. They are present in germinated barley and in the pancreas

diastole the dilatation of the chambers of the heart that follows each contraction, during which they refill with blood

diatomic (of a compound or molecule) **a** containing two atoms **b** containing two characteristic groups or atoms

diatonic *Music* **1** of, relating to, or based upon any scale of five tones and two semitones produced by playing the white keys of a keyboard instrument, esp the natural major or minor scales forming the basis of the key system in Western music **2** not involving the sharpening or flattening of the notes of the major or minor scale nor the use of such notes as modified by accidentals

Diaz 1 Bartholomeu a variant spelling of (Bartholomeu) **Dias 2 Cameron** born 1972, US film actress; films include *The Mask* (1994), *There's Something About Mary* (1998), and *The Gangs of New York* (2003) **3** (José de la Cruz) **Porfirio** 1830–1915, Mexican general and statesman; president of Mexico (1877–80; 1884–1911)

dibble a small hand tool used to make holes in the ground for planting or transplanting bulbs, seeds, or roots

DiCaprio Leonardo born 1974, US film actor; his films include *Romeo and Juliet* (1996), *Titanic* (1997), and *The Gangs of New York* (2003)

dichotomy 1 *Logic* the division of a class into two mutually exclusive subclasses **2** *Botany* a simple method of branching by repeated division into two equal parts **3** the phase of the moon, Venus, or Mercury when half of the disc is visible

dichromatic 1 having or consisting of only two colours **2** (of animal species) having two different colour varieties that are independent of sex and age **3** able to perceive only two (instead of three) primary colours and the mixes of these colours

Dickens Charles (John Huffam), pen name *Boz*. 1812–70, English novelist, famous for the humour and sympathy of his characterization and his criticism of social injustice. His major works include *The Pickwick Papers* (1837), *Oliver Twist* (1839), *Nicholas Nickleby* (1839), *Old Curiosity Shop* (1840–41), *Martin Chuzzlewit* (1844), *David Copperfield* (1850), *Bleak House* (1853), *Little Dorrit* (1857), and *Great Expectations* (1861)

Dickensian grotesquely comic, as some of the characters of Dickens

Dickinson Emily 1830–86, US poet, noted for her short mostly unrhymed mystical lyrics

dicky *or* **dickey 1** a folding outside seat at the rear of some early cars **2** *Indian* an enclosed compartment of a car for holding luggage, etc, usually at the rear

dicotyledon 1 any flowering plant of the class *Dicotyledonae*, normally having two embryonic seed leaves and leaves with netlike veins. The group includes many herbaceous plants and most families of trees and shrubs **2 primitive dicotyledon** any living relative of early angiosperms that branched off before the evolution of monocotyledons and eudicotyledons. The group comprises about 5 per cent of the world's plants

dictator 1 a a ruler who is not effectively restricted by a constitution, laws, recognized opposition, etc. **b** an absolute, esp tyrannical, ruler **2** (in ancient Rome) a person appointed during a crisis to exercise supreme authority

didactic (of works of art or literature) containing a political or moral message to which aesthetic considerations are subordinated

Diderot Denis 1713–84, French philosopher, noted particularly for his direction (1745–72) of the great French *Encyclopédie*

didgeridoo *Music* a deep-toned native Australian wind instrument made from a long hollowed-out piece of wood

die 1 a a shaped block of metal or other hard material used to cut or form metal in a drop forge, press, or similar device **b** a tool of metal, silicon carbide, or other hard material with a conical hole through which wires, rods, or tubes are drawn to reduce their diameter **2** an internally-threaded tool for cutting external threads **3** a casting mould giving accurate dimensions and a good surface to the object cast **4** *Architect* the dado of a pedestal, usually cubic

Diefenbaker John George 1895–1979, Canadian Conservative statesman; prime minister of Canada (1957–63)

dieldrin a crystalline insoluble substance, consisting of a chlorinated derivative of naphthalene: a contact insecticide the use of which is now restricted as it accumulates in the tissues of animals. Formula: $C_{12}H_8OCl_6$

dielectric 1 a substance or medium that can sustain a static electric field within it **2** a substance or body of very low electrical conductivity; insulator

Dien Bien Phu a village in NW Vietnam: French military post during the Indochina War; scene of a major defeat of French forces by the Vietminh (1954)

Dieppe a port and resort in N France, on the English Channel. Pop: 34 653 (1999)

diesel 1 See **diesel engine 2** a ship, locomotive, lorry, etc, driven by a diesel engine **3** *Informal* short for **diesel oil** (*or* **fuel**) **4** *South African, Slang* any cola drink

Diesel Rudolf 1858–1913, German engineer, who invented the diesel engine (1892)

diesel-electric a locomotive fitted with a diesel engine driving an electric generator that feeds electric traction motors

diesel engine *or* **motor** a type of internal-combustion engine in which atomized fuel oil is sprayed into the cylinder and ignited by compression alone

diesel oil *or* **fuel** a fuel obtained from petroleum distillation that is used in diesel engines. It has a relatively low ignition temperature (540°C) and is ignited by the heat of compression

diet¹ a a specific allowance or selection of food, esp prescribed to control weight or in disorders in which certain foods are contraindicated **b** (*as modifier*): *a diet bread*

diet² 1 *Politics* a legislative assembly in various countries, such as Japan 2 *History* the assembly of the estates of the Holy Roman Empire 3 *Scots law* a the date fixed by a court for hearing a case b a single session of a court

dietetics the scientific study and regulation of food intake and preparation

dietician *or* **dietitian** a person who specializes in dietetics

Dietrich Marlene, real name *Maria Magdalene von Losch*. 1901–92, US film actress and cabaret singer, born in Germany

difference 1 *Maths* a the result of the subtraction of one number, quantity, etc, from another b the single number that when added to the subtrahend gives the minuend; remainder 2 *Maths* of two sets a the set of members of the first that are not members of the second. b **symmetric difference** the set of members of one but not both of the given sets.

differential 1 *Maths* of, containing, or involving one or more derivatives or differentials 2 *Physics, Engineering* relating to, operating on, or based on the difference between two effects, motions, forces, etc. 3 *Maths* a an increment in a given function, expressed as the product of the derivative of that function and the corresponding increment in the independent variable b an increment in a given function of two or more variables, $f(x_1, x_2, ...x_n)$, expressed as the sum of the products of each partial derivative and the increment in the corresponding variable 4 *Engineering* an epicyclic gear train that permits two shafts to rotate at different speeds while being driven by a third shaft 5 (in commerce) a difference in rates, esp between comparable labour services or transportation routes

differential calculus the branch of calculus concerned with the study, evaluation, and use of derivatives and differentials

differential gear the epicyclic gear mounted in the driving axle of a road vehicle that permits one driving wheel to rotate faster than the other, as when cornering

diffraction 1 *Physics* a deviation in the direction of a wave at the edge of an obstacle in its path 2 any phenomenon caused by diffraction and interference of light, such as the formation of light and dark fringes by the passage of light through a small aperture 3 deflection of sound waves caused by an obstacle or by nonhomogeneity of a medium

diffuse *Botany* 1 (esp of some creeping stems) spreading loosely over a large area 2 (of plant growth) occurring throughout a tissue

diffusion 1 *Physics* a the random thermal motion of atoms, molecules, clusters of atoms, etc, in gases, liquids, and some solids b the transfer of atoms or molecules by their random motion from one part of a medium to another 2 *Physics* the transmission or reflection of electromagnetic radiation, esp light, in which the radiation is scattered in many directions and not directly reflected or refracted; scattering 3 *Physics* the degree to which the directions of propagation of reverberant sound waves differ from point to point in an enclosure 4 *Anthropol* the transmission of social institutions, skills, and myths from one culture to another

dig *Informal* an archaeological excavation

digest a compilation of rules of law based on decided cases

digestion 1 the act or process in living organisms of breaking down ingested food material into easily absorbed and assimilated substances by the action of enzymes and other agents 2 mental assimilation, esp of ideas 3 *Chem* the treatment of material with heat, solvents, chemicals, etc, to cause softening or decomposition

digger a tool or part of a machine used for excavation, esp a mechanical digger fitted with a head for digging trenches

digit 1 a finger or toe 2 any of the ten Arabic numerals from 0 to 9 3 another name for **finger** 4 *Astronomy* one twelfth of the diameter of the sun or moon, used to express the magnitude of an eclipse

digital 1 of, relating to, resembling, or possessing a digit or digits 2 representing data as a series of numerical values 3 *Electronics* responding to discrete values of input voltage and producing discrete output voltage levels, as in a logic circuit 4 a less common word for **digitate** 5 *Music* one of the keys on the manuals of an organ or on a piano, harpsichord, etc.

digital audio tape magnetic tape on which sound is recorded digitally, giving high-fidelity reproduction

digital computer an electronic computer in which the input is discrete rather than continuous, consisting of combinations of numbers, letters, and other characters written in an appropriate programming language and represented internally in binary notation

digitalis 1 any Eurasian scrophulariaceous plant of the genus *Digitalis*, such as the foxglove, having bell-shaped flowers and a basal rosette of leaves 2 a a drug prepared from the dried leaves or seeds of the foxglove: a mixture of glycosides used medicinally to treat heart failure and some abnormal heart rhythms b any cardiac glycoside, whatever its origin

digital recording a sound recording process that converts audio or analogue signals into a series of pulses that correspond to the voltage level. These can be stored on tape or on any other memory system

digital television a television set that can decode digital picture information and convert it into visible images

▷www.digitaltelevision.gov.uk

digitate *or* **digitated** 1 (of compound leaves) having the leaflets in the form of a spread hand 2 (of animals) having digits or corresponding parts

dihedral 1 having or formed by two intersecting planes; two-sided 2 the figure formed by two intersecting planes 3 the upward inclination of an aircraft wing in relation to the lateral axis

Dijon a city in E France: capital of the former duchy of Burgundy. Pop: 149 867 (1999)

dildo *or* **dildoe** an object used as a substitute for an erect penis

dilemma *Logic* a form of argument one of whose premises is the conjunction of two conditional statements and the other of which affirms the disjunction of their antecedents, and whose conclusion is the disjunction of their consequents. Its form is *if p then q and if r then s; either p or r so either q or s*

dilettante a person who loves the arts

dill an umbelliferous aromatic Eurasian plant, *Anethum graveolens*, with finely dissected leaves and umbrella-shaped clusters of yellow flowers

dilute *Chem* **a** (of a solution, suspension, mixture, etc) having a low concentration or a concentration that has been reduced by admixture **b** (of a substance) present in solution, esp a weak solution in water

diluvial *or* **diluvian** of or connected with a deluge, esp with the great Flood described in Genesis

Dimbleby Richard 1913–65, British broadcaster

dime a coin of the US and Canada, worth one tenth of a dollar or ten cents

dimension **1** *Maths* the number of coordinates required to locate a point in space **2** *Physics* **a** the product or the quotient of the fundamental physical quantities (such as mass, length, or time) raised to the appropriate power in a derived physical quantity **b** the power to which such a fundamental quantity has to be raised in a derived quantity

dimer *Chem* **a** a molecule composed of two identical simpler molecules (monomers) **b** a compound consisting of dimers

diminuendo *Music* **1 a** a gradual decrease in loudness or the musical direction indicating this **b** a musical passage affected by a diminuendo **2** gradually decreasing in loudness **3** with a diminuendo

diminution *Music* the presentation of the subject of a fugue, etc, in which the note values are reduced in length

dimmer **1** a device, such as a rheostat, for varying the current through an electric light and thus changing the illumination **2** *US* **a** a dipped headlight on a road vehicle **b** a parking light on a car

din¹ *Judaism* **1** a particular religious law; the halacha about something **2** the ruling of a Beth Din or religious court

din² *Islam* religion in general, esp the beliefs and obligations of Islam

dinar **1** the standard monetary unit of the following countries or territories. Algeria: divided into 100 centimes. Bahrain: divided into 1000 fils. Iraq: divided into 1000 fils. Jordan: divided into 1000 fils. Kuwait: divided into 1000 fils. Libya: divided into 1000 dirhams. Serbia: divided into 100 paras (formerly the standard monetary unit of Yugoslavia). Sudan, Tunisia: divided into 1000 millimes. **2** a monetary unit of the United Arab Emirates worth one tenth of a dirham **3** a coin, esp one of gold, formerly used in the Middle East

diner **1** a person eating a meal, esp in a restaurant **2** *Chiefly US and Canadian* a small restaurant, often at the roadside **3** a fashionable bar, or a section of one, where food is served

Dinesen Isak , pen name of *Baroness Karen Blixen*. 1885–1962, Danish author of short stories in Danish and English, including *Seven Gothic Tales* (1934) and *Winter's Tales* (1942). Her life story was told in the film *Out of Africa* (1986)

ding-dong **1** the sound of a bell or bells, esp two bells tuned a fourth or fifth apart **2** an imitation or representation of the sound of a bell

dinghy any small boat, powered by sail, oars, or outboard motor

dingle a small wooded dell

dingo a wild dog, *Canis dingo*, of Australia, having a yellowish-brown coat and resembling a wolf

dining car a railway coach in which meals are served at tables

dinner service a set of matching plates, dishes, etc, suitable for serving a meal to a certain number of people

dinosaur any extinct terrestrial reptile of the orders *Saurischia* and *Ornithischia*, many of which were of gigantic size and abundant in the Mesozoic era

Dio Cassius ?155–?230 AD, Roman historian. His *History of Rome* covers the period of Rome's transition from Republic to Empire

diocese the district under the jurisdiction of a bishop

Dio Chrysostom 2nd century AD, Greek orator and philosopher

Diocletian full name *Gaius Aurelius Valerius Diocletianus*. 245–313 AD, Roman emperor (284–305), who divided the empire into four administrative units (293) and instigated the last severe persecution of the Christians (303)

diode **1** a semiconductor device containing one p-n junction, used in circuits for converting alternating current to direct current **2** the earliest and simplest type of electronic valve having two electrodes, an anode and a cathode, between which a current can flow only in one direction. It was formerly widely used as a rectifier and detector but has now been replaced in most electrical circuits by the more efficient and reliable semiconductor diode

dioecious, diecious, *or* **dioicous** (of some plants) having the male and female reproductive organs in separate flowers on separate plants

Diogenes ?412–?323 BC, Greek Cynic philosopher, who rejected social conventions and advocated self-sufficiency and simplicity of life

Dionysian (in the philosophy of Nietzsche) of or relating to the set of creative qualities that encompasses spontaneity, irrationality, the rejection of discipline, etc.

Dionysius called *the Elder*. ?430–367 BC, tyrant of Syracuse (405–367), noted for his successful campaigns against Carthage and S Italy

Dionysus *or* **Dionysos** the Greek god of wine, fruitfulness, and vegetation, worshipped in orgiastic rites. He was also known as the bestower of ecstasy and god of the drama, and identified with Bacchus

Diophantus 3rd century AD, Greek mathematician, noted for his treatise on the theory of numbers, *Arithmetica*

dioptre *or US* **diopter** a unit for measuring the refractive power of a lens: the reciprocal of the focal length of the lens expressed in metres

Dior Christian 1905–57, French couturier, noted for his New Look of narrow waist with a long full skirt (1947); he also created the waistless sack dress

diorama **1** a miniature three-dimensional scene, in which models of figures are seen against a background **2** a picture made up of illuminated translucent curtains, viewed through an aperture **3** a museum display, as of an animal, of a specimen in its natural setting **4** *Films* a scene produced by the rearrangement of lighting effects

dioxide **1** any oxide containing two oxygen atoms per molecule, both of which are bonded to an atom of another element **2** another name for a **peroxide**

dip **1** a depression, esp in a landscape **2** the angle of slope of rock strata, fault planes, etc, from the horizontal plane **3** the angle between the direction of the earth's magnetic field and the plane of the horizon; the angle that a magnetic needle free to swing in a vertical plane makes with the horizontal **4** a candle made by plunging a wick repeatedly into wax **5** a momentary loss of altitude when flying **6** (in gymnastics) a chinning exercise on the parallel bars

diphtheria an acute contagious disease caused by the bacillus *Corynebacterium diphtheriae*, producing fever, severe prostration, and difficulty in breathing and swallowing as the result of swelling of the throat and formation of a false membrane

diploid *Biology* (of cells or organisms) having pairs of homologous chromosomes so that twice the haploid number is present

diploma a document conferring a qualification, recording success in examinations or successful completion of a course of study

diplomacy **1** the conduct of the relations of one state with another by peaceful means **2** skill in the management of international relations

diplomat an official, such as an ambassador or first secretary, engaged in diplomacy

diplomatic immunity the immunity from local jurisdiction and exemption from taxation in the country to which they are accredited afforded to diplomats

dipole **1** two electric charges or magnetic poles that have equal magnitudes but opposite signs and are separated by a small distance **2** a molecule in which the centre of positive charge does not coincide with the centre of negative charge

dipper **1** any aquatic songbird of the genus *Cinclus* and family *Cinclidae*, esp *C. cinclus*. They inhabit fast-flowing streams and resemble large wrens **2** *Archaic* an Anabaptist

dipsomania a compulsive desire to drink alcoholic beverages

dipstick a graduated rod or strip dipped into a container to indicate the fluid level

dip switch a device for dipping car headlights

dipterous **1** of, relating to, or belonging to the *Diptera*, a large order of insects having a single pair of wings and sucking or piercing mouthparts. The group includes flies, mosquitoes, craneflies, and midges **2** *Botany* having two winglike parts

diptych **1** a pair of hinged wooden tablets with waxed surfaces for writing **2** a painting or carving on two panels, usually hinged like a book

Dirac **Paul Adrien Maurice** 1902–84, English physicist, noted for his work on the application of relativity to quantum mechanics and his prediction of electron spin and the positron: shared the Nobel prize for physics 1933

direct **1** (of government, decisions, etc) by or from the electorate rather than through representatives **2** *Logic, Maths* (of a proof) progressing from the premises to the conclusion, rather than eliminating the possibility of the falsehood of the conclusion **3** *Astronomy* moving from west to east on the celestial sphere **4 a** of or relating to direct current **b** (of a secondary induced current) having the same direction as the primary current **5** *Music* **a** (of motion) in the same direction **b** (of an interval or chord) in root position; not inverted

direct access a method of reading data from a computer file without reading through the file from the beginning as on a disk or drum

direct current a continuous electric current that flows in one direction only, without substantial variation in magnitude

direction **1** the work of a stage or film director **2** the course along which a ship, aircraft, etc, is travelling, expressed as the angle between true or magnetic north and an imaginary line through the main fore-and-aft axis of the vessel **3** *Music* the process of conducting an orchestra, choir, etc. **4** *Music* an instruction in the form of a word or symbol heading or occurring in the body of a passage, movement, or piece to indicate tempo, dynamics, mood, etc. **5** *Maths* (of an angle) being any one of the three angles that a line in space makes with the three positive directions of the coordinate axes. Usually given as α, β, and γ with respect to the x-, y-, and z-axes **b** (of a cosine) being the cosine of any of the direction angles

directional **1** *Electronics* **a** having or relating to an increased sensitivity to radio waves, sound waves, nuclear particles, etc, coming from a particular direction **b** (of an aerial) transmitting or receiving radio waves more effectively in some directions than in others **2** *Physics, Electronics* **a** concentrated in, following, or producing motion in a particular direction **b** indicating direction

director **1** a member of the governing board of a business concern who may or may not have an executive function **2** the person responsible for the artistic and technical aspects of making a film or television programme **3** *Music* another word (esp US) for **conductor**

directorate a board of directors

directory **1** a book containing the rules to be observed in the forms of worship used in churches **2** *Computing* an area of a disk, Winchester disk, or floppy disk that contains the names and locations of files currently held on that disk

direct tax a tax paid by the person or organization on which it is levied

dirge **1** a chant of lamentation for the dead **2** the funeral service in its solemn or sung forms **3** any mourning song or melody

dirt **a** packed earth, gravel, cinders, etc, used to make a racetrack **b** *(as modifier): a dirt track*

dirty **1** (of a colour) not clear and bright; impure **2** (of an aircraft) having projections into the airstream, such as lowered flaps

disability **1** the condition of being unable to perform a task or function because of a physical or mental impairment **2** an incapacity in the eyes of the law to

enter into certain transactions
▷www.disabilityworld.org

disadvantaged socially or economically deprived or discriminated against

discard *Cards* a discarded card

disc brake a type of brake in which two calliper-operated pads rub against a flat disc attached to the wheel hub when the brake is applied

discharge 1 the act of removing a load, as of cargo 2 *Law* a a release, as of a person held under legal restraint b an annulment, as of a court order 3 *Physics* a the act or process of removing or losing charge or of equalizing a potential difference b a transient or continuous conduction of electricity through a gas by the formation and movement of electrons and ions in an applied electric field 4 a the volume of fluid flowing along a pipe or a channel in unit time b the output rate of a plant or piece of machinery, such as a pump

disciple 1 a follower of the doctrines of a teacher or a school of thought 2 one of the personal followers of Christ (including his 12 apostles) during his earthly life

discipline 1 systematic training in obedience to regulations and authority 2 a branch of learning or instruction 3 the laws governing members of a Church

discontinuous *Maths* (of a function or curve) changing suddenly in value for one or more values of the variable or at one or more points

discord *Music* a combination of musical notes containing one or more dissonant intervals

discount 1 at a discount a below the regular price b (of share values) below par c held in low regard; not sought after or valued 2 offering or selling at reduced prices

discourse a formal treatment of a subject in speech or writing, such as a sermon or dissertation

discovery *Law* the compulsory disclosure by a party to an action of relevant documents in his possession

discrimination *Electronics* the selection of a signal having a particular frequency, amplitude, phase, etc, effected by the elimination of other signals by means of a discriminator

discursive *Philosophy* of or relating to knowledge obtained by reason and argument rather than intuition

discus 1 (originally) a circular stone or plate used in throwing competitions by the ancient Greeks 2 *Athletics* a a similar disc-shaped object with a heavy middle thrown by athletes b (*as modifier*): *a discus thrower* 3 the event or sport of throwing the discus 4 a South American cichlid fish, *Symphysodon discus*, that has a compressed coloured body and is a popular aquarium fish

disease any impairment of normal physiological function affecting all or part of an organism, esp a specific pathological change caused by infection, stress, etc, producing characteristic symptoms; illness or sickness in general

diseconomy *Economics* disadvantage, such as lower efficiency or higher average costs, resulting from the scale on which an enterprise produces goods or services

disequilibrium a loss or absence of equilibrium, esp in an economy

dishwasher an electrically operated machine for washing, rinsing, and drying dishes, cutlery, etc.

disinfectant an agent that destroys or inhibits the activity of microorganisms that cause disease

disjunctive 1 *Logic* relating to, characterized by, or containing disjunction 2 *Logic* a disjunctive proposition; disjunction

disk drive *Computing* the controller and mechanism for reading and writing data on computer disks

Disney Walt(**er Elias**). 1901–66, US film producer, who pioneered animated cartoons: noted esp for his creations *Mickey Mouse* and *Donald Duck* and films such as *Fantasia* (1940)

disorderly *Law* violating public peace or order

dispensable (of a law, vow, etc) able to be relaxed

dispensary a place where medicine and medical supplies are dispensed

dispensation 1 *Chiefly RC Church* a permission to dispense with an obligation of church law b the document authorizing such permission 2 *Christianity* a the ordering of life and events by God b a divine decree affecting an individual or group c a religious system or code of prescriptions for life and conduct regarded as of divine origin

disperse *Chemistry* of or consisting of the particles in a colloid or suspension

displaced person a person forced from his home or country, esp by war or revolution

displacement 1 the weight or volume displaced by a floating or submerged body in a fluid 2 the volume displaced by the piston of a reciprocating pump or engine 3 *Psychoanal* the transferring of emotional feelings from their original object to one that disguises their real nature 4 *Geology* the distance any point on one side of a fault plane has moved in relation to a corresponding point on the opposite side 5 *Astronomy* an apparent change in position of a body, such as a star 6 *Maths* the distance measured in a particular direction from a reference point.

display 1 *Electronics* a a device capable of representing information visually, as on a cathode-ray tube screen b the information so presented 2 *Zoology* a pattern of behaviour in birds, fishes, etc, by which the animal attracts attention while it is courting the female, defending its territory, etc.

disposal a means of destroying waste products, as by grinding into particles

disposition *Philosophy, Logic* a property that consists not in the present state of an object, but in its propensity to change in a certain way under certain conditions, as brittleness which consists in the propensity to break when struck

disquisition a formal written or oral examination of a subject

Disraeli Benjamin, 1st Earl of Beaconsfield. 1804–81, British Tory statesman and novelist; prime minister (1868; 1874–80). He gave coherence to the Tory principles of protectionism and imperialism, was responsible for the Reform Bill (1867) and, as prime minister, bought a controlling interest in the Suez Canal. His novels include *Coningsby* (1844) and *Sybil* (1845)

disregard *Social welfare* capital or income which is not counted in calculating the amount payable to a claimant for a means-tested benefit

dissent 1 *Christianity* separation from an established church; Nonconformism **2** the voicing of a minority opinion in announcing the decision on a case at law; dissenting judgment

Dissenter *Christianity, chiefly Brit* a Nonconformist or a person who refuses to conform to the established church

dissertation a written thesis, often based on original research, usually required for a higher degree

dissident a person who disagrees, esp one who disagrees with the government

dissolution 1 the termination of a meeting or assembly, such as Parliament **2** the termination of a formal or legal relationship, such as a business enterprise, marriage, etc.

dissolve *Films, Television* a scene filmed or televised by dissolving

dissonance *or* **dissonancy** *Music* a sensation commonly associated with all intervals of the second and seventh, all diminished and augmented intervals, and all chords based on these intervals

distaff the rod on which flax is wound preparatory to spinning

distance 1 *Geometry* **a** the length of the shortest line segment joining two points **b** the length along a straight line or curve **2** *Horse racing* **a** *Brit* a point on a racecourse 240 yards from the winning post **b** *Brit* any interval of more than 20 lengths between any two finishers in a race **c** *US* the part of a racecourse that a horse must reach in any heat before the winner passes the finishing line in order to qualify for later heats **3 go the distance** *Boxing* to complete a bout without being knocked out **4** the distant parts of a picture, such as a landscape **5 middle distance a** (in a picture) halfway between the foreground and the horizon **b** (in a natural situation) halfway between the observer and the horizon **6** *Athletics* relating to or denoting the longer races, usually those longer than a mile

distance learning a teaching system consisting of video, audio, and written material designed for a person to use in studying a subject at home

distemper[1] any of various infectious diseases of animals, esp **canine distemper**, a highly contagious viral disease of dogs, characterized initially by high fever and a discharge from the nose and eyes

distemper[2] *Art* **1** a technique of painting in which the pigments are mixed with water, glue, size, etc, used for poster, mural, and scene painting **2** the paint used in this technique or any of various water-based paints, including, in Britain, whitewash

distich *Prosody* a unit of two verse lines, usually a couplet

distillation 1 the process of evaporating or boiling a liquid and condensing its vapour **2** purification or separation of mixture by using different evaporation rates or boiling points of their components **3** the process of obtaining the essence or an extract of a substance, usually by heating it in a solvent

distiller a person or organization that distils, esp a company that makes spirits

distillery a place where alcoholic drinks, etc, are made by distillation

distinct 1 *Maths, Logic* (of a pair of entities) not identical **2** *Botany* (of parts of a plant) not joined together; separate

distress 1 mental pain; anguish **2** physical or financial trouble **3 in distress** (of a ship, aircraft, etc) in dire need of help **4** *Law* **a** the seizure and holding of property as security for payment of or in satisfaction of a debt, claim, etc.; distraint **b** the property thus seized **c** *US* (*as modifier*): *distress merchandise*

distressed 1 in financial straits; poor **2** *Economics* another word for **depressed**

distribution 1 *Commerce* the process of physically satisfying the demand for goods and services **2** *Economics* the division of the total income of a community among its members, esp between labour incomes (wages and salaries) and property incomes (rents, interest, and dividends) **3** *Law* the apportioning of the estate of a deceased intestate among the persons entitled to share in it **4** *Law* the lawful division of the assets of a bankrupt among his creditors **5** *Engineering* the way in which the fuel-air mixture is supplied to each cylinder of a multicylinder internal-combustion engine

distributive *Maths* able to be distributed

distributor *or* **distributer 1** *Commerce* a wholesaler or middleman engaged in the distribution of a category of goods, esp to retailers in a specific area **2** the device in a petrol engine that distributes the high-tension voltage to the sparking plugs in the sequence of the firing order

district 1 a locality separated by geographical attributes; region **2** (in England from 1974 and in Wales 1974–96) any of the subdivisions of the nonmetropolitan counties that elects a council responsible for local planning, housing, rates, etc. **3** (in Scotland until 1975) a landward division of a county **4** (in Scotland 1975–96) any of the subdivisions of the regions that elected a council responsible for environmental health services, housing, etc. **5** any of the 26 areas into which Northern Ireland has been divided since 1973. Elected district councils are responsible for environmental health services, etc.

district nurse (in Britain) a nurse employed within the National Health Service to attend patients in a particular area, usually by visiting them in their own homes

District of Columbia a federal district of the eastern US, coextensive with the federal capital, Washington. Pop: 564 326 (2003 est). Area: 178 sq km (69 sq miles)

disturbance 1 *Law* an interference with another's rights **2** *Geology* **a** a minor movement of the earth causing a small earthquake **b** a minor mountain-building event **3** *Meteorol* a small depression **4** *Psychiatry* a mental or emotional disorder

disturbed *Psychiatry* emotionally upset, troubled, or maladjusted

ditch 1 a narrow channel dug in the earth, usually used for drainage, irrigation, or as a boundary marker **2** any small, natural waterway **3** *Irish* a bank made of earth excavated from and placed alongside a drain or stream **4** *Informal* either of the gutters at the side of a tenpin bowling lane

dithyramb 1 (in ancient Greece) a passionate choral

hymn in honour of Dionysus; the forerunner of Greek drama **2** any utterance or a piece of writing that resembles this

ditty a short simple song or poem

Diu a small island off the NW coast of India: together with a mainland area, it formed a district of Portuguese India (1535–1961); formerly part of the Indian Union Territory of Goa, Daman, and Diu (1962–87)

diuretic a drug or agent that increases the flow of urine

diurnal 1 (of flowers) open during the day and closed at night **2** (of animals) active during the day **3** a service book containing all the canonical hours except matins

diva a highly distinguished female singer; prima donna

divalent _Chem_ **1** having a valency of two **2** having two valencies

divan 1 a a Muslim law court, council chamber, or counting house **b** a Muslim council of state **2** a collection of poems **3** (in Muslim law) an account book

dive 1 a headlong plunge into water, esp one of several formalized movements executed as a sport **2** an act or instance of diving **3** a steep nose-down descent of an aircraft **4** _Boxing, slang_ the act of a boxer pretending to be knocked down or out **5** _Soccer, slang_ the act of a player pretending to have been tripped or impeded

dive bomber a military aircraft designed to release its bombs on a target during a steep dive

diver 1 any aquatic bird of the genus _Gavia_, family _Gaviidae_, and order _Gaviiformes_ of northern oceans, having a straight pointed bill, small wings, and a long body: noted for swiftness and skill in swimming and diving **2** any of various other diving birds

diversion _Chiefly Brit_ an official detour used by traffic when a main route is closed

diversity _Logic_ the relation that holds between two entities when and only when they are not identical; the property of being numerically distinct

diverticulitis inflammation of one or more diverticula, esp of the colon

divertimento 1 a piece of entertaining music in several movements, often scored for a mixed ensemble and having no fixed form **2** an episode in a fugue

Dives a rich man in the parable in Luke 16:19–31

divide _Chiefly US and Canadian_ an area of relatively high ground separating drainage basins; watershed

dividend 1 _Maths_ a number or quantity to be divided by another number or quantity **2** _Law_ the proportion of an insolvent estate payable to the creditors **3** _Finance_ **a** a distribution from the net profits of a company to its shareholders **b** a pro-rata portion of this distribution received by a shareholder **4** the share of a cooperative society's surplus allocated at the end of a period to members **5** _Insurance_ a sum of money distributed from a company's net profits to the holders of certain policies

divider _Electronics_ an electrical circuit with an output that is a well-defined fraction of the given input

divination the art, practice, or gift of discerning or discovering future events or unknown things, as though by supernatural powers

divine 1 of, relating to, or characterizing God or a deity **2** of, relating to, or associated with religion or worship **3** another term for **God 4** a priest, esp one learned in theology

diving bell an early diving submersible having an open bottom and being supplied with compressed air

diving board a platform or springboard from which swimmers may dive

division 1 a part of a government, business, country, etc, that has been made into a unit for administrative, political, or other reasons **2** a formal vote in Parliament or a similar legislative body **3** a mathematical operation, the inverse of multiplication, in which the quotient of two numbers or quantities is calculated. Usually written: $a \div b$, a/b **4** _Biology_ (in traditional classification systems) a major category of the plant kingdom that contains one or more related classes **5** _Horticulture_ any type of propagation in plants in which a new plant grows from a separated part of the original **6** _Logic_ the fallacy of inferring that the properties of the whole are also true of the parts, as _Britain is in debt, so John Smith is in debt_ **7** (esp in 17th-century English music) the art of breaking up a melody into quick phrases, esp over a ground bass

division sign the symbol ÷, placed between the dividend and the divisor to indicate division, as in $12 \div 6 = 2$

divisor 1 a number or quantity to be divided into another number or quantity (the dividend) **2** a number that is a factor of another number

divorce 1 the dissolution of a marriage by judgment of a court or by accepted custom **2** a judicial decree declaring a marriage to be dissolved

Diwali a major Hindu religious festival, honouring Lakshmi, the goddess of wealth. Held over the New Year according to the Vikrama calendar, it is marked by feasting, gifts, and the lighting of lamps

Dixie 1 the southern states of the US; the states that joined the Confederacy during the Civil War **2** a song adopted as a marching tune by the Confederate states during the American Civil War

Dixieland 1 a form of jazz that originated in New Orleans, becoming popular esp with White musicians in the second decade of the 20th century **2** a revival of this style in the 1950s

Dixon Willie, full name _William James Dixon._ 1915–92, US blues musician, songwriter, and record producer, whose songs have been recorded by many other artists

Djibouti _or_ **Jibouti 1** a republic in E Africa, on the Gulf of Aden: a French overseas territory (1946–77); became independent in 1977; mainly desert. Official languages: Arabic and French. Religion: Muslim majority. Currency: Djibouti franc. Capital: Djibouti. Pop: 712 000 (2004 est). Area: 23 200 sq km (8950 sq miles) **2** the capital of Djibouti, a port on the Gulf of Aden: an outlet for Ethiopian goods. Pop: 523 000 (2005 est)

DNA deoxyribonucleic acid; a nucleic acid that is the main constituent of the chromosomes of all organisms (except some viruses). The DNA molecule consists of two polynucleotide chains in the form of a double helix, containing phosphate and the sugar deoxyribose and linked by hydrogen bonds between the complementary bases adenine and thymine or cytosine and guanine. DNA is self-replicating, plays a central role in protein synthesis, and is responsible for the transmission of hereditary characteristics from parents to offspring

Dnepropetrovsk a city in E central Ukraine on the Dnieper River: a major centre of the metallurgical industry. Pop: 1 036 000 (2005 est)

Dnieper a river in NE Europe, rising in Russia, in the Valdai Hills NE of Smolensk and flowing south to the Black Sea: the third longest river in Europe; a major navigable waterway. Length: 2200 km (1370 miles)

Dniester a river in E Europe, rising in Ukraine, in the Carpathian Mountains and flowing generally southeast to the Black Sea. Length: 1411 km (877 miles)

Dobell Sir William 1899–1970, Australian portrait and landscape painter. Awarded the Archibald prize (1943) for his famous painting of *Joshua Smith* which resulted in a heated clash between the conservatives and the moderns and led to a lawsuit. His other works include *The Cypriot* (1940), *The Billy Boy* (1943), and *Portrait of a strapper* (1941)

Doberman pinscher *or* **Doberman** a fairly large slender but muscular breed of dog, originally from Germany, with a glossy black-and-tan coat, a short tail, and erect ears

Dobruja a region of E Europe, between the River Danube and the Black Sea: the north passed to Romania and the south to Bulgaria after the Berlin Congress (1878)

DOC 1 Denominazione di Origine Controllata: used of wines 2 (in New Zealand) Department of Conservation

dock¹ 1 a wharf or pier 2 a space between two wharves or piers for the mooring of ships 3 an area of water that can accommodate a ship and can be closed off to allow regulation of the water level 4 short for **dry dock** 5 *Chiefly US and Canadian* a platform from which lorries, goods trains, etc, are loaded and unloaded

dock² 1 the bony part of the tail of an animal, esp a dog or sheep 2 the part of an animal's tail left after the major part of it has been cut off

dock³ an enclosed space in a court of law where the accused sits or stands during his trial

dock⁴ 1 any of various temperate weedy plants of the polygonaceous genus *Rumex*, having greenish or reddish flowers and typically broad leaves 2 any of several similar or related plants

docket 1 *Chiefly Brit* a piece of paper accompanying or referring to a package or other delivery, stating contents, delivery instructions, etc, sometimes serving as a receipt 2 *Law* an official summary of the proceedings in a court of justice 3 *Brit* **a** a customs certificate declaring that duty has been paid **b** a certificate giving particulars of a shipment and allowing its holder to obtain a delivery order 4 *US, Law* **a** a list of cases awaiting trial **b** the names of the parties to pending litigation

doctor 1 a person licensed to practise medicine 2 a person who has been awarded a higher academic degree in any field of knowledge 3 *Chiefly US and Canadian* a person licensed to practise dentistry or veterinary medicine 4 a title given to any of several of the leading Fathers or theologians in the history of the Christian Church down to the late Middle Ages whose teachings have greatly influenced orthodox Christian thought 5 *Angling* any of various gaudy artificial flies 6 *Archaic* a man, esp a teacher, of learning 7 a device used for local repair of electroplated surfaces, consisting of an anode of the plating material embedded in an absorbent material containing the solution

doctorate the highest academic degree in any field of knowledge

doctrine a creed or body of teachings of a religious, political, or philosophical group presented for acceptance or belief; dogma

document *Computing* a piece of text or text and graphics stored in a computer as a file for manipulation by document processing software

documentation 1 the furnishing and use of documentary evidence, as in a court of law 2 *Computing* the written comments, graphical illustrations, flowcharts, manuals, etc, supplied with a program or software system

dodder any rootless parasitic plant of the convolvulaceous genus *Cuscuta*, lacking chlorophyll and having slender twining stems with suckers for drawing nourishment from the host plant, scalelike leaves, and whitish flowers

Dodge City a city in SW Kansas, on the Arkansas River: famous as a frontier town on the Santa Fe Trail. Pop: 25 568 (2003 est)

dodger 1 *Nautical* a canvas shelter, mounted on a ship's bridge or over the companionway of a sailing yacht to protect the helmsman from bad weather 2 *Archaic, US and Austral* a handbill

dodo any flightless bird, esp *Raphus cucullatus*, of the recently extinct family *Raphidae* of Mauritius and adjacent islands: order *Columbiformes* (pigeons, etc). They had a hooked bill, short stout legs, and greyish plumage

Dodoma a city in central Tanzania, the legislative capital of the country. Pop: 169 000 (2005 est)

Dodona an ancient Greek town in Epirus: seat of an ancient sanctuary and oracle of Zeus and later the religious centre of Pyrrhus' kingdom

doe the female of the deer, hare, rabbit, and certain other animals

dog 1 **a** a domesticated canine mammal, *Canis familiaris*, occurring in many breeds that show a great variety in size and form **b** (*as modifier*): *dog biscuit* 2 **a** any other carnivore of the family *Canidae*, such as the dingo and coyote **b** (*as modifier*): *the dog family* 3 **a** the male of animals of the dog family **b** (*as modifier*): *a dog fox* 4 a mechanical device for gripping or holding, esp one of the axial slots by which gear wheels or shafts are engaged to transmit torque 5 any of various atmospheric phenomena

dog box *Austral, informal* a compartment in a railway carriage with no corridor

dogcart a light horse-drawn two-wheeled vehicle: originally, one containing a box or section for transporting gun dogs

doge (formerly) the chief magistrate in the republics of Venice (until 1797) and Genoa (until 1805)

dogfish 1 any of several small spotted European sharks, esp *Scyliorhinus caniculus* (**lesser spotted dogfish**): family *Scyliorhinidae* 2 any small shark of the family *Squalidae*, esp *Squalus acanthias* (**spiny dogfish**), typically having a spine on each dorsal fin 3 any small smooth-skinned shark of the family *Triakidae*, esp *Mustelus canis* (**smooth dogfish** or **smooth hound**)

Dogger Bank an extensive submerged sandbank in the

North Sea between N England and Denmark: fishing ground

doggerel *or* **dogrel a** comic verse, usually irregular in measure **b** (*as modifier*): *a doggerel rhythm*

dogma 1 a religious doctrine or system of doctrines proclaimed by ecclesiastical authority as true **2** a belief, principle, or doctrine or a code of beliefs, principles, or doctrines

Dogs Isle of a district in the East End of London, bounded on three sides by the River Thames

dogwatch either of two two-hour watches aboard ship, from four to six pm or from six to eight p.m

doh *Music* (in tonic sol-fa) the first degree of any major scale

Doha the capital and chief port of Qatar, on the E coast of the peninsula. Pop: 370 000 (2002 est)

Dolby *Trademark* any of various specialized electronic circuits, esp those used for noise reduction in tape recorders by functioning as companders on high-frequency signals

doldrums the a a belt of light winds or calms along the equator **b** the weather conditions experienced in this belt, formerly a hazard to sailing vessels

dole 1 a small portion or share, as of money or food, given to a poor person **2** the act of giving or distributing such portions **3** *Brit, informal* money received from the state while out of work **4 on the dole** *Brit, informal* receiving such money

Dolgellau a market town and tourist centre in NW Wales, in Gwynedd. Pop: 2407 (2001)

Dolin Sir **Anton**, real name *Sydney Healey-Kay*. 1904–83, British ballet dancer and choreographer: with Alicia Markova he founded (1949) the London Festival Ballet

dollar 1 the standard monetary unit of the US and its dependencies, divided into 100 cents **2** the standard monetary unit, comprising 100 cents, of the following countries or territories: Antigua and Barbuda, Australia, the Bahamas, Barbados, Belize, Bermuda, the British Virgin Islands, Brunei, Canada, the Cayman Islands, Dominica, East Timor, Ecuador, El Salvador, Fiji, Grenada, Guatemala, Guyana, Hong Kong, Jamaica, Kiribati, Liberia, Malaysia, the Marshall Islands, Micronesia, Namibia, Nauru, New Zealand, Saint Kitts and Nevis, Saint Lucia, Saint Vincent and the Grenadines, Singapore, Solomon Islands, Taiwan, Trinidad and Tobago, Tuvalu, and Zimbabwe **3** *Brit, informal* (formerly) five shillings or a coin of this value

Dollfuss Engelbert 1892–1934, Austrian statesman, chancellor (1932–34), who was assassinated by Austrian Nazis

dolly 1 *Films, Television* a wheeled support on which a camera may be mounted **2** a cup-shaped anvil held against the head of a rivet while the other end is being hammered **3** a shaped block of lead used to hammer dents out of sheet metal **4** a distance piece placed between the head of a pile and the pile-driver to form an extension to the length of the pile **5** *Cricket* a simple catch

dolmen 1 (in British archaeology) a Neolithic stone formation, consisting of a horizontal stone supported by several vertical stones, and thought to be a tomb **2** (in French archaeology) any megalithic tomb

Dolmetsch Arnold 1858–1940, British musician, born in France. He contributed greatly to the revival of interest in early music and instruments

dolomite 1 a white mineral often tinted by impurities, found in sedimentary rocks and veins. It is used in the manufacture of cement and as a building stone (marble). Composition: calcium magnesium carbonate. Formula: $CaMg(CO_3)_2$. Crystal structure: hexagonal (rhombohedral) **2** a sedimentary rock resembling limestone but consisting principally of the mineral dolomite. It is an important source of magnesium and its compounds, and is used as a building material and refractory

dolphin 1 any of various marine cetacean mammals of the family *Delphinidae*, esp *Delphinus delphis*, that are typically smaller than whales and larger than porpoises and have a beaklike snout **2 river dolphin** any freshwater cetacean of the family *Platanistidae*, inhabiting rivers of North and South America and S Asia. They are smaller than marine dolphins and have a longer narrower snout **3** either of two large marine percoid fishes, *Coryphaena hippurus* or *C. equisetis*, that resemble the cetacean dolphins and have an iridescent coloration **4** *Nautical* a post or buoy for mooring a vessel

dolphinarium a pool or aquarium for dolphins, esp one in which they give public displays

Domagk Gerhard 1895–1964, German biochemist: Nobel prize for medicine (1939) for isolating sulphanilamide for treating bacterial infections

domain 1 land governed by a ruler or government **2** a region having specific characteristics or containing certain types of plants or animals **3** *Austral and NZ* a park or recreation reserve maintained by a public authority, often the government **4** *Law* the absolute ownership and right to dispose of land **5** *Maths* **a** the set of values of the independent variable of a function for which the functional value exists **b** any open set containing at least one point **6** *Philosophy* range of significance (esp in the phrase **domain of definition**) **7** *Physics* one of the regions in a ferromagnetic solid in which all the atoms have their magnetic moments aligned in the same direction **8** *Computing* a group of computers that have the same suffix (**domain name**) in their names on the internet, specifying the country, type of institution, etc where they are located **9** *Biology* the highest level of classification of living organisms. Three domains are recognized: *Archaea* (see **archaean**), *Bacteria* (see **bacteria**), and *Eukarya* (see **eukaryote**) **10** *Biochem* a structurally compact portion of a protein molecule

dome 1 a hemispherical roof or vault or a structure of similar form **2** *Crystallog* a crystal form in which two planes intersect along an edge parallel to a lateral axis **3** *Geology* a structure in which rock layers slope away in all directions from a central point

domestic *Informal* (esp in police use) an incident of violence in the home, esp between a man and a woman

domestic science the study of cooking, needlework, and other subjects concerned with household skills

domicile *or* **domicil** *Formal* **1** a permanent legal residence **2** *Commerce, Brit* the place where a bill of exchange is to be paid

dominant 1 *Genetics* **a** (of an allele) producing the same phenotype in the organism irrespective of whether the allele of the same gene is identical or dissimilar **b** (of a character) controlled by such a gene 2 *Music* of or relating to the fifth degree of a scale 3 *Ecology* (of a plant or animal species within a community) more prevalent than any other species and determining the appearance and composition of the community 4 *Genetics* **a** a dominant allele or character **b** an organism having such an allele or character 5 *Music* **a** the fifth degree of a scale and the second in importance after the tonic **b** a key or chord based on this 6 *Ecology* a dominant plant or animal in a community

dominee (in South Africa) a minister in any of the Afrikaner Churches

Domingo Placido born 1941, Spanish operatic tenor

Dominic Saint original name *Domingo de Guzman*. ?1170–1221, Spanish priest; founder of the Dominican order. Feast day: Aug 7

Dominica a republic in the E Caribbean, comprising a volcanic island in the Windward Islands group; a former British colony; became independent as a member of the Commonwealth in 1978. Official language: English. Religion: Roman Catholic majority. Currency: East Caribbean dollar. Capital: Roseau. Pop: 79 000 (2003 est). Area: 751 sq km (290 sq miles)

Dominican a a member of an order of preaching friars founded by Saint Dominic (original name *Domingo de Guzman*; ?1170–1221), the Spanish priest, in 1215; a Blackfriar **b** a nun of one of the orders founded under the patronage of Saint Dominic

Dominican Republic a republic in the Caribbean, occupying the eastern half of the island of Hispaniola: colonized by the Spanish after its discovery by Columbus in 1492; gained independence from Spain in 1821. It is generally mountainous, dominated by the Cordillera Central, which rises over 3000 m (10 000 ft), with fertile lowlands. Language: Spanish. Religion: Roman Catholic majority. Currency: peso. Capital: Santo Domingo. Pop: 8 873 000 (2004 est). Area: 48 441 sq km (18 703 sq miles)

dominion 1 the land governed by one ruler or government 2 a name formerly applied to self-governing divisions of the British Empire 3 (capital) the New Zealand

domino a small rectangular block used in dominoes, divided on one side into two equal areas, each of which is either blank or marked with from one to six dots

Domino Fats real name *Antoine Domino*. born 1928, US rhythm-and-blues and rock-and-roll pianist, singer, and songwriter. His singles include "Ain't that a Shame" (1955) and "Blueberry Hill" (1956)

dominoes any of several games in which matching halves of dominoes are laid together
▷www.idf.statecraft.net/idf.htm

Domitian full name *Titus Flavius Domitianus*. 51–96 AD, Roman emperor (81–96): instigated a reign of terror (93); assassinated

don *Brit* a member of the teaching staff at a university or college, esp at Oxford or Cambridge

Don 1 a river rising in W Russia, southeast of Tula and flowing generally south, to the Sea of Azov: linked by canal to the River Volga. Length: 1870 km (1162 miles) 2 a river in NE Scotland, rising in the Cairngorm Mountains and flowing east to the North Sea. Length: 100 km (62 miles) 3 a river in N central England, rising in S Yorkshire and flowing northeast to the Humber. Length: about 96 km (60 miles)

Donatello real name *Donato di Betto Bardi*. 1386–1466, Florentine sculptor, regarded as the greatest sculptor of the quattrocento, who was greatly influenced by classical sculpture and contemporary humanist theories. His marble relief of *St George Killing the Dragon* (1416–17) shows his innovative use of perspective. Other outstanding works are the classic bronze *David*, and the bronze equestrian monument to Gattamelatta, which became the model of subsequent equestrian sculpture

Donatus 1 Auelius 4th century AD, Latin grammarian, who taught Saint Jerome; his textbook *Ars Grammatica* was used throughout the Middle Ages 2 4th century AD, bishop of Carthage; leader of the Donatists, a heretical Christian sect originating in N Africa in 311 AD

Donbass *or* **Donbas** an industrial region in E Ukraine in the plain of the Rivers Donets and lower Dnieper: the site of a major coalfield

Doncaster 1 an industrial town in N England, in Doncaster unitary authority, South Yorkshire, on the River Don. Pop: 67 977 (2001) 2 a unitary authority in N England, in South Yorkshire. Pop: 288 400 (2003 est). Area: 582 sq km (225 sq miles)

Donegal a county in NW Republic of Ireland, on the Atlantic: mountainous, with a rugged coastline and many offshore islands. County town: Lifford. Pop: 137 575 (2002). Area: 4830 sq km (1865 sq miles)

Donets a river rising in SW Russia, in the Kursk steppe and flowing southeast, through Ukraine, to the Don River. Length: about 1078 km (670 miles)

Donetsk a city in E Ukraine: the chief industrial centre of the Donbass; first ironworks founded by a Welshman, John Hughes (1872), after whom the town was named Yuzovka (Hughesovka). Pop: 992 000 (2005 est)

Dongola a small town in the N Sudan, on the Nile: built on the site of Old Dongola, the capital of the Christian Kingdom of Nubia (6th to 14th centuries). Pop: 5937 (latest est)

Dongting, Tungting, *or* **Tung-t'ing** a lake in S China, in NE Hunan province: main outlet flows to the Yangtze; rice-growing in winter. Area: (in winter) 3900 sq km (1500 sq miles)

Donizetti Gaetano 1797–1848, Italian operatic composer: his works include *Lucia di Lammermoor* (1835), *La Fille du régiment* (1840), and *Don Pasquale* (1843)

Don Juan a legendary Spanish nobleman and philanderer: hero of many poems, plays, and operas, including treatments by de Molina, Molière, Goldoni, Mozart, Byron, and Shaw

donkey 1 a long-eared domesticated member of the horse family (*Equidae*), descended from the African wild ass (*Equus asinus*) 2 *Brit, slang, derogatory* a footballer known for his or her lack of skill

Donne John 1573–1631, English metaphysical poet and preacher. He wrote love and religious poems, sermons, epigrams, and elegies

Donnelly Declan born 1975, British television presenter, who appears with Antony McPartlin as Ant and Dec

donor 1 *Med* any person who voluntarily gives blood, skin, a kidney etc, for use in the treatment of another person 2 *Law* a a person who makes a gift of property b a person who bestows upon another a power of appointment over property 3 *Chemistry* the atom supplying both electrons in a coordinate bond 4 *Physics* an impurity, such as antimony or arsenic, that is added to a semiconductor material in order to increase its n-type conductivity by contributing free electrons

donor card a card carried by a person to show that the bodily organs specified on it may be used for transplants after the person's death

Doohan Michael K (Mick). born 1965, Australian racing motorcyclist; 500 cc world champion 1994–98

Doolittle Hilda known as H.D. 1886–1961, US imagist poet and novelist, living in Europe

doomsday *or* **domesday** the day on which the Last Judgment will occur

doona *Austral.* a quilt, stuffed with down or a synthetic material and containing pockets of air, used as a bed cover in place of the top sheet and blankets

Doorn a town in the central Netherlands, in Utrecht province: residence of Kaiser William II of Germany from his abdication (1919) until his death (1941)

dop *South African South African, informal* a tot or small drink, usually alcoholic

dope 1 any of a number of preparations made by dissolving cellulose derivatives in a volatile solvent, applied to fabric in order to improve strength, tautness, etc. 2 an additive used to improve the properties of something, such as an antiknock compound added to petrol 3 *Slang* a any illegal drug, usually cannabis b *(as modifier): a dope fiend* 4 a drug administered to a racehorse or greyhound to affect its performance 5 *US and Canadian, informal* a photographic developing solution

Doppler effect a phenomenon, observed for sound waves and electromagnetic radiation, characterized by a change in the apparent frequency of a wave as a result of relative motion between the observer and the source

Dorcas a charitable woman of Joppa (Acts 9:36–42)

Dorchester a town in S England, administrative centre of Dorset: associated with Thomas Hardy, esp as the Casterbridge of his novels. Pop: 16 171 (2001)

Dordogne 1 a river in SW France, rising in the Auvergne Mountains and flowing southwest and west to join the Garonne river and form the Gironde estuary. Length: 472 km (293 miles) 2 a department of SW France, in Aquitaine region. Capital: Périgueux. Pop: 392 291 (2003 est). Area: 9224 sq km (3597 sq miles)

Dordrecht a port in the SW Netherlands, in South Holland province: chief port of the Netherlands until the 17th century. Pop: 120 000 (2003 est)

Doric 1 of or relating to the Dorians, esp the Spartans, or their dialect of Ancient Greek 2 of, denoting, or relating to one of the five classical orders of architecture: characterized by a column having no base, a heavy fluted shaft, and a capital consisting of an ovolo moulding beneath a square abacus 3 one of four chief dialects of Ancient Greek, spoken chiefly in the Peloponnese 4 any rural dialect, esp that spoken in the northeast of Scotland

▷www.hellenism.net/eng/doric.htm

Doris in ancient Greece 1 a small landlocked area north of the Gulf of Corinth. Traditionally regarded as the home of the Dorians, it was perhaps settled by some of them during their southward migration 2 the coastal area of Caria in SW Asia Minor, settled by Dorians

dormant 1 (of a volcano) neither extinct nor erupting 2 *Biology* alive but in a resting torpid condition with suspended growth and reduced metabolism

dormer a construction with a gable roof and a window at its outer end that projects from a sloping roof

dormitory 1 *US* a building, esp at a college or camp, providing living and sleeping accommodation 2 *Brit* denoting or relating to an area from which most of the residents commute to work (esp in the phrase **dormitory suburb**)

Dormobile *Trademark* a vanlike vehicle specially equipped for living in while travelling

dormouse any small Old World rodent of the family *Gliridae*, esp the Eurasian *Muscardinus avellanarius*, resembling a mouse with a furry tail

dorp *Archaic except in South Africa* a small town or village

dorsal 1 *Anatomy, Zoology* relating to the back or spinal part of the body 2 *Botany* of, relating to, or situated on the side of an organ that is directed away from the axis

Dorset a county in SW England, on the English Channel: mainly hilly but low-lying in the east: the geographical and ceremonial county includes Bournemouth and Poole, which became independent unitary authorities in 1997. Administrative centre: Dorchester. Pop. (excluding unitary authorities): 398 200 (2003 est). Area (excluding unitary authorities): 2544 sq km (982 sq miles)

Dortmund an industrial city in W Germany, in North Rhine-Westphalia at the head of the **Dortmund–Ems Canal**: university (1966). Pop: 589 661 (2003 est)

dory[1] 1 any spiny-finned marine teleost food fish of the family *Zeidae*, esp the John Dory, having a deep compressed body 2 another name for **walleye** (the fish)

dory[2] *US and Canadian* a flat-bottomed rowing boat with a high bow, stern, and sides

DOS *Trademark, Computing* disk-operating system, often prefixed, as in MS-DOS and PC-DOS; a computer operating system

dose 1 *Med* a specific quantity of a therapeutic drug or agent taken at any one time or at specified intervals 2 *Physics* the total energy of ionizing radiation absorbed by unit mass of material, esp of living tissue; usually measured in grays (SI unit) or rads 3 a small amount of syrup added to wine, esp sparkling wine, when the sediment is removed and the bottle is corked

dosing strip (in New Zealand) an area set aside for treating dogs suspected of having hydatid disease

Dos Passos John (Roderigo). 1896–1970, US novelist of the Lost Generation; author of *Three Soldiers* (1921), *Manhattan Transfer* (1925), and the trilogy *USA*. (1930–36)

dosshouse *Brit, slang* a cheap lodging house, esp one used by tramps

Dostoevsky, Dostoyevsky, Dostoevski *or* **Dostoyevski** Fyodor Mikhailovich 1821–81, Russian novelist, the psychological perception of whose works has greatly influenced the subsequent development of the novel. His best-known works are *Crime and Punishment* (1866), *The Idiot* (1868), *The Possessed* (1871), and *The Brothers Karamazov* (1879–80)

dot¹ 1 *Music* **a** the symbol (.) placed after a note or rest to increase its time value by half **b** this symbol written above or below a note indicating that it must be played or sung staccato 2 *Maths, Logic* **a** the symbol (·) indicating multiplication or logical conjunction **b** a decimal point

dot² *Civil law* a woman's dowry

dotterel *or* **dottrel** 1 a rare Eurasian plover, *Eudromias morinellus*, with reddish-brown underparts and white bands around the head and neck 2 *Austral* any similar and related bird, esp of the genus *Charadrius*

Douai an industrial city in N France: the political and religious centre of exiled English Roman Catholics in the 16th and 17th centuries. Pop: 42 796 (1999)

Douala *or* **Duala** the chief port and largest city in W Cameroon, on the Bight of Bonny: capital of the German colony of Kamerun (1901–16). Pop: 1 980 000 (2005 est)

Douay Bible *or* **Version** an English translation of the Bible from the Latin Vulgate text completed by Roman Catholic scholars at Douai in 1610

double 1 (of flowers) having more than the normal number of petals 2 *Maths* **a** (of a root) being one of two equal roots of a polynomial equation **b** (of an integral) having an integrand containing two independent variables requiring two integrations, in each of which one variable is kept constant 3 *Music* **a** (of an instrument) sounding an octave lower than the pitch indicated by the notation **b** (of time) duple, usually accompanied by the direction *alla breve* 4 an actor who plays two parts in one play 5 *Bridge* a call that increases certain scoring points if the last preceding bid becomes the contract 6 *Billiards, Snooker* a strike in which the object ball is struck so as to make it rebound against the cushion to an opposite pocket 7 a bet on two horses in different races in which any winnings from the horse in the first race are placed on the horse in the later race 8 *Chiefly RC Church* one of the higher-ranking feasts on which the antiphons are recited both before and after the psalms 9 *Music* an ornamented variation in 16th and 17th century music 10 **a** the narrow outermost ring on a dartboard **b** a hit on this ring

double agent a spy employed by two mutually antagonistic countries, companies, etc.

double bass 1 a stringed instrument, the largest and lowest member of the violin family. Range: almost three octaves upwards from E in the space between the fourth and fifth leger lines below the bass staff. It is normally bowed in classical music, but it is very common in a jazz or dance band, where it is practically always played pizzicato 2 of or relating to an instrument whose pitch lies below that regarded as the bass; contrabass

double-check *Chess* a simultaneous check from two pieces brought about by moving one piece to give check and thereby revealing a second check from another piece

double-decker *Chiefly Brit* a bus with two passenger decks

double entendre 1 a word, phrase, etc, that can be interpreted in two ways, esp one having one meaning that is indelicate 2 the type of humour that depends upon such ambiguity

double-jointed having unusually flexible joints permitting an abnormal degree of motion of the parts

double pneumonia pneumonia affecting both lungs

doubles **a** a game between two pairs of players, as in tennis, badminton, etc. **b** (*as modifier*): *a doubles player*

doublet 1 *Physics* **a** a multiplet that has two members **b** a closely spaced pair of related spectral lines 2 two dice each showing the same number of spots on one throw 3 *Physics* two simple lenses designed to be used together, the optical distortion in one being balanced by that in the other

double take (esp in comedy) a delayed reaction by a person to a remark, situation, etc.

double time *Music* **a** a time twice as fast as an earlier section **b** two beats per bar

doubloon *or* **doblón** a former Spanish gold coin

Doubs 1 a department of E France, in Franche-Comté region. Capital: Besançon. Pop: 505 557 (2003 est). Area: 5258 sq km (2030 sq miles) 2 a river in E France, rising in the Jura Mountains, becoming part of the border between France and Switzerland and flowing generally southwest to the Saône River. Length: 430 km (267 miles)

doubt *Philosophy* the methodical device, esp in the philosophy of Descartes, of identifying certain knowledge as the residue after rejecting any proposition which might, however improbably, be false

douche 1 a stream of water or air directed onto the body surface or into a body cavity, for cleansing or medical purposes 2 the application of such a stream of water or air 3 an instrument, such as a special syringe, for applying a douche

doughnut *or esp US* **donut** anything shaped like a ring, such as the reaction vessel of a thermonuclear reactor

Douglas¹ 1 C(lifford) H(ugh). 1879–1952, British economist, who originated the theory of social credit 2 **Gavin** ?1474–1522, Scottish poet, the first British translator of the *Aeneid* 3 **Keith** (**Castellain**). 1920–44, British poet, noted for his poems of World War II: killed in action 4 **Michael K**(irk). born 1944, US film actor; his films include *Romancing the Stone* (1984), *Wall Street* (1987), *Basic Instinct* (1992), and *Wonder Boys* (2000) 5 (**George**) **Norman** 1868–1952, British writer, esp of books on southern Italy such as *South Wind* (1917)

Douglas² a town and resort on the Isle of Man, capital of the island, on the E coast. Pop: 25 347 (2001)

Dounreay the site in N Scotland of a nuclear power station, which contained the world's first fast-breeder reactor (1962–77). A prototype fast-breeder operated from 1974 until 1994: a nuclear fuel re-processing plant has also operated at the site

dove 1 any of various birds of the family *Columbidae*, having a heavy body, small head, short legs, and long pointed wings: order *Columbiformes*. They are typically smaller than pigeons 2 *Politics* a person opposed to war

dovecote *or* **dovecot** a structure for housing pigeons, often raised on a pole or set on a wall, containing compartments for the birds to roost and lay eggs

Dover 1 a port in SE England, in E Kent on the Strait of Dover: the only one of the Cinque Ports that is still important; a stronghold since ancient times and Caesar's first point of attack in the invasion of Britain (55 BC). Pop: 34 087 (2001) **2 Strait of** a strait between SE England and N France, linking the English Channel with the North Sea. Width: about 32 km (20 miles) **3** a city in the US, the capital of Delaware, founded in 1683: 18th-century buildings. Pop: 32 808 (2003 est)

Dowding Baron **Hugh Caswall Tremenheere**, nicknamed *Stuffy*. 1882–1970, British air chief marshal. As commander in chief of Fighter Command (1936–40), he contributed greatly to the British victory in the Battle of Britain (1940)

dower the life interest in a part of her husband's estate allotted to a widow by law

dower house a house set apart for the use of a widow, often on her deceased husband's estate

Dowland John ?1563–1626, English lutenist and composer of songs and lute music

down¹ *American football* one of a maximum of four consecutive attempts by one team to advance the ball a total of at least ten yards

down² **1** the soft fine feathers with free barbs that cover the body of a bird and prevent loss of heat. In the adult they lie beneath and between the contour feathers **2** another name for **eiderdown 3** *Botany* a fine coating of soft hairs, as on certain leaves, fruits, and seeds **4** any growth or coating of soft fine hair, such as that on the human face

down *Archaic* a hill, esp a sand dune

Down 1 a district of SE Northern Ireland, in Co. Down. Pop: 65 195 (2003 est). Area: 649 sq km (250 sq miles) **2** a historical county of SE Northern Ireland, on the Irish Sea: generally hilly, rising to the Mountains of Mourne: in 1973 it was replaced for administrative purposes by the districts of Ards, Banbridge, Castlereagh, Down, Newry and Mourne, North Down, and part of Lisburn. Area: 2466 sq km (952 sq miles)

downbeat *Music* the first beat of a bar or the downward gesture of a conductor's baton indicating this

downer *Slang* **1** a barbiturate, tranquillizer, or narcotic **2** a state of depression

downfall a fall of rain, snow, etc, esp a sudden heavy one

downgrade *Chiefly US and Canadian* a downward slope, esp in a road

downhill 1 the downward slope of a hill; descent **2** a competitive event in which skiers are timed in a downhill run

Downing Street 1 a street in W central London, in Westminster: official residences of the British prime minister and the chancellor of the exchequer **2** *Informal* the prime minister or the British Government

download 1 a file transferred onto a computer from another computer or the internet **2** a file obtained in this way

Downpatrick a market town in Northern Ireland: reputedly the burial place of Saint Patrick. Pop: 10 316 (2001)

down payment the deposit paid on an item purchased on hire-purchase, mortgage, etc.

Downs the 1 any of various ranges of low chalk hills in S England, esp the **South Downs** in Sussex **2** a roadstead off the SE coast of Kent, protected by the Goodwin Sands

downstream in or towards the lower part of a stream; with the current

downtime *Commerce* time during which a machine or plant is not working because it is incapable of production, as when under repair: the term is sometimes used to include all nonproductive time

downtown *US, Canadian, and NZ* the central or lower part of a city, esp the main commercial area

downturn a drop or reduction in the success of a business or economy

down under *Informal* Australia or New Zealand

downwind 1 in the same direction towards which the wind is blowing; with the wind from behind **2** towards or on the side away from the wind; leeward

dowry *Christianity* a sum of money required on entering certain orders of nuns

Dowson Ernest (**Christopher**). 1867–1900, English Decadent poet noted for his lyric *Cynara*

doxology a hymn, verse, or form of words in Christian liturgy glorifying God

DPB in New Zealand domestic purposes benefit: an allowance paid to solo parents

drab 1 a light olive-brown colour **2** a fabric of a dull grey or brown colour

drachm 1 *Brit* one eighth of a fluid ounce **2** *US* another name for **dram 3** another name for **drachma**

drachma 1 the former standard monetary unit of Greece, divided into 100 lepta; replaced by the euro in 2002 **2** *US* another name for **dram 3** a silver coin of ancient Greece **4** a unit of weight in ancient Greece

Draco 7th century BC, Athenian statesman and lawmaker, whose code of laws (621) prescribed death for almost every offence

draft 1 *Engineering* the divergent duct leading from a water turbine to its tailrace **2** *Commerce* an allowance on merchandise sold by weight **3** the usual US spelling of **draught**

drag 1 an implement, such as a dragnet, dredge, etc, used for dragging **2** a sporting coach with seats inside and out, usually drawn by four horses **3** a braking or retarding device, such as a metal piece fitted to the underside of the wheel of a horse-drawn vehicle **4** *Aeronautics* the resistance to the motion of a body passing through a fluid, esp through air: applied to an aircraft in flight, it is the component of the resultant aerodynamic force measured parallel to the direction of air flow **5** the trail of scent left by a fox or other animal hunted with hounds **6** an artificial trail of a strong-smelling substance, sometimes including aniseed, drawn over the ground for hounds to follow **7** *Angling* unnatural movement imparted to a fly, esp a dry fly, by tension on the angler's line **8** short for **drag race**

dragnet 1 a heavy or weighted net used to scour the bottom of a pond, river, etc, as when searching for something **2** any system of coordinated efforts by police forces to track down wanted persons

dragoman (in some Middle Eastern countries, esp formerly) a professional interpreter or guide

dragon 1 any of various very large lizards, esp the Komodo dragon 2 *Christianity* a manifestation of Satan or an attendant devil 3 a yacht of the International Dragon Class, 8.88m long (29.2 feet), used in racing 4 any of various North American aroid plants, esp the green dragon 5 **chase the dragon** *Slang* to smoke opium or heroin

dragonfly 1 any predatory insect of the suborder *Anisoptera*, having a large head and eyes, a long slender body, two pairs of iridescent wings that are outspread at rest, and aquatic larvae: order *Odonata* 2 any other insect of the order *Odonata*

dragoon a domestic fancy pigeon

drag race a type of motor race in which specially built or modified cars or motorcycles are timed over a measured course

drain 1 a pipe or channel that carries off water, sewage, etc. 2 *Surgery* a device, such as a tube, for insertion into a wound, incision, or bodily cavity to drain off pus, etc. 3 *Electronics* the electrode region in a field-effect transistor into which majority carriers flow from the inter-electrode conductivity channel

drainage a system of watercourses or drains

drake¹ the male of any duck

drake² *Angling* an artificial fly resembling a mayfly

Drake Sir Francis ?1540–96, English navigator and buccaneer, the first Englishman to sail around the world (1577–80). He commanded a fleet against the Spanish Armada (1588) and contributed greatly to its defeat

Drakensberg a mountain range in southern Africa, extending through Lesotho, E South Africa, and Swaziland. Highest peak: Thabana Ntlenyana, 3482 m (11 425 ft)

dram 1 one sixteenth of an ounce (avoirdupois). 1 dram is equivalent to 0.0018 kilogram 2 *US* one eighth of an apothecaries' ounce; 60 grains. 1 dram is equivalent to 0.0039 kilogram 3 a small amount of an alcoholic drink, esp a spirit; tot 4 the standard monetary unit of Armenia, divided into 100 lumas

drama 1 a work to be performed by actors on stage, radio, or television; play 2 the genre of literature represented by works intended for the stage 3 the art of the writing and production of plays
▷http://vl-theatre.com

dramatic *Music* (of a voice) powerful and marked by histrionic quality

dramatics a the art of acting or producing plays b dramatic productions

dramatist a writer of plays; playwright

drape 1 a cloth or hanging that covers something in folds; drapery 2 the way in which fabric hangs

draper *Brit* a dealer in fabrics and sewing materials

drapery 1 fabric or clothing arranged and draped 2 curtains or hangings that drape 3 *Brit* the occupation or shop of a draper 4 fabrics and cloth collectively

draught *or US* **draft** 1 a beer, wine, etc, stored in bulk, esp in a cask, as opposed to being bottled b (*as modifier*): *draught beer* c **on draught** drawn from a cask or keg 2 any one of the 12 flat thick discs used by each player in the game of draughts 3 the depth of a loaded vessel in the water, taken from the level of the waterline to the lowest point of the hull

draughtboard a square board divided into 64 squares of alternating colours, used for playing draughts or chess

draughts a game for two players using a draughtboard and 12 draughtsmen each. The object is to jump over and capture the opponent's pieces
▷www.fmjd.nl

draughtsman *or US* **draftsman** 1 a person skilled in drawing 2 *Brit* any of the 12 flat thick discs used by each player in the game of draughts

draw 1 *US and Canadian* a small natural drainage way or gully 2 a defect found in metal castings due to the contraction of the metal on solidification

drawback *Economics* a refund of customs or excise duty paid on goods that are being exported or used in the production of manufactured exports

drawbridge a bridge that may be raised to prevent access or to enable vessels to pass

drawer 1 a person who draws up a commercial paper 2 *Archaic* a person who draws beer, etc, in a bar

drawing 1 a picture or plan made by means of lines on a surface, esp one made with a pencil or pen without the use of colour 2 the art of making drawings; draughtsmanship

drawing pin *Brit* a short tack with a broad smooth head for fastening papers to a drawing board, etc.

dray 1 a low cart without fixed sides, used for carrying heavy loads 2 any other vehicle or sledge used to carry a heavy load

Drayton Michael 1563–1631, English poet. His work includes odes and pastorals, and *Poly-Olbion* (1613–22), on the topography of England

dread *Slang* a Rastafarian

dreadnought *or* **dreadnaught** a battleship armed with heavy guns of uniform calibre

dream 1 a mental activity, usually in the form of an imagined series of events, occurring during certain phases of sleep b (*as modifier*): *a dream sequence* 2 a a sequence of imaginative thoughts indulged in while awake; daydream; fantasy b (*as modifier*): *a dream world*

dredge a machine, in the form of a bucket ladder, grab, or suction device, used to remove material from a riverbed, channel, etc.

drench 1 the act or an instance of drenching 2 a dose of liquid medicine given to an animal

Drenthe a province of the NE Netherlands: a low plateau, with many raised bogs, partially reclaimed; agricultural, with oil deposits. Capital: Assen. Pop: 481 000 (2003 est). Area: 2647 sq km (1032 sq miles)

Dresden an industrial city in SE Germany, the capital of Saxony on the River Elbe: it was severely damaged in the Seven Years' War (1760); the baroque city was almost totally destroyed in World War II by Allied bombing (1945). Pop: 483 632 (2003 est)

dressage 1 the method of training a horse to perform manoeuvres in response to the rider's body signals 2 the manoeuvres performed by a horse trained in this method

dress circle a tier of seats in a theatre or other auditorium, usually the first gallery above the ground floor

dresser 1 *Theatre* a person employed to assist actors in putting on and taking off their costumes 2 a tool used for dressing stone or other materials 3 *Brit* a person who assists a surgeon during operations

dressing 1 a covering for a wound, sore, etc. 2 size used for stiffening textiles

dressing room *Theatre* a room backstage for an actor to change clothing and to make up

dress rehearsal the last complete rehearsal of a play or other work, using costumes, scenery, lighting, etc, as for the first night

drey *or* **dray** a squirrel's nest

Dreyfus Alfred 1859–1935, French army officer, a Jew whose false imprisonment for treason (1894) raised issues of anti-semitism and militarism that dominated French politics until his release (1906)

drift 1 the extent to which a vessel, aircraft, projectile, etc is driven off its course by adverse winds, tide, or current 2 a general tendency of surface ocean water to flow in the direction of the prevailing winds 3 a controlled four-wheel skid, used by racing drivers to take bends at high speed 4 *Geography* a loose unstratified deposit of sand, gravel, etc, esp one transported and deposited by a glacier or ice sheet 5 a tapering steel tool driven into holes to enlarge or align them before bolting or riveting 6 an uncontrolled slow change in some operating characteristic of a piece of equipment, esp an electronic circuit or component 7 *South African* a ford 8 *Engineering* a copper or brass bar used as a punch

drifter 1 a boat used for drift-net fishing 2 *Nautical* a large jib of thin material used in light breezes

drift net a large fishing net supported by floats or attached to a drifter that is allowed to drift with the tide or current

driftwood wood floating on or washed ashore by the sea or other body of water

drill¹ 1 a rotating tool that is inserted into a drilling machine or tool for boring cylindrical holes 2 a hand tool, either manually or electrically operated, for drilling holes 3 strict and often repetitious training or exercises used as a method of teaching 4 a marine gastropod mollusc, *Urosalpinx cinera*, closely related to the whelk, that preys on oysters

drill² a small furrow in which seeds are sown

drill³ *or* **drilling** a hard-wearing twill-weave cotton cloth, used for uniforms, etc.

drill⁴ an Old World monkey, *Mandrillus leucophaeus*, of W Africa, related to the mandrill but smaller and less brightly coloured

drink the drink *Informal* the sea

drink-driving of or relating to driving a car after drinking alcohol

Drinkwater John 1882–1937, English dramatist, poet, and critic; author of chronicle plays such as *Abraham Lincoln* (1918) and *Mary Stuart* (1921)

drip *Med* a the usually intravenous drop-by-drop administration of a therapeutic solution, as of salt or sugar b the solution administered c the equipment used to administer a solution in this way

drip-dry designating clothing or a fabric that will dry relatively free of creases if hung up when wet

drive 1 a road for vehicles, esp a private road leading to a house 2 *Brit* a large gathering of persons to play cards, etc. 3 *Psychol* a motive or interest, such as sex, hunger, or ambition, that actuates an organism to attain a goal 4 a the means by which force, torque, motion, or power is transmitted in a mechanism b (*as modifier*): *a drive shaft* 5 a search for and chasing of game towards waiting guns 6 *Electronics* the signal applied to the input of an amplifier

drive-in *Chiefly US and Canadian* a a cinema designed to be used by patrons seated in their cars b a public facility or service designed for use in such a manner

drivel saliva flowing from the mouth; slaver

driver 1 a mechanical component that exerts a force on another to produce motion 2 *Golf* a club, a No. 1 wood, with a large head and deep face for tee shots 3 *Electronics* a circuit whose output provides the input of another circuit 4 *Computing* a computer program that controls a device

drive-thru a a takeaway restaurant, bank, etc designed so that customers can use it without leaving their cars b (*as modifier*): *a drive-thru restaurant*

driveway a private road for vehicles, often connecting a house or garage with a public road; drive

driving licence an official document or certificate authorizing a person to drive a motor vehicle

drizzle very light rain, specifically consisting of droplets less than 0.5 mm in diameter

Drogheda a port in NE Republic of Ireland, in Co. Louth near the mouth of the River Boyne: captured by Cromwell in 1649 and its inhabitants massacred. Pop: 31 020 (2002)

dromedary a type of Arabian camel bred for racing and riding, having a single hump and long slender legs

drone¹ 1 a male bee in a colony of social bees, whose sole function is to mate with the queen 2 a pilotless radio-controlled aircraft

drone² 1 *Music* a a sustained bass note or chord of unvarying pitch accompanying a melody b (*as modifier*): *a drone bass* 2 *Music* one of the single-reed pipes in a set of bagpipes, used for accompanying the melody played on the chanter

drongo any insectivorous songbird of the family *Dicruridae*, of the Old World tropics, having a glossy black plumage, a forked tail, and a stout bill

drop 1 a steep or sheer incline or slope 2 *Military* the act of unloading troops, equipment, or supplies by parachute 3 *Theatre* See **drop curtain** 4 *Nautical* the midships height of a sail bent to a fixed yard 5 *Austral, Cricket, slang* a fall of the wicket See also **drop off** *or* **dropout**

drop curtain *Theatre* a curtain that is suspended from the flies and can be raised and lowered onto the stage

drop off a steep or vertical descent

dropout 1 a student who fails to complete a school or college course 2 *Rugby* a drop kick taken by the defending team to restart play, as after a touchdown 3 *Electronics* a momentary loss of signal in a magnetic recording medium as a result of an imperfection in its magnetic coating

dropper 1 a small tube having a rubber bulb at one end for drawing up and dispensing drops of liquid 2 *Angling* a short length of monofilament by which a fly is attached to the main trace or leader above the tail fly

dropsy *Pathol* a condition characterized by an accumulation of watery fluid in the tissues or in a body cavity

dross the scum formed, usually by oxidation, on the surfaces of molten metals

drought a prolonged period of scanty rainfall

drove 1 a narrow irrigation channel 2 a chisel with a broad edge used for dressing stone

drug 1 any synthetic, semisynthetic, or natural chemical substance used in the treatment, prevention, or diagnosis of disease, or for other medical reasons 2 a chemical substance, esp a narcotic, taken for the pleasant effects it produces 3 **drug on the market** a commodity available in excess of the demands of the market

drug addict any person who is abnormally dependent on narcotic drugs

druggist *US and Canadian* a person qualified to prepare and dispense drugs

drugstore *US and Canadian* a shop where medical prescriptions are made up and a wide variety of goods and sometimes light meals are sold

drum¹ 1 *Music* a percussion instrument sounded by striking a membrane stretched across the opening of a hollow cylinder or hemisphere 2 the sound produced by a drum or any similar sound 3 *Architect* a one of a number of cylindrical blocks of stone used to construct the shaft of a column b the wall or structure supporting a dome or cupola 4 any of various North American marine and freshwater sciaenid fishes, such as *Equetus pulcher* (**striped drum**), that utter a drumming sound 5 a type of hollow rotor for steam turbines or axial compressors 6 *Computing* a rotating cylindrical device on which data may be stored for later retrieval: now mostly superseded by disks

drum² *Scot, Irish* a narrow ridge or hill

drumbeat the sound made by beating a drum

drumhead 1 *Music* the part of a drum that is actually struck with a stick or the hand 2 the head of a capstan, pierced with holes for the capstan bars

drum machine *Music* a synthesizer specially programmed to reproduce the sound of drums and other percussion instruments in variable rhythms and combinations selected by the musician; the resulting beat is produced continually until stopped or changed

drumstick a stick used for playing a drum

drupe an indehiscent fruit consisting of outer epicarp, fleshy or fibrous mesocarp, and stony endocarp enclosing a single seed, as in the peach, plum, and cherry

dry 1 having little or no rainfall 2 not providing milk 3 (of a wine, cider, etc) not sweet 4 *Pathol* not accompanied by or producing a mucous or watery discharge 5 *Electronics* (of a soldered electrical joint) imperfect because the solder has not adhered to the metal, thus reducing conductance 6 *Brit, informal* a Conservative politician who is considered to be a hard-liner 7 **the dry** *Austral, informal* the dry season

dryad *Greek myth* a nymph or divinity of the woods

dry battery an electric battery consisting of two or more dry cells

dry cell a primary cell in which the electrolyte is in the form of a paste or is treated in some way to prevent it from spilling

Dryden John 1631–1700, English poet, dramatist, and critic of the Augustan period, commonly regarded as the chief exponent of heroic tragedy. His major works include the tragedy *All for Love* (1677), the verse satire *Absalom and Achitophel* (1681), and the *Essay of Dramatick Poesie* (1668)

dry dock a basin-like structure that is large enough to admit a ship and that can be pumped dry for work on the ship's bottom

dryer any of certain chemicals added to oils such as linseed oil to accelerate their drying when used as bases in paints, etc.

dry ice solid carbon dioxide, which sublimes at –78.5°C: used as a refrigerant, and to create billows of smoke in stage shows

dry rot 1 crumbling and drying of timber, bulbs, potatoes, or fruit, caused by saprotrophic basidiomycetous fungi 2 any fungus causing this decay, esp of the genus *Merulius*

Drysdale Sir **George Russell** 1912–81, Australian painter, esp of landscapes

dual *Maths, Logic* (of structures or expressions) having the property that the interchange of certain pairs of terms, and usually the distribution of negation, yields equivalent structures or expressions

dual carriageway *Brit* a road on which traffic travelling in opposite directions is separated by a central strip of turf, etc.

dub the sound of a drum

Dubai a sheikhdom in the NE United Arab Emirates, consisting principally of the port of Dubai, on the Persian Gulf: oilfields. Pop: 1 026 000 (2005 est)

du Barry Comtesse , original name *Marie Jeanne Bécu*. ?1743–93, mistress of Louis XV, guillotined in the French Revolution

dubbin *or* **dubbing** *Brit* a greasy mixture of tallow and oil applied to leather to soften it and make it waterproof

Dubček Alexander 1921–92, Czechoslovak statesman. His reforms as first secretary of the Czechoslovak Communist Party (1968–69) prompted the Russian occupation (1968) and his enforced resignation. Following the uprising of 1989 he was elected chairman of the new Czechoslovak Federal Assembly

Dublin 1 the capital of the Republic of Ireland, on Dublin Bay: under English rule from 1171 until 1922; commercial and cultural centre; contains one of the world's largest breweries and exports whiskey, stout, and agricultural produce. Pop: 1 004 614 (2002) 2 a county in E Republic of Ireland, in Leinster on the Irish Sea: mountainous in the south but low-lying in the north and centre. County seat: Dublin. Pop: 1 122 821 (2002). Area: 922 sq km (356 sq miles)

dubnium a synthetic transactinide element produced in minute quantities by bombarding plutonium with high-energy neon ions. Symbol: Du; atomic no. 105

Dubrovnik a port in W Croatia, on the Dalmatian coast: an important commercial centre in the Middle Ages; damaged in 1991 when it was shelled by Serbian artillery. Pop: 49 730 (1991)

Dubuffet Jean 1901–85, French painter, inspired by graffiti and the untrained art of children and psychotics

ducat 1 any of various former European gold or silver coins, esp those used in Italy or the Netherlands 2 any coin or money

Duccio di Buoninsegna ?1255–?1318, Italian painter; founder of the Sienese school

Duchamp **Marcel** 1887–1968, US painter and sculptor, born in France; noted as a leading exponent of Dada. His best-known work is *Nude Descending a Staircase* (1912)

duck¹ **1** any of various small aquatic birds of the family *Anatidae*, typically having short legs, webbed feet, and a broad blunt bill: order *Anseriformes* **2** the female of such a bird, as opposed to the male (drake) **3** any other bird of the family *Anatidae*, including geese, and swans **4** *Cricket* a score of nothing by a batsman

duck² a heavy cotton fabric of plain weave, used for clothing, tents, etc.

duck-billed platypus an amphibious egg-laying mammal, *Ornithorhynchus anatinus*, of E Australia, having dense fur, a broad bill and tail, and webbed feet: family *Ornithorhynchidae*

duckling a young duck

ducks and drakes a game in which a flat stone is bounced across the surface of water

duct **1** any bodily passage, esp one conveying secretions or excretions **2** a narrow tubular cavity in plants, often containing resin or some other substance **3** a channel or pipe carrying electric cable or wires

ductile (of a metal, such as gold or copper) able to be drawn out into wire

dudgeon *Obsolete* a wood used in making the handles of knives, daggers, etc.

Dudley **1** a town in W central England, in Dudley unitary authority, West Midlands: wrought-iron industry. Pop: 194 919 (2001) **2** a unitary authority in W central England, in West Midlands. Pop: 304 800 (2003 est). Area: 98 sq km (38 sq miles)

duel a prearranged combat with deadly weapons between two people following a formal procedure in the presence of seconds and traditionally fought until one party was wounded or killed, usually to settle a quarrel involving a point of honour

duet a musical composition for two performers or voices

duff *Slang* the rump or buttocks

duffel *or* **duffle** a heavy woollen cloth with a thick nap

duffer **1** *Austral, slang* a mine that proves unproductive **2** a person who steals cattle

Duffy **Carol Ann** born 1955, British poet and writer; her collections include *Standing Female Nude* (1985) and *The World's Wife* (1999)

Dufy **Raoul** 1877–1953, French painter and designer whose style is characterized by swift calligraphic draughtsmanship and bright colouring

dug the nipple, teat, udder, or breast of a female mammal

dugong a whalelike sirenian mammal, *Dugong dugon*, occurring in shallow tropical waters from E Africa to Australia: family *Dugongidae*

duiker *or* **duyker** **1** any small antelope of the genera *Cephalophus* and *Sylvicapra*, occurring throughout Africa south of the Sahara, having short straight backward-pointing horns, pointed hooves, and an arched back **2** *South African* any of several cormorants, esp the long-tailed shag (*Phalacrocorax africanus*)

Duisburg an industrial city in NW Germany, in North Rhine-Westphalia at the confluence of the Rivers Rhine and Ruhr: one of the world's largest and busiest inland ports; university (1972). Pop: 506 496 (2003 est)

Duisenberg **Willem Frederik**, known as *Wim*. born 1935, Dutch economist; president of the European Central Bank from 1998

Dukas **Paul** 1865–1935, French composer best known for the orchestral scherzo *The Sorcerer's Apprentice* (1897)

dulcimer *Music* **1** a tuned percussion instrument consisting of a set of strings of graduated length stretched over a sounding board and struck with a pair of hammers **2** an instrument used in US folk music, consisting of an elliptical body, a fretted fingerboard, and usually three strings plucked with a goose quill

dull **1** (of weather) not bright or clear; cloudy **2** (of colour) lacking brilliance or brightness; sombre **3** *Med* (of sound elicited by percussion, esp of the chest) not resonant

dulse any of several seaweeds, esp *Rhodymenia palmata*, that occur on rocks and have large red edible fronds

Dulwich a residential district in the Greater London borough of Southwark: site of an art gallery and the public school, Dulwich College

Dumas **1** **Alexandre** , known as *Dumas père*. 1802–70, French novelist and dramatist, noted for his historical romances *The Count of Monte Cristo* (1844) and *The Three Musketeers* (1844) **2** his son, **Alexandre**, known as *Dumas fils*. 1824–95, French novelist and dramatist, noted esp for the play he adapted from an earlier novel, *La Dame aux camélias* (1852) **3** **Jean-Baptiste André** 1800–84, French chemist, noted for his research on vapour density and atomic weight

Du Maurier **1** Dame **Daphne** 1907–89, English novelist; author of *Rebecca* (1938) and *My Cousin Rachel* (1951) **2** her grandfather, **George Louis Palmella Busson** 1834–96, English novelist, caricaturist, and illustrator; author of *Peter Ibbetson* (1891) and *Trilby* (1894) **3** his son, Sir **Gerald** (**Hubert Edward**). 1873–1934, British actor-manager: father of Daphne Du Maurier

dumb lacking the power to speak, either because of defects in the vocal organs or because of hereditary deafness; mute

Dumbarton a town in W Scotland, in West Dunbartonshire near the confluence of the Rivers Leven and Clyde: centred around the **Rock of Dumbarton**, an important stronghold since ancient times; engineering and distilling. Pop: 20 527 (2001)

Dumbarton Oaks an estate in the District of Columbia in the US: scene of conferences in 1944 concerned with creating the United Nations

dumbbell *Gymnastics, Weightlifting* an exercising weight consisting of a single bar with a heavy ball or disc at either end

dumb show a part of a play acted in pantomime, popular in early English drama

Dumfries a town in S Scotland on the River Nith, administrative centre of Dumfries and Galloway. Pop: 31 146 (2001)

Dumfries and Galloway a council area in SW Scotland: created in 1975 from the counties of Dumfries, Kirkcudbright, and Wigtown; became a unitary authority in 1996; chiefly agricultural. Administrative centre: Dumfries. Pop: 147 210 (2003 est). Area: 6439 sq km (2486 sq miles)

Dumfriesshire (until 1975) a county in S Scotland, on the Solway Firth, now part of Dumfries and Galloway

dummy 1 *Bridge* **a** the hand exposed on the table by the declarer's partner and played by the declarer **b** the declarer's partner **2** a feigned pass or move in a sport such as football or rugby **3** (of a card game) played with one hand exposed or unplayed

Du Mont Allen Balcom 1901–65, US inventor and electronics manufacturer. He developed the cathode-ray tube used in television sets and oscilloscopes

dump¹ 1 a place or area where waste materials are dumped **2** *Slang, chiefly US* an act of defecation

dump² *Obsolete* a mournful song; lament

dun 1 a brownish-grey colour **2** a horse of this colour **3** *Angling* **a** an immature adult mayfly (the subimago), esp one of the genus *Ephemera* **b** an artificial fly imitating this or a similar fly

Dunant Jean Henri 1828–1910, Swiss humanitarian, founder of the International Red Cross (1864): shared the Nobel peace prize 1901

Dunbar¹ William ?1460–?1520, Scottish poet, noted for his satirical, allegorical, and elegiac works

Dunbar² a port and resort in SE Scotland, in East Lothian: scene of Cromwell's defeat of the Scots (1650). Pop: 6354 (2001)

Dunbartonshire a historical county of W Scotland: became part of Strathclyde region in 1975; administered since 1996 by the council areas of East Dunbartonshire and West Dunbartonshire

Duncan Isadora 1878–1927, US dancer and choreographer, who influenced modern ballet by introducing greater freedom of movement

Duncan I died 1040, king of Scotland (1034–40); killed by Macbeth

Duncan Smith (George) Iain born 1954, British politician; leader of the Conservative Party (2001–03)

Dundalk a town in NE Republic of Ireland, on Dundalk Bay: county town of Co. Louth. Pop: 32 505 (2002)

Dundee¹ 1st Viscount, title of *John Graham of Claverhouse*. ?1649–89, Scottish Jacobite leader, who died from his wounds after winning the battle of Killiecrankie

Dundee² 1 a port in E Scotland, in City of Dundee council area, on the Firth of Tay: centre of the former British jute industry; university (1967). Pop: 154 674 (2001) **2** City of a council area in E Scotland. Pop: 143 090 (2003 est). Area: 65 sq km (25 sq miles)

dune a mound or ridge of drifted sand, occurring on the sea coast and in deserts

Dunedin a port in New Zealand, on SE South Island: founded (1848) by Scottish settlers. Pop: 121 900 (2004 est)

Dunfermline a city in E Scotland, in SW Fife: ruined palace, a former residence of Scottish kings. Pop: 39 229 (2001)

dung a excrement, esp of animals; manure **b** (*as modifier*): *dung cart*

Dungannon a district of S Northern Ireland, in Co. Tyrone. Pop: 48 695 (2003 est). Area: 783 sq km (302 sq miles)

Dungeness a low shingle headland on the S coast of

England, in Kent: two nuclear power stations: automatic lighthouse

Dunkerque a port in N France, on the Strait of Dover: scene of the evacuation of British and other Allied troops after the fall of France in 1940; industrial centre with an oil refinery and naval shipbuilding yards. Pop: 70 850 (1999)

dunlin a small sandpiper, *Calidris* (or *Erolia*) *alpina*, of northern and arctic regions, having a brown back and black breast in summer

Dunlop John Boyd 1840–1921, Scottish veterinary surgeon, who devised the first successful pneumatic tyre, which was manufactured by the company named after him

Dunsinane a hill in central Scotland, in the Sidlaw Hills: the ruined fort at its summit is regarded as Macbeth's castle. Height: 308 m (1012 ft)

Duns Scotus John ?1265–1308, Scottish scholastic theologian and Franciscan priest: opposed the theology of St. Thomas Aquinas

Dunstable¹ John died 1453, English composer, esp of motets and mass settings, noted for his innovations in harmony and rhythm

Dunstable² an industrial town in SE central England, in Bedfordshire. Pop: 50 775 (2001)

Dunstan Saint ?909–988 AD, English prelate and statesman; archbishop of Canterbury (959–988). He revived monasticism in England on Benedictine lines and promoted education. Feast day: May 19

duo 1 *Music* **a** a pair of performers **b** another word for **duet** **2** a pair of actors, entertainers, etc.

duodecimal 1 relating to twelve or twelfths **2** a twelfth **3** one of the numbers used in a duodecimal number system

duodenum the first part of the small intestine, between the stomach and the jejunum

duologue *or sometimes US* **duolog** a part or all of a play in which the speaking roles are limited to two actors

duple *Music* (of time or music) having two beats in a bar

duplex 1 *US and Canadian* a duplex apartment or house **2** *Chemistry* a double-stranded region in a nucleic acid molecule **3** *Machinery* having pairs of components of independent but identical function **4** *Electronics* permitting the transmission of simultaneous signals in both directions in a radio, telecommunications, or computer channel

Duque de Caxias a city in SE Brazil, near Rio de Janeiro. Pop: 116 000 (2005 est)

Durango 1 a state in N central Mexico: high plateau, with the Sierra Madre Occidental in the west; irrigated agriculture (esp cotton) and rich mineral resources. Capital: Durango. Pop: 1 448 661 (2000). Area: 119 648 sq km (46 662 sq miles) **2** a city in NW central Mexico, capital of Durango state: mining centre. Pop: 520 000 (2005 est)

Durante Jimmy, known as *Schnozzle*. 1893–1980, US comedian

Duras Marguerite, real name *Marguerite Donnadieu*. 1914–96, French novelist born in Giadinh, Indochina (now in Vietnam). Her works include *The Sea Wall* (1950), *Practicalities* (1990), *Écrire* (1993), and the script for the film *Hiroshima mon amour* (1960)

Durban a port in E South Africa, in E KwaZulu/Natal province on the Indian Ocean: University of Natal (1909); resort and industrial centre, with oil refineries, shipbuilding yards, etc. Pop: 536 644 (2001)

durbar a (formerly) the court of a native ruler or a governor in India and British Colonial West Africa b a levee at such a court

duress *Law* the illegal exercise of coercion

Durham 1 a county of NE England, on the North Sea: rises to the N Pennines in the west: the geographical and ceremonial county includes the unitary authorities of Hartlepool and Stockton-on-Tees (both part of Cleveland until 1996) and Darlington (created in 1997). Administrative centre: Durham. Pop. (excluding unitary authorities): 494 200 (2003 est). Area (excluding unitary authorities): 2434 sq km (940 sq miles) 2 a city in NE England, administrative centre of Co. Durham, on the River Wear: Norman cathedral; 11th-century castle (founded by William the Conqueror), now occupied by the University of Durham (1832). Pop: 42 939 (2001) 3 a rare variety of shorthorn cattle

Durkan (John) **Mark** born 1960, Northern Irish politician; leader of the Social Democratic and Labour Party (SDLP) from 2001

Durkheim Émile 1858–1917, French sociologist, whose pioneering works include *De la Division du travail social* (1893)

Durrell 1 Gerald (Malcolm). 1925–95, British zoologist and writer: his books include *The Bafut Beagles* (1954), *My Family and Other Animals* (1956), and *The Aye-aye and I* (1992) 2 his brother, **Lawrence** (George). 1912–90, British poet and novelist; author of *The Alexandria Quartet* of novels, consisting of *Justine* (1957), *Balthazar* (1958), *Mountolive* (1958), and *Clea* (1960). Later works include *The Avignon Quintet* of novels (1974–85)

Duse Eleonora 1858–1924, Italian actress, noted as a tragedienne

Dushanbe the capital of Tajikistan; a cultural centre. Pop: 551 000 (2005 est)

dust bowl a semiarid area in which the surface soil is exposed to wind erosion and dust storms occur

Dust Bowl the the area of the south central US that became denuded of topsoil by wind erosion during the droughts of the mid-1930s

dustcart a road vehicle for collecting domestic refuse

duster a cloth used for dusting furniture, etc.

dustpan a short-handled hooded shovel into which dust is swept from floors, etc.

dustsheet *Brit* a large cloth or sheet used for covering furniture to protect it from dust

dusty (of a colour) tinged with grey; pale

Dutch 1 the language of the Netherlands, belonging to the West Germanic branch of the Indo-European family and quite closely related to German and English 2 the Dutch the natives, citizens, or inhabitants of the Netherlands

Dutch auction an auction in which the price is lowered by stages until a buyer is found

Dutch barn *Brit* a farm building consisting of a steel frame and a curved roof

Dutch courage 1 false courage gained from drinking alcohol 2 alcoholic drink

Dutchman 1 a native, citizen, or inhabitant of the Netherlands 2 *South African, often derogatory* an Afrikaaner

dutiable (of goods) liable to duty

duty 1 a government tax, esp on imports 2 *Brit* a the quantity or intensity of work for which a machine is designed b a measure of the efficiency of a machine

duty-free 1 with exemption from customs or excise duties 2 goods sold in a duty-free shop

duty-free shop a shop, esp one at an airport or on board a ship, that sells perfume, tobacco, etc, at duty-free prices

Duvalier 1 François , known as *Papa Doc.* 1907–71, president of Haiti (1957–71) 2 his son, **Jean-Claude** , known as *Baby Doc.* born 1951, Haitian statesman; president of Haiti 1971–86; deposed and exiled

Dvina 1 **Northern** a river in NW Russia, formed by the confluence of the Sukhona and Yug Rivers and flowing northwest to *Dvina Bay* in the White Sea. Length: 750 km (466 miles) 2 **Western** a river rising in W Russia, in the Valdai Hills and flowing south and southwest then northwest to the Gulf of Riga. Length: 1021 km (634 miles)

Dvina Bay *or* **Dvina Gulf** an inlet of the White Sea, off the coast of NW Russia

dwarf 1 an abnormally undersized person, esp one with a large head and short arms and legs 2 a an animal or plant much below the average height for the species b (*as modifier*): *a dwarf tree* 3 (in folklore) a small ugly manlike creature, often possessing magical powers

dwell 1 a regular pause in the operation of a machine 2 a flat or constant-radius portion on a linear or rotary cam enabling the cam follower to remain static for a brief time

dyed-in-the-wool (of a fabric) made of dyed yarn

Dyfed a former county in SW Wales: created in 1974 from Cardiganshire, Pembrokeshire, and Carmarthenshire; in 1996 it was replaced by Pembrokeshire, Carmarthenshire, and Ceredigion

dyke *or* **dike** 1 an embankment constructed to prevent flooding, keep out the sea, etc. 2 a ditch or watercourse 3 a bank made of earth excavated for and placed alongside a ditch 4 *Scot* a wall, esp a dry-stone wall 5 a vertical or near-vertical wall-like body of igneous rock intruded into cracks in older rock

Dyke Greg(ory). born 1947, British television executive; director-general of the BBC (2000–04)

Dylan Bob real name *Robert Allen Zimmerman.* born 1941, US rock singer and songwriter, also noted for his acoustic protest songs in the early 1960s. His albums include *The Freewheelin' Bob Dylan* (1963), *Highway 61 Revisited* (1965), *Blonde on Blonde* (1966), *John Wesley Harding* (1968), *Blood on the Tracks* (1974), *Oh Mercy* (1989), *Time Out of Mind* (1997), and *Love and Theft* (2001)

dynamic 1 of or concerned with energy or forces that produce motion, as opposed to *static* 2 of or concerned with dynamics 3 *Music* of, relating to, or indicating dynamics 4 *Computing* (of a memory) needing its contents refreshed periodically

dynamics 1 the branch of mechanics concerned with the forces that change or produce the motions of bodies 2 the branch of mechanics that includes statics and kinetics **3** the branch of any science concerned with forces **4** *Music* **a** the various degrees of loudness called for in performance **b** directions and symbols used to indicate degrees of loudness

dynamism *Philosophy* any of several theories that attempt to explain phenomena in terms of an immanent force or energy

dynamo a device for converting mechanical energy into electrical energy, esp one that produces direct current

dynamoelectric *or* **dynamoelectrical** of or concerned with the interconversion of mechanical and electrical energy

dynamometer any of a number of instruments for measuring power or force

dysentery infection of the intestine with bacteria or amoebae, marked chiefly by severe diarrhoea with the passage of mucus and blood

dysfunction *Med* any disturbance or abnormality in the function of an organ or part

dyslexia a developmental disorder which can cause learning difficulty in one or more of the areas of reading, writing, and numeracy

Dyson James born 1947, British businessman and industrial designer; inventor of the bagless vacuum cleaner (1979–93)

dyspepsia *or* **dyspepsy** indigestion or upset stomach

dysprosium a soft silvery-white metallic element of the lanthanide series: used in laser materials and as a neutron absorber in nuclear control rods. Symbol: Dy; atomic no.: 66; atomic wt.: 162.50; valency: 3; relative density: 8.551; melting pt.: 1412°C; boiling pt.: 2567°C

dystrophy *or* **dystrophia 1** any of various bodily disorders, characterized by wasting of tissues **2** *Ecology* a condition of lake water when it is too acidic and poor in oxygen to support life, resulting from excessive humus content

Dzungaria another name for **Junggar Pendi**

Ee

Eadred died 955 AD, king of England (946–55): regained Northumbria (954) from the Norwegian king Eric Bloodaxe

eagle 1 any of various birds of prey of the genera *Aquila, Harpia*, etc (see **golden eagle**), having large broad wings and strong soaring flight: family *Accipitridae* (hawks, etc) 2 *Golf* a score of two strokes under par for a hole 3 a former US gold coin worth ten dollars: withdrawn from circulation in 1934

eaglet a young eagle

Eakins Thomas 1844–1916, US painter of portraits and sporting life: a noted realist

Ealing a borough of W Greater London, formed in 1965 from Acton, Ealing, and Southall. Pop: 3 050 000 (2003 est). Area: 55 sq km (21 sq miles)

ear¹ 1 the organ of hearing and balance in higher vertebrates and of balance only in fishes. In man and other mammals it consists of three parts (see also **middle ear**) 2 the outermost cartilaginous part of the ear (pinna) in mammals, esp man 3 **by ear** without reading from written music 4 **play by ear** to perform a musical piece on an instrument without written music

ear² the part of a cereal plant, such as wheat or barley, that contains the seeds, grains, or kernels

earache pain in the middle or inner ear

Earhart Amelia 1898–1937, US aviator: the first woman to fly the Atlantic (1928). She disappeared on a Pacific flight (1937)

earl 1 (in the British Isles) a nobleman ranking below a marquess and above a viscount 2 (in Anglo-Saxon England) a royal governor of any of the large divisions of the kingdom, such as Wessex

ear lobe the fleshy lower part of the external ear

Early English a style of architecture used in England in the 12th and 13th centuries, characterized by lancet arches, narrow openings, and plate tracery
　▷www.britainexpress.com/architecture/
　　early-english.htm

earnest *Contract law* something given, usually a nominal sum of money, to confirm a contract

earphone a device for converting electric currents into sound waves, held close to or inserted into the ear

earth 1 the third planet from the sun, the only planet on which life is known to exist. It is not quite spherical, being flattened at the poles, and consists of three geological zones, the core, mantle, and thin outer crust.

The surface, covered with large areas of water, is enveloped by an atmosphere principally of nitrogen (78 per cent), oxygen (21 per cent), and some water vapour. The age is estimated at over four thousand million years. Distance from sun: 149.6 million km; equatorial diameter: 12 756 km; mass: 5.976×10^{24} kg; sidereal period of axial rotation: 23 hours 56 minutes 4 seconds; sidereal period of revolution about sun: 365.256 days 2 the loose soft material that makes up a large part of the surface of the ground and consists of disintegrated rock particles, mould, clay, etc.; soil 3 the hole in which some species of burrowing animals, esp foxes, live 4 *Chem* See **rare earth** 5 a a connection between an electrical circuit or device and the earth, which is at zero potential b a terminal to which this connection is made 6 *Astrology* of or relating to a group of three signs of the zodiac, Taurus, Virgo, and Capricorn
　▷http://earthobservatory.nasa.gov
　▷www.earth.nasa.gov
　▷www.itc.nl

earthen made of baked clay

earthenware vessels, etc, made of baked clay

earthquake a sudden release of energy in the earth's crust or upper mantle, usually caused by movement along a fault plane or by volcanic activity and resulting in the generation of seismic waves which can be destructive

earth science any of various sciences, such as geology, geography, and geomorphology, that are concerned with the structure, age, and other aspects of the earth
　▷www.geologylink.com
　▷www.psigate.ac.uk/newsite/
　　earth-gateway.html
　▷http://personal.cmich.edu/~francim/
　　homepage.htm
　▷www.geologynet.com/indexa.htm
　▷www.iers.org/links/geo/

earthworm any of numerous oligochaete worms of the genera *Lumbricus, Allolobophora, Eisenia*, etc, which burrow in the soil and help aerate and break up the ground

earthy *Electrical engineering* on the earthed side of an electrical circuit, but not necessarily with a direct current connection to earth

earwig any of various insects of the order *Dermaptera*, esp *Forficula auricularia* (**common European earwig**), which typically have an elongated body with small leathery forewings, semicircular membranous hindwings, and curved forceps at the tip of the abdomen

ease *Military* **at ease a** (of a standing soldier, etc) in a relaxed position with the feet apart and hands linked behind the back **b** a command to adopt such a position

easel a frame, usually in the form of an upright tripod, used for supporting or displaying an artist's canvas, blackboard, etc.

east 1 one of the four cardinal points of the compass, 90° clockwise from north and 180° from west **2** the direction along a parallel towards the sunrise, at 90° to north; the direction of the earth's rotation **3 the east** any area lying in or towards the east **4** *Cards* the player or position at the table corresponding to east on the compass

East the 1 the continent of Asia regarded as culturally distinct from Europe and the West; the Orient **2** the countries under Communist rule and formerly under Communist rule, lying mainly in the E hemisphere **3** in the US **a** the area north of the Ohio and east of the Mississippi **b** the area north of Maryland and east of the Alleghenies

East Africa a region of Africa comprising Kenya, Uganda, and Tanzania

East Anglia 1 a region of E England south of the Wash: consists of Norfolk and Suffolk, and parts of Essex and Cambridgeshire **2** an Anglo-Saxon kingdom that consisted of Norfolk and Suffolk in the 6th century AD; became a dependency of Mercia in the 8th century

East Ayrshire a council area of SW Scotland, comprising the E part of the historical county of Ayrshire: part of Strathclyde region from 1975 to 1996: chiefly agricultural. Administrative centre: Kilmarnock. Pop: 119 530 (2003 est). Area: 1252 sq km (483 sq miles)

East Bengal the part of the former Indian province of Bengal assigned to Pakistan in 1947 (now Bangladesh)

East Berlin (formerly) the part of Berlin under East German control

eastbound going or leading towards the east

Eastbourne a resort in SE England, in East Sussex on the English Channel. Pop: 106 592 (2001)

East Cape 1 the easternmost point of New Guinea, on Milne Bay **2** the easternmost point of New Zealand, on North Island **3** the former name for Cape **Dezhnev**

East China Sea part of the N Pacific, between the E coast of China and the Ryukyu Islands

East Dunbartonshire a council area of central Scotland to the N of Glasgow: part of Strathclyde region from 1975 until 1996: mainly agricultural and residential. Administrative centre: Kirkintilloch. Pop: 106 970 (2003 est). Area: 172 sq km (66 sq miles)

East End the a densely populated part of E London containing former industrial and dock areas

Easter the most important festival of the Christian Church, commemorating the Resurrection of Christ: falls on the Sunday following the first full moon after the vernal equinox

Easter egg a bonus or extra feature hidden inside a website, computer game, or DVD, that is only revealed after repeated or lengthy viewing or playing

Easter Island an isolated volcanic island in the Pacific, 3700 km (2300 miles) west of Chile, of which it is a

dependency: discovered on Easter Sunday, 1722; annexed by Chile in 1888; noted for the remains of an aboriginal culture, which includes gigantic stone figures. Pop: 3791 (2002). Area: 166 sq km (64 sq miles)

easterly 1 towards or in the direction of the east **2** a wind from the east

eastern facing or moving towards the east

Eastern Cape a province of S South Africa; formed in 1994 from the E part of the former Cape Province: service industries, agriculture, and mining. Capital: Bisho. Pop: 7 088 547 (2004 est). Area: 169 600 sq km (65 483 sq miles).

eastern hemisphere 1 that half of the globe containing Europe, Asia, Africa, and Australia, lying east of the Greenwich meridian **2** the lands in this, esp Asia

Eastern Townships an area of central Canada, in S Quebec: consists of 11 townships south of the St Lawrence

East Flanders a province of W Belgium: low-lying, with reclaimed land in the northeast: textile industries. Capital: Ghent. Pop: 1 373 720 (2004 est). Area: 2979 sq km (1150 sq miles)

East Germany a former republic in N central Europe: established in 1949 and declared a sovereign state by the Soviet Union in 1954; Communist regime replaced by a multiparty democracy in 1989; reunited with West Germany in 1990

East Kilbride a town in W Scotland, in South Lanarkshire near Glasgow: designated a new town in 1947. Pop: 73 796 (2001)

Eastleigh a town in S England, in S Hampshire: railway engineering industry. Pop: 52 894 (2001)

East London a port in S South Africa, in S Eastern Cape province. Pop: 135 560 (2001)

East Lothian a council area and historical county of E central Scotland, on the Firth of Forth and the North Sea: part of Lothian region from 1975 to 1996: chiefly agricultural. Administrative centre: Haddington. Pop: 91 090 (2003 est). Area: 678 sq km (262 sq miles)

Eastman George 1854–1932, US manufacturer of photographic equipment: noted for the introduction of roll film and developments in colour photography

East Prussia a former province of NE Germany on the Baltic Sea: separated in 1919 from the rest of Germany by the Polish Corridor and Danzig: in 1945 Poland received the south part, the Soviet Union the north

East Renfrewshire a council area of W central Scotland, comprising part of the historical county of Renfrewshire; part of Strathclyde region from 1975 to 1996: chiefly agricultural and residential. Administrative centre: Giffnock. Pop: 89 680 (2003 est). Area: 173 sq km (67 sq miles)

East Riding of Yorkshire a county of NE England, a historical division of Yorkshire on the North Sea and the Humber estuary: became part of Humberside in 1974; reinstated as an independent unitary authority in 1996, with a separate authority for Kingston upon Hull: chiefly agricultural and low-lying, with various industries in Hull. Administrative centre: Beverley. Pop. (excluding Hull): 321 300 (2003 est). Area (excluding Hull): 748 sq km (675 sq miles)

East Sussex a county of SE England comprising part of

the former county of Sussex: mainly undulating agri-cultural land, with the South Downs and seaside resorts in the south: Brighton and Hove became an independent unitary authority in 1997 but is part of the geographical and ceremonial county. Administrative centre: Lewes. Pop. (excluding Brighton and Hove): 496 100 (2003 est). Area (excluding Brighton and Hove): 1795 sq km (693 sq miles)

East Timor a small country in SE Asia, comprising part of the island of Timor: colonized by Portugal in the 19th century; declared independence in 1975 but immediate-ly invaded by Indonesia; under UN administration from 1999 and an independent state from 2002. It is mountainous with a monsoon climate; subsistence agriculture is the main occupation. Languages: Portuguese, Tetun (a lingua franca), and Bahasa Indonesia. Religion: Roman Catholic majority. Currency: US dollar. Capital: Dili. Pop: 820 000 (2004 est). Area: 14 874 sq km (5743 sq miles)

Eastwood Clint born 1930, US film actor and director. His films as an actor include *The Good The Bad and The Ugly* (1966), *Dirty Harry* (1971), and as actor and director *Play Misty for Me* (1971), *Unforgiven* (1993), and *Mystic River* (2003).

easy *Economics* **a** readily obtainable **b** (of a market) characterized by low demand or excess supply with prices tending to fall

eavestrough *Canadian* a gutter at the eaves of a building

ebb **a** the flowing back of the tide from high to low water or the period in which this takes place **b** (*as modifier*): *the ebb tide*

Ebbinghaus Hermann 1850–1909, German experimen-tal psychologist who undertook the first systematic and large-scale studies of memory and devised tests using nonsense syllables

Ebbw Vale a town in S Wales, in Blaenau Gwent county borough: a former coal mining centre. Pop: 18 558 (2001)

Ebert Friedrich 1871–1925, German Social Democratic statesman; first president of the German Republic (1919–25)

ebony **1** any of various tropical and subtropical trees of the genus *Diospyros*, esp *D. ebenum* of S India, that have hard dark wood: family *Ebenaceae* **2** the wood of such a tree, much used for cabinetwork **3** **a** a black colour, sometimes with a dark olive tinge **b** (*as adjective*): *ebony skin*

Ebro the second largest river in Spain, rising in the Cantabrian Mountains and flowing southeast to the Mediterranean. Length: 910 km (565 miles)

Ecbatana an ancient city in Iran, on the site of modern Hamadān; capital of Media and royal residence of the Persians and Parthians

eccentric **1** situated away from the centre or the axis **2** not having a common centre **3** a device for converting rotary motion to reciprocating motion

eccentricity **1** deviation from a circular path or orbit **2** a measure of the noncircularity of an elliptical orbit, the distance between the foci divided by the length of the major axis **3** *Geometry* a number that expresses the shape of a conic section: the ratio of the distance of a point on the curve from a fixed point (the focus) to the distance of the point from a fixed line (the directrix) **4** the degree of displacement of the geometric centre of a

rotating part from the true centre, esp of the axis of rotation of a wheel or shaft

Eccles[1] Sir John Carew 1903–97, Australian physiologist: shared the Nobel prize for physiology (1963) with A. L. Hodgkin and A. F. Huxley for their work on conduction of nervous impulses

Eccles[2] a town in NW England, in Salford unitary authority, Greater Manchester. Pop: 36 610 (2001)

ecclesiastic **1** a clergyman or other person in holy orders **2** of or associated with the Christian Church or clergy

ecclesiastical of or relating to the Christian Church

Ecclestone Bernard, known as *Bernie*. born 1930, British businessman and sports administrator; head of Formula One motor racing from 1995

Ecevit Bülent born 1925, Turkish politician and journal-ist: prime minister of Turkey (1974, 1977, 1978–79, 1998–2002)

echelon *Physics* a type of diffraction grating used in spectroscopy consisting of a series of plates of equal thickness arranged stepwise with a constant offset

echidna any of the spine-covered monotreme mam-mals of the genera *Tachyglossus* of Australia and *Zaglossus* of New Guinea: family *Tachyglossidae*. They have a long snout and claws for hunting ants and termites

echinoderm any of the marine invertebrate animals constituting the phylum *Echinodermata*, characterized by tube feet, a calcite body-covering (test), and a five-part symmetrical body. The group includes the starfish, sea urchins, and sea cucumbers

echo **1** **a** the reflection of sound or other radiation by a reflecting medium, esp a solid object **b** the sound so reflected **2** **a** the signal reflected by a radar target **b** the trace produced by such a signal on a radar screen **3** the repetition of certain sounds or syllables in a verse line **4** the quiet repetition of a musical phrase **5** a manual or stop on an organ that controls a set of quiet pipes that give the illusion of sounding at a distance **6** an electronic effect in recorded music that adds vibra-tion or resonance

echo chamber a room with walls that reflect sound. It is used to make acoustic measurements and as a source of reverberant sound to be mixed with direct sound for recording or broadcasting

echolocation determination of the position of an object by measuring the time taken for an echo to return from it and its direction

echo sounder a navigation and position-finding device that determines depth by measuring the time taken for a pulse of high-frequency sound to reach the sea bed or a submerged object and for the echo to return

Eck Johann , original name *Johann Mayer*. 1486–1543, German Roman Catholic theologian; opponent of Luther and the Reformation

Eckert John Presper 1919–95, US electronics engineer: built the first electronic computer with John W. Mauchly in 1946

eclampsia *Pathol* a toxic condition of unknown cause that sometimes develops in the last three months of pregnancy, characterized by high blood pressure, abnormal weight gain and convulsions

eclectic (in art, philosophy, etc) selecting what seems

best from various styles, doctrines, ideas, methods, etc.

eclipse 1 the total or partial obscuring of one celestial body by another. A **solar eclipse** occurs when the moon passes between the earth and the sun; a **lunar eclipse** when the earth passes between the sun and the moon **2** the period of time during which such a phenomenon occurs

ecliptic 1 *Astronomy* **a** the great circle on the celestial sphere representing the apparent annual path of the sun relative to the stars. It is inclined at 23.45° to the celestial equator. The **poles of the ecliptic** lie on the celestial sphere due north and south of the plane of the ecliptic **b** (*as modifier*): *the ecliptic plane* **2** an equivalent great circle, opposite points of which pass through the Tropics of Cancer and Capricorn, on the terrestrial globe **3** of or relating to an eclipse

Eco Umberto born 1932, Italian semiologist and writer. His novels include *The Name of the Rose* (1981) and *Foucault's Pendulum* (1988)

ecological (of a practice, policy, product, etc) tending to benefit or cause minimal damage to the environment

ecology 1 the study of the relationships between living organisms and their environment **2** the set of relationships of a particular organism with its environment

e-commerce *or* **ecommerce** business transactions conducted on the internet

economic 1 *Brit* capable of being produced, operated, etc, for profit; profitable **2** concerning or affecting material resources or welfare

economics the social science concerned with the production and consumption of goods and services and the analysis of the commercial activities of a society
▷http://economics.about.com
▷www.res.org.uk
▷http://allserv.rug.ac.be/~gdegeest

economist a specialist in economics

economy 1 a the complex of human activities concerned with the production, distribution, and consumption of goods and services **b** a particular type or branch of such production, distribution, and consumption **2** the management of the resources, finances, income, and expenditure of a community, business enterprise, etc. **3 a** a class of travel in aircraft, providing less luxurious accommodation than first class at a lower fare **b** (*as modifier*): *economy class* **4** *Philosophy* the principle that, of two competing theories, the one with less ontological presupposition is to be preferred

economy of scale *Economics* a fall in average costs resulting from an increase in the scale of production

ecosystem *Ecology* a system involving the interactions between a community of living organisms in a particular area and its nonliving environment

ecotourism tourism which is designed to contribute to the protection of the environment or at least minimize damage to it, often involving travel to areas of natural interest in developing countries or participation in environmental projects

ecru a greyish-yellow to a light greyish colour; the colour of unbleached linen

ecstasy 1 *Psychol* overpowering emotion characterized by loss of self-control and sometimes a temporary loss of consciousness: often associated with orgasm, religious mysticism, and the use of certain drugs **2** *Slang* 3,4-methylenedioxymethamphetamine; MDMA: a powerful drug that acts as a stimulant and can produce hallucinations

ectoplasm 1 *Cytology* the outer layer of cytoplasm in some cells, esp protozoa, which differs from the inner cytoplasm in being a clear gel **2** *Spiritualism* the substance supposedly emanating from the body of a medium during trances

Ecuador a republic in South America, on the Pacific: under the Incas when Spanish colonization began in 1532; gained independence in 1822; declared a republic in 1830. It consists chiefly of a coastal plain in the west, separated from the densely forested upper Amazon basin (Oriente) by ranges and plateaus of the Andes. Official language: Spanish; Quechua is also widely spoken. Religion: Roman Catholic majority. Currency: US dollar. Capital: Quito. Pop: 13 193 000 (2004 est). Area: 283 560 sq km (109 483 sq miles)

ecumenical, oecumenical, ecumenic *or* **oecumenic 1** of or relating to the Christian Church throughout the world, esp with regard to its unity **2 a** tending to promote unity among Churches **b** of or relating to the international movement initiated among non-Catholic Churches in 1910 aimed at Christian unity: embodied, since 1937, in the World Council of Churches
▷http://ecumenism.net/

eczema *Pathol* a skin inflammation with lesions that scale, crust, or ooze a serous fluid, often accompanied by intense itching or burning

Edam a town in the NW Netherlands, in North Holland province, on the IJsselmeer: cheese, light manufacturing. Pop: 28 000 (2003 est.; includes Volendam)

Eddington Sir Arthur Stanley 1882–1944, English astronomer and physicist, noted for his research on the motion, internal constitution, and luminosity of stars and for his elucidation of the theory of relativity

eddy a movement in a stream of air, water, or other fluid in which the current doubles back on itself causing a miniature whirlwind or whirlpool

Eddy Mary Baker 1821–1910, US religious leader; founder of the Christian Science movement (1866)

Eddystone Rocks a dangerous group of rocks at the W end of the English Channel, southwest of Plymouth: lighthouse

Ede a city in the central Netherlands, in Gelderland province. Pop: 105 000 (2003 est)

Edelman Gerald Maurice born 1929, US biochemist: he shared the Nobel prize for physiology or medicine (1972) with Rodney Porter for determining the structure of antibodies

edelweiss a small alpine flowering plant, *Leontopodium alpinum*, having white woolly oblong leaves and a tuft of attractive floral leaves surrounding the flowers: family *Asteraceae* (composites)

Eden¹ Sir (Robert) Anthony, Earl of Avon. 1897–1977, British Conservative statesman; foreign secretary (1935–38; 1940–45; 1951–55) and prime minister (1955–57). He resigned after the controversy caused by the occupation of the Suez Canal zone by British and French forces (1956)

Eden² *Old Testament* the garden in which Adam and Eve

were placed at the Creation

edentate any of the placental mammals that constitute the order *Edentata*, which inhabit tropical regions
of Central and South America. The order includes
anteaters, sloths, and armadillos

Edessa 1 an ancient city on the N edge of the Syrian
plateau, founded as a Macedonian colony by Seleucus I:
a centre of early Christianity 2 a market town in
Greece: ancient capital of Macedonia. Pop: 15 980 (latest
est)

Edgar 1 944–975 AD, king of Mercia and Northumbria
(957–975) and of England (959–975) 2 ?1074–1107, king of
Scotland (1097–1107), fourth son of Malcolm III. He overthrew his uncle Donald to gain the throne 3 **David** born
1948, British dramatist, noted for political plays such as
Destiny (1976), *Maydays* (1983), and *Albert Speer* (1999): he
adapted (1980) *Nicholas Nickleby* and (1991) *Dr Jekyll and Mr
Hyde* for the RSC

Edgar Atheling ?1050–?1125, grandson of Edmund II;
Anglo-Saxon pretender to the English throne in 1066

edge *Maths* **a** a line along which two faces or surfaces of
a solid meet **b** a line joining two vertices of a graph

Edgehill a ridge in S Warwickshire: site of the indecisive
first battle between Charles I and the Parliamentarians
(1642) in the Civil War

Edgeworth Maria 1767–1849, Anglo-Irish novelist: her
works include *Castle Rackrent* (1800) and *The Absentee*
(1812)

edgy *Art* (of paintings, drawings, etc) excessively
defined

edict a decree, order, or ordinance issued by a sovereign,
state, or any other holder of authority

Edinburgh¹ Duke of, title of Prince *Philip Mountbatten*.
born 1921, husband of Elizabeth II of Great Britain and
Northern Ireland

Edinburgh² 1 the capital of Scotland and seat of the
Scottish Parliament (from 1999), in City of Edinburgh
council area on the S side of the Firth of Forth: became
the capital in the 15th century; castle; three universities (including University of Edinburgh,1583); commercial and cultural centre, noted for its annual festival.
Pop: 430 082 (2001) 2 **City of** a council area in central
Scotland, created from part of Lothian region in 1996.
Pop: 448 370 (2003 est). Area: 262 sq km (101 sq miles)

Edirne a city in NW Turkey: a Thracian town, rebuilt and
renamed by the Roman emperor Hadrian. Pop: 126 000
(2005 est)

Edison Thomas Alva 1847–1931, US inventor. He patented
more than a thousand inventions, including the
phonograph, the incandescent electric lamp, the
microphone, and the kinetoscope

editor 1 *Films* **a** a person who makes a selection and
arrangement of individual shots in order to construct
the flowing sequence of images for a film **b** a device for
editing film, including a viewer and a splicer 2 a computer program that facilitates the deletion or insertion
of data within information already stored in a computer

Edmonton a city in W Canada, capital of Alberta: oil
industry. Pop: 782 101 (2001)

Edmund Saint, also called *Saint Edmund Rich*. 1175–1240,
English churchman: archbishop of Canterbury

(1234–40). Feast day: Nov 16.

Edmund I ?922–946 AD, king of England (940–946)

Edmund II called *Edmund Ironside*. ?980–1016, king of
England in 1016. His succession was contested by
Canute and they divided the kingdom between them

education 1 the act or process of acquiring knowledge,
esp systematically during childhood and adolescence 2
the knowledge or training acquired by this process 3
the act or process of imparting knowledge, esp at a
school, college, or university 4 the theory of teaching
and learning 5 a particular kind of instruction or training

▷www.dfes.gov.uk/index.htm
▷www.sosig.ac.uk/education
▷http://canada.gc.ca/azind/eindex_e.html
▷www.fed.gov.au/KSP
▷www.minedu.govt.nz
▷http://education.pwv.gov.za/

Edward¹ 1 known as *the Black Prince*. 1330–76, Prince of
Wales, the son of Edward III of England. He won victo-
ries over the French at Crécy (1346) and Poitiers (1356) in
the Hundred Years' War 2 **Prince** born 1964, Earl of
Wessex, third son of Elizabeth II of Great Britain and
Northern Ireland. In 1999 he married Sophie Rhys-
Jones (born 1965); their daughter Louise was born in
2003

Edward² Lake a lake in central Africa, between Uganda
and the Democratic Republic of Congo (formerly Zaïre)
in the Great Rift Valley: empties through the Semliki
River into Lake Albert. Area: about 2150 sq km (830 sq
miles)

Edward I 1239–1307, king of England (1272–1307); son of
Henry III. He conquered Wales (1284) but failed to sub-
due Scotland

Edwardian denoting, relating to, or having the style of
life, architecture, dress, etc, current in Britain during
the reign (1901–10) of Edward VII (1841–1910)

Edward II 1284–1327, king of England (1307–27); son of
Edward I. He invaded Scotland but was defeated by
Robert Bruce at Bannockburn (1314). He was deposed by
his wife Isabella and Roger Mortimer; died in prison

Edward III 1312–77, king of England (1327–77); son of
Edward II. His claim to the French throne in right of his
mother Isabella provoked the Hundred Years' War (1337)

Edward IV 1442–83, king of England (1461–70; 1471–83);
son of Richard, duke of York. He defeated Henry VI in
the Wars of the Roses and became king (1461). In 1470
Henry was restored to the throne, but Edward recovered the crown by his victory at Tewkesbury

Edward V 1470–?83, king of England in 1483; son of
Edward IV. He was deposed by his uncle, Richard, Duke
of Gloucester (Richard III), and is thought to have been
murdered with his brother in the Tower of London

Edward VI 1537–53, king of England (1547–53), son of
Henry VIII and Jane Seymour. His uncle the Duke of
Somerset was regent until 1552, when he was executed.
Edward then came under the control of Dudley, Duke of
Northumberland

Edward VII 1841–1910, king of Great Britain and Ireland
(1901–10); son of Queen Victoria

Edward VIII 1894–1972, king of Great Britain and Ireland
in 1936; son of George V and brother of George VI. He

abdicated in order to marry an American divorcée, Mrs Wallis Simpson (1896–1986); created Duke of Windsor (1937)

Edwards 1 Gareth (Owen). born 1947, Welsh Rugby Union footballer: halfback for Wales (1967–78) and the British Lions (1968–74) **2 Jonathan** 1703–58, American Calvinist theologian and metaphysician; author of *The Freedom of the Will* (1754) **3 Jonathan** born 1966, British athlete: gold medallist in the Olympic triple jump (2000)

Edward the Confessor Saint ?1002–66, king of England (1042–66); son of Ethelred II; founder of Westminster Abbey. Feast day: Oct 13

Edward the Elder died 924 AD, king of England (899–924), son of Alfred the Great

Edward the Martyr Saint ?963–978 AD, king of England (975–78), son of Edgar: murdered. Feast day: March 18

Edwin ?585–633 AD, king of Northumbria (617–633) and overlord of all England except Kent

eel 1 any teleost fish of the order *Apodes* (or *Anguilliformes*), such as the European freshwater species *Anguilla anguilla*, having a long snakelike body, a smooth slimy skin, and reduced fins **2** any of various other animals with a long body and smooth skin, such as the mud eel and the electric eel

effective *Physics* (of an alternating quantity) having a value that is the square root of the mean of the squares of the magnitude measured at each instant over a defined period of time, usually one cycle

effectual (of documents, agreements, etc) having legal force

effervescent (of a liquid) giving off bubbles of gas; bubbling

effete (of animals or plants) no longer capable of reproduction

efficient *Philosophy* producing a direct effect; causative

effigy *Art* a portrait of a person, esp as a monument or architectural decoration

efflorescence 1 *Chem, Geology* **a** the process of efflorescing **b** the powdery substance formed as a result of this process, esp on the surface of rocks **2** any skin rash or eruption

effluent 1 liquid discharged as waste, as from an industrial plant or sewage works **2** radioactive waste released from a nuclear power station **3** a stream that flows out of another body of water

effort *Physics* an applied force acting against inertia

effusion 1 the flow of a gas through a small aperture under pressure, esp when the density is such that the mean distance between molecules is large compared to the diameter of the aperture **2** *Med* **a** the escape of blood or other fluid into a body cavity or tissue **b** the fluid that has escaped

effusive (of rock) formed by the solidification of magma

EFTA European Free Trade Association; established in 1960 to eliminate trade tariffs on industrial products; now comprises Norway, Switzerland, Iceland, and Liechtenstein. Free trade was established between EFTA and the EC (now EU) in 1984. In 1994 EFTA (excluding Switzerland) and the EU together created the European Economic Area (EEA)
▷www.efta.int

EFTPOS electronic funds transfer at point of sale

egalitarian of, relating to, or upholding the doctrine of the equality of mankind and the desirability of political, social, and economic equality

Egbert ?775–839 AD, king of Wessex (802–839); first overlord of all England (829–830)

Eger 1 a city in N central Hungary. Pop: 56 696 (2003 est) **2** the German name for **Cheb**

egg 1 the oval or round reproductive body laid by the females of birds, reptiles, fishes, and some other animals, consisting of a developing embryo, its food store, and sometimes jelly or albumen, all surrounded by an outer shell or membrane **2** any female gamete; ovum

eggplant 1 a tropical Old World solanaceous plant, *Solanum melongena*, widely cultivated for its egg-shaped typically dark purple fruit **2** the fruit of this plant, which is cooked and eaten as a vegetable

eggshell 1 the hard porous protective outer layer of a bird's egg, consisting of calcite and protein **2** a yellowish-white colour **3** (of paint) having a very slight sheen **4** of a yellowish-white colour

Egham a town in S England, in N Surrey on the River Thames. Pop: 27 666 (2001)

Egmont¹ Lamoral, Count of Egmont, Prince of Gavre. 1522–68, Flemish statesman and soldier. He attempted to secure limited reforms and religious tolerance in the Spanish government of the Netherlands, refused to join William the Silent's rebellion, but was nevertheless executed for treason by the Duke of Alva

Egmont² an extinct volcano in New Zealand, in W central North Island in the **Egmont National Park**: an almost perfect cone. Height: 2518 m (8261 ft)

ego *Psychoanal* the conscious mind, based on perception of the environment from birth onwards: responsible for modifying the antisocial instincts of the id and itself modified by the conscience (superego)

egocentric *Philosophy* pertaining to a theory in which everything is considered in relation to the self

egomania *Psychiatry* **1** obsessive love for oneself and regard for one's own needs **2** any action dictated by this point of view

egret any of various wading birds of the genera *Egretta*, *Hydranassa*, etc, that are similar to herons but usually have a white plumage and, in the breeding season, long feathery plumes: family *Ardeidae*, order *Ciconiiformes*

Egypt a republic in NE Africa, on the Mediterranean and Red Sea: its history dates back about 5000 years. Occupied by the British from 1882, it became an independent kingdom in 1922 and a republic in 1953. Over 96 per cent of the total area is desert, with the chief areas of habitation and cultivation in the Nile delta and valley. Cotton is the main export. Official language: Arabic. Official religion: Muslim; Sunni majority. Currency: pound. Capital: Cairo. Pop: 73 389 000 (2004 est). Area: 997 739 sq km (385 229 sq miles)

Egyptian 1 of, relating to, or characteristic of Egypt, its inhabitants, or their dialect of Arabic **2** of, relating to, or characteristic of the ancient Egyptians, their language, or culture **3** *Archaic* of or relating to the Gypsies **4** a member of an indigenous non-Semitic people who established an advanced civilization in Egypt that flourished from the late fourth millennium BC 5 the extinct language of the ancient Egyptians, belonging to the Afro-Asiatic family of languages. It is recorded in hieroglyphic inscriptions, the earliest of which date from before 3000 BC. It was extinct by the fourth century AD

Egyptology the study of the archaeology and language of ancient Egypt

Ehrenburg or **Erenburg** Ilya Grigorievich 1891–1967, Soviet novelist and journalist. His novel *The Thaw* (1954) was the first published in the Soviet Union to deal with repression under Stalin

Ehrlich Paul 1854–1915, German bacteriologist, noted for his pioneering work in immunology and chemotherapy and for his discovery of a remedy for syphilis: Nobel prize for physiology or medicine 1908

Eichler August Wilhelm 1839–87, German botanist: devised the system on which modern plant classification is based

Eichmann Karl Adolf 1902–62, Austrian Nazi official, who took a leading role in organizing the extermination of the European Jews. He escaped to Argentina after World War II, but was captured and executed in Israel as a war criminal

eider or **eider duck** any of several sea ducks of the genus *Somateria*, esp *S. mollissima*, and related genera, which occur in the N hemisphere. The male has black and white plumage, and the female is the source of eiderdown

eiderdown 1 the breast down of the female eider duck, with which it lines the nest, used for stuffing pillows, quilts, etc. 2 US a warm cotton fabric having a woollen nap

Eid-ul-Adha an annual Muslim festival marking the end of the pilgrimage to Mecca. Animals are sacrificed and their meat shared among the poor

Eid-ul-Fitr an annual Muslim festival marking the end of Ramadan, involving the exchange of gifts and a festive meal

Eifel a plateau region in W Germany, between the River Moselle and the Belgian frontier: quarrying

Eiffel Alexandre Gustave 1832–1923, French engineer

Eiffel Tower a tower in Paris: designed by A. G. Eiffel; erected for the 1889 Paris Exposition. Height: 300 m (984 ft), raised in 1959 to 321 m (1052 ft)

Eigen Manfred born 1927, German physical chemist: shared the Nobel prize for chemistry (1967) for developing his relaxation technique for studying fast reactions

Eiger a mountain in central Switzerland, in the Bernese Alps. Height: 3970 m (13 025 ft)

eight 1 the cardinal number that is the sum of one and seven and the product of two and four 2 a numeral, 8, VIII, etc, representing this number 3 *Music* the numeral 8 used as the lower figure in a time signature to indicate that the beat is measured in quavers 4 the amount or quantity that is one greater than seven 5 *Rowing* a a racing shell propelled by eight oarsmen b the crew of such a shell

eighteen 1 the cardinal number that is the sum of ten and eight and the product of two and nine 2 a numeral, 18, XVIII, etc, representing this number 3 the amount or quantity that is eight more than ten 4 a

team of 18 players in Australian Rules football

eightfold 1 equal to or having eight times as many or as much 2 composed of eight parts

eightsome reel a Scottish dance for eight people

eighty 1 the cardinal number that is the product of ten and eight 2 a numeral, 80, LXXX, etc, representing this number 3 the numbers 80-89, esp a person's age or the year of a particular century 4 the amount or quantity that is eighty times as big as ten

Eilat, Elat, or **Elath** a port in S Israel, on the Gulf of Aqaba: Israel's only outlet to the Red Sea. Pop: 43 500 (2003 est)

Eindhoven a city in the SE Netherlands, in North Brabant province: radio and electrical industry. Pop: 206 000 (2003 est)

Einstein Albert 1879–1955, US physicist and mathematician, born in Germany. He formulated the special theory of relativity (1905) and the general theory of relativity (1916), and made major contributions to the quantum theory, for which he was awarded the Nobel prize for physics in 1921. He was noted also for his work for world peace

einsteinium a metallic transuranic element artificially produced from plutonium. Symbol: Es; atomic no.: 99; half-life of most stable isotope, ^{252}Es: 276 days

Einthoven Willem 1860–1927, Dutch physiologist. A pioneer of electrocardiography, he was awarded the Nobel prize for physiology or medicine in 1924

Eire 1 the Irish Gaelic name for **Ireland**: often used to mean the Republic of Ireland 2 a former name for the **Republic of Ireland** (1937–49)

Eisenach a city in central Germany, in Thuringia: birthplace of Johann Sebastian Bach. Pop: 44 081 (2003 est)

Eisenhower Dwight David, known as *Ike*. 1890–1969, US general and Republican statesman; Supreme Commander of the Allied Expeditionary Force (1943–45) and 34th president of the US (1953–61). He commanded Allied forces in Europe and North Africa (1942), directed the invasion of Italy (1943), and was Supreme Commander of the combined land forces of NATO (1950–52)

Eisenstadt a town in E Austria, capital of Burgenland province: Hungarian until 1921. Pop: 11 334 (2001)

Eisenstein Sergei Mikhailovich 1898–1948, Soviet film director. His films include *Battleship Potemkin* (1925), *Alexander Nevsky* (1938), and *Ivan the Terrible* (1944)

Ekman Vagn Walfrid 1874–1954, Swedish oceanographer: discoverer of the **Ekman Spiral** (a complex interaction on the surface of the sea between wind, rotation of the earth, and friction forces) and the **Ekman layer** (the thin top layer of the sea that flows at 90° to the wind direction)

El Alamein or **Alamein** a village on the N coast of Egypt, about 112 km (70 miles) west of Alexandria: scene of a decisive Allied victory over the Axis forces (1942)

Elam an ancient kingdom east of the River Tigris: established before 4000 BC; probably inhabited by a non-Semitic people

eland 1 a large spiral-horned antelope, *Taurotragus oryx*, inhabiting bushland in eastern and southern Africa. It has a dewlap and a hump on the shoulders and is light brown with vertical white stripes 2 **giant eland** a similar but larger animal, *T. derbianus*, living in wooded areas of central and W Africa

elastane a synthetic fibre characterized by its ability to revert to its original shape after being stretched

elastic 1 (of a body or material) capable of returning to its original shape after compression, expansion, stretching, or other deformation 2 (of gases) capable of expanding spontaneously 3 *Physics* (of collisions) involving no overall change in translational kinetic energy 4 made of elastic 5 tape, cord, or fabric containing interwoven strands of flexible rubber or similar substance allowing it to stretch and return to its original shape 6 *Chiefly US and Canadian* something made of elastic, such as a rubber band or a garter

Elba a mountainous island off the W coast of Italy, in the Mediterranean: Napoleon Bonaparte's first place of exile (1814–15). Pop: 27 722 (1991 est). Area: 223 sq km (86 sq miles)

Elbe a river in central Europe, rising in the N Czech Republic and flowing generally northwest through Germany to the North Sea at Hamburg. Length: 1165 km (724 miles)

Elbert **Mount** a mountain in central Colorado, in the Sawatch range. Height: 4399 m (14 431 ft)

Elblag a port in N Poland: metallurgical industries. Pop: 129 000 (2005 est)

elbow 1 the joint between the upper arm and the forearm, formed by the junction of the radius and ulna with the humerus 2 the corresponding joint or bone of birds or mammals

Elbrus a mountain in SW Russia, on the border with Georgia, in the Caucasus Mountains, with two extinct volcanic peaks: the highest mountain in Europe. Height: 5642 m (18 510 ft)

El Capitan a mountain in E central California, in the Sierra Nevada: a monolith with a precipice rising over 1100 m (3600 ft) above the floor of the Yosemite Valley. Height: 2306 m (7564 ft)

Elche a town in S Spain, in Valencia: noted for Iberian and Roman archaeological finds and the medieval religious drama performed there annually: fruit growing, esp dates, pomegranates, figs. Pop: 207 163 (2003 est)

elder[1] 1 (in piquet and similar card games) denoting or relating to the nondealer (the **elder hand**), who has certain advantages in the play 2 *Anthropol* a senior member of a tribe who has influence or authority 3 (in certain Protestant Churches) a lay office having teaching, pastoral, or administrative functions 4 another word for **presbyter**

elder[2] 1 any of various caprifoliaceous shrubs or small trees of the genus *Sambucus*, having clusters of small white flowers and red, purple, or black berry-like fruits 2 any of various unrelated plants, such as box elder and marsh elder

Elder **Mark Philip** born 1947, British conductor; musical director of the English National Opera (1979–93) and of the Hallé Orchestra from 2000

elderberry 1 the berry-like fruit of the elder, used for making wines, jellies, etc. 2 another name for **elder**

El Dorado a fabled city in South America, rich in treasure and sought by Spanish explorers in the 16th century

Elea (in ancient Italy) a Greek colony on the Tyrrhenian coast of Lucana

Eleanor of Aquitaine ?1122–1204, queen of France (1137–52) by her marriage to Louis VII and queen of England (1154–89) by her marriage to Henry II; mother of the English kings Richard I and John

Eleanor of Castile 1246–90, Spanish wife of Edward I of England. **Eleanor Crosses** were erected at each place at which her body rested between Nottingham, where she died, and London, where she is buried

elect 1 voted into office but not yet installed 2 *Christianity* **a** selected or predestined by God to receive salvation; chosen **b** (*as collective noun; preceded by the*): *the elect*

election 1 the selection by vote of a person or persons from among candidates for a position, esp a political office 2 *Christianity* **a** the doctrine of Calvin that God chooses certain individuals for salvation without reference to their faith or works **b** the doctrine of Arminius and others that God chooses for salvation those who, by grace, persevere in faith and works

▷www.electionworld.org/
▷www.ifes.org/eguide/elecguide.htm

elective 1 of or based on selection by vote 2 selected by vote 3 having the power to elect 4 open to choice; optional 5 an optional course or hospital placement undertaken by a medical student

elector 1 someone who is eligible to vote in the election of a government 2 a member of the US electoral college 3 (in the Holy Roman Empire) any of the German princes entitled to take part in the election of a new emperor

electorate 1 the body of all qualified voters 2 *History* the rank, position, or territory of an elector of the Holy Roman Empire 3 *Austral and NZ* the area represented by a Member of Parliament

electric 1 of, derived from, produced by, producing, transmitting, or powered by electricity 2 (of a musical instrument) amplified electronically

electrical of, relating to, or concerned with electricity

electrical engineering the branch of engineering concerned with the practical applications of electricity

▷http://webdiee.cem.itesm.mx/wwwvlee

electric blanket a blanket that contains an electric heating element, used to warm a bed

electric eel an eel-like freshwater cyprinoid fish, *Electrophorus electricus*, of N South America, having electric organs in the body: family *Electrophoridae*

electric field a field of force surrounding a charged particle within which another charged particle experiences a force

electric guitar an electrically amplified guitar, used mainly in pop music

electricity 1 any phenomenon associated with stationary or moving electrons, ions, or other charged particles 2 the science concerned with electricity 3 an electric current or charge

electric shock the physiological reaction, characterized by pain and muscular spasm, to the passage of an electric current through the body. It can affect the respiratory system and heart rhythm

electrocardiograph an instrument for recording the

electrical activity of the heart

electrode 1 a conductor through which an electric current enters or leaves an electrolyte, an electric arc, or an electronic valve or tube 2 an element in a semiconducting device that emits, collects, or controls the movement of electrons or holes

electrodynamics the branch of physics concerned with the interactions between electrical and mechanical forces

electroencephalograph an instrument for recording the electrical activity of the brain, usually by means of electrodes placed on the scalp: used to diagnose tumours of the brain, to study brain waves, etc.

electrolysis 1 the conduction of electricity by a solution or melt, esp the use of this process to induce chemical changes 2 the destruction of living tissue, such as hair roots, by an electric current, usually for cosmetic reasons

electrolyte 1 a solution or molten substance that conducts electricity 2 **a** a chemical compound that dissociates in solution into ions **b** any of the ions themselves

electromagnet a magnet consisting of an iron or steel core wound with a coil of wire, through which a current is passed

electromagnetic 1 of, containing, or operated by an electromagnet 2 of, relating to, or consisting of electromagnetism 3 of or relating to electromagnetic radiation

electromagnetism 1 magnetism produced by an electric current 2 the branch of physics concerned with magnetism produced by electric currents and with the interaction of electric and magnetic fields

electromotive of, concerned with, producing, or tending to produce an electric current

electromotive force *Physics* **a** a source of energy that can cause a current to flow in an electrical circuit or device **b** the rate at which energy is drawn from this source when unit current flows through the circuit or device, measured in volts.

electron a stable elementary particle present in all atoms, orbiting the nucleus in numbers equal to the atomic number of the element in the neutral atom; a lepton with a negative charge of $1.602\ 176\ 462 \times 10^{-19}$ coulomb, a rest mass of $9.109\ 381\ 88 \times 10^{-31}$ kilogram, a radius of $2.817\ 940\ 285 \times 10^{-15}$ metre, and a spin of ½

electronegative 1 having a negative electric charge 2 (of an atom, group, molecule, etc) tending to gain or attract electrons and form negative ions or polarized bonds

electronic 1 of, concerned with, using, or operated by devices in which electrons are conducted through a semiconductor, free space, or gas 2 of or concerned with electronics 3 of or concerned with electrons or an electron 4 involving or concerned with the representation, storage, or transmission of information by electronic systems

electronics 1 the science and technology concerned with the development, behaviour, and applications of electronic devices and circuits 2 the circuits and devices of a piece of electronic equipment

▷www.eskimo.com/~billb/amateur/elehob.html

▷http://webdiee.cem.itesm.mx/wwwvlee
▷www.eetuk.com

electron microscope a powerful type of microscope that uses electrons, rather than light, and electron lenses to produce a magnified image

electronvolt a unit of energy equal to the work done on an electron accelerated through a potential difference of 1 volt. 1 electronvolt is equivalent to 1.602×10^{-19} joule.

electroplate coated with metal by electrolysis; electroplated

electropositive 1 having a positive electric charge 2 (of an atom, group, molecule, etc) tending to release electrons and form positive ions or polarized bonds

electrostatics the branch of physics concerned with static charges and the electrostatic field

elegiac 1 resembling, characteristic of, relating to, or appropriate to an elegy 2 denoting or written in elegiac couplets or elegiac stanzas 3 an elegiac couplet or stanza

elegy 1 a mournful or plaintive poem or song, esp a lament for the dead 2 poetry or a poem written in elegiac couplets or stanzas

element 1 any of the 118 known substances (of which 93 occur naturally) that consist of atoms with the same number of protons in their nuclei 2 the most favourable environment for an animal or plant 3 the resistance wire and its former that constitute the electrical heater in a cooker, heater, etc. 4 *Electronics* another name for **component** 5 one of the four substances thought in ancient and medieval cosmology to constitute the universe (earth, air, water, or fire) 6 atmospheric conditions or forces, esp wind, rain, and cold 7 *Geometry* a point, line, plane, or part of a geometric figure 8 *Maths* **a** any of the terms in a determinant or matrix **b** one of the infinitesimally small quantities summed by an integral, often represented by the expression following the integral sign 9 *Maths, Logic* one of the objects or numbers that together constitute a set 10 *Christianity* the bread or wine consecrated in the Eucharist 11 *Astronomy* any of the numerical quantities, such as the major axis or eccentricity, used in describing the orbit of a planet, satellite, etc. 12 *Physics* a component of a compound lens

elemental 1 of or relating to atmospheric forces, esp wind, rain, and cold 2 of, relating to, or denoting a chemical element 3 *Rare* a spirit or force that is said to appear in physical form

elementary 1 *Maths* (of a function) having the form of an algebraic, exponential, trigonometric, or a logarithmic function, or any combination of these 2 *Chem* another word for **elemental**

elementary particle any of several entities, such as electrons, neutrons, or protons, that are less complex than atoms and are regarded as the constituents of all matter

elementary school 1 *Brit* a former name for **primary school** 2 *US and Canadian* a state school in which instruction is given for the first six to eight years of a child's education

elephant either of the two proboscidean mammals of the family *Elephantidae*. The **African elephant** (*Loxodonta* *africana*) is the larger species, with large flapping ears and a less humped back than the **Indian elephant** (*Elephas maximus*), of S and SE Asia

elephantiasis *Pathol* a complication of chronic filariasis, in which nematode worms block the lymphatic vessels, usually in the legs or scrotum, causing extreme enlargement of the affected area

Eleusis a town in Greece, in Attica about 23 km (14 miles) west of Athens, of which it is now an industrial suburb

elevation 1 a drawing to scale of the external face of a building or structure 2 the external face of a building or structure 3 a ballet dancer's ability to leap high 4 *RC Church* the lifting up of the Host at Mass for adoration 5 *Astronomy* another name for **altitude**

elevator 1 *Chiefly US* a mechanical hoist for raising something, esp grain or coal, often consisting of a chain of scoops linked together on a conveyor belt 2 *chiefly US and Canadian* a platform, compartment, or cage raised or lowered in a vertical shaft to transport persons or goods in a building 3 any muscle that raises a part of the body 4 a surgical instrument for lifting a part of the body 5 a control surface on the tailplane of an aircraft, for making it climb or descend

eleven 1 the cardinal number that is the sum of ten and one 2 a numeral 11, XI, etc, representing this number 3 a team of 11 players in football, cricket, hockey, etc.

eleven-plus (esp formerly) an examination, taken by children aged 11 or 12, that determines the type of secondary education a child will be given

elf (in folklore) one of a kind of legendary beings, usually characterized as small, manlike, and mischievous

El Ferrol a port in NW Spain, on the Atlantic: fortified naval base, with a deep natural harbour. Pop: 78 764 (2003 est)

Elgar Sir **Edward (William)**. 1857–1934, English composer, whose works include the *Enigma Variations* (1899), the oratorio *The Dream of Gerontius* (1900), two symphonies, a cello concerto, and a violin concerto

Elgin a market town in NE Scotland, the administrative centre of Moray, on the River Lossie: ruined 13th-century cathedral: distilling, engineering. Pop: 20 829 (2001)

Elgon Mount an extinct volcano in E Africa, on the Kenya-Uganda border. Height: 4321m (14 178 ft)

El Greco real name *Domenikos Theotocopoulos*. 1541–1614, Spanish painter, born in Crete; noted for his elongated human forms and dramatic use of colour

Eli *Old Testament* the highest priest at Shiloh and teacher of Samuel (I Samuel 1–3)

Elia *or* **Eleia** a department of SW Greece, in the W Peloponnese: in ancient times most of the region formed the state of Elis. Pop: 183 521 (2001). Area: 2681 sq km (1035 sq miles)

Elijah *Old Testament* a Hebrew prophet of the 9th century BC, who was persecuted for denouncing Ahab and Jezebel. (I Kings 17–21: 21; II Kings 1–2:18)

Eliot 1 **George**, real name *Mary Ann Evans*. 1819–80, English novelist, noted for her analysis of provincial Victorian society. Her best-known novels include *Adam Bede* (1859), *The Mill on the Floss* (1860), *Silas Marner* (1861), and *Middlemarch* (1872) 2 Sir **John** 1592–1632, English statesman, a leader of parliamentary opposition to Charles I 3 **T(homas) S(tearns)**. 1888–1965, British poet,

dramatist, and critic, born in the US His poetry includes *Prufrock and Other Observations* (1917), *The Waste Land* (1922), *Ash Wednesday* (1930), and *Four Quartets* (1943). Among his verse plays are *Murder in the Cathedral* (1935), *The Family Reunion* (1939), *The Cocktail Party* (1950), and *The Confidential Clerk* (1954): Nobel prize for literature 1948

Elis an ancient city-state of SW Greece, in the NW Peloponnese: site of the ancient Olympic games

Elisha *Old Testament* a Hebrew prophet of the 9th century BC: successor of Elijah (II Kings 3–9)

elitism *Politics* the belief that society should be governed by a select group of gifted and highly educated individuals

elixir 1 an alchemical preparation supposed to be capable of prolonging life indefinitely (**elixir of life**) or of transmuting base metals into gold 2 a liquid containing a medicinal drug with syrup, glycerine, or alcohol added to mask its unpleasant taste

Elizabeth¹ 1 Saint *New Testament* the wife of Zacharias, mother of John the Baptist, and kinswoman of the Virgin Mary. Feast day: Nov 5 or 8 2 pen name *Carmen Sylva*. 1843–1916, queen of Romania (1881–1914) and author 3 Russian name *Yelizaveta Petrovna*. 1709–62, empress of Russia (1741–62); daughter of Peter the Great 4 title *the Queen Mother*; original name Lady *Elizabeth Bowes-Lyon*. 1900–2002, queen of Great Britain and Northern Ireland (1936–52) as the wife of George VI; mother of Elizabeth II

Elizabeth² 1 a city in NE New Jersey, on Newark Bay. Pop: 123 215 (2003 est) 2 a town in SE South Australia, near Adelaide. Pop: 34 000 (latest est)

Elizabethan 1 of, characteristic of, or relating to England or its culture in the age of Elizabeth I (1533–1603; reigned 1558–1603) or to the United Kingdom or its culture in the age of Elizabeth II (born 1926; queen from 1952) 2 of, relating to, or designating a style of architecture used in England during the reign of Elizabeth I, characterized by moulded and sculptured ornament based on German and Flemish models

Elizabeth I 1533–1603, queen of England (1558–1603); daughter of Henry VIII and Anne Boleyn. She established the Church of England (1559) and put an end to Catholic plots, notably by executing Mary Queen of Scots (1587) and defeating the Spanish Armada (1588). Her reign was notable for commercial growth, maritime expansion, and the flourishing of literature, music, and architecture

Elizabeth II born 1926, queen of Great Britain and Northern Ireland from 1952; daughter of George VI

Elizabeth of Hungary Saint 1207–31, Hungarian princess who devoted herself to charity and asceticism. Feast day: Nov 17 and 19

elk 1 a large deer, *Alces alces*, of N Europe and Asia, having large flattened palmate antlers: also occurs in North America, where it is called a moose 2 **American elk** another name for **wapiti**

Ellesmere Island a Canadian island in the Arctic Ocean: part of Nunavut; mountainous, with many glaciers. Area: 212 688 sq km (82 119 sq miles)

Ellesmere Port a port in NW England, in NW Cheshire on the Mersey estuary and Manchester Ship Canal. Pop: 66 265 (2001)

Ellington Duke, nickname of *Edward Kennedy Ellington*. 1899–1974, US jazz composer, pianist, and conductor, famous for such works as "Mood Indigo" and "Creole Love Call"

ellipse a closed conic section shaped like a flattened circle and formed by an inclined plane that does not cut the base of the cone. Standard equation $x^2/a^2 + y^2/b^2 = 1$, where $2a$ and $2b$ are the lengths of the major and minor axes. Area: πab

ellipsoid a geometric surface, symmetrical about the three coordinate axes, whose plane sections are ellipses or circles. Standard equation: $x^2/a^2 + y^2/b^2 + z^2/c^2 = 1$, where $\pm a$, $\pm b$, $\pm c$ are the intercepts on the x-, y-, and z-axes

elliptical of speech, literary style, etc **a** very condensed or concise, often so as to be obscure or ambiguous **b** circumlocutory or long-winded

Ellis 1 1814–90, English philologist: made the first systematic survey of the phonology of British dialects 2 (**Henry**) **Havelock** 1859–1939, English essayist: author of works on the psychology of sex

elm 1 any ulmaceous tree of the genus *Ulmus*, occurring in the N hemisphere, having serrated leaves and winged fruits (samaras): cultivated for shade, ornament, and timber 2 the hard heavy wood of this tree

El Minya a river port in central Egypt on the Nile. Pop: 225 000 (2005 est)

El Misti a volcano in S Peru, in the Andes. Height: 5852 m (19 199 ft)

El Obeid a city in the central Sudan, in Kordofan province: scene of the defeat of a British and Egyptian army by the Mahdi (1883). Pop: 423 000 (2005 est)

Elohim *Old Testament* a Hebrew word for God or gods

Elohist *Old Testament* the supposed author or authors of one of the four main strands of text of the Pentateuch, identified chiefly by the use of the word *Elohim* for God instead of YHVH (Jehovah)

El Paso a city in W Texas, on the Rio Grande opposite Ciudad Juárez, Mexico. Pop: 584 113 (2003 est)

El Salvador a republic in Central America, on the Pacific: colonized by the Spanish from 1524; declared independence in 1841, becoming a republic in 1856. It consists of coastal lowlands rising to a central plateau. Coffee constitutes over a third of the total exports. Official language: Spanish. Religion: Roman Catholic majority. Currency: US dollar. Capital: San Salvador. Pop: 6 614 000 (2004 est). Area: 21 393 sq km (8236 sq miles)

ELT English Language Teaching: the teaching of English specifically to students whose native language is not English

Elton 1 Ben(jamin) (**Charles**). born 1959, British comedian, scriptwriter, playwright, and novelist; his work includes the *Blackadder* series for television (1987–89), the play *Gasping* (1990), and the novel *High Society* (2002) 2 **Charles Sutherland** 1900–91, British zoologist: initiated the study of animal ecology

elver a young eel, esp one migrating up a river from the sea

Ely 1 a cathedral city in E England, in E Cambridgeshire on the River Ouse. Pop: 13 954 (2001) 2 a former county of E England, part of Cambridgeshire since 1965

Elysium *Greek myth* the dwelling place of the blessed after death

Elytis Odysseus, real name *Odysseus Alepoudelis*. 1912–96, Greek poet, author of the long poems *Axion Est* (1959) and *Maria Nefeli* (1978): Nobel prize for literature 1979

embankment a man-made ridge of earth or stone that carries a road or railway or confines a waterway

embargo 1 a government order prohibiting the departure or arrival of merchant ships in its ports 2 any legal stoppage of commerce

embassy 1 the residence or place of official business of an ambassador 2 an ambassador and his entourage collectively 3 the position, business, or mission of an ambassador

emblem an allegorical picture containing a moral lesson, often with an explanatory motto or verses, esp one printed in an **emblem book**

embolism 1 the occlusion of a blood vessel by an embolus 2 *Botany* the blocking of a xylem vessel by an air bubble 3 *RC Church* a prayer inserted in the canon of the Mass between the Lord's Prayer and the breaking of the bread 4 another name (not in technical use) for **embolus**

embolus material, such as part of a blood clot or an air bubble, that is transported by the blood stream until it becomes lodged within a small vessel and impedes the circulation

embrasure an opening forming a door or window, having splayed sides that increase the width of the opening in the interior

embrocation a drug or agent for rubbing into the skin; liniment

embryo 1 an animal in the early stages of development following cleavage of the zygote and ending at birth or hatching 2 a plant in the early stages of development: in higher plants, the plumule, cotyledons, and radicle within the seed

embryology 1 the branch of science concerned with the study of embryos 2 the structure and development of the embryo of a particular organism

embryonic *or* **embryonal** of or relating to an embryo

Emden a port in NW Germany, in Lower Saxony at the mouth of the River Ems. Pop: 51 445 (2003 est)

emerald 1 a green transparent variety of beryl: highly valued as a gem 2 **a** the clear green colour of an emerald **b** (*as adjective*): *an emerald carpet*

emergency **a** a patient requiring urgent treatment **b** (*as modifier*): *an emergency ward*

Emerson Ralph Waldo 1803–82, US poet, essayist, and transcendentalist

emery **a** a hard greyish-black mineral consisting of corundum with either magnetite or haematite: used as an abrasive and polishing agent, esp as a coating on paper, cloth, etc. Formula: Al_2O_3 **b** (*as modifier*): *emery paper*

emetic 1 causing vomiting 2 an emetic agent or drug

Emilia-Romagna a region of N central Italy, on the Adriatic: rises from the plains of the Po valley in the north to the Apennines in the south. Capital: Bologna. Pop: 4 030 220 (2003 est). Area: 22 123 sq km (8628 sq miles)

Emin Tracey born 1963, British artist, noted for provocative multimedia works such as *Everyone I Have Ever Slept With* (1995) and *My Bed* (1999)

Eminem real name *Marshall Mathers III*. born 1972, US White rap performer noted for his controversial lyrics; recordings include *The Slim Shady LP* (1999) and *The Eminem Show* (2002); he also starred in the film *8 Mile* (2002)

eminence *Anatomy* a projection of an organ or part

Eminence *or* **Eminency** a title used to address or refer to a cardinal

emir in the Islamic world **1** an independent ruler or chieftain **2** a military commander or governor **3** a descendant of Mohammed

emissary 1 a an agent or messenger sent on a mission, esp one who represents a government or head of state **b** (*as modifier*): *an emissary delegation* **2** (of veins) draining blood from sinuses in the dura mater to veins outside the skull

emission 1 energy, in the form of heat, light, radio waves, etc, emitted from a source **2** a measure of the number of electrons emitted by a cathode or electron gun **3** *Physiol* any bodily discharge, esp an involuntary release of semen during sleep

Emmen a city in the NE Netherlands, in Drenthe province: a new town developed since World War II. Pop: 108 000 (2003 est)

Emmet **Robert** 1778–1803, Irish nationalist, executed for leading an uprising for Irish independence

emollient any preparation or substance that has a softening or soothing effect, esp when applied to the skin

Empedocles ?490–430 BC, Greek philosopher and scientist, who held that the world is composed of four elements, air, fire, earth, and water, which are governed by the opposing forces of love and discord

emperor 1 a monarch who rules or reigns over an empire **2** any of several large saturniid moths with eye-like markings on each wing, esp *Saturnia pavonia* of Europe

emperor penguin an Antarctic penguin, *Aptenodytes forsteri*, with orange-yellow patches on the neck: the largest penguin, reaching a height of 1.3 m (4 ft)

emphysema *Pathol* **1** a condition in which the air sacs of the lungs are grossly enlarged, causing breathlessness and wheezing **2** the abnormal presence of air in a tissue or part

empire 1 an aggregate of peoples and territories, often of great extent, under the rule of a single person, oligarchy, or sovereign state **2** any monarchy that for reasons of history, prestige, etc, has an emperor rather than a king as head of state **3** the period during which a particular empire exists **4** supreme power; sovereignty **5** a large industrial organization with many ramifications, esp a multinational corporation

Empire State nickname of New York (state)

empirical 1 (of medical treatment) based on practical experience rather than scientific proof **2** *Philosophy* **a** (of knowledge) derived from experience rather than by logic from first principles **b** (of a proposition) subject, at least theoretically, to verification **3** of or relating to medical quackery

empiricism 1 *Philosophy* the doctrine that all knowledge of matters of fact derives from experience and that the mind is not furnished with a set of concepts in advance of experience **2** medical quackery; charlatanism
▷http://www.utm.edu/research/iep/e/emp-brit.htm

emporium a large and often ostentatious retail shop offering for sale a wide variety of merchandise

empowerment *Politics* (in South Africa) a policy of providing special opportunities in employment, training, etc for Blacks and others disadvantaged under apartheid

empress 1 the wife or widow of an emperor **2** a woman who holds the rank of emperor in her own right

Empson Sir **William** 1906–84, English poet and critic; author of *Seven Types of Ambiguity* (1930)

empty 1 *Maths, Logic* (of a set or class) containing no members **2** *Philosophy, Logic* (of a name or description) having no reference

empyrean *Archaic* the highest part of the (supposedly spherical) heavens, thought in ancient times to contain the pure element of fire and by early Christians to be the abode of God and the angels

Ems *or* **Bad Ems 1** a town in W Germany, in the Rhineland-Palatinate: famous for the **Ems Telegram** (1870), Bismarck's dispatch that led to the outbreak of the Franco-Prussian War. Pop: 9666 (2003 est) **2** a river in W Germany, rising in the Teutoburger Wald and flowing generally north to the North Sea. Length: about 370 km (230 miles)

emu a large Australian flightless bird, *Dromaius novaehollandiae*, similar to the ostrich but with three-toed feet and grey or brown plumage: order *Casuariiformes*

emulsifier an agent that forms or preserves an emulsion, esp any food additive, such as lecithin, that prevents separation of sauces or other processed foods

emulsion 1 *Photog* a light-sensitive coating on a base, such as paper or film, consisting of fine grains of silver bromide suspended in gelatine **2** *Chem* a colloid in which both phases are liquids **3** a type of paint in which the pigment is suspended in a vehicle, usually a synthetic resin, that is dispersed in water as an emulsion. It usually gives a mat finish **4** *Pharmacol* a mixture in which an oily medicine is dispersed in another liquid

enabling act a legislative act conferring certain specified powers on a person or organization

enamel 1 a coloured glassy substance, translucent or opaque, fused to the surface of articles made of metal, glass, etc, for ornament or protection **2** an article or articles ornamented with enamel **3** an enamel-like paint or varnish **4** any smooth glossy coating resembling enamel **5** the hard white calcified substance that covers the crown of each tooth

encephalitis inflammation of the brain

encephalogram an X-ray photograph of the brain, esp one (a **pneumoencephalogram**) taken after replacing some of the cerebrospinal fluid with air or oxygen so that the brain cavities show clearly

enclave a part of a country entirely surrounded by foreign territory: viewed from the position of the surrounding territories

encomium a formal expression of praise; eulogy; panegyric

encumbrance or **incumbrance** Law a burden or charge upon property, such as a mortgage or lien

encyclical a letter sent by the pope to all Roman Catholic bishops throughout the world

end 1 Sport either of the two defended areas of a playing field, rink, etc. **2** Bowls, Curling a section of play from one side of the rink to the other **3** American football a player at the extremity of the playing line; wing

endangered Ecology in danger: used esp of animals in danger of extinction

endemic an endemic disease or plant

Enderby Land part of the coastal region of Antarctica, between Kemp Land and Queen Maud Land: the westernmost part of the Australian Antarctic Territory (claims are suspended under the Antarctic Treaty); discovered in 1831

endive a plant, Cichorium endivia, cultivated for its crisp curly leaves, which are used in salads: family Asteraceae (composites)

endocrine gland Med any of the glands that secrete hormones directly into the bloodstream, including the pituitary, pineal, thyroid, parathyroid, adrenal, testes, ovaries, and the pancreatic islets of Langerhans

endogenous Biology developing or originating within an organism or part of an organism

endometrium the mucous membrane that lines the uterus

endorphin any of a class of polypeptides, including enkephalin, occurring naturally in the brain, that bind to pain receptors and so block pain sensation

endoskeleton the internal skeleton of an animal, esp the bony or cartilaginous skeleton of vertebrates

endothermic or **endothermal** (of a chemical reaction or compound) occurring or formed with the absorption of heat

enema Med **1** the introduction of liquid into the rectum to evacuate the bowels, medicate, or nourish **2** the liquid so introduced

energy Physics **a** the capacity of a body or system to do work **b** a measure of this capacity, expressed as the work that it does in changing to some specified reference state. It is measured in joules (SI units).

Enesco Georges , original name George Enescu. 1881–1955, Romanian violinist and composer

Enfield a borough of Greater London: a N residential suburb. Pop: 280 300 (2003 est). Area: 55 sq km (31 sq miles)

Engadine the upper part of the valley of the River Inn in Switzerland, in Graubünden canton: tourist and winter sports centre

engaged Architect built against or attached to a wall or similar structure

Engels Friedrich 1820–95, German socialist leader and political philosopher, in England from 1849. He collaborated with Marx on The Communist Manifesto (1848) and his own works include Condition of the Working Classes in England (1844) and The Origin of the Family, Private Property and the State (1884)

engine 1 any machine designed to convert energy, esp heat energy, into mechanical work **2 a** a railway locomotive **b** (as modifier): the engine cab

engineer 1 a person trained in any branch of the profession of engineering **2** a mechanic; one who repairs or services machines **3** US and Canadian the driver of a railway locomotive **4** an officer responsible for a ship's engines

England the largest division of Great Britain, bordering on Scotland and Wales: unified in the mid-tenth century and conquered by the Normans in 1066; united with Wales in 1536 and Scotland in 1707; monarchy overthrown in 1649 but restored in 1660. Capital: London. Pop: 49 855 700 (2003 est). Area: 130 439 sq km (50 352 sq miles)

English 1 the official language of Britain, the US, most parts of the Commonwealth, and certain other countries. It is the native language of over 280 million people and is acquired as a second language by many more. It is an Indo-European language belonging to the West Germanic branch **2 the English** the natives or inhabitants of England collectively **3** the usual US and Canadian term for **side** (in billiards)

English Channel an arm of the Atlantic Ocean between S England and N France, linked with the North Sea by the Strait of Dover. Length: about 560 km (350 miles). Width: between 32 km (20 miles) and 161 km (100 miles)

engraving 1 the art of a person who engraves **2** a block, plate, or other surface that has been engraved

Eniwetok an atoll in the W Pacific Ocean, in the NW Marshall Islands: taken by the US from Japan in 1944; became a naval base and later a testing ground for atomic weapons. Pop: 715 (latest est)

enlightenment 1 Buddhism the awakening to ultimate truth by which man is freed from the endless cycle of personal reincarnations to which all men are otherwise subject **2** Hinduism a state of transcendent divine experience represented by Vishnu: regarded as a goal of all religion

Enlightenment Philosophy the an 18th-century philosophical movement stressing the importance of reason and the critical reappraisal of existing ideas and social institutions

Ennerdale Water a lake in NW England, in Cumbria in the Lake District. Length: 4 km (2.5 miles)

Ennis a town in the W Republic of Ireland, county town of Co. Clare. Pop: 22 051 (2002)

Enniskillen or formerly **Inniskilling** a town in SW Northern Ireland, in Fermanagh, on an island in the River Erne: scene of the defeat of James II's forces in 1689. Pop: 13 599 (2001)

Ennius Quintus 239–169 BC, Roman epic poet and dramatist

Enoch Old Testament **1** the eldest son of Cain after whom the first city was named (Genesis 4:17) **2** the father of Methuselah: said to have walked with God and to have been taken by God at the end of his earthly life (Genesis 5:24)

Enos Old Testament a son of Seth (Genesis 4:26; 5:6)

Enright D(ennis) J(oseph). 1920–2002, British poet, essayist, and editor

Enschede a city in the E Netherlands, in Overijssel province: a major centre of the Dutch cotton industry. Pop: 152 000 (2003 est)

ensemble 1 a the cast of a play other than the principals; supporting players **b** (as modifier): an ensemble role **2**

Music **a** a group of soloists singing or playing together **b** (*as modifier*): *an ensemble passage* **3** *Music* the degree of precision and unity exhibited by a group of instrumentalists or singers performing together **4** *Physics* **a** a set of systems (such as a set of collections of atoms) that are identical in all respects apart from the motions of their constituents **b** a single system (such as a collection of atoms) in which the properties are determined by the statistical behaviour of its constituents **5** (of a film or play) involving several separate but often interrelated story lines **6** involving no individual star but several actors whose roles are of equal importance

entablature *Architect* **1** the part of a classical temple above the columns, having an architrave, a frieze, and a cornice **2** any construction of similar form

entail *Property law* **a** the restriction imposed by entailing an estate **b** an estate that has been entailed

Entebbe a town in S Uganda, on Lake Victoria: British administrative centre of Uganda (1893–1958); international airport. Pop: 57 518 (2002 est)

entente **1** short for **entente cordiale** **2** the parties to an entente cordiale collectively

entente cordiale **1** a friendly understanding between political powers: less formal than an alliance **2** the understanding reached by France and Britain in April 1904, which settled outstanding colonial disputes

enteric *or* **enteral** intestinal

enteritis inflammation of the small intestine

enterprise **1** **a** initiative in business **b** (*as modifier*): *the enterprise culture* **2** a business unit; a company or firm

entertainer a professional singer, comedian, or other performer who takes part in public entertainments

enthusiasm *Archaic* extravagant or unbalanced religious fervour

enthusiast *Archaic* a religious visionary, esp one whose zeal for religion is extravagant or unbalanced

entire **1** (of leaves, petals, etc) having a smooth margin not broken up into teeth or lobes **2** not castrated **3** an uncastrated horse **4** *Philately* **a** a complete item consisting of an envelope, postcard, or wrapper with stamps affixed **b** **on entire** (of a stamp) placed on an envelope, postcard, etc, and bearing postal directions

entity something having real or distinct existence; a thing, esp when considered as independent of other things

entomology the branch of science concerned with the study of insects

entozoon *or* **entozoan** any animal, such as a tapeworm, that lives within another animal, usually as a parasite

entrance *Theatre* the coming of an actor or other performer onto a stage

entropy **1** a thermodynamic quantity that changes in a reversible process by an amount equal to the heat absorbed or emitted divided by the thermodynamic temperature. It is measured in joules per kelvin. **2** a statistical measure of the disorder of a closed system expressed by $S = k \log P + c$ where P is the probability that a particular state of the system exists, k is the Boltzmann constant, and c is another constant

entry **1** **a** a person, horse, car, etc, entering a competition or contest; competitor **b** (*as modifier*): *an entry fee* **2**

the competitors entering a contest considered collectively **3** the people admitted at one time to a school, college, or course of study, etc, considered collectively; intake **4** *Theatre* the action of an actor in going on stage or his manner of doing this **5** *Criminal law* the act of unlawfully going onto the premises of another with the intention of committing a crime **6** *Property law* the act of going upon another person's land with the intention of asserting the right to possession **7** any point in a piece of music, esp a fugue, at which a performer commences or resumes playing or singing **8** *Cards* a card that enables one to transfer the lead from one's own hand to that of one's partner or to the dummy hand

Enugu a city in S Nigeria, capital of Enugu state: capital of the former Eastern region and of the breakaway state of Biafra during the Civil War (1967–70): coal-mining. Pop: 549 000 (2005 est)

enuresis involuntary discharge of urine, esp during sleep

envelope **1** *Biology* any enclosing structure, such as a membrane, shell, or skin **2** the bag enclosing the gas in a balloon **3** *Maths* a curve or surface that is tangent to each one of a group of curves or surfaces **4** *Electronics* the sealed glass or metal housing of a valve, electric light, etc. **5** *Telecomm* the outer shape of a modulated wave, formed by the peaks of successive cycles of the carrier wave

Enver Pasha 1881–1922, Turkish soldier and leader of the Young Turks: minister of war (1914–18)

environment **1** *Ecology* the external surroundings in which a plant or animal lives, which tend to influence its development and behaviour **2** *Computing* an operating system, program, or integrated suite of programs that provides all the facilities necessary for a particular application

▷www.conservation.org
▷www.doc.mmu.ac.uk/aric/eae/english.html
▷http://personal.cmich.edu/~francm/ homepage.htm

environmentalist **1** an adherent of environmentalism **2** a person who is concerned with the maintenance of ecological balance and the conservation of the environment **3** a person concerned with issues that affect the environment, such as pollution

envoy[1] a diplomat of the second class, ranking between an ambassador and a minister resident

envoy[2] *or* **envoi** **1** a brief dedicatory or explanatory stanza concluding certain forms of poetry, notably ballades **2** a postscript in other forms of verse or prose

Enzed *Austral and NZ, informal* **1** New Zealand **2** a New Zealander

enzyme any of a group of complex proteins or conjugated proteins that are produced by living cells and act as catalysts in specific biochemical reactions

Eocene *Geology* of, denoting, or formed in the second epoch of the Tertiary period, which lasted for 20 000 000 years, during which hooved mammals appeared

Eolithic *Geology* denoting, relating to, or characteristic of the early part of the Stone Age, characterized by the use of crude stone tools

Epaminondas ?418–362 BC, Greek Theban statesman and general: defeated the Spartans at Leuctra (371) and Mantinea (362) and restored power in Greece to Thebes

ephedrine *or* **ephedrin** a white crystalline alkaloid obtained from plants of the genus *Ephedra*: used for the treatment of asthma and hay fever; l-phenyl-2-methy-laminopropanol. Formula: $C_6H_5CH(OH)CH(NHCH_3)CH_3$

ephemera 1 a mayfly, esp one of the genus *Ephemera* 2 a class of collectable items not originally intended to last for more than a short time, such as tickets, posters, postcards, or labels

ephemeral *Biology* 1 a short-lived organism, such as the mayfly 2 a plant that completes its life cycle in less than one year, usually less than six months

Ephesus (in ancient Greece) a major trading city on the W coast of Asia Minor: famous for its temple of Artemis (Diana); sacked by the Goths (262 AD)

Ephraim *Old Testament* 1 a the younger son of Joseph, who received the principal blessing of his grandfather Jacob (Genesis 48:8–22) b the tribe descended from him c the territory of this tribe, west of the River Jordan 2 the northern kingdom of Israel after the kingdom of Solomon had been divided into two

Ephraimite a member of the tribe of Ephraim

epic 1 a long narrative poem recounting in elevated style the deeds of a legendary hero, esp one originating in oral folk tradition 2 the genre of epic poetry 3 any work of literature, film, etc, having heroic deeds for its subject matter or having other qualities associated with the epic

epicentre *or* US **epicenter** the point on the earth's surface directly above the focus of an earthquake or underground nuclear explosion

Epictetus ?50–?120 AD, Greek Stoic philosopher, who stressed self-renunciation and the brotherhood of man

Epicurus 341–270 BC, Greek philosopher, who held that the highest good is pleasure and that the world is a series of fortuitous combinations of atoms

Epidaurus an ancient port in Greece, in the NE Peloponnese, in Argolis on the Saronic Gulf

epidemic 1 (esp of a disease) attacking or affecting many persons simultaneously in a community or area 2 a widespread occurrence of a disease

epidemiology the branch of medical science concerned with the occurrence, transmission, and control of epidemic diseases

epidermis 1 the thin protective outer layer of the skin, composed of stratified epithelial tissue 2 the outer layer of cells of an invertebrate 3 the outer protective layer of cells of a plant, which may be thickened by a cuticle

epidural 1 upon or outside the dura mater 2 a injection of anaesthetic into the space outside the dura mater enveloping the spinal cord b anaesthesia induced by this method

epiglottis a thin cartilaginous flap that covers the entrance to the larynx during swallowing, preventing food from entering the trachea

epigram a short, pungent, and often satirical poem, esp one having a witty and ingenious ending

epigraph a quotation at the beginning of a book, chap-ter, etc, suggesting its theme

epilepsy a disorder of the central nervous system characterized by periodic loss of consciousness with or without convulsions. In some cases it is due to brain damage but in others the cause is unknown
▷www.apa.org/science/efa.html

epileptic a person who has epilepsy

epilogue 1 a a speech, usually in verse, addressed to the audience by an actor at the end of a play b the actor speaking this 2 a short postscript to any literary work, such as a brief description of the fates of the characters in a novel

epiphany the manifestation of a supernatural or divine reality

Epiphany a Christian festival held on Jan 6, commemorating, in the Western Church, the manifestation of Christ to the Magi and, in the Eastern Church, the baptism of Christ

Epirus 1 a region of NW Greece, part of ancient Epirus ceded to Greece after independence in 1830 2 (in ancient Greece) a region between the Pindus mountains and the Ionian Sea, straddling the modern border with Albania

episcopacy 1 government of a Church by bishops 2 another word for episcopate

episcopal of, denoting, governed by, or relating to a bishop or bishops

Episcopal Church an autonomous branch of the Anglican Communion in Scotland and the US

episcopalian 1 practising or advocating the principle of Church government by bishops 2 an advocate of such Church government

Episcopalian 1 belonging to or denoting the Episcopal Church 2 a member or adherent of this Church
▷http://www.wikipedia.org/wiki/Episcopalian
▷http://www.holycross.net/anonline.htm
▷http://www.episcopalian.org/

episcopate 1 the office, status, or term of office of a bishop 2 bishops collectively

episiotomy surgical incision into the perineum during the late stages of labour to prevent its laceration during childbirth and to make delivery easier

episode 1 an incident, sequence, or scene that forms part of a narrative but may be a digression from the main story 2 (in ancient Greek tragedy) a section between two choric songs 3 *Music* a contrasting section between statements of the subject, as in a fugue or rondo

epistemology the theory of knowledge, esp the critical study of its validity, methods, and scope
▷http://pespmc1.vub.ac.be/EPISTEMI.html

epistle a literary work in letter form, esp a dedicatory verse letter of a type originated by Horace

Epistle 1 *New Testament* any of the apostolic letters of Saints Paul, Peter, James, Jude, or John 2 a reading from one of the Epistles, forming part of the Eucharistic service in many Christian Churches

epistolary *or archaic* **epistolatory** (of a novel or other work) constructed in the form of a series of letters

epithelium an animal tissue consisting of one or more layers of closely packed cells covering the external and internal surfaces of the body. The cells vary in structure according to their function, which may be protective, secretory, or absorptive

epitome a summary of a written work; abstract

epoch 1 *Astronomy* a precise date to which information, such as coordinates, relating to a celestial body is referred 2 *Geology* a unit of geological time within a period during which a series of rocks is formed 3 *Physics* the displacement of an oscillating or vibrating body at zero time

EPOS electronic point of sale

epoxy *Chem* 1 of, consisting of, or containing an oxygen atom joined to two different groups that are themselves joined to other groups 2 short for **epoxy resin**

epoxy *or* **epoxide resin** any of various tough resistant thermosetting synthetic resins containing epoxy groups: used in surface coatings, laminates, and adhesives

Epping a town in E England, in Essex, on the edge of Epping Forest: a residential centre for London. Pop: 9889 (2001)

Epping Forest a forest in E England, northeast of London: formerly a royal hunting ground

EPROM *Computing* erasable programmable read-only memory

Epsom a town in SE England, in Surrey: famous for its mineral springs and for horse racing. Pop. (with Ewell): 64 492 (2001)

Epsom salts a medicinal preparation of hydrated magnesium sulphate, used as a purgative

Epstein Sir Jacob 1880–1959, British sculptor, born in the US of Russo-Polish parents

equality *Maths* a statement, usually an equation, indicating that quantities or expressions on either side of an equal sign are equal in value

equation a mathematical statement that two expressions are equal: it is either an **identity** in which the variables can assume any value, or a **conditional equation** in which the variables have only certain values (roots)

equator 1 the great circle of the earth with a latitude of 0°, lying equidistant from the poles; dividing the N and S hemispheres 2 a circle dividing a sphere or other surface into two equal symmetrical parts 3 *Astronomy* See **celestial equator**

equatorial 1 of, like, or existing at or near the equator 2 *Astronomy* of or referring to the celestial equator

Equatorial Guinea a republic of W Africa, consisting of Río Muni on the mainland and the island of Bioko in the Gulf of Guinea, with four smaller islands: ceded by Portugal to Spain in 1778; gained independence in 1968. Official languages: Spanish and French. Religion: Roman Catholic majority. Currency: franc. Capital: Malabo. Pop: 507 000 (2004 est). Area: 28 049 sq km (10 830 sq miles)

equerry 1 an officer attendant upon the British sovereign 2 (formerly) an officer in a royal household responsible for the horses

equestrian 1 of or relating to horses and riding 2 on horseback; mounted 3 depicting or representing a person on horseback 4 *History* of, relating to, or composed of knights, esp the imperial free knights of the Holy Roman Empire 5 a person skilled in riding and horse-

manship

equilateral 1 having all sides of equal length 2 a geometric figure having all its sides of equal length 3 a side that is equal in length to other sides

equilibrium 1 any unchanging condition or state of a body, system, etc, resulting from the balance or cancelling out of the influences or processes to which it is subjected 2 *Physics* a state of rest or uniform motion in which there is no resultant force on a body 3 *Chem* the condition existing when a chemical reaction and its reverse reaction take place at equal rates 4 *Physics* the condition of a system that has its total energy distributed among its component parts in the statistically most probable manner 5 *Physiol* a state of bodily balance, maintained primarily by special receptors in the inner ear 6 the economic condition in which there is neither excess demand nor excess supply in a market

equine of, relating to, or belonging to the family *Equidae*, which comprises horses, zebras, and asses

equinoctial 1 relating to or occurring at either or both equinoxes 2 (of a plant) having flowers that open and close at specific regular times 3 *Astronomy* of or relating to the celestial equator 4 a storm or gale at or near an equinox 5 another name for **celestial equator**

equinox either of the two occasions, six months apart, when day and night are of equal length

equitable 1 *Law* relating to or valid in equity, as distinct from common law or statute law 2 *Law* (formerly) recognized in a court of equity only, as claims, rights, etc.

equitation the study and practice of riding and horsemanship

equity 1 *Law* a system of jurisprudence founded on principles of natural justice and fair conduct. It supplements the common law and mitigates its inflexibility, as by providing a remedy where none exists at law 2 *Law* an equitable right or claim

Equity the actors' trade union

equivalent 1 *Maths* a having a particular property in common; equal b (of two equations or inequalities) having the same set of solutions c (of two sets) having the same cardinal number 2 *Maths, Logic* (of two propositions) having an equivalence between them

era *Geology* a major division of geological time, divided into several periods

eraser an object, such as a piece of rubber or felt, used for erasing something written, typed, etc.

Erasmus Desiderius , real name *Gerhard Gerhards*. ?1466–1536, Dutch humanist, the leading scholar of the Renaissance in northern Europe. He published the first Greek edition of the New Testament in 1516; his other works include the satirical *Encomium Moriae* (1509); *Colloquia* (1519), a series of dialogues; and an attack on the theology of Luther, *De Libero Arbitrio* (1524)

Erato *Greek myth* the Muse of love poetry

Eratosthenes ?276–?194 BC, Greek mathematician and astronomer, who calculated the circumference of the earth by observing the angle of the sun's rays at different places

Erbil, **Irbil**, *or* **Arbil** a city in N Iraq: important in Assyrian times. Pop: 870 000 (2005 est)

erbium a soft malleable silvery-white element of the lanthanide series of metals: used in special alloys, room-temperature lasers, and as a pigment. Symbol: Er; atomic no.: 68; atomic wt.: 167.26; valency: 3; relative density: 9.006; melting pt.: 1529°C; boiling pt.: 2868°C

Erciyas Daği an extinct volcano in central Turkey. Height 3916 m (12 848 ft)

Erebus Mount a volcano in Antarctica, on Ross Island: discovered by Sir James Ross in 1841 and named after his ship. Height: 3794 m (12 448 ft)

Erechtheum or **Erechtheion** a temple on the Acropolis at Athens, which has a porch of caryatids

erect 1 (of an optical image) having the same orientation as the object; not inverted 2 *Physiol* (of the penis, clitoris, or nipples) firm or rigid after swelling with blood, esp as a result of sexual excitement 3 (of plant parts) growing vertically or at right angles to the parts from which they arise

erectile *Physiol* (of tissues or organs, such as the penis or clitoris) capable of becoming rigid or erect as the result of being filled with blood

eremite a Christian hermit or recluse

Eretria an ancient city in Greece, on the S coast of Euboea: founded as an Ionian colony; destroyed by the Persians in 490 BC following which it never regained its former significance

Erfurt an industrial city in central Germany, the capital of Thuringia: university (1392). Pop: 201 645 (2003 est)

ergonomics the study of the relationship between workers and their environment, esp the equipment they use

ergot the dried sclerotia of C. *purpurea*, used as the source of certain alkaloids used to treat haemorrhage, facilitate uterine contraction in childbirth, etc.

Erhard Ludwig 1897–1977, German statesman: chief architect of the *Wirtschaftswunder* ("economic miracle") of West Germany's recovery after World War II; chancellor (1963–66)

Ericson or **Ericsson Leif** 10th–11th centuries AD, Norse navigator, who discovered Vinland (?1000), variously identified as the coast of New England, Labrador, or Newfoundland; son of Eric the Red

Eric the Red ?940–?1010 AD, Norse navigator: discovered and colonized Greenland; father of Leif Ericson

Erie 1 **Lake** a lake between the US and Canada: the southernmost and the shallowest of the Great Lakes; empties by the Niagara River into Lake Ontario. Area: 25 718 sq km (9930 sq miles) 2 a port in NW Pennsylvania, on Lake Erie. Pop: 101 373 (2003 est)

Erie Canal a canal in New York State between Albany and Buffalo, linking the Hudson River with Lake Erie. Length: 579 km (360 miles)

Eriksson Sven-Goran born 1948, Swedish football manager; head coach of the England team from 2001

Eritrea a small country in NE Africa, on the Red Sea: became an Italian colony in 1890; federated with Ethiopia (1952–93); an independence movement was engaged in war with the Ethiopian government from 1961 until independence was gained in 1993; consists of hot and arid coastal lowlands, rising to the foothills of the Ethiopian highlands. Languages: Tigrinya, Arabic, English, Afar, and others. Religions: Muslim and Christian. Currency: nakfa. Capital: Asmara. Pop: 4 296 000 (2004 est). Area: 117 400 sq km (45 300 sq miles)

Erlangen a town in central Germany, in Bavaria: university (1743). Pop: 102 449 (2003 est)

Erlanger Joseph 1874–1965, US physiologist. He shared a Nobel prize for physiology or medicine (1944) with Gasser for their work on the electrical signs of nervous activity

ermine 1 the stoat in northern regions, where it has a white winter coat with a black-tipped tail 2 the fur of this animal 3 the dignity or office of a judge, noble, or king

Erne a river in N central Republic of Ireland, rising in County Cavan and flowing north across the border, through **Upper Lough Erne** and **Lower Lough Erne** and then west to Donegal Bay. Length: about 96 km (60 miles)

Ernst Max 1891–1976, German painter, resident in France and the US, a prominent exponent of Dada and surrealism: developed the technique of collage

erogenous or **erogenic** 1 sensitive to sexual stimulation 2 arousing sexual desire or giving sexual pleasure

erosion the wearing away of rocks and other deposits on the earth's surface by the action of water, ice, wind, etc.

erratic a piece of rock that differs in composition, shape, etc, from the rock surrounding it, having been transported from its place of origin, esp by glacial action

Er Rif a mountainous region of N Morocco, near the Mediterranean coast

Erse another name for Irish **Gaelic**

Erymanthus Mount a mountain in SW Greece, in the NW Peloponnese. Height: 2224 m (7297 ft)

erysipelas an acute streptococcal infectious disease of the skin, characterized by fever, headache, vomiting, and purplish raised lesions, esp on the face

erythrocyte a blood cell of vertebrates that transports oxygen and carbon dioxide, combined with the red pigment haemoglobin, to and from the tissues

Erzurum a city in E Turkey: a strategic centre; scene of two major battles against Russian forces (1877 and 1916); important military base and a closed city to unofficial visitors. Pop: 436 000 (2005 est)

Esau *Bible* son of Isaac and Rebecca and twin brother of Jacob, to whom he sold his birthright (Genesis 25)

Esbjerg a port in SW Denmark, in Jutland on the North Sea: Denmark's chief fishing port. Pop: 72 550 (2004 est)

escalator a moving staircase consisting of stair treads fixed to a conveyor belt, for transporting passengers between levels, esp between the floors of a building

escape 1 a valve that releases air, steam, etc, above a certain pressure; relief valve or safety valve 2 *Botany* a plant that was originally cultivated but is now growing wild

escapement 1 any similar mechanism that regulates movement, usually consisting of toothed wheels engaged by rocking levers 2 (in a piano) the mechanism that allows the hammer to clear the string after striking, so that the string can vibrate 3 an overflow channel

escape road a road, usually ending in a pile of sand, provided on a hill for a driver to drive into if his brakes fail or on a bend if he loses control of the turn

escape velocity the minimum velocity that a body must have in order to escape from the gravitational field of the earth or other celestial body

escarpment a the long continuous steep face of a ridge or plateau formed by erosion; scarp **b** any steep slope, such as one resulting from faulting

eschatology the branch of theology or biblical exegesis concerned with the end of the world

escheat *Law* **1** (in England before 1926) the reversion of property to the Crown in the absence of legal heirs **2** (in feudal times) the reversion of property to the feudal lord in the absence of legal heirs or upon outlawry of the tenant **3** the property so reverting

Escoffier (Georges) Auguste 1846–1935, French chef at the Savoy Hotel, London (1890–99)

Escorial *or* **Escurial** a village in central Spain, northwest of Madrid: site of an architectural complex containing a monastery, palace, and college, built by Philip II between 1563 and 1584

escudo **1** the standard monetary unit of Cape Verde, divided into 100 centavos **2** the former standard monetary unit of Portugal, divided into 100 centavos; replaced by the euro in 2002 **3** a former monetary unit of Chile, divided into 100 centesimos **4** an old Spanish silver coin worth 10 reals

escutcheon the place on the stern or transom of a vessel where the name is shown

Esdraelon a plain in N Israel, east of Mount Carmel

Esher a town in SE England, in NE Surrey near London: racecourse. Pop: 25 172 (2001)

Eskilstuna an industrial city in SE Sweden. Pop: 91 137 (2004 est)

Eskimo **1** a member of a group of peoples inhabiting N Canada, Greenland, Alaska, and E Siberia, having a material culture adapted to an extremely cold climate **2** the language of these peoples **3** a family of languages that includes Eskimo and Aleut

Eskişehir an industrial city in NW Turkey: founded around hot springs in Byzantine times. Pop: 519 000 (2005 est)

espalier **1** an ornamental shrub or fruit tree that has been trained to grow flat, as against a wall **2** the trellis, framework, or arrangement of stakes on which such plants are trained **3** the method used to produce such plants

esparto *or* **esparto grass** any of various grasses, esp *Stipa tenacissima* of S Europe and N Africa, that yield a fibre used to make ropes, mats, etc.

Esperanto an international artificial language based on words common to the chief European languages, invented in 1887

Espoo a city in S Finland. Pop: 224 231 (2003 est)

Esquiline one of the seven hills on which ancient Rome was built

esquire (in medieval times) the attendant and shield bearer of a knight, subsequently often knighted himself

Essaouira a port in SW Morocco on the Atlantic. Pop: 84 000 (2003)

essay a short literary composition dealing with a subject analytically or speculatively

Essen a city in W Germany, in North Rhine-Westphalia: the leading administrative centre of the Ruhr; university. Pop: 589 499 (2003 est)

essence **1** *Philosophy* **a** the unchanging and unchangeable nature of something which is necessary to its being the thing it is; its necessary properties **b** the properties in virtue of which something is called by its name **c** the nature of something as distinct from, and logically prior to, its existence **2** *Theol* an immaterial or spiritual entity **3 a** the constituent of a plant, usually an oil, alkaloid, or glycoside, that determines its chemical or pharmacological properties **b** an alcoholic solution of such a substance **4** a substance, usually a liquid, containing the properties of a plant or foodstuff in concentrated form

essential **1** *Biochem* (of an amino acid or a fatty acid) necessary for the normal growth of an organism but not synthesized by the organism and therefore required in the diet **2** derived from or relating to an extract of a plant, drug, etc. **3** *Logic* (of a property) guaranteed by the identity of the subject; necessary. Thus, if having the atomic number 79 is an essential property of gold, nothing can be gold unless it has that atomic number **4** *Music* denoting or relating to a note that belongs to the fundamental harmony of a chord or piece **5** *Pathol* (of a disease) having no obvious external cause **6** *Geology* (of a mineral constituent of a rock) necessary for defining the classification of a rock. Its absence alters the rock's name and classification **7** *Music* an essential note

essential oil any of various volatile organic oils present in plants, usually containing terpenes and esters and having the odour or flavour of the plant from which they are extracted: used in flavouring and perfumery

Essequibo a river in Guyana, rising near the Brazilian border and flowing north to the Atlantic: drains over half of Guyana. Length: 1014 km (630 miles)

Essex[1] 2nd Earl of, title of *Robert Devereux*. ?1566–1601, English soldier and favourite of Queen Elizabeth I; executed for treason

Essex[2] **1** a county of SE England, on the North Sea and the Thames estuary; the geographical and ceremonial county includes Thurrock and Southend-on-Sea, which became independent unitary authorities in 1998. Administrative centre: Chelmsford. Pop. (excluding unitary authorities): 1 324 100 (2003 est). Area (excluding unitary authorities): 3446 sq km (1310 sq miles) **2** an Anglo-Saxon kingdom that in the early 7th century AD comprised the modern county of Essex and much of Hertfordshire and Surrey. By the late 8th century, Essex had become a dependency of the kingdom of Mercia

Esslingen a town in SW Germany, on the River Neckar: Gothic church, medieval buildings: wines, light industry. Pop: 91 980 (2003 est)

Essonne a department of N France, south of Paris in Île-de-France region: formed in 1964. Capital: Évry. Pop: 1 153 434 (2003 est). Area: 1811 sq km (706 sq miles)

Established Church a Church that is officially recognized as a national institution, esp the Church of England

estate **1** *Property law* **a** property or possessions **b** the nature of interest that a person has in land or other property, esp in relation to the right of others **c** the total extent of the real and personal property of a deceased person or bankrupt **2** an order or class of persons in a political community, regarded collectively as a part of the body politic: usually regarded as being the lords temporal (peers), lords spiritual and commons

estate car *Brit* a car with a comparatively long body containing a large carrying space, reached through a rear door: usually the back seats can be folded forward to increase the carrying space

Este a noble family of Italy founded by Alberto Azzo II (996–1097), who was invested with the town of Este in NE Italy as a fief of the Holy Roman Empire. The family governed Ferrara (13th–16th centuries), Modena, and Reggio (13th–18th centuries)

ester *Chem* any of a class of compounds produced by reaction between acids and alcohols with the elimination of water. Esters with low molecular weights, such as ethyl acetate, are usually volatile fragrant liquids; fats are solid esters

Esther *Old Testament* **1** a beautiful Jewish woman who became queen of Persia and saved her people from massacre **2** the book in which this episode is recounted

estimate *Business* a statement indicating the likely charge for or cost of certain work

Estonia *or* **Esthonia** a republic in NE Europe, on the Gulf of Finland and the Baltic: low-lying with many lakes and forests, it includes numerous islands in the Baltic Sea. It was under Scandinavian and Teutonic rule from the 13th century to 1721, when it passed to Russia: it was an independent republic from 1920 to 1940, when it was annexed by the Soviet Union; became independent in 1991 and joined the EU in 2004. Official language: Estonian. Religion: believers are mostly Christian. Currency: kroon. Capital: Tallinn. Pop: 1 308 000 (2004 est). Area: 45 227 sq km (17 462 sq miles)

Estonian *or* **Esthonian** the official language of Estonia: belongs to the Finno-Ugric family

Estoril a resort in W Portugal, near Lisbon, on the Atlantic Ocean: noted esp for a famous avenue of palm trees leading to the seafront. Pop: 24 850 (1991)

Estremadura a region of W Spain: arid and sparsely populated except in the valleys of the Tagus and Guardiana rivers. Area: 41 593 sq km (16 059 sq miles).

estuary 1 the widening channel of a river where it nears the sea, with a mixing of fresh water and salt (tidal) water **2** an inlet of the sea

ET (in Britain) Employment Training: a government scheme offering training in technological and business skills to unemployed people

ETA Euzkadi ta Askatsuna: an organization of militant Basque nationalists attempting to gain independence for the Basques, esp those ruled by Spain, until a ceasefire in 1998, by means of guerrilla warfare

e-tail *or* **e-tailing** retail conducted via the internet

etching 1 the art, act, or process of preparing etched surfaces or of printing designs from them **2** an etched plate **3** an impression made from an etched plate

eternal denoting or relating to that which is without beginning and end, regarded as an attribute of God

Eternal City the Rome

eternity *Theol* the condition of timeless existence,

believed by some to characterize the afterlife

ethane a colourless odourless flammable gaseous alkane obtained from natural gas and petroleum: used as a fuel and in the manufacture of organic chemicals. Formula: C_2H_6

Ethelbert *or* **Æthelbert** Saint ?552–616 AD, king of Kent (560–616): converted to Christianity by St Augustine; issued the earliest known code of English laws. Feast day: Feb 24 or 25

Ethelred I *or* **Æthelred** died 871, king of Wessex (866–71). He led resistance to the Danish invasion of England; died following his victory at Ashdown

Ethelred II *or* **Æthelred** known as *Ethelred the Unready*. ?968–1016 AD, king of England (978–1016). He was temporarily deposed by the Danish king Sweyn (1013) but was recalled on Sweyn's death (1014)

Ethelwulf *or* **Æthelwulf** died 858 AD, king of Wessex (839–858)

ether 1 a colourless volatile highly flammable liquid with a characteristic sweetish odour, made by the reaction of sulphuric acid with ethanol: used as a solvent and anaesthetic. Formula: $C_2H_5OC_2H_5$ **2** any of a class of organic compounds with the general formula ROR′ where R and R′ are alkyl groups, as in diethyl ether $C_2H_5OC_2H_5$ **3 the ether** the hypothetical medium formerly believed to fill all space and to support the propagation of electromagnetic waves **4** *Greek myth* the upper regions of the atmosphere; clear sky or heaven

ethereal *Chem* of, containing, or dissolved in an ether, esp diethyl ether

ethic a moral principle or set of moral values held by an individual or group

ethical 1 of or relating to ethics **2** (of a medicinal agent) available legally only with a doctor's prescription or consent

ethics the philosophical study of the moral value of human conduct and of the rules and principles that ought to govern it; moral philosophy

  ▷http://ethics.acusd.edu/
  ▷http://www.ethics.org/

Ethiopia a state in NE Africa, on the Red Sea: consolidated as an empire under Menelik II (1889–1913); federated with Eritrea from 1952 until 1993; Emperor Haile Selassie was deposed by the military in 1974 and the monarchy was abolished in 1975; an independence movement in Eritrea was engaged in war with the government from 1961 until 1993. It lies along the Great Rift Valley and consists of deserts in the southeast and northeast and a high central plateau with many rivers (including the Blue Nile) and mountains rising over 4500 m (15 000 ft); the main export is coffee. Language: Amharic. Religion: Christian majority. Currency: birr. Capital: Addis Ababa. Pop: 72 420 000 (2004 est). Area: 1 128 215 sq km (435 614 sq miles)

Ethiopian 1 of or denoting a zoogeographical region consisting of Africa south of the Sahara **2** *Anthropol, obsolete* of or belonging to a postulated racial group characterized by dark skin, an oval elongated face, and thin lips, living chiefly in Africa south of the Sahara **3** any of the languages of Ethiopia, esp Amharic **4** an archaic word for **Black**

ethnic *or* **ethnical 1** relating to or characteristic of a human group having racial, religious, linguistic, and certain other traits in common **2** relating to the classification of mankind into groups, esp on the basis of racial characteristics

ethnic cleansing *Euphemistic* the violent removal by one ethnic group of other ethnic groups from the population of a particular area: used esp of the activities of Serbs against Croats and Muslims in the former Yugoslavia

ethnology the branch of anthropology that deals with races and peoples, their relations to one another, their origins, and their distinctive characteristics

ethyl of, consisting of, or containing the monovalent group C_2H_5.

ethylene a colourless flammable gaseous alkene with a sweet odour, obtained from petroleum and natural gas and used in the manufacture of polythene and many other chemicals. Formula: $CH_2:CH_2$

Etna Mount an active volcano in E Sicily: the highest volcano in Europe and the highest peak in Italy south of the Alps. Height: 3323 m (10 902 ft)

Eton 1 a town in S England, in Windsor and Maidenhead unitary authority, Berkshire, near the River Thames: site of **Eton College,** a public school for boys founded in 1440. Pop: 3821 (2001 est) **2** this college

Etruria 1 an ancient country of central Italy, between the Rivers Arno and Tiber, roughly corresponding to present-day Tuscany and part of Umbria **2** a factory established in Staffordshire by Josiah Wedgwood in 1769

étude a short musical composition for a solo instrument, esp one designed as an exercise or exploiting technical virtuosity

Euboea an island in the W Aegean Sea: the largest island after Crete of the Greek archipelago; linked with the mainland by a bridge across the Euripus channel. Capital: Chalcis. Pop: 198 130 (2001). Area: 3908 sq km (1509 sq miles)

eucalyptus *or* **eucalypt** any myrtaceous tree of the mostly Australian genus *Eucalyptus*, such as the blue gum and ironbark, widely cultivated for the medicinal oil in their leaves (**eucalyptus oil**), timber, and ornament

Eucharist 1 the Christian sacrament in which Christ's Last Supper is commemorated by the consecration of bread and wine **2** the consecrated elements of bread and wine offered in the sacrament **3** Mass, esp when regarded as the service where the sacrament of the Eucharist is administered

Euclid 1 3rd century BC, Greek mathematician of Alexandria; author of *Elements*, which sets out the principles of geometry and remained a text until the 19th century at least **2** the works of Euclid, esp his system of geometry

eugenics the study of methods of improving the quality of the human race, esp by selective breeding

Euler 1 Leonhard 1707–83, Swiss mathematician, noted esp for his work on the calculus of variation: considered the founder of modern mathematical analysis **2** Ulf (Svante) von 1905–83, Swedish physiologist: shared the Nobel prize (1970) for physiology or medicine with Julius Axelrod and Bernard Katz for their work on the

catecholamines: son of Hans von Euler-Chelpin

Euler-Chelpin Hans (Karl August) von 1873–1964, Swedish biochemist, born in Germany: shared the Nobel prize for chemistry (1929) with Sir Arthur Harden for their work on enzymes: father of Ulf von Euler

eulogy a formal speech or piece of writing praising a person or thing, esp a person who has recently died

euphonium a brass musical instrument with four valves; the tenor of the tuba family. It is used mainly in brass bands

Euphrates a river in SW Asia, rising in E Turkey and flowing south across Syria and Iraq to join the Tigris, forming the Shatt-al-Arab, which flows to the head of the Persian Gulf: important in ancient times for the extensive irrigation of its valley (in Mesopotamia). Length: 3598 km (2235 miles)

Eurasia the continents of Europe and Asia considered as a whole

Eurasian of mixed European and Asian descent

Eure a department of N France, in Haute-Normandie region. Capital: Évreux. Pop: 550 056 (2003 est). Area: 6037 sq km (2354 sq miles)

Eure-et-Loir a department of N central France, in Centre region. Capital: Chartres. Pop: 412 094 (2003 est). Area: 5940 sq km (2317 sq miles)

Euripides ?480–406 BC, Greek tragic dramatist. His plays, 18 of which are extant, include *Alcestis, Medea, Hippolytus, Hecuba, Trojan Women, Electra, Iphigeneia in Tauris, Iphigeneia in Aulis,* and *Bacchae*

euro the official currency unit, divided into 100 cents, of the member countries of the European Union who have adopted European Monetary Union; these are Austria, Belgium, Finland, France, Germany, Greece, Ireland, Italy, Luxembourg, the Netherlands, Portgual, and Spain; also used by Andorra, Bosnia and Hercegovina, French Guiana, Guadeloupe, Kosovo, Martinique, Mayotte, Monaco, Montenegro, Réunion, San Marino, and the Vatican City

Eurocentric chiefly concerned with or concentrating on Europe and European culture

Euroland the geographical area containing the countries that have joined the European single currency

Europe 1 the second smallest continent, forming the W extension of Eurasia: the border with Asia runs from the Urals to the Caspian and the Black Sea. The coastline is generally extremely indented and there are several peninsulas (notably Scandinavia, Italy, and Iberia) and offshore islands (including the British Isles and Iceland). It contains a series of great mountain systems in the south (Pyrenees, Alps, Apennines, Carpathians, Caucasus), a large central plain, and a N region of lakes and mountains in Scandinavia. Pop: 724 722 000 (2005 est). Area: about 10 400 000 sq km (4 000 000 sq miles) **2** *Brit* the European Union

European 1 a native or inhabitant of Europe **2** a person of European descent **3** a supporter of the European Union or of political union of the countries of Europe or a part of it

European Community *or* **Communities** an economic and political association of European States that came into being in 1967, when the legislative and executive bodies of the European Economic Community merged with those of the European Coal and Steel Community and the European Atomic Energy Community: subsumed into the **European Union** in 1993

European Union an organization created in 1993 with the aim of achieving closer economic and political union between member states of the European Community. The current members are Austria, Belgium, Cyprus, the Czech Republic, Denmark, Estonia, Finland, France, Germany, Greece, Hungary, Ireland, Italy, Latvia, Lithuania, Luxembourg, Malta, the Netherlands, Poland, Portugal, Slovakia, Slovenia, Spain, Sweden, and the UK.

▷www.europa.eu.int/index_en.htm
▷www.eia.org.uk/websites.htm

europium a soft ductile reactive silvery-white element of the lanthanide series of metals: used as the red phosphor in colour television and in lasers. Symbol: Eu; atomic no.: 63; atomic wt.: 151.965; valency: 2 or 3; relative density: 5.244; melting pt.: 822°C; boiling pt.: 1527°C

Europoort a port in the Netherlands near Rotterdam: developed in the 1960s; handles chiefly oil

Euro-sceptic in Britain **1** a person who is opposed to closer links with the European Union **2** opposing closer links with the European Union

Eusebio Silva Ferreira da born 1942, Portuguese footballer

Eusebius ?265–?340 AD, bishop of Caesarea: author of a history of the Christian Church to 324 AD

Eustachian tube a tube that connects the middle ear with the nasopharynx and equalizes the pressure between the two sides of the eardrum

Euterpe *Greek myth* the Muse of lyric poetry and music

euthanasia the act of killing someone painlessly, esp to relieve suffering from an incurable illness

evangel **1** *Archaic* the gospel of Christianity **2** any of the four Gospels of the New Testament **3** any body of teachings regarded as central or basic **4** US an evangelist

evangelical *Christianity* **1** of, based upon, or following from the Gospels **2** denoting or relating to any of certain Protestant sects or parties, which emphasize the importance of personal conversion and faith in atonement through the death of Christ as a means of salvation **3** an upholder of evangelical doctrines or a member of an evangelical sect or party, esp the Low-Church party of the Church of England

▷http://www.wikipedia.org/wiki/
   Evangelicalism
▷http://dict.die.net/evangelical/

evangelism **1** (in Protestant churches) the practice of spreading the Christian gospel **2** the work, methods, or characteristic outlook of a revivalist or evangelist preacher

evangelist **1** an occasional preacher, sometimes itinerant and often preaching at meetings in the open air **2** a preacher of the Christian gospel

Evangelist **1** any of the writers of the New Testament Gospels: Matthew, Mark, Luke, or John **2** a senior official or dignitary of the Mormon Church

Evans **1** Sir Arthur (John). 1851–1941, British archaeologist, whose excavations of the palace of Knossos in Crete provided evidence for the existence of the Minoan civilization **2** Dame Edith (Mary Booth). 1888–1976,

British actress **3** Sir Geraint (Llewellyn). 1922–92, Welsh operatic baritone **4** Herbert McLean 1882–1971, US anatomist and embryologist; discoverer of vitamin E (1922) **5** Oliver 1755–1819, US engineer: invented the continuous production line and a high-pressure steam engine **6** Walker 1903–75, US photographer, noted esp for his studies of rural poverty in the Great Depression

Evanston a city in NE Illinois, on Lake Michigan north of Chicago: Northwestern University (1851). Pop: 74 360 (2003 est)

Evansville a city in SW Indiana, on the Ohio River. Pop: 117 881 (2003 est)

Eve *OldTestament* the first woman; mother of the human race, fashioned by God from the rib of Adam (Genesis 2:18-25)

Evelyn John 1620–1706, English author, noted chiefly for his diary (1640–1706)

even **1 a** (of a number) divisible by two **b** characterized or indicated by such a number **2** *Maths* (of a function) unchanged in value when the sign of the independent variable is changed, as in $y = z^2$ **3 even money a** a bet in which the winnings are the same as the amount staked **b** (*as modifier*): *the even-money favourite*

evening class a class held in the evenings at certain colleges, normally for adults

evening primrose any onagraceous plant of the genus *Oenothera*, native to North America but widely cultivated and naturalized, typically having yellow flowers that open in the evening

evening star a planet, usually Venus, seen just after sunset during the time that the planet is east of the sun

evensong **1** *Church of England* the daily evening service of Bible readings and prayers prescribed in the Book of Common Prayer **2** *Archaic* another name for **vespers**

event *Philosophy* **a** an occurrence regarded as a bare instant of space-time as contrasted with an object which fills space and has endurance **b** an occurrence regarded in isolation from, or contrasted with, human agency

eventing the sport of taking part in equestrian competitions (esp **three-day events**), usually consisting of three sections: dressage, cross-country riding, and showjumping

Everest Mount a mountain in S Asia on the border between Nepal and Tibet, in the Himalayas: the highest mountain in the world; first climbed by members of a British-led expedition (1953). Height: established as 8848 m (29 028 ft) for many years, but the latest of a series of more recent reassessments (in 1999), not currently accepted by all authorities or by either of the controlling governments, puts it at 8850 m (29 035 ft)

evergreen (of certain trees and shrubs) bearing foliage throughout the year; continually shedding and replacing leaves

everlasting another name for **immortelle**

Everyman a medieval English morality play in which the central figure represents mankind, whose earthly destiny is dramatized from the Christian viewpoint

Evesham a town in W central England, in W Worcestershire, on the River Avon: scene of the Battle of Evesham in 1265 (Lord Edward's defeat of Simon de Montfort and the barons); centre of the **Vale of**

Evesham, famous for market gardens and orchards.
Pop: 22 179 (2001)

evidence *Law* **1** matter produced before a court of law in
an attempt to prove or disprove a point in issue, such as
the statements of witnesses, documents, material
objects, etc. **2 turn queen's (king's, state's) evidence** (of
an accomplice) to act as witness for the prosecution and
testify against those associated with him in crime

evil *Archaic* an illness or disease, esp scrofula (the **king's
evil**)

evil eye the 1 a look or glance superstitiously supposed
to have the power of inflicting harm or injury **2** the
power to inflict harm, etc, by such a look

evocation 1 *French law* the transference of a case from
an inferior court for adjudication by a higher tribunal **2**
another word for **induction**

evolution 1 *Biology* a gradual change in the characteristics of a population of animals or plants over successive
generations: accounts for the origin of existing species
from ancestors unlike them **2** the act of throwing off,
as heat, gas, vapour, etc. **3** an algebraic operation in
which the root of a number, expression, etc, is extracted

e-voting the application of electronic technology to
cast and count votes in an election

ewe a a female sheep **b** *(as modifier): a ewe lamb*

examination 1 *Education* **a** written exercises, oral questions, or practical tasks, set to test a candidate's knowledge and skill **b** *(as modifier): an examination paper* **2** *Med* **a**
physical inspection of a patient or parts of his body, in
order to verify health or diagnose disease **b** laboratory
study of secretory or excretory products, tissue samples, etc, esp in order to diagnose disease **3** *Law* the formal interrogation of a person on oath, esp of an accused
or a witness

exasperate *Botany* having a rough prickly surface
because of the presence of hard projecting points

ex cathedra *RC Church* (of doctrines of faith or morals)
defined by the pope as infallibly true, to be accepted by
all Catholics

Excellency *or* **Excellence** *RC Church* a title of bishops
and archbishops in many non-English-speaking countries

exception 1 *Law* (formerly) a formal objection in the
course of legal proceedings **2** *Law* a clause or term in a
document that restricts the usual legal effect of the
document

excerpt a part or passage taken from a book, speech,
play, etc, and considered on its own; extract

excess 1 *Chem* a quantity of a reagent that is greater
than the quantity required to complete a reaction **2**
Commerce payable as a result of previous underpayment

excess luggage *or* **baggage** luggage that is greater in
weight or in number of pieces than an airline, etc, will
carry free

exchange 1 *Commerce* **a** the system by which commercial debts between parties in different places are settled
by commercial documents, esp bills of exchange,
instead of by direct payment of money **b** the percentage or fee charged for accepting payment in this manner **2** *Chess* the capture by both players of pieces of
equal value, usually on consecutive moves **3 win** (*or*

lose) **the exchange** *Chess* to win (or lose) a rook in return
for a bishop or knight **4** *Med* another word for **transfusion 5** *Physics* a process in which a particle is transferred
between two nucleons, such as the transfer of a meson
between two nucleons

excise 1 a tax on goods, such as spirits, produced for the
home market **2** a tax paid for a licence to carry out various trades, sports, etc. **3** *Brit* that section of the government service responsible for the collection of excise,
now the Board of Customs and Excise

excitable *Physiology* (esp of a nerve) ready to respond to a
stimulus

exclusive 1 *Commerce* (of a contract, agreement, etc)
binding the parties to do business only with each other
with respect to a class of goods or services **2** *Logic* (of a
disjunction) true if only one rather than both of its
component propositions is true

excommunicate *RC Church* **1** having incurred such a
sentence **2** an excommunicated person

excrescence a projection or protuberance, esp an outgrowth from an organ or part of the body

excursion 1 *Transport* of or relating to special reduced
rates offered on certain journeys by rail **2** *Physics* **a** a
movement from an equilibrium position, as in an oscillation **b** the magnitude of this displacement **3** the normal movement of a movable bodily organ or part from
its resting position, such as the lateral movement of
the lower jaw **4** *Machinery* the locus of a point on a moving part, esp the deflection of a whirling shaft

executable 1 (of a computer program) able to be run **2** a
file containing a program that will run as soon as it is
opened

execution 1 the carrying out or undergoing of a sentence of death **2 a** the enforcement of the judgment of
a court of law **b** the writ ordering such enforcement

executive a the branch of government responsible for
carrying out laws, decrees, etc.; administration **b** any
administration

executor *Law* a person appointed by a testator to carry
out the wishes expressed in his will

exegesis explanation or critical interpretation of a text,
esp of the Bible

exercise 1 *US and Canadian* a ceremony or formal routine,
esp at a school or college **2** *Gymnastics* a particular type
of event, such as performing on the horizontal bar

Exeter a city in SW England, administrative centre of
Devon; university (1955). Pop: 106 772 (2001)

exhaust 1 gases ejected from an engine as waste products **2 a** the expulsion of expanded gas or steam from
an engine **b** *(as modifier): exhaust stroke* **3 a** the parts of an
engine through which the exhausted gases or steam
pass **b** *(as modifier): exhaust valve*

exhibit *Law* a document or object produced in court and
referred to or identified by a witness in giving evidence

exhibition *Brit* an allowance or scholarship awarded to
a student at a university or school

exhibitionism *Psychiatry* a compulsive desire to expose
one's genital organs publicly

exile the expulsion of a person from his native land by
official decree

existential 1 *Philosophy* pertaining to what exists, and is
thus known by experience rather than reason; empiri-

cal as opposed to theoretical **2** *Logic* denoting or relating to a formula or proposition asserting the existence of at least one object fulfilling a given condition; containing an existential quantifier **3** *Logic* an existential statement or formula

existentialism a modern philosophical movement stressing the importance of personal experience and responsibility and the demands that they make on the individual, who is seen as a free agent in a deterministic and seemingly meaningless universe

▷http://tameri.com/csw/exist/
▷http://connect.net/ron/exist.html
▷http://thecry.com/existentialism/

exit 1 *Theatre* the act of going offstage **2** *Bridge* **a** the act of losing the lead deliberately **b** a card enabling one to do this

Exmoor 1 a high moorland in SW England, in W Somerset and N Devon: chiefly grazing ground for Exmoor ponies, sheep, and red deer **2** a small stocky breed of pony with a fawn-coloured nose, originally from Exmoor

Exmouth a town in SW England, in Devon, at the mouth of the River Exe: tourism, fishing. Pop: 32 972 (2001)

exocrine gland *Med* any gland, such as a salivary or sweat gland, that secretes its products through a duct onto an epithelial surface

Exodus 1 the the departure of the Israelites from Egypt led by Moses **2** the second book of the Old Testament, recounting the events connected with this and the divine visitation of Moses at Mount Sinai

exoskeleton the protective or supporting structure covering the outside of the body of many animals, such as the thick cuticle of arthropods

exothermic *or* **exothermal** (of a chemical reaction or compound) occurring or formed with the evolution of heat

expansion 1 *Maths* **a** the form of an expression or function when it is written as the sum or product of its terms **b** the act or process of determining this expanded form **2** the part of an engine cycle in which the working fluid does useful work by increasing in volume **3** *Physics* the increase in the dimensions of a body or substance when subjected to an increase in temperature, internal pressure, etc.

expansionism the doctrine or practice of expanding the economy or territory of a country

expansive *Psychiatry* lacking restraint in the expression of feelings, esp in having delusions of grandeur or being inclined to overvalue oneself or one's work

expectancy *or* **expectance** the prospect of a future interest or possession, esp in property

expectant *Obsolete* a candidate for office, esp for ecclesiastical preferment

expectorant *Med* **1** promoting the secretion, liquefaction, or expulsion of sputum from the respiratory passages **2** an expectorant drug or agent

expense money needed for individual purchases; cost; charge

experience *Philosophy* **a** the content of a perception regarded as independent of whether the apparent object actually exists **b** the faculty by which a person

acquires knowledge of contingent facts about the world, as contrasted with reason **c** the totality of a person's perceptions, feelings, and memories

experiential *Philosophy* relating to or derived from experience; empirical

expiration the act, process, or sound of breathing out

explicit[1] *Maths* (of a function) having an equation of the form $y = f(x)$, in which y is expressed directly in terms of x, as in $y = x^4 + x + z$

explicit[2] the end; an indication, used esp by medieval scribes, of the end of a book, part of a manuscript, etc.

explosion a violent release of energy resulting from a rapid chemical or nuclear reaction, esp one that produces a shock wave, loud noise, heat, and light

explosive a substance that decomposes rapidly under certain conditions with the production of gases, which expand by the heat of the reaction. The energy released is used in firearms, blasting, and rocket propulsion

exponent *Maths* a number or variable placed as a superscript to the right of another number or quantity indicating the number of times the number or quantity is to be multiplied by itself

exponential 1 *Maths* (of a function, curve, series, or equation) of, containing, or involving one or more numbers or quantities raised to an exponent, esp e^x **2** *Maths* raised to the power of e, the base of natural logarithms. **3** *Maths* an exponential function, etc.

export a goods (**visible exports**) or services (**invisible exports**) sold to a foreign country or countries **b** (*as modifier*): *an export licence*

exposed *Mountaineering* (of a climb, pitch, or move) performed on a high, sheer, and unsheltered rock face

exposition 1 a large public exhibition, esp of industrial products or arts and crafts **2** *Lit* the part of a play, novel, etc, in which the theme and main characters are introduced **3** *Music* the first statement of the subjects or themes of a movement in sonata form or a fugue **4** *RC Church* the exhibiting of the consecrated Eucharistic Host or a relic for public veneration

exposure 1 *Archit* the position or outlook of a house, building, etc.; aspect **2** *Mountaineering* the degree to which a climb, etc is exposed (see **exposed** (sense 4)) **3** *Photog* **a** the act of exposing a photographic film or plate to light, X-rays, etc. **b** an area on a film or plate that has been exposed to light, etc. **c** (*as modifier*): *exposure control* **4** *Photog* **a** the intensity of light falling on a photographic film or plate multiplied by the time for which it is exposed **b** a combination of lens aperture and shutter speed used in taking a photograph **5** See **indecent exposure**

exposure meter *Photog* an instrument for measuring the intensity of light, usually by means of a photocell, so that the suitable camera settings of shutter speed and f-number (or lens aperture) can be determined

express *Transport* a fast train stopping at none or only a few of the intermediate stations between its two termini

expression 1 communication of emotion through music, painting, etc. **2** *Maths* a variable, function, or some combination of constants, variables, or functions **3** *Genetics* the effect of a particular gene on the phenotype

expressionism an artistic and literary movement originating in Germany at the beginning of the 20th century, which sought to express emotions rather than to represent external reality: characterized by the use of symbolism and of exaggeration and distortion
▷www.artlex.com/ArtLex/e/ Expressionism.html
▷www.ibiblio.org/wm/paint/tl/20th/ expressionism.html

expression mark *Music* one of a set of musical directions, usually in Italian, indicating how a piece or passage is to be performed

expressway a motorway

extemporaneous *or* **extemporary** spoken, performed, etc, without planning or preparation; impromptu; extempore

extension 1 *Commerce* a delay, esp one agreed by all parties, in the date originally set for payment of a debt or completion of a contract 2 the property of matter by which it occupies space; size 3 *Med* a steady pull applied to a fractured or dislocated arm or leg to restore it to its normal position 4 a a service by which some of the facilities of an educational establishment, library, etc, are offered to outsiders b (*as modifier*): *a university extension course* 5 *Logic* a the class of entities to which a given word correctly applies: thus, the extension of *satellite of Mars* is the set containing only Deimos and Phobos b **conservative extension** a formal theory that includes among its theorems all the theorems of a given theory

extensive 1 *Physics* of or relating to a property, measurement, etc, of a macroscopic system that is proportional to the size of the system 2 *Logic* a of or relating to logical extension b (of a definition) in terms of the objects to which the term applies rather than its meaning

extensor *Anatomy* any muscle that stretches or extends an arm, leg, or other bodily part

extent *US, Law* a writ authorizing a person to whom a debt is due to assume temporary possession of his debtor's lands

exterior 1 *Film* a film or scene shot outside a studio 2 *Politics* of or involving foreign nations

exterior angle 1 an angle of a polygon contained between one side extended and the adjacent side 2 any of the four angles made by a transversal that are outside the region between the two intersected lines

external 1 *Politics* of or involving foreign nations; foreign 2 of, relating to, or designating a medicine that is applied to the outside of the body 3 *Anatomy* situated on or near the outside of the body 4 *Education* denoting assessment by examiners who are not employed at the candidate's place of study 5 *Austral and NZ* (of a student) studying a university subject extramurally 6 *Philosophy* (of objects, etc) taken to exist independently of a perceiving mind 7 *Austral and NZ* a student taking an extramural subject

extinct 1 (of an animal or plant species) having no living representative; having died out 2 (of a volcano) no longer liable to erupt; inactive

extinction 1 *Physics* reduction of the intensity of radiation as a result of absorption or scattering by matter 2 *Astronomy* the dimming of light from a celestial body as it passes through an absorbing or scattering medium, such as the earth's atmosphere or interstellar dust 3 *Psychol* a process in which the frequency or intensity of a learned response is decreased as a result of reinforcement being withdrawn

extra 1 *Films* an actor or person temporarily engaged, usually for crowd scenes 2 *Cricket* a run not scored from the bat, such as a wide, no-ball, bye, or leg bye

extract 1 a preparation containing the active principle or concentrated essence of a material 2 *Pharmacol* a solution of plant or animal tissue containing the active principle

extraction *Dentistry* a the act or an instance of extracting a tooth or teeth b a tooth or teeth extracted

extractor fan *or* **extraction fan** a fan used in kitchens, bathrooms, workshops, etc, to remove stale air or fumes

extracurricular taking place outside the normal school timetable

extramural connected with but outside the normal courses or programme of a university, college, etc.

extraordinary *Politics* (of an official, etc) additional or subordinate to the usual one

extrasensory perception the supposed ability of certain individuals to obtain information about the environment without the use of normal sensory channels

extravaganza *Theatre, Film, etc* an elaborately staged and costumed light entertainment

extreme 1 *Meteorol* of, relating to, or characteristic of a continental climate 2 *Maths* a the first or last term of a series or a proportion b a maximum or minimum value of a function 3 *Logic* the subject or predicate of the conclusion of a syllogism

extreme sport a sport that is physically hazardous, such as bungee jumping or snowboarding

extremist a person who favours or resorts to immoderate, uncompromising, or fanatical methods or behaviour, esp in being politically radical

extremity a limb, such as a leg, arm, or wing, or the part of such a limb farthest from the trunk

extroversion *or* **extraversion** 1 *Psychol* the directing of one's interest outwards, esp towards social contacts 2 *Pathol* a turning inside out of an organ or part

extrovert *or* **extravert** *Psychol* 1 a person concerned more with external reality than inner feelings 2 of or characterized by extroversion

Eyam a village in N central England, in Derbyshire. When plague reached the village in 1665 the inhabitants, led by the Rev. Mompesson, isolated themselves to prevent it spreading further: as a result most of them died, including Mompesson's family

eye 1 the organ of sight of animals, containing light-sensitive cells associated with nerve fibres, so that light entering the eye is converted to nervous impulses that reach the brain. In man and other vertebrates the iris controls the amount of light entering the eye and the lens focuses the light onto the retina 2 the visible external part of an eye, often including the area around it 3 a structure or marking having the appearance of an eye, such as the bud on a twig or potato tuber or a spot on a butterfly wing 4 a small area of low pressure and calm in the centre of a tornado or cyclone 5 See **photo-**

cell 6 **the eye of the wind** *Nautical* the direction from which the wind is blowing

eyeball the entire ball-shaped part of the eye

eyebrow 1 the transverse bony ridge over each eye 2 the arch of hair that covers this ridge

eye dog NZ a dog trained to control sheep by staring fixedly at them

eyeglass 1 a lens for aiding or correcting defective vision, esp a monocle 2 another word for **eyepiece**

eyelash 1 any one of the short curved hairs that grow from the edge of the eyelids 2 a row or fringe of these hairs

eyelet a small metal ring or tube with flared ends bent back, reinforcing an eyehole in fabric

eyelid 1 either of the two muscular folds of skin that can be moved to cover the exposed portion of the eyeball 2 *Aeronautics* a set of movable parts at the rear of a jet engine that redirect the exhaust flow to assist braking during landing

eyepiece the lens or combination of lenses in an optical instrument nearest the eye of the observer

eyestrain fatigue or irritation of the eyes, resulting from excessive use, as from prolonged reading of small print, or uncorrected defects of vision

eyetooth either of the two canine teeth in the upper jaw

eyewash a mild solution for applying to the eyes for relief of irritation, etc.

Eyre[1] 1 **Edward John** 1815–1901, British explorer and colonial administrator. He was governor of Jamaica (1864–66) until his authorization of 400 executions to suppress an uprising led to his recall 2 **Sir Richard** born 1943, British theatre director: director of the Royal National Theatre (1988–97)

Eyre[2] **Lake** a shallow salt lake or salt flat in NE central South Australia, about 11 m (35 ft) below sea level, divided into two areas (North and South); it usually contains little or no water. Maximum area: 9600 sq km (3700 sq miles)

Eyre Peninsula a peninsula of South Australia, between the Great Australian Bight and Spencer Gulf

eyrie *or* **aerie** 1 the nest of an eagle or other bird of prey, built in a high inaccessible place 2 the brood of a bird of prey, esp an eagle

Eysenck Hans Jürgen 1916–97, British psychologist, born in Germany, who developed a dimensional theory of personality that stressed the influence of heredity

Ezekiel *Old Testament* 1 a Hebrew prophet of the 6th century BC, exiled to Babylon in 597 BC 2 the book containing his oracles, which describe the downfall of Judah and Jerusalem and their subsequent restoration

Ezra *Old Testament* 1 a Jewish priest of the 5th century BC, who was sent from Babylon by the Persian king Artaxerxes I to reconstitute observance of the Jewish law and worship in Jerusalem after the captivity 2 the book recounting his efforts to perform this task

Ff

Fabian 1 of, relating to, or resembling the delaying tactics of the Roman general Q. Fabius Maximus (died 203 BC) who withstood Hannibal while avoiding a pitched battle; cautious; circumspect 2 a member of or sympathizer with the Fabian Society, an association of British socialists founded in 1884

Fabius Maximus full name *Quintus Fabius Maximus Verrucosus*, called *Cunctator* (the delayer). died 203 BC, Roman general and statesman. As commander of the Roman army during the Second Punic War, he withstood Hannibal by his strategy of harassing the Carthaginians while avoiding a pitched battle

fable 1 a short moral story, esp one with animals as characters 2 a story or legend about supernatural or mythical characters or events 3 legends or myths collectively 4 *Archaic* the plot of a play or of an epic or dramatic poem

Fabre Jean Henri 1823–1915, French entomologist; author of many works on insect life, remarkable for their vivid and minute observation, esp *Souvenirs Entomologiques* (1879–1907). Nobel prize for literature 1910

fabric 1 any cloth made from yarn or fibres by weaving, knitting, felting, etc. 2 the texture of a cloth 3 the texture, arrangement, and orientation of the constituents of a rock

▷www.fabriclink.com

Fabry Charles 1867–1945, French physicist: discovered ozone in the upper atmosphere

face 1 *Mountaineering* a steep side of a mountain, bounded by ridges 2 *Nautical, aeronautics* the aft or near side of a propeller blade

face card (in a pack of playing cards) a king, queen, or jack of any suit

face-lift a cosmetic surgical operation for tightening sagging skin and smoothing unwanted wrinkles on the face

facer a lathe tool used to turn a face perpendicular to the axis of rotation

facet 1 *Architect* the raised surface between the flutes of a column 2 *Zoology* any of the lenses that make up the compound eye of an insect or other arthropod 3 *Anatomy* any small smooth area on a hard surface, as on a bone

fact 1 *Law* an actual event, happening, etc, as distinguished from its legal consequences. Questions of fact are decided by the jury, questions of law by the court or judge 2 *Philosophy* a proposition that may be either true or false, as contrasted with an evaluative statement 3 **after** (*or* **before**) **the fact** *Criminal law* after (or before) the commission of the offence

factor 1 *Maths* **a** one of two or more integers or polynomials whose product is a given integer or polynomial **b** an integer or polynomial that can be exactly divided into another integer or polynomial 2 *Med* any of several substances that participate in the clotting of blood 3 *Law, Commerce* a person who acts on another's behalf, esp one who transacts business for another 4 former name for a **gene** 5 *Commercial law* a person to whom goods are consigned for sale and who is paid a factorage 6 (in Scotland) the manager of an estate

factorial *Maths* the product of all the positive integers from one up to and including a given integer. Factorial zero is assigned the value of one: *factorial four is* $1 \times 2 \times 3 \times 4$. Symbol: $n!$, where n is the given integer

factory 1 **a** a building or group of buildings containing a plant assembly for the manufacture of goods **b** (*as modifier*): *a factory worker* 2 *Rare* a trading station maintained by factors in a foreign country

factory ship a fishing boat that processes the fish that are caught

faculty 1 **a** a department within a university or college devoted to a particular branch of knowledge **b** the staff of such a department **c** *Chiefly US and Canadian* all the teaching staff at a university, college, school, etc. 2 all members of a learned profession

Fadden Sir Arthur William 1895–1973, Australian statesman; prime minister of Australia (1941)

Faenza a city in N Italy, in Emilia-Romagna: famous in the 15th and 16th centuries for its majolica earthenware, esp faïence. Pop: 53 641 (2001)

Faeroese *or* **Faroese** the chief language of the Faeroes, closely related to Icelandic, although they are not mutually intelligible

fag *Brit* (esp formerly) a young public school boy who performs menial chores for an older boy or prefect

faggot *or esp US* **fagot** a bundle of iron bars, esp a box formed by four pieces of wrought iron and filled with scrap to be forged into wrought iron

fah *or* **fa** *Music* 1 (in the fixed system of solmization) the note F 2 (in tonic sol-fa) the fourth degree of any major scale; subdominant

Fahd ibn Abdul Aziz born 1923, king of Saudi Arabia

from 1982

Fahrenheit¹ Gabriel Daniel 1686–1736, German physicist, who invented the mercury thermometer and devised the temperature scale that bears his name

Fahrenheit² of or measured according to the Fahrenheit scale of temperature.

Faial or **Fayal** an island in the central Azores archipelago. Chief town: Horta. Area: 171 sq km (66 sq miles)

fail *Education* a failure to attain the required standard, as in an examination

fail-safe designed to return to a safe condition in the event of a failure or malfunction

faint a sudden spontaneous loss of consciousness, usually momentary, caused by an insufficient supply of blood to the brain

fair¹ 1 (of the tide or wind) favourable to the passage of a vessel 2 sunny, fine, or cloudless

fair² a gathering of producers of and dealers in a given class of products to facilitate business

Fairbanks¹ 1 Douglas (Elton), real name *Julius Ullman*. 1883–1939, US film actor and producer 2 his son, Douglas, Jnr 1909–2000, US film actor

Fairbanks² a city in central Alaska, at the terminus of the Alaska Highway. Pop: 30 970 (2003 est)

Fairfax Thomas, 3rd Baron Fairfax. 1612–71, English general and statesman: commanded the Parliamentary army (1645–50), defeating Charles I at Naseby (1645). He was instrumental in restoring Charles II to the throne (1660)

fair game *Hunting, archaic* quarry that may legitimately be pursued according to the rules of a particular sport

fairing an external metal structure fitted around parts of an aircraft, car, vessel, etc, to reduce drag

fairway 1 (on a golf course) the areas of shorter grass between the tees and greens, esp the avenue approaching a green bordered by rough 2 *Nautical* a the navigable part of a river, harbour, etc. b the customary course followed by vessels

fairy penguin a small penguin, *Eudyptula minor*, with a bluish head and back, found on the Australian coast

fairy ring a ring of dark luxuriant vegetation in grassy ground corresponding to the edge of an underground fungal mycelium: popularly associated with the dancing of fairies: seasonally marked by a ring of mushrooms

fairy tale or **story** a story about fairies or other mythical or magical beings, esp one of traditional origin told to children

Faisalabad a city in NE Pakistan: commercial and manufacturing centre of a cotton- and wheat-growing region; university (1961). Pop: 2 533 000 (2005 est)

Faisal I or **Feisal I** 1885–1933, king of Syria (1920) and first king of Iraq (1921–33): a leader of the Arab revolt against the Turks (1916–18)

Faisal II or **Feisal II** 1935–58, last king of Iraq (1939–58)

Faisal Ibn Abdul Aziz 1905–75, king of Saudi Arabia (1964–75)

faith 1 *Christianity* trust in God and in his actions and promises 2 a conviction of the truth of certain doctrines of religion, esp when this is not based on reason

faithful the faithful a the believers in and loyal adherents of a religious faith, esp Christianity b any group of

loyal and steadfast followers

fake *Nautical* one round of a coil of rope

fakir, faqir, or **fakeer** 1 a Muslim ascetic who rejects wordly possessions 2 a Hindu ascetic mendicant or holy man

falcon 1 any diurnal bird of prey of the family *Falconidae*, esp any of the genus *Falco* (gyrfalcon, peregrine falcon, etc), typically having pointed wings and a long tail 2 a any of these or related birds, trained to hunt small game b the female of such a bird

falconry 1 the art of keeping falcons and training them to return from flight to a lure or to hunt quarry 2 the sport of causing falcons to return from flight to their trainer and to hunt quarry under his direction ▷www.falconry.com

Faldo Nick born 1957, British golfer: winner of the British Open Championship (1987, 1990, 1992) and the US Masters (1989, 1990, 1996)

Falerii an ancient city of S Italy, in Latium: important in pre-Roman times

Faliraki a coastal resort in SE Greece, on Rhodes. Pop: 400 (2000 est)

Falkirk 1 a town in Scotland, the administrative centre of Falkirk council area: scene of Edward I's defeat of Wallace (1298) and Prince Charles Edward's defeat of General Hawley (1746); iron works. Pop: 32 379 (2001) 2 a council area in central Scotland, on the Firth of Forth: created in 1996 from part of Central Region: largely agricultural, with heavy industry in Falkirk and Grangemouth. Administrative centre: Falkirk. Pop: 145 920 (2003 est). Area: 299 sq km (115 sq miles)

fall 1 *Machinery, nautical* the end of a tackle to which power is applied to hoist it 2 *Nautical* one of the lines of a davit for holding, lowering, or raising a boat 3 *Wrestling* a scoring move, pinning both shoulders of one's opponent to the floor for a specified period

Fall the *Theol* Adam's sin of disobedience and the state of innate sinfulness ensuing from this for himself and all mankind

Falla Manuel de 1876–1946, Spanish composer and pianist, composer of the opera *La Vida Breve* (1905), the ballet *The Three-Cornered Hat* (1919), guitar and piano music, and songs

fallacy *Logic* an error in reasoning that renders an argument logically invalid

Fall Line a natural junction, running parallel to the E coast of the US, between the hard rocks of the Appalachians and the softer coastal plain, along which rivers form falls and rapids

fallout 1 the descent of solid material in the atmosphere onto the earth, esp of radioactive material following a nuclear explosion 2 any solid particles that so descend

fallow of a light yellowish-brown colour

fallow deer either of two deer, *Dama dama* or *D. mesopotamica*, native to the Mediterranean region and Persia respectively. The antlers are flattened and the summer coat is reddish with white spots

Falmouth a port and resort in SW England, in S Cornwall. Pop: 21 635 (2001)

false 1 (esp of plants) superficially resembling the species specified 2 *Music* a (of a note, interval, etc) out of tune b (of the interval of a perfect fourth or fifth) decreased by a semitone **c** (of a cadence) interrupted or imperfect

falsetto a form of vocal production used by male singers to extend their range upwards beyond its natural compass by limiting the vibration of the vocal cords

Falster an island in the Baltic Sea, part of SE Denmark. Chief town: Nykøbing. Pop: 43 537 (2003 est). Area: 513 sq km (198 sq miles)

Falun a city in central Sweden: iron and pyrites mines. Pop: 55 009 (2004 est)

Famagusta a port in E Cyprus, on **Famagusta Bay**: became one of the richest cities in Christendom in the 14th century. Pop: 67 167 (1994)

familiar 1 a supernatural spirit often assuming animal form, supposed to attend and aid a witch, wizard, etc. 2 a person, attached to the household of the pope or a bishop, who renders service in return for support 3 *History* an officer of the Inquisition who arrested accused persons

family 1 a group of persons related by blood; a group descended from a common ancestor 2 *Biology* any of the taxonomic groups into which an order is divided and which contains one or more genera. *Felidae* (cat family) and *Canidae* (dog family) are two families of the order *Carnivora* 3 *Ecology* a group of organisms of the same species living together in a community 4 *Chiefly US* an independent local group of the Mafia 5 *Maths* a group of curves or surfaces whose equations differ from a given equation only in the values assigned to one or more constants in each curve 6 *Physics* the isotopes, collectively, that comprise a radioactive series

family planning the control of the number of children in a family and of the intervals between them, esp by the use of contraceptives
▷www.icea.org

family tree a chart showing the genealogical relationships and lines of descent of a family

fan *Engineering* a any device for creating a current of air by movement of a surface or number of surfaces, esp a rotating device consisting of a number of blades attached to a central hub b a machine that rotates such a device

fan belt any belt that drives a fan, esp the belt that drives a cooling fan together with a dynamo or alternator in a car engine

fancy 1 (of a domestic animal) bred for particular qualities 2 *Lit* the power to conceive and represent decorative and novel imagery, esp in poetry. Fancy was held by Coleridge to be more casual and superficial than imagination 3 *Music* a composition for solo lute, keyboard, etc, current during the 16th and 17th centuries

fandango 1 an old Spanish courtship dance in triple time between a couple who dance closely and provocatively 2 a piece of music composed for or in the rhythm of this dance

fanfare a flourish or short tune played on brass instruments, used as a military signal, at a ceremonial event, etc.

fang 1 the long pointed hollow or grooved tooth of a venomous snake through which venom is injected 2 any large pointed tooth, esp the canine or carnassial tooth of a carnivorous mammal 3 the root of a tooth

Fangio Juan Manuel 1911–95, Argentinian racing driver who won the World Championship five times between 1951 and 1957

Fang Lizhi born 1936, Chinese astrophysicist and human-rights campaigner, living in the US from 1990

fanlight 1 a semicircular window over a door or window, often having sash bars like the ribs of a fan 2 a small rectangular window over a door

fantail 1 a breed of domestic pigeon having a large tail that can be opened like a fan 2 any Old World flycatcher of the genus *Rhipidura*, of Australia, New Zealand, and SE Asia, having a broad fan-shaped tail 3 *Architect* a part or structure having a number of components radiating from a common centre 4 a burner that ejects fuel to produce a wide flat flame in a lamp or furnace 5 a flat jet of air and coal dust projected into the air stream of a pulverized-coal furnace 6 an auxiliary sail on the upper portion of a windmill that turns the mill to face the wind 7 *US* a curved part of the deck projecting aft of the sternpost of a ship

fantasia 1 any musical composition of a free or improvisatory nature 2 another word for **fancy**

fantasy *or* **phantasy** 1 *Psychol* a a series of pleasing mental images, usually serving to fulfil a need not gratified in reality b the activity of forming such images 2 *Music* another word for **fantasia** *or* **fancy** *or* **development** 3 a literature having a large fantasy content b a prose or dramatic composition of this type

Fantin-Latour (Ignace) Henri (Joseph Théodore). 1836–1904, French painter, noted for his still lifes and portrait groups

fan vaulting *Architect* vaulting having ribs that radiate like those of a fan and spring from the top of a capital or corbel

farad *Physics* the derived SI unit of electrical capacitance; the capacitance of a capacitor between the plates of which a potential of 1 volt is created by a charge of 1 coulomb.

Faraday Michael 1791–1867, English physicist and chemist who discovered electromagnetic induction, leading to the invention of the dynamo. He also carried out research into the principles of electrolysis

farce 1 a broadly humorous play based on the exploitation of improbable situations 2 the genre of comedy represented by works of this kind

fare *Transport* the sum charged or paid for conveyance in a bus, train, aeroplane, etc.

Far East the countries of E Asia, usually including China, Japan, North and South Korea, Indonesia, Malaysia, and the Philippines: sometimes extended to include all territories east of Afghanistan

fare stage 1 a section of a bus journey for which a set charge is made 2 a bus stop marking the end of such a section

Fargo William 1818–81, US businessman: founded (1852) with Henry Wells the express mail service Wells, Fargo and Company

Farhi Nicole born 1946, French fashion designer based in Britain: married to Sir David Hare

farinaceous 1 having a mealy texture or appearance 2 containing starch

Farmer John ?1565–1605, English madrigal composer

and organist

Farnborough a town in S England, in NE Hampshire: military base, with an aeronautical research centre. Pop: 57 147 (2001)

Farnese 1 **Alesandro** original name of (Pope) **Paul III** 2 **Alessandro**, duke of Parma and Piacenza. 1545–92, Italian general, statesman, and diplomat in the service of Philip II of Spain. As governor of the Netherlands (1578–92), he successfully suppressed revolts against Spanish rule

Far North the the Arctic and sub-Arctic regions of the world

Farouk I or **Faruk I** 1920–65, last king of Egypt (1936–52). He was forced to abdicate (1952)

Farquhar George 1678–1707, Irish-born dramatist; author of comedies such as *The Recruiting Officer* (1706) and *The Beaux' Stratagem* (1707)

Farrell 1 **Colin (James)** born 1976, Irish film actor; he appeared in the TV series *Ballykissangel* before starring in the films *Tigerland* (2000), *Minority Report* (2002), and *Alexander* (2004). 2 **J(ames) G(ordon)** 1935–79, British novelist: author of *Troubles* (1970), *The Siege of Krishnapur* (1973), and *The Singapore Grip* (1978) 3 **James T(homas)** 1904–79, US writer. His works include the trilogy *Young* (1932), *The Young Manhood of Studs Lonigan* (1934), and *Judgment Day* (1935)

farrier *Chiefly Brit* 1 a person who shoes horses 2 *Archaic* another name for **veterinary surgeon**

farrow a litter of piglets

far-sighted *Med* of, relating to, or suffering from hyperopia

fascia or **facia** 1 the flat surface above a shop window 2 *Architect* a flat band or surface, esp a part of an architrave or cornice 3 *Anatomy* fibrous connective tissue occurring in sheets beneath the surface of the skin and between muscles and groups of muscles 4 *Biology* a distinctive band of colour, as on an insect or plant 5 *Brit* a less common name for **dashboard**

Fascism the political movement, doctrine, system, or regime (1922–43) in Italy of the dictator Benito Mussolini (1883–1945). Fascism encouraged militarism and nationalism, organizing the country along hierarchical authoritarian lines

▷www.fordham.edu/halshall/mod/
modsbook42.html

▷www.remember.org/hist.root.what.html

Fassbinder Rainer Werner 1946–82, West German film director. His films include *The Bitter Tears of Petra von Kant* (1972), *Fear Eats the Soul* (1974), and *The Marriage of Maria Braun* (1978)

fast 1 *Sport* (of a playing surface, running track, etc) conducive to rapid speed, as of a ball used on it or of competitors playing or racing on it 2 *Photog* **a** requiring a relatively short time of exposure to produce a given density **b** permitting a short exposure time 3 *Cricket* (of a bowler) characteristically delivering the ball rapidly

fast-breeder reactor a nuclear reactor that uses little or no moderator and produces more fissionable material than it consumes

fast lane the outside lane on a motorway or dual carriageway for vehicles overtaking or travelling at high speed

fat 1 any of a class of naturally occurring soft greasy solids that are esters of glycerol and certain fatty acids. They are present in some plants and in the adipose tissue of animals, forming a reserve energy source, and are used in making soap and paint and in the food industry 2 vegetable or animal tissue containing fat 3 *Theatre* a part in a play that gives an actor a good opportunity to show his talents 4 having a high content of a particular material or ingredient, such as resin in wood or oil in paint

fatalism 1 the philosophical doctrine that all events are predetermined so that man is powerless to alter his destiny 2 the acceptance of and submission to this doctrine

father *History* a senator or patrician in ancient Rome

Father 1 God, esp when considered as the first person of the Christian Trinity 2 any of the writers on Christian doctrine of the pre-Scholastic period 3 a title used for Christian priests

fathom 1 a unit of length equal to six feet (1.829 metres), used to measure depths of water 2 *Forestry* a unit of volume equal to six cubic feet, used for measuring timber

fatigue 1 *Physiol* the temporary inability of an organ or part to respond to a stimulus because of overactivity 2 *Mechanics* the progressive cracking of a material subjected to alternating stresses, esp vibrations

Fatima ?606–632 AD daughter of Mohammed; wife of Ali

fat stock livestock fattened and ready for market

fatty 1 containing, consisting of, or derived from fat 2 (esp of tissues, organs, etc) characterized by the excessive accumulation of fat

fatty acid any of a class of aliphatic carboxylic acids, such as palmitic acid, stearic acid, and oleic acid, that form part of a lipid molecule

Faulkner or **Falkner** William 1897–1962, US novelist and short-story writer. Most of his works portray the problems of the southern US, esp the novels set in the imaginary county of Yoknapatawpha in Mississippi. Other novels include *The Sound and the Fury* (1929) and *Light in August* (1932): Nobel prize for literature 1949

fault 1 *Electronics* a defect in a circuit, component, or line, such as a short circuit 2 *Geology* a fracture in the earth's crust resulting in the relative displacement and loss of continuity of the rocks on either side of it 3 *Tennis, squash, badminton* an invalid serve, such as one that lands outside a prescribed area 4 (in showjumping) a penalty mark given for failing to clear or refusing a fence, exceeding a time limit, etc. 5 *Hunting* an instance of the hounds losing the scent 6 **at fault a** (of hounds) having temporarily lost the scent

fault-finding the systematic investigation of malfunctions in electronic apparatus

faun (in Roman legend) a rural deity represented as a man with a goat's ears, horns, tail, and hind legs

fauna 1 all the animal life of a given place or time, esp when distinguished from the plant life (flora) 2 a descriptive list of such animals

favour or US **favor** *History* a badge or ribbon worn or given to indicate loyalty, often bestowed on a knight by a lady

favourite or US **favorite** 1 *Sport* a competitor thought likely to win 2 *Computing* a place on certain browsers that allows internet users to list the addresses of websites they find and like with a click of the mouse so that they can revisit them merely by opening the list and clicking on the address

Fawcett Dame **Millicent Garrett** 1847–1929, British suffragette

Fawkes Guy 1570–1606, English conspirator, executed for his part in the Gunpowder Plot to blow up King James I and the Houses of Parliament (1605). Effigies of him (guys) are burnt in Britain on Guy Fawkes Day (Nov 5)

fawn 1 a young deer of either sex aged under one year 2 a a light greyish-brown colour b *(as adjective): a fawn raincoat* 3 **in fawn** (of deer) pregnant

fealty (in feudal society) the loyalty sworn to one's lord on becoming his vassal

feather 1 any of the flat light waterproof epidermal structures forming the plumage of birds, each consisting of a hollow shaft having a vane of barbs on either side. They are essential for flight and help maintain body temperature 2 *Archery* a a bird's feather or artificial substitute fitted to an arrow to direct its flight b the feathered end of an arrow, opposite the head 3 *Nautical* the wake created on the surface of the water by the raised periscope of a submarine 4 *Rowing* the position of an oar turned parallel to the water between strokes 5 a step in ballroom dancing in which a couple maintain the conventional hold but dance side by side

featherweight 1 a a professional boxer weighing 118–126 pounds (53.5–57 kg) b an amateur boxer weighing 54–57 kg (119–126 pounds) c *(as modifier): the featherweight challenger* 2 a wrestler in a similar weight category (usually 126–139 pounds (57–63 kg))

feature *TV, Radio* a programme given special prominence on radio or television as indicated by attendant publicity

febrile of or relating to fever; feverish

Fechner Gustav Theodor 1801–87, German physicist, philosopher, and psychologist, noted particularly for his work on psychophysics, *Elemente der Psychophysik* (1860)

fed *US, slang* an agent of the FBI

federal 1 of or relating to a form of government or a country in which power is divided between one central and several regional governments 2 of or relating to a treaty between provinces, states, etc, that establishes a political unit in which power is so divided 3 of or relating to the central government of a federation 4 (of a university) comprised of relatively independent colleges 5 a supporter of federal union or federation

Federal 1 characteristic of or supporting the Union government during the American Civil War 2 a supporter of the Union government during the American Civil War

Federal Government the national government of a federated state, such as that of Australia located in Canberra

federate federal; federated

federation 1 the union of several provinces, states, etc, to form a federal union 2 a political unit formed in such a way 3 any league, alliance, or confederacy
▷www.nga.gov.au/federation

Federation of Rhodesia and Nyasaland a federation (1953–63) of Northern Rhodesia, Southern Rhodesia, and Nyasaland

fee 1 *Property law* a an interest in land capable of being inherited b the land held in fee 2 (in feudal Europe) the land granted by a lord to his vassal 3 **in fee** a *Law* (of land) in absolute ownership b *Archaic* in complete subjection

feed 1 *Engineering* the process of supplying a machine or furnace with a material or fuel 2 *Engineering* the quantity of material or fuel so supplied 3 *Engineering* the rate of advance of a cutting tool in a lathe, drill, etc. 4 *Engineering* a mechanism that supplies material or fuel or controls the rate of advance of a cutting tool 5 *Theatre, informal* a performer, esp a straight man, who provides cues

feedback 1 a the return of part of the output of an electronic circuit, device, or mechanical system to its input, so modifying its characteristics. In **negative feedback** a rise in output energy reduces the input energy; in **positive feedback** an increase in output energy reinforces the input energy b that part of the output signal fed back into the input 2 the whistling noise so produced 3 a the effect of the product of a biological pathway on the rate of an earlier step in that pathway b the substance or reaction causing such an effect, such as the release of a hormone in a biochemical pathway

feeder 1 *Engineering* a person or device that feeds the working material into a system or machine 2 *Geography* a tributary channel, esp one that supplies a reservoir or canal with water 3 *Transport* a a road, service, etc, that links secondary areas to the main traffic network b *(as modifier): a feeder bus* 4 *Electronics* a a transmission line connecting an aerial to a transmitter or receiver b a power line for transmitting electrical power from a generating station to a distribution network

feeler *Zoology* an organ in certain animals, such as an antenna or tentacle, that is sensitive to touch

feeling 1 the sense of touch 2 a the ability to experience physical sensations, such as heat, pain, etc. b the sensation so experienced 3 a state of mind

Feininger Lyonel 1871–1956, US artist, who worked at the Bauhaus, noted for his use of superimposed translucent planes of colour

feldspar *or* **felspar** any of a group of hard rock-forming minerals consisting of aluminium silicates of potassium, sodium, calcium, or barium: the principal constituents of igneous rocks. The group includes orthoclase, microcline, and the plagioclase minerals

felicity *Philosophy* appropriateness (of a speech act). The performative *I appoint you ambassador* can only possess felicity if uttered by one in whom the authority for such appointments is vested

feline of, relating to, or belonging to the *Felidae*, a family of predatory mammals, including cats, lions, leopards, and cheetahs, typically having a round head and retractile claws: order *Carnivora* (carnivores)

Felixstowe a port and resort in E England, in Suffolk: ferry connections to Rotterdam and Zeebrugge. Pop: 29 349 (2001)

fell[1] *US and Canadian* the timber felled in one season

fell² *Northern English and Scot* a mountain, hill, or tract of upland moor

Felling a town in NE England, in Gateshead unitary authority, Tyne and Wear; formerly noted for coal mining. Pop: 34 196 (2001)

Fellini Federico 1920–93, Italian film director. His films include *La Dolce Vita* (1959), *8½* (1963), *Satyricon* (1969), and *Intervista* (1987)

felloe *or* **felly** a segment or the whole rim of a wooden wheel to which the spokes are attached and onto which a metal tyre is usually shrunk

fellow 1 (at Oxford and Cambridge universities) a member of the governing body of a college, who is usually a member of the teaching staff 2 a member of the governing body or established teaching staff at any of various universities or colleges 3 a postgraduate student employed, esp for a fixed period, to undertake research and, often, to do some teaching

Fellow a member of any of various learned societies

fellowship 1 a mutual trust and charitableness between Christians b a Church or religious association 2 *Education* a a financed research post providing study facilities, privileges, etc, often in return for teaching services b a foundation endowed to support a postgraduate research student c an honorary title carrying certain privileges awarded to a postgraduate student 3 the body of fellows in a college, university, etc.

fellow traveller *Politics* a non-Communist who sympathizes with Communism

felon¹ *Criminal law* (formerly) a person who has committed a felony

felon² a purulent inflammation of the end joint of a finger, sometimes affecting the bone

felony (formerly) a serious crime, such as murder or arson. All distinctions between felony and misdemeanour were abolished in England and Wales in 1967

felt 1 a a matted fabric of wool, hair, etc, made by working the fibres together under pressure or by heat or chemical action b (*as modifier*): *a felt hat* 2 any material, such as asbestos, made by a similar process of matting

female 1 of, relating to, or designating the sex producing gametes (ova) that can be fertilized by male gametes (spermatozoa) 2 (of reproductive organs such as the ovary and carpel) capable of producing female gametes 3 (of gametes such as the ovum) capable of being fertilized by a male gamete in sexual reproduction 4 (of flowers) lacking, or having nonfunctional, stamens 5 *Engineering* having an internal cavity into which a projecting male counterpart can be fitted

feminism a doctrine or movement that advocates equal rights for women

femur 1 the longest thickest bone of the human skeleton, articulating with the pelvis above and the knee below 2 the corresponding bone in other vertebrates 3 the segment of an insect's leg nearest to the body

fen¹ low-lying flat land that is marshy or artificially drained

fen² a monetary unit of the People's Republic of China, worth one hundredth of a yuan

fence 1 an obstacle for a horse to jump in steeplechasing or showjumping 2 *Machinery* a guard or guide, esp in a circular saw or plane 3 *Aeronautics* a projection usually fitted to the top surface of a sweptback aircraft wing to prevent movement of the airflow towards the wing tips

fencing the practice, art, or sport of fighting with swords, esp the sport of using foils, épées, or sabres under a set of rules to score points
▷www.fencing.net
▷www.foilcommittee.pwp.blueyonder.co.uk

fender 1 *Chiefly US* a metal frame fitted to the front of locomotives to absorb shock, clear the track, etc. 2 a cushion-like device, such as a car tyre hung over the side of a vessel to reduce damage resulting from accidental contact or collision 3 *US and Canadian* the part of a car body that surrounds the wheels

fenestration 1 *Architecture* the arrangement and design of windows in a building 2 *Med* a surgical operation to restore hearing by making an artificial opening into the labyrinth of the ear

feng shui the Chinese art of determining the most propitious design and placement of a grave, building, room, etc, so that the maximum harmony is achieved between the flow of chi of the environment and that of the user, believed to bring good fortune
▷http://www.wofs.com/
▷http://www.fengshuisociety.org.uk/
▷http://www.fengshui-magazine.com/

Fenian (formerly) a member of an Irish revolutionary organization founded in the US in the 19th century to fight for an independent Ireland

fennel a strong-smelling yellow-flowered umbelliferous plant, *Foeniculum vulgare*, whose seeds and feathery leaves are used to season and flavour food

Fenton James (Martin). born 1949, British poet, journalist, and critic. His poetry includes the collections *A German Requiem* (1980) and *Out of Danger* (1993)

fenugreek an annual heavily scented Mediterranean leguminous plant, *Trigonella foenum-graecum*, with hairy stems and white flowers: cultivated for forage and for its medicinal seeds

feral¹ (of animals and plants) existing in a wild or uncultivated state, esp after being domestic or cultivated

feral² *Archaic, Astrology* associated with death

Ferdinand I 1 known as *Ferdinand the Great*. ?1016–65, king of Castile (1035–65) and León (1037–65): achieved control of the Moorish kings of Saragossa, Seville, and Toledo 2 1503–64, king of Hungary and Bohemia (1526–64); Holy Roman Emperor (1558–64), bringing years of religious warfare to an end 3 1751–1825, king of the Two Sicilies (1816–25); king of Naples (1759–1806; 1815–25), as Ferdinand IV, being dispossessed by Napoleon (1806–15) 4 1793–1875, king of Hungary (1830–48) and emperor of Austria (1835–48); abdicated after the Revolution of 1848 in favour of his nephew, Franz Josef I 5 1861–1948, ruling prince of Bulgaria (1887–1908) and tsar from 1908 until his abdication in 1918 6 1865–1927, king of Romania (1914–27); sided with the Allies in World War I

Ferdinand II 1578–1637, Holy Roman Emperor (1619–37); king of Bohemia (1617–19; 1620–37) and of Hungary (1617–37). His anti-Protestant policies led to the Thirty Years' War

Ferdinand III 1608–57, Holy Roman Emperor (1637–57) and king of Hungary (1625–57); son of Ferdinand II

FerdinandV known as *Ferdinand the Catholic*. 1452–1516, king of Castile (1474–1504); as Ferdinand II, king of Aragon (1479–1516) and Sicily (1468–1516); as Ferdinand III, king of Naples (1504–16). His marriage to Isabella I of Castile (1469) led to the union of Aragon and Castile and his reconquest of Granada from the Moors (1492) completed the unification of Spain. He introduced the Inquisition (1478), expelled the Jews from Spain (1492), and financed Columbus' voyage to the New World

FerdinandVII 1784–1833, king of Spain (1808; 1814–33). He precipitated the Carlist Wars by excluding his brother Don Carlos as his successor

Fergana *or* **Ferghana** 1 a region of W central Asia, surrounded by high mountains and accessible only from the west; mainly in Uzbekistan and partly in Tajikistan and Kyrgyzstan 2 the chief city of this region, in E Uzbekistan. Pop: 230 000 (2005 est)

Ferlinghetti Lawrence born 1920, US poet of the Beat Generation. His poetry includes the collections *Pictures of the Gone World* (1955) and *When I Look at Pictures* (1990)

Fermanagh a district and historical county of SW Northern Ireland: contains the Upper and Lower Lough Erne. Pop: 58 705 (2003 est). Area (excluding water): 1700 sq km (656 sq miles)

Fermat Pierre de 1601–65, French mathematician, regarded as the founder of the modern theory of numbers. He studied the properties of whole numbers and, with Pascal, investigated the theory of probability

ferment *Chemistry* 1 any agent or substance, such as a bacterium, mould, yeast, or enzyme, that causes fermentation 2 another word for **fermentation**

fermentation a chemical reaction in which a ferment causes an organic molecule to split into simpler substances, esp the anaerobic conversion of sugar to ethyl alcohol by yeast

Fermi Enrico 1901–54, Italian nuclear physicist, in the US from 1939. He was awarded a Nobel prize for physics in 1938 for his work on radioactive substances and nuclear bombardment and headed the group that produced the first controlled nuclear reaction (1942)

fermium a transuranic element artificially produced by neutron bombardment of plutonium. Symbol: Fm; atomic no.: 100; half-life of most stable isotope, ^{257}Fm: 80 days (approx.)

Fermor Patrick (Michael) Leigh born 1915, British traveller and author, noted esp for the travel books *A Time of Gifts* (1977) and *Between the Woods and the Water* (1986)

fern 1 any tracheophyte plant of the phylum *Filicinophyta*, having roots, stems, and fronds and reproducing by spores formed in structures (sori) on the fronds 2 any of certain similar but unrelated plants, such as the sweet fern

Fernandel real name *Fernand Joseph Désiré Contandin*. 1903–71, French comic film actor

Fernando de Noronha a volcanic island in the S Atlantic northeast of Cape São Roque: constitutes a federal territory of Brazil; a penal colony since the 18th century; inhabited by military personnel. Area: 26 sq km (10 sq miles)

Ferrara a city in N Italy, in Emilia-Romagna: a centre of the Renaissance under the House of Este; university (1391). Pop: 130 992 (2001)

Ferrari Enzo 1898–1988, Italian designer and manufacturer of racing cars

ferret[1] 1 a domesticated albino variety of the polecat *Mustela putorius*, bred for hunting rats, rabbits, etc. 2 **black-footed ferret** a musteline mammal, *Mustela nigripes*, of W North America, closely related to the weasels

ferret[2] *or* **ferreting** silk binding tape

ferric of or containing iron in the trivalent state: *ferric oxide*; designating an iron(III) compound

Ferrier Kathleen 1912–53, British contralto; noted for her expressive voice

ferrous of or containing iron in the divalent state; designating an iron(II) compound

ferruginous (of minerals, rocks, etc) containing iron

ferrule *or* **ferule** 1 a metal ring, tube, or cap placed over the end of a stick, handle, or post for added strength or stability or to increase wear 2 a side opening in a pipe that gives access for inspection or cleaning 3 a bush, gland, small length of tube, etc, esp one used for making a joint

ferry 1 a vessel for transporting passengers and usually vehicles across a body of water, esp as a regular service 2 a legal right to charge for transporting passengers by boat 3 the act or method of delivering aircraft by flying them to their destination

▷http://routesinternational.com/ships.htm

fertile 1 capable of producing offspring 2 *Biology* a capable of undergoing growth and development b (of plants) capable of producing gametes, spores, seeds, or fruits 3 *Physics* (of a substance) able to be transformed into fissile or fissionable material, esp in a nuclear reactor

Fertile Crescent an area of fertile land in the Middle East, extending around the Rivers Tigris and Euphrates in a semicircle from Israel to the Persian Gulf, where the Sumerian, Babylonian, Assyrian, Phoenician, and Hebrew civilizations flourished

fertilizer *or* **fertiliser** an object or organism such as an insect that fertilizes an animal or plant

fescue *or* **fescue grass** any grass of the genus *Festuca*: widely cultivated as pasture and lawn grasses, having stiff narrow leaves

fester a small ulcer or sore containing pus

Festival Hall a concert hall in London, on the South Bank of the Thames: constructed for the 1951 Festival of Britain; completed 1964–65

festoon 1 a decorative chain of flowers, ribbons, etc, suspended in loops; garland 2 a carved or painted representation of this, as in architecture, furniture, or pottery 3 *Dentistry* a the scalloped appearance of the gums where they meet the teeth b a design carved on the base material of a denture to simulate this 4 a either of two *Zerynthia* species of white pierid butterfly of southern Europe, typically mottled red, yellow, and brown b an ochreous brown moth, *Apoda avellana* the unusual sluglike larvae of which feed on oak leaves

fetal alcohol syndrome a condition in newborn babies caused by excessive intake of alcohol by the mother during pregnancy: characterized by various defects including mental retardation

fetch 1 *Engineering* the reach, stretch, etc, of a mechanism **2** *Geography* the distance in the direction of the prevailing wind that air or water can travel continuously without obstruction

fetish *or* **fetich** *Anthropology* something, esp an inanimate object, that is believed in certain cultures to be the embodiment or habitation of a spirit or magical powers

fetlock *or* **fetterlock** **1** a projection behind and above a horse's hoof: the part of the leg between the cannon bone and the pastern **2** the joint at this part of the leg **3** the tuft of hair growing from this part

fetus *or* **foetus** the embryo of a mammal in the later stages of development, when it shows all the main recognizable features of the mature animal, esp a human embryo from the end of the second month of pregnancy until birth

feu **1** *Scot, Legal history* **a** a feudal tenure of land for which rent was paid in money or grain instead of by the performance of military service **b** the land so held **2** *Scots Law* a right to the use of land in return for a fixed annual payment (**feu duty**)

Feuchtwanger Lion 1884–1958, German novelist and dramatist, lived in the US (1940–58): noted for his historical novels, including *Die hässliche Herzogin* (1923) and *Jud Süss* (1925)

feud *or* **feod** *Feudal law* land held in return for service

feudalism **1** the legal and social system that evolved in W Europe in the 8th and 9th centuries, in which vassals were protected and maintained by their lords, usually through the granting of fiefs, and were required to serve under them in war **2** any social system or society, such as medieval Japan or Ptolemaic Egypt, that resembles medieval European feudalism

Feuerbach Ludwig Andreas 1804–72, German materialist philosopher: in *The Essence of Christianity* (1841), translated into English by George Eliot (1853), he maintained that God is merely an outward projection of man's inner self

fever **1** an abnormally high body temperature, accompanied by a fast pulse rate, dry skin, etc. **2** any of various diseases, such as yellow fever or scarlet fever, characterized by a high temperature

feverish *or* **feverous** suffering from fever, esp a slight fever

Feydeau Georges 1862–1921, French dramatist, noted for his farces, esp *La Dame de chez Maxim* (1899) and *Occupe-toi d'Amélie* (1908)

Feynman Richard 1918–88, US physicist, noted for his research on quantum electrodynamics; shared the Nobel prize for physics in 1965

Fezzan a region of SW Libya, in the Sahara: a former province (until 1963)

Ffestiniog a town in N Wales, in Gwynedd: tourist attractions include former slate quarries and a narrow-gauge railway at nearby Blaenau Ffestiniog. Pop: 800 (latest est)

Fibonacci Leonardo , also called *Leonardo of Pisa*. ?1170–?1250, Italian mathematician: popularized the decimal system in Europe

fibre *or* US **fiber** **1** a natural or synthetic filament that may be spun into yarn, such as cotton or nylon **2** cloth or other material made from such yarn **3** *Botany* **a** a

narrow elongated thick-walled cell: a constituent of sclerenchyma tissue **b** such tissue extracted from flax, hemp, etc, used to make linen, rope, etc. **c** a very small root or twig **4** *Anatomy* any thread-shaped structure, such as a nerve fibre

fibreglass *or* US **fiberglass** **1** material consisting of matted fine glass fibres, used as insulation in buildings, in fireproof fabrics, etc. **2** a fabric woven from this material or a light strong material made by bonding fibreglass with a synthetic resin; used for car bodies, boat hulls, etc.

fibre optics the transmission of information modulated on light carried down very thin flexible fibres of glass

fibril *or* **fibrilla** *Biology* a threadlike structure, such as a root hair or a thread of muscle tissue

fibrillation **1** a local and uncontrollable twitching of muscle fibres, esp of the heart, not affecting the entire muscle. **Atrial fibrillation** results in rapid and irregular heart and pulse rate. In **ventricular fibrillation**, the heart stops beating **2** irregular twitchings of the muscular wall of the heart, often interfering with the normal rhythmic contractions

fibrin a white insoluble elastic protein formed from fibrinogen when blood clots: forms a network that traps red cells and platelets

fibrinogen a soluble protein, a globulin, in blood plasma, converted to fibrin by the action of the enzyme thrombin when blood clots

fibroid **1** *Anatomy* (of structures or tissues) containing or resembling fibres **2** a benign tumour, composed of fibrous and muscular tissue, occurring in the wall of the uterus and often causing heavy menstruation

fibrosis the formation of an abnormal amount of fibrous tissue in an organ or part as the result of inflammation, irritation, or healing

fibrositis inflammation of white fibrous tissue, esp that of muscle sheaths

fibula **1** the outer and thinner of the two bones between the knee and ankle of the human leg **2** the corresponding bone in other vertebrates **3** *History* a metal brooch resembling a safety pin, often highly decorated, common in Europe after 1300 BC

fiction **1** literary works invented by the imagination, such as novels or short stories **2** *Law* something assumed to be true for the sake of convenience, though probably false

fiddle **1** a violin played as a folk instrument **2** *Nautical* a small railing around the top of a table to prevent objects from falling off it in bad weather

fidelity *Electronics* the degree to which the output of a system, such as an amplifier or radio, accurately reproduces the characteristics of the input signal

fiduciary *Law* **1** a person bound to act for another's benefit, as a trustee in relation to his beneficiary **2 a** having the nature of a trust **b** of or relating to a trust or trustee

fief *or* **feoff** (in feudal Europe) the property or fee granted to a vassal for his maintenance by his lord in return for service

field **1** *Sport* a limited or marked off area, usually of mown grass, on which any of various sports, athletic competitions, etc, are held **2** *Earth Sciences* an area that is rich in minerals or other natural resources **3** *Hunting* the mounted followers that hunt with a pack of hounds **4** *Sport* **a** all the runners in a particular race or competitors in a competition **b** the runners in a race or competitors in a competition excluding the favourite **5** *Cricket* the fielders collectively, esp with regard to their positions **6** the area within which an object may be observed with a telescope, microscope, etc. **7** *Physics* **a** a region of space that is a vector field **b** a region of space under the influence of some scalar quantity, such as temperature **8** *Maths* a set of entities subject to two binary operations, addition and multiplication, such that the set is a commutative group under addition and the set, minus the zero, is a commutative group under multiplication and multiplication is distributive over addition **9** *Maths, logic* the set of elements that are either arguments or values of a function; the union of its domain and range **10** *Computing* **a** a set of one or more characters comprising a unit of information **b** a predetermined section of a record **11** in the field *Military* in an area in which operations are in progress

Field John 1782–1837, Irish composer and pianist, lived in Russia from 1803: invented the nocturne

fielder *Cricket, Baseball* **a** a player in the field **b** a member of the fielding rather than the batting side

field event a competition, such as the discus, high jump, etc, that takes place on a field or similar area as opposed to those on the running track

fieldfare a large Old World thrush, *Turdus pilaris*, having a pale grey head and rump, brown wings and back, and a blackish tail

field hockey *US and Canadian* hockey played on a field, as distinguished from ice hockey

Fielding Henry 1707–54, English novelist and dramatist, noted particularly for his picaresque novel *Tom Jones* (1749) and for *Joseph Andrews* (1742), which starts as a parody of Richardson's *Pamela*: also noted as an enlightened magistrate and a founder of the Bow Street runners (1749)

fieldmouse **1** any nocturnal mouse of the genus *Apodemus*, inhabiting woods, fields, and gardens of the Old World: family *Muridae*. They have yellowish-brown fur and feed on fruit, vegetables, seeds, etc. **2** a former name for **vole**

Fields **1** Dame **Gracie** real name *Grace Stansfield*. 1898–1979, English popular singer and entertainer **2** W. C real name *William Claude Dukenfield*. 1880–1946, US film actor, noted for his portrayal of comic roles

field trip an expedition, as by a group of students or research workers, to study something at first hand

Fiennes **1** Ralph (**Nathanial**). born 1962, British actor; his films include *Schindler's List* (1993), *The English Patient* (1997), *The End of the Affair* (2000), and *Spider* (2002) **2** Sir Ranulph (**Twistleton-Wykeham-**). born 1944, British explorer; led the first surface journey around the earth's polar axis (1979–82); unsupported crossing of Antarctica (1992–93)

fiery **1** (of the skin or a sore) inflamed **2** flammable or containing flammable gas **3** (of a cricket pitch) making the ball bounce dangerously high

Fiesole a town in central Italy, in Tuscany near Florence:

Etruscan and Roman remains. Pop: 14 085 (2001)

fiesta (esp in Spain and Latin America) **1** a religious festival or celebration, esp on a saint's day **2** a holiday or carnival

FIFA Fédération Internationale de Football Association ▷www.fifa.com

fife a small high-pitched flute similar to the piccolo and usually having no keys, used esp in military bands

Fife a council area and historical county of E central Scotland, bordering on the North Sea between the Firths of Tay and Forth: coastal lowlands in the north and east, with several ranges of hills; mainly agricultural. Administrative centre: Glenrothes. Pop: 352 040 (2003 est). Area: 1323 sq km (511 sq miles)

fifteen **1** the cardinal number that is the sum of ten and five **2** a numeral, 15, XV, etc, representing this number **3** a rugby football team

fifth **1 a** one of five equal or nearly equal parts of an object, quantity, measurement, etc. **b** (*as modifier*): *a fifth part* **2** the fraction equal to one divided by five (1/5) **3** *Music* **a** the interval between one note and another five notes away from it counting inclusively along the diatonic scale **b** one of two notes constituting such an interval in relation to the other **4** an additional high gear fitted to some motor vehicles

fifth column **1** (originally) a group of Falangist sympathizers in Madrid during the Spanish Civil War who were prepared to join the four columns of insurgents marching on the city **2** any group of hostile or subversive infiltrators

fifty **1** the cardinal number that is the product of ten and five **2** a numeral, 50, L, etc, representing this number

fig **1** any moraceous tree or shrub of the tropical and subtropical genus *Ficus*, in which the flowers are borne inside a pear-shaped receptacle **2** the fruit of any of these trees, esp of *F. carica*, which develops from the receptacle and has sweet flesh containing numerous seedlike structures **3** any of various plants or trees having a fruit similar to this **4** **Hottentot** *or* **sour fig** a succulent plant, *Mesembryanthemum edule*, of southern Africa, having a capsular fruit containing edible pulp: family *Aizoaceae*

fig leaf **1** a leaf from a fig tree **2** a representation of a leaf, usually a vine leaf rather than an actual fig leaf, used in painting or sculpture to cover the genitals of nude figures

figuration **1** *Music* **a** the employment of characteristic patterns of notes, esp in variations on a theme **b** decoration or florid ornamentation in general **2** *Art* a figurative or emblematic representation

figurative **1** representing by means of an emblem, likeness, figure, etc. **2** (in painting, sculpture, etc) of, relating to, or characterized by the naturalistic representation of the external world

figure **1** any written symbol other than a letter, esp a whole number **2** another name for **digit 3** an amount expressed numerically **4** a representation in painting or sculpture, esp of the human form **5** a pattern or design, as on fabric or in wood **6** a predetermined set of movements in dancing or skating **7** *Geometry* any combination of points, lines, curves, or planes. A **plane fig-**

ure, such as a circle, encloses an area; a **solid figure** such as a sphere, encloses a volume **8** *Logic* one of the four possible arrangements of the three terms in the premises of a syllogism **9** *Music* **a** a numeral written above or below a note in a part **b** a characteristic short pattern of notes

figured 1 depicted as a figure in graphic art, painting, or sculpture **2** *Music* **a** ornamental **b** (of a bass part) provided with numerals indicating accompanying harmonies

figurehead a carved bust or full-length figure at the upper end of the stems of some sailing vessels

figure skating ice skating in which the skater traces outlines of selected patterns

figurine a small carved or moulded figure; statuette

Fiji 1 an independent republic, consisting of 844 islands (chiefly Viti Levu and Vanua Levu) in the SW Pacific: a British colony (1874–1970); a member of the Commonwealth (1970–87 and from 1997); the large islands are of volcanic origin, surrounded by coral reefs; smaller ones are of coral. Official language: English. Religion: Christian and Hindu. Currency: dollar. Capital: Suva. Pop: 847 000 (2004 est). Area: 18 272 sq km (7055 sq miles) **2** another word for **Fijian**

Fijian 1 a member of the indigenous people of mixed Melanesian and Polynesian descent inhabiting Fiji **2** the language of this people, belonging to the Malayo-Polynesian family

filament 1 the thin wire, usually tungsten, inside a light bulb that emits light when heated to incandescence by an electric current **2** *Electronics* a high-resistance wire or ribbon, forming the cathode in some valves **3** a single strand of a natural or synthetic fibre; fibril **4** *Botany* **a** the stalk of a stamen **b** any of the long slender chains of cells into which some algae and fungi are divided **5** *Ornithol* the barb of a down feather **6** *Anatomy* any slender structure or part, such as the tail of a spermatozoon; filum **7** *Astronomy* **a** a long structure of relatively cool material in the solar corona **b** a long large-scale cluster of galaxies

filbert 1 any of several N temperate shrubs of the genus *Corylus*, esp *C. maxima*, that have edible rounded brown nuts: family *Corylaceae* **2** the nut of any of these shrubs

file¹ 1 *Chess* any of the eight vertical rows of squares on a chessboard **2** *Computing* a named collection of information, in the form of text, programs, graphics, etc, held on a permanent storage device such as a magnetic disk

file² a hand tool consisting essentially of a steel blade with small cutting teeth on some or all of its faces. It is used for shaping or smoothing metal, wood, etc.

filial *Genetics* designating any of the generations following the parental generation. Abbrev.: F; F_1 indicates the first filial generation, F_2 the second, etc.

filibuster 1 *Politics* the process or an instance of obstructing legislation by means of long speeches and other delaying tactics **2** *History* a buccaneer, freebooter, or irregular military adventurer, esp a revolutionary in a foreign country

filigree, filagree, *or* **fillagree 1** delicate ornamental work of twisted gold, silver, or other wire **2** any fanciful delicate ornamentation

Filipino 1 a native or inhabitant of the Philippines **2**

another name for **Tagalog**

fill *Building* material such as gravel, stones, etc, used to bring an area of ground up to a required level

filler *Entertainment* something, such as a musical selection, to fill time in a broadcast or stage presentation

fillet 1 a thin strip of ribbon, lace, etc, worn in the hair or around the neck **2** a narrow flat moulding, esp one between other mouldings **3** a narrow band between two adjacent flutings on the shaft of a column **4** a narrow strip of welded metal of approximately triangular cross-section used to join steel members at right angles **5** the top member of a cornice **6** *Anatomy* a band of sensory nerve fibres in the brain connected to the thalamus **7** another name for **fairing**

filling 1 *Dentistry* **a** any of various substances (metal, plastic, etc) for inserting into the prepared cavity of a tooth **b** the cavity of a tooth so filled **2** *Textiles* another term for **weft**

filling station a place where petrol and other supplies for motorists are sold

Fillmore Millard 1800–74, 13th president of the US (1850–53); a leader of the Whig Party

filly a female horse or pony under the age of four

film 1 a a sequence of images of moving objects photographed by a camera and providing the optical illusion of continuous movement when projected onto a screen **b** a form of entertainment, information, etc, composed of such a sequence of images and shown in a cinema, etc. **c** (*as modifier*): *film techniques* **2** a thin flexible strip of cellulose coated with a photographic emulsion, used to make negatives and transparencies **3** *Pathol* an abnormally opaque tissue, such as the cornea in some eye diseases

filmic having characteristics that are suggestive of films or the cinema

film strip a strip of film composed of different images projected separately as slides

filter 1 a porous substance, such as paper or sand, that allows fluid to pass but retains suspended solid particles: used to clean fluids or collect solid particles **2** any device containing such a porous substance for separating suspensions from fluids **3** any of various porous substances built into the mouth end of a cigarette or cigar for absorbing impurities such as tar **4** any electronic, optical, or acoustic device that blocks signals or radiations of certain frequencies while allowing others to pass **5** any transparent disc of gelatine or glass used to eliminate or reduce the intensity of given frequencies from the light leaving a lamp, entering a camera, etc. **6** *Brit* a traffic signal at a road junction consisting of a green arrow which when illuminated permits vehicles to turn either left or right when the main signals are red

filter paper a porous paper used for filtering liquids

filter tip 1 an attachment to the mouth end of a cigarette for trapping impurities such as tar during smoking. It consists of any of various dense porous substances, such as cotton **2** a cigarette having such an attachment

filtrate a liquid or gas that has been filtered

fin 1 any of the firm appendages that are the organs of locomotion and balance in fishes and some other aquatic animals. Most fishes have paired and unpaired fins, the former corresponding to the limbs of higher vertebrates **2 a** *Brit* a vertical surface to which the rudder is attached, usually placed at the rear of an aeroplane to give stability about the vertical axis **b** a tail surface fixed to a rocket or missile to give stability **3** *Nautical* a fixed or adjustable blade projecting under water from the hull of a vessel to give it stability or control **4** a projecting rib to dissipate heat from the surface of an engine cylinder, motor casing, or radiator **5** another name for **flipper**

final 1 *Music* another word for **perfect 2** *Sport* a deciding contest between the winners of previous rounds in a competition **3** *Music* the tonic note of a church mode

finale 1 the concluding part of any performance or presentation **2** the closing section or movement of a musical composition

finalist a contestant who has reached the last and decisive stage of a sports or other competition

finance 1 funds or the provision of funds **2** funds; financial condition

financial year *Brit* the annual period ending April 5, over which Budget estimates are made by the British Government and which functions as the income-tax year

finch 1 any songbird of the family *Fringillidae*, having a short stout bill for feeding on seeds and, in most species, a bright plumage in the male. Common examples are the goldfinch, bullfinch, chaffinch, siskin, and canary **2** any of various similar or related birds

Finchley a residential district of N London, part of the Greater London borough of Barnet from 1965

finder 1 *Physics* a small low-power wide-angle telescope fitted to a more powerful larger telescope, used to locate celestial objects to be studied by the larger instrument **2** *Photog* short for **viewfinder**

finding 1 *Law* the conclusion reached after a judicial inquiry; verdict **2** *US* the tools and equipment of an artisan

fine¹ 1 (of precious metals) pure or having a high or specified degree of purity **2** *Cricket* (of a fielding position) oblique to and behind the wicket

fine² 1 a payment made by a tenant at the start of his tenancy to reduce his subsequent rent; premium **2** *Feudal law* a sum of money paid by a man to his lord, esp for the privilege of transferring his land to another **3** a method of transferring land in England by bringing a fictitious law suit: abolished 1833

fine *Music* **1** the point at which a piece is to end, usually after a *da capo* or *dal segno* **2** an ending or finale

fine art 1 art produced chiefly for its aesthetic value, as opposed to applied art **2** any of the fields in which such art is produced, such as painting, sculpture, and engraving

▷www.fine-art.com
▷www.tate.org.uk
▷www.vam.ac.uk
▷www.royalacademy.org.uk
▷www.nationalgallery.org.uk
▷www.metmuseum.org
▷www.louvre.fr/louvrea.htm
▷www.rijksmuseum.nl

▷www.guggenheim.org

fine-drawn (of wire) drawn out until very fine; attenuated

finery *Engineering* a hearth for converting cast iron into wrought iron

finesse *Bridge, whist* an attempt to win a trick when opponents hold a high card in the suit led by playing a lower card, hoping the opponent who has already played holds the missing card

finger 1 a any of the digits of the hand, often excluding the thumb **b** (as modifier): a finger bowl **2** the length or width of a finger used as a unit of measurement **3** a quantity of liquid in a glass, etc, as deep as a finger is wide; tot **4** a projecting machine part, esp one serving as an indicator, guide, or guard

fingerboard the long strip of hard wood on a violin, guitar, or related stringed instrument upon which the strings are stopped by the fingers

fingering 1 the technique or art of using one's fingers in playing a musical instrument, esp the piano **2** the numerals in a musical part indicating this

fingernail a thin horny translucent plate covering part of the dorsal surface of the end joint of each finger

fingerprint 1 an impression of the pattern of ridges on the palmar surface of the end joint of each finger and thumb **2** *Biochem* the pattern of fragments obtained when a protein is digested by a proteolytic enzyme, usually observed following two-dimensional separation by chromatography and electrophoresis

fingerstall a protective covering for a finger

fingertip 1 the end joint or tip of a finger **2** another term for **fingerstall**

finis the end; finish: used at the end of books, films, etc.

finish *Sport* ability to sprint at the end of a race

finishing school a private school for girls that prepares them for society by teaching social graces and accomplishments

Finisterre Cape a headland in NW Spain: the westernmost point of the Spanish mainland

finite 1 bounded in magnitude or spatial or temporal extent **2** *Maths, logic* having a number of elements that is a natural number; able to be counted using the natural numbers less than some natural number

Finland 1 a republic in N Europe, on the Baltic Sea: ceded to Russia by Sweden in 1809; gained independence in 1917; Soviet invasion successfully withstood in 1939–40, with the loss of Karelia; a member of the European Union. It is generally low-lying, with about 50 000 lakes, extensive forests, and peat bogs. Official languages: Finnish and Swedish. Religion: Christian, Lutheran majority. Currency: euro. Capital: Helsinki. Pop: 5 216 000 (2004 est). Area: 337 000 sq km (130 120 sq miles) **2 Gulf of** an arm of the Baltic Sea between Finland, Estonia, and Russia

Finlay Carlos Juan 1833–1915, Cuban physician: discovered that the mosquito was the vector of yellow fever

Finn¹ 1 a native, inhabitant, or citizen of Finland **2** a speaker of a Finnic language, esp one of the original inhabitants of Russia, who were pushed northwards during the Slav migrations

Finn² known as *Finn MacCool*. (in Irish legend) chief of the Fianna, father of the heroic poet Ossian

Finney 1 **Albert** born 1936, British stage and film actor 2 **Tom** born 1922, English footballer: won 76 international caps as a winger

Finnish the official language of Finland, also spoken in Estonia and NW Russia, belonging to the Finno-Ugric family

Finnmark a county of N Norway: the largest, northernmost, and least populated county; mostly a barren plateau. Capital: Vadsø. Pop: 73 210 (2004 est). Area: 48 649 sq km (18 779 sq miles)

fino a very dry sherry

Finsen Niels Ryberg 1860–1904, Danish physician; founder of phototherapy: Nobel prize for physiology or medicine 1903

Finsteraarhorn a mountain in S central Switzerland: highest peak in the Bernese Alps. Height: 4274 m (14 022 ft)

fipple flute an end-blown flute provided with a fipple, such as the recorder or flageolet

fir 1 any pyramidal coniferous tree of the N temperate genus *Abies*, having single needle-like leaves and erect cones: family *Pinaceae* 2 any of various other trees of the family *Pinaceae*, such as the Douglas fir 3 the wood of any of these trees

Firbank (Arthur Annesley) Ronald 1886–1926, English novelist, whose works include *Valmouth* (1919), *The Flower beneath the Foot* (1923), and *Concerning the Eccentricities of Cardinal Pirelli* (1926)

Firdausi or **Firdusi** pen name of *Abul Qasim Mansur* ?935–1020 AD, Persian epic poet; author of *Shah Nama* (*The Book of Kings*), a chronicle of the legends and history of Persia

fire *Astrology* of or relating to a group of three signs of the zodiac, Aries, Leo, and Sagittarius

fire alarm a device to give warning of fire, esp a bell, siren, or hooter

fireball 1 a ball-shaped discharge of lightning 2 the bright spherical region of hot ionized gas at the centre of a nuclear explosion

firebreak a strip of open land in forest or prairie, to arrest the advance of a fire

firebrick a refractory brick made of fire clay, used for lining furnaces, flues, etc.

fire clay a heat-resistant clay used in the making of firebricks, furnace linings, etc.

fire-eater a performer who simulates the swallowing of fire

fire engine a heavy road vehicle that carries firemen and fire-fighting equipment to a fire

fire-extinguisher a portable device for extinguishing fires, usually consisting of a canister with a directional nozzle used to direct a spray of water, chemically generated foam, inert gas, or fine powder onto the fire

firefly 1 any nocturnal beetle of the family *Lampyridae*, common in warm and tropical regions, having luminescent abdominal organs 2 any tropical American click beetle of the genus *Pyrophorus*, esp *P. noctiluca*, that have luminescent thoracic organs

fire hydrant a hydrant for use as an emergency supply for fighting fires, esp one in a street

fireman *Railways* a (on steam locomotives) the man who stokes the fire and controls the injectors feeding water to the boiler b (on diesel and electric locomotives) the driver's assistant

fire ship a vessel loaded with explosives and used, esp formerly, as a bomb by igniting it and directing it to drift among an enemy's warships

firewall *Computing* a computer system that isolates another computer from the internet in order to prevent unauthorized access

firewater any strong spirit, esp whisky

firework a device, such as a Catherine wheel, Roman candle, or rocket, in which combustible materials are ignited and produce coloured flames, sparks, and smoke, sometimes accompanied by bangs

firing 1 the process of baking ceramics, etc, in a kiln or furnace 2 *US* a scorching of plants, as a result of disease, drought, or heat

firm[1] (of prices, markets, etc) tending to rise

firm[2] 1 a business partnership 2 any commercial enterprise 3 a team of doctors and their assistants

first 1 preceding all others in numbering or counting order; the ordinal number of *one*. Often written: 1st 2 denoting the lowest forward ratio of a gearbox in a motor vehicle 3 *Music* a denoting the highest part assigned to one of the voice parts in a chorus or one of the sections of an orchestra b denoting the principal player in a specific orchestral section 4 *Education, chiefly Brit* an honours degree of the highest class 5 the lowest forward ratio of a gearbox in a motor vehicle; low gear 6 *Music* a the highest part in a particular section of a chorus or orchestra b the instrument or voice taking such a part c the chief or leading player in a section of an orchestra; principal 7 *Music* a rare word for **prime**

first aid 1 a immediate medical assistance given in an emergency b (*as modifier*): *first-aid box* 2 (in Barbados) a small shop that sells domestic items after hours

first class 1 a (in Britain) of or relating to mail that is processed most quickly b (in the US and Canada) of or relating to mail that consists mainly of written letters, cards, etc. 2 *Education* See **first** (sense 4)

first-day cover *Philately* a cover, usually an envelope, postmarked on the first day of the issue of its stamps

first mate an officer second in command to the captain of a merchant ship

First Minister 1 the chief minister of the Northern Ireland Assembly 2 the chief minister of the Scottish Parliament

first night a the first public performance of a play or other production b (*as modifier*): *first-night nerves*

first offender a person convicted of any criminal offence for the first time

first officer 1 another name for **first mate** 2 the member of an aircraft crew who is second in command to the captain

First Secretary the chief minister of the National Assembly for Wales

firth or **frith** a relatively narrow inlet of the sea, esp in Scotland

fiscal 1 of or relating to government finances, esp tax revenues 2 (in some countries) a public prosecutor

Fischer 1 **Emil Hermann** 1852–1919, German chemist, noted particularly for his work on synthetic sugars and the purine group: Nobel prize for chemistry 1902 2

Ernst Otto 1918–94, German chemist: shared the Nobel prize for chemistry in 1973 with Geoffrey Wilkinson for his work on inorganic complexes **3 Hans** 1881–1945, German chemist, noted particularly for his work on chlorophyll, haemin, and the porphyrins: Nobel prize for chemistry 1930 **4 Robert James**, known as *Bobby*. born 1943, US chess player; world champion 1972–75

Fischer-Dieskau Dietrich born 1925, German baritone, noted particularly for his interpretation of Schubert's song cycles

fish 1 any of a large group of cold-blooded aquatic vertebrates having jaws, gills, and usually fins and a skin covered in scales: includes the sharks and rays (class *Chondrichthyes*: **cartilaginous fishes**) and the teleosts, lungfish, etc (class *Osteichthyes*: **bony fishes**) **2** any of various similar but jawless vertebrates, such as the hagfish and lamprey **3** any of various aquatic invertebrates, such as the cuttlefish, jellyfish, and crayfish **4** short for **fishplate**

▷http://recipe-fish-seafood.com
▷http://fishing.about.com/cs/fishrecipes
▷www.fish4fun.com/seafoodrecipes.htm

Fisher 1 Andrew 1862–1928, Australian statesman, born in Scotland: prime minister of Australia (1908–09; 1910–13; 1914–15) **2 Saint John** ?1469–1535, English prelate and scholar: executed for refusing to acknowledge Henry VIII as supreme head of the church. Feast day: June 22 **3 John Arbuthnot** 1st Baron Fisher of Kilverstone. 1841–1920, British admiral; First Sea Lord (1904–10; 1914–15); introduced the dreadnought

fisherman a vessel used for fishing

fishery 1 a the industry of catching, processing, and selling fish **b** a place where this is carried on **2** a place where fish are reared **3** a fishing ground

Fishguard a port and resort in SW Wales, in Pembrokeshire: ferry connections to Cork and Rosslare. Pop: 3193 (2001)

fishing rod a long tapered flexible pole, often in jointed sections, for use with a fishing line and, usually, a reel

fishmonger *Chiefly Brit* a retailer of fish

fishnet 1 *Chiefly US and Canadian* a net for catching fish **2 a** an open mesh fabric resembling netting **b** (*as modifier*): *fishnet tights*

fishplate a flat piece of metal joining one rail, stanchion, or beam to another

fishtail 1 *Aeronautics* an aeroplane manoeuvre in which the tail is moved from side to side to reduce speed **2** *Engineering* a nozzle having a long narrow slot at the top, placed over a Bunsen burner to produce a thin fanlike flame

fissile 1 *Brit* capable of undergoing nuclear fission as a result of the impact of slow neutrons **2** *US and Canadian* capable of undergoing nuclear fission as a result of any process

fission 1 *Biology* a form of asexual reproduction in single-celled animals and plants involving a division into two or more equal parts that develop into new cells **2** short for **nuclear fission**

fissure 1 *Anatomy* a narrow split or groove that divides an organ such as the brain, lung, or liver into lobes **2** a small unnatural crack in the skin or mucous membrane, as between the toes or at the anus **3** a minute

crack in the surface of a tooth, caused by imperfect joining of enamel during development

fistula *Pathol* an abnormal opening between one hollow organ and another or between a hollow organ and the surface of the skin, caused by ulceration, congenital malformation, etc.

fit¹ *Pathol* a sudden attack or convulsion, such as an epileptic seizure

fit² *Archaic* a story or song or a section of a story or song

fitment *Machinery* an accessory attached to an assembly of parts

fitter a person who supplies something for an expedition, activity, etc.

fitting 1 an accessory or part **2** work carried out by a fitter

Fittipaldi Emerson born 1946, Brazilian motor-racing driver: world champion in 1972 and 1974

Fitzgerald 1 Edward 1809–83, English poet, noted particularly for his free translation of the *Rubáiyát of Omar Khayyám* (1859) **2 Ella** 1918–96, US jazz singer, noted esp for her vocal range and scat singing **3 F(rancis) Scott (Key)**. 1896–1940, US novelist and short-story writer, noted particularly for his portrayal of the 1920s in *The Great Gatsby* (1925) and *Tender is the Night* (1934) **4 Garret** born 1926, Irish politician: leader of Fine Gael Party (1977–87); prime minister of the Republic of Ireland (1981–82; and 1982–87)

Fitzpatrick Sean born 1963, New Zealand Rugby Union footballer; captain of the All Blacks (1992–98)

Fitzrovia *Informal* the district north of Oxford Street, London, around Fitzroy Square and its pubs, noted in the 1930s and 40s as a haunt of poets

Fitzsimmons Bob 1862–1917, New Zealand boxer, born in England: world middleweight (1891–97), heavyweight (1897–99), and light-heavyweight (1903–05) champion

five 1 the cardinal number that is the sum of four and one **2** a numeral, 5, V, etc, representing this number **3** the amount or quantity that is one greater than four **4** something representing, represented by, or consisting of five units, such as a playing card with five symbols on it

five-eighth 1 *Austral* (in rugby) a player positioned between the scrum-half and the inside -centre **2** *NZ* (in rugby) either of two players positioned between the halfback and the centre

fivefold 1 equal to or having five times as many or as much **2** composed of five parts

fivepins a bowling game using five pins, played esp in Canada

fiver *Informal* **1** (in Britain) a five-pound note **2** (in the US) a five-dollar bill

fives a ball game similar to squash but played with bats or the hands
▷www.etonfives.co.uk

Five Towns the the name given in his fiction by Arnold Bennett to the Potteries towns (actually six in number) of Burslem, Fenton, Hanley, Longton, Stoke-upon-Trent, and Tunstall, now part of the city of Stoke-on-Trent

fix *Nautical, etc* the ascertaining of the navigational position, as of a ship, by radar, observation, etc.

fixation 1 *Psychol* **a** the act of fixating **b** (in psychoanalytical schools) a strong attachment of a person to another person or an object in early life **2** *Chem* **a** the conversion of nitrogen in the air into a compound, esp a fertilizer **b** the conversion of a free element into one of its compounds **3** the reduction of a substance from a volatile or fluid form to a nonvolatile or solid form

fixative 1 a fluid usually consisting of a transparent resin, such as shellac, dissolved in alcohol and sprayed over drawings to prevent smudging **2** *Cytology* a fluid, such as formaldehyde or ethanol, that fixes tissues and cells for microscopic study **3** a substance added to a liquid, such as a perfume, to make it less volatile

fixed 1 (of an element) held in chemical combination **2** (of a substance) nonvolatile **3** *Astrology* of, relating to, or belonging to the group consisting of the four signs of the zodiac Taurus, Leo, Scorpio, and Aquarius, which are associated with stability

fixed star 1 any of the stars in the Ptolemaic system, all of which were thought to be attached to an outer crystal sphere thus explaining their apparent lack of movement **2** an extremely distant star whose position appears to be almost stationary over a long period of time

fixer *Photog* a solution containing one or more chemical compounds that is used, in fixing, to dissolve unexposed silver halides. It sometimes has an additive to stop the action of developer

fixture 1 *Property law* an article attached to land and regarded as part of it **2** a device to secure a workpiece in a machine tool **3** *Chiefly Brit* a sports match or social occasion

fizz the bubbly quality of a drink; effervescence

fjord *or* **fiord** (esp on the coast of Norway) a long narrow inlet of the sea between high steep cliffs formed by glacial action

flag¹ 1 an indicator, that may be set or unset, used to indicate a condition or to stimulate a particular reaction in the execution of a computer program **2** *Informal* short for **flagship 3** the fringe of long hair, tapering towards the tip, on the underside of the tail of certain breeds of dog, such as setters **4** the conspicuously marked tail of a deer **5** *Austral and NZ* the part of a taximeter that is raised when a taxi is for hire **6** *Economics* the pennant-shaped pattern that is formed when a price fluctuation is plotted on a chart, interrupting the steady rise or fall that precedes and then follows it **7 show the flag** to assert a claim, as to a territory or stretch of water, by military presence

flag² 1 any of various plants that have long swordlike leaves, esp the iris *Iris pseudacorus* (**yellow flag**) **2** the leaf of any such plant

flagellate 1 resembling a flagellum; whiplike **2** a flagellate organism, esp any protozoan of the phylum *Zoomastigina*

flagellum 1 *Biology* a long whiplike outgrowth from a cell that acts as an organ of locomotion: occurs in some protozoans, gametes, spores, etc. **2** *Botany* a long thin supple shoot or runner **3** *Zoology* the terminal whiplike part of an arthropod's appendage, esp of the antenna of many insects

flageolet¹ a high-pitched musical instrument of the recorder family having six or eight finger holes

flageolet² *or* **flageolet bean** the pale green immature seed of a haricot bean, cooked and eaten as a vegetable

flag of convenience a national flag flown by a ship registered in that country to gain financial or legal advantage

flagon 1 a large bottle of wine, cider, etc. **2** a vessel having a handle, spout, and narrow neck

flagship 1 a ship, esp in a fleet, aboard which the commander of the fleet is quartered **2** the most important ship belonging to a shipping company

Flagstad Kirsten 1895–1962, Norwegian operatic soprano, noted particularly for her interpretations of Wagner

flagstone *or* **flag** a hard fine-textured rock, such as a sandstone or shale, that can be split up into slabs for paving

Flaherty Robert (Joseph) 1884–1951, US film director, a pioneer of documentary film; his work includes *Nanook of the North* (1922) and *Elephant Boy* (1935)

flair *Hunting, rare* **a** the scent left by quarry **b** the sense of smell of a hound

flake *Archaeol* **a** a fragment removed by chipping or hammering from a larger stone used as a tool or weapon **b** (*as modifier*): *flake tool*

Flamborough Head a chalk promontory in NE England, on the coast of the East Riding of Yorkshire

flamboyant *Architecture* of, denoting, or relating to the French Gothic style of architecture characterized by flamelike tracery and elaborate carving

flame 1 a hot usually luminous body of burning gas often containing small incandescent particles, typically emanating in flickering streams from burning material or produced by a jet of ignited gas **2** the state or condition of burning with flames **3** a strong reddish-orange colour

flamenco 1 a type of dance music for vocal soloist and guitar, characterized by elaborate melody and sad mood **2** the dance performed to such music

flamingo 1 any large wading bird of the family *Phoenicopteridae*, having a pink-and-red plumage and downward-bent bill and inhabiting brackish lakes: order *Ciconiiformes* **2** a reddish-orange colour

Flaminian Way an ancient road in Italy, extending north from Rome to Rimini: constructed in 220 BC by Gaius Flaminius. Length: over 322 km (200 miles)

Flamininus Titus Quinctius ?230–?174 BC, Roman general and statesman: defeated Macedonia (197) and proclaimed the independence of the Greek states (196)

Flaminius Gaius died 217 BC, Roman statesman and general: built the Flaminian Way; defeated by Hannibal at Trasimene (217)

Flamsteed John 1646–1719, English astronomer: the first Astronomer Royal and first director of the Royal Observatory, Greenwich (1675). He increased the accuracy of existing stellar catalogues, greatly aiding navigation

flan a piece of metal ready to receive the die or stamp in the production of coins; shaped blank; planchet

Flanders a powerful medieval principality in the SW part of the Low Countries, now in the Belgian provinces of East and West Flanders, the Netherlands province of Zeeland, and the French department of the Nord; scene of battles in many wars

flange 1 a projecting disc-shaped collar or rim on an object for locating or strengthening it or for attaching it to another object 2 a flat outer face of a rolled-steel joist, esp of an I- or H-beam 3 a tool for forming a flange

flank 1 the side of a man or animal between the ribs and the hip 2 (loosely) the outer part of the human thigh

flannel a soft light woollen fabric with a slight nap, used for clothing

flannelette a cotton imitation of flannel

flap 1 *Aviation* a movable surface fixed to the trailing edge of an aircraft wing that increases lift during take-off and drag during landing 2 *Surgery* a piece of tissue partially connected to the body, either following an amputation or to be used as a graft

flapper (in the 1920s) a young woman, esp one flaunting her unconventional dress and behaviour

flare 1 *Optics* a the unwanted light reaching the image region of an optical device by reflections inside the instrument, etc. b the fogged area formed on a negative by such reflections 2 *Aeronautics* the final transition phase of an aircraft landing, from the steady descent path to touchdown

flash 1 *Chemistry* a volatile mixture of inorganic salts used to produce a glaze on bricks or tiles 2 a a sudden rush of water down a river or watercourse b a device, such as a sluice, for producing such a rush 3 *Photog, informal* short for **flashlight** 4 *Engineering* a ridge of thin metal or plastic formed on a moulded object by the extrusion of excess material between dies

flashback a transition in a novel, film, etc, to an earlier scene or event

flashbulb *Photog* a small expendable glass light bulb formerly used to produce a bright flash of light

flash flood a sudden short-lived torrent, usually caused by a heavy storm, esp in desert regions

flashlight 1 *chiefly US and Canadian* a small portable electric lamp powered by one or more dry batteries 2 *Photog* the brief bright light emitted by an electronic flash unit 3 *Chiefly US and Canadian* a light that flashes, used for signalling, in a lighthouse, etc.

flash point or **flashing point** the lowest temperature at which the vapour above a liquid can be ignited in air

flask 1 a container packed with sand to form a mould in a foundry 2 *Engineering* a container used for transporting irradiated nuclear fuel

flat 1 *Chiefly Brit* a (of races, racetracks, or racecourses) not having obstacles to be jumped b of, relating to, or connected with flat racing as opposed to steeplechasing and hurdling 2 (of trade, business, a market, etc) commercially inactive; sluggish 3 (of a print, photograph, or painting) lacking contrast or shading between tones 4 (of a painting) lacking perspective 5 *Music* a denoting a note of a given letter name (or the sound it represents) that has been lowered in pitch by one chromatic semitone b (of an instrument, voice, etc) out of tune by being too low in pitch 6 a low-lying tract of land, esp a marsh or swamp 7 a mud bank exposed at low tide 8 *Music* an accidental that lowers the pitch of the following note by one chromatic semitone. b a note affected by this accidental 9 *Theatre* a rectangular wooden frame covered with painted canvas, etc, used to form part of a stage setting 10 *often cap*; preceded by the *Chiefly Brit* a flat racing, esp as opposed to steeplechasing and hurdling b the season of flat racing 11 *Nautical* a flatboat or lighter 12 *US and Canadian* a shallow box or container, used for holding plants, growing seedlings, etc.

flatboat any boat with a flat bottom, usually for transporting goods on a canal or river

flatfish any marine spiny-finned fish of the order *Heterosomata*, including the halibut, plaice, turbot, and sole, all of which (when adult) swim along the sea floor on one side of the body, which is highly compressed and has both eyes on the uppermost side

flathead any Pacific scorpaenoid food fish of the family *Platycephalidae*, which resemble gurnards

flat racing a the racing of horses on racecourses without jumps b (*as modifier*): *the flat-racing season*

flat spin an aircraft spin in which the longitudinal axis is more nearly horizontal than vertical

flatter 1 a blacksmith's tool, resembling a flat-faced hammer, that is placed on forged work and struck to smooth the surface of the forging 2 a die with a narrow rectangular orifice for drawing flat sections

flattie *NZ, informal* a flounder or other flatfish

flatulent 1 suffering from or caused by an excessive amount of gas in the alimentary canal, producing uncomfortable distension 2 generating excessive gas in the alimentary canal

flatworm any parasitic or free-living invertebrate of the phylum *Platyhelminthes*, including planarians, flukes, and tapeworms, having a flattened body with no circulatory system and only one opening to the intestine

Flaubert Gustave 1821–80, French novelist and short-story writer, regarded as a leader of the 19th-century naturalist school. His most famous novel, *Madame Bovary* (1857), for which he was prosecuted (and acquitted) on charges of immorality, and *L'Éducation sentimentale* (1869) deal with the conflict of romantic attitudes and bourgeois society. His other major works include *Salammbô* (1862), *La Tentation de Saint Antoine* (1874), and *Trois contes* (1877)

flautist or *US and Canadian* **flutist** a player of the flute

flavour or *US* **flavor** *Physics* a property of quarks that enables them to be differentiated into six types: up, down, strange, charm, bottom (or beauty), and top (or truth)

flaw[1] *Law* an invalidating fault or defect in a document or proceeding

flaw[2] a a sudden short gust of wind; squall b a spell of bad, esp windy, weather

flax 1 any herbaceous plant or shrub of the genus *Linum*, esp *L. usitatissimum*, which has blue flowers and is cultivated for its seeds (flaxseed) and for the fibres of its stems: family *Linaceae* 2 the fibre of this plant, made into thread and woven into linen fabrics 3 any of various similar plants 4 *NZ* a swamp plant producing a fibre that is used by Māoris for decorative work, baskets, etc.

flaxen or **flaxy** 1 of, relating to, or resembling flax 2 of a soft yellow colour

Flaxman John 1755–1826, English neoclassical sculptor and draughtsman, noted particularly for his monuments and his engraved illustrations for the *Iliad*, the *Odyssey*, and works by Dante and Aeschylus

flea 1 any small wingless parasitic blood-sucking insect of the order *Siphonaptera*, living on the skin of mammals and birds and noted for its power of leaping 2 any of various invertebrates that resemble fleas, such as the water flea and flea beetle

flea-bitten 1 bitten by or infested with fleas 2 (of the coat of a horse) having reddish-brown spots on a lighter background

flea market an open-air market selling cheap and often second-hand goods

fleapit *Informal* a shabby cinema or theatre

Flecker James Elroy 1884–1915, English poet and dramatist; author of *Hassan* (1922)

fledgling *or* **fledgeling** a young bird that has just fledged

fleece sheepskin or a fabric with soft pile, used as a lining for coats, etc.

fleet¹ 1 a number of warships organized as a tactical unit 2 all the warships of a nation 3 a number of aircraft, ships, buses, etc, operating together or under the same ownership

fleet² *Chiefly Southeastern Brit* a small coastal inlet; creek

Fleet the 1 a stream that formerly ran into the Thames between Ludgate Hill and Fleet Street and is now a covered sewer 2 (formerly) a London prison, esp used for holding debtors

Fleet Street a street in central London in which many newspaper offices were formerly situated

Fleetwood a fishing port in NW England, in Lancashire. Pop: 26 841 (2001)

Fleming¹ 1 Sir Alexander 1881–1955, Scottish bacteriologist: discovered lysozyme (1922) and penicillin (1928): shared the Nobel prize for physiology or medicine in 1945 2 Ian (Lancaster). 1908–64, English author of spy novels; creator of the secret agent James Bond 3 Sir John Ambrose 1849–1945, English electrical engineer: invented the thermionic valve (1904)

Fleming² a native or inhabitant of Flanders or a Flemish-speaking Belgian

Flemish one of the two official languages of Belgium, almost identical in form with Dutch

Flemish Brabant a province of central Belgium, formed in 1995 from the N part of Brabant province: densely populated and intensively farmed, with large industrial centres. Pop: 1 031 904 (2004 est). Area: 2106 sq km (813 sq miles)

Flensburg a port in N Germany, in Schleswig-Holstein: taken from Denmark by Prussia in 1864; voted to remain German in 1920. Pop: 85 300 (2003 est)

flesh 1 the soft part of the body of an animal or human, esp muscular tissue, as distinct from bone and viscera 2 the thick usually soft part of a fruit or vegetable, as distinct from the skin, core, stone, etc. 3 a yellowish-pink to greyish-yellow colour 4 *Christian Science* belief on the physical plane which is considered erroneous, esp the belief that matter has sensation

fleshly worldly as opposed to spiritual

flesh wound a wound affecting superficial tissues

fleshy *Botany* (of some fruits, leaves, etc) thick and pulpy

Fletcher John 1579–1625, English Jacobean dramatist,

noted for his romantic tragicomedies written in collaboration with Francis Beaumont, esp *Philaster* (1610) and *The Maid's Tragedy* (1611)

Fleury André Hercule de 1653–1743, French cardinal and statesman: Louis XV's chief adviser and virtual ruler of France (1726–43)

flex *Brit* a flexible insulated electric cable, used esp to connect appliances to mains

flicker¹ *Television* a visual sensation, often seen in a television image, produced by periodic fluctuations in the brightness of light at a frequency below that covered by the persistence of vision

flicker² any North American woodpecker of the genus *Colaptes*, esp *C. auratus* (**yellow-shafted flicker**), which has a yellow undersurface to the wings and tail

flight 1 a a scheduled airline journey b an aircraft flying on such a journey 2 the basic tactical unit of a military air force 3 a journey through space, esp of a spacecraft 4 *Athletics* a a single line of hurdles across a track in a race b a series of such hurdles 5 a bird's wing or tail feather; flight feather 6 a feather or plastic attachment fitted to an arrow or dart to give it stability in flight 7 the distance covered by a flight arrow 8 *Sport, esp cricket* a a flighted movement imparted to a ball, dart, etc. b the ability to flight a ball 9 *Angling* a device on a spinning lure that revolves rapidly 10 a large enclosed area attached to an aviary or pigeon loft where the birds may fly but not escape

flight deck 1 the crew compartment in an airliner 2 the upper deck of an aircraft carrier from which aircraft take off and on which they land

flightless (of certain birds and insects) unable to fly

flight recorder an electronic device fitted to an aircraft for storing information concerning its performance in flight. It is often used to determine the cause of a crash

flinch a card game in which players build sequences

Flinders Island an island off the coast of NE Tasmania: the largest of the Furneaux Islands. Pop: 850 (2004 est). Area: 2077 sq km (802 sq miles)

Flinders Range a mountain range in E South Australia, between Lake Torrens and Lake Frome. Highest peak: 1188 m (3898 ft)

fling *Dance* any of various vigorous Scottish reels full of leaps and turns, such as the Highland fling

flint 1 an impure opaque microcrystalline greyish-black form of quartz that occurs in chalk. It produces sparks when struck with steel and is used in the manufacture of pottery, flint glass, and road-construction materials. Formula: SiO_2 2 colourless glass other than plate glass

Flint 1 a town in NE Wales, in Flintshire, on the Dee estuary. Pop: 11 936 (2001) 2 a city in SE Michigan: closure of the car production plants led to a high level of unemployment. Pop: 120 292 (2003 est)

Flintshire a county of NE Wales, on the Irish Sea and the Dee estuary: became part of Clwyd in 1974, reinstated with reduced borders in 1996: includes the industrialized Deeside region in the E and the Clwydian Hills in the SW. Administrative centre: Mold. Pop: 149 400 (2003 est). Area: 437 sq km (169 sq miles)

flip 1 a somersault, esp one performed in the air, as in a dive, rather than from a standing position 2 same as **nog**

flip-flop 1 *Gymnastics* a backward handspring 2 *Electronics* an electronic device or circuit that can assume either of two stable states by the application of a suitable pulse

flipper 1 the flat broad limb of seals, whales, penguins, and other aquatic animals, specialized for swimming 2 either of a pair of rubber paddle-like devices worn on the feet as an aid in swimming, esp underwater 3 *Cricket* a ball bowled with topspin imparted by the action of the bowler's wrist

float 1 *Angling* an indicator attached to a baited line that sits on the water and moves when a fish bites 2 *Chiefly US* any buoyant object, such as a platform or inflated tube, used offshore by swimmers or, when moored alongside a pier, as a dock by vessels 3 a blade of a paddle wheel 4 *Brit* a buoyant garment or device to aid a person in staying afloat 5 a hollow watertight structure fitted to the underside of an aircraft to allow it to land on water 6 a motor vehicle used to carry a tableau or exhibit in a parade, esp a civic parade 7 a small delivery vehicle, esp one powered by batteries 8 *Austral and NZ* a vehicle for transporting horses 9 a sum of money used by shopkeepers to provide change at the start of the day's business, this sum being subtracted from the total at the end of the day when calculating the day's takings 10 *Engineering* a hollow cylindrical structure in a carburettor that actuates the fuel valve 11 (in textiles) a single thread brought to or above the surface of a woven fabric, esp to form a pattern 12 *Forestry* a measure of timber equal to eighteen loads

floating 1 (of an organ or part) displaced from the normal position or abnormally movable 2 *Politics* not definitely attached to one place or policy; uncommitted or unfixed 3 *Machinery* operating smoothly through being free from external constraints 4 (of an electronic circuit or device) not connected to a source of voltage

floating rib any rib of the lower two pairs of ribs in man, which are not attached to the breastbone

flocculent 1 *Chem* aggregated in woolly cloudlike masses 2 *Biology* covered with tufts or flakes of a waxy or wool-like substance

flock¹ a body of Christians regarded as the pastoral charge of a priest, a bishop, the pope, etc.

flock² very small tufts of wool applied to fabrics, wallpaper, etc, to give a raised pattern

Flodden a hill in Northumberland where invading Scots were defeated by the English in 1513 and James IV of Scotland was killed

flood 1 a the inundation of land that is normally dry through the overflowing of a body of water, esp a river b the state of a river that is at an abnormally high level (esp in the phrase **in flood**) 2 a the rising of the tide from low to high water b (*as modifier*): *the flood tide* 3 *Theatre* short for **floodlight** (sense 1)

Flood¹ Henry 1732–91, Anglo-Irish politician: leader of the parliamentary opposition to English rule

Flood² *Old Testament* the the flood extending over all the earth from which Noah and his family and livestock were saved in the ark. (Genesis 7–8); the Deluge

floodgate a gate in a sluice that is used to control the flow of water

floodlight 1 a broad intense beam of artificial light, esp

as used in the theatre or to illuminate the exterior of buildings 2 the lamp or source producing such light

flood plain the flat area bordering a river, composed of sediment deposited during flooding

floor 1 a flat bottom surface in or on any structure 2 *Nautical* the bottom, or the lowermost framing members at the bottom, of a vessel 3 *Politics* that part of a legislative hall in which debate and other business is conducted 4 *Politics* the right to speak in a legislative or deliberative body (esp in the phrases **get, have,** or **be given the floor**) 5 a minimum price charged or paid 6 **take the floor** to begin dancing on a dance floor

floor plan a drawing to scale of the arrangement of rooms on one floor of a building

floppy disk a flexible removable magnetic disk that stores information and can be used to store data for use in a microprocessor

flora 1 all the plant life of a given place or time 2 a descriptive list of such plants, often including a key for identification

Florence a city in central Italy, on the River Arno in Tuscany: became an independent republic in the 14th century; under Austrian and other rule intermittently from 1737 to 1859; capital of Italy 1865–70. It was the major cultural and artistic centre of the Renaissance and is still one of the world's chief art centres. Pop: 356 118 (2001)

Florentine a type of domestic fancy pigeon somewhat resembling the Modena

Flores 1 an island in Indonesia, one of the Lesser Sunda Islands, between the Flores Sea and the Savu Sea: mountainous, with active volcanoes and unexplored forests. Chief town: Ende. Area: 17 150 sq km (6622 sq miles) 2 an island in the Atlantic, the westernmost of the Azores. Chief town: Santa Cruz. Area: 142 sq km (55 sq miles)

Flores Sea a part of the Pacific Ocean in Indonesia between Celebes and the Lesser Sunda Islands

floret a small flower, esp one of many making up the head of a composite flower

Florey Howard Walter, Baron Florey. 1898–1968, British pathologist: shared the Nobel prize for physiology or medicine (1945) with E. B. Chain and Alexander Fleming for their work on penicillin

floribunda any of several varieties of cultivated hybrid roses whose flowers grow in large sprays

Florida 1 a state of the southeastern US, between the Atlantic and the Gulf of Mexico: consists mostly of a low-lying peninsula ending in the **Florida Keys** a chain of small islands off the coast of S Florida, extending southwest for over 160 km (100 miles). Capital: Tallahassee. Pop: 17 019 068 (2003 est). Area: 143 900 sq km (55 560 sq miles) 2 **Straits of** a sea passage between the Florida Keys and Cuba, linking the Atlantic with the Gulf of Mexico

florin 1 a former British coin, originally silver and later cupronickel, equivalent to ten (new) pence 2 the standard monetary unit of Aruba, divided into 100 cents 3 (formerly) another name for **guilder**

floss 1 the mass of fine silky fibres obtained from cotton and similar plants 2 any similar fine silky material, such as the hairlike styles and stigmas of maize or the fibres prepared from silkworm cocoons 3 See **dental floss**

flotation or **floatation** 1 power or ability to float; buoyancy 2 a process to concentrate the valuable ore in low-grade ores. The ore is ground to a powder, mixed with water containing surface-active chemicals, and vigorously aerated. The bubbles formed trap the required ore fragments and carry them to the surface froth, which is then skimmed off

flotilla a small fleet or a fleet of small vessels

flotsam wreckage from a ship found floating

flounder 1 a European flatfish, *Platichthys flesus* having a greyish-brown body covered with prickly scales: family *Pleuronectidae*: an important food fish 2 *US and Canadian* any flatfish of the families *Bothidae* (turbot, etc) and *Pleuronectidae* (plaice, halibut, sand dab, etc)

flourish a grandiose passage of music

flow 1 the advancing of the tide 2 a stream of molten or solidified lava 3 an informal word for **menstruation** 4 *Scot* **a** a marsh or swamp **b** an inlet or basin of the sea

flow chart or **sheet** a diagrammatic representation of the sequence of operations or equipment in an industrial process, computer program, etc.

Flow Country an area of moorland and peat bogs in northern Scotland known for its wildlife, now partly afforested

flower 1 the reproductive structure of angiosperm plants, consisting normally of stamens and carpels surrounded by petals and sepals all borne on the receptacle (one or more of these structures may be absent). In some plants it is conspicuous and brightly coloured and attracts insects or other animals for pollination 2 any similar reproductive structure in other plants 3 an embellishment or ornamental symbol depicting a flower 4 *Chemistry* fine powder, usually produced by sublimation

▷www.garden.org
▷www.ontariogardening.com/Tips/flowers.jsp
▷www.bbc.co.uk/gardening/basics/techniques
▷www.anbg.gov.au
▷www.sis.agr.gc.ca/cansis/nsdb/climate/hardiness/intro.html

flowerpot a pot in which plants are grown

flown relating to coloured (usually blue) decoration on porcelain that, during firing, has melted into the surrounding glaze giving a halo-like effect

flu *Informal* 1 short for **influenza** 2 any of various viral infections, esp a respiratory or intestinal infection

flue¹ *Music* the passage in an organ pipe or flute within which a vibrating air column is set up

flue² or **flew** a type of fishing net

fluff soft light particles, such as the down or nap of cotton or wool

fluid 1 a substance, such as a liquid or gas, that can flow, has no fixed shape, and offers little resistance to an external stress 2 capable of flowing and easily changing shape

fluid ounce a unit of capacity equal to the volume of one avoirdupois ounce of distilled water at 62°F: there are twenty fluid ounces in an Imperial pint and sixteen in a US pint

fluke¹ 1 a flat bladelike projection at the end of the arm

of an anchor 2 either of the two lobes of the tail of a whale or related animal 3 the barb or barbed head of a harpoon, arrow, etc.

fluke² 1 any parasitic flatworm, such as the blood fluke and liver fluke, of the classes *Monogenea* and *Digenea* (formerly united in a single class *Trematoda*) 2 another name for **flounder** (sense 1)

flume 1 a ravine through which a stream flows 2 a narrow artificial channel made for providing water for power, floating logs, etc. 3 a slide in the form of a long and winding tube with a stream of water running through it that descends into a purpose-built pool

flunk *Education, Informal, chiefly US, Canadian, and NZ* a low grade below the pass standard

fluorescence 1 *Physics* **a** the emission of light or other radiation from atoms or molecules that are bombarded by particles, such as electrons, or by radiation from a separate source. The bombarding radiation produces excited atoms, molecules, or ions and these emit photons as they fall back to the ground state **b** such an emission of photons that ceases as soon as the bombarding radiation is discontinued **c** such an emission of photons for which the average lifetime of the excited atoms and molecules is less than about 10^{-8} seconds 2 the radiation emitted as a result of fluorescence

fluorescent lamp 1 a type of lamp in which an electrical gas discharge is maintained in a tube with a thin layer of phosphor on its inside surface. The gas, which is often mercury vapour, emits ultraviolet radiation causing the phosphor to fluoresce 2 a type of lamp in which an electrical discharge is maintained in a tube containing a gas such as neon, mercury vapour, or sodium vapour at low pressure. Gas atoms in the discharge are struck by electrons and fluoresce

fluoride 1 any salt of hydrofluoric acid, containing the fluoride ion, F^- 2 any compound containing fluorine, such as methyl fluoride

fluorine or **fluorin** a toxic pungent pale yellow gas of the halogen group that is the most electronegative and reactive of all the elements, occurring principally in fluorspar and cryolite: used in the production of uranium, fluorocarbons, and other chemicals. Symbol: F; atomic no.: 9; atomic wt.: 18.9984032; valency: 1; density: 1.696 kg/m³; relative density: 1.108; freezing pt.: –219.62°C; boiling pt.: –188.13°C

fluoroscopy examination of a person or object by means of a fluoroscope

fluorspar, fluor, or *US and Canadian* **fluorite** a white or colourless mineral sometimes fluorescent and often tinted by impurities, found in veins and as deposits from hot gases. It is used in the manufacture of glass, enamel, and jewellery, and is the chief ore of fluorine. Composition: calcium fluoride. Formula: CaF_2. Crystal structure: cubic

flurry *Hunting* the death spasms of a harpooned whale

flush¹ 1 redness of the skin, esp of the face, as from the effects of a fever, alcohol, etc. 2 *Ecology* an area of boggy land fed by ground water

flush² 1 (of a vessel) having no superstructure built above the flat level of the deck 2 *Botany* a period of fresh growth of leaves, shoots, etc.

flush³ (in poker and similar games) a hand containing

only one suit

Flushing a port in the SW Netherlands, in Zeeland province, on Walcheren Island, at the mouth of the West Scheldt river: the first Dutch city to throw off Spanish rule (1572). Pop: 45 000 (2003 est)

flute 1 a wind instrument consisting of an open cylindrical tube of wood or metal having holes in the side stopped either by the fingers or by pads controlled by keys. The breath is directed across a mouth hole cut in the side, causing the air in the tube to vibrate. Range: about three octaves upwards from middle C 2 any pipe blown directly on the principle of a flue pipe, either by means of a mouth hole or through a fipple 3 *Architect* a rounded shallow concave groove on the shaft of a column, pilaster, etc.

fluting a design or decoration of flutes on a column, pilaster, etc.

flutter 1 *Pathol* an abnormally rapid beating of the auricles of the heart (200 to 400 beats per minute), esp in a regular rhythm, sometimes resulting in heart block 2 *Electronics* a slow variation in pitch in a sound-reproducing system, similar to wow but occurring at higher frequencies 3 *Aeronautics* a potentially dangerous oscillation of an aircraft, or part of an aircraft, caused by the interaction of aerodynamic forces, structural elastic reactions, and inertia 4 *Music* a method of sounding a wind instrument, esp the flute, with a rolling movement of the tongue

fluvial *or* **fluviatile** of, relating to, or occurring in a river

flux 1 a substance, such as borax or salt, that gives a low melting-point mixture with a metal oxide. It is used for cleaning metal surfaces during soldering, etc, and for protecting the surfaces of liquid metals 2 *Metallurgy* a chemical used to increase the fluidity of refining slags in order to promote the rate of chemical reaction 3 a similar substance used in the making of glass 4 *Physics* a the rate of flow of particles, energy, or a fluid, through a specified area, such as that of neutrons (**neutron flux**) or of light energy (**luminous flux**) b the strength of a field in a given area expressed as the product of the area and the component of the field strength at right angles to the area 5 *Pathol* an excessive discharge of fluid from the body, such as watery faeces in diarrhoea 6 (in the philosophy of Heraclitus) the state of constant change in which all things exist

fly¹ 1 a a flap forming the entrance to a tent b a piece of canvas drawn over the ridgepole of a tent to form an outer roof 2 a small air brake used to control the chiming of large clocks 3 the horizontal weighted arm of a fly press 4 *Brit* a light one-horse covered carriage formerly let out on hire 5 *Theatre* the space above the stage out of view of the audience, used for storing scenery, etc.

fly² 1 any dipterous insect, esp the housefly, characterized by active flight 2 any of various similar but unrelated insects, such as the caddis fly, firefly, dragonfly, and chalcid fly 3 *Angling* a lure made from a fish-hook dressed with feathers, tinsel, etc, to resemble any of various flies or nymphs: used in fly-fishing 4 (in southern Africa) an area that is infested with the tsetse fly

flyblown covered with flyblows

flycatcher 1 any small insectivorous songbird of the Old World subfamily *Muscicapinae*, having small slender bills fringed with bristles: family *Muscicapidae* 2 any American passerine bird of the family *Tyrannidae*

flyer *or* **flier** 1 an aviator or pilot 2 a fast-moving machine part, esp one having periodic motion

flying 1 *Nautical* (of a sail) not hauled in tight against the wind 2 the act of piloting, navigating, or travelling in an aircraft

flying boat a seaplane in which the fuselage consists of a hull that provides buoyancy in the water

flying buttress a buttress supporting a wall or other structure by an arch or part of an arch that transmits the thrust outwards and downwards

flying fish any marine teleost fish of the family *Exocoetidae*, common in warm and tropical seas, having enlarged winglike pectoral fins used for gliding above the surface of the water

flying fox 1 any large fruit bat, esp any of the genus *Pteropus* of tropical Africa and Asia: family *Pteropodidae* 2 *Austral and NZ* a cable mechanism used for transportation across a river, gorge, etc.

flying start 1 (in sprinting) a start by a competitor anticipating the starting signal 2 a start to a race or time trial in which the competitor is already travelling at speed as he passes the starting line

Flynn 1 Errol 1909–59, Australian-born Hollywood actor, who was noted for his swashbuckling roles; his films included *Captain Blood* (1935), *The Adventures of Robin Hood* (1938), and *Too Much Too Soon* (1958) 2 Rev. John 1880–1951, founder of the Australian flying doctor service

flyover 1 *Brit* a an intersection of two roads at which one is carried over the other by a bridge b such a bridge 2 the US name for a **fly-past**

fly-past a ceremonial flight of aircraft over a given area

flyweight 1 a a professional boxer weighing not more than 112 pounds (51 kg) b an amateur boxer weighing 48–51 kg (106–112 pounds) c (*as modifier*): *a flyweight contest* 2 (in Olympic wrestling) a wrestler weighing not more than 115 pounds (52 kg)

flywheel a heavy wheel that stores kinetic energy and smooths the operation of a reciprocating engine by maintaining a constant speed of rotation over the whole cycle

f-number *or* **f number** *Photog* the numerical value of the relative aperture. If the relative aperture is f8, 8 is the f-number and indicates that the focal length of the lens is 8 times the size of the lens aperture

Fo Dario born 1926, Italian playwright and actor. His plays include *The Accidental Death of an Anarchist* (1970), *Trumpets and Raspberries* (1984), and *The Tricks of the Trade* (1991): Nobel prize for literature 1997

foal the young of a horse or related animal

foam 1 a mass of small bubbles of gas formed on the surface of a liquid, such as the froth produced by agitating a solution of soap or detergent in water 2 frothy saliva sometimes formed in and expelled from the mouth, as in rabies 3 the frothy sweat of a horse or similar animal 4 a any of a number of light cellular solids made by creating bubbles of gas in the liquid material and solidifying it: used as insulators and in packaging b (*as modifi-*

er): *foam rubber* **5** a colloid consisting of a gas suspended in a liquid **6** a mixture of chemicals sprayed from a fire extinguisher onto a burning substance to create a stable layer of bubbles which smothers the flames

focal length *or* **distance** the distance from the focal point of a lens or mirror to the reflecting surface of the mirror or the centre point of the lens

focal point the point on the axis of a lens or mirror to which parallel rays of light converge or from which they appear to diverge after refraction or reflection

Foch Ferdinand 1851–1929, marshal of France; commander in chief of Allied armies on the Western front in World War I (1918)

focus **1** a point of convergence of light or other electromagnetic radiation, particles, sound waves, etc, or a point from which they appear to diverge **2** another name for **focal point** *or* **focal length** **3** *Optics* the state of an optical image when it is distinct and clearly defined or the state of an instrument producing this image **4** *Geometry* a fixed reference point on the concave side of a conic section, used when defining its eccentricity **5** the point beneath the earth's surface at which an earthquake or underground nuclear explosion originates **6** *Pathol* the main site of an infection or a localized region of diseased tissue

fog¹ **1** a mass of droplets of condensed water vapour suspended in the air, often greatly reducing visibility, corresponding to a cloud but at a lower level **2** a cloud of any substance in the atmosphere reducing visibility **3** *Photog* a blurred or discoloured area on a developed negative, print, or transparency caused by the action of extraneous light, incorrect development, etc. **4** a colloid or suspension consisting of liquid particles dispersed in a gas

fog² **a** a second growth of grass after the first mowing **b** grass left to grow long in winter

Fogarty Carl (George). born 1965, British racing motorcyclist; Superbike world champion 1994, 1995, 1998, 1999

fog bank a distinct mass of fog, esp at sea

Foggia a city in SE Italy, in Apulia: seat of Emperor Frederick II; centre for Carbonari revolutionary societies in the revolts of 1820, 1848, and 1860. Pop: 155 203 (2001)

foghorn a mechanical instrument sounded at intervals to serve as a warning to vessels in fog

foil¹ *Hunting* any scent that obscures the trail left by a hunted animal

foil² **1** metal in the form of very thin sheets **2** the thin metallic sheet forming the backing of a mirror **3** *Architect* a small arc between cusps, esp as used in Gothic window tracery **4** short for **aerofoil** *or* **hydrofoil**

Fokine Michel 1880–1942, US choreographer, born in Russia, regarded as the creator of modern ballet. He worked with Diaghilev as director of the Ballet Russe (1909–15), producing works such as *Les Sylphides* and *Petrushka*

Fokker Anthony Herman Gerard 1890–-1939, Dutch designer and builder of aircraft, born in Java

fold¹ **1** a hollow in undulating terrain **2** *Geology* a bend in stratified rocks that results from movements within the earth's crust and produces such structures as anticlines and synclines

fold² a church or the members of it

foliaceous **1** having the appearance of the leaf of a plant **2** bearing leaves or leaflike structures **3** *Geology* (of certain rocks, esp schists) consisting of thin layers; foliated

foliage **1** the green leaves of a plant **2** an ornamental leaflike design

foliation **1** *Botany* **a** the process of producing leaves **b** the state of being in leaf **c** the arrangement of leaves in a leaf bud; vernation **2** *Architect* **a** ornamentation consisting of foliage **b** ornamentation consisting of cusps and foils **3** any decoration with foliage **4** *Geology* the arrangement of the constituents of a rock in leaflike layers, as in schists

folio *Law* a unit of measurement of the length of legal documents, determined by the number of words, generally 72 or 90 in Britain and 100 in the US

folk dance **1** any of various traditional rustic dances often originating from festivals or rituals **2** a piece of music composed for such a dance

Folkestone a port and resort in SE England, in E Kent. Pop: 45 273 (2001)

folklore **1** the unwritten literature of a people as expressed in folk tales, proverbs, riddles, songs, etc. **2** the body of stories and legends attached to a particular place, group, activity, etc. **3** the anthropological discipline concerned with the study of folkloric materials

folk music **1** music that is passed on from generation to generation by oral tradition **2** any music composed in the idiom of this oral tradition
▷www.folkmusic.org
▷www.allmusic.com

folk song **1** a song of which the music and text have been handed down by oral tradition among the common people **2** a modern song which employs or reflects the folk idiom

follow *Billiards, Snooker* **a** a forward spin imparted to a cue ball causing it to roll after the object ball **b** a shot made in this way

follower *Engineering* a machine part that derives its motion by following the motion of another part

following (of winds, currents, etc) moving in the same direction as the course of a vessel

follow-on *Cricket* an immediate second innings forced on a team scoring a prescribed number of runs fewer than its opponents in the first innings

follow through *Sport* **a** the act of following through **b** the part of the stroke after the ball has been hit

follow up *Med* a routine examination of a patient at various intervals after medical or surgical treatment

folly **1** *Architecture* a building in the form of a castle, temple, etc, built to satisfy a fancy or conceit, often of an eccentric kind **2** *Theatre* an elaborately costumed revue

Fonda **1** Henry 1905–82, US film actor. His many films include *Young Mr Lincoln* (1939), *The Grapes of Wrath* (1940), *Twelve Angry Men* (1957), and *On Golden Pond* (1981) for which he won an Oscar **2** his daughter Jane born 1937, US film actress. Her films include *Klute* (1971) for which she won an Oscar, *Julia* (1977), *The China Syndrome* (1979), *On Golden Pond* (1981), and *The Old Gringo* (1989) **3** her brother, Peter born 1939, US film actor, who made his name in *Easy Rider* (1969); later films include *Ulee's Gold*

(1997)

fondant (of a colour) soft; pastel

Fonseca Gulf of an inlet of the Pacific Ocean in W Central America

font a a large bowl for baptismal water, usually mounted on a pedestal **b** a receptacle for holy water
▷www.fontscape.com
▷http://babel.uoregon.edu/yamada/ altfonts.html

Fontainebleau a town in N France, in the **Forest of Fontainebleau**: famous for its palace (now a museum), one of the largest royal residences in France, built largely by Francis I (16th century). Pop: 15 942 (1999)

fontanelle or chiefly US **fontanel** Anatomy any of several soft membranous gaps between the bones of the skull in a fetus or infant

Fonteyn Dame **Margot** real name Margaret Hookham. 1919–91, English classical ballerina

food any substance containing nutrients, such as carbohydrates, proteins, and fats, that can be ingested by a living organism and metabolized into energy and body tissue

food chain Ecology a sequence of organisms in an ecosystem in which each species is the food of the next member of the chain

food poisoning an acute illness typically characterized by gastrointestinal inflammation, vomiting, and diarrhoea, caused by food that is either naturally poisonous or contaminated by pathogenic bacteria (esp Salmonella)

fool (formerly) a professional jester living in a royal or noble household

foot 1 the part of the vertebrate leg below the ankle joint that is in contact with the ground during standing and walking **2** any of various organs of locomotion or attachment in invertebrates, including molluscs **3** Botany the lower part of some plant structures, as of a developing moss sporophyte embedded in the parental tissue **4 a** a unit of length equal to one third of a yard or 12 inches. 1 Imperial foot is equivalent to 0.3048 metre **b** any of various units of length used at different times and places, typically about 10 per cent greater than the Imperial foot **5** Music a unit used in classifying organ pipes according to their pitch, in terms of the length of an equivalent column of air **b** this unit applied to stops and registers on other instruments **6** Prosody a group of two or more syllables in which one syllable has the major stress, forming the basic unit of poetic rhythm

footage 1 a length or distance measured in feet **2 a** the extent of film material shot and exposed **b** the sequences of filmed material

foot-and-mouth disease an acute highly infectious viral disease of cattle, pigs, sheep, and goats, characterized by the formation of vesicular eruptions in the mouth and on the feet, esp around the hoofs

football 1 a any of various games played with a round or oval ball and usually based on two teams competing to kick, head, carry, or otherwise propel the ball into each other's goal, territory, etc. **b** (as modifier): a football ground **2** the ball used in any of these games or their variants
▷www.fifa.com

footbridge a narrow bridge for the use of pedestrians

footing 1 the lower part of a foundation of a column, wall, building, etc. **2** Rare a fee paid upon entrance into a craft, society, etc, or such an entrance itself

footman any of several arctiid moths related to the tiger moths, esp the **common footman** (Eilema lurideola), with yellowish hind wings and brown forewings with a yellow front stripe; they produce woolly bear larvae

footpad Archaic a robber or highwayman, on foot rather than horseback

footplate Chiefly Brit **a** a platform in the cab of a locomotive on which the crew stand to operate the controls **b** (as modifier): a footplate man

footprint 1 Computing the amount of resources such as disk space and memory, that an application requires **2** an identifying characteristic on land or water, such as the area in which an aircraft's sonic boom can be heard or the area covered by the down-blast of a hovercraft

foramen a natural hole, esp one in a bone through which nerves and blood vessels pass

Forbes George William 1869–1947, New Zealand statesman; prime minister of New Zealand (1930–35)

Forbidden City the 1 Lhasa, Tibet: once famed for its inaccessibility and hostility to strangers **2** a walled section of Beijing, China, enclosing the Imperial Palace and associated buildings of the former Chinese Empire

force 1 Physics **a** a dynamic influence that changes a body from a state of rest to one of motion or changes its rate of motion. The magnitude of the force is equal to the product of the mass of the body and its acceleration **b** a static influence that produces an elastic strain in a body or system or bears weight. **2** Physics any operating influence that produces or tends to produce a change in a physical quantity **3** Criminal law violence unlawfully committed or threatened **4** Philosophy, Logic that which an expression is normally used to achieve **5 in force** (of a law) having legal validity or binding effect

forced Physics caused by an external agency

force-feed Engineering a method of lubrication in which a pump forces oil into the bearings of an engine, etc.

forceps 1 a a surgical instrument in the form of a pair of pincers, used esp in the delivery of babies **b** (as modifier): a forceps baby **2** any part or structure of an organism shaped like a forceps

ford a shallow area in a river that can be crossed by car, horseback, etc.

Ford 1 Ford Maddox original name Ford Madox Hueffer. 1873–1939, English novelist, editor, and critic; works include The Good Soldier (1915) and the war tetralogy Parade's End (1924–28). **2 Gerald R(udolph).** born 1913, US politician; 38th president of the US (1974–77) **3 Harrison** born 1942, US film actor. His films include Star Wars (1977) and its sequels, Raiders of the Lost Ark (1981) and its sequels, Bladerunner (1982), Clear and Present Danger (1994), and What Lies Beneath (2000) **4 Henry** 1863–1947, US car manufacturer, who pioneered mass production **5 John** 1586–?1639, English dramatist; author of revenge tragedies such as 'Tis Pity She's a Whore (1633) **6 John**, real name Sean O'Feeney. 1895–1973, US film director, esp of Westerns such as Stagecoach (1939) and She Wore a Yellow Ribbon (1949)

fore 1 short for **foremast 2 fore and aft** located at or directed towards both ends of a vessel

forearm the part of the arm from the elbow to the wrist

forecast a statement of probable future weather conditions calculated from meteorological data

forecastle, fo'c's'le, *or* **fo'c'sle** the part of a vessel at the bow where the crew is quartered and stores, machines, etc, may be stowed

forecourt *Sport* the front section of the court in tennis, badminton, etc, esp area between the service line and the net

forefinger the finger next to the thumb

forefoot 1 either of the front feet of a quadruped **2** *Nautical* the forward end of the keel

foreground the area of space in a perspective picture, depicted as nearest the viewer

forehand the part of a horse in front of the saddle

forehead the part of the face between the natural hairline and the eyes, formed skeletally by the frontal bone of the skull; brow

foreign *Law* outside the jurisdiction of a particular state; alien

foreign minister *or* **secretary** a cabinet minister who is responsible for a country's dealings with other countries

foreign office the ministry of a country or state that is concerned with dealings with other states

foreleg either of the front legs of a horse, sheep, or other quadruped

forelock¹ a lock of a horse's mane that grows forwards between the ears

forelock² a wedge or peg passed through the tip of a bolt to prevent withdrawal

foreman *Law* the principal juror, who presides at the deliberations of a jury

Foreman George born 1949, US boxer: WBA world heavyweight champion (1973-74); he regained the title in 1994 but refused to fight the WBA's top-ranked challenger and was stripped of the title in 1995; recognized as WBU champion until 1997

foremast the mast nearest the bow on vessels with two or more masts

forensic relating to, used in, or connected with a court of law

forensic medicine the applied use of medical knowledge or practice, esp pathology, to the purposes of the law, as in determining the cause of death

forepaw either of the front feet of most land mammals that do not have hoofs

foresail *Nautical* **1** the aftermost headsail of a fore-and-aft rigged vessel **2** the lowest sail set on the foremast of a square-rigged vessel

foreshore 1 the part of the shore that lies between the limits for high and low tides **2** the part of the shore that lies just above the high-water mark

forest 1 a large wooded area having a thick growth of trees and plants **2** the trees of such an area **3** NZ an area planted with exotic pines or similar trees **4** *Law* (formerly) an area of woodland, esp one owned by the sovereign and set apart as a hunting ground with its own laws and officers

forestation the planting of trees over a wide area

forester 1 a person skilled in forestry or in charge of a forest **2** any of various Old World moths of the genus *Ino*, characterized by brilliant metallic green wings: family *Zygaenidae* **3** a member of the Ancient Order of Foresters, a friendly society

Forester C(ecil) S(cott) 1899–1966, English novelist; creator of Captain Horatio Hornblower in a series of novels on the Napoleonic Wars

forestry 1 the science of planting and caring for trees **2** the planting and management of forests
▷www.metla.fi/info/vlib/Forestry
▷www.forestry.gov.uk

Forfar a market town in E Scotland, the administrative centre of Angus: site of a castle, residence of Scottish kings between the 11th and 14th centuries. Pop: 13 206 (2001)

forfeit 1 *Law* something confiscated as a penalty for an offence, breach of contract, etc. **2 a** a game in which a player has to give up an object, perform a specified action, etc, if he commits a fault **b** an object so given up

forge 1 a place in which metal is worked by heating and hammering; smithy **2** a hearth or furnace used for heating metal **3** a machine used to shape metals by hammering

forgery 1 *Criminal law* the false making or altering of any document, such as a cheque or character reference (and including a postage stamp), or any tape or disc on which information is stored, intending that anyone shall accept it as genuine and so act to his or another's prejudice **2** *Criminal law* the counterfeiting of a seal or die with intention to defraud

forget-me-not any temperate low-growing plant of the mainly European boraginaceous genus *Myosotis*, having clusters of small typically blue flowers

fork 1 a small usually metal implement consisting of two, three, or four long thin prongs on the end of a handle, used for lifting food to the mouth or turning it in cooking, etc. **2** an agricultural tool consisting of a handle and three or four metal prongs, used for lifting, digging, etc. **3** *Chess* a position in which two pieces are forked

fork-lift truck a vehicle having two power-operated horizontal prongs that can be raised and lowered for loading, transporting, and unloading goods, esp goods that are stacked on wooden pallets

form 1 *Sport* the previous record of a horse, athlete, etc, esp with regard to fitness **2** style, arrangement, or design in the arts, as opposed to content **3** a fixed mode of artistic expression or representation in literary, musical, or other artistic works **4** *Education, chiefly Brit* a group of children who are taught together; class **5** *Philosophy* **a** the structure of anything as opposed to its constitution or content **b** essence as opposed to matter **c** (in the philosophy of Plato) the ideal universal that exists independently of the particulars which fall under it **d** (in the philosophy of Aristotle) the constitution of matter to form a substance; by virtue of this its nature can be understood **6** the nest or hollow in which a hare lives **7** a group of organisms within a species that differ from similar groups by trivial differences, as of colour **8** *Taxonomy* a group distinguished from other groups by a single characteristic: ranked below a variety

formal 1 acquired by study in academic institutions 2 logically deductive 3 *Philosophy* **a** of or relating to form as opposed to matter or content **b** pertaining to the essence or nature of something **c** (in the writings of Descartes) pertaining to the correspondence between an image or idea and its object **d** being in the formal mode

formaldehyde a colourless poisonous irritating gas with a pungent characteristic odour, made by the oxidation of methanol and used as formalin and in the manufacture of synthetic resins. Formula: HCHO

formalin *or* **formol** a 40 per cent solution of formaldehyde in water, used as a disinfectant, preservative for biological specimens, etc.

formalism 1 *Arts* scrupulous or excessive adherence to outward form at the expense of inner reality or content 2 **a** the mathematical or logical structure of a scientific argument as distinguished from its subject matter **b** the notation, and its structure, in which information is expressed 3 *Theatre* a stylized mode of production 4 (in Marxist criticism) excessive concern with artistic technique at the expense of social values, etc. 5 the philosophical theory that a mathematical statement has no meaning but that its symbols, regarded as physical objects, exhibit a structure that has useful applications

Forman Miloš born 1932, Czech film director working in the USA. since 1968. His films include *One Flew over the Cuckoo's Nest* (1976), *Amadeus* (1985), and *The People vs Larry Flynt* (1996)

format *Computing* **a** the defined arrangement of data encoded in a file or for example on magnetic disk or CD-ROM, essential for the correct recording and recovery of data on different devices **b** the arrangement of text on printed output or a display screen, or a coded description of such an arrangement

formation 1 *Geology* **a** the fundamental lithostratigraphic unit **b** a series of rocks with certain characteristics in common 2 *Ecology* a community of plants, such as a tropical rainforest, extending over a very large area

formative (of tissues and cells in certain parts of an organism) capable of growth and differentiation

Formby George. Real name *George Booth*. 1904–61, British comedian. He made many musical films in the 1930s, accompanying his songs on the ukulele

former *Electrical engineering* a tool for giving a coil or winding the required shape, sometimes consisting of a frame on which the wire can be wound, the frame then being removed

formic acid a colourless corrosive liquid carboxylic acid found in some insects, esp ants, and many plants: used in dyeing textiles and the manufacture of insecticides and refrigerants. Formula: HCOOH

Formosa Strait an arm of the Pacific between Taiwan and mainland China, linking the East and South China Seas

formula 1 *Maths, physics* a general relationship, principle, or rule stated, often as an equation, in the form of symbols 2 *Chem* a representation of molecules, radicals, ions, etc, expressed in the symbols of the atoms of their constituent elements 3 **a** a prescription for making up a medicine, baby's food, etc. **b** a substance pre-

pared according to such a prescription 4 *Motor racing* the specific category in which a particular type of car competes, judged according to engine size, weight, and fuel capacity

formulary 1 a book or system of prescribed formulas, esp relating to religious procedure or doctrine 2 *Pharmacol* a book containing a list of pharmaceutical products, with their formulas and means of preparation

fornicate *or* **fornicated** *Biology* arched or hoodlike in form

fornication 1 *Law* voluntary sexual intercourse between two persons of the opposite sex, where one is or both are unmarried 2 *Bible* sexual immorality in general, esp adultery

Forrest John, 1st Baron Forrest. 1847–1918, Australian statesman and explorer; first premier of Western Australia (1890–1901)

Forster E(dward) M(organ). 1879–1970, English novelist, short-story writer, and essayist. His best-known novels are *A Room with a View* (1908), *Howard's End* (1910), and *A Passage to India* (1924), in all of which he stresses the need for sincerity and sensitivity in human relationships and criticizes English middle-class values

Forsyth 1 Bill born 1947, Scottish writer and director. His films include *Gregory's Girl* (1981), *Local Hero* (1983), and *Gregory's Two Girls* (1999) 2 **Frederick** born 1938, British thriller writer. His books include *The Day of the Jackal* (1970), *The Odessa File* (1972), and *The Fourth Protocol* (1984)

forsythia any oleaceous shrub of the genus *Forsythia*, native to China, Japan, and SE Europe but widely cultivated for its showy yellow bell-shaped flowers, which appear in spring before the foliage

Fortaleza a port in NE Brazil, capital of Ceará state. Pop: 3 261 000 (2005 est)

Fort-de-France the capital of Martinique, a port on the W coast: commercial centre of the French Antilles. Pop: 94 049 (1999 est)

forte¹ *Fencing* the stronger section of a sword blade, between the hilt and the middle

forte² *Music* 1 loud or loudly. 2 a loud passage in music

Forth 1 Firth of an inlet of the North Sea in SE Scotland: spanned by a cantilever railway bridge 1600 m (almost exactly 1 mile) long (1889), and by a road bridge (1964) 2 a river in S Scotland, flowing generally east to the Firth of Forth. Length: about 104 km (65 miles)

fortissimo *Music* 1 very loud. 2 a very loud passage in music

Fort Knox a military reservation in N Kentucky: site of the US Gold Bullion Depository. Pop: 38 280 (latest est)

Fort Sumter a fort in SE South Carolina, guarding Charleston Harbour. Its capture by Confederate forces (1861) was the first action of the Civil War

fortune a power or force, often personalized, regarded as being responsible for human affairs; chance

fortune-teller a person who makes predictions about the future as by looking into a crystal ball, reading palms, etc.

Fort William a town in W Scotland, in Highland at the head of Loch Linnhe: tourist centre; the fort itself, built in 1655 and renamed after William III in 1690, was demolished in 1866. Pop: 9908 (2001)

Fort Worth a city in N Texas, at the junction of the Clear and West forks of the Trinity River: aircraft works, electronics. Pop: 585 122 (2003 est)

forty 1 the cardinal number that is the product of ten and four 2 a numeral, 40, XL, etc, representing this number

forty-ninth parallel *Canadian* an informal name for the border with the USA, which is in part delineated by the parallel line of latitude at 49°N

forum 1 (in South Africa) a pressure group of leaders or representatives, esp Black leaders or representatives 2 (in ancient Italy) an open space, usually rectangular in shape, serving as a city's marketplace and centre of public business

forward a an attacking player in any of various sports, such as soccer, hockey, or basketball b (in American football) a lineman

Foshan *or* **Fatshan** a city in SE China, in W Guangdong province. Pop: 483 000 (2005 est)

Fosse Way a Roman road in Britain between Lincoln and Exeter, with a fosse on each side

fossil a relic, remnant, or representation of an organism that existed in a past geological age, or of the activity of such an organism, occurring in the form of mineralized bones, shells, etc, as casts, impressions, and moulds, and as frozen perfectly preserved organisms

fossil fuel any naturally occurring carbon or hydrocarbon fuel, such as coal, petroleum, peat, and natural gas, formed by the decomposition of prehistoric organisms

Foster 1 **Jodie** born 1962, US film actress and director: her films include *Taxi Driver* (1976), *The Accused* (1988), *The Silence of the Lambs* (1990), *Little Man Tate* (1991; also directed), *Nell* (1995), and *Panic Room* (2002) 2 **Norman**, Baron. born 1935, British architect. His works include the Willis Faber building (1978) in Ipswich, Stansted Airport, Essex (1991), Chek Lap Kok Airport, Hong Kong (1998), the renovation of the Reichstag, Berlin (1999), and City Hall, London (2002) 3 **Stephen Collins** 1826–64, US composer of songs such as *The Old Folks at Home* and *Oh Susanna*

Fotheringhay a village in E England, in NE Northamptonshire: ruined castle, scene of the imprisonment and execution of Mary Queen of Scots (1587)

Foucault 1 **Jean Bernard Léon** 1819–68, French physicist. He determined the velocity of light and proved that light travels more slowly in water than in air (1850). He demonstrated by means of the pendulum named after him the rotation of the earth on its axis (1851) and invented the gyroscope (1852) 2 **Michel** 1926–84, French philosopher and historian of ideas. His publications include *Histoire de la folie* (1961) and *Les Mots et les choses* (1966)

foul 1 *Nautical* (of the bottom of a vessel) covered with barnacles and other growth that slow forward motion 2 *Sport* a a violation of the rules b (*as modifier*): *a foul shot*

Foulness a flat marshy island in SE England, in Essex north of the Thames estuary

foul play a violation of the rules in a game or sport

foundation 1 the charter incorporating or establishing a society or institution and the statutes or rules governing its affairs 2 *Cards* a card on which a sequence may be built

foundry 1 a place in which metal castings are produced 2 the science or practice of casting metal 3 cast-metal articles collectively

fountainhead a spring that is the source of a stream

Fouquet 1 **Jean** ?1420–?80, French painter and miniaturist 2 **Nicolas**, *Marquis de Belle-Isle*. 1615–80, French statesman; superintendent of finance (1653–61) under Louis XIV. He was imprisoned for embezzlement, having been denounced by Colbert

Fouquier-Tinville Antoine Quentin 1746–95, French revolutionary; as public prosecutor (1793–94) during the Reign of Terror, he sanctioned the guillotining of Desmoulins, Danton, and Robespierre

four 1 the cardinal number that is the sum of three and one 2 a numeral, 4, IV, etc, representing this number 3 something representing, represented by, or consisting of four units, such as a playing card with four symbols on it 4 *Cricket* a a shot that crosses the boundary after hitting the ground b the four runs scored for such a shot 5 *Rowing* a a racing shell propelled by four oarsmen pulling one oar each, with or without a cox b the crew of such a shell

four-by-four a vehicle equipped with four-wheel drive

fourfold 1 equal to or having four times as many or as much 2 composed of four parts

Fourier 1 (**François Marie**) **Charles** 1772–1837, French social reformer: propounded a system of cooperatives known as Fourierism, esp in his work *Le Nouveau monde industriel* (1829–30) 2 **Jean Baptiste Joseph** 1768–1830, French mathematician, Egyptologist, and administrator, noted particularly for his research on the theory of heat and the method of analysis named after him

four-in-hand 1 a road vehicle drawn by four horses and driven by one driver 2 a four-horse team in a coach or carriage

foursome *Sport* a game between two pairs of players, esp a form of golf in which each partner in a pair takes alternate strokes at the same ball

four-stroke relating to or designating an internal-combustion engine in which the piston makes four strokes for every explosion

fourteen 1 the cardinal number that is the sum of ten and four 2 a numeral, 14, XIV, etc, representing this number

fourth 1 denoting the fourth forward ratio of a gearbox in motor vehicles 2 *Music* a the interval between one note and another four notes away from it counting inclusively along the diatonic scale b one of two notes constituting such an interval in relation to the other 3 the fourth forward ratio of a gearbox in a motor vehicle 4 a less common word for **quarter**

fourth dimension 1 the dimension of time, which is necessary in addition to three spatial dimensions to specify fully the position and behaviour of a point or particle 2 the concept in science fiction of a dimension in addition to three spatial dimensions, used to explain supranatural phenomena, events, etc.

four-wheel drive a system used in motor vehicles in which all four wheels are connected to the source of power

Fowey a resort and fishing village in SW England, in Cornwall, linked administratively with St Austell from

1968 to 1974. Pop: 2064 (2001)

fowl 1 any bird, esp any gallinaceous bird, that is used as food or hunted as game 2 an archaic word for any **bird**

Fowler **Henry Watson** 1858–1933, English lexicographer and grammarian; compiler of *Modern English Usage* (1926)

fox 1 any canine mammal of the genus *Vulpes* and related genera. They are mostly predators that do not hunt in packs and typically have large pointed ears, a pointed muzzle, and a bushy tail 2 the fur of any of these animals, usually reddish-brown or grey in colour 3 *Bible* a a jackal b an image of a false prophet 4 *Nautical* small stuff made from yarns twisted together and then tarred

Fox 1 **Charles James** 1749–1806, British Whig statesman and orator. He opposed North over taxation of the American colonies and Pitt over British intervention against the French Revolution. He advocated parliamentary reform and the abolition of the slave trade 2 **George** 1624–91, English religious leader; founder (1647) of the Society of Friends (Quakers) 3 **Vicente** born 1942, Mexican politician; president of Mexico from 2000 4 Sir **William** 1812–93, New Zealand statesman, born in England: prime minister of New Zealand (1856; 1861–62; 1869–72; 1873)

Foxe **John** 1516–87, English Protestant clergyman; author of *History of the Acts and Monuments of the Church* (1563), popularly known as the *Book of Martyrs*

Foxe Basin an arm of the Atlantic in NE Canada, between Melville Peninsula and Baffin Island

foxglove any Eurasian scrophulariaceous plant of the genus *Digitalis*, esp *D. purpurea*, having spikes of purple or white thimble-like flowers. The soft wrinkled leaves are a source of digitalis

foxhound either of two breeds (the English and the American) of dog having a short smooth coat and pendent ears. Though not large (height about 60 cm or 23 in.) they have great stamina and are usually kept for hunting foxes

Fox Talbot **William Henry** 1800–77, English physicist; a pioneer of photography

foxtrot a ballroom dance in quadruple time, combining short and long steps in various sequences

foxy 1 of a reddish-brown colour 2 (of wine) having the flavour of fox grapes 3 (of oats) having a musty smell as a result of getting wet, fermenting, and drying out

foyer (in Britain) a centre providing accommodation and employment training, etc for homeless young people

fr. franc

fraction 1 *Maths* a a ratio of two expressions or numbers other than zero b any rational number that is not an integer 2 *Chem* a component of a mixture separated by a fractional process, such as fractional distillation 3 *Christianity* the formal breaking of the bread in Communion

fractional distillation 1 the process of separating the constituents of a liquid mixture by heating it and condensing separately the components according to their different boiling points 2 a distillation in which the vapour is brought into contact with a countercurrent of condensed liquid to increase the purity of the final products

fracture 1 *Med* a the breaking or cracking of a bone or the tearing of a cartilage b the resulting condition 2 *Mineralogy* a the characteristic appearance of the surface of a freshly broken mineral or rock b the way in which a mineral or rock naturally breaks

Fragonard **Jean-Honoré** 1732–1806, French artist, noted for richly coloured paintings typifying the frivolity of 18th-century French court life

frail a quantity of raisins or figs equal to between 50 and 75 pounds

frame 1 a one of a series of individual exposures on a strip of film used in making motion pictures b an individual exposure in still photography c an individual picture in a comic strip 2 a a television picture scanned by one or more electron beams at a particular frequency b the area of the picture so formed 3 *Billiards, snooker* a the wooden triangle used to set up the balls b the balls when set up c a single game finished when all the balls have been potted 4 *Computing* (on a website) a self-contained section that functions independently from other parts; by using frames, a website designer can make some areas of a website remain constant while others change according to the choices made by the internet user 5 short for **cold frame** 6 a machine or part of a machine over which yarn is stretched in the production of textiles 7 (in telecommunications, computers, etc) one cycle of a regularly recurring number of pulses in a pulse train

Frame **Janet** 1924–2004, and New Zealand writer: author of the novels *Owls Do Cry* (1957) and *Faces in the Water* (1961), the collection of verse *The Pocket* (1967), and volumes of autobiography including *An Angel at My Table* (1984), which was made into a film in 1990

frame of reference *Geometry* any set of planes or curves, such as the three coordinate axes, used to locate or measure movement of a point in space

franc 1 the former standard monetary unit of France, most French dependencies, Andorra, and Monaco, divided into 100 centimes; replaced by the euro in 2002 2 the former standard monetary unit of Belgium (**Belgian franc**) and Luxembourg (**Luxembourg franc**), divided into 100 centimes; replaced by the euro in 2002 3 the standard monetary unit of Switzerland and Liechtenstein, divided into 100 centimes 4 the standard monetary unit, comprising 100 centimes, of the following countries: Benin, Burkina-Faso, Cameroon, the Central African Republic, Chad, Congo-Brazzaville, Côte d'Ivoire, Equatorial Guinea, Gabon, Guinea-Bissau, Mali, Niger, Senegal, and Togo 5 the standard monetary unit of Burundi (**Burundi franc**), Comoros (**Comorian franc**), Democratic Republic of Congo (formerly Zaïre; **Congolese franc**), Djibouti (**Djibouti franc**), Guinea (**Guinea franc**), Madagascar (**franc malgache**), Rwanda (**Rwanda franc**), and French Polynesia and New Caledonia (**French Pacific franc**)

France[1] **Anatole**, real name *Anatole François Thibault*. 1844–1924, French novelist, short-story writer, and critic. His works include *Le Crime de Sylvestre Bonnard* (1881), *L'Île des Pingouins* (1908), and *La Révolte des anges* (1914): Nobel prize for literature 1921

France[2] a republic in W Europe, between the English Channel, the Mediterranean, and the Atlantic: the largest country wholly in Europe; became a republic in 1793 after the French Revolution and an empire in 1804 under Napoleon; reverted to a monarchy (1815–48), followed by the Second Republic (1848–52), the Second Empire (1852–70), the Third Republic (1870–1940), and the Fourth and Fifth Republics (1946 and 1958); a member of the European Union. It is generally flat or undulating in the north and west and mountainous in the south and east. Official language: French. Religion: Roman Catholic majority. Currency: euro. Capital: Paris. Pop: 60 434 000 (2004 est). Area: (including Corsica) 551 600 sq km (212 973 sq miles)

franchise 1 the right to vote, esp for representatives in a legislative body; suffrage 2 any exemption, privilege, or right granted to an individual or group by a public authority, such as the right to use public property for a business 3 *Commerce* authorization granted by a manufacturing enterprise to a distributor to market the manufacturer's products 4 the full rights of citizenship 5 *Films* a film that is or has the potential to be part of a series and lends itself to merchandising

Francis 1 Dick, full name *Richard Stanley Francis*. born 1920, British thriller writer, formerly a champion jockey. His books include *Dead Cert* (1962), *The Edge* (1988), and *Come to Grief* (1995) 2 Sir **Philip** 1740–1818, British politician; probable author of the *Letters of Junius* (1769–72). He played an important part in the impeachment of Warren Hastings (1788–95)

Franciscan a member of any of several Christian religious orders of mendicant friars or nuns tracing their origins back to Saint Francis of Assisi; a Grey Friar

Francis I 1 1494–1547, king of France (1515–47). His reign was dominated by his rivalry with Emperor Charles V for the control of Italy. He was a noted patron of the arts and learning 2 1708–65, duke of Lorraine (1729–37), grand duke of Tuscany (1737–65), and Holy Roman Emperor (1745–65). His marriage (1736) to Maria Theresa led to the War of the Austrian Succession (1740–48)

Francis II 1 1544–60, king of France (1559–60); son of Henry II and Catherine de' Medici; first husband of Mary, Queen of Scots 2 1768–1835, last Holy Roman Emperor (1792–1806) and, as Francis I, first emperor of Austria (1804–35). The Holy Roman Empire was dissolved (1806) following his defeat by Napoleon at Austerlitz

Francis of Assisi Saint original name *Giovanni di Bernardone*. ?1181–1226, Italian monk; founder of the Franciscan order of friars. He is remembered for his humility and love for all creation and was the first person to exhibit stigmata (1224). Feast day: Oct 4

Francis of Sales Saint 1567–1622, French ecclesiastic and theologian; bishop of Geneva (1602–22) and an opponent of Calvinism; author of *Introduction to a Devout Life* (1609) and founder of the Order of the Visitation (1610). Feast day: Jan 24

francium an unstable radioactive element of the alkali-metal group, occurring in minute amounts in uranium ores. Symbol: Fr; atomic no.: 87; half-life of most stable isotope, ^{223}Fr: 22 minutes; valency: 1; melting pt.: 27°C; boiling pt.: 677°C

Franck 1 César (**Auguste**). 1822–90, French composer, organist, and teacher, born in Belgium. His works,

some of which make use of cyclic form, include a violin sonata, a string quartet, the *Symphony in D Minor* (1888), and much organ music 2 **James** 1882–1964, US physicist, born in Germany: shared a Nobel prize for physics with Gustav Hertz (1925) for work on the quantum theory, particularly the effects of bombarding atoms with electrons

Franco Francisco, called *el Caudillo*. 1892–1975, Spanish general and statesman; head of state (1939–1975). He was commander-in-chief of the Falangists in the Spanish Civil War (1936–39), defeating the republican government and establishing a dictatorship (1939). He kept Spain neutral in World War II

Franconia a medieval duchy of Germany, inhabited by the Franks from the 7th century, now chiefly in Bavaria, Hesse, and Baden-Württemberg

Franconian a group of medieval Germanic dialects spoken by the Franks in an area from N Bavaria and Alsace to the mouth of the Rhine. **Low Franconian** developed into Dutch, while **Upper Franconian** contributed to High German, of which it remains a recognizable dialect

frangipani 1 any tropical American apocynaceous shrub of the genus *Plumeria*, esp *P. rubra*, cultivated for its waxy typically white or pink flowers, which have a sweet overpowering scent 2 **native frangipani** *Austral* an Australian evergreen tree, *Hymenosporum flavum*, with large fragrant yellow flowers: family *Pittosporaceae*

Frank[1] 1 **Anne** 1929–45, German Jewess, whose *Diary* (1947) recorded the experiences of her family while in hiding from the Nazis in Amsterdam (1942–44). They were betrayed and she died in a concentration camp 2 **Robert** born 1924, US photographer and film maker, born in Switzerland; best known for his photographic book *The Americans* (1959)

Frank[2] a member of a group of West Germanic peoples who spread from the east bank of the middle Rhine into the Roman Empire in the late 4th century AD, gradually conquering most of Gaul and Germany. The Franks achieved their greatest power under Charlemagne

Frankfort a city in N Kentucky: the state capital. Pop: 27 408 (2003 est)

Frankfurt (**am Main**) a city in central Germany in Hesse on the Main River: a Roman settlement in the 1st century; a free imperial city (1273–1806); seat of the federal assembly (1815–66); university (1914); trade fairs since the 13th century Pop.: 644 700 (1999 est.)

Frankfurt (**an der Oder**) a city in E Germany on the Polish border: member of the Hanseatic League (1368–1450). Pop.: 85 360 (1991)

frankincense an aromatic gum resin obtained from trees of the burseraceous genus *Boswellia*, which occur in Asia and Africa

Frankish the ancient West Germanic language of the Franks, esp the dialect that contributed to the vocabulary of modern French

Franklin 1 **Aretha** born 1942, US soul, pop, and gospel singer 2 **Benjamin** 1706–90, American statesman, scientist, and author. He helped draw up the Declaration of Independence (1776) and, as ambassador to France

(1776–85), he negotiated an alliance with France and a peace settlement with Britain. As a scientist, he is noted particularly for his researches in electricity, esp his invention of the lightning conductor **3** Sir **John** 1786–1847, English explorer of the Arctic: lieutenant-governor of Van Diemen's Land (now Tasmania) (1836–43): died while on a voyage to discover the Northwest Passage **4** **Rosalind** 1920–58, British x-ray crystallographer. She contributed to the discovery of the structure of DNA, before her premature death from cancer

Franz Ferdinand English name *Francis Ferdinand*. 1863–1914, archduke of Austria; heir apparent of Franz Josef I. His assassination contributed to the outbreak of World War I

Franz Josef I English name *Francis Joseph I*. 1830–1916, emperor of Austria (1848–1916) and king of Hungary (1867–1916)

Franz Josef Land an archipelago of over 100 islands in the Arctic Ocean, administratively part of Russia. Area: about 21 000 sq km (8000 sq miles)

Fraser¹ **1** (John) **Malcolm** born 1930, Australian states-man; prime minister of Australia (1975–83) **2** **Peter** 1884–1950, New Zealand statesman, born in Scotland; prime minister (1940–49)

Fraser² a river in SW Canada, in S central British Columbia, flowing northwest, south, and west through spectacular canyons in the Coast Mountains to the Strait of Georgia. Length: 1370 km (850 miles)

fraternal designating either or both of a pair of twins of the same or opposite sex that developed from two sepa-rate fertilized ova

fraternity *US and Canadian* a secret society joined by male students, usually functioning as a social club

Frauenfeld a town in NE Switzerland, capital of Thurgau canton. Pop: 21 954 (2000)

Fraunhofer Joseph von 1787–1826, German physicist and optician, who investigated spectra of the sun, planets, and fixed stars, and improved telescopes and other optical instruments

Fray Bentos a port in W Uruguay, on the River Uruguay: noted for meat-packing. Pop: 21 400 (1995 est)

Frazer Sir **James George** 1854–1941, Scottish anthropolo-gist; author of many works on primitive religion, and magic, esp *The Golden Bough* (1890)

Frazier Joe born 1944, US boxer: won the world heavy-weight title in 1970 and was the first to beat Muhammad Ali professionally (1971)

frazil small pieces of ice that form in water moving tur-bulently enough to prevent the formation of a sheet of ice

freak a person, animal, or plant that is abnormal or deformed; monstrosity

freckle 1 a small brownish spot on the skin: a localized deposit of the pigment melanin, developed by exposure to sunlight **2** *Austral, slang* the anus

Fredericia a port in Denmark, in E Jutland at the N end of the Little Belt. Pop: 37 054 (2004 est)

Frederick I 1657–1713, first king of Prussia (1701–13); son of Frederick William

Frederick II 1194–1250, Holy Roman Emperor (1220–50), king of Germany (1212–50), and king of Sicily (1198–1250)

Frederick III 1 1415–93, Holy Roman Emperor (1452–93) and, as Frederick IV, king of Germany (1440–93) **2** called *the Wise*. 1463–1525, elector of Saxony (1486–1525). He pro-tected Martin Luther in Wartburg Castle after the Diet of Worms (1521)

Frederick V called *the Winter King*. 1596–1632, elector of the Palatinate (1610–23) and king of Bohemia (1619–20). He led the revolt of Bohemian Protestants at the begin-ning of the Thirty Years' War

Frederick IX 1899–1972, king of Denmark (1947–72)

Frederick Barbarossa official title *Frederick I*. ?1123–90, Holy Roman Emperor (1155–90), king of Germany (1152–90). His attempt to assert imperial rights in Italy ended in his defeat at Legnano (1176) and the indepen-dence of the Lombard cities (1183)

Frederick the Great official title *Frederick II*. 1712–86, king of Prussia (1740–86); son of Frederick William I. He gained Silesia during the War of Austrian Succession (1740–48) and his military genius during the Seven Years' War (1756–63) established Prussia as a European power. He was also a noted patron of the arts

Frederick William called *the Great Elector*. 1620–88, elec-tor of Brandenburg (1640–88)

Frederick William I 1688–1740, king of Prussia (1713–40); son of Frederick I: reformed the Prussian army

Frederick William III 1770–1840, king of Prussia (1797–1840)

Frederick William IV 1795–1861, king of Prussia (1840–61). He submitted to the 1848 Revolution but refused the imperial crown offered by the Frankfurt Parliament (1849). In 1857 he became insane and his brother, William I, became regent (1858–61)

Fredericton a city in SE Canada, capital of New Brunswick, on the St John River. Pop: 54 068 (2001)

Frederiksberg a city in E Denmark, within the area of greater Copenhagen: founded in 1651 by King Frederick III. Pop: 91 721 (2004 est)

Fredrikstad a port in SE Norway at the entrance to Oslo Fjord. Pop: 69 867 (2004 est)

free 1 (of a country, etc) autonomous or independent **2** (of jazz) totally improvised, with no preset melodic, harmonic, or rhythmic basis **3** *Law* of property **a** not subject to payment of rent or performance of services; freehold **b** not subject to any burden or charge, such as a mortgage or lien; unencumbered **4** *Chem* chemically uncombined **5** *Logic* denoting an occurrence of a vari-able not bound by a quantifier **6** *Nautical* (of the wind) blowing from the quarter

freeboard the space or distance between the deck of a vessel and the waterline

Free Church *Chiefly Brit* **a** any Protestant Church, esp the Presbyterian, other than the Established Church **b** (*as modifier*): *Free-Church attitudes*

freedom 1 the quality or state of being free, esp to enjoy political and civil liberties **2** autonomy, self-govern-ment, or independence **3** *Philosophy* the quality, esp of the will or the individual, of not being totally con-strained; able to choose between alternative actions in identical circumstances

free enterprise an economic system in which commer-cial organizations compete for profit with little state control

free fall 1 free descent of a body in which the gravitational force is the only force acting on it **2** the part of a parachute descent before the parachute opens

freehold *Property law* **a** tenure by which land is held in fee simple, fee tail, or for life **b** an estate held by such tenure

free house *Brit* a public house not bound to sell only one brewer's products

free kick *Soccer* a place kick awarded for a foul or infringement, either direct, from which a goal may be scored, or indirect, from which the ball must be touched by at least one other player for a goal to be allowed

freelance 1 *Politics* a person, esp a politician, who supports several causes or parties without total commitment to any one **2** (in medieval Europe) a mercenary soldier or adventurer

freeman 1 a person who enjoys political and civil liberties; citizen **2** a person who enjoys a privilege or franchise, such as the freedom of a city

Freeman Cathy, full name *Catherine Astrid Salome Freeman*. born 1973, Australian sprinter; winner of the 200m and 400m in the 1994 Commonwealth Games and the 400m in the 2000 Olympic Games

freesia any iridaceous plant of the genus *Freesia*, of southern Africa, cultivated for their white, yellow, or pink tubular fragrant flowers

free space a region that has no gravitational and electromagnetic fields: used as an absolute standard

Free State 1 a province of central South Africa; replaced the former province of Orange Free State in 1994: gold and uranium mining. Capital: Bloemfontein. Pop: 2 950 661 (2004 est). Area: 129 480 sq km (49 992 sq miles) **2** *US, History* (before the Civil War) any state prohibiting slavery **3** short for the **Irish Free State**

freestyle 1 a competition or race, as in swimming, in which each participant may use a style of his or her choice instead of a specified style **2 a** an amateur style of wrestling with an agreed set of rules **b** a style of professional wrestling with no internationally agreed set of rules **3** a series of acrobatics performed in skiing, etc. **4** (*as modifier*): *a freestyle event*

Freetown the capital and chief port of Sierra Leone: founded in 1787 for slaves freed and destitute in England. Pop: 1 007 000 (2005 est)

free trade 1 international trade that is free of such government interference as import quotas, export subsidies, protective tariffs, etc. **2** *Archaic* illicit trade; smuggling

free verse unrhymed verse without a metrical pattern

freeway *US* **1** another name for **expressway 2** a major road that can be used without paying a toll

freewheel 1 a ratchet device in the rear hub of a bicycle wheel that permits the wheel to rotate freely while the pedals are stationary **2** a device in the transmission of some vehicles that automatically disengages the drive shaft when it rotates more rapidly than the engine shaft, so that the drive shaft can turn freely

free will a the apparent human ability to make choices that are not externally determined **b** the doctrine that such human freedom of choice is not illusory **c** (*as modifier*): *a free-will decision*

Free World the the non-Communist countries collectively, esp those that are actively anti-Communist

freeze 1 *Meteorol* a spell of temperatures below freezing point, usually over a wide area **2** the fixing of incomes, prices, etc, by legislation

freezer a device that freezes or chills, esp an insulated cold-storage cabinet for long-term storage of perishable foodstuffs

freezing point the temperature below which a liquid turns into a solid. It is equal to the melting point

Frege Gottlob 1848–1925, German logician and philosopher, who laid the foundations of modern formal logic and semantics in his *Begriffsschrift* (1879)

Freiburg 1 a city in SW Germany, in SW Baden-Württemberg: under Austrian rule (1368–1805); university (1457). Pop: 212 495 (2003 est) **2** the German name for **Fribourg**

freight 1 a commercial transport that is slower and cheaper than express **b** the price charged for such transport **c** goods transported by this means **d** (*as modifier*): *freight transport* **2** *Chiefly Brit* a ship's cargo or part of it

freighter 1 a ship or aircraft designed for transporting cargo **2** a person concerned with the loading or chartering of a ship

Fremantle a port in SW Western Australia, on the Indian Ocean. Pop: 25 197 (2001)

French[1] Sir John Denton Pinkstone, 1st Earl of Ypres. 1852–1925, British field marshal in World War I: commanded the British Expeditionary Force in France and Belgium (1914–15); Lord Lieutenant of Ireland (1918–21)

French[2] 1 the official language of France: also an official language of Switzerland, Belgium, Canada, and certain other countries. It is the native language of approximately 70 million people; also used for diplomacy. Historically, French is an Indo-European language belonging to the Romance group **2 the French** the natives, citizens, or inhabitants of France collectively **3** relating to, denoting, or characteristic of France, the French, or their language **4** (in Canada) of or relating to French Canadians

French Canada the areas of Canada, esp in the province of Quebec, where French Canadians predominate

French Canadian 1 a Canadian citizen whose native language is French **2** of or relating to French Canadians or their language

French chalk a compact variety of talc used to mark cloth or remove grease stains from materials

French Equatorial Africa the former French overseas territories of Chad, Gabon, Middle Congo, and Ubangi-Shari (1910–58)

French Guiana a French overseas region in NE South America, on the Atlantic: colonized by the French in about 1637; tropical forests. Capital: Cayenne. Pop: 183 000 (2004 est). Area: about 91 000 sq km (23 000 sq miles)

French Guinea a former French territory of French West Africa: became independent as Guinea in 1958

French horn *Music* a valved brass instrument with a funnel-shaped mouthpiece and a tube of conical bore coiled into a spiral. It is a transposing instrument in F. Range: about three and a half octaves upwards from B on the second leger line below the bass staff

French India a former French overseas territory in India, including Chandernagore and Pondicherry: restored to India between 1949 and 1954

French Indochina the territories of SE Asia that were colonized by France and held mostly until 1954: included Cochin China, Annam, and Tonkin (now largely Vietnam), Cambodia, Laos, and Kuang-Chou Wan (returned to China in 1945, now Zhanjiang)

French Morocco a former French protectorate in NW Africa, united in 1956 with Spanish Morocco and Tangier to form the kingdom of Morocco

French North Africa the former French possessions of Algeria, French Morocco, and Tunisia

French polish a varnish for wood consisting of shellac dissolved in alcohol

French Polynesia a French Overseas Country (formerly Territory) in the S Pacific Ocean, including the Society Islands, the Tuamotu group, the Gambier group, the Tubuai Islands, and the Marquesas Islands. Capital: Papeete, on Tahiti. Pop: 248 000 (2004 est). Area: about 4000 sq km (1500 sq miles)

French Togoland a former United Nations Trust Territory in W Africa, administered by France (1946–60), now the independent republic of Togo

French West Africa a former group (1895–1958) of French Overseas Territories: consisted of Senegal, Mauritania, French Sudan, Burkina-Faso, Niger, French Guinea, the Ivory Coast, and Dahomey

Freon *Trademark* any of a group of chemically unreactive chlorofluorocarbons used as aerosol propellants, refrigerants, and solvents

frequency 1 *Physics* the number of times that a periodic function or vibration repeats itself in a specified time, often 1 second. It is usually measured in hertz. 2 *Ecology* a the number of individuals of a species within a given area b the percentage of quadrats that contains individuals of a species

fresco 1 a very durable method of wall-painting using watercolours on wet plaster or, less properly, dry plaster (**fresco secco**), with a less durable result 2 a painting done in this way

Frescobaldi Girolamo 1583–1643, Italian organist and composer, noted esp for his organ and harpsichord music

fresher *or* **freshman** a first-year student at college or university

freshet 1 the sudden overflowing of a river caused by heavy rain or melting snow 2 a stream of fresh water emptying into the sea

freshwater 1 of, relating to, or living in fresh water 2 (esp of a sailor who has not sailed on the sea) unskilled or inexperienced

Fresnel Augustin Jean 1788–1827, French physicist: worked on the interference of light, contributing to the wave theory of light

Fresno a city in central California, in the San Joaquin Valley. Pop: 451 455 (2003 est)

fret[1] the result of fretting; corrosion

fret[2] any of several small metal bars set across the fingerboard of a musical instrument of the lute, guitar, or viol family at various points along its length so as to

produce the desired notes when the strings are stopped by the fingers

fret saw a fine-toothed saw with a long thin narrow blade, used for cutting designs in thin wood or metal

fretwork 1 decorative geometrical carving or openwork 2 any similar pattern of light and dark

Freud 1 **Anna** 1895–1982, Austrian psychiatrist: daughter of Sigmund Freud and pioneer of child psychoanalysis 2 **Lucian** born 1922, British painter, esp of nudes and portraits; grandson of Sigmund Freud 3 **Sigmund** 1856–1939, Austrian psychiatrist; originator of psychoanalysis, based on free association of ideas and analysis of dreams. He stressed the importance of infantile sexuality in later development, evolving the concept of the Oedipus complex. His works include *The Interpretation of Dreams* (1900) and *The Ego and the Id* (1923)

Freudian slip any action, such as a slip of the tongue, that may reveal an unconscious thought

Freytag Gustav 1816–95, German novelist and dramatist; author of the comedy *Die Journalisten* (1853) and *Soll und Haben* (1855), a novel about German commercial life

friar a member of any of various chiefly mendicant religious orders of the Roman Catholic Church, the main orders being the **Black Friars** (Dominicans), **Grey Friars** (Franciscans), **White Friars** (Carmelites), and **Austin Friars** (Augustinians)

friary *Christianity* a convent or house of friars

Fribourg 1 a canton in W Switzerland. Capital: Fribourg. Pop: 242 700 (2002 est). Area: 1676 sq km (645 sq miles) 2 a town in W Switzerland, capital of Fribourg canton: university (1889). Pop: 35 547 (2000)

friction a resistance encountered when one body moves relative to another body with which it is in contact

Friedan Betty born 1921, US feminist, founder and first president (1966–70) of the National Organization for Women. Her books include *The Feminine Mystique* (1963), *The Second Stage* (1982), and *The Fountain of Life* (1993)

Friedman Milton born 1912, US economist, particularly associated with monetarism; a forceful advocate of free market capitalism

Friedrich Caspar David 1774–1840, German romantic landscape painter, noted for his skill in rendering changing effects of light

Friend[1] a member of the Religious Society of Friends; Quaker

Friend[2] *Trademark, Mountaineering* a device consisting of a shaft with double-headed spring-loaded cams that can be wedged in a crack to provide an anchor point

friendly *Sport* a match played for its own sake, and not as part of a competition, etc.

Friese-Greene William 1855–1921, British photographer. He invented (with Mortimer Evans) the first practicable motion-picture camera

Friesian *Brit* any of several breeds of black-and-white dairy cattle having a high milk yield

Friesland 1 a province of the N Netherlands, on the IJsselmeer and the North Sea: includes four of the West Frisian Islands; flat, with sand dunes and fens (under reclamation), canals, and lakes. Capital: Leeuwarden. Pop: 640 000 (2003 est). Area: 3319 sq km (1294 sq miles) 2 an area comprising the province of Friesland in the Netherlands along with the regions of **East Friesland**

and **North Friesland** in Germany

frieze[1] 1 *Architect* **a** the horizontal band between the architrave and cornice of a classical entablature, esp one that is decorated with sculpture **b** the upper part of the wall of a room, below the cornice, esp one that is decorated **2** any ornamental band or strip on a wall

frieze[2] a heavy woollen fabric with a long nap, used for coats, etc.

frigate 1 a medium-sized square-rigged warship of the 18th and 19th centuries **2 a** *Brit* a warship larger than a corvette and smaller than a destroyer **b** *US* (formerly) a warship larger than a destroyer and smaller than a cruiser **c** *US* a small escort vessel

frill 1 a ruff of hair or feathers around the neck of a dog or bird or a fold of skin around the neck of a reptile or amphibian **2** a variety of domestic fancy pigeon having a ruff of curled feathers on the chest and crop **3** *Photog* a wrinkling or loosening of the emulsion at the edges of a negative or print

fringe *Physics* any of the light and dark or coloured bands produced by diffraction or interference of light

Frink Dame **Elisabeth** 1930–93, British sculptor

Frisbee *Trademark* a light plastic disc, usually 20–25 centimetres in diameter, thrown with a spinning motion for recreation or in competition

Frisch 1 **Karl** von 1886–1982, Austrian zoologist; studied animal behaviour, esp of bees; shared the Nobel prize for physiology or medicine 1973 **2 Max** 1911–91, Swiss dramatist and novelist. His works are predominantly satirical and include the plays *Biedermann und die Brandstifter* (1953) and *Andorra* (1961), and the novel *Stiller* (1954) **3 Otto** 1904–79, British nuclear physicist, born in Austria, who contributed to the development of the first atomic bomb **4 Ragnar** (**Anton Kittil**). 1895–1973, Norwegian economist, who pioneered the study of econometrics and greatly influenced the management of the Norwegian economy from 1945: shared the first Nobel prize for economics (1969) with Jan Tinbergen

Frisian *or* **Friesian** a language spoken in the NW Netherlands, parts of N Germany, and adjacent islands, belonging to the West Germanic branch of the Indo-European family: the nearest relative of the English language; it has three main dialects

Friuli a historic region of SW Europe, between the Carnic Alps and the Gulf of Venice: the W part (**Venetian Friuli**) was ceded by Austria to Italy in 1866 and **Eastern Friuli** in 1919; in 1947 Eastern Friuli (except Gorizia) was ceded to Yugoslavia

Friulian the Rhaetian dialect spoken in parts of Friuli

Friuli-Venezia Giulia a region of NE Italy, formed in 1947 from **Venetian Friuli** and part of **Eastern Friuli**. Capital: Trieste. Pop: 1 191 588 (2003 est). Area: 7851 sq km (3031 sq miles)

Frobisher Sir **Martin** ?1535–94, English navigator and explorer: made three unsuccessful voyages in search of the Northwest Passage (1576; 1577; 1578), visiting Labrador and Baffin Island

Frobisher Bay 1 an inlet of the Atlantic in NE Canada, in the SE coast of Baffin Island **2** the former name of **Iqaluit**

frock a coarse wide-sleeved outer garment worn by members of some religious orders

Froebel *or* **Fröbel** 1 **Friedrich** (**Wilhelm August**). 1782–1852, German educator: founded the first kindergarten (1840) **2** of, denoting, or relating to a system of kindergarten education developed by him or to the training and qualification of teachers to use this system

frog[1] 1 any insectivorous anuran amphibian of the family *Ranidae*, such as *Rana temporaria* of Europe, having a short squat tailless body with a moist smooth skin and very long hind legs specialized for hopping **2** any of various similar amphibians of related families, such as the tree frog

frog[2] *Music, US and Canadian* **a** the ledge or ridge at the upper end of the fingerboard of a violin, cello, etc, over which the strings pass to the tuning pegs **b** the end of a violin bow that is held by the player

frog[3] a tough elastic horny material in the centre of the sole of a horse's foot

frog[4] a grooved plate of iron or steel placed to guide train wheels over an intersection of railway lines

frogman a swimmer equipped with a rubber suit, flippers, and breathing equipment for working underwater

frogspawn a mass of fertilized frogs' eggs or developing tadpoles, each egg being surrounded by a protective nutrient jelly

Froissart Jean ?1333–?1400, French chronicler and poet, noted for his *Chronique*, a vivid history of Europe from 1325 to 1400

Frome Lake a shallow salt lake in NE South Australia: intermittently filled with water. Length: 100 km (60 miles). Width: 48 km (30 miles)

Fromm Erich 1900–80, US psychologist and philosopher, born in Germany. His works include *The Art of Loving* (1956) and *To Have and To Be* (1976)

frond 1 a large compound leaf, esp of a fern **2** the thallus of a seaweed or a lichen

front 1 *Meteorol* the dividing line or plane between two air masses or water masses of different origins and having different characteristics **2** *Archaic* the forehead or the face

frontal 1 of or relating to the forehead **2** of or relating to the anterior part of a body or organ **3** *Meteorol* of, relating to, or resulting from a front or its passage **4** a decorative hanging for the front of an altar

front bench *Brit* **a** the foremost bench of either the Government or Opposition in the House of Commons **b** the leadership (**frontbenchers**) of either group, who occupy this bench **c** (*as modifier*): *a front-bench decision*

frontier **a** the region of a country bordering on another or a line, barrier, etc, marking such a boundary **b** (*as modifier*): *a frontier post*

frontispiece 1 the principal façade of a building; front **2** a pediment, esp an ornamented one, over a door, window, etc.

frost 1 a white deposit of ice particles, esp one formed on objects out of doors at night **2** an atmospheric temperature of below freezing point, characterized by the production of this deposit **3** degrees below freezing point: *eight degrees of frost indicates a temperature of either* −8°C or 24°F

Frost 1 Sir **David** (**Paradine**). born 1939, British television presenter and executive, noted esp for political interviews **2 Robert (Lee)**. 1874–1963, US poet, noted for his lyrical verse on country life in New England. His books include *A Boy's Will* (1913), *North of Boston* (1914), and *New Hampshire* (1923)

frostbite 1 destruction of tissues, esp those of the fingers, ears, toes, and nose, by freezing, characterized by tingling, blister formation, and gangrene **2** NZ a type of small sailing dinghy

frosted (of glass, etc) having a surface roughened, as if covered with frost, to prevent clear vision through it

frosting 1 a rough or matt finish on glass, silver, etc. **2** *Slang* the practice of stealing a car while the owner has left it idling in order to defrost the windows and heat the engine

froth a mixture of saliva and air bubbles formed at the lips in certain diseases, such as rabies

Froude 1 James Anthony 1818–94, English historian; author of a controversial biography (1882–84) of Carlyle. **2** his brother **William** 1810–79, English civil engineer

frozen 1 (of a region or climate) icy or snowy **2** a (of prices, wages, etc) arbitrarily pegged at a certain level **b** (of business assets) not convertible into cash, as by government direction or business conditions

fructose a white crystalline water-soluble sugar occurring in honey and many fruits. Formula: $C_6H_{12}O_6$

fruit 1 *Botany* the ripened ovary of a flowering plant, containing one or more seeds. It may be dry, as in the poppy, or fleshy, as in the peach **2** any fleshy part of a plant, other than the above structure, that supports the seeds and is edible, such as the strawberry **3** the specialized spore-producing structure of plants that do not bear seeds **4** any plant product useful to man, including grain, vegetables, etc.

▷www.backyardgardener.com/plants/
gfruittree.html
▷www.doityourself.com/fruits
▷www.ourbrisbane.com/home_garden/
gardening/plants/fruit.htm
▷www.gardentimeonline.com/Fruit.html

fruiterer *Chiefly Brit* a fruit dealer or seller

fruit fly 1 any small dipterous fly of the family *Trypetidae*, which feed on and lay their eggs in plant tissues **2** any dipterous fly of the genus *Drosophila*

frustum 1 *Geometry* **a** the part of a solid, such as a cone or pyramid, contained between the base and a plane parallel to the base that intersects the solid **b** the part of such a solid contained between two parallel planes intersecting the solid **2** *Architect* a single drum of a column or a single stone used to construct a pier

Fry 1 Christopher born 1907, English dramatist; author of the verse dramas *A Phoenix Too Frequent* (1946), *The Lady's Not For Burning* (1948), and *Venus Observed* (1950) **2 Elizabeth** 1780–1845, English prison reformer and Quaker **3 Roger Eliot** 1866–1934, English art critic and painter who helped to introduce the postimpressionists to Britain. His books include *Vision and Design* (1920) and *Cézanne* (1927) **4 Stephen (John)**. born 1957, British writer, actor, and comedian; his novels include *The Liar* (1991) and *The Stars' Tennis Balls* (2000)

f-stop any of the settings for the f-number of a camera

Fuad I original name *Ahmed Fuad Pasha*. 1868–1936, sultan of Egypt (1917–22) and king (1922–36)

Fuchs 1 Klaus Emil. 1911–88, East German physicist. He was born in Germany, became a British citizen (1942), and was imprisoned (1950–59) for giving secret atomic research information to the Soviet Union **2** Sir **Vivian Ernest** 1908–99, English explorer and geologist: led the Commonwealth Trans-Antarctic Expedition (1955–58)

fuchsia 1 any onagraceous shrub of the mostly tropical genus *Fuchsia*, widely cultivated for their showy drooping purple, red, or white flowers **2** a North American onagraceous plant, *Zauschneria californica*, with tubular scarlet flowers **3 a** a reddish-purple to purplish-pink colour **b** (*as adjective*): *a fuchsia dress*

Fuegian 1 of or relating to Tierra del Fuego or its indigenous Indians **2** an Indian of Tierra del Fuego

fuel 1 any substance burned as a source of heat or power, such as coal or petrol **2 a** the material, containing a fissile substance, such as uranium-235, that produces energy in a nuclear reactor **b** a substance that releases energy in a fusion reactor

fuel cell a cell in which the energy produced by oxidation of a fuel is converted directly into electrical energy

Fuentes Carlos born 1928, Mexican novelist and writer. His novels include *A Change of Skin* (1967), *Terra Nostra* (1975), and *Cristóbal Nonato* (1987)

Fugard Athol born 1932, South African dramatist and theatre director. His plays include *The Blood-Knot* (1961), *Sizwe Bansi is Dead* (1972), *Statements after an Arrest under the Immorality Act* (1974), and *The Captain's Tiger* (1999)

fugue 1 a musical form consisting essentially of a theme repeated a fifth above or a fourth below the continuing first statement **2** *Psychiatry* a dreamlike altered state of consciousness, lasting from a few hours to several days, during which a person loses his memory for his previous life and often wanders away from home

Fuji Mount an extinct volcano in central Japan, in S central Honshu: the highest mountain in Japan, famous for its symmetrical snow-capped cone. Height: 3776 m (12 388 ft)

Fujian *or* **Fukien 1** a province of SE China: mountainous and forested, drained chiefly by the Min River; noted for the production of flower-scented teas. Capital: Fuzhou. Pop: 34 880 000 (2003 est). Area: 123 000 sq km (47 970 sq miles) **2** any of the Chinese dialects of this province

Fukuoka an industrial city and port in SW Japan, in N Kyushu: an important port in ancient times; site of Kyushu university. Pop: 1 302 454 (2002 est)

fulcrum 1 the pivot about which a lever turns **2** a spine-like scale occurring in rows along the anterior edge of the fins in primitive bony fishes such as the sturgeon

Fulham a district of the Greater London borough of Hammersmith and Fulham (since 1965): contains **Fulham Palace** (16th century), residence of the Bishop of London

full 1 of, relating to, or designating a relationship established by descent from the same parents **2** *Music* **a** powerful or rich in volume and sound **b** completing a piece or section; concluding **3** (of sails, etc) distended by wind **4** (of wine, such as a burgundy) having a heavy body **5** (of a colour) containing a large quantity of pure hue as opposed to white or grey; rich; saturated **6 in full cry** (esp of a pack of hounds) in hot pursuit of quarry **7**

Brit a ridge of sand or shingle along a seashore

fullback 1 *Soccer, hockey* one of two defensive players positioned in front of the goalkeeper 2 *Rugby* a defensive player positioned close to his own line

full-blooded (esp of horses) of unmixed ancestry; thoroughbred

Fuller 1 (Richard) Buckminster 1895–1983, US architect and engineer: developed the geodesic dome 2 Roy (Broadbent). 1912–91, British poet and writer, whose collections include *The Middle of a War* (1942) and *A Lost Season* (1944), both of which are concerned with World War II, *Epitaphs and Occasions* (1949), and *Available for Dreams* (1989) 3 Thomas 1608–61, English clergyman and antiquarian; author of *The Worthies of England* (1662)

full house 1 *Poker* a hand with three cards of the same value and another pair 2 a theatre, etc, filled to capacity 3 (in bingo, etc) the set of numbers needed to win

full moon 1 one of the four phases of the moon, occurring when the earth lies between the sun and the moon so that the moon is visible as a fully illuminated disc 2 the moon in this phase 3 the time at which this occurs

full-scale (of a plan, etc) of actual size; having the same dimensions as the original

full toss *or* **full pitch** *Cricket* a bowled ball that reaches the batsman without bouncing

fulmar any heavily built short-tailed oceanic bird of the genus *Fulmarus* and related genera, of polar regions: family *Procellariidae*, order *Procellariiformes* (petrels)

fulminate any salt or ester of fulminic acid, esp the mercury salt, which is used as a detonator

Fulton Robert 1765–1815, US engineer: designed the first successful steamboat (1807) and steam warship (1814)

fume *Chem* a pungent or toxic vapour

Funchal the capital and chief port of the Madeira Islands, on the S coast of Madeira. Pop: 103 962 (2001)

function *Maths, logic* a relation between two sets that associates a unique element (the value) of the second (the range) with each element (the argument) of the first (the domain): a many-one relation. Symbol: f(x) The value of f(x) for x = 2 is f(2)

functional 1 *Psychol* a relating to the purpose or context of a behaviour b denoting a psychosis such as schizophrenia assumed not to have a direct organic cause, like deterioration or poisoning of the brain 2 *Maths* a function whose domain is a set of functions and whose range is a set of functions or a set of numbers

functionalism 1 the theory of design that the form of a thing should be determined by its use 2 *Psychol* a system of thought based on the premise that all mental processes derive from their usefulness to the organism in adapting to the environment

fundamental 1 *Music* denoting or relating to the principal or lowest note of a harmonic series 2 of or concerned with the component of lowest frequency in a complex vibration 3 a the principal or lowest note of a harmonic series b the bass note of a chord in root position 4 *Physics* a the component of lowest frequency in a complex vibration b the frequency of this component

fundamentalism 1 *Christianity* (esp among certain Protestant sects) the belief that every word of the Bible is divinely inspired and therefore true 2 *Islam* a movement favouring strict observance of the teachings of

the Koran and Islamic law

fundholding (formerly, in the National Health Service in Britain) the system enabling general practitioners to receive a fixed budget from which to pay for primary care, drugs, and nonurgent hospital treatment for patients

Fundy Bay of an inlet of the Atlantic in SE Canada, between S New Brunswick and W Nova Scotia: remarkable for its swift tides of up to 21 m (70 ft)

Funen the second largest island of Denmark, between the Jutland peninsula and the island of Zealand. Pop: 441 795 (2003 est). Area: 3481 sq km (1344 sq miles)

fungicide a substance or agent that destroys or is capable of destroying fungi

fungoid resembling a fungus or fungi

fungus 1 any member of a kingdom of organisms (Fungi) that lack chlorophyll, leaves, true stems, and roots, reproduce by spores, and live as saprotrophs or parasites. The group includes moulds, mildews, rusts, yeasts, and mushrooms 2 *Pathol* any soft tumorous growth

▷www.agarics.org/Index.jsp
▷www.fungaljungal.org
▷www.botanical.com
▷www.ucmp.berkeley.edu/fungi/fungi.html
▷www.elib.cs.berkeley.edu/photos/fungi

funicular 1 a railway up the side of a mountain, consisting of two counterbalanced cars at either end of a cable passing round a driving wheel at the summit 2 relating to or operated by a rope, cable, etc.

▷www.funimag.com/Funimag-funi03.html

Funk Casimir 1884–1967, US biochemist, born in Poland: studied and named vitamins

funnel 1 a hollow utensil with a wide mouth tapering to a small hole, used for pouring liquids, powders, etc, into a narrow-necked vessel 2 a smokestack for smoke and exhaust gases, as on a steamship or steam locomotive

funnel-web *Austral* any large poisonous black spider of the family *Dipluridae*, constructing funnel-shaped webs

funny bone the area near the elbow where the ulnar nerve is close to the surface of the skin: when it is struck, a sharp tingling sensation is experienced along the forearm and hand

fur 1 the dense coat of fine silky hairs on such mammals as the cat, seal, and mink 2 a a pile fabric made in imitation of animal fur b a garment made from such a fabric 3 *Informal* a whitish coating of cellular debris on the tongue, caused by excessive smoking, an upset stomach, etc.

furlong a unit of length equal to 220 yards (201.168 metres)

furnace an enclosed chamber in which heat is produced to generate steam, destroy refuse, smelt or refine ores, etc.

Furness a region in NW England in Cumbria, forming a peninsula between the Irish Sea and Morecambe Bay

Furnivall Frederick James 1825–1910, English philologist: founder of the Early English Text Society and one of the founders of the *Oxford English Dictionary*

Furphy Joseph, pen name *Tom Collins*. 1843–1912, Australian author. His works include the classic

Australian novel *Such is Life* (1903) and *The Buln-Buln and the Brolga* (1948)

furry (of the tongue) coated with whitish cellular debris

further education (in Britain) formal education beyond school other than at a university or polytechnic

furze another name for **gorse**

fuse a protective device for safeguarding electric circuits, etc, containing a wire that melts and breaks the circuit when the current exceeds a certain value

fuselage the main body of an aircraft, excluding the wings, tailplane, and fin

Fushun a city in NE China, in central Liaoning province near Shenyang: situated on one of the richest coalfields in the world; site of the largest thermal power plant in NE Asia. Pop: 1 425 000 (2005 est)

fusion 1 See **nuclear fusion** 2 a coalition of political parties or other groups, esp to support common candidates at an election 3 *Psychol* the processing by the mind of elements falling on the two eyes so that they yield a single percept

fustian a a hard-wearing fabric of cotton mixed with flax or wool with a slight nap b (*as modifier*): *a fustian jacket*

futurism an artistic movement that arose in Italy in 1909 to replace traditional aesthetic values with the characteristics of the machine age
▷www.unknown.nu/futurism
▷www.futurism.org.uk/futurism.htm

futuristic denoting or relating to design, technology, etc, that is thought likely to be current or fashionable at some future time; ultramodern

futurology the study or prediction of the future of mankind

Fuzhou, Foochow, *or* **Fuchou** a port in SE China, capital of Fujian province on the Min Jiang: one of the original five treaty ports (1842). Pop: 1 398 000 (2005 est)

fuzzy 1 *Maths* of or relating to a form of set theory in which set membership depends on a likelihood function 2 (of a computer program or system) designed to operate according to the principles of fuzzy logic, so as to be able to deal with data which is imprecise or has uncertain boundaries

Fylde a region in NW England in Lancashire between the Wyre and Ribble estuaries

Gg

Ga *or* **Gã** 1 a member of a Negroid people of W Africa living chiefly in S Ghana 2 the language of this people, belonging to the Kwa branch of the Niger-Congo family

gab 1 a hook or open notch in a rod or lever that drops over the spindle of a valve to form a temporary connection for operating the valve 2 a pointed tool used in masonry

gabardine *or* **gaberdine** a twill-weave worsted, cotton, or spun-rayon fabric

gable 1 the triangular upper part of a wall between the sloping ends of a pitched roof (**gable roof**) 2 a triangular ornamental feature in the form of a gable, esp as used over a door or window 3 the triangular wall on both ends of a gambrel roof

Gable (William) **Clark** 1901–60, US film actor. His films include *It Happened One Night* (1934), *San Francisco* (1936), *Gone with the Wind* (1939), *Mogambo* (1953), and *The Misfits* (1960)

Gabo Naum , original name *Naum Neemia Pevsner*. 1890–1977, US sculptor, born in Russia: a leading constructivist

Gabon a republic in W central Africa, on the Atlantic: settled by the French in 1839; made part of the French Congo in 1888; became independent in 1960; almost wholly forested. Official language: French. Religion: Christian majority; significant animist minority. Currency: franc. Capital: Libreville. Pop: 1 352 000 (2004 est). Area: 267 675 sq km (103 350 sq miles)

Gabor Dennis 1900–79, British electrical engineer, born in Hungary. He invented holography: Nobel prize for physics 1971

Gaborone the capital of Botswana (since 1964), in the extreme southeast. Pop: 186 007 (2001)

Gabriel¹ Jacques-Ange 1698–1782, French architect: designed the Petit Trianon at Versailles

Gabriel² *Bible* one of the archangels, the messenger of good news (Daniel 8:16–26; Luke 1:11–20, 26–38) ·

Gabrieli *or* **Gabrielli** 1 Andrea 1520–86, Italian organist and composer; chief organist of St Mark's, Venice 2 his nephew, **Giovanni** 1558–1612, Italian organist and composer

Gad *Old Testament* 1 a Jacob's sixth son, whose mother was Zilpah, Leah's maid b the Israelite tribe descended from him c the territory of this tribe, lying to the east of the Jordan and extending southwards from the Sea of Galilee 2 a prophet and admonisher of David (I

Samuel 22; II Samuel 24)

Gaddafi *or* **Qaddafi** Mu'ammar Muhammad al- born 1942, Libyan army officer and statesman; head of state from 1969

gadfly any of various large dipterous flies, esp the horsefly, that annoy livestock by sucking their blood

gadoid of, relating to, or belonging to the *Anacanthini*, an order of marine soft-finned fishes typically having the pectoral and pelvic fins close together and small cycloid scales. The group includes gadid fishes and hake

gadolinium a ductile malleable silvery-white ferromagnetic element of the lanthanide series of metals: occurs principally in monazite and bastnaesite. Symbol: Gd; atomic no.: 64; atomic wt.: 157.25; valency: 3; relative density: 7.901; melting pt.: 1313±°C; boiling pt.: 3273°C (approx.)

Gadsden Purchase an area of about 77 000 sq km (30 000 sq miles) in present-day Arizona and New Mexico, bought by the US from Mexico for 10 million dollars in 1853. The purchase was negotiated by James Gadsden (1788–1858), US diplomat

Gael a person who speaks a Gaelic language, esp a Highland Scot or an Irishman

Gaelic 1 any of the closely related languages of the Celts in Ireland, Scotland, or (formerly) the Isle of Man 2 of, denoting, or relating to the Celtic people of Ireland, Scotland, or the Isle of Man or their language or customs

Gaeltacht *or* **Gaedhealtacht** any of the regions in Ireland in which Irish Gaelic is the vernacular speech. The form *Gaeltacht* is sometimes also used to mean the region of Scotland in which Scottish Gaelic is spoken

gaff 1 *Angling* a stiff pole with a stout prong or hook attached for landing large fish 2 *Nautical* a boom hoisted aft of a mast to support a gaffsail 3 a metal spur fixed to the leg of a gamecock

gaffer *Film, TV, etc* the senior electrician on a television or film set

gag 1 *Med* a surgical device for keeping the jaws apart, as during a tonsillectomy 2 *Parliamentary procedure* another word for **closure**

Gagarin Yuri 1934–68, Soviet cosmonaut: made the first manned space flight (1961)

gage 1 something deposited as security against the fulfilment of an obligation; pledge 2 (formerly) a glove or other object thrown down to indicate a challenge to combat

Gage Thomas 1721–87, British general and governor in America; commander in chief of British forces at Bunker Hill (1775)

Gaillard Cut the SE section of the Panama Canal, cut through Culebra Mountain. Length: about 13 km (8 miles)

gain *Electronics* the ratio of the output signal of an amplifier to the input signal, usually measured in decibels

Gainsborough Thomas 1727–88, English painter, noted particularly for his informal portraits and for his naturalistic landscapes

gait (used esp of horses and dogs) the pattern of footsteps at various speeds, as the walk, trot, canter, etc, each pattern being distinguished by a particular rhythm and footfall

Gaitskell Hugh (Todd Naylor). 1906–63, British politician; leader of the Labour Party (1955–63)

Gaius *or* **Caius** ?110–?180 AD, Roman jurist. His *Institutes* were later used as the basis for those of Justinian

gal a unit of acceleration equal to 1 centimetre per second per second

gala *Chiefly Brit* a sporting occasion involving competitions in several events

galactic 1 *Astronomy* of or relating to a galaxy, esp the Galaxy 2 *Med* of or relating to milk

Galashiels a town in SE Scotland, in central Scottish Borders. Pop: 14 361 (2001)

Galata a port in NW Turkey, a suburb and the chief business section of Istanbul

Galaţi an inland port in SE Romania, on the River Danube. Pop: 251 000 (2005 est)

Galatia an ancient region in central Asia Minor, conquered by Gauls 278–277 BC; later a Roman province

galaxy any of a vast number of star systems held together by gravitational attraction in an asymmetric shape (an **irregular galaxy**) or, more usually, in a symmetrical shape (a **regular galaxy**), which is either a spiral or an ellipse

Galaxy the the spiral galaxy, approximately 100 000 light years in diameter, that contains the solar system about three fifths of the distance from its centre

Galbraith John Kenneth born 1908, US economist and diplomat born in Canada; author of *The Affluent Society* (1958), *The New Industrial State* (1967), and *The Culture of Contentment* (1992)

gale a strong wind, specifically one of force seven to ten on the Beaufort scale or from 45 to 90 kilometres per hour

Galen Latin name *Claudius Galenus*. ?130–?200 AD, Greek physician, anatomist, and physiologist. He codified existing medical knowledge and his authority continued until the Renaissance

galena *or* **galenite** a grey mineral, found in hydrothermal veins. It is the chief source of lead. Composition: lead sulphide. Formula: PbS. Crystal structure: cubic

Galicia 1 a region of E central Europe on the N side of the Carpathians, now in SE Poland and Ukraine 2 an autonomous region and former kingdom of NW Spain, on the Bay of Biscay and the Atlantic. Pop: 1 969 000 (2003 est)

Galician the Romance language or dialect of Spanish

Galicia, sometimes regarded as a dialect of Spanish, although historically it is more closely related to Portuguese

Galilean a the an epithet of Jesus Christ (?4 BC–?29 AD), the founder of Christianity b a Christian

Galilee 1 **Sea of** Also called: Lake **Tiberias**, Lake **Kinneret** a lake in NE Israel, 209 m (686 ft) below sea level, through which the River Jordan flows. Area: 165 sq km (64 sq miles) 2 a northern region of Israel: scene of Christ's early ministry

Galileo full name *Galileo Galilei*. 1564–1642, Italian mathematician, astronomer, and physicist. He discovered the isochronism of the pendulum and demonstrated that falling bodies of different weights descend at the same rate. He perfected the refracting telescope, which led to his discovery of Jupiter's satellites, sunspots, and craters on the moon. He was forced by the Inquisition to recant his support of the Copernican system

gall a sore on the skin caused by chafing

gall bladder a muscular pear-shaped sac, lying underneath the right lobe of the liver, that stores bile and ejects it into the duodenum through the common bile duct

Galle a port in SW Sri Lanka; along with other coastal settlements, it suffered badly in the Indian Ocean tsunami of December 2004. Pop: 123 616 (1997 est)

galleon *Nautical* a large sailing ship having three or more masts, lateen-rigged on the after masts and square-rigged on the foremast and mainmast, used as a warship or trader from the 15th to the 18th centuries

gallery 1 a room or building for exhibiting works of art 2 a covered passageway open on one side or on both sides 3 a a balcony running along or around the inside wall of a church, hall, etc. b a covered balcony, sometimes with columns on the outside 4 *Theatre* a an upper floor that projects from the rear over the main floor and contains the cheapest seats b the seats there c the audience seated there 5 a long narrow room, esp one used for a specific purpose 6 *Chiefly US* a building or room where articles are sold at auction 7 *Theatre* a narrow raised platform at the side or along the back of the stage for the use of technicians and stagehands 8 *Nautical* a balcony or platform at the quarter or stern of a ship, sometimes used as a gun emplacement

galley 1 any of various kinds of ship propelled by oars or sails used in ancient or medieval times as a warship or as a trader 2 the kitchen of a ship, boat, or aircraft 3 any of various long rowing boats

galley slave a criminal or slave condemned to row in a galley

Gallic *History* of or relating to ancient Gaul or the Gauls

gallinaceous 1 of, relating to, or belonging to the *Galliformes*, an order of birds, including domestic fowl, pheasants, grouse, etc, having a heavy rounded body, short bill, and strong legs 2 of, relating to, or resembling the domestic fowl

Gallinas Point a cape in NE Colombia: the northernmost point of South America

Gallipoli 1 a peninsula in NW Turkey, between the Dardanelles and the Gulf of Saros: scene of a costly but unsuccessful Allied campaign in 1915 2 a port in NW Turkey, at the entrance to the Sea of Marmara: historically important for its strategic position. Pop: 16 751 (latest est)

gallium a silvery metallic element that is liquid for a wide temperature range. It occurs in trace amounts in some ores and is used in high-temperature thermometers and low-melting alloys. **Gallium arsenide** is a semiconductor. Symbol: Ga; atomic no.: 31; atomic wt.: 69.723; valency: 2 or 3; relative density: 5.904; melting pt.: 29.77°C; boiling pt.: 2205°C

gallon 1 *Brit* a unit of capacity equal to 277.42 cubic inches. 1 Brit gallon is equivalent to 1.20 US gallons or 4.55 litres 2 *US* a unit of capacity equal to 231 cubic inches. 1 US gallon is equivalent to 0.83 imperial gallon or 3.79 litres

gallop the fast two-beat gait of horses and other quadrupeds

Gallovidian 1 a native or inhabitant of Galloway 2 of or relating to Galloway

Galloway 1 an area of SW Scotland, on the Solway Firth: consists of the former counties of Kirkcudbright and Wigtown, now part of Dumfries and Galloway; in the west is a large peninsula, the **Rhinns of Galloway**, with the **Mull of Galloway**, a promontory, at the south end of it (the southernmost point of Scotland) 2 a breed of hardy beef cattle, usually black, originally bred in Galloway

gallstone *Pathol* a small hard concretion of cholesterol, bile pigments, and lime salts, formed in the gall bladder or its ducts

Gallup George Horace 1901–84, US statistician: devised the Gallup Poll; founded the American Institute of Public Opinion (1935) and its British counterpart (1936)

Gallup Poll a sampling by the American Institute of Public Opinion or its British counterpart of the views of a representative cross section of the population, used esp as a means of forecasting voting

galop 1 a 19th-century couple dance in quick duple time 2 a piece of music composed for this dance

Galsworthy John 1867–1933, English novelist and dramatist, noted for *The Forsyte Saga* (1906–28): Nobel prize for literature 1932

Galton Sir Francis 1822–1911, English explorer and scientist, a cousin of Charles Darwin, noted for his researches in heredity, meteorology, and statistics. He founded the study of eugenics and the theory of anticyclones

Galvani Luigi 1737–98, Italian physiologist: observed that muscles contracted on contact with dissimilar metals. This led to the galvanic cell and the electrical theory of muscle control by nerves

galvanic *or* **galvanical** of, producing, or concerned with an electric current, esp a direct current produced chemically

galvanometer any sensitive instrument for detecting or measuring small electric currents

Galway 1 a county of W Republic of Ireland, in S Connacht, on **Galway Bay** and the Atlantic: it has a deeply indented coastline and many offshore islands, including the Aran Islands. County town: Galway. Pop: 209 077 (2002). Area: 5939 sq km (2293 sq miles) 2 a port in W Republic of Ireland, county town of Co. Galway, on Galway Bay: important fisheries (esp for salmon). Pop: 66 163 (2002) 3 a breed of sheep with long wool, origi-

nally from W Ireland

Galwegian 1 another word for **Gallovidian** 2 a native or inhabitant of the town or county of Galway in W Republic of Ireland

Gama Vasco da ?1469–1524, Portuguese navigator, who discovered the sea route from Portugal to India around the Cape of Good Hope (1498)

Gambetta Léon 1838–82, French statesman; prime minister (1881–82). He organized resistance during the Franco-Prussian War (1870–71) and was a founder of the Third Republic (1871)

Gambia The a republic in W Africa, entirely surrounded by Senegal except for an outlet to the Atlantic: sold to English merchants by the Portuguese in 1588; became a British colony in 1843; gained independence and became a member of the Commonwealth in 1965; joined with Senegal to form the Confederation of Senegambia (1982–89); consists of a strip of land about 16 km (10 miles) wide, on both banks of the **Gambia River**, extending inland for about 480 km (300 miles). Official language: English. Religion: Muslim majority. Currency: dalasi. Capital: Banjul. Pop: 1 462 000 (2004 est). Area: 11 295 sq km (4361 sq miles)

gambit *Chess* an opening move in which a chessman, usually a pawn, is sacrificed to secure an advantageous position

gamble a bet, wager, or other risk or chance taken for possible monetary gain
 ▷www.betinf.com

gamboge 1 **gamboge tree** any of several tropical Asian trees of the genus *Garcinia*, esp *G. hanburyi*, that yield this resin: family *Clusiaceae* 2 a a gum resin used as the source of a yellow pigment and as a purgative b the pigment made from this resin 3 a strong yellow colour

game 1 an event consisting of various sporting contests, esp in athletics 2 short for **computer game** 3 a wild animals, including birds and fish, hunted for sport, food, or profit b (*as modifier*): *game laws*

gamer a person who plays computer games or participates in a role-playing game

gamester a person who habitually plays games for money; gambler

gamete a haploid germ cell, such as a spermatozoon or ovum, that fuses with another germ cell during fertilization

gaming a gambling on games of chance b (*as modifier*): *gaming house*

gamma 1 the third letter in the Greek alphabet (Γ, γ), a consonant, transliterated as *g*. When double, it is transcribed and pronounced as *ng* 2 the third highest grade or mark, as in an examination 3 a unit of magnetic field strength equal to 10^{-5} oersted. 1 gamma is equivalent to $0.795\ 775 \times 10^{-3}$ ampere per metre 4 *Photog, Television* the numerical value of the slope of the characteristic curve of a photographic emulsion or television camera; a measure of the contrast reproduced in a photographic or television image 5 a involving or relating to photons of very high energy b relating to one of two or more allotropes or crystal structures of a solid c relating to one of two or more isomeric forms of a chemical compound, esp one in which a group is attached to the carbon atom next but one to the atom to which the principal group is attached

gamma radiation 1 electromagnetic radiation emitted by atomic nuclei; the wavelength is generally in the range 1×10^{-10} to 2×10^{-13} metres **2** electromagnetic radiation of very short wavelength emitted by any source, esp the portion of the electromagnetic spectrum with a wavelength less than about 1×10^{-11} metres

gammon 1 a double victory in backgammon in which one player throws off all his pieces before his opponent throws any **2** *Archaic* the game of backgammon

gamut 1 *Music* **a** a scale, esp (in medieval theory) one starting on the G on the bottom line of the bass staff **b** the whole range of notes **2** *Physics* the range of chromaticities that can be obtained by mixing three colours

Gance Abel 1889–1981, French film director, whose works include *J'accuse* (1919, 1937) and *Napoléon* (1927), which introduced the split-screen technique

gander a male goose

Gandhi 1 Indira (**Priyadarshini**) , daughter of Jawaharlal Nehru. 1917–84, Indian stateswoman; prime minister of India (1966–77; 1980–84); assassinated **2 Mohandas Karamchand** , known as *Mahatma Gandhi*. 1869–1948, Indian political and spiritual leader and social reformer. He played a major part in India's struggle for home rule and was frequently imprisoned by the British for organizing acts of civil disobedience. He advocated passive resistance and hunger strikes as means of achieving reform, campaigned for the untouchables, and attempted to unite Muslims and Hindus. He was assassinated by a Hindu extremist **3 Rajiv** , son of Indira Gandhi. 1944–91, Indian statesman; prime minister of India (1984–89); assassinated

Gandzha *or* **Gäncä** a city in NW Azerbaijan: annexed by the Russians in 1804; centre of a cotton-growing region. Pop: 314 000 (2005 est)

gang 1 a herd of buffaloes or elks or a pack of wild dogs **2 a** a series of similar tools arranged to work simultaneously in parallel **b** (*as modifier*): *a gang saw*

Ganges the great river of N India and central Bangladesh: rises in two headstreams in the Himalayas and flows southeast to Allahabad, where it is joined by the Jumna; continues southeast into Bangladesh, where it enters the Bay of Bengal in a great delta; the most sacred river to Hindus, with many places of pilgrimage, esp Varanasi. Length: 2507 km (1557 miles)

ganglion 1 an encapsulated collection of nerve-cell bodies, usually located outside the brain and spinal cord **2** a cystic tumour on a tendon sheath or joint capsule

gangplank *or* **gangway** *Nautical* a portable bridge for boarding and leaving a vessel at dockside

gangrene death and decay of tissue as the result of interrupted blood supply, disease, or injury

Gangtok a town in NE India: capital of Sikkim state. Pop: 29 162 (2001)

gangue *or* **gang** valueless and undesirable material, such as quartz in small quantities, in an ore

gangway 1 an opening in a ship's side to take a gangplank **2** *Chiefly US* a ramp for logs leading into a sawmill

gannet any of several heavily built marine birds of the

genus *Morus* (or *Sula*), having a long stout bill and typically white plumage with dark markings: family *Sulidae*, order *Pelecaniformes* (pelicans, cormorants, etc)

ganoid 1 (of the scales of certain fishes) consisting of an inner bony layer and an outer layer of an enamel-like substance (ganoin) **2** denoting fishes, including the sturgeon and bowfin, having such scales **3** a ganoid fish

Gansu *or* **Kansu** a province of NW China, between Tibet and Inner Mongolia: mountainous, with desert regions; forms a corridor, the Old Silk Road, much used in early and medieval times for trade with Turkestan, India, and Persia. Capital: Lanzhou. Pop: 26 030 000 (2003 est). Area: 366 500 sq km (141 500 sq miles)

gantry *or* **gauntry 1** a bridgelike framework used to support a travelling crane, signals over a railway track, etc. **2** the framework tower used to attend to a large rocket on its launching pad **3** a supporting framework for a barrel or cask

Gao a town in E Mali, on the River Niger: a small river port. Pop: 54 903 (1998 est)

Gao Xingjian born 1940, Chinese dramatist, novelist, and dissident, living in France from 1987; his works include the play *Chezhan* (*Bus Stop*, 1983) and the novel *Lingshan* (*Soul Mountain*, 1989): Nobel prize for literature 2000

gap 1 a break in a line of hills or mountains affording a route through **2** *Chiefly US* a gorge or ravine **3** *Electronics* a break in a magnetic circuit that increases the inductance and saturation point of the circuit

gape the width of the widely opened mouth of a vertebrate

gap year *Brit* a year's break taken by a student between leaving school and starting further education

garage 1 a building or part of a building used to house a motor vehicle **2** a commercial establishment in which motor vehicles are repaired, serviced, bought, and sold, and which usually also sells motor fuels

garbage *Computing* invalid data

Garbo Greta , real name *Greta Lovisa Gustafson*. 1905–90, US film actress, born in Sweden. Her films include *Grand Hotel* (1932), *Queen Christina* (1933), *Anna Karenina* (1935), *Camille* (1936), and *Ninotchka* (1939)

Gard a department of S France, in Languedoc-Roussillon region. Capital: Nîmes. Pop: 648 522 (2003 est). Area: 5881 sq km (2294 sq miles)

Garda Lake a lake in N Italy: the largest lake in the country. Area: 370 sq km (143 sq miles)

garden 1 *Brit* **a** an area of land, usually planted with grass, trees, flowerbeds, etc, adjoining a house **b** (*as modifier*): *a garden chair* **2 a** an area of land used for the cultivation of ornamental plants, herbs, fruit, vegetables, trees, etc. **b** (*as modifier*): *garden tools* **3** such an area of land that is open to the public, sometimes part of a park

▷www.garden.org
▷www.gardenadvice.co.uk
▷www.uk.gardenweb.com
▷www.ngs.org.uk
▷www.greenfingers.com
▷www.bbc.co.uk/gardening
▷www.abc.net.au/gardening

▷www.bestgardening.co.nz/bgc/default.htm
▷www.canadiangardening.com/home.shtml
▷www.global-garden.com.au

garden centre a place where gardening tools and equipment, plants, seeds, etc, are sold

garden city *Brit* a planned town of limited size with broad streets and spacious layout, containing trees and open spaces and surrounded by a rural belt

gardenia 1 any evergreen shrub or tree of the Old World tropical rubiaceous genus *Gardenia*, cultivated for their large fragrant waxlike typically white flowers **2** the flower of any of these shrubs

Gardiner 1 Sir John Eliot born 1943, British conductor, noted for performances using period instruments; founded the Monteverdi Choir in 1965 and the Orchestre Révolutionnaire et Romantique in 1990 **2** Stephen ?1483–1555, English bishop and statesman; lord chancellor (1553–55). He opposed Protestantism, supporting the anti-Reformation policies of Mary I

Gardner Ava 1922–90, US film actress. Her films include *The Killers* (1946), *The Sun also Rises* (1957), and *The Night of the Iguana* (1964)

Garfield James Abram 1831–81, 20th president of the US (1881); assassinated in office

garfish 1 an elongated European marine teleost fish, *Belone belone*, with long toothed jaws: related to the flying fishes **2** any of various marine or estuarine fish with a long needle-like lower jaw

gargoyle 1 a waterspout carved in the form of a grotesque face or creature and projecting from a roof gutter, esp of a Gothic church **2** any grotesque ornament or projection, esp on a building

Garibaldi Giuseppe 1807–82, Italian patriot; a leader of the Risorgimento. He fought against the Austrians and French in Italy (1848– 49; 1859) and, with 1000 volunteers, conquered Sicily and Naples for the emerging kingdom of Italy (1860)

garland 1 a representation of such a wreath, as in painting, sculpture, etc. **2** a collection of short literary pieces, such as ballads or poems; miscellany or anthology **3** *Nautical* a ring or grommet of rope

Garland Judy, real name *Frances Gumm*. 1922–69, US singer and film actress. Already a child star, she achieved international fame with *The Wizard of Oz* (1939). Later films included *Meet Me in St Louis* (1944) and *A Star is Born* (1954)

garlic 1 a hardy widely cultivated Asian alliaceous plant, *Allium sativum*, having a stem bearing whitish flowers and bulbils **2** any of various other plants of the genus *Allium*

Garner Erroll 1921–77, US jazz pianist and composer

garnet¹ any of a group of hard glassy red, yellow, or green minerals consisting of the silicates of calcium, iron, manganese, chromium, magnesium, and aluminium in cubic crystalline form: used as a gemstone and abrasive. Formula: $A_3B_2(SiO_4)_3$ where A is a divalent metal and B is a trivalent metal

garnet² *Nautical* a tackle used for lifting cargo

Garonne a river in SW France, rising in the central Pyrenees in Spain and flowing northeast then northwest into the Gironde estuary. Length: 580 km (360 miles)

Garrett Lesley born 1955, British soprano; principal soprano with the English National Opera from 1984

Garrick David 1717–79, English actor and theatre manager

garrotte, garrote, *or* **garotte 1** a Spanish method of execution by strangulation or by breaking the neck **2** the device, usually an iron collar, used in such executions **3** *Obsolete* strangulation of one's victim while committing robbery

Gary a port in NW Indiana, on Lake Michigan: a major world steel producer. Pop: 99 961 (2003 est)

gas 1 a substance in a physical state in which it does not resist change of shape and will expand indefinitely to fill any container. If very high pressure is applied a gas may become liquid or solid, otherwise its density tends towards that of the condensed phase **2** any substance that is gaseous at room temperature and atmospheric pressure **3** any gaseous substance that is above its critical temperature and therefore not liquefiable by pressure alone **4 a** a fossil fuel in the form of a gas, used as a source of domestic and industrial heat **b** (*as modifier*): *a gas cooker* **5** a gaseous anaesthetic, such as nitrous oxide **6** the usual US, Canadian, and New Zealand word for **petrol**, a shortened form of **gasoline**

Gascony a former province of SW France

gaseous of, concerned with, or having the characteristics of a gas

gasholder 1 a large tank for storing coal gas or natural gas prior to distribution to users **2** any vessel for storing or measuring a gas

Gaskell Mrs married name of *Elizabeth Cleghorn Stevenson*. 1810–65, English novelist. Her novels include *Mary Barton* (1848), an account of industrial life in Manchester, and *Cranford* (1853), a social study of a country village

gasket a compressible packing piece of paper, rubber, asbestos, etc, sandwiched between the faces or flanges of a joint to provide a seal **2** *Nautical* a piece of line used as a sail stop

gaslight a type of lamp in which the illumination is produced by an incandescent mantle heated by a jet of gas

gas meter an apparatus for measuring and recording the amount of gas passed through it

gasoline *or* **gasolene** *US and Canadian* any one of various volatile flammable liquid mixtures of hydrocarbons, mainly hexane, heptane, and octane, obtained from petroleum and used as a solvent and a fuel for internal-combustion engines. Usually petrol also contains additives such as antiknock compounds and corrosion inhibitors

Gasser Herbert Spencer 1888–1963, US physiologist: shared a Nobel prize for physiology or medicine (1944) with Erlanger for work on electrical signs of nervous activity

gastric of, relating to, near, or involving the stomach

gastric juice a digestive fluid secreted by the stomach, containing hydrochloric acid, pepsin, rennin, etc.

gastric ulcer an ulcer of the mucous membrane lining the stomach

gastritis inflammation of the lining of the stomach

gastroenteritis inflammation of the stomach and

intestines

gastropod *or* **gasteropod** any mollusc of the class *Gastropoda*, typically having a flattened muscular foot for locomotion and a head that bears stalked eyes. The class includes the snails, whelks, limpets, and slugs

gasworks a plant in which gas, esp coal gas, is made

gate[1] **1** a mountain pass or gap, esp one providing entry into another country or region **2** (in a large airport) any of the numbered exits leading to the airfield or aircraft **3** *Electronics* **a** a logic circuit having one or more input terminals and one output terminal, the output being switched between two voltage levels determined by the combination of input signals **b** a circuit used in radar that allows only a fraction of the input signal to pass **4** the electrode region or regions in a field-effect transistor that is biased to control the conductivity of the channel between the source and drain **5** a component in a motion-picture camera or projector that holds each frame flat and momentarily stationary behind the lens **6** a slotted metal frame that controls the positions of the gear lever in a motor vehicle **7** *Rowing* a hinged clasp to prevent the oar from jumping out of a rowlock **8** a frame surrounding the blade or blades of a saw

gate[2] *Dialect* **1** the channels by which molten metal is poured into a mould **2** the metal that solidifies in such channels

gatehouse 1 a small house at the entrance to the grounds of a country mansion **2** a structure that houses the controls operating lock gates or dam sluices

Gates 1 Bill, full name *William Henry Gates*. born 1955, US computer-software executive; founder (1976) of Microsoft Corporation **2 Henry Louis** born 1950, US scholar and critic, who pioneered African-American studies in such works as *Figures in Black* (1987) **3** Horatio ?1728–1806, American Revolutionary general: defeated the British at Saratoga (1777)

Gateshead 1 a port in NE England, in Gateshead unitary authority, Tyne and Wear: engineering works, cultural centre. Pop: 78 403 (2001) **2** a unitary authority in NE England, in Tyne and Wear. Pop: 191 000 (2003 est). Area: 142 sq km (55 sq miles)

gateway 1 *Computing* hardware and software that connect incompatible computer networks, allowing information to be passed from one to another **2** *Telecom* a software utility that enables text messages to be sent and received over digital cellular telephone networks

Gath *Old Testament* one of the five cities of the Philistines, from which Goliath came (I Samuel 17:4) and near which Saul fell in battle (II Samuel 1:20)

gathering *Pathol* **a** the formation of pus in a boil **b** the pus so formed

GATT General Agreement on Tariffs and Trade: a multilateral international treaty signed in 1947 to promote trade, esp by means of the reduction and elimination of tariffs and import quotas; replaced in 1995 by the World Trade Organization

Gaudier-Brzeska Henri , original name *Henri Gaudier*. 1891–1915, French vorticist sculptor

gaudy *Brit* a celebratory festival or feast held at some schools and colleges

gauge *or* **gage 1** a standard measurement, dimension, capacity, or quantity **2** any of various instruments for measuring a quantity **3** any of various devices used to check for conformity with a standard measurement **4** the thickness of sheet metal or the diameter of wire **5** the distance between the rails of a railway track: in Britain 4 ft 8½ in. (1.435 m) **6** the distance between two wheels on the same axle of a vehicle, truck, etc. **7** *Nautical* the position of a vessel in relation to the wind and another vessel. One vessel may be windward (**weather gauge**) or leeward (**lee gauge**) of the other **8** a measure of the fineness of woven or knitted fabric, usually expressed as the number of needles used per inch **9** the width of motion-picture film or magnetic tape **10** (of a pressure measurement) measured on a pressure gauge that registers zero at atmospheric pressure; above or below atmospheric pressure

Gauguin Paul 1848–1903, French postimpressionist painter, who worked in the South Pacific from 1891. Inspired by primitive art, his work is characterized by flat contrasting areas of pure colours

Gauhati a city in NE India, in Assam on the River Brahmaputra: centre of British administration in Assam (1826–74). Pop: 808 021 (2001)

Gaul an ancient region of W Europe corresponding to N Italy, France, Belgium, part of Germany, and the S Netherlands: divided into Cisalpine Gaul, which became a Roman province before 100 BC, and Transalpine Gaul, which was conquered by Julius Caesar (58–51 BC)

gauss the cgs unit of magnetic flux density; the flux density that will induce an emf of 1 abvolt (10^{-8} volt) per centimetre in a wire moving across the field at a velocity of 1 centimetre per second. 1 gauss is equivalent to 10^{-4} tesla

Gauss Karl Friedrich 1777–1855, German mathematician: developed the theory of numbers and applied mathematics to astronomy, electricity and magnetism, and geodesy

Gauteng a province of N South Africa; formed in 1994 from part of the former province of Transvaal: service industries, mining, and manufacturing. Capital: Johannesburg. Pop: 8 847 740 (2004 est). Area: 18 810 sq km (7262 sq miles)

Gautier Théophile 1811–72, French poet, novelist, and critic. His early extravagant romanticism gave way to a preoccupation with poetic form and expression that anticipated the Parnassians

gauze 1 a a transparent cloth of loose plain or leno weave **b** (*as modifier*): *a gauze veil* **2** a surgical dressing of muslin or similar material **3** a fine mist or haze

Gavaskar Sunil Manohar born 1949, Indian cricketer. He captained India 1978–83 and 1984–85

gavotte *or* **gavot 1** an old formal dance in quadruple time **2** a piece of music composed for or in the rhythm of this dance

Gay John 1685–1732, English poet and dramatist; author of *The Beggar's Opera* (1728)

Gaya a city in NE India, in Bihar: Hindu place of pilgrimage and one of the holiest sites of Buddhism. Pop: 383 197 (2001)

Gay-Lussac Joseph Louis 1778–1850, French physicist and chemist: discovered the law named after him (1808), investigated the effects of terrestrial magnetism, isolated boron and cyanogen, and discovered methods of manufacturing sulphuric and oxalic acids

Gaza a city in the Gaza Strip: a Philistine city in biblical times. It was under Egyptian administration from 1949 until occupied by Israel (1967). Pop: 787 000 (2005 est)

Gazankulu (formerly) a Bantu homeland in South Africa; abolished in 1993. Capital: Giyani

Gaza Strip a coastal region on the SE corner of the Mediterranean: administered by Egypt from 1949; occupied by Israel from 1967; granted autonomy in 1993 and administered by the Palestinian National Authority from 1994. Pop: 1 406 423 (2004 est)

gazebo a summerhouse, garden pavilion, or belvedere, sited to command a view

gazelle any small graceful usually fawn-coloured antelope of the genera *Gazella* and *Procapra*, of Africa and Asia, such as *G. thomsoni* (**Thomson's gazelle**)

Gaziantep a city in S Turkey: base for Ibrahim Pasha's campaign against the Turks (1839) and centre of Turkish resistance to French forces (1921). Pop: 1 004 000 (2005 est)

GCE General Certificate of Education: a public examination in specified subjects taken in English and Welsh schools at the ages of 17 and 18. The GCSE has replaced the former GCE O-level for 16-year-olds

GCSE in Britain General Certificate of Secondary Education: a public examination in specified subjects for 16-year-old schoolchildren. It replaced the GCE O-level and CSE

Gdańsk 1 the chief port of Poland, on the Baltic: a member of the Hanseatic league; under Prussian rule (1793–1807 and 1814–1919); a free city under the League of Nations from 1919 until annexed by Germany in 1939; returned to Poland in 1945. Pop: 851 000 (2005 est) **2 Bay of** a wide inlet of the Baltic Sea on the N coast of Poland

Gdynia a port in N Poland, near Gdańsk: developed 1924–39 as the outlet for trade through the Polish Corridor; naval base. Pop: 253 521 (1999 est)

gear 1 a toothed wheel that engages with another toothed wheel or with a rack in order to change the speed or direction of transmitted motion **2** a mechanism for transmitting motion by gears, esp for a specific purpose **3** the engagement or specific ratio of a system of gears **4** *Nautical* all equipment or appurtenances belonging to a certain vessel, sailor, etc. **5** a less common word for **harness**

gearbox 1 the metal casing within which a train of gears is sealed **2** this metal casing and its contents, esp in a motor vehicle

gearing 1 an assembly of gears designed to transmit motion **2** the act or technique of providing gears to transmit motion

gear lever *or US and Canadian* **gearshift** a lever used to move gearwheels relative to each other, esp in a motor vehicle

Geber Latinized form of Jabir, assumed in honour of Jabir ibn Hayyan by a 14th-century alchemist, probably Spanish: he described the preparation of nitric and sulphuric acids

Gebrselassie Haile born 1973, Ethiopian athlete; Olympic gold medallist in the 10 000 metres in 1996 and 2000

gecko any small insectivorous terrestrial lizard of the family *Gekkonidae*, of warm regions. The digits have adhesive pads, which enable these animals to climb on smooth surfaces

Gee Maurice born 1931, New Zealand novelist

geebung 1 any of various trees and shrubs of the genus *Persoonia* of Australia having an edible but tasteless fruit **2** the fruit of these trees

geelbek *South African* a yellow-jawed edible marine fish

Geelong a port in SE Australia, in S Victoria on Port Phillip Bay. Pop: 130 194 (2001)

Gehenna 1 *Old Testament* the valley below Jerusalem, where children were sacrificed and where idolatry was practised (II Kings 23:10; Jeremiah 19:6) and where later offal and refuse were slowly burned **2** *New Testament, Judaism* a place where the wicked are punished after death

Gehry Frank O(wen). born 1929, US architect and furniture designer, born in Canada; best known for the Guggenheim Museum in Bilbao, Spain (1997)

Geiger counter *or* **Geiger-Müller counter** an instrument for detecting and measuring the intensity of ionizing radiation. It consists of a gas-filled tube containing a fine wire anode along the axis of a cylindrical cathode with a potential difference of several hundred volts. Any particle or photon which ionizes any number of gas molecules in the tube causes a discharge which is registered by electronic equipment. The magnitude of the discharge does not depend upon the nature or the energy of the ionizing particle

gelatine *or* **gelatin 1** a colourless or yellowish water-soluble protein prepared by boiling animal hides and bones: used in foods, glue, photographic emulsions, etc. **2** any of various substances that resemble gelatine **3** a translucent substance used for colour effects in theatrical lighting

gelatinous 1 consisting of or resembling jelly; viscous **2** of, containing, or resembling gelatine

geld *History* a tax on land levied in late Anglo-Saxon and Norman England

Gelderland *or* **Guelderland** a province of the E Netherlands: formerly a duchy, belonging successively to several different European powers. Capital: Arnhem. Pop: 1 960 000 (2003 est). Area: 5014 sq km (1955 sq miles)

gelding a castrated male horse

Geldof Bob Full name *Robert Frederick Zenon Geldof*. born 1954, Irish rock singer and philanthropist: formerly lead vocalist with the Boomtown Rats (1977–86): organizer of the Band Aid charity for famine relief in Africa. He received an honorary knighthood in 1986

gelignite a type of dynamite in which the nitrogelatine is absorbed in a base of wood pulp and potassium or sodium nitrate

Gelligaer a town in S Wales, in Caerphilly county borough. Pop. (including Ystrad Mynach): 17 185 (2001)

Gell-Mann Murray born 1929, US physicist, noted for his research on the interaction and classification of elementary particles: Nobel prize for physics in 1969

Gelsenkirchen an industrial city in W Germany, in North Rhine-Westphalia. Pop: 272 445 (2003 est)

Gemini 1 *Astronomy* a zodiacal constellation in the N hemisphere lying between Taurus and Cancer on the ecliptic and containing the stars Castor and Pollux **2** *Astrology* **a** the third sign of the zodiac, symbol ♊, having a mutable air classification and ruled by the planet Mercury. The sun is in this sign between about May 21 and June 20 **b** a person born when the sun is in this sign **3** *Astrology* born under or characteristic of Gemini

gendarme 1 a slang word for a **policeman 2** a sharp pinnacle of rock on a mountain ridge, esp in the Alps

gene a unit of heredity composed of DNA occupying a fixed position on a chromosome (some viral genes are composed of RNA). A gene may determine a characteristic of an individual by specifying a polypeptide chain that forms a protein or part of a protein (**structural gene**); or encode an RNA molecule; or regulate the operation of other genes or repress such operation

genealogy 1 the direct descent of an individual or group from an ancestor **2** the study of the evolutionary development of animals and plants from earlier forms **3** a chart showing the relationships and descent of an individual, group, genes, etc.

general 1 *Education* designating a degree awarded at some universities, studied at a lower academic standard than an honours degree **2** *Med* relating to or involving the entire body or many of its parts; systemic **3** *Logic* (of a statement) not specifying an individual subject but quantifying over a domain **4** a title for the head of a religious order, congregation, etc. **5** *Med* short for **general anaesthetic**

general anaesthetic a drug producing anaesthesia of the entire body, with loss of consciousness

general election 1 an election in which representatives are chosen in all constituencies of a state **2** *US* a final election from which successful candidates are sent to a legislative body **3** *US and Canadian* (in the US) a national or state election or (in Canada) a federal or provincial election in contrast to a local election

generalization *or* **generalisation 1** *Psychol* the evoking of a response learned to one stimulus by a different but similar stimulus **2** *Logic* the derivation of a general statement from a particular one, formally by prefixing a quantifier and replacing a subject term by a bound variable. If the quantifier is universal (**universal generalization**) the argument is not in general valid; if it is existential (**existential generalization**) it is valid **3** *Logic* any statement ascribing a property to every member of a class (**universal generalization**) or to one or more members (**existential generalization**)

general practitioner a physician who does not specialize but has a medical practice (**general practice**) in which he deals with all illnesses

general strike a strike by all or most of the workers of a country, province, city, etc, esp (*caps.*) such a strike that took place in Britain in 1926

generation 1 the act or process of bringing into being; production or reproduction, esp of offspring **2 a** a successive stage in natural descent of organisms: the time between when an organism comes into being and when it reproduces **b** the individuals produced at each stage **3** the normal or average time between two such generations of a species: about 35 years for humans **4** a

phase or form in the life cycle of a plant or animal characterized by a particular type of reproduction **5** production of electricity, heat, etc. **6** *Physics* a set of nuclei formed directly from a preceding set in a chain reaction

generative of or relating to the production of offspring, parts, etc.

generator 1 *Physics* **a** any device for converting mechanical energy into electrical energy by electromagnetic induction, esp a large one as in a power station **b** a device for producing a voltage electrostatically **c** any device that converts one form of energy into another form **2** an apparatus for producing a gas

generic *or* **generical 1** *Biology* of, relating to, or belonging to a genus **2** denoting the nonproprietary name of a drug, food product, etc. **3** a drug, food product, etc that does not have a trademark

generous (of wine) rich in alcohol

Genesis the first book of the Old Testament recounting the events from the Creation of the world to the sojourning of the Israelites in Egypt

Genet Jean 1910–86, French dramatist and novelist; his novels include *Notre-Dame des Fleurs* (1944) and his plays *Les Bonnes* (1947) and *Le Balcon* (1956)

genetically modified denoting or derived from an organism whose DNA has been altered for the purpose of improvement or correction of defects: *genetically modified food*.

genetic code *Biochem* the order in which the nitrogenous bases of DNA are arranged in the molecule, which determines the type and amount of protein synthesized in the cell. The four bases are arranged in groups of three in a specific order, each group acting as a unit (codon), which specifies a particular amino acid

genetic engineering alteration of the DNA of a cell for purposes of research, as a means of manufacturing animal proteins, correcting genetic defects, or making improvements to plants and animals bred by man

genetics 1 the branch of biology concerned with the study of heredity and variation in organisms **2** the genetic features and constitution of a single organism, species, or group

▷www.geneticalliance.org
▷www.ornl.gov/TechResources/
    Human_Genome/
▷www.genetics.org
▷http://ghr.nlm.nih.gov
▷www.hgc.gov.uk

Geneva 1 a city in SW Switzerland, in the Rhône valley on Lake Geneva: centre of Calvinism; headquarters of the International Red Cross (1864), the International Labour Office (1925), the League of Nations (1929–46), the World Health Organization, and the European office of the United Nations; banking centre. Pop: 177 500 (2002 est) **2** a canton in SW Switzerland. Capital: Geneva. Pop: 419 300 (2002 est). Area: 282 sq km (109 sq miles) **3 Lake** a lake between SW Switzerland and E France: fed and drained by the River Rhône, it is the largest of the Alpine lakes; the surface is subject to considerable changes of level. Area: 580 sq km (224 sq miles)

Genevan *or* **Genevese 1** of, relating to, or characteristic of Geneva **2** of, adhering to, or relating to the teachings of Calvin or the Calvinists **3** a native or inhabitant of Geneva

Genghis Khan original name *Temuchin* or *Temujin*. ?1162–1227, Mongol ruler, whose empire stretched from the Black Sea to the Pacific

genial *Anatomy* of or relating to the chin

genie 1 (in fairy tales and stories) a servant who appears by magic and fulfils a person's wishes **2** another word for **jinni**

genital 1 of or relating to the sexual organs or to reproduction **2** *Psychoanal* relating to the mature stage of psychosexual development in which an affectionate relationship with one's sex partner is established

genius 1 *Roman myth* **a** the guiding spirit who attends a person from birth to death **b** the guardian spirit of a place, group of people, or institution **2** *Arabic myth* a demon; jinn

Genk *or* **Genck** a town in NE Belgium, in Limburg province: coal-mining. Pop: 106 213 (2004 est)

Genoa a port in NW Italy, capital of Liguria, on the **Gulf of Genoa**: Italy's main port; an independent commercial city with many colonies in the Middle Ages; university (1243); heavy industries. Pop: 610 307 (2001)

genocide the policy of deliberately killing a nationality or ethnic group

genome *or* **genom 1** the full complement of genetic material within an organism **2** all the genes comprising a haploid set of chromosomes

genomics the branch of molecular genetics concerned with the study of genomes, specifically the identification and sequencing of their constituent genes and the application of this knowledge in medicine, pharmacy, agriculture, etc

genre a category of painting in which domestic scenes or incidents from everyday life are depicted

Genseric *or* **Gaiseric** ?390–477 AD, king of the Vandals (428–77). He seized Roman lands, esp extensive parts of N Africa, and sacked Rome (455)

gentian 1 any gentianaceous plant of the genera *Gentiana* or *Gentianella*, having blue, yellow, white, or red showy flowers **2** the bitter-tasting dried rhizome and roots of *Gentiana lutea* (**European** or **yellow gentian**), which can be used as a tonic **3** any of several similar plants, such as the horse gentian

gentian violet a greenish crystalline substance, obtained from rosaniline, that forms a violet solution in water, used as an indicator, antiseptic, and in the treatment of burns

Gentile[1] Giovanni 1875–1944, Italian Idealist philosopher and Fascist politician: minister of education (1922–24)

Gentile[2] **1** a person who is not a Jew **2** a Christian, as contrasted with a Jew **3** a person who is not a member of one's own church: used esp by Mormons **4** a heathen or pagan **5** of or relating to a race or religion that is not Jewish **6** Christian, as contrasted with Jewish **7** not being a member of one's own church: used esp by Mormons **8** pagan or heathen

Gentile da Fabriano original name *Niccolo di Giovanni di Massio*. ?1370–1427, Italian painter. His works, in the International Gothic style, include the *Adoration of the Magi* (1423)

gentle *Angling* a maggot, esp when used as bait in fishing

gentleman *Brit, History* a man of gentle birth, who was entitled to bear arms, ranking above a yeoman in social position

genus 1 *Biology* any of the taxonomic groups into which a family is divided and which contains one or more species. For example, *Vulpes* (foxes) is a genus of the dog family (*Canidae*) **2** *Logic* a class of objects or individuals that can be divided into two or more groups or species **3** *Maths* a number characterizing a closed surface in topology equal to the number of handles added to a sphere to form the surface. A sphere has genus 0, a torus, genus 1, etc.

geocentric 1 having the earth at its centre **2** measured from or relating to the centre of the earth

geodesic 1 relating to or involving the geometry of curved surfaces **2** the shortest line between two points on a curved or plane surface

geodesy *or* **geodetics** the branch of science concerned with determining the exact position of geographical points and the shape and size of the earth

Geoffrey of Monmouth ?1100–54, Welsh bishop and chronicler; author of *Historia Regum Britanniae*, the chief source of Arthurian legends

geography 1 the study of the natural features of the earth's surface, including topography, climate, soil, vegetation, etc, and man's response to them **2** the natural features of a region

  ▷www.sosig.ac.uk/geography
  ▷www.colorado.edu/geography/virtdept/ resources/contents.htm
  ▷http://oceanworld.tamu.edu/
  ▷www.geoexplorer.co.uk
  ▷http://plasma.nationalgeographic.com/ mapmachine/
  ▷www.library.wisc.edu/libraries/Geography/ offcamp.htm

geology 1 the scientific study of the origin, history, structure, and composition of the earth **2** the geological features of a district or country

  ▷www.psigate.ac.uk/newsite/ earth-gateway.html
  ▷http://personal.cmich.edu/~francim/ homepage.htm
  ▷www.earthquakes.bgs.ac.uk
  ▷http://nsidc.org/glaciers/information.html
  ▷http://pubs.usgs.gov/gip/fossils/

geometric *or* **geometrical 1** consisting of, formed by, or characterized by points, lines, curves, or surfaces **2** (of design or ornamentation) composed predominantly of simple geometric forms, such as circles, rectangles, triangles, etc.

geometric progression a sequence of numbers, each of which differs from the succeeding one by a constant ratio, as 1, 2, 4, 8, ...

geometry 1 the branch of mathematics concerned with the properties, relationships, and measurement of points, lines, curves, and surfaces **2 a** any branch of geometry using a particular notation or set of assumptions **b** any branch of geometry referring to a particular set of objects **3** *Arts* the shape of a solid or a surface

geophysics the study of the earth's physical properties

and of the physical processes acting upon, above, and within the earth. It includes seismology, geomagnetism, meteorology, and oceanography

Geordie *Brit* **1** a person who comes from or lives in Tyneside **2** the dialect spoken by these people

George 1 Sir **Edward** (**Alan John**), known as *Eddie*. born 1938, British economist, governor of the Bank of England (1993–2003) **2 Henry** 1839–97, US economist: advocated a single tax on land values, esp in *Progress and Poverty* (1879) **3 Saint** died ?303 AD, Christian martyr, the patron saint of England; the hero of a legend in which he slew a dragon. Feast day: April 23 **4 Stefan** (**Anton**). 1868–1933, German poet and aesthete. Influenced by the French Symbolists, esp Mallarmé and later by Nietzsche, he sought for an idealized purity of form in his verse. He refused Nazi honours and went into exile in 1933

George Cross a British award for bravery, esp of civilians: instituted 1940

George I 1660–1727, first Hanoverian king of Great Britain and Ireland (1714–27) and elector of Hanover (1698–1727). His dependence in domestic affairs on his ministers led to the emergence of Walpole as the first prime minister

George II 1683–1760, king of Great Britain and Ireland and elector of Hanover (1727–60); son of George I. His victory over the French at Dettingen (1743) in the War of the Austrian Succession was the last appearance on a battlefield by a British king **2** 1890–1947, king of Greece (1922–24; 1935–47). He was overthrown by the republicans (1924) and exiled during the German occupation of Greece (1941–45)

George III 1738–1820, king of Great Britain and Ireland (1760–1820) and of Hanover (1814–20). During his reign the American colonies were lost. He became insane in 1811, and his son acted as regent for the rest of the reign

George IV 1762–1830, king of Great Britain and Ireland and also of Hanover (1820–30); regent (1811–20). His father (George III) disapproved of his profligate ways, which undermined the prestige of the crown, and of his association with the Whig opposition

Georgetown 1 the capital and chief port of Guyana, at the mouth of the Demerara River: became capital of the Dutch colonies of Essequibo and Demerara in 1784; seat of the University of Guyana. Pop: 237 000 (2005 est) **2** the capital of the Cayman Islands: a port on Grand Cayman Island. Pop: 20 626 (1999)

George Town a port in NW Malaysia, capital of Penang state, in NE Penang Island: the first chartered city of the Malayan federation. Pop: 162 000 (2005 est)

georgette *or* **georgette crepe a** a thin silk or cotton crepe fabric with a mat finish **b** (*as modifier*): *a georgette blouse*

George V 1865–1936, king of Great Britain and Northern Ireland and emperor of India (1910–36)

George VI 1895–1952, king of Great Britain and Northern Ireland (1936–52) and emperor of India (1936–47). The second son of George V, he succeeded to the throne after the abdication of his brother, Edward VIII

Georgia 1 a republic in NW Asia, on the Black Sea: an independent kingdom during the middle ages, it was divided by Turkey and Persia in 1555; became part of

Russia in 1918 and a separate Soviet republic in 1936; its independence was recognized internationally in 1992. It is rich in minerals and has hydroelectric resources. Official language: Georgian. Religion: believers are mainly Christian or Muslim. Currency: lari. Capital: Tbilisi. Pop: 5 074 000 (2004 est). Area: 69 493 sq km (26 831 sq miles) **2** a state of the southeastern US, on the Atlantic: consists of coastal plains with forests and swamps, rising to the Cumberland Plateau and the Appalachians in the northwest. Capital: Atlanta. Pop: 8 684 715 (2003 est). Area: 152 489 sq km (58 876 sq miles)

Georgian 1 of, characteristic of, or relating to any or all of the four kings who ruled Great Britain and Ireland from 1714 to 1830, or to their reigns **2** of or relating to George V of Great Britain and Northern Ireland or his reign (1910–36) **3** the official language of Georgia, belonging to the South Caucasian family **4** a native or inhabitant of Georgia **5** an aboriginal inhabitant of the Caucasus **6** a native or inhabitant of the American State of Georgia **7** a person belonging to or imitating the styles of either of the Georgian periods in England

Georgian Bay a bay in S central Canada, in Ontario, containing many small islands: the NE part of Lake Huron. Area: 15 000 sq km (5800 sq miles)

geothermal *or* **geothermic** of or relating to the heat in the interior of the earth

Gera an industrial city in E central Germany, in Thuringia. Pop: 106 365 (2003 est)

geranium 1 any cultivated geraniaceous plant of the genus *Pelargonium*, having scarlet, pink, or white showy flowers **2** any geraniaceous plant of the genus *Geranium*, such as cranesbill and herb Robert, having divided leaves and pink or purplish flowers **3** a strong red to a moderate or strong pink colour

gerbil *or* **gerbille** any burrowing rodent of the subfamily *Gerbillinae*, inhabiting hot dry regions of Asia and Africa and having soft pale fur: family *Cricetidae*

Gergiev Valery Abesalovich born 1953, Russian conductor; musical director of the Kirov (now the Mariinsky) Opera from 1988

geriatrics the branch of medical science concerned with the diagnosis and treatment of diseases affecting elderly people

▷www.asaging.org

Gerlachovka a mountain in N Slovakia, in the Tatra Mountains: the highest peak of the Carpathian Mountains. Height: 2663 m (8737 ft)

germ 1 a microorganism, esp one that produces disease in animals or plants **2** a simple structure, such as a fertilized egg, that is capable of developing into a complete organism

German the official language of Germany and Austria and one of the official languages of Switzerland; the native language of approximately 100 million people. It is an Indo-European language belonging to the West Germanic branch, closely related to English and Dutch. There is considerable diversity of dialects; modern standard German is a development of Old High German, influenced by Martin Luther's translation of the Bible

▷www.goethe.de/enindex.htm

German East Africa a former German territory in E

Africa, consisting of Tanganyika and Ruanda-Urundi: divided in 1919 between Great Britain and Belgium; now in Tanzania, Rwanda, and Burundi

Germanic 1 a branch of the Indo-European family of languages that includes English, Dutch, German, the Scandinavian languages, and Gothic 2 the unrecorded language from which all of these languages developed; Proto-Germanic

Germanicus Caesar 15 BC–19 AD, Roman general; nephew of the emperor Tiberius; waged decisive campaigns against the Germans (14–16)

germanium a brittle crystalline grey element that is a semiconducting metalloid, occurring principally in zinc ores and argyrodite: used in transistors, as a catalyst, and to strengthen and harden alloys. Symbol: Ge; atomic no.: 32; atomic wt.: 72.61; valency: 2 or 4; relative density: 5.323; melting pt.: 938.35°C; boiling pt.: 2834°C

Germany a country in central Europe: in the Middle Ages the centre of the Holy Roman Empire; dissolved into numerous principalities; united under the leadership of Prussia in 1871 after the Franco-Prussian War; became a republic with reduced size in 1919 after being defeated in World War I; under the dictatorship of Hitler from 1933 to 1945; defeated in World War II and divided by the Allied Powers into four zones, which became established as East and West Germany in the late 1940s; reunified in 1990: a member of the European Union. It is flat and low-lying in the north with plateaus and uplands (including the Black Forest and the Bavarian Alps) in the centre and south. Official language: German. Religion: Christianity, Protestant majority. Currency: euro. Capital: Berlin. Pop: 82 526 000 (2004 est). Area: 357 041 sq km (137 825 sq miles)

germ cell a sexual reproductive cell; gamete

germicide any substance that kills germs or other microorganisms

Germiston a city in South Africa, southeast of Johannesburg: industrial centre, with the world's largest gold refinery, serving the Witwatersrand mines. Pop: 139 721 (2001)

Gerona a city in NE Spain: city walls and 14th-century cathedral; often besieged, in particular by the French (1809). Pop: 81 220 (2003 est)

Geronimo 1829–1909, Apache Indian chieftain: led a campaign against the White settlers until his final capture in 1886

gerontology the scientific study of ageing and the problems associated with elderly people

Gers a department of SW France, in Midi-Pyrénées region. Capital: Auch. Pop: 175 055 (2003 est). Area: 6291 sq km (2453 sq miles)

Gershwin 1 George, original name *Jacob Gershvin*. 1898–1937, US composer: incorporated jazz into works such as *Rhapsody in Blue* (1924) for piano and jazz band and the opera *Porgy and Bess* (1935) 2 his brother, **Ira**, original name *Israel Gershvin*. 1896–1983, US song lyricist, noted esp for his collaboration with George Gershwin

Gervais Ricky born 1962, British comedian and actor, best known for his starring role in the TV series *The Office* (2001–02), which he also co-wrote and co-directed

gesso 1 a white ground of plaster and size, used esp in the Middle Ages and Renaissance to prepare panels or canvas for painting or gilding 2 any white substance, esp plaster of Paris, that forms a ground when mixed with water

Gestapo the secret state police in Nazi Germany, noted for its brutal methods of interrogation

gestation a the development of the embryo of a viviparous mammal, between conception and birth: about 266 days in humans, 624 days in elephants, and 63 days in cats b (*as modifier*): *gestation period*

get *Informal* (in tennis) a successful return of a shot that was difficult to reach

Gethsemane *New Testament* the garden in Jerusalem where Christ was betrayed on the night before his Crucifixion (Matthew 26:36–56)

get in *Theatre* the process of moving into a theatre the scenery, props, and costumes for a production

get out *Theatre* the process of moving out of a theatre the scenery, props, and costumes after a production

Getty J(ean) Paul 1892–1976, US oil executive, millionaire, and art collector

Gettysburg a small town in S Pennsylvania, southwest of Harrisburg: scene of a crucial battle (1863) during the American Civil War, in which Meade's Union forces defeated Lee's Confederate army; site of the national cemetery dedicated by President Lincoln. Pop: 7825 (2003 est)

Getz Stanley, known as *Stan*. 1927–91, US jazz saxophonist: leader of his own group from 1949

geyser a spring that discharges steam and hot water

Gezira a region of the E central Sudan between the Blue and White Niles: site of a large-scale irrigation system

Ghana a republic in W Africa, on the Gulf of Guinea: a powerful empire from the 4th to the 13th centuries; a major source of gold and slaves for Europeans after 1471; British colony of the Gold Coast established in 1874; united with British Togoland in 1957 and became a republic and a member of the Commonwealth in 1960. Official language: English. Religions: Christian, Muslim, and animist. Currency: cedi. Capital: Accra. Pop: 21 377 000 (2004 est). Area: 238 539 sq km (92 100 sq miles)

ghat in India 1 a mountain pass or mountain range 2 a place of cremation

Ghazali al–1058–1111, Muslim theologian, philosopher, and mystic

Ghent an industrial city and port in NW Belgium, capital of East Flanders province, at the confluence of the Rivers Lys and Scheldt: formerly famous for its cloth industry; university (1816). Pop: 229 344 (2004 est)

Gheorghiu Angela born 1965, Romanian soprano: married to Roberto Alagna

gherkin a a tropical American cucurbitaceous climbing plant, *Cucumis anguria* b the small edible fruit of this plant

Ghiberti Lorenzo 1378–1455, Italian sculptor, painter, and goldsmith of the quattrocento: noted esp for the bronze doors of the baptistry of Florence Cathedral

Ghirlandaio or **Ghirlandajo** Domenico original name *Domenico Bigordi*. 1449–94, Italian painter of frescoes

ghost *Physics* a a faint secondary image produced by an optical system b a similar image on a television screen, formed by reflection of the transmitting waves or by a defect in the receiver

ghost gum *Austral* a eucalyptus tree with white trunk and branches

ghoul (in Muslim legend) an evil demon thought to eat human bodies, either stolen corpses or children

Giacometti Alberto 1901–66, Swiss sculptor and painter, noted particularly for his long skeletal statues of isolated figures

Giambologna original name *Giovanni da Bologna* or *Jean de Boulogne*. 1529–1608, Italian mannerist sculptor, born in Flanders: noted for his fountains and such works as *Samson Slaying a Philistine* (1565)

giant 1 *Greek myth* any of the large and powerful offspring of Uranus (sky) and Gaea (earth) who rebelled against the Olympian gods but were defeated in battle **2** *Pathol* a person suffering from gigantism

gibber *Austral* **1** a stone or boulder **2** of or relating to a dry flat area of land covered with wind-polished stones

Gibberd Sir Frederick 1908–84, British architect and town planner. His buildings include the Liverpool Roman Catholic cathedral (1960–67) and the Regent's Park Mosque in London (1977). Harlow in the U.K. and Santa Teresa in Venezuela were built to his plans

gibbet a a wooden structure resembling a gallows, from which the bodies of executed criminals were formerly hung to public view **b** a gallows

gibbon any small agile arboreal anthropoid ape of the genus *Hylobates*, inhabiting forests in S Asia

Gibbon 1 Edward 1737–94, English historian; author of *The History of the Decline and Fall of the Roman Empire* (1776–88), controversial in its historical criticism of Christianity **2** Lewis Grassic, real name *James Leslie Mitchell*. 1901–35, Scottish writer: best known for his trilogy of novels *Scots Quair* (1932–34)

Gibbons 1 Grinling 1648–1721, English sculptor and woodcarver, noted for his delicate carvings of fruit, flowers, birds, etc. **2** Orlando 1583–1625, English organist and composer, esp of anthems, motets, and madrigals

gibbous *or* **gibbose** (of the moon or a planet) more than half but less than fully illuminated

Gibbs 1 James 1682–1754, British architect; his buildings include St Martin's-in-the-Fields, London (1722–26), and the Radcliffe Camera, Oxford (1737–49) **2** Josiah Willard 1839–1903, US physicist and mathematician: founder of chemical thermodynamics

Gibeon an ancient town of Palestine: the excavated site thought to be its remains lies about 9 kilometres (6 miles) northwest of Jerusalem

Gibraltar 1 City of a city on the Rock of Gibraltar, a limestone promontory at the tip of S Spain: settled by Moors in 711 and taken by Spain in 1462; ceded to Britain in 1713; a British crown colony (1830–1969), still politically associated with Britain; a naval and air base of strategic importance. Pop: 27 000 (2003 est). Area: 6.5 sq km (2.5 sq miles) **2** Strait of a narrow strait between the S tip of Spain and the NW tip of Africa, linking the Mediterranean with the Atlantic

Gibran Kahlil 1883–1931, Syro-Lebanese poet, mystic, and painter, resident in the US after 1910; author of *The Prophet* (1923)

Gibson Mel born 1956, Australian film actor and director: his films include *Mad Max* (1979), *Hamlet* (1990), *Braveheart* (1996; also directed), *What Women Want* (2000), and *The Passion of the Christ* (2004; director only)

Gibson Desert a desert in W central Australia, between the Great Sandy Desert and the Victoria Desert: salt marshes, salt lakes, and scrub. Area: about 220 000 sq km (85 000 sq miles)

Gide André 1869–1951, French novelist, dramatist, critic, diarist, and translator, noted particularly for his exploration of the conflict between self-fulfilment and conventional morality. His novels include *L'Immoraliste* (1902), *La Porte étroite* (1909), and *Les Faux-Monnayeurs* (1926): Nobel prize for literature 1947

Gideon *Old Testament* a Hebrew judge who led the Israelites to victory over their Midianite oppressors (Judges 6:11–8:35)

Gielgud Sir John 1904–2000, English stage, film, and television actor and director

Giessen a city in central Germany, in Hesse: university (1607). Pop: 74 001 (2003 est)

GIF *Computing* **a** a standard compressed file format used for pictures **b** a picture held in this format

Gifu a city in Japan, on central Honshu: hot springs, textile and paper lantern manufacturing. Pop: 401 269 (2002 est)

gig¹ 1 a light two-wheeled one-horse carriage without a hood **2** *Nautical* a light tender for a vessel, often for the personal use of the captain **3** a long light rowing boat, used esp for racing **4** a machine for raising the nap of a fabric

gig² a cluster of barbless hooks drawn through a shoal of fish to try to impale them

Gigli Beniamino 1890–1957, Italian operatic tenor

Gilbert 1 Grove Karl 1843–1918, US geologist who pioneered the study of river development and valley erosion **2** Sir Humphrey ?1539–83, English navigator: founded the colony at St John's, Newfoundland (1583) **3** William 1540–1603, English physician and physicist, noted for his study of terrestrial magnetism in *De Magnete* (1600) **4** Sir W(illiam) S(chwenck). 1836–1911, English dramatist, humorist, and librettist. He collaborated (1871–96) with Arthur Sullivan on the famous series of comic operettas, including *The Pirates of Penzance* (1879), *Iolanthe* (1882), and *The Mikado* (1885)

Gilead¹ a historic mountainous region east of the River Jordan, rising over 1200 m (4000 ft)

Gilead² *Old Testament* a grandson of Manasseh; ancestor of the Coileadites (Numbers 26: 29–30)

Giles 1 Saint 7th century AD, Greek hermit in France; patron saint of cripples, beggars, and lepers. Feast day: Sept 1 **2** William Ernest Powell 1835–97, Australian explorer, born in England. He was noted esp for his exploration of the western desert (1875–76)

gill¹ 1 the respiratory organ in many aquatic animals, consisting of a membrane or outgrowth well supplied with blood vessels. **External gills** occur in tadpoles, some molluscs, etc.; **internal gills**, within gill slits, occur in most fishes **2** any of the radiating leaflike spore-producing structures on the undersurface of the cap of a mushroom

gill² a unit of liquid measure equal to one quarter of a pint

gill³ or **ghyll** *Dialect* **1** a narrow stream; rivulet **2** a wooded ravine **3** a deep natural hole in rock; pothole

gill⁴ *Dialect* a female ferret

Gill (Arthur) Eric (Rowton). 1882–1940, British sculptor, engraver, and typographer: his sculptures include the *Stations of the Cross* in Westminster Cathedral, London

Gillespie Dizzy, nickname of *John Birks Gillespie.* 1917–93, US jazz trumpeter

gillie, ghillie, or **gilly** *Scot* **1** an attendant or guide for hunting or fishing **2** (formerly) a Highland chieftain's male attendant or personal servant

Gillingham a town in SE England, in Medway unitary authority, Kent, on the Medway estuary: former dockyards. Pop: 98 403 (2001)

Gillray James 1757–1815, English caricaturist

gilt¹ gold or a substance simulating it, applied in gilding

gilt² a young female pig, esp one that has not had a litter

gimlet 1 a small hand tool consisting of a pointed spiral tip attached at right angles to a handle, used for boring small holes in wood **2** a eucalyptus of W Australia having a twisted bole

gimmick *Chiefly US* a device or trick of legerdemain that enables a magician to deceive the audience

gin¹ 1 an alcoholic drink obtained by distillation and rectification of the grain of malted barley, rye, or maize, flavoured with juniper berries **2** any of various grain spirits flavoured with other fruit or aromatic essences **3** an alcoholic drink made from any rectified spirit

gin² 1 a primitive engine in which a vertical shaft is turned by horses driving a horizontal beam or yoke in a circle **2** a machine of this type used for separating seeds from raw cotton **3** a trap for catching small mammals, consisting of a noose of thin strong wire **4** a hand-operated hoist that consists of a drum winder turned by a crank

ginger 1 any of several zingiberaceous plants of the genus *Zingiber,* esp *Z. officinale* of the East Indies, cultivated throughout the tropics for its spicy hot-tasting underground stem **2** any of certain related plants **3** a a reddish-brown or yellowish-brown colour **b** (*as adjective*): *ginger hair*

ginger ale a sweetened effervescent nonalcoholic drink flavoured with ginger extract

ginger beer a slightly alcoholic drink made by fermenting a mixture of syrup and root ginger

ginger group *Politics, chiefly Brit* a group within a party, association, etc, that enlivens or radicalizes its parent body

gingham *Textiles* **a** a cotton fabric, usually woven of two coloured yarns in a checked or striped design **b** (*as modifier*): *a gingham dress*

gingivitis inflammation of the gums

gin rummy a version of rummy in which a player may go out if the odd cards outside his sequences total less than ten points

Ginsberg Allen 1926–97, US poet of the Beat Generation. His poetry includes *Howl* (1956) and *Kaddish* (1960)

ginseng 1 either of two araliaceous plants, *Panax schinseng* of China or *P. quinquefolius* of North America, whose forked aromatic roots are used medicinally **2** the root of either of these plants or a substance obtained from the roots, believed to possess stimulant, tonic, and energy-giving properties

Ginzburg Natalia 1916–91, Italian writer and dramatist. Her books include *The Road to the City* (1942), *Voices in the Evening* (1961), and *Family Sayings* (1963)

Giorgione II original name *Giorgio Barbarelli.* ?1478–1511, Italian painter of the Venetian school, who introduced a new unity between figures and landscape

Giotto also known as *Giotto di Bondone.* ?1267–1337, Florentine painter, who broke away from the stiff linear design of the Byzantine tradition and developed the more dramatic and naturalistic style characteristic of the Renaissance: his work includes cycles of frescoes in Assisi, the Arena Chapel in Padua, and the Church of Santa Croce, Florence

Gippsland a fertile region of SE Australia, in SE Victoria, extending east along the coast from Melbourne to the New South Wales border. Area: 35 200 sq km (13 600 sq miles)

giraffe a large ruminant mammal, *Giraffa camelopardalis,* inhabiting savannas of tropical Africa: the tallest mammal, with very long legs and neck and a colouring of regular reddish-brown patches on a beige ground: family *Giraffidae*

Giraldus Cambrensis literary name of *Gerald de Barri.* ?1146–?1223, Welsh chronicler and churchman, noted for his accounts of his travels in Ireland and Wales

Giraud Henri Honoré 1879–1949, French general, who commanded French forces in North Africa (1942–43)

Giraudoux (Hyppolyte) Jean 1882–1944, French dramatist. His works include the novel *Suzanne et le Pacifique* (1921) and the plays *Amphitryon 38* (1929) and *La Guerre de Troie n'aura pas lieu* (1935)

girder *Botany* the structure composed of tissue providing mechanical support for a stem or leaf

girdle 1 *Anatomy* any encircling structure or part **2** the mark left on a tree trunk after the removal of a ring of bark

giro *Brit, informal* an unemployment or income support payment by giro cheque, posted fortnightly

Gironde 1 a department of SW France, in Aquitaine region. Capital: Bordeaux. Pop: 1 330 683 (2003 est). Area: 10 726 sq km (4183 sq miles) **2** an estuary in SW France, formed by the confluence of the Rivers Garonne and Dordogne. Length: 72 km (45 miles)

girt *Nautical* moored securely to prevent swinging

girth *Riding* a band around a horse's belly to keep the saddle in position

Gisborne a port in N New Zealand, on E North Island on Poverty Bay. Pop: 44 900 (2004 est)

Gish 1 Dorothy 1898–1968, US film actress, chiefly in silent films **2** her sister, **Lillian** 1896–1993, US film and stage actress, noted esp for her roles in such silent films as *The Birth of a Nation* (1915) and *Intolerance* (1916)

Gissing George (Robert). 1857–1903, English novelist, noted for his depiction of middle-class poverty. His works include *Demos* (1886) and *New Grub Street* (1891)

gist *Law* the essential point of an action

Giulini Carlo Maria born 1914, Italian orchestral conductor, esp of opera

Giulio Romano ?1499–1546, Italian architect and

painter; a founder of mannerism

given 1 *Maths* known or determined independently 2 (on official documents) issued or executed, as on a stated date 3 *Philosophy* the supposed raw data of experience

gizzard 1 the thick-walled part of a bird's stomach, in which hard food is broken up by muscular action and contact with grit and small stones 2 a similar structure in many invertebrates

glacial 1 characterized by the presence of masses of ice 2 relating to, caused by, or deposited by a glacier 3 (of a chemical compound) of or tending to form crystals that resemble ice

glacial period 1 any period of time during which a large part of the earth's surface was covered with ice, due to the advance of glaciers, as in the late Carboniferous period, and during most of the Pleistocene; glaciation 2 the Pleistocene epoch

glacier a slowly moving mass of ice originating from an accumulation of snow. It can either spread out from a central mass (**continental glacier**) or descend from a high valley (**alpine glacier**)

Gladbeck a city in NW Germany, in North Rhine-Westphalia. Pop: Pop: 77 166 (2003 est)

glade an open place in a forest; clearing

gladiator (in ancient Rome and Etruria) a man trained to fight in arenas to provide entertainment

gladiolus 1 any iridaceous plant of the widely cultivated genus *Gladiolus*, having sword-shaped leaves and spikes of funnel-shaped brightly coloured flowers 2 *Anatomy* the large central part of the breastbone

Gladstone William Ewart 1809–98, British statesman. He became leader of the Liberal Party in 1867 and was four times prime minister (1868–74; 1880–85; 1886; 1892–94). In his first ministry he disestablished the Irish Church (1869) and introduced educational reform (1870) and the secret ballot (1872). He succeeded in carrying the Reform Act of 1884 but failed to gain support for a Home Rule Bill for Ireland, to which he devoted much of the latter part of his career

Glamorgan *or* **Glamorganshire** a former county of SE Wales: divided into West Glamorgan, Mid Glamorgan, and South Glamorgan in 1974; since 1996 administered by the county of Swansea and the county boroughs of Neath Port Talbot, Bridgend, Rhondda Cynon Taff, Vale of Glamorgan, Merthyr Tydfil, and part of Caerphilly

glance[1] *Cricket* a stroke in which the ball is deflected off the bat to the leg side; glide

glance[2] *Mineralogy* any mineral having a metallic lustre, esp a simple sulphide

gland[1] 1 a cell or organ in man and other animals that synthesizes chemical substances and secretes them for the body to use or eliminate, either through a duct (see **exocrine gland**) or directly into the bloodstream (see **endocrine gland**) 2 a structure, such as a lymph node, that resembles a gland in form 3 a cell or organ in plants that synthesizes and secretes a particular substance

gland[2] *Engineering* a device that prevents leakage of fluid along a rotating shaft or reciprocating rod passing through a boundary between areas of high and low pressure. It often consists of a flanged metal sleeve bedding into a stuffing box

glandular *or* **glandulous** of, relating to, containing, functioning as, or affecting a gland

Glarus 1 an Alpine canton of E central Switzerland. Capital: Glarus. Pop: 38 400 (2002 est). Area 684 sq km (264 sq miles) 2 a town in E central Switzerland, the capital of Glarus canton. Pop: 5556 (2000)

Glaser Donald Arthur born 1926, US physicist: invented the bubble chamber; Nobel prize for physics 1960

Glasgow 1 a city in W central Scotland, in City of Glasgow council area on the River Clyde: the largest city in Scotland; centre of a major industrial region, formerly an important port; universities (1451, 1964, 1992). Pop: 629 501 (2001) 2 **City of** a council area in W central Scotland. Pop: 577 090 (2003 est). Area: 175 sq km (68 sq miles)

glasnost *History* the policy of public frankness and accountability developed in the former Soviet Union under the leadership of Mikhail Gorbachov

glass 1 a a hard brittle transparent or translucent non-crystalline solid, consisting of metal silicates or similar compounds. It is made from a fused mixture of oxides, such as lime, silicon dioxide, etc, and is used for making windows, mirrors, bottles, etc. b *(as modifier): a glass bottle* 2 any compound that has solidified from a molten state into a noncrystalline form 3 See **fibreglass**

Glass Philip born 1937, US avant-garde composer noted for his minimalist style: his works include *Music in Fifths* (1970), *Akhnaten* (1984), *The Voyage* (1992), and *Monsters of Grace* (1998)

glass-blowing the process of shaping a mass of molten or softened glass into a vessel, shape, etc, by blowing air into it through a tube

glasshouse *Brit* a glass building, esp a greenhouse, used for growing plants in protected or controlled conditions

Glastonbury a town in SW England, in Somerset: remains of prehistoric lake villages; the reputed burial place of King Arthur; site of a ruined Benedictine abbey, probably the oldest in England. Pop: 8429 (2001)

glaucoma a disease of the eye in which pressure within the eyeball damages the optic disc, impairing vision, sometimes progressing to blindness

glaze 1 *Ceramics* a a vitreous or glossy coating b the substance used to produce such a coating 2 a semitransparent coating applied to a painting to modify the tones 3 a smooth lustrous finish on a fabric produced by applying various chemicals

Glazunov Aleksandr Konstantinovich 1865–1936, Russian composer, in France from 1928. A pupil of Rimsky-Korsakov, he wrote eight symphonies and concertos for piano and for violin among other works

glebe *Brit* land granted to a clergyman as part of his benefice

glee a type of song originating in 18th-century England, sung by three or more unaccompanied voices

glen a narrow and deep mountain valley, esp in Scotland or Ireland

Glencoe a glen in W Scotland, in S Highland: site of a massacre of Macdonalds by Campbells and English troops (1692)

Glendower Owen, Welsh name *Owain Glyndŵr*.

?1350–?1416, Welsh chieftain, who led a revolt against Henry IV's rule in Wales (1400–15)

Glenn John born 1921, US astronaut and politician. The first American to orbit the earth (Feb, 1962), he later became a senator (1975–99) and in 1998 returned to space at the age of 77

Glennie Evelyn (Elizabeth Ann). born 1965, British percussionist

Glenrothes a new town in E central Scotland, the administrative centre of Fife: founded in 1948. Pop: 38 679 (2001)

glide 1 any of various dances featuring gliding steps **b** a step in such a dance **2** a manoeuvre in which an aircraft makes a gentle descent without engine power **3** the act or process of gliding **4** *Music* **a** a long portion of tubing slipped in and out of a trombone to increase its length for the production of lower harmonic series **b** a portamento or slur **5** *Crystallog* another name for **slip 6** *Cricket* another word for **glance¹**

glider an aircraft capable of gliding and soaring in air currents without the use of an engine
▷www.gliding.co.uk
▷www.fai.org/gliding

Glinka Mikhail Ivanovich 1803–57, Russian composer who pioneered the Russian national school of music. His works include the operas *A Life for the Tsar* (1836) and *Russlan and Ludmila* (1842)

glissade a gliding step in ballet, in which one foot slides forwards, sideways, or backwards

glissando 1 a rapidly executed series of notes on the harp or piano, each note of which is discretely audible **2** a portamento, esp as executed on the violin, viola, etc.

glitch 1 *Electronics* a sudden instance of malfunctioning or irregularity in an electronic system **2** *Astronomy* a change in the rotation rate of a pulsar

glitter *Canadian* ice formed from freezing rain

Gliwice an industrial city in S Poland. Pop: 212 164 (1999 est)

global warming an increase in the average temperature worldwide believed to be caused by the greenhouse effect

globe 1 a sphere on which a map of the world or the heavens is drawn or represented **2** a planet or some other astronomical body **3** *Austral, NZ, and South African* an electric light bulb

globule *Astronomy* a small dark nebula thought to be a site of star formation

globulin any of a group of simple proteins, including gamma globulin, that are generally insoluble in water but soluble in salt solutions and coagulated by heat

glockenspiel a percussion instrument consisting of a set of tuned metal plates played with a pair of small hammers

Glomma a river in SE Norway, rising near the border with Sweden and flowing generally south to the Skagerrak: the largest river in Scandinavia; important for hydroelectric power and floating timber. Length: 588 km (365 miles)

glory hole *Informal* a room, cupboard, or other storage space that contains an untidy and miscellaneous collection of objects

glossy a photograph printed on paper that has a smooth shiny surface

glottis the vocal apparatus of the larynx, consisting of the two true vocal cords and the opening between them

Gloucester¹ Humphrey, Duke of. 1391–1447, English soldier and statesman; son of Henry IV. He acted as protector during Henry VI's minority (1422–29) and was noted for his patronage of humanists

Gloucester² a city in SW England, administrative centre of Gloucestershire, on the River Severn; cathedral (founded 1100). Pop: 123 205 (2001)

Gloucestershire a county of SW England, situated around the lower Severn valley: contains the Forest of Dean and the main part of the Cotswold Hills: the geographical and ceremonial county includes the unitary authority of South Gloucestershire (part of Avon county from 1974 to 1996). Administrative centre: Gloucester. Pop. (excluding South Gloucestershire): 568 500 (2003 est). Area (excluding South Gloucestershire): 2643 sq km (1020 sq miles)

glove *Sport* any of various large protective hand covers worn in sports, such as a boxing glove

glow light emitted by a substance or object at a high temperature

glow-worm 1 a European beetle, *Lampyris noctiluca*, the females and larvae of which bear luminescent organs producing a greenish light: family Lampyridae **2** any of various other beetles or larvae of the family Lampyridae

gloxinia any of several tropical plants of the genus *Sinningia*, esp the South American *S. speciosa*, cultivated for its large white, red, or purple bell-shaped flowers: family *Gesneriaceae*

Gluck Christoph Willibald von 1714–87, German composer, esp of operas, including *Orfeo ed Euridice* (1762) and *Alceste* (1767)

glucose 1 a white crystalline monosaccharide sugar that has several optically active forms, the most abundant being dextrose: a major energy source in metabolism. Formula: $C_6H_{12}O_6$ **2** a yellowish syrup (or, after desiccation, a solid) containing dextrose, maltose, and dextrin, obtained by incomplete hydrolysis of starch: used in confectionery, fermentation, etc.

glue any natural or synthetic adhesive, esp a sticky gelatinous substance prepared by boiling animal products such as bones, skin, and horns

glue ear accumulation of fluid in the middle ear in children, caused by infection and sometimes resulting in deafness

gluten a protein consisting of a mixture of glutelin and gliadin, present in cereal grains, esp wheat. A gluten-free diet is necessary in cases of coeliac disease

gluteus *or* **glutaeus** any one of the three large muscles that form the human buttock and move the thigh, esp the **gluteus maximus**

glycerol a colourless or pale yellow odourless sweet-tasting syrupy liquid; 1,2,3-propanetriol: a by-product of soap manufacture, used as a solvent, antifreeze, plasticizer, and sweetener (**E422**). Formula: $C_3H_8O_3$

glycogen a polysaccharide consisting of glucose units: the form in which carbohydrate is stored in the liver and muscles in man and animals. It can easily be hydrolysed to glucose

glycolysis *Biochem* the breakdown of glucose by

enzymes into pyruvic and lactic acids with the liberation of energy

Glyndebourne an estate in SE England, in East Sussex: site of a famous annual festival of opera founded in 1934 by John Christie

G-man 1 *US, slang* an FBI agent 2 *Irish* a political detective

gnat any of various small fragile biting dipterous insects of the suborder *Nematocera*, esp *Culex pipiens* (**common gnat**), which abounds near stagnant water

gneiss any coarse-grained metamorphic rock that is banded and foliated: represents the last stage in the metamorphism of rocks before melting

gnome one of a species of legendary creatures, usually resembling small misshapen old men, said to live in the depths of the earth and guard buried treasure

Gnosticism a religious movement characterized by a belief in gnosis, through which the spiritual element in man could be released from its bondage in matter: regarded as a heresy by the Christian Church

gnu either of two sturdy antelopes, *Connochaetes taurinus* (**brindled gnu**) or the much rarer *C. gnou* (**white-tailed gnu**), inhabiting the savannas of Africa, having an oxlike head and a long tufted tail

go or **I-go** a game for two players in which stones are placed on a board marked with a grid, the object being to capture territory on the board

Goa a state on the W coast of India: a Portuguese overseas territory from 1510 until annexed by India in 1961. Pop: 1 343 998 (2001). Area: 3702 sq km (1430 sq miles)

goal 1 (in various sports) the net, basket, etc into or over which players try to propel the ball, puck, etc, to score 2 *Sport* **a** a successful attempt at scoring **b** the score so made 3 (in soccer, hockey, etc) the position of goalkeeper

goal line *Sport* the line marking each end of the pitch, on which the goals stand

goalpost either of two upright posts supporting the crossbar of a goal

goanna any of various Australian monitor lizards

goat any sure-footed agile bovid mammal of the genus *Capra*, naturally inhabiting rough stony ground in Europe, Asia, and N Africa, typically having a brown-grey colouring and a beard. Domesticated varieties (*C. hircus*) are reared for milk, meat, and wool

goatsucker *US and Canadian* any nocturnal bird of the family *Caprimulgidae*, esp *Caprimulgus europaeus* (**European nightjar**): order *Caprimulgiform es*.

go-away bird *South African* a common name for a grey-plumaged **lourie** of the genus *Corythaixoides*

gob a lump of molten glass used to make a piece of glassware

Gobbi Tito 1915–84, Italian operatic baritone

gobbler *Informal* a male turkey

Gobi a desert in E Asia, mostly in Mongolia and the Inner Mongolian Autonomous Region of China: sometimes considered to include all the arid regions east of the Pamirs and north of the plateau of Tibet and the Great Wall of China: one of the largest deserts in the world. Length: about 1600 km (1000 miles). Width: about 1000 km (625 miles). Average height: 900 m (3000 ft)

Gobind Singh or **Govind Singh** 1666–1708, tenth and last guru of the Sikhs (1675–1708): assassinated

goblet a vessel for drinking, usually of glass or metal, with a base and stem but without handles

goblin (in folklore) a small grotesque supernatural creature, regarded as malevolent towards human beings

goby 1 any small spiny-finned fish of the family *Gobiidae*, of coastal or brackish waters, having a large head, an elongated tapering body, and the ventral fins modified as a sucker 2 any other gobioid fish

god 1 a supernatural being, who is worshipped as the controller of some part of the universe or some aspect of life in the world or is the personification of some force 2 an image, idol, or symbolic representation of such a deity 3 the gallery of a theatre

God *Theol* the sole Supreme Being, eternal, spiritual, and transcendent, who is the Creator and ruler of all and is infinite in all attributes; the object of worship in monotheistic religions

Godard Jean-Luc born 1930, French film director and writer associated with the New Wave of the 1960s. His works include *À bout de souffle* (1960), *Weekend* (1967), *Sauve qui peut* (1980), *Nouvelle Vague* (1990), and *Éloge de l'amour* (2003)

Godavari a river in central India, rising in the Western Ghats and flowing southeast to the Bay of Bengal: extensive delta, linked by canal with the Krishna delta; a sacred river to Hindus. Length: about 1500 km (900 miles)

godchild a person, usually an infant, who is sponsored by adults at baptism

Goddard Robert Hutchings 1882–1945, US physicist. He made the first workable liquid-fuelled rocket

goddaughter a female godchild

Goderich Viscount, title of *Frederick John Robinson*, 1st Earl of Ripon. 1782–1859, British statesman; prime minister (1827–28)

Godesberg a town and spa in W Germany, in North Rhine-Westphalia on the Rhine: a SE suburb of Bonn

godetia any plant of the American onagraceous genus *Godetia*, esp one grown as a showy-flowered annual garden plant

godfather a male godparent

Godhead 1 the essential nature and condition of being God 2 **the Godhead** God

Godiva Lady ?1040–1080, wife of Leofric, Earl of Mercia. According to legend, she rode naked through Coventry in order to obtain remission for the townspeople from the heavy taxes imposed by her husband

godmother a female godparent

Godolphin Sidney 1st Earl of Godolphin. 1645–1712, English statesman; as Lord Treasurer, he managed the financing of Marlborough's campaigns in the War of the Spanish Succession

godparent a person who stands sponsor to another at baptism

godson a male godchild

Godunov Boris Fyodorovich ?1551–1605, Russian regent (1584–98) and tsar (1598–1605)

Godwin 1 died 1053, Earl of Wessex. He was chief adviser to Canute and Edward the Confessor. His son succeeded Edward to the throne as Harold II 2 **William** 1756–1836,

British political philosopher and novelist. In *An Enquiry concerning Political Justice* (1793), he rejected government and social institutions, including marriage. His views greatly influenced English romantic writers

Goebbels Paul Joseph 1897–1945, German Nazi politician; minister of propaganda (1933–45)

Goethe Johann Wolfgang von 1749–1832, German poet, novelist, and dramatist, who settled in Weimar in 1775. His early works of the *Sturm und Drang* period include the play *Götz von Berlichingen* (1773) and the novel *The Sorrows of Young Werther* (1774). After a journey to Italy (1786–88) his writings, such as the epic play *Iphigenie auf Tauris* (1787) and the epic idyll *Hermann und Dorothea* (1797), showed the influence of classicism. Other works include the *Wilhelm Meister* novels (1796–1829) and his greatest masterpiece *Faust* (1808; 1832)

Gog and Magog 1 *Old Testament* a hostile prince and the land from which he comes to attack Israel (Ezekiel 38) 2 *New Testament* two kings, who are to attack the Church in a climactic battle, but are then to be destroyed by God (Revelation 20:8–10) 3 *Brit folklore* two giants, the only survivors of a race of giants destroyed by Brutus, the legendary founder of Britain

gogga *South African, informal* any small animal that crawls or flies, esp an insect

Gogol Nikolai Vasilievich 1809–52, Russian novelist, dramatist, and short-story writer. His best-known works are *The Government Inspector* (1836), a comedy satirizing bureaucracy, and the novel *Dead Souls* (1842)

Gogra a river in N India, rising in Tibet, in the Himalayas, and flowing southeast through Nepal as the Karnali, then through Uttar Pradesh to join the Ganges. Length: about 1000 km (600 miles)

Goidelic, Goidhelic, *or* **Gadhelic** the N group of Celtic languages, consisting of Irish Gaelic, Scottish Gaelic, and Manx

goitre *or US* **goiter** *Pathol* a swelling of the thyroid gland, in some cases nearly doubling the size of the neck, usually caused by under- or overproduction of hormone by the gland

Golconda a ruined town and fortress in S central India, in W Andhra Pradesh near Hyderabad city: capital of one of the five Muslim kingdoms of the Deccan from 1512 to 1687, then annexed to the Mogul empire; renowned for its diamonds

gold 1 a a dense inert bright yellow element that is the most malleable and ductile metal, occurring in rocks and alluvial deposits: used as a monetary standard and in jewellery, dentistry, and plating. The radioisotope gold-198 (**radiogold**), with a half-life of 2.69 days, is used in radiotherapy. Symbol: Au; atomic no.: 79; atomic wt.: 196.96654; valency: 1 or 3; relative density: 19.3; melting pt.: 1064.43°C; boiling pt.: 2857°C b (*as modifier*): *a gold mine* 2 a deep yellow colour, sometimes with a brownish tinge 3 *Archery* the bull's eye of a target, scoring nine points 4 short for **gold medal**

Gold Thomas born 1920, Austrian-born astronomer, working in England and the US: with Bondi and Hoyle he proposed the steady-state theory of the universe

Gold Coast 1 the former name (until 1957) of **Ghana** 2 a line of resort towns and beaches in E Australia, extending for over 30 km (20 miles) along the SE coast of Queensland and the NE coast of New South Wales

goldcrest a small Old World warbler, *Regulus regulus*, having a greenish plumage and a bright yellow-and-black crown

golden age 1 *Classical myth* the first and best age of mankind, when existence was happy, prosperous, and innocent 2 the great classical period of Latin literature, occupying approximately the 1st century BC and represented by such writers as Cicero and Virgil

golden eagle a large eagle, *Aquila chrysaetos*, of mountainous regions of the N hemisphere, having a plumage that is golden brown on the back and brown elsewhere

Golden Gate a strait between the Pacific and San Francisco Bay: crossed by the **Golden Gate Bridge,** with a central span of 1280 m (4200 ft)

golden goal *Soccer* (in certain matches) the first goal scored in extra time, which wins the match for the side scoring it

Golden Horn an inlet of the Bosporus in NW Turkey, forming the harbour of Istanbul

golden hour the first hour after a serious accident, when it is crucial that the victim receives medical treatment in order to have a chance of surviving

golden retriever a compact large breed of dog having a silky coat of flat or wavy hair of a gold or dark-cream colour, well-feathered on the legs and tail

goldenrod 1 any plant of the genus *Solidago*, of North America, Europe, and Asia, having spikes made up of inflorescences of minute yellow florets: family *Asteraceae* (composites) 2 any of various similar related plants, such as *Brachychaeta sphacelata* (**false goldenrod**) of the southern US

golden rule any of a number of rules of fair conduct, such as *Whatsoever ye would that men should do to you, do ye even so to them* (Matthew 7:12) or *thou shalt love thy neighbour as thyself* (Leviticus 19:28)

golden wattle 1 an Australian yellow-flowered leguminous plant, *Acacia pycnantha*, that yields a useful gum and bark 2 any of several similar and related plants, esp *Acacia longifolia* of Australia

goldfinch 1 a common European finch, *Carduelis carduelis*, the adult of which has a red-and-white face and yellow-and-black wings 2 any of several North American finches of the genus *Spinus*, esp the yellow-and-black species *S. tristis*

goldfish 1 a freshwater cyprinid fish, *Carassius auratus*, of E Europe and Asia, esp China, widely introduced as a pond or aquarium fish. It resembles the carp and has a typically golden or orange-red coloration 2 any of certain similar ornamental fishes, esp the golden orfe

gold foil thin gold sheet that is thicker than gold leaf

Golding Sir William (Gerald) 1911–93, English novelist noted for his allegories of man's proclivity for evil. His novels include *Lord of the Flies* (1954), *Darkness Visible* (1979), *Rites of Passage* (1980), *Close Quarters* (1987), and *Fire Down Below* (1989). Nobel prize for literature 1983

gold leaf very thin gold sheet with a thickness usually between 0.076 and 0.127 micrometre, produced by rolling or hammering gold and used for gilding woodwork, etc.

gold medal a medal of gold, awarded to the winner of a

competition or race

Goldoni Carlo 1707–93, Italian dramatist; author of over 250 plays in Italian or French, including *La Locandiera* (1753). His work introduced realistic Italian comedy, superseding the commedia dell'arte

Goldschmidt Richard Benedikt 1878–1958, US geneticist, born in Germany. He advanced the theory that heredity is determined by the chemical configuration of the chromosome molecule rather than by the qualities of the individual genes
▷www.gold.org/goldwork

goldsmith 1 a a dealer in articles made of gold b an artisan who makes such articles 2 (formerly) a dealer or manufacturer of gold articles who also engaged in banking or other financial business

Goldsmith Oliver ?1730–74, Irish poet, dramatist, and novelist. His works include the novel *The Vicar of Wakefield* (1766), the poem *The Deserted Village* (1770), and the comedy *She Stoops to Conquer* (1773)

gold standard a monetary system in which the unit of currency is defined with reference to gold

golf a a game played on a large open course, the object of which is to hit a ball using clubs, with as few strokes as possible, into each of usually 18 holes b *(as modifier)*: a *golf bag*
▷www.pga.com
▷www.randa.org

golf club 1 any of various long-shafted clubs with wood or metal heads used to strike a golf ball 2 a an association of golf players, usually having its own course and facilities b the premises of such an association

golf course a general term for an area of ground, either inland or beside the sea, laid out for the playing of golf

Golgi Camillo 1844–1926, Italian neurologist and histologist, noted for his work on the central nervous system and his discovery in animal cells of the bodies known by his name: shared the Nobel prize for physiology or medicine 1906

Goliath *Old Testament* a Philistine giant from Gath who terrorized the Hebrews until he was killed by David with a stone from his sling (I Samuel 17)

Gomel an industrial city in SE Belarus, on the River Sozh; an industrial centre. Pop: 480 000 (2005 est)

Gomorrah or **Gomorrha** *Old Testament* one of two ancient cities near the Dead Sea, the other being Sodom, that were destroyed by God as a punishment for the wickedness of their inhabitants (Genesis 19:24)

Gomulka Wladyslaw 1905–82, Polish statesman; first secretary of the Polish Communist Party (1956–70)

gonad an animal organ in which gametes are produced, such as a testis or an ovary

Goncharov Ivan Aleksandrovich 1812–91, Russian novelist: his best-known work is *Oblomov* (1859)

Goncourt Edmond Louis Antoine Huot de , 1822–96, and his brother, Jules Alfred Huot de , 1830–70, French writers, noted for their collaboration, esp on their *Journal*, and for the Académie Goncourt founded by Edmond's will

Gondar a city in NW Ethiopia: capital of Ethiopia from the 17th century until 1868. Pop: 191 000 (2005 est)

gondola 1 a long narrow flat-bottomed boat with a high ornamented stem and a platform at the stern where an oarsman stands and propels the boat by sculling or punting: traditionally used on the canals of Venice 2 a a car or cabin suspended from an airship or balloon b a moving cabin suspended from a cable across a valley, etc. 3 a flat-bottomed barge used on canals and rivers of the US as far west as the Mississippi 4 *US and Canadian* a low open flat-bottomed railway goods wagon 5 a set of island shelves in a self-service shop: used for displaying goods

gondolier a man who propels a gondola

gong 1 a percussion instrument of indefinite pitch, consisting of a metal platelike disc struck with a soft-headed drumstick 2 a rimmed metal disc, hollow metal hemisphere, or metal strip, tube, or wire that produces a note when struck. It may be used to give alarm signals when operated electromagnetically

gonorrhoea or *esp US* **gonorrhea** an infectious venereal disease caused by a gonococcus, characterized by a burning sensation when urinating and a mucopurulent discharge from the urethra or vagina

good *Economics* a commodity or service that satisfies a human need

Good Friday the Friday before Easter, observed as a commemoration of the Crucifixion of Jesus

Goodman Benny, full name *Benjamin David Goodman*. 1909–86, US jazz clarinetist and bandleader, whose treatment of popular songs created the jazz idiom known as swing

Good Samaritan *New Testament* a figure in one of Christ's parables (Luke 10:30–37) who is an example of compassion towards those in distress

Goodwood an area in SE England, in Sussex: site of a famous racecourse and of **Goodwood House**, built 1780–1800

Goodyear Charles 1800–60, US inventor of vulcanized rubber

googly *Cricket* an off break bowled with a leg break action

Goole an inland port in NE England, in the East Riding of Yorkshire at the confluence of the Ouse and Don Rivers, 75 km (47 miles) from the North Sea. Pop: 18 741 (2001)

goosander a common merganser (a duck), *Mergus merganser*, of Europe and North America, having a dark head and white body in the male

goose 1 any of various web-footed long-necked birds of the family *Anatidae*: order *Anseriformes*. They are typically larger and less aquatic than ducks and are gregarious and migratory 2 the female of such a bird, as opposed to the male (gander)

gooseberry 1 a Eurasian shrub, *Ribes uva-crispa* (or *R. grossularia*), having greenish, purple-tinged flowers and ovoid yellow-green or red-purple berries: family *Grossulariaceae* 2 a the berry of this plant b *(as modifier)*: *gooseberry jam* 3 **Cape gooseberry** a tropical American solanaceous plant, *Physalis peruviana*, naturalized in southern Africa, having yellow flowers and edible yellow berries

goose flesh the bumpy condition of the skin induced by cold, fear, etc, caused by contraction of the muscles at the base of the hair follicles with consequent erection of papillae: so called because of the resemblance to the skin of a freshly-plucked fowl

Goossens 1 Sir **Eugene** 1893–1962, British composer and conductor, born in Belgium 2 his brother, **Leon** 1896–1988, British oboist

gopher 1 any burrowing rodent of the family *Geomyidae*, of North and Central America, having a thickset body, short legs, and cheek pouches 2 any burrowing tortoise of the genus *Gopherus*, of SE North America

Gorakhpur a city in N India, in SE Uttar Pradesh: formerly an important Muslim garrison. Pop: 624 570 (2001)

Gorbachov or **Gorbachev** Mikhail Sergeevich born 1931, Soviet statesman; general secretary of the Soviet Communist Party (1985– 91): president (1988–91). Nobel peace prize 1990. His reforms ended the Communist monopoly of power and led to the break-up of the Soviet Union

Gorbals the a district of Glasgow, formerly known for its slums

Gordian knot (in Greek legend) a complicated knot, tied by King Gordius of Phrygia, that Alexander the Great cut with a sword

Gordimer Nadine born 1923, South African novelist. Her books include *The Lying Days* (1952), *The Conservationist* (1974), which won the Booker prize, *None to Accompany Me* (1994), and *The House Gun* (1998). Her works were banned in South Africa for their condemnation of apartheid. Nobel prize for literature 1991

Gordon 1 **Adam Lindsay** 1833–70, Australian poet and horseman, born in the Azores, who developed the bush ballad as a literary form, esp in *Bush Ballads and Galloping Rhymes* (1870) 2 **Charles George**, known as *Chinese Gordon*. 1833–85, British general and administrator. He helped to crush the Taiping rebellion (1863–64), and was governor of the Sudan (1877–80), returning in 1884 to aid Egyptian forces against the Mahdi. He was killed in the siege of Khartoum 3 **Dexter (Keith)**. 1923–90, US jazz tenor saxophonist 4 Lord **George** 1751–93, English religious agitator. He led the Protestant opposition to legislation relieving Roman Catholics of certain disabilities, which culminated in the Gordon riots (1780)

Gore Al(bert) Jr born 1948, US Democrat politician; vice president of the US (1993–2001); defeated in the disputed presidential election of 2000

Gorey Edward St. John 1925–2000, US illustrator and author, noted for his bizarre humour in such works as *The Unstrung Harp* (1953) and *The Wuggly Ump* (1963)

gorge 1 a deep ravine, esp one through which a river runs 2 the contents of the stomach 3 *Archaic* the throat or gullet

Gorgon *Greek myth* any of three winged monstrous sisters, Stheno, Euryale, and Medusa, who had live snakes for hair, huge teeth, and brazen claws

gorilla the largest anthropoid ape, *Gorilla gorilla*, inhabiting the forests of central W Africa. It is stocky and massive, with a short muzzle and coarse dark hair

Gorizia a city in NE Italy, in Friuli-Venezia Giulia, on the Isonzo River: cultural centre under the Hapsburgs. Pop: 35 667 (2001)

Gorki or **Gorky** Maxim , pen name of *Aleksey Maximovich Peshkov.* 1868–1936, Russian novelist, dramatist, and short-story writer, noted for his depiction of the out-

casts of society. His works include the play *The Lower Depths* (1902), the novel *Mother* (1907), and an autobiographical trilogy (1913–23)

Gorky Arshile 1904–48, US abstract expressionist painter, born in Armenia. Influenced by Picasso and Miró, his style is characterized by fluid lines and resonant colours

Gorlovka a city in SE Ukraine in the centre of the Donets Basin: a major coal-mining centre. Pop: 280 000 (2005 est)

Gorno-Altai Republic a constituent republic of S Russia: mountainous, rising over 4350 m (14 500 ft) in the Altai Mountains of the south. Capital: Gorno-Altaisk. Pop: 202 900 (2002). Area: 92 600 sq km (35 740 sq miles)

Gorno-Badakhshan Autonomous Republic an administrative division of Tajikistan: generally mountainous and inaccessible. Capital: Khorog. Pop: 206 000 (2000 est). Area: 63 700 sq km (24 590 sq miles)

gorse any evergreen shrub of the leguminous genus *Ulex*, esp the European species *U. europeaus*, which has yellow flowers and thick green spines instead of leaves

Gorton Sir John Grey 1911–2002, Australian statesman; prime minister (1968–71)

goshawk a large hawk, *Accipiter gentilis*, of Europe, Asia, and North America, having a bluish-grey back and wings and paler underparts: used in falconry

Goshen a region of ancient Egypt, east of the Nile delta: granted to Jacob and his descendants by the king of Egypt and inhabited by them until the Exodus (Genesis 45:10)

gosling a young goose

gospel 1 Black religious music originating in the churches of the Southern states of the United States 2 the message or doctrine of a religious teacher 3 a the story of Christ's life and teachings as narrated in the Gospels b the good news of salvation in Jesus Christ c *(as modifier)*: *the gospel story*

▷www.gospelmusic.org

▷www.allmusic.com

Gospel 1 any of the first four books of the New Testament, namely Matthew, Mark, Luke, and John 2 a reading from one of these in a religious service

Gosport a town in S England, in Hampshire on Portsmouth harbour: naval base since the 16th century. Pop: 69 348 (2001)

gossamer a gauze or silk fabric of the very finest texture

Gosse Sir Edmund William 1849–1928, English critic and poet, noted particularly for his autobiographical work *Father and Son* (1907)

Goth a member of an East Germanic people from Scandinavia who settled south of the Baltic early in the first millennium AD. They moved on to the Ukrainian steppes and raided and later invaded many parts of the Roman Empire from the 3rd to the 5th century

Gotha a town in central Germany, in Thuringia on the N edge of the Thuringian forest: capital of Saxe-Coburg-Gotha (1826–1918); noted for the *Almanach de Gotha* (a record of the royal and noble houses of Europe, first published in 1764). Pop: 47 158 (2003 est)

Gothic 1 denoting, relating to, or resembling the style of architecture that was used in W Europe from the 12th to the 16th centuries, characterized by the lancet arch, the ribbed vault, and the flying buttress **2** of or relating to the style of sculpture, painting, or other arts as practised in W Europe from the 12th to the 16th centuries **3** of or relating to a literary style characterized by gloom, the grotesque, and the supernatural, popular esp in the late 18th century: when used of modern literature, films, etc, sometimes spelt: **Gothick 4** of, relating to, or characteristic of the Goths or their language **5** of or relating to the Middle Ages **6** Gothic architecture or art **7** the extinct language of the ancient Goths, known mainly from fragments of a translation of the Bible made in the 4th century by Bishop Wulfila
▷www.artlex.com/ArtLex/g/gothic.html
▷www.greatbuildings.com/types/styles/ gothic.html
▷www.artcyclopedia.com/history/gothic.html

Gotland, Gothland, or **Gottland** an island in the Baltic Sea, off the SE coast of Sweden: important trading centre since the Bronze Age; long disputed between Sweden and Denmark, finally becoming Swedish in 1645; tourism and agriculture now important. Capital: Visby. Pop: (including associated islands) 57 677 (2004 est). Area: 3140 sq km (1212 sq miles)

Gottfried von Strassburg early 13th-century German poet; author of the incomplete epic *Tristan and Isolde*, the version of the legend that served as the basis of Wagner's opera

gouache 1 a painting technique using opaque watercolour paint in which the pigments are bound with glue and the lighter tones contain white **2** the paint used in this technique **3** a painting done by this method

Gouda a town in the W Netherlands, in South Holland province: important medieval cloth trade; famous for its cheese. Pop: 72 000 (2003 est)

gouge 1 a type of chisel with a blade that has a concavo-convex section **2** *Geology* a fine deposit of rock fragments, esp clay, occurring between the walls of a fault or mineral vein

goulash *Bridge* a method of dealing in threes and fours without first shuffling the cards, to produce freak hands

Gould 1 Benjamin Apthorp 1824–96, US astronomer: the first to use the telegraph to determine longitudes; founded the *Astronomical Journal* (1849) **2** Glenn 1932–82, Canadian pianist

Gounod Charles François 1818–93, French composer of the operas *Faust* (1859) and *Romeo and Juliet* (1867)

gourd 1 the fruit of any of various cucurbitaceous or similar plants, esp the bottle gourd and some squashes, whose dried shells are used for ornament, drinking cups, etc **2** any plant that bears this fruit **3** a bottle or flask made from the dried shell of the bottle gourd

gout a metabolic disease characterized by painful inflammation of certain joints, esp of the big toe and foot, caused by deposits of sodium urate in them

governess a woman teacher employed in a private household to teach and train the children

government 1 the exercise of political authority over the actions, affairs, etc, of a political unit, people, etc, as well as the performance of certain functions for this unit or body; the action of governing; political rule and administration **2** the system or form by which a community, etc, is ruled **3** the executive policy-making body of a political unit, community, etc.; ministry or administration **4 a** the state and its administration **b** (*as modifier*): *a government agency*
▷www.lib.umich.edu/govdocs/index.html
▷www.library.northwestern.edu/govpub/ resource/internat
▷www.wto.org/english/res_e/statis_e/ natl_e.pdf
▷www.politicalresources.net
▷www.lib.berkeley.edu/doemoff/ gov_intlgen.html
▷www.psa.ac.uk/www/archives.htm

governor 1 the ruler or chief magistrate of a colony, province, etc. **2** the representative of the Crown in a British colony **3** *Brit* the senior administrator or head of a society, prison, etc. **4** the chief executive of any state in the US **5** *Engineering* a device that controls the speed of an engine, esp by regulating the supply of fuel, etc, either to limit the maximum speed or to maintain a constant speed

governor general 1 the representative of the Crown in a dominion of the Commonwealth or a British colony; vicegerent **2** *Brit* a governor with jurisdiction or precedence over other governors

Gower¹ 1 David (Ivon), born 1957, English cricketer **2** John ?1330–1408, English poet, noted particularly for his tales of love, the *Confessio Amantis*

Gower² the peninsula in S Wales, in Swansea county on the Bristol Channel: mainly agricultural with several resorts

gown the members of a university as opposed to the other residents of the university town

goy a Jewish word for a gentile

Goya Francisco de , full name *Francisco José de Goya y Lucientes*. 1746–1828, Spanish painter and etcher; well known for his portraits, he became court painter to Charles IV of Spain (1799). He recorded the French invasion of Spain in a series of etchings *The Disasters of War* (1810–14) and two paintings *2 May 1808* and *3 May 1808* (1814)

Graafian follicle a fluid-filled vesicle in the mammalian ovary containing a developing egg cell

grab *Tools* a mechanical device for gripping objects, esp the hinged jaws of a mechanical excavator

Gracchus Tiberius Sempronius ?163–133 BC, and his younger brother, Gaius Sempronius , 153–121 BC, known as the *Gracchi*. Roman tribunes and reformers. Tiberius attempted to redistribute public land among the poor but was murdered in the ensuing riot. Violence again occurred when the reform was revived by Gaius, and he too was killed

grace 1 *Christianity* **a** the free and unmerited favour of God shown towards man **b** the divine assistance and power given to man in spiritual rebirth and sanctification **c** the condition of being favoured or sanctified by God **d** an unmerited gift, favour, etc, granted by God **2** a short prayer recited before or after a meal to invoke a blessing upon the food or give thanks for it **3** *Music* a melodic ornament or decoration

Grace¹ W(illiam) G(ilbert). 1848–1915, English cricketer

Grace² a title used to address or refer to a duke, duchess, or archbishop

grace note *Music* a note printed in small type to indicate that it is melodically and harmonically nonessential

gradation 1 (in painting, drawing, or sculpture) transition from one colour, tone, or surface to another through a series of very slight changes **2** *Geology* the natural levelling of land as a result of the building up or wearing down of pre-existing formations

grade 1 a mark or rating indicating achievement or the worth of work done, as at school **2** *US and Canadian* a unit of pupils of similar age or ability taught together at school **3** *US and Canadian* a part of a railway, road, etc, that slopes upwards or downwards; inclination **b** a measure of such a slope, esp the ratio of the vertical distance between two points on the slope to the horizontal distance between them **4** a unit of angle equal to one hundredth of a right angle or 0.9 degree **5** *Stockbreeding* **a** an animal with one purebred parent and one of unknown or unimproved breeding **b** (*as modifier*): *a grade sheep* **6 at grade** (of a river profile or land surface) at an equilibrium level and slope, because there is a balance between erosion and deposition

gradient 1 a part of a railway, road, etc, that slopes upwards or downwards; inclination **2** a measure of such a slope, esp the ratio of the vertical distance between two points on the slope to the horizontal distance between them **3** *Physics* a measure of the change of some physical quantity, such as temperature or electric potential, over a specified distance **4** *Maths* **a** (of a curve) the slope of the tangent at any point on a curve with respect to the horizontal axis **b** (of a function, $f(x, y, z)$) the vector whose components along the axes are the partial derivatives of the function with respect to each variable, and whose direction is that in which the derivative of the function has its maximum value. Usually written: grad **f**, ∇f or ∇**f**

gradual *Christianity* **a** an antiphon or group of several antiphons, usually from the Psalms, sung or recited immediately after the epistle at Mass **b** a book of plainsong containing the words and music of the parts of the Mass that are sung by the cantors and choir

gradualism *Geology* the theory that explains major changes in rock strata, fossils, etc in terms of gradual evolutionary processes rather than sudden violent catastrophes

graduate 1 a a person who has been awarded a first degree from a university or college **b** (*as modifier*): *a graduate profession* **2** *US and Canadian* a student who has completed a course of studies at a high school and received a diploma **3** *US* a container, such as a flask, marked to indicate its capacity

Graeco-Roman *or esp US* **Greco-Roman 1** of, characteristic of, or relating to Greek and Roman influences, as found in Roman sculpture **2** denoting a style of wrestling in which the legs may not be used to obtain a fall and no hold may be applied below the waist

Graf Steffi born 1969, German tennis player: Wimbledon

champion 1988, 1989, 1991, 1992, 1993, 1995, and 1996

graft 1 *Horticulture* **a** a piece of plant tissue (the scion), normally a stem, that is made to unite with an established plant (the stock), which supports and nourishes it **b** the plant resulting from the union of scion and stock **c** the point of union between the scion and the stock **2** *Surgery* a piece of tissue or an organ transplanted from a donor or from the patient's own body to an area of the body in need of the tissue

Graham 1 Martha 1893–1991, US dancer and choreographer **2** Thomas 1805–69, British physicist: proposed **Graham's law** (1831) of gaseous diffusion and coined the terms osmosis, crystalloids, and colloids **3** William Franklin, known as *Billy Graham*. born 1918, US evangelist

Grahame Kenneth 1859–1932, Scottish author, noted for the children's classic *The Wind in the Willows* (1908)

Graham Land the N part of the Antarctic Peninsula: became part of the British Antarctic Territory in 1962 (formerly part of the Falkland Islands Dependencies). (Claims are suspended under the Antarctic Treaty)

grain 1 the small hard seedlike fruit of a grass, esp a cereal plant **2** a mass of such fruits, esp when gathered for food **3** the plants, collectively, from which such fruits are harvested **4 a** the granular texture of a rock, mineral, etc. **b** the appearance of a rock, mineral, etc, determined by the size and arrangement of its constituents **5** the smallest unit of weight in the avoirdupois, Troy, and apothecaries' systems, based on the average weight of a grain of wheat: in the avoirdupois system it equals 1/7000 of a pound, and in the Troy and apothecaries' systems it equals 1/5760 of a pound. 1 grain is equal to 0.0648 gram **6** a metric unit of weight used for pearls or diamonds, equal to 50 milligrams or one quarter of a carat **7** the threads or direction of threads in a woven fabric **8** *Photog* any of a large number of particles in a photographic emulsion, the size of which limit the extent to which an image can be enlarged without serious loss of definition **9** *Chem* any of a large number of small crystals forming a polycrystalline solid, each having a regular array of atoms that differs in orientation from that of the surrounding crystallites

Grainger Percy Aldridge 1882–1961, Australian pianist, composer, and collector of folk music on which many of his works are based

gram¹ a metric unit of mass equal to one thousandth of a kilogram. It is equivalent to 15.432 grains or 0.002 205 pounds.

gram² **1** any of several leguminous plants, such as the beans *Phaseolus mungo* (**black gram** or **urd**) and *P. aureus* (**green gram**), whose seeds are used as food in India **2** the seed of any of these plants

graminivorous (of animals) feeding on grass

grammar school 1 *Brit* (esp formerly) a state-maintained secondary school providing an education with an academic bias for children who are selected by the eleven-plus examination, teachers' reports, or other means **2** *US* another term for **elementary school 3** *NZ* a secondary school forming part of the public education system

gramophone 1 a a device for reproducing the sounds stored on a record: now usually applied to the nearly obsolete type that uses a clockwork motor and acoustic horn **b** (*as modifier*): *a gramophone record* **2** the technique and practice of recording sound on disc

Grampian Region a former local government region in NE Scotland, formed in 1975 from Aberdeenshire, Kincardineshire, and most of Banffshire and Morayshire; replaced in 1996 by the council areas of Aberdeenshire, City of Aberdeen, and Moray

grampus **1** a widely distributed slaty-grey dolphin, *Grampus griseus*, with a blunt snout **2** another name for **killer whale**

Granada **1** a former kingdom of S Spain, in Andalusia: founded in the 13th century and divided in 1833 into the present-day provinces of Granada, Almería, and Málaga, in Andalusia **2** a city in S Spain, in Andalusia: capital of the Moorish kingdom of Granada from 1238 to 1492 and a great commercial and cultural centre, containing the Alhambra palace (13th and 14th centuries); university (1531). Pop: 237 663 (2003 est) **3** a city in SW Nicaragua, on the NW shore of Lake Nicaragua: the oldest city in the country, founded in 1523 by Córdoba; attacked frequently by pirates in the 17th century. Pop: 95 000 (2005 est)

Granados Enrique , full name *Enrique Granados y Campina*. 1867–1916, Spanish composer, noted for the *Goyescas* (1911) for piano, which formed the basis for an opera of the same name

Gran Chaco a plain of S central South America, between the Andes and the Paraguay River in SE Bolivia, E Paraguay, and N Argentina: huge swamps and scrub forest. Area: about 780 000 sq km (300 000 sq miles)

Grand Bahama an island in the Atlantic, in the W Bahamas. Pop: 46 994 (2000). Area: 1114 sq km (430 sq miles)

Grand Canal **1** a canal in E China, extending north from Hangzhou to Tianjin: the longest canal in China, now partly silted up; central section, linking the Yangtze and Yellow Rivers, finished in 486 BC; north section finished by Kublai Khan between 1282 and 1292. Length: about 1600 km (1000 miles) **2** a canal in Venice, forming the main water thoroughfare: noted for its bridges, the Rialto, and the fine palaces along its banks

Grand Canary an island in the Atlantic, in the Canary Islands: part of the Spanish province of Las Palmas. Capital: Las Palmas. Pop: 771 333 (2002 est). Area: 1533 sq km (592 sq miles)

Grand Canyon a gorge of the Colorado River in N Arizona, extending from its junction with the Little Colorado River to Lake Mead; cut by vertical river erosion through the multicoloured strata of a high plateau; partly contained in the **Grand Canyon National Park**, covering 2610 sq km (1008 sq miles). Length: 451 km (280 miles). Width: 6 km (4 miles) to 29 km (18 miles). Greatest depth: over 1.5 km (1 mile)

Grand Coulee a canyon in central Washington State, over 120 m (400 ft) deep, at the N end of which is situated the **Grand Coulee Dam**, on the Columbia River. Height of dam: 168 m (550 ft). Length of dam: 1310 m (4300 ft)

grand duke *History* **1** a prince or nobleman who rules a territory, state, or principality **2** a son or a male descendant in the male line of a Russian tsar **3** a medieval

Russian prince who ruled over other princes

grandee a Spanish or Portuguese prince or nobleman of the highest rank

Grande-Terre a French island in the Caribbean, in the Lesser Antilles: one of the two main islands which constitute Guadeloupe. Chief town: Pointe-à-Pitre

grand jury *Law* (esp in the US and, now rarely, in Canada) a jury of between 12 and 23 persons summoned to inquire into accusations of crime and ascertain whether the evidence is adequate to found an indictment. Abolished in Britain in 1948

grand mal a form of epilepsy characterized by loss of consciousness for up to five minutes and violent convulsions

Grand Manan a Canadian island, off the SW coast of New Brunswick: separated from the coast of Maine by the **Grand Manan Channel** Area: 147 sq km (57 sq miles)

grandmaster **1** *Chess* one of the top chess players of a particular country **2** *Chess* a player who has been awarded the highest title by the Fédération Internationale des Échecs

Grand National the an annual steeplechase run at Aintree, Liverpool, since 1839

grand opera an opera that has a serious plot and is entirely in musical form, with no spoken dialogue

grand piano a form of piano in which the strings are arranged horizontally. Grand pianos exist in three sizes: baby grand, boudoir grand, and concert grand

Grand Prix **1 a** any of a series of formula motor races held to determine the annual Drivers' World Championship **b** (*as modifier*): *a Grand Prix car* **2** *Horse racing* a race for three-year-old horses run at Maisons Lafitte near Paris **3** a very important competitive event in various other sports, such as athletics, snooker, or powerboating

Grand Rapids a city in SW Michigan: electronics, car parts. Pop: 195 601 (2003 est)

grandsire *Bell-ringing* a well-established method used in change-ringing

grand slam **1** *Bridge* the winning of 13 tricks by one player or side or the contract to do so **2** the winning of all major competitions in a season, esp in tennis and golf **3** *Rugby Union* the winning of all five games in the annual Six Nations Championship involving England, Scotland, Wales, Ireland, France, and Italy

grandstand **1 a** a terraced block of seats, usually under a roof, commanding the best view at racecourses, football pitches, etc. **b** (*as modifier*): *grandstand tickets* **2** the spectators in a grandstand

grand tour (formerly) an extended tour through the major cities of Europe, esp one undertaken by a rich or aristocratic Englishman to complete his education

Grand Union Canal a canal in S England linking London and the Midlands: opened in 1801

grange *History* an outlying farmhouse in which a religious establishment or feudal lord stored crops and tithes in kind

Grangemouth a port in Scotland, in Falkirk council area: now Scotland's second port, with oil refineries, shipyards, and chemical industries. Pop: 17 771 (2001)

Granicus an ancient river in NW Asia Minor where Alexander the Great won his first major battle against the Persians (334 BC)

granite 1 a light-coloured coarse-grained acid plutonic igneous rock consisting of quartz, feldspars, and such ferromagnesian minerals as biotite or hornblende: widely used for building 2 another name for a **stone**

granivorous (of animals) feeding on seeds and grain

granny or **grannie** 1 *Engineering* a revolving cap on a chimneypot that keeps out rain, etc. 2 *Southern US* a midwife or nurse

granny flat self-contained accommodation within or built onto a house, suitable for an elderly parent

Gran Paradiso a mountain in NW Italy, in NW Piedmont: the highest peak of the Graian Alps. Height: 4061 m (13 323 ft)

grant 1 a sum of money provided by a government, local authority, or public fund to finance educational study, overseas aid, building repairs, etc. 2 a transfer of property by deed or other written instrument; conveyance 3 *US* a territorial unit in Maine, New Hampshire, and Vermont, originally granted to an individual or organization

Grant 1 **Cary**, real name *Alexander Archibald Leach*. 1904–86, US film actor, born in England. His many films include *Bringing up Baby* (1938), *The Philadelphia Story* (1940), *Arsenic and Old Lace* (1944), and *Mr Blandings Builds his Dream House* (1948) 2 **Duncan (James Corrowr)**. 1885–1978, British painter and designer 3 **Ulysses S(impson)**, real name *Hiram Ulysses Grant*. 1822–85, 18th president of the US (1869–77); commander in chief of Union forces in the American Civil War (1864–65)

Granta the original name, still in use locally, for the River Cam

Grantham a town in E England, in Lincolnshire: birthplace of Sir Isaac Newton and Margaret Thatcher. Pop: 34 592 (2001)

granule *Geology* a single rock fragment in gravel, smaller than a pebble but larger than a sand grain

Granville 1 **1st Earl**, title of *John Carteret*. 1690–1763, British statesman: secretary of state (1742–44); a leading opponent of Walpole 2 **2nd Earl**, title of *Granville George Leveson-Gower*. 1815–91, British Liberal politician: Gladstone's foreign secretary (1870–74; 1880–85) and a supporter of Irish Home Rule

Granville-Barker Harley 1877–1946, English dramatist, theatre director, and critic, noted particularly for his *Prefaces to Shakespeare* (1927–47)

grape 1 the fruit of the grapevine, which has a purple or green skin and sweet flesh: eaten raw, dried to make raisins, currants, or sultanas, or used for making wine 2 any of various plants that bear grapelike fruit, such as the Oregon grape 3 See **grapevine**

grapefruit 1 a tropical or subtropical cultivated evergreen rutaceous tree, *Citrus paradisi* 2 the large round edible fruit of this tree, which has yellow rind and juicy slightly bitter pulp

grapevine 1 any of several vitaceous vines of the genus *Vitis*, esp *V. vinifera* of E Asia, widely cultivated for its fruit (grapes): family *Vitaceae* 2 a wrestling hold in which a wrestler entwines his own leg around his opponent's and exerts pressure against various joints

graph *Maths* 1 a drawing depicting the relation between certain sets of numbers or quantities by means of a series of dots, lines, etc, plotted with reference to a set of axes 2 a drawing depicting a functional relation between two or three variables by means of a curve or surface containing only those points whose coordinates satisfy the relation 3 a structure represented by a diagram consisting of points (vertices) joined by lines (edges)

graphic or **graphical** *Geology* having or denoting a texture formed by intergrowth of the crystals to resemble writing

graphics 1 the process or art of drawing in accordance with mathematical principles 2 the information displayed on a visual display unit or on a computer printout in the form of diagrams, graphs, pictures, and symbols

graphite a blackish soft allotropic form of carbon in hexagonal crystalline form: used in pencils, crucibles, and electrodes, as a lubricant, as a moderator in nuclear reactors, and, in a carbon fibre form, as a tough lightweight material for sporting equipment

graphology the study of handwriting, esp to analyse the writer's character

graph paper paper printed with intersecting lines, usually horizontal and vertical and equally spaced, for drawing graphs, diagrams, etc.

grapnel 1 a device with a multiple hook at one end and attached to a rope, which is thrown or hooked over a firm mooring to secure an object attached to the other end of the rope 2 a light anchor for small boats

Grappelli or **Grappelly Stéphane** 1908–97, French jazz violinist: with Django Reinhardt, he led the Quintet of the Hot Club of France between 1934 and 1939

grapple *Tools* any form of hook or metal instrument by which something is secured, such as a grapnel

grappling iron or **hook** a grapnel, esp one used for securing ships

Grasmere a village in NW England, in Cumbria at the head of **Lake Grasmere**: home of William Wordsworth and of Thomas de Quincey

grass any monocotyledonous plant of the family *Poaceae* (formerly *Gramineae*), having jointed stems sheathed by long narrow leaves, flowers in spikes, and seedlike fruits. The family includes cereals, bamboo, etc.
▷www.doityourself.com/lawn
▷www.grasses.co.uk
▷http://forums.gardenweb.com/forums/grasses

Grass Günter (Wilhelm). born 1927, German novelist, dramatist, and poet. His novels include *The Tin Drum* (1959), *Dog Years* (1963), *The Rat* (1986), *Toad Croaks* (1992), and *Crabwalk* (2002). Nobel prize for literature 1999

grass hockey *Canadian* field hockey, as contrasted with ice hockey

grasshopper any orthopterous insect of the families *Acrididae* (**short-horned grasshoppers**) and *Tettigoniidae* (**long-horned grasshoppers**), typically terrestrial, feeding on plants, and producing a ticking sound by rubbing the hind legs against the leathery forewings

grassland land, such as a prairie, on which grass predominates

grass snake 1 a harmless nonvenomous European colubrid snake, *Natrix natrix*, having a brownish-green body with variable markings **2** any of several similar related European snakes, such as *Natrix maura* (**viperine grass snake**)

grass tree 1 any plant of the Australian genus *Xanthorrhoea*, having a woody stem, stiff grasslike leaves, and a spike of small white flowers: family *Xanthorrhoeaceae*. Some species produce fragrant resins **2** any of several similar Australasian plants

Gratian Latin name *Flavius Gratianus*. 359–383 AD, Roman emperor (367–383): ruled with his father Valentinian I (367–375); ruled the Western Roman Empire with his brother Valentinian II (375-83); appointed Theodosius I emperor of the Eastern Roman Empire (379)

gratis without payment; free of charge

gratuitous *Law* given or made without receiving any value in return

gratuity a gift or reward, usually of money, for services rendered; tip

grave¹ (of colours) sober or dull

grave² *Music* to be performed in a solemn manner

gravel 1 an unconsolidated mixture of rock fragments that is coarser than sand **2** *Geology* a mixture of rock fragments with diameters in the range 4–76 mm **3** *Pathol* small rough calculi in the kidneys or bladder

graven image *Chiefly Bible* a carved image used as an idol

Graves Robert (Ranke). 1895–1985, English poet, novelist, and critic, whose works include his World War I autobiography, *Goodbye to All That* (1929), and the historical novels *I, Claudius* (1934) and *Claudius the God* (1934)

Gravesend a river port in SE England, in NW Kent on the Thames. Pop: 53 045 (2001)

graveyard a place for graves; a burial ground, esp a small one or one in a churchyard

gravimeter 1 an instrument for measuring the earth's gravitational field at points on its surface **2** an instrument for measuring relative density

gravitation 1 the force of attraction that bodies exert on one another as a result of their mass **2** any process or result caused by this interaction, such as the fall of a body to the surface of the earth

gravity 1 the force of attraction that moves or tends to move bodies towards the centre of a celestial body, such as the earth or moon **2** the property of being heavy or having weight **3** another name for **gravitation 4** lowness in pitch

gray the derived SI unit of absorbed ionizing radiation dose or kerma equivalent to an absorption per unit mass of one joule per kilogram of irradiated material. 1 gray is equivalent to 100 rads.

Gray 1 Simon (James Holiday). born 1936, British writer: his plays include *Butley* (1971), *The Common Pursuit* (1988), *Life Support* (1997), and *Japes* (2001) **2** Thomas 1716–71, English poet, best known for his *Elegy written in a Country Churchyard* (1751)

Graz an industrial city in SE Austria, capital of Styria province: the second largest city in the country. Pop: 226 244 (2001)

grease 1 any thick fatty oil, esp one used as a lubricant for machinery, etc. **2** *Vet science* inflammation of the skin of horses around the fetlocks, usually covered with an oily secretion

greasepaint 1 a waxy or greasy substance used to make-up by actors **2** theatrical make-up

great auk a large flightless auk, *Pinguinus impennis*, extinct since the middle of the 19th century

Great Australian Bight a wide bay of the Indian Ocean, in S Australia, extending from Cape Pasley to the Eyre Peninsula: notorious for storms

Great Barrier Reef a coral reef in the Coral Sea, off the NE coast of Australia, extending for about 2000 km (1250 miles) from the Torres Strait along the coast of Queensland; the largest coral reef in the world

Great Basin a semiarid region of the western US, between the Wasatch and the Sierra Nevada Mountains, having no drainage to the ocean: includes Nevada, W Utah, and parts of E California, S Oregon, and Idaho. Area: about 490 000 sq km (189 000 sq miles)

Great Bear Lake a lake in NW Canada, in the Northwest Territories: the largest freshwater lake entirely in Canada; drained by the Great Bear River, which flows to the Mackenzie River. Area: 31 792 sq km (12 275 sq miles)

Great Belt a strait in Denmark, between Zealand and Funen islands, linking the Kattegat with the Baltic

Great Britain England, Wales, and Scotland including those adjacent islands governed from the mainland (i.e. excluding the Isle of Man and the Channel Islands). The United Kingdom of Great Britain was formed by the Act of Union (1707), although the term Great Britain had been in use since 1603, when James VI of Scotland became James I of England (including Wales). Later unions created the United Kingdom of Great Britain and Ireland (1801) and the United Kingdom of Great Britain and Northern Ireland (1922). Pop: 57 851 100 (2003 est). Area: 229 523 sq km (88 619 sq miles)

great circle *Geometry* a circular section of a sphere that has a radius equal to that of the sphere

Great Dane one of a very large powerful yet graceful breed of dog with a short smooth coat

Greater (of a city) considered with the inclusion of the outer suburbs

Greater Manchester a metropolitan county of NW England, administered since 1986 by the unitary authorities of Wigan, Bolton, Bury, Rochdale, Salford, Manchester, Oldham, Trafford, Stockport, and Tameside. Area: 1286 sq km (496 sq miles)

Great Glen the a fault valley across the whole of Scotland, extending southwest from the Moray Firth in the east to Loch Linnhe and containing Loch Ness and Loch Lochy

Great Rift Valley the most extensive rift in the earth's surface, extending from the Jordan valley in Syria to Mozambique; marked by a chain of steep-sided lakes, volcanoes, and escarpments

Great Salt Lake a shallow salt lake in NW Utah, in the Great Basin at an altitude of 1260 m (4200 ft): the area has fluctuated from less than 2500 sq km (1000 sq miles) to over 5000 sq km (2000 sq miles)

Great Sandy Desert a desert in NW Australia. Area: about 415 000 sq km (160 000 sq miles)

Great Slave Lake a lake in NW Canada, in the

Northwest Territories: drained by the Mackenzie River into the Arctic Ocean. Area: 28 440 sq km (10 980 sq miles)

Great Stour another name for **Stour** (sense 1)

Great Victoria Desert a desert in S Australia, in SE Western Australia and W South Australia. Area: 323 750 sq km (125 000 sq miles)

Great Wall of China a defensive wall in N China, extending from W Gansu to the Gulf of Liaodong: constructed in the 3rd century BC as a defence against the Mongols; substantially rebuilt in the 15th century. Length: over 2400 km (1500 miles). Average height: 6 m (20 ft). Average width: 6 m (20 ft)

Great Yarmouth a port and resort in E England, in E Norfolk. Pop: 58 032 (2001)

grebe any aquatic bird, such as *Podiceps cristatus* (**great crested grebe**), of the order *Podicipediformes*, similar to the divers but with lobate rather than webbed toes and a vestigial tail

Grecian 1 (esp of beauty or architecture) conforming to Greek ideals, esp in being classically simple 2 a scholar of or expert in the Greek language or literature

Greece a republic in SE Europe, occupying the S part of the Balkan Peninsula and many islands in the Ionian and Aegean Seas; site of two of Europe's earliest civilizations (the Minoan and Mycenaean); in the classical era divided into many small independent city-states, the most important being Athens and Sparta; part of the Roman and Byzantine Empires; passed under Turkish rule in the late Middle Ages; became an independent kingdom in 1827; taken over by a military junta (1967–74); the monarchy was abolished in 1973; became a republic in 1975; a member of the European Union. Official language: Greek. Official religion: Eastern (Greek) Orthodox. Currency: euro. Capital: Athens. Pop: 10 977 000 (2004 est). Area: 131 944 sq km (50 944 sq miles)

Greek the official language of Greece, constituting the Hellenic branch of the Indo-European family of languages

Greek Orthodox Church 1 Also called: **Greek Church** the established Church of Greece, governed by the holy synod of Greece, in which the Metropolitan of Athens has primacy of honour 2 another name for **Orthodox Church**

green 1 any of a group of colours, such as that of fresh grass, that lie between yellow and blue in the visible spectrum in the wavelength range 575–500 nanometres. Green is the complementary colour of magenta and with red and blue forms a set of primary colours 2 a person, esp a politician, who supports environmentalist issues (see sense 13) 3 concerned with or relating to conservation of the world's natural resources and improvement of the environment 4 denoting a unit of account that is adjusted in accordance with fluctuations between the currencies of the EU nations and is used to make payments to agricultural producers within the EU 5 (of pottery) not fired 6 *Metallurgy* (of a product, such as a sand mould or cermet) compacted but not yet fired; ready for firing 7 (of timber) freshly felled; not dried or seasoned 8 (of concrete) not having matured to design strength

green 1 a the edible leaves and stems of certain plants, eaten as a vegetable b freshly cut branches of ornamental trees, shrubs, etc, used as a decoration 2 *Slang* marijuana of low quality

Green 1 **Henry**, real name *Henry Vincent Yorke*. 1905–73, British novelist: author of *Living* (1929), *Loving* (1945), and *Back* (1946) 2 **John Richard** 1837–83, British historian; author of *A Short History of the English People* (1874) 3 **T(homas) H(ill)**. 1836–82, British idealist philosopher. His chief work, *Prolegomena to Ethics*, was unfinished at his death

Greenaway 1 **Kate** 1846–1901, English painter, noted as an illustrator of children's books 2 **Peter** born 1942, British film director; noted for such cerebral films as *The Draughtsman's Contract* (1982), *Prospero's Books* (1990), and *Eight and a Half Women* (1999)

green belt a zone of farmland, parks, and open country surrounding a town or city: usually officially designated as such and preserved from urban development

Green Cross Code (in Britain) a code for children giving rules for road safety: first issued in 1971

Greene 1 **Graham** 1904–91, English novelist and dramatist; his works include the novels *Brighton Rock* (1938), *The Power and the Glory* (1940), *The End of the Affair* (1951), and *Our Man in Havana* (1958), and the film script *The Third Man* (1949) 2 **Robert** ?1558–92, English poet, dramatist, and prose writer, noted for his autobiographical tract *A Groatsworth of Wit bought with a Million of Repentance* (1592), which contains an attack on Shakespeare

greenfield denoting or located in a rural area which has not previously been built on

greenfinch a common European finch, *Carduelis chloris*, the male of which has a dull green plumage with yellow patches on the wings and tail

greenfly a greenish aphid commonly occurring as a pest on garden and crop plants

greengage 1 a cultivated variety of plum tree, *Prunus domestica italica*, with edible green plumlike fruits 2 the fruit of this tree

greengrocer *Chiefly Brit* a retail trader in fruit and vegetables

Greenham Common a village in West Berkshire unitary authority, Berkshire; site of a US cruise missile base, and, from 1981, a camp of women protesters against nuclear weapons; although the base had closed by 1991 a small number of women remained until 2000

greenhouse 1 a building with transparent walls and roof, usually of glass, for the cultivation and exhibition of plants under controlled conditions 2 relating to or contributing to the greenhouse effect: *greenhouse gases such as carbon dioxide*

greenhouse effect 1 an effect occurring in greenhouses, etc, in which radiant heat from the sun passes through the glass warming the contents, the radiant heat from inside being trapped by the glass 2 the application of this effect to a planet's atmosphere; carbon dioxide and some other gases in the planet's atmosphere can absorb the infrared radiation emitted by the planet's surface as a result of exposure to solar radiation, thus increasing the mean temperature of the planet

Greenland a large island, lying mostly within the Arctic

Circle off the NE coast of North America: first settled by Icelanders in 986; resettled by Danes from 1721 onwards; integral part of Denmark (1953–79); granted internal autonomy 1979; mostly covered by an icecap up to 3300 m (11 000 ft) thick, with ice-free coastal strips and coastal mountains; the population is largely Inuit, with a European minority; fishing, hunting, and mining. Capital: Nuuk. Pop: 57 000 (2003 est). Area: 175 600 sq km (840 000 sq miles)

Greenlandic the dialect of Inuktitut spoken in Greenland

Greenland Sea the S part of the Arctic Ocean, off the NE coast of Greenland

Greenock a port in SW Scotland, in Inverclyde on the Firth of Clyde: shipbuilding and other marine industries. Pop: 45 467 (2001)

Greenough George Bellas 1778–1855, English geologist, founder of the Geological Society of London

green paper (in Britain) a command paper containing policy proposals to be discussed, esp by Parliament

green pepper 1 the green unripe fruit of the sweet pepper, eaten raw or cooked 2 the unripe fruit of various other pepper plants, eaten as a green vegetable

Green River a river in the western US, rising in W central Wyoming and flowing south into Utah, east through NW Colorado, re-entering Utah before joining the Colorado River. Length: 1175 km (730 miles)

greenroom (esp formerly) a backstage room in a theatre where performers may rest or receive visitors

Greensboro a city in N central North Carolina. Pop: 229 110 (2003 est)

greenstick fracture a fracture in children in which the bone is partly bent and splinters only on the convex side of the bend

greenstone 1 any basic igneous rock that is dark green because of the presence of chlorite, actinolite, or epidote 2 a variety of jade used in New Zealand for ornaments and tools

Greenwich a Greater London borough on the Thames: site of a Royal Naval College and of the original Royal Observatory designed by Christopher Wren (1675), accepted internationally as the prime meridian of longitude since 1884, and the basis of Greenwich Mean Time; also site of the Millennium Dome. Pop: 223 700 (2003 est). Area: 46 sq km (18 sq miles)

Greenwich Mean Time or **Greenwich Time** mean solar time on the 0° meridian passing through Greenwich, England, measured from midnight: formerly a standard time in Britain and a basis for calculating times throughout most of the world, it has been replaced by an atomic timescale

Greenwich Village a part of New York City in the lower west side of Manhattan; traditionally the home of many artists and writers

Greer Germaine born 1939, Australian writer and feminist. Her books include *The Female Eunuch* (1970), *Sex and Destiny* (1984), and *The Whole Woman* (1998)

gregarious 1 (of animals) living together in herds or flocks 2 (of plants) growing close together but not in dense clusters

Gregory Lady (Isabella) Augusta (Persse). 1852–1932, Irish dramatist; a founder and director of the Abbey

Theatre, Dublin

Gregory I Saint, known as *Gregory the Great.* ?540–604 AD, pope (590–604), who greatly influenced the medieval Church. He strengthened papal authority by centralizing administration, tightened discipline, and revised the liturgy. He appointed Saint Augustine missionary to England. Feast day: March 12 or Sept 3

Gregory VII Saint, monastic name *Hildebrand.* ?1020–85, pope (1073–85), who did much to reform abuses in the Church. His assertion of papal supremacy and his prohibition (1075) of lay investiture was opposed by the Holy Roman Emperor Henry IV, whom he excommunicated (1076). He was driven into exile when Henry captured Rome (1084). Feast day: May 25

Gregory XIII 1502–85, pope (1572–85). He promoted the Counter-Reformation and founded seminaries. His reformed (Gregorian) calendar was issued in 1582

Gregory of Tours Saint ?538–?594 AD, Frankish bishop and historian. His *Historia Francorum* is the chief source of knowledge of 6th-century Gaul. Feast day: Nov 17

Grenada an island state in the Caribbean, in the Windward Islands: formerly a British colony (1783–1967); since 1974 an independent state within the Commonwealth; occupied by US troops (1983–85); mainly agricultural. Official language: English. Religion: Christian majority. Currency: East Caribbean dollar. Capital: St George's. Pop: 80 000 (2003 est). Area: 344 sq km (133 sq miles)

grenade 1 a small container filled with explosive thrown by hand or fired from a rifle 2 a sealed glass vessel that is thrown and shatters to release chemicals, such as tear gas or a fire extinguishing agent

grenadier 1 any deep-sea gadoid fish of the family *Macrouridae,* typically having a large head and trunk and a long tapering tail 2 any of various African weaver-birds of the genus *Estrilda*

grenadine¹ a light thin leno-weave fabric of silk, wool, rayon, or nylon, used esp for dresses

grenadine² a a moderate reddish-orange colour b (*as adjective*): *a grenadine coat*

Grenfell Joyce, real name *Joyce Irene Phipps.* 1910–79, British comedy actress and writer

Grenoble a city in SE France, on the Isère River: university (1339). Pop: 153 317 (1999)

Grenville 1 George 1712–70, British statesman; prime minister (1763–65). His policy of taxing the American colonies precipitated the War of Independence 2 Sir Richard ?1541–91, English naval commander. He was fatally wounded aboard his ship, the *Revenge,* during a lone battle with a fleet of Spanish treasure ships 3 William Wyndham, Baron Grenville, son of George Grenville. 1759–1834, British statesman; prime minister (1806–07) of the coalition government known as the "ministry of all the talents"

Gresham Sir Thomas ?1519–79, English financier, who founded the Royal Exchange in London (1568)

Gretna Green a village in S Scotland, in Dumfries and Galloway on the border with England: famous smithy where eloping couples were married by the blacksmith from 1754 until 1940, when such marriages became illegal. Pop: 2705 (2001)

Gretzky Wayne born 1961, Canadian ice-hockey player,

based in the US

Greville Fulke, 1st Baron Brooke. 1554–1628, English poet, writer, politician, and diplomat: Chancellor of the Exchequer (1614–22); author of *The Life of the Renowned Sir Philip Sidney* (1652)

grevillea any of a large variety of evergreen trees and shrubs that comprise the genus *Grevillea*, native to Australia, Tasmania, and New Caledonia: family *Proteaceae*

grey *or now esp US* **gray** 1 of a neutral tone, intermediate between black and white, that has no hue and reflects and transmits only a little light 2 greyish in colour or having parts or marks that are greyish 3 (of textiles) natural, unbleached, undyed, and untreated 4 any of a group of grey tones 5 grey cloth or clothing 6 an animal, esp a horse, that is grey or whitish

Grey 1 Charles, 2nd Earl Grey. 1764–1845, British statesman. As Whig prime minister (1830–34), he carried the Reform Bill of 1832 and the bill for the abolition of slavery throughout the British Empire (1833) 2 Sir **Edward**, 1st Viscount Grey of Fallodon. 1862–1933, British statesman; foreign secretary (1905–16) 3 Sir **George** 1812–98, British statesman and colonial administrator; prime minister of New Zealand (1877–79) 4 Lady **Jane** 1537–54, queen of England (July 9–19, 1553); great-granddaughter of Henry VII. Her father-in-law, the Duke of Northumberland, persuaded Edward VI to alter the succession in her favour, but after ten days as queen she was imprisoned and later executed 5 **Zane** 1875–1939, US author of Westerns, including *Riders of the Purple Sage* (1912)

Grey Friar a Franciscan friar

greyhound a tall slender fast-moving dog of an ancient breed originally used for coursing
▷www.thedogs.co.uk
▷www.gra-america.org
▷www.graq.org.au

greylag *or* **greylag goose** a large grey Eurasian goose, *Anser anser*: the ancestor of many domestic breeds of goose

grey matter the greyish tissue of the brain and spinal cord, containing nerve cell bodies, dendrites, and bare (unmyelinated) axons

grey squirrel a grey-furred squirrel, *Sciurus carolinensis*, native to E North America but now widely established

Grey-Thompson Tanni (Carys Davina). born 1969, British wheelchair athlete; eleven gold medals in the Paralympics (1988–2004)

grid 1 a network of horizontal and vertical lines superimposed over a map, building plan, etc, for locating points 2 **the grid** the national network of transmission lines, pipes, etc, by which electricity, gas, or water is distributed 3 *Electronics* **a** an electrode situated between the cathode and anode of a valve usually consisting of a cylindrical mesh of wires, that controls the flow of electrons between cathode and anode **b** (*as modifier*): *the grid bias* 4 a plate in an accumulator that carries the active substance

gridiron 1 a framework above the stage in a theatre from which suspended scenery, lights, etc, are manipulated 2 **a** the field of play in American football **b** an informal name for American football **c** (*as modifier*): *a*

gridiron hero

gridlock obstruction of urban traffic caused by queues of vehicles forming across junctions and causing further queues to form in the intersecting streets

Grieg Edvard (Hagerup). 1843–1907, Norwegian composer. His works, often inspired by Norwegian folk music, include the incidental music for *Peer Gynt* (1876), a piano concerto, and many songs

Grierson John 1898–1972, Scottish film director. He coined the noun *documentary*, of which genre his *Industrial Britain* (1931) and *Song of Ceylon* (1934) are notable examples

grievous bodily harm *Criminal law* really serious injury caused by one person to another

griffin¹, griffon, *or* **gryphon** a winged monster with an eagle-like head and the body of a lion

griffin² a newcomer to the Orient, esp one from W Europe

Griffith 1 Arthur 1872–1922, Irish journalist and nationalist: founder of Sinn Féin (1905); president of the Free State assembly (1922) 2 D(avid Lewelyn) W(ark). 1875–1948, US film director and producer. He introduced several cinematic techniques, including the flashback and the fade-out, in his masterpiece *The Birth of a Nation* (1915)

Griffith-Joyner Florence, known as *Flojo.* 1959–98, US sprinter, winner of two gold medals at the 1988 Olympic Games

griffon 1 any of various small wire-haired breeds of dog, originally from Belgium 2 any large vulture of the genus *Gyps*, of Africa, S Europe, and SW Asia, having a pale plumage with black wings: family *Accipitridae* (hawks)

grille *or* **grill** 1 *Engineering* a grating, often chromium-plated, that admits cooling air to the radiator of a motor vehicle 2 *Electronics* a protective screen, usually plastic or metal, in front of the loudspeaker in a radio, record player, etc. 3 *Real Tennis* the opening in one corner of the receiver's end of the court 4 *Philately* a group of small pyramidal marks impressed in parallel rows into a stamp to prevent reuse

grilse a young salmon that returns to fresh water after one winter in the sea

Grimaldi Joseph 1779–1837, English actor, noted as a clown in pantomime

Grimm Jakob Ludwig Karl, 1785–1863, and his brother, **Wilhelm Karl**, 1786–1859, German philologists and folklorists, who collaborated on *Grimm's Fairy Tales* (1812–22) and began a German dictionary. Jakob is noted also for his philological work *Deutsche Grammatik* (1819–37), in which he formulated the law named after him

Grimsby a port in E England, in North East Lincolnshire unitary authority, formerly important for fishing. Pop: 87 574 (2001)

Grindelwald a valley and resort in central Switzerland, in the Bernese Oberland: mountaineering centre, with the Wetterhorn and the Eiger nearby

grinder 1 a person who grinds, esp one who grinds cutting tools 2 a machine for grinding 3 a molar tooth

grindstone 1 **a** a machine having a circular block of stone or composite abrasive rotated for sharpening tools or grinding metal **b** the stone used in this machine **c** any stone used for sharpening; whetstone **2** another name for **millstone**

grip 1 *Tools* any device that holds by friction, such as certain types of brake **2** *TV, Cinema* a worker in a camera crew or a stagehand who shifts sets and props, etc. **3** *Engineering* a small drainage channel cut above an excavation to conduct surface water away from the excavation

gripe 1 a sudden intense pain in the intestines; colic **2** *Nautical* the lashings that secure a boat

Griqualand East an area of central South Africa: settled in 1861 by Griquas led by Adam Kok III; annexed to the Cape Colony in 1879; part of the Transkei in 1903–94. Chief town: Kokstad. Area: 17 100 sq km (6602 sq miles)

Griqualand West an area of N South Africa, north of the Orange river: settled after 1803 by the Griquas; annexed by the British in 1871 following a dispute with the Orange Free State; became part of the Cape Colony in 1880. Chief town: Kimberley. Area: 39 360 sq km (15 197 sq miles)

Gris Juan 1887–1927, Spanish cubist painter, resident in France from 1906

Grisham John born 1955, US novelist and lawyer; his legal thrillers, many of which have been filmed, include *A Time to Kill* (1989), *The Pelican Brief* (1992), and *The Summons* (2002)

grist *Brewing* malt grains that have been cleaned and cracked

grit 1 any coarse sandstone that can be used as a grindstone or millstone **2** *Engineering* an arbitrary measure of the size of abrasive particles used in a grinding wheel or other abrasive process

grizzle a grey colour

grizzly bear a variety of the brown bear, *Ursus arctos horribilis*, formerly widespread in W North America; its brown fur has cream or white hair tips on the back, giving a grizzled appearance Often shortened to: **grizzly**

groat *History* an English silver coin worth four pennies, taken out of circulation in the 17th century

grocer a dealer in foodstuffs and other household supplies

grocery the business or premises of a grocer

Grodno a city in W Belarus on the Neman River: part of Poland (1921–39); an industrial centre. Pop: 318 000 (2005 est)

Groening Matt(hew). born 1954, US cartoonist and writer, creator and producer of *The Simpsons* television series from 1989

grog 1 diluted spirit, usually rum, as an alcoholic drink **2** *Informal, chiefly Austral and NZ* alcoholic drink in general, esp spirits

grommet *or* **grummet 1** a ring of rubber or plastic or a metal eyelet designed to line a hole to prevent a cable or pipe passed through it from chafing **2** a ring of rope hemp used to stuff the gland of a pipe joint **3** *Med* a small tube inserted into the eardrum in cases of glue ear in order to allow air to enter the middle ear **4** *Austral, informal* a young or inexperienced surfer

Gromyko Andrei Andreyevich 1909–89, Soviet statesman and diplomat; foreign minister (1957–85); president (1985–88)

Groningen 1 a province in the NE Netherlands: mainly

agricultural. Capital: Groningen. Pop: 573 000 (2003 est). Area: 2336 sq km (902 sq miles) **2** a city in the NE Netherlands, capital of Groningen province. Pop: 177 000 (2003 est)

groom 1 a person employed to clean and look after horses **2** any of various officers of a royal or noble household

groove 1 the spiral channel, usually V-shaped, in a gramophone record **2** *Anatomy* any furrow or channel on a bodily structure or part; sulcus **3** *Mountaineering* a shallow fissure in a rock face or between two rock faces, forming an angle of more than 120°

Gropius Walter 1883–1969, US architect, designer, and teacher, born in Germany. He founded (1919) and directed (1919–28) the Bauhaus in Germany. His influence stemmed from his adaptation of architecture to modern social needs and his pioneering use of industrial materials, such as concrete and steel. His buildings include the Fagus factory at Alfeld (1911) and the Bauhaus at Dessau (1926)

Gros Baron Antoine Jean 1771–1835, French painter, noted for his battle scenes

gross a unit of quantity equal to 12 dozen

gross domestic product the total value of all goods and services produced domestically by a nation during a year. It is equivalent to gross national product minus net investment incomes from foreign nations

Grosseteste Robert ?1175–1253, English prelate and scholar; bishop of Lincoln (1235–53). He attacked ecclesiastical abuses and wrote commentaries on Aristotle and treatises on theology, philosophy, and science

gross national product the total value of all final goods and services produced annually by a nation

Grosz George 1893–1959, German painter, in the US from 1932, whose works satirized German militarism and bourgeois society

Grote George 1794–1871, English historian, noted particularly for his *History of Greece* (1846–56)

grotesque 1 a 16th-century decorative style in which parts of human, animal, and plant forms are distorted and mixed **2** a decorative device, as in painting or sculpture, in this style

Grotius Hugo, original name *Huig de Groot*. 1583–1645, Dutch jurist and statesman, whose *De Jure Belli ac Pacis* (1625) is regarded as the foundation of modern international law

grotto 1 a small cave, esp one with attractive features **2** a construction in the form of a cave, esp as in landscaped gardens during the 18th century

ground¹ 1 the land surface **2** *Arts* **a** the prepared surface applied to the support of a painting, such as a wall, canvas, etc, to prevent it reacting with or absorbing the paint **b** the support of a painting **c** the background of a painting or main surface against which the other parts of a work of art appear superimposed **3** **a** the first coat of paint applied to a surface **b** *(as modifier)*: *ground colour* **4** the bottom of a river or the sea **5** *Cricket* **a** the area from the popping crease back past the stumps, in which a batsman may legally stand **b** ground staff **6** See **ground bass 7** a mesh or network supporting the main pattern of a piece of lace **8** *Electrical, US and Canadian* **a** a connection between an electrical circuit or device and the earth, which is at zero potential **b** a terminal to which this connection is made **9** **touch ground** (of a ship) to strike the sea bed **10** (used in names of plants) low-growing and often trailing or spreading

ground² **1** having the surface finished, thickness reduced, or an edge sharpened by grinding **2** reduced to fine particles by grinding

ground bass *or* **ground** *Music* a short melodic bass line that is repeated over and over again

ground control **1** the personnel, radar, computers, etc, on the ground that monitor the progress of aircraft or spacecraft **2** a system for feeding continuous radio messages to an aircraft pilot to enable him to make a blind landing

ground cover a dense low herbaceous plants and shrubs that grow over the surface of the ground, esp, in a forest, preventing soil erosion or, in a garden, stifling weeds **b** (*as modifier*): *ground-cover plants*

ground floor the floor of a building level or almost level with the ground

groundnut **1** a North American climbing leguminous plant, *Apios tuberosa*, with fragrant brown flowers and small edible underground tubers **2** the tuber of this plant **3** any of several other plants having underground nutlike parts **4** *Brit* another name for **peanut**

groundsel **1** any of certain plants of the genus *Senecio*, esp *S. vulgaris*, a Eurasian weed with heads of small yellow flowers: family *Asteraceae* (composites) **2** **groundsel tree** a shrub, *Baccharis halimifolia*, of E North America, with white plumelike fruits: family *Asteraceae*

groundsheet *or* **ground cloth** **1** a waterproof rubber, plastic, or polythene sheet placed on the ground in a tent, etc, to keep out damp **2** a similar sheet put over a sports field to protect it against rain

groundsman a person employed to maintain a sports ground, park, etc.

groundswell a considerable swell of the sea, often caused by a distant storm or earthquake or by the passage of waves into shallow water

ground water underground water that has come mainly from the seepage of surface water and is held in pervious rocks

groundwork the ground or background of a painting, etc.

ground zero the name given to the devastated site of the collapsed World Trade Center towers in New York after September 11 2001

group **1** a small band of players or singers, esp of pop music **2** a number of animals or plants considered as a unit because of common characteristics, habits, etc. **3** two or more figures or objects forming a design or unit in a design, in a painting or sculpture **4** *Chem* two or more atoms that are bound together in a molecule and behave as a single unit **5** a vertical column of elements in the periodic table that all have similar electronic structures, properties, and valencies **6** *Geology* any stratigraphical unit, esp the unit for two or more formations **7** *Maths* a set that has an associated operation that combines any two members of the set to give another member and that also contains an identity element and an inverse for each element **8** See **blood**

group

group therapy *Psychol* the simultaneous treatment of a number of individuals who are members of a natural group or who are brought together to share their problems in group discussion

grouse any gallinaceous bird of the family *Tetraonidae*, occurring mainly in the N hemisphere, having a stocky body and feathered legs and feet. They are popular game birds

grove a small wooded area or plantation

Groves Sir **Charles** 1915–92, English orchestral conductor

growl *Jazz* an effect resembling a growl, produced at the back of the throat when playing a wind instrument

growth **1** *Biology* the process or act of growing, esp in organisms following assimilation of food **2** *Pathology* any abnormal tissue, such as a tumour

groyne *or esp US* **groin** a wall or jetty built out from a riverbank or seashore to control erosion

Grozny a city in S Russia, capital of the Chechen Republic: a major oil centre: it was badly damaged during fighting between separatists and Russian troops (1994–95, 1999–2000). Pop: 199 000 (2005 est)

grub the short legless larva of certain insects, esp beetles

grunge a style of rock music originating in the US in the late 1980s, featuring a distorted guitar sound ▷www.wikipedia.org/wiki/Grunge_music

grunt any of various mainly tropical marine sciaenid fishes, such as *Haemulon macrostomum* (**Spanish grunt**), that utter a grunting sound when caught

G-string *Music* a string tuned to G, such as the lowest string of a violin

G-suit a close-fitting garment covering the legs and abdomen that is worn by the crew of high-speed aircraft and can be pressurized to prevent blackout during certain manoeuvres

GT gran turismo: a high-performance luxury sports car with a hard fixed roof, designed for covering long distances

Guadalajara **1** a city in W Mexico, capital of Jalisco state: the second largest city of Mexico: centre of the Indian slave trade until its abolition, declared here in 1810; two universities (1792 and 1935). Pop: 3 905 000 (2005 est) **2** a city in central Spain, in New Castile. Pop: 70 732 (2003 est)

Guadalcanal a mountainous island in the SW Pacific, the largest of the Solomon Islands: under British protection until 1978; occupied by the Japanese (1942–43). Pop: 60 275 (1999). Area: 6475 sq km (2500 sq miles)

Guadalquivir the chief river of S Spain, rising in the Sierra de Segura and flowing west and southwest to the Gulf of Cádiz: navigable by ocean-going vessels to Seville. Length: 560 km (348 miles)

Guadeloupe an overseas region of France in the E Caribbean, in the Leeward Islands, formed by the islands of Basse-Terre and Grande-Terre and five dependencies. Capital: Basse-Terre. Pop: 443 000 (2004 est). Area: 1780 sq km (687 sq miles)

Guadiana a river in SW Europe, rising in S central Spain and flowing west, then south as part of the border between Spain and Portugal, to the Gulf of Cádiz. Length: 578 km (359 miles)

Guam an island in the N Pacific, the largest and southernmost of the Marianas: belonged to Spain from the 17th century until 1898, when it was ceded to the US; site of naval and air force bases. Capital: Agaña. Pop: 165 000 (2004 est). Area: 541 sq km (209 sq miles)

Guanabara (until 1975) a state of SE Brazil, on the Atlantic and **Guanabara Bay**, now amalgamated with the state of Rio de Janeiro

Guanajuato 1 a state of central Mexico, on the great central plateau: mountainous in the north, with fertile plains in the south; important mineral resources. Capital: Guanajuato. Pop: 4 656 761 (2000). Area: 30 588 sq km (11 810 sq miles) 2 a city in central Mexico, capital of Guanajuato state: founded in 1554, it became one of the world's richest silver-mining centres. Pop: 80 000 (2005 est)

Guangdong *or* **Kwangtung** a province of SE China, on the South China Sea: includes the Leizhou Peninsula, with densely populated river valleys; traditionally also including Macao and Hong Kong; the only true tropical climate in China. Capital: Canton. Pop: Pop: 79 540 000 (2003 est). Area: 197 100 sq km (76 100 sq miles)

Guangxi Zhuang Autonomous Region *or* **Kwangsi-Chuang Autonomous Region** an administrative division of S China. Capital: Nanning. Pop: 48 570 000 (2003 est). Area: 220 400 sq km (85 100 sq miles)

guano 1 a the dried excrement of fish-eating sea birds, deposited in rocky coastal regions of South America: contains the urates, oxalates, and phosphates of ammonium and calcium; used as a fertilizer b the accumulated droppings of bats and seals 2 any similar but artificial substance used as a fertilizer

guarantor a person who gives or is bound by a guarantee or guaranty; surety

guaranty a person who acts as a guarantor

guard 1 *Brit* the official in charge of a train 2 *Sport* an article of light tough material worn to protect any of various parts of the body 3 *Basketball* a the position of the two players in a team who play furthest from the basket b a player in this position 4 the posture of defence or readiness in fencing, boxing, cricket, etc. 5 **take guard** *Cricket* (of a batsman) to choose a position in front of the wicket to receive the bowling, esp by requesting the umpire to indicate his position relative to the stumps 6 **give guard** *Cricket* (of an umpire) to indicate such a position to a batsman

Guardafui Cape a cape at the NE tip of Somalia, extending into the Indian Ocean

Guardi Francesco 1712–93, Venetian landscape painter

guardian a *Law* someone legally appointed to manage the affairs of a person incapable of acting for himself, as a minor or person of unsound mind b *Social welfare* (in England) a local authority, or person accepted by it, named under the Mental Health Act 1983 as having the powers to require a mentally disordered person to live at a specified place, attend for treatment, and be accessible to a doctor or social worker

Guarneri, Guarnieri, *or* **Guarnerius** 1 an Italian family of 17th- and 18th-century violin-makers 2 any violin made by a member of this family

Guatemala a republic in Central America: original Maya Indians conquered by the Spanish in 1523; became the centre of Spanish administration in Central America; gained independence and was annexed to Mexico in 1821, becoming an independent republic in 1839. Official language: Spanish. Religion: Roman Catholic majority. Currency: quetzal and US dollar. Capital: Guatemala City. Pop: 12 661 000 (2004 est). Area: 108 889 sq km (42 042 sq miles)

Guatemala City the capital of Guatemala, in the southeast: founded in 1776 to replace the former capital, Antigua Guatemala, after an earthquake; university (1676). Pop: 982 000 (2005 est)

guava 1 any of various tropical American trees of the myrtaceous genus *Psidium*, esp *P. guajava*, grown in tropical regions for their edible fruit 2 the fruit of such a tree, having yellow skin and pink pulp: used to make jellies, jams, etc.

Guayaquil a port in W Ecuador: the largest city in the country and its chief port; university (1867). Pop: 2 387 000 (2005 est)

gubernatorial *Chiefly US, politics* of or relating to a governor

gudgeon¹ 1 a small slender European freshwater cyprinid fish, *Gobio gobio*, with a barbel on each side of the mouth: used as bait by anglers 2 any of various other fishes, such as the goby

gudgeon² 1 a a pivot at the end of a beam or axle b the female or socket portion of a pinned hinge 2 *Nautical* one of two or more looplike sockets, fixed to the transom of a boat, into which the pintles of a rudder are fitted

Guelph a city in Canada, in SE Ontario. Pop: 106 920 (2001)

Guernica a town in N Spain: formerly the seat of a Basque parliament; destroyed in 1937 by German bombers during the Spanish Civil War, an event depicted in one of Picasso's most famous paintings. Pop: 15 454 (2003 est)

Guernsey 1 an island in the English Channel: the second largest of the Channel Islands, which, with Alderney and Sark, Herm, Jethou, and some islets, forms the bailiwick of Guernsey; finance, market gardening, dairy farming, and tourism. Capital: St Peter Port. Pop: 59 710 (2001). Area: 63 sq km (24.5 sq miles) 2 a breed of dairy cattle producing rich creamy milk, originating from the island of Guernsey

Guerrero a mountainous state of S Mexico, on the Pacific: rich mineral resources. Capital: Chilpancingo. Pop: 3 075 083 (2000 est). Area: 63 794 sq km (24 631 sq miles)

guerrilla *or* **guerilla** *Botany* a form of vegetative spread in which the advance is from several individual rhizomes or stolons growing rapidly away from the centre, as in some clovers

guesthouse a private home or boarding house offering accommodation, esp to travellers

Guevara Ernesto , known as *Che Guevara*. 1928–67, Latin American politician and soldier, born in Argentina. He developed guerrilla warfare as a tool for revolution and was instrumental in Castro's victory in Cuba (1959), where he held government posts until 1965. He was killed while training guerrillas in Bolivia

Guggenheim Museum an international chain of art

museums, some of which are architecturally important buildings in their own right, most notably one in New York, designed by Frank Lloyd Wright (1956–59), and one in Bilbao, designed by Frank O Gehry (1997)

Guiana *or* **The Guianas** a region of NE South America, including Guyana, Surinam, French Guiana, and the **Guiana Highlands** (largely in SE Venezuela and partly in N Brazil). Area: about 1 787 000 sq km (690 000 sq miles)

guide 1 *Engineering* any device that directs the motion of a tool or machine part **2** *Spiritualism* a spirit believed to influence a medium so as to direct what he utters and convey messages through him

Guide a member of an organization for girls equivalent to the Scouts

guide dog a dog that has been specially trained to live with and accompany someone who is blind, enabling the blind person to move about safely

Guienne *or* **Guyenne** a former province of SW France: formed, with Gascony, the duchy of Aquitaine during the 12th century

guild *or* **gild 1** (esp in medieval Europe) an association of men sharing the same interests, such as merchants or artisans: formed for mutual aid and protection and to maintain craft standards or pursue some other purpose such as communal worship **2** *Ecology* a group of plants, such as a group of epiphytes, that share certain habits or characteristics

guilder, gilder, *or* **gulden 1** the former standard monetary unit of the Netherlands, divided into 100 cents; replaced by the euro in 2002 **2** the standard monetary unit of the Netherlands Antilles and Surinam, divided into 100 cents **3** any of various former gold or silver coins of Germany, Austria, or the Netherlands

Guildford a city in S England, in Surrey: cathedral (1936–68); seat of the University of Surrey (1966). Pop: 69 400 (2001)

guildhall 1 *Brit* **a** the hall of a guild or corporation **b** a town hall **2** the meeting place of a medieval guild

Guilin, Kweilin, *or* **Kuei-lin** a city in S China, in Guangxi Zhuang AR on the Li River: noted for the unusual caves and formations of the surrounding karst scenery; trade and manufacturing centre. Pop: 631 000 (2005 est)

Guillaume de Lorris 13th century, French poet who wrote the first 4058 lines of the allegorical romance, the *Roman de la rose*, continued by Jean de Meung

Guillem **Sylvie** born 1965, French ballet dancer based in Britain; with the Royal Ballet from 1989

guillemot any northern oceanic diving bird of the genera *Uria* and *Cepphus*, having a black-and-white plumage and long narrow bill: family *Alcidae* (auks, etc), order *Charadriiformes*

guillotine 1 a a device for beheading persons, consisting of a weighted blade set between two upright posts **b** the **guillotine** execution by this instrument **2** a device for cutting or trimming sheet material, such as paper or sheet metal, consisting of a blade inclined at a small angle that descends onto the sheet **3** *Med* a surgical instrument for removing tonsils, growths in the throat, etc. **4** (in Parliament, etc) a form of closure under which a bill is divided into compartments,

groups of which must be completely dealt with each day

guilt *Law* responsibility for a criminal or moral offence deserving punishment or a penalty

guilty 1 *Law* having committed an offence or adjudged to have done so **2 plead guilty** *Law* (of a person charged with an offence) to admit responsibility; confess

guinea 1 a a British gold coin taken out of circulation in 1813, worth 21 shillings **b** the sum of 21 shillings (£1.05), still used in some contexts, as in quoting professional fees **2** See **guinea fowl**

Guinea 1 a republic in West Africa, on the Atlantic: established as the colony of French Guinea in 1890 and became an independent republic in 1958. Official language: French. Religion: Muslim majority and animist. Currency: franc. Capital: Conakry. Pop: 8 620 000 (2004 est). Area: 245 855 sq km (94 925 sq miles) **2** (formerly) the coastal region of West Africa, between Cape Verde and Namibe (formerly Moçâmedes; Angola): divided by a line of volcanic peaks into **Upper Guinea** (between The Gambia and Cameroon) and **Lower Guinea** (between Cameroon and S Angola) **3** **Gulf of** a large inlet of the S Atlantic on the W coast of Africa, extending from Cape Palmas, Liberia, to Cape Lopez, Gabon: contains two large bays, the Bight of Bonny and the Bight of Benin, separated by the Niger delta

Guinea-Bissau a republic in West Africa, on the Atlantic: first discovered by the Portuguese in 1446 and of subsequent importance in the slave trade; made a colony in 1879; became an independent republic in 1974. Official language: Portuguese; Cape Verde creole is widely spoken. Religion: animist majority and Muslim. Currency: franc. Capital: Bissau. Pop: 1 537 000 (2004 est). Area: 36 125 sq km (13 948 sq miles)

guinea fowl *or* **guinea** any gallinaceous bird, esp *Numida meleagris*, of the family *Numididae* of Africa and SW Asia, having a dark plumage mottled with white, a naked head and neck, and a heavy rounded body

guinea pig a domesticated cavy, probably descended from *Cavia porcellus*, commonly kept as a pet and used in scientific experiments

Guinness Sir **Alec** 1914–2000, British stage and film actor. His films include *Kind Hearts and Coronets* (1949), *The Bridge on the River Kwai* (1957), for which he won an Oscar, and *Star Wars* (1977); TV roles include Le Carré's George Smiley

guipure 1 any of many types of heavy lace that have their pattern connected by brides, rather than supported on a net mesh **2** a heavy corded trimming; gimp

guitar *Music* a plucked stringed instrument originating in Spain, usually having six strings, a flat sounding board with a circular sound hole in the centre, a flat back, and a fretted fingerboard. Range: more than three octaves upwards from E on the first leger line below the bass staff

Guitry **Sacha** 1885–1957, French actor, dramatist, and film director, born in Russia: plays include *Nono* (1905)

Guiyang, Kweiyang, *or* **Kuei-yang** a city in S China, capital of Guizhou province: reached by rail in 1959, with subsequent industrial growth. Pop: 2 467 000 (2005 est)

Guizhou, Kweichow, *or* **Kueichow** a province of SW

China, between the Yangtze and Xi Rivers: a high plateau. Capital: Guiyang. Pop: 38 700 000 (2003 est). Area: 174 000 sq km (69 278 sq miles)

Guizot François Pierre Guillaume 1787–1874, French statesman and historian. As chief minister (1840–48), his reactionary policies contributed to the outbreak of the revolution of 1848

Gujarat *or* **Gujerat 1** a state of W India: formed in 1960 from the N and W parts of Bombay State; one of India's most industrialized states. Capital: Gandhinagar. Pop: 50 596 992 (2001). Area: 196 024 sq km (75 268 sq miles) **2** a region of W India, north of the Narmada River: generally includes the areas north of Bombay city where Gujarati is spoken

Gujarati *or* **Gujerati** the state language of Gujarat, belonging to the Indic branch of the Indo-European family

Gujranwala a city in NE Pakistan: textile manufacturing. Pop: 1 466 000 (2005 est)

Gulag (formerly) the central administrative department of the Soviet security service, established in 1930, responsible for maintaining prisons and forced labour camps

Gulbenkian 1 Calouste Sarkis 1869–1955, British industrialist, born in Turkey. He endowed the international Gulbenkian Foundation for the advancement of the arts, science, and education **2** his son, **Nubar Sarkis** 1896–1972, British industrialist, diplomat, and philanthropist

gulch *US and Canadian* a narrow ravine cut by a fast stream

gulf 1 a large deep bay **2** a deep chasm

Gulf the **1** the Persian Gulf **2** *Austral* **a** the Gulf of Carpentaria **b** of, relating to, or adjoining the Gulf **3** *NZ* the Hauraki Gulf

Gulf War syndrome a group of various debilitating symptoms experienced by many soldiers who served in the Gulf War of 1991. It is claimed to be associated with damage to the central nervous system, caused by exposure to pesticides containing organophosphates

gull any aquatic bird of the genus *Larus* and related genera, such as *L. canus* (**common gull** or **mew**) having long pointed wings, short legs, and a mostly white plumage: family *Laridae*, order *Charadriiformes*

gullet 1 a less formal name for the **oesophagus 2** the throat or pharynx

gully¹ *or* **gulley 1** a channel or small valley, esp one cut by heavy rainwater **2** *NZ* a small bush-clad valley **3** a deep, wide fissure between two buttresses in a mountain face, sometimes containing a stream or scree **4** *Cricket* **a** a fielding position between the slips and point **b** a fielder in this position **5** either of the two channels at the side of a tenpin bowling lane

gully² *Scot* a large knife, such as a butcher's knife

gum¹ 1 any of various sticky substances that exude from certain plants, hardening on exposure to air and dissolving or forming viscous masses in water **2** any of various products, such as adhesives, that are made from such exudates

gum² the fleshy tissue that covers the jawbones around the bases of the teeth

gum arabic a gum exuded by certain acacia trees, esp

Acacia senegal: used in the manufacture of ink, food thickeners, pills, emulsifiers, etc.

gumboil an abscess on the gums, often at the root of a decayed tooth

gummy 1 *Austral* a small crustacean-eating shark, *Mustelus antarcticus*, with bony ridges resembling gums in its mouth **2** *NZ* an old ewe that has lost its incisor teeth

gumtree 1 any of various trees that yield gum, such as the eucalyptus, sweet gum, and sour gum **2** the wood of the eucalyptus tree

gunboat a small shallow-draft vessel carrying mounted guns and used by coastal patrols, etc.

gunboat diplomacy diplomacy conducted by threats of military intervention, esp by a major power against a militarily weak state

gun dog 1 a dog trained to work with a hunter or gamekeeper, esp in retrieving, pointing at, or flushing game **2** a dog belonging to any breed adapted to these activities

gunmetal 1 a type of bronze containing copper (88 per cent), tin (8–10 per cent), and zinc (2–4 per cent): used for parts that are subject to wear or to corrosion, esp by sea water **2** any of various dark grey metals used for toys, belt buckles, etc. **3** a dark grey colour with a purplish or bluish tinge

Gunn Thom(son William). 1929–2004, British poet who lived in the USA. His works include *Fighting Terms* (1954), *My Sad Captains* (1961), *Jack Straw's Castle* (1976), *The Man with the Night Sweats* (1992), and *Boss Cupid* (2000)

gunnel any eel-like blennioid fish of the family *Pholidae*, occurring in coastal regions of northern seas

gunner a person who hunts with a rifle or shotgun

gunny *Chiefly US* **1** a coarse hard-wearing fabric usually made from jute and used for sacks, etc. **2** a sack made from this fabric

Gunter Edmund 1581–1626, English mathematician and astronomer, who invented various measuring instruments, including Gunter's chain

Guntur a city in E India, in central Andhra Pradesh: founded by the French in the 18th century; ceded to Britain in 1788. Pop: 514 707 (2001)

gunwale *or* **gunnel** *Nautical* the top of the side of a boat or the topmost plank of a wooden vessel

guppy a small brightly coloured freshwater viviparous cyprinodont fish, *Lebistes reticulatus*, of N South America and the Caribbean: a popular aquarium fish

Gurdjieff Georgei Ivanovitch ?1877–1949, Russian mystic: founded a teaching centre in Paris (1922)

Gurkha a member of a Hindu people, descended from Brahmins and Rajputs, living chiefly in Nepal, where they achieved dominance after being driven from India by the Muslims

gurnard *or* **gurnet** any European marine scorpaenoid fish of the family *Triglidae*, such as *Trigla lucerna* (**tub** or **yellow gurnard**), having a heavily armoured head and finger-like pectoral fins

guru a Hindu or Sikh religious teacher or leader, giving personal spiritual guidance to his disciples

Gustavo A. Madero a city in central Mexico, northeast of Mexico City: became a pilgrimage centre after an Indian convert had a vision of the Virgin Mary here in

1531. Pop: 668 500 (2000 est)

Gustavus I called *Gustavus Vasa*. ?1496–1560, king of Sweden (1523–60). He was elected king after driving the Danes from Sweden (1520–23)

Gustavus VI title of *Gustaf Adolf*. 1882–1973, king of Sweden (1950–73)

Gustavus Adolphus *or* **Gustavus II** 1594–1632, king of Sweden (1611–32). A brilliant general, he waged successful wars with Denmark, Russia, and Poland and in the Thirty Years' War led a Protestant army against the Catholic League and the Holy Roman Empire (1630–32). He defeated Tilly at Leipzig (1631) and Lech (1632) but was killed at the battle of Lützen

gut **1 a** the lower part of the alimentary canal; intestine **b** the entire alimentary canal **2** the bowels or entrails, esp of an animal **3** a silky fibrous substance extracted from silkworms, used in the manufacture of fishing tackle **4** a narrow channel or passage

Gutenberg Johann , original name *Johannes Gensfleisch*. ?1398–1468, German printer; inventor of printing by movable type

Guthrie **1** Samuel 1782–1848, US chemist: invented percussion priming powder and a punch lock for exploding it, and discovered chloroform (1831) **2** Sir (**William**) **Tyrone** 1900–71, English theatrical director **3** Woody, full name *Woodrow Wilson Guthrie*. 1912–67, US folk singer and songwriter. His songs include "So Long, it's been Good to Know you" (1940) and "This Land is your Land" (1944)

gutta-percha **1** any of several tropical trees of the sapotaceous genera *Palaquium* and *Payena*, esp *Palaquium gutta* **2** a whitish rubber substance derived from the coagulated milky latex of any of these trees: used in electrical insulation and dentistry

gutter **1** a channel running along the kerb or the centre of a road to collect and carry away rainwater **2** a trench running beside a canal lined with clay puddle **3** either of the two channels running parallel to a tenpin bowling lane **4** the space left between stamps on a sheet in order to separate them **5** *Surfing* a dangerous deep channel formed by currents and waves

guttural *Anatomy* of or relating to the throat

guy a rope, chain, wire, etc, for anchoring an object, such as a radio mast, in position or for steadying or guiding it while being hoisted or lowered

Guy Buddy, real name *George Guy*. born 1936, US blues singer and guitarist

Guyana a republic in NE South America, on the Atlantic: colonized chiefly by the Dutch in the 17th and 18th centuries; became a British colony in 1831 and an independent republic within the Commonwealth in 1966. Official language: English. Religions: Christian and Hindu. Currency: dollar. Capital: Georgetown. Pop: 767 000 (2004 est). Area: about 215 000 sq km (83 000 sq miles)

Gwalior **1** a city in N central India, in Madhya Pradesh: built around the fort, which dates from before 525; industrial and commercial centre. Pop: 826 919 (2001) **2** a former princely state of central India, established in the 18th century: merged with Madhya Bharat in 1948,

which in turn merged with Madhya Pradesh in 1956

Gwent a former county of SE Wales: formed in 1974 from most of Monmouthshire and part of Breconshire; replaced in 1996 by Monmouthshire and the county boroughs of Newport, Torfaen, Blaenau Gwent, and part of Caerphilly

Gweru a city in central Zimbabwe. Pop: 140 000 (2005 est)

Gwyn Nell, original name *Eleanor Gwynne*. 1650–87, English actress; mistress of Charles II

Gwynedd a county of NW Wales, formed in 1974 from Anglesey, Caernarvonshire, part of Denbighshire, and most of Merionethshire; lost Anglesey and part of the NE in 1996: generally mountainous with many lakes, much of it lying in Snowdonia National Park. Administrative centre: Caernarfon. Pop: 117 500 (2003 est). Area: 2550 sq km (869 sq miles)

gybe *or* **jibe** *Nautical* an instance of gybing

gymkhana **1** *Chiefly Brit* an event in which horses and riders display skill and aptitude in various races and contests **2** (esp in Anglo-India) a place providing sporting and athletic facilities

gymnasium **1** a large room or hall equipped with bars, weights, ropes, etc, for games or physical training **2** (in various European countries) a secondary school that prepares pupils for university

gymnast a person who is skilled or trained in gymnastics

gymnastics **1** practice or training in exercises that develop physical strength and agility or mental capacity **2** gymnastic exercises
▷www.fig-gymnastics.com

gyp a college servant at the universities of Cambridge and Durham

gypsophila any caryophyllaceous plant of the mainly Eurasian genus *Gypsophila*, such as baby's-breath, having small white or pink flowers

gypsum a colourless or white mineral sometimes tinted by impurities, found in beds as an evaporite. It is used in the manufacture of plaster of Paris, cement, paint, school chalk, glass, and fertilizer. Composition: hydrated calcium sulphate. Formula: $CaSO_4.2H_2O$. Crystal structure: monoclinic

Gypsy *or* **Gipsy** **1 a** a member of a people scattered throughout Europe and North America, who maintain a nomadic way of life in industrialized societies. They migrated from NW India from about the 9th century onwards **b** (*as modifier*): *a Gypsy fortune-teller* **2** the language of the Gypsies; Romany

gyrate *Biology* curved or coiled into a circle; circinate

gyrfalcon *or* **gerfalcon** a very large rare falcon, *Falco rusticolus*, of northern and arctic regions: often used for hunting

gyrocompass *Navigation* a nonmagnetic compass that uses a motor-driven gyroscope to indicate true north

gyroscope *or* **gyrostat** a device containing a disc rotating on an axis that can turn freely in any direction so that the disc resists the action of an applied couple and tends to maintain the same orientation in space irrespective of the movement of the surrounding structure

Hh

Haakon VII 1872–1957, king of Norway (1905–57). During the Nazi occupation of Norway (1940–45) he led the Norwegian resistance from England

Haarlem a city in the W Netherlands, capital of North Holland province. Pop: 147 000 (2003 est)

Habakkuk *Old Testament* **1** a Hebrew prophet **2** the book containing his oracles and canticle

habeas corpus *Law* a writ ordering a person to be brought before a court or judge, esp so that the court may ascertain whether his detention is lawful

Haber process an industrial process for producing ammonia by reacting atmospheric nitrogen with hydrogen at about 200 atmospheres (2×10^7 pascals) and 500°C in the presence of a catalyst, usually iron

habit **1** *Psychol* a learned behavioural response that has become associated with a particular situation, esp one frequently repeated **2** *Botany, Zoology* the method of growth, type of existence, behaviour, or general appearance of a plant or animal

habitant **a** an early French settler in Canada or Louisiana, esp a small farmer **b** a descendant of these settlers, esp a farmer

habitat the environment in which an animal or plant normally lives or grows

hachure shading of short lines drawn on a relief map to indicate gradients

hacienda in Spain or Spanish-speaking countries the main house on such a ranch or plantation

hack¹ **1** a dry spasmodic cough **2** a kick on the shins, as in rugby

hack² **1** a horse kept for riding or (more rarely) for driving **2** an old, ill-bred, or overworked horse **3** a horse kept for hire **4** *Brit* a country ride on horseback **5** *US* a coach or carriage that is for hire **6** *US, informal* **a** a cab driver **b** a taxi

hack³ a board on which meat is placed for a hawk

hacker *Slang* a computer fanatic, esp one who through a personal computer breaks into the computer system of a company, government, etc.

hacking (of a cough) harsh, dry, and spasmodic

Hackman Gene born 1930, US film actor; his films include *The French Connection* (1971), *Mississippi Burning* (1988), *Absolute Power* (1997), and *The Royal Tenenbaums* (2001)

hackney **1** a compact breed of harness horse with a high-stepping trot **2 a** a coach or carriage that is for hire **b** (*as modifier*): *a hackney carriage*

Hackney a borough of NE Greater London: formed in 1965 from the former boroughs of Shoreditch, Stoke Newington, and Hackney; nearby are **Hackney Marshes**, the largest recreation ground in London. Pop: 208 400 (2003 est). Area: 19 sq km (8 sq miles)

hacksaw a handsaw for cutting metal, with a hard-steel blade in a frame under tension

haddock a North Atlantic gadoid food fish, *Melanogrammus aeglefinus*: similar to but smaller than the cod

hadedah *South African* a large greyish-green ibis, *Hagedeshia hagedash*, having a greenish metallic sheen on the wing coverts and shoulders

Haden Charles (**Edward**). born 1937, US jazz bassist

Hades **1** *Greek myth* **a** the underworld abode of the souls of the dead **b** Pluto, the god of the underworld, brother of Zeus and husband of Persephone **2** *New Testament* the abode or state of the dead

Hadhramaut or **Hadramaut** a plateau region of the S Arabian Peninsula, in SE Yemen on the Indian Ocean; formerly in South Yemen: corresponds roughly to the former East Aden Protectorate. Area: about 151 500 sq km (58 500 sq miles)

Hadlee Sir Richard (**John**). born 1951, New Zealand cricketer

Hadrian or **Adrian** Latin name *Publius Aelius Hadrianus*. 76–138 AD, Roman emperor (117–138); adopted son and successor of Trajan. He travelled throughout the Roman Empire, strengthening its frontiers and encouraging learning and architecture, and in Rome he reorganized the army and codified Roman law

Haeckel Ernst Heinrich 1834–1919, German biologist and philosopher. He formulated the recapitulation theory of evolution and was an exponent of the philosophy of materialistic monism

haemal or *US* **hemal** **1** of or relating to the blood or the blood vessels **2** denoting or relating to the region of the body containing the heart

haematic or *US* **hematic** relating to, acting on, having the colour of, or containing blood

haematology or *US* **hematology** the branch of medical science concerned with diseases of the blood and blood-forming tissues

haemoglobin or *US* **hemoglobin** a conjugated protein, consisting of haem and the protein globin, that gives red blood cells their characteristic colour. It combines reversibly with oxygen and is thus very important in the transportation of oxygen to tissues

haemophilia *or US* **hemophilia** an inheritable disease, usually affecting only males but transmitted by women to their male children, characterized by loss or impairment of the normal clotting ability of blood so that a minor wound may result in fatal bleeding
▷www.hemophilia.org

haemorrhage *or US* **hemorrhage** profuse bleeding from ruptured blood vessels

hafnium a bright metallic element found in zirconium ores: used in tungsten filaments and as a neutron absorber in nuclear reactors. Symbol: Hf; atomic no.: 72; atomic wt.: 178.49; valency: 4; relative density: 13.31; melting pt.: 2231±20°C; boiling pt.: 4603°C

hag *Scot and northern English, dialect* 1 a firm spot in a bog 2 a soft place in a moor

Hagar *Old Testament* an Egyptian maid of Sarah, who bore Ishmael to Abraham, Sarah's husband

Hagen[1] Walter 1892–1969, US golfer

Hagen[2] an industrial city in NW Germany, in North Rhine-Westphalia. Pop: 200 039 (2003 est)

Haggai *Old Testament* 1 a Hebrew prophet, whose oracles are usually dated between August and December of 520 BC 2 the book in which these oracles are contained, chiefly concerned with the rebuilding of the Temple after the Exile

haggard 1 (of a hawk) having reached maturity in the wild before being caught 2 *Falconry* a hawk that has reached maturity before being caught

Haggard Sir (Henry) Rider 1856–1925, British author of romantic adventure stories, including *King Solomon's Mines* (1885)

Hagiographa the third of the three main parts into which the books of the Old Testament are divided in Jewish tradition (the other two parts being the Law and the Prophets), comprising Psalms, Proverbs, Job, the Song of Solomon, Ruth, Lamentations, Ecclesiastes, Esther, Daniel, Ezra, Nehemiah, and Chronicles

hagiography 1 the writing of the lives of the saints 2 biography of the saints 3 any biography that idealizes or idolizes its subject

hagiology 1 literature concerned with the lives and legends of saints 2 a a biography of a saint b a collection of such biographies 3 an authoritative canon of saints 4 a history of sacred writings

Hague[1] William Jefferson born 1961, British politician; leader of the Conservative party (1997–2001)

Hague[2] The the seat of government of the Netherlands and capital of South Holland province, situated about 3 km (2 miles) from the North Sea. Pop: 464 000 (2003 est)

Hahn 1 Kurt 1886–1974, German educationalist. During the Nazi era he escaped to Britain, where he founded Gordonstoun School (1935) and helped to establish the Duke of Edinburgh's award scheme 2 Otto 1879–1968, German physicist: discovered the radioactive element protactinium with Meitner (1917); with Strassmann, demonstrated the nuclear fission of uranium, when it is bombarded with neutrons: Nobel prize for chemistry 1944

Hahnemann (Christian Friedrich) Samuel 1755–1843,

German physician; founder of homeopathy

hahnium a name once advanced by the American Chemical Society for a transuranic element, artificially produced from californium, atomic no.: 105; half-life of most stable isotope, [262]Ha: 40 seconds

Haifa a port in NW Israel, near Mount Carmel, on the Bay of Acre: Israel's chief port, with an oil refinery and other heavy industry. Pop: 269 400 (2003 est)

Haig Douglas, 1st Earl Haig. 1861–1928, British field marshal; commander in chief of the British forces in France and Flanders (1915–18)

haiku *or* **hokku** an epigrammatic Japanese verse form in 17 syllables

hail 1 small pellets of ice falling from cumulonimbus clouds when there are very strong rising air currents 2 a shower or storm of such pellets

Haile Selassie title of *Ras Tafari Makonnen*. 1892–1975, emperor of Ethiopia (1930–36; 1941–74). During the Italian occupation of Ethiopia (1936–41), he lived in exile in England. He was a prominent figure in the Pan-African movement: deposed 1974

Hail Mary 1 *RC Church* a prayer to the Virgin Mary, based on the salutations of the angel Gabriel (Luke 1:28) and Elizabeth (Luke 1:42) to her 2 *American football, Slang* a very long high pass into the end zone, made in the final seconds of a half or of a game

hailstone a pellet of hail

hailstorm a storm during which hail falls

Hailwood Mike, full name *Stanley Michael Bailey Hailwood*. 1940–81, English racing motorcyclist: world champion (250 cc.) 1961 and 1966–67; (350 cc.) 1966–67; and (500 cc.) 1962–65

Hainan *or* **Hainan Tao** an island and province in the South China Sea, separated from the mainland of S China by the Hainan Strait: part of Guangdong province until 1988; mainland China's largest offshore island. Pop: 8 110 000 (2003 est). Area: 33 572 sq km (12 962 sq miles)

Hainaut *or* **Hainault** a province of SW Belgium: stretches from the Flanders Plain in the north to the Ardennes in the south. Capital: Mons. Pop: 1 283 200 (2004 est). Area: 3797 sq km (1466 sq miles)

Haiphong a port in N Vietnam, on the Red River delta: a major industrial centre. Pop: 1 817 000 (2005 est)

hair 1 any of the threadlike pigmented structures that grow from follicles beneath the skin of mammals and consist of layers of dead keratinized cells 2 a growth of such structures, as on the human head or animal body, which helps prevent heat loss from the body 3 *Botany* any threadlike outgrowth from the epidermis, such as a root hair 4 a fabric or material made from the hair of some animals

hairline the natural margin formed by hair on the head

Haiti 1 a republic occupying the W part of the island of Hispaniola in the Caribbean, the E part consisting of the Dominican Republic: ceded by Spain to France in 1697 and became one of the richest colonial possessions in the world, with numerous plantations; slaves rebelled under Toussaint L'Ouverture in 1791 and defeated the French; taken over by the US (1915–41) after long political and economic chaos; under the authoritarian regimes of François Duvalier (Papa Doc) (1957–71) and his son Jean-Claude Duvalier (Baby Doc) (1971–86); returned to civilian rule in 1990, but another coup in 1991 brought military rule, which was ended in 1994 with US intervention. Official languages: French and Haitian creole. Religions: Roman Catholic and voodoo. Currency: gourde. Capital: Port-au-Prince. Pop: 8 437 000 (2004 est). Area: 27 749 sq km (10 714 sq miles) **2** a former name for **Hispaniola**

Haitian *or* **Haytian** the creolized French spoken in Haiti

Haitink Bernard born 1929, Dutch orchestral conductor; received an honorary knighthood in 1977

Haji-Ioannou Stelios born 1967, British businessman, born in Greece; founder (1995) and chairman (until 2002) of the low-cost airline company Easyjet

hajj *or* **hadj** the pilgrimage to Mecca that every Muslim is required to make at least once in his life, provided he has enough money and the health to do so

hajji, hadji, *or* **haji** **1** a Muslim who has made a pilgrimage to Mecca: also used as a title **2** a Christian of the Greek Orthodox or Armenian Churches who has visited Jerusalem

haka *NZ* **1** a Māori war chant accompanied by gestures **2** a similar performance by a rugby team

hake **1** any gadoid food fish of the genus *Merluccius*, such as *M. merluccius* (European hake), of the N hemisphere, having an elongated body with a large head and two dorsal fins **2** any North American fish of the genus *Urophycis*, similar and related to *Merluccius* species

hakea any shrub or tree of the Australian genus *Hakea*, having a hard woody fruit and often yielding a useful wood: family *Proteaceae*

Hakluyt Richard ?1552–1616, English geographer, who compiled *The Principal Navigations, Voyages, and Discoveries of the English Nation* (1589)

Hakodate a port in N Japan, on S Hokkaido: fishing industry and shipbuilding. Pop: 284 690 (2002 est)

Halabja a Kurdish town in NE Iraq; in March 1988 Iraqi forces used poison gas on the population, killing hundreds of civilians. Pop: 80 000 (latest est)

halal *or* **hallal** **1** meat from animals that have been killed according to Muslim law **2** of or relating to such meat

Halberstadt a town in central Germany, in Saxony-Anhalt: industrial centre noted for its historic buildings. Pop: 40 014 (2003 est)

halcyon **1** *Greek myth* a fabulous bird associated with the winter solstice **2** a poetic name for the **kingfisher**

Haldane **1** J(ohn) B(urdon) S(anderson) 1892–1964, Scottish biochemist, geneticist, and writer on science **2** his father, **John Scott** 1860–1936, Scottish physiologist, noted particularly for his research into industrial diseases **3** his brother, **Richard Burdon**, 1st Viscount Haldane of Cloan. 1856–1928, British statesman and jurist. As secretary of state for war (1905–12) he reorganized the army and set up the territorial reserve

Hale **1** George Ellery 1868–1938, US astronomer: undertook research into sunspots and invented the spectroheliograph **2** Sir **Matthew** 1609–76, English judge and scholar; Lord Chief Justice (1671–76)

Haleakala a volcano in Hawaii, on E Maui Island. Height: 3057 m (10 032 ft). Area of crater: 49 sq km (19 sq miles). Depth of crater: 829 m (2720 ft)

Halesowen a town in W central England, in Dudley unitary authority, West Midlands. Pop: 55 273 (2001)

Haley Bill, full name *William John Clifton Haley*. 1925–81, US rock and roll singer, best known for his recording of "Rock Around the Clock" (1955)

half **1** half a pint, esp of beer **2** *Scot* a small drink of spirits, esp whisky **3** *Golf* an equal score on a hole or round with an opponent **4** (in various games) either of two periods of play separated by an interval (the **first half** and **second half**) **5** short for **halfpenny 6** *Sport* short for **halfback**

half-and-half a drink consisting of equal parts of beer and stout, or equal parts of bitter and mild

halfback **1** *Rugby* either the scrum half or the stand-off half **2** *Soccer, old-fashioned* any of three players positioned behind the line of forwards and in front of the fullbacks **3** any of certain similar players in other team sports **4** the position of a player who is halfback

half board **a** the daily provision by a hotel of bed, breakfast, and one main meal **b** *(as modifier)*: *half-board accommodation*

half-breed 1 *Offensive* a person whose parents are of different races, esp the offspring of a White person and an American Indian **2** of, relating to, or designating offspring of people or animals of different races or breeds

half-caste *Offensive* a person having parents of different races, esp the offspring of a European and an Indian

half-crown a British silver or cupronickel coin worth two shillings and sixpence (now equivalent to 12½p), taken out of circulation in 1970

half-hour a a period of 30 minutes **b** *(as modifier)*: *a half-hour stint*

half-life 1 the time taken for half of the atoms in a radioactive material to undergo decay. **2** the time required for half of a quantity of radioactive material absorbed by a living tissue or organism to be naturally eliminated (**biological half-life**) or removed by both elimination and decay (**effective half-life**)

half-moon 1 the moon at first or last quarter when half its face is illuminated **2** the time at which a half-moon occurs

half-nelson a wrestling hold in which a wrestler places an arm under one of his opponent's arms from behind and exerts pressure with his palm on the back of his opponent's neck

halfpenny *or* **ha'penny 1** a small British coin worth half a new penny, withdrawn from circulation in 1985 **2** an old British coin worth half an old penny

half-pipe a structure with a U-shaped cross-section, used in performing stunts in skateboarding, snowboarding, rollerblading, etc.

half term *Brit, Education* **a** a short holiday midway through an academic term **b** *(as modifier)*: *a half-term holiday*

half-timbered *or* **half-timber** (of a building, wall, etc) having an exposed timber framework filled with brick, stone, or plastered laths, as in Tudor architecture

half-time *Sport* **a** a rest period between the two halves of a game **b** *(as modifier)*: *the half-time score*

halftone *Art* a tonal value midway between highlight and dark shading

half volley *Sport* a stroke or shot in which the ball is hit immediately after it bounces

halfway house a centre or hostel designed to facilitate the readjustment to private life of released prisoners, mental patients, etc.

halibut *or* **holibut** 1 the largest flatfish: a dark green North Atlantic species, *Hippoglossus hippoglossus*, that is a very important food fish: family *Pleuronectidae* 2 any of several similar and related flatfishes, such as *Reinhardtius hippoglossoides* (**Greenland halibut**)

Halicarnassus a Greek colony on the SW coast of Asia Minor: one of the major Hellenistic cities

Halifax¹ 1 Charles Montagu, Earl of Halifax. 1661–1715, British statesman; founder of the National Debt (1692) and the Bank of England (1694) 2 Edward Frederick Lindley Wood, Earl of Halifax. 1881–1959, British Conservative statesman. He was viceroy of India (1926–31), foreign secretary (1938–40), and ambassador to the US (1941–46) 3 George Savile, 1st Marquess of Halifax, known as *the Trimmer*. 1633–95, British politician, noted for his wavering opinions. He opposed the exclusion of the Catholic James II from the throne but later supported the Glorious Revolution

Halifax² 1 a port in SE Canada, capital of Nova Scotia, on the Atlantic: founded in 1749 as a British stronghold. Pop: 276 221 (2001) 2 a town in N England, in Calderdale unitary authority, West Yorkshire: textiles. Pop: 83 570 (2001)

halitosis the state or condition of having bad breath

hall 1 a room serving as an entry area within a house or building 2 a building for public meetings 3 the great house of an estate; manor 4 a large building or room used for assemblies, worship, concerts, dances, etc. 5 a residential building, esp in a university; hall of residence 6 a a large room, esp for dining, in a college or university b a meal eaten in this room 7 the large room of a house, castle, etc. 8 *US and Canadian* a passage or corridor into which rooms open 9 *Informal* short for **music hall**

Hall 1 Charles Martin 1863–1914, US chemist: discovered the electrolytic process for producing aluminium 2 Sir John 1824–1907, New Zealand statesman, born in England: prime minister of New Zealand (1879–82) 3 Sir Peter born 1930, English stage director: director of the Royal Shakespeare Company (1960–73) and of the National Theatre (1973–88) 4 (Margueritte) Radclyffe 1883–1943, British novelist and poet. Her frank treatment of a lesbian theme in the novel *The Well of Loneliness* (1928) led to an obscenity trial

Halle a city in E central Germany, in Saxony-Anhalt, on the River Saale: early saltworks; a Hanseatic city in the late Middle Ages; university (1694). Pop: 240 119 (2003 est)

hallelujah, halleluiah, *or* **alleluia** a musical composition that uses the word *Hallelujah* as its text

Haller Albrecht von 1708–77, Swiss biologist: founder of experimental physiology

Halley Edmund 1656–1742, English astronomer and mathematician. He predicted the return of the comet now known as **Halley's comet**, constructed charts of magnetic declination, and produced the first wind maps

Hall-Jones Sir William 1851–1936, New Zealand statesman, born in England: prime minister of New Zealand (1906)

hallmark *Brit* an official series of marks, instituted by statute in 1300, and subsequently modified, stamped by the Guild of Goldsmiths at one of its assay offices on gold, silver, or platinum (since 1975) articles to guarantee purity, date of manufacture, etc.

hallowed 1 set apart as sacred 2 consecrated or holy

Halloween *or* **Hallowe'en** the eve of All Saints' Day celebrated on Oct 31 by masquerading; Allhallows Eve

hallucination the alleged perception of an object when no object is present, occurring under hypnosis, in some mental disorders, etc.

hallucinogen any drug, such as LSD or mescaline, that induces hallucinations

Halmahera an island in NE Indonesia, the largest of the Moluccas: consists of four peninsulas enclosing three bays; mountainous and forested. Area: 17 780 sq km (6865 sq miles)

Halmstad a port in SW Sweden, on the Kattegat. Pop: 88 032 (2004 est)

halo 1 a disc or ring of light around the head of an angel, saint, etc, as in painting or sculpture 2 a circle of light around the sun or moon, caused by the refraction of light by particles of ice 3 *Astronomy* a spherical cloud of stars surrounding the Galaxy and other spiral galaxies

halogen any of the chemical elements fluorine, chlorine, bromine, iodine, and astatine. They are all monovalent and readily form negative ions

Hals Frans ?1580–1666, Dutch portrait and genre painter: his works include *The Laughing Cavalier* (1624)

halt *Chiefly Brit* a minor railway station, without permanent buildings

halter a rope or canvas headgear for a horse, usually with a rope for leading

Halton a unitary authority in NW England, in N Cheshire. Pop: 118 400 (2003 est). Area: 75 sq km (29 sq miles)

halyard *or* **halliard** *Nautical* a line for hoisting or lowering a sail, flag, or spar

ham¹ 1 the part of the hindquarters of a pig or similar animal between the hock and the hip 2 *Informal* a the back of the leg above the knee b the space or area behind the knee 3 *Needlework* a cushion used for moulding curves

ham² *Theatre, informal* a an actor who overacts or relies on stock gestures or mannerisms b overacting or clumsy acting c (*as modifier*): *a ham actor*

Hama a city in W Syria, on the Orontes River: an early Hittite settlement; famous for its huge water wheels, used for irrigation since the Middle Ages. Pop: 439 000 (2005 est)

Hamadān *or* **Hamedān** city in W central Iran, at an altitude of over 1830 m (6000 ft): changed hands several times from the 17th century between Iraq, Persia, and Turkey; trading centre. Pop: 508 000 (2005 est)

Hamamatsu a city in central Japan, in S central Honshu: cotton textiles and musical instruments. Pop: 573 504 (2002 est)

Hamburg a city-state and port in NW Germany, on the River Elbe: the largest port in Germany; a founder member of the Hanseatic League; became a free imperial city in 1510 and a state of the German empire in 1871; university (1919); extensive shipyards. Pop: 1 734 083 (2003 est)

Hameln an industrial town in N Germany, in Lower Saxony on the Weser River: famous for the legend of the Pied Piper (supposedly took place in 1284). Pop: 58 902 (2003 est)

Hamersley Range a mountain range in N Western Australia: iron-ore deposits. Highest peak: 1236 m (4056 ft)

Hamhung *or* **Hamheung** an industrial city in central North Korea: commercial and governmental centre of NE Korea during the Yi dynasty (1392–1910). Pop: 753 000 (2005 est)

Hamilcar Barca died ?228 BC, Carthaginian general; father of Hannibal. He held command (247–41) during the first Punic War and established Carthaginian influence in Spain (237–?228)

Hamilton¹ 1 Alexander ?1757–1804, American statesman. He was a leader of the Federalists and as first secretary of the Treasury (1789–95) established a federal bank 2 Lady Emma ?1765–1815, mistress of Nelson 3 James, 1st Duke of Hamilton. 1606–49, Scottish supporter of Charles I in the English Civil War: defeated by Cromwell at the Battle of Preston and executed 4 Richard born 1922, British artist: a pioneer of the pop art style 5 Sir William Rowan 1805–65, Irish mathematician: founded Hamiltonian mechanics and formulated the theory of quaternions

Hamilton² 1 a port in central Canada, in S Ontario on Lake Ontario: iron and steel industry. Pop: 618 820 (2001) 2 a city in New Zealand, on central North Island. Pop: 129 300 (2004 est) 3 a town in S Scotland, in South Lanarkshire near Glasgow. Pop: 48 546 (2001) 4 the capital and chief port of Bermuda. Pop: 3461 (2000) 5 the former name of the **Churchill²** River in Labrador

Hamm an industrial city in NW Germany, in North Rhine-Westphalia: a Hanse town from 1417; severely damaged in World War II. Pop: 184 961 (2003 est)

hammer 1 a hand tool consisting of a heavy usually steel head held transversely on the end of a handle, used for driving in nails, beating metal, etc. 2 any tool or device with a similar function, such as the moving part of a door knocker, the striking head on a bell, etc. 3 a power-driven striking tool, esp one used in forging. A **pneumatic hammer** delivers a repeated blow from a pneumatic ram, a **drop hammer** uses the energy of a falling weight 4 *Athletics* a a heavy metal ball attached to a flexible wire: thrown in competitions b the event or sport of throwing the hammer 5 a device on a piano that is made to strike a string or group of strings causing them to vibrate 6 *Curling* the last stone thrown in an end 7 **go** (*or* **come**) **under the hammer** to be offered for sale by an auctioneer

hammer and sickle a symbolic representation of the former Soviet Union or of Communism in general

Hammerfest a port in N Norway, on the W coast of Kvalöy Island: the northernmost town in Europe, with uninterrupted daylight from May 17 to July 29 and no sun between Nov 21 and Jan 21; fishing and tourist centre. Pop: 9157 (2004 est)

hammerhead 1 any shark of the genus *Sphyrna* and family *Sphyrnidae*, having a flattened hammer-shaped head 2 a heavily built tropical African wading bird, *Scopus umbretta*, related to the herons, having a dark plumage and a long backward-pointing crest: family *Scopidae*, order *Ciconiiformes* 3 a large African fruit bat, *Hypsignathus monstrosus*, with a large square head and hammer-shaped muzzle

Hammersmith and Fulham a borough of Greater London on the River Thames: established in 1965 by the amalgamation of Fulham and Hammersmith. Pop: 174 200 (2003 est). Area: 16 sq km (6 sq miles)

Hammerstein II Oscar 1895–1960, US librettist and songwriter: collaborated with the composer Richard Rodgers in musicals such as *South Pacific* (1949) and *The Sound of Music* (1959)

hammertoe 1 a deformity of the bones of a toe causing the toe to be bent in a clawlike arch 2 such a toe

Hammett Dashiell 1894–1961, US writer of detective novels. His books include *The Maltese Falcon* (1930) and *The Thin Man* (1932)

Hammond¹ 1 Dame Joan 1912–96, Australian operatic singer, born in New Zealand 2 Walter Reginald, known as *Wally*. 1903–65, English cricketer. An all-rounder, he played for England 85 times between 1928 and 1946

Hammond² a city in NW Indiana, adjacent to Chicago. Pop: 80 547 (2003 est)

Hammurabi *or* **Hammurapi** ?18th century BC, king of Babylonia; promulgator of one of the earliest known codes of law

Hampden John 1594–1643, English statesman; one of the leaders of the Parliamentary opposition to Charles I

hamper *Nautical* gear aboard a vessel that, though essential, is often in the way

Hampshire¹ Sir Stuart 1914–2004, British philosopher: his publications include *Thought and Action* (1959), *Two Theories of Morality* (1977), and *Innocence and Experience* (1989)

Hampshire² a county of S England, on the English Channel: crossed by the **Hampshire Downs** and the South Downs, with the New Forest in the southwest and many prehistoric and Roman remains: the geographical and ceremonial county includes Portsmouth and Southampton, which became independent unitary authorities in 1997. Administrative centre: Winchester. Pop. (excluding unitary authorities): 1 251 000 (2003 est). Area (excluding unitary authorities): 3679 sq km (1420 sq miles)

Hampstead a residential district in N London: part of the Greater London borough of Camden since 1965; nearby is **Hampstead Heath**, a popular recreation area

Hampton¹ 1 Christopher James born 1946, British playwright: his works include *When Did You Last See My Mother?* (1964), the screenplay for the films *Dangerous Liaisons* (1988), and the book for the musical *Sunset Boulevard* (1993) 2 Lionel 1913–2002, US jazz-band leader and vibraphone player

Hampton² 1 a city in SE Virginia, on the harbour of Hampton Roads on Chesapeake Bay. Pop: 146 878 (2003 est) 2 a district of the Greater London borough of Richmond-upon-Thames, on the River Thames: famous for **Hampton Court Palace** (built in 1515 by Cardinal Wolsey)

hamster any Eurasian burrowing rodent of the tribe *Cricetini*, such as *Mesocricetus auratus* (**golden hamster**), having a stocky body, short tail, and cheek pouches: family *Cricetidae*. They are popular pets

hamstring 1 *Anatomy* any of the tendons at the back of the knee 2 the large tendon at the back of the hock in the hind leg of a horse, etc.

Hamsun Knut, , pen name of *Knut Pedersen*. 1859–1952, Norwegian novelist, whose works include *The Growth of the Soil* (1917): Nobel prize for literature 1920

Han¹ 1 the imperial dynasty that ruled China for most of the time from 206 BC to 221 AD, expanding its territory and developing its bureaucracy 2 the Chinese people as contrasted to Mongols, Manchus, etc.

Han² a river in E central China, rising in S Shaanxi and flowing southeast through Hubei to the Yangtze River at Wuhan. Length: about 1450 km (900 miles)

Hanau a city in central Germany, in Hesse east of Frankfurt am Main: a centre of the jewellery industry. Pop: 88 897 (2003 est)

Hancock 1 Anthony John, known as *Tony*. 1924–68, British comedian, noted for his radio series *Hancock's Half Hour* 2 John 1737–93, American statesman; first signatory of the Declaration of Independence

hand 1 a the prehensile part of the body at the end of the arm, consisting of a thumb, four fingers, and a palm b the bones of this part 2 the corresponding or similar part in animals 3 a the cards dealt to one or all players in one round of a card game b a player holding such cards c one round of a card game 4 a member of a ship's crew 5 a unit of length measurement equalling four inches, used for measuring the height of horses, usually from the front hoof to the withers

handbag *Pop music* a commercial style of House music

handball 1 a game in which two teams of seven players try to throw a ball into their opponent's goal 2 a game in which two or four people strike a ball against a wall or walls with the hand, usually gloved 3 the small hard rubber ball used in this game 4 *Soccer* the offence committed when a player other than a goalkeeper in his own penalty area touches the ball with a hand
▷www.ihf.info

handbrake 1 a brake operated by a hand lever 2 the lever that operates the handbrake

handcart a simple cart, usually with one or two wheels, pushed or drawn by hand

handcuff a pair of locking metal rings joined by a short bar or chain for securing prisoners, etc.

Handel George Frederick German name *Georg Friedrich Händel*. 1685–1759, German composer, resident in England, noted particularly for his oratorios, including the *Messiah* (1741) and *Samson* (1743). Other works include over 40 operas, 12 concerti grossi, organ concertos, chamber and orchestral music, esp *Water Music* (1717)

handicap 1 *Sport* a a contest, esp a race, in which competitors are given advantages or disadvantages of weight, distance, time, etc, in an attempt to equalize their chances of winning b the advantage or disadvantage prescribed 2 *Golf* the number of strokes by which a player's averaged score exceeds the standard scratch score for the particular course: used as the basis for handicapping in competitive play 3 any physical disability or disadvantage resulting from physical, mental, or social impairment or abnormality

handicapped 1 physically disabled 2 *Psychol* denoting a person whose social behaviour or emotional reactions are in some way impaired 3 *Sport* (of a competitor) assigned a handicap

handicraft 1 a particular skill or art performed with the hands, such as weaving, pottery, etc. 2 the work produced by such a skill or art

handiwork work performed or produced by hand, such as embroidery or pottery

handle 1 the quality, as of textiles, perceived by touching or feeling 2 *Gambling* the total amount of a bet on a horse race or similar event

handler 1 a person, esp a police officer, in charge of a specially trained dog 2 a person who holds or incites a dog, gamecock, etc, esp in a race or contest 3 the trainer or second of a boxer

Handler Daniel born 1970, US writer for older children, best known for the macabre humour of his *A Series of Unfortunate Events*, a sequence of books written in the persona of Lemony Snicket

handrail a rail alongside a stairway, etc, at a convenient height to be grasped to provide support

handspring a gymnastic feat in which a person starts from a standing position and leaps forwards or backwards into a handstand and then onto his feet

handstand the act or instance of supporting the body on the hands alone in an upside down position

Handy W(illiam) C(hristopher). 1873–1958, US blues musician and songwriter, esp noted for the song "St Louis Blues"

hangar a large workshop or building for storing and maintaining aircraft

hanger 1 a bracket designed to attach one part of a mechanical structure to another, such as the one that attaches the spring shackle of a motor car to the chassis 2 a wood on a steep hillside, characteristically beech growing on chalk in southern England

hang-glider an unpowered aircraft consisting of a large cloth wing stretched over a light framework from which the pilot hangs in a harness, using a horizontal bar to control the flight
▷www.bhpa.co.uk
▷www.fai.org/hang-gliding

hanging 1 a the putting of a person to death by suspending the body by the neck from a noose b (as modifier): *a hanging offence* 2 a decorative textile such as a tapestry or drapery hung on a wall or over a window 3 situated on a steep slope or in a high place

Hanging Gardens of Babylon (in ancient Babylon) gardens, probably planted on terraces of a ziggurat: one of the Seven Wonders of the World

hanging valley *Geography* a tributary valley entering a main valley at a much higher level because of overdeepening of the main valley, esp by glacial erosion

hangman an official who carries out a sentence of hanging on condemned criminals

hangover the delayed aftereffects of drinking too much alcohol in a relatively short period of time, characterized by headache and sometimes nausea and dizziness

Hangzhou or **Hangchow** a port in E China, capital of

Zhejiang province, on **Hangzhou Bay** (an inlet of the East China Sea), at the foot of the Eye of Heaven Mountains: regarded by Marco Polo as the finest city in the world; seat of two universities (1927, 1959). Pop: 1 955 000 (2005 est)

hank 1 a loop, coil, or skein, as of rope, wool, or yarn 2 *Nautical* a ringlike fitting that can be opened to admit a stay for attaching the luff of a sail 3 a unit of measurement of cloth, yarn, etc, such as a length of 840 yards (767 m) of cotton or 560 yards (512 m) of worsted yarn

Hankow *or* **Han-k'ou** a former city in SE China, in SE Hubei at the confluence of the Han and Yangtze Rivers: one of the Han Cities; merged with Hanyang and Wuchang in 1950 to form the conurbation of Wuhan

Hanks Tom born 1956, US film actor: his films include *Splash* (1984), *Philadelphia* (1993), *Forrest Gump* (1994), *Saving Private Ryan* (1998), and *The Terminal* (2004)

Hanna William 1910–2001, US animator and film producer who with **Joseph Barbera** (born 1911) created the cartoon characters Tom and Jerry in the 1940s; the Hanna–Barbera company later produced numerous cartoon series for television.

Hannah *Old Testament* the woman who gave birth to Samuel (I Samuel 1–2)

Hannibal 247–182 BC, Carthaginian general; son of Hamilcar Barca. He commanded the Carthaginian army in the Second Punic War (218–201). After capturing Sagunto in Spain, he invaded Italy (218), crossing the Alps with an army of about 40 000 men and defeating the Romans at Trasimene (217) and Cannae (216). In 203 he was recalled to defend Carthage and was defeated by Scipio at Zama (202). He was later forced into exile and committed suicide to avoid capture

Hannover a city in N Germany, capital of Lower Saxony: capital of the kingdom of Hannover (1815–66); situated on the Mittelland canal. Pop: 516 160 (2003 est)

Hanoi the capital of Vietnam, on the Red River: became capital of Tonkin in 1802, of French Indochina in 1887, of Vietnam in 1945, and of North Vietnam (1954–75); university (1917); industrial centre. Pop: 4 147 000 (2005 est)

Hanover 1 a princely house of Germany (1692–1815), the head of which succeeded to the British throne as George I in 1714 2 the royal house of Britain (1714–1901)

Hanoverian 1 of, relating to, or situated in Hannover 2 of or relating to the princely house of Hanover or to the monarchs of England or their reigns from 1714 to 1901 3 a member or supporter of the house of Hanover

Hansard 1 the official report of the proceedings of the British Parliament 2 a similar report kept by other legislative bodies

Hanseatic League a commercial association of towns in N Germany formed in the mid-14th century to protect and control trade. It was at its most powerful in the 15th century

hansom a two-wheeled one-horse carriage with a fixed hood. The driver sits on a high outside seat at the rear

Hanukkah, Hanukah, *or* **Chanukah** the eight-day Jewish festival of lights beginning on the 25th of Kislev and commemorating the rededication of the temple by Judas Maccabaeus in 165 BC

Hanyang *or* **Han-yang** a former city in SE China, in SE Hubei at the confluence of the Han and Yangtze Rivers: one of the Han Cities; merged with Hankow and Wuchang in 1950 to form the conurbation of Wuhan

haploid *Biology* 1 (esp of gametes) having a single set of unpaired chromosomes 2 a haploid cell or organism

Hapsburg a German princely family founded by Albert, count of Hapsburg (1153). From 1440 to 1806, the Hapsburgs wore the imperial crown of the Holy Roman Empire almost uninterruptedly. They also provided rulers for Austria, Spain, Hungary, Bohemia, etc. The line continued as the royal house of **Hapsburg-Lorraine,** ruling in Austria (1806–48) and Austria-Hungary (1848–1918)

hara-kiri *or* **hari-kari** (formerly, in Japan) ritual suicide by disembowelment with a sword when disgraced or under sentence of death

Harald I called *Harald Fairhair.* ?850–933, first king of Norway: his rule caused emigration to the British Isles

Harald III surname *Hardraade.* 1015–66, king of Norway (1047–66); invaded England (1066) and died at the battle of Stamford Bridge

Harappa an ancient city in the Punjab in NW Pakistan: one of the centres of the Indus civilization that flourished from 2500 to 1700 BC; probably destroyed by Indo-European invaders

Harar *or* **Harrer** a city in E Ethiopia: former capital of the Muslim state of Adal. Pop: 96 000 (2005 est)

Harare the capital of Zimbabwe, in the northeast: University of Zimbabwe (1957); industrial and commercial centre. Pop: 1 527 000 (2005 est)

Harbin a city in NE China, capital of Heilongjiang province on the Songhua River: founded by the Russians in 1897; centre of tsarist activities after the October Revolution in Russia (1917). Pop: 2 989 000 (2005 est)

harbinger *Obsolete* a person sent in advance of a royal party or army to obtain lodgings for them

harbour *or US* **harbor** a sheltered port

harbour master an official in charge of a harbour

hard 1 *Chem* (of water) impairing the formation of a lather by soap 2 (of alcoholic drink) being a spirit rather than a wine, beer, etc. 3 (of a drug such as heroin, morphine, or cocaine) highly addictive 4 *Physics* (of radiation, such as gamma rays and X-rays) having high energy and the ability to penetrate solids 5 *Physics* (of a vacuum) almost complete 6 *Chiefly US* (of goods) durable 7 politically extreme 8 *Brit* a roadway across a foreshore

hard copy computer output printed on paper, as contrasted with machine-readable output such as magnetic tape

hardcore *Pop music* 1 a style of rock music characterized by short fast numbers with minimal melody and aggressive delivery 2 a type of dance music with a very fast beat

hard core *Engineering* material, such as broken bricks, stones, etc, used to form a foundation for a road, paving, building, etc.

hard disk a disk of rigid magnetizable material that is used to store data for computers: it is permanently mounted in its disk drive and usually has a storage capacity of a few gigabytes

harden a rough fabric made from hards

Hardenberg Friedrich von the original name of **Novalis**

Hardie (James) Keir 1856–1915, British Labour leader and politician, born in Scotland; the first parliamentary leader of the Labour Party

Harding Warren G(amaliel). 1865–1923, 29th president of the US (1921–23)

hard labour *Criminal law* (formerly) the penalty of compulsory physical labour imposed in addition to a sentence of imprisonment: abolished in England in 1948

hard pad (in dogs) an abnormal increase in the thickness of the foot pads: one of the clinical signs of canine distemper

hard palate the anterior bony portion of the roof of the mouth, extending backwards to the soft palate

hard sell an aggressive insistent technique of selling or advertising

hard shoulder *Brit* a surfaced verge running along the edge of a motorway for emergency stops

hardware 1 *Computing* the physical equipment used in a computer system, such as the central processing unit, peripheral devices, and memory 2 mechanical equipment, components, etc.

hard-wired 1 (of a circuit or instruction) permanently wired into a computer, replacing separate software 2 (of human behaviour) innate; not learned

hardwood 1 the wood of any of numerous broad-leaved dicotyledonous trees, such as oak, beech, ash, etc, as distinguished from the wood of a conifer 2 any tree from which this wood is obtained

hardy¹ (of plants) able to live out of doors throughout the winter

hardy² any blacksmith's tool made with a square shank so that it can be lodged in a square hole in an anvil

Hardy 1 Thomas 1840–1928, British novelist and poet. Most of his novels are set in his native Dorset (part of his fictional Wessex) and include *Far from the Madding Crowd* (1874), *The Return of the Native* (1878), *The Mayor of Casterbridge* (1886), *Tess of the d'Urbervilles* (1891), and *Jude the Obscure* (1895), after which his work consisted chiefly of verse 2 Sir **Thomas Masterman** 1769–1839, British naval officer, flag captain under Nelson (1799–1805): 1st Sea Lord (1830)

hare any solitary leporid mammal of the genus *Lepus*, such as *L. europaeus* (**European hare**). Hares are larger than rabbits, having longer ears and legs, and live in shallow nests (forms)

Hare 1 Sir **David** born 1947, British dramatist and theatre director: his plays include *Plenty* (1978), *Pravda* (with Howard Brenton, 1985), *The Secret Rapture* (1989), *Racing Demon* (1990), and *The Permanent Way* (2003) 2 **William** 19th century, Irish murderer and bodysnatcher: associate of William Burke

harebell a N temperate campanulaceous plant, *Campanula rotundifolia*, having slender stems and leaves, and bell-shaped pale blue flowers

harelip a congenital cleft or fissure in the midline of the upper lip, resembling the cleft upper lip of a hare, often occurring with cleft palate

harem or **hareem** a group of female animals of the same species that are the mates of a single male

Harfleur a port in N France, in Seine-Maritime department: important centre in the Middle Ages. Pop: 8517 (1999)

Hargeisa a city in NW Somalia: former capital of British Somaliland (1941–60); trading centre for nomadic herders. Pop: 400 000 (latest est)

Hargreaves James died 1778, English inventor of the spinning jenny

Haringey a borough of N Greater London. Pop: 224 700 (2003 est). Area: 30 sq km (12 sq miles)

Harlech a town in N Wales, in Gwynedd: noted for its ruined 13th-century castle overlooking Cardigan Bay: tourism. Pop: 1233 (2001)

Harlem a district of New York City, in NE Manhattan: now largely a Black ghetto

harlequin 1 *Theatre* a stock comic character originating in the commedia dell'arte; the foppish lover of Columbine in the English harlequinade. He is usually represented in diamond-patterned multicoloured tights, wearing a black mask 2 (of certain animals) having a white coat with irregular patches of black or other dark colour

harlequinade *Theatre* a play or part of a pantomime in which harlequin has a leading role

Harley Robert, 1st Earl of Oxford. 1661–1724, British statesman; head of the government (1710–14), negotiated the treaty of Utrecht (1713)

Harley Street a street in central London famous for its large number of medical specialists' consulting rooms

Harlow¹ Jean, real name *Harlean Carpentier*. 1911–37, US film actress, whose films include *Hell's Angels* (1930), *Red Dust* (1932), and *Bombshell* (1933)

Harlow² a town in SE England, in W Essex: designated a new town in 1947. Pop: 78 389 (2001 est)

harmonic 1 *Music* of, relating to, or belonging to harmony 2 *Maths* **a** capable of expression in the form of sine and cosine functions **b** of or relating to numbers whose reciprocals form an arithmetic progression 3 *Physics* of or concerned with an oscillation that has a frequency that is an integral multiple of a fundamental frequency 4 *Physics, Music* a component of a periodic quantity, such as a musical tone, with a frequency that is an integral multiple of the fundamental frequency. The **first harmonic** is the fundamental, the **second harmonic** (twice the fundamental frequency) is the **first overtone**, the **third harmonic** (three times the fundamental frequency) is the **second overtone**, etc. 5 *Music* (not in technical use) overtone: in this case, the first overtone is the first harmonic, etc.

harmonica a small wind instrument of the reed family in which reeds of graduated lengths set into a metal plate enclosed in a narrow oblong box are made to vibrate by blowing and sucking

harmonics 1 the science of musical sounds and their acoustic properties 2 the overtones of a fundamental note, as produced by lightly touching the string of a stringed instrument at one of its node points while playing

harmonist 1 a person skilled in the art and techniques of harmony 2 a person who combines and collates parallel narratives

harmonium a musical keyboard instrument of the reed organ family, in which air from pedal-operated bellows causes the reeds to vibrate

harmony 1 *Music* **a** any combination of notes sounded simultaneously **b** the vertically represented structure of a piece of music **c** the art or science concerned with the structure and combinations of chords **2** a collation of the material of parallel narratives, esp of the four Gospels

harness 1 an arrangement of leather straps buckled or looped together, fitted to a draught animal in order that the animal can be attached to and pull a cart **2** *Mountaineering* an arrangement of webbing straps that enables a climber to attach himself to the rope so that the impact of a fall is minimized **3** the total system of electrical leads for a vehicle or aircraft

Harney Peak a mountain in SW South Dakota: the highest peak in the Black Hills. Height: 2207 m (7242 ft)

Harnoncourt Nikolaus born 1929, Austrian conductor and cellist, noted for his performances using period instruments

Harold I surname *Harefoot.* died 1040, king of England (1037–40); son of Canute

Harold II ?1022–66, king of England (1066); son of Earl Godwin and successor of Edward the Confessor. His claim to the throne was disputed by William the Conqueror, who defeated him at the Battle of Hastings (1066)

harp 1 a large triangular plucked stringed instrument consisting of a soundboard connected to an upright pillar by means of a curved crossbar from which the strings extend downwards. The strings are tuned diatonically and may be raised in pitch either one or two semitones by the use of pedals (**double-action harp**). Basic key: B major; range: nearly seven octaves **2** an informal name (esp in pop music) for **harmonica**

harpoon a a barbed missile attached to a long cord and hurled or fired from a gun when hunting whales, etc. **b** (*as modifier*): *a harpoon gun*

harpsichord a horizontally strung stringed keyboard instrument, triangular in shape, consisting usually of two manuals controlling various sets of strings plucked by pivoted plectrums mounted on jacks. Some harpsichords have a pedal keyboard and stops by which the tone colour may be varied

harrier¹ any diurnal bird of prey of the genus *Circus*, having broad wings and long legs and tail and typically preying on small terrestrial animals: family *Accipitridae* (hawks, etc)

harrier² 1 a smallish breed of hound used originally for hare-hunting **2** a cross-country runner

Harriman W(illiam) Averell 1891–1986, US diplomat: negotiated the Nuclear Test Ban Treaty with the Soviet Union (1963); governor of New York (1955–58)

Harris¹ 1 Sir Arthur Travers, known as *Bomber Harris.* 1892–1984, British air marshal. He was commander-in-chief of Bomber Command of the RAF (1942–45) **2** Frank 1856–1931, British writer and journalist; his books include his autobiography *My Life and Loves* (1923–27) and *Contemporary Portraits* (1915–30) **3** Joel Chandler 1848–1908, US writer; creator of Uncle Remus **4** Roy 1898–1979, US composer, esp of orchestral and choral music incorporating American folk tunes

Harris² the S part of the island of Lewis with Harris, in

the Outer Hebrides. Pop: (including Lewis) 23 390 (latest est). Area: 500 sq km (190 sq miles)

Harrisburg a city in S Pennsylvania, on the Susquehanna River: the state capital. Pop: 48 322 (2003 est)

Harrison 1 Benjamin 1833–1901, 23rd president of the US (1889–93) **2** George 1943–2001, British rock singer, guitarist, and songwriter: a member of the Beatles (1962–70). His solo recordings include *All Things Must Pass* (1970) and *Cloud Nine* (1987) **3** Rex (Carey). 1908–90, British actor. His many films include *Major Barbara* (1940), *Blithe Spirit* (1945), and *My Fair Lady* (1964) **4** Tony born 1937, British poet, dramatist, and translator: best known for his poems for television and his translations for the stage **5** grandfather of Benjamin, **William Henry** 1773–1841, 9th president of the US (1841)

Harrogate a town in N England, in North Yorkshire: a former spa, now a centre for tourism and conferences. Pop: 70 811 (2001 est)

Harrow a borough of NW Greater London; site of an English boys' public school founded in 1571 at **Harrow-on-the-Hill**, a part of this borough. Pop: 210 700 (2003 est). Area: 51 sq km (20 sq miles)

hart the male of the deer, esp the red deer aged five years or more

Hart 1 Lorenz 1895–1943, US lyricist: collaborated with Richard Rodgers in writing musicals **2** Moss 1904–61, US dramatist: collaborated with George Kaufman on Broadway comedies and wrote libretti for musicals

Harte (Francis) Bret 1836–1902, US poet and short-story writer, noted for his sketches of Californian gold miners, such as *The Luck of Roaring Camp* (1870)

hartebeest *or* **hartbeest** 1 either of two large African antelopes, *Alcelaphus buselaphus* or *A. lichtensteini*, having an elongated muzzle, lyre-shaped horns, and a fawn-coloured coat **2** any similar and related animal, such as *Damaliscus hunteri* (**Hunter's hartebeest**)

Hartford a port in central Connecticut, on the Connecticut River: the state capital. Pop: 124 387 (2003 est)

Harthacanute, Hardecanute, *or* **Hardicanute** ?1019–42, king of Denmark (1035–42) and of England (1040–42); son of Canute

Hartlepool 1 a port in NE England, in Hartlepool unitary authority, Co. Durham, on the North Sea: greatly enlarged in 1967 by its amalgamation with West Hartlepool; engineering, clothing, food processing. Pop: 86 075 (2001) **2** a unitary authority in NE England, in Co. Durham: formerly (1974–96) part of the county of Cleveland. Pop: 90 200 (2003 est). Area: 93 sq km (36 sq miles)

Hartley 1 David 1705–57, English philosopher and physician. In *Observations of Man* (1749) he introduced the theory of psychological associationism **2** L(eslie) P(oles). 1895–1972, British novelist. His novels include the trilogy *The Shrimp and the Anemone* (1944), *The Sixth Heaven* (1946), and *Eustace and Hilda* (1947) as well as *The Go-Between* (1953)

Hartnell Sir Norman 1901–79, English couturier

Harun al-Rashid ?763–809 AD, Abbasid caliph of Islam (786–809), whose court at Baghdad was idealized in the *Arabian Nights*

harvest moon the full moon occurring nearest to the autumnal equinox

harvest mouse 1 a very small reddish-brown Eurasian mouse, *Micromys minutus,* inhabiting cornfields, hedgerows, etc, and feeding on grain and seeds: family *Muridae* **2 American harvest mouse** any small greyish mouse of the American genus *Reithrodontomys:* family *Cricetidae*

Harvey William 1578–1657, English physician who discovered the mechanism of blood circulation, expounded in *On the motion of the heart* (1628)

Harwell a village in S England, in Oxfordshire: atomic research station (1947)

Harwich a port in SE England, in NE Essex on the North Sea. Pop: 20 130 (2001)

Haryana a state of NE India, formed in 1966 from the Hindi-speaking parts of the state of Punjab. Capital: Chandigarh (shared with Punjab). Pop: 21 082 989 (2001 est). Area: 44 506 sq km (17 182 sq miles)

Hasdrubal died 207 BC, Carthaginian general: commanded the Carthaginian army in Spain (218–211); joined his brother Hannibal in Italy and was killed at the Metaurus

Hašek Jaroslav 1883–1923, Czech novelist and short-story writer; author of *The Good Soldier Schweik* (1923)

hashish *or* **hasheesh 1** a purified resinous extract of the dried flower tops of the female hemp plant, used as a hallucinogenic **2** any hallucinogenic substance prepared from this resin

Hassan II 1929–1999, king of Morocco (1961–99)

Hasselt a market town in E Belgium, capital of Limburg province. Pop: 69 127 (2004 est)

hassium a synthetic element produced in small quantities by high-energy ion bombardment. Symbol: Hs; atomic no. 108

hassock 1 a firm upholstered cushion used for kneeling on, esp in church **2** a thick clump of grass

Hastings[1] **1** Gavin born 1962, Scottish Rugby Union footballer; played for Scotland 1986–95 **2** Warren 1732–1818, British administrator in India; governor general of Bengal (1773–85). He implemented important reforms but was impeached by parliament (1788) on charges of corruption; acquitted in 1795

Hastings[2] **1** a port in SE England, in East Sussex on the English Channel: near the site of the **Battle of Hastings** (1066), in which William the Conqueror defeated King Harold; chief of the Cinque Ports. Pop: 85 828 (2001) **2** a town in New Zealand, on E North Island: centre of a rich agricultural and fruit-growing region. Pop: 71 100 (2004 est)

hatch[1] a group of newly hatched animals

hatch[2] **1** a covering for a hatchway **2** short for **hatchway 3** an opening in a wall between a kitchen and a dining area **4** the lower half of a divided door **5** a sluice or sliding gate in a dam, dyke, or weir

hatchback 1 a a sloping rear end of a car having a single door that is lifted to open **b** (*as modifier*): *a hatchback model* **2** a car having such a rear end

hatchet a short axe used for chopping wood, etc.

hatchling a young animal that has newly emerged from an egg

hatchway 1 an opening in the deck of a vessel to provide access below **2** a similar opening in a wall, floor, ceiling, or roof, usually fitted with a lid or door

Hatfield a market town in S central England, in Hertfordshire, with a new town of the same name built on the outskirts: university (1992); site of **Hatfield House** (1607–11), the seat of the Cecil family. Pop: 32 281 (2001)

Hathaway Anne ?1557–1623, wife of William Shakespeare

Hathor (in ancient Egyptian religion) the mother of Horus and goddess of creation

Hatshepsut *or* **Hatshepset** queen of Egypt of the 18th dynasty (?1512–1482 BC). She built a great mortuary temple at Deir el Bahri near Thebes

Hatteras Cape a promontory off the E coast of North Carolina, on **Hatteras Island,** which is situated between Pamlico Sound and the Atlantic: known as the "Graveyard of the Atlantic" for its danger to shipping

Hattersley Roy (**Sydney George**), Baron Hattersley of Sparkbrook. born 1932, British Labour politician; deputy leader of the Labour Party (1983–92); shadow home secretary (1980–83; 1987–92)

Haughey Charles James born 1925, Irish politician; leader of the Fianna Fáil party; prime minister of the Republic of Ireland (1979–81; 1982; 1987–92)

haulage a rate or charge levied for the transportation of goods, esp by rail

haulier *or US* **hauler** a person or firm that transports goods by lorry; one engaged in road haulage

haulm *or* **halm 1** the stems or stalks of beans, peas, potatoes, grasses, etc, collectively, as used for thatching, bedding, etc. **2** a single stem of such a plant

haunch 1 the human hip or fleshy hindquarter of an animal, esp a horse or similar quadruped **2** *Architect* the part of an arch between the impost and the apex

Hauptmann Gerhart 1862–1946, German naturalist, dramatist, novelist, and poet. His works include the historical drama *The Weavers* (1892): Nobel prize for literature 1912

Hauraki Gulf an inlet of the Pacific in New Zealand, on the N coast of North Island

Haussmann Georges-Eugène, Baron. 1809–91, French town planner, noted for his major rebuilding of Paris in the reign of Napoleon III

hautboy a strawberry, *Fragaria moschata*, of central Europe and Asia, with large fruit

Haute-Garonne a department of SW France, in Midi-Pyrénées region. Capital: Toulouse. Pop: 1 102 919 (2003 est). Area: 6367 sq km (2483 sq miles)

Haute-Loire a department of S central France, in Auvergne region. Capital: Le Puy. Pop: 213 993 (2003 est). Area: 5001 sq km (1950 sq miles)

Haute-Marne a department of NE France, in Champagne-Ardenne region. Capital: Chaumont. Pop: 190 983 (2003 est). Area: 6257 sq km (2440 sq miles)

Haute-Normandie a region of NW France, on the English Channel: generally fertile and flat

Hautes-Alpes a department of SE France in Provence-Alpes-Côte d'Azur region. Capital: Gap. Pop: 126 810 (2003 est). Area: 5643 sq km (2201 sq miles)

Haute-Savoie a department of E France, in Rhône-Alpes region. Capital: Annecy. Pop: 663 810 (2003 est).

Area: 4958 sq km (1934 sq miles)

Haute-Vienne a department of W central France, in Limousin region. Capital: Limoges. Pop: 353 788 (2003 est). Area: 5555 sq km (2166 sq miles)

Haut-Rhin a department of E France in Alsace region. Capital: Colmar. Pop: 722 692 (2003 est). Area: 3566 sq km (1377 sq miles)

Hauts-de-Seine a department of N central France, in Île-de-France region just west of Paris: formed in 1964. Capital: Nanterre. Pop: 1 470 706 (2003 est). Area: 175 sq km (68 sq miles)

Havana the capital of Cuba, a port in the northwest on the Gulf of Mexico: the largest city in the Caribbean; founded in 1514 as San Cristóbal de la Habana by Diego Velásquez. Pop: 2 192 000 (2005 est)

Havant a market town in S England, in SE Hampshire. Pop: 45 435 (2001)

Havel¹ Václav born 1936, Czech dramatist and statesman: founder of the Civil Forum movement for political change: president of Czechoslovakia (1989–92) and of the Czech Republic (1993–2003). His plays include *The Garden Party* (1963) and *Redevelopment* (1989)

Havel² a river in E Germany, flowing south to Berlin, then west and north to join the River Elbe. Length: about 362 km (225 miles)

haven a port, harbour, or other sheltered place for shipping

Havering a borough of NE Greater London, formed in 1965 from Romford and Hornchurch (both previously in Essex). Pop: 224 600 (2003 est). Area: 120 sq km (46 sq miles)

haw¹ 1 the round or oval fruit (a pome) of the hawthorn, usually red or yellow, containing one to five seeds 2 another name for **hawthorn**

haw² the nictitating membrane of a horse or other domestic animal

Hawaii a state of the US in the central Pacific, consisting of over 20 volcanic islands and atolls, including Hawaii, Maui, Oahu, Kauai, and Molokai: discovered by Captain Cook in 1778; annexed by the US in 1898; naval base at Pearl Harbor attacked by the Japanese in 1941, a major cause of US entry into World War II; became a state in 1959. Capital: Honolulu. Pop: 1 257 608 (2003 est). Area: 16 640 sq km (6425 sq miles)

Hawaiian 1 a native or inhabitant of Hawaii, esp one descended from Melanesian or Tahitian immigrants 2 a language of Hawaii belonging to the Malayo-Polynesian family

Hawaiki NZ a legendary Pacific island from which the Māoris migrated to New Zealand by canoe

Hawes Water a lake in NW England, in the Lake District: provides part of Manchester's water supply; extended by damming from 4 km (2.5 miles) to 6 km (4 miles)

Haw-Haw Lord See (William) **Joyce**

Hawick a town in SE Scotland, in S central Scottish Borders: knitwear industry. Pop: 14 573 (2001)

hawk 1 any of various diurnal birds of prey of the family Accipitridae, such as the goshawk and Cooper's hawk, typically having short rounded wings and a long tail 2 US and Canadian any of various other falconiform birds, including the falcons but not the eagles or vultures 3

Politics a person who advocates or supports war or warlike policies

Hawke 1 Edward, 1st Baron. 1705–81, British admiral. He destroyed the French fleet in Quiberon Bay (1759), preventing a French invasion of England 2 Robert (James Lee), known as *Bob*. born 1929, Australian statesman; prime minister of Australia (1983–91)

hawker¹ a person who travels from place to place selling goods

hawker² a person who hunts with hawks, falcons, etc.

Hawking Stephen William born 1942, British physicist. Stricken with a progressive nervous disease since the 1960s, he has nevertheless been a leader in cosmological theory. His *A Brief History of Time* (1987) was a bestseller

Hawkins 1 Coleman 1904–69, US pioneer of the tenor saxophone for jazz 2 Sir John 1532–95, English naval commander and slave trader, treasurer of the navy (1577–89); commander of a squadron in the fleet that defeated the Spanish Armada (1588)

Hawks Howard (Winchester). 1896–1977, US film director. His films include *Sergeant York* (1941) and *The Big Sleep* (1946)

Hawksmoor Nicholas 1661–1736, English architect. His designs include All Souls', Oxford, and a number of London churches, notably St Anne's, Limehouse

Haworth¹ Sir Walter Norman 1883–1950, British biochemist, who shared the Nobel prize for chemistry (1937) for being the first to synthesize ascorbic acid (vitamin C)

Haworth² a village in N England, in Bradford unitary authority, West Yorkshire: home of Charlotte, Emily, and Anne Brontë. Pop: 6078 (2001)

hawser *Nautical* a large heavy rope

hawthorn any of various thorny trees or shrubs of the N temperate rosaceous genus *Crataegus*, esp *C. oxyacantha*, having white or pink flowers and reddish fruits (haws)

Hawthorne Nathaniel 1804–64, US novelist and short-story writer: his works include the novels *The Scarlet Letter* (1850) and *The House of the Seven Gables* (1851) and the children's stories *Tanglewood Tales* (1853)

hay or **hey** 1 a circular figure in country dancing 2 a former country dance in which the dancers wove in and out of a circle

Hay Will 1888–1949, British music-hall comedian, who later starred in films, such as *Oh, Mr Porter!* (1937)

Haydn 1 (Franz) Joseph 1732–1809, Austrian composer, who played a major part in establishing the classical forms of the symphony and the string quartet. His other works include the oratorios *The Creation* (1796–98) and *The Seasons* (1798–1801) 2 his brother, Johann Michael 1737–1806, Austrian composer, esp of Church music

Hayek Friedrich August von 1899–1992, British economist and political philosopher, born in Austria: noted for his advocacy of free-market ideas; shared the Nobel prize for economics 1974

Hayes Rutherford B(irchard). 1822–93, 19th president of the US (1877–81)

hay fever an allergic reaction to pollen, dust, etc, characterized by sneezing, runny nose, and watery eyes due to inflammation of the mucous membranes of the eyes and nose

hazard 1 *Golf* an obstacle such as a bunker, a road, rough, water, etc. **2** a gambling game played with two dice **3** *Real Tennis* **a** the receiver's side of the court **b** one of the winning openings **4** *Billiards* a scoring stroke made either when a ball other than the striker's is pocketed (**winning hazard**) or the striker's cue ball itself (**losing hazard**)

hazard lights the indicator lights of a motor vehicle when flashing simultaneously to indicate that the vehicle is stationary and temporarily obstructing the traffic

haze *Meteorol* **a** reduced visibility in the air as a result of condensed water vapour, dust, etc, in the atmosphere **b** the moisture or dust causing this

hazel 1 any of several shrubs of the N temperate genus *Corylus*, esp *C. avellana*, having oval serrated leaves and edible rounded brown nuts: family *Corylaceae* **2** the wood of any of these trees **3** short for **hazelnut 4 a** a light yellowish-brown colour **b** (*as adjective*): *a pair of hazel eyes*

hazelnut the nut of a hazel shrub, having a smooth shiny hard shell

Hazlitt **William** 1778–1830, English critic and essayist: works include *Characters of Shakespeare's Plays* (1817), *Table Talk* (1821), and *The Plain Speaker* (1826)

he¹ a a children's game in which one player chases the others in an attempt to touch one of them, who then becomes the chaser **b** the person chasing

he² the fifth letter of the Hebrew alphabet (ה), transliterated as *h*

head 1 the upper or front part of the body in vertebrates, including man, that contains and protects the brain, eyes, mouth, and nose and ears when present **2** the corresponding part of an invertebrate animal **3** the froth on the top of a glass of beer **4** *Botany* **a** a dense inflorescence such as that of the daisy and other composite plants **b** any other compact terminal part of a plant, such as the leaves of a cabbage or lettuce **5** the pus-filled tip or central part of a pimple, boil, etc. **6** the source or origin of a river or stream **7** a headland or promontory, esp a high one **8** the obverse of a coin, usually bearing a portrait of the head or a full figure of a monarch, deity, etc. **9** *Nautical* **a** the front part of a ship or boat **b** (in sailing ships) the upper corner or edge of a sail **c** the top of any spar or derrick **d** any vertical timber cut to shape **e** 10 the taut membrane of a drum, tambourine, etc. **11 a** the height of the surface of liquid above a specific point, esp when considered or used as a measure of the pressure at that point **b** pressure of water, caused by height or velocity, measured in terms of a vertical column of water **c** any pressure **12** *Slang* **a** a person who regularly takes drugs, esp LSD or cannabis **b** (*in combination*): *an acid head* **13** a device on a turning or boring machine, such as a lathe, that is equipped with one or more cutting tools held to the work by this device **14** an electromagnet that can read, write, or erase information on a magnetic medium such as a magnetic tape, disk, or drum, used in computers, tape recorders, etc. **15** *Informal* short for **headmaster 16 a** the head of a horse considered as a narrow margin in the outcome of a race (in the phrase **win by a head**) **b** any narrow margin of victory (in the phrase (**win**) **by a**

head) **17** *Informal* short for **headache 18** *Curling* the stones lying in the house after all 16 have been played **19** *Bowls* the jack and the bowls that have been played considered together as a target area **20 against the head** *Rugby* from the opposing side's put-in to the scrum

Head Edith 1907–81, US dress designer: won many Oscars for her Hollywood film costume designs

headache pain in the head, caused by dilation of cerebral arteries, muscle contraction, insufficient oxygen in the cerebral blood, reaction to drugs, etc.

head-banger *Slang* a heavy-metal rock fan

header 1 a reservoir, tank, or hopper that maintains a gravity feed or a static fluid pressure in an apparatus **2** a manifold for distributing a fluid supply amongst a number of passages **3** a machine that trims the heads from castings, forgings, etc, or one that forms heads, as in wire, to make nails **4** a person who operates such a machine **5** the action of striking a ball with the head **6** *Computing* a block of data on a tape or disk providing information about the size, location, etc, of a file

headgear any part of a horse's harness that is worn on the head

head-hunting 1 the practice among certain peoples of removing the heads of slain enemies and preserving them as trophies **2** *US, slang* the destruction or neutralization of political opponents

heading 1 the angle between the direction of an aircraft and a specified meridian, often due north **2** the compass direction parallel to the keel of a vessel

headland a narrow area of land jutting out into a sea, lake, etc.

headlight *or* **headlamp** a powerful light, equipped with a reflector and attached to the front of a motor vehicle, locomotive, etc.

headmaster a male principal of a school

headship *Education, Brit* the position of headmaster or headmistress of a school

headshrinker a head-hunter who shrinks the heads of his victims

headway 1 motion in a forward direction **2** the distance or time between consecutive trains, buses, etc, on the same route

headwind a wind blowing directly against the course of an aircraft or ship

health 1 the state of being bodily and mentally vigorous and free from disease **2** the general condition of body and mind

health centre (in Britain) premises, owned by a local authority, providing health care for the local community and usually housing a group practice, nursing staff, a child-health clinic, X-ray facilities, etc.

health farm a residential establishment, often in the country, visited by those who wish to improve their health by losing weight, eating healthy foods, taking exercise, etc.

health visitor (in Britain) a nurse employed by a district health authority to visit people in their homes and give help and advice on health and social welfare, esp to mothers of preschool children, to the handicapped, and to elderly people

Heaney Seamus (**Justin**). born 1939, Irish poet and critic, born in Northern Ireland. His collections include *Death*

of a Naturalist (1966), *North* (1975), *The Haw Lantern* (1987), *The Spirit Level* (1996), and *Electric Light* (2001). Nobel prize for literature 1995

hearing 1 the faculty or sense by which sound is perceived 2 the range within which sound can be heard; earshot 3 the investigation of a matter by a court of law, esp the preliminary inquiry into an indictable crime by magistrates 4 a formal or official trial of an action or lawsuit

hearing aid a device for assisting the hearing of partially deaf people, typically consisting of a small battery-powered electronic amplifier with microphone and earphone, worn by a deaf person in or behind the ear

hearing dog a dog that has been specially trained to help deaf or partially deaf people by alerting them to sounds such as a ringing doorbell, an alarm, etc.

hearse a vehicle, such as a specially designed car or carriage, used to carry a coffin to a place of worship and ultimately to a cemetary or crematorium

Hearst William Randolph 1863–1951, US newspaper publisher, whose newspapers were noted for their sensationalism

heart 1 the hollow muscular organ in vertebrates whose contractions propel the blood through the circulatory system. In mammals it consists of a right and left atrium and a right and left ventricle 2 the corresponding organ or part in invertebrates 3 the core of a tree 4 a a red heart-shaped symbol on a playing card b a card with one or more of these symbols or (*when pl.*) the suit of cards so marked

▷www.americanheart.org

heart attack any sudden severe instance of abnormal heart functioning, esp coronary thrombosis

heartburn a burning sensation beneath the breastbone caused by irritation of the oesophagus, as from regurgitation of the contents of the stomach

heart failure 1 a condition in which the heart is unable to pump an adequate amount of blood to the tissues, usually resulting in breathlessness, swollen ankles, etc. 2 sudden and permanent cessation of the heartbeat, resulting in death

hearth the bottom part of a metallurgical furnace in which the molten metal is produced or contained

heartland the central region of a country or continent

heartwood the central core of dark hard wood in tree trunks, consisting of nonfunctioning xylem tissue that has become blocked with resins, tannins, and oils

heat 1 a the energy transferred as a result of a difference in temperature b the random kinetic energy of the atoms, molecules, or ions in a substance or body 2 the sensation caused in the body by heat energy; warmth 3 a period or condition of sexual excitement in female mammals that occurs at oestrus 4 *Sport* a a preliminary eliminating contest in a competition b a single section of a contest 5 **on** *or* **in heat** a (of some female mammals) sexually receptive b in a state of sexual excitement

heater 1 any device for supplying heat, such as a hot-air blower, radiator, convector, etc. 2 *Electronics* a conductor carrying a current that indirectly heats the cathode in some types of valve

heath 1 *Brit* a large open area, usually with sandy soil

and scrubby vegetation, esp heather 2 any low-growing evergreen ericaceous shrub of the Old World genus *Erica* and related genera, having small bell-shaped typically pink or purple flowers 3 any of several nonericaceous heathlike plants, such as sea heath 4 *Austral* any of various heathlike plants of the genus *Epacris*: family *Epacridaceae* 5 any of various small brown satyrid butterflies of the genus *Coenonympha*, with coppery-brown wings, esp the **large heath** (*C. tullia*)

Heath Sir **Edward** (**Richard George**). born 1916, British statesman; leader of the Conservative Party (1965–75); prime minister (1970–74)

heathen a person who does not acknowledge the God of Christianity, Judaism, or Islam; pagan

heather 1 a low-growing evergreen Eurasian ericaceous shrub, *Calluna vulgaris*, that grows in dense masses on open ground and has clusters of small bell-shaped typically pinkish-purple flowers 2 any of certain similar plants 3 a purplish-red to pinkish-purple colour 4 of or relating to interwoven yarns of mixed colours

Heath Robinson (of a mechanical device) absurdly complicated in design and having a simple function

heatstroke a condition resulting from prolonged exposure to intense heat, characterized by high fever and in severe cases convulsions and coma

heat wave 1 a continuous spell of abnormally hot weather 2 an extensive slow-moving air mass at a relatively high temperature

heave the horizontal displacement of rock strata at a fault

heaven 1 *Christianity* a the abode of God and the angels b a place or state of communion with God after death 2 the sky, firmament or space surrounding the earth 3 (in any of various mythologies) a place, such as Elysium or Valhalla, to which those who have died in the gods' favour are brought to dwell in happiness

Heaviside Oliver 1850–1925, English physicist. Independently of Kennelly, he predicted (1902) the existence of an ionized gaseous layer in the upper atmosphere (the **Heaviside layer**); he also contributed to telegraphy

heavy 1 having a relatively high density 2 (of soil) having a high clay content; cloggy 3 (of an industry) engaged in the large-scale complex manufacture of capital goods or extraction of raw materials 4 cloudy or overcast, esp threatening rain 5 (of an element or compound) being or containing an isotope with greater atomic weight than that of the naturally occurring element 6 *Horse racing* (of the going on a racecourse) soft and muddy 7 a a villainous role b an actor who plays such a part 8 *Scot* strong bitter beer

heavy-duty subject to high import or export taxes

heavy metal a metal with a high specific gravity
▷www.heavymetal.about.com
▷www.metal-rules.com

heavy water water that has been electrolytically decomposed to enrich it in the deuterium isotope in the form HDO or D_2O

heavyweight 1 a a professional boxer weighing more than 175 pounds (79 kg) b an amateur boxer weighing more than 81 kg (179 pounds) c (*as modifier*): *the world heavyweight championship* 2 a wrestler in a similar weight category (usually over 214 pounds (97 kg))

Hebbel Christian Friedrich 1813–63, German dramatist and lyric poet, whose historical works were influenced by Hegel; his major plays are *Maria Magdalena* (1844), *Herodes und Marianne* (1850), and the trilogy *Die Nibelungen* (1862)

Hebei, Hopeh, *or* **Hopei** a province of NE China, on the Gulf of Chihli: important for the production of winter wheat, cotton, and coal. Capital: Shijiazhuang. Pop: 67 690 000 (2003 est). Area: 202 700 sq km (79 053 sq miles)

Hebrew 1 the ancient language of the Hebrews, revived as the official language of Israel. It belongs to the Canaanitic branch of the Semitic subfamily of the Afro-Asiatic family of languages **2** a member of an ancient Semitic people claiming descent from Abraham; an Israelite

▷www.wsu.edu.8080/~dee/HEBREWS/
HEBREWS.HTM

Hebrews a book of the New Testament

Hebron a city in the West Bank: famous for the Haram, which includes the cenotaphs of Abraham and Sarah, Isaac and Rebecca, and Jacob and Leah. Pop: 168 000 (2005 est)

heck *Northern English, dialect* a frame for obstructing the passage of fish in a river

heckle an instrument for combing flax or hemp

hectare one hundred ares. 1 hectare is equivalent to 10 000 square metres or 2.471 acres.

hectic 1 associated with, peculiar to, or symptomatic of tuberculosis (esp in the phrases **hectic fever, hectic flush**) **2** a hectic fever or flush **3** *Rare* a person who is consumptive or who experiences a hectic fever or flush

hedge a row of shrubs, bushes, or trees forming a boundary to a field, garden, etc.

hedgehog 1 any small nocturnal Old World mammal of the genus *Erinaceus*, such as *E. europaeus*, and related genera, having a protective covering of spines on the back: family *Erinaceidae*, order *Insectivora* (insectivores) **2** any other insectivores of the family *Erinaceidae*, such as the moon rat **3** *US* any of various other spiny animals, esp the porcupine

hedgerow a hedge of shrubs or low trees growing along a bank, esp one bordering a field or lane

hedge sparrow a small brownish European songbird, *Prunella modularis*: family *Prunellidae* (accentors)

hedonism *Ethics* **a** the doctrine that moral value can be defined in terms of pleasure **b** the doctrine that the pursuit of pleasure is the highest good

heel¹ 1 the back part of the human foot from the instep to the lower part of the ankle **2** the corresponding part in other vertebrates **3** *Horticulture* the small part of the parent plant that remains attached to a young shoot cut for propagation and that ensures more successful rooting **4** *Nautical* **a** the bottom of a mast **b** the after end of a ship's keel **5** the back part of a golf club head where it bends to join the shaft **6** *Rugby* possession of the ball as obtained from a scrum (esp in the phrase **get the heel**)

heel² inclined position from the vertical

Heerlen a city in the SE Netherlands, in Limburg province: industrial centre of a coal-mining region.

Pop: 94 000 (2003 est)

Hefei *or* **Hofei** a city in SE China, capital of Anhui province: administrative and commercial centre in a rice- and cotton-growing region. Pop: 1 320 000 (2005 est)

Hegel Georg Wilhelm Friedrich 1770–1831, German philosopher, who created a fundamentally influential system of thought. His view of man's mind as the highest expression of the Absolute is expounded in *The Phenomenology of Mind* (1807). He developed his concept of dialectic, in which the contradiction between a proposition (thesis) and its antithesis is resolved at a higher level of truth (synthesis), in *Science of Logic* (1812–16)

hegemony ascendancy or domination of one power or state within a league, confederation, etc, or of one social class over others

Hegira *or* **Hejira 1** the departure of Mohammed from Mecca to Medina in 622 AD; the starting point of the Muslim era **2** the Muslim era itself

Heidegger Martin 1889–1976, German existentialist philosopher: he expounded his ontological system in *Being and Time* (1927)

Heidelberg a city in SW Germany, in NW Baden-Württemberg on the River Neckar: capital of the Palatinate from the 13th century until 1719; famous castle (begun in the 12th century) and university (1386), the oldest in Germany. Pop: 142 959 (2003 est)

heifer a young cow

Heifetz Jascha 1901–87, US violinist, born in Russia

height *Astronomy* the angular distance of a celestial body above the horizon

height of land *US and Canadian* a watershed

Heilbronn a city in SW Germany, in N Baden-Württemberg on the River Neckar. Pop: 120 705 (2003 est)

Heilongjiang *or* **Heilungkiang** a province of NE China, in Manchuria: coal-mining, with placer gold in some rivers. Capital: Harbin. Pop: 38 150 000 (2003 est). Area: 464 000 sq km (179 000 sq miles)

Heine Heinrich 1797–1856, German poet and essayist, whose chief poetic work is *Das Buch der Lieder* (1827). Many of his poems have been set to music, notably by Schubert and Schumann

Heinkel Ernst Heinrich 1888–1958, German aircraft designer. His company provided many military aircraft in World Wars I and II, including the first jet-powered plane

heir *Civil law* the person legally succeeding to all property of a deceased person, irrespective of whether such person died testate or intestate, and upon whom devolves as well as the rights the duties and liabilities attached to the estate

heir apparent *Property law* a person whose right to succeed to certain property cannot be defeated, provided such person survives his ancestor

heirloom *Property law* a chattel inherited by special custom or in accordance with the terms of a will

heir presumptive *Property law* a person who expects to succeed to an estate but whose right may be defeated by the birth of one nearer in blood to the ancestor

Heisenberg Werner Karl 1901–76, German physicist. He contributed to quantum mechanics and formulated the uncertainty principle (1927): Nobel prize for physics 1932

Heitler Walter 1904–81, German physicist, noted for his work on chemical bonds

Hejaz, Hedjaz, *or* **Hijaz** a region of W Saudi Arabia, along the Red Sea and the Gulf of Aqaba: formerly an independent kingdom; united with Nejd in 1932 to form Saudi Arabia. Area: about 348 600 sq km (134 600 sq miles)

Hekla a volcano in SW Iceland: several craters, subject to fairly frequent eruptions in recent times. Height: 1491 m (4892 ft)

Helena¹ Saint ?248–?328 AD, Roman empress, mother of Constantine I. After converting to Christianity (313) she made a pilgrimage to the Holy Land (?326) where she supposedly discovered the cross on which Christ died. Feast day: May 21

Helena² a city in W Montana: the state capital. Pop: 26 718 (2003 est)

Helicon a mountain in Greece, in Boeotia: location of the springs of Hippocrene and Aganippe, believed by the Ancient Greeks to be the source of poetic inspiration and the home of the Muses. Height: 1749 m (5738 ft)

helicopter an aircraft capable of hover, vertical flight, and horizontal flight in any direction. Most get all of their lift and propulsion from the rotation of overhead blades

▷www.helicoptermuseum.org/museum/
   links.htm
▷www.helikopter.li

Heligoland a small island in the North Sea, one of the North Frisian Islands, separated from the coast of NW Germany by the **Heligoland Bight**: administratively part of the German state of Schleswig-Holstein: a large island in early medieval times, now eroded to an area of about 150 hectares (380 acres); ceded by Britain to Germany in 1890 in exchange for Zanzibar

Heliogabalus *or* **Elagabalus** original name *Varius Avitus Bassianus*. ?204–222 AD, Roman emperor (218–222). His reign was notorious for debauchery and extravagance

heliograph 1 an instrument with mirrors and a shutter used for sending messages in Morse code by reflecting the sun's rays 2 a device used to photograph the sun

Heliopolis 1 (in ancient Egypt) a city near the apex of the Nile delta: a centre of sun worship 2 the Ancient Greek name for **Baalbek**

heliotrope 1 any boraginaceous plant of the genus *Heliotropium*, esp the South American *H. arborescens*, cultivated for its small fragrant purple flowers 2 **garden heliotrope** a widely cultivated valerian, *Valeriana officinalis*, with clusters of small pink, purple, or white flowers 3 any of various plants that turn towards the sun 4 **a** a bluish-violet to purple colour **b** (*as adjective*): *a heliotrope dress*

heliport an airport for helicopters

helium a very light nonflammable colourless odourless element that is an inert gas, occurring in certain natural gases: used in balloons and in cryogenic research. Symbol: He; atomic no.: 2; atomic wt.: 4.002602; density: 0.1785 kg/m³; at normal pressures it is liquid down to absolute zero; melting pt.: below –272.2°C; boiling pt.: –268.90°C

helix 1 a curve that lies on a cylinder or cone, at a constant angle to the line segments making up the surface; spiral 2 the incurving fold that forms the margin of the external ear 3 another name for **volute** 4 any terrestrial gastropod mollusc of the genus *Helix*, which includes the garden snail (*H. aspersa*)

hell 1 *Christianity* **a** the place or state of eternal punishment of the wicked after death, with Satan as its ruler **b** forces of evil regarded as residing there 2 (in various religions and cultures) the abode of the spirits of the dead 3 *Now rare* a gambling house, booth, etc.

hellebore 1 any plant of the Eurasian ranunculaceous genus *Helleborus*, esp *H. niger* (black hellebore), typically having showy flowers and poisonous parts 2 any of various liliaceous plants of the N temperate genus *Veratrum*, esp *V. album*, that have greenish flowers and yield alkaloids used in the treatment of heart disease

Hellenic 1 of or relating to the ancient or modern Greeks or their language 2 of or relating to ancient Greece or the Greeks of the classical period (776–323 BC) 3 another word for **Greek** 4 a branch of the Indo-European family of languages consisting of Greek in its various ancient and modern dialects

Hellenism 1 the principles, ideals, and pursuits associated with classical Greek civilization 2 the spirit or national character of the Greeks 3 conformity to, imitation of, or devotion to the culture of ancient Greece 4 the cosmopolitan civilization of the Hellenistic world

Hellenistic *or* **Hellenistical** 1 characteristic of or relating to Greek civilization in the Mediterranean world, esp from the death of Alexander the Great (323 BC) to the defeat of Antony and Cleopatra (30 BC) 2 of or relating to the Greeks or to Hellenism

▷www.isidore-of-seville.com/hellenistic
▷www.hapcdt.plus.com/ebooks/
   hellenisticworld.html

Heller Joseph 1923–99, US novelist. His works include *Catch 22* (1961), *God Knows* (1984), *Picture This* (1988), and *Closing Time* (1994)

Helles Cape a cape in NW Turkey, at the S end of the Gallipoli Peninsula

hellfire 1 the torment and punishment of hell, envisaged as eternal fire 2 characterizing sermons or preachers that emphasize this aspect of Christian belief

Hellman Lillian 1905–84, US dramatist. Her works include the plays *The Little Foxes* (1939), *The Searching Wind* (1944), and the autobiographical *Scoundrel Time* (1976)

helm *Nautical* **a** the wheel, tiller, or entire apparatus by which a vessel is steered **b** the position of the helm: that is, on the side of the keel opposite from that of the rudder

Helmand a river in S Asia, rising in E Afghanistan and flowing generally southwest to a marshy lake, Hamun Helmand, on the border with Iran. Length: 1400 km (870 miles)

helmet *Biology* a part or structure resembling a helmet, esp the upper part of the calyx of certain flowers

Helmholtz Baron Hermann Ludwig Ferdinand von 1821–94, German physiologist, physicist, and mathematician: helped to found the theory of the conservation of energy; invented the ophthalmoscope (1850);

and investigated the mechanics of sight and sound

Helmont Jean Baptiste van 1577–1644, Flemish chemist and physician. He was the first to distinguish gases and claimed to have coined the word *gas*

Helpmann Sir Robert 1909–86, Australian ballet dancer and choreographer: his ballets include *Miracle in the Gorbals* (1944), *Display* (1965), and *Yugen* (1965)

Helsingborg a port in SW Sweden, on the Sound opposite Helsingør, Denmark: changed hands several times between Denmark and Sweden, finally becoming Swedish in 1710; shipbuilding. Pop: 121 097 (2004 est)

Helsinki the capital of Finland, a port in the south on the Gulf of Finland: founded by Gustavus I of Sweden in 1550; replaced Turku as capital in 1812, while under Russian rule; university. Pop: 559 330 (2003 est)

Helvellyn a mountain in NW England, in the Lake District. Height: 949 m (3114 ft)

Helvetia 1 the Latin name for Switzerland 2 a Roman province in central Europe (1st century BC to the 5th century AD), corresponding to part of S Germany and parts of W and N Switzerland

Helvetian 1 another word for **Swiss** 2 a native or citizen of Switzerland

Hemel Hempstead a town in SE England, in W Hertfordshire: designated a new town in 1947. Pop: 83 118 (2001)

Hemingway Ernest 1899–1961, US novelist and short-story writer. His novels include *The Sun Also Rises* (1926), *A Farewell to Arms* (1929), *For Whom the Bell Tolls* (1940), and *The Old Man and the Sea* (1952): Nobel prize for literature 1954

hemipterous *or* **hemipteran** of, relating to, or belonging to the *Hemiptera*, a large order of insects having sucking or piercing mouthparts specialized as a beak (rostrum). The group is divided into the suborders *Homoptera* (aphids, cicadas, etc) and *Heteroptera* (water bugs, bedbugs, etc)

hemisphere 1 one half of a sphere 2 a half of the terrestrial globe, divided by the equator into **northern** and **southern** hemispheres or into **eastern** and **western** hemispheres by some meridians, usually 0° and 180° b a map or projection of one of the hemispheres 3 either of the two halves of the celestial sphere that lie north or south of the celestial equator

hemlock 1 an umbelliferous poisonous Eurasian plant, *Conium maculatum*, having finely divided leaves, spotted stems, and small white flowers 2 a poisonous drug derived from this plant 3 any coniferous tree of the genus *Tsuga*, of North America and E Asia, having short flat needles: family *Pinaceae* 4 the wood of any of these trees, used for lumber and as a source of wood pulp

hemp 1 an annual strong-smelling Asian plant, *Cannabis sativa*, having tough fibres, deeply lobed leaves, and small greenish flowers: family *Cannabidaeceae* 2 the fibre of this plant, used to make canvas, rope, etc. 3 any of several narcotic drugs obtained from some varieties of this plant, esp from Indian hemp

hen 1 the female of any bird, esp the adult female of the domestic fowl 2 the female of certain other animals, such as the lobster

Henan *or* **Honan** a province of N central China: the chief centre of early Chinese culture; mainly agricultural (the largest wheat-producing province in China). Capital: Zhengzhou. Pop: 96 670 000 (2003 est)

henbane a poisonous solanaceous European plant, *Hyoscyamus niger*, with sticky hairy leaves and funnel-shaped greenish flowers: yields the drug hyoscyamine

Henderson Arthur 1863–1935, British Labour politician. As foreign secretary (1929–31) he supported the League of Nations and international disarmament; Nobel peace prize 1934

Hendrix Jimi, full name *James Marshall Hendrix*. 1942–70, US rock guitarist, singer, and songwriter, noted for his innovative guitar technique. His recordings include "Purple Haze" (1967) and *Are you Experienced?* (1967)

Hendry Stephen born 1969, British snooker player: world champion 1990, 1992–96, and 1999

henge a circular area, often containing a circle of stones or sometimes wooden posts, dating from the Neolithic and Bronze Ages

Hengelo a city in the E Netherlands, in Overijssel province on the Twente Canal: industrial centre, esp for textiles. Pop: 81 000 (2003 est)

Hengist died ?488 AD, a leader, with his brother Horsa, of the first Jutish settlers in Britain; he is thought to have conquered Kent (?455)

Hengyang a city in SE central China, in Hunan province on the Xiang River. Pop: 853 000 (2005 est)

Henie Sonja 1912–69, Norwegian figure-skater

Henley-on-Thames a town in S England, in SE Oxfordshire on the River Thames: a riverside resort with an annual regatta. Pop: 10 513 (2001)

henna 1 a lythraceous shrub or tree, *Lawsonia inermis*, of Asia and N Africa, with white or reddish fragrant flowers 2 a reddish-brown or brown colour

Henrietta Maria 1609–69, queen of England (1625–49), the wife of Charles I; daughter of Henry IV of France. Her Roman Catholicism contributed to the unpopularity of the crown in the period leading to the Civil War

henry the derived SI unit of electric inductance; the inductance of a closed circuit in which an emf of 1 volt is produced when the current varies uniformly at the rate of 1 ampere per second.

Henry 1 Joseph 1797–1878, US physicist. He discovered the principle of electromagnetic induction independently of Faraday and constructed the first electromagnetic motor (1829). He also discovered self-induction and the oscillatory nature of electric discharges (1842) 2 Patrick 1736–99, American statesman and orator, a leading opponent of British rule during the War of American Independence 3 Prince, known as **Harry** born 1984, second son of Charles, Prince of Wales, and Diana, Princess of Wales

Henry I 1 known as *Henry the Fowler*. ?876–936 AD, duke of Saxony (912–36) and king of Germany (919–36): founder of the Saxon dynasty (918–1024) 2 1068–1135, king of England (1100–35) and duke of Normandy (1106–35); son of William the Conqueror: crowned in the absence of his elder brother, Robert II, duke of Normandy; conquered Normandy (1106)

Henry II 1 known as *Henry the Saint*. 973–1024, king of Germany and Holy Roman Emperor (1014–24): canonized in 1145 2 1133–89, first Plantagenet king of England (1154–89): extended his Anglo-French domains and instituted judicial and financial reforms. His attempts to control the church were opposed by Becket **3** 1519–59, king of France (1547–59); husband of Catherine de' Medici. He recovered Calais from the English (1558) and suppressed the Huguenots

Henry III 1 1017–56, king of Germany and Holy Roman Emperor (1046–56). He increased the power of the Empire but his religious policy led to rebellions **2** 1207–72, king of England (1216–72); son of John. His incompetent rule provoked the Barons' War (1264–67), during which he was captured by Simon de Montfort **3** 1551–89, king of France (1574–89). He plotted the massacre of Huguenots on St. Bartholomew's Day (1572) with his mother Catherine de' Medici, thus exacerbating the religious wars in France

Henry IV 1 1050–1106, Holy Roman Emperor (1084–1105) and king of Germany (1056–1105). He was excommunicated by Pope Gregory VII, whom he deposed (1084) **2** surnamed *Bolingbroke*. 1367–1413, first Lancastrian king of England (1399–1413); son of John of Gaunt: deposed Richard II (1399) and suppressed rebellions led by Owen Glendower and the Earl of Northumberland **3** known as *Henry of Navarre*. 1553–1610, first Bourbon king of France (1589–1610). He obtained toleration for the Huguenots with the Edict of Nantes (1598) and restored prosperity to France following the religious wars (1562–98)

Henry V 1 1081–1125, king of Germany (1089–1125) and Holy Roman Emperor (1111–25) **2** 1387–1422, king of England (1413–22); son of Henry IV. He defeated the French at the Battle of Agincourt (1415), conquered Normandy (1419), and was recognized as heir to the French throne (1420)

Henry VI 1 1165–97, king of Germany (1169–97) and Holy Roman Emperor (1190–97): added Sicily to the Empire **2** 1421–71, last Lancastrian king of England (1422–61; 1470–71); son of Henry V. His weak rule was blamed for the loss by 1453 of all his possessions in France except Calais; from 1454 he suffered periods of insanity which contributed to the outbreak of the Wars of the Roses (1455–85). He was deposed by Edward IV (1461) but was briefly restored to the throne (1470)

Henry VII 1 ?1275–1313, Holy Roman Emperor (1312–13) and, as Henry VI, count of Luxembourg (1288–1313). He became king of the Lombards in 1313 **2** 1457–1509, first Tudor king of England (1485–1509). He came to the throne (1485) after defeating Richard III at the Battle of Bosworth Field, ending the Wars of the Roses. Royal power and the prosperity of the country greatly increased during his reign

Henry VIII 1491–1547, king of England (1509–47); second son of Henry VII. The declaration that his marriage to Catherine of Aragon was invalid and his marriage to Anne Boleyn (1533) precipitated the Act of Supremacy, making Henry supreme head of the Church in England. Anne Boleyn was executed (1536) and Henry subsequently married Jane Seymour, Anne of Cleves, Catherine Howard, and Catherine Parr. His reign is also noted for the fame of his succession of advisers, Cardinal Wolsey, Sir Thomas More, and Thomas Cromwell

Henryson Robert ?1430–?1506, Scottish poet. His works

include *Testament of Cresseid* (1593), a sequel to Chaucer's *Troilus and Cressida*, the 13 *Moral Fables of Esope the Phrygian*, and the pastoral dialogue *Robene and Makyne*

Henry the Navigator 1394–1460, prince of Portugal, noted for his patronage of Portuguese voyages of exploration of the W coast of Africa

Henslowe Philip died 1616, English theatre manager, noted also for his diary

Henze Hans Werner born 1926, German composer, whose works, in many styles, include the operas *The Stag King* (1956), *The Bassarids* (1965), *The English Cat* (1983), and *Das verratene Meer* (1990) and the oratorio *The Raft of the Medusa* (1968)

hepatic 1 of or relating to the liver **2** *Botany* of or relating to the liverworts **3** having the colour of liver **4** *Obsolete* any of various drugs for use in treating diseases of the liver

hepatitis inflammation of the liver, characterized by fever, jaundice, and weakness

Hepburn 1 Audrey 1929–93, US actress, born in Belgium. Her films include *Roman Holiday* (1955), *Funny Face* (1957), and *My Fair Lady* (1964) **2 Katharine** 1907–2003, US film actress, whose films include *The Philadelphia Story* (1940), *Adam's Rib* (1949), *The African Queen* (1951), *The Lion in Winter* (1968) for which she won an Oscar, and *On Golden Pond* (1981)

Hephaestus *or* **Hephaistos** *Greek myth* the lame god of fire and metal-working

heptagon a polygon having seven sides

heptathlon an athletic contest for women in which each athlete competes in seven different events

Hepworth Dame Barbara 1903–75, British sculptor of abstract works

Hera *or* **Here** *Greek myth* the queen of the Olympian gods and sister and wife of Zeus

Heraclea any of several ancient Greek colonies. The most famous is the S Italian site where Pyrrhus of Epirus defeated the Romans (280 BC)

Heracleides *or* **Heraclides of Pontus** ?390–?322 BC, Greek astronomer and philosopher: the first to state that the earth rotates on its axis

Heraclitus ?535–?475 BC, Greek philosopher, who held that fire is the primordial substance of the universe and that all things are in perpetual flux

Heraclius ?575–641 AD, Byzantine emperor, who restored the Holy Cross to Jerusalem (629)

herald (in the Middle Ages) an official at a tournament

Herat a city in NW Afghanistan, on the Hari Rud River: on the site of several ancient cities; at its height as a cultural centre in the 15th century. Pop: 344 000 (2005 est)

herb 1 a seed-bearing plant whose aerial parts do not persist above ground at the end of the growing season; herbaceous plant **2 a** any of various usually aromatic plants, such as parsley, rue, and rosemary, that are used in cookery and medicine **b** (*as modifier*): *a herb garden* **3** *Caribbean* a slang term for **marijuana**
▷www.culinarycafe.com/Spices_Herbs
▷www.herbs.org
▷www.herbsforafrica.co.za
▷www.theherbcottage.com/herbs.html

herbaceous 1 designating or relating to plants or plant

parts that are fleshy as opposed to woody **2** (of petals and sepals) green and leaflike

herbaceous border a flower bed that primarily contains nonwoody perennials rather than annuals

herbage herbaceous plants collectively, esp the edible parts on which cattle, sheep, etc, graze

herbalist 1 a person who grows, collects, sells, or specializes in the use of herbs, esp medicinal herbs **2** (formerly) a descriptive botanist

Herbert 1 Edward, 1st Baron Herbert of Cherbury. 1583–1648, English philosopher and poet, noted for his deistic views **2** his brother, **George** 1593–1633, English Metaphysical poet. His chief work is *The Temple: Sacred Poems and Private Ejaculations* (1633) **3** Zbigniew , 1924–98, Polish poet and dramatist, noted esp for his dramatic monologues

herbicide a chemical that destroys plants, esp one used to control weeds

herbivore an animal that feeds on grass and other plants

Herculaneum an ancient city in SW Italy, of marked Greek character, on the S slope of Vesuvius: buried along with Pompeii by an eruption of the volcano (79 AD). Excavation has uncovered well preserved streets, houses, etc.

herd a large group of mammals living and feeding together, esp a group of cattle, sheep, etc.

herd instinct *Psychol* the inborn tendency to associate with others and follow the group's behaviour

hereditary 1 of, relating to, or denoting factors that can be transmitted genetically from one generation to another **2** *Law* **a** descending or capable of descending to succeeding generations by inheritance **b** transmitted or transmissible according to established rules of descent **3** *Maths, Logic* **a** (of a set) containing all those elements which have a given relation to any element of the set **b** (of a property) transferred by the given relation, so that if *x* has the property P and *x*R*y*, then *y* also has the property P

heredity 1 the transmission from one generation to another of genetic factors that determine individual characteristics: responsible for the resemblances between parents and offspring **2** the sum total of the inherited factors or their characteristics in an organism

Hereford 1 a city in W England, in Herefordshire on the River Wye: trading centre for agricultural produce; cathedral (begun 1079). Pop: 56 373 (2001) **2** a hardy breed of beef cattle characterized by a red body, red and white head, and white markings

Hereford and Worcester a former county of the W Midlands of England, created in 1974 from the historic counties of Herefordshire and (most of) Worcestershire: abolished in 1998 when Herefordshire became an independent unitary authority

Herefordshire a county of W England: from 1974 to 1998 part of Hereford and Worcester: drained chiefly by the River Wye; agricultural (esp fruit and cattle). Administrative centre: Hereford. Pop: 176 900 (2003 est). Area: 2180 sq km (842 sq miles)

heresy a an opinion or doctrine contrary to the orthodox tenets of a religious body or church **b** the act of maintaining such an opinion or doctrine

heretic *Now chiefly RC Church* a person who maintains beliefs contrary to the established teachings of the Church

Hereward called *Hereward the Wake*. 11th-century Anglo-Saxon rebel, who defended the Isle of Ely against William the Conqueror (1070–71): a subject of many legends

Herisau a town in NE Switzerland, capital of Appenzell Outer Rhodes demicanton. Pop: 15 882 (2000)

heritable 1 capable of being inherited; inheritable **2** *Chiefly law* capable of inheriting

heritage 1 a the evidence of the past, such as historical sites, buildings, and the unspoilt natural environment, considered collectively as the inheritance of present-day society **b** (*as modifier; cap. as part of name*): *Bannockburn Heritage Centre* **2** *Law* any property, esp land, that by law has descended or may descend to an heir **3** *Bible* **a** the Israelites regarded as belonging inalienably to God **b** the land of Canaan regarded as God's gift to the Israelites

hermaphrodite 1 *Biology* an individual animal or flower that has both male and female reproductive organs **2** a person having both male and female sexual characteristics and genital tissues

hermeneutics 1 the science of interpretation, esp of Scripture **2** the branch of theology that deals with the principles and methodology of exegesis **3** *Philosophy* **a** the study and interpretation of human behaviour and social institutions **b** (in existentialist thought) discussion of the purpose of life

Hermes[1] *Greek myth* the messenger and herald of the gods; the divinity of commerce, cunning, theft, travellers, and rascals. He was represented as wearing winged sandals

Hermes[2] a small asteroid some 800 m in diameter that passed within 670 000 kilometres of the earth in 1937, and is now lost

hermetic *or* **hermetical** sealed so as to be airtight

hermit one of the early Christian recluses

hermitage the abode of a hermit

hermit crab any small soft-bodied decapod crustacean of the genus *Pagurus* and related genera, living in and carrying about the empty shells of whelks or similar molluscs

Hermon Mount a mountain on the border between Lebanon and SW Syria, in the Anti-Lebanon Range: represented the NE limits of Israeli conquests under Moses and Joshua. Height: 2814 m (9232 ft)

Hermosillo a city in NW Mexico, capital of Sonora state, on the Sonora River: university (1938); winter resort and commercial centre for an agricultural and mining region. Pop: 668 000 (2005 est)

Hermoupolis a port in Greece, capital of Cyclades department, on the E coast of Syros Island. Pop: 14 115 (latest est)

Herne an industrial city in W Germany, in North Rhine-Westphalia, in the Ruhr on the Rhine-Herne Canal. Pop: 172 870 (2003 est)

hernia the projection of an organ or part through the lining of the cavity in which it is normally situated, esp the protrusion of intestine through the front wall of the abdominal cavity. It is caused by muscular strain, injury, etc.

hero *Classical myth* a being of extraordinary strength and courage, often the offspring of a mortal and a god, who is celebrated for his exploits

Hero *or* **Heron** 1st century AD, Greek mathematician and inventor

Herod called *the Great*. ?73–4 BC, king of Judaea (37–4). The latter part of his reign was notable for his cruelty: according to the New Testament he ordered the Massacre of the Innocents

Herod Agrippa I 10 BC–44 AD, king of Judaea (41–44), grandson of Herod (the Great). A friend of Caligula and Claudius, he imprisoned Saint Peter and executed Saint James

Herod Agrippa II died ?93 AD, king of territories in N Palestine (50–?93 AD). He presided (60) at the trial of Saint Paul and sided with the Roman authorities in the Jewish rebellion of 66

Herod Antipas died ?40 AD, tetrarch of Galilee and Peraea (4 BC–40 AD); son of Herod the Great. At the instigation of his wife Herodias, he ordered the execution of John the Baptist

Herodias ?14 BC–?40 AD, niece and wife of Herod Antipas and mother of Salome, whom she persuaded to ask for the head of John the Baptist. Her ambition led to the banishment of her husband

Herodotus called *the Father of History*. ?485–?425 BC, Greek historian, famous for his *History* dealing with the causes and events of the wars between the Greeks and the Persians (490–479)

heroic *or* **heroical** **1** of, relating to, or resembling the heroes of classical mythology **2** *Prosody* of, relating to, or resembling heroic verse **3** (of the arts, esp sculpture) larger than life-size; smaller than colossal **4** *RC Church* **a** held to such a degree as to enable a person to perform virtuous actions with exceptional promptness, ease and pleasure, and with self-abnegation and self-control **b** performed or undergone by such a person

heroin a white odourless bitter-tasting crystalline powder related to morphine: a highly addictive narcotic. Formula: $C_{21}H_{23}NO_5$

heron any of various wading birds of the genera *Butorides*, *Ardea*, etc, having a long neck, slim body, and a plumage that is commonly grey or white: family *Ardeidae*, order *Ciconiiformes*

Heron Patrick 1920–99, British abstract painter and art critic

heronry a colony of breeding herons

Herophilus died ?280 BC, Greek anatomist in Alexandria. He was the first to distinguish sensory from motor nerves

herpes any of several inflammatory diseases of the skin, esp herpes simplex, characterized by the formation of small watery blisters

herpes simplex an acute viral disease characterized by formation of clusters of watery blisters, esp on the margins of the lips and nostrils or on the genitals. It can be sexually transmitted and may recur fitfully

Herr a German man: used before a name as a title equivalent to *Mr*

Herrick Robert 1591–1674, English poet. His chief work is the *Hesperides* (1648), a collection of short, delicate, sacred, and pastoral lyrics

herring any marine soft-finned teleost fish of the family *Clupeidae*, esp *Clupea harengus*, an important food fish of northern seas, having an elongated body covered, except in the head region, with large fragile silvery scales

herringbone **1 a** a pattern used in textiles, brickwork, etc, consisting of two or more rows of short parallel strokes slanting in alternate directions to form a series of parallel Vs or zigzags **b** (*as modifier*): *a herringbone jacket* **2** *Skiing* a method of ascending a slope by walking with the skis pointing outwards and one's weight on the inside edges

herring gull a common gull, *Larus argentatus*, that has a white plumage with black-tipped wings and pink legs

Herriot 1 Édouard 1872–1957, French Radical statesman and writer; premier (1924–25; 1932) **2** James real name *James Alfred Wight*. 1916–95, British veterinary surgeon and writer. His books based on his experiences in Yorkshire have been adapted for television and films

Herschel 1 Caroline Lucretia 1750–1848, British astronomer, born in Germany, noted for her catalogue of nebulae and star clusters: sister of Sir William Herschel **2** Sir John Frederick William 1792–1871, British astronomer. He discovered and catalogued over 525 nebulae and star clusters **3** his father, Sir (**Frederick**) **William**, original name *Friedrich Wilhelm Herschel*. 1738–1822, British astronomer, born in Germany. He constructed a reflecting telescope, which led to his discovery of the planet Uranus (1781), two of its satellites, and two of the satellites of Saturn. He also discovered the motions of binary stars

Herstmonceux *or* **Hurstmonceux** a village in S England, in E Sussex north of Eastbourne: 15th-century castle, site of the Royal Observatory, which was transferred from Greenwich between 1948 and 1958, until 1990

Hertford a town in SE England, administrative centre of Hertfordshire. Pop: 24 460 (2001)

Hertfordshire a county of S England, bordering on Greater London in the south: mainly low-lying, with the Chiltern Hills in the northwest; largely agricultural; expanding light industries, esp in the new towns. Administrative centre: Hertford. Pop: 1 040 900 (2003 est). Area: 1634 sq km (631 sq miles)

hertz the derived SI unit of frequency; the frequency of a periodic phenomenon that has a periodic time of 1 second; 1 cycle per second.

Hertz 1 Gustav 1887–1975, German atomic physicist. He provided evidence for the quantum theory by his research with Franck on the effects produced by bombarding atoms with electrons: they shared the Nobel prize for physics (1925) **2** Heinrich Rudolph 1857–94, German physicist. He was the first to produce electromagnetic waves artificially

Hertzog James Barry Munnik 1866–1942, South African statesman; prime minister (1924–39): founded the Nationalist Party (1913), advocating complete South African independence from Britain; opposed South African participation in World Wars I and II

Herzegovina *or* **Hercegovina** a region in Bosnia-

Herzegovina: originally under Austro-Hungarian rule; became part of the province of Bosnia-Herzegovina (1878), which was a constituent republic of Yugoslavia (1946–92)

Herzl Theodor 1860–1904, Austrian writer, born in Hungary; founder of the Zionist movement. In *The Jewish State* (1896), he advocated resettlement of the Jews in a state of their own

Herzog 1 **Roman** born 1934, German politician; president of Germany (1994–2004) 2 **Werner** born 1942, German film director. His films include *Signs of Life* (1967), *Fata Morgana* (1970), *Fitzcarraldo* (1982), and *Little Dieter Needs to Fly* (1997)

Heseltine 1 **Michael (Ray Dibden)** Baron. born 1933, British Conservative politician; secretary of state for defence (1983–86); secretary of state for the environment (1990–92); secretary of state for trade and industry (1992–95); deputy prime minister (1995–97) 2 **Philip Arnold** See (Peter) **Warlock**

Hesiod 8th century BC, Greek poet and the earliest author of didactic verse. His two complete extant works are the *Works and Days*, dealing with the agricultural seasons, and the *Theogony*, concerning the origin of the world and the genealogies of the gods

Hesperia a poetic name used by the ancient Greeks for Italy and by the Romans for Spain or beyond

Hess 1 Dame **Myra** 1890–1965, English pianist 2 **(Walther Richard) Rudolf** 1894–1987, German Nazi leader. He made a secret flight to Scotland (1941) to negotiate peace with Britain but was held as a prisoner of war; later sentenced to life imprisonment at the Nuremberg trials (1946); committed suicide 3 **Victor Francis** 1883–1964, US physicist, born in Austria: pioneered the investigation of cosmic rays: shared the Nobel prize for physics (1936)

Hesse¹ Hermann 1877–1962, German novelist, short-story writer, and poet. His novels include *Der Steppenwolf* (1927) and *Das Glasperlenspiel* (1943): Nobel prize for literature 1946

Hesse² a state of central Germany, formed in 1945 from the former Prussian province of Hesse-Nassau and part of the former state of Hesse; part of West Germany until 1990. Capital: Wiesbaden. Pop: 6 089 000 (2003 est). Area: 21 111 sq km (8151 sq miles)

Hesse-Nassau a former province of Prussia, now part of the state of Hesse, Germany

hessian a coarse jute fabric similar to sacking, used for bags, upholstery, etc.

Hessian 1 a native or inhabitant of Hesse 2 a a Hessian soldier in any of the mercenary units of the British Army in the War of American Independence or the Napoleonic Wars b US any German mercenary in the British Army during the War of American Independence

heterodox at variance with established, orthodox, or accepted doctrines or beliefs

heterodyne produced by, operating by, or involved in heterodyning two signals

heterogeneous *Chem* of, composed of, or concerned with two or more different phases

heteromorphic *or* **heteromorphous** *Biology* 1 differing from the normal form in size, shape, and function

2 (of pairs of homologous chromosomes) differing from each other in size or form 3 (esp of insects) having different forms at different stages of the life cycle

heterosexual 1 a person who is sexually attracted to the opposite sex 2 of or relating to heterosexuality

heterozygous *Genetics* (of an organism) having different alleles for any one gene

heuristic 1 (of a method of teaching) allowing pupils to learn things for themselves 2 a *Maths, Science, Philosophy* using or obtained by exploration of possibilities rather than by following set rules b *Computing* denoting a rule of thumb for solving a problem without the exhaustive application of an algorithm

Hevesy Georg von 1885–1966, Hungarian chemist. He worked on radioactive tracing and, with D. Coster, discovered the element hafnium (1923): Nobel prize for chemistry 1943

Hewish Antony born 1924, British radio astronomer, noted esp for his role in the discovery of pulsars (1967): shared the Nobel prize for physics 1974

Hewitt Lleyton born 1981, Australian tennis player; US Open champion 2001, Wimbledon singles champion 2002

hex a short for **hexadecimal notation** *or* **hexadecimal b** *(as modifier)*: *hex code*

hexadecimal notation *or* **hexadecimal** a number system having a base 16; the symbols for the numbers 0–9 are the same as those used in the decimal system, and the numbers 10–15 are usually represented by the letters A–F. The system is used as a convenient way of representing the internal binary code of a computer

hexagon a polygon having six sides

hexagram 1 a star-shaped figure formed by extending the sides of a regular hexagon to meet at six points 2 a group of six broken or unbroken lines which may be combined into 64 different patterns, as used in the I Ching

hexameter *Prosody* 1 a verse line consisting of six metrical feet 2 (in Greek and Latin epic poetry) a verse line of six metrical feet, of which the first four are usually dactyls or spondees, the fifth almost always a dactyl, and the sixth a spondee or trochee

hexapla an edition of the Old Testament compiled by Origen, containing six versions of the text

Heyer Georgette 1902–74, British historical novelist and writer of detective stories, noted esp for her romances of the Regency period

Heyerdahl Thor 1914–2002, Norwegian anthropologist. In 1947 he demonstrated that the Polynesians could originally have been migrants from South America, by sailing from Peru to the Pacific Islands of Tuamotu in the *Kon-Tiki*, a raft made of balsa wood. DNA testing in the late 1990s indicated that such a migration did not actually take place

Heysham a port in NW England, in NW Lancashire. Pop. (with Morecambe): 46 657 (1991)

Heywood¹ 1 **John** ?1497–?1580, English dramatist, noted for his comic interludes 2 **Thomas** ?1574–1641, English dramatist, noted esp for his domestic drama *A Woman Killed with Kindness* (1607)

Heywood² a town in NW England, in Rochdale unitary authority, Greater Manchester, near Bury. Pop: 28 024

(2001))

Hezekiah a king of Judah ?715–?687 BC, noted for his religious reforms (II Kings 18–19)

Hialeah a city in SE Florida, near Miami: racetrack. Pop: 226 401 (2003 est)

hiatus *Anatomy* 1 a natural opening or aperture; foramen 2 a less common word for **vulva**

hiatus hernia *or* **hiatal hernia** protrusion of part of the stomach through the diaphragm at the oesophageal opening

Hiawatha a 16th-century Onondaga Indian chief: credited with the organization of the Five Nations

Hib *Haemophilus influenzae* type b: a vaccine against a type of bacterial meningitis, administered to children

Hibernia the Roman name for **Ireland**: used poetically in later times

hibiscus any plant of the chiefly tropical and subtropical malvaceous genus *Hibiscus*, esp *H. rosa-sinensis*, cultivated for its large brightly coloured flowers

hiccup 1 a spasm of the diaphragm producing a sudden breathing in followed by a closing of the glottis, resulting in a sharp sound 2 the state or condition of having such spasms

Hickok James Butler, known as *Wild Bill Hickok*. 1837–76, US frontiersman and marshal

hickory 1 any juglandaceous tree of the chiefly North American genus *Carya*, having nuts with edible kernels and hard smooth shells 2 the hard tough wood of any of these trees 3 the nut of any of these trees

Hickox Richard (Sidney). born 1948, British conductor; musical director of the City of London Sinfonia and Singers since 1971

Hidalgo a state of central Mexico: consists of a high plateau, with the Sierra Madre Oriental in the north and east; ancient remains of Teltec culture (at Tula); rich mineral resources. Capital: Pachuca. Pop: 2 231 392 (2000). Area: 20 987 sq km (8103 sq miles)

hide[1] *Brit* a place of concealment, usually disguised to appear as part of the natural environment, used by hunters, birdwatchers, etc.

hide[2] the skin of an animal, esp the tough thick skin of a large mammal, either tanned or raw

hide[3] an obsolete Brit unit of land measure, varying in magnitude from about 60 to 120 acres

hide-and-seek *or US and Canadian* **hide-and-go-seek** a game in which one player covers his eyes and waits while the others hide, and then he tries to find them

hidebound 1 (of cattle, etc) having the skin closely attached to the flesh as a result of poor feeding 2 (of trees) having a very tight bark that impairs growth

hierarchy 1 *Religion* a body of persons in holy orders organized into graded ranks 2 *Taxonomy* a series of ordered groupings within a system, such as the arrangement of plants and animals into classes, orders, families, etc. 3 *Linguistics, Maths* a formal structure, usually represented by a diagram of connected nodes, with a single uppermost element 4 government by an organized priesthood

hieroglyphic 1 of or relating to a form of writing using picture symbols, esp as used in ancient Egypt 2 written with hieroglyphic symbols 3 a picture or symbol representing an object, concept, or sound

Hieronymus Eusebius the Latin name of (Saint) **Jerome**

hi-fi *Informal* 1 a short for **high fidelity** b (*as modifier*): *hi-fi equipment* 2 a set of high-quality sound-reproducing equipment

Higgins 1 Alex, known as *Hurricane Higgins*. born 1949, Northern Irish snooker player 2 Jack, real name *Harry Patterson*. born 1929, British novelist; his thrillers include *The Eagle Has Landed* (1975), *Confessional* (1985), and *Midnight Runner* (2002)

high 1 *Music* (of sound) acute in pitch; having a high frequency 2 *Geography* (of latitudes) situated relatively far north or south from the equator 3 *Informal* being in a state of altered consciousness, characterized esp by euphoria and often induced by the use of alcohol, narcotics, etc. 4 (of a gear) providing a relatively great forward speed for a given engine speed 5 of or relating to the High Church 6 *Cards* a having a relatively great value in a suit b able to win a trick 7 *Informal* a state of altered consciousness, often induced by alcohol, narcotics, etc. 8 another word for **anticyclone** 9 short for **high school** 10 (esp in Oxford) the High Street 11 *Electronics* the voltage level in a logic circuit corresponding to logical one

High Arctic the regions of Canada, esp the northern islands, within the Arctic Circle

highball *Chiefly US* (originally in railway use) a signal that the way ahead is clear and one may proceed

High Church the party or movement within the Church of England stressing continuity with Catholic Christendom, the authority of bishops, and the importance of sacraments, rituals, and ceremonies

high commissioner 1 the senior diplomatic representative sent by one Commonwealth country to another instead of an ambassador 2 the head of an international commission 3 the chief officer in a colony or other dependency

High Court 1 a (in England and Wales) a shortened form of High Court of Justice b (in Scotland) a shortened form of High Court of Justiciary 2 (in New Zealand) a court of law inferior to the Court of Appeal

higher education education and training at colleges, universities, polytechnics, etc.

highest common factor the largest number or quantity that is a factor of each member of a group of numbers or quantities

high explosive an extremely powerful chemical explosive, such as TNT or gelignite

high fidelity a the reproduction of sound using electronic equipment that gives faithful reproduction with little or no distortion b (*as modifier*): *a high-fidelity amplifier*

high frequency a radio-frequency band or radio frequency lying between 3 and 30 megahertz

High German 1 the standard German language, historically developed from the form of West Germanic spoken in S Germany 2 any of the German dialects of S Germany, Austria, or Switzerland

high jump a an athletic event in which a competitor has to jump over a high bar set between two vertical supports b (*as modifier*): *high-jump techniques*

Highland 1 a council area in N Scotland, formed in 1975 (as Highland Region) from Caithness, Sutherland, Nairnshire, most of Inverness-shire, and Ross and

Cromarty except for the Outer Hebrides. Administrative centre: Inverness. Pop: 209 080 (2003 est). Area: 25 149 sq km (9710 sq miles) **2** of, relating to, or denoting the Highlands of Scotland

Highland cattle a breed of cattle with shaggy hair, usually reddish-brown in colour, and long horns

Highland fling a vigorous Scottish solo dance

Highlands the **1 a** the part of Scotland that lies to the northwest of the great fault that runs from Dumbarton to Stonehaven **b** a smaller area consisting of the mountainous north of Scotland: distinguished by Gaelic culture **2** the Highland region of any country

high-level language a computer programming language that resembles natural language or mathematical notation and is designed to reflect the requirements of a problem; examples include Ada, BASIC, C, COBOL, FORTRAN, Pascal

highlight *Art, etc* an area of the lightest tone in a painting, drawing, photograph, etc.

High Mass a solemn and elaborate sung Mass

high-octane (of petrol) having a high octane number

high-pitched 1 pitched high in volume or tone **2** (of a roof) having steeply sloping sides

high-powered (of an optical instrument or lens) having a high magnification

high-pressure *Physics, Engineering* having, using, involving, or designed to withstand a pressure above normal pressure

high priest 1 *Judaism* the priest of highest rank who alone was permitted to enter the holy of holies of the tabernacle and Temple **2** *Mormon Church* a priest of the order of Melchizedek priesthood **3** the head of a group or cult

highroad a main road; highway

high school 1 *Brit* another term for **grammar school 2** *US and NZ* a secondary school from grade 7 to grade 12 **3** *Canadian* a secondary school, the grades covered depending on the province

Highsmith Patricia 1921–95, US author of crime fiction. Her novels include *Strangers on a Train* (1950) and *Ripley's Game* (1974)

High Street 1 *Brit* the main street of a town, usually where the principal shops are situated **2** the market constituted by the general public **3** *Commerce* geared to meet the requirements of, and readily available for purchase by, the general public

high technology highly sophisticated, often electronic, techniques used in manufacturing and other processes

high-tension subjected to, carrying, or capable of operating at a relatively high voltage

high tide a the tide at its highest level **b** the time at which it reaches this

high treason an act of treason directly affecting a sovereign or state

high-water mark a the level reached by sea water at high tide or by other stretches of water in flood **b** the mark indicating this level

High Wycombe a town in S central England, in S Buckinghamshire: furniture industry. Pop: 77 178 (2001)

Hilary of Poitiers Saint ?315–?367 AD, French bishop, an opponent of Arianism. Feast day: Jan 13 or 14

Hilbert David 1862–1943, German mathematician, who made outstanding contributions to the theories of number fields and invariants and to geometry

Hildegard of Bingen Saint 1098–1179, German abbess, poet, composer, and mystic

Hildesheim a city in N central Germany, in Lower Saxony: a member of the Hanseatic League. Pop: 103 245 (2003 est)

hill 1 a conspicuous and often rounded natural elevation of the earth's surface, less high or craggy than a mountain **2** *over the hill Military, slang* absent without leave or deserting

Hill 1 Archibald Vivian 1886–1977, British biochemist, noted for his research into heat loss in muscle contraction: shared the Nobel prize for physiology or medicine (1922) **2** Damon Graham Devereux, son of Graham Hill. born 1960, British motor-racing driver; Formula One world champion (1996) **3** David Octavius 1802–70, Scottish painter and portrait photographer, noted esp for his collaboration with the chemist Robert Adamson (1821– 48) **4** Geoffrey (William). born 1932, British poet: his books include *King Log* (1968), *Mercian Hymns* (1971), *The Mystery of the Charity of Charles Péguy* (1983), and *The Orchards of Syon* (2002) **5** Graham 1929–75, British motor-racing driver: world champion (1962, 1968) **6** Octavia 1838–1912, British housing reformer; a founder of the National Trust **7** Sir Rowland 1795–1879, British originator of the penny postage **8** Susan (Elizabeth). born 1942, British novelist and writer of short stories: her books include *I'm the King of the Castle* (1970) *The Woman in Black* (1983), and *Felix Derby* (2002)

Hilla a market town in central Iraq, on a branch of the Euphrates: built partly of bricks from the nearby site of Babylon. Pop: 364 000 (2005 est)

Hillary Sir Edmund born 1919, New Zealand explorer and mountaineer. He and his Sherpa guide, Tenzing Norgay, were the first to reach the summit of Mount Everest (1953); New Zealand ambassador to India (1984–89)

Hillel ?60 BC–?9 AD, rabbi, born in Babylonia; president of the Sanhedrin. He was the first to formulate principles of biblical interpretation

Hilliard Nicholas 1537–1619, English miniaturist, esp of portraits

Hillingdon a residential borough of W Greater London. Pop: 247 600 (2003 est). Area: 110 sq km (43 sq miles)

hillock a small hill or mound

hilum 1 *Botany* **a** a scar on the surface of a seed marking its point of attachment to the seed stalk (funicle) **b** the nucleus of a starch grain **2** *Anatomy* a deep fissure or depression on the surface of a bodily organ around the point of entrance or exit of vessels, nerves, or ducts

Hilversum a city in the central Netherlands, in North Holland province: Dutch radio and television centre. Pop: 83 000 (2003 est))

Himachal Pradesh a state of N India, in the W Himalayas: rises to about 6700 m (22 000 ft) and is densely forested. Capital: Simla. Pop: 6 077 248 (2001). Area: 55 658 sq km (21 707 sq miles)

Himalayas the a vast mountain system in S Asia, extending 2400 km (1500 miles) from Kashmir (west) to Assam (east), between the valleys of the Rivers Indus and Brahmaputra: covers most of Nepal, Sikkim, Bhutan, and the S edge of Tibet; the highest range in the world, with several peaks over 7500 m (25 000 ft). Highest peak: Mount Everest, 8848 m (29 028 ft)

Himeji a city in central Japan, on W Honshu: cotton textile centre. Pop: 475 892 (2002 est)

Himmler Heinrich 1900–45, German Nazi leader, head of the SS and the Gestapo (1936–45); committed suicide

Himyarite a member of an ancient people of SW Arabia, sometimes regarded as including the Sabeans

Hinckley a town in central England, in Leicestershire. Pop: 43 246 (2001)

hind 1 the female of the deer, esp the red deer when aged three years or more 2 any of several marine serranid fishes of the genus *Epinephelus*, closely related and similar to the gropers

Hindemith Paul 1895–1963, German composer and musical theorist, who opposed the twelve-tone technique. His works include the song cycle *Das Marienleben* (1923) and the opera *Mathis der Maler* (1938)

Hindenburg Paul von Beneckendorff und von 1847–1934, German field marshal and statesman; president (1925–34). During World War I he directed German strategy together with Ludendorff (1916–18)

Hindi 1 a language or group of dialects of N central India. It belongs to the Indic branch of the Indo-European family and is closely related to Urdu 2 a formal literary dialect of this language, the official language of India, usually written in Nagari script 3 a person whose native language is Hindi

Hindu or **Hindoo** 1 a person who adheres to Hinduism 2 an inhabitant or native of Hindustan or India, esp one adhering to Hinduism

Hinduism or **Hindooism** the complex of beliefs, values, and customs comprising the dominant religion of India, characterized by the worship of many gods, including Brahma as supreme being, a caste system, belief in reincarnation, etc.
▷www.himalayanacademy.com
▷www.hindunet.org

Hindustan 1 the land of the Hindus, esp India north of the Deccan and excluding Bengal 2 the general area around the Ganges where Hindi is the predominant language 3 the areas of India where Hinduism predominates, as contrasted with those areas where Islam predominates

Hindustani, Hindoostani, or **Hindostani** 1 the dialect of Hindi spoken in Delhi: used as a lingua franca throughout India 2 a group of languages or dialects consisting of all spoken forms of Hindi and Urdu considered together

Hines Earl, known as Earl "Fatha" Hines. 1905–83, US jazz pianist, conductor, and songwriter

hinge 1 a device for holding together two parts such that one can swing relative to the other, typically having two interlocking metal leaves held by a pin about which they pivot 2 *Anatomy* a type of joint, such as the knee joint, that moves only backwards and forwards; a joint that functions in only one plane 3 a similar structure in invertebrate animals, such as the joint between the two halves of a bivalve shell 4 *Philately* a small thin transparent strip of gummed paper for affixing a stamp to a page

hinny the sterile hybrid offspring of a male horse and a female donkey or ass

hinterland 1 land lying behind something, esp a coast or the shore of a river 2 remote or undeveloped areas of a country

hip¹ 1 either side of the body below the waist and above the thigh, overlying the lateral part of the pelvis and its articulation with the thighbones 2 another name for **pelvis** 3 the angle formed where two sloping sides of a roof meet or where a sloping side meets a sloping end

hip² the berry-like brightly coloured fruit of a rose plant: a swollen receptacle, rich in vitamin C, containing several small hairy achenes

Hipparchus 1 2nd century BC, Greek astronomer. He discovered the precession of the equinoxes, calculated the length of the solar year, and developed trigonometry 2 died 514 BC, tyrant of Athens (527–514)

Hippocrates ?460–?377 BC, Greek physician, commonly regarded as the father of medicine

Hippocratic oath an oath taken by a doctor to observe a code of medical ethics supposedly derived from that of Hippocrates (?460–?337), Greek physician commonly regarded as the father of medicine

hippodrome 1 a music hall, variety theatre, or circus 2 (in ancient Greece or Rome) an open-air course for horse and chariot races

hippopotamus 1 a very large massive gregarious artiodactyl mammal, *Hippopotamus amphibius*, living in or around the rivers of tropical Africa: family *Hippopotamidae*. It has short legs and a thick skin sparsely covered with hair 2 **pigmy hippopotamus** a related but smaller animal, *Choeropsis liberiensis*

Hippo Regius an ancient Numidian city, adjoining present-day Annaba, Algeria

Hiram 10th century BC, king of Tyre, who supplied Solomon with materials and craftsmen for the building of the Temple (II Samuel 5:11; I Kings 5:1–18)

hire 1 a the act of hiring or the state of being hired b (as modifier): *a hire car* 2 a the price paid or payable for a person's services or the temporary use of something b (as modifier): *the hire charge* 3 **for** or **on hire** available for service or temporary use in exchange for payment

hire-purchase Brit, Austral, NZ, & South African a a system for purchasing merchandise, such as cars or furniture, in which the buyer takes possession of the merchandise on payment of a deposit and completes the purchase by paying a series of regular instalments while the seller retains ownership until the final instalment is paid b (as modifier): *hire-purchase legislation*

Hirohito 1901–89, emperor of Japan 1926–89. In 1946 he became a constitutional monarch

Hiroshige Ando 1797–1858, Japanese artist, esp of colour wood-block prints

Hiroshima a port in SW Japan, on SW Honshu on the delta of the Ota River: largely destroyed on August 6, 1945, by the first atomic bomb to be used in warfare, dropped by the US, which killed over 75 000 of its inhabitants. Pop: 1 113 786 (2002 est)

Hirst Damien born 1965, British artist, noted for his works featuring dead animals preserved in tanks of formaldehyde

hirsute (of plants or their parts) covered with long but not stiff hairs

Hispania the Iberian peninsula in the Roman world

Hispanic 1 relating to, characteristic of, or derived from Spain or the Spanish 2 *US* a US citizen of Spanish or Latin-American descent

Hispaniola the second largest island in the Caribbean, in the Greater Antilles: divided politically into Haiti and the Dominican Republic; discovered in 1492 by Christopher Columbus, who named it La Isla Española. Area: 18 703 sq km (29 418 sq miles)

hiss *Electronics* receiver noise with a continuous spectrum, caused by thermal agitation, shot noise, etc.

Hiss Alger 1904–96, US government official: imprisoned (1950–54) for perjury in connection with alleged espionage activities

histamine an amine formed from histidine and released by the body tissues in allergic reactions, causing irritation. It also stimulates gastric secretions, dilates blood vessels, and contracts smooth muscle. Formula: $C_5H_9N_3$

histology 1 the study, esp the microscopic study, of the tissues of an animal or plant 2 the structure of a tissue or organ

historian a person who writes or studies history, esp one who is an authority on it

historicism 1 the belief that natural laws govern historical events which in turn determine social and cultural phenomena 2 the doctrine that each period of history has its own beliefs and values inapplicable to any other, so that nothing can be understood independently of its historical context 3 the conduct of any enquiry in accordance with these views 4 excessive emphasis on history, historicism, past styles, etc.

historiographer 1 a historian, esp one concerned with historical method and the writings of other historians 2 a historian employed to write the history of a group or public institution

history 1 a a record or account, often chronological in approach, of past events, developments, etc. b (*as modifier*): *a history book* 2 all that is preserved or remembered of the past, esp in written form 3 the discipline of recording and interpreting past events involving human beings 4 past events, esp when considered as an aggregate 5 a play that depicts or is based on historical events 6 a narrative relating the events of a character's life

▷www.hyperhistory.com

▷www.historychannel.com

hit *Computing* a single visit to a website

Hitachi a city in Japan, in E Honshu: a centre of the electronics industry. Pop: 193 080 (2002 est)

hit-and-run 1 a involved in or denoting a motor-vehicle accident in which the driver leaves the scene without stopping to give assistance, inform the police, etc. b (*as noun*) 2 *Baseball* denoting a play in which a base runner begins to run as the pitcher throws the ball to the batter

Hitchcock Sir Alfred (Joseph). 1899–1980, English film director, noted for his mastery in creating suspense. His films include *The Thirty-Nine Steps* (1935), *Rebecca*

(1940), *Psycho* (1960), and *The Birds* (1963)

Hitler Adolf. Grandmother's maiden name and father's original surname *Schicklgrüber*. 1889–1945, German dictator, born in Austria. After becoming president of the National Socialist German Workers' Party (Nazi party), he attempted to overthrow the government of Bavaria (1923). While in prison he wrote *Mein Kampf*, expressing his philosophy of the superiority of the Aryan race and the inferiority of the Jews. He was appointed chancellor of Germany (1933), transforming it from a democratic republic into the totalitarian Third Reich, of which he became Führer in 1934. He established concentration camps to exterminate the Jews, rearmed the Rhineland (1936), annexed Austria (1938) and Czechoslovakia, and invaded Poland (1939), which precipitated World War II. He committed suicide

hit wicket *Cricket* an instance of a batsman breaking the wicket with the bat or a part of the body while playing a stroke and so being out

hive 1 a structure in which social bees live and rear their young 2 a colony of social bees

hoar 1 short for **hoarfrost** 2 *Rare* covered with hoarfrost

hoarfrost a deposit of needle-like ice crystals formed on the ground by direct condensation at temperatures below freezing point

hoary white or whitish-grey in colour

hob[1] 1 a steel pattern used in forming a mould or die in cold metal 2 a hard steel rotating cutting tool used in machines for cutting gears

hob[2] 1 a hobgoblin or elf 2 a male ferret

Hobart a port in Australia, capital of the island state of Tasmania on the estuary of the Derwent: excellent natural harbour; University of Tasmania (1890). Pop: 126 048 (2001)

Hobbema Meindert 1638–1709, Dutch painter of peaceful landscapes, usually including a watermill

Hobbes Thomas 1588–1679, English political philosopher. His greatest work is the *Leviathan* (1651), which contains his defence of absolute sovereignty

hobble 1 a strap, rope, etc, used to hobble a horse 2 a castrated ferret

Hobbs Sir John Berry, known as *Jack Hobbs*. 1882–1963, English cricketer: scored 197 centuries

hobby[1] 1 an activity pursued in spare time for pleasure or relaxation 2 *Archaic or dialect* a small horse or pony 3 an early form of bicycle, without pedals

hobby[2] any of several small Old World falcons, esp the European *Falco subbuteo*, formerly used in falconry

hobbyhorse a figure of a horse attached to a performer's waist in a pantomime, morris dance, etc.

hobgoblin 1 an evil or mischievous goblin 2 a bogey; bugbear

Hoboken a city in N Belgium, in Antwerp province, on the River Scheldt. Pop: 33 476 (2002 est)

Hochhuth Rolf born 1933, Swiss dramatist. His best-known works are the controversial documentary drama *The Representative* (1963), on the papacy's attitude to the Jews in World War II, *Soldiers* (1967), *German Love Story* (1980), and *Wessis in Weimar* (1992)

Ho Chi Minh original name *Nguyen That Tan*. 1890–1969, Vietnamese statesman; president of North Vietnam (1954–69). He headed the Vietminh (1941), which won independence for Vietnam from the French (1954)

Ho Chi Minh City a port in S Vietnam, 97 km (60 miles) from the South China Sea, on the Saigon River: captured by the French in 1859; merged with adjoining Cholon in 1932; capital of the former Republic of Vietnam (South Vietnam) from 1954 to 1976; university (1917); US headquarters during the Vietnam War. Pop: 5 030 000 (2005 est)

hock¹ 1 the joint at the tarsus of a horse or similar animal, pointing backwards and corresponding to the human ankle 2 the corresponding joint in domestic fowl

hock² 1 any of several white wines from the German Rhine 2 (not in technical usage) any dry white wine

hockey 1 a a game played on a field by two opposing teams of 11 players each, who try to hit a ball into their opponents' goal using long sticks curved at the end **b** (as modifier): hockey stick 2 See **ice hockey**
▷www.fihockey.org

Hockney David born 1937, English painter, best known for his etchings, such as those to Cavafy's poems (1966), naturalistic portraits such as Mr and Mrs Clark and Percy (1971), and for paintings of water, swimmers, and swimming pools

Hodeida a port in N Yemen, on the Red Sea. Pop: 547 000 (2005 est)

Hodgkin 1 Sir Alan Lloyd 1914–98, English physiologist. With A. F. Huxley, he explained the conduction of nervous impulses in terms of the physical and chemical changes involved: shared the Nobel prize for physiology or medicine (1963) 2 Dorothy Crowfoot 1910–94, English chemist and crystallographer, who determined the three-dimensional structure of insulin: Nobel prize for chemistry (1964) 3 Sir Howard born 1932, British painter, noted for his brightly coloured semi-abstract works

Hoffman Dustin (Lee). born 1937, US stage and film actor. His films include The Graduate (1967), Midnight Cowboy (1969), All the President's Men (1976), Kramer vs Kramer (1979), Rain Man (1989), Accidental Hero (1992), and Moonlight Mile (2002)

Hofmannsthal Hugo von 1874–1929, Austrian lyric poet and dramatist, noted as the librettist for Richard Strauss' operas, esp Der Rosenkavalier (1911), Elektra (1909), and Ariadne auf Naxos (1912)

hog 1 a domesticated pig, esp a castrated male weighing more than 102 kg 2 US and Canadian any artiodactyl mammal of the family Suidae; pig 3 Nautical a stiff brush, for scraping a vessel's bottom 4 Nautical the amount or extent to which a vessel is hogged 5 Slang, chiefly US a large powerful motorcycle

Hogan Ben, full name William Benjamin Hogan. 1912–97, US golfer

Hogarth William 1697–1764, English engraver and painter. He is noted particularly for his series of engravings satirizing the vices and affectations of his age, such as A Rake's Progress (1735) and Marriage à la Mode (1745)

Hogg James, known as the Ettrick Shepherd. 1770–1835, Scottish poet and writer. His works include the volume of poems The Queen's Wake (1813) and the novel The Confessions of a Justified Sinner (1824)

hogshead 1 a unit of capacity, used esp for alcoholic beverages. It has several values, being 54 imperial gallons in the case of beer and 52.5 imperial gallons in the case of wine 2 a large cask used for shipment of wines and spirits

Hogwood Christopher (Jarvis Haley). born 1941, British harpsichordist, conductor, and musicologist; founder and director of the Academy of Ancient Music from 1973

Hohenlohe Chlodwig , Prince of Hohenlohe-Schillingsfürst. 1819–1901, Prussian statesman; chancellor of the German empire (1894–1900)

Hohenstaufen a German princely family that provided rulers of Germany (1138–1208, 1215–54), Sicily (1194–1268), and the Holy Roman Empire (1138–1254)

Hohenzollern a German noble family, the younger (Franconian) branch of which provided rulers of Brandenburg (1417–1701) and Prussia (1701–1918). The last kings of Prussia (1871–1918) were also emperors of Germany

Hohhot, Huhehot, or **Hu-ho-hao-t'e** a city in N China, capital of Inner Mongolia Autonomous Region (since 1954); previously capital of the former Suiyüan province; Inner Mongolia University (1957). Pop: 998 000 (2005 est)

hoist 1 any apparatus or device for hoisting 2 Nautical a the amidships height of a sail bent to the yard with which it is hoisted **b** the difference between the set and lowered positions of this yard 3 Nautical the length of the luff of a fore-and-aft sail 4 Nautical a group of signal flags

Hokkaido the second largest and northernmost of the four main islands of Japan, separated from Honshu by the Tsugaru Strait and from the island of Sakhalin, Russia, by La Pérouse Strait: constitutes an autonomous administrative division. Capital: Sapporo. Pop: 5 670 000 (2002 est). Area: 78 508 sq km (30 312 sq miles)

Hokusai Katsushika 1760–1849, Japanese artist, noted for the draughtsmanship of his colour wood-block prints, which influenced the impressionists

Holbein 1 Hans , known as Holbein the Elder. 1465–1524, German painter 2 his son, Hans, known as Holbein the Younger. 1497–1543, German painter and engraver; court painter to Henry VIII of England (1536–43). He is noted particularly for his portraits, such as those of Erasmus (1524; 1532) and Sir Thomas More (1526)

hold¹ 1 Wrestling a way of seizing one's opponent 2 Music a pause or fermata 3 a a tenure or holding, esp of land **b** (in combination): leasehold; freehold

hold² the space in a ship or aircraft for storing cargo

hold back a strap of the harness joining the breeching to the shaft, so that the horse can hold back the vehicle

holding 1 land held under a lease and used for agriculture or similar purposes 2 property to which the holder has legal title, such as land, stocks, shares, and other investments 3 Sport the obstruction of an opponent with the hands or arms, esp in boxing

hold over US and Canadian, informal 1 Politics an elected official who continues in office after his term has expired 2 Theatre a performer or performance continuing beyond the original engagement

hole 1 an animal's hiding place or burrow 2 the cavity in various games into which the ball must be thrust 3 on a golf course **a** the cup on each of the greens **b** each of the divisions of a course (usually 18) represented by the distance between the tee and a green **c** the score made in striking the ball from the tee into the hole **4** *Physics* **a** a vacancy in a nearly full band of quantum states of electrons in a semiconductor or an insulator. Under the action of an electric field holes behave as carriers of positive charge **b** *(as modifier)*: *hole current* **c** a vacancy in the nearly full continuum of quantum states of negative energy of fermions. A hole appears as the antiparticle of the fermion **5** **in the hole** *Chiefly US* **a** (of a card, the **hole card**, in stud poker) dealt face down in the first round

hole in the heart a a defect of the heart in which there is an abnormal opening in any of the walls dividing the four heart chambers **b** *(as modifier): a hole-in-the-heart operation*

Holi a Hindu spring festival, celebrated for two to five days, commemorating Krishna's dalliance with the cowgirls. Bonfires are lit and coloured powder and water thrown over celebrants

Holiday **Billie** real name *Eleanora Fagan;* known as *Lady Day*. 1915–59, US jazz singer

Holiness a title once given to all bishops, but now reserved for the pope

Holinshed or **Holingshed** **Raphael** died ?1580, English chronicler. His *Chronicles of England, Scotland, and Ireland* (1577) provided material for Shakespeare's historical and legendary plays

holism **1** any doctrine that a system may have properties over and above those of its parts and their organization **2** the treatment of any subject as a whole integrated system, esp, in medicine, the consideration of the complete person, physically and psychologically, in the treatment of a disease **3** *Philosophy* one of a number of methodological theses holding that the significance of the parts can only be understood in terms of their contribution to the significance of the whole and that the latter must therefore be epistemologically prior

Holkar State a former state of central India, ruled by the Holkar dynasty of Maratha rulers of Indore (18th century until 1947)

Holland[1] **1** **Henry** 1745–1806, British neoclassical architect. His work includes Brooks's Club (1776) and Carlton House (1783), both in London **2** **Sir Sidney George** 1893–1961, New Zealand statesman; prime minister of New Zealand (1949–57)

Holland[2] **1** another name for the **Netherlands** **2** a county of the Holy Roman Empire, corresponding to the present-day North and South Holland provinces of the Netherlands **3** **Parts of** an area in E England constituting a former administrative division of Lincolnshire

holly **1** any tree or shrub of the genus *Ilex*, such as the Eurasian *I. aquifolium*, having bright red berries and shiny evergreen leaves with prickly edges **2** branches of any of these trees, used for Christmas decorations **3** **holly oak** another name for **holm oak**

Holly **Buddy** real name *Charles Harden Holley*. 1936–59, US rock-and-roll singer, guitarist, and songwriter. His hits (all 1956–59) include "That'll be the Day", "Maybe Baby", "Peggy Sue", "Oh, Boy", "Think it over", and "It doesn't Matter anymore"

hollyhock a tall widely cultivated malvaceous plant, *Althaea rosea*, with stout hairy stems and spikes of white, yellow, red, or purple flowers

Hollywood **1** a NW suburb of Los Angeles, California: centre of the American film industry. Pop: 250 000 (latest est) **2 a** the American film industry **b** *(as modifier): a Hollywood star*

Holmes **1** **Oliver Wendell** 1809–94, US author, esp of humorous essays, such as *The Autocrat of the Breakfast Table* (1858) and its sequels **2** his son, **Oliver Wendell** 1841–1935, US jurist, noted for his liberal judgments

holmium a malleable silver-white metallic element of the lanthanide series. Symbol: Ho; atomic no.: 67; atomic wt.: 164.93032; valency: 3; relative density: 8.795; melting pt.: 1474°C; boiling pt.: 2700°C

holm oak an evergreen Mediterranean oak tree, *Quercus ilex*, widely planted for ornament: the leaves are holly-like when young but become smooth-edged with age

holocaust **the** Also called: **Churban, Shoah** the mass murder by the Nazis of the Jews of continental Europe between 1940 and 1945
▷www.holocaust-history.org
▷www.nizkor.org

Holocene of, denoting, or formed in the second and most recent epoch of the Quaternary period, which began 10 000 years ago at the end of the Pleistocene

Holofernes the Assyrian general, who was killed by the biblical heroine Judith

hologram a photographic record produced by illuminating the object with coherent light (as from a laser) and, without using lenses, exposing a film to light reflected from this object and to a direct beam of coherent light. When interference patterns on the film are illuminated by the coherent light a three-dimensional image is produced

holography the science or practice of producing holograms

Holst **1** **Alison**. born 1938, New Zealand chef. **2** **Gustav (Theodore)**. 1874–1934, English composer. His works include operas, choral music, and orchestral music such as the suite *The Planets* (1917)

Holstein a region of N Germany, in S Schleswig-Holstein: in early times a German duchy of Saxony; became a duchy of Denmark in 1474; finally incorporated into Prussia in 1866

holster *Mountaineering* a similar case for an ice axe or piton hammer

holt[1] *Archaic or poetic* a wood or wooded hill

holt[2] the burrowed lair of an animal, esp an otter

Holt **Harold Edward** 1908–67, Australian statesman; prime minister (1966–67); believed drowned

holy **1** of, relating to, or associated with God or a deity; sacred **2** endowed or invested with extreme purity or sublimity **3** devout, godly, or virtuous **4 a** a sacred place **b** **the holy** persons or things invested with holiness

Holy Communion **1** the celebration of the Eucharist **2** the consecrated elements of the Eucharist

Holy Grail (in medieval legend) the bowl used by Jesus at the Last Supper. It was allegedly brought to Britain by Joseph of Arimathea, where it became the quest of many knights **b** (in modern spirituality) a symbol of the spiritual wholeness that leads a person to union with the divine

Holyhead a town in NW Wales, in Anglesey, the chief town of Holy Island: a port on the N coast. Pop: 11 237 (2001)

Holy Island 1 an island off the NE coast of Northumberland, linked to the mainland by road but accessible only at low water: site of a monastery founded by St Aidan in 635 **2** an island off the NW coast of Anglesey. Area: about 62 sq km (24 sq miles)

Holyoake Sir Keith Jacka 1904–83, New Zealand politician; prime minister (1957; 1960–72); governor general (1977–80)

holy of holies the innermost compartment of the Jewish tabernacle, and later of the Temple, where the Ark was enshrined

Holy See *RC Church* **1** the see of the pope as bishop of Rome and head of the Church **2** the Roman curia

Holy Spirit *or* **Ghost** *Christianity* the third person of the Trinity

Holy Week the week preceding Easter Sunday

homage (in feudal society) **a** the act of respect and allegiance made by a vassal to his lord **b** something done in acknowledgment of vassalage

home 1 the environment or habitat of a person or animal **2** a building or organization set up to care for orphans, the aged, etc **3** *Sport* one's own ground **4 a** the objective towards which a player strives in certain sports **b** an area where a player is safe from attack **5** *Lacrosse* **a** one of two positions of play nearest the opponents' goal **b** a player assigned to such a position **6** *Sport* relating to one's own ground

Home Baron See (Baron) **Home of the Hirsel**

home-brew a beer or other alcoholic drink brewed at home rather than commercially

homecoming *US* an annual celebration held by a university, college, or school, for former students

home economics the study of diet, budgeting, child care, textiles, and other subjects concerned with running a home

home help *Social welfare* in Britain and New Zealand **1** a person who is paid to do domestic chores for persons unable to look after themselves adequately **2** such a service provided by a local authority social services department to those whom it judges most need it

Home Office *Brit, Government* the national department responsible for the maintenance of law and order, immigration control, and all other domestic affairs not specifically assigned to another department

Home of the Hirsel Baron, title of *Sir Alec Douglas-Home*, formerly 14th Earl of Home. 1903–95, British Conservative statesman: he renounced his earldom to become prime minister of Great Britain and Northern Ireland (1963–64); foreign secretary (1970–74)

homeopathy *or* **homoeopathy** a method of treating disease by the use of small amounts of a drug that, in healthy persons, produces symptoms similar to those of the disease being treated
   ▷www.homeopathy.org

homeostasis *or* **homoeostasis** the maintenance of metabolic equilibrium within an animal by a tendency to compensate for disrupting changes

home page *Computing* (on a website) the main document relating to an individual or institution that provides introductory information about a website with links to the actual details of services or information provided

Homer 1 c. 800 BC, Greek poet to whom are attributed the *Iliad* and the *Odyssey*. Almost nothing is known of him, but it is thought that he was born on the island of Chios and was blind **2** Winslow 1836–1910, US painter, noted for his seascapes and scenes of working life

Homeric *or* **Homerian** of or relating to the archaic form of Greek used by Homer

home rule 1 self-government, esp in domestic affairs **2** *US, Government* the partial autonomy of cities and (in some states) counties, under which they manage their own affairs, with their own charters, etc, within the limits set by the state constitution and laws **3** the partial autonomy sometimes granted to a national minority or a colony

Home Secretary *Brit, Government* short for **Secretary of State for the Home Department**; the head of the Home Office

homespun 1 cloth made at home or made of yarn spun at home **2** a cloth resembling this but made on a power loom

homestead 1 (in the US) a house and adjoining land designated by the owner as his fixed residence and exempt under the homestead laws from seizure and forced sale for debts **2** (in western Canada) a piece of land, usually 160 acres, granted to a settler by the federal government

homesteader 1 a person owning a homestead **2** *US and Canadian* a person who acquires or possesses land under a homestead law **3** a person taking part in a homesteading scheme

homestead law (in the US and Canada) any of various laws conferring certain privileges on owners of homesteads

homework 1 school work done out of lessons, esp at home **2** any preparatory study

homicide 1 the killing of a human being by another person **2** a person who kills another

homily a sermon or discourse on a moral or religious topic

homing 1 *Zoology* relating to the ability to return home after travelling great distances **2** (of an aircraft, a missile, etc) capable of guiding itself onto a target or to a specified point

homing pigeon any breed of pigeon developed for its homing instinct, used for carrying messages or for racing

hominid any primate of the family *Hominidae*, which includes modern man (*Homo sapiens*) and the extinct precursors of man

hominoid of, relating to, or belonging to the primate superfamily *Hominoidea*, which includes the anthropoid apes and man

homogeneous 1 having a constant property, such as density, throughout **2** *Maths* **a** (of a polynomial) containing terms of the same degree with respect to all the variables, as in $x^2 + 2xy + y^2$ **b** (of a function) containing a set of variables such that when each is multiplied by a constant, this constant can be eliminated without altering the value of the function, as in $\cos x/y + x/y$ **c** (of an equation) containing a homogeneous function made equal to o **3** *Chem* of, composed of, or concerned with a single phase

homologous, homological, *or* **homologic 1** *Chem* (of a series of organic compounds) having similar characteristics and structure but differing by a number of CH_2 groups **2** *Med* **a** (of two or more tissues) identical in structure **b** (of a vaccine) prepared from the infecting microorganism **3** *Biology* (of organs and parts) having the same evolutionary origin but different functions **4** *Maths* (of elements) playing a similar role in distinct figures or functions

homology 1 *Chem* the similarities in chemical behaviour shown by members of a homologous series **2** *Zoology* the measurable likenesses between animals, as used in grouping them according to the theory of cladistics

homonym *Biology* a name for a species or genus that should be unique but has been used for two or more different organisms

homophobia intense hatred or fear of homosexuals or homosexuality

homophone a written letter or combination of letters that represents the same speech sound as another

homosexual 1 a person who is sexually attracted to members of the same sex **2** of or relating to homosexuals or homosexuality **3** of or relating to the same sex

homozygous *Genetics* (of an organism) having identical alleles for any one gene

Homs *or* **Hums** a city in W Syria, near the Orontes River: important in Roman times as the capital of Phoenicia-Lebanesia. Pop: 915 000 (2005 est)

Honduras 1 a republic in Central America: an early centre of Mayan civilization; colonized by the Spanish from 1524 onwards; gained independence in 1821. Official language: Spanish; English is also widely spoken. Religion: Roman Catholic majority. Currency: lempira. Capital: Tegucigalpa. Pop: 7 100 000 (2004 est). Area: 112 088 sq km (43 277 sq miles) **2 Gulf of** an inlet of the Caribbean, on the coasts of Honduras, Guatemala, and Belize

hone 1 a fine whetstone, esp for sharpening razors **2** a tool consisting of a number of fine abrasive slips held in a machine head, rotated and reciprocated to impart a smooth finish to cylinder bores, etc.

Honecker Erich 1912–94, German statesman; head of state of East Germany (1976–89)

Honegger Arthur 1892–1955, French composer, one of Les Six. His works include the oratorios *King David* (1921) and *Joan of Arc at the Stake* (1935), and *Pacific 231* (1924) for orchestra

honesty a purple-flowered SE European plant, *Lunaria annua*, cultivated for its flattened silvery pods, which are used for indoor decoration: family *Brassicaceae* (crucifers)

honey any similar sweet substance, esp the nectar of flowers

honeybee any of various social honey-producing bees of the genus *Apis*, esp *A. mellifera*, which has been widely domesticated as a source of honey and beeswax

honeycomb a waxy structure, constructed by bees in a hive, that consists of adjacent hexagonal cells in which honey is stored, eggs are laid, and larvae develop

honeydew 1 a sugary substance excreted by aphids and similar insects **2** a similar substance exuded by certain plants

honeydew melon a variety of muskmelon with a smooth greenish-white rind and sweet greenish flesh

honeysuckle 1 any temperate caprifoliaceous shrub or vine of the genus *Lonicera*: cultivated for their fragrant white, yellow, or pink tubular flowers **2** any of several similar plants **3** any of various Australian trees or shrubs of the genus *Banksia*, having flowers in dense spikes: family *Proteaceae*

Hong Kong 1 a Special Administrative Region of S China, with some autonomy; formerly a British Crown Colony: consists of Hong Kong Island, leased by China to Britain from 1842 until 1997, Kowloon Peninsula, Stonecutters Island, the New Territories (mainland), leased by China in 1898 for a 99-year period, and over 230 small islands; important entrepôt trade and manufacturing centre, esp for textiles and other consumer goods; university (1912). It retains its own currency, the Hong Kong dollar. Administrative centre: Victoria. Pop: 7 182 000 (2005 est). Area: 1046 sq km (404 sq miles) **2** an island in Hong Kong region, south of Kowloon Peninsula: contains the capital, Victoria. Pop: 1 337 800 (2001). Area: 75 sq km (29 sq miles)

Hong-wu *or* **Hung-wu** title of *Chu Yuan-Zhang* (or *Chu Yüan-Chang*), 1328–98, first emperor (1368–98) of the Ming dynasty, uniting China under his rule by 1382

Hong Xiu Quan *or* **Hung Hsiu-Ch'uan** 1814–64, Chinese religious leader and revolutionary. Claiming (1851) to be Christ's brother, he led the Taiping rebellion; committed suicide when it was defeated

Honiara the capital of the Solomon Islands, on NW Guadalcanal Island. Pop: 61 000 (2005 est)

honky-tonk 1 a style of ragtime piano-playing, esp on a tinny-sounding piano **2** a type of country music, usually performed by a small band with electric and steel guitars

Honolulu a port in Hawaii, on S Oahu Island: the state capital. Pop: 380 149 (2003 est)

honorarium a fee paid for a nominally free service

honour *or US* **honor 1 a** *Bridge, Poker* any of the top five cards in a suit or any of the four aces at no trumps **b** *Whist* any of the top four cards **2** *Golf* the right to tee off first

Honour a a title used to or of certain judges **b** (in Ireland) a form of address in general use

Honourable *or US* **Honorable** the a title of respect placed before a name: employed before the names of various officials in the English-speaking world, as a courtesy title in Britain for the children of viscounts and barons and the younger sons of earls, and in Parliament by one member speaking of another

Honshu the largest of the four main islands of Japan, between the Pacific and the Sea of Japan; regarded as the Japanese mainland; includes a number of offshore islands and contains most of the main cities. Pop: 100 995 000 (1995). Area: 230 448 sq km (88 976 sq miles)

hooch *or* **hootch** *Informal, chiefly US and Canadian* alcoholic drink, esp illicitly distilled spirits

Hooch or **Hoogh** Pieter de 1629–?1684, Dutch genre painter, noted esp for his light effects

hood 1 the US and Canadian name for **bonnet** (of a car) 2 the folding roof of a convertible car 3 *Falconry* a close-fitting cover, placed over the head and eyes of a falcon to keep it quiet when not hunting 4 *Biology* a structure or marking, such as the fold of skin on the head of a cobra, that covers or appears to cover the head or some similar part

Hood 1 Robin See **Robin Hood** 2 **Samuel**, 1st Viscount. 1724–1816, British admiral. He fought successfully against the French during the American Revolution and the French Revolutionary Wars 3 **Thomas** 1799–1845, British poet and humorist: his work includes protest poetry, such as *The Song of the Shirt* (1843) and *The Bridge of Sighs* (1844)

hooded crow a subspecies of the carrion crow, *Corvus corone cornix*, that has a grey body and black head, wings, and tail

hoodoo 1 a variant of **voodoo** 2 (in the western US and Canada) a strangely shaped column of rock

hoof 1 the horny covering of the end of the foot in the horse, deer, and all other ungulate mammals 2 the foot of an ungulate mammal 3 a hoofed animal

Hooghly a river in NE India, in West Bengal: the westernmost and commercially most important channel by which the River Ganges enters the Bay of Bengal. Length: 232 km (144 miles)

hook 1 a piece of material, usually metal, curved or bent and used to suspend, catch, hold, or pull something 2 a a sharp bend or angle in a geological formation, esp a river b a sharply curved spit of land 3 *Boxing* a short swinging blow delivered from the side with the elbow bent 4 *Cricket* a shot in which the ball is hit square on the leg side with the bat held horizontally 5 *Golf* a shot that causes the ball to swerve sharply from right to left 6 *Surfing* the top of a breaking wave 7 *Ice hockey* the act of hooking an opposing player 8 *Music* a stroke added to the stem of a written or printed note to indicate time values shorter than a crotchet 9 another name for a **sickle** 10 a nautical word for **anchor**

hookah or **hooka** an oriental pipe for smoking marijuana, tobacco, etc, consisting of one or more long flexible stems connected to a container of water or other liquid through which smoke is drawn and cooled

Hooke Robert 1635–1703, English physicist, chemist, and inventor. He formulated Hooke's law (1678), built the first Gregorian telescope, and invented a balance spring for watches

hooker¹ 1 a commercial fishing boat using hooks and lines instead of nets 2 a sailing boat of the west of Ireland formerly used for cargo and now for pleasure sailing and racing

hooker² *Rugby* the central forward in the front row of a scrum whose main job is to hook the ball

Hooker 1 **John Lee** 1917–2001, US blues singer and guitarist 2 Sir **Joseph Dalton** 1817–1911, British botanist; director of Kew Gardens (1865–85) 3 **Richard** 1554–1600, British theologian, who influenced Anglican theology with *The Laws of Ecclesiastical Polity* (1593–97) 4 Sir **William Jackson** 1785–1865, British botanist; first director of Kew

Gardens: father of Sir Joseph Dalton Hooker

Hook of Holland the 1 a cape on the SW coast of the Netherlands, in South Holland province 2 a port on this cape

hook-up the contact of an aircraft in flight with the refuelling hose of a tanker aircraft

hookworm any parasitic blood-sucking nematode worm of the family *Ancylostomatidae*, esp *Ancylostoma duodenale* or *Necator americanus*, both of which cause disease. They have hooked mouthparts and enter their hosts by boring through the skin

hoop 1 a rigid circular band of metal or wood 2 a a band of iron that holds the staves of a barrel or cask together b (*as modifier*): *hoop iron* 3 *Croquet* any of the iron arches through which the ball is driven 4 *Basketball* the round metal frame to which the net is attached to form the basket 5 *Austral, informal* a jockey

hoopla *Brit* a fairground game in which a player tries to throw a hoop over an object and so win it

hoopoe an Old World bird, *Upupa epops*, having a pinkish-brown plumage with black-and-white wings and an erectile crest: family *Upupidae*, order *Coraciiformes* (kingfishers, etc)

hoop pine a fast-growing timber tree of Australia, *Araucaria cunninghamii*, having rough bark with hoop-like cracks around the trunk and branches: family *Araucariaceae*

Hoover¹ 1 **Herbert (Clark)**. 1874–1964, US statesman; 31st president of the US (1929–33). He organized relief for Europe during and after World War I, but as president he lost favour after his failure to alleviate the effects of the Depression 2 **J(ohn) Edgar** 1895–1972, US lawyer: director of the FBI (1924–72). He used new scientific methods to combat crime, including the first fingerprint file

Hoover² *Trademark* a type of vacuum cleaner

Hoover Dam a dam in the western US, on the Colorado River on the border between Nevada and Arizona; forms Lake Mead. Height: 222 m (727 ft). Length: 354 m (1180 ft)

hop¹ *Old-fashioned informal* a dance, esp one at which popular music is played

hop² *Obsolete slang* opium or any other narcotic drug

hop³ 1 any climbing plant of the N temperate genus *Humulus*, esp H. *lupulus*, which has green conelike female flowers and clusters of small male flowers: family *Cannabiaceae* (or *Cannabidaceae*) 2 **hop garden** a field of hops

Hope 1 **Anthony**, real name *Sir Anthony Hope Hawkins*. 1863–1933, English novelist; author of *The Prisoner of Zenda* (1894) 2 **Bob**, real name *Leslie Townes Hope*. 1903–2003, US comedian and comic actor, born in England. His films include *The Cat and the Canary* (1939), *Road to Morocco* (1942), and *The Paleface* (1947). He was awarded an honorary knighthood in 1998 3 **David (Michael)**. born 1940, British churchman, Archbishop of York from 1995

Hopkins 1 Sir **Anthony** born 1937, Welsh actor: his films include *Bounty* (1984), *The Silence of the Lambs* (1991), *Shadowlands* (1994), and *Hannibal* (2000) 2 Sir **Frederick Gowland** 1861–1947, British biochemist, who pioneered research into what came to be called vitamins: shared the Nobel prize for physiology or medicine (1929) 3

Gerald Manley 1844–89, British poet and Jesuit priest, who experimented with sprung rhythm in his highly original poetry 4 Harry L(loyd). 1890–1946, US administrator. During World War II he was a personal aide to President Roosevelt and administered the lend-lease programme

hopper 1 a funnel-shaped chamber or reservoir from which solid materials can be discharged under gravity into a receptacle below, esp for feeding fuel to a furnace, loading a railway truck with grain, etc. 2 any of various long-legged hopping insects, esp the grasshopper, leaf hopper, and immature locust 3 an open-topped railway truck for bulk transport of loose minerals, etc, unloaded through doors on the underside 4 *Computing* a device formerly used for holding punched cards and feeding them to a card punch or card reader

hopscotch a children's game in which a player throws a small stone or other object to land in one of a pattern of squares marked on the ground and then hops over to it to pick it up

Horace Latin name *Quintus Horatius Flaccus*. 65–8 BC, Roman poet and satirist: his verse includes the lyrics in the *Epodes* and the *Odes*, the *Epistles* and *Satires*, and the *Ars Poetica*

Horatius Cocles a legendary Roman hero of the 6th century BC, who defended a bridge over the Tiber against Lars Porsena

horde 1 a local group of people in a nomadic society 2 a nomadic group of people, esp an Asiatic group 3 a large moving mass of animals, esp insects

Horeb *Bible* a mountain, probably Mount Sinai

horehound *or* **hoarhound** a downy perennial herbaceous Old World plant, *Marrubium vulgare*, with small white flowers that contain a bitter juice formerly used as a cough medicine and flavouring: family *Lamiaceae* (labiates)

horizon 1 the apparent line that divides the earth and the sky 2 *Astronomy* **a** the circular intersection with the celestial sphere of the plane tangential to the earth at the position of the observer **b** the great circle on the celestial sphere, the plane of which passes through the centre of the earth and is parallel to the sensible horizon 3 a thin layer of rock within a stratum that has a distinct composition, esp of fossils, by which the stratum may be dated 4 a layer in a soil profile having particular characteristics

horizontal 1 measured or contained in a plane parallel to that of the horizon 2 *Economics* relating to identical stages of commercial activity

hormone 1 a chemical substance produced in an endocrine gland and transported in the blood to a certain tissue, on which it exerts a specific effect 2 an organic compound produced by a plant that is essential for growth 3 any synthetic substance having the same effects

Hormuz *or* **Ormuz** an island off the SE coast of Iran, in the **Strait of Hormuz**: ruins of the ancient city of Hormuz, a major trading centre in the Middle Ages. Area: about 41 sq km (16 sq miles)

horn 1 either of a pair of permanent outgrowths on the heads of cattle, antelopes, sheep, etc, consisting of a central bony core covered with layers of keratin 2 the

outgrowth from the nasal bone of a rhinoceros, consisting of a mass of fused hairs 3 any hornlike projection or process, such as the eyestalk of a snail 4 the antler of a deer 5 the constituent substance, mainly keratin, of horns, hooves, etc. 6 a primitive musical wind instrument made from the horn of an animal 7 any musical instrument consisting of a pipe or tube of brass fitted with a mouthpiece, with or without valves 8 *Jazz, slang* any wind instrument 9 a device for producing a warning or signalling noise 10 an extension of an aircraft control surface that projects in front of the hinge providing aerodynamic assistance in moving the control 11 **a** a hollow conical device coupled to the diaphragm of a gramophone to control the direction and quality of the sound **b** any such device used to spread or focus sound, such as the device attached to an electrical loudspeaker in a public address system **c** a microwave aerial, formed by flaring out the end of a waveguide 12 a stretch of land or water shaped like a horn 13 *Bible* a symbol of power, victory, or success

Horn Cape See **Cape Horn**

hornbeam 1 any tree of the betulaceous genus *Carpinus*, such as *C. betulus* of Europe and Asia, having smooth grey bark and hard white wood 2 the wood of any of these trees

hornbill any bird of the family *Bucerotidae* of tropical Africa and Asia, having a very large bill with a basal bony protuberance: order *Coraciiformes* (kingfishers, etc)

hornblende a black or greenish-black mineral of the amphibole group, found in igneous and metamorphic rocks. Composition: calcium magnesium iron sodium aluminium aluminosilicate. General formula: $(Ca,Na)_{2.3}(Mg,Fe,Al)_5Si_6(Si,Al)_2O_{22}(OH)_2$

Hornby Nick born 1958, British writer; his books include the memoir *Fever Pitch* (1992; filmed 1997) and the bestselling novels *About a Boy* (1998; filmed 2002) and *How To Be Good* (2001)

hornet any of various large social wasps of the family *Vespidae*, esp *Vespa crabro* of Europe, that can inflict a severe sting

Horn of Africa a region of NE Africa, comprising Somalia and adjacent territories

horn of plenty an edible basidiomycetous fungus, *Craterellus cornucopioides*, related to the chanterelle and like it funnel shaped but dark brown inside and dark grey outside: found in broad-leaved woodland

hornpipe 1 an obsolete reed instrument with a mouthpiece made of horn 2 an old British solo dance to a hornpipe accompaniment, traditionally performed by sailors 3 a piece of music for such a dance

horoscope 1 the prediction of a person's future based on a comparison of the zodiacal data for the time of birth with the data from the period under consideration 2 the configuration of the planets, the sun, and the moon in the sky at a particular moment 3 a diagram showing the positions of the planets, sun, moon, etc, at a particular time and place

Horowitz Vladimir 1904–89, Russian virtuoso pianist, in the US from 1928

Horsa died ?455 AD, leader, with his brother Hengist, of the first Jutish settlers in Britain

horse 1 a domesticated perissodactyl mammal, *Equus*

caballus, used for draught work and riding: family *Equidae* **2** the adult male of this species; stallion **3 wild horse** a horse (*Equus caballus*) that has become feral **4 a** any other member of the family *Equidae*, such as the zebra or ass **b** (*as modifier*): *the horse family* **5** *Gymnastics* a padded apparatus on legs, used for vaulting, etc. **6** a slang word for **heroin 7** *Nautical* a rod, rope, or cable, fixed at the ends, along which something may slide by means of a thimble, shackle, or other fitting; traveller **8** *Chess* an informal name for **knight 9** *Informal* short for **horsepower**

horsebox *Brit* a van or trailer used for carrying horses

horse brass a decorative brass ornament, usually circular, originally attached to a horse's harness

horse chestnut 1 any of several trees of the genus *Aesculus*, esp the Eurasian *A. hippocastanum*, having palmate leaves, erect clusters of white, pink, or red flowers, and brown shiny inedible nuts enclosed in a spiky bur: family *Hippocastanaceae* **2** the nut of this tree

horseflesh horses collectively

horsefly any large stout-bodied dipterous fly of the family *Tabanidae*, the females of which suck the blood of mammals, esp horses, cattle, and man

horsehair a hair taken chiefly from the tail or mane of a horse, used in upholstery and for fabric, etc. **b** (*as modifier*): *a horsehair mattress*

Horsens a port in Denmark, in E Jutland at the head of Horsens Fjord Pop: 49 652 (2004 est)

horsepower 1 an fps unit of power, equal to 550 foot-pounds per second (equivalent to 745.7 watts) **2** a US standard unit of power, equal to 746 watts

horseradish 1 a coarse Eurasian plant, *Armoracia rusticana*, cultivated for its thick white pungent root: family *Brassicaceae* (crucifers) **2** the root of this plant, which is ground and combined with vinegar, etc, to make a sauce

horseshoe a piece of iron shaped like a U with the ends curving inwards that is nailed to the underside of the hoof of a horse to protect the soft part of the foot from hard surfaces: commonly thought to be a token of good luck

horsetail any tracheophyte plant of the genus *Equisetum*, having jointed stems with whorls of small dark tooth-like leaves and producing spores within conelike structures at the tips of the stems: phylum *Sphenophyta*

horsewhip a whip, usually with a long thong, used for managing horses

Horta¹ Victor 1861–1947, Belgian architect, best known for his early buildings in Art Nouveau style

Horta² a port in the Azores, on the SE coast of Fayal Island

Horthy Miklós , full name *Horthy de Nagybánya*. 1868–1957, Hungarian admiral: suppressed Kun's Communist republic (1919); regent of Hungary (1920–44)

horticulture the art or science of cultivating gardens
▷www.horticulture.org.uk/IoHLinks.htm
▷www.ishs.org/

Horus a solar god of Egyptian mythology, usually depicted with a falcon's head

Hosea *Old Testament* **1** a Hebrew prophet of the 8th century BC **2** the book containing his oracles

hospice a nursing home that specializes in caring for the terminally ill

hospital 1 an institution for the medical, surgical, obstetric, or psychiatric care and treatment of patients **2** having the function of a hospital

Hospitalet a city in NE Spain, a SW suburb of Barcelona. Pop: 246 415 (2003 est)

hospitaller *or US* **hospitaler** a person, esp a member of certain religious orders, dedicated to hospital work, ambulance services, etc.

host 1 *Biology* **a** an animal or plant that nourishes and supports a parasite **b** an animal, esp an embryo, into which tissue is experimentally grafted **2** *Computing* a computer connected to a network and providing facilities to other computers and their users **3** the owner or manager of an inn

Host *Christian Church* the bread consecrated in the Eucharist

hot 1 having a relatively high temperature **2** *Ball games* (of a ball) thrown or struck hard, and so difficult to respond to **3** *Informal* having a dangerously high level of radioactivity **4** (of a colour) intense; striking **5** *Informal* at a dangerously high electric potential **6** *Physics* having an energy level higher than that of the ground state **7** *Jazz, slang* arousing great excitement or enthusiasm by inspired improvisation, strong rhythms, etc. **8** (in various searching or guessing games) very near the answer or object to be found **9** *Metallurgy* (of a process) at a sufficiently high temperature for metal to be in a soft workable state

Hotan, Hotien, *or* **Ho-t'ien 1** an oasis in W China, in the Taklimakan Shamo desert of central Xinjiang Uygur Autonomous Region, around the seasonal Hotan River **2** the chief town of this oasis, situated at the foot of the Kunlun Mountains. Pop: 71 600 (latest est)

hotbed a glass-covered bed of soil, usually heated by fermenting material, used for propagating plants, forcing early vegetables, etc.

hot-blooded (of a horse) being of thoroughbred stock

hot dog *Chiefly US* a person who performs showy acrobatic manoeuvres when skiing or surfing

hotel a commercially run establishment providing lodging and usually meals for guests, and often containing a public bar

hotelier an owner or manager of one or more hotels

Hotere Ralph born 1931, New Zealand artist of Māori origin, noted esp for his minimalist *Black Paintings*

hothouse a greenhouse in which the temperature is maintained at a fixed level above that of the surroundings **b** (*as modifier*): *a hothouse plant*

hot key *Computing* a single key or combination of keys on the keyboard of a computer that carries out a series of commands

hot pool a pool or spring that is heated geothermally

hot rod a car with an engine that has been radically modified to produce increased power

hot spot 1 an area of potential violence or political unrest **2 a** any local area of high temperature in a part of an engine, etc. **b** part of the inlet manifold of a paraffin engine that is heated by exhaust gases to vaporize the fuel **3** *Computing* a company that provides wireless access to the internet for users of portable computers or the places from which the internet can be accessed in this manner **4** *Med* **a** a small area on the surface of or within a body with an exceptionally high concentration of radioactivity or of some chemical or mineral considered harmful **b** a similar area that generates an abnormal amount of heat, as revealed by thermography **5** *Genetics* a part of a chromosome that has a tendency for mutation or recombination

Hotspur Harry nickname of (Sir Henry) **Percy**

hotting *Informal* the practice of stealing fast cars and putting on a show of skilful but dangerous driving

hot-water bottle a receptacle, now usually made of rubber, designed to be filled with hot water, used for warming a bed or parts of the body

Houdini Harry, real name *Ehrich Weiss*. 1874–1926, US magician and escapologist

Houdon Jean Antoine 1741–1828, French neoclassical portrait sculptor

Houghton-le-Spring a town in N England, in Sunderland unitary authority, Tyne and Wear: coalmining. Pop: 36 746 (2001)

hound[1] **1 a** any of several breeds of dog used for hunting **b** (*in combination*) **2 the hounds** a pack of foxhounds, etc. **3** (in hare and hounds) a runner who pursues a hare **4 ride to hounds** *or* **follow the hounds** to take part in a fox hunt with hounds

hound[2] **1** either of a pair of horizontal bars that reinforce the running gear of a horse-drawn vehicle **2** *Nautical* either of a pair of fore-and-aft braces that serve as supports for a topmast

Hounslow a borough of Greater London, on the River Thames: site of London's first civil airport (1919). Pop: 212 900 (2003 est). Area: 59 sq km (23 sq miles)

Houphouet-Boigny Félix 1905–93, Côte d'Ivoire statesman; president of the Côte d'Ivoire (1960–93)

hour 1 a period of time equal to 3600 seconds; 1/24th of a calendar day **2** *Astronomy* an angular measurement of right ascension equal to 15° or a 24th part of the celestial equator

houri (in Muslim belief) any of the nymphs of Paradise

house 1 *Genealogy* a family line including ancestors and relatives, esp a noble one **2** a commercial company; firm **3** *Politics* an official deliberative or legislative body, such as one chamber of a bicameral legislature **4** a quorum in such a body (esp in the phrase **make a house**) **5** a dwelling for a religious community **6** *Astrology* any of the 12 divisions of the zodiac **7** any of several divisions, esp residential, of a large school **8** a hotel, restaurant, bar, inn, club, etc, or the management of such an establishment **9** the audience in a theatre or cinema **10** a hall in which an official deliberative or legislative body meets **11** See **full house 12** *Curling* the 12-foot target circle around the tee **13** *Nautical* any structure or shelter on the weather deck of a vessel

house arrest confinement to one's own home

houseboat a stationary boat or barge used as a home

housebreaking *Criminal law* the act of entering a building as a trespasser for an unlawful purpose. Assimilated with burglary, 1968

housefly a common dipterous fly, *Musca domestica*, that frequents human habitations, spreads disease, and lays its eggs in carrion, decaying vegetables, etc.: family *Muscidae*

housekeeping *Computing* the general maintenance of a computer storage system, including removal of obsolete files, documentation, security copying, etc.

house martin a Eurasian swallow, *Delichon urbica*, with a slightly forked tail and a white and bluish-black plumage

House music *or* **House** a type of disco music originating in the late 1980s, based on funk, with fragments of other recordings edited in electronically
▷www.house-music-inyourface.com

House of Commons (in Britain, Canada, etc) the lower chamber of Parliament

House of Keys the lower chamber of the legislature of the Isle of Man

House of Lords (in Britain) the upper chamber of Parliament, composed of the peers of the realm

House of Representatives 1 (in the US) the lower chamber of Congress **2** (in Australia) the lower chamber of Parliament **3** the sole chamber of New Zealand's Parliament: formerly the lower chamber **4** (in the US) the lower chamber in many state legislatures

housing *Engineering* a part designed to shelter, cover, contain, or support a component, such as a bearing, or a mechanism, such as a pump or wheel

Housman A(lfred) E(dward). 1859–1936, English poet and classical scholar, author of *A Shropshire Lad* (1896) and *Last Poems* (1922)

Houston an inland port in SE Texas, linked by the **Houston Ship Canal** to the Gulf of Mexico and the Gulf Intracoastal Waterway: capital of the Republic of Texas (1837–39; 1842–45); site of the Manned Spacecraft Center (1964). Pop: 2 009 690 (2003 est)

Hove a town and coastal resort in S England, in Brighton and Hove unitary authority, East Sussex. Pop: 72 335 (2001)

hovea any of various plants of the Australian genus *Hovea*, having clusters of small purple flowers

hovel the conical building enclosing a kiln

hovercraft a vehicle that is able to travel across both land and water on a cushion of air. The cushion is produced by a fan continuously forcing air under the vehicle

Howard 1 Catherine ?1521–42, fifth wife of Henry VIII of England; beheaded **2 Charles**, Lord Howard of Effingham and 1st Earl of Nottingham. 1536–1624, Lord High Admiral of England (1585–1618). He commanded the fleet that defeated the Spanish Armada (1588) **3** Sir Ebenezer 1850–1928, English town planner, who introduced garden cities **4** Henry See (Earl of) **Surrey 5** John 1726–90, English prison reformer **6** John Winston born 1939, Australian politician; prime minister of Australia from 1996 **7 Leslie** real name *Leslie Howard Stainer*. 1890–1943, British actor of Hungarian descent. His many films included *The Scarlet Pimpernel* (1938), *Pygmalion* (1938), and *Gone With the Wind* (1939) **8** Trevor 1916-88, British actor. His many films include *Brief Encounter* (1946), *The Third Man* (1949), *Ryan's Daughter* (1970), and *White Mischief* (1987)

Howe 1 Elias 1819–67, US inventor of the sewing machine (1846) **2** Gordon, known as *Gordie*. born 1928, US ice-hockey player, who scored a record 1071 goals in a professional career lasting 32 years. **3** Howe of

Aberavon, Baron, title of (*Richard Edward) Geoffrey Howe*. born 1926, British Conservative politician; Chancellor of the Exchequer (1979–83); foreign secretary (1983–89); deputy prime minister (1989–90) **4 Richard,** 4th Viscount Howe. 1726–99, British admiral: served (1776–78) in the War of American Independence and commanded the Channel fleet against France, winning the Battle of the Glorious First of June (1794) **5** his brother, **William,** 5th Viscount Howe. 1729–1814, British general; commander in chief (1776–78) of British forces in the War of American Independence

howl *Electronics* an unwanted prolonged high-pitched sound produced by a sound-producing system as a result of feedback

Howland Island a small island in the central Pacific, near the equator northwest of Phoenix Island: US airfield. Area: 2.6 sq km (1 sq mile)

howler any large New World monkey of the genus *Alouatta*, inhabiting tropical forests in South America and having a loud howling cry

Howrah an industrial city in E India, in West Bengal on the Hooghly River opposite Calcutta. Pop: 1 008 704 (2001)

Hoxha Enver 1908–85, Albanian statesman: founded the Albanian Communist Party in 1941 and was its first secretary (1954–85)

hoy *Nautical* **1** a freight barge **2** a coastal fishing and trading vessel, usually sloop-rigged, used during the 17th and 18th centuries

Hoylake a town and resort in NW England, in Wirral unitary authority, Merseyside, on the Irish Sea. Pop: 25 524 (2001)

Hoyle Sir Fred 1915–2001, English astronomer and writer: his books include *The Nature of the Universe* (1950) and *Frontiers of Astronomy* (1955), and science-fiction writings

HTML hypertext markup language: a text description language that is used for electronic publishing, esp on the World Wide Web

Hua Guo Feng *or* **Hua Kuo-feng** born c. 1920, Chinese Communist statesman; prime minister of China 1976–80

Huainan a city in E China, in Anhui province north of Hefei. Pop: 1 422 000 (2005 est)

Huambo a town in central Angola: designated at one time by the Portuguese as the future capital of the country. Pop: 756 000 (2005 est)

hub 1 the central portion of a wheel, propeller, fan, etc, through which the axle passes **2** *Computing* a device for connecting computers in a network

Hubble Edwin Powell 1889–1953, US astronomer, noted for his investigations of nebulae and the recession of the galaxies

hubcap a metal cap fitting onto the hub of a wheel, esp a stainless steel or chromium-plated one

Hubei, Hupeh, *or* **Hupei** a province of central China: largely low-lying with many lakes. Capital: Wuhan. Pop: 60 020 000 (2003 est). Area: 187 500 sq km (72 394 sq miles)

Hubli a city in W India, in NW Mysore: incorporated with Dharwar in 1961; educational and trading centre. Pop. (with Dharwar): 786 018 (2001)

hubris *or* **hybris** (in Greek tragedy) an excess of ambition, pride, etc, ultimately causing the transgressor's ruin

huckster 1 a person who uses aggressive or questionable methods of selling **2** *Now rare* a person who sells small articles or fruit in the street

Huddersfield a town in N England, in Kirklees unitary authority, West Yorkshire, on the River Colne: former textile centre, now with varied manufacturing and services; university 1992. Pop: 146 234 (2001)

Hudson 1 Henry died 1611, English navigator: he explored the Hudson River (1609) and Hudson Bay (1610), where his crew mutinied and cast him adrift to die **2** W(illiam) H(enry). 1841–1922, British naturalist and novelist, born in Argentina, noted esp for his romance *Green Mansions* (1904) and the autobiographical *Far Away and Long Ago* (1918)

Hudson Bay an inland sea in NE Canada: linked with the Atlantic by **Hudson Strait;** the S extension forms James Bay; discovered in 1610 by Henry Hudson. Area (excluding James Bay): 647 500 sq km (250 000 sq miles)

Hudson River a river in E New York State, flowing generally south into Upper New York Bay: linked to the Great Lakes, the St Lawrence Seaway, and Lake Champlain by the New York State Barge Canal and the canalized Mohawk River. Length: 492 km (306 miles)

hue the attribute of colour that enables an observer to classify it as red, green, blue, purple, etc, and excludes white, black, and shades of grey

hue and cry (formerly) the pursuit of a suspected criminal with loud cries in order to raise the alarm

Huelva a port in SW Spain, between the estuaries of the Odiel and Tinto Rivers: exports copper and other ores. Pop: 144 831 (2003 est)

Huesca a city in NE Spain: Roman town, site of Quintus Sertorius' school (76 BC); 15th-century cathedral and ancient palace of Aragonese kings. Pop: 47 609 (2003 est)

Huggins Sir William 1824–1910, British astronomer. He pioneered the use of spectroscopy in astronomy and discovered the red shift in the lines of a stellar spectrum

Hughes 1 Howard 1905–76, US industrialist, aviator, and film producer. He became a total recluse during the last years of his life **2** (James Mercer) Langston 1902–67, US Black poet and writer. His collections include *The Weary Blues* (1926) and *The Panther and the Lash* (1967) **3** Richard (Arthur Warren). 1900–76, British novelist. He wrote *A High Wind in Jamaica* (1929), *In Hazard* (1938), and *The Fox in the Attic* (1961) **4** Robert (Studley Forrest). born 1938, Australian art critic, writer, and broadcaster; his work includes the television series *The Shock of the New* (1981) and the book *The Culture of Complaint* (1993) **5** Ted, full name *Edward James Hughes*. 1930–98, British poet: his works include *The Hawk in the Rain* (1957), *Crow* (1970), and *Birthday Letters* (1998). Poet laureate (1984–98) **6** Thomas 1822–96, British novelist; author of *Tom Brown's Schooldays* (1857) **7** William Morris 1864–1952, Australian statesman, born in England: prime minister of Australia (1915–23)

Hugo Victor (Marie). 1802–85, French poet, novelist, and dramatist; leader of the romantic movement in France.

His works include the volumes of verse *Les Feuilles d'automne* (1831) and *Les Contemplations* (1856), the novels *Notre-Dame de Paris* (1831) and *Les Misérables* (1862), and the plays *Hernani* (1830) and *Ruy Blas* (1838)

Huguenot 1 a French Calvinist, esp of the 16th or 17th centuries 2 designating the French Protestant Church

hula *or* **hula-hula** a Hawaiian dance performed by a woman

Hula Hoop *Trademark* a light hoop that is whirled around the body by movements of the waist and hips

hulk 1 the body of an abandoned vessel 2 *Disparaging* a large or unwieldy vessel 3 the frame or hull of a ship, used as a storehouse, etc, or (esp in 19th-century Britain) as a prison

hull 1 the main body of a vessel, tank, flying boat, etc. 2 the shell or pod of peas or beans; the outer covering of any fruit or seed; husk 3 the persistent calyx at the base of a strawberry, raspberry, or similar fruit

Hull¹ Cordell 1871–1955, US statesman; secretary of state (1933–44). He helped to found the U.N.: Nobel peace prize 1945

Hull² 1 a city and port in NE England, in Kingston upon Hull unitary authority, East Riding of Yorkshire: fishing, food processing; two universities. Pop: 301 416 (2001). Official name: **Kingston upon Hull** 2 a city in SE Canada, in SW Quebec on the River Ottawa: a centre of the timber trade and associated industries. Pop: 66 246 (2001)

hum *Electronics* an undesired low-frequency noise in the output of an amplifier or receiver, esp one caused by the power supply

humanism 1 the denial of any power or moral value superior to that of humanity; the rejection of religion in favour of a belief in the advancement of humanity by its own efforts 2 a philosophical position that stresses the autonomy of human reason in contradistinction to the authority of the Church 3 a cultural movement of the Renaissance, based on classical studies

humanitarian of or relating to ethical or theological humanitarianism

humanity 1 the study of literature, philosophy, and the arts 2 the study of Ancient Greek and Roman language, literature, etc.

humanoid 1 a being with human rather than anthropoid characteristics 2 (in science fiction) a robot or creature resembling a human being

Humber an estuary in NE England, into which flow the Rivers Ouse and Trent: flows east into the North Sea; navigable for large ocean-going ships as far as Hull; crossed by the **Humber Bridge** (1981), a single-span suspension bridge with a main span of 1410 m (4626 ft). Length: 64 km (40 miles)

Humberside a former county of N England around the Humber estuary, formed in 1974 from parts of the East and West Ridings of Yorkshire and N Lincolnshire: replaced in 1996 by the unitary authorities of East Riding of Yorkshire, Kingston upon Hull, North Lincolnshire, and North East Lincolnshire

Humboldt 1 Baron (Friedrich Heinrich) Alexander von 1769–1859, German scientist, who made important scientific explorations in Central and South America (1799–1804). In *Kosmos* (1845–62), he provided a compre-

hensive description of the physical universe 2 his brother, Baron (**Karl**) **Wilhelm von** 1767–1835, German philologist and educational reformer

Hume 1 (**George**) **Basil** 1923–99, English Roman Catholic Benedictine monk and cardinal; archbishop of Westminster (1976–99) 2 **David** 1711–76, Scottish empiricist philosopher, economist, and historian, whose sceptic philosophy restricted human knowledge to that which can be perceived by the senses. His works include *A Treatise of Human Nature* (1740), *An Enquiry concerning the Principles of Morals* (1751), *Political Discourses* (1752), and *History of England* (1754–62) 3 **John** born 1937, Northern Ireland politician; leader of the Social Democratic and Labour Party (SDLP) (1979–2001). Nobel peace prize jointly with David Trimble in 1998

humerus 1 the bone that extends from the shoulder to the elbow 2 the corresponding bone in other vertebrates

humidex *Canadian* a scale indicating the levels of heat and humidity in current weather conditions

humidity a measure of the amount of moisture in the air

Hummel Johann Nepomuk 1778–1837, German composer and pianist

hummingbird any very small American bird of the family *Trochilidae*, having a brilliant iridescent plumage, long slender bill, and wings specialized for very powerful vibrating flight: order *Apodiformes*

hummock 1 a hillock; knoll 2 a ridge or mound of ice in an ice field 3 *Chiefly southern* US a wooded area lying above the level of an adjacent marsh

humour *or* US **humor** 1 any of various fluids in the body, esp the aqueous humour and vitreous humour 2 *Archaic* any of the four bodily fluids (blood, phlegm, choler or yellow bile, melancholy or black bile) formerly thought to determine emotional and physical disposition

hump 1 *Pathol* a rounded deformity of the back in persons with kyphosis, consisting of a convex spinal curvature 2 a rounded protuberance on the back of a camel or related animal

humpback 1 another word for hunchback 2 a large whalebone whale, *Megaptera novaeangliae*, closely related and similar to the rorquals but with a humped back and long flippers: family *Balaenopteridae* 3 a Pacific salmon, *Oncorhynchus gorbuscha*, the male of which has a humped back and hooked jaws 4 *Brit* a road bridge having a sharp incline and decline and usually a narrow roadway

Humperdinck Engelbert 1854–1921, German composer, esp of operas, including *Hansel and Gretel* (1893)

Humphrey 1 Duke See (Humphrey, Duke of) Gloucester 2 Hubert Horatio 1911–78, US statesman; vice-president of the US under President Johnson (1965–69)

Humphreys Peak a mountain in N central Arizona, in the San Francisco Peaks: the highest peak in the state. Height: 3862 m (12 670 ft)

Humphries (John) Barry born 1934, Australian comic actor and writer, best known for creating the character Dame Edna Everage

humus a dark brown or black colloidal mass of partially decomposed organic matter in the soil. It improves the fertility and water retention of the soil and is therefore important for plant growth

Hun a member of any of several Asiatic nomadic peoples speaking Mongoloid or Turkic languages who dominated much of Asia and E Europe from before 300 BC, invading the Roman Empire in the 4th and 5th centuries AD

Hunan a province of S China, between the Yangtze River and the Nan Ling Mountains: drained chiefly by the Xiang and Yüan Rivers; valuable mineral resources. Capital: Changsha. Pop: 66 630 000 (2003 est). Area: 210 500 sq km (82 095 sq miles)

hunchback 1 a person having an abnormal convex curvature of the thoracic spine 2 such a curvature

hundred 1 the cardinal number that is the product of ten and ten; five score 2 a numeral, 100, C, etc, representing this number 3 *Maths* the position containing a digit representing that number followed by two zeros 4 *History* an ancient division of a county in England, Ireland, and parts of the US

hundredweight 1 *Brit* a unit of weight equal to 112 pounds or 50.802 35 kilograms 2 *US and Canadian* a unit of weight equal to 100 pounds or 45.359 24 kilograms 3 a metric unit of weight equal to 50 kilograms

hung a (of a legislative assembly) not having a party with a working majority b unable to reach a decision c (of a situation) unable to be resolved

Hungarian the official language of Hungary, also spoken in Romania and elsewhere, belonging to the Finno-Ugric family and most closely related to the Ostyak and Vogul languages of NW Siberia

Hungary a republic in central Europe: Magyars first unified under Saint Stephen, the first Hungarian king (1001–38); taken by the Hapsburgs from the Turks at the end of the 17th century; gained autonomy with the establishment of the dual monarchy of Austria-Hungary (1867) and became a republic in 1918; passed under Communist control in 1949; a popular rising in 1956 was suppressed by Soviet troops; a multi-party democracy replaced Communism in 1989 after mass protests; joined the EU in 2004. It consists chiefly of the Middle Danube basin and plains. Official language: Hungarian. Religion: Christian majority. Currency: forint. Capital: Budapest. Pop: 9 831 000 (2004 est). Area: 93 030 sq km (35 919 sq miles)

Hungnam a port in E North Korea, on the Sea of Japan southeast of Hamhung. Pop: 260 000 (latest est)

Hunt 1 Henry, known as *Orator Hunt*. 1773–1835, British radical, who led the mass meeting that ended in the Peterloo Massacre (1819) 2 (**William**) Holman 1827–1910, British painter; a founder of the Pre-Raphaelite Brotherhood (1848) 3 James 1947–93, British motor-racing driver: world champion 1976 4 (**Henry Cecil**) John, Baron. 1910–98, British army officer and mountaineer. He planned and led the expedition that first climbed Mount Everest (1953) 5 (**James Henry**) Leigh 1784–1859, British poet and essayist: a founder of *The Examiner* (1808) in which he promoted the work of Keats and Shelley

hunter 1 a specially bred horse used in hunting, usually characterized by strength and stamina 2 a specially bred dog used to hunt game

Huntingdon¹ Selina, Countess of Huntingdon. 1707–91,

English religious leader, who founded a Calvinistic Methodist sect

Huntingdon² a town in E central England, in Cambridgeshire: birthplace of Oliver Cromwell. Pop. (with Godmanchester): 20 600 (2001))

Huntingdonshire (until 1974) a former county of E England, now part of Cambridgeshire

huntsman 1 a person who hunts 2 a person who looks after and trains hounds, beagles, etc, and manages them during a hunt

Huntsville a city in NE Alabama: space-flight and guided-missile research centre. Pop: 164 237 (2003 est)

hurdle 1 a *Athletics* one of a number of light barriers over which runners leap in certain events b a low barrier used in certain horse races 2 *Brit* a sledge on which criminals were dragged to their executions

hurdy-gurdy 1 any mechanical musical instrument, such as a barrel organ 2 a medieval instrument shaped like a viol in which a rosined wheel rotated by a handle sounds the strings

hurling a traditional Irish game resembling hockey and lacrosse, played with sticks and a ball between two teams of 15 players each

▷www.gaa.ie/sports/hurling

Huron 1 Lake a lake in North America, between the US and Canada: the second largest of the Great Lakes. Area: 59 570 sq km (23 000 sq miles) 2 a member of a North American Indian people formerly living in the region east of Lake Huron 3 the Iroquoian language of this people

hurricane 1 a severe, often destructive storm, esp a tropical cyclone 2 a a wind of force 12 or above on the Beaufort scale b (*as modifier*): *a wind of hurricane force*

hurricane lamp a paraffin lamp, with a glass covering to prevent the flame from being blown out

Hus Jan the Czech name of (John) Huss

Husain ?629–680 AD, Islamic caliph, the son of Ali and Fatima and the grandson of Mohammed

Husein ibn-Ali 1856–1931, first king of Hejaz (1916–24): initiated the Arab revolt against the Turks (1916–18); forced to abdicate by ibn-Saud

husk¹ the external green or membranous covering of certain fruits and seeds

husk² bronchitis in cattle, sheep, and goats, usually caused by lungworm infestation

husky a breed of Arctic sled dog with a thick dense coat, pricked ears, and a curled tail

Huss John, Czech name *Jan Hus*. ?1372–1415, Bohemian religious reformer. Influenced by Wycliffe, he anticipated the Reformation in denouncing doctrines and abuses of the Church. His death at the stake precipitated the Hussite wars in Bohemia and Moravia

Hussein 1 1935–99, king of Jordan (1952–99) 2 Saddam born 1937, Iraqi politician: president (1979–2003) and prime minister (1994–2003) of Iraq. He led Iraq into the Iran-Iraq War (1980–88) and the Gulf War (1991) but was deposed and captured in the US-led invasion of 2003

Husserl Edmund 1859–1938, German philosopher; founder of phenomenology

hustings 1 *Brit* (before 1872) the platform on which candidates were nominated for Parliament and from which they addressed the electors 2 the proceedings at a parliamentary election 3 political campaigning

Huston John 1906–87, US film director. His films include *The Treasure of the Sierra Madre* (1947), for which he won an Oscar, *The African Queen* (1951), *The Man Who Would Be King* (1975), *Prizzi's Honour* (1985), and *The Dead* (1987)

hutch a cage, usually of wood and wire mesh, for small animals

Hutton 1 James 1726–97, Scottish geologist, regarded as the founder of modern geology 2 Sir **Leonard**, known as *Len Hutton*. 1916–90, English cricketer; the first professional captain of England (1953)

Huxley 1 Aldous (**Leonard**). 1894–1963, British novelist and essayist, noted particularly for his his novel *Brave New World* (1932), depicting a scientifically controlled civilization of human robots 2 his half-brother, Sir **Andrew Fielding,** born 1917, English biologist: noted for his research into nerve cells and the mechanism by which nerve impulses are transmitted; Nobel prize for physiology or medicine shared with Alan Hodgkin and John Eccles 1963; president of the Royal Society (1980–85) 3 brother of Aldous, Sir **Julian** (**Sorrel**). 1887–1975, English biologist; first director-general of UNESCO (1946–48). His works include *Essays of a Biologist* (1923) and *Evolution: the Modern Synthesis* (1942) 4 their grandfather, **Thomas Henry** 1825–95, English biologist, the leading British exponent of Darwin's theory of evolution; his works include *Man's Place in Nature* (1863) and *Evolution and Ethics* (1893)

Hu Yaobang 1915–89, Chinese statesman; leader of the Chinese Communist Party (1981–87)

Huygens Christiaan 1629–95, Dutch physicist: first formulated the wave theory of light

Huysmans Joris Karl 1848–1907, French novelist of the Decadent school, whose works include *À rebours* (1884)

Hwange a town in W Zimbabwe: coal mines. Pop: 40 000 (latest est)

Hwang Hai a variant transliteration of the Chinese name for the **Yellow Sea**

Hwang Ho a variant transliteration of the Chinese name for the **Yellow River**

hyacinth 1 any liliaceous plant of the Mediterranean genus *Hyacinthus*, esp any cultivated variety of *H. orientalis*, having a thick flower stalk bearing white, blue, or pink fragrant flowers 2 the flower or bulb of such a plant 3 any similar or related plant, such as the grape hyacinth 4 a red or reddish-brown transparent variety of the mineral zircon, used as a gemstone 5 *Greek myth* a flower which sprang from the blood of the dead Hyacinthus 6 any of the varying colours of the hyacinth flower or stone

hybrid 1 an animal or plant resulting from a cross between genetically unlike individuals. Hybrids between different species are usually sterile 2 a vehicle that is powered by an internal-combustion engine and another source of power such as a battery 3 (of a vehicle) powered by more than one source 4 *Physics* (of an electromagnetic wave) having components of both electric and magnetic field vectors in the direction of propagation 5 *Electronics* **a** (of a circuit) consisting of transistors and valves **b** (of an integrated circuit) consisting of one or more fully integrated circuits and other components, attached to a ceramic substrate

Hyde¹ 1 Douglas 1860–1949, Irish scholar and author; first president of Eire (1938–45) 2 **Edward** See (1st Earl of) **Clarendon**

Hyde² a town in NW England, in Tameside unitary authority, Greater Manchester; textiles, footwear, engineering. Pop: 31 253 (2001)

Hyde Park a park in W central London: popular for open-air meetings

Hyderabad 1 a city in S central India, capital of Andhra Pradesh state and capital of former Hyderabad state; university (1918). Pop: 3 449 878 (2001) 2 a former state of S India: divided in 1956 between the states of Andhra Pradesh, Mysore, and Maharashtra 3 a city in SW Pakistan, on the River Indus: seat of the University of Sind (1947). Pop: 1 392 000 (2005 est)

Hyder Ali *or* **Haidar Ali** 1722–82, Indian ruler of Mysore (1766–82), who waged two wars against the British in India (1767–69; 1780–82)

hydra any solitary freshwater hydroid coelenterate of the genus *Hydra*, in which the body is a slender polyp with tentacles around the mouth

hydrangea any shrub or tree of the Asian and American genus *Hydrangea*, cultivated for their large clusters of white, pink, or blue flowers: family *Hydrangeaceae*

hydrant an outlet from a water main, usually consisting of an upright pipe with a valve attached, from which water can be tapped for fighting fires

hydrate 1 a chemical compound containing water that is chemically combined with a substance and can usually be expelled without changing the constitution of the substance 2 a chemical compound that can dissociate reversibly into water and another compound. For example sulphuric acid (H_2SO_4) dissociates into sulphur trioxide (SO_3) and water (H_2O) 3 a chemical compound, such as a carbohydrate, that contains hydrogen and oxygen atoms in the ratio two to one

hydraulic 1 operated by pressure transmitted through a pipe by a liquid, such as water or oil 2 of, concerned with, or employing liquids in motion

hydride any compound of hydrogen with another element, including ionic compounds such as sodium hydride (NaH), covalent compounds such as borane (B_2H_6), and the transition metal hydrides formed when certain metals, such as palladium, absorb hydrogen

hydro¹ *Brit* (esp formerly) a hotel or resort, often near a spa, offering facilities for hydropathic treatment

hydro² 1 short for **hydroelectric** 2 a Canadian name for **electricity** as supplied to a residence, business, institution, etc.

hydrocarbon any organic compound containing only carbon and hydrogen, such as the alkanes, alkenes, alkynes, terpenes, and arenes

hydrocephalus *or* **hydrocephaly** accumulation of cerebrospinal fluid within the ventricles of the brain because its normal outlet has been blocked by congenital malformation or disease. In infancy it usually results in great enlargement of the head

hydrochloric acid the colourless or slightly yellow aqueous solution of hydrogen chloride: a strong acid used in many industrial and laboratory processes

hydrodynamics the branch of science concerned with

the mechanical properties of fluids, esp liquids

hydroelectric 1 generated by the pressure of falling water 2 of or concerned with the generation of electricity by water pressure

hydrofoil a fast light vessel the hull of which is raised out of the water on one or more pairs of fixed vanes

hydrogen a a flammable colourless gas that is the lightest and most abundant element in the universe. It occurs mainly in water and in most organic compounds and is used in the production of ammonia and other chemicals, in the hydrogenation of fats and oils, and in welding. Symbol: H; atomic no.: 1; atomic wt.: 1.00794; valency: 1; density: 0.08988 kg/m³; melting pt.: –259.34°C; boiling pt.: –252.87°C **b** (as modifier): hydrogen bomb

hydrogen peroxide a colourless oily unstable liquid, usually used in aqueous solution. It is a strong oxidizing agent used as a bleach for textiles, wood pulp, hair, etc, and as an oxidizer in rocket fuels. Formula: H_2O_2

hydrogen sulphide a colourless poisonous soluble flammable gas with an odour of rotten eggs: used as a reagent in chemical analysis. Formula: H_2S

hydrography 1 the study, surveying, and mapping of the oceans, seas, and rivers 2 the oceans, seas, and rivers as represented on a chart
▷www.imo.org/home.asp

hydrology the study of the distribution, conservation, use, etc, of the water of the earth and its atmosphere, particularly at the land surface

hydrolysis a chemical reaction in which a compound reacts with water to produce other compounds

hydrometer an instrument for measuring the relative density of a liquid, usually consisting of a sealed graduated tube with a weighted bulb on one end, the relative density being indicated by the length of the unsubmerged stem

hydropathy a pseudoscientific method of treating disease by the use of large quantities of water both internally and externally

hydrophilic Chem tending to dissolve in, mix with, or be wetted by water

hydrophobia 1 another name for **rabies** 2 a fear of drinking fluids, esp that of a person with rabies, because of painful spasms when trying to swallow

hydroplane 1 a motorboat equipped with hydrofoils or with a shaped bottom that raises its hull out of the water at high speeds 2 an attachment to an aircraft to enable it to glide along the surface of water 3 another name (esp US) for a **seaplane** 4 a horizontal vane on the hull of a submarine for controlling its vertical motion

hydrosphere the watery part of the earth's surface, including oceans, lakes, water vapour in the atmosphere, etc.

hydrostatics the branch of science concerned with the mechanical properties and behaviour of fluids that are not in motion

hydrotherapy Med the treatment of certain diseases by the external use of water, esp by exercising in water in order to mobilize stiff joints or strengthen weakened muscles

hydrous 1 containing water 2 (of a chemical compound) combined with water molecules

hydroxide 1 a base or alkali containing the ion OH⁻ 2 any compound containing an -OH group

hydroxyl of, consisting of, or containing the monovalent group -OH or the ion OH⁻

hyena or **hyaena** any of several long-legged carnivorous doglike mammals of the genera Hyaena and Crocuta, such as C. crocuta (**spotted** or **laughing hyena**), of Africa and S Asia: family Hyaenidae, order Carnivora (carnivores)

hygiene 1 the science concerned with the maintenance of health 2 clean or healthy practices or thinking

hygrometer any of various instruments for measuring humidity

hygroscope any device that indicates the humidity of the air without necessarily measuring it

hygroscopic (of a substance) tending to absorb water from the air

hymen Anatomy a fold of mucous membrane that partly covers the entrance to the vagina and is usually ruptured when sexual intercourse takes place for the first time

hymenopterous or **hymenopteran** of, relating to, or belonging to the Hymenoptera, an order of insects, including bees, wasps, ants, and sawflies, having two pairs of membranous wings and an ovipositor specialized for stinging, sawing, or piercing

Hymettus a mountain in SE Greece, in Attica east of Athens: famous for its marble and for honey. Height: 1032 m (3386 ft)

hymn 1 a Christian song of praise sung to God or a saint 2 a similar song praising other gods, a nation, etc.

hymnal a book of hymns

hymnody 1 the composition or singing of hymns 2 hymns collectively

hymnology 1 the study of hymn composition 2 another word for **hymnody**

Hypatia died 415 AD, Neo-Platonist philosopher and politician, who lectured at Alexandria. She was murdered by a Christian mob

hype¹ Slang a hypodermic needle or injection

hype² 1 intensive or exaggerated publicity or sales promotion 2 the person or thing so publicized

hyperactive abnormally active

hyperbola a conic section formed by a plane that cuts both bases of a cone; it consists of two branches asymptotic to two intersecting fixed lines and has two foci. Standard equation: $x^2/a^2 - y^2/b^2 = 1$ where $2a$ is the distance between the two intersections with the x-axis and $b = a\sqrt{(e^2 - 1)}$, where e is the eccentricity

hyperbolic or **hyperbolical** of or relating to a hyperbola

hyperglycaemia or US **hyperglycemia** Pathol an abnormally large amount of sugar in the blood

hyperlink a word, phrase, picture, icon, etc, in a computer document on which a user may click to move to another part of the document or to another document

hypermarket Brit a huge self-service store, usually built on the outskirts of a town

hypersensitive abnormally sensitive to an allergen, a drug, or other agent

hypersonic concerned with or having a velocity of at least five times that of sound in the same medium under the same conditions

hypertension *Pathol* abnormally high blood pressure

hypertext computer software and hardware that allows users to create, store, and view text and move between related items easily and in a nonsequential way; a word or phrase can be selected to link users to another part of the same document or to a different document

hypertrophy enlargement of an organ or part resulting from an increase in the size of the cells

hyperventilation an increase in the depth, duration, and rate of breathing, sometimes resulting in cramp and dizziness

hypnosis an artificially induced state of relaxation and concentration in which deeper parts of the mind become more accessible: used clinically to reduce reaction to pain, to encourage free association, etc.

hypnotherapy the use of hypnosis in the treatment of emotional and psychogenic problems

hypnotic a drug or agent that induces sleep

hypnotism 1 the scientific study and practice of hypnosis 2 the process of inducing hypnosis

hypoallergenic (of cosmetics, earrings, etc) not likely to cause an allergic reaction

hypocaust an ancient Roman heating system in which hot air circulated under the floor and between double walls

hypochondria chronic abnormal anxiety concerning the state of one's health, even in the absence of any evidence of disease on medical examination

hypodermic 1 of or relating to the region of the skin beneath the epidermis 2 injected beneath the skin 3 a hypodermic syringe or needle 4 a hypodermic injection

hypodermic syringe *Med* a type of syringe consisting of a hollow cylinder, usually of glass or plastic, a tightly fitting piston, and a hollow needle (**hypodermic needle**), used for withdrawing blood samples, injecting medicine, etc.

hypotension *Pathol* abnormally low blood pressure

hypotenuse the side in a right-angled triangle that is opposite the right angle

hypothermia 1 *Pathol* an abnormally low body temperature, as induced in the elderly by exposure to cold weather 2 *Med* the intentional reduction of normal body temperature, as by ice packs, to reduce the patient's metabolic rate: performed esp in heart and brain surgery

hypothesis an unproved theory; a conjecture

hyrax any agile herbivorous mammal of the family *Procaviidae* and order *Hyracoidea*, of Africa and SW Asia, such as *Procavia capensis* (**rock hyrax**). They resemble rodents but have feet with hooflike toes

Hyrcania an ancient district of Asia, southeast of the Caspian Sea

hyssop 1 a widely cultivated Asian plant, *Hyssopus officinalis*, with spikes of small blue flowers and aromatic leaves, used as a condiment and in perfumery and folk medicine: family *Lamiaceae* (labiates) 2 any of several similar or related plants such as the hedge hyssop 3 a Biblical plant, used for sprinkling in the ritual practices of the Hebrews

hysterectomy surgical removal of the uterus

hysteria a mental disorder characterized by emotional outbursts, susceptibility to autosuggestion, and, often, symptoms such as paralysis that mimic the effects of physical disorders

hysterics an attack of hysteria

Hywel Dda *or* **Howel Dda** known as *Hywel the Good*. died 950 AD, Welsh prince. He united S and N Wales and codified Welsh law

Ii

iamb *or* **iambus** *Prosody* **1** a metrical foot consisting of two syllables, a short one followed by a long one (˘–) **2** a line of verse of such feet

iambic *Prosody* **1** (in Greek literature) denoting a type of satirical verse written in iambs **2** a metrical foot, line, or stanza of verse consisting of iambs **3** a type of ancient Greek satirical verse written in iambs

Iaşi a city in NE Romania: capital of Moldavia (1565–1859); university (1860). Pop: 280 000 (2005 est)

Ibadan a city in SW Nigeria, capital of Oyo state: university (1948). Pop: 2 375 000 (2005 est)

Iberia **1** the Iberian Peninsula **2** an ancient region in central Asia, south of the Caucasus corresponding approximately to present-day Georgia

Iberian **1** a member of a group of ancient Caucasoid peoples who inhabited the Iberian Peninsula in preclassical and classical times **2** a native or inhabitant of the Iberian Peninsula; a Spaniard or Portuguese **3** a native or inhabitant of ancient Iberia in the Caucasus **4** denoting, or relating to the pre-Roman peoples of the Iberian Peninsula or of Caucasian Iberia

Iberian Peninsula a peninsula of SW Europe, occupied by Spain and Portugal

Ibert Jacques (François Antoine). 1890–1962, French composer; his works include the humorous orchestral *Divertissement* (1930)

ibex any of three wild goats, *Capra ibex*, *C. caucasica*, or *C. pyrenaica*, of mountainous regions of Europe, Asia, and North Africa, having large backward-curving horns

ibis any of various wading birds of the family *Threskiornithidae*, such as *Threskiornis aethiopica* (**sacred ibis**), that occur in warm regions and have a long thin down-curved bill: order *Ciconiiformes* (herons, storks, etc)

Ibiza, Iviza, *or* **Eivissa 1** a Spanish island in the W Mediterranean, one of the Balearic Islands: hilly, with a rugged coast; tourism. Pop: 40 175 (2003 est). Area: 541 sq km (209 sq miles) **2** the capital of Ibiza, a port on the south of the island. Pop: 16 000 (latest est)

ibn-Saud Abdul-Aziz 1880–1953, first king of Saudi Arabia (1932–53)

Ibo *or* **Igbo 1** a member of a Negroid people of W Africa, living chiefly in S Nigeria **2** the language of this people, belonging to the Kwa branch of the Niger-Congo family: one of the chief literary and cultural languages of S Nigeria

Ibrahim Pasha 1789–1848, Albanian general; son of Mehemet Ali, whom he succeeded as viceroy of Egypt (1848)

Ibsen Henrik 1828–1906, Norwegian dramatist and poet. After his early verse plays *Brand* (1866) and *Peer Gynt* (1867), he began the series of social dramas in prose, including *A Doll's House* (1879), *Ghosts* (1881), and *The Wild Duck* (1886), which have had a profound influence on modern drama. His later plays, such as *Hedda Gabler* (1890) and *The Master Builder* (1892), are more symbolic

Icaria a Greek island in the Aegean Sea, in the Southern Sporades group. Area: 256 sq km (99 sq miles)

Icarian Sea the part of the Aegean Sea between the islands of Patmos and Leros and the coast of Asia Minor, where, according to legend, Icarus fell into the sea

ice 1 *Sport* the field of play in ice hockey **2** **the Ice** NZ, *informal* Antarctica

iceberg a large mass of ice floating in the sea, esp a mass that has broken off a polar glacier

icebreaker 1 a vessel with a reinforced bow for breaking up the ice in bodies of water to keep channels open for navigation **2** any tool or device for breaking ice into smaller pieces

icecap a thick mass of glacial ice and snow that permanently covers an area of land, such as either of the polar regions or the peak of a mountain

ice field 1 a very large flat expanse of ice floating in the sea; large ice floe **2** a large mass of ice permanently covering an extensive area of land

ice floe a sheet of ice, of variable size, floating in the sea

ice hockey a game played on ice by two opposing teams of six players each, who wear skates and try to propel a flat puck into their opponents' goal with long sticks having an offset flat blade at the end
▷www.iihf.com
▷www.nhl.com

Iceland an island republic in the N Atlantic, regarded as part of Europe: settled by Norsemen, who established a legislative assembly in 930; under Danish rule (1380–1918); gained independence in 1918 and became a republic in 1944; contains large areas of glaciers, snowfields, and lava beds with many volcanoes and hot springs (the chief source of domestic heat); inhabited chiefly along the SW coast. The economy is based largely on fishing and tourism. Official language: Icelandic. Official religion: Evangelical Lutheran. Currency:

króna. Capital: Reykjavik. Pop: 291 000 (2004 est). Area: 102 828 sq km (39 702 sq miles)

Icelandic the official language of Iceland, belonging to the North Germanic branch of the Indo-European family

ice skate 1 a boot having a steel blade fitted to the sole to enable the wearer to glide swiftly over ice **2** the steel blade on such a boot or shoe

icewine *Canadian* a dessert wine made from grapes that have frozen before being harvested

I Ching an ancient Chinese book of divination and a source of Confucian and Taoist philosophy. Answers to questions and advice may be obtained by referring to the text accompanying one of 64 hexagrams, selected at random

▷http://www.zhouyi.com/

ichneumon a mongoose, *Herpestes ichneumon*, of Africa and S Europe, having greyish-brown speckled fur

ichthyology the study of the physiology, history, economic importance, etc, of fishes

icon *or* **ikon 1** *Art* a representation of Christ, the Virgin Mary, or a saint, esp one painted in oil on a wooden panel, depicted in a traditional Byzantine style and venerated in the Eastern Church **2** *Computing* a pictorial representation of a facility available on a computer system, that enables the facility to be activated by means of a screen cursor rather than by a textual instruction

icosahedron a solid figure having 20 faces. The faces of a **regular icosahedron** are equilateral triangles

Ictinus 5th century BC, Greek architect, who designed the Parthenon with Callicrates

id *Psychoanal* the mass of primitive instincts and energies in the unconscious mind that, modified by the ego and the superego, underlies all psychic activity

Ida, Mount 1 a mountain in central Crete: the highest on the island; in ancient times associated with the worship of Zeus. Height: 2456 m (8057 ft) **2** a mountain in NW Turkey, southeast of the site of ancient Troy. Height: 1767 m (5797 ft)

Idaho a state of the northwestern US: consists chiefly of ranges of the Rocky Mountains, with the Snake River basin in the south; important for agriculture (**Idaho potatoes**), livestock, and silver-mining. Capital: Boise. Pop: 1 366 332 (2003 est). Area: 216 413 sq km (83 557 sq miles)

idea 1 *Philosophy* **a** a private mental object, regarded as the immediate object of thought or perception **b** a Platonic Idea or Form. **2** *Music* a thematic phrase or figure; motif

ideal *Philosophy* **a** of or relating to a highly desirable and possible state of affairs **b** of or relating to idealism

idealism any of a group of philosophical doctrines that share the monistic view that material objects and the external world do not exist in reality independently of the human mind but are variously creations of the mind or constructs of ideas

▷http://www.stfx.ca/arpa/BI-RP.html
▷http://pratt.edu/~arch543p/help/idealism.html

identical designating either or both of a pair of twins of the same sex who developed from a single fertilized ovum that split into two

identification parade a group of persons including one suspected of having committed a crime assembled for the purpose of discovering whether a witness can identify the suspect

Identikit *Trademark* a set of transparencies of various typical facial characteristics that can be superimposed on one another to build up, on the basis of a description, a picture of a person sought by the police

identity 1 *Logic* **a** that relation that holds only between any entity and itself **b** an assertion that that relation holds, as *Cicero is Tully* **2** *Maths* **a** an equation that is valid for all values of its variables, as in $(x-y)(x+y) = x^2 - y^2$. Often denoted by the symbol ≡ **b** a member of a set that when operating on another member, x, produces that member x: the identity for multiplication of numbers is 1 since $x.1 = 1.x = x$

ideology 1 a body of ideas that reflects the beliefs and interests of a nation, political system, etc and underlies political action **2** *Philosophy, Sociol* the set of beliefs by which a group or society orders reality so as to render it intelligible **3** the study of the nature and origin of ideas

ides (in the Roman calendar) the 15th day in March, May, July, and October and the 13th day of each other month

idiom *Arts* the characteristic artistic style of an individual, school, period, etc.

idiosyncrasy *Med* an abnormal reaction of an individual to specific foods, drugs, or other agents

idol 1 a material object, esp a carved image, that is worshipped as a god **2** *Christianity, Judaism* any being (other than the one God) to which divine honour is paid

idyll *or sometimes US* **idyl 1** a poem or prose work describing an idealized rural life, pastoral scenes, etc. **2** any simple narrative or descriptive piece in poetry or prose **3** a piece of music with a calm or pastoral character

Ife a town in W central Nigeria: one of the largest and oldest Yoruba towns; university (1961); centre of the cocoa trade. Pop: 229 000 (2005 est)

Ifni a former Spanish province in S Morocco, on the Atlantic: returned to Morocco in 1969

igloo *or* **iglu** a hollow made by a seal in the snow over its breathing hole in the ice

Ignatius Saint, surnamed *Theophorus*. died ?110 AD, bishop of Antioch. His seven letters, written on his way to his martyrdom in Rome, give valuable insight into the early Christian Church. Feast day: Oct 17 or Dec 17 or 20

Ignatius Loyola Saint 1491–1556, Spanish ecclesiastic. He founded the Society of Jesus (1534) and was its first general (1541–56). His *Spiritual Exercises* (1548) remains the basic manual for the training of Jesuits. Feast day: July 31

igneous (of rocks) derived by solidification of magma or molten lava emplaced on or below the earth's surface

ignition 1 the process of igniting the fuel in an internal-combustion engine **2** the devices used to ignite the fuel in an internal-combustion engine

ignoble *Falconry* **a** designating short-winged hawks that capture their quarry by swiftness and adroitness of flight **b** designating quarry which is inferior or unworthy of pursuit by a particular species of hawk or falcon

iguana 1 either of two large tropical American arboreal herbivorous lizards of the genus *Iguana*, esp *I. iguana* (**common iguana**), having a greyish-green body with a row of spines along the back: family *Iguanidae* 2 any other lizard of the tropical American family *Iguanidae*

Ihimaera Witi, full name *Witi Tame Ihimaera-Smiler*. born 1944, New Zealand Māori novelist and short-story writer; his novels include *The Whale Rider* (1987) and *The Uncle's Story* (2002)

IJssel *or* **Yssel** a river in the central Netherlands: a distributary of the Rhine, flowing north to the IJsselmeer. Length: 116 km (72 miles)

ikebana the Japanese decorative art of flower arrangement

  ▷www.jinjapan.org
  ▷www.ikebana.com.au/history

Ikeja a town in SW Nigeria, capital of Lagos state: residential and industrial suburb of Lagos. Pop: 63 870 (latest est)

Ilesha a town in W Nigeria. Pop: 500 000 (2005 est)

ileum 1 the part of the small intestine between the jejunum and the caecum 2 the corresponding part in insects

ilex 1 any of various trees or shrubs of the widely distributed genus *Ilex*, such as the holly and inkberry: family *Aquifoliaceae* 2 another name for the **holm oak**

Iliamna 1 a lake in SW Alaska: the largest lake in Alaska. Length: about 130 km (80 miles). Width: 40 km (25 miles) 2 a volcano in SW Alaska, northwest of Iliamna Lake. Height: 3076 m (10 092 ft)

Iligan a city in the Philippines, a port on the N coast of Mindanao. Pop: 306 000 (2005 est)

ilium the uppermost and widest of the three sections of the hipbone

Ilkeston a town in N central England, in SE Derbyshire. Pop: 37 270 (2001)

Ilkley a town in N England, in Bradford unitary authority, West Yorkshire: nearby is **Ilkley Moor** (to the south). Pop: 13 472 (2001)

Illampu one of the two peaks of Mount **Sorata**

Illawarra 1 a coastal district of E Australia, in S New South Wales. Pop: 404 626 (2002 est) 2 an Australian breed of shorthorn dairy cattle noted for its high milk yield and ability to survive on poor pastures

Ille-et-Vilaine a department of NW France, in E Brittany. Capital: Rennes. Pop: 894 625 (2003 est). Area: 6992 sq km (2727 sq miles)

Illich Ivan 1926–2002. US teacher and writer, born in Austria. His books include *Deschooling Society* (1971), *Medical Nemesis* (1975), and *In the Mirror of the Past* (1991)

Illimani a mountain in W Bolivia, in the Andes near La Paz. Height: 6882 m (22 580 ft)

Illinois 1 a state of the N central US, in the Midwest: consists of level prairie crossed by the Illinois and Kaskaskia Rivers; mainly agricultural. Capital: Springfield. Pop: 12 653 544 (2003 est). Area: 144 858 sq km (55 930 sq miles) 2 a river in Illinois, flowing SW to the Mississippi. Length: 439 km (273 miles)

illusion 1 *Psychol* a perception that is not true to reality, having been altered subjectively in some way in the mind of the perceiver 2 a very fine gauze or tulle used for trimmings, veils, etc.

Illyria an ancient region of uncertain boundaries on the E shore of the Adriatic Sea, including parts of present-day Croatia, Montenegro, and Albania

Illyricum a Roman province founded after 168 BC, based on the coastal area of Illyria

Ilmen Lake a lake in NW Russia, in the Novgorod Region: drains through the Volkhov River into Lake Ladoga. Area: between 780 sq km (300 sq miles) and 2200 sq km (850 sq miles), according to the season

Iloilo a port in the W central Philippines, on SE Panay Island. Pop: 408 000 (2005 est)

Ilorin a city in W Nigeria, capital of Kwara state: agricultural trade centre. Pop: 714 000 (2005 est)

Ilyushin Sergei Vladimirovich 1894–1977, Soviet aircraft designer. He designed the dive bomber Il-2 Stormovik and the jet airliner Il-62

image 1 an optically formed reproduction of an object, such as one formed by a lens or mirror 2 the pattern of light that is focused on to the retina of the eye 3 *Psychol* the mental experience of something that is not immediately present to the senses, often involving memory 4 a mental picture or association of ideas evoked in a literary work, esp in poetry 5 a figure of speech, such as a simile or metaphor 6 *Maths* **a** (of a point) the value of a function, $f(x)$, corresponding to the point x **b** the range of a function

imagery 1 figurative or descriptive language in a literary work 2 *Psychol* **a** the materials or general processes of the imagination **b** the characteristic kind of mental images formed by a particular individual

imaginary *Maths* involving or containing imaginary numbers. The imaginary part of a complex number, z, is usually written Imz

imagination (in romantic literary criticism, esp that of S. T. Coleridge) a creative act of perception that joins passive and active elements in thinking and imposes unity on the poetic material

imago 1 an adult sexually mature insect produced after metamorphosis 2 *Psychoanal* an idealized image of another person, usually a parent, acquired in childhood and carried in the unconscious in later life

imam *or* **imaum** *Islam* 1 a leader of congregational prayer in a mosque 2 a caliph, as leader of a Muslim community 3 an honorific title applied to eminent doctors of Islam, such as the founders of the orthodox schools 4 any of a succession of either seven or twelve religious leaders of the Shiites, regarded by their followers as divinely inspired

IMAX *Trademark* a process of film projection using a giant screen on which an image approximately ten times larger than standard is projected

imbecile *Psychol* a person of very low intelligence (IQ of 25 to 50), usually capable only of guarding himself against danger and of performing simple mechanical tasks under supervision

Imbros a Turkish island in the NE Aegean Sea, west of the Gallipoli Peninsula: occupied by Greece (1912–14) and Britain (1914–23). Area: 280 sq km (108 sq miles)

Imhotep *c.* 2600 BC, Egyptian physician and architect. After his death he was worshipped as a god; the Greeks identified him with Asclepius

imitation 1 (in contrapuntal or polyphonic music) the

repetition of a phrase or figure in one part after its appearance in another, as in a fugue **2** a literary composition that adapts the style of an older work to the writer's own purposes

immaculate *Biology* of only one colour, with no spots or markings

immanent of or relating to the pantheistic conception of God, as being present throughout the universe

Immanuel *or* **Emmanuel** *Bible* the child whose birth was foretold by Isaiah (Isaiah 7:14) and who in Christian tradition is identified with Jesus

immediate 1 *Philosophy* of or relating to an object or concept that is directly known or intuited **2** *Logic* (of an inference) deriving its conclusion from a single premise, esp by conversion or obversion of a categorial statement

immigrant an animal or plant that lives or grows in a region to which it has recently migrated

Immingham a port in NE England, in North East Lincolnshire unitary authority, Lincolnshire: docks opened in 1912, principally for the exporting of coal; now handles chiefly bulk materials, esp imported iron ore. Pop: 11 090 (2001)

immovable *or* **immoveable** *Law* **a** (of property) not liable to be removed; fixed **b** of or relating to immoveables

immune *Med* protected against a specific disease by inoculation or as the result of innate or acquired resistance

immunity 1 the ability of an organism to resist disease, either through the activities of specialized blood cells or antibodies produced by them in response to natural exposure or inoculation (**active immunity**) or by the injection of antiserum or the transfer of antibodies from a mother to her baby via the placenta or breast milk (**passive immunity**) **2** freedom from obligation or duty, esp exemption from tax, duty legal liability, etc **3** the exemption of ecclesiastical persons or property from various civil obligations or liabilities

immunodeficiency a deficiency in or breakdown of a person's immune system

immunology the branch of biological science concerned with the study of immunity

Imo a state of SE Nigeria, formed in 1976 from part of East-Central State. Capital: Owerri. Pop: 2 779 028 (1995 est). Area: 5530 sq km (2135 sq miles)

imp a small demon or devil; mischievous sprite

impacted 1 (of a tooth) unable to erupt, esp because of being wedged against another tooth below the gum **2** (of a fracture) having the jagged broken ends wedged into each other

impala an antelope, *Aepyceros melampus*, of southern and eastern Africa, having lyre-shaped horns and able to move with enormous leaps when disturbed

impasto 1 paint applied thickly, so that brush and palette knife marks are evident **2** the technique of applying paint in this way

impedance 1 a measure of the opposition to the flow of an alternating current equal to the square root of the sum of the squares of the resistance and the reactance, expressed in ohms. **2** a component that offers impedance **3** the ratio of the sound pressure in a medium to

the rate of alternating flow of the medium through a specified surface due to the sound wave. **4** the ratio of the mechanical force, acting in the direction of motion, to the velocity of the resulting vibration.

impediment *Law* an obstruction to the making of a contract, esp a contract of marriage by reason of closeness of blood or affinity

impenetrable *Physics* (of a body) incapable of occupying the same space as another body

imperfect 1 *Botany* **a** (of flowers) lacking functional stamens or pistils **b** (of fungi) not undergoing sexual reproduction **2** *Law* (of a trust, an obligation, etc) lacking some necessary formality to make effective or binding; incomplete; legally unenforceable **3** *Music* **a** (of a cadence) proceeding to the dominant from the tonic, subdominant, or any chord other than the dominant **b** of or relating to all intervals other than the fourth, fifth, and octave

imperial 1 of or relating to an empire, emperor, or empress **2** (esp of products and commodities) of a superior size or quality **3** (of weights, measures, etc) conforming to standards or definitions legally established in Britain **4** (formerly) a Russian gold coin originally worth ten roubles **5** *Architect* a dome that has a point at the top **6** a member of an imperial family, esp an emperor or empress **7** a red deer having antlers with fourteen points

imperialism 1 the policy or practice of extending a state's rule over other territories **2** an instance or policy of aggressive behaviour by one state against another **3** a system of imperial government or rule by an emperor

impermeable (of a substance) not allowing the passage of a fluid through interstices; not permeable

impetigo a contagious bacterial skin disease characterized by the formation of pustules that develop into yellowish crusty sores

impetus *Physics* the force that sets a body in motion or that tends to resist changes in a body's motion

Imphal a city in NE India, capital of Manipur Territory, on the Manipur River: formerly the seat of the Manipur kings: site of a major Anglo-Indian victory over the Japanese (1944), which was a turning point in the British recovery of Burma (now called Myanmar). Pop: 217 275 (2001)

implant *Med* anything implanted, esp surgically, such as a tissue graft or hormone

implication *Logic* **a** the operator that forms a sentence from two given sentences and corresponds to the English *if ... then ...* **b** a sentence so formed. Usually written p→q or p!hq, where p,q are the component sentences, it is true except when p (the antecedent) is true and q (the consequent) is false **c** the relation between such sentences

implicit *Maths* (of a function) having an equation of the form $f(x,y) = 0$, in which y cannot be directly expressed in terms of x, as in $xy + x^2 + y^3x^2 = 0$

import 1 a goods (**visible imports**) or services (**invisible imports**) that are bought from foreign countries **b** (*as modifier*): *an import licence* **2** *Canadian, Informal* a sportsman or -woman who is not native to the country in which he or she plays

impotent (esp of males) unable to perform sexual intercourse

impresario 1 a producer or sponsor of public entertainments, esp musical or theatrical ones 2 the director or manager of an opera, ballet, or other performing company

impression *Dentistry* an imprint of the teeth and gums, esp in wax or plaster, for use in preparing crowns, inlays, or dentures

imprimatur *RC Church* a licence granted by a bishop certifying the Church's approval of a book to be published

impromptu a short piece of instrumental music, sometimes improvisatory in character

improper fraction a fraction in which the numerator has a greater absolute value or degree than the denominator, as $7/6$ or $(x^2 + 3)/(x + 1)$

impulse 1 *Physics* a the product of the average magnitude of a force acting on a body and the time for which it acts b the change in the momentum of a body as a result of a force acting upon it for a short period of time 2 *Electronics* a less common word for **pulse**

impulsive 1 (of physical forces) acting for a short time; not continuous 2 (of a sound) brief, loud, and having a wide frequency range

impure 1 (in certain religions) a (of persons) ritually unclean and as such debarred from certain religious ceremonies b (of foodstuffs, vessels, etc) debarred from certain religious uses 2 (of a colour) mixed with another colour or with black or white 3 of more than one origin or style, as of architecture or other design

impurity *Electronics* a small quantity of an element added to a pure semiconductor crystal to control its electrical conductivity

inactive 1 *Chem* (of a substance) having little or no reactivity 2 (of an element, isotope, etc) having little or no radioactivity

inanition exhaustion resulting from lack of food

inaugural a speech made at an inauguration, esp by a president of the US

inboard 1 (esp of a boat's motor or engine) situated within the hull 2 situated between the wing tip of an aircraft and its fuselage

Inca 1 a member of a South American Indian people whose great empire centred on Peru lasted from about 1100 AD to the Spanish conquest in the early 1530s and is famed for its complex culture 2 the ruler or king of this empire or any member of his family 3 the language of the Incas

▷www.wsu.edu/~dee/CIVAMRCA/INCAS.HTM
▷www.incaconquest.com

incandescent lamp a source of light that contains a heated solid, such as an electrically heated filament

incapacity *Law* a legal disqualification or ineligibility b a circumstance causing this

incarnate (esp of plant parts) flesh-coloured or pink

Incarnation 1 *Christian theol* the assuming of a human body by the Son of God 2 *Christianity* the presence of God on Earth in the person of Jesus

incendiary 1 of or relating to the illegal burning of property, goods, etc. 2 tending to create strife, violence, etc.; inflammatory 3 (of a substance) capable of catching fire, causing fires, or burning readily 4 a person who illegally sets fire to property, goods, etc.; arsonist 5

(esp formerly) a person who stirs up civil strife, violence, etc, for political reasons; agitator 6 an incendiary substance, such as phosphorus

incense 1 any of various aromatic substances burnt for their fragrant odour, esp in religious ceremonies 2 the odour or smoke so produced

incentive a an additional payment made to employees as a means of increasing production b (*as modifier*): *an incentive scheme*

inch 1 a unit of length equal to one twelfth of a foot or 0.0254 metre 2 *Meteorol* a an amount of precipitation that would cover a surface with water one inch deep b a unit of pressure equal to a mercury column one inch high in a barometer

inchoate (of a legal document, promissory note, etc) in an uncompleted state; not yet made specific or valid

Inchon *or* **Incheon** a port in W South Korea, on the Yellow Sea: the chief port for Seoul: site of a major strategic amphibious assault by UN troops, liberating Seoul (Sept 15, 1950). Pop: 2 642 000 (2005 est)

incidence 1 *Physics* the arrival of a beam of light or particles at a surface 2 *Geometry* the partial coincidence of two configurations, such as a point that lies on a circle

incident 1 a relatively insignificant event that might have serious consequences, esp in international politics 2 a public disturbance 3 (esp of a beam of light or particles) arriving at or striking a surface

incision 1 a cut made with a knife during a surgical operation 2 any indentation in an incised leaf

incisor a chisel-edged tooth at the front of the mouth. In man there are four in each jaw

inclination 1 *Maths* a the angle between a line on a graph and the positive limb of the x-axis b the smaller dihedral angle between one plane and another 2 *Astronomy* the angle between the plane of the orbit of a planet or comet and another plane, usually that of the ecliptic 3 *Physics* another name for **dip**

inclusion 1 *Geology* a solid fragment, liquid globule, or pocket of gas enclosed in a mineral or rock 2 *Maths* a the relation between two sets that obtains when all the members of the first are members of the second. b **strict** *or* **proper inclusion** the relation that obtains between two sets when the first includes the second but not vice versa. 3 *Engineering* a foreign particle in a metal, such as a particle of metal oxide

inclusive 1 not excluding any particular groups of people 2 *Logic* (of a disjunction) true if at least one of its component propositions is true

incoherent *Physics* (of two or more waves) having the same frequency but not the same phase

income 1 the amount of monetary or other returns, either earned or unearned, accruing over a given period of time 2 receipts; revenue

income support (in Britain, formerly) a social security payment for people on very low incomes

income tax a personal tax, usually progressive, levied on annual income subject to certain deductions

incoming *Finance* 1 (of interest, dividends, etc) being received; accruing 2 income or revenue

incommensurable *Maths* a (of two numbers) having an irrational ratio b not having units of the same dimension c unrelated to another measurement by integral multiples

incompatible 1 *Med* (esp of two drugs or two types of blood) incapable of being combined or used together; antagonistic 2 *Logic* (of two propositions) unable to be both true at the same time 3 (of plants a not capable of forming successful grafts b incapable of fertilizing each other 4 *Maths* another word for **inconsistent**

incompetent 1 *Law* not legally qualified 2 (of rock strata, folds, etc) yielding readily to pressure so as to undergo structural deformation

incomplete *Logic* a (of a formal theory) not so constructed that the addition of a non-theorem to the axioms renders it inconsistent **b** (of an expression) not having a reference of its own but requiring completion by another expression

inconnu a North American freshwater food and game fish, *Stenodus leucichthys*, related to the salmon

inconsistent 1 *Maths* (of two or more equations) not having one common set of values of the variables: $x + 2y = 5$ and $x + 2y = 6$ are inconsistent 2 *Logic* (of a set of propositions) enabling an explicit contradiction to be validly derived

incontinent relating to or exhibiting involuntary urination or defecation

incorporeal 1 spiritual or metaphysical 2 *Law* having no material existence but existing by reason of its annexation of something material, such as an easement, touchline, copyright, etc.

incorrigible *Philosophy* (of a belief) having the property that whoever honestly believes it cannot be mistaken

increment *Maths* a small positive or negative change in a variable or function. Symbol: Δ, as in Δx or Δf

incubator 1 *Med* an enclosed transparent boxlike apparatus for housing prematurely born babies under optimum conditions until they are strong enough to survive in the normal environment 2 a container kept at a constant temperature in which birds' eggs can be artificially hatched or bacterial cultures grown 3 a commercial property, divided into small work units, which provides equipment and support to new businesses

incubus a demon believed in folklore to lie upon sleeping persons, esp to have sexual intercourse with sleeping women

incumbent a person who holds an office, esp a clergyman holding a benefice

incurable 1 (esp of a disease) not curable; unresponsive to treatment 2 a person having an incurable disease

indecent assault the act of taking indecent liberties with a person without his or her consent

indecent exposure the offence of indecently exposing parts of one's body in public, esp the genitals

indefinite *Botany* a too numerous to count b capable of continued growth at the tip of the stem, which does not terminate in a flower

indemnity 1 legal exemption from penalties or liabilities incurred through one's acts or defaults 2 (in Canada) the salary paid to a member of Parliament or of a legislature 3 **act of indemnity** an act of Parliament granting exemption to public officers from technical penalties that they may have been compelled to incur

indent 1 *Chiefly Brit* (in foreign trade) an order for foreign merchandise, esp one placed with an agent 2 *Chiefly*

Brit an official order for goods 3 (in the late 18th-century US) a certificate issued by federal and state governments for the principal or interest due on the public debt

indenture 1 any deed, contract, or sealed agreement between two or more parties 2 (formerly) a deed drawn up in duplicate, each part having correspondingly indented edges for identification and security 3 a contract between an apprentice and his master

Independence a city in W Missouri, near Kansas City: starting point for the Santa Fe, Oregon, and California Trails (1831–44). Pop: 112 079 (2003 est)

independent 1 *Maths* (of a system of equations) not linearly dependent 2 *Logic* of a set of propositions a not validly derivable from one another, so that if the propositions are the axioms of some theory none can be dispensed with b not logically related, so that in no case can the truth value of one be inferred from those of the others 3 a person who is not affiliated to or who acts independently of a political party

independent school (in Britain) a school that is neither financed nor controlled by the government or local authorities

indeterminate 1 *Physics* (of an effect) not obeying the law of causality; noncausal 2 *Maths* a having no numerical meaning, as o/o b (of an equation) having more than one variable and an unlimited number of solutions 3 *Botany* another word for **indefinite** 4 (of a structure, framework, etc) comprising forces that cannot be fully analysed, esp by vector analysis

index 1 *Maths* a another name for **exponent** b a number or variable placed as a superscript to the left of a radical sign indicating by its value the root to be extracted, as in $\sqrt[3]{8} = 2$ c a subscript or superscript to the right of a variable to express a set of variables, as in using x_i for x_1, x_2, x_3, etc 2 a number or ratio indicating a specific characteristic, property, etc.

indexation *or* **index-linking** the act of making wages, interest rates, etc, index-linked

index finger the finger next to the thumb

index-linked (of wages, interest rates, etc) directly related to the cost-of-living index and rising or falling accordingly

India a republic in S Asia: history dates from the Indus Valley civilization (3rd millennium BC); came under British supremacy in 1763 and passed to the British Crown in 1858; nationalist movement arose under Gandhi (1869–1948); Indian subcontinent divided into Pakistan (Muslim) and India (Hindu) in 1947; became a republic within the Commonwealth in 1950. It consists chiefly of the Himalayas, rising over 7500 m (25 000 ft) in the extreme north, the Ganges plain in the north, the Thar Desert in the northwest, the Chota Nagpur plateau in the northeast, and the Deccan Plateau in the south. Official and administrative languages: Hindi and English; each state has its own language. Parts of the SE coast suffered badly in the Indian Ocean tsunami of December 2004. Religion: Hindu majority, Muslim minority. Currency: rupee. Capital: New Delhi. Pop: 1 081 229 000 (2004 est). Area: 3 268 100 sq km (1 261 813 sq miles)

Indiaman (formerly) a large merchant ship engaged in

trade with India

Indian 1 a native, citizen, or inhabitant of the Republic of India 2 an American Indian 3 any of the languages of the American Indians

Indiana a state of the N central US, in the Midwest: consists of an undulating plain, with sand dunes and lakes in the north and limestone caves in the south. Capital: Indianapolis. Pop: 6 195 643 (2003 est). Area: 93 491 sq km (36 097 sq miles)

Indianapolis a city in central Indiana: the state capital. Pop: 783 438 (2003 est)

Indian club a bottle-shaped club, usually used in pairs by gymnasts, jugglers, etc.

Indian Empire British India and the Indian states under indirect British control, which gained independence as India and Pakistan in 1947

Indian hemp 1 another name for **hemp** (esp the variety *Cannabis indica*, from which several narcotic drugs are obtained) 2 a perennial American apocynaceous plant, *Apocynum cannabinum*, whose fibre was formerly used by the Indians to make rope

Indian Ocean an ocean bordered by Africa in the west, Asia in the north, and Australia in the east and merging with the Antarctic Ocean in the south. Average depth: 3900 m (13 000 ft). Greatest depth (off the Sunda Islands): 7450 m (24 442 ft). In December 2004 a major undersea earthquake off Sumatra triggered a tsunami which affected large areas of the ocean as far away as east Africa, and killed around 275 900 people. Area: about 73 556 000 sq km (28 400 000 sq miles)

Indian summer a period of unusually settled warm weather after the end of summer proper

Indic denoting, belonging to, or relating to a branch of Indo-European consisting of the Indo-European languages of India, including Sanskrit, Hindi and Urdu, Punjabi, Gujerati, Bengali, and Sinhalese

indicator 1 a device to attract attention, such as the pointer of a gauge or a warning lamp 2 an instrument that displays certain operating conditions in a machine, such as a gauge showing temperature, speed, pressure, etc. 3 a device for indicating that a motor vehicle is about to turn left or right, esp two pairs of lights that flash when operated or a pair of trafficators 4 a delicate measuring instrument used to determine small differences in the height of mechanical components. It consists of a spring-loaded plunger that operates a pointer moving over a circular scale 5 *Chem* **a** a substance used in titrations to indicate the completion of a chemical reaction, usually by a change of colour **b** a substance, such as litmus, that indicates the presence of an acid or alkali 6 *Ecology* **a** a plant or animal species that thrives only under particular environmental conditions and therefore indicates these conditions where it is found **b** a species of plant or animal whose well-being confirms the well-being of other species in the area

indictment *Criminal law* 1 a formal written charge of crime formerly referred to and presented on oath by a grand jury 2 any formal accusation of crime 3 *Scot* a charge of crime brought at the instance of the Lord Advocate

Indies the 1 the territories of S and SE Asia included in the East Indies, India, and Indochina 2 See **West Indies**

indifferent *Biology* **a** (of cells or tissues) not differentiated or specialized **b** (of a species) not found in any particular community

indigestible incapable of being digested or difficult to digest

indigo 1 any of various tropical plants of the leguminous genus *Indigofera*, such as the anil, that yield this dye 2 **a** any of a group of colours that have the same blue-violet hue; a spectral colour **b** (*as adjective*): *an indigo carpet*

indirect tax a tax levied on goods or services rather than on individuals or companies

indium a rare soft silvery metallic element associated with zinc ores: used in alloys, electronics, and electroplating. Symbol: In; atomic no.: 49; atomic wt.: 114.82; valency: 1, 2, or 3; relative density: 7.31; melting pt.: 156.63°C; boiling pt.: 2073°C

individual 1 *Biology* **a** a single animal or plant, esp as distinct from a species **b** a single member of a compound organism or colony 2 *Logic* **a** an object as opposed to a property or class **b** an element of the domain of discourse of a theory

individualism 1 another word for **laissez faire** 2 *Philosophy* the doctrine that only individual things exist and that therefore classes or properties have no reality

indivisible *Maths* leaving a remainder when divided by a given number

Indochina or **Indo-China** 1 a peninsula in SE Asia, between China and India: consists of Myanmar, Thailand, Laos, Cambodia, Vietnam, and Malaysia 2 the former French colonial possessions of Cochin China, Annam, Tonkin, Laos, and Cambodia

Indo-European 1 denoting, belonging to, or relating to a family of languages that includes English and many other culturally and politically important languages of the world: a characteristic feature, esp of the older languages such as Latin, Greek, and Sanskrit, is inflection showing gender, number, and case 2 denoting or relating to the hypothetical parent language of this family, primitive Indo-European 3 denoting, belonging to, or relating to any of the peoples speaking these languages 4 the Indo-European family of languages 5 the reconstructed hypothetical parent language of this family 6 a member of the prehistoric people who spoke this language 7 a descendant of this people or a native speaker of an Indo-European language

indolent 1 *Pathol* causing little pain 2 (esp of a painless ulcer) slow to heal

Indonesia a republic in SE Asia, in the Malay Archipelago, consisting of the main islands of Sumatra, Java and Madura, Bali, Sulawesi (Celebes), Lombok, Sumbawa, Flores, the Moluccas, part of Timor, part of Borneo (Kalimantan), Papua (formerly Irian Jaya), and over 3000 small islands in the Indian and Pacific Oceans: became the Dutch East Indies in 1798; declared independence in 1945; became a republic in 1950; East Timor (illegally annexed in 1975) became independent in 2002. Parts of Sumatra suffered badly in the Indian Ocean tsunami of December 2004. Official language: Bahasa Indonesia. Religion: Muslim majority. Currency: rupiah. Capital: Jakarta. Pop: 222 611 000

(2004 est). Area: 1 919 317 sq km (741 052 sq miles)

Indore 1 a city in central India, in W Madhya Pradesh. Pop: 1 597 441 (2001) 2 a former state of central India: became part of Madhya Bharat in 1948, which in turn became part of Madhya Pradesh in 1956

Indre a department of central France in the Centre region. Capital: Châteauroux. Pop: 230 954 (2003 est). Area: 6906 sq km (2693 sq miles)

Indre-et-Loire a department of W central France in the Centre region: contains many famous châteaux along the Loire. Capital: Tours. Pop: 563 062 (2003 est). Area: 6158 sq km (2402 sq miles)

inducement *Law* (in pleading) the introductory part that leads up to and explains the matter in dispute

inductance 1 the property of an electric circuit as a result of which an electromotive force is created by a change of current in the same circuit or in a neighbouring circuit. It is usually measured in henries. 2 another name for **inductor**

induction 1 (in an internal-combustion engine) the part of the action of a piston by which mixed air and fuel are drawn from the carburettor to the cylinder 2 *Logic* a a process of reasoning, used esp in science, by which a general conclusion is drawn from a set of premises, based mainly on experience or experimental evidence. The conclusion goes beyond the information contained in the premises, and does not follow necessarily from them. Thus an inductive argument may be highly probable, yet lead from true premises to a false conclusion b a conclusion reached by this process of reasoning 3 the process by which electrical or magnetic properties are transferred, without physical contact, from one circuit or body to another 4 *Biology* the effect of one tissue, esp an embryonic tissue, on the development of an adjacent tissue 5 *Biochem* the process by which synthesis of an enzyme is stimulated by the presence of its substrate 6 *Maths, Logic* a a method of proving a proposition that all integers have a property, by first proving that 1 has the property and then that if the integer n has it so has $n+1$ b the application of recursive rules

induction coil a transformer for producing a high voltage from a low voltage. It consists of a cylindrical primary winding of few turns, a concentric secondary winding of many turns, and often a common soft-iron core

inductive 1 relating to, involving, or operated by electrical or magnetic induction 2 *Logic, Maths* of, relating to, or using induction 3 *Biology* producing a reaction within an organism, esp induction in embryonic tissue

inductor a component, such as a coil, in an electrical circuit the main function of which is to produce inductance

indulgence 1 *RC Church* a remission of the temporal punishment for sin after its guilt has been forgiven 2 *Commerce* an extension of time granted as a favour for payment of a debt or as fulfilment of some other obligation 3 *History* a royal grant during the reigns of Charles II and James II of England giving Nonconformists and Roman Catholics a measure of religious freedom

Indus a river in S Asia, rising in SW Tibet in the Kailas Range of the Himalayas and flowing northwest through Kashmir, then southwest across Pakistan to the Arabian Sea: important throughout history, esp for the Indus Civilization (about 3000 to 1500 BC), and for irrigation. Length: about 2900 km (1800 miles)

industrialist a person who has a substantial interest in the ownership or control of industrial enterprise

Industrial Revolution the the transformation in the 18th and 19th centuries of first Britain and then other W European countries and the US into industrial nations

▷http://members.aol.com/TeacherNet/ Industrial.html

▷www.bergen.org/technology/industrial

industry 1 organized economic activity concerned with manufacture, extraction and processing of raw materials, or construction 2 a branch of commercial enterprise concerned with the output of a specified product or service

Ine died after 726, king of Wessex (688–726)

inequality 1 *Maths* a a statement indicating that the value of one quantity or expression is not equal to another, as in $x \neq y$ b a relationship between real numbers involving inequality: x may be greater than y, denoted by $x > y$, or less than y, denoted by $x < y$ 2 *Astronomy* a departure from uniform orbital motion

inert *Chem* having only a limited ability to react chemically; unreactive

inertia *Physics* a the tendency of a body to preserve its state of rest or uniform motion unless acted upon by an external force b an analogous property of other physical quantities that resist change

inertia selling (in Britain) the illegal practice of sending unrequested goods to householders followed by a bill for the price of the goods if they do not return them

infamous *Criminal law*, formerly a (of a person) deprived of certain rights of citizenship on conviction of certain offences b (of a crime or punishment) entailing such deprivation

infancy the period of life prior to attaining legal majority (reached at 21 under common law, at 18 by statute); minority nonage

infant 1 *Law* another word for **minor** 2 *Brit* a young schoolchild, usually under the age of seven 3 *Law* of or relating to the legal status of infancy

infanta formerly 1 a daughter of a king of Spain or Portugal 2 the wife of an infante

infante (formerly) a son of a king of Spain or Portugal, esp one not heir to the throne

infant school (in England and Wales) a school for children aged between 5 and 7

infection 1 invasion of the body by pathogenic microorganisms 2 the resulting condition in the tissues 3 an infectious disease

infectious 1 (of a disease) capable of being transmitted 2 (of a disease) caused by microorganisms, such as bacteria, viruses, or protozoa 3 causing or transmitting infection 4 *International law* a tainting or capable of tainting with illegality b rendering liable to seizure or forfeiture

infectious mononucleosis an acute infectious disease, caused by Epstein-Barr virus, characterized by fever, sore throat, swollen and painful lymph nodes, and abnormal lymphocytes in the blood

inference 1 any process of reasoning from premises to a conclusion 2 *Logic* the specific mode of reasoning used

inferior 1 *Botany* (of a plant ovary) enclosed by and fused with the receptacle so that it is situated below the other floral parts 2 *Astronomy* a orbiting or occurring between the sun and the earth b lying below the horizon

inferiority complex *Psychiatry* a disorder arising from the conflict between the desire to be noticed and the fear of being humiliated, characterized by aggressiveness or withdrawal into oneself

infield 1 *Cricket* the area of the field near the pitch 2 *Baseball* a the area of the playing field enclosed by the base lines and extending beyond them towards the outfield b the positions of the first baseman, second baseman, shortstop, third baseman, and sometimes the pitcher, collectively

infighting *Boxing* combat at close quarters in which proper blows are inhibited and the fighters try to wear down each other's strength

infiltrate 1 *Pathol* any substance that passes into and accumulates within cells, tissues, or organs 2 *Pathol* a local anaesthetic solution injected into the tissues to cause local anaesthesia

infinite *Maths* a having an unlimited number of digits, factors, terms, members, etc. b (of a set) able to be put in a one-to-one correspondence with part of itself c (of an integral) having infinity as one or both limits of integration

infinitesimal 1 *Maths* of, relating to, or involving a small change in the value of a variable that approaches zero as a limit 2 *Maths* an infinitesimal quantity

infinity 1 *Optics, Photog* a point that is far enough away from a lens, mirror, etc, for the light emitted by it to fall in parallel rays on the surface of the lens, etc. 2 *Physics* a dimension or quantity of sufficient size to be unaffected by finite variations 3 *Maths* the concept of a value greater than any finite numerical value 4 a distant ideal point at which two parallel lines are assumed to meet

infirm *Law* (of a law, custom, etc) lacking legal force; invalid

infirmary a place for the treatment of the sick or injured; dispensary; hospital

inflammation the reaction of living tissue to injury or infection, characterized by heat, redness, swelling, and pain

inflation 1 *Economics* a progressive increase in the general level of prices brought about by an expansion in demand or the money supply (**demand-pull inflation**) or by autonomous increases in costs (**cost-push inflation**) 2 *Informal* the rate of increase of prices

inflection *or* **inflexion** *Maths* a change in curvature from concave to convex or vice versa

inflorescence 1 the part of a plant that consists of the flower-bearing stalks 2 the arrangement of the flowers on the stalks 3 the process of flowering; blossoming

influence *Astrology* an ethereal fluid or occult power regarded as emanating from the stars and affecting a person's actions, future, etc.

influenza a highly contagious and often epidemic viral disease characterized by fever, prostration, muscular aches and pains, and inflammation of the respiratory passages

influx *Geography* the mouth of a stream or river

information 1 *Law* a a charge or complaint made before justices of the peace, usually on oath, to institute summary criminal proceedings b a complaint filed on behalf of the Crown, usually by the attorney general 2 *Computing* the meaning given to data by the way in which it is interpreted

information theory a collection of mathematical theories, based on statistics, concerned with methods of coding, transmitting, storing, retrieving, and decoding information

infra dig *Informal* beneath one's dignity

infrared the part of the electromagnetic spectrum with a longer wavelength than light but a shorter wavelength than radio waves; radiation with wavelength between 0.8 micrometres and 1 millimetre

infrasound soundlike waves having a frequency below the audible range, that is, below about 16Hz

infrastructure the stock of fixed capital equipment in a country, including factories, roads, schools, etc, considered as a determinant of economic growth

infusion *Med* introduction of a liquid, such as a saline solution, into a vein or the subcutaneous tissues of the body

Inge William Ralph, known as *the Gloomy Dean*. 1860–1954, English theologian, noted for his pessimism; dean of St Paul's Cathedral (1911–34)

Ingenhousz Jan 1730–99, Dutch plant physiologist and physician, who discovered photosynthesis

Ingleborough a mountain in N England, in North Yorkshire: potholes. Height: 723 m (2373 ft)

ingoing *English law* the sum paid by a new tenant for fixtures left behind by the outgoing tenant

Ingolstadt a city in S central Germany, in Bavaria on the River Danube: oil-refining. Pop: 119 528 (2003 est)

ingot a piece of cast metal obtained from a mould in a form suitable for storage, transporting, and further use

Ingres Jean Auguste Dominique 1780– 1867, French classical painter, noted for his draughtsmanship

ingrowing (esp of a toenail) growing abnormally into the flesh

Ingush Republic a constituent republic of S Russia: part of the Checheno-Ingush Autonomous Republic from 1936 until 1992. Capital: Magas (formerly at Nazran). Pop: 468 900 (2002). Area: 3600 sq km (1390 sq miles)

inhalant 1 (esp of a volatile medicinal formulation) inhaled for its soothing or therapeutic effect 2 an inhalant medicinal formulation

inhaler a device for breathing in therapeutic vapours through the nose or mouth, esp one for relieving nasal congestion or asthma

Inhambane a port in SE Mozambique on an inlet of the Mozambique Channel (**Inhambane Bay**). Pop: 64 274 (latest est)

inheritable *Biology* capable of being transmitted by heredity from one generation to a later one

inheritance 1 *Law* a hereditary succession to an estate, title, etc. b the right of an heir to succeed to property on the death of an ancestor **c** something that may legally be transmitted to an heir **2** the derivation of characteristics of one generation from an earlier one by heredity **3** *Obsolete* hereditary rights

inheritance tax 1 (in Britain) a tax introduced in 1986 to replace capital transfer tax, consisting of a percentage levied on that part of an inheritance exceeding a specified allowance, and scaled charges on gifts made within seven years of death **2** (in the US) a state tax imposed on an inheritance according to its size and the relationship of the beneficiary to the deceased

inhibition 1 *Psychol* **a** a mental state or condition in which the varieties of expression and behaviour of an individual become restricted **b** the weakening of a learned response usually as a result of extinction or because of the presence of a distracting stimulus **c** (in psychoanalytical theory) the unconscious restraining of an impulse **2** the process of stopping or retarding a chemical reaction **3** *Physiol* the suppression of the function or action of an organ or part, as by stimulation of its nerve supply **4** *Church of England* an episcopal order suspending an incumbent

initial *Botany* a cell from which tissues and organs develop by division and differentiation; a meristematic cell

initiative *Government* **a** the right or power to introduce legislation, etc, in a legislative body **b** the procedure by which citizens originate legislation, as in many American states and Switzerland

injunction *Law* an instruction or order issued by a court to a party to an action, esp to refrain from some act, such as causing a nuisance

injury *Law* a violation or infringement of another person's rights that causes him harm and is actionable at law

ink a dark brown fluid ejected into the water for self-concealment by an octopus or related mollusc from a gland (**ink sac**) near the anus

Inkerman a village in Ukraine, in the S Crimea east of Sevastopol: scene of a battle during the Crimean War in which British and French forces defeated the Russians (1854)

inland 1 of, concerning, or located in the interior of a country or region away from a sea or border **2** the interior of a country or region

Inland Revenue (in Britain and New Zealand) a government board that administers and collects major direct taxes, such as income tax, corporation tax, and capital gains tax

Inland Sea a sea in SW Japan, between the islands of Honshu, Shikoku, and Kyushu

inlay 1 *Dentistry* a filling, made of gold, porcelain, etc, inserted into a cavity and held in position by cement **2** *Art* decoration made by inlaying **3** an inlaid article, surface, etc.

inlet 1 a narrow inland opening of the coastline **2 a** a passage, valve, or part through which a substance, esp a fluid, enters a device or machine **b** (*as modifier*): *an inlet valve*

inn 1 a pub or small hotel providing food and accommodation **2** (formerly, in England) a college or hall of residence for students, esp of law, now only in the names of such institutions as the **Inns of Court**

Inn a river in central Europe, rising in Switzerland in Graubünden and flowing northeast through Austria and Bavaria to join the River Danube at Passau: forms part of the border between Austria and Germany. Length: 514 km (319 miles)

innate 1 *Botany* (of anthers) joined to the filament by the base only **2** (in rationalist philosophy) (of ideas) present in the mind before any experience and knowable by pure reason

inner 1 *Chem* (of a compound) having a cyclic structure formed or apparently formed by reaction of one functional group in a molecule with another group in the same molecule **2** *Archery* **a** the red innermost ring on a target **b** a shot which hits this ring

inner child *Psychol* the part of the psyche believed to retain feelings as they were experienced in childhood

Inner Mongolia an autonomous region of NE China: consists chiefly of the Mongolian plateau, with the Gobi Desert in the north and the Great Wall of China in the south. Capital: Hohhot. Pop: 23 800 000 (2003 est). Area: 1 177 500 sq km (459 225 sq miles)

inner tube an inflatable rubber tube that fits inside a pneumatic tyre casing

innings *Cricket* **a** the batting turn of a player or team **b** the runs scored during such a turn

Innocent II original name *Gregorio Papareschi*. died 1143, pope (1130–43). He condemned Abelard's teachings

Innocent III original name *Giovanni Lotario de' Conti*. ?1161–1216, pope (1198–1216), under whom the temporal power of the papacy reached its height. He instituted the Fourth Crusade (1202) and a crusade against the Albigenses (1208), and called the fourth Lateran Council (1215)

Innocent IV original name *Sinibaldo de' Fieschi*. died 1254, pope (1243–54); an unrelenting enemy of Emperor Frederick II and his heirs

Innsbruck a city in W Austria, on the River Inn at the foot of the Brenner Pass: tourist centre. Pop: 113 392 (2001)

Innu 1 a member of an Algonquian people living in Labrador and northern Quebec **2** the Algonquian language of this people

innuendo 1 *Law* (in pleading) a word introducing an explanatory phrase, usually in parenthesis **2** *Law* in an action for defamation **a** an explanation of the construction put upon words alleged to be defamatory where the defamatory meaning is not apparent **b** the words thus explained

innumerate having neither knowledge nor understanding of mathematics or science

inoperable *Surgery* not suitable for operation without risk, esp (of a malignant tumour) because metastasis has rendered surgery useless

inorganic 1 not having the structure or characteristics of living organisms; not organic **2** relating to or denoting chemical compounds that do not contain carbon

inorganic chemistry the branch of chemistry concerned with the elements and all their compounds except those containing carbon. Some simple carbon compounds, such as oxides, carbonates, etc, are treated as inorganic

inpatient a hospital patient who occupies a bed for at

least one night in the course of treatment, examination, or observation

input 1 *Economics* a resource required for industrial production, such as capital goods, labour services, raw materials, etc. 2 *Electronics* **a** the signal or current fed into a component or circuit **b** the terminals, or some other point, to which the signal is applied 3 *Computing* the data fed into a computer from a peripheral device

inquest an inquiry into the cause of an unexplained, sudden, or violent death, or as to whether or not property constitutes treasure trove, held by a coroner, in certain cases with a jury

inquiry *or* **enquiry** an investigation, esp a formal one conducted into a matter of public concern by a body constituted for that purpose by a government, local authority, or other organization

inquisition 1 an official inquiry, esp one held by a jury before an officer of the Crown 2 another word for **inquest**

Inquisition *History* a judicial institution of the Roman Catholic Church (1232–1820) founded to discover and suppress heresy
▷www.fordham.edu/halsall/source/ inquisition.html
▷www.catholic.com/library/inquisition.asp
▷http://bibletopics.com/biblestudy/64.htm

inquisitor an official of the ecclesiastical court of the Inquisition

inquisitorial *Law* denoting criminal procedure in which one party is both prosecutor and judge, or in which the trial is held in secret

insanity 1 relatively permanent disorder of the mind; state or condition of being insane 2 *Law* a defect of reason as a result of mental illness, such that a defendant does not know what he or she is doing or that it is wrong

insect 1 any small air-breathing arthropod of the class *Insecta*, having a body divided into head, thorax, and abdomen, three pairs of legs, and (in most species) two pairs of wings. Insects comprise about five sixths of all known animal species, with a total of over one million named species 2 (loosely) any similar invertebrate, such as a spider, tick, or centipede

insectivore 1 any placental mammal of the order *Insectivora*, being typically small, with simple teeth, and feeding on invertebrates. The group includes shrews, moles, and hedgehogs 2 any animal or plant that derives nourishment from insects

insertion 1 *Anatomy* the point or manner of attachment of a muscle to the bone that it moves 2 *Botany* the manner or point of attachment of one part to another

inset *Geography* a flowing in, as of the tide

insight 1 *Psychol* **a** the capacity for understanding one's own or another's mental processes **b** the immediate understanding of the significance of an event or action 2 *Psychiatry* the ability to understand one's own problems, sometimes used to distinguish between psychotic and neurotic disorders

insoluble incapable of being dissolved; incapable of forming a solution, esp in water

insolvent (of a person, company, etc) having insufficient assets to meet debts and liabilities; bankrupt

inspector a police officer ranking below a superintendent or chief inspector and above a sergeant

inspiration *Biology* the act or process of inhaling; breathing in

instability 1 tendency to variable or unpredictable behaviour 2 *Physics* a fast growing disturbance or wave in a plasma

installation *Art* an art exhibit often involving video or moving parts where the relation of the parts to the whole is important to the interpretation of the piece

installment plan *or esp Canadian* **instalment plan** *US and Canadian* a system for purchasing merchandise, such as cars or furniture, in which the buyer takes possession of the merchandise on payment of a deposit and completes the purchase by paying a series of regular instalments while the seller retains ownership until the final instalment is paid

instalment *or US* **installment** one of the portions, usually equal, into which a debt is divided for payment at specified intervals over a fixed period

instance *Logic* an expression derived from another by instantiation

instantaneous *Maths* **a** occurring at or associated with a particular instant **b** equal to the limit of the average value of a given variable as the time interval over which the variable is considered approaches zero

instep the middle section of the human foot, forming the arch between the ankle and toes

instinct *Biology* the innate capacity of an animal to respond to a given stimulus in a relatively fixed way

institution 1 *Christian Church* the appointment or admission of an incumbent to an ecclesiastical office or pastoral charge 2 *Christian theol* the creation of a sacrament by Christ, esp the Eucharist

instruction *Computing* a part of a program consisting of a coded command to the computer to perform a specified function

instructor *US and Canadian* a university teacher ranking below assistant professor

instrument 1 *Music* any of various contrivances or mechanisms that can be played to produce musical tones or sounds 2 a measuring device, such as a pressure gauge or ammeter 3 **a** a device or system for use in navigation or control, esp of aircraft **b** (*as modifier*): *instrument landing* 4 a formal legal document

instrumental a piece of music composed for instruments rather than for voices

instrumentalist 1 a person who plays a musical instrument 2 *Philosophy* a person who believes in the doctrines of instrumentalism

instrumentation 1 the instruments specified in a musical score or arrangement 2 the study of the characteristics of musical instruments

instrument panel *or* **board** 1 a panel on which instruments are mounted, as on a car 2 an array of instruments, gauges, etc, mounted to display the condition or performance of a machine or process

insulation material used to insulate a body, device, or region

insulin a protein hormone, secreted in the pancreas by the islets of Langerhans, that controls the concentration of glucose in the blood. Insulin deficiency results

355

in diabetes mellitus

insurgent *International law* a person or group that rises in revolt against an established government or authority but whose conduct does not amount to belligerency

insurrection the act or an instance of rebelling against a government in power or the civil authorities; insurgency

intaglio 1 the art or process of incised carving 2 a design, figure, or ornamentation carved, engraved, or etched into the surface of the material used 3 any of various printing techniques using an etched or engraved plate. The whole plate is smeared with ink, the surface wiped clean, and the ink in the recesses then transferred to the paper or other material 4 an incised die used to make a design in relief

intake *Engineering* the opening through which fluid enters a duct or channel, esp the air inlet of a jet engine

integer any rational number that can be expressed as the sum or difference of a finite number of units, being a member of the set ...-3, -2, -1, 0, 1, 2, 3...

integral 1 *Maths* a of or involving an integral b involving or being an integer 2 *Maths* the limit of an increasingly large number of increasingly smaller quantities, related to the function that is being integrated (the integrand). The independent variables may be confined within certain limits (**definite integral**) or in the absence of limits (**indefinite integral**).

integral calculus the branch of calculus concerned with the determination of integrals and their application to the solution of differential equations, the determination of areas and volumes, etc.

integrand a mathematical function to be integrated

integrated circuit a very small electronic circuit consisting of an assembly of elements made from a chip of semiconducting material, such as crystalline silicon

integument 1 the protective layer around an ovule that becomes the seed coat 2 the outer protective layer or covering of an animal, such as skin or a cuticle

intellect the capacity for understanding, thinking, and reasoning, as distinct from feeling or wishing

intelligence quotient a measure of the intelligence of an individual derived from results obtained from specially designed tests. The quotient is traditionally derived by dividing an individual's mental age by his chronological age and multiplying the result by 100

intelligent (of computerized functions) able to modify action in the light of ongoing events

intelligible *Philosophy* a capable of being apprehended by the mind or intellect alone b (in metaphysical systems such as those of Plato or Kant) denoting that metaphysical realm which is accessible to the intellect as opposed to the world of mere phenomena accessible to the senses

intensifier *Chem* a substance, esp one containing silver or uranium, used to increase the density of a photographic film or plate

intensity 1 *Physics* a a measure of field strength or of the energy transmitted by radiation b (of sound in a specified direction) the average rate of flow of sound energy, usually in watts, for one period through unit area at right angles to the specified direction. 2 *Geology* a measure of the size of an earthquake based on observa-

tion of the effects of the shock at the earth's surface. Specified on the Mercalli scale

intensive 1 *Business* using one factor of production proportionately more than others, as specified 2 *Physics* of or relating to a local property, measurement, etc, that is independent of the extent of the system

intensive care extensive and continuous care and treatment provided for an acutely ill patient, usually in a specially designated section (**intensive care unit**) of a hospital

intent *Law* the will or purpose with which one does an act

intention 1 *Law* the resolve or design with which a person does or refrains from doing an act, a necessary ingredient of certain offences 2 *Med* a natural healing process, as by **first intention**, in which the edges of a wound cling together with no tissue between, or by **second intention**, in which the wound edges adhere with granulation tissue

intentional *Philosophy* a of or relating to the capacity of the mind to refer to different kinds of objects b (of an object) existing only as the object of some mental attitude rather than in reality, as *a unicorn* in *she hopes to meet a unicorn*

intercept 1 *Maths* a a point at which two figures intersect b the distance from the origin to the point at which a line, curve, or surface cuts a coordinate axis c an intercepted segment 2 *Sport, US and Canadian* the act of intercepting an opponent's pass

intercession 1 the act of interceding or offering petitionary prayer to God on behalf of others 2 such petitionary prayer 3 *Roman history* the interposing of a veto by a tribune or other magistrate

interchange a motorway junction of interconnecting roads and bridges designed to prevent streams of traffic crossing one another

Intercity *Trademark* (in Britain) denoting a fast train or passenger rail service, esp between main towns

intercommunion association between Churches, involving esp mutual reception of Holy Communion

interdict 1 *RC Church* the exclusion of a person or all persons in a particular place from certain sacraments and other benefits, although not from communion 2 *Civil law* any order made by a court or official prohibiting an act 3 *Scots law* an order having the effect of an injunction 4 *Roman history* a an order of a praetor commanding or forbidding an act b the procedure by which this order was sought

interface 1 *Chem* a surface that forms the boundary between two bodies, liquids, or chemical phases 2 an electrical circuit linking one device, esp a computer, with another

interference 1 *Physics* the process in which two or more coherent waves combine to form a resultant wave in which the displacement at any point is the vector sum of the displacements of the individual waves. If the individual waves converge the resultant is a system of fringes. Two waves of equal or nearly equal intensity moving in opposite directions combine to form a standing wave 2 *Aeronautics* the effect on the flow pattern around a body of objects in the vicinity

interferon *Biochem* any of a family of proteins made by cells in response to virus infection that prevent the growth of the virus. Some interferons can prevent cell growth and have been tested for use in cancer therapy

interior 1 *Film, TV* a film or scene shot inside a building, studio, etc. 2 *Art* a picture of the inside of a room or building, as in a painting or stage design 3 *Politics* of or involving a nation's domestic affairs; internal

interior angle 1 an angle of a polygon contained between two adjacent sides 2 any of the four angles made by a transversal that lie inside the region between the two intersected lines

Interlaken a town and resort in central Switzerland, situated between Lakes Brienz and Thun on the River Aar. Pop: 5119 (2000)

interleukin a substance extracted from white blood cells that stimulates their activity against infection and may be used to combat some forms of cancer

interlock a device, esp one operated electromechanically, used in a logic circuit or electrical safety system to prevent an activity being initiated unless preceded by certain events

interlocutor *Scots law* a decree by a judge

interlocutory *Law* pronounced during the course of proceedings; provisional

interloper *Commerce* a person who trades unlawfully

interlude 1 *Theatre* a short dramatic piece played separately or as part of a longer entertainment, common in 16th-century England 2 a brief piece of music, dance, etc, given between the sections of another performance

intermediary a person who acts as a mediator or agent between parties

intermediate 1 (of a class, course, etc) suitable for learners with some degree of skill or competence 2 *Physics* (of a neutron) having an energy between 100 and 100 000 electronvolts 3 *Geology* (of such igneous rocks as syenite) containing between 55 and 66 per cent silica 4 a substance formed during one of the stages of a chemical process before the desired product is obtained

intermezzo 1 a short piece of instrumental music composed for performance between the acts or scenes of an opera, drama, etc. 2 an instrumental piece either inserted between two longer movements in an extended composition or intended for independent performance 3 another name for **interlude** (sense 2)

intern 1 another word for **internee** 2 *Med, US and Canadian* a graduate in the first year of practical training after medical school, resident in a hospital and under supervision by senior doctors

internal 1 *Politics* of or involving a nation's domestic as opposed to foreign affairs 2 *Education* denoting assessment by examiners who are employed at the candidate's place of study 3 situated within, affecting, or relating to the inside of the body 4 a medical examination of the vagina, uterus, or rectum

internal-combustion engine a heat engine in which heat is supplied by burning the fuel in the working fluid (usually air)

international 1 of, concerning, or involving two or more nations or nationalities 2 established by, controlling, or legislating for several nations 3 available for use by all nations 4 *Sport* **a** a contest between two national teams **b** a member of these teams

International any of several international socialist organizations

International Date Line the line approximately following the 180° meridian from Greenwich on the east side of which the date is one day earlier than on the west

internationalism the ideal or practice of cooperation and understanding between nations

International Style *or* **Modernism** a 20th-century architectural style characterized by undecorated rectilinear forms and the use of glass, steel, and reinforced concrete

internee a person who is interned, esp an enemy citizen in wartime or a terrorism suspect

internist *Chiefly US* a physician who specializes in internal medicine

Interpol International Criminal Police Organization, an association of over 100 national police forces, devoted chiefly to fighting international crime
▷www.interpol.int

interpretation *Logic* an allocation of significance to the terms of a purely formal system, by specifying ranges for the variables, denotations for the individual constants, etc.; a function from the formal language to such elements of a possible world

interregnum 1 an interval between two reigns, governments, incumbencies, etc. 2 any period in which a state lacks a ruler, government, etc.

interrupt the signal to initiate the stopping of the running of one computer program in order to run another, after which the running of the original program is usually continued

interrupter *or* **interruptor** an electromechanical device for opening and closing an electric circuit

interscholastic 1 (of sports events, competitions, etc) occurring between two or more schools 2 representative of various schools

intersection *Maths* **a** a point or set of points common to two or more geometric configurations **b** the set of elements that are common to two sets **c** the operation that yields that set from a pair of given sets. Symbol: ∩, as in $A \cap B$

interstellar conducted, or existing between two or more stars

interstice *Physics* the space between adjacent atoms in a crystal lattice

interval 1 *Music* the difference of pitch between two notes, either sounded simultaneously (**harmonic interval**) or in succession as in a musical part (**melodic interval**). An interval is calculated by counting the (inclusive) number of notes of the diatonic scale between the two notes 2 the ratio of the frequencies of two sounds 3 *Maths* the set containing all real numbers or points between two given numbers or points, called the endpoints. A **closed interval** includes the endpoints, but an **open interval** does not

intervention 1 *Politics* any interference in the affairs of others, esp by one state in the affairs of another 2 *Economics* the action of a central bank in supporting the international value of a currency by buying large quantities of the currency to keep the price up 3 *Commerce* the action of the EU in buying up surplus produce when the market price drops to a certain value

interwar of or happening in the period between World War I and World War II

intestate 1 a (of a person) not having made a will b (of property) not disposed of by will 2 a person who dies without having made a will

intestine the part of the alimentary canal between the stomach and the anus

intifada the Palestinian uprising against Israel in the West Bank and Gaza Strip that started at the end of 1987

intonation 1 *Music* the opening of a piece of plainsong, sung by a soloist 2 *Music* a the correct or accurate pitching of intervals b the capacity to play or sing in tune

intramural 1 *Education, chiefly US and Canadian* operating within or involving those in a single establishment 2 *Anatomy* within the walls of a cavity or hollow organ

intranet *Computing* an internal network that makes use of internet technology

intransitive *Logic, Maths* (of a relation) having the property that if it holds between one argument and a second, and between the second and a third, it must fail to hold between the first and the third

intrapreneur a person who while remaining within a larger organization uses entrepreneurial skills to develop a new product or line of business as a subsidiary of the organization

intrauterine within the womb

intravenous *Anatomy* within a vein

intrinsic *or* **intrinsical** *Anatomy* situated within or peculiar to a part

introduction 1 *Music* an instrumental passage preceding the entry of a soloist, choir, etc. b an opening passage in a movement or composition that precedes the main material 2 *Logic* (qualified by the name of an operation) a syntactic rule specifying the conditions under which a formula or statement containing the specified operator may be derived from others

introit *RC Church, Church of England* a short prayer said or sung as the celebrant is entering the sanctuary to celebrate Mass or Holy Communion

introversion 1 *Psychol* the directing of interest inwards towards one's own thoughts and feelings rather than towards the external world or making social contacts 2 *Pathol* the turning inside out of a hollow organ or part

intrusion 1 *Geology* a the movement of magma from within the earth's crust into spaces in the overlying strata to form igneous rock b any igneous rock formed in this way 2 *Property law* an unlawful entry onto land by a stranger after determination of a particular estate of freehold and before the remainderman or reversioner has made entry

intuition *Philosophy* immediate knowledge of a proposition or object such as Kant's account of our knowledge of sensible objects

Inuit *or* **Innuit** any of several Native peoples of N America or Greenland, as distinguished from those from Asia or the Aleutian Islands (who are still generally referred to as Eskimos); the preferred term for *Eskimo* in N America

Inuk a member of any Inuit people

Inuktitut *Canadian* the language of the Inuit

invalid *Logic* (of an argument) having a conclusion that does not follow from the premises: it may be false when the premises are all true; not valid

invariable a mathematical quantity having an unchanging value; a constant

invasion 1 *Pathol* the spread of cancer from its point of origin into surrounding tissues 2 *Ecology* the movement of plants to a new area or to an area to which they are not native

invention 1 *Patent law* the discovery or production of some new or improved process or machine that is both useful and is not obvious to persons skilled in the particular field 2 *Music* a short piece consisting of two or three parts usually in imitative counterpoint

Inveraray a town in W Scotland, in Argyll and Bute: Inveraray Castle is the seat of the Dukes of Argyll. Pop: 512 (1991)

Invercargill a city in New Zealand, on South Island: regional trading centre for sheep and agricultural products. Pop: 51 700 (2004 est)

Inverclyde a council area of W central Scotland: created in 1996 from part of Strathclyde region. Administrative centre: Greenock. Pop: 83 050 (2003 est). Area: 162 sq km (63 sq miles)

Inverness a city in N Scotland, administrative centre of Highland: tourism and specialized engineering. Pop: 40 949 (2001)

Inverness-shire (until 1975) a county of NW Scotland, now part of Highland

inverse 1 *Maths* a (of a relationship) containing two variables such that an increase in one results in a decrease in the other b (of an element) operating on a specified member of a set to produce the identity of the set: *the additive inverse element of x is –x, the multiplicative inverse element of x is 1/x* 2 *Maths* a another name for **reciprocal** b an inverse element 3 *Logic* a categorial proposition derived from another by changing both the proposition and its subject from affirmative to negative, or vice versa, as *all immortals are angels* from *no mortals are angels*

inversion 1 *Chem* a the conversion of a dextrorotatory solution of sucrose into a laevorotatory solution of glucose and fructose by hydrolysis b any similar reaction in which the optical properties of the reactants are opposite to those of the products 2 *Music* a the process or result of transposing the notes of a chord (esp a triad) such that the root, originally in the bass, is placed in an upper part. When the bass note is the third of the triad, the resulting chord is the **first inversion**; when it is the fifth, the resulting chord is the **second inversion** b (in counterpoint) the modification of a melody or part in which all ascending intervals are replaced by corresponding descending intervals and vice versa c the modification of an interval in which the higher note becomes the lower or the lower one the higher 3 *Pathol* abnormal positioning of an organ or part, as in being upside down or turned inside out 4 *Psychiatry* the adoption of the role or characteristics of the opposite sex 5 *Meteorol* an abnormal condition in which the layer of air next to the earth's surface is cooler than an overlying layer 6 *Computing* an operation by which each digit of a binary number is changed to the alternative digit, as 10110 to 01001 **7** *Genetics* a type of chromosomal mutation in which a section of a chromosome, and hence the order of its genes, is reversed **8** *Logic* the process of deriving the inverse of a categorial proposition **9** *Maths* a transformation that takes a point P to a point P′ such that $OP \cdot OP' = a^2$, where *a* is a constant and P and P′ lie on a straight line through a fixed point O and on the same side of it

invert 1 *Psychiatry* **a** a person who adopts the role of the opposite sex **b** another word for **homosexual 2** *Architect* **a** the lower inner surface of a drain, sewer, etc. **b** an arch that is concave upwards, esp one used in foundations

invertebrate any animal lacking a backbone, including all species not classified as vertebrates

investiture (in feudal society) the formal bestowal of the possessory right to a fief or other benefice

investment 1 *Economics* the amount by which the stock of capital (plant, machinery, materials, etc) in an enterprise or economy changes **2** *Biology* the outer layer or covering of an organ, part, or organism

invisible 1 *Economics* of or relating to services rather than goods in relation to the invisible balance **2** *Economics* an invisible item of trade; service

in vitro (of biological processes or reactions) made to occur outside the living organism in an artificial environment, such as a culture medium

invocation 1 a prayer asking God for help, forgiveness, etc, esp as part of a religious service **2** an appeal for inspiration and guidance from a Muse or deity at the beginning of a poem **3 a** the act of summoning a spirit or demon from another world by ritual incantation or magic **b** the incantation used in this act

involuntary *Physiol* (esp of a movement or muscle) performed or acting without conscious control

involute 1 *Botany* (esp of petals, leaves, etc, in bud) having margins that are rolled inwards **2** (of certain shells) closely coiled so that the axis is obscured **3** *Geometry* the curve described by the free end of a thread as it is wound around another curve, the **evolute**, such that its normals are tangential to the evolute

inwrought worked or woven into material, esp decoratively

Io¹ *Greek myth* a maiden loved by Zeus and turned into a white heifer by either Zeus or Hera

Io² the innermost of the four Galilean satellites of Jupiter, displaying intense volcanic activity. Diameter: 3640 km; orbital radius: 422 000 km

iodide 1 a salt of hydriodic acid, containing the iodide ion, I^- **2** a compound containing an iodine atom, such as methyl iodide, CH_3I

iodine a bluish-black element of the halogen group that sublimates into a violet irritating gas. Its compounds are used in medicine and photography and in dyes. The radioisotope **iodine-131** (**radioiodine**), with a half-life of 8 days, is used in the diagnosis and treatment of thyroid disease. Symbol: I; atomic no.: 53; atomic wt.: 126.90447; valency: 1, 3, 5, or 7; relative density: 4.93; melting pt.: 113.5°C; boiling pt.: 184.35°C

ion an electrically charged atom or group of atoms formed by the loss or gain of one or more electrons

Iona an island off the W coast of Scotland, in the Inner Hebrides: site of St Columba's monastery (founded in 563) and an important early centre of Christianity. Area: 854 ha (2112 acres)

Ionesco Eugène 1912–94, French dramatist, born in Romania; a leading exponent of the theatre of the absurd. His plays include *The Bald Prima Donna* (1950) and *Rhinoceros* (1960)

ion exchange the process in which ions are exchanged between a solution and an insoluble solid, usually a resin. It is used to soften water, to separate radioactive isotopes, and to purify certain industrial chemicals

Ionia an ancient region of W central Asia Minor, including adjacent Aegean islands: colonized by Greeks in about 1100 BC

Ionian Sea the part of the Mediterranean Sea between SE Italy, E Sicily, and Greece

Ionic 1 of, denoting, or relating to one of the five classical orders of architecture, characterized by fluted columns and capitals with scroll-like ornaments **2** of or relating to Ionia, its inhabitants, or their dialect of Ancient Greek **3** *Prosody* of, relating to, designating, or employing Ionics in verse **4** one of four chief dialects of Ancient Greek; the dialect spoken in Ionia **5** (in classical prosody) a type of metrical foot having either two long followed by two short syllables (**greater Ionic**), or two short followed by two long syllables (**lesser Ionic**)
▷www.hellenism.net/eng/arts.htm

ionosphere a region of the earth's atmosphere, extending from about 60 kilometres to 1000 km above the earth's surface, in which there is a high concentration of free electrons formed as a result of ionizing radiation entering the atmosphere from space

iota the ninth letter in the Greek alphabet (I, ι), a vowel or semivowel, transliterated as *i* or *j*

Iowa a state of the N central US, in the Midwest: consists of rolling plains crossed by many rivers, with the Missouri forming the western border and the Mississippi the eastern. Capital: Des Moines. Pop: 2 944 062 (2003 est). Area: 144 887 sq km (55 941 sq miles)

ipecacuanha *or* **ipecac 1** a low-growing South American rubiaceous shrub, *Cephaelis ipecacuanha* **2** a drug prepared from the dried roots of this plant, used as a purgative and emetic

Ipoh a city in Malaysia, capital of Perak state: tin-mining centre. Pop: 643 000 (2005 est)

Ipsus an ancient town in Asia Minor, in S Phrygia: site of a decisive battle (301 BC) in the Wars of the Diadochi in which Lysimachus and Seleucus defeated Antigonus and Demetrius

Ipswich a town in E England, administrative centre of Suffolk, a port at the head of the Orwell estuary: financial services, telecommunications. Pop: 138 718 (2001)

Iqaluit a town in N Canada, capital of Nunavut. Pop: 5236 (2001)

Iqbal Sir **Muhammad** 1875–1938, Indian Muslim poet, philosopher, and political leader, who advocated the establishment of separate nations for Indian Hindus and Muslims and is generally regarded as the originator of Pakistan

Iquique a port in N Chile: oil refineries. Pop: 243 000 (2005 est)

Iquitos an inland port in NE Peru, on the Amazon 3703

km (2300 miles) from the Atlantic: head of navigation for large steamers. Pop: 389 000 (2005 est)

Iran a republic in SW Asia, between the Caspian Sea and the Persian Gulf: a monarchy until an Islamic revolution in 1979 headed by the Ayatollah Khomeini when the Shah was obliged to leave the country. Consists chiefly of a high central desert plateau almost completely surrounded by mountains, a semitropical fertile region along the Caspian coast, and a hot and dry area beside the Persian Gulf. Oil is the most important export. Official language: Farsi (Persian). Official religion: Muslim majority. Currency: rial. Capital: Tehran. Pop: 68 789 000 (2004 est). Area: 1 647 050 sq km (635 932 sq miles)

Iranian 1 a branch of the Indo-European family of languages, divided into **West Iranian** (including Old Persian, Pahlavi, modern Persian, Kurdish, Baluchi, and Tajik) and **East Iranian** (including Avestan, Sogdian, Pashto, and Ossetic) 2 the modern Persian language 3 belonging to or relating to the Iranian branch of Indo-European

Iraq a republic in SW Asia, on the Persian Gulf: coextensive with ancient Mesopotamia; became a British mandate in 1920, independent in 1932, and a republic in 1958. The Iraqi invasion of Kuwait (1990) led to their defeat in the first Gulf War (1991) by US-led UN forces. The second Gulf War (2003) took place when Iraq was invaded by a coalition of US, UK and other forces. Iraq consists chiefly of the mountains of Kurdistan in the northeast, part of the Syrian Desert, and the lower basin of the Rivers Tigris and Euphrates. Oil is the major export. Official language: Arabic; Kurdish is official in the Kurdish Autonomous Region only. Official religion: Muslim. Currency: dinar. Capital: Baghdad. Pop: 25 856 000 (2004 est). Area: 438 446 sq km (169 284 sq miles)

Irbid a town in NW Jordan. Pop: 280 000 (2005 est)

ire *Literary* anger; wrath

Ireland¹ John (**Nicholson**). 1879–1962, English composer, esp of songs

Ireland² 1 an island off NW Europe: part of the British Isles, separated from Britain by the North Channel, the Irish Sea, and St George's Channel; contains large areas of peat bog, with mountains that rise over 900 m (3000 ft) in the southwest and several large lakes. It was conquered by England in the 16th and early 17th centuries and ruled as a dependency until 1801, when it was united with Great Britain until its division in 1921 into the Irish Free State and Northern Ireland 2 **Republic of Ireland** a republic in NW Europe occupying most of Ireland: established as the Irish Free State (a British dominion) in 1921 and declared a republic in 1949; joined the European Community (now the European Union) in 1973. Official languages: Irish (Gaelic) and English. Currency: euro. Capital: Dublin. Pop: 3 999 000 (2004 est). Area: 70 285 sq km (27 137 sq.miles)

Ireton Henry 1611–51, English Parliamentarian general in the Civil War; son-in-law of Oliver Cromwell. His plan for a constitutional monarchy was rejected by Charles I (1647), whose death warrant he signed; lord deputy of Ireland (1650–51)

iridaceous of, relating to, or belonging to the *Iridaceae*, a

family of monocotyledonous plants, including iris, crocus, and gladiolus, having swordlike leaves and showy flowers

iridium a very hard inert yellowish-white transition element that is the most corrosion-resistant metal known. It occurs in platinum ores and is used as an alloy with platinum. Symbol: Ir; atomic no.: 77; atomic wt.: 192.22; valency: 3 or 4; relative density: 22.42; melting pt.: 2447°C; boiling pt.: 4428°C

iris 1 the coloured muscular diaphragm that surrounds and controls the size of the pupil 2 any plant of the iridaceous genus *Iris*, having brightly coloured flowers composed of three petals and three drooping sepals 3 a form of quartz that reflects light polychromatically from internal fractures

Irish 1 another name for **Irish Gaelic**

Irish Free State a former name for the (Republic of) Ireland (1921–37)

Irish Gaelic the Goidelic language of the Celts of Ireland, now spoken mainly along the west coast; an official language of the Republic of Ireland since 1921

Irish Sea an arm of the North Atlantic Ocean between Great Britain and Ireland

Irkutsk a city in S Russia; situated on the Trans-Siberian railway; university (1918); one of the largest industrial centres in Siberia, esp for heavy engineering. Pop: 587 000 (2005 est)

iron 1 a a malleable ductile silvery-white ferromagnetic metallic element occurring principally in haematite and magnetite. It is widely used for structural and engineering purposes. See also **steel, cast iron, wrought iron, pig iron**. Symbol: Fe; atomic no.: 26; atomic wt.: 55.847; valency: 2,3,4, or 6; relative density: 7.874; melting pt.: 1538°C; boiling pt.: 2862°C b *(as modifier)*: *iron railings* 2 any of certain tools or implements made of iron or steel, esp for use when hot 3 an appliance for pressing fabrics using dry heat or steam, esp a small electrically heated device with a handle and a weighted flat bottom 4 any of various golf clubs with narrow metal heads, numbered from 1 to 9 according to the slant of the face, used esp for approach shots 5 an informal word for **harpoon**

Iron Age the period following the Bronze Age characterized by the extremely rapid spread of iron tools and weapons, which began in the Middle East about 1100 BC

ironbark any of several Australian eucalyptus trees that have hard rough bark

ironclad a large wooden 19th-century warship with armoured plating

Iron Curtain a (formerly) the guarded border between the countries of the Soviet bloc and the rest of Europe b *(as modifier)*: *Iron Curtain countries*

Iron Gate or **Iron Gates** a gorge of the River Danube on the border between Romania and Serbia and Montenegro. Length: 3 km (2 miles)

iron lung an airtight metal cylinder enclosing the entire body up to the neck and providing artificial respiration when the respiratory muscles are paralysed, as by poliomyelitis

iron maiden a medieval instrument of torture, consisting of a hinged case (often shaped in the form of a woman) lined with iron spikes, which was forcibly closed on the victim

ironmaster *Brit* a manufacturer of iron, esp (formerly) the owner of an ironworks

ironmonger *Brit* a dealer in metal utensils, hardware, locks, etc.

Ironside nickname of **Edmund II** of England

ironstone 1 any rock consisting mainly of an iron-bearing ore 2 a tough durable earthenware

ironwood 1 any of various betulaceous trees, such as hornbeam, that have very hard wood 2 a Californian rosaceous tree, *Lyonothamnus floribundus*, with very hard wood 3 any of various other trees with hard wood, such as the mopani

ironwork 1 work done in iron, esp decorative work 2 the craft or practice of working in iron

ironworks a building in which iron is smelted, cast, or wrought

irrational 1 *Maths* a not rational b (*as noun*) 2 *Prosody* in Greek or Latin verse a of or relating to a metrical irregularity, usually the occurrence of a long syllable instead of a short one b denoting a metrical foot where such an irregularity occurs

irrational number any real number that cannot be expressed as the ratio of two integers, such as π

Irrawaddy the main river in Myanmar, rising in the north in two headstreams and flowing south through the whole length of Myanmar, to enter the Andaman Sea by nine main mouths. Length: 2100 km (1300 miles)

irredentist a person who favours the acquisition of territory that once was part of his country or is considered to have been

irreducible *Maths* a (of a polynomial) unable to be factorized into polynomials of lower degree, as (x^2+1) b (of a radical) incapable of being reduced to a rational expression, as $\sqrt{(x+1)}$

irregular 1 (of flowers) having any of their parts, esp petals, differing in size, shape, etc.; asymmetric 2 US (of merchandise) not up to the manufacturer's standards or specifications; flawed; imperfect 3 US imperfect or flawed merchandise

irreversible 1 *Chem, Physics* capable of changing or producing a change in one direction only 2 *Thermodynamics* (of a change, process, etc) occurring through a number of intermediate states that are not all in thermodynamic equilibrium

irritable 1 *Biology* (of all living organisms) capable of responding to such stimuli as heat, light, and touch 2 *Pathol* abnormally sensitive

Irtysh or **Irtish** a river in central Asia, rising in China in the Altai Mountains and flowing west through Kazakhstan, then northwest into Russia to join the Ob River as its chief tributary. Length: 4444 km (2760 miles)

Irvine¹ **Alexander Andrew Mackay,** Baron, known as *Derry.* born 1940, British lawyer and Labour politician; Lord Chancellor (1997–2003)

Irvine² a town on the W coast of Scotland, the administrative centre of North Ayrshire: designated a new town in 1966. Pop: 33 090 (2001)

Irving 1 Sir **Henry** real name *John Henry Brodribb.* 1838–1905, English actor and manager of the Lyceum Theatre in London (1878–1902) 2 **Washington** 1783–1859,

US essayist and short-story writer, noted for *The Sketch Book of Geoffrey Crayon* (1820), which contains the stories *Rip Van Winkle* and *The Legend of Sleepy Hollow*

Isaac an Old Testament patriarch, the son of Abraham and Sarah and father of Jacob and Esau (Genesis 17; 21–27)

Isabella original name *Elizabeth Farnese.* 1692–1766, second wife (1714–46) of Philip V of Spain and mother of Charles III of Spain

Isabella I known as *Isabella the Catholic.* 1451–1504, queen of Castile (1474–1504) and, with her husband, Ferdinand V, joint ruler of Castile and Aragon (1479–1504)

Isabella II 1830–1904, queen of Spain (1833–68), whose accession precipitated the first Carlist war (1833–39). She was deposed in a revolution

Isabella of France 1292–1358, wife (1308–27) of Edward II of England, whom, aided by her lover, Roger de Mortimer, she deposed; mother of Edward III

Isaiah *Old Testament* 1 the first of the major Hebrew prophets, who lived in the 8th century BC 2 the book of his and others' prophecies

isallobar *Meteorol* a line on a map running through places experiencing equal pressure changes

Isar a river in central Europe, rising in W Austria and flowing generally northeast through S Germany into the Danube. Length: over 260 km (160 miles)

Isauria an ancient district of S central Asia Minor, chiefly on the N slopes of the W Taurus Mountains

Iscariot See **Judas** (sense 1)

Ischia a volcanic island in the Tyrrhenian Sea, at the N end of the Bay of Naples. Area: 47 sq km (18 sq miles)

Isfahan or **Eşfahān** a city in central Iran: the second largest city in the country; capital of Persia in the 11th century and from 1598 to 1722. Pop: 1 547 000 (2005 est)

Isherwood **Christopher,** full name *Christopher William Bradshaw-Isherwood.* 1904–86, US novelist and dramatist, born in England. His works include the novel *Goodbye to Berlin* (1939) and three verse plays written in collaboration with W.H. Auden

Ishiguro **Kazuo** born 1954, British novelist, born in Japan. His novels include *An Artist of the Floating World* (1986), the Booker-prizewinning *The Remains of the Day* (1989), and *When We Were Orphans* (2000)

Ishmael 1 the son of Abraham and Hagar, Sarah's handmaid: the ancestor of 12 Arabian tribes (Genesis 21:8–21; 25:12–18) 2 a bandit chieftain, who defied the Babylonian conquerors of Judah and assassinated the governor appointed by Nebuchadnezzar (II Kings 25:25; Jeremiah 40:13–41:18) 3 *Rare* an outcast

Isidore of Seville Saint, Latin name *Isidorus Hispalensis.* ?560–636 AD, Spanish archbishop and scholar, noted for his *Etymologies,* an encyclopedia. Feast day: April 4

isinglass a gelatine made from the air bladders of freshwater fish, used as a clarifying agent and adhesive

Isis¹ the local name for the River Thames at Oxford

Isis² an ancient Egyptian fertility goddess, depicted as a woman with a cow's horns, between which was the disc of the sun; wife and sister of Osiris

Iskenderun a port in S Turkey, on the **Gulf of Iskenderun.** Pop: 161 000 (2005 est)

Islam 1 the religion of Muslims, having the Koran as its sacred scripture and teaching that there is only one God and that Mohammed is his prophet; Mohammedanism **2 a** Muslims collectively and their civilization **b** the countries where the Muslim religion is predominant

▷http://www.islamworld.net/

Islamabad the capital of Pakistan, in the north on the Potwar Plateau: site chosen in 1959; surrounded by the Capital Territory of Islamabad for 909 sq km (351 sq miles). Pop: 770 000 (2005 est)

island 1 a mass of land that is surrounded by water and is smaller than a continent **2** See **traffic island 3** *Anatomy* a part, structure, or group of cells distinct in constitution from its immediate surroundings

Islay an island off the W coast of Scotland: the southernmost of the Inner Hebrides; separated from the island of Jura by the **Sound of Islay**. Pop: 3457 (2001). Area: 606 sq km (234 sq miles)

Isle Royale an island in the northeast US, in NW Lake Superior: forms, with over 100 surrounding islands, **Isle Royale National Park**. Area: 541 sq km (209 sq miles)

islet a small island

Islington a borough of N Greater London. Pop: 180 100 (2003 est). Area: 16 sq km (6 sq miles)

Ismailia a city in NE Egypt, on the Suez Canal: founded in 1863 by the former Suez Canal Company; devastated by Israeli troops in the October War (1973). Pop: 299 000 (2005 est)

Ismail Pasha 1830–95, viceroy (1863–66) and khedive (1867–79) of Egypt, who brought his country close to bankruptcy. He was forced to submit to Anglo-French financial control (1876) and to abdicate (1879)

isobar 1 *Meteorology* a line on a map connecting places of equal atmospheric pressure, usually reduced to sea level for purposes of comparison, at a given time or period **2** *Physics* any of two or more atoms that have the same mass number but different atomic numbers

isochronal *or* **isochronous** occurring at equal time intervals; having a uniform period of vibration or oscillation

Isocrates 436–338 BC, Athenian rhetorician and teacher

isohel a line on a map connecting places with an equal period of sunshine

isohyet a line on a map connecting places having equal rainfall

isomer 1 *Chem* a compound that exhibits isomerism with one or more other compounds **2** *Physics* a nuclide that exhibits isomerism with one or more other nuclides

isometric 1 *Physiol* of or relating to muscular contraction that does not produce shortening of the muscle **2** (of a crystal or system of crystallization) having three mutually perpendicular equal axes **3** *Crystallog* another word for **cubic 4** *Prosody* having or made up of regular feet **5** (of a method of projecting a drawing in three dimensions) having the three axes equally inclined and all lines drawn to scale **6** a drawing made in this way **7** a line on a graph showing variations of pressure with temperature at constant volume

isomorphism 1 *Biology* similarity of form, as in different generations of the same life cycle **2** *Chem* the existence of two or more substances of different composi-

tion in a similar crystalline form **3** *Maths* a one-to-one correspondence between the elements of two or more sets, such as those of Arabic and Roman numerals, and between the sums or products of the elements of one of these sets and those of the equivalent elements of the other set or sets

isotherm 1 a line on a map linking places of equal temperature **2** *Physics* a curve on a graph that connects points of equal temperature

isotonic 1 *Physiol* (of two or more muscles) having equal tension **2** (of two solutions) having the same osmotic pressure, commonly having physiological osmotic pressure **3** *Music* of, relating to, or characterized by the equal intervals of the well-tempered scale

isotope one of two or more atoms with the same atomic number that contain different numbers of neutrons

isotropic *or* **isotropous 1** having uniform physical properties in all directions **2** *Biology* not having predetermined axes

Israel 1 a republic in SW Asia, on the Mediterranean Sea: established in 1948, in the former British mandate of Palestine, as a primarily Jewish state; 8 disputes with Arab neighbours (who did not recognize the state of Israel), erupted into full-scale wars in 1948, 1956, 1967 (the Six Day War), and 1973 (the Yom Kippur War). In 1993 Israel agreed to grant autonomous status to the Gaza Strip and the West Bank, according to the terms of a peace agreement with the P.L.O. Official languages: Hebrew and Arabic. Religion: Jewish majority, Muslim and Christian minorities. Currency: shekel. Capital: Jerusalem (international recognition withheld as East Jerusalem was annexed (1967) by Israel: UN recognized capital: Tel Aviv). Pop: 6 560 000 (2004 est). Area (including Golan Heights and East Jerusalem): 21 946 sq km (8473 sq miles) **2 a** the ancient kingdom of the 12 Hebrew tribes at the SE end of the Mediterranean **b** the kingdom in the N part of this region formed by the ten northern tribes of Israel in the 10th century BC and destroyed by the Assyrians in 721 BC **3** *Informal* the Jewish community throughout the world

Israelite 1 *Bible* a member of the ethnic group claiming descent from Jacob; a Hebrew **2** *Bible* a citizen of the kingdom of Israel (922 to 721BC) as opposed to Judah **3** a member of any of various Christian sects who regard themselves as God's chosen people

Issachar *Old Testament* **1** the fifth son of Jacob by his wife Leah (Genesis 30:17–18) **2** the tribe descended from this patriarch **3** the territory of this tribe

Isserlis Steven (John). born 1958, British cellist

Issigonis Sir Alec (Arnold Constantine). 1906–88, British car designer born in Smyrna. He is noted for his designs for the Morris Minor (1948) and the Mini (1959)

issue 1 *Pathol* **a** a suppurating sore **b** discharge from a wound **2** *Law* the matter remaining in dispute between the parties to an action after the pleadings **3** the yield from or profits arising out of land or other property

Issus an ancient town in S Asia Minor, in Cilicia north of present-day Iskenderun: scene of a battle (333 BC) in which Alexander the Great defeated the Persians

Issyk-Kul a lake in NE Kyrgyzstan in the Tian Shan mountains, at an altitude of 1609 m (5280 ft): one of the largest mountain lakes in the world. Area: 6200 sq km (2390 sq miles)

Istanbul a port in NW Turkey, on the western (European) shore of the Bosporus: the largest city in Turkey; founded in about 660 BC by Greeks; refounded by Constantine the Great in 330 AD as the capital of the Eastern Roman Empire; taken by the Turks in 1453 and remained capital of the Ottoman Empire until 1922; industrial centre for shipbuilding, textiles, etc. Pop: 9 760 000 (2005 est))

isthmus 1 a narrow strip of land connecting two relatively large land areas 2 *Anatomy* a a narrow band of tissue connecting two larger parts of a structure b a narrow passage connecting two cavities

Istria a peninsula in the N Adriatic Sea: passed from Italy to Yugoslavia (except for Trieste) in 1947 and to Croatia in 1991

Italian the official language of Italy and one of the official languages of Switzerland: the native language of approximately 60 million people. It belongs to the Romance group of the Indo-European family, and there is a considerable diversity of dialects

Italian East Africa a former Italian territory in E Africa, formed in 1936 from the possessions of Eritrea, Italian Somaliland, and Ethiopia: taken by British forces in 1941

Italian Somaliland a former Italian colony in E Africa, united with British Somaliland in 1960 to form the independent republic of Somalia

Italy a republic in S Europe, occupying a peninsula in the Mediterranean between the Tyrrhenian and the Adriatic Seas, with the islands of Sardinia and Sicily to the west: first united under the Romans but became fragmented into numerous political units in the Middle Ages; united kingdom proclaimed in 1861; under the dictatorship of Mussolini (1922–43); became a republic in 1946; a member of the European Union. It is generally mountainous, with the Alps in the north and the Apennines running the length of the peninsula. Official language: Italian. Religion: Roman Catholic majority. Currency: euro. Capital: Rome. Pop: 57 346 000 (2004 est) Area: 301 247 sq km (116 312 sq miles)

itch any skin disorder, such as scabies, characterized by intense itching

Ithaca a Greek island in the Ionian Sea, the smallest of the Ionian Islands: regarded as the home of Homer's Odysseus. Area: 93 sq km (36 sq miles)

Ito Prince **Hirobumi** 1841–1909, Japanese statesman; premier (1884–88; 1892–96; 1898; 1900–01). He led the movement to modernize Japan and helped to draft the Meiji constitution (1889); assassinated

Ivan III known as *Ivan the Great*. 1440–1505, grand duke of Muscovy (1462–1505). He expanded Muscovy, defeated the Tatars (1480), and assumed the title of Ruler of all Russia (1472)

Ivan IV known as *Ivan the Terrible*. 1530–84, grand duke of Muscovy (1533–47) and first tsar of Russia (1547–84). He conquered Kazan (1552), Astrakhan (1556), and Siberia (1581), but was defeated by Poland in the Livonian War (1558–82) after which his rule became increasingly oppressive

Ivanovo a city in W central Russia, on the Uvod River: textile centre. Pop: 423 000 (2005 est)

Ives 1 **Charles Edward** 1874–1954, US composer, noted for his innovative use of polytonality, polyrhythms, and quarter tones. His works include *Second Piano Sonata: Concord* (1915), five symphonies, chamber music, and songs 2 **Frederick Eugene** 1856–1937, US inventor of halftone photography

ivory 1 a a hard smooth creamy white variety of dentine that makes up a major part of the tusks of elephants, walruses, and similar animals b (*as modifier*): *ivory ornaments* 2 a tusk made of ivory 3 a a yellowish-white colour; cream b (*as adjective*): *ivory shoes* 4 **black ivory** *Obsolete* Black slaves collectively

Ivory **James** born 1928, US film director. With the producer Ismael Merchant, his films include *Shakespeare Wallah* (1964), *Heat and Dust* (1983), *A Room With a View* (1986), and *The Golden Bowl* (2000)

ivy 1 any woody climbing or trailing araliaceous plant of the Old World genus *Hedera*, esp *H. helix*, having lobed evergreen leaves and black berry-like fruits 2 any of various other climbing or creeping plants, such as Boston ivy, poison ivy, and ground ivy

iwi NZ a Māori tribe

Iwo a city in SW Nigeria. Pop: 479 000 (2005 est)

Iwo Jima an island in the W Pacific, about 1100 km (700 miles) south of Japan: one of the Volcano Islands; scene of prolonged fighting between US and Japanese forces until taken by the US in 1945; returned to Japan in 1968. Area: 20 sq km (8 sq miles)

ixia any plant of the iridaceous genus *Ixia*, of southern Africa, having showy ornamental funnel-shaped flowers

Ixtaccihuatl or **Iztaccihuatl** a dormant volcano in central Mexico, southeast of Mexico City. Height: (central peak) 5286 m (17 342 ft)

Iyeyasu or **Ieyasu** Tokugawa 1542–1616, Japanese general and statesman; founder of the Tokugawa shogunate (1603–1867)

Izetbegović Alija 1925–2003, Bosnia and Herzegovinian politician: president (1992–2000), he led the country to independence and during the subsequent civil war

Izhevsk an industrial city in central Russia, capital of the Udmurt Republic. Pop: 632 000 (2005 est)

Izmir a port in W Turkey, on the **Gulf of Izmir**: the third largest city in the country; university (1955). Pop: 2 500 000 (2005 est)

Izmit a town in NW Turkey, on the **Gulf of Izmit** Pop: 306 000 (2005 est)

Iznik the modern Turkish name of **Nicaea**

J j

jab 1 a quick short blow, esp (in boxing) a straight punch with the leading hand 2 *Informal* an injection

Jabalpur *or* **Jubbulpore** a city in central India, in central Madhya Pradesh. Pop: 951 469 (2001)Pop: 741 927 (1991)

Jabir ibn Hayyan ?721–?815. Arab alchemist, whose many works enjoyed enormous esteem among later alchemists, such as Geber

jabiru 1 a large white tropical American stork, *Jabiru mycteria*, with a dark naked head and a dark bill 2 a large Australian stork, *Xenorhyncus asiaticus*, having a white plumage, dark green back and tail, and red legs

jacaranda 1 any bignoniaceous tree of the tropical American genus *Jacaranda*, having fernlike leaves and pale purple flowers and widely cultivated in temperate areas of Australia 2 the fragrant ornamental wood of any of these trees 3 any of several related or similar trees or their wood

jack¹ 1 a sailor 2 the male of certain animals, esp of the ass or donkey 3 a mechanical or hydraulic device for exerting a large force, esp to raise a heavy weight such as a motor vehicle 4 one of four playing cards in a pack, one for each suit, bearing the picture of a young prince; knave 5 *Bowls* a small usually white bowl at which the players aim with their own bowls 6 *Electrical engineering* a female socket with two or more terminals designed to receive a male plug (**jack plug**) that either makes or breaks the circuit or circuits 7 a flag, esp a small flag flown at the bow of a ship indicating the ship's nationality 8 *Nautical* either of a pair of crosstrees at the head of a topgallant mast used as standoffs for the royal shrouds 9 a part of the action of a harpsichord, consisting of a fork-shaped device on the end of a pivoted lever on which a plectrum is mounted 10 any of various tropical and subtropical carangid fishes, esp those of the genus *Caranx*, such as *C. hippos* (**crevalle jack**) 11 one of the pieces used in the game of jacks

jack² *Archaic* a drinking vessel, often of leather

jackal any of several African or S Asian canine mammals of the genus *Canis*, closely related to the dog, having long legs and pointed ears and muzzle: predators and carrion-eaters

jackanapes *Archaic* a monkey

jackass 1 a male donkey 2 **laughing jackass** another name for **kookaburra**

jackdaw a large common Eurasian passerine bird,

Corvus monedula, in which the plumage is black and dark grey: noted for its thieving habits: family *Corvidae* (crows)

jacket *Engineering* 1 any exterior covering or casing, such as the insulating cover of a boiler 2 the part of the cylinder block of an internal-combustion engine that encloses the coolant

Jack Frost a personification of frost or winter

jack-in-the-box a toy consisting of a figure on a compressed spring in a box, which springs out when the lid is opened

jackknife 1 a knife with the blade pivoted to fold into a recess in the handle 2 a former name for a type of dive in which the diver bends at the waist in midair, with his legs straight and his hands touching his feet, finally straightening out and entering the water headfirst: forward pike dive

jackpot any large prize, kitty, or accumulated stake that may be won in gambling, such as a pool in poker that accumulates until the betting is opened with a pair of jacks or higher

jack rabbit any of various W North American hares, such as *Lepus townsendi* (**white-tailed jack rabbit**), having long hind legs and large ears

jacks a game in which bone, metal, or plastic pieces (**jackstones**) are thrown and then picked up in various groups between bounces or throws of a small ball

Jackson¹ 1 **Andrew** 1767–1845, US statesman, general, and lawyer; seventh president of the US (1829–37). He became a national hero after successfully defending New Orleans from the British (1815). During his administration the spoils system was introduced and the national debt was fully paid off 2 **Colin** (**Ray**). born 1967, British athlete, broke world record for 110 m hurdles in 1993 (12.91 seconds) and for the 60 m hurdles in 1994 (7.3 seconds) 3 **Glenda** born 1936, British stage, film, and television actress, and Labour politician. Her films include *Women in Love* (1969) for which she won an Oscar, *The Music Lovers* (1970), *Sunday Bloody Sunday* (1971), and *Turtle Diary* (1985); became a member of parliament in 1992 4 **Jesse** (**Louis**). born 1941, US Democrat politician and clergyman; Black campaigner for minority rights 5 **Michael** (**Joe**). born 1958, US pop singer, lead vocalist with the Jacksons (originally the Jackson 5) (1969–86). His solo albums include *Thriller* (1982), *Bad* (1989), and *Invincible* (2001) 6 **Peter** born 1961, US film director, screenwriter, and producer; his films include *Heavenly Creatures* (1994) and *The Lord of the Rings* trilogy (2001–03). **7 Thomas Jonathan,** known as *Stonewall Jackson*. 1824–63, Confederate general in the American Civil War, noted particularly for his command at the first Battle of Bull Run (1861)

Jackson² a city in and state capital of Mississippi, on the Pearl River. Pop: 179 599 (2003 est)

Jacksonville a port in NE Florida: the leading commercial centre of the southeast. Pop: 773 781 (2003 est)

Jack Tar *Now chiefly literary* a sailor

Jack the Ripper an unidentified murderer who killed at least seven prostitutes in London's East End between August and November 1888

Jacob 1 *Old Testament* the son of Isaac, twin brother of Esau, and father of the twelve patriarchs of Israel **2** any of an ancient breed of sheep having a fleece with dark brown patches and two or four horns

Jacobean 1 *History* characteristic of or relating to James I (1566–1625) of England or to the period of his rule (1603–25) **2** denoting, relating to, or having the style of architecture used in England during this period, characterized by a combination of late Gothic and Palladian motifs

▷www.building-history.pwp.blueyonder.co.uk
▷www.probertencyclopaedia.com/T8.HTM

Jacobi 1 Sir Derek(George). born 1938, British actor **2 Karl Gustav Jacob** 1804–51, German mathematician. Independently of N. H. Abel, he discovered elliptic functions (1829). He also made important contributions to the study of determinants and differential equations

Jacobite 1 *Brit, History* an adherent of James II (1633–1701), king of England, Ireland, and, as James VII, of Scotland, 1685–88) after his overthrow in 1688, or of his descendants in their attempts to regain the throne **2** a member of the Monophysite Church of Syria, which became a schismatic church in 451 AD

Jacobsen Arne 1902–71, Danish architect and designer. His buildings include the Town Hall at Rodovre (1955)

jade¹ a a semiprecious stone consisting of either jadeite or nephrite. It varies in colour from white to green and is used for making ornaments and jewellery **b** *(as modifier): jade ornaments*

jade² an old overworked horse; nag; hack

Jael *Old Testament* the woman who killed Sisera when he took refuge in her tent (Judges 4:17–21)

Jaffa 1 a port in W Israel, on the Mediterranean: incorporated into Tel Aviv in 1950; an old Canaanite city **2** a large variety of orange, having a thick skin

Jaffna a port in N Sri Lanka: for many centuries the capital of a Tamil kingdom. Pop: 149 000 (2005 est)

Jagger Sir Mick, full name *Michael Philip Jagger*. born 1943, English rock singer and songwriter: lead vocalist with the Rolling Stones

jaguar a large feline mammal, *Panthera onca*, of S North America, Central America, and N South America, similar to the leopard but with a shorter tail and larger spots on its coat

jail *or* **gaol** a place for the confinement of persons convicted and sentenced to imprisonment or of persons awaiting trial to whom bail is not granted

Jaipur a city of great beauty in N India, capital of

Rajasthan state: University of Rajasthan (1947). Pop: 2 324 319 (2001)

Jakarta *or* **Djakarta** the capital of Indonesia, in N West Java: founded in 1619 and ruled by the Dutch until 1945; the chief trading centre of the East in the 17th century; University of Indonesia (1947). Pop: 8 347 083 (2000)

Jalalabad a city in NE Afghanistan, capital of Nangarhar province; a trading, military, and tourist centre on the main route between Kabul and the Khyber Pass. Pop: 140 611 (1991 est)

Jalandhar a city in NW India, in central Punjab. Pop: 701 223 (2001)

Jalapa a city in E central Mexico, capital of Veracruz State, at an altitude of 1427 m (4681 ft): resort. Pop: 525 000 (2005 est)

Jalisco a state of W Mexico, on the Pacific: crossed by the Sierra Madre; valuable mineral resources. Capital: Guadalajara. Pop: 6 321 278 (2000). Area: 80 137 sq km (30 934 sq miles)

Jamaica an island and state in the Caribbean: colonized by the Spanish from 1494 onwards, large numbers of Black slaves being imported; captured by the British in 1655 and established as a colony in 1866; gained full independence in 1962; a member of the Commonwealth. Exports: chiefly bauxite and alumina, sugar, and bananas. Official language: English. Religion: Protestant majority. Currency: Jamaican dollar. Capital: Kingston. Pop: 2 676 000 (2004 est). Area: 10 992 sq km (4244 sq miles)

Jambi *or* **Djambi** a port in W Indonesia, in SE Sumatra on the Hari River. Pop: 417 507 (2000)

James¹ 1 Henry 1843–1916, British novelist, short-story writer, and critic, born in the US Among his novels are *Washington Square* (1880), *The Portrait of a Lady* (1881), *The Bostonians* (1886), *The Wings of the Dove* (1902), *The Ambassadors* (1903), and *The Golden Bowl* (1904) **2 Jesse (Woodson).** 1847–82, US outlaw **3 P(hyllis) D(orothy),** Baroness James of Holland Park. born 1920, British detective novelist. Her books include *Death of an Expert Witness* (1977), *Original Sin* (1994), and *Death in Holy Orders* (2001) **4 William,** brother of Henry James. 1842–1910, US philosopher and psychologist, whose theory of pragmatism is expounded in *Essays in Radical Empiricism* (1912). His other works include *The Will to Believe* (1897), *The Principles of Psychology* (1890), and *The Varieties of Religious Experience* (1902) **5** *New Testament* **a** known as *James the Great.* one of the twelve apostles, a son of Zebedee and brother to John the apostle (Matthew 4:21). Feast day: July 25 or April 30 **b** known as *James the Less.* one of the twelve apostles, son of Alphaeus (Matthew 10:3). Feast day: May 3 or Oct 9 **c** known as *James the brother of the Lord.* a brother or close relative of Jesus (Mark 6:3; Galatians 1:19). Feast day: Oct 23 **d** the book ascribed to his authorship (in full **The Epistle of James**)

James² *New Testament* an epistle traditionally ascribed to James, a brother or close relative of Jesus (in full **The Epistle of James**)

James I 1 called *the Conqueror*. 1208–76, king of Aragon (1216–76). He captured the Balearic Islands and Valencia from the Muslims, thus beginning Aragonese expansion in the Mediterranean **2** 1394–1437, king of Scotland (1406–37), second son of Robert III **3** 1566–1625, king of

England and Ireland (1603–25) and, as James VI, king of Scotland (1567–1625), in succession to Elizabeth I of England and his mother, Mary Queen of Scots, respectively. He alienated Parliament by his assertion of the divine right of kings, his favourites, esp the Duke of Buckingham, and his subservience to Spain

James II 1 1430–60, king of Scotland (1437–60), son of James I 2 1633–1701, king of England, Ireland, and, as James VII, of Scotland (1685–88); son of Charles I. His pro-Catholic sympathies and arbitrary rule caused the Whigs and Tories to unite in inviting his eldest surviving daughter, Mary, and her husband, William of Orange, to take the throne as joint monarchs. James was defeated at the Boyne (1690) when he attempted to regain the throne

James III 1451–88, king of Scotland (1460–88), son of James II

James IV 1473–1513, king of Scotland (1488–1513), son of James III; he invaded England (1496) in support of Perkin Warbeck; he was killed at Flodden

James V 1512–42, king of Scotland (1513–42), son of James IV

James VI title as king of Scotland of **James I** of England and Ireland

James VII title as king of Scotland of **James II** of England and Ireland

James Bay the S arm of Hudson Bay, in central Canada. Area: 108 780 sq km (42 000 sq miles)

Jameson Sir **Leander Starr** 1853–1917, British administrator in South Africa, who led an expedition into the Transvaal in 1895 in an unsuccessful attempt to topple its Boer regime (the **Jameson Raid**); prime minister of Cape Colony (1904–08)

Jamestown a ruined village in E Virginia, on **Jamestown Island** (a peninsula in the James River): the first permanent settlement by the English in America (1607); capital of Virginia (1607–98); abandoned in 1699

Jammu a city in N India, winter capital of the state of Jammu and Kashmir. Pop: 378 431 (2001)

Jammu and Kashmir the official name for the part of Kashmir under Indian control

Jamnagar a city in India, in Gujarat: noted for its palaces and temples: cement, pottery, textiles. Pop: 447 734 (2001)

jam session *Slang* an unrehearsed or improvised jazz or rock performance

Jamshedpur a city in NE India, in Jharkhand: large iron and steel works (1907–11); a major industrial centre. Pop: 570 349 (2001)

Janet **Pierre Marie Félix** 1859–1947, French psychologist and neurologist, noted particularly for his work on the origins of hysteria

Janiculum a hill in Rome across the River Tiber from the Seven Hills

Jan Mayen an island in the Arctic Ocean, between Greenland and N Norway: volcanic, with large glaciers; former site of Dutch whaling stations; annexed to Norway in 1929. Area: 373 sq km (144 sq miles)

Jansen Cornelis . Latin name *Cornelius Jansenius*. 1585–1638, Dutch Roman Catholic theologian. In *Augustinus* (1640) he defended the teachings of St. Augustine, esp on free will, grace, and predestination

japan 1 a glossy durable black lacquer originally from the Orient, used on wood, metal, etc. 2 work decorated and varnished in the Japanese manner 3 a liquid used as a paint drier

Japan an archipelago and empire in E Asia, extending for 3200 km (2000 miles) between the Sea of Japan and the Pacific and consisting of the main islands of Hokkaido, Honshu, Shikoku, and Kyushu and over 3000 smaller islands: feudalism abolished in 1871, followed by industrialization and expansion of territories, esp during World Wars I and II, when most of SE Asia came under Japanese control; dogma of the emperor's divinity abolished in 1946 under a new democratic constitution; rapid economic growth has made Japan the most industrialized nation in the Far East. Official language: Japanese. Religion: Shintoist majority, large Buddhist minority. Currency: yen. Capital: Tokyo. Pop: 127 799 000 (2004 est). Area: 369 660 sq km (142 726 sq miles)

Japan Current a warm ocean current flowing northeastwards off the E coast of Japan towards the North Pacific

Japanese the official language of Japan: the native language of approximately 100 million people: considered by some scholars to be part of the Altaic family of languages

Japheth *Old Testament* the second son of Noah, traditionally regarded as the ancestor of a number of non-Semitic nations (Genesis 10:1–5)

japonica 1 a Japanese rosaceous shrub, *Chaenomeles japonica*, cultivated for its red flowers and yellowish fruit 2 another name for the **camellia**

Jaques-Dalcroze **Émile** 1865–1950, Swiss composer and teacher: invented eurythmics

jar *Obsolete* a measure of electrical capacitance

jargon *or* **jargoon** *Mineralogy, rare* a golden yellow, smoky, or colourless variety of zircon

Jarman **Derek** 1942–94, British film director and writer; his films include *Jubilee* (1977), *Caravaggio* (1986), and *Wittgenstein* (1993)

jarrah a widely planted Australian eucalyptus tree, *Eucalyptus marginata*, that yields a valuable timber

Jarrett **Keith** born 1945, US jazz pianist and composer

Jarrow a port in NE England, in South Tyneside unitary authority, Tyne and Wear: ruined monastery where the Venerable Bede lived and died; its unemployed marched on London in the 1930s; shipyards, oil installations, iron and steel works. Pop: 27 526 (2001)

Jarry **Alfred** 1873–1907, French dramatist and poet, who anticipated the theatre of the absurd with his play *Ubu Roi* (1896)

Jaruzelski **Wojciech** born 1923, Polish statesman and soldier; prime minister (1981–85); head of state 1985–90 (as president from 1989)

jasmine 1 any oleaceous shrub or climbing plant of the tropical and subtropical genus *Jasminum*, esp *J. officinalis*: widely cultivated for their white, yellow, or red fragrant flowers, which are used in making perfume and in flavouring tea 2 any of several other shrubs with fragrant flowers, such as the Cape jasmine, yellow jasmine, and frangipani (**red jasmine**) 3 a light to moderate yellow colour

jasper 1 an opaque impure microcrystalline form of quartz, red, yellow, brown, or dark green in colour, used as a gemstone and for ornamental decoration 2 a dense hard stoneware, invented in 1775 by Wedgwood, capable of being stained throughout its substance with metallic oxides and used as background for applied classical decoration

Jasper National Park a national park in SW Canada, in W Alberta in the Rockies: wildlife sanctuary. Area: 10 900 sq km (4200 sq miles)

Jaspers Karl 1883–1969, German existentialist philosopher

jaundice yellowing of the skin and whites of the eyes due to the abnormal presence of bile pigments in the blood, as in hepatitis

Java[1] an island of Indonesia, south of Borneo, from which it is separated by the **Java Sea**: politically the most important island of Indonesia; it consists chiefly of active volcanic mountains and is densely forested. It came under Dutch control in 1596 and became part of Indonesia in 1949. It is one of the most densely populated areas in the world. Capital: Jakarta. Pop. (with Madura): 121 193 000 (1999 est). Area: 132 174 sq km (51 032 sq miles)

Java[2] *Trademark* a programming language especially applicable to the World Wide Web

Javanese a Malayo-Polynesian language of Central and Eastern Java

Javari or **Javary** a river in South America, flowing northeast as part of the border between Peru and Brazil to join the Amazon. Length: about 1050 km (650 miles)

javelin 1 a long pointed spear thrown as a weapon or in competitive field events 2 **the javelin** the event or sport of throwing the javelin

jaw 1 the part of the skull of a vertebrate that frames the mouth and holds the teeth. In higher vertebrates it consists of the **upper jaw** (maxilla) fused to the cranium and the **lower jaw** (mandible) 2 the corresponding part of an invertebrate, esp an insect 3 a pair or either of a pair of hinged or sliding components of a machine or tool designed to grip an object

jay any of various passerine birds of the family *Corvidae* (crows), esp the Eurasian *Garrulus glandarius*, with a pinkish-brown body, blue-and-black wings, and a black-and-white crest

Jay John 1745–1829, American statesman, jurist, and diplomat; first chief justice of the Supreme Court (1789–95). He negotiated the treaty with Great Britain (**Jay's treaty**, 1794), that settled outstanding disputes

Jaya or **Djaja** Mount a mountain in E Indonesia, in Papua (formerly Irian Jaya) in the Sudirman Range: the highest mountain in New Guinea. Height: 5039 m (16 532 ft)

Jayapura or **Djajapura** a port in NE Indonesia, capital of Papua (formerly Irian Jaya), on the N coast. Pop: 155 548 (2000)

Jayawardene Junius Richard 1906–96, Sri Lankan statesman; prime minister (1977–78) and first president of Sri Lanka (1978–89)

jazz a a kind of music of African-American origin, characterized by syncopated rhythms, solo and group improvisation, and a variety of harmonic idioms and instrumental techniques. It exists in a number of styles b (*as modifier*): *a jazz band*
▷www.apassion4jazz.net
▷www.jazzreview.com
▷www.allmusic.com
▷www.jazzonln.com
▷www.jazzinamerica.org

JCB *Trademark* a type of construction machine with a hydraulically operated shovel on the front and an excavator arm on the back

Jean born 1921, grand duke of Luxembourg from 1964

Jean de Meung real name *Jean Clopinel*. ?1250–?1305, French poet, who continued Guillaume de Lorris' *Roman de la Rose*. His portion of the poem consists of some 18 000 lines and contains satirical attacks on women and the Church

Jean Paul real name *Johann Paul Friedrich Richter*. 1763–1825, German novelist

Jeans Sir James Hopwood 1877–1946, English astronomer, physicist, and mathematician, best known for his popular books on astronomy. He made important contributions to the kinetic theory of gases and the theory of stellar evolution

Jebel Musa a mountain in NW Morocco, near the Strait of Gibraltar: one of the Pillars of Hercules. Height: 850 m (2790 ft)

Jefferson Thomas 1743–1826, US statesman: secretary of state (1790–93); third president (1801–09). He was the chief drafter of the Declaration of Independence (1776), the chief opponent of the centralizing policies of the Federalists under Hamilton, and effected the Louisiana Purchase (1803)

Jefferson City a city in central Missouri, the state capital, on the Missouri River. Pop: 37 550 (2003 est)

Jeffrey Francis, Lord. 1773–1850, Scottish judge and literary critic. As editor of the *Edinburgh Review* (1803–29), he was noted for the severity of his criticism of the romantic poets, esp Wordsworth

Jeffreys George, 1st Baron Jeffreys of Wem. ?1645–89, English judge, notorious for his brutality at the "Bloody Assizes" (1685), where those involved in Monmouth's rebellion were tried

Jehol 1 a former province of NE China, north of the Great Wall: divided among Hebei, Liaoning, and Inner Mongolia in 1956. Area: 192 380 sq km (74 278 sq miles) 2 a region of NE China, in Hebei and Liaoning provinces: mountainous

Jehoshaphat *Old Testament* 1 the king of Judah (?873–?849 BC) (I Kings 22:41–50) 2 the site of Jehovah's apocalyptic judgment upon the nations (Joel 4:14)

Jehovah *Old Testament* the personal name of God, revealed to Moses on Mount Horeb (Exodus 3)

Jehu *Old Testament* the king of Israel (?842–?815 BC); the slayer of Jezebel (II Kings 9:11–30)

jejunum the part of the small intestine between the duodenum and the ileum

Jekyll Gertrude 1843–1932, British landscape gardener: noted for her simplicity of design and use of indigenous plants

Jekyll and Hyde a a person with two distinct personalities, one good, the other evil b (*as modifier*): *a Jekyll-and-Hyde personality*

Jellicoe John Rushworth, 1st Earl Jellicoe. 1859–1935, British admiral, who commanded the Grand Fleet at the Battle of Jutland (1916), which incapacitated the German fleet for the rest of World War I

jellyfish 1 any marine medusoid coelenterate of the class *Scyphozoa*, having a gelatinous umbrella-shaped body with trailing tentacles 2 any other medusoid coelenterate

Jemappes a town in SW Belgium, in Hainaut province west of Mons: scene of a battle (1792) during the French Revolutionary Wars, in which the French defeated the Austrians. Pop: 18 100 (latest est)

jemmy *or US* **jimmy** a short steel crowbar used, esp by burglars, for forcing doors and windows

Jena a city in E central Germany, in Thuringia: university (1558), at which Hegel and Schiller taught; site of the battle (1806) in which Napoleon Bonaparte defeated the Prussians; optical and precision instrument industry. Pop: 102 634 (2003 est)

Jenner 1 Edward 1749–1823, English physician, who discovered vaccination by showing that injections of cowpox virus produce immunity against smallpox (1796) 2 Sir **William** 1815–98, English physician and pathologist, who differentiated between typhus and typhoid fevers (1849)

jenny 1 a hand-operated machine for turning up the edge of a piece of sheet metal in preparation for making a joint 2 the female of certain animals or birds, esp a donkey, ass, or wren 3 short for **spinning jenny** 4 *Billiards, Snooker* an in-off

Jensen Johannes Vilhelm 1873–1950, Danish novelist, poet, and essayist: best known for his novel sequence about the origins of mankind *The Long Journey* (1908–22). Nobel prize for literature 1944

jeopardy *Law* danger of being convicted and punished for a criminal offence

Jephthah *Old Testament* a judge of Israel, who sacrificed his daughter in fulfilment of a vow (Judges 11:12–40)

jerboa any small nocturnal burrowing rodent of the family *Dipodidae*, inhabiting dry regions of Asia and N Africa, having pale sandy fur, large ears, and long hind legs specialized for jumping

Jeremiah *Old Testament* a a major prophet of Judah from about 626 to 587 BC b the book containing his oracles

Jerez a town in SW Spain: famous for the making of sherry. Pop: 191 002 (2003 est)

Jericho a town in the West Bank near the N end of the Dead Sea, 251 m (825 ft) below sea level: on the site of an ancient city, the first place to be taken by the Israelites under Joshua after entering the Promised Land in the 14th century BC (Joshua 6)

Jeroboam *Old Testament* 1 the first king of the northern kingdom of Israel (?922–?901 BC) 2 king of the northern kingdom of Israel (?786–?746 BC)

Jerome 1 Latin name *Eusebius Hieronymus*. ?347–?420 AD, Christian monk and scholar, whose outstanding work was the production of the Vulgate. Feast day: Sept 30 2 Jerome K(lapka). 1859–1927, English humorous writer; author of *Three Men in a Boat* (1889)

jerry can a flat-sided can with a capacity of between 4.5 and 5 gallons used for storing or transporting liquids, esp motor fuel: originally a German design adopted by the British Army during World War II

jersey a a machine-knitted slightly elastic cloth of wool, silk, nylon, etc, used for clothing b (*as modifier*): *a jersey suit*

Jersey 1 an island in the English Channel, the largest of the Channel Islands: forms, with two other islands, the bailiwick of Jersey; colonized from Normandy in the 11th century and still officially French-speaking; noted for finance, market gardening, dairy farming, and tourism. Capital: St Helier. Pop: 87 500 (2003 est). Area: 116 sq km (45 sq miles) 2 a breed of dairy cattle producing milk with a high butterfat content, originating from the island of Jersey

Jersey City an industrial city in NE New Jersey, opposite Manhattan on a peninsula between the Hudson and Hackensack Rivers: part of the Port of New York; site of one of the greatest railway terminals in the world. Pop: 239 097 (2003 est)

Jerusalem 1 the de facto capital of Israel (recognition of this has been withheld by the United Nations), situated in the Judaean hills: became capital of the Hebrew kingdom after its capture by David around 1000 BC; destroyed by Nebuchadnezzar of Babylon in 586 BC; taken by the Romans in 63 BC; devastated in 70 AD and 135 AD during the Jewish rebellions against Rome; fell to the Arabs in 637 and to the Seljuk Turks in 1071; ruled by Crusaders from 1099 to 1187 and by the Egyptians and Turks until conquered by the British (1917); centre of the British mandate of Palestine from 1920 to 1948, when the Arabs took the old city and the Jews held the new city; unified after the Six Day War (1967) under the Israelis; the holy city of Jews, Christians, and Muslims. Pop: 693 200 (2003 est) 2 **the New Jerusalem** *Christianity* Heaven

Jerusalem artichoke 1 a North American sunflower, *Helianthus tuberosus*, widely cultivated for its underground edible tubers 2 the tuber of this plant, which is cooked and eaten as a vegetable

Jervis Bay an inlet of the Pacific in SE Australia, on the coast of S New South Wales: part of the Australian Capital Territory (though for some purposes regarded as a separate entity): site of the Royal Australian Naval College

Jespersen (Jens) Otto (Harry). 1860–1943, Danish philologist: author of *Modern English Grammar* (1909–31)

Jesse *Old Testament* the father of David (I Samuel 16)

Jesuit a member of a Roman Catholic religious order (the **Society of Jesus**) founded by the Spanish ecclesiastic Saint Ignatius Loyola (1491–1556) in 1534 with the aims of defending the papacy and Catholicism against the Reformation and to undertake missionary work among the heathen

Jesus 1 ?4 BC–?29 AD, founder of Christianity, born in Bethlehem and brought up in Nazareth as a Jew. He is believed by Christians to be the Son of God and to have been miraculously conceived by the Virgin Mary, wife of Joseph. With 12 disciples, he undertook two missionary journeys through Galilee, performing miracles, teaching, and proclaiming the coming of the Kingdom of God. His revolutionary Sermon on the Mount (Matthew 5–8), which preaches love, humility, and charity, the essence of his teaching, aroused the hostility of the Pharisees. After the Last Supper with his disciples, he was betrayed by Judas and crucified. He is believed by Christians to have risen from his tomb after three days, appeared to his disciples several times, and ascended to Heaven after 40 days **2** *Son of Sirach*. 3rd century BC, author of the Apocryphal book of Ecclesiasticus

jet¹ 1 a jet-propelled aircraft **2** *Astronomy* a long thin feature extending from an active galaxy and usually observed at radio wavelengths

jet² **a** a hard black variety of coal that takes a brilliant polish and is used for jewellery, ornaments, etc. **b** (*as modifier*): *jet earrings*

jet engine a gas turbine, esp one fitted to an aircraft

Jethro *Old Testament* a Midianite priest, the father-in-law of Moses (Exodus 3:1; 4:18)

jet propulsion 1 propulsion by means of a jet of fluid **2** propulsion by means of a gas turbine, esp when the exhaust gases provide the propulsive thrust

jetsam *or* **jetsom 1** that portion of the equipment or cargo of a vessel thrown overboard to lighten her, as during a storm **2** another word for **flotsam**

Jevons *William Stanley* 1835–82, English economist and logician: introduced the concept of final or marginal utility in *The Theory of Political Economy* (1871)

Jew 1 a member of the Semitic people who are notionally descended from the ancient Israelites, are spread throughout the world, and are linked by loose cultural or religious ties **2** a person whose religion is Judaism

jewel an ornamental glass boss, sometimes faceted, used in stained glasswork

Jewess *Offensive* a Jewish girl or woman

jewfish 1 any of various large dark serranid fishes, such as *Mycteroperca bonaci*, of warm or tropical seas **2** *Austral* any of various marine sciaenid food and game fish, esp the mulloway **3** *Austral* a large food fish of W Australian waters *Glaucosama hebraicum*

Jewish 1 of, relating to, or characteristic of Jews **2** a less common word for **Yiddish**

Jewish Autonomous Region an administrative division of SE Russia, in E Siberia: colonized by Jews in 1928; largely agricultural. Capital: Birobidzhan. Pop: 190 900 (2002). Area: 36 000 sq km (13 895 sq miles)

Jewry 1 Jews collectively **b** the Jewish religion or culture **2** *Archaic* (sometimes found in street names in England) a quarter of a town inhabited by Jews **3** *Archaic* the land of Judaea

Jezebel *Old Testament* the wife of Ahab, king of Israel: she fostered the worship of Baal and tried to destroy the prophets of Israel (I Kings 18:4–13); she was killed by Jehu (II Kings 9:29–37)

Jhansi a city in central India, in SW Uttar Pradesh: scene of a mutiny against the British in 1857. Pop: 383 248 (2001)

Jhelum a river in Pakistan and Kashmir, rising in W central Kashmir and flowing northwest through the Vale of Kashmir, then southwest into NW Punjab to join the Chenab River: important for irrigation, having the Mangla Dam (Pakistan), completed in 1967. Length: about 720 km (450 miles)

Jiang Qing *or* **Chiang Ch'ing** 1913–91, Chinese Communist actress and politician; widow of Mao Tsetung. She was a leading member of the Gang of Four

Jiangsu *or* **Kiangsu** a province of E China, on the Yellow Sea: consists mostly of the marshy delta of the Yangtze River, with some of China's largest cities and most densely populated areas. Capital: Nanjing. Pop: 74 060 000 (2003 est). Area: 102 200 sq km (39 860 sq miles)

Jiangxi *or* **Kiangsi** a province of SE central China, in the basins of the Kan River and Poyang Lake: mineral resources include coal and tungsten. Capital: Nanchang. Pop: 42 220 000 (2003 est). Area: 164 800 sq km (64 300 sq miles)

Jiang Zemin born 1926, Chinese Communist politician: president (1993–2003)

Jiazhou *or* **Kiaochow** a territory of NE China, in SE Shandong province, surrounding **Jiazhou Bay** (an inlet of the Yellow Sea): leased to Germany from 1898 to 1914. Area: about 520 sq km (200 sq miles)

jib¹ *Nautical* any triangular sail set forward of the foremast of a vessel

jib² the projecting arm of a crane or the boom of a derrick, esp one that is pivoted to enable it to be raised or lowered

Jidda *or* **Jedda** a port in W Saudi Arabia, on the Red Sea: the diplomatic capital of the country; the port of entry for Mecca, 80 km (50 miles) east. Pop: 3 807 000 (2005 est)

jig 1 any of several old rustic kicking and leaping dances **2** a piece of music composed for or in the rhythm of this dance, usually in six-eight time **3** a mechanical device designed to hold and locate a component during machining and to guide the cutting tool **4** *Angling* any of various spinning lures that wobble when drawn through the water

Jigawa a state of N Nigeria. Capital: Dutse. Pop: 3 164 134 (1995 est). Area (including Kano state): 43 285 sq km (16 712 sq miles)

jigger 1 *Golf* an iron, now obsolete, with a thin blade, used for hitting long shots from a bare lie **2** any of a number of mechanical devices having a vibratory or jerking motion **3** a light lifting tackle used on ships **4** a small glass, esp for whisky, with a capacity of about one and a half ounces **5** *Engineering* a type of hydraulic lift in which a hydraulic ram operates the lift through a block and tackle which increases the length of the stroke **6** *Canadian* a device used when setting a gill net beneath ice

jigsaw *Tools* a mechanical saw with a fine steel blade for cutting intricate curves in sheets of material

jihad *or* **jehad 1** *Islam* a holy war against infidels undertaken by Muslims in defence of the Islamic faith **2** *Islam* the personal struggle of the individual believer against evil and persecution

Jilin *or* **Kirin 1** a province of NE China, in central Manchuria. Capital: Changchun. Pop: 27 040 000 (2003 est). Area: 187 000 sq km (72 930 sq miles) **2** a river port in NE China, in N central Jilin province on the Songhua River. Pop: 1 496 000 (2005 est)

Jinan, Chinan, *or* **Tsinan** an industrial city in NE China, capital of Shandong province; probably over 3000 years old. Pop: 2 654 000 (2005 est)

Jingdezhen, Fowliang, *or* **Fou-liang** a city in SE China, in NE Jiangxi province east of Poyang Lake:

famous for its porcelain industry, established in the sixth century. Pop: 416 000 (2005 est)

jingoism the belligerent spirit or foreign policy of jingoes; chauvinism

Jinja a town in Uganda, on the N shore of Lake Victoria. Pop: 86 520 (2002 est)

Jinjiang, Chinkiang, *or* **Cheng-chiang** a port in E China, in S Jiangsu at the confluence of the Yangtze River and the Grand Canal. Pop: 620 000 (2005 est)

Jinnah Mohammed Ali 1876–1948, Indian Muslim statesman. He campaigned for the partition of India into separate Hindu and Muslim states, becoming first governor general of Pakistan (1947–48)

jinni, jinnee, djinni *or* **djinny** a being or spirit in Muslim belief who could assume human or animal form and influence man by supernatural powers

Jinzhou, Chin-Chou, *or* **Chin-chow** a city in NE China, in SW Liaoning province. Pop: 888 000 (2005 est)

jitterbug 1 a fast jerky American dance, usually to a jazz accompaniment, that was popular in the 1940s 2 a person who dances the jitterbug

jive a style of lively and jerky dance performed to jazz and, later, to rock and roll, popular esp in the 1940s and 1950s

Joab *Old Testament* the successful commander of King David's forces and the slayer of Abner and Absalom (II Samuel 2:18–23; 3:24–27; 18:14–15)

Joachim 1 Joseph 1831–1907, Hungarian violinist and composer 2 *Saint* 1st century BC, traditionally the father of the Virgin Mary; feast day: July 25 or Sept 9

Joan 1 known as *the Fair Maid of Kent.* 1328–85, wife of Edward the Black Prince; mother of Richard II 2 *Pope* legendary female pope, first mentioned in the 13th century: said to have been elected while disguised as a man and to have died in childbirth

Joan of Arc *Saint* known as *the Maid of Orléans;* French name *Jeanne d'Arc.* ?1412–31, French national heroine, who led the army that relieved Orléans in the Hundred Years' War, enabling Charles VII to be crowned at Reims (1429). After being captured (1430), she was burnt at the stake as a heretic. She was canonized in 1920. Feast day: May 30

job *Computing* a unit of work for a computer consisting of a single complete task submitted by a user

Job *Old Testament* a a Jewish patriarch, who maintained his faith in God in spite of the afflictions sent by God to test him b the book containing Job's pleas to God under these afflictions, attempted explanations of them by his friends, and God's reply to him

Jobcentre *Brit* any of a number of government offices having premises usually situated in or near the main shopping area of a town in which people seeking jobs can consult displayed advertisements in informal surroundings

Jobclub a group of unemployed people organized through a Jobcentre, which meets every day and is given advice on job seeking to increase its members' chances of finding employment

Jochum Eugen 1902–87, German orchestral conductor

jockey a person who rides horses in races, esp as a profession or for hire

Jodhpur 1 a former state of NW India, one of the W

Rajputana states: now part of Rajasthan 2 a walled city in NW India, in W Rajasthan: university (1962). Pop: 846 408 (2001)

Jodl Alfred 1890–1946, German general, largely responsible for German strategy during World War II: executed as a war criminal

Joel *Old Testament* 1 a Hebrew prophet 2 the book containing his oracles

joey *Austral, informal* a young kangaroo or possum

Joffre Joseph Jacques Césaire 1852–1931, French marshal. He commanded the French army (1914–16) and was largely responsible for the Allies' victory at the Marne (1914), which halted the German advance on Paris

jog trot an easy bouncy gait, esp of a horse, midway between a walk and a trot

Johannesburg a city in N South Africa; the capital of Gauteng province: South Africa's largest city and chief industrial centre; grew with the establishment in 1886 of the gold-mining industry; University of Witwatersrand (1922). Pop: 1 009 036 (2001)

John 1 *New Testament* a the apostle John, the son of Zebedee, identified with the author of the fourth Gospel, three epistles, and the book of Revelation. Feast day: Dec 27 or Sept 26 b the fourth Gospel c any of three epistles (in full **The First, Second,** and **Third Epistles of John**) 2 known as *John Lackland.* 1167–1216, king of England (1199–1216); son of Henry II. He succeeded to the throne on the death of his brother Richard I, having previously tried to usurp the throne. War with France led to the loss of most of his French possessions. After his refusal to recognize Stephen Langton as archbishop of Canterbury an interdict was imposed on England (1208–14). In 1215 he was compelled by the barons to grant the Magna Carta 3 called *the Fearless.* 1371–1419, duke of Burgundy (1404–19). His attempt to control the mad king Charles VI and his murder of the king's brother led to civil war: assassinated 4 **Augustus** (**Edwin**). 1878–1961, British painter, esp of portraits 5 **Barry** born 1945, Welsh Rugby Union footballer: halfback for Wales (1966–72) and the British Lions (1968–71) 6 Sir **Elton** (**Hercules**). original name *Reginald Dwight.* born 1947, British rock pianist, composer, and singer; his hits include "Goodbye Yellow Brick Road" (1973) and "Candle in the Wind 1997" (1997), a tribute to Diana, Princess of Wales 7 **Gwen**, sister of Augustus John. 1876–1939, British painter, working in France: noted esp for her portraits of women

John Bull a personification of England or the English people

John I 1 surnamed *Tzimisces.* 925–976 AD, Byzantine emperor (969–976): extended Byzantine power into Bulgaria and Syria 2 called *the Great.* 1357–1433, king of Portugal (1385–1433). He secured independence for Portugal by his victory over Castile (1385) and initiated Portuguese overseas expansion

John II 1 called *the Good.* 1319–64, king of France (1350–64): captured by the English at Poitiers (1356) and forced to sign treaties (1360) surrendering SW France to England 2 called *the Perfect.* 1455–95, king of Portugal (1481–95): sponsored Portuguese expansion in the New World and reduced the power of the aristocracy 3 surnamed *Casimir Vasa.* 1609–72, king of Poland (1648–68), who lost

much territory to neighbouring countries: abdicated
John III 1 1507–57, king of Portugal (1521–57): his reign
saw the expansion of the Portuguese empire overseas
but the start of economic decline at home **2** surnamed
Sobieski. 1624–96, king of Poland (1674–96). He raised the
Turkish siege of Vienna (1683)

John IV called *the Fortunate*. 1604–56, king of Portugal
(1640–56). As duke of Braganza he led a revolt against
Spanish rule and became king: lost most of Portugal's
Asian possessions to the Dutch

Johnson 1 Earvin, known as *Magic*. born 1959, US basketball player **2 Eyvind** 1900–76, Swedish novelist and
writer, whose novels include the *Krilon* trilogy (1941–43):
joint winner of the Nobel prize for literature 1974 **3
Martin** born 1970, English Rugby Union footballer; captain of the England team that won the World Cup in
2003. **4 Philip (Cortelyou)**. born 1906, US architect and
writer; his buildings include the New York State
Theater (1964) and the American Telephone and
Telegraph building (1978–83), both in New York

John XXII original name *Jacques Duèse*. ?1244–1334, pope
(1316–34), residing at Avignon; involved in a long conflict with the Holy Roman Emperor Louis IV and
opposed the Franciscan Spirituals

John XXIII original name *Angelo Giuseppe Roncalli*.
1881–1963, pope (1958–63). He promoted ecumenism and
world peace and summoned the second Vatican Council
(1962–65)

John Chrysostom Saint ?345–407 AD, Greek bishop and
theologian; one of the Fathers of the Greek Church,
noted for his eloquence. Feast day: Sept 13

John of Austria called *Don John*. 1547–78, Spanish general: defeated the Turks at Lepanto (1571)

John of Damascus Saint ?675–749 AD, Syrian theologian, who defended the veneration of icons and images
against the iconoclasts. Feast day: Dec 4

John of Gaunt Duke of Lancaster. 1340–99, son of
Edward III: virtual ruler of England during the last
years of his father's reign and during Richard II's
minority

John of Leyden original name *Jan Bockelson*. ?1509–36,
Dutch Anabaptist leader. He established a theocracy in
Münster (1534) but was tortured to death after the city
was recaptured (1535) by its prince bishop

John of Salisbury died 1180, English ecclesiastic and
scholar; bishop of Chartres (1176–80). He supported
Thomas à Becket against Henry II

John of the Cross Saint original name *Juan de Yepis y
Alvarez*. 1542–91, Spanish Carmelite monk, poet, and
mystic. He founded the Discalced Carmelites with
Saint Teresa (1568). Feast day: Dec 14

John Paul I original name *Albino Luciani*. 1912–78, pope
(1978) whose brief 33-day reign was characterized by a
simpler papal style and anticipated an emphasis on
pastoral rather than administrative priorities

John Paul II original name *Karol Wojtyla*. 1920–2005, pope
from 1978 to 2005, born in Poland: the first non-Italian
to be elected since 1522

Johns Jasper born 1930, US artist, noted for his collages
and constructions

Johnson 1 Amy 1903–41, British aviator, who made several record flights, including those to Australia (1930)

and to Cape Town and back (1936) **2 Andrew** 1808–75, US
Democrat statesman who was elected vice president
under the Republican Abraham Lincoln; 17th president
of the US (1865–69), became president after Lincoln's
assassination. His lenience towards the South after the
American Civil War led to strong opposition from radical Republicans, who tried to impeach him **3 Jack**
1878–1946, US boxer; world heavyweight champion
(1908–15) **4 Lionel (Pigot)** 1867–1902, British poet and
critic, best known for his poems "Dark Angel" and "By
the Statue of King Charles at Charing Cross" **5 Lyndon
Baines** known as *LBJ*. 1908–73, US Democrat statesman;
36th president of the US (1963–69). His administration
carried the Civil Rights Acts of 1964 and 1965, but he lost
popularity by increasing US involvement in the
Vietnam war **6 Michael (Duane)** born 1967, US athlete:
world (1995) and Olympic (1996) 200- and 400-metre
gold medallist **7 Robert** ?1898–1937, US blues singer and
guitarist **8 Samuel** known as *Dr. Johnson*. 1709–84,
British lexicographer, critic, and conversationalist,
whose greatest works are his *Dictionary* (1755), his edition of Shakespeare (1765), and his *Lives of the Most
Eminent English Poets* (1779–81). His fame, however, rests as
much on Boswell's biography of him as on his literary
output

John the Baptist Saint *New Testament* the son of
Zacharias and Elizabeth and the cousin and forerunner
of Jesus, whom he baptized. He was beheaded by Herod
(Matthew 14:1–2). Feast day: June 24

Johore a state of Malaysia, on the S Malay Peninsula:
mostly forested, with large swamps; bauxite- and iron-
mining. Capital: Johore Bahru. Pop: 2 740 625 (2000).
Area: 18 984 sq km (7330 sq miles)

Johore Bahru a city in S Malaysia, capital of Johore
state: important trading centre, situated at the sole
crossing point of Johore Strait (between Malaya and
Singapore Island). Pop: 719 000 (2005 est)

joint 1 *Anatomy* the junction between two or more bones,
usually formed of connective tissue and cartilage **2** the
point of connection between movable parts in invertebrates, esp insects and other arthropods **3** the part of a
plant stem from which a branch or leaf grows **4** *Geology*
a crack in a rock along which no displacement has
occurred **5 out of joint a** dislocated **b** out of order or
disorganized **6** *Law* (of persons) combined in ownership or obligation; regarded as a single entity in law

joint-stock company 1 *Brit* a business enterprise characterized by its separate legal existence and the sharing of ownership between shareholders, whose liability is limited **2** *US* a business enterprise whose owners
are issued shares of transferable stock but do not enjoy
limited liability

Joinville Jean de ?1224–1317, French chronicler, noted for
his *Histoire de Saint Louis* (1309)

jojoba a shrub or small tree of SW North America,
Simmondsia californica, that has edible seeds containing a
valuable oil used in cosmetics

joker 1 an extra playing card in a pack, which in many
card games can substitute for or rank above any other
card **2** *Chiefly US* a clause or phrase inserted in a legislative bill in order to make the bill inoperative or to alter
its apparent effect

Joliot-Curie Jean-Frédéric, 1900–58, and his wife, Irène, 1897–1956, French physicists: shared the Nobel prize for chemistry in 1935 for discovering artificial radioactivity

Jolly Roger the traditional pirate flag, consisting of a white skull and crossbones on a black field

Jolo an island in the SW Philippines: the main island of the Sulu Archipelago. Pop: 87 998 (2000). Area: 893 sq km (345 sq miles)

Jolson Al, real name *Asa Yoelson*. 1886–1950, US singer and film actor, born in Russia: star of the first talking picture *The Jazz Singer* (1927)

Jonah or **Jonas** *Old Testament* **a** a Hebrew prophet who, having been thrown overboard from a ship in which he was fleeing from God, was swallowed by a great fish and vomited onto dry land **b** the book in which his adventures are recounted

Jonathan *Old Testament* the son of Saul and David's close friend, who was killed in battle (I Samuel 31; II Samuel 1:19–26)

Jones 1 Daniel 1881–1967, British phonetician 2 Daniel 1912–93, Welsh composer. He wrote nine symphonies and much chamber music 3 David 1895–1974, British artist and writer: his literary works, which combine poetry and prose, include *In Parenthesis* (1937), an account of World War I, and *The Anathemata* (1952) 4 Digby (**Marritt**). born 1956, British businessman; director-general of the Confederation of British Industry from 2000 5 Inigo 1573–1652, English architect and theatrical designer, who introduced Palladianism to England. His buildings include the Banqueting Hall of Whitehall. He also designed the settings for court masques, being the first to use the proscenium arch and movable scenery in England 6 John Paul, original name *John Paul*. 1747–92, US naval commander, born in Scotland: noted for his part in the War of American Independence 7 (**Everett**) Le Roi, Muslim name *Imanu Amiri Baraka*. born 1934, US Black poet, dramatist, and political figure 8 Quincy born 1933, US composer, arranger, conductor, record producer, and trumpeter, noted esp for his film scores 9 Robert Tyre, known as *Bobby Jones*. 1902–71, US golfer

Jongkind Johann Barthold 1819–91, Dutch landscape painter and etcher, working in Paris: best known for his atmospheric seascapes

jonquil 1 a Eurasian amaryllidaceous plant, *Narcissus jonquilla* with long fragrant yellow or white short-tubed flowers 2 any of various other small daffodil-like plants

Jonson Ben 1572–1637, English dramatist and poet, who developed the "comedy of humours", in which each character is used to satirize one particular humour or temperament. His plays include *Volpone* (1606), *The Alchemist* (1610), and *Bartholomew Fair* (1614), and he also wrote court masques

Joplin 1 Janis 1943–70, US rock singer, noted for her hoarse and passionate style. Her albums include *Cheap Thrills* (1968) and *Pearl* (1971) 2 Scott 1868–1917, US pianist and composer: creator of ragtime

Jordaens Jacob 1593–1678, Flemish painter, noted for his naturalistic depiction of peasant scenes

Jordan¹ 1 Michael (**Jeffrey**). born 1963, US basketball player 2 Neil born 1950, Irish film director and writer;

his films include *The Company of Wolves* (1984), *Mona Lisa* (1986), *The Crying Game* (1992), *Michael Collins* (1996), and *The End of the Affair* (2000)

Jordan² 1 a kingdom in SW Asia: coextensive with the biblical Moab, Gilead, and Edom; made a League of Nations mandate and emirate under British control in 1922 and became an independent kingdom in 1946; territories west of the River Jordan and the Jordanian part of Jerusalem (intended to be part of an autonomous Palestine) were occupied by Israel after the war of 1967. It contains part of the Great Rift Valley and consists mostly of desert. Official language: Arabic. Official religion: (Sunni) Muslim. Currency: dinar. Capital: Amman. Pop: 5 613 000 (2004 est). Area: 89 185 sq km (34 434 sq miles) 2 the chief and only perennial river of Israel and Jordan, rising in several headstreams in Syria and Lebanon, and flowing south through the Sea of Galilee to the Dead Sea: occupies the N end of the Great Rift Valley system and lies mostly below sea level. Length: over 320 km (200 miles)

Jos a city in central Nigeria, capital of Plateau state on the **Jos Plateau**: major centre of the tin-mining industry. Pop: 685 000 (2005 est)

Joseph 1 *Old Testament* **a** the eleventh son of Jacob and one of the 12 patriarchs of Israel (Genesis 30:2–24) **b** either or both of two tribes descended from his sons Ephraim and Manasseh 2 **Saint** *New Testament* the husband of Mary the mother of Jesus (Matthew 1:16–25). Feast day: Mar 19

Joseph Bonaparte Gulf an inlet of the Timor Sea in N Australia. Width: 360 km (225 miles)

Joseph II 1741–90, Holy Roman emperor (1765–90); son of Francis I. He ruled Austria jointly with his mother, Maria Theresa, until her death (1780). He reorganized taxation, abolished serfdom, curtailed the feudal power of the nobles, and asserted his independence from the pope

Josephine Empress, previous name *Joséphine de Beauharnais*; real name *Marie Joséphine Tascher de la Pagerie*. 1763–1814, empress of France as wife of Napoleon Bonaparte (1796–1809)

Joseph of Arimathea Saint *New Testament* a wealthy member of the Sanhedrin, who obtained the body of Jesus after the Crucifixion and laid it in his own tomb (Matthew 27:57–60). Feast day: Mar 17 or July 31

Josephus Flavius real name *Joseph ben Matthias*. ?37–?100 AD, Jewish historian and general; author of *History of the Jewish War* and *Antiquities of the Jews*

Joshua *Old Testament* 1 Moses' successor, who led the Israelites in the conquest of Canaan 2 the book recounting his deeds

Josiah died ?609 BC, king of Judah (?640–?609). After the discovery of a book of law (probably Deuteronomy) in the Temple he began a programme of religious reform

joual nonstandard Canadian French dialect, esp as associated with ill-educated speakers

joule the derived SI unit of work or energy; the work done when the point of application of a force of 1 newton is displaced through a distance of 1 metre in the direction of the force. 1 joule is equivalent to 1 watt-second, 10^7 ergs, 0.2390 calories, or 0.738 foot-pound

Joule James Prescott 1818–89, English physicist, who

evaluated the mechanical equivalent of heat and contributed to the study of heat and electricity

journal 1 an official record of the proceedings of a legislative body 2 the part of a shaft or axle in contact with or enclosed by a bearing 3 a plain cylindrical bearing to support a shaft or axle

journeyman 1 a craftsman, artisan, etc, who is qualified to work at his trade in the employment of another 2 a competent workman 3 (formerly) a worker hired on a daily wage

joust *History* a combat between two mounted knights tilting against each other with lances. A tournament consisted of a series of such engagements

Jovian full name *Flavius Claudius Jovianus*. ?331–364 AD, Roman emperor (363–64): he made peace with Persia, relinquishing Roman provinces beyond the Tigris, and restored privileges to the Christians

Jowett Benjamin 1817–93, British classical scholar and educator: translated the works of Plato

jowl¹ 1 the jaw, esp the lower one 2 a cheek, esp a prominent one

jowl² 1 fatty flesh hanging from the lower jaw 2 a similar fleshy part in animals, such as the wattle of a fowl or the dewlap of a bull

Joyce 1 James (Augustine Aloysius). 1882–1941, Irish novelist and short-story writer. He profoundly influenced the development of the modern novel by his use of complex narrative techniques, esp stream of consciousness and parody, and of compound and coined words. His works include the novels *Ulysses* (1922) and *Finnegans Wake* (1939) and the short stories *Dubliners* (1914) 2 William, known as *Lord Haw-Haw*. 1906–46, British broadcaster of Nazi propaganda to Britain, who was executed for treason

joystick 1 *Informal* the control stick of an aircraft or of any of various machines 2 *Computing* a lever by means of which the display on a screen may be controlled used esp for games, flight simulators, etc

JPEG *Computing* a standard file format for compressing pictures by disposing of redundant pixels

Juan de Fuca Strait of a strait between Vancouver Island (Canada) and NW Washington (US). Length: about 129 km (80 miles). Width: about 24 km (15 miles)

Juba a river in NE Africa, rising in S central Ethiopia and flowing south across Somalia to the Indian Ocean: the chief river of Somalia. Length: about 1660 km (1030 miles)

Jubal *Old Testament* the alleged inventor of musical instruments (Genesis 4:21)

jube a gallery or loft over the rood screen in a church or cathedral

jubilee *RC Church* a specially appointed period, now ordinarily every 25th year, in which special indulgences are granted

Judaea or **Judea** the S division of ancient Palestine, succeeding the kingdom of Judah: a Roman province during the time of Christ

Judah *Old Testament* 1 the fourth son of Jacob, one of whose descendants was to be the Messiah (Genesis 29:35; 49:8–12) 2 the tribe descended from him 3 the tribal territory of his descendants which became the nucleus of David's kingdom and, after the kingdom

had been divided into Israel and Judah, the southern kingdom of Judah, with Jerusalem as its centre

Judah ha-Levi ?1075–1141, Jewish poet and philosopher, born in Spain; his major works include the collection in *Diwan* and the prose work *Sefer ha-Kuzari*, which presented his philosophy of Judaism in dialogue form

Judah ha-Nasi ?135–?220 AD, rabbi and patriarch of the Sanhedrin, who compiled the Mishnah

Judaic or **Judaical** 1 of or relating to the Jews or Judaism 2 a less common word for **Jewish**

Judaism 1 the religion of the Jews, based on the Old Testament and the Talmud and having as its central point a belief in the one God as transcendent creator of all things and the source of all righteousness 2 the religious and cultural traditions, customs, attitudes, and way of life of the Jews

▷http://jewfaq.org/
▷http://judaism.about.com/

Judas 1 *New Testament* the apostle who betrayed Jesus to his enemies for 30 pieces of silver (Luke 22:3–6, 47–48) 2 a brother or relative of James (Matthew 13:55). This figure, Thaddaeus, and Jude were probably identical 3 *Hunting* denoting an animal or bird used to lure others of its kind or lead them to slaughter

Judas Maccabaeus Jewish leader, whose revolt (166–161 BC) against the Seleucid kingdom of Antiochus IV (Epiphanes) enabled him to recapture Jerusalem and rededicate the Temple

judder *Informal, chiefly Brit* abnormal vibration in a mechanical system, esp due to grabbing between friction surfaces, as in the clutch of a motor vehicle

judder bar *NZ* a bump built across roads, esp in housing estates, to deter motorists from speeding

Jude 1 a book of the New Testament (in full **The Epistle of Jude**) 2 *Saint* the author of this, stated to be the brother of James (Jude 1) and almost certainly identical with Thaddaeus (Matthew 10:2–4). Feast day: Oct 28 or June 19

judge a leader of the peoples of Israel from Joshua's death to the accession of Saul

judgment or **judgement** 1 a the decision or verdict pronounced by a court of law b an obligation arising as a result of such a decision or verdict, such as a debt c the document recording such a decision or verdict 2 *Logic* a the act of establishing a relation between two or more terms, esp as an affirmation or denial b the expression of such a relation

Judgment Day the occasion of the Last (or General) Judgment by God at the end of the world

judiciary 1 the branch of the central authority in a state concerned with the administration of justice 2 the system of courts in a country 3 the judges collectively; bench

Judith 1 the heroine of one of the books of the Apocrypha, who saved her native town by decapitating Holofernes 2 the book recounting this episode

judo a the modern sport derived from jujitsu, in which the object is to throw, hold to the ground, or otherwise force an opponent to submit, using the minimum of physical effort b (*as modifier*): *a judo throw*

▷www.ijf.org
▷http://worldjudo.org

juggernaut *Brit* a very large lorry for transporting goods by road, esp one that travels throughout Europe

jugular 1 of, relating to, or situated near the throat or neck **2** of, having, or denoting pelvic fins situated in front of the pectoral fins

Jugurtha died 104 BC, king of Numidia (?112–104), who waged war against the Romans (the **Jugurthine War,** 112–105) and was defeated and executed

juice any liquid that occurs naturally in or is secreted by plant or animal tissue

Juiz de Fora a city in SE Brazil, in Minas Gerais state on the Rio de Janeiro–Belo Horizonte railway: textiles. Pop: 502 000 (2005 est)

jujitsu, jujutsu, *or* **jiujutsu** the traditional Japanese system of unarmed self-defence perfected by the samurai

juju 1 an object superstitiously revered by certain W African peoples and used as a charm or fetish **2** the power associated with a juju **3** a taboo effected by a juju

jujube 1 any of several Old World spiny rhamnaceous trees of the genus *Ziziphus*, esp *Z. jujuba*, that have small yellowish flowers and dark red edible fruits **2** the fruit of any of these trees

jukskei *South African* a game in which a peg is thrown over a fixed distance at a stake driven into the ground

Julian known as *Julian the Apostate*; Latin name *Flavius Claudius Julianus*. 331–363 AD, Roman emperor (361–363), who attempted to revive paganism in the Roman empire while remaining tolerant to Christians and Jews

Julian calendar the calendar introduced by Julius Caesar in 46 BC, identical to the present calendar in all but two aspects: the beginning of the year was not fixed on Jan 1 and leap years occurred every fourth year and in every centenary year

Julian of Norwich ?1342–?1413, English mystic and anchoress: best known for the *Revelations of Divine Love* describing her visions

Julius II original name *Guiliano della Rovere*. 1443–1513, pope (1503–13). He completed the restoration of the Papal States to the Church, began the building of St Peter's, Rome (1506), and patronized Michelangelo, Raphael, and Bramante

jumbo jet *Informal* a type of large jet-propelled airliner that carries several hundred passengers

Jumna a river in N India, rising in Uttaranchal in the Himalayas and flowing south and southeast to join the Ganges just below Allahabad (a confluence held sacred by Hindus). Length: 1385 km (860 miles)

jump 1 *Sport* any of several contests involving a jump **2** *Draughts* a move that captures an opponent's piece by jumping over it **3** *Films* **a** a break in continuity in the normal sequence of shots **b** (*as modifier*): *a jump cut* **4** *Computing* another name for **branch**

jumper 1 *Engineering* a boring tool that works by repeated impact, such as a steel bit in a hammer drill used in boring rock **2** *Electronics* a short length of wire used to make a connection, usually temporarily, between terminals or to bypass a component **3** a type of sled with a high crosspiece

jump jet a fixed-wing jet aircraft that is capable of landing and taking off vertically

Junagadh a town in India, in Gujarat: noted for its Buddhist caves and temples. Pop: 168 686 (2001)

junction 1 *Electronics* **a** a contact between two different metals or other materials **b** a transition region between regions of differing electrical properties in a semiconductor **2** a connection between two or more conductors or sections of transmission lines

Juneau a port in SE Alaska: state capital. Pop: 31 187 (2003 est)

Jung Carl Gustav 1875–1961, Swiss psychologist. His criticism of Freud's emphasis on the sexual instinct ended their early collaboration. He went on to found analytical psychology, developing the concepts of the collective unconscious and its archetypes and of the extrovert and introvert as the two main psychological types

Jungfrau a mountain in S Switzerland, in the Bernese Alps south of Interlaken. Height: 4158 m (13 642 ft)

Junggar Pendi, Dzungaria, *or* **Zungaria** an arid region of W China, in N Xinjiang Uygur between the Altai Mountains and the Tian Shan

jungle an equatorial forest area with luxuriant vegetation, often almost impenetrable

junior 1 *Brit* of or relating to schoolchildren between the ages of 7 and 11 approximately **2** *US* of, relating to, or designating the third year of a four-year course at college or high school **3** *Law* (in England) any barrister below the rank of Queen's Counsel **4** *Brit* a junior schoolchild **5** *US* a junior student

junior lightweight a a professional boxer weighing 126–130 pounds (57–59 kg) **b** (*as modifier*): *a junior-lightweight bout*

juniper 1 any coniferous shrub or small tree of the genus *Juniperus*, of the N hemisphere, having purple berry-like cones. The cones of *J. communis* (**common** or **dwarf juniper**) are used as a flavouring in making gin **2** any of various similar trees, grown mainly as ornamentals **3** *Old Testament* one of the trees used in the building of Solomon's temple (I Kings 6:15, 34) and for shipbuilding (Ezekiel 27:5)

junk a sailing vessel used in Chinese waters and characterized by a very high poop, flat bottom, and square sails supported by battens

Junkers Hugo 1859–1935, German aircraft designer. His military aircraft were used in both World Wars

Juno¹ (in Roman tradition) the queen of the Olympian gods

Juno² *Astronomy* the fourth largest known asteroid (approximate diameter 240 kilometres) and one of the four brightest

junta 1 a group of military officers holding the power in a country, esp after a coup d'état **2** a legislative or executive council in some parts of Latin America

Jupiter¹ (in Roman tradition) the king and ruler of the Olympian gods

Jupiter² the largest of the planets and the fifth from the sun. It has 16 satellites and is surrounded by a transient planar ring system consisting of dust particles. Mean distance from sun: 778 million km; period of revolution around sun: 11.86 years; period of axial rotation: 9.83 hours; diameter and mass: 11.2 and 317.9 times that of earth respectively

Jura 1 a department of E France, in Franche-Comté region. Capital: Lons-le-Saunier. Pop: 253 309 (2003 est)). Area: 5055 sq km (1971 sq miles) 2 a canton of Switzerland, bordering the French frontier: formed in 1979 from part of Bern. Capital: Delémont. Pop: 69 200 (2002 est). Area: 838 sq km (323 sq miles) 3 an island off the W coast of Scotland, in the Inner Hebrides, separated from the mainland by the **Sound of Jura**. Pop: 200 (2004 est). Area: 381 sq km (147 sq.miles) 4 a mountain range in W central Europe, between the Rivers Rhine and Rhône: mostly in E France, extending into W Switzerland 5 a range of mountains in the NE quadrant of the moon lying on the N border of the Mare Imbrium

Jurassic of, denoting, or formed in the second period of the Mesozoic era, between the Triassic and Cretaceous periods, lasting for 55 million years during which dinosaurs and ammonites flourished

jurisdiction 1 the right or power to administer justice and to apply laws 2 the exercise or extent of such right or power 3 power or authority in general

jurisprudence 1 the science or philosophy of law 2 a system or body of law 3 a branch of law
▷www.iisj.es

jurist a student or graduate of law

juror 1 a member of a jury 2 a person whose name is included on a panel from which a jury is selected 3 a person who takes an oath

jury[1] a group of, usually twelve, people sworn to deliver a true verdict according to the evidence upon a case presented in a court of law

jury[2] *Chiefly nautical* makeshift

jury-rigged *Chiefly nautical* set up in a makeshift manner, usually as a result of the loss of regular gear

justice 1 *Ethics* **a** the principle of fairness that like cases should be treated alike **b** a particular distribution of benefits and burdens fairly in accordance with a particular conception of what are to count as like cases **c** the principle that punishment should be proportionate to the offence 2 the administration of law according to prescribed and accepted principles 3 conformity to the law; legal validity

justice of the peace 1 (in Britain) a lay magistrate, appointed by the crown or acting *ex officio*, whose function is to preserve the peace in his area, try summarily such cases as are within his jurisdiction, and perform miscellaneous administrative duties 2 (in Australia and New Zealand) a person authorised to administer oaths, attest instruments, and take declarations

Justinian I called *the Great*; Latin name *Flavius Anicius Justinianus*. 483–565 AD, Byzantine emperor (527–565). He recovered North Africa, SE Spain, and Italy, largely owing to the brilliance of generals such as Belisarius. He sponsored the Justinian Code

Justin Martyr Saint ?100–?165 AD,Christian apologist and philosopher. Feast day: June 1

jute 1 either of two Old World tropical yellow-flowered herbaceous plants, *Corchorus capsularis* or *C. olitorius*, cultivated for their strong fibre: family *Tiliaceae* 2 this fibre, used in making sacks, rope, etc.

Jutland a peninsula of N Europe: forms the continental portion of Denmark and geographically includes the N part of the German province of Schleswig-Holstein, while politically it includes only the mainland of Denmark and the islands north of Limfjorden; a major but inconclusive naval battle was fought off its NW coast in 1916 between the British and German fleets

Juvenal Latin name *Decimus Junius Juvenalis*. ?60–?140 AD, Roman satirist. In his 16 verse satires, he denounced the vices of imperial Rome

juvenile 1 (of animals or plants) not yet fully mature 2 of or denoting young birds that have developed their first plumage of adult feathers 3 *Geology* occurring at the earth's surface for the first time; new 4 a juvenile person, animal, or plant 5 an actor who performs youthful roles 6 a book intended for young readers

juvenile delinquent a child or young person guilty of some offence, act of vandalism, or antisocial behaviour or whose conduct is beyond parental control and who may be brought before a juvenile court

Jylland the Danish name for **Jutland**

Kk

K or **K.** Köchel: indicating the serial number in the catalogue (1862) of the works of Mozart made by Ludwig von Köchel, (1800–1877)

K2 a mountain in the Karakoram Range on the Kashmir-Xinjiang Uygur AR border: the second highest mountain in the world. Height: 8611 m (28 250 ft)

kabaddi a game played between two teams of seven players, in which individuals take turns to chase and try to touch members of the opposing team without being captured by them

▷http://punjabsportsclub.com

Kabardino-Balkar Republic a constituent republic of S Russia, on the N side of the Caucasus Mountains. Capital: Nalchik. Pop: 900 500 (2002). Area: 12 500 sq km (4825 sq miles)

Kabila Laurent 1940–2001, Congolese politician and guerrilla leader: he overthrew the Mobutu regime in Zaïre, becoming president of the renamed Democratic Republic of Congo (1997–2001): assassinated

Kabul or **Kabol 1** the capital of Afghanistan, in the northeast of the country at an altitude of 1800 m (5900 ft) on the **Kabul River**: over 3000 years old, with a strategic position commanding passes through the Hindu Kush and main routes to the Khyber Pass; destroyed and rebuilt many times; capital of the Mogul Empire from 1504 until 1738 and of Afghanistan from 1773; university (1932). Pop: 3 288 000 (2005 est) **2** a river in Afghanistan and Pakistan, rising in the Hindu Kush and flowing east into the Indus at Attock, Pakistan. Length: 700 km (435 miles)

Kaduna 1 a state of N Nigeria. Capital: Kaduna. Pop: 4 438 007 (1995 est). Area: 46 053 sq km (17 781 sq miles) **2** a city in N central Nigeria, capital of Kaduna state on the **Kaduna River** (a principal tributary of the Niger). Pop: 1 329 000 (2005 est)

Kaesŏng a city in SW North Korea: former capital of Korea (938–1392). Pop: 621 000 (2005 est)

Kaffir or **Kafir 1** a former name for the **Xhosa** language **2** *Offensive* (among Muslims) a non-Muslim or infidel

Kaffraria a former region of S central South Africa: inhabited chiefly by people then known as the Kaffirs; British Kaffraria was a crown colony established in 1853 in the southwest of the region and annexed to Cape Colony in 1865

Kafka Franz 1883–1924, Czech novelist writing in German. In his two main novels *The Trial* (1925) and *The Castle* (1926), published posthumously against his wishes, he portrays man's fear, isolation, and bewilderment in a nightmarish dehumanized world

Kagera a river in E Africa, rising in headstreams on the border between Tanzania and Rwanda and flowing east to Lake Victoria: the most remote headstream of the Nile and largest tributary of Lake Victoria. Length: about 480 km (300 miles)

Kagoshima a port in SW Japan, on S Kyushu. Pop: 544 840 (2002 est)

kahawai a large food and game fish of Australian and New Zealand coastal waters, *Arripis trutta*, that is greenish grey to silvery underneath and spotted with brown: resembles a salmon but is in fact a marine perch

Kahn 1 Herman 1922–83, US mathematician and futurologist; director of the Hudson Institute (1961–83) **2 Louis I(sadore)** .1901–74, US architect, noted for his art museums at Yale (1951–53), Fort Worth (1966–72), and New Haven (1969–74)

Kaifeng a city in E China, in N Henan on the Yellow River: one of the oldest cities in China and its capital (as Pien-liang) from 907 to 1126. Pop: 810 000 (2005 est)

Kairouan, Kairwan, or **Qairwan** a city in NE Tunisia: one of the holy cities of Islam; pilgrimage and trading centre. Pop: 124 000 (2005 est)

Kaiser Georg 1878–1945, German expressionist dramatist

Kaiserslautern a city in W Germany, in S Rhineland-Palatinate. Pop: 999 095 (2003 est)

kaka a New Zealand parrot, *Nestor meridionalis*, with a long compressed bill

kakapo a ground-living nocturnal parrot, *Strigops habroptilus*, of New Zealand, resembling an owl

Kalahari the an extensive arid plateau of South Africa, Namibia, and Botswana. Area: 260 000 sq km (100 000 sq miles)

Kalamazoo a city in SW Michigan, midway between Detroit and Chicago: aircraft, missile parts. Pop: 75 312 (2003 est)

Kalat or **Khelat** a region of SW Pakistan, in S Baluchistan: formerly a princely state ruled by the Khan of Kalat, which joined Pakistan in 1948

kale or **kail** a cultivated variety of cabbage, *Brassica oleracea acephala*, with crinkled leaves: used as a potherb

kaleidoscope an optical toy for producing symmetrical patterns by multiple reflections in inclined mirrors enclosed in a tube. Loose pieces of coloured glass, paper, etc, are placed between transparent plates at the far end of the tube, which is rotated to change the pattern

Kalgoorlie a city in Western Australia, adjoining the town of Boulder: a centre of the Coolgardie gold rushes of the early 1890s; declining gold resources superseded by the discovery of nickel ore in 1966. Pop: 28 281 (including Boulder) (2001)

Kalidasa ?5th century AD, Indian dramatist and poet, noted for his romantic verse drama *Sakuntala*

Kalimantan the Indonesian name for Borneo: applied to the Indonesian part of the island only, excluding the Malaysian states of Sabah and Sarawak and the sultanate of Brunei. Pop: 11 341 558 (2000)

Kalinin Mikhail Ivanovich 1875–1946, Soviet statesman: titular head of state (1919–46); a founder of *Pravda* (1912)

Kaliningrad a port in W Russia, on the Pregolya River: severely damaged in World War II as the chief German naval base on the Baltic; ceded to the Soviet Union in 1945 and is now Russia's chief Baltic naval base. Pop: 436 000 (2005 est)

Kalisz a town in central Poland, on an island in the Prosna River: textile industry. Pop: 110 000 (2005 est)

Kalmar a port in SE Sweden, partly on the mainland and partly on a small island in the **Sound of Kalmar** opposite Öland: scene of the signing of the Union of Kalmar, which united Sweden, Denmark, and Norway into a single monarchy (1397–1523). Pop: 60 734 (2004 est)

Kalmuck Republic *or* **Kalmyk Republic** a constituent republic of S Russia, on the Caspian Sea: became subject to Russia in 1646. Capital: Elista. Pop: 292 400 (2002). Area: 76 100 sq km (29 382 sq miles)

Kaluga a city in central Russia, on the Oka River. Pop: 340 000 (2005 est)

Kama a river in central Russia, rising in the Ural Mountains and flowing to the River Volga, of which it is the largest tributary. Length: 2030 km (1260 miles)

Kamakura a city in central Japan, on S Honshu: famous for its Great Buddha (Daibutsu), a 13th-century bronze, 15 m (49 ft) high. Pop: 169 714 (2002 est)

Kamchatka a peninsula in E Russia, between the Sea of Okhotsk and the Bering Sea. Length: about 1200 km (750 miles)

Kamensk-Uralski an industrial city in S Russia. Pop: 183 000 (2005 est)

Kamerlingh-Onnes Heike 1853–1926, Dutch physicist: a pioneer of the physics of low-temperature materials and discoverer (1911) of superconductivity. Nobel prize for physics 1913

Kamet a mountain on the border of China and India, west of Nepal in the Himalayas. Height: 7756 m (25 447 ft)

kamikaze (in World War II) one of a group of Japanese pilots who performed suicidal missions by crashing their aircraft, loaded with explosives, into an enemy target, esp a ship

Kamloops trout *Canadian* a variety of rainbow trout found in Canadian lakes

Kampala the capital and largest city of Uganda, in Central region on Lake Victoria: Makerere University (1961). Pop: 1 208 544 (2002 est)

Kampuchea the name of **Cambodia** from 1976 until 1989.

Kampuchean 1 of or relating to Kampuchea, a former name for Cambodia, or its inhabitants 2 a native or inhabitant of Kampuchea

Kananga a city in the SW Democratic Republic of Congo (formerly Zaïre): a commercial centre on the railway from Lubumbashi to Port Francqui. Pop: 424 000 (2005 est)

Kanara *or* **Canara** a region of SW India, in Karnataka on the Deccan Plateau and the W Coast. Area: about 155 000 sq km (60 000 sq miles)

Kanazawa a port in central Japan, on W Honshu: textile and porcelain industries. Pop: 439 892 (2002 est)

Kanchipuram a city in SE India, in Tamil Nadu: a sacred Hindu town known as "the Benares of the South"; textile industries. Pop: 152 984 (2001)

Kandahar a city in S Afghanistan: an important trading centre, built by Ahmad Shah Durrani (1724–73) as his capital on the site of several former cities. Pop: 436 000 (2005 est)

Kandinsky Vasili 1866–1944, Russian expressionist painter and theorist, regarded as the first to develop an entirely abstract style: a founder of *der Blaue Reiter*

Kandy a city in central Sri Lanka: capital of the kingdom of Kandy from 1480 until 1815, when occupied by the British; sacred Buddhist temple; University of Sri Lanka. Pop: 112 000 (2005 est)

kangaroo any large herbivorous marsupial of the genus *Macropus* and related genera, of Australia and New Guinea, having large powerful hind legs, used for leaping, and a long thick tail: family *Macropodidae*

Kangaroo Island an island in the Indian Ocean, off South Australia. Area: 4350 sq km (1680 sq miles)

kangaroo paw any plant of the Australian genus *Anigozanthos*, resembling a kangaroo's paw, esp the red-and-green flowered *A. manglesii*, which is the floral emblem of Western Australia: family *Haemodoraceae*

Kangchenjunga, Kanchenjunga, *or* **Kinchinjunga** a mountain on the border between Nepal and Sikkim, in the Himalayas: the third highest mountain in the world. Height: 8598 m (28 208 ft)

Kano 1 a state of N Nigeria: consists of wooded savanna in the south and scrub vegetation in the north. Capital: Kano. Pop: 2 884 000 (2005 est). Area: 20 131 sq km (7773 sq miles) 2 a city in N Nigeria, capital of Kano state: transport and market centre. Pop: 674 100 (1996 est)

Kanpur an industrial city in NE India, in S Uttar Pradesh on the River Ganges: scene of the massacre by Nana Sahib of British soldiers and European families and his later defeat by British forces in 1857. Pop: 2 532 138 (2001)

Kansas a state of the central US: consists of undulating prairie, drained chiefly by the Arkansas, Kansas, and Missouri Rivers; mainly agricultural. Capital: Topeka. Pop: 2 723 507 (2003 est). Area: 213 096 sq km (82 277 sq miles)

Kansas City 1 a city in W Missouri, at the confluence of the Missouri and Kansas Rivers: important centre of livestock and meat-packing industry. Pop: 442 768 (2003 est) 2 a city in NE Kansas, adjacent to Kansas City, Missouri. Pop: 145 757 (2003 est)

Kant Immanuel 1724–1804, German idealist philosopher.

He sought to determine the limits of man's knowledge in *Critique of Pure Reason* (1781) and propounded his system of ethics as guided by the categorical imperative in *Critique of Practical Reason* (1788)

Kaohsiung, Kao-hsiung, *or* **Gaoxiong** a port in SW Taiwan, on the South China Sea: the chief port of the island. Pop: 1 506 000 (2005 est)

Kaolack a port in SW Senegal, on the Saloum River. Pop: 299 000 (2005 est)

kaolin *or* **kaoline** a fine white clay used for the manufacture of hard-paste porcelain and bone china and in medicine as a poultice and gastrointestinal absorbent

kapa haka *NZ* the traditional Māori performing arts, often performed competitively

Kapfenberg an industrial town in E Austria, in Styria. Pop: 22 234 (2001)

Kapil Dev (**Ramlal**) **Nikhanj** born 1959, Indian cricketer: captain of India (1983–84)

Kapitza **Piotr Leonidovich** 1894–1984, Russian physicist. He worked in England and the USSR, doing research in several areas, particularly cryogenics; Nobel prize for physics in 1978

kapok a silky fibre obtained from the hairs covering the seeds of a tropical bombacaceous tree, *Ceiba pentandra* (**kapok tree** or **silk-cotton tree**): used for stuffing pillows, etc, and for sound insulation

Karachai-Cherkess Republic *or* **Karachayevo-Cherkess Republic** a constituent republic of W Russia, on the N side of the Caucasus Mountains. Capital: Cherkessk. Pop: 439 700 (2002). Area: 14 100 sq km (5440 sq miles)

Karachi a city in S Pakistan, on the Arabian Sea: capital of Pakistan (1947–60); university (1950); chief port: commercial and industrial centre. Pop: 11 819 000 (2005 est)

Karadžić **Radovan** born 1945, Bosnian Serb political leader and psychiatrist; charged with genocide by the International War Crimes Tribunal for his role in the Bosnian civil war of 1992–95; in hiding

Karaganda a city in E central Kazakhstan, founded in 1857: a major coal-mining and industrial centre. Pop: 412 000 (2005 est)

Karajan **Herbert von** 1908–89, Austrian conductor

Kara-Kalpak Autonomous Republic an administrative division in NW Uzbekistan, on the Aral Sea: came under Russian rule by stages from 1873 until Uzbekistan became independent in 1991. Capital: Nukus. Pop: 1 633 900 (2002 est). Area: 165 600 sq km (63 900 sq miles)

Karakoram *or* **Karakorum** a mountain system in N Kashmir, extending for about 480 km (300 miles) from northwest to southeast: contains the second highest peak in the world (K2); crossed by several high passes, notably the **Karakoram Pass** 5575 m (18 290 ft)

Karakorum a ruined city in Mongolia: founded in 1220 by Ghenghis Khan; destroyed by Kublai Khan when his brother rebelled against him, after Kublai Khan had moved his capital to Peking (now Beijing)

karakul *or* **caracul** 1 a breed of sheep of central Asia having coarse black, grey, or brown hair: the lambs have soft curled usually black hair 2 the fur prepared from these lambs

Kara Kum a desert in Turkmenistan, covering most of

the country: extensive areas now irrigated. Area: about 300 000 sq km (120 000 sq miles)

Karamanlis **Konstantinos** 1907–98, Greek statesman: prime minister of Greece (1955–58; 1958–61; 1961–63; 1974–80): president of Greece (1980–85; 1990–95)

Karan **Donna** born 1948, US fashion designer

Kara Sea a shallow arm of the Arctic Ocean off the N coast of Russia: ice-free for about three months of the year

karate a a traditional Japanese system of unarmed combat, employing smashes, chops, kicks, etc, made with the hands, feet, elbows, or legs b (*as modifier*): *karate chop*
▷www.wkf.net
▷www.itkf.org

Karbala *or* **Kerbela** a town in central Iraq: the chief holy city of Iraq and centre of Shiah Muslim pilgrimage; burial place of Mohammed's grandson Husain. Pop: 460 000 (2005 est)

Karelia 1 a region of NE Europe comprising areas of both Finland and Russia. Following the Russo-Finnish War (1939–40) a large part of what had been Finnish Karelia was annexed by the former Soviet Union; together with the part of Karelia which already belonged to Russia at that time, it corresponds roughly to the modern Karelian Republic in Russia 2 another name for the **Karelian Republic**

Karelian Isthmus a strip of land, now in Russia, between the Gulf of Finland and Lake Ladoga: annexed by the former Soviet Union after the Russo-Finnish War (1939–40)

Karelian Republic a constituent republic of NW Russia between the White Sea and Lakes Onega and Ladoga. Capital: Petrozavodsk. Pop: 716 700 (2002). Area: 172 400 sq km (66 560 sq miles)

Kariba, Lake a lake on the Zambia-Zimbabwe border, created by the building of the **Kariba Dam** across the Zambezi for hydroelectric power. Length: 282 km (175 miles)

Karloff **Boris,** real name *William Pratt* 1887–1969, English film actor, famous for his roles in horror films, esp *Frankenstein* (1931)

Karlovy Vary a city in the W Czech Republic, at the confluence of the Tepla and Ohře Rivers: warm mineral springs. Pop: 56 290 (1991)

Karlskrona a port in S Sweden: Sweden's main naval base since 1680. Pop: 61 097 (2004 est)

Karlsruhe a city in SW Germany, in Baden-Württemberg: capital of the former Baden state. Pop: 282 595 (2003 est)

karma 1 *Hinduism, Buddhism* the principle of retributive justice determining a person's state of life and the state of his reincarnations as the effect of his past deeds 2 *Theosophy* the doctrine of inevitable consequence

Karnak a village in E Egypt, on the Nile: site of the N part of the ruins of ancient Thebes

Karnataka a state of S India, on the Arabian Sea: consists of a narrow coastal plain rising to the South Deccan plateau; mainly agricultural. Capital: Bangalore. Pop: 52 733 958 (2001). Area: 191 791 sq km (74 051 sq miles)

Karoo *or* **Karroo** 1 any of several high arid plateaus in

South Africa, esp the **Central Karoo** and the **Little Karoo**. The highveld, north of the Central Karoo, is sometimes called the **Northern Karoo** **2** a period or rock system in Southern Africa equivalent to the period or system extending from the Upper Carboniferous to the Lower Jurassic: divided into **Lower** and **Upper Karoo**

Karpov Anatoly born 1951, Russian chess player: world champion (1975–85); FIDE world champion (1993–)

karri **1** an Australian eucalyptus tree, *Eucalyptus diversifolia* **2** the durable wood of this tree, used esp for construction

kart a light low-framed vehicle with small wheels and engine used for recreational racing

Karzai Hamid born 1957, Afghan military and political leader: president from 2002

Kasai a river in southwestern Africa, rising in central Angola and flowing east then north as part of the border between Angola and the Democratic Republic of Congo (formerly Zaïre), continuing northwest through the Democratic Republic of Congo to the River Congo. Length: 2154 km (1338 miles)

kasbah *or* **casbah** the citadel of any of various North African cities

Kashi *or* **Kashgar** an oasis city in W China, in W Xinjiang Uygur AR. Pop: 318 000 (2005 est)

Kashmir a region of SW central Asia: from the 16th century ruled by the Moguls, Afghans, Sikhs, and British successively; since 1947 disputed between India, Pakistan, and China; 84 000 sq km (33 000 sq miles) in the northwest are held by Pakistan and in part known as Azad Kashmir (Free Kashmir), part as the Northern Areas; an area of 42 735 sq km (16 496 sq miles) in the east (the Aksai Chin) is held by China; the remainder was in 1956 officially incorporated into India as the state of Jammu and Kashmir; traversed by the Himalaya and Karakoram mountain ranges and the Rivers Jhelum and Indus; a fruit-growing and cattle-grazing region, with a woollen industry. Capitals: (Jammu and Kashmir) Srinagar (summer), Jammu (winter); (Azad Kashmir) Muzaffarabad; (Northern Areas) Gilgit

Kasparov Garry , real name *Garik Weinstein*. born 1963, Armenian-Jewish chess player, born in Azerbaijan: world champion (1985–93); PCA world champion (1993–2000)

Kassala a city in the E Sudan: founded as a fort by the Egyptians in 1834. Pop: 430 000 (2005 est)

Kassel *or* **Cassel** a city in central Germany, in Hesse; capital of Westphalia (1807–13) and of the Prussian province of Hesse-Nassau (1866–1945). Pop: 194 322 (2003 est)

Katanga a region of SE Democratic Republic of Congo (formerly Zaïre): site of a secessionist movement during the 1960s and again in 1993; important for hydroelectric power and rich mineral resources (copper and tin ore). Pop: 4 125 000 (1998 est). Area: 496 964 sq km (191 878 sq miles)

Kathiawar a large peninsula of W India, in Gujarat between the Gulf of Kutch and the Gulf of Cambay. Area: about 60 690 sq km (23 430 sq miles)

katipo a small venomous spider, *Latrodectus katipo*, of New Zealand, commonly black with a red or orange stripe on the abdomen

Katmai Mount a volcano in SW Alaska, in the Aleutian Range: erupted in 1912 forming the Valley of Ten Thousand Smokes, a region with numerous fumaroles; established as **Katmai National Monument**, 10 917 sq km (4215 sq miles), in 1918. Height: 2100 m (7000 ft). Depth of crater: 1130 m (3700 ft). Width of crater: about 4 km (2.5 miles)

Katmandu *or* **Kathmandu** the capital of Nepal, in the east at the confluence of the Baghmati and Vishnumati Rivers. Pop: 814 000 (2005 est)

Katowice an industrial city in S Poland. Pop: 2 914 000 (2005 est)

Katrine, Loch a lake in central Scotland, east of Loch Lomond: noted for its associations with Sir Walter Scott's *Lady of the Lake*. Length: about 13 km (8 miles)

Katsina a city in N Nigeria, in Kaduna state: a major intellectual and cultural centre of the Hausa people (16th–18th centuries). Pop: 530 000 (2005 est)

Kattegat a strait between Denmark and Sweden: linked by the Sound, the Great Belt, and the Little Belt with the Baltic Sea and by the Skagerrak with the North Sea

katydid any typically green long-horned grasshopper of the genus *Microcentrum* and related genera, living among the foliage of trees in North America

Katz Sir Bernard born 1911, British neurophysiologist, born in Germany. Shared the Nobel prize for physiology or medicine (1970) with Julius Axelrod and Ulf von Euler

Kauai a volcanic island in NW Hawaii, northwest of Oahu. Chief town: Lihue. Pop. (Kauai county): 60 747 (2003 est). Area (island): 1433 sq km (553 sq miles)

Kauffmann Angelica 1741–1807, Swiss painter, who worked chiefly in England

Kaufman George S(imon). 1889–1961, US dramatist who, with Moss Hart, collaborated on many Broadway comedy hits

Kaunas a city in central Lithuania at the confluence of the Neman and Viliya Rivers: ceded by Poland to Russia in 1795; became the provisional capital of Lithuania (1920–40); incorporated into the Soviet Union 1944–91; university (1922). Pop: 364 000 (2005 est)

Kaunda Kenneth (David). born 1924, Zambian statesman. He became Zambia's first president (1964–91)

kauri **1** a New Zealand coniferous tree, *Agathis australis*, with oval leaves and round cones: family Araucariaceae **2** the wood or resin of this tree

Kawabata Yasunari 1899–1972, Japanese novelist, author of *Yukiguni (Snow Country*, 1948) and *Yama no oto (The Sound of the Mountain*, 1954): Nobel prize for literature 1968

Kawasaki an industrial port in central Japan, on SE Honshu, between Tokyo and Yokohama. Pop: 1 245 780 (2002 est)

kayak *or* **kaiak** **1** a small light canoe-like boat used by the Inuit, consisting of a light frame covered with watertight animal skins **2** a fibreglass or canvas-covered canoe of similar design

Kayseri a city in central Turkey: trading centre since ancient times as the chief city of Cappadocia. Pop: 605 000 (2005 est)

Kazakhstan *or* **Kazakstan** a republic in central Asia:

conquered by Mongols in the 13th century; came under Russian control in the 18th and 19th centuries; was a Soviet republic from 1936 until it gained independence in 1991. It has rich mineral deposits and agriculture is important. Official language: Kazakh. Religion: nonreligious, Muslim, and Christian. Official currency: tenge. Capital: Astana (formerly Akmola); capital functions moved from Almaty (formerly Alma-Ata) in 1997. Pop: 15 403 000 (2004 est). Area: 2 715 100 sq km (1 048 030 sq miles)

Kazan¹ Elia , real name *Elia Kazanjoglous* 1909–2003, US stage and film director and writer, born in Turkey. His films include *Gentleman's Agreement* (1947) and *On the Waterfront* (1954) for both of which he won Oscars, and *East of Eden* (1955).

Kazan² a city in W Russia, capital of the Tatar Autonomous Republic on the River Volga: capital of an independent khanate in the 15th century; university (1804); a major industrial centre. Pop: 1 108 000 (2005 est)

Kazantzakis Nikos 1885–1957, Greek novelist, poet, and dramatist, noted esp for his novels *Zorba the Greek* (1946) and *Christ Recrucified* (1954) and his epic poem *The Odyssey* (1938).

Kazbek Mount an extinct volcano in N Georgia in the central Caucasus Mountains. Height: 5047 m (16 558 ft)

kazoo a cigar-shaped musical instrument of metal or plastic with a membranous diaphragm of thin paper that vibrates with a nasal sound when the player hums into it

kea a large New Zealand parrot, *Nestor notabilis*, with brownish-green plumage

Kean Edmund ?1789–1833, English actor, noted for his Shakespearean roles

Keating Paul born 1944, Australian Labor politician; prime minister of Australia (1991–96)

Keaton Buster, real name *Joseph Francis Keaton* 1895–1966, US film comedian who starred in silent films such as *The Navigator* (1924), *The General* (1926), and *Steamboat Bill Junior* (1927)

Keats John 1795–1821, English poet. His finest poetry is contained in *Lamia and other Poems* (1820), which includes *The Eve of St Agnes*, *Hyperion*, and the odes *On a Grecian Urn*, *To a Nightingale*, *To Autumn*, and *To Psyche*

Keble John 1792–1866, English clergyman. His sermon on national apostasy (1833) is considered to have inspired the Oxford Movement

Kedah a state of NW Malaysia: under Thai control until it came under the British in 1909; the chief exports are rice, tin, and rubber. Capital: Alor Star. Pop: 1 648 756 (2000). Area: 9425 sq km (3639 sq miles)

kedge *Nautical* a light anchor, used esp for kedging

Kediri a city in Indonesia, in E Java: commercial centre. Pop: 244 519 (2000)

Kedron *or* **Kidron** *Bible* a ravine under the eastern wall of Jerusalem

keel¹ 1 one of the main longitudinal structural members of a vessel to which the frames are fastened and that may extend into the water to provide lateral stability 2 any structure corresponding to or resembling the keel of a ship, such as the central member along the bottom of an aircraft fuselage 3 *Biology* a ridgelike part;

carina

keel² *Eastern English, dialect* 1 a flat-bottomed vessel, esp one used for carrying coal 2 a measure of coal equal to about 21 tons

keel a fatal disease of young ducks, characterized by intestinal bleeding caused by Salmonella bacteria

keelson *or* **kelson** a longitudinal beam fastened to the keel of a vessel for strength and stiffness

keep *Architecture* the main tower within the walls of a medieval castle or fortress

keeper *Physics* a soft iron or steel bar placed across the poles of a permanent magnet to close the magnetic circuit when it is not in use

Keewatin a former administrative district of the Northwest Territories of Canada stretching from the district of Mackenzie to Hudson Bay; became part of Nunavut in 1999: mostly tundra.

keg *Brit* a an aluminium container in which beer is transported and stored b beer kept in a keg: it is infused with gas and served under pressure

Keighley a town in N England, in Bradford unitary authority, West Yorkshire, on the River Aire: textile industry. Pop: 49 453 (2001)

Keitel Wilhelm 1882–1946, German field marshal; chief of the supreme command of the armed forces (1938–45). He was convicted at the Nuremberg trials and executed

Kekkonen Urho (1900–86), Finnish statesman; president (1956–81)

Kelantan a state of NE Malaysia: under Thai control until it came under the British in 1909; produces rice and rubber. Capital: Kota Bharu. Pop: 1 313 014 (2000). Area: 14 930 sq km (5765 sq miles)

Keller 1 Gottfried 1819–90, Swiss novelist and short-story writer, who wrote in German: noted esp for the novel *Der Grüne Heinrich* (1855, rewritten 1880) 2 Helen (Adams). 1880–1968, US author and lecturer. Blind and deaf from infancy, she was taught to read, write, and speak and became noted for her work for handicapped people

Kells a town in the Republic of Ireland, in Co. Meath: *The Book of Kells*, an illuminated manuscript of the Gospels, was produced at the monastery here in the 8th century. Pop: 4421 (2002)

Kelly 1 Gene, full name *Eugene Curran Kelly*. 1912–96, US dancer, choreographer, film actor, and director. His many films include *An American in Paris* (1951) and *Singin' in the Rain* (1952) 2 Grace 1929–82, US film actress. Her films included *High Noon* (1952) and *High Society* (1956). She married Prince Rainier III of Monaco in 1956 and died following a car crash 3 Ned 1855–80, Australian horse and cattle thief and bushranger, active in Victoria: captured by the police and hanged

kelp any large brown seaweed, esp any in the order *Laminariales*

kelpie¹ *or* **kelpy** an Australian breed of sheepdog, originally developed from Scottish collies, having a smooth coat of various colours and erect ears

kelpie² (in Scottish folklore) a water spirit in the form of a horse that drowned its riders

kelt a salmon that has recently spawned and is usually in poor condition

kelvin the basic SI unit of thermodynamic temperature;

the fraction 1/273.16 of the thermodynamic temperature of the triple point of water.

Kelvin William Thomson, 1st Baron Kelvin. 1824–1907, British physicist, noted for his work in thermodynamics, inventing the Kelvin scale, and in electricity, pioneering undersea telegraphy

Kelvin scale a thermodynamic temperature scale based upon the efficiencies of ideal heat engines. The zero of the scale is absolute zero. Originally the degree was equal to that on the Celsius scale but it is now defined so that the triple point of water is exactly 273.16 kelvins. The International Practical Temperature Scale (1968, revised 1990) realizes the Kelvin scale over a wide range of temperatures

Kemerovo a city in S Russia: a major coal-mining centre of the Kuznetsk Basin, with important chemical plants. Pop: 479 000 (2005 est)

Kempe 1 ?1373–?1440, English mystic. Her autobiography, *The Book of Margery Kempe*, describes her mystical experiences and pilgrimages in Europe and Palestine 2 **Rudolf** 1910–76, German orchestral conductor, noted esp for his interpretations of Wagner

Kempis Thomas à ?1380–1471, German Augustinian monk, generally regarded as the author of the devotional work *The Imitation of Christ*

Kendal a town in NW England, in Cumbria: a gateway town to the Lake District, with an ancient woollen industry. Pop: 28 030 (2001)

Kendall Edward Calvin 1886–1972, US biochemist, who isolated the hormone thyroxine (1916). He shared the Nobel prize for physiology or medicine (1950) with Phillip Hench and Tadeus Reichstein for their work on hormones

kendo the Japanese art of fencing with pliable bamboo staves or, sometimes, real swords: strict conventions are observed

Kendrew Sir John Cowdery 1917–97, British biochemist. Using X-ray diffraction he discovered the structure of myoglobin, for which he shared a Nobel Prize (1962) with Max Perutz

Keneally Thomas (**Michael**). born 1935, Australian writer. His novels include the Booker prizewinner *Schindler's Ark* (1982); other works are *The Playmaker* (1987), *The Great Shame* (1998), and *The Office of Innocence* (2002)

Kenilworth a town in central England, in Warwickshire: ruined 12th-century castle, subject of Sir Walter Scott's novel *Kenilworth*. Pop: 22 218 (2001)

Kennedy 1 Charles Peter born 1959, British politician, leader of the Liberal Democrats from 1999 2 **Edward** (**Moore**), known as *Ted*. born 1932, US Democrat politician; senator since 1962 3 his brother, **John** (**Fitzgerald**), known as *JFK*. 1917–63, US Democrat statesman; 35th president of the US (1961–63), the first Roman Catholic and the youngest man ever to be president. He demanded the withdrawal of Soviet missiles from Cuba (1962) and prepared civil rights reforms; assassinated 4 **Nigel** (**Paul**). born 1956, British violinist, noted for his flamboyant style 5 **Robert** (**Francis**), known as *Bobby*, brother of John Kennedy. 1925–68, US Democrat statesman; attorney general (1961–64) and senator for New York (1965–68); assassinated

kennel 1 the lair of a fox or other animal 2 a pack of hounds

Kennelly Arthur Edwin 1861–1939, US electrical engineer: independently of Heaviside, he predicted the existence of an ionized layer in the upper atmosphere, known as the Kennelly-Heaviside layer or E region

Kenneth I surnamed *MacAlpine*. died 858, king of the Scots of Dalriada and of the Picts (?844–858): considered the first Scottish king

Kenny 1 **Brett** born 1961, Australian rugby league player 2 **Yvonne**, born 1950, Australian opera singer

Kensington and Chelsea a borough of Greater London, on the River Thames: **Kensington Palace** (17th century) and gardens. Pop: 174 400 (2003 est). Area: 12 sq km (5 sq miles)

Kent¹ William ?1685–1748, English architect, landscape gardener, and interior designer

Kent² a county of SE England, on the English Channel: the first part of Great Britain to be colonized by the Romans; one of the seven kingdoms of Anglo-Saxon England until absorbed by Wessex in the 9th century AD. Apart from the Downs it is mostly low-lying and agricultural, specializing in fruit and hops. The Medway towns of Rochester and Gillingham became an independent unitary authority in 1998. Administrative centre: Maidstone. Pop. (excluding Medway): 1 348 800 (2003 est). Area (excluding Medway): 3526 sq km (1361 sq miles)

Kentucky 1 a state of the S central US: consists of an undulating plain in the west, the Bluegrass region in the centre, the Tennessee and Ohio River basins in the southwest, and the Appalachians in the east. Capital: Frankfort. Pop: 4 117 827 (2003 est). Area: 102 693 sq km (39 650 sq miles) 2 a river in central Kentucky, rising in the Cumberland Mountains and flowing northwest to the Ohio River. Length: 417 km (259 miles)

Kenya 1 a republic in E Africa, on the Indian Ocean: became a British protectorate in 1895 and a colony in 1920; gained independence in 1963 and is a member of the Commonwealth. Tea and coffee constitute about a third of the total exports. Official languages: Swahili and English. Religions: Christian majority, animist minority. Currency: shilling. Capital: Nairobi. Pop: 32 420 000 (2004 est). Area: 582 647 sq km (224 960 sq miles) 2 **Mount** an extinct volcano in central Kenya: the second highest mountain in Africa; girth at 2400 m (8000 ft) is about 150 km (95 miles). The regions above 3200 m (10 500 ft) constitute **Mount Kenya National Park**. Height: 5199 m (17 058 ft)

Kenyatta Jomo ?1891–1978, Kenyan statesman: imprisoned as a suspected leader of the Mau Mau revolt (1953–59); elected president of the Kenya African National Union (1961); prime minister of independent Kenya (1963) and president (1964–78)

Keos an island in the Aegean Sea, in the NW Cyclades. Pop: 2412 (2001). Area: 174 sq km (67 sq miles)

Kepler Johannes 1571–1630, German astronomer. As discoverer of Kepler's laws of planetary motion he is regarded as one of the founders of modern astronomy

Kerala a state of SW India, on the Arabian Sea: formed in 1956, it includes the former state of Travancore-Cochin; has the highest population density of any Indian state. Capital: Trivandrum. Pop: 31 838 619

(2001). Area: 38 863 sq km (15 005 sq miles)

keratin *or* **ceratin** a fibrous protein that occurs in the outer layer of the skin and in hair, nails, feathers, hooves, etc.

kerb *or* *US and Canadian* **curb** a line of stone or concrete forming an edge between a pavement and a roadway, so that the pavement is some 15 cm above the level of the road

Kerch a port in S Ukraine on the **Kerch Peninsula** and the **Strait of Kerch** (linking the Black Sea with the Sea of Azov): founded as a Greek colony in the 6th century BC; ceded to Russia in 1774; iron-mining, steel production, and fishing. Pop: 153 000 (2005 est)

Kerenski *or* **Kerensky** Aleksandr Fyodorovich 1881–1970, Russian liberal revolutionary leader; prime minister (July–October 1917): overthrown by the Bolsheviks

Kerguelen an archipelago in the S Indian Ocean: consists of one large volcanic island (Kerguelen or Desolation Island) and 300 small islands; part of the French Southern and Antarctic Territories

Kerkrade a town in the SE Netherlands, in Limburg: one of the oldest coal-mining centres in Europe. Pop: 50 000 (2003 est)

Kerman a city in SE Iran: carpet-making centre. Pop: 546 000 (2005 est)

kermes a small evergreen Eurasian oak tree, *Quercus coccifera*, with prickly leaves resembling holly: the host plant of kermes scale insects

Kern Jerome (David). 1885–1945, US composer of musical comedies, esp *Show Boat* (1927)

kernel 1 the edible central part of a seed, nut, or fruit within the shell or stone 2 the grain of a cereal, esp wheat, consisting of the seed in a hard husk

kerosene *or* **kerosine** 1 a liquid mixture consisting mainly of alkane hydrocarbons with boiling points in the range 150°–300°C, used as an aircraft fuel, in domestic heaters, and as a solvent 2 the general name for paraffin as a fuel for jet aircraft

Kerouac Jack, real name *Jean-Louis Lebris de Kérouac*. 1922–69, US novelist and poet of the Beat Generation. His works include *On the Road* (1957) and *Big Sur* (1962)

Kerr Sir John Robert 1914–91, Australian public servant. As governor general of Australia (1974–77), he dismissed the Labor prime minister Gough Whitlam (1975) amid great controversy

Kerry¹ 1 a county of SW Republic of Ireland, in W Munster province: mostly mountainous (including the highest peaks in Ireland), with a deeply indented coast and many offshore islands. County town: Tralee. Pop: 132 527 (2002). Area: 4701 sq km (1815 sq miles) 2 a small black breed of dairy cattle, originally from Kerry

Kerry² John Forbes born 1943, US politician; Democratic Party candidate in the presidential election of 2004

Kesey Ken 1935–2001, US novelist, best-known for *One Flew Over the Cuckoo's Nest* (1962)

Kesselring Albert 1885–1960, German field marshal. He commanded the Luftwaffe attacks on Poland, France, and Britain (1939–40), and was supreme commander in Italy (1943–45) and on the western front (1945)

Kesteven Parts of an area in E England constituting a former administrative division of Lincolnshire

kestrel any of several small falcons, esp the European *Falco tinnunculus*, that tend to hover against the wind and feed on small mammals on the ground

Keswick a market town in NW England, in Cumbria in the Lake District: tourist centre. Pop: 4984 (2001)

ketch a two-masted sailing vessel, fore-and-aft rigged, with a tall mainmast and a mizzen stepped forward of the rudderpost

ketone any of a class of compounds with the general formula R′COR, where R and R′ are alkyl or aryl groups

Kettering a town in central England, in Northamptonshire: footwear industry. Pop: 51 063 (2001)

kettledrum a percussion instrument of definite pitch, consisting of a hollow bowl-like hemisphere covered with a skin or membrane, supported on a tripod or stand. The pitch may be adjusted by means of screws or pedals, which alter the tension of the skin

Kew part of the Greater London borough of Richmond-upon-Thames, on the River Thames: famous for **Kew Gardens** (the Royal Botanic Gardens), established in 1759 and given to the nation in 1841

key 1 a metal instrument, usually of a specifically contoured shape, that is made to fit a lock and, when rotated, operates the lock's mechanism 2 any instrument that is rotated to operate a valve, clock winding mechanism, etc. 3 a small metal peg or wedge inserted into keyways 4 any of a set of levers operating a typewriter, computer, etc. 5 any of the visible parts of the lever mechanism of a musical keyboard instrument that when depressed set in motion the action that causes the instrument to sound 6 a any of the 24 major and minor diatonic scales considered as a corpus of notes upon which a piece of music draws for its tonal framework b the main tonal centre in an extended composition c the tonic of a major or minor scale 7 *Biology* a systematic list of taxonomic characteristics, used to identify animals or plants 8 *Photog, Painting* the dominant tonal value and colour intensity of a picture 9 *Electrical engineering* a a hand-operated device for opening or closing a circuit or for switching circuits b a hand-operated switch that is pressed to transmit coded signals, esp Morse code 10 *Railways* a wooden wedge placed between a rail and a chair to keep the rail firmly in place 11 *Botany* any dry winged fruit, esp that of the ash 12 *Photog* determining the tonal value of a photograph

keyboard 1 a a complete set of keys, usually hand-operated, as on a piano, organ, typewriter, or typesetting machine b (*as modifier*): *a keyboard instrument* 2 a musical instrument, esp an electronic one, played by means of a keyboard

key grip *Chiefly US* the person in charge of moving and setting up camera tracks and scenery in a film or television studio

keyhole 1 an aperture in a door or a lock case through which a key may be passed to engage the lock mechanism 2 a transient column of vapour or plasma formed during the welding or cutting of materials, using high energy beams, such as lasers

keyhole surgery surgery carried out through a very small incision

Keynes John Maynard, 1st Baron Keynes. 1883–1946,

English economist. In *The General Theory of Employment, Interest and Money* (1936) he argued that unemployment was characteristic of an unregulated market economy and therefore to achieve a high level of employment it was necessary for governments to manipulate the overall level of demand through monetary and fiscal policies (including, when appropriate, deficit financing). He helped to found the International Monetary Fund and the World Bank

keynote *Music* the note upon which a scale or key is based; tonic

keypad *Computing* a data input device consisting of a limited number of keys, each with nominated functions

key signature *Music* a group of sharps or flats appearing at the beginning of each stave line to indicate the key in which a piece, section, etc, is to be performed

Khabarovsk a port in E Russia, on the Amur River: it was the administrative centre of the whole Soviet Far Eastern territory until 1938; a major industrial centre. Pop: 579 000 (2005 est)

Khachaturian Aram Ilich 1903–78, Russian composer. His works, which often incorporate Armenian folk tunes, include a piano concerto and the ballets *Gayaneh* (1942) and *Spartacus* (1954)

Khakass Republic a constituent republic of S central Russia, formerly in Krasnoyarsk Territory: formed in 1930. Capital: Abakan. Pop: 546 100 (2002). Area: 61 900 sq km (23 855 sq miles)

khaki 1 a dull yellowish-brown colour **2 a** a hard-wearing fabric of this colour, used esp for military uniforms **b** (*as modifier*): *a khaki jacket*

Khalid ibn Abdul Aziz 1913–82, king and President of the Council of Ministers of Saudi Arabia (1975–82)

Khama Sir Seretse 1921–80, Botswana statesman; the first president of Botswana (1966–80)

Khamenei Ayatollah Seyed Ali born 1940, Iranian political and religious leader: president of Iran (1981–89); leader of the Islamic Republic from 1989

khan 1 a (formerly) a title borne by medieval Chinese emperors and Mongol and Turkic rulers: usually added to a name **b** such a ruler **2** a title of respect borne by important personages in Afghanistan and central Asia

Kharkov a city in E Ukraine: capital of the Ukrainian Soviet Socialist Republic (1917–34); university (1805). Pop: 1 436 000 (2005 est)

Khartoum *or* **Khartum** the capital of the Sudan, at the junction of the Blue and the White Nile: with adjoining Khartoum North and Omdurman, the largest conurbation in the country; destroyed by the Mahdists in 1885 when General Gordon was killed; seat of the Anglo-Egyptian government of the Sudan until 1954, then capital of the new republic. Pop: 4 495 000 (2005 est)

Khatami Seyed Mohammad born 1943, Iranian politician: president of Iran from 1997

Kherson a port in S Ukraine on the Dnieper River near the Black Sea: shipyards. Pop: 320 000 (2005 est)

Khirbet Qumran an archaeological site in NW Jordan, near the NW shore of the Dead Sea: includes the caves where the Dead Sea Scrolls were found

Khomeini Ruholla , known as *Ayatollah Khomeini*. 1900–89, Iranian Shiite Muslim religious and political leader. Following the overthrow of the shah of Iran (1979) he returned from exile and instituted an Islamic republic. His rule saw deteriorating relations with the West and war (1980–88) with Iraq

Khrushchev Nikita Sergeyevich 1894–1971, Soviet statesman; premier of the Soviet Union (1958–64). After Stalin's death he became first secretary of the Soviet Communist Party (1953–64) and initiated a policy to remove the influence of Stalin (1956). As premier, he pursued a policy of peaceful coexistence with the West, but alienated Communist China

Khulna a city in S Bangladesh. Pop: 1 497 000 (2005 est)

Khyber Pass a narrow pass over the Safed Koh Range between Afghanistan and Pakistan, over which came the Persian, Greek, Tatar, Mogul, and Afghan invasions of India; scene of bitter fighting between the British and Afghans (1838–42, 1878–80). Length: about 53 km (33 miles). Highest point: 1072 m (3518 ft)

kick off a a place kick from the centre of the field in a game of football **b** the time at which the first such kick is due to take place

Kid Thomas a variant spelling of (Thomas) Kyd

Kidd William, known as *Captain Kidd*. 1645–1701, Scottish privateer, pirate, and murderer; hanged

Kidderminster 1 a town in W central England, in N Worcestershire on the River Stour: carpet industry. Pop: 55 610 (2001) **2** a type of ingrain reversible carpet originally made at Kidderminster

Kidman Nicole born 1967, Australian film actress, born in Hawaii. Her films include *Far and Away* (1992), *To Die For* (1995), *Eyes Wide Shut* (1999), and *The Hours* (2002): formerly married to Tom Cruise

kidney 1 either of two bean-shaped organs at the back of the abdominal cavity in man, one on each side of the spinal column. They maintain water and electrolyte balance and filter waste products from the blood, which are excreted as urine **2** the corresponding organ in other animals
▷www.kidney.org

kidney bean any of certain bean plants having kidney-shaped seeds, esp the French bean and scarlet runner

Kiel a port in N Germany, capital of Schleswig-Holstein state, on the **Kiel Canal** (connecting the North Sea with the Baltic): joined the Hanseatic League in 1284; became part of Denmark in 1773 and passed to Prussia in 1866; an important naval base in World Wars I and II; shipbuilding and engineering industries. Pop: 233 039 (2003 est)

Kielce an industrial city in S Poland. Pop: 212 383 (1999 est)

Kierkegaard Søren Aabye 1813–55, Danish philosopher and theologian. He rejected organized Christianity and anticipated the existentialists in emphasizing man's moral responsibility and freedom of choice. His works include *Either/Or* (1843), *The Concept of Dread* (1844), and *The Sickness unto Death* (1849)

Kieślowski Krzysztof 1941–96, Polish film director, whose later films were made in France; his work includes the television series *Decalogue* (1988–89) and the film trilogy *Three Colours* (1993–94)

Kiev the capital of Ukraine, on the Dnieper River: formed the first Russian state by the late 9th century;

university (1834). Pop: 2 623 000 (2005 est)

Kigali the capital of Rwanda, in the central part. Pop: 782 000 (2005 est)

Kilauea a crater on the E side of Mauna Loa volcano, on SE Hawaii Island: the world's largest active crater. Height: 1247 m (4090 ft). Width: 3 km (2 miles)

Kildare a county of E Republic of Ireland, in Leinster province: mostly low-lying and fertile. County town: Naas. Pop: 163 944 (2002). Area: 1694 sq km (654 sq miles)

Kilimanjaro a volcanic massif in N Tanzania: the highest peak in Africa; extends from east to west for 80 km (50 miles). Height: 5895 m (19 340 ft)

Kilkenny 1 a county of SE Republic of Ireland, in Leinster province: mostly agricultural. County town: Kilkenny. Pop: 80 339 (2002). Area: 2062 sq km (796 sq miles) 2 a market town in SE Republic of Ireland, county town of Co. Kilkenny: capital of the ancient kingdom of Ossory. Pop: 9500 (latest est)

kill US a channel, stream, or river (chiefly as part of place names)

Killarney a town in SW Republic of Ireland, in Co. Kerry: a tourist centre near the Lakes of Killarney. Pop: 13 137 (2002)

killer whale a predatory black-and-white toothed whale, *Orcinus orca*, with a large erect dorsal fin, most common in cold seas: family *Delphinidae*

Killiecrankie a pass in central Scotland, in the Grampians: scene of a battle (1689) in which the Jacobites defeated William III's forces but lost their leader, Viscount Dundee

Kilmarnock a town in SW Scotland, the administrative centre of East Ayrshire: associations with Robert Burns; engineering and textile industries; whisky blending. Pop: 43 588 (2001)

kiln a large oven for burning, drying, or processing something, such as porcelain or bricks

kilobyte *Computing* 1024 bytes

kilocycle short for kilocycle per second: a former unit of frequency equal to 1 kilohertz

kilogram 1 one thousand grams 2 the basic SI unit of mass, equal to the mass of the international prototype held by the *Bureau International des Poids et Mesures*. One kilogram is equivalent to 2.204 62 pounds.

kilohertz one thousand hertz; one thousand cycles per second.

kilometre *or US* **kilometer** one thousand metres, equal to 0.621371 miles.

kiloton 1 one thousand tons 2 an explosive power, esp of a nuclear weapon, equal to the power of 1000 tons of TNT

kilovolt one thousand volts.

kilowatt one thousand watts.

kilowatt-hour a unit of energy equal to the work done by a power of 1000 watts in one hour.

Kilvert Francis 1840–79, British clergyman and diarist. His diary (published 1938–40) gives a vivid account of life in the Welsh Marches in the 1870s

Kimberley 1 a city in central South Africa; the capital of Northern Cape province: besieged (1899–1900) for 126 days during the Boer War; diamond-mining and -marketing centre, with heavy engineering works. Pop: 62 526 (2001) 2 a plateau region of NW Australia, in N

Western Australia: consists of rugged mountains surrounded by grassland. Area: about 360 000 sq km (140 000 sq miles)

Kim Il Sung 1912–94, North Korean statesman and marshal; prime minister (1948–72) and president (1972–94) of North Korea

Kim Jong Il born 1942, Korean politician; ruler of North Korea from 1994, official head of state from 1998: son of Kim Il Sung

Kinabalu a mountain in Malaysia, on N Borneo in central Sabah: the highest peak in Borneo. Height: 4125 m (13 533 ft)

Kincardineshire a former county of E Scotland: became part of Grampian region in 1975 and part of Aberdeenshire in 1996

kindergarten a class or small school for young children, usually between the ages of four and six to prepare them for primary education. Often shortened (in Australia) to **kinder** or (in Australia and New Zealand) to **kindy** or **kindie**

kinematics the study of the motion of bodies without reference to mass or force

kinetic art art, esp sculpture, that moves or has moving parts

kinetic energy the energy of motion of a body, equal to the work it would do if it were brought to rest. The translational kinetic energy depends on motion through space, and for a rigid body of constant mass is equal to the product of half the mass times the square of the speed. The rotational kinetic energy depends on rotation about an axis, and for a body of constant moment of inertia is equal to the product of half the moment of inertia times the square of the angular velocity. In relativistic physics kinetic energy is equal to the product of the increase of mass caused by motion times the square of the speed of light. The SI unit is the joule but the electronvolt is often used in atomic physics.

kinetics 1 another name for **dynamics** 2 the branch of mechanics, including both dynamics and kinematics, concerned with the study of bodies in motion 3 the branch of dynamics that excludes the study of bodies at rest 4 the branch of chemistry concerned with the rates of chemical reactions

king 1 a male sovereign prince who is the official ruler of an independent state; monarch 2 any of four playing cards in a pack, one for each suit, bearing the picture of a king 3 the most important chess piece, although theoretically the weakest, being able to move only one square at a time in any direction 4 *Draughts* a piece that has moved entirely across the board and has been crowned, after which it may move backwards as well as forwards

King 1 BB, real name *Riley B. King*. born 1925, US blues singer and guitarist 2 Billie Jean (née*Moffitt*). born 1943, US tennis player: Wimbledon champion 1966–68, 1972–73, and 1975; US champion 1967, 1971–72, and 1974 3 Martin Luther 1929–68, US Baptist minister and civil-rights leader. He advocated nonviolence in his campaigns against the segregation of Blacks in the South: assassinated; Nobel Peace Prize 1964 4 Stephen (Edwin). born 1947, US writer esp of horror novels; his books, many of which have been filmed, include *Carrie* (1974), *The Shining* (1977), *Misery* (1988), and *Everything's Eventual* (2002) **5 William Lyon Mackenzie** 1874–1950, Canadian Liberal statesman; prime minister (1921–26; 1926–30; 1935–48)

King Country the an area in the centre of North Island, New Zealand: home of the King Movement, a nineteenth-century Māori separatist movement

kingcup *Brit* any of several yellow-flowered ranunculaceous plants, esp the marsh marigold

kingdom 1 a territory, state, people, or community ruled or reigned over by a king or queen **2** *Biology* any of the major categories into which living organisms of the domain *Eukarya* are classified. Modern systems recognize four kingdoms: *Protoctista* (algae, protozoans, etc), *Fungi*, *Plantae*, and *Animalia* **3** *Theol* the eternal sovereignty of God

kingfisher any coraciiform bird of the family *Alcedinidae*, esp the Eurasian *Alcedo atthis*, which has a greenish-blue and orange plumage. Kingfishers have a large head, short tail, and long sharp bill and tend to live near open water and feed on fish

kingklip *South African* an edible eel-like marine fish

kingpin 1 a pivot pin that provides a steering joint in a motor vehicle by securing the stub axle to the axle beam **2** *Tenpin bowling* the front pin in the triangular arrangement of the ten pins **3** (in ninepins) the central pin in the diamond pattern of the nine pins

Kingsford-Smith Sir Charles (**Edward**). 1897–1935, Australian aviator and pioneer (with Charles Ulm) of trans-Pacific and trans-Tasman flights

Kingsley 1 Sir Ben born 1943, British actor. He won an Oscar for his performance in the title role of the film *Gandhi* (1982) **2 Charles** 1819–75, British clergyman and author. His works include the historical romances *Westward Ho!* (1855) and *Hereward the Wake* (1866) and the children's story *The Water Babies* (1863) **3** his brother, **Henry** 1830–76, British novelist, editor, and journalist, who spent some time in Australia. His works include *Ravenshoe* (1861) and the Anglo-Australian novels *The Recollections of Geoffrey Hamlyn* (1859) and *The Hillyars and the Burtons* (1865)

King-Smith Ronald Gordon, known as *Dick*. born 1922, British writer for children; his numerous books include *The Sheep Pig* (1984) and the *Sophie* series

Kingston 1 the capital and chief port of Jamaica, on the SE coast: University of the West Indies. Pop: 574 000 (2005 est) **2** a port in SE Canada, in SE Ontario: the chief naval base of Lake Ontario and a large industrial centre; university (1841). Pop: 108 158 (2001) **3** short for **Kingston upon Thames**

Kingston upon Hull 1 the official name of **Hull 2** a unitary authority in NE England, in the East Riding of Yorkshire: formerly (1974–96) part of the county of Humberside. Pop: 247 900 (2003 est). Area: 71 sq km (27 sq miles)

Kingston upon Thames a borough of SW Greater London, on the River Thames: formed in 1965 by the amalgamation of several former boroughs of Surrey; administrative centre of Surrey. Pop: 150 400 (2003 est). Area: 38 sq km (15 sq miles)

Kingstown the capital of St Vincent and the Grenadines: a port and resort. Pop: 31 000 (2005 est)

Kinnock Neil (**Gordon**). born 1942, British Labour politician, born in Wales; leader of the Labour Party (1983–92); a European commissioner from 1994 and vice-president of the European Commission (1999–2004)

Kinross-shire a former county of E central Scotland: became part of Tayside region in 1975 and part of Perth and Kinross in 1996

Kinsey Alfred Charles 1894–1956, US zoologist, who directed a survey of human sexual behaviour

Kinshasa the capital of the Democratic Republic of Congo (formerly Zaïre), on the River Congo opposite Brazzaville: became capital of the Belgian Congo in 1929 and of Zaïre in 1960; university (1954). Pop: 5 717 000 (2005 est)

kip¹ a unit of weight equal to one thousand pounds

kip² the standard monetary unit of Laos, divided into 100 at

kip³ *Austral* a small board used to spin the coins in two-up

Kipling (Joseph) Rudyard 1865–1936, English poet, short-story writer, and novelist, born in India. His works include *Barrack-Room Ballads* (1892), the two *Jungle Books* (1894, 1895), *Stalky and Co.* (1899), *Kim* (1901), and the *Just So Stories* (1902): Nobel prize for literature 1907

kipper a male salmon during the spawning season

Kirchhoff Gustav Robert 1824–87, German physicist. With Bunsen he developed the method of spectrum analysis that led to their discovery of caesium (1860) and rubidium (1861): also worked on electrical networks

Kiribati an independent republic in the W Pacific: comprises 33 islands including Banaba (Ocean Island), the Gilbert and Phoenix Islands, and eight of the Line Islands; part of the British colony of the Gilbert and Ellice Islands until 1975; became self-governing in 1977 and gained full independence in 1979 as the Republic of Kiribati; a member of the Commonwealth. Official languages: English, I-Kiribati (Gilbertese) is widely spoken. Religion: Christian majority. Currency: Australian dollar. Capital: Bairiki islet, in Tarawa atoll. Pop: 88 000 (2003 est). Area: 684 sq km (264 sq miles)

Kiritimati an island in the central Pacific, in Kiribati: one of the Line Islands; the largest atoll in the world. Pop: 3225 (1995)

Kirk Norman 1923–74, prime minister of New Zealand (1972–74)

Kirkby¹ Emma born 1949, British soprano, specializing in performances of early music with period instruments

Kirkby² a town in NW England, in Knowsley unitary authority, Merseyside. Pop: 40 006 (2001)

Kirkcaldy a port in E Scotland, in SE Fife on the Firth of Forth. Pop: 46 912 (2001)

Kirkcudbrightshire a former county of SW Scotland, part of Dumfries and Galloway since 1975

Kirklees a unitary authority in N England, in West Yorkshire. Pop: 391 400 (2003 est). Area: 410 sq km (158 sq miles)

Kirkpatrick Mount a mountain in Antarctica, in S Victoria Land in the Queen Alexandra Range. Height: 4528 m (14 856 ft)

Kirkuk a city in NE Iraq: centre of a rich oilfield with pipelines to the Mediterranean. Pop: 548 000 (2005 est)

Kirkwall a town on the N coast of Mainland in the Orkney Islands: administrative centre of the island authority of Orkney: cathedral built by Norsemen (begun in 1137). Pop: 6206 (2001)

Kirov[1] Sergei Mironovich 1888–1934, Soviet politician; one of Stalin's chief aides. His assassination was the starting point for Stalin's purge of the Communist Party (1934–38)

Kirov[2] a city in NW Russia, on the Vyatka River: an early trading centre; engineering industries. Pop: 454 000 (2005 est)

Kirovograd a city in S central Ukraine on the Ingul River: manufacturing centre of a rich agricultural area. Pop: 250 000 (2005 est)

Kirribilli House the official Sydney residence of the Australian Prime Minister

Kirsch or **Kirschwasser** a brandy distilled from cherries, made chiefly in the Black Forest in Germany and in the Jura and Vosges districts of France

Kiruna a town in N Sweden: iron-mining centre. Pop: 23 273 (2004 est)

Kisangani a city in the N Democratic Republic of Congo (formerly Zaïre), at the head of navigation of the River Congo below Stanley Falls: Université Libre du Congo (1963). Pop: 475 000 (2005 est)

Kishinev the capital of Moldova on the Byk River: manufacturing centre of a rich agricultural region; university (1945). Pop: 662 000 (2005 est)

kismet *Islam* the will of Allah

Kissinger Henry (**Alfred**). born 1923, US academic and diplomat, born in Germany; assistant to President Nixon for national security affairs (1969–75); Secretary of State (1973–77): shared the Nobel peace prize 1973

kiss of life the mouth-to mouth or mouth-to-nose resuscitation in which a person blows gently into the mouth or nose of an unconscious person, allowing the lungs to deflate after each blow

Kisumu a port in W Kenya, in Nyanza province on the NE shore of Lake Victoria: fishing and trading centre. Pop: 433 000 (2005 est)

kit[1] *NZ* a flax basket

kit[2] a kind of small violin, now obsolete, used esp by dancing masters in the 17th–18th centuries

kit[3] a cub of various small mammals, such as the ferret or fox

Kitaj R. B born 1932, US painter working in Britain, noted for such large figurative works as *If Not, Not* (1976)

Kitakyushu a port in Japan, on N Kyushu: formed in 1963 by the amalgamation of the cities of Wakamatsu, Yahata, Tobata, Kokura, and Moji; one of Japan's largest industrial centres. Pop: 999 806 (2002 est)

Kitchener[1] Horatio Herbert, 1st Earl Kitchener of Khartoum. 1850–1916, British field marshal. As head of the Egyptian army (1892–98), he expelled the Mahdi from the Sudan (1898), occupying Khartoum; he also commanded British forces (1900–02) in the Boer War and (1902–09) in India. He conducted the mobilization of the British army for World War I as war minister (1914–16); he was drowned on his way to Russia

Kitchener[2] an industrial town in SE Canada, in S Ontario: founded in 1806 as Dutch Sand Hills, it was renamed Berlin in 1830 and Kitchener in 1916. Pop: 190 399 (2001)

kite 1 *Nautical* any of various light sails set in addition to the working sails of a vessel 2 any diurnal bird of prey of the genera *Milvus*, *Elanus*, etc, typically having a long forked tail and long broad wings and usually preying on small mammals and insects: family *Accipitridae* (hawks, etc) 3 *Commerce* a negotiable paper drawn without any actual transaction or assets and designed to obtain money on credit, give an impression of affluence, etc.

▷www.kiteflyers.org

kitten a young cat

kittiwake either of two oceanic gulls of the genus *Rissa*, esp *R. tridactyla*, having a white plumage with pale grey black-tipped wings and a square-cut tail

kitty 1 the pool of bets in certain gambling games 2 (in bowls) the jack

Kitty Hawk a village in NE North Carolina, near Kill Devil Hill, where the Wright brothers made the world's first aeroplane flight (1903)

Kitwe a city in N Zambia: commercial centre of the Copper Belt. Pop: 545 000 (2005 est)

Kivu Lake a lake in central Africa, between the Democratic Republic of Congo (formerly Zaïre) and Rwanda at an altitude of 1460 m (4790 ft). Area: 2698 sq km (1042 sq miles). Depth: (maximum) 475 m (1558 ft)

kiwi any nocturnal flightless New Zealand bird of the genus *Apteryx*, having a long beak, stout legs, and weakly barbed feathers: order *Apterygiformes*

kiwi fruit the edible oval fruit of the kiwi plant, *Actinidia chinensis*, a climbing plant native to Asia but grown extensively in New Zealand; it has a brown furry skin and pale green flesh

Kizil Irmak a river in Turkey, rising in the Kizil Dag and flowing southwest, northwest, and northeast to the Black Sea: the longest river in Asia Minor. Length: about 1150 km (715 miles)

Klagenfurt a city in S Austria, capital of Carinthia province: tourist centre. Pop: 90 141 (2001)

Klaipeda a port in Lithuania on the Baltic: shipbuilding and fish canning. Pop: 190 000 (2005 est)

Klee Paul 1879–1940, Swiss painter and etcher. A founder member of *der Blaue Reiter*, he subsequently evolved an intensely personal style of unusual fantasy and wit

Klein 1 Calvin (**Richard**). born 1942, US fashion designer 2 Melanie 1882–1960, Austrian psychoanalyst resident in England (from 1926), noted for her work on child behaviour

Kleist (**Bernd**) Heinrich (**Wilhelm**) von 1777–1811, German dramatist, poet, and short-story writer. His plays include *The Broken Pitcher* (1808), *Penthesilea* (1808), and *The Prince of Homburg* (published 1821)

Klemperer Otto 1885–1973, orchestral conductor, born in Germany. He was best known for his interpretations of Beethoven

kleptomania *Psychol* a strong impulse to steal, esp when there is no obvious motivation

Kline Franz 1910–62, US abstract expressionist painter. His works are characterized by heavy black strokes on a white or grey background

klipspringer a small agile antelope, *Oreotragus oreotragus*, inhabiting rocky regions of Africa south of the Sahara

Klondike 1 a region of NW Canada, in the Yukon in the basin of the Klondike River: site of rich gold deposits, discovered in 1896 but largely exhausted by 1910. Area: about 2100 sq km (800 sq miles) 2 a river in NW Canada, rising in the Yukon and flowing west to the Yukon River. Length: about 145 km (90 miles)

kloof a mountain pass or gorge in southern Africa

knapweed any of several plants of the genus *Centaurea*, having purplish thistle-like flowers: family *Asteraceae* (composites)

knave another word for **jack**¹ (the playing card)

knee 1 the joint of the human leg connecting the tibia and fibula with the femur and protected in front by the patella 2 a the area surrounding and above this joint b reaching or covering the knee 3 a corresponding or similar part in other vertebrates 4 anything resembling a knee in action, such as a device pivoted to allow one member angular movement in relation to another 5 anything resembling a knee in shape, such as an angular bend in a pipe 6 any of the hollow rounded protuberances that project upwards from the roots of the swamp cypress: thought to aid respiration in waterlogged soil

knees-up a boisterous dance involving the raising of alternate knees

Kneller Sir Godfrey ?1646–1723, portrait painter at the English court, born in Germany

knife edge a sharp-edged wedge of hard material on which the beam of a balance pivots or about which a pendulum is suspended

knight 1 in medieval Europe a (originally) a person who served his lord as a mounted and heavily armed soldier b (later) a gentleman invested by a king or other lord with the military and social standing of this rank 2 (in modern times) a person invested by a sovereign with a nonhereditary rank and dignity usually in recognition of personal services, achievements, etc. A British knight bears the title *Sir* placed before his name, as in *Sir Winston Churchill* 3 a chess piece, usually shaped like a horse's head, that moves either two squares horizontally and one square vertically or one square horizontally and two squares vertically 4 *History* a member of the Roman class of the equites

Knight Dame Laura 1887–1970, British painter, noted for her paintings of Gypsies, the ballet, and the circus

knight errant (esp in medieval romance) a knight who wanders in search of deeds of courage, chivalry, etc.

knob *Geography* a round hill or knoll or morainic ridge

knock 1 the sound of knocking in an engine or bearing 2 *Informal* (in cricket) an innings or a spell of batting

knock about *or* **around** a sailing vessel, usually slooprigged, without a bowsprit and with a single jib

knock-on *Rugby* the infringement of playing the ball forward with the hand or arm

knockout 1 a blow that renders an opponent unconscious 2 a series of absurd invented games, esp obstacle races, involving physical effort or skill

knock up a practice session at tennis, squash, or a similar game

knoll a small rounded hill

Knossos *or* **Cnossus** a ruined city in N central Crete: remains of the Minoan Bronze Age civilization

knot¹ 1 a protuberance or lump of plant tissues, such as that occurring on the trunks of certain trees 2 a *Pathol* a lump of vessels or fibres formed in a part, as in a muscle b *Anatomy* a protuberance on an organ or part 3 a unit of speed used by nautical vessels and aircraft, being one nautical mile (about 1.15 statute miles or 1.85 km) per hour 4 one of a number of equally spaced knots on a log line used to indicate the speed of a ship in nautical miles per hour

knot² a small northern sandpiper, *Calidris canutus*, with a short bill and grey plumage

Knowles Beyoncé born 1981, US singer, songwriter, and actress. A member of the hugely successful Destiny's Child, she later found solo success with *Dangerously in Love* (2003) and the single "Crazy in Love" (2003)

Knowsley a unitary authority of NW England, in Merseyside. Pop: 150 200 (2003 est). Area: 97 sq km (38 sq miles)

Knox 1 John ?1514–72, Scottish theologian and historian. After exile in England and on the Continent (1547–59), he returned to Scotland in 1559 and established the Presbyterian Church of Scotland (1560). His chief historical work was the *History of the Reformation in Scotland* (1586) 2 Ronald (Arbuthnott). 1888–1957, British priest and author. A convert to Roman Catholicism, he is noted for his translation of the Vulgate (1945–49)

Knox-Johnston Sir Robin (William Robert Patrick). born 1939, British yachtsman. He was the first to sail round the world alone nonstop (1968–69)

Knoxville an industrial city in E Tennessee, on the Tennessee River: state capital (1796–1812; 1817–19). Pop: 173 278 (2003 est)

knuckle 1 a joint of a finger, esp that connecting a finger to the hand 2 the cylindrical portion of a hinge through which the pin passes 3 an angle joint between two members of a structure

knuckle-duster a metal bar fitted over the knuckles, often with holes for the fingers, for inflicting injury by a blow with the fist

knurl *or* **nurl** a small ridge, esp one of a series providing a rough surface that can be gripped

koala *or* **koala bear** a slow-moving Australian arboreal marsupial, *Phascolarctus cinereus*, having dense greyish fur and feeding on eucalyptus leaves and bark

Kobarid a village in Slovenia on the Isonzo River: part of Italy until 1947; scene of the defeat of the Italians by Austro-German forces (1917)

Kobe a port in S Japan, on S Honshu on Osaka Bay: formed in 1889 by the amalgamation of Hyogo and Kobe; a major industrial complex, producing ships, steel, and rubber goods. Pop: 1 478 380 (2002 est)

Koblenz *or* **Coblenz** a city in W central Germany, in the Rhineland-Palatinate at the confluence of the Rivers Moselle and Rhine: ruled by the archbishop-electors of Trier from 1018 until occupied by the French in 1794; passed to Prussia in 1815, becoming capital of the Rhine Province (1824–1945) and of the Rhineland-Palatinate (1946–50); wine trade centre. Pop: 107 608 (2003 est)

Koch Robert 1843–1910, German bacteriologist, who isolated the anthrax bacillus (1876), the tubercle bacillus (1882), and the cholera bacillus (1883): Nobel prize for physiology or medicine 1905

Kochi 1 a port in SW Japan, on central Shikoku on Urado Bay. Pop: 326 490 (2002 est) 2 another name for **Cochin**

Kodiak an island in S Alaska, in the Gulf of Alaska: site of the first European settlement in Alaska, made by Russians in 1784. Pop: 13 466 (2004 est). Area: 8974 sq km (3465 sq miles)

Koestler Arthur 1905–83, British writer, born in Hungary. Of his early antitotalitarian novels *Darkness at Noon* (1940) is outstanding. His later works, *The Sleepwalkers* (1959), *The Act of Creation* (1964), and *The Ghost in the Machine* (1967) reflect his interest in science, philosophy, and psychology. He committed suicide

Kofu a city in central Japan, on S Honshu: textiles. Pop: 190 098 (2002 est)

Kogi a state of W Nigeria. Capital: Lokoja. Pop: 2 346 946 (1995 est)

Kohima a city in NE India, capital of Nagaland, near the Burmese border: centre of fierce fighting in World War II, when it was surrounded by the Japanese but not captured (1944). Pop: 78 584 (2001)

Kohl Helmut born 1930, German statesman: chancellor of West Germany (1982–90) and of Germany (1990–98)

kohlrabi a cultivated variety of cabbage, *Brassica oleracea caulorapa* (or *gongylodes*), whose thickened stem is eaten as a vegetable

Koizumi Junichiro born 1941, Japanese politician; prime minister from 2001

Kokand a city in NE Uzbekistan, in the Fergana valley. Pop: 211 000 (2005 est)

kokanee a landlocked salmon, *Oncorhynchus nerka kennerlyi*, of lakes in W North America: a variety of sockeye

Koko Nor or **Kuku Nor** a lake in W China, in Qinghai province in the NE Tibetan Highlands at an altitude of about 3000 m (10 000 ft): the largest lake in China. Area: about 4100 sq km (1600 sq miles)

Kokoschka Oskar 1886–1980, Austrian expressionist painter and dramatist, noted for his landscapes and portraits

Kokura a former city in SW Japan, on N Kyushu: merged with adjacent townships in 1963 to form the new city of **Kitakyushu**

Kola Peninsula a peninsula in NW Russia, between the Barents and White Seas: forms most of the Murmansk region. Area: about 130 000 sq km (50 000 sq miles)

Kolar Gold Fields a city in S India, in SE Karnataka: a major gold-mining centre since 1881. Pop: 72 481 (1991)

Kolding a port in Denmark, in E Jutland at the head of **Kolding Fjord** (an inlet of the Little Belt). Pop: 54 941 (2004 est)

Kolhapur a city in W India, in S Maharashtra: university (1963). Pop: 485 183 (2001)

Kolmogorov Andrei Nikolaevich (1903–87), Soviet mathematician, who made important contributions to the theoretical foundations of probability

Kolomna a city in the W central Russia, at the confluence of the Moskva and Oka Rivers: railway engineering centre. Pop: 151 500 (1999 est)

Kolyma a river in NE Russia, rising in the Kolyma Mountains north of the Sea of Okhotsk and flowing generally north to the East Siberian Sea. Length: 2600 km (1615 miles)

Kolyma Range a mountain range in NE Russia, in NE Siberia, extending about 1100 km (700 miles) between the Kolyma River and the Sea of Okhotsk. Highest peak: 1862 m (6109 ft)

Komati a river in southern Africa, rising in E South Africa and flowing east through Swaziland and Mozambique to the Indian Ocean at Delagoa Bay. Length: about 800 km (500 miles)

komatik a sledge having wooden runners and crossbars bound with rawhide, used by the Inuit and other related peoples

Komi Republic a constituent republic of NW Russia: annexed by the princes of Moscow in the 14th century. Capital: Syktyvkar. Pop: 1 019 000 (2002). Area: 415 900 sq km (160 540 sq miles)

Kommunizma Peak a mountain in SE Tajikistan in the Pamirs: the highest mountain in the former Soviet Union. Height: 7495 m (24 590 ft)

Komsomolsk an industrial city in W Russia, on the Amur River: built by members of the Komsomol (Communist youth league) in 1932. Pop: 275 000 (2005 est)

Kongur Shan, Kungur, or **Qungur** a mountain in China, in W Xinjiang Uygur: the highest peak in the Pamirs. Height: 7719 m (25 325 ft)

Konya or **Konia** a city in SW central Turkey: in ancient times a Phrygian city and capital of Lycaonia. Pop: 883 000 (2005 est)

kookaburra 1 a large arboreal Australian kingfisher, *Dacelo novaeguineae* (or *gigas*), with a cackling cry 2 a related smaller bird *D. Leachii*, of tropical Australia and New Guinea

Koolhaas Rem Dutch architect and theorist, co-founder of the Office for Metropolitan Architecture (1975); buildings include the Grand Palais and associated developments in Lille, France (1989–96); books include *S, M, L, XL* (1996)

Kooning Willem de 1904–97, US abstract expressionist painter, born in Holland

Kootenay or **Kootenai** a river in W North America, rising in SE British Columbia and flowing south into NW Montana, then north into Idaho before re-entering British Columbia, broadening into **Kootenay Lake**, then flowing to the Columbia River. Length: 655 km (407 miles)

kopeck, kopek, or **copeck** a monetary unit of Russia and Belarus worth one hundredth of a rouble: coins are still used as tokens for coin-operated machinery although the kopeck itself is virtually valueless

Kopeisk or **Kopeysk** a city in SW central Russia, in Chelyabinsk province: lignite mining. Pop: 24 000 (2005 est)

Koran the sacred book of Islam, believed by Muslims to be the infallible word of God dictated to Mohammed through the medium of the angel Gabriel
▷http://www.quran.org.uk/

Korbut Olga born 1955, Soviet gymnast: noted for her highly individualistic style, which greatly increased the popularity of the sport, esp following her performance in the 1972 Olympic Games

Korchnoi Victor born 1931, Soviet-born chess player: Soviet champion 1960, 1962, and 1964: defected to the West in 1976

Korda Sir Alexander, real name *Sandor Kellner*. 1893–1956, British film producer and director, born in Hungary: his films include *The Scarlet Pimpernel* (1934), *Anna Karenina* (1948), and *The Third Man* (1949)

Kordofan a region of the central Sudan: consists of a plateau with rugged uplands (the Nuba Mountains). Area: 380 548 sq km (146 930 sq miles)

Korea a former country in E Asia, now divided into two separate countries, North Korea and South Korea. Korea occupied the peninsula between the Sea of Japan and the Yellow Sea: an isolated vassal of Manchu China for three centuries until the opening of ports to Japanese trade in 1876; gained independence in 1895; annexed to Japan in 1910 and divided in 1945 into two occupation zones (Russian in the north, American in the south), which became North Korea and South Korea in 1948

Korean the official language of North and South Korea, considered by some scholars to be part of the Altaic family of languages

Korea Strait a strait between South Korea and SW Japan, linking the Sea of Japan with the East China Sea

Korzybski Alfred (Habdank Skarbek). 1879–1950, US originator of the theory and study of general semantics, born in Poland

Kos *or* **Cos** an island in the SE Aegean Sea, in the Greek Dodecanese Islands: separated from SW Turkey by the **Kos Channel**; settled in ancient times by Dorians and became famous for literature and medicine. Pop: 30 947 (2001). Area: 282 sq km (109 sq miles)

Kosciusko Thaddeus, Polish name *Tadeusz Kościuszko*. 1746–1817, Polish general: fought for the colonists in the American War of Independence and led an unsuccessful revolt against the partitioning of Poland (1794)

kosher *Judaism* conforming to religious law; fit for use: esp, (of food) prepared in accordance with the dietary laws

Košice a city in E Slovakia: passed from Hungary to Czechoslovakia in 1920 and to Slovakia in 1993. Pop: 236 093 (2001)

Kosovo *or* **Kosova** an autonomous province of Serbia and Montenegro, in SW Serbia: chiefly Albanian in population since the 13th century, it declared independence in 1990; Serb suppression of separatists escalated to a policy of ethnic cleansing in 1998, provoking NATO airstrikes against Serbia in 1999: now under UN administration: mainly a plateau. Capital: Priština. Pop: 2 325 000 (2001 est). Area: 10 887 sq km (4203 sq miles)

Kossoff Leon born 1926, British painter, esp of London scenes

Kossuth Lajos 1802–94, Hungarian statesman. He led the revolution against Austria (1848) and was provisional governor (1849), but he fled when the revolt was suppressed (1849)

Kostroma a city in W central Russia, on the River Volga: fought over bitterly by Novgorod, Tver, and Moscow, until annexed by Moscow in 1329; textile centre. Pop: 280 000 (2005 est)

Kostunica Vojislav born 1944, Serbian politician; president of the Federal Republic of Yugoslavia (2000–03);

prime minister of Serbia and Montenegro from 2004

Kosygin Aleksei Nikolayevich 1904–80, Soviet statesman; premier of the Soviet Union (1964–80)

Kota *or* **Kotah** a city in NW India, in Rajasthan on the Chambal River: textile industry. op.: 695 899 (2001)

Kota Bharu *or* **Bahru** a port in NE Peninsular Malaysia: capital of Kelantan state on the delta of the Kelantan River. Pop: 263 000 (2005 est)

Kota Kinabalu a port in Malaysia, capital of Sabah state on the South China Sea: exports timber and rubber. Pop: 439 000 (2005 est)

Kovrov a city in W central Russia, on the Klyazma River: textiles and heavy engineering. Pop: 155 000 (2005 est)

kowhai NZ a small leguminous tree, *Sophora tetraptera*, of New Zealand and Chile, with clusters of yellow flowers

Kowloon 1 a peninsula of SE China, opposite Hong Kong Island: part of the former British colony of Hong Kong. Area: 10 sq km (3.75 sq miles) 2 a port in Hong Kong, on Kowloon Peninsula. Pop: 2 025 800 (2001)

Kozhikode a port in SW India, in W Kerala on the Malabar coast: important European trading post (1511–1765): formerly calico-manufacturing. Pop: 436 527 (2001)

Kra Isthmus of an isthmus of SW Thailand, between the Bay of Bengal and the Gulf of Siam: the narrowest part of the Malay Peninsula. Width: about 56 km (35 miles)

kraal *South African* 1 a hut village in southern Africa, esp one surrounded by a stockade 2 denoting or relating to the tribal aspects of the Black African way of life

Krafft-Ebing Richard , Baron von Krafft-Ebing. 1840–1902, German neurologist and psychiatrist who pioneered the systematic study of sexual behaviour in *Psychopathia Sexualis* (1886)

Kragujevac a town in E central Serbia and Montenegro, in Serbia; capital of Serbia (1818–39); automobile industry. Pop: 145 890 (2002)

Krakatoa *or* **Krakatau** a volcanic island in Indonesia, in the Sunda Strait between Java and Sumatra: partially destroyed by its eruption in 1883, the greatest in recorded history. Further eruptions 44 years later formed a new island, **Anak Krakatau** ("Child of Krakatau")

kraken a legendary sea monster of gigantic size believed to dwell off the coast of Norway

Kramatorsk a city in Ukraine: a major industrial centre of the Donets Basin. Pop: 177 000 (2005 est)

krans *South African* a sheer rock face; precipice

Krasnodar an industrial city in SW Russia, on the Kuban River. Pop: 650 000 (2005 est)

Krasnoyarsk a city in E central Russia, on the Yenisei River: the country's largest hydroelectric power station is nearby. Pop: 912 000 (2005 est)

Krebs Sir Hans Adolf 1900–81, British biochemist, born in Germany, who shared a Nobel prize for physiology or medicine (1953) for the discovery of the **Krebs cycle**

Krefeld a city in Germany, in W North Rhine-Westphalia: textile industries. Pop: 238 565 (2003 est)

Kreisler Fritz 1875–1962, US violinist, born in Austria

Kremenchug an industrial city in E central Ukraine on the Dnieper River. Pop: 234 000 (2005 est)

Kremer Gidon born 1947, Latvian violinist, now based in the US

Kremlin 1 the 12th-century citadel in Moscow, containing the former Imperial Palace, three Cathedrals, and the offices of the Russian government 2 (formerly) the central government of the Soviet Union

Krems a town in NE Austria, in Lower Austria on the River Danube. Pop: 23 713 (2001)

krill any small shrimplike marine crustacean of the order *Euphausiacea*: the principal food of whalebone whales

Krishna[1] a river in S India, rising in the Western Ghats and flowing generally southeast to the Bay of Bengal. Length: 1300 km (800 miles)

Krishna[2] *Hinduism* the most celebrated of the Hindu deities, whose life story is told in the *Mahabharata*

Krishna Menon Vengalil Krishnan . See (Vengalil Krishnan Krishna) **Menon**

Kristiansand or **Christiansand** a port in S Norway, on the Skagerrak: shipbuilding. Pop: 75 280 (2004 est)

Kristiansen Ingrid born 1956, Norwegian long-distance runner: former London marathon winner: world 10 000 metres record holder (1986–93)

Kristianstad a town in S Sweden: founded in 1614 as a Danish fortress, it was finally acquired by Sweden in 1678. Pop: 75 590 (2004 est)

Krivoy Rog a city in SE Ukraine: founded in the 17th century by Cossacks; iron-mining centre; iron- and steelworks. Pop: 658 000 (2005 est)

krona the standard monetary unit of Sweden, divided into 100 öre

krone[1] 1 the standard monetary unit of Denmark, the Faeroe Islands, and Greenland, divided into 100 øre 2 the standard monetary unit of Norway, divided into 100 øre

krone[2] a former Austrian monetary unit

Kronstadt 1 a port in NW Russia, on Kotlin island in the Gulf of Finland: naval base. Pop: 44 400 (1994 est) 2 the German name for **Braşov**

Kropotkin Prince Peter, Russian name *Pyotr Alexeyevich*. 1842–1921, Russian anarchist: his books include *Mutual Aid* (1902) and *Modern Science and Anarchism* (1903)

Kruger Stephanus Johannes Paulus , known as *Oom Paul*. 1825–1904, Boer statesman; president of the Transvaal (1883–1900). His opposition to Cecil Rhodes and his denial of civil rights to the Uitlanders led to the Boer War (1899–1902)

Kruger National Park a wildlife sanctuary in NE South Africa: the world's largest game reserve. Area: over 21 700 sq km (8400 sq miles)

Krugersdorp a city in NE South Africa, on the Witwatersrand, at an altitude of 1720 m (5650 ft): a gold-, manganese-, and uranium-mining centre. Pop: 86 618 (2001)

Krupp a German family of steel and armaments manufacturers, including **Alfred**, 1812–87, his son **Friedrich Alfred**, 1854–1902, and the latter's son-in-law, **Gustav Krupp von Bohlen und Halbach**, 1870–1950

krypton an inert gaseous element occurring in trace amounts in air and used in fluorescent lights and lasers. Symbol: Kr; atomic no.: 36; atomic wt.: 83.80; valency: 0; density: 3.733 kg/m^3; melting pt.: –157.37°C; boiling pt.: –153.23±0.10°C

Kuala Lumpur a city in Malaysia, in the SW Malay Peninsula: formerly (until 1999) the capital of Malaysia; became capital of the Federated Malay States in 1895, and of Malaysia in 1963; capital of Selangor state from 1880 to 1973, when it was made a federal territory. Pop: 1 392 000 (2005 est)

Kuban a river in SW Russia, rising in the Caucasus Mountains and flowing north and northwest to the Sea of Azov. Length: 906 km (563 miles)

Kubelik Raphael 1914–96, Czech conductor and composer

Kublai Khan ?1216–94, Mongol emperor of China: grandson of Genghis Khan. He completed his grandfather's conquest of China by overthrowing the Sung dynasty (1279) and founded the Yuan dynasty (1279–1368)

Kubrick Stanley 1928–99, US film writer, director, and producer. He directed *Lolita* (1962), *Dr Strangelove* (1963), *2001: A Space Odyssey* (1968), *A Clockwork Orange* (1971), *The Shining* (1980), *Full Metal Jacket* (1987), and *Eyes Wide Shut* (1999)

Kuching a port in E Malaysia, capital of Sarawak state, on the Sarawak River 24 km (15 miles) from its mouth. Pop: 152 310 (2000)

kudu or **koodoo** either of two spiral-horned antelopes, *Tragelaphus strepsiceros* (**greater kudu**) or *T. imberbis* (**lesser kudu**), which inhabit the bush of Africa

Ku Klux Klan 1 a secret organization of White Southerners formed after the US Civil War to fight Black emancipation and Northern domination 2 a secret organization of White Protestant Americans, mainly in the South, who use violence against Blacks, Jews, and other minority groups

kulak (in Russia after 1906) a member of the class of peasants who became proprietors of their own farms. After the October Revolution the kulaks opposed collectivization of land, but in 1929 Stalin initiated their liquidation

Kumamoto a city in SW Japan, on W central Kyushu: Kumamoto Medical University (1949). Pop: 653 835 (2002 est)

Kumasi a city in S Ghana: seat of Ashanti kings since 1663; university (1961); market town for a cocoa-producing region. Pop: 862 000 (2005 est)

Kumayri a city in NW Armenia: textile centre. Pop: 144 000 (2005 est)

kumquat or **cumquat** 1 any of several small Chinese trees of the rutaceous genus *Fortunella* 2 the small round orange fruit of such a tree, with a sweet rind, used in preserves and confections

Kun Béla 1886–?1937, Hungarian Communist leader, president of the short-lived Communist republic in Hungary (1919). He was forced into exile and died in a Stalinist purge

Kundera Milan born 1929, Czech novelist living in France. His novels include *The Book of Laughter and Forgetting* (1979), *The Unbearable Lightness of Being* (1984), and *Ignorance* (2002)

kung fu any of various Chinese martial arts, some focusing on unarmed combat, others involving the use of weapons

Kunlun, Kuenlun, or **Kwenlun** a mountain range in China, between the Tibetan plateau and the Tarim

Basin, extending over 1600 km (1000 miles) east from the Pamirs: the largest mountain system of Asia. Highest peak: Ulugh Muztagh, 7723 m (25 338 ft)

Kunming *or* **K'un-ming** a city in SW China, capital of Yunnan province, near Lake Tien: important during World War II as a Chinese military centre, American air base, and transport terminus for the Burma Road; Yunnan University (1934). Pop: 1 748 000 (2005 est)

Kuopio a city in S central Finland. Pop: 88 250 (2003 est)

Kura a river in W Asia, rising in NE Turkey and flowing across Georgia and Azerbaijan to the Caspian Sea. Length: 1515 km (941 miles)

Kurdistan, Kurdestan, *or* **Kordestan** a large plateau and mountainous region, between the Caspian Sea and the Black Sea, south of the Caucasus. Area: over 29 000 sq km (74 000 sq miles)

Kure a port in SW Japan, on SW Honshu: a naval base; shipyards. Pop: 202 628 (2002 est)

Kurgan a city in W Russia, on the Tobol River: industrial centre for an agricultural region. Pop: 344 000 (2005 est)

Kurosawa Akira 1910–99, Japanese film director. His works include *Rashomon* (1950), *The Seven Samurai* (1954), *The Throne of Blood* (1957), *Kagemusha* (1980), *Ran* (1985), and *Madadayo* (1993)

kurrajong *or* **currajong** any of various Australian trees or shrubs, esp *Brachychiton populneum*, a sterculiaceous tree that yields a tough durable fibre

Kursk a city in W Russia: industrial centre of an agricultural region: scene of a major Soviet military victory (1943). Pop: 410 000 (2005 est)

Kuskokwim a river in SW Alaska, rising in the Alaska Range and flowing generally southwest to **Kuskokwim Bay** an inlet of the Bering Sea. Length: about 970 km (600 miles)

Kutaisi an industrial city in W Georgia on the Rioni River: one of the oldest towns of the Caucasus. Pop: 175 000 (2005 est)

Kutch *or* **Cutch** 1 a former state of W India, on the **Gulf of Kutch** (an inlet of the Arabian Sea): part of Gujarat state since 1960 2 **Rann of** an extensive salt waste in W central India, and S Pakistan: consists of the Great Rann in the north and the Little Rann in the southeast; seasonal alternation between marsh and desert; some saltworks. In 1968 an international tribunal awarded about 10 per cent of the border area to Pakistan. Area: 23 000 sq km (9000 sq miles)

Kutuzov Prince Mikhail Ilarionovich 1745–1813, Russian field marshal, who harried the French army under Napoleon throughout their retreat from Moscow (1812–13)

Kuwait *or* **Koweit** 1 a state on the NW coast of the Persian Gulf: came under British protection in 1899 and gained independence in 1961; invaded by Iraq in 1990; liberated by US-led UN forces 1991 in the Gulf War: mainly desert. The economy is dependent on oil. Official language: Arabic. Official religion: Muslim. Currency: dinar. Capital: Kuwait. Pop: 2 595 000 (2004 est). Area: 24 280 sq km (9375 sq miles) 2 the capital of Kuwait: a port on the Persian Gulf. Pop: 1 225 000 (2005 est)

Kuznets Simon 1901–85, US economist born in Russia.

His books include *National Income and its Composition* (1919–1938) (1941) and *Economic Growth of Nations* (1971). He was awarded the Nobel Prize for economics in 1971

Kuznetsk Basin *or* **Kuzbass** a region of S Russia, in the Kemerovo Region of W Siberia: the richest coalfield in the country, with reserves of iron ore. Chief industrial centre: Novokuznetsk. Area: about 69 900 sq km (27 000 sq miles)

Kwajalein an atoll in the W Pacific, in the W Marshall Islands, in the central part of the Ralik Chain. Length: about 125 km (78 miles)

Kwangchowan a territory of SE China, in SW Kwantung province: leased to France as part of French Indochina from 1898 to 1945. Area: 842 sq km (325 sq miles)

Kwangju a city in SW South Korea: an important military base during the Korean War; cotton textile industry. Pop: 1 448 000 (2005 est)

Kwantung Leased Territory a strategic territory of NE China, at the S tip of the Liaodong Peninsula of Manchuria: leased forcibly by Russia in 1898; taken over by Japan in 1905; occupied by the Soviet Union in 1945 and subsequently returned to China on the condition of shared administration; made part of Liaoning province by China in 1954. Area: about 3400 sq km (1300 sq miles)

Kwara a state of W Nigeria: mainly wooded savanna. Capital: Ilorin. Pop: 1 751 464 (1995 est). Area: 36 825 sq km (14 218 sq miles)

kwashiorkor severe malnutrition of infants and young children, esp soon after weaning, resulting from dietary deficiency of protein

KwaZulu/Natal a province of NE South Africa; replaced the former province of Natal in 1994: service industries. Capital: Pietermaritzburg. Pop: 9 665 875 (2004 est). Area: 92 180 sq km (35 591 sq miles)

Ky Nguyen Kao born 1930, Vietnamese military and political leader: premier of South Vietnam (1965–67); vice president (1967–71)

Kyd *or* **Kid** Thomas 1558–94, English dramatist, noted for his revenge play *The Spanish Tragedy* (1586)

kyle *Scot* (esp in place names) a narrow strait or channel

Kyoto *or* **Kioto** a city in central Japan, on S Honshu: the capital of Japan from 794 to 1868; cultural centre, with two universities (1875, 1897). Pop: 1 387 264 (2002 est)

Kyrgyzstan, Kirghizstan, *or* **Kirgizstan** a republic in central Asia: came under Russian rule in the 19th century, became a Soviet republic in 1936 and gained independence in 1991; it has deposits of minerals, oil, and gas. Official languages: Kyrgyz and Russian. Religion: nonreligious, Muslim. Currency: som. Capital: Bishkek. Pop: 5 208 000 (2004 est). Area: 198 500 sq km (76 460 sq miles)

Kyrgyz Steppe a vast steppe region in central Kazakhstan

Kyushu *or* **Kiushu** an island of SW Japan: the southernmost of Japan's four main islands, with over 300 surrounding small islands; coalfield and chemical industries. Chief cities: Fukuoka, Kitakyushu, and Nagasaki. Pop: 14 786 000 (2002 est). Area: 35 659 sq km (13 768 sq miles)

Kyzyl Kum a desert in Kazakhstan and Uzbekistan

Ll

Laban *Old Testament* the father-in-law of Jacob, father of Leah and Rachel (Genesis 29:16)

label 1 *Computing* a group of characters, such as a number or a word, appended to a particular statement in a program to allow its unique identification 2 *Chem* a radioactive element used in a compound to trace the mechanism of a chemical reaction

labial 1 of, relating to, or near lips or labia 2 *Music* producing sounds by the action of an air stream over a narrow liplike fissure, as in a flue pipe of an organ 3 *Music* an organ pipe with a liplike fissure

labiate any plant of the family *Lamiaceae* (formerly *Labiatae*), having square stems, aromatic leaves, and a two-lipped corolla: includes mint, thyme, sage, rosemary, etc.

Labiche *Eugène Marin* 1815–88, French dramatist, noted for his farces of middle-class life, which include *Le Chapeau de paille d'Italie* (1851) and *Le Voyage de Monsieur Perrichon* (1860)

labium 1 a lip or liplike structure 2 any one of the four lip-shaped folds of the female vulva 3 the fused pair of appendages forming the lower lip of insects 4 the lower lip of the corolla of labiate flowers

Labor Party one of the chief political parties of Australia, generally supporting the interests of organized labour

Labour Party 1 a British political party, formed in 1900 as an amalgam of various trade unions and socialist groups, generally supporting the interests of organized labour and advocating democratic socialism and social equality 2 any similar party in any of various other countries

Labrador 1 a large peninsula of NE Canada, on the Atlantic, the Gulf of St. Lawrence, Hudson Strait, and Hudson Bay: contains most of Quebec and the mainland part of the province of Newfoundland and Labrador; geologically part of the Canadian Shield. Area: 1 619 000 sq km (625 000 sq miles) 2 a region of NE Canada, on the Atlantic and consisting of the mainland part of Newfoundland and Labrador province

Labuan an island in Malaysia, off the NW coast of Borneo: part of the Straits Settlements until 1946, when transferred to North Borneo. Chief town: Victoria (or Labuan). Area: 98 sq km (38 sq miles)

laburnum any leguminous tree or shrub of the Eurasian genus *Laburnum*, having clusters of yellow drooping flowers: all parts of the plant are poisonous

labyrinth 1 any system of interconnecting cavities, esp those comprising the internal ear 2 *Electronics* an enclosure behind a high-performance loudspeaker, consisting of a series of air chambers designed to absorb unwanted sound waves

lac a resinous substance secreted by certain lac insects, used in the manufacture of shellac

Lacan *Jacques* 1901–81, French psychoanalyst, who reinterpreted Freud in terms of structural linguistics: an important influence on poststructuralist thought

lace 1 a delicate decorative fabric made from cotton, silk, etc, woven in an open web of different symmetrical patterns and figures 2 a dash of spirits added to a beverage
▷ www.legacyoflace.com
▷ www.laceguild.demon.co.uk

Lachlan a river in SE Australia, rising in central New South Wales and flowing northwest then southwest to the Murrumbidgee River. Length: about 1450 km (900 miles)

Laclos *Pierre Choderlos de* 1741–1803, French soldier and writer, noted for his novel in epistolary form *Les Liaisons dangereuses* (1782)

Laconia an ancient country of S Greece, in the SE Peloponnese, of which Sparta was the capital: corresponds to the present-day department of Lakonia

lacquer 1 a hard glossy coating made by dissolving cellulose derivatives or natural resins in a volatile solvent 2 a black resinous substance, obtained from certain trees, used to give a hard glossy finish to wooden furniture 3 **lacquer tree** an E Asian anacardiaceous tree, *Rhus verniciflua*, whose stem yields a toxic exudation from which black lacquer is obtained 4 *Art* decorative objects coated with such lacquer, often inlaid

lacrimal, lachrymal, *or* **lacrymal** of or relating to tears or to the glands that secrete tears

lacrosse a ball game invented by American Indians, now played by two teams who try to propel a ball into each other's goal by means of long-handled hooked sticks that are loosely strung with a kind of netted pouch
▷ www.lacrosse.ca

lactate an ester or salt of lactic acid

lactation 1 the secretion of milk from the mammary glands after parturition 2 the period during which milk is secreted

lacteal 1 (of lymphatic vessels) conveying or containing chyle 2 any of the lymphatic vessels conveying chyle from the small intestine to the thoracic duct

lactic acid a colourless syrupy carboxylic acid found in sour milk and many fruits and used as a preservative (**E270**) for foodstuffs, such as soft margarine, and for making pharmaceuticals and adhesives. Formula: $CH_3CH(OH)COOH$

lactose a white crystalline disaccharide occurring in milk and used in the manufacture of pharmaceuticals and baby foods. Formula: $C_{12}H_{22}O_{11}$

lacuna 1 *Biology* a cavity or depression, such as any of the spaces in the matrix of bone 2 another name for **coffer**

lad *Brit* a boy or man who looks after horses

lade *Scot* a watercourse, esp a millstream

Ladislaus I or **Ladislas** Saint 1040–95, king of Hungary (1077–95). He extended his country's boundaries and suppressed paganism. Feast day: June 27

ladle a large bucket-shaped container for transferring molten metal

Ladoga Lake a lake in NW Russia, in the SW Karelian Republic: the largest lake in Europe; drains through the River Neva into the Gulf of Finland. Area: about 18 000 sq km (7000 sq miles)

lady *History* a woman with proprietary rights and authority, as over a manor

Lady 1 (in Britain) a title of honour borne by various classes of women of the peerage 2 **Our Lady** a title of the Virgin Mary

ladybird any of various small brightly coloured beetles of the family *Coccinellidae*, such as *Adalia bipunctata* (**two-spotted ladybird**), which has red elytra marked with black spots

Lady Day March 25, the feast of the Annunciation of the Virgin Mary; one of the four quarter days in England, Wales and Ireland

Ladysmith a city in E South Africa: besieged by Boers for four months (1899–1900) during the Boer War. Pop: 41 427 (2001)

lady's-slipper any of various orchids of the Eurasian genus *Cypripedium*, esp *C. calceolus*, having reddish or purple flowers

Lafayette or **La Fayette** 1 Marie Joseph Paul Yves Roch Gilbert du Motier, Marquis de Lafayette. 1757–1834, French general and statesman. He fought on the side of the colonists in the War of American Independence and, as commander of the National Guard (1789–91; 1830), he played a leading part in the French Revolution and the revolution of 1830 2 **Marie-Madeleine**, Comtesse de Lafayette. 1634–93, French novelist, noted for her historical romance *La Princesse de Clèves* (1678)

La Fontaine Jean de 1621–95, French poet, famous for his *Fables* (1668–94)

Laforgue Jules 1860–87, French symbolist poet. An originator of free verse, he had a considerable influence on modern poetry

lager a light-bodied effervescent beer, fermented in a closed vessel using yeasts that sink to the bottom of the brew

Lagerfeld Karl (Otto). born 1938, German fashion designer working mainly in Paris

Lagerkvist Pär (Fabian). 1891–1974, Swedish novelist and dramatist. His works include the novels *The Dwarf* (1944) and *Barabbas* (1950): Nobel prize for literature 1951

lagoon 1 a body of water cut off from the open sea by coral reefs or sand bars 2 any small body of water, esp one adjoining a larger one

Lagos 1 the former capital and chief port of Nigeria, on the Bight of Benin: first settled in the sixteenth century; a slave market until the nineteenth century; ceded to Britain (1861); university (1962). Pop: 11 135 000 (2005 est) 2 a state of SW Nigeria. Capital: Ikeja. Pop: 6 357 253 (1995 est). Area: 3345 sq km (1292 sq miles)

Lagrange Comte Joseph Louis 1736–1813, French mathematician and astronomer, noted particularly for his work on harmonics, mechanics, and the calculus of variations

La Guaira or **La Guayra** the chief seaport of Venezuela, on the Caribbean. Pop: 26 669 (1990 est)

La Guardia Fiorello H(enry). 1882–1947, US politician. As mayor of New York (1933–45), he organized slum-clearance and labour safeguard schemes and suppressed racketeering

lah *Music* (in tonic sol-fa) the sixth note of any major scale; submediant

Lahore 1 a city in NE Pakistan: capital of the former province of West Pakistan (1955–70); University of the Punjab (1882). Pop: 6 373 000 (2005 est) 2 a variety of large domestic fancy pigeon having a black-and-white plumage

Lahti a town in S Finland: site of the main Finnish radio and television stations; furniture industry. Pop: 98 253 (2003 est)

Laing R(onald) D(avid). 1927–89, Scottish psychiatrist; his best known books include *The Divided Self* (1960), *The Politics of Experience and the Bird of Paradise* (1967), and *Knots* (1970)

lair the resting place of a wild animal

laissez faire or **laisser faire** a the doctrine of unrestricted freedom in commerce, esp for private interests b (*as modifier*): *a laissez-faire economy*

laity laymen, as distinguished from clergymen

lake an expanse of water entirely surrounded by land and unconnected to the sea except by rivers or streams

Lake District a region of lakes and mountains in NW England, in Cumbria: includes England's largest lake (Windermere) and highest mountain (Scafell Pike); national park; literary associations (the Lake Poets); tourist region

Lakeland another name for the **Lake District**

Lake of the Woods a lake in N central North America, mostly in W Northern Ontario, Canada: fed chiefly by the Rainy River; drains into Lake Winnipeg by the Winnipeg River; many islands; tourist region. Area: 3846 sq km (1485 sq miles)

Lake Success a village in SE New York State, on W Long Island: headquarters of the United Nations Security Council from 1946 to 1951. Pop: 2832 (2003 est)

lakh or **lac** (in India and Pakistan) the number 100 000, esp when referring to this sum of rupees

Lalique René (Jules). 1860–1945, French Art- Nouveau jeweller, glass-maker, and designer: noted esp for his frosted glassware

Lallans *or* **Lallan** a literary version of the variety of English spoken and written in the Lowlands of Scotland

Lalo (Victor-Antoine-)Édouard 1823–92, French composer of Spanish descent. His works include the *Symphonie espagnole* (1873) and the ballet *Namouna* (1882)

lama a priest or monk of Lamaism

La Mancha a plateau of central Spain, between the mountains of Toledo and the hills of Cuenca: traditionally associated with episodes in *Don Quixote*. Average height: 600 m (2000 ft)

Lamarck Jean Baptiste Pierre Antoine de Monet, Chevalier de Lamarck. 1744–1829, French naturalist. He outlined his theory of organic evolution (Lamarckism) in *Philosophie zoologique* (1809)

Lamartine Alphonse Marie Louis de Prat de 1790–1869, French romantic poet, historian, and statesman: his works include *Méditations poétiques* (1820) and *Histoire des Girondins* (1847)

lamb the young of a sheep

Lamb¹ 1 Charles, pen name *Elia*. 1775–1834, English essayist and critic. He collaborated with his sister Mary on *Tales from Shakespeare* (1807). His other works include *Specimens of English Dramatic Poets* (1808) and the largely autobiographical essays collected in *Essays of Elia* (1823; 1833) 2 Willis Eugene born 1913, US physicist. He detected the small difference in energy between two states of the hydrogen atom (**Lamb shift**). Nobel prize for physics 1955

Lamb² the a title given to Christ in the New Testament

Lambert Constant 1905–51, English composer and conductor. His works include much ballet music and *The Rio Grande* (1929), a work for chorus, orchestra, and piano, using jazz idioms

Lambeth 1 a borough of S Greater London, on the Thames: contains **Lambeth Palace** (the London residence of the Archbishop of Canterbury). Pop: 268 500 (2003 est). Area: 27 sq km (11 sq miles) 2 the Archbishop of Canterbury in his official capacity

Lamb of God a title given to Christ in the New Testament, probably with reference to his sacrificial death

lambskin 1 the skin of a lamb, esp with the wool still on 2 a cotton or woollen fabric resembling this skin

lame disabled or crippled in the legs or feet

lame duck 1 *Business* a company with a large workforce and high prestige that is unable to meet foreign competition without government support 2 *US* a an elected official or body of officials remaining in office in the interval between the election and inauguration of a successor b *(as modifier): a lame-duck president* 3 *US* designating a term of office after which the officeholder will not run for re-election

lament a poem or song in which a death is lamented

lamina 1 a thin plate or layer, esp of bone or mineral 2 *Botany* the flat blade of a leaf, petal, or thallus

laminate a material made by bonding together two or more sheets

Lammas 1 *RC Church* Aug 1, held as a feast, commemorating St. Peter's miraculous deliverance from prison 2 the same day formerly observed in England as a harvest festival. In Scotland Lammas is a quarter day

lampblack a finely divided form of almost pure carbon produced by the incomplete combustion of organic compounds, such as natural gas, used in making carbon electrodes and dynamo brushes and as a pigment

Lampedusa¹ Giuseppe Tomasi di 1896–1957, Italian novelist: author of the historical novel *The Leopard* (1958)

Lampedusa² an island in the Mediterranean, between Malta and Tunisia. Area: about 21 sq km (8 sq miles)

lampoon a satire in prose or verse ridiculing a person, literary work, etc.

lamprey any eel-like cyclostome vertebrate of the family *Petromyzonidae*, having a round sucking mouth for clinging to and feeding on the blood of other animals

Lanai an island in central Hawaii, west of Maui Island. Pop: 3193 (2000). Area: 363 sq km. (140 sq miles)

Lanarkshire a historical county of S Scotland: became part of Strathclyde region in 1975; since 1996 administered by the council areas of North Lanarkshire, South Lanarkshire, and Glasgow

Lancashire a county of NW England, on the Irish Sea: became a county palatine in 1351 and a duchy attached to the Crown; much reduced in size after the 1974 boundary changes, losing the Furness district to Cumbria and much of the south to Greater Manchester, Merseyside, and Cheshire: Blackburn with Darwen and Blackpool became independent unitary authorities in 1998. It was traditionally a cotton textiles manufacturing region. Administrative centre: Preston. Pop. (excluding unitary authorities): 1 147 000 (2003 est). Area (excluding unitary authorities): 2889 sq km (1115 sq miles)

Lancaster a city in NW England, former county town of Lancashire, on the River Lune: castle (built on the site of a Roman camp); university (1964). Pop: 45 952 (2001)

Lancastrian 1 a native or resident of Lancashire or Lancaster 2 an adherent of the house of Lancaster in the Wars of the Roses

lance *Surgery* another name for **lancet**

lanceolate narrow and tapering to a point at each end

lancet 1 a pointed surgical knife with two sharp edges 2 short for **lancet arch** *or* **lancet window**

lancet arch a narrow acutely pointed arch having two centres of equal radii

lancet window a narrow window having a lancet arch

lancewood 1 any of various tropical trees, esp *Oxandra lanceolata*, yielding a tough elastic wood: family *Annonaceae* 2 a New Zealand forest tree, *Pseudopanax crassifolius*, with a small round head and a slender trunk 3 the wood of any of these trees

land 1 the solid part of the surface of the earth as distinct from seas, lakes, etc. 2 ground, esp with reference to its use, quality, etc. 3 *Law* a any tract of ground capable of being owned as property, together with any buildings on it, extending above and below the surface b any hereditament, tenement, or other interest; realty 4 a a country, region, or area b the people of a country, etc. 5 *Economics* the factor of production consisting of all natural resources

Land Edwin Herbert 1909–91, US inventor of the Polaroid Land camera

Landau Lev Davidovich 1908–68, Soviet physicist, noted for his researches on quantum theory and his work on the theories of solids and liquids: Nobel prize for physics 1962

Landes 1 a department of SW France, in Aquitaine region. Capital: Mont-de-Marsan. Pop: 341 254 (2003 est). Area: 9364 sq km (3652 sq miles) 2 a region of SW France, on the Bay of Biscay: occupies most of the Landes department and parts of Gironde and Lot-et-Garonne; consists chiefly of the most extensive forest in France. Area: 14 000 sq km (5400 sq miles)

landfall 1 the act of sighting or nearing land, esp from the sea 2 the land sighted or neared

landfill a disposal of waste material by burying it under layers of earth b (*as modifier*): *landfill sites*

landing the floor area at the top of a flight of stairs or between two flights of stairs

landing field an area of land on which aircraft land and from which they take off

landlocked 1 (of a country) completely surrounded by land 2 (esp of lakes) completely or almost completely surrounded by land 3 (esp of certain salmon) living in fresh water that is permanently isolated from the sea

landlubber *Nautical* any person having no experience at sea

landmass a large continuous area of land, as opposed to seas or islands

land of milk and honey *Old Testament* the land of natural fertility promised to the Israelites by God (Ezekiel 20:6)

land of Nod *Old Testament* a region to the east of Eden to which Cain went after he had killed Abel (Genesis 4:14)

Landor Walter Savage 1775–1864, English poet, noted also for his prose works, including *Imaginary Conversations* (1824–29)

Landowska Wanda 1877–1959, US harpsichordist, born in Poland

landscape 1 an extensive area of land regarded as being visually distinct 2 a painting, drawing, photograph, etc, depicting natural scenery 3 a the genre including such pictures b (*as modifier*): *landscape painter*

landscape gardening the art of laying out grounds in imitation of natural scenery

  ▷www.landscaping.about.com
  ▷http://panther.bsc.edu/~jtatter/glossary.html
  ▷www.thegardenhelper.com/
  gardeningguides.html

Landseer Sir Edwin Henry 1802–73, English painter, noted for his studies of animals

Landshut a city in SE Germany, in Bavaria: Trausnitz castle (13th century); manufacturing centre for machinery and chemicals. Pop: 60 282 (2003 est)

landside 1 the part of an airport farthest from the aircraft, the boundary of which is the security check, customs, passport control, etc. 2 the part of a plough that slides along the face of the furrow wall on the opposite side to the mouldboard

landslide 1 a the sliding of a large mass of rock material, soil, etc, down the side of a mountain or cliff b the material dislodged in this way 2 a an overwhelming electoral victory b (*as modifier*): *a landslide win*

Landsteiner Karl 1868–1943, Austrian immunologist, who discovered (1900) human blood groups and introduced the ABO classification system. He also discovered (1940) the Rhesus (Rh) factor in blood and researched into poliomyelitis. Nobel prize for physiology or medicine (1930)

lane 1 a narrow road or way between buildings, hedges, fences, etc. 2 a any of the parallel strips into which the carriageway of a major road or motorway is divided b any narrow well-defined route or course for ships or aircraft 3 the long strip of wooden flooring down which balls are bowled in a bowling alley

Lanfranc ?1005–89, Italian ecclesiastic and scholar; archbishop of Canterbury (1070–89) and adviser to William the Conqueror. He instituted many reforms in the English Church

Lang 1 Cosmo Gordon, 1st Baron Lang of Lambeth. 1864–1945, British churchman; archbishop of Canterbury (1928–42) 2 Fritz 1890–1976, Austrian film director, later in the US, most notable for his silent films, such as *Metropolis* (1926), *M* (1931), and *The Testament of Dr. Mabuse* (1932) 3 Jack (John Thomas). 1876–1975, controversial Labor premier of New South Wales from 1925–27 and from 1930–32, who introduced much social welfare legislation and was dismissed by the governor, Sir Philip Game, in 1932 for acting unconstitutionally

Lange David (Russell). born 1942, New Zealand statesman: leader of the Labour Party from 1983: prime minister (1984–89)

Langland William ?1332–?1400, English poet. The allegorical religious poem in alliterative verse, *The Vision of William concerning Piers the Plowman*, is attributed to him

Langley Samuel Pierpont 1834–1906, US astronomer and physicist: invented the bolometer (1878) and pioneered the construction of heavier-than-air flying machines

Langmuir Irving 1881–1957, US chemist. He developed the gas-filled tungsten lamp and the atomic hydrogen welding process: Nobel prize for chemistry 1932

Langres Plateau a calcareous plateau of E France north of Dijon between the Seine and the Saône, reaching over 580 m (1900 ft): forms a watershed between rivers flowing to the Mediterranean and to the English Channel

Langton Stephen ?1150–1228, English cardinal; archbishop of Canterbury (1213–28). He was consecrated archbishop by Pope Innocent III in 1207 but was kept out of his see by King John until 1213. He was partly responsible for the Magna Carta (1215)

Langtry Lillie, known as *the Jersey Lily*, real name Émilie Charlotte le Breton. 1852–1929, English actress, noted for her beauty and for her friendship with Edward VII

Languedoc 1 a former province of S France, lying between the foothills of the Pyrenees and the River Rhône: formed around the countship of Toulouse in the 13th century; important production of bulk wines 2 a wine from this region

Languedoc-Roussillon a region of S France, on the Gulf of Lions: consists of the departments of Lozère, Gard, Hérault, Aude, and Pyrénées-Orientales; mainly mountainous with a coastal plain

Lankester Sir Edwin Ray 1847–1929, English zoologist, noted particularly for his work in embryology and study of protozoans

lanolin *or* **lanoline** a yellowish viscous substance extracted from wool, consisting of a mixture of esters of fatty acids: used in some ointments

Lansbury George 1859–1940, British Labour politician, who led the Labour Party in opposition (1931–35). A committed pacifist, he resigned over the party's reaction to Mussolini's seizure of Ethiopia

Lansing a city in S Michigan, on the Grand River: the state capital. Pop: 118 379 (2003 est)

lantana any verbenaceous shrub or herbaceous plant of the tropical American genus *Lantana*, esp *L. camara*, having spikes or umbels of yellow or orange flowers. It has been widely introduced and is regarded as a troublesome weed in some places

lantern jaw a long hollow jaw that gives the face a drawn appearance

lanthanum a silvery-white ductile metallic element of the lanthanide series, occurring principally in bastnaesite and monazite: used in pyrophoric alloys, electronic devices, and in glass manufacture. Symbol: La; atomic no.: 57; atomic wt.: 138.9055; valency: 3; relative density: 6.145; melting pt.: 918°C; boiling pt.: 3464°C

lanyard *or* **laniard** *Nautical* a line rove through deadeyes for extending or tightening standing rigging

Lanzarote the most easterly of the Canary Islands; mountainous, with a volcanic landscape; tourism, fishing. Pop: 109 942 (2002 est). Area: 795 sq km (307 sq miles)

Lanzhou, Lanchow, *or* **Lan-chou** a city in N China, capital of Gansu province, on the Yellow River: situated on the main route between the West and China. op.: 1 788 000 (2005 est)

Laoag a city in the N Philippines, on NW Luzon: trade centre for an agricultural region. Pop: 94 466 (2000)

Laodicea the ancient name of several Greek cities in W Asia, notably of **Latakia**

Laois a county of central Republic of Ireland, in Leinster province: formerly boggy but largely reclaimed for agriculture. County town: Portlaoise. Pop: 58 774 (2002). Area: 1719 sq km (664 sq miles)

Laos a republic in SE Asia: first united as the kingdom of Lan Xang ("million elephants") in 1353, after being a province of the Khmer Empire for about four centuries; made part of French Indochina in 1893 and gained independence in 1949; became a republic in 1975. It is generally forested and mountainous, with the Mekong River running almost the whole length of the W border. Official language: Laotian. Religion: Buddhist majority, tribal religions. Currency: kip. Capital: Vientiane. Pop: 5 787 000 (2004 est). Area: 236 800 sq km (91 429 sq miles)

Lao Zi *or* **Lao-tzu** ?604–?531 BC, Chinese philosopher, traditionally regarded as the founder of Taoism and the author of the *Tao-te Ching*

lap[1] the area formed by the upper surface of the thighs of a seated person

lap[2] 1 a rotating disc coated with fine abrasive for polishing gemstones 2 any device for holding a fine abrasive to polish materials 3 *Metallurgy* a defect in rolled metals caused by the folding of a fin onto the surface 4 a sheet or band of fibres, such as cotton, prepared for further processing

La Palma an island in the N Atlantic, in the NW Canary Islands: administratively part of Spain. Chief town: Santa Cruz de la Palma. Pop: 85 547 (2002 est). Area: 725 sq km (280 sq miles)

La Paz a city in W Bolivia, at an altitude of 3600 m (12 000 ft): seat of government since 1898 (though Sucre is still the official capital); the country's largest city; founded in 1548 by the Spaniards; university (1830). Pop: 1 533 000 (2005 est)

lapdog a pet dog small and docile enough to be cuddled in the lap

lapis lazuli *or* **lazuli** 1 a brilliant blue variety of the mineral lazurite, used as a gemstone 2 the deep blue colour of lapis lazuli

Laplace Pierre Simon , Marquis de Laplace. 1749–1827, French mathematician, physicist, and astronomer. He formulated the nebular hypothesis (1796). He also developed the theory of probability

Lapland an extensive region of N Europe, mainly within the Arctic Circle: consists of the N parts of Norway, Sweden, Finland, and the Kola Peninsula of the extreme NW of Russia

La Plata 1 a port in E Argentina, near the Río de la Plata estuary: founded in 1882 and modelled on Washington DC; university (1897). Pop: 758 000 (2005 est) 2 See (Río de la) **Plata**

Lapp 1 a member of a nomadic people living chiefly in N Scandinavia and the Kola Peninsula of Russia 2 the language of this people, belonging to the Finno-Ugric family

lappet *Zoology* a lobelike hanging structure, such as the wattle on a bird's head

lapse *Law* the termination of some right, interest, or privilege, as by neglecting to exercise it or through failure of some contingency

Laptev Sea a shallow arm of the Arctic Ocean, along the N coast of Russia between the Taimyr Peninsula and the New Siberian Islands

laptop *or* **laptop computer** a personal computer that is small and light enough to be operated on the user's lap

lapwing any of several plovers of the genus *Vanellus*, esp *V. vanellus*, typically having a crested head, wattles, and spurs

Lara Brian Charles born 1970, Trinidadian cricketer: holder of records for highest individual score in first-class cricket and for highest Test innings score

larch 1 any coniferous tree of the genus *Larix*, having deciduous needle-like leaves and egg-shaped cones: family *Pinaceae* 2 the wood of any of these trees

Lardner Ring(old Wilmer). 1885–1933, US short-story writer and journalist, whose best-known works are collected in *How to Write Short Stories* (1924) and *The Love Nest* (1926)

Laredo a city in the US, in Texas, on the Mexican border: founded by the Spanish in 1755 on the Rio Grande. Pop: 197 488 (2003 est)

large *Nautical* (of the wind) blowing from a favourable direction

large intestine the part of the alimentary canal consisting of the caecum, colon, and rectum. It extracts moisture from food residues, which are later excreted as faeces

largo *Music* 1 to be performed slowly and broadly 2 a piece or passage to be performed in this way

Larisa *or* **Larissa** a city in E Greece, in E Thessaly: fortified by Justinian; annexed to Greece in 1881. Pop: 130 000 (2005 est). Area: 336 sq km (130 sq miles)

lark 1 any brown songbird of the predominantly Old World family *Alaudidae*, esp the skylark: noted for their singing 2 any of various slender but powerful fancy pigeons, such as the **Coburg Lark**

Larkin Philip 1922–85, English poet: his verse collections include *The Less Deceived* (1955) and *The Whitsun Weddings* (1964)

larkspur any of various ranunculaceous plants of the genus *Delphinium*, with spikes of blue, pink, or white irregular spurred flowers

Larne a district of NE Northern Ireland, in Co. Antrim. Pop: 30 948 (2003 est). Area: 336 sq km (130 sq miles)

La Rochefoucauld François , Duc de La Rochefoucauld. 1613–80, French writer. His best-known work is *Réflexions ou sentences et maximes morales* (1665), a collection of epigrammatic and cynical observations on human nature

La Rochelle a port in W France, on the Bay of Biscay: a Huguenot stronghold until its submission through famine to Richelieu's forces after a long siege (1627–28). Pop: 76 584 (1999)

Larousse Pierre Athanase 1817–75, French grammarian, lexicographer, and encyclopedist. He edited and helped to compile the *Grand Dictionnaire universel du XIX siècle* (1866–76)

larva an immature free-living form of many animals that develops into a different adult form by metamorphosis

laryngeal *or* **laryngal** of or relating to the larynx

laryngitis inflammation of the larynx

larynx a cartilaginous and muscular hollow organ forming part of the air passage to the lungs: in higher vertebrates it contains the vocal cords

La Salle¹ Sieur Robert Cavelier de 1643–87, French explorer and fur trader in North America; founder of Louisiana (1682)

La Salle² a city in SE Canada, in Quebec: a S suburb of Montreal. Pop: 73 804 (1991)

La Scala the chief opera house in Italy, in Milan (opened 1776)

Lascaux the site of a cave in SW France, in the Dordogne: contains Palaeolithic wall drawings and paintings

Lasdun Sir Denys 1914–2001, British architect. He is best known for the University of East Anglia (1968) and the National Theatre in London (1976)

laser 1 a source of high-intensity optical, infrared, or ultraviolet radiation produced as a result of stimulated emission maintained within a solid, liquid, or gaseous medium. The photons involved in the emission process all have the same energy and phase so that the laser beam is monochromatic and coherent, allowing it to be brought to a fine focus 2 any similar source producing a beam of any electromagnetic radiation, such as infrared or microwave radiation

laser printer a quiet high-quality computer printer

that uses a laser beam shining on a photoconductive drum to produce characters, which are then transferred to paper

Lashio a town in NE central Myanmar: starting point of the Burma Road to Chongqing, China

Lashkar a former city in N India, in Madhya Pradesh: capital of the former states of Gwalior and Madhya Bharat; now part of the city of Gwalior

Lasker Emanuel 1868–1941, German chess player: world champion (1894– 1921)

Laski Harold (Joseph). 1893–1950, English political scientist and socialist leader

Las Palmas a port in the central Canary Islands, on NE Grand Canary: a major fuelling port on the main shipping route between Europe and South America. Pop: 377 600 (2003 est)

La Spezia a port in NW Italy, in Liguria, on the **Gulf of Spezia**: the chief naval base in Italy. Pop: 91 391 (2001)

Lassa fever a serious viral disease of Central West Africa, characterized by high fever and muscular pains

Lassalle Ferdinand 1825–64, German socialist and writer: a founder of the first German workers' political party (1863), which later became the Social Democratic Party

Lassen Peak a volcano in S California, in the S Cascade Range. An area of 416 sq km (161 sq miles) was established as **Lassen Volcanic National Park** in 1916. Height: 3187 m (10 457 ft)

Lassus Roland de Italian name *Orlando di Lasso*. ?1532–94, Flemish composer, noted for his mastery in both sacred and secular music

last¹ the wooden or metal form on which a shoe or boot is fashioned or repaired

last² a unit of weight or capacity having various values in different places and for different commodities. Commonly used values are 2 tons, 2000 pounds, 80 bushels, or 640 gallons

lasting a strong durable closely woven fabric used for shoe uppers, etc.

Last Judgment the the occasion, after the resurrection of the dead at the end of the world, when, according to biblical tradition, God will decree the final destinies of all men according to the good and evil in their earthly lives

Last Supper the the meal eaten by Christ with his disciples on the night before his Crucifixion, during which he is believed to have instituted the Eucharist

Las Vegas a city in SE Nevada: famous for luxury hotels and casinos. Pop: 517 017 (2003 est)

Latakia *or* **Lattakia** the chief port of Syria, in the northwest: tobacco industry. Pop: 486 000 (2005 est)

latch 1 a fastening for a gate or door that consists of a bar that may be slid or lowered into a groove, hole, etc. 2 a spring-loaded door lock that can be opened by a key from outside 3 *Electronics* a logic circuit that transfers the input states to the output states when signalled, the output thereafter remaining insensitive to changes in input status until signalled again

lateen *Nautical* denoting a rig with a triangular sail (**lateen sail**) bent to a yard hoisted to the head of a low mast, used esp in the Mediterranean

Late Greek the Greek language from about the 3rd to

the 8th centuries AD

Late Latin the form of written Latin used from the 3rd to the 7th centuries AD

latent 1 (of buds, spores, etc) dormant **2** *Pathol* (esp of an infectious disease) not yet revealed or manifest **3** (of a virus) inactive in the host cell, its nucleic acid being integrated into, and replicated with, the host cell's DNA **4** *Psychoanal* relating to that part of a dream expressive of repressed desires

lateral thinking a way of solving problems by rejecting traditional methods and employing unorthodox and apparently illogical means

latex 1 a whitish milky fluid containing protein, starch, alkaloids, etc, that is produced by many plants. Latex from the rubber tree is used in the manufacture of rubber **2** a suspension of synthetic rubber or plastic in water, used in the manufacture of synthetic rubber products, etc.

lathe¹ a machine for shaping, boring, facing, or cutting a screw thread in metal, wood, etc, in which the workpiece is turned about a horizontal axis against a fixed tool

lathe² *Brit, History* any of the former administrative divisions of Kent

Latimer Hugh ?1485–1555, English Protestant bishop: burnt at the stake for refusing to disavow his Protestant beliefs when Mary I assumed the throne

Latin 1 the language of ancient Rome and the Roman Empire and of the educated in medieval Europe, which achieved its classical form during the 1st century BC. Having originally been the language of Latium, belonging to the Italic branch of the Indo-European family, it later formed the basis of the Romance group **2** a member of any of those peoples whose languages are derived from Latin **3** an inhabitant of ancient Latium **4** of or relating to the Latin language, the ancient Latins, or Latium **5** characteristic of or relating to those peoples in Europe and Latin America whose languages are derived from Latin **6** of or relating to the Roman Catholic Church

Latina a city in W central Italy, in Lazio: built as a planned town in 1932 on reclaimed land of the Pontine Marshes. Pop: 107 898 (2001)

Latin America those areas of America whose official languages are Spanish and Portuguese, derived from Latin: South America, Central America, Mexico, and certain islands in the Caribbean

Latin Quarter an area of Paris, on the S bank of the River Seine: contains the city's main educational establishments; centre for students and artists

latitude 1 a an angular distance in degrees north or south of the equator (latitude 0°), equal to the angle subtended at the centre of the globe by the meridian between the equator and the point in question **b** a region considered with regard to its distance from the equator **2** *Photog* the range of exposure over which a photographic emulsion gives an acceptable negative

latitudinarian of or relating to a school of thought within the Church of England in the 17th century that minimized the importance of divine authority in matters of doctrine and stressed the importance of reason and personal judgment

Latium an ancient territory in W central Italy, in modern Lazio, on the Tyrrhenian Sea: inhabited by the Latin people from the 10th century BC until dominated by Rome (4th century BC)

Latour Maurice Quentin de 1704–88, French pastelist noted for the vivacity of his portraits

La Tour Georges de ?1593–1652, French painter, esp of candlelit religious scenes

lattice 1 an open framework of strips of wood, metal, etc, arranged to form an ornamental pattern **2 a** a gate, screen, etc, formed of such a framework **b** (*as modifier*): *a lattice window* **3** something, such as a decorative or heraldic device, resembling such a framework **4** an array of objects or points in a periodic pattern in two or three dimensions, esp an array of atoms, ions, etc, in a crystal or an array of points indicating their positions in space

Latvia a republic in NE Europe, on the Gulf of Riga and the Baltic Sea: ruled by Poland, Sweden, and Russia since the 13th century, Latvia was independent from 1919 until 1940 and was a Soviet republic (1940–91), gaining its independence after conflict with Soviet forces; it joined the EU in 2004. Latvia is mostly forested. Official language: Latvian. Religion: nonreligious, Christian. Currency: lats. Capital: Riga. Pop: 2 286 000 (2004 est). Area: 63 700 sq km (25 590 sq miles)

Latvian the official language of Latvia: closely related to Lithuanian and belonging to the Baltic branch of the Indo-European family

Laud William 1573–1645, English prelate; archbishop of Canterbury (1633–45). His persecution of Puritans and his High Church policies in England and Scotland were a cause of the Civil War; he was impeached by the Long Parliament (1640) and executed

laudanum 1 a tincture of opium **2** (formerly) any medicine of which opium was the main ingredient

Lauder Sir Harry real name *Hugh MacLennan*. 1870–1950, Scottish ballad singer and music-hall comedian

Laue Max Theodor Felix von 1879–1960, German physicist. He pioneered the technique of measuring the wavelengths of X-rays by their diffraction by crystals and contributed to the theory of relativity: Nobel prize for physics 1914

Laughton Charles 1899–1962, US actor, born in England: noted esp for his films of the 1930s, such as *The Private Life of Henry VIII* (1933), for which he won an Oscar, and *Mutiny on the Bounty* (1935)

Launceston a city in Australia, the chief port of the island state of Tasmania on the Tamar River, 64 km (40 miles) from Bass Strait. Pop: 68 443 (2001)

launch 1 a motor driven boat used chiefly as a transport boat **2** the largest of the boats of a man-of-war

Laurasia one of the two ancient supercontinents produced by the first split of the even larger supercontinent Pangaea about 200 million years ago, comprising what are now North America, Greenland, Europe, and Asia (excluding India)

laureate *Archaic* made of laurel

laurel 1 any lauraceous tree of the genus *Laurus*, such as the bay tree (see **bay⁴**) and *L. canariensis*, of the Canary Islands and Azores **2** any lauraceous plant **3** spurge laurel a European thymelaeaceous evergreen shrub,

Daphne laureola, with glossy leaves and small green flowers **4 spotted** or **Japan laurel** an evergreen coriaceous shrub, *Aucuba japonica*, of S and SE Asia, the female of which has yellow-spotted leaves

Laurel and Hardy a team of US film comedians, **Stan Laurel**, 1890–1965, born in Britain, the thin one, and his partner, **Oliver Hardy**, 1892–1957, the fat one

Lauren Ralph born 1939, US fashion designer

Laurentian 1 of or resembling the style of D. H. Lawrence (1885–1930), the British novelist, poet, and short-story writer, or T. E. *Lawrence* "of Arabia" (1885–1935), the British soldier and writer 2 of, relating to, or situated near the St Lawrence River

Laurier Sir Wilfrid 1841–1919, Canadian Liberal statesman; the first French-Canadian prime minister (1896–1911)

Lausanne a city in W Switzerland, capital of Vaud canton, on Lake Geneva; cultural and commercial centre; university (1537). Pop: 116 300 (2002 est)

lava 1 magma emanating from volcanoes and other vents 2 any extrusive igneous rock formed by the cooling and solidification of molten lava

Laval¹ Pierre 1883–1945, French statesman. He was premier of France (1931–32; 1935–36) and premier of the Vichy government (1942–44). He was executed for collaboration with Germany

Laval² a city in SE Canada, in Quebec: a NW suburb of Montreal. Pop: 343 005 (2001)

lavender 1 any of various perennial shrubs or herbaceous plants of the genus *Lavandula*, esp *L. vera*, cultivated for its mauve or blue flowers and as the source of a fragrant oil (**oil of lavender**): family *Lamiaceae* (labiates) 2 the dried parts of *L. vera*, used to perfume clothes 3 a pale or light bluish-purple to a very pale violet colour 4 perfume scented with lavender

laver 1 *Old Testament* a large basin of water used by the priests for ritual ablutions 2 the font or the water of baptism

Laver Rod(ney) (George). born 1938, Australian tennis player: Wimbledon champion 1961, 1962, 1968, 1969; US champion 1962, 1969

Lavoisier Antoine Laurent 1743–94, French chemist; one of the founders of modern chemistry. He disproved the phlogiston theory, named oxygen, and discovered its importance in respiration and combustion

law¹ 1 a rule or set of rules, enforceable by the courts, regulating the government of a state, the relationship between the organs of government and the subjects of the state, and the relationship or conduct of subjects towards each other 2 **a** a rule or body of rules made by the legislature **b** a rule or body of rules made by a municipal or other authority 3 the condition and control enforced by such rules 4 **the law a** the legal or judicial system **b** the profession or practice of law **c** *Informal* the police or a policeman 5 the science or knowledge of law; jurisprudence 6 the principles originating and formerly applied only in courts of common law 7 *Judaism* the English term for *Torah* 8 **go to law** to resort to legal proceedings on some matter 9 **reading (of) the Law** *Judaism* that part of the morning service on Sabbaths, festivals, and Mondays and Thursdays during which a passage is read from the Torah scrolls

▷www.worldlii.org
▷www.britac.ac.uk/portal/ bysection.asp?section=S1
▷www.lcd.gov.uk/rlinksfr.htm
▷www.llrx.com/features/uk2.htm
▷www.law.gla.ac.uk/scot_guide/guide.html
▷www.llrx.com/features/canadian3.htm
▷www.llrx.com/features/australian2.htm
▷www.llrx.com/features/newzealand.htm
▷www.llrx.com/features/southafrica.htm

law² *Scot* a hill, esp one rounded in shape

Law 1 **Andrew Bonar** 1858–1923, British Conservative statesman, born in Canada; prime minister (1922–23) 2 **Denis** born 1940, Scottish footballer and television and radio commentator on the sport 3 **John** 1671–1729, Scottish financier. He founded the first bank in France (1716) and the Mississippi Scheme for the development of Louisiana (1717), which collapsed due to excessive speculation 4 **Jude** born 1972, British film actor, who starred in *The Talented Mr Ripley* (1999) and *Cold Mountain* (2003). 5 **William** 1686–1761, British Anglican divine, best known for *A Serious Call to a Holy and Devout Life* (1728)

Lawes 1 **Henry** 1596–1662, English composer, noted for his music for Milton's masque *Comus* (1634) and for his settings of some of Robert Herrick's poems 2 his brother, **William** 1602–45, English composer, noted for his harmonically experimental instrumental music

lawn¹ 1 a flat and usually level area of mown and cultivated grass 2 an archaic or dialect word for **glade**

lawn² a fine linen or cotton fabric, used for clothing

lawn mower a hand-operated or power-operated machine with rotary blades for cutting grass on lawns

lawn tennis 1 tennis played on a grass court 2 the formal name for **tennis**

Lawrence 1 **Saint** died 258 AD, Roman martyr: according to tradition he was roasted to death on a gridiron. Feast day: Aug 10 2 **D(avid) H(erbert)**. 1885–1930, British novelist, poet, and short-story writer. Many of his works deal with the destructiveness of modern industrial society, contrasted with the beauty of nature and instinct, esp the sexual impulse. His novels include *Sons and Lovers* (1913), *The Rainbow* (1915), *Women in Love* (1920), and *Lady Chatterley's Lover* (1928) 3 **Ernest Orlando** 1901–58, US physicist, who invented the cyclotron (1931): Nobel prize for physics 1939 4 **Gertrude** 1898–1952, British actress, noted esp for her roles in comedies such as Noël Coward's *Private Lives* (1930) 5 **Sir Thomas** 1769–1830, British portrait painter 6 **T(homas) E(dward)**, known as *Lawrence of Arabia*. 1888–1935, British soldier and writer. He took a major part in the Arab revolt against the Turks (1916–18), proving himself an outstanding guerrilla leader. He described his experiences in *The Seven Pillars of Wisdom* (1926)

lawrencium a transuranic element artificially produced from californium. Symbol: Lr; atomic no.: 103; half-life of most stable isotope, ^{256}Lr: 35 seconds; valency: 3

Lawson Henry Archibald 1867–1922, Australian poet and short-story writer, whose work is taken as being most representative of the Australian outback, esp in *While the Billy Boils* (1896) and *Joe Wilson and his Mates* (1901) 1 **Nigel**, Baron. born 1932, British Conservative politician;

Chancellor of the Exchquer (1983–89). **2** his daughter, **Nigella** born 1959, British journalist, broadcaster, and cookery writer

lawsuit a proceeding in a court of law brought by one party against another, esp a civil action

lawyer 1 a member of the legal profession, esp a solicitor **2** a popular name for **burbot** (a fish)

lax (of flower clusters) having loosely arranged parts

laxative an agent stimulating evacuation of faeces

Laxness Halldór (Kiljan) ('hald•ur). 1902–98, Icelandic novelist, noted for his treatment of rural working life in Iceland. His works include *Salka Valka* (1932) and *Independent People* (1935). Nobel prize for literature 1955

lay¹ a portion of the catch or the profits from a whaling or fishing expedition

lay² of, involving, or belonging to people who are not clergy

lay³ 1 a ballad or short narrative poem, esp one intended to be sung **2** a song or melody

Layamon or **Lawman** 12th-century English poet and priest; author of the *Brut*, a chronicle providing the earliest version of the Arthurian story in English

Layard Sir **Austen Henry** 1817–94, English archaeologist, noted for his excavations at Nimrud and Nineveh

lay-by 1 *Nautical* an anchorage in a narrow waterway, away from the channel **2** a small railway siding where rolling stock may be stored or parked **3** *Austral and NZ* a system of payment whereby a buyer pays a deposit on an article, which is reserved for him until he has paid the full price

layer 1 one of four or more levels of vegetation defined in ecological studies: the ground or moss layer, the field or herb layer, the shrub layer, and one or more tree layers **2** a laying hen **3** *Horticulture* **a** a shoot or branch rooted during layering **b** a plant produced as a result of layering

lay figure an artist's jointed dummy, used in place of a live model, esp for studying effects of drapery

lay out the formation of cards on the table in various games, esp in patience

lay reader 1 *Church of England* a person licensed by a bishop to conduct religious services other than the Eucharist **2** *RC Church* a layman chosen from among the congregation to read the epistle at Mass and sometimes other prayers

Lazarus *New Testament* 1 the brother of Mary and Martha, whom Jesus restored to life (John 11–12) **2** the beggar who lay at the gate of the rich man Dives in Jesus' parable (Luke 16:19–31)

Lazio 1 a region of W central Italy, on the Tyrrhenian Sea: includes the plain of the lower Tiber, the reclaimed Pontine Marshes, and Campagna. Capital: Rome. Pop: 5 145 805 (2003 est) **2** the Italian name for **Latium**

lea 1 a unit for measuring lengths of yarn, usually taken as 80 yards for wool, 120 yards for cotton and silk, and 300 yards for linen **2** a measure of yarn expressed as the length per unit weight, usually the number of leas per pound

Leach Bernard (Howell). 1887–1979, British potter, born in Hong Kong

Leacock Stephen Butler 1869–1944, Canadian humorist

and economist: his comic works include *Literary Lapses* (1910) and *Frenzied Fiction* (1917)

lead¹ 1 the act or prerogative of playing the first card in a round of cards or the card so played **2** the principal role in a play, film, etc, or the person playing such a role **3** *Music* an important entry assigned to one part usually at the beginning of a movement or section **4** a wire, cable, or other conductor for making an electrical connection **5** *Boxing* **a** one's habitual attacking punch **b** a blow made with this **6** *Nautical* the direction in which a rope runs **7** a deposit of metal or ore; lode **8** the firing of a gun, missile, etc, ahead of a moving target to correct for the time of flight of the projectile

lead² 1 a heavy toxic bluish-white metallic element that is highly malleable: occurs principally as galena and used in alloys, accumulators, cable sheaths, paints, and as a radiation shield. Symbol: Pb; atomic no.: 82; atomic wt.: 207.2; valency: 2 or 4; relative density: 11.35; melting pt.: 327.502°C; boiling pt.: 1750°C **2** a lead weight suspended on a line used to take soundings of the depth of water **3 a** graphite or a mixture containing graphite, clay, etc, used for drawing **b** a thin stick of this material, esp the core of a pencil

Leadbelly real name *Huddie Ledbetter*. 1888–1949, US blues singer and guitarist

leaded (of petrol) containing tetraethyl lead in order to improve combustion

leader 1 *Music* **a** the principal first violinist of an orchestra, who plays solo parts, and acts as the conductor's deputy and spokesman for the orchestra **b** *US* a conductor or director of an orchestra or chorus **2 a** the first man on a climbing rope **b** the leading horse or dog in a team **3** a statistic or index that gives an advance indication of the state of the economy **4** *Angling* another word for **trace** or **cast 5** a strip of blank film or tape used to facilitate threading a projector, developing machine, etc, and to aid identification **6** *Botany* any of the long slender shoots that grow from the stem or branch of a tree: usually removed during pruning **7** *Brit* a member of the Government having primary authority in initiating legislative business (esp in the phrases **Leader of the House of Commons** and **Leader of the House of Lords**) **8** the senior barrister, usually a Queen's Counsel, in charge of the conduct of a case

leading *Maths* (of a coefficient) associated with the term of highest degree in a polynomial containing one variable

lead poisoning acute or chronic poisoning by lead or its salts, characterized by abdominal pain, vomiting, convulsions, and coma

lead time 1 *Manufacturing* the time between the design of a product and its production **2** *Commerce* the time from the placing of an order to the delivery of the goods

leaf 1 the main organ of photosynthesis and transpiration in higher plants, usually consisting of a flat green blade attached to the stem directly or by a stalk **2** foliage collectively **3 in leaf** (of shrubs, trees, etc) having a full complement of foliage leaves **4** metal in the form of a very thin flexible sheet **5** a foil or thin strip of metal in a composite material; lamina **6** a metal strip forming one of the laminations in a leaf spring

leaflet 1 any of the subdivisions of a compound leaf

such as a fern leaf **2** (loosely) any small leaf or leaflike part

leaf mould a nitrogen-rich material consisting of decayed leaves, etc, used as a fertilizer

league an obsolete unit of distance of varying length. It is commonly equal to 3 miles

Leah *Old Testament* the first wife of Jacob and elder sister of Rachel, his second wife (Genesis 29)

leak the loss of current from an electrical conductor because of faulty insulation, etc.

leakage 1 *Commerce* an allowance made for partial loss (of stock, etc) due to leaking **2** *Physics* **a** an undesired flow of electric current, neutrons, etc **b** (*as modifier*): *leakage current*

Leakey 1 Louis Seymour Bazett 1903–72, British anthropologist and archaeologist, settled in Kenya. He discovered fossil remains of manlike apes in E Africa **2** his son **Richard** born 1944, Kenyan anthropologist, who discovered the remains of primitive man over 2 million years old in E Africa

Leamington Spa a town in central England, in central Warwickshire: saline springs. Pop: 61 595 (2001)

lean 1 (of a mixture of fuel and air) containing insufficient fuel and too much air **2** (of concrete) made with a small amount of cement

Lean Sir David 1908–91, English film director. His films include *In Which We Serve* (1942), *Blithe Spirit* (1945), *Brief Encounter* (1946), *Great Expectations* (1946), *Oliver Twist* (1948), *The Bridge on the River Kwai* (1957), *Lawrence of Arabia* (1962), *Dr Zhivago* (1965), and *A Passage to India* (1984)

lean-to 1 a roof that has a single slope with its upper edge adjoining a wall or building **2** a shed or outbuilding with such a roof

leap *Music* a relatively large melodic interval, esp in a solo part

leapfrog a children's game in which each player in turn leaps over the others' bent backs, leaning on them with the hands and spreading the legs wide

leap year a calendar year of 366 days, February 29 (**leap day**) being the additional day, that occurs every four years (those whose number is divisible by four) except for century years whose number is not divisible by 400. It offsets the difference between the length of the solar year (365.2422 days) and the calendar year of 365 days

Lear Edward 1812–88, English humorist and painter, noted for his illustrated nonsense poems and limericks

learned a title applied in referring to a member of the legal profession, esp to a barrister

learning *Psychol* any relatively permanent change in behaviour that occurs as a direct result of experience

lease 1 a contract by which property is conveyed to a person for a specified period, usually for rent **2** the instrument by which such property is conveyed **3** the period of time for which it is conveyed

leasehold 1 land or property held under a lease **2** the tenure by which such property is held **3** held under a lease

leash *Hunting* three of the same kind of animal, usually hounds, foxes, or hares

leather 1 a a material consisting of the skin of an animal made smooth and flexible by tanning, removing the hair, etc. **b** (*as modifier*): *leather goods* **2** the flap of a

dog's ear

▷www.leathertown.com/info_hist_leather.htm

Leatherhead a town in S England, in Surrey. Pop: 42 885 (2001)

leatherjacket 1 any of various tropical carangid fishes of the genera *Oligoplites* and *Scomberoides*, having a leathery skin **2** any of various brightly coloured tropical trigerfishes of the genus *Monacanthus* and related genera **3** the greyish-brown tough-skinned larva of certain craneflies, esp of the genus *Tipula*, which destroy the roots of grasses, etc.

leaven 1 any substance that produces fermentation in dough or batter, such as yeast, and causes it to rise **2** a piece of such a substance kept to ferment a new batch of dough

Leavenworth a city in NE Kansas, on the Missouri River: the state's oldest city, founded in 1854 by proslavery settlers from Missouri. Pop: 35 211 (2003 est)

Leavis F(rank) R(aymond). 1895–1978, English literary critic. He edited *Scrutiny* (1932–53) and his books include *The Great Tradition* (1948) and *The Common Pursuit* (1952)

Lebanon a republic in W Asia, on the Mediterranean: an important centre of the Phoenician civilization in the third millennium BC; part of the Ottoman Empire from 1516 until 1919; gained independence in 1941 (effective by 1945). Official language: Arabic; French and English are also widely spoken. Religion: Muslim and Christian. Currency: Lebanese pound. Capital: Beirut. Pop: 3 708 000 (2004 est). Area: 10 400 sq km (4015 sq miles)

Lebensraum territory claimed by a nation or state on the grounds that it is necessary for survival or growth

Leblanc Nicolas ?1742–1806, French chemist, who invented a process for the manufacture of soda from common salt

Lebrun 1 Albert 1871–1950, French statesman; president (1932–40) **2** Charles 1619–90, French historical painter. He was court painter to Louis XIV and executed much of the decoration of the palace of Versailles

Lecce a walled city in SE Italy, in Puglia: Greek and Roman remains. Pop: 83 303 (2001)

Lech a river in central Europe, rising in SW Austria and flowing generally north through S Germany to the River Danube. Length: 285 km (177 miles)

lecithin *Biochem* any of a group of phospholipids that are found in many plant and animal tissues, esp egg yolk: used in making candles, cosmetics, and inks, and as an emulsifier and stabilizer in foods (**E322**)

Lecky William Edward Hartpole 1838–1903, Irish historian; author of *The History of England in the 18th Century* (1878–90)

Leconte de Lisle Charles Marie René 1818–94, French Parnassian poet

Le Corbusier real name *Charles Édouard Jeanneret*. 1887–1965, French architect and town planner, born in Switzerland. He is noted for his use of reinforced concrete and for his modular system, which used units of a standard size. His works include Unité d'Habitation at Marseilles (1946–52) and the city of Chandigarh, India (1954)

Le Creusot a town in E central France: metal, machinery, and armaments industries. Pop: 26 283 (1999)

lecture 1 a discourse on a particular subject given or read to an audience 2 the text of such a discourse 3 a method of teaching by formal discourse

Lederberg Joshua born 1925, US geneticist, who discovered the phenomenon of transduction in bacteria. Nobel prize for physiology or medicine 1958 with George Beadle and Edward Tatum

ledge 1 a ridge of rock that lies beneath the surface of the sea 2 a narrow shelflike rock projection on a cliff or mountain

ledger 1 a flat horizontal slab of stone 2 a horizontal scaffold pole fixed to two upright poles for supporting the outer ends of putlogs 3 *Angling* a a wire trace that allows the weight to rest on the bottom and the bait to float freely b *(as modifier)*: *ledger tackle*

ledger line 1 *Music* a short line placed above or below the staff to accommodate notes representing pitches above or below the staff 2 *Angling* a line using ledger tackle

Led Zeppelin British rock group (1968–80); comprised Jimmy Page (born 1944), Robert Plant (born 1948), John Paul Jones (born 1946), and John Bonham (1948–80): recordings include *Led Zeppelin I* (1969), *Led Zeppelin IV* (1971), and *Physical Graffiti* (1975)

lee 1 by the lee *Nautical* so that the wind is blowing on the wrong side of the sail 2 under the lee *Nautical* towards the lee 3 *Nautical* on, at, or towards the side or part away from the wind

Lee¹ 1 Ang born 1954, Taiwanese film director; his films include *Sense and Sensibility* (1995), *The Ice Storm* (1997), and *Crouching Tiger, Hidden Dragon* (2000) 2 Bruce, original name *Lee Yuen Kam*. 1940–73, US film actor and kung fu expert who starred in such films as *Enter the Dragon* (1973) 3 Gypsy Rose, original name *Rose Louise Hovick*. 1914–70, US striptease and burlesque artiste, who appeared in the Ziegfeld Follies (1936) and in films 4 Laurie 1914–97, British poet and writer, best known for the autobiographical *Cider with Rosie* (1959) 5 Richard Henry 1732–94, American Revolutionary statesman, who moved the resolution in favour of American independence (1776) 6 Robert E(dward). 1807–70, American general; commander-in-chief of the Confederate armies in the Civil War 7 Spike, real name *Shelton Jackson Lee*. born 1957, US film director: his films include *She's Gotta Have It* (1985), *Malcolm X* (1992), and *25th Hour* (2002) 8 T(sung)-D(ao). born 1926, US physicist, born in China. With Yang he disproved the principle that that parity is always conserved and shared the Nobel prize for physics in 1957

Lee² a river in SW Republic of Ireland, flowing east into Cork Harbour. Length: about 80 km (50 miles)

leech¹ 1 any annelid worm of the class *Hirudinea*, which have a sucker at each end of the body and feed on the blood or tissues of other animals 2 an archaic word for physician

leech² *or* **leach** *Nautical* the after edge of a fore-and-aft sail or either of the vertical edges of a squaresail

Leeds 1 a city in N England, in Leeds unitary authority, West Yorkshire on the River Aire; linked with Liverpool and Goole by canals; a former centre of the clothing industry; two universities (1904, 1992). Pop: 443 247 (2001) 2 a unitary authority in N England, in West Yorkshire. Pop: 715 200 (2003 est). Area 562 sq km (217 sq miles)

leek 1 an alliaceous plant, *Allium porrum*, with a slender white bulb, cylindrical stem, and broad flat overlapping leaves: used in cooking 2 any of several related species, such as *A. ampeloprasum* (wild leek) 3 a leek, or a representation of one, as a national emblem of Wales

leet¹ *English history* 1 a special kind of manorial court that some lords were entitled to hold 2 the jurisdiction of this court

leet² *Scot* a list of candidates for an office

Leeuwarden a city in the N Netherlands, capital of Friesland province. Pop: 91 000 (2003 est)

Leeuwenhoek Anton van 1632–1723, Dutch microscopist, whose microscopes enabled him to give the first accurate description of blood corpuscles, spermatozoa, and microbes

leeward *Chiefly nautical* 1 of, in, or moving to the quarter towards which the wind blows 2 the point or quarter towards which the wind blows 3 the side towards the lee

leeway sideways drift of a boat or aircraft

Le Fanu (Joseph) Sheridan 1814–73, Irish writer, best known for his stories of mystery and the supernatural, esp *Uncle Silas* (1864) and the collection *In a Glass Darkly* (1872)

left the supporters or advocates of varying degrees of social, political, or economic change, reform, or revolution designed to promote the greater freedom, power, welfare, or comfort of the common people

Left Bank a district of Paris, on the S bank of the River Seine; frequented by artists, students, etc.

leg 1 a either of the two lower limbs, including the bones and fleshy covering of the femur, tibia, fibula, and patella b *(as modifier)*: *leg guard* 2 any similar or analogous structure in animals that is used for locomotion or support 3 something similar to a leg in appearance or function, such as one of the four supporting members of a chair 4 either the opposite or adjacent side of a right-angled triangle 5 *Nautical* a the distance travelled without tacking b (in yacht racing) the course between any two marks 6 *Cricket* a the side of the field to the left of a right-handed batsman as he faces the bowler b *(as modifier)*: *a leg slip*

legacy 1 a gift by will, esp of money or personal property 2 something handed down or received from an ancestor or predecessor 3 surviving computer systems, hardware, or software

legal 1 established by or founded upon law; lawful 2 of or relating to law 3 recognized, enforceable, or having a remedy at law rather than in equity 4 relating to or characteristic of the profession of law

legal aid a means-tested benefit in the form of financial assistance for persons to meet the cost of advice and representation in legal proceedings

legalese the conventional language in which legal documents, etc, are written

legalism strict adherence to the law, esp the stressing of the letter of the law rather than its spirit

legal tender currency in specified denominations that a creditor must by law accept in redemption of a debt

Legaspi a port in the Philippines, on SE Luzon on the Gulf of Albay. Pop: 178 000 (2005 est)

legate 1 a messenger, envoy, or delegate 2 *RC Church* an emissary to a foreign state representing the Pope

legatee a person to whom a legacy is bequeathed

legation 1 a diplomatic mission headed by a minister 2 the official residence and office of a diplomatic minister 3 the act of sending forth a diplomatic envoy 4 the mission or business of a diplomatic envoy 5 the rank or office of a legate

legato *Music* 1 to be performed smoothly and connectedly 2 a style of playing in which no perceptible gaps are left between notes b (*as modifier*): *a legato passage*

leg before wicket *Cricket* a manner of dismissal on the grounds that a batsman has been struck on the leg by a bowled ball that otherwise would have hit the wicket

leg break *Cricket* a bowled ball that spins from leg to off on pitching

legend *Christian religion* a a story of the life of a saint b a collection of such stories

Legendre Adrien Marie 1752–1833, French mathematician, noted for his work on the theory of numbers, the theory of elliptical functions, and the method of least squares

leggy (of a plant) having an unusually long and weak stem

leghorn a type of Italian wheat straw that is woven into hats

Leghorn 1 the English name for **Livorno** 2 a breed of domestic fowl laying white eggs

legislation 1 the act or process of making laws; enactment 2 the laws so made

legislative 1 of or relating to legislation 2 having the power or function of legislating 3 of or relating to a legislature 4 *Rare* another word for **legislature**

legislature a body of persons vested with power to make, amend, and repeal laws

legitimate 1 authorized, sanctioned by, or in accordance with law 2 of, relating to, or ruling by hereditary right 3 of or relating to a body of famous long-established plays as distinct from films, television, vaudeville, etc.

Legnica an industrial town in SW Poland. Pop: 109 335 (1999 est)

Lego *Trademark* a construction toy consisting of plastic bricks and other standardized components that fit together with studs

legume 1 the long dry dehiscent fruit produced by leguminous plants; a pod 2 any table vegetable of the family *Fabaceae* (formerly *Leguminosae*), esp beans or peas 3 any leguminous plant

leguminous of, relating to, or belonging to the *Fabaceae* (formerly *Leguminosae*), a family of flowering plants having pods (or legumes) as fruits and root nodules enabling storage of nitrogen-rich material: includes peas, beans, clover, gorse, acacia, and carob

Le Havre a port in N France, on the English Channel at the mouth of the River Seine: transatlantic trade; oil refining. Pop: 190 905 (1999)

Lehmann 1 Lilli 1848–1929, German soprano 2 Lotte 1888–1976, US soprano, born in Germany 3 Rosamond (Nina). 1903–90, British novelist. Her books include *Dusty Answer* (1927), *Invitation to the Waltz* (1932), and *The Echoing Grove* (1953)

Lehmbruck Wilhelm 1881–1919, German sculptor and graphic artist

Leibnitz *or* **Leibniz** Baron Gottfried Wilhelm von 1646–1716, German rationalist philosopher and mathematician. He conceived of the universe as a hierarchy of independent units or monads, synchronized by pre-established harmony. His works include *Théodicée* (1710) and *Monadologia* (1714). He also devised a system of calculus, independently of Newton

Leibovitz Annie born 1949, US photographer, known for her portraits of celebrities

Leicester[1] Earl of title of *Robert Dudley.* ?1532–88, English courtier; favourite of Elizabeth I. He led an unsuccessful expedition to the Netherlands (1585–87)

Leicester[2] 1 a city in central England, in Leicester unitary authority, on the River Soar: administrative centre of Leicestershire: Roman remains and a ruined Norman castle; two universities (1957, 1992); light engineering, hosiery, and footwear industries. Pop: 283 900 (2003 est) 2 a unitary authority in central England, in Leicestershire. Pop: 330 574 (2001). Area: 73 sq km (28 sq miles) 3 short for **Leicestershire** 4 a breed of sheep with long wool, originally from Leicestershire

Leicestershire a county of central England: absorbed the small historical county of Rutland in 1974; Rutland and Leicester city became independent unitary authorities in 1997: largely agricultural. Administrative centre: Leicester. Pop. (excluding Leicester city): 619 200 (2003 est). Area (excluding Leicester city): 2084 sq km (804 sq miles)

Leichhardt Friedrich Wilhelm Ludwig 1813–48, Australian explorer, born in Prussia. He disappeared during an attempt to cross Australia from East to West

Leiden *or* **Leyden** a city in the W Netherlands, in South Holland province: residence of the Pilgrim Fathers for 11 years before they sailed for America in 1620; university (1575). Pop: 118 000 (2003 est)

Leigh[1] 1 Mike born 1943, British dramatist and theatre, film, and television director, noted for his use of improvisation. His plays include *Abigail's Party* (1977), and his films include *High Hopes* (1988), *Secrets and Lies* (1996), and *All or Nothing* (2002) 2 Vivien, real name Vivian Hartley. 1913–67, English stage and film actress. Her films include *Gone with the Wind* (1939) and *A Streetcar Named Desire* (1951), for both of which she won Oscars

Leigh[2] a town in NW England, in Wigan unitary authority, Greater Manchester: engineering industries. Pop: 43 006 (2001)

Leighton Frederic, 1st Baron Leighton of Stretton. 1830–96, British painter and sculptor of classical subjects: president of the Royal Academy (1878)

Leinster a province of E and SE Republic of Ireland: it consists of the counties of Carlow, Dublin, Kildare, Kilkenny, Laois, Longford, Louth, Meath, Offaly, Westmeath, Wexford, and Wicklow. Pop: 2 105 579 (2002). Area: 19 632 sq km (7580 sq miles)

Leipzig a city in E central Germany, in Saxony: famous fairs, begun about 1170; publishing and music centre; university (1409); scene of a decisive defeat for Napoleon Bonaparte in 1813. Pop: 497 531 (2003 est)

Leiria a city in central Portugal: site of the first printing press in Portugal (1466). Pop: 119 870 (2001)

Leith a port in SE Scotland, on the Firth of Forth: part of

Edinburgh since 1920

leitmotif or **leitmotiv** 1 *Music* a recurring short melodic phrase or theme used, esp in Wagnerian music dramas, to suggest a character, thing, etc. 2 an often repeated word, phrase, image, or theme in a literary work

Leitrim a county of N Republic of Ireland in Connacht province, on Donegal Bay: agricultural. County town: Carrick-on-Shannon. Pop: 25 799 (2002). Area: 1525 sq km (589 sq miles)

Leizhou or **Luichow Peninsula** a peninsula of SE China, in SW Guangdong province, separated from Hainan Island by Hainan Strait

Lely Sir Peter Dutch name *Pieter van der Faes*. 1618–80, Dutch portrait painter in England

Lemalu Jonathan (Fa'afetai). born 1976, New Zealand singer of Samoan descent; a bass-baritone noted esp for his lieder recitals

Le Mans a city in NW France: scene of the first experiments in motoring and flying; annual motor race. Pop: 146 105 (1999)

lemming any of various volelike rodents of the genus *Lemmus* and related genera, of northern and arctic regions of Europe, Asia, and North America: family *Cricetidae*. The Scandinavian variety, *Lemmus lemmus*, migrates periodically when its population reaches a peak

Lemnos a Greek island in the N Aegean Sea: famous for its medicinal earth (**Lemnian seal**). Chief town: Kastron. Pop: 18 104 (2001). Area: 477 sq km (184 sq miles)

lemon 1 a small Asian evergreen tree, *Citrus limon*, widely cultivated in warm and tropical regions, having pale green glossy leaves and edible fruits 2 a the yellow oval fruit of this tree, having juicy acidic flesh rich in vitamin C b (*as modifier*): *a lemon jelly* 3 a a greenish-yellow or strong yellow colour b (*as adjective*): *lemon wallpaper*

lemon sole a European flatfish, *Microstomus kitt*, with a variegated brown body: highly valued as a food fish: family *Pleuronectidae*

Lemper Ute born 1963, German singer and actress, noted esp for her performances of songs by Kurt Weill

lemur 1 any Madagascan prosimian primate of the family *Lemuridae*, such as *Lemur catta* (the **ring-tailed lemur**). They are typically arboreal, having foxy faces and long tails 2 any similar or closely related animal, such as a loris or indris

Lena a river in Russia, rising in S Siberia and flowing generally north through the Sakha Republic to the Laptev Sea by an extensive delta: the longest river in Russia. Length: 4271 km (2653 miles)

Lenglen Suzanne 1899–1938, French tennis player: Wimbledon champion (1919-25)

length 1 *Prosody, Phonetics* the metrical quantity or temporal duration of a vowel or syllable 2 the distance from one end of a rectangular swimming bath to the other 3 *Prosody* the quality of a vowel, whether stressed or unstressed, that distinguishes it from another vowel of similar articulatory characteristics. Thus in English *beat* is of greater length than in English *bit* 4 *Cricket* the distance from the batsman at which the ball pitches 5 *Bridge* a holding of four or more cards in a suit

Lenin Vladimir Ilyich, original surname *Ulyanov*. 1870–1924, Russian statesman and Marxist theoretician; first premier of the Soviet Union. He formed the Bolsheviks (1903) and led them in the October Revolution (1917), which established the Soviet Government. He adopted the New Economic Policy (1921) after the Civil War had led to the virtual collapse of the Russian economy, formed the Comintern (1919), and was the originator of the guiding doctrine of the Soviet Union, Marxism-Leninism. After the Soviet Union broke up in 1991, many statues of Lenin were demolished

Lenin Peak a mountain in Tajikistan; the highest peak in the Trans Alai Range. Height: 7134 m (23 406 ft)

Lennon John (Ono), original name *John Winston Lennon*. 1940--80, English rock guitarist, singer, and songwriter: member of the Beatles (1962–70). His subsequent recordings, many in collaboration with his wife Yoko Ono, include "Instant Karma" (1970), *Imagine* (1971), and *Double Fantasy* (1980). He was shot dead by a demented fan

Leno Dan, original name *George Galvin*. 1860–1904, British music-hall entertainer, noted esp for his pantomime performances: he died insane

lens 1 a piece of glass or other transparent material, used to converge or diverge transmitted light and form optical images 2 a combination of such lenses for forming images or concentrating a beam of light 3 a device that diverges or converges a beam of electromagnetic radiation, sound, or particles

Lent *Christianity* the period of forty weekdays lasting from Ash Wednesday to Holy Saturday, observed as a time of penance and fasting commemorating Jesus' fasting in the wilderness

lentil 1 a small annual leguminous plant, *Lens culinaris*, of the Mediterranean region and W Asia, having edible brownish convex seeds 2 any of the seeds of this plant, which are cooked and eaten as a vegetable, in soups, etc.

lento *Music* 1 to be performed slowly 2 a movement or passage performed in this way

Lenya Lotte, original name *Caroline Blamauer*. 1900–81, Austrian singer and actress, associated esp with the songs of her husband Kurt Weill

Leo¹ a name for a lion, used in children's tales, fables, etc.

Leo² 1 *Astronomy* a zodiacal constellation in the N hemisphere, lying between Cancer and Virgo on the ecliptic, that contains the star Regulus and the radiant of the Leonid meteor shower 2 *Astrology* a the fifth sign of the zodiac, symbol ♌, having a fixed fire classification and ruled by the sun. The sun is in this sign between about July 23 and Aug 22 b a person born during a period when the sun is in this sign 3 *Astrology* born under or characteristic of Leo

Leoben a city in E central Austria, in Styria on the Mur River: lignite mining. Pop: 25 804 (2001)

Leo I Saint, known as *Leo the Great*. ?390–461 AD, pope (440–461). He extended the authority of the papacy in the West and persuaded Attila not to attack Rome (452). Feast day: Nov 10 or Feb 18

Leo III 1 called *the Isaurian*. ?675–741 AD, Byzantine emperor (717–41): he checked Arab expansionism and began the policy of iconoclasm, which divided the empire for the next century **2 Saint** ?750–816 AD, pope (795–816). He crowned Charlemagne emperor of the Romans (800). Feast day: June 12

Leonine 1 connected with one of the popes called Leo **2 Leonine City** a district of Rome on the right bank of the Tiber fortified by Pope Leo IV **3** of or relating to certain prayers in the Mass prescribed by Pope Leo XIII (1810–1903) **4 a** a type of medieval hexameter or elegiac verse having internal rhyme **b** a type of English verse with internal rhyme

leopard 1 a large feline mammal, *Panthera pardus*, of forests of Africa and Asia, usually having a tawny yellow coat with black rosette-like spots **2** any of several similar felines, such as the snow leopard and cheetah **3 clouded leopard** a feline, *Neofelis nebulosa*, of SE Asia and Indonesia with a yellowish-brown coat marked with darker spots and blotches

Leo X original name *Giovanni de' Medici*. 1475–1521, pope (1513–21): noted for his patronage of Renaissance art and learning; excommunicated Luther (1521)

Leo XIII original name *Gioacchino Pecci*. 1810–1903, pope (1878–1903). His many important encyclicals include *Rerum novarum* (1891) on the need for Roman Catholics to take action on various social problems

Leonardo da Vinci 1452–1519, Italian painter, sculptor, architect, and engineer: the most versatile talent of the Italian Renaissance. His most famous paintings include *The Virgin of the Rocks* (1483–85), the *Mona Lisa* (or *La Gioconda*, 1503), and the *Last Supper* (?1495–97). His numerous drawings, combining scientific precision in observation with intense imaginative power, reflect the breadth of his interests, which ranged over biology, physiology, hydraulics, and aeronautics. He invented the first armoured tank and foresaw the invention of aircraft and submarines

Leoncavallo Ruggiero 1858–1919, Italian composer of operas, notably I *Pagliacci* (1892)

Leonidas died 480 BC, king of Sparta (?490–480), hero of the Battle of Thermopylae, in which he was killed by the Persians under Xerxes

Leopardi Count Giacomo 1798–1837, Italian poet and philosopher, noted esp for his lyrics, collected in I *Canti* (1831)

Leopold I 1 1640–1705, Holy Roman Emperor (1658–1705). His reign was marked by wars with Louis XIV of France and with the Turks **2** 1790–1865, first king of the Belgians (1831–65)

Leopold II 1 1747–92, Holy Roman Emperor (1790–92). He formed an alliance with Prussia against France (1792) after the downfall of his brother-in-law Louis XVI **2** 1835–1909, king of the Belgians (1865–1909); son of Leopold I. He financed Stanley's explorations in Africa, becoming first sovereign of the Congo Free State (1885)

Leopold III 1901–83, king of the Belgians (1934–51); son of Albert I. His surrender to the Nazis (1940) forced his eventual abdication in favour of his son, Baudouin

Lepanto 1 a port in W Greece, between the Gulfs of Corinth and Patras: scene of a naval battle (1571) in which the Turkish fleet was defeated by the fleets of the Holy League. Pop: 8170 (latest est) **2 Gulf of** another

name for the (Gulf of) **Corinth**

Le Pen Jean-Marie born 1928, French politician; leader of the extreme right-wing Front National from 1972; runner-up in the presidential election of 2002

leper a person who has leprosy

lepidopteran any of numerous insects of the order *Lepidoptera*, typically having two pairs of wings covered with fragile scales, mouthparts specialized as a suctorial proboscis, and caterpillars as larvae: comprises the butterflies and moths

Lepidus Marcus Aemilius died ?13 BC, Roman statesman: formed the Second Triumvirate with Octavian (later Augustus) and Mark Antony

leprechaun (in Irish folklore) a mischievous elf, often believed to have a treasure hoard

leprosy *Pathol* a chronic infectious disease occurring mainly in tropical and subtropical regions, characterized by the formation of painful inflamed nodules beneath the skin and disfigurement and wasting of affected parts, caused by the bacillus *Mycobacterium leprae*

lepton¹ 1 a former Greek monetary unit worth one hundredth of a drachma **2** a small coin of ancient Greece

lepton² *Physics* any of a group of elementary particles and their antiparticles, such as an electron, muon, or neutrino, that participate in electromagnetic and weak interactions and have a half-integral spin

Lermontov Mikhail Yurievich 1814–41, Russian novelist and poet: noted esp for the novel *A Hero of Our Time* (1840)

Lerner Alan Jay 1914–86, US songwriter and librettist. With Frederick Loewe he wrote *My Fair Lady* (1956) and *Camelot* (1960) as well as a number of film scripts, including *Gigi* (1958)

Lerwick a town in Shetland, administrative centre of the island authority of Shetland, on the island of Mainland: the most northerly town in the British Isles; knitwear, oil refining. Pop: 6830 (2001)

Le Sage *or* **Lesage** Alain-René 1668–1747, French novelist and dramatist, author of the picaresque novel *Gil Blas* (1715–35)

Lesbos an island in the E Aegean, off the NW coast of Turkey: a centre of lyric poetry, led by Alcaeus and Sappho (6th century BC); annexed to Greece in 1913. Chief town: Mytilene. Pop: 90 642 (2001). Area: 1630 sq km (630 sq miles)

Les Cayes a port in SW Haiti, on the S Tiburon Peninsula. Pop: 45 904 (1992)

lese-majesty any of various offences committed against the sovereign power in a state; treason

lesion any structural change in a bodily part resulting from injury or disease

Lesotho a kingdom in southern Africa, forming an enclave in the Republic of South Africa: annexed to British Cape Colony in 1871; made a protectorate in 1884; gained independence in 1966; a member of the Commonwealth. It is generally mountainous, with temperate grasslands throughout. Languages: Sesotho and English. Religion: Christian majority. Currency: loti and South African rand. Capital: Maseru. Pop: 1 800 000 (2004 est). Area: 30 344 sq km (11 716 sq miles)

lessee a person to whom a lease is granted; a tenant under a lease

Lesseps Vicomte **Ferdinand Marie de** 1805–94, French diplomat: directed the construction of the Suez Canal (1859–69) and the unsuccessful first attempt to build the Panama Canal (1881–89)

Lessing 1 Doris (May), born 1919, English novelist and short-story writer, brought up in Rhodesia: her novels include the five-novel sequence *Children of Violence* (1952–69), *The Golden Notebook* (1962), a series of science-fiction works (1979–83), *The Good Terrorist* (1985), and *The Sweetest Dream* (2001) **2 Gotthold Ephraim** 1729–81, German dramatist and critic. His plays include *Miss Sara Sampson* (1755), the first German domestic tragedy, and *Nathan der Weise* (1779). He is noted for his criticism of French classical dramatists, and for his treatise on aesthetics *Laokoon* (1766)

lesson 1 a a unit, or single period of instruction in a subject; class **b** the content of such a unit **2** material assigned for individual study **3** a portion of Scripture appointed to be read at divine service

lessor a person who grants a lease of property

let *Tennis, Squash* **a** a minor infringement or obstruction of the ball, requiring a point to be replayed **b** the point so replayed

Letchworth a town in SE England, in N Hertfordshire: the first garden city in Great Britain (founded in 1903). Pop: 32 932 (2001)

let down 1 the gliding descent of an aircraft in preparation for landing **2** the release of milk from the mammary glands following stimulation by the hormone oxytocin

lethargy an abnormal lack of energy, esp as the result of a disease

Lethbridge a city in Canada, in S Alberta: coal-mining. Pop: 67 374 (2001)

letters 1 literary knowledge, ability, or learning **2** literary culture in general **3** an official title, degree, etc, indicated by an abbreviation

lettuce 1 any of various plants of the genus *Lactuca*, esp *L. sativa*, which is cultivated in many varieties for its large edible leaves: family *Asteraceae* (composites) **2** the leaves of any of these varieties, which are eaten in salads **3** any of various plants that resemble true lettuce, such as lamb's lettuce and sea lettuce

Leucippus 5th century BC. Greek philosopher, who originated the atomist theory of matter, developed by his disciple, Democritus

leucocyte *or esp US* **leukocyte** any of the various large unpigmented cells in the blood of vertebrates

Leuctra an ancient town in Greece southwest of Thebes in Boeotia: site of a victory of Thebes over Sparta (371BC), which marked the end of Spartan military supremacy in Greece

leukaemia *or esp US* **leukemia** an acute or chronic disease characterized by a gross proliferation of leucocytes, which crowd into the bone marrow, spleen, lymph nodes, etc, and suppress the blood-forming apparatus

Levant the a former name for the area of the E Mediterranean now occupied by Lebanon, Syria, and Israel

levee¹ *US* an embankment alongside a river, produced naturally by sedimentation or constructed by man to prevent flooding

levee² **1** a formal reception held by a sovereign just after rising from bed **2** (in Britain) a public court reception for men, held in the early afternoon

level 1 *Engineering* a device, such as a spirit level, for determining whether a surface is horizontal **2** *Geography* any of the successive layers of material that have been deposited with the passage of time to build up and raise the height of the land surface **3** *Physics* the ratio of the magnitude of a physical quantity to an arbitrary magnitude

level crossing *Brit* a point at which a railway and a road cross, esp one with barriers that close the road when a train is scheduled to pass

Leven, Loch 1 a lake in E central Scotland: one of the shallowest of Scottish lochs, with seven islands, on one of which Mary, Queen of Scots was imprisoned (1567–8). Length: 6 km (3.7 miles). Width: 4 km (2.5 miles) **2** a sea loch in W Scotland, extending for about 14 km (9 miles) east from Loch Linnhe

lever 1 a rigid bar pivoted about a fulcrum, used to transfer a force to a load and usually to provide a mechanical advantage **2** any of a number of mechanical devices employing this principle

leverage 1 the action of a lever **2** the mechanical advantage gained by employing a lever **3** the enhanced power available to a large company **4** the use made by a company of its limited assets to guarantee the substantial loans required to finance its business

leveret a young hare, esp one less than one year old

Leverhulme **William Hesketh**, 1st Viscount. 1851–1925, English soap manufacturer and philanthropist, who founded (1881) the model industrial town Port Sunlight

Leverkusen a town in NW Germany, in North Rhine-Westphalia on the Rhine: chemical industries. Pop: 161 543 (2003 est)

Leverrier **Urbain Jean Joseph** 1811–77, French astronomer: calculated the existence and position of the planet Neptune

Levi¹ 1 Carlo 1902–75, Italian physician, painter, and writer. Best known for his novel *Christ Stopped at Eboli* (1947), his other works include *The Watch* (1952) and *Words are Stones* (1958) **2 Primo** 1919–87, Italian novelist. His book *If This is a Man* (1947) relates his experiences in Auschwitz. Other books include *The Periodic Table* (1956) and *The Drowned and the Saved* (1988), published after his suicide

Levi² **1** *Old Testament* **a** the third son of Jacob and Leah and the ancestor of the tribe of Levi (Genesis 29:34) **b** the priestly tribe descended from this patriarch (Numbers 18:21–24) **2** *New Testament* another name for **Matthew** (the apostle)

leviathan *Bible* a monstrous beast, esp a sea monster

levy **a** the act of imposing and collecting a tax, tariff, etc. **b** the money so raised

Lewes a market town in S England, administrative centre of East Sussex, on the River Ouse: site of a battle (1264) in which Henry III was defeated by Simon de Montfort. Pop: 15 988 (2001)

Lewis¹ 1 Carl full name *Frederick Carleton Lewis*. born 1961, US athlete; winner of the long jump, 100 metres, 200 metres, and 4 × 100 metres relay at the 1984 Olympic

Games; winner of the 100 metres in the 1988 Olympic Games; winner of the long jump in the 1992 and 1996 Olympic Games **2** C(**live**) S(**taples**). 1898–1963, English novelist, critic, and Christian apologist, noted for his critical work, *Allegory of Love* (1936), his theological study, *The Screwtape Letters* (1942), and for his children's books chronicling the land of Narnia **3** Lennox born 1965, British boxer; undisputed world heavyweight champion (2000–01) **4** Matthew Gregory, known as *Monk Lewis*. 1775–1818, English novelist and dramatist, noted for his Gothic horror story *The Monk* (1796) **5** Meriwether 1774–1807, American explorer who, with William Clark, led an overland expedition from St. Louis to the Pacific Ocean (1804–06) **6** (John) Saunders 1893–1995, Welsh poet, dramatist, critic, and politician: founder (1926) and president (1926–39) of the Welsh Nationalist Party **7** (Harry) Sinclair 1885–1951, US novelist. He satirized the complacency and philistinism of American small-town life, esp in *Main Street* (1920) and *Babbitt* (1922): Nobel prize for literature 1930 **8** Wally born 1959, Australian rugby league player **9** (Percy) Wyndham 1884–1957, British painter, novelist, and critic, born in the US: a founder of vorticism. His writings include *Time and Western Man* (1927), *The Apes of God* (1930), and the trilogy *The Human Age* (1928–55)

Lewis[2] the N part of the island of Lewis with Harris, in the Outer Hebrides. Area: 1634 sq km (631 sq miles)

Lewisham a borough of S Greater London, on the River Thames. Pop: 248 300 (2003 est). Area: 35 sq km (13 sq miles)

Lewis with Harris *or* **Lewis and Harris** an island in the Outer Hebrides, separated from the NW coast of Scotland by the Minch: consists of Lewis in the north and Harris in the south; many lakes and peat moors; economy based chiefly on the Harris tweed industry, with some fishing. Chief town: Stornoway. Pop: 19 918 (2001). Area: 2134 sq km (824 sq miles)

Lexington 1 a city in NE central Kentucky, in the bluegrass region: major centre for horse-breeding. Pop. (including Fayette): 266 798 (2003 est) **2** a city in Massachusetts, northwest of Boston: site of the first action (1775) of the War of American Independence. Pop: 30 631 (2003 est)

ley a line joining two prominent points in the landscape, thought to be the line of a prehistoric track

Leyden jar *Physics* an early type of capacitor consisting of a glass jar with the lower part of the inside and outside coated with tin foil

Leyte an island in the central Philippines, in the Visayan Islands. Chief town: Tacloban. Pop: 1 362 050 (1990). Area: 7215 sq km (2786 sq miles)

Leyte Gulf an inlet of the Pacific in the E Philippines, east of Leyte and south of Samar: scene of a battle (Oct 23–26, 1944) during World War II, in which the Americans defeated almost the entire Japanese navy, thereby ensuring ultimate Allied victory

Lhasa *or* **Lassa** a city in SW China, capital of Tibet AR, at an altitude of 3606 m (11 830 ft): for centuries the sacred city of Lamaism and residence of the Dalai Lamas from the 17th century until 1950; known as the Forbidden City because it was closed to Westerners until the beginning of the 20th century; annexed by China in 1951. The Dalai Lama fled after an unsuccessful revolt against Chinese rule in 1959. Pop: 131 000 (2005 est)

liana *or* **liane** any of various woody climbing plants mainly of tropical forests

Lianyungang, Sinhailien, *or* **Hsin-hai-lien** a city in E China, near the coast of Jiangsu. Pop: 645 000 (2005 est)

Liao a river in NE China, rising in SE Inner Mongolia and flowing northeast then southwest to the Gulf of Liaodong. Length: about 1100 km (700 miles)

Liaoning a province of NE China, in S Manchuria. Capital: Shenyang. Pop: 42 100 000 (2003 est). Area: 150 000 sq km (58 500 sq miles)

Liaoyang a city in NE China, in S Manchuria, in Liaoning province: a regional capital in the early dynasties. Pop: 752 000 (2005 est)

Liard a river in W Canada, rising in the SE Yukon and flowing east and then northwest to the Mackenzie River. Length: 885 km (550 miles)

Libby Willard Frank 1908–80, US chemist, who devised the technique of radiocarbon dating: Nobel prize for chemistry 1960

libel 1 *Law* **a** the publication of defamatory matter in permanent form, as by a written or printed statement, picture, etc. **b** the act of publishing such matter **2** *Ecclesiastical law* a claimant's written statement of claim **3** *Scots law* the formal statement of a charge

liberal 1 relating to or having social and political views that favour progress and reform **2** relating to or having policies or views advocating individual freedom **3** of or relating to an education that aims to develop general cultural interests and intellectual ability

Liberal Democrat a member or supporter of the Liberal Democrats

Liberal Party 1 one of the former major political parties in Britain; in 1988 merged with the Social Democratic Party to form the Social and Liberal Democrats; renamed the Liberal Democrats in 1989 **2** one of the major political parties in Australia, a conservative party, generally opposed to the Labor Party **3** one of the major political parties in Canada, generally representing viewpoints between those of the Progressive Conservative Party and the New Democratic Party

Liberec a city in the N Czech Republic, on the Neisse River: a centre of the German Sudeten movement in 1938. Pop: 97 000 (2005 est)

Liberia a republic in W Africa, on the Atlantic: originated in 1822 as a home for freed Afro-American slaves, with land purchased by the American Colonization Society; republic declared in 1847; exports are predominantly rubber and iron ore. Official language: English. Religion: Christian majority, also animist. Currency: dollar. Capital: Monrovia. Pop: 3 487 000 (2004 est). Area: 111 400 sq km (43 000 sq miles)

libertarian 1 a believer in freedom of thought, expression, etc. **2** *Philosophy* a believer in the doctrine of free will

Liberty Island a small island in upper New York Bay: site of the Statue of Liberty. Area: 5 hectares (12 acres)

Libeskind Daniel born 1946, US architect, born in Poland. Based in Berlin, he designed the Jewish Museum there (1999), the Imperial War Museum in

Manchester (2000), the proposed spiral extension to London's Victoria and Albert Museum, and the "Freedom Tower" that will replace the World Trade Center in New York

libido *Psychoanal* psychic energy emanating from the id

Libra 1 *Astronomy* a small faint zodiacal constellation in the S hemisphere, lying between Virgo and Scorpius on the ecliptic 2 *Astrology* **a** the seventh sign of the zodiac, symbol ♎, having a cardinal air classification and ruled by the planet Venus. The sun is in this sign between about Sept 23 and Oct 22 **b** a person born under this sign 3 *Astrology* born under or characteristic of Libra

library *Computing* a collection of standard programs and subroutines for immediate use, usually stored on disk or some other storage device
▷http://sunsite.berkeley.edu/Libweb/
▷www.bl.uk/index.shtml
▷www.loc.gov

libretto a text written for and set to music in an opera, etc.

Libreville the capital of Gabon, in the west on the estuary of the Gabon River: founded as a French trading post in 1843 and expanded with the settlement of freed slaves in 1848. Pop: 649 000 (2005 est)

Libya a republic in N Africa, on the Mediterranean: became an Italian colony in 1912; divided after World War II into Tripolitania and Cyrenaica (under British administration) and Fezzan (under French); gained independence in 1951; monarchy overthrown by a military junta in 1969. It consists almost wholly of desert and is a major exporter of oil. Official language: Arabic. Official religion: (Sunni) Muslim. Currency: Libyan dinar. Capital: Tripoli. Pop: 5 659 000 (2004 est). Area: 1 760 000 sq km (680 000 sq miles)

Libyan the extinct Hamitic language of ancient Libya

Libyan Desert a desert in N Africa, in E Libya, W Egypt, and the NW Sudan: the NE part of the Sahara

licence *or US* **license** a certificate, tag, document, etc, giving official permission to do something

licensee a person who holds a licence, esp one to sell alcoholic drink

licentiate 1 a person who has received a formal attestation of professional competence to practise a certain profession or teach a certain skill or subject 2 a degree between that of bachelor and doctor awarded now only by certain chiefly European universities 3 *Chiefly Presbyterian Church* a person holding a licence to preach

lichen 1 an organism that is formed by the symbiotic association of a fungus and an alga or cyanobacterium and occurs as crusty patches or bushy growths on tree trunks, bare ground, etc. Lichens are now classified as a phylum of fungi (*Mycophycophyta*) 2 *Pathol* any of various eruptive disorders of the skin

Lichfield a city in central England, in SE Staffordshire: cathedral with three spires (13th-14th century); birthplace of Samuel Johnson, during whose lifetime the **Lichfield Group** (a literary circle) flourished. Pop: 28 435 (2001)

Lichtenstein Roy 1923–97, US pop artist

lick 1 a block of compressed salt or chemical matter provided for domestic animals to lick for medicinal and nutritional purposes 2 a place to which animals go to

lick exposed natural deposits of salt 3 *Slang* a short musical phrase, usually on one instrument

Liddell Hart Sir Basil Henry 1895–1970, British military strategist and historian: he advocated the development of mechanized warfare before World War II

Lidice a mining village in the Czech Republic: destroyed by the Germans in 1942 in reprisal for the assassination of Reinhard Heydrich; rebuilt as a national memorial

lie 1 the hiding place or lair of an animal 2 *Golf* **a** the position of the ball after a shot **b** the angle made by the shaft of the club before the upswing

Lie Trygve Halvdan 1896–1968, Norwegian statesman; first secretary-general of the United Nations (1946–52)

Liebig Justus , Baron von Liebig. 1803–73, German chemist, who founded agricultural chemistry. He also contributed to organic chemistry, esp to the concept of radicals, and discovered chloroform

Liebknecht 1 Karl 1871–1919, German socialist leader: with Rosa Luxemburg he led an unsuccessful Communist revolt (1919) and was assassinated 2 his father, **Wilhelm** 1826–1900, German socialist leader and journalist, a founder (1869) of what was to become (1891) the German Social Democratic Party

Liechtenstein a small mountainous principality in central Europe on the Rhine: formed in 1719 by the uniting of the lordships of Schellenburg and Vaduz, which had been purchased by the Austrian family of Liechtenstein; customs union formed with Switzerland in 1924. Official language: German. Religion: Roman Catholic majority. Currency: Swiss franc. Capital: Vaduz. Pop: 34 000 (2003 est). Area: 160 sq km (62 sq miles)

lied *Music* any of various musical settings for solo voice and piano of a romantic or lyrical poem, for which composers such as Schubert, Schumann, and Wolf are famous

liege 1 (of a lord) owed feudal allegiance (esp in the phrase **liege lord**) 2 (of a vassal or servant) owing feudal allegiance 3 of or relating to the relationship or bond between liege lord and liegeman 4 a liege lord 5 a liegeman or true subject

lien *Law* a right to retain possession of another's property pending discharge of a debt

Liepāja *or* **Lepaya** a port in W Latvia on the Baltic Sea; founded by the Teutonic Knights in 1263: a naval and industrial centre, with a fishing fleet. Pop: 86 985 (2002 est)

Liestal a city in NW Switzerland, capital of Basel-Land demicanton. Pop: 12 930 (2000)

lieutenant 1 a military officer holding commissioned rank immediately junior to a captain 2 a naval officer holding commissioned rank immediately junior to a lieutenant commander

lieutenant commander an officer holding commissioned rank in certain navies immediately junior to a commander

lieutenant governor 1 a deputy governor 2 (in the US) an elected official who acts as deputy to a state governor and succeeds him if he dies 3 (in Canada) the representative of the Crown in a province: appointed by the federal government acting for the Crown

Lifar Serge 1905–86, Russian ballet dancer and choreographer: ballet master at the Paris Opera Ballet (1932–58). His ballets include *Prométhée* (1929), *Icare* (1935), and *Phèdre* (1950)

life 1 the state or quality that distinguishes living beings or organisms from dead ones and from inorganic matter, characterized chiefly by metabolism, growth, and the ability to reproduce and respond to stimuli **2 a** a biography **b** (*as modifier*): *a life story* **3** all living things, taken as a whole **4** sparkle, as of wines **5** *Arts* drawn or taken from a living model **6** (in certain games) one of a number of opportunities of participation

life belt a ring filled with buoyant material or air, used to keep a person afloat when in danger of drowning

lifeblood the blood, considered as vital to sustain life

lifeboat a boat, propelled by oars or a motor, used for rescuing people at sea, escaping from a sinking ship, etc.

life buoy any of various kinds of buoyant device for keeping people afloat in an emergency

life cycle the series of changes occurring in an animal or plant between one development stage and the identical stage in the next generation

life jacket an inflatable sleeveless jacket worn to keep a person afloat when in danger of drowning

lifeline 1 a line thrown or fired aboard a vessel for hauling in a hawser for a breeches buoy **2** any rope or line attached to a vessel or trailed from it for the safety of passengers, crew, swimmers, etc. **3** a line by which a deep-sea diver is raised or lowered

life peer *Brit* a peer whose title lapses at his death

life preserver *US and Canadian* a life belt or life jacket

life raft a raft for emergency use at sea

lifestyle (of a drug) designed to treat problems, such as impotence or excess weight, which affect a person's quality of life rather than their health

lifetime 1 a the length of time a person or animal is alive **b** (*as modifier*): *a lifetime supply* **2** *Physics* the average time of existence of an unstable or reactive entity, such as a nucleus, excited state, elementary particle, etc.; mean life

Liffey a river in E Republic of Ireland, rising in the Wicklow Mountains and flowing west, then northeast through Dublin into Dublin Bay. Length: 80 km (50 miles)

Lifford the county town of Donegal, Republic of Ireland; market town. Pop: 1395 (2002)

lift 1 *Brit* a platform, compartment, or cage raised or lowered in a vertical shaft to transport persons or goods in a building **2** the force required to lift an object **3 a** the component of the aerodynamic forces acting on a wing, etc, at right angles to the airflow **b** the upward force exerted by the gas in a balloon, airship, etc. **4** See **airlift**

ligament *Anatomy* any one of the bands or sheets of tough fibrous connective tissue that restrict movement in joints, connect various bones or cartilages, support muscles, etc.

ligature 1 *Surgery* a thread or wire for tying around a vessel, duct, etc, as for constricting the flow of blood to a part **2** *Music* a slur or the group of notes connected by it **b** (in plainsong notation) a symbol indicating two or more notes grouped together

Ligeti György born 1923, Hungarian composer, resident in Vienna. His works, noted for their experimentalism,

include *Atmospheres* (1961) for orchestra, *Volumina* (1962) for organ, and a requiem mass (1965)

light¹ electromagnetic radiation that is capable of causing a visual sensation and has wavelengths from about 380 to about 780 nanometres

light² 1 having relatively low density **2** relatively low in alcoholic content **3** (of an industry) engaged in the production of small consumer goods using light machinery **4** *Aeronautics* (of an aircraft) having a maximum take-off weight less than 5670 kilograms (12 500 pounds) **5** *Chem* (of an oil fraction obtained from coal tar) having a boiling range between about 100° and 210°C **6** (of a railway) having a narrow gauge, or in some cases a standard gauge with speed or load restrictions not applied to a main line **7** *Bridge* **a** (of a bid) made on insufficient values **b** (of a player) having failed to take sufficient tricks to make his contract

light bulb a glass bulb containing a gas, such as argon or nitrogen, at low pressure and enclosing a thin metal filament that emits light when an electric current is passed through it

lighter¹ a small portable device for providing a naked flame or red-hot filament to light cigarettes, etc.

lighter² a flat-bottomed barge used for transporting cargo, esp in loading or unloading a ship

light flyweight a an amateur boxer weighing not more than 48 kg (106 pounds) **b** (*as modifier*): *a light-flyweight fight*

light heavyweight 1 a a professional boxer weighing 160–175 pounds (72.5–79.5 kg) **b** an amateur boxer weighing 75–81 kg (165–179 pounds) **c** (*as modifier*): *a light-heavyweight bout* **2** a wrestler in a similar weight category (usually 192–214 pounds (87–97 kg))

lighting 1 the apparatus for supplying artificial light effects to a stage, film, or television set **2** the distribution of light on an object or figure, as in painting, photography, etc.

light middleweight a an amateur boxer weighing 67–71 kg (148–157 pounds) **b** (*as modifier*): *a light-middleweight bout*

lightning a flash of light in the sky, occurring during a thunderstorm and caused by a discharge of electricity, either between clouds or between a cloud and the earth

lightning conductor *or* **rod** a metal strip terminating in a series of sharp points, attached to the highest part of a building, etc, to discharge the electric field before it can reach a dangerous level and cause a lightning strike

light pen *Computing* **a** a rodlike device which, when applied to the screen of a cathode-ray tube, can detect the time of passage of the illuminated spot across that point thus enabling a computer to determine the position on the screen being pointed at **b** a penlike device, used to read bar codes, that emits light and determines the intensity of that light as reflected from a small area of an adjacent surface

light rail a transport system using small trains or trams, often serving parts of a large metropolitan area
▷www.lrta.org
▷http://routesinternational.com/
rail.htm?#light

lightship a ship equipped as a lighthouse and moored

409

where a fixed structure would prove impracticable

lightweight 1 a a professional boxer weighing 130–135 pounds (59–61 kg) **b** an amateur boxer weighing 57–60 kg (126–132 pounds) **c** (as modifier): the lightweight contender **2** a wrestler in a similar weight category (usually 115–126 pounds (52–57 kg))

light welterweight a an amateur boxer weighing 60–63.5 kg (132–140 pounds) **b** (as modifier): the light welterweight champion

light year a unit of distance used in astronomy, equal to the distance travelled by light in one year, i.e. 9.4607×10^{12} kilometres or 0.3066 parsecs

ligneous of or resembling wood

lignite a brown carbonaceous sedimentary rock with woody texture that consists of accumulated layers of partially decomposed vegetation: used as a fuel. Fixed carbon content: 46–60 per cent; calorific value: 1.28×10^7 to 1.93×10^7 J/kg (5500 to 8300 Btu/lb)

lignum vitae 1 either of two zygophyllaceous tropical American trees, Guaiacum officinale or G. sanctum, having blue or purple flowers **2** the heavy resinous wood of either of these trees, which is used in machine bearings, casters, etc.: formerly thought to have medicinal properties

Liguria a region of NW Italy, on the **Ligurian Sea** (an arm of the Mediterranean): the third smallest of the regions of Italy. Pop: 1 572 197 (2003 est). Area: 5410 sq km (2089 sq miles)

Likasi a city in the S Democratic Republic of Congo (formerly Zaïre): a centre of copper and cobalt production. Pop: 345 000 (2005 est)

likeness Art a painted, carved, moulded, or graphic image of a person or thing

lilac 1 any of various Eurasian oleaceous shrubs or small trees of the genus Syringa, esp S. vulgaris (**common lilac**) which has large sprays of purple or white fragrant flowers **2** a light or moderate purple colour, sometimes with a bluish or reddish tinge

Lilburne John ?1614-57, English Puritan pamphleteer and leader of the Levellers, a radical group prominent during the Civil War

Lilienthal Otto 1848-96, German aeronautical engineer, a pioneer of glider design

Lilith 1 (in the Old Testament and in Jewish folklore) a female demon, who attacks children **2** (in Talmudic literature) Adam's first wife **3** a witch notorious in medieval demonology

Liliuokalani Lydia Kamekeha 1838-1917, queen and last sovereign of the Hawaiian Islands (1891-95)

Lille an industrial city in N France: the medieval capital of Flanders; forms with Roubaix and Tourcoing one of the largest conurbations in France. Pop: 184 657 (1999)

Lillee Dennis (Keith). born 1949, Australian cricketer who, by the end of the 1982–83 season, had taken what was then world record total of 355 wickets in 65 tests

Lilongwe the capital of Malawi, in the central part west of Lake Malawi. Pop: 655 000 (2005 est)

lilt (in music) a jaunty rhythm

lily 1 any liliaceous perennial plant of the N temperate genus Lilium, such as the Turk's-cap lily and tiger lily, having scaly bulbs and showy typically pendulous flowers **2** the bulb or flower of any of these plants **3**

any of various similar or related plants, such as the water lily, plantain lily, and day lily

lily of the valley a small liliaceous plant, Convallaria majalis, of Eurasia and North America cultivated as a garden plant, having two long oval leaves and spikes of white bell-shaped flowers

Lima the capital of Peru, near the Pacific coast on the Rímac River: the centre of Spanish colonization in South America; university founded in 1551 (the oldest in South America); an industrial centre with a port at nearby Callao. Pop: 8 180 000 (2005 est)

Limassol a port in S Cyprus: trading centre. Pop: 163 000 (2005 est)

Limavady a district of N Northern Ireland, in Co. Londonderry. Pop: 33 571 (2003 est). Area: 586 sq km (226 sq miles)

limb¹ 1 an arm or leg, or the analogous part on an animal, such as a wing **2** any of the main branches of a tree

limb² 1 the edge of the apparent disc of the sun, a moon, or a planet **2** Botany **a** the expanded upper part of a bell-shaped corolla **b** the expanded part of a leaf, petal, or sepal **3** either of the two halves of a bow **4** either of the sides of a geological fold

limber Nautical (in the bilge of a vessel) a fore-and-aft channel through a series of holes in the frames (**limber holes**) where water collects and can be pumped out

limbo¹ Christianity the supposed abode of infants dying without baptism and the just who died before Christ

limbo² a Caribbean dance in which dancers pass, while leaning backwards, under a bar

Limburg¹ or **Limbourg** de active ?1400–?1416, a Dutch family of manuscript illuminators. The three brothers Pol, Herman, and Jehanequin are best known for illustrating the Très Riches Heures du Duc de Berry, one of the finest examples of the International Gothic style

Limburg² 1 a medieval duchy of W Europe: divided between the Netherlands and Belgium in 1839 **2** a province of the SE Netherlands: contains a coalfield and industrial centres. Capital: Maastricht. Pop: 1 142 000 (2003 est). Area: 2253 sq km (809 sq miles) **3** a province of NE Belgium: contains the industrial regions of the Kempen coalfield. Capital: Hasselt. Pop: 805 786 (2004 est). Area: 2422 sq km (935 sq miles)

lime¹ 1 any of certain calcium compounds, esp calcium hydroxide, spread as a dressing on lime-deficient land

lime² 1 a small Asian citrus tree, Citrus aurantifolia, with stiff sharp spines and small round or oval greenish fruits **2 a** the fruit of this tree, having acid fleshy pulp rich in vitamin C **b** (as modifier): lime juice

lime³ any linden tree, such as Tilia europaea, planted in many varieties for ornament

limelight a a type of lamp, formerly used in stage lighting, in which light is produced by heating lime to white heat **b** brilliant white light produced in this way

limerick a form of comic verse consisting of five anapaestic lines of which the first, second, and fifth have three metrical feet and rhyme together and the third and fourth have two metrical feet and rhyme together

Limerick 1 a county of SW Republic of Ireland, in N Munster province: consists chiefly of an undulating plain with rich pasture and mountains in the south.

County town: Limerick. Pop: 175 304 (2002). Area: 2686 sq km (1037 sq miles) **2** a port in SW Republic of Ireland, county town of Limerick, at the head of the Shannon estuary. Pop: 86 998 (2002)

limestone a sedimentary rock consisting mainly of calcium carbonate, deposited as the calcareous remains of marine animals or chemically precipitated from the sea: used as a building stone and in the manufacture of cement, lime, etc.

limey *US and Canadian, slang* a British sailor or ship

limit **1** *Maths* **a** a value to which a function f(x) approaches as closely as desired as the independent variable approaches a specified value (x = a) or approaches infinity **b** a value to which a sequence a_n approaches arbitrarily close as n approaches infinity **c** the limit of a sequence of partial sums of a convergent infinite series **2** *Maths* one of the two specified values between which a definite integral is evaluated

limitation **1** *Law* a certain period of time, legally defined, within which an action, claim, etc, must be commenced **2** *Property law* a restriction upon the duration or extent of an estate

limited **1** (of governing powers, sovereignty, etc) restricted or checked, by or as if by a constitution, laws, or an assembly **2** *US and Canadian* (of a train) stopping only at certain stations and having only a set number of cars for passengers **3** *Chiefly Brit* (of a business enterprise) owned by shareholders whose liability for the enterprise's debts is restricted **4** *US and Canadian* a limited train, bus, etc.

Limoges a city in S central France, on the Vienne River: a centre of the porcelain industry since the 18th century. Pop: 133 968 (1999)

Limousin a region and former province of W central France, in the W part of the Massif Central

limousine **1** any large and luxurious car, esp one that has a glass division between the driver and passengers **2** a former type of car in which the roof covering the rear seats projected over the driver's compartment

limpet **1** any of numerous marine gastropods, such as *Patella vulgata* (**common limpet**) and *Fissurella* (or *Diodora*) *apertura* (**keyhole limpet**), that have a conical shell and are found clinging to rocks **2** any of various similar freshwater gastropods, such as *Ancylus fluviatilis* (**river limpet**) **3** a small open caisson shaped to fit against a dock wall, used mainly in repair work

limpid *Lit* (esp of writings, style, etc) free from obscurity

Limpopo **1** a province of NE South Africa, comprising the N part of the former province of Transvaal: agriculture and service industries. Capital: Polokwane (formerly Pietersburg). Pop: 5 511 962 (2004 est). Area: 123 910 sq km (47 842 sq miles). Former name (1994–2002): **Northern Province 2** a river in SE Africa, rising in E South Africa and flowing northeast, then southeast as the border between South Africa and Zimbabwe and through Mozambique to the Indian Ocean. Length: 1770 km (1100 miles)

Linacre Thomas ?1460–1524, English humanist and physician: founded the Royal College of Physicians (1518)

Linares a city in S Spain: site of Scipio Africanus' defeat of the Carthaginians (208 BC); lead mines. Pop: 58 257

(2003 est)

linchpin *or* **lynchpin** a pin placed transversely through an axle to keep a wheel in position

Lincoln[1] Abraham 1809–65, US Republican statesman; 16th president of the US His fame rests on his success in saving the Union in the Civil War (1861–65) and on his emancipation of slaves (1863); assassinated by Booth

Lincoln[2] **1** a city in E central England, administrative centre of Lincolnshire: an important ecclesiastical and commercial centre in the Middle Ages; Roman ruins, a castle (founded by William the Conqueror) and a famous cathedral (begun in 1086). Pop: 85 963 (2001) **2** a city in SE Nebraska: state capital; University of Nebraska (1869). Pop: 235 594 (2003 est) **3** short for **Lincolnshire 4** a breed of long-woolled sheep, originally from Lincolnshire

Lincolnshire a county of E England, on the North Sea and the Wash: mostly low-lying and fertile, with fenland around the Wash and hills (the **Lincoln Wolds**) in the east; one of the main agricultural counties of Great Britain: the geographical and ceremonial county includes the unitary authorities of North Lincolnshire and North East Lincolnshire (both part of Humberside county from 1974 to 1996). Administrative centre: Lincoln. Pop. (excluding unitary authorities): 665 300 (2003 est). Area (excluding unitary authorities): 5880 sq km (2270 sq miles)

linctus a syrupy medicinal formulation taken to relieve coughs and sore throats

Lind 1 James 1716–94, British physician. He demonstrated (1754) that citrus fruits can cure and prevent scurvy, a remedy adopted by the British navy in 1796 **2** Jenny, original name *Johanna Maria Lind Goldschmidt*. 1820–87, Swedish coloratura soprano

Lindbergh Charles Augustus 1902–74, US aviator, who made the first solo nonstop flight across the Atlantic (1927)

Lindemann Frederick Alexander, 1st Viscount Cherwell. 1886–1957, British physicist, born in Germany; Churchill's scientific adviser during World War II

linden any of various tiliaceous deciduous trees of the N temperate genus *Tilia*, having heart-shaped leaves and small fragrant yellowish flowers: cultivated for timber and as shade trees

Lindesnes a cape at the S tip of Norway, projecting into the North Sea

Lindsay 1 (Nicholas) Vachel 1879–1931, US poet; best known for *General William Booth* (1913) and *The Congo* (1914) **2** Norman Alfred William 1879–1969, Australian artist and writer

Lindsey Parts of an area in E England constituting a former administrative division of Lincolnshire

Lindwall Ray(mond Russell). 1921–96, Australian cricketer. A fast bowler, he played for Australia 61 times between 1946 and 1958

line 1 *Maths* **a** any straight one-dimensional geometrical element whose identity is determined by two points. A **line segment** lies between any two points on a line **b** a set of points (x, y) that satisfies the equation $y = mx + c$, where m is the gradient and c is the intercept with the y-axis **2** *American football* the players arranged in a row on either side of the line of scrimmage at the start of each play **3 a** the edge or contour of a shape, as in sculpture or architecture, or a mark on a painting, drawing, etc, defining or suggesting this **b** the sum or type of such contours or marks, characteristic of a style or design **4 a** a conducting wire, cable, or circuit for making connections between pieces of electrical apparatus, such as a cable for electric-power transmission, telecommunications, etc. **b** (*as modifier*): *the line voltage* **5** a route between two points on a railway **6** *Chiefly Brit* **a** a railway track, including the roadbed, sleepers, etc. **b** one of the rails of such a track **7** one kind of product or article **8** a unit of verse consisting of the number of feet appropriate to the metre being used and written or printed with the words in a single row **9** *Physics* a narrow band in an electromagnetic spectrum, resulting from a transition in an atom, ion, or molecule of a gas or plasma **10** *Music* **a** any of the five horizontal marks that make up the stave **b** the musical part or melody notated on one such set **c** a discernible shape formed by sequences of notes or musical sounds **d** (in polyphonic music) a set of staves that are held together with a bracket or brace **11** a unit of magnetic flux equal to 1 maxwell **12 line ahead** *or* **line abreast** a formation adopted by a naval unit for manoeuvring **13** the combatant forces of certain armies and navies, excluding supporting arms **14** *Fencing* one of four divisions of the target on a fencer's body, considered as areas to which specific attacks are made **15** the scent left by a fox **16 a** the equator (esp in the phrase **crossing the line**) **b** any circle or arc on the terrestrial or celestial sphere **17 above the line a** *Bridge* denoting bonus points, marked above the horizontal line on the score card **18 below the line a** *Bridge* denoting points scored towards game and rubber, marked below the horizontal line on the score card

lineament 1 a facial outline or feature **2** *Geology* any long natural feature on the surface of the earth, such as a fault, esp as revealed by aerial photography

linear 1 designating a style in the arts, esp painting, that obtains its effects through line rather than colour or light and in which the edges of forms and planes are sharply defined **2** *Maths* of or relating to the first degree **3** *Electronics* **a** (of a circuit, etc) having an output that is directly proportional to input **b** having components arranged in a line

linear measure a unit or system of units for the measurement of length

lineation *Geology* any linear arrangement involving rocks or minerals, such as a parallel arrangement of elongated mineral grains

line dancing a form of dancing performed by rows of people to country and western music
  ▷www.knowledgehound.com/topics/
   linedanc.htm
  ▷www.ourworld.compuserve.com/
   homepages/jgothard
  ▷www.uk250.co.uk/linedancing

line drawing a drawing made with lines only, gradations in tone being provided by the spacing and thickness of the lines

linen 1 a a hard-wearing fabric woven from the spun fibres of flax **b** (*as modifier*): *a linen tablecloth* **2** yarn or thread spun from flax fibre **3** clothes, sheets, tablecloths, etc, made from linen cloth or from a substitute such as cotton
  ▷www.irishlinen.co.uk
  ▷www.ulsterlinen.com/2.htm

line printer an electromechanical device that prints a line of characters at a time rather than a character at a time, at speeds from about 200 to 3000 lines per minute: used in printing and in computer systems

liner¹ a passenger ship or aircraft, esp one that is part of a commercial fleet

liner² **1** a material used as a lining **2** *Engineering* a sleeve, usually of a metal that will withstand wear or corrosion, fixed inside or outside a structural component or vessel

ling 1 any of several gadoid food fishes of the northern coastal genus *Molva*, esp *M. molva*, having an elongated body with long fins **2** another name for **burbot** (a fish)

Lingayen Gulf a large inlet of the South China Sea in the Philippines, on the NW coast of Luzon: site of the Japanese landing in the 1941 invasion

lingual *Anatomy* of or relating to the tongue or a part or structure resembling a tongue

liniment a medicated liquid, usually containing alcohol, camphor, and an oil, applied to the skin to relieve pain, stiffness, etc.

lining 1 a material used to line a garment, curtain, etc. **b** (*as modifier*): *lining satin* **2** *Civil engineering* a layer of concrete, brick, or timber, etc, used in canals to prevent them leaking or in tunnels or shafts to prevent them falling in

link 1 a connecting piece in a mechanism, often having pivoted ends **2** a unit of length equal to one hundredth of a chain. 1 link of a Gunter's chain is equal to 7.92 inches, and of an engineer's chain to 1 foot

linkage 1 *Engineering* a system of interconnected levers or rods for transmitting or regulating the motion of a mechanism **2** *Electronics* the product of the total number of lines of magnetic flux and the number of turns in a coil or circuit through which they pass **3** *Genetics* the occurrence of two genes close together on the same chromosome so that they are unlikely to be separated during crossing over and tend to be inherited as a single unit **4** the fact of linking separate but related issues in the course of political negotiations

Linlithgow 1 a town in SE Scotland, in West Lothian: ruined palace, residence of Scottish kings and birthplace of Mary, Queen of Scots. Pop: 13 370 (2001) **2** the former name of **West Lothian**

Linnaeus Carolus, original name *Carl von Linné*. 1707–78, Swedish botanist, who established the binomial system of biological nomenclature that forms the basis of modern classification

linnet 1 a brownish Old World finch, *Acanthis cannabina*: the male has a red breast and forehead **2** a similar and related North American bird, *Carpodacus mexicanus*

Linnhe Loch a sea loch of W Scotland, at the SW end of the Great Glen. Length: about 32 km (20 miles)

linocut 1 a design cut in relief on linoleum mounted on a wooden block **2** a print made from such a design

Lin Piao *or* **Lin Biao** 1908–71, Chinese Communist general and statesman. He became minister of defence

(1959) and second in rank to Mao Tse-tung (1966). He fell from grace and is reported to have died in an air crash while attempting to flee to the Soviet Union

linseed oil a yellow oil extracted from seeds of the flax plant. It has great drying qualities and is used in making oil paints, printer's ink, linoleum, etc.

lint 1 an absorbent cotton or linen fabric with the nap raised on one side, used to dress wounds, etc. **2** shreds of fibre, yarn, etc. **3** *Chiefly US* staple fibre for making cotton yarn

lintel a horizontal beam, as over a door or window

Linz a port in N Austria, capital of Upper Austria, on the River Danube: cultural centre; steelworks. Pop: 183 504 (2001)

lion a large gregarious predatory feline mammal, *Panthera leo*, of open country in parts of Africa and India, having a tawny yellow coat and, in the male, a shaggy mane

Lions Gulf of a wide bay of the Mediterranean off the S coast of France, between the Spanish border and Toulon

lip 1 *Anatomy* **a** either of the two fleshy folds surrounding the mouth, playing an important role in the production of speech sounds, retaining food in the mouth, etc. **b** *(as modifier): lip salve* **2** the corresponding part in animals, esp mammals **3** a nontechnical word for **labium 4** the embouchure and control in the lips needed to blow wind and brass instruments

lipase any of a group of fat-digesting enzymes produced in the stomach, pancreas, and liver and also occurring widely in the seeds of plants

Lipchitz Jacques 1891–1973, US sculptor, born in Lithuania: he pioneered cubist sculpture

Lipetsk a city in central Russia, on the Voronezh River: steelworks. Pop: 518 000 (2005 est)

lipid *or* **lipide** *Biochem* any of a large group of organic compounds that are esters of fatty acids (**simple lipids**, such as fats and waxes) or closely related substances (**compound lipids**, such as phospholipids): usually insoluble in water but soluble in alcohol and other organic solvents. They are important structural materials in living organisms

Li Po *or* **Li T'ai-po** ?700–762 AD, Chinese poet. His lyrics deal mostly with wine, nature, and women and are remarkable for their imagery

liposuction a cosmetic surgical operation in which subcutaneous fat is removed from the body by suction

Lippe 1 a former state of NW Germany, now part of the German state of North Rhine-Westphalia **2** a river in NW Germany, flowing west to the Rhine. Length: about 240 km (150 miles)

Lippi 1 Filippino ?1457–1504, Italian painter of the Florentine school **2** his father, **Fra Filippo** ?1406–69, Italian painter of the Florentine school, noted particularly for his frescoes at Prato Cathedral (1452–64)

Lippmann Gabriel 1845–1921, French physicist. He devised the earliest process of colour photography: Nobel prize for physics 1908

lip-reading a method used by deaf people to comprehend spoken words by interpreting movements of the speaker's lips

liqueur any of several highly flavoured sweetened spirits such as kirsch or cointreau, intended to be drunk after a meal **b** *(as modifier): liqueur glass*
▷www.liqueurweb.com
▷www.thatsthespirit.com/mixology/liqueurs.asp
▷www.webtender.com

liquidation *Business* **a** the process of terminating the affairs of a business firm, etc, by realizing its assets to discharge its liabilities **b** the state of a business firm, etc, having its affairs so terminated (esp in the phrase **to go into liquidation**)

liquid-crystal display a flat-screen display in which an array of liquid-crystal elements can be selectively activated to generate an image, an electric field applied to each element altering its optical properties; it is used, for example, in portable computers, digital watches, and calculators

liquid measure a unit or system of units for measuring volumes of liquids or their containers

liquid oxygen the clear pale blue liquid state of oxygen produced by liquefying air and allowing the nitrogen to evaporate: used in rocket fuels

liquid paraffin a colourless almost tasteless oily liquid obtained from petroleum distillation and used as a laxative

liquor 1 any alcoholic drink, esp spirits, or such drinks collectively **2** *Pharmacol* a solution of a pure substance in water **3** *Brewing* warm water added to malt to form wort

liquorice *or US and Canadian* **licorice 1** a perennial Mediterranean leguminous shrub, *Glycyrrhiza glabra*, having spikes of pale blue flowers and flat red-brown pods **2** the dried root of this plant, used as a laxative and in confectionery

lira 1 the former standard monetary unit of Italy, San Marino, and the Vatican City, divided into 100 centesimi; replaced by the euro in 2002 **2** the standard monetary unit of Turkey, divided into 100 kuruş **3** the standard monetary unit of Malta, divided into 100 cents or 1000 mils

Lisbon the capital and chief port of Portugal, in the southwest on the Tagus estuary: became capital in 1256; subject to earthquakes and severely damaged in 1755; university (1911). Pop: 1 892 891 (2001)

Lisburn 1 a city in Northern Ireland in Lisburn district, Co. Antrim, noted for its linen industry: headquarters of the British Army in Northern Ireland. Pop: 71 465 (2001) **2** a district of S Northern Ireland, in Co. Antrim and Co. Down. Pop: 109 565 (2003 est). Area: 446 sq km (172 sq miles)

Lisieux a town in NW France: Roman Catholic pilgrimage centre, for its shrine of St Thérèse, who lived there. Pop: 23 166 (1999)

lisle a a strong fine cotton thread or fabric **b** *(as modifier): lisle stockings*

list[1] *Computing* a linearly ordered data structure

list[2] **1** a strip of bark, sapwood, etc, trimmed from a board or plank **2** another word for **fillet**

list[3] the act or an instance of a ship leaning to one side

listed building (in Britain) a building officially recognized as having special historical or architectural interest and therefore protected from demolition or alteration

Lister Joseph, 1st Baron Lister. 1827–1912, British surgeon, who introduced the use of antiseptics

listeriosis a serious form of food poisoning, caused by bacteria of the genus *Listeria*. Its symptoms can include meningitis and in pregnant women it may cause damage to the fetus

Liston Sonny, real name *Charles*. 1922–70, US boxer: former world heavyweight champion

list price the selling price of merchandise as quoted in a catalogue or advertisement

Liszt Franz 1811–86, Hungarian composer and pianist. The greatest piano virtuoso of the 19th century, he originated the symphonic poem, pioneered the one-movement sonata form, and developed new harmonic combinations. His works include the symphonies *Faust* (1861) and *Dante* (1867), piano compositions and transcriptions, songs, and church music

litany *Christianity* **a** a form of prayer consisting of a series of invocations, each followed by an unvarying response **b the Litany** the general supplication in this form included in the Book of Common Prayer

litchi, lichee, lichi *or* **lychee 1** a Chinese sapindaceous tree, *Litchi chinensis*, cultivated for its round edible fruits **2** the fruit of this tree, which has a whitish juicy edible aril

literal 1 *Maths* containing or using coefficients and constants represented by letters: $ax^2 + b$ is a literal expression **2** *Publishing* a misprint or misspelling in a text

literalism literal or realistic portrayal in art or literature

lithium a soft silvery element of the alkali metal series: the lightest known metal, used as an alloy hardener, as a reducing agent, and in batteries. Symbol: Li; atomic no.: 3; atomic wt.: 6.941; valency: 1; relative density: 0.534; melting pt.: 180.6°C; boiling pt.: 1342°C

Lithuania a republic in NE Europe, on the Baltic Sea: a grand duchy in medieval times; united with Poland in 1569; occupied by Russia in 1795 and by Germany during World War I; independent Lithuania formed in 1918, but occupied by Soviet troops in 1919 and then by Poland; became a Soviet republic in 1940; unilaterally declared independence from the Soviet Union in 1990; recognized as independent in 1991; joined the EU in 2004. Official language: Lithuanian. Religion: Roman Catholic majority. Currency: litas. Capital: Vilnius. Pop: 3 422 000 (2004 est). Area: 65 200 sq km (25 174 sq miles)

Lithuanian the official language of Lithuania: belonging to the Baltic branch of the Indo-European family

litigant 1 a party to a lawsuit **2** engaged in litigation

litigation 1 the act or process of bringing or contesting a legal action in court **2** a judicial proceeding or contest

litigious 1 excessively ready to go to law **2** of or relating to litigation

litmus a soluble powder obtained from certain lichens. It turns red under acid conditions and blue under basic conditions and is used as an indicator

litre *or US* **liter 1** one cubic decimetre **2** (formerly) the volume occupied by 1 kilogram of pure water at 4°C and 760 millimetres of mercury. This is equivalent to 1.000 028 cubic decimetres or about 1.76 pints

litter 1 a group of offspring produced at one birth by a mammal such as a sow **2** a layer of partly decomposed leaves, twigs, etc, on the ground in a wood or forest

Little Belt a strait in Denmark, between Jutland and Funen Island, linking the Kattegat with the Baltic. Length: about 48 km (30 miles). Width: up to 29 km (18 miles)

Little Bighorn a river in the W central US, rising in N Wyoming and flowing north to the Bighorn River. Its banks were the scene of the defeat (1876) and killing of General Custer and his command by Indians

Little Diomede the smaller of the two Diomede Islands in the Bering Strait: administered by the US Area: about 10 sq km (4 sq miles)

Little Rock a city in central Arkansas, on the Arkansas River: state capital. Pop: 184 053 (2003 est)

Little Russia a region of the former SW Soviet Union, consisting chiefly of Ukraine

Little St Bernard Pass a pass over the Savoy Alps, between Bourg-Saint-Maurice, France, and La Thuile, Italy: 11th-century hospice. Height: 2187 m (7177 ft)

Littlewood (Maud) Joan 1914–2002, British theatre director, who founded the Theatre Workshop Company (1945) with the aim of bringing theatre to the working classes: noted esp for her production of *Oh, What a Lovely War!* (1963)

littoral 1 of or relating to the shore of a sea, lake, or ocean **2** *Biology* inhabiting the shore of a sea or lake or the shallow waters near the shore **3** a coastal or shore region

liturgy 1 the forms of public services officially prescribed by a Church **2** *Chiefly Eastern Churches* the Eucharistic celebration **3** a particular order or form of public service laid down by a Church

Liu Shao Qi *or* **Liu Shao-ch'i** 1898–1974, Chinese Communist statesman; chairman of the People's Republic of China (1959–68); deposed during the Cultural Revolution

live 1 (esp of a volcano) not extinct **2** of a record **a** recorded in concert **b** recorded in one studio take, without overdubs or splicing **3** connected to a source of electric power **4** being in a state of motion or transmitting power; positively connected to a driving member

lively (of a boat or ship) readily responsive to the helm

liver 1 a multilobed highly vascular reddish-brown glandular organ occupying most of the upper right part of the human abdominal cavity immediately below the diaphragm. It secretes bile, stores glycogen, detoxifies certain poisons, and plays an important part in the metabolism of carbohydrates, proteins, and fat, helping to maintain a correct balance of nutrients **2** the corresponding organ in animals **3** a reddish-brown colour, sometimes with a greyish tinge

Liverpool[1] Robert Banks Jenkinson, 2nd Earl of Liverpool. 1770–1828, British Tory statesman; prime minister (1812–27). His government was noted for its repressive policies until about 1822, when more liberal measures were introduced by such men as Peel and Canning

Liverpool[2] **1** a city in NW England, in Liverpool unitary authority, Merseyside, on the Mersey estuary: second largest seaport in Great Britain; developed chiefly in the 17th century with the industrialization of S Lancashire; Liverpool University (1881) and John Moores University (1992). Pop: 469 017 (2001) **2** a unitary authority in NW England, in Merseyside. Pop: 441 800 (2003 est). Area: 113 sq km (44 sq miles)

liverwort any bryophyte plant of the phylum *Hepatophyta*, growing in wet places and resembling green seaweeds or leafy mosses

livery 1 a the stabling, keeping, or hiring out of horses for money b (*as modifier*): *a livery horse* 2 at livery being kept in a livery stable 3 *Legal history* an ancient method of conveying freehold land

live wire *Electronics* a wire carrying an electric current

Livia Drusilla 58 BC–29 AD, Roman noblewoman: wife (from 39 BC) of Emperor Augustus and mother of Emperor Tiberius

livid 1 (of the skin) discoloured, as from a bruise or contusion 2 of a greyish tinge or colour

living 1 (of animals or plants) existing in the present age; extant 2 presented by actors before a live audience 3 *Church of England* another term for **benefice**

Livingston a town in SE Scotland, the administrative centre of West Lothian: founded as a new town in 1962. Pop: 50 826 (2001)

Livingstone 1 David 1813–73, Scottish missionary and explorer in Africa. After working as a missionary in Botswana, he led a series of expeditions and was the first European to discover Lake Ngami (1849), the Zambezi River (1851), the Victoria Falls (1855), and Lake Malawi (1859). In 1866 he set out to search for the source of the Nile and was found in dire straits and rescued (1871) by the journalist H. M. Stanley 2 **Kenneth Robert**, known as *Ken*. born 1945, mayor of London from 2000; Labour leader of the Greater London Council (1981–86)

living wage a wage adequate to permit a wage earner to live and support a family in reasonable comfort

living will a document stating that if its author becomes terminally ill, his or her life should not be prolonged by artificial means, such as a life-support machine

Livonia 1 a former Russian province on the Baltic, north of Lithuania: became Russian in 1721; divided between Estonia and Latvia in 1918 2 a city in SE Michigan, west of Detroit. Pop: 99 487 (2003 est)

Livorno a port in W central Italy, in Tuscany on the Ligurian Sea: shipyards; oil-refining. Pop: 156 274 (2001)

Livy Latin name *Titus Livius*. 59 BC–17 AD, Roman historian; of his history of Rome in 142 books, only 35 survive

lizard any reptile of the suborder *Lacertilia* (or *Sauria*), esp those of the family *Lacertidae* (Old World lizards), typically having an elongated body, four limbs, and a long tail: includes the geckos, iguanas, chameleons, monitors, and slow worms

Lizard the a promontory in SW England, in SW Cornwall: the southernmost point in Great Britain

Ljubljana the capital of Slovenia: capital of Illyria (1816–49); part of Yugoslavia (1918–91); university (1595). Pop: 265 881 (2002)

llama 1 a domesticated South American cud-chewing mammal, *Lama glama* (or *L. peruana*), that is used as a beast of burden and is valued for its hair, flesh, and hide: family *Camelidae* (camels) 2 the cloth made from the wool of this animal 3 any other animal of the genus *Lama*

Llandaff or **Llandaf** a town in SE Wales, now a suburb

of Cardiff; the oldest bishopric in Wales (6th century)

Llandudno a town and resort in NW Wales, in Conwy county borough on the Irish Sea. Pop: 14 872 (2001)

Llanelli or **Llanelly** an industrial town in S Wales, in SE Carmarthenshire on an inlet of Carmarthen Bay. Pop: 46 357 (2001)

Llanfairpwllgwyngyll, Llanfairpwll, or **Llanfair P. G.** a village in NW Wales, in SE Anglesey: reputed to be the longest place name in Great Britain when unabbreviated; means: St. Mary's Church in the hollow of the white hazel near the rapid whirlpool of Llandysilio of the red cave

Llangollen a town in NE Wales, in Denbighshire on the River Dee: International Musical Eisteddfod held annually since 1946. Pop: 2930 (2001)

Llano Estacado the S part of the Great Plains of the US, extending over W Texas and E New Mexico: oil and natural gas resources. Chief towns: Lubbock and Amarillo. Area: 83 700 sq km (30 000 sq miles)

Lleyn Peninsula a peninsula in NW Wales between Cardigan Bay and Caernarvon Bay

Lloyd 1 **Clive** (**Hubert**). born 1944, West Indian (Guyanese) cricketer; captained the West Indies (1974–88) 2 **Harold** (**Clayton**). 1893–1971, US comic film actor 3 **Marie**, real name *Matilda Alice Victoria Wood*. 1870–1922, English music-hall entertainer

Lloyd George David, 1st Earl Lloyd George of Dwyfor. 1863–1945, British Liberal statesman: prime minister (1916–22). As chancellor of the exchequer (1908–15) he introduced old age pensions (1908), a radical budget (1909), and an insurance scheme (1911)

Lloyd Webber Andrew, Baron Lloyd-Webber. born 1948, British composer. His musicals include *Joseph and the Amazing Technicolour Dreamcoat* (1968), *Jesus Christ Superstar* (1970), and *Evita* (1978), all with lyrics by Tim Rice, and *Cats* (1981), *Phantom of the Opera* (1986), *Sunset Boulevard* (1993), and *The Beautiful Game* (2000) his brother, **Julian** born 1951, British cellist

Llywelyn ap Gruffudd died 1282, prince of Wales (1258–82): the only Welsh ruler to be recognized as such by the English

loach any carplike freshwater cyprinoid fish of the family *Cobitidae*, of Eurasia and Africa, having a long narrow body with barbels around the mouth

Loach Ken(neth). born 1936, British television and film director; his works for television include *Cathy Come Home* (1966) and his films include *Kes* (1970), *Riff-Raff* (1991), *Bread and Roses* (2000), and *Ae Fond Kiss* (2004)

load 1 the weight that is carried by a structure 2 *Electrical engineering, Electronics* a a device that receives or dissipates the power from an amplifier, oscillator, generator, or some other source of signals b the power delivered by a machine, generator, circuit, etc. 3 the force acting on a component in a mechanism or structure 4 the resistance overcome by an engine or motor when it is driving a machine, etc. 5 an external force applied to a component or mechanism

loaded 1 (of dice, a roulette wheel, etc) weighted or otherwise biased 2 (of concrete) containing heavy metals, esp iron or lead, for use in making radiation shields

loam 1 rich soil consisting of a mixture of sand, clay, and decaying organic material 2 a paste of clay and sand used for making moulds in a foundry, plastering walls, etc.

lob 1 *Sport* a ball struck in a high arc 2 *Cricket* a ball bowled in a slow high arc

Lobachevsky Nikolai Ivanovich 1793–1856, Russian mathematician; a founder of non-Euclidean geometry

lobate *or* **lobated** 1 having or resembling lobes 2 (of birds) having separate toes that are each fringed with a weblike lobe

lobby 1 a room or corridor used as an entrance hall, vestibule, etc. 2 *Chiefly Brit* a hall in a legislative building used for meetings between the legislators and members of the public 3 *Chiefly Brit* one of two corridors in a legislative building in which members vote 4 a group of persons who attempt to influence legislators on behalf of a particular interest

lobbyist a person employed by a particular interest to lobby

lobe 1 any of the subdivisions of a bodily organ or part, delineated by shape or connective tissue 2 short for **ear lobe** 3 any of the loops that form part of the graphic representation in cylindrical coordinates of the radiation pattern of a transmitting aerial 4 any of the parts, not entirely separate from each other, into which a flattened plant part, such as a leaf, is divided

lobelia any plant of the campanulaceous genus *Lobelia*, having red, blue, white, or yellow five-lobed flowers with the three lower lobes forming a lip

Lobengula ?1836–94, last Matabele king (1870–93); his kingdom was destroyed by the British

Lobito the chief port in Angola, in the west on **Lobito Bay**: terminus of the railway through Benguela to Mozambique. Pop: 70 000 (latest est)

lobola *or* **lobolo** (in southern Africa) an African custom by which a bridegroom's family makes a payment in cattle or cash to the bride's family shortly before the marriage

lobotomy 1 surgical incision into a lobe of any organ 2 surgical interruption of one or more nerve tracts in the frontal lobe of the brain: used in the treatment of intractable mental disorders

lobster 1 any of several large marine decapod crustaceans of the genus *Homarus*, esp *H. vulgaris*, occurring on rocky shores and having the first pair of limbs modified as large pincers 2 any of several similar crustaceans, esp the spiny lobster

lobster pot *or* **trap** a round basket or trap made of open slats used to catch lobsters

local 1 *Med* of, affecting, or confined to a limited area or part 2 *Med* short for **local anaesthetic**

local anaesthetic *Med* a drug that produces local anaesthesia

local authority *Brit and NZ* the governing body of a county, district, etc.

local government 1 government of the affairs of counties, towns, etc, by locally elected political bodies 2 the US equivalent of **local authority**

Locarno a town in S Switzerland, in Ticino canton at the N end of Lake Maggiore: tourist resort. Pop: 14 561 (2000)

location 1 a place outside a studio where filming is done 2 *Computing* a position in a memory capable of

holding a unit of information, such as a word, and identified by its address 3 *Roman and Scots law* the letting out on hire of a chattel or of personal services

loch 1 a Scot word for **lake** 2 a long narrow bay or arm of the sea in Scotland

lock 1 a device fitted to a gate, door, drawer, lid, etc, to keep it firmly closed and often to prevent access by unauthorized persons 2 a similar device attached to a machine, vehicle, etc, to prevent use by unauthorized persons 3 a a section of a canal or river that may be closed off by gates to control the water level and the raising and lowering of vessels that pass through it b (*as modifier*): *a lock gate* 4 *Brit* the extent to which a vehicle's front wheels will turn to the right or left 5 any wrestling hold in which a wrestler seizes a part of his opponent's body and twists it or otherwise exerts pressure upon it 6 *Rugby* either of two players who make up the second line of the scrum and apply weight to the forwards in the front line 7 a gas bubble in a hydraulic system or a liquid bubble in a pneumatic system that stops or interferes with the fluid flow in a pipe, capillary, etc.

Locke 1 John 1632–1704, English philosopher, who discussed the concept of empiricism in his *Essay Concerning Human Understanding* (1690). He influenced political thought, esp in France and America, with his *Two Treatises on Government* (1690), in which he sanctioned the right to revolt 2 Matthew ?1630–77, English composer, esp of works for the stage

Lockerbie a town in SW Scotland, in Dumfries and Galloway: scene (1988) of the UK's worst air disaster when a jumbo jet was brought down by a terrorist bomb, killing 270 people, including eleven residents of the town

lockjaw *Pathol* a nontechnical name for **trismus** and (often) **tetanus**

lock up *Brit* a small shop with no attached quarters for the owner or shopkeeper

Lockyer Sir Joseph Norman 1836–1920, English astronomer: a pioneer in solar spectroscopy, he was the first to observe helium in the sun's atmosphere (1868)

loco denoting a price for goods, esp goods to be exported, that are in a place specified or known, the buyer being responsible for all transport charges from that place

locomotive a a self-propelled engine driven by steam, electricity, or diesel power and used for drawing trains along railway tracks b (*as modifier*): *a locomotive shed*

Locris *or* **Lokris** an ancient region of central Greece

locus 1 (in many legal phrases) a place or area, esp the place where something occurred 2 *Maths* a set of points whose location satisfies or is determined by one or more specified conditions 3 *Genetics* the position of a particular gene on a chromosome

locust 1 any of numerous orthopterous insects of the genera *Locusta, Melanoplus*, etc, such as *L. migratoria*, of warm and tropical regions of the Old World, which travel in vast swarms, stripping large areas of vegetation 2 a North American leguminous tree, *Robinia pseudoacacia*, having prickly branches, hanging clusters of white fragrant flowers, and reddish-brown seed pods 3 the yellowish durable wood of this tree 4 any of several similar trees, such as the honey locust and carob

Lod a town in central Israel, southeast of Tel Aviv: Israel's chief airport. Pop: 66 800 (2003 est)

lodestar *or* **loadstar** a star, esp the North Star, used in navigation or astronomy as a point of reference

lodestone *or* **loadstone** a a rock that consists of pure or nearly pure magnetite and thus is naturally magnetic b a piece of such rock, which can be used as a magnet and which was formerly used as a primitive compass

lodge 1 *Chiefly Brit* a small house at the entrance to the grounds of a country mansion, usually occupied by a gatekeeper or gardener 2 a house or cabin used occasionally, as for some seasonal activity 3 *US and Canadian* a central building in a resort, camp, or park 4 a large house or hotel 5 the dwelling place of certain animals, esp the dome-shaped den constructed by beavers 6 a hut or tent of certain North American Indian peoples

Lodge¹ the official Canberra residence of the Australian Prime Minister

Lodge² 1 **David (John)**. born 1935, British novelist and critic. His books include *Changing Places* (1975), *Small World* (1984), *Nice Work* (1988), *Therapy* (1995), and *Thinks...* (2001) 2 **Sir Oliver (Joseph)**. 1851–1940, British physicist, who made important contributions to electromagnetism, radio reception, and attempted to detect the ether. He also studied allegedly psychic phenomena 3 **Thomas** ?1558–1625, English writer. His romance *Rosalynde* (1590) supplied the plot for Shakespeare's *As You Like It*

Lodi a town in N Italy, in Lombardy: scene of Napoleon's defeat of the Austrians in 1796. Pop: 40 805 (2001)

loess a light-coloured fine-grained accumulation of clay and silt particles that have been deposited by the wind

Loewi **Otto** 1873–1961, US pharmacologist, born in Germany. He shared a Nobel prize for physiology or medicine (1936) with Dale for their work on the chemical transmission of nerve impulses

loft 1 the space inside a roof 2 a gallery, esp one for the choir in a church 3 a room over a stable used to store hay 4 an upper storey of a warehouse or factory, esp when converted into living space 5 a raised house or coop in which pigeons are kept 6 *Sport* a (in golf) the angle from the vertical made by the club face to give elevation to a ball b elevation imparted to a ball c a lofting stroke or shot

log 1 a a detailed record of a voyage of a ship or aircraft b a record of the hours flown by pilots and aircrews c a book in which these records are made; logbook 2 a a device consisting of a float with an attached line, formerly used to measure the speed of a ship b **heave the log** to determine a ship's speed with such a device

Logan **Mount** a mountain in NW Canada, in SW Yukon in the St. Elias Range: the highest peak in Canada and the second highest in North America. Height (after a re-survey in 1993): 5959 m (19 550 ft)

loganberry 1 a trailing prickly hybrid rosaceous plant, *Rubus loganobaccus*, cultivated for its edible fruit: probably a hybrid between an American blackberry and a raspberry 2 a the purplish-red acid fruit of this plant b (*as modifier*): loganberry pie

logarithm the exponent indicating the power to which a fixed number, the base, must be raised to obtain a

given number or variable. It is used esp to simplify multiplication and division: if $a^x = M$, then the logarithm of M to the base a (written $\log_a M$) is x

logbook a book containing the official record of trips made by a ship or aircraft; log

loggerhead 1 a large-headed turtle, *Caretta caretta*, occurring in most seas: family *Chelonidae* 2 **loggerhead shrike** a North American shrike, *Lanius ludovicianus*, having a grey head and body, black-and-white wings and tail, and black facial stripe 3 a tool consisting of a large metal sphere attached to a long handle, used for warming liquids, melting tar, etc. 4 a strong round upright post in a whaleboat for belaying the line of a harpoon

loggia 1 a covered area on the side of a building, esp one that serves as a porch 2 an open balcony in a theatre

logging the work of felling, trimming, and transporting timber

logic 1 the branch of philosophy concerned with analysing the patterns of reasoning by which a conclusion is properly drawn from a set of premises, without reference to meaning or context 2 any particular formal system in which are defined axioms and rules of inference 3 **chop logic** to use excessively subtle or involved logic or argument 4 *Electronics, Computing* a the principles underlying the units in a computer system that perform arithmetical and logical operations b (*as modifier*): a logic element
  ▷http://pvspade.com/Logic/
  ▷http://www.philosophypages.com/lg/

logical 1 relating to, used in, or characteristic of logic 2 using, according to, or deduced from the principles of logic 3 *Computing* of, performed by, used in, or relating to the logic circuits in a computer

logician a person who specializes in or is skilled at logic

log in *Computing* the process by which a computer user logs in

logistics the management of materials flow through an organization, from raw materials through to finished goods

log jam *Chiefly US and Canadian* blockage caused by the crowding together of a number of logs floating in a river

log out *Computing* the process by which a computer user logs out

loin *Anatomy* the part of the lower back and sides between the pelvis and the ribs

Loire 1 a department of E central France, in Rhône-Alpes region. Capital: St. Étienne. Pop: 726 613 (2003 est). Area: 4799 sq km (1872 sq miles) 2 a river in France, rising in the Massif Central and flowing north and west in a wide curve to the Bay of Biscay: the longest river in France. Its valley is famous for its wines and châteaux. Length: 1020 km (634 miles)

Loire-Atlantique a department of W France, in Pays de la Loire region. Capital: Nantes. Pop: 1 174 120 (2003 est). Area: 6980 sq km (2722 sq miles)

Loiret a department of central France, in Centre region. Capital: Orléans. Pop: 629 377 (2003 est). Area: 6812 sq km (2657 sq miles)

Loir-et-Cher a department of N central France, in Centre region. Capital: Blois. Pop: 318 853 (2003 est). Area: 6422 sq km (2505 sq miles)

Lolland *or* **Laaland** an island of Denmark in the Baltic Sea, south of Sjælland. Pop: 69 796 (2003 est). Area: 1240 sq km (480 sq miles)

Lomax **Alan** born 1915, and his father **John Avery** (1867–1948), US folklorists

Lombard¹ **Peter** ?1100–?60, Italian theologian, noted for his *Sententiarum libri quatuor*

Lombard² 1 a native or inhabitant of Lombardy 2 a member of an ancient Germanic people who settled in N Italy after 568 AD

Lombardy a region of N central Italy, bordering on the Alps: dominated by prosperous lordships and city-states during the Middle Ages; later ruled by Spain and then by Austria before becoming part of Italy in 1859; intensively cultivated and in parts highly industrialized. Pop: 9 108 645 (2003 est). Area: 23 804 sq km (9284 sq miles)

Lombok an island of Indonesia, in the Nusa Tenggara Islands east of Java: came under Dutch rule in 1894; important biologically as being transitional between Asian and Australian in flora and fauna, the line of demarcation beginning at **Lombok Strait** (a channel between Lombok and Bali, connecting the Flores Sea with the Indian Ocean). Chief town: Mataram. Pop: 2 500 000 (1991). Area: 4730 sq km (1826 sq miles)

Lomond 1 **Loch** a lake in W Scotland, north of Glasgow: the largest Scottish lake; designated a national park in 2002. Length: about 38 km (24 miles). Width: up to 8 km (5 miles) 2 See **Ben Lomond**

Lomu **Jonah** born 1975, New Zealand Rugby Union football player

London¹ **Jack**, full name *John Griffith London*. 1876–1916, US novelist, short-story writer, and adventurer. His works include *Call of the Wild* (1903), *The Sea Wolf* (1904), *The Iron Heel* (1907), and the semiautobiographical *John Barleycorn* (1913)

London² 1 the capital of the United Kingdom, a port in S England on the River Thames near its estuary on the North Sea: consists of the **City** (the financial quarter), the **West End** (the entertainment and major shopping centre), the **East End** (the industrial and former dock area), and extensive suburbs 2 **Greater** the administrative area of London, consisting of the City of London and 32 boroughs (13 Inner London boroughs and 19 Outer London boroughs): formed in 1965 from the City, parts of Surrey, Kent, Essex, and Hertfordshire, and almost all of Middlesex, and abolished for administrative purposes in 1996: a Mayor of London and a new London Assembly took office in 2000. Pop: 7 387 900 (2003 est). Area: 1579 sq km (610 sq miles) 3 a city in SE Canada, in SE Ontario on the Thames River: University of Western Ontario (1878). Pop: 337 318 (2001)

Londonderry *or* **Derry** 1 a historical county of NW Northern Ireland, on the Atlantic: in 1973 replaced for administrative purposes by the districts of Coleraine, Derry, Limavady, and Magherafelt. Area: 2108 sq km (814 sq miles) 2 a port in N Northern Ireland, second city of Northern Ireland: given to the City of London in 1613 to be colonized by Londoners; besieged by James II's forces (1688–89). Pop: 83 699 (2001)

London pride a saxifragaceous plant, a hybrid between *Saxifraga spathularis* and *S. umbrosa*, having a basal rosette of leaves and pinkish-white flowers

Londrina a city in S Brazil, in Paraná: centre of a coffee-growing area. Pop: 679 000 (2005 est)

long 1 (of drinks) containing a large quantity of nonalcoholic beverage 2 *Prosody* a denoting a vowel of relatively great duration or (esp in classical verse) followed by more than one consonant b denoting a syllable containing such a vowel c (in verse that is not quantitative) carrying the emphasis or ictus 3 *Cricket* (of a fielding position) near the boundary 4 *Music* a note common in medieval music but now obsolete, having the time value of two breves

Long **Crawford Williamson** 1815–78, US surgeon. He was the first to use ether as an anaesthetic

Long Beach a city in SW California, on San Pedro Bay: resort and naval base; oil-refining. Pop: 475 460 (2003 est)

Longbenton a town in N England, in North Tyneside unitary authority, Tyne and Wear. Pop: 34 878 (2001)

longboat 1 the largest boat carried aboard a commercial sailing vessel 2 another term for **longship**

Long Eaton a town in N central England, in SE Derbyshire. Pop: 46 490 (2001)

Longfellow **Henry Wadsworth** 1807–82, US poet, noted particularly for his long narrative poems *Evangeline* (1847) and *The Song of Hiawatha* (1855)

Longford 1 a county of N Republic of Ireland, in Leinster province. County town: Longford. Pop: 31 068 (2002). Area: 1043 sq km (403 sq miles) 2 a town in N Republic of Ireland, county town of Co. Longford. Pop: 7557 (2002)

longhorn 1 a long-horned breed of beef cattle, usually red or variegated, formerly common in SW US 2 a now rare British breed of beef cattle with long curved horns

Longinus **Dionysius** ?2nd century AD, supposed author of the famous Greek treatise on literary criticism, *On the Sublime*

Long Island an island in SE New York State, separated from the S shore of Connecticut by **Long Island Sound** (an arm of the Atlantic): contains the New York City boroughs of Brooklyn and Queens in the west, many resorts (notably Coney Island), and two large airports (La Guardia and John F. Kennedy). Area: 4462 sq km (1723 sq miles)

longitude distance in degrees east or west of the prime meridian at 0° measured by the angle between the plane of the prime meridian and that of the meridian through the point in question, or by the corresponding time difference

longitudinal 1 of or relating to longitude or length 2 *Psychol* (of a study of behaviour) carried on over a protracted period of time

long jump an athletic contest in which competitors try to cover the farthest distance possible with a running jump from a fixed board or mark

long-playing of or relating to an LP (long-playing record)

longship a narrow open vessel with oars and a square sail, used esp by the Vikings during medieval times

longshore drift the process whereby beach material is gradually shifted laterally as a result of waves meeting the shore at an oblique angle

long shot 1 a bet against heavy odds 2 *Films, Television* a shot where the camera is or appears to be distant from the object to be photographed

long-sighted related to or suffering from hyperopia

Longs Peak a mountain in N Colorado, in the Front Range of the Rockies: the highest peak in the Rocky Mountain National Park. Height: 4345 m (14 255 ft)

Longueuil a city in SE Canada, in S Quebec: a suburb of Montreal. Pop: 128 016 (2001)

Longus ?3rd century AD, Greek author of the prose romance *Daphnis and Chloe*

Longyearbyen a village on Spitsbergen island, administrative centre of the Svalbard archipelago: coal-mining

Lons-le-Saunier a town in E France: saline springs; manufactures sparkling wines. Pop: 25 867 (1999)

loo 1 a gambling card game 2 a stake used in this game

loom¹ 1 an apparatus, worked by hand or mechanically (**power loom**), for weaving yarn into a textile 2 the middle portion of an oar, which acts as a fulcrum swivelling in the rowlock

loom² *Archaic or dialect* 1 another name for **diver** (the bird) 2 any of various other birds, esp the guillemot

loon¹ the US and Canadian name for **diver** (the bird)

loon² *Archaic* a person of low rank or occupation (esp in the phrase **lord and loon**)

loonie *Canadian, slang* a a Canadian dollar coin with a loon bird on one of its faces b the Canadian currency

loop 1 *Electronics* a closed electric or magnetic circuit through which a signal can circulate 2 a flight manoeuvre in which an aircraft flies one complete circle in the vertical plane 3 *Chiefly Brit* a railway branch line which leaves the main line and rejoins it after a short distance 4 *Maths, Physics* a closed curve on a graph 5 *Anatomy* a the most common basic pattern of the human fingerprint, formed by several sharply rising U-shaped ridges b a bend in a tubular structure, such as the U-shaped curve in a kidney tubule (**Henle's loop** or **loop of Henle**) 6 *Computing* a series of instructions in a program, performed repeatedly until some specified condition is satisfied 7 *Skating* a jump in which the skater takes off from a back outside edge, makes one, two, or three turns in the air, and lands on the same back outside edge

Loos Adolf 1870–1933, Austrian architect: a pioneer of modern architecture, noted for his plain austere style in such buildings as Steiner House, Vienna (1910)

loose 1 a (of the bowels) emptying easily, esp excessively; lax b (of a cough) accompanied by phlegm, mucus, etc. 2 the loose *Rugby* the part of play when the forwards close round the ball in a ruck or loose scrum

lop-eared (of animals) having ears that droop

Lope de Vega full name *Lope Felix de Vega Carpio*. 1562–1635, Spanish dramatist, novelist, and poet. He established the classic form of Spanish drama and was a major influence on European, esp French, literature. Some 500 of his 1800 plays are extant

Lopez Jennifer born 1970, Puerto Rican singer and film actress, known as *J-Lo*; her films include *Selena* (1997) and *The Wedding Planner* (2001) and her records include *On the 6* (1999) and *This is Me...Then* (2002)

Lorca¹ Federico García 1898–1936, Spanish poet and dramatist. His poetry, such as *Romancero gitano* (1928),

shows his debt to Andalusian folk poetry. His plays include the trilogy *Bodas de sangre* (1933), *Yerma* (1934), and *La Casa de Bernarda Alba* (1936)

Lorca² *Brit*, a town in SE Spain, on the Guadalentín River. Pop: 82 511 (2003 est)

lord 1 a person who has power or authority over others, such as a monarch or master 2 a male member of the nobility, esp in Britain 3 (in medieval Europe) a feudal superior, esp the master of a manor 4 *Astrology* a planet having a dominating influence

Lord 1 a title given to God or Jesus Christ 2 *Brit* a a title given to men of high birth, specifically to an earl, marquess, baron, or viscount b a courtesy title given to the · younger sons of a duke or marquess c the ceremonial title of certain high officials or of a bishop or archbishop

Lord Chancellor *Brit*, *Government* the cabinet minister who is head of the judiciary in England and Wales and Speaker of the House of Lords

Lord Howe Island an island in the Tasman Sea, south- · east of Australia: part of New South Wales. Area: 17 sq km (6 sq miles). Pop: 401 (2001)

Lord Lieutenant 1 (in Britain) the representative of the Crown in a county 2 (formerly) the British viceroy in Ireland

Lord Mayor the mayor in the City of London and in certain other important boroughs and large cities

Lord Privy Seal (in Britain) the senior cabinet minister without official duties

Lordship *Brit* a title used to address or refer to a bishop, a judge of the high court, or any peer except a duke

lore 1 the surface of the head of a bird between the eyes and the base of the bill 2 the corresponding area in a snake or fish

Lorentz Hendrik Antoon 1853–1928, Dutch physicist: shared the Nobel prize for physics (1902) with Zeeman for their work on electromagnetic theory

Lorenz Konrad Zacharias 1903–89, Austrian zoologist, who founded ethology. His works include *On Aggression* (1966): shared the Nobel prize for physiology or medicine 1973

Lorient a port in W France, on the Bay of Biscay. Pop: 59 189 (1999)

lorikeet any of various small lories, such as *Glossopsitta versicolor* (**varied lorikeet**) or *Trichoglossus moluccanus* (**rainbow lorikeet**)

Lorraine 1 a region and former province of E France; ceded to Germany in 1871 after the Franco-Prussian war and regained by France in 1919; rich iron-ore deposits 2 **Kingdom of** an early medieval kingdom on the Meuse, Moselle, and Rhine rivers: later a duchy 3 a former duchy in E France, once the S half of this kingdom

lorry 1 a large motor vehicle designed to carry heavy loads, esp one with a flat platform 2 any of various vehicles with a flat load-carrying surface, esp one designed to run on rails

Los Alamos a town in the US, in New Mexico: the first atomic bomb was developed here. Pop: 18 343 (2000 est)

Los Angeles a city in SW California, on the Pacific: the second largest city in the US, having absorbed many adjacent townships; industrial centre and port, with several universities. Pop: 3 819 951 (2003 est)

loser *Bridge* a card that will not take a trick

Losey Joseph 1909–84, US film director, in Britain from 1952. His films include *The Servant* (1963), *The Go-Between* (1971), and *Don Giovanni* (1979)

loss 1 *Electronics* a measure of the power lost in an electrical system expressed as the ratio of or difference between the input power and the output power 2 **at a loss** at less than the cost of buying, producing, or maintaining (something)

lot 1 an item or set of items for sale in an auction 2 *Chiefly US and Canadian* a film studio and the site on which it is located

Lot¹ 1 a department of S central France, in Midi-Pyrénées region. Capital: Cahors. Pop: 164 413 (2003 est). Area: 5226 sq km (2038 sq miles) 2 a river in S France, rising in the Cévennes and flowing west into the Garonne River. Length: about 483 km (300 miles)

Lot² *Old Testament* Abraham's nephew: he escaped the destruction of Sodom, but his wife was changed into a pillar of salt for looking back as they fled (Genesis 19)

Lot-et-Garonne a department of SW France, in Aquitaine. Capital: Agen. Pop: 309 993 (2003 est). Area: 5385 sq km (2100 sq miles)

Lothair I ?795–855 AD, Frankish ruler and Holy Roman Emperor (823–30, 833–34, 840–55); son of Louis I, whom he twice deposed from the throne

Lothair II called *the Saxon*. ?1070–1137, German king (1125–37) and Holy Roman Emperor (1133–37). He was elected German king over the hereditary Hohenstaufen claimant

Lothian Region a former local government region in SE central Scotland, formed in 1975 from East Lothian, most of Midlothian, and West Lothian; replaced in 1996 by the council areas of East Lothian, Midlothian, West Lothian, and Edinburgh

lottery 1 a method of raising money by selling numbered tickets and giving a proportion of the money raised to holders of numbers drawn at random 2 a similar method of raising money in which players select a small group of numbers out of a larger group printed on a ticket. If a player's selection matches some or all of the numbers drawn at random the player wins a proportion of the prize fund

lotto 1 a children's game in which numbered discs, counters, etc, are drawn at random and called out, while the players cover the corresponding numbers on cards, the winner being the first to cover all the numbers, a particular row, etc. 2 a lottery

lotus 1 (in Greek mythology) a fruit that induces forgetfulness and a dreamy languor in those who eat it 2 the plant bearing this fruit, thought to be the jujube, the date, or any of various other plants 3 any of several water lilies of tropical Africa and Asia, esp the white lotus (*Nymphaea lotus*), which was regarded as sacred in ancient Egypt 4 a similar plant, *Nelumbo nucifera*, which is the sacred lotus of India, China, and Tibet and also sacred in Egypt: family *Nelumbonaceae* 5 a representation of such a plant, common in Hindu, Buddhist, and ancient Egyptian carving and decorative art 6 any leguminous plant of the genus *Lotus*, of the Old World and North America, having yellow, pink, or white pealike flowers

lotus-eater *Greek myth* one of a people encountered by Odysseus in North Africa who lived in indolent forgetfulness, drugged by the fruit of the legendary lotus

lotus position a seated cross-legged position used in yoga, meditation, etc.

loud-hailer a portable loudspeaker having a built-in amplifier and microphone

loudspeaker a device for converting audio-frequency signals into the equivalent sound waves by means of a vibrating conical diaphragm

lough 1 an Irish word for **lake** 2 a long narrow bay or arm of the sea in Ireland

Loughborough a town in central England, in N Leicestershire: university (1966). Pop: 55 258 (2001)

Louis Joe, real name *Joseph Louis Barrow*, nicknamed *the Brown Bomber*. 1914–81, US boxer; world heavyweight champion (1937–49)

Louisbourg a fortress in Canada, in Nova Scotia on SE Cape Breton Island: founded in 1713 by the French and strongly fortified (1720–40); captured by the British (1758) and demolished; reconstructed as a historic site

Louis I known as *Louis the Pious* or *Louis the Debonair*. 778–840 AD, king of France and Holy Roman Emperor (814–23, 830–33, 834–40): he was twice deposed by his sons

Louisiana a state of the southern US, on the Gulf of Mexico: originally a French colony; bought by the US in 1803 as part of the Louisiana Purchase; chiefly lowlying. Capital: Baton Rouge. Pop: 4 496 334 (2003 est). Area: 116 368 sq km (44 930 sq miles)

Louis II 1 known as *Louis the German*. ?804–876 AD, king of Germany (843–76); son of Louis I 2 1845–86, king of Bavaria (1864–86): noted for his extravagant castles and his patronage of Wagner. Declared insane (1886), he drowned himself

Louis IV known as *Louis the Bavarian*. ?1287–1347, king of Germany (1314–47) and Holy Roman Emperor (1328–47)

Louis V known as *Louis le Fainéant*. ?967–987 AD, last Carolingian king of France (986–87)

Louis VIII known as *Coeur-de-Lion*. 1187–1226, king of France (1223–26). He was offered the English throne by opponents of King John but his invasion failed (1216)

Louis IX known as *Saint Louis*. 1214–70, king of France (1226–70): led the Sixth Crusade (1248–54) and was held to ransom (1250); died at Tunis while on another crusade

Louisville a port in N Kentucky, on the Ohio River: site of the annual Kentucky Derby; university (1837). Pop: 248 762 (2003 est)

Louis XI 1423–83, king of France (1461–83); involved in a struggle with his vassals, esp the duke of Burgundy, in his attempt to unite France under an absolute monarchy

Louis XII 1462–1515, king of France (1498–1515), who fought a series of unsuccessful wars in Italy

Louis XIII 1601–43, king of France (1610–43). His mother (Marie de Médicis) was regent until 1617; after 1624 he was influenced by his chief minister Richelieu

Louis XIV known as *le roi soleil* (the Sun King). 1638–1715, king of France (1643–1715); son of Louis XIII and Anne of Austria. Effective ruler from 1661, he established an absolute monarchy. His attempt to establish French supremacy in Europe, waging almost continual wars from 1667 to 1714, ultimately failed. But his reign is regarded as a golden age of French literature and art

Louis XV 1710–74, king of France (1715–74); great-grandson of Louis XIV. He engaged France in a series of wars, esp the disastrous Seven Years' War (1756–63), which undermined the solvency and authority of the crown

Louis XVI 1754–93, king of France (1774–92); grandson of Louis XV. He married Marie Antoinette in 1770 and they were guillotined during the French Revolution

Louis XVII 1785–95, titular king of France (1793–95) during the Revolution, after the execution of his father Louis XVI; he died in prison

Louis XVIII 1755–1824, king of France (1814–24); younger brother of Louis XVI. He became titular king after the death of Louis XVII (1795) and ascended the throne at the Bourbon restoration in 1814. He was forced to flee during the Hundred Days

Louis Philippe known as the *Citizen King*. 1773–1850, king of the French (1830–48). His régime became excessively identified with the bourgeoisie and he was forced to abdicate by the revolution of 1848

Lourdes a town in SW France: a leading place of pilgrimage for Roman Catholics after a peasant girl, Bernadette Soubirous, had visions of the Virgin Mary in 1858. Pop: 15 203 (1999)

lourie *or* **loerie** *South African* any of several species of touraco: louries are divided into two groups, the arboreal species having a mainly green plumage and crimson wings and the species which inhabits the more open savanna areas having a plain grey plumage

louse 1 any wingless bloodsucking insect of the order *Anoplura*: includes *Pediculus capitis* (**head louse**), *Pediculus corporis* (**body louse**), and the crab louse, all of which infest man 2 biting *or* **bird louse** any wingless insect of the order *Mallophaga*, such as the chicken louse: external parasites of birds and mammals with biting mouthparts 3 any of various similar but unrelated insects, such as the plant louse and book louse

Louth a county of NE Republic of Ireland, in Leinster province on the Irish Sea: the smallest of the counties. County town: Dundalk. Pop: 101 821 (2002). Area: 821 sq km (317 sq miles)

Louvain a town in central Belgium, in Flemish Brabant province: capital of the duchy of Brabant (11th–15th centuries) and centre of the cloth trade; university (1426). Pop: 89 777 (2004 est)

louvre *or US* **louver** 1 **a** any of a set of horizontal parallel slats in a door or window, sloping outwards to throw off rain and admit air **b** the slats together with the frame supporting them 2 *Architect* a lantern or turret that allows smoke to escape

Louvre the national museum and art gallery of France, in Paris: formerly a royal palace, begun in 1546; used for its present purpose since 1793

lovage 1 a European umbelliferous plant, *Levisticum officinale*, with greenish-white flowers and aromatic fruits, which are used for flavouring food 2 **Scotch lovage** a similar and related plant, *Ligusticum scoticum*, of N Europe

love 1 *Christianity* **a** God's benevolent attitude towards man **b** man's attitude of reverent devotion towards

God 2 (in tennis, squash, etc) a score of zero

lovebird 1 any of several small African parrots of the genus *Agapornis*, often kept as cage birds 2 another name for **budgerigar**

Lovelace 1 **Countess of**, title of *Ada Augusta King*. 1815–52, English mathematician and personal assistant to Charles Babbage: daughter of Lord Byron. She wrote the first computer program 2 **Richard** 1618–58, English Cavalier poet, noted for *To Althea from Prison* (1642) and *Lucasta* (1649)

love-lies-bleeding any of several amaranthaceous plants of the genus *Amaranthus*, esp *A. caudatus*, having drooping spikes of small red flowers

Lovell Sir **Bernard** born 1913, English radio astronomer; founder (1951) and director of Jodrell Bank

low 1 *Biology* not advanced in evolution 2 of relatively small price or monetary value 3 *Music* relating to or characterized by a relatively low pitch 4 (of latitudes) situated not far north or south of the equator 5 (of a gear) providing a relatively low forward speed for a given engine speed 6 of or relating to the Low Church 7 *Meteorology* an area of relatively low atmospheric pressure, esp a depression 8 *Electronics* the voltage level in a logic circuit corresponding to logical zero

Low Sir **David** 1891–1963, British political cartoonist, born in New Zealand: created Colonel Blimp

low-alcohol (of beer or wine) containing only a small amount of alcohol

Low Church the school of thought in the Church of England stressing evangelical beliefs and practices

Lowell 1 **Amy** (**Lawrence**). 1874–1925, US imagist poet and critic 2 **James Russell** 1819–91, US poet, essayist, and diplomat, noted for his series of poems in Yankee dialect, *Biglow Papers* (1848; 1867) 3 **Robert** (**Traill Spence**). 1917–77, US poet. His volumes of verse include *Lord Weary's Castle* (1946), *Life Studies* (1959), *For the Union Dead* (1964), and a book of free translations of European poems, *Imitations* (1961)

lower 1 *Maths* (of a limit or bound) less than or equal to one or more numbers or variables 2 *Geology* denoting the early part or division of a period, system, formation, etc.

Lower Austria a state of NE Austria: the largest Austrian province, containing most of the Vienna basin. Capital: Sankt Pölten. Pop: 1 552 848 (2003 est). Area: 19 170 sq km (7476 sq miles)

Lower California a mountainous peninsula of NW Mexico, between the Pacific and the Gulf of California: administratively divided into the states of Baja California (or Baja California Norte) and Baja California Sur

Lower Canada (from 1791 to 1841) the official name of the S region of the present-day province of Quebec

Lower Egypt one of the two main administrative districts of Egypt: consists of the Nile Delta

lower house *Politics* one of the two houses of a bicameral legislature: usually the larger and more representative house

Lower Hutt an industrial town in New Zealand on the S coast of North Island. Pop: 100 300 (2004 est)

Lower Saxony a state of N Germany, on the North Sea and including the E Frisian Islands; formerly in West

Germany: a leading European producer of petroleum. Capital: Hanover. Pop: 7 993 000 (2003 est). Area: 47 408 sq km (18 489 sq miles)

lowest common denominator the smallest integer or polynomial that is exactly divisible by each denominator of a set of fractions

lowest common multiple the smallest number or quantity that is exactly divisible by each member of a set of numbers or quantities

Lowestoft a fishing port and resort in E England, in NE Suffolk on the North Sea. Pop: 68 340 (2001)

Low German a language of N Germany, spoken esp in rural areas: more closely related to Dutch than to standard High German

low-key *or* **low-keyed** (of a photograph, painting, etc) having a predominance of dark grey tones or dark colours with few highlights

lowland 1 relatively low ground 2 a low generally flat region

Lowland of or relating to the Lowlands of Scotland or the dialect of English spoken there

Low Mass a Mass that has a simplified ceremonial form and is spoken rather than sung

low-pitched 1 pitched low in tone 2 (of a roof) having sides with a shallow slope

low profile (of a tyre) wide in relation to its height

Lowry 1 L(awrence) S(tephen). 1887–1976, English painter, noted for his bleak northern industrial scenes, often containing primitive or stylized figures 2 (**Clarence**) **Malcolm** 1909–57, British novelist and writer, best known for his semiautobiographical novel *Under the Volcano* (1947)

low technology simple unsophisticated technology, often that used for centuries, that is limited to the production of basic necessities

low tide the tide when it is at its lowest level or the time at which it reaches this

low water 1 another name for **low tide** 2 the state of any stretch of water at its lowest level

loyalist a patriotic supporter of his sovereign or government

Loyalist 1 (in Northern Ireland) any of the Protestants wishing to retain Ulster's link with Britain 2 (in North America) an American colonist who supported Britain during the War of American Independence 3 (during the Spanish Civil War) a supporter of the republican government

loyalty card a swipe card issued by a supermarket or chain store to a customer, used to record credit points awarded for money spent in the store

lozenge 1 *Med* a medicated tablet held in the mouth until it has dissolved 2 *Geometry* another name for **rhombus**

LP 1 a a long-playing gramophone record: usually one 12 inches (30 cm) or 10 inches (25 cm) in diameter, designed to rotate at 33⅓ revolutions per minute b (*as modifier*): *an LP sleeve* 2 long play: a slow-recording facility on a VCR which allows twice the length of material to be recorded on a tape from that of standard play

L-plate *Brit* a white rectangle with an "L" sign fixed to the back and front of a motor vehicle; a red "L" sign is used to show that a driver using it is a learner who has

not passed the driving test; a green "L" sign may be displayed by new drivers for up to a year after passing the driving test

LSD lysergic acid diethylamide; a crystalline compound prepared from lysergic acid, used in experimental medicine and taken illegally as a hallucinogenic drug

Lualaba a river in the SE Democratic Republic of Congo (formerly Zaïre), rising in Katanga province and flowing north as the W headstream of the River Congo. Length: about 1800 km (1100 miles)

Luanda *or* **Loanda** the capital of Angola, a port in the west, on the Atlantic: founded in 1576, it became a centre of the slave trade to Brazil in the 17th and 18th centuries; oil refining. Pop: 2 839 000 (2005 est)

Luang Prabang a market town in N Laos, on the Mekong River: residence of the monarch of Laos (1946–75). Pop: 26 400 (2003 est)

Lubbock a city in NW Texas: cotton market. Pop: 206 481 (2003 est)

Lublin an industrial city in E Poland: provisional seat of the government in 1918 and 1944. Pop: 397 000 (2005 est)

Lubumbashi a city in the S Democratic Republic of Congo (formerly Zaïre): founded in 1910 as a copper-mining centre; university (1955). Pop: 1 102 000 (2005 est)

Lucan[1] Latin name *Marcus Annaeus Lucanus*. 39–65 AD, Roman poet. His epic poem *Pharsalia* describes the civil war between Caesar and Pompey

Lucan[2] of or relating to St. Luke, a fellow worker of Paul and a physician (Colossians 4:14), or St. Luke's gospel

Lucas George born 1944, US film director, producer, and writer of screenplays. Films include *American Graffiti* (1973) and *Star Wars* (1977) and its prequels *The Phantom Menace* (1999) and *Attack of the Clones* (2002)

Lucas van Leyden ?1494–1533, Dutch painter and engraver

Lucca a city in NW Italy, in Tuscany: centre of a rich agricultural region, noted for the production of olive oil. Pop: 81 862 (2001)

Lucerne 1 a canton in central Switzerland, northwest of Lake Lucerne: joined the Swiss Confederacy in 1332. Pop: 352 300 (2002 est). Area: 1494 sq km (577 sq miles) 2 a city in central Switzerland, capital of Lucerne canton, on Lake Lucerne: tourist centre. Pop: 59 496 (2000) 3 **Lake** a lake in central Switzerland: fed and drained chiefly by the River Reuss. Area: 115 sq km (44 sq miles)

Lucian 2nd century AD, Greek writer, noted esp for his satirical *Dialogues of the Gods* and *Dialogues of the Dead*

lucid *Psychiatry* of or relating to a period of normality between periods of insane or irresponsible behaviour

Lucifer 1 the leader of the rebellion of the angels: usually identified with Satan 2 the planet Venus when it rises as the morning star

Lucilius Gaius ?180–102 BC, Roman satirist, regarded as the originator of poetical satire

Lucknow a city in N India, capital of Uttar Pradesh: capital of Oudh (1775–1856); the British residency was besieged (1857) during the Indian Mutiny. Pop: 2 207 340 (2001)

Lucretius full name *Titus Lucretius Carus*. ?96–55 BC, Roman poet and philosopher. In his didactic poem *De*

rerum natura, he expounds Epicurus' atomist theory of the universe

Lucullus Lucius Licinius ?110–56 BC, Roman general and consul, famous for his luxurious banquets. He fought Mithradates VI (74–66)

Lucy Saint died ?303 AD, a virgin martyred by Diocletian in Syracuse. Feast day: Dec 13

Luddite *English history* any of the textile workers opposed to mechanization who rioted and organized machine-breaking between 1811 and 1816

Ludendorff Erich Friedrich Wilhelm von 1865–1937, German general, Hindenburg's aide in World War I

Ludhiana a city in N India, in the central Punjab: Punjab Agricultural University (1962). Pop: 1 395 053 (2001)

Ludlow a market town in W central England, in Shropshire: castle (11th–16th century). Pop: 9548 (2001)

ludo *Brit* a simple board game in which players advance counters by throwing dice

Ludwigsburg a city in SW Germany, in Baden-Württemberg north of Stuttgart: expanded in the 18th century around the palace of the dukes of Württemberg. Pop: 87 581 (2003 est)

Ludwigshafen a city in SW Germany, in the Rhineland-Palatinate, on the Rhine: chemical industry. Pop: 162 836 (2003 est)

luff 1 *Nautical* the leading edge of a fore-and-aft sail 2 tackle consisting of a single and a double, block for use with rope having a large diameter

Lugano a town in S Switzerland, on Lake Lugano: a financial centre and tourist resort. Pop: 26 560 (2000)

Lugansk an industrial city in E Ukraine, in the Donbass mining region: established in 1795 as an iron-founding centre. Pop: 454 000 (2005 est)

lugger *Nautical* a small working boat rigged with a lug-sail

Lugo a city in NW Spain: Roman walls; Romanesque cathedral. Pop: 91 158 (2003 est)

lugworm any polychaete worm of the genus *Arenicola*, living in burrows on sandy shores and having tufted gills: much used as bait by fishermen

Luhrmann Baz (Mark Anthony). born 1962, Australian film director and screenwriter; his films include *Strictly Ballroom* (1992), *Romeo and Juliet* (1996), and *Moulin Rouge* (2001)

Luke *New Testament* 1 Saint a fellow worker of Paul and a physician (Colossians 4:14). Feast day: Oct 18 2 the third Gospel, traditionally ascribed to Luke

lullaby 1 a quiet song to lull a child to sleep 2 the music for such a song

Lully 1 Jean Baptiste , Italian name *Giovanni Battista Lulli*. 1632–87, French composer, born in Italy; founder of French opera. With Philippe Quinault as librettist, he wrote operas such as *Alceste* (1674) and *Armide* (1686); as superintendent of music at the court of Louis XIV, he wrote incidental music to comedies by Molière 2 Raymond *or* Ramón ?1235–1315, Spanish philosopher, mystic, and missionary. His chief works are *Ars generalis sive magna* and the Utopian novel *Blaquerna*

lumbago pain in the lower back; backache affecting the lumbar region

lumbar of, near, or relating to the part of the body

between the lowest ribs and the hipbones

lumbar puncture *Med* insertion of a hollow needle into the lower region of the spinal cord to withdraw cerebrospinal fluid, introduce drugs, etc.

lumber *Chiefly US and Canadian* a logs; sawn timber b cut timber, esp when sawn and dressed ready for use in joinery, carpentry, etc. c (*as modifier*): *the lumber trade*

lumberjack (esp in North America) a person whose work involves felling trees, transporting the timber, etc.

luminescence *Physics* a the emission of light at low temperatures by any process other than incandescence, such as phosphorescence or chemiluminescence b the light emitted by such a process

luminous (of a physical quantity in photometry) evaluated according to the visual sensation produced in an observer rather than by absolute energy measurements

lump *Pathol* any small swelling or tumour

lumpectomy the surgical removal of a tumour in a breast

lumpy (esp of the sea) rough

Lumumba Patrice 1925–61, Congolese statesman; first prime minister of the Democratic Republic of Congo (1960); assassinated

lunacy (formerly) any severe mental illness

lunar 1 of or relating to the moon 2 occurring on, used on, or designed to land on the surface of the moon 3 relating to, caused by, or measured by the position or orbital motion of the moon 4 of or containing silver

Lund a city in SE Sweden, northeast of Malmö: founded in about 1020 by the Danish King Canute; the archbishopric for all Scandinavia in the Middle Ages; university (1668). Pop: 101 427 (2004 est)

Lundy an island in SW England, in Devon, in the Bristol Channel: now a bird sanctuary. Pop: 50 (latest est)

lung 1 either one of a pair of spongy saclike respiratory organs within the thorax of higher vertebrates, which oxygenate the blood and remove its carbon dioxide 2 any similar or analogous organ in other vertebrates or in invertebrates

lunge[1] *Fencing* a thrust made by advancing the front foot and straightening the back leg, extending the sword arm forwards

lunge[2] a rope used in training or exercising a horse

lungfish any freshwater bony fish of the subclass *Dipnoi*, having an air-breathing lung, fleshy paired fins, and an elongated body. The only living species are those of the genera *Lepidosiren* of South America, *Protopterus* of Africa, and *Neoceratodus* of Australia

Luoyang *or* **Loyang** a city in E China, in N Henan province on the Luo River near its confluence with the Yellow River; an important Buddhist centre in the 5th and 6th centuries; a commercial and industrial centre. Pop: 1 594 000 (2005 est)

lupin *or US* **lupine** any leguminous plant of the genus *Lupinus*, of North America, Europe, and Africa, with large spikes of brightly coloured flowers and flattened pods

lupine of, relating to, or resembling a wolf

lupus any of various ulcerative skin diseases

lurch *Cribbage* the state of a losing player with less than

30 points at the end of a game (esp in the phrase **in the lurch**)

lure 1 *Angling* any of various types of brightly-coloured artificial spinning baits, usually consisting of a plastic or metal body mounted with hooks and trimmed with feathers, etc. 2 *Falconry* a feathered decoy to which small pieces of meat can be attached and which is equipped with a long thong

Lusaka the capital of Zambia, in the southeast at an altitude of 1280 m (4200 ft): became capital of Northern Rhodesia in 1932 and of Zambia in 1964; University of Zambia (1966). Pop: 1 450 000 (2005 est)

Lusatia a region of central Europe, lying between the upper reaches of the Elbe and Oder Rivers: now mostly in E Germany, extending into SW Poland; inhabited chiefly by Sorbs

Lusitania an ancient region of the W Iberian Peninsula: a Roman province from 27 BC to the late 4th century AD; corresponds to most of present-day Portugal and the Spanish provinces of Salamanca and Cáceres

lustre *or US* **luster** 1 a a shiny metallic surface on some pottery and porcelain b *(as modifier)*: *lustre decoration* 2 *Mineralogy* the way in which light is reflected from the surface of a mineral. It is one of the properties by which minerals are defined

lute¹ an ancient plucked stringed instrument, consisting of a long fingerboard with frets and gut strings, and a body shaped like a sliced pear

lute² *Dentistry* a thin layer of cement used to fix a crown or inlay in place on a tooth

Lutetia *or* **Lutetia Parisiorum** an ancient name for **Paris** (the French city)

lutetium *or* **lutecium** a silvery-white metallic element of the lanthanide series, occurring in monazite and used as a catalyst in cracking, alkylation, and polymerization. Symbol: Lu; atomic no.: 71; atomic wt.: 174.967; valency: 3; relative density: 9.841; melting pt.: 1663°C; boiling pt.: 3402°C

Luther Martin 1483–1546, German leader of the Protestant Reformation. As professor of biblical theology at Wittenberg University from 1511, he began preaching the crucial doctrine of justification by faith rather than by works, and in 1517 he nailed 95 theses to the church door at Wittenberg, attacking Tetzel's sale of indulgences. He was excommunicated and outlawed by the Diet of Worms (1521) as a result of his refusal to recant, but he was protected in Wartburg Castle by Frederick III of Saxony (1521–22). He translated the Bible into German (1521–34) and approved Melanchthon's Augsburg Confession (1530), defining the basic tenets of Lutheranism

Lutheran 1 a follower of Martin Luther (1483–1546), German leader of the Protestant Reformation, or a member of a Lutheran Church 2 of or relating to Luther or his doctrines, the most important being justification by faith alone, consubstantiation, and the authority of the Bible 3 of or denoting any Protestant Church that follows Luther's doctrines
▷http://www.lhm.org/

Luthuli *or* **Lutuli** Chief Albert John 1899–1967, South African political leader. As president of the African National Congress (1952–60), he campaigned for nonvi-

olent resistance to apartheid: Nobel peace prize 1961

Luton 1 a town in SE central England, in Luton unitary authority, S Bedfordshire: airport; motor-vehicle industries; university (1993). Pop: 185 543 (2001) 2 a unitary authority in SE central England, in Bedfordshire. Pop: 185 200 (2003 est). Area: 43 sq km (17 sq miles)

Lutyens 1 Sir Edwin 1869–1944, British architect, noted for his neoclassical country houses and his planning of New Delhi, India 2 his daughter, Elisabeth 1906–83, British composer

luvvie *or* **luvvy** *Facetious* a person who is involved in the acting profession or the theatre, esp one with a tendency to affectation

lux the derived SI unit of illumination equal to a luminous flux of 1 lumen per square metre. 1 lux is equivalent to 0.0929 foot-candle.

Luxembourg 1 a grand duchy in W Europe: it formed the Benelux customs union with the Belgium and the Netherlands in 1948 and was a founder member of the Common Market, now the European Union . Languages: French, German, and Luxemburgish. Religion: Roman Catholic majority. Currency: euro. Capital: Luxembourg. Pop: 459 000 (2004 est). Area: 2586 sq km (999 sq miles) 2 the capital of Luxembourg, on the Alzette River: an industrial centre. Pop: 77 300 (2003 est) 3 a province in SE Belgium, in the Ardennes. Capital: Arlon. Pop: 254 120 (2004 est). Area: 4416 sq km (1705 sq miles)

Luxemburg Rosa 1871–1919, German socialist leader, led an unsuccessful Communist revolt (1919) with Karl Liebknecht and was assassinated

Luxor a town in S Egypt, on the River Nile: the southern part of the site of ancient Thebes; many ruins and tombs, notably the temple built by Amenhotep III (about 1411–1375 BC). Pop: 183 000 (2005 est)

Luzon the main and largest island of the Philippines, in the N part of the archipelago, separated from the other islands by the Sibuyan Sea: important agriculturally, producing most of the country's rice, with large forests and rich mineral resources; industrial centres at Manila and Batangas. Capital: Quezon City. Pop: 32 558 000 (1995 est). Area: 108 378 sq km (41 845 sq miles)

Lviv an industrial city in W Ukraine: it has belonged to Poland (1340–1772; 1919–39), Austria (1772–1918), Germany (1939–45), and the Soviet Union (1945–91); Ukrainian cultural centre, with a university (1661). Pop: 719 000 (2005 est)

Lycaonia an ancient region of S Asia Minor, north of the Taurus Mountains; corresponds to present-day S central Turkey

lych gate *or* **lich gate** a roofed gate to a churchyard, formerly used during funerals as a temporary shelter for the bier

Lycia an ancient region on the coast of SW Asia Minor: a Persian, Rhodian, and Roman province

Lycra *Trademark* a type of synthetic elastic fabric and fibre used for tight-fitting garments, such as swimming costumes

Lycurgus 9th century BC, Spartan lawgiver. He is traditionally regarded as the founder of the Spartan constitution, military institutions, and educational system

Lydgate John ?1370–?1450, English poet and monk. His vast output includes devotional works and translations, such as that of a French version of Boccaccio's *The Fall of Princes* (1430–38)

Lydia an ancient region on the coast of W Asia Minor: a powerful kingdom in the century and a half before the Persian conquest (546 BC). Chief town: Sardis

lye 1 any solution obtained by leaching, such as the caustic solution obtained by leaching wood ash 2 a concentrated solution of sodium hydroxide or potassium hydroxide

Lyell Sir Charles 1797–1875, Scottish geologist. In *Principles of Geology* (1830–33) he advanced the theory of uniformitarianism, refuting the doctrine of catastrophism

Lyly John ?1554–1606, English dramatist and novelist, noted for his two romances, *Euphues, or the Anatomy of Wit* (1578) and *Euphues and his England* (1580), written in an elaborate style

Lyme Regis a resort in S England, in Dorset, on the English Channel: noted for finds of prehistoric fossils. Pop: 4406 (2001)

Lymington a market town in S England, in SW Hampshire, on the Solent: yachting centre and holiday resort. Pop: 14 227 (2001)

lymph the almost colourless fluid, containing chiefly white blood cells, that is collected from the tissues of the body and transported in the lymphatic system

lymphatic system an extensive network of capillary vessels that transports the interstitial fluid of the body as lymph to the venous blood circulation

lymph node any of numerous bean-shaped masses of tissue, situated along the course of lymphatic vessels, that help to protect against infection by killing bacteria and neutralizing toxins and are the source of lymphocytes

lymphocyte a type of white blood cell formed in lymphoid tissue

Lynagh Michael born 1963, Australian Rugby Union football player; captain of Australia 1987, 1992–95

Lynch 1 David born 1946, US film director; his work includes the films *Eraserhead* (1977), *Blue Velvet* (1986), *Wild at Heart* (1990), and *Mulholland Drive* (2001) and the television series *Twin Peaks* (1990) 2 John, known as Jack Lynch. 1917–99, Irish statesman; prime minister of the Republic of Ireland (1966–73; 1977–79)

Lynn Dame Vera, original name *Vera Margaret Lewis*. born 1917, British singer popular during World War II and known as "the forces' sweetheart". Her best-known

songs are "We'll Meet Again" and "White Cliffs of Dover"

lynx 1 a feline mammal, *Felis lynx* (or *canadensis*), of Europe and North America, with grey-brown mottled fur, tufted ears, and a short tail 2 the fur of this animal 3 **desert lynx** another name for **caracal** 4 a large fancy pigeon from Poland, with spangled or laced markings

Lyon a city in SE central France, capital of Rhône department, at the confluence of the Rivers Rhône and Saône: the third largest city in France; a major industrial centre and river port. Pop: 445 452 (1999)

Lyonnais a former province of E central France, on the Rivers Rhône and Saône: occupied by the present-day departments of Rhône and Loire. Chief town: Lyon

Lyons Joseph Aloysius 1879–1939, Australian statesman; prime minister of Australia (1931–39)

lyre 1 an ancient Greek stringed instrument consisting of a resonating tortoise shell to which a crossbar was attached by two projecting arms. It was plucked with a plectrum and used for accompanying songs 2 any ancient instrument of similar design 3 a medieval bowed instrument of the violin family

lyrebird either of two pheasant-like Australian birds, *Menura superba* and *M. alberti*, constituting the family *Menuridae*: during courtship displays, the male spreads its tail into the shape of a lyre

lyric 1 (of poetry) a expressing the writer's personal feelings and thoughts b having the form and manner of a song 2 (of a singing voice) having a light quality and tone 3 intended for singing, esp (in classical Greece) to the accompaniment of the lyre 4 a short poem of songlike quality

lyricism the quality or style of lyric poetry

lyricist 1 a person who writes the words for a song, opera, or musical play 2 a lyric poet

Lysander died 395 BC, Spartan naval commander of the Peloponnesian War

Lysenko Trofim Denisovich 1898–1976, Russian biologist and geneticist

Lysias ?450–?380 BC, Athenian orator

Lysimachus ?360–281 BC, Macedonian general under Alexander the Great; king of Thrace (323–281); killed in battle by Seleucus I

Lysippus 4th century BC, Greek sculptor. He introduced a new naturalism into Greek sculpture

Lytton 1st Baron, title of *Edward George Earle Lytton Bulwer-Lytton*. 1803–73, British novelist, dramatist, and statesman, noted particularly for his historical romances

Lyublin transliteration of the Russian name for **Lublin**

Mm

Maastricht or **Maestricht** a city in the SE Netherlands near the Belgian and German borders: capital of Limburg province, on the River Maas (Meuse); a European Community treaty (**Maastricht Treaty**) was signed here in 1992, setting out the terms for the creation of the European Union. Pop: 122 000 (2003 est)

Mabuse Jan original name *Jan Gossaert*. ?1478– ?1533, Flemish painter

macadam a road surface made of compressed layers of small broken stones, esp one that is bound together with tar or asphalt

macadamia 1 any tree of the Australian proteaceous genus *Macadamia*, esp *M. ternifolia*, having clusters of small white flowers and edible nutlike seeds 2 **macadamia nut** the seed of this tree

Macao a special administrative region of S China, across the estuary of the Zhu Jiang from Hong Kong: chief centre of European trade with China in the 18th century; attained partial autonomy in 1976; formerly (until 1999) a Portuguese overseas province under a long-term lease from China, as with Hong Kong (a UK territory until 1997); transit trade with rest of China; tourism and financial services. It retains its own currency, the pataca. Pop: 448 500 (2003 est). Area: 16 sq km (6 sq miles)

macaque any of various Old World monkeys of the genus *Macaca*, inhabiting wooded or rocky regions of Asia and Africa. Typically the tail is short or absent and cheek pouches are present

macaroni or **maccaroni** (in 18th-century Britain) a dandy who affected foreign manners and style

Macarthur John 1767–1834, Australian military officer, pastoralist, and entrepreneur, born in England. He established the breeding of merino sheep in Australia and was influential in founding the Australian wool industry

MacArthur Douglas 1880–1964, US general. During World War II he became commanding general of US armed forces in the Pacific (1944) and accepted the surrender of Japan, the Allied occupation of which he commanded (1945–51). He was commander in chief of United Nations forces in Korea (1950–51) until dismissed by President Truman

Macaulay 1 Dame Rose 1881–1958, British novelist. Her books include *Dangerous Ages* (1921) and *The Towers of Trebizond* (1956) 2 Thomas Babington, 1st Baron.

1800–59, English historian, essayist, and statesman. His *History of England from the Accession of James the Second* (1848–61) is regarded as a classic of the Whig interpretation of history

macaw any large tropical American parrot of the genera *Ara* and *Anodorhynchus*, having a long tail and brilliant plumage

Macbeth died 1057, king of Scotland (1040–57): succeeded Duncan, whom he killed in battle; defeated and killed by Duncan's son Malcolm III

MacBride Sean 1904–88, Irish statesman; minister for external affairs (1948–51); chairman of Amnesty International (1961–75); Nobel Peace Prize 1974; UN commissioner for Namibia (1974–76)

McCarthy 1 Joseph R(aymond). 1908-57, US Republican senator, who led (1950-54) the notorious investigations of alleged Communist infiltration into the US government 2 Mary (Therese). 1912–89, US novelist and critic; her works include *The Group* (1963)

McCartney 1 Sir Paul born 1942, English rock musician and songwriter; member of the Beatles (1961–70); leader of Wings (1971–81). His recordings include *Band on the Run* (1973), "Mull of Kintyre" (1977), *Flowers in the Dirt* (1989), and *Driving Rain* (2001) 2 his daughter, Stella born 1971, British fashion designer.

Macclesfield a market town in NW England, in Cheshire: former centre of the silk industry; pharmaceuticals, services. Pop: 50 688 (2001)

McCormack John 1884–1945, Irish tenor: became US citizen 1919

McCoy Tony, full name *Anthony Peter McCoy*. born 1974, Northern Irish jockey; winner of seven consecutive riders' titles in 2001–02

McCullers Carson 1917–67, US writer, whose novels include *The Heart is a Lonely Hunter* (1940)

Macdonald 1 Flora 1722–90, Scottish heroine, who helped the Young Pretender to escape to Skye after his defeat at the battle of Culloden (1746) 2 Sir John Alexander 1815–91, Canadian statesman, born in Scotland, who was the first prime minister of the Dominion of Canada (1867–73; 1878–91)

McDonald Sir Trevor born 1939, British television journalist, born in Trinidad; presenter of ITV's *News at Ten* (1990–99)

MacDonald (James) Ramsay 1866–1937, British statesman, who led the first and second Labour Governments

(1924 and 1929–31). He also led a coalition (1931–35), which the majority of the Labour Party refused to support

mace 1 *Military* a club, usually having a spiked metal head, used esp in the Middle Ages 2 a ceremonial staff of office carried by certain officials 3 *Sport* an early form of billiard cue

Macedon *or* **Macedonia** a region of the S Balkans, now divided among Greece, Bulgaria, and Macedonia (Former Yugoslav Republic of Macedonia). As a kingdom in the ancient world it achieved prominence under Philip II (359–336 BC) and his son Alexander the Great

Macedonia 1 a country in SE Europe, comprising the NW half of ancient Macedon: it became part of the kingdom of Serbs, Croats, and Slovenes (subsequently Yugoslavia) in 1913; it declared independence in 1992, but Greece objected to the use of the historical name Macedonia; in 1993 it was recognized by the UN under its current official name. Official language: Macedonian. Religion: Christian majority, Muslim, nonreligious, and Jewish minorities. Currency: denar. Capital: Skopje. Pop: 2 066 000 (2004 est). Area: 25 713 sq km (10 028 sq miles). Official name: Former Yugoslav Republic of Macedonia (FYROM) 2 an area of N Greece, comprising the regions of Macedonia Central, Macedonia West, and part of Macedonia East and Thrace 3 a district of SW Bulgaria, now occupied by Blagoevgrad province. Area: 6465 sq km (2496 sq miles)

McEnroe John (Patrick Jr). born 1959, US tennis player: US singles champion (1979–81; 1984) and doubles champion (1979; 1981; 1989): Wimbledon singles champion (1981; 1983; 1984) and doubles champion (1979; 1981; 1983; 1984; 1992)

McEwan Ian (Russell). born 1948, British novelist and short-story writer. His books include *First Love, Last Rites* (1975), *The Child in Time* (1987), *The Innocent* (1990), *Amsterdam* (1998), and *Atonement* (2001)

McGonagall William 1830–71902, Scottish writer of doggerel, noted for its bathos, repetitive rhymes, poor scansion, and ludicrous effect

McGrath Glenn (Donald). born 1970, Australian cricketer; played for Australia from 1993

MacGregor Joanna (Clare). born 1959, British concert pianist and broadcaster; recordings include the "crossover" album *Play* (2001)

McGwire Mark (David). born 1963, US baseball player

Mach Ernst 1838–1916, Austrian physicist and philosopher. He devised the system of speed measurement using the Mach number. He also founded logical positivism, asserting that the validity of a scientific law is proved only after empirical testing

Machado Joaquim Maria 1839–1908, Brazilian author of novels and short stories, whose novels include *Epitaph of a Small Winner* (1881) and *Dom Casmurro* (1899)

Machel Samora (Moises). 1933–86, Mozambique statesman; president of Mozambique from 1975–86

Machiavelli Niccolò 1469–1527, Florentine statesman and political philosopher; secretary to the war council of the Florentine republic (1498–1512). His most famous work is *Il Principe* (*The Prince*, 1532)

machine 1 an assembly of interconnected components

arranged to transmit or modify force in order to perform useful work 2 a device for altering the magnitude or direction of a force, esp a lever, screw, wedge, or pulley 3 a mechanically operated device or means of transport, such as a car, aircraft, etc. 4 any mechanical or electrical device that automatically performs tasks or assists in performing tasks 5 (esp in the classical theatre) a device such as a pulley to provide spectacular entrances and exits for supernatural characters 6 an event, etc, introduced into a literary work for special effect

machine code *or* **language** instructions for the processing of data in a binary, octal, or hexadecimal code that can be understood and executed by a computer

machinery 1 machines, machine parts, or machine systems collectively 2 a particular machine system or set of machines 3 literary devices used for effect in epic poetry

machine shop a workshop in which machine tools are operated

machine tool a power-driven machine, such as a lathe, miller, or grinder, that is used for cutting, shaping, and finishing metals or other materials

machinist 1 a person who operates machines to cut or process materials 2 a maker or repairer of machines

Mach number the ratio of the speed of a body in a particular medium to the speed of sound in that medium. Mach number 1 corresponds to the speed of sound

Machu Picchu a ruined Incan city in S Peru

Mackay a port in E Australia, in Queensland: artificial harbour. Pop: 57 649 (2001)

Mackellar Dorothea 1885–1968, Australian poet, who wrote "My Country", Australia's best known poem

McKellen Sir Ian (Murray). born 1939, British actor, noted esp for his Shakespearean roles; films include *The Lord of the Rings* trilogy (2001–03)

McKenna Siobhán 1923–86, Irish actress, whose notable roles included Pegeen Mike in Synge's *The Playboy of the Western World* and Shaw's Saint Joan

Mackenzie[1] 1 Sir Alexander ?1755–1820, Scottish explorer and fur trader in Canada. He explored the Mackenzie River (1789) and was the first European to cross America north of Mexico (1793) 2 Alexander 1822–92, Canadian statesman; first Liberal prime minister (1873–78) 3 Sir Compton 1883–1972, English author. His works include *Sinister Street* (1913–14) and the comic novel *Whisky Galore* (1947) 4 Sir Thomas 1854–1930, New Zealand statesman born in Scotland: prime minister of New Zealand (1912) 5 William Lyon 1795–1861, Canadian journalist and politician, born in Scotland. He led an unsuccessful rebellion against the oligarchic Family Compact (1837)

Mackenzie[2] a river in NW Canada, in the Northwest Territories and Nunavut, flowing northwest from Great Slave Lake to the Beaufort Sea: the longest river in Canada; navigable in summer. Length: 1770 km (1100 miles)

mackerel 1 a spiny-finned food fish, *Scomber scombrus*, occurring in northern coastal regions of the Atlantic and in the Mediterranean: family *Scombridae*. It has a deeply forked tail and a greenish-blue body marked with wavy dark bands on the back 2 any of various other fishes of the family *Scombridae*, such as *Scomber col-*

ias (**Spanish mackerel**) and *S. japonicus* (**Pacific mackerel**)

Mackerras Charles born 1925, Australian conductor, esp of opera; resident in England

Mackinac a wooded island in N Michigan, in the **Straits of Mackinac** (a channel between the lower and upper peninsulas of Michigan): an ancient Indian burial ground; state park. Length: 5 km (3 miles)

McKinley¹ William 1843–1901, 25th president of the US (1897–1901). His administration was marked by high tariffs and by expansionist policies. He was assassinated

McKinley² Mount a mountain in S central Alaska, in the Alaska Range: the highest peak in North America. Height: 6194 m (20 320 ft)

McKinnon Don(ald) (Charles). born 1939, New Zealand politician; secretary-general of the Commonwealth from 2000; deputy prime minister of New Zealand (1990–96)

Mackintosh 1 Sir Cameron (Anthony). born 1946, British producer of musicals and theatre owner; his productions include *Cats* (1981), *Les Misérables* (1985), *Miss Saigon* (1987), and *My Fair Lady* (2001) **2** Charles Rennie 1868–1928, Scottish architect and artist, exponent of the Art Nouveau style; designer of the Glasgow School of Art (1896)

Maclean 1 Donald 1913–83, British civil servant, who spied for the Russians: fled to the former Soviet Union (with Guy Burgess) in 1951 **2** Sorley 1911–96, Scottish Gaelic poet. His works include *Dàin do Eimhir agus Dàin Eile* (1943) and *Spring Tide and Neap Tide* (1977)

Macleod John James Rickard 1876–1935, Scottish physiologist: shared the Nobel prize for physiology or medicine (1923) with Banting for their part in discovering insulin

McLuhan (Herbert) Marshall 1911–80, Canadian author of works analysing the mass media, including *Understanding Media* (1964) and *The Medium is the Message* (1967)

Macmahon Marie Edme Patrice Maurice , Comte de Macmahon. 1808–93, French military commander. He commanded the troops that suppressed the Paris Commune (1871) and was elected president of the Third Republic (1873–79)

McMahon Sir William 1908–88, Australian statesman; prime minister of Australia (1971–72)

Macmillan (Maurice) Harold, 1st Earl of Stockton. 1894–1986, British statesman; Conservative prime minister (1957–63)

MacMillan 1 James (Loy). born 1959, Scottish composer and conductor; his works include two symphonies, the orchestral work *Confession of Isobel Gowdie* (1990), and the opera *Ines de Castro* (1996) **2** Sir Kenneth 1929–92, British choreographer, dancer, and ballet director; chief choreographer for the Royal Ballet from 1970

McMillan Edwin M(attison). 1907–91, US physicist; Nobel prize for chemistry 1951 (with Glenn Seaborg) for the discovery of transuranic elements

MacNeice Louis 1907–63, British poet, born in Northern Ireland. His works include *Autumn Journal* (1939) and *Solstices* (1961) and a translation of *Agamemnon* (1936)

Macon a city in the US, in central Georgia, on the Ocmulgee River. Pop: 95 267 (2003 est)

Maconchy Dame Elizabeth, married name *Elizabeth*

LeFanu. 1907–94, British composer of Irish parentage; noted esp for her chamber music, which includes 13 string quartets and *Romanza* (1980) for viola and ensemble

McPartlin Antony born 1975, British television presenter, who appears with Declan Donnelly as Ant and Dec

Macpherson James 1736–96, Scottish poet and translator. He published supposed translations of the legendary Gaelic poet Ossian, in reality largely his own work

McPherson Conor born 1972, Irish playwright and theatre director; his plays include *The Weir* (1997) and *Port Authority* (2001)

Macquarie¹ Lachlan 1762–1824, Australian colonial administrator; Governor of New South Wales (1809–21), noted for his reformist policies towards ex- convicts and for his record in public works such as road-building in the colony

Macquarie² **1** an Australian island in the Pacific, SE of Tasmania: noted for its species of albatross and penguin. Area: about 168 sq km (65 sq miles) **2** a river in SE Australia, in E central New South Wales, rising in the Blue Mountains and flowing NW to the Darling. Length: about 1200 km (750 miles)

McQueen 1 Alexander born 1969, British fashion designer and master tailor. **2** Steve 1930–80, US film actor, noted for his portrayal of tough characters

Macready William Charles 1793–1873, English actor and theatre manager

macrocarpa a large coniferous tree of New Zealand, *Cupressus macrocarpa*, used for shelter belts on farms and for rough timber

macroeconomics the branch of economics concerned with aggregates, such as national income, consumption, and investment

▷www.elsevier.com/homepage/sae/
econworld/econbase/jmacro/frame.htm
▷www.stern.nyu.edu/globalmacro

macromolecule any very large molecule, such as a protein or synthetic polymer

macron a diacritical mark (¯) placed over a letter, used in prosody, in the orthography of some languages, and in several types of phonetic respelling systems, to represent a long vowel

macroscopic 1 large enough to be visible to the naked eye **2** *Physics* capable of being described by the statistical properties of a large number of parts

macula *or* **macule** *Anatomy* **1** a small spot or area of distinct colour, esp the macula lutea **2** any small discoloured spot or blemish on the skin, such as a freckle

Madagascar an island republic in the Indian Ocean, off the E coast of Africa: made a French protectorate in 1895; became autonomous in 1958 and fully independent in 1960; contains unique flora and fauna. Languages: Malagasy and French. Religions: animist and Christian. Currency: franc. Capital: Antananarivo. Pop: 17 901 000 (2004 est). Area: 587 041 sq km (266 657 sq miles)

madder 1 any of several rubiaceous plants of the genus *Rubia*, esp the Eurasian *R. tinctoria*, which has small yellow flowers and a red fleshy root **2** the root of this plant

Madeira 1 a group of volcanic islands in the N Atlantic, west of Morocco: since 1976 an autonomous region of Portugal; consists of the chief island, Madeira, Porto Santo, and the uninhabited Deserta and Selvagen Islands. Capital: Funchal. Pop: 245 012 (2001). Area: 797 sq km (311 sq miles) **2** a river in W Brazil, flowing northeast to the Amazon below Manaus. Length: 3241 km (2013 miles) **3** a rich strong fortified white wine made on Madeira

made-up (of a road) surfaced with asphalt, concrete, etc.

Madhya Bharat a former state of central India: part of Madhya Pradesh since 1956

Madhya Pradesh a state of central India, situated on the Deccan Plateau: rich in mineral resources, with several industrial cities: formerly the largest Indian state, it lost much of the SE to the new state of Chhattisgarh in 2000. Capital: Bhopal. Pop: 60 385 118 (2001). Area: 308 332 sq km (119 016 sq miles)

Madison¹ James 1751–1836, US statesman; 4th president of the US (1809–17). He helped to draft the US Constitution and Bill of Rights. His presidency was dominated by the War of 1812

Madison² a city in the US, in S central Wisconsin, on an isthmus between Lakes Mendota and Monona: the state capital. Pop: 218 432 (2003 est)

Madison Avenue a street in New York City: a centre of American advertising and public-relations firms and a symbol of their attitudes and methods

Madonna¹ full name *Madonna Louise Veronica Ciccone*. born 1958, US rock singer and film actress. Her records include "Like a Virgin" (1985), "Like a Prayer" (1989), *Ray of Light* (1998), and *Music* (2000). Her films include *Desperately Seeking Susan* (1985), and *Evita* (1996)

Madonna² **1** *Chiefly RC Church* a designation of the Virgin Mary **2** a picture or statue of the Virgin Mary

madras **a** a strong fine cotton or silk fabric, usually with a woven stripe **b** *(as modifier): madras cotton*

Madras **1** a port in SE India, capital of Tamil Nadu, on the Bay of Bengal: founded in 1639 by the English East India Company as **Fort St George**; traditional burial place of St Thomas; university (1857). Pop: 4 216 268 (2001) **2** the former name (until 1968) for the state of Tamil Nadu

Madre de Dios a river in NE South America, rising in SE Peru and flowing northeast to the Beni River in N Bolivia. Length: about 965 km (600 miles)

Madrid the capital of Spain, situated centrally in New Castile: the highest European capital, at an altitude of about 700 m (2300 ft); a Moorish fortress in the 10th century, captured by Castile in 1083 and made capital of Spain in 1561; university (1836). Pop: 3 092 759 (2003 est)

madrigal **1** *Music* a type of 16th- or 17th-century part song for unaccompanied voices with an amatory or pastoral text **2** a 14th-century Italian song, related to a pastoral stanzaic verse form

Madura an island in Indonesia, off the NE coast of Java: extensive forests and saline springs. Capital: Pamekasan. Area: 5472 sq km (2113 sq miles)

Madurai a city in S India, in S Tamil Nadu: centre of Dravidian culture for over 2000 years; cotton industry. Pop: 922 913 (2001)

Maebashi a city in central Japan, on central Honshu:

centre of sericulture and silk-spinning; university (1949). Pop: 283 005 (2002 est)

Maecenas 1 Gaius ?70–8 BC, Roman statesman; adviser to Augustus and patron of Horace and Virgil **2** a wealthy patron of the arts

maelstrom a large powerful whirlpool

Maelstrom a strong tidal current in a restricted channel in the Lofoten Islands off the NW coast of Norway

maenad *or* **menad** *Classical myth* a woman participant in the orgiastic rites of Dionysus; bacchante

maestro a distinguished music teacher, conductor, or musician

Maeterlinck Comte Maurice 1862–1949, Belgian poet and dramatist, noted particularly for his symbolist plays, such as *Pelléas et Mélisande* (1892), which served as the basis for an opera by Debussy, and *L'Oiseau bleu* (1909). Nobel prize for literature 1911

Maewo an almost uninhabited island in Vanuatu

Mafikeng a town in N South Africa: besieged by the Boers for 217 days (1899–1900) during the second Boer War: administrative headquarters of the British protectorate of Bechuanaland until 1965, although outside its borders. Pop: 23 650 (2001)

magazine 1 *Engineering* a device for continuously recharging a handling system, stove, or boiler with solid fuel **2** *Photog* another name for **cartridge**

Magdalena a river in SW Colombia, rising on the E slopes of the Andes and flowing north to the Caribbean near Barranquilla. Length: 1540 km (956 miles)

Magdalena Bay an inlet of the Pacific on the coast of NW Mexico, in Lower California

Magdeburg an industrial city and port in central Germany, on the River Elbe, capital of Saxony-Anhalt: a leading member of the Hanseatic League, whose local laws, the **Magdeburg Laws** were adopted by many European cities. Pop: 227 535 (2003 est)

Magellan¹ Ferdinand Portuguese name *Fernão de Magalhães*. ?1480–1521, Portuguese navigator in the service of Spain. He commanded an expedition of five ships that set out to sail to the East Indies via the West. He discovered the Strait of Magellan (1520), crossed the Pacific, and reached the Philippines (1521), where he was killed by natives. One of his ships reached Spain (1522) and was therefore the first to circumnavigate the world

Magellan² Strait of a strait between the mainland of S South America and Tierra del Fuego, linking the S Pacific with the S Atlantic. Length: 600 km (370 miles). Width: up to 32 km (20 miles)

magenta a deep purplish red that is the complementary colour of green and, with yellow and cyan, forms a set of primary colours

Maggiore Lake a lake in N Italy and S Switzerland, in the S Lepontine Alps

maggot the soft limbless larva of dipterous insects, esp the housefly and blowfly, occurring in decaying organic matter

Magherafelt a district of N Northern Ireland, in Co. Londonderry. Pop: 40 837 (2003 est). Area: 572 sq km (221 sq miles)

Maghreb *or* **Maghrib** NW Africa, including Morocco, Algeria, Tunisia, and sometimes Libya

magic lantern an early type of slide projector

magistracy *or* **magistrature** 1 the office or function of a magistrate 2 magistrates collectively 3 the district under the jurisdiction of a magistrate

magistrate 1 a public officer concerned with the administration of law 2 another name for **justice of the peace**

magma 1 a paste or suspension consisting of a finely divided solid dispersed in a liquid 2 hot molten rock, usually formed in the earth's upper mantle, some of which finds its way into the crust and onto the earth's surface, where it solidifies to form igneous rock

Magna Carta *or* **Magna Charta** *English history* the charter granted by King John at Runnymede in 1215, recognizing the rights and privileges of the barons, church, and freemen
▷www.bl.uk/collections/treasures/magna.html

Magna Graecia (in the ancient world) S Italy, where numerous colonies were founded by Greek cities

magnate 1 *History* a great nobleman 2 (formerly) a member of the upper chamber in certain European parliaments, as in Hungary

magnesium a light silvery-white metallic element of the alkaline earth series that burns with an intense white flame, occurring principally in magnesite, dolomite, and carnallite: used in light structural alloys, flashbulbs, flares, and fireworks. Symbol: Mg; atomic no.: 12; atomic wt.: 24.3050; valency: 2; relative density: 1.738; melting pt.: 650°C; boiling pt.: 1090°C

magnet a body that can attract certain substances, such as iron or steel, as a result of a magnetic field; a piece of ferromagnetic substance

magnetic field a field of force surrounding a permanent magnet or a moving charged particle, in which another permanent magnet or moving charge experiences a force

magnetic needle a slender magnetized rod used in certain instruments, such as the magnetic compass, for indicating the direction of a magnetic field

magnetic north the direction in which a compass needle points, at an angle (the declination) from the direction of true (geographic) north

magnetic pole 1 either of two regions in a magnet where the magnetic induction is concentrated 2 either of two variable points on the earth's surface towards which a magnetic needle points, where the lines of force of the earth's magnetic field are vertical

magnetic storm a sudden severe disturbance of the earth's magnetic field, caused by emission of charged particles from the sun

magnetic tape a long narrow plastic or metal strip coated or impregnated with a ferromagnetic material such as iron oxide, used to record sound or video signals or to store information in computers

magnetism 1 the property of attraction displayed by magnets 2 any of a class of phenomena in which a field of force is caused by a moving electric charge 3 the branch of physics concerned with magnetic phenomena

magnetite a black magnetic mineral, found in igneous and metamorphic rocks and as a separate deposit. It is a source of iron. Composition: iron oxide. Formula: Fe_3O_4. Crystal structure: cubic

magneto a small electric generator in which the magnetic field is produced by a permanent magnet, esp one for providing the spark in an internal-combustion engine

magnetron an electronic valve with two coaxial electrodes used with an applied magnetic field to generate high-power microwave oscillations, esp for use in radar

Magnificat *Christianity* the hymn of the Virgin Mary (Luke 1:46-55), used as a canticle

magnification a measure of the ability of a lens or other optical instrument to magnify, expressed as the ratio of the size of the image to that of the object

magnifying glass *or* **magnifier** a convex lens used to produce an enlarged image of an object

Magnitogorsk a city in central Russia, on the Ural River: founded in 1930 to exploit local magnetite ores; site of one of the world's largest, metallurgical plants. Pop: 415 000 (2005 est)

magnitude 1 *Maths* a number assigned to a quantity, such as weight, and used as a basis of comparison for the measurement of similar quantities 2 *Astronomy* the apparent brightness of a celestial body expressed on a numerical scale on which bright stars have a low value. Values are measured by eye (**visual magnitude**) or more accurately by photometric or photographic methods, and range from –26.7 (the sun), through 1.5 (Sirius), down to about +30. Each integral value represents a brightness 2.512 times greater than the next highest integral value 3 *Geology* a measure of the size of an earthquake based on the quantity of energy released: specified on the Richter scale

magnolia 1 any tree or shrub of the magnoliaceous genus *Magnolia* of Asia and North America: cultivated for their white, pink, purple, or yellow showy flowers 2 the flower of any of these plants 3 a very pale pinkish-white or purplish-white colour

magnox an alloy consisting mostly of magnesium with small amounts of aluminium and other metals, used in fuel elements of nuclear reactors

magnum a wine bottle holding the equivalent of two normal bottles (approximately 52 fluid ounces)

magnum opus a great work of art or literature, esp the greatest single work of an artist

magpie 1 any of various passerine birds of the genus *Pica*, esp *P. pica*, having a black-and-white plumage, long tail, and a chattering call: family *Corvidae* (crows, etc) 2 any of various similar birds of the Australian family *Cracticidae* 3 any of various other similar or related birds 4 a variety of domestic fancy pigeon typically having black-and-white markings 5 a the outmost ring but one on a target b a shot that hits this ring

Magritte René 1898–1967, Belgian surrealist painter. By juxtaposing incongruous objects, depicted with meticulous realism, his works create a bizarre and disturbing impression

magus a Zoroastrian priest

Magus Simon *New Testament* a sorcerer who tried to buy spiritual powers from the apostles (Acts 8:9-24)

Magyar 1 a member of the predominant ethnic group of Hungary, also found in NW Siberia 2 the Hungarian language

Mahajanga a port in NW Madagascar, on Bombetoka Bay. Pop: 147 000 (2005 est)

Mahalla el Kubra a city in N Egypt, on the Nile delta: one of the largest diversified textile centres in Egypt. Pop: 433 000 (2005 est)

Mahanadi a river in E India, rising in Chhattisgarh and flowing north, then south and east to the Bay of Bengal. Length: 885 km (550 miles)

maharani *or* **maharanee** 1 the wife of a maharajah 2 a woman holding the rank of maharajah

Maharashtra a state of W central India, formed in 1960 from the Marathi-speaking S and E parts of former Bombay state: lies mainly on the Deccan plateau; mainly agricultural. Capital: Bombay. Pop: 96 752 247 (2001). Area: 307 690 sq km (118 800 sq miles)

maharishi *Hinduism* a Hindu teacher of religious and mystical knowledge

mahatma 1 *Hinduism* a Brahman sage 2 *Theosophy* an adept or sage

Mahdi 1 the title assumed by *Mohammed Ahmed*. ?1843–85, Sudanese military leader, who led a revolt against Egypt (1881) and captured Khartoum (1885) 2 *Islam* any of a number of Muslim messiahs expected to forcibly convert all mankind to Islam

Mahfouz *or* **Mahfuz Naguib** born 1911, Egyptian novelist and writer, author of the trilogy of novels *Bain al-Kasrain* (1945–57). His novel *Children of Gebelawi* (1959) was banned by the Muslim authorities in Egypt. Nobel prize for literature 1988

mah jong *or* **mah-jongg** a game of Chinese origin, usually played by four people, in which tiles bearing various designs are drawn and discarded until one player has an entire hand of winning combinations

Mahler Gustav 1860–1911, Austrian composer and conductor, whose music links the romantic tradition of the 19th century with the music of the 20th century. His works include nine complete symphonies for large orchestras, the symphonic song cycle *Das Lied von der Erde* (1908), and the song cycle *Kindertotenlieder* (1902)

mahogany 1 any of various tropical American trees of the meliaceous genus *Swietenia*, esp *S. mahogani* and *S. macrophylla*, valued for their hard reddish-brown wood 2 any of several trees with similar wood, such as African mahogany (genus *Khaya*) and Philippine mahogany (genus *Shorea*) 3 a the wood of any of these trees b *(as modifier): a mahogany table* 4 a reddish-brown colour

Mahy Margaret born 1936, New Zealand writer for children. Her books include *A Lion in the Meadow* (1969), *The Changeover* (1984), and *Alchemy* (2002)

maiden 1 *Horse racing* a horse that has never won a race b *(as modifier): a maiden race* 2 *Cricket* See **maiden over**

maidenhair fern *or* **maidenhair** any fern of the cosmopolitan genus *Adiantum*, esp *A. capillis-veneris*, having delicate fan-shaped fronds with small pale-green leaflets: family *Adiantaceae*

Maidenhead a town in S England, in Windsor and Maidenhead unitary authority, Berkshire, on the River Thames. Pop: 58 848 (2001)

maiden over *Cricket* an over in which no runs are scored

Maidstone a town in SE England, administrative centre of Kent, on the River Medway. Pop: 89 684 (2001)

Maiduguri a city in NE Nigeria, capital of Bornu State;

agricultural trade centre. Pop: 828 000 (2005 est)

Maikop a city in SW Russia, capital of the Adygei Republic: extensive oilfields to the southwest; mineral springs. Pop: 165 000 (2005 est)

mail the hard protective shell of such animals as the turtle and lobster

mailbox (on a computer) the directory in which e-mail messages are stored; also used of the icon that can be clicked to provide access to e-mails

Mailer Norman born 1923, US author. His works, which are frequently critical of modern American society, include the war novel *The Naked and the Dead* (1948), *An American Dream* (1965), his account of the 1967 peace march on Washington *The Armies of the Night* (1968), *The Executioner's Song* (1979), and *Barbary Shore* (1998)

Maillol Aristide 1861–1944, French sculptor, esp of monumental female nudes

mail order 1 an order for merchandise sent by post 2 a a system of buying and selling merchandise through the post b *(as modifier): a mail-order firm*

Maimonides also called Rabbi *Moses ben Maimon*. 1135–1204, Jewish philosopher, physician, and jurist, born in Spain. He codified Jewish law in *Mishneh Torah* (1180)

main¹ 1 *Nautical* of, relating to, or denoting any gear, such as a stay or sail, belonging to the mainmast 2 a principal pipe, conduit, duct, or line in a system used to distribute water, electricity, etc. 3 a the main distribution network for water, gas, or electricity b *(as modifier): mains voltage* 4 *Literary* the open ocean 5 *Archaic* short for **Spanish Main** 6 *Archaic* short for **mainland**

main² 1 a throw of the dice in dice games 2 a cockfighting contest

Main a river in central and W Germany, flowing west through Würzburg and Frankfurt to the Rhine. Length: about 515 km (320 miles)

mainbrace *Nautical* a brace attached to the main yard

Maine a state of the northeastern US, on the Atlantic: chiefly hilly, with many lakes, rivers, and forests. Capital: Augusta. Pop: 1 305 728 (2003 est). Area: 86 156 sq km (33 265 sq miles)

Maine-et-Loire a department of W France, in Pays de la Loire region. Capital: Angers. Pop: 745 486 (2003 est). Area: 7218 sq km (2815 sq miles)

mainframe 1 a a high-speed general-purpose computer, usually with a large store capacity b *(as modifier): mainframe systems* 2 the central processing unit of a computer

mainland 1 the main part of a land mass as opposed to an island or peninsula 2 **the mainland** a particular landmass as viewed from a nearby island with which it has close links, such as Great Britain as viewed from Northern Ireland or continental Australia as viewed from Tasmania

Mainland 1 an island off N Scotland: the largest of the Shetland Islands. Chief town: Lerwick. Pop: 17 550 (2001). Area: about 583 sq km (225 sq miles) 2 an island off N Scotland: the largest of the Orkney Islands. Chief town: Kirkwall. Pop: 15 315 (2001). Area: 492 sq km (190 sq miles) 3 **the Mainland** NZ a South Islanders' name for **South Island**

main line 1 *Railways* a the trunk route between two

points, usually fed by branch lines **b** (*as modifier*): *a main-line station* **2** *US* a main road

mainmast *Nautical* the chief mast of a sailing vessel with two or more masts, being the foremast of a yawl, ketch, or dandy and the second mast from the bow of most others

mainsail *Nautical* the largest and lowermost sail on the mainmast

mainspring the principal power spring of a mechanism, esp in a watch or clock

mainstay *Nautical* the forestay that braces the mainmast

mainstream *Music* of or relating to the style of jazz that lies between the traditional and the modern

mainstreeting *Canadian* the practice of a politician walking about the streets of a town or city to gain votes and greet supporters

maintenance **1** *Law* (formerly unlawful) the interference in a legal action by a person having no interest in it, as by providing funds to continue the action **2** *Law* a provision ordered to be made by way of periodical payments or a lump sum, as after a divorce for a spouse **3** *Computing* **a** the correction or prevention of faults in hardware by a programme of inspection and the replacement of parts **b** the removal of existing faults and the modification of software in response to changes in specification or environment

Maintenon Marquise de, title of *Françoise d'Aubigné*. 1635–1719, the mistress and, from about 1685, second wife of Louis XIV

Mainz a port in W Germany, capital of the Rhineland-Palatinate, at the confluence of the Main and Rhine: an archbishopric from about 780 until 1801; important in the 15th century for the development of printing (by Johann Gutenberg). Pop: 185 532 (2003 est)

maisonette *or* **maisonnette** self-contained living accommodation often occupying two floors of a larger house and having its own outside entrance

Maitland¹ Frederic William 1850–1906, English legal historian

Maitland² a town in SE Australia, in E New South Wales: industrial centre of an agricultural region. Pop: 53 470 (2001)

maize **1 a** a tall annual grass, *Zea mays*, cultivated for its yellow edible grains, which develop on a spike **b** the grain of this plant, used for food, fodder, and as a source of oil **2** a yellow colour

majolica *or* **maiolica** a type of porous pottery glazed with bright metallic oxides that was originally imported into Italy via Majorca and was extensively made in Italy during the Renaissance

major **1** *Business* a large or important company **2** *Music* a major key, chord, mode, or scale **3** *US, Canadian, Austral, and NZ* **a** the principal field of study of a student at a university, etc. **b** a student who is studying a particular subject as his principal field **4** *Law* a person who has reached the age of legal majority **5** *Logic* a major term or premise **6** *Music* **a** (of a scale or mode) having notes separated by the interval of a whole tone, except for the third and fourth degrees, and seventh and eighth degrees, which are separated by a semitone **b** relating to or employing notes from the major scale **c** denoting

a specified key or scale as being major **d** denoting a chord or triad having a major third above the root **e** (in jazz) denoting a major chord with a major seventh added above the root **7** *Logic* constituting the major term or major premise of a syllogism **8** *Chiefly US, Canadian, Austral, and NZ* of or relating to a student's principal field of study at a university, etc. **9** *Brit* the elder: used after a schoolboy's surname if he has one or more younger brothers in the same school **10** of full legal age **11** *Bell-ringing* of, relating to, or denoting a method rung on eight bells

Major John born 1943, British Conservative politician: Chancellor of the Exchequer (1989–90); prime minister (1990–97)

Majorca an island in the W Mediterranean: the largest of the Balearic Islands; tourism. Capital: Palma. Pop: 730 778 (2002 est). Area: 3639 sq km (1465 sq miles)

majority **1** (in an election) the number of votes or seats by which the strongest party or candidate beats the combined opposition or the runner-up **2** the largest party or group that votes together in a legislative or deliberative assembly **3** the time of reaching or state of having reached full legal age, when a person is held competent to manage his own affairs, exercise civil rights and duties, etc.

Makalu a massif in NE Nepal, on the border with Tibet in the Himalayas

Makarios III original name *Mikhail Christodoulou Mouskos*. 1913–77, Cypriot archbishop, patriarch, and statesman; first president of the republic of Cyprus (1960–74; 1974–77)

make **1** *Bridge* the contract to be played **2** *Cards* a player's turn to shuffle

Makeba Miriam born 1932, South African singer and political activist; banned from South Africa from 1960 to 1990

Maker a title given to God (as Creator)

make-up **a** the cosmetics, false hair, etc, used by an actor to highlight his features or adapt his appearance **b** the art or result of applying such cosmetics

Makeyevka a city in SE Ukraine: coal-mining centre. Pop: 380 000 (2005 est)

Makhachkala a port in SW Russia, capital of the Dagestan Republic, on the Caspian Sea: fishing fleet; oil refining. Pop: 503 000 (2005 est)

mako¹ any shark of the genus *Isurus*, esp *I. glaucus* of Indo-Pacific and Australian seas: family *Isuridae*

mako² *or* **mako-mako** *NZ* another name for the **bell-bird**, *Anthornis melanura*

mako³ *or* **mako-mako** a small evergreen New Zealand tree, *Aristotelia serrata*: family *Elaeocarpaceae*

Makurdi a port in E central Nigeria, capital of Benue State on the Benue River: agricultural trade centre. Pop: 259 000 (2005 est)

Malabar Coast *or* **Malabar** a region along the SW coast of India, extending from Goa to Cape Comorin: includes most of Kerala state

Malabo the capital and chief port of Equatorial Guinea, on the island of Bioko in the Gulf of Guinea. Pop: 105 000 (2005 est)

Malacca a state of SW Peninsular Malaysia: rubber plantations. Capital: Malacca. Pop: 635 791 (2000). Area:

1650 sq km (637 sq miles)

Malachi *Old Testament* **1** a Hebrew prophet of the 5th century BC **2** the book containing his oracles

malachite a bright green mineral, found in veins and in association with copper deposits. It is a source of copper and is used as an ornamental stone. Composition: hydrated copper carbonate. Formula: $Cu_2CO_3(OH)_2$. Crystal structure: monoclinic

maladjustment *Psychol* a failure to meet the demands of society, such as coping with problems and social relationships: usually reflected in emotional instability

malady any disease or illness

Malagasy 1 a native or inhabitant of Madagascar **2** the official language of Madagascar belonging to the Malayo-Polynesian family **3** of or relating to Madagascar, its people, or their language

malaise a mild sickness, not symptomatic of any disease or ailment

Malamud Bernard 1914–86, US novelist and short-story writer. His works include *The Fixer* (1966) and *Dubin's Lives* (1979)

Malang a city in S Indonesia, on E Java: commercial centre. Pop: 756 982 (2000)

malapropism 1 the unintentional misuse of a word by confusion with one of similar sound, esp when creating a ridiculous effect, as in *I am not under the affluence of alcohol* **2** the habit of misusing words in this manner

malaria an infectious disease characterized by recurring attacks of chills and fever, caused by the bite of an anopheles mosquito infected with any of four protozoans of the genus *Plasmodium* (*P. vivax, P. falciparum, P. malariae,* or *P. ovale*)

Malatesta an Italian family that ruled Rimini from the 13th to the 16th century

Malatya a city in E central Turkey: nearby is the ruined Roman and medieval city of Melitene (Old Malatya). Pop: 448 000 (2005 est)

Malawi 1 a republic in E central Africa: established as a British protectorate in 1891; became independent in 1964 and a republic, within the Commonwealth, in 1966; lies along the Great Rift Valley, with Lake Nyasa (Malawi) along the E border, the Nyika Plateau in the northwest, and the Shire (or Shiré) Highlands in the southeast. Official language: Chichewa; English and various other Bantu languages are also widely spoken. Religion: Christian majority, Muslim, and animist minorities. Currency: kwacha. Capital: Lilongwe. Pop: 12 337 000 (2004 est). Area: 118 484 sq km (45 747 sq miles) **2 Lake** the Malawi name for (Lake) **Nyasa**

Malay 1 a member of a people living chiefly in Malaysia and Indonesia who are descendants of Mongoloid immigrants **2** the language of this people, belonging to the Malayo-Polynesian family

Malaya 1 States of the Federation of part of Malaysia, in the S Malay Peninsula, constituting Peninsular Malaysia: consists of the former Federated Malay States, the former Unfederated Malay States, and the former Straits Settlements. Capital: Kuala Lumpur. Pop: 17 144 322 (2000). Area: 131 587 sq km (50 806 sq miles) **2 Federation of** a federation of the nine Malay States of the Malay Peninsula and two of the Straits Settlements (Malacca and Penang): formed in 1948:

became part of the British Commonwealth in 1957 and joined Malaysia in 1963

Malay Archipelago a group of islands in the Indian and Pacific Oceans, between SE Asia and Australia: the largest group of islands in the world; includes over 3000 Indonesian islands, about 7000 islands of the Philippines, and, sometimes, New Guinea

Malay Peninsula a peninsula of SE Asia, extending south from the Isthmus of Kra in Thailand to Cape Tanjong Piai in Malaysia: consists of SW Thailand and the states of Malaya (Peninsular Malaysia)

Malaysia a federation in SE Asia (within the Commonwealth), consisting of **Peninsular Malaysia** on the Malay Peninsula, and **East Malaysia** (Sabah and Sarawak), occupying the N part of the island of Borneo: formed in 1963 as a federation of Malaya, Sarawak, Sabah, and Singapore (the latter seceded in 1965); densely forested and mostly mountainous. Official language: Malay; English and various Chinese and Indian minority languages are also spoken. Official religion: Muslim. Currency: ringgit. Capital: Putrajaya (the transfer of government from Kuala Lumpur is taking place in stages over several years starting 1999). Pop: 24 876 000 (2004 est). Area: 333 403 sq km (128 727 sq miles)

Malcolm III died 1093, king of Scotland (1057–93). He became king after Macbeth

Malcolm X original name *Malcolm Little.* 1925–65, US Black civil-rights leader: assassinated

Maldon a market town in SE England, in Essex; scene of a battle (991) between the East Saxons and the victorious Danes, celebrated in *The Battle of Maldon,* an Old English poem; notable for Maldon salt, used in cookery. Pop: 20 731 (2001)

male 1 of, relating to, or designating the sex producing gametes (spermatozoa) that can fertilize female gametes (ova) **2** (of gametes) capable of fertilizing an egg cell in sexual reproduction **3** (of reproductive organs, such as a testis or stamen) capable of producing male gametes **4** (of flowers) bearing stamens but lacking a functional pistil **5** *Electronics, Mechanical engineering* having a projecting part or parts that fit into a female counterpart

Malebranche Nicolas 1638–1715, French philosopher. Originally a follower of Descartes, he developed the philosophy of occasionalism, esp in *De la recherche de la vérité* (1674)

Malenkov Georgi Maksimilianovich 1902–88, Soviet politician; prime minister (1953–55). He was removed from the party presidium (1957) for plotting against Khrushchev; expelled from the Communist Party (1961)

Malevich Kasimir 1878–1935, Russian painter. He founded the abstract art movement known as Suprematism

malfeasance *Law* the doing of a wrongful or illegal act, esp by a public official

malformation *Pathol* a deformity in the shape or structure of a part, esp when congenital

Malherbe François de 1555–1628, French poet and critic. He advocated the classical ideals of clarity and concision of meaning

Mali a landlocked republic in West Africa: conquered by the French by 1898 and incorporated (as French Sudan)

into French West Africa; became independent in 1960; settled chiefly in the basins of the Rivers Senegal and Niger in the south. Official language: French. Religion: Muslim majority, also animist. Currency: franc. Capital: Bamako. Pop: 13 408 000 (2004 est). Area: 1 248 574 sq km (482 077 sq miles)

malice *Law* the state of mind with which an act is committed and from which the intent to do wrong may be inferred

malice aforethought *Criminal law* 1 the predetermination to do an unlawful act, esp to kill or seriously injure 2 the intent with which an unlawful killing is effected, which must be proved for the crime to constitute murder

malignant 1 *Pathol* (of a tumour) uncontrollable or resistant to therapy; rapidly spreading 2 *History* (in the English Civil War) a Parliamentarian term for a **royalist**

Malinowski Bronislaw Kasper 1884–1942, Polish anthropologist in England and the US, who researched into the sexual behaviour of primitive people in New Guinea and Melanesia

mall 1 a shaded avenue, esp one that is open to the public 2 short for **shopping mall**

mallard a duck, *Anas platyrhynchos*, common over most of the N hemisphere, the male of which has a dark green head and reddish-brown breast: the ancestor of all domestic breeds of duck

Malle Louis 1932–95, French film director: his films include *Le Feu follet* (1963), *Au revoir les enfants* (1987), and *Vanya on 42nd Street* (1994)

mallee 1 any of several low shrubby eucalyptus trees that flourish in desert regions of Australia 2 *Austral, informal* another name for the **bush**

mallet 1 a tool resembling a hammer but having a large head of wood, copper, lead, leather, etc, used for driving chisels, beating sheet metal, etc. 2 a long stick with a head like a hammer used to strike the ball in croquet or polo 3 *Chiefly US* a very large powerful steam locomotive with a conventional boiler but with two separate articulated engine units

mallow 1 any plant of the malvaceous genus *Malva*, esp *M. sylvestris* of Europe, having purple, pink, or white flowers 2 any of various related plants, such as the marsh mallow, rose mallow, Indian mallow, and tree mallow

malnutrition lack of adequate nutrition resulting from insufficient food, unbalanced diet, or defective assimilation

Malory Sir Thomas 15th-century English author of *Le Morte d'Arthur* (?1470), a prose collection of Arthurian legends, translated from the French

Malouf David born 1934, Australian novelist, short-story writer, and poet. His novels include *An Imaginary Life* (1978), *Remembering Babylon* (1993), and *The Conversations at Curlow Creek* (1996)

Malpighi Marcello 1628–94, Italian physiologist. A pioneer in microscopic anatomy, he identified the capillary system (1661)

Malraux André 1901–76, French writer and statesman. His novels include *La Condition humaine* (1933) on the Kuomintang revolution (1927–28) and *L'Espoir* (1937) on the Spanish Civil War, in both of which events he took

part. He also wrote on art, notably in *Les Voix du silence* (1951)

malt 1 cereal grain, such as barley, that is kiln-dried after it has germinated by soaking in water 2 short for **malt whisky**

Malta a republic occupying the islands of Malta, Gozo, and Comino, in the Mediterranean south of Sicily: governed by the Knights Hospitallers from 1530 until Napoleon's conquest in 1798; French driven out, with British help, 1800; became British dependency 1814; suffered severely in World War II; became independent in 1964 and a republic in 1974; joined the EU in 2004; a member of the Commonwealth. Official languages: Maltese and English. Official religion: Roman Catholic. Currency: Maltese lira. Capital: Valletta. Pop: 396 000 (2004 est). Area: 316 sq km (122 sq miles)

Maltese 1 the official language of Malta, a form of Arabic with borrowings from Italian, etc. 2 a breed of toy dog having a very long straight silky white coat 3 a domestic fancy pigeon having long legs and a long neck

Maltese cross (in a film projector) a cam mechanism of this shape that produces intermittent motion

Malthus Thomas Robert 1766–1834, English economist. He propounded his population theory in *An Essay on the Principle of Population* (1798)

Malthusian of or relating to the theory of the English economist Thomas Robert Malthus (1766–1834) stating that increases in population tend to exceed increases in the means of subsistence and that therefore sexual restraint should be exercised

maltose a disaccharide of glucose formed by the enzymic hydrolysis of starch: used in bacteriological culture media and as a nutrient in infant feeding. Formula: $C_{12}H_{22}O_{11}$

malt whisky whisky made from malted barley

Malvern a town and resort in W England, in S Worcestershire on the E slopes of the **Malvern Hills**: annual dramatic festival; mineral springs. Pop: 35 588 (2001)

mamba any aggressive partly arboreal tropical African venomous elapid snake of the genus *Dendroaspis*, esp *D. angusticeps* (**green** and **black mambas**)

mambo 1 a modern Latin American dance, resembling the rumba, derived from the ritual dance of voodoo 2 a voodoo priestess

Mamet David born 1947, US dramatist and film director. His plays include *Sexual Perversity in Chicago* (1974), *American Buffalo* (1976), *Glengarry Glen Ross* (1983), and *Oleanna* (1992); films include *House of Games* (1987) and *Spartan* (2004)

mammal any animal of the *Mammalia*, a large class of warm-blooded vertebrates having mammary glands in the female, a thoracic diaphragm, and a four-chambered heart. The class includes the whales, carnivores, rodents, bats, primates, etc.

mammary gland any of the milk-producing glands in mammals. In higher mammals each gland consists of a network of tubes and cavities connected to the exterior by a nipple

Mammon *New Testament* the personification of riches and greed in the form of a false god

mammoth any large extinct elephant of the

Pleistocene genus *Mammuthus* (or *Elephas*), such as *M. primigenius* (**woolly mammoth**), having a hairy coat and long curved tusks

man 1 a a member of any of the living races of *Homo sapiens*, characterized by erect bipedal posture, a highly developed brain, and powers of articulate speech, abstract reasoning, and imagination **b** any extinct member of the species *Homo sapiens*, such as Cro-Magnon man **2** a member of any of the extinct species of the genus *Homo*, such as Java man, Heidelberg man, and Solo man **3** *Games* a movable piece in various games, such as draughts **4** *History* a vassal of a feudal lord

Man Isle of an island in the British Isles, in the Irish Sea between Cumbria and Northern Ireland: a UK Crown Dependency (but not part of the United Kingdom), with its own ancient parliament, the Court of Tynwald; a dependency of Norway until 1266, when for a time it came under Scottish rule; its own language, Manx, became extinct in the 19th century but has been revived to some extent. Capital: Douglas. Pop: 75 000 (2003 est). Area: 588 sq km (227 sq miles)

mana *Anthropol* **1** (in Polynesia, Melanesia, etc) a concept of a life force, believed to be seated in the head, and associated with high social status and ritual power **2** any power achieved by ritual means; prestige; authority

manager 1 *Law* a person appointed by a court to carry on a business during receivership **2** *Politics* (in Britain) a member of either House of Parliament appointed to arrange a matter in which both Houses are concerned **3** a computer program that organizes a resource, such as a set of files or a database

Managua 1 the capital of Nicaragua, on the S shore of Lake Managua: chosen as capital in 1857. Pop: 1 159 000 (2005 est) **2 Lake** a lake in W Nicaragua: drains into Lake Nicaragua by the Tipitapa River. Length: 61 km (38 miles). Width: about 26 km (16 miles)

Manama the capital of Bahrain, at the N end of Bahrain Island: transit port. Pop: 142 000 (2005 est)

Manassas a town in NE Virginia, west of Alexandria: site of the victory of Confederate forces in the Battles of Bull Run, or First and Second Manassas (1861; 1862), during the American Civil War. Pop: 37 166 (2003 est)

Manasseh *Old Testament* **1** the elder son of Joseph (Genesis 41:51) **2** the Israelite tribe descended from him **3** the territory of this tribe, in the upper Jordan valley

manatee any sirenian mammal of the genus *Trichechus*, occurring in tropical coastal waters of America, the Caribbean, and Africa: family *Trichechidae*. They resemble whales and have a prehensile upper lip and a broad flattened tail

Manaus *or* **Manáos** a port in N Brazil, capital of Amazonas state, on the Rio Negro 19 km (12 miles) above its confluence with the Amazon: chief commercial centre of the Amazon basin. Pop: 1 673 000 (2005 est)

Manche 1 a department of NW France, in Basse-Normandie region. Capital: St-Lô. Pop: 484 967 (2003 est). Area: 6412 sq km (2501 sq miles) **2 La** the French name for the **English Channel**

Manchester 1 a city in NW England, in Manchester

unitary authority, Greater Manchester: linked to the Mersey estuary by the **Manchester Ship Canal**: commercial, industrial, and cultural centre; formerly the centre of the cotton and textile trades; two universities. Pop: 394 269 (2001) **2** a unitary authority in NW England, in Greater Manchester. Pop: 432 500 (2003 est). Area: 116 sq km (45 sq miles)

Manchu 1 a member of a Mongoloid people of Manchuria who conquered China in the 17th century, establishing an imperial dynasty that lasted until 1912 **2** the language of this people, belonging to the Tungusic branch of the Altaic family

Manchukuo *or* **Manchoukuo** a former state of E Asia (1932–45), consisting of the three provinces of old Manchuria and Jehol

Manchuria a region of NE China, historically the home of the Manchus, rulers of China from 1644 to 1912: includes part of the Inner Mongolian AR and the provinces of Heilongjiang, Jilin, and Liaoning. Area: about 1 300 000 sq km (502 000 sq miles)

Mancunian 1 a native or inhabitant of Manchester **2** of or relating to Manchester

mandala 1 *Hindu and Buddhist art* any of various designs symbolizing the universe, usually circular **2** *Psychol* such a symbol expressing a person's striving for unity of the self

Mandalay a city in central Myanmar, on the Irrawaddy River: the second largest city in the country and former capital of Burma and of Upper Burma; Buddhist religious centre. Pop: 927 000 (2005 est)

mandarin 1 (in the Chinese Empire) a member of any of the nine senior grades of the bureaucracy, entered by examinations **2** a high-ranking official whose powers are extensive and thought to be outside political control

mandarin a a small citrus tree, *Citrus nobilis*, cultivated for its edible fruit **b** the fruit of this tree, resembling the tangerine

Mandarin Chinese *or* **Mandarin** the official language of China since 1917; the form of Chinese spoken by about two thirds of the population and taught in schools throughout China

mandate 1 *Politics* the support or commission given to a government and its policies or an elected representative and his policies through an electoral victory **2** (formerly) any of the territories under the trusteeship of the League of Nations administered by one of its member states **3 a** *Roman law* a contract by which one person commissions another to act for him gratuitously and the other accepts the commission **b** *Contract law* a contract of bailment under which the party entrusted with goods undertakes to perform gratuitously some service in respect of such goods **c** *Scots law* a contract by which a person is engaged to act in the management of the affairs of another

Mandela 1 Nelson (**Rolihlahla**). born 1918, Black South African statesman: president of South Africa (1994–99). Jailed in 1962 for 5 years and, in 1964, for life, he was released in 1990 after a long international campaign; deputy president of the African National Congress (1990–91) and president (1991–97); elected president of South Africa in 1994; Nobel peace prize jointly with F.

W. de Klerk in 1993 **2** (**Numzano**) **Winnie** born 1934, Black South African political activist: campaigned for the release of her husband Nelson Mandela; they divorced in 1996

Mandelstam or **Mandelshtam** **1** Nadezhda (**Yakovlevna**), born *Nadezhda Khazina*. 1899–1980, Soviet writer, wife of Osip Mandelstam: noted for her memoirs *Hope against Hope* (1971) and *Hope Abandoned* (1973) describing life in Stalin's Russia **2** Osip (**Emilyevich**). 1891–?1938, Soviet poet and writer, born in Warsaw; he was persecuted by Stalin and died in a labour camp. His works include *Tristia* (1922), *Poems* (1928), and the autobiographical *Journey to Armenia* (1933)

Mandeville **1** Bernard de ?1670–1733, English author, born in Holland, noted for his satire *The Fable of the Bees* (1723) **2** Sir **John** 14th century, English author of *The Travels of Sir John Mandeville*. The book claims to be an account of the author's journeys in the East but is largely a compilation from other works

mandible **1** the lower jawbone in vertebrates **2** either of a pair of mouthparts in insects and other arthropods that are usually used for biting and crushing food **3** *Ornithol* either the upper or the lower part of the bill, esp the lower part

mandolin or **mandoline** a plucked stringed instrument related to the lute, having four pairs of strings tuned in ascending fifths stretched over a small light body with a fretted fingerboard. It is usually played with a plectrum, long notes being sustained by the tremolo.

mandrake or **mandragora** a Eurasian solanaceous plant, *Mandragora officinarum*, with purplish flowers and a forked root. It was formerly thought to have magic powers and a narcotic was prepared from its root

mandrel or **mandril** **1** a spindle on which a workpiece is supported during machining operations **2** a shaft or arbor on which a machining tool is mounted **3** the driving spindle in the headstock of a lathe **4** *Brit* a miner's pick

mandrill an Old World monkey, *Mandrillus sphinx*, of W Africa. It has a short tail and brown hair, and the ridged muzzle, nose, and hindquarters are red and blue

mane the long coarse hair that grows from the crest of the neck in such mammals as the lion and horse

Manet **Édouard** 1832–83, French painter. His painting *Le Déjeuner sur l'herbe* (1863), which was condemned by the Parisian establishment, was acclaimed by the impressionists, whom he decisively influenced

Mangalore a port in S India, in Karnataka on the Malabar Coast. Pop: 398 745 (2001)

manganese a brittle greyish-white metallic element that exists in four allotropic forms, occurring principally in pyrolusite and rhodonite: used in making steel and ferromagnetic alloys. Symbol: Mn; atomic no.: 25; atomic wt.: 54.93805; valency: 1, 2 ,3, 4, 6, or 7; relative density: 7.21–7.44; melting pt.: 1246±3°C; boiling pt.: 2062°C

mange an infectious disorder mainly affecting domestic animals, characterized by itching, formation of papules and vesicles, and loss of hair: caused by parasitic mites

mangelwurzel or **mangoldwurzel** a Eurasian variety of the beet plant, *Beta vulgaris*, cultivated as a cattle food, having a large yellowish root

manger *Nautical* a basin-like construction in the bows of a vessel for catching water draining from an anchor rode or coming in through the hawseholes

mangetout a variety of garden pea in which the pod is also edible

mangle a machine for pressing or drying wet textiles, clothes, etc, consisting of two heavy rollers between which the cloth is passed

mango **1** a tropical Asian anacardiaceous evergreen tree, *Mangifera indica*, cultivated in the tropics for its fruit **2** the ovoid edible fruit of this tree, having a smooth rind and sweet juicy orange-yellow flesh

mangrove **1 a** any tropical evergreen tree or shrub of the genus *Rhizophora*, having stiltlike intertwining aerial roots and growing below the highest tide levels in estuaries and along coasts, forming dense thickets: family *Rhizophoraceae* **b** (*as modifier*): mangrove swamp **2** any of various similar trees or shrubs of the genus *Avicennia*: family *Avicenniaceae*

Manhattan **1** an island at the N end of New York Bay, between the Hudson, East, and Harlem Rivers: administratively (with adjacent islets) a borough of New York City; a major financial, commercial, and cultural centre. Pop: 1 537 195 (2000). Area: 47 sq km (22 sq miles) **2** a mixed drink consisting of four parts whisky, one part vermouth, and a dash of bitters

Manhire **Bill** born 1946, New Zealand poet and writer. His poetry collections include *How to Take Off Your Clothes at the Picnic* (1977), *Zoetropes* (1984), and *Sunshine* (1996)

manhole **1** a shaft with a removable cover that leads down to a sewer or drain **2** a hole, usually with a detachable cover, through which a man can enter a boiler, tank, etc.

man-hour a unit for measuring work in industry, equal to the work done by one man in one hour

Mani ?216–?276 AD, Persian prophet who founded Manichaeism

mania a mental disorder characterized by great excitement and occasionally violent behaviour

manic-depressive *Psychiatry* denoting a mental disorder characterized either by an alternation between extreme euphoria and deep depression (bipolar manic-depressive disorder or syndrome) or by depression on its own or (rarely) by elation on its own (unipolar disorder)

manifest **1** *Psychoanal* of or relating to the ostensible elements of a dream **2** a customs document containing particulars of a ship, its cargo, and its destination **3 a** a list of cargo, passengers, etc, on an aeroplane **b** a list of railway trucks or their cargo **c** *Chiefly US and Canadian* a fast freight train carrying perishables

manifesto a public declaration of intent, policy, aims, etc, as issued by a political party, government, or movement

manifold *Formal* **1** a chamber or pipe with a number of inlets or outlets used to collect or distribute a fluid. In an internal-combustion engine the **inlet manifold** carries the vaporized fuel from the carburettor to the inlet ports and the **exhaust manifold** carries the exhaust gases away **2** *Maths* **a** a collection of objects or a set **b** a topological space having specific properties **3** (in the philosophy of Kant) the totality of the separate elements of sensation which are then organized by the active mind and conceptualized as a perception of an external object

Manila the chief port of the Philippines, on S Luzon on Manila Bay: capital of the republic until 1948 and from 1976; seat of the Far Eastern University and the University of Santo Tomas (1611). Pop: 10 677 000 (2005 est)

Manila Bay an almost landlocked inlet of the South China Sea in the Philippines, in W Luzon: mostly forms Manila harbour. Area: 1994 sq km (770 sq miles)

Manipur a state in NE India: largely densely forested mountains. Capital: Imphal. Pop: 2 388 634 (2001). Area: 22 327 sq km (8621 sq miles)

Manisa a city in W Turkey: the Byzantine seat of government (1204–1313). Pop: 237 000 (2005 est)

Manitoba 1 a province of W Canada: consists of prairie in the southwest, with extensive forests in the north and tundra near Hudson Bay in the northeast. Capital: Winnipeg. Pop: 1 170 268 (2004 est). Area: 650 090 sq km (251 000 sq miles) **2 Lake** a lake in W Canada, in S Manitoba: fed by the outflow from Lake Winnipegosis; drains into Lake Winnipeg. Area: 4706 sq km (1817 sq miles)

Manitoulin Island an island in N Lake Huron in Ontario: the largest freshwater island in the world. Length: 129 km (80 miles). Width: up to 48 km (30 miles)

Manizales a city in W Colombia, in the Cordillera Central of the Andes at an altitude of 2100 m (7000 ft): commercial centre of a rich coffee-growing area. Pop: 401 000 (2005 est)

Manley Michael Norman 1924–97, Jamaican statesman; prime minister of Jamaica (1972–80; 1989–92)

Mann 1 Heinrich 1871–1950, German novelist: works include *Professor Unrat* (1905), which was filmed as *The Blue Angel* (1928), and *Man of Straw* (1918) **2** his brother, **Thomas** 1875–1955, German novelist, in the US after 1937. His works deal mainly with the problem of the artist in bourgeois society and include the short story *Death in Venice* (1913) and the novels *Buddenbrooks* (1900), *The Magic Mountain* (1924), and *Doctor Faustus* (1947): Nobel prize for literature 1929

manna 1 *Old Testament* the miraculous food which sustained the Israelites in the wilderness (Exodus 16:14–36) **2** a sweet substance obtained from various plants, esp from an ash tree, *Fraxinus ornus* (**manna** or **flowering ash**) of S Europe, used as a mild laxative

Mannar Gulf of the part of the Indian Ocean between SE India and the island of Sri Lanka: pearl fishing

mannered of or having mannerisms of style, as in art or literature

Mannerheim Baron Carl Gustaf Emil 1867–1951, Finnish soldier and statesman; president of Finland (1944–46)

mannerism 1 a principally Italian movement in art and architecture between the High Renaissance and Baroque periods (1520–1600) that sought to represent an ideal of beauty rather than natural images of it, using characteristic distortion and exaggeration of human proportions, perspective, etc. **2** adherence to a distinctive or affected manner, esp in art or literature

▷www.artcyclopedia.com/history/
mannerism.html
▷www.artlex.com/ArtLex/m/mannerism.html
▷www.tigtail.org/TVM/M_View/X1/
c.Mannerism

Mannheim[1] Karl 1893–1947, Hungarian sociologist, living in Britain from 1933: author of *Ideology and Utopia* (1929) and *Man and Society in an Age of Reconstruction* (1941)

Mannheim[2] a city in SW Germany, in Baden-Württemberg at the confluence of the Rhine and Neckar: one of Europe's largest inland harbours; a cultural and musical centre. Pop: 308 353 (2003 est)

Manning 1 Henry Edward 1808–92, British churchman. Originally an Anglican, he was converted to Roman Catholicism (1851) and made archbishop of Westminster (1865) and cardinal (1875) **2 Olivia** 1908–80, British novelist and short-story writer, best known for her novel sequence *Fortunes of War*, comprising the *Balkan Trilogy* (1960–65) and the *Levant Trilogy* (1977–80)

manoeuvre *or US* **maneuver 1** *Aeronautics* a planned movement of an aircraft in flight **2** *Nautical* any change from the straight steady course of a ship

man-of-war *or* **man o' war 1** a warship **2** See Portuguese man-of-war

Manolete original name *Manuel Rodriguez y Sánchez*. 1917–47, Spanish bullfighter

manor 1 (in medieval Europe) the manor house of a lord and the lands attached to it **2** (before 1776 in some North American colonies) a tract of land granted with rights of inheritance by royal charter **3** a manor house

manor house (esp formerly) the house of the lord of a manor

manpower *Physics* a unit of power based on the rate at which a man can work; approximately 75 watts

Manresa a city in NE Spain: contains a cave used as the spiritual retreat of St Ignatius Loyola. Pop: 67 269 (2003 est)

mansard 1 a roof having two slopes on both sides and both ends, the lower slopes being steeper than the upper **2** an attic having such a roof

Mansart 1 François 1598–1666, French architect, who established the classical style in French architecture **2** his great-nephew, **Jules Hardouin** 1646--1708, French architect and town planner, who completed the Palace of Versailles

manse (in certain religious denominations) the house provided for a minister

Mansfield[1] Katherine, real name *Kathleen Mansfield Beauchamp*. 1888--1923, British writer, born in New Zealand, noted for her short stories, such as those in *Bliss* (1920) and *The Garden Party* (1922)

Mansfield[2] a town in central England, in W Nottinghamshire: former coal-mining and cotton-textiles industries. Pop: 69 987 (2001)

Mansholt Sicco Leendert 1908–95, Dutch economist and politician; vice president (1958–72) and president (1972–73) of the European Economic Community Commission. He was the author of the Mansholt Plan for the agricultural organization of the European Economic Community

mansion 1 a large and imposing house **2** a less common word for **manor house 3** *Brit* a block of flats **4** *Astrology* any of 28 divisions of the zodiac each occupied on successive days by the moon

manslaughter *Law* the unlawful killing of one human being by another without malice aforethought

Mantegna Andrea 1431–1506, Italian painter and engraver, noted esp for his frescoes, such as those in the Ducal Palace, Mantua

mantle *or less commonly* **mantle 1** a wooden or stone frame around the opening of a fireplace, together with its decorative facing **2** a shelf above this frame

mantelpiece 1 a shelf above a fireplace often forming part of the mantel **2** another word for **mantel**

Mantinea *or* **Mantineia** (in ancient Greece) a city in E Arcadia; site of several battles

mantis any carnivorous typically green insect of the family *Mantidae*, of warm and tropical regions, having a long body and large eyes and resting with the first pair of legs raised as if in prayer: order *Dictyoptera*

mantissa the fractional part of a common logarithm representing the digits of the associated number but not its magnitude

mantle 1 *Chemistry* a small dome-shaped or cylindrical mesh impregnated with cerium or thorium nitrates, used to increase illumination in a gas or oil lamp **2** *Zoology* **a** a protective layer of epidermis in molluscs that secretes a substance forming the shell **b** a similar structure in brachiopods **3** *Ornithol* the feathers of the folded wings and back, esp when these are of a different colour from the remaining feathers **4** *Geology* the part of the earth between the crust and the core, accounting for more than 82 of the earth's volume (but only 68 of its mass) and thought to be composed largely of peridotite **5** a less common spelling of **mantel 6** a clay mould formed around a wax model which is subsequently melted out

mantra 1 *Hinduism* any of those parts of the Vedic literature which consist of the metrical psalms of praise **2** *Hinduism, Buddhism* any sacred word or syllable used as an object of concentration and embodying some aspect of spiritual power

Mantua a city in N Italy, in E Lombardy, surrounded by lakes: birthplace of Virgil. Pop: 47 790 (2001)

manual *Music* one of the keyboards played by hand on an organ

manufacture 1 the production of goods, esp by industrial processes **2** a manufactured product

manuka a New Zealand myrtaceous tree, *Leptospermum scoparium*, with strong elastic wood and aromatic leaves

Manukau a city in New Zealand, on **Manukau Harbour** (an inlet of the Tasman Sea) near Auckland on NW North Island. Pop: 326 200 (2004 est)

manuscript a book or other document written by hand

Manx 1 of, relating to, or characteristic of the Isle of Man, its inhabitants, their language, or their dialect of English **2** a language of the Isle of Man, belonging to the N Celtic branch of the Indo-European family and closely related to Scottish Gaelic **3** the people of the Isle of Man

Manx cat a short-haired tailless variety of cat, believed to originate on the Isle of Man

Manxman *or feminine* **Manxwoman** a native or inhabi-

tant of the Isle of Man

Manzoni Alessandro 1785–1873, Italian romantic novelist and poet, famous for his historical novel I *Promessi sposi* (1825–27)

Maoism Marxism-Leninism as interpreted by Mao Tsetung (1893–1976), the Chinese Marxist theoretician and statesman: distinguished by its theory of guerrilla warfare and its emphasis on the revolutionary potential of the peasantry

Mao Tse-tung *or* **Mao Ze Dong** 1893–1976, Chinese Marxist theoretician and statesman. The son of a peasant farmer, he helped to found the Chinese Communist Party (1921) and established a soviet republic in SE China (1931–34). He led the retreat of Communist forces to NW China known as the Long March (1935–36), emerging as leader of the party. In opposing the Japanese in World War II, he united with the Kuomintang regime, which he then defeated in the ensuing civil war. He founded the People's Republic of China (1949) of which he was chairman until 1959. As party chairman until his death, he instigated the Cultural Revolution in 1966

map 1 *Surveying* a diagrammatic representation of the earth's surface or part of it, showing the geographical distributions, positions, etc, of natural or artificial features such as roads, towns, relief, rainfall, etc. **2** *Astronomy* a diagrammatic representation of the distribution of stars or of the surface of a celestial body **3** *Maths* another name for **function**

Map *or* **Mapes** Walter ?1140–?1209, Welsh ecclesiastic and satirical writer. His chief work is the miscellany *De Nugis curialium*

maple 1 any tree or shrub of the N temperate genus *Acer*, having winged seeds borne in pairs and lobed leaves: family *Aceraceae* **2** the hard close-grained wood of any of these trees, used for furniture and flooring

Maputo the capital and chief port of Mozambique, in the south on Delagoa Bay: became capital in 1907; the nearest port to the Rand gold-mining and industrial region of South Africa. Pop: 1 316 000 (2005 est)

maquis 1 shrubby mostly evergreen vegetation found in coastal regions of the Mediterranean: includes myrtles, heaths, arbutus, cork oak, and ilex **2 a** the French underground movement that fought against the German occupying forces in World War II **b** a member of this movement

marabou 1 a large black-and-white African carrion-eating stork, *Leptoptilos crumeniferus*, with a very short naked neck and a straight heavy bill **2** a down feather of this bird, used to trim garments **3 a** a fine white raw silk **b** fabric made of this

maraca a percussion instrument, usually one of a pair, consisting of a gourd or plastic shell filled with dried seeds, pebbles, etc. It is used chiefly in Latin American music

Maracaibo 1 a port in NW Venezuela, on the channel from Lake Maracaibo to the Gulf of Venezuela: the second largest city in the country; University of Zulia (1891); major oil centre. Pop: 2 182 000 (2005 est) **2 Lake** a lake in NW Venezuela, linked with the Gulf of Venezuela by a dredged channel: centre of the Venezuelan and South American oil industry. Area:

about 13 000 sq km (500 sq miles)

Maracay a city in N central Venezuela: developed greatly as the headquarters of Juan Vicente Gómez (1857–1935) during his dictatorship; textile industries. Pop: 1 138 000 (2005 est)

Maradona Diego Armando born 1960, Argentinian footballer

marae 1 NZ a traditional Māori tribal meeting place, originally one in the open air, now frequently a purpose-built building 2 (in Polynesia) an open-air place of worship

Maraş a town in S Turkey: noted formerly for the manufacture of weapons but now for carpets and embroidery. Pop: 366 000 (2005 est)

maraschino a liqueur made from marasca cherries and flavoured with the kernels, having a taste like bitter almonds

Marat Jean Paul 1743–93, French revolutionary leader and journalist. He founded the radical newspaper *L'Ami du peuple* and was elected to the National Convention (1792). He was instrumental in overthrowing the Girondists (1793); he was stabbed to death in his bath by Charlotte Corday

marathon a race on foot of 26 miles 385 yards (42.195 kilometres): an event in the modern Olympics

Marathon a plain in Attica northeast of Athens: site of a victory of the Athenians and Plataeans over the Persians (490 BC)

Marbella a coastal resort in S Spain, on the Costa del Sol. Pop: 100 000 (2004 est)

marble 1 a a hard crystalline metamorphic rock resulting from the recrystallization of a limestone: takes a high polish and is used for building and sculpture **b** (*as modifier*): *a marble bust* 2 a block or work of art of marble 3 a small round glass or stone ball used in playing marbles 4 white like some kinds of marble

marbles a game in which marbles are rolled at one another, similar to bowls

Marburg 1 a city in W central Germany, in Hesse: famous for the religious debate between Luther and Zwingli in 1529; Europe's first Protestant university (1527). Pop: 78 511 (2003 est) 2 the German name for **Maribor**

marc 1 the remains of grapes or other fruit that have been pressed for wine-making 2 a brandy distilled from these

Marc Franz 1880–1916, German expressionist painter; cofounder with Kandinsky of the *Blaue Reiter* group (1911). He is noted for his symbolic compositions of animals

marcasite a metallic pale yellow mineral consisting of iron sulphide in orthorhombic crystalline form used in jewellery. Formula: FeS_2

Marceau Marcel born 1923, French mime artist

Marcellus Marcus Claudius ?268–208 BC, Roman general and consul, who captured Syracuse (212) in the Second Punic War

march[1] a piece of music, usually in four beats to the bar, having a strongly accented rhythm

march[2] a frontier, border, or boundary or the land lying along it, often of disputed ownership

Marche a former province of central France

Marches the 1 the border area between England and Wales or Scotland, both characterized by continual feuding (13th–16th centuries) 2 a region of central Italy. Capital: Ancona. Pop: 1 484 601 (2003 est). Area: 9692 sq km (3780 sq miles)

March hare a hare during its breeding season in March, noted for its wild and excitable behaviour (esp in the phrase **mad as a March hare**)

marchioness 1 the wife or widow of a marquis 2 a woman who holds the rank of marquis

Marciano Rocky original name *Rocco Francis Marchegiano*. 1923–69, US heavyweight boxer; world heavyweight champion, 1952–56

Marconi Guglielmo 1874–1937, Italian physicist, who developed radiotelegraphy and succeeded in transmitting signals across the Atlantic (1901): Nobel prize for physics 1909

Marcos Ferdinand (**Edralin**). 1917–89, Filipino statesman; president of the Philippines from 1965; deposed and exiled in 1986

Marcus Aurelius Antoninus original name *Marcus Annius Verus*. 121–180 AD, Roman emperor (161–180) noted particularly for his *Meditations*, propounding his stoic view of life

Marcuse Herbert 1898–1979, US philosopher, born in Germany. In his later works he analysed the situation of man under monopoly capitalism and the dehumanizing effects of modern technology. His works include *Eros and Civilization* (1958) and *One Dimensional Man* (1964)

Mar del Plata a city and resort in E Argentina, on the Atlantic: fishing port. Pop: 552 000 (2005 est)

mare[1] the adult female of a horse or zebra

mare[2] 1 any of a large number of huge dry plains on the surface of the moon, visible as dark markings and once thought to be seas: *Mare Imbrium* (*Sea of Showers*) 2 a similar area on the surface of Mars, such as *Mare Sirenum*

Marengo a village in NW Italy: site of a major battle in which Napoleon decisively defeated the Austrians (1800)

Marenzio Luca 1553–99, Italian composer of madrigals

Margaret 1 called the *Maid of Norway*. ?1282–90, queen of Scotland (1286–90); daughter of Eric II of Norway. Her death while sailing to England to marry the future Edward II led Edward I to declare dominion over Scotland 2 1353–1412, queen of Sweden (1388–1412) and regent of Norway and Denmark (1380–1412), who united the three countries under her rule 3 **Princess** 1930–2002, younger sister of Queen Elizabeth II of Great Britain and Northern Ireland

Margaret of Anjou 1430–82, queen of England. She married the mentally unstable Henry VI of England in 1445 to confirm the truce with France during the Hundred Years' War. She became a leader of the Lancastrians in the Wars of the Roses and was defeated at Tewkesbury (1471) by Edward IV

Margaret of Navarre 1492–1549, queen of Navarre (1544–49) by marriage to Henry II of Navarre; sister of Francis I of France. She was a poet, a patron of humanism, and author of the *Heptaméron* (1558)

Margaret of Scotland Saint 1045–93, queen consort of Malcolm III of Scotland. Her piety and benefactions to the church led to her canonization (1250). Feast days:

439

June 10, Nov 16

Margaret of Valois 1553–1615, daughter of Henry II of France and Catherine de' Medici; queen of Navarre (1572) by marriage to Henry of Navarre. The marriage was dissolved (1599) after his accession as Henry IV of France: noted for her *Mémoires*

Margarita an island in the Caribbean, off the NE coast of Venezuela: pearl fishing. Capital: La Asunción

Margate a town and resort in SE England, in E Kent on the Isle of Thanet. Pop: 58 465 (2001)

margin 1 *Commerce* the profit on a transaction 2 *Economics* the minimum return below which an enterprise becomes unprofitable

marginal 1 *Economics* relating to goods or services produced and sold at the margin of profitability 2 *Politics, chiefly Brit and NZ* of or designating a constituency in which elections tend to be won by small margins 3 *Economics* relating to a small change in something, such as total cost, revenue, or consumer satisfaction

Margolis Donald born 1955, US playwright; plays include *The Loman Family Picnic* (1989) and the Pulitzer Prize-winning *Dinner with Friends* (1999)

margrave a German nobleman ranking above a count. Margraves were originally counts appointed to govern frontier provinces, but all had become princes of the Holy Roman Empire by the 12th century

marguerite 1 a cultivated garden plant, *Chrysanthemum frutescens*, whose flower heads have white or pale yellow rays around a yellow disc: family *Asteraceae* (composites) 2 any of various related plants with daisy-like flowers, esp *C. leucanthemum*

Marianao a city in NW Cuba, adjacent to W Havana city: the chief Cuban military base. Pop: 133 015 (latest est)

Maria Theresa 1717–80, archduchess of Austria and queen of Hungary and Bohemia (1740–80); the daughter and heiress of Emperor Charles VI of Austria; the wife of Emperor Francis I; the mother of Emperor Joseph II. In the War of the Austrian Succession (1740–48) she was confirmed in all her possessions except Silesia, which she attempted unsuccessfully to regain in the Seven Years' War (1756–63)

Maribor an industrial city in N Slovenia on the Drava River: a flourishing Hapsburg trading centre in the 13th century; resort. Pop: 110 668 (2002)

Marie Antoinette 1755–93, queen of France (1774–93) by marriage to Louis XVI of France. Her opposition to reform during the Revolution contributed to the overthrow of the monarchy; guillotined

Marie Galante an island in the E Caribbean southeast of Guadeloupe, of which it is a dependency. Chief town: Grand Bourg. Pop: 13 463 (1990). Area: 155 sq km (60 sq miles)

Mariehamn a city in SW Finland, chief port of the Åland Islands. Pop: 10 693 (2004 est)

Marie Louise 1791–1847, empress of France (1811–15) as the second wife of Napoleon I; daughter of Francis I of Austria. On Napoleon's abdication (1815) she became Duchess of Parma

Mari El Republic a constituent republic of W central Russia, in the middle Volga basin. Capital: Yoshkar-Ola. Pop: 728 000 (2002). Area: 23 200 sq km (8955 sq miles)

marigold 1 any of various tropical American plants of the genus *Tagetes*, esp *T. erecta* (**African marigold**) and *T. patula* (**French marigold**), cultivated for their yellow or orange flower heads and strongly scented foliage: family *Asteraceae* (composites) 2 any of various similar or related plants, such as the marsh marigold, pot marigold, bur marigold, and fig marigold

marijuana *or* **marihuana** 1 the dried leaves and flowers of the hemp plant, used for its euphoric effects, esp in the form of cigarettes 2 another name for **hemp** (the plant)

marimba a Latin American percussion instrument consisting of a set of hardwood plates placed over tuned metal resonators, played with two soft-headed sticks in each hand

Marin John 1870–1953, US painter, noted esp for his watercolour landscapes and seascapes

marina an elaborate docking facility for pleasure boats

Marinduque an island of the central Philippines, east of Mindoro: forms, with offshore islets, a province of the Philippines. Capital: Boac. Pop. (Marinduque province): 217 392 (2000). Area: 960 sq km (370 sq miles)

marine 1 of, found in, or relating to the sea 2 of or relating to shipping, navigation, etc. 3 of or relating to a body of seagoing troops 4 of or relating to a government department concerned with maritime affairs 5 shipping and navigation in general 6 a member of a marine corps or similar body 7 a picture of a ship, seascape, etc.

Marinetti Filippo Tommaso 1876–1944, Italian poet; founder of futurism (1909)

marionette an articulated puppet or doll whose jointed limbs are moved by strings

Maritain Jacques 1882–1973, French neo-Thomist Roman Catholic philosopher

maritime 1 of or relating to navigation, shipping, etc.; seafaring 2 of, relating to, near, or living near the sea 3 (of a climate) having small temperature differences between summer and winter; equable

Maritsa a river in S Europe, rising in S Bulgaria and flowing east into Turkey, then south from Edirne as part of the border between Turkey and Greece to the Aegean. Length: 483 km (300 miles)

Mariupol a port in SE Ukraine, on an estuary leading to the Sea of Azov. Pop: 485 000 (2005 est)

Marius Gaius ?155–86 BC, Roman general and consul. He defeated Jugurtha, the Cimbri, and the Teutons (107–101), but his rivalry with Sulla caused civil war (88). He was exiled but returned (87) and took Rome

Marivaux Pierre Carlet de Chamblain de 1688–1763, French dramatist and novelist, noted particularly for his comedies, such as *Le jeu de l'amour et du hasard* (1730) and *La Vie de Marianne* (1731–41)

marjoram 1 an aromatic Mediterranean plant, *Origanum* (or *Marjorana*) *hortensis*, with small pale purple flowers and sweet-scented leaves, used for seasoning food and in salads: family *Lamiaceae* (labiates) 2 a similar and related European plant, *Origanum vulgare*

mark¹ 1 *Nautical* one of the intervals distinctively marked on a sounding lead 2 *Bowls* another name for the **jack** 3 *Rugby Union* an action in which a player standing inside his own 22m line catches a forward kick by an opponent and shouts "mark", entitling himself to a free kick **4** *Australian Rules football* a catch of the ball from a kick of at least 10 yards, after which a free kick is taken **5 the mark** *Boxing* the middle of the stomach at or above the line made by the boxer's trunks **6** (in medieval England and Germany) a piece of land held in common by the free men of a community **7 on your mark** *or* **marks** a command given to runners in a race to prepare themselves at the starting line

mark² **1** See **Deutschmark 2** a former monetary unit and coin in England and Scotland worth two thirds of a pound sterling **3** a silver coin of Germany until 1924

Mark *New Testament* **1** one of the four Evangelists. Feast day: April 25 **2** the second Gospel, traditionally ascribed to him

markdown a price reduction

market 1 a an event or occasion, usually held at regular intervals, at which people meet for the purpose of buying and selling merchandise **b** *(as modifier)*: *market day* **2** a place, such as an open space in a town, at which a market is held **3** a shop that sells a particular merchandise **4 the market** business or trade in a commodity as specified **5** the trading or selling opportunities provided by a particular group of people **6** demand for a particular product or commodity **7** See **market price 8 at market** at the current price **9 on the market** available for purchase **10 play the market a** to speculate on a stock exchange **b** to act aggressively or unscrupulously in one's own commercial interests **11 seller's** (*or* **buyer's**) **market** a market characterized by excess demand (or supply) and thus favourable to sellers (or buyers)

market garden *Chiefly Brit* an establishment where fruit and vegetables are grown for sale
   ▷http://attra.ncat.org/attra-pub/
      marketgardening.html
   ▷www.cityfarmer.org
   ▷www.marketgardening.com

marketplace 1 a place where a public market is held **2** the commercial world of buying and selling

market price the prevailing price, as determined by supply and demand, at which goods, services, etc, may be bought or sold

market town *Chiefly Brit* a town that holds a market, esp an agricultural centre in a rural area

Markham Mount a mountain in Antarctica, in Victoria Land. Height: 4350 m (14 272 ft)

Markiewicz Constance, Countess, original name *Constance Gore-Booth*. 1868–1927, Irish nationalist, married to a Polish count. She fought in the Easter Rising (1916) and was sentenced to death but reprieved. The first woman elected to the British parliament (1918), she refused to take her seat

marking 1 the arrangement of colours on an animal, plant, etc. **2** assessment and correction of school children's or students' written work by teaching staff

Markova Dame **Alicia** real name *Lilian Alicia Marks*. (1910–2004), English ballerina

marksman a person skilled in shooting

mark-up 1 a percentage or amount added to the cost of a commodity to provide the seller with a profit and to

cover overheads, costs, etc. **2 a** an increase in the price of a commodity **b** the amount of this increase

marl a fine-grained sedimentary rock consisting of clay minerals, calcite or aragonite, and silt: used as a fertilizer

Marlborough¹ 1st Duke of title of *John Churchill*. 1650–1722, English general; commander of British forces in the War of the Spanish Succession (1701–14), in which he won victories at Blenheim (1704), Ramillies (1706), Oudenaarde (1708), and Malplaquet (1709)

Marlborough² a town in S England, in Wiltshire: besieged and captured by Royalists in the Civil War (1642); site of Marlborough College, a public school founded in 1843. Pop: 7713 (2001)

Marley Bob, full name *Robert Nesta Marley*. 1945–81, Jamaican reggae singer, guitarist, and songwriter. With his group, the Wailers, his albums included *Burnin'* (1973), *Natty Dread* (1975), *Rastaman Vibration* (1976), and *Exodus* (1977)

marlin any of several large scombroid food and game fishes of the genera *Makaira*, *Istiompax*, and *Tetrapturus*, of warm and tropical seas, having a very long upper jaw: family *Istiophoridae*

Marlowe Christopher 1564–93, English dramatist and poet, who established blank verse as a creative form of dramatic expression. His plays include *Tamburlaine the Great* (1590), *Edward II* (?1592), and *Dr Faustus* (1604). He was stabbed to death in a tavern brawl

marmalade (of cats) streaked orange or yellow and brown

Marmara *or* **Marmora** Sea of a deep inland sea in NW Turkey, linked with the Black Sea by the Bosporus and with the Aegean by the Dardanelles: separates Turkey in Europe from Turkey in Asia. Area: 11 471 sq km (4429 sq miles)

Marmolada a mountain in NE Italy: highest peak in the Dolomites. Height: 3342 m (10 965 ft)

marmoreal *or less commonly* **marmorean** of, relating to, or resembling marble

marmoset 1 any small South American monkey of the genus *Callithrix* and related genera, having long hairy tails, clawed digits, and tufts of hair around the head and ears: family *Callithricidae* **2 pygmy marmoset** a related form, *Cebuella pygmaea*: the smallest monkey, inhabiting tropical forests of the Amazon

marmot 1 any burrowing sciurine rodent of the genus *Marmota*, of Europe, Asia, and North America. They are heavily built, having short legs, a short furry tail, and coarse fur **2 prairie marmot** another name for **prairie dog**

Marne 1 a department of NE France, in Champagne-Ardenne region. Capital: Châlons-sur-Marne. Pop: 563 027 (2003 est). Area: 8205 sq km (3200 sq miles) **2 a** river in NE France, rising on the plateau of Langres and flowing north, then west to the River Seine, north of Paris: linked by canal with the Rivers Saône, Rhine, and Aisne; scene of two unsuccessful German offensives (1914, 1918) during World War I. Length: 525 km (326 miles)

maroon¹ a descendant of a group of runaway slaves living in the remoter areas of the Caribbean or Guyana

maroon² **a** a dark red to purplish-red colour **b** (*as adjec-*

tive) a maroon carpet

Marprelate Martin, the pen name of the anonymous author or authors of a series of satirical Puritan tracts (1588–89), attacking the bishops of the Church of England

Marquand J(ohn) P(hillips). 1893–1960, US novelist, noted for his stories featuring the Japanese detective Mr Moto and for his satirical comedies of New England life, such as *The Late George Apley* (1937)

marque 1 a brand of product, esp of a car 2 an emblem or nameplate used to identify a product, esp a car

marquee 1 a large tent used for entertainment, exhibition, etc. 2 *Chiefly US and Canadian* a canopy over the entrance to a theatre, hotel, etc.

marquess 1 (in the British Isles) a nobleman ranking between a duke and an earl 2 See **marquis**

marquetry *or* **marqueterie** a pattern of inlaid veneers of wood, brass, ivory, etc, fitted together to form a picture or design, used chiefly as ornamentation in furniture
   ▷www.marquetry.org

Marquette Jacques , known as *Père Marquette*. 1637–75, French Jesuit missionary and explorer, with Louis Jolliet, of the Mississippi river

marquis (in various countries) a nobleman ranking above a count, corresponding to a British marquess. The title of marquis is often used in place of that of marquess

Marquis Don(ald Robert Perry). 1878–1937, US humorist; author of *archy and mehitabel* (1927)

Marrakech *or* **Marrakesh** a city in W central Morocco: several times capital of Morocco; tourist centre. Pop: 672 000 (2003)

marram grass any of several grasses of the genus *Ammophila*, esp *A. arenaria*, that grow on sandy shores and can withstand drying: often planted to stabilize sand dunes

marriage 1 a the legal union or contract made by a man and woman to live as husband and wife b *(as modifier)*: *marriage licence* 2 the religious or legal ceremony formalizing this union; wedding 3 (in certain card games, such as bezique, pinochle) the king and queen of the same suit

Marriner Sir **Neville** born 1924, British conductor and violinist; founder (1956) and director of the Academy of St Martin in the Fields, which specializes in baroque music

marrow *Anatomy* the fatty network of connective tissue that fills the cavities of bones

Marryat Frederick, known as *Captain Marryat*. 1792–1848, English novelist and naval officer; author of novels of sea life, such as *Mr Midshipman Easy* (1836), and children's stories, such as *The Children of the New Forest* (1847)

Mars¹ the Roman god of war, the father of Romulus and Remus

Mars² 1 the fourth planet from the sun, having a reddish-orange surface with numerous dark patches and two white polar caps. It has a thin atmosphere, mainly carbon dioxide, and low surface temperatures. Spacecraft encounters have revealed a history of volcanic activity and running surface water. The planet has two tiny satellites, Phobos and Deimos. Mean dis-

tance from sun: 228 million km; period of revolution around sun: 686.98 days; period of axial rotation: 24.6225 hours; diameter and mass: 53.2 and 10.7 per cent that of earth respectively 2 the alchemical name for iron

Marsala 1 a port in W Sicily: landing place of Garibaldi at the start of his Sicilian campaign (1860). Pop: 77 784 (2001) 2 a dark sweet dessert wine made in Sicily

Marsalis Wynton born 1962, US jazz and classical trumpeter

Marseillaise the the French national anthem. Words and music were composed in 1792 by C. J. Rouget de Lisle as a war song for the Rhine army of revolutionary France

Marseille a port in SE France, on the Gulf of Lions: second largest city in the country and a major port; founded in about 600 BC by Greeks from Phocaea; oil refining. Pop: 798 430 (1999)

marsh low poorly drained land that is sometimes flooded and often lies at the edge of lakes, streams, etc.

Marsh 1 Dame (**Edith**) **Ngaio** 1899–1981, New Zealand crime writer, living in Britain (from 1928). Her many detective novels include *Final Curtain* (1947) and *Last Ditch* (1977) 2 **Rodney** (**William**). born 1947, Australian cricketer. He finished his career with a world record of 355 Test match dismissals

marshal 1 (in England) an officer, usually a junior barrister, who accompanies a judge on circuit and performs miscellaneous secretarial duties 2 in the US a a Federal court officer assigned to a judicial district whose functions are similar to those of a sheriff b (in some states) the chief police or fire officer 3 (formerly in England) an officer of the royal family or court, esp one in charge of protocol 4 an obsolete word for **ostler**

Marshall 1 1842–1924, English economist, author of *Principles of Economics* (1890) 2 **George Catlett** 1880–1959, US general and statesman. He was chief of staff of the US army (1939–45) and, as secretary of state (1947– 49), he proposed the Marshall Plan (1947), later called the European Recovery Programme: Nobel peace prize 1953 3 **John** 1755–1835, US jurist and statesman. As chief justice of the Supreme Court (1801–35), he established the principles of US constitutional law 4 Sir **John Ross** 1912–88, New Zealand politician; prime minister (1972)

marshalling yard *Railways* a place or depot where railway wagons are shunted and made up into trains and where engines, carriages, etc, are kept when not in use

marsh gas a hydrocarbon gas largely composed of methane formed when organic material decays in the absence of air

marsh mallow a malvaceous plant, *Althaea officinalis*, that grows in salt marshes and has pale pink flowers. The roots yield a mucilage formerly used to make marshmallows

Marsilius of Padua Italian name *Marsiglio dei Mainardini*. ?1290–?1343, Italian political philosopher, best known as the author of the *Defensor pacis* (1324), which upheld the power of the temporal ruler over that of the church

Marston John ?1576–1634, English dramatist and satirist. His works include the revenge tragedies *Antonio and Mellida* (1602) and *Antonio's Revenge* (1602) and the satirical comedy *The Malcontent* (1604)

Marston Moor a flat low-lying area in NE England, west of York: scene of a battle (1644) in which the Parliamentarians defeated the Royalists

marsupial any mammal of the order *Marsupialia*, in which the young are born in an immature state and continue development in the marsupium. The order occurs mainly in Australia and South and Central America and includes the opossums, bandicoots, koala, wombats, and kangaroos

mart a market or trading centre

Martaban Gulf of an inlet of the Bay of Bengal in Myanmar

marten 1 any of several agile arboreal musteline mammals of the genus *Martes*, of Europe, Asia, and North America, having bushy tails and golden brown to blackish fur 2 the highly valued fur of these animals, esp that of *M. americana*

Martha Saint *New Testament* a sister of Mary and Lazarus, who lived at Bethany and ministered to Jesus (Luke 10:38–42). Feast day: July 29 or June 4

Martial full name *Marcus Valerius Martialis*. ?40–?104 AD, Latin epigrammatist and poet, born in Spain

martial art any of various philosophies of self-defence and techniques of single combat, such as judo or karate, originating in the Far East
▷www.martialinfo.com
▷http://martialarts.about.com

Martian 1 of, occurring on, or relating to the planet Mars 2 an inhabitant of Mars, esp in science fiction

martin any of various swallows of the genera *Progne, Delichon, Riparia*, etc, having a square or slightly forked tail

Martin 1 Archer John Porter 1910–2002, British biochemist; Nobel prize for chemistry 1952 (with Richard Synge; 1914–94) for developing paper chromatography (1944). He subsequently developed gas chromatography (1953) 2 **Chris** born 1977, British rock musician, lead singer of Coldplay. He is married to the US actress Gwyneth Paltrow. 3 **Frank** 1890–1974, Swiss composer. He used a modified form of the twelve-note technique in some of his works, which include *Petite Symphonie Concertante* (1946) and the oratorio *Golgotha* (1949) 4 Sir **George** (**Henry**). born 1926, British record producer and arranger, noted for his work with the Beatles 5 **John** 1789–1854, British painter, noted for his visionary landscapes and large-scale works with biblical subjects 6 **Michael** (**John**). born 1945, Scottish Labour politician; speaker of the House of Commons from 2000 7 **Saint** called *Saint Martin of Tours*. ?316–?397 AD, bishop of Tours (?371–?397); a patron saint of France. He furthered monasticism in Gaul. Feast day: Nov 11 or 12 8 **Steve(n).** born 1945, US film actor and comedian; his films include *The Jerk* (1979), *Roxanne* (1987), and *Bowfinger* (1999)

martingale 1 a strap from the reins to the girth of a horse preventing it from carrying its head too high 2 any gambling system in which the stakes are raised, usually doubled, after each loss 3 *Nautical* a chain or cable serving to counteract strain

Martinique an island in the E Caribbean, in the Windward Islands of the Lesser Antilles: administratively an overseas region of France. Capital: Fort-de-France. Pop: 395 000 (2004 est). Area: 1090 sq km (420 sq miles)

Martinmas the feast of St Martin on Nov 11; one of the four quarter days in Scotland

Martin du Gard Roger 1881–1958, French novelist, noted for his series of novels, *Les Thibault* (1922–40): Nobel prize for literature 1937

Martini Simone ?1284–1344, Sienese painter

Martinů Bohuslav 1890–1959, Czech composer

martyr a person who suffers death rather than renounce his religious beliefs

Marvell Andrew 1621–78, English poet and satirist. He is noted for his lyrical poems and verse and prose satires attacking the government after the Restoration

Marx Karl 1818–83, German founder of modern communism, in England from 1849. With Engels, he wrote *The Communist Manifesto* (1848). He developed his theories of the class struggle and the economics of capitalism in *Das Kapital* (1867; 1885; 1895). He was one of the founders of the International Workingmen's Association (First International) (1864)

Marx Brothers the a US family of film comedians, esp **Arthur Marx**, known as *Harpo* (1888–1964), **Herbert Marx**, known as *Zeppo* (1901–79), **Julius Marx**, known as *Groucho* (1890–1977), and **Leonard Marx** known as *Chico* (1886–1961). Their films include *Animal Crackers* (1930), *Monkey Business* (1931), *Horsefeathers* (1932), *Duck Soup* (1933), and *A Day at the Races* (1937)

Marxism the economic and political theory and practice originated by the German political philosophers Karl Marx (1818–83) and Friedrich Engels (1820–95), that holds that actions and human institutions are economically determined, that the class struggle is the basic agency of historical change, and that capitalism will ultimately be superseded by communism

Mary¹ 1 *New Testament* a **Saint** Also called: the **Virgin Mary** the mother of Jesus, believed to have conceived and borne him while still a virgin; she was married to Joseph (Matthew 1:18–25). Major feast days: Feb 2, Mar 25, May 31, Aug 15, Sept 8 b the sister of Martha and Lazarus (Luke 10:38–42; John 11:1–2) 2 original name *Princess Mary of Teck*. 1867–1953, queen of Great Britain and Northern Ireland (1910–36) by marriage to George V

Mary² *New Testament* a **Saint** Also called: the **Virgin Mary** the mother of Jesus, believed to have conceived and borne him while still a virgin; she was married to Joseph (Matthew 1:18–25). Major feast days: Feb 2, Mar 25, May 31, Aug 15, Sept 8 b the sister of Martha and Lazarus (Luke 10:38–42; John 11:1–2)

Mary I family name *Tudor*, known as *Bloody Mary*. 1516–58, queen of England (1553–58). The daughter of Henry VIII and Catherine of Aragon, she married Philip II of Spain in 1554. She restored Roman Catholicism to England and about 300 Protestants were burnt at the stake as heretics

Mary II 1662–94, queen of England, Scotland, and Ireland (1689–94), ruling jointly with her husband William III. They were offered the crown by parliament, which objected to the arbitrary rule of her father James II

Maryland a state of the eastern US, on the Atlantic: divided into two unequal parts by Chesapeake Bay: mostly low-lying, with the Alleghenies in the northwest. Capital: Annapolis. Pop: 5 508 909 (2003 est). Area: 31 864 sq km (12 303 sq miles)

Mary Magdalene *New Testament* **Saint** a woman of **Magdala** in Galilee whom Jesus cured of evil spirits (Luke 8:2) and who is often identified with the sinful woman of Luke 7:36–50. In Christian tradition she is usually taken to have been a prostitute. Feast day: July 22

Masaccio original name *Tommaso Guidi*. 1401–28, Florentine painter. He was the first to apply to painting the laws of perspective discovered by Brunelleschi. His chief work is the frescoes in the Brancacci chapel in the church of Sta. Maria del Carmine, Florence

Masada an ancient mountaintop fortress in Israel, 400 m (1300 ft) above the W shore of the Dead Sea: the last Jewish stronghold during a revolt in Judaea (66–73 AD). Besieged by the Romans for a year, almost all of the inhabitants killed themselves rather than surrender. The site is an Israeli national monument

Masan a port in SE South Korea, on an inlet of the Korea Strait: first opened to foreign trade in 1899. Pop: 428 000 (2005 est)

Masaryk 1 Jan 1886–1948, Czech statesman; foreign minister (1941–48). He died in mysterious circumstances after the Communists took control of the government **2** his father, **Tomáš Garrigue** 1850–1937, Czech philosopher and statesman; a founder of Czechoslovakia (1918) and its first president (1918–35)

Masbate 1 an island in the central Philippines, between Negros and SE Luzon: agricultural, with resources of gold, copper, and manganese. Pop. (Masbate province): 707 668 (2000). Area: 4045 sq km (1562 sq miles) **2** the capital of this island, a port in the northeast. Pop: 71 441 (2000)

Mascagni Pietro 1863–1945, Italian composer of operas, including *Cavalleria rusticana* (1890)

Masefield John 1878–1967, English poet, novelist, and critic; poet laureate (1930–67)

maser a device for amplifying microwaves, working on the same principle as a laser

Maseru the capital of Lesotho, in the northwest near the W border with South Africa; established as capital of Basutoland in 1869. Pop: 175 000 (2005 est)

mash (esp in brewing) a mixture of mashed malt grains and hot water, from which malt is extracted

Mashhad *or* **Meshed** a city in NE Iran: an important holy city of Shi'ite Muslims; carpet manufacturing. Pop: 2 147 000 (2005 est)

Masinissa *or* **Massinissa** ?238–?149 BC, king of Numidia (?210–149), who fought as an ally of Rome against Carthage in the Second Punic War

masking tape an adhesive tape used to mask and protect surfaces surrounding an area to be painted

masochism 1 *Psychiatry* an abnormal condition in which pleasure, esp sexual pleasure, is derived from pain or from humiliation, domination, etc, by another person **2** *Psychoanal* the directing towards oneself of any destructive tendencies

masque *or* **mask 1** a dramatic entertainment of the 16th to 17th centuries in England, consisting of pantomime, dancing, dialogue, and song, often performed at court **2** the words and music written for a masque

mass 1 *Physics* a physical quantity expressing the amount of matter in a body. It is a measure of a body's resistance to changes in velocity (**inertial mass**) and also of the force experienced in a gravitational field (**gravitational mass**): according to the theory of relativity, inertial and gravitational masses are equal **2** (in painting, drawing, etc) an area of unified colour, shade, or intensity, usually denoting a solid form or plane **3** *Pharmacol* a pastelike composition of drugs from which pills are made

Mass 1 (in the Roman Catholic Church and certain Protestant Churches) the celebration of the Eucharist **2** a musical setting of those parts of the Eucharistic service sung by choir or congregation

Massa a town in W Italy, in NW Tuscany. Pop: 66 769 (2001)

Massachusetts a state of the northeastern US, on the Atlantic: a centre of resistance to English colonial policy during the War of American Independence; consists of a coastal plain rising to mountains in the west. Capital: Boston. Pop: 6 433 422 (2003 est). Area: 20 269 sq km (7826 sq miles)

Massachusetts Bay an inlet of the Atlantic on the E coast of Massachusetts

massage the act of kneading, rubbing, etc, parts of the body to promote circulation, suppleness, or relaxation

massasauga a North American venomous snake, *Sistrurus catenatus*, that has a horny rattle at the end of the tail: family *Crotalidae* (pit vipers)

Massasoit died 1661, Wampanoag Indian chief, who negotiated peace with the Pilgrim Fathers (1621)

Massawa *or* **Massaua** a port in E central Eritrea, on the Red Sea: capital of Eritrea during Italian occupation, from 1885 until 1900. Pop: 40 000 (1992)

Massenet Jules Émile Frédéric 1842–1912, French composer of operas, including *Manon* (1884), *Werther* (1892), and *Thaïs* (1894)

Massey 1 Raymond 1896–1983, Canadian actor and film star. His films include *The Scarlet Pimpernel* (1934) and *East of Eden* (1955). He also appeared in the television series *Dr Kildare* (1961–65) **2 Vincent** 1887–1967, Canadian statesman: first Canadian governor general of Canada (1952–59) **3 William Ferguson** 1856–1925, New Zealand statesman, born in Ireland: prime minister of New Zealand (1912–25)

massif 1 a geologically distinct mass of rock or a series of connected masses forming the peaks of a mountain range **2** a topographically high part of the earth's crust that is bounded by faults and may be shifted by tectonic movements

Massif Central a mountainous plateau region of S central France, occupying about one sixth of the country: contains several extinct volcanic cones, notably Puy de Dôme, 1465 m (4806 ft). Highest point: Puy de Sancy, 1886 m (6188 ft). Area: about 85 000 sq km (33 000 sq miles)

Massine Léonide 1896–1979, US ballet dancer and choreographer, born in Russia

Massinger Philip 1583–?1640, English dramatist, noted esp for his comedy *A New Way to pay Old Debts* (1633)

massive 1 *Pathol* affecting a large area of the body **2** *Geology* **a** (of igneous rocks) having no stratification, cleavage, etc.; homogeneous **b** (of sedimentary rocks) arranged in thick poorly defined strata **3** *Mineralogy* without obvious crystalline structure

mass number the total number of neutrons and protons in the nucleus of a particular atom.

mass spectrometer *or* **spectroscope** an analytical instrument in which ions, produced from a sample, are separated by electric or magnetic fields according to their ratios of charge to mass. A record is produced (**mass spectrum**) of the types of ion present and their relative amounts

mast¹ 1 *Nautical* any vertical spar for supporting sails, rigging, flags, etc, above the deck of a vessel or any components of such a composite spar **2** *Nautical* a hearing conducted by the captain of a vessel into minor offences of the crew **3** **before the mast** *Nautical* as an apprentice seaman

mast² the fruit of forest trees, such as beech, oak, etc, used as food for pigs

mastaba *or* **mastabah** a mudbrick superstructure above tombs in ancient Egypt from which the pyramid developed

mastectomy the surgical removal of a breast

master 1 a great artist, esp an anonymous but influential artist **2** the principal of some colleges **3** a graduate holding a master's degree **4** the chief executive officer aboard a merchant ship **5** *Chiefly Brit* a male teacher **6** an officer of the Supreme Court of Judicature subordinate to a judge **7** a machine or device that operates to control a similar one **8** the heir apparent of a Scottish viscount or baron

Master of Arts a degree, usually postgraduate and in a nonscientific subject, or the holder of this degree

Master of Science a postgraduate degree, usually in science, or the holder of this degree

Master of the Rolls (in England) a judge of the court of appeal: the senior civil judge in the country and the Keeper of the Records at the Public Record Office

masthead *Nautical* **a** the head of a mast **b** (*as modifier*): *masthead sail*

mastic 1 an aromatic resin obtained from the mastic tree and used as an astringent and to make varnishes and lacquers **2 mastic tree a** a small Mediterranean anacardiaceous evergreen tree, *Pistacia lentiscus*, that yields the resin mastic **b** any of various similar trees, such as the pepper tree

mastiff an old breed of large powerful short-haired dog, usually fawn or brindle with a dark mask

mastitis inflammation of a breast or an udder

mastodon any extinct elephant-like proboscidean mammal of the genus *Mammut* (or *Mastodon*), common in Pliocene times

mastoid 1 shaped like a nipple or breast **2** designating or relating to a nipple-like process of the temporal bone behind the ear **3** the mastoid process **4** *Informal* mastoiditis

mastoiditis inflammation of the mastoid process

Masuria a region of NE Poland: until 1945 part of East Prussia: includes the **Masurian Lakes**, scene of Russian defeats by the Germans (1914, 1915) during World War I

mat¹ a a heavy net of cable or rope laid over a blasting site to prevent the scatter of debris **b** a heavy mesh of

reinforcement in a concrete slab **c** (esp US) a steel or concrete raft serving as a footing to support a post

mat² *Art* a border of cardboard, cloth, etc, placed around a picture to act as a frame or as a contrast between picture and frame

Matabeleland a region of W Zimbabwe, between the Rivers Limpopo and Zambezi, comprises three provinces, Matabeleland North, Matabeleland South, and Bulawayo: rich gold deposits. Chief town: Bulawayo. Area: 181 605 sq km (70 118 sq miles)

Matadi the chief port of the Democratic Republic of Congo (formerly Zaïre), in the west at the mouth of the River Congo. Pop: 256 000 (2005 est)

matador 1 the principal bullfighter who is appointed to kill the bull **2** (in some card games such as skat) one of the highest ranking cards **3** a game played with dominoes in which the dots on adjacent halves must total seven

Mata Hari real name *Gertrud Margarete Zelle*. 1876–1917, Dutch dancer in France, who was executed as a German spy in World War I

matai a coniferous evergreen tree of New Zealand, *Podocarpus spicatus*, having a bluish bark and small linear leaves arranged in two rows: timber used for flooring and weatherboards

Matamoros a port in NE Mexico, on the Río Grande: scene of bitter fighting during the US-Mexican War; centre of a cotton-growing area. Pop: 481 000 (2005 est)

Matanzas a port in W central Cuba: founded in 1693 and developed into the second city of Cuba in the mid-19th century; exports chiefly sugar. Pop: 130 000 (2005 est)

Matapan Cape a cape in S Greece, at the S central tip of the Peloponnese: the southern point of the mainland of Greece

match play *Golf* **a** a scoring according to the number of holes won and lost **b** (*as modifier*): *a matchplay tournament*

match point *Bridge* the unit used for scoring in tournaments

mate 1 the sexual partner of an animal **2** *Nautical* **a** short for **first mate b** any officer below the master on a commercial ship **c** a warrant officer's assistant on a ship

material 1 cloth or fabric **2** *Philosophy* composed of or relating to physical as opposed to mental or spiritual substance **3** *Philosophy* of or relating to matter as opposed to form **4** *Law* relevant to the issue before court: applied esp to facts or testimony of much significance

materialism 1 *Philosophy* the monist doctrine that matter is the only reality and that the mind, the emotions, etc, are merely functions of it **2** *Ethics* the rejection of any religious or supernatural account of things

mathematical *or less commonly* **mathematic 1** of, used in, or relating to mathematics **2** characterized by or using the precision of mathematics; exact **3** using, determined by, or in accordance with the principles of mathematics

mathematician an expert or specialist in mathematics

mathematics 1 a group of related sciences, including algebra, geometry, and calculus, concerned with the study of number, quantity, shape, and space and their interrelationships by using a specialized notation **2**

mathematical operations and processes involved in the solution of a problem or study of some scientific field
▷www.martindalecenter.com/GradMath.html
▷www.math.psu.edu/MathLists/Contents.html
▷http://carbon.cudenver.edu/~hgreenbe/glossary/index.php

Mathura a city in N India, in W Uttar Pradesh on the Jumna River: a place of Hindu pilgrimage, revered as the birthplace of Krishna. Pop: 298 827 (2001)

Matilda known as *the Empress Maud.* 1102–67, only daughter of Henry I of England and wife of Geoffrey of Anjou. After her father's death (1135) she unsuccessfully waged a civil war with Stephen for the English throne; her son succeeded as Henry II

matins *or* **mattins** a *Chiefly RC Church* the first of the seven canonical hours of prayer, originally observed at night but now often recited with lauds at daybreak b the service of morning prayer in the Church of England

Matisse Henri 1869–1954, French painter and sculptor; leader of Fauvism

Matlock a town in England, on the River Derwent, administrative centre of Derbyshire: mineral springs. Pop: 11 265 (2001)

Mato Grosso *or* **Matto Grosso** 1 a high plateau of SW Brazil: forms the watershed separating the Amazon and Plata river systems 2 a state of W central Brazil: mostly on the Mato Grosso Plateau, with the Amazon basin to the north; valuable mineral resources. Capital: Cuiabá. Pop: 2 604 742 (2002). Area: 881 001 sq km (340 083 sq miles)

Mato Grosso do Sul a state of W central Brazil: formed in 1979 from part of Mato Grosso state. Capital: Campo Grande. Pop: 2 140 624 (2002). Area: 350 548 sq km (135 318 sq miles)

matriarch the female head of a tribe or family, esp in a matriarchy

matriarchy 1 a form of social organization in which a female is head of the family or society, and descent and kinship are traced through the female line 2 any society dominated by women

matrilineal relating to descent or kinship through the female line

matrimony a a card game in which the king and queen together are a winning combination b such a combination

matrix 1 *Anatomy* the thick tissue at the base of a nail from which a fingernail or toenail develops 2 the intercellular substance of bone, cartilage, connective tissue, etc. 3 a the rock material in which fossils, pebbles, etc, are embedded b the material in which a mineral is embedded; gangue 4 (formerly) a mould used in the production of gramophone records. It is obtained by electrodeposition onto the master 5 a bed of perforated material placed beneath a workpiece in a press or stamping machine against which the punch operates 6 *Metallurgy* a the shaped cathode used in electroforming b the metal constituting the major part of an alloy c the soft metal in a plain bearing in which the hard particles of surface metal are embedded 7 the main component of a composite material, such as the plastic in a fibre-reinforced plastic 8 *Maths* a rectangular array of elements set out in rows and columns, used to facilitate the solution of problems, such as the transformation of coordinates. Usually indicated by parentheses: $\left(\begin{smallmatrix} abc \\ def \end{smallmatrix}\right)$ 9 *Computing* a rectangular array of circuit elements usually used to generate one set of signals from another 10 *Obsolete* the womb

matron *Brit* the former name for the administrative head of the nursing staff in a hospital

Matsu *or* **Mazu** an island group in Formosa Strait, off the SE coast of mainland China: belongs to Taiwan. Pop: 3145 (1990 est). Area: 44 sq km (17 sq miles)

Matsuyama a port in SW Japan, on NW Shikoku: textile and chemical industries; Ehime University (1949). Pop: 473 039 (2002 est)

matter 1 *Philosophy* (in the writings of Aristotle and the Scholastics) that which is itself formless but can receive form and become substance 2 *Philosophy* (in the Cartesian tradition) one of two basic modes of existence, the other being **mind**: matter being extended in space as well as time 3 a secretion or discharge, such as pus 4 *Law* a something to be proved b statements or allegations to be considered by a court

Matterhorn a mountain on the border between Italy and Switzerland, in the Pennine Alps. Height: 4477 m (14 688 ft)

matter of fact 1 *Law* a statement of facts the truth of which the court must determine on the basis of the evidence before it 2 *Philosophy* a proposition that is amenable to empirical testing, as contrasted with the truths of logic or mathematics

Matthew *New Testament* 1 **Saint** a tax collector of Capernaum called by Christ to be one of the 12 apostles (Matthew 9:9–13; 10:3). Feast day: Sept 21 or Nov 16 2 the first Gospel, traditionally ascribed to him

Matthews Sir Stanley 1915–2002, English footballer

Matthias 1 1557–1619, Holy Roman Emperor (1612–19); king of Hungary (1608–18) and Bohemia (1611–17) 2 **Saint** *New Testament* the disciple chosen by lot to replace Judas as one of the 12 apostles (Acts 1:15–26). Feast day: May 14 or Aug 9

Matthias I Corvinus ?1440–90, king of Hungary (1458–90): built up the most powerful kingdom in Central Europe. A patron of Renaissance art, he founded the Corvina library, one of the finest in Europe

matting a coarsely woven fabric, usually made of a natural fibre such as straw or hemp and used as a floor covering, packing material, etc.

mattock a type of large pick that has one end of its blade shaped like an adze, used for loosening soil, cutting roots, etc.

mattress a woven mat of brushwood, poles, etc, used to protect an embankment, dyke, etc, from scour

maturation *Zoology* the development of ova and spermatozoa from precursor cells in the ovary and testis, involving meiosis

mature 1 *Biology* a fully developed or differentiated b fully grown; adult 2 (of a river valley or land surface) in the middle stage of the cycle of erosion, characterized by meanders, maximum relief, etc.

matzo, matzoh, matza *or* **matzah** a brittle very thin biscuit of unleavened bread, traditionally eaten during Passover

Maubeuge an industrial town in N France, near the

border with Belgium. Pop: 33 546 (1999)

Maugham W(illiam) Somerset 1874–1965, English writer. His works include the novels *Of Human Bondage* (1915) and *Cakes and Ale* (1930), short stories, and comedies

Maui a volcanic island in S central Hawaii: the second largest of the Hawaiian Islands. Pop: 117 644 (2000). Area: 1885 sq km (728 sq miles)

maul 1 a heavy two-handed hammer suitable for driving piles, wedges, etc. **2** *Rugby* a loose scrum that forms around a player who is holding the ball and on his feet

Mauna Kea an extinct volcano in Hawaii, on N central Hawaii Island: the highest island mountain in the world. Height: 4206 m (13 799 ft)

Mauna Loa an active volcano in Hawaii, on S central Hawaii Island. Height: 4171 m (13 684 ft)

Maupassant (Henri René Albert) Guy de 1850–93, French writer, noted esp for his short stories, such as *Boule de suif* (1880), *La Maison Tellier* (1881), and *Mademoiselle Fifi* (1883). His novels include *Bel Ami* (1885) and *Pierre et Jean* (1888)

Maupertuis Pierre Louis Moreau de 1698–1759, French mathematician, who originated the principle of least action (or Maupertuis principle)

Mauretania an ancient region of N Africa, corresponding approximately to the N parts of modern Algeria and Morocco

Mauriac François 1885–1970, French novelist, noted esp for his psychological studies of the conflict between religious belief and human desire. His works include *Le désert de l'amour* (1925), *Thérèse Desqueyroux* (1927), and *Le nœud de vipères* (1932): Nobel prize for literature 1952

Maurice 1 1521–53, duke of Saxony (1541–53) and elector of Saxony (1547–53). He was instrumental in gaining recognition of Protestantism in Germany **2** known as *Maurice of Nassau*. 1567–1625, prince of Orange and count of Nassau; the son of William the Silent, after whose death he led the United Provinces of the Netherlands in their struggle for independence from Spain (achieved by 1609) **3** Frederick Denison 1805–72, English Anglican theologian and pioneer of Christian socialism

Mauritania a republic in NW Africa, on the Atlantic: established as a French protectorate in 1903 and a colony in 1920; gained independence in 1960; lies in the Sahara; contains rich resources of iron ore. Official language: Arabic; Fulani, Soninke, Wolof, and French are also spoken. Official religion: Muslim. Currency: ouguiya. Capital: Nouakchott. Pop: 2 980 000 (2004 est). Area: 1 030 700 sq km (398 000 sq miles)

Mauritius an island and state in the Indian Ocean, east of Madagascar: originally uninhabited, it was settled by the Dutch (1638–1710) then abandoned; taken by the French in 1715 and the British in 1810; became an independent member of the Commonwealth in 1968. It is economically dependent on sugar. Official language: English; a French creole is widely spoken. Religion: Hindu majority, large Christian minority. Currency: rupee. Capital: Port Louis. Pop: 1 233 000 (2004 est). Area: 1865 sq km (720 sq miles)

Maurois André , pen name of *Émile Herzog*. 1885–1967, French writer, best known for his biographies, such as

those of Shelley, Byron, and Proust

Maury Matthew Fontaine 1806–73, US pioneer hydrographer and oceanographer

mauve 1 any of various pale to moderate pinkish-purple or bluish-purple colours **2** a reddish-purple aniline dye

maw the mouth, throat, crop, or stomach of an animal, esp of a voracious animal

Mawson Sir Douglas 1882–1958, Australian Antarctic explorer, born in England

maxi a type of large racing yacht

maxilla 1 the upper jawbone in vertebrates **2** any member of one or two pairs of mouthparts in insects and other arthropods used as accessory jaws

maxim a brief expression of a general truth, principle, or rule of conduct

Maxim Sir Hiram Stevens 1840–1916, British inventor of the first automatic machine gun (1884), born in the US

maximal *Maths* (of a member of an ordered set) being preceded, in order, by all other members of the set

Maximilian full name *Ferdinand Maximilian Joseph*. 1832–67, archduke of Austria and emperor of Mexico (1864–67). After the French had partially conquered Mexico, he was offered the throne but was defeated and shot by the Mexicans under Juárez

Maximilian I 1459–1519, king of Germany (1486–1519) and Holy Roman Emperor (1493–1519)

maximum 1 *Maths* **a** a value of a function that is greater than any neighbouring value **b** a stationary point on a curve at which the tangent changes from a positive value on the left of this point to a negative value on the right **c** the largest number in a set **2** *Astronomy* **a** the time at which the brightness of a variable star has its greatest value **b** the magnitude of the star at that time

maxwell the cgs unit of magnetic flux equal to the flux through one square centimetre normal to a field of one gauss. It is equivalent to 10^{-8} weber.

Maxwell 1 James Clerk 1831–79, Scottish physicist. He made major contributions to the electromagnetic theory, developing the equations (**Maxwell equations**) upon which classical theory is based. He also contributed to the kinetic theory of gases, and colour vision **2** (Ian) Robert, original name *Robert Hoch*. 1923–91, British publisher, born in Slovakia: founder (1949) of Pergamon Press; chairman of Mirror Group Newspapers Ltd. (1984–91); theft from his employees' pension funds and other frauds discovered after his death led to the collapse of his business

May Sir Robert McCredie born 1936, Australian biologist and ecologist

Maya¹ the Hindu goddess of illusion, the personification of the idea that the material world is illusory

Maya² 1 a member of an American Indian people of Yucatan, Belize, and N Guatemala, having an ancient culture once characterized by outstanding achievements in architecture, astronomy, chronology, painting, and pottery **2** the language of this people

Mayakovski *or* **Mayakovsky** Vladimir Vladimirovich 1893–1930, Russian Futurist poet and dramatist. His poems include *150 000 000* (1921) and *At the Top of my Voice* (1930); his plays include *Vladimir Mayakovsky — a Tragedy* (1913) and *The Bedbug* (1929)

Mayenne a department of NW France, in Pays de la

Loire region. Capital: Laval. Pop: 290 780 (2003 est). Area: 5212 sq km (2033 sq miles)

Mayer 1 **Julius Robert von** 1814–78, German physicist whose research in thermodynamics (1842) contributed to the discovery of the law of conservation of energy 2 **Louis B(urt)**. 1885–1957, US film producer, born in Russia; founder and first head (1924–48) of the Metro-Goldwyn-Mayer (MGM) film company

Mayfair a fashionable district of west central London

mayfly 1 any insect of the order *Ephemeroptera* (or *Ephemerida*). The short-lived adults, found near water, have long tail appendages and large transparent wings; the larvae are aquatic 2 *Angling* an artificial fly resembling this

mayhem or **maihem** *Law* the wilful and unlawful infliction of injury upon a person, esp (formerly) the injuring or removing of a limb rendering him less capable of defending himself against attack

Mayhew Henry 1812–87, British social commentator, journalist, and writer; a founder of *Punch* (1841): best known for *London Labour and the London Poor* (1851–62)

Mayo¹ a family of US medical practitioners. They pioneered group practice and established (1903) the **Mayo Clinic** in Rochester, Minnesota. Foremost among them were **William Worrall Mayo** (1819–1911), his sons **William James Mayo** (1861–1939) and **Charles Horace Mayo** (1865–1939), and Charles's son, **Charles William Mayo** (1898–1968)

Mayo² a county of NW Republic of Ireland, in NW Connacht province, on the Atlantic: has many offshore islands and several large lakes. County town: Castlebar. Pop: 117 446 (2002). Area: 5397 sq km (2084 sq miles)

Mayon a volcano in the Philippines, on SE Luzon: Height: 2421 m (7943 ft)

mayor the chairman and civic head of a municipal corporation in many countries

mayoralty the office or term of office of a mayor

mayoress 1 *Chiefly Brit* the wife of a mayor 2 a female mayor

Mayotte an island in the Indian Ocean, northwest of Madagascar; administered by France. Pop. (including Pamanzi): 186 026 (2004 est). Area: 374 sq km (146 sq miles)

Mazar-e-Sharif or **Mazar-i-Sharif** a city in N Afghanistan, reputed burial place of the caliph Ali; trading, agricultural, and military centre. Pop: 254 000 (2005 est)

Mazarin Jules , original name *Giulio Mazarini*. 1602–61, French cardinal and statesman, born in Italy. He succeeded Richelieu (1642) as chief minister to Louis XIII and under the regency of Anne of Austria (1643–61). Despite the disturbances of the Fronde (1648–53), he strengthened the power of France in Europe

mazurka or **mazourka** 1 a Polish national dance in triple time 2 a piece of music composed for this dance

Mazzini Giuseppe 1805–72, Italian nationalist. In 1831, in exile, he established the Young Italy association in Marseille, which sought to unite Italy as a republic. In 1849 he was one of the triumvirate that ruled the short-lived Roman republic

Mbabane the capital of Swaziland, in the northwest: administrative and financial centre, with a large iron mine nearby. Pop: 71 000 (2005 est)

Mbeki Thabo (Mvuyelwa). born 1942, South African politician: a member of the African National Congress (ANC); president of South Africa from 1999; deputy president of South Africa (1994–99)

Mbujimayi a city in S Democratic Republic of Congo (formerly Zaïre): diamond mining. Pop: 821 000 (2005 est)

MDF medium-density fibreboard: a wood-substitute material used in interior decoration

mead an alcoholic drink made by fermenting a solution of honey, often with spices added

Mead¹ Margaret 1901–78, US anthropologist. Her works include *Coming of Age in Samoa* (1928) and *Male and Female* (1949)

Mead² Lake a reservoir in NW Arizona and SE Nevada, formed by the Hoover Dam across the Colorado River: one of the largest man-made lakes in the world. Area: 588 sq km (227 sq miles)

Meade George Gordon 1815–72, Union general in the American Civil War. He commanded the Army of the Potomac, defeating the Confederates at Gettysburg (1863)

meadow 1 an area of grassland, often used for hay or for grazing of animals 2 a low-lying piece of grassland, often boggy and near a river

meadowsweet 1 a Eurasian rosaceous plant, *Filipendula ulmaria*, with dense heads of small fragrant cream-coloured flowers 2 any of several North American rosaceous plants of the genus *Spiraea*, having pyramid-shaped sprays of small flowers

mean *Maths* a the second and third terms of a proportion, as *b* and *c* in $a/b = c/d$ b another name for **average**

meander an ornamental pattern, esp as used in ancient Greek architecture

meaning *Philosophy* a the sense of an expression; its connotation b the reference of an expression; its denotation. In recent philosophical writings meaning can be used in both the above senses

means test a test involving the checking of a person's income to determine whether he qualifies for financial or social aid from a government

mean time or **mean solar time** the time, at a particular place, measured in terms of the passage of the mean sun; the timescale is not precisely constant

measles 1 a highly contagious viral disease common in children, characterized by fever, profuse nasal discharge of mucus, conjunctivitis, and a rash of small red spots spreading from the forehead down to the limbs 2 a disease of cattle, sheep, and pigs, caused by infestation with tapeworm larvae

measure 1 a legislative bill, act, or resolution 2 *Music* another word for **bar** 3 *Prosody* poetic rhythm or cadence; metre 4 a metrical foot 5 *Poetic* a melody or tune 6 *Archaic* a dance

Meath a county of E Republic of Ireland, in Leinster province on the Irish Sea: formerly a kingdom much larger than the present county; livestock farming. County town: Trim. Pop: 134 005 (2002). Area: 2338 sq km (903 sq miles)

Mecca or **Mekka** a city in W Saudi Arabia, joint capital (with Riyadh) of Saudi Arabia: birthplace of

Mohammed; the holiest city of Islam, containing the Kaaba. Pop: 1 529 000 (2005 est)

mechanic a person skilled in maintaining or operating machinery, motors, etc.

mechanical 1 made, performed, or operated by or as if by a machine or machinery 2 concerned with machines or machinery 3 relating to or controlled or operated by physical forces 4 of or concerned with mechanics 5 *Philosophy* accounting for phenomena by physically determining forces

mechanical drawing a drawing to scale of a machine, machine component, architectural plan, etc, from which dimensions can be taken for manufacture

mechanical engineering the branch of engineering concerned with the design, construction, and operation of machines and machinery

▷www.memagazine.org

mechanics 1 the branch of science, divided into statics, dynamics, and kinematics, concerned with the equilibrium or motion of bodies in a particular frame of reference 2 the science of designing, constructing, and operating machines 3 the working parts of a machine

mechanism 1 a system or structure of moving parts that performs some function, esp in a machine 2 any form of mechanical device or any part of such a device 3 *Philosophy* **a** the doctrine that human action can be explained in purely physical terms, whether mechanical or biological **b** the explanation of phenomena in causal rather than teleological or essentialist terms **c** the view that the task of science is to seek such explanations **d** strict determinism 4 *Psychoanal* **a** the ways in which psychological forces interact and operate **b** a structure having an influence on the behaviour of a person, such as a defence mechanism

Mechelen a city in N Belgium, in Antwerp province: capital of the Netherlands from 1507 to 1530; formerly famous for lace-making; now has an important vegetable market. Pop: 76 981 (2004 est)

Mecklenburg a historic region and former state of NE Germany, along the Baltic coast; now part of Mecklenburg-West Pomerania

Mecklenburg-West Pomerania a state of NE Germany, along the Baltic coast: consists of the former state of Mecklenburg and those parts of W Pomerania not incorporated into Poland after World War II: part of East Germany until 1990. Pop: 1 732 000 (2003 est)

Med the *Informal* the Mediterranean region

medallion an oval or circular decorative device resembling a medal, usually bearing a portrait or relief moulding, used in architecture and textile design

Medan a city in Indonesia, in NE Sumatra: seat of the University of North Sumatra (1952) and the Indonesian Islam University (1952). Pop: 1 904 273 (2000)

Medawar Sir Peter Brian 1915–87, English zoologist, who shared the Nobel prize for physiology or medicine (1960) with Sir Macfarlane Burnet for work on immunology

media 1 the middle layer of the wall of a blood or lymph vessel 2 one of the main veins in the wing of an insect

Media an ancient country of SW Asia, south of the Caspian Sea: inhabited by the Medes; overthrew the Assyrian Empire in 612 BC in alliance with Babylonia;

conquered by Cyrus the Great in 550 BC; corresponds to present-day NW Iran

medial 1 *Maths* relating to an average 2 another word for **median** 3 *Zoology* of or relating to a media

median 1 *Biology* of or relating to the plane that divides an organism or organ into symmetrical parts 2 *Geometry* **a** a straight line joining one vertex of a triangle to the midpoint of the opposite side **b** a straight line joining the midpoints of the nonparallel sides of a trapezium 3 *Canadian* the strip, often covered with grass, that separates the two sides of a highway

mediate *Logic* (of an inference) having more than one premise, esp, being syllogistic in form

medic *Informal* a doctor, medical orderly, or medical student

medical 1 of or relating to the science of medicine or to the treatment of patients by drugs, etc, as opposed to surgery 2 a less common word for **medicinal** 3 *Informal* a medical examination

medical certificate a document stating the result of a satisfactory medical examination

medicament a medicine or remedy in a specified formulation

medication 1 treatment with drugs or remedies 2 a drug or remedy

Medici 1 an Italian family of bankers, merchants, and rulers of Florence and Tuscany, prominent in Italian political and cultural history in the 15th, 16th, and 17th centuries, including 2 **Cosimo I**, known as *Cosimo the Great*. 1519–74, duke of Florence and first grand duke of Tuscany (1569–74) 3 **Cosimo de'**, known as *Cosimo the Elder*. 1389–1464, Italian banker, statesman, and patron of arts, who established the political power of the family in Florence (1434) 4 **Lorenzo de'**, known as *Lorenzo the Magnificent*. 1449–92, Italian statesman, poet, and scholar; ruler of Florence (1469–92) and first patron of Michelangelo

medicinal 1 relating to or having therapeutic properties 2 a medicinal substance

medicine 1 any drug or remedy for use in treating, preventing, or alleviating the symptoms of disease 2 the science of preventing, diagnosing, alleviating, or curing disease 3 any nonsurgical branch of medical science 4 the practice or profession of medicine 5 something regarded by primitive people as having magical or remedial properties

▷www.medhelp.org

▷www.medbioworld.com/home/lists/
med-db.html

▷www.ipl.org/div/subject/browse/
hea00.00.00/

medicine man (among certain peoples, esp North American Indians) a person believed to have supernatural powers of healing; a magician or sorcerer

medico a doctor or medical student

medieval *or* **mediaeval** of, relating to, or in the style of the Middle Ages

Medieval Greek the Greek language from the 7th century AD to shortly after the sacking of Constantinople in 1204

Medieval Latin the Latin language as used throughout Europe in the Middle Ages. It had many local forms incorporating Latinized words from other languages

Medina a city in W Saudi Arabia: the second most holy city of Islam (after Mecca), with the tomb of Mohammed; university (1960). Pop: 1 044 000 (2005 est)

Mediterranean 1 short for the **Mediterranean Sea** 2 a native or inhabitant of a Mediterranean country 3 of, relating to, situated or dwelling on or near the Mediterranean Sea 4 denoting a postulated subdivision of the Caucasoid race, characterized by slender build and dark complexion 5 *Meteorol* (of a climate) characterized by hot summers and relatively warm winters when most of the annual rainfall occurs 6 *Obsolete* situated in the middle of a landmass; inland

Mediterranean Sea a large inland sea between S Europe, N Africa, and SW Asia: linked with the Atlantic by the Strait of Gibraltar, with the Red Sea by the Suez Canal, and with the Black Sea by the Dardanelles, Sea of Marmara, and Bosporus; many ancient civilizations developed around its shores. Greatest depth: 4770 m (15 900 ft). Length: (west to east) over 3700 km (2300 miles). Greatest width: about 1368 km (850 miles). Area: (excluding the Black Sea) 2 512 300 sq km (970 000 sq miles)

medium 1 (of a colour) reflecting or transmitting a moderate amount of light 2 a person supposedly used as a spiritual intermediary between the dead and the living 3 the substance in which specimens of animals and plants are preserved or displayed 4 the substance or surroundings in which an organism naturally lives or grows 5 *Art* a the category of a work of art, as determined by its materials and methods of production b the materials used in a work of art 6 any solvent in which pigments are mixed and thinned

medlar 1 a small Eurasian rosaceous tree, *Mespilus germanica* 2 the fruit of this tree, which resembles the crab apple and is not edible until it has begun to decay 3 any of several other rosaceous trees or their fruits

medley 1 a musical composition consisting of various tunes arranged as a continuous whole 2 a *Swimming* a race in which a different stroke is used for each length b *Athletics* a relay race in which each leg has a different distance

medulla 1 *Anatomy* the innermost part of an organ or structure 2 *Botany* another name for **pith**

medusa 1 another name for **jellyfish** 2 one of the two forms in which a coelenterate exists. It has a jelly-like umbrella-shaped body, is free swimming, and produces gametes

Medway 1 a river in SE England, flowing through Kent and the **Medway towns** (Rochester, Chatham, and Gillingham) to the Thames estuary. Length: 110 km (70 miles) 2 a unitary authority in SE England, in Kent. Pop: 251 100 (2003 est). Area: 204 sq km (79 sq miles)

meerkat any of several South African mongooses, esp *Suricata suricatta* (**slender-tailed meerkat** or **suricate**), which has a lemur-like face and four-toed feet

meerschaum 1 a white, yellowish, or pink compact earthy mineral consisting of hydrated magnesium silicate: used to make tobacco pipes and as a building stone. Formula: $Mg_2Si_3O_6(OH)_4$ 2 a tobacco pipe having a bowl made of this mineral

Meerut an industrial city in N India, in W Uttar Pradesh: founded as a military base by the British in 1806 and scene of the first uprising (1857) of the Indian Mutiny. Pop: 1 074 229 (2001)

meet 1 the assembly of hounds, huntsmen, etc, prior to a hunt 2 *US* the place where the paths of two railway trains meet or cross

megahertz one million hertz; one million cycles per second.

megalith a stone of great size, esp one forming part of a prehistoric monument

megalomania a mental illness characterized by delusions of grandeur, power, wealth, etc.

megapode any ground-living gallinaceous bird of the family *Megapodiidae*, of Australia, New Guinea, and adjacent islands. Their eggs incubate in mounds of sand, rotting vegetation, etc, by natural heat

Megara a town in E central Greece: an ancient trading city, founding many colonies in the 7th and 8th centuries BC. Pop: 26 562 (1991 est)

megaton 1 one million tons 2 an explosive power, esp of a nuclear weapon, equal to the power of one million tons of TNT

Meghalaya a state of NE India, created in 1969 from part of Assam. Capital: Shillong. Pop: 2 306 069 (2001). Area: 22 429 sq km (7800 sq miles)

Megiddo an ancient town in N Palestine, strategically located on a route linking Egypt to Mesopotamia: site of many battles, including an important Egyptian victory over rebel chieftains in 1469 or 1468 BC

Mehemet Ali *or* **Mohammed Ali** 1769–1849, Albanian commander in the service of Turkey. He was made viceroy of Egypt (1805) and its hereditary ruler (1841), founding a dynasty that ruled until 1952

Mehta Zubin born 1936, Indian conductor; musical director of the Israel Philharmonic orchestra from 1969

meiosis a type of cell division in which a nucleus divides into four daughter nuclei, each containing half the chromosome number of the parent nucleus: occurs in all sexually reproducing organisms in which haploid gametes or spores are produced

Meir Golda 1898–1978, Israeli stateswoman, born in Russia; prime minister (1969–74)

Meissen a town in E Germany, in Saxony, in Dresden district on the River Elbe: famous for its porcelain (Dresden china), first made here in 1710. Pop: 28 640 (2003 est)

Meitner Lise 1878–1968, Austrian nuclear physicist. With Hahn, she discovered protactinium (1918), and they demonstrated with F. Strassmann the fission of uranium

meitnerium a synthetic element produced in small quantities by high-energy ion bombardment. Symbol: Mt; atomic no.: 109

Mekong a river in SE Asia, rising in SW China in Qinghai province: flows southeast forming the border between Laos and Myanmar, and part of the border between Laos and Thailand, then continues south across Cambodia and Vietnam to the South China Sea by an extensive delta, one of the greatest rice-growing areas in Asia. Length: about 4025 km (2500 miles)

melaleuca any shrub or tree of the mostly Australian

myrtaceous genus *Melaleuca*, found in sandy or swampy regions

melamine 1 a colourless crystalline compound used in making synthetic resins; 2,4,6-triamino-1,3,5-triazine. Formula: $C_3H_6N_6$ 2 melamine resin or a material made from this resin

melancholy *Archaic* a a gloomy character, thought to be caused by too much black bile b one of the four bodily humours; black bile

Melanchthon **Philipp** original surname *Schwarzerd*. 1497–1560, German Protestant reformer. His *Loci Communes* (1521) was the first systematic presentation of Protestant theology and in the Augsburg Confession (1530) he stated the faith of the Lutheran churches. He also reformed the German educational system

Melanesia one of the three divisions of islands in the Pacific (the others being Micronesia and Polynesia); the SW division of Oceania: includes Fiji, New Caledonia, Vanuatu, the Bismarck Archipelago, and the Louisiade, Solomon, Santa Cruz, and Loyalty Islands, which all lie northeast of Australia

melange *or* **mélange** *Geology* a totally disordered mixture of rocks of different shapes, sizes, ages, and origins

melanin any of a group of black or dark brown pigments present in the hair, skin, and eyes of man and animals: produced in excess in certain skin diseases and in melanomas

melanoma *Pathol* a malignant tumour composed of melanocytes, occurring esp in the skin, often as a result of excessive exposure to sunlight

Melba **Dame Nellie,** stage name of *Helen Porter Mitchell*. 1861–1931, Australian operatic soprano

Melbourne[1] **William Lamb,** 2nd Viscount. 1779–1848; Whig prime minister (1834; 1835–41). He was the chief political adviser to the young Queen Victoria

Melbourne[2] a port in SE Australia, capital of Victoria, on Port Phillip Bay: the second largest city in the country; settled in 1835 and developed rapidly with the discovery of rich goldfields in 1851; three universities. Pop: 3 160 171 (2001)

Melchior[1] 1 (in Christian tradition) one of the Magi, the others being Balthazar and Caspar 2 **Lauritz** 1890–1973, US operatic tenor, born in Denmark

Melchior[2] (in Christian tradition) one of the Magi, the others being Balthazar and Caspar

Melchizedek *Old Testament* the priest-king of Salem who blessed Abraham (Genesis 14:18-19) and was taken as a prototype of Christ's priesthood (Hebrews 7)

Melilla the chief town of a Spanish enclave in Morocco, on the Mediterranean coast: founded by the Phoenicians; exports iron ore. Pop: 68 463 (2003 est)

Melitopol a city in SE Ukraine. Pop: 157 000 (2005 est)

Melk a town in N Austria, on the River Danube: noted for its baroque Benedictine abbey. Pop: 5222 (2001)

mellow (esp of wines) well-matured

melodeon *or* **melodion** *Music* 1 a type of small accordion 2 a type of keyboard instrument similar to the harmonium

melodrama 1 a play, film, etc, characterized by extravagant action and emotion 2 (formerly) a romantic drama characterized by sensational incident, music, and song 3 a poem or part of a play or opera spoken to a

musical accompaniment

melody *Music* a a succession of notes forming a distinctive sequence; tune b the horizontally represented aspect of the structure of a piece of music

melon 1 any of several varieties of two cucurbitaceous vines (see **muskmelon**, **watermelon**), cultivated for their edible fruit 2 the fruit of any of these plants, which has a hard rind and juicy flesh

Melos an island in the SW Aegean Sea, in the Cyclades: of volcanic origin, with hot springs; centre of early Aegean civilization, where the Venus de Milo was found. Pop: 4771 (2001). Area: 132 sq km (51 sq miles)

Melpomene *Greek myth* the Muse of tragedy

meltdown (in a nuclear reactor) the melting of the fuel rods as a result of a defect in the cooling system, with the possible escape of radiation into the environment

melting point the temperature at which a solid turns into a liquid. It is equal to the freezing point

Melton Mowbray a town in central England, in Leicestershire: pork pies and Stilton cheese. Pop: 25 554 (2001)

Melville **Herman** 1819–91, US novelist and short-story writer. Among his works, *Moby Dick* (1851) and *Billy Budd* (written 1891, published 1924) are outstanding

Melville Island 1 a Canadian island in the Arctic Ocean, north of Victoria Island: in the Northwest Territories and Nunavut. Area: 41 865 sq km (16 164 sq miles) 2 an island in the Arafura Sea, off the N central coast of Australia, separated from the mainland by Clarence Strait. Area: 6216 sq km (2400 sq miles)

Melville Peninsula a peninsula of N Canada, in Nunavut, between the Gulf of Boothia and Foxe Basin

member 1 any individual plant or animal in a taxonomic group 2 any part of an animal body, such as a limb 3 another word for **penis** 4 any part of a plant, such as a petal, root, etc. 5 *Maths* any individual object belonging to a set or logical class 6 a distinct part of a whole, such as a proposition in a syllogism 7 a component part of a building or construction

Member of Parliament a member of the House of Commons or similar legislative body, as in many Commonwealth countries

membrane 1 a pliable sheetlike usually fibrous tissue that covers, lines, or connects plant and animal organs or cells 2 *Biology* a double layer of lipid, containing some proteins, that surrounds biological cells and some of their internal structures 3 *Physics* a two-dimensional entity postulated as a fundamental constituent of matter in superstring theories of particle physics 4 a skin of parchment forming part of a roll

Memel 1 the German name for **Klaipeda** 2 the lower course of the Neman River

memento *RC Church* either of two prayers occurring during the Mass

memento mori an object, such as a skull, intended to remind people of the inevitability of death

Memling *or* **Memlinc** **Hans** ?1430–94, Flemish painter of religious works and portraits

memoir 1 a biography or historical account, esp one based on personal knowledge 2 an essay or monograph, as on a specialized topic 3 *Obsolete* a memorandum

memorandum 1 an informal diplomatic communication, often unsigned: often summarizing the point of view of a government 2 *Law* a short written summary of the terms of a transaction

memorial 1 a written statement of facts submitted to a government, authority, etc, in conjunction with a petition 2 an informal diplomatic paper

memory a part of a computer in which information is stored for immediate use by the central processing unit

Memphis 1 a port in SW Tennessee, on the Mississippi River: the largest city in the state; a major cotton and timber market; Memphis State University (1909). Pop: 645 978 (2003 est) 2 a ruined city in N Egypt, the ancient centre of Lower Egypt, on the Nile: administrative and artistic centre, sacred to the worship of Ptah

Memphremagog Lake a lake on the border between the US and Canada, in N Vermont and S Quebec. Length: about 43 km (27 miles). Width: up to 6 km (4 miles)

Menado *or* **Manado** a port in NE Indonesia, on NE Sulawesi: founded by the Dutch in 1657. Pop: 372 887 (2000)

menagerie 1 a collection of wild animals kept for exhibition 2 the place where such animals are housed

Menai Strait a channel of the Irish Sea between the island of Anglesey and the mainland of NW Wales: famous suspension bridge (1819–26) designed by Thomas Telford and tubular bridge (1846–50) by Robert Stephenson. Length: 24 km (15 miles). Width: up to 3 km (2 miles)

Menander 1 ?160 BC–?120 BC, Greek king of the Punjab. A Buddhist convert, he reigned over much of NW India 2 ?342–?292 BC, Greek comic dramatist. The *Dyskolos* is his only complete extant comedy but others survive in adaptations by Terence and Plautus

Mencius Chinese name *Mengzi* or *Meng-tze*. ?372–?289 BC, Chinese philosopher, who propounded the ethical system of Confucius

Mencken H(enry) L(ouis). 1880–1956, US journalist and literary critic, noted for *The American Language* (1919): editor of the *Smart Set* and the *American Mercury*, which he founded (1924)

Mendel Gregor Johann 1822–84, Austrian monk and botanist; founder of the science of genetics. He developed his theory of organic inheritance from his experiments on the hybridization of green peas. His findings were published (1865) but remained unrecognized until 1900

mendelevium a transuranic element artificially produced by bombardment of einsteinium. Symbol: Md; atomic no.: 101; half-life of most stable isotope, ^{258}Md: 60 days (approx.); valency: 2 or 3

Mendeleyev *or* **Mendeleev** Dmitri Ivanovich 1834–1907, Russian chemist. He devised the original periodic table of the elements (1869)

Mendelssohn 1 Felix , full name *Jacob Ludwig Felix Mendelssohn-Bartholdy*. 1809–47, German romantic composer. His works include the overtures *A Midsummer Night's Dream* (1826) and *Fingal's Cave* (1832), five symphonies, the oratorio *Elijah* (1846), piano pieces, and songs. He was instrumental in the revival of the music of J. S. Bach in the 19th century 2 his grandfather, Moses 1729–86, German Jewish philosopher. His best-

known work is *Jerusalem* (1783), in which he defends Judaism and appeals for religious toleration

Menderes 1 a river in SW Turkey flowing southwest, then west to the Aegean. Length: about 386 km (240 miles) 2 a river in NW Turkey flowing west and northwest to the Dardanelles. Length: 104 km (65 miles)

Mendes Sam(uel) (Alexander). born 1965, British theatre and film director, who made his name as artistic director of the Donmar Warehouse, London (1992–2002) before directing the films *American Beauty* (1999) and *The Road to Perdition* (2002). He is married to the actress Kate Winslet

mendicant 1 (of a member of a religious order) dependent on alms for sustenance 2 a mendicant friar

Mendoza¹ Pedro de died 1537, Spanish soldier and explorer; founder of Buenos Aires (1536)

Mendoza² a city in W central Argentina, in the foothills of the Sierra de los Paramillos: largely destroyed by an earthquake in 1861; commercial centre of an intensively cultivated irrigated region; University of Cuyo (1939). Pop: 1 072 000 (2005 est)

Menelik II 1844–1913, emperor of Abyssinia (1889–1910). He defeated the Italians at Aduwa (1896), maintaining the independence of Abyssinia in an era of European expansion in Africa

Menes the first king of the first dynasty of Egypt (?3100 BC). He is said to have united Upper and Lower Egypt and founded Memphis

Mengelberg (Josef) Willem 1871–1951, Dutch orchestral conductor, noted for his performances of the music of Mahler

Mengistu Haile Mariam born 1937, Ethiopian soldier and statesman; head of state from 1977 until 1991 when rebels seized power and he fled into exile

menhir a single standing stone, often carved, dating from the middle Bronze Age in the British Isles and from the late Neolithic Age in W Europe

Meninga Mal born 1960, Australian rugby league player

meningitis inflammation of the membranes that surround the brain or spinal cord, caused by infection

meniscus 1 the curved upper surface of a liquid standing in a tube, produced by the surface tension 2 a crescent-shaped fibrous cartilage between the bones at certain joints, esp at the knee 3 a crescent-shaped lens; a concavo-convex or convexo-concave lens

Menon Vengalil Krishnan Krishna 1897–1974, Indian diplomat and politician, who was a close associate of Nehru and played a key role in the Indian nationalist movement

menopause the period during which a woman's menstrual cycle ceases, normally occurring at an age of 45 to 50

menorah *Judaism* 1 a seven-branched candelabrum used in the Temple and now an emblem of Judaism and the badge of the state of Israel 2 a candelabrum having eight branches and a shammes that is lit during the festival of Hanukkah

Menotti Gian Carlo born 1911, Italian composer, in the US from 1928. His works include the operas *The Medium* (1946), *The Consul* (1950), *Amahl and the Night Visitors* (1951), and *Giorno di Nozze* (1988)

menses 1 another name for **menstruation** 2 the period

of time, usually from three to five days, during which menstruation occurs **3** the matter discharged during menstruation

menstruation the approximately monthly discharge of blood and cellular debris from the uterus by nonpregnant women from puberty to the menopause

mensuration the study of the measurement of geometric magnitudes such as length

mental[1] **1** affected by mental illness **2** concerned with care for persons with mental illness **3** *Slang* insane

mental[2] *Anatomy* of or relating to the chin

mental handicap a general or specific intellectual disability, resulting directly or indirectly from injury to the brain or from abnormal neurological development

mental illness any of various disorders in which a person's thoughts, emotions, or behaviour are so abnormal as to cause suffering to himself, herself, or other people

mentality the state or quality of mental or intellectual ability

menthol an optically active organic compound found in peppermint oil and used as an antiseptic, in inhalants, and as an analgesic. Formula: $C_{10}H_{20}O$

Menton a town and resort in SE France, on the Mediterranean: belonged to Monaco from the 14th century until 1848, then an independent republic until purchased by France in 1860. Pop: 28 812 (1999)

menu *Computing* a list of options displayed on a visual display unit from which the operator selects an action to be carried out by positioning the cursor or by depressing the appropriate key

Menuhin Yehudi, Baron. 1916–99, British violinist, born in the US

Menzies Sir Robert Gordon 1894–1978, Australian statesman; prime minister (1939–41; 1949–66)

Mephistopheles *or* **Mephisto** a devil in medieval mythology and the one to whom Faust sold his soul in the Faust legend

Merano a town and resort in NE Italy, in the foothills of the central Alps: capital of the Tyrol (12th–15th century); under Austrian rule until 1919. Pop: 33 656 (2001)

Merca a port in S Somalia on the Indian Ocean. Pop: 189 000 (2005 est)

Mercator Gerardus . Latinized name of *Gerhard Kremer*. 1512–94, Flemish cartographer and mathematician

Mercator projection an orthomorphic map projection on which parallels and meridians form a rectangular grid, scale being exaggerated with increasing distance from the equator

merchandise commercial goods; commodities

merchandising 1 the selection and display of goods in a retail outlet **2** commercial goods, esp ones issued to exploit the popularity of a pop group, sporting event, etc.

merchant 1 *Chiefly US and Canadian* a person engaged in retail trade **2** (esp in historical contexts) any trader **3 a** of the merchant navy **b** of or concerned with trade

Merchant Ismail born 1936, Indian film producer, noted for his collaboration with James Ivory on such films as *Shakespeare Wallah* (1965), *The Europeans* (1979), *A Room with a View* (1986), *The Remains of the Day* (1993), and *The Golden Bowl* (2000)

merchantman a merchant ship

merchant navy *or* **marine** the ships or crew engaged in a nation's commercial shipping
▷www.mna.org.uk

Mercia a kingdom and earldom of central and S England during the Anglo-Saxon period that reached its height under King Offa (757–96)

Merckx Eddy born 1945, Belgian professional cyclist: five times winner of the Tour de France, including four consecutive victories (1969–72)

Mercouri Melina 1925–94, Greek actress and politician: her films include *Never on Sunday* (1960); minister of culture (1981–85 and 1993–94)

mercurial 1 of, like, containing, or relating to mercury **2** of, like, or relating to the god or the planet Mercury **3** *Med* any salt of mercury for use as a medicine

mercuric of or containing mercury in the divalent state; denoting a mercury(II) compound

mercurous of or containing mercury in the monovalent state; denoting a mercury(I) compound. Mercurous salts contain the divalent ion Hg_2^{2+}

mercury 1 a heavy silvery-white toxic liquid metallic element occurring principally in cinnabar: used in thermometers, barometers, mercury-vapour lamps, and dental amalgams. Symbol: Hg; atomic no.: 80; atomic wt.: 200.59; valency: 1 or 2; relative density: 13.546; melting pt.: –38.842°C; boiling pt.: 357°C **2** any plant of the euphorbiaceous genus *Mercurialis*

Mercury[1] *Roman myth* the messenger of the gods

Mercury[2] the second smallest planet and the nearest to the sun. Mean distance from sun: 57.9 million km; period of revolution around sun: 88 days; period of axial rotation: 59 days; diameter and mass: 38 and 5.4 per cent that of earth respectively

mere[1] **1** *Dialect or archaic* a lake or marsh **2** *Obsolete* the sea or an inlet of it

mere[2] *Archaic* a boundary or boundary marker

Meredith George 1828–1909, English novelist and poet. His works, notable for their social satire and analysis of character, include the novels *Beauchamp's Career* (1876) and *The Egoist* (1879) and the long tragic poem *Modern Love* (1862)

merganser any of several typically crested large marine diving ducks of the genus *Mergus*, having a long slender hooked bill with serrated edges

merger 1 *Commerce* the combination of two or more companies, either by the creation of a new organization or by absorption by one of the others **2** *Law* the extinguishment of an estate, interest, contract, right, offence, etc, by its absorption into a greater one

Mergui Archipelago a group of over 200 islands in the Andaman Sea, off the Tenasserim coast of S Myanmar: mountainous and forested

meridian 1 a one of the imaginary lines joining the north and south poles at right angles to the equator, designated by degrees of longitude from 0° at Greenwich to 180° **b** the great circle running through both poles **2** *Astronomy* **a** the great circle on the celestial sphere passing through the north and south celestial poles and the zenith and nadir of the observer **b** (*as modifier*): *a meridian instrument* **3** *Maths* a section of a surface of revolution, such as a paraboloid, that contains the axis of revolution 4 (in acupuncture, etc) any of the channels through which vital energy is believed to circulate round the body 5 *Obsolete* noon 6 along or relating to a meridian

meridional 1 along, relating to, or resembling a meridian 2 characteristic of or located in the south, esp of Europe 3 an inhabitant of the south, esp of France

merino 1 a breed of sheep, originating in Spain, bred for their fleece 2 the long fine wool of this sheep 3 the yarn made from this wool, often mixed with cotton

Merionethshire (until 1974) a county of N Wales, now part of Gwynedd

merit *Christianity* spiritual credit granted or received for good works

meritocracy 1 rule by persons chosen not because of birth or wealth, but for their superior talents or intellect 2 the persons constituting such a group 3 a social system formed on such a basis

merlin a small falcon, *Falco columbarius*, that has a dark plumage with a black-barred tail: used in falconry

mermaid an imaginary sea creature fabled to have a woman's head and upper body and a fish's tail

Merse the a fertile lowland area of SE Scotland, in Scottish Borders, north of the Tweed

Merseburg a city in E Germany, on the Saale River, in Saxony-Anhalt: residence of the dukes of Saxe-Merseburg (1656–1738); chemical industry. Pop: 35 358 (2003 est)

Mersey a river in W England, rising in N Derbyshire and flowing northwest and west to the Irish Sea through a large estuary on which is situated the port of Liverpool. Length: about 112 km (70 miles)

Merseyside a metropolitan county of NW England, administered since 1986 by the unitary authorities of Sefton, Liverpool, St Helens, Knowsley, and Wirral. Area: 652 sq km (252 sq miles)

Mersin a port in S Turkey, on the Mediterranean: oil refinery. Pop: 603 000 (2005 est)

Merthyr Tydfil 1 a town in SE Wales, in Merthyr Tydfil county borough: formerly an important centre for the mining industry. Pop: 30 483 (2001) 2 a county borough in SE Wales, created from part of N Mid Glamorgan in 1996. Pop: 55 400 (2003 est). Area: 111 sq km (43 sq miles)

Merton[1] Thomas (Feverel). 1915–68, US writer, monk, and mystic; noted esp for his autobiography *The Seven Storey Mountain* (1948)

Merton[2] a borough in SW Greater London. Pop: 191 400 (2003 est). Area: 38 sq km (15 sq miles)

mesa a flat tableland with steep edges, common in the southwestern US

Mesa Verde a high plateau in SW Colorado: remains of numerous prehistoric cliff dwellings, inhabited by the Pueblo Indians

mescal 1 a spineless globe-shaped cactus, *Lophophora williamsii*, of Mexico and the southwestern US Its button-like tubercles (**mescal buttons**) contain mescaline and are chewed by certain Indian tribes for their hallucinogenic effects 2 a colourless alcoholic spirit distilled from the fermented juice of certain agave plants

mescaline *or* **mescalin** a hallucinogenic drug derived from mescal buttons. Formula: $C_{11}H_{17}NO_3$

mesembryanthemum any plant of a South African

genus (*Mesembryanthemum*) of succulent-leaved prostrate or erect plants widely grown in gardens and greenhouses: family *Aizoaceae*

mesh *Engineering* the engagement of teeth on interacting gearwheels

Meshach *Old Testament* one of Daniel's three companions who, together with Shadrach and Abednego, was miraculously saved from destruction in Nebuchadnezzar's fiery furnace (Daniel 3:12-30)

Mesolithic the period between the Palaeolithic and the Neolithic, in Europe from about 12 000 to 3000 BC, characterized by the appearance of microliths

meson any of a group of elementary particles, such as a pion or kaon, that usually has a rest mass between those of an electron and a proton, and an integral spin. They are responsible for the force between nucleons in the atomic nucleus

Mesopotamia a region of SW Asia between the lower and middle reaches of the Tigris and Euphrates rivers: site of several ancient civilizations

mesosphere 1 the atmospheric layer lying between the stratosphere and the thermosphere, characterized by a rapid decrease in temperature with height 2 the solid part of the earth's mantle lying between the asthenosphere and the core

Mesozoic of, denoting, or relating to an era of geological time that began 250 000 000 years ago with the Triassic period and lasted about 185 000 000 years until the end of the Cretaceous period

message 1 a formal communiqué 2 an inspired communication of a prophet or religious leader

Messager André (Charles Prosper). 1853–1929, French composer and conductor

messaging the practice of sending and receiving written communications by computer or mobile phone

Messalina Valeria died 48 AD, wife of the Roman emperor Claudius, notorious for her debauchery and cruelty

Messene an ancient Greek city in the SW Peloponnese: founded in 369 BC as the capital of Messenia

messenger 1 a carrier of official dispatches; courier 2 *Nautical* a a light line used to haul in a heavy rope b an endless belt of chain, rope, or cable, used on a powered winch to take off power 3 *Archaic* a herald

Messenia the southwestern area of the Peloponnese in S Greece

Messerschmitt Willy 1898–1978, German aeronautical engineer. His military planes figured prominently in World War II, including the Me-262, the first jet fighter

Messiaen Olivier 1908–92, French composer and organist. His music is distinguished by its rhythmic intricacy; he was influenced by Hindu and Greek rhythms and bird song

Messiah 1 *Judaism* the awaited redeemer of the Jews, to be sent by God to free them 2 Jesus Christ, when regarded in this role 3 an exceptional or hoped for liberator of a country or people

Messina a port in NE Sicily, on the **Strait of Messina**: colonized by Greeks around 730 BC; under Spanish rule (1282–1676 and 1678–1713); university (1549). Pop: 252 026 (2001)

Meštrović Ivan 1883–1962, US sculptor, born in Austria: his works include portraits of Sir Thomas Beecham and

Pope Pius XI

metabolism 1 the sum total of the chemical processes that occur in living organisms, resulting in growth, production of energy, elimination of waste material, etc. 2 the sum total of the chemical processes affecting a particular substance in the body

metacarpus 1 the skeleton of the hand between the wrist and the fingers, consisting of five long bones 2 the corresponding bones in other vertebrates

metal 1 a any of a number of chemical elements, such as iron or copper, that are often lustrous ductile solids, have basic oxides, form positive ions, and are good conductors of heat and electricity b an alloy, such as brass or steel, containing one or more of these elements 2 the substance of glass in a molten state or as the finished product 3 short for **road metal** 4 *Astronomy* any element heavier than helium 5 the rails of a railway

metallic 1 of, concerned with, or consisting of metal or a metal 2 *Chem* (of a metal element) existing in the free state rather than in combination

metalliferous containing a high concentration of metallic elements

metallography the branch of metallurgy concerned with the composition and structure of metals and alloys

metalloid a nonmetallic element, such as arsenic or silicon, that has some of the properties of a metal

metallurgy the scientific study of the extraction, refining, alloying, and fabrication of metals and of their structure and properties

   ▷www.psigate.ac.uk/newsite/
    materials-gateway.html

metalwork 1 the craft of working in metal 2 work in metal or articles made from metal

metamorphic *or* **metamorphous** (of rocks) altered considerably from their original structure and mineralogy by pressure and heat

metamorphism the process by which metamorphic rocks are formed

metamorphosis *Zoology* the rapid transformation of a larva into an adult that occurs in certain animals, for example the stage between tadpole and frog or between chrysalis and butterfly

metaphor a figure of speech in which a word or phrase is applied to an object or action that it does not literally denote in order to imply a resemblance, for example *he is a lion in battle*

metaphysical 1 relating to or concerned with metaphysics 2 (of a statement or theory) having the form of an empirical hypothesis, but in fact immune from empirical testing and therefore (in the view of the logical positivists) literally meaningless

Metaphysical denoting or relating to certain 17th-century poets who combined intense feeling with ingenious thought and often used elaborate imagery and conceits. Notable among them were Donne, Herbert, and Marvell

metaphysics 1 the branch of philosophy that deals with first principles, esp of being and knowing 2 the philosophical study of the nature of reality, concerned with such questions as the existence of God, the external world, etc

   ▷www.foolquest.com/
    metaphysics_for_dummies.htm
   ▷http://pespmc1.vub.ac.be/METAPHI.html
   ▷www.qozi.com/philosophy/metaphysics.html

metastasis 1 *Pathol* the spreading of a disease, esp cancer cells, from one part of the body to another 2 a rare word for **metabolism**

metatarsus 1 the skeleton of the human foot between the toes and the tarsus, consisting of five long bones 2 the corresponding skeletal part in other vertebrates

metazoan any multicellular animal of the group *Metazoa*: includes all animals except sponges

Metchnikoff Élie 1845–1916, Russian bacteriologist in France. He formulated the theory of phagocytosis and shared the Nobel prize for physiology or medicine 1908

meteor 1 a very small meteoroid that has entered the earth's atmosphere. Such objects have speeds approaching 70 kilometres per second 2 the bright streak of light appearing in the sky due to the incandescence of such a body heated by friction at its surface

meteoric 1 of, formed by, or relating to meteors 2 *Rare* of or relating to the weather; meteorological

meteorite a rocklike object consisting of the remains of a meteoroid that has fallen on earth. It may be stony, iron, or stony iron

meteoroid any of the small celestial bodies that are thought to orbit the sun, possibly as the remains of comets. When they enter the earth's atmosphere, they become visible as meteors

meteorology the study of the earth's atmosphere, esp of weather-forming processes and weather forecasting

   ▷http://sciencepolicy.colorado.edu/socasp/
    toc_img.html
   ▷http://personal.cmich.edu/~francim/
    homepage.htm
   ▷www.wmo.ch
   ▷www.worldweather.org

meter 1 any device that measures and records the quantity of a substance, such as gas, that has passed through it during a specified period 2 any device that measures and sometimes records an electrical or magnetic quantity, such as current, voltage, etc. 3 See **parking meter**

-meter *Prosody* indicating a verse having a specified number of feet

methadone *or* **methadon** a narcotic analgesic drug similar to morphine, used to treat opiate addiction. Formula: $C_{21}H_{27}NO$

methane a colourless odourless flammable gas, the simplest alkane and the main constituent of natural gas: used as a fuel. Formula: CH_4

methanol a colourless volatile poisonous liquid compound used as a solvent and fuel. Formula: CH_3OH

Method a a technique of acting based on the theories of Stanislavsky, in which the actor bases his role on the inner motivation of the character he plays b (*as modifier*): *a Method actor*

   ▷www.vtheatre.net/acting/method.html
   ▷www.theatrelinks.com
   ▷www.theatrgroup.com/Method

Methodist 1 a member of any of the Nonconformist denominations that derive from the system of faith and practice initiated by the English preacher John Wesley (1703–91) and his followers **2** of or relating to Methodism or the Church embodying it (the **Methodist Church**)

▷http://www.methodist.org.uk/
▷http://www.methodist.co.za/
▷http://www.methodist.org.nz/

Methodius Saint, with his younger brother Saint Cyril called *the Apostles of the Slavs*. 815–885 AD, Greek Christian theologian sent as a missionary to the Moravians. Feast day: Feb 14 or May 11

methodology the branch of philosophy concerned with the science of method and procedure

Methuselah *Old Testament* a patriarch supposed to have lived 969 years (Genesis 5:21–27) who has come to be regarded as epitomizing longevity

methyl 1 of, consisting of, or containing the monovalent group of atoms CH_3 **2** an organometallic compound in which methyl groups are bound directly to a metal atom

methylated spirits *or* **spirit** alcohol that has been denatured by the addition of methanol and pyridine and a violet dye

methylene of, consisting of, or containing the divalent group of atoms $=CH_2$

metre[1] *or US* **meter 1** a metric unit of length equal to approximately 1.094 yards **2** the basic SI unit of length; the length of the path travelled by light in free space during a time interval of 1/299 792 458 of a second. In 1983 this definition replaced the previous one based on krypton-86, which in turn had replaced the definition based on the platinum-iridium metre bar kept in Paris

metre[2] *or US* **meter 1** *Prosody* the rhythmic arrangement of syllables in verse, usually according to the number and kind of feet in a line **2** *Music* another word (esp US) for **time**

metric 1 of or relating to the metre or metric system **2** *Maths* denoting or relating to a set containing pairs of points for each of which a non-negative real number $\rho(x, y)$ (the distance) can be defined, satisfying specific conditions **3** *Maths* the function $\rho(x, y)$ satisfying the conditions of membership of such a set (a **metric space**)

metric system any decimal system of units based on the metre. For scientific purposes the Système International d'Unités (SI units) is used

metro *or* **métro** an underground, or largely underground, railway system in certain cities, esp in Europe, such as that in Paris

metronome a mechanical device which indicates the exact tempo of a piece of music by producing a clicking sound from a pendulum with an adjustable period of swing

metropolis 1 the main city, esp of a country or region; capital **2** the chief see in an ecclesiastical province

metropolitan 1 constituting a city and its suburbs **2** of, relating to, or designating an ecclesiastical metropolis **3** of or belonging to the home territories of a country, as opposed to overseas territories **4 a** *Eastern Churches* the head of an ecclesiastical province, ranking between archbishop and patriarch **b** *Church of England* an archbishop **c** *RC Church* an archbishop or bishop having authority in certain matters over the dioceses in his

province

Metropolitan Museum of Art the principal museum in New York City: founded in 1870 and housed in its present premises in Central Park since 1880

Metternich Klemens 1773–1859, Austrian statesman. He became foreign minister (1809) and made a significant contribution to the Congress of Vienna (1815). From 1821 to 1848 he was both foreign minister and chancellor of Austria and is noted for his defence of autocracy in Europe

Metz a city in NE France on the River Moselle: a free imperial city in the 13th century; annexed by France in 1552; part of Germany (1871–1918); centre of the Lorraine iron-mining region. Pop: 123 776 (1999)

Meurthe-et-Moselle a department of NE France, in Lorraine region. Capital: Nancy. Pop: 718 250 (2003 est). Area: 5280 sq km (2059 sq miles)

Meuse 1 a department of N France, in Lorraine region: heavy fighting occurred here in World War I. Capital: Bar-le-Duc. Pop: 191 728 (2003 est). Area: 6241 sq km (2434 sq miles) **2** a river in W Europe, rising in NE France and flowing north across E Belgium and the S Netherlands to join the Waal River before entering the North Sea. Length: 926 km (575 miles)

mew[1] any seagull, esp the common gull, *Larus canus*

mew[2] a room or cage for hawks, esp while moulting

mews *Chiefly Brit* a yard or street lined by buildings originally used as stables but now often converted into dwellings

Mexicali a city in NW Mexico, capital of Baja California (Norte) state, on the border with the US adjoining Calexico, California: centre of a rich irrigated agricultural region. Pop: 840 000 (2005 est)

Mexico 1 a republic in North America, on the Gulf of Mexico and the Pacific: early Mexican history includes the Maya, Toltec, and Aztec civilizations; conquered by the Spanish between 1519 and 1525 and achieved independence in 1821; lost Texas to the US in 1836 and California and New Mexico in 1848. It is generally mountainous with three ranges of the Sierra Madre (east, west, and south) and a large central plateau. Official language: Spanish. Religion: Roman Catholic majority. Currency: peso. Capital: Mexico City. Pop: 104 931 000 (2004 est). Area: 1 967 183 sq km (761 530 sq miles) **2** a state of Mexico, on the central plateau surrounding Mexico City, which is not administratively part of the state. Capital: Toluca. Pop: 13 096 686 (2000). Area: 21 460 sq km (8287 sq miles) **3** **Gulf of** an arm of the Atlantic, bordered by the US, Cuba, and Mexico: linked with the Atlantic by the Straits of Florida and with the Caribbean by the Yucatán Channel. Area: about 1 600 000 sq km (618 000 sq miles)

Mexico City the capital of Mexico, on the central plateau at an altitude of 2240 m (7350 ft): founded as the Aztec capital (Tenochtitlán) in about 1300; conquered and rebuilt by the Spanish in 1521; forms, with its suburbs, the federal district of Mexico; the largest industrial complex in the country. Pop: 19 013 000 (2005 est)

Meyerbeer Giacomo, real name *Jakob Liebmann Beer*. 1791–1864, German composer, esp of operas, such as *Robert le diable* (1831) and *Les Huguenots* (1836)

Meyerhof Otto (Fritz). 1884–1951, German physiologist,

noted for his work on the metabolism of muscles. He shared the Nobel prize for physiology or medicine 1922

Meyerhold Vsevolod Emilievich, original name *Karl Theodor Kasimir*. 1874–c 1940, Russian theatre director, noted for his experimental nonrealistic productions. He was arrested in 1939 and died in custody

mezzanine 1 an intermediate storey, esp a low one between the ground and first floor of a building **2** *Theatre, US and Canadian* the first balcony **3** *Theatre, Brit* a room or floor beneath the stage

mezzo-soprano a female voice intermediate between a soprano and contralto and having a range from the A below middle C to the F an eleventh above it

mi *or* **me** *Music* (in tonic sol-fa) the third degree of any major scale; mediant

Miami a city and resort in SE Florida, on Biscayne Bay: developed chiefly after 1896, esp with the Florida land boom of the 1920s; centre of an extensive tourist area. Pop: 376 815 (2003 est)

Miami Beach a resort in SE Florida, on an island separated from Miami by Biscayne Bay. Pop: 89 312 (2003 est)

Miandad Javed born 1957, Pakistani cricketer, a famous batsman; played for Pakistan 1976–94; national team coach 1999–2001

mica any of a group of lustrous rock-forming minerals consisting of hydrous silicates of aluminium, potassium, etc, in monoclinic crystalline form, occurring in igneous and metamorphic rock. Because of their resistance to electricity and heat they are used as dielectrics, in heating elements, etc.

Micah *Old Testament* **1** a Hebrew prophet of the late 8th century BC **2** the book containing his prophecies

Michael 1 1596–1645, tsar of Russia (1613–45); founder of the Romanov dynasty **2** born 1921, king of Romania (1927–30, as part of a three-part regency; 1940–47), who relinquished the throne (1930–40) in favour of his father, Carol II. He led the coup d'état that overthrew (1944) Antonescu but was forced to abdicate (1947) by the Communists **3** **Saint** *Bible* one of the archangels. Feast day: Sept 29 or Nov 8

Michaelmas daisy *Brit* any of various plants of the genus *Aster* that have small autumn-blooming purple, pink, or white flowers: family *Asteraceae* (composites)

Michelangelo full name *Michelangelo Buonarroti*. 1475–1564, Florentine sculptor, painter, architect, and poet; one of the outstanding figures of the Renaissance. Among his creations are the sculptures of *David* (1504) and of *Moses* which was commissioned for the tomb of Julius II, for whom he also painted the ceiling of the Sistine Chapel (1508–12). *The Last Judgment* (1533–41), also in the Sistine, includes a torturous vision of Hell and a disguised self-portrait. His other works include the design of the Laurentian Library (1523–29) and of the dome of St Peter's, Rome

Michelet Jules 1798–1874, French historian, noted esp for his *Histoire de France* (17 vols, 1833–67)

Michelin André 1853–1931, French industrialist; founder, with his brother **Édouard Michelin** (1859–1940), of the Michelin Tyre Company (1888): the first to use demountable pneumatic tyres on motor vehicles

Michelozzo full name *Michelozzo di Bartolommeo*.

1396–1472, Italian architect and sculptor. His most important design was the Palazzo Riccardo for the Medici family in Florence (1444–59)

Michelson Albert Abraham 1852–1931, US physicist, born in Germany: noted for his part in the Michelson-Morley experiment: Nobel prize for physics 1907

Michigan 1 a state of the N central US, occupying two peninsulas between Lakes Superior, Huron, Michigan, and Erie: generally low-lying. Capital: Lansing. Pop: 10 079 985 (2003 est). Area: 147 156 sq km (56 817 sq miles) **2** **Lake** a lake in the N central US between Wisconsin and Michigan: the third largest of the five Great Lakes and the only one wholly in the US; linked with Lake Huron by the Straits of Mackinac. Area: 58 000 sq km (22 400 sq miles)

mickey¹ *or* **micky** *Austral, informal* a young bull, esp one that is wild and unbranded

mickey² *Canadian* a liquor bottle of 0.375 litre capacity, flat on one side and curved on the other to fit into a pocket

Mickiewicz Adam 1798–1855, Polish poet, whose epic *Thaddeus* (1834) is regarded as a masterpiece of Polish literature

microbiology the branch of biology involving the study of microorganisms
  ▷www.microbiol.org/vl_micro
  ▷www.microbes.inf
  ▷www.virology.net

microchemistry chemical experimentation with minute quantities of material

microchip a small piece of semiconductor material carrying many integrated circuits

microcircuit a miniature electronic circuit, esp one in which a number of permanently connected components are contained in one small chip of semiconducting material

microcomputer a small computer in which the central processing unit is contained in one or more silicon chips

microcosm *or* **microcosmos** man regarded as epitomizing the universe

microdot 1 a microcopy about the size of a pinhead, used esp in espionage **2** a tiny tablet containing LSD

microeconomics the branch of economics concerned with particular commodities, firms, or individuals and the economic relationships between them
  ▷www.helsinki.fi/WebEc/webecd.html

microelectronics the branch of electronics concerned with microcircuits

microfiche a sheet of film, usually the size of a filing card, on which books, newspapers, documents, etc, can be recorded in miniaturized form

microfilm a strip of film of standard width on which books, newspapers, documents, etc, can be recorded in miniaturized form

microlight *or* **microlite** a small private aircraft carrying no more than two people, with an empty weight of not more than 150 kg and a wing area not less than 10 square metres: used in pleasure flying and racing

micrometer 1 any of various instruments or devices for the accurate measurement of distances or angles **2** a type of gauge for the accurate measurement of small distances, thicknesses, diameters, etc. The gap between its measuring faces is adjusted by a fine screw, the rotation of the screw giving a sensitive measure of the distance moved by the face

microminiaturization *or* **microminiaturisation** the production and application of very small semiconductor components and the circuits and equipment in which they are used

micron a unit of length equal to 10^{-6} metre. It is being replaced by the micrometre, the equivalent SI unit

Micronesia 1 one of the three divisions of islands in the Pacific (the others being Melanesia and Polynesia); the NW division of Oceania: includes the Mariana, Caroline, Marshall, and Kiribati island groups, and Nauru Island **2 Federated States of** an island group in the W Pacific, formerly within the United States Trust Territory of the Pacific Islands: comprises the islands of Truk, Yap, Ponape, and Kosrae: formed in 1979 when the islands became self-governing: status of free association with the US from 1982. Languages: English and Micronesian languages. Religion: Christian majority. Currency: US dollar. Capital: Palikir. Pop: 111 000 (2004 est)

microphone a device used in sound-reproduction systems for converting sound into electrical energy, usually by means of a ribbon or diaphragm set into motion by the sound waves. The vibrations are converted into the equivalent audio-frequency electric currents

microprocessor *Computing* a single integrated circuit performing the basic functions of the central processing unit in a small computer

microscope 1 an optical instrument that uses a lens or combination of lenses to produce a magnified image of a small, close object. Modern optical microscopes have magnifications of about 1500 to 2000 **2** any instrument, such as the electron microscope, for producing a magnified visual image of a small object

microscopic *or less commonly* **microscopical** not large enough to be seen with the naked eye but visible under a microscope

microscopy 1 the study, design, and manufacture of microscopes **2** investigation by use of a microscope

microsecond one millionth of a second.

microsurgery intricate surgery performed on cells, tissues, etc, using a specially designed operating microscope and miniature precision instruments

microwave a electromagnetic radiation in the wavelength range 0.3 to 0.001 metres: used in radar, cooking, etc. **b** (*as modifier*): *microwave generator*

Middelburg a city in the SW Netherlands, capital of Zeeland province, on Walcheren Island: an important trading centre in the Middle Ages and member of the Hanseatic League; 12th-century abbey; market town. Pop: 46 000 (2003 est)

middle (of a language) intermediate between the earliest and the modern forms

Middle Ages, the *European history* **1** (broadly) the period from the end of classical antiquity (or the deposition of the last W Roman emperor in 476 AD) to the Italian Renaissance (or the fall of Constantinople in 1453) **2** (narrowly) the period from about 1000 AD to the 15th

century
▷www.mnsu.edu/emuseum/history/
middleages
▷http://radiantworks.com/middleages

Middle America 1 the territories between the US and South America: Mexico, Central America, Panama, and the Greater and Lesser Antilles **2** the US middle class, esp those groups that are politically conservative

middle C *Music* the note graphically represented on the first ledger line below the treble staff or the first ledger line above the bass staff and corresponding in pitch to an internationally standardized fundamental frequency of 261.63 hertz

Middle Congo one of the four territories of former French Equatorial Africa, in W central Africa: became an autonomous member of the French Community, as the Republic of the Congo, in 1958

middle ear the sound-conducting part of the ear, containing the malleus, incus, and stapes

Middle East 1 (loosely) the area around the E Mediterranean, esp Israel and the Arab countries from Turkey to North Africa and eastwards to Iran **2** (formerly) the area extending from the Tigris and Euphrates to Myanmar

Middle English the English language from about 1100 to about 1450: main dialects are Kentish, Southwestern (West Saxon), East Midland (which replaced West Saxon as the chief literary form and developed into Modern English), West Midland, and Northern (from which the Scots of Lowland Scotland and other modern dialects developed)

Middle High German High German from about 1200 to about 1500

Middle Low German Low German from about 1200 to about 1500

middleman 1 an independent trader engaged in the distribution of goods from producer to consumer **2** *Theatre* the interlocutor in minstrel shows

Middlesbrough 1 an industrial town in NE England, in Middlesbrough unitary authority, North Yorkshire: on the Tees estuary; university (1992). Pop: 142 691 (2001) **2** a unitary authority in NE England, in North Yorkshire: formerly (1974–96) part of Cleveland county. Pop: 139 000 (2003 est). Area: 54 sq km (21 sq miles)

middle school (in England and Wales) a school for children aged between 8 or 9 and 12 or 13

Middlesex a former county of SE England: became mostly part of N and W Greater London in 1965

Middleton¹ Thomas ?1570–1627, English dramatist. His plays include the tragedies *Women beware Women* (1621) and, in collaboration with William Rowley (?1585–?1642), *The Changeling* (1622) and the political satire *A Game at Chess* (1624)

Middleton² a town in NW England, in Rochdale Unitary Authority, Greater Manchester. Pop: 45 314 (2001)

middleweight 1 a a professional boxer weighing 154–160 pounds (70–72.5 kg) **b** an amateur boxer weighing 71–75 kg (157–165 pounds) **c** (*as modifier*): *a middleweight contest* **2** a wrestler in a similar weight category (usually 172–192 pounds (78–87 kg))

midfield *Soccer* **a** the general area between the two opposing defences **b** *(as modifier)*: *a midfield player*

midge 1 any fragile mosquito-like dipterous insect of the family *Chironomidae*, occurring in dancing swarms, esp near water 2 any similar or related insect, such as the biting midge and gall midge

midget a dwarf whose skeleton and features are of normal proportions

Mid Glamorgan a former county of S Wales, formed in 1974 from parts of Breconshire, Glamorgan, and Monmouthshire: replaced in 1996 by the county boroughs of Bridgend, Rhondda Cynon Taff, Merthyr Tydfil, and part of Caerphilly

Midi 1 the south of France 2 **Canal du** a canal in S France, extending from the River Garonne at Toulouse to the Mediterranean at Sète and providing a link between the Mediterranean and Atlantic coasts: built between 1666 and 1681. Length: 181 km (150 miles)

MIDI a generally accepted specification for the external control of electronic musical instruments

Midian *Old Testament* 1 a son of Abraham (Genesis 25:1–2) 2 a nomadic nation claiming descent from him

midi system a complete set of hi-fi sound equipment designed as a single unit that is more compact than the standard equipment

midland a the central or inland part of a country **b** *(as modifier)*: *a midland region*

Midlands the the central counties of England, including Warwickshire, Northamptonshire, Leicestershire, Nottinghamshire, Derbyshire, Staffordshire, the former West Midlands metropolitan county, and Worcestershire: characterized by manufacturing industries

Midlothian a council area of SE central Scotland: the historical county of Midlothian (including Edinburgh) became part of Lothian region in 1975; separate unitary authorities were created for Midlothian and City of Edinburgh in 1996; mainly agricultural. Administrative centre: Dalkeith. Pop: 79 710 (2003 est). Area: 356 sq km (137 sq miles)

midnight sun the sun visible at midnight during local summer inside the Arctic and Antarctic circles

mid-off *Cricket* 1 the fielding position on the off side closest to the bowler 2 a fielder in this position

mid-on *Cricket* 1 the fielding position on the on side closest to the bowler 2 a fielder in this position

midpoint the point on a line that is at an equal distance from either end

midriff 1 a the middle part of the human body, esp between waist and bust **b** *(as modifier)*: *midriff bulge* 2 *Anatomy* another name for the **diaphragm**

midshipman any of several American toadfishes of the genus *Porichthys*, having small light-producing organs on the undersurface of their bodies

Midwest *or* **Middle West** the N central part of the US; the region consisting of the states from Ohio westwards that border on the Great Lakes, often extended to include the upper Mississippi and Missouri valleys

mid-wicket *Cricket* 1 the fielding position on the on side, approximately midway between square leg and mid-on 2 a fielder in this position

midwinter a the middle or depth of the winter **b** *(as modifier)*: *a midwinter festival*

Mieres a city in N Spain, south of Oviedo: steel and chemical industries; iron and coal mines. Pop: 47 618 (2003 est)

Mies van der Rohe Ludwig 1886–1969, US architect, born in Germany. He directed the Bauhaus (1929–33) and developed a functional style, characterized by geometrical design. His works include the Seagram building, New York (1958)

mifepristone an antiprogestogenic steroid, used in the medical termination of pregnancy. Formula: $C_{29}H_{35}NO_2$

mignonette 1 a type of fine pillow lace 2 of a greyish-green colour; reseda

mignonette any of various mainly Mediterranean plants of the resedaceous genus *Reseda*, such as *R. odorata* (**garden mignonette**), that have spikes of small greenish-white flowers with prominent anthers

migraine a throbbing headache usually affecting only one side of the head and commonly accompanied by nausea and visual disturbances

mikado *Archaic* the Japanese emperor

mil 1 a unit of length equal to one thousandth of an inch 2 an obsolete pharmaceutical unit of volume equal to one millilitre 3 a unit of angular measure, used in gunnery, equal to one sixty-four-hundredth of a circumference

Milan a city in N Italy, in central Lombardy: Italy's second largest city and chief financial and industrial centre; a centre of the Renaissance under the Visconti and Sforza families. Pop: 1 256 211 (2001)

Milazzo a port in NE Sicily: founded in the 8th century BC; scene of a battle (1860), in which Garibaldi defeated the Bourbon forces. Pop: 32 108 (2001)

mild *Brit* draught beer, of darker colour than bitter and flavoured with fewer hops

mild steel any of a class of strong tough steels that contain a low quantity of carbon (0.1–0.25 per cent)

mile 1 a unit of length used in the U.K., the US, and certain other countries, equal to 1760 yards. 1 mile is equivalent to 1.609 34 kilometres 2 See **nautical mile** 3 any of various units of length used at different times and places, esp the Roman mile, equivalent to 1620 yards

mileage *or* **milage** 1 a distance expressed in miles 2 the total number of miles that a motor vehicle has travelled 3 allowance for travelling expenses, esp as a fixed rate per mile 4 the number of miles a motor vehicle will travel on one gallon of fuel

mileometer *or* **milometer** a device that records the number of miles that a bicycle or motor vehicle has travelled

milepost 1 *Horse racing* a marking post on a racecourse a mile before the finishing line 2 *Chiefly US and Canadian* a signpost that shows the distance in miles to or from a place

Miles Bernard, Baron Miles of Blackfriars. 1907–91, British actor and theatre manager. He founded the Mermaid Theatre in London, and was known as a character actor

milestone a stone pillar that shows the distance in miles to or from a place

Miletus an ancient city on the W coast of Asia Minor: a major Ionian centre of trade and learning in the ancient world

Milford Haven a port in SW Wales, in Pembrokeshire on Milford Haven (a large inlet of St George's Channel): major oil port. Pop: 12 830 (2001)

Milhaud Darius 1892–1974, French composer; member of Les Six. A notable exponent of polytonality, his large output includes operas, symphonies, ballets, string quartets, and songs

militarism 1 domination by the military in the formulation of policies, ideals, etc, esp on a political level **2** a policy of maintaining a strong military organization in aggressive preparedness for war

milk 1 a a whitish nutritious fluid produced and secreted by the mammary glands of mature female mammals and used for feeding their young until weaned **b** the milk of cows, goats, or other animals used by man as a food or in the production of butter, cheese, etc. **2** any similar fluid in plants, such as the juice of a coconut **3** any of various milklike pharmaceutical preparations, such as milk of magnesia

milk bar 1 a snack bar at which milk drinks and light refreshments are served **2** (in Australia) a shop selling, in addition to milk, basic provisions and other items

milk float Brit a small motor vehicle used to deliver milk to houses

milk of magnesia a suspension of magnesium hydroxide in water, used as an antacid and laxative

milk round Brit **1** a route along which a milkman regularly delivers milk **2 a** a regular series of visits, esp as made by recruitment officers from industry to universities **b** (as modifier): milk-round recruitment

milk tooth any of the first teeth to erupt; a deciduous tooth

Milky Way the **1** the diffuse band of light stretching across the night sky that consists of millions of faint stars, nebulae, etc, within our Galaxy **2** another name for the **Galaxy**

mill[1] 1 a factory, esp one which processes raw materials **2** any of various processing or manufacturing machines, esp one that grinds, presses, or rolls **3** a hard roller for impressing a design, esp in a textile-printing machine or in a machine for printing banknotes

mill[2] a US and Canadian monetary unit used in calculations, esp for property taxes, equal to one thousandth of a dollar

Mill 1 James 1773–1836, Scottish philosopher, historian, and economist. He expounded Bentham's utilitarian philosophy in Elements of Political Economy (1821) and Analysis of the Phenomena of the Human Mind (1829) and also wrote a History of British India (1817–18) **2** his son, **John Stuart** 1806–73, English philosopher and economist. He modified Bentham's utilitarian philosophy in Utilitarianism (1861) and in his treatise On Liberty (1859) he defended the rights and freedom of the individual. Other works include A System of Logic (1843) and Principles of Political Economy (1848)

Millais Sir John Everett 1829–96, English painter, who was a founder of the Pre-Raphaelite Brotherhood. His works include The Order of Release (1853) and The Blind Girl (1856)

Millay Edna St Vincent 1892–1950, US poet, noted esp for her sonnets; her collections include The Buck in the Snow (1928) and Fatal Interview (1931)

millennium the Christianity the period of a thousand years of Christ's awaited reign upon earth

millennium bug Computing any software problem arising from the change in date at the start of the 21st century

miller 1 another name for **milling machine 2** a person who operates a milling machine **3** any of various pale coloured or white moths, especially the medium-sized noctuid Apatele leporina **o4** an edible basidiomycetous fungus, Clitopilus prunulus, with a white funnel-shaped cap and pinkish spores, often forming rings in grass

Miller 1 Arthur 1915–2005, US dramatist. His plays include Death of a Salesman (1949), The Crucible (1953), A View from the Bridge (1955), and Mr Peters' Connections (1998) **2** (**Alton**) **Glenn** 1904–44, US composer, trombonist, and band leader. His popular compositions include "Moonlight Serenade". During World War II he was leader of the US Air Force band in Europe. He disappeared without trace on a flight between England and France **3** Henry (**Valentine**). 1891–1980, US novelist, author of Tropic of Cancer (1934) and Tropic of Capricorn (1938) **4** Hugh 1802–56, Scottish geologist and writer **5** Sir **Jonathan** (**Wolfe**). born 1934, British doctor, actor, and theatre director. His productions include Shakespeare, Ibsen, and Chekhov as well as numerous operas. He has also presented many television medical programmes

millesimal 1 denoting a thousandth **2** of, consisting of, or relating to a thousandth

millet 1 a cereal grass, Setaria italica, cultivated for grain and animal fodder **2 a** an East Indian annual grass, Panicum miliaceum, cultivated for grain and forage, having pale round shiny seeds **b** the seed of this plant **3** any of various similar or related grasses, such as pearl millet and Indian millet

Millet Jean François 1814–75, French painter of the Barbizon school, noted for his studies of peasants at work

milliard Brit (no longer in technical use) a thousand million

millibar a cgs unit of atmospheric pressure equal to 10^{-3} bar, 100 newtons per square metre or 0.7500617 millimetre of mercury

Milligan Spike, real name Terence Alan Milligan. 1918–2002, British radio, stage, and film comedian and author, born in India. He appeared in The Goon Show (with Peter Sellers and Harry Secombe; BBC Radio, 1952–60) and his films include Postman's Knock (1962), Adolf Hitler, My Part in his Downfall (1972), The Three Musketeers (1974), The Last Remake of Beau Geste (1977), and Yellowbeard (1982). He was awarded an honorary knighthood in 2000

milligram or **milligramme** one thousandth of a gram.

Millikan Robert Andrews 1868–1953, US physicist. He measured the charge of an electron (1910), verified Einstein's equation for the photoelectric effect (1916), and studied cosmic rays; Nobel prize for physics 1923

millilitre or US **milliliter** one thousandth of a litre.

millimetre or US **millimeter** one thousandth of a metre.

million 1 the cardinal number that is the product of 1000 multiplied by 1000 **2** a numeral, 1 000 000, 10^6,

M, etc, representing this number

millipede, millepede, *or* **milleped** any terrestrial herbivorous arthropod of the class *Diplopoda*, having a cylindrical body made up of many segments, each of which bears two pairs of walking legs

millisecond one thousandth of a second.

millpond a pool formed by damming a stream to provide water to turn a millwheel

millrace *or* **millrun 1** the current of water that turns a millwheel **2** the channel for this water

Mills 1 Hayley born 1946, British actress. Her films include *Pollyanna* (1960) and *The Parent Trap* (1961) **2** her father, Sir **John** 1908–2005, British actor. His films include *This Happy Breed* (1944), *Great Expectations* (1946), and *Ryan's Daughter* (1971)

millstone one of a pair of heavy flat disc-shaped stones that are rotated one against the other to grind grain

millwheel a wheel, esp a waterwheel, that drives a mill

Milne A(lan) A(lexander). 1882–1956, English writer, noted for his books and verse for children, including *When We Were Very Young* (1924) and *Winnie the Pooh* (1926)

Milošević Slobodan born 1941, Serbian politician, president of Serbia (1989–97) and of the Federal Republic of Yugoslavia (1997–2000). He supported ethnic cleansing in Bosnia-Herzegovina (1992–95) and Kosovo (1998–99). He was ousted in 2000 and brought to trial (2001) for war crimes

Miłosz Czesław 1911–2004, US poet and writer, born in Lithuania, writing in Polish; author of *The Captive Mind* (1953). Nobel prize for literature 1980

milt 1 the testis of a fish **2** the spermatozoa and seminal fluid produced by a fish **3** *Rare* the spleen of certain animals, esp fowls and pigs

Miltiades ?540–?489 BC, Athenian general, who defeated the Persians at Marathon (490)

Milton John 1608–74, English poet. His early works, notably *L'Allegro* and *Il Penseroso* (1632), the masque *Comus* (1634), and the elegy *Lycidas* (1637), show the influence of his Christian humanist education and his love of Italian Renaissance poetry. A staunch Parliamentarian and opponent of episcopacy, he published many pamphlets during the Civil War period, including *Areopagitica* (1644), which advocated freedom of the press. His greatest works were the epic poems *Paradise Lost* (1667; 1674), and *Paradise Regained* (1671) and the verse drama *Samson Agonistes* (1671)

Milton Keynes 1 a new town in central England, in Milton Keynes unitary authority, N Buckinghamshire: founded in 1967: electronics, clothing, machinery; seat of the Open University. Pop: 215 700 (2003 est) **2** a unitary authority in central England, in Buckinghamshire. Pop: 184 506 (2001). Area: 310 sq km (119 sq miles)

Milwaukee a port in SE Wisconsin, on Lake Michigan: the largest city in the state; established as a trading post in the 18th century; an important industrial centre. Pop: 586 941 (2003 est)

mime 1 the theatrical technique of expressing an idea or mood or portraying a character entirely by gesture and bodily movement without the use of words **2** a performer specializing in such a technique, esp a comic actor **3** a dramatic presentation using such a technique

4 in the classical theatre **a** a comic performance depending for effect largely on exaggerated gesture and physical action **b** an actor in such a performance

mimetic *Biology* of or exhibiting mimicry

mimicry *Zoology* the resemblance shown by one animal species, esp an insect, to another, which protects it from predators

mimosa 1 any tropical shrub or tree of the leguminous genus *Mimosa*, having ball-like clusters of yellow or pink flowers and compound leaves that are often sensitive to touch or light **2** any similar or related tree

minaret 1 a slender tower of a mosque having one or more balconies from which the muezzin calls the faithful to prayer **2** any structure resembling this

Minas Basin a bay in E Canada, in central Nova Scotia: the NE arm of the Bay of Fundy, with which it is linked by **Minas Channel**

Minas Gerais an inland state of E Brazil: situated on the high plateau of the Brazilian Highlands; large reserves of iron ore and manganese. Capital: Belo Horizonte. Pop: 18 343 517 (2002). Area: 587 172 sq km (226 707 sq miles)

Minch the a channel of the Atlantic divided into the **North Minch** between the mainland of Scotland and the Isle of Lewis, and the **Little Minch** between the Isle of Skye and Harris and North Uist

mind 1 the human faculty to which are ascribed thought, feeling, etc.; often regarded as an immaterial part of a person **2** intelligence or the intellect, esp as opposed to feelings or wishes **3** (in Cartesian philosophy) one of two basic modes of existence, the other being matter

Mindanao the second largest island of the Philippines, in the S part of the archipelago: mountainous and volcanic. Chief towns: Davao, Zamboanga. Pop: 13 626 338 (2000). Area: (including offshore islands) 94 631 sq km (36 537 sq miles)

Mindoro a mountainous island in the central Philippines, south of Luzon. Pop: 912 000 (1995 est). Area: 9736 sq km (3759 sq miles)

Mindszenty Joseph 1892–1975, Hungarian cardinal. He was sentenced to life imprisonment on a charge of treason (1949) but released during the 1956 Revolution

mine *Zoology* a groove or tunnel made by certain insects, esp in a leaf

miner *Zoology* **1** any of various insects or insect larvae that bore into and feed on plant tissues **2** *Austral* any of several honey-eaters of the genus *Manorina*, esp *M. melanocephala* (**noisy miner**), of scrub regions

mineral any of a class of naturally occurring solid inorganic substances with a characteristic crystalline form and a homogeneous chemical composition
  ▷www.psigate.ac.uk/newsite/
    earth-gateway.html
  ▷http://un2sg4.unige.ch/athena/mineral/
    mineral.html
  ▷www.minerals.net/glossary/glossary.htm
  ▷http://homepage.boku.ac.at/h9440283/
    eetymol.htm

mineralogy the branch of geology concerned with the study of minerals

mineral water water containing dissolved mineral

salts or gases, usually having medicinal properties

Minerva the Roman goddess of wisdom

Ming 1 the imperial dynasty of China from 1368 to 1644 **2** of or relating to Chinese porcelain produced during the Ming dynasty, characterized by the use of brilliant colours and a fine-quality body

Mingus Charles, known as *Charlie Mingus.* 1922–79, US jazz double bassist, composer, and band leader

miniature *Art* a very small painting, esp a portrait, showing fine detail on ivory or vellum

minibus a small bus able to carry approximately ten passengers

minicab *Brit* a small saloon car used as a taxi

minicomputer a small comparatively cheap digital computer

minidisc a small recordable compact disc

minim 1 a unit of fluid measure equal to one sixtieth of a drachm. It is approximately equal to one drop. **2** *Music* a note having the time value of half a semibreve

minimalism a type of music based on simple elements and avoiding elaboration or embellishment

▷www.nortexinfo.net/McDaniel/
minimalist_music.htm

▷www.sbgmusic.com/html/teacher/reference/
styles/minimal.html

minimum *Maths* a value of a function that is less than any neighbouring value

minister 1 (esp in Presbyterian and some Nonconformist Churches) a member of the clergy **2** a person appointed to head a government department **3** any diplomatic agent accredited to a foreign government or head of state

minister of state 1 (in the British Parliament) a minister, usually below cabinet rank, appointed to assist a senior minister with heavy responsibilities **2** any government minister

Minister of the Crown *Brit* any Government minister of cabinet rank

ministry 1 a the profession or duties of a minister of religion **b** the performance of these duties **2 a** a government department headed by a minister **b** the buildings of such a department

mink 1 any of several semiaquatic musteline mammals of the genus *Mustela,* of Europe, Asia, and North America, having slightly webbed feet **2** the highly valued fur of these animals, esp that of the American mink (*M. vison*)

Minkowski Hermann 1864–1909, German mathematician, born in Russia. His concept of a four-dimensional space-time continuum (1907) proved crucial for the general theory of relativity developed by Einstein

Minna a city in W central Nigeria, capital of Niger state. Pop: 278 000 (2005 est)

Minneapolis a city in SE Minnesota, on the Mississippi River adjacent to St Paul: the largest city in the state; important centre for the grain trade. Pop: 373 188 (2003 est)

minneola a juicy citrus fruit that is a cross between a tangerine and a grapefruit

Minnesota 1 a state of the N central US: chief US producer of iron ore. Capital: St Paul. Pop: 5 059 375 (2003 est). Area: 218 600 sq km (84 402 sq miles) **2** a river in S

Minnesota, flowing southeast and northeast to the Mississippi River near St Paul. Length: 534 km (332 miles)

minnow 1 a small slender European freshwater cyprinid fish, *Phoxinus phoxinus* **2** any other small cyprinid **3** *Angling* a spinning lure imitating a minnow

Minoan 1 denoting the Bronze Age culture of Crete from about 3000 BC to about 1100 BC **2** of or relating to the linear writing systems used in Crete and later in mainland Greece **3** a Cretan belonging to the Minoan culture

▷www.historywiz.com/minoans-mm.htm

▷www.dragonridge.com/greece/minoam.htm

Minogue Kylie born 1968, Australian singer and actress: appeared in the television series *Neighbours* from 1986; records include "I Should Be So Lucky" (1988), *Kylie Minogue* (1994), and *Fever* (2001)

minor 1 *Law* below the age of legal majority **2** *Music* **a** (of a scale) having a semitone between the second and third and fifth and sixth degrees (**natural minor**) **b** (of a key) based on the minor scale **c** denoting a specified key based on the minor scale **d** (of an interval) reduced by a semitone from the major **e** (of a chord, esp a triad) having a minor third above the root **f** (esp in jazz) of or relating to a chord built upon a minor triad and containing a minor seventh **3** *Logic* (of a term or premise) having less generality or scope than another term or proposition **4** *US, education* of or relating to an additional secondary subject taken by a student **5** *Bell-ringing* of, relating to, or denoting a set of changes rung on six bells **6** a person below the age of legal majority **7** *US and Canadian, education* a subsidiary subject in which a college or university student needs fewer credits than in his or her major **8** *Music* a minor key, chord, mode, or scale **9** *Logic* a minor term or premise **10** *Maths* **a** a determinant associated with a particular element of a given determinant and formed by removing the row and column containing that element **b** the number equal to this reduced determinant

Minorca 1 an island in the W Mediterranean, northeast of Majorca: the second largest of the Balearic Islands. Chief town: Mahón. Pop: 78 796 (2002 est). Area: 702 sq km (271 sq miles) **2** a breed of light domestic fowl with glossy white, black, or blue plumage

Minotaur *Greek myth* a monster with the head of a bull and the body of a man. It was kept in the Labyrinth in Crete, feeding on human flesh, until destroyed by Theseus

Minsk the capital of Belarus: an industrial city and educational and cultural centre, with a university (1921). Pop: 1 709 000 (2005 est)

minster *Brit* any of certain cathedrals and large churches, usually originally connected to a monastery

minstrel 1 *History* a medieval wandering musician who performed songs or recited poetry with instrumental accompaniment **2** a performer in a minstrel show

minstrel show a theatrical entertainment consisting of songs, dances, comic turns, etc, performed by a troupe of actors wearing black face make-up

mint¹ 1 a place where money is coined by governmental authority **2** (of coins, postage stamps, etc) in perfect condition as issued

mint² any N temperate plant of the genus *Mentha*, having aromatic leaves and spikes of small typically mauve flowers: family *Lamiaceae* (labiates). The leaves of some species are used for seasoning and flavouring

minuet 1 a stately court dance of the 17th and 18th centuries in triple time **2** a piece of music composed for or in the rhythm of this dance, sometimes as a movement in a suite, sonata, or symphony

minus 1 a indicating or involving subtraction **b** having a value or designating a quantity less than zero **2** on the negative part of a scale or coordinate axis **3** *Education* slightly below the standard of a particular grade **4** *Botany* designating the strain of a fungus that can only undergo sexual reproduction with a plus strain **5** denoting a negative electric charge **6** short for **minus sign 7** a negative quantity

minus sign the symbol –, indicating subtraction or a negative quantity

minute 1 a period of time equal to 60 seconds; one sixtieth of an hour **2** a unit of angular measure equal to one sixtieth of a degree

Miocene of, denoting, or formed in the fourth epoch of the Tertiary period, between the Oligocene and Pliocene epochs, which lasted for 19 million years

Mirabeau Comte de, title of *Honoré-Gabriel Riqueti*. 1749–91, French Revolutionary politician

miracle 1 an event that is contrary to the established laws of nature and attributed to a supernatural cause **2** short for **miracle play**

miracle play a medieval play based on a biblical story or the life of a saint

Miraflores Lake an artificial lake in Panama, in the S Canal Zone of the Panama Canal

mirage an image of a distant object or sheet of water, often inverted or distorted, caused by atmospheric refraction by hot air

mire a boggy or marshy area

Miriam *Old Testament* the sister of Moses and Aaron. (Numbers 12:1–15)

misadventure *Law* accidental death not due to crime or negligence

miscarriage 1 *Med* spontaneous expulsion of a fetus from the womb, esp prior to the 20th week of pregnancy **2** *Brit* the failure of freight to reach its destination

miscegenation interbreeding of races, esp where differences of pigmentation are involved

miscellany a miscellaneous collection of essays, poems, etc, by different authors in one volume

miscreant 1 *Archaic* an unbeliever or heretic **2** *Archaic* unbelieving or heretical

misdemeanour *or US* **misdemeanor** *Criminal law* (formerly) an offence generally less heinous than a felony and which until 1967 involved a different form of trial

Miseno a cape in SW Italy, on the N shore of the Bay of Naples: remains of the town of **Misenum**, a naval base constructed by Agrippa in 31 BC

miser *Civil engineering* a large hand-operated auger used for loose soils

misericord *or* **misericorde 1** a ledge projecting from the underside of the hinged seat of a choir stall in a church, on which the occupant can support himself while standing **2** *Christianity* **a** a relaxation of certain monastic rules for infirm or aged monks or nuns **b** a monastery where such relaxations can be enjoyed

Mishima Yukio 1925–70, Japanese novelist and short-story writer, whose works reflect a preoccupation with homosexuality and death. He committed harakiri in protest at the decline of traditional Japanese values

Miskolc a city in NE Hungary: the second most important industrial centre in Hungary; iron and steel industries. Pop: 180 282 (2003 est)

misprision a a failure to inform the proper authorities of the commission of an act of treason **b** the deliberate concealment of the commission of a felony

misrule inefficient or inhumane government

missal *RC Church* a book containing the prayers, rites, etc, of the Masses for a complete year

missing link a hypothetical extinct animal or animal group, formerly thought to be intermediate between the anthropoid apes and man

mission 1 a group of persons representing or working for a particular country, business, etc, in a foreign country **2 a** a special embassy sent to a foreign country for a specific purpose **b** *US* a permanent legation **3 a** a group of people sent by a religious body, esp a Christian church, to a foreign country to do religious and social work **b** the campaign undertaken by such a group **4 a** the work or calling of a missionary **b** a building or group of buildings in which missionary work is performed **c** the area assigned to a particular missionary **5** the dispatch of aircraft or spacecraft to achieve a particular task **6** a church or chapel that has no incumbent of its own **7** a charitable centre that offers shelter, aid, or advice to the destitute or underprivileged

missionary a member of a religious mission

Missionary Ridge a ridge in NW Georgia and SE Tennessee: site of a battle (1863) during the Civil War: Northern victory leading to the campaign in Georgia

Mississauga a town in SE Ontario: a SW suburb of Toronto. Pop: 612 925 (2001)

Mississippi 1 a state of the southeastern US, on the Gulf of Mexico: consists of a largely forested undulating plain, with swampy regions in the northwest and on the coast, the Mississippi River forming the W border; cotton, rice, and oil. Capital: Jackson. Pop: 2 881 281 (2003 est). Area: 122 496 sq km (47 296 sq miles) **2** a river in the central US, rising in NW Minnesota and flowing generally south to the Gulf of Mexico through several mouths, known as the Passes: the second longest river in North America (after its tributary, the Missouri), with the third largest drainage basin in the world (after the Amazon and the Congo). Length: 3780 km (2348 miles)

Mississippian 1 of or relating to the state of Mississippi or the Mississippi River **2** (in North America) of, denoting, or formed in the lower of two subdivisions of the Carboniferous period (see also **Pennsylvanian** (sense 2)), which lasted for 30 million years **3 the** the Mississippian period or rock system equivalent to the lower Carboniferous of Europe

Missolonghi *or* **Mesolonghi** a town in W Greece, near the Gulf of Patras: famous for its defence against the Turks in 1822–23 and 1825–26 and for its association with Lord Byron, who died here in 1824. Pop: 11 275 (latest est)

Missouri 1 a state of the central US: consists of rolling prairies in the north, the Ozark Mountains in the south, and part of the Mississippi flood plain in the southeast, with the Mississippi forming the E border; chief US producer of lead and barytes. Capital: Jefferson City. Pop: 5 704 484 (2003 est). Area: 178 699 sq km (68 995 sq miles) 2 a river in the W and central US, rising in SW Montana: flows north, east, and southeast to join the Mississippi above St Louis; the longest river in North America; chief tributary of the Mississippi. Length: 3970 km (2466 miles)

mist 1 a thin fog resulting from condensation in the air near the earth's surface 2 *Meteorol* such an atmospheric condition with a horizontal visibility of 1–2 kilometres 3 *Chem* a colloidal suspension of a liquid in a gas

Mistassini *Lake* a lake in E Canada, in N Quebec: the largest lake in the province; drains through the Rupert River into James Bay. Area: 2175 sq km (840 sq miles). Length: about 160 km (100 miles)

mister *Brit* the form of address for a surgeon

mistle thrush *or* **missel thrush** a large European thrush, *Turdus viscivorus*, with a brown back and spotted breast, noted for feeding on mistletoe berries

mistletoe 1 a Eurasian evergreen shrub, *Viscum album*, with leathery leaves, yellowish flowers, and waxy white berries: grows as a partial parasite on various trees: used as a Christmas decoration: family *Viscaceae* 2 any of several similar and related American plants in the families *Loranthaceae* or *Viscaceae*, esp *Phoradendron flavescens* 3 **mistletoe cactus** an epiphytic cactus, *Rhipsalis cassytha*, that grows in tropical America

mistral 1 a strong cold dry wind that blows through the Rhône valley and S France to the Mediterranean coast, mainly in the winter 2 the class of board used in international windsurfing competitions, weighing 15kg and measuring 372cm × 64cm

Mistral 1 Frédéric 1830–1914, French Provençal poet, who led a movement to revive Provençal language and literature: shared the Nobel prize for literature 1904 2 Gabriela , pen name of *Lucila Godoy de Alcayaga*. 1889–1957, Chilean poet, educationalist, and diplomatist. Her poetry includes the collection *Desolación* (1922): Nobel prize for literature 1945

mistrial 1 a trial made void because of some error, such as a defect in procedure 2 (in the US) an inconclusive trial, as when a jury cannot agree on a verdict

Mitchell 1 Joni, original name *Roberta Joan Anderson*. born 1943, Canadian folk-rock singer and songwriter. Her albums include *Blue* (1971), *Court and Spark* (1974), *Mingus* (1979), *Turbulent Indigo* (1994), and *Travelogue* (2002) 2 Margaret 1900–49, US novelist; author of *Gone with the Wind* (1936) 3 Reginald Joseph 1895–1937, British aeronautical engineer; designer of the Spitfire fighter 4 Sir Thomas Livingstone, known as *Major Mitchell*. 1792–1855, Australian explorer born in Scotland

Mitchum Robert 1917–97, US film actor. His many films include *Night of the Hunter* (1955) and *Farewell my Lovely* (1975)

mite¹ any of numerous small free-living or parasitic arachnids of the order *Acarina* (or *Acari*) that can occur in terrestrial or aquatic habitats

mite² a former Flemish coin of small value

Mithridates VI *or* **Mithradates VI** called *the Great*. ?132–63 BC, king of Pontus (?120–63). He waged three wars against Rome (88–84; 83–81; 74–64) and was finally defeated by Pompey: committed suicide

mitochondrion a small spherical or rodlike body, bounded by a double membrane, in the cytoplasm of most cells: contains enzymes responsible for energy production

mitosis a method of cell division, in which the nucleus divides into daughter nuclei, each containing the same number of chromosomes as the parent nucleus

mitre *or* US **miter** *Christianity* the liturgical headdress of a bishop or abbot, in most western churches consisting of a tall pointed cleft cap with two bands hanging down at the back

mitt *Baseball* a large round thickly padded leather mitten worn by the catcher

Mittelland Canal a canal in Germany, linking the Rivers Rhine and Elbe. Length: 325 km (202 miles)

Mitterrand François Maurice Marie 1916–96, French statesman; first secretary of the socialist party (1971–95); president (1981–95)

mixed economy an economy in which some industries are privately owned and others are publicly owned or nationalized

mixed metaphor a combination of incongruous metaphors, as *when the Nazi jackboots sing their swan song*

mixer *Electronics* a device in which two or more input signals are combined to give a single output signal

mixture 1 *Chem* a substance consisting of two or more substances mixed together without any chemical bonding between them 2 *Pharmacol* a liquid medicine in which an insoluble compound is suspended in the liquid 3 *Music* an organ stop that controls several ranks of pipes sounding the upper notes in a harmonic series 4 the mixture of petrol vapour and air in an internal-combustion engine

Mizoguchi Kenji 1898–1956, Japanese film director. His films include *A Paper Doll's Whisper of Spring* (1925), *Woman of Osaka* (1940), and *Ugetsu Monogatari* (1952)

Mizoram a state (since 1986) in NE India, created in 1972 from the former Mizo Hills District of Assam. Capital: Aijal. Pop: 891 058 (2001). Area: about 21 081 sq km (8140 sq miles)

mizzenmast *or* **mizenmast** *Nautical* 1 (on a yawl, ketch, or dandy) the after mast 2 (on a vessel with three or more masts) the third mast from the bow

Mladic Ratko born 1943, Bosnian military figure, commander of the Bosnian Serb forces during the civil war of 1992–95; indicted by the U.N. for war crimes, including the massacre of 6000 Bosnian Muslims at Srebrenica (1995)

MMR a combined vaccine against measles, mumps, and rubella, given to young children

moa any large flightless bird of the recently extinct order *Dinornithiformes* of New Zealand

Moab *Old Testament* an ancient kingdom east of the Dead Sea, in what is now the SW part of Jordan: flourished mainly from the 9th to the 6th centuries BC

mobile *Art* a a sculpture suspended in midair with delicately balanced parts that are set in motion by air currents b (*as modifier*): *mobile sculpture*

Mobile a port in SW Alabama, on **Mobile Bay** (an inlet of the Gulf of Mexico): the state's only port and its first permanent settlement, made by French colonists in 1711. Pop: 193 464 (2003 est)

mobile home living quarters mounted on wheels and capable of being towed by a motor vehicle

Mobutu Sese Seko , original name *Joseph*. 1930–97, Zaïrese statesman; president of Zaïre (now the Democratic Republic of Congo) (1970–97); accused of corruption and overthrown by rebels in 1997; died in exile

mocha a a dark brown colour b (*as adjective*): *mocha shoes*

Mocha *or* **Mokha** a port in Yemen, on the Red Sea; in the former North Yemen until 1990: formerly important for the export of Arabian coffee. Pop: about 2000 (1990 est)

mock-heroic 1 (of a literary work, esp a poem) imitating the style of heroic poetry in order to satirize an unheroic subject, as in Pope's *The Rape of the Lock* 2 burlesque imitation of the heroic style or of a single work in this style

mockingbird 1 any American songbird of the family *Mimidae*, having a long tail and grey plumage: noted for their ability to mimic the song of other birds *Austral* 2 a small scrb bird, *Atrichornis rufescens*, noted for its mimicry

mock orange 1 any shrub of the genus *Philadelphus*, esp *P. coronarius*, with white fragrant flowers that resemble those of the orange: family *Philadelphaceae* 2 any other shrub or tree that resembles the orange tree

mock-up a working full-scale model of a machine, apparatus, etc, for testing, research, etc.

mod an annual Highland Gaelic meeting with musical and literary competitions

modal 1 *Philosophy, logic* a qualifying or expressing a qualification of the truth of some statement, for example, as necessary or contingent b relating to analogous qualifications such as that of rules as obligatory or permissive 2 *Metaphysics* of or relating to the form of a thing as opposed to its attributes, substance, etc.

mode 1 *Music* a any of the various scales of notes within one octave, esp any of the twelve natural diatonic scales taken in ascending order used in plainsong, folk song, and art music until 1600 b (in the music of classical Greece) any of the descending diatonic scales from which the liturgical modes evolved c either of the two main scale systems in music since 1600 2 *Philosophy* a complex combination of ideas the realization of which is not determined by the component ideas 3 the quantitative mineral composition of an igneous rock 4 *Physics* one of the possible configurations of a travelling or stationary wave 5 *Physics* one of the fundamental vibrations

model 1 a a representation, usually on a smaller scale, of a device, structure, etc. b (*as modifier*): *a model train* 2 a person who poses for a sculptor, painter, or photographer 3 a preparatory sculpture in clay, wax, etc, from which the finished work is copied 4 a design or style, esp one of a series of designs of a particular product 5 a simplified representation or description of a system or complex entity, esp one designed to facilitate calculations and predictions 6 *Logic* a an interpretation of a formal system under which the theorems derivable in

that system are mapped onto truths b a theory in which a given sentence is true
▷www.modelmaking.co.uk
▷www.ukmodelrailways.freeserve.co.uk

modem *Computing* a device for connecting two computers by a telephone line, consisting of a modulator that converts computer signals into audio signals and a corresponding demodulator

Modena 1 a city in N Italy, in Emilia-Romagna: ruled by the Este family (18th–19th century); university (1678). Pop: 175 502 (2001 2 a popular variety of domestic fancy pigeon originating in Modena

moderator 1 *Presbyterian Church* a minister appointed to preside over a Church court, synod, or general assembly 2 a presiding officer at a public or legislative assembly 3 a material, such as heavy water or graphite, used for slowing down neutrons in the cores of nuclear reactors so that they have more chance of inducing nuclear fission 4 an examiner at Oxford or Cambridge Universities in first public examinations 5 (in Britain and New Zealand) one who is responsible for consistency of standards in the grading of some educational assessments 6 a person who moniters the conversations in an on-line chatroom for bad language, inappropriate content, etc

modern 1 of, relating to, or characteristic of contemporary styles or schools of art, literature, music, etc, esp those of an experimental kind 2 belonging or relating to the period in history from the end of the Middle Ages to the present

Modern English the English language since about 1450, esp any of the standard forms developed from the S East Midland dialect of Middle English

modernism 1 a 20th-century divergence in the arts from previous traditions, esp in architecture 2 *RC Church* the movement at the end of the 19th and beginning of the 20th centuries that sought to adapt doctrine to the supposed requirements of modern thought
▷www.artsmia.org/modernism
▷www.bc.edu/bc_org/avp/cas/fnart/HP/20th_mod.html

modern pentathlon an athletic contest consisting of five different events: horse riding with jumps, fencing with electric épée, freestyle swimming, pistol shooting, and cross-country running

Modigliani Amedeo 1884–1920, Italian painter and sculptor, noted esp for the elongated forms of his portraits

module 1 a self-contained unit or item, such as an assembly of electronic components and associated wiring or a segment of computer software, which itself performs a defined task and can be linked with other such units to form a larger system 2 a standard unit of measure, esp one used to coordinate the dimensions of buildings and components; in classical architecture, half the diameter of a column at the base of the shaft 3 *Education* a short course of study, esp of a vocational or technical subject, that together with other such completed courses can count towards a particular qualification

modulus 1 *Physics* a coefficient expressing a specified property of a specified substance 2 *Maths* the number

465

by which a logarithm to one base is multiplied to give the corresponding logarithm to another base **3** *Maths* an integer that can be divided exactly into the difference between two other integers

Moers a city in W Germany, in North Rhine-Westphalia: coalmining centre. Pop: 107 903 (2003 est)

Mogadishu *or* **Mogadiscio** the capital and chief port of Somalia, on the Indian Ocean: founded by Arabs around the 10th century; taken by the Sultan of Zanzibar in 1871 and sold to Italy in 1905. Pop: 1 257 000 (2005 est)

Mogilev *or* **Mohilev** an industrial city in E Belarus on the Dnieper River: passed to Russia in 1772 after Polish rule. Pop: 353 000 (2005 est)

mogul¹ a type of steam locomotive with a wheel arrangement of two leading wheels, six driving wheels, and no trailing wheels

mogul² a mound of hard snow on a ski slope

Mogul 1 a member of the Muslim dynasty of Indian emperors established by Baber in 1526 **2** a Muslim Indian, Mongol, or Mongolian
  ▷www.wikipedia.org/wiki/Mogul_Empire
  ▷www.nationmaster.com/encyclopedia/
     Mogul-Empire

mohair 1 the long soft silky hair that makes up the outer coat of the Angora goat **2 a** a fabric made from the yarn of this hair and cotton or wool **b** (*as modifier*): *a mohair suit*

Mohammed *or* **Muhammad** ?570–632 AD, the prophet believed by Muslims to be the channel for the final unfolding of God's revelation to mankind: popularly regarded as the founder of Islam. He began to teach in Mecca in 610 but persecution forced him to flee with his followers to Medina in 622. After several battles, he conquered Mecca (630), establishing the principles of Islam (embodied in the Koran) over all Arabia

Mohammed II ?1430–81, Ottoman sultan of Turkey (1451–81). He captured Constantinople (1453) and conquered large areas of the Balkans

Mohawk¹ 1 a member of a North American Indian people formerly living along the Mohawk River; one of the Iroquois peoples **2** the language of this people, belonging to the Iroquoian family

Mohawk² a river in E central New York State, flowing south and east to the Hudson River at Cohoes: the largest tributary of the Hudson. Length: 238 km (148 miles)

Mohenjo-Daro an excavated city in SE Pakistan, southwest of Sukkur near the River Indus: flourished during the third millennium BC

Moholy-Nagy Laszlo *or* Ladislaus 1895–1946, US painter and teacher, born in Hungary. He worked at the Bauhaus (1923–29)

moire a fabric, usually silk, having a watered effect

Mojave Desert *or* **Mohave Desert** a desert in S California, south of the Sierra Nevada: part of the Great Basin. Area: 38 850 sq km (15 000 sq miles)

mojo *US, slang* **1 a** an amulet, charm, or magic spell **b** (*as modifier*): *ancient mojo spells* **2** the art of casting magic spells

moke 1 *Brit* a slang name for **donkey 2** *Austral, slang* an inferior type of horse

Mokpo a port in SW South Korea, on the Yellow Sea. Pop: 253 000 (2005 est)

molar¹ 1 any of the 12 broad-faced grinding teeth in man **2** a corresponding tooth in other mammals

molar² 1 (of a physical quantity) per unit amount of substance **2** (not recommended in technical usage) (of a solution) containing one mole of solute per litre of solution

Moldavia 1 another name for **Moldova 2** a former principality of E Europe, consisting of the basins of the Rivers Prut and Dniester: the E part (Bessarabia) became Moldova; the W part remains a province of Romania

Moldova a republic in SE Europe: comprising the E part of the former principality of Moldavia, the E part of which (Bessarabia) was ceded to the Soviet Union in 1940 and formed the Moldavian Soviet Socialist Republic until it gained independence in 1991; an agricultural region with many vineyards. Official language: Romanian. Religion: nonreligious and Christian. Currency: leu. Capital: Kishinev. Pop: 4 263 000 (2004 est). Area: 33 670 sq km (13 000 sq miles)

mole¹ 1 any small burrowing mammal, of the family *Talpidae*, of Europe, Asia, and North and Central America: order *Insectivora* (insectivores). They have velvety, typically dark fur and forearms specialized for digging **2 golden mole** any small African burrowing molelike mammal of the family *Chrysochloridae*, having copper-coloured fur: order *Insectivora* (insectivores) **3** *Informal* a spy who has infiltrated an organization and, often over a long period, become a trusted member of it

mole² the basic SI unit of amount of substance; the amount that contains as many elementary entities as there are atoms in 0.012 kilogram of carbon-12. The entity must be specified and may be an atom, a molecule, an ion, a radical, an electron, a photon, etc.

mole³ 1 a breakwater **2** a harbour protected by a breakwater **3** a large tunnel excavator for use in soft rock

mole⁴ *Pathol* a fleshy growth in the uterus formed by the degeneration of fetal tissues

molecular 1 of or relating to molecules **2** *Logic* (of a sentence, formula, etc) capable of analysis into atomic formulae of the appropriate kind

molecular formula a chemical formula indicating the numbers and types of atoms in a molecule

molecule the simplest unit of a chemical compound that can exist, consisting of two or more atoms held together by chemical bonds

molehill the small mound of earth thrown up by a burrowing mole

Molise a region of S central Italy, the second smallest of the regions: separated from **Abruzzi e Molise** in 1965. Capital: Campobasso. Pop: 321 047 (2003 est). Area: 4438 sq km (1731 sq miles)

mollusc *or US* **mollusk** any invertebrate of the phylum *Mollusca*, having a soft unsegmented body and often a shell, secreted by a fold of skin (the mantle). The group includes the gastropods (snails, slugs, etc), bivalves (clams, mussels, etc), and cephalopods (cuttlefish, octopuses, etc)

Moloch *or* **Molech** *Old Testament* a Semitic deity to whom parents sacrificed their children

Molokai an island in central Hawaii. Pop: 7404 (2000). Area: 676 sq km (261 sq miles)

Molopo a seasonal river rising in N South Africa and flowing west and southwest to the Orange river. Length: about 1000 km (600 miles)

Molotov Vyacheslav Mikhailovich , original surname *Skriabin*. 1890–1986, Soviet statesman. As commissar and later minister for foreign affairs (1939–49; 1953–56) he negotiated the nonaggression pact with Nazi Germany and attended the founding conference of the United Nations and the Potsdam conference (1945)

Moltke 1 Count **Helmuth Johannes Ludwig von** 1848–1916, German general; chief of the German general staff (1906–14) 2 his uncle Count **Helmuth Karl Bernhard von** 1800–91, German field marshal; chief of the Prussian general staff (1858–88)

molybdenum a very hard ductile silvery-white metallic element occurring principally in molybdenite: used mainly in alloys, esp to harden and strengthen steels. Symbol: Mo; atomic no.: 42; atomic wt.: 95.94; valency: 2–6; relative density: 10.22; melting pt.: 2623°C; boiling pt.: 4639°C

Mombasa a port in S Kenya, on a coral island in a bay of the Indian Ocean: the chief port for Kenya, Uganda, and NE Tanzania; became British in 1887, capital of the East African Protectorate until 1907. Pop: 828 000 (2005 est)

moment *Physics* a a tendency to produce motion, esp rotation about a point or axis b the product of a physical quantity, such as force or mass, and its distance from a fixed reference point

moment of truth the point in a bullfight when the matador is about to kill the bull

momentum 1 *Physics* the product of a body's mass and its velocity. 2 the impetus of a body resulting from its motion

Mommsen Theodor 1817–1903, German historian, noted esp for *The History of Rome* (1854–56): Nobel prize for literature 1902

Monaco a principality in SW Europe, on the Mediterranean and forming an enclave in SE France: the second smallest sovereign state in the world (after the Vatican); consists of **Monaco-Ville** (the capital) on a rocky headland, **La Condamine** (a business area and port), **Monte Carlo** (the resort centre), and **Fontvieille**, a light industrial area. Language: French. Religion: Roman Catholic. Currency: euro. Pop: 34 000 (2003 est). Area: 189 hectares (476 acres)

monad 1 *Philosophy* a any fundamental singular metaphysical entity, esp if autonomous b (in the metaphysics of Leibnitz) a simple indestructible nonspatial element regarded as the unit of which reality consists c (in the pantheistic philosophy of Giordano Bruno) a fundamental metaphysical unit that is spatially extended and psychically aware 2 a single-celled organism, esp a flagellate protozoan 3 an atom, ion, or radical with a valency of one

Monaghan 1 a county of NE Republic of Ireland, in Ulster province: many small lakes. County town: Monaghan. Pop: 52 593 (2002). Area: 1292 sq km (499 sq miles) 2 a town in NE Republic of Ireland, county town

of Co. Monaghan. Pop: 5717 (2002)

monandrous 1 having or preferring only one male sexual partner over a period of time 2 (of plants) having flowers with only one stamen 3 (of flowers) having only one stamen

Mona Passage a strait between Puerto Rico and the Dominican Republic, linking the Atlantic with the Caribbean

monarch 1 a sovereign head of state, esp a king, queen, or emperor, who rules usually by hereditary right 2 a large migratory butterfly, *Danaus plexippus*, that has orange-and-black wings and feeds on the milkweed plant: family *Danaidae*

monarchy 1 a form of government in which supreme authority is vested in a single and usually hereditary figure, such as a king, and whose powers can vary from those of an absolute despot to those of a figurehead 2 a country reigned over by a king, prince, or other monarch

monastery the residence of a religious community, esp of monks, living in seclusion from secular society and bound by religious vows

monatomic *or* **monoatomic** *Chem* 1 (of an element) having or consisting of single atoms 2 (of a compound or molecule) having only one atom or group that can be replaced in a chemical reaction 3 a less common word for **monovalent**

Monck George 1st Duke of Albemarle. 1608–70, English general. In the Civil War he was a Royalist until captured (1644) and persuaded to support the Commonwealth. After Cromwell's death he was instrumental in the restoration of Charles II (1660)

Moncton a city in E Canada, in SE New Brunswick. Pop: 90 359 (2001)

Mondrian Piet 1872–1944, Dutch painter, noted esp as an exponent of the abstract art movement De Stijl

Monet Claude 1840–1926, French landscape painter; the leading exponent of impressionism. His interest in the effect of light on colour led him to paint series of pictures of the same subject at different times of day. These include *Haystacks* (1889–93), *Rouen Cathedral* (1892–94), the *Thames* (1899–1904), and *Water Lilies* (1899–1906)

monetarism 1 the theory that inflation is caused by an excess quantity of money in an economy 2 an economic policy based on this theory and on a belief in the efficiency of free market forces, that gives priority to achieving price stability by monetary control, balanced budgets, etc, and maintains that unemployment results from excessive real wage rates and cannot be controlled by Keynesian demand management

▷www.econlib.org/library/Enc/ Monetarism.html

money 1 a medium of exchange that functions as legal tender 2 the official currency, in the form of banknotes, coins, etc, issued by a government or other authority

Mongolia 1 a republic in E central Asia: made a Chinese province in 1691; became autonomous in 1911 and a republic in 1924; multiparty democracy introduced in 1990. It consists chiefly of a high plateau, with the Gobi Desert in the south, a large lake district in the northwest, and the Altai and Khangai Mountains in the west. Official language: Khalkha. Religion: nonreligious majority. Currency: tugrik. Capital: Ulan Bator. Pop: 2 630 000 (2004 est). Area: 1 565 000 sq km (604 095 sq miles) **2** a vast region of central Asia, inhabited chiefly by Mongols: now divided into the republic of Mongolia, the Inner Mongolian Autonomous Region of China, and the Tuva Republic of S Russia; at its height during the 13th century under Genghis Khan

Mongoloid denoting, relating to, or belonging to one of the major racial groups of mankind, characterized by yellowish complexion, straight black hair, slanting eyes, short nose, and scanty facial hair, including most of the peoples of Asia, the Inuit, and the North American Indians

mongoose any small predatory viverrine mammal of the genus *Herpestes* and related genera, occurring in Africa and from S Europe to SE Asia, typically having a long tail and brindled coat

mongrel **1** a plant or animal, esp a dog, of mixed or unknown breeding; a crossbreed or hybrid **2** *Derogatory* a person of mixed race

monism **1** *Philosophy* the doctrine that the person consists of only a single substance, or that there is no crucial difference between mental and physical events or properties **2** *Philosophy* the doctrine that reality consists of an unchanging whole in which change is mere illusion **3** the epistemological theory that the object and datum of consciousness are identical

monition **1** a warning or caution; admonition **2** *Christianity* a formal notice from a bishop or ecclesiastical court requiring a person to refrain from committing a specific offence

monitor **1** *Education* **a** a senior pupil with various supervisory duties **b** a pupil assisting a teacher in classroom organization, etc. **2** a television screen used to display certain kinds of information in a television studio, airport, etc. **3** the unit in a desk computer that contains the screen **4** **a** a loudspeaker used in a recording studio control room to determine quality or balance **b** a loudspeaker used on stage to enable musicians to hear themselves **5** a device for controlling the direction of a water jet in fire fighting **6** any large predatory lizard of the genus *Varanus* and family *Varanidae*, inhabiting warm regions of Africa, Asia, and Australia

monk **1** a male member of a religious community bound by vows of poverty, chastity, and obedience **2** a fancy pigeon having a bald pate and often large feathered feet

Monk Thelonious (Sphere). 1920–82, US jazz pianist and composer

monkey **1** any of numerous long-tailed primates excluding the prosimians (lemurs, tarsiers, etc): comprise the families *Cercopithecidae, Cebidae,* and *Callithricidae* (marmosets) **2** any primate except man **3** the head of a pile-driver (**monkey engine**) or of some similar mechanical device **4** *Nautical* denoting a small light structure or piece of equipment contrived to suit an immediate purpose **5** *Slang* (esp in bookmaking) £500 **6** *US and Canadian, slang* $500 **7** *Austral, slang, archaic* a sheep

monkey puzzle a South American coniferous tree,

Araucaria araucana, having branches shaped like a candelabrum and stiff sharp leaves: family *Araucariaceae*

monkey wrench a wrench with adjustable jaws

monkshood any of several poisonous N temperate plants of the ranunculaceous genus *Aconitum*, esp *A. napellus*, that have hooded blue-purple flowers

Monmouth¹ James Scott, Duke of Monmouth. 1649–85, the illegitimate son of Charles II of England, he led a rebellion against James II in support of his own claim to the Crown; captured and beheaded

Monmouth² a market town in E Wales, in Monmouthshire: Norman castle, where Henry V was born in 1387. Pop: 8547 (2001)

Monmouthshire a county of E Wales: administratively part of England for three centuries (until 1830); mainly absorbed into the county of Gwent in 1974; reinstated with reduced boundaries in 1996: chiefly agricultural, with the Black Mountains in the N. Administrative centre: Cwmbran. Pop: 86 200 (2003 est). Area: 851 sq km (329 sq miles)

Monnet Jean 1888–1979, French economist and public servant, regarded as founding father of the European Economic Community. He was first president (1952–55) of the European Coal and Steel Community

mono **1** short for **monophonic 2** monophonic sound; monophony

monobasic *Chem* (of an acid, such as hydrogen chloride) having only one replaceable hydrogen atom per molecule

monochromatic *or* **monochroic** **1** (of light or other electromagnetic radiation) having only one wavelength **2** *Physics* (of moving particles) having only one kinetic energy **3** of or relating to monochromatism **4** a person who is totally colour-blind

monochrome **1** a black-and-white photograph or transparency **2** *Photog* black and white **3** **a** a painting, drawing, etc, done in a range of tones of a single colour **b** the technique or art of this **4** executed in or resembling monochrome

monocle a lens for correcting defective vision of one eye, held in position by the facial muscles

monocline a local steepening in stratified rocks with an otherwise gentle dip

monoclinic *Crystallog* relating to or belonging to the crystal system characterized by three unequal axes, one pair of which are not at right angles to each other

monoclonal antibody an antibody, produced by a single clone of cells grown in culture, that is both pure and specific and is capable of proliferating indefinitely to produce unlimited quantities of identical antibodies: used in diagnosis, therapy, and biotechnology

monocoque **1** a type of aircraft fuselage, car body, etc, in which all or most of the loads are taken by the skin **2** a type of racing-car, racing-cycle, or powerboat design with no separate chassis and body

monocotyledon any flowering plant of the class *Monocotyledonae*, having a single embryonic seed leaf, leaves with parallel veins, and flowers with parts in threes: includes grasses, lilies, palms, and orchids

monocular a device for use with one eye, such as a field glass

monody **1** (in Greek tragedy) an ode sung by a single

actor **2** any poem of lament for someone's death **3** *Music* a style of composition consisting of a single vocal part, usually with accompaniment

monoecious, monecious, *or* **monoicous 1** (of some flowering plants) having the male and female reproductive organs in separate flowers on the same plant **2** (of some animals and lower plants) hermaphrodite

monogamy *Zoology* the practice of having only one mate

monograph a paper, book, or other work concerned with a single subject or aspect of a subject

monolith 1 a large block of stone or anything that resembles one in appearance, intractability, etc. **2** a statue, obelisk, column, etc, cut from one block of stone **3** a large hollow foundation piece sunk as a caisson and having a number of compartments that are filled with concrete when it has reached its correct position

monologue 1 a long speech made by one actor in a play, film, etc, esp when alone **2** a dramatic piece for a single performer

monomania an excessive mental preoccupation with one thing, idea, etc.

monomer *Chem* a compound whose molecules can join together to form a polymer

monomial 1 *Maths* an expression consisting of a single term, such as 5*ax* **2** consisting of a single algebraic term **3** *Biology* of, relating to, or denoting a taxonomic name that consists of a single term

Monongahela a river in the northeastern US, flowing generally north to the Allegheny River at Pittsburgh, Pennsylvania, forming the Ohio River. Length: 206 km (128 miles)

mononucleosis 1 *Pathol* the presence of a large number of monocytes in the blood **2** See **infectious mononucleosis**

monophonic 1 (of a system of broadcasting, recording, or reproducing sound) using only one channel between source and loudspeaker **2** *Music* of or relating to a style of musical composition consisting of a single melodic line

monoplane an aeroplane with only one pair of wings

monopoly 1 exclusive control of the market supply of a product or service **2 a** an enterprise exercising this control **b** the product or service so controlled **3** *Law* the exclusive right or privilege granted to a person, company, etc, by the state to purchase, manufacture, use, or sell some commodity or to carry on trade in a specified country or area

Monopoly *Trademark* a board game for two to six players who throw dice to advance their tokens around a board, the object being to acquire the property on which their tokens land
  ▷www.hasbro.com/monopoly

monorail a single-rail railway, often elevated and with suspended cars
  ▷http://faculty.washington.edu/~jbs/itrans/itrans2.htm

monosaccharide a simple sugar, such as glucose or fructose, that does not hydrolyse to yield other sugars

monosodium glutamate a white crystalline substance, the sodium salt of glutamic acid, that has little flavour itself but enhances the flavour of proteins

either by increasing the amount of saliva produced in the mouth or by stimulating the taste buds: used as a food additive, esp in Chinese foods. Formula: $NaC_5H_8O_4$

monotheism the belief or doctrine that there is only one God

monotone *Maths* (of a sequence or function) consistently increasing or decreasing in value

monounsaturated of or relating to a class of vegetable oils, such as olive oil, the molecules of which have long chains of carbon atoms containing only one double bond

monovalent *Chem* **a** having a valency of one **b** having only one valency

monoxide an oxide that contains one oxygen atom per molecule

Monroe 1 James 1758–1831, US statesman; fifth president of the US (1817–25). He promulgated the Monroe Doctrine (1823) **2** Marilyn, real name *Norma Jean Baker* or *Mortenson*. 1926–62, US film actress. Her films include *Niagara* (1952), *Gentlemen Prefer Blondes* (1953), and *Some Like It Hot* (1959)

Monrovia the capital and chief port of Liberia, on the Atlantic: founded in 1822 as a home for freed American slaves; University of Liberia (1862). Pop: 614 000 (2005 est)

Mons a town in SW Belgium, capital of Hainaut province: scene of the first battle (1914) of the British Expeditionary Force during World War I. Pop: 91 185 (2004 est)

Monsignor *RC Church* an ecclesiastical title attached to certain offices or distinctions usually bestowed by the Pope

monsoon 1 a seasonal wind of S Asia that blows from the southwest in summer, bringing heavy rains, and from the northeast in winter **2** the rainy season when the SW monsoon blows, from about April to October **3** any wind that changes direction with the seasons

mons pubis the fatty cushion of flesh in human males situated over the junction of the pubic bones

monster 1 an imaginary beast, such as a centaur, usually made up of various animal or human parts **2** a person, animal, or plant with a marked structural deformity

monstrance *RC Church* a receptacle, usually of gold or silver, with a transparent container in which the consecrated Host is exposed for adoration

monstrous (of plants and animals) abnormal in structure

mons veneris the fatty cushion of flesh in human females situated over the junction of the pubic bones

montage 1 the art or process of composing pictures by the superimposition or juxtaposition of miscellaneous elements, such as other pictures or photographs **2** such a composition **3** a method of film editing involving the juxtaposition or partial superimposition of several shots to form a single image **4** a rapidly cut film sequence of this kind

Montagu Lady Mary Wortley 1689–1762, English writer, noted for her *Letters from the East* (1763)

Montaigne Michel Eyquem de 1533–92, French writer. His life's work, the *Essays* (begun in 1571), established the essay as a literary genre and record the evolution of his moral ideas

Montale Eugenio 1896–1981, Italian poet: Nobel prize for literature 1975

Montana¹ Joe born 1958, American football quarterback

Montana² a state of the western US: consists of the Great Plains in the east and the Rocky Mountains in the west. Capital: Helena. Pop: 917 621 (2003 est). Area: 377 070 sq km (145 587 sq miles)

Montauban a city in SW France: a stronghold in the 16th and 17th centuries, taken by Richelieu in 1629. Pop: 51 855 (1999)

Mont Blanc a massif in SW Europe, mainly between France and Italy: the highest mountain in the Alps; beneath it is **Mont Blanc Tunnel**, 12 km (7.5 miles) long. Highest peak (in France): 4807 m (15 771 ft)

Montcalm Louis Joseph , Marquis de Montcalm de Saint-Véran. 1712–59, French general in Canada (1756); killed in Quebec by British forces under General Wolfe

Monte Carlo a town and resort forming part of the principality of Monaco, on the Riviera: famous casino and the destination of an annual car rally (the **Monte Carlo Rally**). Pop: 15 507 (2000)

Monte Cassino a hill above Cassino in central Italy: site of intense battle during World War II: site of Benedictine monastery (530 AD), destroyed by Allied bombing in 1944, later restored

Montego Bay a port and resort in NW Jamaica: the second largest town on the island Pop: 83 446 (1991)

Montenegro a constituent republic of the Union of Serbia and Montenegro, bordering on the Adriatic: declared a kingdom in 1910 and united with Serbia, Croatia, and other territories in 1918 to form Yugoslavia; remained united with Serbia as the Federal Republic of Yugoslavia when the other Yugoslav constituent republics became independent in 1991–92; Union of Serbia and Montenegro formed in 2002. Capital: Podgorica. Pop: 658 000 (2001 est). Area: 13 812 sq km (5387 sq miles)

Monterey a city in W California: capital of Spain's Pacific empire from 1774 to 1825; taken by the US (1846). Pop: 29 960 (2003 est)

Monterrey a city in NE Mexico, capital of Nuevo Léon state: the third largest city in Mexico; a major industrial centre, esp for metals. Pop: 1 353 000 (2005 est)

Montespan Marquise de, title of *Françoise Athénaïs de Rochechouart*. 1641–1707, French noblewoman; mistress of Louis XIV of France

Montesquieu Baron de la Brède et de , title of *Charles Louis de Secondat*. 1689–1755, French political philosopher. His chief works are the satirical *Lettres persanes* (1721) and *L'Esprit des lois* (1748), a comparative analysis of various forms of government, which had a profound influence on political thought in Europe and the US

Montessori Maria 1870–1952, Italian educational reformer, who evolved the Montessori method of teaching children

Monteux Pierre 1875–1964, US conductor, born in France

Monteverdi Claudio ?1567–1643, Italian composer, noted esp for his innovations in opera and for his expressive use of dissonance. His operas include *Orfeo* (1607) and *L'Incoronazione di Poppea* (1642) and he also wrote many motets and madrigals

Montevideo the capital and chief port of Uruguay, in the south on the Río de la Plata estuary: the largest city in the country: University of the Republic (1849); resort. Pop: 1 378 707 (1996)

Montezuma II 1466–1520, Aztec emperor of Mexico (?1502–20). He was overthrown and killed by the Spanish conquistador Cortés

Montfort Simon de, Earl of Leicester. ?1208–65, English soldier, born in Normandy. He led the baronial rebellion against Henry III and ruled England from 1264 to 1265; he was killed at Evesham

Montgolfier Jacques Étienne , 1745–99, and his brother Joseph Michel , 1740–1810, French inventors, who built (1782) and ascended in (1783) the first practical hot-air balloon

Montgomery¹ Bernard Law, 1st Viscount Montgomery of Alamein, nicknamed *Monty*. 1887–1976, British field marshal. As commander of the 8th Army in North Africa, he launched the offensive, beginning with the victory at El Alamein (1942), that drove Rommel's forces back to Tunis. He also commanded the ground forces in the invasion of Normandy (1944) and accepted Germany's surrender at Lüneburg Heath (May 7, 1945)

Montgomery² a city in central Alabama, on the Alabama River: state capital; capital of the Confederacy (1861). Pop: 200 123 (2003 est)

Montgomeryshire (until 1974) a county of central Wales, now part of Powys

month 1 one of the twelve divisions (**calendar months**) of the calendar year 2 the period of time (**tropical month**) taken by the moon to return to the same longitude after one complete revolution around the earth; 27.321 58 days (approximately 27 days, 7 hours, 43 minutes, 4.5 seconds) 3 the period of time (**sidereal month**) taken by the moon to make one complete revolution around the earth, measured between two successive conjunctions with a distant star; 27.321 66 days (approximately 27 days, 7 hours, 43 minutes, 11 seconds) 4 the period of time (**lunar** or **synodic month**) taken by the moon to make one complete revolution around the earth, measured between two successive new moons; 29.530 59 days (approximately 29 days, 12 hours, 44 minutes, 3 seconds)

Montherlant Henri (Millon) de 1896–1972, French novelist and dramatist: his novels include *Les Jeunes Filles* (1935–39) and *Le Chaos et la nuit* (1963)

Montmartre a district of N Paris, on a hill above the Seine: the highest point in the city; famous for its associations with many artists

Montparnasse a district of S Paris, on the left bank of the Seine: noted for its cafés, frequented by artists, writers, and students

Montpelier a city in N central Vermont, on the Winooski River: the state capital. Pop: 7945 (2003 est)

Montpellier a city in S France, the chief town of Languedoc: its university was founded by Pope Nicholas IV in 1289; wine trade. Pop: 225 392 (1999)

Montreal a city and major port in central Canada, in S Quebec on **Montreal Island** at the junction of the Ottawa and St Lawrence Rivers. Pop: 1 039 534 (2001)

Montreuil an E suburb of Paris: formerly famous for peaches, but now increasingly industrialized. Pop:

90 674 (1999)

Montreux a town and resort in W Switzerland, in Vaud canton on Lake Geneva annual television festival. Pop: 22 454 (2000)

Montrose James Graham, 1st Marquess and 5th Earl of Montrose. 1612–50, Scottish general, noted for his victories in Scotland for Charles I in the Civil War. He was later captured and hanged

Mont-Saint-Michel a rocky islet off the coast of NW France, accessible at low tide by a causeway, in the **Bay of St Michel** (an inlet of the Gulf of St Malo): Benedictine abbey (966), used as a prison from the Revolution until 1863; reoccupied by Benedictine monks since 1966. Area: 1 hectare (3 acres)

Montserrat 1 a volcanic island in the Caribbean, in the Leeward Islands: a UK Overseas Territory: much of the island rendered uninhabitable by volcanic eruptions in 1997. Capital: Plymouth (effectively destroyed by the eruption). Pop: 4000 (2003 est). Area: 103 sq km (40 sq miles) **2** a mountain in NE Spain, northwest of Barcelona: famous Benedictine monastery. Height: 1235 m (4054 ft)

monument 1 an obelisk, statue, building, etc, erected in commemoration of a person or event or in celebration of something **2** a notable building or site, esp one preserved as public property **3** a literary or artistic work regarded as commemorative of its creator or a particular period

Monza a city in N Italy, northeast of Milan: the ancient capital of Lombardy; scene of the assassination of King Umberto I in 1900; motor-racing circuit. Pop: 120 204 (2001)

mood *Logic* one of the possible arrangements of the syllogism, classified solely by whether the component propositions are universal or particular and affirmative or negative

Moody Dwight Lyman 1837–99, US evangelist and hymnodist, noted for his revivalist campaigns in Britain and the US with I. D. Sankey

Moog *Trademark, Music* a type of synthesizer

Moomba *Austral* **1** a festival held annually in Melbourne since 1954, named in the belief that *moomba* was an Aboriginal word meaning "Let's get together and have fun" **2** a natural gas field in South Australia

moon 1 the natural satellite of the earth. Diameter: 3476 km; mass: 7.35×10^{22} kg; mean distance from earth: 384 400 km; periods of rotation and revolution: 27.32 days **2** the face of the moon as it is seen during its revolution around the earth, esp at one of its phases **3** any natural satellite of a planet **4** moonlight; moonshine **5** a month, esp a lunar one

Moon William 1818–94, British inventor of the Moon writing system in 1847, who, himself blind, taught blind children in Brighton and printed mainly religious works from stereotyped plates of his own designing

moonlight light from the sun received on earth after reflection by the moon

moonscape the general surface of the moon or a representation of it

moonshine 1 another word for **moonlight 2** *US and Canadian* illegally distilled or smuggled whisky or other spirit

moonshot the launching of a spacecraft, rocket, etc, to the moon

moonstone a gem variety of orthoclase or albite that is white and translucent with bluish reflections

moor a tract of unenclosed ground, usually having peaty soil covered with heather, coarse grass, bracken, and moss

Moor a member of a Muslim people of North Africa, of mixed Arab and Berber descent. In the 8th century they were converted to Islam and established power in North Africa and Spain, where they established a civilization (756–1492)
▷www.vivagranada.com/alhambra
▷www.spanish-fiestas.com/andalucia/
  history-moorish-spain.htm

Moore 1 Bobby full name *Robert Frederick Moore*. 1941–93, English footballer, captain of the England team that won the World Cup in 1966 **2** Dudley (Stuart John). 1935–2002, British actor, comedian, and musician noted for his comedy partnership (1960–73) with Peter Cook and such films as *10* (1979) and *Arthur* (1981) **3** George 1852–1933, Irish novelist. His works include *Esther Waters* (1894) and *The Brook Kerith* (1916) **4** G(eorge) E(dward). 1873–1958, British philosopher, noted esp for his *Principia Ethica* (1903) **5** Gerald 1899–1987, British pianist, noted as an accompanist esp to lieder singers **6** Henry 1898–1986, British sculptor. His works are characterized by monumental organic forms and include the *Madonna and Child* (1943) at St Matthew's Church, Northampton **7** Sir John 1761–1809, British general; commander of the British army (1808–09) in the Peninsular War: killed at Corunna **8** Marianne (Craig). 1887–1972, US poet: her works include *Observations* (1924) and *Selected Poems* (1935) **9** Thomas 1779–1852, Irish poet, best known for *Irish Melodies* (1807–34)

moorhen 1 a bird, *Gallinula chloropus*, inhabiting ponds, lakes, etc, having a black plumage, red bill, and a red shield above the bill: family *Rallidae* (rails) **2** the female of the red grouse

mooring 1 a place for mooring a vessel **2** a permanent anchor, dropped in the water and equipped with a floating buoy, to which vessels can moor

moorland *Brit* an area of moor

moose a large North American deer, *Alces alces*, having large flattened palmate antlers: also occurs in Europe and Asia where it is called an elk

Moose Jaw a city in W Canada, in S Saskatchewan. Pop: 32 631 (2001)

moot 1 a discussion or debate of a hypothetical case or point, held as an academic activity **2** (in Anglo-Saxon England) an assembly, mainly in a shire or hundred, dealing with local legal and administrative affairs

mop¹ an implement with a wooden handle and a head made of twists of cotton or a piece of synthetic sponge, used for polishing or washing floors, or washing dishes

mop² (in various parts of England) an annual fair at which formerly servants were hired

moped *Brit* a light motorcycle, not over 50cc

mopoke a small spotted owl, *Ninox novaeseelandiae*, of Australia and New Zealand. In Australia the tawny frogmouth, *Podargus strigoides*, is very often wrongly identified as the mopoke

moquette a thick velvety fabric used for carpets, uphol-stery, etc.

Moradabad a city in N India, in N Uttar Pradesh. Pop: 641 240 (2001)

moraine a mass of debris, carried by glaciers and form-ing ridges and mounds when deposited

moral *Law* (of evidence, etc) based on a knowledge of the tendencies of human nature

moralist 1 a person who seeks to regulate the morals of others or to imbue others with a sense of morality 2 a person who lives in accordance with moral principles 3 a philosopher who is concerned with casuistic discus-sions of right action, or who seeks a general characteri-zation of right action, often contrasted with a moral philosopher whose concern is with general philosophi-cal questions about ethics

morality 1 a system of moral principles 2 an instruc-tion or lesson in morals 3 short for **morality play**

morality play a type of drama written between the 14th and 16th centuries concerned with the conflict between personified virtues and vices

moral philosophy the branch of philosophy dealing with both argument about the content of morality and meta-ethical discussion of the nature of moral judg-ment, language, argument, and value

Morar *Loch* a lake in W Scotland, in the SW Highlands: the deepest in Scotland Length: 18 km (11 miles). Depth: 296 m (987 ft)

morass a tract of swampy low-lying land

moratorium a legally authorized postponement of the fulfilment of an obligation

Morava 1 a river in central Europe, rising in the Sudeten Mountains, in the Czech Republic, and flowing south through Slovakia to the Danube: forms part of the bor-der between the Czech Republic, Slovakia, and Austria. Length: 370 km (230 miles) 2 a river in E Serbia and Montenegro, formed by the confluence of the Southern Morava and the Western Morava near Stalac: flows north to the Danube. Length: 209 km (130 miles) 3 the Czech name for **Moravia²**

Moravia¹ *Alberto*, pen name of *Alberto Pincherle*. 1907–90, Italian novelist and short-story writer: his works include *The Time of Indifference* (1929), *The Woman of Rome* (1949), *The Lie* (1966), and *Erotic Tales* (1985)

Moravia² a region of the Czech Republic around the Morava River, bounded by the Bohemian-Moravian Highlands, the Sudeten Mountains, and the W Carpathians: became a separate Austrian crownland in 1848; part of Czechoslovakia 1918–92; valuable mineral resources

Moravian 1 of or relating to Moravia, its people, or their dialect of Czech 2 of or relating to the Moravian Church 3 the Moravian dialect 4 a native or inhabitant of Moravia 5 a member of the Moravian Church

moray any voracious marine coastal eel of the family *Muraenidae*, esp *Muraena helena*, marked with brilliant patterns and colours

Moray¹ *or* **Murray** *1st Earl of*, title of *James Stuart*. ?1531–70, regent of Scotland (1567–70) following the abdication of Mary, Queen of Scots, his half-sister. He defeated Mary and Bothwell at Langside (1568); assassi-nated by a follower of Mary

Moray² a council area and historical county of NE Scotland: part of Grampian region from 1975 to 1996: mainly hilly, with the Cairngorm mountains in the S. Administrative centre: Elgin. Pop: 87 460 (2003 est). Area: 2238 sq km (874 sq miles)

Moray Firth an inlet of the North Sea on the NE coast of Scotland. Length: about 56 km (35 miles)

morbid 1 having an unusual interest in death or unpleasant events 2 relating to or characterized by dis-ease; pathologic

Morbihan a department of NW France, in S Brittany. Capital: Vannes. Pop: 665 540 (2003 est). Area: 7092 sq km (2766 sq miles)

Mordecai¹ *Old Testament* the cousin of Esther who avert-ed a massacre of the Jews (Esther 2–9)

Mordecai² *Old Testament* the cousin of Esther who avert-ed a massacre of the Jews (Esther 2–9)

Mordvinian Republic a constituent republic of W cen-tral Russia, in the middle Volga basin. Capital: Saransk. Pop: 888 700 (2002). Area: 26 200 sq km (10 110 sq miles)

More 1 *Hannah* 1745–1833, English writer, noted for her religious tracts, esp *The Shepherd of Salisbury Plain* 2 *Sir Thomas* 1478–1535, English statesman, humanist, and Roman Catholic Saint; Lord Chancellor to Henry VIII (1529–32). His opposition to the annulment of Henry's marriage to Catherine of Aragon and his refusal to rec-ognize the Act of Supremacy resulted in his execution on a charge of treason. In *Utopia* (1516) he set forth his concept of the ideal state. Feast day: June 22 or July 6

Moreau 1 *Gustave* 1826–98, French symbolist painter 2 *Jean Victor* 1763–1813, French general in the Revolutionary and Napoleonic Wars 3 *Jeanne* born 1928, French stage and film actress. Her films include *Jules et Jim* (1961), *Diary of a Chambermaid* (1964), and *The Proprietor* (1996)

Morecambe¹ *Eric*, real name *John Eric Bartholomew*. 1926–84, British comedian and actor, noted esp for his comedy partnership (from 1941) with Ernie Wise (real name Ernest Wiseman, 1925–99)

Morecambe² a port and resort in NW England, in NW Lancashire on **Morecambe Bay** (an inlet of the Irish Sea). Pop: (with Heysham): 49 569 (2001)

morel any edible saprotrophic ascomycetous fungus of the genus *Morchella*, in which the mushroom has a pit-ted cap: order *Pezizales*

Morelia a city in central Mexico, capital of Michoacán state: a cultural centre during colonial times; two uni-versities. Pop: 668 000 (2005 est)

morello a variety of small very dark sour cherry, *Prunus cerasus austera*

Morelos an inland state of S central Mexico, on the S slope of the great plateau. Capital: Cuernavaca. Pop: 1 552 878 (2000 est). Area: 4988 sq km (1926 sq miles)

morepork NZ 1 a small spotted owl, *Ninox novaeseelandiae*, of Australia and New Zealand 2 *slang* a slow or lugubri-ous person

Morgan¹ 1 *Edwin* (**George**). born 1920, Scottish poet, noted esp for his collection *The Second Life* (1968) and his many concrete and visual poems 2 (**Hywel**) *Rhodri* born 1939, Welsh Labour politician; first secretary of Wales from 2000

Morgan² 1 Sir **Henry** 1635–88, Welsh buccaneer, who raided Spanish colonies in the West Indies for the English 2 **John Pierpont** 1837–1913, US financier, philanthropist, and art collector 3 **Thomas Hunt** 1866–1945, US biologist. He formulated the chromosome theory of heredity. Nobel prize for physiology or medicine 1933

morganatic of or designating a marriage between a person of high rank and a person of low rank, by which the latter is not elevated to the higher rank and any issue have no rights to the succession of the higher party's titles, property, etc.

Morisot Berthe 1841–95, French impressionist painter; noted for her studies of women and children

Morley¹ 1 **Edward Williams** 1838–1923, US chemist who collaborated with A. A. Michelson in the Michelson-Morley experiment 2 **John,** Viscount Morley of Blackburn. 1838–1923, British Liberal statesman and writer; secretary of state for India (1905–10) 3 **Robert** 1908–92, British actor. His many films include *Major Barbara* (1940), *Oscar Wilde* (1960), and *The Blue Bird* (1976) 4 **Thomas** ?1557–?1603, English composer and organist, noted for his madrigals and his textbook on music, *A Plaine and Easie Introduction to Practicall Musicke* (1597)

Morley² an industrial town in N England, in Leeds unitary authority, West Yorkshire. Pop: 54 051 (2001)

Mormon 1 a member of the Church of Jesus Christ of Latter-day Saints, founded in 1830 at La Fayette, New York, by Joseph Smith (1805–44) 2 a prophet whose supposed revelations were recorded by Joseph Smith in the Book of Mormon

▷http://www.mormon.org/

Mornay Philippe de, Seigneur du Plessis-Marly. 1549–1623, French Huguenot leader

morning-glory any of various mainly tropical convolvulaceous plants of the genus *Ipomoea* and related genera, with trumpet-shaped blue, pink, or white flowers, which close in late afternoon

morning star a planet, usually Venus, seen just before sunrise during the time that the planet is west of the sun

Moro Aldo 1916–78, Italian Christian Democrat statesman; prime minister of Italy (1963–68; 1974–76) and minister of foreign affairs (1965–66; 1969–72; 1973–74). He negotiated the entry of the Italian Communist Party into coalition government before being kidnapped by the Red Brigades in 1978 and murdered

Morocco a kingdom in NW Africa, on the Mediterranean and the Atlantic: conquered by the Arabs in about 683, who introduced Islam; at its height under Berber dynasties (11th–13th centuries); became a French protectorate in 1912 and gained independence in 1956. It is mostly mountainous, with the Atlas Mountains in the centre and the Rif range along the Mediterranean coast, with the Sahara in the south and southeast; an important exporter of phosphates. Official language: Arabic; Berber and French are also widely spoken. Official religion: (Sunni) Muslim. Currency: dirham. Capital: Rabat. Pop: 31 064 000 (2004 est). Area: 458 730 sq km (177 117 sq miles)

Moroni the capital of the Comoros, on the island of Njazidja (Grande Comore). Pop: 59 000 (2005 est)

morphine *or* **morphia** an alkaloid extracted from opium: used in medicine as an analgesic and sedative, although repeated use causes addiction. Formula: $C_{17}H_{19}NO_3$

morphing a computer technique used for graphics and in films, in which one image is gradually transformed into another image without individual changes being noticeable in the process

morphology the branch of biology concerned with the form and structure of organisms

Morphy Paul 1837–84, US chess player, widely considered to have been the world's greatest player

Morris William 1834–96, English poet, designer, craftsman, and socialist writer. He founded the Kelmscott Press (1890)

morris dance any of various old English folk dances usually performed by men (**morris men**) to the accompaniment of violin, concertina, etc. The dancers are adorned with bells and often represent characters from folk tales

▷www.streetswing.com/histmain/z3moris.htm
▷http://web.syr.edu/~rsholmes/morris/rich

Morrison 1 **Herbert Stanley,** Baron Morrison of Lambeth. 1888–1965, British Labour statesman, Home Secretary and Minister for Home Security in Churchill's War Cabinet (1942–45) 2 **Jim,** full name *James Douglas Morrison.* 1943–71, US rock singer and songwriter, lead vocalist with the Doors 3 **Toni,** full name *Chloe Anthony Morrison.* born 1931, US novelist, whose works include *Sula* (1974), *Song of Solomon* (1977), *Beloved* (1987), *Jazz* (1992), and *Paradise* (1998): awarded the Nobel Prize for literature in 1993 4 **Van,** full name *George Ivan Morrison.* born 1945, Northern Irish rock singer and songwriter. His albums include *Astral Weeks* (1968), *Moondance* (1970), *Avalon Sunset* (1989), and *Days Like These* (1995)

Morse Samuel Finley Breese 1791–1872, US inventor and painter. He invented the first electric telegraph and the Morse code

mortal 1 (of living beings, esp human beings) subject to death 2 of or involving life or the world 3 ending in or causing death; fatal

mortality 1 great loss of life, as in war or disaster 2 the number of deaths in a given period

mortal sin *Christianity* a sin regarded as involving total loss of grace

mortar a vessel, usually bowl-shaped, in which substances are pulverized with a pestle

mortgagee *Law* 1 the party to a mortgage who makes the loan 2 a person who holds mortgaged property as security for repayment of a loan

mortgagor *or* **mortgager** *Property law* a person who borrows money by mortgaging his property to the lender as security

Mortimer 1 Sir **John (Clifford).** born 1923, British barrister, playwright, and novelist, best known for the television series featuring the barrister Horace Rumpole. His novels include *Paradise Postponed* (1985) and *The Sound of Trumpets* (1998) 2 **Roger de,** 8th Baron of Wigmore and 1st Earl of March. 1287–1330, lover of Isabella, the wife of Edward II of England: they invaded England in 1326 and compelled the king to abdicate in favour of his son, Edward III; executed

Morton 1 **4th Earl of,** title of *James Douglas.* 1516–81, regent of Scotland (1572–78) for the young James VI. He was implicated in the murders of Rizzio (1566) and Darnley (1567) and played a leading role in ousting Mary, Queen of Scots; executed **2 Jelly Roll,** real name *Ferdinand Joseph La Menthe Morton*. 1885–1941, US jazz pianist, singer, and songwriter; one of the creators of New Orleans jazz

mortuary a building where dead bodies are kept before cremation or burial

mosaic 1 a design or decoration made up of small pieces of coloured glass, stone, etc. **2** the process of making a mosaic **3** *Genetics* another name for **chimera 4** a light-sensitive surface on a television camera tube, consisting of a large number of granules of photoemissive material deposited on an insulating medium

Mosaic *or* **Mosaical** of or relating to Moses or the laws and traditions ascribed to him

Mosaic law *Old Testament* the laws of the Hebrews ascribed to Moses and contained in the Pentateuch

Moscow the capital of Russia and of the Moscow Autonomous Region, on the Moskva River: dates from the 11th century; capital of the grand duchy of Russia from 1547 to 1712; capital of the Soviet Union 1918–91; centres on the medieval Kremlin; chief political, cultural, and industrial centre of Russia, with two universities. Pop: 10 672 000 (2005 est)

Moseley Henry Gwyn-Jeffreys 1887–1915, English physicist. He showed that the wavelengths of X-rays emitted from the elements are related to their atomic numbers

Moselle 1 a department of NE France, in Lorraine region. Capital: Metz. Pop: 1 027 854 (2003 est). Area: 6253 sq km (2439 sq miles) **2** a river in W Europe, rising in NE France and flowing northwest, forming part of the border between Luxembourg and Germany, then northeast to the Rhine: many vineyards along its lower course. Length: 547 km (340 miles) **3** a German white wine from the Moselle valley

Moses¹ 1 *Old Testament* the Hebrew prophet who led the Israelites out of Egypt to the Promised Land and gave them divinely revealed laws **2 Ed** born 1956, US hurdler; winner of the 400 m hurdles in the 1976 and 1984 Olympic Games **3 Grandma,** real name *Anna Mary Robertson Moses*. 1860–1961, US painter of primitives, who began to paint at the age of 75

Moses² *Old Testament* the Hebrew prophet who led the Israelites out of Egypt to the Promised Land and gave them divinely revealed laws

Moshesh *or* **Moshoeshoe** died 1870, African chief, who founded the Basotho nation, now Lesotho

Moskva 1 transliteration of the Russian name for Moscow **2** a river in W central Russia, rising in the Smolensk-Moscow upland, and flowing southeast through Moscow to the Oka River: linked with the River Volga by the Moscow Canal. Length: about 500 km (310 miles)

Mosley Sir Oswald Ernald 1896–1980, British politician; founder of the British Union of Fascists (1932)

mosque a Muslim place of worship, usually having one or more minarets and often decorated with elaborate tracery and texts from the Koran

mosquito any dipterous insect of the family *Culicidae:* the females have a long proboscis adapted for piercing the skin of man and animals to suck their blood

mosquito net *or* **netting** a fine curtain or net put in windows, around beds, etc, to keep mosquitoes out

moss 1 any bryophyte of the phylum *Bryophyta,* typically growing in dense mats on trees, rocks, moist ground, etc. **2** a clump or growth of any of these plants **3** any of various similar but unrelated plants, such as club moss, Spanish moss, Ceylon moss, rose moss, and reindeer moss

Moss 1 Kate born 1974, British supermodel. **2** Sir Stirling born 1929, English racing driver

moss rose a variety of rose, *Rosa centifolia muscosa,* that has a mossy stem and calyx and fragrant pink flowers

Mostaganem a port in NW Algeria, on the Mediterranean Sea: exports wine, fruit, and vegetables. Pop: 133 000 (2005 est)

Most Reverend (in Britain) a courtesy title applied to Anglican and Roman Catholic archbishops

Mosul a city in N Iraq, on the River Tigris opposite the ruins of Nineveh: an important commercial centre with nearby Ayn Zalah oilfield; university. Pop: 1 236 000 (2005 est)

motel a roadside hotel for motorists, usually having direct access from each room or chalet to a parking space or garage

motet a polyphonic choral composition used as an anthem in the Roman Catholic service

moth any of numerous insects of the order *Lepidoptera* that typically have stout bodies with antennae of various shapes (but not clubbed), including large brightly coloured species, such as hawk moths, and small inconspicuous types, such as the clothes moths

mothball a small ball of camphor or naphthalene used to repel clothes moths in stored clothing, blankets, etc.

mother¹ 1 a a female who has given birth to offspring **b** (*as modifier*): *a mother bird* **2** a title given to certain members of female religious orders **3** *Christian Science* God as the eternal Principle

mother² a stringy slime containing various bacteria that forms on the surface of liquids undergoing acetous fermentation. It can be added to wine, cider, etc to promote vinegar formation

mother-of-pearl a hard iridescent substance, mostly calcium carbonate, that forms the inner layer of the shells of certain molluscs, such as the oyster. It is used to make buttons, inlay furniture, etc.

mother superior the head of a community of nuns

Motherwell a town in S central Scotland, the administrative centre of North Lanarkshire on the River Clyde: industrial centre. Pop: 30 311 (2001)

motif 1 a distinctive idea, esp a theme elaborated on in a piece of music, literature, etc. **2** a recurring form or shape in a design or pattern

motile 1 capable of moving spontaneously and independently **2** *Psychol* a person whose mental imagery strongly reflects movement, esp his own

motion 1 the process of continual change in the physical position of an object; movement **2** a movement or action, esp of part of the human body; a gesture **3 a** the capacity for movement **b** a manner of movement, esp walking; gait **4** a mental impulse **5** *Politics* a formal proposal to be discussed and voted on in a debate, meeting, etc. **6** *Law* an application made to a judge or court for an order or ruling necessary to the conduct of legal proceedings **7** *Brit* **a** the evacuation of the bowels **b** excrement **8 a** part of a moving mechanism **b** the action of such a part **9** *Music* the upward or downward course followed by a part or melody. Parts whose progressions are in the same direction exhibit **similar motion**, while two parts whose progressions are in opposite directions exhibit **contrary motion**

Motion Andrew born 1952, British poet and biographer; his collections include *Pleasure Steamers* (1978) and *Public Property* (2002): poet laureate from 1999

motion picture *US and Canadian* **a** a sequence of images of moving objects photographed by a camera and providing the optical illusion of continuous movement when projected onto a screen **b** a form of entertainment, information, etc, composed of such a sequence of images and shown in a cinema, etc.

motive power 1 any source of energy used to produce motion **2** the means of supplying power to an engine, vehicle, etc. **3** any driving force

motocross 1 a motorcycle race across very rough ground **2** another name for **rallycross**. See also **autocross**

motor 1 a the engine, esp an internal-combustion engine, of a vehicle **b** *(as modifier)*: *a motor scooter* **2 a** a machine that converts electrical energy into mechanical energy by means of the forces exerted on a current-carrying coil placed in a magnetic field **3** any device that converts another form of energy into mechanical energy to produce motion **4 a** *Chiefly Brit* a car or other motor vehicle **b** *as modifier*: *motor spares* **5** producing or causing motion **6** *Physiol* **a** of or relating to nerves or neurons that carry impulses that cause muscles to contract **b** of or relating to movement or to muscles that induce movement

▷www.formula1.com
▷www.fia.com
▷www.imca.com

motorbicycle 1 a motorcycle **2** a moped

motorboat any boat powered by a motor

motorcade a parade of cars or other motor vehicles

motorcar 1 a more formal word for **car 2** a self-propelled electric railway car

motorcycle a two-wheeled vehicle, having a stronger frame than a bicycle, that is driven by a petrol engine, usually with a capacity of between 125 cc and 1000 cc

▷www.bmrc.co.uk
▷www.fim.ch
▷http://motorcycles.about.com/
▷www.crmc.co.uk/links.htm

motorist a driver of a car, esp when considered as a car-owner

motorman 1 the driver of an electric train **2** the operator of a motor

motor scooter a light motorcycle with small wheels and an enclosed engine

motor vehicle a road vehicle driven by a motor or engine, esp an internal-combustion engine

motorway *Brit* a main road for fast-moving traffic, having limited access, separate carriageways for vehicles travelling in opposite directions, and usually a total of four or six lanes

Motown *Trademark* music combining rhythm and blues and pop, or gospel rhythms and modern ballad harmony

▷www.motown.com

motte *History* a natural or man-made mound on which a castle was erected

motto 1 a short explanatory phrase inscribed on or attached to something **2** a verse or maxim contained in a paper cracker **3** a quotation prefacing a book or chapter of a book **4** a recurring musical phrase

mould¹ *or US* **mold 1** a shaped cavity used to give a definite form to fluid or plastic material **2** something shaped in or made on a mould

mould² *or US* **mold 1** a coating or discoloration caused by various saprotrophic fungi that develop in a damp atmosphere on the surface of stored food, fabrics, wallpaper, etc. **2** any of the fungi that causes this growth

mould *or US* **mold** loose soil, esp when rich in organic matter

moulder *or US* **molder** a person who moulds or makes moulds

moulding *or US* **molding** *Architect* **a** a shaped outline, esp one used on cornices, etc. **b** a shaped strip made of wood, stone, etc.

Moulin Jean 1899–1943, French lawyer and Resistance hero; Chairman of the National Council of the Resistance (1943): tortured to death by the Nazis

Moulins a market town in central France, on the Allier River. Pop: 21 892 (1999)

Moulmein *or* **Maulmain** a port in S Myanmar, near the mouth of the Salween River: exports teak and rice. Pop: 390 000 (2005 est)

moult *or US* **molt** the periodic process of moulting

mound 1 a small natural hill **2** *Archaeol* another word for **barrow 3** an artificial ridge of earth, stone, etc, as used for defence

mount¹ 1 a horse for riding **2** a slide used in microscopy **3** *Philately* **a** a small transparent pocket in an album for a postage stamp **b** another word for **hinge**

mount² 1 a mountain or hill: used in literature and (when cap.) in proper names **2** (in palmistry) any of the seven cushions of flesh on the palm of the hand

mountain 1 a natural upward projection of the earth's surface, higher and steeper than a hill and often having a rocky summit **2** a surplus of a commodity, esp in the European Union

mountain ash 1 any of various trees of the rosaceous genus *Sorbus*, such as *S aucuparia* (**European mountain ash** or **rowan**), having clusters of small white flowers and bright red berries **2** any of several Australian eucalyptus trees, such as *Eucalyptus regnans*

mountain bike a type of sturdy bicycle with at least 16 and up to 21 gears, straight handlebars, and heavy-duty tyres

▷www.imba.com

mountain cat any of various wild feline mammals, such as the bobcat, lynx, or puma

mountain goat any wild goat inhabiting mountainous regions

mountain sickness 1 nausea, headache, and shortness of breath caused by climbing to high altitudes (usually above 12 000 ft) **2** *Vet science* a disease of cattle kept at high altitude in S and N America, characterized by congestive heart failure

Mountbatten Louis (Francis Albert Victor Nicholas), 1st Earl Mountbatten of Burma 1900–79, British naval commander; great-

grandson of Queen Victoria. During World War II he was supreme allied commander in SE Asia (1943–46). He was the last viceroy of India (1947) and governor general (1947–48); killed by an IRA bomb

Mount Desert Island an island off the coast of Maine: lakes and granite peaks. Area: 279 sq km (108 sq miles)

mountebank (formerly) a person who sold quack medicines in public places

Mountie *or* **Mounty** *Informal* a member of the Royal Canadian Mounted Police

Mount Isa a city in NE Australia in NW Queensland: mining of copper and other minerals. Pop: 20 525 (2001)

Mount McKinley National Park a national park in S central Alaska: contains part of the Alaska Range Area: 7847 sq km (3030 sq miles)

Mount Rainier National Park a national park in W Washington, in the Cascade Range. Area: 976 sq km (377 sq miles)

mouse 1 any of numerous small long-tailed rodents of the families *Muridae* and *Cricetidae* that are similar to but smaller than rats **2** any of various related rodents, such as the jumping mouse **3** *Computing* a hand-held device used to control the cursor movement and select computing functions without keying

mouth 1 the opening through which many animals take in food and issue vocal sounds **2** the system of organs surrounding this opening, including the lips, tongue, teeth, etc. **3** the visible part of the lips on the face **4** the point where a river issues into a sea or lake **5** the opening of a container, such as a jar **6** the opening of or place leading into a cave, tunnel, volcano, etc. **7** that part of the inner lip of a horse on which the bit acts, esp when specified as to sensitivity **8** *Music* the narrow slit in an organ pipe **9** the opening between the jaws of a vice or other gripping device

mouthpiece the part of a wind instrument into which the player blows

mouthwash a medicated aqueous solution, used for gargling and for cleansing the mouth

movable *or* **moveable 1** (esp of religious festivals such as Easter) varying in date from year to year **2** *Law* denoting or relating to personal property as opposed to realty

move (in board games) **a** a player's turn to move his piece or take other permitted action **b** a permitted manoeuvre of a piece

movement 1 a the evacuation of the bowels **b** the matter evacuated **2** *Music* a principal self-contained section of a symphony, sonata, etc, usually having its own structure **3** tempo or pace, as in music or literature **4** *Fine arts* the appearance of motion in painting, sculpture, etc. **5** *Prosody* the rhythmic structure of verse **6** *Commerce* a change in the market price of a security or commodity

Moya (John) Hidalgo 1920–94, British architect: in partnership with Philip Powell, his designs include Skylon, Festival of Britain (1950), Wolfson College, Oxford

(1974), and the Queen Elizabeth Conference Centre, Westminster (1986)

Moyle a district of NE Northern Ireland, in Co. Antrim. Pop: 16 302 (2003 est). Area: 494 sq km (191 sq miles)

Mozambique a republic in SE Africa: colonized by the Portuguese from 1505 onwards and a slave-trade centre until 1878; made an overseas province of Portugal in 1951; became an independent republic in 1975; became a member of the Commonwealth in 1995. Official language: Portuguese. Religion: animist majority. Currency: metical. Capital: Maputo. Pop: 19 183 000 (2004 est). Area: 812 379 sq km (313 661 sq miles)

Mozambique Channel a strait between Mozambique and Madagascar. Length: about 1600 km (1000 miles). Width: 400 km (250 miles)

Mozart Wolfgang Amadeus 1756–91, Austrian composer. A child prodigy and prolific genius, his works include operas, such as *The Marriage of Figaro* (1786), *Don Giovanni* (1787), and *The Magic Flute* (1791), symphonies, concertos for piano, violin, clarinet, and French horn, string quartets and quintets, sonatas, songs, and Masses, such as the unfinished *Requiem* (1791)

MP3 1 MPEG-1 Audio Layer-3: tradename for software created by the Motion Picture Experts Group that enables files to be compressed quickly to 10% or less of their original size for storage on disk or hard drive or esp for transfer across the internet **2** an audio or video file created in this way

MPEG *Computing* a standard file format for compressing video images and audio sounds

Mpumalanga a province of E South Africa; formed in 1994 from part of the former province of Transvaal: agriculture and service industries. Capital: Nelspruit. Pop: 3 244 306 (2004 est). Area: 78 370 sq km (30 259 sq miles)

Mr a title placed before the surname of a surgeon

Mubarak (Muhammad) Hosni born 1928, Egyptian statesman; president of Egypt from 1981

mucilage 1 a sticky preparation, such as gum or glue, used as an adhesive **2** a complex glutinous carbohydrate secreted by certain plants

mucous membrane a mucus-secreting membrane that lines body cavities or passages that are open to the external environment

mucus the slimy protective secretion of the mucous membranes, consisting mainly of mucin

mud a fine-grained soft wet deposit that occurs on the ground after rain, at the bottom of ponds, lakes, etc.

mud bath a medicinal bath in heated mud

mud flat a tract of low muddy land, esp near an estuary, that is covered at high tide and exposed at low tide

mudguard a curved part of a motorcycle, bicycle, etc, attached above the wheels to reduce the amount of water or mud thrown up by them

mudslinging casting malicious slurs on an opponent, esp in politics

muezzin *Islam* the official of a mosque who calls the faithful to prayer five times a day from the minaret

muff the tuft on either side of the head of certain fowls

muffle[1] a kiln with an inner chamber for firing porcelain, enamel, etc, at a low temperature

muffle[2] the fleshy hairless part of the upper lip and

nose in ruminants and some rodents

muffler *US and Canadian* any device designed to reduce noise, esp the tubular device containing baffle plates in the exhaust system of a motor vehicle

mufti 1 a Muslim legal expert and adviser on the law of the Koran 2 (in the former Ottoman empire) the leader of the religious community

Mufulira a mining town in the Copper Belt of Zambia. Pop: 220 000 (2005 est)

Mugabe Robert born 1925, Zimbabwean politician; leader of one wing of the Patriotic Front against the government of Ian Smith of Rhodesia, and of the Zanu party; prime minister (1980–87); president from 1988

muggins 1 a variation on the game of dominoes 2 a card game

muggy (of weather, air, etc) unpleasantly warm and humid

Muhammad Ali, Muhammed Ali, *or* **Mohammed Ali** original name *Cassius (Marcellus) Clay*. born 1942, US boxer, who was world heavyweight champion three times (1964–67; 1974–78; 1978)

Muir Edwin 1887–1959, Scottish poet, novelist, and critic

Muir Glacier a glacier in SE Alaska, in the St Elias Mountains, flowing southeast from Mount Fairweather. Area: about 900 sq km (350 sq miles)

mulatto 1 a person having one Black and one White parent 2 of a light brown colour

mulberry 1 any moraceous tree of the temperate genus *Morus*, having edible blackberry-like fruit, such as *M. alba* (**white mulberry**), the leaves of which are used to feed silkworms 2 any of several similar or related trees, such as the paper mulberry and Indian mulberry 3 a a dark purple colour b (*as adjective*): *a mulberry dress*

Muldoon Sir Robert David 1921–92, New Zealand statesman; prime minister of New Zealand (1975–84)

mule 1 the sterile offspring of a male donkey and a female horse, used as a beast of burden 2 any hybrid animal 3 a machine invented by Samuel Crompton that spins cotton into yarn and winds the yarn on spindles 4 *Slang* a person who is paid to transport illegal drugs for a dealer

mulga *Austral* 1 scrub comprised of a dense growth of acacia 2 the outback; bush

mulga *Austral* any of various Australian acacia shrubs, esp *Acacia aneura*, which grows in the central desert regions and has leaflike leafstalks

Mulhouse a city in E France, on the Rhône-Rhine canal; under German rule (1871–1918); textiles. Pop: 110 359 (1999)

mull¹ a light muslin fabric of soft texture

mull² a layer of nonacidic humus formed in well drained and aerated soils

mull³ *Scot* a promontory

Mull a mountainous island off the west coast of Scotland, in the Inner Hebrides, separated from the mainland by the **Sound of Mull**. Chief town: Tobermory. Pop: 2667 (2001). Area: 909 sq km (351 sq miles)

mullah, mulla, *or* **mollah** (formerly) a Muslim scholar, teacher, or religious leader: also used as a title of respect

Muller Hermann Joseph 1890–1967, US geneticist, noted

for his work on the transmutation of genes by X-rays: Nobel prize for physiology or medicine 1946

mullet any of various teleost food fishes belonging to the families *Mugilidae* or *Mullidae*

Mulligan Gerry, full name *Gerald Joseph Mulligan*. 1927–96, US jazz saxophonist, who pioneered the cool jazz style of the 1950s

Mulliken Robert Sanderson 1896–1986, US physicist and chemist, who won the Nobel prize for chemistry (1966) for his work on bonding and the electronic structure of molecules

Mullingar a town in N central Republic of Ireland, the county town of Co. Westmeath; site of cathedral; cattle raised. Pop: 15 621 (2002)

mullion 1 a vertical member between the casements or panes of a window or the panels of a screen 2 one of the ribs on a rock face

mulloway a large Australian marine sciaenid fish, *Sciaena antarctica*, valued for sport and food

Mulroney (Martin) Brian born 1939, Canadian statesman; Conservative prime minister (1984–93)

Multan a city in central Pakistan, near the Chenab River. Pop: 1 459 000 (2005 est)

multiflora rose an Asian climbing shrubby rose, *Rosa multiflora*, having clusters of small fragrant flowers: the source of many cultivated roses

multilateral of or involving more than two nations or parties

multimedia *Computing* of or relating to any of various systems which can manipulate data in a variety of forms, such as sound, graphics, or text

multinational 1 (of a large business company) operating in several countries 2 such a company

multiparous (of certain species of mammal) producing many offspring at one birth

multiple 1 *Electronics, US and Canadian* (of a circuit) having a number of conductors in parallel 2 *Maths* the product of a given number or polynomial and any other one

multiple-choice having a number of possible given answers out of which the correct one must be chosen

multiple sclerosis a chronic progressive disease of the central nervous system characterized by loss of some of the myelin sheath surrounding certain nerve fibres and resulting in speech and visual disorders, tremor, muscular incoordination, partial paralysis, etc.

multiplex a a purpose-built complex containing a number of cinemas and usually a restaurant or bar b (*as modifier*): *a multiplex cinema*

multiplicand a number to be multiplied by another number, the **multiplier**

multiplication 1 an arithmetical operation, defined initially in terms of repeated addition, usually written $a \times b$, $a.b$, or ab, by which the product of two quantities is calculated: to multiply a by positive integral b is to add a to itself b times. Multiplication by fractions can then be defined in the light of the associative and commutative properties; multiplication by $1/n$ is equivalent to multiplication by 1 followed by division by n: for example $0.3 \times 0.7 = 0.3 \times 7/10 = (0.3 \times 7)/10 = 2.1/10 = 0.21$ 2 the act or process in animals, plants, or people of reproducing or breeding

multiplication sign the symbol ×, placed between

numbers to be multiplied, as in $3 \times 4 \times 5 = 60$

multiplication table one of a group of tables giving the results of multiplying two numbers together

multiplicity *Physics* the number of levels into which the energy of an atom, molecule, or nucleus splits as a result of coupling between orbital angular momentum and spin angular momentum

multiplier 1 a person or thing that multiplies 2 the number by which another number, the **multiplicand**, is multiplied 3 *Physics* any device or instrument, such as a photomultiplier, for increasing an effect 4 *Economics* **a** the ratio of the total change in income (resulting from successive rounds of spending) to an initial autonomous change in expenditure **b** (*as modifier*): *multiplier effects*

multipurpose vehicle a large car, similar to a van, designed to carry up to eight passengers

multistage *Engineering* (of a turbine, compressor, or supercharger) having more than one rotor

multistorey 1 (of a building) having many storeys 2 a multistorey car park

multitrack (in sound recording) using tape containing two or more tracks, usually four to twenty-four

multi-user (of a computer) capable of being used by several people at once

Mumford Lewis 1895–1990, US sociologist, whose works are chiefly concerned with the relationship between man and his environment. They include *The City in History* (1962) and *Roots of Contemporary Architecture* (1972)

mummer 1 one of a group of masked performers in folk play or mime 2 a mime artist 3 *Humorous or derogatory* an actor

mummy 1 an embalmed or preserved body, esp as prepared for burial in ancient Egypt 2 *Obsolete* the substance of such a body used medicinally

mumps an acute contagious viral disease of the parotid salivary glands, characterized by swelling of the affected parts, fever, and pain beneath the ear: usually affects children

Munch Edvard 1863–1944, Norwegian painter and engraver, whose works, often on the theme of death, include *The Scream* (1893); a major influence on the expressionists, esp on *die Brücke*

mung bean an E Asian bean plant, *Phaseolus aureus*, grown for forage and as the source of bean sprouts used in oriental cookery

Munich a city in S Germany, capital of the state of Bavaria, on the Isar River: became capital of Bavaria in 1508; headquarters of the Nazi movement in the 1920s; a major financial, commercial, and manufacturing centre. Pop: 1 247 873 (2003 est)

municipality 1 a city, town, or district enjoying some degree of local self-government 2 the governing body of such a unit

Munro 1 Alice, original name *Alice Laidlaw*. born 1931, Canadian short-story writer; her books include *Lives of Girls and Women* (1971), *The Moons of Jupiter* (1982), and *The Love of a Good Woman* (1999) 2 H(ector) H(ugh), pen name Saki. 1870–1916, Scottish author, born in Burma (now Myanmar), noted for his collections of satirical short stories, such as *Reginald* (1904) and *Beasts and Superbeasts* (1914)

Munster a province of SW Republic of Ireland: the largest of the four provinces and historically a kingdom; consists of the counties of Clare, Cork, Kerry, Limerick, Tipperary, and Waterford. Capital: Cork. Pop: 1 100 614 (2002). Area: 24 125 sq km (9315 sq miles)

muon a positive or negative elementary particle with a mass 207 times that of an electron and spin ½. It was originally called the **mu meson** but is now classified as a lepton

mural a large painting or picture on a wall

Muralitharan Muttiah born 1972, Sri Lankan cricketer, a famous spin bowler; has played for Sri Lanka since 1992

Murasaki Shikibu 11th-century Japanese court lady, author of *The Tale of Genji*, perhaps the world's first novel

Murat Joachim 1767–1815, French marshal, during the Napoleonic Wars; king of Naples (1808–15)

Murchison Sir Roderick Impey 1792–1871, Scottish geologist: played a major role in establishing parts of the geological time scale, esp the Silurian, Permian, and Devonian periods

Murcia 1 a region and ancient kingdom of SE Spain, on the Mediterranean: taken by the Moors in the 8th century; an independent Muslim kingdom in the 11th and 12th centuries 2 a city in SE Spain, capital of Murcia province: trading centre for a rich agricultural region; silk industry; university (1915). Pop: 391 146 (2003 est)

murder the unlawful premeditated killing of one human being by another

Murdoch 1 Dame (Jean) Iris 1919–99, British writer. Her books include *The Bell* (1958), *A Severed Head* (1961), *The Sea, The Sea* (1978), which won the Booker Prize, *The Philosopher's Pupil* (1983), and *Existentialists and Mystics* (1997) 2 (Keith) Rupert born 1931, US publisher and media entrepreneur, born in Australia; chairman of News International Ltd (including Times Newspapers Ltd), 20th Century-Fox, and HarperCollins

Mureş a river in SE central Europe, rising in central Romania in the Carpathian Mountains and flowing west to the Tisza River at Szeged, Hungary. Length: 885 km (550 miles)

Murillo Bartolomé Esteban 1618–82, Spanish painter, esp of religious subjects and beggar children

Murman Coast *or* **Murmansk Coast** a coastal region of NW Russia, in the north of the Kola Peninsula within the Arctic Circle, but ice-free

Murmansk a port in NW Russia, on the Kola Inlet of the Barents Sea: founded in 1915; the world's largest town north of the Arctic Circle, with a large fishing fleet. Pop: 316 000 (2005 est)

murmur *Med* any abnormal soft blowing sound heard within the body, usually over the chest

Murphy 1 Alex born 1939, British rugby league player and coach 2 Eddie, full name *Edward Regan Murphy*. born 1951, US film actor and comedian. His films include *48 Hours* (1982), *Beverly Hills Cop* (1984), *Coming to America* (1988), and *Dr Dolittle* (1998) 3 William Parry 1892–1987, US physician: with G. R. Minot, he discovered the liver treatment for anaemia and they shared, with G. H. Whipple, the Nobel prize for physiology or medicine in 1934

Murray[1] 1 Sir (George) Gilbert (Aimé). 1866–1957, British classical scholar, born in Australia: noted for his verse translations of Greek dramatists, esp Euripides **2** Sir James Augustus Henry 1837–1915, Scottish lexicographer; one of the original editors (1879–1915) of what became the *Oxford English Dictionary* **3 Les,** full name *Leslie Allan Murray.* born 1938, Australian poet; his collections include *The Weatherboard Cathedral* (1969), *The Daylight Moon* (1987), and *Subhuman Redneck Poems* (1996). **4 Murray of Epping Forest,** Baron, title of *Lionel Murray,* known as *Len.* 1922–2004, British trades union leader; general secretary of the Trades Union Congress (1973–84)

Murray² a river in SE Australia, rising in New South Wales and flowing northwest into SE South Australia, then south into the sea at Encounter Bay: the main river of Australia, important for irrigation and power. Length: 2590 km (1609 miles)

Murrumbidgee a river in SE Australia, rising in S New South Wales and flowing north and west to the Murray River: important for irrigation. Length: 1690 km (1050 miles)

mus. of, relating to, or belonging to the *Musaceae,* a family of tropical flowering plants having large leaves and clusters of elongated berry fruits: includes the banana, edible plantain, and Manila hemp

Muscat the capital of the Sultanate of Oman, a port on the Gulf of Oman: a Portuguese port from the early 16th century; controlled by Persia (1650–1741). Pop: 689 000 (2005 est)

muscle **1** a tissue composed of bundles of elongated cells capable of contraction and relaxation to produce movement in an organ or part **2** an organ composed of muscle tissue

Muscovite **1** a native or inhabitant of Moscow **2** an archaic word for **Russian**

Muscovy **1** a Russian principality (13th to 16th centuries), of which Moscow was the capital **2** an archaic name for **Russia** and **Moscow**

muscular dystrophy a genetic disease characterized by progressive deterioration and wasting of muscle fibres, causing difficulty in walking

musculature **1** the arrangement of muscles in an organ or part **2** the total muscular system of an organism

muse a goddess that inspires a creative artist, esp a poet

museum a place or building where objects of historical, artistic, or scientific interest are exhibited, preserved, or studied

museum piece an object of sufficient age or interest to be kept in a museum

Musharraf Pervez born 1943, Pakistani general and politician; became military leader of Pakistan following a coup in 2001; president from 2002

mushroom **1** the fleshy spore-producing body of any of various basidiomycetous fungi, typically consisting of a cap at the end of a stem arising from an underground mycelium. Some species, such as the field mushroom, are edible **2** the fungus producing any of these structures

mushroom cloud the large mushroom-shaped cloud of dust, debris, etc produced by a nuclear explosion

music **1** an art form consisting of sequences of sounds in time, esp tones of definite pitch organized melodically, harmonically, rhythmically and according to tone colour **2** such an art form characteristic of a particular people, culture, or tradition **3** the sounds so produced, esp by singing or musical instruments **4** written or printed music, such as a score or set of parts

▷www.allmusic.com
▷www.musicsearch.com
▷www.dotmusic.com
▷www.music.ucc.ie/wrrm
▷www.classical.net
▷www.essentialsofmusic.com/glossary/n.html
▷www.nme.com

musical chairs a party game in which players walk around chairs while music is played, there being one fewer chair than players. Whenever the music stops, the player who fails to find a chair is eliminated

music centre a single hi-fi unit containing e.g. a turntable, amplifier, radio, cassette player, and compact disc player

music hall *Chiefly Brit* **1 a** a variety entertainment consisting of songs, comic turns, etc. **b** (*as modifier*): *a music-hall song* **2** a theatre at which such entertainments are staged

▷www.rfwilmut.clara.net
▷www.theatrelinks.com

musicology the scholarly study of music

▷www.societymusictheory.org/mto
▷www.music.ucc.ie/wrrm

Musil Robert 1880–1942, Austrian novelist, whose novel *The Man Without Qualities* (1930–42) is an ironic examination of contemporary ills

musk **1** a strong-smelling glandular secretion of the male musk deer, used in perfumery **2** a similar substance produced by certain other animals, such as the civet and otter, or manufactured synthetically

musk any of several scrophulariaceous plants of the genus *Mimulus,* esp the North American *M. moschatus,* which has yellow flowers and was formerly cultivated for its musky scent

musk deer a small central Asian mountain deer, *Moschus moschiferus.* The male has long tusklike canine teeth and secretes musk

muskeg *Chiefly Canadian* **1** undrained boggy land characterized by sphagnum moss vegetation **2** a bog or swamp of this nature

muskmelon any of several varieties of the melon *Cucumis melo,* such as the cantaloupe and honeydew

musk ox a large bovid mammal, *Ovibos moschatus,* which has a dark shaggy coat, short legs, and widely spaced downward-curving horns and emits a musky smell: now confined to the tundras of Canada and Greenland

muskrat **1** a North American beaver-like amphibious rodent, *Ondatra zibethica,* closely related to but larger than the voles: family *Cricetidae* **2** the brown fur of this animal **3** either of two closely related rodents, *Ondatra obscurus* or *Neofiber alleni* (**round-tailed muskrat**)

musk rose a prickly shrubby Mediterranean rose, *Rosa moschata,* cultivated for its white musk-scented flowers

Muslim *or* **Moslem** **1** a follower of the religion of Islam **2** of or relating to Islam, its doctrines, culture, etc.

muslin a fine plain-weave cotton fabric

mussel **1** any of various marine bivalves of the genus *Mytilus* and related genera, esp *M. edulis* (**edible mussel**), having a dark slightly elongated shell and living attached to rocks, etc, **2** any of various freshwater bivalves of the genera *Anodonta*, *Unio*, etc, attached to rocks, sand, etc having a flattened oval shell (a source of mother-of-pearl). The **zebra mussel**, *Dreissena polymorpha*, can be a serious nuisance in water mains

Musset Alfred de 1810–57, French romantic poet and dramatist: his works include the play *Lorenzaccio* (1834) and the lyrics *Les Nuits* (1835–37), tracing his love affair with George Sand

Mussolini Benito known as *il Duce*. 1883–1945, Italian Fascist dictator. After the Fascist march on Rome, he was appointed prime minister by King Victor Emmanuel III (1922) and assumed dictatorial powers. He annexed Abyssinia and allied Italy with Germany (1936), entering World War II in 1940. He was forced to resign following the Allied invasion of Sicily (1943) and was eventually shot by Italian partisans

Mussorgsky or **Moussorgsky Modest Petrovich** 1839–81, Russian composer. He translated inflections of speech into melody in such works as the song cycle *Songs and Dances of Death* (1875–77) and the opera *Boris Godunov* (1874). His other works include *Pictures at an Exhibition* (1874) for piano

must *Winemaking* the newly pressed juice of grapes or other fruit ready for fermentation

mustang a small breed of horse, often wild or half wild, found in the southwestern US

mustard 1 any of several Eurasian plants of the genus *Brassica*, esp black mustard and white mustard, having yellow or white flowers and slender pods and cultivated for their pungent seeds: family *Brassicaceae* (crucifers) **2 a** a brownish-yellow colour **b** (*as adjective*): *a mustard carpet*

mustard gas an oily liquid vesicant compound used in chemical warfare. Its vapour causes blindness and burns. Formula: $(ClCH_2CH_2)_2S$

mustard plaster *Med* a mixture of powdered black mustard seeds and an adhesive agent applied to the skin for its relaxing, stimulating, or counterirritant effects

muster a flock of peacocks

mutable *Astrology* of or relating to four of the signs of the zodiac, Gemini, Virgo, Sagittarius, and Pisces, which are associated with the quality of adaptability

mutagen a substance or agent that can induce genetic mutation

mutagenesis *Genetics* the generation, usually intentional, of mutations

mutant an animal, organism, or gene that has undergone mutation

Mutare a city in E Zimbabwe, near the Mozambique border: rail and trade centre in a mining and tobacco-growing region. Pop: 160 000 (2005 est)

mutation 1 the act or process of mutating; change; alteration **2** a change in the chromosomes or genes of a cell. When this change occurs in the gametes the structure and development of the resultant offspring may be affected **3** another word for **mutant 4** a physical characteristic of an individual resulting from this type of chromosomal change

mute¹ 1 unable to speak; dumb **2** *Law* (of a person arraigned on indictment) refusing to answer a charge

3 a person who is unable to speak **4** *Law* a person who refuses to plead when arraigned on indictment for an offence **5** any of various devices used to soften the tone of stringed or brass instruments **6** an actor in a dumb show

mute² *Archaic* birds' faeces

mute swan a Eurasian swan, *Cygnus olor*, with a pure white plumage, an orange-red bill with a black base, and a curved neck

muti *South African, informal* medicine, esp herbal medicine

mutiny open rebellion against constituted authority, esp by seamen or soldiers against their officers

mutt *Slang* a mongrel dog; cur

Mutter Anne-Sophie born 1963, German violinist

mutton bird 1 any of several shearwaters, having a dark plumage with greyish underparts, esp the sooty shearwater (*Puffinus griseus*) of New Zealand, which is collected for food by Māoris. It inhabits the Pacific Ocean and in summer nests in Australia and New Zealand *Austral* **2** any of various petrols esp the short tailed shearwater, *Puffinus tenuirostris*, which inhabits the Pacific Ocean and in summer nests in S Australia

Muzak *Trademark* recorded light music played in shops, restaurants, factories, etc, to entertain, increase sales or production, etc.

Muzorewa Abel (Tendekayi). born 1925, Zimbabwean Methodist bishop and politician; president of the African National Council (1971–85). He was one of the negotiators of an internal settlement (1978–79); prime minister of Rhodesia (1979)

muzzle 1 the projecting part of the face, usually the jaws and nose, of animals such as the dog and horse **2** a guard or strap fitted over an animal's nose and jaws to prevent it biting or eating

Mweru a lake in central Africa, on the border between Zambia and the Democratic Republic of Congo (formerly Zaïre). Area: 4196 sq km (1620 sq miles)

myall any of several Australian acacias, esp *Acacia pendula*, having hard scented wood used for fences

Myanmar or **Myanma** a republic in SE Asia, on the Bay of Bengal and the Andaman Sea: unified from small states in 1752; annexed by Britain (1823–85) and made a province of India in 1886; became independent in 1948. It is generally mountainous, with the basins of the Chindwin and Irrawaddy Rivers in the central part and the Irrawaddy delta in the south. Official language: Burmese. Religion: Buddhist majority. Currency: kyat. Capital: Yangon. Pop: 50 101 000 (2004 est). Area: 676 577 sq km (261 228 sq miles). Former name (until 1989): **Burma**

mycelium the vegetative body of fungi: a mass of branching filaments (hyphae) that spread throughout the nutrient substratum

Mycenae an ancient Greek city in the NE Peloponnesus on the plain of Argos

Mycenaean 1 of or relating to ancient Mycenae or its inhabitants **2** of or relating to the Aegean civilization of Mycenae (1400 to 1100BC)
▷www.archaeonia.com/history/
mycenaean.htm

mycology 1 the branch of biology concerned with the

study of fungi **2** the fungi of a particular region

myelin or **myeline** a white tissue forming an insulating sheath (**myelin sheath**) around certain nerve fibres. Damage to the myelin sheath causes neurological disease, as in multiple sclerosis

myeloma a usually malignant tumour of the bone marrow or composed of cells normally found in bone marrow

Myers L(eopold) H(amilton). 1881–1944, British novelist, best known for his novel sequence *The Near and the Far* (1929– 40)

Mykonos a Greek island in the S Aegean Sea, one of the Cyclades: a popular tourist resort with many churches. Pop: 9306 (2001)

My Lai a village in S Vietnam where in 1968 US troops massacred over 400 civilians

mynah or **myna** any of various tropical Asian starlings of the genera *Acridotheres*, *Gracula*, etc, esp *G. religiosa* (see **hill mynah**), some of which can mimic human speech

myocardium the muscular tissue of the heart

myopia inability to see distant objects clearly because the images are focused in front of the retina; shortsightedness

myriapod any terrestrial arthropod of the group *Myriapoda*, having a long segmented body and many walking limbs: includes the centipedes and millipedes

Myron 5th century BC, Greek sculptor. He worked mainly in bronze and introduced a greater variety of pose into Greek sculpture, as in his *Discobolus*

myrrh 1 any of several burseraceous trees and shrubs of the African and S Asian genus *Commiphora*, esp *C. myrrha*, that exude an aromatic resin **2** the resin obtained from such a plant, used in perfume, incense, and medicine

myrtle 1 any evergreen shrub or tree of the myrtaceous genus *Myrtus*, esp *M. communis*, a S European shrub with pink or white flowers and aromatic blue-black berries **2** **creeping** or **trailing myrtle** *US and Canadian* another name for **periwinkle** (the plant)

Mysia an ancient region in the NW corner of Asia Minor

Mysore 1 a city in S India, in S Karnataka state: former capital of the state of Mysore; manufacturing and trading centre; university (1916). Pop: 742 261 (2001) **2** the former name (until 1973) of **Karnataka**

mystery[1] 1 a story, film, etc, which arouses suspense and curiosity because of facts concealed **2** *Christianity* any truth that is divinely revealed but otherwise unknowable **3** *Christianity* a sacramental rite, such as the Eucharist, or (*when pl.*) the consecrated elements of the Eucharist **4** any of various rites of certain ancient Mediterranean religions **5** short for **mystery play**

mystery[2] *Archaic* a guild of craftsmen

mystery play (in the Middle Ages) a type of drama based on the life of Christ

mystic a person who achieves mystical experience or an apprehension of divine mysteries

mystical 1 relating to or characteristic of mysticism **2** *Christianity* having a divine or sacred significance that surpasses natural human apprehension **3** having occult or metaphysical significance, nature, or force

mysticism a system of contemplative prayer and spirituality aimed at achieving direct intuitive experience of the divine

myth 1 **a** a story about superhuman beings of an earlier age taken by preliterate society to be a true account, usually of how natural phenomena, social customs, etc, came into existence **b** another word for **mythology** **2** (in modern literature) a theme or character type embodying an idea **3** *Philosophy* (esp in the writings of Plato) an allegory or parable

mythology 1 a body of myths, esp one associated with a particular culture, institution, person, etc. **2** a body of stories about a person, institution, etc. **3** myths collectively **4** the study or collecting of myths

▷http://ugcs.caltech.edu/~cherryne/ mythology.html

▷http://members.bellatlantic.net/~vze33gpz/ myth.html

Mytilene 1 a port on the Greek island of Lesbos: Roman remains; Byzantine fortress. Pop: 25 000 (latest est) **2** a former name for **Lesbos**

myxoedema or *US* **myxedema** a disease resulting from underactivity of the thyroid gland characterized by puffy eyes, face, and hands and mental sluggishness

myxomatosis an infectious and usually fatal viral disease of rabbits characterized by swelling of the mucous membranes and formation of skin tumours; transmitted by flea bites

Nn

Nablus a town in the West Bank: near the site of ancient Shechem. Pop: 136 000 (2005 est)

nabob 1 (formerly) a European who made a fortune in the Orient, esp in India 2 another name for a **nawab**

Nabokov Vladimir Vladimirovich 1899–1977, US novelist, born in Russia. His works include *Lolita* (1955), *Pnin* (1957), *Pale Fire* (1962), and *Ada* (1969)

Naboth *Old Testament* an inhabitant of Jezreel, murdered by King Ahab at the instigation of his wife Jezebel for refusing to sell his vineyard (I Kings 21)

nacelle a streamlined enclosure on an aircraft, not part of the fuselage, to accommodate an engine, passengers, crew, etc.

Nader Ralph born 1934, US lawyer and campaigner for consumer rights and the environment: a candidate for president in 1996, 2000, and 2004

nadir the point on the celestial sphere directly below an observer and diametrically opposite the zenith

naevus *or US* **nevus** any congenital growth or pigmented blemish on the skin; birthmark or mole

Nagaland a state of NE India: formed in 1962 from parts of Assam and the North-East Frontier Agency; inhabited chiefly by Naga tribes; consists of almost inaccessible forested hills and mountains (the **Naga Hills**); shifting cultivation predominates. Capital: Kohima. Pop: 1 988 636 (2001). Area: 16 579 sq km (6401 sq miles)

Nagano a city in central Japan, on central Honshu: Buddhist shrine; two universities. Pop: 359 045 (2002 est)

Nagasaki a port in SW Japan, on W Kyushu: almost completely destroyed in 1945 by the second atomic bomb dropped on Japan by the US; shipbuilding industry. Pop: 419 901 (2002 est)

Nagorno-Karabakh Autonomous Region an administrative division in S Azerbaijan. In 1990–94 Armenian claims to the region led to violent unrest and fighting between national forces. Capital: Stepanakert. Pop: 143 000 (2000 est). Area: 4400 sq km (1700 sq miles)

Nagoya a city in central Japan, on S Honshu on Ise Bay: a major industrial centre. Pop: 2 109 681 (2002 est)

Nagpur a city in central India, in NE Maharashtra state: became capital of the kingdom of Nagpur (1743); capital of the Central Provinces (later Madhya Pradesh) from 1861 to 1956. Pop: 2 051 320 (2001)

Nagy Imre 1896–1958, Hungarian statesman; prime minister (1953–55; 1956). He was removed from office and later executed when Soviet forces suppressed the revolution of 1956; reburied with honours in 1989

Naha a port in S Japan, on the SW coast of Okinawa Island: chief city of the Ryukyu Islands. Pop: 303 146 (2002 est)

Nahum *Old Testament* 1 a Hebrew prophet of the 7th century BC 2 the book containing his oracles

naiad 1 *Greek myth* a nymph dwelling in a lake, river, spring, or fountain 2 the aquatic larva of the dragonfly, mayfly, and related insects 3 any of certain freshwater mussels of the genus *Unio* 4 any monocotyledonous submerged aquatic plant of the genus *Naias* (or *Najas*), having narrow leaves and small flowers: family *Naiadaceae* (or *Najadaceae*)

nail 1 a fastening device usually made from round or oval wire, having a point at one end and a head at the other 2 the horny plate covering part of the dorsal surface of the fingers or toes 3 the claw of a mammal, bird, or reptile 4 a unit of length, formerly used for measuring cloth, equal to two and a quarter inches

Naipaul Sir V(idiadhar) S(urajprasad). born 1932, Trinidadian novelist of Indian descent, living in Britain. His works include *A House for Mr Biswas* (1961), *In a Free State* (1971), which won the Booker Prize, *A Bend in the River* (1979), *The Enigma of Arrival* (1987), and *Beyond Belief* (1998): Nobel prize for literature 2001

Nairnshire (until 1975) a county of NE Scotland, now part of Highland

Nairobi the capital of Kenya, in the southwest at an altitude of 1650 m (5500 ft): founded in 1899; became capital in 1905; commercial and industrial centre; the **Nairobi National Park** (a game reserve) is nearby. Pop: 2 818 000 (2005 est)

Najaf a holy city in central Iraq, near the River Euphrates; burial place of the Caliph Ali and a centre of the Shiite faith. Pop: 639 000 (2005 est)

naked 1 (of the seeds of gymnosperms) not enclosed in a pericarp 2 (of flowers) lacking a perianth 3 (of stems) lacking leaves and other appendages 4 (of animals) lacking hair, feathers, scales, etc. 5 *Law* a unsupported by authority or financial or other consideration b lacking some essential condition to render valid; incomplete

Nakhichevan a city in W Azerbaijan, capital of the Nakhichevan Autonomous Republic: an ancient trading town; ceded to Russia in 1828. Pop: 66 800 (1994)

Nakhichevan Autonomous Republic a region belonging to Azerbaijan, from which it is separated by part of Armenia; annexed by Russia in 1828; unilaterally declared secession from the Soviet Union in 1990. Capital: Nakhichevan. Pop: 363 000 (2000 est). Area: 5500 sq km (2120 sq miles)

Nakuru a town in W Kenya, on Lake Nakuru: commercial centre of an agricultural region. Pop: 264 000 (2005 est)

Nalchik a city in SW Russia, capital of the Kabardino-Balkar Republic, in a valley of the Greater Caucasus: health resort. Pop: 283 000 (2005 est)

Nam or **'Nam** *Chiefly US, informal* Vietnam

Namangan a city in E Uzbekistan. Pop: 471 000 (2005 est)

Namaqualand a semiarid coastal region of SW Africa, extending from near Windhoek, Namibia, into W South Africa: divided by the Orange River into **Little Namaqualand** in South Africa, and **Great Namaqualand** in Namibia; rich mineral resources. Area: 47 961 sq km (18 518 sq miles)

Nam Co or **Nam Tso** a salt lake in SW China, in SE Tibet at an altitude of 4629 m (15 186 ft). Area: about 1800 sq km (700 sq miles)

name day *RC Church* the feast day of a saint whose name one bears

Namibe a port in SW Angola: fishing industry. Pop: 77 000 (latest est)

Namibia a country in southern Africa bordering on South Africa: annexed by Germany in 1884 and mandated by the League of Nations to South Africa in 1920. The mandate was terminated by the UN in 1966 but this was ignored by South Africa, as was the 1971 ruling by the International Court of Justice that the territory be surrendered. Independence was achieved in 1990 and Namibia became a member of the Commonwealth; Walvis Bay remained a South African enclave until 1994 when it was returned to Namibia. Official language: English; Afrikaans and German also spoken. Religion: mostly animist, with some Christians. Currency: dollar. Capital: Windhoek. Pop: 2 011 000 (2004 est). Area: 823 328 sq km (317 887 sq miles)

Namier Sir **Lewis Bernstein**, original name *Ludwik Bernsztajn vel Niemirowski*. 1888–1960, British historian, born in Poland: noted esp for his studies of 18th-century British politics

Namur 1 a province of S Belgium. Capital: Namur. Pop: 452 856 (2004 est). Area: 3660 sq km (1413 sq miles) 2 a town in S Belgium, capital of Namur province: strategically situated on a promontory between the Sambre and Meuse Rivers, besieged and captured many times. Pop: 106 213 (2004 est)

Nanchang or **Nan-ch'ang** a walled city in SE China, capital of Jiangxi province, on the Kan River: largest city in the Poyang basin. Pop: 1 742 000 (2005 est)

Nancy a city in NE France: became the capital of the dukes of Lorraine in the 12th century, becoming French in 1766; administrative and financial centre. Pop: 103 605 (1999)

Nanda Devi a mountain in N India, in Uttaranchal in the Himalayas. Height: 7817 m (25 645 ft)

Nanga Parbat a mountain in N India, in NW Kashmir in the W Himalayas. Height: 8126 m (26 660 ft)

Nanjing, Nanking, or **Nan-ching** a port in E central China, capital of Jiangsu province, on the Yangtze River: capital of the Chinese empire and a literary centre from the 14th to 17th centuries; capital of Nationalist China (1928–37); site of a massacre of about 300 000 civilians by the invading Japanese army in 1937; university (1928). Pop: 2 806 000 (2005 est)

Nanning or **Nan-ning** a port in S China, capital of Guanxi Zhuang AR, on the Xiang River: rail links with Vietnam. Pop: 1 395 000 (2005 est)

Nansen **Fridtjof** 1861–1930, Norwegian arctic explorer, statesman, and scientist. He crossed Greenland (1888–89) and attempted to reach the North Pole (1893–96), attaining a record 86° 14' N (1895). He was the League of Nations' high commissioner for refugees (1920–22): Nobel peace prize 1922

Nanterre a town in N France, on the Seine: an industrial suburb of Paris. Pop: 84 281 (1999)

Nantes a port in W France, at the head of the Loire estuary: scene of the signing of the Edict of Nantes and of the Noyades (drownings) during the French Revolution; extensive shipyards, and large metallurgical and food processing industries. Pop: 270 251 (1999)

Nantong or **Nantung** a city in E China, in Jiangsu province on the Yangtze estuary. Pop: 898 000 (2005 est)

Nantucket an island off SE Massachusetts: formerly a centre of the whaling industry; now a resort. Length: nearly 24 km (15 miles). Width: 5 km (3 miles). Pop. (county and town): 10 724 (2003 est)

Naomi *Old Testament* the mother-in-law of Ruth (Ruth 1:2)

nap[1] **a** the raised fibres of velvet or similar cloth **b** the direction in which these fibres lie when smoothed down

nap[2] 1 a card game similar to whist, usually played for stakes 2 a call in this card game, undertaking to win all five tricks 3 *Horse racing* a tipster's choice for an almost certain winner 4 **go nap a** to undertake to win all five tricks at nap **b** to risk everything on one chance

napalm a thick and highly incendiary liquid, usually consisting of petrol gelled with aluminium soaps, used in firebombs, flame-throwers, etc.

Naphtali *Old Testament* 1 Jacob's sixth son, whose mother was Rachel's handmaid (Genesis 30:7–8) 2 the tribe descended from him 3 the territory of this tribe, between the Sea of Galilee and the mountains of central Galilee

naphtha 1 a distillation product from coal tar boiling in the approximate range 80–170°C and containing aromatic hydrocarbons 2 a distillation product from petroleum boiling in the approximate range 100–200°C and containing aliphatic hydrocarbons: used as a solvent and in petrol 3 an obsolete name for **petroleum**

naphthalene, naphthaline, or **naphthalin** a white crystalline volatile solid with a characteristic penetrating odour: an aromatic hydrocarbon used in mothballs and in the manufacture of dyes, explosives, etc. Formula: $C_{10}H_8$

Napier[1] 1 Sir **Charles James** 1782–1853, British general and colonial administrator: conquered Sind (1843): governor of Sind (1843–47) 2 **John** 1550–1617, Scottish mathe-

matician: invented logarithms and pioneered the decimal notation used today **3 Robert (Cornelis),** 1st Baron
Napier of Magdala. 1810–90, British field marshal, who
commanded in India during the Sikh Wars (1845,
1848–49) and the Indian Mutiny (1857–59). He captured
Magdala (1868) while rescuing British diplomats from
Ethiopia

Napier² a port in New Zealand, on E North Island on
Hawke Bay: wool trade centre. Pop: 56 100 (2004 est)

Naples 1 a port in SW Italy, capital of Campania region,
on the Bay of Naples: the third largest city in the country; founded by Greeks in the 6th century BC; incorporated into the Kingdom of the Two Sicilies in 1140 and
its capital (1282–1503); university (1224). Pop: 1 004 500
(2001) **2 Bay of** an inlet of the Tyrrhenian Sea in the SW
coast of Italy

Napoleon I full name *Napoleon Bonaparte.* 1769–1821,
Emperor of the French (1804–15). He came to power as
the result of a coup in 1799 and established an extensive
European empire. A brilliant general, he defeated every
European coalition against him until, irreparably
weakened by the Peninsular War and the Russian cam-
paign (1812), his armies were defeated at Leipzig (1813).
He went into exile but escaped and ruled as emperor
during the Hundred Days. He was finally defeated at
Waterloo (1815). As an administrator, his achievements
were of lasting significance and include the *Code
Napoléon,* which remains the basis of French law

Napoleon II Duke of Reichstadt. 1811–32, son of
Napoleon Bonaparte and Marie Louise. He was known
as the *King of Rome* during the first French empire and
was entitled Napoleon II by Bonapartists after
Napoleon I's death (1821)

Napoleon III full name *Charles Louis Napoleon Bonaparte,*
known as *Louis-Napoleon.* 1808–73, Emperor of the French
(1852–70); nephew of Napoleon I. He led two abortive
Bonapartist risings (1836; 1840) and was elected president of the Second Republic (1848), establishing the
Second Empire in 1852. Originally successful in foreign
affairs, he was deposed after the disastrous Franco-
Prussian War

nappy 1 (of alcoholic drink, esp beer) **a** having a head;
frothy **b** strong or heady **2** (of a horse) jumpy or irritable; nervy **3** any strong alcoholic drink, esp heady beer

Nara a city in central Japan, on S Honshu: the first permanent capital of Japan (710–784). Pop: 364 411 (2002
est)

Narayan R(asipuram) K(rishnaswamy). 1906–2001,
Indian novelist writing in English. His books include
Swami and Friends (1938), *The Man-Eater of Malgudi* (1961),
Under the Banyan Tree (1985), and *Grandmother's Tale* (1993)

Narayanganj a city in central Bangladesh, on the
Ganges delta just southeast of Dhaka. Pop: 276 549
(1991)

Narbonne a city in S France: capital of the Roman
province of **Gallia Narbonensis;** harbour silted up in the
14th century. Pop: 46 510 (1999)

narcissism *or* **narcism 1** an exceptional interest in or
admiration for oneself, esp one's physical appearance
2 sexual satisfaction derived from contemplation of
one's own physical or mental endowments

narcissus any amaryllidaceous plant of the Eurasian

genus *Narcissus,* esp *N. poeticus,* whose yellow, orange, or
white flowers have a crown surrounded by spreading
segments

narcosis unconsciousness induced by narcotics or general anaesthetics

narcotic any of a group of drugs, such as heroin, morphine, and pethidine, that produce numbness and stupor. They are used medicinally to relieve pain but are
sometimes also taken for their pleasant effects; prolonged use may cause addiction

Narmada *or* **Narbada** a river in central India, rising in
Madhya Pradesh and flowing generally west to the Gulf
of Cambay in a wide estuary: the second most sacred
river in India. Length: 1290 km (801 miles)

Narragansett Bay an inlet of the Atlantic in SE Rhode
Island: contains several islands, including Rhode
Island, Prudence Island, and Conanicut Island

narrow gauge a railway track with a smaller distance
between the lines than the standard gauge of 56½ inches

Narva a port in Estonia on the Narva River near the Gulf
of Finland: developed around a Danish fortress in the
13th century; textile centre. Pop: 77 770 (1995)

Narvik a port in N Norway: scene of two naval battles in
1940; exports iron ore from Kiruna and Gällivare
(Sweden). Pop: 18 542 (2004 est)

narwhal, narwal, *or* **narwhale** an arctic toothed
whale, *Monodon monoceros,* having a black-spotted
whitish skin and, in the male, a long spiral tusk: family
Monodontidae

nascent *Chem* (of an element or simple compound, esp
hydrogen) created within the reaction medium in the
atomic form and having a high activity

Naseby a village in Northamptonshire: site of a major
Parliamentarian victory (1645) in the Civil War, when
Cromwell routed Prince Rupert's force

Nash 1 John 1752–1835, English town planner and architect. He designed Regent's Park, Regent Street, and the
Marble Arch in London **2 Ogden** 1902–71, US humorous
poet **3 Paul** 1889–1946, English painter, noted esp as a
war artist in both World Wars and for his landscapes **4
Richard,** known as *Beau Nash.* 1674–1762, English dandy **5**
Sir **Walter** 1882–1968, New Zealand Labour statesman,
born in England: prime minister of New Zealand
(1957–60)

Nashe *or* **Nash Thomas** 1567–1601, English pamphleteer, satirist, and novelist, author of the first picaresque
novel in English, *The Unfortunate Traveller, or the Life of Jack
Wilton* (1594)

Nashville a city in central Tennessee, the state capital,
on the Cumberland River: an industrial and commercial centre, noted for its recording industry. Pop.
(including Davidson): 544 765 (2003 est)

Nasik a city in W India, in Maharashtra: a centre for
Hindu pilgrims. Pop: 1 076 967 (2001)

Nasiriyah a city in S Iraq, on the River Euphrates; agricultural and trading centre. Pop: 425 000 (2005 est)

Nassau 1 a region of W central Germany: formerly a
duchy (1816–66), from which a branch of the House of
Orange arose (represented by the present rulers of the
Netherlands and Luxembourg); annexed to the
Prussian province of Hesse-Nassau in 1866; corresponds

to present-day W Hesse and NE Rhineland-Palatinate states **2** the capital and chief port of the Bahamas, on the NE coast of New Providence Island: resort. Pop: 229 000 (2005 est)

Nasser *Gamal Abdel* 1918–70, Egyptian soldier and statesman; president of Egypt (1956–70). He was one of the leaders of the coup that deposed King Farouk (1952) and became premier (1954). His nationalization of the Suez Canal (1956) led to an international crisis, and during his presidency Egypt was twice defeated by Israel (1956; 1967)

nasturtium any of various plants of the genus *Tropaeolum*, esp *T. major*, having round leaves and yellow, red, or orange trumpet-shaped spurred flowers: family *Tropaeolaceae*

natal¹ of or relating to birth

natal² *Anatomy* of or relating to the buttocks

Natal 1 a former province of E South Africa, between the Drakensberg and the Indian Ocean: set up as a republic by the Boers in 1838; became a British colony in 1843; joined South Africa in 1910; replaced by KwaZulu/Natal in 1994. Capital: Pietermaritzburg **2** a port in NE Brazil, capital of Rio Grande do Norte state, near the mouth of the Potengi River. Pop: 1 049 000 (2005 est)

Nathan *Old Testament* a prophet at David's court (II Samuel 7:1–17; 12:1–15)

Nathanael *New Testament* a Galilean who is perhaps to be identified with Bartholomew among the apostles (John 1:45–51; 21:1)

nation an aggregation of people or peoples of one or more cultures, races, etc, organized into a single state

National Curriculum (in England and Wales) the curriculum of subjects taught in state schools progressively from 1989. There are ten foundation subjects: English, maths, and science (the core subjects); art, design and technology, geography, history, music, physical education, and a foreign language. Pupils are assessed according to specified attainment targets throughout each of four key stages. Schools must also provide religious education and from 1999 lessons in citizenship
▷www.nc.uk.net/index.html

national debt the total outstanding borrowings of a nation's central government

national grid a grid of metric coordinates used by the Ordnance Survey in Britain and Ireland and in New Zealand by the New Zealand Lands and Survey Department and printed on their maps

National Health Service (in Britain) the system of national medical services since 1948, financed mainly by taxation

national hunt *Brit* **a** the racing of horses on racecourses with jumps **b** *(as modifier): a National Hunt jockey*

nationalism a sentiment based on common cultural characteristics that binds a population and often produces a policy of national independence or separatism

national park an area of countryside for public use designated by a national government as being of notable scenic, environmental, or historical importance

National Park a mountainous volcanic region in New Zealand, in the central North Island: ski resort

national service compulsory military service

National Socialism *German history* the doctrines and practices of the Nazis, involving the supremacy of the Austrian-born German dictator Adolf Hitler (1889–1945) as Führer (1934–45), anti-Semitism, state control of the economy, and national expansion
▷www.phoenixpress.co.uk/articles/ institution/national-socialism-pp.asp
▷www.tiscali.co.uk/reference/encyclopaedia/ hutchinson/M0010979.html
▷http://en.wikipedia.org/wiki/Nazism

national superannuation *NZ* a means-related pension paid to elderly people

native (of chemical elements, esp metals) found naturally in the elemental form

native dog *Austral* a dingo

Nativity 1 the birth of Jesus Christ **2** the feast of Christmas as a commemoration of this **3 a** an artistic representation of the circumstances of the birth of Christ **b** *(as modifier): a Nativity play*

NATO *or* **Nato** North Atlantic Treaty Organization, an international organization composed of the US, Canada, Britain, and a number of European countries: established by the **North Atlantic Treaty** (1949) for purposes of collective security. In 1994 it launched the partnerships for peace initiative, in order to forge alliances with former Warsaw Pact countries; in 1997 a treaty of cooperation with Russia was signed and in 1999 Hungary, Poland, and the Czech Republic became full NATO members
▷www.nato.int

natterjack a European toad, *Bufo calamita*, of sandy regions, having a greyish-brown body marked with reddish warty processes: family *Bufonidae*

natural 1 *Music* **a** not sharp or flat **b** denoting a note that is neither sharp nor flat **c** (of a key or scale) containing no sharps or flats **2** *Music* of or relating to a trumpet, horn, etc, without valves or keys, on which only notes of the harmonic series of the keynote can be obtained **3** *Cards* **a** (of a card) not a joker or wild card **b** (of a canasta or sequence) containing no wild cards **c** (of a bid in bridge) describing genuine values; not conventional **4** based on the principles and findings of human reason and what is to be learned of God from nature rather than on revelation **5** *Music* **a** an accidental cancelling a previous sharp or flat. **b** a note affected by this accidental **6** *Pontoon* the combination of an ace with a ten or court card when dealt to a player as his or her first two cards

natural gas a gaseous mixture consisting mainly of methane trapped below ground; used extensively as a fuel

natural history 1 the study of animals and plants in the wild state **2** the study of all natural phenomena **3** the sum of these phenomena in a given place or at a given time

naturalism 1 a a movement, esp in art and literature, advocating detailed realistic and factual description, esp that in 19th-century France in the writings of the novelists Emile Zola (1840–1902), Gustave Flaubert (1821–80), etc. **b** the characteristics or effects of this movement **2** a school of painting or sculpture characterized by the faithful imitation of appearances for their own sake **3** the belief that all religious truth is based not on revelation but rather on the study of natural causes and processes **4** *Philosophy* **a** a scientific account of the world in terms of causes and natural forces that rejects all spiritual, supernatural, or teleological explanations **b** the meta-ethical thesis that moral properties are reducible to natural ones, or that ethical judgments are derivable from nonethical ones

naturalist 1 a person who is expert or interested in botany or zoology, esp in the field **2** a person who advocates or practises naturalism, esp in art or literature

natural logarithm a logarithm to the base e (see **e**). Usually written log_e or ln

natural number any of the numbers 0,1,2,3,4,... that can be used to count the members of a set; the nonnegative integers

natural philosophy (now only used in Scottish universities) physical science, esp physics

natural selection a process resulting in the survival of those individuals from a population of animals or plants that are best adapted to the prevailing environmental conditions. The survivors tend to produce more offspring than those less well adapted, so that the characteristics of the population change over time, thus accounting for the process of evolution

nature 1 all natural phenomena and plant and animal life, as distinct from man and his creations **2** *Biology* the complement of genetic material that partly determines the structure of an organism; genotype

nature reserve an area of land that is protected and managed in order to preserve a particular type of habitat and its flora and fauna which are often rare or endangered

nature study the study of the natural world, esp animals and plants, by direct observation at an elementary level

Naucratis an ancient Greek city in N Egypt, in the Nile delta: founded in the 7th century BC

Nauru an island republic in the SW Pacific, west of Kiribati: administered jointly by Australia, New Zealand, and Britain as a UN trust territory before becoming independent in 1968; a member of the Commonwealth (formerly a special member not represented at all meetings, until 1999). The economy is based on export of phosphates. Languages: Nauruan (a Malayo-Polynesian language) and English. Religion: Christian. Currency: Australian dollar. Pop: 13 000 (2003 est). Area: 2130 hectares (5263 acres)

nausea the sensation that precedes vomiting

nautical mile 1 a unit of length, used esp in navigation, equivalent to the average length of a minute of latitude, and corresponding to a latitude of 45°, i.e. 1852 m (6076.12 ft) **2** a former British unit of length equal to 1853.18 m (6080 ft), which was replaced by the international nautical mile in 1970

nautilus any cephalopod mollusc of the genus *Nautilus*, esp the pearly nautilus

Navarino 1 the Italian name for **Pylos 2** a sea battle (Oct 20, 1827) in which the defeat of the Turkish-Egyptian fleet by a combined British, French, and Russian fleet decided Greek independence

Navarre a former kingdom of SW Europe: established in the 9th century by the Basques; the parts south of the Pyrenees joined Spain in 1515 and the N parts passed to France in 1589. Capital: Pamplona

nave the central space in a church, extending from the narthex to the chancel and often flanked by aisles

navel the scar in the centre of the abdomen, usually forming a slight depression, where the umbilical cord was attached

navigable 1 wide, deep, or safe enough to be sailed on or through **2** capable of being steered or controlled

Navratilova Martina born 1956, Czech-born US tennis player: Wimbledon champion 1978, 1979, 1982–87, 1990; world champion 1980 and 1984

nawab (formerly) a Muslim ruling prince or powerful landowner in India

Naxos a Greek island in the S Aegean, the largest of the Cyclades: ancient centre of the worship of Dionysius. Pop: 18 188 (2001). Area: 438 sq km (169 sq miles)

Nayarit a state of W Mexico, on the Pacific: includes the offshore Tres Marías Islands. Capital: Tepic. Pop: 919 739 (2000). Area: 27 621 sq km (10 772 sq miles)

Nazarene 1 an early name for a **Christian** (Acts 24:5) or (when preceded by *the*) for Jesus Christ (?4 BC–?29 AD), the founder of Christianity **2** a member of one of several groups of Jewish-Christians found principally in Syria **3** a member of an association of German artists called the Nazarenes or Brotherhood of St Luke, including Friedrich Overbeck (1789–1869) and Peter von Cornelius (1783–1867), founded (1809) in Vienna to revive German religious art after the examples of the Middle Ages and early Renaissance

Nazareth a town in N Israel, in Lower Galilee: the home of Jesus in his youth. Pop: 62 700 (2003 est)

Naze the 1 a flat marshy headland in SE England, in Essex on the North Sea coast **2** another name for **Lindesnes**

Nazi a member of the fascist National Socialist German Workers' Party, which was founded in 1919 and seized political control in Germany in 1933 under the Austrian-born German dictator Adolf Hitler (1889–1945)

Ndjamena *or* **N'djamena** the capital of Chad, in the southwest, at the confluence of the Shari and Logone Rivers: trading centre for livestock. Pop: 866 000 (2005 est)

Ndola a city in N Zambia: copper, cobalt, and sugar refineries. Pop: 478 000 (2005 est)

Neagh Lough a lake in Northern Ireland, in SW Co. Antrim: the largest lake in the British Isles. Area: 388 sq km (150 sq miles)

neap 1 of, relating to, or constituting a neap tide **2** short for **neap tide**

Neapolitan 1 a native or inhabitant of Naples **2** of or relating to Naples

neap tide either of the two tides that occur at the first or last quarter of the moon when the tide-generating forces of the sun and moon oppose each other and produce the smallest rise and fall in tidal level

Near East 1 another term for the **Middle East 2** (formerly) the Balkan States and the area of the Ottoman Empire

nearside *Chiefly Brit* **a** the side of a vehicle normally nearer the kerb (in Britain, the left side) **b** (*as modifier*):

the nearside door

near-sighted relating to or suffering from myopia

neat (of alcoholic drinks) without added water, lemonade, etc.; undiluted

Neath Port Talbot a county borough in S Wales, created from part of West Glamorgan in 1996. Administrative centre: Port Talbot. Pop: 135 300 (2003 est). Area: 439 sq km (169 sq miles)

neb *Archaic or dialect* **a** a peak, esp in N England **b** a prominent gritstone overhang

Nebo *Mount* a mountain in Jordan, northeast of the Dead Sea: the highest point of a ridge known as Pisgah, from which Moses viewed the Promised Land just before his death (Deuteronomy 34:1). Height: 802 m (2631 ft)

Nebraska a state of the western US: consists of an undulating plain. Capital: Lincoln. Pop: 1 739 291 (2003 est). Area: 197 974 sq km (76 483 sq miles)

Nebuchadnezzar *or* **Nebuchadrezzar** *Old Testament* a king of Babylon, 605–562 BC, who conquered and destroyed Jerusalem and exiled the Jews to Babylon (II Kings 24–25)

nebula 1 *Astronomy* a diffuse cloud of particles and gases (mainly hydrogen) that is visible either as a hazy patch of light (either an **emission** or a **reflection nebula**) or an irregular dark region against a brighter background (**dark nebula**) **2** *Pathol* **a** an opacity of the cornea **b** cloudiness of the urine **3** any substance for use in an atomizer spray

nebulizer *or* **nebuliser** a device for converting a drug in liquid form into a mist or fine spray which is inhaled through a mask to provide medication for the respiratory system

necessary 1 *Logic* **a** (of a statement, formula, etc) true under all interpretations or in all possible circumstances **b** (of a proposition) determined to be true by its meaning, so that its denial would be self-contradictory **c** (of a property) essential, so that without it its subject would not be the entity it is **d** (of an inference) always yielding a true conclusion when its premises are true; valid **e** (of a condition) entailed by the truth of some statement or the obtaining of some state of affairs **2** *Philosophy* (in a nonlogical sense) expressing a law of nature, so that if it is in this sense necessary that all As are B, even although it is not contradictory to conceive of an A which is not B, we are licensed to infer that if something were an A it would have to be B

necessity 1 *Philosophy* **a** a condition, principle, or conclusion that cannot be otherwise **b** the constraining force of physical determinants on all aspects of life **2** *Logic* **a** the property of being necessary **b** a statement asserting that some property is essential or statement is necessarily true **c** the operator that indicates that the expression it modifies is true in all possible worlds.

neck 1 the part of an organism connecting the head with the rest of the body **2** *Anatomy* a constricted portion of an organ or part, such as the cervix of the uterus **3** a narrow or elongated projecting strip of land; a peninsula or isthmus **4** a strait or channel **5** the part of a violin, cello, etc, that extends from the body to the tuning pegs and supports the fingerboard **6** a solid block of lava from the opening of an extinct volcano,

exposed after erosion of the surrounding rock **7** *Botany* the upper, usually tubular, part of the archegonium of mosses, ferns, etc. **8** the length of a horse's head and neck taken as an approximate distance by which one horse beats another in a race **9** *Architect* the narrow band at the top of the shaft of a column between the necking and the capital, esp as used in the Tuscan order

Neckar a river in SW Germany, rising in the Black Forest and flowing generally north into the Rhine at Mannheim. Length: 394 km (245 miles)

necromancy the art or practice of supposedly conjuring up the dead, esp in order to obtain from them knowledge of the future

necrophilia sexual attraction for or sexual intercourse with dead bodies

necrosis 1 the death of one or more cells in the body, usually within a localized area, as from an interruption of the blood supply to that part **2** death of plant tissue due to disease, frost, etc.

nectar 1 a sugary fluid secreted in the nectaries of plants and collected by bees and other animals **2** *Classical myth* the drink of the gods

nectarine a variety of peach tree, *Prunus persica nectarina*

needle 1 a another name for **stylus b** a small thin pointed device, esp one made of stainless steel, used to transmit the vibrations from a gramophone record to the pick-up **2** *Med* **a** the long hollow pointed part of a hypodermic syringe, which is inserted into the body **b** an informal name for **hypodermic syringe 3** *Surgery* a pointed steel instrument, often curved, for suturing, puncturing, or ligating **4** a long narrow stiff leaf, esp of a conifer, in which water loss is greatly reduced **5** any slender sharp spine, such as the spine of a sea urchin **6** any slender pointer for indicating the reading on the scale of a measuring instrument **7** short for **magnetic needle 8** a crystal resembling a needle in shape **9** a sharp pointed metal instrument used in engraving and etching

needlecord a corduroy fabric with narrow ribs

Nefertiti *or* **Nofretete** 14th century BC, Egyptian queen; wife of Akhenaton

negation *Logic* **a** the operator that forms one sentence from another and corresponds to the English *not* **b** a sentence so formed. It is usually written $-p$, $\neg p$, $\bar{p}$ or $\neg p$, where p is the given sentence, and is false when the given sentence is true, and true when it is false

negative 1 *Biology* indicating movement or growth away from a particular stimulus **2** *Med* (of the results of a diagnostic test) indicating absence of the disease or condition for which the test was made **3** another word for **minus 4** *Physics* **a** (of an electric charge) having the same polarity as the charge of an electron **b** (of a body, system, ion, etc) having a negative electric charge; having an excess of electrons **c** (of a point in an electric circuit) having a lower electrical potential than some other point with an assigned zero potential **5** short for **electronegative 6** of or relating to a photographic negative **7** *Logic* (of a categorial proposition) denying the satisfaction by the subject of the predicate, as in *some men are irrational; no pigs have wings* **8** *Astrology* of, relating to, or governed by the signs of the zodiac of the earth and water classifications, which are thought to be associated with a receptive passive nature **9** *Photog* a piece of photographic film or a plate, previously exposed and developed, showing an image that, in black-and-white photography, has a reversal of tones. In colour photography the image is in complementary colours to the subject so that blue sky appears yellow, green grass appears purple, etc. **10** *Physics* a negative object, such as a terminal or a plate in a voltaic cell **11** a quantity less than zero or a quantity to be subtracted **12** *Logic* a negative proposition

negative equity the state of holding a property the value of which is less than the amount of mortgage still unpaid

negativism 1 any sceptical or derisive system of thought **2** *Psychiatry* refusal to do what is expected or suggested or the tendency to do the opposite

Negev *or* **Negeb** the S part of Israel, on the Gulf of Aqaba: a triangular-shaped semidesert region, with large areas under irrigation; scene of fighting between Israeli and Egyptian forces in 1948. Chief town: Beersheba. Area: 12 820 sq km (4950 sq miles)

negligence *Law* a civil wrong whereby a person or party is in breach of a legal duty of care to another which results in loss or injury to the claimant

Negri Sembilan a state of S Peninsular Malaysia: mostly mountainous, with large areas under paddy and rubber. Capital: Seremban. Pop: 859 924 (2000). Area: 6643 sq km (2565 sq miles)

Negro[1] *Old-fashioned or offensive* a member of any of the dark-skinned indigenous peoples of Africa and their descendants elsewhere

Negro[2] *Río* **1** a river in NW South America, rising in E Colombia (as the Guainía) and flowing east, then south as part of the border between Colombia and Venezuela, entering Brazil and continuing southeast to join the Amazon at Manáus. Length: about 2250 km (1400 miles) **2** a river in S central Argentina, formed by the confluence of the Neuquén and Limay Rivers and flowing east and southeast to the Atlantic. Length: about 1014 km (630 miles) **3** a river in central Uruguay, rising in S Brazil and flowing southwest into the Uruguay River. Length: about 467 km (290 miles)

Negroid denoting, relating to, or belonging to one of the major racial groups of mankind, characterized by brown-black skin, tightly-curled hair, a short nose, and full lips. This group includes the indigenous peoples of Africa south of the Sahara, their descendants elsewhere, and some Melanesian peoples

Negros an island of the central Philippines, one of the Visayan Islands. Capital: Bacolod. Pop: 3 168 000 (1990 est). Area: 12 704 sq km (4904 sq miles)

Nehemiah *Old Testament* **1** a Jewish official at the court of Artaxerxes, king of Persia, who in 444 BC became a leader in the rebuilding of Jerusalem after the Babylonian captivity **2** the book recounting the acts of Nehemiah

Nehru 1 Jawaharlal 1889–1964, Indian statesman and nationalist leader. He spent several periods in prison for his nationalist activities and practised a policy of noncooperation with Britain during World War II. He was the first prime minister of the republic of India (1947–64) **2** his father, **Motilal** , known as *Pandit Nehru.*

1861–1931, Indian nationalist, lawyer, and journalist; first president of the reconstructed Indian National Congress

neighbourhood *or US* **neighborhood** *Maths* the set of all points whose distance from a given point is less than a specified value

Neill A(lexander) S(utherland). 1883–1973, Scottish educationalist and writer, who put his progressive educational theories into practice at Summerhill school (founded 1921)

Neisse 1 a river in SW Poland, rising on the northern Czech border, and flowing northeast to join the Oder near Brzeg. Length: about 193 km (120 miles) **2** a river in E Europe, rising near Liberec in the Czech Republic and flowing north to join the Oder: forms part of the German-Polish border. Length: 225 km (140 miles)

Nejd a region of central Saudi Arabia: formerly an independent sultanate of Arabia; united with Hejaz to form the kingdom of Saudi Arabia (1932)

nelson any wrestling hold in which a wrestler places his arm or arms under his opponent's arm or arms from behind and exerts pressure with his palms on the back of his opponent's neck

Nelson[1] **1** Horatio, Viscount Nelson. 1758–1805, British naval commander during the Revolutionary and Napoleonic Wars. He became rear admiral in 1797 after the battle of Cape St Vincent and in 1798 almost destroyed the French fleet at the battle of the Nile. He was killed at Trafalgar (1805) after defeating Villeneuve's fleet **2** Willie born 1933, US country singer and songwriter

Nelson[2] **1** a town in NW England, in E Lancashire: textile industry. Pop: 28 998 (2001) **2** a port in New Zealand, on N South Island on Tasman Bay. Pop: 45 300 (2004 est) **3** *River* a river in central Canada, in N central Manitoba, flowing from Lake Winnipeg northeast to Hudson Bay. Length: about 650 km (400 miles)

Nelspruit a city in NE South Africa, the capital of Mpumalanga province on the Crocodile River: trading and agricultural centre, esp for fruit, with a growing tourist trade. Pop: 21 541 (2001)

Neman *or* **Nyeman** a river in NE Europe, rising in Belarus and flowing northwest through Lithuania to the Baltic. Length: 937 km (582 miles)

nematode any unsegmented worm of the phylum (or class) *Nematoda*, having a tough outer cuticle. The group includes free-living forms and disease-causing parasites, such as the hookworm and filaria

Nemea (in ancient Greece) a valley in N Argolis in the NE Peloponnese; site of the **Nemean Games,** a Panhellenic festival and athletic competition held every other year

neoclassicism 1 a late 18th- and early 19th-century style in architecture, decorative art, and fine art, based on the imitation of surviving classical models and types **2** *Music* a movement of the 1920s, involving Hindemith, Stravinsky, etc, that sought to avoid the emotionalism of late romantic music by reviving the use of counterpoint, forms such as the classical suite, and small instrumental ensembles
▷www.comcen.com.au/~carowley/
neoclass.htm

▷www.hypermusic.ca/hist/twentieth3.html

neocolonialism (in the modern world) political control by an outside power of a country that is in theory sovereign and independent, esp through the domination of its economy

neodymium a toxic silvery-white metallic element of the lanthanide series, occurring principally in monazite: used in colouring glass. Symbol: Nd; atomic no.: 60; atomic wt.: 144.24; valency: 3; relative density: 6.80 and 7.00 (depending on allotrope); melting pt.: 1024°C; boiling pt.: 3127°C

Neolithic the cultural period that lasted in SW Asia from about 9000 to 6000 BC and in Europe from about 4000 to 2400 BC and was characterized by primitive crop growing and stock rearing and the use of polished stone and flint tools and weapons

neon a colourless odourless rare gaseous element, an inert gas occurring in trace amounts in the atmosphere: used in illuminated signs and lights. Symbol: Ne; atomic no.: 10; atomic wt.: 20.1797; valency: 0; density: 0.899 90 kg/m^3; melting pt.: -248.59°C; boiling pt.: -246.08°C

neonatal of or relating to newborn children, esp in the first week of life and up to four weeks old

neophyte 1 a person newly converted to a religious faith 2 *RC Church* a novice in a religious order

Nepal a kingdom in S Asia: the world's only Hindu kingdom; united in 1768 by the Gurkhas; consists of swampy jungle in the south and great massifs, valleys, and gorges of the Himalayas over the rest of the country, with many peaks over 8000 m (26 000 ft) (notably Everest and Kangchenjunga). A multiparty democracy was instituted in 1990. Official language: Nepali. Official religion: Hinduism; Mahayana Buddhist minority. Currency: rupee. Capital: Katmandu. Pop: 25 724 000 (2004 est). Area: 147 181 sq km (56 815 sq miles)

Nepali the official language of Nepal, also spoken in Sikkim and parts of India. It forms the E group of Pahari and belongs to the Indic branch of Indo-European

nephritis inflammation of a kidney

Neptune[1] the Roman god of the sea

Neptune[2] the eighth planet from the sun, having eight satellites, the largest being Triton and Nereid, and a faint planar system of rings or ring fragments. Mean distance from sun: 4497 million km; period of revolution around sun: 164.8 years; period of rotation: 14 to 16 hours; diameter and mass: 4.0 and 17.2 times that of earth respectively

neptunium a silvery metallic transuranic element synthesized in the production of plutonium and occurring in trace amounts in uranium ores. Symbol: Np; atomic no.: 93; half-life of most stable isotope, ^{237}Np: 2.14 × 10^6 years; valency: 3, 4, 5, or 6; relative density: 20.25; melting pt.: 639±1°C; boiling pt.: 3902°C (est)

Neri Saint Philip Italian name *Filippo de' Neri*. 1515–95, Italian priest; founder of the Congregation of the Oratory (1564). Feast day: May 26

Nernst Walther Hermann 1864–1941, German physical chemist who formulated the third law of thermodynamics: Nobel prize for chemistry 1920

Nero full name *Nero Claudius Caesar Drusus Germanicus*; original name *Lucius Domitius Ahenobarbus*. 37–68 AD, Roman emperor (54–68). He became notorious for his despotism and cruelty, and was alleged to have started the fire (64) that destroyed a large part of Rome

Neruda Pablo , real name *Neftali Ricardo Reyes*. 1904–73, Chilean poet. His works include *Veinte poemas de amor y una canción desesperada* (1924) and *Canto general* (1950), an epic history of the Americas: Nobel prize for literature 1971

Nerva full name *Marcus Cocceius Nerva*. ?30–98 AD, Roman emperor (96–98), who introduced some degree of freedom after the repressive reign of Domitian. He adopted Trajan as his son and successor

Nerval Gérard de , real name *Gérard Labrunie*. 1808–55, French poet, noted esp for the sonnets of mysticism, myth, and private passion in *Les Chimères* (1854)

nervate (of leaves) having veins

nerve 1 any of the cordlike bundles of fibres that conduct sensory or motor impulses between the brain or spinal cord and another part of the body 2 a large vein in a leaf 3 any of the veins of an insect's wing

nerve centre a group of nerve cells associated with a specific function

nerve gas (esp in chemical warfare) any of various poisonous gases that have a paralysing effect on the central nervous system that can be fatal

nervous breakdown any mental illness not primarily of organic origin, in which the patient ceases to function properly, often accompanied by severely impaired concentration, anxiety, insomnia, and lack of self-esteem; used esp of episodes of depression

nervous system the sensory and control apparatus of all multicellular animals above the level of sponges, consisting of a network of nerve cells

ness a *Archaic* a promontory or headland b (*capital as part of a name*): *Orford Ness*

Ness Loch a lake in NW Scotland, in the Great Glen: said to be inhabited by an aquatic monster. Length: 36 km (22.5 miles). Depth: 229 m (754 ft)

nest 1 a place or structure in which birds, fishes, insects, reptiles, mice, etc, lay eggs or give birth to young 2 a number of animals of the same species and their young occupying a common habitat

nestling a a young bird not yet fledged b (*as modifier*): *a nestling thrush*

Nestorius died ?451 AD, Syrian churchman; patriarch of Constantinople (428–431); deposed for heresy by the Council of Ephesus

net[1] 1 a a thin light mesh fabric of cotton, nylon, or other fibre, used for curtains, dresses, etc. b (*as modifier*): *net curtains* 2 *Cricket* a a pitch surrounded by netting, used for practice b a practice session in a net

net[2] or **nett** (of weight) after deducting tare

Netanyahu Benjamin born 1949, Israeli politician: leader of the Likud party (1993–99); prime minister (1996–99)

netball a team game similar to basketball, played mainly by women

▷www.netball.org

Netherlands the 1 a kingdom in NW Europe, on the North Sea: declared independence from Spain in 1581 as the United Provinces; became a major maritime and commercial power in the 17th century, gaining many overseas possessions; it formed the Benelux customs union with Belgium and Luxembourg in 1948 and was a founder member of the Common Market, now the European Union . It is mostly flat and low-lying, with about 40 per cent of the land being below sea level, much of it on polders protected by dykes. Official language: Dutch. Religion: Christian majority, Protestant and Roman Catholic, large nonreligious minority. Currency: euro. Capital: Amsterdam, with the seat of government at The Hague. Pop: 16 227 000 (2004 est). Area: 41 526 sq km (16 033 sq miles) **2** the kingdom of the Netherlands together with the Flemish-speaking part of Belgium, esp as ruled by Spain and Austria before 1581; the Low Countries

nettle 1 any weedy plant of the temperate urticaceous genus *Urtica*, such as *U. dioica* (**stinging nettle**), having serrated leaves with stinging hairs and greenish flowers **2** any of various other urticaceous plants with stinging hairs or spines **3** any of various plants that resemble urticaceous nettles, such as the dead-nettle, hemp nettle, and horse nettle

network 1 *Electronics* a system of interconnected components or circuits **2** *Computing* a system of interconnected computer systems, terminals, and other equipment allowing information to be exchanged

Neubrandenburg a city in NE Germany, in Mecklenburg-West Pomerania: 14th-century city walls. Pop: 69 157 (2003 est)

Neuilly-sur-Seine a town in N France, on the Seine: a suburb of NW Paris. Pop: 59 848 (1999)

Neumann Johann Balthasar 1687–1753, German rococo architect. His masterpiece is the church of Vierzehnheiligen in Bavaria

neural of or relating to a nerve or the nervous system

neuralgia severe spasmodic pain caused by damage to or malfunctioning of a nerve and often following the course of the nerve

neuritis inflammation of a nerve or nerves, often accompanied by pain and loss of function in the affected part

neurology the study of the anatomy, physiology, and diseases of the nervous system

neurosis a relatively mild mental disorder, characterized by symptoms such as hysteria, anxiety, depression, or obsessive behaviour

neurosurgery the branch of surgery concerned with the nervous system

neurotic 1 of, relating to, or afflicted by neurosis **2** a person who is afflicted with a neurosis or who tends to be emotionally unstable or unusually anxious

Neuss an industrial city in W Germany, in North Rhine-Westphalia west of Düsseldorf: founded as a Roman fortress in the 1st century AD. Pop: 152 050 (2003 est)

Neustria the western part of the kingdom of the Merovingian Franks formed in 561 AD in what is now N France

neuter 1 (of animals and plants) having nonfunctional, underdeveloped, or absent reproductive organs **2** a sexually underdeveloped female insect, such as a worker bee **3** a castrated animal, esp a domestic animal **4** a

flower in which the stamens and pistil are absent or nonfunctional

neutral 1 *Politics* of, belonging to, or appropriate to a neutral party, country, etc. **2** (of a colour such as white or black) having no hue; achromatic **3** a less common term for **neuter** (sense 1) **4** *Chem* neither acidic nor alkaline **5** *Physics* having zero charge or potential **6** *Rare* having no magnetism **7** a citizen of a neutral state **8** the position of the controls of a gearbox that leaves the transmission disengaged

neutrino *Physics* a stable leptonic neutral elementary particle with very small or possibly zero rest mass and spin ½ that travels at the speed of light. Three types exist, associated with the electron, the muon, and the tau particle

neutron *Physics* a neutral elementary particle with a rest mass of $1.674\ 92716 \times 10^{-27}$ kilogram and spin ½; classified as a baryon. In the nucleus of an atom it is stable but when free it decays

Neva a river in NW Russia, flowing west to the Gulf of Finland by the delta on which Saint Petersburg stands. Length: 74 km (46 miles)

Nevada a state of the western US: lies almost wholly within the Great Basin, a vast desert plateau; noted for production of gold and copper. Capital: Carson City. Pop: 2 241 154 (2003 est). Area: 284 612 sq km (109 889 sq miles)

Nevers a city in central France: capital of the former duchy of Nivernais; engineering industry. Pop: 40 932 (1999)

Nevis 1 an island in the Caribbean, part of St Kitts-Nevis; the volcanic cone of **Nevis Peak,** which rises to 1002 m (3287 ft), lies in the centre of the island. Capital: Charlestown. Pop: 11 181 (2001. Area: 129 sq km (50 sq miles) **2** See **Ben Nevis**

New Age a **a** philosophy, originating in the late 1980s, characterized by a belief in alternative medicine, astrology, spiritualism, etc. **b** (*as modifier*): *New Age therapies*

▷http://www.xs4all.nl/~wichm/newage3.html

New Amsterdam the Dutch settlement established on Manhattan (1624–26); capital of New Netherlands; captured by the English and renamed New York in 1664

Newark 1 a town in N central England, in Nottinghamshire. Pop: 35 454 (2001) **2** a port in NE New Jersey, just west of New York City, on Newark Bay and the Passaic River: the largest city in the state; founded in 1666 by Puritans from Connecticut; industrial and commercial centre. Pop: 277 911 (2003 est)

New Australia the colony on socialist principles founded by William Lane in Paraguay in 1893

New Bedford a port and resort in SE Massachusetts, near Buzzards Bay: settled by Plymouth colonists in 1652; a leading whaling port (18th–19th centuries). Pop: 94 112 (2003 est)

New Britain an island in the S Pacific, northeast of New Guinea: the largest island of the Bismarck Archipelago; part of Papua New Guinea; mountainous, with several active volcanoes. Capital: Rabaul. Pop: 435 307 (1999 est). Area: 36 519 sq km (14 100 sq miles)

New Brunswick a province of SE Canada on the Gulf of St Lawrence and the Bay of Fundy: extensively forested.

Capital: Fredericton. Pop: 751 384 (2004 est). Area: 72 092 sq km (27 835 sq miles)

Newbury a market town in West Berkshire unitary authority, S England: scene of a Parliamentarian victory (1643) and a Royalist victory (1644) during the Civil War; telecommunications, racecourse. Pop: 32 675 (2001)

New Caledonia an island in the SW Pacific, east of Australia: forms, with its dependencies, a French Overseas Country; discovered by Captain Cook in 1774; rich mineral resources. Capital: Nouméa. Pop: 232 000 (2004 est). Area: 19 103 sq km (7374 miles)

New Castile a region and former province of central Spain. Chief town: Toledo

Newcastle¹ Duke of, the title of *Thomas Pelham Holles*. 1693–1768, English Whig prime minister (1754–56; 1757–62): brother of Henry Pelham

Newcastle² a port in SE Australia, in E New South Wales near the mouth of the Hunter River: important industrial centre, with extensive steel, metalworking, engineering, shipbuilding, and chemical industries. It suffered Australia's first fatal earthquake in 1989. Pop: 279 975 (2001)

Newcastle-under-Lyme a town in W central England, in Staffordshire. Pop: 74 427 (2001)

Newcastle upon Tyne 1 a port in NE England in Newcastle upon Tyne unitary authority, Tyne and Wear, near the mouth of the River Tyne opposite Gateshead: Roman remains; engineering industries, including ship repairs; two universities (1937, 1992). Pop: 189 863 (2001) **2** a unitary authority in NE England, in Tyne and Wear. Pop: 266 600 (2003 est). Area: 112 sq km (43 sq miles)

new chum *Austral* (in the 19th century) a new arrival in a hulk

Newcombe John (David). born 1944, Australian tennis player; winner of seven Grand Slam singles titles (1967–74)

Newcomen Thomas 1663–1729, English engineer who invented a steam engine, which James Watt later modified and developed

newel the central pillar of a winding staircase, esp one that is made of stone

New England 1 the NE part of the US, consisting of the states of Maine, New Hampshire, Vermont, Massachusetts, Rhode Island, and Connecticut: settled originally chiefly by Puritans in the mid-17th century **2** a region in SE Australia, in the northern tablelands of New South Wales

New England Range a mountain range in SE Australia, in NE New South Wales: part of the Great Dividing Range. Highest peak: Ben Lomond, 1520 m (4986 ft)

New English Bible a new Modern English version of the Bible and Apocrypha, published in full in 1970

New Forest a region of woodland and heath in S England, in SW Hampshire: a hunting ground of the West Saxon kings; tourist area, noted for its ponies. Area: 336 sq km (130 sq miles)

Newfoundland 1 an island of E Canada, separated from the mainland by the Strait of Belle Isle: with the Coast of Labrador forms the province of Newfoundland and

Labrador; consists of a rugged plateau with the Long Range Mountains in the west. Area: 110 681 sq km (42 734 sq miles) **2** a very large heavy breed of dog similar to a Saint Bernard with a flat coarse usually black coat

New France the former French colonies and possessions in North America, most of which were lost to England and Spain by 1763: often restricted to the French possessions in Canada

New Georgia 1 a group of islands in the SW Pacific, in the Solomon Islands **2** the largest island in this group. Area: about 1300 sq km (500 sq miles)

New Granada 1 a former Spanish presidency and later viceroyalty in South America. At its greatest extent it consisted of present-day Panama, Colombia, Venezuela, and Ecuador **2** the name of Colombia when it formed, with Panama, part of Great Colombia (1819–30)

New Guinea 1 an island in the W Pacific, north of Australia: divided politically into Papua (formerly Irian Jaya, a province of Indonesia) in the west and Papua New Guinea in the east. There is a central chain of mountains and a lowland area of swamps in the south and along the Sepik River in the north. Area: 775 213 sq km (299 310 sq miles) **2 Trust Territory of** (until 1975) an administrative division of the former Territory of Papua and New Guinea, consisting of the NE part of the island of New Guinea together with the Bismarck Archipelago; now part of Papua New Guinea

Newham a borough of E Greater London, on the River Thames: established in 1965. Pop: 250 600 (2003 est). Area: 36 sq km (14 sq miles)

New Hampshire a state of the northeastern US: generally hilly. Capital: Concord. Pop: 1 287 687 (2003 est). Area: 23 379 sq km (9027 sq miles)

New Harmony a village in SW Indiana, on the Wabash River: scene of two experimental cooperative communities, the first founded in 1815 by George Rapp, a German religious leader, and the second by Robert Owen in 1825

Newhaven a ferry port and resort on the S coast of England, in East Sussex. Pop: 12 276 (2001)

New Haven an industrial city and port in S Connecticut, on Long Island Sound: settled in 1638 by English Puritans, who established it as a colony in 1643; seat of Yale University (1701). Pop: 124 512 (2003 est)

Ne Win U 1911–2002, Burmese statesman and general; prime minister (1958–60), head of the military government (1962–74), and president (1974–81)

New Ireland an island in the S Pacific, in the Bismarck Archipelago, separated from New Britain by St George's Channel: part of Papua New Guinea. Chief town and port: Kavieng. Pop: 87 194 (1990.). Area (including adjacent islands): 9850 sq km (3800 sq miles)

New Jersey a state of the eastern US, on the Atlantic and Delaware Bay: mostly low-lying, with a heavy industrial area in the northeast and many coastal resorts. Capital: Trenton. Pop: 8 638 396 (2003 est). Area: 19 479 sq km (7521 sq miles)

New Jerusalem *Christianity* heaven regarded as the prototype of the earthly Jerusalem; the heavenly city

Newlands John Alexander 1838–98, British chemist:

classified the elements in order of their atomic weight, noticing similarities in every eighth and thus discovering his law of octaves

New Latin the form of Latin used since the Renaissance, esp for scientific nomenclature

Newman 1 Barnet 1905–70, US painter, a founder of Abstract Expressionism: his paintings include the series *Stations of the Cross* (1965–66) **2 John Henry** 1801–90, British theologian and writer. Originally an Anglican minister, he was a prominent figure in the Oxford Movement. He became a Roman Catholic (1845) and a priest (1847) and was made a cardinal (1879). His writings include the spiritual autobiography, *Apologia pro vita sua* (1864), a treatise on the nature of belief, *The Grammar of Assent* (1870), and hymns **3 Paul** born 1925, US film actor and director, who appeared in such films as *Hud* (1963), *Butch Cassidy and the Sundance Kid* (1969), *The Sting* (1973), *The Verdict* (1982), *The Colour of Money* (1986), *Nobody's Fool* (1994), and *Road to Perdition* (2002)

Newmarket a town in SE England, in W Suffolk: a famous horse-racing centre since the reign of James I. Pop: 16 947 (2001)

new maths *Brit* an approach to mathematics in which the basic principles of set theory are introduced at an elementary level

New Mexico a state of the southwestern US: has high semiarid plateaus and mountains, crossed by the Rio Grande and the Pecos River; large Spanish-American and Indian populations; contains over two-thirds of US uranium reserves. Capital: Santa Fé. Pop: 1 874 614 (2003 est). Area: 314 451 sq km (121 412 sq miles)

new moon 1 the moon when it appears as a narrow waxing crescent **2** the time at which this occurs **3** *Astronomy* one of the four principal phases of the moon, occurring when it lies between the earth and the sun

New Netherland a Dutch North American colony of the early 17th century, centred on the Hudson valley. Captured by the English in 1664, it was divided into New York and New Jersey

New Orleans a port in SE Louisiana, on the Mississippi River about 172 km (107 miles) from the sea: the largest city in the state and the second most important port in the US; founded by the French in 1718; belonged to Spain (1763–1803). It is largely below sea level, built around the Vieux Carré (French quarter); famous for its annual Mardi Gras festival and for its part in the history of jazz; a major commercial, industrial, and transportation centre. Pop: 469 032 (2003 est)

New Plymouth a port in New Zealand, on W North Island: founded in 1841. Pop: 69 200 (2004 est)

Newport 1 a city and port in SE Wales, in Newport county borough on the River Usk: electronics. Pop: 116 143 (2001) **2** a county borough in SE Wales, created from part of Gwent in 1996. Pop: 139 300 (2003 est). Area: 190 sq km (73 sq miles) **3** a port in SE Rhode Island: founded in 1639, it became one of the richest towns of colonial America; centre of a large number of US naval establishments. Pop: 26 136 (2003 est) **4** a town in S England, administrative centre of the Isle of Wight. Pop: 22 957 (2001)

Newport News a port in SE Virginia, at the mouth of the James River: an industrial centre, with one of the world's largest shipyards. Pop: 181 647 (2003 est)

New Providence an island in the Atlantic, in the Bahamas. Chief town: Nassau. Pop: 210 832 (2000). Area: 150 sq km (58 sq miles)

New Quebec a region of E Canada, formerly the Ungava district of Northwest Territories (1895–1912), extending from the line of the Eastmain and Hamilton Rivers north between Hudson Bay and Labrador: absorbed by Quebec in 1912: contains extensive iron deposits. Area: about 777 000 sq km (300 000 sq miles)

New Romney a market town in SE England, in Kent on Romney Marsh: of early importance as one of the Cinque Ports, but is now over 1.6 km (1 mile) inland. Pop: 9406 (2001)

Newry a city and port in Northern Ireland, in Newry and Mourne district, Co. Down: close to the border with the Republic of Ireland, it has been the scene of sectarian violence in recent years. Pop: 27 433 (2001)

Newry and Mourne a district of SE Northern Ireland, in Co. Down. Pop: 89 644 (2003 est). Area: 909 sq km (351 sq miles)

newsgroup *Computing* a forum where subscribers exchange information about a specific subject by electronic mail

newsletter *History* a written or printed account of the news

New South Wales a state of SE Australia: originally contained over half the continent, but was reduced by the formation of other states (1825–1911); consists of a narrow coastal plain, separated from extensive inland plains by the Great Dividing Range; the most populous state; mineral resources. Capital: Sydney. Pop: 6 716 277 (2003 est). Area: 801 428 sq km (309 433 sq miles)

New Style the present method of reckoning dates using the Gregorian calendar

newt 1 any of various small semiaquatic urodele amphibians, such as *Triturus vulgaris* (**common newt**) of Europe, having a long slender body and tail and short feeble legs **2** *Chiefly Brit* any other urodele amphibian, including the salamanders

New Testament the collection of writings consisting of the Gospels, Acts of the Apostles, Pauline and other Epistles, and the book of Revelation, composed soon after Christ's death and added to the Jewish writings of the Old Testament to make up the Christian Bible

newton the derived SI unit of force that imparts an acceleration of 1 metre per second per second to a mass of 1 kilogram; equivalent to 10^5 dynes or 7.233 poundals.

Newton Sir **Isaac** 1642–1727, English mathematician, physicist, astronomer, and philosopher, noted particularly for his law of gravitation, his three laws of motion, his theory that light is composed of corpuscles, and his development of calculus independently of Leibnitz. His works include *Principia Mathematica* (1687) and *Opticks* (1704)

Newtown a new town in central Wales, in Powys. Pop: 10 358 (2001)

new town (in Britain) a town that has been planned as a complete unit and built with government sponsorship, esp to accommodate overspill population

Newtownabbey 1 a town in Northern Ireland, in Newtownabbey district, Co. Antrim on Belfast Lough:

the third largest town in Northern Ireland, formed in 1958 by the amalgamation of seven villages; light industrial centre, esp for textiles. Pop: 62 056 (2001) **2** a district of E Northern Ireland, in Co. Antrim. Pop: 80 285 (2003 est). Area: 151 sq km (58 sq miles)

Newtown St Boswells a village in SE Scotland, administrative centre of Scottish Borders: agricultural centre. Pop: 1199 (2001)

New World the the Americas; the western hemisphere

New York **1** a city in SE New York State, at the mouth of the Hudson River: the largest city and chief port of the US; settled by the Dutch as New Amsterdam in 1624 and captured by the British in 1664, when it was named New York; consists of five boroughs (Manhattan, the Bronx, Queens, Brooklyn, and Richmond) and many islands, with its commercial and financial centre in Manhattan; the country's leading commercial and industrial city. Pop: 8 085 742 (2003 est) **2** a state of the northeastern US: consists chiefly of a plateau with the Finger Lakes in the centre, the Adirondack Mountains in the northeast, the Catskill Mountains in the south-east, and Niagara Falls in the west. Capital: Albany. Pop: 19 190 115 (2003 est). Area: 123 882 sq km (47 831 sq miles)

New York Bay an inlet of the Atlantic at the mouth of the Hudson River: forms the harbour of the port of New York

New York State Barge Canal a system of inland waterways in New York State, connecting the Hudson River with Lakes Erie and Ontario and, via Lake Champlain, with the St Lawrence. Length: 845 km (525 miles)

New Zealand an independent dominion within the Commonwealth, occupying two main islands (the North Island and the South Island), Stewart Island, the Chatham Islands, and a number of minor islands in the SE Pacific: original Māori inhabitants ceded sovereignty to the British government in 1840; became a dominion in 1907; a major world exporter of dairy products, wool, and meat. Official languages: English and Māori. Religion: Christian majority, nonreligious and Māori minorities. Currency: New Zealand dollar. Capital: Wellington. Pop: 3 905 000 (2004 est). Area: 270 534 sq km (104 454 sq miles)

Ney Michel , Duc d'Elchingen. 1769–1815, French marshal, who earned the epithet *Bravest of the Brave* at the battle of Borodino (1812) in the Napoleonic Wars. He rallied to Napoleon on his return from Elba and was executed for treason (1815)

Nha Trang a port in SE Vietnam, on the South China Sea: nearby temples of the Cham civilization; fishing industry. Pop: 382 000 (2005 est)

Niagara a river in NE North America, on the border between W New York State and Ontario, Canada, flowing from Lake Erie to Lake Ontario. Length: 45 km (28 miles)

Niagara Falls **1** the falls of the Niagara River, on the border between the US and Canada: divided by Goat Island into the American Falls, 50 m (167 ft) high, and the Horseshoe or Canadian Falls, 47 m (158 ft) high **2** a city in W New York State, situated at the falls of the Niagara River. Pop: 78 815 (2001) **3** a city in S Canada, in SE Ontario on the Niagara River just below the falls:

linked to the city of Niagara Falls in the US by three bridges. Pop: 78 815 (2001)

Niamey the capital of Niger, in the southwest on the River Niger: became capital in 1926; airport and land route centre. Pop: 997 000 (2005 est)

Nicaea an ancient city in NW Asia Minor, in Bithynia: site of the **first council of Nicaea** (325 AD), which composed the Nicene Creed

NICAM near-instantaneous companding system: a technique for coding audio signals into digital form

Nicaragua **1** a republic in Central America, on the Caribbean and the Pacific: colonized by the Spanish from the 1520s; gained independence in 1821 and was annexed by Mexico, becoming a republic in 1838. Official language: Spanish. Religion: Roman Catholic majority. Currency: córdoba. Capital: Managua. Pop: 5 596 000 (2004 est). Area: 131 812 sq km (50 893 sq miles) **2** **Lake** a lake in SW Nicaragua, separated from the Pacific by an isthmus 19 km (12 miles) wide: the largest lake in Central America. Area: 8264 sq km (3191 sq miles)

Nice a city in SE France, on the Mediterranean: a leading resort of the French Riviera; founded by Phocaeans from Marseille in about the 3rd century BC. Pop: 342 738 (1999)

niche **1** a recess in a wall, esp one that contains a statue **2** any similar recess, such as one in a rock face **3** *Commerce* relating to or aimed at a small specialized group or market **4** *Ecology* the role of a plant or animal within its community and habitat, which determines its activities, relationships with other organisms, etc.

Nicholas Saint 4th-century AD bishop of Myra, in Asia Minor; patron saint of Russia and of children, sailors, merchants, and pawnbrokers. Feast day: Dec 6

Nicholas I **1** Saint, called *the Great.* died 867 AD, Italian ecclesiastic; pope (858–867). He championed papal supremacy. Feast day: Nov 13 **2** 1796–1855, tsar of Russia (1825–55). He gained notoriety for his autocracy and his emphasis on military discipline and bureaucracy

Nicholas II 1868–1918, tsar of Russia (1894–1917). After the disastrous Russo- Japanese War (1904–05), he was forced to summon a representative assembly, but his continued autocracy and incompetence precipitated the Russian Revolution (1917): he abdicated and was shot

Nicholas V original name *Tommaso Parentucelli.* 1397–1455, Italian ecclesiastic; pope (1447–55). He helped to found the Vatican Library

Nicholas of Cusa 1401–64, German cardinal, philosopher, and mathematician: anticipated Copernicus in asserting that the earth revolves around the sun

Nicholson **1** Ben 1894–1982, English painter, noted esp for his abstract geometrical works **2** Jack born 1937, US film actor. His films include *Easy Rider* (1969), *One Flew Over the Cuckoo's Nest* (1974), *Terms of Endearment* (1983), *Batman* (1989), *As Good As It Gets* (1998), and *About Schmidt* (2002) **3** John 1821–57, British general and administrator, born in Ireland: deputy commissioner in the Punjab (1851–56), where he became the object of hero-worship among the natives and kept the Punjab loyal during the Indian Mutiny: played a major role in the capture of Delhi

Nicias died 414 BC, Athenian statesman and general. He ended the first part of the Peloponnesian War by making peace with Sparta (421)

nickel 1 a malleable ductile silvery-white metallic element that is strong and corrosion-resistant, occurring principally in pentlandite and niccolite: used in alloys, esp in toughening steel, in electroplating, and as a catalyst in organic synthesis. Symbol: Ni; atomic no.: 28; atomic wt.: 58.6934; valency: 0, 1, 2, or 3; relative density: 8.902; melting pt.: 1455°C; boiling pt.: 2914°C **2** a US and Canadian coin and monetary unit worth five cents

nickelodeon US **1** an early form of jukebox **2** (formerly) a cinema charging five cents for admission **3** (formerly) a Pianola, esp one operated by inserting a five-cent piece

nickel silver any of various white alloys containing copper (46–63 per cent), zinc (18–36 per cent), and nickel (6–30 per cent): used in making tableware, etc.

Nicklaus Jack born 1940, US professional golfer: won the British Open Championship (1966; 1970; 1978) and the US Open Championship (1962; 1967; 1972; 1980)

Nicodemus *New Testament* a Pharisee and a member of the Sanhedrin, who supported Jesus against the other Pharisees (John 8:50–52)

Nicolai Carl Otto Ehrenfried 1810–49, German composer: noted for his opera *The Merry Wives of Windsor* (1849)

Nicosia the capital of Cyprus, in the central part on the Pedieos River: capital since the 10th century. Pop. (Greek and Turkish): Pop: 211 000 (2005 est)

nicotine a colourless oily acrid toxic liquid that turns yellowish-brown in air and light: the principal alkaloid in tobacco, used as an agricultural insecticide. Formula: $C_{10}H_{14}N_2$

nictitating membrane (in reptiles, birds, and some mammals) a thin fold of skin beneath the eyelid that can be drawn across the eye

Nielsen Carl (August). 1865–1931, Danish composer. His works include six symphonies and the opera *Masquerade* (1906)

Niemeyer Oscar born 1907, Brazilian architect. His work includes many buildings in Brasília, esp the president's palace (1959) and the cathedral (1964)

Niepce Joseph-Nicéphore 1765–1833, French inventor. He produced the first photographic image (1816) and the first permanent camera photograph (1826)

Nietzsche Friedrich Wilhelm 1844–1900, German philosopher, poet, and critic, noted esp for his concept of the superman and his rejection of traditional Christian values. His chief works are *The Birth of Tragedy* (1872), *Thus Spake Zarathustra* (1883– 91), and *Beyond Good and Evil* (1886)

Niger 1 a landlocked republic in West Africa: important since earliest times for its trans-Saharan trade routes; made a French colony in 1922 and became fully independent in 1960; exports peanuts and livestock. Official language: French. Religion: Muslim majority. Currency: franc. Capital: Niamey. Pop: 12 415 000 (2004 est). Area: 1 267 000 sq km (489 000 sq miles) **2** a river in West Africa, rising in S Guinea and flowing in a great northward curve through Mali, then southwest through Niger and Nigeria to the Gulf of Guinea: the third longest river in Africa, with the largest delta, covering an area of 36 260 sq km (14 000 sq miles). Length: 4184 km (2600 miles) **3** a state of W central Nigeria, formed in 1976 from part of North-Western State. Capital: Minna. Pop: 2 775 526 (1995 est). Area: 76 363 sq km (29 476 sq miles)

Nigeria a republic in West Africa, on the Gulf of Guinea: Lagos annexed by the British in 1861; protectorates of Northern and Southern Nigeria formed in 1900 and united as a colony in 1914; gained independence as a member of the Commonwealth in 1960 (membership suspended from 1995 to 1999 following human rights violations); Eastern Region seceded as the Republic of Biafra for the duration of the severe civil war (1967–70); ruled by military governments from 1966. It consists of a belt of tropical rain forest in the south, with semi-desert in the extreme north and highlands in the east; the main export is petroleum. Official language: English; Hausa, Ibo, and Yoruba are the chief regional languages. Religion: animist, Muslim, and Christian. Currency: naira. Capital: Abuja. Pop: 127 117 000 (2004 est). Area: 923 773 sq km (356 669 sq miles)

nightingale 1 a brownish European songbird, *Luscinia megarhynchos*, with a broad reddish-brown tail: well known for its musical song, usually heard at night **2** any of various similar or related birds, such as *Luscinia luscinia* (**thrush nightingale**)

Nightingale Florence, known as *the Lady with the Lamp*. 1820–1910, English nurse, famous for her work during the Crimean War. She helped to raise the status and quality of the nursing profession and founded a training school for nurses in London (1860)

nightjar any nocturnal bird of the family *Caprimulgidae*, esp *Caprimulgus europaeus* (**European nightjar**): order *Caprimulgiformes*. They have a cryptic plumage and large eyes and feed on insects

night school an educational institution that holds classes in the evening for those who are not free during the day

nightshade any of various solanaceous plants, such as deadly nightshade, woody nightshade, and black nightshade

night watchman *Cricket* a batsman sent in to bat to play out time when a wicket has fallen near the end of a day's play

nihilism 1 *Philosophy* an extreme form of scepticism that systematically rejects all values, belief in existence, the possibility of communication, etc. **2** a revolutionary doctrine of destruction for its own sake **3** the practice or promulgation of terrorism

Niigata a port in central Japan, on NW Honshu at the mouth of the Shinano River: the chief port on the Sea of Japan. Pop: 514 678 (2002 est)

Nijinsky Waslaw *or* Vaslaw 1890–1950, Russian ballet dancer and choreographer, who was associated with Diaghilev. His creations include settings of Stravinsky's *Petrushka* and *The Rite of Spring*

Nijmegen an industrial town in the E Netherlands, in Gelderland province on the Waal River: the oldest town in the country; scene of the signing (1678) of the peace treaty between Louis XIV, the Netherlands, Spain, and the Holy Roman Empire. Pop: 156 000 (2003 est)

Nikko a town in central Japan, on NE Honshu: a major

pilgrimage centre, with a 4th-century Shinto shrine, a Buddhist temple (767), and the shrines and mausoleums of the Tokugawa shoguns. Pop: 17 527 (2002 est)

Nikolayev a city in S Ukraine on the Southern Bug about 64 km (40 miles) from the Black Sea: founded as a naval base in 1788; one of the leading Black Sea ports. Pop: 518 000 (2005 est)

Nile a river in Africa, rising in S central Burundi in its remotest headstream, the **Luvironza:** flows into Lake Victoria and leaves the lake as the **Victoria Nile,** flowing to Lake Albert, which is drained by the **Albert Nile,** becoming the White Nile on the border between Uganda and the Sudan; joined by its chief tributary, the **Blue Nile** (which rises near Lake Tana, Ethiopia) at Khartoum, and flows north to its delta on the Mediterranean; the longest river in the world. Length: (from the source of the Luvironza to the Mediterranean) 6741 km (4187 miles)

Nilotic 1 of or relating to the Nile 2 of, relating to, or belonging to a tall Negroid pastoral people inhabiting the S Sudan, parts of Kenya and Uganda, and neighbouring countries 3 relating to or belonging to the group of languages spoken by the Nilotic peoples 4 a group of languages of E Africa, including Luo, Dinka, and Masai, now generally regarded as belonging to the Chari-Nile branch of the Nilo-Saharan family

Nilsson Birgit born 1918, Swedish operatic soprano

nimbus 1 a a dark grey rain-bearing cloud b (*in combination*): *cumulonimbus clouds* 2 a an emanation of light surrounding a saint or deity b a representation of this emanation

Nimrod *Old Testament* a hunter, who was famous for his prowess (Genesis 10:8–9)

Nimrud an ancient city in Assyria, near the present-day city of Mosul (Iraq): founded in about 1250 BC and destroyed by the Medes in 612 BC; excavated by Sir Austen Henry Layard

nine 1 the cardinal number that is the sum of one and eight 2 a numeral, 9, IX, etc, representing this number 3 **nine to five** normal office hours

ninefold 1 equal to or having nine times as many or as much 2 composed of nine parts

ninepins 1 another name for **skittles** (see skittle (sense 2)) 2 one of the pins used in this game

nineteen 1 the cardinal number that is the sum of ten and nine and is a prime number 2 a numeral, 19, XIX, etc, representing this number 3 something represented by, representing, or consisting of 19 units

nineteenth hole *Golf, slang* the bar in a golf clubhouse

ninety 1 the cardinal number that is the product of ten and nine 2 a numeral, 90, XC, etc, representing this number

Nineveh the ancient capital of Assyria, on the River Tigris opposite the present-day city of Mosul (N Iraq): at its height in the 8th and 7th centuries BC; destroyed in 612 BC by the Medes and Babylonians

Ningbo *or* **Ningpo** a port in E China, in NE Zhejiang, on the Yung River, about 20 km (12 miles) from its mouth at Hangzhou Bay: one of the first sites of European settlement in China. Pop: 1 188 000 (2005 est)

Ningsia *or* **Ninghsia** 1 a former province of NW China: mostly included in the Inner Mongolian AR in 1956,

with the smaller part constituted as the Ningxia Hui AR in 1958 2 the former name of **Yinchuan**

Ningxia Hui Autonomous Region an administrative division of NW China, south of the Inner Mongolian AR. Capital: Yinchuan. Pop: 5 800 000 (2003 est). Area: 66 400 sq km (25 896 sq miles)

Ninian Saint ?360–?432 AD, the first known apostle of Scotland; built a stone church (*candida casa*) at Whithorn on his native Solway; preached to the Picts. Feast day: Sept 16

ninja a person skilled in **ninjutsu,** a Japanese martial art characterized by stealthy movement and camouflage

Ninus a king of Assyria and the legendary founder of Nineveh, husband of Semiramis

niobium a ductile white superconductive metallic element that occurs principally in columbite and tantalite: used in steel alloys. Symbol: Nb; atomic no.: 41; atomic wt.: 92.90638; valency: 2, 3, or 5; relative density: 8.57; melting pt.: 2469±10°C; boiling pt.: 4744°C

nip[1] nip and tuck *Informal* plastic surgery performed for cosmetic reasons

nip[2] *Chiefly Brit* a measure of spirits usually equal to one sixth of a gill

Nipigon Lake a lake in central Canada, in NW Ontario, draining into Lake Superior via the **Nipigon River** Area: 4843 sq km (1870 sq miles)

Nipissing Lake a lake in central Canada, in E Ontario between the Ottawa River and Georgian Bay. Area: 855 sq km (330 sq miles)

nipper the large pincer-like claw of a lobster, crab, or similar crustacean

nipple 1 the small conical projection in the centre of the areola of each breast, which in women contains the outlet of the milk ducts 2 a small drilled bush, usually screwed into a bearing, through which grease is introduced

Nippur an ancient Sumerian and Babylonian city, the excavated site of which is in SE Iraq: an important religious centre, abandoned in the 12th or 13th century

Nirenberg Marshall Warren born 1927, US biochemist; shared the Nobel prize for physiology or medicine (1968) for his role in deciphering the genetic code

nirvana *Buddhism, Hinduism* final release from the cycle of reincarnation attained by extinction of all desires and individual existence, culminating (in Buddhism) in absolute blessedness, or (in Hinduism) in absorption into Brahman

Niš *or* **Nish** an industrial town in E Serbia and Montenegro, in SE Serbia: situated on routes between central Europe and the Aegean. Pop: 203 670 (2002)

Nishapur a town in NE Iran, at an altitude of 1195 m (3920 ft): birthplace and burial place of Omar Khayyám. Pop: 208 000 (2005 est)

Nishinomiya an industrial city in central Japan, on S Honshu, northwest of Osaka. Pop: 436 877 (2002 est)

nisi *Law* (of a court order) coming into effect on a specified date unless cause is shown within a certain period why it should not

Nissen hut a military shelter of semicircular cross section, made of corrugated steel sheet

nit[1] 1 the egg of a louse, usually adhering to human hair 2 the larva of a louse or similar insect

nit² a unit of luminance equal to 1 candela per square metre

nit³ a unit of information equal to 1.44 bits

nitrate any salt or ester of nitric acid, such as sodium nitrate, $NaNO_3$

nitric of or containing nitrogen, esp in the pentavalent state

nitric acid a colourless or yellowish fuming corrosive liquid usually used in aqueous solution. It is an oxidizing agent and a strong monobasic acid: important in the manufacture of fertilizers, explosives, and many other chemicals. Formula: HNO_3

nitride a compound of nitrogen with a more electropositive element, for example magnesium nitride, Mg_3N_2

nitrite any salt or ester of nitrous acid

nitrogen a a colourless odourless relatively unreactive gaseous element that forms 78 per cent (by volume) of the air, occurs in many compounds, and is an essential constituent of proteins and nucleic acids: used in the manufacture of ammonia and other chemicals and as a refrigerant. Symbol: N; atomic no.: 7; atomic wt.: 14.00674; valency: 3 or 5; density: 1/2506 kg/m³; melting pt.: –210.00°C; boiling pt.: –195.8°C **b** (as modifier): nitrogen cycle

nitrogen cycle the natural circulation of nitrogen by living organisms. Nitrates in the soil, derived from dead organic matter by bacterial action (see **nitrogen fixation**), are absorbed and synthesized into complex organic compounds by plants and reduced to nitrates again when the plants and the animals feeding on them die and decay

nitrogen fixation 1 the conversion of atmospheric nitrogen into nitrogen compounds by certain bacteria, such as Rhizobium in the root nodules of legumes 2 a process, such as the Haber process, in which atmospheric nitrogen is converted into a nitrogen compound, used esp for the manufacture of fertilizer

nitroglycerine or **nitroglycerin** a pale yellow viscous explosive liquid substance made from glycerol and nitric and sulphuric acids and used in explosives and in medicine as a vasodilator. Formula: $CH_2NO_3CHNO_3CH_2NO_3$

nitrous of, derived from, or containing nitrogen, esp in a low valency state

nitrous acid a weak monobasic acid known only in solution and in the form of nitrite salts. Formula: HNO_2

nitrous oxide a colourless nonflammable slightly soluble gas with a sweet smell: used as an anaesthetic in dentistry and surgery. Formula: N_2O

Niue an island in the S Pacific, between Tonga and the Cook Islands: annexed by New Zealand (1901); achieved full internal self-government in 1974. Chief town and port: Alofi. Pop: 2000 (2003 est). Area: 260 sq km (100 sq miles)

Niven David 1909–83, British film actor and author. His films include The Prisoner of Zenda (1937), Around the World in 80 Days (1956), Casino Royale (1967), and Paper Tiger (1975). He wrote the autobiographical The Moon's a Balloon (1972) and Bring on the Empty Horses (1975)

Nivernais a former province of central France, around Nevers

Nixon Richard M(ilhous). 1913–94, US Republican politician; 37th president from 1969 until he resigned over the Watergate scandal in 1974

Nizhni Novgorod a city and port in central Russia, at the confluence of the Volga and Oka Rivers: situated on the Volga route from the Baltic to central Asia; birthplace of Maxim Gorki. Pop: 1 288 000 (2005 est)

Nizhni Tagil a city in central Russia, on the E slopes of the Ural Mountains: a major metallurgical centre. Pop: 382 000 (2005 est)

Nkomo Joshua 1917–99, Zimbabwean politician; coleader, with Robert Mugabe, of the Patriotic Front (1976–80) against the government of Ian Smith in Rhodesia; minister (1980–82; 1988–99) and vice-president (1990–96).

Nkrumah Kwame 1909–72, Ghanaian statesman, prime minister (1957-60) and president (1960-66). He led demands for self- government in the 1950s, achieving Ghanaian independence in 1957. He was overthrown by a military coup (1966)

No¹ or **Noh** the stylized classic drama of Japan, developed in the 15th century or earlier, using music, dancing, chanting, elaborate costumes, and themes from religious stories or myths

No² Lake a lake in the S central Sudan, where the Bahr el Jebel (White Nile) is joined by the Bahr el Ghazal. Area: about 103 sq km (40 sq miles)

Noah Old Testament a Hebrew patriarch, who saved himself, his family, and specimens of each species of animal and bird from the Flood by building a ship (**Noah's Ark**) in which they all survived (Genesis 6–8)

nob Cribbage 1 the jack of the suit turned up 2 **one for his nob** the call made with this jack, scoring one point

no-ball 1 Cricket an illegal ball, as for overstepping the crease, throwing, etc, for which the batting side scores a run, and from which the batsman can be out only by being run out 2 Rounders an illegal ball, esp one bowled too high or too low

Nobel Alfred Bernhard 1833–96, Swedish chemist and philanthropist, noted for his invention of dynamite (1866) and his bequest founding the Nobel prizes

nobelium a transuranic element produced artificially from curium. Symbol: No; atomic no.: 102; half-life of most stable isotope, ^{255}No: 180 seconds (approx.); valency: 2 or 3

nobility 1 a socially or politically privileged class whose titles are conferred by descent or by royal decree 2 (in the British Isles) the class of people holding the title of dukes, marquesses, earls, viscounts, or barons and their feminine equivalents collectively; peerage

noble 1 of or relating to a hereditary class with special social or political status, often derived from a feudal period 2 Chem **a** (of certain elements) chemically unreactive **b** (of certain metals, esp copper, silver, and gold) resisting oxidation 3 Falconry **a** designating longwinged falcons that capture their quarry by stooping on it from above **b** designating the type of quarry appropriate to a particular species of falcon 4 a person belonging to a privileged social or political class whose status is usually indicated by a title conferred by sovereign authority or descent 5 (in the British Isles) a person holding the title of duke, marquess, earl, viscount, or baron, or a feminine equivalent 6 a former Brit gold coin having the value of one third of a pound

nock 1 a notch on an arrow that fits on the bowstring 2 either of the grooves at each end of a bow that hold the bowstring

nocturnal 1 (of animals) active at night 2 (of plants) having flowers that open at night and close by day

nocturne 1 a short, lyrical piece of music, esp one for the piano 2 a painting or tone poem of a night scene

nod the nod *Boxing, informal* the award of a contest to a competitor on the basis of points scored

noddy any of several tropical terns of the genus *Anous*, esp *A. stolidus* (**common noddy**), typically having a dark plumage

node 1 the point on a plant stem from which the leaves or lateral branches grow 2 *Physics* a point at which the amplitude of one of the two kinds of displacement in a standing wave has zero or minimum value. Generally the other kind of displacement has its maximum value at this point 3 *Maths* a point at which two branches of a curve intersect, each branch having a distinct tangent 4 *Maths, Linguistics* one of the objects of which a graph or a tree consists; vertex 5 *Astronomy* either of the two points at which the orbit of a body intersects the plane of the ecliptic. When the body moves from the south to the north side of the ecliptic it passes the **ascending node** and from the north to the south side it passes the **descending node** 6 *Anatomy* a any natural bulge or swelling of a structure or part, such as those that occur along the course of a lymphatic vessel (**lymph node**) b a finger joint or knuckle 7 *Computing* an interconnection point on a computer network

nodule 1 any of the knoblike outgrowths on the roots of clover and many other legumes: contain bacteria involved in nitrogen fixation 2 *Anatomy* any small node or knoblike protuberance 3 a small rounded lump of rock or mineral substance, esp in a matrix of different rock material

Noel *or* **Noël** *Rare* a Christmas carol

nog *or* **nogg** 1 a drink, esp an alcoholic one, containing beaten egg 2 *East Anglian, dialect* strong local beer

noggin a small quantity of spirits, usually 1 gill

no-go area a district in a town that is barricaded off, usually by a paramilitary organization, within which the police, army, etc, can only enter by force

noise 1 any undesired electrical disturbance in a circuit, degrading the useful information in a signal 2 undesired or irrelevant elements in a visual image 3 **noises off** *Theatre* sounds made offstage intended for the ears of the audience: used as a stage direction

noise pollution annoying or harmful noise in an environment

Nolan 1 Michael Patrick, Baron. born 1928, British judge; chairman of the Committee on Standards in Public Life (1994–97) 2 Sir Sidney 1917–92, Australian painter, whose works explore themes in Australian folklore

nomad a member of a people or tribe who move from place to place to find pasture and food

nominal *Bell-ringing* the harmonic an octave above the strike tone of a bell

nominalism the philosophical theory that the variety of objects to which a single general word, such as *dog*, applies have nothing in common but the name

nonage *Law* the state of being under any of various ages at which a person may legally enter into certain transactions, such as the making of binding contracts, marrying, etc.

nonagon a polygon having nine sides

nonaligned (of states) not part of a major alliance or power bloc, esp not allied to the US, China, or formerly the Soviet Union

Nonconformist a member of a Protestant denomination that dissents from an Established Church, esp the Church of England

nonferrous 1 denoting any metal other than iron 2 not containing iron

nonintervention refusal to intervene, esp the abstention by a state from intervening in the affairs of other states or in its own internal disputes

nonmetal any of a number of chemical elements that form negative ions, have acidic oxides, and are generally poor conductors of heat and electricity

Nono Luigi 1924–90, Italian composer of 12- tone music

non-profit-making not yielding a profit, esp because organized or established for some other reason

non sequitur *Logic* a conclusion that does not follow from the premises

nonstarter a horse that fails to run in a race for which it has been entered

nonunion *Pathol* failure of broken bones or bone fragments to heal

Nord a department of N France, in Nord-Pas-de-Calais region. Capital: Lille. Pop: 2 561 800 (2003 est). Area: 5774 sq km (2252 sq miles)

nordic *Skiing* of or relating to competitions in cross-country racing and ski-jumping

Nordic of, relating to, or belonging to a subdivision of the Caucasoid race typified by the tall blond blue-eyed long-headed inhabitants of N Britain, Scandinavia, N Germany, and the Netherlands

Nordkyn Cape a cape in N Norway: the northernmost point of the European mainland

Nord-Pas-de-Calais a region of N France, on the Straits of Dover (the **Pas de Calais**): coal-mining, textile, and metallurgical industries

Norfolk 1 a county of E England, on the North Sea and the Wash: low-lying, with large areas of fens in the west and the Broads in the east; rich agriculturally. Administrative centre: Norwich. Pop: 810 700 (2003 est). Area: 5368 sq km (2072 sq miles) 2 a port in SE Virginia, on the Elizabeth River and Hampton Roads: headquarters of the US Atlantic fleet; shipbuilding. Pop: 241 727 (2003 est)

Norfolk Island an island in the S Pacific, between New Caledonia and N New Zealand: an Australian external territory; discovered by Captain Cook in 1774; a penal settlement in early years. Pop: 2601 (2001). Area: 36 sq km (14 sq miles)

Noricum an Alpine kingdom of the Celts, south of the Danube: comprises present-day central Austria and parts of Bavaria; a Roman province from about 16 BC

norm 1 *Maths* a the length of a vector expressed as the square root of the sum of the square of its components b another name for **mode** 2 *Geology* the theoretical standard mineral composition of an igneous rock

normal 1 *Psychol* **a** being within certain limits of intelligence, educational success or ability, etc. **b** conforming to the conventions of one's group 2 *Biology, Med* (of laboratory animals) maintained in a natural state for purposes of comparison with animals treated with drugs, etc. 3 *Chem* (of a solution) containing a number of grams equal to the equivalent weight of the solute in each litre of solvent. 4 *Chem* denoting a straight-chain hydrocarbon: *a normal alkane*. Prefix: **n-**, e.g. *n*-octane 5 *Geometry* another word for **perpendicular** 6 *Geometry* a line or plane perpendicular to another line or plane or to the tangent of a curved line or plane at the point of contact

Norman¹ 1 *Greg* born 1955, Australian golfer 2 *Jessye* born 1945, US Black soprano

Norman² 1 (in the Middle Ages) a member of the people of Normandy descended from the 10th-century Scandinavian conquerors of the country and the native French 2 a native or inhabitant of Normandy 3 another name for **Norman French** 4 of, relating to, or characteristic of the Normans, esp the Norman kings of England, the Norman people living in England, or their dialect of French 5 denoting, relating to, or having the style of Romanesque architecture used in Britain from the Norman Conquest until the 12th century. It is characterized by the rounded arch, the groin vault, massive masonry walls, etc.

Normandy a former province of N France, on the English Channel: settled by Vikings under Rollo in the 10th century; scene of the Allied landings in 1944. Chief town: Rouen

Norman French the medieval Norman and English dialect of Old French

Norn¹ *Norse myth* any of the three virgin goddesses of fate, who predestine the lives of the gods and men

Norn² the medieval Norse language of the Orkneys, Shetlands, and parts of N Scotland. It was extinct by 1750

Norrington Sir *Roger* (*Arthur Carver*). born 1934, British conductor; noted for period performances of early music

Norse 1 of, relating to, or characteristic of Norway 2 **a** the N group of Germanic languages, spoken in Scandinavia; Scandinavian **b** any one of these languages, esp in their ancient or medieval forms 3 **the Norse a** the Norwegians **b** the Vikings

north 1 one of the four cardinal points of the compass, at 0° or 360°, that is 90° from east and west and 180° from south 2 the direction along a meridian towards the North Pole 3 the direction in which a compass needle points; magnetic north 4 **the North** any area lying in or towards the north 5 *Cards* the player or position at the table corresponding to north on the compass

North¹ 1 *Frederick*, 2nd Earl of Guildford, called *Lord North*. 1732–92, British statesman; prime minister (1770–82), dominated by George III. He was held responsible for the loss of the American colonies 2 Sir *Thomas* ?1535–?1601, English translator of Plutarch's *Lives* (1579), which was the chief source of Shakespeare's Roman plays

North² **the** 1 the northern area of England, generally regarded as reaching approximately the southern boundaries of Yorkshire and Lancashire 2 (in the US) the area approximately north of Maryland and the Ohio River, esp those states north of the Mason-Dixon Line that were known as the Free States during the Civil War 3 the northern part of North America, esp the area consisting of Alaska, the Yukon, the Northwest Territories, and Nunavut; the North Country 4 the countries of the world that are economically and technically advanced

North Africa the part of Africa between the Mediterranean and the Sahara: consists chiefly of Morocco, Algeria, Tunisia, Libya, and N Egypt

Northallerton a market town in N England, administrative centre of North Yorkshire. Pop: 15 517 (2001)

North America the third largest continent, linked with South America by the Isthmus of Panama and bordering on the Arctic Ocean, the N Pacific, the N Atlantic, the Gulf of Mexico, and the Caribbean. It consists generally of a great mountain system (the Western Cordillera) extending along the entire W coast, actively volcanic in the extreme north and south, with the Great Plains to the east and the Appalachians still further east, separated from the Canadian Shield by an arc of large lakes (Great Bear, Great Slave, Winnipeg, Superior, Michigan, Huron, Erie, Ontario); reaches its greatest height of 6194 m (20 320 ft) in Mount McKinley, Alaska, and its lowest point of 85 m (280 ft) below sea level in Death Valley, California, and ranges from snowfields, tundra, and taiga in the north to deserts in the southwest and tropical forests in the extreme south. Pop: 332 156 000 (2005 est). Area: over 24 000 000 sq km (9 500 000 sq miles)

Northampton 1 a town in central England, administrative centre of Northamptonshire, on the River Nene: footwear and engineering industries. Pop: 189 474 (2001) 2 short for **Northamptonshire**

Northamptonshire a county of central England: agriculture, food processing, engineering, and footwear industries. Administrative centre: Northampton. Pop: 642 700 (2003 est). Area: 2367 sq km (914 sq miles)

North Ayrshire a council area of W central Scotland, on the Firth of Clyde: comprises the N part of the historical county of Ayrshire, including the Isle of Arran; formerly part of Strathclyde Region (1975–96): chiefly agricultural, with fishing and tourism. Administrative centre: Irvine. Pop: 136 030 (2003 est). Area: 884 sq km (341 sq miles)

North Brabant a province of the S Netherlands: formed part of the medieval duchy of Brabant. Capital: 's Hertogenbosch. Pop: 2 400 000 (2003 est). Area: 4965 sq km (1917 sq miles)

North Cape 1 a cape on N Magerøy Island, in the Arctic Ocean off the N coast of Norway 2 a cape on N North Island, New Zealand

North Carolina a state of the southeastern US, on the Atlantic: consists of a coastal plain rising to the Piedmont Plateau and the Appalachian Mountains in the west. Capital: Raleigh. Pop: 8 407 248 (2003 est). Area: 126 387 sq km (48 798 sq miles)

North Channel a strait between NE Ireland and SW Scotland, linking the North Atlantic with the Irish Sea

Northcliffe Viscount title of *Alfred Charles William*

Harmsworth. 1865--1922, British newspaper proprietor. With his brother, 1st Viscount Rothermere, he built up a vast chain of newspapers. He founded the *Daily Mail* (1896), the *Daily Mirror* (1903), and acquired *The Times* (1908)

North Country 1 another name for **North²** (sense 1) **2** the geographic region formed by Alaska, the Yukon, the Northwest Territories, and Nunavut

North Dakota a state of the western US: mostly undulating prairies and plains, rising from the Red River valley in the east to the Missouri plateau in the west, with the infertile Bad Lands in the extreme west. Capital: Bismarck. Pop: 633 837 (2003 est). Area: 183 019 sq km (70 664 sq miles)

North Down a district of E Northern Ireland, in Co. Down. Pop: 77 110 (2003 est). Area: 82 sq km (32 sq miles)

northeast 1 the point of the compass or direction midway between north and east, 45° clockwise from north **2** any area lying in or towards this direction **3** of or denoting the northeastern part of a specified country, area, etc. **4** (esp of the wind) from the northeast

Northeast the northeastern part of England, esp Northumberland, Durham, and the Tyneside area

northeaster a strong wind or storm from the northeast

North East Lincolnshire a unitary authority in E England, in Lincolnshire: formerly (1974–96) part of the county of Humberside. Pop: 157 400 (2003 est). Area: 192 sq km (74 sq miles)

northerly a wind from the north

northern 1 situated in or towards the north **2** directed or proceeding towards the north **3** (esp of winds) proceeding from the north **4** *Astronomy* north of the celestial equator

Northern Cape the largest but least populated province in South Africa, in the NW part of the country; created in 1994 from part of Cape Province: agriculture, mining (esp diamonds). Capital: Kimberley. Pop: 899 349 (2004 est). Area: 139 703 sq km (361 830 sq miles)

northern hemisphere 1 that half of the globe lying north of the equator **2** *Astronomy* that half of the celestial sphere north of the celestial equator

Northern Ireland that part of the United Kingdom occupying the NE part of Ireland: separated from the rest of Ireland, which became independent in law in 1920; it remained part of the United Kingdom, with a separate Parliament (Stormont), inaugurated in 1921, and limited self-government: scene of severe conflict between Catholics and Protestants, including terrorist bombing from 1969: direct administration from Westminster from 1972: assembly and powersharing executive established in 1998–99 following the Good Friday Agreement of 1998 and suspended indefinitely in 2002. Capital: Belfast. Pop: 1 702 628 (2003 est). Area: 14 121 sq km (5452 sq miles)

Northern Territory an administrative division of N central Australia, on the Timor and Arafura Seas: includes Ashmore and Cartier Islands; the Arunta Desert lies in the east, the Macdonnell Ranges in the south, and Arnhem Land in the north (containing Australia's largest Aboriginal reservation). Capital: Darwin. Pop: 198 700 (2003 est). Area: 1 347 525 sq km (520 280 sq miles)

North Holland a province of the NW Netherlands, on the peninsula between the North Sea and IJsselmeer: includes the West Frisian Island of Texel. Capital: Haarlem. Pop: 2 573 000 (2003 est). Area: 2663 sq km (1029 sq miles)

North Island the northernmost of the two main islands of New Zealand. Pop: 3 087 200 (2004 est). Area: 114 729 sq km (44 297 sq miles)

North Korea a republic in NE Asia, on the Sea of Japan and the Yellow Sea: established in 1948 as a people's republic; mostly rugged and mountainous, with fertile lowlands in the west. Language: Korean. Currency: won. Capital: Pyongyang. Pop: 22 776 000 (2004 est). Area: 122 313 sq km (47 225 sq miles)

North Lanarkshire a council area of central Scotland: consists mainly of the NE part of the historical county of Lanarkshire; formerly (1974–96) part of Strathclyde Region: engineering and metalworking industries. Administrative centre: Motherwell. Pop: 321 820 (2003 est). Area: 1771 sq km (684 sq miles)

Northland 1 the peninsula containing Norway and Sweden **2** (in Canada) the far north

North Lincolnshire a unitary authority of NE England, in Lincolnshire: formerly (1975–96) part of the county of Humberside. Pop: 155 000 (2003 est). Area: 1497 sq km (578 sq miles)

North Ossetian Republic a constituent republic of S Russia, on the N slopes of the central Caucasus Mountains. Capital: Vladikavkaz. Pop: 709 900 (2002). Area: about 8000 sq km (3088 sq miles)

North Pole 1 the northernmost point on the earth's axis, at a latitude of 90°N **2** *Astronomy* the point of intersection of the earth's extended axis and the northern half of the celestial sphere, lying about 1° from Polaris **3** the pole of a freely suspended magnet, which is attracted to the earth's magnetic North Pole

North Rhine-Westphalia a state of W Germany: formed in 1946 by the amalgamation of the Prussian province of Westphalia with the N part of the Prussian Rhine province and later with the state of Lippe; part of West Germany until 1990: highly industrialized. Capital: Düsseldorf. Pop: 18 080 000 (2003 est). Area: 34 039 sq km (13 142 sq miles)

North Riding (until 1974) an administrative division of Yorkshire, now constituting most of North Yorkshire

North Saskatchewan a river in W Canada, rising in W Alberta and flowing northeast, east, and southeast to join the South Saskatchewan River and form the Saskatchewan River. Length: 1223 km (760 miles)

North Sea an arm of the Atlantic between Great Britain and the N European mainland. Area: about 569 800 sq km (220 000 sq miles)

North Somerset a unitary authority of SW England, in Somerset: formerly (1974–96) part of the county of Avon. Pop: 191 400 (2003 est). Area: 375 sq km (145 sq miles)

North Tyneside a unitary authority of NE England, in Tyne and Wear. Pop: 190 800 (2003 est). Area: 84 sq km (32 sq miles)

Northumberland¹ 1st Duke of, title of *John Dudley*. 1502–53, English statesman and soldier, who governed England (1549–53) during the minority of Edward VI. His attempt (1553) to gain the throne for his daughter-in-law, Lady Jane Grey, led to his execution

Northumberland² the northernmost county of England, on the North Sea: hilly in the north (the Cheviots) and west (the Pennines), with many Roman remains, notably Hadrian's Wall; shipbuilding, coal mining. Administrative centre: Morpeth. Pop: 309 200 (2003 est). Area: 5032 sq km (1943 sq miles)

Northumbria 1 (in Anglo-Saxon Britain) a region that stretched from the Humber to the Firth of Forth: formed in the 7th century AD, it became an important intellectual centre; a separate kingdom until 876 AD **2** an area of NE England roughly corresponding to the Anglo-Saxon region of Northumbria

North Vietnam a region of N Vietnam, on the Gulf of Tonkin: an independent Communist state from 1954 until 1976. Area: 164 061 sq km (63 344 sq miles)

northwest 1 the point of the compass or direction midway between north and west, clockwise 315° from north **2** any area lying in or towards this direction **3** of or denoting the northwestern part of a specified country, area, etc. **4** in, to, towards, or (esp of the wind) from the northwest

Northwest 1 the northwestern part of England, esp Lancashire and the Lake District **2** the northwestern part of the US, consisting of the states of Washington, Oregon, and sometimes Idaho **3** (in Canada) the region north and west of the Great Lakes

North West a province in N South Africa, created in 1994 from the NE part of Cape Province and part of Transvaal: agriculture and service industries. Capital: Mafikeng. Pop: 3 807 469 (2004 est). Area: 116 320 sq km (44 911 sq miles)

northwester a strong wind or storm from the northwest

North-West Frontier Province a province in N Pakistan between Afghanistan and Jammu and Kashmir: part of British India from 1901 until 1947; of strategic importance, esp for the Khyber Pass. Capital: Peshawar. Pop: 20 170 000 (2003 est). Area: 74 522 sq km (28 773 sq miles)

Northwich a town in NW England, in Cheshire: salt and chemical industries. Pop: 39 568 (2001)

North Yemen a former republic in SW Arabia, on the Red Sea; now part of Yemen: declared a republic in 1962: united with South Yemen in 1990

North Yorkshire a county in N England, formed in 1974 from most of the North Riding of Yorkshire and parts of the East and West Ridings: the geographical and ceremonial county includes the unitary authorities of Middlesbrough, Redcar and Cleveland, and part of Stockton on Tees (all within Cleveland until 1996), and York (created in 1997). Administrative centre: Northallerton. Pop. (excluding unitary authorities): 576 100 (2003 est). Area (excluding unitary authorities): 8037 sq km (3102 sq miles)

Norton Graham, real name *Graham Walker*. born 1963, Irish comedian noted for his camp humour

Norway a kingdom in NW Europe, occupying the W part of the Scandinavian peninsula: first united in the Viking age (800–1050); under the rule of Denmark (1523–1814) and Sweden (1814–1905); became an independent monarchy in 1905. Its coastline is deeply indented by fjords and fringed with islands, rising inland to plateaus and mountains. Norway has a large fishing fleet and its merchant navy is among the world's largest. Official language: Norwegian. Official religion: Evangelical Lutheran. Currency: krone. Capital: Oslo. Pop: 4 552 000 (2004 est). Area: 323 878 sq km (125 050 sq miles)

Norwegian any of the various North Germanic languages of Norway

Norwegian Sea part of the Arctic Ocean between Greenland and Norway

Norwich a city in E England, administrative centre of Norfolk: cathedral (founded 1096); University of East Anglia (1963); traditionally a centre of the footwear industry, now has engineering, financial services. Pop: 174 047 (2001)

nose 1 the organ of smell and entrance to the respiratory tract, consisting of a prominent structure divided into two hair-lined air passages by a median septum **2** **on the nose** *Slang* (in horse-race betting) to win only

nosebag a bag, fastened around the head of a horse and covering the nose, in which feed is placed

noseband the detachable part of a horse's bridle that goes around the nose

nosebleed bleeding from the nose, as the result of injury, etc.

nose dive a sudden plunge with the nose or front pointing downwards, esp of an aircraft

Nostradamus Latinized name of *Michel de Notredame*. 1503–66, French physician and astrologer; author of a book of prophecies in rhymed quatrains, *Centuries* (1555)

nostril either of the two external openings of the nose

notary (formerly) a clerk licensed to prepare legal documents

notch *US and Canadian* a narrow pass or gorge

note 1 any of a series of graphic signs representing a musical sound whose pitch is indicated by position on the stave and whose duration is indicated by the sign's shape **2** a musical sound of definite fundamental frequency or pitch **3** a key on a piano, organ, etc.

notebook computer a portable computer smaller than a laptop model, often approximately the size of a sheet of A4 paper

notice *Arts* a theatrical or literary review

notifiable 1 denoting certain infectious diseases of humans, such as smallpox and tuberculosis, outbreaks of which must be reported to the public health authorities **2** denoting certain infectious diseases of animals, such as BSE, foot-and-mouth disease, and rabies, outbreaks of which must be reported to the appropriate veterinary authority

not proven a third verdict available to Scottish courts, returned when there is evidence against the defendant but insufficient to convict

no-trump *Bridge* **1** a bid or contract to play without trumps **2** (of a hand) of balanced distribution suitable for playing without trumps

Nottingham 1 a city in N central England, administrative centre of Nottinghamshire, on the River Trent: scene of the outbreak of the Civil War (1642); famous for its associations with the Robin Hood legend; two universities. Pop: 249 584 (2001) **2** a unitary authority in N central England, in Nottinghamshire. Pop: 273 900 (2003 est). Area: 78 sq km (30 sq miles)

Nottinghamshire an inland county of central England: generally low-lying, with part of the S Pennines and the remnant of Sherwood Forest in the east. Nottingham became an independent unitary authority in 1998. Administrative centre: Nottingham. Pop. (excluding Nottingham): 755 400 (2003 est). Area (excluding Nottingham): 2086 sq km (805 sq miles)

Nouakchott the capital of Mauritania, near the Atlantic coast: replaced St Louis as capital in 1957; situated on important caravan routes. Pop: 559 000 (2002 est)

noughts and crosses a game in which two players, one using a nought, "O", the other a cross, "X", alternately mark one square out of nine formed by two pairs of crossed lines, the winner being the first to get three of his symbols in a row

nous *Metaphysics* mind or reason, esp when regarded as the principle governing all things

nova a variable star that undergoes a cataclysmic eruption, observed as a sudden large increase in brightness with a subsequent decline over months or years; it is a close binary system with one component a white dwarf

Novalis real name *Friedrich von Hardenberg.* 1772–1801, German romantic poet. His works include the mystical *Hymnen an die Nacht* (1797; published 1800) and *Geistliche Lieder* (1799)

Novara a city in NW Italy, in NE Piedmont: scene of the Austrian defeat of the Piedmontese in 1849. Pop: 100 910 (2001)

Nova Scotia 1 a peninsula in E Canada, between the Gulf of St Lawrence and the Bay of Fundy 2 a province of E Canada, consisting of the Nova Scotia peninsula and Cape Breton Island: first settled by the French as Acadia. Capital: Halifax. Pop: 936 960 (2004 est). Area: 52 841 sq km (20 402 sq miles)

Novaya Zemlya an archipelago in the Arctic Ocean, off the NE coast of Russia: consists of two large islands and many islets. Area: about 81 279 sq km (31 382 sq miles)

novel¹ 1 an extended work in prose, either fictitious or partly so, dealing with character, action, thought, etc, esp in the form of a story 2 the the literary genre represented by novels 3 *Obsolete* a short story or novella, as one of those in the *Decameron* of Boccaccio

novel² *Roman law* a new decree or an amendment to an existing statute

novelette 1 an extended prose narrative story or short novel 2 a novel that is regarded as being slight, trivial, or sentimental 3 a short piece of lyrical music, esp one for the piano

novella 1 (formerly) a short narrative tale, esp a popular story having a moral or satirical point, such as those in Boccaccio's *Decameron* 2 a short novel; novelette

Novello Ivor, real name *Ivor Novello Davies.* 1893–1951, Welsh actor, composer, songwriter, and dramatist

novena *RC Church* a devotion consisting of prayers or services on nine consecutive days

Novgorod a city in NW Russia, on the Volkhov River; became a principality in 862 under Rurik, an event regarded as the founding of the Russian state; a major trading centre in the Middle Ages; destroyed by Ivan

the Terrible in 1570. Pop: 215 000 (2005 est)

novice 1 a probationer in a religious order 2 a racehorse, esp a steeplechaser or hurdler, that has not won a specified number of races

Novi Sad a port in NE Serbia and Montenegro, in Serbia, on the River Danube: founded in 1690 as the seat of the Serbian patriarch; university (1960). Pop: 234 151 (2002)

novitiate *or* **noviciate** 1 the state of being a novice, esp in a religious order, or the period for which this lasts 2 the part of a religious house where the novices live

Novokuznetsk a city in S central Russia: iron and steel works. Pop: 542 000 (2005 est)

Novosibirsk a city in W central Russia, on the River Ob: the largest town in Siberia; developed with the coming of the Trans-Siberian railway in 1893; important industrial centre. Pop: 1 425 000 (2005 est)

Noyon a town in N France: scene of the coronations of Charlemagne (768) and Hugh Capet (987); birthplace of John Calvin. Pop: 14 471 (1999)

nozzle *Engineering* a pipe or duct, esp in a jet engine or rocket, that directs the effluent and accelerates or diffuses the flow to generate thrust

nth *Maths* of or representing an unspecified ordinal number, usually the greatest in a series of values

Nu U, original name *Thakin Nu.* 1907–95, Burmese statesman and writer; prime minister (1948–56, 1957–58, 1960–62). He attempted to establish parliamentary democracy, but was ousted (1962) by Ne Win

nub a small fibrous knot in yarn

Nubia an ancient region of NE Africa, on the Nile, extending from Aswan to Khartoum

Nubian 1 a native or inhabitant of Nubia, an ancient region of NE Africa 2 the language spoken by the people of Nubia

Nubian Desert a desert in the NE Sudan, between the Nile valley and the Red Sea: mainly a sandstone plateau

nuclear 1 of, concerned with, or involving the nucleus of an atom 2 *Biology* of, relating to, or contained within the nucleus of a cell 3 of, concerned with, or operated by energy from fission or fusion of atomic nuclei

nuclear energy energy released during a nuclear reaction as a result of fission or fusion

nuclear fission the splitting of an atomic nucleus into approximately equal parts, either spontaneously or as a result of the impact of a particle usually with an associated release of energy

nuclear fusion a reaction in which two nuclei combine to form a nucleus with the release of energy

nuclear physics the branch of physics concerned with the structure and behaviour of the nucleus and the particles of which it consists

▷http://ie.lbl.gov/education/glossary/ glossaryf.htm
▷www.atomicarchive.com
▷www.visionlearning.com/library/ module_viewer.php?mid=59
▷www.iaea.org/inis/ws/

nuclear power power, esp electrical or motive, produced by a nuclear reactor

nuclear reaction a process in which the structure and energy content of an atomic nucleus is changed by interaction with another nucleus or particle

nuclear reactor a device in which a nuclear reaction is maintained and controlled for the production of nuclear energy

nuclear winter a period of extremely low temperatures and little light that has been suggested would occur as a result of a nuclear war

nucleic acid *Biochem* any of a group of complex compounds with a high molecular weight that are vital constituents of all living cells

nucleon a proton or neutron, esp one present in an atomic nucleus

nucleonics the branch of physics concerned with the applications of nuclear energy

nucleus 1 *Biology* (in the cells of eukaryotes) a large compartment, bounded by a double membrane, that contains the chromosomes and associated molecules and controls the characteristics and growth of the cell 2 *Anatomy* any of various groups of nerve cells in the central nervous system 3 *Astronomy* the central portion in the head of a comet, consisting of small solid particles of ice and frozen gases, which vaporize on approaching the sun to form the coma and tail 4 *Physics* the positively charged dense region at the centre of an atom, composed of protons and neutrons, about which electrons orbit 5 *Chem* a fundamental group of atoms in a molecule serving as the base structure for related compounds and remaining unchanged during most chemical reactions 6 *Botany* the central point of a starch granule 7 *Logic* the largest individual that is a mereological part of every member of a given class

nude 1 *Law* a lacking some essential legal requirement, esp supporting evidence b (of a contract, agreement, etc) made without consideration and void unless under seal 2 a naked figure, esp in painting, sculpture, etc.

Nuevo Laredo a city and port of entry in NE Mexico, in Tamaulipas state on the Rio Grande opposite Laredo, Texas: oil industries. Pop: 353 000 (2005 est)

Nuffield William Richard Morris, 1st Viscount Nuffield. 1877–1963, English motorcar manufacturer and philanthropist. He endowed Nuffield College at Oxford (1937) and the Nuffield Foundation (1943), a charitable trust for the furtherance of medicine and education

nuisance *Law* something unauthorized that is obnoxious or injurious to the community at large (**public nuisance**) or to an individual, esp in relation to his ownership or occupation of property (**private nuisance**)

Nukus a city in Uzbekistan, capital of the Kara-Kalpak Autonomous Republic, on the Amu Darya River. Pop: 325 000 (2005 est)

null 1 *Maths* a quantitatively zero b relating to zero c (of a set) having no members d (of a sequence) having zero as a limit 2 *Physics* involving measurement in which an instrument has a zero reading, as with a Wheatstone bridge

Nullarbor Plain a vast low plateau of S Australia: extends north from the Great Australian Bight to the Great Victoria Desert; has no surface water or trees. Area: 260 000 sq km (100 000 sq miles)

Numantia an ancient city in N Spain: a centre of Celtic resistance to Rome in N Spain: captured by Scipio the Younger in 133 BC

Numa Pompilius the legendary second king of Rome

(?715–?673 BC), said to have instituted religious rites

numbat a small Australian marsupial, *Myrmecobius fasciatus*, having a long snout and tongue and strong claws for hunting and feeding on termites: family *Dasyuridae*

number 1 a concept of quantity that is or can be derived from a single unit, the sum of a collection of units, or zero. Every number occupies a unique position in a sequence, enabling it to be used in counting. It can be assigned to one or more sets that can be arranged in a hierarchical classification: every number is a **complex number**; a complex number is either an **imaginary number** or a **real number**, and the latter can be a **rational number** or an **irrational number**; a rational number is either an **integer** or a **fraction**, while an irrational number can be a **transcendental number** or an **algebraic number** 2 the symbol used to represent a number; numeral 3 a a self-contained part of an opera or other musical score, esp one for the stage

number crunching *Computing* the large-scale processing of numerical data

numberplate a plate mounted on the front and back of a motor vehicle bearing the registration number

Number Ten 10 Downing Street, the British prime minister's official London residence

numeral a symbol or group of symbols used to express a number: for example, 6 (*Arabic*), VI (*Roman*), 110 (*binary*)

numerate able to use numbers, esp in arithmetical operations

numeration 1 the act or process of writing, reading, or naming numbers 2 a system of numbering or counting

numerator *Maths* the dividend of a fraction

numerical *or* **numeric** *Maths* a containing or using constants, coefficients, terms, or elements represented by numbers b another word for **absolute**

numerology the study of numbers, such as the figures in a birth date, and of their supposed influence on human affairs

Numidia an ancient country of N Africa, corresponding roughly to present-day Algeria: flourished until its invasion by Vandals in 429; chief towns were Cirta and Hippo Regius

numismatics the study or collection of coins, medals, etc.

▷www.numis.org

nun¹ 1 a female member of a religious order 2 a variety of domestic fancy pigeon usually having a black-and-white plumage with a ridged peak or cowl of short white feathers

nun² the 14th letter in the Hebrew alphabet (נ or, at the end of a word, ן), transliterated as *n*

Nunavut a territory of NW Canada, formed in 1999 from part of the Northwest Territories as a semiautonomous region for the Inuit; includes Baffin Island and Ellesmere Island. Capital: Iqaluit. Pop: 29 644 (2004 est). Area: 2 093 190 sq km (808 185 sq miles)

Nunc Dimittis 1 the Latin name for the Canticle of Simeon (Luke 2:29–32) 2 a musical setting of this

nuncio *RC Church* a diplomatic representative of the Holy See, ranking above an internuncio and esp having ambassadorial status

Nuneaton a town in central England, in Warwickshire. Pop: 70 721 (2001)

Nunn Sir Trevor (**Robert**). born 1940, British theatre director; artistic director (1968–86) and chief executive (1968–86) of the Royal Shakespeare Company; artistic director of the Royal National Theatre (1997–2003). His productions include *Nicholas Nickleby* (1980), *Cats* (1981), and *Les Misérables* (1985)

nunnery the convent or religious house of a community of nuns

nuptial *Zoology* of or relating to mating

Nuremberg a city in S Germany, in N Bavaria: scene of annual Nazi rallies (1933–38), the anti-Semitic Nuremberg decrees (1935), and the trials of Nazi leaders for their war crimes (1945–46); important metalworking and electrical industries. Pop: 493 553 (2003 est)

Nureyev Rudolf 1938–93, Austrian ballet dancer, born in the Soviet Union: he lived in England (1961–83) and France (1983–89). He became an Austrian citizen in 1982

Nuristan a region of E Afghanistan: consists mainly of high mountains (including part of the Hindu Kush), steep narrow valleys, and forests. Area: about 13 000 sq km (5000 sq miles)

nurse 1 a person, usually a woman, who tends the sick, injured, or infirm 2 *Zoology* a worker in a colony of social insects that takes care of the larvae

nursery 1 a place where plants, young trees, etc, are grown commercially 2 an establishment providing residential or day care for babies and very young children; crèche 3 short for **nursery school** 4 *Billiards* **a** a series of cannons with the three balls adjacent to a cushion, esp near a corner pocket **b** a cannon in such a series

nurseryman a person who owns or works in a nursery in which plants are grown

nursery school a school for young children, usually from three to five years old

nursing home 1 a private hospital or residence staffed and equipped to care for aged or infirm persons 2 *Brit* a private maternity home

nurture *Biology* the environmental factors that partly determine the structure of an organism

Nusa Tenggara an island chain east of Java, mostly in Indonesia: the main islands are Bali, Lombok, Sumbawa, Sumba, Flores, Alor, and Timor. Pop: 7 237 600 (1995 est). Area: 73 144 sq km (28 241 sq miles)

nut 1 a dry one-seeded indehiscent fruit that usually possesses a woody wall 2 the edible kernel of such a fruit 3 a small square or hexagonal block, usu. metal, with a threaded hole through the middle for screwing on the end of a bolt 4 *Mountaineering* a variously shaped small metal block, usually a wedge or hexagonal prism (originally an ordinary engineer's nut) with a wire or rope loop attached, for jamming into a crack to provide security 5 *Music* **a** the ledge or ridge at the upper end of the fingerboard of a violin, cello, etc, over which the strings pass to the tuning pegs **b** the end of a violin bow that is held by the player

▷www.treenuts.org
▷www.users.globalnet.co.uk/~aair/nuts.htm
▷www.cooks.com

nutcracker either of two birds, *Nucifraga caryocatactes* of the Old World or *N. columbianus* (**Clark's nutcracker**) of North America, having speckled plumage and feeding on nuts, seeds, etc.: family *Corvidae* (crows)

nuthatch any songbird of the family *Sittidae*, esp *Sitta europaea*, having strong feet and bill, and feeding on insects, seeds, and nuts

nutmeg 1 an East Indian evergreen tree, *Myristica fragrans*, cultivated in the tropics for its hard aromatic seed: family *Myristicaceae* 2 the seed of this tree, used as a spice 3 any of several similar trees or their fruit 4 a greyish-brown colour

nutria 1 another name for **coypu** (esp the fur) 2 a brown colour with a grey tinge

nutrient 1 any of the mineral substances that are absorbed by the roots of plants for nourishment 2 any substance that nourishes an organism 3 providing or contributing to nourishment

nutrition 1 a process in animals and plants involving the intake of nutrient materials and their subsequent assimilation into the tissues 2 the study of nutrition, esp in humans

▷www.crnusa.org

nutritive a nutritious food

nutshell the shell around the kernel of a nut

Nuuk the capital of Greenland, in the southwest: the oldest Danish settlement in Greenland, founded in 1721. Pop: 14 350 (2004 est)

nux vomica 1 an Indian spiny loganiaceous tree, *Strychnos nux-vomica*, with orange-red berries containing poisonous seeds 2 any of the seeds of this tree, which contain strychnine and other poisonous alkaloids 3 a medicine manufactured from the seeds of this tree, formerly used as a heart stimulant

Nyasa *or* **Nyassa** Lake a lake in central Africa at the S end of the Great Rift Valley: the third largest lake in Africa, drained by the Shire River into the Zambezi. Area: about 28 500 sq km (11 000 sq miles)

Nyerere Julius Kambarage 1922–99, Tanzanian statesman; president (1964–85). He became prime minister of Tanganyika in 1961 and president in 1962, negotiating the union of Tanganyika and Zanzibar to form Tanzania (1964)

nylon 1 a class of synthetic polyamide materials made by copolymerizing dicarboxylic acids with diamines. They can be moulded into a variety of articles, such as combs and machine parts. Nylon monofilaments are used for bristles, etc, and nylon fibres can be spun into yarn 2 **a** yarn or cloth made of nylon, used for clothing, stockings, etc. **b** (*as modifier*): *a nylon dress*

Nyman Michael born 1944, British composer; works include the opera *The Man Who Mistook His Wife For a Hat* (1986) and scores for films, including *The Piano* (1992) and several films by Peter Greenaway

nymph 1 *Myth* a spirit of nature envisaged as a beautiful maiden 2 the larva of insects such as the dragonfly and mayfly. It resembles the adult, apart from having underdeveloped wings and reproductive organs, and develops into the adult without a pupal stage

Oo

Oahu an island in central Hawaii: the third largest of the Hawaiian Islands. Chief town: Honolulu. Pop: 876 151 (2000). Area: 1574 sq km (608 sq miles)

oak 1 any deciduous or evergreen tree or shrub of the fagaceous genus *Quercus*, having acorns as fruits and lobed leaves 2 a the wood of any of these trees, used esp as building timber and for making furniture b (*as modifier*): *an oak table* 3 any of various trees that resemble the oak, such as the poison oak, silky oak, and Jerusalem oak 4 *Austral* any of various species of casuarina, such as desert oak, swamp oak, or she-oak

oak apple *or* **gall** any of various brownish round galls on oak trees, containing the larva of certain wasps

Oakham a market town in E central England, the administrative centre of Rutland. Pop: 9620 (2001)

Oakland a port and industrial centre in W California, on San Francisco Bay; damaged by earthquake in 1989. Pop: 398 844 (2003 est)

Oakley Annie, real name *Phoebe Anne Oakley Mozee*. 1860–1926, US markswoman

Oaks the 1 a horse race for fillies held annually at Epsom since 1779: one of the classics of English flat racing 2 any of various similar races

oakum loose fibre obtained by unravelling old rope, used esp for caulking seams in wooden ships

Oakville a city in SE Canada, in SE Ontario on Lake Ontario southwest of Toronto: motor-vehicle industry. Pop: 144 738 (2001)

oar 1 a long shaft of wood for propelling a boat by rowing, having a broad blade that is dipped into and pulled against the water. Oars were also used for steering certain kinds of ancient sailing boats 2 short for **oarsman**

oarsman a man who rows, esp one who rows in a racing boat

oasis a fertile patch in a desert occurring where the water table approaches or reaches the ground surface

oat 1 an erect annual grass, *Avena sativa*, grown in temperate regions for its edible seed 2 the seeds or fruits of this grass 3 any of various other grasses of the genus *Avena*, such as the wild oat 4 *Poetic, Music* a flute made from an oat straw

Oates 1 Captain **Lawrence Edward Grace** 1880–1912, English explorer. He died on Scott's second Antarctic expedition 2 **Titus** 1649–1705, English conspirator. He fabricated the Popish Plot (1678), a supposed Catholic conspiracy to kill Charles II, burn London, and massacre Protestants. His perjury caused the execution of many innocent Catholics

oath 1 on, upon, *or* under oath a *Law* having sworn to tell the truth, usually with one's hand on the Bible 2 take an oath to declare formally with an oath or pledge, esp before giving evidence

oatmeal a a greyish-yellow colour b (*as adjective*): *an oatmeal coat*

Oaxaca 1 a state of S Mexico, on the Pacific: includes most of the Isthmus of Tehuantepec; inhabited chiefly by Indians. Capital: Oaxaca de Juárez. Pop: 3 432 180 (2000). Area: 95 363 sq km (36 820 sq miles) 2 a city in S Mexico, capital of Oaxaca state: founded in 1486 by the Aztecs and conquered by Spain in 1521. Pop: 483 000 (2005 est)

Ob a river in N central Russia, formed at Bisk by the confluence of the Biya and Katun Rivers and flowing generally north to the **Gulf of Ob** (an inlet of the Arctic Ocean): one of the largest rivers in the world, with a drainage basin of about 2 930 000 sq km (1 131 000 sq miles). Length: 3682 km (2287 miles)

Obadiah *Old Testament* 1 a Hebrew prophet 2 the book containing his oracles, chiefly directed against Edom

Oban a small port and resort in W Scotland, in Argyll and Bute on the Firth of Lorne. Pop: 8120 (2001)

Obasanjo Olusegun born 1937, Nigerian politician and general; head of the military government (1976–79); president from 1999

obbligato *or* **obligato** *Music* 1 not to be omitted in performance 2 an essential part in a score

obelisk a stone pillar having a square or rectangular cross section and sides that taper towards a pyramidal top, often used as a monument in ancient Egypt

Oberammergau a village in S Germany, in Bavaria in the foothills of the Alps: famous for its Passion Play, performed by the villagers every ten years (except during the World Wars) since 1634, in thanksgiving for the end of the Black Death. Pop: 5363 (2003 est)

Oberhausen an industrial city in W Germany, in North Rhine-Westphalia on the Rhine-Herne Canal: site of the first ironworks in the Ruhr. Pop: 220 033 (2003 est)

Oberland the lower parts of the Bernese Alps in central Switzerland, mostly in S Bern canton

obese excessively fat or fleshy; corpulent

object 1 *Philosophy* that towards which cognition is directed, as contrasted with the thinking subject; anything regarded as external to the mind, esp in the external world **2** *Computing* a self-contained identifiable component of a software system or design

objective 1 existing independently of perception or an individual's conceptions **2** *Med* (of disease symptoms) perceptible to persons other than the individual affected **3** *Optics* **a** the lens or combination of lenses nearest to the object in an optical instrument **b** the lens or combination of lenses forming the image in a camera or projector

object lesson (esp formerly) a lesson in which a material object forms the basis of the teaching and is available to be inspected

oblate[1] having an equatorial diameter of greater length than the polar diameter

oblate[2] a person dedicated to a monastic or religious life

oblation *Christianity* the offering of the bread and wine of the Eucharist to God

obligation 1 *Law* a legally enforceable agreement to perform some act, esp to pay money, for the benefit of another party **2** *Law* **a** a written contract containing a penalty **b** an instrument acknowledging indebtedness to secure the repayment of money borrowed

oblique 1 *Geometry* **a** (of lines, planes, etc) neither perpendicular nor parallel to one another or to another line, plane, etc. **b** not related to or containing a right angle **2** *Biology* having asymmetrical sides or planes **3** (of a map projection) constituting a type of zenithal projection in which the plane of projection is tangential to the earth's surface at some point between the equator and the poles **4** *Navigation* the act of changing course by less than 90° **5** an aerial photograph taken at an oblique angle

oblique angle an angle that is not a right angle or any multiple of a right angle

oblivion *Law* an intentional overlooking, esp of political offences; amnesty; pardon

oblong a figure or object having an elongated, esp rectangular, shape

oboe a woodwind instrument of the family that includes the bassoon and cor anglais, consisting of a conical tube fitted with a mouthpiece having a double reed. It has a penetrating nasal tone. Range: about two octaves plus a sixth upwards from B flat below middle C

Obote (Apollo) **Milton** born 1924, Ugandan politician; prime minister of Uganda (1962–66) and president (1966–71; 1980–85). He was deposed by Amin in 1971 and remained in exile until 1980; deposed again in 1985 by the Acholi army

obscene *Law* (of publications) having a tendency to deprave or corrupt

observance the degree of strictness of a religious order or community in following its rule

observation *Navigation* **a** a sight taken with an instrument to determine the position of an observer relative to that of a given heavenly body **b** the data so taken

observatory an institution or building specially designed and equipped for observing meteorological and astronomical phenomena

obsession *Psychiatry* a persistent idea or impulse that continually forces its way into consciousness, often associated with anxiety and mental illness

obsidian a dark volcanic glass formed by very rapid solidification of lava

obsolete *Biology* (of parts, organs, etc) vestigial; rudimentary

obstacle *Brit* a fence or hedge used in showjumping

obstruction *Politics* delay of business, esp in a legislature by means of procedural devices

obstructionist a a person who deliberately obstructs business, esp in a legislature **b** (*as modifier*): *obstructionist tactics*

obtuse 1 *Maths* **a** (of an angle) lying between 90° and 180° **b** (of a triangle) having one interior angle greater than 90° **2** (of a leaf or similar flat part) having a rounded or blunt tip

obverse 1 (of certain plant leaves) narrower at the base than at the top **2** *Logic* a categorial proposition derived from another by replacing the original predicate by its negation and changing the proposition from affirmative to negative or vice versa, as *no sum is correct* from *every sum is incorrect*

ocarina an egg-shaped wind instrument with a protruding mouthpiece and six to eight finger holes, producing an almost pure tone

Occident 1 the countries of Europe and America **2** the western hemisphere

occiput the back part of the head or skull

occluded front *Meteorol* the line or plane occurring where the cold front of a depression has overtaken the warm front, raising the warm sector from ground level

occupancy 1 *Law* the possession and use of property by or without agreement and without any claim to ownership **2** *Law* the act of taking possession of unowned property, esp land, with the intent of thus acquiring ownership

occupant 1 *Law* a person who has possession of something, esp an estate, house, etc.; tenant **2** *Law* a person who acquires by occupancy the title to something previously without an owner

occupational therapy *Med* treatment of people with physical, emotional, or social problems, using purposeful activity to help them overcome or learn to deal with their problems

ocean 1 a very large stretch of sea, esp one of the five oceans of the world, the Atlantic, Pacific, Indian, Arctic, and Antarctic **2** the body of salt water covering approximately 70 per cent of the earth's surface

ocean-going (of a ship, boat, etc) suited for travel on the open ocean

Oceania the islands of the central and S Pacific, including Melanesia, Micronesia, and Polynesia: sometimes also including Australasia and the Malay Archipelago

oceanography the branch of science dealing with the physical, chemical, geological, and biological features of the oceans and ocean basins

ocelot a feline mammal, *Felis pardalis*, inhabiting the forests of Central and South America and having a dark-spotted buff-brown coat

oche *Darts* the mark or ridge on the floor behind which a player must stand to throw

ochre *or US* **ocher a** a moderate yellow-orange to orange colour **b** (*as adjective*): *an ochre dress*

Ockham *or* **Occam William of** died ?1349, English nominalist philosopher, who contested the temporal power of the papacy and ended the conflict between nominalism and realism

octagon *or less commonly* **octangle** a polygon having eight sides

octahedron a solid figure having eight plane faces

octane a liquid alkane hydrocarbon found in petroleum and existing in 18 isomeric forms, esp the isomer *n*-octane. Formula: C_8H_{18}

octane number *or* **rating** a measure of the quality of a petrol expressed as the percentage of isooctane in a mixture of isooctane and *n*-heptane that gives a fuel with the same antiknock qualities as the given petrol

octave **1 a** the interval between two musical notes one of which has twice the pitch of the other and lies eight notes away from it counting inclusively along the diatonic scale **b** one of these two notes, esp the one of higher pitch **c** (*as modifier*): *an octave leap* **2** *Prosody* a rhythmic group of eight lines of verse **3 a** a feast day and the seven days following **b** the final day of this period **4** the eighth of eight basic positions in fencing

Octavian the name of **Augustus** before he became emperor (27 BC)

octet 1 any group of eight, esp eight singers or musicians **2** a piece of music composed for such a group **3** *Prosody* another word for **octave** (sense 2) **4** *Chem* a group of eight electrons forming a stable shell in an atom

octopus 1 any cephalopod mollusc of the genera *Octopus, Eledone*, etc, having a soft oval body with eight long suckered tentacles and occurring at the sea bottom: order *Octopoda* (octopods) **2** another name for **spider**

ocular 1 of or relating to the eye **2** another name for **eyepiece**

OD *Informal* an overdose of a drug

odd 1 a not divisible by two **b** represented or indicated by a number that is not divisible by two **2** *Maths* (of a function) changing sign but not absolute value when the sign of the independent variable is changed, as in $y=x^3$ **3** *Golf* **a** one stroke more than the score of one's opponent **b** an advantage or handicap of one stroke added to or taken away from a player's score

odds-on (of a chance, horse, etc) rated at even money or less to win

ode 1 a lyric poem, typically addressed to a particular subject, with lines of varying lengths and complex rhythms **2** (formerly) a poem meant to be sung

Odense a port in S Denmark, on Funen Island: cathedral founded by King Canute in the 11th century. Pop: 145 554 (2004 est)

Oder a river in central Europe, rising in the NE Czech Republic and flowing north and west, forming part of the border between Germany and Poland, to the Baltic. Length: 913 km (567 miles)

Oder-Neisse Line the present-day boundary between Germany and Poland along the Rivers Oder and Neisse. Established in 1945, it originally separated the Soviet Zone of Germany from the regions under Polish administration

Odessa a port in S Ukraine on the Black Sea: the chief Russian grain port in the 19th century; university (1865); industrial centre and important naval base. Pop:

1 010 000 (2005 est)

Odin *or* **Othin** *Norse myth* the supreme creator god; the divinity of wisdom, culture, war, and the dead

Odoacer *or* **Odovacar** ?434–493 AD, barbarian ruler of Italy (476–493); assassinated by Theodoric

odometer *US and Canadian* a device that records the number of miles that a bicycle or motor vehicle has travelled

oedema *or* **edema** *Pathol* an excessive accumulation of serous fluid in the intercellular spaces of tissue

Oedipus complex *Psychoanal* a group of emotions, usually unconscious, involving the desire of a child, esp a male child, to possess sexually the parent of the opposite sex while excluding the parent of the same sex

oesophagus *or US* **esophagus** the part of the alimentary canal between the pharynx and the stomach; gullet

oestrogen *or US* **estrogen** any of several steroid hormones, that are secreted chiefly by the ovaries and placenta, that induce oestrus, stimulate changes in the female reproductive organs during the oestrous cycle, and promote development of female secondary sexual characteristics

oestrus, *US* **estrus,** *or* **estrum** a regularly occurring period of sexual receptivity in most female mammals, except humans, during which ovulation occurs and copulation can take place; heat

off *Cricket* **a** the part of the field on that side of the pitch to which the batsman presents his bat when taking strike: thus for a right-hander, off is on the right-hand side **b** a fielding position in this part of the field **c** (*as modifier*): *the off stump*

Offa died 796 AD, king of Mercia (757–796), who constructed an earthwork (**Offa's Dyke**) between Wales and Mercia

Offaly an inland county of E central Republic of Ireland, in Leinster province: formerly an ancient kingdom, which also included parts of Tipperary, Leix, and Kildare. County town: Tullamore. Pop: 63 663 (2002). Area: 2000 sq km (770 sq miles)

offbeat *Music* any of the normally unaccented beats in a bar, such as the second and fourth beats in a bar of four-four time. They are stressed in most rock and some jazz and dance music, such as the bossa nova

Offenbach[1] Jacques 1819–80, German-born French composer of many operettas, including *Orpheus in the Underworld* (1858), and of the opera *The Tales of Hoffmann* (1881)

Offenbach[2] a city in central Germany, on the River Main in Hesse opposite Frankfurt am Main: leather-goods industry. Pop: 119 208 (2003 est)

offence *or US* **offense** *American football* **a** the team that has possession of the ball **b** the members of a team that play in such circumstances

offer 1 *Contract law* a proposal made by one person that will create a binding contract if accepted unconditionally by the person to whom it is made **2 on offer** for sale at a reduced price

offering 1 a contribution to the funds of a religious organization **2** a sacrifice, as of an animal, to a deity

offertory 1 the oblation of the bread and wine at the Eucharist **2** the offerings of the worshippers at this service **3** the prayers said or sung while the worshippers' offerings are being received

Offiah Martin born 1965, British Rugby League football player

office 1 (in Britain) a department of the national government **2** in the US **a** a governmental agency, esp of the Federal government **b** a subdivision of such an agency or of a department **3** a place where tickets, information, etc, can be obtained **4** *Christianity* **a** a ceremony or service, prescribed by ecclesiastical authorities, esp one for the dead **b** the order or form of these **c** *RC Church* the official daily service

officer 1 a person in the armed services who holds a position of responsibility, authority, and duty, esp one who holds a commission **2** (on a non-naval ship) any person including the captain and mate, who holds a position of authority and responsibility **3** a government official

Official Receiver an officer appointed by the Department of Trade and Industry to receive the income and manage the estate of a bankrupt pending the appointment of a trustee in bankruptcy

officious *Diplomacy* informal or unofficial

offing the part of the sea that can be seen from the shore

off key *Music* **a** not in the correct key **b** out of tune

off-road (of a motor vehicle) designed or built for use away from public roads, esp on rough terrain

off-roader 1 a motor vehicle designed for use away from public roads, esp on rough terrain **2** an owner or driver of an off-road vehicle

offset 1 *Botany* **a** a short runner in certain plants, such as the houseleek, that produces roots and shoots at the tip **b** a plant produced from such a runner **2** a ridge projecting from a range of hills or mountains **3** the horizontal component of displacement on a fault **4** a narrow horizontal or sloping surface formed where a wall is reduced in thickness towards the top **5** a person or group descended collaterally from a particular group or family; offshoot

offshoot *Botany* a shoot or branch growing from the main stem of a plant

offshore based or operating abroad in places where the tax system is more advantageous than that of the home country

Ofgem in Britain Office of Gas and Electricity Markets: a government body formed in 1999 by the merger of the separate regulatory bodies for gas and electricity; its functions are to promote competition and protect consumers' interests

Ofili Chris(topher). born 1968, British painter, noted esp for his brightly coloured collages using elephant dung: Turner Prize 1998

Ogaden the a region of SE Ethiopia, bordering on Somalia: consists of a desert plateau, inhabited by Somali nomads; a secessionist movement, supported by Somalia, has existed within the region since the early 1960s and led to bitter fighting between Ethiopia and Somalia (1977–78)

Ogbomosho a city in SW Nigeria: the third largest town in Nigeria; trading centre for an agricultural region. Pop: 959 000 (2005 est)

Ogden C(harles) K(ay). 1889–1957, English linguist, who, with I. A. Richards, devised Basic English

ogee arch *Architect* a pointed arch having an S-shaped curve on both sides

Oglethorpe James Edward 1696–1785, English general and colonial administrator; founder of the colony of Georgia (1733)

O grade formerly, in Scotland **1 a** the basic level of the Scottish Certificate of Education, now replaced by **Standard Grade b** (*as modifier*): *O grade history* **2** a pass in a particular subject at O grade

ogre (in folklore) a giant, usually given to eating human flesh

Ogun a state of SW Nigeria, formed in 1976 from part of Western State. Capital: Abeokuta. Pop: 2 614 747 (1995 est). Area: 16 762 sq km (6472 sq miles)

Ohio 1 a state of the central US, in the Midwest on Lake Erie: consists of prairies in the W and the Allegheny plateau in the E, the Ohio River forming the S and most of the E borders. Capital: Columbus. Pop: 11 435 798 (2003 est). Area: 107 044 sq km (41 330 sq miles) **2** a river in the eastern US, formed by the confluence of the Allegheny and Monongahela Rivers at Pittsburgh: flows generally W and SW to join the Mississippi at Cairo, Illinois, as its chief E tributary. Length: 1570 km (975 miles)

ohm the derived SI unit of electrical resistance; the resistance between two points on a conductor when a constant potential difference of 1 volt between them produces a current of 1 ampere.

Ohm Georg Simon 1787–1854, German physicist, who formulated the law named after him

oil 1 any of a number of viscous liquids with a smooth sticky feel. They are usually flammable, insoluble in water, soluble in organic solvents, and are obtained from plants and animals, from mineral deposits, and by synthesis. They are used as lubricants, fuels, perfumes, foodstuffs, and raw materials for chemicals. See also **essential oil 2 a** another name for **petroleum b** (*as modifier*): *an oil engine* **3 a** any of a number of substances usually derived from petroleum and used for lubrication **b** (*as modifier*): *an oil pump* **4** a petroleum product used as a fuel in domestic heating, industrial furnaces, marine engines, etc. **5** *Brit* **a** paraffin, esp when used as a domestic fuel **b** (*as modifier*): *an oil lamp* **6** the solvent, usually linseed oil, with which pigments are mixed to make artists' paints **7 a** oil colour or paint **b** (*as modifier*): *an oil painting* **8** an oil painting **9 strike oil** to discover petroleum while drilling for it

oilcloth waterproof material made by treating one side of a cotton fabric with a drying oil, or a synthetic resin

oilfield an area containing reserves of petroleum, esp one that is already being exploited

oil paint *or* **colour** paint made of pigment ground in oil, usually linseed oil, used for oil painting

oil painting 1 a picture painted with oil paints **2** the art or process of painting with oil paints

oilskin a a cotton fabric treated with oil and pigment to make it waterproof **b** (*as modifier*): *an oilskin hat*

ointment 1 a fatty or oily medicated formulation applied to the skin to heal or protect **2** a similar substance used as a cosmetic

Oise 1 a department of N France, in Picardy region.

Capital: Beauvais. Pop: 776 999 (2003 est). Area: 5887 sq km (2296 sq miles) **2** a river in N France, rising in Belgium, in the Ardennes, and flowing southwest to join the Seine at Conflans. Length: 302 km (188 miles)

Oistrakh 1 David 1908–74, Russian violinist 2 his son, Igor born 1931, Russian violinist

Oita an industrial city in SW Japan, on NE Kyushu: dominated most of Kyushu in the 16th century. Pop: 437 699 (2002 est)

Okanagan 1 a river in North America that flows south from Okanagan Lake in Canada into the Columbia River in NE Washington, US Length: about 483 km (300 miles) **2** a member of a North American Indian people living in the Okanagan River valley in British Columbia and Washington **3** the language of this people, belonging to the Salish family

Okanagan Lake a lake in SW Canada, in S British Columbia: drained by the Okanagan River into the Columbia River. Length: about 111 km (69 miles). Width: from 3.2–6.4 km (2–4 miles)

okapi a ruminant mammal, *Okapia johnstoni*, of the forests of central Africa, having a reddish-brown coat with horizontal white stripes on the legs and small horns: family *Giraffidae*

Okavango *or* **Okovango** a river in SW central Africa, rising in central Angola and flowing southeast, then east as part of the border between Angola and Namibia, then southeast across the Caprivi Strip into Botswana to form a great marsh known as the **Okavango Basin, Delta or Swamp**. Length: about 1600 km (1000 miles)

Okayama a city in SW Japan, on W Honshu on the Inland Sea. Pop: 621 809 (2002 est)

Okeechobee Lake a lake in S Florida, in the Everglades: second largest freshwater lake wholly within the US. Area: 1813 sq km (700 sq miles)

Okefenokee Swamp a swamp in the US, in SE Georgia and N Florida: protected flora and fauna. Area: 1554 sq km (600 sq miles)

Okhotsk Sea of part of the NW Pacific, surrounded by the Kamchatka Peninsula, the Kurile Islands, Sakhalin Island, and the E coast of Siberia. Area: 1 589 840 sq km (613 838 sq miles)

Okinawa a coral island of SW Japan, the largest of the Ryukyu Islands in the N Pacific: scene of heavy fighting in World War II; administered by the US (1945–72); agricultural. Chief town: Naha City. Pop: 1 273 508 (1995). Area: 1176 sq km (454 sq miles)

Oklahoma a state in the S central US: consists of plains in the west, rising to mountains in the southwest and east; important for oil. Capital: Oklahoma City. Pop: 3 511 532 (2003 est). Area: 181 185 sq km (69 956 sq miles)

Oklahoma City a city in central Oklahoma: the state capital and a major agricultural and industrial centre. Pop: 523 303 (2003 est)

okra 1 an annual malvaceous plant, *Hibiscus esculentus*, of the Old World tropics, with yellow-and-red flowers and edible oblong sticky green pods **2** the pod of this plant, eaten in soups, stews, etc.

Olaf I *or* **Olav I** known as *Olaf Tryggvesson*. ?965–?1000 AD, king of Norway (995–?1000). He began the conversion of Norway to Christianity

Olaf II *or* **Olav II** Saint 995–1030 AD, king of Norway

(1015–28), who worked to complete the conversion of Norway to Christianity; deposed by Canute; patron saint of Norway. Feast day: July 29

Olaf V *or* **Olav V** 1903–91, king of Norway 1957–91; son of Haakon VII

old *Geography* (of a river, valley, or land surface) in the final stage of the cycle of erosion, characterized by flat extensive flood plains and minimum relief

Old Bailey the chief court exercising criminal jurisdiction in London; the Central Criminal Court of England

Old Castile a region of N Spain, on the Bay of Biscay: formerly a province

Oldcastle Sir John, Baron Cobham. ?1378–1417, Lollard leader. In 1411 he led an English army in France but in 1413 he was condemned as a heretic and later hanged and burnt. He is thought to have been a model for Shakespeare's character Falstaff in *Henry IV*

Oldenbarneveldt Johan van 1547–1619, Dutch statesman, regarded as a founder of Dutch independence; the leading figure (from 1586) in the United Provinces of the Netherlands: executed by Maurice of Nassau

Oldenburg¹ Claes born 1929, US pop sculptor and artist, born in Sweden

Oldenburg² 1 a city in NW Germany, in Lower Saxony: former capital of Oldenburg state. Pop: 158 340 (2003 est) **2** a former state of NW Germany: became part of Lower Saxony in 1946

Old English the English language from the time of the earliest settlements in the fifth century AD to about 1100. The main dialects were West Saxon (the chief literary form), Kentish, and Anglian

Old English sheepdog a breed of large bobtailed sheepdog with a profuse shaggy coat

Old French the French language in its earliest forms, from about the 9th century up to about 1400

Oldham 1 a town in NW England, in Oldham unitary authority, Greater Manchester. Pop: 103 544 (2001) **2** a unitary authority in NW England, in Greater Manchester. Pop: 218 100 (2003 est). Area: 141 sq km (54 sq miles)

Old High German a group of West Germanic dialects that eventually developed into modern German; High German up to about 1200: spoken in the Middle Ages on the upper Rhine, in Bavaria, Alsace, and elsewhere, including Alemannic, Bavarian, Langobardic, and Upper Franconian

old lady a large noctuid moth, *Mormo maura*, that has drab patterned wings originally thought to resemble an elderly Victorian lady's shawl

old maid a card game using a pack from which one card has been removed, in which players try to avoid holding the unpaired card at the end of the game

old master 1 *Art* one of the great European painters of the period 1500 to 1800 **2** a painting by one of these

old moon 1 a phase of the moon lying between last quarter and new moon, when it appears as a waning crescent **2** the moon when it appears as a waning crescent **3** the time at which this occurs

Old Northwest (in the early US) the land between the Great Lakes, the Mississippi, and the Ohio River. Awarded to the US in 1783, it was organized into the **Northwest Territory** in 1787 and now forms the states of

Ohio, Indiana, Illinois, Wisconsin, Michigan, and part of Minnesota

Old Style the former method of reckoning dates using the Julian calendar

Old Testament the collection of books comprising the sacred Scriptures of the Hebrews and essentially recording the history of the Hebrew people as the chosen people of God; the first part of the Christian Bible

Olduvai Gorge a gorge in N Tanzania, north of the Ngorongoro Crater: fossil evidence of early man and other closely related species, together with artefacts

Old World that part of the world that was known before the discovery of the Americas, comprising Europe, Asia, and Africa; the eastern hemisphere

oleaginous 1 resembling or having the properties of oil 2 containing or producing oil

oleander a poisonous evergreen Mediterranean apocynaceous shrub or tree, *Nerium oleander*, with fragrant white, pink, or purple flowers

O level formerly, in Britain 1 a the basic level of the General Certificate of Education, now replaced by **GCSE** b *(as modifier): O level maths* 2 a pass in a particular subject at O level

olfactory 1 of or relating to the sense of smell 2 an organ or nerve concerned with the sense of smell

oligarchy 1 government by a small group of people 2 a state or organization so governed 3 a small body of individuals ruling such a state 4 *Chiefly US* a small clique of private citizens who exert a strong influence on government

Oligocene of, denoting, or formed in the third epoch of the Tertiary period, which lasted for 10 000 000 years

oligopoly *Economics* a market situation in which control over the supply of a commodity is held by a small number of producers each of whom is able to influence prices and thus directly affect the position of competitors

Oliphant Sir Mark Laurence Elwin 1901–2000, British nuclear physicist, born in Australia

olive 1 an evergreen oleaceous tree, *Olea europaea*, of the Mediterranean region but cultivated elsewhere, having white fragrant flowers, and edible shiny black fruits 2 the fruit of this plant, eaten as a relish and used as a source of olive oil 3 the wood of the olive tree, used for ornamental work 4 any of various trees or shrubs resembling the olive 5 a a yellow-green colour b *(as modifier): an olive coat* 6 an angler's name for the dun of various mayflies or an artificial fly in imitation of this

Oliver 1 one of Charlemagne's 12 paladins 2 **Isaac** ?1556–1617, English portrait miniaturist, born in France: he studied under Hilliard and worked at James I's court 3 **Jamie (Trevor)**. born 1975, British chef and presenter of television cookery programmes 4 **Joseph,** known as *King Oliver*. 1885–1938, US pioneer jazz cornetist

Olives Mount of a hill to the east of Jerusalem: in New Testament times the village Bethany (Mark 11:11) was on its eastern slope and Gethsemane on its western one

Olivier Laurence (Kerr), Baron Olivier of Brighton. 1907–89, English stage, film, and television actor and director: director of the National Theatre Company (1961–73): films include the Shakespeare adaptations

Henry V (1944), *Hamlet* (1948), and *Richard III* (1956)

Olomouc a city in the Czech Republic, in North Moravia on the Morava River: capital of Moravia until 1640; university (1576). Pop: 102 000 (2005 est)

oloroso a full-bodied golden-coloured sweet sherry

Olsen Mary-Kate and Ashley born 1986, US twin juvenile act who became famous sharing a role in the sitcom *Full House* (1987–95); now known for their videos, CDs, and numerous branded products

Olsztyn a town in NE Poland: founded in 1334 by the Teutonic Knights; communications centre. Pop: 176 000 (2005 est)

Olympia 1 a plain in Greece, in the NW Peloponnese: in ancient times a major sanctuary of Zeus and site of the original Olympic Games 2 a port in W Washington, the state capital, on Puget Sound. Pop: 43 963 (2003 est)

Olympiad the four-year period between consecutive celebrations of the Olympic Games; a unit of ancient Greek chronology dating back to 776 BC

Olympian 1 of or relating to Mount Olympus or to the classical Greek gods 2 of or relating to ancient Olympia or its inhabitants 3 a god of Olympus 4 an inhabitant or native of ancient Olympia

Olympic Games the greatest Panhellenic festival, held every fourth year in honour of Zeus at ancient Olympia. From 472 BC, it consisted of five days of games, sacrifices, and festivities

▷www.olympics.org

Olympic Peninsula a large peninsula of W Washington

Olympus 1 Mount a mountain in NE Greece: the highest mountain in Greece, believed in Greek mythology to be the dwelling place of the greater gods. Height: 2911 m (9550 ft) 2 Mount a mountain in NW Washington: highest peak of the Olympic Mountains. Height: 2427 m (7965 ft)

Olynthus an ancient city in N Greece: the centre of Chalcidice

Omagh 1 a market town in Northern Ireland. Pop: 19 910 (2001) 2 a district of W Northern Ireland, in Co. Tyrone. Pop: 49 560 (2003 est). Area: 1130 sq km (436 sq miles)

Omaha a city in E Nebraska, on the Missouri River opposite Council Bluffs, Iowa: the largest city in the state; the country's largest livestock market and meatpacking centre. Pop: 404 267 (2003 est)

Oman a sultanate in SE Arabia, on the Gulf of Oman and the Arabian Sea: the most powerful state in Arabia in the 19th century, ruling Zanzibar, much of the Persian coast, and part of Pakistan. Official language: Arabic. Official religion: Muslim. Currency: rial. Capital: Muscat. Pop: 2 935 000 (2004 est). Area: about 306 000 sq km (118 150 sq miles)

Omar or **Umar** died 644 AD, the second caliph of Islam (634–44). During his reign Islamic armies conquered Syria and Mesopotamia: murdered

Omayyad or **Ommiad** 1 a caliph of the dynasty ruling (661–750 AD) from its capital at Damascus 2 an emir (756–929 AD) or caliph (929–1031 AD) of the Omayyad dynasty in Spain

ombudsman 1 a commissioner who acts as independent referee between individual citizens and their government or its administration 2 (in Britain) an official, without power of sanction or mechanism of appeal, who investigates complaints of maladministration by members of the public against national or local government or its servants

Omdurman a city in the central Sudan, on the White Nile, opposite Khartoum: the largest town in the Sudan; scene of the **Battle of Omdurman** (1898), in which the Mahdi's successor was defeated by Lord Kitchener's forces. Pop: 1 267 077 (1993)

omega the 24th and last letter of the Greek alphabet (Ω, ω), a long vowel, transliterated as *o* or *ō*

omnivorous eating food of both animal and vegetable origin, or any type of food indiscriminately

Omsk a city in W central Russia, at the confluence of the Irtysh and Om Rivers: a major industrial centre, with pipelines from the second Baku oilfield. Pop: 1 132 000 (2005 est)

Omuta a city in SW Japan, on W Kyushu on Ariake Bay: former coal-mining centre; chemical industries and manufacturing. Pop: 139 345 (2002 est)

on 1 *Cricket* (of a bowler) bowling 2 *Cricket* a relating to or denoting the leg side of a cricket field or pitch b used to designate certain fielding positions on the leg side

onager a Persian variety of the wild ass, *Equus hemionus*

Onassis Aristotle (Socrates). 1906–75, Argentinian (formerly Greek) shipowner, born in Turkey. In 1968 he married **Jacqueline,** 1929–94, the widow of US President John F. Kennedy

oncogene any of several genes, first identified in viruses but present in all cells, that when abnormally activated can cause cancer

Ondaatje Michael born 1943, Sri Lankan-born Canadian writer: his works include the poetry collection *There's a Trick with a Knife I'm Learning to Do* (1979), the Bookerprizewinning novel *The English Patient* (1992, filmed 1997), and *Anil's Ghost* (2000)

Ondo a state of SW Nigeria, on the Bight of Benin: formed in 1976 from part of Western State. Capital: Akure. Pop: 4 343 230 (1995 est). Area: 20 959 sq km (8092 sq miles)

one 1 the smallest whole number and the first cardinal number; unity 2 a numeral (1, I, i, etc) representing this number 3 *Music* the numeral 1 used as the lower figure in a time signature to indicate that the beat is measured in semibreves 4 **the one** (in Neo-Platonic philosophy) the ultimate being 5 **the Holy One** *or* **the One above** God 6 **the Evil One** Satan; the devil

one-armed bandit a fruit machine operated by pulling down a lever at one side

Onega a lake in NW Russia, mostly in the Karelian Republic: the second largest lake in Europe. Area: 9891 sq km (3819 sq miles)

Oneida 1 **Lake** a lake in central New York State: part of the New York State Barge Canal system. Length: about 35 km (22 miles). Greatest width: 9 km (6 miles) 2 a North American Indian people formerly living east of Lake Ontario; one of the Iroquois peoples 3 a member of this people 4 the language of this people, belonging to the Iroquoian family

onerous *Law* (of a contract, lease, etc) having or involving burdens or obligations that counterbalance or outweigh the advantages

one-sided denoting a surface on which any two points can be joined without crossing an edge

one-to-one *Maths* characterized by or involving the pairing of each member of one set with only one member of another set, without remainder

onion 1 an alliaceous plant, *Allium cepa*, having greenish-white flowers: cultivated for its rounded edible bulb 2 the bulb of this plant, consisting of concentric layers of white succulent leaf bases with a pungent odour and taste 3 any of several related plants similar to *A. cepa*, such as *A. fistulosum* (Welsh onion)

Onitsha a port in S Nigeria, in Anambra State on the Niger River: industrial centre. Pop: 565 000 (2005 est)

onomatopoeia 1 the formation of words whose sound is imitative of the sound of the noise or action designated, such as *hiss, buzz,* and *bang* 2 the use of such words for poetic or rhetorical effect

Onondaga 1 **Lake** a salt lake in central New York State. Area: about 13 sq km (5 sq miles) 2 a member of a North American Indian Iroquois people formerly living between Lake Champlain and the St Lawrence River 3 the language of this people, belonging to the Iroquoian family

onshore towards the land

Ontario 1 a province of central Canada: lies mostly on the Canadian Shield and contains the fertile plain of the lower Great Lakes and the St Lawrence River, one of the world's leading industrial areas; the second largest and the most populous province. Capital: Toronto. Pop: 12 392 721 (2004 est). Area: 891 198 sq km (344 092 sq miles) 2 **Lake** a lake between the US and Canada, bordering on New York State and Ontario province: the smallest of the Great Lakes; linked with Lake Erie by the Niagara River and Welland Canal; drained by the St Lawrence. Area: 19 684 sq km (7600 sq miles)

ontology 1 *Philosophy* the branch of metaphysics that deals with the nature of being 2 *Logic* the set of entities presupposed by a theory

onyx 1 a variety of chalcedony with alternating black and white parallel bands, used as a gemstone. Formula: SiO_2 2 a compact variety of calcite used as an ornamental stone; onyx marble. Formula: $CaCO_3$

oolite any sedimentary rock, esp limestone, consisting of tiny spherical concentric grains within a fine matrix

ooze a fine-grained calcareous or siliceous marine deposit consisting of the hard parts of planktonic organisms

opacity 1 the state or quality of being opaque 2 an opaque object or substance 3 *Physics, Photog* the ratio of the intensity of light incident on a medium, such as a photographic film, to that transmitted through the medium 4 *Logic, Philosophy* the property of being an opaque context

opal an amorphous, usually iridescent, mineral that can be of almost any colour, found in igneous rocks and around hot springs. It is used as a gemstone. Composition: hydrated silica. Formula: $SiO_2.nH_2O$

opaque 1 not transmitting radiant energy, such as electromagnetic or corpuscular radiation, or sound 2 *Photog* an opaque pigment used to block out particular areas on a negative

OPEC Organization of Petroleum-Exporting Countries:

an organization formed in 1961 to administer a common policy for the sale of petroleum. Its members are Algeria, Indonesia, Iran, Iraq, Kuwait, Libya, Nigeria, Qatar, Saudi Arabia, the United Arab Emirates, and Venezuela. Ecuador and Gabon were members but withdrew in 1992 and 1995 respectively
▷www.opec.org

open 1 *Nautical* free from navigational hazards, such as ice, sunken ships, etc. 2 *Music* **a** (of a violin or guitar string) not stopped with the finger **b** (of a pipe, such as an organ pipe) not closed at either end **c** (of a note) played on such a string or pipe 3 *Commerce* **a** in operation; active **b** unrestricted; unlimited 4 (of a wound) exposed to the air 5 (esp of the large intestine) free from obstruction 6 *Chess* (of a file) having no pawns on it 7 *Maths* (of a set) containing points whose neighbourhood consists of other points of the same set 8 *Computing* (of software or a computer system) designed to an internationally agreed standard in order to allow communication between computers, irrespective of size, maufacturer, etc.

open-heart surgery surgical repair of the heart during which the blood circulation is often maintained mechanically

opening 1 *Chiefly US* a tract in a forest in which trees are scattered or absent 2 **a** the first performance of something, esp a theatrical production **b** (*as modifier*): *the opening night* 3 a specific or formal sequence of moves at the start of any of certain games, esp chess or draughts 4 *Law* the preliminary statement made by counsel to the court or jury before adducing evidence in support of his case

open market *Economics* **a** a market in which prices are determined by supply and demand, there are no barriers to entry, and trading is not restricted to a specific area **b** (*as modifier*): *open-market value*

open source a intellectual property, esp computer source code, that is made freely available to the general public by its creators **b** (*as modifier*): *open source software*

Open University the (in Britain) a university founded in 1969 for mature students studying by television and radio lectures, correspondence courses, local counselling, and summer schools

open verdict a finding by a coroner's jury of death without stating the cause

opera 1 an extended dramatic work in which music constitutes a dominating feature, either consisting of separate recitatives, arias, and choruses, or having a continuous musical structure 2 the branch of music or drama represented by such works 3 the score, libretto, etc, of an opera

operable *Med* capable of being treated by a surgical operation

opera house a theatre designed for opera

operand a quantity or function upon which a mathematical or logical operation is performed

operating system the set of software that controls the overall operation of a computer system, typically by performing such tasks as memory allocation, job scheduling, and input/output control

operating theatre a room in which surgical operations are performed

operation 1 *Surgery* any manipulation of the body or one of its organs or parts to repair damage, arrest the progress of a disease, remove foreign matter, etc. 2 *Maths* **a** any procedure, such as addition, multiplication, involution, or differentiation, in which one or more numbers or quantities are operated upon according to specific rules **b** a function from a set onto itself

operations research the analysis of problems in business and industry involving the construction of models and the application of linear programming, critical path analysis, and other quantitative techniques

operative *Med* of or relating to a surgical procedure

operator *Maths* any symbol, term, letter, etc, used to indicate or express a specific operation or process, such as Δ (the differential operator)

operculum 1 *Zoology* **a** the hard bony flap covering the gill slits in fishes **b** the bony plate in certain gastropods covering the opening of the shell when the body is withdrawn 2 *Botany* the covering of the sporebearing capsule of a moss 3 *Biology* any other covering or lid in various organisms

operetta a type of comic or light-hearted opera
▷www.operetta.org

Ophir *Bible* a region, probably situated on the SW coast of Arabia on the Red Sea, renowned, esp in King Solomon's reign, for its gold and precious stones (I Kings 9:28; 10:10)

ophthalmia inflammation of the eye, often including the conjunctiva

ophthalmic of or relating to the eye

ophthalmology the branch of medicine concerned with the eye and its diseases

ophthalmoscope an instrument for examining the interior of the eye

opiate 1 any of various narcotic drugs, such as morphine and heroin, that act on opioid receptors 2 any other narcotic or sedative drug 3 containing or consisting of opium

opinion *Law* the advice given by a barrister or counsel on a case submitted to him or her for a view on the legal points involved

opium the dried juice extracted from the unripe seed capsules of the opium poppy that contains alkaloids such as morphine and codeine: used in medicine as an analgesic

Oporto a port in NW Portugal, near the mouth of the Douro River: the second largest city in Portugal, famous for port wine (begun in 1678). Pop: 263 131 (2001)

opossum 1 any thick-furred marsupial, esp *Didelphis marsupialis* (**common opossum**), of the family Didelphidae of S North, Central, and South America, having an elongated snout and a hairless prehensile tail 2 any of various similar animals, esp the phalanger, *Trichosurus vulpecula*, of the New Zealand bush

Oppenheimer J(ulius) Robert 1904–67, US nuclear physicist. He was director of the Los Alamos laboratory (1943–45), which produced the first atomic bomb. He opposed the development of the hydrogen bomb (1949) and in 1953 was alleged to be a security risk. He was later exonerated

opponent *Anatomy* 1 an opponent muscle 2 (of a muscle) bringing two parts into opposition

opposable (of the thumb of primates, esp man) capable of being moved into a position facing the other digits so as to be able to touch the ends of each

opposite 1 *Botany* a (of leaves, flowers, etc) arranged in pairs on either side of the stem b (of parts of a flower) arranged opposite the middle of another part 2 *Maths* a (of two vertices or sides in an even-sided polygon) separated by the same number of vertices or sides in both a clockwise and anticlockwise direction b (of a side in a triangle) facing a specified angle 3 *Maths* the side facing a specified angle in a right-angled triangle

opposition 1 a a political party or group opposed to the ruling party or government b **in opposition** (of a political party) opposing the government 2 *Astronomy* a the position of an outer planet or the moon when it is in line or nearly in line with the earth as seen from the sun and is approximately at its nearest to the earth b the position of two celestial bodies when they appear to be diametrically opposite each other on the celestial sphere 3 *Astrology* an exact aspect of 180° between two planets, etc, an orb of 8° being allowed 4 *Logic* a the relation between propositions having the same subject and predicate but differing in quality, quantity, or both, as with *all men are wicked; no men are wicked; some men are not wicked* b **square of opposition** a diagram representing these relations with the contradictory propositions at diagonally opposite corners 5 **the opposition** *Chess* a relative position of the kings in the endgame such that the player who has the move is at a disadvantage

optic 1 of or relating to the eye or vision 2 a less common word for **optical**

optical 1 of, relating to, producing, or involving light 2 of or relating to the eye or to the sense of sight; optic 3 (esp of a lens) aiding vision or correcting a visual disorder

optician a a general name used to refer to **ophthalmic optician**, a person qualified to examine the eyes and prescribe and supply spectacles and contact lenses b a general name used to refer to **dispensing optician**, a person who supplies and fits spectacle frames but is not qualified to prescribe lenses

optics the branch of science concerned with vision and the generation, nature, propagation, and behaviour of electromagnetic light

optimism 1 the doctrine of the ultimate triumph of good over evil 2 the philosophical doctrine that this is the best of all possible worlds

option *Commerce* an exclusive opportunity, usually for a limited period, to buy something at a future date

optometrist a person who is qualified to examine the eyes and prescribe and supply spectacles and contact lenses

opus (usually followed by a number) a musical composition by a particular composer, generally catalogued in order of publication

oracle 1 a prophecy, often obscure or allegorical, revealed through the medium of a priest or priestess at the shrine of a god 2 a shrine at which an oracular god is consulted 3 an agency through which a prophecy is transmitted 4 *Bible* a a message from God b the holy of holies in the Israelite temple

Oradea an industrial city in NW Romania, in Transylvania: ceded by Hungary (1919). Pop: 182 000 (2005 est)

oral 1 relating to, affecting, or for use in the mouth 2 of or relating to the surface of an animal, such as a jellyfish, on which the mouth is situated 3 denoting a drug to be taken by mouth 4 *Psychoanal* a relating to a stage of psychosexual development during which the child's interest is concentrated on the mouth b denoting personality traits, such as dependence, selfishness, and aggression, resulting from fixation at the oral stage 5 an examination in which the questions and answers are spoken rather than written

Oran a port in NW Algeria: the second largest city in the country; scene of the destruction by the British of most of the French fleet in the harbour in 1940 to prevent its capture by the Germans. Pop: 744 000 (2005 est)

orange 1 any of several citrus trees, esp *Citrus sinensis* (**sweet orange**) and the Seville orange, cultivated in warm regions for their round edible fruit. See also **tangerine** 2 a the fruit of any of these trees, having a yellowish-red bitter rind and segmented juicy flesh b (*as modifier*): *orange peel* 3 the hard wood of any of these trees 4 any of several trees or herbaceous plants that resemble the orange, such as mock orange 5 any of a group of colours, such as that of the skin of an orange, that lie between red and yellow in the visible spectrum in the approximate wavelength range 620–585 nanometres

Orange[1] 1 a princely family of Europe. Its possessions, originally centred in S France, passed in 1544 to the count of Nassau, who became William I of Orange and helped to found the United Provinces of the Netherlands. Since 1815 it has been the name of the reigning house of the Netherlands. It was the ruling house of Great Britain and Ireland under William III and Mary (1689–94) and under William III as sole monarch (1694–1702) 2 of or relating to the Orangemen 3 of or relating to the royal dynasty of Orange

Orange[2] 1 a river in S Africa, rising in NE Lesotho and flowing generally west across the South African plateau to the Atlantic: the longest river in South Africa. Length: 2093 km (1300 miles) 2 a town in SE France: a small principality in the Middle Ages, the descendants of which formed the House of Orange. Pop: 27 989 (1999)

orange blossom the flowers of the orange tree, traditionally worn by brides

Orange Free State a former province of central South Africa, between the Orange and Vaal rivers: settled by Boers in 1836 after the Great Trek; annexed by Britain in 1848; became a province of South Africa in 1910; replaced in 1994 by the new province of Free State; economy based on agriculture and mineral resources (esp gold and uranium). Capital: Bloemfontein

Orangeman a member of a society founded in Ireland (1795) to uphold the Protestant religion, the Protestant dynasty, and the Protestant constitution. **Orange Lodges** have since spread to many parts of the former British Empire

orangery a building, such as a greenhouse, in which orange trees are grown

orang-utan or **orang-utang** a large anthropoid ape, *Pongo pygmaeus*, of the forests of Sumatra and Borneo, with shaggy reddish-brown hair and strong arms

oration an academic exercise or contest in public speaking

orator *Obsolete* the claimant in a cause of action in chancery

oratorio a dramatic but unstaged musical composition for soloists, chorus, and orchestra, based on a religious theme

oratory a small room or secluded place, set apart for private prayer

orb *Obsolete or poetic* **a** a celestial body, esp the earth or sun **b** the orbit of a celestial body

orbit 1 *Astronomy* the curved path, usually elliptical, followed by a planet, satellite, comet, etc, in its motion around another celestial body under the influence of gravitation 2 *Anatomy* the bony cavity containing the eyeball 3 *Zoology* **a** the skin surrounding the eye of a bird **b** the hollow in which lies the eye or eyestalk of an insect or other arthropod 4 *Physics* the path of an electron in its motion around the nucleus of an atom

Orcadian a native or inhabitant of Orkney

Orcagna Andrea , original name *Andrea di Cione.* ?1308–68, Florentine painter, sculptor, and architect

orchestra 1 a large group of musicians, esp one whose members play a variety of different instruments 2 a group of musicians, each playing the same type of instrument 3 the space reserved for musicians in a theatre, immediately in front of or under the stage 4 *Chiefly US and Canadian* the stalls in a theatre 5 (in the ancient Greek theatre) the semicircular space in front of the stage

orchid any terrestrial or epiphytic plant of the family *Orchidaceae*, often having flowers of unusual shapes and beautiful colours, specialized for pollination by certain insects

Orczy Baroness Emmuska 1865–1947, British novelist, born in Hungary; author of *The Scarlet Pimpernel* (1905)

Ord a river in NE Western Australia, rising on the Kimberley Plateau and flowing generally north to the Timor Sea: subject of a major irrigation scheme. Length: about 500 km (300 miles)

ordeal *History* a method of trial in which the guilt or innocence of an accused person was determined by subjecting him to physical danger, esp by fire or water. The outcome was regarded as an indication of divine judgment

order 1 *Biology* any of the taxonomic groups into which a class is divided and which contains one or more families. *Carnivora*, *Primates*, and *Rodentia* are three orders of the class *Mammalia* 2 a decision or direction of a court or judge entered on the court record but not included in the final judgment 3 a commission or instruction to produce or supply something in return for payment **b** the commodity produced or supplied **c** (*as modifier*): *order form* 4 a group of persons who bind themselves by vows in order to devote themselves to the pursuit of religious aims 5 *History* a society of knights constituted as a fraternity, such as the Knights Templars 6 **a** any of the five major classical styles of architecture classified by the style of columns and entablatures used **b** any style of architecture 7 *Christianity* **a** the sacrament by which bishops, priests, etc, have their offices conferred upon

them **b** any of the degrees into which the ministry is divided **c** the office of an ordained Christian minister 8 a form of Christian Church service prescribed to be used on specific occasions 9 *Judaism* one of the six sections of the Mishna or the corresponding tractates of the Talmud 10 *Maths* **a** the number of times a function must be differentiated to obtain a given derivative **b** the order of the highest derivative in a differential equation **c** the number of rows or columns in a determinant or square matrix **d** the number of members of a finite group

orderly *Med* a male hospital attendant

order paper *Politics* a list indicating the order in which business is to be conducted, esp in Parliament

ordinal number 1 a number denoting relative position in a sequence, such as *first, second, third* 2 *Logic, Maths* a measure of not only the size of a set but also the order of its elements

ordinary 1 *Law* having regular or ex officio jurisdiction 2 *Maths* (of a differential equation) containing two variables only and derivatives of one of the variables with respect to the other 3 *Civil law* a judge who exercises jurisdiction in his own right 4 an ecclesiastic, esp a bishop, holding an office to which certain jurisdictional powers are attached 5 *RC Church* **a** the parts of the Mass that do not vary from day to day **b** a prescribed form of divine service, esp the Mass 6 *History* a clergyman who visited condemned prisoners before their death

ordinary seaman a seaman of the lowest rank, being insufficiently experienced to be an able-bodied seaman

ordinate the vertical or *y*-coordinate of a point in a two-dimensional system of Cartesian coordinates

ordination **a** the act of conferring holy orders **b** the reception of holy orders

Ordnance Survey the official map-making body of the British or Irish government

Ordovician of, denoting, or formed in the second period of the Palaeozoic era, between the Cambrian and Silurian periods, which lasted for 45 000 000 years during which marine invertebrates flourished

ore any naturally occurring mineral or aggregate of minerals from which economically important constituents, esp metals, can be extracted

oregano a Mediterranean variety of wild marjoram (*Origanum vulgare*), with pungent leaves

Oregon a state of the northwestern US, on the Pacific: consists of the Coast and Cascade Ranges in the west and a plateau in the east; important timber production. Capital: Salem. Pop: 3 559 596 (2003 est). Area: 251 418 sq km (97 073 sq miles)

Oregon trail an early pioneering route across the central US, from Independence, W Missouri, to the Columbia River country of N Oregon: used chiefly between 1804 and 1860. Length: about 3220 km (2000 miles)

Orel *or* **Oryol** a city in W Russia; founded in 1564 but damaged during World War II. Pop: 333 000 (2005 est)

Orenburg a city in W Russia, on the Ural River. Pop: 550 000 (2005 est)

Orense a city in NW Spain, in Galicia on the Miño River: warm springs. Pop: 109 475 (2003 est)

Orff Carl 1895–1982, German composer. His works include the secular oratorio *Carmina Burana* (1937) and the opera *Antigone* (1949)

organ 1 a a large complex musical keyboard instrument in which sound is produced by means of a number of pipes arranged in sets or stops, supplied with air from a bellows. The largest instruments possess three or more manuals and one pedal keyboard and have the greatest range of any instrument **b** (*as modifier*): *organ pipe* **2** any instrument, such as a harmonium, in which sound is produced in this way **3** *Biology* a fully differentiated structural and functional unit, such as a kidney or a root, in an animal or plant

organdie *or esp US* **organdy** a fine and slightly stiff cotton fabric used esp for dresses

organic 1 of, relating to, derived from, or characteristic of living plants and animals **2** of or relating to animal or plant constituents or products having a carbon basis **3** of or relating to one or more organs of an animal or plant **4** of, relating to, or belonging to the class of chemical compounds that are formed from carbon **5** of or relating to the essential constitutional laws regulating the government of a state

organic chemistry the branch of chemistry concerned with the compounds of carbon: originally confined to compounds produced by living organisms but now extended to include man-made substances based on carbon, such as plastics

organism any living biological entity, such as an animal, plant, fungus, or bacterium

organist a person who plays the organ

organization *or* **organisation** a body of administrative officials, as of a political party, a government department, etc.

organza a thin stiff fabric of silk, cotton, nylon, rayon, etc.

orgasm the most intense point during sexual excitement, characterized by extremely pleasurable sensations and in the male accompanied by ejaculation of semen

orgy *History* secret religious rites of Dionysus, Bacchus, etc, marked by drinking, dancing, and songs

oriel window a bay window, esp one that is supported by one or more brackets or corbels

Orient 1 the countries east of the Mediterranean **2** the eastern hemisphere

Oriental 1 of or relating to the Orient **2** of or denoting a zoogeographical region consisting of southeastern Asia from India to Borneo, Java, and the Philippines **3** a breed of slender muscular cat with large ears, long legs, and a long tail

orientation 1 position or positioning with relation to the points of the compass or other specific directions **2** *Chiefly US and Canadian* **a** a course, programme, lecture, etc, introducing a new situation or environment **b** (*as modifier*): *an orientation talk* **3** *Psychol* the knowledge of one's own temporal, social, and practical circumstances in life **4** *Biology* the change in position of the whole or part of an organism in response to a stimulus, such as light **5** *Chem* the relative dispositions of atoms, ions, or groups in molecules or crystals **6** *Archit* the siting of a church on an east-west axis, usually with the altar at the E end

orienteering a sport in which contestants race on foot over a course consisting of checkpoints found with the aid of a map and a compass
▷www.orienteering.org

origami the art or process, originally Japanese, of paper folding
▷www.origami.com
▷www.paperfolding.com
▷www.origami-usa.org

Origen ?185–?254 AD, Christian theologian, born in Alexandria. His writings include *Hexapla*, a synopsis of the Old Testament, *Contra Celsum*, a defence of Christianity, and *De principiis*, a statement of Christian theology

origin 1 *Anatomy* **a** the end of a muscle, opposite its point of insertion **b** the beginning of a nerve or blood vessel or the site where it first starts to branch out **2** *Maths* **a** the point of intersection of coordinate axes or planes **b** the point whose coordinates are all zero **3** *Commerce* the country from which a commodity or product originates

original sin a state of sin held to be innate in mankind as the descendants of Adam

Orinoco a river in N South America, rising in S Venezuela and flowing west, then north as part of the border between Colombia and Venezuela, then east to the Atlantic by a great delta: the third largest river system in South America, draining an area of 945 000 sq km (365 000 sq miles); reaches a width of 22 km (14 miles) during the rainy season. Length: about 2575 km (1600 miles)

oriole 1 any songbird of the mainly tropical Old World family *Oriolidae*, such as *Oriolus oriolus* (**golden oriole**), having a long pointed bill and a mostly yellow-and-black plumage **2** any American songbird of the family *Icteridae*, esp those of the genus *Icterus*, such as the Baltimore oriole, with a typical male plumage of black with either orange or yellow

Orissa a state of E India, on the Bay of Bengal: part of the province of Bihar and Orissa (1912–36); enlarged by the addition of 25 native states in 1949. Capital: Bhubaneswar. Pop: 36 706 920 (2001). Area: 155 707 sq km (60 119 sq miles)

Orizaba a city and resort in SE Mexico, in Veracruz state. Pop: 327 000 (2005 est)

Orlando a city in the US, in Florida: site of Walt Disney World. Pop: 199 336 (2003 est)

Orly a suburb of SE Paris, France, with an international airport

Ormandy Eugene 1899–1985, US conductor, born in Hungary

ormolu 1 a a gold-coloured alloy of copper, tin, or zinc used to decorate furniture, mouldings, etc. **b** (*as modifier*): *an ormolu clock* **2** gold prepared to be used for gilding

ornament *Music* any of several decorations, such as the trill, mordent, etc, occurring chiefly as improvised embellishments in baroque music

Orne a department of NW France, in Basse-Normandie. Capital: Alençon. Pop: 291 274 (2003 est). Area: 6144 sq km (2396 sq miles)

ornithology the study of birds, including their physiology, classification, ecology, and behaviour

Orontes a river in SW Asia, rising in Lebanon and flowing north through Syria into Turkey, where it turns west to the Mediterranean. Length: 571 km (355 miles)

Orozco José Clemente 1883–1949, Mexican painter, noted for his monumental humanistic murals

Orpington a district of SE London, part of the Greater London borough of Bromley from 1965

Orr Robert Gordon, known as *Bobby*. born 1948, Canadian ice-hockey player

orrery a mechanical model of the solar system in which the planets can be moved at the correct relative velocities around the sun

orris¹ or **orrice** the rhizome of such a plant, prepared and used as perfume

orris² a kind of lace made of gold or silver, used esp in the 18th century

orris or **orrice** any of various irises, esp *Iris florentina*, that have fragrant rhizomes

Orsini an Italian aristocratic family that was prominent in Rome from the 12th to the 18th century

Orsk a city in W Russia, on the Ural River: a major railway and industrial centre, with an oil refinery linked by pipeline with the Emba field (on the Caspian). Pop: 247 000 (2005 est)

Ortegal Cape a cape in NW Spain, projecting into the Bay of Biscay

Ortega y Gasset José 1883–1955, Spanish essayist and philosopher. His best-known work is *The Revolt of the Masses* (1930)

orthodontics or **orthodontia** the branch of dentistry concerned with preventing or correcting irregularities of the teeth

orthodox *Religion* conforming to the Christian faith as established by the early Church

Orthodox 1 of or relating to the Orthodox Church of the East **2 a** of or relating to Orthodox Judaism **b** (of an individual Jew) strict in the observance of Talmudic law and in personal devotions

Orthodox Church the collective body of those Eastern Churches that were separated from the western Church in the 11th century and are in communion with the Greek patriarch of Constantinople

orthography 1 a writing system **2** the study of spelling

orthopaedics or US **orthopedics 1** the branch of surgery concerned with disorders of the spine and joints and the repair of deformities of these parts **2** dental orthopaedics another name for **orthodontics**

ortolan 1 a brownish Old World bunting, *Emberiza hortulana*, regarded as a delicacy **2** any of various other small birds eaten as delicacies, esp the bobolink

Orton Joe (Kingsley). 1933–67, British dramatist, noted for his black comedies: these include *Entertaining Mr Sloane* (1964), *Loot* (1966), and *What the Butler Saw* (1969)

Oruro a city in W Bolivia: a former silver-mining centre; university (1892); tin, copper, and tungsten. Pop: 206 000 (2005 est)

Orvieto 1 a market town in central Italy, in Umbria: Etruscan remains. Pop: 20 705 (2001) **2** a light white wine from this region

Orwell George, real name *Eric Arthur Blair*. 1903–50, English novelist and essayist, born in India. He is notable for his social criticism, as in *The Road to Wigan Pier* (1932); his account of his experiences of the Spanish Civil War *Homage to Catalonia* (1938); and his satirical novels *Animal Farm* (1945), an allegory on the Russian Revolution, and *1984* (1949), in which he depicts an authoritarian state of the future

oryx any large African antelope of the genus *Oryx*, typically having long straight nearly upright horns

Osaka a port in S Japan, on S Honshu on **Osaka Bay** (an inlet of the Pacific): the third largest city in Japan (the chief commercial city during feudal times); university (1931); an industrial and commercial centre. Pop: 2 484 326 (2002 est)

Osborne John (James). 1929–94, British dramatist. His plays include *Look Back in Anger* (1956), containing the prototype of the angry young man, Jimmy Porter, *The Entertainer* (1957), and *Inadmissible Evidence* (1964)

Oscar a any of several small gold statuettes awarded annually in the United States by the Academy of Motion Picture Arts and Sciences for outstanding achievements in films **b** an award made in recognition of outstanding endeavour in any of various other fields
▷www.oscars.org
▷www.oscar.com
▷www.howstuffworks.com/oscar.htm

Oscar II 1829–1907, king of Sweden (1872–1907) and of Norway (1872–1905)

oscilloscope an instrument for producing a representation of a quantity that rapidly changes with time on the screen of a cathode-ray tube. The changes are converted into electric signals, which are applied to plates in the cathode-ray tube. Changes in the magnitude of the potential across the plates deflect the electron beam and thus produce a trace on the screen

Oshawa a city in central Canada, in SE Ontario on Lake Ontario: motor-vehicle industry. Pop: 139 051 (2001)

Oshogbo a city in SW Nigeria: trade centre. Pop: 629 000 (2005 est)

osier 1 any of various willow trees, esp *Salix viminalis*, whose flexible branches or twigs are used for making baskets, etc. a twig or branch from such a tree **2** any of several North American dogwoods, esp the red osier

Osijek 3 a town in NE Croatia on the Drava River: under Turkish rule from 1526 to 1687. Pop: 85 000 (2005 est)

Osiris an ancient Egyptian god, ruler of the underworld and judge of the dead

Oslo the capital and chief port of Norway, in the southeast at the head of **Oslo Fjord** (an inlet of the Skagerrak): founded in about 1050; university (1811); a major commercial and industrial centre, producing about a quarter of Norway's total output. Pop: 521 886 (2004 est)

Osman I or **Othman I** 1259–1326, Turkish sultan; founder of the Ottoman Empire

osmium a very hard brittle bluish-white metal occurring with platinum and alloyed with iridium in osmiridium: used to produce platinum alloys, mainly for pen tips and instrument pivots, as a catalyst, and in electric-light filaments. Symbol: Os; atomic no.: 76; atomic wt.: 190.2; valency: 0 to 8; relative density: 22.57; melting pt.: 3033±30°C; boiling pt.: 5012±100°C

osmoregulation *Zoology* the adjustment of the osmotic

pressure of a cell or organism in relation to the surrounding fluid

osmosis 1 the passage of a solvent through a semipermeable membrane from a less concentrated to a more concentrated solution until both solutions are of the same concentration 2 diffusion through any membrane or porous barrier, as in dialysis '

osprey a large broad-winged fish-eating diurnal bird of prey, *Pandion haliaetus*, with a dark back and whitish head and underparts: family *Pandioridae*

Ossa a mountain in NE Greece, in E Thessaly: famous in mythology for the attempt of the twin giants, Otus and Ephialtes, to reach heaven by piling Ossa on Olympus and Pelion on Ossa. Height: 1978 m (6489 ft)

osseous consisting of or containing bone, bony

Ossetia a region of central Asia, in the Caucasus: consists administratively of the North Ossetian Republic in Russia and the South Ossetian Autonomous Region in Georgia

Ossian a legendary Irish hero and bard of the 3rd century AD

Ossietzky Carl von 1889–1938, German pacifist leader. He was imprisoned for revealing Germany's secret rearmament (1931–32) and again under Hitler (1933–36): Nobel peace prize 1935

Ostend a port and resort in NW Belgium, in West Flanders on the North Sea. Pop: 68 273 (2004 est)

ostensive 1 obviously or manifestly demonstrative 2 *Philosophy* (of a definition) given by demonstrative means, esp by pointing

osteoarthritis chronic inflammation of the joints, esp those that bear weight, with pain and stiffness

osteopathy a system of healing based on the manipulation of bones or other parts of the body

osteoporosis porosity and brittleness of the bones due to loss of calcium from the bone matrix

Ostia an ancient town in W central Italy, originally at the mouth of the Tiber but now about 6 km (4 miles) inland: served as the port of ancient Rome; harbours built by Claudius and Trajan; ruins excavated since 1854

ostinato a continuously reiterated musical phrase b (*as modifier*): *an ostinato passage*

ostler *or* **hostler** *Archaic* a stableman, esp one at an inn

Ostrava an industrial city in the E Czech Republic, on the River Oder: the chief coal-mining area in the Czech Republic, in Upper Silesia. Pop: 316 000 (2005 est)

ostrich 1 a fast-running flightless African bird, *Struthio camelus*, that is the largest living bird, with stout two-toed feet and dark feathers, except on the naked head, neck, and legs: order *Struthioniformes* 2 **American ostrich** another name for **rhea**

Ostwald Wilhelm 1853–1932, German chemist, noted for his pioneering work in catalysis. He also invented a process for making nitric acid from ammonia and developed a new theory of colour: Nobel prize for chemistry 1909

Oswald 1 Lee Harvey 1939–63, presumed assassin (1963) of US president John F. Kennedy; murdered by Jack Ruby two days later 2 **Saint** ?605–41 AD, king of Northumbria (634–41); with St Aidan he restored Christianity to the region. He was killed in battle by Penda of Mercia. Feast day: Aug 5

Otago a council region of New Zealand, formerly a province, founded by Scottish settlers in the south of South Island. The University of Otago (1869) in Dunedin is the oldest university in New Zealand. Chief town: Dunedin. Pop: 195 000 (2004 est)

OTE on-target earnings: referring to the salary a salesperson should be able to achieve

Otranto a small port in SE Italy, in Apulia on the **Strait of Otranto**: the most easterly town in Italy; dates back to Greek times and was an important Roman port; its ruined castle was the setting of Horace Walpole's *Castle of Otranto*. Pop: 5282 (2001)

Ottawa 1 the capital of Canada, in E Ontario on the Ottawa River: name changed from Bytown to Ottawa in 1854. Pop: 774 072 (2001) 2 a river in central Canada, rising in W Quebec and flowing west, then southeast to join the St Lawrence River as its chief tributary at Montreal; forms the border between Quebec and Ontario for most of its length. Length: 1120 km (696 miles)

otter 1 any freshwater carnivorous musteline mammal of the subfamily *Lutrinae*, esp *Lutra lutra* (**Eurasian otter**), typically having smooth fur, a streamlined body, and webbed feet 2 the fur of any of these animals 3 a type of fishing tackle consisting of a weighted board to which hooked and baited lines are attached

Otterburn a village in NE England, in central Northumberland: scene of a battle (1388) in which the Scots, led by the earl of Douglas, defeated the English, led by Hotspur

Otto Rudolf 1869–1937, German theologian: his best-known work is *The Idea of the Holy* (1923)

Otto I *or* **Otho I** called *the Great*. 912–73 AD, king of Germany (936–73); Holy Roman Emperor (962–73)

ottoman a corded fabric

Ottoman *or* **Othman** 1 *History* of or relating to the Ottomans or the Ottoman Empire 2 denoting or relating to the Turkish language 3 a member of a Turkish people who invaded the Near East in the late 13th century

Otway Thomas 1652–85, English dramatist, noted for *The Orphan* (1680) and *Venice Preserv'd* (1682)

Ouachita *or* **Washita** a river in the S central US, rising in the **Ouachita Mountains** and flowing east, south, and southeast into the Red River in E Louisiana. Length: 974 km (605 miles)

Ouagadougou the capital of Burkina-Faso, on the central plateau: terminus of the railway from Abidjan (Côte d'Ivoire). Pop: 870 000 (2005 est)

oubliette a dungeon the only entrance to which is through the top

Oudh a region of N India, in central Uttar Pradesh: annexed by Britain in 1856 and a centre of the Indian Mutiny (1857–58); joined with Agra in 1877, becoming the United Provinces of Agra and Oudh in 1902, which were renamed Uttar Pradesh in 1950

Ouija board *Trademark* a board on which are marked the letters of the alphabet. Answers to questions are spelt out by a pointer or glass held by the fingertips of the participants, and are supposedly formed by spiritual forces

Oujda a city in NE Morocco, near the border with Algeria: frontier post. Pop: 454 000 (2003)

Oulu an industrial city and port in W Finland, on the Gulf of Bothnia: university (1959). Pop: 125 928 (2003 est)

ounce 1 a unit of weight equal to one sixteenth of a pound (avoirdupois); 1 ounce is equal to 437.5 grains or 28.349 grams 2 a unit of weight equal to one twelfth of a Troy or Apothecaries' pound; 1 ounce is equal to 480 grains or 31.103 grams 3 short for **fluid ounce**

Ouse 1 a river in E England, rising in Northamptonshire and flowing northeast to the Wash near King's Lynn; for the last 56 km (35 miles) follows mainly artificial channels. Length: 257 km (160 miles) 2 a river in NE England, in Yorkshire, formed by the confluence of the Swale and Ure Rivers: flows southeast to the Humber. Length: 92 km (57 miles) 3 a river in S England, rising in Sussex and flowing south to the English Channel. Length: 48 km (30 miles)

ouster *Property law* the act of dispossessing of freehold property; eviction; ejection

out 1 *Politics* not in office or authority 2 *Baseball* an instance of the putting out of a batter; putout

outage *Commerce* a quantity of goods missing or lost after storage or shipment

outbuilding a building subordinate to but separate from a main building; outhouse

outcrop part of a rock formation or mineral vein that appears at the surface of the earth

outer *Archery* a the white outermost ring on a target b a shot that hits this ring

outer space any region of space beyond the atmosphere of the earth

outfield 1 *Cricket* the area of the field relatively far from the pitch; the deep 2 *Baseball* a the area of the playing field beyond the lines connecting first, second, and third bases b the positions of the left fielder, centre fielder, and right fielder taken collectively

outfit *Canadian* (formerly) the annual shipment of trading goods and supplies sent by a fur company to its trading posts

outhouse a building near to, but separate from, a main building; outbuilding

outlaw 1 (formerly) a person excluded from the law and deprived of its protection 2 any fugitive from the law, esp a habitual transgressor 3 a wild or untamed beast

outlet 1 a a market for a product or service b a commercial establishment retailing the goods of a particular producer or wholesaler 2 a point in a wiring system from which current can be taken to supply electrical devices 3 *Anatomy* the beginning or end of a passage, esp the lower opening of the pelvis (**pelvic outlet**)

outline a a drawing or manner of drawing consisting only of external lines b (*as modifier*): *an outline map*

outpatient a nonresident hospital patient

output 1 *Electronics* a the power, voltage, or current delivered by a circuit or component b the point at which the signal is delivered 2 the power, energy, or work produced by an engine or a system 3 *Computing* a the information produced by a computer b the operations and devices involved in producing this information

outrigger 1 a framework for supporting a pontoon outside and parallel to the hull of a boat to provide stability 2 a boat equipped with such a framework, esp one of the canoes of the South Pacific

outsider *Sport* a contestant, esp a horse, thought unlikely to win in a race

outstation 1 a station or post in a remote region 2 *Austral* a station set up independently of the head station of a large sheep or cattle farm 3 **outstation movement** *Austral* the programme to resettle native Australians on their tribal lands

out-tray (in an office) a tray for outgoing correspondence, documents, etc.

outward (of a ship, part of a voyage, etc) leaving for a particular destination

ouzel *or* **ousel** 1 short for **water ouzel** (see **dipper**) 2 an archaic name for the (European) **blackbird**

ouzo a strong aniseed-flavoured spirit from Greece

Oval the a cricket ground in south London, in the borough of Lambeth

ovary 1 either of the two female reproductive organs, which produce ova and secrete oestrogen hormones 2 the corresponding organ in vertebrate and invertebrate animals 3 *Botany* the hollow basal region of a carpel containing one or more ovules. In some plants the carpels are united to form a single compound ovary

ovate 1 shaped like an egg 2 (esp of a leaf) shaped like the longitudinal section of an egg, with the broader end at the base

ovation *History* a victory procession less glorious than a triumph awarded to a Roman general

over *Cricket* a a series of six balls bowled by a bowler from the same end of the pitch b the play during this

overburden *Geology* the sedimentary rock material that covers coal seams, mineral veins, etc.

overcast 1 *Meteorol* (of the sky) more than 95 per cent cloud-covered 2 *Meteorol* the state of the sky when more than 95 per cent of it is cloud-covered

overcharge 1 an excessive price or charge 2 an excessive load

overdrive a very high gear in a motor vehicle used at high speeds to reduce wear and save fuel

overdub in multitrack recording the addition of new sound to a recording; the blending of various layers of sound in one recording

overflow *Computing* a condition that occurs when numeric operations produce results too large to store in the register available

overhang *Aeronautics* a half the difference in span of the main supporting surfaces of a biplane or other multiplane b the distance from the outer supporting strut of a wing to the wing tip

overhead *Nautical* the interior lining above one's head below decks in a vessel

Overijssel a province of the E Netherlands: generally low-lying. Capital: Zwolle. Pop: 1 101 000 (2003 est). Area: 3929 sq km (1517 sq miles)

overlap *Geology* the horizontal extension of the upper beds in a series of rock strata beyond the lower beds, usually caused by submergence of the land

overlay an applied decoration or layer, as of gold leaf

overman *Philosophy* the Nietzschean superman

overprint additional matter, other than a change in face value, applied to a finished postage stamp by printing, stamping, etc.

overrun the cleared level area at the end of an airport runway

overshoot a momentary excessive response of an electrical or mechanical system

overshot 1 having or designating an upper jaw that projects beyond the lower jaw, esp when considered as an abnormality **2** (of a water wheel) driven by a flow of water that passes over the wheel rather than under it

overstrung (of a piano) having two sets of strings crossing each other at an oblique angle

overt *Law* open; deliberate. Criminal intent may be inferred from an overt act

overthrow *Cricket* **a** a ball thrown back too far by a fielder **b** a run scored because of this

overtone *Music, Acoustics* any of the tones, with the exception of the fundamental, that constitute a musical sound and contribute to its quality, each having a frequency that is a multiple of the fundamental frequency

overture 1 *Music* **a** a piece of orchestral music containing contrasting sections that is played at the beginning of an opera or oratorio, often containing the main musical themes of the work **b** a similar piece preceding the performance of a play **c** a one-movement orchestral piece, usually having a descriptive or evocative title **d** a short piece in three movements (**French overture** or **Italian overture**) common in the 17th and 18th centuries **2** something that introduces what follows

overwrought *Art* with the surface decorated or adorned

Ovid Latin name *Publius Ovidius Naso*. 43 BC–?17 AD, Roman poet. His verse includes poems on love, *Ars Amatoria*, on myths, *Metamorphoses*, and on his sufferings in exile, *Tristia*

oviduct the tube through which ova are conveyed from an ovary

Oviedo a city in NW Spain: capital of Asturias from 810 until 1002; centre of a coal- and iron-mining area. Pop: 207 699 (2003 est)

oviform *Biology* shaped like an egg

ovine of, relating to, or resembling a sheep

oviparous (of fishes, reptiles, birds, etc) producing eggs that hatch outside the body of the mother

ovoid *Botany* (of a fruit or similar part) egg-shaped with the broader end at the base

ovule 1 a small body in seed-bearing plants that consists of the integument(s), nucellus, and embryosac (containing the egg cell) and develops into the seed after fertilization **2** *Zoology* an immature ovum

ovum an unfertilized female gamete; egg cell

Owen 1 David (**Anthony Llewellyn**), Baron. born 1938, British politician: Labour foreign secretary (1977–79); cofounder of the Social Democratic Party (1981) and its leader (1983–87): leader (1988–92) of the section of the Social Democratic Party that did not merge with the Liberal Party in 1988; peace envoy to Bosnia-Herzegovina (1992–94) **2** Michael (**James**). born 1979, British footballer; plays for Real Madrid and England (from 1997) **3** Sir **Richard** 1804–92, English comparative

anatomist and palaeontologist **4** Robert 1771–1858, Welsh industrialist and social reformer. He formed a model industrial community at New Lanark, Scotland, and pioneered cooperative societies. His books include *New View of Society* (1813) **5** Wilfred 1893–1918, English poet of World War I, who was killed in action

Owens Jesse, real name *John Cleveland Owens*. 1913–80, US Black athlete: won four gold medals at the Berlin Olympics (1936)

Owen Stanley Range a mountain range in SE New Guinea. Highest peak: Mount Victoria, 4073 m (13 363 ft)

Owerri a market town in S Nigeria, capital of Imo state. Pop: 35 010 (latest est)

owl 1 any nocturnal bird of prey of the order *Strigiformes*, having large front-facing eyes, a small hooked bill, soft feathers, and a short neck **2** any of various breeds of owl-like fancy domestic pigeon (esp the **African owl, Chinese owl,** and **English owl**)

ox 1 an adult castrated male of any domesticated species of cattle, esp *Bos taurus*, used for draught work and meat **2** any bovine mammal, esp any of the domestic cattle

oxalic acid a colourless poisonous crystalline dicarboxylic acid found in many plants: used as a bleach and a cleansing agent for metals. Formula: $(COOH)_2$

Oxbridge a the British universities of Oxford and Cambridge, esp considered as ancient and prestigious academic institutions, bastions of privilege and superiority, etc. **b** (*as modifier*): *Oxbridge graduates*

Oxford 1 a city in S England, administrative centre of Oxfordshire, at the confluence of the Rivers Thames and Cherwell: Royalist headquarters during the Civil War; seat of Oxford University, consisting of 40 separate colleges, the oldest being University College (1249), and Oxford Brookes University (1993); motor-vehicle industry. Pop: 143 016 (2001) **2** a breed of sheep with middle-length wool and a dark brown face and legs **3** a lightweight fabric of plain or twill weave used esp for men's shirts

Oxfordshire an inland county of S central England: situated mostly in the basin of the Upper Thames, with the Cotswolds in the west and the Chilterns in the southeast. Administrative centre: Oxford. Pop: 615 200 (2003 est). Area: 2608 sq km (1007 sq miles)

oxide 1 any compound of oxygen with another element **2** any organic compound in which an oxygen atom is bound to two alkyl or aryl groups; an ether or epoxide

Oxonian 1 of or relating to Oxford or Oxford University **2** a member of Oxford University **3** an inhabitant or native of Oxford

oxyacetylene a a mixture of oxygen and acetylene; used in a blowpipe for cutting or welding metals at high temperatures **b** (*as modifier*): *an oxyacetylene burner*

oxygen a a colourless odourless highly reactive gaseous element: the most abundant element in the earth's crust (49.2 per cent). It is essential for aerobic respiration and almost all combustion and is widely used in industry. Symbol: O; atomic no.: 8; atomic wt.: 15.9994; valency: 2; density: 1.429 kg/m³; melting pt.: –218.79°C; boiling pt.: –182.97°C **b** (*as modifier*): *an oxygen mask*

oxygen tent *Med* a transparent enclosure covering a bedridden patient, into which oxygen is released to help maintain respiration

oxymoron *Rhetoric* an epigrammatic effect, by which contradictory terms are used in conjunction

Oyo a state of SW Nigeria, formed in 1976 from part of Western State. Capital: Ibadan. Pop: 3 900 803 (1995 est). Area: 28 454 sq km (10 986 sq miles)

oyster 1 a any edible marine bivalve mollusc of the genus *Ostrea*, having a rough irregularly shaped shell and occurring on the sea bed, mostly in coastal waters b (*as modifier*): *oyster farm* 2 any of various similar and related molluscs, such as the pearl oyster and the **saddle oyster** (*Anomia ephippium*)

oystercatcher any shore bird of the genus *Haematopus* and family *Haematopodidae*, having a black or black-and-white plumage and a long stout laterally compressed red bill

ozone a colourless gas with a chlorine-like odour, formed by an electric discharge in oxygen: a strong oxidizing agent, used in bleaching, sterilizing water, purifying air, etc. Formula: O_3; density: 2.14 kg/m^3; melting pt.: −192°C; boiling pt.: −110.51°C

ozone layer the region of the stratosphere with the highest concentration of ozone molecules, which by absorbing high-energy solar ultraviolet radiation protects organisms on earth

Pp

P pharmacy only: used to label medicines that can be obtained without a prescription, but only at a shop at which there is a pharmacist

pa *or* **pah** NZ **1** a Māori village or settlement **2** *History* a Māori defensive position and settlement on a hilltop

Pabst G(eorge) W(ilhelm). 1885–1967, German film director, whose films include *Joyless Street* (1925), *Pandora's Box* (1929), and *The Last Act* (1954)

pace 1 a measure of length equal to the average length of a stride, approximately 3 feet **2** any of the manners in which a horse or other quadruped walks or runs, the three principal paces being the walk, trot, and canter (or gallop) **3** a manner of moving, natural to the camel and sometimes developed in the horse, in which the two legs on the same side of the body are moved and put down at the same time **4** *Architect* a step or small raised platform

pacemaker 1 *Anatomy* a small area of specialized tissue within the wall of the right atrium of the heart whose spontaneous electrical activity initiates and controls the beat of the heart **2** *Med* an electronic device for use in certain cases of heart disease to assume the functions of the natural cardiac pacemaker

Pachelbel Johann 1653–1706, German organist and composer, noted esp for his popular *Canon in D Major*

Pachuca a city in central Mexico, capital of Hidalgo state, in the Sierra Madre Oriental: silver mines; university (1961). Pop: 333 000 (2005 est)

pachyderm any very large thick-skinned mammal, such as an elephant, rhinoceros, or hippopotamus

Pacific Northwest the region of North America lying north of the Columbia River and west of the Rockies

Pacific Ocean the world's largest and deepest ocean, lying between Asia and Australia and North and South America: almost landlocked in the north, linked with the Arctic Ocean only by the Bering Strait, and extending to Antarctica in the south; has exceptionally deep trenches, and a large number of volcanic and coral islands. Area: about 165 760 000 sq km (64 000 000 sq miles). Average depth: 4215 m (14 050 ft). Greatest depth: Challenger Deep (in the Marianas Trench), 11 033 m (37 073 ft). Greatest width: (between Panama and Mindanao, Philippines) 17 066 km (10 600 miles)

Pacino Al, full name *Alfredo James Pacino.* born 1940, US film actor; his films include *The Godfather* (1972), *Dog Day Afternoon* (1975), *Scent of a Woman* (1992), for which he won an Oscar, and *Insomnia* (2002)

pack 1 a complete set of similar things, esp a set of 52 playing cards **2** a group of animals of the same kind, esp hunting animals **3** *Rugby* the forwards of a team or both teams collectively, as in a scrum or in rucking **4** a small package, carton, or container, used to retail commodities, esp foodstuffs, cigarettes, etc. **5** short for **pack ice 6** *Med* **a** a sheet or blanket, either damp or dry, for wrapping about the body, esp for its soothing effect **b** a material such as cotton or gauze for temporarily filling a bodily cavity, esp to control bleeding **7** a parachute folded and ready for use **8** *Computing* another name for **deck**

package *Computing* a set of programs designed for a specific type of problem in statistics, production control, etc, making it unnecessary for a separate program to be written for each problem

packet 1 a small or medium-sized container of cardboard, paper, etc, often together with its contents **2** a boat that transports mail, passengers, goods, etc, on a fixed short route **3** *Computing* a unit into which a larger piece of data is broken down for more efficient transmission

packhorse a horse used to transport goods, equipment, etc.

pack ice a large area of floating ice, usually occurring in polar seas, consisting of separate pieces that have become massed together

packing 1 the packaging of foodstuffs **2** *Med* **a** the application of a medical pack **b** gauze or other absorbent material for packing a wound **3** any substance or material used to make watertight or gastight joints, esp in a stuffing box **4** *Engineering* pieces of material of various thicknesses used to adjust the position of a component or machine before it is secured in its correct position or alignment

pact an agreement or compact between two or more parties, nations, etc, for mutual advantage

pad 1 a the fleshy ike underpart of the foot of a cat, dog, etc. **b** any of the parts constituting such a structure **2** the large flat floating leaf of the water lily **3** *Electronics* a resistive attenuator network inserted in the path of a signal to reduce amplitude or to match one circuit to another

Padang a port in W Indonesia, in W Sumatra at the foot of the **Padang Highlands** on the Indian Ocean. Pop:

713 242 (2000)

paddle 1 a short light oar with a flat blade at one or both ends, used without a rowlock to propel a canoe or small boat 2 a blade of a water wheel or paddle wheel 3 a period of paddling 4 a a paddle wheel used to propel a boat b (as modifier): a paddle steamer 5 the sliding panel in a lock or sluicegate that regulates the level or flow of water 6 a table-tennis bat 7 the flattened limb of a seal, turtle, or similar aquatic animal, specialized for swimming

paddle wheel a large wheel fitted with paddles, turned by an engine to propel a vessel on the water

paddock¹ 1 (in horse racing) the enclosure in which horses are paraded and mounted before a race, together with the accompanying rooms 2 (in motor racing) an area near the pits where cars are worked on before races 3 Austral and NZ a playing field

paddock² Archaic or dialect a frog or toad

pademelon or **paddymelon** a small wallaby of the genus Thylogale, of coastal scrubby regions of Australia

Paderborn a market town in NW Germany, in North Rhine-Westphalia: scene of the meeting between Charlemagne and Pope Leo III (799 AD) that led to the foundation of the Holy Roman Empire. Pop: 141 800 (2003 est)

Paderewski Ignace Jan 1860–1941, Polish pianist, composer, and statesman; prime minister (1919)

padre Informal father: used to address or refer to a clergyman, esp a priest

Padua a city in NE Italy, in Veneto: important in Roman and Renaissance times; university (1222); botanical garden (1545). Pop: 204 870 (2001)

paean or sometimes US **pean** a hymn sung in ancient Greece in invocation of or thanksgiving to a deity

paediatrician or chiefly US **pediatrician** a medical practitioner who specializes in paediatrics

paediatrics or chiefly US **pediatrics** the branch of medical science concerned with children and their diseases

paedophilia or esp US **pedophilia** the condition of being sexually attracted to children

Paestum an ancient Greek colony on the coast of Lucania in S Italy

pagan a member of a group professing a polytheistic religion or any religion other than Christianity, Judaism, or Islam

▷www.paganfed.demon.co.uk/
▷www.pagansunite.com/

Paganini Niccolò 1782–1840, Italian violinist and composer

page 1 Medieval history a a boy in training for knighthood in personal attendance on a knight b a youth in the personal service of a person of rank, esp in a royal household 2 Canadian a person employed in the debating chamber of the House of Commons, the Senate, or a legislative assembly to carry messages for members

Page 1 Sir Earle (Christmas Grafton). 1880–1961, Australian statesman; co-leader, with S. M. Bruce, of the federal government of Australia (1923–29) 2 Sir Frederick Handley 1885–1962, English pioneer in the design and manufacture of aircraft

Paglia Camille born 1947, US writer and academic, noted for provocative cultural studies such as Sexual Personae

(1990) and Vamps and Tramps (1995)

Pagnol Marcel (Paul). 1895–1974, French dramatist, film director, and novelist, noted for his depiction of Provençal life in such films as Manon des Sources (1952; remade 1986)

pagoda an Indian or Far Eastern temple, esp a tower, usually pyramidal and having many storeys

Pago Pago a port in American Samoa, on SE Tutuila Island. Pop: 4278 (2000)

Pahang a state of Peninsular Malaysia, on the South China Sea: the largest Malayan state; mountainous and heavily forested. Capital: Kuantan. Pop: 1 288 376 (2000). Area: 35 964 sq km (13 886 sq miles)

Pahlavi 1 Mohammed Reza 1919–80, shah of Iran (1941–79); forced into exile (1979) during civil unrest following which an Islamic republic was established led by the Ayatollah Khomeini 2 his father, **Reza** 1877–1944, shah of Iran (1925–41). Originally an army officer, he gained power by a coup d'état (1921) and was chosen shah by the National Assembly. He reorganized the army and did much to modernize Iran

Paignton a town and resort in SW England, in Devon: administratively part of Torbay since 1968

Paine Thomas 1737–1809, American political pamphleteer, born in England. His works include the pamphlets Common Sense (1776) and Crisis (1776–83), supporting the American colonists' fight for independence; The Rights of Man (1791–92), a justification of the French Revolution; and The Age of Reason (1794–96), a defence of deism

painkiller 1 an analgesic drug or agent 2 anything that relieves pain

Painted Desert a section of the high plateau country of N central Arizona, along the N side of the Little Colorado River Valley: brilliant-coloured rocks; occupied largely by Navaho and Hopi Indians. Area: about 20 000 sq km (7500 sq miles)

painted lady a migratory nymphalid butterfly, Vanessa cardui, with pale brownish-red mottled wings

painter Nautical a line attached to the bow of a boat for tying it up

painting 1 the art or process of applying paints to a surface such as canvas, to make a picture or other artistic composition 2 a composition or picture made in this way

pair 1 a male and a female animal of the same species, esp such animals kept for breeding purposes 2 Parliamentary procedure a two opposed members who both agree not to vote on a specified motion or for a specific period of time b the agreement so made 3 two playing cards of the same rank or denomination 4 Logic, Maths a a set with two members b an ordered set with two members

Paisley¹ 1 Bob 1919–96, English footballer and manager 2 Rev. Ian (Richard Kyle). born 1926, Northern Ireland politician and Presbyterian minister; cofounder (1972) and leader of the Ulster Democratic Unionist Party

Paisley² an industrial town in SW Scotland, the administrative centre of Renfrewshire: one of the world's chief centres for the manufacture of thread, linen, and gauze in the 19th century. Pop: 74 170 (2001)

Pakistan 1 a republic in S Asia, on the Arabian Sea: the

Union of Pakistan, formed in 1947, comprised West and East Pakistan; East Pakistan gained independence as Bangladesh in 1971 and West Pakistan became Pakistan; a member of the Commonwealth from 1947, it withdrew from 1972 until 1989; contains the fertile plains of the Indus valley rising to mountains in the north and west. Official language: Urdu. Official religion: Muslim. Currency: rupee. Capital: Islamabad. Pop: 157 315 000 (2004 est). Area: 801 508 sq km (309 463 sq miles) **2** a former republic in S Asia consisting of the provinces of West Pakistan and East Pakistan (now Bangladesh), 1500 km (900 miles) apart: formed in 1947 from the predominantly Muslim parts of India

paladin History **1** one of the legendary twelve peers of Charlemagne's court **2** a knightly champion

Palaeocene of, denoting, or formed in the first epoch of the Tertiary period, which lasted for 10 million years

palaeography 1 the study of the handwritings of the past, and often the manuscripts as well, so that they may be dated, read, etc, and may serve as historical and literary sources **2** a handwriting of the past

Palaeolithic the period of the emergence of primitive man and the manufacture of unpolished chipped stone tools, about 2.5 million to 3 million years ago until about 12 000 BC

palaeontology the study of fossils to determine the structure and evolution of extinct animals and plants and the age and conditions of deposition of the rock strata in which they are found
▷www.ucmp.berkeley.edu/index.html
▷www.dinosauria.com

Palaeozoic of, denoting, or relating to an era of geological time that began 600 million years ago with the Cambrian period and lasted about 375 million years until the end of the Permian period

palanquin or **palankeen** a covered litter, formerly used in the Orient, carried on the shoulders of four men

palate 1 the roof of the mouth, separating the oral and nasal cavities **2** Botany (in some two-lipped corollas) the projecting part of the lower lip that closes the opening of the corolla

palatinate a territory ruled by a palatine prince or noble or count palatine

palatine¹ 1 (of an individual) possessing royal prerogatives in a territory **2** of, belonging to, characteristic of, or relating to a count palatine, county palatine, palatinate, or palatine **3** Feudal history the lord of a palatinate **4** any of various important officials at the late Roman, Merovingian, or Carolingian courts **5** (in Colonial America) any of the proprietors of a palatine colony, such as Carolina

palatine² 1 of or relating to the palate **2** either of two bones forming the hard palate

Palatine one of the Seven Hills of Rome: traditionally the site of the first settlement of Rome

Palawan an island of the SW Philippines between the South China Sea and the Sulu Sea: the westernmost island in the country; mountainous and forested. Capital: Puerto Princesa. Pop: 311 550 (latest est). Area: 11 785 sq km (4550 sq miles)

paleface a derogatory term for a White person, said to have been used by North American Indians

Palembang a port in W Indonesia, in S Sumatra; oil refineries; university (1955). Pop: 1 451 419 (2000)

Palencia a city in N central Spain: earliest university in Spain (1208); seat of Castilian kings (12th–13th centuries); communications centre. Pop: 81 378 (2003 est)

Palenque the site of an ancient Mayan city in S Mexico famous for its architectural ruins

Palermo the capital of Sicily, on the NW coast: founded by the Phoenicians in the 8th century BC. Pop: 686 722 (2001)

Palestine 1 the area between the Jordan River and the Mediterranean Sea in which most of the biblical narrative is located **2** the province of the Roman Empire in this region **3** the former British mandatory territory created by the League of Nations in 1922 (but effective from 1920), and including all of the present territories of Israel and Jordan between whom it was partitioned by the UN in 1948

Palestinian a native or inhabitant of the former British mandate, or their descendants, esp such Arabs now living in the Palestinian Administered Territories, Jordan, Lebanon, or Israel, or as refugees from Israeli-occupied territory

Palestrina Giovanni Pierluigi da ?1525–94, Italian composer and master of counterpoint. His works, nearly all for unaccompanied choir and religious in nature, include the *Missa Papae Marcelli* (1555)

palette 1 a flat piece of wood, plastic, etc, used by artists as a surface on which to mix their paints **2** the range of colours characteristic of a particular artist, painting, or school of painting **3** the available range of colours or patterns that can be displayed by a computer on a visual display unit

Paley William 1743–1805, English theologian and utilitarian philosopher. His chief works are *The Principles of Moral and Political Philosophy* (1785), *Horae Paulinae* (1790), *A View of the Evidences of Christianity* (1794), and *Natural Theology* (1802)

palisade Botany a layer of elongated mesophyll cells containing many chloroplasts, situated below the outer epidermis of a leaf blade

Palk Strait a channel between SE India and N Ceylon. Width: about 64 km (40 miles)

pall Christianity a small square linen cloth with which the chalice is covered at the Eucharist

Palladian¹ denoting, relating to, or having the neoclassical style of architecture created by Palladio
▷www.britainexpress.com/architecture

Palladian² 1 of or relating to the goddess Pallas Athena **2** Literary wise or learned
▷www.britainexpress.com/architecture

Palladio Andrea 1508–80, Italian architect who revived and developed classical architecture, esp the ancient Roman ideals of symmetrical planning and harmonic proportions. His treatise *Four Books on Architecture* (1570) and his designs for villas and palaces profoundly influenced 18th-century domestic architecture in England and the US

palladium a ductile malleable silvery-white element of the platinum metal group occurring principally in nickel-bearing ores: used as a hydrogenation catalyst and, alloyed with gold, in jewellery. Symbol: Pd; atomic no.: 46; atomic wt.: 106.42; valency: 2, 3, or 4; relative density: 1202; melting pt.: 1555°C; boiling pt.: 2964°C

Pall Mall a street in London, noted for its many clubs

palm¹ 1 the inner part of the hand from the wrist to the base of the fingers 2 a corresponding part in animals, esp apes and monkeys 3 a linear measure based on the breadth or length of a hand, equal to three to four inches or seven to ten inches respectively 4 a hard leather shield worn by sailmakers to protect the palm of the hand 5 a the side of the blade of an oar that faces away from the direction of a boat's movement during a stroke b the face of the fluke of an anchor 6 a flattened or expanded part of the antlers of certain deer

palm² any treelike plant of the tropical and subtropical monocotyledonous family *Arecaceae* (formerly *Palmae* or *Palmaceae*), usually having a straight unbranched trunk crowned with large pinnate or palmate leaves

Palma¹ Jacopo , known as *Palma Vecchio*, original name *Jacopo Negretti*. ?1480–1528, Venetian painter, noted esp for his portraits of women

Palma² the capital of the Balearic Islands, on the SW coast of Majorca: a tourist centre. Pop: 367 277 (2003 est)

palmate *or* **palmated** 1 shaped like an open hand 2 *Botany* having more than three lobes or segments that spread out from a common point 3 (of the feet of most water birds) having three toes connected by a web

Palm Beach a town in SE Florida, on an island between Lake Worth (a lagoon) and the Atlantic: major resort and tourist centre. Pop: 9759 (2003 est)

Palme (Sven) Olof (Joachim). 1927–86, Swedish Social Democratic statesman; prime minister (1969–76, 1982–86); assassinated

Palmer 1 Arnold born 1929, US professional golfer: won the US Open Championship (1960) and the British Open Championship (1961; 1962) 2 **Samuel** 1805–81, English painter of visionary landscapes, influenced by William Blake

Palmer Archipelago a group of islands between South America and Antarctica: part of the British Antarctic Territory (formerly the British colony of the Falkland Islands and Dependencies). (Claims are suspended under the Antarctic Treaty)

Palmer Land the S part of the Antarctic Peninsula

Palmerston Henry John Temple, 3rd Viscount Palmerston. 1784–1865, British statesman; foreign secretary (1830–34; 1835–41; 1846–51); prime minister (1855–58; 1859–65). His talent was for foreign affairs, in which he earned a reputation as a British nationalist and for high-handedness and gunboat diplomacy

Palmerston North a city in New Zealand, in the S North Island on the Manawatu River. Pop: 78 100 (2004 est)

palmetto 1 any of several small chiefly tropical fan palms, esp any of the genus *Sabal*, of the southeastern US 2 any of various other fan palms such as palms of the genera *Serenoa*, *Thrinax*, and *Chamaerops*

Palmira a city in W Colombia: agricultural trading centre. Pop: 253 000 (2005 est)

palmistry the process or art of interpreting character, telling fortunes, etc, by the configuration of lines, marks, and bumps on a person's hand

palm oil a yellow butter-like oil obtained from the fruit

of the oil palm, used as an edible fat and in soap

Palm Springs a city in the US, in California: a popular tourist resort. Pop: 45 228 (2003 est)

Palm Sunday the Sunday before Easter commemorating Christ's triumphal entry into Jerusalem

Palmyra 1 an ancient city in central Syria: said to have been built by Solomon 2 an island in the central Pacific, in the Line Islands: under US administration

Palo Alto 1 a city in W California, southeast of San Francisco: founded in 1891 as the seat of Stanford University. Pop: 57 233 (2003 est) 2 a battlefield in E Mexico, northwest of Monterrey, where the first battle (1846) of the Mexican War took place, in which the Mexicans under General Mariano Arista were defeated by the Americans under General Zachary Taylor

Palomar Mount a mountain in S California, northeast of San Diego: site of Mount Palomar Observatory, which has a large (200-inch) reflecting telescope. Height: 1871 m (6140 ft)

palomino a golden horse with a cream or white mane and tail

Palos a village and former port in SW Spain: starting point of Columbus' voyage of discovery to America (1492)

palpable *Med* capable of being discerned by the sense of touch

palpate *Zoology* of, relating to, or possessing a palp or palps

palsy *Pathol* paralysis, esp of a specified type

Paltrow Gwyneth (Kate). born 1973, US film actress; her films include *Emma* (1996), *Sliding Doors* (1998), *Shakespeare in Love* (1998), and *Sylvia* (2003)

Pamlico Sound an inlet of the Atlantic between the E coast of North Carolina and its chain of offshore islands. Length: 130 km (80 miles)

pampas a the extensive grassy plains of temperate South America, esp in Argentina b (*as modifier*): *pampas dwellers*

pampas grass any of various large grasses of the South American genus *Cortaderia* and related genera, widely cultivated for their large feathery silver-coloured flower branches

Pamphylia an area on the S coast of ancient Asia Minor

Pamplona a city in N Spain in the foothills of the Pyrenees: capital of the kingdom of Navarre from the 11th century until 1841. Pop: 190 937 (2003 est)

pan¹ 1 either of the two dishlike receptacles on a balance 2 a a natural or artificial depression in the ground where salt can be obtained by the evaporation of brine b a natural depression containing water or mud 3 *Caribbean* the indented top from an oil drum used as the treble drum in a steel band 4 a small ice floe 5 a hard substratum of soil

pan² 1 the leaf of the betel tree 2 a preparation of this leaf which is chewed, together with betel nuts and lime, in India and the East Indies

Panama 1 a republic in Central America, occupying the Isthmus of Panama: gained independence from Spain in 1821 and joined Greater Colombia; became independent in 1903, with the immediate area around the canal forming the Canal Zone under US jurisdiction; Panama assumed sovereignty over the Canal Zone in 1979 and full control in 1999. Official language: Spanish; English is also widely spoken. Religion: Roman Catholic majority. Currency: balboa. Capital: Panama City. Pop: 3 178 000 (2004 est). Area: 75 650 sq km (29 201 sq miles) **2 Isthmus of** an isthmus linking North and South America, between the Pacific and the Caribbean. Length: 676 km (420 miles). Width (at its narrowest point): 50 km (31 miles) **3 Gulf of** a wide inlet of the Pacific in Panama

Panama Canal a canal across the Isthmus of Panama, linking the Atlantic and Pacific Oceans: extends from Colón on the Caribbean Sea southeast to Balboa on the Gulf of Panama; built by the US (1904–14), after an unsuccessful previous attempt (1880–89) by the French under de Lesseps. Length: 64 km (40 miles)

Panama City the capital of Panama, near the Pacific entrance of the Panama Canal: developed rapidly with the building of the Panama Canal; seat of the University of Panama (1935). Pop: 950 000 (2005 est)

Pan-American of, relating to, or concerning North, South, and Central America collectively or the advocacy of political or economic unity among American countries

Panay an island in the central Philippines, the westernmost of the Visayan Islands. Pop: 2 595 315 (latest est). Area: 12 300 sq km (4750 sq miles)

pancake *Aeronautics* an aircraft landing made by levelling out a few feet from the ground and then dropping onto it

panchromatic *Photog* (of an emulsion or film) made sensitive to all colours by the addition of suitable dyes to the emulsion

pancreas a large elongated glandular organ, situated behind the stomach, that secretes insulin and pancreatic juice

panda 1 a large black-and-white herbivorous bearlike mammal, *Ailuropoda melanoleuca*, related to the raccoons and inhabiting the high mountain bamboo forests of China: family *Procyonidae* 2 **lesser** or **red panda** a closely related smaller animal resembling a raccoon, *Ailurus fulgens*, of the mountain forests of S Asia, having a reddish-brown coat and ringed tail

pandemic (of a disease) affecting persons over a wide geographical area; extensively epidemic

pane *Philately* **a** any of the rectangular marked divisions of a sheet of stamps made for convenience in selling **b** a single page in a stamp booklet

panegyric a formal public commendation; eulogy

panel 1 *Law* **a** a list of persons summoned for jury service **b** the persons on a specific jury 2 *Scots law* a person indicted or accused of crime after appearing in court 3 **a** a thin board used as a surface or backing for an oil painting **b** a painting done on such a panel 4 any picture with a length much greater than its breadth 5 See **instrument panel** 6 formerly, in Britain **a** a list of patients insured under the National Health Insurance Scheme **b** a list of medical practitioners within a given area available for consultation by these patients

panel beater a person who beats out the bodywork of motor vehicles

panel van 1 *Austral* a small van with two rear doors, esp one having windows and seats in the rear 2 NZ a small

enclosed delivery van

pangolin any mammal of the order *Pholidota* found in tropical Africa, S Asia, and Indonesia, having a body covered with overlapping horny scales and a long snout specialized for feeding on ants and termites

panicle 1 a compound raceme, occurring esp in grasses 2 any branched inflorescence

Panjim or **Panaji** the capital of the Indian state of Goa (formerly capital of the union territory of Goa, Daman, and Diu until 1987): a port on the Arabian Sea on the coast of Goa. Pop: 58 785 (2001)

Pankhurst 1 Dame **Christabel** 1880–1958, English suffragette 2 her mother, **Emmeline** 1858–1928, English suffragette leader, who founded the militant Women's Social and Political Union (1903) 3 **Sylvia**, daughter of Emmeline Pankhurst. 1882–1960, English suffragette and pacifist

Panmunjom a village in the demilitarized zone of Korea: site of truce talks leading to the end of the Korean War (1950–53)

Pannonia a region of the ancient world south and west of the Danube: made a Roman province in 6 AD

panorama a large extended picture or series of pictures of a scene, unrolled before spectators a part at a time so as to appear continuous

pansy 1 any violaceous garden plant that is a variety of *Viola tricolor*, having flowers with rounded velvety petals, white, yellow, or purple in colour 2 **a** a strong violet colour **b** (as adjective): a pansy carpet

Pantelleria an Italian island in the Mediterranean, between Sicily and Tunisia: of volcanic origin; used by the Romans as a place of banishment. Pop: 7316 (1991 est). Area: 83 sq km (32 sq miles)

pantheism 1 the doctrine that God is the transcendent reality of which man, nature, and the material universe are manifestations 2 any doctrine that regards God as identical with the material universe or the forces of nature 3 readiness to worship all or a large number of gods

pantheon 1 (esp in ancient Greece or Rome) a temple to all the gods 2 all the gods collectively of a religion

Pantheon a circular temple in Rome dedicated to all the gods, built by Agrippa in 27 BC, rebuilt by Hadrian 120–24 AD, and used since 609 AD as a Christian church

panther 1 another name for **leopard** (esp the black variety (**black panther**)) 2 *US and Canadian* any of various related animals, esp the puma

pantograph 1 an instrument consisting of pivoted levers for copying drawings, maps, etc, to any desired scale 2 a sliding type of current collector, esp a diamond-shaped frame mounted on a train roof in contact with an overhead wire

pantomime 1 (in Britain) **a** a kind of play performed at Christmas time characterized by farce, music, lavish sets, stock roles, and topical jokes **b** (as modifier): a pantomime horse 2 a theatrical entertainment in which words are replaced by gestures and bodily actions 3 (in ancient Rome) an actor in a dumb show

Panufnik Sir **Andrzej** 1914–91, British composer and conductor, born in Poland. His works include nine symphonies, the cantata *Winter Solstice* (1972), Polish folksong settings, and ballet music

Paolozzi Sir Eduardo (Luigi), 1924–2005, British sculptor and designer, noted esp for his semiabstract metal figures

pap 1 *Scot and northern English, dialect* a nipple or teat 2 a something resembling a breast or nipple, such as (formerly) one of a pair of rounded hilltops b (*capital as part of a name*): *the Pap of Glencoe*

papa *NZ rare.* a soft blue-grey clay of marine siltstone or sandstone

papacy 1 the office or term of office of a pope 2 the system of government in the Roman Catholic Church that has the pope as its head
▷www.wayoflife.org/papacy

Papandreou Andreas (George). 1919–96, Greek economist and socialist politician; prime minister (1981–89; 1993–96)

papaya a Caribbean evergreen tree, *Carica papaya*, with a crown of large dissected leaves and large green hanging fruit: family *Caricaceae*

Papeete the capital of French Polynesia, on the NW coast of Tahiti: one of the largest towns in the S Pacific. Pop: 130 000 (2005 est)

Papen Franz von 1879–1969, German statesman; chancellor (1932) and vice chancellor (1933–34) under Hitler, whom he was instrumental in bringing to power

paper 1 official documents relating to the ownership, cargo, etc, of a ship 2 collected diaries, letters, etc. 3 *Government* See **white paper, green paper** 4 a lecture or short published treatise on a specific subject 5 a short essay, as by a student 6 a a set of written examination questions b the student's answers 7 *Theatre, slang* a free ticket

paper chase a former type of cross-country run in which a runner laid a trail of paper for others to follow

paperknife a knife with a comparatively blunt blade, esp one of wood, bone, etc, for opening sealed envelopes

Paphlagonia an ancient country and Roman province in N Asia Minor, on the Black Sea

Paphos a village in SW Cyprus, near the sites of two ancient cities: famous as the centre of Aphrodite worship and traditionally the place at which she landed after her birth among the waves. Pop: 32 575 (1992 est)

papilla 1 the small projection of tissue at the base of a hair, tooth, or feather 2 any other similar protuberance 3 any minute blunt hair or process occurring in plants

paprika 1 a mild powdered seasoning made from a sweet variety of red pepper 2 the fruit or plant from which this seasoning is obtained

Pap test *or* **smear** *Med* a similar test for precancerous cells in other organs

Papua 1 Territory of a former territory of Australia, consisting of SE New Guinea and adjacent islands: now part of Papua New Guinea 2 the W part of the island of New Guinea: formerly under Dutch rule, becoming a province of Indonesia in 1963. Capital: Jayapura. Pop: 2 220 934 (2000). Area: 416 990 sq km (161 000 sq miles) 3 Gulf of an inlet of the Coral Sea in the SE coast of New Guinea

Papua New Guinea a country in the SW Pacific; consists of the E half of New Guinea, the Bismarck Archipelago, the W Solomon Islands, Trobriand Islands, the

D'Entrecasteaux Islands, Woodlark Island, and the Louisiade Archipelago; administered by Australia from 1949 until 1975, when it became an independent member of the Commonwealth. Official language: English; Tok Pisin (English Creole) and Motu are widely spoken. Religion: Christian majority. Currency: kina. Capital: Port Moresby. Pop: 5 836 000 (2004 est). Area: 461 693 sq km (178 260 sq miles)

papyrus a tall aquatic cyperaceous plant, *Cyperus papyrus*, of S Europe and N and central Africa with small green-stalked flowers arranged like umbrella spokes around the stem top

par *Golf* an estimated standard score for a hole or course that a good player should make

para¹ a monetary unit of Serbia worth one hundredth of a dinar; formerly a monetary unit of Yugoslavia

para² a New Zealand fern, *Marattia salicina*, with long heavy fronds

parable 1 a short story that uses familiar events to illustrate a religious or ethical point 2 any of the stories of this kind told by Jesus Christ

parabola a conic section formed by the intersection of a cone by a plane parallel to its side. Standard equation: $y^2 = 4ax$, where $2a$ is the distance between focus and directrix

Paracelsus Philippus Aureolus , real name *Theophrastus Bombastus von Hohenheim*. 1493–1541, Swiss physician and alchemist, who pioneered the use of specific treatment, based on observation and experience, to remedy particular diseases

paracetamol a mild analgesic and antipyretic drug used as an alternative to aspirin

parachute a device used to retard the fall of a man or package from an aircraft, consisting of a large fabric canopy connected to a harness b (*as modifier*): *parachute troops*

parade *Sport* a parry in fencing

paradigm (in the philosophy of science) a very general conception of the nature of scientific endeavour within which a given enquiry is undertaken

paradise 1 heaven as the ultimate abode or state of the righteous 2 *Islam* the sensual garden of delights that the Koran promises the faithful after death 3 (according to some theologians) the intermediate abode or state of the just prior to the Resurrection of Jesus, as in Luke 23:43 4 the place or state of happiness enjoyed by Adam before the first sin; the Garden of Eden

paradise duck a large duck, *Casarca variegata*, of New Zealand, having a brightly coloured plumage

paradox a self-contradictory proposition, such as *I always tell lies*

paraffin *or less commonly* **paraffine** 1 a liquid mixture consisting mainly of alkane hydrocarbons with boiling points in the range 150°–300°C, used as an aircraft fuel, in domestic heaters, and as a solvent 2 another name for **alkane** 3 See **paraffin wax** 4 See **liquid paraffin**

paraffin wax a white insoluble odourless waxlike solid consisting mainly of alkane hydrocarbons with melting points in the range 50°–60°C, used in candles, waterproof paper, and as a sealing agent

Paraguay 1 an inland republic in South America: colonized by the Spanish from 1537, gaining independence in 1811; lost 142 500 sq km (55 000 sq miles) of territory and over half its population after its defeat in the war against Argentina, Brazil, and Uruguay (1865–70). It is divided by the Paraguay River into a sparsely inhabited semiarid region (Chaco) in the west, and a central region of wooded hills, tropical forests, and rich grasslands, rising to the Paraná plateau in the east. Official languages: Spanish and Guarani. Religion: Roman Catholic majority. Currency: guarani. Capital: Asunción. Pop: 6 018 000 (2004 est). Area: 406 750 sq km (157 047 sq miles) **2** a river in South America flowing south through Brazil and Paraguay to the Paraná River. Length: about 2400 km (1500 miles)

parakeet *or* **parrakeet** any of numerous small usually brightly coloured long-tailed parrots, such as *Psittacula krameri* (**ring-necked parakeet**), of Africa

parallax 1 an apparent change in the position of an object resulting from a change in position of the observer **2** *Astronomy* the angle subtended at a celestial body, esp a star, by the radius of the earth's orbit. **Annual** or **heliocentric parallax** is the apparent displacement of a nearby star resulting from its observation from the earth. **Diurnal** or **geocentric parallax** results from the observation of a planet, the sun, or the moon from the surface of the earth

parallel 1 separated by an equal distance at every point; never touching or intersecting **2** *Music* **a** (of two or more parts or melodies) moving in similar motion but keeping the same interval apart throughout **b** denoting successive chords in which the individual notes move in parallel motion **3** *Computing* operating on several items of information, instructions, etc, simultaneously **4** *Maths* one of a set of parallel lines, planes, etc. **5** any of the imaginary lines around the earth parallel to the equator, designated by degrees of latitude ranging from 0° at the equator to 90° at the poles **6 a** a configuration of two or more electrical components connected between two points in a circuit so that the same voltage is applied to each (esp in the phrase **in parallel**) **b** (*as modifier*): *a parallel circuit*

parallelepiped, parallelopiped, *or* **parallelepipedon** a geometric solid whose six faces are parallelograms

parallelism *Philosophy* the dualistic doctrine that mental and physical processes are regularly correlated but are not causally connected, so that, for example, pain always accompanies, but is not caused by, a pin-prick

parallelogram a quadrilateral whose opposite sides are parallel and equal in length

paralysis *Pathol* **a** impairment or loss of voluntary muscle function or of sensation (**sensory paralysis**) in a part or area of the body, usually caused by a lesion or disorder of the muscles or the nerves supplying them **b** a disease characterized by such impairment or loss; palsy

paralytic 1 of, relating to, or of the nature of paralysis **2** afflicted with or subject to paralysis **3** *Brit, informal* very drunk **4** a person afflicted with paralysis

Paramaribo the capital and chief port of Surinam, 27 km (17 miles) from the Atlantic on the Surinam River: the only large town in the country. Pop: 261 000 (2005 est)

paramecium any freshwater protozoan of the genus *Paramecium*, having an oval body covered with cilia and a

ventral ciliated groove for feeding: phylum *Ciliophora* (ciliates)

paramedic *or* **paramedical 1** a person, such as a laboratory technician, who supplements the work of the medical profession **2** a member of an ambulance crew trained in a number of life-saving skills, including infusion and cardiac care

parameter 1 one of a number of auxiliary variables in terms of which all the variables in an implicit functional relationship can be explicitly expressed **2** a variable whose behaviour is not being considered and which may for present purposes be regarded as a constant, as *y* in the partial derivative $\partial f(x,y)/\partial x$

paramilitary 1 denoting or relating to a group of personnel with military structure functioning either as a civil force or in support of military forces **2** denoting or relating to a force with military structure conducting armed operations against a ruling or occupying power **3 a** a paramilitary force **b** a member of such a force

paramount *Rare* a supreme ruler

paranoia 1 a form of schizophrenia characterized by a slowly progressive deterioration of the personality, involving delusions and often hallucinations **2** a mental disorder characterized by any of several types of delusions, in which the personality otherwise remains relatively intact **3** *Informal* intense fear or suspicion, esp when unfounded

paranormal 1 beyond normal explanation **2** the paranormal happenings generally
  ▷www.paraseek.com/
  ▷http://paranormal.com/

parapet a low wall or railing along the edge of a balcony, roof, etc.

paraphrase 1 an expression of a statement or text in other words, esp in order to clarify **2** the practice of making paraphrases

paraplegia *Pathol* paralysis of the lower half of the body, usually as the result of disease or injury of the spine

parapsychology the study of mental phenomena, such as telepathy, which are beyond the scope of normal physical explanation
  ▷www.parapsychology.org/
  ▷www.psiresearch.org/para1.html

Paraquat *Trademark* a yellow extremely poisonous soluble solid used in solution as a weedkiller

parasite an animal or plant that lives in or on another (the host) from which it obtains nourishment. The host does not benefit from the association and is often harmed by it

paratyphoid fever *Pathol* a disease resembling but less severe than typhoid fever, characterized by chills, headache, nausea, vomiting, and diarrhoea, caused by bacteria of the genus *Salmonella*

parcel 1 a quantity of some commodity offered for sale; lot **2** a distinct portion of land

pardon 1 *Law* **a** release from punishment for an offence **b** the warrant granting such release **2** a Roman Catholic indulgence

Pardubice a city in the central Czech Republic, on the Elbe River: 13th-century cathedral; oil refinery. Pop: 163 000 (1993)

parent 1 a father or mother **2** *Rare* an ancestor **3 a** an organism or organization that has produced one or more organisms or organizations similar to itself **b** (*as modifier*): *a parent organism* **4** *Physics, Chem* **a** a precursor, such as a nucleus or compound, of a derived entity **b** (*as modifier*): *a parent nucleus*

parent company a company that owns more than half the shares of another company

Pareto 1 Vilfredo 1848–1923, Italian sociologist and economist. He anticipated Fascist principles of government in his *Mind and Society* (1916) **2** denoting a law, mathematical formula, etc, originally used by Pareto to express the frequency distribution of incomes in a society

parietal 1 *Anatomy, Biology* of, relating to, or forming the walls or part of the walls of a bodily cavity or similar structure **2** of or relating to the side of the skull **3** (of plant ovaries) having ovules attached to the walls **4** *US* living or having authority within a college **5** a parietal bone

Paris¹ 1 *Greek myth* a prince of Troy, whose abduction of Helen from her husband Menelaus started the Trojan War **2** **Matthew** ?1200–59, English chronicler, whose principal work is the *Chronica Majora*

Paris² 1 the capital of France, in the north on the River Seine: constitutes a department; dates from the 3rd century BC, becoming capital of France in 987; centre of the French Revolution; centres around its original site on an island in the Seine, the **Île de la Cité**, containing Notre Dame; university (1150). Pop: 2 125 246 (1999) **2** **Treaty of Paris a** a treaty of 1783 between the US, Britain, France, and Spain, ending the War of American Independence **b** a treaty of 1763 signed by Britain, France, and Spain that ended their involvement in the Seven Years' War **c** a treaty of 1898 between Spain and the US bringing to an end the Spanish-American War

parish 1 a subdivision of a diocese, having its own church and a clergyman **2** the churchgoers of such a subdivision **3** (in England and, formerly, Wales) the smallest unit of local government in rural areas **4** (in Louisiana) a unit of local government corresponding to a county in other states of the US **5** the people living in a parish **6** **on the parish** *History* receiving parochial relief

parish clerk a person designated to assist in various church duties

parish council (in England and, formerly, Wales) the administrative body of a parish

parish register a book in which the births, baptisms, marriages, and deaths in a parish are recorded

parity 1 *Physics* **a** a property of a physical system characterized by the behaviour of the sign of its wave function when all spatial coordinates are reversed in direction. The wave function either remains unchanged (**even parity**) or changes in sign (**odd parity**) **b** a quantum number describing this property, equal to +1 for even parity systems and –1 for odd parity systems. **2** *Maths* a relationship between two integers. If both are odd or both even they have the same parity; if one is odd and one even they have different parity

park 1 a large area of land preserved in a natural state for recreational use by the public **2** a piece of open land in a town with public amenities **3** *NZ* an area, esp of

mountain country, reserved for recreational purposes **4** a large area of land forming a private estate **5** *English law* an enclosed tract of land where wild beasts are protected, acquired by a subject by royal grant or prescription **6** an area designed and landscaped to accommodate a group of related enterprises, businesses, research establishments, etc. **7** **the park** *Brit, informal* a soccer pitch **8** a gear selector position on the automatic transmission of a motor vehicle that acts as a parking brake **9** a high valley surrounded by mountains in the western US

Park 1 **Mungo** 1771–1806, Scottish explorer. He led two expeditions (1795–97; 1805–06) to trace the course of the Niger in Africa. He was drowned during the second expedition **2** **Nick**, full name *Nicholas Wulstan Park*. born 1958, British animator and film director; his films include *A Grand Day Out* (1992), which introduced the characters Wallace and Gromit, and the feature-length *Chicken Run* (2000) **3** **Chung Hee** 1917–79, South Korean politician; president of the Republic of Korea (1963–79); assassinated

parkade *Canadian* a building used as a car park

Parker 1 **Alan** (**William**). born 1944, British film director and screenwriter; his films include *Midnight Express* (1978), *Mississippi Burning* (1988), *The Commitments* (1991), and *Angela's Ashes* (2000); chairman of the British Film Institute (1998–99) and of the Film Council from 1999 **2** **Charlie** nickname *Bird* or *Yardbird*. 1920–55, US jazz alto saxophonist and composer; the leading exponent of early bop **3** **Dorothy** (**Rothschild**). 1893–1967, US writer, noted esp for the ironical humour of her short stories **4** **Matthew** 1504–75, English prelate. As archbishop of Canterbury (1559–75), he supervised Elizabeth I's religious settlement

Parker Bowles **Camilla** (née *Shand*). born 1947, married Prince Charles (2005). Duchess of Cornwall

Parkes Sir Henry 1815–96, Australian journalist and politician born in England, five times premier of New South Wales, advocate of free trade and Federation, and a founder of the public education system

parkette *Canadian* a small public park

parking lot *US and Canadian* an area or building reserved for parking cars

parking meter a timing device, usually coin-operated, that indicates how long a vehicle may be left parked

parking ticket a summons served for a parking offence

parkland grassland with scattered trees

parliament 1 an assembly of the representatives of a political nation or people, often the supreme legislative authority **2** any legislative or deliberative assembly, conference, etc. **3** (in France before the Revolution) any of several high courts of justice in which royal decrees were registered

▷www.ipu.org/english/parlweb.htm

Parliament 1 the highest legislative authority in Britain, consisting of the House of Commons, which exercises effective power, the House of Lords, and the sovereign **2** a similar legislature in another country **3** the two chambers of a Parliament **4** the lower chamber of a Parliament **5** any of the assemblies of such a body created by a general election and royal summons and dissolved before the next election

parliamentary 1 of or characteristic of a parliament or Parliament 2 proceeding from a parliament or Parliament 3 conforming to or derived from the procedures of a parliament or Parliament 4 having a parliament or Parliament 5 of or relating to Parliament or its supporters during the English Civil War

parlour or US **parlor** 1 Old-fashioned a living room, esp one kept tidy for the reception of visitors 2 a reception room in a priest's house, convent, etc. 3 Chiefly US, Canadian, and NZ a room or shop equipped as a place of business 4 Caribbean a small shop, esp one selling cakes and nonalcoholic drinks

Parma 1 a city in N Italy, in Emilia-Romagna: capital of the duchy of Parma and Piacenza from 1545 until it became part of Italy in 1860; important food industry (esp Parmesan cheese). Pop: 163 457 (2001) 2 a city in NE Ohio, south of Cleveland. Pop: 83 861 (2003 est)

Parmenides 5th century BC, Greek Eleatic philosopher, born in Italy. He held that the universe is single and unchanging and denied the existence of change and motion. His doctrines are expounded in his poem On Nature, of which only fragments are extant

Parmigianino real name Girolamo Francesco Maria Mazzola. 1503–40, Italian painter, one of the originators of mannerism

Parnassus 1 Mount a mountain in central Greece, in NW Boeotia: in ancient times sacred to Dionysus, Apollo, and the Muses, with the Castalian Spring and Delphi on its slopes. Height: 2457 m (8061 ft) 2 a the world of poetry b a centre of poetic or other creative activity 3 a collection of verse or belles-lettres

Parnell Charles Stewart 1846–91, Irish nationalist, who led the Irish Home Rule movement in Parliament (1880–90) with a calculated policy of obstruction. Although Gladstone was converted to Home Rule (1886), Parnell's career was ruined by the scandal over his adultery with Mrs O'Shea

parody a musical, literary, or other composition that mimics the style of another composer, author, etc, in a humorous or satirical way

parotid gland a large salivary gland, in man situated in front of and below each ear

paroxysm Pathol a a sudden attack or recurrence of a disease b any fit or convulsion

parquet 1 a floor covering of pieces of hardwood fitted in a decorative pattern; parquetry 2 a floor so covered 3 US the stalls of a theatre 4 (in France) the department of government responsible for the prosecution of crimes

parquetry a geometric pattern of inlaid pieces of wood, often of different kinds, esp as used to cover a floor or to ornament furniture

parr a salmon up to two years of age, with dark spots and transverse bands

Parr Catherine 1512–48, sixth wife of Henry VIII of England

parricide 1 the act of killing either of one's parents 2 a person who kills his parent

parrot any bird of the tropical and subtropical order Psittaciformes, having a short hooked bill, compact body, bright plumage, and an ability to mimic sounds

parrotfish 1 any brightly coloured tropical marine per-

coid fish of the family Scaridae, having parrot-like jaws 2 Austral any of various brightly coloured marine fish of the family Labridae 3 any of various similar fishes

parry an act of parrying, esp (in fencing) using a stroke or circular motion of the blade

Parry 1 Sir (Charles) Hubert (Hastings). 1848–1918, English composer, noted esp for his choral works 2 Sir William Edward 1790–1855, English arctic explorer, who searched for the Northwest Passage (1819–25) and attempted to reach the North Pole (1827)

parsec a unit of astronomical distance equal to the distance from earth at which stellar parallax would be 1 second of arc; equivalent to 3.0857×10^{16} m or 3.262 light years

parsley 1 a S European umbelliferous plant, Petroselinum crispum, widely cultivated for its curled aromatic leaves, which are used in cooking 2 any of various similar and related plants, such as fool's-parsley, stone parsley, and cow parsley

parsnip 1 a strong-scented umbelliferous plant, Pastinaca sativa, cultivated for its long whitish root 2 any of several similar plants, esp the cow parsnip

parson 1 a parish priest in the Church of England, formerly applied only to those who held ecclesiastical benefices 2 any clergyman 3 NZ a nonconformist minister

parsonage the residence of a parson who is not a rector or vicar, as provided by the parish

Parsons 1 Sir Charles Algernon 1854–1931, English engineer, who developed the steam turbine 2 Gram, real name Cecil Connor. 1946–73. US country-rock singer and songwriter; founder of the Flying Burrito Brothers (1968–70), he later released the solo albums G.P. (1973) and Grievous Angel (1974) 3 Talcott 1902–79, US sociologist, author of The Structure of Social Action (1937) and The Social System (1951)

part 1 a an actor's role in a play b the speech and actions which make up such a role c a written copy of these 2 Anatomy any portion of a larger structure 3 a component that can be replaced in a machine, engine, etc. 4 Music a one of a number of separate melodic lines making up the texture of music b one of such melodic lines, which is assigned to one or more instrumentalists or singers c such a line performed from a separately written or printed copy

parterre 1 a formally patterned flower garden 2 Brit, Irish the pit in a theatre

Parthia a country in ancient Asia, southeast of the Caspian Sea, that expanded into a great empire dominating SW Asia in the 2nd century BC. It was destroyed by the Sassanids in the 3rd century AD

partial 1 Botany a constituting part of a larger structure b used for only part of the life cycle of a plant c (of a parasite) not exclusively parasitic 2 Maths designating or relating to an operation in which only one of a set of independent variables is considered at a time 3 Music, Acoustics any of the component tones of a single musical sound, including both those that belong to the harmonic series of the sound and those that do not 4 Maths a partial derivative

particle 1 Physics a body with finite mass that can be treated as having negligible size, and internal structure 2 See **elementary particle** 3 *RC Church* a small piece broken off from the Host at Mass

parti-coloured *or* **party-coloured** having different colours in different parts; variegated

particular 1 (of the solution of a differential equation) obtained by giving specific values to the arbitrary constants in a general equation 2 *Logic* (of a proposition) affirming or denying something about only some members of a class of objects, as in *some men are not wicked* 3 *Property law* denoting an estate that precedes the passing of the property into ultimate ownership 4 *Logic* another name for **individual** 5 *Philosophy* an individual object, as contrasted with a universal

parting *Chem* a division of a crystal along a plane that is not a cleavage plane

partisan *or* **partizan** 1 an adherent or devotee of a cause, party, etc. 2 relating to or excessively devoted to one party, faction, etc.; one-sided

partition 1 a division of a country into two or more separate nations 2 *Property law* a division of property, esp realty, among joint owners 3 *Maths* any of the ways by which an integer can be expressed as a sum of integers 4 *Logic, Maths* a the division of a class into a number of disjoint and exhaustive subclasses b such a set of subclasses 5 *Biology* a structure that divides or separates

partner 1 a member of a partnership 2 one of a pair of dancers or players on the same side in a game

partnership a a contractual relationship between two or more persons carrying on a joint business venture with a view to profit, each incurring liability for losses and the right to share in the profits b the deed creating such a relationship c the persons associated in such a relationship

Parton Dolly born 1946, US country and pop singer and songwriter

partridge 1 any of various small Old World gallinaceous game birds of the genera *Perdix, Alectoris*, etc, esp *P. perdix* (**common** or **European partridge**): family *Phasianidae* (pheasants) 2 *US and Canadian* any of various other gallinaceous birds, esp the bobwhite and ruffed grouse

part song 1 a song composed in harmonized parts 2 a piece of homophonic choral music in which the topmost part carries the melody

party 1 a a group of people organized together to further a common political aim, such as the election of its candidates to public office b (*as modifier*): *party politics* 2 the practice of taking sides on public issues 3 the person or persons taking part in legal proceedings, such as plaintiff or prosecutor

party line 1 the policies or dogma of a political party, to which all members are expected to subscribe 2 *Chiefly US* the boundary between adjoining property

party wall *Property law* a wall separating two properties or pieces of land and over which each of the adjoining owners has certain rights

Pasadena a city in SW California, east of Los Angeles. Pop: 144 413 (2003 est)

Pasargadae an ancient city in Persia, northeast of Persepolis in present-day Iran: built by Cyrus the Great

Pasay a city in the Philippines, on central Luzon just south of Manila, on Manila Bay. Pop: 364 000 (2005 est)

pascal the derived SI unit of pressure; the pressure

exerted on an area of 1 square metre by a force of 1 newton; equivalent to 10 dynes per square centimetre or 1.45×10^{-4} pound per square inch.

Pascal¹ Blaise 1623–62, French philosopher, mathematician, and physicist. As a scientist, he made important contributions to hydraulics and the study of atmospheric pressure and, with Fermat, developed the theory of probability. His chief philosophical works are *Lettres provinciales* (1656–57), written in defence of Jansenism and against the Jesuits, and *Pensées* (1670), fragments of a Christian apologia

Pascal² a high-level computer programming language developed as a teaching language: used for general-purpose programming

paschal 1 of or relating to Passover 2 of or relating to Easter

Pas-de-Calais a department of N France, in Nord-Pas-de-Calais region, on the Straits of Dover (the **Pas de Calais**): the part of France closest to the British Isles. Capital: Arras. Pop: 1 451 307 (2003 est). Area: 6752 sq km (2633 sq miles)

pas de deux *Ballet* a sequence for two dancers

pasha *or* **pacha** (formerly) a provincial governor or other high official of the Ottoman Empire or the modern Egyptian kingdom: placed after a name when used as a title

Pasionaria La , real name *Dolores Ibarruri*. 1895–1989, Spanish Communist leader, who lived in exile in the Soviet Union (1939–75)

Pasmore Victor 1908–98, British artist. Originally a figurative painter, he devoted himself to abstract paintings and reliefs after 1947

paso doble 1 a modern ballroom dance in fast duple time 2 a piece of music composed for or in the rhythm of this dance

Pasolini Pier Paolo 1922–75, Italian film director. His films include *The Gospel according to St. Matthew* (1964), *Oedipus Rex* (1967), *Theorem* (1968), *Pigsty* (1969), and *Decameron* (1970)

paspalum any of various grasses of the genus *Paspalum* of Australia and New Zealand having wide leaves

pasqueflower 1 a purple-flowered herbaceous ranunculaceous plant, *Anemone pulsatilla* (or *Pulsatilla vulgaris*), of N and Central Europe and W Asia 2 any of several related North American plants, such as *A. patens*

pass 1 a route through a range of mountains where the summit is lower or where there is a gap between peaks 2 a way through any difficult region 3 a permit, licence, or authorization to do something without restriction 4 *Brit* a the passing of a college or university examination to a satisfactory standard but not as high as honours b (*as modifier*): *a pass degree* 5 a dive, sweep, or bombing or landing run by an aircraft 6 a motion of the hand or of a wand as a prelude to or part of a conjuring trick 7 *Sport* the transfer of a ball from one player to another 8 *Fencing* a thrust or lunge with a sword 9 *Bridge* the act of passing (making no bid)

passable (of a proposed law) able to be ratified or enacted

passage¹ 1 *Music* a section or division of a piece, movement, etc. 2 a section of a written work, speech, etc, esp one of moderate length 3 a journey, esp by ship 4 the enactment of a law or resolution by a legislative or deliberative body **5** an evacuation of the bowels

passage² *Dressage* **1** a sideways walk in which diagonal pairs of feet are lifted alternately **2** a cadenced lofty trot, the moment of suspension being clearly defined

Passamaquoddy Bay an inlet of the Bay of Fundy between New Brunswick (Canada) and Maine (US) at the mouth of the St Croix River

passbook 1 a customer's book in which is recorded by a trader a list of credit sales to that customer **2** (formerly in South Africa) an official document serving to identify the bearer, his race, his residence, and his employment

Passchendaele a village in NW Belgium, in West Flanders province: the scene of heavy fighting during the third battle of Ypres in World War I during which 245 000 British troops were lost

passerine of, relating to, or belonging to the *Passeriformes*, an order of birds characterized by the perching habit: includes the larks, finches, crows, thrushes, starlings, etc.

passion 1 *Philosophy* **a** any state of the mind in which it is affected by something external, such as perception, desire, etc, as contrasted with action **b** feelings, desires or emotions, as contrasted with reason **2** the sufferings and death of a Christian martyr

Passion 1 the sufferings of Christ from the Last Supper to his death on the cross **2** any of the four Gospel accounts of this **3** a musical setting of this

passionflower any passifloraceous plant of the tropical American genus *Passiflora*, cultivated for their red, yellow, greenish, or purple showy flowers: some species have edible fruit

passion fruit the edible fruit of any of various passionflowers, esp granadilla

Passion play a play depicting the Passion of Christ

passive 1 *Chem* (of a substance, esp a metal) apparently chemically unreactive, usually as a result of the formation of a thin protective layer that prevents further reaction **2** *Electronics, Telecomm* **a** containing no source of power and therefore capable only of attenuating a signal **b** not capable of amplifying a signal or controlling a function

passive resistance resistance to a government, law, etc, made without violence, as by fasting, demonstrating peacefully, or refusing to cooperate

passive smoking the inhalation of smoke from other people's cigarettes by a nonsmoker

passkey any of various keys, esp a latchkey

pass law (formerly, in South Africa) a law restricting the movement of Black Africans, esp from rural to urban areas

Passover an eight-day Jewish festival beginning on Nisan 15 and celebrated in commemoration of the passing over or sparing of the Israelites in Egypt, when God smote the firstborn of the Egyptians (Exodus 12)

passport 1 an official document issued by a government, identifying an individual, granting him permission to travel abroad, and requesting the protection of other governments for him **2** a licence granted by a state to a foreigner, allowing the passage of his person or goods through the country

password a sequence of characters used to gain access to a computer system

paste 1 a mixture or material of a soft or malleable consistency, such as toothpaste **2** the combined ingredients of porcelain

pastel 1 a a substance made of ground pigment bound with gum, used for making sticks for drawing **b** a crayon of this **c** a drawing done in such crayons **2** the medium or technique of pastel drawing **3** a pale delicate colour **4** a light prose work, esp a poetic one **5** (of a colour) pale; delicate

pastern 1 the part of a horse's foot between the fetlock and the hoof **2** either of the two bones that constitute this part

Pasternak **Boris Leonidovich** 1890–1960, Russian lyric poet, novelist, and translator, noted particularly for his novel of the Russian Revolution, *Dr. Zhivago* (1957). He was awarded the Nobel prize for literature in 1958, but was forced to decline it

Pasteur **Louis** 1822–95, French chemist and bacteriologist. His discovery that the fermentation of milk and alcohol was caused by microorganisms resulted in the process of pasteurization. He also devised methods of immunization against anthrax and rabies and pioneered stereochemistry

pastiche *or* **pasticcio 1** a work of art that mixes styles, materials, etc. **2** a work of art that imitates the style of another artist or period

pastille *or* **pastil 1** an aromatic substance burnt to fumigate the air **2** *Med* a small coated paper disc formerly used to estimate the dose or intensity of radiation (esp of X-rays): it changes colour when exposed **3** a variant of **pastel** (sense 1)

Pasto a city in SE Colombia, at an altitude of 2590 m (8500 ft). Pop: 404 000 (2005 est)

pastor 1 a clergyman or priest in charge of a congregation **2** a person who exercises spiritual guidance over a number of people **3** a S Asian starling, *Sturnus roseus*, having glossy black head and wings and a pale pink body

pastoral 1 (of a literary work) dealing with an idealized form of rural existence in a conventional way **2** denoting or relating to the branch of theology dealing with the duties of a clergyman or priest to his congregation **3** of or relating to a clergyman or priest in charge of a congregation or his duties as such **4** of or relating to a teacher's responsibility for the personal, as the distinct from the educational, development of pupils **5** a literary work or picture portraying rural life, esp the lives of shepherds in an idealizing way **6** *Music* a variant of **pastorale** **7** *Christianity* **a** a letter from a clergyman to the people under his charge **b** the letter of a bishop to the clergy or people of his diocese **c** the crosier or staff carried by a bishop as a symbol of his pastoral responsibilities

pastorale *Music* **1** a composition evocative of rural life, characterized by moderate compound duple or quadruple time and sometimes a droning accompaniment **2** a musical play based on a rustic story, popular during the 16th century

Patagonia 1 the southernmost region of South America, in Argentina and Chile extending from the

Andes to the Atlantic. Area: about 777 000 sq km (300 000 sq miles) **2** an arid tableland in the southernmost part of Argentina, rising towards the Andes in the west

patch 1 a a small plot of land **b** its produce **2** a district for which particular officials, such as social workers or policemen, have responsibility **3** *Pathol* any discoloured area on the skin, mucous membranes, etc, usually being one sign of a specific disorder **4** *Med* **a** a protective covering for an injured eye **b** any protective dressing **5** *Computing* a small set of instructions to correct or improve a computer program

pate the head, esp with reference to baldness or (in facetious use) intelligence

patella 1 *Anatomy* a small flat triangular bone in front of and protecting the knee joint **2** *Biology* a cuplike structure, such as the spore-producing body of certain ascomycetous fungi **3** *Archaeol* a small pan

paten, patin, *or* **patine** a plate, usually made of silver or gold, esp the plate on which the bread is placed in the Eucharist

patent 1 a a government grant to an inventor assuring him the sole right to make, use, and sell his invention for a limited period **b** a document conveying such a grant **2** an invention, privilege, etc, protected by a patent **3 a** an official document granting a right **b** any right granted by such a document **4** in the US **a** a grant by the government of title to public lands **b** the instrument by which such title is granted **c** the land so granted **5** open or available for inspection (esp in the phrases **letters patent, patent writ**) **6** concerning protection, appointment, etc, of or by a patent or patents **7** (esp of a bodily passage or duct) being open or unobstructed **8** *Biology* spreading out widely **9** (of plate glass) ground and polished on both sides

patent medicine a medicine protected by a patent and available without a doctor's prescription

Patent Office a government department that issues patents

Pater Walter (Horatio). 1839–94, English essayist and critic, noted for his prose style and his advocation of the "love of art for its own sake". His works include the philosophical romance *Marius the Epicurean* (1885), *Studies in the History of the Renaissance* (1873), and *Imaginary Portraits* (1887)

paternal *Biology* inherited or derived from the male parent

paternalism the attitude or policy of a government or other authority that manages the affairs of a country, company, community, etc, in the manner of a father, esp in usurping individual responsibility and the liberty of choice

paternity descent or derivation from a father

Paternoster *RC Church* **1** the Lord's Prayer, esp in Latin **2** the recital of this as an act of devotion

Paterson[1] 1 Andrew Barton, known as *Banjo Paterson*. 1864–1941, Australian poet. His works include "Waltzing Matilda" and "The Man from Snowy River" **2** William 1658–1719, Scottish merchant and banker: founded the Bank of England (1694)

Paterson[2] a city in NE New Jersey: settled by the Dutch in the late 17th century. Pop: 150 782 (2003 est)

path *Computing* the directions for reaching a particular file or directory, as traced hierarchically through each of the parent directories usually from the root; the file or directoryand all parent directories are separated from one another in the path by slashes

pathetic fallacy (in literature) the presentation of inanimate objects in nature as possessing human feelings

pathname *Computing* the name of a file or directory together with its position in relation to other directories traced back in a line to the root; the names of the file and each of the parent directories are separated from one another by slashes

pathogen *or* **pathogene** any agent that can cause disease

pathological *or less commonly* **pathologic 1** of or relating to pathology **2** relating to, involving, or caused by disease **3** *Informal* compulsively motivated

pathology 1 the branch of medicine concerned with the cause, origin, and nature of disease, including the changes occurring as a result of disease **2** the manifestations of disease, esp changes occurring in tissues or organs

  ▷www.medbioworld.com/home/lists/
    diseases.html
  ▷www.cdc.gov/health

pathway 1 *Education* courses taken by a student to gain entry to a higher course or towards a final qualification **2** *Biochem* a chain of reactions associated with a particular metabolic process

Patiala a city in N India, in E Punjab: seat of the Punjabi University (1962). Pop: 302 870 (2001)

patience *Chiefly Brit* any of various card games for one player only, in which the cards may be laid out in various combinations as the player tries to use up the whole pack

patient a person who is receiving medical care

patina[1] a film of oxide formed on the surface of a metal, esp the green oxidation of bronze or copper

patina[2] a broad shallow dish used in ancient Rome

patio 1 an open inner courtyard, esp one in a Spanish or Spanish-American house **2** an area adjoining a house, esp one that is paved and used for outdoor activities

Patmore Coventry (Kersey Dighton). 1823–96, English poet. His works, celebrating both conjugal and divine love, include *The Angel in the House* (1854–62) and *The Unknown Eros* (1877)

Patmos a Greek island in the Aegean, in the NW Dodecanese: St John's place of exile (about 95 AD), where he wrote the Apocalypse. Pop: 2984 (2001). Area: 34 sq km (13 sq miles)

Patna a city in NE India, capital of Bihar state, on the River Ganges: founded in the 5th century BC; university (1917); centre of a rice-growing region. Pop: 1 376 950 (2001)

Paton Alan (Stewart). 1903–88, South African writer, noted esp for his novel dealing with racism and apartheid in South Africa, *Cry, the Beloved Country* (1965)

Patras a port in W Greece, in the NW Peloponnese on the **Gulf of Patras** (an inlet of the Ionian Sea): one of the richest cities in Greece until the 3rd century BC; under Turkish rule from 1458 to 1687 and from 1715 until the

War of Greek Independence, which began here in 1821. Pop: 193 000 (2005 est)

patrial (in Britain formerly) a person having by statute the right of abode in the United Kingdom, and so not subject to immigration control

patriarch 1 the male head of a tribe or family **2** *Old Testament* any of a number of persons regarded as the fathers of the human race, divided into the antediluvian patriarchs, from Adam to Noah, and the postdiluvian, from Noah to Abraham **3** *Old Testament* any of the three ancestors of the Hebrew people: Abraham, Isaac, or Jacob **4** *Old Testament* any of Jacob's twelve sons, regarded as the ancestors of the twelve tribes of Israel **5** *Early Christian Church* the bishop of one of several principal sees, esp those of Rome, Antioch, and Alexandria **6** *Eastern Orthodox Church* the bishops of the four ancient principal sees of Constantinople, Antioch, Alexandria, and Jerusalem, and also of Russia, Romania, and Serbia, the bishop of Constantinople (the **ecumenical Patriarch**) being highest in dignity among these **7** *RC Church* **a** a title given to the pope **b** a title given to a number of bishops, esp of the Uniat Churches, indicating their rank as immediately below that of the pope **8** *Mormon Church* another word for **Evangelist 9** *Eastern Christianity* the head of the Coptic, Armenian, Syrian Jacobite, or Nestorian Churches, and of certain other non-Orthodox Churches in the East

patriarchate 1 the office, jurisdiction, province, or residence of a patriarch **2** a family or people under male domination or government

patrician 1 a member of the hereditary aristocracy of ancient Rome. In the early republic the patricians held almost all the higher offices **2** a high nonhereditary title awarded by Constantine and his eastern Roman successors for services to the empire **3** in medieval Europe **a** a title borne by numerous princes including several emperors from the 8th to the 12th centuries **b** a member of the upper class in numerous Italian republics and German free cities **4** (esp in ancient Rome) of, relating to, or composed of patricians

Patrick Saint 5th century AD, Christian missionary to Ireland, probably born in Britain; patron saint of Ireland. Feast day: March 17

patrimony the endowment of a church

patrol car a police car with a radio telephone used for patrolling streets and motorways

patron 1 a customer of a shop, hotel, etc, esp a regular one **2** See **patron saint 3** (in ancient Rome) the protector of a dependant or client, often the former master of a freedman still retaining certain rights over him **4** *Christianity* a person or body having the right to present a clergyman to a benefice

patronage 1 in politics **a** the practice of making appointments to office, granting contracts, etc. **b** the favours so distributed **2** *Christianity* the right to present a clergyman to a benefice

patron saint a saint regarded as the particular guardian of a country, church, trade, person, etc.

pattern *Manufacturing* a wooden or metal shape or model used in a foundry to make a mould

Patti Adelina 1843–1919, Italian operatic coloratura soprano, born in Spain

Patton George Smith 1885–1945, US general, who successfully developed tank warfare as an extension of cavalry tactics in World War II: captured Palermo, Sicily (1942) and much of France (1944)

Pau a city in SW France: residence of the French kings of Navarre; tourist centre for the Pyrenees. Pop: 78 732 (1999)

paua an edible abalone, *Haliotis iris*, of New Zealand, having an iridescent shell used esp for jewellery

Paul 1 Saint Also called: **Paul the Apostle, Saul of Tarsus** original name *Saul*. died ?67 AD, one of the first Christian missionaries to the Gentiles, who died a martyr in Rome. Until his revelatory conversion he had assisted in persecuting the Christians. He wrote many of the Epistles in the New Testament. Feast day: June 29 **2 Les,** real name *Lester Polfuss*. born 1915, US guitarist: creator of the solid-body electric guitar and pioneer in multitrack recording

Paul III original name *Alessandro Farnese*. 1468–1549, Italian ecclesiastic; pope (1534–49). He excommunicated Henry VIII of England (1538) and inaugurated the Counter-Reformation by approving the establishment of the Jesuits (1540), instituting the Inquisition in Italy, and convening the Council of Trent (1545)

Paul VI original name *Giovanni Battista Montini*. 1897–1978, Italian ecclesiastic; pope (1963–1978)

Pauli Wolfgang 1900–58, US physicist, born in Austria. He formulated the exclusion principle (1924) and postulated the existence of the neutrino (1931), later confirmed by Fermi: Nobel prize for physics 1945

Pauling Linus Carl 1901–94, US chemist, noted particularly for his work on the nature of the chemical bond and his opposition to nuclear tests: Nobel prize for chemistry 1954; Nobel peace prize 1962

Paulinus Saint died 644 AD, Roman missionary to England; first bishop of York and archbishop of Rochester. Feast day: Oct 10

paunch *Nautical* a thick mat that prevents chafing

pauper (formerly) a destitute person supported by public charity

Pausanias 2nd century AD, Greek geographer and historian. His *Description of Greece* gives a valuable account of the topography of ancient Greece

pause 1 *Prosody* another word for **caesura 2** *Music* a continuation of a note or rest beyond its normal length.

pavane *or* **pavan 1** a slow and stately dance of the 16th and 17th centuries **2** a piece of music composed for or in the rhythm of this dance, usually characterized by a slow stately triple time

Pavarotti Luciano born 1935, Italian operatic tenor, specializing in works by Verdi and Puccini

pavement 1 a hard-surfaced path for pedestrians alongside and a little higher than a road **2** a paved surface, esp one that is a thoroughfare **3** the material used in paving **4** *Civil engineering* the hard-layered structure that forms a road carriageway, airfield runway, vehicle park, or other paved areas **5** *Geology* a level area of exposed rock resembling a paved road

Pavese Cesare 1908–50, Italian writer and translator. His works include collections of poems, such as *Verrà la morte e avrà i tuoi occhi* (1953), short stories, such as the collection *Notte di festa* (1953), and the novel *La Luna e i falò*

(1950)

Pavia a town in N Italy, in Lombardy: noted for its Roman and medieval remains, including the tomb of St Augustine. Pop: 71 214 (2001)

pavilion 1 a summerhouse or other decorative shelter 2 a building or temporary structure, esp one that is open and ornamental, for housing exhibitions 3 a large ornate tent, esp one with a peaked top, as used by medieval armies 4 one of a set of buildings that together form a hospital or other large institution

paving 1 a paved surface; pavement 2 material used for a pavement, such as paving stones, bricks, or asphalt

Pavlodar a port in NE Kazakhstan on the Irtysh River: major industrial centre with an oil refinery. Pop: 303 000 (2005 est)

Pavlov Ivan Petrovich 1849–1936, Russian physiologist. His study of conditioned reflexes in dogs influenced behaviourism. He also made important contributions to the study of digestion: Nobel prize for physiology or medicine 1904

Pavlova Anna 1885–1931, Russian ballerina

paw any of the feet of a four-legged mammal, bearing claws or nails

pawl a pivoted lever shaped to engage with a ratchet wheel to prevent motion in a particular direction

pawn a chessman of the lowest theoretical value, limited to forward moves of one square at a time with the option of two squares on its initial move: it captures with a diagonal move only

pawnbroker a dealer licensed to lend money at a specified rate of interest on the security of movable personal property, which can be sold if the loan is not repaid within a specified period

pawnshop the premises of a pawnbroker

pax *Chiefly RC Church* a a greeting signifying Christian love transmitted from one to another of those assisting at the Eucharist; kiss of peace b a small metal or ivory plate, often with a representation of the Crucifixion, formerly used to convey the kiss of peace from the celebrant at Mass to those attending it, who kissed the plate in turn

Paxman Jeremy (Dickson). born 1950, British journalist, broadcaster, and author, noted esp for his political interviews

Paxton Sir Joseph 1801–65, English architect, who designed Crystal Palace (1851), the first large structure of prefabricated glass and iron parts

payable 1 capable of being profitable 2 (of a debt) imposing an obligation on the debtor to pay, esp at once

payload 1 that part of a cargo earning revenue 2 a the passengers, cargo, or bombs carried by an aircraft b the equipment carried by a rocket, satellite, or spacecraft

paymaster an official of a government, business, etc, responsible for the payment of wages and salaries

Pays de la Loire a region of W France, on the Bay of Biscay: generally low-lying, drained by the River Loire and its tributaries; agricultural

Paz Octavio 1914–98, Mexican poet and essayist. His poems include the cycle *Piedra de Sol* (1957) and *Blanco* (1967). Nobel prize for literature 1990

PDF *Computing* portable document format: a format in which documents may be viewed

pea 1 an annual climbing leguminous plant, *Pisum sativum*, with small white flowers and long green pods containing edible green seeds: cultivated in temperate regions 2 a the seed of this plant, eaten as a vegetable b (*as modifier*): *pea soup* 3 any of several other leguminous plants, such as the sweet pea, chickpea, and cowpea

Peabody George 1795–1869, US merchant, banker, and philanthropist in the US and England

peace dividend additional money available to a government from cuts in defence expenditure because of the end of a period of hostilities

peace offering *Judaism* a sacrificial meal shared between the offerer and Jehovah to intensify the union between them

peace pipe a long decorated pipe smoked by North American Indians on ceremonial occasions, esp as a token of peace

Peace River a river in W Canada, rising in British Columbia as the Finlay River and flowing northeast into the Slave River. Length: 1715 km (1065 miles)

peach 1 a small rosaceous tree, *Prunus persica*, with pink flowers and rounded edible fruit: cultivated in temperate regions 2 the soft juicy fruit of this tree, which has a downy reddish-yellow skin, yellowish-orange sweet flesh, and a single stone 3 a a pinkish-yellow to orange colour b (*as adjective*): *a peach dress*

peacock 1 a male peafowl, having a crested head and a very large fanlike tail marked with blue and green eye-like spots 2 another name for **peafowl**

Peacock Thomas Love 1785–1866, English novelist and poet, noted for his satirical romances, including *Headlong Hall* (1816) and *Nightmare Abbey* (1818)

peafowl 1 either of two large pheasants, *Pavo cristatus* (**blue peafowl**) of India and Ceylon and *P. muticus* (**green peafowl**) of SE Asia. The males (see **peacock** (sense 1)) have a characteristic bright plumage 2 a rare closely related African species, *Afropavo congensis* (**Congo peafowl**), both sexes of which are brightly coloured

peak 1 the pointed summit of a mountain 2 a mountain with a pointed summit 3 a a sharp increase in a physical quantity followed by a sharp decrease b the maximum value of this quantity c (*as modifier*): *peak voltage* 4 *Nautical* a the extreme forward (**forepeak**) or aft (**afterpeak**) part of the hull b (of a fore-and-aft quadrilateral sail) the after uppermost corner c the after end of a gaff

Peak District a region of N central England, mainly in N Derbyshire at the S end of the Pennines: consists of moors in the north and a central limestone plateau; many caves. Highest point: 727 m (2088 ft)

Peake Mervyn 1911–68, English novelist, poet, and illustrator. In his trilogy *Gormenghast* (1946–59), he creates, with vivid imagination, a grotesque Gothic world

peak load the maximum load on an electrical power-supply system

peal¹ 1 *Bell-ringing* a series of changes rung in accordance with specific rules, consisting of not fewer than 5000 permutations in a ring of eight bells 2 the set of bells in a belfry

peal² a dialect name for a grilse or a young sea trout

peanut a a leguminous plant, *Arachis hypogaea*, of tropical America: widely cultivated for its edible seeds. The seed pods are forced underground where they ripen. **b** the edible nutlike seed of this plant, used for food and as a source of oil

pear 1 a widely cultivated rosaceous tree, *Pyrus communis*, having white flowers and edible fruits 2 the sweet gritty-textured juicy fruit of this tree, which has a globular base and tapers towards the apex 3 the wood of this tree, used for making furniture

pearl 1 See **mother-of-pearl** 2 a pale greyish-white colour, often with a bluish tinge

Pearl Harbor an almost landlocked inlet of the Pacific on the S coast of the island of Oahu, Hawaii: site of a US naval base attacked by the Japanese in 1941, resulting in the US entry into World War II

Pearl River 1 a river in central Mississippi, flowing southwest and south to the Gulf of Mexico. Length: 789 km (490 miles) 2 the English name for the **Zhu Jiang**

Pears Sir Peter 1910–86, British tenor, associated esp with the works of Benjamin Britten

Pearse Patrick (Henry), Irish name *Pádraic*. 1879–1916, Irish nationalist, who planned and led the Easter Rising (1916): executed by the British

Pearson 1 Karl 1857–1936, British mathematician, noted for his work in statistics, esp as applied to biological problems 2 Lester B(owles). 1897–1972, Canadian Liberal statesman; prime minister (1963–68): Nobel peace prize 1957 for helping to resolve the Suez crisis (1956)

Peary Robert Edwin 1856–1920, US arctic explorer, generally regarded as the first man to reach the North Pole (1909)

pebble a a transparent colourless variety of rock crystal, used for making certain lenses b such a lens

pecan 1 a hickory tree, *Carya pecan* (or *C. illinoensis*), of the southern US, having deeply furrowed bark and edible nuts 2 the smooth oval nut of this tree, which has a sweet oily kernel

peccary either of two piglike artiodactyl mammals, *Tayassu tajacu* (**collared peccary**) or *T. albirostris* (**white-lipped peccary**) of forests of southern North America, Central and South America: family *Tayassuidae*

Pechora a river in N Russia, rising in the Ural Mountains and flowing north in a great arc to the **Pechora Sea** (the SE part of the Barents Sea). Length: 1814 km (1127 miles)

peck 1 a unit of dry measure equal to 8 quarts or one quarter of a bushel 2 a container used for measuring this quantity

Peck Gregory 1916–2003, US film actor; his films include *Keys of the Kingdom* (1944), *The Gunfighter* (1950), *The Big Country* (1958), *To Kill a Mockingbird* (1963), *The Omen* (1976), and *Other People's Money* (1991)

pecking order a natural hierarchy in a group of gregarious birds, such as domestic fowl

Peckinpah Sam(uel David). 1926–84, US film director, esp of Westerns, such as *The Wild Bunch* (1969). Among his other films are *Straw Dogs* (1971), *Bring me the Head of Alfredo Garcia* (1974), and *Cross of Iron* (1977)

Pecos a river in the southwestern US, rising in N central New Mexico and flowing southeast to the Rio Grande. Length: about 1180 km (735 miles)

pectin *Biochem* any of the acidic hemicelluloses that occur in ripe fruit and vegetables: used in the manufacture of jams because of their ability to solidify to a gel when heated in a sugar solution (may be referred to on food labels as **E440(a)**)

pectoral 1 of or relating to the chest, breast, or thorax 2 a pectoral organ or part, esp a muscle or fin 3 a medicine or remedy for disorders of the chest or lungs

pectoral fin either of a pair of fins, situated just behind the head in fishes, that help to control the direction of movement during locomotion

peculiar *Church of England* a church or parish that is exempt from the jurisdiction of the ordinary in whose diocese it lies

pecuniary *Law* (of an offence) involving a monetary penalty

pedagogue *or sometimes US* **pedagog** 1 a teacher or educator 2 a pedantic or dogmatic teacher

pedagogy the principles, practice, or profession of teaching

pedal[1] 1 any foot-operated lever or other device, esp one of the two levers that drive the chain wheel of a bicycle, the foot brake, clutch control, or accelerator of a car, one of the levers on an organ controlling deep bass notes, or one of the levers on a piano used to create a muted effect or sustain tone b *(as modifier): a pedal cycle*

pedal[2] of or relating to the foot or feet

pedestal a base that supports a column, statue, etc, as used in classical architecture

pedestrian crossing *Brit* a path across a road marked as a crossing for pedestrians

pedicure professional treatment of the feet, either by a medical expert or a cosmetician

pedigree 1 a the line of descent of a purebred animal b *(as modifier): a pedigree bull* 2 a document recording this

pediment 1 a low-pitched gable, esp one that is triangular, as used in classical architecture 2 a gently sloping rock surface, formed through denudation under arid conditions

pedlar, *esp US* **peddler,** *or* **pedler** a person who peddles; hawker

pedometer a device containing a pivoted weight that records the number of steps taken in walking and hence the distance travelled

peduncle 1 the stalk of a plant bearing an inflorescence or solitary flower 2 *Anatomy* a stalklike structure, esp a large bundle of nerve fibres within the brain 3 *Pathol* a slender process of tissue by which a polyp or tumour is attached to the body

Peebles a town in SE Scotland, in Scottish Borders. Pop: 8065 (2001)

Peeblesshire (until 1975) a county of SE Scotland, now part of Scottish Borders

peel a long-handled shovel used by bakers for moving bread, in an oven

Peel 1 John, real name *John Robert Parker Ravenscroft*. 1939–2005, British broadcaster; noted for his Radio 1 music programme and Radio 4's *Home Truths* 2 Sir Robert 1788–1850, British statesman; Conservative prime minister (1834–35; 1841–46). As Home Secretary (1828–30) he founded the Metropolitan Police and in his second ministry carried through a series of free-trade budgets culminating in the repeal of the Corn Laws (1846), which split the Tory party

Peele George ?1556–?96, English dramatist and poet. His works include the pastoral drama *The Arraignment of Paris* (1584) and the comedy *The Old Wives' Tale* (1595)

peen the end of a hammer head opposite the striking face, often rounded or wedge-shaped

peep *US* any of various small sandpipers of the genus *Calidris* (or *Erolia*) and related genera, such as the pectoral sandpiper

peer 1 a member of a nobility; nobleman 2 a person who holds any of the five grades of the British nobility: duke, marquess, earl, viscount, and baron

peerage 1 the whole body of peers; aristocracy 2 the position, rank, or title of a peer 3 (esp in the British Isles) a book listing the peers and giving genealogical and other information about them

peeress 1 the wife or widow of a peer 2 a woman holding the rank of a peer in her own right

peg 1 *Informal* a person's leg 2 *Northern English, dialect* a tooth 3 *Brit* a small drink of wine or spirits, esp of brandy or whisky and soda 4 a mountaineering piton 5 *Croquet* a post that a player's ball must strike to win the game 6 *Angling* a fishing station allotted to an angler in a competition, marked by a peg in the ground

pegboard 1 a board having a pattern of holes into which small pegs can be fitted, used for playing certain games or keeping a score 2 another name for **solitaire**

Pegu a city in S Myanmar: capital of a united Burma (16th century). Pop: 307 000 (2005 est)

Pei I(eòh) M(ing). born 1917, US architect, born in China. His buildings include the E wing of the National Museum of Art, Washington DC (1978), a glass and steel pyramid at the Louvre, Paris (1989), and the Rock and Roll Hall of Fame, Cleveland, USA (1995)

Peipus a lake in W Russia, on the boundary with Estonia: drains into the Gulf of Finland. Area: 3512 sq km (1356 sq miles)

Peirce Charles Sanders 1839–1914, US logician, philosopher, and mathematician: pioneer of pragmatism

peke *Informal* a Pekingese dog

Pekingese *or* **Pekinese** 1 a small breed of pet dog with a profuse straight coat, curled plumed tail, and short wrinkled muzzle 2 the dialect of Mandarin Chinese spoken in Beijing (formerly Peking), the pronunciation of which serves as a standard for the language

Pelagius ?360–?420 AD, British monk, who originated the body of doctrines known as Pelagianism and was condemned for heresy (417)

pelargonium any plant of the chiefly southern African geraniaceous genus *Pelargonium*, having circular or lobed leaves and red, pink, or white aromatic flowers: includes many cultivated geraniums

Pelham Henry 1696–1754, British statesman: prime minister (1743–54); brother of Thomas Pelham Holles, 1st Duke of Newcastle

pelican any aquatic bird of the tropical and warm water family *Pelecanidae*, such as *P. onocrotalus* (**white pelican**): order *Pelecaniformes*. They have a long straight flattened bill, with a distensible pouch for engulfing fish

pelican crossing a type of road crossing marked by black-and-white stripes or by two rows of metal studs

and consisting of a pedestrian-operated traffic-light system

Pelion a mountain in NE Greece, in E Thessaly. In Greek mythology it was the home of the centaurs. Height: 1548 m (5079 ft)

Pella an ancient city in N Greece: the capital of Macedonia under Philip II

pellagra *Pathol* a disease caused by a dietary deficiency of nicotinic acid, characterized by burning or itching often followed by scaling of the skin, inflammation of the mouth, diarrhoea, mental impairment, etc.

pellet 1 *Ornithol* a mass of undigested food, including bones, fur, feathers, etc, that is regurgitated by certain birds, esp birds of prey 2 a small pill 3 a raised area on coins and carved or moulded ornaments

Pelletier Pierre Joseph 1788–1842, French chemist, who isolated quinine, chlorophyll, and other chemical substances

pellucid 1 transparent or translucent 2 extremely clear in style and meaning; limpid

Peloponnese the the S peninsula of Greece, joined to central Greece by the Isthmus of Corinth: chief cities in ancient times were Sparta and Corinth, now Patras. Pop: 503 300 (2001). Area: 21 439 sq km (8361 sq miles)

pelota any of various games played in Spain, Spanish America, SW France, etc, by two players who use a basket strapped to their wrists or a wooden racket to propel a ball against a specially marked wall
  ▷www.fipv.com

Pelotas a port in S Brazil, in Rio Grande do Sul on the Canal de São Gonçalo. Pop: 323 000 (2005 est)

pelt the skin of a fur-bearing animal, such as a mink, esp when it has been removed from the carcass

pelvis 1 the large funnel-shaped structure at the lower end of the trunk of most vertebrates: in man it is formed by the hipbones and sacrum 2 the bones that form this structure 3 any anatomical cavity or structure shaped like a funnel or cup

Pemba an island in the Indian Ocean, off the E coast of Africa north of Zanzibar: part of Tanzania; produces most of the world's cloves. Chief town: Chake Chake. Pop: 362 166 (2002). Area: 984 sq km (380 sq miles)

Pembroke 1 a town in SW Wales, in Pembrokeshire on Milford Haven: 11th-century castle where Henry VII was born. Pop. (with Pembroke Dock): 15 890 (2001) 2 the smaller variety of corgi, usually having a short tail

Pembrokeshire a county of SW Wales, on the Irish Sea and the Bristol Channel: formerly (1974–96) part of Dyfed: a hilly peninsula with a deeply indented coast: tourism, agriculture, oil refining. Administrative centre: Haverfordwest. Pop: 116 300 (2003 est). Area: 1589 sq km (614 sq miles)

pen[1] the long horny internal shell of a squid

pen[2] a dock for servicing submarines, esp one having a bombproof roof

pen[3] a female swan

penal code the codified body of the laws in any legal system that relate to crime and its punishment

penalty box 1 *Soccer* a rectangular area in front of the goal, within which the goalkeeper may handle the ball and within which a penalty is awarded for a foul by the defending team 2 *Ice hockey* a bench for players serving time penalties

penalty corner *Hockey* a free hit from the goal line taken by the attacking side

penalty shoot-out *Soccer* a method of deciding the winner of a drawn match, in which players from each team attempt to score with a penalty kick

penance *Christianity* **a** a punishment usually consisting of prayer, fasting, etc, undertaken voluntarily as an expression of penitence for sin **b** a punishment of this kind imposed by church authority as a condition of absolution

Penang **1** a state of Peninsular Malaysia: consists of the island of Penang and the province Wellesley on the mainland, which first united administratively in 1798 as a British colony. Capital: George Town. Pop: 1 313 449 (2000). Area: 1031 sq km (398 sq miles) **2** a forested island off the NW coast of Malaya, in the Strait of Malacca. Area: 293 sq km (113 sq miles) **3** another name for **George Town**

pencil **1** a narrow set of lines or rays, such as light rays, diverging from or converging to a point **2** *Archaic* an artist's fine paintbrush **3** *Rare* an artist's individual style or technique in drawing

Penderecki **Krzystof** born 1933, Polish composer, noted for his highly individual orchestration. His works include *Threnody for the Victims of Hiroshima* for strings (1960), *Stabat Mater* (1962), *Polish Requiem* (1983–84), and the opera *Ubu Rex* (1991)

pendulum a body mounted so that it can swing freely under the influence of gravity. It is either a bob hung on a light thread (**simple pendulum**) or a more complex structure (**compound pendulum**)

penetration *Marketing* the proportion of the total number of potential purchasers of a product or service who either are aware of its existence or actually buy it

penguin **1** any flightless marine bird, such as *Aptenodytes patagonica* (king penguin) and *Pygoscelis adeliae* (Adélie penguin), of the order *Sphenisciformes* of cool southern, esp Antarctic, regions: they have wings modified as flippers, webbed feet, and feathers lacking barbs **2** an obsolete name for **great auk**

penicillin any of a group of antibiotics with powerful bactericidal action, used to treat many types of infections, including pneumonia, gonorrhoea, and infections caused by streptococci and staphylococci: originally obtained from the fungus *Penicillium*, esp *P. notatum*. Formula: $R-C_9H_{11}N_2O_4S$ where R is one of several side chains

peninsula a narrow strip of land projecting into a sea or lake from the mainland

penis the male organ of copulation in higher vertebrates, also used for urine excretion in many mammals

penitent *Christianity* **a** a person who repents his sins and seeks forgiveness for them **b** *RC Church* a person who confesses his sins to a priest and submits to a penance imposed by him

penitential *Chiefly RC Church* a book or compilation of instructions for confessors

penitentiary **1** (in the US and Canada) a state or federal prison: in Canada, esp a federal prison for offenders convicted of serious crimes **2** *RC Church* **a** a cleric appointed to supervise the administration of the sacrament of penance in a particular area **b** a priest who has special faculties to absolve particularly grave sins **c** a cardinal who presides over a tribunal that decides all matters affecting the sacrament of penance **d** this tribunal itself **3** *US and Canadian* (of an offence) punishable by imprisonment in a penitentiary

penknife a small knife with one or more blades that fold into the handle; pocketknife

Penn **1** **Irving** born 1917, US photographer, noted for his portraits and his innovations in colour photography **2** **William** 1644–1718, English Quaker and founder of Pennsylvania

pen name an author's pseudonym

pennant **1** a type of pennon, esp one flown from vessels as identification or for signalling **2** same as **flag**

Penney **William George**, Baron Penney of East Hendred. 1909–91, British mathematician. He worked on the first atomic bomb and became chairman of the UK Atomic Energy Authority (1964–67)

Pennine Way a long-distance footpath extending from Edale, Derbyshire, for 402 km (250 miles) to Kirk Yetholm, Scottish Borders

pennon a small tapering or triangular flag borne on a ship or boat

Pennsylvania a state of the northeastern US: almost wholly in the Appalachians, with the Allegheny Plateau to the west and a plain in the southeast; the second most important US state for manufacturing. Capital: Harrisburg. Pop: 12 365 455 (2003 est). Area: 116 462 sq km (44 956 sq miles)

Pennsylvanian **1** of the state of Pennsylvania **2** (in North America) of, denoting, or formed in the upper of two divisions of the Carboniferous period (see also **Mississippian** (sense 2)), which lasted 30 million years, during which coal measures were formed **3** an inhabitant or native of the state of Pennsylvania **4** **the** the Pennsylvanian period or rock system, equivalent to the Upper Carboniferous of Europe

penny **1** (in Britain) a bronze coin having a value equal to one hundredth of a pound **2** (in Britain before 1971) a bronze or copper coin having a value equal to one twelfth of a shilling or one two-hundred-and-fortieth of a pound **3** a former monetary unit of the Republic of Ireland worth one hundredth of a pound **4** (in the US and Canada) a cent **5** a coin of similar value, as used in several other countries

Penny Black the first adhesive postage stamp, issued in Britain in 1840; an imperforate stamp bearing the profile of Queen Victoria on a dark background

penny-farthing *Brit* an early type of bicycle with a large front wheel and a small rear wheel, the pedals being attached to the front wheel

pennyroyal **1** a Eurasian plant, *Mentha pulegium*, with hairy leaves and small mauve flowers, that yields an aromatic oil used in medicine: family *Lamiaceae* (labiates) **2** a similar and related plant, *Hedeoma pulegioides*, of E North America

pennywort **1** a crassulaceous Eurasian rock plant, *Umbilicus rupestris* (or *Cotyledon umbilicus*), with whitish-green tubular flowers and rounded leaves **2** a marsh plant, *Hydrocotyle vulgaris*, of Europe and North Africa, having circular leaves and greenish-pink flowers: family *Hydrocotylaceae* **3** a gentianaceous plant, *Obolaria virginica*, of E North America, with fleshy scalelike leaves and small white or purplish flowers **4** any of various other plants with rounded penny-like leaves

penology the science of prison management

Penrith a market town in NW England, in Cumbria. Pop: 14 471 (2001)

Penrose Sir *Roger* born 1931, British mathematician and theoretical physicist, noted for his investigation of black holes

pension 1 a regular payment made by the state to people over a certain age to enable them to subsist without having to work **2** a regular payment made by an employer to former employees after they retire **3** a regular payment made to a retired person as the result of his or her contributions to a personal pension scheme **4** any regular payment made on charitable grounds, by way of patronage, or in recognition of merit, service, etc.

pentagon a polygon having five sides

Pentagon 1 the five-sided building in Arlington, Virginia, that houses the headquarters of the US Department of Defense **2** the military leadership of the US

pentagram 1 a star-shaped figure formed by extending the sides of a regular pentagon to meet at five points **2** such a figure used as a magical or symbolic figure by the Pythagoreans, black magicians, etc.

pentameter 1 a verse line consisting of five metrical feet **2** (in classical prosody) a verse line consisting of two dactyls, one stressed syllable, two dactyls, and a final stressed syllable **3** designating a verse line consisting of five metrical feet

Pentateuch the first five books of the Old Testament regarded as a unity

pentathlon an athletic contest consisting of five different events, based on a competition in the ancient Greek Olympics

pentatonic scale *Music* any of several scales consisting of five notes, the most commonly encountered one being composed of the first, second, third, fifth, and sixth degrees of the major diatonic scale

pentavalent *Chem* having a valency of five

Pentecost 1 a Christian festival occurring on Whit Sunday commemorating the descent of the Holy Ghost on the apostles **2** *Judaism* the harvest festival celebrated fifty days after the second day of Passover on the sixth and seventh days of Sivan, and commemorating the giving the Torah on Mount Sinai

Pentecostal 1 of or relating to any of various Christian groups that emphasize the charismatic aspects of Christianity and adopt a fundamental attitude to the Bible **2** of or relating to Pentecost or the influence of the Holy Ghost **3** a member of a Pentecostal Church

▷http://pentecostalevangel.ag.org/
▷http://www.oru.edu/university/library/
   holyspirit/pentorg1.html
▷http://www.upci.org/
▷http://www.paoc.org/
▷http://www.iphc.org/
▷http://www.pentecostalworldconf.org/
▷http://www.wikipedia.org/wiki/Pentecostal

Pentelikon a mountain in SE Greece, near Athens: famous for its white marble, worked regularly from the 6th century BC, from which the chief buildings and sculptures in Athens are made. Height: 1109 m (3638 ft)

penthouse 1 a flat or maisonette built onto the top floor or roof of a block of flats **2** a construction on the roof of a building, esp one used to house machinery **3** a shed built against a building, esp one that has a sloping roof **4** *Real Tennis* the roofed corridor that runs along three sides of the court

Pentland Firth a channel between the mainland of N Scotland and the Orkney Islands: notorious for rough seas. Length: 32 km (20 miles). Width: up to 13 km (8 miles)

penumbra 1 a fringe region of half shadow resulting from the partial obstruction of light by an opaque object **2** *Astronomy* the lighter and outer region of a sunspot **3** *Painting* the point or area in which light and shade blend

Penza a city in W Russia: manufacturing centre. Pop: 514 000 (2005 est)

Penzance a town in SW England, in SW Cornwall: the westernmost town in England; resort and fishing port. Pop: 20 255 (2001)

Penzias *Arno Allan* born 1933, US astrophysicist, who shared the Nobel prize for physics (1978) with Robert W. Wilson for their discovery of cosmic microwave background radiation

peon[1] (formerly in Spanish America) a debtor compelled to work off his debts

peon[2] (in India, Sri Lanka, etc, esp formerly) **1** a messenger or attendant, esp in an office **2** a native policeman

peony or **paeony 1** any of various ranunculaceous shrubs and plants of the genus *Paeonia*, of Eurasia and North America, having large pink, red, white, or yellow flowers **2** the flower of any of these plants

people mover any of various automated forms of transport for large numbers of passengers over short distances, such as a moving pavement, driverless cars, etc.

Peoria a port in N central Illinois, on the Illinois River. Pop: 112 907 (2003 est)

Pepin the Short died 768 AD, king of the Franks (751–768); son of Charles Martel and father of Charlemagne. He deposed the Merovingian king (751) and founded the Carolingian dynasty

pepper 1 a woody climbing plant, *Piper nigrum*, of the East Indies, having small black berry-like fruits: family *Piperaceae* **2** the dried fruit of this plant, which is ground to produce a sharp hot condiment **3** any of various other plants of the genus *Piper* **4** any of various tropical plants of the solanaceous genus *Capsicum*, esp *C. frutescens*, the fruits of which are used as a vegetable and a condiment **5** the fruit of any of these capsicums, which has a mild or pungent taste **6** any of various similar but unrelated plants, such as water pepper

pepper-and-salt (of cloth) marked with a fine mixture of black and white

peppercorn the small dried berry of the pepper plant (*Piper nigrum*)

peppermint a temperate mint plant, *Mentha piperita*, with purple or white flowers: cultivated for its downy leaves, which yield a pungent oil

pep pill *Informal* a tablet containing a stimulant drug

pepsin *or* **pepsine** a proteolytic enzyme produced in the stomach in the inactive form pepsinogen, which, when activated by acid, splits proteins into peptones

peptic 1 of, relating to, or promoting digestion 2 of, relating to, or caused by pepsin or the action of the digestive juices

peptic ulcer *Pathol* an ulcer of the mucous membrane lining those parts of the alimentary tract exposed to digestive juices. It can occur in the oesophagus, the stomach, the duodenum, the jejunum, or in parts of the ileum

peptide any of a group of compounds consisting of two or more amino acids linked by chemical bonding between their respective carboxyl and amino groups

Pepys Samuel 1633–1703, English diarist and naval administrator. His diary, which covers the period 1660–69, is a vivid account of London life through such disasters as the Great Plague, the Fire of London, and the intrusion of the Dutch fleet up the Thames

Peraea *or* **Perea** a region of ancient Palestine, east of the River Jordan and the Dead Sea

Perak a state of NW Peninsular Malaysia, on the Strait of Malacca: tin mining. Capital: Ipoh. Pop: 2 051 236 (2000). Area: 20 680 sq km (8030 sq miles)

percentage *Commerce* the interest, tax, commission, or allowance on a hundred items

perception 1 *Biology* the process by which an organism detects and interprets information from the external world by means of the sensory receptors 2 *Law* the collection, receipt, or taking into possession of rents, crops, etc.

Perceval Spencer 1762–1812, British statesman; prime minister (1809–12); assassinated

perch¹ 1 another name for **rod** 2 a solid measure for stone, usually taken as 198 inches by 18 inches by 12 inches 3 a pole joining the front and rear axles of a carriage 4 a frame on which cloth is placed for inspection 5 *Obsolete or dialect* a pole

perch² 1 any freshwater spiny-finned teleost fish of the family Percidae, esp those of the genus Perca, such as P. *fluviatilis* of Europe and P. *flavescens* (**yellow perch**) of North America: valued as food and game fishes 2 any of various similar or related fishes

percussion 1 the act, an instance, or an effect of percussing 2 *Music* the family of instruments in which sound arises from the striking of materials with sticks, hammers, or the hands 3 *Music* a instruments of this family constituting a section of an orchestra, band, etc. b (*as modifier*): *a percussion ensemble* 4 *Med* the act of percussing a body surface

percussion instrument any of various musical instruments that produce a sound when their resonating surfaces are struck directly, as with a stick or mallet, or by leverage action. They may be of definite pitch (as a kettledrum or xylophone), indefinite pitch (as a gong or rattle), or a mixture of both (as various drums)

percussionist *Music* a person who plays any of several percussion instruments, esp in an orchestra

Percy 1 Sir Henry, known as *Harry Hotspur*. 1364–1403, English rebel, who was killed leading an army against Henry IV 2 Thomas 1729–1811, English bishop and anti-

quary. His *Reliques of Ancient English Poetry* (1765) stimulated the interest of Romantic writers in old English and Scottish ballads

Perdido Monte a mountain in NE Spain, in the central Pyrenees. Height: 3352 m (10 997 ft)

perdition 1 *Christianity* a final and irrevocable spiritual ruin b this state as one that the wicked are said to be destined to endure for ever 2 another word for **hell**

peregrine falcon a falcon, *Falco peregrinus*, occurring in most parts of the world, having a dark plumage on the back and wings and lighter underparts

Pereira a town in W central Colombia: cattle trading and coffee processing. Pop: 656 000 (2005 est)

Perelman S(idney) J(oseph). 1904–79, US humorous writer. After scriptwriting for the Marx Brothers, he published many collections of articles, including *Crazy Like a Fox* (1944) and *Eastward, Hi!* (1977)

peremptory *Law* a admitting of no denial or contradiction; precluding debate b obligatory rather than permissive

perennial a woody or herbaceous plant that can continue its growth for at least two years

Peres Shimon born 1923, Israeli statesman, born in Poland: prime minister (1984–86; 1995–96); Nobel peace prize 1994 jointly with Yasser Arafat and Yitzhak Rabin

perfect 1 *Maths* exactly divisible into equal integral or polynomial roots 2 *Botany* a (of flowers) having functional stamens and pistils b (of plants) having all parts present 3 *Music* a of or relating to the intervals of the unison, fourth, fifth, and octave b (of a cadence) ending on the tonic chord, giving a feeling of conclusion

perfectionism *Philosophy* the doctrine that man can attain perfection in this life

perforate *Biology* a pierced by small holes b marked with small transparent spots

perfumer *or* **perfumier** a person who makes or sells perfume

Pergamum an ancient city in NW Asia Minor, in Mysia: capital of a major Hellenistic monarchy of the same name that later became a Roman province

pergola a horizontal trellis or framework, supported by posts, that carries climbing plants and may form a covered walk

Pergolesi Giovanni Battista 1710–36, Italian composer: his works include the operetta *La Serva padrona* (1733) and the *Stabat Mater* (1736) for women's voices

perianth the outer part of a flower, consisting of the calyx and corolla

pericardium the membranous sac enclosing the heart

pericarp 1 the part of a fruit enclosing the seeds that develops from the wall of the ovary 2 a layer of tissue around the reproductive bodies of some algae and fungi

Pericles ?495–429 BC, Athenian statesman and leader of the popular party, who contributed greatly to Athens' political and cultural supremacy in Greece. In power from about 460 BC, he was responsible for the construction of the Parthenon. He conducted the Peloponnesian War (431–404 BC) successfully until his death

perigee the point in its orbit around the earth when the moon or an artificial satellite is nearest the earth

perihelion the point in its orbit when a planet or comet is nearest the sun

perimeter 1 *Maths* **a** the curve or line enclosing a plane area **b** the length of this curve or line 2 a medical instrument for measuring the limits of the field of vision

perinatal of, relating to, or occurring in the period from about three months before to one month after birth

perineum 1 the region of the body between the anus and the genital organs, including some of the underlying structures 2 the nearly diamond-shaped surface of the human trunk between the thighs

period 1 a nontechnical name for an occurrence of menstruation 2 *Geology* a unit of geological time during which a system of rocks is formed 3 a division of time, esp of the academic day 4 *Physics, Maths* **a** the time taken to complete one cycle of a regularly recurring phenomenon; the reciprocal of frequency. **b** an interval in which the values of a periodic function follow a certain pattern that is duplicated over successive intervals 5 *Astronomy* **a** the time required by a body to make one complete rotation on its axis **b** the time interval between two successive maxima or minima of light variation of a variable star 6 *Chem* one of the horizontal rows of elements in the periodic table. Each period starts with an alkali metal and ends with a rare gas 7 a complete sentence, esp a complex one with several clauses 8 *Music* a passage or division of a piece of music, usually consisting of two or more contrasting or complementary musical phrases and ending on a cadence 9 (in classical prosody) a unit consisting of two or more cola

periodic law the principle that the chemical properties of the elements are periodic functions of their atomic weights (also called: **Mendeleev's law**) or, more accurately, of their atomic numbers

periodic table a table of the elements, arranged in order of increasing atomic number, based on the periodic law. Elements having similar chemical properties and electronic structures appear in vertical columns (groups)

▷www.psigate.ac.uk/newsite/reference/ periodic-table.html

▷www.colorado.edu/physics/2000/applets/ a2.html

peripatetic *Brit* employed in two or more educational establishments and travelling from one to another

peripheral *Anatomy* of, relating to, or situated near the surface of the body

periphery *Anatomy* the surface or outermost part of the body or one of its organs or parts

peristalsis *Physiol* the succession of waves of involuntary muscular contraction of various bodily tubes, esp of the alimentary tract, where it effects transport of food and waste products

peritoneum a thin translucent serous sac that lines the walls of the abdominal cavity and covers most of the viscera

peritonitis inflammation of the peritoneum

periwinkle[1] any of various edible marine gastropods of the genus *Littorina*, esp *L. littorea*, having a spirally coiled shell

periwinkle[2] 1 any of several Eurasian apocynaceous evergreen plants of the genus *Vinca*, such as *V. minor*

(lesser periwinkle) and *V. major* (greater periwinkle), having trailing stems and blue flowers 2 **a** a light purplish-blue colour **b** (*as adjective*): *a periwinkle coat*

perjury *Criminal law* the offence committed by a witness in judicial proceedings who, having been lawfully sworn or having affirmed, wilfully gives false evidence

Perl a computer language that is used for text manipulation, esp on the World Wide Web

Perlis a state of NW Peninsular Malaysia, on the Andaman Sea: a dependency of Thailand until 1909. Capital: Kangar. Pop: 204 450 (2000). Area: 803 sq km (310 sq miles)

Perlman Itzhak born 1945, Israeli violinist; polio victim

Perm a port in W Russia, on the Kama River: oil refinery; university (1916). Pop: 984 000 (2005 est)

permafrost ground that is permanently frozen, often to great depths, the surface sometimes thawing in the summer

permanent way *Chiefly Brit* the track of a railway, including the ballast, sleepers, rails, etc.

permanganate a salt of permanganic acid

Permian of, denoting, or formed in the last period of the Palaeozoic era, between the Carboniferous and Triassic periods, which lasted for 60 000 000 years

permit 1 an official certificate or document granting authorization; licence 2 permission, esp written permission

permutation 1 *Maths* **a** an ordered arrangement of the numbers, terms, etc, of a set into specified groups **b** a group formed in this way. The number of permutations of n objects taken r at a time is $n! / (n–r)!$ 2 a fixed combination for selections of results on football pools

Pernambuco 1 a state of NE Brazil, on the Atlantic: consists of a humid coastal plain rising to a high inland plateau. Capital: Recife. Pop: 8 084 667 (2002). Area: 98 280 sq km (37 946 sq miles) 2 the former name of **Recife**

pernicious anaemia a form of anaemia characterized by lesions of the spinal cord, weakness, sore tongue, numbness in the arms and legs, diarrhoea, etc.: associated with inadequate absorption of vitamin B_{12}

Pernik an industrial town in W Bulgaria, on the Struma River. Pop: 84 000 (2005 est)

peroxide 1 short for **hydrogen peroxide** (esp when used for bleaching hair) 2 any of a class of metallic oxides, such as sodium peroxide, Na_2O_2, that contain the divalent ion $^-O–O^-$ 3 any of certain dioxides, such as manganese peroxide, MnO_2, that resemble peroxides in their formula but do not contain the $^-O–O^-$ ion 4 any of a class of organic compounds whose molecules contain two oxygen atoms bound together. They tend to be explosive

perpendicular 1 at right angles to a horizontal plane 2 denoting, relating to, or having the style of Gothic architecture used in England during the 14th and 15th centuries, characterized by tracery having vertical lines, a four-centred arch, and fan vaulting 3 *Geometry* a line or plane perpendicular to another 4 any instrument used for indicating the vertical line through a given point 5 *Mountaineering* a nearly vertical face

▷www.britainexpress.com/architecture

perpetual 1 *Horticulture* blooming throughout the growing season or year **2** a plant that blooms throughout the growing season

perpetuity *Property law* a limitation preventing the absolute disposal of an estate for longer than the period allowed by law

Perpignan a town in S France: historic capital of Roussillon. Pop: 105 115 (1999)

perquisite an incidental benefit gained from a certain type of employment, such as the use of a company car

Perrault Charles 1628–1703, French author, noted for his *Contes de ma mère l'oye* (1697), which contains the fairy tales *Little Red Riding Hood*, *Cinderella*, and *The Sleeping Beauty*

Perrin Jean Baptiste 1870–1942, French physicist. His researches on the distribution and diffusion of particles in colloids (1911) gave evidence for the physical reality of molecules, confirmed the explanation of Brownian movement in terms of kinetic theory, and determined the magnitude of the Avogadro constant. He also studied cathode rays: Nobel prize for physics 1926

perry alcoholic drink made of pears, similar in taste to cider

Perry 1 Fred(erick John). 1909–95, English tennis and table-tennis player; world singles table-tennis champion (1929); Wimbledon singles champion (1934–36) **2 Grayson** born 1960, British potter. A transvestite, he won the Turner Prize (2003). **3 Matthew Calbraith** 1794–1858, US naval officer, who led a naval expedition to Japan that obtained a treaty (1854) opening up Japan to western trade **4** his brother, **Oliver Hazard** 1785–1819, US naval officer. His defeat of a British squadron on Lake Erie (1813) was the turning point in the War of 1812, leading to the recapture of Detroit

Perse Saint-John, real name *Alexis Saint-Léger*. 1887–1975, French poet, born in Guadeloupe. His works include *Anabase* (1922) and *Chronique* (1960). Nobel prize for literature 1960

Persepolis the capital of ancient Persia in the Persian Empire and under the Seleucids: founded by Darius; sacked by Alexander the Great in 330 BC

perseverance *Christianity* persistence in remaining in a state of grace until death

Pershing John Joseph, nickname *Black Jack*. 1860–1948, US general. He was commander in chief of the American Expeditionary Force in Europe (1917–19)

Persian 1 of or relating to ancient Persia or modern Iran, their inhabitants, or their languages **2** a native, citizen, or inhabitant of modern Iran; an Iranian **3** a member of an Indo-European people of West Iranian speech who established a great empire in SW Asia in the 6th century BC **4** (loosely) the language of Iran or Persia in any of its ancient or modern forms, belonging to the West Iranian branch of the Indo-European family

Persian carpet or **rug** a carpet or rug made in Persia or other countries of the Near East by knotting silk or wool yarn by hand onto a woven backing, characterized by rich colours and flowing or geometric designs

Persian cat a long-haired variety of domestic cat with a stocky body, round face, short nose, and short thick legs

Persian Gulf a shallow arm of the Arabian Sea between SW Iran and Arabia: linked with the Arabian Sea by the Strait of Hormuz and the Gulf of Oman; important for the oilfields on its shores. Area: 233 000 sq km (90 000 sq miles)

Persian lamb 1 a black loosely curled fur obtained from the skin of the karakul lamb **2** a karakul lamb

persimmon 1 any of several tropical trees of the genus *Diospyros*, typically having hard wood and large orange-red fruit: family *Ebenaceae* **2** the sweet fruit of any of these trees, which is edible when completely ripe

persistent 1 (of plant parts) remaining attached to the plant after the normal time of withering **2** *Zoology* **a** (of parts normally present only in young stages) present in the adult **b** continuing to grow or develop after the normal period of growth **3** (of a chemical, esp when used as an insecticide) slow to break down; not easily degradable

persistent vegetative state *Med* an irreversible condition, resulting from brain damage, characterized by lack of consciousness, thought, and feeling, although reflex activities (such as breathing) continue

person 1 *Law* a human being or a corporation recognized in law as having certain rights and obligations **2** *Philosophy* a being characterized by consciousness, rationality, and a moral sense, and traditionally thought of as consisting of both a body and a mind or soul

persona 1 a character in a play, novel, etc. **2** (in Jungian psychology) the mechanism that conceals a person's true thoughts and feelings, esp in his adaptation to the outside world

personal 1 *Law* of or relating to movable property, such as money **2** *Law* an item of movable property

personal computer a small inexpensive computer used in word processing, playing computer games, etc.

personality *Psychol* the sum total of all the behavioural and mental characteristics by means of which an individual is recognized as being unique

personal organizer a pocket-sized electronic device that performs the same functions

personal stereo a very small audio cassette player designed to be worn attached to a belt and used with lightweight headphones

personate (of the corollas of certain flowers) having two lips in the form of a face

perspective *Art* **1** the theory or art of suggesting three dimensions on a two-dimensional surface, in order to recreate the appearance and spatial relationships that objects or a scene in recession present to the eye **2** a picture showing perspective

perspiration 1 the act or process of insensibly eliminating fluid through the pores of the skin, which evaporates immediately **2** the sensible elimination of fluid through the pores of the skin, which is visible as droplets on the skin **3** the salty fluid secreted through the pores of the skin; sweat

Perth 1 a city in central Scotland, in Perth and Kinross on the River Tay: capital of Scotland from the 12th century until the assassination of James I there in 1437. Pop: 43 450 (2001) **2** a city in SW Australia, capital of Western Australia, on the Swan River: major industrial centre; University of Western Australia (1911). Pop: 1 176 542 (2001)

Perth and Kinross a council area of N central Scotland,

corresponding mainly to the historical counties of Perthshire and Kinross-shire: part of Tayside Region from 1975 until 1996: chiefly mountainous, with agriculture, tourism, and forestry. Administrative centre: Perth. Pop: 135 990 (2003 est). Area: 5321 sq km (2019 sq miles)

Perthshire (until 1975) a county of central Scotland, now part of Perth and Kinross council area

perturbation 1 *Physics* a secondary influence on a system that modifies simple behaviour, such as the effect of the other electrons on one electron in an atom **2** *Astronomy* a small continuous deviation in the inclination and eccentricity of the orbit of a planet or comet, due to the attraction of neighbouring planets

Peru a republic in W South America, on the Pacific: the centre of the great Inca Empire when conquered by the Spanish in 1532; gained independence in 1824 by defeating Spanish forces with armies led by San Martín and Bolívar; consists of a coastal desert, rising to the Andes; an important exporter of minerals and a major fishing nation. Official languages: Spanish, Quechua, and Aymara. Official religion: Roman Catholic. Currency: nuevo sol. Capital: Lima. Pop: 27 567 000 (2004 est). Area: 1 285 215 sq km (496 222 sq miles)

Perugia 1 a city in central Italy, in Umbria: centre of the Umbrian school of painting (15th century); university (1308); Etruscan and Roman remains. Pop: 149 125 (2001) **2 Lake** another name for (Lake) **Trasimene**

Perugino II, real name *Pietro Vannucci*. 1446–1523, Italian painter; master of Raphael. His works include the fresco *Christ giving the Keys to Peter* in the Sistine Chapel, Rome

Perutz Max Ferdinand 1914–2002, British biochemist, born in Austria. With J. C. Kendrew, he worked on the structure of haemoglobin and shared the Nobel prize for chemistry 1962

Peruzzi Baldassare Tommaso 1481–1536, Italian architect and painter of the High Renaissance. The design of the Palazzo Massimo, Rome, is attributed to him

perversion any abnormal means of obtaining sexual satisfaction

pervert a person who practises sexual perversion

Pesaro a port and resort in E central Italy, in the Marches on the Adriatic. Pop: 91 086 (2001)

Pescara a city and resort in E central Italy, on the Adriatic. Pop: 116 286 (2001)

peseta the former standard monetary unit of Spain and Andorra, divided into 100 céntimos; replaced by the euro in 2002

Peshawar a city in N Pakistan, at the E end of the Khyber Pass: one of the oldest cities in Pakistan and capital of the ancient kingdom of Gandhara; university (1950). Pop: 1 255 000 (2005 est)

peso 1 the standard monetary unit, comprising 100 centavos, of Argentina, Chile, Colombia, Cuba, the Dominican Republic, Mexico, and the Philippines; formerly also of Guinea-Bissau, where it was replaced by the CFA franc **2** the standard monetary unit of Uruguay, divided into 100 centesimos **3** another name for **piece of eight**

pessary *Med* **1** a device for inserting into the vagina, either as a support for the uterus or (**diaphragm pessary**) to deliver a drug, such as a contraceptive **2** a medicated vaginal suppository

pessimism *Philosophy, Religion* **1** the doctrine of the ultimate triumph of evil over good **2** the doctrine that this world is corrupt and that man's sojourn in it is a preparation for some other existence

Pessoa Fernando 1888–1935, Portuguese poet, who ascribed much of his work to three imaginary poets, Alvaro de Campos, Alberto Caeiro, and Ricardo Reis

Pestalozzi Johann Heinrich 1746–1827, Swiss educational reformer. His emphasis on learning by observation exerted a wide influence on elementary education

pesticide a chemical used for killing pests, esp insects and rodents

pestilence a any epidemic outbreak of a deadly and highly infectious disease, such as the plague **b** such a disease

pestilent infected with or likely to cause epidemic or infectious disease

petal any of the separate parts of the corolla of a flower: often brightly coloured

Peter¹ *New Testament* **1 Saint** Also called: **Simon Peter** died ?67 AD, a fisherman of Bethsaida, who became leader of the apostles and is regarded by Roman Catholics as the first pope; probably martyred at Rome. Feast day: June 29 or Jan 18 **2** either of two epistles traditionally ascribed to Peter (in full **The First Epistle** and **The Second Epistle of Peter**)

Peter² *New Testament* either of the two epistles traditionally ascribed to the apostle Peter (in full **The First Epistle** and **The Second Epistle of Peter**)

Peterborough 1 a city in central England, in Peterborough unitary authority, N Cambridgeshire on the River Nene: industrial centre; under development as a new town since 1968. Pop: 136 292 (2001). **2** a unitary authority in central England, in Cambridgeshire. Pop: 158 800 (2003 est). Area: 402 sq km (155 sq miles) **3 Soke of** a former administrative unit of E central England, generally considered part of Northamptonshire or Huntingdonshire: absorbed into Cambridgeshire in 1974 **4** a city in SE Canada, in SE Ontario: manufacturing centre. Pop: 73 303 (2001) **5** a traditional type of wooden canoe formerly made in Peterborough, SE Ontario

Peter I known as *Peter the Great*. 1672–1725, tsar of Russia (1682–1725), who assumed sole power in 1689. He introduced many reforms in government, technology, and the western European ideas. He also acquired new territories for Russia in the Baltic and founded the new capital of St Petersburg (1703)

Peter III 1728–62, grandson of Peter I and tsar of Russia (1762): deposed in a coup d'état led by his wife (later Catherine II); assassinated

Peterlee a new town in Co. Durham, founded in 1948. Pop: 29 936 (2001)

Petermann Peak a mountain in E Greenland. Height: 2932 m (9645 ft)

Petersburg a city in SE Virginia, on the Appomattox River: scene of prolonged fighting (1864–65) during the final months of the American Civil War. Pop: 33 091 (2003 est)

Peterson Oscar (Emmanuel). born 1925, Canadian jazz pianist and singer, who led his own trio from the early

1950s

Peter the Hermit ?1050–1115, French monk and preacher of the First Crusade

pethidine a white crystalline water-soluble drug used as an analgesic. Formula: $C_{15}H_{21}NO_2.HCl$

petiole 1 the stalk by which a leaf is attached to the rest of the plant **2** *Zoology* a slender stalk or stem, such as the connection between the thorax and abdomen of ants

Petit Roland born 1924, French ballet dancer and choreographer. His innovative ballets include *Carmen* (1949), *Kraanerg* (1969), and *The Blue Angel* (1985); he also choreographed films, such as *Anything Goes* (1956) and *Black Tights* (1960)

petit bourgeois the section of the middle class with the lowest social status, generally composed of shopkeepers, lower clerical staff, etc.

petition 1 a written document signed by a large number of people demanding some form of action from a government or other authority **2** *Law* a formal application in writing made to a court asking for some specific judicial action

petit mal a mild form of epilepsy characterized by periods of impairment or loss of consciousness for up to 30 seconds

Petra an ancient city in the south of present-day Jordan; capital of the Nabataean kingdom

Petrarch Italian name *Francesco Petrarca*. 1304–74, Italian lyric poet and scholar, who greatly influenced the values of the Renaissance. His collection of poems *Canzoniere*, inspired by his ideal love for Laura, was written in the Tuscan dialect. He also wrote much in Latin, esp the epic poem *Africa* (1341) and the *Secretum* (1342), a spiritual self-analysis

petrel any oceanic bird of the order *Procellariiformes*, having a hooked bill and tubular nostrils: includes albatrosses, storm petrels, and shearwaters

Petri dish a shallow circular flat-bottomed dish, often with a fitting cover, used in laboratories, esp for producing cultures of microorganisms

Petrie Sir (William Matthew) Flinders 1853–1942, British Egyptologist and archaeologist

Petrified Forest a national park in E Arizona, containing petrified coniferous trees about 170 000 000 years old

petrochemical 1 any substance, such as acetone or ethanol, obtained from petroleum or natural gas **2** of, concerned with, or obtained from petrochemicals or related to petrochemistry

petrol any one of various volatile flammable liquid mixtures of hydrocarbons, mainly hexane, heptane, and octane, obtained from petroleum and used as a solvent and a fuel for internal-combustion engines. Usually petrol also contains additives such as antiknock compounds and corrosion inhibitors

petrolatum a translucent gelatinous substance obtained from petroleum; used as a lubricant and in medicine as an ointment base and protective dressing

petroleum a dark-coloured thick flammable crude oil occurring in sedimentary rocks around the Persian Gulf, in parts of North and South America, and below the North Sea, consisting mainly of hydrocarbons. Fractional distillation separates the crude oil into petrol, paraffin, diesel oil, lubricating oil, etc. Fuel oil, paraffin wax, asphalt, and carbon black are extracted from the residue

Petronius Gaius , known as *Petronius Arbiter.* died 66 AD, Roman satirist, supposed author of the *Satyricon*, a picaresque account of the licentiousness of contemporary society

Petropavlovsk a city in N Kazakhstan on the Ishim River. Pop: 190 000 (2005 est)

Petrozavodsk a city in NW Russia, capital of the Karelian Autonomous Republic, on Lake Onega: developed around ironworks established by Peter the Great in 1703; university (1940). Pop: 265 000 (2005 est.

petty *Law* of lesser importance

petty cash a small cash fund kept on a firm's premises for the payment of minor incidental expenses

petunia any solanaceous plant of the tropical American genus *Petunia*: cultivated for their white, pink, blue, or purple funnel-shaped flowers

Pevsner 1 Antoine 1886–1962, French constructivist sculptor and painter, born in Russia; brother of Naum Gabo **2 Sir Nikolaus** 1902–83, British architectural historian, born in Germany: his series *Buildings of England* (1951–74) describes every structure of account in the country

pewter 1 a any of various alloys containing tin (80–90 per cent), lead (10–20 per cent), and sometimes small amounts of other metals, such as copper and antimony **b** (*as modifier*): *pewter ware* **2 a** a bluish-grey colour **b** (*as adjective*): *pewter tights*

pfennig 1 a former German monetary unit worth one hundredth of a Deutschmark **2** (formerly) a monetary unit worth one hundredth of an East German ostmark

Pforzheim a city in SW Germany, in W Baden-Württemberg: centre of the German watch and jewellery industry. Pop: 119 046 (2003 est)

pH potential of hydrogen; a measure of the acidity or alkalinity of a solution equal to the common logarithm of the reciprocal of the concentration of hydrogen ions in moles per cubic decimetre of solution. Pure water has a pH of 7, acid solutions have a pH less than 7, and alkaline solutions a pH greater than 7

Phaedrus ?15 BC–?50 AD, Roman author of five books of Latin verse fables, based chiefly on Aesop

phagocyte an amoeboid cell or protozoan that engulfs particles, such as food substances or invading microorganisms

phalanger any of various Australasian arboreal marsupials, such as *Trichosurus vulpecula* (**brush-tailed phalanger**), having dense fur and a long tail: family *Phalangeridae*

phalanx 1 (in Fourierism) a group of approximately 1800 persons forming a commune in which all property is collectively owned **2** *Anatomy* any of the bones of the fingers or toes **3** *Botany* **a** a bundle of stamens, joined together by their stalks (filaments) **b** a form of vegetative spread in which the advance is on a broad front, as in the common reed

phallic *Psychoanal* **a** relating to a stage of psychosexual development during which a male child's interest is concentrated on the genital organs **b** designating personality traits, such as conceit and self-assurance, due to fixation at the phallic stage of development **c** (in Freudian theory) denoting a phase of early childhood in which there is a belief that both sexes possess a phallus

phallus 1 another word for **penis** 2 an image of the penis, esp as a religious symbol of reproductive power

phantasm (in the philosophy of Plato) objective reality as distorted by perception

phantasmagoria or **phantasmagory** *Films* a sequence of pictures made to vary in size rapidly while remaining in focus

Pharaoh the title of the ancient Egyptian kings

Pharisee *Judaism* a member of an ancient Jewish sect that was opposed to the Sadducees, teaching strict observance of Jewish tradition as interpreted rabbinically and believing in life after death and in the coming of the Messiah

pharmaceutics 1 another term for **pharmacy** 2 pharmaceutical remedies

pharmacist or *less commonly* **pharmaceutist** a person qualified to prepare and dispense drugs

pharmacology the science of drugs, including their characteristics and uses
▷www.pharmacy.org
▷www.pharmweb.net
▷www.medbioworld.com/home/lists/
  medications.html

pharmacopoeia or *sometimes US* **pharmacopeia** an authoritative book containing a list of medicinal drugs with their uses, preparation, dosages, formulas, etc.

pharmacy the practice or art of preparing and dispensing drugs

Pharsalus an ancient town in Thessaly in N Greece. Several major battles were fought nearby, including Caesar's victory over Pompey (48 BC)

pharyngitis inflammation of the pharynx

pharynx the part of the alimentary canal between the mouth and the oesophagus

phase 1 *Astronomy* one of the recurring shapes of the portion of the moon or an inferior planet illuminated by the sun 2 *Physics* **a** the fraction of a cycle of a periodic quantity that has been completed at a specific reference time, expressed as an angle **b** (*as modifier*): *a phase shift* 3 *Physics* a particular stage in a periodic process or phenomenon 4 **in phase** (of two waveforms) reaching corresponding phases at the same time 5 **out of phase** (of two waveforms) not in phase 6 *Chem* a distinct state of matter characterized by homogeneous composition and properties and the possession of a clearly defined boundary 7 *Zoology* a variation in the normal form of an animal, esp a colour variation, brought about by seasonal or geographical change 8 *Biology* a stage in mitosis or meiosis 9 *Electrical engineering* one of the circuits in a system in which there are two or more alternating voltages displaced by equal amounts in phase (sense 5)

pheasant 1 any of various long-tailed gallinaceous birds of the family *Phasianidae*, esp *Phasianus colchicus* (**ring-necked pheasant**), having a brightly-coloured plumage in the male: native to Asia but introduced elsewhere 2 any of various other galli-

naceous birds of the family *Phasianidae*, including the quails and partridges 3 *US and Canadian* any of several other gallinaceous birds, esp the ruffed grouse

Pheidippides or **Phidippides** 5th century BC Athenian athlete, who ran to Sparta to seek help against the Persians before the Battle of Marathon (490 BC)

phenol 1 a white crystalline soluble poisonous acidic derivative of benzene, used as an antiseptic and disinfectant and in the manufacture of resins, nylon, dyes, explosives, and pharmaceuticals; hydroxybenzene. Formula: C_6H_5OH 2 *Chem* any of a class of weakly acidic organic compounds whose molecules contain one or more hydroxyl groups bound directly to a carbon atom in an aromatic ring

phenomenal *Philosophy* known or perceived by the senses rather than the mind

phenomenalism *Philosophy* the doctrine that statements about physical objects and the external world can be analysed in terms of possible or actual experiences, and that entities, such as physical objects, are only mental constructions out of phenomenal appearances

phenomenon *Philosophy* **a** the object of perception, experience, etc. **b** (in the writings of Kant) a thing as it appears and is interpreted in perception and reflection, as distinguished from its real nature as a thing-in-itself

phenotype the physical and biochemical characteristics of an organism as determined by the interaction of its genetic constitution and the environment

phenyl of, containing, or consisting of the monovalent group C_6H_5, derived from benzene

Phidias 5th century BC, Greek sculptor, regarded as one of the greatest of sculptors. He executed the sculptures of the Parthenon and the colossal statue of Zeus at Olympia, one of the Seven Wonders of the World: neither survives in the original

Philadelphia a city and port in SE Pennsylvania, at the confluence of the Delaware and Schuylkill Rivers: the fourth largest city in the US; founded by Quakers in 1682; cultural and financial centre of the American colonies and the federal capital (1790–1800); scene of the Continental Congresses (1774–83) and the signing of the Declaration of Independence (1776). Pop: 1 479 339 (2003 est)

philadelphus any shrub of the N temperate genus *Philadelphus*, cultivated for their strongly scented showy flowers: family *Hydrangeaceae*

Philae an island in Upper Egypt, in the Nile north of the Aswan Dam: of religious importance in ancient times; almost submerged since the raising of the level of the dam

philately the collection and study of postage stamps and all related material concerned with postal history
▷www.philately.com

Philby 1 **Harold Adrian Russell**, known as *Kim*. 1912–88, English double agent; defected to the Soviet Union (1963) 2 his father, **H(arry) Saint John (Bridger)**. 1885–1960, British explorer, civil servant, and Arabist

Philemon *New Testament* 1 a Christian of Colossae whose escaped slave came to meet Paul 2 the book (in full **The Epistle of Paul the Apostle to Philemon**), asking

Philemon to forgive the slave for escaping

philharmonic 1 fond of music **2** denoting an orchestra, choir, society, etc, devoted to the performance, appreciation, and study of music **3** a specific philharmonic choir, orchestra, or society

Philip 1 *New Testament* **a b** one of the seven deacons appointed by the early Church **c** one of the sons of Herod the Great, who was ruler of part of former Judaea (4 BC–34 AD) (Luke 3:1) **2 King,** American Indian name *Metacomet.* died 1676, American Indian chief, the son of Massasoit. He waged King Philip's War against the colonists of New England (1675–76) and was killed in battle

Philip II 1 382–336 BC, king of Macedonia (359–336); the father of Alexander the Great **2** known as *Philip Augustus.* 1165–1223, Capetian king of France (1180–1223); set out on the Third Crusade with Richard I of England (1190) **3** 1527–98, king of Spain (1556–98) and, as Philip I, king of Portugal (1580–98); the husband of Mary I of England (1554–58). He championed the Counter-Reformation, sending the Armada against England (1588)

Philip IV known as *Philip the Fair.* 1268–1314, king of France (1285–1314): he challenged the power of the papacy, obtaining the elevation of Clement V as pope residing at Avignon (the beginning of the Babylonian captivity of the papacy)

Philippi an ancient city in NE Macedonia: scene of the victory of Antony and Octavian over Brutus and Cassius (42 BC)

philippic a bitter or impassioned speech of denunciation; invective

Philippines Republic of the a republic in SE Asia, occupying an archipelago of about 7100 islands (including Luzon, Mindanao, Samar, and Negros): became a Spanish colony in 1571 but ceded to the US in 1898 after the Spanish-American War; gained independence in 1946. The islands are generally mountainous and volcanic. Official languages: Filipino, based on Tagalog, and English. Religion: Roman Catholic majority. Currency: peso. Capital: Manila. Pop: 81 408 000 (2004 est). Area: 300 076 sq km (115 860 sq miles)

Philippine Sea part of the NW Pacific Ocean, east and north of the Philippines

Philip V 1683–1746, king of Spain (1700–46) and founder of the Bourbon dynasty in Spain. His accession began the War of Spanish Succession (1701–13)

Philip VI 1293–1350, first Valois king of France (1328–50). Edward III of England claimed his throne, which with other disputes led to the beginning of the Hundred Years' War (1337)

Philip the Good 1396–1467, duke of Burgundy (1419–67), under whose rule Burgundy was one of the most powerful states in Europe

Philistia an ancient country on the coast of SW Palestine

Philistine a member of the non-Semitic people who inhabited ancient Philistia

Phillip Arthur 1738–1814, English naval commander; captain general of the First Fleet, which carried convicts from Portsmouth to Sydney Cove, Australia, where he founded New South Wales

Philo Judaeus ?20 BC–?50 AD, Jewish philosopher, born in Alexandria. He sought to reconcile Judaism with Greek philosophy

philology 1 the scientific analysis of written records and literary texts **2** (no longer in scholarly use) the study of literature in general
▷www.britac.ac.uk/portal/

philosopher 1 a student, teacher, or devotee of philosophy **2** (formerly) an alchemist or devotee of occult science

philosophical *or* **philosophic** of or relating to philosophy or philosophers

philosophy 1 the academic discipline concerned with making explicit the nature and significance of ordinary and scientific beliefs and investigating the intelligibility of concepts by means of rational argument concerning their presuppositions, implications, and interrelationships; in particular, the rational investigation of the nature and structure of reality (metaphysics), the resources and limits of knowledge (epistemology), the principles and import of moral judgment (ethics), and the relationship between language and reality (semantics) **2** the particular doctrines relating to these issues of some specific individual or school **3** the critical study of the basic principles and concepts of a discipline **4** *Archaic or literary* the investigation of natural phenomena, esp alchemy, astrology, and astronomy
▷http://users.ox.ac.uk/~worc0337/
   phil_index.html
▷www.philosophypages.com
▷www.utm.edu/research/iep/
▷http://n-e-x-u-s.com/philosophy/

Phiz real name *Hablot Knight Browne.* 1815–82, English painter, noted for his illustrations for Dickens' novels

phlebitis inflammation of a vein

phlegm 1 the viscid mucus secreted by the walls of the respiratory tract **2** *Archaic* one of the four bodily humours

phloem tissue in higher plants that conducts synthesized food substances to all parts of the plant

phlox any polemoniaceous plant of the chiefly North American genus *Phlox:* cultivated for their clusters of white, red, or purple flowers

Phnom Penh *or* **Pnom Penh** the capital of Cambodia, a port in the south at the confluence of the Mekong and Tonle Sap Rivers: capital of the country since 1865; university (1960). Pop: 1 174 000 (2005 est)

phobia *Psychiatry* an abnormal intense and irrational fear of a given situation, organism, or object

Phocaea an ancient port in Asia Minor, the northernmost of Ionian cities on the W coast of Asia Minor: an important maritime state (about 1000–600 BC)

Phocis an ancient district of central Greece, on the Gulf of Corinth: site of the Delphic oracle

Phoenicia an ancient maritime country extending from the Mediterranean Sea to the Lebanon Mountains, now occupied by the coastal regions of Lebanon and parts of Syria and Israel: consisted of a group of city-states, at their height between about 1200 and 1000 BC, that were leading traders of the ancient world

Phoenician 1 a member of an ancient Semitic people of

NW Syria who dominated the trade of the ancient world in the first millennium BC and founded colonies throughout the Mediterranean **2** the extinct language of this people, belonging to the Canaanitic branch of the Semitic subfamily of the Afro-Asiatic family
▷www.fordham.edu/halsall/ancient/ 43ophoenicia.html

phoenix *or US* **phenix** a legendary Arabian bird said to set fire to itself and rise anew from the ashes every 500 years

Phoenix a city in central Arizona, capital city of the state, on the Salt River. Pop: 1 388 416 (2003 est)

Phomvihane Kaysone 1920–92, Laotian Communist statesman; prime minister of Laos (1975–91); president (1991–92)

phonograph 1 an early form of gramophone capable of recording and reproducing sound on wax cylinders **2** *US and Canadian* a device for reproducing the sounds stored on a record: now usually applied to the nearly obsolete type that uses a clockwork motor and acoustic horn

phosgene a colourless easily liquefied poisonous gas, carbonyl chloride, with an odour resembling that of new-mown hay: used in chemical warfare as a lethal choking agent and in the manufacture of pesticides, dyes, and polyurethane resins. Formula: $COCl_2$

phosphate any salt or ester of any phosphoric acid, esp a salt of orthophosphoric acid

phosphor a substance, such as the coating on a cathode-ray tube, capable of emitting light when irradiated with particles or electromagnetic radiation

phosphorescence 1 *Physics* **a** a fluorescence that persists after the bombarding radiation producing it has stopped **b** a fluorescence for which the average lifetime of the excited atoms is greater than 10^{-8} seconds **2** the light emitted in phosphorescence **3** the emission of light during a chemical reaction, such as biolumi-nescence, in which insufficient heat is evolved to cause fluorescence

phosphoric of or containing phosphorus in the pen-tavalent state

phosphorous of or containing phosphorus in the triva-lent state

phosphorus 1 an allotropic nonmetallic element occurring in phosphates and living matter. Ordinary phosphorus is a toxic flammable phosphorescent white solid; the red form is less reactive and nontoxic: used in matches, pesticides, and alloys. The radioisotope **phosphorus-32 (radiophosphorus)**, with a half-life of 14.3 days, is used in radiotherapy and as a tracer. Symbol: P; atomic no.: 15; atomic wt.: 30.973 762; valency: 3 or 5; relative density: 1.82 (white), 2.20 (red); melting pt.: 44.1°C (white); boiling pt.: 280°C (white) **2** a less common name for a **phosphor**

photocell a device in which the photoelectric or photovoltaic effect or photoconductivity is used to produce a current or voltage when exposed to light or other electromagnetic radiation. They are used in exposure meters, burglar alarms, etc.

photoelectric *or* **photoelectrical** of or concerned with electric or electronic effects caused by light or other electromagnetic radiation

Photofit *Trademark* **a** a method of combining photographs of facial features, hair, etc, into a composite picture of a face: formerly used by the police to trace suspects from witnesses' descriptions **b** *(as modifier)*: *a Photofit picture*

photogenic *Biology* producing or emitting light

photograph an image of an object, person, scene, etc, in the form of a print or slide recorded by a camera on photosensitive material

photography 1 the process of recording images on sensitized material by the action of light, X-rays, etc, and the chemical processing of this material to produce a print, slide, or cine film **2** the art, practice, or occupation of taking and printing photographs, making cine films, etc.
▷www.photolinks.net
▷www.nyip.com

photolithography *Electronics* a process used in the manufacture of semiconductor devices, thin-film circuits, optical devices, and printed circuits in which a particular pattern is transferred from a photograph onto a substrate, producing a pattern that acts as a mask during an etching or diffusion process

photometer an instrument used in photometry, usually one that compares the illumination produced by a particular light source with that produced by a standard source

photometry 1 the measurement of the intensity of light **2** the branch of physics concerned with such measurements

photomontage 1 the technique of producing a composite picture by combining several photographs: used esp in advertising **2** the composite picture so produced

photon a quantum of electromagnetic radiation, regarded as a particle with zero rest mass and charge, unit spin, and energy equal to the product of the frequency of the radiation and the Planck constant

photosensitive sensitive to electromagnetic radiation, esp light

photosynthesis (in plants) the synthesis of organic compounds from carbon dioxide and water (with the release of oxygen) using light energy absorbed by chlorophyll

phototropism 1 the growth response of plant parts to the stimulus of light, producing a bending towards the light source **2** the response of animals to light

phrase 1 *Music* a small group of notes forming a coherent unit of melody **2** (in choreography) a short sequence of dance movements

phrasing *Music* the division of a melodic line, part, etc, into musical phrases

phrenology (formerly) the branch of science concerned with localization of function in the human brain, esp determination of the strength of the faculties by the shape and size of the skull overlying the parts of the brain thought to be responsible for them

Phrygia an ancient country of W central Asia Minor

Phryne real name *Muesarete*. 4th century BC, Greek courtesan; lover of Praxiteles and model for Apelles' painting *Aphrodite Rising from the Waves*

Phuket 1 an island and province of S Thailand, in the Andaman Sea: mainly flat; suffered badly in the Indian

Ocean tsunami of December 2004. Area: 534 sq km (206 sq miles) **2** the chief town of the island of Phuket; a popular tourist resort

Phyfe *or* **Fife** Duncan ?1768–1854, US cabinet-maker, born in Scotland

phylactery *Judaism* either of the pair of blackened square cases containing parchments inscribed with biblical passages, bound by leather thongs to the head and left arm, and worn by Jewish men during weekday morning prayers

phylum a major taxonomic division of living organisms that contain one or more classes. An example is the phylum *Arthropoda* (insects, crustaceans, arachnids, etc, and myriapods)

physical 1 of or concerned with matter and energy **2** of or relating to physics

physical education training and practice in sports, gymnastics, etc, as in schools and colleges

physical geography the branch of geography that deals with the natural features of the earth's surface

physical science any of the sciences concerned with nonliving matter, energy, and the physical properties of the universe, such as physics, chemistry, astronomy, and geology

physician 1 a person legally qualified to practise medicine, esp one specializing in areas of treatment other than surgery; doctor of medicine **2** *Archaic* any person who treats diseases; healer

physicist a person versed in or studying physics

physics 1 the branch of science concerned with the properties of matter and energy and the relationships between them. It is based on mathematics and traditionally includes mechanics, optics, electricity and magnetism, acoustics, and heat. Modern physics, based on quantum theory, includes atomic, nuclear, particle, and solid-state studies. It can also embrace applied fields such as geophysics and meteorology **2** physical properties of behaviour **3** *Archaic* natural science or natural philosophy

▷www.physlink.com
▷www.physicsweb.org
▷www.vlib.org/Physics.html

physiology 1 the branch of science concerned with the functioning of organisms **2** the processes and functions of all or part of an organism

▷www.physoc.org/links/

physiotherapy the therapeutic use of physical agents or means, such as massage, exercises, etc.

pi 1 the 16th letter in the Greek alphabet (Π, π), a consonant, transliterated as *p* **2** *Maths* a transcendental number, fundamental to mathematics, that is the ratio of the circumference of a circle to its diameter. Approximate value: 3.141 592...; symbol: π

Piacenza a town in N Italy, in Emilia-Romagna on the River Po. Pop: 95 594 (2001)

Piaf Edith, real name *Edith Giovanna Gassion*, known as *the Little Sparrow*, 1915–63, French singer

Piaget Jean 1896–1980, Swiss psychologist, noted for his work on the development of the cognitive functions in children

pianissimo *Music* (to be performed) very quietly.

piano¹ a musical stringed instrument resembling a

harp set in a vertical or horizontal frame, played by depressing keys that cause hammers to strike the strings and produce audible vibrations

piano² *Music* (to be performed) softly.

Piano Renzo born 1937, Italian architect; buildings include the Pompidou Centre, Paris (1977; with Richard Rogers) and the Potsdamer Platz redevelopment, Berlin (1998)

piano accordion an accordion in which the right hand plays a piano-like keyboard

Pianola *Trademark* a type of mechanical piano in which the keys are depressed by air pressure from bellows, this air flow being regulated by perforations in a paper roll

Piave a river in NE Italy, rising near the border with Austria and flowing south and southeast to the Adriatic: the main line of Italian defence during World War I. Length: 220 km (137 miles)

piazza 1 a large open square in an Italian town **2** *Chiefly Brit* a covered passageway or gallery

pibroch 1 a form of music for Scottish bagpipes, consisting of a theme and variations **2** a piece of such music

pica *Pathol* an abnormal craving to ingest substances such as clay, dirt, or hair, sometimes occurring during pregnancy, in persons with chlorosis, etc.

Picabia Francis 1879–1953, French painter, designer, and writer, associated with the cubist, Dadaist, and surrealist movements

picador *Bullfighting* a horseman who pricks the bull with a lance in the early stages of a fight to goad and weaken it

Picard Jean 1620–82, French astronomer. He was the first to make a precise measurement of a longitude line, enabling him to estimate the earth's radius

Picardy a region of N France: mostly low-lying; scene of heavy fighting in World War I

picaresque of or relating to a type of fiction in which the hero, a rogue, goes through a series of episodic adventures. It originated in Spain in the 16th century

Picasso Pablo 1881–1973, Spanish painter and sculptor, resident in France: a highly influential figure in 20th-century art and a founder, with Braque, of cubism. A prolific artist, his works include *The Dwarf Dancer* (1901), belonging to his blue period; the first cubist painting *Les Demoiselles d'Avignon* (1907); *Three Dancers* (1925), which appeared in the first surrealist exhibition; and *Guernica* (1937), inspired by an event in the Spanish Civil War

picayune *US and Canadian, informal* **1** the half real, an old Spanish-American coin **2** *US* any coin of little value, esp a five-cent piece

Piccadilly one of the main streets of London, running from Piccadilly Circus to Hyde Park Corner

Piccard 1 Auguste 1884–1962, Swiss physicist, whose study of cosmic rays led to his pioneer balloon ascents in the stratosphere (1931–32) **2** his twin brother, Jean Félix 1884–1963, US chemist and aeronautical engineer, born in Switzerland, noted for his balloon ascent into the stratosphere (1934)

piccolo a woodwind instrument, the smallest member of the flute family, lying an octave above that of the flute

pick¹ 1 a tool with a handle carrying a long steel head

curved and tapering to a point at one or both ends, used for loosening soil, breaking rocks, etc. **2** any of various tools used for picking, such as an ice pick or toothpick **3** a plectrum

pick² (in weaving) **1** one casting of a shuttle **2** a weft or filling thread

pickaxe or US **pickax** a large pick or mattock

Pickering 1 Edward Charles 1846–1919, US astronomer, who invented the meridian photometer **2** his brother, William Henry 1858–1938, US astronomer, who discovered Phoebe, the ninth satellite of Saturn, and predicted (1919) the existence and position of Pluto

Pickford Mary, real name *Gladys Mary Smith*. 1893–1979, US actress in silent films, born in Canada

pick-up 1 another name for **cartridge 2** a small truck with an open body and low sides, used for light deliveries

Pico della Mirandola Count Giovanni 1463–94, Italian Platonist philosopher. His attempt to reconcile the ideas of classical, Christian, and Arabic writers in a collection of 900 theses, prefaced by his *Oration on the Dignity of Man* (1486), was condemned by the pope

Pict a member of any of the peoples who lived in Britain north of the Forth and Clyde in the first to the fourth centuries AD: later applied chiefly to the inhabitants of NE Scotland. Throughout Roman times the Picts carried out border raids

picture window a large window having a single pane of glass, usually placed so that it overlooks a view

pidgin English a pidgin in which one of the languages involved is English

pie¹ a very small former Indian coin worth one third of a pice

pie² or **pye** *History* a book for finding the Church service for any particular day

piebald 1 marked or spotted in two different colours, esp black and white **2** a black-and-white pied horse

piece 1 a length by which a commodity is sold, esp cloth, wallpaper, etc. **2** a literary, musical, or artistic composition **3** a coin having a value as specified **4** a small object, often individually shaped and designed, used in playing certain games, esp board games **5** any chessman other than a pawn **6** *Austral and NZ* fragments of fleece wool

piece of eight a former Spanish coin worth eight reals; peso

piecework work paid for according to the quantity produced

pied having markings of two or more colours

Piedmont 1 a region of NW Italy: consists of the upper Po Valley; mainly agricultural. Chief town: Turin. Pop: 4 231 334 (2003 est). Area: 25 399 sq km (9807 sq miles) **2** a low plateau of the eastern US, between the coastal plain and the Appalachian Mountains

Pienaar (Jacobus) Francois born 1967, South African Rugby Union footballer; captain of the South African team that won the Rugby World Cup in 1995

pier 1 a structure with a deck that is built out over water, and used as a landing place, promenade, etc. **2** a pillar that bears heavy loads, esp one of rectangular cross section **3** the part of a wall between two adjacent openings **4** another name for **buttress**

Pierce Franklin 1804–69, US statesman; 14th president of the US (1853–57)

Pieria a region of ancient Macedonia, west of the Gulf of Salonika: site of the Pierian Spring

Piero della Francesca ?1420–92, Italian painter, noted particularly for his frescoes of the *Legend of the True Cross* in San Francesco, Arezzo

Piero di Cosimo 1462–1521, Italian painter, noted for his mythological works

Pierre a city in central South Dakota, capital of the state, on the Missouri River. Pop: 13 939 (2003 est)

Pierrot a male character from French pantomime with a whitened face, white costume, and pointed hat

Pietermaritzburg a city in E South Africa, the capital of KwaZulu/Natal: founded in 1839 by the Boers: gateway to Natal's mountain resorts. Pop: 223 519 (2001)

pietism 1 a less common word for **piety 2** excessive, exaggerated, or affected piety or saintliness

Pietro da Cortona real name *Pietro Berrettini*. 1596–1669, Italian baroque painter and architect

piety dutiful devotion to God and observance of religious principles

piezoelectric effect or **piezoelectricity** *Physics* **a** the production of electricity or electric polarity by applying a mechanical stress to certain crystals **b** the converse effect in which stress is produced in a crystal as a result of an applied potential difference

pig 1 any artiodactyl mammal of the African and Eurasian family *Suidae*, esp *Sus scrofa* (**domestic pig**), typically having a long head with a movable snout, a thick bristle-covered skin, and, in wild species, long curved tusks **2 a** a mass of metal, such as iron, copper, or lead, cast into a simple shape for ease of storing or transportation **b** a mould in which such a mass of metal is formed **3** an automated device propelled through a duct or pipeline to clear impediments or check for faults, leaks, etc.

pigeon any of numerous birds of the family *Columbidae*, having a heavy body, small head, short legs, and long pointed wings: order *Columbiformes*

pigeonhole a hole or recess in a dovecote for pigeons to nest in

pigeon-toed having the toes turned inwards

Piggott Lester (Keith). born 1935, English flat-racing jockey: he won the Derby nine times

piggy 1 a child's word for a pig, esp a piglet **2 piggy in the middle a** a children's game in which one player attempts to retrieve a ball thrown over him or her by at least two other players **b** a situation in which a person or group is caught up in a disagreement between other people or groups

piggyback or **pickaback 1** a ride on the back and shoulders of another person **2** *Med* of or relating to a type of heart transplant in which the transplanted heart functions in conjunction with the patient's own heart

pig iron crude iron produced in a blast furnace and poured into moulds in preparation for making wrought iron, steels, alloys, etc.

Pig Island *NZ, informal* New Zealand

piglet a young pig

pigment a substance occurring in plant or animal tissue and producing a characteristic colour, such as chlorophyll in green plants and haemoglobin in red blood

pigmentation 1 coloration in plants, animals, or man caused by the presence of pigments 2 the deposition of pigment in animals, plants, or man

pigskin 1 leather made of this skin 2 *US and Canadian, informal* a football 3 made of pigskin

pigtail a twisted roll of tobacco

pike¹ 1 any of several large predatory freshwater teleost fishes of the genus *Esox*, esp E. *lucius* (**northern pike**), having a broad flat snout, strong teeth, and an elongated body covered with small scales: family *Esocidae* 2 any of various similar fishes

pike² *Northern English, dialect* a pointed or conical hill

pike³ *or* **piked** (of the body position of a diver) bent at the hips but with the legs straight

piker *Slang Austral* a wild bullock

Pikes Peak a mountain in central Colorado, in the Rockies. Height: 4300 m (14 109 ft)

pilaster a shallow rectangular column attached to the face of a wall

Pilate Pontius . Roman procurator of Judaea (?26–?36 AD), who ordered the crucifixion of Jesus, allegedly against his better judgment

Pilatus a mountain in central Switzerland, in Unterwalden canton: derives its name from the legend that the body of Pontius Pilate lay in a former lake on the mountain. Height: 2122 m (6962 ft)

pilchard 1 a European food fish, *Sardina* (or *Clupea*) *pilchardus*, with a rounded body covered with large scales: family *Clupeidae* (herrings) 2 a related fish, *Sardinops neopilchardus*, of S Australian waters

Pilcomayo a river in S central South America, rising in W central Bolivia and flowing southeast, forming the border between Argentina and Paraguay, to the Paraguay River at Asunción. Length: about 1600 km (1000 miles)

pile¹ 1 *Physics* a structure of uranium and a moderator used for producing atomic energy; nuclear reactor 2 *Metallurgy* an arrangement of wrought-iron bars that are to be heated and worked into a single bar 3 the point of an arrow

pile² a long column of timber, concrete, or steel that is driven into the ground to provide a foundation for a vertical load (a bearing pile) or a group of such columns to resist a horizontal load from earth or water pressure (a sheet pile)

pile³ 1 *Textiles* a the yarns in a fabric that stand up or out from the weave, as in carpeting, velvet, etc. b one of these yarns 2 soft fine hair, fur, wool, etc.

pile-driver a machine that drives piles into the ground either by repeatedly allowing a heavy weight to fall on the head of the pile or by using a steam hammer

pill 1 a small spherical or ovoid mass of a medicinal substance, intended to be swallowed whole 2 **the** *Informal* an oral contraceptive

pillar 1 an upright structure of stone, brick, metal, etc, that supports a superstructure or is used for ornamentation 2 a tall, slender, usually sheer rock column, forming a separate top

pillory a wooden framework into which offenders were formerly locked by the neck and wrists and exposed to public abuse and ridicule

pilot 1 a a person who is qualified to operate an aircraft or spacecraft in flight b (*as modifier*): *pilot error* 2 a a person who is qualified to steer or guide a ship into or out of a port, river mouth, etc. b (*as modifier*): *a pilot ship* 3 a person who steers a ship 4 *Machinery* a guide, often consisting of a tongue or dowel, used to assist in joining two mating parts together 5 *Machinery* a plug gauge for measuring an internal diameter 6 *Films* a colour test strip accompanying black-and-white rushes from colour originals

pilot light 1 a small auxiliary flame that ignites the main burner of a gas appliance when the control valve opens 2 a small electric light used as an indicator

pimiento a Spanish pepper, *Capsicum annuum*, with a red fruit used raw in salads, cooked as a vegetable, and as a stuffing for green olives

pimpernel 1 any of several plants of the primulaceous genus *Anagallis*, such as the scarlet pimpernel, typically having small star-shaped flowers 2 any of several similar and related plants, such as *Lysimachia nemorum* (**yellow pimpernel**)

pimple 1 a small round usually inflamed swelling of the skin 2 any of the bumps on the surface of a table tennis bat

pin 1 short for **cotter pin** 2 (in various bowling games) a usually club-shaped wooden object set up in groups as a target 3 *Nautical* a the axle of a sheave b the sliding closure for a shackle 4 *Music* a metal tuning peg on a piano, the end of which is inserted into a detachable key by means of which it is turned 5 *Surgery* a metal rod, esp of stainless steel, for holding together adjacent ends of fractured bones during healing 6 *Chess* a position in which a piece is pinned against a more valuable piece or the king 7 *Golf* the flagpole marking the hole on a green 8 a the cylindrical part of a key that enters a lock b the cylindrical part of a lock where this part of the key fits 9 *Wrestling* a position in which a person is held tight or immobile, esp with both shoulders touching the ground 10 (in Britain) a miniature beer cask containing 4½ gallons

pinball a game in which the player shoots a small ball through several hazards on a table, electrically operated machine, etc. b (*as modifier*): *a pinball machine*

pince-nez eyeglasses that are held in place only by means of a clip over the bridge of the nose

pinch 1 the quantity of a substance, such as salt, that can be taken between a thumb and finger 2 a very small quantity

Pinckney 1 Charles 1757–1824, US statesman, who was a leading member of the convention that framed the US Constitution (1787) 2 his cousin, **Charles Cotesworth** 1746–1825, US soldier, statesman, and diplomat, who also served at the Constitutional Convention 3 his brother, **Thomas** 1750–1828, US soldier and politician. He was US minister to Britain (1792–96) and special envoy to Spain (1795–96)

Pincus Gregory Goodwin 1903–67, US physiologist, whose work on steroid hormones led to the development of the first contraceptive pill

Pindar ?518–?438 BC, Greek lyric poet, noted for his *Epinikia*, odes commemorating victories in the Greek games

Pindus a mountain range in central Greece between Epirus and Thessaly. Highest peak: Mount Smólikas, 2633 m (8639 ft)

pine 1 any evergreen resinous coniferous tree of the genus *Pinus*, of the N hemisphere, with long needle-shaped leaves and brown cones: family *Pinaceae* 2 any other tree or shrub of the family *Pinaceae* 3 the wood of any of these trees

Pine Courtney born 1964, British jazz saxophonist

pineal gland *or* **body** a pea-sized organ in the brain, situated beneath the posterior part of the corpus callosum, that secretes melatonin into the bloodstream

pineapple 1 a tropical American bromeliaceous plant, *Ananas comosus*, cultivated in the tropics for its large fleshy edible fruit 2 the fruit of this plant, consisting of an inflorescence clustered around a fleshy axis and surmounted by a tuft of leaves

pine cone the seed-producing structure of a pine tree

pine marten a marten, *Martes martes*, of N European and Asian coniferous woods, having dark brown fur with a creamy-yellow patch on the throat

Pinero Sir Arthur Wing 1855–1934, English dramatist. His works include the farce *Dandy Dick* (1887) and the problem play *The Second Mrs Tanqueray* (1893)

ping *Computing* a system for testing whether internet systems are responding and how long in milliseconds it takes them to respond

pinhole *Archery* the exact centre of an archery target, in the middle of the gold zone

pinion¹ 1 *Chiefly poetic* a bird's wing 2 the part of a bird's wing including the flight feathers

pinion² a cogwheel that engages with a larger wheel or rack, which it drives or by which it is driven

pink¹ 1 any of a group of colours with a reddish hue that are of low to moderate saturation and can usually reflect or transmit a large amount of light; a pale reddish tint 2 pink cloth or clothing 3 of the colour pink 4 *Brit, informal* left-wing 5 *US, derogatory* **a** sympathetic to or influenced by Communism **b** leftist or radical, esp half-heartedly 6 (of a huntsman's coat) scarlet or red

pink² a sailing vessel with a narrow overhanging transom

pink 1 any of various Old World plants of the caryophyllaceous genus *Dianthus*, such as *D. plumarius* (**garden pink**), cultivated for their fragrant flowers 2 any of various plants of other genera, such as the moss pink 3 the flower of any of these plants

Pinkerton Allan 1819–84, US private detective, born in Scotland. He founded the first detective agency in the US (1850) and organized an intelligence system for the Federal States of America (1861)

Pink Floyd British rock group, formed in 1966: originally comprised Syd Barrett (born 1946), Roger Waters (born 1944), Rick Wright (born 1945), and Nick Mason (born 1945); Barrett was replaced by Dave Gilmour (born 1944) in 1968 and Waters left in 1986. Recordings include *The Piper at the Gates of Dawn* (1967), *Dark Side of the Moon* (1973), *Wish You Were Here* (1975), and *The Division Bell* (1994)

pinkie *or* **pinky** *Scot, US, and Canadian* the little finger

pinna 1 any leaflet of a pinnate compound leaf 2 *Zoology* a feather, wing, fin, or similarly shaped part 3 another name for **auricle**

pinnace any of various kinds of ship's tender

pinnacle 1 a towering peak, as of a mountain 2 a slender upright structure in the form of a cone, pyramid, or spire on the top of a buttress, gable, or tower

pinnate *or* **pinnated** 1 like a feather in appearance 2 (of compound leaves) having the leaflets growing opposite each other in pairs on either side of the stem

Pinsk a city in SW Belarus: capital of a principality (13th–14th centuries). Pop: 134 000 (2005 est)

pinstripe (in textiles) **a** a very narrow stripe in fabric or the fabric itself, used esp for men's suits **b** (*as modifier*): *a pinstripe suit*

pint 1 a unit of liquid measure of capacity equal to one eighth of a gallon. 1 Brit pint is equal to 0.568 litre, 1 US pint to 0.473 litre 2 a unit of dry measure of capacity equal to one half of a quart. 1 US dry pint is equal to one sixty-fourth of a US bushel or 0.5506 litre

pinta a tropical infectious skin disease caused by the bacterium *Treponema carateum* and characterized by the formation of papules and loss of pigmentation in circumscribed areas

pintail a greyish-brown duck, *Anas acuta*, with slender pointed wings and a pointed tail

Pinter Harold born 1930, English dramatist. His plays, such as *The Caretaker* (1959), *The Homecoming* (1964), *No Man's Land* (1974), *Moonlight* (1993), and *Celebration* (2000), are noted for their equivocal and halting dialogue

pintle 1 a pin or bolt forming the pivot of a hinge 2 the link bolt, hook, or pin on a vehicle's towing bracket 3 the needle or plunger of the injection valve of an oil engine

pinto *US and Canadian* 1 marked with patches of white; piebald 2 a pinto horse

Pinturicchio *or* **Pintoricchio** real name *Bernardino di Betto*. ?1454–1513, Italian painter of the Umbrian school

pinwheel a cogwheel whose teeth are formed by small pins projecting either axially or radially from the rim of the wheel

pion *or* **pi meson** *Physics* a meson having a positive or negative charge and a rest mass 273.13 times that of the electron, or no charge and a rest mass 264.14 times that of the electron

pioneer *Ecology* the first species of plant or animal to colonize an area of bare ground

pip¹ 1 the seed of a fleshy fruit, such as an apple or pear 2 any of the segments marking the surface of a pineapple 3 a rootstock or flower of the lily of the valley or certain other plants

pip² 1 a short high-pitched sound, a sequence of which can act as a time signal, esp on radio 2 a radar blip 3 **a** a spot or single device, such as a spade, diamond, heart, or club on a playing card **b** any of the spots on dice or dominoes

pip³ a contagious disease of poultry characterized by the secretion of thick mucus in the mouth and throat

pipe¹ 1 a long tube of metal, plastic, etc, used to convey water, oil, gas, etc. 2 **a** an object made in any of various shapes and sizes, consisting of a small bowl with an attached tubular stem, in which tobacco or other substances are smoked **b** (*as modifier*): *a pipe bowl* 3 the amount of tobacco that fills the bowl of a pipe **4** *Zoology, Botany* any of various hollow organs, such as the respiratory passage of certain animals **5 a** any musical instrument whose sound production results from the vibration of an air column in a simple tube **b** any of the tubular devices on an organ, in which air is made to vibrate either directly, as in a flue pipe, or by means of a reed **6** an obsolete three-holed wind instrument, held in the left hand while played and accompanied by the tabor **7 a** a boatswain's pipe **b** the sound it makes **8** *Informal* the respiratory tract or vocal cords **9** *Metallurgy* a conical hole in the head of an ingot, made by escaping gas as the metal cools **10** a vertical cylindrical passage in a volcano through which molten lava is forced during eruption

pipe² a measure of capacity for wine equal to four barrels. 1 pipe is equal to 126 US gallons or 105 Brit gallons

pipeclay a fine white pure clay, used in the manufacture of tobacco pipes and pottery and for whitening leather and similar materials

piped music light popular music prerecorded and played through amplifiers in a shop, restaurant, factory, etc, as background music

pipeline a long pipe, esp underground, used to transport oil, natural gas, etc, over long distances

pipe organ another name for **organ** (the musical instrument)

Piper John 1903–92, British artist. An official war artist in World War II, he is known esp for his watercolours of bombed churches and his stained glass in Coventry Cathedral

pipette a calibrated glass tube drawn to a fine bore at one end, filled by sucking liquid into the bulb, and used to transfer or measure known volumes of liquid

pipi any of various shellfishes, esp *Plebidonax deltoides* of Australia or *Mesodesma novae-zelandiae* of New Zealand

piping *Music* **1** the sound of a pipe or a set of bagpipes **2** the art or technique of playing a pipe or bagpipes

pipistrelle any of numerous small brownish insectivorous bats of the genus *Pipistrellus*, occurring in most parts of the world: family *Vespertilionidae*

pipit any of various songbirds of the genus *Anthus* and related genera, having brownish speckled plumage and a long tail: family *Motacillidae*

pippin **1** any of several varieties of eating apple with a rounded oblate shape **2** the seed of any of these fruits

pique *Piquet* a score of 30 points made by a player from a combination of cards held before play begins and from play while his opponent's score is nil

piquet a card game for two people playing with a reduced pack and scoring points for card combinations and tricks won

piracy **1** *Brit* robbery on the seas within admiralty jurisdiction **2** a felony, such as robbery or hijacking, committed aboard a ship or aircraft

Piraeus *or* **Peiraeus** a port in SE Greece, adjoining Athens: the country's chief port; founded in the 5th century BC as the port of Athens. Pop: 169 622 (1991)

Pirandello Luigi 1867–1936, Italian short-story writer, novelist, and dramatist. His plays include *Right you are (If you think so)* (1917), *Six Characters in Search of an Author* (1921), and *Henry IV* (1922): Nobel prize for literature 1934

Piranesi Giambattista 1720–78, Italian etcher and architect: etchings include *Imaginary Prisons* and *Views of Rome*

piranha *or* **piraña** any of various small freshwater voracious fishes of the genus *Serrasalmus* and related genera, of tropical America, having strong jaws and sharp teeth: family *Characidae* (characins)

pirate **1** a person who commits piracy **2 a** a vessel used by pirates **b** (*as modifier*): *a pirate ship*

pirouette a body spin, esp in dancing, on the toes or the ball of the foot

Pisa a city in Tuscany, NW Italy, near the mouth of the River Arno: flourishing maritime republic (11th–12th centuries), contains a university (1343), a cathedral (1063), and the Leaning Tower (begun in 1174 and about 5 m (17 ft) from perpendicular); tourism. Pop: 89 694 (2001)

Pisanello Antonio ?1395–?1455, Italian painter and medallist; a major exponent of the International Gothic style. He is best known for his portrait medals and drawings of animals

Pisano **1** Andrea , real name *Andrea de Pontedera*. ?1290–1348, Italian sculptor and architect, noted for his bronze reliefs on the door of the baptistry in Florence **2** Giovanni ?1250–?1320, Italian sculptor, who successfully integrated classical and Gothic elements in his sculptures, esp in his pulpit in St Andrea, Pistoia **3** his father, Nicola ?1220–?84, Italian sculptor, who pioneered the classical style and is often regarded as a precursor of the Italian Renaissance: noted esp for his pulpit in the baptistry of Pisa Cathedral

piscatorial *or* **piscatory** **1** of or relating to fish, fishing, or fishermen **2** devoted to fishing

Pisces **1** *Astronomy* a faint extensive zodiacal constellation lying between Aquarius and Aries on the ecliptic **2** *Astrology* **a** the twelfth sign of the zodiac, symbol ♓, having a mutable water classification and ruled by the planets Jupiter and Neptune. The sun is in this sign between about Feb 19 and March 20 **b** a person born when the sun is in this sign **3 a** a taxonomic group that comprises all fishes **b** a taxonomic group that comprises the bony fishes only **4** *Astrology* born under or characteristic of Pisces

pisciculture the rearing and breeding of fish under controlled conditions

piscine of, relating to, or resembling a fish

Pisgah Mount *Old Testament* the mountain slopes to the northeast of the Dead Sea, from one of which, Mount Nebo, Moses viewed Canaan

Pisistratus ?600–527 BC, tyrant of Athens: he established himself in firm control of the city following his defeat of his aristocratic rivals at Pallene (546)

Pissarro Camille 1830–1903, French impressionist painter, esp of landscapes

pistachio **1** an anacardiaceous tree, *Pistacia vera*, of the Mediterranean region and W Asia, with small hard-shelled nuts **2** the nut of this tree, having an edible green kernel **3** of a yellowish-green colour

piste **1** a trail, slope, or course for skiing **2** a rectangular area for fencing bouts

pistil the female reproductive part of a flower, consisting of one or more separate or fused carpels; gynoecium

pistillate of plants **1** having pistils but no anthers **2**

having or producing pistils

Pistoia a city in N Italy, in N Tuscany: scene of the defeat and death of Catiline in 62 BC. Pop: 84 274 (2001)

piston a disc or cylindrical part that slides to and fro in a hollow cylinder. In an internal-combustion engine it is forced to move by the expanding gases in the cylinder head and is attached by a pivoted connecting rod to a crankshaft or flywheel, thus converting reciprocating motion into rotation

pit 1 **the pit** hell 2 the area that is occupied by the orchestra in a theatre, located in front of the stage 3 *Anatomy* a a small natural depression on the surface of a body, organ, structure, or part; fossa b the floor of any natural bodily cavity 4 *Pathol* a small indented scar at the site of a former pustule; pockmark 5 any of various small areas in a plant cell wall that remain unthickened when the rest of the cell becomes lignified, esp the vascular tissue 6 a working area at the side of a motor-racing track for servicing or refuelling vehicles 7 a rowdy card game in which players bid for commodities 8 an area of sand or other soft material at the end of a long-jump approach, behind the bar of a pole vault, etc, on which an athlete may land safely 9 the ground floor of the auditorium of a theatre 10 another word for pitfall

pit *Chiefly US and Canadian* the stone of a cherry, plum, etc.

pit bull terrier a dog resembling the Staffordshire bull terrier but somewhat larger: developed for dog-fighting; it is not recognized by kennel clubs and is regarded as dangerous. It is not allowed in some countries, including the UK

Pitcairn Island an island in the S Pacific: forms with the islands of Ducie, Henderson and Oeno (all uninhabited) a UK Overseas Territory; Pitcairn itself was uninhabited until the landing in 1790 of the mutineers of H.M.S. *Bounty* and their Tahitian companions. Pop: 47 (2004 est). Area: 4.6 sq km (1.75 sq miles)

pitch¹ 1 *Mountaineering* a section of a route between two belay points, sometimes equal to the full length of the rope but often shorter 2 the degree of slope of a roof, esp when expressed as a ratio of height to span 3 the distance between corresponding points on adjacent members of a body of regular form, esp the distance between teeth on a gearwheel or between threads on a screw thread 4 the distance between regularly spaced objects such as rivets, bolts, etc. 5 a the distance a propeller advances in one revolution, assuming no slip b the blade angle of a propeller or rotor 6 *Music* a the auditory property of a note that is conditioned by its frequency relative to other notes b an absolute frequency assigned to a specific note, fixing the relative frequencies of all other notes. The fundamental frequencies of the notes A–G, in accordance with the frequency A = 440 hertz, were internationally standardized and accepted in 1939 7 *Cricket* the rectangular area between the stumps, 22 yards long and 10 feet wide; the wicket 8 *Geology* the inclination of the axis of an anticline or syncline or of a stratum or vein from the horizontal 9 the act or manner of pitching a ball, as in cricket 10 *Chiefly Brit* a vendor's station, esp on a pavement 11 *Golf* an approach shot in which the ball is struck in a high arc

pitch² 1 any of various heavy dark viscid substances obtained as a residue from the distillation of tars 2 any of various similar substances, such as asphalt, occurring as natural deposits 3 any of various similar substances obtained by distilling certain organic substances so that they are incompletely carbonized 4 crude turpentine obtained as sap from pine trees

pitch-black of a deep black colour

pitchblende a blackish mineral that is a type of uraninite and occurs in veins, frequently associated with silver: the principal source of uranium and radium. Formula: UO_2

pitcher¹ *Botany* any of the urn-shaped leaves of the pitcher plant

pitcher² 1 *Baseball* the player on the fielding team who pitches the ball to the batter 2 a granite stone or sett used in paving

pitcher plant any of various insectivorous plants of the genera *Sarracenia*, *Darlingtonia*, *Nepenthes*, and *Cephalotus*, having leaves modified to form pitcher-like organs that attract and trap insects, which are then digested

pitchfork a long-handled fork with two or three long curved tines for lifting, turning, or tossing hay

pitch pine 1 any of various coniferous trees of the genus *Pinus*, esp P. *rigida*, of North America, having red-brown bark and long lustrous light brown cones: valued as a source of turpentine and pitch 2 the wood of any of these trees

pitch pipe a small pipe, esp one having a reed like a harmonica, that sounds a note or notes of standard frequency. It is used for establishing the correct starting note for unaccompanied singing

pitfall a trap in the form of a concealed pit, designed to catch men or wild animals

pith 1 the soft fibrous tissue lining the inside of the rind in fruits such as the orange and grapefruit 2 *Botany* the central core of unspecialized cells surrounded by conducting tissue in stems 3 the soft central part of a bone, feather, etc.

Pitman Sir Isaac 1813–97, English inventor of a system of phonetic shorthand (1837)

piton *Mountaineering* a metal spike that may be driven into a crevice of rock or into ice and used to secure a rope

Pitt 1 William, known as *Pitt the Elder*, 1st Earl of Chatham. 1708–78, British statesman. He was first minister (1756–57; 1757–61; 1766–68) and achieved British victory in the Seven Years' War (1756–63) 2 his son William, known as *Pitt the Younger*. 1759–1806, British statesman. As prime minister (1783–1801; 1804–06), he carried through important fiscal and tariff reforms. From 1793, his attention was focused on the wars with revolutionary and Napoleonic France

Pittsburgh a port in SW Pennsylvania, at the confluence of the Allegheny and Monongahela Rivers, which form the Ohio River: settled around Fort Pitt in 1758; developed rapidly with the discovery of iron deposits and one of the world's richest coalfields; the largest river port in the US and an important industrial centre, formerly with large steel mills. Pop: 325 337 (2003 est)

pituitary gland *or* **body** the master endocrine gland, attached by a stalk to the base of the brain. Its two lobes (see **adenohypophysis** and **neurohypophysis**) secrete hormones affecting skeletal growth, development of the sex glands, and the functioning of the other endocrine glands Also called: **hypophysis, hypophysis cerebri**

Piura a city in NW Peru: the oldest colonial city in Peru, founded by Pizarro in 1532; commercial centre of an agricultural district. Pop: 357 000 (2005 est)

Pius II pen name *Aeneas Silvius*, original name *Enea Silvio de' Piccolomini*. 1405–64, Italian ecclesiastic, humanist, poet, and historian; pope (1458–64)

Pius IV original name *Giovanni Angelo de' Medici*. 1499–1565, pope (1559–65). He reconvened the Council of Trent (1562), confirming its final decrees

Pius V Saint original name *Michele Ghislieri*. 1504–72, Italian ecclesiastic; pope (1566–72). He attempted to enforce the reforms decreed by the Council of Trent, excommunicated Elizabeth I of England (1570), and organized the alliance that defeated the Turks at Lepanto (1571). Feast day: 30 April

Pius VII original name *Luigi Barnaba Chiaramonti*. 1740–1823, Italian ecclesiastic; pope (1800–23). He concluded a concordat with Napoleon (1801) and consecrated him as emperor of France (1804), but resisted his annexation of the Papal States (1809)

Pius IX original name *Giovanni Maria Mastai-Ferretti*. 1792–1878, Italian ecclesiastic; pope (1846–78). He refused to recognize the incorporation of Rome and the Papal States in the kingdom of Italy, confining himself to the Vatican after 1870. He decreed the dogma of the Immaculate Conception (1854) and convened the Vatican Council, which laid down the doctrine of papal infallibility (1870)

Pius X Saint original name *Giuseppe Sarto*. 1835–1914, Italian ecclesiastic; pope (1903–14). He condemned Modernism (1907) and initiated a new codification of canon law. Feast day: Aug 21

Pius XI original name *Achille Ratti*. 1857–1939, Italian ecclesiastic; pope (1922–39). He signed the Lateran Treaty (1929), by which the Vatican City was recognized as an independent state. His encyclicals condemned Nazism and Communism

Pius XII original name *Eugenio Pacelli*. 1876–1958, Italian ecclesiastic; pope (1939–58): his attitude towards Nazi German anti-Semitism has been a matter of controversy

pivot 1 a short shaft or pin supporting something that turns; fulcrum **2** the end of a shaft or arbor that terminates in a bearing

pixie *or* **pixy** (in folklore) a fairy or elf

Pizarro Francisco ?1475–1541, Spanish conqueror of Peru. He landed in Peru (1532), murdered the Inca King Atahualpa (1533), and founded Lima as the new capital of Peru (1535). He was murdered by his own followers

pizzicato *Music* **1** (in music for the violin family) to be plucked with the finger **2** the style or technique of playing a normally bowed stringed instrument in this manner

place 1 a geographical point, such as a town, city, etc. **2 a** an open square lined with houses of a similar type in a city or town **b** (*capital when part of a street name*): *Grosvenor Place* **3** *Maths* the relative position of a digit in a number **4** *Horse racing* **a** *Brit* the first, second, or third position at the finish **b** *US and Canadian* the first or usually the second position at the finish **c** (*as modifier*): *a place bet* **5** *Theatre* one of the three unities **6** **another place** *Brit, Parliamentary procedure* **a** (in the House of Commons) the House of Lords **b** (in the House of Lords) the House of Commons **7** **the other place** *Facetious* **a** (at Oxford University) Cambridge University **b** (at Cambridge University) Oxford University

placebo 1 *Med* an inactive substance or other sham form of therapy administered to a patient usually to compare its effects with those of a real drug or treatment, but sometimes for the psychological benefit to the patient through his believing he is receiving treatment **2** *RC Church* a traditional name for the vespers of the office for the dead

place kick *Football* a kick in which the ball is placed in position before it is kicked

placenta 1 the vascular organ formed in the uterus during pregnancy, consisting of both maternal and embryonic tissues and providing oxygen and nutrients for the fetus and transfer of waste products from the fetal to the maternal blood circulation **2** the corresponding organ or part in certain mammals **3** *Botany* **a** the part of the ovary of flowering plants to which the ovules are attached **b** the mass of tissue in nonflowering plants that bears the sporangia or spores

plague 1 any widespread and usually highly contagious disease with a high fatality rate **2** an infectious disease of rodents, esp rats, transmitted to man by the bite of the rat flea (*Xenopsylla cheopis*) **3** See **bubonic plague 4** a pestilence, affliction, or calamity on a large scale, esp when regarded as sent by God

plaice 1 a European flatfish, *Pleuronectes platessa*, having an oval brown body marked with red or orange spots and valued as a food fish: family *Pleuronectidae* **2** *US and Canadian* any of various other fishes of the family *Pleuronectidae*, esp *Hippoglossoides platessoides*

plaid a a crisscross weave or cloth **b** (*as modifier*): *a plaid scarf*
▷www.tartans.scotland.net

Plaid Cymru the Welsh nationalist party

plain 1 (of fabric) without pattern or of simple untwilled weave **2** a level or almost level tract of country, esp an extensive treeless region **3** in billiards **a** the unmarked white ball, as distinguished from the spot balls **b** the player using this ball **4** (in Ireland) short for plain porter (a light porter)

plain sailing *Nautical* sailing in a body of water that is unobstructed; clear sailing

Plains of Abraham a field in E Canada between Quebec City and the St Lawrence River: site of an important British victory (1759) in the Seven Years' War, which cost the French their possession of Canada

plainsong the style of unison unaccompanied vocal music used in the medieval Church, esp in Gregorian chant
▷www.1upinfo.com/encyclopedia/P/plainson.html

plaint 1 *Archaic* a complaint or lamentation **2** *Law* a statement in writing of grounds of complaint made to a court of law and asking for redress of the grievance

plaintiff (formerly) a person who brings a civil action in a court of law

plan 1 a drawing to scale of a horizontal section through a building taken at a given level; a view from above an object or an area in orthographic projection 2 (in perspective drawing) any of several imaginary planes perpendicular to the line of vision and between the eye and object depicted

planchette a heart-shaped board on wheels, on which messages are written under supposed spirit guidance

Planck Max (**Karl Ernst Ludwig**). 1858–1947, German physicist who first formulated the quantum theory (1900): Nobel prize for physics 1918

plane¹ 1 *Maths* a flat surface in which a straight line joining any two of its points lies entirely on that surface 2 a short for **aeroplane** b a wing or supporting surface of an aircraft or hydroplane 3 *Maths* (of a curve, figure, etc) lying entirely in one plane

plane² 1 a tool with an adjustable sharpened steel blade set obliquely in a wooden or iron body, for levelling or smoothing timber surfaces, cutting mouldings or grooves, etc. 2 a flat tool, usually metal, for smoothing the surface of clay or plaster in a mould

planet 1 any of the nine celestial bodies, Mercury, Venus, Earth, Mars, Jupiter, Saturn, Uranus, Neptune, or Pluto, that revolve around the sun in elliptical orbits and are illuminated by light from the sun 2 any other celestial body revolving around a star, illuminated by light from that star 3 *Astrology* any of the planets of the solar system, excluding the earth but including the sun and moon, each thought to rule one or sometimes two signs of the zodiac

planetarium 1 an instrument for simulating the apparent motions of the sun, moon, and planets against a background of stars by projecting images of these bodies onto the inside of a domed ceiling 2 a building in which such an instrument is housed 3 a model of the solar system, sometimes mechanized to show the relative motions of the planets

plane tree *or* **plane** any tree of the genus *Platanus*, having ball-shaped heads of fruits and leaves with pointed lobes: family *Platanaceae*. The hybrid *P.* × *acerifolia* (**London plane**) is frequently planted in towns

plank *Politics* one of the policies in a political party's programme

plankton the organisms inhabiting the surface layer of a sea or lake, consisting of small drifting plants and animals, such as diatoms

planning permission (in Britain) formal permission that must be obtained from a local authority before development or a change of use of land or buildings

plant¹ 1 any living organism that typically synthesizes its food from inorganic substances, possesses cellulose cell walls, responds slowly and often permanently to a stimulus, lacks specialized sense organs and nervous system, and has no powers of locomotion 2 such an organism that is green, terrestrial, and smaller than a shrub or tree; a herb 3 a cutting, seedling, or similar structure, esp when ready for transplantation 4 *Billiards, Snooker* a position in which the cue ball can be made to strike an intermediate which then pockets another ball

plant² 1 a the land, buildings, and equipment used in carrying on an industrial, business, or other undertaking or service b (*as modifier*): *plant costs* 2 a factory or workshop 3 mobile mechanical equipment for construction, road-making, etc.

Plantagenet a line of English kings, ruling from the ascent of Henry II (1154) to the death of Richard III (1485)

plantain¹ any of various N temperate plants of the genus *Plantago*, esp *P. major* (**great plantain**), which has a rosette of broad leaves and a slender spike of small greenish flowers: family *Plantaginaceae*

plantain² 1 a large tropical musaceous plant, *Musa paradisiaca* 2 the green-skinned banana-like fruit of this plant, eaten as a staple food in many tropical regions

plantation 1 an estate, esp in tropical countries, where cash crops such as rubber, oil palm, etc, are grown on a large scale 2 a group of cultivated trees or plants 3 (formerly) a colony or group of settlers

plantigrade 1 walking with the entire sole of the foot touching the ground, as, for example, man and bears 2 a plantigrade animal

plaque *Pathol* any small abnormal patch on or within the body, such as the typical lesion of psoriasis

plasma *or* **plasm** 1 the clear yellowish fluid portion of blood or lymph in which the red blood cells, white blood cells, and platelets are suspended 2 a former name for **protoplasm** 3 *Physics* a a hot ionized material consisting of nuclei and electrons. It is sometimes regarded as a fourth state of matter and is the material present in the sun, most stars, and fusion reactors b the ionized gas in an electric discharge or spark, containing positive ions and electrons and a small number of negative ions together with un-ionized material 4 a green slightly translucent variety of chalcedony, used as a gemstone

Plassey a village in NE India, in W Bengal: scene of Clive's victory (1757) over Siraj-ud-daula, which established British supremacy over India

plastic 1 any one of a large number of synthetic usually organic materials that have a polymeric structure and can be moulded when soft and then set, esp such a material in a finished state containing plasticizer, stabilizer, filler, pigments, etc. Plastics are classified as thermosetting (such as Bakelite) or thermoplastic (such as PVC) and are used in the manufacture of many articles and in coatings, artificial fibres, etc. 2 *Fine arts* a of or relating to moulding or modelling b produced or apparently produced by moulding 3 *Biology* of or relating to any formative process; able to change, develop, or grow

Plasticine *Trademark* a soft coloured material used, esp by children, for modelling

plastic surgery the branch of surgery concerned with therapeutic or cosmetic repair or re-formation of missing, injured, or malformed tissues or parts

Plata Río de la an estuary on the SE coast of South America, between Argentina and Uruguay, formed by the Uruguay and Paraná Rivers. Length: 275 km (171 miles). Width: (at its mouth) 225 km (140 miles)

Plataea an ancient city in S Boeotia, traditionally an ally of Athens: scene of the defeat of a great Persian army by the Greeks in 479 BC

plate 1 any shallow or flat receptacle, esp for receiving a collection in church 2 flat metal of uniform thickness obtained by rolling, usually having a thickness greater than about three millimetres 3 a thin coating of metal usually on another metal, as produced by electrodeposition, chemical action, etc. 4 *Photog* a a sheet of glass, or sometimes metal, coated with photographic emulsion on which an image can be formed by exposure to light b (*as modifier*): *a plate camera* 5 an orthodontic device, esp one used for straightening children's teeth 6 an informal word for **denture** 7 *Anatomy* any flat platelike structure or part 8 any of the rigid layers of the earth's lithosphere of which there are believed to be at least 15 9 *Electronics* a *Chiefly US* the anode in an electronic valve b an electrode in an accumulator or capacitor 10 a light horseshoe for flat racing 11 *RC Church* a flat plate held under the chin of a communicant in order to catch any fragments of the consecrated Host 12 *Archaic* a coin, esp one made of silver

plateau a wide mainly level area of elevated land

Plateau a state of central Nigeria, formed in 1976 from part of Benue-Plateau State: tin mining. Capital: Jos. Pop. (including Nassarawa state): 3 671 498 (1995 est). Area (including Nassarawa state): 58 030 sq km (22 405 sq miles)

plated 1 a coated with a layer of metal b (*in combination*): *gold-plated* 2 (of a fabric) knitted in two different yarns so that one appears on the face and the other on the back

platelayer *Brit* a workman who lays and maintains railway track

platelet a minute cell occurring in the blood of vertebrates and involved in clotting of the blood

platen the worktable of a machine tool, esp one that is slotted to enable T-bolts to be used

platform 1 a raised floor or other horizontal surface, such as a stage for speakers 2 a raised area at a railway station, from which passengers have access to the trains 3 the declared principles, aims, etc, of a political party, an organization, or an individual 4 a level raised area of ground 5 a specific type of computer hardware or computer operating system

platform ticket a ticket for admission to railway platforms but not for travel

Plath Sylvia 1932–63, US poet living in England. She wrote two volumes of verse, *The Colossus* (1960) and *Ariel* (1965), and a novel, *The Bell Jar* (1963): she was married to Ted Hughes

plating 1 a coating or layer of material, esp metal 2 a layer or covering of metal plates

Platini Michel born 1955, French football player and sports administrator

platinum 1 a ductile malleable silvery-white metallic element, very resistant to heat and chemicals. It occurs free and in association with other platinum metals, esp in osmiridium: used in jewellery, laboratory apparatus, electrical contacts, dentistry, electroplating, and as a catalyst. Symbol: Pt; atomic no.: 78; atomic wt.: 195.08; valency: 1–4; relative density: 21.45; melting pt.: 1769°C; boiling pt.: 3827±100°C 2 a a medium to light grey colour b (*as adjective*): *a platinum carpet*

Plato ?427–?347 BC, Greek philosopher: with his teacher Socrates and his pupil Aristotle, he is regarded as the initiator of western philosophy. His influential theory of ideas, which makes a distinction between objects of sense perception and the universal ideas or forms of which they are an expression, is formulated in such dialogues as *Phaedo, Symposium*, and *The Republic*. Other works include *The Apology* and *Laws*

Platonic of or relating to the Greek philosopher Plato (?427–?347 BC) or his teachings

Platonism 1 the teachings of the Greek philosopher Plato (?427–?347 BC) and his followers, esp the philosophical theory that the meanings of general words are real existing abstract entities (Forms) and that particular objects have properties in common by virtue of their relationship with these Forms 2 the realist doctrine that mathematical entities have real existence and that mathematical truth is independent of human thought

Platte a river system of the central US, formed by the confluence of the **North Platte** and **South Platte** at North Platte, Nebraska: flows generally east to the Missouri River. Length: 499 km (310 miles)

platteland the (in South Africa) the country districts or rural areas

Plauen a city in E central Germany, in Saxony: textile centre. Pop: 70 070 (2003 est)

Plautus Titus Maccius ?254–?184 BC, Roman comic dramatist. His 21 extant works, adapted from Greek plays, esp those by Menander, include *Menaechmi* (the basis of Shakespeare's *The Comedy of Errors*), *Miles Gloriosus, Rudens*, and *Captivi*

play 1 a dramatic composition written for performance by actors on a stage, on television, etc.; drama 2 a the performance of a dramatic composition b (*in combination*): *playreader*

playback 1 the act or process of reproducing a recording, esp on magnetic tape 2 the part of a tape recorder serving to reproduce or used for reproducing recorded material 3 of or relating to the reproduction of signals from a recording

playbill 1 a poster or bill advertising a play 2 the programme of a play

player 1 a person who plays a musical instrument 2 an actor 3 See **record player** 4 the playing mechanism in a Pianola

Player Gary born 1935, South African professional golfer: won the British Open Championship (1959; 1968; 1974) and the US Open Championship (1965)

player piano a mechanical piano; Pianola

playgoer a person who goes to theatre performances, esp frequently

playgroup a regular meeting of small children arranged by their parents or a welfare agency to give them an opportunity of supervised creative play

playhouse a theatre where live dramatic performances are given

playschool an informal nursery group taking preschool children in half-day sessions

playwright a person who writes plays

plaza 1 an open space or square, esp in Spain or a Spanish-speaking country 2 *Chiefly US and Canadian* a a modern complex of shops, buildings, and parking areas b (*capital when part of a name*): *Rockefeller Plaza*

plea a *Law* something alleged or pleaded by or on behalf of a party to legal proceedings in support of his claim or defence **b** *Criminal law* the answer made by an accused to the charge **c** (in Scotland and formerly in England) a suit or action at law

Pleasence Donald 1919–95, British actor. His films include *Dr Crippen* (1962) and *Cul de Sac* (1966)

plebeian 1 of, relating to, or characteristic of the common people, esp those of Rome **2** one of the common people, esp one of the Roman plebs

plebiscite 1 a direct vote by the electorate of a state, region, etc, on some question of usually national importance, such as union with another state or acceptance of a government programme **2** any expression or determination of public opinion on some matter

plectrum any implement for plucking a string, such as a small piece of plastic, wood, etc, used to strum a guitar, or the quill that plucks the string of a harpsichord

pledge 1 *Law* a person who binds himself, as by becoming bail or surety for another **2** **take** *or* **sign the pledge** to make a vow to abstain from alcoholic drink

Pleistocene of, denoting, or formed in the first epoch of the Quaternary period, which lasted for about 1 600 000 years. It was characterized by extensive glaciations of the N hemisphere and the evolutionary development of humans

plenary 1 (of assemblies, councils, etc) attended by all the members **2** a book of the gospels or epistles and homilies read at the Eucharist

plenipotentiary 1 (esp of a diplomatic envoy) invested with or possessing full power or authority **2** conferring full power or authority **3** a person invested with full authority to transact business, esp a diplomat authorized to represent a country

Plenty Bay of a large bay of the Pacific on the NE coast of the North Island, New Zealand

pleonasm *Rhetoric* **1** the use of more words than necessary or an instance of this, such as *a tiny little child* **2** a word or phrase that is superfluous

plethora *Pathol, obsolete* a condition caused by dilation of superficial blood vessels, characterized esp by a reddish face

pleura the thin transparent serous membrane enveloping the lungs and lining the walls of the thoracic cavity

pleurisy inflammation of the pleura, characterized by pain that is aggravated by deep breathing or coughing

Pleven *or* **Plevna** a town in N Bulgaria: taken by Russia from the Turks in 1877 after a siege of 143 days. Pop: 102 000 (2005 est)

plexus any complex network of nerves, blood vessels, or lymphatic vessels

plinth 1 the rectangular slab or block that forms the lowest part of the base of a column, statue, pedestal, or pier **2** the lowest part of the wall of a building that appears above ground level, esp one that is formed of a course of stone or brick **3** a flat block on either side of a doorframe, where the architrave meets the skirting

Pliny 1 known as *Pliny the Elder*. Latin name *Gaius Plinius Secundus*. 23–79 AD, Roman writer, the author of the encyclopedic *Natural History* (77) **2** his nephew, known as *Pliny the Younger*. Latin name *Gaius Plinius Caecilius Secundus*. ?62–?113 AD, Roman writer and administrator, noted for his letters

Pliocene *or* **Pleiocene** of, denoting, or formed in the last epoch of the Tertiary period, which lasted for three million years, during which many modern mammals appeared

Płock a town in central Poland, on the River Vistula: several Polish kings are buried in the cathedral: oil refining, petrochemical works. Pop: 130 000 (2005 est)

plod *Brit, slang* a policeman

Ploeşti a city in SE central Romania: centre of the Romanian petroleum industry. Pop: 204 000 (2005 est)

plonk *Brit, Austral, and NZ, informal* alcoholic drink, usually wine, esp of inferior quality

Plotinus ?205–?270 AD, Roman Neo-Platonist philosopher, born in Egypt

plough *or esp US* **plow 1** an agricultural implement with sharp blades, attached to a horse, tractor, etc., for cutting or turning over the earth **2** any of various similar implements, such as a device for clearing snow **3** a plane with a narrow blade for cutting grooves in wood

Plough the the group of the seven brightest stars in the constellation Ursa Major

Plovdiv a city in S Bulgaria on the Maritsa River: the second largest town in Bulgaria; conquered by Philip II of Macedonia in 341 BC; capital of Roman Thracia; commercial centre of a rich agricultural region. Pop: 339 000 (2005 est)

plover 1 any shore bird of the family *Charadriidae*, typically having a round head, pointed bill, and large pointed wings: order *Charadriiformes* **2** any of similar and related birds, such as the Egyptian plover and the upland plover **3** **green plover** another name for **lapwing**

plug 1 a device having one or more pins to which an electric cable is attached: used to make an electrical connection when inserted into a socket **2** a mass of solidified magma filling the neck of an extinct volcano **3 a** a cake of pressed or twisted tobacco, esp for chewing **b** a small piece of such a cake **4** *Angling* a weighted artificial lure with one or more sets of hooks attached, used in spinning **5** a seedling with its roots encased in potting compost, grown in a tray with compartments for each individual plant

plug in *Computing* a module or piece of software that can be added to a system to provide extra functions or features, esp software that enhances the capabilities of a web browser

plum 1 a small rosaceous tree, *Prunus domestica*, with white flowers and an edible oval fruit that is purple, yellow, or green and contains an oval stone **2** the fruit of this tree **3 a** a dark reddish-purple colour **b** (*as adjective*): *a plum carpet*

plumage the layer of feathers covering the body of a bird

plumber a person who installs and repairs pipes, fixtures, etc, for water, drainage, and gas

plumb line a string with a metal weight at one end that, when suspended, points directly towards the earth's centre of gravity and so is used to determine verticality, the depth of water, etc.

plume 1 *Biology* any feathery part, such as the structure on certain fruits and seeds that aids dispersal by wind **2** *Geology* a rising column of hot, low viscosity material within the earth's mantle, which is believed to be responsible for linear oceanic island chains and flood basalts

plummet a lead plumb used by anglers to determine the depth of water

plunger 1 a rubber suction cup fixed to the end of a rod, used to clear blocked drains **2** a device or part of a machine that has a plunging or thrusting motion; piston

Plunket or **Plunkett** Saint Oliver 1629–81, Irish Roman Catholic churchman and martyr; wrongly executed as a supposed conspirator in the Popish Plot (1678). Feast day: July 11

pluralism 1 the holding by a single person of more than one ecclesiastical benefice or office **2** Philosophy **a** the metaphysical doctrine that reality consists of more than two basic types of substance **b** the metaphysical doctrine that reality consists of independent entities rather than one unchanging whole

plurality 1 Maths a number greater than one **2** US and Canadian the excess of votes or seats won by the winner of an election over the runner-up when no candidate or party has more than 50 per cent **3** another word for **pluralism** (sense 1)

plus 1 indicating or involving addition **2** on the positive part of a scale or coordinate axis **3** indicating the positive side of an electrical circuit **4** slightly above a specified standard on a particular grade or percentage **5** Botany designating the strain of fungus that can only undergo sexual reproduction with a minus strain **6** a positive quantity

plush a a fabric with a cut pile that is longer and softer than velvet **b** (as modifier): a plush chair

Plutarch ?46–?120 AD, Greek biographer and philosopher, noted for his Parallel Lives of distinguished Greeks and Romans

Pluto[1] Classical myth the god of the underworld; Hades

Pluto[2] the smallest planet and the farthest known from the sun. Discovered in 1930 by Clyde Tombaugh (1906–97), it has one known satellite, Charon. Mean distance from sun: 5907 million km; period of revolution around sun: 248.6 years; period of axial rotation: 6.4 days; diameter and mass: 18 and 0.3 per cent that of earth respectively

plutocracy 1 the rule or control of society by the wealthy **2** a state or government characterized by the rule of the wealthy **3** a class that exercises power by virtue of its wealth

plutonic (of igneous rocks) derived from magma that has cooled and solidified below the surface of the earth

plutonium a highly toxic metallic transuranic element. It occurs in trace amounts in uranium ores and is produced in a nuclear reactor by neutron bombardment of uranium-238. The most stable and important isotope, **plutonium-239**, readily undergoes fission and is used as a reactor fuel in nuclear power stations and in nuclear weapons. Symbol: Pu; atomic no.: 94; half-life of ^{239}Pu: 24 360 years; valency: 3, 4, 5, or 6; relative density (alpha modification): 19.84; melting pt.: 640°C; boiling pt.: 3230°C

pluvial Geology **1** of or relating to rainfall or precipitation **2** a climate characterized by persistent heavy rainfall,

esp one occurring in unglaciated regions during the Pleistocene epoch

ply one of the strands twisted together to make rope, yarn, etc.

Plymouth 1 a port in SW England, in Plymouth unitary authority, SW Devon, on **Plymouth Sound** (an inlet of the English Channel): Britain's chief port in Elizabethan times; the last port visited by the Pilgrim Fathers in the Mayflower before sailing to America; naval base; university (1992). Pop: 243 795 (2001). **2** a unitary authority in SW England, in Devon. Pop: 241 500 (2003 est). Area: 76 sq km (30 sq miles) **3** a city in SE Massachusetts, on **Plymouth Bay**: the first permanent European settlement in New England; founded by the Pilgrim Fathers. Pop: 54 109 (2003 est)

Plzeň an industrial city in the Czech Republic. Pop: 163 000 (2005 est)

pneumatic 1 of or concerned with air, gases, or wind **2** (of a machine or device) operated by compressed air or by a vacuum **3** containing compressed air **4** Theol **a** of or relating to the soul or spirit **b** of or relating to the Holy Ghost or other spiritual beings **5** (of the bones of birds) containing air spaces which reduce their weight as an adaptation to flying

pneumatics the branch of physics concerned with the mechanical properties of gases, esp air

pneumonia inflammation of one or both lungs, in which the air sacs (alveoli) become filled with liquid, which renders them useless for breathing. It is usually caused by bacterial (esp pneumococcal) or viral infection

Po a river in N Italy, rising in the Cottian Alps and flowing northeast to Turin, then east to the Adriatic: the longest river in Italy. Length: 652 km (405 miles)

Pocahontas original name Matoaka; married name Rebecca Rolfe. ?1595–1617, American Indian, who allegedly saved the colonist Captain John Smith from being killed

pock any pustule resulting from an eruptive disease, esp from smallpox

pocket 1 Billiards, Snooker any of the six holes with pouches or nets let into the corners and sides of a billiard table **2** Australian Rules football a player in one of two side positions at the ends of the ground

pocket borough (before the Reform Act of 1832) an English borough constituency controlled by one person or family who owned the land

pocketknife a small knife with one or more blades that fold into the handle; penknife

pod[1] 1 a the fruit of any leguminous plant, consisting of a long two-valved case that contains seeds and splits along both sides when ripe **b** the seedcase as distinct from the seeds **2** any similar fruit **3** a streamlined structure attached by a pylon to an aircraft and used to house a jet engine (**podded engine**), fuel tank, armament, etc. **4** an enclosed cabin suspended from a cable or a big wheel, for carrying passengers

pod[2] a small group of animals, esp seals, whales, or birds

pod[3] 1 a straight groove along the length of certain augers and bits **2** the socket that holds the bit in a boring tool

Podgorica *or* **Podgoritsa** a city in Serbia and Montenegro, the capital of Montenegro: under Turkish rule (1474–1878). Pop: 230 000 (2005 est)

podium 1 a plinth that supports a colonnade or wall 2 a low wall surrounding the arena of an ancient amphitheatre 3 *Zoology* a the terminal part of a vertebrate limb b any footlike organ, such as the tube foot of a starfish

Podolsk an industrial city in W Russia, near Moscow. Pop: 177 000 (2005 est)

Poe Edgar Allan 1809–49, US short-story writer, poet, and critic. Most of his short stories, such as *The Fall of the House of Usher* (1839) and the *Tales of the Grotesque and Arabesque* (1840), are about death, decay, and madness. *The Murders in the Rue Morgue* (1841) is regarded as the first modern detective story

poem 1 a composition in verse, usually characterized by concentrated and heightened language in which words are chosen for their sound and suggestive power as well as for their sense, and using such techniques as metre, rhyme, and alliteration 2 a literary composition that is not in verse but exhibits the intensity of imagination and language common to it

poesy 1 an archaic word for **poetry** 2 *Poetic* the art of writing poetry 3 *Archaic or poetic* a poem or verse, esp one used as a motto

poet *or sometimes when feminine* **poetess** a person who writes poetry

poetaster a writer of inferior verse

poetic *or* **poetical** 1 of or relating to poetry 2 characteristic of poetry, as in being elevated, sublime, etc. 3 characteristic of a poet 4 recounted in verse

poet laureate *Brit* the poet appointed as court poet of Britain who is given a post as an officer of the Royal Household. The first was Ben Jonson in 1616

poetry 1 literature in metrical form; verse 2 the art or craft of writing verse
▷www.bartleby.com/verse
▷www.bbc.co.uk/bbcfour/audiointerviews/
   professions

pogey *or* **pogy** *Canadian, slang* 1 financial or other relief given to the unemployed by the government; dole 2 unemployment insurance 3 a the office distributing relief to the unemployed b *(as modifier): pogey clothes*

pogrom an organized persecution or extermination of an ethnic group, esp of Jews

poi *NZ* a ball of woven flax swung rhythmically in poi dances

poi dance *NZ* a women's formation dance that involves singing and manipulating a poi

poinsettia a euphorbiaceous shrub, *Euphorbia* (or *Poinsettia*) *pulcherrima*, of Mexico and Central America, widely cultivated for its showy scarlet bracts, which resemble petals

point 1 the sharp tapered end of a pin, knife, etc 2 a pin, needle, or other object having such a point 3 *Maths* a a geometric element having no dimensions and whose position in space is located by means of its coordinates b a location 4 a promontory, usually smaller than a cape 5 a distinctive characteristic or quality of an animal, esp one used as a standard in judging livestock 6 any of the extremities, such as the tail, ears, or feet, of a domestic animal 7 *Ballet* the tip of the toes 8 *Australian Rules football* an informal name for **behind** 9 *Navigation* a one of the 32 marks on the circumference of a compass card indicating direction b the angle of 11°15′ between two adjacent marks c a point on the horizon indicated by such a mark 10 *Cricket* a a fielding position at right angles to the batsman on the off side and relatively near the pitch b a fielder in this position 11 any of the numbers cast in the first throw in craps with which one neither wins nor loses by throwing them: 4, 5, 6, 8, 9, or 10 12 either of the two electrical contacts that make or break the current flow in the distributor of an internal-combustion engine 13 *Brit* a junction of railway tracks in which a pair of rails can be moved so that a train can be directed onto either of two lines 14 a piece of ribbon, cord, etc, with metal tags at the end: used during the 16th and 17th centuries to fasten clothing 15 *Backgammon* a place or position on the board 16 *Brit* a short for **power point** b an informal name for **socket** 17 the position of the body of a pointer or setter when it discovers game 18 *Boxing* a mark awarded for a scoring blow, knockdown, etc. 19 *Ice hockey* the position just inside the opponents' blue line

point duty the stationing of a policeman or traffic warden at a road junction to control and direct traffic

pointed 1 (of an arch or style of architecture employing such an arch) Gothic 2 *Music* (of a psalm text) marked to show changes in chanting 3 (of Hebrew text) with vowel points marked

Pointe-Noire a port in S Congo-Brazzaville, on the Atlantic: the country's chief port and former capital (1950–58). Pop: 638 000 (2005 est)

pointer 1 an indicator on a measuring instrument 2 a long rod or cane used by a lecturer to point to parts of a map, blackboard, etc. 3 one of a breed of large swift smooth-coated dogs, usually white with black, liver, or lemon markings: when on shooting expeditions it points to the bird with its nose, body, and tail in a straight line

pointillism the technique of painting elaborated from impressionism, in which dots of unmixed colour are juxtaposed on a white ground so that from a distance they fuse in the viewer's eye into appropriate intermediate tones
▷www.artcyclopedia.com/history/
   pointillism.html

pointing a the insertion of marks to indicate the chanting of a psalm or the vowels in a Hebrew text b the sequence of marks so inserted

point of order a question raised in a meeting or deliberative assembly by a member as to whether the rules governing procedures are being breached

point-to-point *Brit* a a steeplechase organized by a recognized hunt or other body, usually restricted to amateurs riding horses that have been regularly used in hunting b *(as modifier): a point-to-point race*

poise the cgs unit of viscosity; the viscosity of a fluid in which a tangential force of 1 dyne per square centimetre maintains a difference in velocity of 1 centimetre per second between two parallel planes 1 centimetre apart. It is equivalent to 0.1 newton second per square metre.

poison 1 any substance that can impair function, cause structural damage, or otherwise injure the body 2 *Chemistry* a substance that retards a chemical reaction or destroys or inhibits the activity of a catalyst 3 *Physics* a substance that absorbs neutrons in a nuclear reactor and thus slows down the reaction. It may be added deliberately or formed during fission

poison ivy any of several North American anacardiaceous shrubs or vines of the genus *Rhus* (or *Toxicodendron*), esp *R. radicans*, which has small green flowers and whitish berries that cause an itching rash on contact

Poitiers a city in S central France: capital of the former province of Poitou until 1790; scene of the battle (1356) in which the English under the Black Prince defeated the French; university (1432). Pop: 83 448 (1999)

Poitou a former province of W central France, on the Atlantic. Chief town: Poitiers

Poitou-Charentes a region of W central France, on the Bay of Biscay: mainly low-lying

poker¹ a metal rod, usually with a handle, for stirring a fire

poker² a card game of bluff and skill in which bets are made on the hands dealt, the highest-ranking hand (containing the most valuable combinations of sequences and sets of cards) winning the pool

pokerwork 1 the art of decorating wood or leather by burning a design with a heated metal point; pyrography 2 artefacts decorated in this way

poky *or* **pokey** the *Chiefly US and Canadian, slang* prison

Poland a republic in central Europe, on the Baltic: first united in the 10th century; dissolved after the third partition effected by Austria, Russia, and Prussia in 1795; re-established independence in 1918; invaded by Germany in 1939; ruled by a Communist government from 1947 to 1989, when a multiparty system was introduced. It consists chiefly of a low undulating plain in the north, rising to a low plateau in the south, with the Sudeten and Carpathian Mountains along the S border. Official language: Polish. Religion: Roman Catholic majority. Currency: zloty. Capital: Warsaw. Pop: 38 551 000 (2004 est). Area: 311 730 sq km (120 359 sq miles)

Polanski Roman born 1933, Polish film director with a taste for the macabre, as in *Repulsion* (1965) and *Rosemary's Baby* (1968): later films include *Tess* (1980), *Death and the Maiden* (1995), and *The Pianist* (2002)

polar 1 situated at or near, coming from, or relating to either of the earth's poles or the area inside the Arctic or Antarctic Circles 2 having or relating to a pole or poles 3 *Chem* **a** (of a molecule or compound) being or having a molecule in which there is an uneven distribution of electrons and thus a permanent dipole moment **b** (of a crystal or substance) being or having a crystal that is bound by ionic bonds

polar bear a white carnivorous bear, *Thalarctos maritimus*, of coastal regions of the North Pole

polarity the condition of a body or system in which it has opposing physical properties at different points, esp magnetic poles or electric charge

polarization *or* **polarisation** *Physics* the process or phenomenon in which the waves of light or other electro-

magnetic radiation are restricted to certain directions of vibration, usually specified in terms of the electric field vector

Polaroid *Trademark* 1 a type of plastic sheet that can polarize a transmitted beam of normal light because it is composed of long parallel molecules. It only transmits plane-polarized light if these molecules are parallel to the plane of polarization and, since reflected light is partly polarized, it is often used in sunglasses to eliminate glare 2 **Polaroid Land Camera** any of several types of camera yielding a finished print by means of a special developing and processing technique that occurs inside the camera and takes only a few seconds to complete

polder a stretch of land reclaimed from the sea or a lake, esp in the Netherlands

pole¹ 1 a long slender usually round piece of wood, metal, or other material 2 the piece of timber on each side of which a pair of carriage horses are hitched 3 another name for **rod** 4 *Horse racing, chiefly US and Canadian* **a** the inside lane of a racecourse **b** (*as modifier*): *the pole position* **c** one of a number of markers placed at intervals of one sixteenth of a mile along the side of a racecourse 5 *Nautical* **a** any light spar **b** the part of a mast between the head and the attachment of the uppermost shrouds 6 **under bare poles** *Nautical* (of a sailing vessel) with no sails set

pole² 1 either of the two antipodal points where the earth's axis of rotation meets the earth's surface 2 *Physics* **a** either of the two regions at the extremities of a magnet to which the lines of force converge or from which they diverge **b** either of two points or regions in a piece of material, system, etc, at which there are opposite electric charges, as at the two terminals of a battery 3 *Maths* an isolated singularity of an analytical function 4 *Biology* **a** either end of the axis of a cell, spore, ovum, or similar body **b** either end of the spindle formed during the metaphase of mitosis and meiosis 5 *Physiol* the point on a neuron from which the axon or dendrites project from the cell body 6 *Geometry* the origin in a system of polar or spherical coordinates

Pole Reginald 1500–58, English cardinal; last Roman Catholic archbishop of Canterbury (1556–58)

polecat 1 a dark brown musteline mammal, *Mustela putorius*, of woodlands of Europe, Asia, and N Africa, that is closely related to but larger than the weasel and gives off an unpleasant smell 2 any of various related animals, such as the **marbled polecat**, *Vormela peregusna* 3 *US* a nontechnical name for **skunk**

pole position (in motor racing) the starting position on the inside of the front row, generally considered the best one

Pole Star the the star closest to the N celestial pole at any particular time. At present this is Polaris, but it will eventually be replaced by some other star owing to precession of the earth's axis

pole vault 1 the a field event in which competitors attempt to clear a high bar with the aid of an extremely flexible long pole 2 a single attempt in the pole vault

Poliakoff Stephen born 1952, British playwright and film director; work includes the stage plays *Breaking the Silence* (1984) and *Blinded by the Sun* (1996) and the television serial *The Lost Prince* (2003)

police 1 a the organized civil force of a state, concerned with maintenance of law and order, the detection and prevention of crime, etc. **b** (*as modifier*): *a police inquiry* **2** the members of such a force collectively **3** *Archaic* **a** the regulation and control of a community, esp in regard to the enforcement of law, the prevention of crime, etc. **b** the department of government concerned with this
▷www.police.uk
▷www.ipa-iac.org/index2.htm

police dog a dog, often an Alsatian, trained to help the police, as in tracking

policeman *or feminine* **policewoman** a member of a police force, esp one holding the rank of constable

police procedural a novel, film, or television drama that deals realistically with police work

police state a state or country in which a repressive government maintains control through the police

police station the office or headquarters of the police force of a district

policy a plan of action adopted or pursued by an individual, government, party, business, etc.

Polignac Prince de, title of *Auguste Jules Armand Marie de Polignac*. 1780–1847, French statesman; prime minister (1829–30) to Charles X: his extreme royalist and ultramontane policies provoked the 1830 revolution

poliomyelitis an acute infectious viral disease, esp affecting children. In its paralytic form (**acute anterior poliomyelitis**) the brain and spinal cord are involved, causing weakness, paralysis, and wasting of muscle

polish a substance used to produce a smooth and shiny, often protective surface

Polish the official language of Poland, belonging to the West Slavonic branch of the Indo-European family

Polish Corridor the strip of land through E Pomerania providing Poland with access to the sea (1919–39), given to her in 1919 in the Treaty of Versailles, and separating East Prussia from the rest of Germany. It is now part of Poland

Politburo 1 the executive and policy-making committee of a Communist Party **2** the supreme policy-making authority in most Communist countries

Politian Italian name *Angelo Polliziano*; original name *Angelo Ambrogini*. 1454–94, Florentine humanist and poet

political 1 of or relating to the state, government, the body politic, public administration, policy-making, etc. **2 a** of, involved in, or relating to government policy-making as distinguished from administration or law **b** of or relating to the civil aspects of government as distinguished from the military **3** of, dealing with, or relating to politics **4** of, characteristic of, or relating to the parties and the partisan aspects of politics **5** organized or ordered with respect to government
▷www.lib.umich.edu/govdocs/polisci.html
▷www.political-theory.org/
▷www.psr.keele.ac.uk/theory.htm
▷www.psr.keele.ac.uk/thought.htm

political prisoner someone imprisoned for holding, expressing, or acting in accord with particular political beliefs

political science (esp as an academic subject) the study of the state, government, and politics: one of the social sciences
▷www.bubl.ac.uk/link/p/politicalscience.htm
▷www.sosig.ac.uk/politics
▷www.apsanet.org/PS/
▷www.britac.ac.uk/portal/
bysection.asp?section=S5

politician 1 a person actively engaged in politics, esp a full-time professional member of a deliberative assembly **2** a person who is experienced or skilled in the art or science of politics, government, or administration; statesman **3** *Disparaging, chiefly US* a person who engages in politics out of a wish for personal gain, as realized by holding a public office

politics 1 the practice or study of the art and science of forming, directing, and administrating states and other political units; the art and science of government; political science **2** the complex or aggregate of relationships of people in society, esp those relationships involving authority or power **3** political activities or affairs **4** the business or profession of politics **5** opinions, principles, sympathies, etc, with respect to politics **6 a** the policy-formulating aspects of government as distinguished from the administrative, or legal **b** the civil functions of government as distinguished from the military

polity 1 a form of government or organization of a state, church, society, etc.; constitution **2** a politically organized society, state, city, etc. **3** the management of public or civil affairs **4** political organization

Polk James Knox 1795–1849, US statesman; 11th president of the US (1845–49). During his administration, Texas and territory now included in New Mexico, Colorado, Utah, Nevada, Arizona, Oregon, and California were added to the Union

polka 1 a 19th-century Bohemian dance with three steps and a hop, in fast duple time **2** a piece of music composed for or in the rhythm of this dance

poll 1 the casting, recording, or counting of votes in an election; a voting **2** the result or quantity of such a voting **3** short for **poll tax 4** a list or enumeration of people, esp for taxation or voting purposes **5** the striking face of a hammer **6** the occipital or back part of the head of an animal

pollack *or* **pollock** a gadoid food fish, *Pollachius pollachius*, that has a dark green back and a projecting lower jaw and occurs in northern seas, esp the North Atlantic Ocean

Pollaiuolo 1 Antonio , ?1432–98, Florentine painter, sculptor, goldsmith, and engraver: his paintings include the *Martyrdom of St Sebastian* **2** his brother **Piero** ?1443–96, Florentine painter and sculptor

pollard 1 an animal, such as a sheep or deer, that has either shed its horns or antlers or has had them removed **2** a tree that has had its top cut off to encourage the formation of a crown of branches

pollen a fine powdery substance produced by the anthers of seed-bearing plants, consisting of numerous fine grains containing the male gametes

Pollen Daniel 1813–96, New Zealand statesman, born in Ireland: prime minister of New Zealand (1876)

polling booth a semienclosed space in which a voter stands to mark a ballot paper during an election

polling station a building, such as a school, designated as the place to which voters go during an election to cast their votes

Pollock 1 Sir **Frederick** 1845–1937, English legal scholar: with Maitland, he wrote *History of English Law before the Time of Edward I* (1895) **2** **Jackson** 1912–56, US abstract expressionist painter; chief exponent of action painting in the US

poll tax 1 a tax levied per head of adult population **2** an informal name for (the former) **community charge**

pollutant a substance that pollutes, esp a chemical or similar substance that is produced as a waste product of an industrial process

polo 1 a game similar to hockey played on horseback using long-handled mallets (**polo sticks**) and a wooden ball **2** any of several similar games, such as one played on bicycles **3** short for **water polo**
▷www.fippolo.com

Polo Marco 1254–1324, Venetian merchant, famous for his account of his travels in Asia. After travelling overland to China (1271–75), he spent 17 years serving Kublai Khan before returning to Venice by sea (1292–95)

Polokwane a town in NE South Africa, the capital of Limpopo province: commercial and agricultural centre. Pop: 90 398 (2001)

polonaise 1 a ceremonial marchlike dance in three-four time from Poland **2** a piece of music composed for or in the rhythm of this dance

polonium a very rare radioactive element that occurs in trace amounts in uranium ores. The isotope **polonium-210** is produced artificially and is used as a lightweight power source in satellites and to eliminate static electricity in certain industries. Symbol: Po; atomic no.: 84; half-life of most stable isotope, ^{209}Po: 103 years; valency: –2, 0, 2, 4, or 6; relative density (alpha modification): 9.32; melting pt.: 254°C; boiling pt.: 962°C

Pol Pot original name *Kompong Thom*. 1925–98, Cambodian Communist statesman; prime minister of Kampuchea (1976; 1977–79); his policies led to the deaths of thousands in labour camps before he was overthrown by Vietnamese forces; in 1997 his former supporters in the Khmer Rouge captured him and claimed to have tried and sentenced him to life imprisonment

Poltava a city in E Ukraine: scene of the victory (1709) of the Russians under Peter the Great over the Swedes under Charles XII; centre of an agricultural region. Pop: 319 000 (2005 est)

poltergeist a spirit believed to manifest its presence by rappings and other noises and also by acts of mischief, such as throwing furniture about

polyandry 1 the practice or condition of being married to more than one husband at the same time **2** the practice in animals of a female mating with more than one male during one breeding season **3** the condition in flowers of having a large indefinite number of stamens

polyanthus 1 any of several hybrid garden primroses, esp *Primula polyantha*, which has brightly coloured flowers **2** **polyanthus narcissus** a Eurasian amaryllidaceous plant, *Narcissus tazetta*, having clusters of small yellow or white fragrant flowers

Polybius ?205–?123 BC, Greek historian. Under the patronage of Scipio the Younger, he wrote in 40 books a history of Rome from 264 BC to 146 BC

Polycarp Saint ?69–?155 AD, Christian martyr and bishop of Smyrna, noted for his letter to the church at Philippi. Feast day: Feb 23

polychromatic, polychromic, *or* **polychromous 1** having various or changing colours **2** (of light or other electromagnetic radiation) containing radiation with more than one wavelength

Polyclitus, Polycleitus, *or* **Polycletus** 5th-century BC. Greek sculptor, noted particularly for his idealized bronze sculptures of the male nude, such as the *Doryphoros*

Polycrates died ?522 BC, Greek tyrant of Samos, who was crucified by a Persian satrap

polycystic ovary syndrome a hormonal disorder in which the Graafian follicles in the ovary fail to develop completely so that they are unable to ovulate, remaining as multiple cysts that distend the ovary. The result is infertility, obesity, and hirsutism

polyester any of a large class of synthetic materials that are polymers containing recurring -COO- groups: used as plastics, textile fibres, and adhesives

polygamy 1 the practice of having more than one wife or husband at the same time **2 a** the condition of having male, female, and hermaphrodite flowers on the same plant **b** the condition of having these different types of flower on separate plants of the same species **3** the practice in male animals of having more than one mate during one breeding season

Polygnotus 5th century BC, Greek painter: associated with Cimon in rebuilding Athens

polygon a closed plane figure bounded by three or more straight sides that meet in pairs in the same number of vertices, and do not intersect other than at these vertices. The sum of the interior angles is $(n–2) \times 180°$ for n sides; the sum of the exterior angles is 360°. A **regular polygon** has all its sides and angles equal. Specific polygons are named according to the number of sides, such as triangle, pentagon, etc.

polygraph an instrument for the simultaneous electrical or mechanical recording of several involuntary physiological activities, including blood pressure, skin resistivity, pulse rate, respiration, and sweating, used esp as a would-be lie detector

polygyny 1 the practice or condition of being married to more than one wife at the same time **2** the practice in animals of a male mating with more than one female during one breeding season **3** the condition in flowers of having many carpels

polyhedron a solid figure consisting of four or more plane faces (all polygons), pairs of which meet along an edge, three or more edges meeting at a vertex. In a **regular polyhedron** all the faces are identical regular polygons making equal angles with each other. Specific polyhedrons are named according to the number of faces, such as tetrahedron, icosahedron, etc.

Polyhymnia *Greek myth* the Muse of singing, mime, and sacred dance

polymer a naturally occurring or synthetic compound, such as starch or Perspex, that has large molecules made up of many relatively simple repeated units

polymerization *or* **polymerisation** the act or process of forming a polymer or copolymer, esp a chemical reaction in which a polymer is formed

polymorphous *or* **polymorphic** 1 (of a substance) exhibiting polymorphism 2 (of an animal or plant) displaying or undergoing polymorphism

Polynesia one of the three divisions of islands in the Pacific, the others being Melanesia and Micronesia: includes Samoa, Society, Marquesas, Mangareva, Tuamotu, Cook, and Tubuai Islands, and Tonga

Polynesian 1 of or relating to Polynesia, its people, or any of their languages 2 a member of the people that inhabit Polynesia, generally of Caucasoid features with light skin and wavy hair 3 a branch of the Malayo-Polynesian family of languages, including Māori and Hawaiian and a number of other closely related languages of the S and central Pacific

polynomial 1 a a mathematical expression consisting of a sum of terms each of which is the product of a constant and one or more variables raised to a positive or zero integral power. For one variable, x, the general form is given by: $a_0x^n + a_1x^{n-1} + ... + a_{n-1}x + a_n$, where a_0, a_1, etc, are real numbers b any mathematical expression consisting of the sum of a number of terms 2 *Biology* a taxonomic name consisting of more than two terms, such as *Parus major minor* in which *minor* designates the subspecies

polyp 1 *Zoology* one of the two forms of individual that occur in coelenterates. It usually has a hollow cylindrical body with a ring of tentacles around the mouth 2 *Pathol* a small vascularized growth arising from the surface of a mucous membrane, having a rounded base or a stalklike projection

polyphonic *Music* composed of relatively independent melodic lines or parts; contrapuntal

polyphony polyphonic style of composition or a piece of music utilizing it

polysaccharide *or* **polysaccharose** any one of a class of carbohydrates whose molecules contain linked monosaccharide units: includes starch, inulin, and cellulose. General formula: $(C_6H_{10}O_5)_n$

polystyrene a synthetic thermoplastic material obtained by polymerizing styrene; used as a white rigid foam (**expanded polystyrene**) for insulating and packing and as a glasslike material in light fittings and water tanks

polytechnic 1 *Brit* a college offering advanced full- and part-time courses, esp vocational courses, in many fields at and below degree standard 2 of or relating to technical instruction and training

polytheism the worship of or belief in more than one god

polythene any one of various light thermoplastic materials made from ethylene with properties depending on the molecular weight of the polymer. The common forms are a waxy flexible plastic (**low-density polythene**) and a tougher rigid more crystalline form (**high-density polythene**). Polythene is used for packaging, moulded articles, pipes and tubing, insulation, textiles, and coatings on metal

polyunsaturated of or relating to a class of animal and vegetable fats, the molecules of which consist of long carbon chains with many double bonds.

Polyunsaturated compounds are less likely to be converted into cholesterol in the body. They are widely used in margarines and in the manufacture of paints and varnishes

polyurethane *or* **polyurethan** a class of synthetic materials made by copolymerizing an isocyanate and a polyhydric alcohol and commonly used as a foam (**polyurethane foam**) for insulation and packing, as fibres and hard inert coatings, and in a flexible form (**polyurethane rubber**) for diaphragms and seals

pomander 1 a mixture of aromatic substances in a sachet or an orange, formerly carried as scent or as a protection against disease 2 a container for such a mixture

Pombal Marquês de title of *Sebastião José de Carvalho e Mello*. 1699–1782, Portuguese statesman, who dominated Portuguese government from 1750 to 1777 and instituted many administrative and economic reforms

pomegranate 1 an Asian shrub or small tree, *Punica granatum*, cultivated in semitropical regions for its edible fruit: family *Punicaceae* 2 the many-chambered globular fruit of this tree, which has tough reddish rind, juicy red pulp, and many seeds

pomelo 1 a tropical rutaceous tree, *Citrus maxima* (or *C. decumana*), grown widely in oriental regions for its large yellow grapefruit-like edible fruit 2 the fruit of this tree 3 *Chiefly US* another name for **grapefruit**

Pomerania a region of N central Europe, extending along the S coast of the Baltic Sea from Stralsund to the Vistula River: now chiefly in Poland, with a small area in NE Germany

Pomeranian 1 of or relating to Pomerania or its inhabitants 2 a native or inhabitant of Pomerania, esp a German 3 a breed of toy dog of the spitz type with a long thick straight coat

pomfret 1 any of various fishes of the genus *Stromateidae* of the Indian and Pacific oceans: valued as food fishes 2 any of various scombroid fishes, esp *Brama raii*, of northern oceans: valued as food fishes

pommel the raised part on the front of a saddle

Pomona another name for **Mainland** (in Orkney)

Pompadour Marquise de, title of *Jeanne Antoinette Poisson*. 1721–64, mistress of Louis XV of France (1745–64), whom she greatly influenced

Pompeii an ancient city in Italy, southeast of Naples: buried by an eruption of Vesuvius (79 AD); excavation of the site, which is extremely well preserved, began in 1748

Pompey called *Pompey the Great*; Latin name *Gnaeus Pompeius Magnus*. 106–48 BC, Roman general and statesman; a member with Caesar and Crassus of the first triumvirate (60). He later quarrelled with Caesar, who defeated him at Pharsalus (48). He fled to Egypt and was murdered

Pompidou Georges 1911–74, French statesman; president of France (1969–74)

pompom *or* **pompon** a the small globelike flower head of certain cultivated varieties of dahlia and chrysanthemum b *(as modifier)*: *pompom dahlia*

Ponce a port in S Puerto Rico, on the Caribbean: the second largest town on the island; settled in the 16th century. Pop: 185 930 (2003 est)

Pondicherry 1 a Union Territory of SE India: transferred from French to Indian administration in 1954 and made a Union Territory in 1962. Capital: Pondicherry. Pop: 973 829 (2001 est). Area: 479 sq km (185 sq miles) 2 a port in SE India, capital of the Union Territory of Pondicherry, on the Coromandel Coast. Pop: 220 749 (2001)

pondok or **pondokkie** (in southern Africa) a crudely made house built of tin sheet, reeds, etc.

Pondoland an area in SE central South Africa: inhabited chiefly by the Pondo people

pondweed 1 any of various water plants of the genus *Potamogeton*, which grow in ponds and slow streams: family *Potamogetonaceae* 2 *Brit* any of various unrelated water plants, such as Canadian pondweed, mare's-tail, and water milfoil, that have thin or much divided leaves

ponga a tall tree fern, *Cyathea dealbata*, of New Zealand, with large feathery leaves

Ponta Delgada a port in the E Azores, on S São Miguel Island: chief commercial centre of the archipelago. Pop: 65 853 (2001)

Pontchartrain Lake a shallow lagoon in SE Louisiana, linked with the Gulf of Mexico by a narrow channel, the Rigolets: resort and fishing centre. Area: 1620 sq km (625 sq miles)

Pontefract an industrial town in N England, in Wakefield unitary authority, West Yorkshire: castle (1069), in which Richard II was imprisoned and murdered (1400). Pop: 28 250 (2001)

Pontevedra a port in NW Spain: takes its name from a 12-arched Roman bridge, the Pons Vetus. Pop: 77 993 (2003 est)

Pontiac died 1769, chief of the Ottawa Indians, who led a rebellion against the British (1763–66)

Pontianak a port in Indonesia, on W coast of Borneo almost exactly on the equator. Pop: 464 534 (2000)

Pontic denoting or relating to the Black Sea

pontiff a former title of the pagan high priest at Rome, later used of popes and occasionally of other bishops, and now confined exclusively to the pope

pontifical 1 of, relating to, or characteristic of a pontiff, the pope, or a bishop 2 *RC Church, Church of England* a book containing the prayers and ritual instructions for ceremonies restricted to a bishop

pontificate the office or term of office of a pontiff, now usually the pope

pontoon[1] *Nautical* a float, often inflatable, for raising a vessel in the water

pontoon[2] 1 a gambling game in which players try to obtain card combinations worth 21 points 2 (in this game) the combination of an ace with a ten or court card when dealt to a player as his first two cards

Pontoppidan Henrik 1857–1943, Danish novelist and short-story writer, author of the novel sequences *The Promised Land* (1891–95), *Lykke-Per* (1898–1904), and *The Empire of Death* (1912–16). Nobel prize for literature 1917

Pontormo Jacopo da original name *Jacopo Carrucci*. 1494–1556, Italian mannerist painter

Pontus an ancient region of NE Asia Minor, on the Black Sea: became a kingdom in the 4th century BC; at its height under Mithridates VI (about 115–63 BC), when it controlled all Asia Minor; defeated by the Romans in the mid-1st century BC

Pontypool an industrial town in E Wales, in Torfaen county borough: famous for lacquered ironware in the 18th century. Pop: 35 447 (2001)

Pontypridd an industrial town in S Wales, in Rhondda Cynon Taff county borough. Pop: 29 781 (2001)

pony 1 any of various breeds of small horse, usually under 14.2 hands 2 *Brit, slang* a sum of £25, esp in book-making 3 *US, slang* a literal translation used by students, often illicitly, in preparation for foreign language lessons or examinations; crib

pony trekking the act of riding ponies cross-country, esp as a pastime

poodle a breed of dog, with varieties of different sizes, having curly hair, which is often clipped from ribs to tail for showing: originally bred to hunt waterfowl

pool[1] 1 a deep part of a stream or river where the water runs very slowly 2 an underground accumulation of oil or gas, usually forming a reservoir in porous sedimentary rock 3 See swimming pool

pool[2] 1 the combined stakes of the betters in many gambling sports or games; kitty 2 *Commerce* a group of producers who conspire to establish and maintain output levels and high prices, each member of the group being allocated a maximum quota; price ring 3 any of various billiard games in which the object is to pot all the balls with the cue ball, esp that played with 15 coloured and numbered balls; pocket billiards

Poole 1 a port and resort in S England, in Poole unitary authority, Dorset, on **Poole Harbour**; seat of Bournemouth University (1992). Pop: 144 800 (2001) 2 a unitary authority in S England, in Dorset. Pop: 137 500 (2003 est). Area: 37 sq km (14 sq miles)

Poona or **Pune** a city in W India, in W Maharashtra: under British rule served as the seasonal capital of the Bombay Presidency. Pop: 2 540 069 (2001)

poop *Nautical* a raised structure at the stern of a vessel, esp a sailing ship

poorhouse (formerly) a publicly maintained institution offering accommodation to the poor

poor law *English history* a law providing for the relief or support of the poor from public, esp parish, funds

poor White *Often offensive* a a poverty-stricken and underprivileged White person, esp in the southern US and South Africa **b** (*as modifier*): poor White trash

POP 1 *Internet* post office protocol: a protocol which brings e-mail to and from a mail server 2 *Environment* persistent organic pollutant

pop art a movement in modern art that imitates the methods, styles, and themes of popular culture and mass media, such as comic strips, advertising, and science fiction

▷www.artchive.com/ftp_site_reg.htm
▷www.artcyclopedia.com/history/pop.html

popcorn a variety of maize having hard pointed kernels that puff up when heated

Pope Alexander 1688–1744, English poet, regarded as the most brilliant satirist of the Augustan period, esp with his *Imitations of Horace* (1733–38). His technical virtuosity is most evident in *The Rape of the Lock* (1712–14). Other works include *The Dunciad* (1728; 1742), the *Moral Essays*

(1731–35), and *An Essay on Man* (1733–34)

popinjay 1 an archaic word for **parrot** 2 the figure of a parrot used as a target

popish *Derogatory* belonging to or characteristic of Roman Catholicism

poplar 1 any tree of the salicaceous genus *Populus*, of N temperate regions, having triangular leaves, flowers borne in catkins, and light soft wood 2 any of various trees resembling the true poplars, such as the tulip tree 3 the wood of any of these trees

poplin a a strong fabric, usually of cotton, in plain weave with fine ribbing, used for dresses, children's wear, etc. **b** *(as modifier): a poplin shirt*

Popov 1 **Alexander Stepanovich** 1859–1906, Russian physicist, the first to use an aerial in experiments with radio waves 2 **Oleg (Konstantinovich)**. born 1930, Russian clown, a member of the Moscow Circus

popper *Slang* an amyl nitrite capsule, which is crushed and its contents inhaled by drug users as a stimulant

Popper Sir **Karl** 1902–94, British philosopher, born in Vienna. In *The Logic of Scientific Discovery* (1934), he proposes that knowledge cannot be absolutely confirmed, but rather that science progresses by the experimental refutation of the current theory and its consequent replacement by a new theory, equally provisional but covering more of the known data. *The Open Society and its Enemies* (1945) is a critique of dogmatic political philosophies, such as Marxism. Other works are *The Poverty of Historicism* (1957), *Conjectures and Refutations* (1963), and *Objective Knowledge* (1972)

poppet 1 a mushroom-shaped valve that is lifted from its seating against a spring by applying an axial force to its stem: commonly used as an exhaust or inlet valve in an internal-combustion engine 2 *Nautical* a temporary supporting brace for a vessel hauled on land or in a dry dock

popping crease *Cricket* a line four feet in front of and parallel with the bowling crease, at or behind which the batsman stands

poppy 1 any of numerous papaveraceous plants of the temperate genus *Papaver*, having red, orange, or white flowers and a milky sap 2 any of several similar or related plants, such as the California poppy, prickly poppy, horned poppy, and Welsh poppy 3 *Obsolete* any of the drugs, such as opium, that are obtained from these plants 4 a strong red to reddish-orange colour

popular front *History* any of the left-wing groups or parties that were organized from 1935 onwards to oppose the spread of fascism

population 1 *Ecology* a group of individuals of the same species inhabiting a given area 2 *Astronomy* either of two main groups of stars classified according to age and location. **Population I** consists of younger metal-rich hot white stars, many occurring in galactic clusters and forming the arms of spiral galaxies. Stars of **population II** are older, the brightest being red giants, and are found in the centre of spiral and elliptical galaxies in globular clusters

populism a political strategy based on a calculated appeal to the interests or prejudices of ordinary people

porbeagle any of several voracious sharks of the genus *Lamna*, esp *L. nasus*, of northern seas: family *Isuridae*

porcelain 1 a more or less translucent ceramic material, the principal ingredients being kaolin and petuntse (hard paste) or other clays, ground glassy substances, soapstone, bone ash, etc. 2 an object made of this or such objects collectively

▷www.gotheborg.com

▷www.porcelainpainters.com

porch 1 a low structure projecting from the doorway of a house and forming a covered entrance 2 *US and Canadian* an exterior roofed gallery, often partly enclosed; veranda

porcine of, connected with, or characteristic of pigs

porcupine any of various large hystricomorph rodents of the families *Hystricidae*, of Africa, Indonesia, S Europe, and S Asia, and *Erethizontidae*, of the New World. All species have a body covering of protective spines or quills

pore 1 *Anatomy, Zoology* any small opening in the skin or outer surface of an animal 2 *Botany* any small aperture, esp that of a stoma through which water vapour and gases pass 3 any other small hole, such as a space in a rock, soil, etc.

Pori a port in SW Finland, on the Gulf of Bothnia. Pop: 76 189 (2003 est)

poriferan any invertebrate of the phylum *Porifera*, which comprises the sponges

Porirua a city in New Zealand, on the North Island just north of Wellington. Pop: 50 600 (2004 est)

porous *Botany, Geology* having pores; poriferous

porphyry 1 any igneous rock with large crystals embedded in a finer groundmass of minerals 2 *Obsolete* a reddish-purple rock consisting of large crystals of feldspar in a finer groundmass of feldspar, hornblende, etc.

Porphyry original name *Malchus*. 232–305 AD, Greek Neo-Platonist philosopher, born in Syria; disciple and biographer of Plotinus

porpoise 1 any of various small cetacean mammals of the genus *Phocaena* and related genera, having a blunt snout and many teeth: family *Delphinidae* (or *Phocaenidae*) 2 any of various related cetaceans, esp the dolphin

port¹ a town or place alongside navigable water with facilities for the loading and unloading of ships

port² a the left side of an aircraft or vessel when facing the nose or bow **b** *(as modifier): the port bow*

port³ a sweet fortified dessert wine

port⁴ 1 *Nautical* a an opening in the side of a ship, fitted with a watertight door, for access to the holds **b** See **porthole** 2 an aperture, esp one controlled by a valve, by which fluid enters or leaves the cylinder head of an engine, compressor, etc. 3 *Electronics* a logic circuit for the input and ouput of data

portable (of software, files, etc) able to be transferred from one type of computer system to another

Port Adelaide the chief port of South Australia, near Adelaide on St Vincent Gulf. Pop: 101 225 (1998 est)

Portadown a town in S Northern Ireland, in the district of Armagh. Pop: 21 299 (1991)

portage the cost of carrying or transporting

portal 1 an entrance, gateway, or doorway, esp one that is large and impressive 2 *Anatomy* a of or relating to a portal vein **b** of or relating to a porta

Port Arthur a former penal settlement (1833–70) in

Australia, on the S coast of the Tasman Peninsula, Tasmania

Port-au-Prince the capital and chief port of Haiti, in the south on the Gulf of Gonaïves: founded in 1749 by the French; university (1944). Pop: 2 090 000 (2005 est)

Port Blair the capital of the Indian Union Territory of the Andaman and Nicobar Islands, a port on the SE coast of South Andaman Island: a former penal colony. Pop: 100 186 (2001)

portcullis an iron or wooden grating suspended vertically in grooves in the gateway of a castle or fortified town and able to be lowered so as to bar the entrance

Port Elizabeth a port in S South Africa, on Algoa Bay: motor-vehicle manufacture, fruit canning; resort. Pop: 237 502 (2001)

porter¹ *US and Canadian* a railway employee who waits on passengers, esp in a sleeper

porter² *RC Church* a person ordained to what was formerly the lowest in rank of the minor orders

porter³ *Brit* a dark sweet ale brewed from black malt

Porter 1 **Cole** 1893–1964, US composer and lyricist of musical comedies. His most popular songs include *Night and Day* and *Let's do It* 2 **George**, Baron Porter of Luddenham. 1920–2002, British chemist, who shared a Nobel prize for chemistry in 1967 for his work on flash photolysis 3 **Katherine Anne** 1890–1980, US short-story writer and novelist. Her best-known collections of stories are *Flowering Judas* (1930) and *Pale Horse, Pale Rider* (1939) 4 **Peter** born 1929, Australian poet, living in Britain 5 **Rodney Robert** 1917–85, British biochemist: shared the Nobel prize for physiology or medicine 1972 for determining the structure of an antibody

porterhouse (formerly) a place in which porter, beer, etc, and sometimes chops and steaks, were served

portfolio 1 a flat case, esp of leather, used for carrying maps, drawings, etc. 2 the contents of such a case, such as drawings, paintings, or photographs, that demonstrate recent work 3 such a case used for carrying ministerial or state papers 4 the responsibilities or role of the head of a government department 5 **Minister without portfolio** a cabinet minister who is not responsible for any government department

Port-Gentil the chief port of Gabon, in the west near the mouth of the Ogooué River: oil refinery. Pop: 80 841 (1993)

Port Harcourt a port in S Nigeria, capital of Rivers state on the Niger delta: the nation's second largest port; industrial centre. Pop: 942 000 (2005 est)

porthole a small aperture in the side of a vessel to admit light and air, usually fitted with a watertight glass or metal cover, or both

portico 1 a covered entrance to a building; porch 2 a covered walkway in the form of a roof supported by columns or pillars, esp one built on to the exterior of a building

portion *Law* a a share of property, esp one coming to a child from the estate of his parents b the property given by a woman to her husband at marriage; dowry

Port Jackson an inlet of the Pacific on the coast of SE Australia, forming a fine natural harbour: site of the city of Sydney, spanned by Sydney Harbour Bridge

Portland¹ 3rd Duke of title of *William Henry Cavendish*

Bentinck. 1738–1809, British statesman; prime minister (1783; 1807–09); father of Lord William Cavendish Bentinck

Portland² 1 **Isle of** a rugged limestone peninsula in SW England, in Dorset, connected to the mainland by a narrow isthmus and by Chesil Bank: the lighthouse of **Portland Bill** lies at the S tip; famous for the quarrying of **Portland stone**, a fine building material. Pop. (town): 12 000 (latest est) 2 an inland port in NW Oregon, on the Willamette River: the largest city in the state; shipbuilding and chemical industries. Pop: 538 544 (2003 est) 3 a port in SW Maine, on Casco Bay: the largest city in the state; settled by the English in 1632, destroyed successively by French, Indian, and British attacks, and rebuilt; capital of Maine (1820–32). Pop: 63 635 (2003 est)

Portlaoise a town in central Republic of Ireland, county town of Laois: site of a top-security prison. Pop: 12 127 (2002)

Port Louis the capital and chief port of Mauritius, on the NW coast on the Indian Ocean. Pop: 146 876 (2002 est)

Port Moresby the capital and chief port of Papua New Guinea, on the SE coast on the Gulf of Papua: important Allied base in World War II. Pop: 290 000 (2005 est)

Port Nicholson 1 the first British settlement in New Zealand, established on Wellington Harbour in 1840: grew into Wellington 2 the former name for Wellington Harbour

Portobello a small port in Panama, on the Caribbean northeast of Colón: the most important port in South America in colonial times; declined with the opening of the Panama Canal. Pop: 3026 (1990 est)

Port of Spain the capital and chief port of Trinidad and Tobago, on the W coast of Trinidad. Pop: 56 000 (2005 est)

Porto Novo the capital of Benin, in the southwest on a coastal lagoon: formerly a centre of Portuguese settlement and the slave trade. Pop: 253 000 (2005 est)

Port Phillip Bay *or* **Port Phillip** a bay in SE Australia, which forms the harbour of Melbourne

portrait a a painting, drawing, sculpture, photograph, or other likeness of an individual, esp of the face b (*as modifier*): *a portrait gallery*

portraiture 1 the practice or art of making portraits 2 a another term for **portrait** (sense a) b portraits collectively

Port Royal 1 a fortified town in SE Jamaica, at the entrance to Kingston harbour: capital of Jamaica in colonial times 2 the former name (until 1710) of **Annapolis Royal** 3 an educational institution about 27 km (17 miles) west of Paris that flourished from 1638 to 1704, when it was suppressed by papal bull as it had become a centre of Jansenism. Its teachers were noted esp for their work on linguistics: their *Grammaire générale et raisonnée* exercised much influence

Port Said a port in NE Egypt, at the N end of the Suez Canal: founded in 1859 when the Suez Canal was begun; became the largest coaling station in the world and later an oil-bunkering port; damaged in the Arab-Israeli wars of 1967 and 1973. Pop: 546 000 (2005 est)

Portsmouth 1 a port in S England, in Portsmouth unitary authority, Hampshire, on the English Channel: Britain's chief naval base; university (1992). Pop: 187 056 (2001) **2** a unitary authority in S England, in Hampshire. Pop: 188 700 (2003 est). Area: 37 sq km (14 sq miles) **3** a port in SE Virginia, on the Elizabeth River: naval base; shipyards. Pop: 99 617 (2003 est)

Port Sudan the chief port of the Sudan, in the NE on the Red Sea. Pop: 499 000 (2005 est)

Port Talbot a port in SE Wales, in Neath Port Talbot county borough on Swansea Bay: established as a coal port in the mid-19th century; large steelworks; ore terminal. Pop: 35 633 (2001)

Portugal a republic in SW Europe, on the Atlantic: became an independent monarchy in 1139 and expelled the Moors in 1249 after more than four centuries of Muslim rule; became a republic in 1910; under the dictatorship of Salazar from 1932 until 1968, when he was succeeded by Dr Caetano, who was overthrown by a junta in 1974; constitutional government restored in 1976. Portugal is a member of the European Union. Official language: Portuguese. Religion: Roman Catholic majority. Currency: euro. Capital: Lisbon. Pop: 10 072 000 (2004 est). Area: 91 831 sq km (35 456 sq miles)

Portuguese the official language of Portugal, its overseas territories, and Brazil: the native language of approximately 110 million people. It belongs to the Romance group of the Indo-European family and is derived from the Galician dialect of Vulgar Latin

Portuguese India a former Portuguese overseas province on the W coast of India, consisting of Goa, Daman, and Diu: established between 1505 and 1510; annexed by India in 1961

Portuguese man-of-war any of several large complex colonial hydrozoans of the genus *Physalia*, esp *P. physalis*, having an aerial float and long stinging tentacles: order *Siphonophora*

pose *Art* a physical attitude, esp one deliberately adopted for or represented by an artist or photographer

Poseidon *Greek myth* the god of the sea and of earthquakes; brother of Zeus, Hades, and Hera. He is generally depicted in art wielding a trident

position **1** *Music* **a** the vertical spacing or layout of the written notes in a chord. Chords arranged with the three upper voices close together are in **close position**. Chords whose notes are evenly or widely distributed are in **open position** **b** one of the points on the fingerboard of a stringed instrument, determining where a string is to be stopped **2** in classical prosody **a** the situation in which a short vowel may be regarded as long, that is, when it occurs before two or more consonants **b** **make position** (of a consonant, either on its own or in combination with other consonants, such as x in Latin) to cause a short vowel to become metrically long when placed after it

positive vetting the checking of a person's background, political affiliation, etc, to assess his suitability for a position that may involve national security

positivism **1** a strong form of empiricism, esp as established in the philosophical system of Auguste Comte, the French mathematician and philosopher (1798–1857), that rejects metaphysics and theology as seeking knowledge beyond the scope of experience, and holds that experimental investigation and observation are the only sources of substantial knowledge **2** the jurisprudential doctrine that the legitimacy of a law depends on its being enacted in proper form, rather than on its content

positron *Physics* the antiparticle of the electron, having the same mass but an equal and opposite charge. It is produced in certain decay processes and in pair production, annihilation occurring when it collides with an electron

posse **1** *US* short for **posse comitatus**, the able-bodied men of a district assembled together and forming a group upon whom the sheriff may call for assistance in maintaining law and order **2** *Law* possibility (esp in the phrase **in posse**)

possession *Politics* a territory subject to a foreign state or to a sovereign prince

possible *Logic* (of a statement, formula, etc) capable of being true under some interpretation, or in some circumstances. Usual symbol: Mp or $\Diamond p$, where p is the given expression

possum **1** an informal name for **opossum 2** *Austral. and NZ* any of various Australasian arboreal marsupials, such as *Trichosurus vulpecula* (**brush-tailed phalanger**), having dense fur and a long tail: family *Phalangeridae*

post[1] *Horse racing* **a** either of two upright poles marking the beginning (**starting post**) and end (**winning post**) of a racecourse **b** the finish of a horse race

post[2] **1** *Brit* an official system of mail delivery **2** (formerly) any of a series of stations furnishing relays of men and horses to deliver mail over a fixed route **3** a rider who carried mail between such stations

postage stamp **1** a printed paper label with a gummed back for attaching to mail as an official indication that the required postage has been paid **2** a mark directly printed or embossed on an envelope, postcard, etc, serving the same function

posterior **1** *Zoology* (of animals) of or near the hind end **2** *Botany* (of a flower) situated nearest to the main stem **3** *Anatomy* dorsal or towards the spine **4** the buttocks; rump

postern **1** a back door or gate, esp one that is for private use **2** situated at the rear or the side

postgraduate a student who has obtained a degree from a university, etc, and is pursuing studies for a more advanced qualification

postilion *or* **postillion** a person who rides the near horse of the leaders in order to guide a team of horses drawing a coach

postimpressionism a movement in painting in France at the end of the 19th century, begun by Paul Cézanne (1839–1906) and exemplified by Paul Gauguin (1848–1903), Vincent Van Gogh (1853–90), and Henri Matisse (1869–1954), which rejected the naturalism and momentary effects of impressionism but adapted its use of pure colour to paint subjects with greater subjective emotion

▷www.artchive.com/ftp_site_reg.htm
▷www.artcyclopedia.com/history

posting *Sport* a wrestling attack in which the opponent is hurled at the post in one of the corners of the ring

postmaster general the executive head of the postal service in certain countries

postmortem 1 occurring after death **2** dissection and examination of a dead body to determine the cause of death

Post Office a government department or authority in many countries responsible for postal services and often telecommunications

postoperative of, relating to, or occurring in the period following a surgical operation

post-traumatic stress disorder a psychological condition, characterized by anxiety, withdrawal, and a proneness to physical illness, that may follow a traumatic experience

postulate *Logic, Maths* an unproved and indemonstrable statement that should be taken for granted: used as an initial premise or underlying hypothesis in a process of reasoning

pot¹ 1 the amount that a pot will hold; potful **2** a handmade piece of pottery **3** a large mug or tankard, as for beer **4** the money or stakes in the pool in gambling games, esp poker **5** a wicker trap for catching fish, esp crustaceans **6** *Billiards, Snooker* a shot by which a ball is pocketed **7** *US, informal* a joint fund created by a group of individuals or enterprises and drawn upon by them for specified purposes **8** *Hunting* See **pot shot 9** See **potbelly**

pot² *Scot and northern English, dialect* a deep hole or pothole **b** (*capital when part of a name*): *Pen-y-Ghent Pot*

pot³ *Slang* cannabis used as a drug in any form, such as leaves (marijuana or hemp) or resin (hashish)

potassium a light silvery element of the alkali metal group that is highly reactive and rapidly oxidizes in air; occurs principally in carnallite and sylvite. It is used when alloyed with sodium as a cooling medium in nuclear reactors and its compounds are widely used, esp in fertilizers. Symbol: K; atomic no.: 19; atomic wt.: 39.0983; valency: 1; relative density: 0.862; melting pt.: 63.71°C; boiling pt.: 759°C

potassium nitrate a colourless or white crystalline compound used in gunpowders, pyrotechnics, fertilizers, and as a preservative for foods, esp as a curing salt for ham, sausages, etc (**E252**). Formula: KNO_3

potato 1 a a solanaceous plant, *Solanum tuberosum*, of South America: widely cultivated for its edible tubers **b** the starchy oval tuber of this plant, which has a brown or red skin and is cooked and eaten as a vegetable **2** any of various similar plants, esp the sweet potato
▷www.indepthinfo.com/potato
▷www.potatohelp.com
▷www.bigspud.com

potbelly a protruding or distended belly

potboiler *Informal* a literary or artistic work of little merit produced quickly in order to make money

pot-bound (of a pot plant) having grown to fill all the available root space and therefore lacking room for continued growth

poteen *or* **poitín** (in Ireland) illicit spirit, often distilled from potatoes

Potemkin *or* **Potyomkin 1** Grigori Aleksandrovich 1739–91, Russian soldier and statesman; lover of Catherine II, whose favourite he remained until his death **2** apparently impressive but actually sham or artificial

potentate a person who possesses great power or authority, esp a ruler or monarch

potential difference the difference in electric potential between two points in an electric field; the work that has to be done in transferring unit positive charge from one point to the other, measured in volts.

potential energy the energy of a body or system as a result of its position in an electric, magnetic, or gravitational field. It is measured in joules (SI units), electronvolts, ergs, etc.

potherb any plant having leaves, flowers, stems, etc, that are used in cooking for seasoning and flavouring or are eaten as a vegetable

pothole 1 *Geography* **a** a deep hole in limestone areas resulting from action by running water **b** a circular hole in the bed of a river produced by abrasion **2** a deep hole, esp one produced in a road surface by wear or weathering

potholing *Brit* a sport in which participants explore underground caves
▷www.caveinfo.org.uk

pothook a long hook used for lifting hot pots, lids, etc.

Potiphar *Old Testament* one of Pharaoh's officers, who bought Joseph as a slave (Genesis 37:36)

Potomac a river in the E central US, rising in the Appalachian Mountains of West Virginia: flows northeast, then generally southeast to Chesapeake Bay. Length (from the confluence of headstreams): 462 km (287 miles)

potpourri *Music* a medley of popular tunes

Potsdam a city in Germany, the capital of Brandenburg on the Havel River: residence of Prussian kings and German emperors and scene of the **Potsdam Conference** of 1945, at which the main Allied powers agreed on a plan to occupy Germany at the end of the Second World War. Pop: 144 979 (2003 est)

pot shot 1 a chance shot taken casually, hastily, or without careful aim **2** a shot fired to kill game in disregard of the rules of sport **3** a shot fired at quarry within easy range, often from an ambush

Potter 1 (**Helen**) Beatrix 1866–1943, British author and illustrator of children's animal stories, such as *The Tale of Peter Rabbit* (1902) **2** Dennis (**Christopher George**). 1935–94, British dramatist. His TV plays include *Pennies from Heaven* (1978), *The Singing Detective* (1986), and *Blackeyes* (1989) **3** Paulus 1625–54, Dutch painter, esp of animals **4** Stephen 1900–70, British humorist and critic. Among his best-known works are *Gamesmanship* (1947) and *One-Upmanship* (1952), on the art of achieving superiority over others

pottery 1 articles, vessels, etc, made from earthenware and dried and baked in a kiln **2** a place where such articles are made **3** the craft or business of making such articles
▷www.potterymaking.org/pmionline.html
▷www.ceramicstoday.com
▷www.studiopottery.com

potting shed a building in which plants are set in flowerpots and in which empty pots, potting compost, etc, are stored

pouch 1 *Zoology* a saclike structure in any of various animals, such as the abdominal receptacle marsupium in marsupials or the cheek fold in rodents **2** *Anatomy* any sac, pocket, or pouchlike cavity or space in an organ or part

Poulenc Francis 1899–1963, French composer; a member of Les Six. His works include the operas *Les Mamelles de Tirésias* (1947) and *Dialogues des Carmélites* (1957), and the ballet *Les Biches* (1924)

poultice *Med* a local moist and often heated application for the skin consisting of substances such as kaolin, linseed, or mustard, used to improve the circulation, treat inflamed areas, etc.

pounce¹ the claw of a bird of prey

pounce² **1** a very fine resinous powder, esp of cuttlefish bone, formerly used to dry ink or sprinkled over parchment or unsized writing paper to stop the ink from running **2** a fine powder, esp of charcoal, that is tapped through perforations in paper corresponding to the main lines of a design in order to transfer the design to another surface

pound¹ **1** an avoirdupois unit of weight that is divided into 16 ounces and is equal to 0.453 592 kilograms **2** a troy unit of weight divided into 12 ounces equal to 0.373 242 kilograms **3** an apothecaries' unit of weight, used in the US, that is divided into 5760 grains and is equal to one pound troy **4** a unit of force equal to the mass of 1 pound avoirdupois where the acceleration of free fall is 32.174 feet per second per second **5** **a** the standard monetary unit of the United Kingdom, the Channel Islands, the Isle of Man, and various UK overseas territories, divided into 100 pence **b** (*as modifier*): *a pound coin* **6** the standard monetary unit of the following countries **a** Cyprus: divided into 100 cents **b** Egypt: divided into 100 piastres **c** Lebanon: divided into 100 piastres **d** Syria: divided into 100 piastres **7** another name for **lira** **8** a former Scottish monetary unit originally worth an English pound but later declining in value to 1 shilling 8 pence **9** the former standard monetary unit of the Republic of Ireland, divided into 100 pence; replaced by the euro in 2002 **10** a former monetary unit of the Sudan replaced by the dinar in 1992

pound² an enclosure, esp one maintained by a public authority, for keeping officially removed vehicles or distrained goods or animals, esp stray dogs

Pound Ezra (**Loomis**). 1885–1972, US poet, translator, and critic, living in Europe. Indicted for treason by the US government (1945) for pro-Fascist broadcasts during World War II, he was committed to a mental hospital until 1958. He was a founder of imagism and championed the early work of such writers as T. S. Eliot, Joyce, and Hemingway. His life work, the *Cantos* (1925–70), is an unfinished sequence of poems, which incorporates mythological and historical materials in several languages as well as political, economic, and autobiographical elements

poundage a weight expressed in pounds

Poussin Nicolas 1594–1665, French painter, regarded as a leader of French classical painting. He is best known for the austere historical and biblical paintings and landscapes of his later years

pout 1 any of various gadoid food fishes, esp the bib

(also called **whiting pout**) **2** any of certain other stout-bodied fishes

pouter a breed of domestic pigeon with a large crop capable of being greatly puffed out

pow¹ *Scot* the head or a head of hair

pow² *Scot* a creek or slow stream

powder 1 a solid substance in the form of tiny loose particles **2** any of various preparations in this form, such as gunpowder, face powder, or soap powder **3** fresh loose snow, esp when considered as skiing terrain

Powell 1 Anthony (**Dymoke**). 1905–2000, British novelist, best known for his sequence of novels under the general title *A Dance to the Music of Time* (1951–75) **2 Cecil Frank** 1903–69, British physicist, who was awarded the Nobel prize for physics in 1950 for his discovery of the pi-meson **3 Colin** (**Luther**). born 1937, US politician and general; Republican secretary of state from 2001 **4 Earl**, known as **Bud Powell**. 1924–1966, US modern-jazz pianist **5** (**John**) **Enoch** 1912–98, British politician. An outspoken opponent of Commonwealth immigration into Britain and of British membership of the Common Market (now the European Union), in 1974 he resigned from the Conservative Party, returning to Parliament as a United Ulster Unionist Council member (1974–87) **6 Michael** 1905–90, British film writer, producer, and director, best known for his collaboration (1942–57) with Emeric Pressburger. Films include *The Life and Death of Colonel Blimp* (1943), *A Matter of Life and Death* (1946), *The Red Shoes* (1948), and *Peeping Tom* (1960)

power 1 control or dominion or a position of control, dominion, or authority **2** a state or other political entity with political, industrial, or military strength **3** a legal authority to act, esp in a specified capacity, for another **b** the document conferring such authority **4** *Maths* **a** the value of a number or quantity raised to some exponent **b** another name for **exponent 5** *Physics, Engineering* a measure of the rate of doing work expressed as the work done per unit time. It is measured in watts, horsepower, etc. **6** **a** the rate at which electrical energy is fed into or taken from a device or system. It is expressed, in a direct-current circuit, as the product of current and voltage and, in an alternating-current circuit, as the product of the effective values of the current and voltage and the cosine of the phase angle between them. It is measured in watts **b** (*as modifier*): *a power amplifier* **7** **a** mechanical energy as opposed to manual labour **b** (*as modifier*): *a power mower* **8** **a** a measure of the ability of a lens or optical system to magnify an object, equal to the reciprocal of the focal length. It is measured in dioptres **b** another word for **magnification 9** the sixth of the nine orders into which the angels are traditionally divided in medieval angelology

powerboat a boat propelled by an inboard or outboard motor

power cut a temporary interruption or reduction in the supply of electrical power to a particular area

powerful extremely effective or efficient in action

powerhouse an electrical generating station or plant

power of attorney 1 legal authority to act for another person in certain specified matters **2** the document conferring such authority

power point 1 an electrical socket mounted on or recessed into a wall **2** such a socket, esp one installed before the introduction of 13 ampere ring mains, that is designed to provide a current of up to 15 amperes for supplying heaters, etc, rather than lights

power-sharing a political arrangement in which opposing groups in a society participate in government

power station an electrical generating station

power steering a form of steering used on vehicles, where the torque applied to the steering wheel is augmented by engine power

Powhatan American Indian name *Wahunsonacock*. died 1618, American Indian chief of a confederacy of tribes; father of Pocahontas

powwow 1 a magical ceremony of certain North American Indians, usually accompanied by feasting and dancing **2** (among certain North American Indians) a medicine man **3** a meeting of or negotiation with North American Indians

Powys¹ 1 John Cowper 1872–1963, British novelist, essayist, and poet, who spent much of his life in the US. His novels include *Wolf Solent* (1929), *A Glastonbury Romance* (1932), and *Owen Glendower* (1940) **2** his brother, **Llewelyn** 1884–1939, British essayist and journalist **3** his brother, **T(heodore) F(rancis)**. 1875–1953, British novelist and short-story writer, noted for such religious fables as *Mr Weston's Good Wine* (1927) and *Unclay* (1931)

Powys² a county in E Wales, formed in 1974 from most of Breconshire, Montgomeryshire, and Radnorshire. Administrative centre: Llandrindod Wells. Pop: 129 300 (2003 est). Area: 5077 sq km (1960 sq miles)

pox 1 any disease characterized by the formation of pustules on the skin that often leave pockmarks when healed **2** an informal name for **syphilis**

Poznań a city in W Poland, on the Warta River: the centre of Polish resistance to German rule (1815–1918, 1939–45). Pop: 661 000 (2005 est)

Pozzuoli a port in SW Italy, in Campania on the **Gulf of Pozzuoli** (an inlet of the Bay of Naples): in a region of great volcanic activity; founded in the 6th century BC by the Greeks. Pop: 78 754 (2001)

practical *Education* an examination in the practical skills of a subject

practice *Law* the established method of conducting proceedings in a court of law

practitioner *Christian Science* a person authorized to practise spiritual healing

Prado an art gallery in Madrid housing an important collection of Spanish paintings

praetor *or* **pretor** (in ancient Rome) any of several senior magistrates ranking just below the consuls

Praetorius Michael 1571–1621, German composer and musicologist, noted esp for his description of contemporary musical practices and instruments, *Syntagma musicum* (1615–19)

pragmatism *Philosophy* **a** the doctrine that the content of a concept consists only in its practical applicability **b** the doctrine that truth consists not in correspondence with the facts but in successful coherence with experience

Prague the capital and largest city of the Czech Republic, on the Vltava River: a rich commercial centre during the Middle Ages; site of Charles University (1348) and a technical university (1707); scene of defenestrations (1419 and 1618) that contributed to the outbreak of the Hussite Wars and the Thirty Years' War respectively. Pop: 1 164 000 (2005 est)

prairie a treeless grassy plain of the central US and S Canada

prairie dog any of several gregarious sciurine rodents of the genus *Cynomys*, such as *C. ludovicianus*, that live in large complex burrows in the prairies of North America

praise *Religion* the extolling of a deity or the rendering of homage and gratitude to a deity

pram *Nautical* a light tender with a flat bottom and a bow formed from the ends of the side and bottom planks meeting in a small raised transom

praseodymium a malleable ductile silvery-white element of the lanthanide series of metals. It occurs principally in monazite and bastnaesite and is used with other rare earths in carbon-arc lights and as a pigment in glass. Symbol: Pr; atomic no.: 59; atomic wt.: 140.90765; valency: 3; relative density: 6.773; melting pt.: 931°C; boiling pt.: 3520°C

Pratchett Terence (David John), known as *Terry*. born 1948, British writer, noted for his comic fantasy novels in the *Discworld* series

Prato a walled city in central Italy, in Tuscany: woollen industry. Pop: 172 499 (2001)

prawn any of various small edible marine decapod crustaceans of the genera *Palaemon*, *Penaeus*, etc, having a slender flattened body with a long tail and two pairs of pincers

praxis 1 the practice and practical side of a profession or field of study, as opposed to the theory **2** a practical exercise

Praxiteles 4th-century BC. Greek sculptor: his works include statues of Hermes at Olympia, which survives, and of Aphrodite at Cnidus

prayer 1 a a personal communication or petition addressed to a deity, esp in the form of supplication, adoration, praise, contrition, or thanksgiving **b** any other form of spiritual communion with a deity **2** a similar personal communication that does not involve adoration, addressed to beings venerated as being closely associated with a deity, such as angels or saints **3** a form of devotion, either public or private, spent mainly or wholly praying **4** a form of words used in praying **5** *Law* a request contained in a petition to a court for the relief sought by the petitioner

prayer wheel *Buddhism* (esp in Tibet) a wheel or cylinder inscribed with or containing prayers, each revolution of which is counted as an uttered prayer, so that such prayers can be repeated by turning it

preacher a person who has the calling and function of preaching the Christian Gospel, esp a Protestant clergyman

prebend 1 the stipend assigned by a cathedral or collegiate church to a canon or member of the chapter **2** the land, tithe, or other source of such a stipend **3** a less common word for **prebendary 4** *Church of England* the office, formerly with an endowment, of a prebendary

prebendary 1 a canon or member of the chapter of a cathedral or collegiate church who holds a prebend **2**

Church of England an honorary canon with the title of prebendary

Precambrian *or* **Pre-Cambrian** of, denoting, or formed in the earliest geological era, which lasted for about 4 000 000 000 years before the Cambrian period

precancerous (esp of cells) displaying characteristics that may develop into cancer

precedent *Law* a judicial decision that serves as an authority for deciding a later case

precentor 1 a cleric who directs the choral services in a cathedral 2 a person who leads a congregation or choir in the sung parts of church services

precept *Law* a a writ or warrant b a written order to a sheriff to arrange an election, the empanelling of a jury, etc. c (in England) an order to collect money under a rate

preceptor *US* a practising physician giving practical training to a medical student

precession the motion of a spinning body, such as a top, gyroscope, or planet, in which it wobbles so that the axis of rotation sweeps out a cone

precinct 1 an area in a town, often closed to traffic, that is designed or reserved for a particular purpose 2 *US* a a district of a city for administrative or police purposes b the police responsible for such a district 3 *US* a polling or electoral district

precious stone any of certain rare minerals, such as diamond, ruby, sapphire, emerald, or opal, that are highly valued as gemstones

precipice a the steep sheer face of a cliff or crag b the cliff or crag itself

precipitant *Chem* a substance or agent that causes a precipitate to form

precipitate *Chem* a precipitated solid in its suspended form or after settling or filtering

precipitation 1 *Meteorol* a rain, snow, sleet, dew, etc, formed by condensation of water vapour in the atmosphere b the deposition of these on the earth's surface c the amount precipitated 2 the production or formation of a chemical precipitate 3 *Spiritualism* the appearance of a spirit in bodily form; materialization

precocious *Botany* (of plants, fruit, etc) flowering or ripening early

precognition *Psychol* the alleged ability to foresee future events

precursor a chemical substance that gives rise to another more important substance

predacious *or* **predaceous** (of animals) habitually hunting and killing other animals for food

predator any carnivorous animal

predestination *Theol* a the act of God foreordaining every event from eternity b the doctrine or belief, esp associated with Calvin, that the final salvation of some of mankind is foreordained from eternity by God

predicable *Logic, obsolete* one of the five Aristotelian classes of predicates (**the five heads of predicables**), namely genus, species, difference, property, and relation

predicament *Logic, obsolete* one of Aristotle's ten categories of being

predicate *Logic* a an expression that is derived from a sentence by the deletion of a name b a property, characteristic, or attribute that may be affirmed or denied of something. The categorial statement *all men are mortal* relates two predicates, *is a man* and *is mortal* c the term of a categorial proposition that is affirmed or denied of its subject. In this example *all men* is the subject, and *mortal* is the predicate d a function from individuals to truth values, the truth set of the function being the extension of the predicate

predikant *or* **predicant** a minister in the Dutch Reformed Church, esp in South Africa

pre-emption 1 *Law* the purchase of or right to purchase property in advance of or in preference to others 2 *International law* the right of a government to intercept and seize for its own purposes goods or property of the subjects of another state while in transit, esp in time of war

pre-emptive *Bridge* (of a high bid) made to shut out opposition bidding

preface 1 a statement written as an introduction to a literary or other work, typically explaining its scope, intention, method, etc.; foreword 2 *RC Church* a prayer of thanksgiving and exhortation serving as an introduction to the canon of the Mass

prefect 1 (in France, Italy, etc) the chief administrative officer in a department 2 (in France, etc) the head of a police force 3 *Brit* a schoolchild appointed to a position of limited power over his fellows 4 (in ancient Rome) any of several magistrates or military commanders 5 *RC Church* an official having jurisdiction over a missionary district that has no ordinary 6 *RC Church* one of two senior masters in a Jesuit school or college (the **prefect of studies** and the **prefect of discipline** or **first prefect**) 7 *RC Church* a cardinal in charge of a congregation of the Curia

prefecture 1 the office, position, or area of authority of a prefect 2 the official residence of a prefect in France, Italy, etc.

preference 1 *Law* a the settling of the claims of one or more creditors before or to the exclusion of those of the others b a prior right to payment, as of a dividend or share in the assets of a company in the event of liquidation 2 *Commerce* the granting of favour or precedence to particular foreign countries, as by levying differential tariffs

prehensile adapted for grasping, esp by wrapping around a support

prehistoric *or* **prehistorical** of or relating to man's development before the appearance of the written word

prejudice without prejudice *Law* without dismissing or detracting from an existing right or claim

prelacy 1 a the office or status of a prelate b prelates collectively 2 *Often derogatory* government of the Church by prelates

prelate a Church dignitary of high rank, such as a cardinal, bishop, or abbot

prelude a a piece of music that precedes a fugue, or forms the first movement of a suite, or an introduction to an act in an opera, etc. b (esp for piano) a self-contained piece of music

premature (of an infant) weighing less than 2500 g (5½ lbs) and usually born before the end of the full period of gestation

premedication *Surgery* any drugs administered to sedate and otherwise prepare a patient for general anaesthesia

premenstrual syndrome *or* **tension** a group of symptoms, including nervous tension and fluid retention, any of which may be experienced as a result of hormonal changes in the days before a menstrual period starts

premier 1 another name for **prime minister** 2 any of the heads of governments of the Canadian provinces and the Australian states

premiere 1 the first public performance of a film, play, opera, etc. 2 the leading lady in a theatre company

Preminger Otto (**Ludwig**). 1906–86, US film director, born in Austria. His films include *Carmen Jones* (1954) and *Anatomy of a Murder* (1959)

premise *Logic* a statement that is assumed to be true for the purpose of an argument from which a conclusion is drawn

premium 1 an amount paid in addition to a standard rate, price, wage, etc.; bonus 2 the amount above nominal or par value at which something sells 3 a an offer of something free or at a specially reduced price as an inducement to buy a commodity or service b (*as modifier*): *a premium offer* 4 a fee, now rarely required, for instruction or apprenticeship in a profession or trade

premolar 1 situated before a molar tooth 2 any one of eight bicuspid teeth in the human adult, two situated on each side of both jaws between the first molar and the canine

prenatal *Informal* a prenatal examination

preparation 1 something that is prepared, esp a medicinal formulation 2 esp in a boarding school a homework b the period reserved for this 3 *Music* a the anticipation of a dissonance so that the note producing it in one chord is first heard in the preceding chord as a consonance b a note so employed 4 the preliminary prayers at Mass or divine service

preparatory school 1 (in Britain) a private school, usually single-sex and for children between the ages of 6 and 13, generally preparing pupils for public school 2 (in the US) a private secondary school preparing pupils for college

prepuce 1 the retractable fold of skin covering the tip of the penis 2 a similar fold of skin covering the tip of the clitoris

Pre-Raphaelite a member of the Pre-Raphaelite Brotherhood, an association of British painters and writers including Dante Gabriel Rossetti (1828–82), Holman Hunt (1827–1910), and Sir John Everett Millais (1829–96), founded in 1848 to combat the shallow conventionalism of academic painting and revive the fidelity to nature and the vivid realistic colour that they considered typical of Italian painting before Raphael (1483–1520)

▷www.artchive.com/ftp_site_reg.htm

prerogative a power, privilege, or immunity restricted to a sovereign or sovereign government

presbyopia a progressively diminishing ability of the eye to focus, noticeable from middle to old age, caused by loss of elasticity of the crystalline lens

presbyter 1 a an elder of a congregation in the early

Christian Church b (in some Churches having episcopal politics) an official who is subordinate to a bishop and has administrative, teaching, and sacerdotal functions 2 (in some hierarchical Churches) another name for **priest** 3 in the Presbyterian Church a a teaching elder b a ruling elder

presbyterian 1 of, relating to, or designating Church government by presbyters or lay elders 2 an upholder of this type of Church government

Presbyterian of or relating to any of various Protestant Churches governed by presbyters or lay elders and adhering to various modified forms of Calvinism

▷http://www.wikipedia.org/wiki/Presbyterian

presbytery 1 *Presbyterian Church* a a local Church court composed of ministers and elders b the congregations or churches within the jurisdiction of any such court 2 the part of a cathedral or church east of the choir, in which the main altar is situated; sanctuary 3 presbyters or elders collectively 4 government of a church by presbyters or elders 5 *RC Church* the residence of a parish priest

Prescott 1 John Leslie born 1938, British politician: deputy leader of the Labour Party from 1994; deputy prime minister from 1997; secretary of state for the environment, transport, and the regions (1997–2001); minister for local government and the regions (2002–) 2 William Hickling 1796–1859, US historian, noted for his work on the history of Spain and her colonies

prescription 1 a written instructions from a physician, dentist, etc, to a pharmacist stating the form, dosage strength, etc, of a drug to be issued to a specific patient b the drug or remedy prescribed 2 (of drugs) available legally only with a doctor's prescription 3 a written instructions from an optician specifying the lenses needed to correct defects of vision b (*as modifier*): *prescription glasses* 4 *Law* a the uninterrupted possession of property over a stated period of time, after which a right or title is acquired (**positive prescription**) b the barring of adverse claims to property, etc, after a specified period of time has elapsed, allowing the possessor to acquire title (**negative prescription**) c the right or title acquired in either of these ways

presence 1 an invisible spirit felt to be nearby 2 *Electronics* a recording control that boosts mid-range frequencies 3 (of a recording) a quality that gives the impression that the listener is in the presence of the original source of the sound

presentation 1 a verbal report presented with illustrative material, such as slides, graphs, etc. 2 *Church* the act or right of nominating a clergyman to a benefice 3 *Med* the position of a baby relative to the birth canal at the time of birth 4 *Philosophy* a sense datum 5 another name for (feast of) **Candlemas**

preserve areas where game is reared for private hunting or fishing

preset *Electronics* a control, such as a variable resistor, that is not as accessible as the main controls and is used to set initial conditions

preshrunk (of fabrics, garments, etc) having undergone a shrinking process during manufacture so that further shrinkage will not occur

presidency 1 a the office, dignity, or term of a president

b the office of president of a republic, esp the office of the President of the US **2** *Mormon Church* **a** a local administrative council consisting of a president and two executive members **b** the supreme administrative body composed of the Prophet and two councillors

president 1 the chief executive or head of state of a republic, esp the US **2** (in the US) the chief executive officer of a company, corporation, etc. **3** the chief executive officer of certain establishments of higher education

presidium *or* **praesidium 1** (in Communist countries) a permanent committee of a larger body, such as a legislature, that acts for it when it is in recess **2** a collective presidency, esp of a nongovernmental organization

Presley Elvis (**Aaron** *or* **Aron**). 1935–77, US rock and roll singer. His recordings include "That's all Right (Mama)" (1954), "Heartbreak Hotel" (1956), "Hound Dog" (1956), numbers from the films *Loving You* and *Jailhouse Rock* (both 1957), and "Suspicious Minds" (1970)

press¹ 1 any machine that exerts pressure to form, shape, or cut materials or to extract liquids, compress solids, or hold components together while an adhesive joint is formed **2** *Weightlifting* a lift in which the weight is raised to shoulder level and then above the head

press² 1 recruitment into military service by forcible measures, as by a press gang

Pressburger Emeric 1902–88, Hungarian film writer and producer, living in Britain: best known for his collaboration (1942–57) with Michael Powell. Films include *The Life and Death of Colonel Blimp* (1943), *I Know Where I'm Going* (1945), and *A Matter of Life and Death* (1946)

press gang (formerly) a detachment of men used to press civilians for service in the navy or army

pressing 1 a large specified number of gramophone records produced at one time from a master record **2** a component formed in a press **3** *Football* the tactic of trying to stay very close to the opposition when they are in possession of the ball

press-up an exercise in which the body is alternately raised from and lowered to the floor by the arms only, the trunk being kept straight with the toes and hands resting on the floor

pressure 1 the normal force applied to a unit area of a surface, usually measured in pascals (newtons per square metre), millibars, torr, or atmospheres. **2** short for **atmospheric pressure** *or* **blood pressure**

pressure group a group of people who seek to exert pressure on legislators, public opinion, etc, in order to promote their own ideas or welfare

presto 1 *Music* to be played very fast **2** *Music* a movement or passage directed to be played very quickly

Preston a city in NW England, administrative centre of Lancashire, on the River Ribble: developed as a weaving centre (17th–18th centuries); university (1992). Pop: 184 836 (2001)

Prestonpans a small town and resort in SE Scotland, in East Lothian on the Firth of Forth: scene of the battle (1745) in which the Jacobite army of Prince Charles Edward defeated government forces under Sir John Cope. Pop: 7153 (2001)

Prestwich a town in NW England, in Bury unitary authority, Greater Manchester. Pop: 31 693 (2001)

Prestwick a town in SW Scotland, in South Ayrshire on the Firth of Clyde; international airport, golf course: tourism. Pop: 14 934 (2001)

presumption *Law* an inference of the truth of a fact from other facts proved, admitted, or judicially noticed

pretender *History* a person who mounts a claim, as to a throne or title

Pretoria a city in N South Africa, the administrative capital of South Africa; formerly capital of Transvaal province: two universities (1873, 1930); large steelworks. Pop: 525 384 (2001)

Pretorius 1 Andries Wilhelmus Jacobus 1799–1853, a Boer leader in the Great Trek (1838) to escape British sovereignty; he also led an expedition to the Transvaal (1848). The town Pretoria was named after him **2** his son, Marthinus Wessels 1819–1901, first president of the South African Republic (1857–71) and of the Orange Free State (1859–63)

preventive 1 *Med* **a** tending to prevent disease; prophylactic **b** of or relating to the branch of medicine concerned with prolonging life and preventing disease **2** (in Britain) of, relating to, or belonging to the customs and excise service or the coastguard **3** *Med* any drug or agent that tends to prevent or protect against disease

preview *or US* **prevue** a public performance of a play before the official first night

Previn André born 1929, US orchestral conductor, born in Germany; living in Britain

prey 1 an animal hunted or captured by another for food **2 bird** *or* **beast of prey** a bird or animal that preys on others for food

price-fixing the setting of prices by agreement among producers and distributors

prick 1 a taboo slang word for **penis 2** the footprint or track of an animal, esp a hare

prickle *Botany* a pointed process arising from the outer layer of a stem, leaf, etc, and containing no woody or conducting tissue

prickly pear 1 any of various tropical cacti of the genus *Opuntia*, having flattened or cylindrical spiny joints and oval fruit that is edible in some species **2** the fruit of any of these plants

pride 1 a group (of lions) **2** the mettle of a horse; courage; spirit **3** *Archaic* sexual desire, esp in a female animal

Pride Thomas died 1658, English soldier on the Parliamentary side during the Civil War. He expelled members of the Long Parliament hostile to the army (**Pride's Purge**, 1648) and signed Charles I's death warrant

priest *or feminine* **priestess 1** *Christianity* a person ordained to act as a mediator between God and man in administering the sacraments, preaching, blessing, guiding, etc. **2** (in episcopal Churches) a minister in the second grade of the hierarchy of holy orders, ranking below a bishop but above a deacon **3** a minister of any religion **4** *Judaism* a descendant of the family of Aaron who has certain privileges in the synagogue service **5** (in some non-Christian religions) an official who offers sacrifice on behalf of the people and performs other religious ceremonies **6** a variety of fancy pigeon having a bald pate with a crest or peak at the back of the head **7** *Angling* a small club used to kill fish caught

Priestley 1 J(ohn) B(oynton). 1894–1984, English author. His works include the novels *The Good Companions* (1929) and *Angel Pavement* (1930) and the play *An Inspector Calls* (1946) **2** Joseph 1733–1804, English chemist, political theorist, and clergyman, in the US from 1794. He discovered oxygen (1774) independently of Scheele and isolated and described many other gases

Prigogine Viscount Ilya 1917–2003, Belgian chemist, born in Russia: Nobel prize for chemistry 1977 for his work on nonequilibrium thermodynamics

prima ballerina a leading female ballet dancer

primacy *Christianity* the office, rank, or jurisdiction of a primate or senior bishop or (in the Roman Catholic Church) the pope

prima donna a female operatic star; diva

primary 1 of or relating to the education of children up to the age of 11 **2** (of the flight feathers of a bird's wing) growing from the manus **3 a** being the part of an electric circuit, such as a transformer or induction coil, in which a changing current induces a current in a neighbouring circuit **b** (of a current) flowing in such a circuit **4 a** (of a product) consisting of a natural raw material; unmanufactured **b** (of production or industry) involving the extraction or winning of such products. Agriculture, fishing, forestry, hunting, and mining are primary industries **5** *Chem* **a** (of an organic compound) having a functional group attached to a carbon atom that is attached to at least two hydrogen atoms **b** (of an amine) having only one organic group attached to the nitrogen atom; containing the group NH_2 **c** (of a salt) derived from a tribasic acid by replacement of one acidic hydrogen atom with a metal atom or electropositive group **6** *Geology* relating to magmas that have not experienced fractional crystallization or crystal contamination **7** in the US **a** a preliminary election in which the voters of a state or region choose a party's convention delegates, nominees for office, etc. **b** a local meeting of voters registered with one party to nominate candidates, select convention delegates, etc. **8** any of the flight feathers growing from the manus of a bird's wing **9** a primary coil, winding, inductance, or current in an electric circuit **10** *Astronomy* a celestial body around which one or more specified secondary bodies orbit

primary school 1 (in Britain) a school for children below the age of 11. It is usually divided into an infant and a junior section **2** (in the US and Canada) a school equivalent to the first three or four grades of elementary school, sometimes including a kindergarten

primate¹ any placental mammal of the order *Primates*, typically having flexible hands and feet with opposable first digits, good eyesight, and, in the higher apes, a highly developed brain: includes lemurs, lorises, monkeys, apes, and man

primate² **1** another name for **archbishop 2 Primate of all England** the Archbishop of Canterbury **3 Primate of England** the Archbishop of York

prime 1 *Maths* **a** having no factors except itself or one **b** having no common factors (with) **2** *Maths* short for **prime number 3** *Music* **a** unison **b** the tonic of a scale **4**

Chiefly RC Church the second of the seven canonical hours of the divine office, originally fixed for the first hour of the day, at sunrise **5** the first of eight basic positions from which a parry or attack can be made in fencing

prime meridian the 0° meridian from which the other meridians or lines of longitude are calculated, usually taken to pass through Greenwich

prime minister 1 the head of a parliamentary government **2** the chief minister of a sovereign or a state

prime mover 1 a the source of power, such as fuel, wind, electricity, etc, for a machine **b** the means of extracting power from such a source, such as a steam engine, electric motor, etc. **2** (in the philosophy of Aristotle) that which is the cause of all movement

prime number an integer that cannot be factorized into other integers but is only divisible by itself or 1, such as 2, 3, 5, 7, and 11

primer¹ an introductory text, such as a school textbook

primer² a substance, such as paint, applied to a surface as a base, sealer, etc.

primitive 1 *Anthropol* denoting or relating to a preliterate and nonindustrial social system **2** *Biology* **a** of, relating to, or resembling an early stage in the evolutionary development of a particular group of organisms **b** another word for **primordial 3** showing the characteristics of primitive painters; untrained, childlike, or naive **4** *Geology* pertaining to magmas that have experienced only small degrees of fractional crystallization or crystal contamination **5** *Obsolete* of, relating to, or denoting rocks formed in or before the Palaeozoic era **6** *Protestant theol* of, relating to, or associated with a minority group that breaks away from a sect, denomination, or Church in order to return to what is regarded as the original simplicity of the Gospels **7 a** an artist whose work does not conform to traditional, academic, or avant-garde standards of Western painting, such as a painter from an African or Oceanic civilization **b** a painter of the pre-Renaissance era in European painting **c** a painter of any era whose work appears childlike or untrained **8** a work by such an artist **9** *Maths* a curve, function, or other form from which another is derived

Primo de Rivera 1 José Antonio 1903–36, Spanish politician; founded Falangism **2** his father, **Miguel** 1870–1930, Spanish general; dictator of Spain (1923–30)

primogeniture *Law* the right of an eldest son to succeed to the estate of his ancestor to the exclusion of all others

primordial *Biology* of or relating to an early stage of development

primrose 1 any of various temperate primulaceous plants of the genus *Primula*, esp *P. vulgaris* of Europe, which has pale yellow flowers **2** short for **evening primrose 3** a light to moderate yellow, sometimes with a greenish tinge

primula any primulaceous plant of the N temperate genus *Primula*, having white, yellow, pink, or purple funnel-shaped flowers with five spreading petals: includes the primrose, oxlip, cowslip, and polyanthus

prince 1 (in Britain) a son of the sovereign or of one of the sovereign's sons **2** a nonreigning male member of a sovereign family **3** the monarch of a small territory, such as Monaco, usually called a principality, that was at some time subordinate to an emperor or king **4** any sovereign; monarch **5** a nobleman in various countries, such as Italy and Germany

prince consort the husband of a female sovereign, who is himself a prince

Prince Edward Island an island in the Gulf of St Lawrence that constitutes the smallest Canadian province. Capital: Charlottetown. Pop: 137 864 (2004 est). Area: 5656 sq km (2184 sq miles)

princely of, belonging to, or characteristic of a prince

Prince of Peace *Bible* the future Messiah (Isaiah 9:6): held by Christians to be Christ

Prince of Wales¹ the eldest son and heir apparent of the British sovereign

Prince of Wales² Cape a cape in W Alaska, on the Bering Strait opposite the coast of the extreme northeast of Russia: the westernmost point of North America

Prince of Wales Island 1 an island in N Canada, in Nunavut. Area: about 36 000 sq km (14 000 sq miles) **2** an island in SE Alaska, the largest island in the Alexander Archipelago. Area: about 4000 sq km (1500 sq miles) **3** an island in NE Australia, in N Queensland in the Torres Strait **4** the former name (until about 1867) of the island of **Penang**

Prince Regent George IV as regent of Great Britain and Ireland during the insanity of his father (1811–20)

Prince Rupert a port in W Canada, on the coast of British Columbia: one of the W termini of the Canadian National transcontinental railway. Pop: 14 643 (2001)

princess 1 (in Britain) a daughter of the sovereign or of one of the sovereign's sons **2** a nonreigning female member of a sovereign family **3** the wife and consort of a prince

Princeton a town in central New Jersey: settled by Quakers in 1696; an important educational centre, seat of Princeton University (founded at Elizabeth in 1747 and moved here in 1756); scene of the battle (1777) during the War of American Independence in which Washington's troops defeated the British on the university campus. Pop: 13 577 (2003 est)

principal 1 (in Britain) a civil servant of an executive grade who is in charge of a section **2** *Law* **a** a person who engages another to act as his agent **b** an active participant in a crime **c** the person primarily liable to fulfil an obligation **3** the head of a school or other educational institution **4** (in Scottish schools) a head of department **5** *Music* **a** the chief instrumentalist in a section of the orchestra **b** one of the singers in an opera company **c** either of two types of open diapason organ stops, one of four-foot length and pitch and the other of eight-foot length and pitch **6** the leading performer in a play

principal boy the leading male role in a pantomime, played by a woman

principality 1 a a territory ruled by a prince **b** a territory from which a prince draws his title **2** the dignity or authority of a prince

principle 1 a rule or law concerning a natural phenomenon or the behaviour of a system **2** *Chem* a constituent of a substance that gives the substance its characteris-

tics and behaviour

print 1 a positive photographic image in colour or black and white produced, usually on paper, from a negative image on film **2 a** a fabric with a printed design **b** (*as modifier*): *a print dress*

printed circuit an electronic circuit in which certain components and the connections between them are formed by etching a metallic coating or by electrodeposition on one or both sides of a thin insulating board

printer *Computing* an output device for printing results on paper

prior 1 the superior of a house and community in certain religious orders **2** the deputy head of a monastery or abbey, ranking immediately below the abbot **3** (formerly) a chief magistrate in medieval Florence and other Italian republics

Prior Matthew 1664–1721, English poet and diplomat, noted for his epigrammatic occasional verse

priory a religious house governed by a prior, sometimes being subordinate to an abbey

Pripet a river in E Europe, rising in NW Ukraine and flowing northeast into Belarus across the **Pripet Marshes** (the largest swamp in Europe), then east into the Dnieper River. Length: about 800 km (500 miles)

Priscian Latin name *Priscianus Caesariensis*. 6th century AD, Latin grammarian

prise *or* **prize** *Rare or dialect* a tool involving leverage in its use or the leverage so employed

prism 1 a transparent polygonal solid, often having triangular ends and rectangular sides, for dispersing light into a spectrum or for reflecting and deviating light. They are used in spectroscopes, binoculars, periscopes, etc. **2** a form of crystal with faces parallel to the vertical axis **3** *Maths* a polyhedron having parallel, polygonal, and congruent bases and sides that are parallelograms

prismatic 1 concerned with, containing, or produced by a prism **2** exhibiting bright spectral colours

prison a public building used to house convicted criminals and accused persons remanded in custody and awaiting trial

 ▷www.hmprisonservice.gov.uk/
 link_bottom.asp?#sixth

 ▷www.homeoffice.gov.uk/justice/prisons/
 index.html

 ▷www.kcl.ac.uk/depsta/rel/icps/home.html

prisoner a person deprived of liberty and kept in prison or some other form of custody as a punishment for a crime, while awaiting trial, or for some other reason

Priština a city in S Serbia and Montenegro, the capital of Kosovo: under Turkish control until 1912; severely damaged in the Kosovo conflict of 1999; nearby is the 14th-century Gračanica monastery. Pop: 261 000 (2005 est)

Pritchett Sir V(ictor) **S**(awdon). 1900–97, British short-story writer, novelist, essayist, and autobiographer; his works include *Mr Beluncle* (1951) and *A Careless Widow* (1989)

privacy *Philosophy* the condition of being necessarily restricted to a single person

private *Law, Politics* of, relating to, or provided by a private individual or organization, rather than by the state or a public body

private bill a bill presented to Parliament or Congress on behalf of a private individual, corporation, etc.

private company a limited company that does not issue shares for public subscription and whose owners do not enjoy an unrestricted right to transfer their shareholdings

private detective an individual privately employed to investigate a crime, keep watch on a suspected person, or make other inquiries

privateer 1 an armed, privately owned vessel commissioned for war service by a government 2 a commander or member of the crew of a privateer

private member a member of a legislative assembly, such as the House of Commons, not having an appointment in the government

private school a school under the financial and managerial control of a private body or charitable trust, accepting mostly fee-paying pupils

private sector the part of a country's economy that consists of privately owned enterprises

privation *Logic, obsolete* the absence from an object of what ordinarily or naturally belongs to such objects

privative *Logic, obsolete* (of a proposition) that predicates a logical privation

privet a any oleaceous shrub of the genus *Ligustrum*, esp *L. vulgare* or *L. ovalifolium*, having oval dark green leaves, white flowers, and purplish-black berries b (*as modifier*): a privet hedge

privilege 1 any of the fundamental rights guaranteed to the citizens of a country by its constitution 2 a the right of a lawyer to refuse to divulge information obtained in confidence from a client b the right claimed by any of certain other functionaries to refuse to divulge information 3 the rights and immunities enjoyed by members of most legislative bodies, such as freedom of speech, freedom from arrest in civil cases during a session, etc.

privileged 1 *Law* a not actionable as a libel or slander b (of a communication, document, etc) that a witness cannot be compelled to divulge 2 *Nautical* (of a vessel) having the right of way

privy *Law* a person in privity with another

Privy Council the private council of the British sovereign, consisting of all current and former ministers of the Crown and other distinguished subjects, all of whom are appointed for life

privy purse 1 a (in Britain) an allowance voted by Parliament for the private expenses of the monarch: part of the civil list b (in other countries) a similar sum of money for the monarch 2 an official of the royal household responsible for dealing with the monarch's private expenses

privy seal (in Britain) a seal affixed to certain documents issued by royal authority: of less rank and importance than the great seal

prize 1 something given to the winner of any game of chance, lottery, etc. 2 any valuable property captured in time of war, esp a vessel

prizefight a boxing match for a prize or purse, esp one of the fights popular in the 18th and 19th centuries

proactive *Psychol* of or denoting a mental process that affects a subsequent process

probate 1 the act or process of officially proving the authenticity and validity of a will 2 a the official certificate stating a will to be genuine and conferring on the executors power to administer the estate b the probate copy of a will 3 (in the US) all matters within the jurisdiction of a probate court

probation 1 a system of dealing with offenders by placing them under the supervision of a probation officer 2 on probation a under the supervision of a probation officer b undergoing a test period

probation officer an officer of a court who supervises offenders placed on probation and assists and befriends them

probe 1 *Surgery* a slender and usually flexible instrument for exploring a wound, sinus, etc. 2 *Electronics* a lead connecting to or containing a measuring or monitoring circuit used for testing 3 *Electronics* a conductor inserted into a waveguide or cavity resonator to provide coupling to an external circuit 4 any of various devices that provide a coupling link, esp a flexible tube extended from an aircraft to link it with another so that it can refuel

probiotic 1 a harmless bacterium that helps to protect the body from harmful bacteria 2 a substance that encourages the growth of natural healthy bacteria in the gut

problem 1 *Maths* a statement requiring a solution usually by means of one or more operations or geometric constructions 2 designating a literary work that deals with difficult moral questions

problematic *or* **problematical** *Logic, obsolete* (of a proposition) asserting that a property may or may not hold

proboscis 1 a long flexible prehensile trunk or snout, as of an elephant 2 the elongated mouthparts of certain insects, adapted for piercing or sucking food 3 any similar part or organ

procedure 1 the established mode or form of conducting the business of a legislature, the enforcement of a legal right, etc. 2 *Computing* another name for **subroutine**

proceeding 1 a the institution of a legal action b any step taken in a legal action 2 legal action; litigation

process 1 *Law* a a summons, writ, etc, commanding a person to appear in court b the whole proceedings in an action at law 2 *Biology* a natural outgrowth or projection of a part, organ, or organism 3 *Computing* a distinct subtask of a computer system which can be regarded as proceeding in parallel with other subtasks of the system 4 *Film, TV* denoting a film, film scene, shot, etc, made by techniques that produce unusual optical effects

procession 1 a hymn, litany, etc, sung in a procession 2 *Christianity* the emanation of the Holy Spirit

processional *Christianity* a a book containing the prayers, hymns, litanies, and liturgy prescribed for processions b a hymn, litany, etc, used in a procession

Proclus ?410–485 AD, Greek Neo-Platonist philosopher

Procopius ?490–?562 AD, Byzantine historian, noted for his account of the wars of Justinian I against the Persians, Vandals, and Ostrogoths

Procrustean tending or designed to produce conformity by violent or ruthless methods

proctor 1 a member of the teaching staff of any of certain universities having the duties of enforcing discipline 2 *US* (in a college or university) a supervisor or monitor who invigilates examinations, enforces discipline, etc. 3 (formerly) an agent, esp one engaged to conduct another's case in a court 4 (formerly) an agent employed to collect tithes 5 *Church of England* one of the elected representatives of the clergy in Convocation and the General Synod

procurator fiscal (in Scotland) a legal officer who performs the functions of public prosecutor and coroner

Prodi *Romano* born 1939, Italian politician; prime minister (1996–98); president of the European Commission from 1999

producer 1 *Brit* a person responsible for the artistic direction of a play, including interpretation of the script, preparation of the actors, and overall design 2 *US and Canadian* a person who organizes the stage production of a play, including the finance, management, etc. 3 the person who supervises the arrangement, recording, and mixing of a record 4 *Economics* a person or business enterprise that generates goods or services for sale 5 *Chem* an apparatus or plant for making producer gas 6 *Ecology* an organism, esp a green plant, that builds up its own tissues from simple inorganic compounds

product 1 a substance formed in a chemical reaction 2 *Maths* the result of the multiplication of two or more numbers, quantities, etc

production 1 *Economics* the creation or manufacture for sale of goods and services with exchange value 2 the organization and presentation of a film, play, opera, etc. 3 *Brit* the artistic direction of a play 4 a the supervision of the arrangement, recording, and mixing of a record b the overall sound quality or character of a recording 5 manufactured by a mass-production process

production line a factory system in which parts or components of the end product are transported by a conveyor through a number of different sites at each of which a manual or machine operation is performed on them without interrupting the flow of production

productive *Economics* a producing or capable of producing goods and services that have monetary or exchange value b of or relating to such production

proem an introduction or preface, such as to a work of literature

profane 1 not designed or used for religious purposes; secular 2 not initiated into the inner mysteries or sacred rites

profession a a declaration of faith in a religion, esp as made on entering the Church of that religion or an order belonging to it b the faith or the religion that is the subject of such a declaration

professor 1 the principal lecturer or teacher in a field of learning at a university or college; a holder of a university chair 2 *Chiefly US and Canadian* any teacher in a university or college

profile 1 a view or representation of an object, esp a building, in contour or outline 2 a vertical section of soil from the ground surface to the parent rock show-

ing the different horizons 3 a a vertical section of part of the earth's crust showing the layers of rock b a representation of such a section 4 the outline of the shape of a river valley either from source to mouth (**long profile**) or at right angles to the flow of the river (**cross profile**)

profit 1 the monetary gain derived from a transaction 2 *Economics* a the income or reward accruing to a successful entrepreneur and held to be the motivating factor of all economic activity in a capitalist economy b (*as modifier*): *the profit motive*

profiteer a person who makes excessive profits, esp by charging exorbitant prices for goods in short supply

profit-sharing a system in which a portion of the net profit of a business is distributed to its employees, usually in proportion to their wages or their length of service

Profumo *John (Dennis)*. born 1915, British Conservative politician; secretary of state for war (1960–63). He resigned after a scandal that threatened the government of Harold Macmillan

progesterone a steroid hormone, secreted mainly by the corpus luteum in the ovary, that prepares and maintains the uterus for pregnancy. Formula: $C_{21}H_{30}O_2$

prognathous *or* **prognathic** having a projecting lower jaw

prognosis *Med* a a prediction of the course or outcome of a disease or disorder b the chances of recovery from a disease

program *or sometimes* **programme** a sequence of coded instructions fed into a computer, enabling it to perform specified logical and arithmetical operations on data

programmable *or* **programable** (esp of a device or operation) capable of being programmed for automatic operation or computer processing

programming language a simple language system designed to facilitate the writing of computer programs

progress 1 *Biology* increasing complexity, adaptation, etc, during the development of an individual or evolution of a group 2 *Brit* a stately royal journey

progression 1 *Maths* a sequence of numbers in which each term differs from the succeeding term by a constant relation 2 *Music* movement, esp of a logical kind, from one note to the next (**melodic progression**) or from one chord to the next (**harmonic progression**) 3 *Astrology* one of several calculations, based on the movement of the planets, from which it is supposed that one can find the expected developments in a person's birth chart and the probable trends of circumstances for a year in his life

progressive 1 favouring or promoting political or social reform through government action, or even revolution, to improve the lot of the majority 2 denoting or relating to an educational system that allows flexibility in learning procedures, based on activities determined by the needs and capacities of the individual child, the aim of which is to integrate academic with social development 3 (of a tax or tax system) graduated so that the rate increases relative to the amount taxed 4 (esp of a disease) advancing in severity, complexity, or extent 5 (of a dance, card game, etc) involving a regular change of partners after one figure, one game, etc.

prohibition 1 (esp in the US) a policy of legally forbidding the manufacture, transportation, sale, or consumption of alcoholic beverages except for medicinal or scientific purposes 2 *Law* an order of a superior court (in Britain the High Court) forbidding an inferior court to determine a matter outside its jurisdiction

Prohibition the period (1920–33) when the manufacture, sale, and transportation of intoxicating liquors was banned by constitutional amendment in the US

projection 1 the representation of a line, figure, or solid on a given plane as it would be seen from a particular direction or in accordance with an accepted set of rules 2 a the process of showing film on a screen b the image or images shown 3 *Psychol* a the belief, esp in children, that others share one's subjective mental life b the process of projecting one's own hidden desires and impulses 4 the mixing by alchemists of powdered philosopher's stone with molten base metals in order to transmute them into gold

projectionist a person responsible for the operation of film projection machines

projector 1 an optical instrument that projects an enlarged image of individual slides onto a screen or wall 2 an optical instrument in which a strip of film is wound past a lens at a fixed speed so that the frames can be viewed as a continuously moving sequence on a screen or wall 3 a device for projecting a light beam

Prokofiev Sergei Sergeyevich 1891–1953, Soviet composer. His compositions include the orchestral fairy tale *Peter and the Wolf* (1936), the opera *The Love for Three Oranges* (1921), and seven symphonies

Prokopyevsk a city in S Russia: the chief coal-mining centre of the Kuznetsk Basin. Pop: 216 000 (2005 est)

prolapse *Pathol* the sinking or falling down of an organ or part, esp the womb

prolate having a polar diameter of greater length than the equatorial diameter

proletariat 1 all wage-earners collectively 2 the lower or working class 3 (in Marxist theory) the class of wage-earners, esp industrial workers, in a capitalist society, whose only possession of significant material value is their labour 4 (in ancient Rome) the lowest class of citizens, who had no property

prologue *or often US* **prolog** 1 a the prefatory lines introducing a play or speech b the actor speaking these lines 2 in early opera a an introductory scene in which a narrator summarizes the main action of the work b a brief independent play preceding the opera, esp one in honour of a patron

PROM *Computing* programmable read only memory

promenade 1 a marchlike step in dancing 2 a marching sequence in a square or country dance

promenade concert a concert at which some of the audience stand rather than sit

promethium a radioactive element of the lanthanide series artificially produced by the fission of uranium. Symbol: Pm; atomic no.: 61; half-life of most stable isotope, ^{145}Pm: 17.7 years; valency: 3; melting pt.: 1042°C; boiling pt.: 2460°C (approx.)

Promised Land 1 *Old Testament* the land of Canaan, promised by God to Abraham and his descendants as their heritage (Genesis 12:7) 2 heaven, esp when considered as the goal towards which Christians journey in their earthly lives

promo a *Informal* something that is used to promote a product, esp a videotape film used to promote a pop record b (*as modifier*): *a promo video*

promontory 1 a high point of land, esp of rocky coast, that juts out into the sea 2 *Anatomy* any of various projecting structures

promoter 1 *Chem* a substance added in small amounts to a catalyst to increase its activity 2 *Genetics* a sequence of nucleotides, associated with a structural gene, that must bind with messenger RNA polymerase before transcription can proceed

prompt 1 *Commerce* a the time limit allowed for payment of the debt incurred by purchasing goods or services on credit b the contract specifying this time limit c a memorandum sent to a purchaser to remind him of the time limit and the sum due 2 an aid to the operator of a computer in the form of a question or statement that appears on the screen showing that the equipment is ready to proceed and indicating the options available

prompter a person offstage who reminds the actors of forgotten lines or cues

proof 1 *Law* the whole body of evidence upon which the verdict of a court is based 2 *Maths, logic* a sequence of steps or statements that establishes the truth of a proposition 3 *Scots law* trial before a judge without a jury 4 (in engraving, etc) a print made by an artist or under his supervision for his own satisfaction before he hands the plate over to a professional printer 5 *Photog* a trial print from a negative 6 a the alcoholic strength of proof spirit b the strength of a beverage or other alcoholic liquor as measured on a scale in which the strength of proof spirit is 100 degrees 7 having the alcoholic strength of proof spirit

proof spirit 1 (in Britain and Canada) a mixture of alcohol and water or an alcoholic beverage that contains 49.28 per cent of alcohol by weight, 57.1 per cent by volume at 51°F: up until 1980 used as a standard of alcoholic liquids 2 (in the US) a similar standard mixture containing 50 per cent of alcohol by volume at 60°F

prop *Rugby* either of the forwards at either end of the front row of a scrum

propaganda 1 the organized dissemination of information, allegations, etc, to assist or damage the cause of a government, movement, etc. 2 such information, allegations, etc.

propane a colourless flammable gaseous alkane found in petroleum and used as a fuel. Formula: $CH_3CH_2CH_3$

propeller a device having blades radiating from a central hub that is rotated to produce thrust to propel a ship, aircraft, etc.

propene a colourless gaseous alkene obtained by cracking petroleum: used in synthesizing many organic compounds. Formula: $CH_3CH:CH_2$

proper 1 *Maths, logic* (of a relation) distinguished from a weaker relation by excluding the case where the relata are identical. For example, every set is a subset of itself, but a **proper subset** must exclude at least one member of the containing set 2 the parts of the Mass that vary according to the particular day or feast on which the Mass is celebrated

proper fraction a fraction in which the numerator has a lower absolute value than the denominator, as $\frac{1}{2}$ or $x/(3+x^2)$

Propertius Sextus ?50–?15 BC, Roman elegiac poet

property 1 *Law* the right to possess, use, and dispose of anything **2** a quality, attribute, or distinctive feature of anything, esp a characteristic attribute such as the density or strength of a material **3** any movable object used on the set of a stage play or film

prophecy 1 a a message of divine truth revealing God's will **b** the act of uttering such a message **2** the function, activity, or charismatic endowment of a prophet or prophets

prophet 1 a person who supposedly speaks by divine inspiration, esp one through whom a divinity expresses his will **2** *Christian Science* **a** a seer in spiritual matters **b** the vanishing of material sense to give way to the conscious facts of spiritual truth

Prophet the 1 the principal designation of Mohammed as the founder of Islam **2** a name for Joseph Smith as founder of the Mormon Church

prophylactic 1 protecting from or preventing disease **2** a prophylactic drug or device, esp a condom

proponent *Law* a person who seeks probate of a will

proportion 1 *Maths* a relationship that maintains a constant ratio between two variable quantities **2** *Maths* a relationship between four numbers or quantities in which the ratio of the first pair equals the ratio of the second pair

proportional 1 *Maths* having or related by a constant ratio **2** *Maths* an unknown term in a proportion

proportional representation *Politics* representation of parties in an elective body in proportion to the votes they win

proposition 1 *Philosophy* **a** the content of a sentence that affirms or denies something and is capable of being true or false **b** the meaning of such a sentence: *I am warm* always expresses the same proposition whoever the speaker is **2** *Maths* a statement or theorem, usually containing its proof

proprietary 1 of, relating to, or belonging to property or proprietors **2** *Med* of or denoting a drug or agent manufactured and distributed under a trade name **3** *Med* a proprietary drug or agent **4** a proprietor or proprietors collectively **5 a** a right to property **b** property owned **6** (in Colonial America) an owner, governor, or grantee of a proprietary colony

proprietor 1 an owner of an unincorporated business enterprise **2** a person enjoying exclusive right of ownership to some property **3** *US, history* a governor or body of governors of a proprietary colony

proscenium 1 the arch or opening separating the stage from the auditorium together with the area immediately in front of the arch **2** (in ancient theatres) the stage itself

prose 1 spoken or written language as in ordinary usage, distinguished from poetry by its lack of a marked metrical structure **2** a passage set for translation into a foreign language **3** *RC Church* a hymn recited or sung after the gradual at Mass

prosecution 1 a the institution and conduct of legal proceedings against a person **b** the proceedings brought in the name of the Crown to put an accused on trial **2** the lawyers acting for the Crown to put the case against a person

proselyte a person newly converted to a religious faith or sect; a convert, esp a gentile converted to Judaism

prosody 1 the study of poetic metre and of the art of versification, including rhyme, stanzaic forms, and the quantity and stress of syllables **2** a system of versification

prospectus a pamphlet or brochure giving details of courses, as at a college or school

Prost Alain born 1955, French motor-racing driver: world champion 1985, 1986, 1989, and 1993

prostate a gland in male mammals that surrounds the neck of the bladder and urethra and secretes a liquid constituent of the semen

prosthesis *Surgery* **a** the replacement of a missing bodily part with an artificial substitute **b** an artificial part such as a limb, eye, or tooth

prostrate (of a plant) growing closely along the ground

protactinium a toxic radioactive metallic element that occurs in uranium ores and is produced by neutron irradiation of thorium. Symbol: Pa; atomic no.: 91; half-life of the most stable isotope, ^{231}Pa: 32 500 years; valency: 4 or 5; relative density: 15.37 (calc.); melting pt.: 1572°C

protagonist the principal character in a play, story, etc.

Protagoras ?485–?411 BC, Greek philosopher and sophist, famous for his dictum "Man is the measure of all things."

protea any shrub or small tree of the genus *Protea*, of tropical and southern Africa, having flowers with coloured bracts arranged in showy heads: family *Proteaceae*

protection 1 a the imposition of duties or quotas on imports, designed for the protection of domestic industries against overseas competition, expansion of domestic employment, etc. **b** the system, policy, or theory of such restrictions **2** a document that grants protection or immunity from arrest or harassment to a person, esp a traveller **3** *Mountaineering* security on a climb provided by running belays, etc.

protective *Economics* of, relating to, or intended for protection of domestic industries

protector *History* a person who exercised royal authority during the minority, absence, or incapacity of the monarch

protectorate 1 a a territory largely controlled by but not annexed to a stronger state **b** the relation of a protecting state to its protected territory **2** the office or period of office of a protector

protein any of a large group of nitrogenous compounds of high molecular weight that are essential constituents of all living organisms. They consist of one or more chains of amino acids linked by peptide bonds and are folded into a specific three-dimensional shape maintained by further chemical bonding

protest a statement made by the master of a vessel attesting to the circumstances in which his vessel was damaged or imperilled

Protestant a an adherent of Protestantism b (as modifier): the Protestant Church

Protestantism the religion or religious system of any of the Churches of Western Christendom that are separated from the Roman Catholic Church and adhere substantially to principles established by Luther, Calvin, etc, in the Reformation

protium the most common isotope of hydrogen, having a mass number of 1

protocol 1 the formal etiquette and code of behaviour, precedence, and procedure for state and diplomatic ceremonies 2 a memorandum or record of an agreement, esp one reached in international negotiations, a meeting, etc. 3 a an amendment to a treaty or convention b an annexe appended to a treaty to deal with subsidiary matters or to render the treaty more lucid c a formal international agreement or understanding on some matter 4 Philosophy a statement that is immediately verifiable by experience 5 Computing the set form in which data must be presented for handling by a particular computer configuration, esp in the transmission of information between different computer systems

proton a stable, positively charged elementary particle, found in atomic nuclei in numbers equal to the atomic number of the element. It is a baryon with a charge of $1.602176462 \times 10^{-19}$ coulomb, a rest mass of $1.672 \ 62159 \times 10^{-27}$ kilogram, and spin ½

protoplasm Biology the living contents of a cell, differentiated into cytoplasm and nucleoplasm

prototype 1 one of the first units manufactured of a product, which is tested so that the design can be changed if necessary before the product is manufactured commercially 2 Biology the ancestral or primitive form of a species or other group; an archetype

protozoan Also called: **protozoon** any of various minute unicellular organisms formerly regarded as invertebrates of the phylum Protozoa but now usually classified in certain phyla of protoctists. Protozoans include flagellates, ciliates, sporozoans, amoebas, and foraminifers

protractor 1 an instrument for measuring or drawing angles on paper, usually a flat semicircular transparent plastic sheet graduated in degrees 2 a surgical instrument for removing a bullet from the body 3 Anatomy a former term for **extensor**

proud (of animals) restive or excited, esp sexually; on heat

Proudhon Pierre Joseph 1809–65, French socialist, whose pamphlet What is Property? (1840) declared that property is theft

Proust 1 Joseph Louis 1754–1826, French chemist, who formulated the law of constant proportions 2 Marcel 1871–1922, French novelist whose long novel la recherche du temps perdu (1913–27) deals with the relationship of the narrator to themes such as art, time, memory, and society

provenance or chiefly US **provenience** a place of origin, esp that of a work of art or archaeological specimen

Provence a former province of SE France, on the Mediterranean, and the River Rhône: forms part of the administrative region of Provence-Alpes-Côte d'Azur

proverb 1 a short, memorable, and often highly condensed saying embodying, esp with bold imagery, some commonplace fact or experience 2 Ecclesiast a wise saying or admonition providing guidance

providence 1 a Christianity God's foreseeing protection and care of his creatures b such protection and care as manifest by some other force 2 a supposed manifestation of such care and guidance

Providence[1] Christianity God, esp as showing foreseeing care and protection of his creatures

Providence[2] a port in NE Rhode Island, capital of the state, at the head of Narragansett Bay: founded by Roger Williams in 1636. Pop: 176 365 (2003 est)

province 1 a territory governed as a unit of a country or empire 2 a district, territory, or region 3 those parts of a country lying outside the capital and other large cities and regarded as outside the mainstream of sophisticated culture 4 Ecology a subdivision of a region, characterized by a particular fauna and flora 5 an area or branch of learning, activity, etc. 6 RC Church, Church of England an ecclesiastical territory, usually consisting of several dioceses, and having an archbishop or metropolitan at its head 7 a major administrative and territorial subdivision of a religious order 8 History a region of the Roman Empire outside Italy ruled by a governor from Rome

Provincetown a village in SE Massachusetts, at the tip of Cape Cod: scene of the first landing place of the Pilgrims (1620) and of the signing of the Mayflower Compact (1620). Pop: 3472 (2003 est)

provincial 1 NZ denoting a football team representing a province, one of the historical administrative areas of New Zealand 2 the head of an ecclesiastical province 3 the head of a major territorial subdivision of a religious order

provision the conferring of and induction into ecclesiastical offices

provisional or less commonly **provisionary** a postage stamp surcharged during an emergency to alter the stamp's denomination or significance until a new or regular issue is printed

Provisional of, designating, or relating to the unofficial factions of the IRA and Sinn Féin that became increasingly dominant following a split in 1969. The Provisional movement remained committed to a policy of terrorism until its ceasefires of the mid-1990s

provocation English criminal law words or conduct that incite a person to attack another

provost 1 the head of certain university colleges or schools 2 (in Scotland) the chairman and civic head of certain district councils or (formerly) of a burgh council 3 Church of England the senior dignitary of one of the more recent cathedral foundations 4 RC Church a the head of a cathedral chapter in England and some other countries b (formerly) the member of a monastic community second in authority under the abbot 5 (in medieval times) an overseer, steward, or bailiff in a manor 6 Obsolete a prison warder

prow the bow of a vessel

proxy 1 a person authorized to act on behalf of someone else; agent 2 the authority, esp in the form of a document, given to a person to act on behalf of someone else 3 Computing short for **proxy server**

proxy server *Computing* a computer that acts as an intermediary between a client machine and a server, caching information to save access time

Prozac *Trademark* fluoxetine; a drug that prolongs the action of serotonin in the brain; used as an antidepressant

Prudentius Aurelius Clemens 348–410 AD, Latin Christian poet, born in Spain. His works include the allegory *Psychomachia*

prurient unusually or morbidly interested in sexual thoughts or practices

Prussia a former German state in N and central Germany, extending from France and the Low Countries to the Baltic Sea and Poland: developed as the chief military power of the Continent, leading the North German Confederation from 1867–71, when the German Empire was established; dissolved in 1947 and divided between East and West Germany, Poland, and the former Soviet Union. Area: (in 1939) 294 081 sq km (113 545 sq miles)

Prussian 1 of, relating to, or characteristic of Prussia or its people, esp of the Junkers and their formal military tradition 2 a German native or inhabitant of Prussia 3 a member of a Baltic people formerly inhabiting the coastal area of the SE Baltic

prussic acid the weakly acidic extremely poisonous aqueous solution of hydrogen cyanide

Prut a river in E Europe, rising in SW Ukraine and flowing generally southeast, forming part of the border between Romania and Moldova, to join the River Danube. Length: 853 km (530 miles)

Prynne William 1600–69, English Puritan leader and pamphleteer, whose ears were cut off in punishment for his attacks on Laud

Przemyśl a city in SE Poland, near the border with Ukraine on the San River: a fortress in the early Middle Ages; belonged to Austria (1722–1918). Pop: 67 000 (latest est)

PSA 1 prostatic specific antigen: an enzyme secreted by the prostate gland, increased levels of which are found in the blood of patients with cancer of the prostate 2 (in New Zealand) Public Service Association

psalm 1 any of the 150 sacred songs, lyric poems, and prayers that together constitute a book (Psalms) of the Old Testament 2 a musical setting of one of these poems 3 any sacred song or hymn

psalmist the composer of a psalm or psalms, esp (when *capital* and preceded by *the*) David, traditionally regarded as the author of The Book of Psalms

psalmody 1 the act of singing psalms or hymns 2 the art or practice of the setting to music or singing of psalms

Psalms the collection of 150 psalms in the Old Testament, the full title of which is **The Book of Psalms**

Psalter 1 another name for **Psalms** (esp in the version in the Book of Common Prayer) 2 a translation, musical, or metrical version of the Psalms 3 a devotional or liturgical book containing a version of Psalms, often with a musical setting

psaltery *Music* an ancient stringed instrument similar to the lyre, but having a trapezoidal sounding board over which the strings are stretched

PSBR in Britain public sector borrowing requirement: the excess of government expenditure over receipts (mainly from taxation) that has to be financed by borrowing from the banks or the public

psephology the statistical and sociological study of elections

psittacosis a disease of parrots, caused by the obligate intracellular parasite *Chlamydia psittaci*, that can be transmitted to man, in whom it produces inflammation of the lungs and pneumonia

Pskov 1 a city in NW Russia, on the Velikaya River: one of the oldest Russian cities, at its height in the 13th and 14th centuries. Pop: 203 000 (2005 est) 2 *Lake* the S part of Lake Peipus in NW Russia, linked to the main part by a channel 24 km (15 miles) long. Area: about 1000 sq km (400 sq miles)

psoriasis a skin disease characterized by the formation of reddish spots and patches covered with silvery scales: tends to run in families

psyche the human mind or soul

psychedelic *or* **psychodelic** 1 relating to or denoting new or altered perceptions or sensory experiences, as through the use of hallucinogenic drugs 2 denoting any of the drugs, esp LSD, that produce these effects 3 *Informal* (of painting, fabric design, etc) having the vivid colours and complex patterns popularly associated with the visual effects of psychedelic states

psychiatry the branch of medicine concerned with the diagnosis and treatment of mental disorders
▷www.nmha.org
▷www.psycline.org/journals/psycline.html

psychic 1 a outside the possibilities defined by natural laws, as mental telepathy b (of a person) sensitive to forces not recognized by natural laws 2 mental as opposed to physical; psychogenic 3 *Bridge* (of a bid) based on less strength than would normally be required to make the bid 4 a person who is sensitive to parapsychological forces or influences

psychoactive capable of affecting mental activity

psychoanalysis a method of studying the mind and treating mental and emotional disorders based on revealing and investigating the role of the unconscious mind
▷http://aapsa.org/
▷www.freudfile.org/psychoanalysis

psychogenic *Psychol* (esp of disorders or symptoms) of mental, rather than organic, origin

psychological warfare the military application of psychology, esp to propaganda and attempts to influence the morale of enemy and friendly groups in time of war

psychology 1 the scientific study of all forms of human and animal behaviour, sometimes concerned with the methods through which behaviour can be modified 2 *Informal* the mental make-up or structure of an individual that causes him or her to think or act in the way he or she does
▷www.psych.neu.edu/faclinks
▷www.sosig.ac.uk/psychology
▷www.clas.ufl.edu/users/gthursby/psi

psychopath a person afflicted with a personality disorder characterized by a tendency to commit antisocial and sometimes violent acts and a failure to feel guilt for such acts

psychopathology the scientific study of mental disorders

psychosis any form of severe mental disorder in which the individual's contact with reality becomes highly distorted

psychosomatic of or relating to disorders, such as stomach ulcers, thought to be caused or aggravated by psychological factors such as stress

psychotherapy *or less commonly* **psychotherapeutics** the treatment of nervous disorders by psychological methods

ptarmigan 1 any of several arctic and subarctic grouse of the genus *Lagopus*, esp *L. mutus*, which has a white winter plumage 2 a created domestic fancy pigeon with ruffled or curled feathers on the wings and back

pterodactyl any extinct flying reptile of the genus *Pterodactylus* and related genera, having membranous wings supported on an elongated fourth digit

Ptolemaic 1 of or relating to the 2nd century AD. Greek astronomer, mathematician and geographer Ptolemy (Latin name *Claudius Ptolemaeus*) or to his conception of the universe 2 of or relating to the Macedonian dynasty that ruled Egypt from the death of Alexander the Great (323 BC) to the death of Cleopatra (30 BC)

Ptolemy Latin name *Claudius Ptolemaeus*. 2nd century AD, Greek astronomer, mathematician, and geographer. His *Geography* was the standard geographical textbook until the discoveries of the 15th century. His system of astronomy, as expounded in the *Almagest*, remained undisputed until the Copernican system was evolved

Ptolemy I called *Ptolemy Soter*. ?367–283 BC, king of Egypt (323–285 BC), a general of Alexander the Great, who obtained Egypt on Alexander's death and founded the Ptolemaic dynasty: his capital Alexandria became the centre of Greek culture

Ptolemy II called *Philadelphus*. 309–246 BC, the son of Ptolemy I; king of Egypt (285–246). Under his rule the power, prosperity, and culture of Egypt was at its height

ptomaine *or* **ptomain** any of a group of amines, such as cadaverine or putrescine, formed by decaying organic matter

pub 1 *Chiefly Brit* a building with a bar and one or more public rooms licensed for the sale and consumption of alcoholic drink, often also providing light meals 2 *Austral and NZ* a hotel

pub-crawl *Informal, chiefly Brit* drinking tour of a number of pubs or bars

puberty the period at the beginning of adolescence when the sex glands become functional and the secondary sexual characteristics emerge

pubes 1 the region above the external genital organs, covered with hair from the time of puberty 2 the pubic bones

pubescent 1 arriving or having arrived at puberty 2 (of certain plants and animals or their parts) covered with a layer of fine short hairs or down

pubic of or relating to the pubes or pubis

pubis one of the three sections of the hipbone that forms part of the pelvis

public go public a (of a private company) to issue shares for subscription by the public b to reveal publicly hitherto confidential information

public-address system a system of one or more microphones, amplifiers, and loudspeakers for increasing the sound level of speech or music, used in auditoriums, public gatherings, etc.

publican 1 (in Britain) a person who keeps a public house 2 (in ancient Rome) a public contractor, esp one who farmed the taxes of a province

publication *Law* the act of disseminating defamatory matter, esp by communicating it to a third person

public bar *Brit* a bar in a public house usually serving drinks at a cheaper price than in the saloon bar

public enemy a notorious person, such as a criminal, who is regarded as a menace to the public

public house 1 *Brit* the formal name for **pub** 2 *US and Canadian* an inn, tavern, or small hotel

publicist *Rare* a person learned in public or international law

public prosecutor *Law* an official in charge of prosecuting important cases

public school 1 (in England and Wales) a private independent fee-paying secondary school 2 (in the US) any school that is part of a free local educational system

public sector the part of an economy that consists of state-owned institutions, including nationalized industries and services provided by local authorities

public servant 1 an elected or appointed holder of a public office 2 *Austral. and NZ* a member of the **public service** (sense 3)

public service 1 a government employment b the management and administration of the affairs of a political unit, esp the civil service 2 a a service provided for the community b (*as modifier*): *a public-service announcement* 3 *Austral and NZ* the service responsible for the public administration of the government of a country. It excludes the legislative, judicial, and military branches. Members of the public service have no official political allegiance and are not generally affected by changes of governments

public utility an enterprise concerned with the provision to the public of essentials, such as electricity or water

Puccini Giacomo 1858–1924, Italian operatic composer, noted for the dramatic realism of his operas, which include *Manon Lescaut* (1893), *La Bohème* (1896), *Tosca* (1900), and *Madame Butterfly* (1904)

puce a a colour varying from deep red to dark purplish-brown b (*as adjective*): *a puce carpet*

puck¹ 1 a small disc of hard rubber used in ice hockey 2 a stroke at the ball in hurling

puck² a mischievous or evil spirit

puddle *Rowing* the patch of eddying water left by the blade of an oar after completion of a stroke

Pudsey a town in N England, in Leeds unitary authority, West Yorkshire. Pop: 32 391 (2001)

Puebla 1 an inland state of S central Mexico, situated on the Anáhuac Plateau. Capital: Puebla. Pop: 5 070 346 (2000 est). Area: 33 919 sq km (13 096 sq miles) 2 a city in S Mexico, capital of Puebla state: founded in 1532; university (1537). Pop: 1 880 000 (2005 est)

Pueblo a city in Colorado: a centre of the steel industry. Pop: 103 648 (2003 est)

puerperal fever a serious, formerly widespread, form of blood poisoning caused by infection contracted during childbirth

Puerto Rico an autonomous commonwealth (in association with the US) occupying the smallest and easternmost of the Greater Antilles in the Caribbean: one of the most densely populated areas in the world; ceded by Spain to the US in 1899. Currency: US dollar. Capital: San Juan. Pop: 3 897 000 (2004 est). Area: 9104 sq km (3515 sq miles)

puff adder a large venomous African viper, *Bitis arietans*, that is yellowish-grey with brown markings and inflates its body when alarmed

puffball any of various basidiomycetous saprotrophic fungi of the genera *Calvatia* and *Lycoperdon*, having a round fruiting body that discharges a cloud of brown spores when mature

puffin any of various northern diving birds of the family *Alcidae* (auks, etc), esp *Fratercula arctica* (**common** or **Atlantic puffin**), having a black-and-white plumage and a brightly coloured vertically flattened bill: order *Charadriiformes*

pug 1 a small compact breed of dog with a smooth coat, lightly curled tail, and a short wrinkled nose 2 any of several small geometrid moths, mostly of the genus *Eupithecia*, with slim forewings held outstretched at rest

Puget Sound an inlet of the Pacific in NW Washington. Length: about 130 km (80 miles)

Pugin Augustus (**Welby Northmore**). 1812–52, British architect; a leader of the Gothic Revival. He collaborated with Sir Charles Barry on the Palace of Westminster (begun 1836)

puissance a competition in showjumping that tests a horse's ability to jump a limited number of large obstacles

pukeko a wading bird, *Porphyrio melanotus*, of New Zealand, with a brightly coloured plumage

Pula a port in NW Croatia at the S tip of the Istrian Peninsula: made a Roman military base in 178 BC; became the main Austro-Hungarian naval station and passed to Italy in 1919, to Yugoslavia in 1947, and is now in independent Croatia. Pop: 62 300 (1991)

Pulitzer Joseph 1847–1911, US newspaper publisher, born in Hungary. He established the Pulitzer prizes

pull 1 a period of rowing 2 a single stroke of an oar in rowing 3 the act of pulling the ball in golf, cricket, etc. 4 the act of checking or reining in a horse

pullet a young hen of the domestic fowl, less than one year old

pulley 1 a wheel with a grooved rim in which a rope, chain, or belt can run in order to change the direction or point of application of a force applied to the rope, etc. 2 a number of such wheels pivoted in parallel in a block, used to raise heavy loads 3 a wheel with a flat, convex, or grooved rim mounted on a shaft and driven by or driving a belt passing around it

Pullman¹ a luxurious railway coach, esp a sleeping car

Pullman² Philip born 1946, British author. Writing primarily for older children, he is best known for the fantasy trilogy *His Dark Materials* (1997–2000)

pull-out a flight manoeuvre during which an aircraft levels out after a dive

pull-up an exercise in which the body is raised up by the arms pulling on a horizontal bar fixed above the head

pulmonary 1 of, or relating to or affecting the lungs 2 having lungs or lunglike organs

pulp 1 soft or fleshy plant tissue, such as the succulent part of a fleshy fruit 2 *Dentistry* the soft innermost part of a tooth, containing nerves and blood vessels

pulpit 1 a raised platform, usually surrounded by a barrier, set up in churches as the appointed place for preaching, leading in prayer, etc. 2 a the preaching of the Christian message b the clergy or their message and influence

pulpwood pine, spruce, or any other soft wood used to make paper

pulsar any of a number of very small extremely dense objects first observed in 1967, which rotate very rapidly and emit very regular pulses of polarized radiation, esp radio waves. They are thought to be neutron stars formed following supernova explosions

pulse¹ 1 *Physiol* a the rhythmic contraction and expansion of an artery at each beat of the heart, often discernible to the touch at points such as the wrists b a single pulsation of the heart or arteries 2 *Physics, electronics* a a transient sharp change in voltage, current, or some other quantity normally constant in a system b one of a series of such transient disturbances, usually recurring at regular intervals and having a characteristic geometric shape c (*as modifier*): *a pulse generator*

pulse² 1 the edible seeds of any of several leguminous plants, such as peas, beans, and lentils 2 the plant producing any of these seeds

puma a large American feline mammal, *Felis concolor*, that resembles a lion, having a plain greyish-brown coat and long tail

pumice a light porous acid volcanic rock having the composition of rhyolite, used for scouring and, in powdered form, as an abrasive and for polishing

pump 1 any device for compressing, driving, raising, or reducing the pressure of a fluid, esp by means of a piston or set of rotating impellers 2 *Biology* a mechanism for the active transport of ions, such as protons, calcium ions, and sodium ions, across cell membranes

pumpkin any of several creeping cucurbitaceous plants of the genus *Cucurbita*, esp *C. pepo* of North America and *C. maxima* of Europe

pun the use of words or phrases to exploit ambiguities and innuendoes in their meaning, usually for humorous effect; a play on words. An example is: *"Ben Battle was a soldier bold, And used to war's alarms: But a cannonball took off his legs, So he laid down his arms."* (Thomas Hood)

Punakha *or* **Punaka** a town in W central Bhutan: a former capital of the country

punch¹ 1 a tool or machine for piercing holes in a material 2 any of various tools used for knocking a bolt, rivet, etc, out of a hole 3 a tool or machine used for stamping a design on something or shaping it by impact 4 the solid die of a punching machine for cutting, stamping, or shaping material 5 *Computing* a device, such as a card punch or tape punch, used for making holes in a card or paper tape

punch² any mixed drink containing fruit juice and, usually, alcoholic liquor, generally hot and spiced

punchbag a suspended stuffed bag that is punched for exercise, esp boxing training

punchball 1 a stuffed or inflated ball, supported by a flexible rod, that is punched for exercise, esp boxing training 2 US a game resembling baseball in which a light ball is struck with the fist

punchbowl 1 a large bowl for serving punch, lemonade, etc, usually with a ladle and often having small drinking glasses hooked around the rim 2 Brit a bowl-shaped depression in the land

punch-drunk demonstrating or characteristic of the behaviour of a person who has suffered repeated blows to the head, esp a professional boxer

punched card or esp US **punch card** (formerly) a card on which data can be coded in the form of punched holes. In computing, there were usually 80 columns and 12 rows, each column containing a pattern of holes representing one character

punch line the culminating part of a joke, funny story, etc, that gives it its humorous or dramatic point

punctual Maths consisting of or confined to a point in space

puncture 1 a perforation and loss of pressure in a pneumatic tyre, made by sharp stones, glass, etc. 2 the act of puncturing or perforating

pundit 1 (formerly) a learned person 2 a Brahman learned in Sanskrit and, esp in Hindu religion, philosophy or law

pungent 1 (of wit, satire, etc) biting; caustic 2 Biology ending in a sharp point

punishment 1 a penalty or sanction given for any crime or offence 2 the act of punishing or state of being punished 3 Psychol any aversive stimulus administered to an organism as part of training

Punjab 1 (formerly) a province in NW British India: divided between India and Pakistan in 1947 2 a state of NW India: reorganized in 1966 as a Punjabi-speaking state, a large part forming the new state of Haryana; mainly agricultural. Capital: Chandigarh. Pop: 24 289 296 (2001). Area: 50 255 sq km (19 403 sq miles) 3 a province of W Pakistan: created in 1947. Capital: Lahore. Pop: 82 710 000 (2003 est). Area: 205 344 sq km (127 595 sq miles)

Punjabi or **Panjabi** the state language of the Punjab, belonging to the Indic branch of the Indo-European family

punk 1 dried decayed wood that smoulders when ignited: used as tinder 2 any of various other substances that smoulder when ignited, esp one used to light fireworks

punk rock a fast abrasive style of rock music of the late 1970s, characterized by aggressive or offensive lyrics and performance
  ▷www.punkrock.org
  ▷www.punk77.co.uk

punster a person who is fond of making puns, esp one who makes a tedious habit of this

punt¹ an open flat-bottomed boat with square ends, propelled by a pole

punt² a kick in certain sports, such as rugby, in which the ball is released and kicked before it hits the ground

punt³ Chiefly Brit 1 a gamble or bet, esp against the bank, as in roulette, or on horses 2 a person who bets

punt⁴ (formerly) the Irish pound

Punta Arenas a port in S Chile, on the Strait of Magellan: the southernmost city in the world. Pop: 118 000 (2005 est)

pup 1 a a young dog, esp when under one year of age; puppy b the young of various other animals, such as the seal 2 **in pup** (of a bitch) pregnant

pupa an insect at the immobile nonfeeding stage of development between larva and adult, when many internal changes occur

pupil¹ 1 a student who is taught by a teacher, esp a young student 2 Civil and Scots law a boy under 14 or a girl under 12 who is in the care of a guardian

pupil² the dark circular aperture at the centre of the iris of the eye, through which light enters

puppet a a small doll or figure of a person or animal moved by strings attached to its limbs or by the hand inserted in its cloth body b (as modifier): a puppet theatre

puppy a young dog; pup

puppy fat fatty tissue that develops in childhood or adolescence and usually disappears by maturity

purblind partly or nearly blind

Purcell 1 Edward Mills 1912–97, US physicist, noted for his work on the magnetic moments of atomic nuclei: shared the Nobel prize for physics (1952) 2 Henry ?1659–95, English composer, noted chiefly for his rhythmic and harmonic subtlety in setting words. His works include the opera Dido and Aeneas (1689), music for the theatrical pieces King Arthur (1691) and The Fairy Queen (1692), several choral odes, fantasias, sonatas, and church music

purchase 1 something that is purchased, esp an article bought with money 2 the act of buying 3 acquisition of an estate by any lawful means other than inheritance 4 a rough measure of the mechanical advantage achieved by a lever

purdah or **purda** 1 the custom in some Muslim and Hindu communities of keeping women in seclusion, with clothing that conceals them completely when they go out 2 a screen in a Hindu house used to keep the women out of view 3 a veil worn by Hindu women of high caste

pure 1 of supposedly unmixed racial descent 2 Genetics, biology breeding true for one or more characteristics; homozygous 3 Music a (of a sound) composed of a single frequency without overtones b (of intervals in the system of just intonation) mathematically accurate in respect to the ratio of one frequency to another

purebred denoting a pure strain obtained through many generations of controlled breeding for desirable traits

purgative Med 1 a drug or agent for purging the bowels 2 causing evacuation of the bowels; cathartic

purgatory Chiefly RC Church a state or place in which the souls of those who have died in a state of grace are believed to undergo a limited amount of suffering to expiate their venial sins and become purified of the remaining effects of mortal sin

purge 1 Politics the elimination of opponents or dissidents from a state, political party, etc. 2 Med a purgative drug or agent; cathartic

Puri a port in E India, in Orissa on the Bay of Bengal: 12th-century temple of Jagannath. Pop: 157 610 (2001)

purism insistence on traditional canons of correctness of form or purity of style or content, esp in language, art, or music

Puritan (in the late 16th and 17th centuries) any of the more extreme English Protestants, most of whom were Calvinists, who wished to purify the Church of England of most of its ceremony and other aspects that they deemed to be Catholic

purity *Physics* a measure of the amount of a single-frequency colour in a mixture of spectral and achromatic colours

purl 1 a curling movement of water; eddy 2 a murmuring sound, as of a shallow stream

purlieu 1 *English history* land on the edge of a forest that was once included within the bounds of the royal forest but was later separated although still subject to some of the forest laws, esp regarding hunting 2 a neighbouring area; outskirts 3 *Rare* a district or suburb, esp one that is poor or squalid

purple 1 any of various colours with a hue lying between red and blue and often highly saturated; a nonspectral colour 2 cloth of this colour, often used to symbolize royalty or nobility 3 high rank; nobility 4 a the official robe of a cardinal b the rank, office, or authority of a cardinal as signified by this 5 **the purple** bishops collectively 6 of the colour purple 7 (of writing) excessively elaborate or full of imagery 8 noble or royal

purple heart 1 any of several tropical American leguminous trees of the genus *Peltogyne* 2 the decorative purple heartwood of any of these trees

purser an officer aboard a passenger ship, merchant ship, or aircraft who keeps the accounts and attends to the welfare of the passengers

pursuit 1 an occupation, hobby, or pastime 2 (in cycling) a race in which the riders set off at intervals along the track and attempt to overtake each other

pursuivant 1 *History* a state or royal messenger 2 *History* a follower or attendant

purulent of, relating to, or containing pus

purview *Law* the body of a statute, containing the enacting clauses

pus the yellow or greenish fluid product of inflammation, composed largely of dead leucocytes, exuded plasma, and liquefied tissue cells

Pusan a port in SE South Korea, on the Korea Strait: the second largest city and chief port of the country; industrial centre; two universities. Pop: 3 527 000 (2005 est)

Pusey Edward Bouverie 1800–82, British ecclesiastic; a leader with Keble and Newman of the Oxford Movement

push button an electrical switch operated by pressing a button, which closes or opens a circuit

pusher 1 *Informal* a person who sells illegal drugs, esp narcotics such as heroin and morphine 2 a a type of aircraft propeller placed behind the engine b a type of aircraft using such a propeller

Pushkin¹ Aleksander Sergeyevich 1799–1837, Russian poet, novelist, and dramatist. His works include the romantic verse tale *The Prisoner of the Caucasus* (1822), the

verse novel *Eugene Onegin* (1833), the tragedy *Boris Godunov* (1825), and the novel *The Captain's Daughter* (1836)

Pushkin² a town in NW Russia: site of the imperial summer residence and Catherine the Great's palace. Pop: 97 000 (latest est)

Puskas Ferenc born 1927, Hungarian footballer; played for Hungary (1945–56) and Real Madrid (1958–66)

pussy 1 an informal name for a **cat** 2 a furry catkin, esp that of the pussy willow

pussy willow 1 a willow tree that produces silvery silky catkins, esp *Salix caprea* or *S. cinerea* in Britain or *S. discolor* in North America 2 any of various similar willows

pustulate covered with pustules

pustule 1 a small inflamed elevated area of skin containing pus 2 any small distinct spot resembling a pimple or blister

put *Athletics* a throw or cast, esp in putting the shot

put-in *Rugby* the act of throwing the ball into a scrum

Putin Vladimir (Vladimirovich). born 1952, Russian statesman; president of Russia from 2000

Putnam 1 Israel 1718–90, American general in the War of Independence 2 his cousin **Rufus** 1738–1824, American soldier in the War of Independence; surveyor general of the US (1796–1803)

putout *Baseball* a play in which the batter or runner is put out

putrescent 1 becoming putrid; rotting 2 characterized by or undergoing putrefaction

putrid (of organic matter) in a state of decomposition, usually giving off a foul smell

putsch a violent and sudden uprising; political revolt, esp a coup d'état

putt *Golf* a stroke on the green with a putter to roll the ball into or near the hole

putter¹ *Golf* 1 a club for putting, usually having a solid metal head 2 a golfer who putts

putter² *Athletics* a person who puts the shot

putting green 1 (on a golf course) the area of closely mown grass at the end of a fairway where the hole is 2 an area of smooth grass with several holes for putting games

Puttnam David, Baron. born 1941, British film producer. Films include *Chariots of Fire* (1981), *The Killing Fields* (1984), *Memphis Belle* (1990), and *My Life So Far* (1999)

putty 1 a stiff paste made of whiting and linseed oil that is used to fix glass panes into frames and to fill cracks or holes in woodwork, etc. 2 (*as modifier*): *a putty knife* 3 a a colour varying from a greyish-yellow to a greyish-brown or brownish-grey b (*as adjective*): *putty-coloured*

Putumayo a river in NW South America, rising in S Colombia and flowing southeast as most of the border between Colombia and Peru, entering the Amazon in Brazil: scene of the Putumayo rubber scandal (1910–11) during the rubber boom, in which many Indians were enslaved and killed by rubber exploiters. Length: 1578 km (980 miles)

Puvis de Chavannes Pierre Cécile 1824–98, French mural painter

Puy de Sancy a mountain in S central France: highest peak of the Monts Dore. Height: 1886 m (6188 ft)

Pu-yi Henry 1906–67, last emperor of China as Xuan-Tong (1908–12); emperor of the Japanese puppet state of

Manchukuo as Kang-de (1934–45)

puzzle a toy, game, or question presenting a problem that requires skill or ingenuity for its solution
▷www.puzzles.com

pyaemia or **pyemia** blood poisoning characterized by pus-forming microorganisms in the blood

Pydna a town in ancient Macedonia: site of a major Roman victory over the Macedonians, resulting in the downfall of their kingdom (168 BC)

pye-dog, pie-dog, or **pi-dog** an ownerless half-wild Asian dog

Pygmy or **Pigmy** a member of one of the dwarf peoples of Equatorial Africa, noted for their hunting and forest culture

pylon 1 a large vertical steel tower-like structure supporting high-tension electrical cables 2 a post or tower for guiding pilots or marking a turning point in a race 3 a streamlined aircraft structure for attaching an engine pod, external fuel tank, etc, to the main body of the aircraft 4 a monumental gateway, such as one at the entrance to an ancient Egyptian temple 5 a temporary artificial leg

Pylos a port in SW Greece, in the SW Peloponnese; scene of a defeat of the Spartans by the Athenians (425 BC) during the Peloponnesian War and of the Battle of Navarino (see **Navarino**)

Pym 1 Barbara (**Mary Crampton**). 1913–80, British novelist, noted for such comedies of middle-class English life as *Excellent Women* (1952), *A Glass of Blessings* (1958), and *The Sweet Dove Died* (1978) 2 John ?1584–1643, leading English parliamentarian during the events leading to the Civil War. He took a prominent part in the impeachment of Buckingham (1626) and of Strafford and Laud (1640)

Pynchon Thomas born 1937, US novelist, author of *V* (1963), *The Crying of Lot 49* (1967), *Gravity's Rainbow* (1973), and *Mason and Dixon* (1997)

Pyongyang or **P'yŏng-yang** the capital of North Korea, in the southwest on the Taedong River: industrial centre; university (1946). Pop: 3 284 000 (2005 est)

pyorrhoea or *esp US* **pyorrhea** inflammation of the gums characterized by the discharge of pus and loosening of the teeth; periodontal disease

pyramid 1 a huge masonry construction that has a square base and, as in the case of the ancient Egyptian royal tombs, four sloping triangular sides 2 *Maths* a solid having a polygonal base and triangular sides that meet in a common vertex 3 *Crystallog* a crystal form in which three planes intersect all three axes of the crystal 4 *Anatomy* any pointed or cone-shaped bodily structure or part 5 a game similar to billiards with fifteen

coloured balls

pyramid selling a practice adopted by some manufacturers of advertising for distributors and selling them batches of goods. The first distributors then advertise for more distributors who are sold subdivisions of the original batches at an increased price. This process continues until the final distributors are left with a stock that is unsaleable except at a loss

pyrethrum 1 any of several cultivated Eurasian chrysanthemums, such as *Chrysanthemum coccineum* and *C. roseum*, with white, pink, red, or purple flowers

pyretic *Pathol* of, relating to, or characterized by fever 3 any insecticide prepared from the dried flowers of any of these plants, esp *C. roseum*

Pyrex *Trademark* a any of a variety of borosilicate glasses that have low coefficients of expansion, making them suitable for heat-resistant glassware used in cookery and chemical apparatus b (*as modifier*): *a Pyrex dish*

pyrite a yellow mineral, found in igneous and metamorphic rocks and in veins. It is a source of sulphur and is used in the manufacture of sulphuric acid. Composition: iron sulphide. Formula: FeS_2. Crystal structure: cubic

pyrites 1 another name for **pyrite** 2 any of a number of other disulphides of metals, esp of copper and tin

pyromania *Psychiatry* the uncontrollable impulse and practice of setting things on fire

pyrotechnics 1 the art or craft of making fireworks 2 a firework display

Pyrrho ?365–?275 BC, Greek philosopher; founder of scepticism. He maintained that true wisdom and happiness lie in suspension of judgment, since certain knowledge is impossible to attain

Pyrrhus 319–272 BC, king of Epirus (306–272). He invaded Italy but was ultimately defeated by the Romans (275 BC)

Pythagoras ?580–?500 BC, Greek philosopher and mathematician. He founded a religious brotherhood, which followed a life of strict asceticism and greatly influenced the development of mathematics and its application to music and astronomy

Pytheas 4th century BC, Greek navigator. He was the first Greek to visit and describe the coasts of Spain, France, and the British Isles and may have reached Iceland

python any large nonvenomous snake of the family *Pythonidae* of Africa, S Asia, and Australia, such as *Python reticulatus* (**reticulated python**). They can reach a length of more than 20 feet and kill their prey by constriction

pyx or *less commonly* **pix** 1 *Christianity* any receptacle in which the Eucharistic Host is kept

Qq

Qaboos bin Said born 1940, sultan of Oman from 1970

Qatar *or* **Katar** a state in E Arabia, occupying a peninsula in the Persian Gulf: under Persian rule until the 19th century; became a British protectorate in 1916; declared independence in 1971; exports petroleum and natural gas. Official language: Arabic. Official religion: (Sunni) Muslim. Currency: riyal. Capital: Doha. Pop: 619 000 (2004 est). Area: about 11 000 sq km (4250 sq miles)

Qattara Depression an arid basin in the Sahara, in NW Egypt, impassable to vehicles. Area: about 18 000 sq km (7000 sq miles). Lowest point: 133 m (435 ft) below sea level

Qeshm *or* **Qishm** 1 the largest island in the Persian Gulf: part of Iran. Area: 1336 sq km (516 sq miles) 2 the chief town of this island

Qingdao, Tsingtao, *or* **Chingtao** a port in E China, in E Shandong province on Jiazhou Bay, developed as a naval base and fort in 1891. Shandong university (1926). Pop: 2 431 000 (2005 est)

Qinghai, Tsinghai, *or* **Chinghai** 1 a province of NW China: consists largely of mountains and high plateaus. Capital: Xining. Pop: 5 340 000 (2003 est). Area: 721 000 sq km (278 400 sq miles) 2 the Pinyin transliteration of the Chinese name for **Koko Nor**

Qiqihar, Chichihaerh, Ch'i-ch'i-haerh *or* **Tsitsihar** a city in NE China, in Heilongjiang province on the Nonni River. Pop: 1 452 000 (2005 est)

Qom, Qum, *or* **Kum** a city in NW central Iran: a place of pilgrimage for Shiite Muslims. Pop: 1 045 000 (2005 est)

quack *Brit, Austral, and NZ informal* a doctor; physician or surgeon

quad bike *or* **quad** a vehicle like a motorcycle with four large wheels, designed for agricultural, sporting, and other off-road uses

quadrangle 1 *Geometry* a plane figure consisting of four points connected by four lines. In a **complete quadrangle**, six lines connect all pairs of points 2 a rectangular courtyard, esp one having buildings on all four sides 3 the building surrounding such a courtyard

quadrant 1 *Geometry* **a** a quarter of the circumference of a circle **b** the area enclosed by two perpendicular radii of a circle and its circumference **c** any of the four sections into which a plane is divided by two coordinate axes 2 a piece of a mechanism in the form of a quarter

circle, esp one used as a cam or a gear sector 3 an instrument formerly used in astronomy and navigation for measuring the altitudes of stars, consisting of a graduated arc of 90° and a sighting mechanism attached to a movable arm

quadrate 1 one of a pair of bones of the upper jaw of fishes, amphibians, reptiles, and birds that articulates with the lower jaw. In mammals it forms the incus 2 of or relating to this bone

quadratic *Maths* 1 an equation containing one or more terms in which the variable is raised to the power of two, but no terms in which it is raised to a higher power 2 of or relating to the second power

quadrennial a period of four years

quadrilateral 1 having or formed by four sides 2 a polygon having four sides. A **complete quadrilateral** consists of four lines and their six points of intersection

quadrille¹ 1 a square dance of five or more figures for four or more couples 2 a piece of music for such a dance, alternating between simple duple and compound duple time

quadrille² an old card game for four players

quadrillion 1 (in Britain) the number represented as one followed by 24 zeros (10^{24}) 2 (in the US and Canada) the number represented as one followed by 15 zeros (10^{15})

quadriplegia *Pathol* paralysis of all four limbs, usually as the result of injury to the spine

quadruped 1 an animal, esp a mammal, that has all four limbs specialized for walking 2 having four feet

quadruplet *Music* a group of four notes to be played in a time value of three

quagga a recently extinct member of the horse family (*Equidae*), *Equus quagga*, of southern Africa: it had a sandy brown colouring with zebra-like stripes on the head and shoulders

quagmire a soft wet area of land that gives way under the feet; bog

quail 1 any small Old World gallinaceous game bird of the genus *Coturnix* and related genera, having a rounded body and small tail: family *Phasianidae* (pheasants) 2 any of various similar and related American birds, such as the bobwhite

Quaker a member of the Religious Society of Friends, a Christian sect founded by the English religious leader George Fox (1624–91) about 1650, whose central belief is the doctrine of the Inner Light. Quakers reject sacraments, ritual, and formal ministry, hold meetings at which any member may speak, and have promoted many causes for social reform

▷http://www.quaker.org/

quality 1 *Music* musical tone colour; timbre **2** *Logic* the characteristic of a proposition that is dependent on whether it is affirmative or negative

quandong, quandang, or **quantong 1 a** a small Australian santalaceous tree, *Eucarya acuminata* (or *Fusanus acuminatus*) **b** the edible fruit or nut of this tree, used in preserves **2 silver quandong a** the pale easily worked timber of this tree

quango a semipublic government-financed administrative body whose members are appointed by the government

Quant Mary born 1934, British fashion designer, whose Chelsea Look of miniskirts and geometrically patterned fabrics dominated London fashion in the 1960s

quantitative or **quantitive** *Prosody* denoting or relating to a metrical system, such as that in Latin and Greek verse, that is based on the relative length rather than stress of syllables

quantity 1 *Maths* an entity having a magnitude that may be denoted by a numerical expression **2** *Physics* a specified magnitude or amount; the product of a number and a unit **3** *Logic* the characteristic of a proposition dependent on whether it is a universal or particular statement, considering all or only part of a class **4** *Prosody* the relative duration of a syllable or the vowel in it

quantum *Physics* **a** the smallest quantity of some physical property, such as energy, that a system can possess according to the quantum theory **b** a particle with such a unit of energy

quantum theory a theory concerning the behaviour of physical systems based on Planck's idea that they can only possess certain properties, such as energy and angular momentum, in discrete amounts (quanta). The theory later developed in several equivalent mathematical forms based on De Broglie's theory and on the Heisenberg uncertainty principle

quarantine 1 a period of isolation or detention, esp of persons or animals arriving from abroad, to prevent the spread of disease, usually consisting of the maximum known incubation period of the suspected disease **2** the place or area where such detention is enforced

quark *Physics* any of a set of six hypothetical elementary particles together with their antiparticles thought to be fundamental units of all baryons and mesons but unable to exist in isolation. The magnitude of their charge is either two thirds or one third of that of the electron

Quarles Francis 1592–1644, English poet

quarrel an arrow having a four-edged head, fired from a crossbow

quart 1 a unit of liquid measure equal to a quarter of a gallon or two pints. 1 US quart (0.946 litre) is equal to 0.8326 U.K. quart. 1 U.K. quart (1.136 litres) is equal to 1.2009 US quarts **2** a unit of dry measure equal to 2 pints or one eighth of a peck

quarter 1 one of four equal or nearly equal parts of an object, quantity, amount, etc. **2** the fraction equal to one divided by four (1/4) **3** *US and Canadian* a quarter of a dollar; 25-cent piece **4** a unit of weight equal to a quarter of a hundredweight. 1 US quarter is equal to 25 pounds; 1 Brit quarter is equal to 28 pounds **5** short for **quarter-hour 6** a fourth part of a year; three months **7** *Astronomy* **a** one fourth of the moon's period of revolution around the earth **b** either of two phases of the moon, **first quarter** or **last quarter** when half of the lighted surface is visible from the earth **8** *Informal* a unit of weight equal to a quarter of a pound or 4 ounces **9** *Brit* a unit of capacity for grain, etc, usually equal to 8 U.K. bushels **10** *Nautical* the part of a vessel's side towards the stern, usually aft of the aftermost mast **11** *Nautical* the general direction along the water in the quadrant between the beam of a vessel and its stern **12** a region or district of a town or city **13** a region, direction, or point of the compass **14** any of the four limbs, including the adjacent parts, of the carcass of a quadruped or bird **15** *Vet science* the side part of the wall of a horse's hoof **16** *Military, slang* short for **quartermaster**

quarterback *US and Canadian* a player in American or Canadian football, positioned usually behind the centre, who directs attacking play

quarterdeck *Nautical* the after part of the weather deck of a ship, traditionally the deck on a naval vessel for official or ceremonial use

quarter-hour a period of 15 minutes

quarterlight *Brit* a small pivoted window in the door of a car for ventilation

quartermaster a rating in the navy, usually a petty officer, with particular responsibility for steering a ship and other navigational duties

quarter sessions 1 (in England and Wales, formerly) a criminal court held four times a year before justices of the peace or a recorder, empowered to try all but the most serious offences and to hear appeals from petty sessions. Replaced in 1972 by **crown courts 2** (in Scotland, formerly) a court held by justices of the peace four times a year, empowered to hear appeals from justice of the peace courts and to deal with some licensing matters: abolished in 1975

quartet or **quartette** a group of four singers or instrumentalists or a piece of music composed for such a group

quartile *Astrology* denoting an aspect of two heavenly bodies when their longitudes differ by 90°

quartz a colourless mineral often tinted by impurities, found in igneous, sedimentary, and metamorphic rocks. It is used in the manufacture of glass, abrasives, and cement, and also as a gemstone; the violet-purple variety is amethyst, the brown variety is cairngorm, the yellow variety is citrine, and the pink variety is rose quartz. Composition: silicon dioxide. Formula: SiO_2. Crystal structure: hexagonal

quartz crystal a thin plate or rod cut in certain directions from a piece of piezoelectric quartz and accurately ground so that it vibrates at a particular frequency

quasar any of a class of extragalactic objects that emit an immense amount of energy in the form of light, infrared radiation, etc, from a compact source. They are extremely distant and their energy generation is thought to involve a supermassive black hole located in the centre of a galaxy

Quasimodo 1 a character in Victor Hugo's novel *Notre-Dame de Paris* (1831), a grotesque hunch-backed bell-ringer of the cathedral of Notre Dame 2 **Salvatore** 1901–68, Italian poet, whose early work expresses symbolist ideas and techniques. His later work is more concerned with political and social issues: Nobel prize for literature 1959

quassia 1 the bark and wood of *Quassia amara* and of a related tree, *Picrasma excelsa*, used in furniture making 2 a bitter compound extracted from this bark and wood, formerly used as a tonic and anthelmintic, now used in insecticides

quaternary 1 *Chem* containing or being an atom bound to four other atoms or groups 2 *Maths* having four variables

Quaternary 1 of, denoting, or formed in the most recent period of geological time, which succeeded the Tertiary period nearly two million years ago 2 **the** the Quaternary period or rock system, divided into Pleistocene and Holocene (Recent) epochs or series

quatrain a stanza or poem of four lines, esp one having alternate rhymes

Quatre Bras a village in Belgium near Brussels; site of a battle in June 1815 where Wellington defeated the French under Marshal Ney, immediately preceding the battle of Waterloo

quatrefoil 1 a leaf composed of four leaflets 2 *Architect* a carved ornament having four foils arranged about a common centre, esp one used in tracery

quattrocento the 15th century, esp in reference to Renaissance Italian art and literature

quaver *Music* a note having the time value of an eighth of a semibreve

quay a wharf, typically one built parallel to the shoreline

Quayle Sir (John) Anthony 1913–89, British actor and theatrical producer: director (1948–56) of the Shakespeare Memorial Theatre

Quebec 1 a province of E Canada: the largest Canadian province; a French colony from 1608 to 1763, when it passed to Britain; lying mostly on the Canadian Shield, it has vast areas of forest and extensive tundra and is populated mostly in the plain around the St Lawrence River. Capital: Quebec. Pop: 7 542 760 (2004 est). Area: 1 540 680 sq km (594 860 sq miles) 2 a port in E Canada, capital of the province of Quebec, situated on the St Lawrence River: founded in 1608 by Champlain; scene of the battle of the Plains of Abraham (1759), by which the British won Canada from the French. Pop: 169 076 (2001)

queen 1 a female sovereign who is the official ruler or head of state 2 the wife or widow of a king 3 a the only fertile female in a colony of social insects, such as bees, ants, and termites, from the eggs of which the entire colony develops b (*as modifier*): *a queen bee* 4 an adult female cat 5 one of four playing cards in a pack, one for each suit, bearing the picture of a queen 6 a chess piece, theoretically the most powerful piece, able to

move in a straight line in any direction or diagonally, over any number of squares

Queenborough in Sheppey a town in SE England, in Kent: formed in 1968 by the amalgamation of Queenborough, Sheerness, and Sheppey. Pop: 3471 (2001)

queen consort the wife of a reigning king

Queen Maud Land the large section of Antarctica between Coats Land and Enderby Land: claimed by Norway in 1939. (Claims are suspended under the Antarctic Treaty of 1959)

Queen Maud Range a mountain range in Antarctica, in S Ross Dependency, extending for about 800 km (500 miles)

queen mother the widow of a former king who is also the mother of the reigning sovereign

Queens a borough of E New York City, on Long Island. Pop: 2 225 486 (2003 est)

Queensland a state of NE Australia: fringed on the Pacific side by the Great Barrier Reef; the Great Dividing Range lies in the east, separating the coastal lowlands from the dry Great Artesian Basin in the south. Capital: Brisbane. Pop: 3 840 111 (2003 est). Area: 1 727 500 sq km (667 000 sq miles)

Quemoy an island in Formosa Strait, off the SE coast of China: administratively part of Taiwan. Pop. (with associated islets): 53 237 (1996 est). Area: 130 sq km (50 sq miles)

Queneau Raymond 1903–76. French writer, influenced in the 1920s by surrealism. His novels include *Zazie dans le métro* (1959)

Quesnay François 1694–1774, French political economist, encyclopedist, and physician. He propounded the theory championed by the physiocrats in his *Tableau économique* (1758)

quest (in medieval romance) an expedition by a knight or company of knights to accomplish some prescribed task, such as finding the Holy Grail

question *Law* 1 a matter submitted to a court or other tribunal for judicial or quasi-judicial decision 2 **question of fact** (in English law) that part of the issue before a court that is decided by the jury 3 **question of law** (in English law) that part of the issue before a court that is decided by the judge

question time (in parliamentary bodies of the British type) a period of time set aside each day for members to question government ministers

Quetta a city in W central Pakistan, at an altitude of 1650 m (5500 ft): a summer resort, military station, and trading centre. Pop: 744 000 (2005 est)

queue *Computing* a list in which entries are deleted from one end and inserted at the other

Quezon City a city in the Philippines, on central Luzon adjoining Manila: capital of the Philippines from 1948 to 1976; seat of the University of the Philippines (1908). Pop: 2 173 831 (2000)

Quezon y Molina Manuel Luis 1878–1944, Philippine statesman: first president of the Philippines (from 1935) and head of the government in exile after the Japanese conquest of the islands in World War II

Quiberon a peninsula of NW France, on the S coast of Brittany: a naval battle was fought off its coast in 1759

during the Seven Years' War, in which the British defeated the French

quick *Biology* 1 composed of living plants 2 any area of living flesh that is highly sensitive to pain or touch, esp that under a toenail or fingernail or around a healing wound

quick-change artist an actor or entertainer who undertakes several rapid changes of costume during his performance

quicksand a deep mass of loose wet sand that submerges anything on top of it

quickstep 1 a modern ballroom dance in rapid quadruple time 2 a piece of music composed f or or in the rhythm of this dance

quid *Brit* a slang word for pound¹ (sterling)

quiddity *Philosophy* the essential nature of something

quiet *Astronomy* (of the sun) exhibiting a very low number of sunspots, solar flares, and other surface phenomena; inactive

quietism a form of religious mysticism originating in Spain in the late 17th century, requiring withdrawal of the spirit from all human effort and complete passivity to God's will

quill 1 a any of the large stiff feathers of the wing or tail of a bird b the long hollow central part of a bird's feather; calamus 2 any of the stiff hollow spines of a porcupine or hedgehog 3 a device, formerly usually made from a crow quill, for plucking a harpsichord string 4 *Angling* a length of feather barb stripped of barbules and used for the body of some artificial flies 5 a small roll of bark, esp one of dried cinnamon 6 (in weaving) a bobbin or spindle 7 *Engineering* a hollow shaft that rotates upon an inner spindle or concentrically about an internal shaft

▷www.handcraftersvillage.com/quilling.htm

Quilmes a city in E Argentina: a resort and suburb of Buenos Aires. Pop: 550 069 (1999 est)

Quimper a city in NW France: capital of Finistère department. Pop: 63 238 (1999)

quince 1 a small widely cultivated Asian rosaceous tree, *Cydonia oblonga*, with pinkish-white flowers and edible pear-shaped fruits 2 the acid-tasting fruit of this tree, much used in preserves 3 Japanese *or* flowering quince another name for japonica

quincunx 1 *Botany* a quincuncial arrangement of sepals or petals in the bud 2 *Astrology* an aspect of 150° between two planets

Quine Willard van Orman 1908–2000, US philosopher. His works include *Word and Object* (1960), *Philosophy of Logic* (1970), *The Roots of Reference* (1973), and *The Logic of Sequences* (1990)

Qui Nhong a port in SE Vietnam, on the South China Sea. Pop: 163 385 (1992 est)

quinine a bitter crystalline alkaloid extracted from cinchona bark, the salts of which are used as a tonic, antipyretic, analgesic, etc, and in malaria therapy.

Formula: $C_{20}H_{24}N_2O_2$

quinquereme an ancient Roman galley with five banks of oars on each side

quinsy inflammation of the tonsils and surrounding tissues with the formation of abscesses

quint 1 an organ stop sounding a note a fifth higher than that normally produced by the key depressed 2 *Piquet* a sequence of five cards in the same suit

quintal 1 a unit of weight equal to 100 pounds 2 a unit of weight equal to 100 kilograms

Quintana Roo a state of SE Mexico, on the E Yucatán Peninsula: hot, humid, forested, and inhabited chiefly by Maya Indians. Capital: Chetumal. Pop: 287 000 (2005 est). Area: 50 350 sq km (19 463 sq miles)

quintessence 1 an extract of a substance containing its principle in its most concentrated form 2 (in ancient and medieval philosophy) ether, the fifth and highest essence or element after earth, water, air, and fire, which was thought to be the constituent matter of the heavenly bodies and latent in all things

quintet *or* **quintette** a group of five singers or instrumentalists or a piece of music composed for such a group

quintillion 1 (in Britain, France, and Germany) the number represented as one followed by 30 zeros (10^{30}) 2 (in the US and Canada) the number represented as one followed by 18 zeros (10^{18})

quintuplet *Music* a group of five notes to be played in a time value of three, four, or some other value

Quirinal one of the seven hills on which ancient Rome was built

quirk a continuous groove in an architectural moulding

Quito the capital of Ecuador, in the north at an altitude of 2850 m (9350 ft), just south of the equator: the oldest capital in South America, existing many centuries before the Incan conquest in 1487; a cultural centre since the beginning of Spanish rule (1534); two universities. Pop: 1 514 000 (2005 est)

quittance 1 release from debt or other obligation 2 a receipt or other document certifying this

quiver a case for arrows

quoin, coign, *or* **coigne** 1 an external corner of a wall 2 a stone forming the external corner of a wall

quokka a small wallaby, *Setonix brachyurus*, of Western Australia, occurring mostly on offshore islands

quotation 1 *Commerce* a statement of the current market price of a security or commodity 2 an estimate of costs submitted by a contractor to a prospective client; tender

quotidian 1 (esp of attacks of malarial fever) recurring daily 2 a malarial fever characterized by attacks that recur daily

quotient 1 a the result of the division of one number or quantity by another b the integral part of the result of division 2 a ratio of two numbers or quantities to be divided

Rr

Ra *or* **Re** the ancient Egyptian sun god, depicted as a man with a hawk's head surmounted by a solar disc and serpent

Rabat the capital of Morocco, in the northwest on the Atlantic coast, served by the port of Salé: became a military centre in the 12th century and a Corsair republic in the 17th century. Pop: 673 000 (2003)

Rabaul a port in Papua New Guinea, on NE New Britain Island, in the Bismarck Archipelago: capital of the Territory of New Guinea until 1941; almost surrounded by volcanoes. Pop: 17 022 (1990)

Rabbath Ammon *Old Testament* the ancient royal city of the Ammonites, on the site of modern Amman

rabbi 1 (in Orthodox Judaism) a man qualified in accordance with traditional religious law to expound, teach, and rule in accordance with this law 2 the religious leader of a congregation; the minister of a synagogue 3 **the Rabbis** the early Jewish scholars whose teachings are recorded in the Talmud

rabbit 1 any of various common gregarious burrowing leporid mammals, esp *Oryctolagus cuniculus* of Europe and North Africa and the cottontail of America. They are closely related and similar to hares but are smaller and have shorter ears 2 the fur of such an animal

rabble an iron tool or mechanical device for stirring, mixing, or skimming a molten charge in a roasting furnace

Rabelais François ?1494–1553, French writer. His written works, esp *Gargantua and Pantagruel* (1534), contain a lively mixture of earthy wit, common sense, and satire

Rabi Isidor Isaac 1898–1988, US physicist, born in Austria, who devised the atomic and molecular beam resonance method of observing atomic spectra. Nobel prize for physics 1944

rabid relating to or having rabies

rabies *Pathol* an acute infectious viral disease of the nervous system transmitted by the saliva of infected animals, esp dogs. It is characterized by excessive salivation, aversion to water, convulsions, and paralysis

Rabin Yitzhak 1922–95, Israeli statesman; prime minister of Israel (1974–77; 1992–95); assassinated

raccoon *or* **racoon** 1 any omnivorous mammal of the genus *Procyon*, esp *P. lotor* (**North American raccoon**), inhabiting forests of North and Central America and the Caribbean: family *Procyonidae*, order *Carnivora* (carnivores). Raccoons have a pointed muzzle, long tail, and greyish-black fur with black bands around the tail and across the face 2 the fur of the North American raccoon

race¹ 1 a rapid current of water, esp one through a narrow channel that has a tidal range greater at one end than the other 2 a channel of a stream, esp one for conducting water to or from a water wheel or other device for utilizing its energy 3 a a channel or groove that contains ball bearings or roller bearings or that restrains a sliding component b the inner or outer cylindrical ring in a ball bearing or roller bearing 4 *Austral* a wire tunnel through which footballers pass from the changing room onto a football field 5 another name for **slipstream**

race² 1 a group of people of common ancestry, distinguished from others by physical characteristics, such as hair type, colour of eyes and skin, stature, etc. Principal races are Caucasoid, Mongoloid, and Negroid 2 **the human race** human beings collectively 3 a group of animals or plants having common characteristics that distinguish them from other members of the same species, usually forming a geographically isolated group; subspecies

race³ a ginger root

Race Cape a cape at the SE extremity of Newfoundland, Canada

racecourse a long broad track, usually of grass, enclosed between rails, and with starting and finishing points marked upon it, over which horses are raced

racehorse a horse specially bred for racing

raceme an inflorescence in which the flowers are borne along the main stem, with the oldest flowers at the base. It can be simple, as in the foxglove, or compound (see **panicle**)

race meeting a prearranged fixture for racing horses (or sometimes greyhounds) over a set course at set times

racetrack 1 a circuit or course, esp an oval one, used for motor racing, speedway, etc. 2 *chiefly US and Canadian* a long broad track, usually of grass, enclosed between rails, and with starting and finishing points marked upon it, over which horses are raced

Rachel¹ 1 *Old Testament* the second and best-loved wife of Jacob; mother of Joseph and Benjamin (Genesis 29–35) 2 original name *Elisa Félix*. 1820–58, French tragic actress, famous for her roles in the plays of Racine and Corneille

Rachel² *Old Testament* the second and best-loved wife of Jacob; mother of Joseph and Benjamin (Genesis 29–35)

Rachmaninoff *or* **Rachmaninov** Sergei Vassilievich 1873–1943, Russian piano virtuoso and composer

racial 1 denoting or relating to the division of the human species into races on grounds of physical characteristics 2 characteristic of any such group 3 of or relating to a subspecies

Racine Jean Baptiste 1639–99, French tragic poet and dramatist. His plays include *Andromaque* (1667), *Bérénice* (1670), and *Phèdre* (1677)

rack¹ 1 a toothed bar designed to engage a pinion to form a mechanism that will interconvert rotary and rectilinear motions 2 a framework fixed to an aircraft for carrying bombs, rockets, etc. 3 *History* an instrument of torture that stretched the body of the victim 4 *US and Canadian* in pool, snooker, etc **a** the triangular frame used to arrange the balls for the opening shot **b** the balls so grouped

rack² a group of broken clouds moving in the wind

rack-and-pinion 1 a device for converting rotary into linear motion and vice versa, in which a gearwheel (the pinion) engages with a flat toothed bar (the rack) 2 (of a type of steering gear in motor vehicles) having a track rod with a rack along part of its length that engages with a pinion attached to the steering column

racket *Music* **a** a medieval woodwind instrument of deep bass pitch **b** a reed stop on an organ of deep bass pitch

rackets **a** a game similar to squash played in a large four-walled court by two or four players using rackets and a small hard ball **b** (*as modifier*): *a rackets court*

Rackham Arthur 1867–1939, English artist, noted for his book illustrations, esp of fairy tales

rad a former unit of absorbed ionizing radiation dose equivalent to an energy absorption per unit mass of 0.01 joule per kilogram of irradiated material. 1 rad is equivalent to 0.01 gray

radar 1 a method for detecting the position and velocity of a distant object, such as an aircraft. A narrow beam of extremely high-frequency radio pulses is transmitted and reflected by the object back to the transmitter, the signal being displayed on a radarscope. The direction of the reflected beam and the time between transmission and reception of a pulse determine the position of the object 2 the equipment used in such detection

Radcliffe Ann 1764–1823, British novelist, noted for her Gothic romances *The Mysteries of Udolpho* (1794) and *The Italian* (1797) **Paula** (**Jane**). born 1973, British athlete, winner of the London Marathon (2002, 2003), and European Record Holder for the 10000m.

Radetzky Count Joseph 1766–1858, Austrian field marshal: served in the war against Sardinia (1848–9), winning brilliant victories at Custozza (1848) and Novara (1849): governor of Lombardy-Venetia in N Italy (1849-57)

radial 1 of or relating to the arms of a starfish or similar radiating structures 2 *Anatomy* of or relating to the radius or forearm 3 *Astronomy* (of velocity) in a direction along the line of sight of a celestial object and measured by means of the red shift (or blue shift) of the spectral lines of the object 4 *Zoology* **a** any of the basal fin rays of most bony fishes **b** a radial or radiating structure, such as any of the ossicles supporting the oral disc of a sea star

radial-ply (of a motor tyre) having the fabric cords in the outer casing running radially to enable the sidewalls to be flexible

radian an SI unit of plane angle; the angle between two radii of a circle that cut off on the circumference an arc equal in length to the radius. 1 radian is equivalent to 57.296 degrees and π/2 radians equals a right angle

radiant 1 emitted or propagated by or as radiation; radiated 2 *Physics* (of a physical quantity in photometry) evaluated by absolute energy measurements 3 a point or object that emits radiation, esp the part of a heater that gives out heat 4 *Astronomy* the point in space from which a meteor shower appears to emanate

radiant energy energy that is emitted or propagated in the form of particles or electromagnetic radiation. It is measured in joules.

radiate 1 (of a capitulum) consisting of ray florets 2 (of animals or their parts) showing radial symmetry

radiation 1 *Physics* **a** the emission or transfer of radiant energy as particles, electromagnetic waves, sound, etc. **b** the particles, etc, emitted, esp the particles and gamma rays emitted in nuclear decay 2 *Med* treatment using a radioactive substance 3 *Anatomy* a group of nerve fibres that diverge from their common source

radiation sickness *Pathol* illness caused by overexposure of the body or a part of the body to ionizing radiations from radioactive material or X-rays. It is characterized by vomiting, diarrhoea, and in severe cases by sterility and cancer

radiator 1 a device for heating a room, building, etc, consisting of a series of pipes through which hot water or steam passes 2 a device for cooling an internal-combustion engine, consisting of thin-walled tubes through which water passes. Heat is transferred from the water through the walls of the tubes to the airstream, which is created either by the motion of the vehicle or by a fan 3 *Electronics* the part of an aerial or transmission line that radiates electromagnetic waves 4 an electric space heater

radical 1 favouring or tending to produce extreme or fundamental changes in political, economic, or social conditions, institutions, habits of mind, etc 2 *Med* (of treatment) aimed at removing the source of a disease 3 of, relating to, or arising from the root or the base of the stem of a plant 4 *Maths* of, relating to, or containing roots of numbers or quantities 5 a person who favours extreme or fundamental change in existing institutions or in political, social, or economic conditions 6 *Maths* a root of a number or quantity, such as $^3\sqrt{5}$, $\sqrt{x}$

radical sign the symbol √ placed before a number or quantity to indicate the extraction of a root, esp a square root. The value of a higher root is indicated by a raised digit in front of the symbol, as in $^3\sqrt{}$

radicchio an Italian variety of chicory, having purple leaves streaked with white that are eaten raw in salads

Radiguet Raymond 1903–23, French novelist; the author of *The Devil in the Flesh* (1923) and *Count d'Orgel* (1924)

radio 1 the use of electromagnetic waves, lying in the

radio-frequency range, for broadcasting, two-way communications, etc. 2 an electronic device designed to receive, demodulate, and amplify radio signals from sound broadcasting stations, etc. 3 a similar device permitting both transmission and reception of radio signals for two-way communications

radioactive exhibiting, using, or concerned with radioactivity

radioactivity the spontaneous emission of radiation from atomic nuclei. The radiation can consist of alpha, beta, and gamma radiation

radio astronomy a branch of astronomy in which a radio telescope is used to detect and analyse radio signals received on earth from radio sources in space

radiocarbon a radioactive isotope of carbon, esp carbon-14

radiocarbon dating a technique for determining the age of organic materials, such as wood, based on their content of the radioisotope ^{14}C acquired from the atmosphere when they formed part of a living plant. The ^{14}C decays to the nitrogen isotope ^{14}N with a half-life of 5730 years. Measurement of the amount of radioactive carbon remaining in the material thus gives an estimate of its age

radiochemistry the chemistry of radioactive elements and their compounds

radiogram 1 Brit a unit comprising a radio and record player 2 another name for **radiograph**

radiograph an image produced on a specially sensitized photographic film or plate by radiation, usually by X-rays or gamma rays

radiography the production of radiographs of opaque objects for use in medicine, surgery, industry, etc.

radioisotope an isotope that is radioactive

radiology the use of X-rays and radioactive substances in the diagnosis and treatment of disease

radiosonde an airborne instrument to send meteorological information back to earth by radio

radio telescope an instrument consisting of an antenna or system of antennas connected to one or more radio receivers, used in radio astronomy to detect and analyse radio waves from space

radiotherapy the treatment of disease, esp cancer, by means of alpha or beta particles emitted from an implanted or ingested radioisotope, or by means of a beam of high-energy radiation

radish 1 any of various plants of the genus Raphanus, esp R. sativus of Europe and Asia, cultivated for its edible root: family Brassicaceae (crucifers) 2 the root of this plant, which has a pungent taste and is eaten raw in salads 3 **wild radish** another name for **white charlock**

radium a a highly radioactive luminescent white element of the alkaline earth group of metals. It occurs in pitchblende, carnotite, and other uranium ores, and is used in radiotherapy and in luminous paints. Symbol: Ra; atomic no.: 88; half-life of most stable isotope, ^{226}Ra: 1620 years; valency: 2; relative density: 5; melting pt.: 700°C; boiling pt.: 1140°C b (as modifier): radium needle

radius 1 a straight line joining the centre of a circle or sphere to any point on the circumference or surface 2 the length of this line, usually denoted by the symbol r 3 the distance from the centre of a regular polygon to a

vertex (**long radius**) or the perpendicular distance to a side (**short radius**) 4 Anatomy the outer and slightly shorter of the two bones of the human forearm, extending from the elbow to the wrist 5 a corresponding bone in other vertebrates 6 any of the veins of an insect's wing 7 a group of ray florets, occurring in such plants as the daisy 8 the lateral displacement of a cam or eccentric wheel

Radnorshire or **Radnor** (until 1974) a county of E Wales, now part of Powys

Radom a city in E Poland: under Austria from 1795 to 1815 and Russia from 1815 to 1918. Pop: 232 000 (2005 est)

radon a colourless radioactive element of the rare gas group, the most stable isotope of which, radon-222, is a decay product of radium. It is used as an alpha particle source in radiotherapy. Symbol: Rn; atomic no.: 86; half-life of ^{222}Rn: 3.82 days; valency: 0; density: 9.73 kg/m^3; melting pt.: −71°C; boiling pt.: −61.7°C

Raeburn Sir Henry 1756–1823, Scottish portrait painter

raffia or **raphia** 1 a palm tree, Raphia ruffia, native to Madagascar, that has large plumelike leaves, the stalks of which yield a useful fibre 2 the fibre obtained from this plant, used for tying, weaving, etc. 3 any of several related palms or the fibre obtained from them

Raffles Sir Thomas Stamford 1781–1826, British colonial administrator: founded Singapore (1819) as a station for the British East India Company

raft a buoyant platform of logs, planks, etc, used as a vessel or moored platform

rag¹ 1 a a small piece of cloth, such as one torn from a discarded garment, or such pieces of cloth collectively b (as modifier): a rag doll 2 Brit, slang, esp naval a flag or ensign

rag² in British universities a a period, usually a week, in which various events are organized to raise money for charity, including a procession of decorated floats and tableaux b (as modifier): rag day

rag³ Jazz a piece of ragtime music

ragged robin a caryophyllaceous plant, Lychnis floscuculi, native to Europe and Asia, that has pink or white flowers with ragged petals

Raglan Fitzroy James Henry Somerset, 1st Baron Raglan. 1788–1855, British field marshal, diplomatist, politician, and protégé of Wellington: commanded British troops (1854–55) in the Crimean War

ragtime a style of jazz piano music, developed by Scott Joplin around 1900, having a two-four rhythm base and a syncopated melody
  ▷www.wikipedia.org/wiki/Ragtime
  ▷www.dropbears.com/r/ragtime
  ▷www.jazzinamerica.org

Ragusa 1 an industrial town in SE Sicily. Pop: 68 956 (2001) 2 the Italian name (until 1918) for **Dubrovnik**

ragwort any of several plants of the genus Senecio, esp S. jacobaea of Europe, that have yellow daisy-like flowers: family Asteraceae (composites)

rail¹ 1 one of a pair of parallel bars laid on a prepared track, roadway, etc, that serve as a guide and running surface for the wheels of a railway train, tramcar, etc. 2 a short for **railway** b (as modifier): rail transport 3 Nautical a trim for finishing the top of a bulwark

rail² any of various small wading birds of the genus

Rallus and related genera: family *Rallidae*, order *Gruiformes* (cranes, etc). They have short wings, long legs, and dark plumage

railcard *Brit* an identity card that young people or pensioners in Britain can buy, which allows them to buy train tickets more cheaply

railhead 1 a terminal of a railway 2 the farthest point reached by completed track on an unfinished railway 3 the upper part of a railway rail, on which the traffic wheels run

railway *or US* **railroad** 1 a permanent track composed of a line of parallel metal rails fixed to sleepers, for transport of passengers and goods in trains 2 any track on which the wheels of a vehicle may run 3 the entire equipment, rolling stock, buildings, property, and system of tracks used in such a transport system 4 the organization responsible for operating a railway network
▷http://routesinternational.com/rail.htm
▷http://RAILlinks.com/railfan/pages/

rain 1 a precipitation from clouds in the form of drops of water, formed by the condensation of water vapour in the atmosphere b a fall of rain; shower

rainbird any of various birds, such as (in Britain) the green woodpecker, whose cry is supposed to portend rain

rainbow 1 a bow-shaped display in the sky of the colours of the spectrum, caused by the refraction and reflection of the sun's rays through rain or mist 2 of or relating to a political grouping together by several minorities, esp of different races

Rainbow Bridge a natural stone bridge over a creek in SE Utah. Height: 94 m (309 ft). Span: 85 m (278 ft)

rainbow trout a freshwater trout of North American origin, *Salmo gairdneri*, having a body marked with many black spots and two longitudinal red stripes

rainfall 1 precipitation in the form of raindrops 2 *Meteorol* the amount of precipitation in a specified place and time

rainforest dense forest found in tropical areas of heavy rainfall. The trees are broad-leaved and evergreen, and the vegetation tends to grow in three layers (undergrowth, intermediate trees and shrubs, and very tall trees, which form a canopy)

Rainier Mount a mountain in W Washington State: the highest mountain in the state and in the Cascade Range. Height: 4392 m (14 410 ft)

rainwater water from rain (as distinguished from spring water, tap water, etc)

Rais *or* **Retz** Gilles de 1404–40, French nobleman who fought with Joan of Arc; marshal of France (1429–40). He was executed for the torture and murder of more than 140 children

Rajasthan a state of NW India, bordering on Pakistan: formed in 1958; contains the Thar Desert in the west; now the largest state in India. Capital: Jaipur. Pop: 56 473 122 (2001). Area: 342 239 sq km (132 111 sq miles)

Rajkot a city in W India, in S Gujarat. Pop: 966 642 (2001)

Rajputana a former group of princely states in NW India: now mostly part of Rajasthan

rake[1] 1 a hand implement consisting of a row of teeth set in a headpiece attached to a long shaft and used for

gathering hay, straw, leaves, etc, or for smoothing loose earth 2 any of several mechanical farm implements equipped with rows of teeth or rotating wheels mounted with tines and used to gather hay, straw, etc. 3 any of various implements similar in shape or function, such as a tool for drawing out ashes from a furnace 4 *NZ* a line of wagons coupled together as one unit, used on railways

rake[2] 1 *Nautical* the degree to which an object, such as a ship's mast, inclines from the perpendicular, esp towards the stern 2 *Theatre* the slope of a stage from the back towards the footlights 3 *Aeronautics* a the angle between the wings of an aircraft and the line of symmetry of the aircraft b the angle between the line joining the centroids of the section of a propeller blade and a line perpendicular to the axis 4 the angle between the working face of a cutting tool and a plane perpendicular to the surface of the workpiece 5 a slanting ledge running across a crag in the Lake District

rakish *Nautical* (of a ship or boat) having lines suggestive of speed

Raleigh[1] *or* **Ralegh** Sir Walter ?1552–1618, English courtier, explorer, and writer; favourite of Elizabeth I. After unsuccessful attempts to colonize Virginia (1584–89), he led two expeditions to the Orinoco to search for gold (1595; 1616). He introduced tobacco and potatoes into England, and was imprisoned (1603–16) for conspiracy under James I. He was beheaded in 1618

Raleigh[2] a city in E central North Carolina, capital of the state. Pop: 316 802 (2003 est)

rallentando *Music* becoming slower

rally 1 *Tennis, Squash, Badminton* an exchange of several shots before one player wins the point 2 *Motor sport* a type of motoring competition over public and closed roads

ram 1 an uncastrated adult sheep 2 a piston or moving plate, esp one driven hydraulically or pneumatically 3 the falling weight of a pile driver or similar device 4 a pointed projection in the stem of an ancient warship for puncturing the hull of enemy ships 5 a warship equipped with a ram

RAM *Computing* random access memory: semiconductor memory in which all storage locations can be rapidly accessed in the same amount of time. It forms the main memory of a computer, used by applications to perform tasks while the device is operating

Ramadan, Rhamadhan, *or* **Ramazan** 1 the ninth month of the Muslim year, lasting 30 days, during which strict fasting is observed from sunrise to sunset 2 the fast itself

Ramakrishna Sri 1834–86, Hindu yogi and religious reformer. He preached the equal value of all religions as different paths to God

Ramat Gan a city in Israel, E of Tel Aviv. Pop: 126 500 (2003 est)

Rambert Dame Marie 1888–1982, British ballet dancer and teacher, born in Poland: founded the **Ballet Rambert** (1926)

rambler a weak-stemmed plant, esp any of various cultivated hybrid roses that straggle over other vegetation

rambling (of a plant, esp a rose) profusely climbing and straggling

Rambouillet a town in N France, in the Yvelines department: site of the summer residence of French presidents. Pop: 24 758 (1999)

Rameau Jean Philippe 1683–1764, French composer. His works include the opera *Castor et Pollux* (1737), chamber music, harpsichord pieces, church music, and cantatas. His *Traité de l'harmonie* (1722) was of fundamental importance in the development of modern harmony

Ramillies a village in central Belgium where the Duke of Marlborough defeated the French in 1706

ramjet *or* **ramjet engine** a a type of jet engine in which fuel is burned in a duct using air compressed by the forward speed of the aircraft b an aircraft powered by such an engine

rampant (of an arch) having one abutment higher than the other

Rampur a city in N India, in N Uttar Pradesh. Pop: 281 549 (2001)

Ramsay 1 Allan ?1686–1758, Scottish poet, editor, and bookseller, noted particularly for his pastoral comedy *The Gentle Shepherd* (1725): first person to introduce the circulating library in Scotland 2 his son, **Allan** 1713–84, Scottish portrait painter 3 **James Andrew Broun**. See (1st Marquis and 10th Earl of) **Dalhousie** 4 **Gordon** born 1963, British chef and restaurateur; the only British-born chef to achieve a third Michelin star (2001) 5 Sir **William** 1852–1916, Scottish chemist. He discovered argon (1894) with Rayleigh, isolated helium (1895), and identified neon, krypton, and xenon: Nobel prize for chemistry 1904

Ramses *or* **Rameses** any of 12 kings of ancient Egypt, who ruled from ?1315 to ?1090 BC

Ramses II *or* **Rameses II** died ?1225 BC, king of ancient Egypt (?1292–?25). His reign was marked by war with the Hittites and the construction of many colossal monuments, esp the rock temple at Abu Simbel

Ramses III *or* **Rameses III** died ?1167 BC, king of ancient Egypt (?1198–?67). His reign was marked by wars in Libya and Syria

Ramsey Sir **Alf(red)** (**Ernest**). 1922–99, English footballer and football manager, who played for England 32 times and managed England when they won the World Cup (1966)

Ramsgate a port and resort in SE England, in E Kent on the North Sea coast. Pop: 37 967 (2001)

Rancagua a city in central Chile. Pop: 217 000 (2005 est)

Ranchi an industrial city in E India, between the coal and iron belts of the Chota Nagpur Plateau; the capital of Jharkhand from 2000. Pop: 846 454 (2001)

rand[1] the standard monetary unit of the Republic of South Africa, divided into 100 cents

rand[2] *Dialect* a a strip or margin; border b a strip of cloth; selvage

Rand the short for **Witwatersrand**

Randers a port and industrial centre in Denmark, in E Jutland on **Randers Fjord** (an inlet of the Kattegat). Pop: 55 739 (2004 est)

Randolph 1 **Edmund Jennings**, 1753–1813, US politician. He was a member of the convention that framed the US constitution (1787), attorney general (1789–94), and secretary of state (1794–95) 2 **John**, called *Randolph of Roanoke*. 1773–1833, US politician, noted for his elo-

quence: in 1820 he opposed the Missouri Compromise that outlawed slavery 3 Sir **Thomas**; 1st Earl of Moray. Died 1332, Scottish soldier: regent after the death of Robert the Bruce (1329)

rangatira *NZ* a Māori chief of either sex

range 1 the total products of a manufacturer, designer, or stockist 2 *Physics* the distance that a particle of ionizing radiation, such as an electron or proton, can travel through a given medium, esp air, before ceasing to cause ionization 3 *Maths, Logic* a (of a function) the set of values that the function takes for all possible arguments b (of a variable) the set of values that a variable can take c (of a quantifier) the set of values that the variable bound by the quantifier can take 4 the extent of pitch difference between the highest and lowest notes of a voice, instrument, etc. 5 the geographical region in which a species of plant or animal normally grows or lives 6 a series or chain of mountains 7 *Nautical* a line of sight taken from the sea along two or more navigational aids that mark a navigable channel 8 **range of significance** *Philosophy, Logic* the set of subjects for which a given predicate is intelligible

rangefinder an instrument for determining the distance of an object from the observer, esp in order to sight a gun or focus a camera

rani *or* **ranee** (in oriental countries, esp India) a queen or princess; the wife of a rajah

Ranjit Singh called *the Lion of the Punjab*. 1780–1839; founder of the Sikh kingdom in the Punjab

rank[1] 1 any of the eight horizontal rows of squares on a chessboard 2 *Music* a set of organ pipes controlled by the same stop 3 *Maths* (of a matrix) the largest number of linearly independent rows or columns; the number of rows (or columns) of the nonzero determinant of greatest order that can be extracted from the matrix

rank[2] *Botany* showing vigorous and profuse growth

Rank 1 **J(oseph) Arthur**. 1888–1972, British industrialist and film executive, whose companies dominated the British film industry in the 1940s and 1950s 2 **Otto** 1884–1939, Austrian psychoanalyst, noted for his theory that the trauma of birth may be reflected in certain forms of mental illness

Ransom **John Crowe** 1888–1974, US poet and critic

Ransome **Arthur** 1884–1967, English writer, best known for his books for children, including *Swallows and Amazons* (1930) and *Great Northern?* (1947)

ranunculus any ranunculaceous plant of the genus *Ranunculus*, having finely divided leaves and typically yellow five-petalled flowers. The genus includes buttercup, crowfoot, spearwort, and lesser celandine

rapacious (of animals, esp birds) subsisting by catching living prey

Rapacki **Adam** 1909–70, Polish politician: foreign minister (1956–68): proposed (1957) the denuclearization of Poland, Czechoslovakia, East Germany, and West Germany (the **Rapacki Plan**): rejected by the West because of Soviet predominance in conventional weapons

Rapallo a port and resort in NW Italy, in Liguria on the **Gulf of Rapallo** (an inlet of the Ligurian Sea): scene of the signing of two treaties after World War I. Pop: 29 159 (2001)

rape¹ the offence of forcing a person, esp a woman, to submit to sexual intercourse against that person's will

rape² 1 a Eurasian plant, *Brassica napus*, that has bright yellow flowers and is cultivated for its seeds, which yield a useful oil, and as a fodder plant: family *Brassicaceae* (crucifers) 2 the skins and stalks of grapes left after wine-making: used in making vinegar

Raphael¹ 1 *Bible* one of the archangels; the angel of healing and the guardian of Tobias (Tobit 3:17; 5–12). Feast day: Sept 29 2 original name *Raffaello Santi* or *Sanzio*. 1483–1520, Italian painter and architect, regarded as one of the greatest artists of the High Renaissance. His many paintings include the *Sistine Madonna* (?1513) and the *Transfiguration* (unfinished, 1520)

Raphael² *Bible* one of the archangels; the angel of healing and the guardian of Tobias (Tobit 3:17; 5–12). Feast day: Sept 29

rapid eye movement movement of the eyeballs under closed eyelids during paradoxical sleep, which occurs while the sleeper is dreaming

raptor 1 another name for **bird of prey** 2 *Informal* a carnivorous bipedal dinosaur of the late Cretaceous period

rare (of a gas, esp the atmosphere at high altitudes) having a low density; thin; rarefied

rarefied (of a gas, esp the atmosphere at high altitudes) having a low density; thin

Rarotonga an island in the S Pacific, in the SW Cook Islands: the chief island of the group. Chief settlement: Avarua. Pop: 12 188 (2001). Area: 67 sq km (26 sq miles)

rash *Pathol* any skin eruption

Rashid a town in N Egypt, on the Nile delta. Pop: 52 015 (latest est)

Rasht or **Resht** a city in NW Iran, near the Caspian Sea: agricultural and commercial centre in a rice-growing area. Pop: 586 000 (2005 est)

Rask Rasmus Christian 1787–1832, Danish philologist. He pioneered comparative philology with his work on Old Norse (1818)

Rasmussen Knud Johan Victor 1879–1933, Danish arctic explorer and ethnologist. He led several expeditions through the Arctic in support of his theory that the North American Indians were originally migrants from Asia

rasp a coarse file with rows of raised teeth

raspberry 1 any of the prickly shrubs of the rosaceous genus *Rubus*, such as *R. strigosus* of E North America and *R. idaeus* of Europe, that have pinkish-white flowers and typically red berry-like fruits (drupelets) 2 a the fruit of any such plant b (*as modifier*): raspberry jelly 3 **black raspberry** a a related plant, *Rubus occidentalis*, of E North America, that has black berry-like fruits b the fruit of this plant 4 a a dark purplish-red colour b (*as adjective*): *a raspberry coat*

Rasputin Grigori Efimovich ?1871–1916, Siberian peasant monk, notorious for his debauchery, who wielded great influence over Tsarina Alexandra. He was assassinated by a group of Russian noblemen

Rastafarian a member of an originally Jamaican religion that regards **Ras Tafari** (the former emperor of Ethiopia, Haile Selassie (1892–1975)) as God
  ▷www.rastafarian.net/

raster a pattern of horizontal scanning lines traced by an electron beam, esp on a television screen

rat any of numerous long-tailed murine rodents, esp of the genus *Rattus*, that are similar to but larger than mice and are now distributed all over the world

ratafia or **ratafee** any liqueur made from fruit or from brandy with added fruit

ratchet 1 a device in which a toothed rack or wheel is engaged by a pawl to permit motion in one direction only 2 the toothed rack or wheel forming part of such a device

rate 1 a a price or charge with reference to a standard or scale b (*as modifier*): *a rate card* 2 a charge made per unit for a commodity, service, etc. 3 a wage calculated against a unit of time

Rathenau Walther 1867–1922, German industrialist and statesman: he organized the German war industries during World War I, became minister of reconstruction (1921) and of foreign affairs (1922), and was largely responsible for the treaty of Rapallo with Russia. His assassination by right-wing extremists caused a furore

rating 1 (in certain navies) a sailor who holds neither commissioned nor warrant rank; an ordinary seaman 2 *Sailing* a handicap assigned to a racing boat based on its dimensions, sail area, weight, draught, etc.

ratio *Maths* a quotient of two numbers or quantities

rational *Maths* 1 expressible as a ratio of two integers or polynomials 2 a rational number

rationalism *Philosophy* a the doctrine that knowledge about reality can be obtained by reason alone without recourse to experience b the doctrine that human knowledge can all be encompassed within a single, usually deductive, system c the school of philosophy initiated by René Descartes, the French philosopher and mathematician (1596–1650), which held both the above doctrines
  ▷http://radicalacademy.com/
  adiphilrationalism.htm

rational number any real number of the form *a*/*b*, where *a* and *b* are integers and *b* is not zero, as 7 or 7/3

rattan or **ratan** 1 any of the climbing palms of the genus *Calamus* and related genera, having tough stems used for wickerwork and canes 2 the stems of such plants collectively 3 a stick made from one of these stems

Rattigan Sir Terence Mervyn 1911–77, English playwright. His plays include *The Winslow Boy* (1946), *Separate Tables* (1954), and *Ross* (1960)

rattle 1 a series of loosely connected horny segments on the tail of a rattlesnake, vibrated to produce a rattling sound 2 any of various European scrophulariaceous plants having a capsule in which the seeds rattle, such as *Pedicularis palustris* (**red rattle**) and *Rhinanthus minor* (**yellow rattle**)

Rattle Sir Simon born 1955, British conductor. Principal conductor (1980–91) and music director (1991–98) of the City of Birmingham Symphony Orchestra; chief conductor of the Berlin Philharmonic Orchestra from 2002

rattlesnake any of the venomous New World snakes constituting the genera *Crotalus* and *Sistrurus*, such as *C. horridus* (**black** or **timber rattlesnake**): family *Crotalidae* (pit vipers). They have a series of loose horny segments on the tail that are vibrated to produce a buzzing or whirring sound

Ratushinskaya Irina born 1954, Russian poet and writer, living in Britain: imprisoned (1983–86) in a Soviet labour camp on charges of subversion. Her publications include *Poems* (1984), *Grey is the Colour of Hope* (1988), and *The Odessans* (1992)

Rauschenberg Robert born 1925, US artist; one of the foremost exponents of pop art

Ravel Maurice (Joseph). 1875–1937, French composer, noted for his use of unresolved dissonances and mastery of tone colour. His works include *Gaspard de la Nuit* (1908) and *Le Tombeau de Couperin* (1917) for piano, *Boléro* (1928) for orchestra, and the ballet *Daphnis et Chloé* (1912)

raven 1 a large passerine bird, *Corvus corax*, having a large straight bill, long wedge-shaped tail, and black plumage: family *Corvidae* (crows). It has a hoarse croaking cry 2 **a** a shiny black colour **b** (*as adjective*): *raven hair*

Ravenna a city and port in NE Italy, in Emilia-Romagna: capital of the Western Roman Empire from 402 to 476, of the Ostrogoths from 493 to 526, and of the Byzantine exarchate from 584 to 751; famous for its ancient mosaics. Pop: 134 631 (2001)

ravine a deep narrow steep-sided valley, esp one formed by the action of running water

raw 1 (of the skin, a wound, etc) having the surface exposed or abraded, esp painfully 2 (of spirits) undiluted 3 (of the weather) harshly cold and damp

Rawalpindi an ancient city in N Pakistan: interim capital of Pakistan (1959–67) during the building of Islamabad. Pop: 1 794 000 (2005 est)

Rawsthorne Alan 1905–71, English composer, whose works include three symphonies, several concertos, and a set of *Symphonic Studies* (1939)

ray[1] 1 *Maths* a straight line extending from a point 2 a thin beam of electromagnetic radiation or particles 3 any of the bony or cartilaginous spines of the fin of a fish that form the support for the soft part of the fin 4 any of the arms or branches of a starfish or other radiate animal 5 *Astronomy* any of a number of bright streaks that radiate from the youngest lunar craters, such as Tycho; they are composed of crater ejecta not yet darkened, and extend considerable distances 6 *Botany* any strand of tissue that runs radially through the vascular tissue of some higher plants

ray[2] any of various selachian fishes typically having a flattened body, greatly enlarged winglike pectoral fins, gills on the undersurface of the fins, and a long whiplike tail. They constitute the orders *Torpediniformes* (**electric rays**) and *Rajiformes*

ray *Music* (in tonic sol-fa) the second degree of any major scale; supertonic

Ray[1] 1 John 1627–1705, English naturalist. He originated natural botanical classification and the division of flowering plants into monocotyledons and dicotyledons 2 **Man**, real name *Emmanuel Rudnitsky*. 1890–1976, US surrealist photographer 3 **Satyajit** 1921–92, Indian film director, noted for his *Apu* trilogy (1955–59)

Ray[2] Cape a promontory in SW Newfoundland, Canada

Rayleigh Lord, title of *John William Strutt*. 1842–1919, British physicist. He discovered argon (1894) with Ramsay and made important contributions to the theory of sound, the theory of scattering of radiation, etc.

Nobel prize for physics 1904

rayon 1 any of a number of textile fibres made from wood pulp or other forms of cellulose 2 any fabric made from such a fibre

razorbill *or* **razor-billed auk** a common auk, *Alca torda*, of the North Atlantic, having a thick laterally compressed bill with white markings

reach 1 an open stretch of water, esp on a river 2 *Nautical* the direction or distance sailed by a vessel on one tack 3 a bar on the rear axle of a vehicle connecting it with some part at the front end

reactance 1 the opposition to the flow of alternating current by the capacitance or inductance of an electrical circuit; the imaginary part of the impedance Z, $Z = R + iX$, where R is the resistance, $i = \sqrt{-1}$, and X is the reactance. It is expressed in ohms 2 the opposition to the flow of an acoustic or mechanical vibration, usually due to inertia or stiffness. It is the magnitude of the imaginary part of the acoustic or mechanical impedance

reactant a substance that participates in a chemical reaction, esp a substance that is present at the start of the reaction

reaction 1 opposition to change, esp political change, or a desire to return to a former condition or system 2 a response indicating a person's feelings or emotional attitude 3 *Med* **a** any effect produced by the action of a drug, esp an adverse effect **b** any effect produced by a substance (allergen) to which a person is allergic the simultaneous equal and opposite force that acts on a body whenever it exerts a force on another body 4 short for **nuclear reaction**

reactionary *or* **reactionist** 1 of, relating to, or characterized by reaction, esp against radical political or social change 2 a person opposed to radical change

reactive 1 readily partaking in chemical reactions 2 of, concerned with, or having a reactance 3 (of mental illnesses) precipitated by an external cause

reactor 1 *Chem* a substance, such as a reagent, that undergoes a reaction 2 short for **nuclear reactor** 3 a vessel, esp one in industrial use, in which a chemical reaction takes place 4 a coil of low resistance and high inductance that introduces reactance into a circuit 5 *Med* a person sensitive to a particular drug or agent

Reade Charles 1814–84, English novelist: author of *The Cloister and the Hearth* (1861), a historical romance

reader 1 **a** *Chiefly Brit* at a university, a member of staff having a position between that of a senior lecturer and a professor **b** *US* a teaching assistant in a faculty who grades papers, examinations, etc, on behalf of a professor 2 **a** a book that is part of a planned series for those learning to read **b** a standard textbook, esp for foreign-language learning 3 short for **lay reader** 4 *Judaism, chiefly Brit* another word for **cantor**

readership *Chiefly Brit* the office, position, or rank of university reader

reading 1 the form of a particular word or passage in a given text, esp where more than one version exists 2 *Parliamentary procedure* **a** the formal recital of the body or title of a bill in a legislative assembly in order to begin one of the stages of its passage **b** one of the three stages in the passage of a bill through a legislative assembly 3 the formal recital of something written, esp a will

Reading 1 a town in S England, in Reading unitary authority, Berkshire, on the River Thames: university (1892). Pop: 232 662 (2001) 2 a unitary authority in S England, in Berkshire. Pop: 144 100 (2003 est). Area: 37 sq km (14 sq miles)

read out a the act of retrieving information from a computer memory or storage device b the information retrieved

read-write head *Computing* an electromagnet that can both read and write information on a magnetic medium such as magnetic tape or disk

ready at *or* to the ready (of a rifle) in the position normally adopted immediately prior to aiming and firing

Reagan Ronald 1911–2004, US film actor and Republican statesman: Governor of California (1966–74): 40th president of the US (1981–89)

reagent a substance for use in a chemical reaction, esp for use in chemical synthesis and analysis

real¹ 1 *Philosophy* existent or relating to actual existence (as opposed to nonexistent, potential, contingent, or apparent) 2 *Economics* (of prices, incomes, wages, etc) considered in terms of purchasing power rather than nominal currency value 3 denoting or relating to immovable property such as land and tenements 4 *Physics* See **image** 5 *Maths* involving or containing real numbers alone; having no imaginary part 6 *Music* a (of the answer in a fugue) preserving the intervals as they appear in the subject b denoting a fugue as having such an answer 7 short for **real number**

real² a former small Spanish or Spanish-American silver coin

real³ the standard monetary unit of Brazil, divided into 100 centavos 2 a former coin of Portugal

real ale *or* **beer** any beer which is allowed to ferment in the cask and which when served is pumped up without using carbon dioxide

realism 1 a style of painting and sculpture that seeks to represent the familiar or typical in real life, rather than an idealized, formalized, or romantic interpretation of it 2 any similar school or style in other arts, esp literature 3 *Philosophy* the thesis that general terms such as common nouns refer to entities that have a real existence separate from the individuals which fall under them 4 *Philosophy* the theory that physical objects continue to exist whether they are perceived or not 5 *Logic, Philosophy* the theory that the sense of a statement is given by a specification of its truth conditions, or that there is a reality independent of the speaker's conception of it that determines the truth or falsehood of every statement
▷www.artlex.com/ArtLex/r/realism.html
▷www.artcyclopedia.com/history/realism.html

reality *Philosophy* a that which exists, independent of human awareness b the totality of facts as they are independent of human awareness of them

realm a royal domain; kingdom (now chiefly in such phrases as **Peer of the Realm**)

real number a number expressible as a limit of rational numbers

real tennis an ancient form of tennis played in a four-walled indoor court with various openings, a sloping-roofed corridor along three sides, and a buttress on the fourth side
▷www.real-tennis.com

real-time denoting or relating to a data-processing system in which a computer receives constantly changing data, such as information relating to air-traffic control, travel booking systems, etc, and processes it sufficiently rapidly to be able to control the source of the data

reaper the grim reaper death

rear admiral an officer holding flag rank in any of certain navies, junior to a vice admiral

rear light *or* **lamp** a red light, usually one of a pair, attached to the rear of a motor vehicle

rear-view mirror a mirror on a motor vehicle enabling the driver to see traffic coming behind him or her

reason 1 *Philosophy* the intellect regarded as a source of knowledge, as contrasted with experience 2 *Logic* grounds for a belief; a premise of an argument supporting that belief 3 **reasons of State** political justifications for an immoral act

rebate a refund of a fraction of the amount payable or paid, as for goods purchased in quantity; discount

Rebecca *Old Testament* the sister of Laban, who became the wife of Isaac and the mother of Esau and Jacob (Genesis 24–27)

rebellion organized resistance or opposition to a government or other authority

rebore the process of boring out the cylinders of a worn reciprocating engine and fitting oversize pistons

rebus a puzzle consisting of pictures representing syllables and words; in such a puzzle the word *hear* might be represented by H followed by a picture of an ear

recall US the process by which elected officials may be deprived of office by popular vote

recapitulation 1 *Biology* the apparent repetition in the embryonic development of an animal of the changes that occurred during its evolutionary history 2 *Music* the repeating of earlier themes, esp when forming the final section of a movement in sonata form

recapture 1 the act of recapturing or fact of being recaptured 2 US the seizure by the government of a proportion of the profits of a public-service undertaking

receipt a written acknowledgment by a receiver of money, goods, etc, that payment or delivery has been made

receiver 1 a person appointed by a court to manage property pending the outcome of litigation, during the infancy of the owner, or after the owner(s) has been declared bankrupt or of unsound mind 2 *Chiefly Brit* a person who receives stolen goods knowing that they have been stolen 3 the equipment in a telephone, radio, or television that receives incoming electrical signals or modulated radio waves and converts them into the original audio or video signals 4 the equipment in a radar system, radio telescope, etc, that converts incoming radio signals into a useful form, usually displayed on the screen of a cathode-ray oscilloscope 5 *Chem* a vessel in which the distillate is collected during distillation

receivership *Law* 1 the office or function of a receiver 2 the condition of being administered by a receiver

receptacle *Botany* a the enlarged or modified tip of the flower stalk that bears the parts of the flower **b** the shortened flattened stem bearing the florets of the capitulum of composite flowers such as the daisy **c** the part of lower plants that bears the reproductive organs or spores

reception *Brit* **a** the first class in an infant school **b** a class in a school designed to receive new immigrants, esp those whose knowledge of English is poor **c** (*as modifier*): *a reception teacher*

receptor *Physiol* a sensory nerve ending that changes specific stimuli into nerve impulses

recess 1 *Anatomy* a small cavity or depression in a bodily organ, part, or structure **2** *US and Canadian* a break between classes at a school

recession 1 *Economics* a temporary depression in economic activity or prosperity **2** *Religion* the withdrawal of the clergy and choir in procession from the chancel at the conclusion of a church service

recessional a hymn sung as the clergy and choir withdraw from the chancel at the conclusion of a church service

recessive 1 *Genetics* **a** (of a gene) capable of producing its characteristic phenotype in the organism only when its allele is identical **b** (of a character) controlled by such a gene **2** *Genetics* **a** a recessive gene or character **b** an organism having such a gene or character

recidivism habitual relapse into crime

Recife a port at the easternmost point of Brazil on the Atlantic: capital of Pernambuco state; built partly on an island, with many waterways and bridges. Pop: 3 527 000 (2005 est)

recipe (formerly) a medical prescription

reciprocal 1 *Maths* of or relating to a number or quantity divided into one **2** *Navigation* denoting a course or bearing that is 180° from the previous or assumed one **3** *Maths* a number or quantity that when multiplied by a given number or quantity gives a product of one

recital 1 a musical performance by a soloist or soloists **2** *Law* the preliminary statement in a deed showing the reason for its existence and leading up to and explaining the operative part

recitative a passage in a musical composition, esp the narrative parts in an oratorio, set for one voice with either continuo accompaniment only or full accompaniment, reflecting the natural rhythms of speech

Recklinghausen an industrial city in NW Germany, in North Rhine-Westphalia on the N edge of the Ruhr. Pop: 123 144 (2003 est)

reckoning 1 settlement of an account or bill **2** a bill or account **3** *Navigation* short for **dead reckoning**

recluse a person who lives in solitude to devote himself to prayer and religious meditation; a hermit, anchorite, or anchoress

recognition formal acknowledgment of a government or of the independence of a country

recognizance *or* **recognisance** *Law* a bond entered into before a court or magistrate by which a person binds himself to do a specified act, as to appear in court on a stated day, keep the peace, or pay a debt **b** a monetary sum pledged to the performance of such an act

recoil the motion acquired by a particle as a result of its emission of a photon or other particle

recombinant *Genetics* **1** produced by the combining of genetic material from more than one origin **2** a chromosome, cell, organism, etc, the genetic makeup of which results from recombination

reconnaissance *or* **reconnoissance** a preliminary inspection of an area of land before an engineering survey is made

record 1 a written account of some transaction that serves as legal evidence of the transaction **2** a written official report of the proceedings of a court of justice or legislative body, including the judgments given or enactments made **3** a list of crimes of which an accused person has previously been convicted, which are known to the police but may only be disclosed to a court in certain circumstances **4 have a record** to be a known criminal; have a previous conviction or convictions **5** a thin disc of a plastic material upon which sound has been recorded. Each side has a spiral groove, which undulates in accordance with the frequency and amplitude of the sound. Records were formerly made from a shellac-based compound but were later made from vinyl plastics **6** *Computing* a group of data or piece of information preserved as a unit in machine-readable form **7** (in some computer languages) a data structure designed to allow the handling of groups of related pieces of information as though the group was a single entity

recorder 1 something that records, esp an apparatus that provides a permanent record of experiments, etc. **2** short for **tape recorder 3** *Music* a wind instrument of the flute family, blown through a fipple in the mouth end, having a reedlike quality of tone. There are four usual sizes: bass, tenor, treble, and descant **4** (in England) a barrister or solicitor of at least ten years' standing appointed to sit as a part-time judge in the crown court

recording 1 a the act or process of making a record, esp of sound on a gramophone record or magnetic tape **b** (*as modifier*): *recording studio* **2** the record or tape so produced

record player a device for reproducing the sounds stored on a record, consisting of a turntable, usually electrically driven, that rotates the record at a fixed speed of 33, 45, or (esp formerly) 78 revolutions a minute. A stylus vibrates in accordance with undulations in the groove in the record: these vibrations are converted into electric currents, which, after amplification, are recreated in the form of sound by one or more loudspeakers

recourse 1 the right to demand payment, esp from the drawer or endorser of a bill of exchange or other negotiable instrument when the person accepting it fails to pay **2 without recourse** a qualified endorsement on such a negotiable instrument, by which the endorser protects himself from liability to subsequent holders

recovery 1 *Law* **a** the obtaining of a right, etc, by the judgment of a court **b** (in the US) the final judgment or verdict in a case **2** *Fencing* a return to the position of guard after making an attack **3** *Swimming, Rowing* the action of bringing the arm, oar, etc, forward for another stroke **4** *Golf* a stroke played from the rough or a bunker to the fairway or green

recreation *Education* **a** an interval of free time between school lessons **b** (*as modifier*): *recreation period*

recrimination *Law* a charge made by an accused against his accuser; countercharge

rectal of or relating to the rectum

rectangle a parallelogram having four right angles

rectilinear *or* **rectilineal** **1** in, moving in, or characterized by a straight line or lines **2** consisting of, bounded by, or formed by a straight line or lines

rector **1** *Church of England* a clergyman in charge of a parish in which, as its incumbent, he would formerly have been entitled to the whole of the tithes **2** *RC Church* a cleric in charge of a college, religious house, or congregation **3** *Protestant Episcopal Church, Scottish Episcopal Church* a clergyman in charge of a parish **4** *Chiefly Brit* the head of certain schools or colleges

rectory **1** the official house of a rector **2** *Church of England* the office and benefice of a rector

rectum the lower part of the alimentary canal, between the sigmoid flexure of the colon and the anus

recumbent **1** (of a part or organ) leaning or resting against another organ or the ground **2** (of a fold in a rock formation) in which the axial plane is nearly horizontal

recurring decimal a rational number that contains a pattern of digits repeated indefinitely after the decimal point

recusant **1** (in 16th to 18th century England) a Roman Catholic who did not attend the services of the Church of England, as was required by law **2** (formerly, of Catholics) refusing to attend services of the Church of England

red **1** any of a group of colours, such as that of a ripe tomato or fresh blood, that lie at one end of the visible spectrum, next to orange, and are perceived by the eye when light in the approximate wavelength range 740–620 nanometres falls on the retina. Red is the complementary colour of cyan and forms a set of primary colours with blue and green **2** red cloth or clothing **3** a red ball in snooker, billiards, etc. **4** (in roulette and other gambling games) one of two colours on which players may place even bets, the other being black **5** *Archery* a red ring on a target, between the blue and the gold, scoring seven points **6** of the colour red **7** reddish in colour or having parts or marks that are reddish **8** (of wine) made from black grapes and coloured by their skins

Red *Informal* **1** Communist, Socialist, or Soviet **2** radical, leftist, or revolutionary **3** a member or supporter of a Communist or Socialist Party or a national of a state having such a government, esp the former Soviet Union **4** a radical, leftist, or revolutionary

red admiral a nymphalid butterfly, *Vanessa atalanta*, of temperate Europe and Asia, having black wings with red and white markings

redbreast any of various birds having a red breast, esp the Old World robin (see **robin** (sense 1))

redbrick denoting, relating to, or characteristic of a provincial British university of relatively recent foundation, esp as distinguished from Oxford and Cambridge

Redbridge a borough of NE Greater London: includes part of Epping Forest. Pop: 245 100 (2003 est). Area: 56 sq km (22 sq miles)

Redcar and Cleveland a unitary authority in NE England, in North Yorkshire: formerly (1975–96) part of Cleveland county. Pop: 139 100 (2003 est). Area: 240 sq km (93 sq miles)

redcoat (formerly) a British soldier

Red Crescent a national branch of or the emblem of the Red Cross Society in a Muslim country

Red Cross **1** an international humanitarian organization (**Red Cross Society**) formally established by the Geneva Convention of 1864. It was originally limited to providing medical care for war casualties, but its services now include liaison between prisoners of war and their families, relief to victims of natural disasters, etc. **2** any national branch of this organization **3** the emblem of this organization, consisting of a red cross on a white background

redcurrant **1** a N temperate shrub, *Ribes rubrum*, having greenish flowers and small edible rounded red berries: family *Grossulariaceae* **2 a** the fruit of this shrub **b** (*as modifier*): *redcurrant jelly*

red deer a large deer, *Cervus elaphus*, formerly widely distributed in the woodlands of Europe and Asia. The coat is reddish brown in summer and the short tail is surrounded by a patch of light-coloured hair

Red Deer **1** a town in S Alberta on the Red Deer River: trade centre for mixed farming, dairying region, and natural gas processing. Pop: 67 707 (2001) **2** a river in W Canada, in SW Alberta, flowing southeast into the South Saskatchewan River. Length: about 620 km (385 miles) **3** a river in W Canada, flowing east through **Red Deer Lake** into Lake Winnipegosis. Length: about 225 km (140 miles)

Redding Otis 1941–67, US soul singer and songwriter. His recordings include "Respect" (1965), *Dictionary of Soul* (1966), and "(Sittin' on) The Dock of the Bay" (1968)

Redditch a town in W central England, in N Worcestershire: designated a new town in the mid-1960s; metal-working industries. Pop: 74 803 (2001)

Redeemer The. Jesus Christ as having brought redemption to mankind

redemption *Christianity* **a** deliverance from sin through the incarnation, sufferings, and death of Christ **b** atonement for guilt

redfish **1** a male salmon that has recently spawned **2** any of several red European scorpaenid fishes of the genus *Sebastes*, esp *S. marinus*, valued as a food fish

red flag a symbol of socialism, communism, or revolution

Redford Robert born 1937, US film actor and director. His films include (as actor) *Barefoot in the Park* (1966), *Butch Cassidy and the Sundance Kid* (1969), *The Sting* (1973), *All the President's Men* (1976), *Up Close and Personal* (1996) and (as director) *Ordinary People* (1980), *A River Runs Through It* (1992), and *The Horse Whisperer* (1998)

Redgrave **1** Lynn born 1944, British stage and film actress. Her films include *Georgy Girl* (1966), *The Happy Hooker* (1975), and *Gods and Monsters* (1999) **2** her father, Sir **Michael** 1908–85, British stage and film actor. Among his films are *The Lady Vanishes* (1938), *The Dam Busters* (1955), *The Loneliness of the Long Distance Runner*

(1963), and *The Go-Between* (1971) **3** his elder daughter, **Vanessa** born 1937, British stage and film actress, whose roles include performances in the films *Isadora* (1968), *Julia* (1977), *Howards End* (1992), *Mrs Dalloway* (1998), and *A Rumour of Angels* (2000): noted also for her active commitment to left-wing politics **4** Sir **Steve** born 1962, British oarsman; won five gold medals in rowing events at consecutive Olympic Games (1984, 1988, 1992, 1996, 2000)

red hat 1 the broad-brimmed crimson hat given to cardinals as the symbol of their rank and office **2** the rank and office of a cardinal

redhead a diving duck, *Aythya americana*, of North America, the male of which has a grey-and-black body and a reddish-brown head

red lead a bright-red poisonous insoluble oxide of lead usually obtained as a powder by heating litharge in air. It is used as a pigment in paints. Formula: Pb_3O_4

red light a signal to stop, esp a red traffic signal in a system of traffic lights

Redmond John Edward 1856–1918, Irish politician. He led the Parnellites from 1891 and helped to procure the Home Rule bill of 1912, but was considered too moderate by extreme nationalists

Redon Odilon 1840–1916, French symbolist painter and etcher. He foreshadowed the surrealists in his paintings of fantastic dream images

red pepper 1 any of several varieties of the pepper plant *Capsicum frutescens*, cultivated for their hot pungent red podlike fruits **2** the fruit of any of these plants **3** the ripe red fruit of the sweet pepper

Red River 1 a river in the S central US, flowing east from N Texas through Arkansas into the Mississippi in Louisiana. Length: 1639 km (1018 miles) **2** a river in the northern US, flowing north as the border between North Dakota and Minnesota and into Lake Winnipeg, Canada. Length: 515 km (320 miles) **3** a river in SE Asia, rising in SW China in Yünnan province and flowing southeast across N Vietnam to the Gulf of Tongkin: the chief river of N Vietnam, with an extensive delta. Length: 500 km (310 miles)

red salmon 1 any salmon having reddish flesh, esp the sockeye salmon **2** the flesh of such a fish, esp canned

Red Sea a long narrow sea between Arabia and NE Africa, linked with the Mediterranean in the north by the Suez Canal and with the Indian Ocean in the south: occasionally reddish in appearance through algae. Area: 438 000 sq km (169 000 sq miles)

redshank either of two large common European sandpipers, *Tringa totanus* or *T. erythropus* (**spotted redshank**), having red legs

red squirrel 1 a reddish-brown squirrel, *Sciurus vulgaris*, inhabiting woodlands of Europe and parts of Asia **2** **American red squirrel** either of two reddish-brown squirrels, *Tamiasciurus hudsonicus* or *T. douglasii*, inhabiting forests of North America

redstart 1 any European songbird of the genus *Phoenicurus*, esp *P. phoenicurus*, in which the male has a black throat, orange-brown tail and breast, and grey back: family *Muscicapidae* (thrushes, etc) **2** any North American warbler of the genus *Setophaga*, esp *S. ruticilla*

reduction *Maths* **a** the process of converting a fraction

into its decimal form **b** the process of dividing out the common factors in the numerator and denominator of a fraction; cancellation

redundant (of components, information, etc) duplicated or added as a precaution against failure, error, etc.

reduplicate (of petals or sepals) having the margins curving outwards

redwood a giant coniferous tree, *Sequoia sempervirens*, of coastal regions of California, having reddish fibrous bark and durable timber: family *Taxodiaceae*. The largest specimen is over 120 metres (360 feet) tall

reed 1 any of various widely distributed tall grasses of the genus *Phragmites*, esp *P. communis*, that grow in swamps and shallow water and have jointed hollow stalks **2** the stalk, or stalks collectively, of any of these plants, esp as used for thatching **3** *Music* **a** a thin piece of cane or metal inserted into the tubes of certain wind instruments, which sets in vibration the air column inside the tube **b** a wind instrument or organ pipe that sounds by means of a reed **4** one of the several vertical parallel wires on a loom that may be moved upwards to separate the warp threads **5** a small semicircular architectural moulding **6** an ancient Hebrew unit of length equal to six cubits **7** an archaic word for **arrow**

reed 2 the stalk, or stalks collectively, of any of these plants, esp as used for thatching

Reed 1 Sir **Carol** 1906–76, English film director. His films include *The Third Man* (1949), *An Outcast of the Islands* (1951), and *Oliver!* (1968), for which he won an Oscar **2 Lou** born 1942, US rock singer, songwriter, and guitarist: member of the Velvet Underground (1965–70). His albums include *Transformer* (1972), *Berlin* (1973), *Street Hassle* (1978), *New York* (1989), *Set the Twilight Reeling* (1996), and *The Raven* (2003) **3 Walter** 1851–1902, US physician, who proved that yellow fever is transmitted by mosquitoes (1900)

reef¹ 1 a ridge of rock, sand, coral, etc, the top of which lies close to the surface of the sea **2** a ridge- or moundlike structure built by sedentary calcareous organisms (esp corals) and consisting mainly of their remains

reef² *Nautical* the part gathered in when sail area is reduced, as in a high wind

reefer 1 *Nautical* a person who reefs, such as a midshipman **2** *Slang* a hand-rolled cigarette, esp one containing cannabis

reel¹ 1 *Angling* a device for winding, casting, etc, consisting of a revolving spool with a handle, attached to a fishing rod **2** a roll of celluloid exhibiting a sequence of photographs to be projected

reel² 1 any of various lively Scottish dances, such as the **eightsome reel** and **foursome reel** for a fixed number of couples who combine in square and circular formations **2** a piece of music having eight quavers to the bar composed for or in the rhythm of this dance

reeve¹ 1 *English history* the local representative of the king in a shire (under the ealdorman) until the early 11th century **2** (in medieval England) a manorial steward who supervised the daily affairs of the manor: often a villein elected by his fellows **3** *Canadian government* (in certain provinces) a president of a local council, esp in a rural area **4** (formerly) a minor local official in any of several parts of England and the US

reeve² the female of the ruff (the bird)

reference *Philosophy* **a** the relation between a word, phrase, or symbol and the object or idea to which it refers **b** the object referred to by an expression

referendum **1** submission of an issue of public importance to the direct vote of the electorate **2** a vote on such a measure **3** a poll of the members of a club, union, or other group to determine their views on some matter **4** a diplomatic official's note to his government requesting instructions

refinery a factory for the purification of some crude material, such as ore, sugar, oil, etc.

reflation **1** an increase in economic activity **2** an increase in the supply of money and credit designed to cause such an increase

reflecting telescope a type of telescope in which the initial image is formed by a concave mirror

reflection *or less commonly* **reflexion** **1** *Maths* a transformation in which the direction of one axis is reversed or which changes the sign of one of the variables **2** *Anatomy* the bending back of a structure or part upon itself

reflector **1** a small translucent red disc, strip, etc, with a reflecting backing on the rear of a road vehicle, which reflects the light of the headlights of a following vehicle **2** another name for **reflecting telescope** **3** part of an aerial placed so as to increase the forward radiation of the radiator and decrease the backward radiation

reflex **1** **a** an immediate involuntary response, esp one that is innate, such as coughing or removal of the hand from a hot surface, evoked by a given stimulus **b** (*as modifier*): *a reflex action* **2** **a** a mechanical response to a particular situation, involving no conscious decision **b** (*as modifier*): *a reflex response* **3** a reflection; an image produced by or as if by reflection **4** *Maths* (of an angle) between 180° and 360°

reflex camera a camera in which the image is composed and focused on a large ground-glass viewfinder screen. In a **single-lens reflex** the light enters through the camera lens and falls on the film when the viewfinder mirror is retracted. In a **twin-lens reflex** the light enters through a separate lens and is deflected onto the viewfinder screen

reflexive **1** *Physiol* of or relating to a reflex **2** *Logic, Maths* (of a relation) holding between any member of its domain and itself

reflexology **1** a form of therapy practised as a treatment in alternative medicine in which the soles of the feet are massaged: designed to stimulate the blood supply and nerves and thus relieve tension **2** *Psychol* the belief that behaviour can be understood in terms of combinations of reflexes

reformatory (formerly) a place of instruction where young offenders were sent for corrective training

Reformed **1** of or designating a Protestant Church, esp the Calvinist as distinct from the Lutheran **2** of or designating Reform Judaism

refracting telescope a type of telescope in which the image is formed by a set of lenses

refraction **1** *Physics* the change in direction of a propagating wave, such as light or sound, in passing from one medium to another in which it has a different velocity **2** the amount by which a wave is refracted **3** the ability of the eye to refract light **4** the determination of the refractive condition of the eye **5** *Astronomy* the apparent elevation in position of a celestial body resulting from the refraction of light by the earth's atmosphere

refractory **1** *Med* not responding to treatment **2** (of a material) able to withstand high temperatures without fusion or decomposition **3** a material, such as fireclay or alumina, that is able to withstand high temperatures: used to line furnaces, kilns, etc.

refrain a regularly recurring melody, such as the chorus of a song

refrangible capable of being refracted

refresher course a short educational course for people to review their subject and developments in it

refrigerant **1** a fluid capable of changes of phase at low temperatures: used as the working fluid of a refrigerator **2** a cooling substance, such as ice or solid carbon dioxide **3** *Med* an agent that provides a sensation of coolness or reduces fever

refuge another name for a traffic island

refund return of money to a purchaser or the amount so returned

refusenik *or* **refusnik** **1** (formerly) a Jew in the Soviet Union who had been refused permission to emigrate **2** a person who refuses to cooperate with a system or comply with a law because of a moral conviction

regal¹ of, relating to, or befitting a king or queen; royal

regal² a portable organ equipped only with small reed pipes, popular from the 15th century and recently revived for modern performance

regatta an organized series of races of yachts, rowing boats, etc.

regency **1** government by a regent or a body of regents **2** the office of a regent or body of regents **3** a territory under the jurisdiction of a regent or body of regents

Regency **1** (in the United Kingdom) the period (1811–20) during which the Prince of Wales (later George IV (1762–1830; king 1820–30)) acted as regent during his father's periods of insanity **2** (in France) the period of the regency of Philip, Duke of Orleans, during the minority (1715–23) of Louis XV (1710–74; king 1715–74) **3** characteristic of or relating to the Regency periods in France or the United Kingdom or to the styles of architecture, furniture, art, literature, etc, produced in them

Regensburg a city in SE Germany, in Bavaria on the River Danube: a free Imperial city from 1245 and the leading commercial city of S Germany in the 12th and 13th centuries; the Imperial Diet was held in the town hall from 1663 to 1806. Pop: 128 604 (2003 est)

regent **1** the ruler or administrator of a country during the minority, absence, or incapacity of its monarch **2** (formerly) a senior teacher or administrator in any of certain universities **3** *US and Canadian* a member of the governing board of certain schools and colleges **4** *Rare* any person who governs or rules **5** acting or functioning as a regent **6** *Rare* governing, ruling, or controlling

Reger Max 1873–1916, German composer, noted esp for his organ works

Reggio di Calabria a port in S Italy, in Calabria on the Strait of Messina: founded about 720 BC by Greek colonists. Pop: 180 353 (2001)

regime or **régime** 1 a system of government or a particular administration 2 *Med* another word for **regimen**

regimen 1 a systematic way of life or course of therapy, often including exercise and a recommended diet 2 administration or rule

Regina¹ queen: now used chiefly in documents, inscriptions, etc

Regina² a city in W Canada, capital and largest city of Saskatchewan: founded in 1882 as Pile O'Bones. Pop: 178 225 (2001)

Regiomontanus original name *Johann Müller*. 1436–76, German mathematician and astronomer, who furthered the development of trigonometry

region 1 an area considered as a unit for geographical, functional, social, or cultural reasons 2 an administrative division of a country 3 (in Scotland from 1975 until 1996) any of the nine territorial divisions into which the mainland of Scotland was divided for purposes of local government; replaced in 1996 by council areas

regionalism 1 division of a country into administrative regions having partial autonomy 2 advocacy of such division 3 loyalty to one's home region; regional patriotism 4 the common interests of national groups, people, etc, living in the same part of the world

register 1 a recording device that accumulates data, totals sums of money, etc. 2 a movable plate that controls the flow of air into a furnace, chimney, room, etc. 3 *Computing* one of a set of word-sized locations in the central processing unit in which items of data are placed temporarily before they are operated on by program instructions 4 *Music* a the timbre characteristic of a certain manner of voice production b any of the stops on an organ as classified in respect of its tonal quality

register office *Brit* a government office where civil marriages are performed and births, marriages, and deaths are recorded

registrar 1 an administrative official responsible for student records, enrolment procedure, etc, in a school, college, or university 2 *Brit and NZ* a hospital doctor senior to a houseman but junior to a consultant, specializing in either medicine (**medical registrar**) or surgery (**surgical registrar**)

registration document *Brit* a document giving identification details of a motor vehicle, including its manufacturer, date of registration, engine and chassis numbers, and owner's name

registration number a sequence of letters and numbers assigned to a motor vehicle when it is registered, usually indicating the year and place of registration, displayed on numberplates at the front and rear of the vehicle, and by which the vehicle may be identified

registry 1 a place where registers are kept, such as the part of a church where the bride and groom sign a register after a wedding 2 the registration of a ship's country of origin

Regius professor *Brit* a person appointed by the Crown to a university chair founded by a royal patron

regress *Logic* a supposed explanation each stage of which requires to be similarly explained, as saying that knowledge requires a justification in terms of propositions themselves known to be true

regression 1 *Psychol* the adoption by an adult or adolescent of behaviour more appropriate to a child, esp as a defence mechanism to avoid anxiety 2 *Astronomy* the slow movement around the ecliptic of the two points at which the moon's orbit intersects the ecliptic. One complete revolution occurs about every 19 years 3 *Geology* the retreat of the sea from the land

regular 1 (of flowers) having any of their parts, esp petals, alike in size, shape, arrangement, etc.; symmetrical 2 *Maths* a (of a polygon) equilateral and equiangular b (of a polyhedron) having identical regular polygons as faces that make identical angles with each other c (of a prism) having regular polygons as bases d (of a pyramid) having a regular polygon as a base and the altitude passing through the centre of the base 3 subject to the rule of an established religious order or community 4 *US, Politics* of, selected by, or loyal to the leadership or platform of a political party 5 *Crystallog* another word for **cubic** 6 a member of a religious order or congregation, as contrasted with a secular 7 *US, Politics* a party member loyal to the leadership, organization, platform, etc, of his party

regulation 1 a governmental or ministerial order having the force of law 2 *Embryol* the ability of an animal embryo to develop normally after its structure has been altered or damaged in some way 3 *Electrical engineering* the change in voltage occurring when a load is connected across a power supply, caused by internal resistance (for direct current) or internal impedance (alternating current)

regulator 1 any of various mechanisms or devices, such as a governor valve, for controlling fluid flow, pressure, temperature, voltage, etc. 2 a gene the product of which controls the synthesis of a product from another gene

Regulus Marcus Atilius died ?250 BC, Roman general; consul (267; 256). Captured by the Carthaginians in the First Punic War, he was sent to Rome on parole to deliver the enemy's peace terms, advised the Senate to refuse them, and was tortured to death on his return to Carthage

Reich¹ 1 Steve born 1936, US composer, whose works are characterized by the repetition and modification of small rhythmic motifs. His works include *Drumming* (1971), *The Desert Music* (1984), and *City Life* (1995) 2 Wilhelm 1897–1957, Austrian psychologist, lived in the US. An ardent socialist and advocate of sexual freedom, he proclaimed a cosmic unity of all energy and built a machine (the orgone accumulator) to concentrate this energy on human beings. His books include *The Function of the Orgasm* (1927)

Reich² 1 the Holy Roman Empire (**First Reich**) 2 the Hohenzollern empire from 1871 to 1919 (**Second Reich**) 3 the Weimar Republic from 1919 to 1933 4 the Nazi dictatorship from 1933 to 1945 (**Third Reich**)

Reid 1 Sir George Houston 1845–1918, Australian statesman, born in Scotland: premier of New South Wales (1894–99); prime minister of Australia (1904–05) 2 Thomas 1710–96, Scottish philosopher and founder of what came to be known as the philosophy of common sense

Reigate a town in S England, in Surrey at the foot of the

North Downs. Pop. (including Redhill): Pop: 50 436 (2001)

reign the period during which a monarch is the official ruler of a country

Reims *or* **Rheims** a city in NE France: scene of the coronation of most French monarchs. Pop: 187 206 (1999)

rein 1 one of a pair of long straps, usually connected together and made of leather, used to control a horse, running from the side of the bit or the headstall to the hand of the rider, driver, or trainer 2 the direction in which a rider turns (in phrases such as **on a left** (*or* **right**) **rein, change the rein**) 3 **on a long rein** with the reins held loosely so that the horse is relatively unconstrained 4 **shorten the reins** to take up the reins so that the distance between hand and bit is lessened, in order that the horse may be more collected

reincarnate born again in a new body

reincarnation 1 the belief that on the death of the body the soul transmigrates to or is born again in another body 2 the incarnation or embodiment of a soul in a new body after it has left the old one at physical death

reindeer a large deer, *Rangifer tarandus*, having large branched antlers in the male and female and inhabiting the arctic regions of Greenland, Europe, and Asia. It also occurs in North America, where it is known as a caribou

Reindeer Lake a lake in W Canada, in Saskatchewan and Manitoba: drains into the Churchill River via the Reindeer River. Area: 6390 sq km (2467 sq miles)

Reinhardt 1 Django, real name *Jean Baptiste Reinhardt*. 1910–53, French jazz guitarist, whose work was greatly influenced by Gypsy music. With Stéphane Grappelli, he led the Quintet of the Hot Club of France between 1934 and 1939 2 Max, original name *Max Goldmann*. 1873–1943, Austrian theatre producer and director, in the US after 1933

Reith John (Charles Walsham), 1st Baron. 1889–1971, British public servant: first general manager (1922–27) and first director general (1927–38) of the BBC

rejoinder *Law* (in pleading) the answer made by a defendant to the claimant's reply

relapse the return of ill health after an apparent or partial recovery

related (in diatonic music) denoting or relating to a key that has notes in common with another key or keys

relation 1 *Law* the principle by which an act done at one time is regarded in law as having been done antecedently 2 *Law* the statement of grounds of complaint made by a relator 3 *Logic, Maths* **a** an association between ordered pairs of objects, numbers, etc, such as *... is greater than ...* **b** the set of ordered pairs whose members have such an association 4 *Philosophy* **a internal relation** a relation that necessarily holds between its relata, as *4 is greater than 2* **b external relation** a relation that does not so hold

relative (of a musical key or scale) having the same key signature as another key or scale

relative atomic mass the ratio of the average mass per atom of the naturally occurring form of an element to one-twelfth the mass of an atom of carbon-12.

relativity 1 either of two theories developed by Albert Einstein, the **special theory of relativity**, which

requires that the laws of physics shall be the same as seen by any two different observers in uniform relative motion, and the **general theory of relativity** which considers observers with relative acceleration and leads to a theory of gravitation 2 *Philosophy* dependence upon some variable factor such as the psychological, social, or environmental context

relaxation 1 *Physics* the return of a system to equilibrium after a displacement from this state 2 *Maths* a method by which errors resulting from an approximation are reduced by using new approximations

relay 1 an automatic device that controls the setting of a valve, switch, etc, by means of an electric motor, solenoid, or pneumatic mechanism 2 *Electronics* an electrical device in which a small change in current or voltage controls the switching on or off of circuits or other devices

release 1 *Law* the surrender of a claim, right, title, etc, in favour of someone else 2 a control mechanism for starting or stopping an engine 3 **a** the opening of the exhaust valve of a steam engine near the end of the piston stroke **b** the moment at which this valve opens 4 the electronic control regulating how long a note sounds after a synthesizer key has been released 5 the control mechanism for the shutter in a camera

relic 1 *RC Church, Eastern Church* part of the body of a saint or something supposedly used by or associated with a saint, venerated as holy 2 *Ecology* a less common term for **relict** (sense 1)

relict 1 *Ecology* **a** a group of animals or plants that exists as a remnant of a formerly widely distributed group in an environment different from that in which it originated **b** (*as modifier*): *a relict fauna* 2 *Geology* **a** a mountain, lake, glacier, etc, that is a remnant of a pre-existing formation after a destructive process has occurred **b** a mineral that remains unaltered after metamorphism of the rock in which it occurs

relief 1 **a** help or assistance, as to the poor, needy, or distressed **b** (*as modifier*): *relief work* 2 a road (**relief road**) carrying traffic round an urban area; bypass 3 *Sculpture, Architect* **a** the projection of forms or figures from a flat ground, so that they are partly or wholly free of it **b** a piece of work of this kind 4 variation in altitude in an area; difference between highest and lowest level 5 *Mechanical engineering* the removal of the surface material of a bearing area to allow the access of lubricating fluid 6 *Law* redress of a grievance or hardship 7 *European history* a succession of payments made by an heir to a fief to his lord: the size of the relief was determined by the lord within bounds set by custom 8 **on relief** US and Canadian (of people) in receipt of government aid because of personal need

relief map a map that shows the configuration and height of the land surface, usually by means of contours

religion *Chiefly RC Church* the way of life determined by the vows of poverty, chastity, and obedience entered upon by monks, friars, and nuns

religious 1 *Christianity* of or relating to a way of life dedicated to religion by the vows of poverty, chastity, and obedience, and defined by a monastic rule 2 *Christianity* a member of an order or congregation living by such a rule; a monk, friar, or nun

reliquary a receptacle or repository for relics, esp relics of saints

relish *Music* (in English lute, viol, and keyboard music of the 16th and 17th centuries) a trilling ornament, used esp at cadences

reluctance *or less commonly* **reluctancy** *Physics* a measure of the resistance of a closed magnetic circuit to a magnetic flux, equal to the ratio of the magnetomotive force to the magnetic flux

REM rapid eye movement

remainder 1 *Maths* **a** the amount left over when one quantity cannot be exactly divided by another **b** another name for **difference** 2 *Property law* a future interest in property; an interest in a particular estate that will pass to one at some future date, as on the death of the current possessor

remand 1 the sending of a prisoner or accused person back into custody (or sometimes admitting him to bail) to await trial or continuation of his trial 2 **on remand** in custody or on bail awaiting trial or completion of one's trial

remand centre (in Britain) an institution to which accused persons are sent for detention while awaiting appearance before a court. Until 1967 remand centres were for detaining young people between 14 and 21 years of age

Remarque Erich Maria 1898–1970, US novelist, born in Germany, noted for his novel of World War I, *All Quiet on the Western Front* (1929)

Rembrandt full name *Rembrandt Harmensz* (or *Harmenszoon*) *van Rijn* (or *van Ryn*). 1606–69, Dutch painter, noted for his handling of shade and light, esp in his portraits

remedial 1 affording a remedy; curative 2 denoting or relating to special teaching, teaching methods, or material for backward and slow learners

remedy any drug or agent that cures a disease or controls its symptoms

reminiscence 1 (in the philosophy of Plato) the doctrine that perception and recognition of particulars is possible because the mind has seen the universal forms of all things in a previous disembodied existence 2 *Psychol* the ability to perform a task better when tested some time after the task has been learnt than when tested immediately after learning it

remission *or less commonly* **remittal** 1 the act of remitting or state of being remitted 2 a reduction of the term of a sentence of imprisonment, as for good conduct 3 forgiveness for sin

remit *Law* the transfer of a case from one court or jurisdiction to another, esp from an appeal court to an inferior tribunal

remittance payment for goods or services received or as an allowance, esp when sent by post

remittent (of a fever or the symptoms of a disease) characterized by periods of diminished severity

remix *Music* a remixed version of a recording

remote control control of a system or activity by a person at a different place, usually by means of radio or ultrasonic signals or by electrical signals transmitted by wire

removal *South African* the forced displacement of a community for political or social reasons

remove *Brit* (in certain schools) a class or form, esp one for children of about 14 years, designed to introduce them to the greater responsibilities of a more senior position in the school

removed *Genealogy* separated by a degree of descent or kinship

Remscheid an industrial city in W Germany, in North Rhine-Westphalia. Pop: 117 717 (2003 est)

Renaissance 1 **the** the period of European history marking the waning of the Middle Ages and the rise of the modern world: usually considered as beginning in Italy in the 14th century 2 **a** the spirit, culture, art, science, and thought of this period. Characteristics of the Renaissance are usually considered to include intensified classical scholarship, scientific and geographical discovery, a sense of individual human potentialities, and the assertion of the active and secular over the religious and contemplative life **b** (*as modifier*): *Renaissance writers* 3 of, characteristic of, or relating to the Renaissance, its culture, etc.

▷www.learner.org/exhibits/renaissance
▷www.ibiblio.org/wm/paint/glo/renaissance

renal of, relating to, resembling, or situated near the kidney

Renan (Joseph) Ernest 1823–92, French philosopher, theologian, and historian; best known for his *Life of Jesus* (1863), which discounted the supernatural aspects of the Gospels

Rendell Ruth (Barbara), Baroness. born 1930, British crime writer: author of detective novels, such as *Wolf to the Slaughter* (1967), and psychological thrillers, such as *The Lake of Darkness* (1980) and (under the name **Barbara Vine**) *A Fatal Inversion* (1987) and *The Chimney Sweeper's Boy* (1998)

render *History* a payment in money, goods, or services made by a feudal tenant to his lord

rendition *Lit* a translation of a text

Renfrew an industrial town in W central Scotland, in Renfrewshire, W of Glasgow. Pop: 20 251 (2001)

Renfrewshire 1 a council area of W central Scotland, on the River Clyde W of Glasgow: corresponds to part of the historical county of Renfrewshire; part of Strathclyde region from 1975 to 1996: agricultural and residential, with clothing and manufacturing industries in Paisley. Administrative centre: Paisley. Pop: 170 980 (2003 est). Area: 261 sq km (101 sq miles) 2 a former county of W central Scotland, on the Firth of Clyde: became part of Strathclyde region in 1975; now covered by the council areas of Renfrewshire, East Renfrewshire, and Inverclyde

Reni Guido 1575–1642, Italian baroque painter and engraver

Rennes a city in NW France: the ancient capital of Brittany. Pop: 206 229 (1999)

rennet 1 **a** the membrane lining the fourth stomach (abomasum) of a young calf **b** the stomach of certain other young animals 2 a substance, containing the enzyme rennin, prepared esp from the stomachs of calves and used for curdling milk in making cheese and junket

Reno a city in W Nevada, at the foot of the Sierra Nevada: noted as a divorce, wedding, and gambling centre by reason of its liberal laws. Pop: 193 882 (2003 est)

Renoir 1 Jean 1894–1979, French film director: his films include *La grande illusion* (1937), *La règle du jeu* (1939), and *Diary of a Chambermaid* (1945) 2 his father, **Pierre Auguste** 1841–1919, French painter. One of the initiators of impressionism, he broke away from the movement with his later paintings, esp his many nude studies, which are more formal compositions

renounce *Rare* a failure to follow suit in a card game

rent *Economics* a that portion of the national income accruing to owners of land and real property b the return derived from the cultivation of land in excess of production costs

reo NZ a language

rep¹ *or* **repp** a silk, wool, rayon, or cotton fabric with a transversely corded surface

rep² *Theatre* short for **repertory** (**company**)

repeal an instance or the process of repealing; annulment

repeat 1 *Commerce* an order made out for goods, provisions, etc, that duplicates a previous order 2 *Music* a passage that is an exact restatement of the passage preceding it

repeater 1 *Electrical engineering* a device that amplifies or augments incoming electrical signals and retransmits them, thus compensating for transmission losses 2 *Nautical* one of three signal flags hoisted with others to indicate that one of the top three is to be repeated

repellent a substance with which fabrics are treated to increase their resistance to water

repent *Botany* lying or creeping along the ground; reptant

repercussion *Music* the reappearance of a fugal subject and answer after an episode

repertoire in repertoire denoting the performance of two or more plays, ballets, etc, by the same company in the same venue on different evenings over a period of time

repertory company a theatrical company that performs plays from a repertoire, esp at its own theatre

repetition *Civil and Scots law* the recovery or repayment of money paid or received by mistake, as when the same bill has been paid twice

replacement 1 *Geology* the growth of a mineral within another of different chemical composition by gradual simultaneous deposition and removal 2 a process of fossilization by gradual substitution of mineral matter for the original organic matter

reply *Law* the answer made by a plaintiff or petitioner to a defendant's case

report 1 *Brit* a statement on the progress, academic achievement, etc, of each child in a school, written by teachers and sent to the parents or guardian annually or each term 2 a written account of a case decided at law, giving the main points of the argument on each side, the court's findings, and the decision reached

reporter 1 a person, esp a barrister, authorized to write official accounts of judicial proceedings 2 a person authorized to report the proceedings of a legislature 3

(in Scotland) *Social welfare* an official who arranges and conducts children's panel hearings and who may investigate cases and decide on the action to be taken

reposition *Surgery* the return of a broken or displaced organ, or part to its normal site

repository a place where commodities are kept before being sold; warehouse

representation 1 the principle by which delegates act for a constituency 2 *Contract law* a statement of fact made by one party to induce another to enter into a contract 3 an instance of acting for another, on his authority, in a particular capacity, such as executor or administrator 4 a dramatic production or performance

representative 1 a person representing a constituency in a deliberative, legislative, or executive body, esp (*cap*) a member of the **House of Representatives** (the lower house of Congress) 2 acting for or representing a constituency or the whole people in the process of government 3 of, characterized by, or relating to the political principle of representation of the people

reprieve 1 a postponement or remission of punishment, esp of a person condemned to death 2 a warrant granting a postponement 3 the act of reprieving or the state of being reprieved

reprisal (formerly) the forcible seizure of the property or subjects of one nation by another

reprise *Music* the repeating of an earlier theme

reprobate *Christianity* destined or condemned to eternal punishment in hell

reproduction 1 *Biology* any of various processes, either sexual or asexual, by which an animal or plant produces one or more individuals similar to itself 2 a an imitation or facsimile of a work of art, esp of a picture made by photoengraving b (*as modifier*): *a reproduction portrait* 3 the quality of sound from an audio system 4 a revival of an earlier production, as of a play

reptile any of the cold-blooded vertebrates constituting the class *Reptilia*, characterized by lungs, an outer covering of horny scales or plates, and young produced in amniotic eggs. The class today includes the tortoises, turtles, snakes, lizards, and crocodiles; in Mesozoic times it was the dominant group, containing the dinosaurs and related forms

Repton Humphry 1752–1818, English landscape gardener

republic 1 a form of government in which the people or their elected representatives possess the supreme power 2 a political or national unit possessing such a form of government 3 a constitutional form in which the head of state is an elected or nominated president 4 any community or group that resembles a political republic in that its members or elements exhibit a general equality, shared interests, etc

republican 1 of, resembling, or relating to a republic 2 supporting or advocating a republic 3 a supporter or advocate of a republic

Republican 1 of, belonging to, or relating to a Republican Party 2 of, belonging to, or relating to the Irish Republican Army 3 a member or supporter of a Republican Party 4 a member or supporter of the Irish Republican Army

repulsion *Physics* a force tending to separate two objects, such as the force between two like electric charges or magnetic poles

repulsive *Physics* concerned with, producing, or being a repulsion

Requiem 1 *RC Church* a Mass celebrated for the dead 2 a musical setting of this Mass 3 any piece of music composed or performed as a memorial to a dead person or persons

requisition a formal request by one government to another for the surrender of a fugitive from justice

reredos a screen or wall decoration at the back of an altar, in the form of a hanging, tapestry, painting, or piece of metalwork or sculpture

rerun 1 a film, play, series, etc, that is broadcast or put on again; repeat 2 *Computing* the repeat of a part of a computer program

rescue 1 the forcible removal of a person from legal custody 2 *Law* the forcible seizure of goods or property

reservation 1 an area of land set aside, esp (in the US) for American Indian peoples 2 *Brit* the strip of land between the two carriageways of a dual carriageway 3 *Law* a right or interest retained by the grantor in property granted, conveyed, leased, etc, to another

reserve *Ecology* a tract of land set aside for the protection and conservation of wild animals, flowers, etc.

reserved referring to matters that are the responsibility of the national parliament rather than a devolved regional assembly

reserve price the minimum price acceptable to the owner of property being auctioned or sold

reservoir 1 a natural or artificial lake or large tank used for collecting and storing water, esp for community water supplies or irrigation 2 *Biology* a vacuole or cavity in an organism, containing a secretion or some other fluid

residence the official house of the governor of any of various countries

resident 1 *Social welfare* an occupant of a welfare agency home 2 (esp formerly) a representative of the British government in a British protectorate 3 (esp in the 17th century) a diplomatic representative ranking below an ambassador 4 (in India, formerly) a representative of the British governor general at the court of a native prince 5 a bird or other animal that does not migrate 6 *US and Canadian* a physician who lives in the hospital where he works while undergoing specialist training after completing his internship 7 *Brit and NZ* a junior doctor, esp a house officer, who lives in the hospital in which he works 8 (of birds and other animals) not in the habit of migrating

residential school (in Canada) a boarding school maintained by the Canadian government for Indian and Inuit children from sparsely populated settlements

residual 1 (of deposits, soils, etc) formed by the weathering of pre-existing rocks and the removal of disintegrated material 2 payment made to an actor, actress, musician, etc, for subsequent use of film in which the person appears

residue *Law* what is left of an estate after the discharge of debts and distribution of specific gifts

resilient (of an object or material) capable of regaining its original shape or position after bending, stretching, compression, or other deformation; elastic

resin 1 any of a group of solid or semisolid amorphous compounds that are obtained directly from certain plants as exudations. They are used in medicine and in varnishes 2 any of a large number of synthetic, usually organic, materials that have a polymeric structure, esp such a substance in a raw state before it is moulded or treated with plasticizer, stabilizer, filler, etc

resist a substance used to protect something, esp a coating that prevents corrosion

resistance 1 a the opposition to a flow of electric current through a circuit component, medium, or substance. It is the magnitude of the real part of the impedance and is measured in ohms. b (*as modifier*): *resistance coupling* 2 any force that tends to retard or oppose motion 3 (in psychoanalytical theory) the tendency of a person to prevent the translation of repressed thoughts and ideas from the unconscious to the conscious and esp to resist the analyst's attempt to bring this about 4 *Physics* the magnitude of the real part of the acoustic or mechanical impedance 5 See passive resistance

Resistencia a city in NE Argentina, on the Paraná River. Pop: 423 000 (2005 est)

resistor an electrical component designed to introduce a known value of resistance into a circuit

resit an examination taken again by a person who has not been successful in a previous attempt

Resnais Alain born 1922, French film director, whose films include *Hiroshima mon amour* (1959), *L'Année dernière à Marienbad* (1961), *La Vie est un roman* (1983), and *On Connaît la Chanson* (1998)

resolution 1 a judicial decision on some matter; verdict; judgment 2 *Med* a return from a pathological to a normal condition b subsidence of the symptoms of a disease, esp the disappearance of inflammation without the formation of pus 3 *Music* the process in harmony whereby a dissonant note or chord is followed by a consonant one 4 the ability of a television or film image to reproduce fine detail

resonance 1 sound produced by a body vibrating in sympathy with a neighbouring source of sound 2 the condition of a body or system when it is subjected to a periodic disturbance of the same frequency as the natural frequency of the body or system. At this frequency the system displays an enhanced oscillation or vibration 3 *Electronics* the condition of an electrical circuit when the frequency is such that the capacitive and inductive reactances are equal in magnitude. In a series circuit there is then maximum alternating current whilst in a parallel circuit there is minimum alternating current 4 *Med* the sound heard when percussing a hollow bodily structure, esp the chest or abdomen. Change in the quality of the sound often indicates an underlying disease or disorder 5 *Chem* the phenomenon in which the electronic structure of a molecule can be represented by two or more hypothetical structures involving single, double, and triple chemical bonds. The true structure is considered to be an average of these theoretical structures 6 *Physics* a the condition of a system in which there is a sharp maximum probability for the absorption of electromagnetic radiation or capture of particles b a type of elementary particle of extremely short lifetime. Resonances are regarded as excited states of more stable particles **c** a highly transient atomic state formed during a collision process

Respighi Ottorino 1879–1936, Italian composer, noted esp for his suites *The Fountains of Rome* (1917) and *The Pines of Rome* (1924)

respiration 1 the process in living organisms of taking in oxygen from the surroundings and giving out carbon dioxide (**external respiration**). In terrestrial animals this is effected by breathing air 2 the chemical breakdown of complex organic substances, such as carbohydrates and fats, that takes place in the cells and tissues of animals and plants, during which energy is released and carbon dioxide produced (**internal respiration**)

▷www.osrc.org

respirator an apparatus for providing long-term artificial respiration

respond 1 *Architect* a pilaster or an engaged column that supports an arch or a lintel 2 *Christianity* a choral anthem chanted in response to a lesson read at a church service

respondent *Law* a person against whom a petition, esp in a divorce suit, or appeal is brought

response 1 *Bridge* a bid replying to a partner's bid or double 2 *Christianity* a short sentence or phrase recited or sung by the choir or congregation in reply to the officiant at a church service 3 *Electronics* the ratio of the output to the input level, at a particular frequency, of a transmission line or electrical device 4 any pattern of glandular, muscular, or electrical reactions that arises from stimulation of the nervous system

responsive (of an organism) reacting to a stimulus

rest 1 a mark in a musical score indicating a pause of specific duration 2 *Prosody* a pause in or at the end of a line; caesura 3 *Billiards, Snooker* any of various special poles used as supports for the cue in shots that cannot be made using the hand as a support

restaurant car *Brit* a railway coach in which meals are served

rest-cure a rest taken as part of a course of medical treatment, as for stress, anxiety, etc.

restitution 1 *Law* the act of compensating for loss or injury by reverting as far as possible to the position before such injury occurred 2 the return of an object or system to its original state, esp a restoration of shape after elastic deformation

restorative anything that restores or revives, esp a drug or agent that promotes health or strength

restriction *Logic, Maths* a condition that imposes a constraint on the possible values of a variable or on the domain of arguments of a function

restrictive practice *Brit* a trading agreement against the public interest

result 1 a number, quantity, or value obtained by solving a mathematical problem 2 *US* a decision of a legislative body

resultant *Maths, Physics* a single vector that is the vector sum of two or more other vectors

resurrection 1 a supposed act or instance of a dead person coming back to life 2 belief in the possibility of this as part of a religious or mystical system 3 the condi-

tion of those who have risen from the dead

retail the sale of goods individually or in small quantities to consumers

retainer 1 *History* a supporter or dependant of a person of rank, esp a soldier 2 a clip, frame, or similar device that prevents a part of a machine, engine, etc, from moving 3 a dental appliance for holding a loose tooth or prosthetic device in position

retake 1 *Films* a rephotographed shot or scene 2 a retaped recording

retarded underdeveloped, esp mentally and esp having an IQ of 70 to 85

retch an involuntary spasm of ineffectual vomiting

retention 1 *Pathol* the abnormal holding within the body of urine, faeces, etc, that are normally excreted 2 *Commerce* a sum of money owed to a contractor but not paid for an agreed period as a safeguard against any faults found in the work carried out

reticulate in the form of a network or having a network of parts

retina the light-sensitive membrane forming the inner lining of the posterior wall of the eyeball, composed largely of a specialized terminal expansion of the optic nerve. Images focused here by the lens of the eye are transmitted to the brain as nerve impulses

retirement pension a pension given to a person who has retired from regular employment, whether paid by the state, arising from the person's former employment, or the product of investment in a personal or stakeholder pension scheme

retort 1 a glass vessel with a round bulb and long tapering neck that is bent down, used esp in a laboratory for distillation 2 a vessel in which large quantities of material may be heated, esp one used for heating ores in the production of metals or heating coal to produce gas

retouch 1 the art or practice of retouching 2 a detail that is the result of retouching 3 a photograph, painting, etc, that has been retouched 4 *Archaeol* fine percussion to shape flakes of stone into usable tools

retread 1 another word for **remould** 2 a film, piece of music, etc which is a superficially altered version of an earlier original

retreat an institution, esp a private one, for the care and treatment of the mentally ill, infirm, elderly, etc.

retriever 1 one of a breed of large gun dogs that can be trained to retrieve game: varieties include golden retriever, labrador retriever, Chesapeake Bay retriever, curly-coated retriever, flat-coated retriever 2 any dog used to retrieve shot game

retrograde 1 *Astronomy* a occurring or orbiting in a direction opposite to that of the earth's motion around the sun b occurring or orbiting in a direction around a planet opposite to the planet's rotational direction c appearing to move in a clockwise direction due to the rotational period exceeding the period of revolution around the sun 2 *Biology* tending to retrogress; degenerate 3 *Music* of, concerning, or denoting a melody or part that is played backwards

retrospective an exhibition of an artist's life's work or a representative selection of it

retsina a Greek wine flavoured with resin

return 1 *Politics* a statement of the votes counted at an election or poll 2 *Architect* **a** a part of a building that forms an angle with the façade **b** any part of an architectural feature that forms an angle with the main part 3 *Law* a report by a bailiff or other officer on the outcome of a formal document such as a claim, summons, etc, issued by a court 4 *Cards* a lead of a card in the suit that one's partner has previously led

returning officer (in Britain, Canada, Australia, etc) an official in charge of conducting an election in a constituency or electoral district, who supervises the counting of votes and announces the results

Retz Gilles de. See (Gilles de) **Rais**

Reuben *Old Testament* 1 the eldest son of Jacob and Leah: one of the 12 patriarchs of Israel (Genesis 29:30) 2 the Israelite tribe descended from him 3 the territory of this tribe, lying to the northeast of the Dead Sea

Reus a city in NE Spain, northwest of Tarragona: became commercially important after the establishment of an English colony (about 1750). Pop: 94 407 (2003 est)

Reuter Baron **Paul Julius von** original name *Israel Beer Josaphat*. 1816–99, German telegrapher, who founded a news agency in London (1851)

Reutlingen a city in SW Germany, in Baden-Württemberg: founded in the 11th century; an Imperial free city from 1240 until 1802; textile industry. Pop: 112 346 (2003 est)

rev *Informal* revolution per minute

reveal *Architect* the vertical side of an opening in a wall, esp the side of a window or door between the frame and the front of the wall

revelation *Christianity* **a** God's disclosure of his own nature and his purpose for mankind, esp through the words of human intermediaries **b** something in which such a divine disclosure is contained, such as the Bible

Revelation the last book of the New Testament, containing visionary descriptions of heaven, of conflicts between good and evil, and of the end of the world. Also called: the **Apocalypse**, the **Revelation of Saint John the Divine**

revenue 1 the income accruing from taxation to a government during a specified period of time, usually a year 2 **a** a government department responsible for the collection of government revenue **b** (*as modifier*): *revenue men*

Revere Paul 1735–1818, American patriot and silversmith, best known for his night ride on April 18, 1775, to warn the Massachusetts colonists of the coming of the British troops

Reverence (preceded by *Your* or *His*) a title sometimes used to address or refer to a Roman Catholic priest

reverend 1 relating to or designating a clergyman or the clergy 2 *Informal* a clergyman

Reverend a title of respect for a clergyman

reverie *or* **revery** a piece of instrumental music suggestive of a daydream

reverse **a** the mechanism or gears by which machinery, a vehicle, etc, can be made to reverse its direction **b** (*as modifier*): *reverse gear*

reversible 1 *Chem, Physics* capable of assuming or producing either of two possible states and changing from one to the other 2 *Thermodynamics* (of a change, process, etc) occurring through a number of intermediate states that are all in thermodynamic equilibrium 3 (of a fabric or garment) woven, printed, or finished so that either side may be used as the outer side

reversion 1 *Biology* **a** the return of individuals, organs, etc, to a more primitive condition or type **b** the reappearance of primitive characteristics in an individual or group 2 *Property law* **a** an interest in an estate that reverts to the grantor or his heirs at the end of a period, esp at the end of the life of a grantee **b** an estate so reverting **c** the right to succeed to such an estate

revert a person who, having been converted, has returned to his former beliefs or Church

review 1 *US and Canadian* the process of rereading a subject or notes on it, esp in preparation for an examination 2 *Law* judicial re-examination of a case, esp by a superior court 3 a less common spelling of **revue**

Revised Standard Version a revision by American scholars of the American Standard Version of the Bible. The New Testament was published in 1946 and the entire Bible in 1953

Revised Version a revision of the Authorized Version of the Bible prepared by two committees of British scholars, the New Testament being published in 1881 and the Old in 1885

revision *Brit* the process of rereading a subject or notes on it, esp in preparation for an examination

revisionism 1 **a** a moderate, nonrevolutionary version of Marxism developed in Germany around 1900 **b** (in Marxist-Leninist ideology) any dangerous departure from the true interpretation of the teachings of Karl Marx, the German founder of modern Communism (1818–83) 2 an ultra-nationalist form of Zionism that arose in Palestine in the 1940s

revival 1 a new production of a play that has not been recently performed 2 a reawakening of faith or renewal of commitment to religion 3 an evangelistic meeting or service intended to effect such a reawakening in those present 4 the re-establishment of legal validity, as of a judgment, contract, etc.

revivalism a movement, esp an evangelical Christian one, that seeks to reawaken faith

revoke *Cards* the act of revoking; a renege

revolution 1 the overthrow or repudiation of a regime or political system by the governed 2 (in Marxist theory) the violent and historically necessary transition from one system of production in a society to the next, as from feudalism to capitalism 3 **a** the orbital motion of one body, such as a planet or satellite, around another **b** one complete turn in such motion 4 *Geology, Obsolete* a profound change in conditions over a large part of the earth's surface, esp one characterized by mountain building

revolve *Theatre* a circular section of a stage that can be rotated by electric power to provide a scene change

revue *or less commonly* **review** a form of light entertainment consisting of a series of topical sketches, songs, dancing, comic turns, etc.

revulsion *Obsolete* the diversion of disease or congestion from one part of the body to another by cupping, counterirritants, etc.

reward *Psychol* any pleasant event that follows a response and therefore increases the likelihood of the response recurring in the future

Rex king: part of the official title of a king, now used chiefly in documents, legal proceedings, inscriptions on coins, etc

Reykjavik the capital and chief port of Iceland, situated in the southwest: its buildings are heated by natural hot water. Pop: 112 490 (2003 est)

Reynaud Paul 1878–1966, French statesman: premier during the defeat of France by Germany (1940); later imprisoned by the Germans

Reynolds 1 Albert born 1935, Irish politician: leader of the Fianna Fáil party and prime minister of the Republic of Ireland (1994–96) **2** Sir Joshua 1723–92, English portrait painter. He was the first president of the Royal Academy (1768): the annual lectures he gave there, published as *Discourses*, are important contributions to art theory and criticism

Reynosa a city in E Mexico, in Tamaulipas state on the Rio Grande. Pop: 847 000 (2005 est)

Rhaetia an Alpine province of ancient Rome including parts of present-day Tyrol and E Switzerland

rhapsody 1 *Music* a composition free in structure and highly emotional in character **2** (in ancient Greece) an epic poem or part of an epic recited by a rhapsodist **3** a literary work composed in an intense or exalted style

rhea either of two large fast-running flightless birds, *Rhea americana* or *Pterocnemia pennata*, inhabiting the open plains of S South America: order *Rheiformes*. They are similar to but smaller than the ostrich, having three-toed feet and a completely feathered body

Rhee Syngman 1875–1965, Korean statesman, leader of the campaign for independence from Japan; first president of South Korea (1948–60). Popular unrest forced his resignation

Rhenish 1 of or relating to the River Rhine or the lands adjacent to it, esp the Rhineland-Palatinate **2** another word for **hock²** (the wine)

rhenium a dense silvery-white metallic element that has a high melting point. It occurs principally in gadolinite and molybdenite and is used, alloyed with tungsten or molybdenum, in high-temperature thermocouples. Symbol: Re; atomic no.: 75; atomic wt.: 186.207; valency: –1 or 1–7; relative density: 21.02; melting pt.: 3186°C; boiling pt.: 5596°C (est)

rheostat a variable resistance, usually consisting of a coil of wire with a terminal at one end and a sliding contact that moves along the coil to tap off the current

rhesus monkey a macaque monkey, *Macaca mulatta*, of S Asia: used extensively in medical research

rheum a watery discharge from the eyes or nose

rheumatic fever a disease characterized by sore throat, fever, inflammation, and pain in the joints

rheumatics *Informal* rheumatism

rheumatism any painful disorder of joints, muscles, or connective tissue

rheumatoid (of the symptoms of a disease) resembling rheumatism

rheumatoid arthritis a chronic disease of the musculoskeletal system, characterized by inflammation and swelling of joints (esp joints in the hands, wrists,

knees, and feet), muscle weakness, and fatigue

Rh factor an agglutinogen commonly found in human blood: it may cause a haemolytic reaction, esp during pregnancy or following transfusion of blood that does not contain this agglutinogen

Rhine a river in central and W Europe, rising in SE Switzerland: flows through Lake Constance north through W Germany and west through the Netherlands to the North Sea. Length: about 1320 km (820 miles)

Rhineland the region of Germany surrounding the Rhine

Rhineland-Palatinate a state of W Germany: formed in 1946 from the S part of the Prussian Rhine province, the Palatinate, and parts of Rhine-Hesse and Hesse-Nassau; part of West Germany until 1990: agriculture (with extensive vineyards) and tourism are important. Capital: Mainz. Pop: 4 059 000 (2003 est). Area: 19 832 sq km (7657 sq miles)

rhinoceros any of several perissodactyl mammals constituting the family *Rhinocerotidae* of SE Asia and Africa and having either one horn on the nose, like the Indian rhinoceros (*Rhinoceros unicornis*), or two horns, like the African white rhinoceros (*Diceros simus*). They have a very thick skin, massive body, and three digits on each foot

rhizome a thick horizontal underground stem of plants such as the mint and iris whose buds develop new roots and shoots

Rhode Island a state of the northeastern US, bordering on the Atlantic: the smallest state in the US; mainly low-lying and undulating, with an indented coastline in the east and uplands in the northwest. Capital: Providence. Pop: 1 076 164 (2003 est). Area: 2717 sq km (1049 sq miles)

Rhodes¹ Cecil John 1853–1902, British colonial financier and statesman in South Africa. He made a fortune in diamond and gold mining and, as prime minister of the Cape Colony (1890–96), he helped to extend British territory. He established the annual Rhodes scholarships to Oxford

Rhodes² **1** a Greek island in the SE Aegean Sea, about 16 km (10 miles) off the Turkish coast: the largest of the Dodecanese and the most easterly island in the Aegean. Capital: Rhodes. Pop: 117 007 (2001). Area: 1400 sq km (540 sq miles) **2** a port on this island, in the NE: founded in 408 BC; of great commercial and political importance in the 3rd century BC; suffered several earthquakes, notably in 225, when the Colossus was destroyed. Pop: 41 000 (latest est)

rhodium a hard corrosion-resistant silvery-white element of the platinum metal group, occurring free with other platinum metals in alluvial deposits and in nickel ores. It is used as an alloying agent to harden platinum and palladium. Symbol: Rh; atomic no.: 45; atomic wt.: 102.90550; valency: 2–6; relative density: 12.41; melting pt.: 1963±3°C; boiling pt.: 3697±100°C

rhododendron any ericaceous shrub of the genus *Rhododendron*, native to S Asia but widely cultivated in N temperate regions. They are mostly evergreen and have clusters of showy red, purple, pink, or white flowers

rhombohedron a six-sided prism whose sides are parallelograms

rhomboid 1 a parallelogram having adjacent sides of unequal length 2 having such a shape

rhombus an oblique-angled parallelogram having four equal sides

Rhondda an urban area in S Wales, in Rhondda Cynon Taff county borough on two branches of the **Rhondda Valley**: developed into a major coal-mining centre after 1807 and grew to a population of 167 900 in 1924: the last coal mine closed in 1990. Pop: 59 947 (1991)

Rhondda Cynon Taff a county borough in S Wales, created from part of Mid Glamorgan in 1996. Pop: 231 600 (2003 est). Area: 558 sq km (215 sq miles)

rhubarb 1 any of several temperate and subtropical plants of the polygonaceous genus *Rheum*, esp *R. rhaponticum* (**common garden rhubarb**), which has long green and red acid-tasting edible leafstalks, usually eaten sweetened and cooked 2 the leafstalks of this plant 3 a related plant, *Rheum officinale*, of central Asia, having a bitter-tasting underground stem that can be dried and used medicinally as a laxative or astringent

rhyme *or archaic* **rime** 1 identity of the terminal sounds in lines of verse or in words 2 a word that is identical to another in its terminal sound 3 a verse or piece of poetry having corresponding sounds at the ends of the lines 4 any verse or piece of poetry

rhymester, rimester, rhymer *or* **rimer** a poet, esp one considered to be mediocre or mechanical in diction; poetaster or versifier

Rhys Jean (Ella Gwendolen Rees Williams). ?1890–1979, Welsh novelist and short-story writer, born in Dominica. Her novels include *Voyage in the Dark* (1934), *Good Morning, Midnight* (1939), and *Wide Sargasso Sea* (1966)

rhythm 1 a the arrangement of the relative durations of and accents on the notes of a melody, usually laid out into regular groups (**bars**) of beats, the first beat of each bar carrying the stress b any specific arrangement of such groupings; time 2 (in poetry) a the arrangement of words into a more or less regular sequence of stressed and unstressed or long and short syllables b any specific such arrangement; metre 3 (in painting, sculpture, architecture, etc) a harmonious sequence or pattern of masses alternating with voids, of light alternating with shade, of alternating colours, etc. 4 any sequence of regularly recurring functions or events, such as the regular recurrence of certain physiological functions of the body, as the cardiac rhythm of the heartbeat

Rialto an island in Venice, Italy, linked with San Marco Island by the **Rialto Bridge** (1590) over the Grand Canal: the business centre of medieval and renaissance Venice

rib 1 any of the 24 curved elastic arches of bone that together form the chest wall in humans. All are attached behind to the thoracic part of the spinal column 2 the corresponding bone in other vertebrates 3 a structural member in a wing that extends from the leading edge to the trailing edge and maintains the shape of the wing surface 4 a projecting moulding or band on the underside of a vault or ceiling, which may be structural or ornamental 5 any of the transverse stiffening timbers or joists forming the frame of a ship's hull 6 any of the larger veins of a leaf 7 a projecting ridge of a mountain; spur

Ribbentrop Joachim von 1893–1946, German Nazi politician: foreign minister under Hitler (1938–45). He was hanged after conviction as a war criminal at Nuremberg

Ribble a river in NW England, flowing south and west through Lancashire to the Irish Sea. Length: 121 km (75 miles)

ribbon a long thin flexible band of metal used as a graduated measure, spring, etc.

ribbon development *Brit* the building of houses in a continuous row along a main road: common in England between the two World Wars

ribbonwood a small evergreen malvaceous tree, *Hoheria populnea*, of New Zealand. Its wood is used in furniture making and the tough bark for making cord

ribcage the bony structure consisting of the ribs and their connective tissue that encloses and protects the lungs, heart, etc.

Ribera José de also called *Jusepe de Ribera*, Italian nickname *Lo Spagnoletto* (The Little Spaniard). 1591–1652, Spanish artist, living in Italy. His religious pictures often dwell on horrible suffering, presented in realistic detail

riboflavin *or* **riboflavine** a yellow water-soluble vitamin of the B complex that occurs in green vegetables, germinating seeds, and in milk, fish, egg yolk, liver, and kidney. It is essential for the carbohydrate metabolism of cells. It is used as a permitted food colour, yellow or orange-yellow (**E101**). Formula: $C_{17}H_{20}N_4O_6$

Ricardo David 1772–1823, British economist. His main work is *Principles of Political Economy and Taxation* (1817)

rice 1 an erect grass, *Oryza sativa*, that grows in East Asia on wet ground and has drooping flower spikes and yellow oblong edible grains that become white when polished 2 the grain of this plant

> www.riceweb.org
> www.virtualcities.com/ons/orec/10rice.htm

Rice Elmer, original name *Elmer Reizenstein*. 1892–1967, US dramatist. His plays include *The Adding Machine* (1923) and *Street Scene* (1929), which was made into a musical by Kurt Weill in 1947

rich 1 *Geography* having an abundance of natural resources, minerals, etc. 2 (of colour) intense or vivid; deep 3 (of a fuel-air mixture) containing a relatively high proportion of fuel

Rich 1 Adrienne born 1929, US poet and feminist writer; her volumes of poetry include *Snapshots of a Daughter-in-Law* (1963) and *Diving Into the Wreck* (1973) 2 Buddy, real name *Bernard Rich*. 1917–87, US jazz drummer and band leader

Richard Sir Cliff, real name *Harry Rodger Webb*. born 1940, British pop singer. Film musicals include *The Young Ones* (1961) and *Summer Holiday* (1962)

Richard I nicknamed *Coeur de Lion* or the *Lion-Heart*. 1157–99, king of England (1189–99); a leader of the third crusade (joining it in 1191). On his way home, he was captured in Austria (1192) and held to ransom. After a brief return to England, where he was crowned again (1194), he spent the rest of his life in France

Richard II 1367–1400, king of England (1377–99), whose reign was troubled by popular discontent and baronial opposition. He was forced to abdicate in favour of

Henry Bolingbroke, who became Henry IV

Richard III 1452–85, king of England (1483–85), notorious as the suspected murderer of his two young nephews in the Tower of London. He proved an able administrator until his brief reign was ended by his death at the hands of Henry Tudor (later Henry VII) at the battle of Bosworth Field

Richards 1 I(vor) A(rmstrong). 1893–1979, British literary critic and linguist, who, with C. K. Ogden, wrote *The Meaning of Meaning* (1923) and devised Basic English 2 Sir **Gordon** 1904–86, British jockey 3 Sir **Viv**, full name *Isaac Vivian Alexander Richards*. born 1952, West Indian cricketer; captained the West Indies (1985–91)

Richardson 1 Dorothy M(iller). 1873–1957, British novelist, a pioneer of stream-of-consciousness writing: author of the novel sequence *Pilgrimage* (14 vols, 1915–67) 2 Henry Handel pen name of *Ethel Florence Lindesay Richardson*, 1870–1946, Australian novelist; author of the trilogy *The Fortunes of Richard Mahony* (1917–29) 3 Sir **Owen Willans** 1879–1959, British physicist; a pioneer in the study of atomic physics: Nobel prize for physics 1928 4 Sir **Ralph** (David). 1902–83, British stage and screen actor 5 **Samuel** 1689–1761, British novelist whose psychological insight and use of the epistolary form exerted a great influence on the development of the novel. His chief novels are *Pamela* (1740) and *Clarissa* (1747)

Richelieu Armand Jean du Plessis 1585–1642, French statesman and cardinal, principal minister to Louis XIII and virtual ruler of France (1624–42). He destroyed the power of the Huguenots and strengthened the crown in France and the role of France in Europe

Richelieu River a river in E Canada, in S Quebec, rising in Lake Champlain and flowing north to the St Lawrence River. Length: 338 km (210 miles)

Richler Mordecai born 1931, Canadian novelist. His novels include *St Urbain's Horseman* (1971), *Solomon Gursky Was Here* (1990), and *Barney's Version* (1997)

Richmond 1 a borough of Greater London, on the River Thames: formed in 1965 by the amalgamation of Barnes, Richmond, and Twickenham; site of Hampton Court Palace and the Royal Botanic Gardens at Kew. Pop: 179 200 (2003 est). Area: 55 sq km (21 sq miles) 2 a town in N England, in North Yorkshire: Norman castle. Pop: 8178 (2001) 3 a port in E Virginia, the state capital, at the falls of the James River: developed after the establishment of a trading post (1637); scene of the Virginia Conventions of 1774 and 1775; Confederate capital in the American Civil War. Pop: 194 729 (2003 est) 4 a county of SW New York City: coextensive with Staten Island borough; consists of Staten Island and several smaller islands

Richter 1 **Burton** born 1931, US physicist: shared the 1976 Nobel prize for physics with Samuel Tring for discovering the subatomic particle known as the J/psi particle 2 **Johann Friedrich** , wrote under the name *Jean Paul*. 1763–1825, German romantic novelist. His works include *Hesperus* (1795) and *Titan* (1800–03) 3 **Sviatoslav** 1915–97, Ukrainian concert pianist

Richter scale a scale for expressing the magnitude of an earthquake in terms of the logarithm of the amplitude of the ground wave; values range from 0 to over 9

Richthofen Baron **Manfred von** , nickname *the Red*

Baron. 1892–1918, German aviator; commander during World War I of the 11th Chasing Squadron (**Richthofen's Flying Circus**). He was credited with 80 air victories before he was shot down

rickets *Pathol* a disease mainly of children, characterized by softening of developing bone, and hence bow legs, malnutrition, and enlargement of the liver and spleen, caused by a deficiency of vitamin D

rickrack *or* **ricrac** a zigzag braid used for trimming

riddle a sieve, esp a coarse one used for sand, grain, etc.

rider 1 an additional clause, amendment, or stipulation added to a legal or other document, esp (in Britain) a legislative bill at its third reading 2 *Brit* a statement made by a jury in addition to its verdict, such as a recommendation for mercy 3 a small weight that can be slid along one arm of a chemical balance to make fine adjustments during weighing 4 *Geology* a thin seam, esp of coal or mineral ore, overlying a thicker seam

ridge 1 a long narrow raised land formation with sloping sides esp one formed by the meeting of two faces of a mountain or of a mountain buttress or spur 2 *Anatomy* any elongated raised margin or border on a bone, tooth, tissue membrane, etc. 3 a the top of a roof at the junction of two sloping sides b *(as modifier): a ridge tile* 4 the back or backbone of an animal, esp a whale 5 *Meteorol* an elongated area of high pressure, esp an extension of an anticyclone

riding¹ a the art or practice of horsemanship b *(as modifier): a riding school*

riding² 1 any of the three former administrative divisions of Yorkshire: **North Riding**, **East Riding** and **West Riding** 2 (in Canada) a parliamentary constituency

riding crop a short whip with a thong at one end and a handle for opening gates at the other

Ridley Nicholas ?1500–55, English bishop, who helped to revise the liturgy under Edward VI. He was burnt at the stake for refusing to disavow his Protestant beliefs when Mary I assumed the throne

Riefenstahl Leni 1902–2003, German photographer and film director, best known for her Nazi propaganda films, such as *Triumph of the Will* (1934)

Riemann Georg Friedrich Bernhard 1826–66, German mathematician whose non-Euclidean geometry was used by Einstein as a basis for his general theory of relativity

riff *Music* (in jazz or rock music) a short series of chords

riffle *US and Canadian* a a rapid in a stream b a rocky shoal causing a rapid c a ripple on water

rift¹ *Geology* a long narrow zone of faulting resulting from tensional stress in the earth's crust

rift² *US* 1 a shallow or rocky part in a stream 2 the backwash from a wave that has just broken

rift valley a long narrow valley resulting from the subsidence of land between two parallel faults, often associated with volcanism. The East African Rift Valley is an example

rig 1 *Nautical* the distinctive arrangement of the sails, masts, and other spars of a vessel 2 *Chiefly US and Canadian* an articulated lorry

Riga the capital of Latvia, on the **Gulf of Riga** at the mouth of the Western Dvina on the Baltic Sea: a port and major trading centre since Viking times. Pop:

739 232 (2002 est)

-rigged (of a sailing vessel) having a rig of a certain kind

rigging 1 the shrouds, stays, halyards, etc, of a vessel 2 the bracing wires, struts, and lines of a biplane, balloon, etc. 3 any form of lifting gear, tackle, etc.

right 1 of, designating, supporting, belonging to, or relating to the political or intellectual right (see sense 39) 2 conservative or reactionary 3 *Geometry* a formed by or containing a line or plane perpendicular to another line or plane b having the axis perpendicular to the base c straight 4 the supporters or advocates of social, political, or economic conservatism or reaction, based generally on a belief that things are better left unchanged (opposed to *radical* or *left*) 5 *Boxing* a a punch with the right hand b the right hand

right angle the angle between two radii of a circle that cut off on the circumference an arc equal in length to one quarter of the circumference; an angle of 90° or $\pi/2$ radians

right-angled triangle a triangle one angle of which is a right angle

rightist 1 of, tending towards, or relating to the political right or its principles; conservative, traditionalist, or reactionary 2 a person who supports or belongs to the political right

right of way a the legal right of someone to pass over another's land, acquired by grant or by long usage b the path or road used by this right

Right Reverend (in Britain) a title of respect for an Anglican or Roman Catholic bishop

right whale any large whalebone whale of the family *Balaenidae*. They are grey or black, have a large head, and, in most, no dorsal fin, and are hunted as a source of whalebone and oil

Rigi a mountain in the Alps of N central Switzerland, between Lakes Lucerne, Zug, and Lauerz

rigor mortis *Pathol* the stiffness of joints and muscular rigidity of a dead body, caused by depletion of ATP in the tissues. It begins two to four hours after death and lasts up to about four days, after which the muscles and joints relax

rigorous *Maths, Logic* (of a proof) making the validity of the successive steps completely explicit

rigour *or US* **rigor** *Maths, Logic* logical validity or accuracy

Rijeka a port in Croatia: an ancient town, changing hands many times before passing to Yugoslavia in 1947 until Croatia became independent in 1991. Pop: 135 000 (2005 est)

Rijksmuseum a museum in Amsterdam housing the national art collection of the Netherlands

Rijswijk a town in the SW Netherlands, in South Holland province on the SE outskirts of The Hague: scene of the signing (1697) of the **Treaty of Rijswijk** ending the War of the Grand Alliance. Pop: 48 000 (2003 est)

Riley Bridget (Louise). born 1931, British painter, best known for her black-and-white op art paintings of the 1960s

Rilke Rainer Maria 1875–1926, Austro-German poet, born in Prague. Author of intense visionary lyrics, notably in the *Duino Elegies* (1922) and *Sonnets to Orpheus* (1923)

rill 1 a brook or stream; rivulet 2 a small channel or gulley, such as one formed during soil erosion 3 one of many winding cracks on the moon

rim 1 the peripheral part of a wheel, to which the tyre is attached 2 *Basketball* the hoop from which the net is suspended

Rimbaud Arthur 1854–91, French poet, whose work, culminating in the prose poetry of *Illuminations* (published 1884), greatly influenced the symbolists. *A Season in Hell* (1873) draws on his tempestuous homosexual affair with Verlaine, after which he abandoned writing (aged about 20) and spent the rest of his life travelling

rime frost formed by the freezing of supercooled water droplets in fog onto solid objects

Rimini a port and resort in NE Italy, in Emilia-Romagna on the N Adriatic coast. Pop: 128 656 (2001)

Rimsky-Korsakov Nikolai Andreyevich 1844–1908, Russian composer; noted for such works as the orchestral suite *Scheherazade* (1888) and the opera *Le Coq d'or* (first performed in 1910)

rind 1 the outer layer of a fruit or of the spore-producing body of certain fungi 2 the outer layer of the bark of a tree

ring¹ 1 a square apron or raised platform, marked off by ropes, in which contestants box or wrestle 2 **the ring** the sport of boxing 3 an area reserved for betting at a racecourse 4 a circular strip of bark cut from a tree or branch, esp in order to kill it 5 *Geometry* the area of space lying between two concentric circles 6 *Maths* a set that is subject to two binary operations, addition and multiplication, such that the set is an Abelian group under addition and is closed under multiplication, this latter operation being associative 7 *Chem* a closed loop of atoms in a molecule 8 *Astronomy* any of the thin circular bands of small bodies orbiting a giant planet, esp Saturn

ring² *Electronics* the damped oscillatory wave produced by a circuit that rings

ringer 1 a quoit thrown so as to encircle a peg 2 such a throw

ring finger the third finger, esp of the left hand, on which a wedding ring is traditionally worn

ringlet any of numerous butterflies of the genus *Erebia*, most of which occur in S Europe and have dark brown wings marked with small black-and-white eyespots: family *Satyridae*

ring main a domestic electrical supply in which outlet sockets are connected to the mains supply through a ring circuit

ringmaster the master of ceremonies in a circus

ring road a main road that bypasses a town or town centre

ringside the area immediately surrounding an arena, esp the row of seats nearest a boxing or wrestling ring

ringtail *Austral* any of several possums having curling prehensile tails used to grasp branches while climbing

ringworm any of various fungal infections of the skin (esp the scalp) or nails, often appearing as itching circular patches

rink 1 an expanse of ice for skating on, esp one that is artificially prepared and under cover 2 an area for roller skating on 3 a building or enclosure for ice skating or roller skating **4** *Bowls* a strip of the green, usually about 5–7 metres wide, on which a game is played **5** *Curling* the strip of ice on which the game is played, usually 41 by 4 metres **6** (in bowls and curling) the players on one side in a game

rinkhals a venomous elapid snake, *Hemachatus hemachatus* of southern Africa, which spits venom at its enemies from a distance

rink rat *Canadian, informal* a young person who carries out chores at an ice-hockey rink in return for free skating time

Rio Branco 1 a city in W Brazil, capital of Acre state. Pop: 261 000 (2005 est) **2** a river in Brazil, flowing south to the Rio Negro. Length: 644 km (400 miles)

Rio de Janeiro *or* **Rio 1** a port in SE Brazil, on Guanabara Bay: the country's chief port and its capital from 1763 to 1960; backed by mountains, notably Sugar Loaf Mountain; founded by the French in 1555 and taken by the Portuguese in 1567. Pop: 11 469 000 (2005 est) **2** a state of E Brazil. Capital: Rio de Janeiro. Pop: 14 724 475 (2002). Area: 42 911 sq km (16 568 sq miles)

Rio Grande 1 a river in North America, rising in SW Colorado and flowing southeast to the Gulf of Mexico, forming the border between the US and Mexico. Length: about 3030 km (1885 miles) **2** a port in SE Brazil, in SE Rio Grande do Sul state: serves as the port for Porto Alegre. Pop: 188 000 (2005 est))

Rio Grande do Norte a state of NE Brazil, on the Atlantic: much of it is semiarid plateau. Capital: Natal. Pop: 2 852 784 (2002). Area: 53 014 sq km (20 469 sq miles)

Rio Grande do Sul a state of S Brazil, on the Atlantic. Capital: Porto Alegre. Pop: 10 408 540 (2002). Area: 282 183 sq km (108 951 sq miles)

rioja a red or white wine, with a distinctive vanilla bouquet and flavour, produced around the Ebro river in central N Spain

riot *Hunting* the indiscriminate following of any scent by hounds

rip *Informal, archaic* an old worn-out horse

riparian 1 of, inhabiting, or situated on the bank of a river **2** denoting or relating to the legal rights of the owner of land on a river bank, such as fishing or irrigation **3** *Property law* a person who owns land on a river bank

ripcord 1 a cord that when pulled opens a parachute from its pack **2** a cord on the gas bag of a balloon that when pulled opens a panel, enabling gas to escape and the balloon to descend

ripe (of fruit, grain, etc) mature and ready to be eaten or used; fully developed

Ripon a city in N England, in North Yorkshire: cathedral (12th–16th centuries). Pop: 16 468 (2001)

riposte *or* **ripost** *Fencing* a counterattack made immediately after a successful parry

ripple¹ 1 a slight wave or undulation on the surface of water **2** *Electronics* an oscillation of small amplitude superimposed on a steady value

ripple² a special kind of comb designed to separate the seed from the stalks in flax, hemp, or broomcorn

ripsaw a handsaw for cutting along the grain of timber

rise 1 the appearance of the sun, moon, or other celestial body above the horizon **2** the vertical height of a step or of a flight of stairs **3** the vertical height of a roof above the walls or columns **4** the height of an arch above the impost level **5** *Angling* the act or instance of fish coming to the surface of the water to take flies, etc.

riser 1 the vertical part of a stair or step **2** a vertical pipe, esp one within a building

risk at risk *Social welfare* vulnerable to personal damage, to the extent that a welfare agency might take protective responsibility

rite 1 a formal act or procedure prescribed or customary in religious ceremonies **2** a particular body of such acts or procedures, esp of a particular Christian Church **3** a Christian Church

rite of passage *or* **rite de passage** a ceremony performed in some cultures at times when an individual changes his status, as at puberty and marriage

ritual 1 the prescribed or established form of a religious or other ceremony **2** such prescribed forms in general or collectively **3** *Psychol* any repetitive behaviour, such as hand-washing, performed by a person with a compulsive personality disorder

ritualism 1 emphasis, esp exaggerated emphasis, on the importance of rites and ceremonies **2** the study of rites and ceremonies, esp magical or religious ones

river a a large natural stream of fresh water flowing along a definite course, usually into the sea, being fed by tributary streams **b** (*as modifier*): *river traffic*

Rivera Diego 1886–1957, Mexican painter, noted for his monumental murals in public buildings, which are influenced by Aztec art and depict revolutionary themes

Rivers a state of S Nigeria, in the Niger River Delta on the Gulf of Guinea. Capital: Port Harcourt. Pop: 4 103 372 (1995 est). Area: 21 850 sq km (8436 sq miles)

Riverside a city in SW California. Pop: 281 514 (2003 est)

Riviera the Mediterranean coastal region between Cannes, France, and La Spezia, Italy: contains some of Europe's most popular resorts

rivulet a small stream

Riyadh the joint capital (with Mecca) of Saudi Arabia, situated in a central oasis: the largest city in the country. Pop: 5 514 000 (2005 est)

Rizal Jose 1861–96, Philippine nationalist, executed by the Spanish during the Philippine revolution of 1896

Rizzio *or* **Riccio** David ?1533–66, Italian musician and courtier who became the secretary and favourite of Mary, Queen of Scots. He was murdered at the instigation of a group of nobles, including Mary's husband, Darnley

RNA *Biochem* ribonucleic acid; any of a group of nucleic acids, present in all living cells, that play an essential role in the synthesis of proteins. On hydrolysis they yield the pentose sugar ribose, the purine bases adenine and guanine, the pyrimidine bases cytosine and uracil, and phosphoric acid

roach¹ 1 a European freshwater cyprinid food fish, *Rutilus rutilus*, having a deep compressed body and reddish ventral and tail fins **2** any of various similar fishes

roach² 1 short for **cockroach 2** *Slang* the butt of a cannabis cigarette

roach³ *Nautical* **1** the amount by which the leech of a fore-and-aft sail projects beyond an imaginary straight line between the clew and the head **2** the curve at the foot of a square sail

road 1 a an open way, usually surfaced with asphalt or concrete, providing passage from one place to another **b** (*as modifier*): *road traffic* **2** a street **3** *Nautical* a partly sheltered anchorage

roadholding the extent to which a motor vehicle is stable and does not skid, esp at high speeds, or on sharp bends or wet roads

road metal crushed rock, broken stone, etc, used to construct a road

roadster an open car, esp one seating only two

road tax a tax paid, usually annually, on motor vehicles in use on the roads

road test a test to ensure that a vehicle is roadworthy, esp after repair or servicing, by driving it on roads

roadway 1 the surface of a road **2** the part of a road that is used by vehicles

roadworthy 1 (of a motor vehicle) mechanically sound; fit for use on the roads **2** *South African* a certificate of roadworthiness for a motor vehicle

roan 1 (of a horse) having a bay (**red roan**), chestnut (**strawberry roan**), or black (**blue roan**) coat sprinkled with white hairs **2** a horse having such a coat

Roanoke Island an island off the coast of North Carolina: site of the first attempted English settlement in America. Length: 19 km (12 miles). Average width: 5 km (3 miles)

roar a prolonged loud cry of certain animals, esp lions

roaring *Vet* a debilitating breathing defect of horses characterized by rasping sounds with each breath: caused by inflammation of the respiratory tract or obstruction of the larynx

Robbe-Grillet Alain born 1922, French novelist and screenwriter. Author of *The Voyeur* (1955), *Jealousy* (1957), and *Djinn* (1981): he is one of the leading practitioners of the antinovel

Robben Island a small island in South Africa, 11 km (7 miles) off the Cape Peninsula: formerly used by the South African government to house political prisoners

robbery *Criminal law* the stealing of property from a person by using or threatening to use force

Robbia 1 Andrea della 1435–1525, Florentine sculptor, best known for his polychrome reliefs and his statues of infants in swaddling clothes **2** his uncle, **Luca della** ?1400–82, Florentine sculptor, who perfected a technique of enamelling terra cotta for reliefs

Robbins Jerome 1918–98, US ballet dancer and choreographer. He choreographed the musicals *The King and I* (1951) and *West Side Story* (1957)

Robert I known as *Robert the Bruce*. 1274–1329, king of Scotland (1306–29): he defeated the English army of Edward II at Bannockburn (1314) and gained recognition of Scotland's independence (1328)

Robert II 1316–90, king of Scotland (1371–90)

Robert III ?1337–1406, king of Scotland (1390–1406), son of Robert II

Roberts 1 Frederick Sleigh, 1st Earl. 1832–1914, British field marshal. He was awarded the Victoria Cross (1858) for his service during the Indian Mutiny and was commander in chief (1899–1900) in the second Boer War **2**

Julia born 1967, US film actress; her films include *Pretty Woman* (1990), *Notting Hill* (1999), *Erin Brockovich* (2000), which earned her an Academy Award, and *Mona Lisa Smile* (2003)

Robeson Paul 1898–1976, US bass singer, actor, and leader in the Black civil rights movement

Robespierre Maximilien François Marie Isidore de. 1758–94, French revolutionary and Jacobin leader: established the Reign of Terror as a member of the Committee of Public Safety (1793–94): executed in the coup d'état of Thermidor (1794)

Robey Sir **George**, original name *George Edward Wade*, known as *the prime minister of mirth*. 1869–1954, British music-hall comedian, who also appeared in films

robin 1 a small Old World songbird, *Erithacus rubecula*, related to the thrushes: family *Muscicapidae*. The male has a brown back, orange-red breast and face, and grey underparts **2** a North American thrush, *Turdus migratorius*, similar to but larger than the Old World robin **3** any of various similar birds having a reddish breast

Robin Hood a legendary English outlaw of the reign of Richard I, who according to tradition lived in Sherwood Forest and robbed the rich to give to the poor

Robinson 1 Edward G, real name *Emanuel Goldenberg*. 1893–1973, US film actor, born in Romania, famous esp for gangster roles. His films include *Little Caesar* (1930), *Brother Orchid* (1940), *Double Indemnity* (1944), and *All My Sons* (1948) **2 Edward Arlington** 1869–1935, US poet, author of narrative verse, often based on Arthurian legend. His works include *Collected Poems* (1922), *The Man Who Died Twice* (1924), and *Tristram* (1927) **3** (**William**) **Heath** 1872–1944, British cartoonist and book illustrator, best known for his comic drawings of fantastic machines **4 John** (**Arthur Thomas**) 1919–83, British bishop and theologian, best known for his controversial *Honest to God* (1963), which popularized radical theological discussion. He was suffragan Bishop of Woolwich (1959–69) **5 Mary** born 1944, Irish barrister and politician: president of Ireland 1990–97; U.N. high commissioner for human rights (1997–2001) **6 Smokey**, real name *William Robinson*. born 1940, US Motown singer, songwriter, and producer. His hits include "The Tears of a Clown" (1970) (with the Miracles) and "Being with you" (1981) **7 "Sugar" Ray**, real name *Walker Smith*. 1921–89, US boxer, winner of the world middleweight championship on five separate occasions

robot 1 any automated machine programmed to perform specific mechanical functions in the manner of a man **2** not controlled by man; automatic

robotics the science or technology of designing, building, and using robots

Rob Roy real name *Robert Macgregor*. 1671–1734, Scottish outlaw

Robson[1] 1 Bobby, full name *Robert William*. born 1933, English footballer and manager of England (1982–90) **2 Bryan** born 1957, English footballer and manager: captain of England (1982–90) **3** Dame **Flora** 1902–84, English stage and film actress

Robson[2] Mount a mountain in SW Canada, in E British Columbia: the highest peak in the Canadian Rockies. Height: 3954 m (12 972 ft)

robust (esp of wines) having a rich full-bodied flavour

roc (in Arabian legend) a bird of enormous size and power

Roca Cape a cape in SW central Portugal, near Lisbon: the westernmost point of continental Europe

Rocard Michel born 1930, French politician: prime minister of France (1988–91)

Rochdale 1 a town in NW England, in Rochdale unitary authority, Greater Manchester: former centre of the textile industry. Pop: 95 769 (2001) **2** a unitary authority in NW England, in Greater Manchester. Pop: 206 600 (2003 est). Area: 159 sq km (61 sq miles)

Rochester¹ 2nd Earl of, title of *John Wilmot*. 1647–80, English poet, wit, and libertine. His poems include satires, notably *A Satire against Mankind* (1675), love lyrics, and bawdy verse

Rochester² **1** a city in SE England, in Medway unitary authority, Kent, on the River Medway. Pop: 27 123 (2001) **2** a city in NW New York State, on Lake Ontario. Pop: 215 093 (2003 est) **3** a city in the US, in Minnesota: site of the Mayo Clinic. Pop: 92 507 (2003 est)

rock 1 *Geology* any aggregate of minerals that makes up part of the earth's crust. It may be unconsolidated, such as a sand, clay, or mud, or consolidated, such as granite, limestone, or coal **2** short for **rock salmon 3** *Slang* another name for **crack 4 on the rocks a** in a state of ruin or destitution **b** (of drinks, esp whisky) served with ice

Rock 1 the an informal name for **Gibraltar 2** the a Canadian informal name for **Newfoundland**

Rockall an uninhabited British island in the N Atlantic, 354 km (220 miles) W of the Outer Hebrides. Area: 0.07 ha (0.18 acres)

rock and roll *or* **rock'n'roll** dancing performed to such music, with exaggerated body movements stressing the beat

> ▷www.reasontorock.com
> ▷www.allmusic.com
> ▷www.dotmusic.com

rock crystal a pure transparent colourless quartz, used in electronic and optical equipment. Formula: SiO_2

rock dove *or* **pigeon** a common dove, *Columba livia*, from which domestic and feral pigeons are descended. It has a pale grey plumage with black-striped wings

Rockefeller 1 John D(avison). 1839–1937, US industrialist and philanthropist **2** his son, John D(avison). 1874–1960, US capitalist and philanthropist **3** his son, Nelson (Aldrich). 1908–79, US politician; governor of New York State (1958–74); vice president (1974–76)

rocker 1 any of various devices that transmit or operate with a rocking motion **2** a steel tool with a curved toothed cage, used to roughen the copper plate in engraving a mezzotint **3 a** an ice skate with a curved blade **b** the curve itself **4** *Skating* **a** a figure consisting of three interconnecting circles **b** a half turn in which the skater turns through 180°, so facing about while continuing to move in the same direction

rockery a garden constructed with rocks, esp one where alpine plants are grown

rocket 1 a Mediterranean plant, *Eruca sativa*, having yellowish-white flowers and leaves used as a salad: family *Brassicaceae* (crucifers) **2** any of several plants of the related genus *Sisymbrium*, esp *S. irio* (**London rocket**),

which grow on waste ground and have pale yellow flowers **3 yellow rocket** any of several yellow-flowered plants of the related genus *Barbarea*, esp *B. vulgaris* **4 sea rocket** any of several plants of the related genus *Cakile*, esp *C. maritima*, which grow along the seashores of Europe and North America and have mauve, pink, or white flowers

Rockford a city in N Illinois, on the Rock River. Pop: 151 725 (2003 est)

rock garden a garden featuring rocks or rockeries

Rockhampton a port in Australia, in E Queensland on the Fitzroy River. Pop: 59 475 (2001)

Rockingham Marquess of, title of *Charles Watson-Wentworth*. 1730–82, British statesman and leader of the Whig opposition, whose members were known as the **Rockingham Whigs**; prime minister (1765–66; 1782). He opposed the war with the American colonists

rock salmon *Brit* (formerly) any of several coarse fishes when used as food, esp the dogfish or wolffish: now known as **catfish**

rock tripe *Canadian* any of various edible lichens, esp of the genus *Umbilicaria*, that grow on rocks and are used in the North as a survival food

Rockwell Norman 1894–1978, US illustrator, noted esp for magazine covers

rococo 1 a style of architecture and decoration that originated in France in the early 18th century, characterized by elaborate but graceful, light, ornamentation, often containing asymmetrical motifs **2** an 18th-century style of music characterized by petite prettiness, a decline in the use of counterpoint, and extreme use of ornamentation

> ▷www.artchive.com/ftp_site_reg.htm
> ▷www.artlex.com/ArtLex/r/rococo.htmlm

rod 1 a straight slender shoot, stem, or cane of a woody plant **2** See **fishing rod 3 a** a unit of length equal to 5½ yards **b** a unit of square measure equal to 30¼ square yards **4** a metal shaft that transmits power in axial reciprocating motion **5** any of the elongated cylindrical cells in the retina of the eye, containing the visual purple (rhodopsin), which are sensitive to dim light but not to colour **6** short for **hot rod**

Rodchenko Alexander (Mikhailovich). 1891–1956, Soviet painter, sculptor, designer, and photographer, noted for his abstract geometrical style: a member of the constructivist movement

rode *Nautical* an anchor rope or chain

rodent a any of the relatively small placental mammals that constitute the order *Rodentia*, having constantly growing incisor teeth specialized for gnawing. The group includes porcupines, rats, mice, squirrels, marmots, etc. **b** (*as modifier*): *rodent characteristics*

Rodgers Richard 1902–79, US composer of musical comedies. He collaborated with the librettist Lorenz Hart on such musicals as *A Connecticut Yankee* (1927), *On Your Toes* (1936), and *Pal Joey* (1940). After Hart's death his librettist was Oscar Hammerstein II. Two of their musicals, *Oklahoma!* (1943) and *South Pacific* (1949), received the Pulitzer Prize

Rodin Auguste 1840–1917, French sculptor, noted for his portrayal of the human form. His works include *The Kiss* (1886), *The Burghers of Calais* (1896), and *The Thinker* (1905)

Rodney George Brydges, 1st Baron Rodney. 1719–92, English admiral: captured Martinique (1762): defeated the Spanish at Cape St Vincent (1780) and the French under Admiral de Grasse off Dominica (1782), restoring British superiority in the Caribbean

Rodrigo Joaquín 1902–99, Spanish composer. His works include *Concierto de Aranjuez* (1940) for guitar and orchestra and *Concierto Pastorale* (1978)

roe 1 the ovary of a female fish filled with mature eggs 2 the testis of a male fish filled with mature sperm 3 the ripe ovary of certain crustaceans, such as the lobster

Roeg Nic(olas). born 1928, British film director and cinematographer. Films include *Walkabout* (1970), *Don't Look Now* (1972), *Insignificance* (1984), and *The Witches* (1990)

roentgen *or* **röntgen** a unit of dose of electromagnetic radiation equal to the dose that will produce in air a charge of 0.258×10^{-3} coulomb on all ions of one sign, when all the electrons of both signs liberated in a volume of air of mass one kilogram are stopped completely.

Roentgen *or* **Röntgen** Wilhelm Konrad 1845–1923, German physicist, who in 1895 discovered X-rays: Nobel prize for physics 1901

Roethke Theodore 1908–63, US poet, whose books include *Words for the Wind* (1957) and *The Far Field* (1964)

Rogers 1 Ginger, real name Virginia McMath. 1911–95, US dancer and film actress, who partnered Fred Astaire 2 Richard, Baron Rogers of Riverside. born 1933, British architect. His works include the Pompidou Centre in Paris (1971–77; with Renzo Piano), the Lloyd's building in London (1986), and the Millennium Dome in Greenwich, London 3 William Penn Adair, known as Will. 1879–1935, US actor, newspaper columnist, and humorist in the homespun tradition

Roget Peter Mark 1779–1869, English physician, who on retirement devised a *Thesaurus of English Words and Phrases* (1852), a classified list of synonyms

rogue a an animal of vicious character that has separated from the main herd and leads a solitary life b (*as modifier*): *a rogue elephant*

Roland the greatest of the legendary 12 peers (paladins, of whom Oliver was another) in attendance on Charlemagne; he died in battle at Roncesvalles (778 AD)

role *or* **rôle** 1 a part or character in a play, film, etc, to be played by an actor or actress 2 *Psychol* the part played by a person in a particular social setting, influenced by his expectation of what is appropriate

Rolfe Frederick William, also known as *Baron Corvo*. 1860–1913, British novelist. His best-known work is *Hadrian the Seventh* (1904)

roll 1 a cylinder used to flatten something; roller 2 a very rapid beating of the sticks on a drum 3 a flight manoeuvre in which an aircraft makes one complete rotation about its longitudinal axis without loss of height or change in direction 4 a throw of dice 5 a bookbinder's tool having a brass wheel, used to impress a line or repeated pattern on the cover of a book

Rolland Romain 1866–1944, French novelist, dramatist, and essayist, known for his novels about a musical genius, *Jean-Christophe*, (1904–12): Nobel prize for literature 1915

rolled gold a metal, such as brass, coated with a thin layer of gold, usually above 9 carat purity. It is used in inexpensive jewellery

roller 1 a cylinder having an absorbent surface and a handle, used for spreading paint 2 a heavy cast-iron cylinder or pair of cylinders on an axle to which a handle is attached; used for flattening lawns 3 a long heavy wave of the sea, advancing towards the shore 4 a hardened cylinder of precision-ground steel that forms one of the rolling components of a roller bearing or of a linked driving chain 5 a cylinder fitted on pivots, used to enable heavy objects to be easily moved; castor 6 *Printing* a cylinder, usually of hard rubber, used to ink a forme or plate before impression 7 *Med* a bandage consisting of a long strip of muslin or cheesecloth rolled tightly into a cylindrical form before application 8 a band fastened around a horse's belly to keep a blanket in position 9 any of various Old World birds of the family Coraciidae, such as *Coracias garrulus* (**European roller**), that have a blue, green, and brown plumage, a slightly hooked bill, and an erratic flight: order *Coraciiformes* (kingfishers, etc) 10 a variety of tumbler pigeon that performs characteristic backward somersaults in flight 11 a breed of canary that has a soft trilling song in which the notes are run together

Rollerblade *Trademark* a type of roller skate in which the wheels are set in a single straight line under the boot

roller skate a device having clamps and straps for fastening to a boot or shoe and four small wheels that enable the wearer to glide swiftly over a floor or other surface

rolling mill 1 a mill or factory where ingots of heated metal are passed between rollers to produce sheets or bars of a required cross section and form 2 a machine having rollers that may be shaped to reduce ingots, etc, to a required cross section and form

rolling stock the wheeled vehicles collectively used on a railway, including the locomotives, passenger coaches, freight wagons, guard's vans, etc.

Rollins Sonny, original name *Theodore Walter Rollins*. born 1930, US jazz tenor saxophonist, noted for his improvisation

Rollo ?860–?930 AD, Norse war leader who received from Charles the Simple a fief that formed the basis of the duchy of Normandy

roll-on/roll-off denoting a cargo ship or ferry designed so that vehicles can be driven straight on and straight off

ROM *Computing* read only memory: a storage device that holds data permanently and cannot in normal circumstances be altered by the programmer

Romagna an area of N Italy: part of the Papal States up to 1860

Romains Jules pseudonym of *Louis Farigoule*. 1885–1972, French poet, dramatist, and novelist. His works include the novel *Men of Good Will* (1932–46)

roman a metrical narrative in medieval French literature derived from the *chansons de geste*

Roman 1 of or relating to Rome or its inhabitants in ancient or modern times 2 of or relating to Roman Catholicism or the Roman Catholic Church 3 denoting, relating to, or having the style of architecture used by the ancient Romans, characterized by large-scale masonry domes, barrel vaults, and semicircular arches **4** a citizen or inhabitant of ancient or modern Rome **5** *Informal* short for **Roman Catholic**

Roman alphabet the alphabet evolved by the ancient Romans for the writing of Latin, based upon an Etruscan form derived from the Greeks and ultimately from the Phoenicians. The alphabet serves for writing most of the languages of W Europe and many other languages

Roman Catholic 1 of or relating to the Roman Catholic Church **2** a member of this Church

Roman Catholic Church the Christian Church over which the pope presides, with administrative headquarters in the Vatican
▷http://www.vatican.va/

romance 1 a narrative in verse or prose, written in a vernacular language in the Middle Ages, dealing with strange and exciting adventures of chivalrous heroes **2** any similar narrative work dealing with events and characters remote from ordinary life **3** the literary genre represented by works of these kinds **4** (in Spanish literature) a short narrative poem, usually an epic or historical ballad **5** a lyrical song or short instrumental composition having a simple melody

Romanesque 1 denoting, relating to, or having the style of architecture used in W and S Europe from the 9th to the 12th century, characterized by the rounded arch, the groin vault, massive-masonry wall construction, and a restrained use of mouldings **2** denoting or relating to a corresponding style in painting, sculpture, etc.
▷www.britainexpress.com/architecture

Romania, Rumania, *or* **Roumania** a republic in SE Europe, bordering on the Black Sea: united in 1861; became independent in 1878; Communist government set up in 1945; became a socialist republic in 1965; a more democratic regime was installed after a revolution in 1989. It consists chiefly of a great central arc of the Carpathian Mountains and Transylvanian Alps, with the plains of Walachia, Moldavia, and Dobriya on the south and east and the Pannonian Plain in the west. Official language: Romanian. Religion: Romanian Orthodox (Christian) majority. Currency: leu. Capital: Bucharest. Pop: 22 280 000 (2004 est). Area: 237 500 sq km (91 699 sq miles)

Romanian, Rumanian, *or* **Roumanian** the official language of Romania, belonging to the Romance group of the Indo-European family

Roman nose a nose having a high prominent bridge

Romanov any of the Russian imperial dynasty that ruled from the crowning (1613) of Mikhail Fyodorovich to the abdication (1917) of Nicholas II during the February Revolution

romantic 1 of or relating to a movement in European art, music, and literature in the late 18th and early 19th centuries, characterized by an emphasis on feeling and content rather than order and form, on the sublime, supernatural, and exotic, and the free expression of the passions and individuality **2** a person whose tastes in art, literature, etc, lie mainly in romanticism; romanticist **3** a poet, composer, etc, of the romantic period or whose main inspiration or interest is romanticism

▷http://classicalmus.hispeed.com/romantic.html

romanticism the theory, practice, and style of the romantic art, music, and literature of the late 18th and early 19th centuries, usually opposed to classicism
▷www.artchive.com/ftp_site_reg.htm
▷www.artcyclopedia.com/history/romanticism.html
▷www.artlex.com/ArtLex/r/romanticism.html

Romany *or* **Romani 1 a** another name for a **Gypsy b** (*as modifier*): *Romany customs* **2** the language of the Gypsies, belonging to the Indic branch of the Indo-European family, but incorporating extensive borrowings from local European languages. Most of its 250 000 speakers are bilingual. It is extinct in Britain

Romberg Sigmund 1887–1951, US composer of operettas, born in Hungary. He wrote *The Student Prince* (1924) and *The Desert Song* (1926)

Rome 1 the capital of Italy, on the River Tiber: includes the independent state of the Vatican City; traditionally founded by Romulus on the Palatine Hill in 753 BC, later spreading to six other hills east of the Tiber; capital of the Roman Empire; a great cultural and artistic centre, esp during the Renaissance. Pop: 2 546 804 (2001) **2** the Roman Empire **3** the Roman Catholic Church or Roman Catholicism

Rommel Erwin , nicknamed *the Desert Fox*. 1891–1944, German field marshal, noted for his brilliant generalship in N Africa in World War II. Later a commander in N France, he committed suicide after the officers' plot against Hitler

Romney George 1734–1802, English painter, who painted more than 50 portraits of Lady Hamilton in various historical roles

Romney Marsh 1 a marshy area of SE England, on the Kent coast between New Romney and Rye: includes Dungeness **2** a type of hardy British sheep from this area, with long wool, bred for mutton

Roncesvalles a village in N Spain, in the Pyrenees: a nearby pass was the scene of the defeat of Charlemagne and death of Roland in 778

rondeau a poem consisting of 13 or 10 lines with two rhymes and having the opening words of the first line used as an unrhymed refrain

rondo a piece of music in which a refrain is repeated between episodes: often constitutes the form of the last movement of a sonata or concerto

Ronsard Pierre de 1524–85, French poet, foremost of the *Pléiade*

roo *Austral, informal* a kangaroo

rood 1 a a crucifix, esp one set on a beam or screen at the entrance to the chancel of a church **b** (*as modifier*): *rood beam* **2** the Cross on which Christ was crucified **3** a unit of area equal to one quarter of an acre or 0.10117 hectares **4** a unit of area equal to 40 square rods

roof 1 a a structure that covers or forms the top of a building **b** (*as modifier*): *a roof garden* **2** *Anatomy* any structure that covers an organ or part **3** *Mountaineering* the underside of a projecting overhang

roof garden a garden on a flat roof of a building

roof rack a rack attached to the roof of a motor vehicle for carrying luggage, skis, etc.

rook¹ a large Eurasian passerine bird, *Corvus frugilegus*, with a black plumage and a whitish base to its bill: family *Corvidae* (crows)

rook² a chesspiece that may move any number of unoccupied squares in a straight line, horizontally or vertically.

rookery 1 a group of nesting rooks 2 a clump of trees containing rooks' nests 3 a a breeding ground or communal living area of certain other species of gregarious birds or mammals, esp penguins or seals b a colony of any such creatures

room an area within a building enclosed by a floor, a ceiling, and walls or partitions

Rooney Wayne born 1985, English footballer; he played for Everton (2002–2004) and plays for Manchester United (from 2004) and England (from 2003)

Roosevelt 1 (Anna) Eleanor 1884–1962, US writer, diplomat, and advocate of liberal causes: delegate to the United Nations (1945–52) 2 her husband, **Franklin Delano**, known as FDR. 1882–1945, 32nd president of the US (1933–45); elected four times. He instituted major reforms (the **New Deal**) to counter the economic crisis of the 1930s and was a forceful leader during World War II 3 **Theodore** 1858–1919, 26th president of the US (1901–09). A proponent of extending military power, he won for the US the right to build the Panama Canal (1903). He won the Nobel peace prize (1906), for mediating in the Russo-Japanese war

roost a place, perch, branch, etc, where birds, esp domestic fowl, rest or sleep

rooster *Chiefly US and Canadian* the male of the domestic fowl; a cock

root 1 a the organ of a higher plant that anchors the rest of the plant in the ground, absorbs water and mineral salts from the soil, and does not bear leaves or buds b (loosely) any of the branches of such an organ 2 any plant part, such as a rhizome or tuber, that is similar to a root in structure, function, or appearance 3 *Anatomy* the embedded portion of a tooth, nail, hair, etc. 4 *Bible* a descendant 5 *Maths* a number or quantity that when multiplied by itself a certain number of times equals a given number or quantity 6 *Maths* a number that when substituted for the variable satisfies a given equation 7 *Music* (in harmony) the note forming the foundation of a chord

root canal the passage in the root of a tooth through which its nerves and blood vessels enter the pulp cavity

root mean square *Maths* the square root of the average of the squares of a set of numbers or quantities

rootstock 1 another name for **rhizome** 2 another name for **stock** 3 *Biology* a basic structure from which offshoots have developed

rope 1 a a fairly thick cord made of twisted and intertwined hemp or other fibres or of wire or other strong material b (*as modifier*): *a rope bridge*

Roraima a state of N Brazil: chiefly rainforest. Capital: Boa Vista. Pop: 346 871 (2002). Area: 230 104 sq km (89 740 sq miles)

rorqual any of several whalebone whales of the genus *Balaenoptera*, esp *B. physalus*: family *Balaenopteridae*. They have a dorsal fin and a series of grooves along the throat and chest

Rorschach test *Psychol* a personality test consisting of a number of unstructured ink blots presented for interpretation

Rosa¹ Salvator 1615–73, Italian artist, noted esp for his romantic landscapes

Rosa² Monte a mountain between Italy and Switzerland: the highest in the Pennine Alps. Height: 4634 m (15 204 ft)

rosaceous 1 of, relating to, or belonging to the *Rosaceae*, a family of flowering plants typically having white, yellow, pink, or red five-petalled flowers. The family includes the rose, strawberry, blackberry, and many fruit trees such as apple, cherry, and plum 2 of the colour rose; rose-coloured; rosy

Rosario an inland port in E Argentina, on the Paraná River: the second largest city in the country; industrial centre. Pop: 1 312 000 (2005 est)

rosary 1 *RC Church* a a series of prayers counted on a string of beads, usually consisting of five or 15 decades of Aves, each decade beginning with a Paternoster and ending with a Gloria b a string of 55 or 165 beads used to count these prayers as they are recited 2 (in other religions) a similar string of beads used in praying 3 a bed or garden of roses

Roscius 1 full name *Quintus Roscius Gallus*. died 62 BC, Roman actor 2 any actor

Roscommon 1 an inland county of N central Republic of Ireland, in Connacht: economy based on cattle and sheep farming. County town: Roscommon. Pop: 53 774 (2002). Area: 2463 sq km (951 sq miles) 2 a former name for **Galway**

rose 1 any shrub or climbing plant of the rosaceous genus *Rosa*, typically having prickly stems, compound leaves, and fragrant flowers 2 the flower of any of these plants 3 any of various similar plants, such as the rockrose and Christmas rose 4 a moderate purplish-red colour; purplish pink 5 a perforated cap fitted to the spout of a watering can or the end of a hose, causing the water to issue in a spray 6 *Electrical engineering* a circular boss attached to a ceiling through which the flexible lead of an electric-light fitting passes

Rosebery Earl of, title of *Archibald Philip Primrose*. 1847–1929, British Liberal statesman; prime minister (1894–95)

rosebud the bud of a rose

rosehip the berry-like fruit of a rose plant

rosella any of various Australian parrots of the genus *Platycercus*, such as *P. elegans* (**crimson rosella**), often kept as cage birds

rosemary an aromatic European shrub, *Rosmarinus officinalis*, widely cultivated for its grey-green evergreen leaves, which are used in cookery for flavouring and yield a fragrant oil used in the manufacture of perfumes: family *Lamiaceae* (labiates). It is the traditional flower of remembrance

Rosenberg 1 **Alfred** 1893–1946, German Nazi politician and writer, who devised much of the racial ideology of Nazism: hanged for war crimes 2 **Isaac** 1890–1918, British poet and painter, best known for his poems about life in the trenches during World War I: died in action 3 **Julius** 1918–53, US spy, who, with his wife **Ethel** (1914–53), was executed for passing information about nuclear weapons to the Russians

rosette 1 another name for **rose window** 2 a rose-shaped patch of colour, such as one of the clusters of spots marking a leopard's fur 3 *Botany* a circular cluster of leaves growing from the base of a stem

rose window a circular window, esp one that has ornamental tracery radiating from the centre to form a symmetrical roselike pattern

rosewood 1 the hard dark wood of any of various tropical and subtropical leguminous trees, esp of the genus *Dalbergia*. It has a roselike scent and is used in cabinetwork 2 any of the trees yielding this wood

Rosh Hashanah or **Rosh Hashana** the festival marking the Jewish New Year, celebrated on the first and second days of Tishri, and marked by penitential prayers and by the blowing of the shofar

rosin a translucent brittle amber substance produced in the distillation of crude turpentine oleoresin and used esp in making varnishes, printing inks, and sealing waxes and for treating the bows of stringed instruments

Roskilde a city in Denmark, on NE Zealand west of Copenhagen: capital of Denmark from the 10th century to 1443; scene of the signing (1658) of the **Peace of Roskilde** between Denmark and Sweden. Pop: 44 205 (2004 est)

Ross 1 Diana born 1944, US singer: lead vocalist (1961–69) with Motown group the Supremes, whose hits include "Baby Love" (1964). Her subsequent recordings include *Lady Sings the Blues* (film soundtrack, 1972), and *Chain Reaction* (1986) 2 Sir **James Clark** 1800–62, British naval officer; explorer of the Arctic and Antarctic. He located the north magnetic pole (1831) and discovered the Ross Sea during an Antarctic voyage (1839–43) 3 his uncle, Sir **John** 1777–1856, Scottish naval officer and Arctic explorer 4 Sir **Ronald** 1857–1932, English bacteriologist, who discovered the transmission of malaria by mosquitoes: Nobel prize for physiology or medicine 1902

Ross and Cromarty (until 1975) a county of N Scotland, including the island of Lewis and many islets: now split between the Highland and Western Isles council areas

Ross Dependency a section of Antarctica administered by New Zealand. (Claims are suspended under the Antarctic Treaty of 1959). Includes the coastal regions of Victoria Land and King Edward VII Land, the Ross Sea and islands, and the Ross Ice Shelf. Area: about 414 400 sq km (160 000 sq miles)

Rossellini Roberto 1906–77, Italian film director. His films include *Rome, Open City* (1945), *Paisà* (1946), and *L'Amore* (1948)

Rossetti 1 Christina Georgina 1830–94, British poet 2 her brother, **Dante Gabriel** 1828–82, British poet and painter: a leader of the Pre-Raphaelites

Rossini Gioacchino Antonio 1792–1868, Italian composer, esp of operas, such as *The Barber of Seville* (1816) and *William Tell* (1829)

Ross Island an island in the W Ross Sea: contains the active volcano Mount Erebus

Ross Sea a large arm of the S Pacific in Antarctica, incorporating the Ross Ice Shelf and lying between Victoria Land and the Edward VII Peninsula

Rostand Edmond 1868–1918, French playwright and poet in the romantic tradition; best known for his verse drama *Cyrano de Bergerac* (1897)

Rostock a port in NE Germany, in Mecklenburg-West Pomerania on the Warnow estuary 13 km (8 miles) from the Baltic and its outport, Warnemünde: the chief port of the former East Germany; university (1419). Pop: 198 303 (2003 est)

Rostov or **Rostov-on-Don** a port in S Russia, on the River Don 48 km (30 miles) from the Sea of Azov: industrial centre. Pop: 1 081 000 (2005 est)

Rostropovich Mstislav Leopoldovich born 1927, Soviet cellist, composer, and conductor; became a US citizen in 1978 after losing Soviet citizenship (restored in 1990)

rostrum 1 a platform or dais in front of an orchestra on which the conductor stands 2 another word for **ram** (sense 4) 3 the prow or beak of an ancient Roman ship 4 *Biology, Zoology* a beak or beaklike part

rot 1 the process of rotting or the state of being rotten 2 something decomposed, disintegrated, or degenerate 3 short for **dry rot** 4 *Pathol* any putrefactive decomposition of tissues 5 *Vet science* a contagious fungal disease of the feet of sheep characterized by inflammation, swelling, a foul-smelling discharge, and lameness

rotary 1 a part of a machine that rotates about an axis 2 *US and Canadian* another term for **roundabout** (for traffic)

Rotary Club any of the local clubs that form **Rotary International**, an international association of professional and businessmen founded in the US in 1905 to promote community service

rotate *Botany* designating a corolla the united petals of which radiate from a central point like the spokes of a wheel

Rotavator or **Rotovator** *Trademark* a type of machine with rotating blades that will break up soil

rote an ancient violin-like musical instrument; crwth

rotgut *Facetious slang* alcoholic drink, esp spirits, of inferior quality

Roth Philip born 1933, US novelist. His works include *Goodbye, Columbus* (1959), *Portnoy's Complaint* (1969), *My Life as a Man* (1974), *Sabbath's Theater* (1995), *The Human Stain* (2000), and *The Plot Against America* (2004)

Rotherham 1 an industrial town in N England, in Rotherham unitary authority, South Yorkshire. Pop: 117 262 (2001) 2 a unitary authority in N England, in South Yorkshire. Pop: 251 500 (2003 est). Area: 283 sq km (109 sq miles)

Rothermere Viscount title of *Harold Sidney Harmsworth*. 1868–1940, British newspaper magnate

Rothesay a town in SW Scotland, in Argyll and Bute, on the E coast of the Isle of Bute. Pop: 5017 (2001)

Rothko Mark 1903–70, US abstract expressionist painter, born in Russia

Rothschild a powerful family of European Jewish bankers, prominent members of which were 1 Lionel **Nathan**, Baron de Rothschild. 1809–79, British banker and first Jewish member of Parliament 2 his grandfather **Meyer Amschel** 1743–1812, German financier and founder of the Rothschild banking firm 3 his son, **Nathan Meyer**, Baron de Rothschild. 1777–1836, British banker, born in Germany

rotor 1 the rotating member of a machine or device, esp the armature of a motor or generator or the rotating assembly of a turbine 2 a device having blades radiating from a central hub that is rotated to produce thrust to lift and propel a helicopter 3 the revolving arm of the distributor of an internal-combustion engine 4 a violent rolling wave of air occurring in the lee of a mountain or hill, in which the air rotates about a horizontal axis

Rotorua a city in New Zealand, on N central North Island at the SW end of Lake Rotorua: centre of forestry; noted for volcanic activity. Pop: 67 800 (2004 est)

rotten 1 affected with rot; decomposing, decaying, or putrid 2 (of rocks, soils, etc) soft and crumbling, esp as a result of weathering

Rotterdam a port in the SW Netherlands, in South Holland province: the second largest city of the Netherlands and one of the world's largest ports; oil refineries, shipbuilding yards, etc. Pop: 600 000 (2003 est)

Rottweiler a breed of large robustly built dog with a smooth coat of black with dark tan markings on the face, chest, and legs. It was previously a docked breed

rotunda a building or room having a circular plan, esp one that has a dome

Rouault Georges 1871–1958, French expressionist artist. His work is deeply religious; it includes much stained glass

Roubaix a city in N France near the Belgian border: forms, with Tourcoing, a large industrial conurbation. Pop: 96 984 (1999)

Roubiliac or **Roubillac** Louis-François ?1695–1762, French sculptor: lived chiefly in England: his sculptures include the statue of Handel in Vauxhall Gardens (1737)

rouble or **ruble** 1 the standard monetary unit of Belarus and Russia, divided into 100 kopecks 2 the former standard monetary unit of Tajikistan, divided into 100 tanga

Rouen a city in N France, on the River Seine: the chief river port of France; became capital of the duchy of Normandy in 912; scene of the burning of Joan of Arc (1431); university (1964). Pop: 106 592 (1999)

Rouget de Lisle Claude Joseph 1760–1836, French army officer: composer of the *Marseillaise* (1792), the French national anthem

rough 1 a sketch or preliminary piece of artwork 2 **the rough** *Golf* the part of the course bordering the fairways where the grass is untrimmed 3 *Tennis, Squash, Badminton* the side of a racket on which the binding strings form an uneven line

roughage the coarse indigestible constituents of food or fodder, which provide bulk to the diet and promote normal bowel function

roughshod (of a horse) shod with rough-bottomed shoes to prevent sliding

Roulers a city in NW Belgium, in West Flanders province: electronics. Pop: 55 273 (2004 est)

roulette 1 a gambling game in which a ball is dropped onto a spinning horizontal wheel divided into 37 or 38 coloured and numbered slots, with players betting on the slot into which the ball will fall 2 **a** a toothed

wheel for making a line of perforations **b** a tiny slit made by such a wheel on a sheet of stamps as an aid to tearing it apart 3 a curve generated by a point on one curve rolling on another

round 1 *Maths* **a** forming or expressed by an integer or whole number, with no fraction **b** expressed to the nearest ten, hundred, or thousand 2 **in the round** *Theatre* with the audience all round the stage 3 a playing of all the holes on a golf course 4 *Archery* a specified number of arrows shot from a specified distance 5 *Music* a part song in which the voices follow each other at equal intervals at the same pitch 6 a sequence of bells rung in order of treble to tenor 7 a dance in which the dancers move in a circle

roundabout 1 *Brit* a revolving circular platform provided with wooden animals, seats, etc, on which people ride for amusement; merry-go-round 2 a road junction in which traffic streams circulate around a central island

round dance 1 a dance in which the dancers form a circle 2 a ballroom dance, such as the waltz, in which couples revolve

roundel 1 a form of rondeau consisting of three stanzas each of three lines with a refrain after the first and the third 2 a small ornamental circular window, panel, medallion, plate, disc, etc. 3 another word for **roundelay**

roundelay 1 a slow medieval dance performed in a circle 2 a song in which a line or phrase is repeated as a refrain

rounders *Brit* a ball game in which players run between posts after hitting the ball, scoring a 'rounder' if they run round all four before the ball is retrieved
▷www.roundersonline.net

Roundhead *English history* a supporter of Parliament against Charles I during the Civil War

roundhouse 1 a circular building in which railway locomotives are serviced or housed, radial tracks being fed by a central turntable 2 *Boxing, slang* **a** a swinging punch or style of punching **b** (as modifier): *a roundhouse style* 3 *Pinochle, US* a meld of all four kings and queens 4 *Obsolete* a cabin on the quarterdeck of a sailing ship

round-shouldered denoting a faulty posture characterized by drooping shoulders and a slight forward bending of the back

Round Table **the** 1 (in Arthurian legend) the table of King Arthur, shaped so that his knights could sit around it without any having precedence 2 Arthur and his knights collectively 3 one of an organization of clubs of young business and professional men who meet in order to further social and business activities and charitable work 4 (in New Zealand) an organization of businessmen supporting policies of the New Right

roundworm any nematode worm, esp *Ascaris lumbricoides*, a common intestinal parasite of man and pigs

Rousseau 1 Henri, known as *le Douanier*. 1844–1910, French painter, who created bold dreamlike pictures, often of exotic landscapes in a naive style. Among his works are *Sleeping Gypsy* (1897) and *Jungle with a Lion* (1904–06). He also worked as a customs official 2 Jean

Jacques 1712–78, French philosopher and writer, born in Switzerland, who strongly influenced the theories of the French Revolution and the romantics. Many of his ideas spring from his belief in the natural goodness of man, whom he felt was warped by society. His works include *Du contrat social* (1762), *Émile* (1762), and his *Confessions* (1782) **3 Théodore** 1812–67, French landscape painter: leader of the Barbizon school

Roussillon a former province of S France: united with Aragon in 1172; passed to the French crown in 1659; now forms part of the region of Languedoc-Roussillon

rout *Law* a group of three or more people proceeding to commit an illegal act

route **1** *US* a main road between cities **2** *Mountaineering* the direction or course taken by a climb **3** *Med* the means by which a drug or agent is administered or enters the body, such as by mouth or by injection

router¹ any of various tools or machines for hollowing out, cutting grooves, etc.

router² *Computing* a device that allows packets of data to be moved efficiently between two points on a network

routine **1** *Computing* a program or part of a program performing a specific function **2** a set sequence of dance steps

rove wool, cotton, etc, thus prepared

row **1** *Chiefly Brit* a street, esp a narrow one lined with identical houses **2** *Maths* a horizontal linear arrangement of numbers, quantities, or terms, esp in a determinant or matrix **3** a horizontal rank of squares on a chessboard or draughtboard

Rowe Nicholas 1674–1718, English dramatist, who produced the first critical edition of Shakespeare; poet laureate (1715–18). His plays include *Tamerlane* (1702) and *The Fair Penitent* (1703)

rowel **1** a small spiked wheel attached to a spur **2** *Vet science, Obsolete* a piece of leather or other material inserted under the skin of a horse to act as a seton and allow drainage

rowing boat *Chiefly Brit* a small boat propelled by one or more pairs of oars

Rowlandson Thomas 1756–1827, English caricaturist, noted for the vigour of his attack on sordid aspects of contemporary society and on statesmen such as Napoleon

Rowley Thomas ?1586–?1642, English dramatist, who collaborated with John Ford and Thomas Dekker on *The Witch of Edmonton* (1621) and with Thomas Middleton on *The Changeling* (1622)

Rowling J(oanne) K(athleen). born 1965, British novelist; author of the bestselling series of children's books featuring the boy wizard Harry Potter, which began with *Harry Potter and the Philosopher's Stone* (1995)

rowlock a swivelling device attached to the gunwale of a boat that holds an oar in place and acts as a fulcrum during rowing

Roxburghshire (until 1975) a county of SE Scotland, now part of Scottish Borders council area

royal **1** of, relating to, or befitting a king, queen, or other monarch; regal **2** established, chartered by, under the patronage or in the service of royalty **3** being a member of a royal family **4** *Nautical* just above the topgallant (in the phrase **royal mast**) **5** *Informal* a member of a royal

family **6** a stag with antlers having 12 or more branches **7** *Nautical* a sail set next above the topgallant, on a royal mast

royalist **1** a supporter of a monarch or monarchy, esp a supporter of the Stuarts during the English Civil War **2** *Informal* an extreme reactionary or conservative

royal jelly a substance secreted by the pharyngeal glands of worker bees and fed to all larvae when very young and to larvae destined to become queens throughout their development

Royal Navy the navy of the United Kingdom
▷www.royal-navy.mod.uk

royalty **1** the rank, power, or position of a king or queen **2 a** royal persons collectively **b** one who belongs to the royal family **3** any quality characteristic of a monarch; kingliness or regal dignity

royal warrant an authorization to a tradesman to supply goods to a royal household

Royce Josiah 1855–1916, US philosopher of monistic idealism. In his ethical studies he emphasized the need for individual loyalty to the world community

Ruanda-Urundi a former territory of central Africa: part of German East Africa from 1890; a League of Nations mandate under Belgian administration from 1919; a United Nations trusteeship from 1946; divided into the independent states of Rwanda and Burundi in 1962

rub **1** *Bowls* an uneven patch in the green **2 a** *Golf* an incident of accidental interference with the ball **b** *Informal* a piece of good or bad luck

rubato *Music* **1** flexibility of tempo in performance **2** to be played with a flexible tempo

rubber¹ **1** a cream to dark brown elastic material obtained by coagulating and drying the latex from certain plants, esp the tree *Hevea brasiliensis* **2** any of a large variety of elastomers produced by improving the properties of natural rubber or by synthetic means **3** a coarse file

rubber² *Bridge, Whist* **a** a match of three games **b** the deal that wins such a match

rubber plant **1** a moraceous plant, *Ficus elastica*, with glossy leathery leaves: a tall tree in India and Malaya, it is cultivated as a house plant in Europe and America **2** any of several tropical trees, the sap of which yields rubber

rubber tree a tropical American euphorbiaceous tree, *Hevea brasiliensis*, cultivated throughout the tropics, esp in Malaya, for the latex of its stem, which is the major source of commercial rubber

Rubbra (Charles) Edmund 1901–86, English composer of works in a traditional idiom

rubella a mild contagious viral disease, somewhat similar to measles, characterized by cough, sore throat, skin rash, and occasionally vomiting. It can cause congenital defects if caught during the first three months of pregnancy

Rubens Sir Peter Paul 1577–1640, Flemish painter, regarded as the greatest exponent of the Baroque: appointed (1609) painter to Archduke Albert of Austria, who gave him many commissions, artistic and diplomatic. He was knighted by Charles I of England in 1629. His prolific output includes the triptych in Antwerp

Cathedral, *Descent from the Cross* (1611–14), *The Rape of the Sabines* (1635), and his *Self-Portrait* (?1639)

Rubicon 1 a stream in N Italy: in ancient times the boundary between Italy and Cisalpine Gaul. By leading his army across it and marching on Rome in 49 BC, Julius Caesar broke the law that a general might not lead an army out of the province to which he was posted and so committed himself to civil war with the senatorial party 2 a penalty in piquet by which the score of a player who fails to reach 100 points in six hands is added to his opponent's

rubicund of a reddish colour; ruddy; rosy

rubidium a soft highly reactive radioactive element of the alkali metal group; the 16th most abundant element in the earth's crust (310 parts per million), occurring principally in pollucite, carnallite, and lepidolite. It is used in electronic valves, photocells, and special glass. Symbol: Rb; atomic no.: 37; atomic wt.: 85.4678; half-life of ^{87}Rb: 5×10^{11} years; valency: 1, 2, 3, or 4; relative density: 1.532 (solid), 1.475 (liquid); melting pt.: 39.48°C; boiling pt.: 688°C

Rubinstein 1 Anton Grigorevich 1829–94, Russian composer and pianist 2 Artur 1886–1982, US pianist, born in Poland

rubric 1 a set of directions for the conduct of Christian church services, often printed in red in a prayer book or missal 2 instructions to a candidate at the head of the examination paper

ruby 1 a deep red transparent precious variety of corundum: occurs naturally in Myanmar and Sri Lanka but is also synthesized. It is used as a gemstone, in lasers, and for bearings and rollers in watchmaking. Formula: Al_2O_3 2 the deep-red colour of a ruby

ruck 1 *Rugby* a loose scrum that forms around the ball when it is on the ground 2 *Australian Rules football* the three players, two ruckmen and a rover, that do not have fixed positions but follow the ball closely

Ruda Śląska a town in SW Poland: coalmining. Pop: 159 665 (1999 est)

rudder 1 *Nautical* a pivoted vertical vane that projects into the water at the stern of a vessel and can be controlled by a tiller, wheel, or other apparatus to steer the vessel 2 a vertical control surface attached to the rear of the fin used to steer an aircraft, in conjunction with the ailerons

rudiment *Biology* an organ or part in its earliest recognizable form, esp one in an embryonic or vestigial state

Rudolf¹ or **Rudolph** 1858–89, archduke of Austria, son of emperor Franz Joseph: he and his mistress committed suicide at the royal hunting lodge in Mayerling

Rudolf² **Lake** the former name (until 1979) of (Lake) Turkana

Rudolf I or **Rudolph I** 1218–91, king of Germany (1273–91): founder of the Hapsburg dynasty based on the duchies of Styria and Austria

rue any rutaceous plant of the genus *Ruta*, esp *R. graveolens*, an aromatic Eurasian shrub with small yellow flowers and evergreen leaves which yield an acrid volatile oil, formerly used medicinally as a narcotic stimulant

ruff¹ 1 a natural growth of long or coloured hair or feathers around the necks of certain animals or birds 2 a an Old World shore bird, *Philomachus pugnax*, the male of which has a large erectile ruff of feathers in the breeding season: family *Scolopacidae* (sandpipers, etc), order *Charadriiformes* b the male of this bird

ruff² *Cards* 1 another word for **trump** 2 an old card game similar to whist

ruffle a low continuous drumbeat

rufous reddish-brown

rug 1 a floor covering, smaller than a carpet and made of thick wool or of other material, such as an animal skin 2 *Chiefly Brit* a blanket, esp one used as a wrap or lap robe for travellers

rugby or **rugby football** 1 a form of football played with an oval ball in which the handling and carrying of the ball is permitted 2 *Canadian* another name for **Canadian football** See also **rugby league** or **rugby union**

Rugby a town in central England, in E Warwickshire: famous public school, founded in 1567. Pop: 61 988 (2001)

rugby league a form of rugby football played between teams of 13 players

▷http://world.rleague.com

rugby union a form of rugby football played between teams of 15 players

▷www.irfu.com
▷www.irfb.com

Ruhr the chief coalmining and industrial region of Germany: in North Rhine-Westphalia around the valley of the **River Ruhr** (a tributary of the Rhine 235 km (146 miles) long)

Ruisdael or **Ruysdael** Jacob van ?1628–82, Dutch landscape painter

rule 1 the exercise of governmental authority or control 2 the period of time in which a monarch or government has power 3 a prescribed method or procedure for solving a mathematical problem, or one constituting part of a computer program, usually expressed in an appropriate formalism 4 any of various devices with a straight edge for guiding or measuring; ruler 5 *Christianity* a systematic body of prescriptions defining the way of life to be followed by members of a religious order 6 *Law* an order by a court or judge

ruler 1 a person who rules or commands 2 a strip of wood, metal, or other material, having straight edges graduated usually in millimetres or inches, used for measuring and drawing straight lines

rum spirit made from sugar cane, either coloured brownish-red by the addition of caramel or by maturation in oak containers, or left white

rumba or **rhumba** 1 a rhythmic and syncopated Cuban dance in duple time 2 a ballroom dance derived from this 3 a piece of music composed for or in the rhythm of this dance

Rumford Count. See (Benjamin) Thompson

ruminant 1 any artiodactyl mammal of the suborder *Ruminantia*, the members of which chew the cud and have a stomach of four compartments, one of which is the rumen. The group includes deer, antelopes, cattle, sheep, and goats 2 any other animal that chews the cud, such as a camel 3 of, relating to, or belonging to the suborder *Ruminantia* 4 (of members of this suborder and related animals, such as camels) chewing the cud;

ruminating

rummy *or* **rum** a card game based on collecting sets and sequences

rump 1 the hindquarters of a mammal, not including the legs 2 the rear part of a bird's back, nearest to the tail 3 a person's buttocks

Rumsfeld Donald H born 1932, US Republican politician and businessman: US Secretary of Defense from 2001

run 1 an act, instance, or period of travelling in a vehicle, esp for pleasure 2 **a** a period of time during which a machine, computer, etc, operates **b** the amount of work performed in such a period 3 a continuous sequence of performances 4 *Cards* a sequence of winning cards in one suit, usually more than five 5 US a small stream 6 a steeply inclined pathway or course, esp a snow-covered one used for skiing and bobsleigh racing 7 a track or area frequented by animals 8 a group of animals of the same species moving together 9 the migration of fish upstream in order to spawn 10 *Nautical* **a** the tack of a sailing vessel in which the wind comes from astern **b** part of the hull of a vessel near the stern where it curves upwards and inwards 11 the movement of an aircraft along the ground during take-off or landing 12 *Music* a rapid scalelike passage of notes 13 *Cricket* a score of one, normally achieved by both batsmen running from one end of the wicket to the other after one of them has hit the ball 14 *Baseball* an instance of a batter touching all four bases safely, thereby scoring 15 *Golf* the distance that a ball rolls after hitting the ground 16 **the runs** *Slang* diarrhoea

runabout 1 a small car, esp one for use in a town 2 a light aircraft 3 a light motorboat

Runcorn a town in NW England, in Halton unitary authority, N Cheshire, on the Manchester Ship Canal: port and industrial centre; designated a new town in 1964. Pop: 60 072 (2001)

run down the process of a motor or mechanism coming gradually to a standstill after the source of power is removed

Rundstedt Karl Rudolf Gerd von 1875–1953, German field marshal; directed the conquest of Poland and France in World War II; commander of the Western Front (1942–44); led the Ardennes counteroffensive (Dec 1944)

rune 1 any of the characters of an ancient Germanic alphabet, derived from the Roman alphabet, in use, esp in Scandinavia, from the 3rd century AD to the end of the Middle Ages. Each character was believed to have a magical significance 2 any obscure piece of writing using mysterious symbols 3 a kind of Finnish poem or a stanza in such a poem

rung *Nautical* a spoke on a ship's wheel or a handle projecting from the periphery

runnel *Literary* a small stream

runner 1 a person who runs, esp an athlete 2 an employee of an art or antique dealer who visits auctions to bid on desired lots 3 a person engaged in the solicitation of business 4 **a** either of the strips of metal or wood on which a sledge runs **b** the blade of an ice skate 5 a roller or guide for a sliding component 6 a channel through which molten material enters a casting or moulding 7 the rotating element of a water turbine 8 any of various carangid fishes of temperate and

tropical seas, such as *Caranx crysos* (**blue runner**) of American Atlantic waters 9 *Botany* **a** a slender stem with very long internodes, as of the strawberry, that arches down to the ground and propagates by producing roots and shoots at the nodes or tip **b** a plant that propagates in this way 10 a strip of lace, linen, etc, placed across a table, dressing table, etc for protection and decoration 11 a narrow rug or carpet, as for a passage

running 1 (of a wound, sore, etc) discharging pus or a serous fluid 2 (of certain plants, plant stems, etc) creeping along the ground

running board a footboard along the side of a vehicle, esp an early motorcar

running mate 1 US a candidate for the subordinate of two linked positions, esp a candidate for the vice-presidency 2 a horse that pairs another in a team

Runnymede a meadow on the S bank of the Thames near Windsor, where King John met his rebellious barons in 1215 and acceded to Magna Carta

runoff 1 **a** *Sport* an extra race to decide the winner after a tie **b** *Politics* a contest or election held after a previous one has failed to produce a clear victory for any one person 2 *Geog* that portion of rainfall that runs into streams as surface water rather than being absorbed into ground water or evaporating

run-out 1 *Cricket* dismissal of a batsman by running him out 2 *Mechanical engineering* an imperfection of a rotating component so that not all parts revolve about their intended axes relative to each other

runt 1 the smallest and weakest young animal in a litter, esp the smallest piglet in a litter 2 a large pigeon, originally bred for eating

run-up *Sport* an approach run by an athlete for a long jump, pole vault, etc.

runway 1 a hard level roadway or other surface from which aircraft take off and on which they land 2 *Forestry, US and Canadian* a chute for sliding logs down 3 a narrow ramp extending from the stage into the audience in a theatre, nightclub, etc, esp as used by models in a fashion show

Runyon (**Alfred**) **Damon** 1884–1946, US short-story writer, best known for his humorous tales about racy Broadway characters. His story collections include *Guys and Dolls* (1932), which became the basis of a musical (1950)

rupee the standard monetary unit of India, Nepal, and Pakistan (divided into 100 paise), Sri Lanka, Mauritius, and the Seychelles (divided into 100 cents)

Rupert Prince 1619–82, German-born nephew of Charles I: Royalist general during the Civil War (until 1646) and commander of the Royalist fleet (1648–50). After the Restoration he was an admiral of the English fleet in wars against the Dutch

rupture *Pathol* **a** the breaking or tearing of a bodily structure or part **b** another word for **hernia**

rural dean *Chiefly Brit* a clergyman having authority over a group of parishes

Rurik *or* **Ryurik** died 879. Varangian (Scandinavian Viking) leader who founded the Russian monarchy. He gained control over Novgorod (?862) and his dynasty, the**Rurikids**, ruled until 1598

Ruritania 1 an imaginary kingdom of central Europe: setting of several novels by Anthony Hope, esp *The Prisoner of Zenda* (1894) 2 any setting of adventure, romance, and intrigue

Ruse a city in NE Bulgaria, on the River Danube: the chief river port and one of the largest industrial centres in Bulgaria. Pop: 172 000 (2005 est)

rush 1 any annual or perennial plant of the genus *Juncus*, growing in wet places and typically having grasslike cylindrical leaves and small green or brown flowers: family *Juncaceae* Many species are used to make baskets 2 any of various similar or related plants, such as the woodrush, scouring rush, and spike-rush

Rushdie (Ahmed) Salman born 1947, British writer, born in India, whose novels include *Midnight's Children* (1981), which won the Booker prize, *Shame* (1983), and *The Ground Beneath Her Feet* (1998). His novel *The Satanic Verses* (1988) was regarded as blasphemous by many Muslims and he was forced into hiding (1989) when the Ayatollah Khomeini called for his death

Rushmore Mount a mountain in W South Dakota, in the Black Hills: a national memorial, with the faces of presidents George Washington, Abraham Lincoln, Thomas Jefferson, and Theodore Roosevelt carved into its side by Gutzon Borglum between 1927 and 1941. Height: 1841 m (6040 ft)

Rusk (David) Dean 1909–94, US statesman: secretary of state (1961–69). He defended US military involvement in Vietnam and opposed recognition of communist China

Ruskin John 1819–1900, English art critic and social reformer. He was a champion of the Gothic Revival and the Pre-Raphaelites and saw a close connection between art and morality. From about 1860 he argued vigorously for social and economic planning. His works include *Modern Painters* (1843–60), *The Stones of Venice* (1851–53), *Unto this Last* (1862), *Time and Tide* (1867), and *Fors Clavigera* (1871–84)

Russell 1 Bertrand (Arthur William), 3rd Earl. 1872–1970, British philosopher and mathematician. His books include *Principles of Mathematics* (1903), *Principia Mathematica* (1910–13) with A. N. Whitehead, *Introduction to Mathematical Philosophy* (1919), *The Problems of Philosophy* (1912), *The Analysis of Mind* (1921), and *An Enquiry into Meaning and Truth* (1940): Nobel prize for literature 1950 2 George William pen name *æ*. 1867–1935, Irish poet and journalist 3 Henry Norris 1877–1957, US astronomer and astrophysicist, who originated one form of the Hertzsprung–Russell diagram 4 John, 1st Earl. 1792–1878, British statesman; prime minister (1846–52; 1865–66). He led the campaign to carry the 1832 Reform Act 5 Ken born 1927, British film director. His films include *Women in Love* (1969), *The Music Lovers* (1970), *The Boy Friend* (1971), *Valentino* (1977), *Gothic* (1986), and *The Rainbow* (1989)

russet 1 any of various apples with rough brownish-red skins 2 brown with a yellowish or reddish tinge 3 a a rough homespun fabric, reddish-brown in colour, formerly in use for clothing b *(as modifier)*: *a russet coat*

Russia full name Russian Federation 1 the largest country in the world, covering N Eurasia and bordering on the Pacific and Arctic Oceans and the Baltic, Black, and Caspian Seas: originating from the principality of Muscovy in the 17th century, it expanded to become the Russian Empire; the Tsar was overthrown in 1917 and the Communist Russian Soviet Federative Socialist Republic was created; this merged with neighbouring Soviet Republics in 1922 to form the Soviet Union; on the disintegration of the Soviet Union in 1991 the Russian Federation was established as an independent state. Official language: Russian. Religion: non-religious and Russian orthodox Christian. Currency: rouble. Capital: Moscow. Pop: 142 397 000 (2004 est). Area: 17 074 984 sq km (6 592 658 sq miles) 2 another name for the former Soviet Union 3 another name for the former Russian Soviet Federative Socialist Republic

Russian 1 the official language of Russia: an Indo-European language belonging to the East Slavonic branch 2 the official language of the former Soviet Union

Russian roulette a game of chance in which each player in turn spins the cylinder of a revolver loaded with only one cartridge and presses the trigger with the barrel against his own head

Russian Soviet Federative Socialist Republic (formerly) the largest administrative division of the Soviet Union

rust 1 a reddish-brown oxide coating formed on iron or steel by the action of oxygen and moisture 2 a strong brown colour, sometimes with a reddish or yellowish tinge

rustic 1 (of masonry) having a rusticated finish 2 brick or stone having a rough finish

rut 1 a recurrent period of sexual excitement and reproductive activity in certain male ruminants, such as the deer, that corresponds to the period of oestrus in females 2 another name for **oestrus**

rutabaga *US and Canadian* a Eurasian plant, *Brassica napus* (or *B. napobrassica*), cultivated for its bulbous edible root, which is used as a vegetable and as cattle fodder: family *Brassicaceae* (crucifers)

Ruth¹ 1 *Old Testament* a a Moabite woman, who left her own people to remain with her mother-in-law Naomi, and became the wife of Boaz; an ancestress of David b the book in which these events are recounted 2 George Herman, nicknamed *Babe*. 1895–1948, US professional baseball player from 1914 to 1935

Ruth² *Old Testament* a a Moabite woman, who left her own people to remain with her mother-in-law Naomi, and became the wife of Boaz; an ancestress of David b the book in which these events are recounted

Ruthenia a region of E Europe on the south side of the Carpathian Mountains: belonged to Hungary from the 14th century, to Czechoslovakia from 1918 to 1939, and was ceded to the former Soviet Union in 1945; in 1991 it became part of the newly independent Ukraine

ruthenium a hard brittle white element of the platinum metal group. It occurs free with other platinum metals in pentlandite and other ores and is used to harden platinum and palladium. Symbol: Ru; atomic no.: 44; atomic wt.: 101.07; valency: 0–8; relative density: 12.41; melting pt.: 2334°C; boiling pt.: 4150°C

Rutherford 1 Ernest, 1st Baron. 1871–1937, British physicist, born in New Zealand, who discovered the atomic nucleus (1909). Nobel prize for chemistry 1908 **2** Dame **Margaret** 1892–1972, British stage and screen actress. Her films include *Passport to Pimlico* (1949), *Murder She Said* (1962), and *The VIPs* (1963) **3 Mark**, original name *William Hale White*. 1831–1913, British novelist and writer, whose work deals with his religious uncertainties: best known for *The Autobiography of Mark Rutherford* (1881) and the novel *The Revolution in Tanner's Lane* (1887)

rutherfordium a transactinide element produced by bombarding californium-249 nuclei with carbon-12 nuclei. Symbol: Rf; atomic number.: 104; atomic wt.: 261

Rutland an inland county of central England: the smallest of the historical English counties, it became part of Leicestershire in 1974 but was reinstated as an independent unitary authority in 1997: mainly agricultural. Administrative centre: Oakham. Pop: 35 700 (2003 est). Area: 394 sq km (152 sq miles)

Ruwenzori a mountain range in central Africa, on the border between Uganda and the Democratic Republic of Congo (formerly Zaïre) between Lakes Edward and Albert: generally thought to be Ptolemy's "Mountains of the Moon". Highest peak: Mount Stanley, 5109 m (16 763 ft)

Ruyter **Michiel Adriaanszoon de** 1607–76, Dutch admiral, noted for actions in the Anglo-Dutch wars in 1652–53, 1665–67, 1672, and 1673, when he prevented an Anglo-French invasion

Rwanda a republic in central Africa: part of German East Africa from 1899 until 1917, when Belgium took over the administration; became a republic in 1961 after a Hutu revolt against the Tutsi (1959); fighting between the ethnic groups broke out repeatedly after independence, culminating in the genocide of Tutsis by Hutus in 1994. Official languages: Rwanda, French, and English. Religion: Roman Catholic, African Protestant, Muslim, and animist. Currency: Rwanda franc. Capital: Kigali. Pop: 8 481 000 (2004 est). Area: 26 338 sq km (10 169 sq miles)

Ryazan a city in W central Russia: capital of a medieval principality; oil refineries and engineering industries. Pop: 523 000 (2005 est)

Rybinsk a city in W central Russia, on the River Volga: an important river port, terminal of the Mariinsk Waterway (between Saint Petersburg and the Volga) at the SE end of the **Rybinsk Reservoir** (area: 4700 sq km (1800 sq miles)). Pop: 218 000 (2005 est)

Rydal a village in NW England, in Cumbria on **Rydal Water** (a small lake). **Rydal Mount**, home of Wordsworth from 1813 to 1850, is situated here

Ryder **Susan**, Baroness Ryder of Warsaw. 1923–2000, British philanthropist; founder of the Sue Ryder Foundation for the Sick and Disabled, which is funded by a chain of charity shops: married to Leonard Cheshire

rye 1 a tall hardy widely cultivated annual grass, *Secale cereale*, having soft bluish-green leaves, bristly flower spikes, and light brown grain **2** the grain of this grass, used in making flour and whiskey, and as a livestock food

Rye a resort in SE England, in East Sussex: one of the Cinque Ports. Pop: 4195 (2001)

rye-grass any of various grasses of the genus *Lolium*, esp *L. perenne*, native to Europe, N Africa, and Asia and widely cultivated as forage crops. They have a flattened flower spike and hairless leaves

Ryle 1 Gilbert 1900–76, British philosopher. His works include *The Concept of Mind* (1949) **2** Sir **Martin** 1918–84, British astronomer, noted for his research on radio astronomy: Astronomer Royal 1972–82; shared the Nobel prize for physics in 1974

Ss

Saar 1 a river in W Europe, rising in the Vosges Mountains and flowing north to the Moselle River in Germany. Length: 246 km (153 miles) **2 the Saar** another name for **Saarland**

Saarinen Eero 1910–61, US architect, born in Finland. His works include the US Embassy, London (1960)

Saarland a state of W Germany: formed in 1919; under League of Nations administration until 1935; occupied by France (1945–57); part of West Germany (1957–90): contains rich coal deposits and is a major industrial region. Capital: Saarbrücken. Pop: 1 060 000 (2003 est). Area: 2567 sq km (991 sq miles)

Saba 1 an island in the NE Caribbean, in the Netherlands Antilles. Pop: 2498 (2004 est). Area: 13 sq km (5 sq miles) **2** another name for **Sheba**¹ (sense 1)

Sabadell a town in NE Spain, near Barcelona: textile manufacturing. Pop: 191 057 (2003 est)

Sabaean *or* **Sabean** 1 an inhabitant or native of ancient Saba **2** the ancient Semitic language of Saba **3** of or relating to ancient Saba, its inhabitants, or their language

Sabah a state of Malaysia, occupying N Borneo and offshore islands in the South China and Sulu Seas: became a British protectorate in 1888; gained independence and joined Malaysia in 1963. Capital: Kota Kinabalu. Pop: 2 603 485 (2000). Area: 76 522 sq km (29 545 sq miles)

Sabatier Paul 1854–1941, French chemist, who discovered a process for the hydrogenation of organic compounds: shared the Nobel prize for chemistry (1912)

Sabbath 1 the seventh day of the week, Saturday, devoted to worship and rest from work in Judaism and in certain Christian Churches **2** Sunday, observed by Christians as the day of worship and rest from work in commemoration of Christ's Resurrection **3** a period of rest **4** a midnight meeting or secret rendezvous for practitioners of witchcraft, sorcery, or devil worship

sabbatical 1 denoting a period of leave granted to university staff, teachers, etc, esp approximately every seventh year **2** denoting a post that renders the holder eligible for such leave **3** any sabbatical period

Sabbatical of, relating to, or appropriate to the Sabbath as a day of rest and religious observance

Sabin Albert Bruce 1906–93, US microbiologist, born in Poland. He developed the **Sabin vaccine** (1955), taken orally to immunize against poliomyelitis

sable 1 a marten, *Martes zibellina*, of N Asian forests, with dark brown luxuriant fur **2 a** the highly valued fur of this animal **b** (*as modifier*): *a sable coat* **3 American sable** the brown, slightly less valuable fur of the American marten, *Martes americana* **4** the colour of sable fur: a dark brown to yellowish-brown colour **5** of the colour of sable fur

Sable Cape 1 a cape at the S tip of Florida: the southernmost point of continental US **2** the southernmost point of Nova Scotia, Canada

sable antelope a large black E African antelope, *Hippotragus niger*, with long backward-curving horns

sabot *Austral* a small sailing boat with a shortened bow

sabre *or US* **saber** a sword used in fencing, having a narrow V-shaped blade, a semicircular guard, and a slightly curved hand

sac a pouch, bag, or pouchlike part in an animal or plant

saccharin a very sweet white crystalline slightly soluble powder used as a nonfattening sweetener. Formula: $C_7H_5NO_3S$

saccharine of, relating to, of the nature of, or containing sugar or saccharin

sacerdotal of, relating to, or characteristic of priests

Sachs 1 **Hans** 1494–1576, German master shoemaker and Meistersinger, portrayed by Wagner in *Die Meistersinger von Nürnberg* **2 Nelly** (**Leonie**). 1891–1970, German Jewish poet and dramatist, who escaped from Nazi Germany and settled in Sweden. Her works include *Eli: A Mystery Play of the Sufferings of Israel* (1951) and 'O the Chimneys', a poem about the Nazi extermination camps. Nobel prize for literature 1966 jointly with Shmuel Yosef Agnon

sack¹ *Cricket, Austral.* a run scored off a ball not struck by the batsman: allotted to the team as an extra and not to the individual batsman

sack² *American football* a tackle on a quarterback which brings him down before he has passed the ball

sack³ *Archaic except in trademarks* any dry white wine formerly imported into Britain from SW Europe

sackbut a medieval form of trombone

sackcloth coarse cloth such as sacking

sacking coarse cloth used for making sacks, woven from flax, hemp, jute, etc.

Sacks Jonathan (Henry). born 1948, British rabbi; Commonwealth chief rabbi from 1991

Sackville Thomas, 1st Earl of Dorset. 1536–1608, English poet, dramatist, and statesman. He collaborated with Thomas Norton on the early blank-verse tragedy

Gorboduc (1561)

Sackville-West Victoria (Mary), known as *Vita*. 1892–1962, British writer and gardener, whose works include the novel *The Edwardians* (1930) and the poem *The Land* (1931). She is also noted for the gardens at Sissinghurst Castle, Kent. Married to Harold Nicolson

sacrament 1 an outward sign combined with a pre-scribed form of words and regarded as conferring some specific grace upon those who receive it. The Protestant sacraments are baptism and the Lord's Supper. In the Roman Catholic and Eastern Churches they are baptism, penance, confirmation, the Eucharist, holy orders, matrimony, and the anointing of the sick (formerly extreme unction) 2 the Eucharist 3 the consecrated elements of the Eucharist, esp the bread

Sacramento 1 an inland port in N central California, capital of the state at the confluence of the American and Sacramento Rivers: became a boom town in the gold rush of the 1850s. Pop: 445 335 (2003 est) 2 a river in N California, flowing generally south to San Francisco Bay. Length: 615 km (382 miles)

sacrifice *Chess* the act or an instance of sacrificing a piece

sacristan *or* **sacrist** 1 a person who has charge of the contents of a church, esp the sacred vessels, vestments, etc. 2 a less common word for **sexton**

sacristy a room attached to a church or chapel where the sacred vessels, vestments, etc, are kept and where priests attire themselves

sacrosanct very sacred or holy; inviolable

sacrum 1 (in man) the large wedge-shaped bone, consisting of five fused vertebrae, in the lower part of the back 2 the corresponding part in some other vertebrates

Sadat (Mohammed) Anwar El 1918–81, Egyptian statesman: president of Egypt (1970–81); assassinated; Nobel peace prize jointly with Begin 1978

saddle 1 a seat for a rider, usually made of leather, placed on a horse's back and secured with a girth under the belly 2 a back pad forming part of the harness of a packhorse 3 the part of a horse or similar animal on which a saddle is placed 4 the part of the back of a domestic chicken that is nearest to the tail 5 *Civil engineering* a block on top of one of the towers of a suspension bridge that acts as a bearing surface over which the cables or chains pass 6 *Engineering* the carriage that slides on the bed of a lathe and supports the slide rest, tool post, or turret 7 another name for **col**

saddleback 1 a marking resembling a saddle on the backs of various animals 2 a breed of black pig with a white band across its back 3 a rare bird of New Zealand, *Philesturnus carunculatus*, having a chestnut-coloured saddle-shaped marking across its back and wings 4 another name for **col**

saddlebag *Informal* rolls of fat protruding from the sides of a person's thighs

saddle horse a lightweight horse kept for riding only

saddler a person who makes, deals in, or repairs saddles and other leather equipment for horses

saddlery saddles, harness, and other leather equipment for horses collectively

saddle soap a soft soap containing neat's-foot oil used

to preserve and clean leather

saddletree the frame of a saddle

Sadducee *Judaism* a member of an ancient Jewish sect that was opposed to the Pharisees, denying the resurrection of the dead, the existence of angels, and the validity of oral tradition

Sade Comte **Donatien Alphonse François de** , known as the *Marquis de Sade*. 1740–1814, French soldier and writer, whose exposition of sexual perversion gave rise to the term sadism

sadhu *or* **saddhu** a Hindu wandering holy man

Sadi *or* **Saadi** original name *Sheikh Muslih Addin*. ?1184–1292, Persian poet. His best-known works are *Gulistān* (Flower Garden) and *Būstān* (Tree Garden), long moralistic poems in prose and verse

sadomasochism *Psychol* the combination of sadistic and masochistic elements in one person, characterized by both aggressive and submissive periods in relationships with others

Sadowa a village in the Czech Republic, in NE Bohemia: scene of the decisive battle of the Austro-Prussian war (1866) in which the Austrians were defeated by the Prussians

safari park an enclosed park in which lions and other wild animals are kept uncaged in the open and can be viewed by the public from cars, etc.

safe-conduct 1 a document giving official permission to travel through a region, esp in time of war 2 the protection afforded by such a document

safety *American football* a either of two players who defend the area furthest back in the field b a play in which the offensive team causes the ball to cross its own goal line and then grounds the ball behind that line, scoring two points for the opposing team

safety curtain a curtain made of fireproof material that can be lowered to separate the auditorium and stage in a theatre to prevent the spread of a fire

safety valve a valve in a pressure vessel that allows fluid to escape when a predetermined level of pressure has been reached

safflower a thistle-like Eurasian annual plant, *Carthamus tinctorius*, having large heads of orange-yellow flowers and yielding a dye and an oil used in paints, medicines, etc.: family *Asteraceae* (composites)

saffron an Old World crocus, *Crocus sativus*, having purple or white flowers with orange stigmas

Safi a port in W Morocco, 170 km (105 miles) northwest of Marrakech, to which it is the nearest port. Pop: 470 000 (2003)

Safid Rud a river in N Iran, flowing northeast to a delta on the Caspian Sea. Length: about 785 km (490 miles)

sag 1 *Nautical* the extent to which a vessel's keel sags at the centre 2 a a marshy depression in an area of glacial till, chiefly in the US Middle West b (*as modifier*): *sag and swell topography*

saga 1 any of several medieval prose narratives written in Iceland and recounting the exploits of a hero or a family 2 any similar heroic narrative 3 a series of novels about several generations or members of a family 4 any other artistic production said to resemble a saga

sagacious *Obsolete* (of hounds) having an acute sense of smell

Sagan 1 Carl (Edward) 1934–96, US astronomer and writer on scientific subjects; presenter of the television series *Cosmos* (1980) 2 Françoise , original name *Françoise Quoirez*. 1935–2004, French writer, best-known for the novels *Bonjour Tristesse* (1954) and *Aimez-vous Brahms?* (1959)

sage 1 a perennial Mediterranean plant, *Salvia officinalis*, having grey-green leaves and purple, blue, or white flowers: family *Lamiaceae* (labiates) 2 short for **sage-brush**

sagebrush any of several aromatic plants of the genus *Artemisia*, esp *A. tridentata*, a shrub of W North America, having silver-green leaves and large clusters of small white flowers: family *Asteraceae* (composites)

Sagittarius 1 *Astronomy* a large conspicuous zodiacal constellation in the S hemisphere lying between Scorpius and Capricornus on the ecliptic and crossed by the Milky Way and containing the galactic centre 2 *Astrology* **a** the ninth sign of the zodiac, symbol ♐ , having a mutable fire classification and ruled by the planet Jupiter. The sun is in this sign between Nov 22 and Dec 21 **b** a person born when the sun is in this sign 3 *Astrology* born under or characteristic of Sagittarius

Saguenay a river in SE Canada in S Quebec, rising as the Péribonca River on the central plateau and flowing south, then east to the St. Lawrence. Length: 764 km (475 miles)

Sagunto an industrial town in E Spain, near Valencia: allied to Rome and made a heroic resistance to the Carthaginian attack led by Hannibal (219–218 BC). Pop: 58 287 (2003 est)

Sahara a desert in N Africa, extending from the Atlantic to the Red Sea and from the Mediterranean to central Mali, Niger, Chad, and the Sudan: the largest desert in the world, occupying over a quarter of Africa; rises to over 3300 m (11 000 ft) in the central mountain system of the Ahaggar and Tibesti massifs; large reserves of iron ore, oil, and natural gas. Area: 9 100 000 sq km (3 500 000 sq miles). Average annual rainfall: less than 254 mm (10 in.). Highest recorded temperature: 58°C (136.4°F)

said (in contracts, pleadings, etc) named or mentioned previously; aforesaid

Saida a port in SW Lebanon, on the Mediterranean: on the site of ancient Sidon; terminal of the Trans-Arabian pipeline from Saudi Arabia. Pop: 150 000 (2005 est)

sail 1 an area of fabric, usually Terylene or nylon (formerly canvas), with fittings for holding it in any suitable position to catch the wind, used for propelling certain kinds of vessels, esp over water 2 a voyage on such a vessel 3 a vessel with sails or such vessels collectively 4 a ship's sails collectively 5 the conning tower of a submarine 6 **in sail** having the sail set 7 **make sail a** to run up the sail or to run up more sail **b** to begin a voyage 8 **set sail a** to embark on a voyage by ship **b** to hoist sail 9 **under sail a** with sail hoisted **b** under way ▷www.sailing.org

sailboard the craft used for windsurfing, consisting of a moulded board like a surfboard, to which a mast bearing a single sail is attached by a swivel joint

sailcloth 1 any of various fabrics from which sails are made 2 a lighter cloth used for clothing, etc.

sailfish 1 any of several large scombroid game fishes of

the genus *Istiophorus*, such as *I. albicans* (**Atlantic sailfish**), of warm and tropical seas: family *Istiophoridae*. They have an elongated upper jaw and a long sail-like dorsal fin 2 another name for **basking shark**

sailor any member of a ship's crew, esp one below the rank of officer

sainfoin a Eurasian perennial leguminous plant, *Onobrychis viciifolia*, widely grown as a forage crop, having pale pink flowers and curved pods

Sainsbury David John, Baron. born 1940, British businessman and politician, chief executive of the Sainsbury supermarket chain from 1992; science minister from 1998

saint 1 a person who after death is formally recognized by a Christian Church, esp the Roman Catholic Church, as having attained, through holy deeds or behaviour, a specially exalted place in heaven and the right to veneration 2 *Bible* the collective body of those who are righteous in God's sight

Saint Albans a city in SE England, in W Hertfordshire: founded in 948 AD around the Benedictine abbey first built in Saxon times on the site of the martyrdom (about 303 AD) of St Alban; present abbey built in 1077; Roman ruins. Pop: 82 429 (2001)

Saint Andrews a city in E Scotland, in Fife on the North Sea: the oldest university in Scotland (1411); famous golf links. Pop: 14 209 (2001)

Saint Augustine a resort in NE Florida, on the Intracoastal Waterway: the oldest town in North America (1565); the northernmost outpost of the Spanish colonial empire for over 200 years. Pop: 11 915 (2003 est)

Saint Austell a town in SW England, in S Cornwall on **St Austell Bay** (an inlet of the English Channel): centre for the now-declining china clay industry; the Eden Project, a rainforest environment in the world's largest greenhouse, is nearby; administratively part of St Austell with Fowey 1968-1974. Pop. (with Fowey): 22 658 (2001)

Saint Bernard a large breed of dog with a dense red-and-white coat, formerly used as a rescue dog in mountainous areas

Saint Bernard Pass either of two passes over the Alps: the **Great St Bernard Pass** 2472 m (8110 ft) high, east of Mont Blanc between Italy and Switzerland, or the **Little St Bernard Pass** 2157 m (7077 ft) high, south of Mont Blanc between Italy and France

Saint-Brieuc a market town in NW France, near the N coast of Brittany. Pop: 46 087 (1999)

Saint Catharines an industrial city in S central Canada, in S Ontario on the Welland Canal. Pop: 129 170 (2001)

Saint Clair Lake a lake between SE Michigan and Ontario: linked with Lake Huron by the **St Clair River** and with Lake Erie by the Detroit River. Area: 1191 sq km (460 sq miles)

Saint-Cloud a residential suburb of Paris: former royal palace; Sèvres porcelain factory. Pop: 28 157 (1999)

Saint Croix an island in the Caribbean, the largest of the Virgin Islands of the US: purchased from Denmark by the US in 1917. Chief town: Christiansted. Pop: 53 234 (2000). Area: 207 sq km (80 sq miles)

Saint Croix River a river on the border between the northeast US and SE Canada, flowing from the Chiputneticook Lakes to Passamaquoddy Bay, forming the border between Maine, US, and New Brunswick, Canada. Length: 121 km (75 miles)

Saint-Denis 1 a town in N France, on the Seine: 12th-century Gothic abbey church, containing the tombs of many French monarchs; an industrial suburb of Paris. Pop: 85 832 (1999) **2** the capital of the French overseas region of Réunion, a port on the N coast. Pop: 131 557 (1999)

Sainte-Beuve Charles Augustin 1804–69, French critic, best known for his collections of essays *Port Royal* (1840–59) and *Les Causeries du Lundi* (1851–62)

Sainte Foy a SW suburb of Quebec, on the St Lawrence River. Pop: 72 547 (2001)

Saint Gall 1 a canton of NE Switzerland. Capital: St Gall. Pop: 455 200 (2002 est). Area: 2012 sq km (777 sq miles) **2** a town in NE Switzerland, capital of St Gall canton: an important educational centre in the Middle Ages. Pop: 72 626 (2000)

Saint Gotthard 1 a range of the Lepontine Alps in SE central Switzerland **2** a pass over the St Gotthard mountains, in S Switzerland. Height: 2114 m (6935 ft)

Saint Helena a volcanic island in the SE Atlantic, forming a UK Overseas Territory with its dependencies Tristan da Cunha and Ascension, and the uninhabited Gough, Inaccessible, and Nightingale Islands: discovered by the Portuguese in 1502 and annexed by England in 1651; scene of Napoleon's exile and death. Capital: Jamestown. Pop: 5644 (2003 est). Area: 122 sq km (47 sq miles)

Saint Helens 1 a town in NW England, in St Helens unitary authority, Merseyside: glass industry. Pop: 102 629 (2001) **2** a unitary authority in NW England, in Merseyside. Pop: 176 700 (2003 est). Area: 130 sq km (50 sq miles) **3** a volcanic peak in S Washington state; it erupted in 1980 after lying dormant from 1857

Saint Helier a market town and resort in the Channel Islands, on the S coast of Jersey. Pop: 28 310 (2001)

Saint John 1 a port in E Canada, at the mouth of the St John River: the largest city in New Brunswick; very often not abbreviated to 'St'. Pop: 90 762 (2001) **2** an island in the Caribbean, in the Virgin Islands of the US. Pop: 4197 (2000). Area: 49 sq km (19 sq miles) **3** Lake a lake in Canada, in S Quebec: drained by the Saguenay River. Area: 971 sq km (375 sq miles) **4** a river in E North America, rising in Maine, US, and flowing northeast to New Brunswick, Canada, then generally southeast to the Bay of Fundy. Length: 673 km (418 miles)

Saint John's wort a any of numerous shrubs or herbaceous plants of the temperate genus *Hypericum*, such as *H. perforatum*, having yellow flowers and glandular leaves: family *Hypericaceae* b a preparation of this plant often used to treat mild depression

Saint-Just Louis Antoine Léon de 1767–94, French Revolutionary leader and orator. A member of the Committee of Public Safety (1793–94), he was guillotined with Robespierre

Saint Kilda 1 a group of volcanic islands in the Atlantic, in the Outer Hebrides: uninhabited since 1930; bird sanctuary **2** the main island of this group

Saint Kitts an island in the E Caribbean, in the Leeward Islands: part of the state of St Kitts-Nevis. Capital: Basseterre. Pop: 34 703 (2001). Area: 168 sq km (65 sq miles)

Saint Kitts-Nevis an independent state in the E Caribbean; comprises the two islands of St Kitts and Nevis: with the island of Anguilla formed a colony (1882–1967) and a British associated state (1967–83); Anguilla formally separated from the group in 1983; gained full independence in 1983 as a member of the Commonwealth. Official language: English. Religion: Protestant majority. Currency: E Caribbean dollar. Capital: Basseterre. Pop: 42 000 (2003 est). Area: 262 sq km (101 sq miles)

Saint-Laurent Yves , full name *Yves-Mathieu*. born 1936, French couturier: popularized trousers for women for all occasions

Saint Laurent a W suburb of Montreal, Canada. Pop: 77 391 (2001)

Saint Lawrence 1 a river in SE Canada, flowing northeast from Lake Ontario, forming part of the border between Canada and the US, to the Gulf of St Lawrence: commercially one of the most important rivers in the world as the easternmost link of the St Lawrence Seaway. Length: 1207 km (750 miles). Width at mouth: 145 km (90 miles) **2** Gulf of a deep arm of the Atlantic off the E coast of Canada between Newfoundland and the mainland coasts of Quebec, New Brunswick, and Nova Scotia

Saint Lawrence Seaway an inland waterway of North America, passing through the Great Lakes, the St Lawrence River, and connecting canals and locks: one of the most important waterways in the world. Length: 3993 km (2480 miles)

Saint Leger the an annual horse race run at Doncaster since 1776: one of the classics of the flat-racing season

Saint Leonard a N suburb of Montreal, Canada. Pop: 69 604 (2001)

Saint Louis a port in E Missouri, on the Mississippi River near its confluence with the Missouri: the largest city in the state; university; major industrial centre. Pop: 332 223 (2003 est)

Saint-Louis a port in NW Senegal, on an island at the mouth of the Senegal River: the first French settlement in W Africa (1689); capital of Senegal until 1958. Pop: 183 000 (2005 est)

Saint Lucia an island state in the Caribbean, in the Windward Islands group of the Lesser Antilles: a volcanic island; gained self-government in 1967 as a British Associated State; attained full independence within the Commonwealth in 1979. Official language: English. Religion: Roman Catholic majority. Currency: E Caribbean dollar. Capital: Castries. Pop: 150 000 (2004 est). Area: 616 sq km (238 sq miles)

Saint Martin an island in the E Caribbean, in the Leeward Islands: administratively divided since 1648, the north belonging to France (as a dependency of Guadeloupe) and the south belonging to the Netherlands (as part of the Netherlands Antilles); salt industry. Pop: (French) 29 078 (1999); (Dutch) 33 119 (2004 est). Areas: (French) 52 sq km (20 sq miles); (Dutch) 33 sq km (13 sq miles)

Saint-Mihiel a village in NE France, on the River Meuse: site of a battle in World War I, in which the American army launched its first offensive in France

Saint Moritz a village in E Switzerland, in Graubünden canton in the Upper Engadine, at an altitude of 1856 m (6089 ft): sports and tourist centre. Pop: 5589 (2000)

Saint-Nazaire a port in NW France, at the mouth of the River Loire: German submarine base in World War II; shipbuilding. Pop: 65 874 (1999)

Saint-Ouen a town in N France, on the Seine: an industrial suburb of Paris; famous flea market. Pop: 39 722 (1999)

Saint Paul a port in SE Minnesota, capital of the state, at the head of navigation of the Mississippi: now contiguous with Minneapolis (the Twin Cities). Pop: 280 404 (2003 est)

Saint Petersburg 1 a city and port in Russia, on the Gulf of Finland at the mouth of the Neva River: founded by Peter the Great in 1703 and built on low-lying marshes subject to frequent flooding; capital of Russia from 1712 to 1918; a cultural and educational centre, with a university (1819); a major industrial centre, with engineering, shipbuilding, chemical, textile, and printing industries. Pop: 5 315 000 (2005 est) 2 a city and resort in W Florida, on Tampa Bay. Pop: 247 610 (2003 est)

Saint Pierre and Miquelon an archipelago in the Atlantic, off the S coast of Newfoundland: an overseas department of France, the only remaining French possession in North America; consists of the islands of St Pierre, with most of the population, and Miquelon, about ten times as large; fishing industries. Capital: St Pierre. Pop: 6000 (2003 est). Area: 242 sq km (94 sq miles)

Saint-Quentin a town in N France, on the River Somme: textile industry. Pop: 59 066 (1999)

Saint-Simon 1 **Comte de**, title of *Claude Henri de Rouvroy*. 1760–1825, French social philosopher, generally regarded as the founder of French socialism. He thought society should be reorganized along industrial lines and that scientists should be the new spiritual leaders. His most important work is *Nouveau Christianisme* (1825) 2 **Duc de**, title of *Louis de Rouvroy*. 1675–1755, French soldier, statesman, and writer: his *Mémoires* are an outstanding account of the period 1694–1723, during the reigns of Louis XIV and Louis XV

Saint Thomas 1 an island in the E Caribbean, in the Virgin Islands of the US. Capital: Charlotte Amalie. Pop: 51 181 (2000). Area: 83 sq km (28 sq miles) 2 the former name (1921–37) of **Charlotte Amalie**

Saint Vincent 1 **Cape** a headland at the SW extremity of Portugal: scene of several important naval battles, notably in 1797, when the British defeated the French and Spanish 2 **Gulf** a shallow inlet of SE South Australia, to the east of the Yorke Peninsula: salt industry

Saint Vincent and the Grenadines an island state in the Caribbean, in the Windward Islands of the Lesser Antilles: comprises the island of St Vincent and the Northern Grenadines; formerly a British associated state (1969–79); gained full independence in 1979 as a member of the Commonwealth. Official language: English. Religion: Protestant majority. Currency: Caribbean dollar. Capital: Kingstown. Pop: 121 000 (2004 est). Area: 389 sq km (150 sq miles)

Saipan an island in the W Pacific, administrative centre of the US associated territory of the Northern Mariana Islands; captured by the Americans and used as an air base until the end of World War II. Pop: 62 392 (2000). Area: 180 sq km (70 sq miles)

Sakai a port in S Japan, on S Honshu on Osaka Bay: an industrial satellite of Osaka. Pop: 787 833 (2002 est)

sake, saké, *or* **saki** a Japanese alcoholic drink made from fermented rice

Sakhalin *or* **Saghalien** an island in the Sea of Okhotsk, off the SE coast of Russia north of Japan: fishing, forestry, and mineral resources (coal and petroleum). Capital: Yuzhno-Sakhalinsk. Pop: 546 500 (2002). Area: 76 000 sq km (29 300 sq miles)

Sakha Republic *or* **Yakutia** an administrative division in E Russia, in NE Siberia on the Arctic Ocean: the coldest inhabited region of the world; it has rich mineral resources. Capital: Yakutsk. Pop: 948 100 (2002). Area: 3 103 200 sq km (1 197 760 sq miles)

Sakharov **Andrei** 1921–89, Soviet physicist and human-rights campaigner: Nobel peace prize 1975

salaam 1 a Muslim form of salutation consisting of a deep bow with the right palm on the forehead 2 a salutation signifying peace, used chiefly by Muslims

Saladin Arabic name *Salah-ed-Din Yusuf ibn-Ayyub*. ?1137–93, sultan of Egypt and Syria and opponent of the Crusaders. He defeated the Christians near Tiberias (1187) and captured Acre, Jerusalem, and Ashkelon. He fought against Richard I of England and Philip II of France during the Third Crusade (1189–92)

Salado 1 a river in N Argentina, rising in the Andes as the Juramento and flowing southeast to the Paraná River. Length: 2012 km (1250 miles) 2 a river in W Argentina, rising near the Chilean border as the Desaguadero and flowing south to the Colorado River. Length: about 1365 km (850 miles)

Salamanca a city in W Spain: a leading cultural centre of Europe till the end of the 16th century; market town. Pop: 157 906 (2003 es

salamander 1 any of various urodele amphibians, such as *Salamandra salamandra* (**European fire salamander**) of central and S Europe (family *Salamandridae*). They are typically terrestrial, have an elongated body, and only return to water to breed 2 *Chiefly US and Canadian* any urodele amphibian 3 a mythical reptile supposed to live in fire 4 an elemental fire-inhabiting being 5 *Metallurgy* a residue of metal and slag deposited on the walls of a furnace

Salambria a river in N Greece, in Thessaly, rising in the Pindus Mountains and flowing southeast and east to the Gulf of Salonika. Length: about 200 km (125 miles)

Salamis an island in the Saronic Gulf, Greece: scene of the naval battle in 480 BC, in which the Greeks defeated the Persians. Pop: 20 000 (latest est). Area: 95 sq km (37 sq miles)

Salazar **Antonio de Oliveira** 1889–1970, Portuguese statesman; dictator (1932–68)

sale 1 the exchange of goods, property, or services for an agreed sum of money or credit 2 the amount sold 3 the opportunity to sell; market 4 the rate of selling or being sold **5 a** an event at which goods are sold at reduced prices, usually to clear old stocks **b** *(as modifier)*: *sale bargains* **6** an auction

Sale **1** a town in NW England, in Trafford unitary authority, Greater Manchester: a residential suburb of Manchester. Pop: 55 234 (2001) **2** a city in SE Australia, in SE Victoria: centre of an agricultural region. Pop: 12 854 (2001)

saleable *or US* **salable** fit for selling or capable of being sold

Salem **1** a city in S India, in Tamil Nadu: textile industries. Pop: 693 236 (2001) **2** a city in NE Massachusetts, on the Atlantic: scene of the execution of 19 people after the witch hunts of 1692. Pop: 42 067 (2003 est) **3** a city in the NW USA, the state capital of Oregon: food-processing. Pop: 142 914 (2003 est) **4** an Old Testament name for Jerusalem (Genesis 14:18; Psalms 76:2)

Salerno a port in SW Italy, in Campania on the Gulf of Salerno: first medical school of medieval Europe. Pop: 138 188 (2001)

saleroom *Chiefly Brit* a room where objects are displayed for sale, esp by auction

salesman a person who sells merchandise or services either in a shop or by canvassing in a designated area

salesmanship **1** the technique, skill, or ability of selling **2** the work of a salesman

sales pitch *or* **talk** an argument or other persuasion used in selling

Salford **1** a city in NW England in Salford unitary authority, Greater Manchester, on the Manchester Ship Canal: a major centre of the cotton industry in the 19th century; extensive dock area, now redeveloped, includes the Lowry arts centre; university (1967). Pop: 72 750 (2001) **2** a unitary authority in NW England, in Greater Manchester. Pop: 216 500 (2003 est). Area: 97 sq km (37 sq miles)

salicylic acid a white crystalline slightly water-soluble substance with a sweet taste and bitter aftertaste, used in the manufacture of aspirin, dyes, and perfumes, and as a fungicide. Formula: $C_6H_4(OH)(COOH)$

salient **1** *Geometry* (of an angle) pointing outwards from a polygon and hence less than 180° **2** (esp of animals) leaping **3** a salient angle

Salieri Antonio 1750–1825, Italian composer and conductor, who worked in Vienna (from 1766). The suggestion that he poisoned Mozart has no foundation

saline **1** of, concerned with, consisting of, or containing common salt **2** *Med* of or relating to a saline **3** of, concerned with, consisting of, or containing any chemical salt, esp a metallic salt resembling sodium chloride **4** *Med* an isotonic solution of sodium chloride in distilled water

Salinger J(erome) D(avid) born 1919, US writer, noted particularly for his novel of adolescence *The Catcher in the Rye* (1951). His first novel for 34 years, *Hapworth 16, 1924* was published in 1997

Salisbury[1] Robert Gascoyne Cecil , 3rd Marquess of Salisbury. 1830–1903, British statesman; Conservative prime minister (1885–86; 1886–92; 1895–1902). His greatest interest was in foreign and imperial affairs

Salisbury[2] **1** the former name (until 1982) of **Harare 2** a city in S Australia: an industrial suburb of N Adelaide.

Pop: 112 344 (1998 est) **3** a city in S England, in SE Wiltshire: nearby Old Sarum was the site of an Early Iron Age hill fort; its cathedral (1220–58) has the highest spire in England. Pop: 43 355 (2001)

Salisbury Plain an open chalk plateau in S England, in Wiltshire: site of Stonehenge; military training area. Average height: 120 m (400 ft)

saliva the secretion of salivary glands, consisting of a clear usually slightly acid aqueous fluid of variable composition. It moistens the oral cavity, prepares food for swallowing, and initiates the process of digestion

Salk Jonas Edward 1914–95, US virologist: developed an injected vaccine against poliomyelitis (1954)

sallow **1** any of several small willow trees, esp the Eurasian *Salix cinerea* (**common sallow**), which has large catkins that appear before the leaves **2** a twig or the wood of any of these trees

Sallust full name *Gaius Sallustius Crispus*. 86–?34 BC, Roman historian and statesman, noted for his histories of the Catiline conspiracy and the Roman war against Jugurtha

sally the lower part of a bell rope, where it is caught at handstroke, into which coloured wool is woven to make a grip

salmon **1** any soft-finned fish of the family *Salmonidae*, esp *Salmo salar* of the Atlantic and *Oncorhynchus* species (sockeye, Chinook, etc) of the Pacific, which are important food fishes. They occur in cold and temperate waters and many species migrate to fresh water to spawn **2** *Austral* any of several unrelated fish, esp the Australian salmon

salmon ladder a series of steps in a river designed to enable salmon to bypass a dam and move upstream to their breeding grounds

Salome *New Testament* the daughter of Herodias, at whose instigation she beguiled Herod by her seductive dancing into giving her the head of John the Baptist

salon **1** a commercial establishment in which hairdressers, beauticians, etc, carry on their businesses **2 a** a hall for exhibiting works of art **b** such an exhibition, esp one showing the work of living artists

saloon **1** a large public room on a passenger ship **2** a closed two-door or four-door car with four to six seats

salsa **1** a type of Latin American big-band dance music **2** a dance performed to this kind of music ▷www.salsaweb.com

salsify **1** a Mediterranean plant, *Tragopogon porrifolius*, having grasslike leaves, purple flower heads, and a long white edible taproot: family *Asteraceae* (composites) **2** the root of this plant, which tastes of oysters and is eaten as a vegetable

salt **1** a white powder or colourless crystalline solid, consisting mainly of sodium chloride and used for seasoning and preserving food **2** preserved in, flooded with, containing, or growing in salt or salty water **3** *Chem* any of a class of usually crystalline solid compounds that are formed from, or can be regarded as formed from, an acid and a base by replacement of one or more hydrogen atoms in the acid molecules by positive ions from the base

SALT Strategic Arms Limitation Talks *or* Treaty

Salta a city in NW Argentina: thermal springs. Pop:

504 000 (2005 est)

saltbush any of various chenopodiaceous shrubs of the genus *Atriplex* that grow in alkaline desert regions

Saltillo a city in N Mexico, capital of Coahuila state: resort and commercial centre of a mining region. Pop: 698 000 (2005 est)

Salt Lake City a city in N central Utah, near the Great Salt Lake at an altitude of 1330 m (4300 ft): state capital; founded in 1847 by the Mormons as world capital of the Mormon Church; University of Utah (1850). Pop: 179 894 (2003 est)

salt lick 1 a place where wild animals go to lick naturally occurring salt deposits **2** a block of salt or a salt preparation given to domestic animals to lick

Salto a port in NW Uruguay, on the Uruguay River: Uruguay's second largest city. Pop: 105 000 (2005 est)

Saluki a tall breed of hound with a smooth coat and long fringes on the ears and tail

Salvador a port in E Brazil, capital of Bahia state: founded in 1549 as capital of the Portuguese colony, which it remained until 1763; a major centre of the African slave trade in colonial times. Pop: 3 331 000 (2005 est)

salvage 1 the act, process, or business of rescuing vessels or their cargoes from loss at sea **2** compensation paid for the salvage of a vessel or its cargo

salvation 1 *Christianity* deliverance by redemption from the power of sin and from the penalties ensuing from it **2** *Christian Science* the realization that Life, Truth, and Love are supreme and that they can destroy such illusions as sin, death, etc.

Salvation Army a a Christian body founded in 1865 by William Booth and organized on quasi-military lines for evangelism and social work among the poor **b** (*as modifier*): *the Salvation Army Hymn Book*
▷http://www.salvationarmy.org/

salve an ointment for wounds, sores, etc.

salvia any herbaceous plant or small shrub of the genus *Salvia*, such as the sage, grown for their medicinal or culinary properties or for ornament: family *Lamiaceae* (labiates)

salvo *Rare* (in legal documents) a saving clause; reservation

sal volatile 1 another name for **ammonium** carbonate **2** a solution of ammonium carbonate in alcohol and aqueous ammonia, often containing aromatic oils, used as smelling salts

Salween a river in SW Asia, rising in the Tibetan Plateau and flowing east and south through SW China and Myanmar to the Gulf of Martaban. Length: 2400 km (1500 miles)

Salzburg 1 a city in W Austria, capital of Salzburg province: 7th-century Benedictine abbey; a centre of music since the Middle Ages and birthplace of Mozart; tourist centre. Pop: 142 662 (2001) **2** a state of W Austria. Pop: 521 238 (2003 est). Area: 7154 sq km (2762 sq miles)

Salzgitter an industrial city in central Germany, in SE Lower Saxony. Pop: 109 855 (2003 est)

Samar an island in the E central Philippines, separated from S Luzon by the San Bernardino Strait: the third largest island in the republic. Capital: Catbalogan. Pop: 1 140 000 (2005 est). Area: 13 080 sq km (5050 sq miles)

Samara a port in SW Russia, on the River Volga: centre

of an important industrial complex; oil refining. Pop: 1 168 000 (1999 est)

Samaria 1 the region of ancient Palestine that extended from Judaea to Galilee and from the Mediterranean to the River Jordan; the N kingdom of Israel **2** the capital of this kingdom; constructed northwest of Shechem in the 9th century BC

Samaritan 1 a native or inhabitant of Samaria **2** short for **Good Samaritan 3** the dialect of Aramaic spoken in Samaria

samarium a silvery metallic element of the lanthanide series occurring chiefly in monazite and bastnaesite and used in carbon-arc lighting, as a doping agent in laser crystals, and as a neutron-absorber. Symbol: Sm; atomic no.: 62; atomic wt.: 150.36; valency: 2 or 3; relative density: 7.520; melting pt.: 1074°C; boiling pt.: 1794°C

Samarkand a city in E Uzbekistan: under Tamerlane it became the chief economic and cultural centre of central Asia, on trade routes from China and India (the "silk road"). Pop: 289 000 (2005 est)

samba 1 a lively modern ballroom dance from Brazil in bouncy duple time **2** a piece of music composed for or in the rhythm of this dance

Sambre a river in W Europe, rising in N France and flowing east into Belgium to join the Meuse at Namur. Length: 190 km (118 miles)

Samian a native or inhabitant of Samos

Samnium an ancient country of central Italy inhabited by Oscan-speaking Samnites: corresponds to the present-day regions of Abruzzi, Molise, and part of Campania

Samoa 1 an independent state occupying four inhabited islands and five uninhabited islands in the S Pacific archipelago of the Samoa Islands: established as a League of Nations mandate under New Zealand administration in 1920 and a UN trusteeship in 1946; gained independence as Western Samoa in 1962 as the first fully independent Polynesian state; officially changed its name to Samoa in 1997; a member of the Commonwealth. Languages: Samoan and English. Religion: Christian. Currency: tala. Capital: Apia. Pop: 180 000 (2004 est). Area 2841 sq km (1097 sq miles) **2** a group of islands in the S Pacific, northeast of Fiji: an independent kingdom until the mid 19th century, when it was divided administratively into **American Samoa** (in the east) and **German Samoa** (in the west); the latter was mandated to New Zealand in 1919 and gained full independence in 1962 as Western Samoa, now Samoa (sense 1). Area: 3038 sq km (1173 sq miles)

Samos a Greek island in the E Aegean Sea, off the SW coast of Turkey: a leading commercial centre of ancient Greece. Pop: 33 809 (2001). Area: 492 sq km (190 sq miles)

Samothrace a Greek island in the NE Aegean Sea: mountainous. Pop: 2723 (2001)

Samoyed 1 a member of a group of peoples who migrated along the Russian Arctic coast and now live chiefly in the area of the N Urals: related to the Finns **2** the languages of these peoples, related to Finno-Ugric within the Uralic family **3** a Siberian breed of dog of the spitz type, having a dense white or cream coat with a distinct ruff, and a tightly curled tail

sampan any small skiff, widely used in the Orient, that

is propelled by oars or a scull

samphire 1 an umbelliferous plant, *Crithmum maritimum*, of Eurasian coasts, having fleshy divided leaves and clusters of small greenish-white flowers **2 golden samphire** a Eurasian coastal plant, *Inula crithmoides*, with fleshy leaves and yellow flower heads: family *Asteraceae* (composites) **3** any of several other plants of coastal areas

sampler *Music* a recording comprising a collection of tracks from other albums, intended to stimulate interest in the featured products

Sampras Pete born 1971, US tennis player: US singles champion (1990, 1993, 1995, 1996); Wimbledon singles champion (1993–95, 1997–2000)

Samson a judge of Israel, who performed herculean feats of strength against the Philistine oppressors until he was betrayed to them by his mistress Delilah (Judges 13–16)

Samsun a port in N Turkey, on the Black Sea. Pop: 395 000 (2005 est)

Samuel *Old Testament* **1** a Hebrew prophet, seer, and judge, who anointed the first two kings of the Israelites (I Samuel 1–3; 8–15) **2** either of the two books named after him, I and II **Samuel**

samurai 1 the Japanese warrior caste that provided the administrative and fighting aristocracy from the 11th to the 19th centuries **2** a member of this aristocracy ▷www.samurai-archives.com

San a river in E central Europe, rising in W Ukraine and flowing northwest across SE Poland to the Vistula River. Length: about 450 km (280 miles)

San Antonio a city in S Texas: site of the Alamo; the leading town in Texas until about 1930. Pop: 1 214 725 (2003 est)

sanatorium *or US* **sanitarium 1** an institution for the medical care and recuperation of persons who are chronically ill **2** a health resort

San Bernardino a city in SE California: founded in 1851 by Mormons from Salt Lake City. Pop: 195 357 (2003 est)

San Bernardino Pass a pass over the Lepontine Alps in SE Switzerland. Highest point: 2062 m (6766 ft)

San Blas 1 Isthmus of the narrowest part of the Isthmus of Panama. Width: about 50 km (30 miles) **2** Gulf of an inlet of the Caribbean on the N coast of Panama

sanction 1 the penalty laid down in a law for contravention of its provisions **2** a coercive measure, esp one taken by one or more states against another guilty of violating international law

sanctuary 1 a holy place **2** a consecrated building or shrine **3** *Old Testament* **a** the Israelite temple at Jerusalem, esp the holy of holies **b** the tabernacle in which the Ark was enshrined during the wanderings of the Israelites **4** the chancel, or that part of a sacred building surrounding the main altar **5 a** a sacred building where fugitives were formerly entitled to immunity from arrest or execution **b** the immunity so afforded **6** a place, protected by law, where animals, esp birds, can live and breed without interference

sanctum a sacred or holy place

sand 1 loose material consisting of rock or mineral grains, esp rounded grains of quartz, between 0.05 and 2 mm in diameter **2** a sandy area, esp on the seashore or in a desert **3** a greyish-yellow colour

Sand George , pen name of *Amandine Aurore Lucie Dupin*. 1804–76, French novelist, best known for such pastoral novels as *La Mare au diable* (1846) and *François le Champi* (1847–48) and for her works for women's rights to independence

Sandage Allan Rex born 1926, US astronomer, who discovered the first quasar (1961)

Sandakan a port in Malaysia, on the NE coast of Sabah: capital (until 1947) of North Borneo. Pop: 347 334 (2000)

sandalwood *or* **sandal 1** any of several evergreen hemiparasitic trees of the genus *Santalum*, esp *S. album* (**white sandalwood**), of S Asia and Australia, having hard light-coloured heartwood: family *Santalaceae* **2** the wood of any of these trees, which is used for carving, is burned as incense, and yields an aromatic oil used in perfumery **3** any of various similar trees or their wood, esp *Pterocarpus santalinus* (**red sandalwood**), a leguminous tree of SE Asia having dark red wood used as a dye

sandbank a submerged bank of sand in a sea or river, that may be exposed at low tide

sandblast a jet of sand or grit blown from a nozzle under air, water, or steam pressure

Sandburg Carl 1878–1967, US writer, noted esp for his poetry, often written in free verse

sand castle a mass of sand moulded into a castle-like shape, esp as made by a child on the seashore

sander 1 a power-driven tool for smoothing surfaces, esp wood, plastic, etc, by rubbing with an abrasive disc **2** a person who uses such a device

Sandhurst a village in S England, in Bracknell unitary authority, Berkshire: seat of the Royal Military Academy for the training of officer cadets in the British Army. Pop: 19 546 (2001)

San Diego a port in S California, on the Pacific: naval base; two universities. Pop: 1 266 753 (2003 est)

sandman (in folklore) a magical person supposed to put children to sleep by sprinkling sand in their eyes

sand martin a small brown European songbird, *Riparia riparia*, with white underparts: it nests in tunnels bored in sand, river banks, etc.: family *Hirundinidae* (swallows and martins)

sandpiper 1 any of numerous N hemisphere shore birds of the genera *Tringa*, *Calidris*, etc, typically having a long slender bill and legs and cryptic plumage: family *Scolopacidae*, order *Charadriiformes* **2** any other bird of the family *Scolopacidae*, which includes snipes and woodcocks

Sandringham a village in E England, in Norfolk near the E shore of the Wash: site of **Sandringham House**, a residence of the royal family

sandstone any of a group of common sedimentary rocks consisting of sand grains consolidated with such materials as quartz, haematite, and clay minerals: used widely in building

sandstorm a strong wind that whips up clouds of sand, esp in a desert

Sandwell a unitary authority in central England, in West Midlands. Pop: 285 000 (2003 est). Area: 86 sq km (33 sq miles)

sandwich course any of several courses consisting of alternate periods of study and industrial work

sandy (esp of hair) reddish-yellow

sane sound in mind; free from mental disturbance

San Fernando 1 a port in Trinidad and Tobago, on Trinidad on the Gulf of Paria: the second-largest town in the country. Pop: 55 149 (2000) 2 an inland port in Venezuela, on the Apure River. Pop: 84 180 (latest est) 3 a port in SW Spain, on the Isla de León SE of Cádiz; site of an arsenal (founded 1790) and of the most southerly observatory in Europe. Pop: 88 490 (2003 est)

San Francisco a port in W California, situated around the Golden Gate: developed rapidly during the California gold rush; a major commercial centre and one of the world's finest harbours. Pop: 751 682 (2003 est)

San Francisco Bay an inlet of the Pacific in W California, linked with the open sea by the Golden Gate strait. Length: about 80 km (50 miles). Greatest width: 19 km (12 miles)

Sanger 1 **Frederick** born 1918, English biochemist, who determined the molecular structure of insulin: awarded two Nobel prizes for chemistry (1958; 1980) 2 **Margaret (Higgins)**. 1883–1966, US leader of the birth-control movement

sangoma *South African* a witch doctor, healer, or herbalist

sangria a Spanish drink of red wine, sugar, orange or lemon juice, and iced soda, sometimes laced with brandy

sanguine a red pencil containing ferric oxide, used in drawing

Sanhedrin *Judaism* 1 the supreme judicial, ecclesiastical, and administrative council of the Jews in New Testament times, having 71 members 2 a similar tribunal of 23 members having less important functions and authority

San Ildefonso a town in central Spain, near Segovia: site of the 18th-century summer palace of the kings of Spain

sanitary 1 of or relating to health and measures for the protection of health 2 conducive to or promoting health; free from dirt, germs, etc.; hygienic

sanitation the study and use of practical measures for the preservation of public health

sanity the state of being sane

San Jose a city in W central California: a leading world centre of the fruit drying and canning industry. Pop: 898 349 (2003 est)

San Juan 1 the capital and chief port of Puerto Rico, on the NE coast; University of Puerto Rico; manufacturing centre. Pop: 433 733 (2003 est) 2 a city in W Argentina: almost completely destroyed by an earthquake in 1944. Pop: 455 000 (2005 est)

Sankey **Ira David** 1840–1908, US evangelist and hymnodist, noted for his revivalist campaigns in Britain and the US with D. L. Moody

San Marino a republic in S central Europe in the Apennines, forming an enclave in Italy: the smallest republic in Europe, according to tradition founded by St Marinus in the 4th century. Official language: Italian. Religion: Roman Catholic majority. Currency: euro. Capital: San Marino. Pop: 28 000 (2003 est). Area: 62 sq km (24 sq miles)

Sanmicheli **Michele** ?1484–1559, Italian mannerist architect

San Pedro Sula a city in NW Honduras: the country's chief industrial centre. Pop: 610 000 (2005 est)

San Remo a port and resort in NW Italy, in Liguria on the slopes of the Maritime Alps; flower market. Pop: 50 608 (2001)

San Salvador the capital of El Salvador, situated in the SW central part: became capital in 1841; ruined by earthquakes in 1854 and 1873; university (1841). Pop: 1 472 000 (2005 est)

San Salvador Island an island in the central Bahamas: the first land in the New World seen by Christopher Columbus (1492). Area: 156 sq km (60 sq miles)

sans-culotte 1 during the French Revolution **a** (originally) a revolutionary of the poorer class **b** (later) any revolutionary, esp one having extreme republican sympathies 2 any revolutionary extremist

Sanskrit an ancient language of India, the language of the Vedas, of Hinduism, and of an extensive philosophical and scientific literature dating from the beginning of the first millennium BC. It is the oldest recorded member of the Indic branch of the Indo-European family of languages; recognition of the existence of the Indo-European family arose in the 18th century from a comparison of Sanskrit with Greek and Latin. Although it is used only for religious purposes, it is one of the official languages of India

San Stefano a village in NW Turkey, near Istanbul on the Sea of Marmara: scene of the signing (1878) of the treaty ending the Russo-Turkish War

Santa Ana 1 a city in NW El Salvador: the second largest city in the country; coffee-processing industry. Pop: 172 000 (2005 est) 2 a city in SW California: commercial and processing centre of a rich agricultural region. Pop: 342 510 (2003 est)

Santa Catalina an island in the Pacific, off the coast of SW California: part of Los Angeles county: resort. Area: 181 sq km (70 sq miles)

Santa Catarina a state of S Brazil, on the Atlantic: consists chiefly of the Great Escarpment. Capital: Florianópolis. Pop: 5 527 707 (2002). Area: 95 985 sq km (37 060 sq miles)

Santa Clara a city in W central Cuba: sugar and tobacco industries. Pop: 216 000 (2005 est)

Santa Claus the legendary patron saint of children, commonly identified with Saint Nicholas, who brings presents to children on Christmas Eve or, in some European countries, on Saint Nicholas' Day

Santa Cruz[1] **Alvaro de Bazán** 1526–88, Spanish naval commander, who proposed, assembled, and prepared the Spanish Armada but died shortly before it sailed for England

Santa Cruz[2] 1 a province of S Argentina, on the Atlantic: consists of a large part of Patagonia, with the forested foothills of the Andes in the west. Capital: Río Gallegos. Pop: 206 897 (2000 est). Area: 243 940 sq km (94 186 sq miles) 2 a city in E Bolivia: the second largest town in Bolivia. Pop: 1 352 000 (2005 est) 3 another name for **Saint Croix**

Santa Cruz de Tenerife a port and resort in the W Canary Islands, on NE Tenerife: oil refinery. Pop:

220 022 (2003 est)

Santa Fe 1 a city in N central New Mexico, capital of the state: one of the oldest European settlements in North America, founded in 1610 as the capital of the Kingdom of New Mexico; developed trade with the US by the Santa Fe Trail in the early 19th century. Pop: 66 476 (2003 est) 2 an inland port in E Argentina, on the Salado River: University of the Littoral (1920). Pop: 492 000 (2005 est)

Santa Maria 1 a city in S Brazil, in Rio Grande do Sul state. Pop: 252 000 (2005 est) 2 an active volcano in SW Guatemala. Height: 3768 m (12 362 ft)

Santa Marta a port in NW Colombia, on the Caribbean: the oldest city in Colombia, founded in 1525; terminus of the Atlantic railway from Bogotá (opened 1961). Pop: 454 000 (2005 est)

Santander a port and resort in N Spain, on an inlet of the Bay of Biscay: noted for its prehistoric collection from nearby caves; shipyards and an oil refinery. Pop: 184 778 (2003 est)

Santayana George 1863–1952, US philosopher, poet, and critic, born in Spain. His works include *The Life of Reason* (1905–06) and *The Realms of Being* (1927–40)

Santee a river in SE central South Carolina, formed by the union of the Congaree and Wateree Rivers: flows southeast to the Atlantic; part of the **Santee-Wateree-Catawba River System** an inland waterway 866 km (538 miles) long. Length: 230 km (143 miles)

Santiago 1 the capital of Chile, at the foot of the Andes: commercial and industrial centre; two universities. Pop: 5 623 000 (2005 est) 2 a city in the N Dominican Republic. Pop: 479 000 (2005 est)

Santiago de Compostela a city in NW Spain: place of pilgrimage since the 9th century and the most visited (after Jerusalem and Rome) in the Middle Ages; cathedral built over the tomb of the apostle St. James. Pop: 92 339 (2003 est)

Santiago de Cuba a port in SE Cuba, on **Santiago Bay** (a large inlet of the Caribbean): capital of Cuba until 1589; university (1947); industrial centre. Pop: 456 000 (2005 est)

Santiago del Estero a city in N Argentina: the oldest continuous settlement in Argentina, founded in 1553 by Spaniards from Peru. Pop: 385 000 (2005 est)

Santo Domingo 1 the capital and chief port of the Dominican Republic, on the S coast: the oldest continuous European settlement in the Americas, founded in 1496; university (1538). Pop: 1 920 000 (2005 est) 2 the former name (until 1844) of the **Dominican Republic** 3 another name (esp in colonial times) for **Hispaniola**

Santos a port in S Brazil, in São Paulo state: the world's leading coffee port. Pop: 1 634 000 (2005 est)

sap a solution of mineral salts, sugars, etc, that circulates in a plant

sapling a young tree

Sapper real name *Herman Cyril McNeile*. 1888–1937, British novelist, author of the popular thriller *Bull-dog Drummond* (1920) and its sequels

Sapphira *New Testament* the wife of Ananias, who together with her husband was struck dead for fraudulently concealing their wealth from the Church (Acts 5)

sapphire 1 a any precious corundum gemstone that is not red, esp the highly valued transparent blue variety. A synthetic form is used in electronics and precision apparatus. Formula: Al₂O₃ b (*as modifier*): *a sapphire ring* 2 the blue colour of sapphire

Sappho 6th century BC, Greek lyric poetess of Lesbos

Sapporo a city in N Japan, on W Hokkaido: commercial centre; university (1918). Pop: 1 822 992 (2002 est)

saprophyte any plant that lives and feeds on dead organic matter using mycorrhizal fungi associated with its roots; a saprotrophic plant

sarabande *or* **saraband** 1 a decorous 17th-century courtly dance 2 *Music* a piece of music composed for or in the rhythm of this dance, in slow triple time, often incorporated into the classical suite

Saracen 1 *History* a member of one of the nomadic Arabic tribes, esp of the Syrian desert, that harassed the borders of the Roman Empire in that region 2 a a Muslim, esp one who opposed the crusades b (in later use) any Arab 3 of or relating to Arabs of either of these periods, regions, or types 4 designating, characterizing, or relating to Muslim art or architecture

Sarah *Old Testament* the wife of Abraham and mother of Isaac (Genesis 17:15–22)

Sarajevo *or* **Serajevo** the capital of Bosnia-Herzegovina: developed as a Turkish town in the 15th century; capital of the Turkish and Austro-Hungarian administrations in 1850 and 1878 respectively; scene of the assassination of Archduke Franz Ferdinand in 1914, precipitating World War I; besieged by Bosnian Serbs (1992–95). Pop: 603 000 (2005 est)

Saramago José born 1922, Portuguese novelist and writer; his works include the novel *O ano da morte de Ricardo Reis* (1984): Nobel prize for literature 1998

Saransk a city in W central Russia, capital of the Mordovian Republic: university (1957). Pop: 304 000 (2005 est)

Saratov an industrial city in W Russia, on the River Volga: university (1919). Pop: 868 000 (2005 est)

Sarawak a state of Malaysia, on the NW coast of Borneo on the South China Sea: granted to Sir James Brooke by the Sultan of Brunei in 1841 as a reward for helping quell a revolt; mainly agricultural. Capital: Kuching. Pop: 2 071 506 (2000). Area: about 121 400 sq km (48 250 sq miles)

Sarazen Gene, original name *Eugenio Saraceni*. 1902–99, US golfer; won seven major tournaments between 1922 and 1935

sarcoma *Pathol* a usually malignant tumour arising from connective tissue

sardine any of various small marine food fishes of the herring family, esp a young pilchard

Sardinia the second-largest island in the Mediterranean: forms, with offshore islands, an administrative region of Italy; ceded to Savoy by Austria in 1720 in exchange for Sicily and formed the Kingdom of Sardinia with Piedmont; became part of Italy in 1861. Capital: Cagliari. Pop: 1 637 639 (2003 est). Area: 24 089 sq km (9301 sq miles)

Sardis *or* **Sardes** an ancient city of W Asia Minor: capital of Lydia

sardonyx a variety of chalcedony with alternating reddish-brown and white parallel bands, used as a gemstone. Formula: SiO_2

Sardou Victorien 1831–1908, French dramatist. His plays include *Fédora* (1882) and *La Tosca* (1887), the source of Puccini's opera

Sargasso Sea a calm area of the N Atlantic, between the Caribbean and the Azores, where there is an abundance of floating seaweed of the genus *Sargassum*

sargassum *or* **sargasso** any floating brown seaweed of the genus *Sargassum*, such as gulfweed, of warm seas, having ribbon-like fronds containing air sacs

Sargent 1 Sir (**Harold**) **Malcolm** (**Watts**). 1895–1967, English conductor **2 John Singer** 1856–1925, US painter, esp of society portraits; in London from 1885

Sargeson Frank 1903–82, New Zealand short-story writer and novelist. His work includes the short-story collection *That Summer and Other Stories* (1946) and the novel *I Saw in my Dream* (1949)

Sargodha a city in NE Pakistan: grain market. Pop: 556 000 (2005 est)

Sargon II died 705 BC, king of Assyria (722–705). He developed a policy of transporting conquered peoples to distant parts of his empire

Sark an island in the English Channel in the Channel Islands, consisting of **Great Sark** and **Little Sark**, connected by an isthmus: ruled by a hereditary Seigneur or Dame. Pop: 591 (2000). Area: 5 sq km (2 sq miles)

Sarmatia the ancient name of a region between the Volga and Vistula Rivers now covering parts of Poland, Belarus, and SW Russia

Sarnen a town in central Switzerland, capital of Obwalden demicanton: resort. Pop: 9145 (2000)

Sarnia an inland port in S central Canada, in SW Ontario at the S end of Lake Huron: oil refineries. Pop: 78 577 (2001)

Saronic Gulf an inlet of the Aegean on the SE coast of Greece. Length: about 80 km (50 miles). Width: about 48 km (30 miles)

Saros **Gulf of** an inlet of the Aegean in NW Turkey, north of the Gallipoli Peninsula. Length: 59 km (37 miles). Width: 35 km (22 miles)

Sarraute Nathalie 1900–99, French novelist, noted as an exponent of the antinovel. Her novels include *Portrait of a Man Unknown* (1948), *Martereau* (1953), and *Ici* (1995)

SARS severe acute respiratory syndrome; a severe viral infection of the lungs characterized by high fever, a dry cough, and breathing difficulties. It is contagious, having an airborne mode of transmission

sarsaparilla 1 any of various prickly climbing plants of the tropical American genus *Smilax* having large aromatic roots and heart-shaped leaves: family *Smilacaceae* **2** the dried roots of any of these plants, formerly used as a medicine **3** a nonalcoholic drink prepared from these roots **4** any of various plants resembling true sarsaparilla, esp the araliaceous plant *Aralia nudicaulis* (**wild sarsaparilla**), of North America

Sarthe a department of NW France, in Pays de la Loire region. Capital: Le Mans. Pop: 536 857 (2003 est). Area: 6245 sq km (2436 sq miles)

Sarto Andrea del 1486–1531, Florentine painter. His works include *The Nativity of the Virgin* (1514) in the church of Sant' Annunziata, Florence

sartorial *Anatomy* of or relating to the sartorius

Sartre Jean-Paul 1905–80, French philosopher, novelist, and dramatist; chief French exponent of atheistic existentialism. His works include the philosophical essay *Being and Nothingness* (1943), the novels *Nausea* (1938) and *Les Chemins de la liberté* (1945–49), a trilogy, and the plays *Les Mouches* (1943), *Huis clos* (1944), and *Les Mains sales* (1948)

Sasebo a port in SW Japan, on NW Kyushu on Omura Bay: naval base. Pop: 242 474 (2002 est)

Saskatchewan 1 a province of W Canada: consists of part of the Canadian Shield in the north and open prairie in the south; economy based chiefly on agriculture and mineral resources. Capital: Regina. Pop: 995 391 (2004 est). Area: 651 900 sq km (251 700 sq miles) **2** a river in W Canada, formed by the confluence of the North and South Saskatchewan Rivers: flows east to Lake Winnipeg. Length: 596 km (370 miles)

Saskatoon a city in W Canada, in S Saskatchewan on the South Saskatchewan River: oil refining; university (1907). Pop: 196 816 (2001)

sassafras 1 an aromatic deciduous lauraceous tree, *Sassafras albidum*, of North America, having three-lobed leaves and dark blue fruits **2** the aromatic dried root bark of this tree, used as a flavouring, and yielding sassafras oil **3** *Austral* any of several unrelated trees having a similar fragrant bark

Sassari a city in NW Sardinia, Italy: the second-largest city on the island; university (1565). Pop: 120 729 (2001)

Sassenach *Scot and occasionally Irish* an English person or a Lowland Scot

Sassoon 1 Siegfried (**Lorraine**). 1886–1967, British poet and novelist, best known for his poems of the horrors of war collected in *Counterattack* (1918) and *Satirical Poems* (1926). He also wrote a semi-fictitious autobiographical trilogy *The Memoirs of George Sherston* (1928–36) **2 Vidal** born 1928, British hair stylist: founder and chairman of Vidal Sassoon Inc

Satan the devil, adversary of God, and tempter of mankind: sometimes identified with Lucifer (Luke 4:5–8)

Satanism 1 the worship of Satan **2** a form of such worship which includes blasphemous or obscene parodies of Christian prayers, etc. **3** a satanic disposition or satanic practices

satellite 1 a celestial body orbiting around a planet or star **2** a man-made device orbiting around the earth, moon, or another planet transmitting to earth scientific information or used for communication **3** a country or political unit under the domination of a foreign power **4** a subordinate area or community that is dependent upon a larger adjacent town or city

Satie Erik (**Alfred Leslie**). 1866–1925, French composer, noted for his eccentricity, experimentalism, and his direct and economical style. His music, including numerous piano pieces and several ballets, exercised a profound influence upon other composers, such as Debussy and Ravel

satin a fabric of silk, rayon, etc, closely woven to show much of the warp, giving a smooth glossy appearance

satinwood 1 a rutaceous tree, *Chloroxylon swietenia*, that occurs in the East Indies and has hard wood with a satiny texture **2** the wood of this tree, used in veneering, cabinetwork, marquetry, etc.

satire 1 a novel, play, entertainment, etc, in which topical issues, folly, or evil are held up to scorn by means of ridicule and irony 2 the genre constituted by such works

satirist a person who writes satire

satisfaction 1 *RC Church, Church of England* the performance by a repentant sinner of a penance 2 *Christianity* the atonement for sin by the death of Christ

Sato Eisaku 1901–75, Japanese statesman: prime minister (1964–72). During his term of office Japan became a major economic power. He shared the Nobel peace prize (1974) for opposing the proliferation of nuclear weapons

satrap 1 (in ancient Persia) a provincial governor 2 a subordinate ruler, esp a despotic one

satsuma 1 a small citrus tree, *Citrus nobilis* var. *unshiu*, cultivated, esp in Japan, for its edible fruit 2 the fruit of this tree, which has a loose rind and easily separable segments

Satsuma a former province of SW Japan, on S Kyushu: famous for its porcelain

saturation 1 *Chem* the state of a chemical compound, solution, or vapour when it is saturated 2 *Meteorol* the state of the atmosphere when it can hold no more water vapour at its particular temperature and pressure, the relative humidity then being 100 per cent 3 the attribute of a colour that enables an observer to judge its proportion of pure chromatic colour 4 *Physics* the state of a ferromagnetic material in which it is fully magnetized. The magnetic domains are then all fully aligned 5 *Electronics* the state of a valve or semiconductor device that is carrying the maximum current of which it is capable and is therefore unresponsive to further increases of input signal 6 the level beyond which demand for a product or service is not expected to increase

saturation point *Chem* the point at which no more solute can be dissolved in a solution or gaseous material absorbed in a vapour

Saturn[1] the Roman god of agriculture and vegetation

Saturn[2] 1 one of the **giant planets** the sixth planet from the sun, around which revolve planar concentric rings (**Saturn's rings**) consisting of small frozen particles. The planet has at least 30 satellites. Mean distance from sun: 1425 million km; period of revolution around sun: 29.41 years; period of axial rotation: 10.23 hours; equatorial diameter and mass: 9.26 and 95.3 times that of the earth, respectively 2 a large US rocket used for launching various objects, such as a spaceprobe or an Apollo spacecraft, into space 3 the alchemical name for **lead**

Saturnalia an ancient Roman festival celebrated in December: renowned for its general merrymaking

saturnine *Archaic* a of or relating to lead b having or symptomatic of lead poisoning

satyr 1 *Greek myth* one of a class of sylvan deities, represented as goatlike men who drank and danced in the train of Dionysus and chased the nymphs 2 a man who has satyriasis 3 any of various butterflies of the genus *Satyrus* and related genera, having dark wings often marked with eyespots: family *Satyridae*

Saud full name *Saud ibn Abdul-Aziz*. 1902–69, king of Saudi Arabia (1953–64); son of Ibn Saud. He was deposed by his brother Faisal

Saudi Arabia a kingdom in SW Asia, occupying most of the Arabian peninsula between the Persian Gulf and the Red Sea: founded in 1932 by Ibn Saud, who united Hejaz and Nejd; consists mostly of desert plateau; large reserves of petroleum and natural gas. Official language: Arabic. Official religion: (Sunni) Muslim. Currency: riyal. Capital: Riyadh (royal), Jidda (administrative). Pop: 24 919 000 (2004 est). Area: 2 260 353 sq km (872 722 sq miles)

Saul 1 *Old Testament* the first king of Israel (?1020–1000 BC). He led Israel successfully against the Philistines, but was in continual conflict with the high priest Samuel. He became afflicted with madness and died by his own hand; succeeded by David 2 *New Testament* the name borne by Paul prior to his conversion (Acts 9: 1–30)

Sault Sainte Marie 1 an inland port in central Canada, in Ontario on the St. Mary's River, which links Lake Superior and Lake Huron, opposite Sault Ste Marie, Michigan: canal bypassing the rapids completed in 1895. Pop: 67 385 (2001) 2 an inland port in NE Michigan, opposite Sault Ste Marie, Ontario: canal around the rapids completed in 1855, enlarged and divided in 1896 and 1919 (popularly called **Soo Canals**). Pop: 14 184 (2003 est)

Saunders Dame **Cicely** born 1918, British philanthropist: founded St Christopher's Hospice in 1967 for the care of the terminally ill, upon which the modern hospice movement is modelled. Her books include *Living with Dying* (1983)

saurian 1 of, relating to, or resembling a lizard 2 of, relating to, or belonging to the *Sauria*, a former suborder of reptiles (now called *Lacertilia*), which included the lizards 3 a former name for **lizard**

Saussure **Ferdinand de** 1857–1913, Swiss linguist. He pioneered structuralism in linguistics and the separation of scientific language description from historical philological studies

Sava *or* **Save** a river in SE Europe, rising in NW Slovenia and flowing east and south to the Danube at Belgrade. Length: 940 km (584 miles)

savage 1 (of peoples) nonliterate or primitive 2 (of terrain) rugged and uncultivated 3 a member of a nonliterate society, esp one regarded as primitive

Savage **Michael Joseph** 1872–1940, New Zealand statesman; prime minister of New Zealand (1935–40)

Savaii the largest island in Samoa: mountainous and volcanic. Pop: 42 400 (2001). Area: 1174 sq km (662 sq miles)

Savannah 1 a port in the US, in E Georgia, near the mouth of the Savannah River: port of departure of the *Savannah* for Liverpool (1819), the first steamship to cross the Atlantic. Pop: 127 573 (2003 est) 2 a river in the southeastern US, formed by the confluence of the Tugaloo and Seneca Rivers in NW South Carolina: flows southeast to the Atlantic. Length: 505 km (314 miles)

Savery **Thomas** ?1650–1715, English engineer, who built (1698) the first practical steam engine, used to pump water from mines

saving 1 *Law* denoting or relating to an exception or reservation 2 *Law* an exception or reservation

Saviour *or US* **Savior** *Christianity* Jesus Christ regarded as the saviour of men from sin

Savoie 1 a department of E France, in Rhône-Alpes region. Capital: Chambéry. Pop: 386 246 (2003 est). Area: 6188 sq km (2413 sq miles) 2 the French name for **Savoy**

Savona a port in NW Italy, in Liguria on the Mediterranean: an important centre of the Italian iron and steel industry. Pop: 59 907 (2001)

Savonarola Girolamo 1452–98, Italian religious and political reformer. As a Dominican prior in Florence he preached against contemporary sinfulness and moral corruption. When the Medici were expelled from the city (1494) he instituted a severely puritanical republic but lost the citizens' support after being excommunicated (1497). He was hanged and burned as a heretic

savory 1 any of numerous aromatic plants of the genus *Satureja*, esp *S. montana* (**winter savory**) and *S. hortensis* (**summer savory**), of the Mediterranean region, having narrow leaves and white, pink, or purple flowers: family *Lamiaceae* (labiates) 2 the leaves of any of these plants, used as a potherb

Savoy[1] a noble family of Italy that ruled over the duchy of Savoy and became the royal house of Italy (1861–1946): the oldest reigning dynasty in Europe before the dissolution of the Italian monarchy

Savoy[2] an area of SE France, bordering on Italy, mainly in the Savoy Alps: a duchy in the late Middle Ages and part of the Kingdom of Sardinia from 1720 to 1860, when it became part of France

Savoyard the dialect of French spoken in Savoy

saw 1 any of various hand tools for cutting wood, metal, etc, having a blade with teeth along one edge 2 any of various machines or devices for cutting by use of a toothed blade, such as a power-driven circular toothed wheel or toothed band of metal

sawfish any sharklike ray of the family *Pristidae* of subtropical coastal waters and estuaries, having a serrated bladelike mouth

sawhorse a stand for timber during sawing

sawmill 1 an industrial establishment where timber is sawn into planks, etc. 2 a large sawing machine

sawyer a person who saws timber for a living

sax a tool resembling a small axe, used for cutting roofing slate

Saxe Hermann Maurice, comte de Saxe. 1696–1750, French marshal born in Saxony: he distinguished himself in the War of the Austrian Succession (1740–48)

Saxe-Coburg-Gotha the ruling house of the former German duchy of Saxe-Coburg-Gotha (until 1918) and the name of the British royal family (1901–17) through Prince Albert

saxifrage any saxifragaceous plant of the genus *Saxifraga*, having smallish white, yellow, purple, or pink flowers

Saxo Grammaticus ?1150–?1220, Danish chronicler, noted for his *Gesta Danorum*, a history of Denmark down to 1185, written in Latin, which is partly historical and partly mythological, and contains the Hamlet (Amleth) legend

Saxon 1 a member of a West Germanic people who in Roman times spread from Schleswig across NW Germany to the Rhine. Saxons raided and settled parts of S Britain in the fifth and sixth centuries AD. In Germany they established a duchy and other domin-ions, which changed and shifted through the centuries, usually retaining the name Saxony 2 a native or inhabitant of Saxony 3 a the Low German dialect of Saxony b any of the West Germanic dialects spoken by the ancient Saxons or their descendants 4 of, relating to, or characteristic of the ancient Saxons, the Anglo-Saxons, or their descendants 5 of, relating to, or characteristic of Saxony, its inhabitants, or their Low German dialect

▷www.anglo-saxons.net

▷www.bbc.co.uk/history/ancient/anglo_saxons/index.shtml

Saxony 1 a state in E Germany, formerly part of East Germany. Pop: 4 321 000 (2003 est) 2 a former duchy and electorate in SE and central Germany, whose territory changed greatly over the centuries 3 (in the early Middle Ages) any territory inhabited or ruled by Saxons

Saxony-Anhalt a state of E Germany: created in 1947 from the state of Anhalt and those parts of Prussia formerly ruled by the duchy of Saxony: part of East Germany until 1990. Pop: 2 523 000 (2003 est)

saxophone a keyed wind instrument of mellow tone colour, used mainly in jazz and dance music. It is made in various sizes, has a conical bore, and a single reed

say *Archaic* a type of fine woollen fabric

Sayers Dorothy L(eigh). 1893–1957, English detective-story writer

scab 1 the dried crusty surface of a healing skin wound or sore 2 a contagious disease of sheep, a form of mange, caused by a mite (*Psoroptes communis*)

scabies a contagious skin infection caused by the mite *Sarcoptes scabiei*, characterized by intense itching, inflammation, and the formation of vesicles and pustules

scabious 1 any plant of the genus *Scabiosa*, esp *S. atropurpurea*, of the Mediterranean region, having blue, red, or whitish dome-shaped flower heads: family *Dipsacaceae* 2 any of various similar plants of the related genus *Knautia* 3 **devil's bit scabious** a similar and related Eurasian marsh plant, *Succisa pratensis*

Scafell Pike a mountain in NW England, in Cumbria in the Lake District: the highest peak in England. Height: 977m (3206ft.)

scalar 1 a quantity, such as time or temperature, that has magnitude but not direction 2 *Maths* an element of a field associated with a vector space 3 having magnitude but not direction

scale[1] 1 any of the numerous plates, made of various substances resembling enamel or dentine, covering the bodies of fishes 2 a any of the horny or chitinous plates covering a part or the entire body of certain reptiles and mammals b any of the numerous minute structures covering the wings of lepidoptera 3 a thin flake of dead epidermis shed from the skin: excessive shedding may be the result of a skin disease 4 a specialized leaf or bract, esp the protective covering of a bud or the dry membranous bract of a catkin 5 a flaky black oxide of iron formed on the surface of iron or steel at high temperatures 6 any oxide formed on a metal during heat treatment

scale[2] 1 a machine or device for weighing 2 one of the pans of a balance

scale³ 1 a sequence of marks either at regular intervals or else representing equal steps used as a reference in making measurements 2 a measuring instrument having such a scale 3 *Music* a group of notes taken in ascending or descending order, esp within the compass of one octave 4 *Maths* the notation of a given number system 5 a graded series of tests measuring mental development, etc.

scalene 1 *Maths* (of a triangle) having all sides of unequal length 2 *Anatomy* of or relating to any of the scalenus muscles

scallop 1 any of various marine bivalves of the family *Pectinidae*, having a fluted fan-shaped shell: includes free-swimming species (genus *Pecten*) and species attached to a substratum (genus *Chlamys*) 2 the edible adductor muscle of certain of these molluscs 3 either of the shell valves of any of these molluscs 4 the shape of a scallop shell used as the badge of a pilgrim, esp in the Middle Ages

scallywag (after the US Civil War) a White Southerner who supported the Republican Party and its policy of Black emancipation. Scallywags were viewed as traitors by their fellow Southerners

scalp 1 *Anatomy* the skin and subcutaneous tissue covering the top of the head 2 (among North American Indians) a part of this removed as a trophy from a slain enemy 3 *Hunting, chiefly US* a piece of hide cut from the head of a victim as a trophy or as proof of killing in order to collect a bounty 4 *Informal, chiefly US* a small speculative profit taken in quick transactions 5 *Scot, dialect* a projection of bare rock from vegetation

scalpel a surgical knife with a short thin blade

scan *Med* a the examination of a part of the body by means of a scanner b the image produced by a scanner

scandal *Law* a libellous action or statement

Scandinavia 1 the peninsula of N Europe occupied by Norway and Sweden 2 the countries of N Europe, esp considered as a cultural unit and including Norway, Sweden, Denmark, and often Finland, Iceland, and the Faeroes

Scandinavian the northern group of Germanic languages, consisting of Swedish, Danish, Norwegian, Icelandic, and Faeroese

scandium a rare light silvery-white metallic element occurring in minute quantities in numerous minerals. Symbol: Sc; atomic no.: 21; atomic wt.: 44.955910; valency: 3; relative density: 2.989; melting pt.: 1541°C; boiling pt.: 2836°C

scanner 1 a device, usually electronic, used to measure or sample the distribution of some quantity or condition in a particular system, region, or area 2 any of various devices used in medical diagnosis to obtain an image of an internal organ or part

scansion the analysis of the metrical structure of verse

Scapa Flow an extensive landlocked anchorage off the N coast of Scotland, in the Orkney Islands: major British naval base in both World Wars. Length: about 24 km (15 miles). Width: 13 km (8 miles)

scapegoat *Old Testament* a goat used in the ritual of Yom Kippur (Leviticus 16); it was symbolically laden with the sins of the Israelites and sent into the wilderness to be destroyed

scapula 1 either of two large flat triangular bones, one on each side of the back part of the shoulder in man 2 the corresponding bone in most vertebrates

scapular 1 *Anatomy* of or relating to the scapula 2 part of the monastic habit worn by members of many Christian, esp Roman Catholic, religious orders, consisting of a piece of woollen cloth worn over the shoulders, and hanging down in front and behind to the ankles 3 two small rectangular pieces of woollen cloth joined by tapes passing over the shoulders and worn under secular clothes in token of affiliation to a religious order 4 any of the small feathers that are attached to the humerus of a bird and lie along the shoulder

scar¹ 1 any mark left on the skin or other tissue following the healing of a wound 2 the mark on a plant indicating the former point of attachment of a part, esp the attachment of a leaf to a stem

scar² 1 an irregular enlongated trench-like feature on a land surface that often exposes bedrock 2 a similar formation in a river or sea

scarab 1 any scarabaeid beetle, esp *Scarabaeus sacer* (**sacred scarab**), regarded by the ancient Egyptians as divine 2 the scarab as represented on amulets, etc, of ancient Egypt, or in hieroglyphics as a symbol of the solar deity

Scarborough a fishing port and resort in NE England, in North Yorkshire on the North Sea: developed as a spa after 1660; ruined 12th-century castle. Pop: 38 364 (2001)

scarf *Whaling* an incision made along a whale's body before stripping off the blubber

Scarlatti 1 Alessandro ?1659–1725, Italian composer; regarded as the founder of modern opera 2 his son, (**Giuseppe**) **Domenico** 1685–1757, Italian composer and harpsichordist, in Portugal and Spain from 1720. He wrote over 550 single-movement sonatas for harpsichord, many of them exercises in virtuoso technique

scarlet 1 a vivid red colour, sometimes with an orange tinge 2 of the colour scarlet

scarlet fever an acute communicable disease characterized by fever, strawberry-coloured tongue, and a typical rash starting on the neck and chest and spreading to the abdomen and limbs, caused by all group A haemolytic *Streptococcus* bacteria

scarlet woman *New Testament* a sinful woman described in Revelation 17, interpreted as a figure either of pagan Rome or of the Roman Catholic Church regarded as typifying vice overlaid with gaudy pageantry

scarp a steep slope, esp one formed by erosion or faulting; escarpment

Scarron Paul 1610–60, French comic dramatist and novelist, noted particularly for his picaresque novel *Le Roman comique* (1651–57)

Scart *or* **SCART** *Electronics* a a 21-pin plug-and-socket system which carries picture, sound, and other signals, used especially in home entertainment systems b (*as modifier*): *a Scart cable*

scat¹ a type of jazz singing characterized by improvised vocal sounds instead of words

scat² any marine and freshwater percoid fish of the Asian family *Scatophagidae*, esp *Scatophagus argus*, which has a beautiful coloration

scat³ an animal dropping

scatology the scientific study of excrement, esp in medicine for diagnostic purposes, and in palaeontology of fossilized excrement

scavenger 1 any animal that feeds on decaying organic matter, esp on refuse 2 a substance added to a chemical reaction or mixture to counteract the effect of impurities

SCE in Scotland Scottish Certificate of Education: either of two public examinations in specific subjects taken as school-leaving qualifications or as qualifying examinations for entry into a university, college, etc.

scenario a summary of the plot of a play, etc, including information about its characters, scenes, etc.

scene 1 a a subdivision of an act of a play, in which the time is continuous and the setting fixed b a single event, esp a significant one, in a play 2 *Films* a shot or series of shots that constitutes a unit of the action 3 the backcloths, stage setting, etc, for a play or film set; scenery

scenery *Theatre* the painted backcloths, stage structures, etc, used to represent a location in a theatre or studio

scenic 1 of or relating to the stage or stage scenery 2 (in painting) representing a scene, such as a scene of action or a historical event

sceptic *or archaic and US* **skeptic** 1 a person who habitually doubts the authenticity of accepted beliefs 2 a person who doubts the truth of religion, esp Christianity

Schaerbeek a city in central Belgium: an industrial suburb of Brussels. Pop: 110 253 (2004 est)

Schaffhausen 1 a small canton of N Switzerland. Pop: 73 900 (2002 est). Area: 298 sq km (115 sq miles) 2 a town in N Switzerland, capital of Schaffhausen canton, on the Rhine. Pop: 33 628 (2000)

Schama Simon (**Michael**). born 1945, British historian, art critic, and broadcaster, based in the US; his work includes *The Embarrassment of Riches* (1987), *Landscape and Memory* (1995), and the BBC television series *A History of Britain* (2000–02)

Schaumburg-Lippe a former state of NW Germany, between Westphalia and Hanover: part of Lower Saxony since 1946

schedule *Law* a list or inventory, usually supplementary to a contract, will, etc.

Scheele Karl Wilhelm 1742–86, Swedish chemist. He discovered oxygen, independently of Priestley, and many other substances

Scheldt a river in W Europe, rising in NE France and flowing north and northeast through W Belgium to Antwerp, then northwest to the North Sea in the SW Netherlands. Length: 435 km (270 miles)

Schelling Friedrich Wilhelm Joseph von 1775–1854, German philosopher. He expanded Fichte's idea that there is one reality, the infinite and absolute Ego, by regarding nature as an absolute being working towards self-consciousness. His works include *Ideas towards a Philosophy of Nature* (1797) and *System of Transcendental Idealism* (1800)

schema 1 (in the philosophy of Kant) a rule or principle that enables the understanding to apply its categories and unify experience 2 *Psychol* a mental model of aspects of the world or of the self that is structured in such a way as to facilitate the processes of cognition and perception 3 *Logic* an expression using metavariables that may be replaced by object language expressions to yield a well-formed formula. Thus $A = A$ is an axiom schema for identity, representing the infinite number of axioms, $x = x, y = y, z = z$, etc.

schematic a diagram, esp of an electrical circuit

scheme an astrological diagram giving the aspects of celestial bodies at a particular time

scherzo *Music* a brisk lively movement, developed from the minuet, with a contrastive middle section (a trio)

Schiaparelli 1 Elsa 1896–1973, Italian couturière, noted esp for the dramatic colours of her designs 2 Giovanni Virginio 1835–1910, Italian astronomer, who discovered the asteroid Hesperia (1861) and the so-called canals of Mars (1877)

Schiedam a port in the SW Netherlands, in South Holland province west of Rotterdam: gin distilleries. Pop: 76 000 (2003 est)

Schiele Egon 1890–1918, Austrian painter and draughtsman: a leading exponent of Austrian expressionism

Schiff Andras born 1953, Hungarian concert pianist

Schiller Johann Christoph Friedrich von 1759–1805, German poet, dramatist, historian, and critic. His concern with the ideal freedom of the human spirit to rise above the constraints placed upon it is reflected in his great trilogy *Wallenstein* (1800) and in *Maria Stuart* (1800)

schilling 1 the former standard monetary unit of Austria, divided into 100 groschen; replaced by the euro in 2002 2 an old German coin of low denomination

schism division within or separation from an established Church, esp the Roman Catholic Church, not necessarily involving differences in doctrine

schist any metamorphic rock that can be split into thin layers because its micaceous minerals have become aligned in thin parallel bands

schistosomiasis a disease caused by infestation of the body with blood flukes of the genus *Schistosoma*

schizoid 1 *Psychol* denoting a personality disorder characterized by extreme shyness and oversensitivity to others 2 a person who has a schizoid personality

schizophrenia any of a group of psychotic disorders characterized by progressive deterioration of the personality, withdrawal from reality, hallucinations, delusions, social apathy, emotional instability, etc.

Schlegel 1 August Wilhelm von 1767–1845, German romantic critic and scholar, noted particularly for his translations of Shakespeare 2 his brother, **Friedrich von** 1772–1829, German philosopher and critic; a founder of the romantic movement in Germany

Schlesinger John (**Richard**). 1926–2003, British film and theatre director. Films include *Billy Liar* (1963), *Midnight Cowboy* (1969), *Sunday Bloody Sunday* (1971), and *Eye for an Eye* (1995)

Schleswig 1 a fishing port in N Germany, in Schleswig-Holstein state: on an inlet of the Baltic. Pop: 24 288 (2003 est) 2 a former duchy, in the S Jutland Peninsula: annexed by Prussia in 1864; N part returned to Denmark after a plebiscite in 1920; S part forms part of the German state of Schleswig-Holstein

Schleswig-Holstein a state of N Germany, formerly in West Germany: drained chiefly by the River Elbe; mainly agricultural. Capital: Kiel. Pop: 2 823 000 (2003 est). Area: 15 658 sq km (6045 sq miles)

Schlick Moritz 1882–1936, German philosopher, working in Austria, who founded (1924) the Vienna Circle to develop the doctrine of logical positivism. His works include the *General Theory of Knowledge* (1918) and *Problems of Ethics* (1930)

Schlieffen Alfred , Count von Schlieffen. 1833–1913, German field marshal, who devised the **Schlieffen Plan** (1905): it was intended to ensure German victory over a Franco-Russian alliance by holding off Russia with minimal strength and swiftly defeating France by a massive flanking movement through the Low Countries. In a modified form, it was unsuccessfully employed in World War I (1914)

Schliemann Heinrich 1822–90, German archaeologist, who discovered nine superimposed city sites of Troy (1871–90). He also excavated the site of Mycenae (1876)

Schmidt Helmut (Heinrich Waldemar). born 1918, German Social Democrat statesman; chancellor of West Germany (1974–82)

Schnabel Artur 1882–1951, US pianist and composer, born in Austria

schnapps *or* **schnaps** 1 a Dutch spirit distilled from potatoes 2 (in Germany) any strong spirit

Schnittke Alfred 1934–98, Russian composer: his works include four symphonies, four violin concertos, choral, chamber, and film music

Schoenberg *or* **Schönberg** Arnold 1874–1951, Austrian composer and musical theorist, in the US after 1933. The harmonic idiom of such early works as the string sextet *Verklärte Nacht* (1899) gave way to his development of atonality, as in the song cycle *Pierrot Lunaire* (1912), and later of the twelve-tone technique. He wrote many choral, orchestral, and chamber works and the unfinished opera *Moses and Aaron*

scholar a student of merit at an educational establishment who receives financial aid, esp from an endowment given for such a purpose

scholarship a financial aid provided for a scholar because of academic merit b the position of a student who gains this financial aid c (*as modifier*): *a scholarship student*

scholastic 1 characteristic of or relating to the medieval Schoolmen 2 a disciple or adherent of scholasticism; Schoolman 3 a a Jesuit student who is undergoing a period of probation prior to commencing his theological studies b the status and position of such a student 4 a formalist in art

scholasticism the system of philosophy, theology, and teaching that dominated medieval western Europe and was based on the writings of the Church Fathers and (from the 12th century) Aristotle, the Greek philosopher (384–322 BC)

Schongauer Martin ?1445–91, German painter and engraver

school¹ 1 a an institution or building at which children and young people usually under 19 receive education b (*as modifier*): *school bus* 2 any educational institution or

building 3 a faculty, institution, or department specializing in a particular subject 4 the staff and pupils of a school 5 the period of instruction in a school or one session of this 6 meetings held occasionally for members of a profession, etc. 7 a group of artists, writers, etc, linked by the same style, teachers, or aims

school² a group of porpoises or similar aquatic animals that swim together

schoolmaster 1 a man who teaches in or runs a school 2 a food fish, *Lutjanus apodus*, of the warm waters of the Caribbean and Atlantic: family *Lutjanidae* (snappers)

school year 1 a twelve-month period, (in Britain) usually starting in late summer and continuing for three terms until the following summer, during which pupils remain in the same class 2 the time during this period when the school is open

schooner a sailing vessel with at least two masts, with all lower sails rigged fore-and-aft, and with the main mast stepped aft

Schopenhauer Arthur 1788–1860, German pessimist philosopher. In his chief work, *The World as Will and Idea* (1819), he expounded the view that will is the creative primary factor and idea the secondary receptive factor

schottische 1 a 19th-century German dance resembling a slow polka 2 a piece of music composed for or in the manner of this dance

Schreiner Olive (Emilie Albertina). 1855–1920, South African novelist and feminist writer, whose works include the autobiography *The Story of an African Farm* (1883) and *Women and Labour* (1911)

Schubert Franz (Peter). 1797–1828, Austrian composer; the originator and supreme exponent of the modern German lied. His many songs include the cycles *Die Schöne Müllerin* (1823) and *Die Winterreise* (1827). His other works include symphonies and much piano and chamber music including string quartets and the *Trout* piano quintet (1819)

Schumacher 1 Ernst Friedrich 1911–77, British economist, born in Germany. He is best known for his book *Small is Beautiful* (1973) 2 Michael born 1969, German motor racing driver, who has won more Grand Prix races than any other; Formula One world champion (1994–1995, 2000–2004)

Schuman 1 Robert 1886–1963, French statesman; prime minister (1947–48). He proposed (1950) pooling the coal and steel resources of W Europe 2 William (Howard). 1910–91, US composer

Schumann 1 Elisabeth 1885–1952, German soprano, noted esp for her interpretations of lieder 2 Robert Alexander 1810–56, German romantic composer, noted esp for his piano music, such as *Carneval* (1835) and *Kreisleriana* (1838), his songs, and four symphonies

schuss *Skiing* a straight high-speed downhill run

Schwarzkopf 1 Elisabeth born 1915, Austro-British operatic soprano, born in Germany 2 Norman, nicknamed *Stormin' Norman*. born 1934, US general. As head of Central Command, the US military district covering the Middle East, he became the victorious commander-in-chief of the US-led forces in the Gulf War (1991)

Schweinfurt a city in central Germany, in N Bavaria on the River Main. Pop: 54 601 (2003 est)

Schweitzer Albert 1875–1965, Franco-German medical

missionary, philosopher, theologian, and organist, born in Alsace. He took up medicine in 1905 and devoted most of his life after 1913 to a medical mission at Lambaréné, Gabon: Nobel peace prize 1952

Schwerin a city in N Germany, in Mecklenburg-West Pomerania on **Lake Schwerin**. Pop: 97 694 (2003 est)

Schwitters Kurt 1887–1948, German dadaist painter and poet, noted for his collages composed of discarded materials

Schwyz 1 a canton of central Switzerland: played an important part in the formation of the Swiss confederation, to which it gave its name. Capital: Schwyz. Pop: 133 300 (2002 est). Area: 908 sq km (351 sq miles) 2 a town in E central Switzerland, capital of Schwyz canton: tourism. Pop: 13 802 (2000)

sciatic 1 *Anatomy* of or relating to the hip or the hipbone 2 of, relating to, or afflicted with sciatica

sciatica a form of neuralgia characterized by intense pain and tenderness along the course of the body's longest nerve (**sciatic nerve**), extending from the back of the thigh down to the calf of the leg

science fiction a a literary genre that makes imaginative use of scientific knowledge or conjecture b *(as modifier)*: *a science fiction writer*

science park an area usually linked with a university where scientific research and commercial development are carried on in cooperation

scion *Botany* a shoot or twig of a plant used to form a graft

Scipio 1 full name *Publius Cornelius Scipio Africanus Major.* 237–183 BC, Roman general. He commanded the Roman invasion of Carthage in the Second Punic War, defeating Hannibal at Zama (202) 2 full name *Publius Cornelius Scipio Aemilianus Africanus Minor.* ?185–129 BC, Roman statesman and general; the grandson by adoption of Scipio Africanus Major. He commanded an army against Carthage in the last Punic War and razed the city to the ground (146). He became the leader (132) of the opposition in Rome to popular reforms

sclera the firm white fibrous membrane that forms the outer covering of the eyeball

sclerosis 1 *Pathol* a hardening or thickening of organs, tissues, or vessels from chronic inflammation, abnormal growth of fibrous tissue, or degeneration of the myelin sheath of nerve fibres, or (esp on the inner walls of arteries) deposition of fatty plaques 2 the hardening of a plant cell wall or tissue by the deposition of lignin

sclerotic 1 of or relating to the sclera 2 of, relating to, or having sclerosis 3 *Botany* characterized by the hardening and strengthening of cell walls 4 another name for **sclera**

scollop (in Ireland) a rod, pointed at both ends, used to pin down thatch

sconce a flat candlestick with a handle

Scone a parish in Perth and Kinross, E Scotland, consisting of the two villages of New Scone and Old Scone, formerly the site of the Pictish capital and the stone upon which medieval Scottish kings were crowned. The stone was removed to Westminster Abbey by Edward I in 1296; it was returned to Scotland in 1996 and placed in Edinburgh Castle. Scone Palace was rebuilt in the Neo-Gothic style in the 19th century

scoop 1 anything that resembles a scoop in action, such as the bucket on a dredge 2 a spoonlike surgical instrument for scraping or extracting foreign matter, etc, from the body

scooter 1 a child's vehicle consisting of a low footboard on wheels, steered by handlebars. It is propelled by pushing one foot against the ground 2 See **motor scooter**

Scopas 4th century BC, Greek sculptor and architect

scope 1 *Nautical* slack left in an anchor cable 2 *Logic, linguistics* that part of an expression that is governed by a given operator: *the scope of the negation in PV–(q∧r) is –(q∧r)*

Scopus Mount a mountain in central Israel, east of Jerusalem: a N extension of the Mount of Olives; site of the Hebrew University (1925). Height: 834 m (2736 ft)

scorbutic of, relating to, or having scurvy

score 1 *Music* a the written or printed form of a composition in which the instrumental or vocal parts appear on separate staves vertically arranged on large pages (**full score**) or in a condensed version, usually for piano (**short score**) or voices and piano (**vocal score**) b the incidental music for a film or play c the songs, music, etc, for a stage or film musical 2 *Dancing* notation indicating a dancer's moves

scoria 1 a rough cindery crust on top of solidified lava flows containing numerous vesicles 2 refuse obtained from smelted ore; slag

Scorpio *Astrology* a the eighth sign of the zodiac, symbol ♏ having a fixed water classification and ruled by the planets Mars and Pluto. The sun is in this sign between about Oct 23 and Nov 21 b a person born during a period when the sun is in this sign

scorpion 1 any arachnid of the order *Scorpionida*, of warm dry regions, having a segmented body with a long tail terminating in a venomous sting 2 **false scorpion** any small nonvenomous arachnid of the order *Pseudoscorpionida* (or *Chelonethida*), which superficially resemble scorpions but lack the long tail 3 any of various other similar arachnids, such as the whip scorpion, or other arthropods, such as the water scorpion 4 *Old Testament* a barbed scourge (I Kings 12:11) 5 *History* a war engine for hurling stones; ballista

Scorsese Martin born 1942, US film director, whose films include *Taxi Driver* (1976), *Raging Bull* (1980), the controversial *The Last Temptation of Christ* (1988), *Casino* (1995), and *Gangs of New York* (2002)

Scot 1 a native or inhabitant of Scotland 2 a member of a tribe of Celtic raiders from the north of Ireland who carried out periodic attacks against the British mainland coast from the 3rd century AD, eventually settling in N Britain during the 5th and 6th centuries

scotch a line marked down, as for hopscotch

Scotch[1] 1 another word for **Scottish** 2 the Scots or their language

Scotch[2] 1 whisky distilled esp from fermented malted barley and made in Scotland 2 *Northeast English* a type of relatively mild beer

Scotch mist 1 a heavy wet mist 2 drizzle

Scotland a country that is part of the United Kingdom, occupying the north of Great Britain: the English and Scottish thrones were united under one monarch in

1603 and the parliaments in 1707: a separate Scottish parliament was established in 1999. Scotland consists of the Highlands in the north, the central Lowlands, and hilly uplands in the south; has a deeply indented coastline, about 800 offshore islands (mostly in the west), and many lochs. Capital: Edinburgh. Pop: 5 057 400 (2003 est). Area: 78 768 sq km (30 412 sq miles)

Scotland Yard the headquarters of the police force of metropolitan London, controlled directly by the British Home Office and hence having certain national responsibilities

Scots 1 of, relating to, or characteristic of Scotland, its people, their English dialects, or their Gaelic language 2 any of the English dialects spoken or written in Scotland

Scots pine *or* **Scotch pine** 1 a coniferous tree, *Pinus sylvestris*, of Europe and W and N Asia, having blue-green needle-like leaves and brown cones with a small prickle on each scale: a valuable timber tree 2 the wood of this tree

Scott 1 Sir **George Gilbert** 1811–78, British architect, prominent in the Gothic revival. He restored many churches and cathedrals and designed the Albert Memorial (1863) and St Pancras Station (1865) 2 his grandson, **Sir Giles Gilbert** 1880–1960, British architect, whose designs include the Anglican cathedral in Liverpool (1904–78) and the new Waterloo Bridge (1939–45) 3 **Paul** (**Mark**). 1920–78, British novelist, who is best known for the series of novels known as the "Raj Quartet": *The Jewel in the Crown* (1966), *The Day of the Scorpion* (1968), *The Towers of Silence* (1972), and *A Division of the Spoils* (1975). *Staying On* (1977) won the Booker Prize 4 Sir **Peter** (**Markham**). 1909–89, British naturalist, wildlife artist, and conservationist, noted esp for his paintings of birds. He founded (1946) the Slimbridge refuge for waterfowl in Gloucestershire 5 his father, **Robert Falcon** 1868–1912, British naval officer and explorer of the Antarctic. He commanded two Antarctic expeditions (1901–04; 1910–12) and reached the South Pole on Jan 18, 1912, shortly after Amundsen; he and the rest of his party died on the return journey 6 Sir **Walter** 1771–1832, Scottish romantic novelist and poet. He is remembered chiefly for the "Waverley" historical novels, including *Waverley* (1814), *Rob Roy* (1817), *The Heart of Midlothian* (1818), inspired by Scottish folklore and history, and *Ivanhoe* (1819), *Kenilworth* (1821), *Quentin Durward* (1823), and *Redgauntlet* (1824). His narrative poems include *The Lay of the Last Minstrel* (1805), *Marmion* (1808), and *The Lady of the Lake* (1810)

Scottish 1 of, relating to, or characteristic of Scotland, its people, their Gaelic language, or their English dialect 2 **the** the Scots collectively

Scottish Borders a council area in SE Scotland, on the English border: created in 1996, it has the same boundaries as the former Borders Region: it is mainly hilly, with agriculture (esp sheep farming) the chief economic activity. Administrative centre: Newtown St Boswells. Pop: 108 280 (2003 est). Area: 4734 sq km (1827 sq miles)

scour prolonged diarrhoea in livestock, esp cattle

Scouse *Brit, informal* 1 a person who lives in or comes from Liverpool 2 the dialect spoken by such a person 3 of or from Liverpool; Liverpudlian

scout 1 (esp at Oxford University) a college servant 2 *Obsolete* (in Britain) a patrolman of a motoring organization

scow 1 an unpowered barge used for freight; lighter 2 (esp in the midwestern US) a sailing yacht with a flat bottom, designed to plane

Scrabble *Trademark* a board game in which words are formed by placing lettered tiles in a pattern similar to a crossword puzzle

▷www.scrabble.com

scrag *Informal* the neck of a human being

scram an emergency shutdown of a nuclear reactor

scramble *Brit* a motorcycle rally in which competitors race across rough open ground

scrambler a plant that produces long weak shoots by which it grows over other plants

Scranton an industrial city in NE Pennsylvania: university (1888). Pop: 74 320 (2003 est)

scrap a waste material or used articles, esp metal, often collected and reprocessed b (*as modifier*): *scrap iron*

scratch 1 *Billiards, snooker* a a shot that results in a penalty, as when the cue ball enters the pocket b a lucky shot 2 *poultry food*

scratching a percussive effect obtained by rotating a gramophone record manually: a disc-jockey and dub technique

scree an accumulation of weathered rock fragments at the foot of a cliff or hillside, often forming a sloping heap

screech *Canadian* (esp in Newfoundland) a dark rum

screech owl 1 a small North American owl, *Otus asio*, having ear tufts and a reddish-brown or grey plumage 2 *Brit* any owl that utters a screeching cry

screen 1 a decorated partition, esp in a church around the choir 2 the wide end of a cathode-ray tube, esp in a television set, on which a visible image is formed 3 a white or silvered surface, usually fabric, placed in front of a projector to receive the enlarged image of a film or of slides 4 **the screen** the film industry or films collectively 5 *Photog* a plate of ground glass in some types of camera on which the image of a subject is focused before being photographed 6 *Psychoanal* anything that prevents a person from realizing his true feelings about someone or something

screenplay the script for a film, including instructions for sets and camera work

screenwriter a person who writes screenplays

screw 1 a device used for fastening materials together, consisting of a threaded and usually tapered shank that has a slotted head by which it may be rotated so as to cut its own thread as it bores through the material 2 a threaded cylindrical rod that engages with a similarly threaded cylindrical hole; bolt 3 a thread in a cylindrical hole corresponding with that on the bolt or screw with which it is designed to engage 4 *Billiards, snooker* a a stroke in which the cue ball recoils or moves backward after striking the object ball, made by striking the cue ball below its centre b the motion resulting from this stroke 5 another name for **propeller** 6 *Slang* an old, unsound, or worthless horse

screwdriver 1 a tool used for turning screws, usually

having a handle of wood, plastic, etc, and a steel shank with a flattened square-cut tip that fits into a slot in the head of the screw **2** an alcoholic beverage consisting of orange juice and vodka

Scriabin *or* **Skryabin** Aleksandr Nikolayevich 1872–1915, Russian composer, whose works came increasingly to express his theosophic beliefs. He wrote many piano works; his orchestral compositions include *Prometheus* (1911)

scribe 1 *Old Testament* a recognized scholar and teacher of the Jewish Law **2** *Judaism* a man qualified to write certain documents in accordance with religious requirements

Scribe Augustin Eugène 1791–1861, French author or coauthor of over 350 vaudevilles, comedies, and libretti for light opera

scrimmage *American football* the clash of opposing linemen at every down

scrip *or* **script** *Informal* a medical prescription

script 1 written copy for the use of performers in films and plays **2** *Law* an original or principal document **b** (esp in England) a will or codicil or the draft for one **3** *Computing* a series of instructions that is executed by a computer program **4** an answer paper in an examination

Scripture *Christianity* the Old and New Testaments

scriptwriter a person who prepares scripts, esp for a film

scrofula *Pathol* tuberculosis of the lymphatic glands

scrotum the pouch of skin containing the testes in most mammals

scrub 1 a vegetation consisting of stunted trees, bushes, and other plants growing in an arid area **b** (*as modifier*): *scrub vegetation* **2** an area of arid land covered with such vegetation **3 a** an animal of inferior breeding or condition **b** (*as modifier*): *a scrub bull*

scrubber¹ an apparatus for purifying a gas

scrubber² *Austral* a domestic animal, esp a bullock, that has run wild in the bush

scrum *Rugby* the act or method of restarting play after an infringement when the two opposing packs of forwards group together with heads down and arms interlocked and push to gain ground while the scrum half throws the ball in and the hookers attempt to scoop it out to their own team. A scrum is usually called by the referee (**set scrum**) but may be formed spontaneously (**loose scrum**)

scrum half *Rugby* **1** a player who puts in the ball at scrums and tries to get it away to his three-quarter backs **2** this position in a team

scrumpy a rough dry cider, brewed esp in the West Country

scruple 1 a unit of weight equal to 20 grains (1.296 grams) **2** an ancient Roman unit of weight equivalent to approximately one twenty-fourth of an ounce

scrutiny (in the early Christian Church) a formal testing that catechumens had to undergo before being baptized **b** a similar examination of candidates for holy orders

scuba a apparatus used in skindiving, consisting of a cylinder or cylinders containing compressed air attached to a breathing apparatus **b** (*as modifier*): *scuba diving*

scud *Meteorol* **a** a formation of low fractostratus clouds driven by a strong wind beneath rain-bearing clouds **b** a sudden shower or gust of wind

scuffle US a type of hoe operated by pushing rather than pulling

scull 1 a single oar moved from side to side over the stern of a boat to propel it **2** one of a pair of short-handled oars, both of which are pulled by one oarsman, esp in a racing shell **3** a racing shell propelled by an oarsman or oarsmen pulling two oars **4** a race between racing shells, each propelled by one, two, or four oarsmen pulling two oars

Scullin James Henry 1876–1953, Australian statesman; prime minister of Australia (1929–31)

sculptor *or feminine* **sculptress** a person who practises sculpture

sculpture 1 the art of making figures or designs in relief or the round by carving wood, moulding plaster, etc, or casting metals, etc. **2** the gradual formation of the landscape by erosion
  ▷http://dir.yahoo.com/Arts/Visual_Arts/Sculpture
  ▷www.sculptor.org
  ▷www.bluffton.edu/~sullivanm/index

scum 1 the greenish film of algae and similar vegetation surface of a stagnant pond **2** the skin of oxides or impurities on the surface of a molten metal

Scunthorpe a town in E England, in North Lincolnshire unitary authority, Lincolnshire: developed rapidly after the discovery of local iron ore in the late 19th century; iron and steel industries have declined. Pop: 72 660 (2001)

scupper *Nautical* a drain or spout allowing water on the deck of a vessel to flow overboard

scurry *Horse racing* a short race or sprint

scurvy a disease caused by a lack of vitamin C, characterized by anaemia, spongy gums, bleeding beneath the skin, and (in infants) malformation of bones and teeth

scut the short tail of animals such as the deer and rabbit

scuttle¹ the part of a motor-car body lying immediately behind the bonnet

scuttle² *Nautical* a small hatch or its cover

Scylla *Greek myth* a sea nymph transformed into a sea monster believed to drown sailors navigating the Strait of Messina. She was identified with a rock off the Italian coast

scythe a manual implement for cutting grass, etc, having a long handle held with both hands and a curved sharpened blade that moves in a plane parallel to the ground

Scythia an ancient region of SE Europe and Asia, north of the Black Sea: now part of Ukraine

Scythian 1 of or relating to ancient Scythia, its inhabitants, or their language **2** a member of an ancient nomadic people of Scythia **3** the extinct language of this people, belonging to the East Iranian branch of the Indo-European family

sea 1 a the mass of salt water on the earth's surface as differentiated from the land **b** (*as modifier*): *sea air* **2 a** one of the smaller areas of ocean **b** a large inland area of water **3** turbulence or swell, esp of considerable size

4 *Astronomy* any of many huge dry plains on the surface of the moon

sea anchor *Nautical* any device, such as a bucket or canvas funnel, dragged in the water to keep a vessel heading into the wind or reduce drifting

sea anemone any of various anthozoan coelenterates, esp of the order *Actiniaria*, having a polypoid body with oral rings of tentacles

sea bird a bird such as a gull, that lives on the sea

seaboard a land bordering on the sea; the seashore **b** (*as modifier*): *seaboard towns*

Seaborg Glenn Theodore 1912–99, US chemist and nuclear physicist. With E.M. McMillan, he discovered several transuranic elements, including plutonium (1940), curium, and americium (1944), and shared a Nobel prize for chemistry 1951

seaborgium a synthetic transuranic element, synthesized and identified in 1974. Symbol: Sg; atomic no.: 106

sea breeze a wind blowing from the sea to the land, esp during the day when the land surface is warmer

sea cow 1 any sirenian mammal, such as a dugong or manatee **2** an archaic name for **walrus**

seafaring 1 working as a sailor **2** the act of travelling by sea **3** the career or work of a sailor

seafront a built-up area facing the sea

sea horse 1 any marine teleost fish of the temperate and tropical genus *Hippocampus*, having a bony-plated body, a prehensile tail, and a horselike head and swimming in an upright position: family *Syngnathidae* (pipefishes) **2** an archaic name for the **walrus 3** a fabled sea creature with the tail of a fish and the front parts of a horse

sea kale a European coastal plant, *Crambe maritima*, with broad fleshy leaves and white flowers, cultivated for its edible asparagus-like shoots: family *Brassicaceae* (crucifers)

seal¹ *RC Church* the obligation never to reveal anything said by a penitent in confession

seal² 1 any pinniped mammal of the families *Otariidae* and *Phocidae* that are aquatic but come on shore to breed **2** any earless seal (family *Phocidae*), esp the common or harbour seal or the grey seal (*Halichoerus grypus*)

sealant 1 any substance, such as wax, used for sealing documents, bottles, etc. **2** any of a number of substances used for stopping leaks, waterproofing wood, etc.

sea level the level of the surface of the sea with respect to the land, taken to be the mean level between high and low tide, and used as a standard base for measuring heights and depths

sealing wax a hard material made of shellac, turpentine, and pigment that softens when heated. It is used for sealing documents, parcels, letters, etc.

sea lion any of various large eared seals, such as *Zalophus californianus* (**Californian sea lion**), of the N Pacific, often used as a performing animal

Sea Lord (in Britain) either of the two serving naval officers (**First** and **Second Sea Lords**) who sit on the admiralty board of the Ministry of Defence

sealskin a the skin or pelt of a fur seal, esp when dressed with the outer hair removed and the underfur dyed dark brown **b** (*as modifier*): *a sealskin coat*

seam 1 a stratum of coal, ore, etc. **2** *Surgery* another name for **suture** (sense 1b) **3** *Cricket* of or relating to a style of bowling in which the bowler utilizes the stitched seam round the ball in order to make it swing in flight and after touching the ground

seaman a man who serves as a sailor

seance *or* **séance** a meeting at which spiritualists attempt to receive messages from the spirits of the dead

seaplane any aircraft that lands on and takes off from water

search 1 the examination of a vessel by the right of search **2** *Computing* **a** a review of a file to locate specific information **b** (*as modifier*): *a search routine* **3** **right of search** *International law* the right possessed by the warships of a belligerent state in time of war to board and search merchant vessels to ascertain whether ship or cargo is liable to seizure

search engine *Computing* a service provided on the internet enabling users to search for items of interest

searchlight 1 a device, consisting of a light source and a reflecting surface behind it, that projects a powerful beam of light in a particular direction **2** the beam of light produced by such a device

search warrant a written order issued by a justice of the peace authorizing a constable or other officer to enter and search premises for stolen goods, drugs, etc.

Searle Ronald (**William Fordham**). born 1920, British cartoonist, best known as the creator of the schoolgirls of St Trinian's

seashell the empty shell of a marine mollusc

seashore the land between the marks of high and low water

seasick suffering from nausea and dizziness caused by the motion of a ship at sea

seaside any area bordering on the sea, esp one regarded as a resort **b** (*as modifier*): *a seaside hotel*

season 1 one of the four equal periods into which the year is divided by the equinoxes and solstices, resulting from the apparent movement of the sun north and south of the equator during the course of the earth's orbit around it. These periods (spring, summer, autumn, and winter) have their characteristic weather conditions in different regions, and occur at opposite times of the year in the N and S hemispheres **2** a period of the year characterized by particular conditions or activities **3** the period during which any particular species of animal, bird, or fish is legally permitted to be caught or killed **4** any of the major periods into which the ecclesiastical calendar is divided, such as Lent, Advent, or Easter **5 in season a** (of game) permitted to be caught or killed **b** (of some female mammals) sexually receptive

seat 1 *Politics* a membership or the right to membership in a legislative or similar body **2** *Chiefly Brit* a parliamentary constituency **3** the manner in which a rider sits on a horse **4 on seat** *W African, informal* (of officials) in the office rather than on tour or on leave

seat belt 1 a belt or strap worn in a vehicle to restrain forward motion in the event of a collision **2** a similar belt or strap worn in an aircraft at takeoff and landing and in rough weather

Seaton Valley a region in NE England, in SE Northumberland: consists of a group of former coal-mining villages.

Seattle a port in W Washington, on the isthmus between Lake Washington and Puget Sound: the largest city in the state and chief commercial centre of the Northwest; two universities. Pop: 569 101 (2003 est)

sea urchin any echinoderm of the class *Echinoidea*, such as *Echinus esculentus* (**edible sea urchin**), typically having a globular body enclosed in a rigid spiny test and occurring in shallow marine waters

seaweed 1 any of numerous multicellular marine algae that grow on the seashore, in salt marshes, in brackish water, or submerged in the ocean **2** any of certain other plants that grow in or close to the sea

sebaceous 1 of or resembling sebum, fat, or tallow; fatty **2** secreting fat or a greasy lubricating substance

Sebastian Saint died ?288 AD, Christian martyr. According to tradition, he was first shot with arrows and then beaten to death. Feast day: Jan 20

sebum the oily secretion of the sebaceous glands that acts as a lubricant for the hair and skin and provides some protection against bacteria

sec 1 (of wines) dry **2** (of champagne) of medium sweetness

secant 1 (of an angle) a trigonometric function that in a right-angled triangle is the ratio of the length of the hypotenuse to that of the adjacent side; the reciprocal of cosine **2** a line that intersects a curve

secession *Chiefly US* the withdrawal in 1860–61 of 11 Southern states from the Union to form the Confederacy, precipitating the American Civil War

second¹ 1 coming directly after the first in numbering or counting order, position, time, etc.; being the ordinal number of *two*: often written 2nd **2** denoting the lowest but one forward ratio of a gearbox in a motor vehicle **3** *Music* **a** relating to or denoting a musical part, voice, or instrument lower in pitch than another part, voice, or instrument (the first) **b** of or relating to a part, instrument, or instrumentalist regarded as subordinate to another (the first) **4** *Brit, education* an honours degree of the second class, usually further divided into an upper and lower designation **5** the lowest but one forward ratio of a gearbox in a motor vehicle **6** (in boxing, duelling, etc) an attendant who looks after a competitor **7** a speech seconding a motion or the person making it **8** *Music* **a** the interval between one note and another lying next above or below it in the diatonic scale **b** one of two notes constituting such an interval in relation to the other **9** goods of inferior quality

second² 1 a a 1/60 of a minute of time **b** the basic SI unit of time: the duration of 9 192 631 770 periods of radiation corresponding to the transition between two hyperfine levels of the ground state of caesium-133. **2** 1/60 of a minute of angle.

secondary 1 of or relating to the education of young people between the ages of 11 and 18 **2** (of the flight feathers of a bird's wing) growing from the ulna **3 a** being the part of an electric circuit, such as a transformer or induction coil, in which a current is induced by a changing current in a neighbouring coil **b** (of a current) flowing in such a circuit **4** (of an industry)

involving the manufacture of goods from raw materials **5** *Geology* (of minerals) formed by the alteration of pre-existing minerals **6** *Chem* **a** (of an organic compound) having a functional group attached to a carbon atom that is attached to one hydrogen atom and two other groups **b** (of an amine) having only two organic groups attached to a nitrogen atom; containing the group NH **c** (of a salt) derived from a tribasic acid by replacement of two acidic hydrogen atoms with metal atoms or electropositive groups **7** a secondary coil, winding, inductance, or current in an electric circuit **8** *Ornithol* any of the flight feathers that grow from the ulna of a bird's wing **9** *Astronomy* a celestial body that orbits around a specified primary body **10** *Med* a cancerous growth in some part of the body away from the site of the original tumour **11** *American football* **a** cornerbacks and safeties collectively **b** their area in the field **12** short for **secondary colour**

secondary colour a colour formed by mixing two primary colours

second chamber *Politics* the upper house of a bicameral legislative assembly

second class a (in Britain) of or relating to mail that is processed more slowly than first-class mail **b** (in the US and Canada) of or relating to mail that consists mainly of newspapers, etc.

Second Coming *or less commonly* **Second Advent** the prophesied return of Christ to earth at the Last Judgment

second fiddle *Informal* **a** the second violin in a string quartet or one of the second violins in an orchestra **b** the musical part assigned to such an instrument

second wind the return of the ability to breathe at a comfortable rate, esp following a period of exertion

secret *Liturgy* a variable prayer, part of the Mass, said by the celebrant after the offertory and before the preface

secretariat a an office responsible for the secretarial, clerical, and administrative affairs of a legislative body, executive council, or international organization **b** the staff of such an office **c** the building or rooms in which such an office is housed

secretary 1 (in Britain) a senior civil servant who assists a government minister **2** (in the US and New Zealand) the head of a government administrative department **3** (in Britain) See **secretary of state 4** (in Australia) the head of a public service department **5** *Diplomacy* the assistant to an ambassador or diplomatic minister of certain countries

secretary bird a large African long-legged diurnal bird of prey, *Sagittarius serpentarius*, having a crest and tail of long feathers and feeding chiefly on snakes: family *Sagittariidae*, order *Falconiformes* (hawks, falcons, etc)

secretary-general a chief administrative official, as of the United Nations

secretary of state 1 (in Britain) the head of any of several government departments **2** (in the US) the head of the government department in charge of foreign affairs (**State Department**) **3** (in certain US states) an official with various duties, such as keeping records

secretion 1 a substance that is released from a cell, esp a glandular cell, and is synthesized in the cell **2** the process involved in producing and releasing such a substance from the cell

secret police a police force that operates relatively secretly to check subversion or political dissent

secret service a government agency or department that conducts intelligence or counterintelligence operations

sect 1 a subdivision of a larger religious group (esp the Christian Church as a whole) the members of which have to some extent diverged from the rest by developing deviating beliefs, practices, etc. 2 *Often disparaging* a a schismatic religious body characterized by an attitude of exclusivity in contrast to the more inclusive religious groups called denominations or Churches **b** a religious group regarded as extreme or heretical

section 1 *Transport* the section of a railway track that is maintained by a single crew or is controlled by a particular signal box 2 *Archit* a representation of a portion of a building or object exposed when cut by an imaginary vertical plane so as to show its construction and interior 3 *Geometry* **a** a plane surface formed by cutting through a solid **b** the shape or area of such a plane surface 4 *Surgery* any procedure involving the cutting or division of an organ, structure, or part, such as a Caesarian section 5 a thin slice of biological tissue, mineral, etc, prepared for examination by a microscope 6 a segment of an orange or other citrus fruit 7 *Austral and NZ* a fare stage on a bus, tram, etc. 8 *Music* **a** an extended division of a composition or movement that forms a coherent part of the structure **b** a division in an orchestra, band, etc, containing instruments belonging to the same class

sector 1 *Geometry* either portion of a circle included between two radii and an arc. Area: $\frac{1}{2}r^2\theta$, where r is the radius and θ is the central angle subtended by the arc (in radians) 2 a measuring instrument consisting of two graduated arms hinged at one end 3 *Computing* the smallest addressable portion of the track on a magnetic tape, disk, or drum store

secular 1 of an education, etc **a** having no particular religious affinities **b** not including compulsory religious studies or services 2 (of clerics) not bound by religious vows to a monastic or other order 3 *Astronomy* occurring slowly over a long period of time 4 a member of the secular clergy

secularism *Philosophy* a doctrine that rejects religion, esp in ethics

Secunderabad a former town in S central India, in N Andra Pradesh: one of the largest British military stations in India: now part of Hyderabad city

security 1 something given or pledged to secure the fulfilment of a promise or obligation 2 a person who undertakes to fulfil another person's obligation 3 the protection of data to ensure that only authorized personnel have access to computer files

security risk a person deemed to be a threat to state security in that he could be open to pressure, have subversive political beliefs, etc.

sedan 1 *US, Canadian, and NZ* a closed two-door or four-door car with four to six seats 2 short for **sedan chair**

Sedan a town in NE France, on the River Meuse: passed to France in 1642; a Protestant stronghold (16th–17th centuries); scene of a French defeat (1870) during the Franco-Prussian War and of a battle (1940) in World War II, which began the German invasion of France. Pop: 20 548 (1999)

sedan chair a closed chair for one passenger, carried on poles by two bearers. It was commonly used in the 17th and 18th centuries

sedation 1 a state of calm or reduced nervous activity 2 the administration of a sedative

sedative 1 of or relating to sedation 2 *Med* a sedative drug or agent

Seddon Richard John, known as *King Dick*. 1845–1906, New Zealand statesman, born in England; prime minister of New Zealand (1893–1906)

sedentary 1 (of animals) moving about very little, usually because of attachment to a rock or other surface 2 (of animals) not migratory

sedge 1 any grasslike cyperaceous plant of the genus *Carex*, typically growing on wet ground and having rhizomes, triangular stems, and minute flowers in spikelets 2 any other plant of the family *Cyperaceae*

Sedgemoor a low-lying plain in SW England, in central Somerset: scene of the defeat (1685) of the Duke of Monmouth

sedge warbler a European songbird, *Acrocephalus schoenobaenus*, of reed beds and swampy areas, having a streaked brownish plumage with white eye stripes: family *Muscicapidae* (Old World flycatchers, etc)

Sedgwick Adam 1785–1873, English geologist; played a major role in establishing much of the geological time scale, esp the Cambrian and Devonian periods

sediment material that has been deposited from water, ice, or wind

sedition 1 an offence that tends to undermine the authority of a state 2 an incitement to public disorder

sedum any crassulaceous rock plant of the genus *Sedum*, having thick fleshy leaves and clusters of white, yellow, or pink flowers

see the diocese of a bishop, or the place within it where his cathedral or procathedral is situated

seed 1 *Botany* a mature fertilized plant ovule, consisting of an embryo and its food store surrounded by a protective seed coat (testa) 2 the small hard seedlike fruit of plants such as wheat 3 (loosely) any propagative part of a plant, such as a tuber, spore, or bulb 4 such parts collectively 5 an archaic or dialect term for **sperm** or **semen** 6 the egg cell or cells of the lobster and certain other animals 7 *Chem* a small crystal added to a supersaturated solution or supercooled liquid to induce crystallization 8 **go** or **run to seed** (of plants) to produce and shed seeds

seedbed a plot of land in which seeds or seedlings are grown before being transplanted

seedling a very young plant produced from a seed

seed pod a carpel or pistil enclosing the seeds of a plant, esp a flowering plant

Seeger Pete born 1919. US folk singer and songwriter, noted for his protest songs, which include "We shall Overcome" (1960), "Where have all the Flowers gone" (1961), "If I had a Hammer" (1962), and "Little Boxes" (1962)

seeing *Astronomy* the quality of the observing conditions (especially the turbulence of the atmosphere) during an astronomical observation

seersucker a light cotton, linen, or other fabric with a crinkled surface and often striped

seesaw 1 a plank balanced in the middle so that two people seated on the ends can ride up and down by pushing on the ground with their feet 2 the pastime of riding up and down on a seesaw

Seferis George pen name of *Georgios Seferiades*. 1900–71, Greek poet and diplomat: Nobel prize for literature 1963

Sefton a unitary authority in NW England, in Merseyside. Pop: 281 600 (2003 est). Area: 150 sq km (58 sq miles)

segment 1 *Maths* a a part of a line or curve between two points b a part of a plane or solid figure cut off by an intersecting line, plane, or planes, esp one between a chord and an arc of a circle 2 *Zoology* any of the parts into which the body or appendages of an annelid or arthropod are divided

Segovia[1] Andrés, Marquis of Salobreña. 1893–1987, Spanish classical guitarist

Segovia[2] a town in central Spain: site of a Roman aqueduct, still in use, and the fortified palace of the kings of Castile (the Alcázar). Pop: 55 640 (2003 est)

segregation 1 *Genetics* the separation at meiosis of the two members of any pair of alleles into separate gametes 2 *Metallurgy* the process in which a component of an alloy or solid solution separates in small regions within the solid or on the solid's surface

seigneur 1 a feudal lord, esp in France 2 (in French Canada, until 1854) the landlord of an estate that was subdivided among peasants who held their plots by a form of feudal tenure

seine a large fishing net that hangs vertically in the water by means of floats at the top and weights at the bottom

Seine a river in N France, rising on the Plateau de Langres and flowing northwest through Paris to the English Channel: the second longest river in France, linked by canal with the Rivers Somme, Scheldt, Meuse, Rhine, Saône, and Loire. Length: 776 km (482 miles)

Seine-et-Marne a department of N central France, in Île-de-France region. Capital: Melun. Pop: 1 232 467 (2003 est). Area: 5931 sq km (2313 sq miles)

Seine-Maritime a department of N France, in Haute-Normandie region. Capital: Rouen. Pop: 1 237 263 (2003 est). Area: 6342 sq km (2473 sq miles)

Seine-Saint-Denis a department of N central France, in Île-de-France region. Capital: Bobigny. Pop: 1 396 122 (2003 est). Area: 236 sq km (92 sq miles)

seismic relating to or caused by earthquakes or artificially produced earth tremors

seismograph an instrument that registers and records the features of earthquakes. A **seismogram** is the record from such an instrument

seismology the branch of geology concerned with the study of earthquakes and seismic waves

seizure *Pathol* a sudden manifestation or recurrence of a disease, such as an epileptic convulsion

Sekondi a port in SW Ghana, 8 km (5 miles) northeast of Takoradi: linked administratively with Takoradi in 1946. Pop. (with Takoradi): 335 000 (2005 est)

Selangor a state of Peninsular Malaysia, on the Strait of Malacca: established as a British protectorate in 1874, became a Federated Malay State in 1896 and part of Malaysia in 1946; tin producer. Capital: Shah Alam. Pop: 4 188 876 (2000). Area: 8203 sq km (3167 sq miles)

Selby an inland port in N England, in North Yorkshire, on the River Ouse: centre for a coalfield since 1983: agricultural products. Pop: 15 807 (2001)

select committee (in Britain) a small committee composed of members of parliament, set up by either House of Parliament to investigate and report back on a specified matter of interest

selection *Biology* the natural or artificial process by which certain organisms or characters are reproduced and perpetuated in the species in preference to others

selective *Electronics* occurring at, operating at, or capable of separating out a particular frequency or band of frequencies

selenium a nonmetallic element that exists in several allotropic forms. It occurs free in volcanic areas and in sulphide ores, esp pyrite. The common form is a grey crystalline solid that is photoconductive, photovoltaic, and semiconducting: used in photocells, solar cells, and in xerography. Symbol: Se; atomic no.: 34; atomic wt.: 78.96; valency: –2, 4, or 6; relative density: 4.79 (grey); melting pt.: 221°C (grey); boiling pt.: 685°C (grey)

Seles Monica born 1973, US tennis player, born in Yugoslavia: winner of the US Open (1991, 1992); stabbed while on court in an unprovoked attack

Seleucia 1 an ancient city in Mesopotamia, on the River Tigris: founded by Seleucus Nicator in 312 BC; became the chief city of the Seleucid empire; sacked by the Romans around 162 AD 2 an ancient city in SE Asia Minor, on the River Calycadnus (modern Goksu Nehri): captured by the Turks in the 13th century; site of present-day Silifke (Turkey) 3 an ancient port in Syria, on the River Orontes: the port of Antioch, of military importance during the wars between the Ptolemies and Seleucids; largely destroyed by earthquake in 526; site of present-day Samandağ (Turkey)

Seleucus I surname *Nicator*. ?358–280 BC, Macedonian general under Alexander the Great, who founded the Seleucid kingdom

self 1 an individual's consciousness of his own identity or being 2 *Philosophy* that which is essential to an individual, esp the mind or soul in Cartesian metaphysics; the ego 3 a bird, animal, etc, that is a single colour throughout, esp a self-coloured pigeon

self-absorption *Physics* the process in which some of the radiation emitted by a material is absorbed by the material itself

self-coloured (of cloth, material, etc) a having the natural or original colour b retaining the colour of the thread before weaving

self-conscious conscious of one's existence

self-defence 1 boxing as a means of defending the person (esp in the phrase **noble art of self-defence**) 2 *Law* the right to defend one's person, family, or property against attack or threat of attack by the use of no more force than is reasonable

self-determination the right of a nation or people to determine its own form of government without influence from outside

self-employed earning one's living in one's own business or through freelance work, rather than as the employee of another

self-government the government of a country, nation, etc, by its own people

self-pollination the transfer of pollen from the anthers to the stigma of the same flower or of another flower on the same plant

self-propelled (of a vehicle) provided with its own source of tractive power rather than requiring an external means of propulsion

Selkirk Alexander original name *Alexander Selcraig*. 1676–1721, Scottish sailor, who was marooned on one of the islets of Juan Fernández and is regarded as the prototype of Defoe's *Robinson Crusoe*

Selkirkshire (until 1975) a county of SE Scotland, now part of Scottish Borders

Sella Phillipe . French Rugby Union football player; played 111 internationals for France (1982–95), making him the game's most capped player

Sellafield the site of an atomic power station and nuclear reprocessing plant in NW England, in W Cumbria

sell-by date a date printed on the packaging of perishable goods, indicating the date after which the goods should not be offered for sale

Sellers Peter 1925–80, English radio, stage, and film actor and comedian: noted for his gift of precise vocal mimicry, esp in *The Goon Show* (with Spike Milligan and Harry Secombe; BBC Radio, 1952–60). His films include *I'm All Right, Jack* (1959), *The Millionairess* (1961), *The Pink Panther* (1963), *Dr Strangelove* (1964), and *Being There* (1979)

sell-through 1 the ratio of the quantity of goods sold by a retailer to the quantity originally delivered to it wholesale 2 the sale of prerecorded video cassettes or DVDs, as opposed to their being available for hire only 3 (of prerecorded video cassettes or DVDs) sold in this way

selvage *or* **selvedge** a similar strip of material allowed in fabricating a metal or plastic article, used esp for handling components during manufacture

semantic 1 of or relating to semantics 2 *Logic* concerned with the interpretation of a formal theory, as when truth tables are given as an account of the sentential connectives

semantics 1 the study of the relationships between signs and symbols and what they represent 2 *Logic* **a** the study of interpretations of a formal theory **b** the study of the relationship between the structure of a theory and its subject matter **c** (of a formal theory) the principles that determine the truth or falsehood of sentences within the theory, and the references of its terms

Semarang *or* **Samarang** a port in S Indonesia, in N Java on the Java Sea. Pop: 1 348 803 (2000)

semen 1 the thick whitish fluid containing spermatozoa that is ejaculated from the male genital tract 2 another name for **sperm**

Semeru *or* **Semeroe** a volcano in Indonesia: the highest peak in Java. Height: 3676 m (12 060 ft)

semester 1 (in some universities) either of two divisions of the academic year, ranging from 15 to 18 weeks

2 (in German universities) a session of six months

semiarid characterized by scanty rainfall and scrubby vegetation, often occurring in continental interiors

semibreve *Music* a note, now the longest in common use, having a time value that may be divided by any power of 2 to give all other notes

semicircle a one half of a circle **b** half the circumference of a circle

semiconductor 1 a substance, such as germanium or silicon, that has an electrical conductivity that increases with temperature and is intermediate between that of a metal and an insulator. The behaviour may be exhibited by the pure substance (**intrinsic semiconductor**) or as a result of impurities (**extrinsic semiconductor**) 2 **a** a device, such as a transistor or integrated circuit, that depends on the properties of such a substance **b** (*as modifier*): *a semiconductor diode*

seminal 1 of or relating to semen 2 *Biology* of or relating to seed

seminar 1 a small group of students meeting regularly under the guidance of a tutor, professor, etc, to exchange information, discuss theories, etc. 2 one such meeting or the place in which it is held 3 a higher course for postgraduates

seminary 1 an academy for the training of priests, rabbis, etc. 2 *US* another word for **seminar** (sense 1)

semiotics *or* **semeiotics** the scientific study of the symptoms of disease; symptomatology

Semipalatinsk a city in NE Kazakhstan on the Irtysh River; an important communications centre. Pop: 282 000 (2005 est)

semipermeable (esp of a cell membrane) selectively permeable

semiprecious (of certain stones) having commercial value, but less than a precious stone

semiquaver *Music* a note having the time value of one-sixteenth of a semibreve

Semiramis the legendary founder of Babylon and wife of Ninus, king of Assyria, which she ruled with great skill after his death

semirigid (of an airship) maintaining shape by means of a main supporting keel and internal gas pressure

Semite *or less commonly* **Shemite** 1 a member of the group of Caucasoid peoples who speak a Semitic language, including the Jews and Arabs as well as the ancient Babylonians, Assyrians, and Phoenicians 2 another word for a **Jew**

Semitic *or less commonly* **Shemitic** 1 a branch or subfamily of the Afro-Asiatic family of languages that includes Arabic, Hebrew, Aramaic, Amharic, and such ancient languages as Akkadian and Phoenician 2 denoting, belonging to, or characteristic of any of the peoples speaking a Semitic language, esp the Jews or the Arabs 3 another word for **Jewish**

semitone an interval corresponding to a frequency difference of 100 cents as measured in the system of equal temperament, and denoting the pitch difference between certain adjacent degrees of the diatonic scale (**diatonic semitone**) or between one note and its sharpened or flattened equivalent (**chromatic semitone**); minor second

semitrailer a type of trailer or articulated lorry that has wheels only at the rear, the front end being supported by the towing vehicle

Semmelweis Ignaz Philipp 1818–65, Hungarian obstetrician, who discovered the cause of puerperal infection and pioneered the use of antiseptics

Sempach a village in central Switzerland, in Lucerne canton on **Lake Sempach**: scene of the victory (1386) of the Swiss over the Hapsburgs

senate 1 any legislative or governing body considered to resemble a Senate 2 the main governing body at some colleges and universities

Senate 1 the upper chamber of the legislatures of the US, Canada, Australia, and many other countries 2 the legislative council of ancient Rome. Originally the council of the kings, the Senate became the highest legislative, judicial, and religious authority in republican Rome 3 the ruling body of certain free cities in medieval and modern Europe

senator 1 a member of a Senate or senate 2 any legislator or statesman

Sendai a city in central Japan, on NE Honshu: university (1907). Pop: 986 713 (2002 est)

Seneca 1 **Lucius Annaeus** , called *the Younger*. ?4 BC–65 AD, Roman philosopher, statesman, and dramatist; tutor and adviser to Nero. He was implicated in a plot to murder Nero and committed suicide. His works include Stoical essays on ethical subjects and tragedies that had a considerable influence on Elizabethan drama 2 his father, **Marcus** or **Lucius Annaeus**, called *the Elder* or *the Rhetorician*. ?55 BC–?39 AD, Roman writer on oratory and history

Senegal a republic in West Africa, on the Atlantic: made part of French West Africa in 1895; became fully independent in 1960; joined with The Gambia to form the Confederation of Senegambia (1982–89); mostly lowlying, with semidesert in the north and tropical forest in the southwest. Official language: French. Religion: Muslim majority. Currency: franc. Capital: Dakar. Pop: 10 339 000 (2004 est). Area: 197 160 sq km (76 124 sq miles)

Senegambia a region of W Africa, between the Senegal and Gambia Rivers: now mostly in Senegal

seneschal 1 a steward of the household of a medieval prince or nobleman who took charge of domestic arrangements, etc. 2 *Brit* a cathedral official

senile (of land forms or rivers) at an advanced stage in the cycle of erosion

senior 1 *Education* a of, relating to, or designating more advanced or older pupils b of or relating to a secondary school 2 a a senior pupil, student, etc. b a fellow of senior rank in an English university

Senlac a hill in Sussex: site of the Battle of Hastings in 1066

senna 1 any of various tropical plants of the leguminous genus *Cassia*, esp *C. angustifolia* (**Arabian senna**) and *C. acutifolia* (**Alexandrian senna**), having typically yellow flowers and long pods 2 **senna leaf** the dried leaflets of any of these plants, used as a cathartic and laxative

Senna Ayrton 1960–94, Brazilian racing driver: world champion (1988, 1990, 1991)

Sennacherib died 681 BC, king of Assyria (705–681); son of Sargon II. He invaded Judah twice, defeated Babylon,

and rebuilt Nineveh

Sennar 1 a region of the E Sudan, between the White Nile and the Blue Nile: a kingdom from the 16th to 19th centuries 2 a town in this region, on the Blue Nile: the nearby **Sennar Dam** (1925) supplies irrigation water to Gezira. Pop: 135 000 (2005 est)

sensation 1 the power of perceiving through the senses 2 a physical condition or experience resulting from the stimulation of one of the sense organs

sensationalism 1 *Philosophy* a the doctrine that knowledge cannot go beyond the analysis of experience b *Ethics* the doctrine that the ability to gratify the senses is the only criterion of goodness 2 *Psychol* the theory that all experience and mental life may be explained in terms of sensations and remembered images 3 *Aesthetics* the theory of the beauty of sensuality in the arts

sense 1 any of the faculties by which the mind receives information about the external world or about the state of the body. In addition to the five traditional faculties of sight, hearing, touch, taste, and smell, the term includes the means by which bodily position, temperature, pain, balance, etc, are perceived 2 such faculties collectively; the ability to perceive 3 a feeling perceived through one of the senses 4 *Maths* one of two opposite directions measured on a directed line; the sign as contrasted with the magnitude of a vector 5 *Logic, linguistics* a the import of an expression as contrasted with its referent. Thus *the morning star* and *the evening star* have the same reference, Venus, but different senses b the property of an expression by virtue of which its referent is determined c that which one grasps in understanding an expression

sense organ a structure in animals that is specialized for receiving external or internal stimuli and transmitting them in the form of nervous impulses to the brain

sensibility 1 the ability to perceive or feel 2 the condition of a plant of being susceptible to external influences, esp attack by parasites

sensitive 1 having the power of sensation 2 of or relating to the senses or the power of sensation 3 *Photog* having a high sensitivity 4 connected with matters affecting national security, esp through access to classified information 5 (of a stock market or prices) quickly responsive to external influences and thus fluctuating or tending to fluctuate

sensor anything, such as a photoelectric cell, that receives a signal or stimulus and responds to it

sensory *or less commonly* **sensorial** 1 of or relating to the senses or the power of sensation 2 of or relating to those processes and structures within an organism that receive stimuli from the environment and convey them to the brain

sent a monetary unit of Estonia, worth one hundredth of a kroon

sentence 1 the judgment formally pronounced upon a person convicted in criminal proceedings, esp the decision as to what punishment is to be imposed 2 *Music* another word for **period** 3 any short passage of scripture employed in liturgical use 4 *Logic* a well-formed expression, without variables

sentinel *Computing* a character used to indicate the

beginning or end of a particular block of information

Seoul the capital of South Korea, in the west on the Han River: capital of Korea from 1392 to 1910, then seat of the Japanese administration until 1945; became capital of South Korea in 1948; cultural and educational centre. Pop: 9 592 000 (2005 est)

sepal any of the separate parts of the calyx of a flower

separate designating or relating to a Church or similar institution that has ceased to have associations with an original parent organization

separate school (in Canada) a school for a large religious minority financed by its rates and administered by its own school board but under the authority of the provincial department of education

separation *Family law* the cessation of cohabitation between a man and wife, either by mutual agreement or under a decree of a court

separatist *or* **separationist** a a person who advocates or practises secession from an organization, group, or country b *(as modifier)*: *a separatist movement*

sepia 1 a dark reddish-brown pigment obtained from the inky secretion of the cuttlefish 2 any cuttlefish of the genus *Sepia* 3 a brownish tone imparted to a photograph, esp an early one such as a calotype. It can be produced by first bleaching a print (after fixing) and then immersing it for a short time in a solution of sodium sulphide or of alkaline thiourea 4 a brownish-grey to dark yellowish-brown colour 5 a drawing or photograph in sepia

sepoy (formerly) an Indian soldier in the service of the British

sepsis the presence of pus-forming bacteria in the body

sept 1 *Anthropol* a clan or group that believes itself to be descended from a common ancestor 2 a branch of a tribe or nation, esp in medieval Ireland or Scotland

septet *or* **septette** *Music* a group of seven singers or instrumentalists or a piece of music composed for such a group

septic 1 of, relating to, or caused by sepsis 2 of, relating to, or caused by putrefaction

septicaemia *or US* **septicemia** a condition caused by pus-forming microorganisms in the blood

Septuagint the principal Greek version of the Old Testament, including the Apocrypha, believed to have been translated by 70 or 72 scholars

septum 1 *Biology, anatomy* a dividing partition between two tissues or cavities 2 a dividing partition or membrane between two cavities in a mechanical device

sepulchre *or US* **sepulcher** a separate alcove in some medieval churches in which the Eucharistic elements were kept from Good Friday until the Easter ceremonies

sequence 1 a *Cards* a set of three or more consecutive cards, usually of the same suit b *Bridge* a set of two or more consecutive cards 2 *Music* an arrangement of notes or chords repeated several times at different pitches 3 *Maths* a an ordered set of numbers or other mathematical entities in one-to-one correspondence with the integers 1 to *n* b an ordered infinite set of mathematical entities in one-to-one correspondence with the natural numbers 4 a section of a film constituting a single continuous uninterrupted episode 5 *Biochem* the unique order of amino acids in the polypep-

tide chain of a protein or of nucleotides in the polynucleotide chain of DNA or RNA 6 *RC Church* another word for **prose**

sequin any of various gold coins formerly minted in Italy, Turkey, and Malta

sequoia either of two giant Californian coniferous trees, *Sequoia sempervirens* (**redwood**) or *Sequoiadendron giganteum* (formerly *Sequoia gigantea*) (**big tree** or **giant sequoia**): family *Taxodiaceae*

Sequoia National Park a national park in central California, in the Sierra Nevada Mountains: established in 1890 to protect groves of giant sequoias, some of which are about 4000 years old. Area: 1556 sq km (601 sq miles)

seraglio *or* **serail** 1 the harem of a Muslim house or palace 2 a sultan's palace, esp in the former Turkish empire 3 the wives and concubines of a Muslim

Seram *or* **Ceram** an island in Indonesia, in the Moluccas, separated from New Guinea by the **Ceram Sea**: mountainous and densely forested. Area: 17 150 sq km (6622 sq miles)

seraph 1 *Theol* a member of the highest order of angels in the celestial hierarchies, often depicted as the winged head of a child 2 *Old Testament* one of the fiery six-winged beings attendant upon Jehovah in Isaiah's vision (Isaiah 6)

Serbia a constituent republic of the Union of Serbia and Montenegro: declared a kingdom in 1882; precipitated World War I by the conflict with Austria; became part of the Kingdom of the Serbs, Croats, and Slovenes (later called Yugoslavia) in 1918; with Montenegro formed the Federal Republic of Yugoslavia when the other constituent republics became independent in 1991–92; a new Union of Serbia and Montenegro formed in 2002; the autonomous region of Kosovo has been administered by the U.N. since the conflict of 1999. Capital: Belgrade. Pop: 7 479 437 (2002). Area: 88 361 sq km (34 109 sq miles)

Serbian *or* **Serb** the dialect of Serbo-Croat spoken in Serbia

Serbo-Croat *or* **Serbo-Croatian** the language of the Serbs and the Croats, belonging to the South Slavonic branch of the Indo-European family. The Serbian dialect is usually written in the Cyrillic alphabet, the Croatian in Roman

Seremban a town in Peninsular Malaysia, capital of Negri Sembilan state. Pop: 332 000 (2005 est)

serenade 1 a piece of music appropriate to the evening, characteristically played outside the house of a woman 2 a piece of music indicative or suggestive of this 3 an extended composition in several movements similar to the modern suite or divertimento

serf (esp in medieval Europe) an unfree person, esp one bound to the land. If his lord sold the land, the serf was passed on to the new landlord

serge 1 a twill-weave woollen or worsted fabric used for clothing 2 a similar twilled cotton, silk, or rayon fabric

sergeant 1 a (in Britain) a police officer ranking between constable and inspector b (in the US) a police officer ranking below a captain 2 See **sergeant at arms** 3 a court or municipal officer who has ceremonial duties 4 (formerly) a tenant by military service, not of knightly rank

sergeant at arms (formerly) an officer who served a monarch or noble, esp as an armed attendant

sergeant major a large damselfish, *Abudefduf saxatilis*, having a bluish-grey body marked with black stripes

Sergipe a state of NE Brazil: the smallest Brazilian state; a centre of resistance to Dutch conquest (17th century). Capital: Aracajú. Pop: 1 846 039 (2002). Area: 13 672 sq km (8492 sq miles)

serial 1 *Computing* of or operating on items of information, instructions, etc, in the order in which they occur **2** of, relating to, or using the techniques of serialism **3** *Logic, maths* (of a relation) connected, transitive, and asymmetric, thereby imposing an order on all the members of the domain, as *less than* on the natural numbers

series 1 *Maths* the sum of a finite or infinite sequence of numbers or quantities **2** *Electronics* **a** a configuration of two or more components connected in a circuit so that the same current flows in turn through each of them (esp in the phrase **in series**) **b** (*as modifier*): *a series circuit* **3** *Geology* a stratigraphical unit that is a subdivision of a system and represents the rocks formed during an epoch

Seringapatam a small town in S India, in Karnataka on **Seringapatam Island** in the Cauvery River: capital of Mysore from 1610 to 1799, when it was besieged and captured by the British. Pop: 23 448 (2001)

sermon a an address of religious instruction or exhortation, often based on a passage from the Bible, esp one delivered during a church service **b** a written version of such an address

Sermon on the Mount *New Testament* a major discourse delivered by Christ, including the Beatitudes and the Lord's Prayer (Matthew 5–7)

seropositive (of a person whose blood has been tested for a specific disease, such as AIDS) showing a serological reaction indicating the presence of the disease

serpent 1 a literary or dialect word for **snake 2** *Old Testament* a manifestation of Satan as a guileful tempter (Genesis 3:1–5) **3** an obsolete wind instrument resembling a snake in shape, the bass form of the cornett

serpentine¹ 1 of, relating to, or resembling a serpent **2** *Maths* a curve that is symmetric about the origin of and asymptotic to the *x*-axis

serpentine² 1 a dark green or brown mineral with a greasy or silky lustre, found in igneous and metamorphic rocks. It is used as an ornamental stone; and one variety (chrysotile) is known as asbestos. Composition: hydrated magnesium silicate. Formula: $Mg_3Si_2O_5(OH)_4$ Crystal structure: monoclinic **2** any of a group of minerals having the general formula $(Mg,Fe)_3Si_2O_5(OH)_4$

Sertorius Quintus ?123–72 BC, Roman soldier who fought with Marius in Gaul (102) and led an insurrection in Spain against Sulla until he was assassinated

serum 1 antitoxin obtained from the blood serum of immunized animals **2** *Physiol, zoology* clear watery fluid, esp that exuded by serous membranes

serval a slender feline mammal, *Felis serval*, of the African bush, having an orange-brown coat with black spots, large ears, and long legs

server 1 *Chiefly RC Church* a person who acts as acolyte or assists the priest at Mass **2** *Computing* a computer or program that supplies data or resources to other machines on a network

Servetus Michael, Spanish name *Miguel Serveto*. 1511–53, Spanish theologian and physician. He was burnt at the stake by order of Calvin for denying the doctrine of the Trinity and the divinity of Christ

service 1 the supply, installation, or maintenance of goods carried out by a dealer **2** a department of public employment and its employees **3** the work of a public servant **4** public worship carried out according to certain prescribed forms **5** the prescribed form according to which a specific kind of religious ceremony is to be carried out **6** a unified collection of musical settings of the canticles and other liturgical items prescribed by the Book of Common Prayer as used in the Church of England **7** (in feudal law) the duty owed by a tenant to his lord **8** the serving of a writ, summons, etc, upon a person **9** *Nautical* a length of tarred marline or small stuff used in serving **10** (of male animals) the act of mating

service area a place on a motorway providing garage services, restaurants, toilet facilities, etc.

service road *Brit* a relatively narrow road running parallel to a main road and providing access to houses, shops, offices, factories, etc, situated along its length

service station 1 a place that supplies fuel, oil, etc, for motor vehicles and often carries out repairs, servicing, etc. **2** a place that repairs and sometimes supplies mechanical or electrical equipment

servitude *Law* a burden attaching to an estate for the benefit of an adjoining estate or of some definite person

servomechanism a mechanical or electromechanical system for control of the position or speed of an output transducer. Negative feedback is incorporated to minimize discrepancies between the output state and the input control setting

sesame a tropical herbaceous plant, *Sesamum indicum*, of the East Indies, cultivated, esp in India, for its small oval seeds: family *Pedaliaceae* **2** the seeds of this plant, used in flavouring bread and yielding an edible oil (**benne oil** or **gingili**)

Sesostris I 20th century BC, king of Egypt of the 12th dynasty. He conquered Nubia and brought ancient Egypt to the height of its prosperity. The funerary complex at Lisht was built during his reign

sessile 1 (of flowers or leaves) having no stalk; growing directly from the stem **2** (of animals such as the barnacle) permanently attached to a substratum

session 1 the meeting of a court, legislature, judicial body, etc, for the execution of its function or the transaction of business **2** a single continuous meeting of such a body **3** a series or period of such meetings **4** *Education* **a** the time during which classes are held **b** a school or university term or year **5** *Presbyterian Church* the judicial and administrative body presiding over a local congregation and consisting of the minister and elders **6** a meeting of a group of musicians to record in a studio

Sessions Roger (Huntington). 1896–1985, US composer

sestet 1 *Prosody* the last six lines of a Petrarchan sonnet 2 *Prosody* any six-line stanza 3 another word for **sextet**

Sestos a ruined town in NW Turkey, at the narrowest point of the Dardanelles: N terminus of the bridge of boats built by Xerxes in 481 BC for the crossing of his armies of invasion

set 1 *Maths, logic* a a collection of numbers, objects, etc, that is treated as an entity: {3, the moon} is the set the two members of which are the number 3 and the moon b (in some formulations) a class that can itself be a member of other classes 2 any apparatus that receives or transmits television or radio signals 3 *Tennis, squash, badminton* one of the units of a match, in tennis one in which one player or pair of players must win at least six games 4 a the number of couples required for a formation dance b a series of figures that make up a formation dance 5 a a band's or performer's concert repertoire on a given occasion b a continuous performance

set back 1 a recession in the upper part of a high building, esp one that increases the daylight at lower levels 2 a steplike shelf where a wall is reduced in thickness

Seth *Old Testament* Adam's third son, given by God in place of the murdered Abel (Genesis 4:25)

Seton Ernest Thompson 1860–1946, US author and illustrator of animal books, born in England

set piece *Theatre* a piece of scenery built to stand independently as part of a stage set

set square a thin flat piece of plastic, metal, etc, in the shape of a right-angled triangle, used in technical drawing

sett *or* **set** 1 a small rectangular paving block made of stone, such as granite, used to provide a durable road surface 2 the burrow of a badger

setter any of various breeds of large gun dog, having silky coats and plumed tails

set theory 1 *Maths* the branch of mathematics concerned with the properties and interrelationships of sets 2 *Logic* a theory constructed within first-order logic that yields the mathematical theory of classes, esp one that distinguishes sets from proper classes as a means of avoiding certain paradoxes

setting 1 the scenery, properties, or background, used to create the location for a stage play, film, etc. 2 *Music* a composition consisting of a certain text and music provided or arranged for it 3 any of a series of points on a scale or dial that can be selected to control the level as of temperature, speed, etc, at which a machine functions 4 a clutch of eggs in a bird's nest, esp a clutch of hen's eggs

settlement 1 a place newly settled; colony 2 a collection of dwellings forming a community, esp on a frontier 3 a public building used to provide educational and general welfare facilities for persons living in deprived areas 4 *Law* a a conveyance, usually to trustees, of property to be enjoyed by several persons in succession b the deed or other instrument conveying such property c the determination of a dispute, etc, by mutual agreement without resorting to legal proceedings

setup *Films* the position of the camera, microphones, and performers at the beginning of a scene

Seurat Georges 1859–91, French neoimpressionist painter. He developed the pointillist technique of painting, characterized by brilliant luminosity, as in *Dimanche à la Grande-Jatte* (1886)

Sevan Lake a lake in Armenia at an altitude of 1914 m (6279 ft). Area: 1417 sq km (547 sq miles)

Sevastopol a port, resort, and naval base in S Ukraine, in the Crimea, on the Black Sea: captured and destroyed by British, French, and Turkish forces after a siege of 11 months (1854–55) during the Crimean War; taken by the Germans after a siege of 8 months (1942) during World War II. Pop: 338 000 (2005 est)

seven 1 the cardinal number that is the sum of six and one and is a prime number 2 a numeral, 7, VII, etc, representing this number 3 the amount or quantity that is one greater than six

seventeen 1 the cardinal number that is the sum of ten and seven and is a prime number 2 a numeral, 17, XVII, etc, representing this number 3 the amount or quantity that is seven more than ten

seventh heaven the final state of eternal bliss, esp according to Talmudic and Muslim eschatology

seventy 1 the cardinal number that is the product of ten and seven 2 a numeral, 70, LXX, etc, representing this number 3 the numbers 70–79, esp the 70th to the 79th year of a person's life or of a particular century 4 the amount or quantity that is seven times as big as ten

several *Law* capable of being dealt with separately; not shared

Severn 1 a river in E Wales and W England, rising in Powys and flowing northeast and east into England, then south to the Bristol Channel. Length: about 290 km (180 miles) 2 a river in SE central Canada, in Ontario, flowing northeast to Hudson Bay. Length: about 676 km (420 miles)

Severnaya Zemlya an archipelago in the Arctic Ocean off the coast of N central Russia

Severus Lucius Septimius 146–211 AD, Roman soldier and emperor (193–211). He waged war successfully against the Parthians (197–202) and spent his last years in Britain (208- -11)

Seveso a town in N Italy, near Milan: evacuated in 1976 after contamination by a poisonous cloud of dioxin gas released from a factory

Seville a port in SW Spain, on the Guadalquivir River: chief town of S Spain under the Vandals and Visigoths (5th–8th centuries); centre of Spanish colonial trade (16th–17th centuries); tourist centre. Pop: 709 975 (2003 est)

Seville orange 1 an orange tree, *Citrus aurantium*, of tropical and semitropical regions: grown for its bitter fruit, which is used to make marmalade 2 the fruit of this tree

sewage farm a place where sewage is treated, esp for use as manure

Seward William Henry 1801–72, US statesman; secretary of state (1861–69). He was a leading opponent of slavery and was responsible for the purchase of Alaska (1867)

Seward Peninsula a peninsula of W Alaska, on the Bering Strait. Length: about 290 km (180 miles)

Sewell Henry 1807–79, New Zealand statesman, born in England: first prime minister of New Zealand (1856)

sewer[1] a drain or pipe, esp one that is underground, used to carry away surface water or sewage

sewer² (in medieval England) a servant of high rank in charge of the serving of meals and the seating of guests

sewerage 1 an arrangement of sewers **2** the removal of surface water or sewage by means of sewers

sex 1 the sum of the characteristics that distinguish organisms on the basis of their reproductive function **2** either of the two categories, male or female, into which organisms are placed on this basis **3** short for **sexual intercourse**

sex chromosome either of the chromosomes determining the sex of animals

sexless having or showing no sexual differentiation

sextant 1 an optical instrument used in navigation and consisting of a telescope through which a sighting of a heavenly body is taken, with protractors for determining its angular distance above the horizon or from another heavenly body **2** a sixth part of a circle having an arc which subtends an angle of 60°

sextet or **sextette** Music a group of six singers or instrumentalists or a piece of music composed for such a group

sexton a person employed to act as caretaker of a church and its contents and graveyard, and often also as bell-ringer, gravedigger, etc.

sextuple (of musical time or rhythm) having six beats per bar

sextuplet Music a group of six notes played in a time value of four

sexual (of reproduction) characterized by the union of male and female gametes

sexual intercourse the act carried out for procreation or for pleasure in which the insertion of the male's erect penis into the female's vagina is followed by rhythmic thrusting usually culminating in orgasm; copulation; coitus

Seymour Jane ?1509–37, third wife of Henry VIII of England; mother of Edward VI

Sfax a port in E Tunisia, on the Gulf of Gabès: the second largest town in Tunisia; commercial centre of a phosphate region. Pop: 570 000 (2005 est)

Sforza 1 Count **Carlo** 1873–1952, Italian statesman; leader of the anti-Fascist opposition **2 Francesco** 1401–66, duke of Milan (1450–66) **3** his father **Giacomuzzo** or **Muzio**, original name *Attendolo*. 1369–1424, Italian condottiere and founder of the dynasty that ruled Milan (1450–1535) **4 Lodovico**, called *the Moor*. 1451–1508, duke of Milan (1494–1500), but effective ruler from 1480; patron of Leonardo da Vinci

Shaanxi or **Shensi** a province of NW China: one of the earliest centres of Chinese civilization; largely mountainous. Capital: Xi'an. Pop: 36 900 000 (2003 est). Area: 195 800 sq km (75 598 sq miles)

Shaba a region of SE Democratic Republic of Congo (formerly Zaïre): site of a secessionist movement during the 1960s and again declared itself independent in 1993; important for hydroelectric power and rich mineral resources (copper and tin ore). Pop: 4 125 000 (1998 est). Area: 496 964 sq km (191 878 sq miles)

Shache, Soche, or **So-ch'e** a town in W China, in the W Xinjiang Uygur AR: a centre of the caravan trade between China, India, and Transcaspian areas

shack 1 a roughly built hut **2** South African temporary accommodation put together by squatters

shackle a U-shaped bracket, the open end of which is closed by a bolt (**shackle pin**), used for securing ropes, chains, etc.

Shackleton Sir **Ernest Henry** 1874–1922, British explorer. He commanded three expeditions to the Antarctic (1907–09; 1914–17; 1921–22), during which the south magnetic pole was located (1909)

shad 1 any of various herring-like food fishes of the genus *Alosa* and related genera, such as *A. alosa* (**allis shad**) of Europe, that migrate from the sea to freshwater to spawn: family *Clupeidae* (herrings) **2** any of various similar but unrelated fishes

Shadbolt Maurice born 1932, New Zealand novelist

shade 1 a darker area indicated in a painting, drawing, etc, by shading **2** a colour that varies slightly from a standard colour due to a difference in hue, saturation, or luminosity

shading the graded areas of tone, lines, dots, etc, indicating light and dark in a painting or drawing

shadow 1 the dark portions of a picture **2** Med a dark area on an X-ray film representing an opaque structure or part **3** (in Jungian psychology) the archetype that represents man's animal ancestors **4** Brit designating a member or members of the main opposition party in Parliament who would hold ministerial office if their party were in power

Shadrach Old Testament one of Daniel's three companions, who, together with Meshach and Abednego, was miraculously saved from destruction in Nebuchadnezzar's fiery furnace (Daniel 3:12–30)

Shaffer Sir **Peter** born 1926, British dramatist. His plays include *The Royal Hunt of the Sun* (1964), *Equus* (1973), *Amadeus* (1979), and *The Gift of the Gorgon* (1992)

shaft 1 a revolving rod that transmits motion or power: usually used of axial rotation **2** Anatomy **a** the middle part (diaphysis) of a long bone **b** the main portion of any elongated structure or part **3** the middle part of a column or pier, between the base and the capital **4** a column, obelisk, etc, esp one that forms a monument **5** Architect a column that supports a vaulting rib, sometimes one of a set **6** Ornithol the central rib of a feather **7** an archaic or literary word for **arrow**

Shaftesbury 1 1st Earl of, title of *Anthony Ashley Cooper*. 1621–83, English statesman, a major figure in the Whig opposition to Charles II **2 7th Earl of,** title of *Anthony Ashley Cooper*. 1801–85, English evangelical churchman and social reformer. He promoted measures to improve conditions in mines (1842), factories (1833; 1847; 1850), and schools

shag 1 a napped fabric, usually a rough wool **2** shredded coarse tobacco

shaggy (in textiles) having a nap of long rough strands

shah a ruler of certain Middle Eastern countries, esp (formerly) Iran

Shah Jahan 1592–1666, Mogul emperor (1628–58). During his reign the finest monuments of Mogul architecture in India were built, including the Taj Mahal and the Pearl Mosque at Agra

Shahjahanpur a city in N India, in central Uttar Pradesh: founded in 1647 in the reign of Shah Jahan. Pop: 297 932 (2001)

Shaka or **Chaka** died 1828, Zulu military leader, who founded the Zulu Empire in southern Africa

shake 1 an instance of shaking dice before casting **2** *Music* another word for **trill 3** a dance, popular in the 1960s, in which the body is shaken convulsively in time to the beat **4** an informal name for **earthquake**

shake down *Informal, chiefly US* a voyage to test the performance of a ship or aircraft or to familiarize the crew with their duties **b** *(as modifier): a shakedown run*

Shakespeare William 1564–1616, English dramatist and poet. He was born and died at Stratford-upon-Avon but spent most of his life as an actor and playwright in London. His plays with approximate dates of composition are: *Henry VI, Parts I–III* (1590); *Richard III* (1592); *The Comedy of Errors* (1592); *Titus Andronicus* (1593); *The Taming of the Shrew* (1593); *The Two Gentlemen of Verona* (1594); *Love's Labour's Lost* (1594); *Romeo and Juliet* (1594); *Richard II* (1595); *A Midsummer Night's Dream* (1595); *King John* (1596); *The Merchant of Venice* (1596); *Henry IV, Parts I–II* (1597); *Much Ado about Nothing* (1598); *Henry V* (1598); *Julius Caesar* (1599); *As You Like It* (1599); *Twelfth Night* (1599); *Hamlet* (1600); *The Merry Wives of Windsor* (1600); *Troilus and Cressida* (1601); *All's Well that ends Well* (1602); *Measure for Measure* (1604); *Othello* (1604); *King Lear* (1605); *Macbeth* (1605); *Antony and Cleopatra* (1606); *Coriolanus* (1607); *Timon of Athens* (1607); *Pericles* (1608); *Cymbeline* (1609); *The Winter's Tale* (1610); *The Tempest* (1611); and, possibly in collaboration with John Fletcher, *Two Noble Kinsmen* (1612) and *Henry VIII* (1612). His *Sonnets*, variously addressed to a fair young man and a dark lady, were published in 1609

Shakespearean or **Shakespearian 1** of, relating to, or characteristic of William Shakespeare, the English dramatist and poet (1564–1616), or his works **2** a student of or specialist in Shakespeare's works

Shakhty an industrial city in W Russia: the chief town of the E Donets Basin; a major coal-mining centre. Pop: 219 000 (2005 est)

shale a dark fine-grained laminated sedimentary rock formed by compression of successive layers of clay-rich sediment

shallot 1 an alliaceous plant, *Allium ascalonicum*, cultivated for its edible bulb **2** the bulb of this plant, which divides into small sections and is used in cooking for flavouring and as a vegetable

shaman 1 a priest of shamanism **2** a medicine man of a similar religion, esp among certain tribes of North American Indians

shamanism 1 the religion of certain peoples of northern Asia, based on the belief that the world is pervaded by good and evil spirits who can be influenced or controlled only by the shamans **2** any similar religion involving forms of spiritualism
　▷http://www.shamanism.co.uk/
　▷http://www.faqs.org/faqs/shamanism/
　overview/

shambles *Brit, dialect* a row of covered stalls or shops where goods, originally meat, are sold

Shamir Yitzhak born 1915, Israeli statesman, born in Poland: prime minister (1983–84; 1986–92): foreign minister (1980–83; 1984–86)

shamrock a plant having leaves divided into three leaflets, variously identified as the wood sorrel, red clover, white clover, and black medick: the national emblem of Ireland

Shandong or **Shantung** a province of NE China, on the Yellow Sea and the Gulf of Chihli: part of the earliest organized state of China (1520–1030 BC); consists chiefly of the fertile plain of the lower Yellow River, with mountains over 1500 m (5000 ft) high in the centre. Capital: Jinan. Pop: 91 290 000 (2003 est). Area: 153 300 sq km (59 189 sq miles)

shandy or US **shandygaff** an alcoholic drink made of beer and ginger beer or lemonade

Shang 1 the dynasty ruling in China from about the 18th to the 12th centuries BC **2** of or relating to the pottery produced during the Shang dynasty

Shanghai a port in E China, in SE Jiangsu near the estuary of the Yangtze: the largest city in China and one of the largest ports in the world; a major cultural and industrial centre, with two universities. Pop: 12 665 000 (2005 est)

shank 1 *Anatomy* the shin **2** the corresponding part of the leg in vertebrates other than man **3** *Engineering* a ladle used for molten metal **4** *Music* another word for **crook**

Shankar Ravi born 1920, Indian sitarist

Shankaracharya or **Shankara** 9th century AD, Hindu philosopher and teacher; chief exponent of Vedanta philosophy

Shankly Bill 1913–81, Scottish footballer and manager of Liverpool FC (1959–74)

Shannon¹ Claude (Elwood). 1916–2000, US mathematician, who first developed information theory

Shannon² a river in the Republic of Ireland, rising in NW Co. Cavan and flowing south to the Atlantic by an estuary 113 km (70 miles) long: the longest river in the Republic of Ireland. Length: 260 km (161 miles)

Shan State an administrative division of E Myanmar: formed in 1947 from the joining of the Federation of Shan States with the Wa States; consists of the **Shan plateau** crossed by forested mountain ranges reaching over 2100 m (7000 ft). Pop: 4 416 000 (1994 est). Area: 149 743 sq km (57 816 sq miles)

Shantou or **Shantow** a port in SE China, in E Guangdong near the mouth of the Han River: became a treaty port in 1869. Pop: 1 356 000 (2005 est)

shantung 1 a heavy silk fabric with a knobbly surface **2** a cotton or rayon imitation of this

shanty¹ 1 a ramshackle hut; crude dwelling **2** formerly, in Canada **a** a log bunkhouse at a lumber camp **b** the camp itself

shanty², shantey, chanty or US **chantey** a song originally sung by sailors, esp a rhythmic one forming an accompaniment to work.

shantytown a town or section of a town or city inhabited by very poor people living in shanties

Shanxi or **Shansi** a province of N China: China's richest coal reserves and much heavy industry. Capital: Taiyuan. Pop: 33 140 000 (2003 est). Area: 157 099 sq km (60 656 sq miles)

shape up *US and Canadian* (formerly) a method of hiring dockers for a day or shift by having a union hiring boss select them from a gathering of applicants

shard or **sherd** *Zoology* a tough sheath, scale, or shell, esp the elytra of a beetle

Shari a variant spelling of **Chari** (the river)

sharia *or* **sheria** the body of doctrines that regulate the lives of those who profess Islam

shark any of various usually ferocious selachian fishes, typically marine with a long body, two dorsal fins, rows of sharp teeth, and between five and seven gill slits on each side of the head

sharkskin a smooth glossy fabric of acetate rayon, used for sportswear, etc.

Sharon¹ Plain of a plain in W Israel, between the Mediterranean and the hills of Samaria, extending from Haifa to Tel Aviv

Sharon² Ariel born 1928, Israeli soldier and politician; Likud prime minister from 2001

sharp 1 *Music* **a** denoting a note that has been raised in pitch by one chromatic semitone **b** (of an instrument, voice, etc) out of tune by being or tending to be too high in pitch **2** *Music* **a** an accidental that raises the pitch of the following note by one chromatic semitone. **b** a note affected by this accidental **3** any medical instrument with sharp point or edge, esp a hypodermic needle

Sharp Cecil (James). 1859–1924, British musician, best known for collecting, editing, and publishing English folk songs

Sharpeville a town in E South Africa: scene of riots in 1960 (when 69 demonstrators died), 1984, and 1985 (when 19 died)

Shatt-al-Arab a river in SE Iraq, formed by the confluence of the Tigris and Euphrates Rivers: flows southeast as part of the border between Iraq and Iran to the Persian Gulf. Length: 193 km (120 miles)

shave any tool for scraping

Shavian 1 of, relating to, or like George Bernard Shaw (1856–1950), the Irish dramatist and critic, his works, ideas, etc. **2** an admirer of Shaw or his works

Shaw 1 Artie, original name *Arthur Arshawsky.* born 1910, US jazz clarinetist, band leader, and composer **2** George Bernard, often known as *GBS.* 1856–1950, Irish dramatist and critic, in England from 1876. He was an active socialist and became a member of the Fabian Society but his major works are effective as satiric attacks rather than political tracts. These include *Arms and the Man* (1894), *Candida* (1894), *Man and Superman* (1903), *Major Barbara* (1905), *Pygmalion* (1913), *Back to Methuselah* (1921), and *St. Joan* (1923): Nobel prize for literature 1925 **3** Richard Norman 1831–1912, English architect **4** Thomas Edward the name assumed by (T. E.) **Lawrence** after 1927

sheaf *Archery* the arrows contained in a quiver

shear 1 a form of deformation or fracture in which parallel planes in a body or assembly slide over one another **2** *Physics* the deformation of a body, part, etc, expressed as the lateral displacement between two points in parallel planes divided by the distance between the planes **3** a machine that cuts sheet material by passing a knife blade through it **4** a device for lifting heavy loads consisting of a tackle supported by a framework held steady by guy ropes

sheath 1 *Biology* an enclosing or protective structure, such as a leaf base encasing the stem of a plant **2** the protective covering on an electric cable

Sheba¹ 1 the ancient kingdom of the Sabeans: a rich trading nation dealing in gold, spices, and precious stones (I Kings 10) **2** the region inhabited by this nation, located in the SW corner of the Arabian peninsula: modern Yemen

Sheba² Queen of Sheba *Old Testament* a queen of the Sabeans, who visited Solomon (I Kings 10:1–13)

shebeen *or* **shebean** 1 (in Ireland) alcohol, esp home-distilled whiskey, sold without a licence **2** (in the US and Ireland) weak beer

shed¹ 1 a small building or lean-to of light construction, used for storage, shelter, etc. **2** a large roofed structure, esp one with open sides, used for storage, repairing locomotives, sheepshearing, etc. **3** a large retail outlet in the style of a warehouse

shed² 1 (in weaving) the space made by shedding **2** short for **watershed**

shed³ *Physics* a former unit of nuclear cross section equal to 10^{-52} square metre

sheep any of various bovid mammals of the genus *Ovis* and related genera, esp *O. aries* (**domestic sheep**), having transversely ribbed horns and a narrow face. There are many breeds of domestic sheep, raised for their wool and for meat

sheepdog 1 a dog used for herding sheep **2** any of various breeds of dog reared originally for herding sheep

sheepskin a the skin of a sheep, esp when used for clothing, etc, or with the fleece removed and used for parchment **b** (*as modifier*): *a sheepskin coat*

sheer¹ any transparent fabric used for making garments

sheer² 1 the upward sweep of the deck or bulwarks of a vessel **2** *Nautical* the position of a vessel relative to its mooring

Sheerness a port and resort in SE England, in N Kent at the junction of the Medway estuary and the Thames: administratively part of Queenborough in Sheppey since 1968

sheet¹ 1 a large rectangular piece of cotton, linen, etc, generally one of a pair used as inner bedclothes **2** a page of stamps, usually of one denomination and already perforated **3** any thin tabular mass of rock covering a large area

sheet² *Nautical* a line or rope for controlling the position of a sail relative to the wind

sheet anchor *Nautical* a large strong anchor for use in emergency

sheet metal metal in the form of a sheet, the thickness being intermediate between that of plate and that of foil

sheet music 1 the printed or written copy of a short composition or piece, esp in the form of unbound leaves **2** music in its written or printed form

Sheffield 1 a city in N England, in Sheffield unitary authority, South Yorkshire on the River Don: important centre of steel manufacture and of the cutlery industry; Sheffield university (1905) and Sheffield Hallam University (1992). Pop: 439 866 (2001) **2** a unitary authority in N England, in South Yorkshire. Pop: 512 500 (2003 est). Area: 368 sq km (142 sq miles)

sheikh *or* **sheik** in Muslim countries **a** the head of an Arab tribe, village, etc. **b** a high priest or religious leader, esp a Sufi master

shekel or **sheqel** 1 the standard monetary unit of modern Israel, divided into 100 agorot 2 any of several former coins and units of weight of the Near East

Shelburne 2nd Earl of, title of *William Petty Fitzmaurice*, also called (from 1784) *1st Marquess of Lansdowne*. 1737–1805, British statesman; prime minister (1782–83)

shelduck or masculine **sheldrake** any of various large usually brightly coloured gooselike ducks, such as *Tadorna tadorna* (**common shelduck**), of the Old World

shelf 1 a projecting layer of ice, rock, etc, on land or in the sea 2 *Archery* the part of the hand on which an arrow rests when the bow is grasped

shell 1 the protective calcareous or membranous outer layer of an egg, esp a bird's egg 2 the hard outer covering of many molluscs that is secreted by the mantle 3 any other hard outer layer, such as the exoskeleton of many arthropods 4 the hard outer layer of some fruits, esp of nuts 5 *Rowing* a very light narrow racing boat 6 the basic structural case of something, such as a machine, vehicle, etc. 7 *Physics* **a** a class of electron orbits in an atom in which the electrons have the same principal quantum number and orbital angular momentum quantum number and differences in their energy are small compared with differences in energy between shells **b** an analogous energy state of nucleons in certain theories (**shell models**) of the structure of the atomic nucleus 8 *Brit* (in some schools) a class or form

shellac 1 a yellowish resin secreted by the lac insect, esp a commercial preparation of this used in varnishes, polishes, and leather dressings 2 a varnish made by dissolving shellac in ethanol or a similar solvent

Shelley 1 Mary (**Wollstonecraft**). 1797–1851, British writer; author of *Frankenstein* (1818); the daughter of William Godwin and Mary Wollstonecraft, she eloped with Percy Bysshe Shelley 2 Percy Bysshe 1792–1822, British romantic poet. His works include *Queen Mab* (1813), *Prometheus Unbound* (1820), and *The Triumph of Life* (1824). He wrote an elegy on the death of Keats, *Adonais* (1821), and shorter lyrics, including the odes 'To the West Wind' and 'To a Skylark' (both 1820). He was drowned in the Ligurian Sea while sailing from Leghorn to La Spezia

shellfish any aquatic invertebrate having a shell or shell-like carapace, esp such an animal used as human food. Examples are crustaceans such as crabs and lobsters and molluscs such as oysters

shell shock loss of sight, memory, etc, resulting from psychological strain during prolonged engagement in warfare

Shelta a secret language used by some itinerant tinkers in Ireland and parts of Britain, based on systematically altered Gaelic

sheltered (of buildings) specially designed to provide a safe environment for the elderly, handicapped, or disabled

Shem *Old Testament* the eldest of Noah's three sons (Genesis 10:21)

Shenyang a walled city in NE China in S Manchuria, capital of Liaoning province: capital of the Manchu dynasty from 1644–1912; seized by the Japanese in 1931.

Pop: 4 916 000 (2005 est)

Sheol *Old Testament* 1 the abode of the dead 2 hell

Shepard 1 Alan Bartlett, Jr 1923–98, US naval officer; first US astronaut in space (1961) 2 Sam, original name *Samuel Shepard Rogers*. born 1943, US dramatist, film actor, and director. His plays include *Chicago* (1966), *The Tooth of Crime* (1972), and *Buried Child* (1978): films as actor include *Days of Heaven* (1978) and *The Right Stuff* (1983); films as director include *Far North* (1989) and *Silent Tongue* (1994)

Sheppey Isle of an island in SE England, off the N coast of Kent in the Thames estuary: separated from the mainland by **The Swale**, a narrow channel. Chief towns: Sheerness, Minster. Pop: 31 854 (latest est). Area: 80 sq km (30 sq miles)

Sheraton Thomas 1751–1806, English furniture maker, author of the influential *Cabinet-Maker and Upholsterer's Drawing Book* (1791)

Sherborne a town in S England in Dorset: noted for its medieval abbey, ruined medieval castle, and Sherborne Castle, a mansion built by Sir Walter Raleigh in 1594. Pop: 9350 (2001)

Sherbrooke a city in E Canada, in S Quebec: industrial and commercial centre. Pop: 127 354 (2001)

Sheridan 1 Philip Henry 1831–88, American Union cavalry commander in the Civil War. He forced Lee's surrender to Grant (1865) 2 Richard Brinsley 1751–1816, Irish dramatist, politician, and orator, noted for his comedies of manners *The Rivals* (1775), *School for Scandal* (1777), and *The Critic* (1779)

sheriff 1 (in the US) the chief law-enforcement officer in a county: popularly elected, except in Rhode Island 2 (in England and Wales) the chief executive officer of the Crown in a county, having chiefly ceremonial duties 3 (in Scotland) a judge in any of the sheriff courts 4 (in Australia) an administrative officer of the Supreme Court, who enforces judgments and the execution of writs, empanels juries, etc. 5 (in New Zealand) an officer of the High Court

sheriff court (in Scotland) a court having jurisdiction to try summarily or on indictment all but the most serious crimes and to deal with most civil actions

Sherman William Tecumseh 1820–91, American Union commander during the Civil War. He led the victorious march through Georgia (1864), becoming commander of the army in 1869

Sherpa a member of a people of Mongolian origin living on the southern slopes of the Himalayas in Nepal, noted as mountaineers

Sherrington Sir Charles Scott 1857–1952, English physiologist, noted for his work on reflex action, published in *The Integrative Action of the Nervous System* (1906): shared the Nobel prize for physiology or medicine with Adrian (1932)

sherry a fortified wine, originally from the Jerez region in S Spain, usually drunk as an apéritif

Sherwood Robert Emmet 1896–1955, US dramatist. His plays include *The Petrified Forest* (1935), *Idiot's Delight* (1936), and *There shall be no Night* (1940)

Sherwood Forest an ancient forest in central England, in Nottinghamshire: formerly a royal hunting ground and much more extensive; famous as the home of Robin Hood

Shetland a group of about 100 islands (fewer than 20 inhabited), off the N coast of Scotland, which constitute an island authority of Scotland: a Norse dependency from the 8th century until 1472; noted for the breeding of Shetland ponies, knitwear manufacturing, and fishing; oil-related industries. Administrative centre: Lerwick. Pop: 21 870 (2003 est). Area: 1426 sq km (550 sq miles)

Shetland pony a very small sturdy breed of pony with a long shaggy mane and tail

Shevardnadze Eduard (Amvrosiyevich). born 1928, Georgian statesman; president of Georgia (1992–2003); Soviet minister of foreign affairs (1985–91), who played an important part in arms negotiations with the US

shield 1 the protective outer covering of an animal, such as the shell of a turtle 2 *Physics* a structure of concrete, lead, etc, placed around a nuclear reactor or other source of radiation in order to prevent the escape of radiation 3 a broad stable plateau of ancient Precambrian rocks forming the rigid nucleus of a particular continent 4 *Civil engineering* a hollow steel cylinder that protects men driving a circular tunnel through loose, soft, or water-bearing ground

Shields Carol (Ann). 1935–2003, Canadian novelist and writer, born in the US; her novels include *Happenstance* (1980), *The Stone Diaries* (1995), and *Unless* (2002)

shift the displacement of rocks, esp layers or seams in mining, at a geological fault

Shijiazhuang, Shihchiachuang, *or* **Shihkiachwang** a city in NE China, capital of Hebei province: textile manufacturing. Pop: 1 733 000 (2005 est)

Shikoku the smallest of the four main islands of Japan, separated from Honshu by the Inland Sea: forested and mountainous. Pop: 4 137 000 (2002 est). Area: 17 759 sq km (6857 sq miles)

shilling 1 a former British and Australian silver or cupronickel coin worth one twentieth of a pound: not minted in Britain since 1970 2 the standard monetary unit of Kenya, Somalia, Tanzania, and Uganda: divided into 100 cents 3 an old monetary unit of the US varying in value in different states 4 *Scot* an indication of the strength and character of a beer, referring to the price after duty that was formerly paid per barrel

Shillong a city in NE India, capital of Meghalaya: situated on the **Shillong Plateau** at an altitude of 1520 m (4987 ft); destroyed by earthquake in 1897 and rebuilt. Pop: 132 876 (2001)

Shiloh a town in central ancient Palestine, in Canaan on the E slope of Mount Ephraim: keeping place of the tabernacle and the ark; destroyed by the Philistines

shim 1 a thin packing strip or washer often used with a number of similar washers or strips to adjust a clearance for gears, etc. 2 *Physics* a thin strip of magnetic material, such as soft iron, used to adjust a magnetic field

Shimonoseki a port in SW Japan, on SW Honshu: scene of the peace treaty (1895) ending the Sino-Japanese War; a heavy industrial centre. Pop: 246 924 (2002 est)

shin¹ 1 the front part of the lower leg 2 the front edge of the tibia

shin² the 21st letter in the Hebrew alphabet (ש), transliterated as *sh*

Shinar *Old Testament* the southern part of the valley of the Tigris and Euphrates, often identified with Sumer; Babylonia

shine *Informal* short for **moonshine** (whisky)

shiner 1 any of numerous small North American freshwater cyprinid fishes of the genus *Notropis* and related genera, such as *N. cornutus* (**common shiner**) and *Notemigonus crysoleucas* (**golden shiner**) 2 a popular name for the **mackerel**

shingle 1 coarse gravel, esp the pebbles found on beaches 2 a place or area strewn with shingle

shingles an acute viral disease affecting the ganglia of certain nerves, characterized by inflammation, pain, and skin eruptions along the course of the affected nerve

Shinto the indigenous religion of Japan, polytheistic in character and incorporating the worship of a number of ethnic divinities, from the chief of which the emperor is believed to be descended
  ▷http://www.jinja.or.jp/english/

shinty *or US and Canadian* **shinny** a simple form of hockey of Scottish origin played with a ball and sticks curved at the lower end
  ▷http://shinty.com

ship 1 a vessel propelled by engines or sails for navigating on the water, esp a large vessel that cannot be carried aboard another, as distinguished from a boat 2 *Nautical* a large sailing vessel with three or more square-rigged masts 3 the crew of a ship

shipboard 1 taking place, used, or intended for use aboard a ship 2 **on shipboard** on board a ship

shipbuilder a person or business engaged in the building of ships

Shipka Pass a pass over the Balkan Mountains in central Bulgaria: scene of a bloody Turkish defeat in the Russo-Turkish War (1877–78). Height: 1334 m (4376 ft)

shipmate a sailor who serves on the same ship as another

shipping 1 a the business of transporting freight, esp by ship b (*as modifier*): *a shipping magnate* 2 a ships collectively b the tonnage of a number of ships

shipwreck 1 the partial or total destruction of a ship at sea 2 a wrecked ship or part of such a ship

shipwright an artisan skilled in one or more of the tasks required to build vessels

shipyard a place or facility for the building, maintenance, and repair of ships

Shiraz a city in SW Iran, at an altitude of 1585 m (5200 ft): an important Muslim cultural centre in the 14th century; university (1948); noted for fine carpets. Pop: 1 230 000 (2005 est)

shire 1 one of the British counties 2 (in Australia) a rural district having its own local council 3 See **shire horse** 4 the Midland counties of England, esp Northamptonshire and Leicestershire, famous for hunting, etc.

shire horse a large heavy breed of carthorse with long hair on the fetlocks

shirk *Islam* a the fundamental sin of regarding anything as equal to Allah b any belief that is considered to be in opposition to Allah and Islam

Shittim *Old Testament* the site to the east of the Jordan and northeast of the Dead Sea where the Israelites encamped before crossing the Jordan (Numbers 25:1–9)

Shizuoka a city in central Japan, on S Honshu: a centre for green tea; university (1949). Pop: 468 775 (2002 est)

shoal¹ 1 a stretch of shallow water 2 a sandbank or rocky area in a stretch of water, esp one that is visible at low water 3 *Nautical* (of the draught of a vessel) drawing little water

shoal² a large group of certain aquatic animals, esp fish

shock *Pathol* a state of bodily collapse or near collapse caused by circulatory failure or sudden lowering of the blood pressure, as from severe bleeding, burns, fright, etc.

shock absorber any device designed to absorb mechanical shock, esp one fitted to a motor vehicle to damp the recoil of the suspension springs

Shockley William Bradfield 1910–89, US physicist, born in Britain, who shared the Nobel prize for physics (1956) with John Bardeen and Walter Brattain for developing the transistor. He also held controversial views on the connection between race and intelligence

shock therapy *or* **treatment** the treatment of certain psychotic conditions by injecting drugs or by passing an electric current through the brain (**electroconvulsive therapy**) to produce convulsions or coma

shoddy a yarn or fabric made from wool waste or clippings

shoe 1 a band of metal or wood on the bottom of the runner of a sledge 2 (in baccarat, etc) a boxlike device for holding several packs of cards and allowing the cards to be dispensed singly 3 a base for the supports of a superstructure of a bridge, roof, etc. 4 a metal collector attached to an electric train that slides along the third rail and picks up power for the motor 5 *Engineering* a lining to protect from and withstand wear: see **brake shoe**

shoehorn a smooth curved implement of horn, metal, plastic, etc, inserted at the heel of a shoe to ease the foot into it

Sholapur a city in SW India, in S Maharashtra: major textile centre. Pop: 873 037 (2001)

Sholokhov Mikhail Aleksandrovich 1905–84, Soviet author, noted particularly for *And Quiet flows the Don* (1934) and *The Don flows Home to the Sea* (1940), describing the effect of the Revolution and civil war on the life of the Cossacks: Nobel prize for literature 1965

shoot 1 the first aerial part of a plant to develop from a germinating seed 2 any new growth of a plant, such as a bud, young branch, etc. 3 *Chiefly Brit* a meeting or party organized for hunting game with guns 4 an area or series of coverts and woods where game can be hunted with guns 5 a steep descent in a stream; rapid 6 *Informal* a photographic assignment 7 *Geology, mining* a narrow workable vein of ore
▷www.issf-shooting.org

shooter *Cricket* a ball that unexpectedly travels low on pitching

shop 1 a place, esp a small building, for the retail sale of goods and services 2 **shut up shop** to close business at the end of the day or permanently

shop floor the part of a factory housing the machines and men directly involved in production

shopkeeper a person who owns or manages a shop or small store

shopping centre 1 a purpose-built complex of shops, restaurants, etc, for the use of pedestrians 2 the area of a town where most of the shops are situated

shopping mall a large enclosed shopping centre

shopwalker *Brit* a person employed by a departmental store to supervise sales personnel, assist customers, etc.

shore 1 the land along the edge of a sea, lake, or wide river 2 a land, as opposed to water (esp in the phrase **on shore**) b (*as modifier*): *shore duty* 3 *Law* the tract of coastland lying between the ordinary marks of high and low water

shoreline the edge of a body of water

short 1 *Prosody* a denoting a vowel that is phonetically short or a syllable containing such a vowel. In classical verse short vowels are followed by one consonant only or sometimes one consonant plus a following l or r b (of a vowel or syllable in verse that is not quantitative) not carrying emphasis or accent; unstressed 2 (of a drink of spirits) undiluted; neat 3 a drink of spirits as opposed to a long drink such as beer 4 *Phonetics, Prosody* a short vowel or syllable 5 a short film, usually of a factual nature 6 See **short circuit**

short circuit a faulty or accidental connection between two points of different potential in an electric circuit, bypassing the load and establishing a path of low resistance through which an excessive current can flow. It can cause damage to the components if the circuit is not protected by a fuse

shorthorn a short-horned breed of cattle with several regional varieties

short shrift (formerly) a brief period allowed to a condemned prisoner to make confession

short-termism the tendency to focus attention on short-term gains, often at the expense of long-term success or stability

Shostakovich Dmitri Dmitriyevich 1906–75, Soviet composer, noted esp for his 15 symphonies and his chamber music

shot¹ 1 a a single photograph b a series of frames on cine film concerned with a single event c a length of film taken by a single camera without breaks, used with others to build up a full motion picture or television film 2 *Sport* a heavy metal ball used in the shot put 3 globules of metal occurring in the body of a casting that are harder than the rest of the casting 4 a unit of chain length equal to 75 feet (Brit) or 90 feet (US)

shot² 1 (of textiles) woven to give a changing colour effect 2 streaked with colour

shotgun *American football* an offensive formation in which the quarterback lines up for a snap unusually far behind the line of scrimmage

shot put 1 an athletic event in which contestants hurl or put a heavy metal ball or shot as far as possible 2 a single put of the shot

shoulder 1 the part of the vertebrate body where the arm or a corresponding forelimb joins the trunk: the pectoral girdle and associated structures 2 the joint at the junction of the forelimb with the pectoral girdle 3 the strip of unpaved land that borders a road 4 *Engineering* a substantial projection or abrupt change in shape or diameter designed to withstand thrust 5

Photog the portion of the characteristic curve of a photographic material indicating the maximum density that can be produced on the material

shout *Informal, Brit, Austral, and NZ* **a** a round, esp of drinks **b** one's turn to buy a round of drinks

shovel 1 an instrument for lifting or scooping loose material, such as earth, coal, etc, consisting of a curved blade or a scoop attached to a handle 2 any machine or part resembling a shovel in action

show 1 a theatrical or other entertainment 2 a sporting event consisting of contests in which riders perform different exercises to show their skill and their horses' ability and breeding

show business the entertainment industry, including theatre, films, television, and radio

showdown *Poker* the exposing of the cards in the players' hands on the table at the end of the game

shower 1 a brief period of rain, hail, sleet, or snow 2 a large number of particles formed by the collision of a cosmic-ray particle with a particle in the atmosphere

showjumping the riding of horses in competitions to demonstrate skill in jumping over or between various obstacles

▷www.horsesport.org
▷www.bsja.co.uk

showman a person who presents or produces a theatrical show, etc.

showroom a room in which goods, such as cars, are on display

Shreveport a city in NW Louisiana, on the Red River: centre of an oil and natural-gas region. Pop: 198 364 (2003 est)

shrew any small mouse-like long-snouted mammal, such as *Sorex araneus* (**common shrew**), of the family *Soricidae*: order *Insectivora* (insectivores)

Shrewsbury a town in W central England, administrative centre of Shropshire, on the River Severn: strategically situated near the Welsh border; market town. Pop: 67 126 (2001)

shrike 1 any songbird of the chiefly Old World family *Laniidae*, having a heavy hooked bill and feeding on smaller animals which they sometimes impale on thorns, barbed wire, etc. 2 any of various similar but unrelated birds, such as the cuckoo shrikes 3 **shrike thrush** *or* **tit** another name for **thickhead** (the bird)

shrimp 1 any of various chiefly marine decapod crustaceans of the genus *Crangon* and related genera, having a slender flattened body with a long tail and a single pair of pincers 2 any of various similar but unrelated crustaceans, such as the opossum shrimp and mantis shrimp 3 any of various freshwater shrimplike amphipod crustaceans of the genus *Gammarus*, esp *G. pulex* 4 any of various shrimplike amphipod crustaceans of the genus *Gammarus*, esp *G. locusta*

shrine 1 a place of worship hallowed by association with a sacred person or object 2 a container for sacred relics 3 the tomb of a saint or other holy person 4 *RC Church* a building, alcove, or shelf arranged as a setting for a statue, picture, or other representation of Christ, the Virgin Mary, or a saint

shrinkage *Commerce* the loss of merchandise in a retail store through theft or damage

Shropshire 1 a county of W central England: Telford and Wrekin became an independent unitary authority in 1998; mainly agricultural. Administrative centre: Shrewsbury. Pop. (excluding Telford and Wrekin): 286 700 (2003 est). Area (excluding Telford and Wrekin): 3201 sq km (1236 sq miles) 2 a breed of medium-sized sheep having a dense fleece, originating from Shropshire and Staffordshire, England

shroud 1 *Nautical* one of a pattern of ropes or cables used to stay a mast 2 any of a set of lines running from the canopy of a parachute to the harness

shrub¹ a woody perennial plant, smaller than a tree, with several major branches arising from near the base of the main stem

shrub² 1 a mixed drink of rum, fruit juice, sugar, and spice 2 mixed fruit juice, sugar, and spice made commercially to be mixed with rum or other spirits

shrubbery 1 a place where a number of shrubs are planted 2 shrubs collectively

shunt 1 a railway point 2 *Electronics* a low-resistance conductor connected in parallel across a device, circuit, or part of a circuit to provide an alternative path for a known fraction of the current 3 *Med* a channel that bypasses the normal circulation of the blood: a congenital abnormality or surgically induced 4 *Brit, informal* a collision which occurs when a vehicle runs into the back of the vehicle in front

shut the line along which pieces of metal are welded

shutdown *a* the closing of a factory, shop, etc. *b* (*as modifier*): *shutdown costs*

Shute Nevil, real name *Nevil Shute Norway*. 1899–1960, English novelist, in Australia after World War II: noted for his novels set in Australia, esp *A Town like Alice* (1950) and *On the Beach* (1957)

shutter 1 a hinged doorlike cover, often louvred and usually one of a pair, for closing off a window 2 **put up the shutters** to close business at the end of the day or permanently 3 *Photog* an opaque shield in a camera that, when tripped, admits light to expose the film or plate for a predetermined period, usually a fraction of a second. It is either built into the lens system or lies in the focal plane of the lens (**focal-plane shutter**) 4 *Photog* a rotating device in a film projector that permits an image to be projected onto the screen only when the film is momentarily stationary 5 *Music* one of the louvred covers over the mouths of organ pipes, operated by the swell pedal

shuttle 1 a bobbin-like device used in weaving for passing the weft thread between the warp threads 2 **a** a bus, train, aircraft, etc, that plies between two points, esp one that offers a frequent service over a short route **b** short for **space shuttle**: any of a series of reusable US space vehicles (*Columbia* (exploded 2003), *Challenger* (exploded 1986), *Discovery, Atlantis, Endeavour*) that can be launched into earth orbit transporting astronauts and equipment for a period of observation, research, etc, before re-entry and an unpowered landing on a runway; the first operational flight occurred in 1982 3 **a** the movement between various countries of a diplomat in order to negotiate with rulers who refuse to meet each other **b** (*as modifier*): *shuttle diplomacy* 4 *Badminton* short for **shuttlecock**

shuttlecock a light cone consisting of a cork stub with feathered flights, struck to and fro in badminton and battledore

shy 1 *Poker* (of a player) without enough money to back his bet 2 (of plants and animals) not breeding or producing offspring freely

Sialkot a city in NE Pakistan: shrine of Guru Nanak. Pop: 487 000 (2005 est)

Siam 1 the former name (until 1939 and 1945–49) of **Thailand** 2 **Gulf of** an arm of the South China Sea between the Malay Peninsula and Indochina

Siamese 1 See **Siamese cat** 2 characteristic of, relating to, or being a Siamese twin 3 another word for **Thai**

Siamese cat a short-haired breed of cat with a tapering tail, blue eyes, and dark ears, mask, tail, and paws

Sibelius Jean 1865–1957, Finnish composer, noted for his seven symphonies, his symphonic poems, such as *Finlandia* (1900) and *Tapiola* (1925), and his violin concerto (1905)

Siberia a vast region of Russia and N Kazakhstan: extends from the Ural Mountains to the Pacific and from the Arctic Ocean to the borders with China and Mongolia; colonized after the building of the Trans-Siberian Railway. Area: 13 807 037 sq km (5 330 896 sq miles)

Sibiu an industrial town in W central Romania: originally a Roman city, refounded by German colonists in the 12th century. Pop: 133 000 (2005 est)

sibyl 1 (in ancient Greece and Rome) any of a number of women believed to be oracles or prophetesses, one of the most famous being the sibyl of Cumae, who guided Aeneas through the underworld 2 a witch, fortune-teller, or sorceress

Sichuan, Szechuan, or **Szechwan** a province of SW China: the most populous administrative division in the country, esp in the central Red Basin, where it is crossed by three main tributaries of the Yangtze. Capital: Chengdu. Pop: 81 000 000 (2003 est). Area: about 569 800 sq km (220 000 sq miles)

Sicilian 1 of or relating to Sicily or its inhabitants 2 a native or inhabitant of Sicily

Sicily the largest island in the Mediterranean, separated from the tip of SW Italy by the Strait of Messina: administratively an autonomous region of Italy; settled by Phoenicians, Greeks, and Carthaginians before the Roman conquest of 241 BC; under Normans (12th–13th centuries); formed the **Kingdom of the Two Sicilies** with Naples in 1815; mountainous and volcanic. Capital: Palermo. Pop: 4 972 124 (2003 est). Area: 25 460 sq km (9830 sq miles)

sickbay a room or area for the treatment of the sick or injured, as on board a ship or at a boarding school

Sickert Walter Richard 1860–1942, British impressionist painter, esp of scenes of London music halls

sickle an implement for cutting grass, corn, etc, having a curved blade and a short handle

sickly 1 disposed to frequent ailments; not healthy; weak 2 of, relating to, or caused by sickness

sickness 1 an illness or disease 2 nausea or queasiness 3 the state or an instance of being sick

Sicyon an ancient city in S Greece, in the NE Peloponnese near Corinth: declined after 146 BC

Siddons Sarah 1755–1831, English tragedienne

side 1 *Geometry* a any line segment forming part of the perimeter of a plane geometric figure b another name for **face** 2 either half of a human or animal body, esp the area around the waist, as divided by the median plane 3 *Billiards, snooker* spin imparted to a ball by striking it off-centre with the cue

sidecar 1 a small car attached to one side of a motorcycle, usually for one passenger, the other side being supported by a single wheel 2 a cocktail containing brandy with equal parts of Cointreau and lemon juice

sidelight 1 either of the two navigational running lights used by vessels at night, a red light on the port and a green on the starboard 2 *Brit* either of two small lights on the front of a motor vehicle, used to indicate the presence of the vehicle at night rather than to assist the driver

sideline an auxiliary business activity or line of merchandise

sidereal 1 of, relating to, or involving the stars 2 determined with reference to one or more stars

side-saddle a riding saddle originally designed for women riders in skirts who sit with both legs on the near side of the horse

sideshow a small show or entertainment offered in conjunction with a larger attraction, as at a circus or fair

sidetrack *US and Canadian* a railway siding

sidewalk *US and Canadian* a hard-surfaced path for pedestrians alongside and a little higher than a road

siding 1 a short stretch of railway track connected to a main line, used for storing rolling stock or to enable trains on the same line to pass 2 a short railway line giving access to the main line for freight from a factory, mine, quarry, etc.

Sidney or **Sydney** 1 Algernon 1622–83, English Whig politician, beheaded for his supposed part in the Rye House Plot to assassinate Charles II and the future James II: author of *Discourses Concerning Government* (1689) 2 Sir **Philip** 1554–86, English poet, courtier, and soldier. His works include the pastoral romance *Arcadia* (1590), the sonnet sequence *Astrophel and Stella* (1591), and *The Defence of Poesie* (1595), one of the earliest works of literary criticism in English

Sidon the chief city of ancient Phoenicia: founded in the third millennium BC; wealthy through trade and the making of glass and purple dyes; now the Lebanese city of Saïda

Sidra Gulf of a wide inlet of the Mediterranean on the N coast of Libya

Siegbahn 1 **Kai** born 1918, Swedish physicist who worked on electron spectroscopy: Nobel prize for physics 1981 2 his father, **Karl Manne Georg** 1886–1978, Swedish physicist, who discovered the M series in X-ray spectroscopy: Nobel prize for physics 1924

Siegen a city in NW Germany, in North Rhine-Westphalia: manufacturing centre: birthplace of Rubens. Pop: 107 768 (2003 est)

siemens the derived SI unit of electrical conductance equal to 1 reciprocal ohm.

Siemens 1 Ernst Werner von 1816–92, German engineer, inventor, and pioneer in telegraphy. Among his inventions are the self-excited dynamo and an electrolytic refining process **2** his brother, Sir **William**, original name *Karl Wilhelm Siemens*. 1823–83, British engineer, born in Germany, who invented the open-hearth process for making steel

Siena a walled city in central Italy, in Tuscany: founded by the Etruscans; important artistic centre (13th–14th centuries); university (13th century). Pop: 52 625 (2001)

Sienkiewicz Henryk 1846–1916, Polish novelist. His best-known works are *Quo Vadis?* (1896), set in Nero's Rome, and the war trilogy *With Fire and Sword* (1884), *The Deluge* (1886), and *Pan Michael* (1888), set in 17th-century Poland: Nobel prize for literature 1905

sienna 1 a natural earth containing ferric oxide used as a yellowish-brown pigment when untreated (**raw sienna**) or a reddish-brown pigment when roasted (**burnt sienna**) **2** the colour of this pigment

sierra a range of mountains with jagged peaks, esp in Spain or America

Sierra Leone a republic in W Africa, on the Atlantic: became a British colony in 1808 and gained independence (within the Commonwealth) in 1961; declared a republic in 1971; became a one-party state in 1978; multiparty democracy restored in 1991 but military rule was imposed following a coup in 1992, which led to civil unrest; consists of coastal swamps rising to a plateau in the east. Official language: English. Religion: Muslim majority and animist. Currency: leone. Capital: Freetown. Pop: 5 169 000 (2004 est). Area: 71 740 sq km (27 699 sq miles)

Sierra Madre the main mountain system of Mexico, extending for 2500 km (1500 miles) southeast from the N border: consists of the **Sierra Madre Oriental** in the east, the **Sierra Madre Occidental** in the west, and the **Sierra Madre del Sur** in the south. Highest peak: Citlaltépetl, 5699 m (18 698 ft)

Sierra Morena a mountain range in SW Spain, between the Guadiana and Guadalquivir Rivers. Highest peak: Estrella, 1299 m (4262 ft)

Sierra Nevada 1 a mountain range in E California, parallel to the Coast Ranges. Highest peak: Mount Whitney, 4418 m (14 495 ft) **2** a mountain range in SE Spain, mostly in Granada and Almería provinces. Highest peak: Cerro de Mulhacén, 3478 m (11 411 ft)

sieve a device for separating lumps from powdered material, straining liquids, grading particles, etc, consisting of a container with a mesh or perforated bottom through which the material is shaken or poured

sight 1 the power or faculty of seeing; perception by the eyes; vision **2** any of various devices or instruments used to assist the eye in making alignments or directional observations, esp such a device used in aiming a gun **3** an observation or alignment made with such a device

sightscreen *Cricket* a large white screen placed near the boundary behind the bowler to help the batsman see the ball

Sigismund 1368–1437, king of Hungary (1387–1437) and of Bohemia (1419–37); Holy Roman Emperor (1411–37). He helped to end the Great Schism in the Church; implicated in the death of Huss

sigma 1 the 18th letter in the Greek alphabet (Σ, σ or,

when final, ς, a consonant, transliterated as S **2** *Maths* the symbol Σ, indicating summation of the numbers or quantities indicated

sign 1 *Maths, logic* **a** any symbol indicating an operation **b** the positivity or negativity of a number, quantity, or expression **2** an indication, such as a scent or spoor, of the presence of an animal **3** *Med* any objective evidence of the presence of a disease or disorder **4** *Astrology* See **sign of the zodiac**

Signac Paul 1863–1935, French neoimpressionist painter, influenced by Seurat

signal box 1 a building containing manually operated signal levers for all the railway lines in its section **2** a control point for a large area of a railway system, operated electrically and semiautomatically

signalman 1 a railway employee in charge of the signals and points within a section **2** a man who sends and receives signals, esp in the navy

signatory a person who has signed a document such as a treaty or contract or an organization, state, etc, on whose behalf such a document has been signed

signature 1 *Music* See **key signature** *or* **time signature 2** *US* the part of a medical prescription that instructs a patient how frequently and in what amounts he should take a drug or agent

signature tune *Brit* a melody used to introduce or identify a television or radio programme, a dance band, a performer, etc.

signboard a board carrying a sign or notice, esp one used to advertise a product, event, etc.

signing a specific set of manual signs used to communicate with deaf people

sign of the zodiac any of the 12 equal areas, 30° wide, into which the zodiac can be divided, named after the 12 zodiacal constellations. In astrology, it is thought that a person's psychological type and attitudes to life can be correlated with the sign in which the sun lay at the moment of his birth, with the ascendant sign, and to a lesser extent with the signs in which other planets lay at this time

signor *or* **signior** an Italian man: usually used before a name as a title equivalent to *Mr*

signora a married Italian woman: a title of address equivalent to *Mrs* when placed before a name or *madam* when used alone

Signorelli Luca ?1441–1523, Italian painter, noted for his frescoes

Signoret Simone , original name *Simone Kaminker*. 1921–85, French stage and film actress, whose films include *La Ronde* (1950), *Casque d'Or* (1952), *Room at the Top* (1958), and *Ship of Fools* (1965): married the actor and singer Yves Montand (1921–91)

signorina an unmarried Italian woman: a title of address equivalent to *Miss* when placed before a name or *madam* or *miss* when used alone

Sihanouk King **Norodom** born 1922, Cambodian statesman; king of Cambodia (1941–55 and from 1993); prime minister (1955–60), after which he became head of state. He was deposed in 1970 but reinstated (1975–76) following the victory of the Khmer Rouge in the civil war. He was head of state in exile from 1982; returned in 1991 and became monarch in 1993 under a new constitution

Sikang a former province of W China: established in 1928 from part of W Sichuan and E Tibet; dissolved in 1955

Sikh a member of an Indian religion that separated from Hinduism and was founded in the 16th century, that teaches monotheism and that has the Granth as its chief religious document, rejecting the authority of the Vedas

▷http://www.sikhnet.com/
▷http://www.sikhs.org/
▷http://www.sikhseek.com/

Sikkim a state of NE India. formerly an independent state: under British control (1861–1947); became an Indian protectorate in 1950 and an administrative division of India in 1975; lies in the Himalayas, rising to 8600 m (28 216 ft) at Kanchenjunga in the north. Capital: Gangtok. Pop: 540 493 (2001). Area: 7096 sq km (2740 sq miles)

Sikorski Władysław 1881–1943, Polish general and statesman: prime minister (1922–23) and prime minister of the Polish government in exile during World War II: died in an air crash

Sikorsky Igor 1889–1972, US aeronautical engineer, born in Russia. He designed and flew the first four-engined aircraft (1913) and designed the first successful helicopter (1939)

silencer any device designed to reduce noise, esp the tubular device containing baffle plates in the exhaust system of a motor vehicle

silent *Cinema* denoting a film that has no accompanying soundtrack, esp one made before 1927, when such soundtracks were developed

Silesia a region of central Europe around the upper and middle Oder valley: mostly annexed by Prussia in 1742 but became almost wholly Polish in 1945; rich coal and iron-ore deposits

silhouette an outline drawing filled in with black, often a profile portrait cut out of black paper and mounted on a light ground

silica the dioxide of silicon, occurring naturally as quartz, cristobalite, and tridymite. It is a refractory insoluble material used in the manufacture of glass, ceramics, and abrasives

silicate a salt or ester of silicic acid, esp one of a large number of usually insoluble salts with polymeric negative ions having a structure formed of tetrahedrons of SiO_4 groups linked in rings, chains, sheets, or three dimensional frameworks. Silicates constitute a large proportion of the earth's minerals and are present in cement and glass

silicon a brittle metalloid element that exists in two allotropic forms; occurs principally in sand, quartz, granite, feldspar, and clay. It is usually a grey crystalline solid but is also found as a brown amorphous powder. It is used in transistors, rectifiers, solar cells, and alloys. Its compounds are widely used in glass manufacture, the building industry, and in the form of silicones. Symbol: Si; atomic no.: 14; atomic wt.: 28.0855; valency: 4; relative density: 2.33; melting pt.: 1414°C; boiling pt.: 3267°C

silicone *Chem* a any of a large class of polymeric syn-

thetic materials that usually have resistance to temperature, water, and chemicals, and good insulating and lubricating properties, making them suitable for wide use as oils, water-repellents, resins, etc. Chemically they have alternate silicon and oxygen atoms with the silicon atoms bound to organic groups **b** *(as modifier)*: *silicone rubber*

Silicon Valley **1** an industrial strip in W California, extending S of San Francisco, in which the US information technology industry is concentrated **2** any area in which industries associated with information technology are concentrated

silicosis *Pathol* a form of pneumoconiosis caused by breathing in tiny particles of silica, quartz, or slate, and characterized by shortness of breath and fibrotic changes in the tissues of the lungs

silk **1** the very fine soft lustrous fibre produced by a silkworm to make its cocoon **2 a** thread or fabric made from this fibre **b** *(as modifier)*: *a silk dress* **3** a very fine fibre produced by a spider to build its web, nest, or cocoon **4** the tuft of long fine styles on an ear of maize **5** *Brit* **a** the gown worn by a Queen's (or King's) Counsel **b** *Informal* a Queen's (or King's) Counsel **c take silk** to become a Queen's (or King's) Counsel

▷www.silkroadproject.org/silkroad

silken made of silk

silkworm **1** the larva of the Chinese moth *Bombyx mori*, that feeds on the leaves of the mulberry tree: widely cultivated as a source of silk **2** any of various similar or related larvae **3 silkworm moth** the moth of any of these larvae

silky **1** made of silk **2** *Botany* covered with long fine soft hairs

sill **1** a shelf at the bottom of a window inside a room **2** a horizontal piece along the outside lower member of a window, that throws water clear of the wall below **3** the lower horizontal member of a window or door frame **4** a continuous horizontal member placed on top of a foundation wall in order to carry a timber framework **5** a flat usually horizontal mass of igneous rock, situated between two layers of older sedimentary rock, that was formed by an intrusion of magma

Sillitoe Alan born 1928, British novelist. His best-known works include *Saturday Night and Sunday Morning* (1958) and *The Loneliness of the Long Distance Runner* (1959)

silly *Cricket* (of a fielding position) near the batsman's wicket

Siloam *Bible* a pool in Jerusalem where Jesus cured a man of his blindness (John 9)

Silone Ignazio 1900–78, Italian writer, noted for his humanitarian socialistic novels, *Fontamara* (1933) and *Bread and Wine* (1937)

silt a fine deposit of mud, clay, etc, esp one in a river or lake

Silurian **1** of, denoting, or formed in the third period of the Palaeozoic era, between the Ordovician and Devonian periods, which lasted for 25 million years, during which fishes first appeared **2** of or relating to the Silures

silver **1 a** a very ductile malleable brilliant greyish-white element having the highest electrical and thermal conductivity of any metal t occurs free and in argentite and other ores: used in jewellery, tableware, coinage, electrical contacts, and in electroplating. Its compounds are used in photography. Symbol: Ag; atomic no.: 47; atomic wt.: 107.8682; valency: 1 or 2; relative density: 10.50; melting pt.: 961.93°C; boiling pt.: 2163°C **b** (*as modifier*): *a silver coin* **2** coin made of, or having the appearance of, this metal **3** *Photog* any of a number of silver compounds used either as photosensitive substances in emulsions or as sensitizers **4 a** a brilliant or light greyish-white colour **b** (*as adjective*): *silver hair*

silver birch a betulaceous tree, *Betula pendula*, of N temperate regions of the Old World, having silvery-white peeling bark

silverfish 1 a silver variety of the goldfish *Carassius auratus* **2** any of various other silvery fishes, such as the moonfish *Monodactylus argenteus* **3** any of various small primitive wingless insects of the genus *Lepisma*, esp *L. saccharina*, that have long antennae and tail appendages and occur in buildings, feeding on food scraps, bookbindings, etc.: order *Thysanura* (bristletails)

silver goal *Soccer* (in certain competitions) a goal scored in a full half of extra time that is played if a match is drawn. This goal counts as the winner if it is the only goal scored in the full half or full period of extra time

silver plate a thin layer of silver deposited on a base metal

silver screen, the *Informal* **1** films collectively or the film industry **2** the screen onto which films are projected

silverside any small marine or freshwater teleost fish of the family *Atherinidae*, related to the grey mullets: includes the jacksmelt

silversmith a craftsman who makes or repairs articles of silver

silver thaw *Canadian* **1** a freezing rainstorm **2** another name for **glitter**

silviculture the branch of forestry that is concerned with the cultivation of trees

sim a computer game which simulates an activity such as playing a sport or flying an aircraft

Simbirsk a city in W central Russia on the River Volga: birthplace of Lenin (V. I. Ulyanov). Pop: 639 000 (2005 est)

Simenon Georges 1903–89, Belgian novelist. He wrote over two hundred novels, including the detective series featuring Maigret

Simeon 1 a *Old Testament* the second son of Jacob and Leah **b** the tribe descended from him **c** the territory once occupied by this tribe in the extreme south of the land of Canaan **2** *New Testament* a devout Jew, who recognized the infant Jesus as the Messiah and uttered the canticle *Nunc Dimittis* over him in the Temple (Luke 2:25–35)

Simeon Stylites Saint ?390–459 AD, Syrian monk, first of the ascetics who lived on pillars. Feast day: Jan 5 or Sept 1

Simferopol a city in S Ukraine on the S Crimean Peninsula: a Scythian town in the 1st century BC; seized by the Russians in 1736. Pop: 344 000 (2005 est)

simian 1 of, relating to, or resembling a monkey or ape. **2** a monkey or ape

similar 1 *Geometry* (of two or more figures) having corresponding angles equal and all corresponding sides in the same ratio **2** *Maths* (of two classes) equinumerous

similitude *Archaic* a simile, allegory, or parable

Simla a city in N India, capital of Himachal Pradesh state: summer capital of India (1865–1939); hill resort and health centre. Pop: 142 161 (2001)

Simon 1 *New Testament* **a b** a relative of Jesus, who may have been identical with Simon Zelotes (Matthew 13:55) **c** a Christian of Joppa with whom Peter stayed (Acts of the Apostles 9:43) **2** **John** (**Allsebrook**), 1st Viscount Simon. 1873–1954, British statesman and lawyer. He was Liberal home secretary (1915–16) and, as a leader of the National Liberals, foreign secretary (1931–35), home secretary (1935–37), Chancellor of the Exchequer (1937–40), Lord Chancellor (1940–45) **3** (**Marvin**) **Neil** born 1927, US dramatist and librettist, whose plays include *Barefoot in the Park* (1963), *California Suite* (1976), *Biloxi Blues* (1985), *Lost in Yonkers* (1990), and *London Suite* (1995): many have been made into films **4 Paul** born 1942, US pop singer and songwriter. His albums include: with Art Garfunkel (born 1941), *The Sounds of Silence* (1966), and *Bridge over Troubled Water* (1970); and, solo, *Graceland* (1986), *The Rhythm of the Saints* (1990), and *You're The One* (2000)

Simonides ?556–?468 BC, Greek lyric poet and epigrammatist, noted for his odes to victory

Simon Magus *New Testament* a Samaritan sorcerer, probably from Gitta, of the 1st century AD. After being converted to Christianity, he tried to buy miraculous powers from the apostles (Acts of the Apostles 8:9–24). He is also identified as the founder of a Gnostic sect

Simon Peter *New Testament* the full name of the apostle Peter, a combination of his original name and the name given him by Christ (Matthew 16:17–18)

simony *Christianity* the practice, now usually regarded as a sin, of buying or selling spiritual or Church benefits such as pardons, relics, etc, or preferments

Simon Zelotes Saint one of the 12 apostles, who had probably belonged to the Zealot party before becoming a Christian (Luke 6:15). Owing to a misinterpretation of two similar Aramaic words he is also, but mistakenly, called *the Canaanite* (Matthew 10:4). Feast day: Oct 28 or May 10

simoom *or* **simoon** a strong suffocating sand-laden wind of the deserts of Arabia and North Africa

simple 1 *Chem* (of a substance or material) consisting of only one chemical compound rather than a mixture of compounds **2** *Maths* **a** (of a fraction) containing only integers **b** (of an equation) containing variables to the first power only; linear **c** (of a root of an equation) occurring only once; not multiple **3** *Biology* not divided into parts **4** *Music* relating to or denoting a time where the number of beats per bar may be two, three, or four **5** a plant, esp a herbaceous plant, having medicinal properties

simple fraction a fraction in which the numerator and denominator are both integers expressed as a ratio rather than a decimal

simple fracture a fracture in which the broken bone does not pierce the skin

Simplon Pass a pass over the Lepontine Alps in S Switzerland, between Brig (Switzerland) and Iselle

(Italy). Height: 2009 m (6590 ft)

Simpson Sir James Young 1811–70, Scottish obstetrician, who pioneered the use of chloroform as an anaesthetic

Simpson Desert an uninhabited arid region in central Australia, mainly in the Northern Territory. Area: about 145 000 sq km (56 000 sq miles)

simulator any device or system that simulates specific conditions or the characteristics of a real process or machine for the purposes of research or operator training

simultaneous *Chess* a display in which one player plays a number of opponents at once, walking from board to board

sin¹ *Theol* **a** a transgression of God's known will or any principle or law regarded as embodying this **b** the condition of estrangement from God arising from such transgression

sin² a variant of the 21st letter in the Hebrew alphabet (ש), transliterated as *S*

Sinai 1 a mountainous peninsula of NE Egypt at the N end of the Red Sea, between the Gulf of Suez and the Gulf of Aqaba: occupied by Israel in 1967; fully restored by 1982 **2 Mount** the mountain where Moses received the Law from God (Exodus 19–20): often identified as Jebel Musa, sometimes as Jebel Serbal, both on the S Sinai Peninsula

Sinaloa a state of W Mexico. Capital: Culiacán. Pop: 2 534 835 (2000). Area: 58 092 sq km (22 425 sq miles)

Sinatra Francis Albert, known as *Frank*. 1915–98, US popular singer and film actor. His recordings include "One for My Baby (and One More for the Road)" (1955) and "My Way" (1969)

sin bin 1 *Slang* (in ice hockey, etc) an area off the field of play where a player who has committed a foul can be sent to sit for a specified period **2** *Brit, informal* a special unit on a separate site from a school that disruptive schoolchildren attend until they can be reintegrated into their normal classes

Sinclair 1 Sir Clive (**Marles**). born 1940, British electronics engineer, inventor, and entrepreneur, who produced such electronic goods as pocket calculators and some of the first home computers; however, the Sinclair C5, a small light electric vehicle for one person, proved a commercial failure **2** Upton (**Beall**). 1878–1968, US novelist, whose *The Jungle* (1906) exposed the working and sanitary conditions of the Chicago meat-packing industry and prompted the passage of food inspection laws

Sind a province of SE Pakistan, mainly in the lower Indus valley: formerly a province of British India; became a province of Pakistan in 1947; divided in 1955 between Hyderabad and Khairpur; reunited as a province in 1970. Capital: Karachi. Pop: 34 240 000 (2003 est). Area: 140 914 sq km (54 407 sq miles)

sine of an angle **a** a trigonometric function that in a right-angled triangle is the ratio of the length of the opposite side to that of the hypotenuse **b** a function that in a circle centred at the origin of a Cartesian coordinate system is the ratio of the ordinate of a point on the circumference to the radius of the circle

sinecure a Church benefice to which no spiritual or pastoral charge is attached

sinewy consisting of or resembling a tendon or tendons

Singapore 1 a republic in SE Asia, occupying one main island and over 50 small islands at the S end of the Malay Peninsula: established as a British trading post in 1819 and became part of the Straits Settlements in 1826; occupied by the Japanese (1942–45); a British colony from 1946, becoming self-governing in 1959; part of the Federation of Malaysia from 1963 to 1965, when it became an independent republic (within the Commonwealth). Official languages: Chinese, Malay, English, and Tamil. Religion: Buddhist, Taoist, traditional beliefs, and Muslim. Currency: Singapore dollar. Capital: Singapore. Pop: 4 315 000 (2004 est). Area: 646 sq km (250 sq miles) **2** the capital of the republic of Singapore: a major international port; administratively not treated as a city

singe a superficial burn

Singer 1 Isaac Bashevis 1904–91, US writer of Yiddish novels and short stories; born in Poland. His works include *Satan in Goray* (1935), *The Family Moscat* (1950), the autobiographical *In my Father's Court* (1966), and *The King of the Fields* (1989): Nobel prize for literature 1978 **2** Isaac Merrit 1811–75, US inventor, who originated and developed an improved chain-stitch sewing machine (1852)

singing telegram a greetings service in which a person is employed to present greetings by singing to the person celebrating

single 1 (of a flower) having only one set or whorl of petals **2** *Archaic* (of ale, beer, etc) mild in strength **3** a gramophone record, CD, or cassette with a short recording, usually of pop music, on it **4** *Golf* a game between two players **5** *Cricket* a hit from which one run is scored **6 a** *Brit* a pound note **b** *US and Canadian* a dollar note

single-decker *Brit, informal* a bus with only one passenger deck

singlet 1 *Physics* a multiplet that has only one member **2** *Chem* a chemical bond consisting of one electron

singleton 1 *Bridge* an original holding of one card only in a suit **2** *Maths* a set containing only one member

singular *Logic* of or referring to a specific thing or person as opposed to something general

Sinhalese *or* **Singhalese 1** a member of a people living chiefly in Sri Lanka, where they constitute the majority of the population **2** the language of this people, belonging to the Indic branch of the Indo-European family: the official language of Sri Lanka. It is written in a script of Indian origin

sink 1 an area of ground below that of the surrounding land, where water collects **2** *Physics* a device or part of a system at which energy is removed from the system **3** *Informal* (of a housing estate or school) deprived or having low standards of achievement

sinker 1 a weight attached to a fishing line, net, etc, to cause it to sink in water **2** a person who sinks shafts, etc.

Sinology the study of Chinese history, language, culture, etc.

Sintra a town in central Portugal, near Lisbon, in the Sintra mountains: noted for its castles and palaces and the beauty of its setting: tourism

Sinŭiju a port in North Korea, on the Yalu River opposite Andong, China: developed by the Japanese during their occupation (1910–45); industrial centre. Pop: 349 000 (2005 est)

sinus 1 *Anatomy* **a** any bodily cavity or hollow space **b** a large channel for venous blood, esp between the brain and the skull **c** any of the air cavities in the cranial bones 2 *Pathol* a passage leading to a cavity containing pus 3 *Botany* a small rounded notch between two lobes of a leaf, petal, etc. 4 an irregularly shaped cavity

sinusitis inflammation of the membrane lining a sinus, esp a nasal sinus

Sion 1 a town in SW Switzerland, capital of Valais canton, on the River Rhône. Pop: 27 171 (2000) 2 a variant of **Zion**

Sioux 1 a member of a group of North American Indian peoples formerly ranging over a wide area of the Plains from Lake Michigan to the Rocky Mountains 2 any of the Siouan languages

siphon *or* **syphon** 1 a tube placed with one end at a certain level in a vessel of liquid and the other end outside the vessel below this level, so that atmospheric pressure forces the liquid through the tube and out of the vessel 2 See **soda siphon** 3 *Zoology* any of various tubular organs in different aquatic animals, such as molluscs and elasmobranch fishes, through which a fluid, esp water, passes

Siple Mount a mountain in Antarctica, on the coast of Byrd Land. Height: 3100 m (10 171 ft)

Sir 1 a title of honour placed before the name of a knight or baronet 2 *Archaic* a title placed before the name of a figure from ancient history

Siraj-ud-daula ?1728–57, Indian leader who became the Great Mogul's deputy in Bengal (1756); opponent of English colonization. He captured Calcutta (1756) from the English and many of his prisoners suffocated in a crowded room that became known as the Black Hole of Calcutta. He was defeated (1757) by a group of Indian nobles in alliance with Robert Clive

sire 1 a male parent, esp of a horse or other domestic animal 2 a respectful term of address, now used only in addressing a male monarch

siren 1 a device for emitting a loud wailing sound, esp as a warning or signal, typically consisting of a rotating perforated metal drum through which air or steam is passed under pressure 2 *Greek myth* one of several sea nymphs whose seductive singing was believed to lure sailors to destruction on the rocks the nymphs inhabited 3 any aquatic eel-like salamander of the North American family *Sirenidae*, having external gills, no hind limbs, and reduced forelimbs

Siret a river in SE Europe, rising in Ukraine and flowing southeast through E Romania to the Danube. Length: about 450 km (280 miles)

sirocco 1 a hot oppressive and often dusty wind usually occurring in spring, beginning in N Africa and reaching S Europe 2 any hot southerly wind, esp one moving to a low pressure centre

sisal 1 a Mexican agave plant, *Agave sisalana*, cultivated for its large fleshy leaves, which yield a stiff fibre used for making rope 2 the fibre of this plant 3 any of the fibres of certain similar or related plants

Sisera a defeated leader of the Canaanites, who was assassinated by Jael (Judges 4:17–21)

siskin 1 a yellow-and-black Eurasian finch, *Carduelis spinus* 2 **pine siskin** a North American finch, *Spinus pinus*, having a streaked yellowish-brown plumage

Sisley Alfred 1839–99, French painter, esp of landscapes; one of the originators of impressionism

sister 1 a senior nurse 2 *Chiefly RC Church* a nun or a title given to a nun 3 a woman fellow member of a Church or religious body 4 *Biology* denoting any of the cells or cell components formed by division of a parent cell or cell component

sisterhood a religious body or society of sisters, esp a community, order, or congregation of nuns

sitar a stringed musical instrument, esp of India, having a long neck, a rounded body, and movable frets. The main strings, three to seven in number, overlie other sympathetic strings, the tuning depending on the raga being performed

sit-down a form of civil disobedience in which demonstrators sit down in a public place as a protest or to draw attention to a cause

site **a** the piece of land where something was, is, or is intended to be located **b** (*as modifier*): *site office*

sit-in a form of civil disobedience in which demonstrators occupy seats in a public place and refuse to move as a protest

Sitka a town in SE Alaska, in the Alexander Archipelago on W Baranof Island: capital of Russian America (1804–67) and of Alaska (1867–1906). Pop: 8876 (2003 est)

sitka spruce a tall North American spruce tree, *Picea sitchensis*, having yellowish-green needle-like leaves: yields valuable timber

sitter 1 a person who is posing for his or her portrait to be painted, carved, etc. 2 a broody hen or other bird that is sitting on its eggs to hatch them 3 anyone, other than the medium, taking part in a seance

Sitter Willem de 1872–1934, Dutch astronomer, who calculated the size of the universe and conceived of it as expanding

sitting 1 the act or period of posing for one's portrait to be painted, carved, etc. 2 a meeting, esp of an official body, to conduct business 3 the incubation period of a bird's eggs during which the mother sits on them to keep them warm 4 *Politics, Law* in office

Sitting Bull Indian name *Tatanka Yotanka*. ?1831–90, American Indian chief of the Teton Dakota Sioux. Resisting White encroachment on his people's hunting grounds, he led the Sioux tribes against the US Army in the Sioux War (1876–77) in which Custer was killed. The hunger of the Sioux, whose food came from the diminishing buffalo, forced his surrender (1881). He was killed during renewed strife

sitting tenant a tenant occupying a house, flat, etc.

situate (now used esp in legal contexts) situated; located

sit-up a physical exercise in which the body is brought into a sitting position from one lying on the back

Sitwell 1 Dame Edith 1887–1964, English poet and critic, noted esp for her collection *Façade* (1922) 2 her brother, Sir Osbert 1892–1969, English writer, best known for his five autobiographical books (1944–50) 3 his brother, Sir Sacheverell 1897–1988, English poet and writer of books on art, architecture, music, and travel

SI unit any of the units adopted for international use under the Système International d'Unités, now employed for all scientific and most technical purposes. There are seven fundamental units: the metre, kilogram, second, ampere, kelvin, candela, and mole; and two supplementary units: the radian and the steradian. All other units are derived by multiplication or division of these units without the use of numerical factors

Siva or **Shiva** *Hinduism* the destroyer, one of the three chief divinities of the later Hindu pantheon, the other two being Brahma and Vishnu. Siva is also the god presiding over personal destinies

Sivas a city in central Turkey, at an altitude of 1347 m (4420 ft): one of the chief cities in Asia Minor in ancient times; scene of the national congress (1919) leading to the revolution that established modern Turkey. Pop: 266 000 (2005 est)

six 1 the cardinal number that is the sum of five and one 2 a numeral, 6, VI, etc, representing this number 3 something representing, represented by, or consisting of six units, such as a playing card with six symbols on it 4 *Cricket* a a stroke in which the ball crosses the boundary without bouncing b the six runs scored for such a stroke 5 a division of a Brownie Guide or Cub Scout pack

sixfold 1 equal to or having six times as many or as much 2 composed of six parts

six-pack 1 *Informal* a package containing six units, esp six cans of beer 2 *Austral* arranged in standard sets of six

sixpence a small British cupronickel coin with a face value of six pennies, worth 2½ (new) pence, not minted since 1970

sixteen 1 the cardinal number that is the sum of ten and six 2 a numeral, 16, XVI, etc, representing this number 3 *Music* the numeral 16 used as the lower figure of a time signature to indicate that the beat is measured in semiquavers

sixth form (in England and Wales) the most senior class in a secondary school to which pupils, usually above the legal leaving age, may proceed to take A levels, retake GCSEs, etc.

sixth sense any supposed sense or means of perception, such as intuition or clairvoyance, other than the five senses of sight, hearing, touch, taste, and smell

Sixtus V original name *Felice Peretti*. 1520–90, Italian ecclesiastic; pope (1585–90). He is noted for vigorous administrative reforms that contributed to the Counter-Reformation

sixty 1 the cardinal number that is the product of ten and six 2 a numeral, 60, LX, etc, representing sixty

Skagerrak an arm of the North Sea between Denmark and Norway, merging with the Kattegat in the southeast

Skara Brae a Neolithic village in NE Scotland, in the Orkney Islands: one of Europe's most perfectly preserved Stone Age villages, buried by a sand dune until uncovered by a storm in 1850

skate[1] 1 See **roller skate** or **ice skate** 2 the steel blade or runner of an ice skate 3 such a blade fitted with straps for fastening to a shoe 4 a current collector on an electric railway train that collects its current from a third rail

skate[2] any large ray of the family *Rajidae*, of temperate and tropical seas, having flat pectoral fins continuous with the head, two dorsal fins, a short spineless tail, and a long snout

skateboard a narrow board mounted on roller-skate wheels, usually ridden while standing up
▷http://skateboard.about.com

Skaw the a cape at the N tip of Denmark

skein a flock of geese flying

skeleton a hard framework consisting of inorganic material that supports and protects the soft parts of an animal's body and provides attachment for muscles: may be internal, as in vertebrates (see **endoskeleton**), or external, as in arthropods (see **exoskeleton**)

skeleton key a key with the serrated edge filed down so that it can open numerous locks

Skelmersdale a town in NW England, in Lancashire: designated a new town in 1962. Pop: 39 279 (2001)

Skelton John ?1460–1529, English poet celebrated for his short rhyming lines using the rhythms of colloquial speech

skerry *Chiefly Scot* 1 a small rocky island 2 a reef

sketch 1 a rapid drawing or painting, often a study for subsequent elaboration 2 a brief usually descriptive and informal essay or other literary composition 3 a short play, often comic, forming part of a revue 4 a short evocative piece of instrumental music, esp for piano

sketchbook 1 a book of plain paper containing sketches or for making sketches in 2 a book of literary sketches

skew 1 *Machinery* having a component that is at an angle to the main axis of an assembly or is in some other way asymmetrical 2 *Maths* a composed of or being elements that are neither parallel nor intersecting as, for example, two lines not lying in the same plane in a three-dimensional space b (of a curve) not lying in a plane 3 *Psychol* the system of relationships in a family in which one parent is extremely dominating while the other parent tends to be meekly compliant

skewbald 1 marked or spotted in white and any colour except black 2 a horse with this marking

skewer *Chess* a tactical manoeuvre in which an attacked man is made to move and expose another man to capture

ski 1 a one of a pair of wood, metal, or plastic runners that are used for gliding over snow. Skis are commonly attached to shoes for sport, but may also be used as landing gear for aircraft, etc. b (*as modifier*): *a ski boot* 2 a water-ski
▷www.fis-ski.com

skid 1 *Chiefly US and Canadian* one of the logs forming a skidway 2 a support on which heavy objects may be stored and moved short distances by sliding 3 a shoe or drag used to apply pressure to the metal rim of a wheel to act as a brake

Skien a port in S Norway, on the **Skien River**: one of the oldest towns in Norway; timber industry. Pop: 50 507 (2004 est)

skiff any of various small boats propelled by oars, sail, or motor

ski jump a high ramp overhanging a slope from which

skiers compete to make the longest jump

Skikda a port in NE Algeria, on an inlet of the Mediterranean: founded by the French in 1838 on the site of a Roman city. Pop: 170 000 (2005 est)

ski lift any of various devices for carrying skiers up a slope, such as a chairlift

skin 1 a the tissue forming the outer covering of the vertebrate body: it consists of two layers, the dermis and the epidermis, the outermost of which (epidermis) may be covered with hair, scales, feathers, etc. It is mainly protective and sensory in function **b** (*as modifier*): *a skin disease* **2** any similar covering in a plant or lower animal **3** the outer covering surface of a vessel, rocket, etc. **4** *Informal* (in jazz or pop use) a drum **5** *Slang* a cigarette paper used for rolling a cannabis cigarette

skin diving the sport or activity of diving and underwater swimming without wearing a diver's costume

skin flick *Slang* a film containing much nudity and explicit sex for sensational purposes

skin graft a piece of skin removed from one part of the body and surgically grafted at the site of a severe burn or similar injury

Skinner B(urrhus) F(rederic). 1904–90, US behavioural psychologist. His "laws of learning", derived from experiments with animals, have been widely applied to education and behaviour therapy

skip¹ the captain of a curling or bowls team

skip² a college servant, esp of Trinity College, Dublin

skipper¹ 1 the captain of any vessel **2** the captain of an aircraft

skipper² any small butterfly of the family *Hesperiidae*, having a hairy mothlike body and erratic darting flight

skipping the act of jumping over a rope that is held and swung either by the person jumping or by two other people, as a game or for exercise

skipping-rope *Brit* a cord, usually having handles at each end, that is held in the hands and swung round and down so that the holder or others can jump over it

Skipton a market town in N England, in North Yorkshire: 11th-century castle. Pop: 14 313 (2001)

skirl the sound of bagpipes

skirt 1 a frieze or circular flap, as round the base of a hovercraft **2** the flaps on a saddle that protect a rider's legs **3** *NZ* the lower part of a sheep's fleece

ski stick *or* **pole** a stick, usually with a metal point and a disc to prevent it from sinking into the snow, used by skiers to gain momentum and maintain balance

skit 1 a brief satirical theatrical sketch **2** a short satirical piece of writing

ski tow a device for pulling skiers uphill, usually a motor-driven rope grasped by the skier while riding on his skis

skittle 1 a wooden or plastic pin, typically widest just above the base **2 skittles** a bowling game in which players knock over as many skittles as possible by rolling a wooden ball at them

Skopje the capital of (the Former Yugoslav Republic of) Macedonia, on the Vardar River: became capital of Serbia in 1346 and of Macedonia in 1945; suffered a severe earthquake in 1963; university (1949). Pop: 449 000 (2005 est)

skua any predatory gull-like bird of the family *Stercorariidae*, such as the **great skua** or **bonxie** (*Stercorarius skua*) or **arctic skua** (*S. parasiticus*) both of which harass terns or gulls into dropping or disgorging fish they have caught

skulk *Obsolete* a pack of foxes or other animals that creep about stealthily

skull the bony skeleton of the head of vertebrates

skullcap any of various perennial plants of the genus *Scutellaria*, esp *S. galericulata*, that typically have helmet-shaped flowers: family *Lamiaceae* (labiates)

skunk 1 any of various American musteline mammals of the subfamily *Mephitinae*, esp *Mephitis mephitis* (**striped skunk**), typically having a black and white coat and bushy tail: they eject an unpleasant-smelling fluid from the anal gland when attacked **2** *Slang* a strain of cannabis smoked for its exceptionally powerful psychoactive properties

sky 1 the apparently dome-shaped expanse extending upwards from the horizon that is characteristically blue or grey during the day, red in the evening, and black at night **2** outer space, as seen from the earth **3** weather, as described by the appearance of the upper air

skydiving the sport of parachute jumping, in which participants perform manoeuvres before opening the parachute and attempt to land accurately
▷www.fai.org/parachuting

Skye a mountainous island off the NW coast of Scotland, the largest island of the Inner Hebrides: tourist centre. Chief town: Portree. Pop: 9232 (2001). Area: 1735 sq km (670 sq miles)

skylark 1 an Old World lark, *Alauda arvensis*, noted for singing while hovering at a great height **2** any of various Australian larks

skyline the line at which the earth and sky appear to meet; horizon

Skyros *or* **Scyros** a Greek island in the Aegean, the largest island in the N Sporades. Pop: 2602 (2001). Area: 199 sq km (77 sq miles)

skyscraper a very tall multistorey building

slab 1 any of the outside parts of a log that are sawn off while the log is being made into planks **2** *Mountaineering* a flat sheet of rock lying at an angle of between 30° and 60° from the horizontal **3** *Informal, chiefly Brit* an operating or mortuary table

slack¹ 1 a a patch of water without current **b** a slackening of a current **2** *Prosody* (in sprung rhythm) the unstressed syllable or syllables

slack² small pieces of coal with a high ash content

slag 1 the fused material formed during the smelting or refining of metals by combining the flux with gangue, impurities in the metal, etc. It usually consists of a mixture of silicates with calcium, phosphorus, sulphur, etc. **2** a mass of rough fragments of pyroclastic rock and cinders derived from a volcanic eruption; scoria

slalom 1 *Skiing* a race, esp one downhill, over a winding course marked by artificial obstacles **2** a similar type of obstacle race in canoes

slam¹ 1 a the winning of all (**grand slam**) or all but one (**little** or **small slam**) of the 13 tricks at bridge or whist **b** the bid to do so in bridge **2** an old card game

slam² a poetry contest in which entrants compete with each other by reciting their work and are awarded points by the audience

slammer the *Slang* prison

slander *Law* **a** defamation in some transient form, as by spoken words, gestures, etc. **b** a slanderous statement, etc.

slapstick 1 a comedy characterized by horseplay and physical action **b** (*as modifier*): *slapstick humour* **2** a flexible pair of paddles bound together at one end, formerly used in pantomime to strike a blow to a person with a loud clapping sound but without injury

slash *US and Canadian* **a** a littered wood chips and broken branches that remain after trees have been cut down **b** an area so littered

slasher *Austral and NZ* a wooden-handled cutting tool or tractor-drawn machine used for cutting scrub or undergrowth in the bush

slat¹ a movable or fixed auxiliary aerofoil attached to the leading edge of an aircraft wing to increase lift, esp during landing and takeoff

slat² *Irish* a spent salmon

slate 1 a a compact fine-grained metamorphic rock formed by the effects of heat and pressure on shale. It can be split into thin layers along natural cleavage planes and is used as a roofing and paving material **b** (*as modifier*): *a slate tile* **2** a dark grey colour, often with a purplish or bluish tinge **3** *Chiefly US and Canadian* a list of candidates in an election **4** *Films* **a** the reference information written on a clapperboard **b** *Informal* the clapperboard itself

Slav a member of any of the peoples of E Europe or NW Asia who speak a Slavonic language

slave 1 a person legally owned by another and having no freedom of action or right to property **2 a** a device that is controlled by or that duplicates the action of another similar device (the master device) **b** (*as modifier*): *slave cylinder*

Slave Coast the coast of W Africa between the Volta River and Mount Cameroon, chiefly along the Bight of Benin: the main source of African slaves (16th–19th centuries)

Slave River a river in W Canada, in the Northwest Territories and NE Alberta, flowing from Lake Athabaska northwest to Great Slave Lake. Length: about 420 km (260 miles)

slavery the state or condition of being a slave; a civil relationship whereby one person has absolute power over another and controls his life, liberty, and fortune

slave trade the business of trading in slaves, esp the transportation of Black Africans to America from the 16th to 19th centuries

▷www.spartacus.schoolnet.co.uk/slavery.htm
▷http://webworld.unesco.org/slave_quest/en

Slavonia a region in Croatia, mainly between the Drava and Sava Rivers

Slavonic *or esp US* **Slavic 1** a branch of the Indo-European family of languages, usually divided into three subbranches: **South Slavonic** (including Old Church Slavonic, Serbo-Croat, Bulgarian, etc), **East Slavonic** (including Ukrainian, Russian, etc), and **West Slavonic** (including Polish, Czech, Slovak, etc) **2** the

unrecorded ancient language from which all of these languages developed

sleazy thin or flimsy, as cloth

sledge¹ *or esp US and Canadian* **sled 1** a vehicle mounted on runners, drawn by horses or dogs, for transporting people or goods, esp over snow **2** a light wooden frame used, esp by children, for sliding over snow; toboggan **3** *NZ* a farm vehicle mounted on runners, for use on rough or muddy ground

sledge² an insult aimed at another player during a game of cricket

sledgehammer a large heavy hammer with a long handle used with both hands for heavy work such as forging iron, breaking rocks, etc.

sleek (of an animal or bird) having a shiny healthy coat or feathers

sleep a periodic state of physiological rest during which consciousness is suspended and metabolic rate is decreased

▷www.sleepfoundation.org
▷www.stanford.edu/~dement

sleeper 1 a railway sleeping car or compartment **2** *Brit* one of the blocks supporting the rails on a railway track **3** a wrestling hold in which a wrestler presses the sides of his opponent's neck, causing him to pass out **4** any gobioid fish of the family *Eleotridae*, of brackish or fresh tropical waters, resembling the gobies but lacking a ventral sucker **5** a spy planted in advance for future use, but not currently active

sleeping car a railway car fitted with compartments containing bunks for people to sleep in

sleeping partner a partner in a business who does not play an active role, esp one who supplies capital

sleeping pill a pill or tablet containing a sedative drug, such as a barbiturate, used to induce sleep

sleeping policeman a bump built across roads, esp in housing estates, to deter motorists from speeding

sleeping sickness 1 an African disease caused by infection with protozoans of the genus *Trypanosoma*, characterized by fever, wasting, and sluggishness **2** an epidemic viral form of encephalitis characterized by extreme drowsiness

sleet 1 partly melted falling snow or hail or (esp US) partly frozen rain **2** *Chiefly US* the thin coat of ice that forms when sleet or rain freezes on cold surfaces

sleeve 1 a tubular piece that is forced or shrunk into a cylindrical bore to reduce the diameter of the bore or to line it with a different material; liner **2** a tube fitted externally over two cylindrical parts in order to join them; bush **3** a flat cardboard or plastic container to protect a gramophone record

sleight of hand 1 manual dexterity used in performing conjuring tricks **2** the performance of such tricks

slice 1 any of various utensils having a broad flat blade and resembling a spatula **2** in golf, tennis, etc **a** the flight of a ball that travels obliquely because it has been struck off centre **b** the action of hitting such a shot **c** the shot so hit

slick 1 a chisel or other tool used for smoothing or polishing a surface **2** the tyre of a racing car that has worn treads

slide 1 *Rowing* a sliding seat in a boat or its runners **2** a thin glass plate on which specimens are mounted for microscopic study **3** a positive photograph on a transparent base, mounted in a cardboard or plastic frame or between glass plates, that can be viewed by means of a slide projector **4** *Machinery* **a** a sliding part or member **b** the track, guide, or channel on or in which such a part slides **5** *Music* **a** the sliding curved tube of a trombone that is moved in or out to allow the production of different harmonic series and a wider range of notes **b** a portamento **6** *Music* **a** a metal or glass tube placed over a finger held against the frets of a guitar to produce a portamento **b** the style of guitar playing using a slide **7** *Geology* **a** the rapid downward movement of a large mass of earth, rocks, etc, caused by erosion, faulting, etc. **b** the mass of material involved in this descent

slide rule *Obsolete* a mechanical calculating device consisting of two strips, one sliding along a central groove in the other, each strip graduated in two or more logarithmic scales of numbers, trigonometric functions, etc. It employs the same principles as logarithm tables

sliding scale a variable scale according to which specified wages, tariffs, prices, etc, fluctuate in response to changes in some other factor, standard, or conditions

Sligo **1** a county of NW Republic of Ireland, on the Atlantic: has a deeply indented low-lying coast; livestock and dairy farming. County town: Sligo. Pop: 58 200 (2002). Area: 1795 sq km (693 sq miles) **2** a port in NW Republic of Ireland, county town of Co. Sligo on **Sligo Bay**. Pop: 19 735 (2002)

Slim **William Joseph, 1st Viscount.** 1891–1970, British field marshal, who commanded (1943–45) the 14th Army in the reconquest of Burma (now called Myanmar) from the Japanese; governor general of Australia (1953–60)

slime a mucous substance produced by various organisms, such as fish, slugs, and fungi

sling¹ **1** a rope or strap by which something may be secured or lifted **2** a rope net swung from a crane, used for loading and unloading cargo **3** *Nautical* **a** a halyard for a yard **b** the part of a yard where the sling is attached **4** *Med* a wide piece of cloth suspended from the neck for supporting an injured hand or arm across the front of the body **5** *Mountaineering* a loop of rope or tape used for support in belays, abseils, etc.

sling² a mixed drink with a spirit base, usually sweetened

slink **a** an animal, esp a calf, born prematurely **b** (*as modifier*): *slink veal*

slip¹ **1** *US and Canadian* a narrow space between two piers in which vessels may dock **2** See **slipway** **3** a kind of dog lead that allows for the quick release of the dog **4** a small block of hard steel of known thickness used for measurement, usually forming one of a set **5** *Engineering* the ratio between output speed and input speed of a transmission device when subtracted from unity, esp of a drive belt or clutch that is not transmitting full power **6** *Cricket* **a** the position of the fielder who stands a little way behind and to the offside of the wicketkeeper **b** the fielder himself **7** the relative movement of rocks along a fault plane **8** a landslide, esp one blocking a road or railway line **9** *Metallurgy, crystallog* the deformation of a metallic crystal caused when one part glides

over another part along a plane **10** the deviation of a propeller from its helical path through a fluid, expressed as the difference between its actual forward motion and its theoretical forward motion in one revolution

slip² **1** a part of a plant that, when detached from the parent, will grow into a new plant; cutting; scion **2** *Dialect* a young pig **3** *Chiefly US* a pew or similar long narrow seat **4** a small piece of abrasive material of tapering section used in honing

slip clay mixed with water to a creamy consistency, used for decorating or patching a ceramic piece

slipe *NZ* **a** wool removed from the pelt of a slaughtered sheep by immersion in a chemical bath **b** (*as modifier*): *slipe wool*

slipped disc *Pathol* a herniated intervertebral disc, often resulting in pain because of pressure on the spinal nerves

slip road *Brit* a short road connecting a motorway, etc, to another road

slipstream **a** the stream of air forced backwards by an aircraft propeller **b** a stream of air behind any moving object

slipway **1** the sloping area in a shipyard, containing the ways **2** the ways on which a vessel is launched **3** the ramp of a whaling factory ship **4** a pillowcase; pillowslip

sliver a loose strand or fibre obtained by carding

Sloan **John** 1871–1951, US painter and etcher, a leading member of the group of realistic painters known as the Ash Can School. His pictures of city scenes include *McSorley's Bar* (1912) and *Backyards, Greenwich Village* (1914)

sloe the small sour blue-black fruit of the blackthorn

slogan *Scot, history* a Highland battle cry

sloop a single-masted sailing vessel, rigged fore-and-aft, with the mast stepped about one third of the overall length aft of the bow

slop¹ **1** the beer, cider, etc, spilt from a barrel while being drawn **2** the residue left after spirits have been distilled **3** *Informal* gushing speech or writing

slop² sailors' clothing and bedding issued from a ship's stores

slope **1** hills or foothills **2** *Maths* **a** (of a line) the tangent of the angle between the line and another line parallel to the *x*-axis **b** the first derivative of the equation of a curve at a given point **3** *US, slang, derogatory* a person from Southeast Asia, especially a Vietnamese

slosh a popular dance with a traditional routine of steps, kicks, and turns performed in lines

slot¹ **1** an air passage in an aerofoil to direct air from the lower to the upper surface, esp the gap formed behind a slat **2** a vertical opening between the leech of a foresail and a mast or the luff of another sail through which air spills from one against the other to impart forward motion

slot² the trail of an animal, esp a deer

sloth any of several shaggy-coated arboreal edentate mammals of the family *Bradypodidae*, esp *Bradypus tridactylus* (**three-toed sloth** or **ai**) or *Choloepus didactylus* (**two-toed sloth** or **unau**), of Central and South America. They are slow-moving, hanging upside down by their long arms and feeding on vegetation

slot machine a machine, esp one for selling small articles or for gambling, activated by placing a coin or metal disc in a slot

slough[1] 1 a hollow filled with mud; bog 2 *US and Canadian* a (in the prairies) a large hole where water collects or the water in such a hole b (in the northwest) a sluggish side channel of a river c (on the Pacific coast) a marshy saltwater inlet

slough[2] 1 any outer covering that is shed, such as the dead outer layer of the skin of a snake, the cellular debris in a wound, etc. 2 *Bridge* a discarded card

Slough 1 an industrial town in SE central England, in Slough unitary authority, Berkshire; food products, high-tech industries. Pop: 126 276 (2001) 2 a unitary authority in SE central England, in Berkshire. Pop: 118 800 (2003 est). Area: 28 sq km (11 sq miles)

Slovak the official language of Slovakia, belonging to the West Slavonic branch of the Indo-European family. Slovak is closely related to Czech, they are mutually intelligible

Slovakia a country in central Europe: part of Hungary from the 11th century until 1918, when it united with Bohemia and Moravia to form Czechoslovakia; it became independent in 1993 and joined the EU in 2004. Official language: Slovak. Religion: Roman Catholic majority. Currency: koruna. Capital: Bratislava. Pop: 5 407 000 (2004 est). Area: 49 036 sq km (18 940 sq miles)

Slovene a South Slavonic language spoken in Slovenia, closely related to Serbo-Croat

Slovenia a republic in S central Europe: settled by the Slovenes in the 6th century; joined Yugoslavia in 1918 and became an autonomous republic in 1946; became fully independent in 1992 and joined the EU in 2004; rises over 2800 m (9000 ft) in the Julian Alps. Official language: Slovene. Religion: Roman Catholic majority. Currency: tolar. Capital: Ljubljana. Pop: 1 982 000 (2004 est). Area: 20 251 sq km (7819 sq miles)

slow 1 (of trade, etc) unproductive; slack 2 *Photog* requiring a relatively long time of exposure to produce a given density 3 *Cricket* (of a bowler, etc) delivering the ball slowly, usually with spin

slow motion *Films, television* action that is made to appear slower than normal by passing the film through the taking camera at a faster rate than normal or by replaying a video tape recording more slowly

slow virus any of a class of virus-like disease-causing agents known as prions that are present in the body for a long time before becoming active or infectious and are very resistant to radiation and similar factors: believed to be the cause of BSE and scrapie

slowworm a Eurasian legless lizard, *Anguis fragilis*, with a brownish-grey snakelike body: family *Anguidae*

sludge 1 any deposit or sediment 2 a surface layer of ice that has a slushy appearance 3 (in sewage disposal) the solid constituents of sewage that precipitate during treatment and are removed for subsequent purification

slug[1] 1 any of various terrestrial gastropod molluscs of the genera *Limax, Arion*, etc, in which the body is elongated and the shell is absent or very much reduced 2 any of various other invertebrates having a soft slimy

body, esp the larvae of certain sawflies

slug[2] 1 an fps unit of mass; the mass that will acquire an acceleration of 1 foot per second per second when acted upon by a force of 1 pound. 1 slug is approximately equal to 32.17 pounds 2 *Metallurgy* a metal blank from which small forgings are worked 3 a draught of a drink, esp an alcoholic one 4 a magnetic core that is screwed into or out of an inductance coil to adjust the tuning of a radio frequency amplifier

sluice 1 a channel that carries a rapid current of water, esp one that has a sluicegate to control the flow 2 the body of water controlled by a sluicegate 3 See **sluicegate** 4 an artificial channel through which logs can be floated

sluicegate a valve or gate fitted to a sluice to control the rate of flow of water

slum a squalid section of a city, characterized by inferior living conditions and usually by overcrowding

slump 1 a decline in commercial activity, prices, etc. 2 *Economics* another word for **depression** 3 a slipping of earth or rock; landslide

slur *Music* a a performance or execution of a melodic interval of two or more notes in a part b the curved line (⌣ or ⌢) indicating this

slurry a suspension of solid particles in a liquid, as in a mixture of cement, clay, coal dust, manure, meat, etc with water

slush *Nautical* waste fat from the galley of a ship

slush fund 1 a fund for financing political or commercial corruption 2 *US, nautical* a fund accumulated from the sale of slush from the galley

slut *Archaic* a female dog

Sluter Claus ?1345–1406, Dutch sculptor, working in Burgundy, whose realism influenced many sculptors and painters in 15th-century Europe. He is best known for the portal sculptures and the *Well of Moses* in the Carthusian monastery at Champnol

smack 1 a sailing vessel, usually sloop-rigged, used in coasting and fishing along the British coast 2 a fishing vessel equipped with a well for keeping the catch alive

small *Obsolete* (of beer, etc) of low alcoholic strength

small intestine the longest part of the alimentary canal, consisting of the duodenum, jejunum, and ileum, in which digestion is completed

smallpox an acute highly contagious viral disease characterized by high fever, severe prostration, and a pinkish rash changing in form from papules to pustules, which dry up and form scabs that are cast off, leaving pitted depressions

small print matter in a contract, etc, printed in small type, esp when considered to be a trap for the unwary

small-scale (of a map, model, etc) giving a relatively small representation of something, usually missing out details

smart (of systems) operating as if by human intelligence by using automatic computer control

Smart Christopher 1722–71, British poet, author of *A Song to David* (1763) and *Jubilate Agno* (written 1758–63, published 1939). He was confined (1756–63) for religious mania and died in a debtors' prison

smart card a plastic card with integrated circuits used

for storing and processing computer data

smash *Tennis, squash, badminton* a fast and powerful overhead stroke

smear a preparation of blood, secretions, etc, smeared onto a glass slide for examination under a microscope

smell that sense (olfaction) by which scents or odours are perceived

smelt any marine or freshwater salmonoid food fish of the family *Osmeridae*, such as *Osmerus eperlanus* of Europe, having a long silvery body and occurring in temperate and cold northern waters

Smetana Bedřich 1824–84, Czech composer, founder of his country's national school of music. His works include *My Fatherland* (1874–79), a cycle of six symphonic poems, and the opera *The Bartered Bride* (1866)

Smiles Samuel 1812–1904, British writer: author of the didactic work *Self-Help* (1859)

smiley any of a group of symbols depicting a smile, or other facial expression, used in electronic mail

smith a person who works in metal, esp one who shapes metal by hammering

Smith 1 Adam 1723–90, Scottish economist and philosopher, whose influential book *The Wealth of Nations* (1776) advocated free trade and private enterprise and opposed state interference **2** Bessie, known as *Empress of the Blues*. 1894–1937, US blues singer and songwriter **3** Delia born 1941, British cookery writer and broadcaster: her publications include *The Complete Cookery Course* (1982) **4** Harvey born 1938, British showjumper **5** Ian (**Douglas**). born 1919, Zimbabwean statesman; prime minister of Rhodesia (1964–79). He declared independence from Britain unilaterally (1965) **6** John ?1580–1631, English explorer and writer, who helped found the North American colony of Jamestown, Virginia. He was reputedly saved by the Indian chief's daughter Pocahontas from execution by her tribe. Among his works is a *Description of New England* (1616) **7** John 1938–94, British Labour politician; leader of the Labour Party 1992–94 **8** Joseph 1805–44, US religious leader; founder of the Mormon Church **9** Dame Maggie born 1934, British actress. Her films include *The Prime of Miss Jean Brodie* (1969), *California Suite* (1978), *The Lonely Passion of Judith Hearne* (1988), *The Secret Garden* (1993), and *Gosford Park* (2001) **10** Stevie, real name *Florence Margaret Smith*. 1902–71, British poet. Her works include *Novel on Yellow Paper* (1936), and the poems 'A Good Time was had by All' (1937) and 'Not Waving but Drowning' (1957) **11** Sydney 1771–1845, British clergyman and writer, noted for *The Letters of Peter Plymley* (1807–08), in which he advocated Catholic emancipation **12** Will(**ard**) **Christopher** born 1968, US film actor and rap singer; star of the television series *The Fresh Prince of Bel Air* (1990–96) and the films *Men In Black* (1997), *Wild Wild West* (1999), and *Ali* (2001) **13** William 1769–1839, English geologist, who founded the science of stratigraphy by proving that rock strata could be dated by the fossils they contained

Smithson James original name *James Lewes Macie*. 1765–1829, English chemist and mineralogist, who left a bequest to found the Smithsonian Institution

smithy a place in which metal, usually iron or steel, is worked by heating and hammering; forge

smog a mixture of smoke, fog, and chemical fumes

smoke 1 the product of combustion, consisting of fine particles of carbon carried by hot gases and air **2** any cloud of fine particles suspended in a gas **3 a** the act of smoking tobacco or other substances, esp in a pipe or as a cigarette or cigar **b** the duration of smoking such substances **4** *Informal* **a** a cigarette or cigar **b** a substance for smoking, such as pipe tobacco or marijuana **5** any of various colours similar to that of smoke, esp a dark grey with a bluish, yellowish, or greenish tinge

smokeless zone an area designated by the local authority where only smokeless fuels are permitted

smoker *Oceanography* a vent on the ocean floor from which hot water and minerals erupt

Smolensk a city in W Russia, on the Dnieper River: a major commercial centre in medieval times; scene of severe fighting (1941 and 1943) in World War II. Pop: 323 000 (2005 est)

Smollett Tobias George 1721–71, Scottish novelist, whose picaresque satires include *Roderick Random* (1748), *Peregrine Pickle* (1751), and *Humphry Clinker* (1771)

smolt a young salmon at the stage when it migrates from fresh water to the sea

smooch *Informal Brit* a piece of music played for dancing to slowly and amorously

smooth 1 (of the skin) free from hair **2** not harsh or astringent **3** *Maths* (of a curve) differentiable at every point **4** *Physics* (of a plane, surface, etc) regarded as being frictionless **5** *Tennis, squash, badminton* the side of a racket on which the binding strings form a continuous line

smut *Angling* a minute midge or other insect relished by trout

Smuts Jan Christiaan 1870–1950, South African statesman; prime minister (1919–24; 1939–48). He fought for the Boers during the Boer War, then worked for Anglo-Boer reconciliation and served the Allies during World Wars I and II

Smyrna an ancient city on the W coast of Asia Minor: a major trading centre in the ancient world; a centre of early Christianity

snack bar a place where light meals or snacks can be obtained, often with a self-service system

snaffle a simple jointed bit for a horse

snag 1 a small loop or hole in a fabric caused by a sharp object **2** *Engineering* a projection that brings to a stop a sliding or rotating component **3** *Chiefly US and Canadian* a tree stump in a riverbed that is dangerous to navigation **4** *US and Canadian* a standing dead tree, esp one used as a perch by an eagle

snail 1 any of numerous terrestrial or freshwater gastropod molluscs with a spirally coiled shell, esp any of the family *Helicidae*, such as *Helix aspersa* (**garden snail**) **2** any other gastropod with a spirally coiled shell, such as a whelk

snake 1 any reptile of the suborder *Ophidia* (or *Serpentes*), typically having a scaly cylindrical limbless body, fused eyelids, and a jaw modified for swallowing large prey: includes venomous forms such as cobras and rattlesnakes, large nonvenomous constrictors (boas and pythons), and small harmless types such as the grass snake **2** (in the European Union) a former system of managing a group of currencies by allowing the exchange rate of each of them only to fluctuate within narrow limits **3** a tool in the form of a long flexible wire for unblocking drains

snakebite 1 a bite inflicted by a snake, esp a venomous one **2** a drink of cider and lager

snake charmer an entertainer, esp in Asia, who charms or appears to charm snakes by playing music and by rhythmic body movements

Snake River a river in the northwestern US, rising in NW Wyoming and flowing west through Idaho, turning north as part of the border between Idaho and Oregon, and flowing west to the Columbia River near Pasco, Washington. Length: 1670 km (1038 miles)

snakes and ladders a board game in which players move counters along a series of squares according to throws of a dice. A ladder provides a short cut to a square nearer the finish and a snake obliges a player to return to a square nearer the start

snap 1 *Informal* See **snapshot 2** *Brit* a card game in which the word *snap* is called when two cards of equal value are turned up on the separate piles dealt by each player **3** *American football* the start of each play when the centre passes the ball back from the line of scrimmage to a teammate

snapdragon any of several scrophulariaceous chiefly Old World plants of the genus *Antirrhinum*, esp *A. majus*, of the Mediterranean region, having spikes of showy white, yellow, pink, red, or purplish flowers

snapper 1 any large sharp-toothed percoid food fish of the family *Lutjanidae* of warm and tropical coastal regions **2** a sparid food fish, *Chrysophrys auratus*, of Australia and New Zealand, that has a pinkish body covered with blue spots

snapshot an informal photograph taken with a simple camera

snare¹ 1 a device for trapping birds or small animals, esp a flexible loop that is drawn tight around the prey **2** a surgical instrument for removing certain tumours, consisting of a wire loop that may be drawn tight around their base to sever or uproot them

snare² *Music* a set of gut strings wound with wire fitted against the lower drumhead of a snare drum. They produce a rattling sound when the drum is beaten

snare drum *Music* a cylindrical drum with two drumheads, the upper of which is struck and the lower fitted with a snare

snarl a knot in wood

snatch *Weightlifting* a lift in which the weight is raised in one quick motion from the floor to an overhead position

Snead Sam(uel Jackson). 1912–2002, US golfer; winner of seven major tournaments between 1938 and 1951

sneak thief a person who steals paltry articles from premises, which he enters through open doors, windows, etc.

snick 1 a knot in thread, etc. **2** *Cricket* **a** a glancing blow off the edge of the bat **b** the ball so hit

snicker *chiefly US and Canadian* a sly or disrespectful laugh, esp one partly stifled

sniffer dog a police dog trained to detect drugs or explosives by smell

snifter 1 a pear-shaped glass with a short stem and a bowl that narrows towards the top so that the aroma of brandy or a liqueur is retained **2** *Informal* a small quantity of alcoholic drink

snipe 1 any of various birds of the genus *Gallinago* (or *Capella*) and related genera, such as *G. gallinago* (**common** or **Wilson's snipe**), of marshes and river banks, having a long straight bill: family *Scolopacidae* (sandpipers, etc), order *Charadriiformes* **2** any of various similar related birds, such as certain sandpipers and curlews

snoek a South African edible marine fish, *Thyrsites atun*

snood *Vet science* a long fleshy appendage that hangs over the upper beak of turkeys

snook 1 any of several large game fishes of the genus *Centropomus*, esp *C. undecimalis* of tropical American marine and fresh waters: family *Centropomidae* (robalos) **2** *Austral* the sea pike *Australuzza novaehollandiae*

snooker 1 a game played on a billiard table with 15 red balls, six balls of other colours, and a white cue ball. The object is to pot the balls in a certain order **2** a shot in which the cue ball is left in a position such that another ball blocks the object ball. The opponent is then usually forced to play the cue ball off a cushion
▷www.worldsnooker.com

snorkel 1 a device allowing a swimmer to breathe while face down on the surface of the water, consisting of a bent tube fitting into the mouth and projecting above the surface **2** (on a submarine) a retractable vertical device containing air-intake and exhaust pipes for the engines and general ventilation: its use permits extended periods of submergence at periscope depth

Snorri Sturluson 1179–1241, Icelandic historian and poet; author of *Younger* or *Prose Edda* (?1222), containing a collection of Norse myths and a treatise on poetry, and the *Heimskringla* sagas of the Norwegian kings from their mythological origins to the 12th century

snout 1 the part of the head of a vertebrate, esp a mammal, consisting of the nose, jaws, and surrounding region, esp when elongated **2** the corresponding part of the head of such insects as weevils **3** a brownish noctuid moth, *Hypena proboscidalis*, that frequents nettles: named from the palps that project prominently from the head at rest

snow 1 precipitation from clouds in the form of flakes of ice crystals formed in the upper atmosphere **2** a layer of snowflakes on the ground **3** a fall of such precipitation **4** the random pattern of white spots on a television or radar screen, produced by noise in the receiver and occurring when the signal is weak or absent

Snow C(harles) P(ercy), Baron. 1905–80, British novelist and physicist. His novels include the series *Strangers and Brothers* (1949–70)

snowball 1 a drink made of advocaat and lemonade **2** *Slang* a mixture of heroin and cocaine **3** a dance started by one couple who separate and choose different partners. The process continues until all present are dancing

snowberry 1 any of several caprifoliaceous shrubs of the genus *Symphoricarpos*, esp *S. albus*, cultivated for their small pink flowers and white berries **2** any of the berries of such a plant **3** any of various other white-berried plants

snow-blind temporarily unable to see or having

impaired vision because of the intense reflection of sunlight from snow

snowboard a shaped board, resembling a skateboard without wheels, on which a person can stand to slide across snow

snowcap a cap of snow, as on the top of a mountain

Snowdon¹ 1st Earl of, title of *Antony Armstrong-Jones*. born 1930, British photographer, whose work includes television documentaries, photographic books, and the design of the Snowdon Aviary, London Zoo (1965). His marriage (1960–78) to Princess Margaret ended in divorce

Snowdon² a mountain in NW Wales, in Gwynedd: the highest peak in Wales. Height: 1085 m (3560 ft)

Snowdonia 1 a massif in NW Wales, in Gwynedd, the highest peak being Snowdon 2 a national park in NW Wales, in Gwynedd and Conwy: includes the Snowdonia massif in the north. Area: 2189 sq km (845 sq miles)

snowdrift a bank of deep snow driven together by the wind

snowdrop any of several amaryllidaceous plants of the Eurasian genus *Galanthus*, esp *G. nivalis*, having drooping white bell-shaped flowers that bloom in early spring

snowfall 1 a fall of snow 2 *Meteorol* the amount of snow received in a specified place and time

snowflake 1 one of the mass of small thin delicate arrangements of ice crystals that fall as snow 2 any of various European amaryllidaceous plants of the genus *Leucojum*, such as *L. vernum* (**spring snowflake**), that have white nodding bell-shaped flowers

snow goose a North American goose, *Anser hyperboreus* (or *Chen hyperborea* or *A. caerulescens*), having a white plumage with black wing tips

snow line the altitudinal or latitudinal limit of permanent snow

snowmobile a a small open motor vehicle for travelling on snow, steered by two skis at the front and driven by a caterpillar track underneath b a larger closed motor vehicle with two skis at the front and a track at each side

snowplough 1 an implement or vehicle for clearing away snow 2 *Skiing* a technique of turning the points of the skis inwards to turn or stop

Snowy River a river in SE Australia, rising in SE New South Wales: waters diverted through a system of dams and tunnels across the watershed into the Murray and Murrumbidgee Rivers for hydroelectric power and to provide water for irrigation. Length: 426 km (265 miles)

snub *Nautical* a an elastic shock absorber attached to a mooring line b *(as modifier): a snub rope*

snuff 1 finely powdered tobacco for sniffing up the nostrils or less commonly for chewing 2 a small amount of this 3 any powdered substance, esp one for sniffing up the nostrils

snuffbox a container, often of elaborate ornamental design, for holding small quantities of snuff

snug 1 (in Britain and Ireland) one of the bars in certain pubs, offering intimate seating for only a few persons 2 *Engineering* a small peg under the head of a bolt engaging with a slot in the bolted component to prevent the bolt turning when the nut is tightened

Soane Sir John 1753–1837, British architect. His work includes Dulwich College Art Gallery (1811–14) and his own house in Lincoln's Inn Fields, London (1812–13), which is now the Sir John Soane's Museum

soap 1 a cleaning or emulsifying agent made by reacting animal or vegetable fats or oils with potassium or sodium hydroxide. Soaps often contain colouring matter and perfume and act by emulsifying grease and lowering the surface tension of water, so that it more readily penetrates open materials such as textiles 2 any metallic salt of a fatty acid, such as palmitic or stearic acid

soapbox 1 a box or crate for packing soap 2 a child's homemade racing cart consisting of a wooden box set on a wooden frame with wheels and a steerable front axle

soapstone a massive compact soft variety of talc, used for making tabletops, hearths, ornaments, etc.

Soares Mário born 1924, Portuguese statesman; prime minister of Portugal (1976–77; 1978–80; 1983–86); president of Portugal (1986–96)

Sobers Sir Garfield St. Auburn, known as *Garry*. born 1936, West Indian (Barbadian) cricketer; one of the finest all-rounders of all time

sobriquet *or* **soubriquet** a humorous epithet, assumed name, or nickname

soca a mixture of soul and calypso music typical of the E Caribbean

soccer a a game in which two teams of eleven players try to kick or head a ball into their opponent's goal, only the goalkeeper on either side being allowed to touch the ball with his hands and arms except in the case of throw-ins b *(as modifier): a soccer player*

Sochi a city and resort in SW Russia, in the Krasnodar Territory on the Black Sea: hot mineral springs. Pop: 328 000 (2005 est)

sociable a type of open carriage with two seats facing each other

social 1 relating to or engaged in social services 2 (esp of certain species of insects) living together in organized colonies 3 (of plant species) growing in clumps, usually over a wide area

Social Charter a declaration of the rights, minimum wages, maximum hours, etc, of workers in the European Union, later adopted in the Social Chapter

social contract *or* **compact** (in the theories of Locke, Hobbes, Rousseau, and others) an agreement, entered into by individuals, that results in the formation of the state or of organized society, the prime motive being the desire for protection, which entails the surrender of some or all personal liberties

social democrat 1 any socialist who believes in the gradual transformation of capitalism into democratic socialism 2 a member of a Social Democratic Party

social fund (in Britain) a social security fund from which loans or payments may be made to people in cases of extreme need

socialism 1 an economic theory or system in which the means of production, distribution, and exchange are owned by the community collectively, usually through the state. It is characterized by production for use rather than profit, by equality of individual wealth, by the absence of competitive economic activity, and, usually, by government determination of investment, prices, and production levels **2** any of various social or political theories or movements in which the common welfare is to be achieved through the establishment of a socialist economic system **3** (in Leninist theory) a transitional stage after the proletarian revolution in the development of a society from capitalism to communism: characterized by the distribution of income according to work rather than need

social security 1 public provision for the economic, and sometimes social, welfare of the aged, unemployed, etc, esp through pensions and other monetary assistance **2** a government programme designed to provide such assistance

social welfare 1 the various social services provided by a state for the benefit of its citizens **2** (in New Zealand) a government department concerned with pensions and benefits for the elderly, the sick, etc.
▷www.sosig.ac.uk/social_welfare/
▷www.eswin.net
▷www.unfpa.org

social work any of various social services designed to alleviate the conditions of the poor and aged and to increase the welfare of children

society *Ecology* a small community of plants within a larger association

Society of Jesus the religious order of the Jesuits, founded by Ignatius Loyola

socioeconomic of, relating to, or involving both economic and social factors

sociopolitical of, relating to, or involving both political and social factors

sock 1 a light shoe worn by actors in ancient Greek and Roman comedy, sometimes taken to allude to comic drama in general **2** another name for **windsock**

socket 1 a device into which an electric plug can be inserted in order to make a connection in a circuit **2** *Chiefly Brit* such a device mounted on a wall and connected to the electricity supply **3** a part with an opening or hollow into which some other part, such as a pipe, probe, etc, can be fitted **4** a spanner head having a recess suitable to be fitted over the head of a bolt and a keyway into which a wrench can be fitted **5** *Anatomy* **a** a bony hollow into which a part or structure fits **b** the receptacle of a ball-and-socket joint

Socotra, Sokotra, *or* **Suqutra** an island in the Indian Ocean, about 240 km (150 miles) off Cape Guardafui, Somalia: administratively part of Yemen. Capital: Tamrida. Area: 3100 sq km (1200 sq miles)

Socrates ?470–399 BC, Athenian philosopher, whose beliefs are known only through the writings of his pupils Plato and Xenophon. He taught that virtue was based on knowledge, which was attained by a dialectical process that took into account many aspects of a stated hypothesis. He was indicted for impiety and corruption of youth (399) and was condemned to death. He refused to flee and died by drinking hemlock

Socratic method *Philosophy* the method of instruction by question and answer used by Socrates in order to elicit from his pupils truths he considered to be implicitly known by all rational beings

sod a piece of grass-covered surface soil held together by the roots of the grass; turf

soda 1 any of a number of simple inorganic compounds of sodium, such as sodium carbonate (**washing soda**), sodium bicarbonate (**baking soda**), and sodium hydroxide (**caustic soda**) **2** the top card of the pack in faro

soda fountain *US and Canadian* a counter that serves drinks, snacks, etc.

soda siphon a sealed bottle containing and dispensing soda water. The water is forced up a tube reaching to the bottom of the bottle by the pressure of gas above the water

Soddy Frederick 1877–1956, English chemist, whose work on radioactive disintegration led to the discovery of isotopes: Nobel prize for chemistry 1921

sodium a a very reactive soft silvery-white element of the alkali metal group occurring principally in common salt, Chile saltpetre, and cryolite. Sodium and potassium ions maintain the essential electrolytic balance in living cells. It is used in the production of chemicals, in metallurgy, and, alloyed with potassium, as a cooling medium in nuclear reactors. Symbol: Na; atomic no.: 11; atomic wt.: 22.989768; valency: 1; relative density: 0.971; melting pt.: 97.81±0.03°C; boiling pt.: 892.9°C **b** (*as modifier*): *sodium light*

sodium bicarbonate a white crystalline soluble compound usually obtained by the Solvay process and used in effervescent drinks, baking powders, fire extinguishers, and in medicine as an antacid; sodium hydrogen carbonate. Formula: $NaHCO_3$

sodium carbonate a colourless or white odourless soluble crystalline compound existing in several hydrated forms and used in the manufacture of glass, ceramics, soap, and paper and as an industrial and domestic cleansing agent. It is made by the Solvay process and commonly obtained as the decahydrate (**washing soda** or **sal soda**) or a white anhydrous powder (**soda ash**). Formula: Na_2CO_3

sodium chlorate a colourless crystalline soluble compound used as a bleaching agent, weak antiseptic, and weedkiller. Formula: $NaClO_3$

sodium chloride common table salt; a soluble colourless crystalline compound occurring naturally as halite and in sea water: widely used as a seasoning and preservative for food and in the manufacture of chemicals, glass, and soap. Formula: NaCl

sodium hydroxide a white deliquescent strongly alkaline solid used in the manufacture of rayon, paper, aluminium, soap, and sodium compounds. Formula: NaOH

Sodom *Old Testament* a city destroyed by God for its wickedness that, with Gomorrah, traditionally typifies depravity (Genesis 19:24)

sodomite a person who practises sodomy

sodomy anal intercourse committed by a man with another man or a woman

Sofia the capital of Bulgaria, in the west: colonized by the Romans in 29 AD; became capital of Bulgaria in 1879; university (1880). Pop: 1 045 000 (2005 est)

soft 1 *Dialect* drizzly or rainy **2** (of a diet) consisting of easily digestible foods **3** *Chem* (of water) relatively free of mineral salts and therefore easily able to make soap lather **4** (of a drug such as cannabis) nonaddictive or only mildly addictive **5** (of a currency) in relatively little demand, esp because of a weak balance of payments situation **6** (of radiation, such as X-rays and ultraviolet radiation) having low energy and not capable of deep penetration of materials **7** *Physics* (of valves or tubes) only partially evacuated

softball 1 a variation of baseball using a larger softer ball, pitched underhand **2** the ball used
▷www.internationalsoftball.com

soft palate the posterior fleshy portion of the roof of the mouth. It forms a movable muscular flap that seals off the nasopharynx during swallowing and speech

soft-pedal a foot-operated lever on a piano, the left one of two, that either moves the whole action closer to the strings so that the hammers strike with less force or causes fewer of the strings to sound

soft sell a method of selling based on indirect suggestion or inducement

software 1 *Computing* the programs that can be used with a particular computer system **2** video cassettes and discs for use with a particular video system

softwood 1 the open-grained wood of any of numerous coniferous trees, such as pine and cedar, as distinguished from that of a dicotyledonous tree **2** any tree yielding this wood

Sogdiana a region of ancient central Asia. Its chief city was Samarkand

soh *or* **so** *Music* (in tonic sol-fa) the name used for the fifth note or dominant of any scale

Soho a district of central London, in the City of Westminster: a foreign quarter since the late 17th century, now chiefly known for restaurants, nightclubs, striptease clubs, etc.

soil¹ 1 the top layer of the land surface of the earth that is composed of disintegrated rock particles, humus, water, and air **2** a type of this material having specific characteristics

soil² refuse, manure, or excrement

soiree an evening party or other gathering given usually at a private house, esp where guests are invited to listen to, play, or dance to music

Soissons a city in N France, on the Aisne River: has Roman remains and an 11th-century abbey. Pop: 29 453 (1999)

Sokoto 1 a state of NW Nigeria. Capital: Sokoto. Pop: 4 911 118 (1995 est). Area: 65 735 sq km (25 380 sq miles) **2** a town in NW Nigeria, capital of Sokoto state: capital of the Fulah Empire in the 19th century; Muslim place of pilgrimage. Pop: 444 000 (2005 est)

sol¹ a former French copper or silver coin, usually worth 12 deniers

sol² a colloid that has a continuous liquid phase, esp one in which a solid is suspended in a liquid

sol³ *Astronomy* a solar day as measured on the planet Mars, equal to 24.65 hours

solar 1 of or relating to the sun **2** operating by or utilizing the energy of the sun **3** *Astronomy* determined from the motion of the earth relative to the sun **4** *Astrology* subject to the influence of the sun

solarium 1 a bed equipped with ultraviolet lights used for acquiring an artificial suntan **2** an establishment offering such facilities

solar plexus 1 *Anatomy* the network of sympathetic nerves situated behind the stomach that supply the abdominal organs **2** the part of the stomach beneath the diaphragm; pit of the stomach

solar system the system containing the sun and the bodies held in its gravitational field, including the planets (Mercury, Venus, Earth, Mars, Jupiter, Saturn, Uranus, Neptune, Pluto), the asteroids, and comets
▷www.solarviews.com
▷www.the-solar-system.net
▷http://ssd.jpl.nasa.gov

solder an alloy for joining two metal surfaces by melting the alloy so that it forms a thin layer between the surfaces. **Soft solders** are alloys of lead and tin; **brazing solders** are alloys of copper and zinc

soldering iron a hand tool consisting of a handle fixed to a copper tip that is heated, electrically or in a flame, and used to melt and apply solder

soldier 1 a low-ranking member of the Mafia or other organized crime ring **2** *Zoology* **a** an individual in a colony of social insects, esp ants, that has powerful jaws adapted for defending the colony, crushing large food particles, etc. **b** (*as modifier*): *soldier ant*

sole¹ *Law* having no wife or husband

sole² **1** the underside of the foot **2** the underside of a golf-club head **3** the bottom of an oven, furnace, etc.

sole³ 1 any tongue-shaped flatfish of the family *Soleidae*, esp *Solea solea* (**European sole**): most common in warm seas and highly valued as food fishes **2** any of certain other similar fishes

solecism a the nonstandard use of a grammatical construction **b** any mistake, incongruity, or absurdity

solemnity *Law* a formality necessary to validate a deed, act, contract, etc.

solenoid 1 a coil of wire, usually cylindrical, in which a magnetic field is set up by passing a current through it **2** a coil of wire, partially surrounding an iron core, that is made to move inside the coil by the magnetic field set up by a current: used to convert electrical to mechanical energy, as in the operation of a switch **3** such a device used as a relay, as in a motor vehicle for connecting the battery directly to the starter motor when activated by the ignition switch

Solent the a strait of the English Channel between the coast of Hampshire, on the English mainland, and the Isle of Wight. Width: up to 6 km (4 miles)

solicitor 1 (in Britain) a lawyer who advises clients on matters of law, draws up legal documents, prepares cases for barristers, etc, and who may represent clients in certain courts **2** (in the US) an officer responsible for the legal affairs of a town, city, etc.

Solicitor General 1 (in Britain) the law officer of the Crown ranking next to the Attorney General (in Scotland to the Lord Advocate) and acting as his assistant **2** (in New Zealand) the government's chief lawyer: head of the Crown Law Office and prosecutor for the Crown

solid 1 of, concerned with, or being a substance in a physical state in which it resists changes in size and shape **2** *Geometry* having or relating to three dimensions **3** of or having a single uniform colour or tone **4**

Geometry **a** a closed surface in three-dimensional space **b** such a surface together with the volume enclosed by it **5** a solid substance, such as wood, iron, or diamond

solid geometry the branch of geometry concerned with the properties of three-dimensional geometric figures

solid-state (of an electronic device) activated by a semiconductor component in which current flow is through solid material rather than in a vacuum

solidus *History* a gold coin of the Byzantine empire

Solihull **1** a town in central England, in Solihull unitary authority in the S West Midlands near Birmingham: mainly residential. Pop: 94 753 (2001) **2** a unitary authority in central England, in the West Midlands. Pop: 200 300 (2003 est). Area: 180 sq km (70 sq miles)

soliloquy **1** the act of speaking alone or to oneself, esp as a theatrical device **2** a speech in a play that is spoken in soliloquy

Solingen a city in W Germany, in North Rhine-Westphalia: a major European centre of the cutlery industry. Pop: 164 543 (2003 est)

solipsism *Philosophy* the extreme form of scepticism which denies the possibility of any knowledge other than of one's own existence

solitaire **1** a game played by one person, esp one involving moving and taking pegs in a pegboard or marbles on an indented circular board with the object of being left with only one **2** the US name for **patience** (the card game) **3** any of several extinct birds of the genus *Pezophaps*, related to the dodo **4** any of several dull grey North American songbirds of the genus *Myadestes*: subfamily *Turdinae* (thrushes)

solitary **1** (of animals) not living in organized colonies or large groups **2** (of flowers) growing singly **3** *Informal* short for **solitary confinement**

solitary confinement isolation imposed on a prisoner, as by confinement in a special cell

solo **1** a musical composition for one performer with or without accompaniment **2** any of various card games in which each person plays on his own instead of in partnership with another, such as solo whist **3** a flight in which an aircraft pilot is unaccompanied

Solomon 10th century BC, king of Israel, son of David and Bathsheba, credited with great wisdom

Solomon's seal any of several liliaceous plants of the genus *Polygonatum* of N temperate regions, having greenish or yellow paired flowers, long narrow waxy leaves, and a thick underground stem with prominent leaf scars

Solon ?638–?559 BC, Athenian statesman, who introduced economic, political, and legal reforms

Solothurn **1** a canton of NW Switzerland. Capital: Solothurn. Pop: 246 500 (2002 est). Area: 793 sq km (306 sq miles) **2** a town in NW Switzerland, capital of Solothurn canton, on the Aare River. Pop: 15 489 (2000)

solstice **1** either the shortest day of the year (**winter solstice**) or the longest day of the year (**summer solstice**) **2** either of the two points on the ecliptic at which the sun is overhead at the tropic of Cancer or Capricorn at the summer and winter solstices

Solti Sir **Georg** 1912–97, British conductor, born in Hungary

soluble (of a substance) capable of being dissolved, esp easily dissolved in some solvent, usually water

solute **1** the component of a solution that changes its state in forming the solution or the component that is not present in excess; the substance that is dissolved in another substance **2** *Botany, now rare* loose or unattached; free

solution **1** a homogeneous mixture of two or more substances in which the molecules or atoms of the substances are completely dispersed. The constituents can be solids, liquids, or gases **2** the act or process of forming a solution **3** the state of being dissolved (esp in the phrase **in solution**) **4** a mixture of two or more substances in which one or more components are present as small particles with colloidal dimension; colloid **5** *Maths* **a** the unique set of values that yield a true statement when substituted for the variables in an equation **b** a member of a set of assignments of values to variables under which a given statement is satisfied; a member of a solution set **6** the stage of a disease, following a crisis, resulting in its termination **7** *Law* the payment, discharge, or satisfaction of a claim, debt, etc.

solvent **1** (of a substance, esp a liquid) capable of dissolving another substance **2** a liquid capable of dissolving another substance **3** the component of a solution that does not change its state in forming the solution or the component that is present in excess

solvent abuse the deliberate inhaling of intoxicating fumes given off by certain solvents such as toluene

Solway Firth an inlet of the Irish Sea between SW Scotland and NW England. Length: about 56 km (35 miles)

Solzhenitsyn Alexander Isayevich born 1918, Russian novelist. His books include *One Day in the Life of Ivan Denisovich* (1962), *The First Circle* (1968), *Cancer Ward* (1968), *August 1914* (1971), *The Gulag Archipelago* (1974), and *October 1916* (1985). His works criticize the Soviet regime and he was imprisoned (1945–53) and exiled to Siberia (1953–56). He was deported to the West from the Soviet Union in 1974; all charges against him were dropped in 1991 and he returned to Russia in 1994. Nobel prize for literature 1970

Somali **1** a member of a tall dark-skinned people inhabiting Somalia **2** the language of this people, belonging to the Cushitic subfamily of the Afro-Asiatic family of languages

Somalia a republic in NE Africa, on the Indian Ocean and the Gulf of Aden: the north became a British protectorate in 1884; the east and south were established as an Italian protectorate in 1889; gained independence and united as the Somali Republic in 1960. In 1991 the former British Somaliland region in the north unilaterally declared itself independent as the Republic of Somaliland, and other areas are also operating effectively as separate states, but this has not been recognized officially. Official languages: Arabic and Somali. Official religion: (Sunni) Muslim. Currency: Somali shilling. Capital: Mogadishu. Pop: 10 312 000 (2004 est). Area: 637 541 sq km (246 154 sq miles)

Somaliland a former region of E Africa, between the equator and the Gulf of Aden: includes Somalia, Djibouti, and SE Ethiopia

somatic 1 of or relating to the soma **2** of or relating to an animal body or body wall as distinct from the viscera, limbs, and head **3** of or relating to the human body as distinct from the mind

somersault *or* **summersault 1 a** a forward roll in which the head is placed on the ground and the trunk and legs are turned over it **b** a similar roll in a backward direction **2** an acrobatic feat in which either of these rolls are performed in midair, as in diving or gymnastics

Somerset¹ 1st Duke of, title of *Edward Seymour*. ?1500–52, English statesman, protector of England (1547–49) during Edward VI's minority. He defeated the Scots (1547) and furthered the Protestant Reformation: executed

Somerset² a county of SW England, on the Bristol Channel: the Mendip Hills lie in the north and Exmoor in the west: the geographical and ceremonial county includes the unitary authorities of North Somerset and Bath and North East Somerset (both part of Avon county from 1975 until 1996): mainly agricultural (esp dairying and fruit). Administrative centre: Taunton. Pop. (excluding unitary authorities): 507 500 (2003 est). Area (excluding unitary authorities): 3452 sq km (1332 sq miles)

Somme 1 a department of N France, in Picardy region. Capital: Amiens. Pop: 557 061 (2003 est). Area: 6277 sq km (2448 sq miles) **2** a river in N France, rising in Aisne department and flowing west to Amiens, then northwest to the English Channel: scene of heavy fighting in World War I. Length: 245 km (152 miles)

somnambulism a condition that is characterized by walking while asleep or in a hypnotic trance

Son *Christianity* the second person of the Trinity, Jesus Christ

sonar a communication and position-finding device used in underwater navigation and target detection using echolocation

sonata 1 an instrumental composition, usually in three or more movements, for piano alone (**piano sonata**) or for any other instrument with or without piano accompaniment (**violin sonata**, **cello sonata**, etc) **2** a one-movement keyboard composition of the baroque period

Sondheim Stephen (Joshua). born 1930, US songwriter. He wrote the lyrics for *West Side Story* (1957), the score for *Company* (1971), and both for *A Little Night Music* (1973), *Into the Woods* (1987), and *Passion* (1994)

song 1 a a piece of music, usually employing a verbal text, composed for the voice, esp one intended for performance by a soloist **b** the whole repertory of such pieces **c** (*as modifier*): *a song book* **2** poetical composition; poetry **3** the characteristic tuneful call or sound made by certain birds or insects

songbird 1 any passerine bird of the suborder *Oscines*, having highly developed vocal organs and, in most, a musical call **2** any bird having a musical call

Songhua a river in NE China, rising in SE Jilin province and flowing north and northeast to the Amur River near Tongjiang: the chief river of Manchuria and largest tributary of the Amur; frozen from November to April. Length: over 1300 km (800 miles)

songololo *or* **shongololo** a millipede, *Jurus terrestris*, having a hard shiny dark brown segmented exoskeleton

song thrush a common Old World thrush, *Turdus philomelos*, that has a brown back and spotted breast and is noted for its song

sonic 1 of, involving, or producing sound **2** having a speed about equal to that of sound in air: 331 metres per second (741 miles per hour) at 0°C

sonic boom a loud explosive sound caused by the shock wave of an aircraft, etc, travelling at supersonic speed

sonnet *Prosody* a verse form of Italian origin consisting of 14 lines in iambic pentameter with rhymes arranged according to a fixed scheme, usually divided either into octave and sestet or, in the English form, into three quatrains and a couplet

Son of Man *Bible* a title of Jesus Christ

Sonora a state of NW Mexico, on the Gulf of California: consists of a narrow coastal plain rising inland to the Sierra Madre Occidental; an important mining area in colonial times. Capital: Hermosillo. Pop: 2 213 370 (2000). Area: 184 934 sq km (71 403 sq miles)

Sontag Susan born 1933, US intellectual and essayist, noted esp for her writings on modern culture. Her works include 'Notes on Camp' (1964), 'Against Interpretation' (1968), *On Photography* (1977), *Illness as Metaphor* (1978), and the novel *The Volcano Lover* (1992)

Soong *or* **Song** an influential Chinese family, notably Soong Ch'ing-ling (1890–1981), who married Sun Yat-sen and became a vice-chairman of the People's Republic of China (1959); and Soong Mei-ling (born 1898), who married Chiang Kai-shek

soot finely divided carbon deposited from flames during the incomplete combustion of organic substances such as coal

soothsayer a seer or prophet

Sophia 1630–1714, electress of Hanover (1658–1714), in whom the Act of Settlement (1701) vested the English Crown. She was a granddaughter of James I of England and her son became George I of Great Britain and Ireland

sophist one of the pre-Socratic philosophers who were itinerant professional teachers of oratory and argument and who were prepared to enter into debate on any matter however specious

sophistry a a method of argument that is seemingly plausible though actually invalid and misleading **b** the art of using such arguments

Sophocles ?496–406 BC, Greek dramatist; author of seven extant tragedies: *Ajax, Antigone, Oedipus Rex, Trachiniae, Electra, Philoctetes,* and *Oedipus at Colonus*

sophomore *Chiefly US and Canadian* a second-year student at a secondary (high) school or college

soporific a drug or other agent that induces sleep

soprano 1 the highest adult female voice, having a range approximately from middle C to the A a thirteenth above it **2** the voice of a young boy before puberty **3** a singer with such a voice **4** the highest part of a piece of harmony **5 a** the highest or second highest instrument in a family of instruments **b** (*as modifier*): *a soprano saxophone*

Sopwith Sir Thomas Octave Murdoch 1888–1989, British aircraft designer, who built the Sopwith Camel biplane used during World War I. He was chairman (1935–63) of the Hawker Siddeley Group, which developed the Hurricane fighter and Lancaster bomber

Sorata Mount a mountain in W Bolivia, in the Andes: the highest mountain in the Cordillera Real, with two peaks, Ancohuma, 6550 m (21 490 ft), and Illampu, 6485 m (21 276 ft)

Sorbonne the a part of the University of Paris containing the faculties of science and literature: founded in 1253 by Robert de Sorbon as a theological college; given to the university in 1808

sorcerer or feminine **sorceress** a person who seeks to control and use magic powers; a wizard or magician

sorcery the art, practices, or spells of magic, esp black magic, by which it is sought to harness occult forces or evil spirits in order to produce preternatural effects in the world

sore 1 (esp of a wound, injury, etc) painfully sensitive; tender 2 a painful or sensitive wound, injury, etc.

Sorenstam Annika born 1970, Swedish golfer; winner of the US Women's Open (1995, 1996), the LPGA Championship (2003), and the British Women's Open (2003)

sorghum any grass of the Old World genus Sorghum, having solid stems, large flower heads, and glossy seeds: cultivated for grain, hay, and as a source of syrup

Sorocaba a city in S Brazil, in São Paulo state: industrial centre. Pop: 671 000 (2005 est)

sorority Chiefly US a social club or society for university women

sorrel any of several polygonaceous plants of the genus Rumex, esp R. acetosa, of Eurasia and North America, having acid-tasting leaves used in salads and sauces

Sorrento a port in SW Italy, in Campania on a mountainous peninsula between the Bay of Naples and the Gulf of Salerno: a resort since Roman times. Pop: 16 536 (2001)

Sosnowiec an industrial town in S Poland. Pop: 244 102 (1999 est)

sou a former French coin of low denomination

soubrette a minor female role in comedy, often that of a pert lady's maid

sough Northern English, dialect a sewer or drain or an outlet channel

souk or **suq** (in Muslim countries, esp North Africa and the Middle East) an open-air marketplace

soul 1 the spirit or immaterial part of man, the seat of human personality, intellect, will, and emotions, regarded as an entity that survives the body after death 2 Christianity the spiritual part of a person, capable of redemption from the power of sin through divine grace 3 a a type of Black music resulting from the addition of jazz, gospel, and pop elements to the urban blues style b (as modifier): a soul singer 4 of or relating to Black Americans and their culture

▷www.jazzinamerica.org
▷www.bluesandsoul.co.uk

sound¹ 1 a a periodic disturbance in the pressure or density of a fluid or in the elastic strain of a solid, produced by a vibrating object. It has a velocity in air at sea level at 0°C of 331 metres per second (741 miles per hour) and travels as longitudinal waves b (as modifier): a sound wave 2 the sensation produced by such a periodic disturbance in the organs of hearing 3 Slang music, esp rock, jazz, or pop

sound² 1 Law (of a title, etc) free from defect; legally valid 2 Logic a (of a deductive argument) valid b (of an inductive argument) according with whatever principles ensure the high probability of the truth of the conclusion given the truth of the premises c another word for **consistent**

sound¹ Med an instrument for insertion into a bodily cavity or passage to dilate strictures, dislodge foreign material, etc.

sound² 1 a relatively narrow channel between two larger areas of sea or between an island and the mainland 2 an inlet or deep bay of the sea 3 the air bladder of a fish

Sound the a strait between SW Sweden and Zealand (Denmark), linking the Kattegat with the Baltic: busy shipping lane; spanned by a bridge in 2000. Length: 113 km (70 miles). Narrowest point: 5 km (3 miles)

sound barrier a hypothetical barrier to flight at or above the speed of sound, when a sudden large increase in drag occurs

sounding board a thin wooden board in a piano or comprising the upper surface of a resonating chamber in a violin, cello, etc, serving to amplify the vibrations produced by the strings passing across it

soundtrack 1 the recorded sound accompaniment to a film 2 a narrow strip along the side of a spool of film, which carries the sound accompaniment

sound wave a wave that propagates sound

soup 1 Informal a photographic developer 2 a slang name for **nitroglycerine**

▷www.souprecipe.com/default.asp
▷www.greatrecipesonline.com/dir/Soup

soup kitchen a place or mobile stall where food and drink, esp soup, is served to destitute people

sour 1 made acid or bad, as in the case of milk or alcohol, by the action of microorganisms 2 (esp of the weather or climate) harsh and unpleasant 3 (of oil, gas, or petrol) containing a relatively large amount of sulphur compounds 4 Chiefly US any of several iced drinks usually made with spirits, lemon juice, and ice

source 1 a a spring that forms the starting point of a stream; headspring b the area where the headwaters of a river rise 2 anything, such as a story or work of art, that provides a model or inspiration for a later work 3 Electronics the electrode region in a field-effect transistor from which majority carriers flow into the inter-electrode conductivity channel

source code Computing the original form of a computer program before it is converted into a machine-readable code

Sousa John Philip 1854–1932, US bandmaster and composer of military marches, such as The Stars and Stripes Forever (1897) and The Liberty Bell (1893)

souse Falconry of hawks or falcons a sudden downward swoop

Sousse, Susa, or **Susah** a port in E Tunisia, on the Mediterranean: founded by the Phoenicians in the 9th century BC. Pop: 191 000 (2005 est)

soutane RC Church a priest's cassock

south 1 one of the four cardinal points of the compass,

at 180° from north and 90° clockwise from east and anticlockwise from west **2** the direction along a meridian towards the South Pole **3** **the south** any area lying in or towards the south **4** *Cards* the player or position at the table corresponding to south on the compass **5** (esp of the wind) from the south

South the **1** the southern part of England, generally regarded as lying to the south of an imaginary line between the Wash and the Severn **2** in the US **a** the area approximately south of Pennsylvania and the Ohio River, esp those states south of the Mason-Dixon line that formed the Confederacy during the Civil War **b** the Confederacy itself **3** the countries of the world that are not economically and technically advanced

South Africa **Republic of** a republic occupying the southernmost part of the African continent: the Dutch Cape Colony (1652) was acquired by Britain in 1806 and British victory in the Boer War resulted in the formation of the Union of South Africa in 1910, which became a republic in 1961; implementation of the apartheid system began in 1948 and was abolished, following an intense civil rights campaign, in 1993, with multiracial elections held in 1994; a member of the Commonwealth, it withdrew in 1961 but was re-admitted in 1994. Mainly plateau with mountains in the south and east. Mineral production includes gold, diamonds, coal, and copper. Official languages: Afrikaans; English; Ndebele; Pedi; South Sotho; Swazi; Tsonga; Tswana; Venda; Xhosa; Zulu. Religion: Christian majority. Currency: rand. Capitals: Cape Town (legislative), Pretoria (administrative), Bloemfontein (judicial). Pop: 45 214 000 (2004 est). Area: 1 221 044 sq km (471 445 sq miles)

South America the fourth largest of the continents, bordering on the Caribbean in the north, the Pacific in the west, and the Atlantic in the east and joined to Central America by the Isthmus of Panama. It is dominated by the Andes Mountains, which extend over 7250 km (4500 miles) and include many volcanoes; ranges from dense tropical jungle, desert, and temperate plains to the cold wet windswept region of Tierra del Fuego. Pop. (Latin America and the Caribbean): Pop: 558 281 000 (2005 est). Area: 17 816 600 sq km (6 879 000 sq miles)

Southampton[1] 3rd Earl of, title of *Henry Wriothesley*. 1573–1624, English courtier and patron of Shakespeare, who dedicated *Venus and Adonis* (1593) and *The Rape of Lucrece* (1594) to him: sentenced to death (1601) for his part in the Essex rebellion but reprieved

Southampton[2] **1** a port in S England, in Southampton unitary authority, Hampshire on **Southampton Water** (an inlet of the English Channel): chief English passenger port; university (1952); shipyards and oil refinery. Pop: 234 224 (2001) **2** a unitary authority in S England, in Hampshire. Pop: 221 100 (2003 est). Area: 49 sq km (19 sq miles)

Southampton Island an island in N Canada, in Nunavut at the entrance to Hudson Bay: inhabited chiefly by Inuit. Area: 49 470 sq km (19 100 sq miles)

South Arabia **Federation of** the former name (1963–67) of **South Yemen** (excluding Aden): see **Yemen**

South Australia a state of S central Australia, on the Great Australian Bight: generally arid, with the Great Victoria Desert in the west central part, the Lake Eyre basin in the northeast, and the Flinders Ranges, Murray River basin, and salt lakes in the southeast. Capital: Adelaide. Pop: 1 531 375 (2003 est). Area: 984 395 sq km 380 070 sq miles)

South Ayrshire a council area of SW Scotland, on the Firth of Clyde: comprises the S part of the historical county of Ayrshire; formerly part of Strathclyde Region (1975–96): chiefly agricultural, with fishing and tourism. Administrative centre: Ayr. Pop: 111 580 (2003 est). Area: 1202 sq km (464 sq miles)

South Bend a city in the US, in N Indiana: university (1842). Pop: 105 540 (2003 est)

South Carolina a state of the southeastern US, on the Atlantic: the first state to secede from the Union in 1860: consists largely of low-lying coastal plains, rising in the northwest to the Blue Ridge Mountains; the largest US textile producer. Capital: Columbia. Pop: 4 147 152 (2003 est). Area: 78 282 sq km (30 225 sq miles)

South China Sea part of the Pacific surrounded by SE China, Vietnam, the Malay Peninsula, Borneo, and the Philippines

Southcott Joanna 1750–1814, British religious fanatic, who claimed that she would give birth to the second Messiah

South Dakota a state of the western US: lies mostly in the Great Plains; the chief US producer of gold and beryl. Capital: Pierre. Pop: 764 309 (2003 est). Area: 196 723 sq km (75 955 sq miles)

southeast **1** the point of the compass or the direction midway between south and east, 135° clockwise from north **2** (esp of the wind) from the southeast

Southeast the southeastern part of Britain, esp the London area

Southeast Asia a region including Brunei, Cambodia, Indonesia, Laos, Malaysia, Myanmar, the Philippines, Thailand, and Vietnam

southeaster a strong wind or storm from the southeast

Southend-on-Sea **1** a town in SE England, in SE Essex on the Thames estuary: one of England's largest resorts, extending for about 11 km (7 miles) along the coast. Pop: 160 257 (2001). **2** a unitary authority in SE England, in Essex. Pop: 160 300 (2003 est). Area: 42 sq km (16 sq miles)

southerly **1** towards or in the direction of the south **2** from the south **3** a wind from the south

southern *Astronomy* south of the celestial equator

Southern of, relating to, or characteristic of the south of a particular region or country

Southerner a native or inhabitant of the south of any specified region, esp the South of England or the Southern states of the US

southern hemisphere **1** that half of the earth lying south of the equator **2** *Astronomy* that half of the celestial sphere lying south of the celestial equator

Southey Robert 1774–1843, English poet, a friend of Wordsworth and Coleridge, attacked by Byron; poet laureate (1813–43)

South Georgia an island in the S Atlantic, about 1300 km (800 miles) southeast of the Falkland Islands, part of the UK Overseas Territory of **South Georgia and the**

South Sandwich Islands; no permanent population. Area: 3755 sq km (1450 sq miles)

South Glamorgan a former county of S Wales, formed in 1974 from parts of Glamorgan and Monmouthshire plus the county borough of Cardiff: replaced in 1996 by the county boroughs of Cardiff and Vale of Glamorgan

South Gloucestershire a unitary authority of SW England, in Gloucestershire: formerly (1975–96) part of the county of Avon. Pop: 246 800 (2003 est). Area: 510 sq km (197 sq miles)

South Holland a province of the SW Netherlands, on the North Sea: lying mostly below sea level, it has a coastal strip of dunes and is drained chiefly by distributaries of the Rhine, with large areas of reclaimed land; the most densely populated province in the country, intensively cultivated and industrialized. Capital: The Hague. Pop: 3 440 000 (2003 est). Area: 3196 sq km (1234 sq miles)

South Island the the largest island of New Zealand, separated from the North Island by the Cook Strait. Pop: 973 000 (2004 est). Area: 153 947 sq km (59 439 sq miles)

South Korea a republic in NE Asia: established as a republic in 1948; invaded by North Korea and Chinese Communists in 1950 but division remained unchanged at the end of the war (1953); includes over 3000 islands; rapid industrialization. Language: Korean. Religions: Buddhist, Confucianist, Shamanist, and Chondokyo. Currency: won. Capital: Seoul. Pop: 47 950 000 (2004 est). Area: 98 477 sq km (38 022 sq miles)

South Lanarkshire a council area of S Scotland, comprising the S part of the historical county of Lanarkshire: included within Strathclyde Region from 1975 to 1996: has uplands in the S and part of the Glasgow conurbation in the N: mainly agricultural. Administrative centre: Hamilton. Pop: 303 010 (2003 est). Area: 1771 sq km (684 sq miles)

South Ossetia a region in Georgia on the S slopes of the Caucasus Mountains; in 1990 it voted to join Russia, leading to armed conflict with Georgian forces; it became an autonomous region in 1997. Capital: Tskhinvali. Pop: 99 800 (1990). Area: 3900 sq km (1500 sq miles)

southpaw *Informal* a boxer who leads with his right hand and off his right foot as opposed to the orthodox style of leading with the left

South Pole 1 the southernmost point on the earth's axis, at the latitude of 90°S **2** *Astronomy* the point of intersection, in the constellation Octans, of the earth's extended axis and the southern half of the celestial sphere **3** the south-seeking pole of a freely suspended magnet

Southport a town and resort in NW England, in Sefton unitary authority, Merseyside on the Irish Sea. Pop: 91 404 (2001)

South Saskatchewan a river in S central Canada, rising in S Alberta and flowing east and northeast to join the North Saskatchewan River, forming the Saskatchewan River. Length: 1392 km (865 miles)

South Shields a port in NE England, in South Tyneside unitary authority, Tyne and Wear on the Tyne estuary opposite North Shields. Pop: 82 854 (2001)

South Tyneside a unitary authority of NE England, in

Tyne and Wear. Pop: 151 700 (2003 est). Area: 64 sq km (25 sq miles)

South Tyrol *or* **Tirol** a former part of the Austrian state of Tyrol: ceded to Italy in 1919, becoming the Bolzano and Trento provinces of the Trentino-Alto Adige Autonomous Region. Area: 14 037 sq km (5420 sq miles)

South Vietnam a former republic (1955–76) occupying the S of present-day Vietnam on the South China Sea and the Gulf of Siam

Southwark a borough of S central Greater London, on the River Thames: site of the Globe Theatre, now reconstructed; the former docks and warehouses have been redeveloped. Pop: 253 800 (2003 est). Area: 29 sq km (11 sq miles)

Southwell Saint Robert ?1561–95, English poet and Roman Catholic martyr, who was imprisoned, tortured, and executed for his Jesuit activities. His best known poem is 'The Burning Babe'

southwest 1 the point of the compass or the direction midway between west and south, 225° clockwise from north **2** (esp of the wind) from the southwest

Southwest the southwestern part of Britain, esp Cornwall, Devon, and Somerset

southwester a strong wind or storm from the southwest

South Yemen a former republic in SW Arabia, on the Gulf of Aden; now a part of Yemen: became a republic in 1967; merged with North Yemen in 1990

South Yorkshire a metropolitan county of N England, administered since 1986 by the unitary authorities of Barnsley, Doncaster, Sheffield, and Rotherham. Area: 1560 sq km (602 sq miles)

Soutine Chaim 1893–1943, French expressionist painter, born in Russia; noted for his portraits and still lifes, esp of animal carcasses

sovereign 1 a person exercising supreme authority, esp a monarch **2** a former British gold coin worth one pound sterling

sovereignty 1 supreme and unrestricted power, as of a state **2** the position, dominion, or authority of a sovereign **3** an independent state

Sovetsk a town in W Russia, in the Kaliningrad Region on the Neman River: scene of the signing of the treaty (1807) between Napoleon I and Tsar Alexander I; passed from East Prussia to the Soviet Union in 1945

soviet 1 (in the former Soviet Union) an elected government council at the local, regional, and national levels, which culminated in the Supreme Soviet **2** (in prerevolutionary Russia) a local revolutionary council

Soviet Central Asia the region of the former Soviet Union now occupied by Kazakhstan, Kyrgyzstan, Tajikistan, Turkmenistan, and Uzbekistan

Soviet Russia (formerly) another name for the **Russian Soviet Federative Socialist Republic** or the **Soviet Union**

Soviet Union a former federal republic in E Europe and central and N Asia: the revolution of 1917 achieved the overthrow of the Russian monarchy and the Soviet Union (the USSR) was established in 1922 as a Communist state. It was the largest country in the world, occupying a seventh of the total land surface. The collapse of Communist rule in 1991 was followed by declarations of independence by the constituent republics and the consequent break-up of the Soviet Union.

Soviet Zone that part of Germany occupied by Soviet forces in 1945–49: transformed into the German Democratic Republic in 1949–50

sow 1 a female adult pig 2 the female of certain other animals, such as the mink 3 *Metallurgy* **a** the channels for leading molten metal to the moulds in casting pig iron **b** iron that has solidified in these channels

Soweto a contiguous group of Black African townships southwest of Johannesburg, South Africa: the largest purely Black African urban settlement in southern Africa: scene of riots (1976) following protests against the use of Afrikaans in schools for Black African children. Area: 62 sq km (24 sq miles). Pop: 858 649 (2001)

soya bean *or US and Canadian* **soybean** 1 an Asian bean plant, *Glycine max* (or *G. soja*), cultivated for its nutritious seeds, for forage, and to improve the soil 2 the seed of this plant, used as food, forage, and as the source of an oil

Soyinka Wole born 1934, Nigerian dramatist, novelist, poet, and literary critic. His works include the plays *The Strong Breed* (1963), *The Road* (1965), and *Kongi's Harvest* (1966), the novel *The Interpreters* (1965), and the political essays *The Burden of Memory, the Muse of Forgiveness* (1999); forced into exile by the military regime (1993–98). Nobel prize for literature 1986

spa a mineral spring or a place or resort where such a spring is found

Spa a town in E Belgium, in Liège province: a resort with medicinal mineral springs (discovered in the 14th century). Pop: 10 491 (2004 est)

Spaak Paul Henri 1899–1972, Belgian statesman, first socialist premier of Belgium (1937–38); a leading advocate of European unity, he was president of the consultative assembly of the Council of Europe (1949–51) and secretary-general of NATO (1957–61)

space 1 **a** the region beyond the earth's atmosphere containing the other planets of the solar system, stars, galaxies, etc.; universe **b** *(as modifier): a space probe* 2 **a** the region beyond the earth's atmosphere occurring between the celestial bodies of the universe. The density is normally negligible although cosmic rays, meteorites, gas clouds, etc, can occur. It can be divided into **cislunar space** (between the earth and moon), **interplanetary space**, **interstellar space**, and **intergalactic space b** *(as modifier): a space station* 3 *Music* any of the gaps between the lines that make up the staff 4 *Maths* a collection of unspecified points having properties that obey a specified set of axioms

Space Invaders *Trademark* a video or computer game, the object of which is to destroy attacking alien spacecraft

space-time *or* **space-time continuum** *Physics* the four-dimensional continuum having three spatial coordinates and one time coordinate that together completely specify the location of a particle or an event

Spacey Kevin, original name *Kevin Spacey Fowler*. born 1959, US actor; films include *Glengarry Glen Ross* (1992), *The Usual Suspects* (1995), *American Beauty* (1999), which earned him an Academy Award, and *The Shipping News* (2001)

spade¹ 1 a tool for digging, typically consisting of a flat rectangular steel blade attached to a long wooden handle 2 **a** an object or part resembling a spade in shape **b** *(as modifier): a spade beard* 3 a type of oar blade that is comparatively broad and short 4 a cutting tool for stripping the blubber from a whale or skin from a carcass

spade² **a** the black symbol on a playing card resembling a heart-shaped leaf with a stem **b** a card with one or more of these symbols or *(when pl.)* the suit of cards so marked, usually the highest ranking of the four

spadix a racemose inflorescence having many small sessile flowers borne on a fleshy stem, the whole usually being surrounded by a spathe: typical of aroid plants

spaghetti junction an interchange, usually between motorways, in which there are a large number of underpasses and overpasses and intersecting roads used by a large volume of high-speed traffic

spaghetti western a cowboy film about the American West made, esp by an Italian director, in Europe
▷www.everything2.com/index.pl?node=Spaghetti%20 western
▷www.plume-noire.com/movies/cult/spaghettiwesterns.html

Spain a kingdom of SW Europe, occupying the Iberian peninsula between the Mediterranean and the Atlantic: a leading European power in the 16th century, with many overseas possessions, esp in the New World; became a republic in 1931; under the fascist dictatorship of Franco following the Civil War (1936–39) until his death in 1975; a member of the European Union. It consists chiefly of a central plateau (the Meseta), with the Pyrenees and the Cantabrian Mountains in the north and the Sierra Nevada in the south. Official language: Castilian Spanish, with Catalan, Galician, and Basque official regional languages. Religion: Roman Catholic majority. Currency: euro. Capital: Madrid. Pop: 41 128 000 (2004 est). Area: 504 748 sq km (194 883 sq miles)

Spalding a town in E England, in S Lincolnshire: noted for its bulbfields. Pop: 22 081 (2001)

spam *Computing, slang* unsolicited electronic mail or text messages

span 1 *Psychol* the amount of material that can be processed in a single mental act 2 short for **wingspan** 3 a unit of length based on the width of an expanded hand, usually taken as nine inches

Spaniard a native or inhabitant of Spain

spaniel 1 any of several breeds of gundog with long drooping ears, a silky coat, and formerly a docked tail 2 either of two toy breeds of spaniel: the **King Charles spaniel** and the **cavalier King Charles spaniel**

Spanish the official language of Spain, Mexico, and most countries of South and Central America except Brazil: also spoken in Africa, the Far East, and elsewhere. It is the native language of approximately 200 million people throughout the world. Spanish is an Indo-European language belonging to the Romance group

Spanish America the parts of America colonized by Spaniards from the 16th century onwards and now chiefly Spanish-speaking: includes all of South America (except Brazil, Guyana, French Guiana, and

Surinam), Central America (except Belize), Mexico, Cuba, Puerto Rico, the Dominican Republic, and a number of small Caribbean islands

Spanish-American 1 of or relating to any of the Spanish-speaking countries or peoples of the Americas 2 a native or inhabitant of Spanish America 3 a Spanish-speaking person in the US

Spanish fly a European blister beetle, *Lytta vesicatoria* (family *Meloidae*), the dried bodies of which yield the pharmaceutical product cantharides

Spanish Main 1 the mainland of Spanish America, esp the N coast of South America from the Isthmus of Panama to the mouth of the Orinoco River, Venezuela 2 the Caribbean Sea, the S part of which in colonial times was the route of Spanish treasure galleons and the haunt of pirates

Spanish Morocco a former Spanish colony on the N coast of Morocco: part of the kingdom of Morocco since 1956

Spanish West Africa a former overseas territory of Spain in NW Africa: divided in 1958 into the overseas provinces of Ifni and Spanish Sahara

spanner a steel hand tool with a handle carrying jaws or a hole of particular shape designed to grip a nut or bolt head

spanspek *South African* a sweet rough-skinned melon; a cantaloupe: family *Cucurbitaceae*

spar¹ 1 a any piece of nautical gear resembling a pole and used as a mast, boom, gaff, etc. b (*as modifier*): *a spar buoy* 2 a principal supporting structural member of an aerofoil that runs from tip to tip or root to tip

spar² any of various minerals, such as feldspar or calcite, that are light-coloured, microcrystalline, transparent to translucent, and easily cleavable

spare 1 a spare tyre 2 *Tenpin bowling* a the act of knocking down all the pins with the two bowls of a single frame b the score thus made

spare tyre 1 an additional tyre, usually mounted on a wheel, carried by a motor vehicle in case of puncture 2 *Brit, slang, jocular* a deposit of fat just above the waist

spark 1 a a momentary flash of light accompanied by a sharp crackling noise, produced by a sudden electrical discharge through the air or some other insulating medium between two points b the electrical discharge itself c (*as modifier*): *a spark gap* 2 a small piece of diamond, as used in the cutting of glass

Spark Dame **Muriel (Sarah).** born 1918, British novelist and writer; her novels include *Memento Mori* (1959), *The Prime of Miss Jean Brodie* (1961), *The Takeover* (1976), *A Far Cry from Kensington* (1988), *Symposium* (1990), and *The Finishing School* (2004)

sparkler a type of firework that throws out showers of sparks

sparring partner a person who practises with a boxer during training

sparrow 1 any weaverbird of the genus *Passer* and related genera, esp the house sparrow, having a brown or grey plumage and feeding on seeds or insects 2 *US and Canadian* any of various North American finches, such as the chipping sparrow (*Spizella passerina*), that have a dullish streaked plumage

sparrowhawk any of several small hawks, esp *Accipiter*

nisus, of Eurasia and N Africa that prey on smaller birds

Sparta an ancient Greek city in the S Peloponnese, famous for the discipline and military prowess of its citizens and for their austere way of life

Spartacus died 71 BC, Thracian slave, who led an ultimately unsuccessful revolt of gladiators against Rome (73–71 BC)

Spartan 1 a citizen of Sparta 2 a Canadian variety of eating apple

spasm an involuntary muscular contraction, esp one resulting in cramp or convulsion

spasmodic *or rarely* **spasmodical** of or characterized by spasms

Spassky Boris born 1937, Russian chess player; world champion (1969–72)

spastic 1 a person who is affected by spasms or convulsions, esp one who has cerebral palsy 2 affected by or resembling spasms

spat 1 a larval oyster or similar bivalve mollusc, esp when it settles to the sea bottom and starts to develop a shell 2 such oysters or other molluscs collectively

spate 1 *Chiefly Brit* a sudden flood 2 *Chiefly Brit* a sudden heavy downpour

spathe a large bract, often coloured, that surrounds the inflorescence of aroid plants and palms

spawn 1 the mass of eggs deposited by fish, amphibians, or molluscs 2 *Botany* the nontechnical name for mycelium

speakeasy *US* a place where alcoholic drink was sold illicitly during Prohibition

Speaker the presiding officer in any of numerous legislative bodies, including the House of Commons in Britain and Canada and the House of Representatives in the US, Australia, and New Zealand

spear a shoot, slender stalk or blade, as of grass, asparagus, or broccoli

spearmint a purple-flowered mint plant, *Mentha spicata,* of S and central Europe, cultivated for its leaves, which yield an oil used for flavouring

Spears Britney born 1981, US pop singer; records include the single "Baby One More Time" (1998) and the album *Britney* (2001)

special 1 denoting or relating to the education of physically or mentally handicapped children 2 *Austral, history, slang* a convict given special treatment on account of his education, social class, etc. 3 short for **special constable** 4 *Austral, NZ, US and Canadian, informal* an item in a store that is advertised at a reduced price; a loss leader

Special Branch (in Britain) the department of the police force that is concerned with political security

special constable a person recruited for temporary or occasional police duties, esp in time of emergency

specialist *Ecology* an organism that has special nutritional requirements and lives in a restricted habitat that provides these

special licence *Brit* a licence permitting a marriage to take place by dispensing with the usual legal conditions

specialty *Law* a formal contract or obligation expressed in a deed

specie 1 coin money, as distinguished from bullion or paper money 2 **in specie a** (of money) in coin **b** *Law* in the actual form specified

species 1 *Biology* **a** any of the taxonomic groups into which a genus is divided, the members of which are capable of interbreeding: often containing subspecies, varieties, or races. A species is designated in italics by the genus name followed by the specific name, for example *Felis domesticus* (the domestic cat) **b** the animals of such a group **c** any group of related animals or plants not necessarily of this taxonomic rank 2 denoting a plant that is a natural member of a species rather than a hybrid or cultivar 3 *Logic* a group of objects or individuals, all sharing at least one common attribute, that forms a subdivision of a genus 4 *Chiefly RC Church* the outward form of the bread and wine in the Eucharist

specific 1 of or relating to a biological species 2 (of a disease) caused by a particular pathogenic agent 3 *Physics* **a** characteristic of a property of a particular substance, esp in relation to the same property of a standard reference substance **b** characteristic of a property of a particular substance per unit mass, length, area, volume, etc. **c** (of an extensive physical quantity) divided by mass 4 *International trade* denoting a tariff levied at a fixed sum per unit of weight, quantity, volume, etc, irrespective of value 5 *Med* any drug used to treat a particular disease

specification (in patent law) a written statement accompanying an application for a patent that describes the nature of an invention

specific gravity the ratio of the density of a substance to that of water

specific heat capacity the heat required to raise unit mass of a substance by unit temperature interval under specified conditions, such as constant pressure: usually measured in joules per kelvin per kilogram.

specimen 1 *Med* **a** a sample of tissue, blood, urine, etc, taken for diagnostic examination or evaluation 2 the whole or a part of an organism, plant, rock, etc, collected and preserved as an example of its class, species, etc.

spectacular a lavishly produced performance

Spector Phil born 1940, US record producer and songwriter, noted for the densely orchestrated "Wall of Sound" in his work with groups such as the Ronettes and the Crystals; arrested on a murder charge in 2003

spectre *or US* **specter** a ghost; phantom; apparition

spectrometer any instrument for producing a spectrum, esp one in which wavelength, energy, intensity, etc, can be measured

spectroscope any of a number of instruments for dispersing electromagnetic radiation and thus forming or recording a spectrum

spectrum 1 the distribution of colours produced when white light is dispersed by a prism or diffraction grating. There is a continuous change in wavelength from red, the longest wavelength, to violet, the shortest. Seven colours are usually distinguished: violet, indigo, blue, green, yellow, orange, and red 2 the whole range of electromagnetic radiation with respect to its wavelength or frequency 3 any particular distribution of electromagnetic radiation often showing lines or bands characteristic of the substance emitting the radiation or absorbing it 4 any similar distribution or record of the energies, velocities, masses, etc, of atoms, ions, electrons, etc.

speech day *Brit* (in schools) an annual day on which prizes are presented, speeches are made by guest speakers, etc.

speed 1 *Physics* **a** a scalar measure of the rate of movement of a body expressed either as the distance travelled divided by the time taken (**average speed**) or the rate of change of position with respect to time at a particular point (**instantaneous speed**). It is measured in metres per second, miles per hour, etc. **b** (not in technical usage) another word for **velocity** 2 a rate of rotation, usually expressed in revolutions per unit time 3 a gear ratio in a motor vehicle, bicycle, etc. 4 *Photog* a numerical expression of the sensitivity to light of a particular type of film, paper, or plate 5 *Photog* a measure of the ability of a lens to pass light from an object to the image position, determined by the aperture and also the transmitting power of the lens. It increases as the f-number is decreased and vice versa 6 a slang word for **amphetamine**

speedboat a high-speed motorboat having either an inboard or outboard motor

speed camera a fixed camera that photographs vehicles breaking the speed limit on a certain stretch of road

speed limit the maximum permitted speed at which a vehicle may travel on certain roads

speedo an informal name for **speedometer** or (Austral.) **odometer**

speedometer a device fitted to a vehicle to measure and display the speed of travel

speedway 1 **a** the sport of racing on light powerful motorcycles round cinder tracks **b** (*as modifier*): *a speedway track* 2 the track or stadium where such races are held 3 *US and Canadian* **a** a racetrack for cars **b** a road on which fast driving is allowed
▷www.speedwaygp.com
▷www.british-speedway.co.uk

speedwell any of various temperate scrophulariaceous plants of the genus *Veronica*, such as *V. officinalis* (**heath speedwell**) and *V. chamaedrys* (**germander speedwell**), having small blue or pinkish white flowers

speleology *or* **spelaeology** 1 the scientific study of caves, esp in respect of their geological formation, flora and fauna, etc. 2 the sport or pastime of exploring caves

spell a verbal formula considered as having magical force

spellchecker *Computing* a program that highlights any word in a word-processed document that is not recognized as being correctly spelt

spelt a species of wheat, *Triticum spelta*, that was formerly much cultivated and was used to develop present-day cultivated wheats

Spence Sir Basil (**Unwin**). 1907–76, Scottish architect, born in India; designed Coventry Cathedral (1951)

Spencer 1 Herbert 1820–1903, English philosopher, who applied evolutionary theory to the study of society, favouring laissez-faire doctrines 2 Sir Stanley 1891–1959, English painter, noted esp for his paintings of Christ in a contemporary English setting

Spencer Gulf an inlet of the Indian Ocean in S Australia, between the Eyre and Yorke Peninsulas. Length: about 320 km (200 miles). Greatest width: about 145 km (90 miles)

Spender Sir **Stephen** 1909–95, English poet and critic, who played an important part in the left-wing literary movement of the 1930s. His works include *Journals 1939–83* (1985) and *Collected Poems* (1985)

Spengler Oswald 1880–1936, German philosopher of history, noted for *The Decline of the West* (1918–22), which argues that civilizations go through natural cycles of growth and decay

Spenser Edmund ?1552–99, English poet celebrated for *The Faerie Queene* (1590; 1596), an allegorical romance. His other verse includes the collection of eclogues *The Shephearde's Calendar* (1579) and the marriage poem *Epithalamion* (1594)

spent (of a fish) exhausted by spawning

sperm 1 another name for **semen 2** a male reproductive cell; male gamete

spermaceti a white waxy substance obtained from oil from the head of the sperm whale: used in cosmetics, candles, ointments, etc.

spermatozoon any of the male reproductive cells released in the semen during ejaculation, consisting of a flattened egg-shaped head, a long neck, and a whip-like tail by which it moves to fertilize the female ovum

spermicide any drug or other agent that kills spermatozoa

sperm oil an oil obtained from the head of the sperm whale, used as a lubricant

sperm whale a large toothed whale, *Physeter catodon*, having a square-shaped head and hunted for sperm oil, spermaceti, and ambergris: family *Physeteridae*

Spey a river in E Scotland, flowing generally northeast through the Grampian Mountains to the Moray Firth: salmon fishing; parts of the surrounding area (Speyside) are famous for whisky distilleries. Length: 172 km (107 miles)

Speyer a port in SW Germany, in Rhineland-Palatinate on the Rhine: the scene of 50 imperial diets. Pop: 50 247 (2003 est)

sphagnum any moss of the genus *Sphagnum*, of temperate bogs, having leaves capable of holding much water: layers of these mosses decay to form peat

sphere 1 *Maths* **a** a three-dimensional closed surface such that every point on the surface is equidistant from a given point, the centre **b** the solid figure bounded by this surface or the space enclosed by it. Equation: $(x-a)^2 + (y-b)^2 + (z-c)^2 = r^2$, where r is the radius and (a, b, c) are the coordinates of the centre; surface area: $4\pi r^2$; volume: $4\pi r^3/3$ **2** the night sky considered as a vaulted roof; firmament **3** any heavenly object such as a planet, natural satellite, or star **4** (in the Ptolemaic or Copernican systems of astronomy) one of a series of revolving hollow globes, arranged concentrically, on whose transparent surfaces the sun (or in the Copernican system the earth), the moon, the planets, and fixed stars were thought to be set, revolving around the earth (or in the Copernican system the sun)

spherical *or* **spheric 1** of or relating to a sphere **2** *Geometry* formed on the surface of or inside a sphere **3** a of or relating to heavenly bodies **b** of or relating to the spheres of the Ptolemaic or the Copernican system

sphincter *Anatomy* a ring of muscle surrounding the opening of a hollow organ or body and contracting to close it

sphinx any of a number of huge stone statues built by the ancient Egyptians, having the body of a lion and the head of a man

Sphinx the 1 *Greek myth* a monster with a woman's head and a lion's body. She lay outside Thebes, asking travellers a riddle and killing them when they failed to answer it. Oedipus answered the riddle and the Sphinx then killed herself **2** the huge statue of a sphinx near the pyramids at El Gîza in Egypt, of which the head is a carved portrait of the fourth-dynasty Pharaoh, Chephren

spider 1 any predatory silk-producing arachnid of the order *Araneae*, having four pairs of legs and a rounded unsegmented body consisting of abdomen and cephalothorax **2** any of various similar or related arachnids **3** a hub fitted with radiating spokes or arms that serve to transmit power or support a load **4** any implement or tool having the shape of a spider **5** *Nautical* a metal frame fitted at the base of a mast to which halyards are tied when not in use **6** *Brit* a cluster of elastic straps fastened at a central point and used to hold a load on a car rack, motorcycle, etc. **7** *Billiards, Snooker* a rest having long legs, used to raise the cue above the level of the height of the ball **8** *Angling* an artificial fly tied with a hackle and no wings, perhaps originally thought to imitate a spider

spider monkey 1 any of several arboreal New World monkeys of the genus *Ateles*, of Central and South America, having very long legs, a long prehensile tail, and a small head **2** **woolly spider monkey** a rare related monkey, *Brachyteles arachnoides*, of SE Brazil

Spielberg Steven born 1947, US film director, noted esp for the commercial success of such films as *Jaws* (1975), *Close Encounters of the Third Kind* (1977), *Raiders of the Lost Ark* (1981) and its sequels, *E.T.* (1982), and *Jurassic Park* (1993). Other films include *The Color Purple* (1986), *Schindler's List* (1993), *Saving Private Ryan* (1998), and *The Terminal* (2004)

spigot 1 a stopper for the vent hole of a cask **2** a tap, usually of wood, fitted to a cask **3** a US name for **tap 4** a short cylindrical projection on one component designed to fit into a hole on another, esp the male part of a joint (**spigot and socket joint**) between two pipes

spike¹ 1 a long metal nail **2** *Physics* **a** a transient variation in voltage or current in an electric circuit **b** a graphical recording of this, such as one of the peaks on an electroencephalogram **3** the straight unbranched antler of a young deer

spike² ** *Botany* **1 an inflorescence consisting of a raceme of sessile flowers, as in the gladiolus and sedges **2** an ear of wheat, barley, or any other grass that has sessile spikelets

spikenard 1 an aromatic Indian valerianaceous plant, *Nardostachys jatamans*, having rose-purple flowers **2** any of various similar or related plants **3** a North American araliaceous plant, *Aralia racemosa*, having small green flowers and an aromatic root

spill¹ *Austral* the declaring of several political jobs vacant when one higher up becomes so

spill² a small peg or rod made of metal

Spillane **Mickey**, original name *Frank Morrison Spillane*. born 1918, US detective-story writer, best known for his books featuring the detective Mike Hammer, for example *I, the Jury* (1947) and *The Twisted Thing* (1966)

spillikin, spilikin, *or* **spellican** a thin strip of wood, cardboard, or plastic, esp one used in spillikins

spillikins *Brit* a game in which players try to pick each spillikin from a heap without moving any of the others

spin 1 *Physics* **a** the intrinsic angular momentum of an elementary particle or atomic nucleus, as distinguished from any angular momentum resulting from its motion **b** a quantum number determining values of this angular momentum in units of the Dirac constant, having integral or half-integral values. 2 a condition of loss of control of an aircraft or an intentional flight manoeuvre in which the aircraft performs a continuous spiral descent because the angle of maximum lift is less than the angle of incidence 3 (in skating) any of various movements involving spinning rapidly on the spot 4 *Informal* a short or fast drive, ride, etc, esp in a car, for pleasure 5 *Commerce, informal* a sudden downward trend in prices, values, etc.

spina bifida a congenital condition in which the meninges of the spinal cord protrude through a gap in the backbone, sometimes causing enlargement of the skull (due to accumulation of cerebrospinal fluid) and paralysis

spinach a chenopodiaceous annual plant, *Spinacia oleracea*, cultivated for its dark green edible leaves

spinal column a series of contiguous or interconnecting bony or cartilaginous segments that surround and protect the spinal cord

spinal cord the thick cord of nerve tissue within the spinal canal, which in man gives rise to 31 pairs of spinal nerves, and together with the brain forms the central nervous system

▷www.spinalcord.uab.edu

▷www.spinalcord.org

spin bowler *Cricket* a bowler who specializes in bowling balls with a spinning motion

spindle 1 a rod or stick that has a notch in the top, used to draw out natural fibres for spinning into thread, and a long narrow body around which the thread is wound when spun 2 one of the thin rods or pins bearing bobbins upon which spun thread is wound in a spinning wheel or machine 3 any of various parts in the form of a rod, esp a rotating rod that acts as an axle, mandrel, or arbor 4 a measure of length of yarn equal to 18 hanks (15 120 yards) for cotton or 14 400 yards for linen 5 *Biology* a spindle-shaped structure formed by microtubules during mitosis or meiosis which draws the duplicated chromosomes apart as the cell divides 6 a less common name for a **hydrometer** 7 a tall pole with a marker at the top, fixed to an underwater obstruction as an aid to navigation 8 a device consisting of a sharp upright spike on a pedestal on which bills, order forms, etc, are impaled

spin doctor *Informal* a person who provides a favourable slant to an item of news, potentially unpopular policy, etc, esp on behalf of a political personality or party

spindrift 1 spray blown up from the surface of the sea 2 powdery snow blown off a mountain

spin-dryer a device that extracts water from clothes, linen, etc, by spinning them in a perforated drum

spine 1 the spinal column 2 the sharply pointed tip or outgrowth of a leaf, stem, etc. 3 *Zoology* a hard pointed process or structure, such as the ray of a fin, the quill of a porcupine, or the ridge on a bone 4 a ridge, esp of a hill

spine-chiller a book, film, etc, that arouses terror

spineless 1 lacking a backbone; invertebrate 2 having no spiny processes

spinet a small type of harpsichord having one manual

spinifex 1 *Austral* any of various coarse spiny-leaved inland grasses of the genus *Triodia* 2 any grass of the SE Asian genus *Spinifex*, having pointed leaves and spiny seed heads: often planted to bind loose sand

spinnaker a large light triangular racing sail set from the foremast of a yacht when running or on a broad reach

spinner 1 *Informal* a spin doctor 2 *Cricket* **a** a ball that is bowled with a spinning motion **b** a bowler who specializes in bowling such balls 3 a streamlined fairing that fits over and revolves with the hub of an aircraft propeller 4 a fishing lure with a fin or wing that revolves when drawn through the water 5 an angler's name for the mature adult form (imago) of various flies, especially the mayflies

spinneret 1 any of several organs in spiders and certain insects through which silk threads are exuded 2 a finely perforated dispenser through which a viscous liquid is extruded in the production of synthetic fibres

spinney *Chiefly Brit* a small wood or copse

spinning jenny an early type of spinning frame with several spindles, invented by James Hargreaves in 1764

spinning wheel a wheel-like machine for spinning at home, having one hand- or foot-operated spindle

Spinoza **Baruch** 1632–77, Dutch philosopher who constructed a holistic metaphysical system derived from a series of hypotheses that he judged self-evident. His chief work is *Ethics* (1677)

spinster 1 *Law* (in legal documents) a woman who has never married 2 (formerly) a woman who spins thread for her living

spiny 1 (of animals) having or covered with quills or spines 2 (of plants) covered with spines; thorny

spiracle 1 any of several paired apertures in the cuticle of an insect, by which air enters and leaves the trachea 2 a small paired rudimentary gill slit just behind the head in skates, rays, and related fishes 3 any similar respiratory aperture, such as the blowhole in whales 4 *Geology* a protrusion of sediment into a lava flow, formed by the explosive transition of water into steam

spiraea *or esp US* **spirea** any rosaceous plant of the genus *Spiraea*, having sprays of small white or pink flowers

spiral 1 *Geometry* one of several plane curves formed by a point winding about a fixed point at an ever-increasing distance from it. Polar equation of **Archimedes spiral**: $r = a\theta$; of **logarithmic spiral**: $\log r = a\theta$; of **hyperbolic spiral**: $r\theta = a$, (where a is a constant) 2 another name for **helix** 3 a flight manoeuvre in which an aircraft descends describing a helix of comparatively large radius with the angle of attack within the normal flight range **4** *Economics* a continuous upward or downward movement in economic activity or prices, caused by interaction between prices, wages, demand, and production

spire¹ 1 a tall structure that tapers upwards to a point, esp one on a tower or roof or one that forms the upper part of a steeple **2** a slender tapering shoot or stem, such as a blade of grass

spire² the apical part of a spiral shell

spirit¹ 1 the force or principle of life that animates the body of living things **2 a** an incorporeal being, esp the soul of a dead person **b** (*as modifier*): *spirit world*

spirit² 1 any distilled alcoholic liquor such as brandy, rum, whisky, or gin **2** *Chem* **a** an aqueous solution of ethanol, esp one obtained by distillation **b** the active principle or essence of a substance, extracted as a liquid, esp by distillation **3** *Pharmacol* **a** a solution of a volatile substance, esp a volatile oil, in alcohol **b** (*as modifier*): *a spirit burner* **4** *Alchemy* any of the four substances sulphur, mercury, sal ammoniac, or arsenic

spirit lamp a lamp that burns methylated or other spirits instead of oil

spirit level a device for setting horizontal surfaces, consisting of an accurate block of material in which a sealed slightly curved tube partially filled with liquid is set so that the air bubble rests between two marks on the tube when the block is horizontal

spiritual 1 of, relating to, or characteristic of sacred things, the Church, religion, etc. **2** standing in a relationship based on communication between the souls or minds of the persons involved **3** the sphere of religious, spiritual, or ecclesiastical matters, or such matters in themselves

spiritualism 1 the belief that the disembodied spirits of the dead, surviving in another world, can communicate with the living in this world, esp through mediums **2** the doctrines and practices associated with this belief **3** *Philosophy* the belief that because reality is to some extent immaterial it is therefore spiritual

spirituous 1 characterized by or containing alcohol **2** (of a drink) being a spirit

spirogyra any green freshwater multicellular alga of the genus *Spirogyra*, consisting of minute filaments containing spirally coiled chloroplasts

spit¹ 1 another name for **spittle 2** a light or brief fall of rain, snow, etc.

spit² an elongated often hooked strip of sand or shingle projecting from the shore, deposited by longshore drift, and usually above water

Spithead an extensive anchorage between the mainland of England and the Isle of Wight, off Portsmouth

spittle 1 the fluid secreted in the mouth; saliva or spit **2** the frothy substance secreted on plants by the larvae of certain froghoppers

spitz any of various breeds of dog characterized by very dense hair, a stocky build, a pointed muzzle, erect ears, and a tightly curled tail

Spitz Mark born 1950, US swimmer, who won seven gold medals at the 1972 Olympic Games

splash a small amount of soda water, water, etc, added to an alcoholic drink

splay a surface of a wall that forms an oblique angle to the main flat surfaces, esp at a doorway or window opening

spleen 1 a spongy highly vascular organ situated near the stomach in man. It forms lymphocytes, produces antibodies, aids in destroying worn-out red blood cells, and filters bacteria and foreign particles from the blood **2** the corresponding organ in other animals **3** *Archaic* another word for **melancholy**

spleenwort any of various ferns of the genus *Asplenium*, esp *A. trichomanes*, that often grows on walls, having linear or oblong sori on the undersurface of the fronds

splenetic 1 of or relating to the spleen **2** *Obsolete* full of melancholy

splice the wedge-shaped end of a cricket-bat handle or similar instrument that fits into the blade

splint 1 a rigid support for restricting movement of an injured part, esp a broken bone **2** *Vet science* inflammation of the small metatarsal or metacarpal bones along the side of the cannon bone of a horse

splinter group a number of members of an organization, political party, etc, who split from the main body and form an independent association, usually as the result of dissension

split *Tenpin bowling* a formation of the pins after the first bowl in which there is a large gap between two pins or groups of pins

Split a port and resort in W Croatia on the Adriatic: remains of the palace of Diocletian (295–305). Pop: 188 000 (2005 est)

split-level (of a house, room, etc) having the floor level of one part about half a storey above or below the floor level of an adjoining part

splits (in gymnastics, etc) the act of sinking to the floor to achieve a sitting position in which both legs are straight, pointing in opposite directions, and at right angles to the body

splitting 1 (of a headache) intolerably painful; acute **2** (of the head) assailed by an overpowering unbearable pain **3** *Psychoanal* the Freudian defence mechanism in which an object or idea (or, alternatively, the ego) is separated into two or more parts in order to remove its threatening meaning

Spock Benjamin, known as *Dr Spock*. 1903–98, US paediatrician, noted for his influential work *The Common Sense Book of Baby and Child* (1946), which challenged traditional notions of child care, advocating a more permissive approach

spoiler 1 a device fitted to an aircraft wing to increase drag and reduce lift. It is usually extended into the airflow to assist descent and banking **2** a similar device fitted to a car

Spokane a city in E Washington: commercial centre of an agricultural region. Pop: 196 624 (2003 est)

spoke 1 a radial member of a wheel, joining the hub to the rim **2** a radial projection from the rim of a wheel, as in a ship's wheel

spoliation 1 the authorized seizure or plundering of neutral vessels on the seas by a belligerent state in time of war **2** *Law* the material alteration of a document so as to render it invalid **3** *English ecclesiastical law* the taking of the fruits of a benefice by a person not entitled to them

spondee *Prosody* a metrical foot consisting of two long syllables (– –)

sponge 1 any multicellular typically marine animal of the phylum *Porifera*, usually occurring in complex sessile colonies in which the porous body is supported by a fibrous, calcareous, or siliceous skeletal framework 2 a piece of the light porous highly absorbent elastic skeleton of certain sponges, used in bathing, cleaning, etc. 3 any of a number of light porous elastic materials resembling a sponge 4 porous metal produced by electrolysis or by reducing a metal compound without fusion or sintering and capable of absorbing large quantities of gas

sponger a person or ship employed in collecting sponges

sponsor 1 a legislator who presents and supports a bill, motion, etc. 2 a an authorized witness who makes the required promises on behalf of a person to be baptized and thereafter assumes responsibility for his Christian upbringing b a person who presents a candidate for confirmation

spontaneous (of plants) growing naturally; indigenous

spontaneous combustion the ignition of a substance or body as a result of internal oxidation processes, without the application of an external source of heat, occurring in finely powdered ores, coal, straw, etc.

spool a device around which magnetic tape, film, cotton, etc, can be automatically wound, with plates at top and bottom to prevent it from slipping off

spoon 1 an angling lure for spinning or trolling, consisting of a bright piece of metal which swivels on a trace to which are attached a hook or hooks 2 *Golf* a former name for a No. 3 wood 3 *Rowing* a type of oar blade that is curved at the edges and tip to gain a firm grip on the water

spoonbill any of several wading birds of warm regions, such as *Platalea leucorodia* (**common spoonbill**) and *Ajaia ajaja* (**roseate spoonbill**), having a long horizontally flattened bill: family *Threskiornithidae*, order *Ciconiiformes*

spoor the trail of an animal or person, esp as discernible to the human eye

spore 1 a reproductive body, produced by bacteria, fungi, various plants and some protozoans, that develops into a new individual. A **sexual spore** is formed after the fusion of gametes and an **asexual spore** is the result of asexual reproduction 2 a germ cell, seed, dormant bacterium, or similar body

sport *Biology* a an animal or plant that differs conspicuously in one or more aspects from other organisms of the same species, usually because of a mutation b an anomalous characteristic of such an organism

sports 1 relating to or similar to a sports car 2 *Brit* a meeting held at a school or college for competitions in various athletic events

sports car a production car designed for speed, high acceleration, and manoeuvrability, having a low body and usually adequate seating for only two persons

sporty 1 (of a car) having the performance or appearance of a sports car 2 *Brit, informal* a young person who typically wears sportswear, is competitive about sport , and takes an interest in his or her fitness

spot 1 a geographical area that is restricted in extent 2 a blemish of the skin, esp a pimple or one occurring through some disease 3 a position or length of time in a show assigned to a specific performer 4 short for **spotlight** 5 in billiards a the white ball that is distinguished from the plain by a mark or spot b the player using this ball 6 *Billiards, snooker* one of several small black dots on a table that mark where a ball is to be placed 7 *Commerce* a denoting or relating to goods, currencies, or securities available for immediate delivery and payment b involving immediate cash payment

spotlight a powerful light focused so as to illuminate a small area, usually mounted so that it can be directed at will

spotter 1 a person who makes a hobby of watching for and noting numbers or types of trains, buses, etc. 2 *Films* a a person who checks against irregularities and inconsistencies b a person who searches for new material, performers, etc.

sprain a sudden twisting or wrenching of the ligaments of a joint

sprat 1 a small marine food fish, *Clupea sprattus*, of the NE Atlantic Ocean and North Sea: family *Clupeidae* (herrings) 2 any of various small or young herrings

sprawl a the urban area formed by the expansion of a town or city into surrounding countryside b the process by which this has happened

spray¹ 1 fine particles of a liquid 2 a a liquid, such as perfume, paint, etc, designed to be discharged from an aerosol or atomizer b the aerosol or atomizer itself

spray² *Botany* a single slender shoot, twig, or branch that bears buds, leaves, flowers, or berries, either growing on or detached from a plant

spray gun a device that sprays a fluid in a finely divided form by atomizing the fluid in an air jet

spread 1 *Informal* the wingspan of an aircraft 2 a covering for a table or bed

spreadsheet a computer program that allows easy entry and manipulation of figures, equations, and text, used esp for financial planning and budgeting

sprig 1 a shoot, twig, or sprout of a tree, shrub, etc.; spray 2 an ornamental device resembling a spray of leaves or flowers

spring 1 a a natural outflow of ground water, as forming the source of a stream b (*as modifier*): *spring water* 2 a a device, such as a coil or strip of steel, that stores potential energy when it is compressed, stretched, or bent and releases it when the restraining force is removed b (*as modifier*): *a spring mattress* 3 a the season of the year between winter and summer, astronomically from the March equinox to the June solstice in the N hemisphere and from the September equinox to the December solstice in the S hemisphere b (*as modifier*): *spring showers* 4 one of a set of strips of rubber, steel, etc, running down the inside of the handle of a cricket bat, hockey stick, etc. 5 *Nautical* a mooring line, usually one of a pair that cross amidships 6 a flock of teal

spring balance or *esp US* **spring scale** a device in which an object to be weighed is attached to the end of a helical spring, the extension of which indicates the weight of the object on a calibrated scale

springboard 1 a flexible board, usually projecting low over the water, used for diving 2 a similar board used for gaining height or momentum in gymnastics 3 *Austral and NZ* a board inserted into the trunk of a tree at some height above the ground on which a lumberjack stands to chop down the tree

springbok *or less commonly* **springbuck** an antelope, *Antidorcas marsupialis*, of semidesert regions of southern Africa, which moves in leaps exposing a patch of white erectile hairs on the rump that are usually covered by a fold of skin

Springfield 1 a city in S Massachusetts, on the Connecticut River: the site of the US arsenal and armoury (1794–1968), which developed the Springfield and Garand rifles. Pop: 152 157 (2003 est) 2 a city in SW Missouri. Pop: 150 867 (2003 est) 3 a city in central Illinois, capital of the state: the home and burial place of Abraham Lincoln. Pop: 113 586 (2003 est)

Springs a city in E South Africa: developed around a coal mine established in 1885 and later became a major world gold-mining centre, now with uranium extraction. Pop: 80 776 (2001)

Springsteen Bruce born 1949, US rock singer, songwriter, and guitarist. His albums include *Born to Run* (1975), *Darkness on the Edge of Town* (1978), *Born in the USA* (1984), *The Ghost of Tom Joad* (1995), and *The Rising* (2002)

spring tide either of the two tides that occur at or just after new moon and full moon when the tide-generating force of the sun acts in the same direction as that of the moon, reinforcing it and causing the greatest rise and fall in tidal level. The highest spring tides (**equinoctial springs**) occur at the equinoxes

sprint 1 *Athletics* a short race run at top speed, such as the 100 metres 2 a fast finishing speed at the end of a longer race, as in running or cycling, etc.

sprit *Nautical* a light spar pivoted at the mast and crossing a fore-and-aft quadrilateral sail diagonally to the peak

sprite 1 (in folklore) a nimble elflike creature, esp one associated with water 2 an icon in a computer game which can be manoeuvred around the screen by means of a joystick, etc.

spritsail *Nautical* 1 a rectangular sail mounted on a sprit in some 19th-century small vessels 2 (in medieval rigging) a square sail mounted on a yard on the bowsprit

spritzer a drink, usually white wine, with soda water added

sprocket 1 a relatively thin wheel having teeth projecting radially from the rim, esp one that drives or is driven by a chain 2 an individual tooth on such a wheel 3 a cylindrical wheel with teeth on one or both rims for pulling film through a camera or projector

sprout a newly grown shoot or bud

spruce 1 any coniferous tree of the N temperate genus *Picea*, cultivated for timber and for ornament: family *Pinaceae*. They grow in a pyramidal shape and have needle-like leaves and light-coloured wood 2 the wood of any of these trees

spud 1 a narrow-bladed spade for cutting roots, digging up weeds, etc. 2 a tool, resembling a chisel, for removing bark from trees

spur 1 a pointed device or sharp spiked wheel fixed to

the heel of a rider's boot to enable him to urge his horse on 2 a sharp horny projection from the leg just above the claws in male birds, such as the domestic cock 3 a pointed process in any of various animals; calcar 4 a tubular extension at the base of the corolla in flowers such as larkspur 5 a short or stunted branch of a tree 6 a ridge projecting laterally from a mountain or mountain range 7 another name for **groyne** 8 a railway branch line or siding 9 a short side road leading off a main road 10 a sharp cutting instrument attached to the leg of a gamecock 11 **win one's spurs** *History* to earn knighthood

spurge any of various euphorbiaceous plants of the genus *Euphorbia* that have milky sap and small flowers typically surrounded by conspicuous bracts. Some species have purgative properties

spurious (of a plant part or organ) having the appearance of another part but differing from it in origin, development, or function; false

sputum 1 a mass of salivary matter ejected from the mouth 2 saliva ejected from the mouth mixed with mucus or pus exuded from the respiratory passages, as in bronchitis or bronchiectasis

spy a person employed by a state or institution to obtain secret information from rival countries, organizations, companies, etc.

spyglass a small telescope

SQL structured query language: a computer programming language used for database management

squab 1 a young unfledged bird, esp a pigeon 2 (of birds) recently hatched and still unfledged

squad *Sport* a number of players from which a team is to be selected

squall a sudden strong wind or brief turbulent storm

square 1 a plane geometric figure having four equal sides and four right angles 2 an open area in a town, sometimes including the surrounding buildings, which may form a square 3 *Maths* the product of two equal factors; the second power 4 an instrument having two strips of wood, metal, etc, set in the shape of a T or L, used for constructing or testing right angles 5 *Cricket* the closely-cut area in the middle of a ground on which wickets are prepared 6 *Rowing* the position of the blade of an oar perpendicular to the surface of the water just before and during a stroke 7 *Astrology* an aspect of about 90° between two planets, etc 8 having or forming one or more right angles or being at right angles to something 9 **a** denoting a measure of area of any shape **b** denoting a square having a specified length on each side 10 *Cricket* at right angles to the wicket 11 *Nautical* (of the sails of a square-rigger) set at right angles to the keel 12 (of a horse's gait) sound, steady, or regular 13 *Maths* (of a matrix) having the same number of rows and columns

square bracket either of these characters used as a sign of aggregation in mathematical or logical expressions indicating that the expression contained in the brackets is to be evaluated first and treated as a unit in the evaluation of the whole

square dance *Chiefly US and Canadian* any of various formation dances, such as a quadrille, in which the couples form squares

▷www.squaredanceworld.com

▷www.dosado.com

square leg *Cricket* **1** a fielding position on the on side approximately at right angles to the batsman **2** a person who fields in this position

square-rigged *Nautical* rigged with square sails

square root a number or quantity that when multiplied by itself gives a given number or quantity

squash¹ 1 a game for two or four players played in an enclosed court with a small rubber ball and light long-handled rackets. The ball may be hit against any of the walls but must hit the facing wall at a point above a horizontal line **2** a similar game played with larger rackets and a larger pneumatic ball

squash² *US and Canadian* any of various marrow-like cucurbitaceous plants of the genus *Cucurbita*, esp *C. pepo* and *C. moschata*, the fruits of which have a hard rind surrounding edible flesh

squat *Weightlifting* an exercise in which a person crouches down and rises up repeatedly while holding a barbell at shoulder height

squatter 1 a person who occupies property or land to which he has no legal title **2** (in Australia) **a** (formerly) a person who occupied a tract of land, esp pastoral land, as tenant of the Crown **b** a farmer of sheep or cattle on a large scale **3** (in New Zealand) a 19th-century settler who took up large acreage on a Crown lease

squaw *Offensive* a North American Indian woman

squeegee *or less commonly* **squilgee 1** an implement with a rubber blade used for wiping away surplus water from a surface, such as a windowpane **2** any of various similar devices used in photography for pressing the water out of wet prints or negatives or for squeezing prints onto a glazing surface

squeeze 1 *Chiefly Brit* a condition of restricted credit imposed by a government to counteract price inflation **2** *Commerce* any action taken by a trader or traders on a market that forces buyers to make purchases and prices to rise **3** *Bridge, whist* a manoeuvre that forces opponents to discard potentially winning cards

squelch *Electronics* a circuit that cuts off the audio-frequency amplifier of a radio receiver in the absence of an input signal, in order to suppress background noise

squib 1 a firework, usually having a tube filled with gunpowder, that burns with a hissing noise and culminates in a small explosion **2** a firework that does not explode because of a fault; dud

squid¹ any of various fast-moving pelagic cephalopod molluscs of the genera *Loligo*, *Ommastrephes*, etc, of most seas, having a torpedo-shaped body ranging from about 10 centimetres to 16.5 metres long and a pair of triangular tail fins: order *Decapoda* (decapods)

squid² *Brit, slang* a pound sterling

squill 1 short for **sea squill**, a Mediterranean liliaceous plant, *Urginea maritima*, having dense spikes of small white flowers, and yielding a bulb with medicinal properties **2** the bulb of the sea squill, formerly used medicinally as an expectorant after being sliced and dried **3** any Old World liliaceous plant of the genus *Scilla*, such as *S. verna* (**spring squill**) of Europe, having small blue or purple flowers

squint 1 the nontechnical name for **strabismus 2** a narrow oblique opening in a wall or pillar of a church to permit a view of the main altar from a side aisle or transept **3** having a squint

squire 1 *Feudal history* a young man of noble birth, who attended upon a knight **2** *Austral* an immature snapper (see **snapper** (sense 2))

squirrel 1 any arboreal sciurine rodent of the genus *Sciurus*, such as *S. vulgaris* (**red squirrel**) or *S. carolinensis* (**grey squirrel**), having a bushy tail and feeding on nuts, seeds, etc **2** any other rodent of the family *Sciuridae*, such as a ground squirrel or a marmot **3** the fur of such an animal

Sri Lanka a republic in S Asia, occupying the island of Ceylon: settled by the Sinhalese from S India in about 550 BC; became a British colony 1802; gained independence in 1948, becoming a republic within the Commonwealth in 1972. Exports include tea, cocoa, cinnamon, and copra. Official languages: Sinhalese and Tamil; English is also widely spoken. Religion: Hinayana Buddhist majority. Currency: Sri Lanka rupee. Capital: Colombo (administrative), Sri Jayewardenepura Kotte (legislative). Parts of the coast suffered badly in the Indian Ocean tsunami of December 2004. Pop: 19 218 000 (2004 est). Area: 65 610 sq km (25 332 sq miles)

Srinagar a city in N India, the summer capital of the state of Jammu and Kashmir, at an altitude of 1600 m (5250 ft) on the Jhelum River: seat of the University of Jammu and Kashmir (1948). Pop: 894 940 (2001)

stability 1 the ability of an aircraft to resume its original flight path after inadvertent displacement **2** *Meteorol* **a** the condition of an air or water mass characterized by no upward movement **b** the degree of susceptibility of an air mass to disturbance by convection currents **3** *Ecology* the ability of an ecosystem to resist change **4** *Electrical engineering* the ability of an electrical circuit to cope with changes in the operational conditions **5** a vow taken by every Benedictine monk attaching him perpetually to the monastery where he is professed

stabilizer *or* **stabiliser 1** any device for stabilizing an aircraft **2** a substance added to something to maintain it in a stable or unchanging state, such as an additive to food to preserve its texture during distribution and storage **3** *Nautical* a system of one or more pairs of fins projecting from the hull of a ship and controllable to counteract roll **4** either of a pair of brackets supporting a small wheel that can be fitted to the back wheel of a bicycle to help an inexperienced cyclist to maintain balance **5** an electronic device for producing a direct current supply of constant voltage **6** *Economics* a measure, such as progressive taxation, interest-rate control, or unemployment benefit, used to restrict swings in prices, employment, production, etc, in a free economy

stable¹ a the racehorses belonging to a particular establishment or owner **b** the establishment itself **c** (*as modifier*): *stable companion*

stable² 1 (of an elementary particle, atomic nucleus, etc) not undergoing decay; not radioactive **2** (of a chemical compound) not readily partaking in a chemical change **3** (of electronic equipment) with no tendency to self-oscillation

staccato *Music* (of notes) short, clipped, and separate

stack 1 a number of aircraft circling an airport at different altitudes, awaiting their signal to land 2 *Brit* a measure of coal or wood equal to 108 cubic feet 3 a high column of rock, esp one isolated from the mainland by the erosive action of the sea 4 an area in a computer memory for temporary storage

stadium 1 a sports arena with tiered seats for spectators 2 (in ancient Greece) a course for races, usually located between two hills providing natural slopes for tiers of seats 3 an ancient Greek measure of length equivalent to about 607 feet or 184 metres 4 (in many arthropods) the interval between two consecutive moultings 5 *Obsolete* a particular period or stage in the development of a disease

staff 1 the body of teachers or lecturers of an educational institution, as distinct from the students 2 *Music* a the system of horizontal lines grouped into sets of five (four in the case of plainsong) upon which music is written. The spaces between them are also used, being employed in conjunction with a clef in order to give a graphic indication of pitch b any set of five lines in this system together with its clef

Staffa an island in W Scotland, in the Inner Hebrides west of Mull: site of Fingal's Cave

staff nurse formerly, in Britain a qualified nurse ranking immediately below a sister

Stafford[1] Sir Edward William 1819–1901, New Zealand statesman, born in Scotland: prime minister of New Zealand (1856–61; 1865–69; 1872)

Stafford[2] a market town in central England, administrative centre of Staffordshire. Pop: 63 681 (2001)

Staffordshire a county of central England: lowlands in the east and south rise to the Pennine uplands in the north; important in the history of industry, coal and iron having been worked at least as early as the 13th century. In 1974 the industrial area in the S passed to the new county of West Midlands; Stoke-on-Trent became an independent unitary authority in 1997. Administrative centre: Stafford. Pop. (excluding Stoke-on-Trent): 811 000 (2003 est). Area (excluding Stoke-on-Trent): 2624 sq km (1013 sq miles)

stag the adult male of a deer, esp a red deer

stag beetle any lamellicorn beetle of the family *Lucanidae*, the males of which have large branched mandibles

stage 1 the platform in a theatre where actors perform 2 the the theatre as a profession 3 short for **stagecoach** 4 *Brit* a division of a bus route for which there is a fixed fare 5 any of the various distinct periods of growth or development in the life of an organism, esp an insect 6 the organism itself at such a period of growth 7 a small stratigraphical unit; a subdivision of a rock series or system 8 the platform on a microscope on which the specimen is mounted for examination 9 *Electronics* a part of a complex circuit, esp one of a number of transistors with the associated elements required to amplify a signal in an amplifier 10 a university subject studied for one academic year

stagecoach a large four-wheeled horse-drawn vehicle formerly used to carry passengers, mail, etc, on a regular route between towns and cities

stage direction *Theatre* an instruction to an actor or director, written into the script of a play

stage door a door at a theatre leading backstage

stage fright nervousness or panic that may beset a person about to appear in front of an audience

stagehand a person who sets the stage, moves props, etc, in a theatrical production

stage manager a person who supervises the stage arrangements of a theatrical production

stage whisper a loud whisper from one actor to another onstage intended to be heard by the audience

stagflation *Economics* a situation in which inflation is combined with stagnant or falling output and employment

stagger *Aviation* a staggered arrangement on a biplane, etc

staggers 1 a form of vertigo associated with decompression sickness 2 a disease of horses and some other domestic animals characterized by a swaying unsteady gait, caused by infection, toxins, or lesions of the central nervous system

Stagira an ancient city on the coast of Chalcidice in Macedonia: the birthplace of Aristotle

stagy *or US* **stagey** excessively theatrical or dramatic

stain a dye or similar reagent, used to colour specimens for microscopic study

stained glass a glass that has been coloured in any of various ways, as by fusing with a film of metallic oxide or burning pigment into the surface, used esp for church windows b (*as modifier*): *a stained-glass window*

Stainer Sir John 1840–1901, British composer and organist, noted for his sacred music, esp the oratorio *The Crucifixion* (1887)

Staines a town in SE England, in N Surrey on the River Thames. Pop: 50 538 (2001)

stainless steel a type of steel resistant to corrosion as a result of the presence of large amounts of chromium (12–15 per cent). The carbon content depends on the application, being 0.2–0.4 per cent for steel used in cutlery, etc, and about 1 per cent for use in scalpels and razor blades b (*as modifier*): *stainless-steel cutlery*

stair 1 one of a flight of stairs 2 a series of steps

staircase a flight of stairs, its supporting framework, and, usually, a handrail or banisters

stairway a means of access consisting of stairs; staircase or flight of steps

stairwell a vertical shaft or opening that contains a staircase

stake[1] 1 one of a number of vertical posts that fit into sockets around a flat truck or railway wagon to hold the load in place 2 a method or the practice of executing a person by binding him to a stake in the centre of a pile of wood that is then set on fire 3 *Mormon Church* an administrative district consisting of a group of wards under the jurisdiction of a president

stake[2] 1 the money or valuables that a player must hazard in order to buy into a gambling game or make a bet 2 the money that a player has available for gambling 3 *Horse racing* a race in which all owners of competing horses contribute to the prize money

stakeholder of or relating to policies intended to allow people to participate in and benefit from decisions made by enterprises in which they have a stake

stakeout *Slang, chiefly US and Canadian* **1** a police surveillance of an area, house, or criminal suspect **2** an area or house kept under such surveillance

stalactite a cylindrical mass of calcium carbonate hanging from the roof of a limestone cave: formed by precipitation from continually dripping water

stalagmite a cylindrical mass of calcium carbonate projecting upwards from the floor of a limestone cave: formed by precipitation from continually dripping water

stale **1** (of beer, etc) flat and tasteless from being kept open too long **2** *Law* (of a claim, etc) having lost its effectiveness or force, as by failure to act or by the lapse of time

stalemate a chess position in which any of a player's possible moves would place his king in check: in this position the game ends in a draw

Stalin *Joseph* original name *Iosif Vissarionovich Dzhugashvili*. 1879–1953, Soviet leader; general secretary of the Communist Party of the Soviet Union (1922–53). He succeeded Lenin as head of the party and created a totalitarian state, crushing all opposition, esp in the great purges of 1934–37. He instigated rapid industrialization and the collectivization of agriculture and established the Soviet Union as a world power

Stalinism the theory and form of government associated with the Soviet leader Joseph Stalin (original name *Iosif Vissarionovich Dzhugashvili*; 1879–1953): a variant of Marxism-Leninism characterized by totalitarianism, rigid bureaucracy, and loyalty to the state

stalk¹ **1** the main stem of a herbaceous plant **2** any of various subsidiary plant stems, such as a leafstalk (petiole) or flower stalk (peduncle) **3** a slender supporting structure in animals such as crinoids and certain protozoans, coelenterates, and barnacles

stalk² the act of stalking

stalking-horse **1** a horse or an imitation one used by a hunter to hide behind while stalking his quarry **2** a candidate put forward by one group to divide the opposition or mask the candidacy of another person for whom the stalking-horse would then withdraw

stall **1** a small often temporary stand or booth for the display and sale of goods **2** in a church **a** one of a row of seats, usually divided from the others by armrests or a small screen, for the use of the choir or clergy **b** a pen **3** an instance of an engine stalling **4** a condition of an aircraft in flight in which a reduction in speed or an increase in the aircraft's angle of attack causes a sudden loss of lift resulting in a downward plunge **5** *Brit* **a** a seat in a theatre or cinema that resembles a chair, usually fixed to the floor **b** the area of seats on the ground floor of a theatre or cinema nearest to the stage or screen

stallion an uncastrated male horse, esp one used for breeding

Stambul *or* **Stamboul** the old part of Istanbul, Turkey, south of the Golden Horn: the site of ancient Byzantium; sometimes used as a name for the whole city

stamen the male reproductive organ of a flower, consisting of a stalk (filament) bearing an anther in which pollen is produced

Stamford a city in SW Connecticut, on Long Island Sound: major chemical research laboratories. Pop: 120 107 (2003 est)

Stamford Bridge a village in N England, east of York: site of a battle (1066) in which King Harold of England defeated his brother Tostig and King Harald Hardrada of Norway, three weeks before the Battle of Hastings

stammer a speech disorder characterized by involuntary repetitions and hesitations

stamp **1 a** See **postage stamp b** a mark applied to postage stamps for cancellation purposes **2** a similar piece of gummed paper used for commercial or trading purposes **3** a piece of gummed paper or other mark applied to official documents to indicate payment of a fee, validity, ownership, etc. **4** *Brit, informal* a national insurance contribution, formerly recorded by means of a stamp on an official card **5** an instrument or machine for crushing or pounding ores, etc, or the pestle in such a device

stampede any sudden large-scale movement or other action, such as a rush of people to support a candidate

stance **1** *Sport* the posture assumed when about to play the ball, as in golf, cricket, etc. **2** *Scot* a place where buses or taxis wait **3** *Mountaineering* a place at the top of a pitch where a climber can stand and belay

stanch *or* **staunch** a primitive form of lock in which boats are carried over shallow parts of a river in a rush of water released by the lock

stanchion any vertical pole, rod, etc, used as a support

stand **1** a stall, booth, or counter from which goods may be sold **2** an exhibition area in a trade fair **3** *Cricket* an extended period at the wicket by two batsmen **4** a growth of plants in a particular area, esp trees in a forest or a crop in a field **5** a stop made by a touring theatrical company, pop group, etc, to give a performance (esp in the phrase **one-night stand**) **6** (of a gun dog) the act of pointing at game

standard **1** the commodity or commodities in which is stated the value of a basic monetary unit **2** an authorized model of a unit of measure or weight **3** a unit of board measure equal to 1980 board feet **4 a** a plant, esp a fruit tree, that is trained so that it has an upright stem free of branches **b** (*as modifier*): *a standard cherry* **5** a song or piece of music that has remained popular for many years **6** the largest petal of a leguminous flower, such as a sweetpea **7** (in New Zealand and, formerly, in England and Wales) a class or level of attainment in an elementary school

standard-bearer a leader of a cause or party

standard gauge a railway track with a distance of 4 ft 8½ in. (1.435 m) between the lines; used on most railways

Standard Grade (in Scotland) a type of examination designed to test skills and the application of knowledge, replaced O grade

standard of living a level of subsistence or material welfare of a community, class, or person

standard time the official local time of a region or country determined by the distance from Greenwich of a line of longitude passing through the area

stand-by (of an airline passenger, fare, or seat) not

booked in advance but awaiting or subject to availability

stand-in a person who substitutes for an actor during intervals of waiting or in dangerous stunts

standing *Athletics* **a** (of the start of a race) begun from a standing position without the use of starting blocks **b** (of a jump, leap, etc) performed from a stationary position without a run-up

standing order a rule or order governing the procedure, conduct, etc, of a legislative body

Standish Myles (*or* Miles). ?1584–1656, English military leader of the Pilgrim Fathers at Plymouth, New England

stand-up **1** (of comedy or a comedian) performed or performing solo **2** *Informal* (of a boxer) having an aggressive style without much leg movement **3** a stand-up comedian **4** stand-up comedy

Stanford Sir Charles (**Villiers**). 1852–1924, Anglo-Irish composer and conductor, who as a teacher at the Royal College of Music had much influence on the succeeding generation of composers: noted esp for his church music, oratorios, and cantatas

Stanislavsky *or* **Stanislavski** Konstantin 1863–1938, Russian actor and director, cofounder of the Moscow Art Theatre (1897). He is famous for his theory of acting, known as the Method, which directs the actor to find the truth within himself or herself about the role he or she is playing

Stanisław *or* **Stanislaus** Saint 1030–79, the patron saint of Poland. As Bishop of Cracow (1072–79) he excommunicated King Bolesław II, who arranged his murder. Feast day: May 11

stank¹ **1** a small cofferdam, esp one of timber made watertight with clay **2** *Scot and northern English, dialect* a pond or pool

stank² *Dialect* a drain, as in a roadway

Stanley¹ Sir Henry Morton 1841–1904, British explorer and journalist, who led an expedition to Africa in search of Livingstone, whom he found on Nov 10, 1871. He led three further expeditions in Africa (1874–77; 1879–84; 1887–89) and was instrumental in securing Belgian sovereignty over the Congo Free State

Stanley² **1** the capital of the Falkland Islands, in NE East Falkland Island: scene of fighting in the Falklands War of 1982. Pop: 1989 (2001) **2** a town in NE England, in N Durham. Pop: 19 072 (2001) **3 Mount** a mountain in central Africa, between Uganda and the Democratic Republic of Congo (formerly Zaïre): the highest peak of the Ruwenzori range. Height: 5109 m (16 763 ft)

Stanley knife *Trademark* a type of knife used for carpet fitting, etc, consisting of a thick hollow metal handle with a short, very sharp, replaceable blade inserted at one end

Stanley Pool a lake between the Democratic Republic of Congo (formerly Zaïre) and Congo-Brazzaville, formed by a widening of the River Congo. Area: 829 sq km (320 sq miles)

Stannaries the a tin-mining district of Devon and Cornwall, formerly under the jurisdiction of special courts

Stanovoi Range *or* **Stanovoy Range** a mountain range in SE Russia; forms part of the watershed

between rivers flowing to the Arctic and the Pacific. Highest peak: Mount Skalisty, 2482 m (8143 ft)

Stans a town in central Switzerland, capital of Nidwalden demicanton, 11 km (7 miles) southeast of Lucerne: tourist centre. Pop: 6983 (2000)

stanza **1** *Prosody* a fixed number of verse lines arranged in a definite metrical pattern, forming a unit of a poem **2** *US and Austral* a half or a quarter in an American or Australian rules football match

staple¹ **1** a short length of thin wire bent into a square U-shape, used to fasten papers, cloth, etc. **2** a short length of stiff wire formed into a U-shape with pointed ends, used for holding a hasp to a post, securing electric cables, etc

staple² **1** (of a commodity) forming a predominant element in the product, consumption, or trade of a nation, region, etc. **2** a staple commodity **3** *Chiefly US and Canadian* a principal raw material produced or grown in a region **4** the fibre of wool, cotton, etc, graded as to length and fineness **5** (in medieval Europe) a town appointed to be the exclusive market for one or more major exports of the land

star **1** any of a vast number of celestial objects that are visible in the clear night sky as points of light **2 a** a hot gaseous mass, such as the sun, that radiates energy, esp as light and infrared radiation, usually derived from thermonuclear reactions in the interior, and in some cases as ultraviolet, radio waves, and X-rays. The surface temperature can range from about 2100 to 40 000°C **b** (*as modifier*): *a star catalogue* **3** *Astrology* **a** a celestial body, esp a planet, supposed to influence events, personalities, etc. **b** **4** a small white blaze on the forehead of an animal, esp a horse

Stara Zagora a city in central Bulgaria: ceded to Bulgaria by Turkey in 1877. Pop: 163 000 (2005 est)

starboard the right side of an aeroplane or vessel when facing the nose or bow

starch **1** a polysaccharide composed of glucose units that occurs widely in plant tissues in the form of storage granules, consisting of amylose and amylopectin **2** a starch obtained from potatoes and some grain: it is fine white powder that forms a translucent viscous solution on boiling with water and is used to stiffen fabric and in many industrial processes

stare *Dialect* a starling

starfish any echinoderm of the class *Asteroidea*, such as *Asterias rubens*, typically having a flattened body covered with a flexible test and five arms radiating from a central disc

Stark **1** Dame Freya (**Madeline**). 1893–1993, British traveller and writer, whose many books include *The Southern Gates of Arabia* (1936), *Beyond Euphrates* (1951), and *The Journey's Echo* (1963) **2 Johannes** 1874–1957, German physicist, who discovered the splitting of the lines of a spectrum when the source of light is subjected to a strong electrostatic field (**Stark effect**, 1913): Nobel prize for physics 1919

Starkey David born 1945, British historian and broadcaster, noted for his books and television series on the Tudor period

starlet **1** a young and inexperienced actress who is projected as a potential star **2** a small star

starlight the light emanating from the stars

starling¹ any gregarious passerine songbird of the Old World family *Sturnidae*, esp *Sturnus vulgaris*, which has a blackish plumage and a short tail

starling² an arrangement of piles that surround a pier of a bridge to protect it from debris, etc.

Star of David an emblem symbolizing Judaism and consisting of a six-pointed star formed by superimposing one inverted equilateral triangle upon another of equal size

Starr 1 (Myra) **Belle** 1848–89, US outlaw, a famous rustler of horses and cattle **2 Ringo**, original name *Richard Starkey*. born 1940, British rock musician; drummer (1962–70) with the Beatles

Star-Spangled Banner the the national anthem of the United States of America

starter 1 a device for starting an internal-combustion engine, usually consisting of a powerful electric motor that engages with the flywheel **2** *US* a person who organizes the timely departure of buses, trains, etc.

start-up a business enterprise that has been launched recently

stash *Slang* drugs kept for personal consumption

state 1 a sovereign political power or community **2** the territory occupied by such a community **3** the sphere of power in such a community **4** one of a number of areas or communities having their own governments and forming a federation under a sovereign government, as in the US **5** the body politic of a particular sovereign power, esp as contrasted with a rival authority such as the Church

▷www.sosig.ac.uk/roads/subject-listing/ World-cat/state.html

stateless 1 without nationality **2** without a state or states

stately home *Brit* a large mansion, esp one open to the public

statement 1 *Law* a declaration of matters of fact, esp in a pleading **2** *Music* the presentation of a musical theme or idea, such as the subject of a fugue or sonata **3** a computer instruction written in a source language, such as FORTRAN, which is converted into one or more machine code instructions by a compiler **4** *Logic* the content of a sentence that affirms or denies something and may be true or false; what is thereby affirmed or denied abstracted from the act of uttering it. Thus *I am warm* said by me and *you are warm* said to me make the same statement **5** *Brit, Education* a legally binding account of the needs of a pupil with special educational needs and the provisions that will be made to meet them

Staten Island an island in SE New York State, in New York Harbor: a borough of New York city; heavy industry. Pop: 443 728 (2000). Area: 155 sq km (60 sq miles)

State Registered Nurse (formerly in Britain) a nurse who had extensive training and passed examinations enabling him or her to perform all nursing services

stateroom *Chiefly Brit* a large room in a palace or other building for use on state occasions

States the an informal name for the **United States of America**

state school any school maintained by the state, in which education is free

statesman 1 a political leader whose wisdom, integrity, etc, win great respect **2** a person active and influential in the formulation of high government policy, such as a cabinet member **3** a politician

static 1 (of a weight, force, or pressure) acting but causing no movement **2** of or concerned with forces that do not produce movement **3** relating to or causing stationary electric charges; electrostatic **4** of or concerned with statics **5** *Computing* (of a memory) not needing its contents refreshed periodically **6** electric sparks or crackling produced by friction

statics the branch of mechanics concerned with the forces that produce a state of equilibrium in a system of bodies

station 1 a a place along a route or line at which a bus, train, etc, stops for fuel or to pick up or let off passengers or goods, esp one with ancillary buildings and services **b** (*as modifier*): *a station buffet* **2** (in British India) a place where the British district officials or garrison officers resided **3** *Biology* the type of habitat occupied by a particular animal or plant **4** *RC Church* **a** one of the Stations of the Cross **b** any of the churches (**station churches**) in Rome that have been used from ancient times as points of assembly for religious processions and ceremonies on particular days (**station days**) **5** (in rural Ireland) mass, preceded by confessions, held annually in a parishioner's dwelling and attended by other parishioners

stationer 1 a person who sells stationery or a shop where stationery is sold **2** *Obsolete* a publisher or bookseller

stationmaster *or* **station manager** the senior official in charge of a railway station

station wagon *US, Canadian, Austral., NZ, and South African* a car with a comparatively long body containing a large carrying space, reached through a rear door: usually the back seats can be folded forward to increase the carrying space

Statius Publius Papinius ?45–96 AD, Roman poet; author of the collection *Silvae* and of two epics, *Thebais* and the unfinished *Achilleis*

statuary 1 statues collectively **2** the art of making statues

statue a wooden, stone, metal, plaster, or other kind of sculpture of a human or animal figure, usually life-size or larger

statuette a small statue

status *Law* the legal standing or condition of a person

statute 1 a an enactment of a legislative body expressed in a formal document **b** this document **2** a permanent rule made by a body or institution for the government of its internal affairs

statute law 1 a law enacted by a legislative body **2** a particular example of this

statutory 1 of, relating to, or having the nature of a statute **2** prescribed or authorized by statute **3** of an offence **a** recognized by statute **b** subject to a punishment or penalty prescribed by statute

Stauffenberg Claus, Graf von. 1907–44, German army officer, who tried to assassinate Hitler (1944). He and his fellow conspirators were executed

staunch *Rare* (of a ship, etc) watertight; seaworthy

Stavanger a port in SW Norway: canning and ship-building industries. Pop: 112 405 (2004 est)

stave 1 a stanza or verse of a poem 2 *Music* a *Brit* an individual group of five lines and four spaces used in staff notation b another word for **staff**

Stavropol 1 a city in SW Russia: founded as a fortress in 1777. Pop: 362 000 (2005 est) 2 the former name (until 1964) of **Togliatti**

stay *Law* the suspension of a judicial proceeding, etc.

stay-at-home a person who does not bother to vote in a political election

staysail *Nautical* an auxiliary sail, often triangular, set to catch the wind, as between the masts of a yawl (**mizzen staysail**), aft of a spinnaker (**spinnaker staysail**), etc.

Stead Christina (Ellen). 1902–83, Australian novelist. Her works include *Seven Poor Men of Sydney* (1934), *The Man who Loved Children* (1940), and *Cotters' England* (1966)

steady *Nautical* (of a vessel) keeping upright, as in heavy seas

steady state *Physics* the condition of a system when some or all of the quantities describing it are independent of time but not necessarily in thermodynamic or chemical equilibrium

steakhouse a restaurant that has steaks as its speciality

stealth tax *Brit, informal* an indirect tax, such as that on fuel or pension funds, esp one of which people are unaware or that is felt to be unfair

steam 1 the gas or vapour into which water is changed when boiled 2 the mist formed when such gas or vapour condenses in the atmosphere

steamer 1 a boat or ship driven by steam engines 2 an apparatus for steaming wooden beams and planks to make them pliable for shipbuilding 3 *Austral, slang* a clash of sporting teams characterized by rough play

steam iron an electric iron that emits steam from channels in the iron face to facilitate the pressing and ironing of clothes, etc, the steam being produced from water contained within the iron

steamship a ship powered by one or more steam engines

steed *Archaic or literary* a horse, esp one that is spirited or swift

steel 1 a any of various alloys based on iron containing carbon (usually 0.1–1.7 per cent) and often small quantities of other elements such as phosphorus, sulphur, manganese, chromium, and nickel. Steels exhibit a variety of properties, such as strength, machinability, malleability, etc, depending on their composition and the way they have been treated b (*as modifier*): *steel girders* 2 something that is made of steel 3 a ridged steel rod with a handle used for sharpening knives

Steel 1 Danielle, full name *Danielle Fernande Schüelein-Steel*. born 1950, US writer of romantic fiction 2 Baron **David** (**Martin Scott**). born 1938, British politician; leader of the Liberal Party (1976–88); Presiding Officer of the Scottish Parliament (1999–2003)

steel band *Music* a type of instrumental band, popular in the Caribbean Islands, consisting mainly of tuned percussion instruments made chiefly from the heads

of oil drums, hammered or embossed to obtain different notes

Steele Sir **Richard** 1672–1729, British essayist and dramatist, born in Ireland; with Joseph Addison he was the chief contributor to the periodicals *The Tatler* (1709–11) and *The Spectator* (1711–12)

steel wool a tangled or woven mass of fine steel fibres, used for cleaning or polishing

steelworks a plant in which steel is made from iron ore and rolled or forged into blooms, billets, bars, or sheets

Steen Jan 1626–79, Dutch genre painter

steeple 1 a tall ornamental tower that forms the superstructure of a church, temple, etc. 2 such a tower with the spire above it

steeplechase 1 a horse race over a course equipped with obstacles to be jumped, esp artificial hedges, ditches, water jumps, etc. 2 a track race, usually of 3000 metres, in which the runners have to leap hurdles, a water jump, etc. 3 *Archaic* a a horse race across a stretch of open countryside including obstacles to be jumped b a rare word for **point-to-point**

steer a castrated male ox or bull; bullock

steerage 1 the cheapest accommodation on a passenger ship, originally the compartments containing the steering apparatus 2 an instance or the practice of steering and the effect of this on a vessel or vehicle

steering committee a committee set up to prepare and arrange topics to be discussed, the order of business, etc, for a legislative assembly or other body

steering wheel a wheel turned by the driver of a motor vehicle, ship, etc, when he wishes to change direction. It is connected to the front wheels, rudder, etc.

steersman the helmsman of a vessel

Stefansson Vilhjalmur 1879–1962, Canadian explorer, noted for his books on the Inuit

Steffens (**Joseph**) **Lincoln** 1866–1936, US political analyst, known for his exposure of political corruption

stein an earthenware beer mug, esp of a German design

Stein 1 Gertrude 1874–1946, US writer, resident in Paris (1903–1946). Her works include *Three Lives* (1908) and *The Autobiography of Alice B. Toklas* (1933) 2 Heinrich Friedrich Carl , Baron Stein. 1757–1831, Prussian statesman, who contributed greatly to the modernization of Prussia and played a major role in the European coalition against Napoleon (1813–15) 3 Jock, real name *John*. 1922–85, Scottish footballer and manager: managed Celtic (1965–78) and Scotland (1978–85)

Steinbeck John (**Ernst**). 1902–68, US writer, noted for his novels about agricultural workers, esp *The Grapes of Wrath* (1939): Nobel prize for literature 1962

Steiner Rudolf 1861–1925, Austrian philosopher, founder of anthroposophy. He was particularly influential in education

Steinitz Wilhelm 1836–1900, US chess player, born in Prague; world champion (1866–94)

Steinway Henry (**Engelhard**), original name *Heinrich Engelhardt Steinweg*. 1797–1871, US piano maker, born in Germany

stellar of, relating to, involving, or resembling a star or stars

stem[1] 1 the main axis of a plant, which bears the leaves, axillary buds, and flowers and contains a hollow cylinder of vascular tissue **2** any similar subsidiary structure in such plants that bears a flower, fruit, or leaf **3** a corresponding structure in algae and fungi **4** a banana stalk with several bunches attached **5** a round pin in some locks on which a socket in the end of a key fits and about which it rotates **6** any projecting feature of a component: a shank or cylindrical pin or rod, such as the pin that carries the winding knob on a watch **7** *Electronics* the tubular glass section projecting from the base of a light bulb or electronic valve, on which the filament or electrodes are mounted **8 a** the main upright timber or structure at the bow of a vessel **b** the very forward end of a vessel (esp in the phrase **from stem to stern**)

stem² *Skiing* a technique in which the heel of one ski or both skis is forced outwards from the direction of movement in order to slow down or turn

stem cell *Histology* an undifferentiated cell that gives rise to specialized cells, such as blood cells

Stendhal original name *Marie Henri Beyle*. 1783–1842, French writer, who anticipated later novelists in his psychological analysis of character. His two chief novels are *Le Rouge et le noir* (1830) and *La Chartreuse de Parme* (1839)

stent *Medicine* a tube of plastic or sprung metal mesh placed inside a hollow tube to reopen it or keep it open; uses in surgery include preventing a blood vessel from closing, esp after angioplasty, and assisting healing after an anastomosis

step **1** the act of motion brought about by raising the foot and setting it down again in coordination with the transference of the weight of the body **2** a sequence of foot movements that make up a particular dance or part of a dance **3** any of several paces or rhythmic movements in marching, dancing, etc. **4** a flight of stairs, esp out of doors **5** *Music* a melodic interval of a second **6** a strong block or frame bolted onto the keel of a vessel and fitted to receive the base of a mast

Step **a** a set of aerobic exercises designed to improve the cardiovascular system, which consists of stepping on and off a special box of adjustable height **b** (*as modifier*): *Step aerobics*

step-down (of a transformer) reducing a high voltage applied to the primary winding to a lower voltage on the secondary winding

stephanotis any climbing asclepiadaceous shrub of the genus *Stephanotis*, esp *S. floribunda*, of Madagascar and Malaya: cultivated for their fragrant white waxy flowers

Stephen **1** ?1097–1154, king of England (1135–54); grandson of William the Conqueror. He seized the throne on the death of Henry I, causing civil war with Henry's daughter Matilda. He eventually recognized her son (later Henry II) as his successor **2** *Saint* died ?35 AD, the first Christian martyr. Feast day: Dec 26 or 27 **3** *Saint*, Hungarian name *István*. ?975–1038 AD, first king of Hungary as Stephen I (997–1038). Feast day: Aug 16 or 20 **4** *Sir* **Leslie** 1832–1904, English biographer, critic, and first editor of the *Dictionary of National Biography*; father of the novelist Virginia Woolf

Stephenson **1** *George* 1781–1848, British inventor of the first successful steam locomotive (1814); constructed

the first railway line to carry passengers, the Stockton and Darlington Railway (opened 1825) **2** his son, **Robert** 1803–59, British engineer, noted for his construction of railway bridges and viaducts, esp the tubular bridge over the Menai Strait

step-in (of a ski binding) engaging automatically when the boot is positioned on the ski

stepping stone one of a series of stones acting as footrests for crossing streams, marshes, etc.

step-up (of a transformer) increasing a low voltage applied to the primary winding to a higher voltage on the secondary winding

stereo **1** short for **stereophonic** or **stereoscopic 2** stereophonic sound **3** a stereophonic record player, tape recorder, etc. **4** *Photog* **a** stereoscopic photography **b** a stereoscopic photograph

stereophonic (of a system for recording, reproducing, or broadcasting sound) using two or more separate microphones to feed two or more loudspeakers through separate channels in order to give a spatial effect to the sound

stereoscopic of, concerned with, or relating to seeing space three-dimensionally as a result of binocular disparity

sterile **1** unable to produce offspring; infertile **2** free from living, esp pathogenic, microorganisms; aseptic **3** (of plants or their parts) not producing or bearing seeds, fruit, spores, stamens, or pistils **4** *Economics, US* (of gold) not being used to support credit creation or an increased money supply

sterling **1 a** British money **b** (*as modifier*): *sterling reserves* **2 a** short for **sterling silver b** (*as modifier*): *a sterling bracelet* **3** an article or articles manufactured from sterling silver **4** a former British silver penny

sterling silver **1** an alloy containing not less than 92.5 per cent of silver, the remainder usually being copper **2** sterling-silver articles collectively

Sterlitamak an industrial city in W Russia, in the Bashkir Republic. Pop: 268 000 (2005 est)

stern **1** the rear or after part of a vessel, opposite the bow or stem **2** the tail of certain breeds of dog, such as the foxhound or beagle

Stern *Isaac* 1920–2001, US concert violinist, born in (what is now) Ukraine

Sterne *Laurence* 1713–68, English novelist, born in Ireland, author of *The Life and Opinions of Tristram Shandy, Gentleman* (1759–67) and *A Sentimental Journey through France and Italy* (1768)

sternum **1** (in man) a long flat vertical bone, situated in front of the thorax, to which are attached the collarbone and the first seven pairs of ribs **2** the corresponding part in many other vertebrates **3** a cuticular plate covering the ventral surface of a body segment of an arthropod

steroid *Biochem* any of a large group of fat-soluble organic compounds containing a characteristic chemical ring system. The majority, including the sterols, bile acids, many hormones, and the D vitamins, have important physiological action

sterol *Biochem* any of a group of natural steroid alcohols, such as cholesterol and ergosterol, that are waxy insoluble substances

stertorous 1 marked or accompanied by heavy snoring 2 breathing in this way

stethoscope 1 *Med* an instrument for listening to the sounds made within the body, typically consisting of a hollow disc that transmits the sound through hollow tubes to earpieces 2 a narrow cylinder expanded at both ends to recieve and transmit fetal sounds

stevedore a person employed to load or unload ships

Stevenage a town in SE England, in N Hertfordshire on the Great North Road: developed chiefly as the first of the new towns (1946). Pop: 81 482 (2001)

Stevenson 1 **Adlai Ewing** 1900–68, US statesman: twice defeated as Democratic presidential candidate (1952; 1956); US delegate at the United Nations (1961–65) 2 **Robert Louis (Balfour)**. 1850–94, Scottish writer: his novels include *Treasure Island* (1883), *Kidnapped* (1886), and *The Master of Ballantrae* (1889)

stew *Brit* 1 a fishpond or fishtank 2 an artificial oyster bed

steward a waiter on a ship or aircraft

stewardess a woman who performs a steward's job on an aircraft or ship

Stewart 1 the usual spelling for the royal house of **Stuart** before the reign of Mary Queen of Scots (Mary Stuart) 2 **Sir Jackie**, full name *John Young Stewart*. born 1939, Scottish motor-racing driver: world champion 1969, 1971, and 1973 3 **James (Maitland)**. 1908–97, US film actor, known for his distinctive drawl; appeared in many films including *Destry Rides Again* (1939), *It's a Wonderful Life* (1946), *The Glenn Miller Story* (1953), and *Vertigo* (1958) 4 **Rod** born 1945, British rock singer: vocalist with the Faces (1969–75). His albums include *Gasoline Alley* (1970), *Every Picture Tells a Story* (1971), and *Atlantic Crossing* (1975)

Stewart Island the third largest island of New Zealand, in the SW Pacific off the S tip of South Island. Pop: 387 (2001). Area: 1735 sq km (670 sq miles)

Steyr *or* **Steier** an industrial city in N central Austria, in Upper Austria. Pop: 39 340 (2001)

stick 1 a small thin branch of a tree 2 a any long thin piece of wood b such a piece of wood having a characteristic shape for a special purpose c a baton, wand, staff, or rod 3 *Informal* the lever used to change gear in a motor vehicle 4 *Nautical* a mast or yard 5 *Informal* a rural area considered remote or backward (esp in the phrase **in the sticks**) 6 *W and NW Canadian, informal* the wooded interior part of the country

sticking plaster a thin cloth with an adhesive substance on one side, used for covering slight or superficial wounds

stick insect any of various mostly tropical insects of the family *Phasmidae* that have an elongated cylindrical body and long legs and resemble twigs: order *Phasmida*

stickleback any small teleost fish of the family *Gasterosteidae*, such as *Gasterosteus aculeatus* (**three-spined stickleback**) of rivers and coastal regions and *G. pungitius* (**ten-spined stickleback**) confined to rivers. They have a series of spines along the back and occur in cold and temperate northern regions

sticky 1 (of weather or atmosphere) warm and humid; muggy 2 (of prices) tending not to fall in deflationary conditions

sticky wicket a cricket pitch that is rapidly being dried by the sun after rain and is particularly conducive to spin

Stieglitz Alfred 1864–1946, US photographer, whose work helped to develop photography as an art: among his best photographs are those of his wife Georgia O'Keeffe. He was also well known as a promoter of modern art

stiff *Nautical* (of a sailing vessel) relatively resistant to heeling or rolling

stifle the joint in the hind leg of a horse, dog, etc, between the femur and tibia

stigma 1 a small scar or mark such as a birthmark 2 *Pathol* a any mark on the skin, such as one characteristic of a specific disease b any sign of a mental deficiency or emotional upset 3 *Botany* the receptive surface of a carpel, where deposited pollen germinates 4 *Zoology* a a pigmented eyespot in some protozoans and other invertebrates b the spiracle of an insect 5 *Archaic* a mark branded on the skin 6 *Christianity* marks resembling the wounds of the crucified Christ, believed to appear on the bodies of certain individuals

Stilicho Flavius ?365–408 AD, Roman general and statesman, born a Vandal. As the guardian of Emperor Theodosius' son Honorius, he was effective ruler of the Western Roman Empire (395–408), which he defended against the Visigoths

still¹ a still photograph, esp of a scene from a motion-picture film b (*as modifier*): *a still camera*

still² 1 an apparatus for carrying out distillation, consisting of a vessel in which a mixture is heated, a condenser to turn the vapour back to liquid, and a receiver to hold the distilled liquid, used esp in the manufacture of spirits 2 a place where spirits are made; distillery

stillborn 1 (of a fetus) dead at birth 2 a stillborn fetus or baby

still life 1 a a painting or drawing of inanimate objects, such as fruit, flowers, etc. b (*as modifier*): *a still-life painting* 2 the genre of such paintings

still room *Brit* a room in which distilling is carried out

stilt 1 either of a pair of two long poles with footrests on which a person stands and walks, as used by circus clowns 2 any of several shore birds of the genera *Himantopus* and *Cladorhynchus*, similar to the avocets but having a straight bill

stilted *Architect* (of an arch) having vertical piers between the impost and the springing

Stilwell Joseph W(arren), known as *Vinegar Joe*. 1883–1946, US general, who was (1941–44) Chiang Kai-shek's chief of staff and commander of all US forces in China, Burma (Myanmar), and India

stimulant 1 a drug or similar substance that increases physiological activity, esp of a particular organ 2 increasing physiological activity; stimulating

stimulus 1 any drug, agent, electrical impulse, or other factor able to cause a response in an organism 2 an object or event that is apprehended by the senses 3 *Med* a former name for stimulant

Stine R(obert) L(awrence). born 1943, US writer, noted for his numerous bestselling horror novels for older children, esp those in the *Goosebumps* and *Fear Street*

series

sting 1 a skin wound caused by the poison injected by certain insects or plants 2 pain caused by or as if by the sting of a plant or animal 3 a sharp pointed organ, such as the ovipositor of a wasp, by which poison can be injected into the prey 4 *Slang* a trap set up by the police to entice a person to commit a crime and thereby produce evidence

stingray any ray of the family *Dasyatidae*, having a whip-like tail bearing a serrated venomous spine capable of inflicting painful weals on man

stingy *South Wales, dialect* a stinging nettle

stink bomb a small glass globe, used by practical jokers: it releases a liquid with an offensive smell when broken

stinker *Informal* any of several fulmars or related birds that feed on carrion

stint any of various small sandpipers of the chiefly northern genus *Calidris* (or *Erolia*), such as *C. minuta* (**little stint**)

stipulate (of a plant) having stipules

Stirling[1] Sir James 1926–92, British architect; buildings include the Neue Staatsgalerie in Stuttgart (1977–84)

Stirling[2] 1 a city in central Scotland, in Stirling council area on the River Forth: its castle was a regular residence of many Scottish monarchs between the 12th century and 1603. Pop: 32 673 (2001) 2 a council area of central Scotland, created from part of Central Region in 1996; includes most of the historical county of Stirlingshire: the Forth valley rises to the Grampian Mountains in the N. Administrative centre: Stirling. Pop: 86 370 (2003 est). Area: 2173 sq km (839 sq miles)

Stirlingshire a former county of central Scotland: mostly became part of Central Region in 1975: now covered by the council areas of Stirling, Falkirk, and East Dunbartonshire

stirrer *Austral and NZ, informal* a political activist or agitator

stirrup 1 either of two metal loops on a riding saddle, with a flat footpiece through which a rider puts his foot for support. They are attached to the saddle by **stirrup leathers** 2 *Nautical* one of a set of ropes fastened to a yard at one end and having a thimble at the other through which a footrope is rove for support

stirrup cup a cup containing an alcoholic drink offered to a horseman ready to ride away

stirrup pump a hand-operated vertical reciprocating pump, such as one used in fire-fighting, etc, in which the base of the cylinder is placed in a bucket of water

stitch 1 a sharp spasmodic pain in the side resulting from running or exercising 2 an informal word for suture
  ▷www.petitpoint.com/References/ stitchTypes.htm

stoat a small Eurasian musteline mammal, *Mustela erminea*, closely related to the weasels, having a brown coat and a black-tipped tail: in the northern parts of its range it has a white winter coat and is then known as an ermine

stock 1 a the total goods or raw material kept on the premises of a shop or business b (*as modifier*): *a stock clerk* 2 the trunk or main stem of a tree or other plant 3

Horticulture a a rooted plant into which a scion is inserted during grafting b a plant or stem from which cuttings are taken 4 the original type from which a particular race, family, group, etc, is derived 5 a race, breed, or variety of animals or plants 6 any of the major subdivisions of the human species; race or ethnic group 7 the main body of a tool, such as the block of a plane 8 film material before exposure and processing 9 *Metallurgy* a a portion of metal cut from a bar upon which a specific process, such as forging, is to be carried out b the material that is smelted in a blast furnace 10 any of several plants of the genus *Matthiola*, such as *M. incana* and *M. bicornis* (**evening** or **night-scented stock**), of the Mediterranean region, cultivated for their brightly coloured flowers: *Brassicaceae* (crucifers) 11 **Virginian stock** a similar and related North American plant, *Malcolmia maritima* 12 *Cards* a pile of cards left after the deal in certain games, from which players draw 13 a the repertoire of plays available to a repertory company b (*as modifier*): *a stock play* 14 (on some types of anchors) a crosspiece at the top of the shank under the ring 15 the centre of a wheel 16 an exposed igneous intrusion that is smaller in area than a batholith 17 a log or block of wood

stockbreeder a person who breeds or rears livestock as an occupation

stock car 1 a a car, usually a production saloon, strengthened and modified for a form of racing in which the cars often collide b (*as modifier*): *stock-car racing* 2 *US and Canadian* a railway wagon designed for carrying livestock

Stockhausen Karlheinz born 1928, German composer, whose avant-garde music exploits advanced serialization, electronic sounds, group improvization, and vocal and instrumental timbres and techniques. Works include *Gruppen* (1959) for three orchestras, *Stimmung* (1968) for six vocalists, and the operas *Donnerstag* (1980) and *Freitag* (1996)

stockholder *Austral* a person who keeps livestock

Stockholm the capital of Sweden, a port in the E central part at the outflow of Lake Mälar into the Baltic: situated partly on the mainland and partly on islands; traditionally founded about 1250; university (1877). Pop: 765 582 (2004 est)

stock in trade 1 goods in stock necessary for carrying on a business 2 anything constantly used by someone as a part of his profession, occupation, or trade

stockist *Commerce, Brit* a dealer who undertakes to maintain stocks of a specified product at or above a certain minimum in return for favourable buying terms granted by the manufacturer of the product

Stockport 1 a town in NW England, in Stockport unitary authority, Greater Manchester: an early textile centre and scene of several labour disturbances in the early 19th century; engineering, electronics. Pop: 136 082 (2001) 2 a unitary authority in NW England, in Greater Manchester. Pop: 282 500 (2003 est). Area: 126 sq km (49 sq miles)

stockroom a room in which a stock of goods is kept, as in a shop or factory

stocktaking the examination, counting, and valuing of goods on hand in a shop or business

Stockton an inland port in central California, on the San Joaquin River: seat of the University of the Pacific (1851). Pop: 271 466 (2003 est)

Stockton-on-Tees 1 a former port and industrial centre in NE England, in Stockton-on-Tees unitary authority, Co. Durham, on the River Tees: famous for the **Stockton-Darlington Railway** (1825), the first passenger-carrying railway in the world; now mainly residential. Pop: 80 060 (2001) **2** a unitary authority in NE England, in Co. Durham and North Yorkshire: created in 1996 from part of Cleveland county. Pop: 186 300 (2003 est). Area: 195 sq km (75 sq miles)

Stoic a member of the ancient Greek school of philosophy founded by Zeno of Citium, the Greek philosopher (?336–?264 BC), holding that virtue and happiness can be attained only by submission to destiny and the natural law

stokehold *Nautical* **1** a coal bunker for a ship's furnace **2** the hold for a ship's boilers; fire room

Stoke-on-Trent 1 a city in central England, in Stoke-on-Trent unitary authority, Staffordshire on the River Trent: a centre of the pottery industry; university (1992). Pop: 259 252 (2001) **2** a unitary authority in central England, in N Staffordshire. Pop: 238 000 (2003 est). Area: 93 sq km (36 sq miles)

stoker a person employed to tend a furnace, as on a steamship

Stoker Bram, original name *Abraham Stoker.* 1847–1912, Irish novelist, author of *Dracula* (1897)

Stokowski Leopold 1887–1977, US conductor, born in Britain. He did much to popularize classical music with orchestral transcriptions and film appearances, esp in *Fantasia* (1940)

stole a long narrow scarf worn by various officiating clergymen

Stolypin Petr Arkadievich 1863–1911, Russian conservative statesman: prime minister (1906–11). He instituted agrarian reforms but was ruthless in suppressing rebellion: assassinated

stoma 1 *Botany* an epidermal pore, present in large numbers in plant leaves, that controls the passage of gases into and out of a plant **2** *Zoology, anatomy* a mouth or mouthlike part **3** *Surgery* an artificial opening made in a tubular organ, esp the colon or ileum

stomach 1 (in vertebrates) the enlarged muscular saclike part of the alimentary canal in which food is stored until it has been partially digested and rendered into chyme **2** the corresponding digestive organ in invertebrates

stomachache pain in the stomach or abdominal region, as from acute indigestion

stomach pump *Med* a suction device for removing stomach contents by a tube inserted through the mouth

stone 1 the hard compact nonmetallic material of which rocks are made **2** a small lump of rock; pebble **3** the woody central part of such fruits as the peach and plum, that contains the seed; endocarp **4** any similar hard part of a fruit, such as the stony seed of a date **5** *Brit* a unit of weight, equal to 14 pounds or 6.350 kilograms **6** the rounded heavy mass of granite or iron used in the game of curling **7** *Pathol* a nontechnical name for **calculus 8** *Rare* (in certain games) a piece or man **9** any of various dull grey colours **10** made of stoneware

Stone 1 Oliver born 1946, US film director and screenwriter: his films include *Platoon* (1986), *Born on the Fourth of July* (1989), *JFK* (1991), *Nixon* (1995), and *Alexander* (2004) **2** Sharon born 1958, US film actress: her films include *Basic Instinct* (1991), *Casino* (1995), and *Cold Creek Manor* (2003)

Stone Age a period in human culture identified by the use of stone implements and usually divided into the Palaeolithic, Mesolithic, and Neolithic stages

stonechat an Old World songbird, *Saxicola torquata*, having a black plumage with a reddish-brown breast: subfamily *Turdinae* (thrushes)

Stonehenge a prehistoric ruin in S England, in Wiltshire on Salisbury Plain: constructed over the period of roughly 3000–1600 BC; one of the most important megalithic monuments in Europe; believed to have had religious and astronomical purposes

stoneware 1 a hard opaque pottery, fired at a very high temperature **2** made of stoneware

stooge an actor who feeds lines to a comedian or acts as his foil or butt

stool 1 a rootstock or base of a plant, usually a woody plant, from which shoots, etc, are produced **2** a cluster of shoots growing from such a base **3** *Chiefly US* a decoy used in hunting **4** waste matter evacuated from the bowels **5** (in W Africa, esp Ghana) a chief's throne

stool pigeon 1 a living or dummy pigeon used to decoy others **2** an informer for the police; nark

stoop¹ a downward swoop, esp of a bird of prey

stoop² *US and Canadian* a small platform with steps up to it at the entrance to a building

stop 1 a plug or stopper **2** a block, screw, or other device or object that prevents, limits, or terminates the motion of a mechanism or moving part **3** *Fencing* a counterthrust made without a parry in the hope that one's blade will touch before one's opponent's blade **4** *Music* **a** the act of stopping the string, finger hole, etc, of an instrument **b** a set of organ pipes or harpsichord strings that may be allowed to sound as a group by muffling or silencing all other such sets **c** a knob, lever, or handle on an organ, etc, that is operated to allow sets of pipes to sound **d** an analogous device on a harpsichord or other instrument with variable registers, such as an electrophonic instrument **5** the angle between the forehead and muzzle of a dog or cat, regarded as a point in breeding **6** *Nautical* a short length of line or small stuff used as a tie, esp for a furled sail **7** *Photog* **a** a setting of the aperture of a camera lens, calibrated to the corresponding f-number **b** another name for **diaphragm 8** a block or carving used to complete the end of a moulding **9** *Bridge* a protecting card or winner in a suit in which one's opponents are strong

stopbank *NZ* an embankment to prevent flooding

Stopes Marie Carmichael 1880–1958, English pioneer of birth control, who established the first birth-control clinic in Britain (1921)

Stoppard Sir Tom, original name *Thomas Strausser* born 1937, British playwright, born in Czechoslovakia: his works include *Rosencrantz and Guildenstern are Dead* (1967),

Travesties (1974), *Hapgood* (1988), *The Invention of Love* (1997), and the trilogy *The Coast of Utopia* (2002)

storage 1 a charge made for storing 2 *Computing* **a** the act or process of storing information in a computer memory or on a magnetic tape, disk, etc. **b** (*as modifier*): *a storage device*

storage device a piece of computer equipment, such as a magnetic tape, disk, etc, in or on which data and instructions can be stored, usually in binary form

storage heater an electric device capable of accumulating and radiating heat generated by off-peak electricity

store 1 an establishment for the retail sale of goods and services 2 short for **department store** 3 a storage place such as a warehouse or depository 4 *Computing, chiefly Brit* another name for **memory** 5 a pig that has not yet been weaned and weighs less than 40 kg

storey *or US* **story** 1 a floor or level of a building 2 a set of rooms on one level

Storey David (Malcolm). born 1933, British novelist and dramatist. His best-known works include the novels *This Sporting Life* (1960) and *A Serious Man* (1998) and the plays *In Celebration* (1969), *Home* (1970), and *Stages* (1992)

stork 1 any large wading bird of the family Ciconiidae, chiefly of warm regions of the Old World, having very long legs and a long stout pointed bill, and typically having a white-and-black plumage: order Ciconiiformes 2 a variety of domestic fancy pigeon resembling the fairy swallow

storm 1 **a** a violent weather condition of strong winds, rain, hail, thunder, lightning, blowing sand, snow, etc. **b** (*as modifier*): *storm signal* 2 *Meteorol* a violent gale of force 10 on the Beaufort scale reaching speeds of 55 to 63 mph

storm centre the centre of a cyclonic storm, etc, where pressure is lowest

Stormont a suburb of Belfast: site of Parliament House (1928–30), formerly the seat of the parliament of Northern Ireland (1922–72) and since 1998 of the Northern Ireland assembly, and Stormont Castle, formerly the residence of the prime minister of Northern Ireland and since 1998 the office of the province's first minister

storm trooper *History* a member of the Nazi *Sturmabteilung* (SA)

Stornoway a port in NW Scotland, on the E coast of Lewis in the Outer Hebrides, administrative centre of the Western Isles. Pop: 5602 (2001)

story 1 a narration of a chain of events told or written in prose or verse 2 a piece of fiction, briefer and usually less detailed than a novel 3 the plot of a book, film, etc.

Stoss Viet ?1445–1533, German Gothic sculptor and woodcarver. His masterpiece is the high altar in the Church of St Mary, Cracow (1477–89)

stoup *or* **stoop** 1 a small basin for holy water 2 *Scot and northern English, dialect* a bucket or drinking vessel

Stour 1 a river in S England, in Kent, rising in the Weald and flowing N to the North Sea: separates the Isle of Thanet from the mainland 2 any of several smaller rivers in England

Stourbridge an industrial town in W central England, in Dudley unitary authority, West Midlands. Pop: 55 480 (2001)

stout strong porter highly flavoured with malt

Stout Sir Robert 1844–1930, New Zealand statesman, born in Scotland: prime minister of New Zealand (1884–87)

stove any heating apparatus, such as a kiln

stovepipe a pipe that serves as a flue to a stove

Stow John 1525–1605, English antiquary, noted for his *Survey of London and Westminster* (1598; 1603)

Stowe Harriet Elizabeth Beecher 1811–96, US writer, whose bestselling novel *Uncle Tom's Cabin* (1852) contributed to the antislavery cause

Strabane a district of W Northern Ireland, in Co. Tyrone. Pop: 38 565 (2003 est). Area: 862 sq km (333 sq miles)

strabismus abnormal alignment of one or both eyes, characterized by a turning inwards or outwards from the nose thus preventing parallel vision: caused by paralysis of an eye muscle, etc.

Strabo ?63 BC–?23 AD, Greek geographer and historian, noted for his *Geographica*

Strachey (Giles) Lytton 1880–1932, English biographer and critic, best known for *Eminent Victorians* (1918) and *Queen Victoria* (1921)

straddle 1 *Athletics* a high-jumping technique in which the body is parallel with the bar and the legs straddle it at the highest point of the jump 2 (in poker) the stake put up after the ante in poker by the second player after the dealer 3 *Irish* a wooden frame placed on a horse's back to which panniers are attached

Stradivari Antonio ?1644–1737, Italian violin, viola, and cello maker

Stradivarius any of a number of violins manufactured by Antonio Stradivari (?1644–1737), Italian violin, viola, and cello maker, or his family

Strafford Thomas Wentworth, Earl of. 1593–1641, English statesman. As lord deputy of Ireland (1632–39) and a chief adviser to Charles I, he was a leading proponent of the king's absolutist rule. He was impeached by Parliament and executed

straight 1 (esp of an alcoholic drink) undiluted; neat 2 (of a play, acting style, etc) straightforward or serious 3 US sold at a fixed unit price irrespective of the quantity sold 4 *Boxing* (of a blow) delivered with an unbent arm 5 (of the cylinders of an internal-combustion engine) in line, rather than in a V-formation or in some other arrangement 6 a slang word for **heterosexual** 7 *Slang* not using narcotics; not addicted 8 *Brit* a straight part of a racetrack 9 *Poker* **a** five cards that are in sequence irrespective of suit **b** a hand containing such a sequence **c** (*as modifier*): *a straight flush* 10 *Slang* a cigarette containing only tobacco, without marijuana, etc.

straight man a subsidiary actor who acts as stooge to a comedian

strain[1] 1 *Music* a theme, melody, or tune 2 a feeling of tension and tiredness resulting from overwork, worry, etc.; stress 3 a particular style or recurring theme in speech or writing 4 *Physics* the change in dimension of a body under load expressed as the ratio of the total deflection or change in dimension to the original unloaded dimension. It may be a ratio of lengths, areas, or volumes

strain[2] 1 a group of organisms within a species or variety, distinguished by one or more minor characteristics **2** a variety of bacterium or fungus, esp one used for a culture

strainer 1 a gauze or simple filter used to strain liquids **2** *Austral and NZ* a self-locking device or a tool for tightening fencing wire

strait 1 a a narrow channel of the sea linking two larger areas of sea **b** (*capital as part of a name*) **2** *Archaic* a narrow place or passage *Archaic*

Straits Settlements (formerly) a British crown colony of SE Asia that included Singapore, Penang, Malacca, Labuan, and some smaller islands

Stralsund a port in NE Germany, in Mecklenburg-West Pomerania on a strait of the Baltic: one of the leading towns of the Hanseatic League. Pop: 59 140 (2003 est)

strand¹ *Chiefly poetic* **1** a shore or beach **2** a foreign country

strand² **1** a set of or one of the individual fibres or threads of string, wire, etc, that form a rope, cable, etc. **2** a single length of string, hair, wool, wire, etc.

Strand the a street in W central London, parallel to the Thames: famous for its hotels and theatres

strange *Physics* **a** denoting a particular flavour of quark **b** denoting or relating to a hypothetical form of matter composed of such quarks

stranger *Law* a person who is neither party nor privy to a transaction

stranglehold a wrestling hold in which a wrestler's arms are pressed against his opponent's windpipe

Stranraer a market town in SW Scotland, in W Dumfries and Galloway: fishing port with a ferry service to Northern Ireland. Pop: 10 851 (2001)

strap a loop of leather, rubber, etc, suspended from the roof in a bus or train for standing passengers to hold on to **2** a razor strop

Strasbourg a city in NE France, on the Rhine: the chief French inland port; under German rule (1870–1918); university (1567); seat of the Council of Europe and the European Parliament. Pop: 264 115 (1999)

Stratford-on-Avon *or* **Stratford-upon-Avon** a market town in central England, in SW Warwickshire on the River Avon: the birthplace and burial place of William Shakespeare and home of the Royal Shakespeare Company; tourist centre. Pop: 22 187 (2001)

strath *Scot* a broad flat river valley

Strathclyde Region a former local government region in W Scotland: formed in 1975 from Glasgow, Renfrewshire, Lanarkshire, Buteshire, Dunbartonshire, and parts of Argyllshire, Ayrshire, and Stirlingshire; replaced in 1996 by the council areas of Glasgow, Renfrewshire, East Renfrewshire, Inverclyde, North Lanarkshire, South Lanarkshire, Argyll and Bute, East Dunbartonshire, West Dunbartonshire, North Ayrshire, South Ayrshire, and East Ayrshire

strathspey 1 a Scottish dance with gliding steps, slower than a reel **2** a piece of music in four-four time composed for this dance

stratocumulus *Meteorol* a uniform stretch of cloud containing dark grey globular masses

stratosphere the atmospheric layer lying between the troposphere and the mesosphere, in which temperature generally increases with height

stratum 1 any of the distinct layers into which sedimentary rocks are divided **2** *Biology* a single layer of tissue or cells **3** a layer of ocean or atmosphere either naturally or arbitrarily demarcated

stratus a grey layer cloud

Straus Oscar 1870–1954, French composer, born in Austria, noted for such operettas as *Waltz Dream* (1907) and *The Chocolate Soldier* (1908)

Strauss 1 David Friedrich 1808–74, German Protestant theologian: in his *Life of Jesus* (1835–36) he treated the supernatural elements of the story as myth **2** Johann 1804–49, Austrian composer, noted for his waltzes **3** his son, Johann, called the *Waltz King*. 1825–99, Austrian composer, whose works include *The Blue Danube Waltz* (1867) and the operetta *Die Fledermaus* (1874) **4** Richard 1864–1949, German composer, noted esp for his symphonic poems, including *Don Juan* (1889) and *Till Eulenspiegel* (1895), his operas, such as *Elektra* (1909) and *Der Rosenkavalier* (1911), and his *Four Last Songs* (1948)

Stravinsky Igor Fyodorovich 1882–1971, US composer, born in Russia. He created ballet scores, such as *The Firebird* (1910), *Petrushka* (1911), and *The Rite of Spring* (1913), for Diaghilev. These were followed by neoclassical works, including *Oedipus Rex* (1927) and the *Symphony of Psalms* (1930). The 1950s saw him reconciled to serial techniques, which he employed in such works as the *Canticum Sacrum* (1955), the ballet *Agon* (1957), and *Requiem Canticles* (1966)

straw 1 stalks of threshed grain, esp of wheat, rye, oats, or barley, used in plaiting hats, baskets, etc, or as fodder **b** (*as modifier*): *a straw hat* **2** a single dry or ripened stalk, esp of a grass **3** a pale yellow colour

Straw Jack, full name *John Whitaker Straw*. born 1946, British Labour politician; Home Secretary (1997–2001); Foreign Secretary from 2001

strawberry 1 a any of various low-growing rosaceous plants of the genus *Fragaria*, such as *F. vesca* (**wild strawberry**) and *F. ananassa* (**garden strawberry**), which have white flowers and red edible fruits and spread by runners **b** (*as modifier*): *a strawberry patch* **2** barren strawberry a related Eurasian plant, *Potentilla sterilis*, that does not produce edible fruit **3** a purplish-red colour **4** another name for **strawberry mark**

strawberry mark a soft vascular red birthmark

straw poll *or chiefly US, Canadian, and NZ* **vote** an unofficial poll or vote taken to determine the opinion of a group or the public on some issue

Strawson Sir Peter (Frederick). born 1919, British philosopher. His early work deals with the relationship between language and logic, his later work with metaphysics. His books include *The Bounds of Sense* (1966) and *Freedom and Resentment* (1974)

strawweight a a professional boxer weighing not more than 47.6 kg (105 pounds) **b** (*as modifier*): *the strawweight title*

stray a a domestic animal, fowl, etc, that has wandered away from its place of keeping and is lost **b** (*as modifier*): *stray dogs*

Strayhorn Billy, full name *William Strayhorn*. 1915–67, US jazz composer and pianist, noted esp for his association (1939–67) with Duke Ellington

streak 1 a (of lightning) a sudden flash **b** (*as modifier*):

streak lightning **2** *Mineralogy* the powdery mark made by a mineral when rubbed on a hard or rough surface: its colour is an important distinguishing characteristic

stream 1 a small river; brook **2** *Brit* any of several parallel classes of schoolchildren, or divisions of children within a class, grouped together because of similar ability

streamer a stream of light, esp one appearing in some forms of the aurora

streamline 1 a contour on a body that offers the minimum resistance to a gas or liquid flowing around it **2** an imaginary line in a fluid such that the tangent at any point indicates the direction of the velocity of a particle of the fluid at that point

Streep Meryl, original name *Mary Louise Streep*. born 1949, US actress. Her films include *The Deerhunter* (1978), *Kramer vs Kramer* (1979), *The French Lieutenant's Woman* (1981), *Sophie's Choice* (1982), *Out of Africa* (1986), *Dancing at Lughnasa* (1999), and *The Hours* (2002)

street 1 a a public road that is usually lined with buildings, esp in a town **b** *(as modifier)*: *a street directory* **2** the buildings lining a street **3** the part of the road between the pavements, used by vehicles

streetcar *US and Canadian* an electrically driven public transport vehicle that runs on rails let into the surface of the road, power usually being taken from an overhead wire

street value the monetary worth of a commodity, usually an illicit commodity such as a drug, considered as the price it would fetch when sold to the ultimate user

Streicher Julius 1885–1946, German Nazi journalist and politician, who spread anti-Semitic propaganda as editor of *Der Stürmer* (1923–45). He was hanged as a war criminal

Streisand Barbra born 1942, US singer, actress, and film director: the films she has acted in include *Funny Girl* (1968) and *A Star is Born* (1976); her films as actress and director include *Yentl* (1983), *Prince of Tides* (1990), and *The Mirror has Two Faces* (1996)

streptomycin an antibiotic obtained from the bacterium *Streptomyces griseus*: used in the treatment of tuberculosis and Gram-negative bacterial infections. Formula: $C_{21}H_{39}N_7O_{12}$

Stresemann Gustav 1878–1929, German statesman; chancellor (1923) and foreign minister (1923–29) of the Weimar Republic. He gained (1926) Germany's admission to the League of Nations and shared the Nobel peace prize (1926) with Aristide Briand

stress 1 such emphasis as part of a regular rhythmic beat in music or poetry **2** *Physics* **a** a force or a system of forces producing deformation or strain **b** the force acting per unit area

stretch 1 *Horse racing* the section or sections of a racecourse that are straight, esp the final straight section leading to the finishing line **2** *Slang* a term of imprisonment

stretcher 1 a device for transporting the ill, wounded, or dead, consisting of a frame covered by canvas or other material **2** the wooden frame on which canvas is stretched and fixed for oil painting **3** *Rowing* a fixed board across a boat on which an oarsman braces his feet

stretcher-bearer a person who helps to carry a stretcher, esp in wartime

Stretford an industrial town in NW England, in Trafford unitary authority, Greater Manchester. Pop: 42 103 (2001)

stria 1 *Geology* any of the parallel scratches or grooves on the surface of a rock caused by abrasion resulting from the passage of a glacier, motion on a fault surface, etc. **2** fine ridges and grooves on the surface of a crystal caused by irregular growth **3** *Biology, anatomy* a narrow band of colour or a ridge, groove, or similar linear mark, usually occurring in a parallel series **4** *Architect* a narrow channel, such as a flute on the shaft of a column

striation 1 an arrangement or pattern of striae **2** another word for **stria** (sense 1)

stricken 1 laid low, as by disease or sickness **2** *Archaic* wounded or injured

strict 1 *Logic, maths* of a relation **a** applying more narrowly than some other relation often given the same name, as *strict inclusion*, which holds only between pairs of sets that are distinct, while *simple inclusion* permits the case in which they are identical **b** distinguished from a relation of the same name that is not the subject of formal study **2** *Botany, rare* very straight, narrow, and upright

stricture *Pathol* an abnormal constriction of a tubular organ, structure, or part

stride 1 an act of forward movement by an animal, completed when the legs have returned to their initial relative positions **2** *Rowing* the distance covered between strokes **3** *Jazz* a piano style characterized by single bass notes on the first and third beats and chords on the second and fourth

strike 1 *Baseball* a pitched ball judged good but missed or not swung at, three of which cause a batter to be out **2** *Tenpin bowling* **a** the act or an instance of knocking down all the pins with the first bowl of a single frame **b** the score thus made **3** the horizontal direction of a fault, rock stratum, etc, which is perpendicular to the direction of the dip **4** *Angling* the act or an instance of striking **5** the number of coins or medals made at one time **6** **take strike** *Cricket* (of a batsman) to prepare to play a ball delivered by the bowler

striker 1 any part in a mechanical device that strikes something, such as the firing pin of a gun **2** *Soccer, informal* an attacking player, esp one who generally positions himself near his opponent's goal in the hope of scoring **3** *Cricket* the batsman who is about to play a ball **4 a** a person who harpoons whales or fish **b** the harpoon itself

Strimmer *Trademark* an electrical tool for trimming the edges of lawns

Strindberg August 1849–1912, Swedish dramatist and novelist, whose plays include *The Father* (1887), *Miss Julie* (1888), and *The Ghost Sonata* (1907)

string 1 a thin length of cord, twine, fibre, or similar material used for tying, hanging, binding, etc. **2** a tough fibre or cord in a plant **3** *Music* a tightly stretched wire, cord, etc, found on stringed instruments, such as the violin, guitar, and piano **4** short for **bowstring 5** *Architect* short for **stringer** (sense 1) **6** *Maths, linguistics* a sequence of symbols or words **7** *Physics* a one-dimensional entity postulated to be a fundamental component of matter in some theories of particle physics **8** a group of characters that can be treated as a unit by a computer program **9 a** violins, violas, cellos, and double basses collectively **b** the section of a symphony orchestra constituted by such instruments **10** composed of stringlike strands woven in a large mesh

string bean any of several bean plants, such as the scarlet runner, cultivated for their edible unripe pods

stringed (of musical instruments) having or provided with strings

stringer 1 *Architect* a long horizontal beam that is used for structural purposes **2** *Nautical* a longitudinal structural brace for strengthening the hull of a vessel

string quartet *Music* 1 an instrumental ensemble consisting of two violins, one viola, and one cello **2** a piece of music written for such a group, usually having the form and commonest features of a sonata

stringy-bark *Austral* any of several eucalyptus trees having a fibrous bark

strip 1 short for **airstrip** 2 *Philately* a horizontal or vertical row of three or more unseparated postage stamps **3** NZ short for **dosing strip**

strip lighting electric lighting by means of long glass tubes that are fluorescent lamps or that contain long filaments

stripper a device or substance for removing paint, varnish, etc.

strip-search a search that involves stripping a person naked

strobe lighting 1 a high-intensity flashing beam of light produced by rapid electrical discharges in a tube or by a perforated disc rotating in front of an intense light source: used in discotheques, etc. **2** the use of or the apparatus for producing such light

stroboscope 1 an instrument producing a flashing light, the frequency of which can be synchronized with some multiple of the frequency of rotation, vibration, or operation of an object, etc, making it appear stationary. It is used to determine speeds of rotation or vibration, or to adjust objects or parts **2** a similar device synchronized with the opening of the shutter of a camera so that a series of still photographs can be taken of a moving object

Stroessner Alfredo born 1912, Paraguayan soldier and politician; president (1954–89): deposed in a military coup

stroke 1 *Pathol* apoplexy; rupture of a blood vessel in the brain resulting in loss of consciousness, often followed by paralysis, or embolism or thrombosis affecting a cerebral vessel **2** a pulsation, esp of the heart **3** *Sport* the act or manner of striking the ball with a racket, club, bat, etc. **4** any one of the repeated movements used by a swimmer to propel himself through the water **5** a manner of swimming, esp one of several named styles such as the crawl or butterfly **6 a** any one of a series of linear movements of a reciprocating part, such as a piston **b** the distance travelled by such a part from one end of its movement to the other **7** a single pull on an oar or oars in rowing **8** manner or style of rowing **9** the oarsman who sits nearest the stern of a shell, facing the cox, and sets the rate of striking for the rest of the crew

▷www.neuro.wustl.edu/stroke

▷http://209.107.44.93/NationalStroke/default.htm

Stromboli an island in the Tyrrhenian Sea, in the Lipari Islands off the N coast of Sicily: famous for its active volcano, 927 m (3040 ft) high

strong 1 (of a colour) having a high degree of saturation or purity; being less saturated than a vivid colour but more so than a moderate colour; produced by a concentrated quantity of colouring agent **2** (of a wind, current, etc) moving fast **3** (of a syllable) accented or stressed **4** (of certain acids and bases) producing high concentrations of hydrogen or hydroxide ions in aqueous solution

strontium a soft silvery-white element of the alkaline earth group of metals, occurring chiefly in celestite and strontianite. Its compounds burn with a crimson flame and are used in fireworks. The radioisotope **strontium-90**, with a half-life of 28.1 years, is used in nuclear power sources and is a hazardous nuclear fall-out product. Symbol: Sr; atomic no.: 38; atomic wt.: 87.62; valency: 2; relative density: 2.54; melting pt.: 769°C; boiling pt.: 1384°C

strop 1 a leather strap or an abrasive strip for sharpening razors **2** a rope or metal band around a block or deadeye for support

structural 1 of or relating to the structure and deformation of rocks and other features of the earth's crust **2** of or relating to the structure of organisms; morphological **3** *Chem* of, concerned with, caused by, or involving the arrangement of atoms in molecules

structuralism an approach to anthropology and other social sciences and to literature that interprets and analyses its material in terms of oppositions, contrasts, and hierarchical structures, esp as they might reflect universal mental characteristics or organizing principles

structure 1 *Biology* morphology; form **2** *Chem* the arrangement of atoms in a molecule of a chemical compound **3** *Geology* the way in which a mineral, rock, rock mass or stratum, etc, is made up of its component parts

struggle **the struggle** *S African* the radical and armed opposition to apartheid, especially by the military wings of the ANC and the PAC

Struma a river in S Europe, rising in SW Bulgaria near Sofia and flowing generally southeast through Greece to the Aegean. Length: 362 km (225 miles)

strung a (of a piano, etc) provided with strings, esp of a specified kind or in a specified manner **b** (*in combination*): *gut-strung*

Struve Otto 1897–1963, US astronomer, born in Russia, noted for his work in stellar spectroscopy and his discovery (1937) of interstellar hydrogen

strychnine a white crystalline very poisonous alkaloid, obtained from the plant nux vomica: formerly used in small quantities as a stimulant of the central nervous system and the appetite. Formula: $C_{21}H_{22}O_2N_2$

Stuart 1 the royal house that ruled in Scotland from 1371 to 1714 and in England from 1603 to 1714 **2 Charles Edward**, called *the Young Pretender* or *Bonnie Prince Charlie*. 1720–88, pretender to the British throne. He led the

Jacobite Rebellion (1745–46) in an attempt to re-establish the Stuart succession **3** his father, **James Francis Edward**, called *the Old Pretender*. 1688–1766, pretender to the British throne; son of James II (James VII of Scotland) and his second wife, Mary of Modena. He made two unsuccessful attempts to realize his claim to the throne (1708; 1715)

▷www.royal.gov.uk/output/Page74.asp

▷www.wsu.edu:8080/~dee/Greece/Sparta.htm

stub the stump of a tree or plant

Stubbs George 1724–1806, English painter, noted esp for his pictures of horses

stubby *Austral, slang* a small bottle of beer

stucco 1 a weather-resistant mixture of dehydrated lime, powdered marble, and glue, used in decorative mouldings on buildings **2** decorative work moulded in stucco

stud¹ 1 a large-headed nail or other projection protruding from a surface, usually as decoration **2** a headless bolt that is threaded at both ends, the centre portion being unthreaded **3** any short projection on a machine, such as the metal cylinder that forms a journal for the gears on a screw-cutting lathe **4** the crossbar in the centre of a link of a heavy chain

stud² 1 a group of pedigree animals, esp horses, kept for breeding purposes **2** any male animal kept principally for breeding purposes, esp a stallion **3** a farm or stable where a stud is kept **4** the state or condition of being kept for breeding purposes

student 1 a a person following a course of study, as in a school, college, university, etc. **b** (*as modifier*): *student teacher* **2** a person who makes a thorough study of a subject

studio 1 a room in which an artist, photographer, or musician works **2** a room used to record television or radio programmes, make films, etc. **3** the premises of a radio, television, or film company

study 1 a drawing, sculpture, etc, executed for practice or in preparation for another work **2** a musical composition intended to develop one aspect of performing technique **3** *Theatre* a person who memorizes a part in the manner specified

stump 1 the base part of a tree trunk left standing after the tree has been felled or has fallen **2** *Cricket* any of three upright wooden sticks that, with two bails laid across them, form a wicket (the **stumps**) **3** a short sharply-pointed stick of cork or rolled paper or leather, used in drawing and shading **4** **on the stump** *Chiefly US and Canadian* engaged in campaigning, esp by political speech-making

stunt¹ a person, animal, or plant that has been stunted

stunt² an acrobatic or dangerous piece of action in a film or television programme

stupor a state of unconsciousness

sturdy *Vet science* another name for **staggers** (sense 2)

sturgeon any primitive bony fish of the family *Acipenseridae*, of temperate waters of the N hemisphere, having an elongated snout and rows of spines along the body: valued as a source of caviar and isinglass

Sturt Charles 1795–1869, English explorer, who led three expeditions (1828–29; 1829; 1844–45) into the Australian interior, discovering the Darling River (1828)

Stuttgart an industrial city in W Germany, capital of Baden-Württemberg state, on the River Neckar: developed around a stud farm (*Stuotgarten*) of the Counts of Württemberg. Pop: 589 161 (2003 est)

Stuyvesant Peter ?1610–72, Dutch colonial administrator of New Netherland (later New York) (1646–64)

stye *or* **sty** inflammation of a sebaceous gland of the eyelid, usually caused by bacteria

Stygian 1 of or relating to the river Styx **2** *Chiefly literary* **a** dark, gloomy, or hellish **b** completely inviolable, as a vow sworn by the river Styx

style 1 a distinctive, formal, or characteristic manner of expression in words, music, painting, etc. **2** *Botany* the stalk of a carpel, bearing the stigma **3** *Zoology* a slender pointed structure, such as the piercing mouthparts of certain insects **4** a method of expressing or calculating dates **5** another word for **stylus** (sense 1)

stylist a designer whose job is to coordinate the style of products, advertising material, etc.

stylus 1 a pointed instrument for engraving, drawing, or writing **2** a tool used in ancient times for writing on wax tablets, which was pointed at one end and blunt at the other for erasing mistakes **3** a device attached to the cartridge in the pick-up arm of a record player that rests in the groove in the record, transmitting the vibrations to the sensing device in the cartridge. It consists of or is tipped with a hard material, such as diamond or sapphire

stymie *or* **stymy** *Golf* (formerly) a situation on the green in which an opponent's ball is blocking the line between the hole and the ball about to be played: an obstructing ball may now be lifted and replaced by a marker

styptic 1 contracting the blood vessels or tissues **2** a styptic drug

Styria a mountainous state of SE Austria: rich mineral resources. Capital: Graz. Pop: 1 190 574 (2003 est). Area: 16 384 sq km (6326 sq miles)

Suakin a port in the NE Sudan, on the Red Sea: formerly the chief port of the African Red Sea; now obstructed by a coral reef. Pop: 5511 (latest est)

subaltern *Logic* **a** the relation of one proposition to another when the first is implied by the second, esp the relation of a particular to a universal proposition **b** (*as modifier*): *a subaltern relation*

subaqua of or relating to underwater sport

subatomic 1 of, relating to, or being a particle making up an atom or a process occurring within atoms **2** having dimensions smaller than atomic dimensions

subconscious 1 acting or existing without one's awareness **2** *Psychoanal* that part of the mind which is on the fringe of consciousness and contains material of which it is possible to become aware by redirecting attention

subcontinent a large land mass that is a distinct part of a continent, such as India is of Asia

subcontract a subordinate contract under which the supply of materials, services, or labour is let out to someone other than a party to the main contract

subcutaneous *Med* situated, used, or introduced beneath the skin

subhuman of, relating to, or designating animals that

are below man (*Homo sapiens*) in evolutionary development

subject 1 any branch of learning considered as a course of study **2** a person who lives under the rule of a monarch, government, etc. **3** an object, figure, scene, etc, as selected by an artist or photographer for representation **4** *Philosophy* **a** that which thinks or feels as opposed to the object of thinking and feeling; the self or the mind **b** a substance as opposed to its attributes **5** *Music* a melodic or thematic phrase used as the principal motif of a fugue, the basis from which the musical material is derived in a sonata-form movement, or the recurrent figure in a rondo **6** *Logic* **a** the term of a categorial statement of which something is predicated **b** the reference or denotation of the subject term of a statement. The subject of *John is tall* is not the name *John*, but John himself **7** being under the power or sovereignty of a ruler, government, etc.

subjective 1 existing only as perceived and not as a thing in itself **2** *Med* (of a symptom, condition, etc) experienced only by the patient and incapable of being recognized or studied by anyone else

sub judice before a court of law or a judge; under judicial consideration

sublimate *Chem* the material obtained when a substance is sublimed

subliminal 1 resulting from processes of which the individual is not aware **2** (of stimuli) less than the minimum intensity or duration required to elicit a response

submersible *or* **submergible 1** a vessel designed to operate under water for short periods **2** a submarine taking one or more men that is designed and equipped to carry out work in deep water below the levels at which divers can work

submission 1 *Law* **a** an agreement by the parties to a dispute to refer the matter to arbitration **b** the instrument referring a disputed matter to arbitration **2** (in wrestling) the act of causing such pain to one's opponent that he submits

subnormal having a low intelligence, esp having an IQ of less than 70

Subotica a town in NE Serbia and Montenegro, in Serbia near the border with Hungary: agricultural and industrial centre. Pop: 107 139 (2002)

subplot a subordinate or auxiliary plot in a novel, play, film, etc.

subpoena a writ issued by a court of justice requiring a person to appear before the court at a specified time

subroutine a section of a computer program that is stored only once but can be used when required at several different points in the program, thus saving space

sub-Saharan in, of, or relating to Africa south of the Sahara desert

subscription 1 a the advance purchase of tickets for a series of concerts, operas, etc. **b** (*as modifier*): *a subscription concert* **2** acceptance of a fixed body of articles of faith, doctrines, or principles laid down as universally binding upon all the members of a Church **3** *Med* that part of a written prescription directing the pharmacist how to mix and prepare the ingredients: rarely seen today as modern drugs are mostly prepackaged by the manufac-

turers **4** an advance order for a new product

subset *Maths* **a** a set the members of which are all members of some given class: *A is a subset of B* is usually written $A \subseteq B$ **b** **proper subset** one that is strictly contained within a larger class and excludes some of its members. Symbol: $A \subset B$

subsidiarity 1 (in the Roman Catholic Church) a principle of social doctrine that all social bodies exist for the sake of the individual so that what individuals are able to do, society should not take over, and what small societies can do, larger societies should not take over **2** (in political systems) the principle of devolving decisions to the lowest practical level

subsidy 1 a financial aid supplied by a government, as to industry, for reasons of public welfare, the balance of payments, etc. **2** *English history* a financial grant made originally for special purposes by Parliament to the Crown **3** any monetary contribution, grant, or aid

subsoil a the layer of soil beneath the surface soil and overlying the bedrock **b** (*as modifier*): *a subsoil plough*

subsonic being, having, or travelling at a velocity below that of sound

substance 1 material density **2** *Philosophy* **a** the supposed immaterial substratum that can receive modifications and in which attributes and accidents inhere **b** a thing considered as a continuing whole that survives the changeability of its properties **3** *Christian Science* that which is eternal

substantial *Philosophy* of or relating to substance rather than to attributes, accidents, or modifications

substantive relating to the essential legal principles administered by the courts, as opposed to practice and procedure

substrate 1 *Biochem* the substance upon which an enzyme acts **2** *Electronics* the semiconductor base on which other material is deposited, esp in the construction of integrated circuits

subtenant a person who rents or leases property from a tenant

subtext 1 an underlying theme in a piece of writing **2** a message which is not stated directly but can be inferred

subtitle 1 an additional subordinate title given to a literary or other work **2** *Films* **a** a written translation superimposed on a film that has foreign dialogue **b** explanatory text on a silent film

suburb a residential district situated on the outskirts of a city or town

suburban 1 of, relating to, situated in, or inhabiting a suburb or the suburbs **2** characteristic of or typifying a suburb or the suburbs

suburbia suburbs or the people living in them considered as an identifiable community or class in society

subvention a grant, aid, or subsidy, as from a government to an educational institution

subversion 1 the act or an instance of subverting or overthrowing a legally constituted government, institution, etc. **2** the state of being subverted; destruction or ruin **3** something that brings about an overthrow

subversive 1 liable to subvert or overthrow a government, legally constituted institution, etc. **2** a person engaged in subversive activities, etc.

subway 1 *Brit* an underground passage or tunnel

enabling pedestrians to cross a road, railway, etc. **2** an underground passage or tunnel for traffic, electric power supplies, etc. **3** *Chiefly US and Canadian* an underground railway

succession *Ecology* the sum of the changes in the composition of a community that occur during its development towards a stable climax community

successor *Logic* the element related to a given element by a serial ordering, esp the natural number next larger to a given one. The successor of n is $n + 1$, usually written Sn or n'

succubus 1 a female demon fabled to have sexual intercourse with sleeping men **2** any evil demon

succulent 1 (of plants) having thick fleshy leaves or stems **2** a plant that is able to exist in arid or salty conditions by using water stored in its fleshy tissues

sucker 1 a young animal that is not yet weaned, esp a suckling pig **2** *Zoology* an organ that is specialized for sucking or adhering **3** a cup-shaped device, generally made of rubber, that may be attached to articles allowing them to adhere to a surface by suction **4** *Botany* **a** a strong shoot that arises in a mature plant from a root, rhizome, or the base of the main stem **b** a short branch of a parasitic plant that absorbs nutrients from the host **5** a pipe or tube through which a fluid is drawn by suction **6** any small mainly North American cyprinoid fish of the family *Catostomidae*, having toothless jaws and a large sucking mouth **7** any of certain fishes that have sucking discs, esp the clingfish or sea snail **8** a piston in a suction pump or the valve in such a piston

suckling an infant or young animal that is still taking milk from the mother

Suckling Sir John 1609–42, English Cavalier poet and dramatist

Sucre¹ Antonio José de 1795–1830, South American liberator, born in Venezuela, who assisted Bolivar in the colonial revolt against Spain; first president of Bolivia (1826–28)

Sucre² the legal capital of Bolivia, in the south central part of the country in the E Andes: university (1624). Pop: 231 000 (2005 est)

suction 1 the force or condition produced by a pressure difference, as the force holding a suction cap onto a surface **2** the act or process of producing such a force or condition

Sudan 1 a republic in NE Africa, on the Red Sea: the largest country in Africa; conquered by Mehemet Ali of Egypt (1820–22) and made an Anglo-Egyptian condominium in 1899 after joint forces defeated the Mahdist revolt; became a republic in 1956; civil war has been waged between separatists, in the mainly Christian south, and the government since independence, apart from a period of peace (1972–83). It consists mainly of a plateau, with the Nubian Desert in the north. Official language: Arabic. Official religion: Muslim; there are large Christian and animist minorities. Currency: Sudanese dinar. Capital: Khartoum. Pop: 34 333 000 (2004 est). Area: 2 505 805 sq km (967 491 sq miles) **2** the a region stretching across Africa south of the Sahara and north of the tropical zone: inhabited chiefly by Negroid tribes rather than Arabs

Sudanese 1 of or relating to the republic of Sudan or its

inhabitants **2** of or relating to the African region of the Sudan or its inhabitants **3** a native or inhabitant of the republic of Sudan **4** a native or inhabitant of the African region of the Sudan

Sudbury a city in central Canada, in Ontario: a major nickel-mining centre. Pop: 103 879 (2001)

Sudetenland a mountainous region of the N Czech Republic: part of Czechoslovakia (1919–38; 1945–93); occupied by Germany (1938–45)

sudorific 1 producing or causing sweating; sudatory **2** a sudorific agent

Sue Eugène original name *Marie-Joseph Sue*. 1804–57, French novelist, whose works, notably *Les mystères de Paris* (1842–43) and *Le juif errant* (1844–45), were among the first to reflect the impact of the industrial revolution on France

suet a hard waxy fat around the kidneys and loins in sheep, cattle, etc, used in cooking and making tallow

Suetonius full name *Gaius Suetonius Tranquillus*. 75–150 AD, Roman biographer and historian, whose chief works were *Concerning Illustrious Men* and *The Lives of the Caesars* (from Julius Caesar to Domitian)

Suez 1 a port in NE Egypt, at the head of the Gulf of Suez at the S end of the Suez Canal: an ancient trading site and a major naval station under the Ottoman Empire; port of departure for pilgrims to Mecca; oil-refining centre. It suffered severely in the Arab-Israeli conflicts of 1967 and 1973. Pop: 513 000 (2005 est) **2 Isthmus of** a strip of land in NE Egypt, between the Mediterranean and the Red Sea: links Africa and Asia and is crossed by the Suez Canal **3 Gulf of** the NW arm of the Red Sea: linked with the Mediterranean by the Suez Canal

Suez Canal a sea-level canal in NE Egypt, crossing the Isthmus of Suez and linking the Mediterranean with the Red Sea: built (1854–69) by de Lesseps with French and Egyptian capital; nationalized in 1956 by the Egyptians. Length: 163 km (101 miles)

sufficient *Logic* (of a condition) assuring the truth of a statement; requiring but not necessarily required by some other state of affairs

Suffolk a county of SE England, on the North Sea: its coast is flat and marshy, indented by broad tidal estuaries. Administrative centre: Ipswich. Pop: 678 100 (2003 est). Area: 3800 sq km (1467 sq miles)

suffragan a (of any bishop of a diocese) subordinate to and assisting his superior archbishop or metropolitan **b** (of any assistant bishop) having the duty of assisting the bishop of the diocese to which he is appointed but having no ordinary jurisdiction in that diocese

suffrage 1 the right to vote, esp in public elections; franchise **2** the exercise of such a right; casting a vote **3** a supporting vote **4** a prayer, esp a short intercessory prayer

suffragette a female advocate of the extension of the franchise to women, esp a militant one, as in Britain at the beginning of the 20th century
▷www.cjbooks.demon.co.uk/suffrage.htm
▷www.san.beck.org/GPJ19-Suffragettes.html

suffragist an advocate of the extension of the franchise, esp to women

sugar 1 a white crystalline sweet carbohydrate, a disaccharide, found in many plants and extracted from

sugar cane and sugar beet: it is used esp as a sweetening agent in food and drinks. Formula: $C_{12}H_{22}O_{11}$ **2** any of a class of simple water-soluble carbohydrates, such as sucrose, lactose, and fructose **3** a slang name for **LSD**
▷www.britishsugar.co.uk
▷www.sugar.org

Sugar Sir Alan **(Michael)**. born 1947, British electronics entrepreneur; chairman of Amstrad from 1968

sugar beet a variety of the plant *Beta vulgaris* that is cultivated for its white roots from which sugar is obtained

sugar cane a coarse perennial grass, *Saccharum officinarum*, of Old World tropical regions, having tall stout canes that yield sugar: widely cultivated in tropical regions

sugar glider a common Australian phalanger, *Petaurus breviceps*, that glides from tree to tree feeding on insects and nectar

Sugar Loaf Mountain a mountain in SE Brazil, in Rio de Janeiro on Guanabara Bay. Height: 390 m (1280 ft)

sugar maple a North American maple tree, *Acer saccharum*, that is grown as a source of sugar, which is extracted from the sap, and for its hard wood

Suger 1081–1151, French ecclesiastic and statesman, who acted as adviser to Louis VI and regent (1147–49) to Louis VII. As abbot of Saint-Denis (1122–51) he influenced the development of Gothic architecture

suggestible easily influenced by ideas provided by other persons

suggestion *Psychol* the process whereby the mere presentation of an idea to a receptive individual leads to the acceptance of that idea

Suharto T. N. J born 1921, Indonesian general and statesman; president (1968–98)

suicide 1 the act or an instance of killing oneself intentionally **2** a person who kills himself intentionally

suit 1 any of the four sets of 13 cards in a pack of playing cards, being spades, hearts, diamonds, and clubs. The cards in each suit are two to ten, jack, queen, and king in the usual order of ascending value, with ace counting as either the highest or lowest according to the game **2** a civil proceeding; lawsuit **3** the act or process of suing in a court of law **4** **follow suit** to play a card of the same suit as the card played immediately before it

suite 1 a number of connected rooms in a hotel forming one living unit **2** *Music* **a** an instrumental composition consisting of several movements in the same key based on or derived from dance rhythms, esp in the baroque period **b** an instrumental composition in several movements less closely connected than a sonata **c** a piece of music containing movements based on or extracted from music already used in an opera, ballet, play, etc.

suitor *Law* a person who brings a suit in a court of law; plaintiff

Sukarno *or* **Soekarno** Achmed 1901–70, Indonesian statesman; first president of the Republic of Indonesia (1945–67)

Sukarnoputri Megawati born 1949, Indonesian politician; president of Indonesia from 2001: daughter of Achmed Sukarno

Sukhumi a port and resort in W Georgia, on the Black Sea: site of an ancient Greek colony. Pop: 134 000 (2005 est)

Sukkoth *or* **Succoth** an eight-day Jewish harvest festival beginning on Tishri 15, which commemorates the period when the Israelites lived in the wilderness

Sulawesi an island in E Indonesia: mountainous and forested, with volcanoes and hot springs. Pop: 14 768 400 (1999 est). Area (including adjacent islands): 229 108 sq km (88 440 sq miles)

Suleiman I, **Soliman**, *or* **Solyman** called *the Magnificent*. ?1495–1566, sultan of the Ottoman Empire (1520–66), whose reign was noted for its military power and cultural achievements

sulky a light two-wheeled vehicle for one person, usually drawn by one horse

Sulla full name *Lucius Cornelius Sulla Felix*. 138–78 BC, Roman general and dictator (82–79). He introduced reforms to strengthen the power of the Senate

sullen *Literary* sluggish; slow

Sullivan 1 Sir Arthur **(Seymour)**. 1842–1900, English composer who wrote operettas, such as *H.M.S. Pinafore* (1878) and *The Mikado* (1885), with W. S. Gilbert as librettist **2** Louis **(Henri)**. 1856–1924, US pioneer of modern architecture: he coined the slogan "form follows function"

Sullom Voe a deep coastal inlet in the Shetland Islands, on the N coast of Mainland. It is used for the storage and transshipment of oil

Sully Maximilien de Béthune , Duc de Sully. 1559–1641, French statesman; minister of Henry IV. He helped restore the finances of France after the Wars of Religion

Sully-Prudhomme René François Armand 1839–1907, French poet: Nobel prize for literature 1901

sulphate 1 any salt or ester of sulphuric acid, such as sodium sulphate, Na_2SO_4, sodium hydrogen sulphate, or diethyl sulphate, $(C_2H_5)_2SO_4$ **2** *Slang* amphetamine sulphate

sulphide a compound of sulphur with a more electropositive element

sulphite any salt or ester of sulphurous acid, containing the ions SO_3^{2-} or HSO_3^- (**hydrogen sulphite**) or the groups $-SO_3$ or $-HSO_3$. The salts are usually soluble crystalline compounds

sulphonamide any of a class of organic compounds that are amides of sulphonic acids containing the group $-SO_2NH_2$ or a group derived from this. An important class of sulphonamides are the sulfa drugs

sulphur *or US* **sulfur a** an allotropic nonmetallic element, occurring free in volcanic regions and in combined state in gypsum, pyrite, and galena. The stable yellow rhombic form converts on heating to monoclinic needles. It is used in the production of sulphuric acid, in the vulcanization of rubber, and in fungicides. Symbol: S; atomic no.: 16; atomic wt.: 32.066; valency: 2, 4, or 6; relative density: 2.07 (rhombic), 1.957 (monoclinic); melting pt.: 115.22°C (rhombic), 119.0°C (monoclinic); boiling pt.: 444.674°C **b** (*as modifier*): *sulphur springs*

sulphur dioxide a colourless soluble pungent gas produced by burning sulphur. It is both an oxidizing and a reducing agent and is used in the manufacture of sulphuric acid, the preservation of a wide range of foodstuffs (**E220**), bleaching, and disinfecting. Formula: SO_2

sulphureous 1 another word for **sulphurous 2** of the

yellow colour of sulphur

sulphuric acid a colourless dense oily corrosive liquid produced by the reaction of sulphur trioxide with water and used in accumulators and in the manufacture of fertilizers, dyes, and explosives. Formula: H_2SO_4

sulphurous 1 of, relating to, or resembling sulphur 2 of or containing sulphur with an oxidation state of 4

sultan 1 the sovereign of a Muslim country, esp of the former Ottoman Empire 2 an arbitrary ruler; despot 3 a small domestic fowl with a white crest and heavily feathered legs and feet: originated in Turkey

sultana a wife, concubine, or female relative of a sultan

sultanate 1 the territory or a country ruled by a sultan 2 the office, rank, or jurisdiction of a sultan

sultry (of weather or climate) oppressively hot and humid

Sulu Archipelago a chain of over 500 islands in the SW Philippines, separating the Sulu Sea from the Celebes Sea: formerly a sultanate, ceded to the Philippines in 1940. Capital: Jolo. Pop: 619 668 (2000). Area: 2686 sq km (1037 sq miles)

Sulu Sea part of the W Pacific between Borneo and the central Philippines

sum¹ 1 a the result of the addition of numbers, quantities, objects, etc. b the cardinality of the union of disjoint sets whose cardinalities are the given numbers 2 one or more columns or rows of numbers to be added, subtracted, multiplied, or divided 3 *Maths* the limit of a series of sums of the first *n* terms of a converging infinite series as *n* tends to infinity

sum² the standard monetary unit of Uzbekistan, divided into 100 tiyin

Sumatra a mountainous island in W Indonesia, in the Greater Sunda Islands, separated from the Malay Peninsula by the Strait of Malacca: Dutch control began in the 16th century; joined Indonesia in 1945. Northern coastal areas, esp Aceh province, suffered devastation as a result of the Indian Ocean tsunami of December 2004. Pop: 24 284 400 (1999 est). Area: 473 606 sq km (182 821 sq miles)

Sumba *or* **Soemba** an island in Indonesia, in the Lesser Sunda Islands, separated from Flores by the **Sumba Strait**: formerly important for sandalwood exports. Pop: 355 073 (1990). Area: 11 153 sq km (4306 sq miles)

Sumbawa *or* **Soembawa** a mountainous island in Indonesia, in the Lesser Sunda Islands, between Lombok and Flores Islands. Pop: 373 000 (1990 est). Area: 14 750 sq km (5695 sq miles)

Sumer the S region of Babylonia; seat of a civilization of city-states that reached its height in the 3rd millennium BC

Sumerian 1 a member of a people who established a civilization in Sumer during the 4th millennium BC 2 the extinct language of this people, of no known relationship to any other language

summary 1 (of legal proceedings) short and free from the complexities and delays of a full trial 2 **summary jurisdiction** the right a court has to adjudicate immediately upon some matter arising during its proceedings

summation 1 the act or process of determining a sum; addition 2 the result of such an act or process 3 *US, law* the concluding statements made by opposing counsel

in a case before a court

summer¹ 1 a the warmest season of the year, between spring and autumn, astronomically from the June solstice to the September equinox in the N hemisphere and at the opposite time of year in the S hemisphere b (*as modifier*): *summer flowers* 2 the period of hot weather associated with the summer

summer² 1 a large horizontal beam or girder, esp one that supports floor joists 2 another name for **lintel** 3 a stone on the top of a column, pier, or wall that supports an arch or lintel

summer school a school, academic course, etc, held during the summer

summer solstice 1 the time at which the sun is at its northernmost point in the sky (southernmost point in the S hemisphere), appearing at noon at its highest altitude above the horizon. It occurs about June 21 (December 22 in the S hemisphere) 2 *Astronomy* the point on the celestial sphere, opposite the **winter solstice**, at which the ecliptic is furthest north from the celestial equator. Right ascension: 6 hours; declination: 23.5°

summing-up a direction regarding the law and a summary of the evidence, given by a judge in his address to the jury before they retire to consider their verdict

summit 1 the highest point or part, esp of a mountain or line of communication; top 2 a a meeting of chiefs of governments or other high officials b (*as modifier*): *a summit conference*

summons 1 a an official order requiring a person to attend court, either to answer a charge or to give evidence b the writ making such an order 2 a call or command given to the members of an assembly to convene a meeting

sumo the national style of wrestling of Japan, the object of which is to force one's opponent to touch the ground with any part of his body except the soles of his feet or to step out of the ring

sump 1 a receptacle, such as the lower part of the crankcase of an internal-combustion engine, into which liquids, esp lubricants, can drain to form a reservoir 2 *Brit, dialect* a muddy pool or swamp

Sumy a city in Ukraine, on the River Pysol: site of early Slav settlements. Pop: 294 000 (2005 est)

sun 1 the star at the centre of our solar system. It is a gaseous body having a highly compressed core, in which energy is generated by thermonuclear reactions (at about 15 million kelvins), surrounded by less dense radiative and convective zones serving to transport the energy to the surface (the **photosphere**). The atmospheric layers (the **chromosphere** and **corona**) are normally invisible except during a total eclipse. Mass and diameter: 333 000 and 109 times that of earth respectively; mean distance from earth: 149.6 million km (1 astronomical unit) 2 any star around which a planetary system revolves 3 the sun as it appears at a particular time or place 4 the radiant energy, esp heat and light, received from the sun; sunshine 5 **take** *or* **shoot the sun** *Nautical* to measure the altitude of the sun in order to determine latitude

▷www.solarviews.com/eng/sun.htm
▷www.michielb.nl/sun/kaft.htm

▷www.hao.ucar.edu/public/education/
education.html

sunbeam a beam, ray, or stream of sunlight

Sunbelt the southern states of the USA.

sunburn 1 inflammation of the skin caused by overexposure to the sun **2** another word for **suntan**

Sunbury-on-Thames a town in SE England, in N Surrey. Pop: 27 415 (2001)

Sunda Strait *or* **Soenda Strait** a strait between Sumatra and Java, linking the Java Sea with the Indian Ocean. Narrowest point: about 26 km (16 miles)

Sunday the first day of the week and the Christian day of worship

Sunday school a a school for the religious instruction of children on Sundays, usually held in a church hall and formerly also providing secular education **b** (*as modifier*): *a Sunday-school outing*

Sunderland 1 a city and port in NE England, in Sunderland unitary authority, Tyne and Wear at the mouth of the River Wear: formerly known for shipbuilding now has car manufacturing, chemicals; university (1992). Pop: 177 739 (2001) **2** a unitary authority in NE England, in Tyne and Wear. Pop: 283 100 (2003 est). Area: 138 sq km (53 sq miles)

Sundsvall a port in E Sweden, on the Gulf of Bothnia: icebound in winter; cellulose industries. Pop: 93 623 (2004 est)

sunfish 1 any large plectognath fish of the family *Molidae*, of temperate and tropical seas, esp *Mola mola*, which has a large rounded compressed body, long pointed dorsal and anal fins, and a fringelike tail fin **2** any of various small predatory North American freshwater percoid fishes of the family *Centrarchidae*, typically having a compressed brightly coloured body

sunflower any of several American plants of the genus *Helianthus*, esp *H. annuus*, having very tall thick stems, large flower heads with yellow rays, and seeds used as food, esp for poultry: family *Asteraceae* (composites)

Sung *or* **Song** an imperial dynasty of China (960–1279 AD), notable for its art, literature, and philosophy

Sungkiang a former province of NE China: now part of the Inner Mongolian AR

sun-god 1 the sun considered as a personal deity **2** a deity associated with the sun or controlling its movements

sun lamp 1 a lamp that generates ultraviolet rays, used for obtaining an artificial suntan, for muscular therapy, etc. **2** a lamp used in film studios, etc, to give an intense beam of light by means of parabolic mirrors

sunlight the light emanating from the sun

sun lounge *or US* **sun parlor** a room with large windows positioned to receive as much sunlight as possible

sunrise 1 the daily appearance of the sun above the horizon **2** the atmospheric phenomena accompanying this appearance **3** the time at which the sun rises at a particular locality

sunrise industry any of the high-technology industries, such as electronics, that hold promise of future development

sunroof *or* **sunshine roof** a panel, often translucent, that may be opened in the roof of a car

sunset 1 the daily disappearance of the sun below the horizon **2** the atmospheric phenomena accompanying this disappearance **3** the time at which the sun sets at a particular locality

sunshade a device, esp a parasol or awning, serving to shade from the sun

sunshine the light received directly from the sun

sunspot 1 any of the dark cool patches, with a diameter of up to several thousand kilometres, that appear on the surface of the sun and last about a week. They occur in approximately 11-year cycles and possess a strong magnetic field **2** *Austral* a small cancerous spot produced by overexposure to the sun

sunstroke heatstroke caused by prolonged exposure to intensely hot sunlight

suntan a a brownish colouring of the skin caused by the formation of the pigment melanin within the skin on exposure to the ultraviolet rays of the sun or a sunlamp **b** (*as modifier*): *suntan oil*

Sun Yat-sen 1866–1925, Chinese statesman, who was instrumental in the overthrow of the Manchu dynasty and was the first president of the Republic of China (1911). He reorganized the Kuomintang

super 1 petrol with a high octane rating **2** *Austral and NZ, informal* superphosphate

Super Bowl *American football* the main championship game of the sport, held annually in January between the champions of the American Football Conference and the National Football Conference

supercharger a device, usually a fan or compressor driven by the engine, that increases the mass of air drawn into an internal-combustion engine by raising the intake pressure

superconductivity *Physics* the property of certain substances that have no electrical resistance. In metals it occurs at very low temperatures, but higher temperature superconductivity occurs in some ceramic materials

supercontinent a great landmass thought to have existed in the geological past and to have split into smaller landmasses, which drifted and formed the present continents

superego *Psychoanal* that part of the unconscious mind that acts as a conscience for the ego, developing mainly from the relationship between a child and his parents

supererogation *RC Church* supererogatory prayers, devotions, etc.

superficial (of measurements) involving only the surface area

superglue any of various impact adhesives that quickly make an exceptionally strong bond

supergrass an informer whose information implicates a large number of people in terrorist activities or other major crimes

superintendent 1 (in Britain) a senior police officer higher in rank than an inspector but lower than a chief superintendent **2** (in the US) the head of a police department

superior 1 *Astronomy* **a** (of a planet) having an orbit further from the sun than the orbit of the earth **b** (of a conjunction) occurring when the sun lies between the earth and an inferior planet **2** (of a plant ovary) situated above the calyx and other floral parts **3** *Anatomy* (of one part in relation to another) situated above or higher **4** the head of a community in a religious order

Superior Lake a lake in the N central US and S Canada: one of the largest freshwater lakes in the world and westernmost of the Great Lakes. Area: 82 362 sq km (31 800 sq miles)

superman (in the philosophy of Nietzsche) an ideal man who through integrity and creativity would rise above good and evil and who represents the goal of human evolution

supermarket a large self-service store retailing food and household supplies

supernatural 1 of or relating to things that cannot be explained according to natural laws **2** characteristic of or caused by or as if by a god; miraculous **3** of, involving, or ascribed to occult beings **4** the supernatural forces, occurrences, and beings collectively or their realm

supernova a star that explodes catastrophically owing to either instabilities following the exhaustion of its nuclear fuel or gravitational collapse following the accretion of matter from an orbiting companion star, becoming for a few days up to one hundred million times brighter than the sun. The expanding shell of debris (the **supernova remnant**) creates a nebula that radiates radio waves, X-rays, and light, for hundreds or thousands of years

supernumerary 1 exceeding a regular or proper number; extra **2** an actor who has no lines, esp a nonprofessional one

superphosphate 1 a mixture of the diacid calcium salt of orthophosphoric acid $Ca(H_2PO_4)_2$ with calcium sulphate and small quantities of other phosphates: used as a fertilizer **2** a salt of phosphoric acid formed by incompletely replacing its acidic hydrogen atoms; acid phosphate; hydrogen phosphate

superpower 1 an extremely powerful state, such as the US **2** extremely high power, esp electrical or mechanical

supersonic being, having, or capable of reaching a speed in excess of the speed of sound

superstar a popular singer, film star, etc, who is idolized by fans and elevated to a position of importance in the entertainment industry

superstition 1 irrational belief usually founded on ignorance or fear and characterized by obsessive reverence for omens, charms, etc. **2** a notion, act or ritual that derives from such belief **3** any irrational belief, esp with regard to the unknown

superstore a very large supermarket, often selling household goods, clothes, etc, as well as food

superstructure 1 *Nautical* any structure above the main deck of a ship with sides flush with the sides of the hull **2** the part of a bridge supported by the piers and abutments **3** (in Marxist theory) an edifice of interdependent agencies of the state, including legal and political institutions and ideologies, each possessing some autonomy but remaining products of the dominant mode of economic production

supertanker a large fast tanker of more than 275 000 tons capacity

supertax a tax levied in addition to the basic tax, esp a graduated surtax on incomes above a certain level

Super Twelve an annual international southern hemisphere Rugby Union tournament between teams from South Africa, Australia, and New Zealand

Suppiluliumas I king of the Hittites (?1375–?1335 BC); founder of the Hittite empire

supplement *Geometry* **a** either of a pair of angles whose sum is 180° **b** an arc of a circle that when added to another arc forms a semicircle

supply 1 *Economics* **a** willingness and ability to offer goods and services for sale **b** the amount of a commodity that producers are willing and able to offer for sale at a specified price **2** a grant of money voted by a legislature for government expenses, esp those not covered by other revenues **3** (in Parliament and similar legislatures) the money voted annually for the expenses of the civil service and armed forces **4** a source of electrical energy, gas, etc.

support 1 a band or entertainer not topping the bill **2** an actor or group of actors playing subordinate roles **3** the solid material on which a painting is executed, such as canvas

supporter a garment or device worn to ease the strain on or restrict the movement of a bodily structure or part

suppository *Med* an encapsulated or solid medication for insertion into the vagina, rectum, or urethra, where it melts and releases the active substance

suppressant a suppressant drug or agent

Surabaya, Surabaja, *or* **Soerabaja** a port in Indonesia, on E Java on the **Surabaya Strait**: the country's second port and chief naval base; university (1954); fishing and ship-building industries; oil refinery. Pop: 2 599 796 (2000)

Surakarta a town in Indonesia, on central Java: textile manufacturing. Pop: 516 500 (1995 est)

Surat a port in W India, in W Gujarat: a major port in the 17th century; textile manufacturing. Pop: 2 433 787 (2001)

surcharge 1 a charge in addition to the usual payment, tax, etc. **2** an excessive sum charged, esp when unlawful **3** *Law* the act or an instance of surcharging **4** an overprint that alters the face value of a postage stamp

surd *Maths* an expression containing one or more irrational roots of numbers, such as $2\sqrt{3} + 3\sqrt{2} + 6$

surety 1 a person who assumes legal responsibility for the fulfilment of another's debt or obligation and himself becomes liable if the other defaults **2** security given against loss or damage or as a guarantee that an obligation will be met **3 stand surety** to act as a surety

surf 1 waves breaking on the shore or on a reef **2** foam caused by the breaking of waves

surface 1 *Geometry* **a** the complete boundary of a solid figure **b** a continuous two-dimensional configuration **2 a** the uppermost level of the land or sea **b** (*as modifier*): *surface transportation*

surface tension 1 a property of liquids caused by intermolecular forces near the surface leading to the apparent presence of a surface film and to capillarity, etc. **2** a measure of this property expressed as the force acting normal to one side of a line of unit length on the surface: measured in newtons per metre.

surfboard a long narrow board used in surfing

surfing the sport of riding towards shore on the crest of a wave by standing or lying on a surfboard
▷www.aspeurope.com

surge 1 the rolling swell of the sea, esp after the passage of a large wave 2 *Nautical* a temporary release or slackening of a rope or cable 3 a large momentary increase in the voltage or current in an electric circuit 4 an upward instability or unevenness in the power output of an engine 5 *Astronomy* a short-lived disturbance, occurring during the eruption of a solar flare

surgeon 1 a medical practioner who specializes in surgery 2 a medical officer in the Royal Navy

surgery 1 the branch of medicine concerned with treating disease, injuries, etc, by means of manual or operative procedures, esp by incision into the body 2 the performance of such procedures by a surgeon 3 *Brit* a place where a doctor, dentist, etc, can be consulted 4 *Brit* an occasion when an MP, lawyer, etc, is available for consultation 5 *US and Canadian* an operating theatre where surgical operations are performed
▷www.nlm.nih.gov/medlineplus/surgery.html
▷www.contemporarysurgery.com/links.html

surgical spirit methylated spirit containing small amounts of oil of wintergreen and castor oil: used medically for sterilizing

Suribachi Mount a volcanic hill in the Volcano Islands, on Iwo Jima: site of a US victory (1945) over the Japanese in World War II

Surinam *or* **Suriname** a republic in NE South America, on the Atlantic: became a self-governing part of the Netherlands in 1954 and fully independent in 1975. Official languages: Dutch; English is also widely spoken. Religion: Hindu, Christian, and Muslim. Currency: guilder. Capital: Paramaribo. Pop: 439 000 (2004 est). Area: 163 820 sq km (63 251 sq miles)

surly (of an animal) ill-tempered or refractory

surplus *Economics* a an excess of government revenues over expenditures during a certain financial year b an excess of receipts over payments on the balance of payments

surrealism a movement in art and literature in the 1920s, which developed esp from dada, characterized by the evocative juxtaposition of incongruous images in order to include unconscious and dream elements
▷www.artchive.com/ftp_site_reg.htm

surrender *Law* a the yielding up or restoring of an estate, esp the giving up of a lease before its term has expired b the giving up to the appropriate authority of a fugitive from justice c the act of surrendering or being surrendered to bail d the deed by which a legal surrender is effected

Surrey¹ Earl of, title of *Henry Howard*. ?1517–47, English courtier and poet; one of the first in England to write sonnets. He was beheaded for high treason

Surrey² a county of SE England, on the River Thames: urban in the northeast; crossed from east to west by the North Downs and drained by tributaries of the Thames. Administrative centre: Kingston upon Thames. Pop: 1 064 600 (2003 est). Area: 1679 sq km (648 sq miles)

surrogate 1 *Chiefly Brit* a deputy, such as a clergyman appointed to deputize for a bishop in granting marriage licences 2 *Psychiatry* a person who is a substitute for someone else, esp in childhood when different persons, such as a brother or teacher, can act as substitutes for the parents 3 (in some US states) a judge with jurisdiction over the probate of wills, etc.

surround *Chiefly US* a a method of capturing wild beasts by encircling the area in which they are believed to be b the area so encircled

surtax 1 a tax, usually highly progressive, levied on the amount by which a person's income exceeds a specific level 2 an additional tax on something that has already been taxed

Surtees 1 John born 1934, British racing motorcyclist and motor-racing driver. He was motorcycling world champion (1956, 1958–60) and world champion motor-racing driver (1964), the only man to have been world champion in both sports 2 Robert Smith 1803–64, British journalist and novelist, who satirized the sporting life of the English gentry in such works as *Jorrocks's Jaunts and Jollities* (1838)

surveillance close observation or supervision maintained over a person, group, etc, esp one in custody or under suspicion

Susa an ancient city north of the Persian Gulf: capital of Elam and of the Persian Empire; flourished as a Greek polis under the Seleucids and Parthians

Susanna¹ *Apocrypha* 1 the wife of Joachim, who was condemned to death for adultery because of a false accusation, but saved by Daniel's sagacity 2 the book of the Apocrypha containing this story

Susanna² the book of the Apocrypha containing the story of Susanna, who was condemned to death for adultery because of a false accusation but saved by Daniel's sagacity

susceptibility *Physics* a (of a dielectric) the amount by which the relative permittivity differs from unity. b (of a magnetic medium) the amount by which the relative permeability differs from unity.

suspended animation a temporary cessation of the vital functions, as by freezing an organism

suspended sentence a sentence of imprisonment that is not served by an offender unless he commits a further offence during its currency

suspension 1 *Law* a a postponement of execution of a sentence or the deferring of a judgment, etc. b a temporary extinguishment of a right or title 2 a system of springs, shock absorbers, etc, that supports the body of a wheeled or tracked vehicle and insulates it and its occupants from shocks transmitted by the wheels 3 a device or structure, usually a wire or spring, that serves to suspend or support something, such as the pendulum of a clock 4 *Chem* a dispersion of fine solid or liquid particles in a fluid, the particles being supported by buoyancy 5 the process by which eroded particles of rock are transported in a river 6 *Music* one or more notes of a chord that are prolonged until a subsequent chord is sounded, usually to form a dissonance

suspension bridge a bridge that has a deck suspended by cables or rods from other cables or chains that hang between two towers and are anchored at both ends

Susquehanna a river in the eastern US, rising in Otsego Lake and flowing generally south to Chesapeake Bay at Havre de Grace: the longest river in the eastern US.

Length: 714 km (444 miles)

Sussex 1 (until 1974) a county of SE England, now divided into the separate counties of East Sussex and West Sussex **2** (in Anglo-Saxon England) the kingdom of the South Saxons, which became a shire of the kingdom of Wessex in the early 9th century AD **3** a breed of red beef cattle originally from Sussex **4** a heavy and long-established breed of domestic fowl used principally as a table bird

sustain *Music* the prolongation of a note, by playing technique or electronics

sustainable 1 (of economic development, energy sources, etc) capable of being maintained at a steady level without exhausting natural resources or causing severe ecological damage **2** (of economic growth) non-inflationary

Sutcliffe Herbert 1894–1978, English cricketer, who played for Yorkshire; scorer of 149 centuries and 1000 runs in a season 24 times

Sutherland¹ 1 Graham 1903–80, English artist, noted for his work as an official war artist (1941–44), for his tapestry *Christ in Majesty* (1962) in Coventry Cathedral, and for his portraits **2** Dame **Joan**, known as *La Stupenda*. born 1926, Australian operatic soprano

Sutherland² (until 1975) a county of N Scotland, now part of Highland

Sutherland Falls a waterfall in New Zealand, on SW South Island. Height: 580 m (1904 ft)

Sutlej a river in S Asia, rising in SW Tibet and flowing west through the Himalayas: crosses Himachal Pradesh and the Punjab (India), enters Pakistan, and joins the Chenab west of Bahawalpur: the longest of the five rivers of the Punjab. Length: 1368 km (850 miles)

Sutton a borough of S Greater London. Pop: 178 500 (2003 est). Area: 43 sq km (17 sq miles)

Sutton Coldfield a town in central England, in Birmingham unitary authority, West Midlands; a residential suburb of Birmingham. Pop: 105 452 (2001)

Sutton-in-Ashfield a market town in N central England, in W Nottinghamshire. Pop: 41 951 (2001)

suture 1 *Surgery* **a** catgut, silk thread, or wire used to stitch together two bodily surfaces **b** the surgical seam formed after joining two surfaces **2** *Anatomy* a type of immovable joint, esp between the bones of the skull (**cranial suture**) **3** *Zoology* a line of junction in a mollusc shell, esp the line between adjacent chambers of a nautiloid shell **4** *Botany* a line marking the point of dehiscence in a seed pod or capsule

Suva the capital and chief port of Fiji, on the SE coast of Viti Levu; popular tourist resort; University of the South Pacific (1968). Pop: 219 000 (2005 est)

Suvorov Aleksandr Vasilyevich 1729–1800, Russian field marshal, who fought successfully against the Turks (1787–91), the Poles (1794), and the French in Italy (1798–99)

Suwannee *or* **Swanee** a river in the southeastern US, rising in SE Georgia and flowing across Florida to the Gulf of Mexico at **Suwannee Sound** Length: about 400 km (250 miles)

suzerain 1 a a state or sovereign exercising some degree of dominion over a dependent state, usually controlling its foreign affairs **b** (*as modifier*): *a suzerain power* **2** *History* **a** a feudal overlord **b** (*as modifier*): *suzerain lord*

Suzhou, Su-chou, *or* **Soochow** a city in E China, in S Jiangsu on the Grand Canal: noted for its gardens; produces chiefly silk. Pop: 1 201 000 (2005 est)

Svalbard a Norwegian archipelago in the Arctic Ocean, about 650 km (400 miles) north of Norway: consists of the main group (Spitsbergen, North East Land, Edge Island, Barents Island, and Prince Charles Foreland) and a number of outlying islands; sovereignty long disputed but granted to Norway in 1920; coal mining. Administrative centre: Longyearbyen. Area: 62 050 sq km (23 958 sq miles)

Svevo Italo , original name *Ettore Schmitz*. 1861–1928, Italian novelist and short-story writer, best known for the novel *Confessions of Zeno* (1923)

swab 1 *Med* **a** a small piece of cotton, gauze, etc, for use in applying medication, cleansing a wound, or obtaining a specimen of a secretion, etc. **b** the specimen so obtained **2** a mop for cleaning floors, decks, etc.

Swabia a region and former duchy (from the 10th century to 1313) of S Germany, now part of Baden-Württemberg and Bavaria: part of West Germany until 1990

swag 1 an ornamental festoon of fruit, flowers, or drapery or a representation of this **2** *Midland English, dialect* a depression filled with water, resulting from mining subsidence

Swahili 1 a language of E Africa that is an official language of Kenya and Tanzania and is widely used as a lingua franca throughout E and central Africa. It is a member of the Bantu group of the Niger-Congo family, originally spoken in Zanzibar, and has a large number of loan words taken from Arabic and other languages **2** a member of a people speaking this language, living chiefly in Zanzibar

swallow¹ *Nautical* the opening between the shell and the groove of the sheave of a block, through which the rope is passed

swallow² any passerine songbird of the family Hirundinidae, esp *Hirundo rustica* (**common** or **barn swallow**), having long pointed wings, a forked tail, short legs, and a rapid flight

swallow dive a type of dive in which the diver arches back while in the air, keeping his legs straight and together and his arms oustretched, finally entering the water headfirst

swallowtail 1 any of various butterflies of the genus *Papilio* and related genera, esp *P. machaon* of Europe, having a tail-like extension of each hind wing: family Papilionidae **2** the forked tail of a swallow or similar bird

swami (in India) a title of respect for a Hindu saint or religious teacher

swamp a permanently waterlogged ground that is usually overgrown and sometimes partly forested **b** (*as modifier*): *swamp fever*

swan any large aquatic bird of the genera *Cygnus* and *Coscoroba*, having a long neck and usually a white plumage: family Anatidae, order Anseriformes

Swan¹ Sir Joseph Wilson 1828–1914, English physicist and chemist, who developed the incandescent electric light (1880) independently of Edison

Swan² a river in SW Western Australia, rising as the Avon northeast of Narrogin and flowing northwest and west to the Indian Ocean below Perth. Length: about 240 km (150 miles)

Swansea 1 a port in S Wales, in Swansea county on an inlet of the Bristol Channel (**Swansea Bay**); a metallurgical and oil-refining centre; university (1920). Pop: 169 880 (2001) 2 a county of S Wales on the Bristol Channel, created in 1996 from part of West Glamorgan: includes the Swansea conurbation and the Gower peninsula. Administrative centre: Swansea. Pop: 224 600 (2003 est). Area: 378 sq km (146 sq miles)

swan song the song that a dying swan is said to sing

SWAPO or **Swapo** South-West Africa People's Organization

sward turf or grass or a stretch of turf or grass

swarm 1 a group of social insects, esp bees led by a queen, that has left the parent hive in order to start a new colony 2 a large mass of small animals, esp insects

swash 1 a sandbar washed by the waves 2 a channel of moving water cutting through or running behind a sandbank

swastika this symbol with clockwise arms, officially adopted in 1935 as the emblem of Nazi Germany

Swat 1 a former princely state of NW India: passed to Pakistan in 1947 2 a river in Pakistan, rising in the north and flowing south to the Kabul River north of Peshawar. Length: about 640 km (400 miles)

swatch 1 a sample of cloth 2 a number of such samples, usually fastened together in book form

Swaziland a kingdom in southern Africa: made a protectorate of the Transvaal by Britain in 1894; gained independence in 1968; a member of the Commonwealth. Official languages: Swazi and English. Religion: Christian majority, traditional beliefs. Currency: lilangeni (plural emalangeni) and South African rand. Capital: Mbabane (administrative), Lobamba (legislative). Pop: 1 083 000 (2004 est). Area: 17 363 sq km (6704 sq miles)

sweat 1 the secretion from the sweat glands, esp when profuse and visible, as during strenuous activity, from excessive heat, etc.; commonly also called perspiration 2 *Chiefly US* an exercise gallop given to a horse, esp on the day of a race

swede a Eurasian plant, *Brassica napus* (or *B. napobrassica*), cultivated for its bulbous edible root, which is used as a vegetable and as cattle fodder: family *Brassicaceae* (crucifers)

Sweden a kingdom in NW Europe, occupying the E part of the Scandinavian Peninsula, on the Gulf of Bothnia and the Baltic: first united during the Viking period (8th–11th centuries); a member of the European Union. About 50 per cent of the total area is forest and 9 per cent lakes. Exports include timber, pulp, paper, iron ore, and steel. Official language: Swedish. Official religion: Church of Sweden (Lutheran). Currency: krona. Capital: Stockholm. Pop: 8 886 000 (2004 est). Area: 449 793 sq km (173 665 sq miles)

Swedenborg Emanuel original surname *Svedberg*. 1688–1772, Swedish scientist and theologian, whose mystical ideas became the basis of a religious movement

Swedish the official language of Sweden, belonging to the North Germanic branch of the Indo-European family: one of the two official languages of Finland

Sweelinck Jan Pieterszoon 1562–1621, Dutch composer and organist, whose organ works are important for being the first to incorporate independent parts for the pedals

sweep 1 the distance, arc, etc, through which something, such as a pendulum, moves 2 *Cards* a the winning of every trick in a hand of whist b the taking, by pairing, of all exposed cards in cassino 3 short for **sweepstake** 4 *Cricket* a shot in which the ball is hit more or less square on the leg side from a half-kneeling position with the bat held nearly horizontal 5 a a long oar used on an open boat b *Austral* a person steering a surf boat with such an oar 6 any of the sails of a windmill 7 *Electronics* a steady horizontal or circular movement of an electron beam across or around the fluorescent screen of a cathode-ray tube

sweeper *Informal, Soccer* a player who supports the main defenders, as by intercepting loose balls, etc.

sweepstake or esp US **sweepstakes** 1 a a lottery in which the stakes of the participants constitute the prize b the prize itself 2 any event involving a lottery, esp a horse race in which the prize is the competitors' stakes

sweet 1 (of wine, etc) having a relatively high sugar content; not dry 2 free from unpleasant odours 3 containing no corrosive substances 4 (of petrol) containing no sulphur compounds 5 *Jazz* performed with a regular beat, with the emphasis on clearly outlined melody and little improvisation
▷www.completechocolate.com

Sweet Henry 1845–1912, English philologist; a pioneer of modern phonetics. His books include *A History of English Sounds* (1874)

sweetbrier a Eurasian rose, *Rosa rubiginosa*, having a tall bristly stem, fragrant leaves, and single pink flowers

sweet corn a variety of maize, *Zea mays saccharata*, whose kernels are rich in sugar and eaten as a vegetable when young

sweetener a sweetening agent, esp one that does not contain sugar

sweet pea a climbing leguminous plant, *Lathyrus odoratus*, of S Europe, widely cultivated for its butterfly-shaped fragrant flowers of delicate pastel colours

sweet pepper a pepper plant, *Capsicum frutescens grossum*, with large bell-shaped fruits that are eaten unripe (**green pepper**) or ripe (**red pepper**)

sweet potato a convolvulaceous twining plant, *Ipomoea batatas*, of tropical America, cultivated in the tropics for its edible fleshy yellow root

sweet spot *Sport* the centre area of a racquet, golf club, etc, from which the cleanest shots are made

sweet william a widely cultivated Eurasian caryophyllaceous plant, *Dianthus barbatus*, with flat clusters of white, pink, red, or purple flowers

swell 1 a the undulating movement of the surface of the open sea b a succession of waves or a single large wave 2 a gentle hill 3 *Music* a crescendo followed by an immediate diminuendo 4 *Music* a a set of pipes on an organ housed in a box (**swell box**) fitted with a shutter operated by a pedal, which can be opened or closed to control the volume **b** the manual on an organ controlling this

swelling an abnormal enlargement of a bodily structure or part, esp as the result of injury

Sweyn known as *Sweyn Forkbeard*. died 1014, king of Denmark (?986–1014). He conquered England, forcing Ethelred II to flee (1013); father of Canute

swift 1 any bird of the families *Apodidae* and *Hemiprocnidae*, such as *Apus apus* (**common swift**) of the Old World: order *Apodiformes*. They have long narrow wings and spend most of the time on the wing 2 a variety of domestic fancy pigeon originating in Egypt and Syria and having an appearance somewhat similar to a swift 3 any of certain North American lizards of the genera *Sceloporus* and *Uta* that can run very rapidly: family *Iguanidae* (iguanas) 4 the main cylinder in a carding machine 5 an expanding circular frame used to hold skeins of silk, wool, etc.

Swift 1 **Graham Colin** born 1949, British writer: his novels include *Waterland* (1983), *Last Orders* (1996), which won the Booker prize, and *The Light of Day* (2002) 2 **Jonathan** 1667–1745, Anglo-Irish satirist and churchman, who became dean of St. Patrick's, Dublin, in 1713. His works include *A Tale of a Tub* (1704) and *Gulliver's Travels* (1726)

swimming bath an indoor swimming pool

swimming pool an artificial pool for swimming

Swinburne **Algernon Charles** 1837–1909, English lyric poet and critic

swindle a fraudulent scheme or transaction

Swindon 1 a town in S England, in NE Wiltshire: railway workshops, high technology. Pop: 155 432 (2001). 2 a unitary authority in S England, in Wiltshire. Pop: 181 200 (2003 est). Area: 230 sq km (89 sq miles)

swing 1 *Boxing* a wide punch from the side similar to but longer than a hook 2 *Cricket* the lateral movement of a bowled ball through the air 3 something that swings or is swung, esp a suspended seat on which a person may sit and swing back and forth 4 a a kind of popular dance music influenced by jazz, usually played by big bands and originating in the 1930s b (*as modifier*): *swing music* 5 *Prosody* a steady distinct rhythm or cadence in prose or verse 6 a a fluctuation, as in some business activity, voting pattern etc. b able to bring about a swing in a voting pattern c having a mixed voting history, and thus becoming a target for political election campaigners

▷www.jazzinamerica.org

swing bridge 1 a low bridge that can be rotated about a vertical axis, esp to permit the passage of ships 2 NZ a pedestrian bridge over a river, suspended by heavy wire cables

Swinney **John** (**Ramsay**). born 1964, Scottish politician; leader of the Scottish National Party (2000–04)

swipe a type of lever for raising and lowering a weight, such as a bucket in a well

Swiss of, relating to, or characteristic of Switzerland, its inhabitants, or their dialects of German, French, and Italian

switch 1 a mechanical, electrical, electronic, or optical device for opening or closing a circuit or for diverting

energy from one part of a circuit to another 2 the tassel-like tip of the tail of cattle and certain other animals 3 any of various card games in which the suit is changed during play 4 *US and Canadian* a railway siding 5 *US and Canadian* a railway point

switchback a mountain road, railway, or track which rises and falls sharply many times or a sharp rise and fall on such a road, railway, or track

switchboard an assembly of switchgear for the control of power supplies in an installation or building

Swithin or **Swithun** Saint died 862 AD, English ecclesiastic: bishop of Winchester (?852–862). Feast day: July 15

Switzerland a federal republic in W central Europe: the cantons of Schwyz, Uri, and Unterwalden formed a defensive league against the Hapsburgs in 1291, later joined by other cantons; gained independence in 1499; adopted a policy of permanent neutrality from 1516; a leading centre of the Reformation in the 16th century. It lies in the Jura Mountains and the Alps, with a plateau between the two ranges. Official languages: German, French, and Italian; Romansch minority. Religion: mostly Protestant and Roman Catholic. Currency: Swiss franc. Capital: Bern. Pop: 7 163 000 (2004 est). Area: 41 288 sq km (15 941 sq miles)

swivel 1 a coupling device which allows an attached object to turn freely 2 such a device made of two parts which turn independently, such as a compound link of a chain

swizzle stick a small rod used to agitate an effervescent drink to facilitate the escape of carbon dioxide

sword dance a dance in which the performers dance nimbly over swords on the ground or brandish them in the air

swordfish a large scombroid fish, *Xiphias gladius*, with a very long upper jaw: valued as a food and game fish: family *Xiphiidae*

Sword of Damocles a closely impending disaster

swordplay the action or art of fighting with a sword

swordsman one who uses or is skilled in the use of a sword

Syal **Meera** born 1964, British actress and writer of Punjabi origin, who appeared in the TV comedy series *Goodness Gracious Me* (1998) and *The Kumars at No. 42* (2001–02); her screenplays include *Bhaji on the Beach* (1993)

Sybaris a Greek colony in S Italy, on the Gulf of Taranto: notorious for its luxurious living, founded about 720 BC and sacked in 510

sycamore 1 a Eurasian maple tree, *Acer pseudoplatanus*, naturalized in Britain and North America, having five-lobed leaves, yellow flowers, and two-winged fruits 2 *US and Canadian* an American plane tree, *Platanus occidentalis* 3 a moraceous tree, *Ficus sycomorus*, of N Africa and W Asia, having an edible figlike fruit

Sydney 1 a port in SE Australia, capital of New South Wales, on an inlet of the S Pacific: the largest city in Australia and the first British settlement, established as a penal colony in 1788; developed rapidly after 1820 with the discovery of gold in its hinterland; large wool market; three universities. Pop: 3 502 301 (2001) 2 a port in SE Canada, in Nova Scotia on NE Cape Breton Island: capital of Cape Breton Island until 1820, when the island united administratively with Nova Scotia. Pop: 26 063 (1991)

Syktyvkar a city in NW Russia, capital of the Komi Republic: timber industry. Pop: 230 000 (2005 est)

syllabic 1 denoting a kind of verse line based on a specific number of syllables rather than being regulated by stresses or quantities 2 (of plainsong and similar chanting) having each syllable sung to a different note

syllabub or **sillabub** a spiced drink made of milk with rum, port, brandy, or wine, often hot

syllabus 1 an outline of a course of studies, text, etc. 2 *Brit* a the subjects studied for a particular course b a document which lists these subjects and states how the course will be assessed

syllogism 1 a deductive inference consisting of two premises and a conclusion, all of which are categorial propositions. The subject of the conclusion is the **minor term** and its predicate the **major term**; the **middle term** occurs in both premises but not the conclusion. There are 256 such arguments but only 24 are valid. *Some men are mortal; some men are angelic; so some mortals are angelic* is invalid, while *some temples are in ruins; all ruins are fascinating; so some temples are fascinating* is valid. Here *fascinating*, *in ruins*, and *temples* are respectively major, middle, and minor terms 2 a deductive inference of certain other forms with two premises, such as the **hypothetical syllogism**, *if P then Q; if Q then R; so if P then R*

sylph any of a class of imaginary beings assumed to inhabit the air

sylvan or **silvan** *Chiefly poetic* 1 of, characteristic of, or consisting of woods or forests 2 living or located in woods or forests 3 an inhabitant of the woods, esp a spirit

Sylvester II original name *Gerbert of Aurillac.c* 940–1003 AD, French ecclesiastic and scholar; pope (999–1003): noted for his achievements in mathematics and astronomy

symbiosis a close and usually obligatory association of two organisms of different species that live together, often to their mutual benefit

symbol 1 an object, person, idea, etc, used in a literary work, film, etc, to stand for or suggest something else with which it is associated either explicitly or in some more subtle way 2 a letter, figure, or sign used in mathematics, science, music, etc to represent a quantity, phenomenon, operation, function, etc. 3 *Psychoanal* the end product, in the form of an object or act, of a conflict in the unconscious between repression processes and the actions and thoughts being repressed 4 *Psychol* any mental process that represents some feature of external reality

symbolism 1 a late 19th-century movement in art that sought to express mystical or abstract ideas through the symbolic use of images 2 *Theol* any symbolist interpretation of the Eucharist

symmetry 1 *Maths* an exact correspondence in position or form about a given point, line, or plane 2 *Physics* the independence of a property with respect to direction; isotropy

Symonds John Addington 1840–93, English writer, noted for his *Renaissance in Italy* (1875–86) and for studies

of homosexuality

Symons Arthur 1865–1945, English poet and critic, who helped to introduce the French symbolists to England

sympathetic 1 *Anatomy, physiol* of or relating to the division of the autonomic nervous system that acts in opposition to the parasympathetic system accelerating the heartbeat, dilating the bronchi, inhibiting the smooth muscles of the digestive tract, etc. 2 relating to vibrations occurring as a result of similar vibrations in a neighbouring body

sympathy 1 the condition of a physical system or body when its behaviour is similar or corresponds to that of a different system that influences it, such as the vibration of sympathetic strings 2 *Physiol* the mutual relationship between two organs or parts whereby a change in one has an effect on the other

symphony 1 an extended large-scale orchestral composition, usually with several movements, at least one of which is in sonata form. The classical form of the symphony was fixed by Haydn and Mozart, but the innovations of subsequent composers have freed it entirely from classical constraints. It continues to be a vehicle for serious, large-scale orchestral music 2 a piece of instrumental music in up to three very short movements, used as an overture to or interlude in a baroque opera 3 any purely orchestral movement in a vocal work, such as a cantata or oratorio 4 short for **symphony orchestra** 5 in musical theory, esp of classical Greece: the interval of unison

symphony orchestra *Music* an orchestra capable of performing symphonies, esp the large orchestra comprising strings, brass, woodwind, harp and percussion

symposium 1 a conference or meeting for the discussion of some subject, esp an academic topic or social problem 2 a collection of scholarly contributions, usually published together, on a given subject 3 (in classical Greece) a drinking party with intellectual conversation, music, etc.

symptom *Med* any sensation or change in bodily function experienced by a patient that is associated with a particular disease

synagogue 1 a a building for Jewish religious services and usually also for religious instruction b (*as modifier*): *synagogue services* 2 a congregation of Jews who assemble for worship or religious study 3 the religion of Judaism as organized in such congregations

synapse the point at which a nerve impulse is relayed from the terminal portion of an axon to the dendrites of an adjacent neuron

synchromesh 1 (of a gearbox, etc) having a system of clutches that synchronizes the speeds of the driving and driven members before engagement to avoid shock in gear changing and to reduce noise and wear 2 a gear system having these features

synchronism 1 *History* a chronological usually tabular list of historical persons and events, arranged to show parallel or synchronous occurrence 2 *Art* the representation in a work of art of one or more incidents that occurred at separate times

synchronous *Physics* (of periodic phenomena, such as voltages) having the same frequency and phase

syncline a downward fold of stratified rock in which the strata slope towards a vertical axis

syndic 1 *Brit* a business agent of some universities or other bodies 2 (in several countries) a government administrator or magistrate with varying powers

syndicalism 1 a revolutionary movement and theory advocating the seizure of the means of production and distribution by syndicates of workers through direct action, esp a general strike 2 an economic system resulting from such action

syndicate 1 an association of business enterprises or individuals organized to undertake a joint project requiring considerable capital 2 any association formed to carry out an enterprise or enterprises of common interest to its members 3 a board of syndics or the office of syndic 4 (in Italy under the Fascists) a local organization of employers or employees

syndrome *Med* any combination of signs and symptoms that are indicative of a particular disease or disorder

synergy the potential ability of individual organizations or groups to be more successful or productive as a result of a merger

Synge John Millington 1871–1909, Irish playwright. His plays, marked by vivid colloquial Irish speech, include *Riders to the Sea* (1904) and *The Playboy of the Western World*, produced amidst uproar at the Abbey Theatre, Dublin, in 1907

synod a local or special ecclesiastical council, esp of a diocese, formally convened to discuss ecclesiastical affairs

synonym 1 a word or phrase used as another name for something, such as *Hellene* for a *Greek* 2 *Biology* a taxonomic name that has been superseded or rejected

synopsis a condensation or brief review of a subject; summary

synoptic 1 of or relating to a synopsis 2 *Bible* a (of the Gospels of Matthew, Mark, and Luke) presenting the narrative of Christ's life, ministry, etc from a point of view held in common by all three, and with close similarities in content, order, etc. b of, relating to, or characterizing these three Gospels 3 *Meteorol* showing or concerned with the distribution of meteorological conditions over a wide area at a given time 4 *Bible* a any of the three synoptic Gospels b any of the authors of these three Gospels

synovia a transparent viscid lubricating fluid, secreted by the membrane lining joints, tendon sheaths, etc.

syntax *Logic* a systematic statement of the rules governing the properly formed formulas of a logical system

synthesis 1 the process of producing a compound by a chemical reaction or series of reactions, usually from simpler or commonly available starting materials 2 *Philosophy, archaic* synthetic reasoning 3 *Philosophy* a (in the writings of Kant) the unification of one concept with another not contained in it b the final stage in the Hegelian dialectic, that resolves the contradiction between thesis and antithesis

synthesizer an electrophonic instrument, usually operated by means of a keyboard and pedals, in which sounds are produced by voltage-controlled oscillators, filters, and amplifiers, with an envelope generator module that controls attack, decay, sustain, and release

synthetic 1 (of a substance or material) made artificially by chemical reaction 2 *Philosophy* a (of a proposition) having a truth-value that is not determined solely by virtue of the meanings of the words, as in *all men are arrogant* b contingent 3 a synthetic substance or material

syphilis a venereal disease caused by infection with the microorganism *Treponema pallidum*: characterized by an ulcerating chancre, usually on the genitals and progressing through the lymphatic system to nearly all tissues of the body, producing serious clinical manifestations

Syracuse 1 a port in SW Italy, in SE Sicily on the Ionian Sea: founded in 734 BC by Greeks from Corinth and taken by the Romans in 212 BC, after a siege of three years. Pop: 123 657 (2001) 2 a city in central New York State, on Lake Onondaga: site of the capital of the Iroquois Indian federation. Pop: 144 001 (2003 est)

Syr Darya a river in central Asia, formed from two headstreams rising in the Tian Shan: flows generally west to the Aral Sea: the longest river in central Asia. Length: (from the source of the Naryn) 2900 km (1800 miles)

Syria 1 a republic in W Asia, on the Mediterranean: ruled by the Ottoman Turks (1516–1918); made a French mandate in 1920; became independent in 1944; joined Egypt in the United Arab Republic (1958–61). Official language: Arabic. Religion: Muslim majority. Currency: Syrian pound. Capital: Damascus. Pop: 18 223 000 (2004 est). Area: 185 180 sq km (71 498 sq miles) 2 (formerly) the region between the Mediterranean, the Euphrates, the Taurus, and the Arabian Desert

Syrian 1 of, relating to, or characteristic of Syria, its people, or their dialect of Arabic 2 *Eastern Church* of or relating to Christians who belong to churches with Syriac liturgies 3 a native or inhabitant of Syria 4 *Eastern Church* a Syrian Christian

syringa another name for **mock orange** and **lilac** (sense 1)

syringe 1 *Med* an instrument, such as a hypodermic syringe or a rubber ball with a slender nozzle, for use in withdrawing or injecting fluids, cleaning wounds, etc. 2 any similar device for injecting, spraying, or extracting liquids by means of pressure or suction

syrup a liquid medicine containing a sugar solution for flavouring or preservation

system 1 an organism considered as a functioning entity 2 any of various bodily parts or structures that are anatomically or physiologically related 3 any assembly of electronic, electrical, or mechanical components with interdependent functions, usually forming a self-contained unit 4 *Astron* a group of celestial bodies that are associated as a result of natural laws, esp gravitational attraction 5 *Chem* a sample of matter in which there are one or more substances in one or more phases 6 *Mineralogy* one of a group of divisions into which crystals may be placed on the basis of the lengths and inclinations of their axes 7 *Geology* a stratigraphical unit for the rock strata formed during a period of geological time. It can be subdivided into series

systematic *Biology* of or relating to the taxonomic classification of organisms

systemic *Physiol* (of a poison, disease, etc) affecting the entire body

systems analysis the analysis of the requirements of a task and the expression of those requirements in a form that permits the assembly of computer hardware and software to perform the task

systole contraction of the heart, during which blood is pumped into the aorta and the arteries that lead to the lungs

Syzran a port in W central Russia, on the Volga River: oil refining. Pop: 191 000 (2005 est)

Szczecin a port in NW Poland, on the River Oder: the busiest Polish port and leading coal exporter; shipbuilding. Pop: 435 000 (2005 est)

Szeged an industrial city in S Hungary, on the Tisza River. Pop: 162 860 (2003 est)

Szell George 1897–1970, US conductor, born in Hungary

Szilard Leo 1898–1964, US physicist, born in Hungary, who originated the idea of a self-sustaining nuclear chain reaction (1934). He worked on the atomic bomb during World War II but later pressed for the international control of nuclear weapons

Szombathely a city in W Hungary: site of the Roman capital of Pannonia. Pop: 81 113 (2003 est)

Szymanowski Karol 1882–1937, Polish composer, whose works include the opera *King Roger* (1926), two violin concertos, symphonies, piano music, and songs

Szymborska Wisława born 1923, Polish poet and writer: Nobel prize for literature 1996

Tt

Taal an active volcano in the Philippines, on S Luzon on an island in the centre of **Lake Taal**. Height: 300 m (984 ft). Area of lake: 243 sq km (94 sq miles)

tab¹ a small auxiliary aerofoil on the trailing edge of a rudder, aileron, or elevator, etc, to assist in the control of the aircraft in flight

tab² 1 short for **tabulator** or **tablet** 2 *Slang* a portion of a drug, esp LSD or ecstasy

tabard a sleeveless or short-sleeved jacket, esp one worn by a herald, bearing a coat of arms, or by a knight over his armour

Tabasco a state in SE Mexico, on the Gulf of Campeche: mostly flat and marshy with extensive jungles; hot and humid climate. Capital: Villahermosa. Pop: 1 889 367 (2000). Area: 24 661 sq km (9520 sq miles)

tabby¹ a fabric with a watered pattern, esp silk or taffeta

tabby² 1 (esp of cats) brindled with dark stripes or wavy markings on a lighter background 2 a tabby cat 3 any female domestic cat

tabernacle 1 *Old Testament* **a** the portable sanctuary in the form of a tent in which the ancient Israelites carried the Ark of the Covenant (Exodus 25–27) **b** the Jewish Temple regarded as the shrine of the divine presence 2 a meeting place for worship used by Mormons or Nonconformists 3 a small ornamented cupboard or box used for the reserved sacrament of the Eucharist 4 the human body regarded as the temporary dwelling of the soul 5 *Chiefly RC Church* a canopied niche or recess forming the shrine of a statue 6 *Nautical* a strong framework for holding the foot of a mast stepped on deck, allowing it to be swung down horizontally to pass under low bridges, etc.

tabla a musical instrument of India consisting of a pair of drums whose pitches can be varied

table 1 any flat or level area, such as a plateau 2 a rectangular panel set below or above the face of a wall 3 *Architect* another name for **cordon** 4 *Music* the sounding board of a violin, guitar, or similar stringed instrument 5 a tablet on which laws were inscribed by the ancient Romans, the Hebrews, etc. 6 *Palmistry* an area of the palm's surface bounded by four lines 7 **a** either of the two bony plates that form the inner and outer parts of the flat bones of the cranium **b** any thin flat plate, esp of bone

tableau a pause during or at the end of a scene on stage when all the performers briefly freeze in position

Table Bay the large bay on which Cape Town is situated, on the SW coast of South Africa

tableland flat elevated land; a plateau

Table Mountain a mountain in SW South Africa, overlooking Cape Town and Table Bay: flat-topped and steep-sided. Height: 1087 m (3567 ft)

tablespoon 1 the amount contained in such a spoon 2 a unit of capacity used in cooking, medicine, etc, equal to half a fluid ounce or three teaspoons

tablet 1 a medicinal formulation made of a compressed powdered substance containing an active drug and excipients 2 a slab of stone, wood, etc, esp one formerly used for inscriptions 3 NZ a token giving right of way , to the driver of a train on a single line section

table tennis a miniature form of tennis played on a table with small bats and a light hollow ball
▷www.ittf.com
▷www.ettu.org
▷www.usatt.org

taboo or **tabu** 1 (in Polynesia and other islands of the South Pacific) marked off as simultaneously sacred and forbidden 2 ritual restriction or prohibition, esp of something that is considered holy or unclean

tabor or **tabour** *Music* a small drum used esp in the Middle Ages, struck with one hand while the other held a three-holed pipe

Tabor Mount a mountain in N Israel, near Nazareth: traditionally regarded as the mountain where the Transfiguration took place. Height: 588 m (1929 ft)

Tabriz a city in NW Iran: an ancient city, situated in a volcanic region of hot springs; university (1947); carpet manufacturing. Pop: 1 396 000 (2005 est)

tabulate (of certain corals) having transverse skeletal plates

tabulator *Computing* a machine that reads data from one medium, such as punched cards, producing lists, tabulations, or totals, usually on a continuous sheet of paper

tachograph a tachometer that produces a graphical record (**tachogram**) of its readings, esp a device for recording the speed of and distance covered by a heavy goods vehicle

tachometer any device for measuring speed, esp the rate of revolution of a shaft. Tachometers (rev counters) are often fitted to cars to indicate the number of revolutions per minute of the engine

tacit created or having effect by operation of law, rather than by being directly expressed

Tacitus Publius Cornelius ?55–?120 AD, Roman historian and orator, famous as a prose stylist. His works include the *Histories*, dealing with the period 68–96, and the *Annals*, dealing with the period 14–68

tack¹ 1 a short sharp-pointed nail, usually with a flat and comparatively large head 2 *Nautical* the heading of a vessel sailing to windward, stated in terms of the side of the sail against which the wind is pressing 3 *Nautical* **a** a course sailed by a sailing vessel with the wind blowing from forward of the beam **b** one such course or a zigzag pattern of such courses 4 *Nautical* **a** a sheet for controlling the weather clew of a course **b** the weather clew itself 5 *Nautical* the forward lower clew of a fore-and-aft sail

tack² a riding harness for horses, such as saddles, bridles, etc. **b** (*as modifier*): *the tack room*

tackle 1 any mechanical system for lifting or pulling, esp an arrangement of ropes and pulleys designed to lift heavy weights 2 *Nautical* the halyards and other running rigging aboard a vessel 3 *American football* a defensive lineman

Tacna-Arica a coastal desert region of W South America, long disputed by Chile and Peru: divided in 1929 into the Peruvian department of Tacna and the Chilean department of Arica

Tacoma a port in W Washington, on Puget Sound: industrial centre. Pop: 196 790 (2003 est)

tactical voting (in an election) the practice of casting one's vote not for the party of one's choice but for the second strongest contender in order to defeat the likeliest winner

tactile of, relating to, affecting, or having a sense of touch

tadpole the aquatic larva of frogs, toads, etc, which develops from a limbless tailed form with external gills into a form with internal gills, limbs, and a reduced tail

Taegu a city in SE South Korea: textile and agricultural trading centre. Pop: 2 510 000 (2005 est)

Taejon a city in W South Korea: market centre of an agricultural region. Pop: 1 464 000 (2005 est)

taffeta 1 **a** a crisp lustrous plain-weave silk, rayon, etc, used esp for women's clothes **b** (*as modifier*): *a taffeta petticoat* 2 any of various similar fabrics

taffrail *Nautical* 1 a rail at the stern or above the transom of a vessel 2 the upper part of the transom of a vessel, esp a sailing vessel, often ornately decorated

Tafilelt *or* **Tafilalet** an oasis in SE Morocco, the largest in the Sahara. Area: about 1300 sq km (500 sq miles)

Taft William Howard 1857–1930, US statesman; 27th president of the US (1909–13)

tag¹ 1 an electronic device worn, usually on the wrist or ankle, by an offender serving a noncustodial sentence, which monitors the offender's whereabouts by means of a link to a central computer through the telephone system 2 a brief quotation, esp one in a foreign language 3 the contrastingly coloured tip to an animal's tail 4 *Angling* a strand of tinsel, wire, etc, tied to the body of an artificial fly 5 *Slang* a graffito consisting of a nickname or personal symbol

tag² 1 a children's game in which one player chases the others in an attempt to catch one of them who will then become the chaser 2 denoting or relating to a wrestling contest between two teams of two wrestlers, in which only one from each team may be in the ring at one time. The contestant outside the ring may change places with his team-mate inside the ring after touching his hand

Tagalog 1 a member of a people of the Philippines, living chiefly in the region around Manila 2 the language of this people, belonging to the Malayo-Polynesian family: the official language of the Philippines

Taganrog a port in SW Russia, on the **Gulf of Taganrog** (an inlet of the Sea of Azov): founded in 1698 as a naval base and fortress by Peter the Great: industrial centre. Pop: 281 000 (2005 est)

Tagore Rabindranath 1861–1941, Indian poet and philosopher. His verse collections, written in Bengali and English, include *Gitanjali* (1910; 1912): Nobel prize for literature 1913

Tagus a river in SW Europe, rising in E central Spain and flowing west to the border with Portugal, then southwest to the Atlantic at Lisbon: the longest river of the Iberian Peninsula. Length: 1007 km (626 miles)

Tahiti an island in the S Pacific, in the Windward group of the Society Islands: the largest and most important island in French Polynesia; became a French protectorate in 1842 and a colony in 1880. Capital: Papeete. Pop: 169 674 (2002). Area: 1005 sq km (388 sq miles)

Tahoe Lake a lake between E California and W Nevada, in the Sierra Nevada Mountains at an altitude of 1899 m (6229 ft). Area: about 520 sq km (200 sq miles)

Taichung *or* **T'ai-chung** a city in W Taiwan: commercial centre of an agricultural region. Pop: 1 066 000 (2005 est)

taiga the coniferous forests extending across much of subarctic North America and Eurasia, bordered by tundra to the north and steppe to the south

tail¹ 1 the region of the vertebrate body that is posterior to or above the anus and contains an elongation of the vertebral column, esp forming a flexible movable appendage 2 the rear part of an aircraft including the fin, tail plane, and control surfaces; empennage 3 *Astronomy* the luminous stream of gas and dust particles, up to 200 million kilometres long, driven from the head of a comet, when close to the sun, under the effect of the solar wind and light pressure 4 *Angling* the lowest fly on a wet-fly cast 5 a final short line in a stanza 6 the lower end of a pool or part of a stream

tail² *Property law* 1 the limitation of an estate or interest to a person and the heirs of his body 2 (of an estate or interest) limited in this way

tailboard a board at the rear of a lorry, wagon, etc, that can be removed or let down on a hinge

tailgate 1 another name for **tailboard** 2 a door at the rear of a hatchback vehicle

tailor 1 a person who makes, repairs, or alters outer garments, esp menswear 2 a voracious and active marine food fish, *Pomatomus saltator*, of Australia with scissor-like teeth

tailorbird any of several tropical Asian warblers of the genus *Orthotomus*, which build nests by sewing together large leaves using plant fibres

tailpiece 1 *Music* a piece of wood to which the strings of a violin, etc, are attached at their lower end. It is suspended between the taut strings and the bottom of the violin by a piece of gut or metal 2 *Architect* a short beam or rafter that has one end embedded in a wall

tailpipe a pipe from which the exhaust gases from an internal-combustion engine are discharged, esp the terminal pipe of the exhaust system of a motor vehicle

tailplane a small horizontal wing at the tail of an aircraft to provide longitudinal stability

Taimyr Peninsula a large peninsula of N central Russia, between the Kara Sea and the Laptev Sea

Tainan *or* **T'ai-nan** a city in the SW Taiwan: an early centre of Chinese emigration from the mainland; largest city and capital of the island (1638–1885); Chengkung University. Pop: 754 000 (2005 est)

taipan¹ a large highly venomous elapid snake, *Oxyuranus scutellatus*, of NE Australia

taipan² the foreign head of a business in China

Taipei *or* **T'ai-pei** the capital of Taiwan (the Republic of China), at the N tip of the island: became capital in 1885; industrial centre; two universities. Pop: 2 473 000 (2005 est)

Taisho 1 the period of Japanese history and artistic style associated with the reign of Emperor Yoshihito (1912–26) 2 the throne name of Yoshihito (1879–1926), emperor of Japan (1912–26)

Taiwan an island in SE Asia between the East China Sea and the South China Sea, off the SE coast of the People's Republic of China: the principal territory of the Republic of China; claimed by the People's Republic of China since its political separation from mainland China in the late 1940s. Pop: 22 610 000 (2003 est)

Taiyuan *or* **T'ai-yüan** a city in N China, capital of Shanxi: founded before 450 AD; an industrial centre, surrounded by China's largest reserves of high-grade bituminous coal. Pop: 2 516 000 (2005 est)

Tajikistan, Tadzhikistan, *or* **Tadjikistan** a republic in central Asia: under Uzbek rule from the 15th century until taken over by Russia in the 1860s, it became an autonomous Soviet republic in 1929 and gained full independence from the Soviet Union in 1991; it is mainly mountainous. Official language: Tajik or Tajiki. Religion: believers are mainly Muslim. Currency: somoni. Capital: Dushanbe. Pop: 6 297 000 (2004 est). Area: 143 100 sq km (55 240 sq miles)

Taj Mahal a white marble mausoleum in central India, in Agra on the Jumna River: built (1632–43) by the emperor Shah Jahan in memory of his beloved wife, Mumtaz Mahal; regarded as the finest example of Mogul architecture

Takamatsu a port in SW Japan, on NE Shikoku on the Inland Sea. Pop: 333 387 (2002 est)

take 1 *Hunting* the number of quarry killed or captured on one occasion 2 *Informal, chiefly US* the amount of anything taken, esp money 3 *Films, Music* **a** one of a series of recordings from which the best will be selected for release **b** the process of taking one such recording **c** a scene or part of a scene photographed without interruption 4 *Med, informal* **a** any objective indication of a successful vaccination, such as a local skin reaction **b** a successful skin graft

takeoff 1 the act or process of making an aircraft airborne 2 the stage of a country's economic development when rapid and sustained economic growth is first achieved

takeout *Bridge* of or designating a conventional informatory bid, asking one's partner to bid another suit

take-up *Machinery* the distance through which a part must move to absorb the free play in a system

Takoradi the chief port of Ghana, in the southwest on the Gulf of Guinea: modern harbour opened in 1928. Pop. (with Sekondi): 335 000 (2005 est)

Talavera de la Reina a walled town in central Spain, on the Tagus River: scene of the defeat of the French by British and Spanish forces (1809) during the Peninsular War; agricultural processing centre. Pop: 79 916 (2003 est)

Talbot (William Henry) Fox 1800–77, British scientist, a pioneer of photography, who developed the calotype process

talc a white, grey, brown, or pale green mineral, found in metamorphic rocks. It is used in the manufacture of talcum powder and electrical insulators. Composition: hydrated magnesium silicate. Formula: $Mg_3Si_4O_{10}(OH)_2$. Crystal structure: monoclinic

Talca a city in central Chile: scene of the declaration of Chilean independence (1818). Pop: 206 000 (2005 est)

Talcahuano a port in S central Chile, near Concepción on an inlet of the Pacific: oil refinery. Pop: 251 000 (2005 est)

tale one of a group of short stories connected by an overall narrative framework

talent *History* any of various ancient units of weight and money

talent scout a person whose occupation is the search for talented artists, sportsmen, performers, etc, for engagements as professionals

Taliesin 6th century AD, Welsh bard; supposed author of 12 heroic poems in the *Book of Taliesin*

talisman 1 a stone or other small object, usually inscribed or carved, believed to protect the wearer from evil influences 2 anything thought to have magical or protective powers

talkie *Informal* an early film with a soundtrack

Tallahassee a city in N Florida, capital of the state: two universities. Pop: 153 938 (2003 est)

Tallinn *or* **Tallin** the capital of Estonia, on the Gulf of Finland: founded by the Danes in 1219; a port and naval base. Pop: 384 000 (2005 est)

Tallis Thomas ?1505–85, English composer and organist; noted for his music for the Anglican liturgy

tallow a fatty substance consisting of a mixture of glycerides, including stearic, palmitic, and oleic acids and extracted chiefly from the suet of sheep and cattle: used for making soap, candles, food, etc.

tall ship any square-rigged sailing ship

tally-ho 1 the cry of a participant at a hunt to encourage the hounds when the quarry is sighted 2 another name for a **four-in-hand**

Talmud *Judaism* 1 the primary source of Jewish religious law, consisting of the Mishnah and the Gemara 2 either of two recensions of this compilation, the

Palestinian Talmud of about 375 AD, or the longer and more important Babylonian Talmud of about 500 AD
▷http://www.oru.edu/university/library/guides/talmud.html
▷http://www.aishdas.org/webshas/

talon 1 a sharply hooked claw, esp of a bird of prey 2 *Cards* the pile of cards left after the deal 3 *Architect* another name for **ogee arch**

tamarind 1 a leguminous tropical evergreen tree, *Tamarindus indica*, having pale yellow red-streaked flowers and brown pulpy pods, each surrounded by a brittle shell 2 the acid fruit of this tree, used as a food and to make beverages and medicines 3 the wood of this tree

tamarisk any of various ornamental trees and shrubs of the genus *Tamarix*, of the Mediterranean region and S and SE Asia, having scalelike leaves, slender branches, and feathery clusters of pink or whitish flowers: family *Tamaricaceae*

Tamaulipas a state of NE Mexico, on the Gulf of Mexico. Capital: Ciudad Victoria. Pop: 2 747 114 (2000). Area: 79 829 sq km (30 822 sq miles)

Tambo Oliver 1917–93, South African politician; president (1977–91) of the African National Congress. He was arrested (1956) with Nelson Mandela but released (1957)

Tambora a volcano in Indonesia, on N Sumbawa: violent eruption of 1815 reduced its height from about 4000 m (13 000 ft) to 2850 m (9400 ft)

tambour 1 *Real Tennis* the sloping buttress on one side of the receiver's end of the court 2 *Architect* a wall that is circular in plan, esp one that supports a dome or one that is surrounded by a colonnade 3 a drum

tambourine *Music* a percussion instrument consisting of a single drumhead of skin stretched over a circular wooden frame hung with pairs of metal discs that jingle when it is struck or shaken

Tambov an industrial city in W Russia: founded in 1636 as a Muscovite fort; a major engineering centre. Pop: 293 000 (2005 est)

Tamerlane or **Tamburlaine** Turkic name *Timur*. ?1336–1405, Mongol conqueror of the area from Mongolia to the Mediterranean; ruler of Samarkand (1369–1405). He defeated the Turks at Angora (1402) and died while invading China

Tameside a unitary authority of NW England, in Greater Manchester. Pop: 213 400 (2003 est). Area: 103 sq km (40 sq miles)

Tamil 1 a member of a mixed Dravidian and Caucasoid people of S India and Sri Lanka 2 the language of this people: the state language of Tamil Nadu, also spoken in Sri Lanka and elsewhere, belonging to the Dravidian family of languages

Tamil Nadu a state of SE India, on the Coromandel Coast: reorganized in 1956 and 1960 and made smaller; consists of a coastal plain backed by hills, including the Nilgiri Hills in the west. Capital: Madras. Pop: 62 110 839 (2001). Area: 130 058 sq km (50 216 sq miles)

Tampa a port and resort in W Florida, on **Tampa Bay** (an arm of the Gulf of Mexico): two universities. Pop: 317 647 (2003 est)

Tampere a city in SW Finland: the second largest town in Finland; textile manufacturing. Pop: 200 966 (2003 est)

Tampico a port and resort in E Mexico, in Tamaulipas on the Pánuco River: oil refining. Pop: 702 000 (2005 est)

tampon a plug of lint, cotton wool, cotton, etc, inserted into an open wound or body cavity to stop the flow of blood, absorb secretions, etc, esp one inserted into the vagina to absorb menstrual blood

Tamworth 1 a market town in W central England, in SE Staffordshire. Pop: 71 650 (2001) 2 a city in SE Australia, in E central New South Wales: industrial centre of an agricultural region. Pop: 32 543 (2001)

tan 1 a light or moderate yellowish-brown colour 2 of the colour tan

Tana 1 **Lake** Also called: (Lake) **Tsana** a lake in NW Ethiopia, on a plateau 1800 m (6000 ft) high: the largest lake of Ethiopia; source of the Blue Nile. Area: 3673 sq km (1418 sq miles) 2 a river in E Kenya, rising in the Aberdare Range and flowing in a wide curve east to the Indian Ocean: the longest river in Kenya. Length: 708 km (440 miles) 3 a river in NE Norway, flowing generally northeast as part of the border between Norway and Finland to the Arctic Ocean by Tana Fjord. Length: about 320 km (200 miles)

Tanagra a town in ancient Boeotia, famous for terracotta figurines of the same name, first discovered in its necropolis

Tanana a river in central Alaska, rising in the Wrangell Mountains and flowing northwest to the Yukon River. Length: about 765 km (475 miles)

Tancred died 1112, Norman hero of the First Crusade, who played a prominent part in the capture of Jerusalem (1099)

Tandjungpriok or **Tanjungpriok** a port in Indonesia, on the NW coast of Java adjoining the capital, Jakarta: a major shipping and distributing centre for the whole archipelago

tang the pointed end of a tool, such as a chisel, file, knife, etc, which is fitted into a handle, shaft, or stock

Tanga a port in N Tanzania, on the Indian Ocean: Tanzania's second port. Pop: 190 000 (2005 est)

Tanganyika 1 a former state in E Africa: became part of German East Africa in 1884; ceded to Britain as a League of Nations mandate in 1919 and as a UN trust territory in 1946; gained independence in 1961 and united with Zanzibar in 1964 as the United Republic of Tanzania 2 **Lake** a lake in central Africa between Tanzania and the Democratic Republic of Congo (formerly Zaïre), bordering also on Burundi and Zambia, in the Great Rift Valley: the longest freshwater lake in the world. Area: 32 893 sq km (12 700 sq miles). Length: 676 km (420 miles)

tangata whenua NZ the indigenous Māori people of a particular area of New Zealand or of the country as a whole

Tange Kenzo born 1913, Japanese architect. His buildings include the Kurashiki city hall (1960) and St Mary's Cathedral in Tokyo (1962–64)

tangent 1 a geometric line, curve, plane, or curved surface that touches another curve or surface at one point but does not intersect it 2 (of an angle) a trigonometric function that in a right-angled triangle is the ratio of the length of the opposite side to that of the adjacent side; the ratio of sine to cosine 3 *Music* a part of the action of a clavichord consisting of a small piece of metal that strikes the string to produce a note

tangential 1 of, being, relating to, or in the direction of a tangent 2 *Astronomy* (of velocity) in a direction perpendicular to the line of sight of a celestial object

tangerine 1 an Asian citrus tree, *Citrus reticulata*, cultivated for its small edible orange-like fruits 2 the fruit of this tree, having a loose rind and sweet spicy flesh 3a a reddish-orange colour **b** (*as adjective*): *a tangerine door*

tangi NZ 1 a Māori funeral ceremony 2 *Informal* a lamentation

Tangier a port in N Morocco, on the Strait of Gibraltar: a Phoenician trading post in the 15th century BC; a neutral international zone (1923–56); made the summer capital of Morocco and a free port in 1962; commercial and financial centre. Pop: 526 000 (2003)

tango 1 a Latin American dance in duple time, characterized by long gliding steps and sudden pauses 2 a piece of music composed for or in the rhythm of this dance

Tangshan an industrial city in NE China, in Hebei province. Pop: 1 773 000 (2005 est)

Tanguy Yves 1900–55, US surrealist painter, born in France

Tanis an ancient city located in the E part of the Nile delta: abandoned after the 6th century BC; at one time the capital of Egypt

taniwha NZ a legendary Māori monster

tank 1 *Photog* **a** a light-tight container inside which a film can be processed in daylight, the solutions and rinsing waters being poured in and out without light entering **b** any large dish or container used for processing a number of strips or sheets of film 2 *Slang, chiefly US* **a** a jail **b** a jail cell 3 *Austral* a dam formed by excavation

Tannenberg a village in N Poland, formerly in East Prussia: site of a decisive defeat of the Teutonic Knights by the Poles in 1410 and of a decisive German victory over the Russians in 1914

tannin any of a class of yellowish or brownish solid compounds found in many plants and used as tanning agents, mordants, medical astringents, etc. Tannins are derivatives of gallic acid with the approximate formula $C_{76}H_{52}O_{46}$

tansy 1 any of numerous plants of the genus *Tanacetum*, esp *T. vulgare*, having yellow flowers in flat-topped clusters and formerly used in medicine and for seasoning: family *Asteraceae* (composites) 2 any of various similar plants

Tanta a city in N Egypt, on the Nile delta: noted for its Muslim festivals. Pop: 413 000 (2005 est)

tantalum a hard greyish-white metallic element that occurs with niobium in tantalite and columbite: used in electrical capacitors in most circuit boards and in alloys to increase hardness and chemical resistance, esp in surgical instruments. Symbol: Ta; atomic no.: 73; atomic wt.: 180.9479; valency: 2, 3, 4, or 5; relative density: 16.654; melting pt.: 3020°C; boiling pt.: 5458±100°C

Tanzania a republic in E Africa, on the Indian Ocean: formed by the union of the independent states of Tanganyika and Zanzibar in 1964; a member of the Commonwealth. Exports include coffee, tea, sisal, and cotton. Official languages: Swahili and English. Religions: Christian, Muslim, and animist. Currency: Tanzanian shilling. Capital: Dodoma. Pop: 37 671 000 (2004 est). Area: 945 203 sq km (364 943 sq miles)

Taoiseach the prime minister of the Republic of Ireland

Taoism 1 the philosophy of Lao Zi, the Chinese philosopher (?604–?531 BC), that advocates a simple honest life and noninterference with the course of natural events 2 a popular Chinese system of religion and philosophy claiming to be teachings of Lao Zi but also incorporating pantheism and sorcery
▷http://taopage.org/
▷http://crystalinks.com/taoism.html

tap 1 a particular quality of alcoholic drink, esp when contained in casks 2 the surgical withdrawal of fluid from a bodily cavity 3 a tool for cutting female screw threads, consisting of a threaded steel cylinder with longitudinal grooves forming cutting edges 4 *Electronics, chiefly US and Canadian* a connection made at some point between the end terminals of an inductor, resistor, or some other component

tape 1 a string stretched across the track at the end of a race course 2 **tape recording**: see **magnetic tape, ticker tape**

tape deck 1 a tape recording unit in a hi-fi system 2 the platform supporting the spools, cassettes, or cartridges of a tape recorder, incorporating the motor or motors that drive them and the playback, recording, and erasing heads

tape drive *Computing* a device for reading from or writing to magnetic tape

taper *Engineering* (in conical parts) the amount of variation in the diameter per unit of length

tape recorder an electrical device used for recording sounds on magnetic tape and usually also for reproducing them, consisting of a tape deck and one or more amplifiers and loudspeakers

tape recording 1 the act or process of recording on magnetic tape 2 the speech, music, etc, so recorded

tapestry a heavy ornamental fabric, often in the form of a picture, used for wall hangings, furnishings, etc, and made by weaving coloured threads into a fixed warp
▷www.adorabella.com.au/HistoryTapestry.htm
▷www.bayeuxtapestry.org.uk
▷www.metmuseum.org/explore/Unicorn/unicorn_inside.htm

tapeworm any parasitic ribbon-like flatworm of the class *Cestoda*, having a body divided into many egg-producing segments and lacking a mouth and gut. The adults inhabit the intestines of vertebrates

tapir any perissodactyl mammal of the genus *Tapirus*, such as *T. indicus* (**Malayan tapir**), of South and Central America and SE Asia, having an elongated snout, three-toed hind legs, and four-toed forelegs: family *Tapiridae*

tappet a mechanical part that reciprocates to receive or transmit intermittent motion, esp the part of an internal-combustion engine that transmits motion from the camshaft to the push rods or valves

taproot the large single root of plants such as the dandelion, which grows vertically downwards and bears smaller lateral roots

tar 1 any of various dark viscid substances obtained by the destructive distillation of organic matter such as coal, wood, or peat 2 another name for **coal tar**

Tara a village in Co. Meath near Dublin, by the **Hill of Tara**, the historic seat of the ancient Irish kings

Tarabulus el Gharb transliteration of the Arabic name for **Tripoli** (Libya)

Tarabulus esh Sham transliteration of the Arabic name for **Tripoli** (Lebanon)

tarakihi or **terakihi** a common edible sea fish of New Zealand waters

tarantella 1 a peasant dance from S Italy 2 a piece of music composed for or in the rhythm of this dance, in fast six-eight time

Tarantino Quentin born 1963, US film director and screenwriter, noted for violent quirky crime dramas including *Reservoir Dogs* (1993), *Pulp Fiction* (1994), *Jackie Brown* (1998), and the two parts of *Kill Bill* (2003, 2004)

Taranto a port in SE Italy, in Apulia on the **Gulf of Taranto** (an inlet of the Ionian Sea): the chief city of Magna Graecia; taken by the Romans in 272 BC. Pop: 202 033 (2001)

tarantula 1 any of various large hairy mostly tropical spiders of the American family *Theraphosidae* 2 a large hairy spider, *Lycosa tarentula* of S Europe, the bite of which was formerly thought to cause tarantism

Tarawa an atoll in Kiribati, occupying a chain of islets surrounding a lagoon in the W central Pacific: the capital of Kiribati, Bairiki, is on this atoll. Pop: 32 354 (1995)

Tarbes a town in SW France: noted for the breeding of Anglo-Arab horses. Pop: 46 275 (1999)

tare[1] 1 any of various vetch plants, such as *Vicia hirsuta* (**hairy tare**) of Eurasia and N Africa 2 the seed of any of these plants

tare[2] *Bible* a troublesome weed, thought to be the darnel

tare[3] 1 the weight of the wrapping or container in which goods are packed 2 a deduction from gross weight to compensate for this 3 the weight of a vehicle without its cargo, passengers, etc. 4 an empty container used as a counterbalance in determining net weight

target 1 a an object or area at which an archer or marksman aims, usually a round flat surface marked with concentric rings b (*as modifier*): *target practice* 2 *Physics, Electronics* a a substance, object, or system subjected to bombardment by electrons or other particles, or to irradiation b an electrode in a television camera tube whose surface, on which image information is stored, is scanned by the electron beam 3 *Electronics* an object to be detected by the reflection of a radar or sonar signal, etc.

tariff 1 a a tax levied by a government on imports or occasionally exports for purposes of protection, support of the balance of payments, or the raising of revenue b a system or list of such taxes 2 *Chiefly Brit* a a method of charging for the supply of services, esp public services, such as gas and electricity b a schedule of such charges 3 *Chiefly Brit* a bill of fare with prices listed; menu

Tarim a river in NW China, in Xinjiang Uygur AR: flows east along the N edge of the Taklimakan Shama desert, dividing repeatedly and forming lakes among the dunes, finally disappearing in the Lop Nor depression; the chief river of Xinjiang Uygur AR; drains the great

Tarim Basin between the Tian Shan and Kunlun mountain systems of central Asia, an area of about 906 500 sq km (350 000 sq miles). Length: 2190 km (1360 miles)

Tarkington (Newton) Booth 1869–1946, US novelist. His works include the historical romance *Monsieur Beaucaire* (1900), tales of the Middle West, such as *The Magnificent Ambersons* (1918) and *Alice Adams* (1921), and the series featuring the character Penrod

Tarkovsky Andrei 1932–86, Soviet film director, whose films include *Andrei Rublev* (1966), *Solaris* (1971), *Nostalgia* (1983), and *The Sacrifice* (1986)

tarn a small mountain lake or pool

Tarn 1 a department of S France, in Midi-Pyrénées region. Capital: Albi. Pop: 350 477 (2003 est). Area: 5780 sq km (2254 sq miles) 2 a river in SW France, rising in the Massif Central and flowing generally west to the Garonne River. Length: 375 km (233 miles)

Tarn-et-Garonne a department of SW France, in Midi-Pyrénées region. Capital: Montauban. Pop: 214 488 (2003 est). Area: 3731 sq km (1455 sq miles)

taro 1 an aroid plant, *Colocasia esculenta*, cultivated in the tropics for its large edible rootstock 2 the rootstock of this plant

tarot 1 one of a special pack of cards, now used mainly for fortune-telling, consisting of 78 cards (4 suits of 14 cards each (the minor arcana), and 22 other cards (the major arcana)) 2 a card in a tarot pack with distinctive symbolic design, such as the Wheel of Fortune

tarpaulin 1 a heavy hard-wearing waterproof fabric made of canvas or similar material coated with tar, wax, or paint, for outdoor use as a protective covering against moisture 2 a sheet of this fabric 3 a rare word for **seaman**

tarragon 1 an aromatic perennial plant, *Artemisia dracunculus*, of the Old World, having whitish flowers and small toothed leaves, which are used as seasoning: family *Asteraceae* (composites) 2 the leaves of this plant

Tarragona a port in NE Spain, on the Mediterranean: one of the richest seaports of the Roman Empire; destroyed by the Moors (714). Pop: 121 076 (2003 est)

Tarrasa a city in NE Spain: textile centre. Pop: 184 829 (2003 est)

tarseal *NZ* the bitumen surface of a road

Tarshish *Old Testament* an ancient port, mentioned in I Kings 10:22, situated in Spain or in one of the Phoenician colonies in Sardinia

tarsier any of several nocturnal arboreal prosimian primates of the genus *Tarsius*, of Indonesia and the Philippines, having huge eyes, long hind legs, and digits ending in pads to facilitate climbing: family *Tarsiidae*

tarsus 1 the bones of the ankle and heel, collectively 2 the corresponding part in other mammals and in amphibians and reptiles 3 the dense connective tissue supporting the free edge of each eyelid 4 the part of an insect's leg that lies distal to the tibia

Tarsus 1 a city in SE Turkey, on the Tarsus River: site of ruins of ancient Tarsus, capital of Cilicia, and birthplace of St. Paul. Pop: 231 000 (2005 est) 2 a river in SE Turkey, in Cilicia, rising in the Taurus Mountains and flowing south past Tarsus to the Mediterranean. Length: 153 km (95 miles)

tartan[1] 1 a a design of straight lines, crossing at right angles to give a chequered appearance, esp the distinctive design or designs associated with each Scottish clan **b** (*as modifier*): *a tartan kilt* **2** a woollen fabric or garment with this design

tartan² a single-masted vessel used in the Mediterranean, usually with a lateen sail

tartar 1 *Dentistry* a hard crusty deposit on the teeth, consisting of food, cellular debris, and mineral salts **2** a brownish-red substance consisting mainly of potassium hydrogen tartrate, present in grape juice and deposited during the fermentation of wine

tartaric acid a colourless or white odourless crystalline water-soluble dicarboxylic acid existing in four stereoisomeric forms, the commonest being the dextrorotatory (*d-*) compound which is found in many fruits: used as a food additive (**E334**) in soft drinks, confectionery, and baking powders and in tanning and photography. Formula: HOOCCH(OH)CH(OH)COOH

Tartu a city in SE Estonia: successively under Polish, Swedish, and Russian rule; university (1632). Pop: 95 000 (2005 est)

Tashkent the capital of Uzbekistan: one of the oldest and largest cities in central Asia; cotton textile manufacturing. Pop: 2 160 000 (2005 est)

Tasman Abel Janszoon 1603–59, Dutch navigator, who discovered Tasmania, New Zealand, and the Tonga and Fiji Islands (1642–43)

Tasmania an island in the S Pacific, south of mainland Australia: forms, with offshore islands, the smallest state of Australia; discovered by the Dutch explorer Tasman in 1642; used as a penal colony by the British (1803–53); mostly forested and mountainous. Capital: Hobart. Pop: 479 958 (2003 est). Area: 68 332 sq km (26 383 sq miles)

Tasmanian devil a small ferocious carnivorous marsupial, *Sarcophilus harrisi*, of Tasmania, having black fur with pale markings, strong jaws, and short legs: family *Dasyuridae*

Tasman Sea the part of the Pacific between SE Australia and NW New Zealand

Tass (formerly) the principal news agency of the Soviet Union: replaced in 1992 by **Itar Tass**

tassel anything resembling this tuft, esp the tuft of stamens at the tip of a maize inflorescence

Tassie or **Tassy** *Austral, informal* **1** Tasmania **2** a native or inhabitant of Tasmania

Tasso Torquato 1544–95, Italian poet, noted for his pastoral idyll *Aminta* (1573) and for *Jerusalem Delivered* (1581), dealing with the First Crusade

taste 1 the sense by which the qualities and flavour of a substance are distinguished by the taste buds **2** the sensation experienced by means of the taste buds

taste bud any of the elevated oval-shaped sensory end organs on the surface of the tongue, by means of which the sensation of taste is experienced

taster 1 a person employed, esp formerly, to taste food and drink prepared for a king, etc, to test for poison **2** a sample or preview of a product, experience, etc, intended to stimulate interest in the product, experience, etc, itself

Tatar or **Tartar 1 a** a member of a Mongoloid people who under Genghis Khan established a vast and power-

ful state in central Asia from the 13th century until conquered by Russia in 1552 **b** a descendant of this people, now scattered throughout Russia but living chiefly in the Tatar Republic **2** any of the languages spoken by the present-day Tatars, belonging to various branches of the Turkic family of languages, esp Kazan Tatar

Tatar Republic a constituent republic of W Russia, around the confluence of the Volga and Kama Rivers. Capital: Kazan. Pop: 3 779 800 (2002). Area: 68 000 sq km (26 250 sq miles)

Tatar Strait an arm of the Pacific between the mainland of SE Russia and Sakhalin Island, linking the Sea of Japan with the Sea of Okhotsk. Length: about 560 km (350 miles)

Tatary or **Tartary 1** a historical region (with indefinite boundaries) in E Europe and Asia, inhabited by Bulgars until overrun by the Tatars in the mid-13th century: extended as far east as the Pacific under Genghis Khan **2 Gulf of** another name for the **Tatar Strait**

Tate 1 (John Orley) Allen 1899–1979, US poet and critic **2** Sir Henry 1819–99, British sugar refiner and philanthropist; founder of the Tate Gallery **3** Nahum 1652–1715, British poet, dramatist, and hymn-writer, born in Ireland: poet laureate (1692–1715). He is best known for writing a version of *King Lear* with a happy ending

Tati Jacques , real name *Jacques Tatischeff*. 1908–82, French film director, pantomimist, and comic actor, creator of the character Monsieur Hulot

tattoo a picture or design made on someone's body by pricking small holes in the skin and filling them with indelible dye

Tatum 1 Art, full name *Arthur Tatum*. 1910–56, US jazz pianist **2** Edward Lawrie 1909–75, US biochemist, who showed how genes regulate biochemical processes in an organism and demonstrated that bacteria reproduce sexually; Nobel prize for physiology or medicine (1958) with Beadle and Lederberg

taunt *Nautical* (of the mast or masts of a sailing vessel) unusually tall

Taunton a market town in SW England, administrative centre of Somerset: scene of Judge Jeffreys' "Bloody Assize" (1685) after the Battle of Sedgemoor. Pop: 58 241 (2001)

Taupo Lake a lake in New Zealand, on central North Island: the largest lake of New Zealand. Area: 616 sq km (238 sq miles)

Tauranga a port in New Zealand, on NE North Island on the Bay of Plenty: exports dairy produce, meat, and timber. Pop: 101 300 (2004 est)

Taurus 1 *Astronomy* a zodiacal constellation in the N hemisphere lying close to Orion and between Aries and Gemini. It contains the star Aldebaran, the star clusters Hyades and Pleiades, and the Crab Nebula **2** *Astrology* **a** the second sign of the zodiac, symbol ♉, having a fixed earth classification and ruled by the planet Venus. The sun is in this sign between about April 20 and May 20 **b** a person born when the sun is in this sign **3** born under or characteristic of Taurus

taut *Chiefly nautical* in good order; neat

tautology *Logic* a statement that is always true, esp a truth-functional expression that takes the value true for all combinations of values of its components, as in *either the sun is out or the sun is not out*

Tavener Sir John (**Kenneth**). born 1944, British composer, whose works include the cantata *The Whale* (1966), the opera *Thérèse* (1979), and the choral work *The Last Discourse* (1998); many of his later works are inspired by the liturgy of the Russian Orthodox Church

tavern 1 a less common word for **pub 2** *US, Eastern Canadian, and NZ* a place licensed for the sale and consumption of alcoholic drink

Taverner John ?1495–1545, English composer, esp of church music; best known for the mass *Western Wynde*, based on a secular song

tawny *or* **tawney** a light brown to brownish-orange colour **b** (*as adjective*): *tawny port*

tawny owl a European owl, *Strix aluco*, having a reddish-brown or grey plumage, black eyes, and a round head

tawse *or* **taws** *Chiefly Scot* a leather strap having one end cut into thongs, formerly used as an instrument of punishment by a schoolteacher

tax a compulsory financial contribution imposed by a government to raise revenue, levied on the income or property of persons or organizations, on the production costs or sales prices of goods and services, etc.

tax evasion reduction or minimization of tax liability by illegal methods

taxi a car, usually fitted with a taximeter, that may be hired, along with its driver, to carry passengers to any specified destination

taxonomy a the branch of biology concerned with the classification of organisms into groups based on similarities of structure, origin, etc. **b** the practice of arranging organisms in this way

Tay 1 Firth of the estuary of the River Tay on the North Sea coast of Scotland. Length: 40 km (25 miles) **2** a river in central Scotland, flowing northeast through Loch Tay, then southeast to the Firth of Tay: the longest river in Scotland; noted for salmon fishing. Length: 193 km (120 miles) **3 Loch** a lake in central Scotland, in Stirling council area. Length: 23 km (14 miles)

Taylor 1 A(lan) J(ohn) P(ercivale). 1906–90, British historian whose many works include *The Origins of the Second World War* (1961) **2 Brook** 1685–1731, English mathematician, who laid the foundations of differential calculus **3** Dame **Elizabeth** born 1932, US film actress, born in England: films include *National Velvet* (1944), *Cat on a Hot Tin Roof* (1958), *Suddenly Last Summer* (1959), and *Butterfield 8* (1960) and *Who's Afraid of Virginia Woolf?* (1966), for both of which she won Oscars **4 Frederick Winslow** 1856–1915, US engineer, who pioneered the use of time and motion studies to increase efficiency in industry **5 Jeremy** 1613–67, English cleric, best known for his devotional manuals *Holy Living* (1650) and *Holy Dying* (1651) **6** **Zachary** 1784–1850, 12th president of the US (1849–50); hero of the Mexican War

Tayside Region a former local government region in E Scotland: formed in 1975 from Angus, Kinross-shire, and most of Perthshire; replaced in 1996 by the council areas of Angus, City of Dundee, and Perth and Kinross

Tbilisi the capital of Georgia, on the Kura River: founded in 458; taken by the Russians in 1801; university (1918); a major industrial centre. Pop: 1 042 000 (2005 est)

Tchaikovsky Pyotr Ilyich 1840–93, Russian composer.

His works, which are noted for their expressive melodies, include the *Sixth Symphony* (the *Pathétique;* 1893), ballets, esp *Swan Lake* (1876) and *The Sleeping Beauty* (1889), and operas, including *Eugene Onegin* (1879) and *The Queen of Spades* (1890), both based on works by Pushkin

te *or* **ti** *Music* (in tonic sol-fa) the syllable used for the seventh note or subtonic of any scale

tea 1 an evergreen shrub or small tree, *Camellia sinensis*, of tropical and subtropical Asia, having toothed leathery leaves and white fragrant flowers: family *Theaceae* **2 a** any of various plants that are similar to *Camellia sinensis* or are used to make a tealike beverage **b** any such beverage

▷www.teacouncil.co.uk
▷www.tea.co.uk
▷http://coffeetea.about.com
▷www.nicecupofteaandasitdown.com

teacup the amount a teacup will hold, about four fluid ounces

teahouse a restaurant, esp in Japan or China, where tea and light refreshments are served

teak 1 a large verbenaceous tree, *Tectona grandis*, of the East Indies, having white flowers and yielding a valuable dense wood **2** any of various similar trees or their wood **3** the hard resinous yellowish-brown wood of this tree, used for furniture making, etc. **4** a brown or yellowish-brown colour

teal 1 any of various small ducks, such as the Eurasian *Anas crecca* (**common teal**) that are related to the mallard and frequent ponds, lakes, and marshes **2** a greenish-blue colour

tear a drop of the secretion of the lacrimal glands

tear gas any one of a number of gases or vapours that make the eyes smart and water, causing temporary blindness; usually dispersed from grenades and used in warfare and to control riots

teasel, teazel, *or* **teazle 1** any of various stout biennial plants of the genus *Dipsacus*, of Eurasia and N Africa, having prickly leaves and prickly heads of yellow or purple flowers: family *Dipsacaceae* **2 a** the prickly dried flower head of the fuller's teasel, used for teasing **b** any manufactured implement used for the same purpose

teaser *Vet science* a vasectomized male animal, such as an ox, used to detect oestrus in females

teaspoon a unit of capacity used in cooking, medicine, etc, equal to about one fluid dram

teat a the nipple of a mammary gland **b** (in cows, etc) any of the projections from the udder through which milk is discharged

tea tree any of various myrtaceous trees of the genus *Leptospermum*, of Australia and New Zealand, that yield an oil used as an antiseptic

technetium a silvery-grey metallic element, artificially produced by bombardment of molybdenum by deuterons: used to inhibit corrosion in steel. The radioisotope **technetium-99m**, with a half-life of six hours, is used in radiotherapy. Symbol: Tc; atomic no.: 43; half-life of most stable isotope, ^{97}Tc: 2.6×10^6 years; valency: 0, 2, 4, 5, 6, or 7; relative density: 11.50 (calculated); melting pt.: 2204°C; boiling pt.: 4265°C

technical college *Brit* an institution for further education that provides courses in technology, art, secretarial skills, agriculture, etc.

technical drawing the study and practice, esp as a subject taught in school, of the basic techniques of draughtsmanship, as employed in mechanical drawing, architecture, etc.

technical knockout *Boxing* a judgment of a knockout given when a boxer is in the referee's opinion too badly beaten to continue without risk of serious injury

Technicolor *Trademark* the process of producing colour film by means of superimposing synchronized films of the same scene, each of which has a different colour filter, to obtain the desired mix of colour

technikon *South African* a technical college

technocracy 1 a theory or system of society according to which government is controlled by scientists, engineers, and other experts 2 a body of such experts 3 a state considered to be governed or organized according to these principles

tectonics the study of the processes by which the earth's crust has attained its present structure

Tecumseh ?1768–1813, American Indian chief of the Shawnee tribe. He attempted to unite western Indian tribes against the Whites, but was defeated at Tippecanoe (1811). He was killed while fighting for the British in the War of 1812

Tedder Arthur William, 1st Baron Tedder of Glenguin. 1890–1967, British marshal of the Royal Air Force; deputy commander under Eisenhower of the Allied Expeditionary Force (1944–45)

Te Deum 1 an ancient Latin hymn in rhythmic prose, sung or recited at matins in the Roman Catholic Church and in English translation at morning prayer in the Church of England and used by both Churches as an expression of thanksgiving on special occasions 2 a musical setting of this hymn 3 a service of thanksgiving in which the recital of this hymn forms a central part

tee[1] *Golf* 1 an area, often slightly elevated, from which the first stroke of a hole is made 2 a support for a golf ball, usually a small wooden or plastic peg, used when teeing off or in long grass, etc.

tee[2] a mark used as a target in certain games such as curling and quoits

Tees a river in N England, rising in the N Pennines and flowing southeast and east to the North Sea at Middlesbrough. Length: 113 km (70 miles)

Teesside the industrial region around the lower Tees valley and estuary: a county borough, containing Middlesbrough, from 1968 to 1974

TEFL Teaching (of) English as a Foreign Language

Teflon a trademark used for nonstick coatings on saucepans, etc.

Tegucigalpa the capital of Honduras, in the south on the Choluteca River: founded about 1579; university (1847). Pop: 1 061 000 (2005 est)

Tehran *or* **Teheran** the capital of Iran, at the foot of the Elburz Mountains: built on the site of the ancient capital Ray, destroyed by Mongols in 1220; became capital in the 1790s; three universities. Pop: 7 352 000 (2005 est)

Tehuantepec Isthmus of the narrowest part of S Mexico, with the Bay of Campeche on the north coast and the Gulf of Tehuantepec (an inlet of the Pacific) on the south coast

Teide *or* **Teyde** Pico de a volcanic mountain in the Canary Islands, on Tenerife. Height: 3718 m (12 198 ft)

Teilhard de Chardin Pierre 1881–1955, French Jesuit priest, palaeontologist, and philosopher. *The Phenomenon of Man* (1938–40), uses scientific evolution to prove the existence of God

Te Kanawa Dame Kiri born 1944, New Zealand operatic soprano

Tel Aviv a city in W Israel, on the Mediterranean: the largest city and chief financial centre in Israel; incorporated the city of Jaffa in 1950; university (1953): the capital of Israel according to the UN and international law. Pop: 363 400 (2003 est)

Telemann Georg Philipp 1681–1767, German composer, noted for his prolific output

teleology 1 *Philosophy* **a** the doctrine that there is evidence of purpose or design in the universe, and esp that this provides proof of the existence of a Designer **b** the belief that certain phenomena are best explained in terms of purpose rather than cause **c** the systematic study of such phenomena 2 *Biology* the belief that natural phenomena have a predetermined purpose and are not determined by mechanical laws

telepathy *Psychol* the communication between people of thoughts, feelings, desires, etc, involving mechanisms that cannot be understood in terms of known scientific laws

telephoto lens a compound camera lens in which the focal length is greater than that of a simple lens of the same dimensions and thus produces a magnified image of a distant object

teleprinter 1 a telegraph apparatus consisting of a keyboard transmitter, which converts a typed message into coded pulses for transmission along a wire or cable, and a printing receiver, which converts incoming signals and prints out the message. See also **telex** *or* **radioteletype** 2 a network of such devices, formerly used for communicating information, etc. 3 a similar device used for direct input/output of data into a computer at a distant location

telesales the selling or attempted selling of a particular commodity or service by a salesman who makes his initial approach by telephone

telescope 1 an optical instrument for making distant objects appear larger and brighter by use of a combination of lenses (**refracting telescope**) or lenses and curved mirrors (**reflecting telescope**) 2 any instrument, such as a radio telescope, for collecting, focusing, and detecting electromagnetic radiation from space

televangelist *US* an evangelical preacher who appears regularly on television, preaching the gospel and appealing for donations from viewers

television 1 the system or process of producing on a distant screen a series of transient visible images, usually with an accompanying sound signal. Electrical signals, converted from optical images by a camera tube, are transmitted by UHF or VHF radio waves or by cable and reconverted into optical images by means of a television tube inside a television set 2 a device designed to receive and convert incoming electrical signals into a series of visible images on a screen together with accompanying sound

▷www.emmys.com

teleworking the use of home computers, telephones, etc, to enable a person to work from home while maintaining contact with colleagues, customers, or a central office

Telford¹ **Thomas** 1757–1834, Scottish civil engineer, known esp for his roads and such bridges as the Menai suspension bridge (1825)

Telford² a town in W central England, in Telford and Wrekin unitary authority, Shropshire: designated a new town in 1963. Pop: 138 241 (2001)

Telford and Wrekin a unitary authority in W Central England, in Shropshire. Pop: 160 300 (2003 est). Area: 289 sq km (112 sq miles)

tell a large mound resulting from the accumulation of rubbish on a long-settled site, esp one with mudbrick buildings, particularly in the Middle East

Tell William, German name *Wilhelm Tell.* a legendary Swiss patriot, who, traditionally, lived in the early 14th century and was compelled by an Austrian governor to shoot an apple from his son's head with one shot of his crossbow. He did so without mishap

Tell el Amarna a group of ruins and rock tombs in Upper Egypt, on the Nile below Asyut: site of the capital of Amenhotep IV, built about 1375 BC; excavated from 1891 onwards

teller *Politics* a person appointed to count votes in a legislative body, assembly, etc.

Teller Edward 1908–2003, US nuclear physicist, born in Hungary: a major contributor to the development of the hydrogen bomb (1952)

telltale 1 any of various indicators or recording devices used to monitor a process, machine, etc. 2 *Nautical* one of a pair of light vanes mounted on the main shrouds of a sailing boat to indicate the apparent direction of the wind

tellurium a brittle silvery-white nonmetallic element occurring both uncombined and in combination with metals: used in alloys of lead and copper and as a semiconductor. Symbol: Te; atomic no.: 52; atomic wt.: 127.60; valency: 2, 4, or 6; relative density: 6.24; melting pt.: 449.57±0.3°C; boiling pt.: 988°C

Telukbetung *or* **Teloekbetoeng** a port in Indonesia, in S Sumatra on the Sunda Strait. Pop: 742 749 (2000)

Tema a port in SE Ghana on the Atlantic: new harbour opened in 1962; oil-refining. Pop: 160 000 (2005 est)

temazepam a benzodiazepine sedative; the gel-like capsule formulation is properly taken orally but has also been melted and injected by drug users

Tempe Vale of a wooded valley in E Greece, in Thessaly between the mountains Olympus and Ossa

temper the degree of hardness, elasticity, or a similar property of a metal or metal object

tempera 1 a painting medium for powdered pigments, consisting usually of egg yolk and water 2 a any emulsion used as a painting medium, with casein, glue, wax, etc, as a base b the paint made from mixing this with pigment 3 the technique of painting with tempera

temperament 1 the characteristic way an individual behaves, esp towards other people 2 an adjustment

made to the frequency differences between notes on a keyboard instrument to allow modulation to other keys 3 *Obsolete* the characteristic way an individual behaves, viewed as the result of the influence of the four humours (blood, phlegm, yellow bile, and black bile)

temperate having a climate intermediate between tropical and polar; moderate or mild in temperature

Temperate Zone those parts of the earth's surface lying between the Arctic Circle and the tropic of Cancer and between the Antarctic Circle and the tropic of Capricorn

temperature 1 the degree of hotness of a body, substance, or medium; a physical property related to the average kinetic energy of the atoms or molecules of a substance 2 a measure of this degree of hotness, indicated on a scale that has one or more fixed reference points 3 *Informal* a body temperature in excess of the normal

template *or* **templet** 1 a gauge or pattern, cut out in wood or metal, used in woodwork, etc, to help shape something accurately 2 a pattern cut out in card or plastic, used in various crafts to reproduce shapes 3 *Biochem* the molecular structure of a compound that serves as a pattern for the production of the molecular structure of another specific compound in a reaction

temple¹ 1 a building or place dedicated to the worship of a deity or deities 2 a Mormon church 3 US another name for a **synagogue** 4 any Christian church, esp a large or imposing one 5 any place or object regarded as a shrine where God makes himself present, esp the body of a person who has been sanctified or saved by grace

temple² the region on each side of the head in front of the ear and above the cheek bone

temple³ the part of a loom that keeps the cloth being woven stretched to the correct width

Temple¹ 1 **Shirley,** married name *Shirley Temple Black.* born 1928, US film actress and politician. Her films as a child star include *Little Miss Marker* (1934), *Wee Willie Winkie* (1937), and *Heidi* (1937). She was US ambassador to Ghana (1974–76) and to Czechoslovakia (1989–92) 2 **Sir William** 1628–99, English diplomat and essayist. He negotiated the Triple Alliance (1668) and the marriage of William of Orange to Mary II 3 **William** 1881–1944, English prelate and advocate of social reform; archbishop of Canterbury (1942–44)

Temple² 1 either of two buildings in London and Paris that belonged to the Templars. The one in London now houses two of the chief law societies 2 any of three buildings or groups of buildings erected by the Jews in ancient Jerusalem for the worship of Jehovah

Temple of Artemis the large temple at Ephesus, on the W coast of Asia Minor: one of the Seven Wonders of the World

tempo the speed at which a piece or passage of music is meant to be played, usually indicated by a musical direction (**tempo marking**) or metronome marking

temporal *Anatomy* of, relating to, or near the temple or temples

temporal bone either of two compound bones forming part of the sides and base of the skull: they surround the organs of hearing

Temuco a city in S Chile: agricultural trading centre. Pop: 287 000 (2005 est)

ten 1 the cardinal number that is the sum of nine and one. It is the base of the decimal number system and the base of the common logarithm. **2** a numeral, 10, X, etc, representing this number

tenancy 1 the temporary possession or holding by a tenant of lands or property owned by another **2** the period of holding or occupying such property **3** property held or occupied by a tenant

tenant a person who holds, occupies, or possesses land or property by any kind of right or title, esp from a landlord under a lease

tench a European freshwater cyprinid game fish, *Tinca tinca*, having a thickset dark greenish body with a barbel at each side of the mouth

tendency *Politics* a faction, esp one within a political party

tender¹ (of a sailing vessel) easily keeled over by a wind; crank

tender² *Commerce* a formal offer to supply specified goods or services at a stated cost or rate

tender³ 1 a small boat, such as a dinghy, towed or carried by a yacht or ship **2** a vehicle drawn behind a steam locomotive to carry the fuel and water

tenderfoot (formerly) a beginner in the Scouts or Guides

tenderloin *US* a district of a city that is particularly noted for vice and corruption

tendon a cord or band of white inelastic collagenous tissue that attaches a muscle to a bone or some other part; sinew

tendril a specialized threadlike part of a leaf or stem that attaches climbing plants to a support by twining or adhering

Tendulkar Sachin (Ramesh). born 1973, Indian cricketer

Tenedos an island in the NE Aegean, near the entrance to the Dardanelles: in Greek legend the base of the Greek fleet during the siege of Troy

tenement 1 (now esp in Scotland) a large building divided into separate flats **2** *Property law* any form of permanent property, such as land, dwellings, offices, etc.

Tenerife a Spanish island in the Atlantic, off the NW coast of Africa: the largest of the Canary Islands; volcanic and mountainous; tourism and agriculture. Capital: Santa Cruz. Pop: 778 071 (2002 est). Area: 2058 sq km (795 sq miles)

tenfold 1 equal to or having 10 times as many or as much **2** composed of 10 parts

Tengri Khan a mountain in central Asia, on the border between Kyrgyzstan and the Xinjiang Uygur Autonomous Region of W China. Height: 6995 m (22 951 ft)

Teniers David , called *the Elder*, 1582–1649, and his son David, called *the Younger*, 1610–90, Flemish painters

tenner *Informal* **1** *Brit* **a** a ten-pound note **b** the sum of ten pounds **2** *US* a ten-dollar bill

Tennessee 1 a state of the E central US: consists of a plain in the west, rising to the Appalachians and the Cumberland Plateau in the east. Capital: Nashville. Pop: 5 841 748 (2003 est). Area: 109 412 sq km (42 244 sq miles) **2** a river in the E central US, flowing southwest from E Tennessee into N Alabama, then west and north to the Ohio River at Paducah: the longest tributary of the Ohio; includes a series of dams and reservoirs under the Tennessee Valley Authority. Length: 1049 km (652 miles)

Tenniel Sir John 1820–1914, English caricaturist, noted for his illustrations to Lewis Carroll's *Alice* books and for his political cartoons in *Punch* (1851–1901)

tennis a a racket game played between two players or pairs of players who hit a ball to and fro over a net on a rectangular court of grass, asphalt, clay, etc. **b** (*as modifier*): *tennis court*
▷www.lta.org.uk
▷www.atptennis.com

tennis elbow a painful inflammation of the elbow caused by exertion in playing tennis and similar games

Tennyson Alfred, Lord Tennyson. 1809–92, English poet; poet laureate (1850–92). His poems include *The Lady of Shalott* (1832), *Morte d'Arthur* (1842), the collection *In Memoriam* (1850), *Maud* (1855), and *Idylls of the King* (1859)

tenor 1 *Music* **a** the male voice intermediate between alto and baritone, having a range approximately from the B a ninth below middle C to the G a fifth above it **b** a singer with such a voice **c** a saxophone, horn, recorder, etc, intermediate in compass and size between the alto and baritone or bass **d** (*as modifier*): *a tenor sax* **2 a** (in early polyphonic music) the part singing the melody or the cantus firmus **b** (in four-part harmony) the second lowest part lying directly above the bass **3** *Bell-ringing* **a** the heaviest and lowest-pitched bell in a ring **b** (*as modifier*): *a tenor bell* **4** *Law* **a** the exact words of a deed, etc, as distinct from their effect **b** an exact copy or transcript

tenpin bowling a bowling game in which heavy bowls are rolled down a long lane to knock over the ten target pins at the other end
▷www.bowwwling.com
▷www.btba.org.uk

tensile strength a measure of the ability of a material to withstand a longitudinal stress, expressed as the greatest stress that the material can stand without breaking

tension 1 *Physics* a force that tends to produce an elongation of a body or structure **2** *Physics* voltage, electromotive force, or potential difference **3** a device for regulating the tension in a part, string, thread, etc, as in a sewing machine

tent¹ *Med* a plug of soft material for insertion into a bodily canal, etc, to dilate it or maintain its patency

tent² *Obsolete* a red table wine from Alicante, Spain

tentacle 1 any of various elongated flexible organs that occur near the mouth in many invertebrates and are used for feeding, grasping, etc. **2** any of the hairs on the leaf of an insectivorous plant that are used to capture prey

tenth 1 coming after the ninth in numbering or counting order, position, time, etc.; being the ordinal number of *ten*: often written 10th **2 a** one of 10 approximately equal parts of something **b** (*as modifier*): *a tenth part* **3** one of 10 equal divisions of a particular measurement, etc. **4** the fraction equal to one divided by ten (1/10) **5**

Music **a** an interval of one octave plus a third **b** one of two notes constituting such an interval in relation to the other

tenure 1 *Chiefly US and Canadian* the improved security status of a person after having been in the employ of the same company or institution for a specified period 2 the right to permanent employment until retirement, esp for teachers, lecturers, etc. 3 *Property law* **a** the holding or occupying of property, esp realty, in return for services rendered, etc. **b** the duration of such holding or occupation

Tenzing Norgay 1914–86, Nepalese mountaineer. With Sir Edmund Hillary, he was the first to reach the summit of Mount Everest (1953)

tepee *or* **teepee** a cone-shaped tent of animal skins used by certain North American Indians

Tepic a city in W central Mexico, capital of Nayarit state: agricultural, trading and processing centre. Pop: 341 000 (2005 est)

tequila 1 a spirit that is distilled in Mexico from an agave plant and forms the basis of many mixed drinks 2 the plant, *Agave tequilana*, from which this drink is made

Terai (in India) a belt of marshy land at the foot of mountains, esp at the foot of the Himalayas in N India

teratology 1 the branch of medical science concerned with the development of physical abnormalities during the fetal or early embryonic stage 2 the branch of biology that is concerned with the structure, development, etc, of monsters 3 a collection of tales about mythical or fantastic creatures, monsters, etc.

terbium a soft malleable silvery-grey element of the lanthanide series of metals, occurring in gadolinite and monazite and used in lasers and for doping solid-state devices. Symbol: Tb; atomic no.: 65; atomic wt.: 158.92534; valency: 3 or 4; relative density: 8.230; melting pt.: 1356°C; boiling pt.: 3230°C

Ter Borch *or* **Terborch** Gerard 1617–81, Dutch genre and portrait painter

Terceira an island in the N Atlantic, in the Azores: NATO military air base. Pop: 55 833 (2001). Area: 397 sq km (153 sq miles)

teredo any marine bivalve mollusc of the genus *Teredo*

Terence Latin name *Publius Terentius Afer*. ?190–159 BC, Roman comic dramatist. His six comedies, *Andria, Hecyra, Heauton Timoroumenos, Eunuchus, Phormio*, and *Adelphoe*, are based on Greek originals by Menander

Teresa *or* **Theresa** 1 *Saint*, known as *Teresa of Avila*. 1515–82, Spanish nun and mystic. She reformed the Carmelite order and founded 17 convents. Her writings include a spiritual autobiography and *The Way to Perfection*. Feast day: Oct 15 2 *Mother*, original name *Agnes Gonxha Bojaxhiu*. 1910–97, Indian Roman Catholic missionary, born in Skopje, now in the Former Yugoslav Republic of Macedonia, of Albanian parents: noted for her work among the starving in Calcutta; Nobel peace prize 1979

Tereshkova Valentina Vladimirovna born 1937, Soviet cosmonaut; first woman in space (1963)

Teresina an inland port in NE Brazil, capital of Piauí state, on the Parnaíba River: chief commercial centre of the Parnaíba valley. Pop: 895 000 (2005 est)

Terfel Bryn, real name *Bryn Terfel Jones*. born 1965, Welsh bass baritone

term 1 any of the divisions of the academic year during which a school, college, etc, is in session 2 *Law* **a** an estate or interest in land limited to run for a specified period **b** the duration of an estate, etc. **c** (formerly) a period of time during which sessions of courts of law were held **d** time allowed to a debtor to settle 3 *Maths* either of the expressions the ratio of which is a fraction or proportion, any of the separate elements of a sequence, or any of the individual addends of a polynomial or series 4 *Logic* **a** the word or phrase that forms either the subject or predicate of a proposition **b** a name or variable, as opposed to a predicate **c** one of the relata of a relation **d** any of the three subjects or predicates occurring in a syllogism 5 *Architect* a sculptured post, esp one in the form of an armless bust or an animal on the top of a square pillar 6 *Australian Rules football* the usual word for **quarter**

terminal 1 (of a disease) terminating in death 2 of or relating to the storage or delivery of freight at a warehouse 3 **a** a point at which current enters or leaves an electrical device, such as a battery or a circuit **b** a conductor by which current enters or leaves at such a point 4 *Computing* a device having input/output links with a computer but situated at a distance from the computer 5 *Architect* **a** an ornamental carving at the end of a structure **b** another name for **term** (sense 5) 6 **a** a point or station usually at the end of the line of a railway, serving as an important access point for passengers or freight **b** a less common name for **terminus** 7 *Physiol* **a** the smallest arteriole before its division into capillaries **b** either of two veins that collect blood from the thalamus and surrounding structures and empty it into the internal cerebral vein **c** the portion of a bronchiole just before it subdivides into the air sacs of the lungs

terminal velocity 1 the constant maximum velocity reached by a body falling under gravity through a fluid, esp the atmosphere 2 the maximum velocity that an aircraft can attain, as determined by its total drag

terminus 1 either end of a railway, bus route, etc, or a station or town at such a point 2 *Architect* another name for **term** (sense 5)

termite any whitish ant-like social insect of the order *Isoptera*, of warm and tropical regions. Some species feed on wood, causing damage to furniture, buildings, trees, etc.

tern[1] any aquatic bird of the subfamily *Sterninae*, having a forked tail, long narrow wings, a pointed bill, and a typically black-and-white plumage: family *Laridae* (gulls, etc), order *Charadriiformes*

tern[2] a three-masted schooner

ternary 1 *Maths* **a** (of a number system) to the base three **b** involving or containing three variables 2 (of an alloy, mixture, or chemical compound) having three different components or composed of three different elements

Terni an industrial city in central Italy, in Umbria: site of waterfalls created in Roman times. Pop: 105 018 (2001)

Ternopol a town in W Ukraine, on the River Seret: formerly under Polish rule. Pop: 235 000 (2005 est)

Terpsichore the Muse of the dance and of choral song

terrace 1 a balcony or patio 2 the flat roof of a house built in a Spanish or Oriental style 3 a flat area bounded by a short steep slope formed by the down-cutting of a river or by erosion 4 a unroofed tiers around a football pitch on which the spectators stand b the spectators themselves

terraced house Brit a house that is part of a terrace

terrapin any of various web-footed chelonian reptiles that live on land and in fresh water and feed on small aquatic animals: family *Emydidae*

terrarium 1 an enclosure for keeping small land animals 2 a glass container, often a globe, in which plants are grown

terrestrial (of animals and plants) living or growing on the land

terrier[1] any of several usually small, active, and short-bodied breeds of dog, originally trained to hunt animals living underground

terrier[2] *English legal history* a register or survey of land

territory 1 the geographical domain under the jurisdiction of a political unit, esp of a sovereign state 2 the district for which an agent, etc, is responsible 3 an area inhabited and defended by an individual animal or a breeding group of animals 4 a region of a country, esp of a federal state, that enjoys less autonomy and a lower status than most constituent parts of the state 5 a protectorate or other dependency of a country

terrorism systematic use of violence and intimidation to achieve some goal
▷www.ict.org.il/default.htm
▷www.un.org/terrorism

terry 1 an uncut loop in the pile of towelling or a similar fabric 2 a a fabric with such a pile on both sides b (as modifier): *a terry towel*

Terry 1 Dame Ellen 1847–1928, British actress, noted for her Shakespearean roles opposite Sir Henry Irving and for her correspondence with George Bernard Shaw 2 (John) Quinlan born 1937, British architect, noted for his works in neoclassical style, such as the Richmond riverside project (1984)

tertiary 1 (of education) taking place after secondary school, such as at university, college, etc. 2 (of an industry) involving services as opposed to extraction or manufacture, such as transport, finance, etc. 3 *RC Church* of or relating to a Third Order 4 *Chem* a (of an organic compound) having a functional group attached to a carbon atom that is attached to three other groups b (of an amine) having three organic groups attached to a nitrogen atom c (of a salt) derived from a tribasic acid by replacement of all its acidic hydrogen atoms with metal atoms or electropositive groups 5 *Ornithol, rare* of, relating to, or designating any of the small flight feathers attached to the part of the humerus nearest to the body 6 *Ornithol, rare* any of the tertiary feathers 7 *RC Church* a member of a Third Order

Tertiary 1 of, denoting, or formed in the first period of the Cenozoic era, which lasted for 63 million years, during which mammals became dominant 2 the the Tertiary period or rock system, divided into Palaeocene, Eocene, Oligocene, Miocene, and Pliocene epochs or series

Tertullian Latin name *Quintus Septimius Florens Tertullianus*. ?160–?220 AD, Carthaginian Christian theologian, who wrote in Latin rather than Greek and originated much of Christian terminology

Teruel a city in E central Spain: 15th-century cathedral; scene of fierce fighting during the Spanish Civil War. Pop: 32 304 (2003 est)

Terylene *Trademark* a synthetic polyester fibre or fabric based on terephthalic acid, characterized by lightness and crease resistance and used for clothing, sheets, ropes, sails, etc.

TESL Teaching (of) English as a Second Language

Tesla Nikola 1857–1943, US electrical engineer and inventor, born in Smiljan, now in Croatia. His inventions include a transformer, generators, and dynamos

tessera 1 a small square tile of stone, glass, etc, used in mosaics 2 a die, tally, etc, used in classical times, made of bone or wood

test[1] 1 a series of questions or problems designed to test a specific skill or knowledge 2 a a chemical reaction or physical procedure for testing a substance, material, etc. b a chemical reagent used in such a procedure c the result of the procedure or the evidence gained from it

test[2] 1 the hard or tough outer covering of certain invertebrates and tunicates 2 a variant of **testa**

testa a hard protective outer layer of the seeds of flowering plants; seed coat

testaceous *Biology* 1 of, relating to, or possessing a test or testa 2 of the reddish-brown colour of terra cotta

testament 1 *Law* a will setting out the disposition of personal property (esp in the phrase **last will and testament**) 2 a a covenant instituted between God and man, esp the covenant of Moses or that instituted by Christ b a copy of either the Old or the New Testament, or of the complete Bible

Testament 1 either of the two main parts of the Bible; the Old Testament or the New Testament 2 the New Testament as distinct from the Old

testate 1 *Law* having left a legally valid will at death 2 a person who dies testate

testator *or feminine* **testatrix** a person who makes a will, esp one who dies testate

test case a legal action that serves as a precedent in deciding similar succeeding cases

testicle either of the two male reproductive glands, in most mammals enclosed within the scrotum, that produce spermatozoa and the hormone testosterone

testimony 1 *Law* evidence given by a witness, esp orally in court under oath or affirmation 2 *Old Testament* a the Ten Commandments, as inscribed on the two stone tables b the Ark of the Covenant as the receptacle of these (Exodus 25:16; 16:34)

testosterone a potent steroid hormone secreted mainly by the testes. It can be extracted from the testes of animals or synthesized and used to treat androgen deficiency or promote anabolism. Formula: $C_{19}H_{28}O_2$

test paper 1 *Chem* paper impregnated with an indicator for use in chemical tests 2 *Brit, Education* a the question sheet of a test b the paper completed by a test candidate

test pilot a pilot who flies aircraft of new design to test their performance in the air

test tube 1 a cylindrical round-bottomed glass tube open at one end: used in scientific experiments 2 made synthetically in, or as if in, a test tube

test-tube baby 1 a fetus that has developed from an ovum fertilized in an artificial womb 2 a baby conceived by artificial insemination

tetanus 1 an acute infectious disease in which sustained muscular spasm, contraction, and convulsion are caused by the release of exotoxins from the bacterium, *Clostridium tetani*: infection usually occurs through a contaminated wound 2 *Physiol* any tense contraction of a muscle, esp when produced by electric shocks

Tethys the sea that lay between Laurasia and Gondwanaland, the two supercontinents formed by the first split of the larger supercontinent Pangaea. The Tethys Sea can be regarded as the predecessor of today's smaller Mediterranean

Teton Range a mountain range in the N central US, mainly in NW Wyoming. Highest peak: Grand Teton, 4196 m (13 766 ft)

tetrad 1 a group or series of four 2 the number four 3 *Botany* a group of four cells formed by meiosis from one diploid cell 4 *Genetics* a four-stranded structure, formed during the pachytene stage of meiosis, consisting of paired homologous chromosomes that have each divided into two chromatids 5 *Chem* an element, atom, group, or ion with a valency of four 6 *Ecology* a square of 2×2 km used in distribution mapping

tetraethyl lead a colourless oily insoluble liquid used in petrol to prevent knocking. Formula: $Pb(C_2H_5)_4$

Tetragrammaton *Bible* the Hebrew name for God revealed to Moses on Mount Sinai (Exodus 3), consisting of the four consonants Y H V H (or Y H W H) and regarded by Jews as too sacred to be pronounced. It is usually transliterated as *Jehovah* or *Yahweh*

tetrahedron 1 a solid figure having four plane faces. A regular tetrahedron has faces that are equilateral triangles 2 any object shaped like a tetrahedron

tetralogy 1 a series of four related works, as in drama or opera 2 (in ancient Greece) a group of four dramas, the first three tragic and the last satiric 3 *Pathol* a group of four symptoms present in one disorder, esp Fallot's tetralogy

tetrameter *Prosody* 1 a line of verse consisting of four metrical feet 2 a verse composed of such lines 3 (in classical prosody) a line of verse composed of four dipodies

Tetrazzini Luisa 1871–1940, Italian coloratura soprano

Tetzel *or* **Tezel** Johann ?1465–1519, German Dominican monk. His preaching on papal indulgences provoked Luther's 95 theses at Wittenberg (1517)

Teutoburger Wald a low wooded mountain range in N Germany: possible site of the annihilation of three Roman legions by Germans under Arminius in 9 AD

Teuton 1 a member of an ancient Germanic people from Jutland who migrated to S Gaul in the 2nd century BC: annihilated by a Roman army in 102 BC 2 a member of any people speaking a Germanic language, esp a German 3 Teutonic

Tewkesbury a town in W England, in N Gloucestershire at the confluence of the Rivers Severn and Avon: scene of a decisive battle (1471) of the Wars of the Roses in which the Yorkists defeated the Lancastrians; 12th-century abbey. Pop: 9978 (2001)

Texas a state of the southwestern US, on the Gulf of Mexico: the second largest state; part of Mexico from 1821 to 1836, when it was declared an independent republic; joined the US in 1845; consists chiefly of a plain, with a wide flat coastal belt rising up to the semiarid Sacramento and Davis Mountains of the southwest; a major producer of cotton, rice, and livestock; the chief US producer of oil and gas; a leading world supplier of sulphur. Capital: Austin. Pop: 22 118 509 (2003 est). Area: 678 927 sq km (262 134 sq miles)

text 1 a book prescribed as part of a course of study 2 *Computing* the words printed, written, or displayed on a visual display unit 3 the original exact wording of a work, esp the Bible, as distinct from a revision or translation 4 a short passage of the Bible used as a starting point for a sermon or adduced as proof of a doctrine 5 short for **textbook**

textbook a a book used as a standard source of information on a particular subject b (*as modifier*): *a textbook example*

textile 1 any fabric or cloth, esp woven 2 raw material suitable to be made into cloth; fibre or yarn 3 of or relating to fabrics or the making of fabrics
▷www.textilemuseum.org

texture 1 the structure, appearance, and feel of a woven fabric 2 *Art* the representation of the nature of a surface 3 a music considered as the interrelationship between the horizontally presented aspects of melody and rhythm and the vertically represented aspect of harmony b the nature and quality of the instrumentation of a passage, piece, etc.

TGV in France train à grande vitesse: a high-speed passenger train

Thabana-Ntlenyana a mountain in Lesotho: the highest peak of the Drakensberg Mountains. Height: 3482 m (11 425 ft)

Thackeray William Makepeace 1811–63, English novelist, born in India. His novels, originally serialized, include *Vanity Fair* (1848), *Pendennis* (1850), *Henry Esmond* (1852), and *The Newcomes* (1855)

Thaddeus *or* **Thadeus** *New Testament* one of the 12 apostles (Matthew 10:3; Mark 3:18), traditionally identified with Jude

Thai the language of Thailand, sometimes classified as belonging to the Sino-Tibetan family

Thailand a kingdom in SE Asia, on the Andaman Sea and the Gulf of Siam: united as a kingdom in 1350 and became a major SE Asian power; consists chiefly of a central plain around the Chao Phraya river system, mountains rising over 2400 m (8000 ft) in the northwest, and rainforest the length of the S peninsula. Parts of the SW coast suffered badly in the Indian Ocean tsunami of December 2004. Official language: Thai. Official religion: (Hinayana) Buddhist. Currency: baht. Capital: Bangkok. Pop: 63 465 000 (2004 est). Area: 513 998 sq km (198 455 sq miles)

Thales ?624–?546 BC, Greek philosopher, mathematician, and astronomer, born in Miletus. He held that water was the origin of all things and he predicted the solar eclipse of May 28, 585 BC

Thalia *Greek myth* **1** the Muse of comedy and pastoral poetry **2** one of the three Graces

thalidomide a **a** synthetic drug formerly used as a sedative and hypnotic but withdrawn from the market when found to cause abnormalities in developing fetuses. Formula: $C_{13}H_{10}N_2O_4$ **b** (*as modifier*): *a thalidomide baby*

thallium a soft malleable highly toxic white metallic element used as a rodent and insect poison and in low-melting glass. Its compounds are used as infrared detectors and in photoelectric cells. Symbol: Tl; atomic no.: 81; atomic wt.: 204.3833; valency: 1 or 3; relative density: 11.85; melting pt.: 304°C; boiling pt.: 1473±10°C

Thames **1** a river in S England, rising in the Cotswolds in several headstreams and flowing generally east through London to the North Sea by a large estuary. Length: 346 km (215 miles) **2** a river in SE Canada, in Ontario, flowing south to London, then southwest to Lake St Clair. Length: 217 km (135 miles)

thane *or commonly* **thegn** **1** (in Anglo-Saxon England) a member of an aristocratic class, ranking below an ealdorman, whose status was hereditary and who held land from the king or from another nobleman in return for certain services **2** (in medieval Scotland) **a** a person of rank, often the chief of a clan, holding land from the king **b** a lesser noble who was a Crown official holding authority over an area of land

Thanet Isle of an island in SE England, in NE Kent, separated from the mainland by two branches of the River Stour: scene of many Norse invasions. Area: 109 sq km (42 sq miles)

Thanjavur a city in SE India, in E Tamil Nadu: headquarters of the earliest Protestant missions in India. Pop: 215 725 (2001)

thanksgiving **a** an expression of thanks to God **b** a public act of religious observance or a celebration in acknowledgment of divine favours

Thanksgiving Day an annual day of holiday celebrated in thanksgiving to God on the fourth Thursday of November in the United States, and on the second Monday of October in Canada

Thapsus an ancient town near Carthage in North Africa: site of Caesar's victory over Pompey in 46 BC

Thar Desert a desert in NW India, mainly in NW Rajasthan state and extending into Pakistan. Area: over 260 000 sq km (100 000 sq miles)

Tharp Twyla born 1941, US choreographer, whose work fuses classical ballet with modern dance

thatch any of various palms with leaves suitable for thatching

Thatcher Margaret (Hilda), Baroness (née *Roberts*). born 1925, British stateswoman; leader of the Conservative Party (1975–90); prime minister (1979–90)

thaw a spell of relatively warm weather, causing snow or ice to melt

theatre *or US* **theater** **1 a** a building designed for the performance of plays, operas, etc. **b** (*as modifier*): *a theatre ticket* **2** a room in a hospital or other medical centre

equipped for surgical operations **3** plays regarded collectively as a form of art **4 the theatre** the world of actors, theatrical companies, etc. **5** writing that is suitable for dramatic presentation **6** *US, Austral, NZ* the usual word for **cinema 7** a circular or semicircular open-air building with tiers of seats

▷http://vl-theatre.com
▷www.theatrelinks.com
▷www.uktw.co.uk
▷www.artslynx.org/theatre

Thebaid the territory around ancient Thebes in Egypt, or sometimes around Thebes in Greece

Thebes **1** (in ancient Greece) the chief city of Boeotia, destroyed by Alexander the Great (336 BC) **2** (in ancient Egypt) a city on the Nile: at various times capital of Upper Egypt or of the entire country

theft *Criminal law* the dishonest taking of property belonging to another person with the intention of depriving the owner permanently of its possession

Theiler Max 1899–1972, US virologist, born in South Africa, who developed a vaccine against yellow fever. Nobel prize for physiology or medicine 1951

theism **1** the form of the belief in one God as the transcendent creator and ruler of the universe that does not necessarily entail further belief in divine revelation **2** the belief in the existence of a God or gods

theme **1** *Music* a group of notes forming a recognizable melodic unit, often used as the basis of the musical material in a composition **2** a short essay, esp one set as an exercise for a student **3** (in the Byzantine Empire) a territorial unit consisting of several provinces under a military commander

theme park an area planned as a leisure attraction, in which all the displays, buildings, activities, etc, are based on or relate to one particular subject

Themistocles ?527–?460 BC, Athenian statesman, who was responsible for the Athenian victory against the Persians at Salamis (480). He was ostracized in 470

theocracy **1** government by a deity or by a priesthood **2** a community or political unit under such government

Theocritus ?310–?250 BC, Greek poet, born in Syracuse. He wrote the first pastoral poems in Greek literature and was closely imitated by Virgil

Theodora ?500–548 AD, Byzantine empress; wife and counsellor of Justinian I

Theodoric *or* **Theoderic** called *the Great*. ?454–526 AD, king of the Ostrogoths and founder of the Ostrogothic kingdom in Italy after his murder of Odoacer (493)

Theodosius I called *the Great*. ?346–395 AD, Roman emperor of the Eastern Roman Empire (379–95) and of the Western Roman Empire (392–95)

theologian a person versed in or engaged in the study of theology, esp Christian theology

theology **1** the systematic study of the existence and nature of the divine and its relationship to and influence upon other beings **2** a specific branch of this study, undertaken from the perspective of a particular group **3** the systematic study of Christian revelation concerning God's nature and purpose, esp through the teaching of the Church **4** a specific system, form, or branch of this study, esp for those preparing for the ministry or priesthood

Theophrastus ?372–?287 BC, Greek Peripatetic philosopher, noted esp for his *Characters*, a collection of sketches of moral types

theorem *Maths, Logic* a statement or formula that can be deduced from the axioms of a formal system by means of its rules of inference

theosophy 1 any of various religious or philosophical systems claiming to be based on or to express an intuitive insight into the divine nature 2 the system of beliefs of the Theosophical Society founded in 1875, claiming to be derived from the sacred writings of Brahmanism and Buddhism, but denying the existence of any personal God

Thera a Greek island in the Aegean Sea, in the Cyclades: site of a Minoan settlement and of the volcano that ended Minoan civilization on Crete. Pop: 13 402 (2001)

therapeutics the branch of medicine concerned with the treatment of disease

therapy a the treatment of physical, mental, or social disorders or disease b *(in combination)*: *physiotherapy*; *electrotherapy*

therm *Brit* a unit of heat equal to 100 000 British thermal units. One therm is equal to 1.055 056 × 10^8 joules

thermal 1 of, relating to, caused by, or generating heat or increased temperature 2 (of garments or fabrics) specially designed so as to have exceptional heatretaining properties 3 *Meteorol* a column of rising air caused by local unequal heating of the land surface, and used by gliders and birds to gain height

thermionic valve *or esp US and Canadian* **tube** an electronic valve in which electrons are emitted from a heated rather than a cold cathode

thermistor a semiconductor device having a resistance that decreases rapidly with an increase in temperature. It is used for temperature measurement, to compensate for temperature variations in a circuit, etc.

thermocouple 1 a device for measuring temperature consisting of a pair of wires of different metals or semiconductors joined at both ends. One junction is at the temperature to be measured, the second at a fixed temperature. The electromotive force generated depends upon the temperature difference 2 a similar device with only one junction between two dissimilar metals or semiconductors

thermodynamics the branch of physical science concerned with the interrelationship and interconversion of different forms of energy and the behaviour of macroscopic systems in terms of certain basic quantities, such as pressure, temperature, etc.

thermoelectric *or* **thermoelectrical** 1 of, relating to, used in, or operated by the generation of an electromotive force by the Seebeck effect or the Thomson effect 2 of, relating to, used in, or operated by the production or absorption of heat by the Peltier effect

thermonuclear involving nuclear fusion

thermoplastic 1 (of a material, esp a synthetic plastic or resin) becoming soft when heated and rehardening on cooling without appreciable change of properties 2 a synthetic plastic or resin, such as polystyrene, with these properties

Thermopylae (in ancient Greece) a narrow pass between the mountains and the sea linking Locris and Thessaly: a defensible position on a traditional invasion route from N Greece; scene of a famous battle (480 BC) in which a greatly outnumbered Greek army under Leonidas fought to the death to delay the advance of the Persians during their attempted conquest of Greece

thermosetting (of a material, esp a synthetic plastic or resin) hardening permanently after one application of heat and pressure. Thermosetting plastics, such as phenol-formaldehyde, cannot be remoulded

thermostat a device that maintains a system at a constant temperature. It often consists of a bimetallic strip that bends as it expands and contracts with temperature, thus breaking and making contact with an electrical power supply

Theron Charlize born 1975, South African film actress; her films include *The Cider House Rules* (1999) and *Monster* (2003), which earned her an Oscar

Theroux Paul (Edward). born 1941, US novelist and travel writer. His novels include *Picture Palace* (1978), *The Mosquito Coast* (1981), and *My Other Life* (1996); travel writings include *The Great Railway Bazaar* (1975)

thesaurus 1 a book containing systematized lists of synonyms and related words 2 a dictionary of selected words or topics 3 *Rare* a treasury

Thesiger Wilfred (Patrick). 1910–2003, British writer, who explored the Empty Quarter of Arabia (1945–50) and lived with the Iraqi marsh Arabs (1950–58). His books include *Arabian Sands* (1958), *The Marsh Arabs* (1964), and *My Kenya Days* (1994)

thesis 1 a dissertation resulting from original research, esp when submitted by a candidate for a degree or diploma 2 a subject for a discussion or essay 3 an unproved statement, esp one put forward as a premise in an argument 4 *Music* the downbeat of a bar, as indicated in conducting 5 (in classical prosody) the syllable or part of a metrical foot not receiving the ictus 6 *Philosophy* the first stage in the Hegelian dialectic, that is challenged by the antithesis

Thespian of or relating to drama and the theatre; dramatic

Thespis 6th century BC, Greek poet, regarded as the founder of tragic drama

Thessalonian 1 of or relating to ancient Thessalonica (modern Salonika) 2 an inhabitant of ancient Thessalonica

Thessaly a region of E Central Greece, on the Aegean: an extensive fertile plain, edged with mountains. Pop: 609 100 (2001). Area: 14 037 sq km (5418 sq miles)

Thetford Mines a city in SE Canada, in S Quebec: asbestos industry. Pop: 21 651 (2001)

thiamine *or* **thiamin** *Biochem* a soluble white crystalline vitamin that occurs in the outer coat of rice and other grains. It forms part of the vitamin B complex and is essential for carbohydrate metabolism: deficiency leads to nervous disorders and to the disease beriberi. Formula: $C_{12}H_{17}ON_4SCl.H_2O$

thicket a dense growth of small trees, shrubs, and similar plants

thickhead any of various Australian and SE Asian songbirds of the family *Muscicapidae* (flycatchers, etc)

Thiers Louis Adolphe 1797–1877, French statesman and historian. After the Franco-Prussian war, he suppressed the Paris Commune and became first president of the Third Republic (1871–73). His policies made possible the paying off of the war indemnity exacted by Germany

thigh 1 the part of the leg between the hip and the knee in man 2 the corresponding part in other vertebrates and insects

thimble 1 any small metal cap resembling this 2 *Nautical* a loop of metal having a groove at its outer edge for a rope or cable, for lining the inside of an eye

Thimbu *or* **Thimphu** the capital of Bhutan, in the west in the foothills of the E Himalayas: became the official capital in 1962. Pop: 40 000 (2005 est)

thin 1 (of a photographic negative) having low density, usually insufficient to produce a satisfactory positive 2 *Mountaineering* a climb or pitch on which the holds are few and small

thin client *Computing* a computer on a network where most functions are carried out on a central server

thing¹ *Law* any object or right that may be the subject of property (as distinguished from a person)

thing² a law court or public assembly in the Scandinavian countries

thinner a solvent, such as turpentine, added to paint or varnish to dilute it, reduce its opacity or viscosity, or increase its penetration into the ground

third 1 coming after the second and preceding the fourth in numbering or counting order, position, time, etc.; being the ordinal number of *three*: often written 3rd 2 denoting the third from lowest forward ratio of a gearbox in a motor vehicle 3 a one of three equal or nearly equal parts of an object, quantity, etc. b *(as modifier)*: *a third part* 4 the fraction equal to one divided by three (1/3) 5 the forward ratio above second of a gearbox in a motor vehicle. In some vehicles it is the top gear 6 a the interval between one note and another three notes away from it counting inclusively along the diatonic scale b one of two notes constituting such an interval in relation to the other 7 *Brit* an honours degree of the third and usually the lowest class 8 goods of a standard lower than that of seconds

third class 1 of or denoting the class of accommodation in a hotel, on a ship, etc, next in quality and price to the second: usually the cheapest 2 (in the US and Canada) of or relating to a class of mail consisting largely of unsealed printed matter 3 *Brit* See **third**

third degree *Informal* torture or bullying, esp used to extort confessions or information

third man *Cricket* a a fielding position on the off side near the boundary behind the batsman's wicket b a fielder in this position

third party a person who is involved by chance or only incidentally in a legal proceeding, agreement, or other transaction, esp one against whom a defendant claims indemnity

Third World the less economically advanced countries of Africa, Asia, and Latin America collectively, esp when viewed as underdeveloped and as neutral in the East-West alignment. Also called: **developing world**

Thirlmere a lake in NW England, in Cumbria in the Lake District: provides part of Manchester's water supply. Length: 6 km (4 miles)

thirteen 1 the cardinal number that is the sum of ten and three and is a prime number 2 a numeral, 13, XIII, etc, representing this number 3 the amount or quantity that is three more than ten; baker's dozen

thirty 1 the cardinal number that is the product of ten and three 2 a numeral, 30, XXX, etc, representing this number 3 the amount or quantity that is three times as big as ten

thistle any of numerous plants of the genera *Cirsium*, *Carduus*, and related genera, having prickly-edged leaves, pink, purple, yellow, or white dense flower heads, and feathery hairs on the seeds: family *Asteraceae* (composites)

thistledown the mass of feathery plumed seeds produced by a thistle

thole *or* **tholepin** a wooden pin or one of a pair, set upright in the gunwales of a rowing boat to serve as a fulcrum in rowing

Thomas 1 Saint Also called: **doubting Thomas** one of the twelve apostles, who refused to believe in Christ's resurrection until he had seen his wounds (John 20:24–29). Feast day: July 3 or Dec 21 or Oct 6 2 Ambroise 1811–96, French composer of light operas, including *Mignon* (1866) 3 Dylan (**Marlais**). 1914–53, Welsh poet and essayist. His works include the prose *Portrait of the Artist as a Young Dog* (1940), the verse collection *Deaths and Entrances* (1946), and his play for voices *Under Milk Wood* (1954) 4 (**Philip**) Edward, pen name *Edward Eastaway*. 1878–1917, British poet and critic: killed in World War I 5 R(**onald**) S(**tuart**). 1913–2000, Welsh poet and clergyman. His collections include *Song at the Year's Turning* (1955), *Not that He Brought Flowers* (1968), and *Laboratories of the Spirit* (1975)

Thomas of Woodstock 1355–97, youngest son of Edward III, who led opposition to his nephew Richard II (1386–89); arrested in 1397, he died in prison

Thompson 1 Benjamin, Count Rumford. 1753–1814, Anglo-American physicist, noted for his work on the nature of heat 2 Daley born 1958, British athlete: Olympic decathlon champion (1980, 1984) 3 Emma born 1959, British actress: her films include *Howards End* (1991), *Sense and Sensibility* (1996; also wrote screenplay), *Primary Colors* (1998), and *Love Actually* (2003) 4 Flora (**Jane**). 1876–1947, British writer, author of the autobiographical *Lark Rise to Candleford* (1945) 5 Francis 1859–1907, British poet, best known for the mystical poem *The Hound of Heaven* (1893)

Thomson 1 Sir George Paget, son of Joseph John Thomson. 1892–1975, British physicist, who discovered (1927) the diffraction of electrons by crystals: shared the Nobel prize for physics 1937 2 James 1700–48, Scottish poet. He anticipated the romantics' feeling for nature in *The Seasons* (1726–30) 3 James, pen name B.V. 1834–82, British poet, born in Scotland, noted esp for *The City of Dreadful Night* (1874), reflecting man's isolation and despair 4 Sir Joseph John 1856–1940, British physicist. He discovered the electron (1897) and his work on the nature of positive rays led to the discovery of isotopes: Nobel prize for physics 1906 5 Roy, 1st Baron Thomson of Fleet. 1894–1976, British newspaper proprietor, born in Canada 6 Virgil 1896–1989, US composer, music critic, and conductor, whose works include two operas, *Four Saints in Three Acts* (1928) and *The Mother of Us All* (1947), piano sonatas, a cello concerto, songs, and film music

Thonburi a city in central Thailand, part of Bankok Metropolis on the Chao Phraya River; the national capital (1767–82)

thong a a skimpy article of beachwear, worn by men or women, consisting of thin strips of leather or cloth attached to a piece of material that covers the genitals while leaving the buttocks bare b a similar item of underwear

Thor *Norse myth* the god of thunder, depicted as wielding a hammer, emblematic of the thunderbolt

thorax 1 the part of the human body enclosed by the ribs 2 the corresponding part in other vertebrates 3 the part of an insect's body between the head and abdomen, which bears the wings and legs

Thoreau Henry David 1817–62, US writer, noted esp for *Walden, or Life in the Woods* (1854), an account of his experiment in living in solitude. A powerful social critic, his essay *Civil Disobedience* (1849) influenced such dissenters as Gandhi

thorium a soft ductile silvery-white metallic element. It is radioactive and occurs in thorite and monazite: used in gas mantles, magnesium alloys, electronic equipment, and as a nuclear power source. Symbol: Th; atomic no.: 90; atomic wt.: 232.0381; half-life of most stable isotope, ^{232}Th: 1.41×10^{10} years; valency: 4; relative density: 11.72; melting pt.: 1755°C; boiling pt.: 4788°C

thorn 1 a sharp pointed woody extension of a stem or leaf 2 a any of various trees or shrubs having thorns, esp the hawthorn b the wood of any of these plants 3 a Germanic character of runic origin Þ used in Old and Modern Icelandic to represent the voiceless dental fricative sound of *th*, as in *thin, bath*. Its use in phonetics for the same purpose is now obsolete 4 this same character as used in Old and Middle English as an alternative to *edh*, but indistinguishable from it in function or sound 5 *Zoology* any of various sharp spiny parts

Thorndike 1 Edward Lee 1874–1949, US psychologist, who worked on animals and proposed that all learnt behaviour is regulated by rewards and punishments (**Thorndike's law** or **law of effect**) 2 Dame (**Agnes**) **Sybil** 1882–1976, British actress

thoroughbred a pedigree animal; purebred

Thorpe 1 Ian born 1982, Australian swimmer; won three gold medals at the 2000 Olympic Games and six gold medals at the 2002 Commonwealth Games. 2 James Francis 1888–1953, American football player and athlete: Olympic pentathlon and decathlon champion (1912) 3 Jeremy born 1929, British politician; leader of the Liberal party (1967–76)

Thorshavn or **Tórshavn** the capital of the Faeroes, a port on the northernmost island. Pop: 17 549 (2004 est)

Thorvaldsen Bertel 1770–1844, Danish neoclassical sculptor

thou 1 one thousandth of an inch. 1 thou is equal to 0.0254 millimetre 2 *Informal* short for **thousand**

thousand 1 the cardinal number that is the product of 10 and 100 2 a numeral, 1000, 10^3, M, etc, representing this number 3 the amount or quantity that is one hundred times greater than ten 4 *Maths* the position containing a digit representing that number followed by three zeros

Thrace 1 an ancient country in the E Balkan Peninsula: successively under the Persians, Macedonians, and Romans 2 a region of SE Europe, corresponding to the S part of the ancient country: divided by the Maritsa River into **Western Thrace** (Greece) and **Eastern Thrace** (Turkey)

thread 1 a fine cord of twisted filaments, esp of cotton, used in sewing, weaving, etc. 2 any of the filaments of which a spider's web is made 3 a helical groove in a cylindrical hole (**female thread**), formed by a tap or lathe tool, or a helical ridge on a cylindrical bar, rod, shank, etc (**male thread**), formed by a die or lathe tool 4 the course of an individual's life believed in Greek mythology to be spun, measured, and cut by the Fates

Threadneedle Street a street in the City of London famous for its banks, including the Bank of England, known as **The Old Lady of Threadneedle Street**

threadworm any of various nematodes, esp the pinworm

three 1 the cardinal number that is the sum of two and one and is a prime number 2 a numeral, 3, III, (iii), representing this number 3 the amount or quantity that is one greater than two 4 something representing, represented by, or consisting of three units such as a playing card with three symbols on it

three-decker a warship with guns on three decks

three-dimensional, three-D, or **3-D** 1 of, having, or relating to three dimensions 2 (of a film, transparency, etc) simulating the effect of depth by presenting slightly different views of a scene to each eye 3 having volume

threefold 1 equal to or having three times as many or as much; triple 2 composed of three parts

three-legged race a race in which pairs of competitors run with their adjacent legs tied together

three-point turn a turn reversing the direction of motion of a motor vehicle using forward and reverse gears alternately, and completed after only three movements

three-quarter *Rugby* a any of the four players between the fullback and the halfbacks b this position

threesome 1 *Golf* a match in which a single player playing his own ball competes against two others playing alternate strokes on the same ball 2 any game, etc, for three people

threnody or **threnode** an ode, song, or speech of lamentation, esp for the dead

thresher any of various large sharks of the genus *Alopias*, esp *A. vulpinus*, occurring in tropical and temperate seas: family *Alopiidae*. They have a very long whiplike tail with which they are thought to round up the small fish on which they feed

threshold 1 *Psychol* the strength at which a stimulus is just perceived 2 a the minimum intensity or value of a signal, etc, that will produce a response or specified effect b (*as modifier*): *a threshold current*

thrift *Rare* vigorous thriving or growth, as of a plant

thrift any of numerous perennial plumbaginaceous low-growing plants of the genus *Armeria*, esp *A. maritima*, of Europe, W Asia, and North America, having narrow leaves and round heads of pink or white flowers

thrill *Pathol* an abnormal slight tremor associated with a heart or vascular murmur, felt on palpation

thriller a book, film, play, etc, depicting crime, mystery, or espionage in an atmosphere of excitement and suspense

thrips any of various small slender-bodied insects of the order *Thysanoptera*, typically having piercing mouthparts and narrow feathery wings and feeding on plant sap. Some species are serious plant pests

throat 1 a that part of the alimentary and respiratory tracts extending from the back of the mouth (nasopharynx) to just below the larynx b the front part of the neck 2 *Botany* the gaping part of a tubular corolla or perianth

thrombosis 1 the formation or presence of a thrombus 2 *Informal* short for **coronary thrombosis**

throne 1 the power, duties, or rank ascribed to a royal person 2 a person holding royal rank 3 the third of the nine orders into which the angels are traditionally divided in medieval angelology

throstle 1 a poetic name for **thrush** (esp the song thrush) 2 a spinning machine for wool or cotton in which the fibres are twisted and wound continuously

throttle 1 any device that controls the quantity of fuel or fuel and air mixture entering an engine 2 an informal or dialect word for **throat**

throughput the quantity of raw material or information processed or communicated in a given period, esp by a computer

throw 1 an act or result of throwing dice 2 a the eccentricity of a cam b the radial distance between the central axis of a crankshaft and the axis of a crankpin forming part of the shaft 3 a sheet of fabric used for draping over an easel or unfinished painting, etc, to keep the dust off 4 *Geology* the vertical displacement of rock strata at a fault 5 *Physics* the deflection of a measuring instrument as a result of a sudden fluctuation

throwaway *Chiefly US and Canadian* a handbill or advertisement distributed in a public place

throwback a a person, animal, or plant that has the characteristics of an earlier or more primitive type b a reversion to such an organism

throw-in *Soccer* the method of putting the ball into play after it has gone into touch by throwing it two-handed from behind the head to a teammate, both feet being kept on the ground

thrum *Textiles* 1 a any of the unwoven ends of warp thread remaining on the loom when the web has been removed b such ends of thread collectively 2 a fringe or tassel of short unwoven threads

thrush¹ any songbird of the subfamily *Turdinae*, esp those having a brown plumage with a spotted breast, such as the mistle thrush and song thrush: family *Muscicapidae*

thrush² 1 a a fungal disease of the mouth, esp of infants, and the genitals, characterized by the formation of whitish spots and caused by infection with the fungus *Candida albicans* b another word for **sprue** 2 a softening of the frog of a horse's hoof characterized by degeneration and a thick foul discharge

thrust 1 a force, esp one that produces motion 2 a a propulsive force produced by the fluid pressure or the change of momentum of the fluid in a jet engine, rock-

et engine, etc. b a similar force produced by a propeller 3 a pressure that is exerted continuously by one part of an object, structure, etc, against another, esp the axial force by or on a shaft 4 *Geology* the compressive force in the earth's crust that produces recumbent folds and thrust or reverse faults 5 *Civil engineering* a force exerted in a downwards and outwards direction, as by an arch or rafter, or the horizontal force exerted by retained earth

Thucydides ?460–?395 BC, Greek historian and politician, distinguished for his *History of the Peloponnesian War*

thug (formerly) a member of an organization of robbers and assassins in India who typically strangled their victims

Thule 1 a region believed by ancient geographers to be the northernmost land in the inhabited world: sometimes thought to have been Iceland, Norway, or one of the Shetland Islands 2 an Inuit settlement in NW Greenland: a Danish trading post, founded in 1910, and US air force base

thulium a malleable ductile silvery-grey element occurring principally in monazite. The radioisotope **thulium-170** is used as an electron source in portable X-ray units. Symbol: Tm; atomic no.: 69; atomic wt.: 168.93421; valency: 3; relative density: 9.321; melting pt.: 1545°C; boiling pt.: 1950°C

thumb 1 the first and usually shortest and thickest of the digits of the hand, composed of two short bones 2 the corresponding digit in other vertebrates

thumbnail 1 the nail of the thumb 2 *Computing* a small image which can be expanded

thumbscrew 1 an instrument of torture that pinches or crushes the thumbs 2 a screw with projections on its head enabling it to be turned by the thumb and forefinger

thumbtack *chiefly US and Canadian* a short tack with a broad smooth head for fastening papers to a drawing board, etc.

Thun 1 a town in central Switzerland, in Bern canton on Lake Thun. Pop: 40 377 (2000) 2 a lake in central Switzerland, formed by a widening of the Aar River. Length: about 17 km (11 miles). Width: 3 km (2 miles)

thunder a loud cracking or deep rumbling noise caused by the rapid expansion of atmospheric gases which are suddenly heated by lightning

Thunder Bay a port in central Canada, in Ontario on Lake Superior: formed in 1970 by the amalgamation of Fort William and Port Arthur; the head of the St Lawrence Seaway for Canada. Pop: 103 215 (2001)

thunderbolt 1 a flash of lightning accompanying thunder 2 (in mythology) the destructive weapon wielded by several gods, esp the Greek god Zeus

thundercloud a towering electrically charged cumulonimbus cloud associated with thunderstorms

thunderstorm a storm caused by strong rising air currents and characterized by thunder and lightning and usually heavy rain or hail

Thurber James (Grover). 1894–1961, US humorist and illustrator. He contributed drawings and stories to the *New Yorker* and his books include *Is Sex Necessary?* (1929), written with E. B. White

Thurgau a canton of NE Switzerland, on Lake

Constance: annexed by the confederated Swiss states in 1460. Capital: Frauenfeld. Pop: 229 800 (2002 est). Area: 1007 sq km (389 sq miles)

Thuringia a state of central Germany, formerly in East Germany. Pop: 2 373 000 (2003 est)

Thuringian Forest a forested mountainous region in E central Germany, rising over 900 m (3000 ft)

Thurrock a unitary authority in SE England, in Essex. Pop: 145 300 (2003 est). Area: 163 sq km (63 sq miles)

Thursday Island an island in Torres Strait, between NE Australia and New Guinea: administratively part of Queensland, Australia. Area: 4 sq km (1.5 sq miles)

Thutmose I died c1500 BC, king of Egypt of the 18th dynasty, who extended his territory in Nubia and Syria and enlarged the Temple of Amon at Karnak

Thutmose III died c1450 BC, king of Egypt of the 18th dynasty, who completed the conquest of Syria and dominated the Middle East. He was also a patron of the arts and a famous athlete

thwart *Nautical* **a** a seat lying across a boat and occupied by an oarsman **b** @Headword:**thyme** any of various small shrubs of the temperate genus *Thymus*, having a strong mintlike odour, small leaves, and white, pink, or red flowers: family *Lamiaceae* (labiates)

thymol a white crystalline substance with an aromatic odour, obtained from the oil of thyme and used as a fungicide, antiseptic, and anthelmintic and in perfumery and embalming; 2-isopropylphenol. Formula: $(CH_3)_2CHC_6H_3(CH_3)OH$

thymus a glandular organ of vertebrates, consisting in man of two lobes situated below the thyroid. In early life it produces lymphocytes and is thought to influence certain immunological responses. It atrophies with age and is almost nonexistent in the adult

thyroid **1** of or relating to the thyroid gland **2** of or relating to the largest cartilage of the larynx **3** See **thyroid gland** **4** the powdered preparation made from the thyroid gland of certain animals, used to treat hypothyroidism

▷www.thyroidfoundation.org

thyroid gland an endocrine gland of vertebrates, consisting in man of two lobes near the base of the neck. It secretes hormones that control metabolism and body growth

ti **1** a woody palmlike agave plant, *Cordyline terminalis*, of the East Indies, having white, mauve, or reddish flowers. The sword-shaped leaves are used for garments, fodder, thatch, etc, and the root for food and liquor **2** a similar and related plant, *Cordyline australis*, of New Zealand

Tianjin, Tientsin, *or* **T'ien-ching** an industrial city in NE China, in Hebei province, on the Grand Canal, 51 km (32 miles) from the Yellow Sea: the third largest city in China; seat of Nankai University (1919). Pop: 9 346 000 (2005 est)

Tian Shan *or* **Tien Shan** a great mountain system of central Asia, in Kyrgyzstan and the Xinjiang Uygur Autonomous Region of W China, extending for about 2500 km (1500 miles). Highest peak: Pobeda Peak, 7439 m (24 406 ft)

tiara *RC Church* **a** a headdress worn by the pope, consisting of a beehive-shaped diadem surrounded by three coronets **b** the office or rank of pope

▷www.vam.ac.uk/vastatic/microsites/tiaras/exhibition.html

Tiber a river in central Italy, rising in the Tuscan Apennines and flowing south through Rome to the Tyrrhenian Sea. Length: 405 km (252 miles)

Tiberias **1** a resort in N Israel, on the Sea of Galilee: an important Jewish centre after the destruction of Jerusalem by the Romans. Pop: 40 100 (2003 est) **2 Lake** another name for the (Sea of) **Galilee**

Tiberius full name *Tiberius Claudius Nero Caesar Augustus*. 42 BC–37 AD, Roman emperor (14–37 AD). He succeeded his father-in-law Augustus after a brilliant military career. He became increasingly tyrannical

Tibesti *or* **Tibesti Massif** a mountain range of volcanic origin in NW Chad, in the central Sahara extending for about 480 km (300 miles). Highest peak: Emi Koussi, 3415 m (11 204 ft)

Tibet an autonomous region of SW China: Europeans strictly excluded in the 19th century; invaded by China in 1950; rebellion (1959) against Chinese rule suppressed and the Dalai Lama fled to India; military rule imposed (1989–90) after continued demands for independence; consists largely of a vast high plateau between the Himalayas and Kunlun Mountains; formerly a theocracy and the centre of Lamaism. Capital: Lhasa. Pop: 2 700 000 (2003 est). Area: 1 221 601 sq km (471 660 sq miles)

tibia **1** the inner and thicker of the two bones of the human leg between the knee and ankle **2** the corresponding bone in other vertebrates **3** the fourth segment of an insect's leg, lying between the femur and the tarsus

Tibullus Albius ?54–?19 BC, Roman elegiac poet

tic *Pathol* spasmodic twitching of a particular group of muscles

Ticino **1** a canton in S Switzerland: predominantly Italian-speaking and Roman Catholic; mountainous. Capital: Bellinzona. Pop: 314 600 (2002 est). Area: 2810 sq km (1085 sq miles) **2** a river in S central Europe, rising in S central Switzerland and flowing southeast and west to Lake Maggiore, then southeast to the River Po. Length: 248 km (154 miles)

tick¹ *Commerce* the smallest increment of a price fluctuation in a commodity exchange. Tick size is usually 0.01 of the nominal value of the trading unit

tick² **1** any of various small parasitic arachnids of the families *Ixodidae* (**hard ticks**) and *Argasidae*, (**soft ticks**), typically living on the skin of warm-blooded animals and feeding on the blood and tissues of their hosts: order *Acarina* (mites and ticks) **2** any of certain other arachnids of the order *Acarina* **3** any of certain insects of the dipterous family *Hippoboscidae* that are ectoparasitic on horses, cattle, sheep, etc, esp the sheep ked

tick¹ **1** the strong covering of a pillow, mattress, etc. **2** *Informal* short for **ticking**

tick² *Brit, informal* account or credit (esp in the phrase **on tick**)

ticker tape ticker-tape reception (*or* **parade**) (mainly in New York) the showering of the motorcade of a distinguished politician, visiting head of state, etc, with ticker tape as a sign of welcome

ticket 1 *Chiefly US and NZ* the group of candidates nominated by one party in an election; slate 2 *Chiefly US* the declared policy of a political party at an election

ticking a strong cotton fabric, often striped, used esp for mattress and pillow covers

tick over *Brit* **a** the speed of an engine when it is ticking over **b** (*as modifier*): *tick-over speed*

ticktack *Brit* a system of sign language, mainly using the hands, by which bookmakers transmit their odds to each other at racecourses

Ticonderoga a village in NE New York State, on Lake George: site of Fort Ticonderoga, scene of battles between the British and French (1758–59) and a strategic point in the War of American Independence

tidal 1 relating to, characterized by, or affected by tides 2 dependent on the state of the tide 3 (of a glacier) reaching the sea and discharging floes or icebergs

tidal wave 1 a name (not accepted in technical usage) for **tsunami** 2 an unusually large incoming wave, often caused by high winds and spring tides

tiddler *Brit, informal* a very small fish or aquatic creature, esp a stickleback, minnow, or tadpole

tiddlywinks a game in which players try to flick discs of plastic into a cup by pressing them sharply on the side with other larger discs

tide 1 the cyclic rise and fall of sea level caused by the gravitational pull of the sun and moon. There are usually two high tides and two low tides in each lunar day 2 the current, ebb, or flow of water at a specified place resulting from these changes in level 3 See **ebb** and **flood** (sense 2)

tidemark 1 a mark left by the highest or lowest point of a tide 2 a marker indicating the highest or lowest point reached by a tide

tie 1 a structural member carrying tension, such as a tie beam or tie rod 2 the US and Canadian name for **sleeper** (on a railway track) 3 *Music* a slur connecting two notes of the same pitch indicating that the sound is to be prolonged for their joint time value

tie-break *or* **tie-breaker** *Tennis* a method of deciding quickly the result of a set drawn at six-all, usually involving the playing of one deciding game for the best of twelve points in which the service changes after every two points

tied *Brit* 1 (of a public house, retail shop, etc) obliged to sell only the beer, products, etc of a particular producer 2 (of a house or cottage) rented out to the tenant for as long as he is employed by the owner

tie-in *US* **a** a sale or advertisement offering products of which a purchaser must buy one or more in addition to his purchase **b** an item sold or advertised in this way, esp the extra item **c** (*as modifier*): *a tie-in sale*

Tiepolo **Giovanni Battista** 1696–1770, Italian rococo painter, esp of frescoes as in the Residenz at Würzburg

Tierra del Fuego an archipelago at the S extremity of South America, separated from the mainland by the Strait of Magellan: the west and south belong to Chile, the east to Argentina. Area: 73 643 sq km (28 434 sq miles)

Tiffany **Louis Comfort** 1848–1933, US glass-maker and Art-Nouveau craftsman, best known for creating the Favrile style of stained glass

tiger 1 a large feline mammal, *Panthera tigris*, of forests in most of Asia, having a tawny yellow coat with black stripes 2 any of various other animals, such as the jaguar, leopard, and thylacine 3 **a** a country, esp in E Asia, that is achieving rapid economic growth **b** (*as modifier*): *a tiger economy* 4 *Archaic* a servant in livery, esp a page or groom 5 short for **tiger moth**

tiger lily 1 a lily plant, *Lilium tigrinum*, of China and Japan, cultivated for its flowers, which have black-spotted orange reflexed petals 2 any of various similar lilies

tiger moth any of a group of arctiid moths, mostly boldly marked, often in black, orange, and yellow, of the genera *Arctia*, *Parasemia*, *Euplagia*, etc, producing woolly bear larvae and typified by the **garden tiger** (*Arctia caja*)

tiger snake a highly venomous brown-and-yellow elapid snake, *Notechis scutatus*, of Australia

tight *Economics* **a** (of a commodity) difficult to obtain; in excess demand **b** (of funds, money, etc) difficult and expensive to borrow because of high demand or restrictive monetary policy **c** (of markets) characterized by excess demand or scarcity with prices tending to rise

Tiglath-pileser I king of Assyria (?1116–?1093 BC), who extended his kingdom to the upper Euphrates and defeated the king of Babylonia

Tiglath-pileser III known as *Pulu*. died ?727 BC, king of Assyria (745–727), who greatly extended his empire, subjugating Syria and Palestine

tigress a female tiger

Tigris a river in SW Asia, rising in E Turkey and flowing southeast through Baghdad to the Euphrates in SE Iraq, forming the delta of the Shatt-al-Arab, which flows into the Persian Gulf: part of a canal and irrigation system as early as 2400 BC, with many ancient cities (including Nineveh) on its banks. Length: 1900 km (1180 miles)

Tijuana *or* **Tia Juana** a city in NW Mexico, in Baja California (Norte). Pop: 1 570 000 (2005 est)

tiki an amulet or figurine in the form of a carved representation of an ancestor, worn in some Māori cultures

Tikrit a town in N central Iraq on the River Tigris; birthplace of Saladin and Saddam Hussein. Pop: 28 900 (2002 est)

Tilburg a city in the S Netherlands, in North Brabant: textile industries. Pop: 198 000 (2003 est)

Tilbury an area in Essex, on the River Thames: extensive docks; principal container port of the Port of London

Tilden **Bill**, full name *William Tatem Tilden*, known as *Big Bill*. 1893–1953, US tennis player: won the US singles championship (1920–25, 1929) and the British singles championship (1920–21, 1930)

tile a rectangular block used as a playing piece in mah jong and other games
▷www.tiles.org

till¹ a box, case, or drawer into which the money taken from customers is put, now usually part of a cash register

till² an unstratified glacial deposit consisting of rock fragments of various sizes. The most common is boulder clay

tiller¹ *Nautical* a handle fixed to the top of a rudderpost to serve as a lever in steering it

tiller² 1 a shoot that arises from the base of the stem in grasses **2** a less common name for **sapling**

Tilley Vesta , original name *Matilda Alice Powles*. 1864–1952, British music-hall entertainer, best known as a male impersonator

Tillich Paul Johannes 1886–1965, US Protestant theologian and philosopher, born in Germany. His works include *The Courage to Be* (1952) and *Systematic Theology* (1951–63)

tilt (esp in medieval Europe) **a** a jousting contest **b** a thrust with a lance or pole delivered during a tournament

Timaru a port and resort in S New Zealand, on E South Island. Pop: 43 100 (2004 est)

timber 1 a wood, esp when regarded as a construction material **b** (*as modifier*): *a timber cottage* **2 a** trees collectively **b** *Chiefly US* woodland **3** *Nautical* a frame in a wooden vessel

Timberlake Justin born 1981, US pop singer; a member of the boy band NSYNC, he later found success with the bestselling solo album *Justified* (2002)

timbre *Music* tone colour or quality of sound, esp a specific type of tone colour

Timbuktu a town in central Mali, on the River Niger: terminus of a trans-Saharan caravan route; a great Muslim centre (14th–16th centuries). Pop: 31 925 (latest est)

time 1 *Physics* a quantity measuring duration, usually with reference to a periodic process such as the rotation of the earth or the vibration of electromagnetic radiation emitted from certain atoms (see **second²** (sense 1)). In classical mechanics, time is absolute in the sense that the time of an event is independent of the observer. According to the theory of relativity it depends on the observer's frame of reference. Time is considered as a fourth coordinate required, along with three spatial coordinates, to specify an event **2** indicating a degree or amount calculated by multiplication with the number specified **3 a** the system of combining beats or pulses in music into successive groupings by which the rhythm of the music is established **b** a specific system having a specific number of beats in each grouping or bar **4** *Music* short for **time value 5** *Prosody* a unit of duration used in the measurement of poetic metre; mora **6 beat time** (of a conductor, etc) to indicate the tempo or pulse of a piece of music by waving a baton or a hand, tapping out the beats, etc. **7 in time a** *Music* at a correct metrical or rhythmic pulse **8 keep time** to observe correctly the accent or rhythmic pulse of a piece of music in relation to tempo

time capsule a container holding articles, documents, etc, representative of the current age, buried in the earth or in the foundations of a new building for discovery in the future

time exposure 1 an exposure of a photographic film for a relatively long period, usually a few seconds **2** a photograph produced by such an exposure

time-out *Computing* a condition occurring when the amount of time a computer has been instructed to wait for another device to perform a task has expired, usually indicated by an error message

timer a switch or regulator that causes a mechanism to operate at a specific time or at predetermined intervals

time sharing *Computing* a a system by which users at different terminals of a computer can, because of its high speed, apparently communicate with it at the same time **b** (*as modifier*): *a time-sharing computer*

time signature *Music* a sign usually consisting of two figures, one above the other, the upper figure representing the number of beats per bar and the lower one the time value of each beat. This sign is placed after the key signature at the outset of a piece or section of a piece

Times Square a square formed by the intersection of Broadway and Seventh Avenue in New York City, extending from 42nd to 45th Street

time value *Music* the duration of a given printed note relative to other notes in a composition or section and considered in relation to the basic tempo

time warp a hypothetical distortion of time in which people and events from one age can be imagined to exist in another age

time zone a region throughout which the same standard time is used. There are 24 time zones in the world, demarcated approximately by meridians at 15° intervals, an hour apart

Timişoara a city in W Romania: formerly under Turkish and then Hapsburg rule, being allotted to Romania in 1920; scene of violence during the revolution of 1989. Pop: 296 000 (2005 est)

Timor an island in the Malay Archipelago, the largest and easternmost of the Lesser Sunda Islands: the west was a Dutch possession (part of the Dutch East Indies) until 1949, when it became part of Indonesia: the east was held by Portugal until 1975, when it declared independence but was immediately invaded by Indonesia; East Timor finally became an independent state in 2002. Area: 30 775 sq km (11 883 sq miles)

Timor Sea an arm of the Indian Ocean between Australia and Timor. Width: about 480 km (300 miles)

Timoshenko Semyon Konstantinovich 1895–1970, Soviet general in World War II

Timothy¹ *New Testament* **1 Saint** a disciple of Paul, who became leader of the Christian community at Ephesus. Feast day: Jan 26 or 22 **2** either of the two books addressed to him (in full **The First and Second Epistles of Paul the Apostle to Timothy**), containing advice on pastoral matters

Timothy² either of the two books addressed to St Timothy, a disciple of Paul, who became leader of the Christian community at Ephesus (in full **The First and Second Epistles of Paul the Apostle to Timothy**), containing advice on pastoral matters

tin 1 a metallic element, occurring in cassiterite, that has several allotropes; the ordinary malleable silvery-white metal slowly changes below 13.2°C to a grey powder. It is used extensively in alloys, esp bronze and pewter, and as a noncorroding coating for steel. Symbol: Sn; atomic no.: 50; atomic wt.: 118.710; valency: 2 or 4; relative density: 5.75 (grey), 7.31 (white); melting pt.: 231.9°C; boiling pt.: 2603°C **2** the contents of a tin or the amount a tin will hold

Tinbergen 1 Jan 1903–94, Dutch economist, noted for his work on econometrics. He shared (1969) the first Nobel prize for economics with Ragnar Frisch **2** his brother,

Nikolaas 1907–88, British zoologist, born in the Netherlands; studied animal behaviour, esp instincts, and was one of the founders of ethology; Nobel prize for physiology or medicine 1973

tincture 1 *Pharmacol* a medicinal extract in a solution of alcohol **2** a tint, colour, or tinge

tinder dry wood or other easily combustible material used for lighting a fire

tine any of the sharp terminal branches of a deer's antler

tinfoil thin foil made of tin or an alloy of tin and lead

Ting Samuel Chao Chung born 1936, US physicist, who discovered the J/psi particle independently of Burton Richter, with whom he shared (1976) the Nobel prize for physics

tinker 1 (esp formerly) a travelling mender of pots and pans **2** *Scot and Irish* another name for a **Gypsy 3** any of several small mackerels that occur off the North American coast of the Atlantic

tinned 1 plated, coated, or treated with tin **2** coated with a layer of solder

tinny *Austral, informal* a small fishing or pleasure boat with an aluminium hull

tin plate thin steel sheet coated with a layer of tin that protects the steel from corrosion

tinsel a yarn or fabric interwoven with strands of glittering thread

tint 1 a shade of a colour, esp a pale one **2** a colour that is softened or desaturated by the addition of white

Tintagel Head a promontory in SW England, on the W coast of Cornwall: ruins of **Tintagel Castle**, legendary birthplace of King Arthur

tintinnabulation the act or an instance of the ringing or pealing of bells

Tintoretto Il original name *Jacopo Robusti*. 1518–94, Italian painter of the Venetian school. His works include *Susanna bathing* (?1550) and the fresco cycle in the Scuola di San Rocco, Venice (from 1564)

tip¹ 1 a payment given for services in excess of the standard charge; gratuity **2** a piece of inside information, esp in betting or investing

tip² a glancing hit in cricket

tip-off *Basketball* the act or an instance of putting the ball in play by a jump ball

Tipperary a county of S Republic of Ireland, in Munster province; divided into the North Riding and South Riding: mountainous. County town: Clonmel; Nenagh serves as administrative capital of the North Riding. Pop: 140 131 (2002). Area: 4255 sq km (1643 sq miles)

tippet 1 the long stole of Anglican clergy worn during a service **2** the ruff of a bird **3** a tippet feather or something similar used in dressing some artificial angling flies

Tippett Sir Michael 1905–98, English composer, whose works include the oratorio *A Child of Our Time* (1941) and the operas *The Midsummer Marriage* (1952), *King Priam* (1961), *The Knot Garden* (1970), *The Ice Break* (1976), and *New Year* (1989)

tipple 1 a device for overturning ore trucks, mine cars, etc, so that they discharge their load **2** a place at which such trucks are tipped and unloaded

tipstaff a court official having miscellaneous duties,

mostly concerned with the maintenance of order in court

tirade *Prosody, rare* a speech or passage dealing with a single theme

Tiran Strait of a strait between the Gulf of Aqaba and the Red Sea. Length: 16 km (10 miles). Width: 8 km (5 miles)

Tirana *or* **Tiranë** the capital of Albania, in the central part 32 km (20 miles) from the Adriatic: founded in the early 17th century by Turks; became capital in 1920; the country's largest city and industrial centre. Pop: 390 000 (2005 est)

Tiree an island off the W coast of Scotland, in the Inner Hebrides. Pop: 770 (2001). Area: 78 sq km (30 sq miles)

Tirich Mir a mountain in N Pakistan: highest peak of the Hindu Kush. Height: 7690 m (25 230 ft)

Tirpitz Alfred von 1849–1930, German admiral: as secretary of state for the Imperial Navy (1897–1916), he created the modern German navy, which challenged British supremacy at sea

Tiruchirapalli *or* **Trichinopoly** an industrial city in S India, in central Tamil Nadu on the Cauvery River: dominated by a rock fortress 83 m (273 ft) high. Pop: 746 062 (2001)

Tirunelveli a city in S India, in Tamil Nadu: site of St Francis Xavier's first preaching in India; textile manufacturing. Pop: 411 298 (2001)

Tissot James Joseph Jacques 1836–1902, French painter and etcher, best known for scenes of fashionable Victorian life painted in England

tissue 1 a part of an organism consisting of a large number of cells having a similar structure and function **2** a woven cloth, esp of a light gauzy nature, originally interwoven with threads of gold or silver

Tisza a river in S central Europe, rising in W Ukraine and flowing west, forming part of the border between Ukraine and Romania, then southwest across Hungary into Serbia to join the Danube north of Belgrade

tit 1 any of numerous small active Old World songbirds of the family *Paridae* (titmice), esp those of the genus *Parus* (bluetit, great tit, etc). They have a short bill and feed on insects and seeds **2** any of various similar small birds

titanic of or containing titanium, esp in the tetravalent state

titanium a strong malleable white metallic element, which is very corrosion-resistant and occurs in rutile and ilmenite. It is used in the manufacture of strong lightweight alloys, esp aircraft parts. Symbol: Ti; atomic no.: 22; atomic wt.: 47.88; valency: 2, 3, or 4; relative density: 4.54; melting pt.: 1670±10°C; boiling pt.: 3289°C

tithe 1 *Christianity* a tenth part of agricultural or other produce, personal income, or profits, contributed either voluntarily or as a tax for the support of the church or clergy or for charitable purposes **2** any levy, esp of one tenth

tithe barn a large barn where, formerly, the agricultural tithe of a parish was stored

Titian¹ original name *Tiziano Vecellio*. ?1490–1576, Italian painter of the Venetian school, noted for his religious and mythological works, such as *Bacchus and Ariadne* (1523), and his portraits

Titian² reddish-gold, like the hair colour used in many

of the works of Titian (original name *Tiziano Vecellio*), the Italian painter of the Venetian school (?1490–1576)

Titicaca Lake a lake between S Peru and W Bolivia, in the Andes: the highest large lake in the world; drained by the Desaguadero River flowing into Lake Poopó. Area: 8135 sq km (3141 sq miles). Altitude: 3809 m (12 497 ft). Depth: 370 m (1214 ft)

title 1 an appellation designating nobility **2** *Films* **a** short for **subtitle b** written material giving credits in a film or television programme **3** *Property law* **a** the legal right to possession of property, esp real property **b** the basis of such right **c** the documentary evidence of such right **4** *Law* **a** the heading or a division of a statute, book of law, etc. **b** the heading of a suit or action at law **5 a** any customary or established right **b** a claim based on such a right **6** a definite spiritual charge or office in the church, without appointment to which a candidate for holy orders cannot lawfully be ordained **7** *RC Church* a titular church

title deed a deed or document evidencing a person's legal right or title to property, esp real property

title role the role of the character after whom a play, etc, is named

titmouse any small active songbird of the family *Paridae*, esp those of the genus *Parus* (see **tit**)

Tito Marshal original name *Josip Broz*. 1892–1980, Yugoslav statesman, who led the communist guerrilla resistance to German occupation during World War II; prime minister of Yugoslavia (1945–53) and president (1953–80)

titration an operation, used in volumetric analysis, in which a measured amount of one solution is added to a known quantity of another solution until the reaction between the two is complete. If the concentration of one solution is known, that of the other can be calculated

titular *or* **titulary** *RC Church* designating any of certain churches in Rome to whom cardinals or bishops are attached as their nominal incumbents

Titus¹ 1 *New Testament* **a Saint** a Greek disciple and helper of Saint Paul. Feast day: Jan 26 or Aug 25 **b** the book written to him (in full **The Epistle of Paul the Apostle to Titus**), containing advice on pastoral matters **2** full name *Titus Flavius Sabinus Vespasianus*. ?40–81 AD, Roman emperor (78–81 AD)

Titus² ** *New Testament* the epistle written by Saint Paul to Titus, his Greek disciple and helper (in full **The Epistle of Paul the Apostle to Titus), containing advice on pastoral matters

Tivoli a town in central Italy, east of Rome: a summer resort in Roman times; contains the Renaissance Villa d'Este and the remains of Hadrian's Villa. Pop: 49 342 (2001)

Tjirebon *or* **Cheribon** a port in S central Indonesia, on N Java on the Java Sea: scene of the signing of the **Tjirebon Agreement** of Indonesian independence (1946) by the Netherlands. Pop: 272 263 (2000)

T-junction a road junction in which one road joins another at right angles but does not cross it

Tlaxcala 1 a state of S central Mexico: the smallest Mexican state; formerly an Indian principality, the chief Indian ally of Cortés in the conquest of Mexico.

Capital: Tlaxcala. Pop: 961 912 (2000 est). Area: 3914 sq km (1511 sq miles) **2** a city in E central Mexico, on the central plateau, capital of Tlaxcala state: the church of San Francisco (founded 1521 by Cortés) is the oldest in the Americas. Pop: 25 000 (1990 est)

Tlemcen a city in NW Algeria: capital of an Arab kingdom from the 12th to the late 14th century. Pop: 177 000 (2005 est)

toad 1 any anuran amphibian of the class *Bufonidae*, such as *Bufo bufo* (**common toad**) of Europe. They are similar to frogs but are more terrestrial, having a drier warty skin **2** any of various similar amphibians of different families

toadflax any of various scrophulariaceous plants of the genus *Linaria*, esp *L. vulgaris*, having narrow leaves and spurred two-lipped yellow-orange flowers

toadstool any basidiomycetous fungus with a capped spore-producing body that is not edible

Toamasina a port in E Madagascar, on the Indian Ocean: the country's chief commercial centre. Pop: 198 000 (2005 est)

tobacco 1 any of numerous solanaceous plants of the genus *Nicotiana*, having mildly narcotic properties, tapering hairy leaves, and tubular or funnel-shaped fragrant flowers. The species *N. tabacum* is cultivated as the chief source of commercial tobacco **2** the leaves of certain of these plants dried and prepared for snuff, chewing, or smoking

tobacconist *Chiefly Brit* a person or shop that sells tobacco, cigarettes, pipes, etc.

Tobago an island in the SE Caribbean, northeast of Trinidad: ceded to Britain in 1814; joined with Trinidad in 1888 as a British colony; part of the independent republic of Trinidad and Tobago. Pop: 54 084 (2000)

Tobey Mark 1890–1976, US painter. Influenced by Chinese calligraphy, he devised a style of improvisatory abstract painting called "white writing"

Tobit *Old Testament* **1** a pious Jew who was released from blindness through the help of the archangel Raphael **2** a book of the Apocrypha relating this story

Tobol a river in central Asia, rising in N Kazakhstan and flowing northeast into Russia to join the Irtysh River. Length: about 1300 km (800 miles)

Tobolsk a town in central Russia, at the confluence of the Irtysh and Tobol Rivers: the chief centre for the early Russian colonization of Siberia. Pop: 100 000 (2000 est)

Tobruk a small port in NE Libya, in E Cyrenaica on the Mediterranean coast road: scene of severe fighting in World War II: taken from the Italians by the British in January 1941, from the British by the Germans in June 1942, and finally taken by the British in November 1942

toby a water stopcock at the boundary of a street and house section

Tocantins 1 a state of N Brazil, created from the northern part of Goiás state in 1988. Capital: Palmas. Pop: 1 207 014 (2002). Area: 278 421 sq km (107 499 sq miles) **2** a river in E Brazil, rising in S central Goiás state and flowing generally north to the Pará River. Length: about 2700 km (1700 miles)

toccata a rapid keyboard composition for organ, harpsichord, etc, dating from the baroque period, usually in a rhythmically free style

Toc H a society formed in England after World War I to fight loneliness and hate and to encourage Christian comradeship

Tocqueville Alexis Charles Henri Maurice Clérel de 1805–59, French politician and political writer. His chief works are *De la Démocratie en Amérique* (1835–40) and *L'Ancien régime et la révolution* (1856)

tod *Brit* a unit of weight, used for wool, etc, usually equal to 28 pounds

Todd Baron **Alexander Robertus** 1907–97, Scottish chemist, noted for his research into the structure of nucleic acids: Nobel prize for chemistry 1957

toddy 1 a drink made from spirits, esp whisky, with hot water, sugar, and usually lemon juice 2 a the sap of various palm trees (**toddy** or **wine palms**), used as a beverage b the liquor prepared from this sap 3 (in Malaysia) a milky-white sour alcoholic drink made from fermented coconut milk, drunk chiefly by Indians

toe 1 any one of the digits of the foot 2 the corresponding part in other vertebrates 3 the lower bearing of a vertical shaft assembly 4 the tip of a cam follower that engages the cam profile

toehold 1 a small foothold to facilitate climbing 2 a wrestling hold in which the opponent's toe is held and his leg twisted against the joints

toenail a thin horny translucent plate covering part of the dorsal surface of the end joint of each toe

tog a unit of thermal resistance used to measure the power of insulation of a fabric, garment, quilt, etc. The tog-value of an article is equal to ten times the temperature difference between its two faces, in degrees Celsius, when the flow of heat across it is equal to one watt per m^2 (*as modifier*): *tog-rating*

toga 1 a garment worn by citizens of ancient Rome, consisting of a piece of cloth draped around the body 2 the official vestment of certain offices

toggle 1 a wooden peg or metal rod fixed crosswise through an eye at the end of a rope, chain, or cable, for fastening temporarily by insertion through an eye in another rope, chain, etc. 2 *Machinery* a toggle joint or a device having such a joint

toggle switch 1 an electric switch having a projecting lever that is manipulated in a particular way to open or close a circuit 2 a computer device that is used to turn a feature on or off

Togliatti[1] **Palmiro** 1893–1964, Italian politician; leader of the Italian Communist Party (1926–64). After Mussolini's fall he became a minister (1944) and vice premier (1945)

Togliatti[2] a city in W central Russia, on the Volga River: automobile industry: renamed in honour of Palmiro Togliatti, an Italian communist. Pop: 718 000 (2005 est)

Togo[1] Marquis **Heihachiro** 1847–1934, Japanese admiral, who commanded the Japanese fleet in the war with Russia (1904–05)

Togo[2] a republic in West Africa, on the Gulf of Guinea: became French Togoland (a League of Nations mandate) after the division of German Togoland in 1922; independent since 1960. Official language: French. Religion: animist majority. Currency: franc. Capital: Lomé. Pop: 5 017 000 (2004 est). Area: 56 700 sq km

(20 900 sq miles)

Togoland a former German protectorate in West Africa on the Gulf of Guinea: divided in 1922 into the League of Nations mandates of British Togoland (west) and French Togoland (east); the former joined Ghana in 1957; the latter became independent as Togo in 1960

toheroa a bivalve mollusc, *Amphidesma* (or *Semele*) *ventricosum*, of New Zealand

tohunga *NZ* a Māori priest, the repository of traditional lore

Tojo **Hideki** 1885–1948, Japanese soldier and statesman; minister of war (1940–41) and premier (1941–44); hanged as a war criminal

token 1 a gift voucher that can be used as payment for goods of a specified value 2 *Philosophy* an individual instance: if the same sentence has different truth-values on different occasions of utterance the truth-value may be said to attach to the sentence-token

Tokyo the capital of Japan, a port on SE Honshu on Tokyo Bay (an inlet of the Pacific): part of the largest conurbation in the world (the Tokyo-Yokohama metropolitan area) of over 35 million people; major industrial centre and the chief cultural centre of Japan. Pop. (city proper): 8 025 538 (2002 est)

Toledo 1 a city in central Spain, on the River Tagus: capital of Visigothic Spain, and of Castile from 1087 to 1560; famous for steel and swords since the first century. Pop: 72 549 (2003 est) 2 an inland port in NW Ohio, on Lake Erie: one of the largest coal-shipping ports in the world; transportation and industrial centre; university (1872). Pop: 308 973 (2003 est)

tolerance 1 the permitted variation in some measurement or other characteristic of an object or workpiece 2 *Physiol* the capacity of an organism to endure the effects of a poison or other substance, esp after it has been taken over a prolonged period

tolerant *Med* (of a patient) exhibiting tolerance to a drug

Tolima a volcano in W Colombia, in the Andes. Height: 5215 m (17 110 ft)

Tolkien J(ohn) R(onald) R(euel). 1892–1973, British philologist and writer, born in South Africa. He is best known for *The Hobbit* (1937), the trilogy *The Lord of the Rings* (1954–55), and the posthumously published *The Silmarillion* (1977)

toll (formerly) the right to levy a toll

Tolstoy Leo, Russian name *Count Lev Nikolayevich Tolstoy*. 1828–1910, Russian novelist, short-story writer, and philosopher; author of the two monumental novels *War and Peace* (1865–69) and *Anna Karenina* (1875–77). Following a spiritual crisis in 1879, he adopted a form of Christianity based on a doctrine of nonresistance to evil

tolu an aromatic balsam obtained from a South American tree, *Myroxylon balsamum*

Toluca 1 a city in S central Mexico, capital of Mexico state, at an altitude of 2640 m (8660 ft). Pop: 1 987 000 (2005 est) 2 **Nevado de** a volcano in central Mexico, in Mexico state near Toluca: crater partly filled by a lake. Height: 4577 m (15 017 ft)

toluene a colourless volatile flammable liquid with an odour resembling that of benzene, obtained from petroleum and coal tar and used as a solvent and in the manufacture of many organic chemicals. Formula: $C_6H_5CH_3$

tom a the male of various animals, esp the cat **b** (*as modifier*): *a tom turkey*

tomato 1 a solanaceous plant, *Lycopersicon* (or *Lycopersicum*) *esculentum*, of South America, widely cultivated for its red fleshy many-seeded edible fruits 2 the fruit of this plant, which has slightly acid-tasting flesh and is eaten in salads, as a vegetable, etc.

Tombaugh Clyde William 1906–97, US astronomer, who discovered (1930) the planet Pluto

tombola *Brit* a type of lottery, esp at a fête, in which tickets are drawn from a revolving drum

Tomsk a city in central Russia: formerly an important gold-mining town and administrative centre for a large area of Siberia; university (1888); engineering industries. Pop: 486 000 (2005 est)

Tom Thumb General, stage name of *Charles Stratton*. 1838–83, US midget, exhibited in P. T. Barnum's circus

tomtit *Brit* any of various tits, esp the bluetit

tom-tom 1 a drum associated either with the American Indians or with Eastern cultures, usually beaten with the hands as a signalling instrument 2 a standard cylindrical drum, normally with one drumhead

ton 1 *Brit* a unit of weight equal to 2240 pounds or 1016.046909 kilograms 2 *US* a unit of weight equal to 2000 pounds or 907.184 kilograms 3 a unit of weight equal to 1000 kilograms 4 a unit of volume or weight used for charging or measuring freight in shipping. It depends on the type of material being shipped but is often taken as 40 cubic feet, 1 cubic metre, or 1000 kilograms 5 a unit of volume used in shipping freight, equal to 40 cubic feet, irrespective of the commodity shipped 6 a unit used for measuring the displacement of a ship, equal to 35 cubic feet of sea water or 2240 pounds 7 a unit of internal capacity of ships equal to 100 cubic feet

tonal 1 of, relating to, or utilizing the diatonic system; having an established key 2 a (of an answer in a fugue) not having the same melodic intervals as the subject, so as to remain in the original key **b** denoting a fugue as having such an answer

tonality 1 *Music* a the actual or implied presence of a musical key in a composition **b** the system of major and minor keys prevalent in Western music since the decline of modes 2 the overall scheme of colours and tones in a painting

Tonbridge a market town in SE England, in SW Kent on the River Medway. Pop: 35 833 (2001)

tone 1 *US and Canadian* another word for **note** 2 (in acoustic analysis) a sound resulting from periodic or regular vibrations, composed either of a simple sinusoidal waveform (**pure tone**) or of several such waveforms superimposed upon one main one (**compound tone**) 3 an interval of a major second; whole tone 4 any of several plainsong melodies or other chants used in the singing of psalms 5 the quality of a given colour, as modified by mixture with white or black; shade; tint 6 *Physiol* a the normal tension of a muscle at rest **b** the natural firmness of the tissues and normal functioning of bodily organs in health 7 the overall effect of the colour values and gradations of light and dark in a picture 8 *Photog* a colour or shade of colour, including black or grey, of a particular area on a negative or positive that can be distinguished from surrounding lighter or darker areas

tone-deaf unable to distinguish subtle differences in musical pitch

toner *Photog* a chemical solution that softens or alters the colour of the tones of a photographic image

tong (formerly) a Chinese secret society or association, esp one popularly assumed to engage in criminal activities

Tonga a kingdom occupying an archipelago of more than 150 volcanic and coral islands in the SW Pacific, east of Fiji: inhabited by Polynesians; became a British protectorate in 1900 and gained independence in 1970; a member of the Commonwealth. Official languages: Tongan and English. Religion: Christian majority. Currency: pa'anga. Capital: Nuku'alofa. Pop: 104 000 (2004 est). Area: 750 sq km (290 sq miles)

tongue 1 a movable mass of muscular tissue attached to the floor of the mouth in most vertebrates. It is the organ of taste and aids the mastication and swallowing of food. In man it plays an important part in the articulation of speech sounds 2 an analogous organ in invertebrates 3 a language, dialect, or idiom 4 a promontory or spit of land 5 *Music* the reed of an oboe or similar instrument 6 the clapper of a bell 7 a long and narrow projection on a machine or structural part that serves as a guide for assembly or as a securing device

tongue-tie a congenital condition in which the tongue has restricted mobility as the result of an abnormally short frenulum

tonguing a technique of articulating notes on a wind instrument

tonic 1 a medicinal preparation intended to improve and strengthen the functioning of the body or increase the feeling of wellbeing 2 *Music* a the first degree of a major or minor scale and the tonal centre of a piece composed in a particular key **b** a key or chord based on this 3 *Music* of or relating to the first degree of a major or minor scale 4 of or denoting the general effect of colour and light and shade in a picture 5 *Physiol* of, relating to, characterized by, or affecting normal muscular or bodily tone

tonic sol-fa a method of teaching music, esp singing, used mainly in Britain, by which the syllables of a movable system of solmization are used as names for the notes of the major scale in any key. In this system *sol* is usually replaced by *so* as the name of the fifth degree

Tonkin *or* **Tongking** 1 a former state of N French Indochina (1883–1946), on the Gulf of Tonkin: forms the largest part of N Vietnam 2 **Gulf of** an arm of the South China Sea, bordered by N Vietnam, the Leizhou Peninsula of SW China, and Hainan Island. Length: about 500 km (300 miles)

Tonle Sap a lake in W central Cambodia, linked with the Mekong River by the **Tonle Sap River**. Area: (dry season) about 2600 sq km (1000 sq miles); (rainy season) about 10 000 sq km (3860 sq miles)

tonnage *or* **tunnage** 1 the capacity of a merchant ship expressed in tons, for which purpose a ton is considered as 40 cubic feet of freight or 100 cubic feet of bulk cargo, unless such an amount would weigh more than 2000 pounds in which case the actual weight is used **2** the weight of the cargo of a merchant ship **3** the total amount of shipping of a port or nation, estimated by the capacity of its ships **4** a duty on ships based either on their capacity or their register tonnage

tonne a unit of mass equal to 1000 kg or 2204.6 pounds

tonsil 1 either of two small masses of lymphatic tissue situated one on each side of the back of the mouth **2** *Anatomy* any small rounded mass of tissue, esp lymphatic tissue

tonsillectomy surgical removal of the palatine tonsils

tonsillitis inflammation of the palatine tonsils, causing enlargement, occasionally to the extent that they nearly touch one another

tool 1 a an implement, such as a hammer, saw, or spade, that is used by hand **b** a power-driven instrument; machine tool **2** the cutting part of such an instrument **3 a** any of the instruments used by a bookbinder to impress a design on a book cover **b** a design so impressed **4** anything used as a means of performing an operation or achieving an end

tool-maker a person who specializes in the production or reconditioning of precision tools, cutters, etc.

toonie *or* **twonie** *Canadian, informal* a Canadian two-dollar coin

tooth 1 any of various bonelike structures set in the jaws of most vertebrates and modified, according to the species, for biting, tearing, or chewing **2** any of various similar structures in invertebrates, occurring in the mouth or alimentary canal **3** any of the various small indentations occurring on the margin of a leaf, petal, etc. **4** any one of a number of uniform projections on a gear, sprocket, rack, etc, by which drive is transmitted

toothache a pain in or about a tooth

tooth powder a powder used for cleaning the teeth, applied with a toothbrush

Toowoomba a city in E Australia, in SE Queensland: agricultural and industrial centre. Pop: 89 338 (2001)

top 1 short for **top gear 2** *Cards* the highest card of a suit in a player's hand **3** a platform around the head of a lower mast of a sailing vessel, the edges of which serve to extend the topmast shrouds **4** *Chem* the part of a volatile liquid mixture that distils first **5** the high-frequency content of an audio signal

topaz 1 a white or colourless mineral often tinted by impurities, found in cavities in igneous rocks and in quartz veins. It is used as a gemstone. Composition: hydrated aluminium silicate. Formula: $Al_2SiO_4(F,OH)_2$. Crystal structure: orthorhombic **2 oriental topaz** a yellowish-brown variety of sapphire **3** a yellowish-brown colour, as in some varieties of topaz **4** either of two South American hummingbirds, *Topaza pyra* and *T. pella*

top dressing a thin layer of loose gravel that covers the top of a road surface

tope 1 a small grey requiem shark, *Galeorhinus galeus*, of European coastal waters **2** any of various other small sharks

Topeka a city in E central Kansas, capital of the state, on the Kansas River: university (1865). Pop: 122 008 (2003 est)

Top End the *Austral* the northern part of the Northern Territory

topgallant 1 a mast on a square-rigger above a topmast or an extension of a topmast **2** a sail set on a yard of a topgallant mast

top gear the highest gear in a motor vehicle, often shortened to **top**

top-heavy (of a business enterprise) having too many executives

Tophet *or* **Topheth** *Old Testament* a place in the valley immediately to the southwest of Jerusalem; the Shrine of Moloch, where human sacrifices were offered

topiary the trimming or training of trees or bushes into artificial decorative animal, geometric, or other shapes

topic (in rhetoric, logic, etc) a category or class of arguments or ideas which may be drawn on to furnish proofs

topical (of a drug, ointment, etc) for application to the body surface; local

topknot any of several European flatfishes of the genus *Zeugopterus* and related genera, esp *Z. punctatus*, which has an oval dark brown body marked with darker blotches: family *Bothidae* (turbot, etc)

topmast the mast next above a lower mast on a sailing vessel

topography 1 the study or detailed description of the surface features of a region **2** the detailed mapping of the configuration of a region **3** the land forms or surface configuration of a region

topology 1 the branch of mathematics concerned with generalization of the concepts of continuity, limit, etc. **2** a branch of geometry describing the properties of a figure that are unaffected by continuous distortion, such as stretching or knotting **3** *Maths* a family of subsets of a given set *S*, such that *S* is a topological space **4** the arrangement and interlinking of computers in a computer network **5** the study of the topography of a given place, esp as far as it reflects its history **6** the anatomy of any specific bodily area, structure, or part

Topolski Feliks 1907–89, British painter, born in Poland; best known for his sketches and murals, esp for *Memoir of the Century* (1975–89) painted on viaduct arches on London's South Bank

topping *Angling* part of a brightly-coloured feather, usually from a golden pheasant crest, used to top some artificial flies

topsail a square sail carried on a yard set on a topmast

top-secret containing information whose disclosure would cause exceedingly grave damage to the nation and therefore classified as needing the highest level of secrecy and security

topside a the part of a ship's sides above the waterline **b** the parts of a ship above decks

tor 1 a high hill, esp a bare rocky one **2** *Chiefly southwestern Brit* a prominent rock or heap of rocks, esp on a hill

Torah 1 a the Pentateuch **b** the scroll on which this is written, used in synagogue services **2** the whole body of traditional Jewish teaching, including the Oral Law
▷http://www.jewfaq.org/torah.htm

Torbay 1 a unitary authority in SW England, in Devon, consisting of Torquay and two neighbouring coastal resorts. Pop: 131 300 (2003 est). Area: 63 sq km (24 sq miles) **2** an inlet of the English Channel on the coast of SW England, near Torquay

torch 1 a small portable electric lamp powered by one or more dry batteries **2** any apparatus that burns with a hot flame for welding, brazing, or soldering

toreador a bullfighter

torero a bullfighter, esp one who fights on foot

Torfaen a county borough of SE Wales, created in 1996 from part of Gwent. Administrative centre: Pontypool. Pop: 90 700 (2003 est). Area: 290 sq km (112 sq miles)

tormentil a rosaceous downy perennial plant, *Potentilla erecta*, of Europe and W Asia, having serrated leaves, four-petalled yellow flowers, and an astringent root used in medicine, tanning, and dyeing

tornado 1 a violent storm with winds whirling around a small area of extremely low pressure, usually characterized by a dark funnel-shaped cloud causing damage along its path **2** a small but violent squall or whirlwind, such as those occurring on the West African coast

Toronto a city in S central Canada, capital of Ontario, on Lake Ontario: the major industrial centre of Canada; two universities. Pop: 2 481 494 (2001)

torpedo 1 *US and Canadian* a detonator placed on a railway line as a danger signal **2** any of various electric rays of the genus *Torpedo*

torpedo boat (formerly) a small high-speed warship designed to carry out torpedo attacks in coastal waters

torpid (of a hibernating animal) dormant; having greatly reduced metabolic activity

Torquay a town and resort in SW England, in Torbay unitary authority, S Devon. Pop: 62 968 (2001).

torque 1 a necklace or armband made of twisted metal, worn esp by the ancient Britons and Gauls **2** any force or system of forces that causes or tends to cause rotation **3** the ability of a shaft to cause rotation

Torquemada Tomás de 1420–98, Spanish Dominican monk. As first Inquisitor-General of Spain (1483–98), he was responsible for the burning of some 2000 heretics

torr a unit of pressure equal to one millimetre of mercury (133.322 newtons per square metre)

Torrance a city in SW California, southwest of Los Angeles: developed rapidly with the discovery of oil. Pop: 142 621 (2003 est)

Torre del Greco a city in SW Italy, in Campania near Vesuvius on the Bay of Naples: damaged several times by eruptions. Pop: 90 607 (2001)

Torrens Lake a shallow salt lake in E central South Australia, about 8 m (25 ft) below sea level. Area: 5776 sq km (2230 sq miles)

torrent a fast, voluminous, or violent stream of water or other liquid

Torres Strait a strait between NE Australia and S New Guinea, linking the Arafura Sea with the Coral Sea. Width: about 145 km (90 miles)

Torricelli Evangelista 1608–47, Italian physicist and mathematician, who discovered the principle of the barometer

torsion a the twisting of a part by application of equal and opposite torques at either end b the condition of twist and shear stress produced by a torque on a part or component

torso 1 the trunk of the human body **2** a statue of a nude human trunk, esp without the head or limbs

tort *Law* a civil wrong arising from an act or failure to act, independently of any contract, for which an action for personal injury or property damages may be brought

Tortelier Paul 1914–90, French cellist and composer

tortoise 1 any herbivorous terrestrial chelonian reptile of the family *Testudinidae*, of most warm regions, having a heavy dome-shaped shell and clawed limbs **2** **water tortoise** another name for **terrapin**

tortoiseshell 1 a horny translucent yellow-and-brown mottled substance obtained from the outer layer of the shell of the hawksbill turtle: used for making ornaments, jewellery, etc. **2** a breed of domestic cat, usually female, having black, cream, and brownish markings **3** any of several nymphalid butterflies of the genus *Nymphalis*, and related genera, having orange-brown wings with black markings **4** a yellowish-brown mottled colour

Tortola an island in the NE Caribbean, in the Leeward Islands group: chief island of the British Virgin Islands. Pop: 13 568 (1991). Area: 62 sq km (24 sq miles)

Tortuga an island in the Caribbean, off the NW coast of Haiti: haunt of pirates in the 17th century. Area: 180 sq km (70 sq miles)

Toruń an industrial city in N Poland, on the River Vistula: developed around a castle that was founded by the Teutonic Knights in 1230; under Prussian rule (1793–1919). Pop: 214 000 (2005 est)

Tory 1 a member or supporter of the Conservative Party in Great Britain or Canada **2** a member of the English political party that opposed the exclusion of James, Duke of York from the royal succession (1679–80). Tory remained the label for subsequent major conservative interests until they gave birth to the Conservative Party in the 1830s **3** an American supporter of the British cause; loyalist **4** an ultraconservative or reactionary **5** (in the 17th century) an Irish Roman Catholic, esp an outlaw who preyed upon English settlers

tosa a large dog, usually red in colour, which is a cross between a mastiff and a Great Dane: originally developed for dog-fighting; it is not recognized as a breed by kennel clubs outside Japan

Toscanini Arturo 1867–1957, Italian conductor; musical director of La Scala, Milan, and of the NBC symphony orchestra (1937–57) in New York

totalitarianism a dictatorial one-party state that regulates every realm of life

totality the state or period of an eclipse when light from the eclipsed body is totally obscured

totalizator, totalizer, totalisator or **totaliser 1** a system of betting on horse races in which the aggregate stake, less an administration charge and tax, is paid out to winners in proportion to their stake **2** the machine that records bets in this system and works out odds, pays out winnings, etc. **3** an apparatus for registering totals, as of a particular function or measurement

totem 1 (in some societies, esp among North American Indians) an object, species of animal or plant, or natural phenomenon symbolizing a clan, family, etc, often having ritual associations **2** a representation of such an object

totem pole a pole carved or painted with totemic figures set up by certain North American Indians, esp those of the NW Pacific coast, within a village as a tribal symbol or, sometimes, in memory of a dead person

toucan any tropical American arboreal fruit-eating bird of the family *Ramphastidae*, having a large brightly coloured bill with serrated edges and a bright plumage

touch 1 *Rugby, Soccer* the area outside the touchlines, beyond which the ball is out of play (esp in the phrase **in touch**) **2** *Archaic* **a** an official stamp on metal indicating standard purity **b** the die stamp used to apply this mark **3** a scoring hit in competitive fencing **4** an estimate of the amount of gold in an alloy as obtained by use of a touchstone **5** the technique of fingering a keyboard instrument **6** the quality of the action of a keyboard instrument with regard to the relative ease with which the keys may be depressed **7** *Bell-ringing* any series of changes where the permutations are fewer in number than for a peal

touchdown 1 the moment at which a landing aircraft or spacecraft comes into contact with the landing surface **2** *Rugby* the act of placing or touching the ball on the ground behind the goal line, as in scoring a try **3** *American football* a scoring play worth six points, achieved by being in possession of the ball in the opposing team's end zone

touch judge one of the two linesmen in rugby

touchstone a hard dark siliceous stone, such as basalt or jasper, that is used to test the quality of gold and silver from the colour of the streak they produce on it

Toul a town in NE France: a leading episcopal see in the Middle Ages. Pop: 16 945 (1999)

Toulon a fortified port and naval base in SE France, on the Mediterranean: naval arsenal developed by Henry IV and Richelieu, later fortified by Vauban. Pop: 160 639 (1999)

Toulouse a city in S France, on the Garonne River: scene of severe religious strife in the early 13th and mid-16th centuries; university (1229). Pop: 390 350 (1999)

Toulouse-Lautrec Henri (Marie Raymond) de 1864–1901, French painter and lithographer, noted for his paintings and posters of the life of Montmartre, Paris

toupee (formerly) a prominent lock on a periwig, esp in the 18th century

Touraine a former province of NW central France: at its height in the 16th century as an area of royal residences, esp along the Loire. Chief town: Tours

Tourcoing a town in NE France: textile manufacturing. Pop: 93 540 (1999)

tourism tourist travel and the services connected with it, esp when regarded as an industry

tourist the lowest class of accommodation on a passenger ship

tourmaline any of a group of hard glassy minerals of variable colour consisting of complex borosilicates of aluminium with quantities of lithium, sodium, calcium, potassium, iron, and magnesium in hexagonal crystalline form: used in optical and electrical equipment and in jewellery

Tournai a city in W Belgium, in Hainaut province on the River Scheldt: under several different European rulers until 1814. Pop: 67 341 (2004 est)

tournament *Medieval history* **a** (originally) a martial sport or contest in which mounted combatants fought for a prize **b** (later) a meeting for knightly sports and exercises

Tourneur Cyril ?1575–1626, English dramatist; author of *The Atheist's Tragedy* (1611) and, reputedly, of *The Revenger's Tragedy* (1607)

tourniquet *Med* any instrument or device for temporarily constricting an artery of the arm or leg to control bleeding

Tours a town in W central France, on the River Loire: nearby is the scene of the defeat of the Arabs in 732, which ended the advance of Islam in W Europe. Pop: 132 820 (1999)

tout 1 a a person who spies on racehorses so as to obtain betting information to sell **b** a person who sells information obtained by such spying **2** a person who sells tickets unofficially for a heavily booked sporting event, concert, etc, at greatly inflated prices

tow¹ 1 *Informal* (in motor racing, etc) the act of taking advantage of the slipstream of another car (esp in the phrase **get a tow**) **2** short for **ski tow**

tow² 1 the fibres of hemp, flax, jute, etc, in the scutched state **2** synthetic fibres preparatory to spinning **3** the coarser fibres discarded after combing

towbar a rigid metal bar or frame used for towing vehicles

towelling an absorbent fabric, esp with a nap, used for making towels, bathrobes, etc.

tower 1 a tall, usually square or circular structure, sometimes part of a larger building and usually built for a specific purpose **2** a mobile structure used in medieval warfare to attack a castle, etc.

Tower Hamlets a borough of E Greater London, on the River Thames: contains the main part of the East End. Pop: 206 600 (2003 est). Area: 20 sq km (8 sq miles)

Tower of London a fortress in the City of London, on the River Thames: begun 1078; later extended and used as a palace, the main state prison, and now as a museum containing the crown jewels

town 1 a a densely populated urban area, typically smaller than a city and larger than a village, having some local powers of government and a fixed boundary **b** (*as modifier*): *town life* **2** a city, borough, or other urban area **3** (in the US) a territorial unit of local government that is smaller than a county; township **4** the nearest town or commercial district **5** London or the chief city of an area **6** the inhabitants of a town

town clerk 1 (in Britain until 1974) the secretary and chief administrative officer of a town or city **2** (in the US) the official who keeps the records of a town

town crier (formerly) a person employed by a town to make public announcements in the streets

Townes Charles Hard born 1915, US physicist, noted for his research in quantum electronics leading to the invention of the maser and the laser; shared the Nobel prize for physics in 1964

town hall the chief building in which municipal business is transacted, often with a hall for public meetings

town house 1 a person's town residence as distinct from his country residence **2** another name (now chiefly Scot) for **town hall 3** US and Canadian a house that is part of a terrace

town planning the comprehensive planning of the physical and social development of a town, including the construction of facilities

Townshend 1 Charles, 2nd Viscount, nicknamed *Turnip Townshend.* 1674–1738, English politician and agriculturist **2 Pete** born 1945, British rock guitarist, singer, and songwriter: member of the Who (1964–83) and composer of much of their material

township 1 a small town **2** (in the Scottish Highlands and islands) a small crofting community **3** (in the US and Canada) a territorial area, esp a subdivision of a county: often organized as a unit of local government **4** (formerly, in South Africa) a planned urban settlement of Black Africans or Coloured people **5** *English history* **a** any of the local districts of a large parish, each division containing a village or small town **b** the particular manor or parish itself as a territorial division **c** the inhabitants of a township collectively

townsman 1 an inhabitant of a town **2** a person from the same town as oneself

townspeople or **townsfolk** the inhabitants of a town; citizens

Townsville a port in E Australia, in NE Queensland on the Coral Sea: centre of a vast agricultural and mining hinterland. Pop: 119 504 (2001)

toxaemia or US **toxemia 1** a condition characterized by the presence of bacterial toxins in the blood **2** the condition in pregnancy of pre-eclampsia or eclampsia

toxic harmful or deadly

toxicology the branch of science concerned with poisons, their nature, effects, and antidotes

toxin 1 any of various poisonous substances produced by microorganisms that stimulate the production of neutralizing substances (antitoxins) in the body **2** any other poisonous substance of plant or animal origin

Toyama a city in central Japan, on W Honshu on **Toyama Bay** (an inlet of the Sea of Japan): chemical and textile centre. Pop: 321 049 (2002 est)

Toynbee 1 Arnold 1852–83, British economist and social reformer, after whom **Toynbee Hall,** a residential settlement in East London, is named **2** his nephew, **Arnold Joseph** 1889–1975, British historian. In his chief work, *A Study of History* (1934–61), he attempted to analyse the principles determining the rise and fall of civilizations

toy-toy or **toyi-toyi** *South African* a dance expressing defiance and protest

Trabzon or **Trebizond** a port in NE Turkey, on the Black Sea: founded as a Greek colony in the 8th century BC at the terminus of an important trade route from central Europe to Asia. Pop: 246 000 (2005 est)

trace¹ 1 any line drawn by a recording instrument or a record consisting of a number of such lines **2** the postulated alteration in the cells of the nervous system that occurs as the result of any experience or learning **3** *Geometry* the intersection of a surface with a coordinate plane **4** *Maths* the sum of the diagonal entries of a square matrix **5** *Meteorol* an amount of precipitation

that is too small to be measured

trace² 1 either of the two side straps that connect a horse's harness to the swingletree **2** *Angling* a length of nylon or, formerly, gut attaching a hook or fly to a line

trace element any of various chemical elements, such as iron, manganese, zinc, copper, and iodine, that occur in very small amounts in organisms and are essential for many physiological and biochemical processes

tracer *Med* any radioactive isotope introduced into the body to study metabolic processes, absorption, etc, by following its progress through the body with a gamma camera or other detector

tracery *Archit* a pattern of interlacing ribs, esp as used in the upper part of a Gothic window, etc.

trachea 1 *Anatomy, Zoology* the membranous tube with cartilaginous rings that conveys inhaled air from the larynx to the bronchi **2** any of the tubes in insects and related animals that convey air from the spiracles to the tissues **3** *Botany* another name for **vessel**

tracheotomy surgical incision into the trachea, usually performed when the upper air passage has been blocked

trachoma a chronic contagious disease of the eye characterized by inflammation of the conjunctiva and cornea and the formation of scar tissue, caused by infection with the virus-like bacterium *Chlamydia trachomatis*

track 1 a rail or pair of parallel rails on which a vehicle, such as a locomotive, runs, esp the rails together with the sleepers, ballast, etc, on a railway **2** an endless jointed metal band driven by the wheels of a vehicle such as a tank or tractor to enable it to move across rough or muddy ground **3** *Physics* the path of a particle of ionizing radiation as observed in a cloud chamber, bubble chamber, or photographic emulsion **4 a** a course for running or racing **b** (as modifier): *track events* **5** US and Canadian **a** sports performed on a track **b** track and field events as a whole **6** a path on a magnetic recording medium, esp magnetic tape, on which information, such as music or speech, from a single input channel is recorded **7** any of a number of separate sections in the recording on a record, CD, or cassette **8** a metal path that makes the interconnections on an integrated circuit **9** the distance between the points of contact with the ground of a pair of wheels, such as the front wheels of a motor vehicle or the paired wheels of an aircraft undercarriage **10** a hypothetical trace made on the surface of the earth by a point directly below an aircraft in flight

tracker dog a dog specially trained to hunt fugitives or to search for missing people

track event a competition in athletics, such as relay running or sprinting, that takes place on a running track

track shoe either of a pair of light running shoes fitted with steel spikes for better grip

tract¹ 1 *Anatomy* a system of organs, glands, or other tissues that has a particular function **2** a bundle of nerve fibres having the same function, origin, and termination

tract² *RC Church* an anthem in some Masses

traction 1 *Med* the application of a steady pull on a part during healing of a fractured or dislocated bone, using a system of weights and pulleys or splints **2** the adhesive friction between a wheel and a surface, as between a driving wheel of a motor vehicle and the road

traction engine a steam-powered locomotive used, esp formerly, for drawing heavy loads along roads or over rough ground. It usually has two large rear wheels and a rope drum for haulage purposes

tractor 1 a motor vehicle used to pull heavy loads, esp farm machinery such as a plough or harvester. It usually has two large rear wheels with deeply treaded tyres **2** a short motor vehicle with a powerful engine and a driver's cab, used to pull a trailer, as in an articulated lorry **3** an aircraft with its propeller or propellers mounted in front of the engine

Tracy Spencer 1900–67, US film actor. His films include *The Power and the Glory* (1933), *Captains Courageous* (1937) and *Boys' Town* (1938), for both of which he won Oscars, *Adam's Rib* (1949), and *Bad Day at Black Rock* (1955)

trade 1 the act or an instance of buying and selling goods and services either on the domestic (wholesale and retail) markets or on the international (import, export, and entrepôt) markets **2** a personal occupation, esp a craft requiring skill **3** the people and practices of an industry, craft, or business **4** the regular clientele of a firm or industry **5** amount of custom or commercial dealings; business **6** a specified market or business **7** an occupation in commerce, as opposed to a profession **8** commercial customers, as opposed to the general public

trade-in a a used article given in part payment for the purchase of a new article **b** a transaction involving such part payment **c** the valuation put on the article traded in **d** (*as modifier*): *a trade-in dealer*

trademark the name or other symbol used to identify the goods produced by a particular manufacturer or distributed by a particular dealer and to distinguish them from products associated with competing manufacturers or dealers

trade name 1 the name used by a trade to refer to a commodity, service, etc. **2** the name under which a commercial enterprise operates in business

tradescantia any plant of the American genus *Tradescantia*, widely cultivated for their striped variegated leaves: family *Commelinaceae*

trade secret a secret formula, technique, process, etc, known and used to advantage by only one manufacturer

tradesman 1 a man engaged in trade, esp a retail dealer **2** a skilled worker

Trades Union Congress the major association of British trade unions, which includes all the larger unions

trade wind a wind blowing obliquely towards the equator either from the northeast in the N hemisphere or the southeast in the S hemisphere, approximately between latitudes 30° N and S, forming part of the planetary wind system

trading estate *Chiefly Brit* a large area in which a number of commercial or industrial firms are situated

tradition 1 *Christianity* a doctrine or body of doctrines regarded as having been established by Christ or the apostles though not contained in Scripture **2** *Judaism* a body of laws regarded as having been handed down from Moses orally and only committed to writing in the 2nd century AD **3** the beliefs and customs of Islam supplementing the Koran, esp as embodied in the Sunna **4** *Law, chiefly Roman and Scots* the act of formally transferring ownership of movable property; delivery

traditional of or relating to the style of jazz originating in New Orleans, characterized by collective improvisation by a front line of trumpet, trombone, and clarinet accompanied by various rhythm instruments

Trafalgar Cape a cape on the SW coast of Spain, south of Cádiz: scene of the decisive naval battle (1805) in which the French and Spanish fleets were defeated by the British under Nelson, who was mortally wounded

traffic 1 a the business of commercial transportation by land, sea, or air **b** the freight, passengers, etc, transported **2** trade, esp of an illicit or improper kind **3** *Chiefly US* the number of customers patronizing a commercial establishment in a given time period

traffic island a raised area in the middle of a road, designed as a guide for traffic and to provide a stopping place for pedestrians

traffic warden *Brit* a person who is appointed to supervise road traffic and report traffic offences

Trafford a unitary authority in NW England, in Greater Manchester. Pop: 211 800 (2003 est). Area: 106 sq km (41 sq miles)

tragedian *or feminine* **tragedienne 1** an actor who specializes in tragic roles **2** a writer of tragedy

tragedy 1 (esp in classical and Renaissance drama) a play in which the protagonist, usually a man of importance and outstanding personal qualities, falls to disaster through the combination of a personal failing and circumstances with which he cannot deal **2** (in later drama, such as that of Ibsen) a play in which the protagonist is overcome by a combination of social and psychological circumstances **3** any dramatic or literary composition dealing with serious or sombre themes and ending with disaster **4** (in medieval literature) a literary work in which a great person falls from prosperity to disaster, often through no fault of his own **5** the branch of drama dealing with such themes

tragicomedy a a drama in which aspects of both tragedy and comedy are found **b** the dramatic genre of works of this kind

Traherne Thomas 1637–74, English mystical prose writer and poet. His prose works include *Centuries of Meditations*, which was discovered in manuscript in 1896 and published in 1908

trail 1 the scent left by a moving person or animal that is followed by a hunting animal **2** *Engineering* the distance between the point of contact of a steerable wheel and a line drawn from the swivel pin axis to the ground

trailer 1 a road vehicle, usually two-wheeled, towed by a motor vehicle: used for transporting boats, etc. **2** the part of an articulated lorry that is drawn by the cab **3** a series of short extracts from a film, used to advertise it in a cinema or on television

train 1 a a line of coaches or wagons coupled together and drawn by a railway locomotive **b** (*as modifier*): *a train ferry* **2** a series of interacting parts through which motion is transmitted

trainer *Horse racing* a person who schools racehorses and prepares them for racing

train spotter a person who collects the numbers of railway locomotives

▷www.wikipedia.org/wiki/Train_spotting

Trajan Latin name *Marcus Ulpius Traianus*. ?53–117 AD, Roman emperor (98–117). He extended the empire to the east and built many roads, bridges, canals, and towns

trajectory 1 the path described by an object moving in air or space under the influence of such forces as thrust, wind resistance, and gravity, esp the curved path of a projectile 2 *Geometry* a curve that cuts a family of curves or surfaces at a constant angle

Tralee a market town in SW Republic of Ireland, county town of Kerry, near **Tralee Bay** (an inlet of the Atlantic). Pop: 21 987 (2002)

tram¹ an electrically driven public transport vehicle that runs on rails let into the surface of the road, power usually being taken from an overhead wire

▷http://routesinternational.com/buslines.htm

tram² *Machinery* a fine adjustment that ensures correct function or alignment

tram³ (in weaving) a weft yarn of two or more twisted strands of silk

▷http://routesinternational.com/buslines.htm

trammel 1 a fishing net in three sections, the two outer nets having a large mesh and the middle one a fine mesh 2 *Rare* a fowling net 3 *US* a fetter or shackle, esp one used in teaching a horse to amble 4 a device for drawing ellipses consisting of a flat sheet of metal, plastic, or wood having a cruciform slot in which run two pegs attached to a beam. The free end of the beam describes an ellipse 5 a gauge for setting up machines correctly

tramp a merchant ship that does not run between ports on a regular schedule but carries cargo wherever the shippers desire

trampoline a tough canvas sheet suspended by springs or elasticated cords from a frame, used by acrobats, gymnasts, etc.

trance 1 a hypnotic state resembling sleep 2 *Spiritualism* a state in which a medium, having temporarily lost consciousness, can supposedly be controlled by an intelligence from without as a means of communication with the dead 3 a type of electronic dance music with repetitive rhythms, aiming at a hypnotic effect

tranquillizer, tranquilliser, *or US* **tranquilizer** a drug that calms a person without affecting clarity of consciousness

transaction 1 something that is transacted, esp a business deal or negotiation 2 (in business computing) the act of obtaining and paying for an item or service 3 (in general computing) the transmission and processing of an item of data

transalpine situated in or relating to places beyond the Alps, esp from Italy

Transalpine Gaul (in the ancient world) that part of Gaul northwest of the Alps

Transcaucasia a region in central Asia, south of the Caucasus Mountains between the Black and Caspian Seas in Georgia, Armenia, and Azerbaijan: a con-

stituent republic of the Soviet Union from 1918 until 1936

transcendent 1 a (in the philosophy of Kant) beyond or before experience; a priori b (of a concept) falling outside a given set of categories c beyond consciousness or direct apprehension 2 *Theol* (of God) having continuous existence outside the created world 3 free from the limitations inherent in matter 4 *Philosophy* a transcendent thing

transcendental 1 (in the philosophy of Kant) a (of a judgment or logical deduction) being both synthetic and a priori b of or relating to knowledge of the presuppositions of thought 2 *Philosophy* beyond our experience of phenomena, although not beyond potential knowledge 3 *Theol* surpassing the natural plane of reality or knowledge; supernatural or mystical

transcendentalism 1 a any system of philosophy, esp that of Immanuel Kant, the German philosopher (1724–1804), holding that the key to knowledge of the nature of reality lies in the critical examination of the processes of reason on which depends the nature of experience b any system of philosophy, esp that of Emerson, that emphasizes intuition as a means to knowledge or the importance of the search for the divine 2 vague philosophical speculation

transcript *Education, chiefly US and Canadian* an official record of a student's school progress and achievements

transducer any device, such as a microphone or electric motor, that converts one form of energy into another

transect a sample strip of land used to monitor plant distribution, animal populations, etc, within a given area

transept either of the two wings of a cruciform church at right angles to the nave

transfer 1 a design or drawing that is transferred from one surface to another, as by ironing a printed design onto cloth 2 *Law* the passing of title to property or other right from one person to another by act of the parties or by operation of law; conveyance

transfer station *NZ* a municipal depot where rubbish is sorted for recycling or relocation to a landfill site

Transfiguration 1 *New Testament* the change in the appearance of Christ that took place before three disciples (Matthew 17:1–9) 2 the Church festival held in commemoration of this on Aug 6

transform *Maths* the result of a mathematical transformation, esp (of a matrix or an element of a group) another related to the given one by $B = X^{-1}AX$ for some appropriate X

transformation 1 *Maths* a a change in position or direction of the reference axes in a coordinate system without an alteration in their relative angle b an equivalent change in an expression or equation resulting from the substitution of one set of variables by another 2 *Physics* a change in an atomic nucleus to a different nuclide as the result of the emission of either an alpha-particle or a beta-particle 3 an apparently miraculous change in the appearance of a stage set 4 (in South Africa) a national strategy aimed at attaining national unity, promoting reconciliation through negotiated settlement and non-racism

transformer a device that transfers an alternating current from one circuit to one or more other circuits, usually with an increase (**step-up transformer**) or decrease (**step-down transformer**) of voltage. The input current is fed to a primary winding, the output being taken from a secondary winding or windings inductively linked to the primary

transfusion the injection of blood, blood plasma, etc, into the blood vessels of a patient

transgenic (of an animal or plant) containing genetic material artificially transferred from another species

transient *Physics* a brief change in the state of a system, such as a sudden short-lived oscillation in the current flowing through a circuit

transistor a semiconductor device, having three or more terminals attached to electrode regions, in which current flowing between two electrodes is controlled by a voltage or current applied to one or more specified electrodes. The device is capable of amplification, etc, and has replaced the valve in most circuits since it is much smaller, more robust, and works at a much lower voltage

transit 1 *Astronomy* a the passage of a celestial body or satellite across the face of a relatively larger body as seen from the earth b the apparent passage of a celestial body across the meridian, caused by the earth's diurnal rotation 2 *Astrology* the passage of a planet across some special point on the zodiac

transition 1 *Music* a a movement from one key to another; modulation b a linking passage between two divisions in a composition; bridge 2 a style of architecture that was used in western Europe in the late 11th and early 12th century, characterized by late Romanesque forms combined with early Gothic details 3 *Physics* a any change that results in a change of physical properties of a substance or system, such as a change of phase or molecular structure b a change in the configuration of an atomic nucleus, involving either a change in energy level resulting from the emission of a gamma-ray photon or a transformation to another element or isotope 4 a sentence, passage, etc, that connects a topic to one that follows or that links sections of a written work

transition element *or* **metal** *Chem* any element belonging to one of three series of elements with atomic numbers between 21 and 30, 39 and 48, and 57 and 80. They have an incomplete penultimate electron shell and tend to exhibit more than one valency and to form complexes

transitive *Logic, Maths* having the property that if one object bears a relationship to a second object that also bears the same relationship to a third object, then the first object bears this relationship to the third object

Transkei the largest of South Africa's former Bantu homelands and the first South African self-governing territory (1963); declared an independent state in 1976 but this status was not recognized outside South Africa; abolished in 1993 when South African citizenship was restored to its inhabitants. Capital: Umtata

translation *Maths* a transformation in which the origin of a coordinate system is moved to another position so that each axis retains the same direction or, equivalently, a figure or curve is moved so that it retains the

same orientation to the axes
▷http://babelfish.altavista.com

transmission 1 the extent to which a body or medium transmits light, sound, or some other form of energy 2 the transference of motive force or power 3 a system of shafts, gears, torque converters, etc, that transmits power, esp the arrangement of such parts that transmits the power of the engine to the driving wheels of a motor vehicle

transom *Nautical* a a surface forming the stern of a vessel, either vertical or canted either forwards (**reverse transom**) or aft at the upper side b any of several transverse beams used for strengthening the stern of a vessel

transparency a positive photograph on a transparent base, usually mounted in a frame or between glass plates. It can be viewed by means of a slide projector

transparent (of a substance or object) permitting the free passage of electromagnetic radiation

transplant *Surgery* a the procedure involved in such a transfer b the organ or tissue transplanted

transportation (esp formerly) deportation to a penal colony

transpose *Maths* the matrix resulting from interchanging the rows and columns of a given matrix

transsexual *or* **transexual** 1 a person who permanently acts the part of and completely identifies with the opposite sex 2 a person who has undergone medical and surgical procedures to alter external sexual characteristics to those of the opposite sex

transubstantiation (esp in Roman Catholic theology) a the doctrine that the whole substance of the bread and wine changes into the substance of the body and blood of Christ when consecrated in the Eucharist b the mystical process by which this is believed to take place during consecration

transuranic, transuranian, *or* **transuranium** (of an element) having an atomic number greater than that of uranium

Transvaal former province of NE South Africa: colonized by the Boers after the Great Trek (1836); became a British colony in 1902; joined South Africa in 1910; replaced in 1994 for administrative purposes by a new system of provinces (Eastern Transvaal (later Mpumalanga), Northern Transvaal (later Limpopo), Gauteng, and North West province. Capital: Pretoria

transverse 1 *Geometry* denoting the axis that passes through the foci of a hyperbola 2 (of a flute, etc) held almost at right angles to the player's mouth, so that the breath passes over a hole in the side to create a vibrating air column within the tube of the instrument 3 *Astronomy* another word for **tangential** (sense 2)

transvestite a person who seeks sexual pleasure from wearing clothes that are normally associated with the opposite sex

Transylvania a region of central and NW Romania: belonged to Hungary from the 11th century until 1918; restored to Romania in 1947

trap¹ 1 a mechanical device or enclosed place or pit in which something, esp an animal, is caught or penned 2 a device that hurls clay pigeons into the air to be fired at by trapshooters 3 *Golf* an obstacle or hazard, esp a bunker

trap² *or* **traprock** 1 any fine-grained often columnar dark igneous rock, esp basalt 2 any rock in which oil or gas has accumulated

Trapani a port in S Italy, in NW Sicily: Carthaginian naval base, ceded to the Romans after the First Punic War. Pop: 68 346 (2001)

trap-door spider any of various spiders of the family *Ctenizidae* that construct a silk-lined hole in the ground closed by a hinged door of earth and silk

trapeze 1 a free-swinging bar attached to two ropes, used by circus acrobats, etc. 2 a sling like a bosun's chair at one end of a line attached to the masthead of a light racing sailing boat, used in sitting out

trapezium 1 *Chiefly Brit* a quadrilateral having two parallel sides of unequal length 2 *Now chiefly US and Canadian* a quadrilateral having neither pair of sides parallel 3 a small bone of the wrist near the base of the thumb

trapezoid 1 a quadrilateral having neither pair of sides parallel 2 *US and Canadian* a quadrilateral having two parallel sides of unequal length 3 a small bone of the wrist near the base of the index finger

trapper a person who traps animals, esp for their furs or skins

Trappist a a member of a branch of the Cistercian order of Christian monks, the Reformed Cistercians of the Strict Observance which originated at La Trappe in France in 1664. They are noted for their rule of silence b (*as modifier*): *a Trappist monk*

trash 1 the dry remains of sugar cane after the juice has been extracted 2 bits that are broken or lopped off, esp the trimmings from trees or plants

Trasimene Lake a lake in central Italy, in Umbria: the largest lake in central Italy; scene of Hannibal's victory over the Romans in 217 BC. Area: 128 sq km (49 sq miles)

trauma 1 *Psychol* a powerful shock that may have long-lasting effects 2 *Pathol* any bodily injury or wound

Travancore a former princely state of S India which joined with Cochin in 1949 to form **Travancore-Cochin**: part of Kerala state since 1956

travel *Engineering* the distance moved by a mechanical part, such as the stroke of a piston

travel agency *or* **bureau** an agency that arranges and negotiates flights, holidays, etc, for travellers

traveller *or US* **traveler** 1 a part of a mechanism that moves in a fixed course 2 *Nautical* a a thimble fitted to slide freely on a rope, spar, or rod b the fixed rod on which such a thimble slides

Traven B(en), original name *Albert Otto Max Feige*. ?1882–1969, US novelist, born in Germany and living in Mexico from 1920, who kept his identity secret. His novels, originally written in German, include *The Treasure of Sierra Madre* (1934)

Travers Ben(jamin). 1886–1980, British dramatist, best known for such farces as *Rookery Nook* (1926), *Thark* (1927), and *Plunder* (1928)

traverse 1 a gallery or loft inside a building that crosses it 2 *Maths* another name for **transversal** 3 *Nautical* the zigzag course of a vessel tacking frequently 4 *Law* the formal denial of a fact alleged in the opposite party's pleading 5 *Mountaineering* a horizontal move across a face

travois a sled formerly used by the Plains Indians of North America, consisting of two poles joined by a frame and dragged by an animal

trawl *Sea fishing* 1 a large net, usually in the shape of a sock or bag, drawn at deep levels behind special boats (trawlers) 2 a long line to which numerous shorter hooked lines are attached, suspended between buoys 3 *Angling* another word for **troll** (sense 2)

treacle *Obsolete* any of various preparations used as an antidote to poisoning

tread 1 the outer part of a tyre or wheel that makes contact with the road, esp the grooved surface of a pneumatic tyre 2 the part of a rail that wheels touch 3 *Vet science* an injury to a horse's foot caused by the opposite foot, or the foot of another horse

treadle a a rocking lever operated by the foot to drive a machine b (*as modifier*): *a treadle sewing machine*

treadmill (formerly) an apparatus used to produce rotation, in which the weight of men or animals climbing steps on or around the periphery of a cylinder or wheel caused it to turn

treason violation or betrayal of the allegiance that a person owes his sovereign or his country, esp by attempting to overthrow the government; high treason

treasure hunt a game in which players act upon successive clues and are eventually directed to a prize

treasure-trove in Britain *Law* valuable articles, such as coins, bullion, etc, found hidden in the earth or elsewhere and of unknown ownership. Such articles become the property of the Crown, which compensates the finder if the treasure is declared. In 1996 treasure was defined as any item over 300 years old and containing more than 5% precious metal

treasury 1 the revenues or funds of a government, private organization, or individual 2 a place where funds are kept and disbursed

Treasury (in various countries) the government department in charge of finance. In Britain the Treasury is also responsible for economic strategy

treatment 1 the application of medicines, surgery, psychotherapy, etc, to a patient or to a disease or symptom 2 *Films* an expansion of a script into sequence form, indicating camera angles, dialogue, etc.

treaty 1 a a formal agreement or contract between two or more states, such as an alliance or trade arrangement b the document in which such a contract is written 2 any international agreement 3 an agreement between two parties concerning the purchase of property at a price privately agreed between them 4 (in Canada) a any of the formal agreements between Indian bands and the federal government by which the Indians surrender their land rights in return for various forms of aid b (*as modifier*): *treaty Indians*
  ▷http://fletcher.tufts.edu/multilaterals.html

treble 1 of, relating to, or denoting a soprano voice or part or a high-pitched instrument 2 a soprano voice or part or a high-pitched instrument 3 the highest register of a musical instrument 4 a the high-frequency response of an audio amplifier, esp in a record player or tape recorder b a control knob on such an instrument by means of which the high-frequency gain can be increased or decreased 5 *Bell-ringing* the lightest and highest bell in a ring **6 a** the narrow inner ring on a dartboard **b** a hit on this ring

treble chance a method of betting in football pools in which the chances of winning are related to the number of draws and the number of home and away wins forecast by the competitor

treble clef *Music* the clef that establishes G a fifth above middle C as being on the second line of the staff.

tree 1 any large woody perennial plant with a distinct trunk giving rise to branches or leaves at some distance from the ground **2** any plant that resembles this but has a trunk not made of wood, such as a palm tree **3** See **family tree, shoetree,** *or* **saddletree 4** *Chem* a treelike crystal growth; dendrite **5** *Archaic* the cross on which Christ was crucified

　▷www.british-trees.com
　▷www.wildlifesafari.info
　▷http://homepages.ihug.co.nz/~crysalis
　▷www.ecoworld.org/trees/
　　ecoworld_trees_home.cfm
　▷www.globalforestscience.org

Tree Sir Herbert Beerbohm 1853–1917, English actor and theatre manager; half-brother of Sir Max Beerbohm. He was noted for his lavish productions of Shakespeare

tree creeper any small songbird of the family *Certhiidae* of the N hemisphere, having a brown-and-white plumage and slender downward-curving bill. They creep up trees to feed on insects

tree fern any of numerous large tropical ferns, mainly of the family *Cyatheaceae*, having a trunklike stem bearing fronds at the top

tree kangaroo any of several arboreal kangaroos of the genus *Dendrolagus*, of New Guinea and N Australia, having hind and forelegs of a similar length and a long tail

tree line the zone, at high altitudes or high latitudes, beyond which no trees grow. Trees growing between the timberline and the tree line are typically stunted

tree surgery the treatment of damaged trees by filling cavities, applying braces, etc.

tree tomato 1 an arborescent shrub, *Cyphomandra betacea* or *C. crassifolia*, native to South America but widely cultivated, bearing red egg-shaped edible fruit: family *Solanaceae* **2** the fruit of this plant

trefoil 1 any of numerous leguminous plants of the temperate genus *Trifolium*, having leaves divided into three leaflets and dense heads of small white, yellow, red, or purple flowers **2** any of various related plants having leaves divided into three leaflets, such as bird's-foot trefoil **3** a leaf having three leaflets **4** *Architect* an ornament in the form of three arcs arranged in a circle

trek *South African* a journey or stage of a journey, esp a migration by ox wagon

trellis a structure or pattern of latticework, esp one used to support climbing plants

tremolo *Music* **1 a** (in playing the violin, cello, etc) the rapid repetition of a single note produced by a quick back-and-forth movement of the bow **b** the rapid reiteration of two notes usually a third or greater interval apart (**fingered tremolo**) **2** (in singing) a fluctuation in pitch **3** a vocal ornament of late renaissance music consisting of the increasingly rapid reiteration of a single note

tremor a minor earthquake

Trenchard Hugh Montague, 1st Viscount. 1873–1956, British air marshal, who as chief of air staff (1918, 1919–27) and marshal of the RAF (1927–29) established the RAF as a fully independent service. As commissioner of the Metropolitan Police (1931–35) he founded the police college at Hendon

trencher (esp formerly) a wooden board on which food was served or cut

Trengganu *or* **Terengganu** a state of E Peninsular Malaysia, on the South China Sea: under Thai suzerainty until becoming a British protectorate in 1909; joined the Federation of Malaya in 1948; an isolated forested region; mainly agricultural. Capital: Kuala Trengganu. Pop: 898 825 (2000). Area: 13 020 sq km (5027 sq miles)

Trent 1 a river in central England, rising in Staffordshire and flowing generally northeast into the Humber: the chief river of the Midlands. Length: 270 km (170 miles) **2** the German name for **Trento**

Trentino-Alto Adige a region of N Italy: consists of the part of the Tyrol south of the Brenner Pass, ceded by Austria after World War I. Pop: 950 495 (2003 est). Area: 13 613 sq km (5256 sq miles)

Trento a city in N Italy, in Trentino-Alto Adige region on the Adige River: Roman military base; seat of the Council of Trent (1545-1563). Pop: 104 946 (2001)

Trenton a city in W New Jersey, capital of the state, on the Delaware River: settled by English Quakers in 1679; scene of the defeat of the British by Washington (1776) during the War of American Independence. Pop: 85 314 (2003 est)

trespass *Law* **a** any unlawful act committed with force or violence, actual or implied, which causes injury to another person, his property, or his rights **b** a wrongful entry upon another's land **c** an action to recover damages for such injury or wrongful entry

trestle a a braced structural tower-like framework of timber, metal, or reinforced concrete that is used to support a bridge or ropeway **b** a bridge constructed of such frameworks

trevally any of various marine food and game fishes of the genus *Caranx*: family *Carangidae*

Trevelyan 1 George Macaulay 1876–1962, British historian, noted for his *English Social History* (1944) **2** his father, Sir **George Otto** 1838–1928, British historian and biographer. His works include a biography of his uncle Lord Macaulay (1876)

Trevino Lee born 1939, US professional golfer: winner of the US Open Championship (1968; 1971) and the British Open Championship (1971; 1972)

Treviso a city in N Italy, in Veneto region: agricultural market centre. Pop: 80 144 (2001)

Trevithick Richard 1771–1833, British engineer, who built the first steam-driven passenger carriage (1801) and the first locomotive to run on smooth wheels on smooth rails (1804)

triad 1 *Chem* an atom, element, group, or ion that has a valency of three **2** *Music* a three-note chord consisting of a note and the third and fifth above it **3** an aphoristic literary form used in medieval Welsh and Irish literature

Triad any of several Chinese secret societies, esp one

involved in criminal activities, such as drug trafficking

trial 1 *Law* a the judicial examination of the issues in a civil or criminal cause by a competent tribunal and the determination of these issues in accordance with the law of the land b the determination of an accused person's guilt or innocence after hearing evidence for the prosecution and for the accused and the judicial examination of the issues involved c (*as modifier*): *trial proceedings* 2 a motorcycling competition in which the skills of the riders are tested over rough ground 3 *Ceramics* a piece of sample material used for testing the heat of a kiln and its effects

triangle 1 *Geometry* a three-sided polygon that can be classified by angle, as in an acute triangle, or by side, as in an equilateral triangle. Sum of interior angles: 180°; area: ½ base × height 2 *Music* a percussion instrument consisting of a sonorous metal bar bent into a triangular shape, beaten with a metal stick

triangulate marked with or composed of triangles

triangulation 1 the fixing of an unknown point, as in navigation, by making it one vertex of a triangle, the other two being known 2 *Chess* a key manoeuvre in the endgame in which the king moves thrice in a triangular path to leave the opposing king with the move and at a disadvantage

Triassic of, denoting, or formed in the first period of the Mesozoic era that lasted for 42 million years and during which reptiles flourished

triathlon an athletic contest in which each athlete competes in three different events, swimming, cycling, and running

tribalism 1 the state of existing as a separate tribe or tribes 2 the customs and beliefs of a tribal society 3 loyalty to a tribe or tribal values

tribe 1 a social division of a people, esp of a preliterate people, defined in terms of common descent, territory, culture, etc. 2 an ethnic or ancestral division of ancient cultures, esp of one of the following a any of the three divisions of the ancient Romans, the Latins, Sabines, and Etruscans b one of the later political divisions of the Roman people c any of the 12 divisions of ancient Israel, each of which was named after and believed to be descended from one of the 12 patriarchs d a phyle of ancient Greece 3 *Biology* a taxonomic group that is a subdivision of a subfamily

tribunal 1 a court of justice or any place where justice is administered 2 (in Britain) a special court, convened by the government to inquire into a specific matter 3 a raised platform containing the seat of a judge or magistrate, originally that in a Roman basilica

tribune¹ 1 in ancient Rome a an officer elected by the plebs to protect their interests. Originally there were two of these officers but finally there were ten b a senior military officer 2 a person or institution that upholds public rights; champion

tribune² 1 a the apse of a Christian basilica that contains the bishop's throne b the throne itself 2 a gallery or raised area in a church

tributary 1 a stream, river, or glacier that feeds another larger one 2 a person, nation, or people that pays tribute 3 (of a stream, etc) feeding a larger stream

tribute 1 a a payment by one ruler or state to another,

usually as an acknowledgment of submission b any tax levied for such a payment 2 (in feudal society) homage or a payment rendered by a vassal to his lord 3 the obligation to pay tribute

triceps any muscle having three heads, esp the one (*triceps brachii*) that extends the forearm

trichology the branch of medicine concerned with the hair and its diseases

trichromatic or **trichromic** 1 *Photog, Printing* involving the combination of three primary colours in the production of any colour 2 of, relating to, or having normal colour vision

trick *Cards* a a batch of cards containing one from each player, usually played in turn and won by the player or side that plays the card with the highest value b a card that can potentially win a trick

trickle-down of or concerning the theory that granting concessions such as tax cuts to the rich will benefit all levels of society by stimulating the economy

tricolour or US **tricolor** 1 having or involving three colours 2 the French national flag, having three equal vertical stripes in blue, white, and red

trident (in Greek and Roman mythology) the three-pronged spear that the sea god Poseidon (Neptune) is represented as carrying

Trier a city in W Germany, in the Rhineland-Palatinate on the Moselle River: one of the oldest towns of central Europe, ancient capital of a Celto-Germanic tribe (the **Treveri**); an early centre of Christianity, ruled by powerful archbishops until the 18th century; wine trade; important Roman remains. Pop: 100 180 (2003 est)

Trieste 1 a port in NE Italy, capital of Friuli-Venezia Giulia region, on the **Gulf of Trieste** at the head of the Adriatic Sea: under Austrian rule (1382–1918); capital of the Free Territory of Trieste (1947–54); important transit port for central Europe. Pop: 211 184 (2001) 2 **Free Territory of** a former territory on the N Adriatic: established by the UN in 1947; most of the N part passed to Italy and the remainder to Yugoslavia in 1954

trifle 1 a type of pewter of medium hardness 2 articles made from this pewter

trigger *Machinery* a device that releases a spring-loaded mechanism or a similar arrangement

trigonometry the branch of mathematics concerned with the properties of trigonometric functions and their application to the determination of the angles and sides of triangles. Used in surveying, navigation, etc.

trike a microlight aircraft with three fixed wheels for landing and take-off

trill *Music* a melodic ornament consisting of a rapid alternation between a principal note and the note a whole tone or semitone above it.

trillion 1 the number represented as one followed by twelve zeros (10^{12}); a million million 2 (formerly, in Britain) the number represented as one followed by eighteen zeros (10^{18}); a million million million

trillium any herbaceous plant of the genus *Trillium*, of Asia and North America, having a whorl of three leaves at the top of the stem with a single central white, pink, or purple three-petalled flower: family *Trilliaceae*

trilobite any extinct marine arthropod of the group

Trilobita, abundant in Palaeozoic times, having a segmented exoskeleton divided into three parts

trilogy 1 a series of three related works, esp in literature, etc. 2 (in ancient Greece) a series of three tragedies performed together at the Dionysian festivals

trim 1 the upholstery and decorative facings, as on the door panels, of a car's interior 2 *Nautical* **a** the general set and appearance of a vessel **b** the difference between the draught of a vessel at the bow and at the stern **c** the fitness of a vessel **d** the position of a vessel's sails relative to the wind **e** the relative buoyancy of a submarine 3 the attitude of an aircraft in flight when the pilot allows the main control surfaces to take up their own positions 4 *Films* a section of shot cut out during editing

Trim the county town of Meath, Republic of Ireland; 12th-century castle, medieval cathedral; textiles and machinery. Pop: 5894 (2002)

trimaran a vessel, usually of shallow draught, with two hulls flanking the main hull

Trimble (William) David born 1944, Northern Irish politician; leader of the Ulster Unionist party from 1995, First Minister of Northern Ireland from 1998; Nobel peace prize jointly with John Hume in 1998

Trincomalee a port in NE Sri Lanka, on the **Bay of Trincomalee** (an inlet of the Bay of Bengal); British naval base until 1957. Pop: 51 000 (latest est)

Trinidad an island in the West Indies, off the NE coast of Venezuela: colonized by the Spanish in the 17th century and ceded to Britain in 1802; joined with Tobago in 1888 as a British colony; now part of the independent republic of Trinidad and Tobago. Pop: 1 208 282 (2000)

Trinidad and Tobago an independent republic in the Caribbean, occupying the two southernmost islands of the Lesser Antilles: became a British colony in 1888 and gained independence in 1962; became a republic in 1976; a member of the Commonwealth. Official language: English. Religion: Christian majority, with a large Hindu minority. Currency: Trinidad and Tobago dollar. Capital: Port of Spain. Pop: 1 307 000 (2004 est). Area: 5128 sq km (1980 sq miles)

Trinitarian 1 a person who believes in the doctrine of the Trinity 2 a member of the Holy Trinity

Trinity 1 *Christian theol* the union of three persons, the Father, Son, and Holy Spirit, in one Godhead 2 **Holy Trinity** a religious order founded in 1198

trio 1 *Music* **a** a group of three singers or instrumentalists or a piece of music composed for such a group **b** a subordinate section in a scherzo, minuet, etc, that is contrastive in style and often in a related key 2 *Piquet* three cards of the same rank

trip 1 **a** any catch on a mechanism that acts as a switch **b** (*as modifier*): *trip button* 2 a surge in the conditions of a chemical or other automatic process resulting in an instability 3 *Informal* a hallucinogenic drug experience

tripartite (esp of leaves) consisting of three parts formed by divisions extending almost to the base

triple 1 consisting of three parts; threefold 2 (of musical time or rhythm) having three beats in each bar

triple jump an athletic event in which the competitor has to perform successively a hop, a step, and a jump in continuous movement

triple point *Chem* the temperature and pressure at which the three phases of a substance are in equilibrium. The triple point of water, 273.16 K at a pressure of 611.2 Pa, is the basis of the definition of the kelvin

triplet 1 one of three offspring born at one birth 2 *Music* a group of three notes played in a time value of two, four, etc. 3 *Chem* a state of a molecule or free radical in which there are two unpaired electrons

tripod an adjustable and usually collapsible three-legged stand to which a camera, etc, can be attached to hold it steady

Tripoli 1 the capital and chief port of Libya, in the northwest on the Mediterranean: founded by Phoenicians in about the 7th century BC; the only city that has survived of the three (Oea, Leptis Magna, and Sabratha) that formed the African Tripolis ("three cities"); fishing and manufacturing centre. Pop: 1 223 300 (2002 est) 2 a port in N Lebanon, on the Mediterranean: the second largest town in Lebanon; taken by the Crusaders in 1109 after a siege of five years; oil-refining and manufacturing centre. Pop: 212 000 (2005 est)

Tripolitania the NW part of Libya: established as a Phoenician colony in the 7th century BC; taken by the Turks in 1551 and became one of the Barbary states; under Italian rule from 1912 until World War II

tripos *Brit* the final honours degree examinations in all subjects at Cambridge University

tripper 1 another word for **trip** (sense 1) 2 **a** any device that generates a signal causing a trip to operate **b** the signal so generated

triptych a set of three pictures or panels, usually hinged so that the two wing panels fold over the larger central one: often used as an altarpiece

Tripura a state of NE India: formerly a princely state, ruled by the Maharajahs for over 1300 years; became a union territory in 1956 and a state in 1972; extensive jungles. Capital: Agartala. Pop: 3 191 168 (2001). Area: 10 486 sq km (4051 sq miles)

trireme a galley, developed by the ancient Greeks as a warship, with three banks of oars on each side

trismus *Pathol* the state or condition of being unable to open the mouth because of sustained contractions of the jaw muscles, caused by a form of tetanus

Tristan da Cunha a group of four small volcanic islands in the S Atlantic, about halfway between South Africa and South America: comprises the main island of Tristan and the uninhabited islands of Gough, Inaccessible, and Nightingale; discovered in 1506 by the Portuguese admiral Tristão da Cunha; annexed to Britain in 1816; whole population of Tristan evacuated for two years after the volcanic eruption of 1961. Pop: 284 (2003 est). Area: about 100 sq km (40 sq miles)

tritium a radioactive isotope of hydrogen, occurring in trace amounts in natural hydrogen and produced in a nuclear reactor. Tritiated compounds are used as tracers. Symbol: T or ^{3}H; half-life: 12.5 years

triumph 1 (in ancient Rome) a ritual procession to the Capitoline Hill held in honour of a victorious general 2 *Cards* an obsolete word for **trump**

triumvir (esp in ancient Rome) a member of a triumvirate

triumvirate 1 in ancient Rome **a** a board of three officials jointly responsible for some task **b** the political alliance of Caesar, Crassus, and Pompey, formed in 60 BC (**First Triumvirate**) **c** the coalition and joint rule of the Roman Empire by Antony, Lepidus, and Octavian, begun in 43 BC (**Second Triumvirate**) **2** any joint rule by three men **3** the office of a triumvir

trivalent *Chem* **1** having a valency of three **2** having three valencies

Trivandrum a city in S India, capital of Kerala, on the Malabar Coast: made capital of the kingdom of Travancore in 1745; University of Kerala (1937). Pop: 744 739 (2001)

trivial **1** *Maths* (of the solutions of a set of homogeneous equations) having zero values for all the variables **2** *Biology* denoting the specific name of an organism in binomial nomenclature **3** *Biology, Chem* denoting the popular name of an organism or substance, as opposed to the scientific one **4** of or relating to the trivium

Troas the region of NW Asia Minor surrounding the ancient city of Troy

trochee *Prosody* a metrical foot of two syllables, the first long and the second short (– ᵕ)

troglodyte a cave dweller, esp one of the prehistoric peoples thought to have lived in caves

troika three horses harnessed abreast

Trojan **1** a native or inhabitant of ancient Troy **2** of or relating to ancient Troy or its inhabitants

Trojan Horse **1** *Greek myth* the huge wooden hollow figure of a horse left outside Troy by the Greeks when they feigned retreat and dragged inside by the Trojans. The men concealed inside it opened the city to the final Greek assault **2** *Computing* a bug inserted into a program or system designed to be activated after a certain time or a certain number of operations

troll[1] *Angling* a bait or lure used in trolling, such as a spinner

troll[2] (in Scandinavian folklore) one of a class of supernatural creatures that dwell in caves or mountains and are depicted either as dwarfs or as giants

trolley **1** *Brit* (in a hospital) a bed mounted on casters and used for moving patients who are unconscious, immobilized, etc. **2** a device that collects the current from an overhead wire (**trolley wire**), third rail, etc, to drive the motor of an electric vehicle **3** a pulley or truck that travels along an overhead wire in order to support a suspended load **4** *Chiefly Brit* a low truck running on rails, used in factories, mines, etc, and on railways

Trollope **1** **Anthony** 1815–82, English novelist. His most successful novels, such as *The Warden* (1855), *Barchester Towers* (1857), and *Dr Thorne* (1858), are those in the Barsetshire series of studies of English provincial life. The Palliser series of political novels includes *Phineas Redux* (1874) and *The Prime Minister* (1876) **2** **Joanna** born 1943, British novelist: her works include *The Choir* (1988), *A Village Affair* (1989), *The Rector's Wife* (1991), *The Best of Friends* (1995), and *The Girl From the South* (2002)

trombone **1** a brass instrument, a low-pitched counterpart of the trumpet, consisting of a tube the effective length of which is varied by means of a U-shaped slide. The usual forms of this instrument are the **tenor trombone** (range: about two and a half octaves upwards from E) and the **bass trombone** (pitched a fourth lower) **2** a person who plays this instrument in an orchestra

Trondheim a port in central Norway, on **Trondheim Fjord** (an inlet of the Norwegian Sea): national capital until 1380; seat of the Technical University of Norway. Pop: 154 351 (2004 est)

trooper **1** *US and Austral* a mounted policeman **2** *US* a state policeman

trope an interpolation of words or music into the plainsong settings of the Roman Catholic liturgy

trophy **1** in ancient Greece and Rome **a** a memorial to a victory, usually consisting of captured arms raised on the battlefield or in a public place **b** a representation of such a memorial **2** an ornamental carving that represents a group of weapons, etc.

tropic **1** either of the parallel lines of latitude at about 23½°N (**tropic of Cancer**) and 23½°S (**tropic of Capricorn**) of the equator **2** **the tropics** that part of the earth's surface between the tropics of Cancer and Capricorn; the Torrid Zone **3** *Astronomy* either of the two parallel circles on the celestial sphere having the same latitudes and names as the corresponding lines on the earth

tropical situated in, used in, characteristic of, or relating to the tropics

tropism the response of an organism, esp a plant, to an external stimulus by growth in a direction determined by the stimulus

troposphere the lowest atmospheric layer, about 18 kilometres (11 miles) thick at the equator to about 6 km (4 miles) at the Poles, in which air temperature decreases normally with height at about 6.5°C per km

Trossachs the **1** a narrow wooded valley in central Scotland, between Loch Achray and Loch Katrine: made famous by Sir Walter Scott's descriptions **2** (popularly) the area extending northwards from Loch Ard and Aberfoyle to Lochs Katrine, Achray, and Venachar

trot **1** a gait of a horse or other quadruped, faster than a walk, in which diagonally opposite legs come down together **2** (in harness racing) a race for horses that have been trained to trot fast **3** *Angling* **a** one of the short lines attached to a trotline **b** the trotline

Trot *Informal* a follower of Trotsky; Trotskyist

Trotsky *or* **Trotski** **Leon**, original name *Lev Davidovich Bronstein*. 1879–1940, Russian revolutionary and Communist theorist. He was a leader of the November Revolution (1917) and, as commissar of foreign affairs and war (1917–24), largely created the Red Army. He was ousted by Stalin after Lenin's death and deported from Russia (1929); assassinated by a Stalinist agent

trotter **1** a person or animal that trots, esp a horse that is specially trained to trot fast **2** the foot of certain animals, esp of pigs

troubadour **1** any of a class of lyric poets who flourished principally in Provence and N Italy from the 11th to the 13th centuries, writing chiefly on courtly love in complex metric form **2** a singer

trouble **a** political unrest or public disturbances **b** **the Troubles** political violence in Ireland during the 1920s or in Northern Ireland since the late 1960s

trough **1** a narrow depression either in the land surface, ocean bed, or between two successive waves **2** *Meteorol* an elongated area of low pressure, esp an extension of a depression **3** *Physics* the portion of a wave, such as a light wave, in which the amplitude lies below its average value **4** *Economics* the lowest point or most depressed stage of the trade cycle

troupe a company of actors or other performers, esp one that travels

trout **1** any of various game fishes, esp *Salmo trutta* and related species, mostly of fresh water in northern regions: family *Salmonidae* (salmon). They resemble salmon but are smaller and spotted **2** any of various similar or related fishes, such as a sea trout **3** *Austral* any of various fishes of the *Salmo* or *Oncorhynchus* genera smaller than the salmon, esp European and American varieties naturalized in Australia

Trowbridge a market town in SW England, administrative centre of Wiltshire: woollen manufacturing. Pop: 34 401 (2001)

trowel **1** any of various small hand tools having a flat metal blade attached to a handle, used for scooping or spreading plaster or similar materials **2** a similar tool with a curved blade used by gardeners for lifting plants, etc.

Troy any of nine ancient cities in NW Asia Minor, each of which was built on the ruins of its predecessor. The seventh was the site of the Trojan War (mid-13th century BC)

Troyes an industrial city in NE France: became prosperous through its great fairs in the early Middle Ages. Pop: 60 958 (1999)

troy weight *or* **troy** a system of weights used for precious metals and gemstones, based on the grain, which is identical to the avoirdupois grain. 24 grains = 1 pennyweight; 20 pennyweights = 1 (troy) ounce; 12 ounces = 1 (troy) pound

truant a person who is absent without leave, esp from school

truce an agreement to stop fighting, esp temporarily

truck¹ **1** *Brit* a vehicle for carrying freight on a railway; wagon **2** a frame carrying two or more pairs of wheels and usually springs and brakes, attached under an end of a railway coach, etc. **3** *Nautical* **a** a disc-shaped block fixed to the head of a mast having sheave holes for receiving signal halyards **b** the head of a mast itself

truck² **1** commercial goods **2** commercial exchange **3** *Archaic* payment of wages in kind

trucker *US and Canadian* **1** a market gardener **2** another word for **hawker**

Trudeau Pierre Elliott 1919–2000, Canadian statesman; Liberal prime minister (1968–79; 1980–84)

true **1** *Music* exactly in tune **2** (of a compass bearing) according to the earth's geographical rather than magnetic poles **3** *Biology* conforming to the typical structure of a designated type **4** *Physics* not apparent or relative; taking into account all complicating factors

true-blue *Chiefly Brit* a staunch royalist or Conservative

Trueman Freddy, full name *Frederick Sewards Trueman*. born 1931, English cricketer, a fast bowler for Yorkshire and England

true north the direction from any point along a meridian towards the North Pole

Truffaut François 1932–84, French film director of the New Wave. His films include *Les Quatre cents coups* (1959), *Jules et Jim* (1961), *Baisers volés* (1968), and *Le Dernier Métro* (1980)

truffle any of various edible saprotrophic ascomycetous subterranean fungi of the European genus *Tuber*. They have a tuberous appearance and are regarded as a delicacy

Trujillo¹ Rafael (Léonidas), original name *Rafael Léonidas Trujillo Molina*. 1891–1961, Dominican dictator, who governed the Dominican Republic (1930–61) with the help of a powerful police force: assassinated

Trujillo² a city in NW Peru: founded 1535; university (1824); centre of a district producing rice and sugar cane. Pop: 686 000 (2005 est)

Truman Harry S 1884–1972, US Democratic statesman; 33rd president of the US (1945–53). He approved the dropping of the two atomic bombs on Japan (1945), advocated the postwar loan to Britain, and involved the US in the Korean War

trump¹ **a** any card from the suit chosen as trumps **b** this suit itself; trumps

trump² *Archaic or literary* **1** a trumpet or the sound produced by one **2** **the last trump** the final trumpet call that according to the belief of some will awaken and raise the dead on the Day of Judgment

trumpet **1** a valved brass instrument of brilliant tone consisting of a narrow tube of cylindrical bore ending in a flared bell, normally pitched in B flat. Range: two and a half octaves upwards from F sharp on the fourth line of the bass staff **2** any instrument consisting of a valveless tube ending in a bell, esp a straight instrument used for fanfares, signals, etc. **3** an eight-foot reed stop on an organ

truncate *Biology* having a blunt end, as though cut off at the tip

trundle **1** a small wheel or roller **2** **a** the pinion of a lantern **b** any of the bars in a lantern pinion

trunk **1** the main stem of a tree, usually thick and upright, covered with bark and having branches at some distance from the ground **2** *Anatomy* the body excluding the head, neck, and limbs; torso **3** the elongated prehensile nasal part of an elephant; proboscis **4** *US and Canadian* an enclosed compartment of a car for holding luggage, etc, usually at the rear **5** *Anatomy* the main stem of a nerve, blood vessel, etc. **6** *Nautical* a watertight boxlike cover within a vessel with its top above the waterline, such as one used to enclose a centreboard

trunk line the main route or routes on a railway

trunk road *Brit* a main road, esp one that is suitable for heavy vehicles

Truro a market town in SW England, administrative centre of Cornwall. Pop: 20 920 (2001)

truss **1** *Med* a device for holding a hernia in place, typically consisting of a pad held in position by a belt **2** *Horticulture* a cluster of flowers or fruit growing at the end of a single stalk **3** *Nautical* a metal fitting fixed to a yard at its centre for holding it to a mast while allowing movement **4** *Architect* another name for **corbel** **5** *Chiefly Brit* a bundle of hay or straw, esp one having a fixed weight of 36, 56, or 60 pounds

trust **1** a group of commercial enterprises combined to monopolize and control the market for any commodity: illegal in the US **2 a** an arrangement whereby a person to whom the legal title to property is conveyed (the trustee) holds such property for the benefit of those entitled to the beneficial interest **b** property that is the subject of such an arrangement **c** the confidence put in the trustee **3** (in the British National Health Service) a self-governing hospital, group of hospitals, or other body providing health-care services, which operates as an independent commercial unit within the NHS

trustee **1** a person to whom the legal title to property is entrusted to hold or use for another's benefit **2** a member of a board that manages the affairs and administers the funds of an institution or organization

try **1** *Rugby* the act of an attacking player touching the ball down behind the opposing team's goal line, scoring five or, in Rugby League, four points **2** *American football* an attempt made after a touchdown to score an extra point by kicking a goal or, for two extra points, by running the ball or completing a pass across the opponents' goal line

trysail a small fore-and-aft sail, triangular or square, set on the mainmast of a sailing vessel in foul weather to help keep her head to the wind

tsar *or* **czar** **1** (until 1917) the emperor of Russia **2** *Informal* a public official charged with responsibility for dealing with a certain problem or issue **3** (formerly) any of several S Slavonic rulers, such as any of the princes of Serbia in the 14th century

tsarevitch *or* **czarevitch** a son of a Russian tsar, esp the eldest son

tsarina, czarina, tsaritsa *or* **czaritza** the wife of a Russian tsar; Russian empress

tsetse fly *or* **tzetze fly** any of various bloodsucking African dipterous flies of the genus *Glossina*, which transmit the pathogens of various diseases: family *Muscidae*

Tshombe **Moise** 1919–69, Congolese statesman. He led the secession of Katanga (1960) from the newly independent Congo; forced into exile (1963) but returned (1964–65) as premier of the Congo; died in exile

T-square a T-shaped ruler used in mechanical drawing, consisting of a short crosspiece, which slides along the edge of the drawing board, and a long horizontal piece: used for drawing horizontal lines and to support set squares when drawing vertical and inclined lines

Tsugaru Strait a channel between N Honshu and S Hokkaido islands, Japan. Width: about 30 km (20 miles)

tsunami a large, often destructive, sea wave produced by a submarine earthquake, subsidence, or volcanic eruption. Sometimes incorrectly called a tidal wave

Tsushima a group of five rocky islands between Japan and South Korea, in the Korea Strait: administratively part of Japan; scene of a naval defeat for the Russians (1905) during the Russo-Japanese war. Pop: 50 810 (latest est). Area: 698 sq km (269 sq miles)

Tsvangirai **Morgan** born 1952, Zimbabwean trade unionist and politician; leader of the Movement for Democratic Change, the main opposition party to President Mugabe's Zanu-PF since 1999

Tuamotu Archipelago a group of about 80 coral islands in the S Pacific, in French Polynesia. Pop: 15 973 (2002). Area: 860 sq km (332 sq miles)

tuatara a greenish-grey lizard-like rhynchocephalian

reptile, *Sphenodon punctatus*, occurring only on certain small islands near New Zealand: it is the sole surviving member of a group common in Mesozoic times

tub **1** a clumsy slow boat or ship **2** *Informal* (in rowing) a heavy wide boat used for training novice oarsmen

tuba **1** a valved brass instrument of bass pitch, in which the bell points upwards and the mouthpiece projects at right angles. The tube is of conical bore and the mouthpiece cup-shaped **2** any other bass brass instrument such as the euphonium, helicon, etc. **3** a powerful reed stop on an organ **4** a form of trumpet of ancient Rome

Tubal-cain *Old Testament* a son of Lamech, said in Genesis 4:22 to be the first artificer of metals

tube **1** *Anatomy* **a** short for **Eustachian tube** *or* **Fallopian tube** **b** any hollow cylindrical structure **2** *Botany* **a** the lower part of a gamopetalous corolla or gamosepalous calyx, below the lobes **b** any other hollow structure in a plant **3** *Brit* **the tube** **a** an underground railway system **b** the tunnels through which the railway runs **c** the train itself **d** *Trademark* the London underground railway system **4** *Electronics* another name for **valve b** See **cathode-ray tube** **5** *Surfing* the cylindrical passage formed when a wave breaks and the crest tips forward

tuber **1** a fleshy underground stem (as in the potato) or root (as in the dahlia) that is an organ of vegetative reproduction and food storage **2** *Anatomy* a raised area; swelling

tubercle **1** any small rounded nodule or elevation, esp on the skin, on a bone, or on a plant **2** any small rounded pathological lesion of the tissues, esp one characteristic of tuberculosis

tuberculin a sterile liquid prepared from cultures of attenuated tubercle bacillus and used in the diagnosis of tuberculosis

tuberculin-tested (of milk) produced by cows that have been certified as free of tuberculosis

tuberculosis a communicable disease caused by infection with the tubercle bacillus, most frequently affecting the lungs (**pulmonary tuberculosis**)

tuberous *or* **tuberose** **1** (of plants or their parts) forming, bearing, or resembling a tuber or tubers **2** *Anatomy* of, relating to, or having warty protuberances or tubers

tubing fabric in the form of a tube, used for pillowcases and some cushions; piping

Tubman **William Vacanarat Shadrach** 1895–1971, Liberian statesman; president of Liberia (1944–71)

tubule any small tubular structure, esp one in an animal, as in the kidney, testis, etc.

tuck **1** the part of a vessel where the after ends of the planking or plating meet at the sternpost **2** a position of the body in certain dives in which the legs are bent with the knees drawn up against the chest and tightly clasped

Tucson a city in SE Arizona, at an altitude of 700m (2400 ft): resort and seat of the University of Arizona (1891). Pop: 507 658 (2003 est)

Tudor **1** an English royal house descended from a Welsh squire, **Owen Tudor** (died 1461), and ruling from 1485 to 1603. Monarchs of the Tudor line were Henry VII, Henry VIII, Edward VI, Mary I, and Elizabeth I **2** denoting a style of architecture of the late perpendicular period and characterized by half-timbered houses

▷www.artchive.com/ftp_site_reg.htm
▷www.britainexpress.com/architecture/
tudor.htm
▷www.bbc.co.uk/history/timelines/wales/
tudor.shtml
▷www.2hwy.com/eg/d/dynt.htm

tufa a soft porous rock consisting of calcium carbonate deposited from springs rich in lime

tuff a rock formed by the fusing together on the ground of small rock fragments (less than 2 mm across) ejected from a volcano

tuft 1 a small clump of trees or bushes 2 (formerly) a gold tassel on the cap worn by titled undergraduates at English universities

tug a boat with a powerful engine, used for towing barges, ships, etc.

Tugela a river in E South Africa, rising in the Drakensberg where it forms the **Tugela Falls**, 856 m (2810 ft) high (highest waterfall in Africa), before flowing east to the Indian Ocean: scene of battles during the Zulu War (1879) and the Boer War (1899–1902). Length: about 500 km (312 miles)

tug-of-war a contest in which two people or teams pull opposite ends of a rope in an attempt to drag the opposition over a central line

tuition the payment for instruction, esp in colleges or universities

Tula an industrial city in W central Russia. Pop: 460 000 (2005 est)

tulip 1 any spring-blooming liliaceous plant of the temperate Eurasian genus *Tulipa*, having tapering bulbs, long broad pointed leaves, and single showy bell-shaped flowers 2 the flower or bulb of any of these plants

tulip tree 1 a North American magnoliaceous forest tree, *Liriodendron tulipifera*, having tulip-shaped greenish-yellow flowers and long conelike fruits 2 a similar and related Chinese tree, *L. chinense* 3 any of various other trees with tulip-shaped flowers, such as the magnolia

Tull Jethro 1674–1741, English agriculturalist, who invented the seed drill

Tullamore the county town of Offaly, Republic of Ireland; food processing and brewing. Pop: 11 098 (2002)

tulle a fine net fabric of silk, rayon, etc, used for evening dresses, as a trimming for hats, etc.

Tulsa a city in NE Oklahoma, on the Arkansas River: a major oil centre; two universities. Pop: 387 807 (2003 est)

tumble an acrobatic feat, esp a somersault

tumbler 1 a person, esp a professional entertainer, who performs somersaults and other acrobatic feats 2 a a part that moves a gear in a train of gears into and out of engagement b a single cog or cam that transmits motion to the part with which it engages 3 a breed of domestic pigeon kept for exhibition or flying. The performing varieties execute backward somersaults in flight

tumid bulging or protuberant

tumour *or US* **tumor** *Pathol* a any abnormal swelling b a mass of tissue formed by a new growth of cells, normally independent of the surrounding structures

tumulus *Archaeol* (no longer in technical usage) another word for **barrow²**

tun 1 a measure of capacity, usually equal to 252 wine gallons 2 a cask used during the manufacture of beer

tuna¹ 1 any of various large marine spiny-finned fishes of the genus *Thunnus*, esp *T. thynnus*, chiefly of warm waters: family *Scombridae*. They have a spindle-shaped body and widely forked tail, and are important food fishes 2 any of various similar and related fishes

tuna² 1 any of various tropical American prickly pear cacti, esp *Opuntia tuna*, that are cultivated for their sweet edible fruits 2 the fruit of any of these cacti

Tunbridge Wells a town and resort in SE England, in SW Kent: chalybeate spring discovered in 1606; an important social centre in the 17th and 18th centuries. Pop: 60 095 (2001)

tundra a a vast treeless zone lying between the ice cap and the timberline of North America and Eurasia and having a permanently frozen subsoil b (*as modifier*): *tundra vegetation*

tune 1 a melody, esp one for which harmony is not essential 2 the most important part in a musical texture 3 the condition of producing accurately pitched notes, intervals, etc (esp in the phrases **in tune, out of tune**) 4 accurate correspondence of pitch and intonation between instruments (esp in the phrases **in tune, out of tune**) 5 the correct adjustment of a radio, television, or some other electronic circuit with respect to the required frequency (esp in the phrases **in tune, out of tune**)

tune-up adjustments made to an engine to improve its performance

tungsten a hard malleable ductile greyish-white element. It occurs principally in wolframite and scheelite and is used in lamp filaments, electrical contact points, X-ray targets, and, alloyed with steel, in high-speed cutting tools. Symbol: W; atomic no.: 74; atomic wt.: 183.85; valency: 2–6; relative density: 19.3; melting pt.: 3422±20°C; boiling pt.: 5555°C

Tunguska any of three rivers in Russia, in central Siberia, all tributaries of the Yenisei: the **Lower** (Nizhnyaya) **Tunguska** 2690 km (1670 miles) long; the **Stony** (Podkamennaya) **Tunguska** 1550 km (960 miles) long; the **Upper** (Verkhnyaya) **Tunguska** which is the lower course of the Angara

tunic *Anatomy, Botany, Zoology* a covering, lining, or enveloping membrane of an organ or part

tuning fork a two-pronged metal fork that when struck produces a pure note of constant specified pitch. It is used to tune musical instruments and in acoustics

Tunis the capital and chief port of Tunisia, in the northeast on the **Gulf of Tunis** (an inlet of the Mediterranean): dates from Carthaginian times, the ruins of ancient Carthage lying to the northeast; university (1960). Pop: 2 063 000 (2005 est)

Tunisia a republic in N Africa, on the Mediterranean: settled by the Phoenicians in the 12th century BC; made a French protectorate in 1881 and gained independence in 1955. It consists chiefly of the Sahara in the south, a central plateau, and the Atlas Mountains in the north. Exports include textiles, petroleum, and phosphates. Official language: Arabic; French is also widely spoken.

Official religion: Muslim. Currency: dinar. Capital: Tunis. Pop: 9 937 000 (2004 est). Area: 164 150 sq km (63 380 sq miles)

tunnel an underground passageway, esp one for trains or cars that passes under a mountain, river, or a congested urban area

tunnel vision a condition in which peripheral vision is greatly restricted

tup 1 *Chiefly Brit* an uncastrated male sheep; ram 2 the head of a pile-driver or steam hammer

tupik *or* **tupek** *Canadian* (esp in the Arctic) a tent of animal skins, a traditional type of Inuit summer dwelling

Tupolev Andrei Nikolaievich 1888–1972, Soviet aircraft designer, who designed the first supersonic passenger aircraft, the TU-144 (tested 1969). He also designed supersonic bombers and the TU-104, one of the first passenger jet aircraft (1955)

Tupungato a mountain on the border between Argentina and Chile, in the Andes. Height: 6550 m (21 484 ft)

turbine any of various types of machine in which the kinetic energy of a moving fluid is converted into mechanical energy by causing a bladed rotor to rotate. The moving fluid may be water, steam, air, or combustion products of a fuel

turbocharger a centrifugal compressor which boosts the intake pressure of an internal-combustion engine, driven by an exhaust-gas turbine fitted to the engine's exhaust manifold

turbofan 1 a type of by-pass engine in which a large fan driven by a turbine and housed in a short duct forces air rearwards around the exhaust gases in order to increase the propulsive thrust 2 an aircraft driven by one or more turbofans 3 the ducted fan in such an engine

turbojet 1 a gas turbine in which the exhaust gases provide the propulsive thrust to drive an aircraft 2 an aircraft powered by one or more turbojets

turboprop 1 an aircraft propulsion unit where a propeller is driven by a gas turbine 2 an aircraft powered by turboprops

turbot 1 a European flatfish, *Scophthalmus maximus*, having a pale brown speckled scaleless body covered with tubercles: family *Bothidae*. It is highly valued as a food fish 2 any of various similar or related fishes

turbulence *or rarely* **turbulency** 1 *Meteorol* local instability in the atmosphere, oceans, or rivers 2 turbulent flow in a liquid or gas

turf 1 the surface layer of fields and pastures, consisting of earth containing a dense growth of grasses with their roots; sod 2 a piece cut from this layer, used to form lawns, verges, etc. 3 a a track, usually of grass or dirt, where horse races are run b horse racing as a sport or industry

Turgenev Ivan Sergeyevich 1818–83, Russian novelist and dramatist. In *A Sportsman's Sketches* (1852) he pleaded for the abolition of serfdom. His novels, such as *Rudin* (1856) and *Fathers and Sons* (1862), are noted for their portrayal of country life and of the Russian intelligentsia. His plays include *A Month in the Country* (1850)

Turin a city in NW Italy, capital of Piedmont region, on the River Po: became capital of the Kingdom of Sardinia in 1720; first capital (1861–65) of united Italy; university (1405); a major industrial centre, producing most of Italy's cars. Pop: 865 263 (2001)

Turing Alan Mathison 1912–54, English mathematician, who was responsible for formal description of abstract automata, and speculation on computer imitation of humans: a leader of the Allied codebreakers at Bletchley Park during World War II

Turishcheva Ludmilla born 1952, Soviet gymnast: world champion 1970, 1972 (at the Olympic Games), and 1974

Turk 1 a native, inhabitant, or citizen of Turkey 2 a native speaker of any Turkic language, such as an inhabitant of Turkmenistan or Kyrgyzstan

Turkana Lake a long narrow lake in E Africa, in the Great Rift Valley. Area: 7104 sq km (2743 sq miles)

Turkestan *or* **Turkistan** an extensive region of central Asia between Siberia in the north and Tibet, India, Afghanistan, and Iran in the south: formerly divided into **West** (**Russian**) **Turkestan** (also called Soviet Central Asia), comprising present-day Turkmenistan, Uzbekistan, Tajikistan, and Kyrgyzstan and the S part of Kazakhstan, and **East** (**Chinese**) **Turkestan** consisting of the Xinjiang Uygur Autonomous Region

turkey 1 a large gallinaceous bird, *Meleagris gallopavo*, of North America, having a bare wattled head and neck and a brownish iridescent plumage. The male is brighter and has a fan-shaped tail. A domestic variety is widely bred for its flesh 2 a similar and related bird, *Agriocharis ocellata* (**ocellated turkey**), of Central and N South America 3 any of various Australian birds considered to resemble the turkey, such as the bush turkey 4 *Slang* (in tenpin bowling) three strikes in a row 5 See **cold turkey**

Turkey a republic in W Asia and SE Europe, between the Black Sea, the Mediterranean, and the Aegean: the centre of the Ottoman Empire; became a republic in 1923. The major Asian part, consisting mainly of an arid plateau, is separated from European Turkey by the Bosporus, Sea of Marmara, and Dardanelles. Official languages: Turkish; Kurdish and Arabic minority languages. Religion: Muslim majority. Currency: lira. Capital: Ankara. Pop: 72 320 000 (2004 est). Area: 780 576 sq km (301 380 sq miles)

Turkic a branch or subfamily of the Altaic family of languages, including Turkish, Turkmen, Kirghiz, Tatar, etc, members of which are found from Turkey to NE China, esp in central Asia

Turkish the official language of Turkey, belonging to the Turkic branch of the Altaic family

Turkmenistan a republic in central Asia: the area has been occupied by a succession of empires; a Turkmen state was established in the 15th century but suffered almost continual civil strife and was gradually conquered by Russia; in 1918 it became a Soviet republic and gained independence from the Soviet Union in 1991: deserts including the **Kara Kum** cover most of the region; agricultural communities are concentrated around oases; there are rich mineral deposits. Official language: Turkmen. Religion: believers are mainly Muslim. Currency: manat. Capital: Ashkhabad. Pop: 4 940 000 (2004 est). Area: 488 100 sq km (186 400 sq miles)

Turku a city and port in SW Finland, on the Gulf of Bothnia: capital of Finland until 1812. Pop: 175 059 (2003 est)

turmeric 1 a tropical Asian zingiberaceous plant, *Curcuma longa*, having yellow flowers and an aromatic underground stem **2** any of several other plants with similar roots

turn 1 *Music* a melodic ornament that makes a turn around a note, beginning with the note above, in a variety of sequences **2** *Theatre, chiefly Brit* a short theatrical act, esp in music hall, cabaret, etc.

turnaround 1 a the act or process in which a ship, aircraft, etc, unloads passengers and freight at the end of a trip and reloads for the next trip **b** the time taken for this **2** the total time taken by a ship, aircraft, or other vehicle in a round trip

Turner 1 J(oseph) M(allord) W(illiam). 1775–1851, British landscape painter; a master of water colours. He sought to convey atmosphere by means of an innovative use of colour and gradations of light **2** *Nat* 1800–31, US rebel slave, who led (1831) Turner's Insurrection, the only major slave revolt in US history: executed **3** Robert Edward III, known as *Ted*. born 1938, US broadcasting executive and yachtsman; chairman of Turner Broadcasting (1970–96), founder of Cable News Network (1980), and vice-chairman of Time Warner from 1996 **4** Tina, real name *Annie Mae Bullock*. born 1940, US rock singer who performed (1958–75) with her then husband Ike Turner (born 1931) and later as a solo act. Her recordings include "River Deep, Mountain High" (1966) and "Simply the Best" (1991)

turning an object made on a lathe

turning circle the smallest circle in which a vehicle can turn

turning point *Maths* a stationary point at which the first derivative of a function changes sign, so that typically its graph does not cross a horizontal tangent

turnip 1 a widely cultivated plant, *Brassica rapa*, of the Mediterranean region, with a large yellow or white edible root: family *Brassicaceae* (crucifers) **2** the root of this plant, which is eaten as a vegetable **3** any of several similar or related plants **4** another name for **kohlrabi**

turnkey denoting a project, as in civil engineering, in which a single contractor has responsibility for the complete job from the start to the time of installation or occupancy

turn-off a road or other way branching off from the main thoroughfare

turnover 1 a the amount of business, usually expressed in terms of gross revenue, transacted during a specified period **b** (*as modifier*): *a turnover tax* **2** the rate at which stock in trade is sold and replenished **3 a** the number of workers employed by a firm in a given period to replace those who have left **b** the ratio between this number and the average number of employees during the same period

turnpike 1 (between the mid-16th and late 19th centuries) **a** gates or some other barrier set across a road to prevent passage until a toll had been paid **b** a road on which a turnpike was operated **2** *US* a motorway for use of which a toll is charged

turnstile *Logic* a symbol of the form ⊢, ⊨, or ⊩, used to represent logical consequence when inserted between expressions to form a sequent, or when prefixed to a single expression to indicate its status as a theorem

turntable 1 the circular horizontal platform that rotates a gramophone record while it is being played **2** a flat circular platform that can be rotated about its centre, used for turning locomotives and cars **3** the revolvable platform on a microscope on which specimens are examined

turpentine 1 any of various viscous oleoresins obtained from various coniferous trees, esp from the longleaf pine, and used as the main source of commercial turpentine **2** a brownish-yellow sticky viscous oleoresin that exudes from the terebinth tree **3** a colourless flammable volatile liquid with a pungent odour, distilled from turpentine oleoresin. It is an essential oil containing a mixture of terpenes and is used as a solvent for paints and in medicine as a rubefacient and expectorant **4** any one of a number of thinners for paints and varnishes, consisting of fractions of petroleum

Turpin Dick 1706–39, English highwayman

turps 1 *Brit* short for **turpentine 2** *Austral and NZ, slang* alcoholic drink, esp beer (esp in the phrase **on the turps**)

turquoise 1 a greenish-blue fine-grained secondary mineral consisting of hydrated copper aluminium phosphate. It occurs in igneous rocks rich in aluminium and is used as a gemstone. Formula: $CuAl_6(PO_4)_4(OH)_8.4H_2O$ **2** the colour of turquoise

turret 1 a small tower that projects from the wall of a building, esp a medieval castle **2** (on a machine tool) a turret-like steel structure with tools projecting radially that can be indexed round to select or to bring each tool to bear on the work

turtle 1 any of various aquatic chelonian reptiles, esp those of the marine family *Chelonidae*, having a flattened shell enclosing the body and flipper-like limbs adapted for swimming **2** *US and Canadian* any of the chelonian reptiles, including the tortoises and terrapins **3** *Nautical* a zip bag made as part of a spinnaker for holding the sail so that it can be set rapidly

turtledove any of several Old World doves of the genus *Streptopelia*, having a brown plumage with speckled wings and a long dark tail

Tuscan 1 of or relating to Tuscany, its inhabitants, or their dialect of Italian **2** of, denoting, or relating to one of the five classical orders of architecture: characterized by a column with an unfluted shaft and a capital and base with mouldings but no decoration **3** a native or inhabitant of Tuscany **4** any of the dialects of Italian spoken in Tuscany, esp the dialect of Florence: the standard form of Italian

▷http://ah.bfn.org/a/DCTNRY/t/tuscan.html

Tuscany a region of central Italy, on the Ligurian and Tyrrhenian Seas: corresponds roughly to ancient Etruria; a region of numerous small states in medieval times; united in the 15th and 16th centuries under Florence; united with the rest of Italy in 1861. Capital: Florence. Pop: 3 516 296 (2003 est). Area: 22 990 sq km (8876 sq miles)

Tusculum an ancient city in Latium near Rome

tusk 1 a pointed elongated usually paired tooth in the

elephant, walrus, and certain other mammals that is often used for fighting **2** the canine tooth of certain animals, esp horses

Tussaud Marie 1760–1850, Swiss modeller in wax, who founded a permanent exhibition in London of historical and contemporary figures

tussock a dense tuft of vegetation, esp of grass

Tutankhamen *or* **Tutankhamun** king (1361–1352 BC) of the 18th dynasty of Egypt. His tomb near Luxor, discovered in 1922, contained many material objects

tutelage instruction or guidance, esp by a tutor

tutor 1 a teacher, usually instructing individual pupils and often engaged privately **2** (at universities, colleges, etc) a member of staff responsible for the teaching and supervision of a certain number of students **3** *Scots law* the guardian of a pupil

tutorial a period of intensive tuition given by a tutor to an individual student or to a small group of students

tutti *Music* to be performed by the whole orchestra, choir, etc.

tutu¹ a very short skirt worn by ballerinas, made of projecting layers of stiffened sheer material

tutu² a shrub, *Coriaria arborea*, of New Zealand, having seeds that are poisonous to farm animals

Tutu Desmond born 1931, South African clergyman, noted for his opposition to apartheid: Anglican Bishop of Johannesburg (1984–86) and Archbishop of Cape Town (1986–96); in 1995 he became leader of the Truth and Reconciliation Commission, established to investigate human rights violations during the apartheid era. Nobel peace prize 1984

Tutuila the largest island of American Samoa, in the SW Pacific. Chief town and port: Pago Pago. Pop: 55 876 (2000). Area: 135 sq km (52 sq miles)

Tutuola Amos 1920–97, Nigerian writer: his books include *The Palm-Wine Drinkard* (1952) and *Pauper, Brawler and Slanderer* (1987)

Tuvalu a country in the SW Pacific, comprising a group of nine coral islands: established as a British protectorate in 1892. From 1915 until 1975 the islands formed part of the British colony of the Gilbert and Ellice Islands; achieved full independence in 1978; a member of the Commonwealth (formerly a special member not represented at all meetings, until 2000). Languages: English and Tuvaluan. Religion: Christian majority. Currency: Australian dollar; Tuvalu dollars are also used. Capital: Funafuti. Pop: 11 000 (2003 est). Area: 26 sq km (10 sq miles)

Tuva Republic a constituent republic of S Russia: mountainous. Capital: Kizyl. Pop: 305 500 (2002). Area: 170 500 sq km (65 800 sq miles)

TVEI in Britain technical and vocational educational initiative: a national educational scheme in which pupils gain practical experience in technology and industry often through work placement

Tver a city in central Russia, at the confluence of the Volga and Tversta Rivers: chief port of the upper Volga, linked by canal with Moscow. Pop: 402 000 (2005 est)

Twain 1 Mark, pen name of *Samuel Langhorne Clemens*. 1835–1910, US novelist and humorist, famous for his classics *The Adventures of Tom Sawyer* (1876) and *The Adventures of Huckleberry Finn* (1885) **2** Shania , real name

Eilleen Regina Edwards. born 1965, Canadian country-rock singer; her bestselling recordings include *The Woman In Me* (1995) *Come On Over* (1997), and *UP!* (2002)

tweed a a thick woollen often knobbly cloth produced originally in Scotland **b** (*as modifier*): *a tweed coat*
▷www.harristweed.org/fabric_hist.htm
▷www.irishcultureandcustoms.com/AEmblem/Tweed.html

Tweed a river in SE Scotland and NE England, flowing east and forming part of the border between Scotland and England, then crossing into England to enter the North Sea at Berwick. Length: 156 km (97 miles)

Tweedsmuir Baron title of (John) Buchan

tweeter a loudspeaker used in high-fidelity systems for the reproduction of high audio frequencies. It is usually employed in conjunction with a woofer and a crossover network

Twelfth Day a Jan 6, the twelfth day after Christmas and the feast of the Epiphany, formerly observed as the final day of the Christmas celebrations **b** (*as modifier*): *Twelfth-Day celebrations*

twelfth man a reserve player in a cricket team

Twelfth Night a the evening of Jan 5, the eve of Twelfth Day, formerly observed with various festal celebrations **b** the evening of Twelfth Day itself **c** (*as modifier*): *Twelfth-Night customs*

twelve 1 the cardinal number that is the sum of ten and two **2** a numeral, 12, XII, etc, representing this number

twelve-tone of, relating to, or denoting the type of serial music invented and developed by Arnold Schoenberg, which uses as musical material a tone row formed by the 12 semitones of the chromatic scale, together with its inverted and retrograde versions. The technique has been applied in various ways by different composers and usually results in music in which there are few, if any, tonal centres

twenty 1 the cardinal number that is the product of ten and two; a score **2** a numeral, 20, XX, etc, representing this number

Twickenham a former town in SE England, on the River Thames: part of the Greater London borough of Richmond-upon-Thames since 1965; contains the English Rugby Football Union ground

twig 1 any small branch or shoot of a tree or other woody plant **2** something resembling this, esp a minute branch of a blood vessel

twilight zone 1 an area of a city or town, usually surrounding the central business district, where houses have become dilapidated **2** the lowest level of the ocean to which light can penetrate

twill 1 (in textiles) of or designating a weave in which the weft yarns are worked around two or more warp yarns to produce an effect of parallel diagonal lines or ribs **2** any fabric so woven

twin 1 a either of two persons or animals conceived at the same time **b** (*as modifier*): *a twin brother* **2** a crystal consisting of two parts each of which has a definite orientation to the other

twine string made by twisting together fibres of hemp, cotton, etc.

twin town *Brit* a town that has civic associations, such as reciprocal visits and cultural exchanges, with a foreign town, usually of similar size and sometimes with other similarities, as in commercial activities

twist 1 (in weaving) a specified direction of twisting the yarn 2 **the twist** a modern dance popular in the 1960s, in which couples vigorously twist the hips in time to rhythmic music 3 **a** a cigar made by twisting three cigars around one another **b** chewing tobacco made in the form of a roll by twisting the leaves together 4 *Physics* torsional deformation or shear stress or strain

twitch 1 a sudden muscular spasm, esp one caused by a nervous condition 2 a loop of cord used to control a horse by drawing it tight about its upper lip

twitcher *Informal* a bird-watcher who tries to spot as many rare varieties as possible

two 1 the cardinal number that is the sum of one and one. It is a prime number 2 a numeral, 2, II, (ii), etc, representing this number 3 *Music* the numeral 2 used as the lower figure in a time signature, indicating that the beat is measured in minims

twoccing *or* **twocking** *Brit, slang* the act of breaking into a motor vehicle and driving it away

two-dimensional 1 of, having, or relating to two dimensions, usually describable in terms of length and breadth or length and height 2 lying on a plane; having an area but not enclosing any volume 3 (of painting or drawing) lacking the characteristics of form or depth

twofold 1 equal to twice as many or twice as much; double 2 composed of two parts; dual

twopence *or* **tuppence** *Brit* a former British silver coin, now only coined as Maundy money

twosome *Sport* a match between two people

two-step 1 an old-time dance in duple time 2 a piece of music composed for or in the rhythm of such a dance

two-stroke relating to or designating an internal-combustion engine whose piston makes two strokes for every explosion

Two Thousand Guineas an annual horse race run at Newmarket since 1809

Tyburn (formerly) a place of execution in London, on the **River Tyburn** (a tributary of the Thames, now entirely below ground)

tycoon 1 a business man of great wealth and power 2 an archaic name for a **shogun**

tyke *or* **tike** 1 a dog, esp a mongrel 2 *Austral, slang, offensive* a Roman Catholic

Tyler 1 **John** 1790–1862, US statesman; tenth president of the US (1841–45) 2 **Wat** died 1381, English leader of the Peasants' Revolt (1381)

Tylor Sir **Edward Burnett** 1832–1917, British anthropologist; first professor of anthropology at Oxford (1896). His *Primitive Culture* (1871) became a standard work

tympanic membrane the thin translucent oval membrane separating the external ear from the middle ear. It transmits vibrations produced by sound waves, via the ossicles, to the cochlea

tympanum 1 **a** the cavity of the middle ear **b** another name for **tympanic membrane** 2 any diaphragm resembling that in the middle ear in function 3 *Architect* **a** the recessed space bounded by the cornices of a pediment, esp one that is triangular in shape and ornamented **b** the recessed space bounded by an arch

and the lintel of a doorway or window below it 4 *Music* a tympan or drum 5 a scoop wheel for raising water

Tyndale, Tindal, *or* **Tindale** William ?1492–1536, English Protestant and humanist, who translated the New Testament (1525), the Pentateuch (1530), and the Book of Jonah (1531) into English. He was burnt at the stake as a heretic

Tyndall **John** 1820–93, Irish physicist, noted for his work on the radiation of heat by gases, the transmission of sound through the atmosphere, and the scattering of light

Tyne a river in N England, flowing east to the North Sea. Length: 48 km (30 miles)

Tyne and Wear a metropolitan county of NE England, administered since 1986 by the unitary authorities of Newcastle upon Tyne, North Tyneside, Gateshead, South Tyneside, and Sunderland. Area: 540 sq km (208 sq miles)

Tynemouth a port in NE England, in North Tyneside unitary authority, Tyne and Wear, at the mouth of the River Tyne: includes the port and industrial centre of North Shields; fishing, ship-repairing, and marine engineering. Pop: 17 056 (2001)

Tyneside the conurbation on the banks of the Tyne from Newcastle to the coast

Tynwald the the Parliament of the Isle of Man, consisting of the crown, lieutenant governor, House of Keys, and legislative council

type 1 *Biology* **a** the taxonomic group the characteristics of which are used for defining the next highest group, for example *Rattus norvegicus* (brown rat) is the type species of the rat genus *Rattus* **b** (*as modifier*): *a type genus* 2 *Logic* a class of expressions or of the entities they represent that can all enter into the same syntactic relations. The **theory of types** was advanced by Bertrand Russell to avoid the liar paradox, Russell's paradox, etc. 3 *Philosophy* a universal. If a sentence always has the same meaning whenever it is used, the meaning is said to be a property of the sentence-type 4 *Chiefly Christian theol* a figure, episode, or symbolic factor resembling some future reality in such a way as to foreshadow or prefigure it

typhoid *Pathol* 1 resembling typhus 2 short for **typhoid fever**

typhoid fever an acute infectious disease characterized by high fever, rose-coloured spots on the chest or abdomen, abdominal pain, and occasionally intestinal bleeding. It is caused by the bacillus *Salmonella typhosa* ingested with food or water

typhoon 1 a violent tropical storm or cyclone, esp in the China seas and W Pacific 2 a violent storm of India

typhus any one of a group of acute infectious rickettsial diseases characterized by high fever, skin rash, and severe headache

typical *Biology* having most of the characteristics of a particular taxonomic group

tyrannosaurus *or* **tyrannosaur** any large carnivorous bipedal dinosaur of the genus *Tyrannosaurus*, common in North America in upper Jurassic and Cretaceous times: suborder *Theropoda* (theropods)

tyranny 1 **a** a government by a tyrant or tyrants; despotism **b** similarly oppressive and unjust government by more than one person **2** a political unit ruled by a tyrant **3** (esp in ancient Greece) government by a usurper

tyrant **1** a person who governs oppressively, unjustly, and arbitrarily; despot **2** (esp in ancient Greece) a ruler whose authority lacked the sanction of law or custom; usurper

tyre *or US* **tire** **1** a rubber ring placed over the rim of a wheel of a road vehicle to provide traction and reduce road shocks, esp a hollow inflated ring (**pneumatic tyre**) consisting of a reinforced outer casing enclosing an inner tube **2** a ring of wear-resisting steel shrunk thermally onto a cast-iron railway wheel

Tyre *or* **Tyr** a port in S Lebanon, on the Mediterranean: founded about the 15th century BC; for centuries a major Phoenician seaport, famous for silks and its Tyrian-purple dye; now a small market town. Pop: 141 000 (2005 est)

Tyrol *or* **Tirol** a mountainous state of W Austria: passed to the Hapsburgs in 1363; S part transferred to Italy in 1919. Capital: Innsbruck. Pop: 683 317 (2003 est). Area: 12 648 sq km (4883 sq miles)

Tyrone a historical county of W Northern Ireland, occupying almost a quarter of the total area of Northern Ireland; in 1973 its administrative functions were devolved to several district councils

Tyrrhenian Sea an arm of the Mediterranean between Italy and the islands of Corsica, Sardinia, and Sicily

Tyumen a port in S central Russia, on the Tura River: one of the oldest Russian towns in Siberia; industrial centre with nearby oil and natural gas reserves. Pop: 518 000 (2005 est)

Tzara Tristan, original name *Samuel Rosenstock*. 1896–1963, French poet and essayist, born in Romania, best known as the founder of Dada: author of *The Approximate Man* (1931).

Tzu-po *or* **Tzepo** a variant transliteration of the Chinese name for **Zibo**

Uu

UB40 (in Britain) a registration card issued by the Department of Employment to a person registering as unemployed

Ubangi a river in central Africa, flowing west and south, forming the border between the Democratic Republic of Congo (formerly Zaïre) and the Central African Republic and Congo-Brazzaville, into the River Congo. Length (with the Uele): 2250 km (1400 miles)

U-boat a German submarine, esp in World Wars I and II

UCAS (in Britain) Universities and Colleges Admissions Service
▷www.ucas.co.uk

Ucayali a river in E Peru, flowing north into the Marañón above Iquitos. Length: 1600 km (1000 miles)

UCCA formerly, in Britain Universities Central Council on Admissions

Uccello Paolo 1397–1475, Florentine painter noted esp for three paintings of *The Battle of San Romano*, 1432 (1456–60)

Udaipur 1 a former state of NW India: became part of Rajasthan in 1947 **2** a city in NW India, in S Rajasthan. Pop: 389 317 (2001)

udder the large baglike mammary gland of cows, sheep, etc, having two or more teats

Udine a city in NE Italy, in Friuli-Venezia Giulia region: partially damaged in an earthquake in 1976. Pop: 95 030 (2001)

Udmurt Republic a constituent republic of W central Russia, in the basin of the middle Kama. Capital: Izhevsk. Pop: 1 570 500 (2002). Area: 42 100 sq km (16 250 sq miles)

UEFA Union of European Football Associations
▷www.uefa.com

Uele a river in central Africa, rising near the border between the Democratic Republic of Congo (formerly Zaïre) and Uganda and flowing west to join the Bomu River and form the Ubangi River. Length: about 1100 km (700 miles)

Ufa a city in W central Russia, capital of the Bashkir Republic: university (1957). Pop: 1 035 000 (2005 est)

Uganda a republic in E Africa: British protectorate established in 1894–96; gained independence in 1962 and became a republic in 1963; a member of the Commonwealth. It consists mostly of a savanna plateau with part of Lake Victoria in the southeast and mountains in the southwest, reaching 5109 m (16 763 ft) in the Ruwenzori Range. Official language: English;

Swahili, Luganda, and Luo are also widely spoken. Religion: Christian majority. Currency: Ugandan shilling. Capital: Kampala. Pop: 26 699 000 (2004 est). Area: 235 886 sq km (91 076 sq miles)

UGLI *Trademark* a large juicy yellow-skinned citrus fruit of the Caribbean: a cross between a tangerine, grapefruit, and orange

Uhland Johann Ludwig 1787–1862, German romantic poet, esp of lyrics and ballads

Ujiji a town in W Tanzania, on Lake Tanganyika: a former slave and ivory centre; the place where Stanley found Livingstone in 1871. It merged with the neighbouring town of Kigoma to form Kigoma-Ujiji in the 1960s

Ujjain a city in W central India, in Madhya Pradesh: one of the seven sacred cities of the Hindus; a major agricultural trade centre. Pop: 429 933 (2001)

Ujung Pandang a port in central Indonesia, on SW Sulawesi: an important native port before Portuguese (16th century) and Dutch (17th century) control; capital of the Dutch East Indies (1946–49); a major Indonesian distribution and transshipment port. Pop: 1 100 019 (2000)

ukase 1 (in imperial Russia) an edict of the tsar **2** a rare word for **edict**

Ukraine a republic in SE Europe, on the Black Sea and the Sea of Azov: ruled by the Khazars (7th–9th centuries), by Ruïk princes with the Mongol conquest in the 13th century, then by Lithuania, by Poland, and by Russia; one of the four original republics that formed the Soviet Union in 1922; unilaterally declared independence in 1990, which was recognized in 1991: consists chiefly of lowlands; economy based on rich agriculture and mineral resources and on the major heavy industries of the Donets Basin. Official language: Ukrainian; Russian is also widely spoken. Religion: believers are mainly Christian. Currency: hryvna. Capital: Kiev. Pop: 48 151 000 (2004 est). Area: 603 700 sq km (231 990 sq miles)

Ukrainian the official language of Ukraine: an East Slavonic language closely related to Russian

ukulele *or* **ukelele** a small four-stringed guitar, esp of Hawaii

Ulan Bator the capital of Mongolia, in the N central part: developed in the mid-17th century around the Da Khure monastery, residence until 1924 of successive "living Buddhas" (third in rank of Buddhist-Lamaist leaders), and main junction of caravan routes across Mongolia; university (1942); industrial and commercial centre. Pop: 842 000 (2005 est)

Ulanova Galina (**Sergeyevna**) 1910–98, Russian ballet dancer, who performed with the Leningrad Kirov ballet (1928–44) and the Moscow Bolshoi Ballet (1944–62)

Ulan-Ude an industrial city in SE Russia, capital of the Buryat Republic: an important rail junction. Pop: 361 000 (2005 est)

Ulbricht Walter 1893-1973, East German statesman; largely responsible for the establishment and development of East German communism

ulcer a disintegration of the surface of the skin or a mucous membrane resulting in an open sore that heals very slowly

Ullswater a lake in NW England, in Cumbria in the Lake District. Length: 12 km (7.5 miles)

Ulm an industrial city in S Germany, in Baden-Württemberg on the Danube: a free imperial city (1155–1802). Pop: 119 807 (2003 est)

ulna 1 the inner and longer of the two bones of the human forearm 2 the corresponding bone in other vertebrates

Ulster 1 a province and former kingdom of N Ireland: passed to the English Crown in 1461; confiscated land given to English and Scottish Protestant settlers in the 17th century, giving rise to serious long-term conflict; partitioned in 1921, six counties forming Northern Ireland and three counties joining the Republic of Ireland. Pop. (three Ulster counties of the Republic of Ireland): 46 714 (2002); (six Ulster counties of Northern Ireland): 1 702 628 (2003 est). Area (Republic of Ireland): 8013 sq km (3094 sq miles); (Northern Ireland): 14 121 sq km (5452 sq miles) 2 an informal name for **Northern Ireland**

ultima Thule 1 another name for **Thule** 2 any distant or unknown region

ultimatum a final communication by a party, esp a government, setting forth conditions on which it insists, as during negotiations on some topic

ultramarine a vivid blue colour

ultramontane 1 on the other side of the mountains, esp the Alps, from the speaker or writer 2 of or relating to a movement in the Roman Catholic Church which favours the centralized authority and influence of the pope as opposed to local independence 3 a resident or native from beyond the mountains, esp the Alps 4 a member of the ultramontane party of the Roman Catholic Church

ultrasonic of, concerned with, or producing waves with the same nature as sound waves but frequencies above audio frequencies

ultrasonics the branch of physics concerned with ultrasonic waves

ultrasound ultrasonic waves at frequencies above the audible range (above about 20 kHz), used in cleaning metallic parts, echo sounding, medical diagnosis and therapy, etc.

ultraviolet the part of the electromagnetic spectrum with wavelengths shorter than light but longer than X-rays; in the range 0.4×10^{-6} and 1×10^{-8} metres

ultra vires Law beyond the legal power or authority of a person, corporation, agent, etc.

Uluru a large isolated desert rock, sometimes described as the world's largest monolith, in the Northern Territory of Australia: sacred to local Aboriginal people. Height: 330m (1100 ft). Base circumference: 9 km (5.6 miles)

umbel an inflorescence, characteristic of umbelliferous plants, in which the flowers arise from the same point in the main stem and have stalks of the same length, to give a cluster with the youngest flowers at the centre

umbelliferous of, relating to, or belonging to the Umbelliferae, a family of herbaceous plants and shrubs, typically having hollow stems, divided or compound leaves, and flowers in umbels: includes fennel, dill, parsley, carrot, celery, and parsnip

umber 1 any of various natural brown earths containing ferric oxide together with lime and oxides of aluminium, manganese, and silicon 2 any of the dark brown to greenish-brown colours produced by this pigment

Umberto I 1844–1900, king of Italy (1878–1900); son of Victor Emmanuel II: assassinated at Monza

umbilical 1 of, relating to, or resembling the umbilicus or the umbilical cord 2 in the region of the umbilicus 3 short for **umbilical cord**

umbilical cord the long flexible tubelike structure connecting a fetus with the placenta: it provides a means of metabolic interchange with the mother

umbilicus 1 Biology a hollow or navel-like structure, such as the cavity at the base of a gastropod shell 2 Anatomy a technical name for the **navel**

umbra 1 a region of complete shadow resulting from the total obstruction of light by an opaque object, esp the shadow cast by the moon onto the earth during a solar eclipse 2 the darker inner region of a sunspot

umbrella Zoology the flattened cone-shaped contractile body of a jellyfish or other medusa

Umbria a mountainous region of central Italy, in the valley of the Tiber. Pop: 834 210 (2003 est). Area: 8456 sq km (3265 sq miles)

Umbrian 1 of or relating to Umbria, its inhabitants, their dialect of Italian, or the ancient language once spoken there 2 of or relating to a Renaissance school of painting that included Raphael 3 a native or inhabitant of Umbria 4 an extinct language of ancient S Italy, belonging to the Italic branch of the Indo-European family

umiak or **oomiak** a large open boat made of stretched skins, used by Inuit

Umtata a city in South Africa, in Eastern Cape province; the capital of the former Transkei Bantu homeland. Pop: 94 778 (2001)

Unalaska Island a large volcanic island in SW Alaska, in the Aleutian Islands. Length: 120 km (75 miles). Greatest width: about 40 km (25 miles)

Unamuno Miguel de 1864–1936, Spanish philosopher and writer

unarmed Biology (of animals and plants) having no claws, prickles, spines, thorns, or similar structures

unattached (of property) not seized or held as security or in satisfaction of a judgment

unavoidable Law not capable of being declared null and

void

unbalanced 1 mentally disordered or deranged **2** *Electronics* (of signals or circuitry) not symmetrically disposed about earth or zero reference potential

unbeliever a person who does not believe or withholds belief, esp in religious matters

unbridled (of a horse, etc) wearing no bridle

unbroken 1 (of animals, esp horses) not tamed; wild **2** (of a contract, law, etc) not broken or infringed

uncharted (of a physical or nonphysical region or area) not yet mapped, surveyed, or investigated

uncial 1 of, relating to, or written in majuscule letters, as used in Greek and Latin manuscripts of the third to ninth centuries, that resemble modern capitals, but are characterized by much greater curvature and inclination and general inequality of height **2** pertaining to an inch or an ounce **3** pertaining to the duodecimal system **4** an uncial letter or manuscript

uncivilized *or* **uncivilised** (of a tribe or people) not yet civilized, esp preliterate

Uncle Sam a personification of the government of the United States

unconditional *Maths* (of an equality) true for all values of the variable

unconscious 1 lacking normal sensory awareness of the environment; insensible **2** coming from or produced by the unconscious **3** *Psychoanal* the part of the mind containing instincts, impulses, images, and ideas that are not available for direct examination

unconstitutional at variance with or not permitted by a constitution

unction *Chiefly RC and Eastern Churches* the act of anointing with oil in sacramental ceremonies, in the conferring of holy orders

underage below the required or standard age, esp below the legal age for voting or drinking

underbelly the part of an animal's belly nearest to the ground

undercarriage 1 the assembly of wheels, shock absorbers, struts, etc, that supports an aircraft on the ground and enables it to take off and land **2** the framework that supports the body of a vehicle, carriage, etc.

undercurrent a current that is not apparent at the surface or lies beneath another current

undercut *Forestry, chiefly US and Canadian* a notch cut in a tree trunk, to ensure a clean break in felling

underdeveloped *Photog* (of a film, plate, or print) processed in developer for less than the required time, thus lacking in contrast

underfelt thick felt laid between floorboards and carpet to increase insulation and resilience

undergraduate a person studying in a university for a first degree

underground 1 a a movement dedicated to overthrowing a government or occupation forces, as in the European countries occupied by the German army in World War II **b** (*as modifier*): *an underground group* **2** an electric passenger railway operated in underground tunnels **3 a** any avant-garde, experimental, or subversive movement in popular art, films, music, etc. **b** (*as modifier*): *the underground press*

▷www.reed.edu/~reyn/transport.html

▷www.metropla.net/index2.htm

undergrowth 1 small trees, bushes, ferns, etc, growing beneath taller trees in a wood or forest **2** a growth of short fine hairs beneath longer ones; underfur

underlay felt, rubber, etc, laid beneath a carpet to increase insulation and resilience

underpass 1 a section of a road that passes under another road, railway line, etc. **2** another word for **subway**

underseal *Brit* a coating of a tar or rubber-based material applied to the underside of a motor vehicle to retard corrosion

undersecretary 1 (in Britain) **a** any of various senior civil servants in certain government departments **b** short for **undersecretary of state**: any of various high officials subordinate only to the minister in charge of a department **2** (in the US) a high government official subordinate only to the secretary in charge of a department

undersexed having weaker sex urges or responses than is considered normal

understanding *Philosophy, archaic* the mind, esp the faculty of reason

understudy an actor or actress who studies a part so as to be able to replace the usual actor or actress if necessary

undertaking *Informal* the practice of overtaking on an inner lane a vehicle which is travelling in an outer lane

undertone a pale or subdued colour

undertow 1 the seaward undercurrent following the breaking of a wave on the beach **2** any strong undercurrent flowing in a different direction from the surface current

underwater 1 being, occurring, or going under the surface of the water, esp the sea **2** *Nautical* below the water line of a vessel

under way *Nautical* in motion

Underwood Rory born 1963, British Rugby Union football player; played for England (1984–99), becoming Britain's most capped player

underworld *Greek and Roman myth* the regions below the earth's surface regarded as the abode of the dead; Hades

undine any of various female water spirits

Undset Sigrid 1882–1949, Norwegian novelist, best known for her trilogy *Kristin Lavransdatter* (1920–22): Nobel prize for literature 1928

unemployment benefit 1 (in Britain, formerly) a regular payment to a person who is out of work: replaced by jobseeker's allowance in 1996 **2** (in New Zealand) a means-tested monetary benefit paid weekly by the Social Security Department to the unemployed

UNESCO United Nations Educational, Scientific, and Cultural Organization: an agency of the United Nations that sponsors programmes to promote education, communication, the arts, etc.

▷www.unesco.org

unfinished 1 (of fabric) unbleached or not processed **2** (of fabric) with a short nap

unfledged (of a young bird) not having developed adult feathers

Ungaretti Giuseppe 1888–1970, Italian poet, best known for his collection of war poems *Allegria di naufragi* (1919)

Ungava a sparsely inhabited region of NE Canada, in N Quebec east of Hudson Bay: part of the Labrador peninsula: rich mineral resources. Area: 911 110 sq km (351 780 sq miles)

ungulate any of a large group of mammals all of which have hooves: divided into odd-toed ungulates and even-toed ungulates

unhallowed 1 not consecrated or holy 2 sinful or profane

unicameral *Politics* of or characterized by a single legislative chamber

UNICEF United Nations Children's Fund (formerly, United Nations International Children's Emergency Fund): an agency of the United Nations that administers programmes to aid education and child and maternal health in developing countries
 ▷www.unicef.org

Unicode *Computing* a character set for all languages

unicorn 1 an imaginary creature usually depicted as a white horse with one long spiralled horn growing from its forehead 2 *Old Testament* a two-horned animal, thought to be either the rhinoceros or the aurochs: (Deuteronomy 33:17): mistranslation in the Authorized Version of the original Hebrew

unicycle a one-wheeled vehicle driven by pedals, esp one used in a circus, etc. Also called: **monocycle**

unilateral 1 *Law* (of contracts, obligations, etc) made by, affecting, or binding one party only and not involving the other party in reciprocal obligations 2 *Botany* having or designating parts situated or turned to one side of an axis

Unimak Island an island in SW Alaska, in the Aleutian Islands. Length: 113 km (70 miles)

union 1 an association, alliance, or confederation of individuals or groups for a common purpose, esp political 2 a device on a flag representing union, such as another flag depicted in the top left corner 3 a device for coupling or linking parts, such as pipes 4 a an association of students at a university or college formed to look after the students' interests, provide facilities for recreation, etc. b the building or buildings housing the facilities of such an organization 5 *Maths* a set containing all members of two given sets. Symbol: ∪, as in A∪B 6 in 19th-century England a a number of parishes united for the administration of poor relief b a workhouse supported by such a combination 7 *Textiles* a piece of cloth or fabric consisting of two different kinds of yarn

Union the 1 *Brit* a the union of England and Wales from 1543 b the union of the English and Scottish crowns (1603-1707) c the union of England and Scotland from 1707 d the political union of Great Britain and Ireland (1801-1920) e the union of Great Britain and Northern Ireland from 1920 2 *US* a the United States of America b the northern states of the US during the Civil War c (*as modifier*): *Union supporters*

Unionist 1 a (before 1920) a supporter of the union of all Ireland and Great Britain b (since 1920) a supporter of union between Britain and Northern Ireland 2 a supporter of the US federal Union, esp during the Civil War

Union Jack 1 a common name for **Union flag**: the national flag of the United Kingdom being a composite design composed of St George's Cross (England), St Andrew's Cross (Scotland), and Saint Patrick's Cross (Ireland) 2 a national flag flown at the jackstaff of a vessel

unique *Maths* a leading to only one result b having precisely one value

unisexual (of some organisms) having either male or female reproductive organs but not both

unison *Music* a the interval between two sounds of identical pitch b played or sung at the same pitch

unit 1 a mechanical part or integrated assembly of parts that performs a subsidiary function 2 a complete system, apparatus, or establishment that performs a specific function 3 the amount of a drug, vaccine, etc, needed to produce a particular effect 4 a standard measure used in calculating alcohol intake and its effect 5 *Maths* a the first position in a place-value counting system, representing a single-digit number b having a value defined as one for the system 6 *Maths, logic* a set having a single member 7 *NZ* a self-propelled railcar
 ▷www.psigate.ac.uk/newsite/reference/ units.html
 ▷www.ex.ac.uk/cimt/dictunit/dictunit.htm
 ▷www.unc.edu/~rowlett/units/index.html

Unitarian 1 *Theol* a person who believes that God is one being and rejects the doctrine of the Trinity 2 *Ecclesiast* an upholder of Unitarianism, esp a member of the Church (**Unitarian Church**) that embodies this system of belief
 ▷http://uusc.org/
 ▷http://unitarian.org.uk/
 ▷http://cuc.ca/
 ▷http://anzua.org/
 ▷http://unitarian.co.za/

unitary of or relating to a system of government in which all governing authority is held by the central government

unit cost the actual cost of producing one article

unite an English gold coin minted in the Stuart period, originally worth 20 shillings

United Kingdom a kingdom of NW Europe, consisting chiefly of the island of Great Britain together with Northern Ireland: became the world's leading colonial power in the 18th century: the first country to undergo the Industrial Revolution. It became the **United Kingdom of Great Britain and Northern Ireland** in 1921, after the rest of Ireland became autonomous as the Irish Free State. Primarily it is a trading nation, the chief exports being manufactured goods; joined the Common Market (now the European Union) in January 1973. Official language: English; Gaelic, Welsh, and other minority languages. Religion: Christian majority. Currency: pound sterling. Capital: London. Pop: 59 428 000 (2004 est). Area: 244 110 sq km (94 251 sq miles)
 ▷www.ukonline.gov.uk
 ▷www.visitbritain.com

United Nations 1 an international organization of independent states, with its headquarters in New York City, that was formed in 1945 to promote peace and international cooperation and security 2 (in World War

II) a coalition of 26 nations that signed a joint declaration in Jan 1942, pledging their full resources to defeating the Axis powers
▷www.unsystem.org

United States of America a federal republic mainly in North America consisting of 50 states and the District of Columbia: colonized principally by the English and French in the 17th century, the native Indians being gradually defeated and displaced; 13 colonies under British rule made the Declaration of Independence in 1776 and became the United States after the War of American Independence. The northern states defeated the South in the Civil War (1861–65). It is the world's most productive industrial nation and also exports agricultural products. It participated in World Wars I and II but since the establishment of the United Nations in 1945 has played a major role in international affairs. It consists generally of the Rocky Mountains in the west, the Great Plains in the centre, the Appalachians in the east, deserts in the southwest, and coastal lowlands and swamps in the southeast. Language: predominantly English; Spanish is also widely spoken. Religion: Christian majority. Currency: dollar. Capital: Washington, D.C. Pop: 297 043 000 (2004 est). Area: 9 518 323 sq km (3 675 031 sq miles)

unit price a price for foodstuffs, etc, stated or shown as the cost per unit, as per pound, per kilogram, per dozen, etc.

unity 1 *Maths* a the number or numeral one b a quantity assuming the value of one c the element of a set producing no change in a number following multiplication 2 *Art* the arrangement of the elements in a work of art in accordance with a single overall design or purpose 3 any one of the three principles of dramatic structure deriving from Aristotle's *Poetics* by which the action of a play should be limited to a single plot (unity of action), a single location (unity of place), and the events of a single day (unity of time)

univalent 1 (of a chromosome during meiosis) not paired with its homologue 2 *Chem* another word for **monovalent**

universal 1 *Machinery* designed or adapted for a range of sizes, fittings, or uses 2 *Logic* (of a statement or proposition) affirming or denying something about every member of a class, as in *all men are wicked* 3 *Philosophy* a a general term or concept or the type such a term signifies b a metaphysical entity taken to be the reference of a general term, as distinct from the class of individuals it describes c a Platonic Idea or Aristotelian form 4 *Logic* a a universal proposition, statement, or formula b a universal quantifier 5 short for **universal joint**

universal joint *or* **coupling** a form of coupling between two rotating shafts allowing freedom of angular movement in all directions

universe *Astronomy* the aggregate of all existing matter, energy, and space

university 1 an institution of higher education having authority to award bachelors' and higher degrees, usually having research facilities 2 the buildings, members, staff, or campus of a university
▷www.braintrack.com
▷www.unesco.org/iau

unknown *Maths* a variable, or the quantity it represents, the value of which is to be discovered by solving an equation; a variable in a conditional equation

unleaded 1 (of petrol) containing a reduced amount of tetraethyl lead, in order to reduce environmental pollution 2 petrol containing a reduced amount of tetraethyl lead

unmanned 1 (of aircraft, spacecraft, etc) operated by automatic or remote control 2 *Falconry* (of a hawk or falcon) not yet trained to accept humans

unofficial *Med* (of a medicinal drug) not listed in a pharmacopoeia

unorganized *or* **unorganised** *Biology* nonliving; inorganic

unreactive (of a substance) not readily partaking in chemical reactions

unsafe (of a criminal conviction) based on inadequate or false evidence

unsaturated 1 (of a chemical compound, esp an organic compound) containing one or more double or triple bonds and thus capable of undergoing addition reactions 2 (of a fat, esp a vegetable fat) containing a high proportion of fatty acids having double bonds 3 (of a solution) containing less solute than a saturated solution

unseen 1 (of passages of writing) not previously seen or prepared 2 *Chiefly Brit* a passage, not previously seen, that is presented to students for translation

unsound *Business* of doubtful financial or commercial viability

unstable 1 (of a chemical compound) readily decomposing 2 *Physics* a (of an elementary particle) having a very short lifetime b spontaneously decomposing by nuclear decay; radioactive 3 *Electronics* (of an electrical circuit, mechanical body, etc) having a tendency to self-oscillation

Unter den Linden the main street of Berlin, formerly in East Berlin, extending to the Brandenburg Gate

Unterwalden a canton of central Switzerland, on Lake Lucerne: consists of the demicantons of **Nidwalden** (east) and **Obwalden** (west). Capitals: (Nidwalden) Stans; (Obwalden) Sarnen. Pop: (Nidwalden) 38 900 (2002 est); (Obwalden) 33 000 (2002 est). Areas: (Nidwalden) 274 sq km (107 sq miles); (Obwalden) 492 sq km (192 sq miles)

up *Transport* of or relating to a train or trains to a more important place or one regarded as higher

upbeat *Music* a a usually unaccented beat, esp the last in a bar b the upward gesture of a conductor's baton indicating this

upbringing the education of a person during his formative years

upcountry 1 of or coming from the interior of a country or region 2 the interior part of a region or country

Updike **John** (**Hoyer**). born 1932, US writer. His novels include *Rabbit, Run* (1960), *Couples* (1968), *The Coup* (1979), *Brazil* (1993), *Seek My Face* (2003), and *Rabbit is Rich* (1982) and *Rabbit at Rest* (1990), both of which won Pulitzer prizes

upgrade 1 *US and Canadian* an upward slope 2 *US and Canadian* going or sloping upwards

upland an area of high or relatively high ground

uplift the process or result of land being raised to a higher level, as during a period of mountain building

Upolu an island in the SW central Pacific, in Samoa. Chief town: Apia. Pop: 134 400 (2001). Area: 1114 sq km (430 sq miles)

upper 1 *Geology, archaeol* denoting the late part or division of a period, system, formation, etc. 2 *Maths* (of a limit or bound) greater than or equal to one or more numbers or variables

Upper Austria a state of N Austria: first divided from Lower Austria in 1251. Capital: Linz. Pop: 1 387 086 (2003 est). Area: 11 978 sq km (4625 sq miles)

Upper Canada 1 *History* (from 1791–1841) the official name of the region of Canada lying southwest of the Ottawa River and north of the lower Great Lakes 2 (esp in E Canada) another name for **Ontario**

upper class *US, Education* of or relating to the junior or senior classes of a college or high school

uppercut *Boxing* a short swinging upward blow with the fist delivered at an opponent's chin

Upper Egypt one of the four main traditional administrative districts of Egypt: extends south from Cairo to the Sudan

Upper Peninsula a peninsula in the northern US between Lakes Superior and Michigan, constituting the N part of the state of Michigan

Upper Silesia a region of SW Poland, formerly ruled by Germany: coal mining and other heavy industry

Uppsala *or* **Upsala** a city in E central Sweden: the royal headquarters in the 13th century; Gothic cathedral (the largest in Sweden) and Sweden's oldest university (1477). Pop: 182 124 (2004 est)

upright piano a piano which has a rectangular vertical case

upset 1 a tool used to upset a bar or rivet; swage 2 a forging or bar that has been upset in preparation for further processing

upshot *Archery* the final shot in a match

upstage *Theatre* the back half of the stage

upstanding be upstanding a (in a court of law) a direction to all persons present to rise to their feet before the judge enters or leaves the court b (at a formal dinner) a direction to all persons present to rise to their feet for a toast

upstream 1 in or towards the higher part of a stream; against the current 2 (in the oil industry) of or for any of the stages prior to oil production, such as exploration or research

upswing *Economics* a recovery period in the trade cycle

upthrust *Geology* a violent upheaval of the earth's surface

uptown *US and Canadian* 1 towards, in, or relating to some part of a town that is away from the centre 2 such a part of a town, esp a residential part

upwind 1 going against the wind 2 on the windward side

Ur an ancient city of Sumer located on a former channel of the Euphrates

Ural a river in central Russia, rising in the S Ural Mountains and flowing south to the Caspian Sea. Length: 2534 km (1575 miles)

uranium a radioactive silvery-white metallic element

of the actinide series. It occurs in several minerals including pitchblende, carnotite, and autunite and is used chiefly as a source of nuclear energy by fission of the radioisotope **uranium-235**. Symbol: U; atomic no.: 92; atomic wt.: 238.0289; half-life of most stable isotope, ^{238}U: 451 × 10^9 years; valency: 2-6; relative density: 18.95 (approx.); melting pt.: 1135°C; boiling pt.: 4134°C

Uranus[1] *Greek myth* the personification of the sky, who, as a god, ruled the universe and fathered the Titans and Cyclopes on his wife and mother Gaea (earth). He was overthrown by his son Cronus

Uranus[2] one of the giant planets, the seventh planet from the sun, sometimes visible to the naked eye. It has about 15 satellites, a ring system, and an axis of rotation almost lying in the plane of the orbit. Mean distance from sun: 2870 million km; period of revolution around sun: 84 years; period of axial rotation: 17.23 hours; diameter and mass: 4 and 14.5 times that of earth respectively

urban 1 of, relating to, or constituting a city or town 2 living in a city or town

Urban II original name *Odo* or *Udo*. ?1042–99, French ecclesiastic; pope (1088–99). He inaugurated the First Crusade at the Council of Clermont (1095)

urchin 1 See **sea urchin** *or* **heart urchin** 2 an archaic or dialect name for a **hedgehog** 3 either of the two cylinders in a carding machine that are covered with carding cloth 4 *Obsolete* an elf or sprite

Urdu an official language of Pakistan, also spoken in India. The script derives primarily from Persia. It belongs to the Indic branch of the Indo-European family of languages, being closely related to Hindi but containing many Arabic and Persian loan words

urea a white water-soluble crystalline compound with a saline taste and often an odour of ammonia, produced by protein metabolism and excreted in urine. A synthetic form is used as a fertilizer, animal feed, and in the manufacture of synthetic resins. Formula: $CO(NH_2)_2$

ureter the tube that conveys urine from the kidney to the urinary bladder or cloaca

urethra the canal that in most mammals conveys urine from the bladder out of the body. In human males it also conveys semen

urethritis inflammation of the urethra

Urey Harold Clayton 1893–1981, US chemist, who discovered the heavy isotope of hydrogen, deuterium (1932), and worked on methods of separating uranium isotopes: Nobel prize for chemistry 1934

Urfa a city in SE Turkey: market centre. Pop: 451 000 (2005 est)

Uri one of the original three cantons of Switzerland, in the centre of the country: mainly German-speaking and Roman Catholic. Capital: Altdorf. Pop: 35 200 (2002 est). Area: 1075 sq km (415 sq miles)

Uriah *Old Testament* a Hittite officer, who was killed in battle on instructions from David so that he could marry Uriah's wife Bathsheba (II Samuel 11)

uric of, concerning, or derived from urine

uric acid a white odourless tasteless crystalline product of protein metabolism, present in the blood and urine; 2,6,8-trihydroxypurine. Formula: $C_5H_4N_4O_3$

urinary *Anatomy* of or relating to urine or to the organs and structures that secrete and pass urine
▷www.urolog.nl

urinary bladder a distensible membranous sac in which the urine excreted from the kidneys is stored

urine the pale yellow slightly acid fluid excreted by the kidneys, containing waste products removed from the blood. It is stored in the urinary bladder and discharged through the urethra

Urmia Lake a shallow lake in NW Iran, at an altitude of 1300 m (4250 ft): the largest lake in Iran, varying in area from 4000–6000 sq km (1500–2300 sq miles) between autumn and spring

Urmston a town in NW England, in Salford unitary authority, Greater Manchester. Pop: 40 964 (2001)

urn *Botany* the spore-producing capsule of a moss

urogenital *or* **urinogenital** of or relating to the urinary and genital organs and their functions

urology the branch of medicine concerned with the study and treatment of diseases of the urogenital tract

ursine of, relating to, or resembling a bear or bears

Ursula Saint a legendary British princess of the fourth or fifth century AD, said to have been martyred together with 11 000 virgins to the Huns at Cologne. Feast day: Oct 21

Uruapan a city in SW Mexico, in Michoacán state: agricultural trading centre. Pop: 282 000 (2005 est)

Uruguay a republic in South America, on the Atlantic: Spanish colonization began in 1624, followed by Portuguese settlement in 1680; revolted against Spanish rule in 1820 but was annexed by the Portuguese to Brazil; gained independence in 1825. It consists mainly of rolling grassy plains, low hills, and plateaus. Official language: Spanish. Religion: Roman Catholic majority. Currency: peso. Capital: Montevideo. Pop: 3 439 000 (2004 est). Area: 176 215 sq km (68 037 sq miles)

Urumchi, Urumqi, *or* **Wu-lu-mu-ch'i** a city in NW China, capital of Xinjiang Uygur Autonomous Region: trading centre on a N route between China and central Asia. Pop: 1 562 000 (2005 est)

USB Universal Serial Bus: a standard for connection sockets on computers and other electronic equipment

use 1 *Christianity* a distinctive form of liturgical or ritual observance, esp one that is traditional in a Church or group of Churches **2** the enjoyment of property, land, etc, by occupation or by deriving revenue or other benefit from it **3** *Law* the beneficial enjoyment of property the legal title to which is held by another person as trustee **4** *Law* an archaic word for **trust 5** *Philosophy, logic, linguistics* the occurrence of an expression in such a context that it performs its own linguistic function rather than being itself referred to. In "*Fido*" *refers to Fido*, the name *Fido* is used only on the second occurrence, first being mentioned

Usenet *Computing* a vast collection of newsgroups that follow agreed naming, maintaining, and distribution practices

user-friendly (of a computer system) easily operated and understood by means of a straightforward guide in jargon-free language

username *Computing* a name that someone uses for identification purposes when logging onto a computer, using chatrooms, or as part of his or her e-mail address

Ushant an island off the NW coast of France, at the tip of Brittany: scene of naval battles in 1778 and 1794 between France and Britain. Area: about 16 sq km (6 sq miles)

usher 1 a person who acts as doorkeeper, esp in a court of law **2** (in England) a minor official charged with maintaining order in a court of law **3** *Brit, obsolete* a teacher

Usk a river in SE Wales, flowing southeast and south to the Bristol Channel. Length: 113 km (70 miles)

Uspallata Pass a pass over the Andes in S South America, between Mendoza (Argentina) and Santiago (Chile). Height: 3840 m (12 600 ft)

Ussuri a river in E central Asia, flowing north, forming part of the Chinese border with Russia, to the Amur River. Length: about 800 km (500 miles)

Ust-Kamenogorsk a city in E Kazakhstan: centre of a zinc-, lead-, and copper-mining area. Pop: 307 000 (2005 est)

Ustyurt *or* **Ust Urt** an arid plateau in central Asia, between the Caspian and Aral seas in Kazakhstan and Uzbekistan. Area: about 238 000 sq km (92 000 sq miles)

Utah a state of the western US: settled by Mormons in 1847; situated in the Great Basin and the Rockies, with the Great Salt Lake in the northwest; mainly arid and mountainous. Capital: Salt Lake City. Pop: 2 351 467 (2003 est). Area: 212 628 sq km (82 096 sq miles)

Utamaro Kitagawa , original name *Kitagawa Nebsuyoshi*. 1753–1806, Japanese master of wood-block prints, of the ukiyo-e school; noted esp for his portraits of women

uterus 1 *Anatomy* a hollow muscular organ lying within the pelvic cavity of female mammals. It houses the developing fetus and by contractions aids in its expulsion at parturition **2** the corresponding organ in other animals

Utica an ancient city on the N coast of Africa, northwest of Carthage

utilitarianism *Ethics* **1** the doctrine that the morally correct course of action consists in the greatest good for the greatest number, that is, in maximizing the total benefit resulting, without regard to the distribution of benefits and burdens **2** the theory that the criterion of virtue is utility

utility 1 a a public service, such as the bus system; public utility **b** (*as modifier*): *utility vehicle* **2** *Economics* **a** the ability of a commodity to satisfy human wants **b** the amount of such satisfaction **3** *Austral and NZ* a small truck with an open body and low sides, often with a removable tarpaulin cover; pick-up **4** a piece of computer software designed for a routine task, such as examining or copying files

Utopia any real or imaginary society, place, state, etc, considered to be perfect or ideal

Utrecht 1 a province of the W central Netherlands. Capital: Utrecht. Pop: 1 152 000 (2003 est). Area: 1362 sq km (526 sq miles) **2** a city in the central Netherlands, capital of Utrecht province: scene of the signing (1579) of the **Union of Utrecht** (the foundation of the later kingdom of the Netherlands) and of the **Treaty of Utrecht** (1713), ending the War of the Spanish Succession. Pop: 265 000 (2003 est)

Utrillo Maurice 1883–1955, French painter, noted for his Parisian street scenes

Uttar Pradesh a state of N India: the most populous state; originated in 1877 with the merging of Agra and Oudh as the United Provinces; augmented by the states of Rampur, Benares, and Tehri-Garhwal in 1949; the N Himalayan region passed to the new state of Uttaranchal in 2000; now consists mostly of the Upper Ganges plain; agricultural. Capital: Lucknow. Pop: 166 052 859 (2001). Area: 243 350 sq km (93 933 sq miles)

utterance *Logic, philosophy* an element of spoken language, esp a sentence

Utzon Jørn born 1918, Danish architect known primarily for his unique design for the Sydney Opera House (1966)

uvula a small fleshy finger-like flap of tissue that hangs in the back of the throat and is an extension of the soft palate

Uxbridge a town in SE England, part of the Greater London borough of Hillingdon since 1965; chiefly residential; seat of Brunel University (1966)

Uxmal an ancient ruined city in SE Mexico, in Yucatán: capital of the later Maya empire

Uzbekistan a republic in central Asia: annexed by Russia in the 19th century, it became a separate Soviet Socialist republic in 1924 and gained independence in 1991; mining, textile, and chemical industries are important. Official language: Uzbek. Religion: believers are mainly Muslim. Currency: sum. Capital: Tashkent. Pop: 26 479 000 (2004 est). Area: 449 600 sq km (173 546 sq miles)

V v

Vaal a river in South Africa, rising in the Drakensberg and flowing west to join the Orange River. Length: 1160 km (720 miles)

Vaasa a port in W Finland, on the Gulf of Bothnia: the provisional capital of Finland (1918); textile industries. Pop: 56 953 (2003 est)

vacancy *Physics* a defect in a crystalline solid caused by the absence of an atom, ion, or molecule from its position in the crystal lattice

vacant *Law* (of an estate, etc) having no heir or claimant

vacation *chiefly Brit* a period of the year when the law courts or universities are closed

vaccine *Med* 1 a suspension of dead, attenuated, or otherwise modified microorganisms (viruses, bacteria, or rickettsiae) for inoculation to produce immunity to a disease by stimulating the production of antibodies 2 (originally) a preparation of the virus of cowpox taken from infected cows and inoculated in humans to produce immunity to smallpox 3 of or relating to vaccination or vaccinia 4 *Computing* a piece of software designed to detect and remove computer viruses from a system

vacuous *Logic, maths* (of an operator or expression) having no import; idle: in (x) (John is tall) the quantifier (x) is vacuous

vacuum 1 a region containing no matter; free space 2 a region in which gas is present at a low pressure 3 the degree of exhaustion of gas within an enclosed space 4 of, containing, measuring, producing, or operated by a low gas pressure

Vadodara a city in W India, in SE Gujarat: textile manufacturing. Pop: 1 306 035 (2001)

Vaduz the capital of Liechtenstein, in the Rhine valley: an old market town, dominated by a medieval castle, residence of the prince of Liechtenstein. Pop: 5005 (2003 est)

vagina 1 the moist canal in most female mammals, including humans, that extends from the cervix of the uterus to an external opening between the labia minora 2 *Anatomy, biology* any sheath or sheathlike structure, such as a leaf base that encloses a stem

vagrant 1 a migratory animal that is off course 2 (of plants) showing uncontrolled or straggling growth

vain to use the name of someone, esp God, without due respect or reverence b *Jocular* to mention someone's name

Vajpayee A(tal) B(ihari). born 1926, Indian politician; prime minister of India (1996, from 1998)

Valais a canton of S Switzerland: includes the entire valley of the upper Rhône and the highest peaks in Switzerland; produces a quarter of Switzerland's hydroelectricity. Capital: Sion. Pop: 281 000 (2002 est). Area: 5231 sq km (2020 sq miles)

valance a short piece of drapery hung along a shelf, canopy, or bed, or across a window, to hide structural detail

Valdemar I, II, *or* **IV** a variant spelling of **Waldemar I, II** *or* **IV**

Val-de-Marne a department of N France, in Île-de-France region. Capital: Créteil. Pop: 1 239 352 (2003 est). Area: 244 sq km (95 sq miles)

Valdivia¹ Pedro de ?1500–54, Spanish soldier; conqueror of Chile

Valdivia² a port in S Chile, on the **Valdivia River** about 19 km (12 miles) from the Pacific: developed chiefly by German settlers in the 1850s; university (1954). Pop: 136 000 (2005 est)

valence *Chem* 1 another name (esp US and Canadian) for **valency** 2 the phenomenon of forming chemical bonds

Valence a town in SE France, on the River Rhône. Pop: 64 260 (1999)

Valencia 1 a port in E Spain, capital of Valencia province, on the Mediterranean: the third largest city in Spain; capital of the Moorish kingdom of Valencia (1021–1238); university (1501). Pop: 780 653 (2003 est) 2 a region and former kingdom of E Spain, on the Mediterranean 3 a city in N Venezuela: one of the two main industrial centres in Venezuela. Pop: 2 330 000 (2005 est)

Valenciennes a town in N France, on the River Escaut: a coal-mining and heavy industrial centre. Pop: 41 278 (1999)

valency *or esp US and Canadian* **valence** 1 *Chem* a property of atoms or groups, equal to the number of atoms of hydrogen that the atom or group could combine with or displace in forming compounds 2 *Immunol* a the number of antigen-

binding sites on an antibody molecule b the number of antigen-binding sites with which an antigen can combine

Valens ?328–378 AD, emperor of the Eastern Roman Empire (364–378); appointed by his elder brother

Valentinian I, emperor of the Western Empire

Valentine Saint 3rd century AD, Christian martyr, associated by historical accident with the custom of sending valentines; bishop of Terni. Feast day: Feb 14

Valentinian I or **Valentinianus I** 321–375 AD, emperor of the Western Roman Empire (364–375); appointed his brother Valens to rule the Eastern Empire

Valentinian II or **Valentinianus II** 371–392 AD, emperor of the Western Roman Empire (375–392), reigning jointly with his half brother Gratian until 383

Valentinian III or **Valentinianus III** ?419–455 AD, emperor of the Western Roman Empire (425–455). His government lost Africa to the Vandals. With Pope Leo I he issued (444) an edict giving the bishop of Rome supremacy over the provincial churches

Valentino Rudolph, original name *Rodolpho Guglielmi di Valentina d'Antonguolla*. 1895–1926, US silent-film actor, born in Italy. He is famous for his romantic roles in such films as *The Sheik* (1921)

Vale of Glamorgan a county borough of S Wales, created in 1996 from parts of South Glamorgan and Mid Glamorgan. Administrative centre: Barry. Pop: 121 200 (2003 est). Area: 295 sq km (114 sq miles)

valerian a sedative drug made from the dried roots of *V. officinalis*

valerian any of various Eurasian valerianaceous plants of the genus *Valeriana*, esp *V. officinalis*, having small white or pinkish flowers and a medicinal root

Valerian Latin name *Publius Licinius Valerianus*. died 260 AD, Roman emperor (253–260): renewed persecution of the Christians; defeated by the Persians

valeta or **veleta** a ballroom dance in triple time

Valhalla, Walhalla, Valhall or **Walhall** *Norse myth* the great hall of Odin where warriors who die as heroes in battle dwell eternally

valid 1 legally acceptable 2 a having legal force; effective b having legal authority; binding 3 *Logic* (of an inference or argument) having premises and conclusion so related that whenever the former are true the latter must also be true, esp (**formally valid**) when the inference is justified by the form of the premises and conclusion alone. Thus *Tom is a bachelor; therefore Tom is unmarried* is valid but not formally so, while *today is hot and dry; therefore today is hot* is formally valid

Valium *Trademark* a brand of diazepam used as a tranquillizer

Valkyrie, Walkyrie, or **Valkyr** *Norse myth* any of the beautiful maidens who serve Odin and ride over battlefields to claim the dead heroes and take them to Valhalla

Valladolid 1 a city in NW Spain: residence of the Spanish court in the 16th century; university (1346). Pop: 321 143 (2003 est) 2 the former name (until 1828) of **Morelia**

Valletta or **Valetta** the capital of Malta, on the NE coast: founded by the Knights Hospitallers, after the victory over the Turks in 1565; became a major naval base after Malta's annexation by Britain (1814). Pop: 84 000 (2005 est)

valley 1 a long depression in the land surface, usually containing a river, formed by erosion or by movements in the earth's crust 2 the broad area drained by a single river system 3 the junction of a roof slope with another or with a wall 4 relating to or proceeding by way of a valley

Valley Forge an area in SE Pennsylvania, northwest of Philadelphia: winter camp (1777–78) of Washington and the American Revolutionary Army

Valley of Ten Thousand Smokes a volcanic region of SW Alaska, formed by the massive eruption of Mount Katmai in 1912; jets of steam issue from vents up to 45 m (150 ft) across

Vallombrosa a village and resort in central Italy, in Tuscany region: 11th-century Benedictine monastery

Valois[1] a royal house of France, ruling from 1328 to 1589

Valois[2] Dame **Ninette de** original name *Edris Stannus*. 1898–2001, British ballet dancer and choreographer, born in Ireland: a founder of the Vic-Wells Ballet Company (1931), which under her direction became the Royal Ballet (1956)

Valois a historic region and former duchy of N France

value 1 *Maths* a a particular magnitude, number, or amount b the particular quantity that is the result of applying a function or operation for some given argument 2 *Music* short for **time value** 3 in painting, drawing, etc a a gradation of tone from light to dark or of colour luminosity b the relation of one of these elements to another or to the whole picture

valve 1 any device that shuts off, starts, regulates, or controls the flow of a fluid 2 *Anatomy* a flaplike structure in a hollow organ, such as the heart, that controls the one-way passage of fluid through that organ 3 *Electronics* an evacuated electron tube containing a cathode, anode, and, usually, one or more additional control electrodes. When a positive potential is applied to the anode, electrons emitted from the cathode are attracted to the anode, constituting a flow of current which can be controlled by a voltage applied to the grid to produce amplification, oscillation, etc. 4 *Zoology* any of the separable pieces that make up the shell of a mollusc 5 *Music* a device on some brass instruments by which the effective length of the tube may be varied to enable a chromatic scale to be produced 6 *Botany* a any of the several parts that make up a dry dehiscent fruit, esp a capsule b either of the two halves of a diatom cell wall 7 *Archaic* a leaf of a double door or of a folding door

vamp *Music* an improvised accompaniment, consisting largely of chords

vampire 1 (in European folklore) a corpse that rises nightly from its grave to drink the blood of the living 2 See **vampire bat** 3 *Theatre* a trapdoor on a stage

vampire bat any bat, esp *Desmodus rotundus*, of the family *Desmodontidae* of tropical regions of Central and South America, having sharp incisor and canine teeth and feeding on the blood of birds and mammals

van 1 a covered motor vehicle for transporting goods, etc, by road 2 *Brit* a closed railway wagon in which the guard travels, for transporting goods, mail, etc. 3 *Brit* See **delivery van**

Van 1 a city in E Turkey, on Lake Van. Pop: 377 000 (2005 est) 2 **Lake** a salt lake in E Turkey, at an altitude of 1650 m (5400 ft): fed by melting snow and glaciers. Area: 3737 sq km (1433 sq miles)

vanadium a toxic silvery-white metallic element occurring chiefly in carnotite and vanadinite and used in steel alloys, high-speed tools, and as a catalyst. Symbol: V; atomic no.: 23; atomic wt.: 50.9415; valency: 2–5; relative density: 6.11; melting pt.: 1910±10°C; boiling pt.: 3409°C

Van Allen James Alfred born 1914, US physicist, noted for his use of satellites to investigate cosmic radiation in the upper atmosphere

Van Allen belt either of two regions of charged particles above the earth, the inner one extending from 2400 to 5600 kilometres above the earth and the outer one from 13 000 to 19 000 kilometres. The charged particles result from cosmic rays and are trapped by the earth's magnetic field

Vanbrugh Sir John 1664–1726, English dramatist and baroque architect. His best-known plays are the Restoration comedies *The Relapse* (1697) and *The Provok'd Wife* (1697). As an architect, he is noted esp for Blenheim Palace

Van Buren Martin 1782–1862, US Democratic statesman; 8th president of the US (1837–41)

Vancouver¹ Captain George 1757–98, English navigator, noted for his exploration of the Pacific coast of North America (1792–94)

Vancouver² 1 **Vancouver Island** an island of SW Canada, off the SW coast of British Columbia: separated from the Canadian mainland by the Strait of Georgia and Queen Charlotte Sound, and from the US mainland by Juan de Fuca Strait; the largest island off the W coast of North America. Chief town: Victoria. Pop: 706 243 (2001). Area: 32 137 sq km (12 408 sq miles) 2 a city in SW Canada, in SW British Columbia: Canada's chief Pacific port, named after Captain George Vancouver: university (1908). Pop: 545 671 (2001) 3 **Mount** a mountain on the border between Canada and Alaska, in the St Elias Mountains. Height: 4785 m (15 700 ft)

Vanderbilt Cornelius, known as *Commodore Vanderbilt.* 1794–1877, US steamship and railway magnate and philanthropist

Van der Post Sir Laurens (Jan). 1906–96, South African writer and traveller. His works include the travel books *Venture to the Interior* (1952), *The Lost World of the Kalahari* (1958), and *Testament to the Bushmen* (1984) and the novels *The Hunter and the Whale* (1967) and *The Admiral's Baby* (1996)

van der Waals Johannes Diderik 1837–1923, Dutch physicist, noted for his research on the equations of state of gases and liquids: Nobel prize for physics in 1910

van der Weyden Rogier ?1400–64, Flemish painter, esp of religious works and portraits

Van Diemen Gulf an inlet of the Timor Sea in N Australia, in the Northern Territory

Van Dyck or **Vandyke** Sir Anthony 1599–1641, Flemish painter; court painter to Charles I of England (1632–41). He is best known for his portraits of the aristocracy

vane 1 a flat plate or blade of metal mounted on a vertical axis in an exposed position to indicate wind direction 2 any one of the flat blades or sails forming part of the wheel of a windmill 3 any flat or shaped plate used to direct fluid flow, esp a stator blade in a turbine, etc. 4 a fin or plate fitted to a projectile or missile to provide stabilization or guidance 5 *Ornithol* the flat part of a feather, consisting of two rows of barbs on either side of

the shaft

van Eyck Jan died 1441, Flemish painter; founder of the Flemish school of painting. His most famous work is the altarpiece *The Adoration of the Lamb*, in Ghent, in which he may have been assisted by his brother **Hubert** , died ?1426

Van Gogh Vincent 1853–90, Dutch postimpressionist painter, noted for his landscapes and portraits, in which colour is used essentially for its expressive and emotive value

vanilla 1 any tropical climbing orchid of the genus *Vanilla,* esp *V. plonifolia,* having spikes of large fragrant greenish-yellow flowers and long fleshy pods containing the seeds (beans) 2 the pod or bean of certain of these plants, used to flavour food, etc.

vanishing point the point to which parallel lines appear to converge in the rendering of perspective, usually on the horizon

Vanua Levu the second largest island of Fiji: mountainous. Area: 5535 sq km (2137 sq miles)

Vanuatu a republic comprising a group of islands in the W Pacific, W of Fiji: a condominium under Anglo-French joint rule from 1906; attained partial autonomy in 1978 and full independence in 1980 as a member of the Commonwealth. Its economy is based chiefly on copra. Official languages: Bislama; French; English. Religion: Christian majority. Currency: vatu. Capital: Vila (on Efate). Pop: 217 000 (2004 est). Area: about 14 760 sq km (5700 sq miles)

vapour or US **vapor** 1 particles of moisture or other substance suspended in air and visible as clouds, smoke, etc. 2 a gaseous substance at a temperature below its critical temperature 3 a substance that is in a gaseous state at a temperature below its boiling point

Var 1 a department of SE France, in Provence-Alpes-Côte-d'Azur region. Capital: Toulon. Pop: 946 305 (2003 est). Area: 6023 sq km (2349 sq miles) 2 a river in SE France, flowing southeast and south to the Mediterranean near Nice. Length: about 130 km (80 miles)

Varah (Edward) Chad born 1911, British Anglican clergyman, who founded (1953) the Samaritans counselling service

Varanasi a city in NE India, in SE Uttar Pradesh on the River Ganges: probably dates from the 13th century BC; an early centre of Aryan philosophy and religion; a major place of pilgrimage for Hindus, Jains, Sikhs, and Buddhists, with many ghats along the Ganges; seat of the Banaras Hindu University (1916), India's leading university, and the Sanskrit University (1957). Pop: 1 100 748 (2001)

Vardar a river in S Europe, rising in W Macedonia and flowing northeast, then south past Skopje into Greece, where it is called the Axios and enters the Aegean at Thessaloníki. Length: about 320 km (200 miles)

Varese a historic city in N Italy, in Lombardy near Lake Varese: manufacturing centre, esp for leather goods. Pop: 80 511 (2001)

Vargas Getúlio Dornelles 1883–1954, Brazilian statesman; president (1930–45; 1951–54)

Vargas Llosa (Jorge) Mario (Pedro) born 1936, Peruvian novelist, writer, and political figure. His novels include

The City and the Dogs (1963), Conversation in the Cathedral (1969), The Storyteller (1990), and The Notebook of Don Rigoberto (1998). In 1990 he stood unsuccessfully for the presidency of Peru

variable 1 *Maths* having a range of possible values 2 (of a species, characteristic, etc) liable to deviate from the established type 3 (of a wind) varying its direction and intensity 4 (of an electrical component or device) designed so that a characteristic property, such as resistance, can be varied 5 *Maths* a an expression that can be assigned any of a set of values b a symbol, esp *x*, *y*, or *z*, representing an unspecified member of a class of objects, numbers, etc. 6 *Logic* a symbol, esp *x*, *y*, *z*, representing any member of a class of entities 7 *Computing* a named unit of storage that can be changed to any of a set of specified values during execution of a program

variance 1 a difference or discrepancy between two steps in a legal proceeding, esp between a statement in a pleading and the evidence given to support it 2 (in the US and Canada) a licence or authority issued by the board of variance to contravene the usual rule, esp to build contrary to the provision of a zoning code 3 *Chem* the number of degrees of freedom of a system, used in the phase rule

variation 1 *Music* a a repetition of a musical theme in which the rhythm, harmony, or melody is altered or embellished b (*as modifier*): *variation form* 2 *Biology* a a marked deviation from the typical form or function b a characteristic or an organism showing this deviation 3 *Astronomy* any change in or deviation from the mean motion or orbit of a planet, satellite, etc, esp a perturbation of the moon 4 another word for **magnetic declination** 5 *Ballet* a solo dance

varicoloured *or US* **varicolored** having many colours; variegated; motley

varicose veins a condition in which the superficial veins, esp of the legs, become tortuous, knotted, and swollen: caused by a defect in the venous valves or in the venous pump that normally moves the blood out of the legs when standing for long periods

variegated (of foliage or flowers) having pale patches, usually as a result of mutation, infection, etc.

variety 1 a *Taxonomy* a race whose distinct characters are insufficient to justify classification as a separate species; a subspecies b *Horticulture, stockbreeding* a strain of animal or plant produced by artificial breeding 2 a entertainment consisting of a series of short unrelated performances or acts, such as comedy turns, songs, dances, sketches, etc. b (*as modifier*): *a variety show*

varifocal 1 *Optics* having a focus that can vary 2 relating to a lens that is graduated to permit any length of vision between near and distant

varlet *Archaic* 1 a menial servant 2 a knight's page 3 a rascal

Varna a port in NE Bulgaria, on the Black Sea: founded by Greeks in the 6th century BC; under the Ottoman Turks (1391–1878). Pop: 340 000 (2005 est)

varnish 1 a preparation consisting of a solvent, a drying oil, and usually resin, rubber, bitumen, etc, for application to a surface where it polymerizes to yield a hard glossy, usually transparent, coating 2 a similar preparation consisting of a substance, such as shellac or cel-

lulose ester, dissolved in a volatile solvent, such as alcohol. It hardens to a film on evaporation of the solvent 3 the sap of certain trees used to produce such a coating

Varro Marcus Terentius 116–27 BC, Roman scholar and satirist

varsity *Brit, NZ, and South African, informal* short for **university**: formerly used esp at the universities of Oxford and Cambridge

vas *Anatomy, zoology* a vessel, duct, or tube that carries a fluid

Vasari Giorgio 1511–74, Italian architect, painter, and art historian, noted for his *Lives of the Most Excellent Italian Architects, Painters, and Sculptors* (1550; 1568), a principal source for the history of Italian Renaissance art

vascular *Biology, anatomy* of, relating to, or having vessels that conduct and circulate liquids

vas deferens *Anatomy* the duct that conveys spermatozoa from the epididymis to the urethra

vasectomy surgical removal of all or part of the vas deferens, esp as a method of contraception

Vashti *Old Testament* the wife of the Persian king Ahasuerus: deposed for refusing to display her beauty before his guests (Esther 1–2)

vassal 1 (in feudal society) a man who entered into a personal relationship with a lord to whom he paid homage and fealty in return for protection and often a fief. A **great vassal** was in vassalage to a king and a **rear vassal** to a great vassal 2 of or relating to a vassal

VAT in Britain value-added tax: a tax levied on the difference between the cost of materials and the selling price of a commodity or service

Vatican 1 a the palace of the popes in Rome and their principal residence there since 1377, which includes administrative offices, a library, museum, etc, and is attached to the basilica of St Peter's b (*as modifier*): *the Vatican Council* 2 a the authority of the Pope and the papal curia b (*as modifier*): *a Vatican edict*

Vatican City an independent state forming an enclave in Rome, with extraterritoriality over 12 churches and palaces in Rome: the only remaining Papal State; independence recognized by the Italian government in 1929; contains St Peter's Basilica and Square and the Vatican; the spiritual and administrative centre of the Roman Catholic Church. Languages: Italian and Latin. Currency: euro. Pop: 1000 (2003 est). Area: 44 hectares (109 acres)

Vaucluse a department of SE France, in Provence-Alpes-Côte-d'Azur region. Capital: Avignon. Pop: 517 810 (2003 est). Area: 3578 sq km (1395 sq miles)

Vaud a canton of SW Switzerland: mountainous in the southeast; chief Swiss producer of wine. Capital: Lausanne. Pop: 632 000 (2002 est). Area: 3209 sq km (1240 sq miles)

vaudeville 1 *Chiefly US and Canadian* variety entertainment consisting of short acts such as acrobatic turns, song-and-dance routines, animal acts, etc, popular esp in the early 20th century 2 a light or comic theatrical piece interspersed with songs and dances
▷http://memory.loc.gov/ammem/vshtml/ vshome.html
▷www.theatrelinks.com

Vaughan 1 Henry 1622–95, Welsh mystic poet, best

known for his *Silex Scintillans* (1650; 1655) **2** Dame **Janet** (**Maria**). 1899–1993, British physician and university official: helped set up Britain's first National Blood Transfusion Service (1939): after World War II, became Britain's expert on the effects of radiation on humans; Principal of Somerville College, Oxford (1945–67) **3** **Sarah** (**Lois**). 1924–90, US jazz vocalist and pianist, noted esp for her skill in vocal improvisation

Vaughan Williams Ralph 1872–1958, English composer, inspired by British folk songs and music of the Tudor period. He wrote operas, symphonies, hymns, and choral music

vault¹ **1** an arched structure that forms a roof or ceiling **2** *Anatomy* any arched or domed bodily cavity or space

vault² *Dressage* a low leap; curvet

vaulting one or more vaults in a building or such structures considered collectively

Vauxhall **1** a district in London, on the south bank of the Thames **2** a public garden at Vauxhall, laid out in 1661; a fashionable meeting place and site of lavish entertainments. Closed in 1859

veal a calf, esp one bred for eating

vector **1** *Maths* a variable quantity, such as force, that has magnitude and direction and can be resolved into components that are odd functions of the coordinates. It is represented in print by a bold italic symbol: **F** **2** *Maths* an element of a vector space **3** *Pathol* an organism, esp an insect, that carries a disease-producing microorganism from one host to another, either within or on the surface of its body **4** *Genetics* an agent, such as a bacteriophage or a plasmid, by means of which a fragment of foreign DNA is inserted into a host cell to produce a gene clone in genetic engineering **5** the course or compass direction of an aircraft

Veda any or all of the most ancient sacred writings of Hinduism, esp the Rig-Veda, Yajur-Veda, Sama-Veda, and Atharva-Veda

vegetable **1** any of various herbaceous plants having parts that are used as food, such as peas, beans, cabbage, potatoes, cauliflower, and onions **2** *Rare* any member of the plant kingdom
▷www.vegetablepatch.net
▷www.vegkitchen.com
▷www.vegetarianrecipe.com
▷www.gardenguides.com/Vegetables/
  vegetabl.htm
▷www.doityourself.com/vegetables
▷www.cityfarmer.org
▷http://gardening.about.com/cs/edibles

vegetable marrow **1** a cucurbitaceous plant, *Cucurbita pepo*, probably native to America but widely cultivated for its oblong green striped fruit, which is eaten as a vegetable **2** the fruit of this plant

vegetable oil any of a group of oils that are esters of fatty acids and glycerol and are obtained from plants

vegetal of or relating to processes in plants and animals that do not involve sexual reproduction; vegetative

vegetation **1** plant life as a whole, esp the plant life of a particular region **2** the process of vegetating **3** *Pathol* any abnormal growth, excrescence, etc.

vegetative **1** of, relating to, or denoting the nonreproductive parts of a plant, i.e. the stems, leaves, and roots, or growth that does not involve the reproductive parts **2** (of reproduction) characterized by asexual processes **3** of or relating to functions such as digestion, growth, and circulation rather than sexual reproduction

vehicle **1** any conveyance in or by which people or objects are transported, esp one fitted with wheels **2** *Pharmacol* a therapeutically inactive substance mixed with the active ingredient to give bulk to a medicine **3** a painting medium, such as oil, in which pigments are suspended **4** (in the performing arts) a play, musical composition, etc, that enables a particular performer to display his talents

Veii an ancient Etruscan city, northwest of Rome: destroyed by the Romans in 396 BC

veil **1** the veil the life of a nun in a religious order and the obligations entailed by it **2** *Botany* a membranous structure, esp the thin layer of cells connecting the edge of a young mushroom cap with the stipe **3** *Anatomy* another word for **caul**

vein **1** any of the tubular vessels that convey oxygen-depleted blood to the heart **2** any of the hollow branching tubes that form the supporting framework of an insect's wing **3** any of the vascular strands of a leaf **4** a clearly defined mass of ore, mineral, etc, filling a fault or fracture, often with a tabular or sheetlike shape **5** a natural underground watercourse

Velcro *Trademark* a fastening consisting of two strips of nylon fabric, one having tiny hooked threads and the other a coarse surface, that form a strong bond when pressed together

veld *or* **veldt** elevated open grassland in Southern Africa

Vellore a town in SE India, in NE Tamil Nadu: medical centre. Pop: 177 413 (2001)

velocipede **1** an early form of bicycle propelled by pushing along the ground with the feet **2** any early form of bicycle or tricycle

velocity *Physics* a measure of the rate of motion of a body expressed as the rate of change of its position in a particular direction with time. It is measured in metres per second, miles per hour, etc.

velour *or* **velours** any of various fabrics with a velvet-like finish, used for upholstery, coats, hats, etc.

Velsen a port in the W Netherlands, in North Holland at the mouth of the canal connecting Amsterdam with the North Sea: fishing and heavy industrial centre. Pop: 68 000 (2003 est)

velvet **1** **a** a fabric of silk, cotton, nylon, etc, with a thick close soft usually lustrous pile **b** (*as modifier*): *velvet curtains* **2** the furry covering of the newly formed antlers of a deer **3** *Slang, chiefly US* **a** gambling or speculative winnings **b** a gain, esp when unexpectedly high

velveteen **a** a cotton fabric resembling velvet with a short thick pile, used for clothing, etc. **b** (*as modifier*): *velveteen trousers*

vending machine a machine that automatically dispenses consumer goods such as cigarettes, food, or petrol, when money is inserted

vendor *or* **vender** **1** *Chiefly law* a person who sells something, esp real property **2** another name for **vending machine**

venerable 1 *RC Church* a title bestowed on a deceased person when the first stage of his canonization has been accomplished and his holiness has been recognized in a decree of the official Church **2** *Church of England* a title given to an archdeacon

venereal 1 (of a disease) transmitted by sexual intercourse **2** of, relating to, or involving the genitals

venereal disease any of various diseases, such as syphilis or gonorrhoea, transmitted by sexual intercourse

Venetia 1 the area of ancient Italy between the lower Po valley and the Alps: later a Roman province **2** the territorial possessions of the medieval Venetian republic that were at the head of the Adriatic and correspond to the present-day region of Veneto and a large part of Friuli-Venezia Giulia

Venetian 1 of, relating to, or characteristic of Venice or its inhabitants **2** a native or inhabitant of Venice **3** a cotton or woollen cloth used for linings

Veneto a region of NE Italy, on the Adriatic: mountainous in the north with a fertile plain in the south, crossed by the Rivers Po, Adige, and Piave. Capital: Venice. Pop: 4 577 408 (2003 est). Area: 18 377 sq km (7095 sq miles)

Venezia Giulia a former region of NE Italy at the N end of the Adriatic: divided between Yugoslavia and Italy after World War II; now divided between Italy and Slovenia

Venezuela 1 a republic in South America, on the Caribbean: colonized by the Spanish in the 16th century; independence from Spain declared in 1811 and won in 1819 after a war led by Simón Bolívar. It contains Lake Maracaibo and the northernmost chains of the Andes in the northwest, the Orinoco basin in the central part, and the Guiana Highlands in the south. Exports: petroleum, iron ore, and coffee. Official language: Spanish. Religion: Roman Catholic majority. Currency: bolívar. Capital: Caracas. Pop: 26 170 000 (2004 est). Area: 912 050 sq km (352 142 sq miles) **2** *Gulf of* an inlet of the Caribbean in NW Venezuela: continues south as Lake Maracaibo

Venice a port in NE Italy, capital of Veneto region, built on over 100 islands and mud flats in the **Lagoon of Venice** (an inlet of the **Gulf of Venice** at the head of the Adriatic): united under the first doge in 697 AD; became an independent republic and a great commercial and maritime power, defeating Genoa, the greatest rival, in 1380; contains the Grand Canal and about 170 smaller canals, providing waterways for city transport. Pop: 271 073 (2001)

Venlo *or* **Venloo** a city in the SE Netherlands, in Limburg on the Maas River. Pop: 92 000 (2003 est)

Venn diagram *Maths, logic* a diagram in which mathematical sets or terms of a categorial statement are represented by overlapping circles within a boundary representing the universal set, so that all possible combinations of the relevant properties are represented by the various distinct areas in the diagram

venom a poisonous fluid secreted by such animals as certain snakes and scorpions and usually transmitted by a bite or sting

venous 1 *Physiol* of or relating to the blood circulating in the veins **2** of or relating to the veins

vent 1 the shaft of a volcano or an aperture in the earth's crust through which lava and gases erupt **2** the external opening of the urinary or genital systems of lower vertebrates

ventilator *Med* a machine that maintains a flow of air into and out of the lungs of a patient who is unable to breathe normally

ventral 1 relating to the front part of the body; towards the belly **2** of, relating to, or situated on the upper or inner side of a plant organ, esp a leaf, that is facing the axis

ventricle *Anatomy* **1** a chamber of the heart, having thick muscular walls, that receives blood from the atrium and pumps it to the arteries **2** any one of the four main cavities of the vertebrate brain, which contain cerebrospinal fluid **3** any of various other small cavities in the body

ventriloquism *or* **ventriloquy** the art of producing vocal sounds that appear to come from another source
 ▷www.bbk.ac.uk/eh/dumbstruck/archive
 ▷www.axtell.com/learn.html
 ▷www.comediansusa.com/vents/index.html

Ventris Michael George Francis 1922–56, English architect and scholar, who deciphered the Linear B script, identifying it as an early form of Mycenaean Greek

venture a a commercial undertaking characterized by risk of loss as well as opportunity for profit **b** the merchandise, money, or other property placed at risk in such an undertaking

Venturi Robert born 1925, US architect, a pioneer of the postmodernist style. His writings include *Complexity and Contradiction in Architecture* (1966)

venue *Law* **a** the place in which a cause of action arises **b** the place fixed for the trial of a cause **c** the locality from which the jurors must be summoned to try a particular cause

Venus¹ 1 the Roman goddess of love **2** mount of Venus See **mons veneris**

Venus² 1 one of the inferior planets and the second nearest to the sun, visible as a bright morning or evening star. Its surface is extremely hot (over 400°C) and is completely shrouded by dense cloud. The atmosphere is principally carbon dioxide. Mean distance from sun: 108 million km; period of revolution around sun: 225 days; period of axial rotation: 244.3 days (retrograde motion); diameter and mass: 96.5 and 81.5 per cent that of earth respectively **2** the alchemical name for **copper**

Venusberg a mountain in central Germany: contains caverns that, according to medieval legend, housed the palace of the goddess Venus

Veracruz 1 a state of E Mexico, on the Gulf of Mexico: consists of a hot humid coastal strip with lagoons, rising rapidly inland to the central plateau and Sierra Madre Oriental. Capital: Jalapa. Pop: 630 000 (2005 est). Area: 72 815 sq km (28 114 sq miles) **2** the chief port of Mexico, in Veracruz state on the Gulf of Mexico. Pop: 410 000 (2000 est)

verbena 1 any plant of the verbenaceous genus *Verbena*, chiefly of tropical and temperate America, having red, white, or purple fragrant flowers: much cultivated as garden plants **2** any of various similar or related plants, esp the lemon verbena

Vercelli a city in NW Italy, in Piedmont: an ancient Ligurian and later Roman city; has an outstanding library of manuscripts (notably the *Codex Vercellensis*, dating from the 10th century). Pop: 45 132 (2001)

Vercingetorix died ?45 BC, Gallic chieftain and hero, executed for leading a revolt against the Romans under Julius Caesar (52 BC)

Verde Cape a cape in Senegal, near Dakar: the westernmost point of Africa

Verdi Giuseppe 1813–1901, Italian composer of operas, esp *Rigoletto* (1851), *Il Trovatore* (1853), *La Traviata* (1853), and *Aïda* (1871)

verdict the findings of a jury on the issues of fact submitted to it for examination and trial; judgment

verdigris 1 a green or bluish patina formed on copper, brass, or bronze and consisting of a basic salt of copper containing both copper oxide and a copper salt **2** a green or blue crystalline substance obtained by the action of acetic acid on copper and used as a fungicide and pigment; basic copper acetate

Verdun 1 a fortified town in NE France, on the Meuse: scene of the longest and most severe battle (1916) of World War I, in which the French repelled a powerful German offensive. Pop: 19 624 (1999) **2 Treaty of** an agreement reached in 843 AD by three grandsons of Charlemagne, dividing his empire into an E kingdom (later Germany), a W kingdom (later France), and a middle kingdom (containing what became the Low Countries, Lorraine, Burgundy, and N Italy)

Vereeniging a city in E South Africa: scene of the signing (1902) of the treaty ending the Boer War. Pop: 79 630 (2001)

verge 1 *Architect* the edge of the roof tiles projecting over a gable **2** *Architect* the shaft of a classical column **3** *English legal history* **a** the area encompassing the royal court that is subject to the jurisdiction of the Lord High Steward **b** a rod or wand carried as a symbol of office or emblem of authority, as in the Church **c** a rod held by a person swearing fealty to his lord on becoming a tenant, esp of copyhold land

verger *Chiefly Church of England* **1** a church official who acts as caretaker and attendant, looking after the interior of a church and often the vestments and church furnishings **2** an official who carries the verge or rod of office before a bishop, dean, or other dignitary in ceremonies and processions

Verlaine Paul 1844–96, French poet. His verse includes *Poèmes saturniens* (1866), *Fêtes galantes* (1869) and *Romances sans paroles* (1874). He was closely associated with Rimbaud and was a precursor of the symbolists

Vermeer Jan full name *Jan van der Meer van Delft.* 1632–75, Dutch genre painter, noted esp for his masterly treatment of light

vermiform appendix or **process** a wormlike pouch extending from the lower end of the caecum in some mammals. In man it is vestigial

vermilion or **vermillion 1** a bright red to reddish-orange colour **2** mercuric sulphide, esp when used as a bright red pigment; cinnabar

vermin small animals collectively, esp insects and rodents, that are troublesome to man, domestic animals, etc.

Vermont a state in the northeastern US: crossed from north to south by the Green Mountains; bounded on the east by the Connecticut River and by Lake Champlain in the northwest. Capital: Montpelier. Pop: 619 107 (2003 est). Area: 24 887 sq km (9609 sq miles)

vermouth any of several wines containing aromatic herbs and some other flavourings

vernacular 1 a local style of architecture, in which ordinary houses are built **2** designating or relating to the common name of an animal or plant **3** built in the local style of ordinary houses, rather than a grand architectural style

Verne Jules 1828–1905, French writer, esp of science fiction, such as *Twenty Thousand Leagues under the Sea* (1870) and *Around the World in Eighty Days* (1873)

vernier 1 a small movable scale running parallel to the main graduated scale in certain measuring instruments, such as theodolites, used to obtain a fractional reading of one of the divisions on the main scale **2** an auxiliary device for making a fine adjustment to an instrument, usually by means of a fine screw thread

Verona a city in N Italy, in Veneto on the Adige River: strategically situated at the junction of major routes between Italy and N Europe; became a Roman colony (89 BC); under Austrian rule (1797–1866); many Roman remains. Pop: 253 208 (2001)

Veronese Paolo , original name *Paolo Cagliari* or *Caliari.* 1528–88, Italian painter of the Venetian school. His works include *The Marriage at Cana* (1563) and *The Feast of the Levi* (1573)

veronica¹ *RC Church* **1** the representation of the face of Christ that, according to legend, was miraculously imprinted upon the headcloth that Saint Veronica offered him on his way to his crucifixion **2** the cloth itself **3** any similar representation of Christ's face

veronica² *Bullfighting* a pass in which the matador slowly swings the cape away from the charging bull

veronica³ any scrophulariaceous plant of the genus *Veronica*, esp the speedwells, of temperate and cold regions, having small blue, pink, or white flowers and flattened notched fruits

Verrazano or **Verrazzano** Giovanni da ?1485–?1528, Florentine navigator; the first European to sight what was to become New York (1524)

Verrocchio Andrea del 1435–88, Italian sculptor, painter, and goldsmith of the Florentine school: noted esp for the equestrian statue of Bartolommeo Colleoni in Venice

verruca 1 *Pathol* a wart, esp one growing on the hand or foot **2** *Biology* a wartlike outgrowth, as in certain plants or on the skin of some animals

Versace 1 Donatella born 1955, Italian fashion designer and businesswoman; creative director of the Versace group from 1997 **2** Gianni 1946–97, Italian fashion designer

Versailles 1 a city in N central France, near Paris: site of an elaborate royal residence built for Louis XIV; seat of the French kings (1682–1789). Pop: 85 726 (1999) **2 Treaty of Versailles a** the treaty of 1919 imposed upon Germany by the Allies (except for the US and the Soviet

Union): the most important of the five peace treaties that concluded World War I **b** another name for the (Treaty of) **Paris** of 1783

versatile 1 *Botany* (of an anther) attached to the filament by a small area so that it moves freely in the wind 2 *Zoology* able to turn forwards and backwards

verse 1 (not in technical usage) a stanza or other short subdivision of a poem 2 poetry as distinct from prose 3 **a** a series of metrical feet forming a rhythmic unit of one line **b** (*as modifier*): *verse line* 4 a specified type of metre or metrical structure 5 one of the series of short subsections into which most of the writings in the Bible are divided 6 a metrical composition; poem

version a translation, esp of the Bible, from one language into another

vertebra one of the bony segments of the spinal column

vertebrate 1 any chordate animal of the subphylum *Vertebrata*, characterized by a bony or cartilaginous skeleton and a well-developed brain: the group contains fishes, amphibians, reptiles, birds, and mammals 2 of, relating to, or belonging to the subphylum *Vertebrata*

vertex 1 *Maths* **a** the point opposite the base of a figure **b** the point of intersection of two sides of a plane figure or angle **c** the point of intersection of a pencil of lines or three or more planes of a solid figure 2 *Astronomy* a point in the sky towards which a star stream appears to move 3 *Anatomy* the crown of the head

vertical 1 *Economics* of or relating to associated or consecutive, though not identical, stages of industrial activity 2 *Anatomy* of, relating to, or situated at the top of the head (vertex) 3 a vertical plane, position, or line

vertigo *Pathol* a sensation of dizziness or abnormal motion resulting from a disorder of the sense of balance

vervain any of several verbenaceous plants of the genus *Verbena*, having square stems and long slender spikes of purple, blue, or white flowers

Verwoerd Hendrik Frensch 1901–66, South African statesman, born in the Netherlands: prime minister of South Africa (1958–66) and the principal architect of the apartheid system: assassinated

Vesalius Andreas 1514–64, Flemish anatomist, whose *De Humani Corporis fabrica* (1543) formed the basis of modern anatomical research and medicine

vesicle 1 *Pathol* **a** any small sac or cavity, esp one containing serous fluid **b** a blister 2 *Geology* a rounded cavity within a rock formed during solidification by expansion of the gases present in the magma 3 *Botany* a small bladder-like cavity occurring in certain seaweeds and aquatic plants

Vespasian Latin name *Titus Flavius Sabinus Vespasianus*. 9–79 AD, Roman emperor (69–79), who consolidated Roman rule, esp in Britain and Germany. He began the building of the Colosseum

vespers 1 *Chiefly RC Church* the sixth of the seven canonical hours of the divine office, originally fixed for the early evening and now often made a public service on Sundays and major feast days 2 another word for **evensong**

Vespucci Amerigo , Latin name *Americus Vespucius*. ?1454–1512, Florentine navigator in the New World

(1499–1500; 1501–02), after whom the continent of America was named

vessel 1 a passenger or freight-carrying ship, boat, etc. 2 an aircraft, esp an airship 3 *Anatomy* a tubular structure that transports such body fluids as blood and lymph 4 *Botany* a tubular element of xylem tissue consisting of a row of cells in which the connecting cell walls have broken down

vestal virgin (in ancient Rome) one of the four, later six, virgin priestesses whose lives were dedicated to Vesta and to maintaining the sacred fire in her temple

vested *Property law* having a present right to the immediate or future possession and enjoyment of property

vested interest *Property law* an existing and disposable right to the immediate or future possession and enjoyment of property

vestibule any small bodily cavity or space at the entrance to a passage or canal

vestige *Biology* an organ or part of an organism that is a small nonfunctioning remnant of a functional organ in an ancestor

Vestmannaeyjar a group of islands off the S coast of Iceland: they include the island of Surtsey (emerged 1963) and the volcano Helgafell (erupted 1974). Pop: 4888 (1994)

vestry 1 a room in or attached to a church in which vestments, sacred vessels, etc, are kept 2 a room in or attached to some churches, used for Sunday school, meetings, etc. 3 *Church of England* **a** a meeting of all the members of a parish or their representatives, to transact the official business of the parish **b** the body of members meeting for this; the parish council 4 *Episcopalian (US) and Anglican (Canadian) Churches* a committee of vestrymen chosen by the congregation to manage the temporal affairs of their church

Vesuvius a volcano in SW Italy, on the Bay of Naples: first recorded eruption in 79 AD, which destroyed Pompeii, Herculaneum, and Stabiae; numerous eruptions since then. Average height: 1220 m (4003 ft)

vetch 1 any of various climbing leguminous plants of the temperate genus *Vicia*, esp *V. sativa*, having pinnate leaves, typically blue or purple flowers, and tendrils on the stems 2 any of various similar and related plants, such as *Lathyrus sativus*, cultivated in parts of Europe, and the kidney vetch 3 the beanlike fruit of any of these plants

veteran car *Brit* a car constructed before 1919, esp one constructed before 1905

veterinary medicine *or* **science** the branch of medicine concerned with the health of animals and the treatment of injuries or diseases that affect them
▷www.merckvetmanual.com/mvm/index.jsp
▷http://vetmedicine.about.com/

veterinary surgeon *Brit* a person suitably qualified and registered to practise veterinary medicine

veto *US, Government* a document containing the reasons why a chief executive has vetoed a measure

vexatious *Law* (of a legal action or proceeding) instituted without sufficient grounds, esp so as to cause annoyance or embarrassment to the defendant

VHS *Trademark* video home system: a video cassette recording system using ½″ magnetic tape

viable (of seeds, eggs, etc) capable of normal growth and development

Via Dolorosa the route followed by Christ from the place of his condemnation to Calvary for his crucifixion

Viagra *Trademark* a drug, sildenafil, that allows increased blood flow into the penis; used to treat erectile impotence in men

Viareggio a town and resort in W Italy, in Tuscany on the Ligurian Sea. Pop: 61 103 (2001)

viaticum *Christianity* Holy Communion as administered to a person dying or in danger of death

Viborg 1 the Swedish name for **Vyborg** 2 a town in N central Denmark, in Jutland: formerly a royal town and capital of Jutland. Pop: 33 192 (2004 est)

vibraphone *or esp US* **vibraharp** a percussion instrument, used esp in jazz, consisting of a set of metal bars placed over tubular metal resonators, which are made to vibrate electronically

vibration *Physics* **a** a periodic motion about an equilibrium position, such as the regular displacement of air in the propagation of sound **b** a single cycle of such a motion

vibrato *Music* 1 a slight, rapid, and regular fluctuation in the pitch of a note produced on a stringed instrument by a shaking movement of the hand stopping the strings 2 an oscillatory effect produced in singing by fluctuation in breath pressure or pitch

vibrator 1 **a** a device for producing a vibratory motion, such as one used in massage or in the distribution of wet concrete in moulds **b** such a device with a vibrating part or tip, used as a dildo 2 a device in which a vibrating conductor interrupts a circuit to produce a pulsating current from a steady current, usually so that the current can then be amplified or the voltage transformed

viburnum 1 any of various temperate and subtropical caprifoliaceous shrubs or trees of the genus *Viburnum*, such as the wayfaring tree, having small white flowers and berry-like red or black fruits 2 the dried bark of several species of this tree, sometimes used in medicine

vicar 1 *Church of England* **a** (in Britain) a clergyman appointed to act as priest of a parish from which, formerly, he did not receive tithes but a stipend **b** a clergyman who acts as assistant to or substitute for the rector of a parish at Communion **c** (in the US) a clergyman in charge of a chapel 2 *RC Church* a bishop or priest representing the pope or the ordinary of a diocese and exercising a limited jurisdiction 3 *Church of England* a member of a cathedral choir appointed to sing certain parts of the services

vicarage the residence or benefice of a vicar

vicar apostolic *RC Church* a titular bishop having jurisdiction in non-Catholic or missionary countries where the normal hierarchy has not yet been established

vicar general an official, usually a layman, appointed to assist the bishop of a diocese in discharging his administrative or judicial duties

vicarious *Pathol* (of menstrual bleeding) occurring at an abnormal site

Vicar of Bray 1 a vicar (Simon Aleyn) appointed to the parish of Bray in Berkshire during Henry VIII's reign who changed his faith to Catholic when Mary I was on the throne and back to Protestant when Elizabeth I succeeded and so retained his living 2 a ballad in which the vicar's changes of faith are transposed to the Stuart period

Vicar of Christ *RC Church* the pope when regarded as Christ's earthly representative

vice[1] *Pathol, obsolete* any physical defect or imperfection

vice[2] *or US (often)* **vise** an appliance for holding an object while work is done upon it, usually having a pair of jaws

vice chancellor 1 the chief executive or administrator at some British universities 2 (in the US) a judge in courts of equity subordinate to the chancellor 3 (formerly in England) a senior judge of the court of chancery who acted as assistant to the Lord Chancellor

vicegerent 1 a person appointed to exercise all or some of the authority of another, esp the administrative powers of a ruler; deputy 2 *RC Church* the pope or any other representative of God or Christ on earth, such as a bishop

Vicenza a city in NE Italy, in Veneto: home of the 16th-century architect Andrea Palladio and site of some of his finest works. Pop: 107 223 (2001)

viceregal 1 of or relating to a viceroy or his viceroyalty 2 *Chiefly Austral and NZ* of or relating to a governor or governor general

viceroy a governor of a colony, country, or province who acts for and rules in the name of his sovereign or government

vice squad a police division to which is assigned the enforcement of gaming and prostitution laws

Vichy a town and spa in central France, on the River Allier: seat of the collaborationist government under Marshal Pétain (1940–44); mineral waters bottled for export. Pop: 26 528 (1999)

vicious circle 1 *Logic* **a** a form of reasoning in which a conclusion is inferred from premises the truth of which cannot be established independently of that conclusion **b** an explanation given in terms that cannot be understood independently of that which was to be explained **c** a situation in which some statement is shown to entail its negation and vice versa, as *this statement is false* is true only if false and false only if true 2 *Med* a condition in which one disease or disorder causes another, which in turn aggravates the first condition

Vicksburg a city in W Mississippi, on the Mississippi River: site of one of the most decisive campaigns (1863) of the American Civil War, in which the Confederates were besieged for nearly seven weeks before capitulating. Pop: 26 005 (2003 est)

Vicky professional name of *Victor Weisz*. 1913–66, British left-wing political cartoonist, born in Germany

Vico *Giovanni Battista* 1668–1744, Italian philosopher. In *Scienza Nuova* (1721) he postulated that civilizations rise and fall in evolutionary cycles, making use of myths, poetry, and linguistics as historical evidence

Victor Emmanuel II 1820–78, king of Sardinia-Piedmont (1849–78) and first king of Italy from 1861

Victor Emmanuel III 1869–1947, last king of Italy (1900–46): dominated after 1922 by Mussolini, whom he appointed as premier; abdicated

victoria 1 *Brit* a large sweet variety of plum, red and yellow in colour **2** any South American giant water lily of the genus *Victoria*, having very large floating leaves and large white, red, or pink fragrant flowers: family *Nymphaeaceae*

Victoria¹ 1 1819–1901, queen of the United Kingdom (1837–1901) and empress of India (1876–1901). She married Prince Albert of Saxe-Coburg-Gotha (1840). Her sense of vocation did much to restore the prestige of the British monarchy **2 Tomás Luis de** ?1548–1611, Spanish composer of motets and masses in the polyphonic style

Victoria² 1 a state of SE Australia: part of New South Wales colony until 1851; semiarid in the northwest, with the Great Dividing Range in the centre and east and the Murray River along the N border. Capital: Melbourne. Pop: 4 947 985 (2003 est). Area: 227 620 sq km (87 884 sq miles) **2 Lake** a lake in East Africa, in Tanzania, Uganda, and Kenya, at an altitude of 1134 m (3720 ft): the largest lake in Africa and second largest in the world; drained by the Victoria Nile. Area: 69 485 sq km (26 828 sq miles) **3** a port in SW Canada, capital of British Columbia, on Vancouver Island: founded in 1843 by the Hudson's Bay Company; made capital of British Columbia in 1868; university (1963). Pop: 288 346 (2001) **4** the capital of the Seychelles, a port on NE Mahé. Pop: 24 701 (1997) **5** an urban area in S China, part of Hong Kong, on N Hong Kong Island: financial and administrative district; university (1911). Pop: 595 000 (latest est) **6 Mount** a mountain in SE Papua New Guinea: the highest peak of the Owen Stanley Range. Height: 4073 m (13 363 ft)

Victoria Island a large island in the Canadian Arctic, in Nunavut and the Northwest Territories. Area: about 212 000 sq km (82 000 sq miles)

Victoria Land a section of Antarctica, largely in the Ross Dependency on the Ross Sea

Victorian 1 denoting, relating to, or having the style of architecture used in England during the reign of Queen Victoria, characterized by massive construction and elaborate ornamentation **2** of or relating to Victoria (the state or any of the cities)

Vidal Gore born 1925, US novelist and essayist. His novels include *Julian* (1964), *Myra Breckinridge* (1968), *Burr* (1974), *Lincoln* (1984), and *The Season of Conflict* (1996)

video 1 of, concerned with, or operating at video frequencies **2** a film recorded on a video cassette **3** short for **video cassette 4** *US* an informal name for **television**

video cassette a cassette containing video tape

video game any of various games that can be played by using an electronic control to move points of light or graphical symbols on the screen of a visual display unit

video nasty a film, usually specially made for video, that is explicitly horrific, brutal, and pornographic

video tape magnetic tape used mainly for recording the vision and sound signals of a television programme or film for subsequent transmission

Videotex *Trademark* an information system that displays information from a distant computer on a television screen

videotext a means of providing a written or graphical representation of computerized information on a television screen

Vienna the capital and the smallest state of Austria, in

the northeast on the River Danube: seat of the Hapsburgs (1278-1918); residence of the Holy Roman Emperor (1558–1806); withstood sieges by Turks in 1529 and 1683; political and cultural centre in the 18th and 19th centuries, having associations with many composers; university (1365). Pop: 1 590 242 (2003 est). Area: 1075 sq km (415 sq miles)

Vienne 1 a department of W central France, in Poitou-Charentes region. Capital: Poitiers. Pop: 402 555 (2003 est). Area: 7044 sq km (2747 sq miles) **2** a town in SE France, on the River Rhône: extensive Roman remains **3** a river in SW central France, flowing west and north to the Loire below Chinon. Length: over 350 km (200 miles)

Vientiane the administrative capital of Laos, in the south near the border with Thailand: capital of the kingdom of Vientiane from 1707 until taken by the Thais in 1827. Pop: 776 000 (2005 est)

Vietnam *or* **Viet Nam** a republic in SE Asia: an ancient empire, conquered by France in the 19th century; occupied by Japan (1940–45) when the Communist-led Vietminh began resistance operations that were continued against restored French rule after 1945. In 1954 the country was divided along the 17th parallel, establishing North Vietnam (under the Vietminh) and South Vietnam (under French control), the latter becoming the independent **Republic of Vietnam** in 1955. From 1959 the country was dominated by war between the Communist Vietcong, supported by North Vietnam, and the South Vietnamese government; increasing numbers of US forces were brought to the aid of the South Vietnamese army until a peace agreement (1973) led to the withdrawal of US troops; further fighting led to the eventual defeat of the South Vietnamese government in March 1975 and in 1976 an elected National Assembly proclaimed the reunification of the country. Official language: Vietnamese. Religion: Buddhist majority. Currency: dong. Capital: Hanoi. Pop: 82 481 000 (2004 est). Area: 331 041 sq km (127 816 sq miles)

Vietnamese the language of Vietnam, probably related to the Mon-Khmer languages

view 1 *Law* **a** a formal inspection by a jury of the place where an alleged crime was committed **b** a formal inspection of property in dispute **2** a sight of a hunted animal before or during the chase

Viewdata *Trademark* an interactive form of Videotext that sends information from a distant computer along telephone lines, enabling shopping, booking theatre and airline tickets, and banking transactions to be conducted from the home

viewer 1 any optical device by means of which something is viewed, esp one used for viewing photographic transparencies **2** *Law* a person appointed by a court to inspect and report upon property, etc.

viewfinder a device on a camera, consisting of a lens system and sometimes a ground-glass screen, enabling the user to see what will be included in his photograph

vigil 1 *RC Church, Church of England* the eve of certain major festivals, formerly observed as a night spent in prayer: often marked by fasting and abstinence and a special Mass and divine office **2** a period of sleeplessness;

insomnia

vigilance the abnormal state or condition of being unable to sleep

vignette 1 a short graceful literary essay or sketch 2 a photograph, drawing, etc, with edges that are shaded off 3 *Architect* a carved ornamentation that has a design based upon tendrils, leaves, etc.

Vignola Giacomo Barozzi da 1507–73, Italian architect, whose cruciform design for Il Gesù, Rome, greatly influenced later Church architecture

Vigny Alfred Victor de 1797–1863, French romantic poet, novelist, and dramatist, noted for his pessimistic lyric verse *Poèmes antiques et modernes* (1826) and *Les Destinées* (1864), the novel *Cinq-Mars* (1826), and the play *Chatterton* (1835)

Vigo a port in NW Spain, in Galicia on Vigo Bay (an inlet of the Atlantic): site of a British and Dutch naval victory (1702) over the French and Spanish. Pop: 292 566 (2003 est)

vigour *or US* **vigor** 1 the capacity for survival or strong healthy growth in a plant or animal 2 *Chiefly US* legal force or effectiveness; validity (esp in the phrase **in vigour**)

Vijayawada a town in SE India, in E central Andra Pradesh on the Krishna River: Hindu pilgrimage centre. Pop: 825 436 (2001)

Viking any of the Danes, Norwegians, and Swedes who raided by sea most of N and W Europe from the 8th to the 11th centuries, later often settling, as in parts of Britain
> http://viking.no/e/
> www.pbs.org/wgbh/nova/vikings

villa (in ancient Rome) a country house, usually consisting of farm buildings and residential quarters around a courtyard

Villa Francisco , called *Pancho Villa*, original name *Doroteo Arango.* ?1877–1923, Mexican revolutionary leader

Villach a city in S central Austria, on the Drava River: nearby hot mineral springs. Pop: 57 497 (2002)

village 1 a small group of houses in a country area, larger than a hamlet 2 the inhabitants of such a community collectively 3 an incorporated municipality smaller than a town in various parts of the US and Canada 4 a group of habitats of certain animals 5 *NZ* a self-contained city area having its own shops, etc.

Villahermosa a town in E Mexico, capital of Tabasco state: university (1959). Pop: 583 000 (2005 est)

Villa-Lobos Heitor 1887–1959, Brazilian composer, much of whose work is based on Brazilian folk tunes

villein *or* **villain** (in medieval Europe) a peasant personally bound to his lord, to whom he paid dues and services, sometimes commuted to rents, in return for his land

Villeneuve Pierre Charles Jean Baptiste Silvestre de 1763–1806, French admiral, defeated by Nelson at the Battle of Trafalgar (1805)

Villeurbanne a town in E France: an industrial suburb of E Lyon. Pop: 124 215 (1999)

Villon François born 1431, French poet. His poems, such as those in *Le Petit testament* (?1456) and *Le Grand testament* (1461), are mostly ballades and rondeaux, verse forms that he revitalized. He was banished in 1463, after

which nothing more was heard of him

villus 1 *Zoology, anatomy* any of the numerous finger-like projections of the mucous membrane lining the small intestine of many vertebrates 2 any similar membranous process, such as any of those in the mammalian placenta 3 *Botany* any of various hairlike outgrowths, as from the stem of a moss

Vilnius *or* **Vilnyus** the capital of Lithuania: passed to Russia in 1795; under Polish rule (1920–39); university (1578); an industrial and commercial centre. Pop: 544 000 (2005 est)

Viminal one of the seven hills on which ancient Rome was built

Vincennes a suburb of E Paris: 14th-century castle. Pop: 43 595 (1999)

Vincent de Paul Saint ?1581–1660, French Roman Catholic priest, who founded two charitable orders, the Lazarists (1625) and the Sisters of Charity (1634). Feast day: Sept 27

Vindhya Pradesh a former state of central India: merged with the reorganized Madhya Pradesh in 1956

Vindhya Range *or* **Mountains** a mountain range in central India: separates the Ganges basin from the Deccan, marking the limits of northern and peninsular India. Greatest height: 1113 m (3651 ft)

vindictive *English law* (of damages) in excess of the compensation due to the plaintiff and imposed in punishment of the defendant

vine 1 any of various plants, esp the grapevine, having long flexible stems that creep along the ground or climb by clinging to a support by means of tendrils, leafstalks, etc. 2 the stem of such a plant

vinegar a sour-tasting liquid consisting of impure dilute acetic acid, made by oxidation of the ethyl alcohol in beer, wine, or cider. It is used as a condiment or preservative

viniculture the process or business of growing grapes and making wine

Vinland *or* **Vineland** the stretch of the E coast of North America visited by Leif Ericson and other Vikings from about 1000

Vinnitsa a city in central Ukraine: passed from Polish to Russian rule in 1793. Pop: 353 000 (2005 est)

vinous 1 of, relating to, or characteristic of wine 2 indulging in or indicative of indulgence in wine

vintage 1 the wine obtained from a harvest of grapes, esp in an outstandingly good year, referred to by the year involved, the district, or the vineyard 2 the harvest from which such a wine is obtained 3 a the harvesting of wine grapes b the season of harvesting these grapes or for making wine 4 (of wine) of an outstandingly good year

vintage car *Chiefly Brit* an old car, esp one constructed between 1919 and 1930

vintner a wine merchant

vinyl 1 of, consisting of, or containing the monovalent group of atoms CH_2CH- 2 of, consisting of, or made of a vinyl resin 3 any vinyl polymer, resin, or plastic, esp PVC 4 (collectively) conventional records made of vinyl as opposed to compact discs

viol any of a family of stringed musical instruments that preceded the violin family, consisting of a fretted fingerboard, a body rather like that of a violin but having a flat back and six strings, played with a curved bow. They are held between the knees when played and have a quiet yet penetrating tone; they were much played, esp in consorts, in the 16th and 17th centuries

viola 1 a bowed stringed instrument, the alto of the violin family; held beneath the chin when played. It is pitched and tuned an octave above the cello 2 any of various instruments of the viol family, such as the viola da gamba 3 any temperate perennial herbaceous plant of the violaceous genus *Viola*, the flowers of which have showy irregular petals, white, yellow, blue, or mauve in colour

viola da gamba the second largest and lowest member of the viol family

violet any of a group of colours that vary in saturation but have the same purplish-blue hue. They lie at one end of the visible spectrum, next to blue; approximate wavelength range 445–390 nanometres

violet 1 any of various temperate perennial herbaceous plants of the violaceous genus *Viola*, such as *V. odorata* (**sweet** (or **garden**) **violet**), typically having mauve or bluish flowers with irregular showy petals 2 any other plant of the genus *Viola*, such as the wild pansy 3 any of various similar but unrelated plants, such as the African violet

violin a bowed stringed instrument, the highest member of the violin family, consisting of a fingerboard, a hollow wooden body with waisted sides, and a sounding board connected to the back by means of a soundpost that also supports the bridge. It has two f-shaped sound holes cut in the belly. The instrument, noted for its fine and flexible tone, is the most important of the stringed instruments. It is held under the chin when played. Range: roughly three and a half octaves upwards from G below middle C

violinist a person who plays the violin

violist a person who plays the viol

Viollet-le-Duc Eugène Emmanuel 1814–79, French architect and leader of the Gothic Revival in France, noted for his dictionary of French architecture (1854–68) and for his restoration of medieval buildings

viper 1 any venomous Old World snake of the family *Viperidae*, esp any of the genus *Vipera* (the adder and related forms), having hollow fangs in the upper jaw that are used to inject venom 2 any of various other snakes, such as the horned viper

viral of, relating to, or caused by a virus

Virchow Rudolf Ludwig Karl 1821–1902, German pathologist, who is considered the founder of modern (cellular) pathology

Viren Lasse born 1949, Finnish distance runner: winner of the 5000 metres and the 10 000 metres in the 1972 and 1976 Olympic Games

Virgil or **Vergil** Latin name *Publius Vergilius Maro*. 70–19 BC, Roman poet, patronized by Maecenas. The *Eclogues* (42–37), ten pastoral poems, and the *Georgics* (37–30), four books on the art of farming, established Virgil as the foremost poet of his age. His masterpiece is the *Aeneid* (30–19)

virgin 1 an unmarried woman who has taken a religious vow of chastity in order to dedicate herself totally to

God 2 any female animal that has never mated 3 a female insect that produces offspring by parthenogenesis 4 (of vegetable oils) obtained directly by the first pressing of fruits, leaves, or seeds of plants without applying heat 5 (of a metal) made from an ore rather than from scrap 6 *Physics* (of a neutron) not having experienced a collision

Virgin[1] 1 **the** See **Virgin Mary** 2 a statue or other artistic representation of the Virgin Mary

Virgin[2] **the** the constellation Virgo, the sixth sign of the zodiac

virginal a smaller version of the harpsichord, but oblong in shape, having one manual and no pedals

Virgin Birth the doctrine that Jesus Christ had no human father but was conceived solely by the direct intervention of the Holy Spirit so that Mary remained miraculously a virgin during and after his birth

Virginia a state of the eastern US, on the Atlantic: site of the first permanent English settlement in North America; consists of a low-lying deeply indented coast rising inland to the Piedmont plateau and the Blue Ridge Mountains. Capital: Richmond. Pop: 7 386 330 (2003 est). Area: 103 030 sq km (39 780 sq miles)

Virginia Beach a city and resort in SE Virginia, on the Atlantic. Pop: 439 467 (2003 est)

Virginia creeper 1 a vitaceous woody vine, *Parthenocissus quinquefolia*, of North America, having tendrils with adhesive tips, bluish-black berry-like fruits, and compound leaves that turn red in autumn: widely planted for ornament 2 a similar related plant, *Parthenocissus tricuspidata*, of SE Asia, having trilobed leaves and purple berries

Virgin Mary Mary, the mother of Christ

Virgo 1 *Astronomy* a large zodiacal constellation on the celestial equator, lying between Leo and Libra. It contains the star Spica and a cluster of several thousand galaxies, the **Virgo cluster**, lying 50 million light years away and itself containing the intense radio source Virgo A, which is the closest active galaxy 2 *Astrology* a the sixth sign of the zodiac, symbol ♍, having a mutable earth classification and ruled by the planet Mercury. The sun is in this sign between about Aug 23 and Sept 22 b a person born when the sun is in this sign 3 *Astrology* born under or characteristic of Virgo

virile 1 of, relating to, or having the characteristics of an adult male 2 (of a male) possessing high sexual drive and capacity for sexual intercourse 3 of or capable of copulation or procreation

virology the branch of medicine concerned with the study of viruses and the diseases they cause

virtual 1 *Physics* being, relating to, or involving a virtual image 2 of or relating to a computer technique by which a person, wearing a headset or mask, has the experience of being in an environment created by the computer, and of interacting with and causing changes in it 3 *Physics* designating or relating to a particle exchanged between other particles that are interacting by a field of force

virtual reality a computer-generated environment that, to the person experiencing it, closely resembles reality

virtue any of the cardinal virtues (prudence, justice, fortitude, and temperance) or theological virtues (faith, hope, and charity)

virtuoso 1 a consummate master of musical technique and artistry 2 a connoisseur, dilettante, or collector of art objects

virulent a (of a microorganism) extremely infective b (of a disease) having a rapid course and violent effect

virus 1 any of a group of submicroscopic entities consisting of a single nucleic acid chain surrounded by a protein coat and capable of replication only within the cells of living organisms: many are pathogenic 2 *Computing* an unauthorized program that inserts itself into a computer system and then propagates itself to other computers via networks or disks; when activated it interferes with the operation of the computer
▷www.tulane.edu/~dmsander/ garryfavweb.html

visa an endorsement in a passport or similar document, signifying that the document is in order and permitting its bearer to travel into or through the country of the government issuing it

Visby a port in SE Sweden, on NW Gotland Island in the Baltic: an early member of the Hanseatic League and major N European commercial centre in the Middle Ages. Pop: 22 017 (2000 est)

viscid (esp of a leaf) covered with a sticky substance

Visconti 1 the ruling family of Milan from 1277 to 1447 2 *Luchino*, real name *Luchino Visconti de Modrone*. 1906–76, Italian stage and film director, whose neorealist films include *Ossessione* (1942). His other films include *The Leopard* (1963), *Death in Venice* (1970), and *The Innocents* (1976)

viscose 1 a a viscous orange-brown solution obtained by dissolving cellulose in sodium hydroxide and carbon disulphide. It can be converted back to cellulose by an acid, as in the manufacture of rayon and cellophane b (*as modifier*): *viscose rayon* 2 rayon made from this material

viscosity *Physics* a the extent to which a fluid resists a tendency to flow b a measure of this resistance, equal to the tangential stress on a liquid undergoing streamline flow divided by its velocity gradient. It is measured in newton seconds per metre squared.

viscount 1 (in the British Isles) a nobleman ranking below an earl and above a baron 2 (in various countries) a son or younger brother of a count 3 (in medieval Europe) the deputy of a count

viscountess 1 the wife or widow of a viscount 2 a woman who holds the rank of viscount in her own right

Viseu a city in N central Portugal: 12th-century cathedral. Pop: 93 502 (2001)

Vishakhapatnam, Visakhapatnam, *or* **Vizagapatam** a port in E India, in NE Andhra Pradesh on the Bay of Bengal: shipbuilding and oil-refining industries. Pop: 969 608 (2001)

Vishnu *Hinduism* the Pervader or Sustainer, originally a solar deity occupying a secondary place in the Hindu pantheon, later one of the three chief gods, the second member of the Trimurti, and, later still, the saviour appearing in many incarnations

visible *Economics* 1 of or relating to the balance of trade 2 a visible item of trade; product

visit *International law* the right of an officer of a belligerent state to stop and search neutral ships in war to verify their nationality and ascertain whether they carry contraband

visitant a migratory bird that is present in a particular region only at certain times

visitation 1 an official call or visit for the purpose of inspecting or examining an institution, esp such a visit made by a bishop to his diocese 2 a visiting of punishment or reward from heaven 3 an appearance or arrival of a supernatural being

Visitation 1 a the visit made by the Virgin Mary to her cousin Elizabeth (Luke 1:39–56) b the Church festival commemorating this, held on July 2 2 a religious order of nuns, the **Order of the Visitation**, founded in 1610 by St Francis of Sales and dedicated to contemplation and the cultivation of humility, gentleness, and sisterly love

visor *or* **vizor** a small movable screen used as protection against glare from the sun, esp one attached above the windscreen of a motor vehicle

Vistula 1 a river in central and N Poland, rising in the Carpathian Mountains and flowing generally north and northwest past Warsaw and Torun, then northeast to enter the Baltic via an extensive delta region. Length: 1090 km (677 miles) 2 **Lagoon** a shallow lagoon on the SW coast of the Baltic Sea, between Danzig and Kaliningrad, crossed by the border between Poland and Russia

visual display unit *Computing* a device with a screen that displays characters or graphics representing data in a computer memory. It usually has a keyboard or light pen for the input of information or inquiries

vital 1 essential to maintain life 2 of, relating to, having, or displaying life 3 a the bodily organs, such as the brain, liver, heart, lungs, etc, that are necessary to maintain life b the organs of reproduction, esp the male genitals

vitamin any of a group of substances that are essential, in small quantities, for the normal functioning of metabolism in the body. They cannot usually be synthesized in the body but they occur naturally in certain foods: insufficient supply of any particular vitamin results in a deficiency disease

Vitebsk a city in E Belarus, a port on the Dvina river: taken by Russia in 1772. Pop: 344 000 (2005 est)

Viti Levu the largest island of Fiji: mountainous. Chief town (and capital of the state): Suva. Pop: 340 560 (latest est). Area: 10 386 sq km (4010 sq miles)

Vitoria[1] *Francisco de* ?1486–1546, Spanish theologian, sometimes considered the father of international law. He criticized Spanish colonial policy in the New World and argued that war was only defensible in certain strictly defined circumstances

Vitoria[2] a city in NE Spain: scene of Wellington's decisive victory (1813) over Napoleon's forces in the Peninsular War. Pop: 223 257 (2003 est)

vitreous 1 of, relating to, or resembling glass 2 made of, derived from, or containing glass 3 of or relating to the vitreous humour or vitreous body

vitreous humour the aqueous fluid contained within

the interstices of the vitreous body

vitriol 1 another name for **sulphuric acid** 2 any one of a number of sulphate salts, such as ferrous sulphate (**green vitriol**), copper sulphate (**blue vitriol**), or zinc sulphate (**white vitriol**)

vitriolic (of a substance, esp a strong acid) highly corrosive

Vitruvius Pollio Marcus 1st century BC, Roman architect, noted for his treatise *De architectura*, the only surviving Roman work on architectural theory and a major influence on Renaissance architects

viva *Brit* an oral examination

vivace *Music* to be performed in a brisk lively manner

Vivaldi Antonio ?1675–1741, Italian composer and violinist, noted esp for his development of the solo concerto. His best-known work is *The Four Seasons* (1725)

vivarium a place where live animals are kept under natural conditions for study, research, etc.

viviparous 1 (of animals) producing offspring that as embryos develop within and derive nourishment from the body of the female parent 2 (of plants) producing bulbils or young plants instead of flowers 3 (of seeds) germinating before separating from the parent plant

vivisection the act or practice of performing experiments on living animals, involving cutting into or dissecting the body

vixen a female fox

vizier a high official in certain Muslim countries, esp in the former Ottoman Empire. Viziers served in various capacities, such as that of provincial governor or chief minister to the sultan

Vlaardingen a port in the W Netherlands, in South Holland west of Rotterdam: the third largest port in the Netherlands. Pop: 74 000 (2003 est)

Vladikavkaz a city in S Russia, capital of the North Ossetian Republic on the N slopes of the Caucasus. Pop: 318 000 (2005 est)

Vladimir[1] Saint, called *the Great*. ?956–1015, grand prince of Kiev (980–1015); first Christian ruler of Russia. Feast day: July 15

Vladimir[2] a city in W central Russia: capital of the principality of Vladimir until the court transferred to Moscow in 1328. Pop: 310 000 (2005 est)

Vladivostok a port in SE Russia, on the Sea of Japan: terminus of the Trans-Siberian Railway; the main Russian Pacific naval base since 1872 and chief commercial and civilian Russian port in the Far East; university (1956). Pop: 584 000 (2005 est)

Vlaminck Maurice de 1876–1958, French painter of the Fauve school

Vltava a river in the Czech Republic, rising in the Bohemian Forest and flowing generally southeast and then north to the River Elbe near Melnik. Length: 434 km (270 miles)

vocal 1 a piece of jazz or pop music that is sung 2 a performance of such a piece of music

vocalist a singer, esp one who regularly appears with a jazz band or pop group

vocational of or relating to applied educational courses concerned with skills needed for an occupation, trade, or profession

vodka an alcoholic drink originating in Russia, made

from grain, potatoes, etc, usually consisting only of rectified spirit and water

▷www.ginvodka.org
▷www.ivodka.com
▷www.webtender.com

Vogel Sir Julius 1835–99, New Zealand statesman; prime minister of New Zealand (1873–75; 1876)

voice 1 the sound made by the vibration of the vocal cords, esp when modified by the resonant effect of the tongue and mouth 2 the musical sound of a singing voice, with respect to its quality or tone 3 the ability to speak, sing, etc. 4 *Music* a musical notes produced by vibrations of the vocal cords at various frequencies and in certain registers b (in harmony) an independent melodic line or part

void 1 not legally binding 2 (of a card suit or player) having no cards in a particular suit 3 a lack of any cards in one suit

voile a light semitransparent fabric of silk, rayon, cotton, etc, used for dresses, scarves, shirts, etc.

Voiotia a department of E central Greece: corresponds to ancient Boeotia and part of ancient Phocis. Pop: 123 913 (2001). Area: 3173 sq km (1225 sq miles)

Vojvodina *or* **Voivodina** an autonomous region of NE Serbia and Montenegro, in N Serbia. Capital: Novi Sad. Pop: 2 024 487 (2002). Area: 22 489 sq km (8683 sq miles)

volatile 1 (of a substance) capable of readily changing from a solid or liquid form to a vapour; having a high vapour pressure and a low boiling point 2 *Computing* (of a memory) not retaining stored information when the power supply is cut off 3 a volatile substance

volcano 1 an opening in the earth's crust from which molten lava, rock fragments, ashes, dust, and gases are ejected from below the earth's surface 2 a mountain formed from volcanic material ejected from a vent in a central crater

vole[1] any of numerous small rodents of the genus *Microtus* and related genera, mostly of Eurasia and North America and having a stocky body, short tail, and inconspicuous ears: family *Cricetidae*

vole[2] (in some card games, such as écarté) the taking of all the tricks in a deal, thus scoring extra points

Volga a river in W Russia, rising in the Valdai Range and flowing through a chain of small lakes to the Rybinsk Reservoir and south to the Caspian Sea through Volgograd: the longest river in Europe. Length: 3690 km (2293 miles)

Volgograd a port in SW Russia, on the River Volga: scene of a major engagement (1918) during the civil war and again in World War II (1942–43), in which the German forces were defeated; major industrial centre. Pop: 1 016 000 (2005 est)

volition *Philosophy* an act of will as distinguished from the physical movement it intends to bring about

volley *Cricket* the flight of such a ball or the ball itself

volleyball a game in which two teams hit a large ball back and forth over a high net with their hands
▷www.volleyball.org/iva

Vologda an industrial city in W central Russia. Pop: 295 000 (2005 est)

volt[1] the derived SI unit of electric potential; the potential difference between two points on a conductor carrying a current of 1 ampere, when the power dissipated between these points is 1 watt.

volt² *or* **volte 1** a small circle of determined size executed in dressage **2** a leap made in fencing to avoid an opponent's thrust

Volta¹ Count Alessandro 1745–1827, Italian physicist after whom the volt is named. He made important contributions to the theory of current electricity and invented the voltaic pile (1800), the electrophorus (1775), and an electroscope

Volta² **1** a river in W Africa, formed by the confluence of the **Black Volta** and the **White Volta** in N central Ghana: flows south to the Bight of Benin: the chief river of Ghana. Length: 480 km (300 miles): (including the Black Volta) 1600 km (1000 miles) **2** *Lake* an artificial lake in Ghana, extending 408 km (250 miles) upstream from the **Volta River Dam** on the Volta River: completed in 1966. Area: 8482 sq km (3275 sq miles)

voltage an electromotive force or potential difference expressed in volts

Voltaire pseudonym of *François Marie Arouet*. 1694–1778, French writer, whose outspoken belief in religious, political, and social liberty made him the embodiment of the 18th-century Enlightenment. His major works include *Lettres philosophiques* (1734) and the satire *Candide* (1759). He also wrote plays, such as *Zaïre* (1732), poems, and scientific studies. He suffered several periods of banishment for his radical views

Volta Redonda a city in SE Brazil, in Rio de Janeiro state on the Paraíba River: founded in 1941; site of South America's largest steelworks. Pop: 419 000 (2005 est)

voltmeter an instrument for measuring potential difference or electromotive force

Volturno a river in S central Italy, flowing southeast and southwest to the Tyrrhenian Sea: scene of a battle (1860) during the wars for Italian unity, in which Garibaldi defeated the Neapolitans; German line of defence during World War II. Length: 175 km (109 miles)

volume 1 the magnitude of the three-dimensional space enclosed within or occupied by an object, geometric solid, etc. **2** fullness or intensity of tone or sound **3** *History* a roll or scroll of parchment, papyrus, etc.

voluntary 1 *Law* **a** acting or done without legal obligation, compulsion, or persuasion **b** made without payment or recompense in any form **2** (of the muscles of the limbs, neck, etc) having their action controlled by the will **3** maintained or provided by the voluntary actions or contributions of individuals and not by the state **4** *Music* a composition or improvisation, usually for organ, played at the beginning or end of a church service

volunteer 1 *Law* **a** a person who does some act or enters into a transaction without being under any legal obligation to do so and without being promised any remuneration for his services **b** *Property law* a person to whom property is transferred without his giving any valuable consideration in return, as a legatee under a will **2 a** a plant that grows from seed that has not been deliberately sown **b** (*as modifier*): *a volunteer plant*

volute 1 a carved ornament, esp as used on an Ionic capital, that has the form of a spiral scroll **2** any of the

whorls of the spirally coiled shell of a snail or similar gastropod mollusc **3** any tropical marine gastropod mollusc of the family *Volutidae*, typically having a spiral shell with beautiful markings **4** a tangential part, resembling the volute of a snail's shell, that collects the fluids emerging from the periphery of a turbine, impeller pump, etc. **5** *Machinery* moving in a spiral path

von Braun Wernher 1912–77, US rocket engineer, born in Germany, where he designed the V-2 missile used in World War II. In the US he worked on the Apollo project

Vonnegut Kurt born 1922, US novelist. His works include *Cat's Cradle* (1963), *Slaughterhouse Five* (1969), *Galapagos* (1985), *Hocus Pocus* (1990), and *Timequake* (1997)

von Sternberg Joseph , real name *Jonas Sternberg*. 1894–1969, US film director, born in Austria, whose films include *The Blue Angel* (1930), *Blonde Venus* (1932), *The Scarlet Empress* (1934), and the unfinished *I, Claudius* (1937)

von Stroheim Erich , real name *Hans Erich Maria Stroheim von Nordenwall*. 1885–1957, US film director and actor, born in Austria, whose films include *Foolish Wives* (1921) and *Greed* (1923)

voodoo 1 a religious cult involving witchcraft and communication by trance with ancestors and animistic deities, common in Haiti and other Caribbean islands **2** a person who practises voodoo **3** a charm, spell, or fetish involved in voodoo worship and ritual
▷http://www.religioustolerance.org/voodoo.htm

Vorarlberg a mountainous state of W Austria. Capital: Bregenz. Pop: 356 590 (2003 est). Area: 2601 sq km (1004 sq miles)

Voronezh a city in W Russia: engineering, chemical, and food-processing industries; university (1918). Pop: 842 000 (2005 est)

Vorster Balthazar Johannes, known as *John*. 1915–83, South African statesman; Nationalist prime minister (1966–78); president (1978)

vortex a whirling mass or rotary motion in a liquid, gas, flame, etc, such as the spiralling movement of water around a whirlpool

Vosges 1 a mountain range in E France, west of the Rhine valley. Highest peak: 1423 m (4672 ft) **2** a department of NE France, in Lorraine region. Capital: Épinal. Pop: 381 277 (2003 est). Area: 5903 sq km (2302 sq miles)

votary 1 *RC Church, Eastern Churches* a person, such as a monk or nun, who has dedicated himself or herself to religion by taking vows **2** ardently devoted to the services or worship of God, a deity, or a saint

vote 1 an indication of choice, opinion, or will on a question, such as the choosing of a candidate, by or as if by some recognized means, such as a ballot **2** the opinion of a group of persons as determined by voting **3** a body of votes or voters collectively **4** the total number of votes cast **5** the ticket, ballot, etc, by which a vote is expressed **6 a** the right to vote; franchise; suffrage **b** a person regarded as the embodiment of this right **7** a means of voting, such as a ballot **8** *Chiefly Brit* a grant or other proposition to be voted upon

votive *RC Church* optional; not prescribed; having the nature of a voluntary offering

voucher 1 a document serving as evidence for some

claimed transaction, as the receipt or expenditure of money **2** *Brit* a ticket or card serving as a substitute for cash **3** any of certain documents that various groups of British nationals born outside Britain must obtain in order to settle in Britain **4** *English law, obsolete* **a** the summoning into court of a person to warrant a title to property **b** the person so summoned

vow 1 a solemn promise made to a deity or saint, by which the promiser pledges himself to some future act, course of action, or way of life **2 take vows** to enter a religious order and commit oneself to its rule of life by the vows of poverty, chastity, and obedience, which may be taken for a limited period as **simple vows** or as a perpetual and still more solemn commitment as **solemn vows**

voyageur *Canadian History* a boatman employed by one of the early fur-trading companies, esp in the interior

VSO very superior old: used to indicate that a brandy, port, etc, is between 12 and 17 years old

VSOP very special (or superior) old pale: used to indicate that a brandy, port, etc, is between 20 and 25 years old

VTOL 1 vertical takeoff and landing; a system in which an aircraft can take off and land vertically **2** an aircraft that uses this system

Vuelta Abajo a region of W Cuba: famous for its tobacco

Vuillard Jean Édouard 1868–1940, French painter and lithographer

Vulcan¹ the Roman god of fire and metalworking

Vulcan² a hypothetical planet once thought to lie within the orbit of Mercury

vulcanite a hard usually black rubber produced by vulcanizing natural rubber with large amounts of sul-

phur. It is resistant to chemical attack: used for chemical containers, electrical insulators, etc.

Vulgar Latin any of the dialects of Latin spoken in the Roman Empire other than classical Latin. The Romance languages developed from them

Vulgate a (from the 13th century onwards) the fourth-century version of the Bible produced by Jerome, partly by translating the original languages, and partly by revising the earlier Latin text based on the Greek versions **b** (*as modifier*): *the Vulgate version*

vulnerable *Bridge* (of a side who have won one game towards rubber) subject to increased bonuses or penalties

vulpine of, relating to, or resembling a fox

vulture 1 any of various very large diurnal birds of prey of the genera *Neophron, Gyps, Gypaetus*, etc, of Africa, Asia, and warm parts of Europe, typically having broad wings and soaring flight and feeding on carrion: family *Accipitridae* (hawks) **2** any similar bird of the family *Cathartidae* of North, Central, and South America

vulva the external genitals of human females, including the labia, mons veneris, clitoris, and the vaginal orifice

Vyborg a port in NW Russia, at the head of **Vyborg Bay** (an inlet of the Gulf of Finland): belonged to Finland (1918–40). Pop: 80 000 (latest est)

Vyshinsky *or* **Vishinsky** Andrei Yanuaryevich 1883–1954, Soviet jurist, statesman, and diplomat; foreign minister (1949–53). He was public prosecutor (1935–38) at the trials held to purge Stalin's rivals and was the Soviet representative at the United Nations (1945–49; 1953–54)

Ww

Waal a river in the central Netherlands: the S branch of the Lower Rhine. Length: 84 km (52 miles)

Wabash a river in the E central US, rising in W Ohio and flowing west and southwest to join the Ohio River in Indiana. Length: 764 km (475 miles)

Wace Robert born ?1100, Anglo-Norman poet; author of the *Roman de Brut* and *Roman de Rou*

wad¹ a small mass or ball of fibrous or soft material, such as cotton wool, used esp for packing or stuffing

wad² a soft dark earthy amorphous material consisting of decomposed manganese minerals: occurs in damp marshy areas

Wadai a former independent sultanate of NE central Africa: now the E part of Chad

Waddenzee the part of the North Sea between the Dutch mainland and the West Frisian Islands

wadding any fibrous or soft substance used as padding, stuffing, etc, esp sheets of carded cotton prepared for the purpose

waddy a heavy wooden club used as a weapon by native Australians

wader any of various long-legged birds, esp those of the order *Ciconiiformes* (herons, storks, etc), that live near water and feed on fish, etc.

wadi or **wady** a watercourse in N Africa and Arabia, dry except in the rainy season

Wadi Halfa a town in the N Sudan that was partly submerged by Lake Nasser: an important archaeological site

Wad Medani a town in the E Sudan, on the Blue Nile: headquarters of the Gezira irrigation scheme; agricultural research centre. Pop: 332 000 (2005 est)

wafer 1 *Christianity* a thin disc of unleavened bread used in the Eucharist as celebrated by the Western Church 2 *Pharmacol* an envelope of rice paper enclosing a medicament 3 *Electronics* a large single crystal of semiconductor material, such as silicon, on which numerous integrated circuits are manufactured and then separated

waft *Nautical* (formerly) a signal flag hoisted furled to signify various messages depending on where it was flown

wage *Economics* the portion of the national income accruing to labour as earned income, as contrasted with the unearned income accruing to capital in the form of rent, interest, and dividends

wager 1 an agreement or pledge to pay an amount of money as a result of the outcome of an unsettled matter 2 an amount staked on the outcome of such a matter or event 3 **wager of battle** (in medieval Britain) a pledge to do battle for a cause, esp to decide guilt or innocence by single combat 4 **wager of law** *English legal history* a form of trial in which the accused offered to make oath of his innocence, supported by the oaths of 11 of his neighbours declaring their belief in his statements

Wagga Wagga a city in SE Australia, in New South Wales on the Murrumbidgee River: agricultural trading centre. Pop: 44 451 (2001)

Wagner 1 Otto 1841–1918, Austrian architect, whose emphasis on function and structure in such buildings as the Post Office Savings Bank, Vienna (1904–06), influenced the development of modern architecture 2 (**Wilhelm**) **Richard** 1813–83, German romantic composer noted chiefly for his invention of the music drama. His cycle of four such dramas *The Ring of the Nibelung* was produced at his own theatre in Bayreuth in 1876. His other operas include *Tannhäuser* (1845; revised 1861), *Tristan und Isolde* (1865), and *Parsifal* (1882)

Wagner-Jauregg Julius 1857–1940, Austrian psychiatrist and neurologist; a pioneer of the use of fever therapy in the treatment of mental disorders. Nobel prize for physiology or medicine 1927

wagon or **waggon** 1 any of various types of wheeled vehicles, ranging from carts to lorries, esp a vehicle with four wheels drawn by a horse, tractor, etc, and used for carrying crops, heavy loads, etc. 2 *Brit* a railway freight truck, esp an open one 3 *US and Canadian* a child's four-wheeled cart 4 *US and Canadian* a police van for transporting prisoners and those arrested 5 *Chiefly US and Canadian* See **station wagon**

Wagram a village in NE Austria: scene of the defeat of the Austrians by Napoleon in 1809

wagtail any of various passerine songbirds of the genera *Motacilla* and *Dendronanthus*, of Eurasia and Africa, having a very long tail that wags when the bird walks: family *Motacillidae*

wahine (esp in the Pacific islands) a Polynesian or Māori woman, esp a girlfriend or wife

wahoo¹ an elm, *Ulmus alata*, of SE North America having twigs with winged corky edges

wahoo² an E North American shrub or small tree, *Euonymus atropurpureus*, with scarlet capsules and seeds

wahoo³ a large fast-moving food and game fish, *Acanthocybium solandri*, of tropical seas: family *Scombridae* (mackerels and tunnies)

waif 1 *Nautical* another name for **waft 2** *Law, obsolete* a stolen article thrown away by a thief in his flight and forfeited to the Crown or to the lord of the manor

Waikaremoana Lake a lake in the North Island of New Zealand in a dense bush setting. Area: about 55 sq km (21 sq miles)

Waikato the longest river in New Zealand, flowing northwest across North Island to the Tasman Sea. Length: 350 km (220 miles)

Waikiki a resort area in Hawaii, on SE Oahu: a suburb of Honolulu

waist 1 *Anatomy* the constricted part of the trunk between the ribs and hips **2** the middle part of a ship **3** the middle section of an aircraft fuselage **4** the constriction between the thorax and abdomen in wasps and similar insects

waistline a line or indentation around the body at the narrowest part of the waist

wait 1 *Rare* a band of musicians who go around the streets, esp at Christmas, singing and playing carols **2** an interlude or interval between two acts or scenes in a play, etc.

Waitangi Day the national day of New Zealand (Feb 6), commemorating the signing of the **Treaty of Waitangi** (1840) by Māori chiefs and a representative of the British Government. The treaty provided the basis for the British annexation of New Zealand
▷www.archives.govt.nz/holdings/
  treaty_frame.html
▷www.waitangi.com

waiter 1 a man whose occupation is to serve at table, as in a restaurant **2** a tray or salver on which dishes, etc, are carried

waitress a woman who serves at table, as in a restaurant

waiver 1 the voluntary relinquishment, expressly or by implication, of some claim or right **2** the act or an instance of relinquishing a claim or right **3** a formal statement in writing of such relinquishment

Wajda Andrei or **Andrzej** born 1926, Polish film director. His films include *Ashes and Diamonds* (1958), *The Wedding* (1972), *Man of Iron* (1980), *Danton* (1982), and *Miss Nobody* (1997)

Wakayama an industrial city in S Japan, on S Honshu. Pop: 391 008 (2002 est)

wake¹ 1 a watch or vigil held over the body of a dead person during the night before burial **2** (in Ireland) festivities held after a funeral **3** the patronal or dedication festival of English parish churches

wake² the waves or track left by a vessel or other object moving through water

Wakefield 1 a city in N England, in Wakefield unitary authority, West Yorkshire: important since medieval times as an agricultural and textile centre. Pop: 76 886 (2001) **2** a unitary authority in N England, in West Yorkshire. Pop: 318 300 (2003 est). Area: 333 sq km (129 sq miles)

Wake Island an atoll in the N central Pacific: claimed by the US in 1899; developed as a civil and naval air station in the late 1930s. Area: 8 sq km (3 sq miles)

Waksman Selman Abraham 1888–1973, US microbiologist, born in Russia. He discovered streptomycin: Nobel prize for physiology or medicine 1952

Walachia or **Wallachia** a former principality of SE Europe: a vassal state of the Ottoman Empire from the 15th century until its union with Moldavia in 1859, subsequently forming present-day Romania

Wałbrzych an industrial city in SW Poland. Pop: 176 000 (2005 est)

Walcheren an island in the SW Netherlands, in the Scheldt estuary: administratively part of Zeeland province; suffered severely in World War II, when the dykes were breached, and again in the floods of 1953. Area: 212 sq km (82 sq miles)

Walcott 1 Derek (Alton). born 1930, St Lucian poet and playwright, whose works include the poetry collections *In a Green Night* (1962) and *The Bounty* (1997), the play *The Dream on Monkey Mountain* (1967), and the long poem *Omeros* (1990): Nobel prize for literature 1992 **2 Jersey Joe**, real name *Arnold Raymond Cream*. 1914–94, US boxer: world heavyweight champion 1951–52

Waldemar I or **Valdemar I** known as *Waldemar the Great*. 1131–82, king of Denmark (1157–82). He conquered the Wends (1169), increased the territory of Denmark, and established the hereditary rule of his line

Wales a principality that is part of the United Kingdom, in the west of Great Britain; conquered by the English in 1282; parliamentary union with England took place in 1536: a separate Welsh Assembly with limited powers was established in 1999. Wales consists mainly of moorlands and mountains and has an economy that is chiefly agricultural, with an industrial and former coal-mining area in the south. Capital: Cardiff. Pop: 2 938 000 (2003 est). Area: 20 768 sq km (8017 sq miles)

Wałęsa Lech born 1943, Polish statesman: president of Poland (1990–95); leader of the independent trade union Solidarity 1980–90; Nobel peace prize 1983

walkabout 1 a periodic nomadic excursion into the Australian bush made by a native Australian **2 go walkabout** *Austral* to wander through the bush

Walker 1 Alice (Malsenior). born 1944, US writer: her works include *In Love and Trouble: Stories of Black Women* (1973) and the novels *Meridian* (1976), *The Color Purple* (1982), and *Possessing the Secret of Joy* (1992) **2 John** born 1952, New Zealand middle-distance runner, the first athlete to run one hundred sub-four-minute miles

walking stick 1 a stick or cane carried in the hand to assist walking **2** the usual US name for **stick insect**

Walkman *Trademark* a small portable cassette player with light headphones

walk-on 1 a a small part in a play or theatrical entertainment, esp one without any lines **b** (*as modifier*): *a walk-on part* **2** (of an aircraft or air service) having seats to be booked immediately before departure rather than in advance

walkover *Horse racing* **a** the running or walking over the course by the only contestant entered in a race at the time of starting **b** a race won in this way

walkway a path designed, and sometimes landscaped, for pedestrian use

wall 1 *Anatomy* any lining, membrane, or investing part that encloses or bounds a bodily cavity or structure 2 *Mountaineering* a vertical or almost vertical smooth rock face

wallaby any of various herbivorous marsupials of the genera *Lagorchestes* (**hare wallabies**), *Petrogale* (**rock wallabies**), *Protemnodon*, etc, of Australia and New Guinea, similar to but smaller than kangaroos: family *Macropodidae*

Wallace 1 **Alfred Russel** 1823–1913, British naturalist, whose work on the theory of natural selection influenced Charles Darwin 2 **Edgar** 1875–1932, English crime novelist 3 Sir **Richard** 1818–90, English art collector and philanthropist. His bequest to the nation forms the Wallace Collection, London 4 Sir **William** ?1272–1305, Scottish patriot, who defeated the army of Edward I of England at Stirling (1297) but was routed at Falkirk (1298) and later executed

wallaroo a large stocky Australian kangaroo, *Macropus* (or *Osphranter*) *robustus*, of rocky regions

Wallasey a town in NW England, in Wirral unitary authority, Merseyside; near the mouth of the River Mersey, opposite Liverpool. Pop: 58 710 (2001)

Wallenberg Raoul 1912–? Swedish diplomat, who helped (1944–45) thousands of Hungarian Jews to escape from the Nazis. After his arrest (1945) by the Soviets nothing is certainly known of him: despite claims that he is still alive he is presumed to have died in prison

Waller 1 **Edmund** 1606–87, English poet and politician, famous for his poem "Go, Lovely Rose" 2 **Fats**, real name *Thomas Waller*. 1904–43, US jazz pianist and singer

walleye 1 a divergent squint 2 opacity of the cornea 3 an eye having a white or light-coloured iris 4 (in some collies) an eye that is particoloured white and blue 5 a North American pikeperch, *Stizostedion vitreum*, valued as a food and game fish 6 any of various other fishes having large staring eyes

wallflower 1 a plant, *Cheiranthus cheiri*, of S Europe, grown for its clusters of yellow, orange, brown, red, or purple fragrant flowers and naturalized on old walls, cliffs, etc.: family *Brassicaceae* (crucifers) 2 any of numerous other crucifers of the genera *Cheiranthus* and *Erysimum*, having orange or yellow flowers

Wallis Sir **Barnes** (**Neville**). 1887–1979, English aeronautical engineer. He designed the airship R100, the Wellesley and Wellington bombers, and the bouncing bomb (1943), which was used to destroy the Ruhr dams during World War II

Walloon 1 a member of a French-speaking people living chiefly in S Belgium and adjacent parts of France 2 the French dialect of Belgium

Walloon Brabant a province of central Belgium, formed in 1995 from the S part of Brabant province: densely populated and intensively farmed, with large industrial centres. Pop: 360 717 (2004 est). Area: 1091 sq km (421 sq miles)

wallow a muddy place or depression where animals wallow

Wallsend a town in NE England, in North Tyneside unitary authority, Tyne and Wear: situated on the River Tyne at the E end of Hadrian's Wall. Pop: 42 842 (2001)

Wall Street a street in lower Manhattan, New York, where the Stock Exchange and major banks are situated, regarded as the embodiment of American finance

wally *Central Scot, dialect* 1 made of china 2 lined with ceramic tiles

walnut 1 any juglandaceous deciduous tree of the genus *Juglans*, of America, SE Europe, and Asia, esp *J. regia*, which is native to W Asia but introduced elsewhere. They have aromatic leaves and flowers in catkins and are grown for their edible nuts and for their wood 2 the wood of any of these trees, used in making furniture, panelling, etc. 3 a light yellowish-brown colour 4 made from the wood of a walnut tree 5 of the colour walnut

Walpole 1 **Horace**, 4th Earl of Orford. 1717–97, British writer, noted for his letters and for his delight in the Gothic, as seen in his house Strawberry Hill and his novel *The Castle of Otranto* (1764) 2 Sir **Hugh** (**Seymour**). 1884–1941, British novelist, born in New Zealand: best known for *The Herries Chronicle* (1930–33), a sequence of historical novels set in the Lake District 3 Sir **Robert**, 1st Earl of Orford, father of Horace Walpole. 1676–1745, English Whig statesman. As first lord of the Treasury and Chancellor of the Exchequer (1721–42) he was effectively Britain's first prime minister

walrus a pinniped mammal, *Odobenus rosmarus*, of northern seas, having a tough thick skin, upper canine teeth enlarged as tusks, and coarse whiskers and feeding mainly on shellfish: family *Odobenidae*

Walsall 1 an industrial town in central England, in Walsall unitary authority, West Midlands: engineering, electronics. Pop: 170 994 (2001) 2 a unitary authority in central England, in the West Midlands. Pop: 252 400 (2003 est). Area: 106 sq km (41 sq miles)

Walsh **Courtney** (**Andrew**). born 1962, Jamaican cricketer; a fast bowler, he became the highest wicket-taker in test match history in 2000

Walsingham¹ Sir **Francis** ?1530–90, English statesman. As secretary of state (1573–90) to Elizabeth I he developed a system of domestic and foreign espionage and uncovered several plots against the Queen

Walsingham² a village in E England, in Norfolk: remains of a medieval priory; site of the shrine of Our Lady of Walsingham

Walter 1 **Bruno**, real name *Bruno Walter Schlesinger*. 1876–1962, US conductor, born in Germany: famous for his performances of Haydn, Mozart, and Mahler 2 **John** 1739–1812, English publisher; founded *The Daily Universal Register* (1785), which in 1788 became *The Times*

Waltham Forest a borough of NE Greater London. Pop: 221 600 (2003 est). Area: 40 sq km (15 sq miles)

Walton 1 **Ernest Thomas Sinton** 1903–95, Irish physicist. He succeeded in producing the first artificial transmutation of an atomic nucleus (1932) with Sir John Cockcroft, with whom he shared the Nobel prize for physics 1951 2 **Izaak** 1593–1683, English writer, best known for *The Compleat Angler* (1653; enlarged 1676) 3 Sir **William** (**Turner**). 1902–83, English composer. His works include *Façade* (1923), a setting of satirical verses by Edith Sitwell, the *Viola Concerto* (1929), and the oratorio *Belshazzar's Feast* (1931)

waltz 1 a ballroom dance in triple time in which couples spin around as they progress round the room **2** a piece of music composed for or in the rhythm of this dance

Walvis Bay *or* **Walfish Bay** a port in Namibia, on the Atlantic: formed an exclave of South Africa, covering an area of 1124 sq km (434 sq miles) with its hinterland, but has been administered by Namibia since 1992; formally returned to Namibia in 1994; chief port of Namibia and rich fishing centre. Pop: 40 849 (2001)

wampum (formerly) money used by North American Indians, made of cylindrical shells strung or woven together, esp white shells rather than the more valuable black or purple ones

wan 1 unnaturally pale esp from sickness, grief, etc. **2** characteristic or suggestive of ill health, unhappiness, etc. **3** (of light, stars, etc) faint or dim

wand 1 a thin rod carried as a symbol of authority **2** a rod used by a magician, water diviner, etc. **3** *Informal* a conductor's baton **4** *Archery* a marker used to show the distance at which the archer stands from the target **5** a hand-held electronic device, such as a light pen or bar-code reader, which is pointed at or passed over an item to read the data stored there

Wandsworth a borough of S Greater London, on the River Thames. Pop: 274 100 (2003 est). Area: 35 sq km (13 sq miles)

wane 1 the period during which the moon wanes **2** a rounded surface or defective edge of a plank, where the bark was

Wanganui a port in New Zealand, on SW North Island: centre for a dairy-farming and sheep-rearing district. Pop: 43 600 (2004 est)

Wanne-Eickel an industrial town in W Germany, in North Rhine-Westphalia on the Rhine-Herne Canal: formed in 1926 by the merging of two townships. Pop: 98 800 (latest est)

want *English, dialect* a mole

Wanxian, Wanhsien, *or* **Wan-Hsien** an inland port in central China, in E Sichuan province, on the Yangtze River. Pop: 1 963 000 (2005 est)

wapiti a large deer, *Cervus canadensis*, with large much-branched antlers, native to North America and now also common in the South Island of New Zealand

Warangal a city in S central India, in N Andhra Pradesh: capital of a 12th-century Hindu kingdom. Pop: 528 570 (2001)

waratah *Austral* a proteaceous shrub, *Telopea speciosissima*, the floral emblem of New South Wales, having dark green leaves and large clusters of crimson flowers

Warbeck Perkin ?1474–99, Flemish impostor, pretender to the English throne. Professing to be Richard, Duke of York, he led an unsuccessful rising against Henry VII (1497) and was later executed

warble *Vet science* **1** a small lumpy abscess under the skin of cattle caused by infestation with larvae of the war-ble fly **2** a hard tumorous lump of tissue on a horse's back, caused by prolonged friction of a saddle

warbler 1 a person or thing that warbles **2** any small active passerine songbird of the Old World subfamily *Sylviinae*: family *Muscicapidae*. They have a cryptic plumage and slender bill and are arboreal insectivores **3** any small bird of the American family *Parulidae*, simi-

lar to the Old World forms but often brightly coloured

Warburg Otto (Heinrich). 1883–1970, German bio-chemist and physiologist: Nobel prize for physiology or medicine (1931) for his work on respiratory enzymes

war crime a crime committed in wartime in violation of the accepted rules and customs of war, such as geno-cide, ill-treatment of prisoners of war, etc.

ward 1 (in many countries) a district into which a city, town, parish, or other area is divided for administra-tion, election of representatives, etc. **2** a room in a hos-pital, esp one for patients requiring similar kinds of care **3** one of the divisions of a prison **4** *Law* **a** a person, esp a minor or one legally incapable of managing his own affairs, placed under the control or protection of a guardian or of a court **b** guardianship, as of a minor or legally incompetent person **5** the state of being under guard or in custody **6 a** an internal ridge or bar in a lock that prevents an incorrectly cut key from turning **b** a corresponding groove cut in a key

Ward 1 Dame Barbara (Mary), Baroness Jackson. 1914–81, British economist, environmentalist, and writer. Her books include *Spaceship Earth* (1966) **2** Mrs Humphry, married name of *Mary Augusta Arnold*. 1851–1920, English novelist. Her novels include *Robert Elsmere* (1888) and *The Case of Richard Meynell* (1911) **3** Sir Joseph George 1856–1930, New Zealand statesman; prime minister of New Zealand (1906–12; 1928–30)

warden 1 *Archaic* any of various public officials, esp one responsible for the enforcement of certain regulations **2** *Chiefly US and Canadian* the chief officer in charge of a prison **3** *Brit* the principal or president of any of various universities or colleges **4** See churchwarden

warder[1] *or feminine* **wardress** *Chiefly Brit* an officer in charge of prisoners in a jail

warder[2] (formerly) a staff or truncheon carried by a ruler as an emblem of authority and used to signal his wishes or intentions

Wardour Street a street in Soho where many film com-panies have their London offices: formerly noted for shops selling antiques and mock antiques

wardrobe the collection of costumes belonging to a theatre or theatrical company

wardroom 1 the quarters assigned to the officers (except the captain) of a warship **2** the officers of a warship collectively, excepting the captain

ware porcelain or pottery of a specified type

warehouse 1 a place where goods are stored prior to their use, distribution, or sale **2** *Chiefly Brit* a large com-mercial, esp wholesale, establishment

war game a game in which model soldiers are used to create battles, esp past battles, in order to study tactics

Warhol Andy, real name *Andrew Warhola*. ?1926–87, US artist and film maker; one of the foremost exponents of pop art

Warley an industrial town in W central England, in Sandwell unitary authority, West Midlands: formed in 1966 by the amalgamation of Smethwick, Oldbury, and Rowley Regis. Pop: 189 854 (2001)

warlock 1 a man who practises black magic; sorcerer **2** a fortune-teller, conjuror, or magician

Warlock Peter, real name *Philip Arnold Heseltine*. 1894–1930, British composer and scholar of early

English music. His works include song cycles, such as *The Curlew* (1920–22), and the *Capriol Suite* (1926) for strings

warlord a military leader of a nation or part of a nation, esp one who is accountable to nobody when the central government is weak

warm 1 (of colours) predominantly red or yellow in tone 2 (of a scent, trail, etc) recently made; strong 3 near to finding a hidden object or discovering or guessing facts, as in children's games

warm-blooded (of birds and mammals) having a constant body temperature, usually higher than the temperature of the surroundings

warm-down light exercises performed to aid recovery from strenuous physical activity

war memorial a monument, usually an obelisk or cross, to those who die in a war, esp those from a particular locality

warm front *Meteorol* the boundary between a warm air mass and the cold air above which it is rising, at a less steep angle than at the cold front

Warne Shane (Keith). born 1969, Australian cricketer, playing for Australia since 1991

warning (of the coloration of certain distasteful or poisonous animals) having conspicuous markings, which predators recognize and learn to avoid; aposematic

warp 1 a mental or moral deviation 2 the yarns arranged lengthways on a loom, forming the threads through which the weft yarns are woven 3 the heavy threads used to reinforce the rubber in the casing of a pneumatic tyre 4 *Nautical* a rope used for warping a vessel 5 alluvial sediment deposited by water

war paint painted decoration of the face and body applied by certain North American Indians before battle

warpath the route taken by North American Indians on a warlike expedition

warrant 1 a document that certifies or guarantees, such as a receipt for goods stored in a warehouse, a licence, or a commission 2 *Law* an authorization issued by a magistrate or other official allowing a constable or other officer to search or seize property, arrest a person, or perform some other specified act

Warrant of Fitness NZ a six-monthly certificate required for motor vehicles certifying mechanical soundness

warrantor an individual or company that provides a warranty

warranty 1 *Property law* a covenant, express or implied, by which the vendor of real property vouches for the security of the title conveyed 2 *Contract law* an express or implied term in a contract, such as an undertaking that goods contracted to be sold shall meet specified requirements as to quality, etc. 3 *Insurance law* an undertaking by the party insured that the facts given regarding the risk are as stated

warren 1 a series of interconnected underground tunnels in which rabbits live 2 a colony of rabbits 3 an overcrowded area or dwelling 4 a *Chiefly Brit* an enclosed place where small game animals or birds are kept, esp for breeding, or a part of a river or lake enclosed by nets in which fish are kept (esp in the phrase **beasts** or **fowls of warren**) b *English legal history* a

franchise permitting one to keep animals, birds, or fish in this way

Warren[1] Earl 1891–1974, US lawyer; chief justice of the US (1953– 69). He chaired the commission that investigated the murder of President Kennedy

Warren[2] a city in the US, in SE Michigan, northeast of Detroit. Pop: 136 016 (2003 est)

warrigal *Austral* a dingo 2 another word for **brumby**

Warrington 1 an industrial town in NW England, in Warrington unitary authority, Cheshire on the River Mersey: dates from Roman times. Pop: 80 661 (2001) 2 a unitary authority in NW England, in N Cheshire. Pop: 193 200 (2003 est). Area: 176 sq km (68 sq miles)

Warsaw the capital of Poland, in the E central part on the River Vistula: became capital at the end of the 16th century; almost completely destroyed in World War II as the main centre of the Polish resistance movement; rebuilt within about six years; university (1818); situated at the junction of important trans-European routes. Pop: 2 204 000 (2005 est)

wart 1 *Pathol* any firm abnormal elevation of the skin caused by a virus 2 *Botany* a small rounded outgrowth

Warta a river in Poland, flowing generally north and west across the whole W Polish Plain to the River Oder. Length: 808 km (502 miles)

Wartburg a medieval castle in central Germany, in Thuringia southwest of Eisenach: residence of Luther (1521–22) when he began his German translation of the New Testament

warthog a wild pig, *Phacochoerus aethiopicus*, of southern and E Africa, having heavy tusks, wartlike protuberances on the face, and a mane of coarse hair

Warwick[1] Earl of, title of *Richard Neville*, known as *the Kingmaker.* 1428–71, English statesman. During the Wars of the Roses, he fought first for the Yorkists, securing the throne (1461) for Edward IV, and then for the Lancastrians, restoring Henry VI (1470). He was killed at Barnet by Edward IV

Warwick[2] a town in central England, administrative centre of Warwickshire, on the River Avon: 14th-century castle, with collections of armour and waxworks: the university of Warwick (1965) is in Coventry. Pop: 23 350 (2001)

Warwickshire a county of central England: until 1974, when the West Midlands metropolitan county was created, it contained one of the most highly industrialized regions in the world, centred on Birmingham. Administrative centre: Warwick. Pop: 519 300 (2003 est). Area: 1981 sq km (765 sq miles)

Wasatch Range a mountain range in the W central US, in N Utah and SE Idaho. Highest peak: Mount Timpanogos, 3581 m (11 750 ft)

wash 1 *Med* any medicinal or soothing lotion for application to a part of the body 2 the flow of water, esp waves, against a surface, or the sound made by such a flow 3 the technique of making wash drawings 4 the erosion of soil by the action of flowing water 5 a mass of alluvial material transported and deposited by flowing water 6 land that is habitually washed by tidal or river waters 7 an alcoholic liquid resembling strong beer, resulting from the fermentation of wort in the production of whisky

Wash the a shallow inlet of the North Sea on the E coast of England, between Lincolnshire and Norfolk

washer 1 a flat ring or drilled disc of metal used under the head of a bolt or nut to spread the load when tightened **2** any flat ring of rubber, felt, metal, etc, used to provide a seal under a nut or in a tap or valve seat **3** See **washing machine 4** *Chemical engineering* a device for cleaning or washing gases or vapours; scrubber **5** *Austral* a face cloth; flannel

washing 1 something, such as gold dust or metal ore, that has been obtained by washing **2** a thin coat of something applied in liquid form

washing machine a mechanical apparatus, usually powered by electricity, for washing clothing, linens, etc.

washing soda the crystalline decahydrate of sodium carbonate, esp when used as a cleansing agent

Washington[1] **1 Booker T(aliaferro).** 1856–1915, US Black educationalist and writer **2 Denzil .** US film actor; his films include *Glory* (1990), *Malcolm X* (1992), *The Hurricane* (1999), and *John Q.* (2002) **3 George** 1732–99, US general and statesman; first president of the US (1789–97). He was appointed commander in chief of the Continental Army (1775) at the outbreak of the War of American Independence, which ended with his defeat of Cornwallis at Yorktown (1781). He presided over the convention at Philadelphia (1787) that formulated the constitution of the US and elected him president

Washington[2] **1** a state of the northwestern US, on the Pacific: consists of the Coast Range and the Olympic Mountains in the west and the Columbia Plateau in the east. Capital: Olympia. Pop: 6 131 445 (2003 est). Area: 172 416 sq km (66 570 sq miles) **2** the capital of the US, coextensive with the District of Columbia and situated near the E coast on the Potomac River: site chosen by President Washington in 1790; contains the White House and the Capitol; a major educational and administrative centre. Pop: 563 384 (2003 est) **3** a town in Tyne and Wear: designated a new town in 1964. Pop: 53 388 (2001) **4 Mount** a mountain in N New Hampshire, in the White Mountains: the highest peak in the northeast US; noted for extreme weather conditions. Height: 1917 m (6288 ft) **5 Lake** a lake in W Washington, forming the E boundary of the city of Seattle: linked by canal with Puget Sound. Length: about 32 km (20 miles) Width: 6 km (4 miles)

washout 1 *Geology* **a** erosion of the earth's surface by the action of running water **b** a narrow channel produced by this erosion **2** *Aeronautics* a decrease in the angle of attack of an aircraft wing towards the wing tip

Wasim Akram Chaudhry born 1966, Pakistani cricketer; captain of Pakistan 1993–94, 1995–2000

wasp 1 any social hymenopterous insect of the family *Vespidae*, esp *Vespula vulgaris* (**common wasp**), typically having a black-and-yellow body and an ovipositor specialized for stinging **2** any of various solitary hymenopterans, such as the digger wasp and gall wasp

wassail 1 (formerly) a toast or salutation made to a person at festivities **2** a festivity when much drinking takes place **3** alcoholic drink drunk at such a festivity, esp spiced beer or mulled wine **4** the singing of Christmas carols, going from house to house **5** *Archaic* a drinking song

waste 1 a land or region that is devastated or ruined **2** a land or region that is wild or uncultivated **3** *Physiol* **a** the useless products of metabolism **b** indigestible food residue **4** disintegrated rock material resulting from erosion **5** *Law* reduction in the value of an estate caused by act or neglect, esp by a life-tenant

wasteland a barren or desolate area of land, not or no longer used for cultivation or building

waster an article spoiled in manufacture

Wast Water a lake in NW England, in Cumbria in the Lake District. Length: 5 km (3 miles)

watap a stringy thread made by North American Indians from the roots of various conifers and used for weaving and sewing

watch *Nautical* **a** any of the usually four-hour periods beginning at midnight and again at noon during which part of a ship's crew are on duty **b** those officers and crew on duty during a specified watch

watchdog a dog kept to guard property

water 1 a clear colourless tasteless odourless liquid that is essential for plant and animal life and constitutes, in impure form, rain, oceans, rivers, lakes, etc. It is a neutral substance, an effective solvent for many compounds, and is used as a standard for many physical properties. Formula: H_2O **2 a** any body or area of this liquid, such as a sea, lake, river, etc. **b** (*as modifier*): *water sports* **3** any form or variety of this liquid, such as rain **4** See **high water mark** or **low water 5** any of various solutions of chemical substances in water **6** *Physiol* any fluid secreted from the body, such as sweat, urine, or tears **b** the amniotic fluid surrounding a fetus in the womb **7** a wavy lustrous finish on some fabrics, esp silk **8** *Astrology* of or relating to the three signs of the zodiac Cancer, Scorpio, and Pisces

water buffalo or **ox** a member of the cattle tribe, *Bubalus bubalis*, of swampy regions of S Asia, having widely spreading back-curving horns. Domesticated forms are used as draught animals

water chestnut 1 a floating aquatic onagraceous plant, *Trapa natans*, of Asia, having four-pronged edible nut-like fruits **2 Chinese water chestnut** a Chinese cyperaceous plant, *Eleocharis tuberosa*, with an edible succulent corm

watercolour or US **watercolor 1 a** a water-soluble pigment, applied in transparent washes and without the admixture of white pigment in the lighter tones **b** any water-soluble pigment, including opaque kinds such as gouache and tempera **2 a** a painting done in watercolours **b** (*as modifier*): *a watercolour masterpiece* **3** the art or technique of painting with such pigments

watercourse 1 a stream, river, or canal **2** the channel, bed, or route along which this flows

watercress 1 an Old World plant, *Nasturtium officinale*, of clear ponds and streams, having pungent leaves that are used in salads and as a garnish: family *Brassicaceae* (crucifers) **2** any of several similar or related plants

water cycle the circulation of the earth's water, in which water evaporates from the sea into the atmosphere, where it condenses and falls as rain or snow, returning to the sea by rivers or returning to the atmosphere by evapotranspiration

water diviner *Brit* a person able to locate the presence of water, esp underground, with a divining rod

waterfall a cascade of falling water where there is a vertical or almost vertical step in a river

Waterford 1 a county of S Republic of Ireland, in Munster province on the Atlantic: mountainous in the centre and in the northwest. County town: Waterford. Pop: 101 546 (2002). Area: 1838 sq km (710 sq miles) **2** a port in S Republic of Ireland, county town of Co. Waterford: famous glass industry; fishing. Pop: 44 594 (2002)

waterfowl 1 any aquatic freshwater bird, esp any species of the family *Anatidae* (ducks, geese, and swans) **2** such birds collectively

waterfront the area of a town or city alongside a body of water, such as a harbour or dockyard

Waterhouse 1 Alfred 1830–1905, British architect; a leader of the Gothic Revival. His buildings include Manchester Town Hall (1868) and the Natural History Museum, London (1881) **2 George Marsden** 1824–1906, New Zealand statesman, born in England: prime minister of New Zealand (1872–73) **3** Keith (**Spencer**). born 1929, British novelist, dramatist, and journalist: best known for the novel *Billy Liar* (1959) and his collaborations with the dramatist Willis Hall (born 1929)

watering can a container with a handle and a spout with a perforated nozzle used to sprinkle water over plants

watering hole 1 a pool where animals drink; water hole **2** *Facetious slang* a pub

watering place 1 a place where drinking water for men or animals may be obtained **2** *Brit* a spa **3** *Brit* a seaside resort

water jump a ditch, brook, or pond over which athletes or horses must jump in a steeplechase or similar contest

water level the water line of a boat or ship

water lily 1 any of various aquatic plants of the genus *Nymphaea* and related genera, of temperate and tropical regions, having large leaves and showy flowers that float on the surface of the water: family *Nymphaeaceae* **2** any of various similar and related plants, such as the yellow water lily

water line a line marked at the level around a vessel's hull to which the vessel will be immersed when afloat

waterlogged (of a vessel still afloat) having taken in so much water as to be unmanageable

Waterloo a small town in central Belgium, in Walloon Brabant province south of Brussels: battle (1815) fought nearby in which British and Prussian forces under the Duke of Wellington and Blücher routed the French under Napoleon. Pop: 29 003 (2004 est)

water main a principal supply pipe in an arrangement of pipes for distributing water

watermelon an African melon, *Citrullus vulgaris*, widely cultivated for its large edible fruit

water pistol a toy pistol that squirts a stream of water or other liquid

water polo a game played in water by two teams of seven swimmers in which each side tries to throw or propel an inflated ball into the opponents' goal
▷www.fina.org

water power 1 the power latent in a dynamic or static head of water as used to drive machinery, esp for generating electricity **2** a source of such power, such as a drop in the level of a river, etc. **3** the right to the use of water for such a purpose, as possessed by a water mill

water rat 1 any of several small amphibious rodents, esp the water vole or the muskrat **2** any of various amphibious rats of the subfamily *Hydromyinae*, of New Guinea, the Philippines, and Australia

water-resistant (esp of fabrics) designed to resist but not entirely prevent the penetration of water

Waters Muddy, real name *McKinley Morganfield*. 1915–83, US blues guitarist, singer, and songwriter. His songs include "Rollin' Stone" (1948) and "Got my Mojo Working" (1954)

watershed the dividing line between two adjacent river systems, such as a ridge

waterside a the area of land beside a body of water **b** (*as modifier*): *waterside houses*

watersider *Austral and NZ* a wharf labourer

water-ski a type of ski used for planing or gliding over water

water softener 1 any substance that lessens the hardness of water, usually by precipitating or absorbing calcium and magnesium ions **2** a tank, apparatus, or chemical plant that is used to filter or treat water to remove chemicals that cause hardness

waterspout *Meteorol* **a** a tornado occurring over water that forms a column of water and mist extending between the surface and the clouds above **b** a sudden downpour of heavy rain

water table 1 the surface of the water-saturated part of the ground, usually following approximately the contours of the overlying land surface **2** an offset or string course that has a moulding designed to throw rainwater clear of the wall below

water tower a reservoir or storage tank mounted on a tower-like structure at the summit of an area of high ground in a place where the water pressure would otherwise be inadequate for distribution at a uniform pressure

water vapour water in the gaseous state, esp when due to evaporation at a temperature below the boiling point

water vole a large amphibious vole, *Arvicola terrestris*, of Eurasian river banks: family *Cricetidae*

waterway a river, canal, or other navigable channel used as a means of travel or transport

water wheel 1 a simple water-driven turbine consisting of a wheel having vanes set axially across its rim, used to drive machinery **2** a wheel with buckets attached to its rim for raising water from a stream, pond, etc.

waterworks 1 an establishment for storing, purifying, and distributing water for community supply **2** a display of water in movement, as in fountains

Watford a town in SE England, in SW Hertfordshire: light industries, services. Pop: 120 960 (2001)

Watson 1 James Dewey born 1928, US biologist, whose contribution to the discovery of the helical structure of DNA won him a Nobel prize for physiology or medicine shared with Francis Crick and Maurice Wilkins in 1962 **2** John B(**roadus**). 1878–1958, US psychologist; a leading exponent of behaviourism **3 John Christian** 1867–1941, Australian statesman, born in Chile: prime minister of Australia (1904) **4 Russell** born 1973, British tenor, maker of the bestselling albums *The Voice* (2001) and *Encore* (2002) **5 Tom**, full name *Thomas Sturges Watson*. born 1949, US golfer: won the US Open Championship (1982), the British Open Championship (1975, 1977, 1980, 1982, 1983), and the World Series (1975, 1977, 1980)

Watson-Watt Sir Robert Alexander 1892–1973, Scottish physicist, who played a leading role in the development of radar

watt the derived SI unit of power, equal to 1 joule per second; the power dissipated by a current of 1 ampere flowing across a potential difference of 1 volt. 1 watt is equivalent to 1.341×10^{-3} horsepower.

Watt James 1736–1819, Scottish engineer and inventor. His fundamental improvements to the steam engine led to the widespread use of steam power in industry

wattage 1 power, esp electric power, measured in watts 2 the power rating, measured in watts, of an electrical appliance

Watteau Jean-Antoine 1684–1721, French painter, esp of *fêtes champêtres*

Wattenscheid an industrial town in NW Germany, in North Rhine-Westphalia east of Essen. Pop: 81 200 (latest est)

wattle 1 a loose fold of skin, often brightly coloured, hanging from the neck or throat of certain birds, lizards, etc. 2 any of various chiefly Australian acacia trees having spikes of small brightly coloured flowers and flexible branches, which were used by early settlers for making fences 3 a southern African caesalpinaceous tree, *Peltophorum africanum*, with yellow flowers

Watts 1 George Frederick 1817–1904, English painter and sculptor, noted esp for his painting *Hope* (1886) and his sculpture *Physical Energy* (1904) in Kensington Gardens, London 2 Isaac 1674–1748, English hymn-writer

Waugh Evelyn (Arthur St. John). 1903–66, English novelist. His early satirical novels include *Decline and Fall* (1928), *Vile Bodies* (1930), *A Handful of Dust* (1934), and *Scoop* (1938). His later novels include the more sombre *Brideshead Revisited* (1945) and the trilogy of World War II *Men at Arms* (1952), *Officers and Gentlemen* (1955), and *Unconditional Surrender* (1961) 1 Mark (Edward). born 1965, Australian cricketer 2 his twin brother Steve, full name *Stephen Roger Waugh*. born 1965, Australian cricketer; captain of the Australian team that won the 1999 one-day World Cup

wave 1 one of a sequence of ridges or undulations that moves across the surface of a body of a liquid, esp the sea: created by the wind or a moving object and gravity 2 the waves the sea 3 *Physics* an oscillation propagated through a medium or space such that energy is periodically interchanged between two kinds of disturbance. For example, an oscillating electric field generates a magnetic oscillation and vice versa, hence an electromagnetic wave is produced. Similarly a wave on a liquid comprises vertical and horizontal displacements 4 *Physics* a graphical representation of a wave obtained by plotting the magnitude of the disturbance against time at a particular point in the medium or space; waveform 5 a prolonged spell of some weather condition 6 an undulating pattern or finish on a fabric

wavelength the distance, measured in the direction of propagation, between two points of the same phase in consecutive cycles of a wave.

Wavell Archibald (Percival), 1st Earl. 1883–1950, British field marshal. During World War II he was commander in chief in the Middle East (1939–41), defeating the Italians in N Africa. He was commander in chief in India (1941–43) and viceroy of India (1943–47)

wavey *Canadian* a snow goose or other wild goose

wax 1 any of various viscous or solid materials of natural origin: characteristically lustrous, insoluble in water, and having a low softening temperature, they consist largely of esters of fatty acids 2 any of various similar substances, such as paraffin wax or ozocerite, that have a mineral origin and consist largely of hydrocarbons 3 short for **beeswax** *or* **sealing wax** 4 a resinous preparation used by shoemakers to rub on thread 5 **bone wax** a mixture of wax, oil, and carbolic acid applied to the cut surface of a bone to prevent bleeding

waxwork 1 an object reproduced in wax, esp as an ornament 2 a life-size lifelike figure, esp of a famous person, reproduced in wax 3 a museum or exhibition of wax figures or objects

way 1 a route or direction 2 a means or line of passage, such as a path or track 3 a street in or leading out of a town 4 movement of a ship or other vessel 5 a right of way in law 6 a guide along which something can be moved, such as the surface of a lathe along which the tailstock slides 7 the wooden or metal tracks down which a ship slides to be launched 8 **each way** (of a bet) laid on a horse, dog, etc, to win or gain a place

waybill a document attached to goods in transit specifying their nature, point of origin, and destination as well as the route to be taken and the rate to be charged

Wayne John, real name *Marion Michael Morrison*. 1907–79, US film actor, noted esp for his many Westerns, which include *Stagecoach* (1939), *The Alamo* (1960), and *True Grit* (1969), for which he won an Oscar

wayside a the side or edge of a road b situated by the wayside

Waziristan a mountainous region of N Pakistan, on the border with Afghanistan

weak 1 lacking in political or strategic strength 2 (of a syllable) not accented or stressed 3 (of a fuel-air mixture) containing a relatively low proportion of fuel 4 *Photog* having low density or contrast; thin

weak-minded 1 lacking in stability of mind or character 2 another word for **feeble-minded**

weal[1] a raised mark on the surface of the body produced by a blow

weal[2] *Obsolete* the state

Weald the a region of SE England, in Kent, Surrey, and East and West Sussex between the North Downs and the South Downs: formerly forested

wealth 1 a large amount of money and valuable material possessions 2 the state of being rich 3 *Economics* all goods and services with monetary, exchangeable, or productive value

Wear a river in NE England, rising in NW Durham and flowing southeast then northeast to the North Sea at Sunderland. Length: 105 km (65 miles)

weasel 1 any of various small predatory musteline mammals of the genus *Mustela* and related genera, esp *M. nivalis* (**European weasel**), having reddish-brown fur, an elongated body and neck, and short legs **2** *Chiefly US* a motor vehicle for use in snow, esp one with caterpillar tracks

weather 1 a the day-to-day meteorological conditions, esp temperature, cloudiness, and rainfall, affecting a specific place **b** relating to the forecasting of weather **2 make heavy weather** (of a vessel) to roll and pitch in heavy seas
▷http://sciencepolicy.colorado.edu/socasp/ toc_img.html
▷www.wmo.ch
▷www.worldweather.org

weatherboard the windward side of a vessel

weathercock a weather vane in the form of a cock

weather eye the vision of a person trained to observe changes in the weather

weathering the mechanical and chemical breakdown of rocks by the action of rain, snow, cold, etc.

weatherman a person who forecasts the weather, esp one who works in a meteorological office

weather vane a vane designed to indicate the direction in which the wind is blowing

weave the method or pattern of weaving or the structure of a woven fabric
▷www.faculty.de.gcsu.edu/~dvess/ids/fap/ weav.html

web 1 a mesh of fine tough scleroprotein threads built by a spider from a liquid secreted from its spinnerets and used to trap insects **2** a similar network of threads spun by certain insect larvae, such as the silkworm **3** a fabric, esp one in the process of being woven **4** a membrane connecting the toes of some aquatic birds or the digits of such aquatic mammals as the otter **5** the vane of a bird's feather **6** *Architect* the surface of a ribbed vault that lies between the ribs **7** the central section of an I-beam or H-beam that joins the two flanges of the beam **8** any web-shaped part of a casting used for reinforcement **9** the radial portion of a crank that connects the crankpin to the crankshaft **10** a thin piece of superfluous material left attached to a forging; fin **11** the woven edge, without pile, of some carpets **12** short for **World Wide Web**

Webb 1 Sir Aston 1849–1930, British architect. His work includes the Victoria and Albert Museum (1909), the Victoria Memorial (1911), and Admiralty Arch (1911) **2** Mary (Gladys). 1881–1927, British novelist, remembered for her novels of rustic life, notably *Precious Bane* (1924) **3** Sidney (James), Baron Passfield. 1859–1947, British economist, social historian, and Fabian socialist. He and his wife (Martha) Beatrice (née Potter), 1858–1943, British writer on social and economic problems, collaborated in *The History of Trade Unionism* (1894) and *English Local Government* (1906–29), helped found the London School of Economics (1895), and started the *New Statesman* (1913)

webbing 1 a strong fabric of hemp, cotton, jute, etc, woven in strips and used under springs in upholstery or for straps, etc. **2** the skin that unites the digits of a webbed foot

webcam a camera that transmits still or moving images over the internet

webcast a broadcast of an event over the World Wide Web

weber the derived SI unit of magnetic flux; the flux that, when linking a circuit of one turn, produces in it an emf of 1 volt as it is reduced to zero at a uniform rate in one second. 1 weber is equivalent to 10^8 maxwells

Weber 1 Baron Carl Maria Friedrich Ernst von 1786–1826, German composer and conductor. His three romantic operas are *Der Freischütz* (1821), *Euryanthe* (1823), and *Oberon* (1826) **2** Ernst Heinrich 1795–1878, German physiologist and anatomist. He introduced the psychological concept of the just noticeable difference between stimuli **3** Max 1864–1920, German economist and sociologist, best known for *The Protestant Ethic and the Spirit of Capitalism* (1904–05) **4** Wilhelm Eduard , brother of Ernst Heinrich Weber. 1804–91, German physicist, who conducted research into electricity and magnetism

Webern Anton von 1883–1945, Austrian composer; pupil of Schoenberg, whose twelve-tone technique he adopted. His works include those for chamber ensemble, such as *Five Pieces for Orchestra* (1911–13)

web-footed *or* **web-toed** (of certain animals) having webbed feet that facilitate swimming

website a group of connected pages on the World Wide Web containing information on a particular subject

Webster 1 Daniel 1782–1852, US politician and orator **2** John ?1580–?1625, English dramatist, noted for his revenge tragedies *The White Devil* (?1612) and *The Duchess of Malfi* (?1613) **3** Noah 1758–1843, US lexicographer, famous for his *American Dictionary of the English Language* (1828)

Weddell Sea an arm of the S Atlantic in Antarctica

Wedekind Frank 1864–1918, German dramatist, whose plays, such as *The Awakening of Spring* (1891) and *Pandora's Box* (1904), bitterly satirize the sexual repressiveness of society

wedge 1 *Golf* a club with a face angle of more than 50°, used for bunker shots (**sand wedge**) or pitch shots (**pitching wedge**) **2** a wedge-shaped extension of the high pressure area of an anticyclone, narrower than a ridge **3** *Mountaineering* a wedge-shaped device, formerly of wood, now usually of hollow steel, for hammering into a crack to provide an anchor point **4** any of the triangular characters used in cuneiform writing **5** *Photog* a strip of glass coated in such a way that it is clear at one end but becomes progressively more opaque towards the other end: used in making measurements of transmission density

wedge-tailed eagle a large brown Australian eagle, *Aquila audax*, having a wedge-shaped tail and a wingspan of 3 m

Wedgwood¹ *Trademark* **a** pottery produced, esp during the late 18th and early 19th centuries, at the Wedgwood factories **b** such pottery having applied classical decoration in white on a blue or other coloured ground

Wedgwood² Josiah 1730–95, British potter and industrialist, who founded several pottery works near Stoke-on-Trent in Staffordshire

weed 1 any plant that grows wild and profusely, esp one that grows among cultivated plants, depriving them of space, food, etc. **2** *Slang* **a the weed** tobacco **b** marijuana **3** an inferior horse, esp one showing signs of weakness of constitution

weedkiller a substance, usually a chemical or hormone, used for killing weeds

weedy (of a plant) resembling a weed in rapid or straggling growth

weekday any day of the week other than Sunday and, often, Saturday

Weelkes Thomas ?1575–1623, English composer of madrigals

weeping willow a hybrid willow tree, *Salix alba × S. babylonica*, known as *S. alba* var. *tristis*, having long hanging branches: widely planted for ornament

weepy *Informal* a romantic and sentimental film or book

weevil 1 any beetle of the family *Curculionidae*, having an elongated snout (rostrum): they are pests, feeding on plants and plant products **2** any of various beetles of the family *Bruchidae* (or *Lariidae*), the larvae of which live in the seeds of leguminous plants **3** any of various similar or related beetles

weft the yarn woven across the width of the fabric through the lengthwise warp yarn

Wegener Alfred 1880–1930, German meteorologist: regarded as the originator of the theory of continental drift

weighbridge a machine for weighing vehicles, etc, by means of a metal plate set into a road

weigh-in the act of checking a competitor's weight, as in boxing, horse racing, etc.

weight 1 *Physics* the vertical force experienced by a mass as a result of gravitation. It equals the mass of the body multiplied by the acceleration of free fall. Its units are units of force (such as newtons or poundals) but is often given as a mass unit (kilogram or pound). **2** a system of units used to express the weight of a substance **3** a unit used to measure weight

weightless 1 (of a body) having no actual weight; a state in which an object has no actual weight (because it is in space and unaffected by gravitational attraction) or no apparent weight (because the gravitational attraction equals the centripetal force and the object is in free fall) **2** *Business* **a** (of economic activity) based on the supply of information and ideas rather than trade in physical goods **b** (of a company) having very few physical assets

weightlifting the sport of lifting barbells of specified weights in a prescribed manner for competition or exercise

▷www.iwf.net

weight training physical exercise involving lifting weights to improve muscle performance

Weihai *or* **Wei-hai** a port in NE China, in NE Shandong on the Yellow Sea: leased to Britain as a naval base (1898–1930). Pop: 966 000 (2005 est)

Weil Simone 1909–43, French philosopher and mystic, whose works include *Waiting for God* (1951), *The Need for Roots* (1952), and *Notebooks* (1956)

Weill Kurt 1900–50, German composer, in the US from 1935. He wrote the music for Brecht's *The Rise and Fall of the City of Mahagonny* (1927) and *The Threepenny Opera* (1928)

Weimar a city in E central Germany, in Thuringia: a cul-

tural centre in the 18th and early 19th century; scene of the adoption (1919) of the constitution of the Weimar Republic. Pop: 64 409 (2003 est)

Weinberg Steven born 1933, US physicist, who shared the Nobel prize for physics (1979) with Sheldon Glashow and Abdus Salam for his role in formulating the electroweak theory

weir 1 a low dam that is built across a river to raise the water level, divert the water, or control its flow **2** a series of traps or enclosures placed in a stream to catch fish

Weir 1 Judith born 1954, Scottish composer, noted esp for her opera *A Night at the Chinese Opera* (1987) **2** Peter born 1944, Australian film director; his films include *Dead Poets Society* (1989), *The Truman Show* (1998), and *Master and Commander* (2003)

Weisshorn a mountain in S Switzerland, in the Pennine Alps. Height: 4505 m (14 781 ft)

Weissmuller John Peter, known as *Johnny*. 1904–84, US swimmer and film actor, who won Olympic gold medals in 1924 and 1928 and played the title role in the early Tarzan films

Weizmann Chaim 1874–1952, Israeli statesman, born in Russia. As a leading Zionist, he was largely responsible for securing the Balfour Declaration (1917); first president of Israel (1949–52)

Weld Sir Frederick Aloysius 1823–91, New Zealand statesman, born in England: prime minister of New Zealand (1864–65)

Weldon Fay born 1931, British novelist and writer. Her novels include *Praxis* (1978), *Life and Loves of a She-Devil* (1984), *Big Women* (1998), and *Rhode Island Blues* (2003)

welfare 1 a financial and other assistance given to people in need (*as modifier*): *welfare services* **b** plans or work to better the social or economic conditions of various underprivileged groups **3 the welfare** *Informal, chiefly Brit* the public agencies involved with giving such assistance **4 on welfare** *Chiefly US and Canadian* in receipt of financial aid from a government agency or other source

welfare state 1 a system in which the government undertakes the chief responsibility for providing for the social and economic security of its population, usually through unemployment insurance, old-age pensions, and other social-security measures **2** a social system characterized by such policies

Welkom a town in central South Africa; developed rapidly following the discovery of gold. Pop: 34 157 (2001)

well 1 a hole or shaft that is excavated, drilled, bored, or cut into the earth so as to tap a supply of water, oil, gas, etc. **2** a natural pool where ground water comes to the surface **3 a** a bulkheaded compartment built around a ship's pumps for protection and ease of access **b** another word for **cockpit 4** a perforated tank in the hold of a fishing boat for keeping caught fish alive **5** (in England) the open space in the centre of a law court

Welland Canal a canal in S Canada, in Ontario, linking Lake Erie to Lake Ontario: part of the St Lawrence Seaway, with eight locks. Length: 44 km (28 miles)

Welles (George) Orson 1915–85, US film director, actor, producer, and screenwriter. His *Citizen Kane* (1941) and *The Magnificent Ambersons* (1942) are regarded as film classics

Wellesley his brother, **Richard Colley,** Marquis Wellesley. 1760–1842, British administrator. As governor general of Bengal (1797–1805) he consolidated British power in India

wellhead the source of a well or stream

Wellingborough a town in central England, in Northamptonshire. Pop: 46 959 (2001)

Wellington[1] **1st Duke of,** title of *Arthur Wellesley.* 1769–1852, British soldier and statesman; prime minister (1828–30). He was given command of the British forces against the French in the Peninsular War (1808–14) and routed Napoleon at Waterloo (1815)

Wellington[2] **1** an administrative district, formerly a province, of New Zealand, on SW North Island: major livestock producer in New Zealand. Capital: Wellington. Pop: 456 900 (2004 est). Area: 28 153 sq km (10 870 sq miles) **2** the capital city of New Zealand. Its port, historically Port Nicholson, on **Wellington Harbour** has a car and rail ferry link between the North and South Islands; university (1899). Pop: 182 600 (2004 est)

Wells[1] **1** Henry 1805–78, US businessman, who founded (1852) with William Fargo the express mail service Wells, Fargo and Company **2** H(erbert) G(eorge). 1866–1946, British writer. His science-fiction stories include *The Time Machine* (1895), *War of the Worlds* (1898), and *The Shape of Things to Come* (1933). His novels on contemporary social questions, such as *Kipps* (1905), *Tono-Bungay* (1909), and *Ann Veronica* (1909), affected the opinions of his day. His nonfiction works include *The Outline of History* (1920)

Wells[2] a city in SW England, in Somerset: 12th-century cathedral. Pop: 10 406 (2001)

wellspring the source of a spring or stream; fountainhead

Wels an industrial city in N central Austria, in Upper Austria. Pop: 56 478 (2002)

Welsh[1] a language of Wales, belonging to the S Celtic branch of the Indo-European family. Welsh shows considerable diversity between dialects

Welsh[2] a white long-bodied lop-eared breed of pig, kept chiefly for bacon

welterweight 1 a a professional boxer weighing 140–147 pounds (63.5–66.5 kg) **b** an amateur boxer weighing 63.5–67 kg (140–148 pounds) **c** (*as modifier*): *a great welterweight era* **2** a wrestler in a similar weight category (usually 154–172 pounds (70–78 kg))

Welwyn Garden City a town in SE England, in Hertfordshire: established (1920) as a planned industrial and residential community. Pop: 43 512 (2001)

Wembley part of the Greater London borough of Brent: site of the English national soccer stadium

wen[1] **1** *Pathol* a sebaceous cyst, esp one occurring on the scalp **2** a large overcrowded city (esp London in the phrase **the great wen**)

wen[2] a rune having the sound of Modern English *w*

Wenceslaus *or* **Wenceslas 1** 1361–1419, Holy Roman Emperor (1378–1400) and, as **Wenceslaus IV,** king of Bohemia (1378–1419) **2 Saint,** known as *Good King Wenceslaus.* ?907–929, duke of Bohemia (?925–29); patron saint of Bohemia. Feast day: Sept 28

wensleydale a breed of sheep with long woolly fleece

Wentworth William Charles 1790–1872, Australian explorer and statesman who was a member of the exploring party that first crossed the Blue Mountains in 1813 and was later a leader in the movement for self-government in New South Wales

Wenzhou, Wen-chou, *or* **Wenchow** a port in SE China, in Zhejiang province: noted for its historic buildings. Pop: 1 475 000 (2005 est)

werewolf a person fabled in folklore and superstition to have been changed into a wolf by being bewitched or said to be able to assume wolf form at will

Werner Abraham Gottlieb 1749–1817, German geologist. He emphasized the importance of field and laboratory observation for understanding the earth **2 Alfred** 1866–1919, Swiss chemist, born in Germany. He developed a coordination theory of the valency of inorganic complexes: Nobel prize for chemistry 1913

Weser a river in NW Germany: flows northwest to the North Sea at Bremerhaven and is linked by the Mittelland Canal to the Ems, Rhine, and Elbe waterways. Length: 477 km (196 miles)

Wesker Arnold born 1932, British dramatist, whose plays include *Roots* (1959), *Chips With Everything* (1962), *The Merchant* (1976), *Caritas* (1981), and *Break My Heart* (1997)

Wesley 1 Charles 1707–88, English Methodist preacher and writer of hymns **2** his brother, **John** 1703–91, English preacher, who founded Methodism **3 Mary,** pseudonym of *Mary Aline Siepmann.* 1912–2003, British writer: her novels include *The Camomile Lawn* (1984) and *An Imaginative Experience* (1994)

Wessex[1] **Earl of** See Edward[1] (sense 2)

Wessex[2] **1** an Anglo-Saxon kingdom in S and SW England that became the most powerful English kingdom by the 10th century AD **2 a** (in Thomas Hardy's works) the southwestern counties of England, esp Dorset **b** (*as modifier*): *Wessex Poems*

west 1 one of the four cardinal points of the compass, 270° clockwise from north and 180° from east **2** the direction along a parallel towards the sunset, at 270° clockwise from north **3 the west** any area lying in or towards the west **4** *Cards* the player or position at the table corresponding to west on the compass **5** (esp of the wind) from the west

West[1] **1 Benjamin** 1738–1820, US painter, in England from 1763 **2 Mae** 1892–1980, US film actress **3 Nathanael,** real name *Nathan Weinstein.* 1903–40, US novelist: author of *Miss Lonely-Hearts* (1933) and *The Day of the Locust* (1939) **4** Dame **Rebecca,** real name *Cicily Isabel Andrews* (*née Fairfield*). 1892–1983, British journalist, novelist, and critic

West[2] **the 1** the western part of the world contrasted historically and culturally with the East or Orient; the Occident **2** (formerly) the non-Communist countries of Europe and America contrasted with the Communist states of the East **3** (in the US) **a** that part of the US lying approximately to the west of the Mississippi **b** (during the Colonial period) the region outside the 13 colonies, lying mainly to the west of the Alleghenies **4** (in the ancient and medieval world) the Western Roman Empire and, later, the Holy Roman Empire

West Atlantic 1 the W part of the Atlantic Ocean, esp

the N Atlantic around North America **2** a branch of the Niger-Congo family of African languages, spoken in Senegal and in scattered areas eastwards, including Fulani and Wolof

West Bank the a semi-autonomous Palestinian region in the Middle East on the W bank of the River Jordan, comprising the hills of Judaea and Samaria and part of Jerusalem: formerly part of Palestine (the entity created by the League of Nations in 1922 and operating until 1948): became part of Jordan after the ceasefire of 1949: occupied by Israel since the 1967 Arab-Israeli War. In 1993 a peace treaty between Israel and the Palestine Liberation Organization provided for the West Bank to become a self-governing Palestinian area; a new Palestinian National Authority assumed control of parts of the territory in 1994–95, but subsequent talks broke down and Israel reoccupied much of this in 2001–02. Pop: 2 421 491 (2004 est). Area: 5879 sq km (2270 sq miles)

West Bengal a state of E India, on the Bay of Bengal: formed in 1947 from the Hindu area of Bengal; additional territories added in 1950 (Cooch Behar), 1954 (Chandernagor), and 1956 (part of Bihar); mostly low-lying and crossed by the Hooghly River. Capital: Calcutta. Pop: 80 221 171 (2001). Area: 88 752 sq km (34 260 sq miles)

West Berkshire a unitary authority in S England, in Berkshire. Pop: 144 200 (2003 est). Area: 705 sq km (272 sq miles)

West Berlin (formerly) the part of Berlin under US, British, and French control

West Bromwich a town in central England, in Sandwell unitary authority, West Midlands: industrial centre. Pop: 136 940 (2001)

West Country the the southwest of England, esp Cornwall, Devon, and Somerset

West Dunbartonshire a council area of W central Scotland, on Loch Lomond and the Clyde estuary: corresponds to part of the historical county of Dunbartonshire; part of Strathclyde Region from 1975 to 1996: engineering industries. Administrative centre: Dumbarton. Pop: 92 320 (2003 est). Area: 162 sq km (63 sq miles)

West End the a part of W central London containing the main shopping and entertainment areas

Westenra Hayley (Dee). born 1987, New Zealand singer, known for the purity of her voice in many musical genres

westerly **1** (esp of the wind) from the west **2** a wind blowing from the west

western **1** (of a wind, etc) coming or originating from the west **2** *Music* See country and western

Western **1** of, relating to, or characteristic of the West as opposed to the Orient **2** (formerly) of, relating to, or characteristic of the Americas and the parts of Europe not under Communist rule **3** of, relating to, or characteristic of the western states of the US **4** a film, book, etc, concerned with life in the western states of the US, esp during the era of exploration and early development

Western Australia a state of W Australia: mostly an arid undulating plateau, with the Great Sandy Desert,

Gibson Desert, and Great Victoria Desert in the interior; settlement concentrated in the southwest; rich mineral resources. Capital: Perth. Pop: 1 969 046 (2003 est). Area: 2 527 636 sq km (975 920 sq miles)

Western Cape a province of W South Africa, created in 1994 from the SW part of Cape Province: agriculture (esp fruit), wine making, fishing, various industries in Cape Town. Capital: Cape Town. Pop: 4 570 696 (2004 est). Area: 129 370 sq km (49 950 sq miles).

western hemisphere **1** that half of the globe containing the Americas, lying to the west of the Greenwich or another meridian **2** the lands contained in this, esp the Americas

Western Isles an island authority in W Scotland, consisting of the Outer Hebrides; created in 1975. Administrative centre: Stornoway. Pop: 26 100 (2003 est). Area: 2900 sq km (1120 sq miles)

Western Sahara a disputed region of NW Africa, on the Atlantic: mainly desert; rich phosphate deposits; a Spanish overseas province from 1958 to 1975; partitioned in 1976 between Morocco and Mauritania who faced growing resistance from the Polisario Front, an organization aiming for the independence of the region as the Democratic Saharan Arab Republic. Mauritania renounced its claim in 1979 and it was taken over by Morocco. Polisario agreed to a UN-brokered cease-fire in 1991 but attempts to settle the status of the region have failed. Pop: 316 000 (2004 est). Area: 266 000 sq km (102 680 sq miles)

Western Wall *Judaism* a wall in Jerusalem, the last extant part of the Temple of Herod, held sacred by Jews as a place of prayer and pilgrimage

West Flanders a province of W Belgium: the country's chief agricultural province. Capital: Bruges. Pop: 1 135 802 (2004 est). Area: 3132 sq km (1209 sq miles)

West Germany a former republic in N central Europe, on the North Sea: established in 1949 from the zones of Germany occupied by the British, Americans, and French after the defeat of Nazi Germany; a member of the European Community; reunited with East Germany in 1990

West Glamorgan a former county in S Wales, formed in 1974 from part of Glamorgan and the county borough of Swansea: replaced in 1996 by the county of Swansea and the county borough of Neath Port Talbot

West Indies an archipelago off Central America, extending over 2400 km (1500 miles) in an arc from the peninsula of Florida to Venezuela, separating the Caribbean Sea from the Atlantic Ocean: consists of the Greater Antilles, the Lesser Antilles, and the Bahamas; largest island is Cuba. Area: over 235 000 sq km (91 000 sq miles)

West Lothian a council area and historical county of central Scotland, on the Firth of Forth: became part of Lothian region in 1975: reinstated as an independent authority (with revised boundaries) in 1996: agriculture, oil-refining. Administrative centre: Livingston. Pop: 161 020 (2003 est). Area: 425 sq km (164 sq miles)

Westmeath a county of N central Republic of Ireland, in Leinster province: mostly low-lying, with many lakes and bogs. County town: Mullingar. Pop: 71 858 (2002). Area: 1764 sq km (681 sq miles)

West Midlands a metropolitan county of central England, administered since 1986 by the unitary authorities of Wolverhampton, Walsall, Dudley, Sandwell, Birmingham, Solihull, and Coventry. Area: 899 sq km (347 sq miles)

Westminster 1 a borough of Greater London, on the River Thames: contains the Houses of Parliament, Westminster Abbey, and Buckingham Palace. Pop: 222 000 (2003 est). Area: 22 sq km (8 sq miles) 2 the Houses of Parliament at Westminster

Westmorland (until 1974) a county of NW England, now part of Cumbria

Weston-super-Mare a town and resort in SW England, in North Somerset unitary authority, Somerset, on the Bristol Channel. Pop: 78 044 (2001)

Westphalia a historic region of NW Germany, now mostly in the state of North Rhine-Westphalia

West Prussia a former province of NE Prussia, on the Baltic: assigned to Poland in 1945

West Riding (until 1974) an administrative division of Yorkshire, now part of West Yorkshire, North Yorkshire, Cumbria, and Lancashire

West Sussex a county of SE England, comprising part of the former county of Sussex: mainly low-lying, with the South Downs in the S. Administrative centre: Chichester. Pop: 758 600 (2003 est). Area: 1989 sq km (768 sq miles)

West Virginia a state of the eastern US: part of Virginia until the outbreak of the American Civil War (1861); consists chiefly of the Allegheny Plateau; bounded on the west by the Ohio River; coal-mining. Capital: Charleston. Pop: 1 810 354 (2003 est). Area: 62 341 sq km (24 070 sq miles)

Westwood Vivienne (**Isabel**). born 1941, British fashion designer: noted for her punk designs of the late 1970s

West Yorkshire a metropolitan county of N England, administered since 1986 by the unitary authorities of Bradford, Leeds, Calderdale, Kirklees, and Wakefield. Area: 2039 sq km (787 sq miles)

wet 1 rainy, foggy, misty, or humid 2 employing a liquid, usually water 3 *Chiefly US and Canadian* characterized by or permitting the free sale of alcoholic beverages 4 damp or rainy weather 5 *Brit, informal* a Conservative politician who is considered not to be a hard-liner 6 *Chiefly US and Canadian* a person who advocates free sale of alcoholic beverages 7 **the wet** *Austral* (in northern and central Australia) the rainy season

wet dream an erotic dream accompanied by an emission of semen during or just after sleep

wether a male sheep, esp a castrated one

wetland a an area of swampy or marshy land, esp considered as part of an ecological system b (*as modifier*): *wetland species*

Wetterhorn a mountain in S Switzerland, in the Bernese Alps. Height: 3701 m (12 143 ft)

Wexford 1 a county of SE Republic of Ireland, in Leinster province on the Irish Sea: the first Irish county to be colonized from England; mostly low-lying and fertile. County town: Wexford. Pop: 116 596 (2002). Area: 2352 sq km (908 sq miles) 2 a port in SE Republic of Ireland, county town of Co. Wexford: sacked by Oliver Cromwell in 1649. Pop: 17 235 (2002)

Weymouth a port and resort in S England, in Dorset on the English Channel: formerly part of the borough of **Weymouth and Melcombe** Regis. Pop. (with Melcombe Regis): 48 279 (2001)

whale 1 any of the larger cetacean mammals, excluding dolphins, porpoises, and narwhals. They have flippers, a streamlined body, and a horizontally flattened tail and breathe through a blowhole on the top of the head 2 any cetacean mammal 3 *Slang* a gambler who has the capacity to win and lose large sums of money in a casino

whalebone a horny elastic material forming a series of numerous thin plates that hang from the upper jaw on either side of the palate in the toothless (whalebone) whales and strain plankton from water entering the mouth

whalebone whale any whale belonging to the cetacean suborder *Mysticeti*, having a double blowhole and strips of whalebone between the jaws instead of teeth: includes the rorquals, right whales, and the blue whale

whaler 1 a person employed in whaling 2 a vessel engaged in whaling 3 *Austral* a nomad surviving in the bush without working

whaling the work or industry of hunting and processing whales for food, oil, etc.

Whangarei a port in New Zealand, the northernmost city of North Island: oil refinery. Pop: 72 200 (2004 est)

wharf 1 a platform of timber, stone, concrete, etc, built parallel to the waterfront at a harbour or navigable river for the docking, loading, and unloading of ships 2 **the wharves** the working area of a dock 3 an obsolete word for **shore**

wharfie *Austral and NZ* a wharf labourer; docker

Wharton Edith (**Newbold**). 1862–1937, US novelist; author of *The House of Mirth* (1905) and *Ethan Frome* (1911)

wheat any annual or biennial grass of the genus *Triticum*, native to the Mediterranean region and W Asia but widely cultivated, having erect flower spikes and light brown grains

wheatear any small northern songbird of the genus *Oenanthe*, esp *O. oenanthe*, a species having a pale grey back, black wings and tail, white rump, and pale brown underparts: subfamily *Turdinae* (thrushes)

wheaten of a pale yellow colour

wheel 1 a solid disc, or a circular rim joined to a hub by radial or tangential spokes, that is mounted on a shaft about which it can turn, as in vehicles and machines 2 a device consisting of or resembling a wheel or having a wheel as its principal component 3 short for **potter's wheel** 4 a type of firework coiled to make it rotate when let off 5 a set of short rhyming lines, usually four or five in number, forming the concluding part of a stanza 6 the disc in which the ball is spun in roulette 7 *US and Canadian* an informal word for **bicycle** 8 *Archaic* a refrain

wheelbarrow a simple vehicle for carrying small loads, typically being an open container supported by a wheel at the front and two legs and two handles behind

wheelbase the distance between the front and back axles of a motor vehicle

wheelchair *Med* a special chair mounted on large wheels, for use by invalids or others for whom walking is impossible or temporarily inadvisable

wheel clamp a device fixed onto one wheel of an illegally parked car in order to immobilize it. The driver has to pay to have it removed

Wheeler 1 John Archibald born 1911, US physicist, noted for his work on nuclear fission and the development (1949–51) of the hydrogen bomb, also for his work on unified field theory **2** Sir (**Robert Eric**) **Mortimer** 1890–1976, Scottish archaeologist, who did much to increase public interest in archaeology. He is noted esp for his excavations at Mohenjo-Daro and Harappa in the Indus Valley and at Maiden Castle in Dorset

wheelie a manoeuvre on a bicycle or motorbike in which the front wheel is raised off the ground

wheelwright a person who makes or mends wheels as a trade

whelk¹ any carnivorous marine gastropod mollusc of the family *Buccinidae*, of coastal waters and intertidal regions, having a strong snail-like shell

whelk² a raised lesion on the skin; wheal

whelp 1 a young offspring of certain animals, esp of a wolf or dog **2** *Nautical* any of the ridges, parallel to the axis, on the drum of a capstan to keep a rope, cable, or chain from slipping

whetstone 1 a stone used for sharpening edged tools, knives, etc. **2** something that sharpens

whiff¹ a single inhalation or exhalation from the mouth or nose

whiff² *Chiefly Brit* a narrow clinker-built skiff having outriggers, for one oarsman

Whig 1 a member of the English political party or grouping that in 1679–80 opposed the succession to the throne of James, Duke of York (1633–1701; king of England and Ireland as James II, and of Scotland as James VII, 1685–88), on the grounds that he was a Catholic. Standing for a limited monarchy, the Whigs represented the great aristocracy and the moneyed middle class for the next 80 years. In the late 18th and early 19th centuries the Whigs represented the desires of industrialists and Dissenters for political and social reform. The Whigs provided the core of the Liberal Party **2** (in the US) a supporter of the War of American Independence **3** a member of the American political party that opposed the Democrats from about 1834 to 1855 and represented propertied and professional interests **4** a conservative member of the Liberal Party in Great Britain **5** a person who advocates and believes in an unrestricted laissez-faire economy **6** *History* a 17th-century Scottish Presbyterian, esp one in rebellion against the Crown

whip 1 (in a legislative body) **a** a member of a party chosen to organize and discipline the members of his faction, esp in voting and to assist in the arrangement of the business **b** a call issued to members of a party, insisting with varying degrees of urgency upon their presence or loyal voting behaviour **c** (in the British Parliament) a schedule of business sent to members of a party each week. Each item on it is underlined to indicate its importance: one line means that no division is expected, two lines means that the item is fairly important, and three lines means that the item is very important and every member must attend and vote according

to the party line **2** an apparatus for hoisting, consisting of a rope, pulley, and snatch block **3** a windmill vane **4** transient elastic movement of a structure or part when subjected to sudden release of load or dynamic excitation **5** a percussion instrument consisting of two strips of wood, joined forming the shape of a V, and clapped loudly together **6** a ride in a funfair involving bumper cars that move with sudden jerks **7** a wrestling throw in which a wrestler seizes his opponent's arm and spins him to the floor

whip hand (in driving horses) the hand holding the whip

whiplash injury *Med, informal* any injury to the neck resulting from a sudden thrusting forwards and snapping back of the unsupported head

whipper-in a person employed to assist the huntsman managing the hounds

whippet a small slender breed of dog similar to a greyhound in appearance

whirligig 1 any spinning toy, such as a top **2** another name for **windmill** (the toy)

whirlpool a powerful circular current or vortex of water, usually produced by conflicting tidal currents or by eddying at the foot of a waterfall

whirlwind a column of air whirling around and towards a more or less vertical axis of low pressure, which moves along the land or ocean surface

whisk a small brush or broom

whisker 1 any of the stiff sensory hairs growing on the face of a cat, rat, or other mammal **2** any light spar used for extending the clews of a sail, esp in light airs **3** *Chem* a very fine filamentary crystal having greater strength than the bulk material since it is a single crystal. Such crystals often show unusual electrical properties

whisky a spirit made by distilling fermented cereals, which is matured and often blended
▷www.scotchwhisky.net
▷www.smws.com
▷www.whisky-heritage.co.uk
▷www.whiskyportal.com

whist a card game for four in which the two sides try to win the balance of the 13 tricks: forerunner of bridge

whist drive a social gathering where whist is played; the winners of each hand move to different tables to play the losers of the previous hand

whistle 1 a device for making a shrill high-pitched sound by means of air or steam under pressure **2** *Music* any pipe that is blown down its end and produces sounds on the principle of a flue pipe, usually having as a mouthpiece a fipple cut in the side

Whistler James Abbott McNeill 1834–1903, US painter and etcher, living in Europe. He is best known for his sequence of nocturnes and his portraits

Whit See **Whitsuntide**

Whitaker Sir Frederick 1812–91, New Zealand statesman, born in England: prime minister of New Zealand (1863–64; 1882–83)

Whitby a fishing port and resort in NE England, in E North Yorkshire at the mouth of the River Esk: an important ecclesiastical centre in Anglo-Saxon times; site of an abbey founded in 656. Pop: 13 594 (2001)

white 1 having no hue due to the reflection of all or almost all incident light 2 (of light, such as sunlight) consisting of all the colours of the spectrum or produced by certain mixtures of three additive primary colours, such as red, green, and blue 3 comparatively white or whitish-grey in colour or having parts of this colour 4 (of an animal) having pale-coloured or white skin, fur, or feathers 5 bloodless or pale, as from pain, emotion, etc. 6 colourless or transparent 7 counterrevolutionary, very conservative, or royalist 8 (of wine) made from pale grapes or from black grapes separated from their skins 9 *Physics* having or characterized by a continuous distribution of energy, wavelength, or frequency 10 a white colour 11 the condition or quality of being white; whiteness 12 the white or lightly coloured part or area of something 13 the viscous fluid that surrounds the yolk of a bird's egg, esp a hen's egg; albumen 14 *Anatomy* the white part (sclera) of the eyeball 15 any of various butterflies of the family *Pieridae* 16 *Chess, draughts* a a white or light-coloured piece or square b the player playing with such pieces 17 anything that has or is characterized by a white colour, such as a white paint or pigment, a white cloth, a white ball in billiards 18 *Archery* a the outer ring of the target, having the lowest score b a shot or arrow hitting this ring 19 *Poetic* fairness of complexion 20 **in the white** (of wood or furniture) left unpainted or unvarnished

White[1] 1 Gilbert 1720–93, English clergyman and naturalist, noted for his *Natural History and Antiquities of Selborne* (1789) 2 Jimmy born 1962, British snooker player 3 Marco Pierre born 1961, British chef and restaurateur 4 Patrick (Victor Martindale). 1912–90, Australian novelist: his works include *Voss* (1957), *The Eye of the Storm* (1973), and *A Fringe of Leaves* (1976): Nobel prize for literature 1973 5 T(erence) H(anbury). 1906–64, British novelist: author of the Arthurian sequence *The Once and Future King* (1939–58) 6 Willard (Wentworth). born 1946, British operatic bass, born in Jamaica

White[2] 1 a member of the Caucasoid race 2 a person of European ancestry 3 denoting or relating to a White or Whites

whitebait any of various small silvery fishes, such as *Galaxias attenuatus* of Australia and New Zealand and *Allosmerus elongatus* of North American coastal regions of the Pacific

white dwarf one of a large class of small faint stars of enormous density (on average 10^8 kg/m^3) with diameters only about 1 per cent that of the sun, and masses less than the Chandrasekhar limit (about 1.4 solar masses). It is thought to mark the final stage in the evolution of a sun-like star

white elephant a rare albino or pale grey variety of the Indian elephant, regarded as sacred in parts of S Asia

Whitefield George 1714–70, English Methodist preacher, who separated from the Wesleys (?1741) because of his Calvinistic views

white fish (in the British fishing industry) any edible marine fish or invertebrate in which the main reserves of fat are in the liver, excluding herring, trout, sprat, mackerel, salmon, and shellfish

whitefly any hemipterous insect of the family *Aleyrodidae*, typically having a body covered with powdery wax. Many are pests of greenhouse crops

white gold any of various white lustrous hard-wearing alloys containing gold together with platinum and palladium and sometimes smaller amounts of silver, nickel, or copper: used in jewellery

Whitehall 1 a street in London stretching from Trafalgar Square to the Houses of Parliament: site of the main government offices 2 the British Government or its central administration

Whitehead Alfred North 1861–1947, English mathematician and philosopher, who collaborated with Bertrand Russell in writing *Principia Mathematica* (1910–13), and developed a holistic philosophy of science, chiefly in *Process and Reality* (1929)

white heat intense heat or a very high temperature, characterized by emission of white light

Whitehorse a town in NW Canada: capital of the Yukon Territory. Pop: 16 843 (2001)

white-hot at such a high temperature that white light is emitted

White House the 1 the official Washington residence of the president of the US 2 the US presidency

Whitelaw William (Stephen Ian), 1st Viscount Whitelaw of Penrith. 1918–99, British Conservative politician; Home Secretary (1979–83); leader of the House of Lords (1983–88)

Whiteley Brett 1939–1992, Australian artist, who travelled widely in Europe and Asia; his works include landscapes, nudes, and portraits

white light light that contains all the wavelengths of visible light at approximately equal intensities, as in sunlight or the light from white-hot solids

white matter the whitish tissue of the brain and spinal cord, consisting mainly of myelinated nerve fibres

white noise a sound or electrical noise that has a relatively wide continuous range of frequencies of uniform intensity b noise containing all frequencies rising in level by six decibels every octave

white paper an official government report in any of a number of countries, including Britain, Australia, New Zealand, and Canada, which sets out the government's policy on a matter that is or will come before Parliament

White Sea an almost landlocked inlet of the Barents Sea on the coast of NW Russia. Area: 90 000 sq km (34 700 sq miles)

white spirit a colourless liquid obtained from petroleum and used as a substitute for turpentine

White Volta a river in W Africa, rising in N Burkina-Faso flowing southwest and south to join the Black Volta in central Ghana and form the Volta River. Length: about 885 km (550 miles)

whitewash a substance used for whitening walls and other surfaces, consisting of a suspension of lime or whiting in water, often with other substances, such as size, added

whitewood 1 any of various trees with light-coloured wood, such as the tulip tree, basswood, and cottonwood 2 the wood of any of these trees

whiting[1] 1 an important gadoid food fish, *Merlangius* (or *Gadus*) *merlangus*, of European seas, having a dark back with silvery sides and underparts 2 any of various similar fishes, such as *Merluccius bilinearis*, a hake of American Atlantic waters, and any of several Atlantic sciaenid fishes of the genus *Menticirrhus* **3** *Austral* any of several marine food fishes of the genus *Sillago* **4** **whiting pout** another name for **bib** (the fish)

whiting² white chalk that has been ground and washed, used in making whitewash, metal polish, etc.

Whitlam (Edward) Gough born 1916, Australian Labor statesman: prime minister (1972–75)

Whitley Bay a resort in NE England, in North Tyneside unitary authority, Tyne and Wear, on the North Sea. Pop: 36 544 (2001)

whitlow any pussy inflammation of the end of a finger or toe

Whitman Walt(er). 1819–92, US poet, whose life's work is collected in *Leaves of Grass* (1855 and subsequent enlarged editions). His poems celebrate existence and the multiple elements that make up a democratic society

Whitney¹ **1** Eli 1765–1825, US inventor of a mechanical cotton gin (1793) and pioneer manufacturer of interchangeable parts **2** William Dwight 1827–94, US philologist, noted esp for his *Sanskrit Grammar* (1879)

Whitney² Mount a mountain in E California: the highest peak in the Sierra Nevada Mountains and in continental US (excluding Alaska). Height: 4418 m (14 495 ft)

Whitsun short for **Whitsuntide**

Whit Sunday the seventh Sunday after Easter, observed as a feast in commemoration of the descent of the Holy Spirit on the apostles 50 days after Easter

Whitsuntide the week that begins with Whit Sunday, esp the first three days

Whittier John Greenleaf 1807–92, US poet and humanitarian: a leading campaigner in the antislavery movement. His poems include *Snow-Bound* (1866)

Whittington Richard, known as *Dick*. died 1423, English merchant, three times mayor of London. According to legend, he walked to London at the age of 13 with his cat and was prevented from leaving again only by the call of the church bells

whittle *Brit, dialect* a knife, esp a large one

Whittle Sir Frank 1907–96, English engineer, who invented the jet engine for aircraft; flew first British jet aircraft (1941)

whodunnit *or* **whodunit** *Informal* a novel, play, etc, concerned with a crime, usually murder

whole **1** *Maths* having no fractional or decimal part; integral **2** *Biology* of, relating to, or designating a relationship established by descent from the same parents; full

whole number **1** an integer **2** a natural number

wholesale **1** the business of selling goods to retailers in larger quantities than they are sold to final consumers but in smaller quantities than they are purchased from manufacturers **2** **at wholesale a** in large quantities **b** at wholesale prices

wholesome **1** conducive to health or physical wellbeing **2** characteristic or suggestive of health or wellbeing, esp in appearance

whoop *Med* the convulsive crowing sound made during a paroxysm of whooping cough

whooping cough an acute infectious disease characterized by coughing spasms that end with a shrill crowing sound on inspiration: caused by infection with the bacillus *Bordetella pertussis*

whorl **1** *Botany* a radial arrangement of three or more petals, stamens, leaves, etc, around a stem **2** *Zoology* a single turn in a spiral shell **3** one of the basic patterns of the human fingerprint, formed by several complete circular ridges one inside another

Whyalla a port in S South Australia, on Spencer Gulf: iron and steel and shipbuilding industries. Pop: 21 271 (2001)

Wichita a city in S Kansas, on the Arkansas River: the largest city in the state; two universities. Pop: 354 617 (2003 est)

wick¹ a cord or band of loosely twisted or woven fibres, as in a candle, cigarette lighter, etc, that supplies fuel to a flame by capillary action

wick² *Archaic* a village or hamlet

Wick a town in N Scotland, in Highland, at the head of Wick Bay (an inlet of the North Sea). Pop: 7333 (2001)

wicker **1** a slender flexible twig or shoot, esp of willow **2** short for **wickerwork 3** made, consisting of, or constructed from wicker

wickerwork a a material consisting of wicker **b** (*as modifier*): *a wickerwork chair*
  ▷www.wickerweaver.com/bookstore/
  PB_wh_history.html

wicket **1** a small sluicegate, esp one in a canal lock gate or by a water wheel **2** *US* a croquet hoop **3** a *Cricket* either of two constructions, placed 22 yards apart, consisting of three pointed stumps stuck parallel in the ground with two wooden bails resting on top, at which the batsman stands **b** the strip of ground between these **c** a batsman's turn at batting or the period during which two batsmen bat **d** the act or instance of a batsman being got out **4** **keep wicket** to act as a wicketkeeper

wicketkeeper *Cricket* the player on the fielding side positioned directly behind the wicket

Wicklow **1** a county of E Republic of Ireland, in Leinster province on the Irish Sea: consists of a coastal strip rising inland to the **Wicklow Mountains**; mainly agricultural, with several resorts. County town: Wicklow. Pop: 114 676 (2002). Area: 2025 sq km (782 sq miles) **2** a port in E Republic of Ireland, county town of Co. Wicklow. Pop: 9355 (2002)

wide (in cricket) a bowled ball that is outside the batsman's reach and scores a run for the batting side

wide-angle lens a lens system on a camera that can cover an angle of view of 60° or more and therefore has a fairly small focal length

widget **1** *Informal* any small mechanism or device, the name of which is unknown or temporarily forgotten **2** a small device in a beer can which, when the can is opened, releases nitrogen gas into the beer, giving it a head

Widnes a town in NW England, in Halton unitary authority, N Cheshire, on the River Mersey: chemical industry. Pop: 55 686 (2001)

widow **1** a woman who has survived her husband, esp one who has not remarried **2** (in some card games) an additional hand or set of cards exposed on the table

widower a man whose wife has died and who has not

remarried

width the distance across a rectangular swimming bath, as opposed to its length

Wieland Christoph Martin 1733–1813, German writer, noted esp for his verse epic *Oberon* (1780)

Wien Wilhelm 1864–1928, German physicist, who studied black-body radiation: Nobel prize for physics 1911

Wiener Norbert 1894–1964, US mathematician, who developed the concept of cybernetics

Wiener Neustadt a city in E Austria, in Lower Austria. Pop: 37 627 (2002)

Wiesbaden a city in W Germany, capital of Hesse state: a spa resort since Roman times. Pop: 271 995 (2003 est)

Wiesel Elie born 1928, US human rights campaigner: noted esp for his documentaries of wartime atrocities against the Jews; Nobel peace prize 1986

Wiesenthal Simon born 1908, Austrian investigator of Nazi war crimes. A survivor of the concentration camps, he has been active since 1945 in documenting Nazi crimes against the Jews, tracking down their perpetrators, and assisting surviving victims

wife a man's partner in marriage; a married woman

Wi-Fi *Computing* a system of accessing the internet from remote machines such as laptop computers that have wireless connections

Wigan 1 an industrial town in NW England, in Wigan unitary authority, Greater Manchester: former coal-mining centre. Pop: 81 203 (2001) 2 a unitary authority in NW England, in Greater Manchester. Pop: 303 800 (2003 est). Area: 199 sq km (77 sq miles)

wigeon *or* **widgeon** 1 a Eurasian duck, *Anas penelope*, of marshes, swamps, etc, the male of which has a reddish-brown head and chest and grey and white back and wings 2 **American wigeon** a similar bird, *Anas americana*, of North America, the male of which has a white crown

Wight Isle of an island and county of S England in the English Channel. Administrative centre: Newport. Pop: 136 300 (2003 est). Area: 380 sq km (147 sq miles)

Wigner Eugene Paul 1902–95, US physicist, born in Hungary. He is noted for his contributions to nuclear physics: shared the Nobel prize for physics 1963

Wigtownshire (until 1975) a county of SW Scotland, now part of Dumfries and Galloway

wigwam 1 any dwelling of the North American Indians, esp one made of bark, rushes, or skins spread over or enclosed by a set of arched poles lashed together 2 a similar structure for children

Wilberforce 1 Samuel 1805–73, British Anglican churchman; bishop of Oxford (1845–69) and Winchester (1869–73) 2 his father, William 1759–1833, British politician and philanthropist, whose efforts secured the abolition of the slave trade (1807) and of slavery (1833) in the British Empire

wild 1 (of animals) living independently of man; not domesticated or tame 2 (of plants) growing in a natural state; not cultivated 3 living in a savage or uncivilized way 4 (of a card, such as a joker or deuce in some games) able to be given any value the holder pleases 5 a desolate, uncultivated, or uninhabited region

wild card 1 See wild (sense 4) 2 *Computing* a symbol that can represent any character or group of characters, as in a filename

wildcat 1 a wild European cat, *Felis silvestris*, that resembles the domestic tabby but is larger and has a bushy tail 2 any of various other felines, esp of the genus *Lynx*, such as the lynx and the caracal 3 *US and Canadian* an unsound commercial enterprise 4 *US and Canadian* a railway locomotive in motion without drawing any carriages or wagons 5 *US and Canadian* a of or relating to an unsound business enterprise b financially or commercially unsound 6 *US and Canadian* (of a train) running without permission or outside the timetable

Wilde Oscar (Fingal O'Flahertie Wills). 1854–1900, Irish writer and wit, famous for such plays as *Lady Windermere's Fan* (1892) and *The Importance of being Earnest* (1895). *The Picture of Dorian Gray* (1891) is a macabre novel about a hedonist and *The Ballad of Reading Gaol* (1898) relates to his experiences in prison while serving a two-year sentence for homosexuality

Wilder 1 Billy, real name *Samuel Wilder*. 1906–2002, US film director and screenwriter, born in Austria. His films include *Double Indemnity* (1944), *The Lost Weekend* (1945), *Sunset Boulevard* (1950), *The Seven Year Itch* (1955), *Some Like it Hot* (1959), *The Apartment* (1960), and *Buddy Buddy* (1981) 2 Thornton 1897–1975 US novelist and dramatist. His works include the novel *The Bridge of San Luis Rey* (1927) and the play *The Skin of Our Teeth* (1942)

wilderness a wild, uninhabited, and uncultivated region

Wilderness the the barren regions to the south and east of Palestine, esp those in which the Israelites wandered before entering the Promised Land and in which Christ fasted for 40 days and nights

wildfire 1 a highly flammable material, such as Greek fire, formerly used in warfare 2 lightning without audible thunder

wild flower 1 any flowering plant that grows in an uncultivated state 2 the flower of such a plant

wildfowl 1 any bird that is hunted by man, esp any duck or similar aquatic bird 2 such birds collectively

wildlife wild animals and plants collectively

Wild West the western US during its settlement, esp with reference to its frontier lawlessness

Wilhelmina I 1880–1962, queen of the Netherlands from 1890 until her abdication (1948) in favour of her daughter Juliana

Wilhelmshaven a port and resort in NW Germany, in Lower Saxony: founded in 1853; was the chief German North Sea naval base until 1945; a major oil port. Pop: 84 586 (2003 est)

Wilhelmstrasse 1 a street in the centre of Berlin, where the German foreign office and other government buildings were situated until 1945 2 Germany's ministry of foreign affairs until 1945

Wilkes 1 Charles 1798–1877, US explorer of Antarctica 2 John 1727–97, English politician, who was expelled from the House of Commons and outlawed for writing scurrilous articles about the government. He became a champion of parliamentary reform

Wilkes Land a region in Antarctica south of Australia, on the Indian Ocean

Wilkins 1 Sir George Hubert 1888–1958, Australian polar explorer and aviator 2 Maurice Hugh Frederick born

1916, British biochemist, born in New Zealand. With Crick and Watson, he shared the Nobel prize 1962 for his work on the structure of DNA

Wilkinson Jonny born 1979, English Rugby Union player; he scored the last-minute drop goal that won England victory in the final of the 2003 World Cup

will a the declaration of a person's wishes regarding the disposal of his or her property after death b a revocable instrument by which such wishes are expressed

Willemstad the capital of the Netherlands Antilles, a port on the SW coast of Curaçao: important for refining Venezuelan oil. Pop: 137 000 (2005 est)

William 1 known as *William the Lion*. ?1143–1214, king of Scotland (1165–1214) 2 **Prince** born 1982, first son of Prince Charles and Diana, Princess of Wales

William I 1 known as *William the Conqueror*. ?1027–1087, duke of Normandy (1035–87) and king of England (1066–87). He claimed to have been promised the English crown by Edward the Confessor, after whose death he disputed the succession of Harold II, invading England in 1066 and defeating Harold at Hastings. The conquest of England resulted in the introduction to England of many Norman customs, esp feudalism. In 1085 he ordered the Domesday Book to be compiled 2 known as *William the Bad*. 1120–66, Norman king of Sicily (1154–66) 3 known as *William the Silent*. 1533–84, prince of Orange and count of Nassau: led the revolt of the Netherlands against Spain (1568–76) and became first stadholder of the United Provinces of the Netherlands (1579–84); assassinated 4 1772–1843, king of the Netherlands (1815–40): abdicated in favour of his son William II 5 German name *Wilhelm I*. 1797–1888, king of Prussia (1861–88) and first emperor of Germany (1871–88)

William II 1 known as *William Rufus*. ?1056–1100, king of England (1087–1100); the son of William the Conqueror. He was killed by an arrow while hunting in the New Forest 2 known as *William the Good*. 1154–89, last Norman king of Sicily (1166–89) 3 1792–1849, king of the Netherlands (1840–49); son of William I 4 German name *Kaiser Wilhelm*. 1859–1941, German emperor and king of Prussia (1888–1918): asserted Germany's claim to world leadership; forced to abdicate at the end of World War I

William III known as *William of Orange*. 1650–1702, stadholder of the Netherlands (1672–1702) and king of Great Britain and Ireland (1689–1702). He was invited by opponents of James II to accept the British throne (1688) and ruled jointly with his wife Mary II (James' daughter) until her death in 1694

William IV known as the *Sailor King*. 1765–1837, king of the United Kingdom and of Hanover (1830–37), succeeding his brother George IV; the third son of George III

Williams 1 **Hank**, real name *Hiram Williams*. 1923–53, US country singer and songwriter. His songs (all 1948–52) include "Jambalaya", "Your Cheatin' Heart", and "Why Don't you Love me (like you Used to Do?)" 2 **John** born 1941, Australian classical guitarist, living in Britain 3 **John** (**Towner**). born 1932, US composer of film music; his scores include those for *Jaws* (1975), *Star Wars* (1977), *E.T.* (1982), *Schindler's List* (1993), and *Harry Potter and the Philosopher's Stone* (2001) 4 **Raymond** (**Henry**). 1921–88,

British literary critic and novelist, noted esp for such works as *Culture and Society* (1958) and *The Long Revolution* (1961), which offer a socialist analysis of the relationship between society and culture 5 **Robbie**, full name *Robert Peter Williams*. born 1974, British pop singer and songwriter. A member of Take That (1990–95), he later found success with "Angels" (1997) and the albums *Life Thru a Lens* (1997), *Swing When You're Winning* (2001), and *Escapology* (2002) 6 **Robin** (**McLaurim**). born 1951, US film actor and comedian; films include *Good Morning, Vietnam* (1987), *Dead Poets' Society* (1989), *Mrs Doubtfire* (1993), and *Insomnia* (2002) 7 **Rowan** (**Douglas**). born 1950, Archbishop of Canterbury from 2002; formerly Archbishop of Wales (2000–02) 8 **Tennessee**, real name *Thomas Lanier Williams*. 1911–83, US dramatist. His plays include *The Glass Menagerie* (1944), *A Streetcar Named Desire* (1947), *Cat on a Hot Tin Roof* (1955), and *Night of the Iguana* (1961) 9 **William Carlos** 1883–1963, US poet, who formulated the poetic concept "no ideas but in things". His works include *Paterson* (1946–58), which explores the daily life of a man living in a modern city, and the prose work *In the American Grain* (1925)

Williamsburg a city in SE Virginia: the capital of Virginia (1693–1779); the restoration of large sections of the colonial city was begun in 1926. Pop: 11 605 (2003 est)

Williamson 1 **Henry** 1895–1977, British novelist, best known for *Tarka the Otter* (1927) and other animal stories 2 **Malcolm** 1931–2003, Australian composer, living in Britain: Master of the Queen's Music since 1975. His works include operas and music for children

Willis 1 **Norman** (**David**). born 1933, British trade union leader; general secretary of the Trades Union Congress (1984–93) 2 **Ted** Baron Willis of Chislehurst. 1918–92, British author. His works include the play *Hot Summer Night* (1959) and the novel *Death May Surprise Us* (1974)

willow 1 any of numerous salicaceous trees and shrubs of the genus *Salix*, such as the weeping willow and osiers of N temperate regions, which have graceful flexible branches, flowers in catkins, and feathery seeds 2 the whitish wood of certain of these trees 3 something made of willow wood, such as a cricket or baseball bat 4 a machine having a system of revolving spikes for opening and cleaning raw textile fibres

willowherb 1 any of various temperate and arctic onagraceous plants of the genus *Epilobium*, having narrow leaves, terminal clusters of pink, purplish, or white flowers, and willow-like feathery seeds 2 short for **rosebay willowherb**

willow pattern a a pattern incorporating a willow tree, river, bridge, and figures, typically in blue on a white ground, used on pottery and porcelain b (*as modifier*): *a willow-pattern plate*

Willow South a city in S Alaska, about 113 km (70 miles) northwest of Anchorage: chosen as the site of the projected new state capital in 1976

Wills 1 **Helen Newington**, married name *Helen Wills Moody Roark*. 1905–98, US tennis player. She was Wimbledon singles champion eight times between 1927 and 1938. She also won the US title seven times and the French title four times 2 **William John** 1834–61, English explorer: Robert Burke's deputy in an expedition on which both men died after crossing Australia from north to south for the first time

willy wagtail *Austral* a black-and-white flycatcher, *Rhipidura leucophrys*, having white feathers over the brows

willy-willy *Austral* a tropical cyclone or duststorm

Wilmington a port in N Delaware, on the Delaware River: industrial centre. Pop: 72 051 (2003 est)

Wilson 1 **Alexander** 1766–1813, Scottish ornithologist in the US 2 Sir **Angus (Frank Johnstone)** 1913–91, British writer, whose works include the collection of short stories *The Wrong Set* (1949) and the novels *Anglo-Saxon Attitudes* (1956) and *No Laughing Matter* (1967) 3 **Charles Thomson Rees** 1869–1959, Scottish physicist, who invented the cloud chamber: shared the Nobel prize for physics 1927 4 **Edmund** 1895–1972, US critic, noted esp for *Axel's Castle* (1931), a study of the symbolist movement 5 **(James) Harold,** Baron Wilson of Rievaulx. 1916–95, British Labour statesman; prime minister (1964–70; 1974–76) 6 **Jacqueline** born 1945, British writer for older girls; her best-selling books include *The Story of Tracey Beaker* (1991), *The Illustrated Mum* (1998), and *Girls in Tears* (2002). 7 **Richard** 1714–82, Welsh landscape painter 8 **(Thomas) Woodrow** 1856–1924, US Democratic statesman; 28th president of the US (1913–21). He led the US into World War I in 1917 and proposed the Fourteen Points (1918) as a basis for peace. Although he secured the formation of the League of Nations, the US Senate refused to support it: Nobel peace prize 1919

Wiltshire a county of S England, consisting mainly of chalk uplands, with Salisbury Plain in the south and the Marlborough Downs in the north; prehistoric remains (at Stonehenge and Avebury): the geographical and ceremonial county includes Swindon unitary authority (established in 1997). Administrative centre: Trowbridge. Pop. (excluding Swindon): 440 800 (2003 est). Area (excluding Swindon): 3481 sq km (1344 sq miles)

Wimbledon part of the Greater London borough of Merton: headquarters of the All England Lawn Tennis Club since 1877 and the site of the annual international tennis championships

WIMP 1 *Computing* windows, icons, menus (*or* mice), pointers: denoting a type of user-friendly screen display used on small computers 2 *Physics* weakly interacting massive particle

wimple *Scot* a curve or bend, as in a river

winch 1 a windlass driven by a hand- or power-operated crank 2 a hand- or power-operated crank by which a machine is driven

Winchester a city in S England, administrative centre of Hampshire: a Romano-British town; Saxon capital of Wessex; 11th-century cathedral; site of **Winchester College** (1382), English public school. Pop: 41 420 (2001)

Winckelmann Johann Joachim 1717–68, German archaeologist and art historian; one of the founders of neoclassicism

wind 1 a current of air, sometimes of considerable force, moving generally horizontally from areas of high pressure to areas of low pressure 2 *Chiefly poetic* the direction from which a wind blows, usually a cardinal point of the compass 3 air artificially moved, as by a fan,

pump, etc. 4 (often used in sports) the power to breathe normally 5 *Music* a a wind instrument or wind instruments considered collectively b the musicians who play wind instruments in an orchestra c of, relating to, or composed of wind instruments 6 the air on which the scent of an animal is carried to hounds or on which the scent of a hunter is carried to his quarry 7 **between wind and water** the part of a vessel's hull below the water line that is exposed by rolling or by wave action 8 **have in the wind** to be in the act of following (quarry) by scent 9 **off the wind** *Nautical* away from the direction from which the wind is blowing 10 **on the wind** *Nautical* as near as possible to the direction from which the wind is blowing

windbag the bag in a set of bagpipes, which provides a continuous flow of air to the pipes

windblown 1 (of trees, shrubs, etc) growing in a shape determined by the prevailing winds 2 *NZ* (of trees) felled by the wind

windbreak a fence, line of trees, etc, serving as a protection from the wind by breaking its force

Windermere a lake in NW England, in Cumbria in the SE part of the Lake District: the largest lake in England. Length: 17 km (10.5 miles)

windfall 1 something blown down by the wind, esp a piece of fruit 2 *Chiefly US and Canadian* a plot of land covered with trees blown down by the wind

windfall tax a tax levied on an organization considered to have made excessive profits, esp a privatized utility company that has exploited a monopoly

wind farm a large group of wind-driven generators for electricity supply

wind gauge 1 another name for **anemometer** 2 *Music* a device for measuring the wind pressure in the bellows of an organ

Windhoek the capital of Namibia, in the centre, at an altitude of 1654 m (5428 ft): formerly the capital of German South West Africa. Pop: 252 000 (2005 est)

winding sheet a sheet in which a corpse is wrapped for burial; shroud

wind instrument any musical instrument sounded by the breath, such as the woodwinds and brass instruments of an orchestra

windjammer a large merchant sailing ship

windlass a machine for raising weights by winding a rope or chain upon a barrel or drum driven by a crank, motor, etc.

windmill 1 a machine for grinding or pumping driven by a set of adjustable vanes or sails that are caused to turn by the force of the wind 2 the set of vanes or sails that drives such a mill 3 *Brit* a toy consisting of plastic or paper vanes attached to a stick in such a manner that they revolve like the sails of a windmill 4 a small airdriven propeller fitted to a light aircraft to drive auxiliary equipment

window 1 the display space in and directly behind a shop window 2 *Physics* a region of the spectrum in which a medium transmits electromagnetic radiation 3 *Computing* an area of a VDU display that may be manipulated separately from the rest of the display area; typically different files can be displayed simultaneously in different overlapping windows

window box a long narrow box, placed on or outside a windowsill, in which plants are grown

window-dressing the ornamentation of shop windows, designed to attract customers

Wind River Range a mountain range in W Wyoming: one of the highest ranges of the central Rockies. Highest peak: Gannet Peak, 4202 m (13 785 ft)

windscreen *Brit, Austral., NZ, and South African* the sheet of flat or curved glass that forms a window of a motor vehicle, esp the front window

windscreen wiper *Brit* an electrically operated blade with a rubber edge that wipes a windscreen clear of rain, snow, etc.

windshield 1 *US and Canadian* the sheet of flat or curved glass that forms a window of a motor vehicle, esp the front window 2 an object designed to shield something from the wind

windsock a truncated cone of textile mounted on a mast so that it is free to rotate about a vertical axis: used, esp at airports, to indicate the local wind direction

Windsor[1] 1 the official name of the British royal family from 1917 2 **Duke of** the title of **Edward VIII** from 1937

Windsor[2] 1 a town in S England, in Windsor and Maidenhead unitary authority, Berkshire, on the River Thames, linked by bridge with Eton: site of **Windsor Castle**, residence of English monarchs since its founding by William the Conqueror; **Old Windsor**, royal residence in the time of Edward the Confessor, is 3 km (2 miles) southeast. Pop: 26 747 (2001 est) 2 a city in SE Canada, in S Ontario on the Detroit River opposite Detroit: motor-vehicle manufacturing; university (1963). Pop: 208 402 (2001)

Windsor and Maidenhead a unitary authority in S England, in Berkshire. Pop: 135 300 (2003 est). Area: 197 sq km (76 sq miles)

windsurfing the sport of sailing standing up on a sailboard that is equipped with a mast, sail, and wishbone boom

▷www.worldwindsurfing.com

wind tunnel a chamber for testing the aerodynamic properties of aircraft, aerofoils, etc, in which a current of air can be maintained at a constant velocity

windward *Chiefly nautical* 1 of, in, or moving to the quarter from which the wind blows 2 **to windward of** advantageously situated with respect to 3 the windward point 4 the side towards the wind

Windward Passage a strait in the Caribbean, between E Cuba and NW Haiti. Width: 80 km (50 miles)

wine 1 a an alcoholic drink produced by the fermenting of grapes with water and sugar b an alcoholic drink produced in this way from other fruits, flowers, etc. 2 a dark red colour, sometimes with a purplish tinge 3 *Pharmacol, Obsolete* fermented grape juice containing medicaments 4 **Adam's wine** *Brit* a dialect word for water

▷www.intowine.com
▷http://wine.about.com
▷www.wines.com
▷www.upenn.edu/museum/Wine/ wineintro.html

wine bar a bar in a restaurant, etc, or an establishment that specializes in serving wine and usually food

wine box wine sold in a cubic carton, usually of three-litre capacity, having a plastic lining and a tap for dispensing

wine cellar 1 a place, such as a dark cool cellar, where wine is stored 2 the stock of wines stored there

wineglass 1 a glass drinking vessel, typically having a small bowl on a stem, with a flared foot 2 the amount that such a glass will hold

wing 1 either of the modified forelimbs of a bird that are covered with large feathers and specialized for flight in most species 2 one of the organs of flight of an insect, consisting of a membranous outgrowth from the thorax containing a network of veins 3 either of the organs of flight in certain other animals, esp the forelimb of a bat 4 a a half of the main supporting surface on an aircraft, confined to one side of it b the full span of the main supporting surface on both sides of an aircraft c an aircraft designed as one complete wing d a position in flight formation, just to the rear and to one side of an aircraft 5 a an organ or apparatus resembling a wing b *Anatomy* any bodily structure resembling a wing 6 *Botany* a either of the lateral petals of a sweetpea or related flower b any of various outgrowths of a plant part, esp the process on a wind-dispersed fruit or seed 7 *Brit* the part of a car body that surrounds the wheels 8 any affiliate of or subsidiary to a parent organization 9 a faction or group within a political party or other organization 10 the space offstage to the right or left of the acting area in a theatre 11 a surface fitted to a racing car to produce aerodynamic download to hold it on the road at high speed 12 an insignia in the form of stylized wings worn by a qualified aircraft pilot 13 any of various flattened organs or extensions in lower animals, esp when used in locomotion 14 the side of a hold alongside a ship's hull 15 a jetty or dam for narrowing a channel of water

Wingate **Orde** (**Charles**). 1903–44, British soldier. During World War II he organized the Chindits in Burma (Myanmar) to disrupt Japanese communications. He died in an air crash

wing nut a threaded nut tightened by hand by means of two flat lugs or wings projecting from the central body

wingspan *or* **wingspread** the distance between the wing tips of an aircraft, bird, etc.

wink[1] an interrupted flashing of light

wink[2] a disc used in the game of tiddlywinks

Winnebago 1 **Lake** a lake in E Wisconsin, fed and drained by the Fox river: the largest lake in the state. Area: 557 sq km (215 sq miles) 2 a member of a North American Indian people living in Wisconsin and Nebraska 3 the language of this people, belonging to the Siouan family

winning money, prizes, or valuables won, esp in gambling

Winnipeg 1 a city in S Canada, capital of Manitoba at the confluence of the Assiniboine and Red Rivers: University of Manitoba (1877) and University of Winnipeg (1871). Pop: 626 685 (2001) 2 **Lake** a lake in S Canada, in Manitoba: drains through the Nelson River into Hudson Bay. Area: 23 553 sq km (9 094 sq miles)

Winnipegosis **Lake** a lake in S Canada, i W Manitoba.

Area: 5400 sq km (2086 sq miles)

wino *Informal* a person who habitually drinks wine as a means of getting drunk

Winslet Kate born 1975, British film actress; her films include *Sense and Sensibility* (1995), *Titanic* (1997), and *Iris* (2001)

Winston Robert (Maurice Lipson, Baron. born 1940, British obstetrician and gynaecologist, noted for his work on human infertility treatment; also a well-known broadcaster

Winston-Salem a city in N central North Carolina: formed in 1913 by the uniting of Salem and Winston; a major tobacco manufacturing centre. Pop: 190 299 (2003 est)

winter 1 a the coldest season of the year, between autumn and spring, astronomically from the December solstice to the March equinox in the N hemisphere and at the opposite time of year in the S hemisphere b (*as modifier*): *winter pasture* 2 the period of cold weather associated with the winter

wintergreen oil of wintergreen an aromatic compound, formerly made from this and various other plants but now synthesized: used medicinally and for flavouring

wintergreen 1 any of several evergreen ericaceous shrubs of the genus *Gaultheria*, esp *G. procumbens*, of E North America, which has white bell-shaped flowers and edible red berries 2 any of various plants of the genus *Pyrola*, such as *P. minor* (**common wintergreen**), of temperate and arctic regions, having rounded leaves and small pink globose flowers: family *Pyrolaceae* 3 any of several plants of the genera *Orthilia* and *Moneses*: family *Pyrolaceae* 4 **chickweed wintergreen** a primulaceous plant, *Trientalis europaea*, of N Europe and N Asia, having white flowers and leaves arranged in a whorl

winter solstice 1 the time at which the sun is at its southernmost point in the sky (northernmost point in the S hemisphere) appearing at noon at its lowest altitude above the horizon. It occurs about December 22 (June 21 in the S hemisphere) 2 *Astronomy* the point on the celestial sphere, opposite the **summer solstice**, at which the ecliptic is furthest south from the celestial equator. Right ascension: 18 hours; declination: -23.5°

Winterthur an industrial town in NE central Switzerland, in Zürich canton: has the largest technical college in the country. Pop: 90 483 (2000)

wipe (in film editing) an effect causing the transition from one scene to the next in which the image of the first scene appears to be wiped off the screen by that of the second

wiper 1 any piece of cloth, such as a handkerchief, towel, etc, used for wiping 2 a cam rotated to ease a part and allow it to fall under its own weight, as used in stamping machines, etc. 3 See **windscreen wiper** 4 *Electrical engineering* a movable conducting arm, esp one in a switching or selecting device, that makes contact with a row or ring of contacts

wire 1 a slender flexible strand or rod of metal 2 a cable consisting of several metal strands twisted together 3 a flexible metallic conductor, esp one made of copper, usually insulated, and used to carry electric current in a circuit 4 anything made of wire, such as wire netting, a barbed wire fence, etc. 5 a metallic string on a

guitar, piano, etc. 6 *Horse racing, chiefly US and Canadian* the finishing line on a racecourse 7 a wire-gauze screen upon which pulp is spread to form paper during the manufacturing process 8 a snare made of wire for rabbits and similar animals

wireless communicating without connecting wires or other material contacts

wireworm the wormlike larva of various elaterid beetles, which feeds on the roots of many crop plants and is a serious agricultural pest

wiring 1 the network of wires used in an electrical system, device, or circuit 2 the quality or condition of such a network

Wirral 1 the a peninsula in NW England between the estuaries of the Rivers Mersey and Dee 2 a unitary authority in NW England, in Merseyside. Pop: 313 800 (2003 est). Area: 158 sq km (61 sq miles)

wiry (of a sound) produced by or as if by a vibrating wire

Wisbech a town in E England, in N Cambridgeshire: market-gardening. Pop: 26 536 (2001)

Wisconsin 1 a state of the N central US, on Lake Superior and Lake Michigan: consists of an undulating plain, with uplands in the north and west; over 168 m (550 ft) above sea level along the shore of Lake Michigan. Capital: Madison. Pop: 5 472 299 (2003 est). Area: 141 061 sq km (54 464 sq miles) 2 a river in central and SW Wisconsin, flowing south and west to the Mississippi. Length: 692 km (430 miles)

Wisden John 1826–84, English cricketer; publisher of *Wisden Cricketers' Almanack*, which first appeared in 1864

wisdom tooth any of the four molar teeth, one at the back of each side of the jaw, that are the last of the permanent teeth to erupt

Wiseman Nicholas Patrick Stephen 1802–65, British cardinal; first Roman Catholic archbishop of Westminster (1850–65)

wishbone the V-shaped bone above the breastbone in most birds consisting of the fused clavicles; furcula

Wismar a port in NE Germany, on an inlet of the Baltic, in Mecklenburg-West Pomerania: shipbuilding industries. Pop: 45 714 (2003 est)

wisp a flock of birds, esp snipe

wisteria any twining leguminous woody climbing plant of the genus *Wisteria*, of E Asia and North America, having blue, purple, or white flowers in large drooping clusters

wit 1 the talent or quality of using unexpected associations between contrasting or disparate words or ideas to make a clever humorous effect 2 speech or writing showing this quality 3 a person possessing, showing, or noted for such an ability, esp in repartee

witblits *South African* an extremely potent illegally distilled spirit

witch[1] a person, usually female, who practises or professes to practise magic or sorcery, esp black magic, or is believed to have dealings with the devil

witch[2] a flatfish, *Pleuronectes* (or *Glyptocephalus*) *cynoglossus*, of N Atlantic coastal waters, having a narrow greyish-brown body marked with tiny black spots: family *Pleuronectidae* (plaice, flounders, etc)

witchcraft 1 the art or power of bringing magical or preternatural power to bear or the act or practice of attempting to do so **2** the influence of magic or sorcery

witch doctor 1 a man in certain societies, esp preliterate ones, who appears to possess magical powers, used esp to cure sickness but also to harm people **2** a person who seeks out or hunts witches in some African tribal cultures

witchetty grub the wood-boring edible larva of certain Australian moths and beetles

witch hazel *or* **wych-hazel 1** any of several trees and shrubs of the genus *Hamamelis*, esp *H. virginiana*, of North America, having ornamental yellow flowers and medicinal properties: family *Hamamelidaceae* **2** an astringent medicinal solution containing an extract of the bark and leaves of *H. virginiana*, applied to treat bruises, inflammation, etc.

witch-hunt a rigorous campaign to round up or expose dissenters on the pretext of safeguarding the welfare of the public

withdrawal the period a drug addict goes through following abrupt termination in the use of narcotics, usually characterized by physical and mental symptoms (**withdrawal symptoms**)

witness 1 a person or thing giving or serving as evidence **2** a person who testifies, esp in a court of law, to events or facts within his own knowledge **3** a person who attests to the genuineness of a document, signature, etc, by adding his own signature **4** **bear witness a** to give written or oral testimony **b** to be evidence or proof of

witness box *or esp US* **witness stand** the place in a court of law in which witnesses stand to give evidence

Witt Johan de 1625–72, Dutch statesman; chief minister of the United Provinces of the Netherlands (1653–72)

Wittenberg a city in E Germany, on the River Elbe, in Brandenburg: Martin Luther, as a philosophy teacher at Wittenberg university, began the Reformation here in 1517 by nailing his 95 theses to the doors of a church. Pop: 46 295 (2003 est)

Wittgenstein Ludwig Josef Johann 1889–1951, British philosopher, born in Austria. After studying with Bertrand Russell, he wrote the *Tractatus Logico-Philosophicus* (1921), which explores the relationship of language to the world. He was a major influence on logical positivism but later repudiated this, and in *Philosophical Investigations* (1953) he argues that philosophical problems arise from insufficient attention to the variety of natural language use

Witwatersrand a rocky ridge in NE South Africa: contains the richest gold deposits in the world, also coal and manganese; chief industrial centre is Johannesburg. Height: 1500–1800 m (5000–6000 ft)

wizard 1 a male witch or a man who practises or professes to practise magic or sorcery **2** *Computing* a computer program that guides a user through a complex task

wizardry the art, skills, and practices of a wizard, sorcerer, or magician

woad a European plant, *Isatis tinctoria*, formerly cultivated for its leaves, which yield a blue dye: family *Brassicaceae* (crucifers)

wobbegong an Australian carpet shark, *Orectolobus maculatus*, with brown-and-white skin

Wodehouse Sir P(elham) G(renville). 1881–1975, US author, born in England. His humorous novels of upper-class life in England include the *Psmith* and *Jeeves* series

Woking a town in SE England, in central Surrey: mainly residential. Pop: 101 127 (2001)

Wokingham a unitary authority in SE England, in Berkshire. Pop: 151 200 (2003 est). Area: 179 sq km (69 sq miles)

wold *Chiefly literary* a tract of open rolling country, esp upland

wolf 1 a predatory canine mammal, *Canis lupus*, which hunts in packs and was formerly widespread in North America and Eurasia but is now less common **2** any of several similar and related canines, such as the red wolf and the coyote (**prairie wolf**) **3** the fur of any such animal **4** *Informal* the destructive larva of any of various moths and beetles **5** *Music* **a** an unpleasant sound produced in some notes played on the violin, cello, etc, owing to resonant vibrations of the belly **b** an out-of-tune effect produced on keyboard instruments accommodated esp to the system of mean-tone temperament

Wolf 1 Friedrich August 1759–1824, German classical scholar, who suggested that the Homeric poems, esp the *Iliad*, are products of an oral tradition **2** Hugo 1860–1903, Austrian composer, esp of songs, including the *Italienisches Liederbuch* and the *Spanisches Liederbuch* **3**

Wolfe 1 James 1727–59, English soldier, who commanded the British capture of Quebec, in which he was killed **2** Thomas (**Clayton**). 1900–38, US novelist, noted for his autobiographical fiction, esp *Look Homeward, Angel* (1929) **3** Tom, full name *Thomas Kennerly Wolfe*. born 1931, US author and journalist; his books include *The Right Stuff* (1979) and the novels *Bonfire of the Vanities* (1987), and *A Man in Full* (1998)

Wolfensohn James D, known as *Jim*. born 1933, US businessman and international official, born in Australia; president of the International Bank for Reconstruction and Development (the World Bank) from 1995

wolfhound the largest breed of dog, used formerly to hunt wolves

Wolfit Sir Donald 1902–68, English stage actor and manager

Wolfram von Eschenbach died ?1220, German poet: author of the epic *Parzival*, incorporating the story of the Grail

Wolfsburg a city in N central Germany, in Lower Saxony: founded in 1938; motor-vehicle industry. Pop: 122 724 (2003 est)

wolf whistle a whistle made by a man to express admiration of a woman's appearance

Wollongong a city in E Australia, in E New South Wales on the Pacific: an early centre of dairy farming; now a coal-mining and heavy industrial centre. Pop: 228 846 (2001)

Wollstonecraft Mary 1759–97, British feminist and writer, author of *A Vindication of the Rights of Women* (1792); wife of William Godwin and mother of Mary Shelley

Wolsey Thomas ?1475–1530, English cardinal and statesman; archbishop of York (1514–30); lord chancellor (1515–29). He dominated Henry VIII's foreign and domestic policies but his failure to obtain papal consent for the annulment of the king's marriage to Catherine of Aragon led to his arrest for high treason (1530); he died on the journey to face trial

Wolverhampton 1 a city in W central England, in Wolverhampton unitary authority, West Midlands: iron and steel foundries; university (1992). Pop: 251 462 (2001) 2 a unitary authority in W central England, in the West Midlands. Pop: 238 900 (2003 est). Area: 69 sq km (27 sq miles)

wolverine a large musteline mammal, *Gulo gulo*, of northern forests of Eurasia and North America having dark very thick water-resistant fur

woman 1 an adult female human being 2 women collectively; womankind

womankind the female members of the human race; women collectively

womb the nontechnical name for **uterus**

wombat any of various burrowing herbivorous Australian marsupials, esp *Vombatus ursinus*, constituting the family *Vombatidae* and having short limbs, a heavy body, and coarse dense fur

won 1 the standard monetary unit of North Korea, divided into 100 chon 2 the standard monetary unit of South Korea, divided into 100 chon

Wonder Stevie real name *Steveland Judkins Morris*. born 1950, US Motown singer, songwriter, and multi-instrumentalist. His recordings include *Up-Tight* (1966), "Superstition" (1972), *Innervisions* (1973), *Songs in the Key of Life* (1976), and "I Just Called to Say I Love You" (1985)

wood 1 the hard fibrous substance consisting of xylem tissue that occurs beneath the bark in trees, shrubs, and similar plants 2 the trunks of trees that have been cut and prepared for use as a building material 3 a collection of trees, shrubs, herbs, grasses, etc, usually dominated by one or a few species of tree: usually smaller than a forest 4 fuel; firewood 5 *Golf* a a long-shafted club with a broad wooden or metal head, used for driving: numbered from 1 to 7 according to size, angle of face, etc. b (*as modifier*): *a wood shot* 6 *Tennis, squash, badminton* the frame of a racket 7 one of the biased wooden bowls used in the game of bowls 8 *Music* short for **woodwind** 9 a casks, barrels, etc, made of wood b **from the wood** (of a beverage) from a wooden container rather than a metal or glass one

Wood 1 Mrs Henry, married name of *Ellen Price*. 1814–87, British novelist, noted esp for the melodramatic novel *East Lynne* (1861) 2 Sir Henry **(Joseph)**. 1869–1944, English conductor, who founded the Promenade Concerts in London 3 John, known as *the Elder*. 1707–54, British architect and town planner, working mainly in Bath, where he designed the North and South Parades (1728) and the Circus (1754) 4 his son, John, known as *the Younger*. 1727–82, British architect: designed the Royal Crescent (1767–71) and the Assembly Rooms (1769–71), Bath 5 Ralph 1715–72, British potter, working in Staffordshire, who made the first toby jug (1762)

woodbine 1 a honeysuckle, *Lonicera periclymenum*, of Europe, SW Asia, and N Africa, having fragrant creamy flowers 2 **American woodbine** a related North American plant, *L. caprifolium* 3 *US* another name for **Virginia creeper**

woodcarving 1 the act of carving wood, esp as an art

form 2 a work of art produced by carving wood

woodcock 1 an Old World game bird, *Scolopax rusticola*, resembling the snipe but larger and having shorter legs and neck: family *Scolopacidae* (sandpipers, etc), order *Charadriiformes* 2 a related North American bird, *Philohela minor*

woodland a land that is mostly covered with woods or dense growths of trees and shrubs b (*as modifier*): *woodland fauna*

woodlouse any of various small terrestrial isopod crustaceans of the genera *Oniscus*, *Porcellio*, etc, which have a flattened segmented body and occur in damp habitats

woodpecker any climbing bird of the family *Picidae*, typically having a brightly coloured plumage and strong chisel-like bill with which they bore into trees for insects: order *Piciformes*

wood pulp 1 wood that has been ground to a fine pulp for use in making newsprint and other cheap forms of paper, and in the production of hardboard 2 finely pulped wood that has been digested by a chemical, such as caustic soda, and sometimes bleached: used in making paper

woodruff any of several rubiaceous plants of the genus *Galium*, esp *G. odoratum* (**sweet woodruff**), of Eurasia, which has small sweet-scented white flowers and whorls of narrow fragrant leaves used to flavour wine and liqueurs and in perfumery

Woods Tiger, real name *Eldrick Woods*. born 1975, US golfer: youngest US Masters champion (1997) and first Black golfer to win a major championship; in 2001 he became the only player to hold all four major titles at once

woodsman a person who lives in a wood or who is skilled in woodcraft

Woodstock a town in New York State, the site of a large rock festival in August 1969. Pop: 6253 (2003 est)

Woodward 1 Sir Clive born 1956, English Rugby Union player and subsequently (1997–) coach of the England team that won the Rugby World Cup in 2003. 2 R(obert) B(urns). 1917–79, US chemist. For his work on the synthesis of quinine, strychnine, cholesterol, and other organic compounds he won the Nobel prize for chemistry 1965

woodwind *Music* 1 of, relating to, or denoting a type of wind instrument, excluding the brass instruments, formerly made of wood but now often made of metal, such as the flute or clarinet 2 woodwind instruments collectively

woodwork the art, craft, or skill of making things in wood; carpentry
▷www.woodworking.com

woodworm 1 any of various insect larvae that bore into wooden furniture, beams, etc, esp the larvae of the furniture beetle, *Anobium punctatum*, and the deathwatch beetle 2 the condition caused in wood by any of these larvae

woof 1 the crosswise yarns that fill the warp yarns in weaving; weft 2 a woven fabric or its texture

woofer a loudspeaker used in high-fidelity systems for the reproduction of low audio frequencies

Wookey Hole a village in SW England, in Somerset, near Wells: noted for the nearby limestone cave in which prehistoric remains have been found. Pop: 1000 (latest est)

wool 1 the outer coat of sheep, yaks, etc, which consists of short curly hairs 2 yarn spun from the coat of sheep, etc, used in weaving, knitting, etc. 3 **a** cloth or a garment made from this yarn **b** (as modifier): *a wool dress* 4 any of certain fibrous materials 5 a tangled mass of soft fine hairs that occurs in certain plants
▷www.kswpa.com/woolhistory.htm

Woolf 1 **Leonard Sidney** 1880–1969, English publisher and political writer 2 his wife, **Virginia** 1882–1941, English novelist and critic. Her novels, which include *Mrs Dalloway* (1925), *To the Lighthouse* (1927), *The Waves* (1931), and *Between the Acts* (1941), employ such techniques as the interior monologue and stream of consciousness

woollen *or US* **woolen** relating to or consisting partly or wholly of wool

Woolley Sir (**Charles**) **Leonard** 1880–1960, British archaeologist, noted for his excavations at Ur in Mesopotamia (1922–34)

woolly *or sometimes US* **wooly** 1 consisting of, resembling, or having the nature of wool 2 covered or clothed in wool or something resembling it 3 *Botany* covered with long soft whitish hairs 4 *US* recalling the rough and lawless period of the early West of America (esp in the phrase **wild and woolly**) 5 *Western US and Austral* an informal word for **sheep**

Woolworth Frank Winfield 1852–1919, US merchant; founder of an international chain of department stores selling inexpensive goods

Woomera a town in South Australia: site of the Long Range Weapons Establishment. Pop: 602 (2001)

Wootton Barbara (**Frances**), Baroness of Abinger. 1897–1988, English economist, educationalist, social scientist, and criminologist

wop-wops the NZ, *informal* the backblocks; the back of beyond

Worcester 1 a cathedral city in W central England, the administrative centre of Worcestershire on the River Severn: scene of the battle (1651) in which Charles II was defeated by Cromwell. Pop: 94 029 (2001) 2 an industrial city in the US, in central Massachusetts: Clark University (1887). Pop: 175 706 (2003 est) 3 a town in S South Africa; centre of a fruit-growing region. Pop: 66 349 (2001)

Worcestershire a county of W central England, formerly (1974–98) part of Hereford and Worcester. Administrative centre: Worcester. Pop: 549 300 (2003 est). Area: 1742 sq km (674 sq miles)

word *Computing* a set of bits used to store, transmit, or operate upon an item of information in a computer, such as a program instruction

Word the 1 *Christianity* the 2nd person of the Trinity 2 Scripture, the Bible, or the Gospels as embodying or representing divine revelation

word game any game involving the formation, discovery, or alteration of a word or words

word processing the composition of documents using a computer system to input, edit, store, and print them

word processor a computer program that performs word processing **b** a computer system designed for

word processing

Wordsworth 1 **Dorothy** 1771–1855, English writer, whose *Journals* are noted esp for their descriptions of nature 2 her brother, **William** 1770–1850, English poet, whose work, celebrating nature, was greatly inspired by the Lake District, in which he spent most of his life. *Lyrical Ballads* (1798), to which Coleridge contributed, is often taken as the first example of English romantic poetry and includes his *Lines Written above Tintern Abbey*. Among his other works are *The Prelude* (completed in 1805; revised thereafter and published posthumously) and *Poems in Two Volumes* (1807), which includes *The Solitary Reaper* and *Intimations of Immortality*

work 1 something done, made, etc, as a result of effort or exertion 2 any piece of material that is undergoing a manufacturing operation or process; workpiece 3 decoration or ornamentation, esp of a specified kind 4 an engineering structure such as a bridge, building, etc. 5 *Physics* the transfer of energy expressed as the product of a force and the distance through which its point of application moves in the direction of the force.

workaholic a a person obsessively addicted to work **b** (*as modifier*): *workaholic behaviour*

worker a sterile female member of a colony of bees, ants, or wasps that forages for food, cares for the larvae, etc.

work ethic a belief in the moral value of work (often in the phrase **Protestant work ethic**)

workforce the total number of people who could be employed

workhorse a horse used for nonrecreational activities

workhouse 1 (formerly in England) an institution maintained at public expense where able-bodied paupers did unpaid work in return for food and accommodation 2 (in the US) a prison for petty offenders serving short sentences at manual labour

working 1 *Maths* a record of the steps by which the result of a calculation or the solution of a problem is obtained 3 (of a meal or occasion) during which business discussions are carried on

working day *or esp US* **workday** *Commerce* any day of the week except Sunday, public holidays, and, in some cases, Saturday

work of art 1 a piece of fine art, such as a painting or sculpture 2 something that may be likened to a piece of fine art, esp in beauty, intricacy, etc.

worksheet a sheet of paper containing exercises to be completed by a pupil or student

workshop a group of people engaged in study or work on a creative project or subject

Worksop a town in N central England, in N Nottinghamshire. Pop: 39 072 (2001)

work station *Computing* a device or component of an electronic office system consisting of a display screen and keyboard used to handle electronic office work

world 1 the earth as a planet, esp including its inhabitants 2 mankind; the human race 3 the universe or cosmos; everything in existence 4 a complex united whole regarded as resembling the universe 5 any star or planet, esp one that might be inhabited 6 an area, sphere, or realm considered as a complete environment 7 *Logic* See **possible world**

World Cup an international competition held between national teams in various sports, most notably association football

world music popular music of various ethnic origins and styles outside the tradition of Western pop and rock music

▷http://africanmusic.org
▷www.ceolas.org/ceolas.html
▷www.sbgmusic.com/html/teacher/reference/cultures.html
▷www.rootsworld.com/rw

World War I the war (1914–18), fought mainly in Europe and the Middle East, in which the Allies (principally France, Russia, Britain, Italy after 1915, and the US after 1917) defeated the Central Powers (principally Germany, Austria-Hungary, and Turkey). The war was precipitated by the assassination of Austria's crown prince (Archduke Franz Ferdinand) at Sarajevo on June 28, 1914 and swiftly developed its major front in E France, where millions died in static trench warfare. After the October Revolution (1917) the Bolsheviks ended Russian participation in the war (Dec 15, 1917). The exhausted Central Powers agreed to an armistice on Nov 11, 1918 and quickly succumbed to internal revolution, before being forced to sign the Treaty of Versailles (June 28, 1919) and other treaties

▷www.worldwar1.com
▷www.firstworldwar.com

World War II the war (1939–45) in which the Allies (principally Britain, the Soviet Union, and the US) defeated the Axis powers (principally Germany, Italy, and Japan). Britain and France declared war on Germany (Sept 3, 1939) as a result of the German invasion of Poland (Sept 1, 1939). Italy entered the war on June 10, 1940 shortly before the collapse of France (armistice signed June 22, 1940). On June 22, 1941 Germany attacked the Soviet Union and on Dec 7, 1941 the Japanese attacked the US at Pearl Harbor. On Sept 8, 1943 Italy surrendered, the war in Europe ending on May 7, 1945 with the unconditional surrender of the Germans. The Japanese capitulated on Aug 14, 1945 as a direct result of the atomic bombs dropped by the Americans on Hiroshima and Nagasaki

▷www.ibiblio.org/pha

World Wide Web *Computing* a vast network of linked hypertext files, stored on computers throughout the world, that can provide a computer user with information on a huge variety of subjects

worm 1 any of various invertebrates, esp the annelids (earthworms, etc), nematodes (roundworms), and flatworms, having a slender elongated body 2 any of various insect larvae having an elongated body, such as the silkworm and wireworm 3 any of various unrelated animals that resemble annelids, nematodes, etc, such as the glow-worm and shipworm 4 a shaft on which a helical groove has been cut, as in a gear arrangement in which such a shaft meshes with a toothed wheel 5 a spiral pipe cooled by air or flowing water, used as a condenser in a still 6 *Anatomy* any wormlike organ, structure, or part, such as the middle lobe of the cerebellum (*vermis cerebelli*) 7 *Computing* a program that duplicates itself many times in a network and prevents its

destruction. It often carries a logic bomb or virus

WORM *Computing* write once read many times: an optical disk that enables users to store data but not change it

wormcast a coil of earth or sand that has been egested by a burrowing earthworm or lugworm

wormhole 1 a hole made by a worm in timber, plants, etc. 2 *Physics* a tunnel in the geometry of space–time postulated to connect different parts of the universe

worms any disease or disorder, usually of the intestine, characterized by infestation with parasitic worms

Worms a city in SW Germany, in Rhineland-Palatinate on the Rhine: famous as the seat of imperial diets, notably that of 1521, before which Luther defended his doctrines in the presence of Charles V; river port and manufacturing centre with a large wine trade. Pop: 81 100 (2003 est)

wormwood any of various plants of the chiefly N temperate genus *Artemisia*, esp *A. absinthium*, a European plant yielding a bitter extract used in making absinthe: family *Asteraceae* (composites)

wormy 1 worm-infested or worm-eaten 2 (of wood) having irregular small tunnels bored into it and tracked over its surface, made either by worms or artificially

worship 1 religious adoration or devotion 2 the formal expression of religious adoration; rites, prayers, etc.

Worship *Chiefly Brit* a title used to address or refer to a mayor, magistrate, or a person of similar high rank

worshipful *Chiefly Brit* a title used to address or refer to various people or bodies of distinguished rank, such as mayors and certain ancient companies of the City of London

worsted 1 a closely twisted yarn or thread made from combed long-staple wool 2 a fabric made from this, with a hard smooth close-textured surface and no nap

worth 1 having a value of 2 value, price 3 the amount or quantity of something of a specified value

Worthing a resort in S England, in West Sussex on the English Channel. Pop: 96 964 (2001)

wound 1 any break in the skin or an organ or part as the result of violence or a surgical incision 2 an injury to plant tissue

wow a slow variation or distortion in pitch that occurs at very low audio frequencies in sound-reproducing systems, such as a record player, usually due to variation in speed of the turntable, etc.

wowser *Austral and NZ, slang* a teetotaller

wrack 1 seaweed or other marine vegetation that is floating in the sea or has been cast ashore 2 any of various seaweeds of the genus *Fucus*, such as *F. serratus* (**serrated wrack**)

wraith 1 the apparition of a person living or thought to be alive, supposed to appear around the time of his death 2 a ghost or any apparition

Wrangel Island an island in the Arctic Ocean, off the coast of the extreme NE of Russia: administratively part of Russia; mountainous and mostly tundra. Area: about 7300 sq km (2800 sq miles)

Wrangell Mount a mountain in S Alaska, in the W Wrangell Mountains. Height: 4269 m (14 005 ft)

wrap 1 *Brit, slang* a small package of an illegal drug in powder form **2 a** the end of a working day during the filming of a motion picture or television programme **b** the completion of filming of a motion picture or television programme

wrapper 1 the cover, usually of paper or cellophane, in which something is wrapped **2** the ripe firm tobacco leaf forming the outermost portion of a cigar and wound around its body

wrasse any marine percoid fish of the family *Labridae*, of tropical and temperate seas, having thick lips, strong teeth, and usually a bright coloration: many are used as food fishes

Wrath Cape a promontory at the NW extremity of the Scottish mainland

wreath 1 a band of flowers or foliage intertwined into a ring, usually placed on a grave as a memorial or worn on the head as a garland or a mark of honour **2** a spiral or circular defect appearing in porcelain and glassware

wreck 1 a the accidental destruction of a ship at sea **b** the ship so destroyed **2** *Maritime law* goods cast ashore from a wrecked vessel

wrecker 1 *Chiefly US and Canadian* a person whose job is to demolish buildings or dismantle cars **2** (formerly) a person who lures ships to destruction to plunder the wreckage

Wrekin the an isolated hill in the English Midlands in Telford and Wrekin unitary authority, Shropshire. Height: 400 m (1335 ft)

wren 1 any small brown passerine songbird of the chiefly American family *Troglodytidae*, esp *Troglodytes troglodytes* (**wren** in Britain, **winter wren** in the US and Canada). They have a slender bill and feed on insects **2** any of various similar birds of the families *Muscicapidae* (Australian warblers), *Xenicidae* (New Zealand wrens), etc.

Wren Sir Christopher 1632–1723, English architect. He designed St Paul's Cathedral and over 50 other London churches after the Great Fire as well as many secular buildings

wrench 1 an injury to a limb, caused by twisting **2** a spanner, esp one with adjustable jaws

wrest *Archaic* a small key used to tune a piano or harp

wrestling any of certain sports in which the contestants fight each other according to various rules governing holds and usually forbidding blows with the closed fist. The principal object is to overcome the opponent either by throwing or pinning him to the ground or by causing him to submit

▷www.fila-wrestling.com

Wrexham 1 a town in N Wales, in Wrexham county borough: seat of the Roman Catholic bishopric of Wales (except the former Glamorganshire); formerly noted for coal-mining. Pop: 42 576 (2001) **2** a county borough in NE Wales, created in 1996 from part of Clwyd. Pop: 129 700 (2003 est). Area: 500 sq km (193 sq miles)

Wright 1 Frank Lloyd 1869–1959, US architect, whose designs include the Imperial Hotel, Tokyo (1916), the Guggenheim Museum, New York (1943), and many private houses. His "organic architecture" sought a close relationship between buildings and their natural surroundings **2** Joseph, known as *Wright of Derby*. 1734–97, British painter, noted for his paintings of industrial

and scientific subjects, esp *The Orrery* (?1765) and *The Air Pump* (1768) **3** Joseph 1855–1930, British philologist; editor of *The English Dialect Dictionary* (1898–1905) **4** Judith (**Arundel**). 1915–2000, Australian poet, critic, and conservationist. Her collections of poetry include *The Moving Image* (1946), *Woman to Man* (1949), and *A Human Pattern* (1990) **5** Richard 1908–60, US Black novelist and short-story writer, best known for the novel *Native Son* (1940) **6** Wilbur (1867–1912) and his brother, **Orville** (1871–1948), US aviation pioneers, who designed and flew the first powered aircraft (1903) **7** William, known as *Billy*. 1924–94, English footballer: winner of 105 caps

wrist *Anatomy* the joint between the forearm and the hand

writ 1 *Law* (formerly) a document under seal, issued in the name of the Crown or a court, commanding the person to whom it is addressed to do or refrain from doing some specified act **2** *Archaic* a piece or body of writing

write-off *Informal* something damaged beyond repair, esp a car

writer 1 a person who is able to write or write well **2** a composer of music **3** *Scot* a legal practitioner, such as a notary or solicitor **4 Writer to the Signet** (in Scotland) a member of an ancient society of solicitors, now having the exclusive privilege of preparing crown writs

writing 1 a group of letters or symbols written or marked on a surface as a means of communicating ideas by making each symbol stand for an idea, concept, or thing (see **ideogram**), by using each symbol to represent a set of sounds grouped into syllables (syllabic writing), or by regarding each symbol as corresponding roughly or exactly to each of the sounds in the language (alphabetic writing) **2** anything expressed in letters, esp a literary composition **3** the work of a writer **4** literary style, art, or practice

Wrocław an industrial city in SW Poland, on the River Oder: passed to Austria (1527) and to Prussia (1741); returned to Poland in 1945. Pop: 647 000 (2005 est)

wrong 1 (of a side, esp of a fabric) intended to face the inside so as not to be seen **2** *Law* **a** an infringement of another person's rights, rendering the offender liable to a civil action, as for breach of contract or tort **b** a violation of public rights and duties, affecting the community as a whole and actionable at the instance of the Crown

wrought 1 *Metallurgy* shaped by hammering or beating **2** decorated or made with delicate care

wrought iron a a pure form of iron having a low carbon content and a fibrous microstructure. It is made by various processes and is often used for decorative work **b** (*as modifier*): *wrought-iron gates*

wrybill a New Zealand plover, *Anarhynchus frontalis*, having its bill deflected to one side enabling it to search for food beneath stones

wryneck either of two cryptically coloured Old World woodpeckers, *Jynx torquilla* or *J. ruficollis*, which do not drum on trees

Wu Harry, real name *Wu Hongda*. born 1937, Chinese dissident and human-rights campaigner, a US citizen from 1994: held in labour camps (1960–79); exiled to the US in 1985 but returned secretly to document forced labour in

Chinese prisons

Wuchang or **Wu-ch'ang** a former city of E central China: now a part of Wuhan

Wuhan a city in SE China, in Hubei province, at the confluence of the Han and Yangtze Rivers: formed in 1950 by the union of the cities of Hanyang, Hankou, and Wuchang (the Han Cities); river port and industrial centre; university (1913). Pop: 6 003 000 (2005 est)

Wuhu a port in E China, in E Anhui province on the Yangtze River. Pop: 701 000 (2005 est)

Wuppertal a city in W Germany, in North Rhine-Westphalia state on the **Wupper River** (a Rhine tributary): formed in 1929 from the amalgamation of the towns of Barmen and Elberfeld and other smaller towns; textile centre. Pop: 362 137 (2003 est)

Wuxi, Wusih, or **Wu-hsi** a city in E China, in S Jiangsu province on the Grand Canal: textile industry. Pop: 1 192 000 (2005 est)

Wyatt 1 James 1746–1813, British architect; a pioneer of the Gothic Revival 2 Sir **Thomas** ?1503–42, English poet at the court of Henry VIII

wych-elm or **witch-elm** 1 Eurasian elm tree, *Ulmus glabra*, having a rounded shape, longish pointed leaves, clusters of small flowers, and winged fruits 2 the wood of this tree

Wycherley William ?1640–1716, English dramatist. His Restoration comedies include *The Country Wife* (1675) and *The Plain Dealer* (1676)

Wycliffe or **Wyclif** John ?1330–84, English religious reformer. A precursor of the Reformation, whose writings were condemned as heretical, he attacked the doctrines and abuses of the Church. He instigated the first complete translation of the Bible into English. His followers were called Lollards

Wye a river in E Wales and W England, rising in Powys and flowing southeast into Herefordshire, then south to the Severn estuary. Length: 210 km (130 miles)

Wykeham William of 1324–1404, English prelate and statesman, who founded New College, Oxford, and Winchester College: chancellor of England (1367–71; 1389–91); bishop of Winchester (1367–1404)

Wyndham John, pseudonym of *John Wyndham Parkes Lucas Beynon Harris*. 1903–69, British writer of science fiction novels and stories. His works include *The Day of the Triffids* (1951), *The Kraken Wakes* (1953), and *The Midwich Cuckoos* (1957)

Wynette Tammy, original name *Virginia Wynette Pugh*. 1942–98, US country singer; her bestselling records include "Your Good Girl's Gonna Go Bad" (1967) and "Stand By Your Man" (1969)

Wyn Jones Ieuan born 1949, Welsh politician; leader of Plaid Cymru from 2000

Wyoming a state of the western US: consists largely of ranges of the Rockies in the west and north, with part of the Great Plains in the east and several regions of hot springs. Capital: Cheyenne. Pop: 501 242 (2003 est). Area: 253 597 sq km (97 914 sq miles)

WYSIWYG *Computing* what you see is what you get: referring to what is displayed on the screen being the same as what will be printed out

X

Xanthippe or **Xantippe** the wife of Socrates, proverbial as a scolding and quarrelsome woman

Xanthus the chief city of ancient Lycia in SW Asia Minor: source of some important antiquities

Xavier Saint Francis, known as the *Apostle of the Indies*. 1506–52, Spanish missionary, who was a founding member of the Jesuit society (1534) and later preached in Goa, Ceylon, the East Indies, and Japan. Feast day: Dec 3

X-chromosome the sex chromosome that occurs in pairs in the diploid cells of the females of many animals, including humans, and as one of a pair with the Y-chromosome in those of males

Xenakis Yannis 1922–2001, Greek composer and musical theorist, born in Romania: later a French citizen. He was noted for his use of computers in composition: his works include *ST/10-1, 080262* (1962) and *Dox-orkh* (1991)

Xenocrates ?396–314 BC, Greek Platonic philosopher

xenon a colourless odourless gaseous element occurring in trace amounts in air; formerly considered inert it is now known to form compounds and is used in radio valves, stroboscopic and bactericidal lamps, and bubble chambers. Symbol: Xe; atomic no.: 54; atomic wt.: 131.29; valency: 0; density: 5.887 kg/m³; melting pt.: −111.76°C; boiling pt.: −108.0°C

Xenophanes ?570–?480 BC, Greek philosopher and poet, noted for his monotheism and regarded as a founder of the Eleatic school

xenophobia hatred or fear of foreigners or strangers or of their politics or culture

Xenophon 431–?355 BC, Greek general and historian; a disciple of Socrates. He accompanied Cyrus the Younger against Artaxerxes II and, after Cyrus' death at Cunaxa (401), he led his army of 10 000 Greek soldiers to the Black Sea, an expedition described in his *Anabasis*. His other works include *Hellenica*, a history of Greece, and the *Memorabilia*, *Apology*, and *Symposium*, which contain recollections of Socrates

Xerxes I ?519–465 BC, king of Persia (485–465), who led a vast army against Greece. His forces were victorious at Thermopylae but his fleet was defeated at Salamis (480) and his army at Plataea (479)

Xhosa 1 a member of a cattle-rearing Negroid people of southern Africa, living chiefly in South Africa 2 the language of this people, belonging to the Bantu group of the Niger-Congo family: one of the Nguni languages, closely related to Swazi and Zulu and characterized by several clicks in its sound system

Xi, Hsi, or **Si** a river in S China, rising in Yünnan province and flowing east to the Canton delta on the South China Sea: the main river system of S China. Length: about 1900 km (1200 miles)

Xia Gui or **Hsia Kuei** ?1180–1230, Chinese landscape painter of the Sung dynasty; noted for his misty mountain landscapes in ink monochrome

Xiang, Hsiang, or **Siang** 1 a river in SE central China, rising in NE Guangxi Zhuang and flowing northeast and north to Dongting Lake. Length: about 1150 km (715 miles) 2 a river in S China, rising in SE Yünnan and flowing generally east to the Hongxiu (the upper course of the Xi River). Length: about 800 km (500 miles)

Xiangtan or **Siangtan** a city in S central China, in NE Hunan on the Xiang River: centre of a region noted for tea production. Pop: 592 000 (2005 est)

Xining, Hsining, or **Sining** a city in W China, capital of Qinghai province, at an altitude of 2300 m (7500 ft). Pop: 689 000 (2005 est)

Xinjiang Uygur or **Sinkiang-Uighur Autonomous Region** an administrative division of NW China: established in 1955 for the Uygur ethnic minority, with autonomous subdivisions for other small minorities; produces over half China's wool and contains valuable mineral resources. Capital: Urumqi. Pop: 19 340 000 (2003 est). Area: 1 646 799 sq km (635 829 sq miles)

Xochimilco a town in central Mexico, on Lake Xochimilco: noted for its floating gardens. Pop: 271 020 (1990)

X-rated (formerly, in Britain) (of a film) considered suitable for viewing by adults only

X-ray or **x-ray** 1 a electromagnetic radiation emitted when matter is bombarded with fast electrons. X-rays have wavelengths shorter than that of ultraviolet radiation, that is less than about 1×10^{-8} metres. They extend to indefinitely short wavelengths, but below about 1×10^{-11} metres they are often called gamma radiation b (as modifier): *X-ray astronomy* 2 a picture produced by exposing photographic film to X-rays: used in medicine as a diagnostic aid as parts of the body, such as bones, absorb X-rays and so appear as opaque areas on the picture

Xuzhou, Hsü-chou, or **Süchow** a city in N central

China, in NW Jiangsu province: scene of a decisive battle (1949) in which the Communists defeated the Nationalists. Pop: 1 662 000 (2005 est)

xylem a plant tissue that conducts water and mineral salts from the roots to all other parts, provides mechanical support, and forms the wood of trees and shrubs. It is of two types (protoxylem and metaxylem), both of which are made up mainly of vessels and tracheids

xylene an aromatic hydrocarbon existing in three isomeric forms, all three being colourless flammable volatile liquids used as solvents and in the manufacture of synthetic resins, dyes, and insecticides; dimethylbenzene. Formula: $C_6H_4(CH_3)_2$

xylophone *Music* a percussion instrument consisting of a set of wooden bars of graduated length. It is played with hard-headed hammers

Yy

yabby or **yabbie** Austral **1** a small freshwater crayfish of the genus Cherax, esp C. destructor **2** a marine prawn used as bait

yacht a vessel propelled by sail or power, used esp for pleasure cruising, racing, etc.

Yahweh, Jahweh, Yahveh or **Jahveh** Old Testament a vocalization of the Tetragrammaton, used esp by Christian theologians

Yahwism, Jahwism, Yahvism or **Jahvism** the use of the name Yahweh, esp in parts of the Old Testament, as the personal name of God

Yahwist, Jahwist, Yahvist or **Jahvist** Bible **the a** the conjectured author or authors of the earliest of four main sources or strands of tradition of which the Pentateuch is composed and in which God is called Yahweh throughout **b** (as modifier): the Yahwist source

yak a wild and domesticated type of cattle, Bos grunniens, of Tibet, having long horns and long shaggy hair

Yakutsk a port in E Russia, capital of the Sakha Republic, on the Lena River. Pop: 214 000 (2005 est)

Yale lock Trademark a type of cylinder lock using a flat serrated key

Yalta a port and resort in S Ukraine, in the Crimea on the Black Sea: scene of a conference (1945) between Churchill, Roosevelt, and Stalin, who met to plan the final defeat and occupation of Nazi Germany. Pop: 89 000 (latest est)

Yalu a river in E Asia, rising in N North Korea and flowing southwest to Korea Bay, forming a large part of the border between North Korea and NE China. Length: 806 km (501 miles)

yam 1 any of various twining plants of the genus Dioscorea, of tropical and subtropical regions, cultivated for their edible tubers: family Dioscoreaceae **2** Southern US any of certain large varieties of sweet potato **3** a former Scot name for the (common) **potato**

Yamoussoukro the capital of Côte d'Ivoire, situated in the S centre of the country. It replaced Abidjan as capital in 1983. Pop: 468 000 (2005 est)

Yanan or **Yenan** a city in NE China, in N Shaanxi province: political and military capital of the Chinese Communists (1935–49). Pop: 343 000 (2005 est)

Yang Chen Ning born 1922, US physicist, born in China: with Tsung-Dao Lee, he disproved the physical principle known as the conservation of parity and shared the Nobel prize for physics (1957)

Yangon the capital and chief port of Myanmar (formerly Burma): an industrial city and transport centre; dominated by the gold-covered Shwe Dagon pagoda, 112 m (368 ft) high. Pop: 4 082 000 (2005 est)

Yangtze the longest river in China, rising in SE Qinghai province and flowing east to the East China Sea near Shanghai: a major commercial waterway in one of the most densely populated areas of the world. The **Three Gorges dam** near Yichang, the world's biggest hydroelectric and flood-control project, was begun in 1994 and the dam was completed in 2003, with filling expected to take several years thereafter. Length: 5528 km (3434 miles)

Yank 1 a slang word for an American **2** US, informal short for **Yankee**

Yankee or informal **Yank 1** Often disparaging a native or inhabitant of the US; American **2** a native or inhabitant of New England **3** a native or inhabitant of the Northern US, esp a Northern soldier in the Civil War

Yantai, Yentai, or **Yen-t'ai** a port in E China, in NE Shandong. Pop: 1 707 000 (2005 est)

Yap a group of four main islands in the W Pacific, in the W Caroline Islands: administratively a district of the US Trust Territory of the Pacific Islands from 1947; became self-governing in 1979 as part of the Federated States of Micronesia; important Japanese naval base in World War II. Pop: 12 055 (1999 est). Area: 101 sq km (39 sq miles)

Yaqui a river in NW Mexico, rising near the border with the US and flowing south to the Gulf of California. Length: about 676 km (420 miles)

yarborough Bridge, whist a hand of 13 cards in which no card is higher than nine

yard[1] 1 a unit of length equal to 3 feet and defined in 1963 as exactly 0.9144 metre **2** a cylindrical wooden or hollow metal spar, tapered at the ends, slung from a mast of a square-rigged or lateen-rigged vessel and used for suspending a sail **3** short for **yardstick**

yard[2] 1 an enclosed or open area used for some commercial activity, for storage, etc. **2** a US and Canadian word for **garden 3** an area having a network of railway tracks and sidings, used for storing rolling stock, making up trains, etc. **4** US and Canadian the winter pasture of deer, moose, and similar animals **5** NZ short for **saleyard** or **stockyard**

yardarm *Nautical* the two tapering outer ends of a ship's yard

yardstick a graduated stick, one yard long, used for measurement

yarmulke *Judaism* a skullcap worn by orthodox male Jews at all times, and by others during prayer

yarn 1 a continuous twisted strand of natural or synthetic fibres, used in weaving, knitting, etc. **2** *Informal* a long and often involved story or account, usually telling of incredible or fantastic events

Yaroslavl a city in W Russia, on the River Volga: a major trading centre since early times and one of the first industrial centres in Russia; textile industries were established in the 18th century. Pop: 609 000 (2005 est)

Yarra River a river in SE Australia, rising in the Great Dividing Range and flowing west and southwest through Melbourne to Port Phillip Bay. Length: 250 km (155 miles)

yarrow any of several plants of the genus *Achillea*, esp *A. millefolium*, of Eurasia, having finely dissected leaves and flat clusters of white flower heads: family *Asteraceae* (composites)

yashmak *or* **yashmac** the face veil worn by Muslim women when in public

yaw 1 the angular movement of an aircraft, missile, etc, about its vertical axis **2** the deviation of a vessel from a straight course

Yawata *or* **Yahata** a former city in Japan, on N Kyushu: merged with Moji, Kokura, Tobata, and Wakamatsu in 1963 to form **Kitakyushu**

yawl 1 a two-masted sailing vessel, rigged fore-and-aft, with a large mainmast and a small mizzenmast stepped aft of the rudderpost **2** a ship's small boat, usually rowed by four or six oars

yaws an infectious nonvenereal disease of tropical climates with early symptoms resembling syphilis, characterized by red skin eruptions and, later, pain in the joints: it is caused by the spiral bacterium *Treponema pertenue*

Yazd *or* **Yezd** a city in central Iran: a major centre of silk weaving. Pop: 436 000 (2005 est)

Y-chromosome the sex chromosome that occurs as one of a pair with the X-chromosome in the diploid cells of the males of many animals, including humans

year 1 the period of time, the **calendar year**, containing 365 days or in a **leap year** 366 days. It is based on the Gregorian calendar, being divided into 12 calendar months, and is reckoned from January 1 to December 31 **2** the period of time, the **solar year**, during which the earth makes one revolution around the sun, measured between two successive vernal equinoxes: equal to 365.242 19 days **3** the period of time, the **sidereal year**, during which the earth makes one revolution around the sun, measured between two successive conjunctions of a particular distant star: equal to 365.256 36 days **4** the period of time, the **lunar year**, containing 12 lunar months and equal to 354.3671 days **5** the period of time taken by a specified planet to complete one revolution around the sun **6** a group of pupils or students, who are taught or study together, divided into classes at school **7** **year and a day** *English law* a period fixed by law to ensure the completion of a full year. It is applied

for certain purposes, such as to determine the time within which wrecks must be claimed

yearling 1 the young of any of various animals, including the antelope and buffalo, between one and two years of age **2** a thoroughbred racehorse counted for racing purposes as being one year old until the second Jan 1 following its birth

yeast 1 any of various single-celled ascomycetous fungi of the genus *Saccharomyces* and related genera, which reproduce by budding and are able to ferment sugars: a rich source of vitamins of the B complex **2** any yeast-like fungus, esp of the genus *Candida*, which can cause thrush in areas infected with it **3** a preparation containing yeast cells, used to treat diseases caused by vitamin B deficiency

Yeisk, Yeysk, *or* **Eisk** a port and resort in SW Russia, on the Sea of Azov. Pop: 86 300 (1991 est)

Yekaterinburg *or* **Ekaterinburg** a city in NW Russia, in the Ural Mountains: scene of the execution (1918) of Nicholas II and his family; university (1920); one of the largest centres of heavy engineering in Russia. Pop: 1 281 000 (2005 est)

yellow 1 any of a group of colours that vary in saturation but have the same hue. They lie in the approximate wavelength range 585–575 nanometres. Yellow is the complementary colour of blue and with cyan and magenta forms a set of primary colours **2** yellow cloth or clothing **3** the yolk of an egg **4** a yellow ball in snooker, etc. **5** any of a group of pieridine butterflies the males of which have yellow or yellowish wings, esp the clouded yellows (*Colias* spp.) and the brimstone

yellow fever an acute infectious disease of tropical and subtropical climates, characterized by fever, haemorrhages, vomiting of blood, and jaundice: caused by a virus transmitted by the bite of a female mosquito of the species *Aedes aegypti*

yellowhammer 1 a European bunting, *Emberiza citrinella*, having a yellowish head and body and brown streaked wings and tail **2** *US and Canadian* an informal name for the **yellow-shafted flicker**, an American woodpecker (see **flicker²**)

Yellowknife a city in N Canada, capital of the Northwest Territories on Great Slave Lake. Pop: 16 055 (2001)

Yellow River the second longest river in China, rising in SE Qinghai and flowing east, south, and east again to the Gulf of Bohai south of Tianjin; it has changed its course several times in recorded history. Length: about 4350 km (2700 miles)

Yellow Sea a shallow arm of the Pacific between Korea and NE China. Area: about 466 200 sq km (180 000 sq miles)

Yellowstone a river rising in N Wyoming and flowing north through Yellowstone National Park, then east to the Missouri. Length: 1080 km (671 miles)

Yellowstone National Park a national park in the NW central US, mostly in NW Wyoming: the oldest and largest national park in the US, containing unusual geological formations and geysers. Area: 8956 sq km (3458 sq miles)

Yemen a republic in SW Arabia, on the Red Sea and the Gulf of Aden: formed in 1990 from the union of North

Yemen and South Yemen: consists of arid coastal low-lands, rising to fertile upland valleys and mountains in the west and to the Hadhramaut plateau in the SE: the north and east contains part of the Great Sandy Desert. Official language: Arabic. Official religion: Muslim. Currency: riyal. Capital: San'a. Pop: 20 732 000 (2004 est). Area (including territory claimed by Yemen along the undemarcated eastern border with Saudi Arabia): 472 099 sq km (182 278 sq miles)

yen the standard monetary unit of Japan, (notionally) divided into 100 sen

Yenisei or **Yenisey** a river in central Russia, in central Siberia, formed by the confluence of two headstreams in the Tuva Republic: flows west and north to the Arctic Ocean; the largest river in volume in Russia. Length: 4129 km (2566 miles)

yeoman 1 *History* **a** a member of a class of small free-holders of common birth who cultivated their own land **b** an assistant or other subordinate to an official, such as a sheriff, or to a craftsman or trader **c** an attendant or lesser official in a royal or noble household **2** (in Britain) another name for **yeoman of the guard**

yeoman of the guard a member of the bodyguard (**Yeomen of the Guard**) of the English monarch. This unit was founded in 1485 and now retains ceremonial functions only

yeomanry 1 yeomen collectively **2** (in Britain) a volunteer cavalry force, organized in 1761 for home defence: merged into the Territorial Army in 1907

Yerevan the capital of Armenia: founded in the 8th century BC; an industrial city and a main focus of trade routes since ancient times; university. Pop: 1 066 000 (2005 est)

Yeşil Irmak a river in N Turkey, flowing northwest to the Black Sea. Length: 418 km (260 miles)

yew 1 any coniferous tree of the genus *Taxus*, of the Old World and North America, esp *T. baccata*, having flattened needle-like leaves, fine-grained elastic wood, and solitary seeds with a red waxy aril resembling berries: family *Taxaceae* **2** the wood of any of these trees, used to make bows for archery **3** *Archery* a bow made of yew

Yibin or **I-pin** a port in S central China, in Sichuan province: a commercial centre. Pop: 784 000 (2005 est)

Yichang, Ichang, or **I-ch'ang** a port in S central China, in Hubei province on the Yangtze River 1600 km (1000 miles) from the East China Sea: the Three Gorges dam, the world's biggest hydroelectric and flood-control project, is nearby. Pop: 724 000 (2005 est)

Yiddish a language spoken as a vernacular by Jews in Europe and elsewhere by Jewish emigrants, usually written in the Hebrew alphabet. Historically, it is a dialect of High German with an admixture of words of Hebrew, Romance, and Slavonic origin, developed in central and E Europe during the Middle Ages

yield *Chem* the quantity of a specified product obtained in a reaction or series of reactions, usually expressed as a percentage of the quantity that is theoretically obtainable

Yin and Yang two complementary principles of Chinese philosophy: Yin is negative, dark, and feminine, Yang positive, bright, and masculine. Their interaction is thought to maintain the harmony of the universe and to influence everything within it

Yinchuan, Yin-ch'uan, or **Yinchwan** a city in N central China, capital of the Ningxia Hui AR, on the Yellow River. Pop: 642 000 (2005 est)

Yingkou or **Yingkow** a port in NE China, in SW Liaoning province: a major shipping centre for Manchuria. Pop: 723 000 (2005 est)

yodel an effect produced in singing by an abrupt change of register from the chest voice to falsetto, esp in popular folk songs of the Swiss Alps

yoga 1 a Hindu system of philosophy aiming at the mystical union of the self with the Supreme Being in a state of complete awareness and tranquillity through certain physical and mental exercises **2** any method by which such awareness and tranquillity are attained, esp a course of related exercises and postures designed to promote physical and spiritual wellbeing ▷www.yoga.com

yogi a person who is a master of yoga

Yogyakarta, Jogjakarta, Jokjakarta or **Djokjakarta** a city in S Indonesia, in central Java: seat of government of Indonesia (1946–49); university (1949). Pop: 396 711 (2000)

yoke 1 something resembling a yoke in form or function, such as a frame fitting over a person's shoulders for carrying buckets suspended at either end **2** a part, esp one of relatively thick cross section, that secures two or more components so that they move together **3** a crosshead that transmits the drive of an opposed piston engine from the upper of a pair of linked pistons to the crankshaft through a connecting rod **4** *Nautical* a crossbar fixed athwartships to the head of a rudderpost in a small boat, to which are attached ropes or cables for steering **5** a Y-shaped cable, rope, or chain, used for holding, towing, etc. **6** (in the ancient world) a symbolic reconstruction of a yoke, consisting of two upright spears with a third lashed across them, under which conquered enemies were compelled to march, esp in Rome **7** *Irish* any device, unusual object, or gadget

Yokohama a port in central Japan, on SE Honshu on Tokyo Bay: a major port and the country's second largest city situated in the largest and most populous industrial region of Japan. Pop: 3 433 612 (2002 est)

Yokosuka a port in Japan, in SE Honshu: a major naval base with shipbuilding industries. Pop: 434 613 (2002 est)

yolk 1 the substance in an animal ovum consisting of protein and fat that nourishes the developing embryo **2** a greasy substance secreted by the skin of a sheep and present in the fleece

Yom Kippur an annual Jewish holiday celebrated on Tishri 10 as a day of fasting, on which prayers of penitence are recited in the synagogue throughout the day

Yonkers a city in SE New York State, near New York City on the Hudson River. Pop: 197 388 (2003 est)

Yonne 1 a department of N central France, in Burgundy region. Capital: Auxerre. Pop: 335 917 (2003 est). Area: 7461 sq km (2910 sq miles) **2** a river in N France, flowing generally northwest to the Seine at Montereau. Length: 290 km (180 miles)

York¹ 1 the English royal house that reigned from 1461 to 1485 and was descended from Richard Plantagenet,

Duke of York (1411–60), whose claim to the throne precipitated the Wars of the Roses. His sons reigned as Edward IV and Richard III **2 Alvin C(ullum).** 1887–1964, US soldier and hero of World War I **3 Duke of,** full name *Prince Frederick Augustus, Duke of York and Albany.* 1763–1827, second son of George III of Great Britain and Ireland. An undistinguished commander-in-chief of the British army (1798–1809), he is the "grand old Duke of York" of the nursery rhyme **4 Prince Andrew, Duke of** born 1960, second son of Elizabeth II of Great Britain and Northern Ireland. He married (1986) Miss Sarah Ferguson; they divorced in 1996; their first daughter, Princess Beatrice of York, was born in 1988 and their second, Princess Eugenie of York, in 1990

York² **1** a historic city in NE England, in York unitary authority, North Yorkshire, on the River Ouse: the military capital of Roman Britain; capital of the N archiepiscopal province of Britain since 625, with a cathedral (the Minster) begun in 1154; noted for its cycle of medieval mystery plays; unusually intact medieval walls; university (1963). Pop: 137 505 (2001) **2** a unitary authority in NE England, in North Yorkshire. Pop: 183 100 (2003 est). Area: 272 sq km (105 sq miles) **3 Cape** a cape in NE Australia, in Queensland at the N tip of the Cape York Peninsula, extending into the Torres Strait: the northernmost point of Australia

Yorke Peninsula a peninsula in South Australia, between Spencer Gulf and St Vincent Gulf: mainly agricultural with several coastal resorts

yorker *Cricket* a ball bowled so as to pitch just under or just beyond the bat

Yorkist *English history* a member or adherent of the royal house of York, esp during the Wars of the Roses

Yorkshire a historic county of N England: the largest English county, formerly administratively into East, West, and North Ridings. In 1974 it was much reduced in size and divided into the new counties of North, West, and South Yorkshire: in 1996 the East Riding of Yorkshire was reinstated as a unitary authority and parts of the NE were returned to North Yorkshire for geographical and ceremonial purposes

Yorktown a village in SE Virginia: scene of the surrender (1781) of the British under Cornwallis to the Americans under Washington at the end of the War of American Independence

Yosemite National Park a national park in central California, in the Sierra Nevada Mountains: contains the Yosemite Valley, at an altitude of about 1200 m (4000 ft), with sheer walls rising about another 1200 m (4000 ft). Area: 3061 sq km (1182 sq miles)

Yoshkar-Ola a city in Russia, capital of the Mari El Republic. Pop: 260 000 (2005 est)

young **1** *Geography* **a** (of mountains) formed in the Alpine orogeny and still usually rugged in outline **b** another term for **youthful 2** of or relating to a rejuvenated group or movement or one claiming to represent the younger members of the population, esp one adhering to a political ideology **3** offspring, esp young animals **4 with young** (of animals) pregnant

youngster a young animal, esp a horse

Youngstown a city in NE Ohio: a major centre of steel production; university (1908). Pop: 79 271 (2003 est)

Youth Isle of an island in the NW Caribbean, south of Cuba: administratively part of Cuba from 1925. Chief town: Nueva Gerona. Pop: 80 600 (2002 est). Area: 3061 sq km (1182 sq miles)

youthful (of a river, valley, or land surface) in the early stage of the cycle of erosion, characterized by steep slopes, lack of flood plains, and V-shaped valleys

youth hostel one of a chain of inexpensive lodging places for young people travelling cheaply
▷www.iyhf.org

yo-yo a toy consisting of a spool attached to a string, the end of which is held while it is repeatedly spun out and reeled in

Ypres a town in W Belgium, in W Flanders province near the border with France: scene of many sieges and battles, esp in World War I, when it was completely destroyed. Pop: 35 021 (2004 est)

Yser a river in NW central Europe, rising in N France and flowing through SW Belgium to the North Sea: scene of battles in World War I. Length: 77 km (48 miles)

ytterbium a soft malleable silvery element of the lanthanide series of metals that occurs in monazite and is used to improve the mechanical properties of steel. Symbol: Yb; atomic no.: 70; atomic wt.: 173.04; valency: 2 or 3; relative density: 6.903 (alpha), 6.966 (beta); melting pt.: 819°C; boiling pt.: 1196°C

yttrium a silvery metallic element occurring in monazite and gadolinite and used in various alloys, in lasers, and as a catalyst. Symbol: Y; atomic no.: 39; atomic wt.: 88.90585; valency: 3; relative density: 4.469; melting pt.: 1522°C; boiling pt.: 3338°C

yuan the standard monetary unit of China, divided into 10 jiao and 100 fen.

yucca any of several plants of the genus *Yucca,* of tropical and subtropical America, having stiff lancelike leaves and spikes of white flowers: family *Agaraceae*

Yugoslav *or* **Jugoslav** **1** (formerly) a native, inhabitant, or citizen of Yugoslavia (sense 1 or 2) **2** (not in technical use) another name for **Serbo-Croat** (the language) **3** (formerly) of, relating to, or characteristic of Yugoslavia (sense 1 or 2) or its people

Yugoslavia *or* **Jugoslavia** **1** Federal Republic of Yugoslavia a former country of SE Europe, comprising Serbia and Montenegro, that was formed in 1991 but not widely internationally recognized until 2000; it was replaced by the Union of Serbia and Montenegro in 2003 **2** a former country in SE Europe, on the Adriatic: established in 1918 from the independent states of Serbia and Montenegro, and regions that until World War I had belonged to Austria-Hungary (Croatia, Slovenia, and Bosnia-Herzegovina); the name was changed from Kingdom of Serbs, Croats, and Slovenes to Yugoslavia in 1929; German invasion of 1941–44 was resisted chiefly by a Communist group led by Tito, who declared a people's republic in 1945; it became the Socialist Federal Republic of Yugoslavia in 1963; in 1991 Slovenia, Croatia, and Bosnia-Herzegovina declared independence, followed by Macedonia in 1992; Serbia and Montenegro formed the Federal Republic of Yugoslavia, subsequently (2003) replaced by the Union of Serbia and Montenegro

Yukon the territory of NW Canada, on the Beaufort

Sea, between the Northwest Territories and Alaska: arctic and mountainous, reaching 5959 m (19 550 ft) at Mount Logan, Canada's highest peak; mineral resources. Capital: Whitehorse. Pop: 31 209 (2004 est). Area: 536 327 sq km (207 076 sq miles)

Yukon River a river in NW North America, rising in NW Canada on the border between the Yukon Territory and British Columbia: flows northwest into Alaska, US, and then southwest to the Bering Sea; navigable for about 2850 km (1775 miles) to Whitehorse. Length: 3185 km (1979 miles)

Yvelines a department of N France, in Île de France region. Capital: Versailles. Pop: 1 370 443 (2003 est). Area: 2271 sq km (886 sq miles)

Zz

Zaandam a former town in the W Netherlands, in North Holland: an important shipbuilding centre in the 17th century. It became part of Zaanstad in 1974

Zaanstad a port in the W Netherlands, in North Holland: formed (1974) from Zaandam, Koog a/d Zaan, Zaandijk, Wormerveer, Krommenie, Westzaan, and Assendelft; food and machinery industries. Pop: 139 000 (2003 est)

Zabrze a city in SW Poland: a Prussian and German town from 1742 until 1945, when it passed to Poland; industrial centre in a coal-mining region. Pop: 200 177 (1999 est)

Zacatecas 1 a state of N central Mexico, on the central plateau: rich mineral resources. Capital: Zacatecas. Pop: 1 351 207 (2000). Area: 75 040 sq km (28 973 sq miles) 2 a city in N central Mexico, capital of Zacatecas state: silver mines. Pop: 241 000 (2005 est)

Zacharias, Zachariah, *or* **Zachary** *New Testament* John the Baptist's father, who underwent a temporary period of dumbness for his lack of faith (Luke 1)

Zagazig *or* **Zaqaziq** a city in NE Egypt, in the Nile Delta: major cotton market. Pop: 291 000 (2005 est)

Zagreb the capital of Croatia, on the River Sava; gothic cathedral; university (1874); industrial centre. Pop: 685 000 (2005 est)

Zama the name of several ancient cities in N Africa, including the one near the site of Scipio's decisive defeat of Hannibal (202 BC)

Zambezi *or* **Zambese** a river in S central and E Africa, rising in NW Zambia and flowing across E Angola back into Zambia, continuing south to the Caprivi Strip of Namibia, then east forming the Zambia–Zimbabwe border, and finally crossing Mozambique to the Indian Ocean: the fourth longest river in Africa. Length: 2740 km (1700 miles)

Zambia a republic in southern Africa: an early site of human settlement; controlled by the British South Africa Company by 1900 and unified as Northern Rhodesia in 1911; made a British protectorate in 1924; part of the Federation of Rhodesia and Nyasaland (1953–63), gaining independence as a member of the Commonwealth in 1964; important mineral exports, esp copper. Official language: English. Religion: Christian majority, animist minority. Currency: kwacha. Capital: Lusaka. Pop: 10 924 000 (2004 est). Area: 752 617 sq km (290 587 sq miles)

Zamboanga a port in the Philippines, on SW Mindanao

on Basilan Strait: founded by the Spanish in 1635; tourist centre, with fisheries. Pop: 716 000 (2005 est)

Zamenhof Lazarus Ludwig 1859–1917, Polish oculist; invented Esperanto

Zamora a city in NW central Spain, on the Douro River. Pop: 65 639 (2003 est)

Zamyatin Yevgenii Ivanovich 1884–1937, Russian novelist and writer, in Paris from 1931, whose works include satirical studies of provincial life in Russia and England, where he worked during World War I, and the dystopian novel *We* (1924)

Zante an island in the Ionian Sea, off the W coast of Greece: southernmost of the Ionian Islands; traditionally belonged to Ulysses, king of Ithaca. Pop: 38 957 (2001). Area: 402 sq km (155 sq miles)

zany a clown or buffoon, esp one in old comedies who imitated other performers with ludicrous effect

Zanzibar an island in the Indian Ocean, off the E coast of Africa: settled by Persians and Arabs from the 7th century onwards; became a flourishing trading centre for slaves, ivory, and cloves; made a British protectorate in 1890, becoming independent within the Commonwealth in 1963 and a republic in 1964; joined with Tanganyika in 1964 to form the United Republic of Tanzania. Pop: 622 459 (2002)

Zapata Emiliano ?1877–1919, Mexican guerrilla leader

Zaporozhye a city in E Ukraine on the Dnieper River: developed as a major industrial centre after the construction (1932) of the Dnieper hydroelectric station. Pop: 798 000 (2005 est)

Zappa Frank 1940–93, US rock musician, songwriter, and experimental composer: founder and only permanent member of the Mothers of Invention. His recordings include *Freak Out* (1966), *Hot Rats* (1969), and *Sheik Yerbouti* (1979)

Zaragoza a city in NE Spain, on the River Ebro: Roman colony established 25 BC; under Moorish rule (714–1118); capital of Aragon (12th–15th centuries); twice besieged by the French during the Peninsular War and captured (1809); university (1474). Pop: 626 081 (2003 est)

Zaria a city in N central Nigeria: former capital of a Hausa state; agricultural trading centre; university (1962). Pop: 822 000 (2005 est)

Zarqa the second largest town in Jordan, northeast of Amman. Pop: 494 000 (2005 est)

Zealand the largest island of Denmark, separated from the island of Funen by the Great Belt and from S

Sweden by the Sound (both now spanned by road bridges). Chief town: Copenhagen. Pop: 2 096 449 (2003 est). Area: 7016 sq km (2709 sq miles)

Zeami or **Seami** **Motokiyo** 1363–1443, Japanese dramatist, regarded as the greatest figure in the history of No drama

Zebedee *New Testament* the father of the apostles James and John (Matthew 4:21)

zebra any of several mammals of the horse family (*Equidae*), such as *Equus burchelli* (the **common zebra**), of southern and eastern Africa, having distinctive black-and-white striped hides

zebra crossing *Brit* a pedestrian crossing marked on a road by broad alternate black and white stripes. Once on the crossing the pedestrian has right of way

zebu a domesticated ox, *Bos indicus*, having a humped back, long horns, and a large dewlap: used in India and E Asia as a draught animal

Zebulun *Old Testament* **1** the sixth son whom Leah bore to Jacob: one of the 12 patriarchs of Israel (Genesis 30:20) **2** the tribe descended from him **3** the territory of this tribe, lying in lower Galilee to the north of Mount Carmel and to the east of the coastal plain

Zedekiah *Old Testament* the last king of Judah, who died in captivity at Babylon

Zeebrugge a port in NW Belgium, in W Flanders on the North Sea: linked by canal with Bruges; German submarine base in World War I

Zeeland a province of the SW Netherlands: consists of a small area on the mainland together with a number of islands in the Scheldt estuary; mostly below sea level. Capital: Middelburg. Pop: 378 000 (2003 est). Area: 1787 sq km (690 sq miles)

Zeffirelli **Franco** born 1923, Italian stage and film director and designer, noted esp for his work in opera

Zeist a city in the central Netherlands, near Utrecht. Pop: 60 000 (2003 est)

Zellweger **Renée** (**Kathleen**). born 1969, US film actress, best known for her performances in *Nurse Betty* (2000), *Bridget Jones's Diary* (2001) and its sequel *Bridget Jones and the Edge of Reason* (2004), and *Chicago* (2002)

Zen *Buddhism* a Japanese school, of 12th-century Chinese origin, teaching that contemplation of one's essential nature to the exclusion of all else is the only way of achieving pure enlightenment

Zend-Avesta the Avesta together with the traditional interpretative commentary known as the Zend, esp as preserved in the Avestan language among the Parsees

zenith *Astronomy* the point on the celestial sphere vertically above an observer

Zenobia 3rd century AD, queen of Palmyra (?267–272), who was captured by the Roman emperor Aurelian

Zeno of Citium ?336–?264 BC, Greek philosopher, who founded the Stoic school in Athens

Zeno of Elea ?490–?430 BC, Greek Eleatic philosopher; disciple of Parmenides. He defended the belief that motion and change are illusions in a series of paradoxical arguments, of which the best known is that of Achilles and the tortoise

Zephaniah¹ *Old Testament* **1** a Hebrew prophet of the late 7th century BC **2** the book containing his oracles, which are chiefly concerned with the approaching judgment

by God upon the sinners of Judah

Zephaniah² **Benjamin** born 1958, British poet, writer, and activist, born in Jamaica. His poetry collections include *The Dread Affair* (1985) and *Too Black, Too Strong* (2001)

zephyr **1** a soft or gentle breeze **2** any of several delicate soft yarns, fabrics, or garments, usually of wool

Zeppelin **Count Ferdinand von** 1838–1917, German aeronautical pioneer, who designed and manufactured airships (zeppelins)

Zermatt a village and resort in S Switzerland, in Valais canton at the foot of the Matterhorn: cars are not allowed in the area. Pop: 5988 (2000)

zero **1** the symbol 0, indicating an absence of quantity or magnitude; nought **2** the integer denoted by the symbol 0; nought **3** the cardinal number between +1 and –1 **4 a** the temperature, pressure, etc, that registers a reading of zero on a scale **b** the value of a variable, such as temperature, obtained under specified conditions **5** *Maths* **a** the cardinal number of a set with no members **b** the identity element of addition **6** *Meteorol* **a** (of a cloud ceiling) limiting visibility to 15 metres (50 feet) or less **b** (of horizontal visibility) limited to 50 metres (165 feet) or less

zero gravity the state or condition of weightlessness

zero-rated denoting goods on which the buyer pays no value-added tax although the seller can claim back any tax he has paid

Zeta-Jones **Catherine**, original name *Catherine Jones*. born 1969, Welsh actress, who made her name in the TV series *The Darling Buds of May* (1991) before starring in the films *Traffic* (2000), *Chicago* (2002), and *Smoke and Mirrors* (2004). She is married to the US actor Michael Douglas

Zeus the supreme god of the ancient Greeks, who became ruler of gods and men after he dethroned his father Cronus and defeated the Titans. He was the husband of his sister Hera and father by her and others of many gods, demigods, and mortals. He wielded thunderbolts and ruled the heavens, while his brothers Poseidon and Hades ruled the sea and underworld respectively

Zeuxis late 5th century BC, Greek painter, noted for the verisimilitude of his works

Zhangjiakou, Changchiakow, or **Changchiak'ou** a city in NE China, in NW Hebei province: a military centre, controlling the route to Mongolia, under the Ming and Manchu dynasties. Pop: 973 000 (2005 est)

Zhangzhou, Changchow, or **Ch'ang-chou 1** a city in E China, in S Jiangsu province, on the Grand Canal: also known as Wutsin until 1949, when the 7th-century name was officially readopted. Pop: 772 700 (1990 est) **2** a city in SE China, in S Fujian province on the Saikoe River. Pop. 231 333 (1999 est)

Zhejiang or **Chekiang** a province of E China: mountainous and densely populated; a cultural centre since the 12th century. Capital: Hangzhou. Pop: 46 800 000 (2003 est). Area: 102 000 sq km (39 780 sq miles)

Zhengzhou, Chengchow, or **Cheng-chou** a city in E central China, capital of Henan province; an administrative centre. Pop: 2 250 000 (2005 est)

Zhitomir a city in central Ukraine; centre of an agricultural region. Pop: 282 000 (2005 est)

Zhu Jiang, Chu Chiang, or **Chu Kiang** a river in SE

China, in S Guangdong province, flowing southeast from Canton to the South China Sea. Length: about 177 km (110 miles)

Zhukov Georgi Konstantinovich 1896–1974, Soviet marshal. In World War II, he led the offensives that broke the sieges of Stalingrad and Leningrad (1942–43) and later captured Warsaw and Berlin; minister of defence (1955–57)

Zia ul Haq Mohammed 1924–88, Pakistani general: president of Pakistan (1978–88), following the overthrow (1977) of Z. A. Bhutto by a military coup. He was killed in an air crash, possibly through sabotage

Zibo, Tzu-po, *or* **Tzepo** a city in NE China, in Shandong province. Pop: 2 775 000 (2005 est)

Zidane Zinedine born 1972, French football player, known as *Zizou*; scored two goals in the 1998 World Cup final

Ziegfeld Florenz 1869–1932, US theatrical producer, noted for his series of extravagant revues (1907–31), known as the Ziegfeld Follies

ziggurat, zikkurat, *or* **zikurat** a type of rectangular temple tower or tiered mound erected by the Sumerians, Akkadians, and Babylonians in Mesopotamia. The tower of Babel is thought to be one of these

Zigong, Tzekung, *or* **Tzu-kung** an industrial city in W central China, in Sichuan. Pop: 1 123 000 (2005 est)

Zilpah *Old Testament* Leah's maidservant, who bore Gad and Asher to Jacob (Genesis 30:10–13)

Zimbabwe 1 a country in SE Africa, formerly a self-governing British colony founded in 1890 by the British South Africa Company, which administered the country until a self-governing colony was established in 1923; joined with Northern Rhodesia (now Zambia) and Nyasaland (now Malawi) as the Federation of Rhodesia and Nyasaland from 1953 to 1963; made a unilateral declaration of independence (UDI) under the leadership of Ian Smith in 1965 on the basis of White minority rule; proclaimed a republic in 1970; in 1976 the principle of Black majority rule was accepted and in 1978 a transitional government was set up; gained independence under Robert Mugabe in 1980; effectively a one-party state since 1987; a member of the Commonwealth until 2003, when it withdrew as a result of conflict with other members. Official language: English. Religion: Christian majority. Currency: Zimbabwe dollar. Capital: Harare. Pop: 12 932 000 (2004 est). Area: 390 624 sq km (150 820 sq miles) 2 a ruined fortified settlement in Zimbabwe, which at its height, in the 15th century, was probably the capital of an empire covering SE Africa

zinc 1 a brittle bluish-white metallic element that becomes coated with a corrosion-resistant layer in moist air and occurs chiefly in sphalerite and smithsonite. It is a constituent of several alloys, esp brass and nickel-silver, and is used in die-casting, galvanizing metals, and in battery electrodes. Symbol: Zn; atomic no.: 30; atomic wt.: 65.39; valency: 2; relative density: 7.133; melting pt.: 419.58°C; boiling pt.: 907°C 2 *Informal* corrugated galvanized iron

zinc ointment a medicinal ointment consisting of zinc oxide, petrolatum, and paraffin, used to treat certain skin diseases

zinc oxide a white insoluble powder used as a pigment

in paints (**zinc white** or **Chinese white**), cosmetics, glass, and printing inks. It is an antiseptic and astringent and is used in making zinc ointment. Formula: ZnO

zinnia any annual or perennial plant of the genus *Zinnia*, of tropical and subtropical America, having solitary heads of brightly coloured flowers: family *Asteraceae* (composites)

Zinoviev Grigori Yevseevich, original name *Ovsel Gershon Aronov Radomyslsky.* 1883–1936, Soviet politician; chairman of the Comintern (1919–26) executed for supposed complicity in the murder of Kirov. He was the supposed author of the forged 'Zinoviev letter' urging British Communists to revolt, publication of which helped to defeat (1924) the first Labour Government

Zion *or* **Sion** 1 the hill on which the city of Jerusalem stands 2 *Judaism* a the ancient Israelites of the Bible b the modern Jewish nation c Israel as the national home of the Jewish people 3 *Christianity* heaven regarded as the city of God and the final abode of his elect 4 a a religious community or its site, regarded as chosen by God and under his special protection b an ideal theocratic community, esp any of the Christian Churches regarded as such a community

Zionism 1 a political movement for the establishment and support of a national homeland for Jews in Palestine, now concerned chiefly with the development of the modern state of Israel 2 a policy or movement for Jews to return to Palestine from the Diaspora

zircon a reddish-brown, grey, green, blue, or colourless hard mineral consisting of zirconium silicate in tetragonal crystalline form with hafnium and some rare earths as impurities. It occurs principally in igneous rocks and is an important source of zirconium, zirconia, and hafnia: it is used as a gemstone and a refractory. Formula: $ZrSiO_4$

zirconium a greyish-white metallic element, occurring chiefly in zircon, that is exceptionally corrosion-resistant and has low neutron absorption. It is used as a coating in nuclear and chemical plants, as a deoxidizer in steel, and alloyed with niobium in superconductive magnets. Symbol: Zr; atomic no.: 40; atomic wt.: 91.224; valency: 2, 3, or 4; relative density: 6.506; melting pt.: 1855±2°C; boiling pt.: 4409°C

Ziska *or* **Žižka** Jan ?1370–1424, Bohemian soldier, who successfully led the Hussite rebellion (1420–24) against emperor Sigismund

zither a plucked musical instrument consisting of numerous strings stretched over a resonating box, a few of which may be stopped on a fretted fingerboard

Zlatoust a town in W Russia, on the Ay river: one of the chief metallurgical centres of the Urals since the 18th century. Pop: 192 000 (2005 est)

zloty the standard monetary unit of Poland, divided into 100 groszy

zodiac 1 an imaginary belt extending 8° either side of the ecliptic, which contains the 12 zodiacal constellations and within which the moon and planets appear to move. It is divided into 12 equal areas, called **signs of the zodiac,** each named after the constellation which once lay in it 2 *Astrology* a diagram, usually circular, representing this belt and showing the symbols, illustrations, etc, associated with each of the 12 signs of the zodiac, used to predict the future

Zoffany John or Johann ?1733–1810, British painter, esp of portraits; born in Germany

Zog I 1895–1961, king of Albania (1928–39), formerly prime minister (1922–24) and president (1925–28). He allowed Albania to become dominated by Fascist Italy and fled into exile when Mussolini invaded (1939)

Zola Émile 1840–1902, French novelist and critic; chief exponent of naturalism. In *Les Rougon-Macquart* (1871–93), a cycle of 20 novels, he explains the behaviour of his characters in terms of their heredity: it includes *L'Assommoir* (1877), *Nana* (1880), *Germinal* (1885), and *La Terre* (1887). He is also noted for his defence of Dreyfus in his pamphlet *J'accuse* (1898)

Zomba a city in S Malawi: the capital of Malawi until 1971. Pop: 65 915 (1998 est)

zombie *or* **zombi** 1 a supernatural spirit that reanimates a dead body 2 a corpse brought to life in this manner 3 the snake god of voodoo cults in the West Indies, esp Haiti, and in scattered areas of the southern US 4 the python god revered in parts of West Africa 5 a piece of computer code that instructs an infected computer to send a virus on to other computer systems

zone 1 an area subject to a particular political, military, or government function, use, or jurisdiction 2 *Geography* one of the divisions of the earth's surface, esp divided into latitudinal belts according to temperature 3 *Geology* a distinctive layer or region of rock, characterized by particular fossils (**zone fossils**), metamorphism, structural deformity, etc. 4 *Ecology* an area, esp a belt of land, having a particular flora and fauna determined by the prevailing environmental conditions 5 *Maths* a portion of a sphere between two parallel planes intersecting the sphere 6 *NZ* a section on a transport route; fare stage 7 *NZ* a catchment area for pupils for a specific school

zoo a place where live animals are kept, studied, bred, and exhibited to the public

zooid 1 any independent animal body, such as an individual of a coelenterate colony 2 a motile cell or body, such as a gamete, produced by an organism

zoology 1 the study of animals, including their classification, structure, physiology, and history 2 the biological characteristics of a particular animal or animal group 3 the fauna characteristic of a particular region 4 a book, treatise, etc, dealing with any aspect of the study of animals
▷www.biosis.org.uk/zrdocs/zoolinfo/
info_gen.htm
▷www.academicinfo.net/zoo.html

zoom lens a lens system that allows the focal length of a camera lens to be varied continuously without altering the sharpness of the image

zoophyte any animal resembling a plant, such as a sea anemone

Zoroaster ?628–?551 BC, Persian prophet; founder of Zoroastrianism

Zoroastrianism *or* **Zoroastrism** the dualistic religion founded by the Persian prophet Zoroaster in the late 7th or early 6th centuries BC and set forth in the sacred writings of the Zend-Avesta. It is based on the concept

of a continuous struggle between Ormazd (or Ahura Mazda), the god of creation, light, and goodness, and his arch enemy, Ahriman, the spirit of evil and darkness, and it includes a highly developed ethical code
▷http://www.avesta.org/avesta.html

Zorrilla y Moral José 1817–93, Spanish poet and dramatist, noted for his romantic plays based on national legends, esp *Don Juan Tenorio* (1844)

Zsigmondy Richard Adolf 1865–1929, German chemist, born in Austria, noted for his work on colloidal particles and, with H. Siedentopf, his introduction (1903) of the ultramicroscope: Nobel prize for chemistry 1925

zucchetto *RC Church* a small round skullcap worn by certain ecclesiastics and varying in colour according to the rank of the wearer, the Pope wearing white, cardinals red, bishops violet, and others black

zucchini a small variety of vegetable marrow, cooked and eaten as a vegetable

Zug 1 a canton of N central Switzerland: the smallest Swiss canton; mainly German-speaking and Roman Catholic; joined the Swiss Confederation in 1352. Capital: Zug. Pop: 102 200 (2002 est). Area: 239 sq km (92 sq miles) 2 a town in N central Switzerland, the capital of Zug canton, on Lake Zug. Pop: 22 973 (2000) 3 **Lake** a lake in N central Switzerland, in Zug and Schwyz cantons. Area: 39 sq km (15 sq miles)

Zugspitze a mountain peak in S Germany in the Bavarian Alps, on the Austrian border: the highest peak in Germany. Height: 2963 m (9721 ft)

Zuider Zee *or* **Zuyder Zee** a former inlet of the North Sea in the N coast of the Netherlands sealed off from the sea by a dam in 1932, dividing it into the Waddenzee and the freshwater IJsselmeer, with several large areas under reclamation

Zukerman Pinchas born 1948, Israeli violinist

Zulu 1 a member of a tall Negroid people of SE Africa, living chiefly in South Africa, who became dominant during the 19th century due to a warrior-clan system organized by the powerful leader, Shaka 2 the language of this people, belonging to the Bantu group of the Niger-Congo family, closely related to Swazi and Xhosa

Zululand a region of E South Africa, on the Indian Ocean; partly corresponds to KwaZulu/Natal. Chief town: Eshowe

Zweig 1 Arnold 1887–1968, German novelist, famous for his realistic war novel *The Case of Sergeant Grischa* (1927) 2 Stefan 1881–1942, Austrian novelist, dramatist, essayist, and poet

Zwickau a city in E Germany, in Saxony: Anabaptist movement founded here (1521); coal-mining and industrial centre. Pop: 99 846 (2003 est.)

Zwingli Ulrich *or* Huldreich 1484–1531, Swiss leader of the Reformation, based in Zurich. He denied the Eucharistic presence, holding that the Communion was merely a commemoration of Christ's death

Zworykin Vladimir Kosma 1889–1982, US physicist and television pioneer, born in Russia. He developed the first practical television camera

zygote 1 the cell resulting from the union of an ovum and a spermatozoon 2 the organism that develops from such a cell